Cost Accounting

A Managerial Emphasis

Fourteenth Edition

Charles T. Horngren
Stanford University

Srikant M. Datar
Harvard University

Madhav V. Rajan
Stanford University

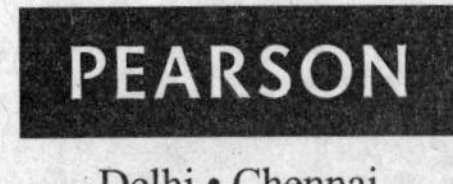

Delhi • Chennai

Photo Credits: **page 3** Oleksiy Maksymenko\Alamy Images; **page 15** BuildPix\Alamy Images Royalty Free; **page 25** DAVID SWANSON/STAFF PHOTOGRAPH/PHILADELPHIA INQUIRER/RAPPORT SYNDICATION; **page 31** Jim Wilson\Redux Pictures; **page 65** Getty Images, Inc.—Liaison; **page 82** Richard Drew\AP Wide World Photos; **page 109** Dana Hoff\Getty Images, Inc.—Liaison; **page 119** BRANDON THIBODEAUX/THE NEW YORK TIMES; **page 155** Ethan Miller\Getty Images, Inc.—Liaison; **page 176** James Leynse\CORBIS-NY; **page 207** Michael Blann\Getty Images, Inc.—Liaison; **page 223** Getty Images, Inc.; **page 255** Eric Gay\AP Wide World Photos; **page 268** Stephen Chernin\Newscom; **page 297** Jason Kempin\Redux Pictures; **page 309** Getty Images, Inc.—Liaison; **page 345** Erin Siegal\Redux Pictures; **page 363** DIANE COLLINS/JORDAN HOLLENDER/GETTY IMAGES; **page 393** Al Seib/Los Angeles Times/MCT/Newscom; **page 410** Kristoffer Tripplaar\Alamy Images; **page 445** © (JAMES LEYNSE) / CORBIS All Rights Reserved; **page 456** mediablitzimages limited\Alamy Images; **page 495** Ajit Solanki\AP Wide World Photos; **page 503** Steven Sheppard\AP Wide World Photos; **page 535** Namas Bhojani\Getty Images, Inc.—Bloomberg News; **page 555** Facebook, Inc.; **page 583** © (GUS RUELAS)/Reuters / CORBIS All Rights Reserved/; **page 598** Rich Schultz\AP Wide World Photos; **page 633** David Zalubowski\AP Wide World Photos; **page 673** Jim West\Alamy Images; **page 688** Jay Laprete\Getty Images, Inc.—Bloomberg News; **page 713** Karen BLEIER\Newscom; **page 732** Adidas Americas; **page 761** Kevin P. Casey\Getty Images, Inc.—Bloomberg News; **page 775** Ed Andrieski\AP Wide World Photos; **page 810** Daniel Heighton\Alamy Images; **page 792** Steven Senne\AP Wide World Photos; **page 851** Diane Bondareff/Picture Group via AP IMAGES; **page 837** Newscom; **page 899** Yoshikazu Tsuno/AFP/Getty Images/Newscom; **page 881** Charles Krupa\AP Wide World Photos; **page 944** Lenscap\Alamy Images; **page 927** Symantec Corporation; **page 985** AFP Photo/Jim Watson/Newscom; **page 967** AFP Photo/Gabriel Bouys/Newscom

Authorized adaptation from the United States edition, entitled *Cost Accounting: A Managerial Emphasis, 14th Edition*, ISBN: 9780132109178 by Horngren, Charles T., Datar, Srikant M., Rajan, Madhav V., published by Pearson Education, Inc., publishing as Prentice Hall © 2012 Pearson Education, Inc.

Indian Subcontinent Adaptation

ISBN 978-81-317-6435-0

First Impression
Second Impression, 2013
Third Impression, 2014

Published by Dorling Kindersley (India) Pvt. Ltd., licensees of Pearson Education in South Asia.

Head Office: 7th Floor, Knowledge Boulevard, A-8(A), Sector 62, Noida, UP 201309, India.
Registered Office: 11 Community Centre, Panchsheel Park, New Delhi 110017, India.

Printed in India by Rahul Print O Pack.

Brief Contents

Contents

About the Authors

Charles T. Horngren is the Edmund W. Littlefield Professor of Accounting, Emeritus, at Stanford University. A Graduate of Marquette University, he received his MBA from Harvard University and his PhD from the University of Chicago. He is also the recipient of honorary doctorates from Marquette University and DePaul University.

A certified public accountant, Horngren served on the Accounting Principles Board for six years, the Financial Accounting Standards Board Advisory Council for five years, and the Council of the American Institute of Certified Public Accountants for three years. For six years, he served as a trustee of the Financial Accounting Foundation, which oversees the Financial Accounting Standards Board and the Government Accounting Standards Board. Horngren is a member of the Accounting Hall of Fame.

A member of the American Accounting Association, Horngren has been its president and its director of research. He received its first Outstanding Accounting Educator Award. The California Certified Public Accountants Foundation gave Horngren its Faculty Excellence Award and its Distinguished Professor Award. He is the first person to have received both awards.

The American Institute of Certified Public Accountants presented its first Outstanding Educator Award to Horngren.

Horngren was named Accountant of the Year, Education, by the national professional accounting fraternity, Beta Alpha Psi.

Professor Horngren is also a member of the Institute of Management Accountants, from whom he received its Distinguished Service Award. He was also a member of the Institutes' Board of Regents, which administers the Certified Management Accountant examinations.

Horngren is the author of other accounting books published by Prentice Hall: *Introduction to Management Accounting*, 15th ed. (2011, with Sundem and Stratton); *Introduction to Financial Accounting*, 10th ed. (2011, with Sundem and Elliott); *Accounting*, 8th ed. (2010, with Harrison and Bamber); and *Financial Accounting*, 8th ed. (2010, with Harrison).

Horngren is the Consulting Editor for the Charles T. Horngren Series in Accounting.

Srikant M. Datar is the Arthur Lowes Dickinson Professor of Business Administration and Senior Associate Dean at Harvard University. A graduate with distinction from the University of Bombay, he received gold medals upon graduation from the Indian Institute of Management, Ahmedabad, and the Institute of Cost and Works Accountants of India. A chartered accountant, he holds two master's degrees and a PhD from Stanford University.

Cited by his students as a dedicated and innovative teacher, Datar received the George Leland Bach Award for Excellence in the Classroom at Carnegie Mellon University and the Distinguished Teaching Award at Stanford University.

Datar has published his research in leading accounting, marketing, and operations management journals, including *The Accounting Review*, *Contemporary Accounting Research*, *Journal of Accounting, Auditing and Finance*, *Journal of Accounting and Economics*, *Journal of Accounting Research*, and *Management Science*. He has also served on the editorial board of several journals and presented his research to corporate executives and academic audiences in North America, South America, Asia, Africa, Australia, and Europe.

Datar is a member of the board of directors of Novartis A.G., ICF International, KPIT Cummins Infosystems Ltd., Stryker Corporation, and Harvard Business Publishing, and has worked with many organizations, including Apple Computer, AT&T, Boeing, Du Pont, Ford, General Motors, HSBC, Hewlett-Packard, Morgan Stanley, PepsiCo, TRW, Visa, and the World Bank. He is a member of the American Accounting Association and the Institute of Management Accountants.

Madhav V. Rajan is the Gregor G. Peterson Professor of Accounting and Senior Associate Dean at Stanford University. From 2002 to 2010, he was the area coordinator for accounting at Stanford's Graduate School of Business.

Rajan received his undergraduate degree in commerce from the University of Madras, India, and his MS in accounting, MBA, and PhD degrees from the Graduate School of Industrial Administration at Carnegie Mellon University. In 1990, his dissertation won the Alexander Henderson Award for Excellence in Economic Theory.

Rajan's primary area of research interest is the economics-based analysis of management accounting issues, especially as they relate to internal control cost allocation, capital budgeting, quality management, supply chain, and performance systems in firms. He has published his research in leading accounting and operations management journals including *The Accounting Review*, *Review of Financial Studies*, *Journal of Accounting Research*, and *Management Science*. In 2004, he received the Notable Contribution to Management Accounting Literature Award.

Rajan has served as the Departmental Editor for Accounting at *Management Science*, as well as associate editor for both the accounting and operations areas. From 2002 to 2008, Rajan served as an editor of *The Accounting Review*. He is also currently an associate editor for the *Journal of Accounting, Auditing and Finance*. Rajan is a member of the management accounting section of the American Accounting Association and has twice been a plenary speaker at the AAA Management Accounting Conference.

Rajan has won several teaching awards at Wharton and Stanford, including the David W. Hauck Award, the highest undergraduate teaching honor at Wharton. Rajan has taught in a variety of executive education programs including the Stanford Executive Program, the National Football League Program for Managers, and the National Basketball Players Association Program, as well as custom programs for firms including nVidia, Genentech, and Google.

Preface

Studying Cost Accounting is one of the best business investments a student can make. Why? Because success in any organization—from the smallest corner store to the largest multinational corporation—requires the use of cost accounting concepts and practices. Cost accounting provides key data to managers for planning and controlling, as well as costing products, services, even customers. This book focuses on how cost accounting helps managers make better decisions, as cost accountants are increasingly becoming integral members of their company's decision-making teams. In order to emphasize this prominence in decision-making, we use the "different costs for different purposes" theme throughout this book. By focusing on basic concepts, analyses, uses, and procedures instead of procedures alone, we recognize cost accounting as a managerial tool for business strategy and implementation.

We also prepare students for the rewards and challenges they face in the professional cost accounting world of today and tomorrow. For example, we emphasize both the development of analytical skills such as Excel to leverage available information technology and the values and behaviors that make cost accountants effective in the workplace.

Hallmark Features of *Cost Accounting*

- Exceptionally strong emphasis on managerial uses of cost information
- Clarity and understandability of the text
- Excellent balance in integrating modern topics with traditional coverage
- Emphasis on human behavior aspects
- Extensive use of real-world examples
- Ability to teach chapters in different sequences
- Excellent quantity, quality, and range of assignment material

The first thirteen chapters provide the essence of a one-term (quarter or semester) course. There is ample text and assignment material in the book's twenty-three chapters for a two-term course. This book can be used immediately after the student has had an introductory course in financial accounting. Alternatively, this book can build on an introductory course in managerial accounting.

Deciding on the sequence of chapters in a textbook is a challenge. Since every instructor has a unique way of organizing his or her course, we utilize a modular, flexible organization that permits a course to be custom tailored. *This organization facilitates diverse approaches to teaching and learning.*

As an example of the book's flexibility, consider our treatment of process costing. Process costing is described in Chapters 17 and 18. Instructors interested in filling out a student's perspective of costing systems can move directly from job-order costing described in Chapter 4 to Chapter 17 without interruption in the flow of material. Other instructors may want their students to delve into activity-based costing and budgeting and more decision-oriented topics early in the course. These instructors may prefer to postpone discussion of process costing.

New to This Edition

Greater Emphasis on Strategy

This edition deepens the book's emphasis on strategy development and execution. Several chapters build on the strategy theme introduced in Chapter 1. Chapter 13 has a greater discussion of strategy maps as a useful tool to implement the balanced scorecard and a simplified presentation of how income statements of companies can be analyzed from the strategic perspective of product differentiation or cost leadership. We also discuss strategy considerations in the design of activity-based costing systems in Chapter 5, the preparation of budgets in Chapter 6, and decision making in Chapters 11 and 12.

Deeper Consideration of Global Issues

Business is increasingly becoming more global. Even small and medium-sized companies across the manufacturing, merchandising, and service sectors are being forced to deal with the effects of globalization. Global considerations permeate many chapters. For example, Chapter 11 discusses the benefits and the challenges that arise when outsourcing products or services outside the United States. Chapter 22 examines the importance of transfer pricing in minimizing the tax burden faced by multinational companies. Several new examples of management accounting applications in companies are drawn from international settings.

Increased Focus on the Service Sector

In keeping with the shifts in the U.S. and world economy this edition makes greater use of service sector examples. For example, Chapter 2 discusses the concepts around the measurement of costs in a software development rather than a manufacturing setting. Chapter 6 provides several examples of the use of budgets and targets in service companies. Several concepts in action boxes focus on the service sector such as activity-based costing at Charles Schwab (Chapter 5) and managing wireless data bottlenecks (Chapter 19).

New Cutting Edge Topics

The pace of change in organizations continues to be rapid. The fourteenth edition of *Cost Accounting* reflects changes occurring in the role of cost accounting in organizations.

- We have introduced foreign currency and forward contract issues in the context of outsourcing decisions.
- We have added ideas based on Six Sigma to the discussion of quality.
- We have rewritten the chapter on strategy and the balanced scorecard and simplified the presentation to connect strategy development, strategy maps, balanced scorecard, and analysis of operating income.
- We discuss current trends towards Beyond Budgeting and the use of rolling forecasts.
- We develop the link between traditional forms of cost allocation and the nascent movement in Europe towards Resource Consumption Accounting.
- We focus more sharply on how companies are simplifying their costing systems with the presentation of value streams and lean accounting.

Opening Vignettes

Each chapter opens with a vignette on a real company situation. The vignettes engage the reader in a business situation, or dilemma, illustrating why and how the concepts in the chapter are relevant in business. For example, Chapter 1 describes how Apple uses cost accounting information to make decisions relating to how they price the most popular songs on iTunes. Chapter 3 explains how the band U2 paid for their extensive new stage by lowering ticket prices. Chapter 7 describes how even the NBA was forced to cut costs after over half of the league's franchises declared losses. Chapter 11 shows how JetBlue uses Twitter and e-mail to help their customers make better pricing decisions. Chapter 12 discusses how Tata Motors designed a car for the Indian masses, priced at only $2,500. Chapter 14 shows how Best Buy boosts profits by analyzing its customers and their buying habits. Chapter 18 describes how Boeing incurred great losses as it reworked its much-anticipated Dreamliner airplane.

Concepts in Action Boxes

Found in every chapter, these boxes cover real-world cost accounting issues across a variety of industries including automobile racing, defense contracting, entertainment, manufacturing, and retailing. New examples include

- How Zipcar Helps Reduce Business Transportation Costs p. 31
- Job Costing at Cowboys Stadium p. 119
- The "Death Spiral" and the End of Landline Telephone Service p. 363
- Transfer Pricing Dispute Temporarily Stops the Flow of Fiji Water p. 944

Streamlined Presentation

We continue to try to simplify and streamline our presentation of various topics to make it as easy as possible for a student to learn the concepts, tools, and frameworks introduced in different chapters. Examples of more streamlined presentations can be found in

- Chapter 3 on the discussion of target net income
- Chapter 5 on the core issues in activity-based costing (ABC)
- Chapter 8, which uses a single comprehensive example to illustrate the use of variance analysis in ABC systems
- Chapter 13, which has a much simpler presentation of the strategic analysis of operating income
- Chapter 15, which uses a simpler, unified framework to discuss various cost-allocation methods
- Chapters 17 and 18, where the material on standard costing has been moved to the appendix, allowing for smoother transitions through the sections in the body of the chapter

Selected Chapter-by-Chapter Content Changes

Thank you for your continued support of Cost Accounting. In every new edition, we strive to update this text thoroughly. To ease your transition from the thirteenth edition, here are selected highlights of chapter changes for the fourteenth edition.

Chapter 1 has been rewritten to focus on strategy, decision-making, and learning emphasizing the managerial issues that animate modern management accounting. It now emphasizes decision making instead of problem solving, performance evaluation instead of scorekeeping and learning instead of attention directing.

Chapter 2 has been rewritten to emphasize the service sector. For example, instead of a manufacturing company context, the chapter uses the software development setting at a company like Apple Inc. to discuss cost measurement. It also develops ideas related to risk when discussing fixed versus variable costs.

Chapter 3 has been rewritten to simplify the presentation of target net income by describing how target net income can be converted to target operating income. This allows students to use the equations already developed for target operating income when discussing target net income. We deleted the section on multiple cost drivers, because it is closely related to the multi-product example discussed in the chapter. The managerial and decision-making aspects of the chapter have also been strengthened.

Chapter 4 has been reorganized to first discuss normal costing and then actual costing because normal costing is much more prevalent in practice. As a result of this change the exhibits in the early part of the chapter tie in more closely to the detailed exhibits of normal job-costing systems in manufacturing later in the chapter. The presentation of actual costing has been retained to help students understand the benefits and challenges of actual costing systems. To focus on job costing, we moved the discussion of responsibility centers and departments to Chapter 6.

Chapter 5 has been reorganized to clearly distinguish design choices, implementation challenges, and managerial applications of ABC systems. The presentation of the ideas has been simplified and streamlined to focus on the core issues.

Chapter 6 now includes ideas from relevant applied research on the usefulness of budgets and the circumstances in which they add the greatest value, as well as the challenges in administering them. It incorporates new material on the Beyond Budgeting movement, and in particular the trend towards the use of rolling forecasts.

Chapters 7 and 8 present a streamlined discussion of direct-cost and overhead variances, respectively. The separate sections on ABC and variance analysis in Chapters 7 and 8 have now been combined into a single integrated example at the end of Chapter 8. A new appendix to Chapter 7 now addresses more detailed revenue variances using the existing Webb Company example. The use of potentially confusing terms such as 2-variance analysis and 1-variance analysis has been eliminated.

We have rewritten Chapter 9 as a single integrated chapter with the same running example rather than as two distinct sub-parts on inventory costing and capacity analysis. The material on the tax and financial reporting implications of various capacity concepts has also been fully revised.

Chapter 10 has been revised to provide a more linear progression through the ideas of cost estimation and the choice of cost drivers, culminating in the use of quantitative analysis (regression analysis, in particular) for managerial decision-making.

Chapter 11 now includes more discussion of global issues such as foreign currency considerations in international outsourcing decisions. There is also greater emphasis on strategy and decision-making.

Chapter 12 has been reorganized to more sharply delineate short-run from long-run costing and pricing and to bring together the various considerations other than costs that affect pricing decisions. This reorganization has helped streamline several sections in the chapter.

Chapter 13 has been substantially rewritten. Strategy maps are presented as a way to link strategic objectives and as a useful first step in developing balanced scorecard measures. The section on strategic analysis of operating income has been significantly simplified by focusing on only one indirect cost and eliminating most of the technical details. Finally, the section on engineered and discretionary costs has been considerably shortened to focus on only the key ideas.

Chapter 14 now discusses the use of "whale curves" to depict the outcome of customer profitability analysis. The last part of the chapter has been rationalized to focus on the decomposition of sales volume variances into quantity and mix variances; and the calculation of sales mix variances has also been simplified.

Chapter 15 has been completely revised and uses a simple, unified conceptual framework to discuss various cost allocation methods (single-rate versus dual-rate, actual costs versus budgeted costs, etc.).

Chapter 16 now provides a more in-depth discussion of the rationale underlying joint cost allocation as well as the reasons why some firms *do not* allocate costs (along with real-world examples).

Chapters 17 and 18 have been reorganized, with the material on standard costing moved to the appendix in both chapters. This reorganization has made the chapters easier to navigate and fully consistent (since all sections in the body of the chapter now use actual costing). The material on multiple inspection points from the appendix to Chapter 18 has been moved into the body of the chapter, but using a variant of the existing example involving Anzio Corp.

Chapter 19 introduces the idea of Six Sigma quality. It also integrates design quality, conformance quality, and financial and nonfinancial measures of quality. The discussion of queues, delays, and costs of time has been significantly streamlined.

Chapter 20's discussion of EOQ has been substantially revised and the ideas of lean accounting further developed. The section on backflush costing has been completely rewritten.

Chapter 21 has been revised to incorporate the payback period method with discounting, and also now includes survey evidence on the use of various capital budgeting methods. The discussion of goal congruence and performance measurement has been simplified and combined, making the latter half of the chapter easier to follow.

Chapter 22 has been fully rewritten with a new section on the use of hybrid pricing methods. The chapter also now includes a fuller description (and a variety of examples) of the use of transfer pricing for tax minimization, and incorporates such developments as the recent tax changes proposed by the Obama administration.

Chapter 23 includes a more thorough description of Residual Income and EVA, as well as a more streamlined discussion of the various choices of accounting-based performance measures.

Resources

In addition to this textbook and MyAccountingLab, the following resources are available for students:

- Student Study Guide—self study aid full of review features.
- Student Solutions Manual—solutions and assistance for even numbered problems.
- Excel Manual—workbook designed for Excel practice.
- Companion website—www.pearsonhighered.com/horngren.

The following resources are available for Instructors:

- Solutions Manual
- Test Gen
- Instructors Manual
- PowerPoint Presentations
- Image Library
- Instructors Resource Center—www.pearsonhighered.com/horngren

Acknowledgments

We are indebted to many people for their ideas and assistance. Our primary thanks go to the many academics and practitioners who have advanced our knowledge of cost accounting. The package of teaching materials we present is the work of skillful and valued team members developing some excellent end-of-chapter assignment material. Tommy Goodwin, Ian Gow (Northwestern), Richard Saouma (UCLA) and Shalin Shah (Berkeley) provided outstanding research assistance on technical issues and current developments. We would also like to thank the dedicated and hard working supplement author team and GEX Publishing Services. The book is much better because of the efforts of these colleagues.

In shaping this edition, we would like to thank a group of colleagues who worked closely with us and the editorial team. This group provided detailed feedback and participated in focus groups that guided the direction of this edition:

Wagdy Abdallah
Seton Hall University

David Alldredge
Salt Lake Community College

Felicia Baldwin
Richard J. Daley College

Molly Brown
James Madison University

Shannon Charles
Brigham Young University

David Franz
San Francisco State University

Anna Jensen
Indiana University

Donna McGovern
Custom Business Results, Inc.

Cindy Nye
Bellevue University

Glenn Pate
Florida Atlantic University

Kelly Pope
DePaul University

Jenice Prather-Kinsey
University of Missouri

Melvin Roush
Pitt State University

Karen Shastri
Pitt University

Frank Stangota
Rutgers University

Patrick Stegman
College of Lake County

We would also like to extend our thanks to those professors who provided detailed written reviews or comments on drafts. These professors include the following:

Robyn Alcock
Central Queensland University

David S. Baglia
Grove City College

Charles Bailey
University of Central Florida

Robert Bauman
Allan Hancock Joint Community College

David Bilker
University of Maryland, University College

Marvin Bouillon
Iowa State University

Dennis Caplan
Columbia University

Donald W. Gribbin
Southern Illinois University

Rosalie Hallbauer
Florida International University

John Haverty
St. Joseph's University

Jean Hawkins
William Jewell College

Rodger Holland
Francis Marion University

Jiunn C. Huang
San Francisco State University

Zafar U. Khan
Eastern Michigan University

Larry N. Killough
Virginia Polytechnic Institute & State University

Keith Kramer
Southern Oregon University

Jay Law
Central Washington University

Sandra Lazzarini
University of Queensland

Gary J. Mann
University of Texas at El Paso

Ronald Marshall
Michigan State University

Maureen Mascha
Marquette University

Pam Meyer
University of Louisiana at Lafayette

Marjorie Platt
Northeastern University

Roy W. Regel
University of Montana

Pradyot K. Sen
University of Cincinnati

Gim S. Seow
University of Connecticut

Rebekah A. Sheely
Northeastern University

Robert J. Shepherd
University of California, Santa Cruz

Kenneth Sinclair
Lehigh University

Vic Stanton
California State University, Hayward

Carolyn Streuly
Marquette University

Gerald Thalmann
North Central College

Peter D. Woodlock
Youngstown State University

James Williamson
San Diego State University

Sung-Soo Yoon
UCLA at Los Angeles

Jennifer Dosch
Metro State University

Joe Dowd
Eastern Washington University

Leslie Kren
University of Wisconsin-Madison

Michele Matherly
Xavier University

Laurie Burney
Mississippi State University

Mike Morris
Notre Dame University

Cinthia Nye
Bellevue University

Roy Regel
University of Montana

Margaret Shackell-Dowel
Notre Dame University

Marvin Bouillon
Iowa State University

Kreag Danvers
Clarion University of Pennsylvania

A.J. Cataldo II
West Chester University

Kenneth Danko
San Francisco State University

T.S. Amer
Northern Arizona University

Robert Hartman
University of Iowa

Diane Satin
California State University East Bay

John Stancil
Florida Southern College

Michael Flores
Wichita University

Ralph Greenberg
Temple University

Paul Warrick
Westwood College

Karen Schoenebeck
Southwestern College

Thomas D. Fields
Washington University in St. Louis

Constance Hylton
George Mason University

Robert Alford
DePaul University

Michael Eames
Santa Clara University

We also would like to thank our colleagues who helped us greatly by accuracy checking the text and supplements including Molly Brown, Barbara Durham, and Anna Jensen.

We thank the people at Prentice Hall for their hard work and dedication, including Donna Battista, Stephanie Wall, Christina Rumbaugh, Brian Reilly, Cindy Zonneveld, Lynne Breitfeller, Natacha Moore, and Kate Thomas and Kelly Morrison at GEX Publishing Services. We must extend special thanks to Deepa Chungi, the development editor on this edition, who took charge of this project and directed it across the finish line. This book would not have been possible without her dedication and skill.

Alexandra Gural, Jacqueline Archer, and others expertly managed the production aspects of all the manuscript preparation with superb skill and tremendous dedication. We are deeply appreciative of their good spirits, loyalty, and ability to stay calm in the most hectic of times. The constant support of Bianca Baggio and Caroline Roop is greatly appreciated.

Appreciation also goes to the American Institute of Certified Public Accountants, the Institute of Management Accountants, the Society of Management Accountants of Canada, the Certified General Accountants Association of Canada, the Financial Executive Institute of America, and many other publishers and companies for their generous permission to quote from their publications. Problems from the Uniform CPA examinations are designated (CPA); problems from the Certified Management Accountant examination are designated (CMA); problems from the Canadian examinations administered by the Society of Management Accountants are designated (SMA); and problems from the Certified General Accountants Association are designated (CGA). Many of these problems are adapted to highlight particular points.

We are grateful to the professors who contributed assignment material for this edition. Their names are indicated in parentheses at the start of their specific problems. Comments from users are welcome.

CHARLES T. HORNGREN
SRIKANT M. DATAR
MADHAV V. RAJAN

To Our Families

The Horngren Family (CH)

Swati, Radhika, Gayatri, Sidharth (SD)

Gayathri, Sanjana, Anupama (MVR)

1 The Manager and Management Accounting

Learning Objectives

1. Distinguish financial accounting from management accounting
2. Understand how management accountants affect strategic decisions
3. Describe the set of business functions in the value chain and identify the dimensions of performance that customers are expecting of companies
4. Explain the five-step decision-making process and its role in management accounting
5. Describe three guidelines management accountants follow in supporting managers
6. Understand how management accounting fits into an organization's structure
7. Understand what professional ethics mean to management accountants

All businesses are concerned about costs. Whether their products are automobiles, fast food, or the latest designer fashions, managers must understand the cost behavior of their operations or risk losing control. Managers use cost accounting information to make decisions—including decisions related to strategy formulation, research and development, budgeting, production planning, and pricing, among others. Sometimes these decisions involve tradeoffs. The following article shows how companies like Xerox make those tradeoffs to increase their profits.

iTunes Variable Pricing: Downloads Are Down, but Profits Are Up[1]

Can selling less of something be more profitable than selling more of it? In 2009, Apple changed the pricing structure for songs sold through iTunes from a flat fee of $0.99 to a three-tier price point system of $0.69, $0.99, and $1.29. The top 200 songs in any given week make up more than one-sixth of digital music sales. Apple now charges the higher price of $1.29 for these hit songs by artists like Taylor Swift and the Black Eyed Peas.

After the first six months of the new pricing model in the iTunes store, downloads of the top 200 tracks were down by about 6%.While the number of downloads dropped, the higher prices generated more revenue than before the new pricing structure was in place. Since Apple's iTunes costs—wholesale song costs, network and transaction fees, and other operating costs—do not vary based on the price of each download, the profits from the 30% increase in price more than made up for the losses from the 6% decrease in volume.

To increase profits beyond those created by higher prices, Apple also began to manage iTunes' costs. Transaction costs (what Apple pays credit-card processors like Visa and MasterCard) have

---

[1] *Sources:* Bruno, Anthony and Glenn Peoples. 2009. Variable iTunes pricing a moneymaker for artists. *Reuters*, June 21. http://www.reuters.com/article/idUSTRE55K0DJ20090621; Peoples, Glenn. 2009. The long tale? *Billboard,* November 14. http://www.billboard.biz/bbbiz/content_display/magazine/features/e3i35ed869fbd929ccdcca52ed7fd9262d3?imw=Y; Savitz, Eric. 2007. Apple: Turns out, iTunes makes money Pacific Crest says; subscription services seems inevitable. *Barron's* "Tech Trader Daily" blog, April 23. http://blogs.barrons.com/techtraderdaily/2007/04/23/apple-turns-out-itunes-makes-money-pacific-crest-says-subscription-service-seems-inevitable/

decreased, and Apple has also reduced the number of people working in the iTunes store.

The study of modern cost accounting yields insights into how managers and accountants can contribute to operations. It also prepares them for leadership roles. Many large companies, such as Teva Sport Sandals, Sony Pictures, and Nike, have senior executives with accounting backgrounds.

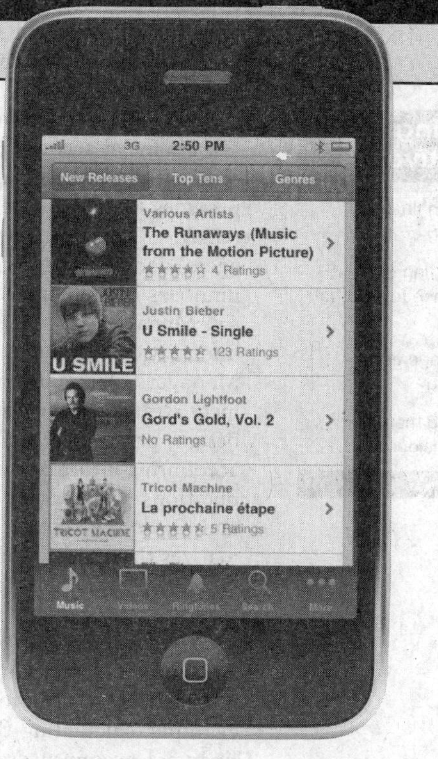

Management Accounting, Financial Accounting, and Cost Accounting

As many of you have already seen in your financial accounting class, accounting systems take economic events and transactions, such as sales and materials purchases, and process the data into information helpful to managers, sales representatives, production supervisors, and others. Processing any economic transaction means collecting, categorizing, summarizing, and analyzing. For example, costs are collected by category, such as materials, labor, and shipping. These costs are then summarized to determine total costs by month, quarter, or year. The results are analyzed to evaluate, say, how costs have changed relative to revenues from one period to the next. Accounting systems provide the information found in the income statement, the balance sheet, and the statement of cash flow and in performance reports, such as the cost of operating a plant or of providing a service. Managers use accounting information to administer the activities, businesses, or functional areas they oversee and to coordinate those activities, businesses, or functions within the framework of the organization. This book focuses on how accounting assists managers in these tasks.

Individual managers often require the information in an accounting system to be presented or reported differently. Consider, for example, sales order information. A sales manager may be interested in the total rupee amount of sales to determine the commissions to be paid. A distribution manager may be interested in the sales order quantities by geographic region and by customer-requested delivery dates to ensure timely deliveries. A manufacturing manager, to schedule production, may be interested in the quantities of various products and their desired delivery dates. An ideal database—sometimes called a data warehouse or infobarn—consists of small, detailed bits of information that can be used for multiple purposes. For instance, the sales order database will contain detailed information about product, quantity ordered, selling price, and delivery details (place and date) for each sales order. The database stores information in a way that allows managers to access the information they need. Many companies are building their own Enterprise Resource Planning (ERP) systems, single databases that collect data and feed it into applications that support the company's business activities, such as purchasing, production, distribution, and sales.

Learning Objective 1

Distinguish financial accounting

.... reporting on past performance to external users

from management accounting

... helping managers make decisions

Financial accounting and management accounting have different goals.

Financial accounting focuses on reporting to external parties such as investors, government agencies, banks, and suppliers. It measures and records business transactions and provides financial statements that are based on generally accepted accounting principles (GAAP). The most important way that financial accounting information affects managers' decisions and actions is through compensation, which is often, in part, based on numbers in financial statements.

Management accounting measures, analyzes, and reports financial and nonfinancial information that helps managers make decisions to fulfill the goals of an organization. Managers use management accounting information to choose, communicate, and implement strategy. They also use management accounting information to coordinate product design, production, and marketing decisions and to evaluate performance. Management accounting information and reports do not have to follow set principles or rules. The key questions are always (1) How will this information help managers do their jobs better, and (2) do the benefits of producing this information exceed the costs? Exhibit 1-1 summarizes the major differences between management accounting and financial accounting. Note, however, that reports such as balance sheets, income statements, and statements of cash flows are common to both management accounting and financial accounting.

Cost accounting provides information for management accounting and financial accounting. **Cost accounting** measures, analyzes, and reports financial and nonfinancial information relating to the costs of acquiring or using resources in an organization. For example, calculating the cost of a product is a cost accounting function that answers financial accounting's inventory-valuation needs and management accounting's decision-making needs (such as choosing which products to offer). Modern cost accounting

Exhibit 1-1

Major Differences Between Management Accounting and Financial Accounting

	Management Accounting	Financial Accounting
Purpose of information	Help managers make decisions to fulfill an organization's goals	Communicate organization's financial position to investors, banks, regulators, and other outside parties
Primary users	Managers of the organization	External users such as investors, banks, regulators, and suppliers
Focus and emphasis	Future-oriented (budget for 2008 prepared in 2007)	Past-oriented (reports on 2007 performance prepared in 2008)
Rules of measurement and reporting	Internal measures and reports do not have to follow GAAP but are based on cost-benefit analysis	Financial statements must be prepared in accordance with GAAP and be certified by external, independent auditors
Time span and type of reports	Varies from hourly information to 15 to 20 years, with financial and nonfinancial reports on products, departments, territories, and strategies	Annual and quarterly financial reports, primarily on the company as a whole
Behavioral implications	Designed to influence the behavior of managers and other employees	Primarily reports economic events but also influences behavior because manager's compensation is often based on reported financial results

takes the perspective that collecting cost information is a function of the management decisions being made. Thus, the distinction between management accounting and cost accounting is not so clear-cut, and we often use these terms interchangeably in the book.

We frequently hear business people use the term *cost management*. Unfortunately, that term has no uniform definition. We use **cost management** to describe the approaches and activities of managers to use resources to increase value to customers and to achieve organizational goals. Cost management decisions include decisions such as the amounts and kinds of materials used, changes in plant processes, and changes in product designs. Information from accounting systems helps managers to manage costs, but the information and the accounting systems themselves are not cost management.

Cost management has a broad focus and should not be interpreted to mean only continuous reduction in costs. Cost management is inextricably linked with revenue and profit planning. As part of cost management, managers often deliberately incur additional costs, for example in advertising and product modifications, to enhance revenues and profits.

Strategic Decisions and the Management Accountant

Learning Objective 2

Understand how management accountants affect strategic decisions

. . . they provide information about competitive advantages and resources

Strategy specifies how an organization matches its own capabilities with the opportunities in the marketplace to accomplish its objectives. In other words, strategy describes how an organization will compete and the opportunities its managers should seek and pursue. Businesses follow one of two broad strategies. Some companies, such as Deccan Airlines and Vanguard (the mutual fund company), have been profitable and have grown over the years on the basis of providing quality products or services at low prices. Other companies such as Pfizer, the pharmaceutical giant, generate their profits and growth on the basis of their ability to offer differentiated or unique products or services that are often priced higher than the products or services of their competitors.

Deciding between these strategies is a critical part of what managers do. Management accountants work closely with managers in formulating strategy by providing information about the sources of competitive advantage—for example, the cost, productivity, or efficiency advantage of their company relative to competitors or the premium prices a company can charge relative to the costs of adding features that make its products or services distinctive. **Strategic cost management** describes cost management that specifically focuses on strategic issues.

Management accountants help formulate strategy by helping managers answer questions such as:

- Who are our most important customers, and how do we deliver value to them? For example, after Amazon.com's success in selling books online, Barnes and Noble developed the capabilities to sell online by building its information and technology infrastructure. Toyota has built flexible computer-integrated manufacturing (CIM) plants that enable it to use the same equipment to produce a variety of cars in response to changing customer tastes.
- What substitute products exist in the marketplace, and how do they differ from our product in terms of price and quality? For example, Hewlett-Packard designs new printers after comparing the functionality, quality, and price of its printers to other printers available in the marketplace.
- What is our most critical capability? Is it technology, production, or marketing? How can we leverage it for new strategic initiatives? Kellogg Company, for example, uses the reputation of its brand to introduce new types of cereal.
- Will adequate cash be available to fund the strategy, or will additional funds need to be raised? Proctor & Gamble, for example, issued new debt and equity to fund its strategic acquisition of Gillette, a maker of shaving products.

The best-designed strategies and the best-developed capabilities are useless unless they are effectively executed. In the next section, we describe actions managers take to create value for their customers and how management accountants help them do it.

Value Chain and Supply Chain Analysis and Key Success Factors

Customers demand from companies much more than a fair price. They expect a quality product or service delivered in a timely way. These multiple factors drive how a customer experiences a product or service and the value or usefulness a customer derives from the product or service. How then does a company go about creating this value?

Value-Chain Analysis

Learning Objective 3

Describe the set of business functions in the value chain and identify the dimensions of performance that customers are expecting of companies

. . . R&D, design, production, marketing, distribution, and customer service to achieve cost and efficiency, quality, time, and innovation

Value chain is the sequence of business functions in which customer usefulness is added to products or services. Exhibit 1-2 shows six business functions: R&D, design, production, marketing, distribution, and customer service. We illustrate these business functions using SONY Corporation's television division.

1. **Research and development**—Generating and experimenting with ideas related to new products, services, or processes. At SONY, this function includes research on alternative television signal transmission (analog, digital, high-definition) and on the clarity of different shapes and thicknesses of television screens.
2. **Design of products, services, or processes**—Detailed planning and engineering of products, services, or processes. Design at Sony includes determining the number of component parts in a television set and the effect of alternative product designs on quality and manufacturing costs.
3. **Production**—Acquiring, coordinating, and assembling resources to produce a product or deliver a service. Production of a SONY television set includes the acquisition and assembly of the electronic parts, the cabinet, and the packaging used for shipping.
4. **Marketing**—Promoting and selling products or services to customers or prospective customers. SONY markets its televisions through trade shows, advertisements in newspapers and magazines, and on the Internet.
5. **Distribution**—Delivering products or services to customers. Distribution for SONY includes shipping to retail outlets, catalog vendors, direct sales via the Internet, and other channels through which customers purchase televisions.
6. **Customer service**—Providing after-sale support to customers. SONY provides customer service on its televisions in the form of customer-help telephone lines, support on the Internet, and warranty repair work.

In addition to the six primary business functions, Exhibit 1-2 shows an administrative function, which includes functions such as accounting and finance, human resource management, and information technology, that support the six primary business functions. When discussing the value chain in subsequent chapters of the book, we include the administrative support function within the primary functions. For example, included in the marketing function is the function of analyzing, reporting, and accounting for resources spent in different marketing channels, while the production function includes the human resource management function of training front-line workers.

Each of these business functions is essential to SONY satisfying its customers and keeping them satisfied (and loyal) over time. Companies use the term *customer relationship management (CRM)* to describe a strategy that integrates people and technology in all business functions to enhance relationships with customers, partners, and distributors. CRM initiatives use technology to coordinate all customer-facing activities (such as marketing, sales

Exhibit 1-2 Different Parts of the Value Chain

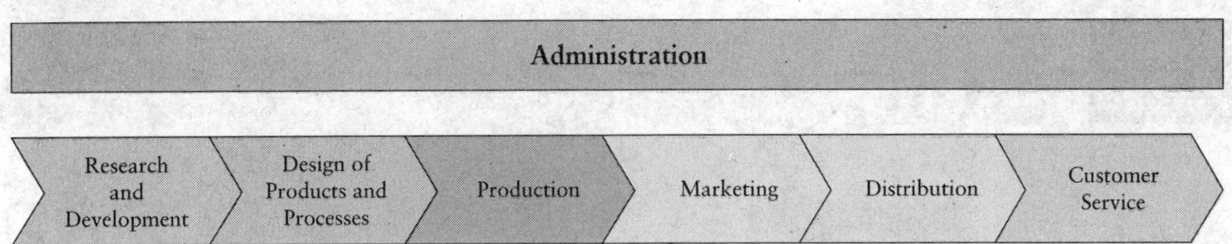

calls, distribution, and postsales support) and the design and production activities necessary to get products to customers.

Exhibit 1-2 depicts the usual order in which different business-function activities physically occur. Do not, however, interpret Exhibit 1-2 as implying that managers should proceed sequentially through the value chain when planning and managing their activities. Companies gain (in terms of cost, quality, and the speed with which new products are developed) if two or more of the individual business functions of the value chain work concurrently as a team. For example, inputs into design decisions by production, marketing, distribution, and customer service managers often lead to design choices that reduce total costs of the company.

Managers track the costs incurred in each value-chain category. Their goal is to reduce costs in each category and to improve efficiency. Cost information also helps managers make cost-benefit tradeoffs. For example, is it cheaper to buy products from outside vendors or to do manufacturing in-house? How does investing resources in design and manufacturing reduce costs of marketing and customer service?

Supply-Chain Analysis

Companies can also implement strategy, cut costs, and create value by enhancing their supply chain. The term **supply chain** describes the flow of goods, services, and information from the initial sources of materials and services to the delivery of products to consumers, regardless of whether those activities occur in the same organization or in other organizations. Consider the soft drinks Coke and Pepsi. Many companies play a role in bringing these products to consumers. Exhibit 1-3 presents an overview of the supply chain. Cost management emphasizes integrating and coordinating activities across all companies in the supply chain, as well as across each business function in an individual company's value chain, to reduce costs. For example, both Coca-Cola Company and Pepsi Bottling Group contract with their suppliers (such as plastic and aluminum companies and sugar refiners) to frequently deliver small quantities of materials directly to the production floor to reduce materials-handling costs. Consider another example: To reduce inventory levels in the supply chain, Reliance Fresh is asking its suppliers such as Coca-Cola to be responsible for and to manage inventory at both the Coca-Cola warehouse and Reliance Fresh.

Key Success Factors

Customers want companies to use the value chain and supply chain to deliver ever improving levels of performance regarding several (or even all) of the following:

- **Cost and efficiency**—Companies face continuous pressure to reduce the cost of the products or services they sell. To calculate and manage the cost of products, the management accountant tries to understand the tasks or activities (such as setting up machines or distributing products) that cause costs to arise. Managers monitor the marketplace to determine prices that customers are willing to pay for products or services. Management accountants calculate a target cost for a product by subtracting the operating income per unit of product that the company thinks it can earn from the "target price." Managers work with management accountants to achieve the target

Exhibit 1-3 Supply Chain for a Cola Bottling Company

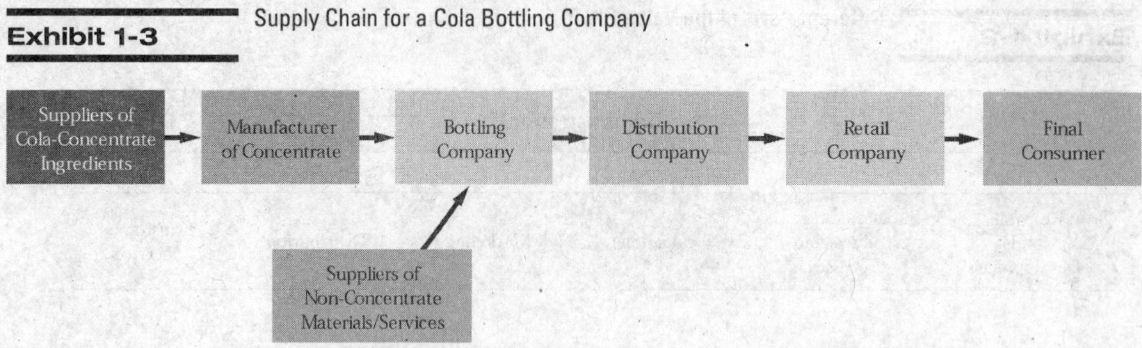

cost by eliminating some activities (such as rework) and by reducing the costs of performing activities in all value-chain functions—from initial R&D to customer service.

Increased global competition is placing even more pressure on companies to lower costs. U.S. companies are cutting costs by outsourcing some of their business functions. Nike, for example, has moved its manufacturing operations to China and Mexico. Citigroup and America Online are increasingly doing their software development in Spain, Eastern Europe, and India.

- **Quality**—Customers expect high levels of quality. Total quality management (TQM) is a philosophy in which management improves operations throughout the value chain to deliver products and services that exceed customer expectations. TQM encompasses designing the product or service to meet the needs and wants of customers, as well as making products with zero (or minimal) defects and waste and with low inventories. Management accountants evaluate the costs and revenue benefits of TQM initiatives.
- **Time**—Time has many components. New-product development time is the time it takes for new products to be created and brought to market. The increasing pace of technological innovation has led to shorter product life cycles and the need for companies to bring new products to market more rapidly. The management accountant measures the costs and benefits of a product over its life cycle.

  Customer-response time describes the speed at which an organization responds to customer requests. To increase customer satisfaction, organizations must complete activities faster and meet promised delivery dates reliably. Delays or bottlenecks occur when the work to be performed exceeds the available capacity. To increase output in these situations, managers need to increase the capacity of the bottleneck operation. The management accountant's role is to quantify the costs and benefits of relieving the bottleneck constraints.
- **Innovation**—A constant flow of innovative products or services is the basis for ongoing company success. The management accountant helps managers evaluate alternative investment decisions and R&D decisions.

Companies are increasingly applying the key success factors of cost and efficiency, quality, time, and innovation to promote sustainability—the development and implementation of strategies to achieve long-term financial, social, and environmental performance. For example, the Japanese copier company Ricoh's sustainability efforts aggressively focus on energy conservation, resource conservation, product recycling, and pollution prevention. By designing products that can be easily recycled, Ricoh simultaneously improves efficiency, cost, and quality. Interest in sustainability appears to be intensifying. Already, government regulations, in countries such as China and India, are impelling companies to develop and report on their sustainability initiatives.

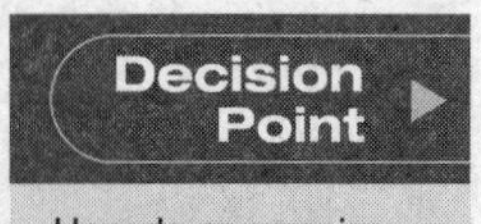

How do companies add value, and what are the dimensions of performance that customers are expecting of companies?

Management accountants help managers track performance on the chosen key success factors relative to the performance of competitors on the same factors. Tracking what is happening in other companies serves as a *benchmark* and alerts managers to the changes their own customers are observing and evaluating. The goal is for a company to *continuously improve* its critical operations—for example, on-time arrival for Deccan

Airlines, customer access for online auctions at eBay, and cost reduction at Tata Electric. Sometimes more-fundamental changes in operations—such as redesigning a manufacturing process to reduce costs—may be necessary. However, successful strategy implementation requires more than value-chain and supply-chain analysis and execution of key success factors. It is the decisions that managers make that help them to develop, integrate, and implement their strategies.

Decision Making, Planning, and Control: The Five-Step Decision-Making Process

We illustrate the five-step decision-making process using the example of the *Daily News*, a newspaper in Mumbai. In subsequent chapters of the book, we describe how managers use this five-step decision-making process to make a variety of decisions.

The *Daily News* has a strategy to differentiate itself from its competitors by focusing on in-depth analyses of news by its highly rated journalists, using color to enhance attractiveness to readers and advertisers, and developing its Web site to deliver up-to-the-minute news, interviews, and analyses. It has substantial capabilities to deliver on this strategy. It owns an automated, computer-integrated, state-of-the-art printing facility and has developed a Web-based information technology infrastructure. Its distribution network is one of the best in the newspaper industry.

A key challenge for Anita Guha, the manager of the *Daily News*, is to increase revenues. To decide what she should do, Anita works through the five-step decision-making process.

Learning Objective 4

Explain the five-step decision-making process and its role in management accounting

. . . identify the problem and uncertainties, obtain information, make predictions about the future, make decisions by choosing among alternatives, and implement the decision, evaluate performance and learn to do planning and control

1. **Identify the problem and uncertainties.** Anita has two main choices:
   a. Increase the selling price per newspaper, or
   b. Increase the rate per page charged to advertisers.

   The key uncertainty is the effect on demand of any increase in price or rates. A decrease in demand could offset any increase in prices or rates and lead to lower overall revenues.
2. **Obtain information.** Gathering information before making a decision helps managers get a better handle on the uncertainties. Anita asks her marketing manager to talk to some representative readers to gauge how they might react to an increase in the newspaper's selling price. She asks her advertising sales manager to talk to current and potential advertisers to get a better understanding of the advertising market. She also reviews the effect that past price increases had on readership. Amit Choksi, the management accountant at the *Daily News*, provides information about past increases or decreases in advertising rates and the subsequent changes in advertising revenues. He also collects and analyzes information on advertising rates charged by competing media outlets, including other newspapers.
3. **Make predictions about the future.** On the basis of information she has obtained, Anita makes predictions about the future. She concludes that readers would be quite upset if she increased prices and is fairly certain that it would lead to a decrease in readership. She has a different view when it comes to advertising rates. She anticipates a marketwide increase in advertising rates and therefore believes that increasing these rates will have little effect on the number of pages of advertising sold.

   Anita recognizes that making predictions requires considerable judgment. She carefully evaluates any biases that she might have. Has she correctly judged readers' sentiment or has her thinking been overly influenced by anticipation of all the negative publicity she would get rather than an actual decline in readership? How sure is she that her competitors will increase advertising rates? Is her thinking in this regard biased by their past actions? Have circumstances changed? How confident is she that her sales representatives can convince advertisers to pay higher rates? Anita retests her assumptions and reviews her thinking. She feels comfortable with her predictions and judgments.

4. **Make decisions by choosing among alternatives.** When making decisions, strategy is a vital guidepost; many individuals in different parts of the organization at different times make decisions. Consistency with strategy binds individuals and timelines together and provides a common purpose for disparate decisions. Aligning decisions with strategy enables an organization to implement its strategy and achieve its goals. Without this alignment, decisions will be uncoordinated, pull the organization in different directions, and produce inconsistent results.

Steps 1 through 4 are collectively referred to as *planning*. **Planning** comprises selecting organization goals, predicting results under various alternative ways of achieving those goals, deciding how to attain the desired goals, and communicating the goals and how to attain them to the entire organization. Management accountants serve as business partners in these planning activities because of their understanding of what creates value and the key success factors.

The most important planning tool is a budget. A **budget** is the quantitative expression of a proposed plan of action by management and is an aid to coordinating what needs to be done to implement that plan. For March 2011, budgeted advertising revenues equal Rs 4,16,00,000. The full budget for March 2011 will include budgeted circulation revenue and the production, distribution, and customer-service costs that would be needed to achieve sales goals; the anticipated cash flows; and the potential financing needs. Because the process of preparing a budget crosses business functions, it forces coordination and communication throughout the company, as well as with the company's suppliers and customers.

5. **Implement the decision, evaluate performance, and learn.** Managers at the *Daily News* take actions to implement the March 2011 budget. Management accountants collect information to follow through on how actual performance compares to planned or budgeted performance (also referred to as scorekeeping). This information is very different from the *predecision* planning information Anita collected in Step 2 to enable her to better understand uncertainties, to make predictions, and to make a decision. The comparison of actual performance to budgeted performance is the *control* or *postdecision* role of information. **Control** comprises taking actions that implement the planning decisions, deciding how to evaluate performance, and providing feedback and learning to help future decision making.

   Measuring actual performance informs managers how well they and their subunits are doing. Linking rewards to performance helps motivate managers. These rewards are both intrinsic (self-satisfaction for a job well done) and extrinsic (salary, bonuses, and promotions linked to performance). A budget serves as much as a control tool as a planning tool. Why? Because a budget is a benchmark against which actual performance can be compared.

Consider performance evaluation at the *Daily News*. During March 2011, the newspaper sold advertising, issued invoices, and received payments. These invoices and receipts were recorded in the accounting system. Exhibit 1-4 shows the *Daily News*'s performance report of advertising revenues for March 2011. This report indicates that 760 pages of advertising (40 pages fewer than the budgeted 800 pages) were sold. The average rate per page was Rs 50,800, compared with the budgeted Rs 52,200 rate, yielding actual advertising revenues of Rs 3,86,08,000. The actual advertising revenues were Rs 29,92,000 less than the budgeted Rs 4,16,00,000. Observe how managers use both financial and nonfinancial information, such as pages of advertising, to evaluate performance.

Exhibit 1-4

Performance Report of Advertising Revenues at the *Daily News* for March 2011

	Actual Result (1)	Budgeted Amount (2)	Difference: (Actual Result – Budgeted Amount) (3) = (1) – (2)	Difference as a Percentage of Budgeted Amount (4) = (3) ÷ (2)
Advertising pages sold	760 pages	800 pages	40 pages Unfavorable	5.0% Unfavorable
Average rate per page	Rs 50,800	Rs 52,000	Rs 1, 200 Unfavorable	2.3% Unfavorable
Advertising revenues	Rs 3,86,08,000	Rs 4,16,00,000	Rs 29,92,000 Unfavorable	7.2% Unfavorable

The performance report in Exhibit 1-4 spurs investigation and learning. **Learning** is examining past performance (the control function) and systematically exploring alternative ways to make better-informed decisions and plans in the future. Learning can lead to changes in goals, changes in the ways decision alternatives are identified, changes in the range of information collected when making predictions, and sometimes changes in managers.

The performance report in Exhibit 1-4 would prompt the management accountant to raise several questions directing the attention of managers to problems and opportunities. Did the marketing and sales department make sufficient efforts to convince advertisers that, even with the new higher rate of Rs 52,000 per page, advertising in the *Daily News* was a good buy? Why was the actual average rate per page Rs 50,800 instead of the budgeted rate of Rs 52,000? Did some sales representatives offer discounted rates? Did economic conditions cause the decline in advertising revenues? Are revenues falling because editorial and production standards have declined? Answers to these questions could prompt the newspaper's publisher to take subsequent actions, including, for example, adding more sales personnel or making changes in editorial policy. Good implementation requires the marketing, editorial, and production departments to coordinate their actions.

The management accountant could go further by identifying the specific advertisers that cut back or stopped advertising after the rate increase went into effect. Managers could then decide when and how sales representatives should follow-up with these advertisers.

The left side of Exhibit 1-5 provides an overview of the decision-making processes at the *Daily News*. The right side of the exhibit highlights how the management accounting system aids in decision making.

Exhibit 1-5

How Accounting Aids Decision Making, Planning, and Control at the *Daily News*

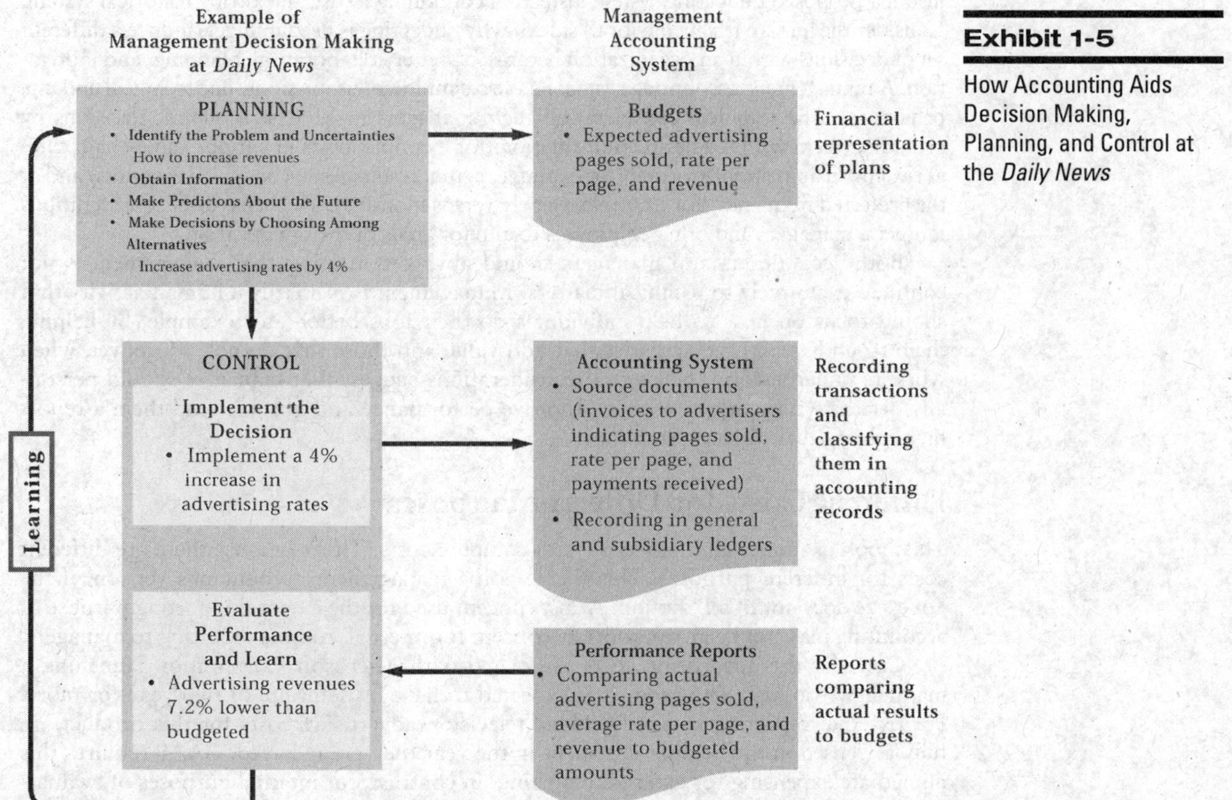

Key Management Accounting Guidelines

Three guidelines help management accountants provide the most value to their companies in strategic and operational decision making: Employ a cost-benefit approach, give full recognition to behavioral considerations as well as technical considerations, and use different costs for different purposes.

Cost-Benefit Approach

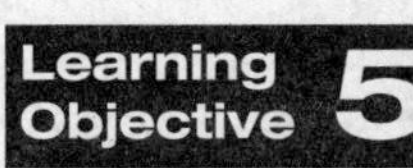

Describe three guidelines management accountants follow in supporting managers

. . . employing a cost-benefit approach, recognizing behavioral as well as technical considerations, and calculating different costs for different purposes

Management accountants continually face resource-allocation decisions, such as whether to purchase a new software package or hire a new employee. The **cost-benefit approach** should be used in making these decisions: Resources should be spent if the expected benefits to the company exceed the expected costs. The expected benefits and costs may not be easy to quantify. Nevertheless, the cost-benefit approach is useful for making resource-allocation decisions.

Consider the installation of a company's first budgeting system. Previously, the company used historical recordkeeping and little formal planning. A major benefit of installing a budgeting system is that it compels managers to plan ahead, compare actual to budgeted information, and take corrective action. These actions lead to different decisions that improve performance relative to decisions that would have been made using the historical system, but the benefits are not easy to measure. On the cost side, some costs, such as investments in software and training are easier to quantify. Others, such as the time spent by managers on the budgeting process, are harder to quantify. Regardless, senior managers compare expected benefits and expected costs, exercise judgment, and reach a decision, in this case to install the budgeting system.

Behavioral and Technical Considerations

The cost-benefit approach is the criterion that assists managers in deciding whether, say, to install a proposed budgeting system instead of continuing to use an existing historical system. Consider the human (the behavioral) side of why budgeting is used. Budgets induce a different set of decisions within an organization because of better collaboration, planning, and motivation. A management accounting system has two simultaneous missions, one technical and one behavioral. The technical considerations help managers make wise economic decisions by providing them with the desired information (for example, costs in various value-chain categories) in an appropriate format (for example, actual results versus budgeted amounts) and at the preferred frequency (for example, weekly versus monthly). The behavioral considerations motivate managers and other employees to aim for goals of the organization.

Both accountants and managers should always remember that management is not confined exclusively to technical matters. Management is primarily a human activity that should focus on how to help individuals do their jobs better—for example, by helping them to understand the activities that add value and those that do not. Moreover, when workers underperform, behavioral considerations suggest that managers should personally discuss with workers ways to improve performance and not just send them a report highlighting their underperformance.

Different Costs for Different Purposes

This book examines alternative ways to compute costs. That's because there are different costs for different purposes. This theme is the management accountant's version of the "one size does not fit all" notion. A cost concept used for the external-reporting purpose of accounting may not be an appropriate concept for internal, routine reporting to managers.

Consider the advertising costs associated with Microsoft Corporation launching a major new product. The product is expected to have a useful life of two years or more. For external reporting to shareholders, television advertising costs for this product are fully expensed in the income statement in the year they are incurred. GAAP requires this immediate expensing for external reporting. In contrast, for internal purposes of evaluating management performance, the television advertising costs could be capitalized and then amortized or written off as expenses over several years. Microsoft could capitalize these advertising costs if it believes doing so results in a more accurate and fairer measure of the performance of the managers that launched the new product.

We now discuss how organization structure affects the reporting responsibilities of the management accountant.

Organization Structure and the Management Accountant

We focus first on broad management functions and then look at the accounting and finance functions in more detail.

Line and Staff Relationships

Learning Objective 6

Understand how management accounting fits into an organization's structure

. . . for example, the responsibilities of the controller

Organizations distinguish between line management and staff management. **Line management**, such as production, marketing, and distribution management, is directly responsible for attaining the goals of the organization. For example, managers of manufacturing divisions may target particular levels of budgeted operating income, certain levels of product quality and safety, and compliance with environmental laws. Similarly, the pediatrics department in a hospital is responsible for patient billings, costs, and quality of service. **Staff management**, such as management accountants and information technology and human-resources management, exists to provide advice and assistance to line management. A plant manager (a line function) may be responsible for investing in new equipment. A management accountant (a staff function) works as a business partner of the plant manager by preparing detailed operating-cost comparisons of alternative pieces of equipment.

Increasingly, organizations such as Toyota and Dell are using teams to achieve their objectives. These teams include both line and staff management so that all inputs into a decision are available simultaneously.

The Chief Financial Officer and the Controller

The **chief financial officer** (**CFO**)—also called the **finance director** in many countries—is the executive responsible for overseeing the financial operations of an organization. The responsibilities of the CFO vary among organizations, but they usually include the following areas:

- **Controllership**—includes providing financial information for reports to managers and shareholders, and overseeing the overall operations of the accounting system
- **Treasury**—includes banking and short- and long-term financing, investments, and cash management
- **Risk management**—includes managing the financial risk of interest-rate and exchange-rate changes and derivatives management
- **Taxation**—includes income taxes, sales taxes, and international tax planning
- **Investor relations**—responding to and interacting with shareholders
- **Internal audit**—includes reviewing and analyzing financial and other records to attest to the integrity of the organization's financial reports and to adherence to its policies and procedures

The **controller** (also called the *chief accounting officer*) is the financial executive primarily responsible for management accounting and financial accounting. This book focuses on the controller as the chief management accounting executive. Modern controllers do not do any controlling in terms of line authority except over their own departments. Yet the modern concept of controllership maintains that the controller does control in a special sense. That is, by reporting and interpreting relevant data, the controller exerts a force or influence that impels line managers toward making better-informed decisions as they implement their strategies.

Exhibit 1-6

Nike: Reporting Relationships for the CFO and the Corporate Controller

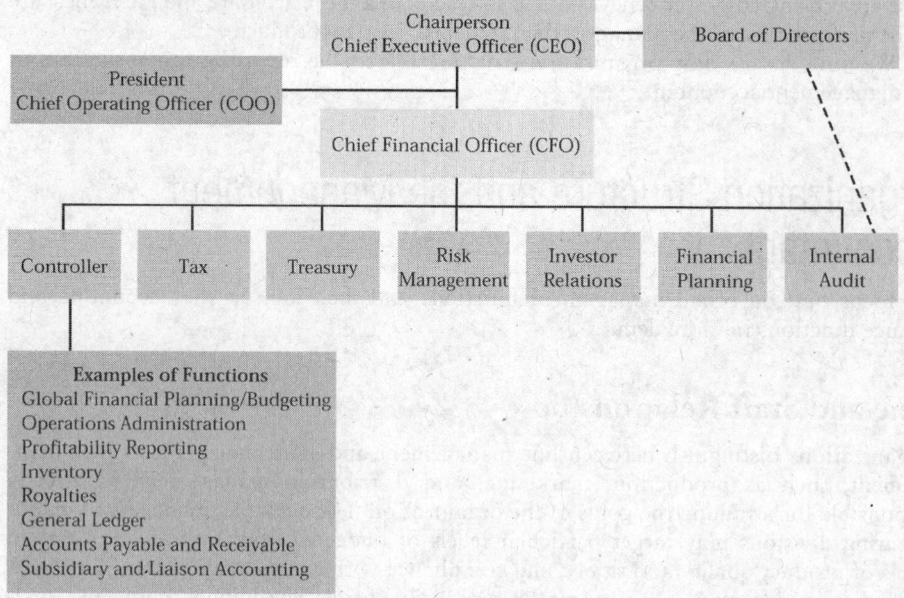

Exhibit 1-6 is an organization chart of the CFO and the corporate controller at Nike, the leading footwear and apparel company. The CFO is a staff manager who reports to the chief operating officer (COO), who reports to the chief executive officer (CEO). As in most organizations, the corporate controller at Nike reports to the CFO. Nike also has regional controllers for the major geographic regions in which it operates, such as the United States, Asia Pacific, Latin America, and Europe. Individual countries sometimes have a country controller. Organization charts such as the one in Exhibit 1-6 show formal reporting relationships. In most organizations, there also are informal relationships that must be understood when managers attempt to implement their decisions. Examples of informal relationships are friendships among managers (friendships of a professional or personal kind) and the personal preferences of top management about the managers they rely on in decision making.

Ponder what managers do to design and implement strategies and the organization structures within which they operate. Then think about the management accountants' and controllers' roles. It should be clear that the successful management accountant must have technical and analytical competence *as well as* behavioral and interpersonal skills. The Concepts in Action box on next page describes some desirable values and behaviors and why they are so critical to the partnership between management accountants and managers. We will elaborate on these values and behaviors as we discuss different topics in subsequent chapters of this book.

Professional Ethics

Understand what professional ethics mean to management accountants

. . . for example, management accountants must maintain integrity and credibility in every aspect of their jobs

At no time has the focus on ethical conduct been sharper than it is today. Corporate scandals at Enron, WorldCom, Arthur Andersen, Ahold, Health South, and Tyco have seriously eroded the public's confidence in corporations. All employees in a company, whether in line management or staff management, must comply with the organization's—and more broadly, society's—expectations of ethical standards.

Institutional Support

Accountants have special obligations regarding ethics, given that they are responsible for the integrity of the financial information provided to internal and external parties. The Sarbanes–Oxley legislation in the United States, passed in 2002 in response to a series of corporate scandals, focuses on improving internal control, corporate governance, monitoring of managers, and disclosure practices of public corporations. These regulations call for tough ethical standards on managers and accountants and provide a process for employees to report violations of illegal and unethical acts.

Concepts in Action

Management Accounting Beyond the Numbers

When you hear the job title "accountant," what comes to mind? The CPA who does your tax return each year? Individuals who prepare budgets at Dell or Unilever? To people outside the profession, it may seem like accountants are just "numbers people." It is true that most accountants are adept financial managers, yet their skills do not stop there. To be successful, management accountants must possess certain values and behaviors that reach well beyond basic analytical abilities.

Working in cross-functional teams and as a business partner of managers. It is not enough that management accountants simply be technically competent about management accounting. They need to be able to work in teams, to learn about business issues, to understand the motivations of different individuals, to respect the views of their colleagues, and to show empathy and trust.

Promoting fact-based analysis and making tough-minded, critical judgments without being adversarial. Management accountants must raise tough questions for managers to consider, especially when preparing budgets. They must do so thoughtfully and with the intent of improving plans and decisions. In the case of Washington Mutual's bank failure, management accountants should have raised questions about whether the company's risky mortgage lending would be profitable if housing prices declined.

Leading and motivating people to change and be innovative. Implementing new ideas, however good they may be, is seldom easy. When the United States Department of Defense sought to consolidate more than 320 finance and accounting systems into a centralized platform, the accounting services director and his team of management accountants made sure that the vision for change was well understood throughout the agency. Ultimately, each individual's performance was aligned with the transformative change and incentive pay was introduced to promote adoption and drive innovation within this new framework.

Communicating clearly, openly, and candidly. Communicating information is a large part of what management accountants do. A few years ago, Pitney Bowes, Inc. (PBI), a $4 billion global provider of integrated mail and document management solutions, implemented a reporting initiative to give managers feedback in key areas. The initiative succeeded because it was clearly designed and openly communicated by PBI's team of management accountants.

Having a strong sense of integrity and of doing the right things. Management accountants must never succumb to pressure from managers to manipulate financial information. They must always remember that their primary commitment is to the organization and its shareholders. At WorldCom, under pressure from senior managers, members of the accounting staff concealed billion of dollars in expenses. Because the accounting staff lacked the integrity and courage to do what was right, WorldCom landed in bankruptcy. Some members of the accounting staff served prison terms for their actions.

Sources: Dash, Eric and Andrew Ross Sorkin. 2008. Government seizes WaMu and sells some assets. *New York Times*, September 25. http://www.nytimes.com/2008/09/26/business/26wamu.html; Garling, Wendy. 2007. Winning the Transformation Battle at the Defense Finance and Accounting Service. *Balanced Scorecard Report*, May–June. http://cb.hbsp.harvard.edu/cb/web/product_detail.seam?R=B0705C-PDF-ENG; Gollakota, Kamala and Vipin Gupta. 2009. *WorldCom Inc.: What went wrong*. Richard Ivey School of Business Case No. 905M43. London, ON: The University of Western Ontario. http://cb.hbsp.harvard.edu/cb/web/product_detail.seam?R=905M43-PDF-ENG; Green, Mark, Jeannine Garrity, Andrea Gumbus, and Bridget Lyons. 2002. Pitney Bowes Calls for New Metrics. *Strategic Finance*, May. http://www.allbusiness.com/accounting-reporting/reports-statements-profit/189988-1.html

Professional accounting organizations, which represent management accountants in many countries, promote high ethical standards.[2] Each of these organizations provides certification programs indicating that the holder has demonstrated the competency of technical knowledge required by that organization in management accounting and financial management, respectively.

In the United States, the Institute of Management Accountants (IMA) has also issued ethical guidelines. Exhibit 1-7 presents the IMA's guidance on issues relating to competence, confidentiality, integrity, and credibility. To provide support to its members to act ethically at all times, the IMA runs an ethics hotline service. Members can call professional counselors at the IMA's Ethics Counseling Service to discuss their ethical dilemmas. The counselors help identify the key ethical issues and possible alternative ways of resolving

[2] See Appendix C: Cost Accounting in Professional Examinations in MyAccountingLab and at www.pearsonhighered.com/horngren for a list of professional management accounting organizations in the United States, Canada, Australia, Japan, and the United Kingdom.

Exhibit 1-7

Ethical Behavior for Practitioners of Management Accounting and Financial Management

Practitioners of management accounting and financial management have an obligation to the public, their profession, the organizations they serve, and themselves to maintain the highest standards of ethical conduct. In recognition of this obligation, the Institute of Management Accountants has promulgated the following standards of ethical professional practice. Adherence to these standards, both domestically and internationally, is integral to achieving the Objectives of Management Accounting. Practitioners of management accounting and financial management shall not commit acts contrary to these standards nor shall they condone the commission of such acts by others within their organizations.

IMA STATEMENT OF ETHICAL PROFESSIONAL PRACTICE

Practitioners of management accounting and financial management shall behave ethically. A commitment to ethical professional practice includes overarching principles that express our values and standards that guide our conduct.

PRINCIPLES

IMA's overarching ethical principles include: Honesty, Fairness, Objectivity, and Responsibility. Practitioners shall act in accordance with these principles and shall encourage others within their organizations to adhere to them.

STANDARDS

A practitioner's failure to comply with the following standards may result in disciplinary action.

COMPETENCE

Each practitioner has a responsibility to:

1. Maintain an appropriate level of professional expertise by continually developing knowledge and skills.
2. Perform professional duties in accordance with relevant laws, regulations, and technical standards.
3. Provide decision support information and recommendations that are accurate, clear, concise, and timely.
4. Recognize and communicate professional limitations or other constraints that would preclude responsible judgment or successful performance of an activity.

CONFIDENTIALITY

Each practitioner has a responsibility to:

1. Keep information confidential except when disclosure is authorized or legally required.
2. Inform all relevant parties regarding appropriate use of confidential information. Monitor subordinates' activities to ensure compliance.
3. Refrain from using confidential information for unethical or illegal advantage.

INTEGRITY

Each practitioner has a responsibility to:

1. Mitigate actual conflicts of interest. Regularly communicate with business associates to avoid apparent conflicts of interest. Advise all parties of any potential conflicts.
2. Refrain from engaging in any conduct that would prejudice carrying out duties ethically.
3. Abstain from engaging in or supporting any activity that might discredit the profession.

CREDIBILITY

Each practitioner has a responsibility to:

1. Communicate information fairly and objectively.
2. Disclose all relevant information that could reasonably be expected to influence an intended user's understanding of the reports, analyses, or recommendations.
3. Disclose delays or deficiencies in information, timeliness, processing, or internal controls in conformance with organization policy and/or applicable law.

Source: Statement on Management Accounting Number 1-C. 2005. *IMA Statement of Ethical Professional Practice.* Montvale, NJ: Institute of Management Accountants. Reprinted with permission from the Institute of Management Accountants, Montvale, NJ, www.imanet.org.

Exhibit 1-8

Resolution of Ethical Conflict

In applying the Standards of Ethical Professional Practice, you may encounter problems identifying unethical behavior or resolving an ethical conflict. When faced with ethical issues, you should follow your organization's established policies on the resolution of such conflict. If these policies do not resolve the ethical conflict, you should consider the following courses of action:

1. Discuss the issue with your immediate supervisor except when it appears that the supervisor is involved. In that case, present the issue to the next level. If you cannot achieve a satisfactory resolution, submit the issue to the next management level. If your immediate superior is the chief executive officer or equivalent, the acceptable reviewing authority may be a group such as the audit committee, executive committee, board of directors, board of trustees, or owners. Contact with levels above the immediate superior should be initiated only with your superior's knowledge, assuming he or she is not involved. Communication of such problems to authorities or individuals not employed or engaged by the organization is not considered appropriate, unless you believe there is a clear violation of the law.
2. Clarify relevant ethical issues by initiating a confidential discussion with an IMA Ethics Counselor or other impartial advisor to obtain a better understanding of possible courses of action.
3. Consult your own attorney as to legal obligations and rights concerning the ethical conflict.

Source: Statement on Management Accounting Number 1-C. 2005. *IMA Statement of Ethical Professional Practice.* Montvale, NJ: Institute of Management Accountants. Reprinted with permission from the Institute of Management Accountants, Montvale, NJ, www.imanet.org.

them, and confidentiality is guaranteed. The IMA is just one of many institutions that help navigate management accountants through what could be turbulent ethical waters.

Typical Ethical Challenges

Ethical issues can confront management accountants in many ways. Here are two examples:

- **Case A:** A management accountant, knowing that reporting a loss for a software division will result in yet another "rightsizing initiative" (a gentler term than "layoffs"), has concerns about the commercial potential of a software product for which development costs are currently being capitalized as an asset rather than being shown as an expense for internal reporting purposes. The division manager argues that showing development costs as an asset is justified because the new product will generate profits. However, the division manager presents little evidence to support his argument. The last two products from this division have been unsuccessful. The management accountant has many friends in the division and wants to avoid a personal confrontation with the division manager.
- **Case B:** A packaging supplier, bidding for a new contract, offers the management accountant of the purchasing company an all-expenses-paid weekend to the Super Bowl. The supplier does not mention the new contract when giving the invitation. The accountant is not a personal friend of the supplier. He knows cost issues are critical in approving the new contract and is concerned that the supplier will ask for details about bids by competing packaging companies.

In each case the management accountant is faced with an ethical dilemma. Case A involves competence, credibility, and integrity. The management accountant should request that the division manager provide credible evidence that the new product is commercially viable. If the manager does not provide such evidence, expensing development costs in the current period is appropriate. Case B involves confidentiality and integrity.

Ethical issues are not always clear-cut. The supplier in Case B may have no intention of raising issues associated with the bid. However, the appearance of a conflict of interest in Case B is sufficient for many companies to prohibit employees from accepting "favors" from suppliers.

Problem for Self-Study

Campbell Soup Company incurs the following costs:

a. Purchase of tomatoes by a canning plant for Campbell's tomato soup products
b. Materials purchased for redesigning Pepperidge Farm biscuit containers to make biscuits stay fresh longer
c. Payment to Backer, Spielvogel, Bates, the advertising agency, for advertising work on Healthy Request line of soup products
d. Salaries of food technologists researching feasibility of a Prego pizza sauce that has minimal calories
e. Payment to Safeway for redeeming coupons on Campbell's food products
f. Cost of a toll-free telephone line used for customer inquiries about using Campbell's soup products
g. Cost of gloves used by line operators on the Swanson Fiesta breakfast-food production line
h. Cost of handheld computers used by Pepperidge Farm delivery staff serving major supermarket accounts

Required Classify each cost item (a–h) as one of the business functions in the value chain in Exhibit 1-2.

Solution

a. Production
b Design of products, services, or processes
c. Marketing
d. Research and development
e. Marketing
f. Customer service
g. Production
h. Distribution

Decision Points

The following question-and-answer format summarizes the chapter's learning objectives. Each decision presents a key question related to a learning objective. The guidelines are the answer to that question.

Decision	Guidelines
1. How is management accounting different from financial accounting?	Financial accounting reports to external users on past financial performance using GAAP. Management accounting provides future-oriented information in formats that help managers (internal users) make decisions and achieve organizational goals.
2. How do management accountants support strategic decisions?	Management accountants contribute to strategic decisions by providing information about the sources of competitive advantage.
3. How do companies add value, and what are the dimensions of performance that customers are expecting of companies?	Companies add value through R&D; design of products, services, or processes; production; marketing; distribution; and customer service. Customers want companies to deliver performance through cost and efficiency, quality, timeliness, and innovation.
4. How do managers make decisions to implement strategy?	Managers use a five-step decision-making process to implement strategy: (1) identify the problem and uncertainties; (2) obtain information; (3) make predictions about the future; (4) make decisions by choosing among alternatives; and (5) implement the decision, evaluate performance, and

learn. The first four steps are the planning decisions, which include deciding on organization goals, predicting results under various alternative ways of achieving those goals, and deciding how to attain the desired goals. Step 5 is the control decision, which includes taking actions to implement the planning decisions and deciding on performance evaluation and feedback that will help future decision making.

5. What guidelines do management accountants use?

Three guidelines that help management accountants increase their value to managers are (a) employ a cost-benefit approach, (b) recognize behavioral as well as technical considerations, and (c) identify different costs for different purposes.

6. Where does the management accounting function fit into an organization's structure?

Management accounting is an integral part of the controller's function in an organization. In most organizations, the controller reports to the chief financial officer, who is a key member of the top management team.

7. What are the ethical responsibilities of management accountants?

Management accountants have ethical responsibilities that are related to competence, confidentiality, integrity, and credibility.

TERMS TO LEARN

Each chapter will include this section. Like all technical terms, accounting terms have precise meanings. Learn the definitions of new terms when you initially encounter them. The meaning of each of the following terms is given in this chapter and in the Glossary at the end of this book.

budget (**p. 10**)
chief financial officer (CFO) (**p. 13**)
control (**p. 10**)
controller (**p. 13**)
cost accounting (**p. 4**)
cost-benefit approach (**p. 12**)
cost management (**p. 5**)
customer service (**p. 6**)
design of products, services, or processes (**p. 6**)
distribution (**p. 6**)
finance director (**p. 13**)
financial accounting (**p. 4**)
learning (**p. 11**)
line management (**p. 13**)
management accounting (**p. 4**)
marketing (**p. 6**)
planning (**p. 10**)
production (**p. 6**)
research and development (**p. 6**)
staff management (**p. 13**)
strategic cost management (**p. 5**)
strategy (**p. 5**)
supply chain (**p. 7**)
value chain (**p. 6**)

ASSIGNMENT MATERIAL

Questions

1-1 How does management accounting differ from financial accounting?

1-2 "Management accounting should not fit the straitjacket of financial accounting." Explain and give an example.

1-3 How can a management accountant help formulate a strategy?

1-4 Describe the business functions in the value chain.

1-5 Explain the term "supply chain" and its importance to cost management.

1-6 "Management accounting deals only with costs." Do you agree? Explain.

1-7 How can management accountants help improve quality and achieve timely product deliveries?

1-8 Describe the five-step decision-making process.

1-9 Distinguish planning decisions from control decisions.

1-10 What three guidelines help management accountants provide the most value to managers?

1-11 "Knowledge of technical issues such as computer technology is a necessary but not sufficient condition to becoming a successful management accountant." Do you agree? Why?

1-12 As a new controller, reply to this comment by a plant manager: "As I see it, our accountants may be needed to keep records for shareholders and Uncle Sam, but I don't want them sticking their noses in my day-to-day operations. I do the best I know how. No bean counter knows enough about my responsibilities to be of any use to me."

1-13 As used in accounting, what do IMA and CMA stand for?

1-14 Name the four areas in which standards of ethical conduct exist for management accountants in the United States. What organization sets forth these standards?

1-15 What steps should a management accountant take if established written policies provide insufficient guidance on how to handle an ethical conflict?

Solved Examples

1-16 Planning and control decisions. Rupa is a book retailing company. Most of its sales are made at its own stores, located in shopping malls or in central business districts. A small but increasing percentage of sales is made via BarnesandNoble.com, in which its major competitor is Amazon.com.

The following five reports were recently prepared by the management accounting group at Rupa:

1. Annual financial statements.
2. Weekly report to Vice President of operations for each Rupa store – includes revenues, gross margin, and operating costs.
3. Study for Vice President of new business development of the expected revenues and costs of BarnesandNoble.com, selling music products (CDs, cassettes, etc.) as well as books.
4. Weekly report to book publishers and trade magazines on the sales of the top 10 selling fiction and non-fiction books at both its own stores and BarnesandNoble.com.
5. Report to insurance company on losses Rupa suffered at its three Gujarat stores due to an earthquake.

Required For each report, identify both a planning-decision and a control-decision used by a Rupa manager.

Solution

Planning and control decisions

1. (a) Planning—decision by Rupa about cash needs for the future.
   (b) Control—performance evaluation of Rupa for the year.
2. (a) Planning—decision to increase or decrease local marketing support.
   (b) Control—decision on whether recent sales promotion led to an increase in revenues.
3. (a) Planning—decision about whether or not to expand Rupa's internet lines of business.
   (b) Control—evaluation by Vice President of New Business Development of the performance of managers of individual lines of business.
4. (a) Planning—decision on which books to advertise more or which books to include in a special chat-room site.
   (b) Control—decision by publisher to pay additional bonuses to authors due to their book being on a bestseller list.
5. (a) Planning—decision by Rupa on the amount and type of insurance to purchase next year.
   (b) Control—follow up by Rupa with the insurance company regarding cash payment to Rupa.

1-17 Problem solving, scorekeeping, and attention direction. For each of the following activities, identify the main role the accountant is performing—problem solving, scorekeeping, or attention directing.

Required

1. Preparing a monthly statement of Indian sales for the IBM marketing Vice President.
2. Interpreting differences between actual results and budgeted amounts on a performance report for the Customer Warranty Department of General Electric.
3. Analyzing, for a Mitsubishi international-manufacturing manager, the desirability of having some auto parts made in India.
4. Interpreting why a New Delhi distribution center exceeded its delivery-costs budget.
5. Explaining a Xerox Corporation Shipping Department's performance report.
6. Preparing for the manager of production control of an Indian steel plant, a cost comparison of two computerized-manufacturing control systems.
7. Preparing a scrap report for the Finishing Department of a Toyota parts plant.
8. Preparing the budget for the Maintenance Department of Appolo Hospital.
9. Analyzing for a General Motors product designer the impact on product costs of a new headlight.

Solution

Problem solving, scorekeeping, and sttention directing.

1. Scorekeeping
2. Attention directing
3. Problem solving
4. Attention directing
5. Attention directing
6. Problem solving

7. Scorekeeping (depending on the extent of the report) or attention directing
8. This question is intentionally vague. The give-and-take of the budgetary process usually encompasses all three functions, but it emphasizes scorekeeping the least. The main function is attention directing, but problem solving is also involved.
9. Problem solving

Note: Because the accountant's duties are often not sharply defined, some of these answers might be challenged.

1-18 Value chain and classification of costs, computer company. HCL incurs the following costs:

1. Electricity costs for the plant assembling the HCL computer line of products.
2. Salary of computer scientist working on the next generation of minicomputers.
3. Cost of HCL employees visit to a major customer to demonstrate HCL's ability to interconnect with other computers.
4. Purchase of products of competitors for testing against potential HCL products.
5. Payment to television network for running HCL advertisements.
6. Cost of cables purchased from outside supplier to be sued with the HCL printer.

Solution

Value chain and classification of costs, computer company.

Cost Item	Value Chain Business Function
1.	Production
2.	Research and Development
3.	Customer Service
4.	Design (or Research and Development)
5.	Marketing
6.	Production

1-19 Management accounting guidelines. For each of the following items, identify which of the management guidelines applies-cost-benefit approach, behavioral and technical considerations, or different costs for different purposes.

1. Analyzing whether to keep the billing function within the organization or outsourcing it.
2. Deciding to give bonuses for superior performance to the employees in an Indian subsidiary and extra vacation time to the employees in a Swedish subsidiary.
3. Including costs of all the value-chain functions before deciding to launch a new product but including only its manufacturing costs in determining its inventory valuation.
4. Considering the desirability of hiring one more salesperson.
5. Giving each salesperson the compensation option of choosing either from a low salary and a high-percentage sales commission or a high salary and a low-percentage sales commission.
6. Selecting the costlier computer system after considering two systems.
7. Installing a participatory budgeting system in which managers set their own performance targets, instead of top management imposing performance targets on them.
8. Recording research costs as a revenue expense for financial reporting purpose but capitalizing and expensing them over a longer period for management performance-evaluation purposes.
9. Introducing a profit-sharing plan for employees.

Solution

Management accounting guidelines.

1. Cost-benefit approach
2. Behavioral and technical considerations
3. Different costs for different purposes
4. Cost-benefit approach
5. Behavioral and technical considerations
6. Cost-benefit approach
7. Behavioral and technical considerations
8. Different costs for different purposes
9. Behavioral and technical considerations

1-20 Planning and control decisions, Internet company. WebNews.com is an Internet company. It offers subscribers multiple online services ranging from an annotated TV guide to local-area information on restaurants and movie theaters. It has two main revenue sources:

■ Monthly fees from subscribers. Recent data are:

Month/Year	Actual Number of Subscribers	Actual Monthly Fee per Subscriber
June 2010	28,642	Rs 50
December 2010	54,813	200
June 2011	58,178	200
December 2011	86,437	200
June 2012	1,46,581	200

■

Month/Year	Advertising Revenues
June 2010	Rs 40,00,000
December 2010	83,00,000
June 2011	86,00,000
December 2011	1,47,80,000
June 2012	2,91,70,000

The following decisions were made from June to October 2012:

a. June. Decision to raise the monthly subscription fee from Rs 200 per month to Rs 250 per month in July. The Rs 200 fee began in December 2010.
b. June. Decision to inform existing subscribers that the July subscription fee would be Rs 250.
c. July. Decision to upgrade the content of its online services and to offer better Internet mail services.
d. October. Demotion of Vice President of marketing after significant slowing of subscriber growth in accounts and revenues. Results include:

Month/Year	Actual Number of Subscribers	Actual Monthly Fee per Subscriber
July 2012	1,28,900	Rs 250
August 2012	1,39,500	250
September 2012	1,43,100	250

Budgeted amounts (set in June 2012) for the number of subscribers were 1,40,000 for July 2012, 1,50,000 for August 2012, and 1,60,000 for September 2012.

e. October 2012. Decision to reduce the monthly subscription fee from Rs 250 per month in September 2012 to Rs 220 in October 2012.

Required

1. Distinguish between planning decisions and control decisions at WebNews.com.
2. Classify each of the (a) to (e) decisions as a planning or a control decision.
3. What was the role of feedback in the decisions made in the period?
4. What further action might WebNews.com take based on feedback from the July to September subscription information?

Solution

1. **Planning decisions**
   a. Decision to raise monthly subscription fee.
   c. Decision to upgrade content of online services.
   e. Decision to decrease monthly subscription fee.
2. **Control decisions**
   b. Decision to inform existing subscribers about the rate of increase—an implementation part of control decisions.
   d. Demotion of VP of Marketing—performance evaluation and feedback aspect of control decisions.
3. As a result of the feedback, WebNews.com made the following decisions:
   a. Decision to change subscription fee from Rs 250 per month in September 2012 to Rs 220 in October 2012.
   b. Demotion of Vice President of Marketing after significant slowing of subscriber growth in accounts and revenues.
4. WebNews.com overestimated the number of subscribers for the July to September 2012 period. It might examine the methodology it uses to estimate the sensitivity of subscriptions to price changes and upgradation of its services.

Exercises

1-21 Problem solving, scorekeeping, and attention directing. For each of the following activities, identify the main role the accountant is performing—problem solving, scorekeeping, or attention directing.

1. Interpreting differences between actual results and budgeted amounts on a shipping manager's performance report at a Maruti distribution center.
2. Preparing a report showing the benefits from leasing motor vehicles rather than owning them.
3. Preparing journal entries for depreciation on the personnel manager's office equipment at Citibank.
4. Preparing a customer's monthly statement for a Ranbaxy store.
5. Processing the weekly payroll for the Bombay University Maintenance Department.
6. Analyzing the costs of different ways to blend materials in the foundry of a TISCO plant.
7. Tallying sales, by branches, for the Vice President of Hindustan Levers, sales.
8. Analyzing, for the President of Microsoft, the impact of a contemplated new product on the net income.
9. Interpreting why an IBM sales district did not meet its sales quota.

1-22 Value chain and classification of costs, pharmaceutical company. Indian Drugs and Pharmaceutical Corp., a pharmaceutical company, incurs the following costs:

1. Cost of redesigning blister packs to make drug containers more tamper-proof.
2. Cost of videos sent to doctors to promote sales of a new drug.
3. Cost of a toll-free telephone line used for customer inquiries about usage, side effects of drugs, and so on.
4. Equipment purchased to conduct experiments on drugs yet to be approved by the government.
5. Payment to actors on an infomercial to be shown on television promoting a new hair-growing product for balding men.
6. Labor costs of workers in the packaging area of a production facility.
7. Bonus paid to a salesperson for exceeding monthly sales quota.
8. Cost of Desk to Desk Courier service to deliver drugs to hospitals.

Required

Classify each of the cost items (1-8) as one of the business functions of the value chain shown in Exhibit 1-4.

1-23 Management themes and changes in management accounting. A survey on ways organizations are changing their management accounting systems reported the following:

1. Company A now prepares a value-chain income statement for each brand it sells.
2. Company B now presents in a single report all costs related to achieving high quality levels of its products.
3. Company C now presents in its performance report estimates of the manufacturing costs of its two most important competitors, in addition to its own manufacturing costs.
4. Company D reduces by 1 per cent each month the budgeted labor-assembly cost of a product while evaluating the performance of a plant manager.
5. Company E now reports profitability and satisfaction measure (as assessed by a third party) on a customer-by-customer basis.

Required

Link each of these changes to one of the key themes that are important to managers attaining success (see Exhibit 1-3).

2 An Introduction to Cost Terms and Purposes

Learning Objectives

1. Define and illustrate a cost object
2. Distinguish between direct costs and indirect costs
3. Explain variable costs and fixed costs
4. Interpret unit costs cautiously
5. Distinguish inventoriable costs from period costs
6. Explain why product costs are computed in different ways for different purposes
7. Describe a framework for cost accounting and cost management

What does the word cost mean to you? Is it the price you pay for something of value? A cash outflow? Something that affects profitability? There are many different types of costs, and at different times organizations put more or less emphasis on them. When times are good companies often focus on selling as much as they can, with costs taking a backseat. But when times get tough, the emphasis usually shifts to costs and cutting them, as General Motors tried to do. Unfortunately, when times became really bad GM was unable to cut costs fast enough leading to Chapter 11 bankruptcy.

GM Collapses Under the Weight of Its Fixed Costs[1]

After nearly 80 years as the world's largest automaker, General Motors (GM) was forced to file for bankruptcy protection in 2009. Declining sales and the rise of Japanese competitors, such as Toyota and Honda, affected GM's viability given its high fixed costs—costs that did not decrease as the number of cars that GM made and sold declined.

A decade of belt-tightening brought GM's variable costs—costs such as material costs that vary with the number of cars that GM makes—in line with those of the Japanese. Unfortunately for GM, a large percentage of its operating costs were fixed because union contracts made it difficult for the company to close its factories or reduce pensions and health benefits owed to retired workers.

To cover its high fixed costs, GM needed to sell a lot of cars. Starting in 2001, it began offering sales incentives and rebates, which for a few years were somewhat successful. GM also expanded aggressively into China and Europe.

But in 2005, growth efforts slowed, and GM lost $10.4 billion. As a result, GM embarked on a reorganization plan that closed more than a dozen plants, eliminated tens of thousands of jobs, slashed retirement plan benefits for its 40,000-plus salaried employees, and froze its pension program.

Despite these cuts, GM could not reduce its costs fast enough to keep up with the steadily declining market for new cars and trucks. In the United States, as gas prices rose above $40 a gallon, GM's product mix was too heavily weighted toward gas-guzzling trucks,

[1] *Sources:* Loomis, Carol. 2006. The tragedy of General Motors. *Fortune*, February 6; *New York Times*. 2009. Times topics: Automotive industry crisis. December 6. http://topics.nytimes.com/top/reference/timestopics/subjects/c/credit_crisis/auto_industry/index.html; Taylor, III, Alex. 2005. GM hits the skids. *Fortune*, April 4; Vlasic, Bill and Nick Bunkley. 2008. G.M. says U.S. cash is its best hope. *New York Times*, November 8.

pickup trucks, and sport utility vehicles, all of which were experiencing sharp decreases in sales.

In late 2008, as the economic crisis worsened, GM announced plans to cut $15 billion in costs and raise $5 billion through the sale of assets, like its Hummer brand of off-road vehicles. "We're cutting to the bone," said Fritz Henderson, GM's president. "But given the situation, we think that's appropriate."

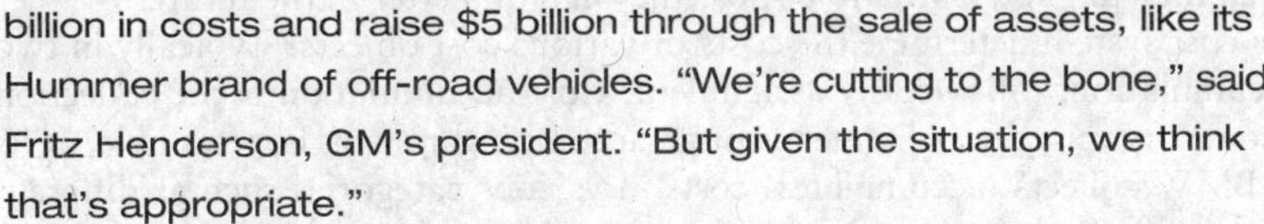

It was appropriate, but it wasn't enough. By November 2008, GM had lost more than $18 billion for the year, and the government loaned the company $20 billion to continue operations. Ultimately, its restructuring efforts fell short, and the weight of GM's fixed costs drove the company into bankruptcy. In court papers, the company claimed $82.3 billion in assets and $172.8 billion in debt.

When it emerges from bankruptcy, GM will be a much smaller company with only four brands of cars (down from eight), more than 20,000 fewer hourly union workers, and as many as 20 additional shuttered factories.

As the story of General Motors illustrates, managers must understand costs in order to interpret and act on accounting information. Organizations as varied as the United Way, the Mayo Clinic, and Sony generate reports containing a variety of cost concepts and terms that managers need to run their businesses. Managers must understand these concepts and terms to effectively use the information provided. This chapter discusses cost concepts and terms that are the basis of accounting information used for internal and external reporting.

Costs and Cost Terminology

Learning Objective 1

Define and illustrate a cost object

. . . examples of cost objects are products, services, activities, processes, and customers

Accountants define **cost** as a resource sacrificed or forgone to achieve a specific objective. A cost (such as direct materials or advertising) is usually measured as the monetary amount that must be paid to acquire goods or services. An **actual cost** is the cost incurred (a historical or past cost), as distinguished from a **budgeted cost**, which is a predicted or forecasted cost (a future cost).

When you think of cost, you invariably think of it in the context of finding the cost of a particular thing. We call this thing a **cost object,** which is anything for which a measurement of costs is desired. Suppose that you were a manager at BMW's Chennai plant. BMW makes several different types of cars and sport activity vehicles (SAVs) at this plant. What cost objects can you think of? Now look at Exhibit 2-1.

Exhibit 2-1

Examples of Cost Objects at BMW

Cost Object	Illustration
Product	A BMW X5 sports activity vehicle
Service	Telephone hotline providing information and assistance to BMW dealers
Project	R&D project on enhancing the DVD system in BMW cars
Customer	Herb Chambers Motors, the BMW dealer that purchases a broad range of BMW vehicles
Activity	Setting up machines for production or maintaining production equipment
Department	Environmental, Health, and Safety Department

You will see that BMW managers want to know the cost of various products, such as the BMW X5, but that they also want to know the costs of things such as projects, services, and departments. Managers use their knowledge of these costs to guide decisions, for example, about product innovation, quality, and customer service.

Now think about whether a manager at BMW might want to know the *budgeted cost* of a cost object, or the *actual cost*. Managers almost always need to know both types of costs when making decisions. Comparing budgeted costs to actual costs helps managers evaluate how well they did and learn about how they can do better in the future.

How does a cost system determine the costs of various cost objects? Typically in two basic stages: accumulation, followed by assignment. **Cost accumulation** is the collection of cost data in some organized way by means of an accounting system. For example, at its Chennai plant, BMW collects (accumulates) costs in various categories such as different types of materials, different classifications of labor, and costs incurred for supervision. Managers and management accountants then *assign* these accumulated costs to designated cost objects, such as the different models of cars that BMW manufactures at that plant. BMW managers use this cost information in two main ways:

1. when *making* decisions, for instance, on how to price different models of cars or how much to invest in R&D and marketing and
2. for *implementing* decisions, by influencing and motivating employees to act and learn, for example, by rewarding employees for reducing costs.

Now that we know why it is useful to assign costs, we turn our attention to some concepts that will help us do it. Again, think of the different types of costs that we just discussed—materials, labor, and supervision. You are probably thinking that some costs, such as costs of materials, are easier to assign to a cost object than others, such as costs of supervision. As you will see, this is indeed the case.

Direct Costs and Indirect Costs

We now describe how costs are classified as direct and indirect costs and the methods used to assign these costs to cost objects.

Distinguish between direct costs

. . . costs that are traced directly to the cost object and indirect costs

. . . costs that are allocated to the cost object

- **Direct costs of a cost object** are related to the particular cost object and can be traced to it in an economically feasible (cost-effective) way. For example, the cost of steel or tires is a direct cost of BMW X5s. The cost of the steel or tires can be easily traced to or identified with the BMW X5. The workers on the BMW X5 line request materials from the warehouse and the material requisition document identifies the cost of the materials supplied to the X5. In a similar vein, individual workers record the time spent working on the X5 on time sheets. The cost of this labor can easily be traced to the X5 and is another example of a direct cost. The term **cost tracing** is used to describe the assignment of direct costs to a particular cost object.
- **Indirect costs of a cost object** are related to the particular cost object but cannot be traced to it in an economically feasible (cost-effective) way. For example, the salaries of plant administrators (including the plant manager) who oversee production of the many different types of cars produced at the Spartanburg plant are an indirect cost of the X5s. Plant administration costs are related to the cost object (X5s) because plant administration is necessary for managing the production of X5s. Plant administration costs are

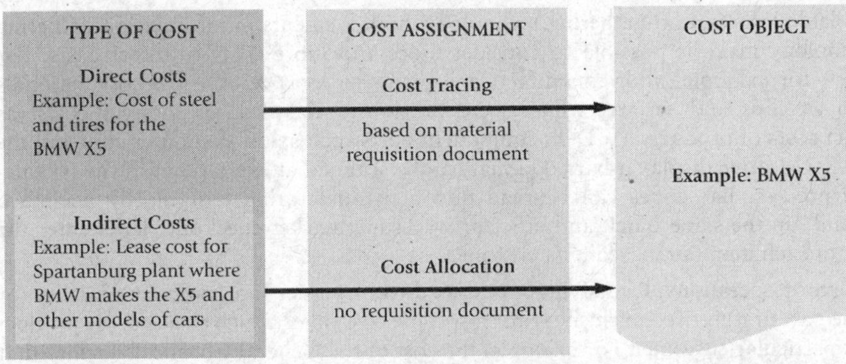

TYPE OF COST	COST ASSIGNMENT	COST OBJECT
Direct Costs Example: Cost of steel and tires for the BMW X5	**Cost Tracing** → based on material requisition document	Example: BMW X5
Indirect Costs Example: Lease cost for Spartanburg plant where BMW makes the X5 and other models of cars	**Cost Allocation** → no requisition document	

Exhibit 2-2

Cost Assignment to a Cost Object

indirect costs because plant administrators also oversee the production of other products, such as the Z4 Roadster. Unlike the cost of steel or tires, there is no requisition of plant administration services and it is virtually impossible to trace plant administration costs to the X5 line. The term **cost allocation** is used to describe the assignment of indirect costs to a particular cost object. **Cost assignment** is a general term that encompasses both (1) tracing direct costs to a cost object and (2) allocating indirect costs to a cost object. Exhibit 2-2 depicts direct costs and indirect costs and both forms of cost assignment—cost tracing and cost allocation—using the example of the BMW X5.

Challenges in Cost Allocation

Consider the cost to lease the Chennai plant. This cost is an indirect cost of the X5—there is no separate lease agreement for the space used to make the X5. But BMW *allocates* to the X5 a part of the lease cost of the building—for example, on the basis of an estimate of the percentage of the building's total floor space occupied for the production of the X5 relative to the total floor space used to produce all models of cars.

Managers want to assign costs accurately to cost objects. Inaccurate product costs will mislead managers about the profitability of different products. Consequently, managers might unknowingly promote unprofitable products while deemphasizing profitable products. Generally, managers are more confident about the accuracy of direct costs of cost objects, such as the cost of steel and tires of the X5.

Identifying indirect costs of cost objects, on the other hand, can be more challenging. Consider the lease. Allocating the cost of the lease on the basis of the total floor space occupied by each car model makes sense. This approach measures the building resources used by each car model reasonably and accurately. The more floor space that a car model occupies, the greater the lease costs that should be assigned to it. Accurately allocating other indirect costs, such as plant administration to the X5, however, is more difficult. Should these costs be allocated on the basis of the number of workers working on each car model? The number of cars produced of each model? Some other measure? How to measure the share of plant administration used by each car model is not clearcut.

Factors Affecting Direct/Indirect Cost Classifications

Several factors affect the classification of a cost as direct or indirect:

- **The materiality of the cost in question.** The smaller the amount of a cost—that is, the more immaterial the cost is—the less likely that it is economically feasible to trace that cost to a particular cost object. Consider a mail-order catalog company. It would be economically feasible to trace the courier charge for delivering a package to an individual customer as a direct cost. In contrast, the cost of the invoice paper included in the package would be classified as an indirect cost. Why? Because although the cost of the paper can be traced to each customer, it is not cost-effective to do so. The benefits of knowing that, say, exactly Rs 0.50 worth of paper is included in each package do not exceed the data processing and administrative costs of tracing the cost to each package.

- **Available information-gathering technology.** Improvements in information-gathering technology make it possible to consider more and more costs as direct costs. Bar codes, for example, allow manufacturing plants to treat certain low-cost materials such as clips and screws, which were previously classified as indirect costs, as direct costs of products. At Dell, component parts such as the computer chip and the CD-ROM drive display a bar code that can be scanned at every point in the production process. Bar codes can be read into a manufacturing cost file by waving a "wand" in the same quick and efficient way supermarket checkout clerks enter the cost of each item purchased by a customer.
- **Design of operations.** Classifying a cost as direct is easier if a company's facility (or some part of it) is used exclusively for a specific cost object, such as a specific product or a particular customer. For example, the cost of the General Chemicals facility that is dedicated to manufacturing soda ash is a direct cost of soda ash.

Be aware that a specific cost may be both a direct cost of one cost object and an indirect cost of another cost object. *That is, the direct/indirect classification depends on the choice of the cost object.* For example, the salary of an Assembly Department supervisor at BMW is a direct cost if the cost object is the Assembly Department, but it is an indirect cost if the cost object is a product such as the BMW X5 SAV because the Assembly Department assembles many different models. A useful rule to remember is that the broader the definition of the cost object—the Assembly Department rather than the X5 SAV—the higher the proportion of total costs that are direct costs and the more confidence that a manager has in the accuracy of the resulting cost amounts.

Cost-Behavior Patterns: Variable Costs and Fixed Costs

Explain variable costs and fixed costs

. . . the two basic ways in which costs behave

Costing systems record the cost of resources acquired, such as materials, labor, and equipment, and track how those resources are used to produce and sell products or services. Recording the costs of resources acquired and used allows managers to see how costs behave. Consider two basic types of cost-behavior patterns found in many accounting systems. A **variable cost** changes *in total* in proportion to changes in the related level of total activity or volume. A **fixed cost** remains unchanged *in total* for a given time period, despite wide changes in the related level of total activity or volume. Costs are defined as *variable or fixed with respect to a specific activity* and for *a given time period.* Surveys of practice repeatedly show that identifying a cost as variable or fixed provides valuable information for making many management decisions and is an important input when evaluating performance. To illustrate these two basic types of costs, again consider costs at the Chennai plant of BMW.

1. **Variable costs:** If BMW buys a steering wheel at Rs 600 for each of its BMW X5 vehicles, then the total cost of steering wheels should be Rs 600 times the number of vehicles produced, as the following table illustrates.

Number of X5s Produced (1)	Variable Cost per Steering Wheel (2)	Total Variable Cost of Steering Wheels (3) = (1) × (2)
1	Rs 600	Rs 600
1,000	600	6,00,000
3,000	600	18,00,000

The steering wheel cost is an example of a variable cost because *total cost* changes in proportion to changes in the number of vehicles produced. The cost per unit of a variable cost is constant. It is precisely because the variable cost per steering wheel in column 2 is the same for each steering wheel that the total variable cost of steering wheels in column 3

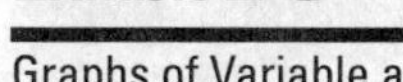

Exhibit 2-3

Graphs of Variable and Fixed Costs

PANEL A: Variable Cost of Steering Wheels at RS 600 per BMW X5 Assembled

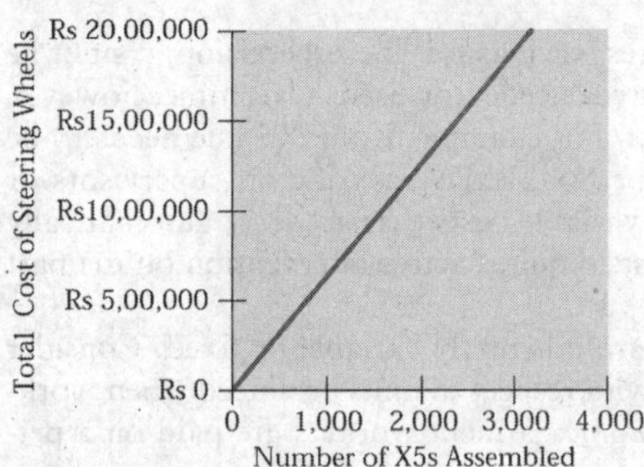

PANEL B: Supervision Costs for the BMW X5 assembly line (in millions)

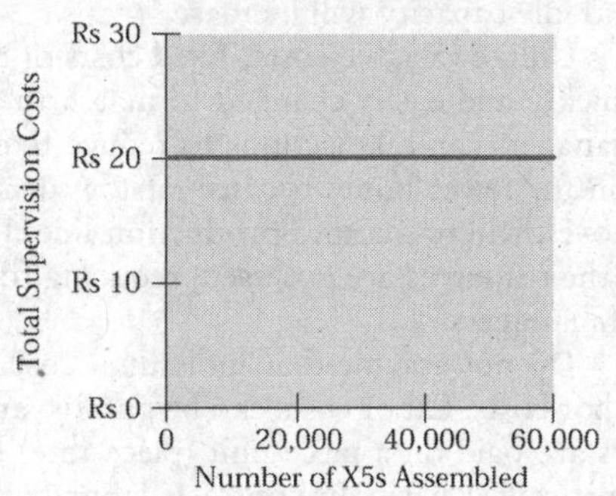

changes proportionately with the number of X5s produced in column 1. When considering how variable costs behave, always focus on total costs.

Exhibit 2-3, Panel A, graphically illustrates the total variable cost of steering wheels. The cost is represented by a straight line that climbs from left to right. The phrases "strictly variable" and "proportionately variable" are sometimes used to describe the variable cost in Panel A.

Consider an example of a variable cost with respect to a different activity—the Rs 200 hourly wage paid to each worker to set up machines at the Chennai plant. Setup labor cost is a variable cost with respect to setup hours because setup cost changes in total in proportion to the number of setup hours used.

2. **Fixed costs:** Suppose BMW incurs a total cost of Rs 2,00,00,000 per year for supervisors who work exclusively on the X5 line. These costs are unchanged in total over a designated range of the number of vehicles produced during a given time span (see Exhibit 2-3, Panel B). Fixed costs become smaller and smaller on a per unit basis as the number of vehicles assembled increases, as the following table shows.

Annual Total Fixed Supervision Costs for BMW X5 Assembly Line (1)	Number of X5s Produced (2)	Fixed Supervision Cost per X5 (3) = (1) ÷ (2)
Rs 2,00,00,000	10,000	Rs 2,000
Rs 2,00,00,000	25,000	800
Rs 2,00,00,000	50,000	400

It is precisely because *total* line supervision costs are fixed at Rs 2,00,00,000 that fixed supervision cost per X5 decreases as the number of X5s produced increases; the same fixed cost is spread over a larger number of X5s. Do not be misled by the change in fixed cost per unit. Just as in the case of variable costs, when considering fixed costs, always focus on total costs. Costs are fixed when total costs remain unchanged despite significant changes in the level of total activity or volume.

Why are some costs variable and other costs fixed? Recall that a cost is usually measured as the amount of money that must be paid to acquire goods and services. Total cost of steering wheels is a variable cost because BMW buys the steering wheels only when they are needed. As more X5s are produced, proportionately more steering wheels are acquired and proportionately more costs are incurred.

Contrast the description of variable costs with the Rs 2,00,00,000 of fixed costs per year incurred by BMW for supervision of the X5 assembly line. This level of supervision is acquired and put in place well before BMW uses it to produce X5s and before BMW even knows how many X5s it will produce. Suppose that BMW puts in place supervisors capable of supervising the production of 60,000 X5s each year. If the demand is for only 55,000 X5s, there will be idle capacity. Supervisors on the X5 line could have supervised the production of 60,000 X5s but will supervise only 55,000 X5s because of the lower demand. However, BMW must pay for the unused line supervision capacity because the cost of supervision cannot be reduced in the short run. If demand is even lower—say only 50,000 X5s—line supervision costs will not change; they will continue to be Rs 2,00,00,000, and idle capacity will increase.

Unlike variable costs, fixed costs of resources (such as for line supervision) cannot be quickly and easily changed to match the resources needed or used. Over time, however, managers can take actions to reduce fixed costs. For example, if the X5 line needs to be run for fewer hours because of low demand for X5s, BMW may lay off supervisors or move them to another production line. Unlike variable costs that go away automatically if the resources are not used, reducing fixed costs requires active intervention on the part of managers.

Do not assume that individual cost items are inherently variable or fixed. Consider labor costs. Labor costs can be purely variable with respect to units produced when workers are paid on a piece-unit (piece-rate) basis. Some garment workers are paid on a per-shirt-sewed basis. In contrast, labor costs at a plant in the coming year are sometimes appropriately classified as fixed.

For instance, a labor union agreement might set annual salaries and conditions, contain a no-layoff clause, and severely restrict a company's flexibility to assign workers to any other plant that has demand for labor. Indian companies have for a long time had a policy of lifetime employment for their workers. Although such a policy entails higher labor costs, particularly in economic downturns, the benefits are increased loyalty and dedication to the company and higher productivity. The Concepts in Action following describes how a car-sharing service offers companies the opportunity to convert the fixed costs of owning corporate cars into variable costs by renting cars on an as-needed basis.

A particular cost item could be variable with respect to one level of activity and fixed with respect to another. Consider annual registration and license costs for a fleet of planes owned by an airline company. Registration and license costs would be a variable cost with respect to the number of planes owned. But registration and license costs for a particular plane are fixed with respect to the miles flown by that plane during a year.

To focus on key concepts, we have classified the behavior of costs as variable or fixed. Some costs have both fixed and variable elements and are called *mixed* or *semivariable* costs. For example, a company's telephone costs may have a fixed monthly payment and a charge per phone-minute used. We discuss mixed costs and techniques to separate out their fixed and variable components in Chapter 10.

Cost Drivers

A **cost driver** is a variable, such as the level of activity or volume, that causally affects costs over a given time span. That is, there is a cause-and-effect relationship between a change in the level of activity or volume and a change in the level of total costs. For example, if product-design costs change with the number of parts in a product, the number of parts is a cost driver of product-design costs. Similarly, miles driven is often a cost driver of distribution costs.

The cost driver of a variable cost is the level of activity or volume whose change causes proportionate changes in the variable cost. For example, the number of vehicles assembled is the cost driver of the total cost of steering wheels. If setup workers are paid an hourly wage, the number of setup hours is the cost driver of total (variable) setup costs.

Costs that are fixed in the short run have no cost driver in the short run but may have a cost driver in the long run. Consider the costs of testing, say, 0.1% of the color printers at Hewlett-Packard. These costs consist equipment and staff costs of Testing Department that are difficult to change and, hence, are fixed in the short run with respect to changes in the volume of production. In this case, volume of production is not a cost driver of testing costs in the short run. In the long run, however, Hewlett-Packard will increase or decrease the Testing Department's equipment and staff to the levels needed to support future production volumes. In the long run, volume of production is a cost driver of testing costs. Costing systems that identify the cost of each activity such as testing, design, or set up are called *activity-based costing systems*.

Concepts in Action

How Zipcar Helps Reduce Twitter's Transportation Costs

Soaring gas prices, high insurance costs, and hefty parking fees have forced many businesses to reexamine whether owning corporate cars is economical. In some cities, Zipcar has emerged as an attractive alternative. Zipcar provides an "on demand" option for urban individuals and businesses to rent a car by the week, the day, or even the hour. Zipcar members make a reservation by phone or Internet, go to the parking lot where the car is located (usually by walking or public transportation), use an electronic card or iPhone application that unlocks the car door via a wireless sensor, and then simply climb in and drive away. Rental fees begin around $70 per hour and $66 per day, and include gas, insurance, and some mileage (usually around 180 miles per day). Currently, business customers account for 15% of Zipcar's revenues, but that number is expected to double in the coming years.

Let's think about what Zipcar means for companies. Many small businesses own a company car or two for getting to meetings, making deliveries, and running errands. Similarly, many large companies own a fleet of cars to shuttle visiting executives and clients back and forth from appointments, business lunches, and the airport. Traditionally, owning these cars has involved very high fixed costs, including buying the asset (car), costs of the maintenance department, and insurance for multiple drivers. Unfortunately, businesses had no other options.

Now, however, companies like Twitter can use Zipcar for on-demand mobility while reducing their transportation and overhead costs. Based in downtown San Francisco, Twitter managers use Zipcar's fleet of Mini Coopers and Toyota Priuses to meet venture capitalists and partners in Silicon Valley. "We would get in a Zipcar to drive down to San Jose to pitch investors or go across the city," says Jack Dorsey, the micro-blogging service's co-founder. "Taxis are hard to find and unreliable here." Twitter also uses Zipcar when traveling far away from its headquarters, like when visiting advertisers in New York and technology vendors in Boston, forgoing the traditional black sedans and long taxi rides from the airport.

From a business perspective, Zipcar allows companies to convert the fixed costs of owning a company car to variable costs. If business slows, or a car isn't required to visit a client, Zipcar customers are not saddled with the fixed costs of car ownership. Of course, if companies use Zipcar too frequently, they can end up paying more overall than they would have paid if they purchased and maintained the car themselves.

Along with cutting corporate spending, car sharing services like Zipcar reduce congestion on the road and promote environmental sustainability. Users report reducing their vehicle miles traveled by 44%, and surveys show CO_2 emissions are being cut by up to 50% per user. Beyond that, each shared car takes up to 20 cars off the road as members sell their cars or decide not to buy new ones—challenging the whole principle of owning a car. "The future of transportation will be a blend of things like Zipcar, public transportation, and private car ownership," says Bill Ford, Ford's executive chairman. But the automaker isn't worried. "Not only do I not fear that, but I think it's a great opportunity for us to participate in the changing nature of car ownership."

Sources: Keegan, Paul. 2009. Zipcar – the best new idea in business. *Fortune*, August 27. http://money.cnn.com/2009/08/26/news/companies/zipcar_car_rentals.fortune/; Olsen, Elizabeth. 2009. Car sharing reinvents the company wheels. *New York Times*, May 7. http://www.nytimes.com/2009/05/07/business/businessspecial/07CAR.html; Zipcar, Inc. Zipcar for business case studies. http://www.zipcar.com/business/is-it/case-studies (accessed October 8, 2009)

Relevant Range

Relevant range is the band of normal activity level or volume in which there is a specific relationship between the level of activity or volume and the cost in question. For example, a fixed cost is fixed only in relation to a given wide range of total activity or volume (at which the company is expected to operate) and only for a given time span (usually a particular budget period). Suppose that BMW contracts with Jaipur Golden Transport Company (JGTC) to transport X5s to BMW dealers. Jaipur Golden Transport Company (JGTC), rents two trucks. Each truck has annual fixed rental costs of Rs 4,00,000. The maximum annual usage of each truck is 120,000 kms. In the current year (2011), the predicted combined total hauling of the two trucks is 170,000 kms.

Exhibit 2-4 shows how annual fixed costs behave at different levels of miles of hauling. Up to 120,000 kms, JGTC can operate with one truck; from 120,001 to 240,000 kms, it operates with two trucks; from 240,001 to 360,000 kms, it operates with three trucks. This

Exhibit 2-4

Fixed-Cost Behavior at Thomas Transport Company

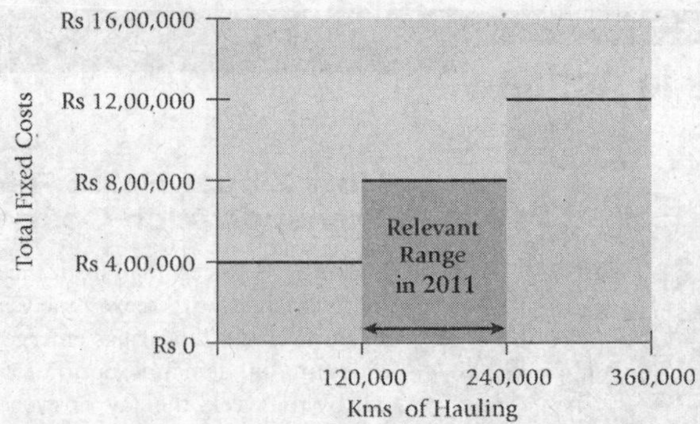

pattern will continue as JGTC adds trucks to its fleet to provide more miles of hauling. Given the predicted 170,000-km usage for 2011, the range from 120,001 to 240,000 kms hauled is the range in which JGTC expects to operate, resulting in fixed rental costs of Rs 8,00,000. Within this relevant range, changes in miles hauled will not affect the annual fixed costs.

Fixed costs may change from one year to the next. For example, if the total rental fee of the two trucks is increased by Rs 20,000 for 2012, the total level of fixed costs will increase to Rs 8,20,000 (all else remaining the same). If that increase occurs, total rental costs will be fixed at this new level of Rs 8,20,000 for 2012 for kms hauled in the 120,001 to 240,000 range.

The basic assumption of the relevant range also applies to variable costs. That is, outside the relevant range, variable costs, such as direct materials, may not change proportionately with changes in production volume. For example, above a certain volume, direct material costs may increase at a lower rate because of price discounts on purchases greater than a certain quantity.

Relationships of Types of Costs

We have introduced two major classifications of costs: direct/indirect and variable/fixed. Costs may simultaneously be:

- Direct and variable
- Direct and fixed
- Indirect and variable
- Indirect and fixed

Exhibit 2-5 shows examples of costs in each of these four cost classifications for the BMW X5.

Exhibit 2-5

Examples of Costs in Combinations of the Direct/Indirect and Variable/Fixed Cost Classifications for a Car Manufacturer

Cost-Behavior Pattern	Assignment of Costs to Cost Object: Direct Costs	Assignment of Costs to Cost Object: Indirect Costs
Variable Costs	• Cost object: BMW X5s produced Example: Tires used in assembly of automobile	• Cost object: BMW X5s produced Example: Power costs at Chennai plant. Power usage is metered only to the plant, where multiple products are assembled.
Fixed Costs	• Cost object: BMW X5s produced Example: Salary of supervisor on BMW X5 assembly line	• Cost object: BMW X5s produced Example: Annual lease costs at Chennai plant. Lease is for whole plant, where multiple products are produced.

Total Costs and Unit Costs

The preceding section concentrated on the behavior patterns of total costs in relation to activity or volume levels. We now consider unit costs.

Unit Costs

Learning Objective 4

Interpret unit costs cautiously

. . . for many decisions, managers should use total costs, not unit costs

Generally, the decision maker should think in terms of total costs rather than unit costs. In many decision contexts, however, calculating a unit cost is essential. Consider the chairman of the social committee of a Welfare Association of a locality, who is trying to decide whether to hire a musical group for an upcoming party. He estimates the cost of hiring the group to be Rs 10,000. This knowledge is helpful for the decision, but it is not enough.

Before a decision can be reached, the chairman also must predict the number of people who will attend. Without knowledge of both total cost and number of attendees, he cannot make an informed decision on a possible admission price to recover the cost of the party or even on whether to have a party at all. So he computes the unit cost of hiring the musical group by dividing the total cost (Rs 4,00,00,000) by the expected number of people who will attend. If 50,000 people attend, the unit cost is Rs 800 (Rs 4,00,00,000 ÷ 50,000) per person; if 20,000 attend, the unit cost increases to Rs 2,000 (Rs 4,00,00,000 ÷ 20,000).

Unless the total cost is "unitized" (that is, averaged with respect to the level of activity or volume), the Rs 4,00,00,000 cost is difficult to interpret. The unit cost combines the total cost and the number of people in a handy, communicative way.

Accounting systems typically report both total-cost amounts and average-cost-per-unit amounts. A **unit cost**, also called an **average cost**, is computed by dividing total cost by the number of units. The units might be expressed in various ways. Examples are automobiles assembled, packages delivered, or hours worked. Suppose that, in 2011, its first year of operations, Rs 40,00,00,000 of manufacturing costs are incurred to produce 5,00,000 speaker systems at the Pune plant of LG Products. Then the unit cost is Rs 800:

$$\frac{\text{Total manufacturing costs}}{\text{Number of units manufactured}} = \frac{\text{Rs } 40{,}00{,}00{,}000}{5{,}00{,}000 \text{ units}} = \text{Rs } 800 \text{ per unit}$$

If 480,000 units are sold and 20,000 units remain in ending inventory, the unit-cost concept helps in the determination of total costs in the income statement and balance sheet and, hence, the financial results reported by LG Products to shareholders, banks, and the government.

Cost of goods sold in the income statement, 480,000 units × Rs 800 per unit	Rs 38,40,00,000
Ending inventory in the balance sheet, 20,000 units × Rs 800 per unit	1,60,00,000
Total manufacturing costs of 500,000 units	Rs 40,00,00,000

Unit costs are found in all areas of the value chain—for example, unit cost of product design, of sales visits, and of customer-service calls. By summing unit costs throughout the value chain, managers calculate the unit cost of the different products or services they deliver and determine the profitability of each product or service. Managers use this information, for example, to decide the products in which they should invest more resources, such as R&D and marketing, and the prices they should charge.

Use Unit Costs Cautiously

Although unit costs are regularly used in financial reports and for making product mix and pricing decisions, *managers should think in terms of total costs rather than unit costs for many decisions*. Consider the manager of the Pune plant of LG Products. Assume the Rs 40,00,00,000 in costs in 2011 consist of Rs 10,00,00,000 of fixed costs and Rs 30,00,00,000 of variable costs (at Rs 600 variable cost per speaker system produced). Suppose the total fixed cost and the variable cost per speaker system in 2012 are expected to be unchanged from 2011. The budgeted costs for 2012 at different production levels, calculated on the basis of total variable costs, total fixed costs, and total costs, are:

Units Produced (1)	Variable Cost per Unit (2)	Total Variable Costs (3) = (1) × (2)	Total Fixed Costs (4)	Total Costs (5) = (3) + (4)	Unit Cost (6) = (5) ÷ (1)
1,00,000	Rs 600	Rs 6,00,00,000	Rs 10,00,00,000	Rs 16,00,00,000	Rs 1,600.00
2,00,000	Rs 600	Rs 12,00,00,000	Rs 10,00,00,000	Rs 22,00,00,000	Rs 1,100.00
5,00,000	Rs 600	Rs 30,00,00,000	Rs 10,00,00,000	Rs 40,00,00,000	Rs 800.00
8,00,000	Rs 600	Rs 48,00,00,000	Rs 10,00,00,000	Rs 58,00,00,000	Rs 725.00
10,00,000	Rs 600	Rs 60,00,00,000	Rs 10,00,00,000	Rs 70,00,00,000	Rs 700.00

A plant manager who uses the 2011 unit cost of Rs 800 per unit will underestimate actual total costs if 2012 output is below the 2011 level of 500,000 units. If actual volume is 200,000 units due to, say, the presence of a new competitor, actual costs would be Rs 22,00,00,000. The unit cost of Rs 800 times 200,000 units equals Rs 16,00,00,000, which underestimates the actual total costs by Rs 6,00,00,000 (Rs 22,00,00,000−Rs 16,00,00,000). *The unit cost of Rs 800 applies only when 500,000 units are produced.*

An overreliance on unit cost in this situation could lead to insufficient cash being available to pay costs if volume declines to 200,000 units. As the table indicates, for making this decision, managers should think in terms of total variable costs, total fixed costs, and total costs rather than unit cost. As a general rule, first calculate total costs, then compute a unit cost, if it is needed for a particular decision.

Business Sectors, Types of Inventory, Inventoriable Costs, and Period Costs

In this section, we describe the different sectors of the economy, the different types of inventory that companies hold, and some commonly used classifications of manufacturing costs.

Manufacturing-, Merchandising-, and Service-Sector Companies

Distinguish among manufacturing companies, merchandising companies, and service-sector companies

. . . different types of companies face different accounting issues

We define three sectors of the economy and provide examples of companies in each sector.

1. **Manufacturing-sector companies** purchase materials and components and convert them into various finished goods. Examples are automotive companies such as Jaguar, cellular phone producers such as Nokia, food-processing companies such as Heinz, and computer companies such as Toshiba.
2. **Merchandising-sector companies** purchase and then sell tangible products without changing their basic form. This sector includes companies engaged in retailing (for example, bookstores such as Barnes and Noble or department stores such as Target), distribution (for example, a supplier of hospital products, such as Owens and Minor), or wholesaling (for example, a supplier of electronic components, such as Arrow Electronics).
3. **Service-sector companies** provide services (intangible products)—for example, legal advice or audits—to their customers. Examples are law firms, such as Wachtell, Lipton, Rosen & Katz, accounting firms such as Ernst and Young, banks such as Barclays, mutual fund companies such as Fidelity, insurance companies such as Aetna, transportation companies such as Singapore Airlines, advertising agencies such as Saatchi & Saatchi, television stations such as Turner Broadcasting, Internet service providers such as Comcast, travel agencies such as American Express, and brokerage firms such as Merrill Lynch.

Types of Inventory, Inventoriable Costs, and Period Costs

In this section, we describe the different types of inventory that companies hold and some commonly used classifications of manufacturing costs.

Learning Objective 6

Describe the three categories of inventories commonly found in manufacturing companies

. . . the categories are direct materials, work in process, and finished goods

Types of Inventory

Manufacturing-sector companies purchase materials and components and convert them into various finished goods. These companies typically have one or more of the following three types of inventory:

1. **Direct materials inventory.** Direct materials in stock and awaiting use in the manufacturing process (for example, computer chips and components needed to manufacture cellular phones).
2. **Work-in-process inventory.** Goods partially worked on but not yet completed (for example, cellular phones at various stages of completion in the manufacturing process). Also called **work in progress.**
3. **Finished goods inventory.** Goods (for example, cellular phones) completed but not yet sold.

Merchandising-sector companies purchase tangible products and then sell them without changing their basic form. They hold only one type of inventory, which is products in their original purchased form, called *merchandise inventory*. Service-sector companies provide only services or intangible products and so do not hold inventories of tangible products.

Commonly Used Classifications of Manufacturing Costs

Three terms commonly used when describing manufacturing costs are direct material costs, direct manufacturing labor costs, and indirect manufacturing costs.

1. **Direct material costs** are the acquisition costs of all materials that eventually become part of the cost object (work in process and then finished goods) and can be traced to the cost object in an economically feasible way. Acquisition costs of direct materials include freight-in (inward delivery) charges, sales taxes, and custom duties. Examples of direct material costs are the steel and tires used to make the BMW X5, and the computer chips used to make cellular phones.
2. **Direct manufacturing labor costs** include the compensation of all manufacturing labor that can be traced to the cost object (work in process and then finished goods) in an economically feasible way. Examples include wages and fringe benefits paid to machine operators and assembly-line workers who convert direct materials purchased to finished goods.
3. **Indirect manufacturing costs** are all manufacturing costs that are related to the cost object (work in process and then finished goods) but cannot be traced to that cost object in an economically feasible way. Examples include supplies, indirect materials such as lubricants, indirect manufacturing labor such as plant maintenance and cleaning labor, plant rent, plant insurance, property taxes on the plant, plant depreciation, and the compensation of plant managers. This cost category is also referred to as **manufacturing overhead costs** or **factory overhead costs.** We use *indirect manufacturing costs* and *manufacturing overhead costs* interchangeably in this book.

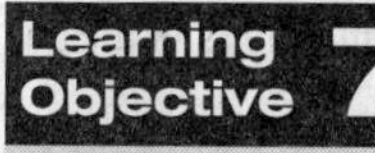

Learning Objective 7

Distinguish inventoriable costs

. . . assets when incurred, then cost of goods sold from period costs

. . . expenses of the period when incurred

We now describe the distinction between inventoriable costs and period costs.

Inventoriable Costs

Inventoriable costs are all costs of a product that are considered as assets in the balance sheet when they are incurred and that become cost of goods sold only when the product is sold. For manufacturing-sector companies, all manufacturing costs are inventoriable costs. Consider Cellular Products, a manufacturer of cellular phones. Costs of direct materials, such as computer chips, issued to production (from direct material inventory), direct manufacturing labor costs, and manufacturing overhead costs create new assets, starting as work in process and becoming finished goods (the cellular phones). Hence, manufacturing costs are included in work-in-process inventory and in finished goods inventory (they are "inventoried") to accumulate the costs of creating these assets.

When the cellular phones are sold, the cost of manufacturing them is matched against **revenues**, which are inflows of assets (usually cash or accounts receivable) received for products or services provided to customers. The cost of goods sold includes all manufacturing costs (direct materials, direct manufacturing labor, and manufacturing overhead costs) incurred to produce them. The cellular phones may be sold during a different accounting period than the period in which they were manufactured. Thus, inventorying manufacturing costs in the balance sheet during the accounting period when goods are manufactured and expensing the manufacturing costs in a later income statement when the goods are sold matches revenues and expenses.

For merchandising-sector companies such as Bharti Wal-Mart, inventoriable costs are the costs of purchasing the goods that are resold in their same form. These costs comprise the costs of the goods themselves plus any incoming freight, insurance, and handling costs for those goods. Service-sector companies provide only services or intangible products. The absence of inventories of tangible products for sale means there are no inventoriable costs.

Period Costs

Period costs are all costs in the income statement other than cost of goods sold. Period costs are treated as expenses of the accounting period in which they are incurred because they are expected to benefit revenues in that period and are not expected to benefit revenues in future periods (because there is not sufficient evidence to conclude that such future benefit exists). Expensing these costs in the period they are incurred matches expenses to revenues.

For manufacturing-sector companies, period costs in the income statement are all nonmanufacturing costs (for example, design costs and distribution costs). For merchandising-sector companies, period costs in the income statement are all costs not related to the cost of goods purchased for resale. Examples of these period costs are labor costs of sales floor personnel and advertising costs. Because there are no inventoriable costs for service-sector companies, all costs in the income statement are period costs.

Exhibit 2-5 showed examples of inventoriable costs in direct/indirect and variable/fixed cost classifications for a car manufacturer. Exhibit 2-6 shows examples of period costs in direct/indirect and variable/fixed cost classifications at a bank.

Exhibit 2-6

Examples of Period Costs in Combinations of the Direct/Indirect and Variable/Fixed Cost Classifications at a Bank

Cost-Behavior Pattern	Assignment of Costs to Cost Object: Direct Costs	Assignment of Costs to Cost Object: Indirect Costs
Variable Costs	• Cost object: Number of mortgage loans Example: Fees paid to property appraisal company for each mortgage loan	• Cost object: Number of mortgage loans Example: Postage paid to deliver mortgage-loan documents to lawyers/homeowners
Fixed Costs	• Cost object: Number of mortgage loans Example: Salary paid to executives in mortgage loan department to develop new mortgage-loan products	• Cost object: Number of mortgage loans Example: Cost to the bank of sponsoring annual golf tournament

Illustrating the Flow of Inventoriable Costs and Period Costs

We illustrate the flow of inventoriable costs and period costs through the income statement of a manufacturing company, for which the distinction between inventoriable costs and period costs is most detailed.

Manufacturing-Sector Example

Follow the flow of costs for Cellular Products in Exhibit 2-7 and Exhibit 2-8. Exhibit 2-7 visually highlights the differences in the flow of inventoriable and period costs for a manufacturing-sector company. Note how, as described in the previous section, inventoriable costs go through the balance sheet accounts of work-in-process inventory and finished goods inventory before entering cost of goods sold in the income statement. Period costs are expensed directly in the income statement. Exhibit 2-8 takes the visual presentation in Exhibit 2-7 and shows how inventoriable costs and period expenses would appear in the income statement and schedule of cost of goods manufactured of a manufacturing company.

We start by tracking the flow of direct materials shown on the left of Exhibit 2-7 and in Panel B of Exhibit 2-8.

Step 1: Cost of direct materials used. Note how the arrows in Exhibit 2-7 for beginning inventory, Rs, 1,10,000, and direct material purchases, Rs 7,30,000, "fill up" the direct material inventory box and how direct material used, Rs 7,60,000 "empties out" direct material inventory leaving an ending inventory of direct materials of Rs 80,000 that becomes the beginning inventory for the next year.

The cost of direct materials used is calculated in Exhibit 2-8, Panel B (light blue shaded area) as

Beginning inventory of direct materials, January 1, 2011	Rs 1,10,000
+ Purchases of direct materials in 2011	7,30,000
− Ending inventory of direct materials, December 31, 2011	80,000
= Direct materials used in 2011	Rs 7,60,000

Exhibit 2-7 Flow of Revenue and Costs for a Manufacturing-Sector Company, Cellular Products (in thousands)

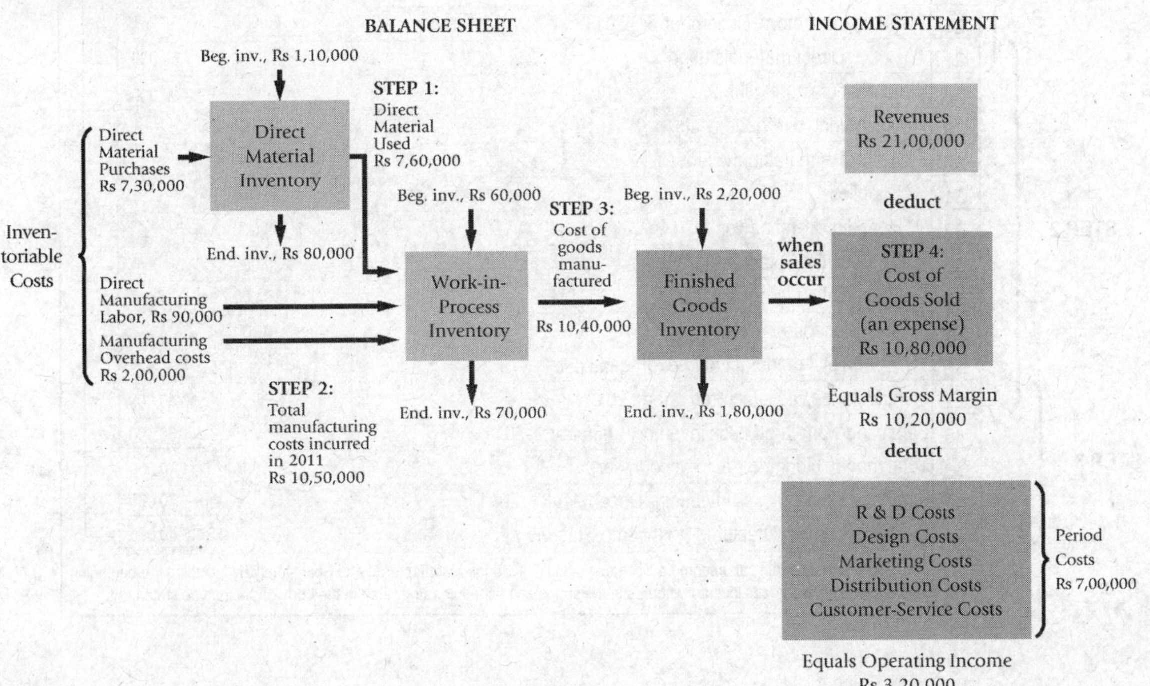

Exhibit 2-8 Income Statement and Schedule of Cost of Goods Manufactured of a Manufacturing-Sector Company, Cellular Products

		A	B	C	D
	1	**PANEL A: INCOME STATEMENT**			
	2	**Cellular Products**			
	3	**Income Statement**			
	4	**For the Year Ended December 31, 2011 (in thousands)**			
	5	Revenues		Rs 21,00,000	
	6	Cost of goods sold:			
	7	Beginning finished goods inventory, January 1, 2011	Rs 2,20,000		
STEP 4	8	Cost of goods manufactured (see Panel B)	Rs 10,40,000		
	9	Cost of goods available for sale	Rs 12,60,000		
	10	Ending finished goods inventory, December 31, 2011	Rs 1,80,000		
	11	Cost of goods sold		Rs 10,80,000	
	12	Gross margin (or gross profit)		Rs 10,20,000	
	13	Operating costs:			
	14	R&D, design, mktg., dist., & cust.-service cost	Rs 7,00,000		
	15	Total operating costs		Rs 7,00,000	
	16	Operating income		Rs 3,20,000	
	17				
	18	**PANEL B: COST OF GOODS MANUFACTURED**			
	19	**Cellular Products**			
	20	**Schedule of Cost of Goods Manufactured[a]**			
	21	**For the Year Ended December 31, 2011 (in thousands)**			
	22	Direct materials:			
	23	Beginning inventory, January 1, 2011	Rs 1,10,000		
STEP 1	24	Purchases of direct materials	7,30,000		
	25	Cost of direct materials available for use	8,40,000		
	26	Ending inventory, December 31, 2011	80,000		
	27	Direct materials used		Rs 7,60,000	
	28	Direct manufacturing labor		90,000	
	29	Manufacturing overhead costs:			
	30	Indirect manufacturing labor	Rs 70,000		
	31	Supplies	20,000		
STEP 2	32	Heat, light, and power	50,000		
	33	Depreciation--plant building	20,000		
	34	Depreciation--plant equipment	30,000		
	35	Miscellaneous	10,000		
	36	Total manufacturing overhead costs		2,00,000	
	37	Manufacturing costs incurred during 2011		10,50,000	
	38	Beginning work-in-process inventory, January 1, 2011		60,000	
STEP 3	39	Total manufacturing costs to account for		11,10,000	
	40	Ending work-in-process inventory, December 31, 2011		70,000	
	41	Cost of goods manufactured (to Income Statement)		Rs 10,40,000	
	42	[a]Note that this schedule can become a Schedule of Cost of Goods Manufactured and Sold simply by including the beginning and ending finished goods inventory figures in the supporting schedule rather than in the body of the income statement.			

Step 2: Total manufacturing costs incurred in 2011. Total manufacturing costs refers to all direct manufacturing costs and manufacturing overhead costs incurred during 2011 for all goods worked on during the year. Cellular Products classifies its manufacturing costs into the three categories described earlier.

(i) Direct materials used in 2011 (shaded light blue in Exhibit 2-8, Panel B)	Rs 7,60,000
(ii) Direct manufacturing labor in 2011 (shaded blue in Exhibit 2-8, Panel B)	90,000
(iii) Manufacturing overhead costs (shaded dark blue in Exhibit 2-8, Panel B)	2,00,000
Total manufacturing costs incurred in 2011	Rs 10,50,000

Note how in Exhibit 2-7, these costs increase work-in-process inventory.

Step 3: Cost of goods manufactured in 2011. Cost of goods manufactured refers to the cost of goods brought to completion, whether they were started before or during the current accounting period.

Note how the work-in-process inventory box in Exhibit 2-7 has a very similar structure to the direct material inventory box described in Step 1. Beginning work-in-process inventory of Rs 60,000 and total manufacturing costs incurred in 2011 of Rs 10,50,000 "fill-up" the work-in-process inventory box. Some of the manufacturing costs incurred during 2011 are held back as the cost of the ending work-in-process inventory. The ending work-in-process inventory of Rs 70,000 becomes the beginning inventory for the next year, and the cost of goods manufactured during 2011 of Rs 10,40,000 "empties out" the work-in-process inventory while "filling up" the finished goods inventory box.

The cost of goods manufactured in 2011 (shaded teal) is calculated in Exhibit 2-8, Panel B as:

Beginning work-in-process inventory, January 1, 2011	Rs 60,000
+ Total manufacturing costs incurred in 2011	10,50,000
= Total manufacturing costs to account for	11,10,000
− Ending work-in-process inventory, December 31, 2011	70,000
= Cost of goods manufactured in 2011	Rs 10,40,000

Step 4: Cost of goods sold in 2011. The cost of goods sold is the cost of finished goods inventory sold to customers during the current accounting period. Looking at the finished goods inventory box in Exhibit 2-7, we see that the beginning inventory of finished goods of Rs 2,20,000 and cost of goods manufactured in 2011 of Rs 10,40,000 "fill up" the finished goods inventory box. The ending inventory of finished goods of Rs 1,80,000 becomes the beginning inventory for the next year, and the cost of goods sold during 2011 of Rs 10,80,000 "empties out" the finished goods inventory.

This cost of goods sold is an expense that is matched against revenues. The cost of goods sold for Cellular Products (shaded brown) is computed in Exhibit 2-8, Panel A, as:

Beginning inventory of finished goods, January 1, 2011	Rs 2,20,000
+ Cost of goods manufactured in 2011	10,40,000
− Ending inventory of finished goods, December 31, 2011	1,80,000
= Cost of goods sold in 2011	Rs 10,80,000

Exhibit 2-9 shows related general-ledger T-accounts for Cellular Products' manufacturing cost flow. Note how the cost of goods manufactured (Rs 10,40,000) is the cost of all goods completed during the accounting period. These costs are all inventoriable costs. Goods completed during the period are transferred to finished goods inventory. These costs become cost of goods sold in the accounting period when the goods are sold. Also note that the direct materials, direct manufacturing labor, and manufacturing overhead costs of the units in work-in-process inventory (Rs 70,000) and finished goods inventory (Rs 1,80,000) as of December 31, 2011, will appear as an asset in the balance sheet. These costs will become expenses next year, when these units are sold.

We are now in a position to prepare Cellular Products' income statement for 2011. The income statement of Cellular Products is shown on the right-hand side of Exhibit 2-7 and in Exhibit 2-8, Panel A. Revenues of Cellular Products are (in thousands) Rs 21,00,000. Inventoriable costs expensed during 2011 equal cost of goods sold of Rs 10,80,000. Gross margin = Revenues − Cost of goods sold = Rs 21,00,000 − Rs 10,80,000 = Rs10,20,000.

Exhibit 2-9

General-Ledger T-Accounts for Cellular Products' Manufacturing Cost Flow

Work-in-Process Inventory				Finished Goods Inventory				Cost of Goods Sold
Bal. Jan. 1, 2011	60,000	Cost of goods manufactured	10,40,000 →	Bal. Jan. 1, 2011	2,20,000	Cost of goods sold	10,80,000 →	10,80,000
Direct materials used	7,60,000				→ 10,40,000			
Direct manuf. labor	90,000			Bal. Dec. 31, 2011	1,80,000			
Indirect manuf. costs	2,00,000							
Bal. Dec. 31, 2011	70,000							

The Rs 7,00,000 comprising R&D, design, marketing, distribution, and customer-service costs are period costs of Cellular Products. These period costs include, for example, salaries of salespersons, depreciation on computers and other equipment used in marketing, and the cost of leasing warehouse space for distribution. Period costs help to calculate **operating income**, which is total revenues from operations minus cost of goods sold and operating costs (excluding interest expense and income taxes). The operating income of Cellular Products is Rs 3,20,000 (gross margin, Rs 10,20,000 – period costs, Rs 7,00,000).

Newcomers to cost accounting frequently assume that indirect costs such as rent, telephone, and depreciation are always costs of the period in which they are incurred and are not associated with inventories. When these costs are incurred in marketing or in corporate headquarters, they are period costs. However, when these costs are incurred in manufacturing, they are manufacturing overhead costs and are inventoriable.

Recap of Inventoriable Costs and Period Costs

Exhibit 2-7 highlights the differences between inventoriable costs and period costs for a manufacturing company. The manufacturing costs of finished goods include direct materials, other direct manufacturing costs such as direct manufacturing labor, and manufacturing overhead costs such as supervision, production control, and machine maintenance. All these costs are inventoriable: They are assigned to work-in-process inventory until the goods are completed and then to finished goods inventory until the goods are sold. All nonmanufacturing costs, such as R&D, design, and distribution costs, are period costs.

Inventoriable costs and period costs flow through the income statement at a merchandising company similar to the way costs flow at a manufacturing company. At a merchandising company, however, the flow of costs is much simpler to understand and track. Exhibit 2-10 shows the distribution between inventoriable costs and period costs for a retailer or wholesaler who buys goods for resale. The only inventoriable cost is the cost of merchandise. (This corresponds to the cost of finished goods manufactured for a manufacturing company.)

Exhibit 2-10

Merchandising Company (Retailer or Wholesaler)

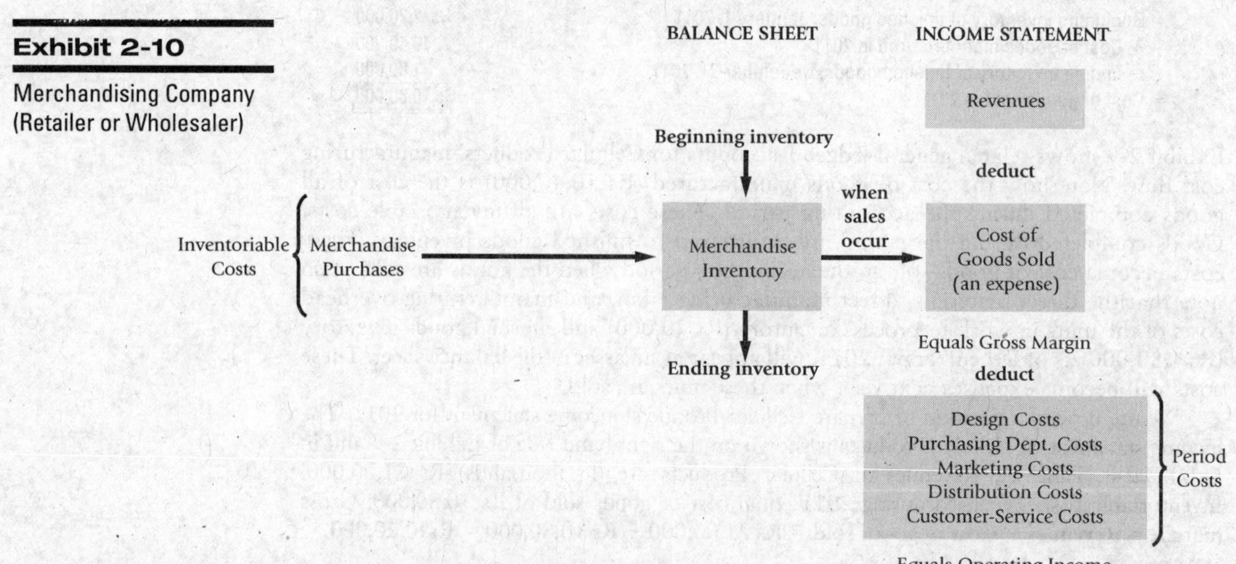

Purchased goods are held as merchandise inventory, the cost of which is shown as an asset in the balance sheet. As the goods are sold, their costs are shown in the income statement as cost of goods sold. A retailer or wholesaler also has a variety of marketing, distribution, and customer-service costs, which are period costs. In the income statement, period costs are deducted from revenues without ever having been included as part of inventory.

Prime Costs and Conversion Costs

Two terms used to describe cost classifications in manufacturing costing systems are prime costs and conversion costs. **Prime costs** are all direct manufacturing costs. For Cellular Products,

$$\text{Prime costs} = \text{Direct material costs} + \text{Direct manufacturing labor} = \text{Rs } 7{,}60{,}000 + \text{Rs } 90{,}000 = \text{Rs } 8{,}50{,}000$$

As we have already discussed, the greater the proportion of prime costs in a company's cost structure, the more confident managers can be about the accuracy of the costs of products. As information-gathering technology improves, companies can add more and more direct-cost categories. For example, power costs might be metered in specific areas of a plant and identified with specific products. In this case, prime costs would include direct materials, direct manufacturing labor, and direct metered power. Furthermore, if a production line were dedicated to the manufacture of a specific product, the depreciation on the production equipment would be a direct manufacturing cost and would be included in prime costs. Computer software companies often have a "purchased technology" direct manufacturing cost item. This item, which represents payments to suppliers who develop software algorithms for a product, is also included in prime costs. **Conversion costs** are all manufacturing costs other than direct material costs. Conversion costs represent all manufacturing costs incurred to convert direct materials into finished goods. For Cellular Products,

$$\text{Conversion costs} = \begin{matrix}\text{Direct manufacturing}\\ \text{labor costs}\end{matrix} + \begin{matrix}\text{manufacturing}\\ \text{overhead costs}\end{matrix} = \text{Rs } 90{,}000 + \text{Rs } 2{,}00{,}000 = \text{Rs } 2{,}90{,}000$$

Note that direct manufacturing labor costs are a part of both prime costs and conversion costs.

Some manufacturing operations, such as computer-integrated manufacturing (CIM) plants, have very few workers. The workers' roles are to monitor the manufacturing process and to maintain the equipment that produces multiple products. Costing systems in CIM plants do not have a direct manufacturing labor cost category because direct manufacturing labor cost is relatively small and because it is difficult to trace this cost to products. In CIM plants, the only prime cost is direct material costs, and conversion costs consist only of manufacturing overhead costs.

Measuring Costs Requires Judgment

Measuring costs requires judgment. That's because there are alternative ways in which costs can be defined and classified. Different companies or sometimes even different subunits within the same company may define and classify costs differently. Be careful to define and understand the ways costs are measured in a company or situation. We first illustrate this point with respect to labor cost measurement.

Measuring Labor Costs

Although manufacturing labor cost classifications vary among companies, most companies have the following categories:

- Direct manufacturing labor (labor that can be traced to individual products)
- Manufacturing overhead (examples of prominent labor components of manufacturing overhead follow):
  - Indirect labor (compensation)

    Forklift truck operators (internal handling of materials)
    Plant janitors
    Plant guards

Rework labor (time spent by direct laborers redoing defective work)
Overtime premium paid to plant workers (explained next)
Idle time (explained next)

- Managers', department heads', and supervisors' salaries
- Payroll fringe costs, for example, health care premiums and pension costs (explained later)

Note how *indirect labor costs* are commonly divided into many subclassifications, for example, forklift operators and plant guards, to retain information on different categories of indirect labor. Note also that managers' salaries usually are not classified as indirect labor costs. Instead, the compensation of supervisors, department heads, and all others who are regarded as manufacturing management is placed in a separate classification of labor-related manufacturing overhead.

Overtime Premium and Idle Time

The purpose of classifying costs in detail is to associate an individual cost with a specific cause or reason for why it was incurred. Two classes of indirect labor—overtime premium and idle time—need special mention. **Overtime premium** is the wage rate paid to workers (for both direct labor and indirect labor) in *excess* of their straight-time wage rates. Overtime premium is usually considered to be a part of indirect costs or overhead. Consider an example from the service sector. Govind Chopra does home repairs for Godrej Appliance Services. He is paid Rs 200 per hour for straight-time and Rs 300 per hour (time and a half) for overtime. His overtime premium is Rs 100 per overtime hour. If he works 44 hours, including 4 overtime hours, in one week, his gross compensation would be classified as follows:

Direct service labor: 44 hours × Rs 200 per hour	Rs 8,800
Overtime premium: 4 hours × Rs 100 per hour	400
Total compensation for 44 hours	Rs 9,200

In this example, why is the overtime premium of direct labor usually considered an overhead cost rather than a direct cost? After all, it can be traced to specific repair jobs. Overtime premium is generally not considered a direct charge because the scheduling of repair jobs is usually either random or in accordance with minimizing overall travel time. For example, assume that jobs 1 through 5 are scheduled to be completed on a specific workday of 10 hours, including 2 overtime hours. Each job (service call) requires 2 hours. Should the job scheduled during hours 9 and 10 be assigned the overtime premium? Or should the premium be prorated over all five jobs? Prorating the overtime premium does not "penalize"—add to the cost of—a particular batch of work solely because it happened to be worked on during the overtime hours. *Instead, the overtime premium is considered to be attributable to the heavy overall volume of work. Its cost is regarded as part of overhead, which is borne by both products.*

Sometimes overtime is not random. For example, a customer demanding a "rush job" may clearly be the sole source of overtime. In such instances, the overtime premium is regarded as a direct cost of that job.

Another subclassification of indirect labor is the idle time of both direct and indirect manufacturing or service labor. **Idle time** is wages paid for unproductive time caused by lack of orders, machine breakdowns, material shortages, poor scheduling, and the like. For example, if the Godrej repair truck broke down for 3 hours, Govind earnings would be classified as follows:

Direct service labor: 41 hours × Rs 200/hour	Rs 8,200
Idle time (service overhead): 3 hours × Rs 200/hour	600
Overtime premium (service overhead): 4 hours × Rs 100/hour	400
Total earnings for 44 hours	Rs 9,200

Clearly, the idle time is not related to a particular job, nor, as we have already discussed, is the overtime premium. Both overtime premium and idle time are considered overhead costs.

Benefits of Defining Accounting Terms

Managers, accountants, suppliers, and others will avoid many problems if they thoroughly understand and agree on the classifications and meanings of the cost terms introduced in this chapter and later in this book.

Consider the classification of manufacturing labor *payroll fringe costs* (for example, employer payments for employee benefits such as Social Security, life insurance, health insurance, and pensions). Some companies classify these costs as manufacturing overhead costs. In other companies, the fringe benefits related to direct manufacturing labor are treated as an additional direct manufacturing labor cost. Consider, for example, a direct laborer, such as a lathe operator, whose gross wages are computed on the basis of a stated wage rate of Rs 200 an hour and fringe benefits totaling, say, Rs 50 per hour. Some companies classify the Rs 200 as direct manufacturing labor cost and the Rs 50 as manufacturing overhead cost. Other companies classify the entire Rs 250 as direct manufacturing labor cost. The latter approach is preferable because the stated wage and the fringe benefit costs together are a fundamental part of acquiring direct manufacturing labor services.

Caution: In every situation, pinpoint clearly what direct manufacturing labor includes and what direct manufacturing labor excludes. Achieving clarity may prevent disputes regarding cost-reimbursement contracts, income tax payments, and labor union matters. Consider that some countries such as Mauritius offer substantial income tax savings to companies that locate plants within their borders. In some cases, to qualify for the tax benefits, the direct manufacturing labor costs of the plant must at least equal a specified percentage of the total manufacturing costs.

When direct manufacturing labor costs are not precisely defined, disputes have arisen as to whether payroll fringe costs should be included in direct manufacturing labor when calculating the direct manufacturing labor percentage for qualifying for such tax benefits. Companies have sought to classify payroll fringe costs as part of direct manufacturing labor costs to make direct manufacturing labor costs a higher percentage of total manufacturing costs. Tax authorities have argued that payroll fringe costs are part of manufacturing overhead. In addition to fringe benefits, other debated items are compensation for training time, idle time, vacations, sick leave, and overtime premium. To prevent disputes, contracts and laws should be as specific as possible regarding definitions and measurements.

Learning Objective 8

Explain why product costs are computed in different ways for different purposes

. . . examples are pricing and product-mix decisions, government contracts, and financial statements

Different Meanings of Product Costs

Many cost terms found in practice have ambiguous meanings. Consider the term *product cost*. A **product cost** is the sum of the costs assigned to a product for a specific purpose. Different purposes can result in different measures of product cost, as the brackets on the value chain in Exhibit 2-11 illustrate:

- **Pricing and product-mix decisions.** For the purposes of making decisions about pricing and which products provide the most profits, the manager is interested in the

Exhibit 2-11

Different Product Costs for Different Purposes

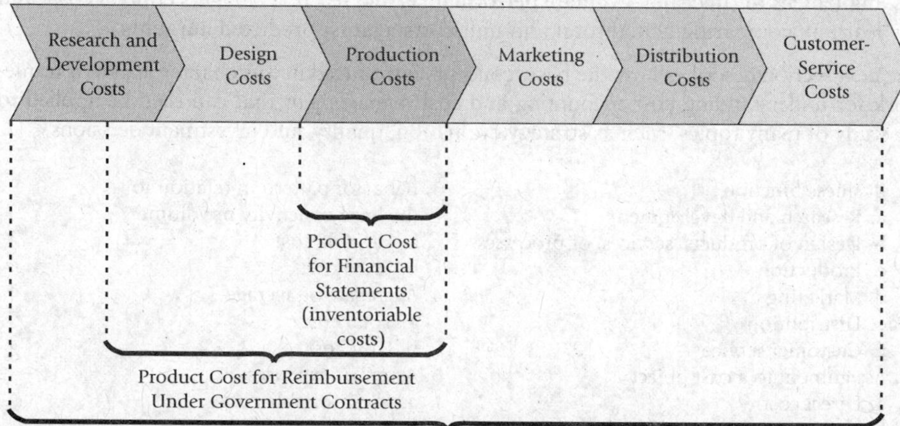

overall (total) profitability of different products and, consequently, assigns costs incurred in all business functions of the value chain to the different products.

- **Contracting with government agencies.** Government contracts often reimburse contractors on the basis of the "cost of a product" plus a prespecified margin of profit. Because of the cost-plus profit margin nature of the contract, government agencies provide detailed guidelines on the cost items they will allow and disallow when calculating the cost of a product. For example, some government agencies explicitly exclude marketing, distribution, and customer-service costs from the product costs that qualify for reimbursement, and they may only partially reimburse R&D costs. These agencies want to reimburse contractors for only those costs most closely related to delivering products under the contract. The second bracket in Exhibit 2-11 shows how the product-cost calculations for a specific contract may allow for all design and production costs but only part of R&D costs.
- **Preparing financial statements for external reporting under GAAP.** Under GAAP, only manufacturing costs can be assigned to inventories in the financial statements. For purposes of calculating inventory costs, product costs include only inventoriable (manufacturing) costs.

As Exhibit 2-11 illustrates, product-cost measures range from a narrow set of costs for financial statements—a set that includes only inventoriable costs—to a broader set of costs for reimbursement under a government contract to a still broader set of costs for pricing and product-mix decisions.

This section focused on how different purposes result in the inclusion of different cost items of the value chain of business functions when product costs are calculated. The same caution about the need to be clear and precise about cost concepts and their measurement applies to each cost classification introduced in this chapter. Exhibit 2-12 summarizes the key cost classifications.

Using the five-step process described in Chapter 1, think about how these different classifications of costs are helpful to managers when making decisions and evaluating performance.

1. **Identify the problem and uncertainties.** Consider a decision about how much to price a product. This decision often depends on how much it costs to make the product.
2. **Obtain information.** Managers identify direct and indirect costs of a product in each business function. Managers also gather other information about customers, competitors, and prices of substitute products.
3. **Make predictions about the future.** Managers estimate what it will cost to make the product in the future. This requires predictions about the quantity of product that managers expect to sell and an understanding of fixed and variable costs.
4. **Make decisions by choosing among alternatives.** Managers choose a price to charge based on a thorough understanding of costs and other information.
5. **Implement the decision, evaluate performance, and learn.** Managers control costs and learn by comparing actual total and unit costs against predicted amounts.

The next section describes how the basic concepts introduced in this chapter lead to a framework for understanding cost accounting and cost management that can then be applied to the study of many topics, such as strategy evaluation, quality, and investment decisions.

Exhibit 2-12

Alternative Classifications of Costs

1. Business function
   a. Research and development
   b. Design of products, services, or processes
   c. Production
   d. Marketing
   e. Distribution
   f. Customer service
2. Assignment to a cost object
   a. Direct cost
   b. Indirect cost
3. Behavior pattern in relation to the level of activity or volume
   a. Variable cost
   b. Fixed cost
4. Aggregate or average
   a. Total cost
   b. Unit cost
5. Assets or expenses
   a. Inventoriable cost
   b. Period cost

A Framework for Cost Accounting and Cost Management

Three features of cost accounting and cost management across a wide range of applications are:

1. Calculating the cost of products, services, and other cost objects
2. Obtaining information for planning and control and performance evaluation
3. Analyzing the relevant information for making decisions

We develop these ideas in Chapters 3 through 12. The ideas also form the foundation for the study of various topics later in the book.

Learning Objective 9

Describe a framework for cost accounting and cost management

. . . three features that help managers make decisions

Calculating the Cost of Products, Services, and Other Cost Objects

We have already seen the different purposes and measures of product costs. Whatever the purpose, the costing system traces direct costs and allocates indirect costs to products. Chapters 4 and 5 describe systems, such as activity-based costing systems, used to calculate total costs and unit costs of products and services. The chapters also discuss how managers use this information to formulate strategy and make pricing, product-mix, and cost-management decisions.

Obtaining Information for Planning and Control and Performance Evaluation

Budgeting is the most commonly used tool for planning and control. A budget forces managers to look ahead, to translate strategy into plans, to coordinate and communicate within the organization, and to provide a benchmark for evaluating performance. Budgeting often plays a major role in affecting behavior and decisions because managers strive to meet budget targets. Chapter 6 describes budgeting systems.

At the end of a reporting period, managers compare actual results to planned performance. The manager's tasks are to understand why differences (called variances) between actual and planned performances arise and to use the information provided by these variances as feedback to promote learning and future improvement. Managers also use variances as well as nonfinancial measures, such as defect rates and customer satisfaction ratings, to control and evaluate the performance of various departments, divisions, and managers. Chapters 7 and 8 discuss variance analysis. Chapter 9 describes planning, control, and inventory-costing issues relating to capacity. Chapters 6, 7, 8, and 9 focus on the management accountant's role in implementing strategy.

Analyzing the Relevant Information for Making Decisions

When making decisions about strategy design and strategy implementation, managers must understand which revenues and costs to consider and which ones to ignore. Management accountants help managers identify what information is relevant and what information is irrelevant. Consider a decision about whether to buy a product from an outside vendor or to make it in-house. The costing system indicates that it costs Rs 250 per unit to make the product in-house. A vendor offers the product for Rs 220 per unit. At first glance, it seems it will cost less for the company to buy the product rather than make it. Suppose, however, that of the Rs 250 to make the product in-house, Rs 50 consists of plant lease costs that the company will have to pay whether the product is made or bought. That is, if the product is bought, the plant will remain idle and the Rs 50 in lease costs will still be incurred. Under this condition, it will cost less to make the product than to buy it. That's because making the product costs only an *additional* Rs 200 per unit (Rs 250−Rs 50), compared with an *additional* Rs 220 per unit if it is bought. The Rs 50 per unit of lease cost is irrelevant to the decision because it will be incurred whether the product is made or bought. Analyzing relevant information is a key aspect of making decisions.

When making strategic decisions about which products to produce, managers must know how revenues and costs vary with changes in output levels. For this purpose, managers need to distinguish fixed costs from variable costs. Chapter 3 analyzes how operating income changes with changes in units sold and how managers use this information to make decisions such as how much to spend on advertising. Chapter 10 describes methods to estimate the fixed and variable components of costs. Chapter 11 applies the concept of relevance to decision making in many different situations and describes methods managers use to maximize income given the resource constraints that they face. Chapter 12 describes how management accountants help managers determine prices and manage costs across the value chain and over a product's life cycle.

Later chapters in the book discuss topics such as strategy evaluation, customer profitability, quality, just-in-time systems, investment decisions, transfer pricing, and performance evaluation. Each of these topics invariably has product costing, planning and control, and decision-making perspectives. A command of the first 12 chapters will help you master these topics. For example, Chapter 13 on strategy describes the balanced scorecard, a set of financial and nonfinancial measures used to implement strategy that builds on the planning and control functions. The section on strategic analysis of operating income builds on ideas of product costing and variance analysis. The section on downsizing and managing capacity builds on ideas of relevant revenues and relevant costs.

Problem for Self-Study

Campbell Company is a metal- and woodcutting manufacturer, selling products to the home construction market. Consider the following data for 2011:

Sandpaper	Rs 20,000
Materials-handling costs	7,00,000
Lubricants and coolants	50,000
Miscellaneous indirect manufacturing labor	4,00,000
Direct manufacturing labor	30,00,000
Direct materials inventory Jan. 1, 2011	4,00,000
Direct materials inventory Dec. 31, 2011	50,00,000
Finished goods inventory Jan. 1, 2011	10,00,000
Finished goods inventory Dec. 31, 2011	15,00,000
Work in process inventory Jan. 1, 2011	1,00,000
Work in process inventory Dec. 31, 2011	1,40,000
Plant-leasing costs	5,40,000
Depreciation—plant equipment	3,60,000
Property taxes on plant equipment	40,000
Fire insurance on plant equipment	Rs 30,000
Direct materials purchased	46,00,000
Revenues	1,36,00,000
Marketing promotions	6,00,000
Marketing salaries	10,00,000
Distribution costs	7,00,000
Customer-service costs	10,00,000

Required

1. Prepare an income statement with a separate supporting schedule of cost of goods manufactured. For all manufacturing items, classify costs as direct costs or indirect costs and indicate by V or F whether each is basically a variable cost or a fixed cost (when the cost object is a product unit). If in doubt, decide on the basis of whether the total cost will change substantially over a wide range of units produced.
2. Suppose that both the direct material costs and the plant-leasing costs are for the production of 900,000 units. What is the direct material cost of each unit produced? What is the plant-leasing cost per unit? Assume that the plant-leasing cost is a fixed cost.
3. Suppose Campbell Company manufactures 1,000,000 units next year. Repeat the computation in requirement 2 for direct materials and plant-leasing costs. Assume the implied cost-behavior patterns persist.

4. As a management consultant, explain concisely to the company president why the unit cost for direct materials did not change in requirements 2 and 3 but the unit cost for plant-leasing costs did change.

Solution

1.

Campbell Company
Income Statement
For the Year Ended December 31, 2011

Revenues	Rs 1,36,00,000	
Cost of goods sold		
Beginning finished goods inventory January 1, 2011	Rs 10,00,000	
Cost of goods manufactured (see schedule below)	96,00,000	
Cost of goods available for sale	1,06,00,000	
Deduct ending finished goods inventory December 31, 2011	15,00,000	91,00,000
Gross margin (or gross profit)		45,00,000
Operating costs		
Marketing promotions	6,00,000	
Marketing salaries	10,00,000	
Distribution costs	7,00,000	
Customer-service costs	10,00,000	33,00,000
Operating income		Rs 12,00,000

Campbell Company
Schedule of Cost of Goods Manufactured
For the Year Ended December 31, 2011

Direct materials		
Beginning inventory, January 1, 2011		Rs 4,00,000
Purchases of direct materials		46,00,000
Cost of direct materials available for use		50,00,000
Ending inventory, December 31, 2011		5,00,000
Direct materials used		45,00,000 (V)
Direct manufacturing labor		30,00,000 (V)
Indirect manufacturing costs		
Sandpaper	Rs 20,000 (V)	
Materials-handling costs	7,00,000 (V)	
Lubricants and coolants	50,000 (V)	
Miscellaneous indirect manufacturing labor	4,00,000 (V)	
Plant-leasing costs	5,40,000 (F)	
Depreciation—plant equipment	3,60,000 (F)	
Property taxes on plant equipment	40,000 (F)	
Fire insurance on plant equipment	30,000 (F)	21,40,000
Manufacturing costs incurred during 2011		96,40,000
Beginning work in process inventory, January 1, 2011		1,00,000
Total manufacturing costs to account for		97,40,000
Ending work in process inventory, December 31, 2011		1,40,000
Cost of goods manufactured (to Income Statement)		Rs 96,00,000

2. Direct material unit cost = Direct materials used ÷ Units produced
= 45,00,000 ÷ 900,000 units = Rs 5 per unit

Plant-leasing unit cost = Plant-leasing costs ÷ Units produced
= 5,40,000 ÷ 900,000 units = Rs 6 per unit

3. The direct material costs are variable, so they would increase in total from Rs 45,00,000 to Rs 50,00,000 (1,000,000 units × Rs 5 per unit). However, their unit cost would be unaffected: Rs.50,00,000 ÷ 1,000,000 units = Rs 5 per unit.

   In contrast, the plant-leasing costs of Rs 5,40,000 are fixed, so they would not increase in total. However, the plant-leasing cost per unit would decline from Rs 6 to Rs 5.40: Rs 5,40,000 ÷ 1,000,000 units = Rs 5.4 per unit.
4. The explanation would begin with the answer to requirement 3. As a consultant, you should stress that the unitizing (averaging) of costs that have different behavior patterns can be misleading. A common error is to assume that a total unit cost, which is often a sum of variable unit cost and fixed unit cost, is an indicator that total costs change in proportion to changes in production levels. The next chapter demonstrates the necessity for distinguishing between cost-behavior patterns. You must be wary, especially about average fixed cost per unit. Too often, unit fixed cost is erroneously regarded as being indistinguishable from unit variable cost.

Decision Points

The following question-and-answer format summarizes the chapter's learning objectives. Each decision presents a key question related to a learning objective. The guidelines are the answer to that question.

Decision	Guidelines
1. How do managers choose a cost object?	A cost object is anything for which a separate measurement of cost is needed. Examples include a product, a service, a project, a customer, a brand category, an activity, and a department.
2. How do managers decide whether a cost is a direct or an indirect cost?	A direct cost is any cost that is related to a particular cost object and can be traced to that cost object in an economically feasible way. Indirect costs are related to the particular cost object but cannot be traced in an economically feasible way. The same cost can be direct for one cost object and indirect for other cost objects. This book uses *cost tracing* to describe the assignment of direct costs to a cost object and *cost allocation* to describe the assignment of indirect costs to a cost object.
3. How do managers decide whether a cost is a variable or a fixed cost?	A variable cost changes *in total* in proportion to changes in the related level of total activity or volume. A fixed cost remains unchanged *in total* for a given time period despite wide changes in the related level of total activity or volume.
4. How should costs be estimated?	In general, focus on total costs, not unit costs. When making total cost esti mates, think of variable costs as an amount per unit and fixed costs as a total amount. The unit cost of a cost object should be interpreted cautiously when it includes a fixed-cost component.
5. How do you distinguish among manufacturing-, merchandising-, and service-sector companies?	Manufacturing-sector companies purchase materials and components and convert them into finished goods. Merchandising-sector companies purchase and then sell tangible products without changing their basic form. Service-sector companies provide services (intangible products) to their customers.
6. How do manufacturing companies categorize inventories?	The three categories of inventories found in many manufacturing companies depict stages in the conversion process: direct materials, work in process, and finished goods.
7. Which costs are initially treated as assets for external reporting, and which costs are expensed as they are incurred?	Inventoriable costs are all costs of a product that are regarded as an asset in the accounting period when they are incurred and then become cost of goods sold in the accounting period when the product is sold. Period costs are expensed in the accounting period in which they are incurred and are all of the costs in an income statement other than cost of goods sold.

8. How do managers assign costs to cost objects?	Managers can assign different costs to the same cost object depending on the purpose. For example, for the external reporting purpose in a manufacturing company, the inventoriable cost of a product includes only manufacturing costs. In contrast, costs from all business functions of the value chain often are assigned to a product for pricing and product-mix decisions.
9. What are the features of cost accounting and cost management?	Three features of cost accounting and cost management are (1) calculating the cost of products, services, and other cost objects; (2) obtaining information for planning and control and performance evaluation; and (3) analyzing the relevant information for making decisions.

TERMS TO LEARN

This chapter contains more basic terms than any other in this book. Do not proceed before you check your understanding of the following terms. Both the chapter and the Glossary at the end of the book contain definitions.

actual cost **(p. 25)**
average cost **(p. 33)**
budgeted cost **(p. 25)**
conversion costs **(p. 41)**
cost **(p. 25)**
cost accumulation **(p. 26)**
cost allocation **(p. 27)**
cost assignment **(p. 27)**
cost driver **(p. 30)**
cost object **(p. 25)**
cost of goods manufactured **(p. 37)**
cost tracing **(p. 26)**
direct costs of a cost object **(p. 26)**
direct manufacturing labor costs **(p. 35)**
direct material costs **(p. 35)**
direct materials inventory **(p. 35)**
factory overhead costs **(p. 35)**
finished goods inventory **(p. 35)**
fixed cost **(p. 28)**
idle time **(p. 42)**
indirect costs of a cost object **(p. 26)**
indirect manufacturing costs **(p. 35)**
inventoriable costs **(p. 35)**
manufacturing overhead costs **(p. 35)**
manufacturing-sector companies **(p. 34)**
merchandising-sector companies **(p. 34)**
operating income **(p. 40)**
overtime premium **(p. 42)**
period costs **(p. 36)**
prime costs **(p. 41)**
product cost **(p. 43)**
relevant range **(p. 31)**
revenues **(p. 36)**
service-sector companies **(p. 34)**
unit cost **(p. 33)**
variable cost **(p. 28)**
work-in-process inventory **(p. 35)**
work in progress **(p. 35)**

ASSIGNMENT MATERIAL

Questions

2-1 Define cost object and give three examples.

2-2 Define direct costs and indirect costs.

2-3 Why do managers consider direct costs to be more accurate than indirect costs?

2-4 Name three factors that will affect the classification of a cost as direct or indirect.

2-5 Define variable cost and fixed cost. Give an example of each.

2-6 What is a cost driver? Give one example.

2-7 What is the relevant range? What role does the relevant-range concept play in explaining how costs behave?

2-8 Explain why unit costs must often be interpreted with caution.

2-9 Describe how manufacturing-, merchandising-, and service-sector companies differ from each other.

2-10 What are three different types of inventory that manufacturing companies hold?

2-11 Distinguish between inventoriable costs and period costs.

2-12 Do service-sector companies have inventoriable costs? Explain.

2-13 Define the following: direct material costs, direct manufacturing-labor costs, manufacturing overhead costs, prime costs, and conversion costs.

2-14 Describe the overtime-premium and idle-time categories of indirect labor.

2-15 Define product cost. Describe three different purposes for computing product costs.

Solved Examples

2-16 Computing and interpreting manufacturing unit costs. J.K. Paper Products (JKPP) produces three different paper products - Supreme, Deluxe, and Regular. Each product has its own dedicated production line at the plant. It currently uses the following three-part classification for its manufacturing costs: direct materials, direct manufacturing labor, and indirect manufacturing costs. Total indirect manufacturing costs of the plant for July, current year are Rs 150 million (Rs 20 million of which is fixed). This total amount is allocated to each product line on the basis of direct manufacturing labor costs of each line. Summary data (in millions) for July are as follows:

Particulars	Supreme	Deluxe	Regular
Direct material costs	Rs 84.00	Rs 54.00	Rs 62.00
Direct manufacturing labor costs	14.00	28.00	8.00
Manufacturing overhead costs	42.00	84.00	24.00
Units produced	80	120	100

Required

1. Compute the manufacturing cost per unit for each product produced in July.
2. Suppose that in August production was 120 million units of Supreme, 160 million units of Deluxe, and 180 million units of Regular. Why might the July manufacturing unit cost information be misleading when predicting total manufacturing costs in August?

Solution

1. **Computation of manufacturing cost per unit (in millions)**

Particulars	Supreme	Deluxe	Regular
Direct materials costs	Rs 84.00	Rs 54.00	Rs 62.00
Direct manufacturing labor costs	14.00	28.00	8.00
Indirect manufacturing costs	42.00	84.00	24.00
Total manufacturing costs	140.00	166.00	94.00
Units produced (millions)	80	120	100
Cost per unit (Total manufacturing costs ÷ Units produced)	Rs 1.7500	Rs 1.3833	Rs 0.9400

2. The unit costs in requirement 1 includes Rs 20 million of indirect manufacturing costs that are fixed irrespective of changes in the volume of output per month, while the remaining variable indirect manufacturing costs change with the production volume. Given the unit volume changes for August, the use of unit costs from the past month at a different unit volume level (both in aggregate and at the individual product level) will yield incorrect estimates of total costs in August.

2-17 Direct, indirect, fixed and variable costs. J.K. Paper Products (JKPP) employs a consultant to help reduce energy costs at its plant. Currently, JKPP does not trace energy costs to each of its three different paper products–Supreme, Deluxe, and Regular. The energy consultant notes that each production line at the plant has multiple energy meters and that tracing of energy costs to each line is possible. Of the Rs 150 million of indirect manufacturing costs in July, Rs 90 million is for energy costs traceable to individual production lines. The remaining Rs 60 million of indirect manufacturing costs of the plant (including the Rs 20 million fixed costs) is allocated to each product line on the basis of direct manufacturing-labor costs at each line. Using this information, JKPP's cost analyst reports the following numbers (in millions) for July.

Particulars	Supreme	Deluxe	Regular
Direct materials costs	Rs 84.0	Rs 54.0	Rs 62.0
Direct manufacturing labor costs	14.0	28.0	8.0
Direct energy costs	39.8	40.7	9.5
Indirect manufacturing costs	16.8	33.6	9.6
Units produced (millions)	80	120	100

Required

1. Why might JKPP's managers prefer energy costs to be a direct cost rather than an indirect manufacturing cost?
2. Compute the manufacturing cost per unit for each of the product lines.

Solution

1. Energy costs of Rs 90 million can be traced to each individual production line. This tracing will result in a more accurate assignment of costs to products than when the Rs 150 million of indirect manufacturing costs (Rs 20 million of which is fixed) is allocated. Accurate product costing results in assignment of costs to different products in a manner that avoids undercosting and overcosting of the product lines.

2.	Supreme	Deluxe	(in millions) Regular
Direct materials costs	Rs 84.0	Rs 54.0	Rs 62.0
Direct manufacturing labor costs	14.0	28.0	8.0
Direct energy costs	39.8	40.7	9.5
Indirect manufacturing costs	16.8	33.6	9.6
Total manufacturing costs	Rs 154.6	Rs 156.3	Rs 89.1
Units produced (millions)	80	120	100
Cost per unit	Rs 1.9325	Rs 1.3025	Rs 0.8910

2-18 Classification of costs, service sector. Consumer Focus is a marketing research firm that organizes focus groups for consumer-product companies. Each focus group has eight individuals who are paid Rs 1,000 per session to provide comments on new products. These focus groups meet in hotels and are led by a trained, independent, marketing specialist hired by Consumer Focus. Each specialist is paid a fixed retainer to conduct a minimum number of sessions and per session fee of Rs 5,000. A Consumer Focus staff member attends each session to ensure that all the logistical aspects run smoothly.

Required

Classify each of the following cost items as:

a. Direct or indirect (D or I) costs with respect to each individual focus group.

b. Variable or fixed (V or F) costs with respect to how the total costs of Consumer Focus change as the number of focus groups conducted changes. (If in doubt, select on the basis of whether the total costs will change substantially if there is a large change in the number of groups conducted.)

You will have two answers (D or I; V or F) for each of the following items:

Cost Item

A. Payment to individuals in each focus group to provide comments on new products.

B. Annual subscription of Consumer Focus to Consumer Reports magazine.

C. Phone calls made by Consumer Focus staff member to confirm individuals will attend a focus group session (records of individual calls are not kept).

D. Retainer paid to focus group leader to conduct 20 focus groups per year on new medical products.

E. Meals provided to participants in each focus group.

F. Lease payment by Consumer Focus for corporate office.

G. Cost of tapes used to record comments made by individuals in a focus group session. (These tapes are sent to the company whose products are being tested.)

H. Petrol/diesel costs of Consumer Focus staff for company-owned vehicles (staff members submit monthly bills with no mileage breakdowns).

Solution

Cost object: Each individual focus group.

Cost variability: With respect to changes in the number of focus groups.

There may be some debate over classifications of individual items. Debate is more likely as regards to cost variability.

Cost Item	D or I	V or F
A	D	V
B	I	F
C	I	V[a]
D	I	F
E	D	V
F	I	F
G	D	V
H	I	V[b]

[a]Some students will note that phone call costs are variable when each call has a separate charge. It may be a fixed cost if Consumer Focus has a flat monthly charge for a line, irrespective of the amount of usage.

[b]Petrol/diesel costs are likely to vary with the number of focus groups. However, vehicles are likely to serve multiple purposes, and detailed records may be required to examine how costs vary with changes in one of the many purposes served.

2-19 Classification of costs, manufacturing sector. Skoda Octavia, plant of New United Motor Manufacturing, Ltd. (NUMML), a joint venture of General Motors and Toyota, assembles two types of cars (Corollas and Geo Prisms). Separate assembly lines are used for each type of car.

a. Direct or indirect (D or I) costs with respect to the type of car assembled (Corolla or Geo Prism).
b. Variable or fixed (V or F) costs with respect to how the total costs of the plant change as the number of cars assembled changes. (If in doubt, select on the basis of whether the total costs will change substantially if there is a large change in the number of cars assembled.)

You will have two answers (D or I; V or F) for each of the following items:

Cost Item	D or I	V or F
A. Cost of tires used on Geo Prisms		
B. Salary of public relations manager for NUMML plant		
C. Annual awards dinner for Corolla suppliers		
D. Salary of engineer who monitors design changes on Geo Prism		
E. Freight costs of Corolla engines shipped from Toyota City, Japan, to Fremont, California		
F. Electricity costs for NUMML plant (single bill covers entire plant)		
G. Wages paid to temporary assembly-line workers hired in periods of high production (paid on hourly basis)		
H. Annual fire-insurance policy cost for NUMML plant		

Solution

Cost object: Type of car assembled (Corolla or Geo Prism)

Cost variability: With respect to changes in the number of cars assembled

There may be some debate over classifications of individual items. Debate is more likely as regards cost variability.

Cost Item	D or I	V or F
A	D	V
B	I	F
C	D	F
D	D	F
E	D	V
F	I	V
G	D	V
H	I	F

2-20 Variable costs and fixed costs. Coal India Ltd. (CI) owns the rights to extract minerals from Jharkhand state. CI has costs in three areas:

a. Payment to a mining subcontractor who charges Rs 4,000 per ton of coal mined and returned to the beach (after being processed on the mainland to extract three minerals — ilmenite, rutile, and zircon).
b. Payment of a government mining and environmental tax of Rs 3,000 per ton of coal mined.
c. Payment to a barge operator. This operator charges Rs 1,50,000 per month to transport each batch of coal up to 100 tons per batch per day to the mainland and then return to Jharkhand State (That is, 0-100 tons per day Rs 1,50,000 per month; 101-200 tons per day = Rs 3,00,000 per month, and so on.) Each barge operates 25 days per month. The Rs 50,000 monthly charge must be paid even if fewer than 100 tons are transported on any day and even if Coal India Ltd. requires fewer than 25 days of barge transportation in that month.

Required CI is currently mining 180 tons of coal per day for 25 days per month.

1. What is the variable cost per ton of coal mined? What is the fixed cost to CI per month?
2. Plot a graph of the variable costs and another graph of the fixed costs of Coal India Ltd. (CI). Is the concept of relevant range applicable to your graphs? Explain.
3. What is the unit cost per ton of coal mined (a) if 180 tons are mined each day, or (b) if 220 tons are mined each day? Explain the difference in the unit-cost figures.

Solution

1. **Variable cost per ton of coal mined in Jharkhand state:**

Subcontractor	Rs 4,000 per ton
Government tax	3,000
Total	7,000 per ton

Fixed mosts per month:

0 to 100 tons of capacity per day	Rs 1,50,000
101 to 200 tons of capacity per day	3,00,000
201 to 300 tons of capacity per day	4,50,000

2.

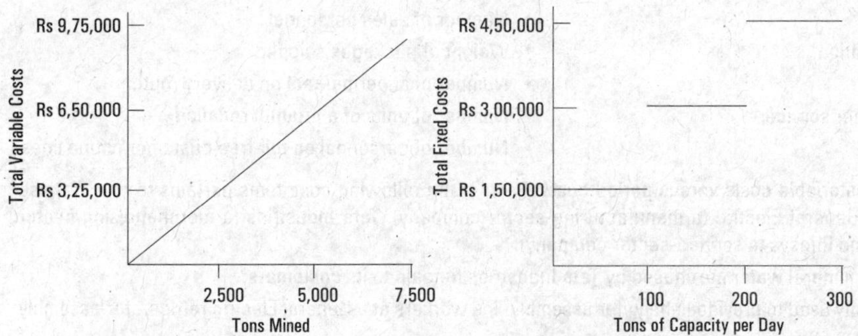

The concept of relevant range is potentially relevant for both graphs. However, the question does not place restrictions on the unit variable costs. The relevant range for the total fixed costs is from 0 to 100 tons; 101 to 200 tons; 201 to 300 tons, and so on. Within these ranges, the total fixed costs do not change in total.

3.	Tons Mined per Day (1)	Tons Mined per Month (2) = (1) × 25	Fixed Unit Cost per Ton (3) = FC ÷ (2)	Variable Unit Cost per Ton (4)	Total Unit Cost per Ton (5) = (3) + (4)
(a)	180	4,500	Rs 3,00,000 ÷ 4,500	Rs 7,000	Rs 7,066.67
		= Rs 66.67			
(b)	220	5,500	Rs 4,50,000 ÷ 5,500	Rs 7,000	Rs 7,081.82
		= Rs 81.82			

The unit cost for 220 tons mined per day is Rs 7,081.82, while for 180 tons it is only Rs 7,066.67. This difference is caused by the fixed cost increment from 101 to 200 tons being spread over an increment of 80 tons, while the fixed cost increment from 201 to 300 tons is spread over an increment of only 20 tons.

2-21 Cost drivers and the value chain. A Ranbaxy analyst is preparing a presentation on cost drives at its pharmaceutical drug subsidiary. Unfortunately, both the list of its business functions and the accompanying list of representative cost drivers are accidentally randomized. The two lists now on the computer screen are:

Business Function	Representative Cost Driver
A. Production	1. Minutes of T.V. advertising time on "60 Minutes"
B. Research and development	2. Number of calls to toll-free customer phone line
C. Marketing	3. Hours the Tylenol packaging line is in operation
D. Distribution	4. Number of packages shipped
E. Design of products/processes	5. Hours spent designing tamper-proof bottles
F. Customer service	6. Number of patents filed with India Patent office

Required

1. Match each business function with its representative cost driver.
2. Give a second example of a cost driver for each business function of Ranbaxy pharmaceutical drug subsidiary.

Solution

1.

Business Function	Representative Cost Driver
Production	• Hours the Tylenol packaging line is in operation
Research and development	• Number of patents filed with U.S. Patent office
Marketing	• Minutes of TV advertising time on "60 Minutes"
Distribution	• Number of packages shipped
Design of products/processes	• Hours spent designing tamper-proof bottles
Customer service	• Number of calls to toll-free customer phone line

2.

Business Function	Representative Cost Driver
Research and development	• Hours of laboratory work
	• Number of new drugs in development
Design of products/processes	• Number of focus groups on alternative package designs
	• Hours of process engineering work
Production	• Number of units packaged
	• Number of tablets manufactured

Marketing	• Number of promotion packages mailed
	• Number of sales personnel
Distribution	• Weight of packages shipped
	• Number of supermarkets on delivery route
Customer service	• Number of units of a product recalled
	• Number of personnel on toll-free customer phone lines

2-22 Inventoriable costs versus period costs. Each of the following cost items pertains to one of these companies. General Electric (a manufacturing-sector company), Tata Industries (a merchandising-sector company), and Infosys (a service-sector company):

a. Perrier mineral water purchased by Tata Industries for sale to its customers.
b. Electricity used to provide lighting for assembly-line workers at a General Electric refrigerator-assembly plant.
c. Depreciation on Infosys computer equipment used to update directories of Web sites.
d. Electricity used to provide lighting for Tata Industries store aisles.
e. Depreciation on General Electric's computer equipment used for quality testing of refrigerator components during the assembly process.
f. Salaries of Tata Industries marketing personnel planning local-newspaper advertising campaigns.
g. Perrier mineral water purchased by Infosys for consumption by its software engineers.
h. Salaries of Infosys marketing personnel selling banner advertising.

Required

1. Distinguish between manufacturing-sector, merchandising-sector, and service-sector companies.
2. Distinguish between inventoriable costs and period costs.
3. Classify each of the cost items (a-h) as an inventoriable cost or a period cost. Explain your answers.

Solution

1. **Manufacturing—sector companies** purchase materials and components and convert them into different finished goods.

   Merchandising—sector companies purchase and then sell tangible products without changing their basic form.

   Service—sector companies provide services or intangible products to their customers–for example, legal advice or audits.

   Only manufacturing and merchandising companies have inventories of goods for sale.

2. **Inventoriable costs** are all costs of a product that are regarded as an asset when they are incurred and then become cost of goods sold when the product is sold. These costs for a manufacturing company are included in work-in-process and finished goods inventory (they are "inventoried") to build up the costs of creating these assets.

   Period costs are all costs in the income statement other than cost of goods sold. These costs are treated as expenses of the period in which they are incurred because they are presumed not to benefit future periods (or because there is not sufficient evidence to conclude that such benefit exists). Expensing these costs immediately best matches expenses to revenues.

3.
   (a) Mineral water purchased for resale by Tata Industries–inventoriable cost of a merchandising company. It becomes part of cost of goods sold when the mineral water is sold.

   (b) Electricity used at GE assembly plant–inventoriable cost of a manufacturing company. It is part of the manufacturing overhead that is included in the manufacturing cost of a refrigerator finished good.

   (c) Depreciation on Infosys computer equipment–period cost of a service company. Infosys has no inventory of goods for sale and, hence, no inventoriable cost.

   (d) Electricity for Tata Industries store aisles–period cost of a merchandising company. It is a cost that benefits the current period and is not traceable to goods purchased for resale.

   (e) Depreciation on GE's assembly testing equipment–inventoriable cost of a manufacturing company. It is part of the manufacturing overhead that is included in the manufacturing cost of a refrigerator finished good.

   (f) Salaries of Tata Industries marketing personnel–period cost of a merchandising company. It is a cost that is not traceable to goods purchased for resale. It is presumed not to benefit future periods (or at least not to have sufficiently reliable evidence to estimate such future benefits).

   (g) Water consumed by Infosys engineers–period cost of a service company. Infosys has no inventory of goods for sale and, hence, no inventoriable cost.

(h) Salaries of Infosys marketing personnel–period cost of a service company. Infosys has no inventory of goods for sale and, hence, no inventoriable cost.

2-23 Cost of goods manufactured. Consider the following account balances (in thousands) for the BPL Company:

	Beginning of Current Year	End of Current Year
Direct materials inventory	Rs 22,000	Rs 26,000
Work-in-process inventory	21,000	20,000
Finished goods inventory	18,000	23,000
Purchases of direct materials		75,000
Direct manufacturing labor		25,000
Indirect manufacturing labor		15,000
Plant insurance		9,000
Depreciation—plant building and equipment		11,000
Repairs and maintenance—plant		4,000
Marketing, distribution, and customer-service costs		93,000
General and administrative costs		29,000

Required

1. Prepare a schedule of cost of goods manufactured for current year.
2. Revenues in current year were Rs 300 million. Prepare the income statement, current year.

Solution

(1) BPL Company

Schedule of Cost of Goods Manufactured for Current Year **(in thousands)**

Direct Materials:		
Beginning inventory	Rs 22,000	
Purchases of direct materials	75,000	
Cost of direct materials available for use	97,000	
Ending inventory	26,000	
Direct materials used		Rs 71,000
Direct manufacturing labor costs		25,000
Indirect manufacturing costs:		
Indirect manufacturing labor costs	Rs 15,000	
Plant insurance	9,000	
Depreciation—plant building and equipment	11,000	
Repairs and Maintenance—plant	4,000	39,000
Manufacturing costs incurred during current year		1,35,000
Add beginning work-in-process inventory		21,000
Total manufacturing costs to account for		1,56,000
Deduct ending work-in-process inventory		20,000
Cost of goods manufactured		1,36,000

(2) BPL Company

Income Statement for the Year Ended **(in thousands)**

Revenues		Rs 3,00,000
Cost of goods sold:		
Beginning finished goods	Rs 18,000	
Cost of goods manufactured	1,36,000	
Cost of goods available for sale	1,54,000	
Ending finished goods	23,000	1,31,000
Gross margin		1,69,000
Operating costs:		
Marketing, distribution, and customer service	93,000	
General and administrative costs	29,000	1,22,000
Operating Income		47,000

2-24 Income statement and schedule of cost of goods manufactured. The BHEL Ltd. has the following account balances (in millions):

For Specific Date		For Current Year	
Direct materials, Jan. 1, current year	Rs 150	Purchases of direct materials	Rs 3,250
Work in process, Jan. 1, current year	100	Direct manufacturing labor	1,000
Finished goods, Jan. 1, current year	700	Depreciation-plant building and equipment	800
Direct materials, Dec. 31, current year	200	Plant supervisory salaries	50
Work in process, Dec. 31, current year	50	Miscellaneous plant overhead	350
Finished goods, Dec. 31, current year	550	Revenues	9,500
		Marketing, distribution, and customer-service costs	2,400
		Plant supplies used	100
		Plant utilities	300
		Indirect manufacturing labor	600

Required Prepare an income statement and a supporting schedule of cost of goods manufactured for the current year. (For additional questions regarding these facts, see the next problem.)

Solution

BHEL Corporation Income Statement for Current Year (in millions)

Revenues		Rs 9,500
Cost of goods sold:		
Beginning finished goods	Rs 700	
Cost of goods manufactured	6,450	
Cost of goods available for sale	7,150	
Ending finished goods	550	6,600
Gross margin		2,900
Marketing, distribution, and customer-service costs		2,400
Operating income		Rs 500

BHEL Corporation Schedule of Cost of Goods Manufactured for the Current Year (in millions)

Direct materials costs		
Beginning inventory, for current year	Rs 150	
Purchases of direct materials	3,250	
Cost of direct materials available for use	3,400	
Ending inventory for current year	200	
Direct materials used		Rs 3,200
Direct manufacturing labor costs		100
Indirect manufacturing costs		
Indirect manufacturing labor	600	
Plant supplies used	100	
Plant utilities	300	
Depreciation—plant, building, and equipment	800	
Plant supervisory salaries	50	
Miscellaneous plant overhead	350	2,200
Manufacturing costs incurred during current year		6,400
Add beginning work-in-process inventory		100
Total manufacturing costs		6,500
Deduct ending work-in-process		50
Cost of goods manufactured		6,450

2-25 Interpretation of statements (continuation of 2-24).

Required

1. How would the answer to previous problem be modified if you were asked for a schedule of cost of goods manufactured and sold instead of a schedule of cost of goods manufactured? Be specific.
2. Would the sales manager's salary (included in marketing, distribution, and customer-service costs) be accounted for any differently if the BHEL Corporation were a merchandising-sector company instead of a manufacturing-sector company? Using the flow of manufacturing costs, describe how the wages of an assembler in the plant would be accounted for in this manufacturing company.
3. Plant supervisory salaries are usually regarded as indirect manufacturing costs. When might some of these costs be regarded as direct manufacturing costs? Give an example.
4. Suppose that both the direct materials used and the plant depreciation are related to the manufacturing of 1 million units of product. What is the unit cost for the direct materials assigned to those units? What is the unit cost for plant building and equipment depreciation? Assume that yearly plant depreciation is computed on a straight-line basis.

5. Assume that the implied cost-behavior patterns in requirement 4 persist. That is, direct material costs behave as a variable cost, and depreciation behaves as a fixed cost. Repeat the computations in requirement 4, assuming that the costs are being predicted for the manufacture of 1.2 million units of product. How would the total costs be affected?
6. As a management accountant, explain concisely to the president why the unit costs differed in requirements 4 and 5.

Solution

1. The schedule in previous question can become a schedule of cost of goods manufactured and sold simply by including the beginning and ending finished goods inventory figures in the supporting schedule, rather than directly in the body of the income statement. Note that the term *cost of goods manufactured* refers to the cost of goods brought to completion (finished) during the accounting period, whether they were started before or during the current accounting period. Some of the manufacturing costs incurred are held back as costs of the ending work in process; similarly, the costs of the beginning work in process inventory become a part of the cost of goods manufactured.
2. The sales manager's salary would be charged as a marketing cost as incurred by both manufacturing and merchandising companies. It is basically an operating cost that appears below the gross margin line on an income statement. In contrast, an assembler's wages would be assigned to the products worked on. Thus, the wages cost would be charged to Work in process and would not be expensed until the product is transferred through Finished Goods Inventory to Cost of Goods Sold as the product is sold.
3. The direct-indirect distinction can be resolved only with respect to a particular cost object. For example, in defense contracting, the cost object may be defined as a contract. Then, a plant supervisor working only on that contract will have his or her salary charged directly and wholly to that single contract.
4. Direct materials used = Rs 3,20,00,00,000 ÷ 10,00,000 units = Rs 3,200 per unit
   Depreciation = Rs 80,00,00,000 ÷ 10,00,000 units = Rs 800 per unit
5. Direct materials unit cost would be unchanged at Rs 3,200. Depreciation cost per unit would be Rs 80,00,00,000 × 12,00,000 = Rs 666.67 per unit. Total direct materials costs would rise by 20% to Rs 3,84,00,00,000 (Rs 3,200 per unit × 12,00,000 units), whereas total depreciation would be unaffected at Rs 80,00,00,000.
6. Unit costs are averages, and they must be interpreted with caution. The Rs 3,200 direct materials unit cost is valid for predicting total costs because direct materials is a variable cost; total direct materials costs indeed change as output levels change. However, fixed costs like depreciation must be interpreted quite differently from variable costs. A common error in cost analysis is to regard all unit costs as one-as if all the total costs to which they are related are variable costs. Changes in output levels (the denominator) will affect *total variable costs,* but not *total fixed costs.* Graphs of the two costs may clarify this point; it is safer to think in terms of total costs rather than in terms of unit costs.

2-26 Overtime premium. Varun and Sachin are sales representatives for Electronic Manufacturing Ltd (EML). Each sales representative receives a base salary plus a bonus based on 20% of the actual gross margin of each order they sell. Indirect manufacturing costs excluding overtime premium are determined as 200 per cent of direct manufacturing labor cost.

Summary data for two recent orders (in thousands) are as follows:

Customer **Sales representative**	**Aaj Tak** **Sachin**	**NDTV** **Varun**
Revenues	Rs 4,200	Rs 4,800
Direct materials	2,500	2,700
Direct manufacturing labor	400	400
Indirect manufacturing	800	800
Direct labor-hours	2 hours	2 hours

EML charges an overtime premium to the rush orders that cause work to be done overtime. In cases when overtime is caused by overall heavy production volume, and not due to any rush orders, the overhead premium is allocated to all orders. The direct manufacturing labor straight-time rate is Rs 200 per hour, and the overtime rate is 50% higher.

Required

1. Calculate the gross margin EML would report on each of the two orders if only NDTV was a rush order that caused overtime.
2. Assume that only Aaj Tak was a rush order that caused overtime. Compute the revised gross margin EML would report on each of the two orders.
3. Assume that neither Aaj Tak nor NDTV was a rush order. Calculate the revised gross margin EML would report on each of the two orders. There were no other orders. There was a total of two overtime hours.

Solution

1. **Computation of Gross Margin**

Particulars	**Aaj Tak**	**NDTV**
	(Amount in thousands)	
Revenues	Rs 4,200	Rs 4,800
Direct materials	2,500	2,700
Direct manufacturing labor	400	400
Overtime premium	–	200
Indirect manufacturing	800	800
Total manufacturing costs	3,700	4,100
Gross margin	Rs 500	Rs 700
Gross margin percentage	11.9%	14.6%

2. **Computation of Revised Gross Margin**

Particulars	**Aaj Tak**	**NDTV**
Revenues	Rs 4,200	Rs 4,800
Direct materials	2,500	2,700
Direct manufacturing labor	400	400
Overtime premium	200	–
Indirect manufacturing	800	800
Total manufacturing costs	3,900	3,900
Gross margin percentage	Rs 300	Rs 900
Gross margin percentage	7.1%	18.8%

3.

Particulars	**Aaj Tak**	**NDTV**
Revenues	Rs 4,200	Rs 4,800
Direct materials	2,500	2,700
Direct manufacturing labor	400	400
Overtime premium	100	100
Indirect manufacturing	800	800
Total manufacturing costs	3,800	4,000
Gross margin percentage	Rs 400	Rs 800
Gross margin percentage	9.5%	16.7%

2-27 **Cost analysis, litigation risk, ethics.** Singhania is the manager of new product development of Lakme Lever (LL). Singhania is currently considering Enhance, which would be (LL's) next major product. All LL's current products are cosmetics applied to the skin by the consumer. In contrast, Enhance is inserted via a needle into the skin by a doctor. Each treatment is planned to cost patients Rs 3,000 and will last three months. Enhance fills out the skin so that fewer wrinkles are observable.

LL plans to sell Enhance to doctors for Rs 1,200 per treatment, providing the doctor with a large incentive to promote the product. However, Singhania questions the economics of this product. At present all the costs recognized, including manufacturing by a third party, are Rs 1,000 per treatment. Singhania's main concern is that the current costing proposal excludes potential litigation costs in defending lawsuits related to Enhance. Kareena the CEO of the company, totally disagrees with Singhania. She maintains she has total confidence in her medical research team and directs Singhania not to include any amount from his potential litigation cost of Rs 1,100 per treatment in his upcoming presentation to the board of directors on the economics and pricing of the Enhance product. Singhania was previously controller of LL.

Required

1. What reasons might Kareena have for not wanting Singhania to include potential litigation costs on the product in a presentation on Enhance's economics and pricing?
2. LL sets prices by adding 20 per cent to total costs. What would be the selling price per unit if Singhania's proposal for including pótential litigation costs are also included? How might this price affect promotion of Enhance?
3. Kareena directs Singhania to drop any further discussion of the litigation issue. Singhania is to focus on making Enhance the blockbuster product that field research has suggested it will be. Singhania is uneasy with this directive. He tells Kareena "it is an ostrich approach" (head-in-the-sand) to a real problem that could potentially bankrupt the company. Kareena tells Singhania to go and think about her directive. What should Singhania do next?

Solution

1. Reasons for Kareena not wanting Singhania to include the potential litigation costs include:
   (a) Genuine belief that the product has no risk of future litigation. Note that she asserts "she has total confidence in her medical research team".
   (b) Concern that the uncertainties about litigation are sufficiently high to make any numerical estimate "meaningless".
   (c) Concern that inclusion of future litigation costs would cause the board of directors to vote against the project. Kareena may be "overly committed" to the project and wants to avoid showing information that prompts questions she prefers not to be raised.
   (d) Kareena may believe that if subsequent litigation occurs, the plaintiffs will "inappropriately" use a litigation cost line item as "proof" (LL) "knew the product had health problems" that were known to management at the outset.

2.

Unit costs excluding litigation costs	Rs 1,000
Add unit litigation costs	1,100
Total unit costs	2,100
Add 20% markup	420
Selling price per unit	2,520

Since each treatment is planned to cost patients Rs 3,000, the new selling price of Rs 2,520 will drop the doctors' margin to only Rs 480 from the planned margin of Rs 1,800 based on the planned selling price of Rs 1,200. This would probably result in the doctors not having much incentive to promote the product. In fact, it may be quite possible that the doctors may not attempt to prescribe the treatment at such a low margin because of their own exposure to liability.

3. Singhania has already registered his concern to Kareena. The difficulty is that Kareena asked Singhania not to include the possible litigation in his presentation. If there is no record of this presentation, then Singhania may have several concerns.
   (a) He may be accused at a later stage of not anticipating the costs of litigation. If litigation does occur, some people will try to distance themselves from the problems. It may be to Singhania's advantage to have a record of his early concerns. (Although plaintiffs may make Singhania's life very difficult if they get access to Singhania's files.) Singhania may want to keep some record of his presentation to Kareena.
   (b) He may be portrayed as not being a "team player" if he continues his objections. Kareena may have to silence his concerns if he decides to stay at LL.
   (c) He may have difficult ethical objections with Kareena's behavior. If he thinks she is acting unethically, his main options are to speak to her first (at least one time), speak to her supervisor (probably chairman of the company), or, as a final resort, resign.

Exercises

2-28 Classification of costs, merchandising sector. Home Entertainment Centre (HEC) operates a large store in Mumbai. The store has both a video section and a musical (compact disks, and tapes) section. HEC reports revenues for the video section separately from the musical section.

Required

Classify each of the following cost items as:

a. Direct or indirect (D or I) costs with respect to the video section.
b. Variable or fixed (V or F) costs with respect to how the total costs of the video section change as the number of videos sold changes. (If in doubt, select on the basis of whether the total costs will change substantially if there is a large change in the number of videos sold.)

You will have two answers (D or I; V or F) for each of the following items:

Cost Item	D or I	V or F
A. Annual retainer paid to a video distributor		
B. Electricity costs of HEC store (single bill covers entire store)		
C. Costs of videos purchased for sale to customers		
D. Subscription to video trends magazine		
E. Leasing of computer software used for financial budgeting at HEC		
F. Cost of popcorn provided free to all customers of HEC		
G. Earthquake insurance policy for HEC store		
H. Freight-in costs of videos purchased by HEC		

2-29 Cost drivers and functions. The list of representative cost drivers in the right column below are randomized with respect to the list of functions in the left column. That is, they do not match.

Function	Representative Cost Driver
1. Accounting	A. Number of invoices sent
2. Personnel	B. Number of purchase orders
3. Data Processing	C. Number of research scientists
4. Research and Development	D. Hours of computer processing unit (CPU)
5. Purchasing	E. Number of new hires
6. Billing	F. Number of transactions processed

1. Match each function with its representative cost driver.
2. Give a second example of a cost driver for each function.

2-30 Total cost and unit costs. A student association has hired a musical group for a graduation party. The cost will be a fixed amount of Rs 4,000.

Required

1. Suppose 500 people attend the party. What will be the total cost of the musical group? The unit cost per person?
2. Suppose 2,000 people attend. What will be the total cost of the musical group? The unit cost per person?
3. For prediction of total costs, should the manager of the party use the unit cost in requirement 1? The unit cost in requirement 2? What is the major lesson of this exercise?

2-31 Total costs and unit costs. Ms Thomas is a well-known software engineer. Her specialty is writing software code used in maintaining the security of credit-card information. Thomas is approached by the Electronic Commerce Group (ECG). It offers to pay her Rs 1,00,000 for the right to use her code under license in their e.procurement software package. Thomas rejects this offer because it provides her with no upside if the e.procurement package is a runaway success. Both parties eventually agree to a contract in which ECG pays Thomas a flat fee of Rs 1,00,000 for the right to use her code in up to 10,000 packages. If e.procurement sells more than 10,000 packages, Thomas receives an additional Rs 8 for each package sold beyond the 10,000 level.

1. What is the unit cost to ECG of Thomas software code included in its e.procurement package if it sells (a) 2,000 packages, (b) 6,000 packages, (c) 10,000 packages, and (d) 20,000 packages? Comment on the results.
2. To predict ECG's total cost of using Thomas software code in e.procurement, which unit cost (if any) of (a) to (d) in requirement 1 would you recommend ECG use? Explain.

2-32 Computing cost of goods purchased and cost of goods sold. The data below are for Big Bazaar Department Store. The account balances (in thousands) are for current year.

Marketing, distribution, and customer service costs	Rs 3,70,000
Merchandise inventory, January 1, current year	2,70,000
Utilities	1,70,000
General and administrative costs	4,30,000
Merchandise inventory, December 31, current year	3,40,000
Purchases	15,50,000
Miscellaneous expenses	40,000
Freight on purchases	70,000
Purchase returns and allowances	40,000
Purchase discounts	60,000

Required Compute (a) cost of goods purchased and (b) cost of goods sold.

2-33 Income statement and schedule of cost of goods manufactured. The following items (in millions) pertain to NTPC Ltd.

For Specific Date		For Current Year	
Work in process, Jan. 1. current year	Rs 1,000	Plant utilities	Rs 500
Direct materials, Dec. 31, current year	500	Indirect manufacturing labor	2,000
Finished goods, Dec. 31, current year	1,200	Depreciation-pant, building, and equipment	900
Accounts payable, Dec. 31, current year	2,000	Revenues	35,000
Accounts receivable, Jan. 1. current year	5,000	Miscellaneous manufacturing overhead	1,000
Work in process, Dec. 31, current year	200	Marketing, distribution, and customer-service costs	9,000
Finished goods, Jan. 1. current year	4,000	Direct materials purchased	8,000
Accounts receivable, Dec. 31, current year	3,000	Direct manufacturing labor	4,000
Accounts payable, Jan. 1. current year	4,000	Plant supplies used	600
Direct materials, Jan. 1. current year	3,000	Property taxes on plant	100

NTPC's manufacturing costing system uses a three-part classification of direct materials, direct manufacturing labor, and indirect manufacturing costs.

Required

Prepare an income statement and a supporting schedule of cost of goods manufactured. (For additional questions regarding these facts, see the next problem).

2-34 Terminology, interpretation of statements (continuation of the previous question).

1. Calculate total prime costs and total conversion costs.
2. Compute total inventoriable costs and period costs.
3. Design costs and R&D costs are not considered product costs for financial reporting purposes. When might some of these costs be regarded as product costs? Give an example.
4. Suppose that both the direct materials used and the plant depreciation are related to the manufacture of 1 million units of product. Determine the unit cost for the direct materials assigned to those units and the unit cost for plant, building, and equipment depreciation. Assume that yearly depreciation is computed on a straight-line basis.
5. Assume that the implied cost-behavior patterns in requirement 4 persist. That is, direct materials costs behave as a variable cost and plant depreciation behaves as a fixed cost. Repeat the computations in requirement 4, assuming that the costs are being predicted for the manufacturing of 1.5 million units of product. Determine the effect on total cost.
6. Assume depreciation on the equipment (but not the plant and building) is computed based on number of units produced because the equipment deteriorates with units produced. The depreciation rate is Rs 4 per unit. Calculate the equipment depreciation assuming (a) 1 million units of product are produced and (b) 1.5 million units of product are produced.

2-35 Finding unknown amounts. An author for the Internal Revenue Service is trying to reconstruct some partially destroyed records of two taxpayers. For each of the cases in the accompanying list, find the unknowns designated by the letters A through D.

	Case 1	Case 2 (in thousands)
Accounts receivable, 12/31	Rs 6,000	Rs 2,100
Cost of goods sold	A	20,000
Accounts payable, 1/1	3,000	1,700
Accounts payable, 12/31	1,800	1,500
Finished goods inventory, 12/31	B	5,300
Gross margin	11,300	C
Work in process, 1/1	0	800
Work in process, 12/31	0	3,000
Finished goods inventory, 1/1	4,000	4,000
Direct material used	8,000	12,000
Direct manufacturing labor	3,000	5,000
Indirect manufacturing costs	7,000	D
Purchases of direct material	9,000	7,000
Revenues	32,000	31,800
Accounts receivable, 1/1	2,000	1,400

2-36 Fire loss, computing inventory costs. A distraught employee, Mr. Unsatisfied, put a torch to a manufacturing plant on a blustery February 26. The resulting blaze destroyed the plant and its contents. Fortunately, certain accounting records were kept in another building. They reveal the following for the period from January 1 to February 28, current year.

Direct materials purchased	Rs 1,60,000
Work in process, 1st January	3,40,000
Direct materials, 1st January	1,60,000
Finished goods, 1st January	3,00,000
Indirect manufacturing costs	40% of conversion costs
Revenues	50,00,000
Direct manufacturing labor	18,00,000
Prime costs	29,40,000
Gross margin percentage based on revenues	20%
Cost of goods available for sale	45,00,000

The loss is fully covered by insurance. The insurance company wants to know the historical cost of the inventories as a basis for negotiating a settlement, although the settlement is actually to be based on replacement cost, not historical cost.

Calculate the cost of

Required

1. Finished goods inventory, 28th February.
2. Work-in-process inventory, 28th February.
3. Direct materials inventory, 28th February.

2-37 Comprehensive problem on unit costs, product costs. Godrej office equipment manufactures and sells metal shelving. It began operations on January 1. Costs incurred for the current year are as follows (V stands for variable; F stands for fixed):

Direct material costs	Rs 1,40,000 V
Direct manufacturing-labor costs	30,000 V
Plant energy costs	5,000 V
Indirect manufacturing-labor costs	10,000 V
Indirect manufacturing-labor costs	16,000 F
Other indirect manufacturing costs	8,000 V
Other indirect manufacturing costs	24,000 F
Marketing, distribution, and customer-service costs	1,22,850 V
Marketing, distribution, and customer-service costs	40,000 F
Administrative costs	50,000 F

Variable manufacturing costs are variable with respect to units produced. Variable marketing, distribution, and customer-service costs are variable with respect to units sold.

Inventory data are

	Beginning, January 1	Ending, December 31
Direct materials	0 kg	2,000 kg
Work in process	0 units	0 units
Finished goods	0 units	? units

Production in the current year was 1,00,000 units. Two kgs of direct materials are used to make one unit of finished product.

Revenues in the current year were Rs 4,36,800. The selling price per unit and the purchase price per kg of direct materials were stable throughout the year. The company's ending inventory of finished goods is carried at the average unit manufacturing costs for the current year. Finished-goods inventory at December 31, current year was Rs 20,970.

Required

1. Calculate direct materials inventory, total cost, as on December 31.
2. Calculate finished-goods inventory, total units, as on December 31.
3. Calculate selling price per unit.
4. Calculate operating income.

2-38 Product costs, effect of changing the cost classification (continuation of previous problem). Assume the same facts as in the previous problem, except that fixed indirect manufacturing costs are not considered inventoriable costs. There are 9,000 units of finished goods inventory on December 31.

Required

1. Calculate finished goods inventory, total costs, December 31.
2. Calculate operating income of the year.

2-39 Missing data. Shaheen Plastics, Ltd's selected data for the month of August related to current year are presented below (in millions):

Beginning work-in-process inventory	Rs 2,000
Beginning direct materials inventory	900
Direct materials purchased	3,600
Direct materials used	3,750
Variable manufacturing overhead	2,500
Total manufacturing overhead	4,800
Total manufacturing costs	16,000
Cost of goods manufactured	16,500
Cost of goods sold	17,000
Ending finished goods inventory	1,250

Calculate the following costs:

Required

1. Direct materials inventory as on 31st August.
2. Fixed manufacturing overhead costs for August.
3. Direct manufacturing labor costs for August.
4. Work-in-process inventory as on 31st August.
5. Goods available for sale in August.
6. Finished-goods inventory as on 31st August.

3 Cost-Volume-Profit Analysis

Learning Objectives

1. Explain the features of cost-volume-profit (CVP) analysis
2. Determine the breakeven point and output level needed to achieve a target operating income
3. Understand how income taxes affect CVP analysis
4. Explain how managers use CVP analysis in decision making
5. Explain how sensitivity analysis helps managers cope with uncertainty
6. Use CVP analysis to plan variable and fixed costs
7. Apply CVP analysis to a company producing multiple products

All managers want to know how profits will change as the units sold of a product or service change. Home Depot managers, for example, might wonder how many units of a new product must be sold to break even or make a certain amount of profit. Procter & Gamble managers might ask: If we expand our business into a particular foreign market, how will that affect costs, selling price, and profits? These questions have a common "what-if" theme. Examining the results of these what-if possibilities and alternatives helps managers make better decisions.

Managers must also decide whether to produce more or less of a particular product, change the mix of products they sell, or change their sales prices. The following article explains the dilemma the high-end jeweler Tiffany & Co. recently faced—whether it should increase the prices on one of its best-selling jewelry lines recognizing that it will likely lower the quantity of jewelry sold. Does this sound like a wise strategy to you?

How the "The Biggest Rock Show Ever" Turned a Big Profit[1]

When U2 embarked on its recent world tour, *Rolling Stone* magazine called it "the biggest rock show ever." Visiting large stadiums across the United States and Europe, the Irish quartet performed on an imposing 164-foot high stage that resembled a spaceship, complete with a massive video screen and footbridges leading to ringed catwalks.

With an ambitious 48-date trek planned, U2 actually had three separate stages leapfrogging its global itinerary—each one costing nearly $40 million dollars. As a result, the tour's success was dependent not only on each night's concert, but also recouping its tremendous fixed costs—costs that do not change with the number of fans in the audience.

To cover its high fixed costs and make a profit, U2 needed to sell a lot of tickets. To maximize revenue, the tour employed a unique in-the-round stage configuration, which boosted stadium capacity by roughly 20%, and sold tickets for as little as $300, far less than most large outdoor concerts.

The band's plan worked—despite a broader music industry slump and global recession, U2 shattered attendance records in most of the venues it played. By the end of the tour, the band played to over 3 million fans, racking up almost $300 million in ticket and merchandise sales and

[1] *Source*: Gundersen, Edna. 2009. U2 turns 360 stadium into attendance-shattering sellouts. *USA Today*, October 4. *www.usatoday.com/life/music/news/2009-10-04-u2-stadium-tour_N.htm*

turning a profit. As you read this chapter, you will begin to understand how and why U2 made the decision to lower prices.

Many capital intensive companies, such as US Airways and United Airlines in the airlines industry and Global Crossing and WorldCom in the telecommunications industry, have high fixed costs. They must generate sufficient revenues to cover these costs and turn a profit. When revenues declined at these companies during 2001 and 2002 and fixed costs remained high, these companies declared bankruptcy. The methods of CVP analysis described in this chapter help managers minimize such risks.

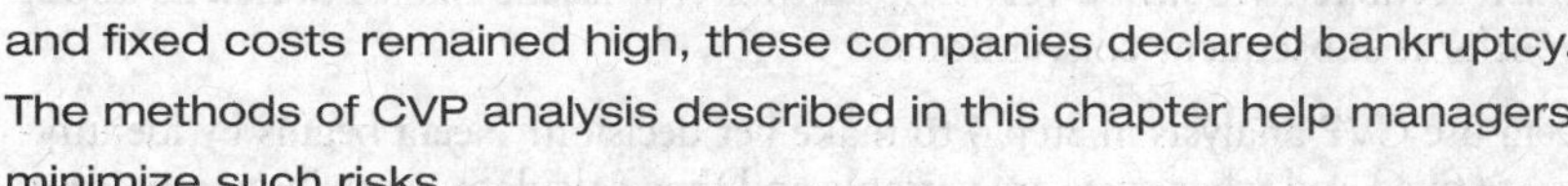

Essentials of CVP Analysis

Learning Objective 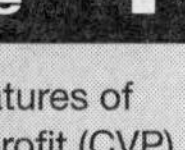

Explain the features of cost-volume-profit (CVP) analysis

. . . how operating income changes with changes in output level, selling prices, variable costs, or fixed costs

Cost-volume-profit (CVP) analysis examines the behavior of total revenues, total costs, and operating income as changes occur in the units sold, the selling price, the variable cost per unit, or the fixed costs of a product. Let's consider an example to illustrate CVP analysis.

> Example: Neeta Ambani is considering selling Do-All Software, a home-office software package, at a computer convention in New Delhi. Neeta knows she can purchase this software from a computer software wholesaler at Rs 1,200 per package, with the privilege of returning all unsold packages and receiving a full Rs 1,200 refund per package. She also knows that she would pay Rs 20,000 to Computer Conventions, Ltd., for the booth rental at the convention. She will incur no other costs. She must decide whether she should rent a booth.

Neeta, like most managers who face such a situation, works through a series of steps.

1. **Identify the problem and uncertainties.** The decision to rent the booth hinges critically on how Neeta resolves two important uncertainties—the price she can charge and the number of packages she can sell at that price. Every decision deals with selecting a course of action. The outcome of the chosen action is uncertain and will only be known in the future.
2. **Obtain information.** When faced with uncertainty, managers obtain information that might help them understand the uncertainties better. For example, Neeta gathers information about the type of individuals likely to attend the convention and other software that might be sold at the convention. She also gathers data on her past experiences selling Do-All Software at conventions very much like the New Delhi convention.
3. **Make predictions about the future.** Using all the information available to them, managers make predictions. Neeta predicts that she can charge a price of Rs 2,000 for Do-All Software. At that price she is reasonably confident that she will be able to sell 30 packages and possibly as many as 60. In making these predictions, Neeta like most managers, must exercise considerable judgment. Her predictions rest on the belief that

her experience at the New Delhi convention will be similar to her experience at the Mumbai convention four months earlier. Yet, Neeta ponders several questions. Is this comparison appropriate? Have conditions and circumstances changed over the last four months? Are there any biases creeping into her thinking? She is keen on selling at the New Delhi convention because sales in the last couple of months have been lower than expected. Is this experience making her predictions overly optimistic? Has she ignored some of the competitive risks? Will the other software vendors at the convention reduce their prices?

Neeta reviews her thinking. She retests her assumptions. She also explores these questions with Dinesh Shah, a close friend, who has extensive experience selling software like Do-All. In the end, she feels quite confident that her predictions are reasonable and carefully thought through.

4. **Make decisions by choosing among alternatives.** Neeta uses CVP analysis, described just below, and decides to rent the booth at the New Delhi convention.
5. **Implement the decision, evaluate performance, and learn.** Thoughtful managers never stop learning. They compare their actual performance to predicted performance to understand why things worked out the way they did and what they might learn. At the end of the New Delhi convention, for example, Neeta would want to evaluate whether her predictions about price and the number of packages she could sell were correct. Such feedback would be very helpful to Neeta as she makes decisions about renting booths at subsequent conventions.

How does Neeta use CVP analysis in Step 4 to make her decision? Neeta begins by identifying what costs are fixed and what costs are variable and then calculates *contribution margin.*

Contribution Margins

The booth-rental cost of Rs 20,000 is a fixed cost because it will not change no matter how many packages Neeta sells. The cost of the package itself is a variable cost because it increases in proportion to the number of packages sold. Neeta will incur a cost of Rs 1,200 for each package that she sells. To get an idea of how operating income will change as a result of selling different quantities of packages, Neeta calculates operating income if sales are 5 packages and if sales are 40 packages.

	5 packages sold	40 packages sold
Revenues	Rs 10,000 (Rs 2,000 per package × 5 packages)	Rs 80,000 (Rs 2,000 per package × 40 packages)
Variable purchase costs	6,000 (Rs 1,200 per package × 5 packages)	48,000 (Rs 1,200 per package × 40 packages)
Fixed costs	20,000	20,000
Operating income	Rs(16,000)	Rs12,000

The only numbers that change from selling different quantities of packages are *total revenues* and *total variable costs*. The difference between total revenues and total variable costs is called **contribution margin.** That is,

$$\text{Contribution margin} = \text{Total revenues} - \text{Total variable costs}$$

Contribution margin indicates why operating income changes as the number of units sold changes. The contribution margin when Neeta sells 5 packages is Rs 4,000 (Rs 10,000 in total revenues minus Rs 6,000 in total variable costs); the contribution margin when Neeta sells 40 packages is Rs 32,000 (Rs 80,000 in total revenues minus Rs 48,000 in total variable costs). When calculating the contribution margin, be sure to subtract all variable costs. For example, if Neeta had variable selling costs because she paid a commission to salespeople for each package they sold at the convention, variable costs would include the cost of each package plus the sales commission.

Contribution margin per unit is a useful tool for calculating contribution margin and operating income. It is defined as,

$$\text{Contribution margin per unit} = \text{Selling price} - \text{Variable cost per unit}$$

In the Do-All Software example, contribution margin per package, or per unit, is Rs 2,000 − Rs 1,200 = Rs 800. Contribution margin per unit recognizes the tight coupling of selling price and variable cost per unit. Unlike fixed costs, Neeta will only incur the variable cost per unit of Rs 1,200 when she sells a unit of Do-All Software for Rs 2,000. Consequently, a second way to calculate contribution margin is:

$$\text{Contribution margin} = \text{Contribution margin per unit} \times \text{Number of units sold}$$

For example, when 40 packages are sold, contribution margin = Rs 800 per unit × 40 units = Rs 32,000.

Even before she gets to the convention, Neeta incurs Rs 20,000 in fixed costs. For each package that Neeta sells at the convention, she recovers Rs 800 of the Rs 20,000. Neeta hopes to sell enough packages to fully recover the Rs 20,000 she spent for renting the booth and to then make a profit.

Exhibit 3-1 presents contribution margins for different quantities of packages sold. The income statement in Exhibit 3-1 is called a **contribution income statement** because it groups costs into variable costs and fixed costs to highlight contribution margin. See how each additional package sold from 0 to 1 to 5 increases contribution margin by Rs 800 per package, recovering more of the fixed costs and reducing the operating loss. If Neeta sells 25 packages, contribution margin equals Rs 20,000 (Rs 800 per packag × 25 packages), exactly recovering fixed costs and resulting in Rs 0 operating income. If Neeta sells 40 packages, contribution margin increases by another Rs 12,000 (Rs 32,000 − Rs 20,000), all of which becomes operating income. As you look across Exhibit 3-1 from left to right, you see that the increase in contribution margin exactly equals the increase in operating income (or the decrease in operating loss).

Instead of expressing contribution margin as a rupee amount per unit, we can express it as a percentage called **contribution margin percentage** (or **contribution margin ratio**):

$$\text{Contribution margin percentage (or contribution margin ratio)} = \frac{\text{Contribution margin per unit}}{\text{Selling price}}$$

In our example,

$$\text{Contribution margin percentage} = \frac{\text{Rs } 800}{\text{Rs } 2{,}000} = 0.40, \text{ or } 40\%$$

Contribution margin percentage is the contribution margin per rupee of revenue. Neeta earns 40% of each rupee of revenue (equal to 40 paise).

Most companies have multiple products. As we shall see later in this chapter, calculating contribution margin per unit when there are multiple products is more cumbersome. In practice, companies routinely use contribution margin percentage as a handy way to calculate contribution margin for different rupee amounts of revenue:

$$\text{Contribution margin} = \text{Contribution margin percentage} \times \text{Revenues (in rupees)}$$

For example, in Exhibit 3-1, if Neeta sells 40 packages, revenues will be Rs 80,000 and contribution margin will equal 40% of Rs 80,000, or 0.40 × Rs 80,000 = Rs 32,000. Neeta earns operating income of Rs 12,000 (Rs 32,000 - Fixed costs, Rs 20,000) by selling 40 packages for Rs 80,000.

Expressing CVP Relationships

How was the Excel spreadsheet in Exhibit 3-1 constructed? Underlying the Exhibit are some equations that express the CVP relationships. To make good decisions using CVP analysis, we must understand these relationships and the structure of the

Exhibit 3-1

Contribution Income Statement for Different Quantities of Do-All Software Packages Sold

File Edit View Insert Format Tools Data Window Help

	A	B	C	D	E	F	G	H
1				Number of Packages Sold				
2				0	1	5	25	40
3	Revenues	Rs 2,000	per package	Rs 0	Rs 2,000	Rs 10,000	Rs 50,000	Rs 80,000
4	Variable costs	Rs 1,200	per package	0	1,200	6,000	30,000	48,000
5	Contribution margin	Rs 800	per package	0	800	4,000	20,000	32,000
6	Fixed costs	Rs 20,000		20,000	20,000	20,000	20,000	20,000
7	Operating income			Rs (20,000)	Rs (19,200)	Rs (16,000)	Rs 0	Rs 12,000

contribution income statement in Exhibit 3-1. There are three related ways (we will call them methods) to think more deeply about and model CVP relationships:

1. The equation method
2. The contribution margin method
3. The graph method

The equation method and the contribution margin method are most useful when managers want to determine operating income at few specific levels of sales (for example – 5, 15, 25, and 40 units sold). The graph method helps managers visualize the relationship between units sold and operating income over a wide range of quantities of units sold. As we shall see later in the chapter, different methods are useful for different decisions.

Equation Method

Each column in Exhibit 3-1 is expressed as an equation.

$$\text{Revenues} = \text{Variable costs} - \text{Fixed costs} = \text{Operating income}$$

How are revenues in each column calculated?

$$\text{Revenues} = \text{Selling price } (SP) \times \text{Quantity of units sold } (Q)$$

How are variable costs in each column calculated?

$$\text{Variable costs} = \text{Variable cost per unit } (VCU) \times \text{Quantity of units sold } (Q)$$

So,

$$\left[\left(\begin{array}{c}\text{Selling}\\\text{price}\end{array} \times \begin{array}{c}\text{Quantity of}\\\text{units sold}\end{array}\right) - \left(\begin{array}{c}\text{Variable cost}\\\text{per unit}\end{array} \times \begin{array}{c}\text{Quantity of}\\\text{units sold}\end{array}\right)\right] - \begin{array}{c}\text{Fixed}\\\text{costs}\end{array} = \begin{array}{c}\text{Operating}\\\text{income}\end{array} \quad \textbf{(Equation 1)}$$

Equation 1 becomes the basis for calculating operating income for different quantities of units sold. For example, if you go to cell F7 in Exhibit 3-1, the calculation of operating income when Neeta sells 5 packages is

$$(\text{Rs } 2{,}000 \times 5) - (\text{Rs } 1{,}200 \times 5) - (\text{Rs } 20{,}000 = \text{Rs } 10{,}000 - \text{Rs } 6{,}000 - \text{Rs } 20{,}000 = -\text{Rs } 16{,}000$$

Contribution Margin Method

Rearranging equation 1,

$$\left[\left(\begin{array}{c}\text{Selling}\\\text{price}\end{array} - \begin{array}{c}\text{Variable cost}\\\text{per unit}\end{array}\right) \times \left(\begin{array}{c}\text{Quantity of}\\\text{units sold}\end{array}\right)\right] - \begin{array}{c}\text{Fixed}\\\text{costs}\end{array} = \begin{array}{c}\text{Operating}\\\text{income}\end{array}$$

$$\left(\begin{array}{c}\text{Contribution margin}\\\text{per unit}\end{array} \times \begin{array}{c}\text{Quantity of}\\\text{units sold}\end{array}\right) - \begin{array}{c}\text{Fixed}\\\text{costs}\end{array} = \begin{array}{c}\text{Operating}\\\text{income}\end{array} \quad \textbf{(Equation 2)}$$

In our Do-All Software example, contribution margin per unit is Rs 800 (Rs 2,000 – Rs 1,200), so when Neeta sells 5 packages,

$$\text{Operating income} = (\text{Rs } 800 \times 5) - \text{Rs } 20{,}000 = -\text{Rs } 16{,}000$$

Equation 2 expresses the basic idea we described earlier—each unit sold helps Neeta recover Rs 800 (in contribution margin) of the Rs 20,000 in fixed costs.

Graph Method

In the graph method, we represent total costs and total revenues graphically. Each is shown as a line on a graph. Exhibit 3-2 illustrates the graph method for Do-All Software. Because we have assumed that total costs and total revenues behave in a linear fashion, we need only two points to plot the line representing each of them.

1. **Total costs line.** The total costs line is the sum of fixed costs and variable costs. Fixed costs are Rs 20,000 at all quantities of units sold within the relevant range. To plot the total costs line, use as one point the Rs 20,000 fixed costs at zero units sold (point A), because variable costs are Rs 0 when no units are sold. Select a second point by choosing any other convenient output level (say, 40 units sold) and determine the corresponding total costs. Total variable costs at this output level are Rs 48,000 (40 units × Rs 1,200 per unit). Remember,

Exhibit 3-2

Cost-Volume Graph for Do-All Software

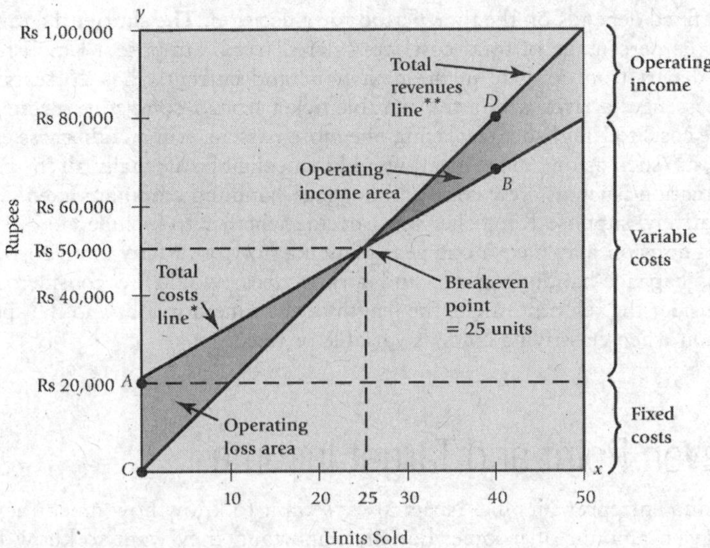

*Slope of the total costs line is the variable cost per unit = Rs 1,200
**Slope of the total revenues line is the selling price = Rs 2,000

fixed costs are Rs 20,000 at all quantities of units sold within the relevant range, so total costs at 40 units sold equal Rs 68,000 (Rs 20,000 +Rs 48,000), which is point B in Exhibit 3-2. The total costs line is the straight line from point A through point B.

2. **Total revenues line.** One convenient starting point is Rs 0 revenues at 0 units sold, which is point C in Exhibit 3-2. Select a second point by choosing any other convenient output level and determining the corresponding total revenues. At 40 units sold, total revenues are Rs 80,000 (Rs 2,000 per unit × 40 units), which is point D in Exhibit 3-2. The total revenues line is the straight line from point C through point D.

Profit or loss at any sales level can be determined by the vertical distance between the two lines at that level in Exhibit 3-2. For quantities fewer than 25 units sold, total costs exceed total revenues, and the purple area indicates operating losses. For quantities greater than 25 units sold, total revenues exceed total costs, and the blue-green area indicates operating incomes. At 25 units sold, total revenues equal total costs. Neeta will break even by selling 25 packages.

Cost-Volume-Profit Assumptions

Now that you have seen how CVP analysis works, think about the following assumptions we made during the analysis:

1. Changes in the levels of revenues and costs arise only because of changes in the number of product (or service) units sold. The number of units sold is the only revenue driver and the only cost driver. Just as a cost driver is any factor that affects costs, a **revenue driver** is a variable, such as volume, that causally affects revenues.
2. Total costs can be separated into two components: a fixed component that does not vary with units sold and a variable component that changes with respect to units sold. Furthermore, you know from Chapter 2 (Exhibit 2-5) that variable costs include both direct variable costs and indirect variable costs of a product. Similarly, fixed costs include both direct fixed costs and indirect fixed costs of a product.
3. When represented graphically, the behaviors of total revenues and total costs are linear (meaning they can be represented as a straight line) in relation to units sold within a relevant range (and time period).
4. Selling price, variable cost per unit, and total fixed costs (within a relevant range and time period) are known and constant.

As the CVP assumptions make clear, an important feature of CVP analysis is distinguishing fixed from variable costs. Always keep in mind, however, that whether a cost is variable or fixed depends on the time period for a decision. The shorter the time horizon, the higher the percentage of total costs considered fixed. Suppose a Kingfisher Airlines plane will depart from its gate in the next hour and currently has 20 seats unsold. A potential passenger arrives with a transferable ticket from a competing airline. What are the variable costs to Kingfisher of placing one more passenger in an otherwise empty seat? Variable costs (such as one more meal) would be negligible. Virtually all the costs in this decision situation (such as crew costs and baggage-handling costs) are fixed.

Alternatively, suppose Kingfisher must decide whether to include another city in its routes. This decision may have a one-year planning horizon. Many more costs, including crew costs, baggage-handling costs, and airport fees, would be considered variable. Always consider the relevant range, the length of the time horizon, and the specific decision situation when classifying costs as variable or fixed.

Breakeven Point and Target Income

Learning Objective 2

Determine the breakeven point and output level needed to achieve a target operating income

. . . compare contribution margin and fixed costs

Managers and entrepreneurs like Neeta always want to know how much they must sell to earn a given amount of income. Equally important, they want to know how much they must sell to avoid a loss.

Breakeven Point

The **breakeven point** (BEP) is that quantity of output sold at which total revenues equal total costs—that is, the quantity of output sold that results in Rs 0 of operating income. Managers are interested in the breakeven point because they want to avoid operating losses. The breakeven point tells them how much output they must sell to avoid a loss. We have already seen how to use the graph method to calculate the breakeven point. Recall from Exhibit 3-1 that operating income was Rs 0 when Neeta sold 25 units, the breakeven point. But by understanding the equations underlying the calculations in Exhibit 3-1, we can calculate the breakeven point directly for Do-All Software rather than trying out different quantities and checking when operating income equals Rs 0.

Recall the equation method (equation 1):

$$\left(\begin{array}{c}\text{Selling}\\\text{price}\end{array}\times\begin{array}{c}\text{Quantity of}\\\text{units sold}\end{array}\right)-\left(\begin{array}{c}\text{Variable cost}\\\text{per unit}\end{array}\times\begin{array}{c}\text{Quantity of}\\\text{units sold}\end{array}\right)-\begin{array}{c}\text{Fixed}\\\text{costs}\end{array}=\begin{array}{c}\text{Operating}\\\text{income}\end{array}$$

Setting operating income equal to Rs 0 and denoting quantity of output units that must be sold by *Q*,

$$(\text{Rs } 2{,}000 \times Q) - (\text{Rs } 1{,}200 \times Q) - \text{Rs } 20{,}000 = \text{Rs } 0$$
$$\text{Rs } 800 \times Q = \text{Rs } 20{,}000$$
$$Q = \text{Rs } 20{,}000 \div \text{Rs } 800 \text{ per unit} = 25 \text{ units}$$

If Neeta sells fewer than 25 units, she will have a loss; if she sells 25 units, she will break even; and if she sells more than 25 units, she will make a profit. While this breakeven point is expressed in units, it can also be expressed in terms of revenues: 25 units × Rs 2,000 selling price = Rs 50,000.

Recall the contribution margin method (equation 2):

$$\left(\begin{array}{c}\text{Contribution}\\\text{margin per unit}\end{array}\times\begin{array}{c}\text{Quantity of}\\\text{units sold}\end{array}\right)-\text{Fixed costs}=\text{Operating income}$$

At the breakeven point, operating income is by definition Rs 0 and so:

$$\text{Contribution margin per unit} \times \text{Breakeven number of units} = \text{Fixed cost} \qquad \textbf{(Equation 3)}$$

Rearranging equation 3 and entering the data,

$$\begin{array}{c}\text{Breakeven}\\\text{number of units}\end{array}=\frac{\text{Fixed costs}}{\text{Contribution margin per unit}}=\frac{\text{Rs } 20{,}000}{\text{Rs } 800 \text{ per unit}}=25 \text{ units}$$

To calculate the breakeven point in terms of revenues, recall that in the Do-All Software example,

$$\frac{\text{Contribution margin}}{\text{Percentage}} = \frac{\text{Contribution margin per unit}}{\text{Selling price}} = \frac{\text{Rs } 800}{\text{Rs } 2{,}000} = 0.40, \text{ or } 40\%$$

That is, 40% of each rupee of revenue, or 40 cents, is contribution margin. To break even, contribution margin must equal fixed costs of Rs 20,000. To earn Rs 20,000 of contribution margin, revenues must equal Rs 20,000 ÷ 0.40 = Rs 50,000.

$$\frac{\text{Breakeven}}{\text{revenues}} = \frac{\text{Fixed costs}}{\text{Contribution margin } \%} = \frac{\text{Rs } 20{,}000}{0.40} = \text{Rs } 50{,}000$$

The breakeven point tells managers how much they must sell to avoid a loss. But managers are equally interested in how they will achieve the operating income targets underlying their strategies and plans. For example, selling 25 units at a price of Rs 2,000 assures Neeta that she will not lose money if she rents the booth. This news is comforting, but Neeta is equally interested in learning how much she needs to sell to achieve a targeted amount of operating income.

Target Operating Income

We illustrate target operating income calculations by asking: How many units must Neeta sell to earn an operating income of Rs 12,000? One approach is to keep plugging in different quantities into Exhibit 3-1 and check when operating income equals Rs 12,000. Exhibit 3-1 shows that operating income is Rs 12,000 when 40 packages are sold. A more convenient approach is to use equation 1.

$$\left[\left(\begin{matrix}\text{Selling}\\ \text{price}\end{matrix} \times \begin{matrix}\text{Quantity of}\\ \text{units sold}\end{matrix}\right) - \left(\begin{matrix}\text{Variable cost}\\ \text{per unit}\end{matrix} \times \begin{matrix}\text{Quantity of}\\ \text{units sold}\end{matrix}\right)\right] - \begin{matrix}\text{Fixed}\\ \text{costs}\end{matrix} = \begin{matrix}\text{Operating}\\ \text{income}\end{matrix} \qquad \textbf{(Equation 1)}$$

We denote by Q the unknown quantity of units Neeta must sell to earn an operating income of Rs 12,000. Selling price is Rs 2,000, variable cost per package is Rs 1,200, fixed costs are Rs 20,000, and target operating income is Rs 12,000. Substituting these values into equation 1, we have

$$(\text{Rs } 2{,}000 \times Q) - (\text{Rs } 1{,}200 \times Q) - \text{Rs } 20{,}000 = \text{Rs } 12{,}000$$
$$\text{Rs } 800 \times Q = \text{Rs } 20{,}000 + \text{Rs } 12{,}000 = \text{Rs } 32{,}000$$
$$Q = \text{Rs } 32{,}000 \div \text{Rs } 800 \text{ per unit} = 40 \text{ units}$$

Alternatively, we could use equation 2,

$$\left(\begin{matrix}\text{Contribution margin}\\ \text{per unit}\end{matrix} \times \begin{matrix}\text{Quantity of}\\ \text{units sold}\end{matrix}\right) - \begin{matrix}\text{Fixed}\\ \text{costs}\end{matrix} = \begin{matrix}\text{Operating}\\ \text{income}\end{matrix} \qquad \textbf{(Equation 2)}$$

Given a target operating income (Rs 12,000 in this case), we can rearrange terms to get equation 4.

$$\frac{\text{Quantity of units}}{\text{required to be sold}} = \frac{\text{Fixed costs} + \text{Target operating income}}{\text{Contribution margin per unit}} \qquad \textbf{(Equation 4)}$$

$$\frac{\text{Quantity of units}}{\text{required to be sold}} = \frac{\text{Rs } 20{,}000 + \text{Rs } 12{,}000}{\text{Rs } 800 \text{ per unit}} = 40 \text{ units}$$

Proof:		
	Revenues, Rs 2,000 per unit × 40 units	Rs 80,000
	Variable costs, Rs 1,200 per unit × 40 units	48,000
	Contribution margin, Rs 800 per unit × 40 units	32,000
	Fixed costs	20,000
	Operating income	Rs 12,000

The revenues needed to earn an operating income of Rs 12,000 can also be calculated directly by recognizing (1) that Rs 32,000 of contribution margin must be earned (fixed costs of Rs 20,000 plus operating income of Rs 12,000) and (2) that each rupee of revenue earns 40 paise of contribution margin. To earn Rs 32,000 of contribution margin, revenues must equal Rs 32,000 ÷ 0.40 = Rs 80,000.

$$\text{Revenues needed to earn Rs 12,000} = \frac{\text{Rs 20,000} + \text{Rs 12,000}}{0.40} = \frac{\text{Rs 32,000}}{0.40} = \text{Rs 80,000}$$

The graph in Exhibit 3-2 is very difficult to use if the question is: How many units must Neeta sell to earn an operating income of Rs 12,000. Why? Because it is not easy to determine from the graph the precise point at which the difference between the total revenues line and the total costs line equals Rs 12,000. However, recasting Exhibit 3-2 in the form of a profit-volume (PV) graph makes it easier to answer this question.

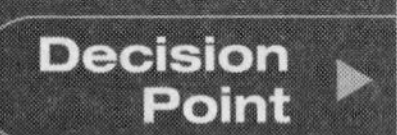

How can managers determine the breakeven point or the output needed to achieve a target operating income?

A **PV graph** shows how changes in the quantity of units sold affect operating income. Exhibit 3-3 is the PV graph for Do-All Software (fixed costs, Rs 20,000; selling price, Rs 2,000; and variable cost per unit, Rs 1,200). The PV line can be drawn using two points. One convenient point (M) is the operating loss at 0 units sold, which is equal to the fixed costs of Rs 20,000, shown at –Rs 20,000 on the vertical axis. A second convenient point (N) is the breakeven point, which is 25 units in our example. The PV line is the straight line from point M through point N. To find the number of units Neeta must sell to earn an operating income of Rs 12,000, draw a horizontal line parallel to the x-axis corresponding to Rs 12,000 on the vertical axis (that's the y-axis). At the point where this line intersects the PV line, draw a vertical line down to the horizontal axis (that's the x-axis). The vertical line intersects the x-axis at 40 units, indicating that by selling 40 units Neeta will earn an operating income of Rs 12,000.

Target Net Income and Income Taxes

Understand how income taxes affect CVP analysis

. . . focus on net income

Net income is operating income plus nonoperating revenues (such as interest revenue) minus nonoperating costs (such as interest cost) minus income taxes. For simplicity, throughout this chapter we assume nonoperating revenues and nonoperating costs are zero. Thus,

$$\text{Net income} = \text{Operating income} - \text{Income taxes}$$

Until now, we have ignored the effect of income taxes in our CVP analysis. In many companies, the income targets for managers in their strategic plans are expressed in terms of net income. That's because top management wants subordinate managers to take into account the effects their decisions have on operating income after income taxes are paid. Some decisions may not result in large operating incomes. But they may have favorable tax consequences and so may be attractive on a net income basis—the measure that drives shareholders' dividends and returns.

To make net income evaluations, CVP calculations for target income must be stated in terms of target net income instead of target operating income. For example, Neeta may be interested in knowing the quantity of units she must sell to earn a net income of Rs 9,600, assuming an income tax rate of 40%.

$$\text{Target net income} = \left(\begin{array}{c}\text{Target}\\ \text{operating income}\end{array}\right) - \left(\begin{array}{c}\text{Target}\\ \text{operating income}\end{array} \times \text{Tax rate}\right)$$

$$\text{Target net income} = (\text{Target operating income}) \times (1 - \text{Tax rate})$$

$$\text{Target operating income} = \frac{\text{Target net income}}{1 - \text{Tax rate}} = \frac{\text{Rs 9,600}}{1 - 0.40} = \text{Rs, 16,000}$$

In other words, to earn a target net income of Rs 9,600, Neeta's target operating income is Rs 16,000.

Proof:

Target operating income	Rs 16,000
Tax at 40% (0.40 × Rs 16,000)	6,400
Target net income	Rs 9,600

The key step is to take the target net income number and convert it into the corresponding target operating income number. We can then use equation 1 for target operating income and substitute numbers from our Do-All Software example.

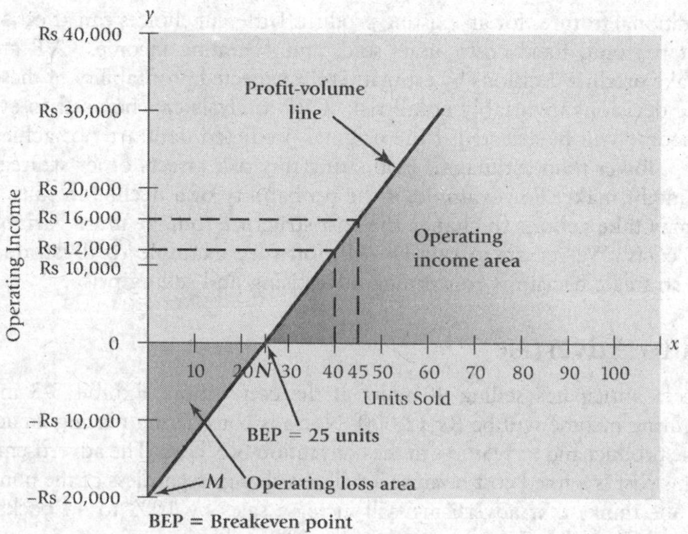

Exhibit 3-3

Profit-Volume Graph for Do-All Software

$$\left[\left(\text{Selling price} \times \text{Quantity of units sold}\right) - \left(\text{Variable cost per unit} \times \text{Quantity of units sold}\right)\right] - \text{Fixed costs} = \text{Operating income} \qquad \textbf{(Equation 1)}$$

$$(\text{Rs } 2{,}000 \times Q) - (\text{Rs } 1{,}200 \times Q) - \text{Rs } 20{,}000 = \frac{\text{Rs } 9{,}600}{1-0.40}$$

$$(\text{Rs } 2{,}000 \times Q) - (\text{Rs } 1{,}200 \times Q) - \text{Rs } 20{,}000 = \text{Rs } 16{,}000$$

$$\text{Rs } 800 \times Q = \text{Rs } 36{,}000$$

$$Q = \text{Rs } 36{,}000 \div \text{Rs } 800 \text{ per unit} = 45 \text{ units}$$

Alternatively we can calculate the number of units Neeta must sell by using the contribution margin method and equation 4:

$$\text{Quantity of units required to be sold} = \frac{\text{Fixed costs} + \text{Target operating income}}{\text{Contribution margin per unit}} \qquad \textbf{(Equation 4)}$$

$$= \frac{\text{Rs } 20{,}000 + \text{Rs } 16{,}000}{\text{Rs } 800 \text{ per unit}} = 45 \text{ units}$$

Proof:

Revenues, Rs 2,000 per unit × 45 units	Rs 90,000
Variable costs, Rs 1,200 per unit × 45 units	54,000
Contribution margin	36,000
Fixed costs	20,000
Operating income	16,000
Income taxes, Rs 16,000 × 0.40	6,400
Net income	Rs 9,600

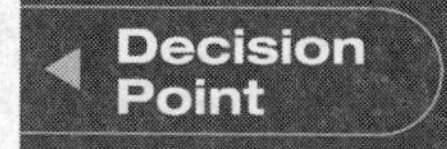
Decision Point

How can managers incorporate income taxes into CVP analysis?

Neeta can also use the PV graph in Exhibit 3-3. To earn target operating income of Rs 16,000, Neeta needs to sell 45 units.

Focusing the analysis on target net income instead of target operating income will not change the breakeven point. That's because, by definition, operating income at the breakeven point is Rs 0, and no income taxes are paid when there is no operating income.

Learning Objective 

4

Explain how managers use CVP analysis in decision making

. . . choose the alternative that maximizes operating income

Using CVP Analysis for Decision Making

We have seen how CVP analysis is useful for calculating the units that need to be sold to break even, or to achieve a target operating income or target net income. Managers also use CVP analysis to guide other decisions, many of them strategic decisions. Consider a decision about choosing additional features for an existing product. Different choices can affect selling prices, variable cost per unit, fixed costs, units sold, and operating income. CVP analysis helps managers make product decisions by estimating the expected profitability of these choices.

Strategic decisions invariably entail risk. CVP analysis can be used to evaluate how operating income will be affected if the original predicted data are not achieved—say, if sales are 10% lower than estimated. Evaluating this risk affects other strategic decisions a company might make. For example, if the probability of a decline in sales seems high, a manager may take actions to change the cost structure to have more variable costs and fewer fixed costs. We return to our Do-All Software example to illustrate using CVP analysis for strategic decisions concerning advertising and selling price.

Decision to Advertise

Suppose Neeta anticipates selling 40 units at the convention. Exhibit 3-3 indicates that Neeta's operating income will be Rs 12,000. Neeta is considering placing an advertisement describing the product and its features in the convention brochure. The advertisement will cost Rs 5,000. This cost is a fixed cost because it will not change regardless of the number of units Neeta sells. She thinks that advertising will increase sales by 10% to 44 packages. Should Neeta advertise? The following table presents the CVP analysis.

	40 Packages Sold with No Advertising (1)	44 Packages Sold with Advertising (2)	Difference (3) = (2) − (1)
Revenues (Rs 2,000 × 40; Rs 2,000 × 44)	Rs 80,000	Rs 88,000	Rs 8,000
Variable costs (Rs 1,200 × 40; Rs 1,200 × 44)	48,000	52,800	4,800
Contribution margin (Rs 800 × 40; Rs 800 × 44)	32,000	35,200	3,200
Fixed costs	− 20,000	− 25,000	5,000
Operating income	Rs 12,000	Rs 10,200	Rs(1,800)

Operating income decreases from Rs 12,000 to Rs 10,200, so Neeta should not advertise. Note that Neeta could focus only on the difference column and come to the same conclusion: If Neeta advertises, contribution margin will increase by Rs 3,200 (revenues, Rs 8,000 – variable costs, Rs 4,800), and fixed costs will increase by Rs 5,000, resulting in a Rs 1,800 decrease in operating income.

As you become more familiar with CVP analysis, try evaluating decisions based on differences rather than mechanically working through the contribution income statement. Analyzing differences gets to the heart of CVP analysis and sharpens intuition by focusing only on the revenues and costs that will change by implementing new decisions.

Decision to Reduce Selling Price

Having decided not to advertise, Neeta is contemplating whether to reduce the selling price to Rs 1,750. At this price, she thinks she will sell 50 units. At this quantity, the software wholesaler who supplies Do-All Software will sell the packages to Neeta for Rs 1,150 per unit instead of Rs 1,200. Should Neeta reduce the selling price?

Contribution margin from lowering price to Rs 1,750: (Rs 1,750 − Rs 1,150) per unit × 50 units	Rs 30,000
Contribution margin from maintaining price at Rs 2,000: (Rs 2,000 − Rs 1,200) per unit × 40 units	32,000
Change in contribution margin from lowering price	Rs (2,000)

Decreasing the price will reduce contribution margin by Rs 2,000 and, because the fixed costs of Rs 20,000 will not change, it will also reduce operating income by Rs 2,000. Neeta should not reduce the selling price.

Neeta could also ask "At what price can I sell 50 units (purchased at Rs 1,150 per unit) and continue to earn an operating income of Rs 12,000?" The answer is Rs 1,790, as the following calculations show.

Target operating income	Rs 12,000
Add fixed costs	20,000
Target contribution margin	Rs 32,000
Divided by number of units sold	÷50 units
Target contribution margin per unit	Rs 640
Add variable cost per unit	1,150
Target selling price	Rs 1,790

Proof:

Revenues, Rs 1,790 per unit × 50 units	Rs 89,500
Variable costs, Rs 1,150 per unit × 50 units	57,500
Contribution margin	32,000
Fixed costs	20,000
Operating income	Rs 12,000

Neeta should also examine the effects of other decisions, such as simultaneously increasing advertising costs and lowering prices. In each case, Neeta will compare the changes in contribution margin (through the effects on selling prices, variable costs, and quantities of units sold) to the changes in fixed costs, and she will choose the alternative that provides the highest operating income.

Decision Point

How do managers use CVP analysis to make decisions?

Sensitivity Analysis and Margin of Safety

Learning Objective 5

Explain how sensitivity analysis helps managers cope with uncertainty

. . . determine the effect on operating income of different assumptions

Before choosing strategies and plans about how to implement strategies, managers frequently analyze the sensitivity of their decisions to changes in underlying assumptions. **Sensitivity analysis** is a "what-if" technique that managers use to examine how an outcome will change if the original predicted data are not achieved or if an underlying assumption changes. In the context of CVP analysis, sensitivity analysis answers questions such as, What will operating income be if the quantity of units sold decreases by 5% from the original prediction? And, What will operating income be if variable cost per unit increases by 10%? The sensitivity of operating income to various possible outcomes broadens managers' perspectives about what might actually occur *before* costs are committed.

Electronic spreadsheets, such as Excel, enable managers to conduct CVP-based sensitivity analyses in a systematic and efficient way. Using spreadsheets, managers can conduct sensitivity analysis to examine the effect and interaction of changes in selling price, variable cost per unit, fixed costs, and target operating income. Exhibit 3-4 displays a

Exhibit 3-4

Spreadsheet Analysis of CVP Relationships for Do-All Software

File Edit View Insert Format Tools Data Window Help

D5 fx =(Rs A5+DRs 3)/(Rs FRs 1-Rs B5)

	A	B	C	D	E	F
1			Number of units required to be sold at Rs			200
2			Selling Price to Earn Target Operating Income of			
3		Variable Costs	Rs 0	Rs 12,000	Rs 16,000	Rs 20,000
4	Fixed Costs	per Unit	(Breakeven point)			
5	Rs 20,000	Rs 1,000	20	32[a]	36	40
6	Rs 20,000	Rs 1,200	25	40	45	50
7	Rs 20,000	Rs 1,500	40	64	72	80
8	Rs 24,000	Rs 1,000	24	36	40	44
9	Rs 24,000	Rs 1,200	30	45	50	55
10	Rs 24,000	Rs 1,500	48	72	80	88
11	Rs 28,000	Rs 1,000	28	40	44	48
12	Rs 28,000	Rs 1,200	35	50	55	60
13	Rs 28,000	Rs 1,500	56	80	88	96
14						

[a]Number of units required to be sold $= \dfrac{\text{Fixed costs + Target operating income}}{\text{Contribution margin per unit}} = \dfrac{\text{Rs } 20{,}000 + \text{Rs } 12{,}000}{\text{Rs } 2{,}000 - \text{Rs } 1{,}000} = 32$

spreadsheet for the Do-All Software example. Using the spreadsheet, Neeta can immediately see how many units she needs to sell to achieve particular operating-income levels, given alternative levels of fixed costs and variable cost per unit that she may face. For example, 32 units must be sold to earn an operating income of Rs 12,000 if fixed costs are Rs 20,000 and variable cost per unit is Rs 1,000. Neeta can also use Exhibit 3-4 to determine that she needs to sell 56 units to break even (earn operating income of Rs 0) if the booth rental at the New Delhi convention is raised to Rs 28,000 (increasing fixed costs to Rs 28,000) and if the software supplier raises its price to Rs 1,500 (increasing variable cost to Rs 1,500 per unit). Neeta can use information about costs and sensitivity analysis, together with realistic predictions about how much she can sell to decide if she should rent a booth at the convention.

Another aspect of sensitivity analysis is **margin of safety:**

$$\text{Margin of safety} = \text{Budgeted (or actual) revenues} - \text{Breakeven revenues}$$
$$\text{Margin of safety (in units)} = \text{Budgeted (or actual) sales quantity} - \text{Breakeven quantity}$$

The margin of safety answers the "what-if" question: If budgeted revenues are above breakeven and drop, how far can they fall below budget before the breakeven point is reached? Such a fall could be a result of a competitor introducing a better product, or poorly executed marketing programs, and so on. Assume that Neeta has fixed costs of Rs 20,000, a selling price of Rs 2,000, and variable cost per unit of Rs 1,200. From Exhibit 3-1, if Neeta sells 40 units, the budgeted revenues are Rs 80,000 and the budgeted operating income is Rs 12,000. The breakeven point is 25 units or Rs 50,000 in total revenues.

$$\text{Margin of safety} = \begin{matrix}\text{Budgeted}\\\text{revenues}\end{matrix} - \begin{matrix}\text{Breakeven}\\\text{revenues}\end{matrix} = \text{Rs } 80{,}000 - \text{Rs } 50{,}000 = \text{Rs } 30{,}000$$

$$\begin{matrix}\text{Margin of}\\\text{safety (in units)}\end{matrix} = \begin{matrix}\text{Budgeted}\\\text{sales (units)}\end{matrix} - \begin{matrix}\text{Breakeven}\\\text{sales (units)}\end{matrix} = 40 - 25 = 15 \text{ units}$$

Sometimes margin of safety is expressed as a percentage:

$$\text{Margin of safety percentage} = \frac{\text{Margin of safety in rupees}}{\text{Budgted (or actual) revenues}}$$

In our example, margin of safety percentage $= \dfrac{\text{Rs } 30{,}000}{\text{Rs } 80{,}000} = 37.5\%$

This result means that revenues would have to decrease substantially, by 37.5%, to reach breakeven revenues. The high margin of safety gives Neeta confidence that she is unlikely to suffer a loss.

If, however, Neeta expected to sell only 30 units, budgeted revenues would be Rs 60,000 (Rs 2,000 per unit × 30 units) and the margin of safety would equal:

Decision Point

What can managers do to cope with uncertainty or changes in underlying assumptions?

$$\text{Budgeted revenues} - \text{Breakeven revenues} = \text{Rs } 60{,}000 - \text{Rs } 50{,}000 = \text{Rs } 10{,}000$$

$$\begin{matrix}\text{Margin of}\\\text{safety percentage}\end{matrix} = \frac{\text{Margin of safety in rupees}}{\text{Budgeted (or actual) revenues}} = \frac{\text{Rs } 10{,}000}{\text{Rs } 60{,}000} = 16.67\%$$

This result means that if revenues decrease by more than 16.67%, Neeta would suffer a loss. A low margin of safety increases the risk of a loss. If Neeta does not have the tolerance for this level of risk, she will prefer not to rent a booth at the convention.

Sensitivity analysis is a simple approach to recognizing **uncertainty**, which is the possibility that an actual amount will deviate from an expected amount. Sensitivity analysis gives managers a good feel for the risks involved. A more comprehensive approach to recognizing uncertainty is to compute expected values using probability distributions. This approach is illustrated in the appendix to this chapter.

Learning Objective 6

Use CVP analysis to plan variable and fixed costs

. . . compare risk of losses versus higher returns

Cost Planning and CVP

Managers have the ability to choose the levels of fixed and variable costs in their cost structures. This is a strategic decision. In this section, we describe various factors that managers and management accountants consider as they make this decision.

Alternative Fixed-Cost/Variable-Cost Structures

CVP-based sensitivity analysis highlights the risks and returns as fixed costs are substituted for variable costs in a company's cost structure. In Exhibit 3-4, compare line 6 and line 11.

	Fixed Cost	Variable Cost	Number of units required to be sold at Rs 2,000 selling price to earn target operating income	
			Rs 0 (Breakeven point)	Rs 20,000
Line 6	Rs 20,000	Rs 1,200	25	50
Line 11	Rs 28,000	Rs 1,000	28	48

Compared to Line 6, Line 11, with higher fixed costs, has more risk of loss (has a higher breakeven point) but requires fewer units to be sold (48 versus 50) to earn operating income of Rs 20,000. CVP analysis can help managers evaluate various fixed-cost/variable-cost structures. We next consider the effects of these choices in more detail. Suppose Computer Conventions, Ltd. offers Neeta three rental alternatives:

Option 1: Rs 20,000 fixed fee

Option 2: Rs 8,000 fixed fee plus 15% of convention revenues

Option 3: 25% of convention revenues with no fixed fee

Neeta's variable cost per unit is Rs 1,200. Neeta is interested in how her choice of a rental agreement will affect the income she earns and the risks she faces. Exhibit 3-5 graphically depicts the profit-volume relationship for each option. The line representing the relationship between units sold and operating income for Option 1 is the same as the line in the PV graph shown in Exhibit 3-3 (fixed costs of Rs 20,000 and contribution margin per unit of Rs 800). The line representing Option 2 shows fixed costs of Rs 8,000 and a contribution margin per unit of Rs 500 [selling price, Rs 2,000, minus variable cost per unit, Rs 1,200, minus variable rental fees per unit, Rs 300, (0.15 × Rs 2,000)]. The line representing Option 3 has fixed costs of Rs 0 and a contribution margin per unit of Rs 300 [Rs 2,000 − Rs 1,200 − Rs 500 (0.25 × Rs 2,000)].

Option 3 has the lowest breakeven point (0 units), and Option 1 has the highest breakeven point (25 units). Option 1 has the highest risk of loss if sales are low, but it also has the highest contribution margin per unit (Rs 800) and hence the highest operating income when sales are high (greater than 40 units).

The choice among Options 1, 2, and 3 is a strategic decision that Neeta faces. As in most strategic decisions, what she decides now will significantly affect her operating income (or loss), depending on the demand for Do-All Software. Faced with this uncertainty, Neeta's choice will be influenced by her confidence in the level of demand for the software package and her willingness to risk losses if demand is low. For example, if Neeta's tolerance for risk is high, she will choose Option 1 with its high potential rewards. If, however, Neeta is averse to taking risk, she will prefer Option 3, where the rewards are smaller if sales are high but where she never suffers a loss if sales are low.

Operating Leverage

The risk-return trade-off across alternative cost structures can be measured as operating leverage. **Operating leverage** describes the effects that fixed costs have on changes in operating income as changes occur in units sold and contribution margin. Organizations with a high proportion of fixed costs in their cost structures, as is the case under Option 1, have high operating leverage. The line representing Option 1 in Exhibit 3-5 is the steepest of the three lines. Small increases in sales lead to large increases in operating income. Small decreases in sales result in relatively large decreases in operating income, leading to a greater risk of operating losses. *At any given level of sales,*

$$\text{Degree of operating leverage} = \frac{\text{Contribution margin}}{\text{Operating income}}$$

Exhibit 3-5

Profit-Volume Graph for Alternative Rental Options for Do-All Software

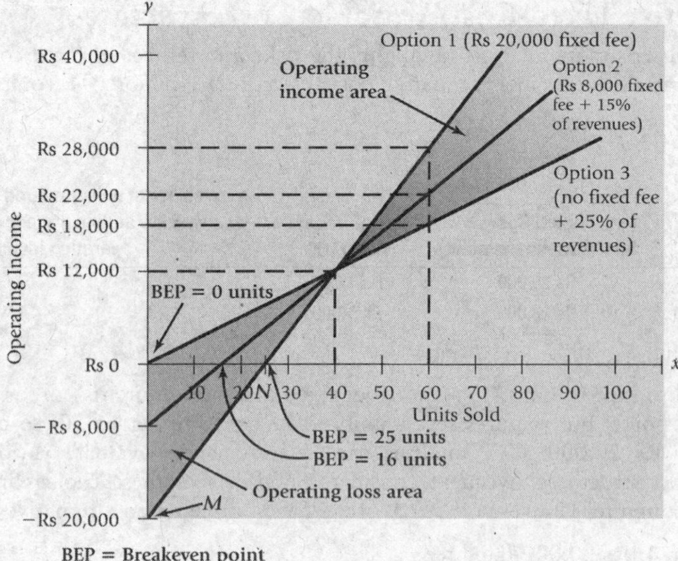

The following table shows the **degree of operating leverage** at sales of 40 units for the three rental options.

	Option 1	Option 2	Option 3
1. Contribution margin per unit	Rs 800	Rs 500	Rs 300
2. Contribution margin (Row 1 × 40 units)	Rs 32,000	Rs 20,000	Rs 12,000
3. Operating income (from Exhibit 3-5)	Rs 12,000	Rs 12,000	Rs 12,000
4. Degree of operating leverage (Row 2 ÷ Row 3)	$\frac{\text{Rs } 32{,}000}{\text{Rs } 12{,}000} = 2.67$	$\frac{\text{Rs } 20{,}000}{\text{Rs } 12{,}000} = 1.67$	$\frac{\text{Rs } 12{,}000}{\text{Rs } 12{,}000} = 1.00$

These results indicate that, when sales are 40 units, a percentage change in sales and contribution margin will result in 2.67 times that percentage change in operating income for Option 1, but the same percentage change (1.00) in operating income for Option 3. Consider, for example, a sales increase of 50% from 40 to 60 units. Contribution margin will increase by 50% under each option. Operating income, however, will increase by 2.67 × 50% = 133% from Rs 12,000 to Rs 28,000 in Option 1, but it will increase by only 1.00 × 50% = 50% from Rs 12,000 to Rs 18,000 in Option 3 (see Exhibit 3-5). The degree of operating leverage at a given level of sales helps managers calculate the effect of fluctuations in sales on operating income.

Keep in mind that, in the presence of fixed costs, the degree of operating leverage is different at different levels of sales. For example, at sales of 60 units, the degree of operating leverage under each of the three options is as follows:

	Option 1	Option 2	Option 3
1. Contribution margin per unit	Rs 800	Rs 500	Rs 300
2. Contribution margin (Row 1 × 60 units)	Rs 48,000	Rs 30,000	Rs 18,000
3. Operating income (from Exhibit 3-5)	Rs 28,000	Rs 22,000	Rs 18,000
4. Degree of operating leverage (Row 2 ÷ Row 3)	$\frac{\text{Rs } 48{,}000}{\text{Rs } 28{,}000} = 1.71$	$\frac{\text{Rs } 30{,}000}{\text{Rs } 22{,}000} = 1.36$	$\frac{\text{Rs } 18{,}000}{\text{Rs } 18{,}000} = 1.00$

The degree of operating leverage decreases from 2.67 (at sales of 40 units) to 1.71 (at sales of 60 units) under Option 1 and from 1.67 to 1.36 under Option 2. In general, whenever there are fixed costs, the degree of operating leverage decreases as the level of sales increases beyond the breakeven point. If fixed costs are Rs 0 as in Option 3, contribution margin equals operating income, and the degree of operating leverage equals 1.00 at all sales levels.

But why must managers monitor operating leverage carefully? Again, consider companies such as General Motors, Global Crossing, US Airways, United Airlines, and WorldCom. Their high operating leverage was a major reason for their financial problems. Anticipating high demand for their services, these companies borrowed money to acquire assets, resulting in high fixed costs. As sales declined, these companies suffered losses and could not generate sufficient cash to service their interest and debt, causing them to seek bankruptcy protection. Managers and management accountants should always evaluate how the level of fixed costs and variable costs they choose will affect the risk-return trade-off. See the following Concepts in Action, for another example of the risks of high fixed costs.

What actions are managers taking to reduce their fixed costs? Many companies are moving their manufacturing facilities from the United States to lower-cost countries, such as Mexico and China. To substitute high fixed costs with lower variable costs, companies are purchasing products from lower-cost suppliers instead of manufacturing products themselves. These actions reduce both costs and operating leverage. More recently, General Electric and Hewlett-Packard began outsourcing service functions, such as post-sales customer service, by shifting their customer call centers to countries, such as India, where costs are lower. These decisions by companies are not without controversy. Some economists argue that outsourcing helps to keep costs, and therefore prices, low and enables U.S. companies to remain globally competitive. Others argue that outsourcing reduces job opportunities in the United States and hurts working-class families.

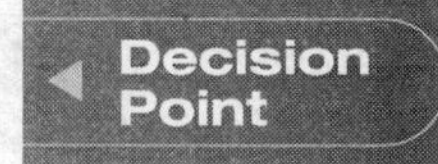

How should managers choose among different variable-cost/fixed-cost structures?

Effects of Sales Mix on Income

Learning Objective 7

Apply CVP analysis to a company producing multiple products

. . . assume sales mix of products remains constant as total units sold changes

Sales mix is the quantities (or proportion) of various products (or services) that constitute total unit sales of a company. Suppose Neeta is now budgeting for a subsequent computer convention in Chennai. She plans to sell two different software products—Do-All and Superword—and budgets the following:

	Do-All	Superword	Total
Expected sales	60	40	100
Revenues, Rs 2,000 and Rs 1,000 per unit	Rs 1,20,000	Rs 40,000	Rs 1,60,000
Variable costs, Rs 1,200 and Rs 700 per unit	72,000	28,000	1,00,000
Contribution margin, Rs 800 and Rs 300 per unit	Rs 48,000	Rs 12,000	60,000
Fixed costs			45,000
Operating income			Rs 15,000

What is the breakeven point? In contrast to the single-product (or service) situation, the number of total units that must be sold to break even in a multiproduct company depends on the sales mix—the combination of the number of units of Do-All sold and the number of units of Superword sold. We assume that the budgeted sales mix (60 units of Do-All sold for every 40 units of Superword sold, that is, 3 units of Do-All sold for every 2 units of Superword sold) will not change at different levels of total unit sales. That is, we think of Neeta selling a bundle of 3 units of Do-All and 2 units of Superword. Note that this does not mean that Neeta physically bundles the two products together into one big package.

Each bundle yields a contribution margin of Rs 3,000 calculated as follows:

	Number of Units of Do-All and Superword in Each Bundle	Contribution Margin per Unit for Do-All and Superword	Contribution Margin of the Bundle
Do-All	3	Rs 800	Rs 2,400
Superword	2	300	600
Total			Rs 3,000

To compute the breakeven point, we calculate the number of bundles Neeta needs to sell.

$$\text{Breakeven point in bundles} = \frac{\text{Fixed costs}}{\text{Contribution margin per bundle}} = \frac{\text{Rs } 45{,}000}{\text{Rs } 3{,}000 \text{ per bundle}} = 15 \text{ bundles}$$

Breakeven point in units of Do-All and Superword is:

Do-All: 15 bundles × 3 units of Do-All per bundle =	45 units
Superword: 15 bundles × 2 units of Superword per bundle =	30 units
Total number of units to breakeven	75 units

Breakeven point in rupees for Do-All and Superword is:

Do-All: 45 units × Rs 2,000 per unit	Rs 90,000
Superword: 30 units × Rs 1,000 per unit	30,000
Breakeven revenues	Rs 1,20,000

We can also calculate the breakeven point in revenues for the multiple-products situation as follows:

	Number of Units of Do-All and Superword in Each Bundle	Selling Price for Do-All and Superword	Revenue of the Bundle
Do-All	3	Rs 2,000	Rs 6,000
Superword	2	1,000	2,000
Total			Rs 8,000

$$\text{Contribution margin percentage for the bundle} = \frac{\text{Contribution margin of the bundle}}{\text{Revenue of the bundle}} = \frac{\text{Rs } 3{,}000}{\text{Rs } 8{,}000} = 0.375 \text{ or } 37.5\%$$

$$\text{Breakeven revenues} = \frac{\text{Fixed costs}}{\text{Contribution margin \% for the bundle}} = \frac{\text{Rs } 45{,}000}{0.375} = \text{Rs } 1{,}20{,}000$$

$$\text{Number of bundles required to be sold to break even} = \frac{\text{Breakeven revenues}}{\text{Revenue per bundle}} = \frac{\text{Rs } 1{,}20{,}000}{\text{Rs } 8{,}000 \text{ per bundle}} = 15 \text{ bundles}$$

The breakeven point in units and rupees for Do-All and Superword are:

Do-All: 15 bundles × 3 units of Do-All per bundle = 45 units × Rs 2,000 per unit = Rs 90,000
Superword: 15 bundles × 2 units of Superword per bundle = 30 units × Rs 1,000 per unit = Rs 30,000

Recall that in all our calculations, we have assumed that the budgeted sales mix (3 units of Do-All for every 2 units of Superword) will not change at different levels of total unit sales.

Of course, there are many different sales mixes (in units) that result in a contribution margin of Rs 45,000 and cause Neeta to break even, as the following table shows:

Sales Mix (Units)		Contribution Margin from		
Do-All (1)	Superword (2)	Do-All (3) = Rs 800 × (1)	Superword (4) = Rs 300 × (2)	Total Contribution Margin (5) = (3) + (4)
48	22	Rs 38,400	Rs 6,600	Rs 45,000
36	54	28,800	16,200	45,000
30	70	24,000	21,000	45,000

If for example, the sales mix changes to 3 units of Do-All for every 7 units of Superword, you can see in the preceding table that the breakeven point increases from 75 units to 100 units, comprising 30 units of Do-All and 70 units of Superword. The breakeven quantity increases because the sales mix has shifted toward the lower-contribution-margin product, Superword (Rs 300 per unit compared to Do-All's Rs 800 per unit). In general, for any given total quantity of units sold, as the sales mix shifts toward units with lower contribution margins (more units of Superword compared to Do-All), operating income will be lower.

How do companies choose their sales mix? They adjust their mix to respond to demand changes. For example, as gasoline prices increase and customers want smaller cars, auto companies shift their production mix to produce additional smaller cars.

The multi-product case has two cost drivers, GMAT Success and GRE Guarantee. It shows how CVP and breakeven analysis can be adapted to the case of multiple cost drivers. The key point is that many different combinations of cost drivers can result in a given contribution margin.

Multiple Cost Drivers

Learning Objective 8

Adapt CVP analysis to situations in which a product has more than one cost driver

. . . basic concepts apply but simple formulas do not

Throughout this chapter, we have assumed that the number of output units is the only revenue driver and the only cost driver. Now we describe how some aspects of CVP analysis can be adapted to the general case of multiple cost drivers.

Consider again the single-product Do-All Software example. Suppose Neeta will incur a variable cost of Rs 100 for preparing documents (including an invoice) for each customer who buys Do-All Software. That is, the cost driver of document-preparation costs is the number of customers who buy Do-All Software. Neeta's operating income can then be expressed in terms of revenues and these costs:

$$\text{Operating Income} = \text{Revenues} - \left(\begin{array}{c}\text{Cost of each}\\ \text{Do-All software}\\ \text{package}\end{array} \times \begin{array}{c}\text{Number of}\\ \text{packages}\\ \text{sold}\end{array}\right) - \left(\begin{array}{c}\text{Cost of preparing}\\ \text{documents for}\\ \text{each customer}\end{array} \times \begin{array}{c}\text{Number of}\\ \text{customers}\end{array}\right) - \text{Fixed costs}$$

If Neeta sells 40 packages to 15 customers, then

$$\begin{aligned}\text{Operating income} &= (\text{Rs } 2{,}000 \text{ per package} \times 40 \text{ packages}) - (\text{Rs } 1{,}200 \text{ per package} \times 40 \text{ packages}) - \\ &\quad (\text{Rs } 100 \text{ per customer} \times 15 \text{ customers}) - \text{Rs } 20{,}000 \\ &= \text{Rs } 80{,}000 - \text{Rs } 48{,}000 - \text{Rs } 1{,}500 - \text{Rs } 20{,}000 = \text{Rs } 10{,}500\end{aligned}$$

If instead Neeta sells 40 packages to 40 customers, then

$$\begin{aligned}\text{Operating income} &= (\text{Rs } 2{,}000 \times 40) - (\text{Rs } 1{,}200 \times 40) - (\text{Rs } 100 \times 40) - \text{Rs } 20{,}000 \\ &= \text{Rs } 80{,}000 - \text{Rs } 48{,}000 - \text{Rs } 4{,}000 - \text{Rs } 20{,}000 = \text{Rs } 8{,}000\end{aligned}$$

The number of packages sold is not the only determinant of Neeta's operating income. For a given number of packages sold, Neeta's operating income will be lower if she sells Do-All Software to more customers. Neeta's costs depend on two cost drivers: the number of packages sold and the number of customers.

Just as in the case of multiple products, there is no unique breakeven point when there are multiple cost drivers. For example, Neeta will break even if she sells 26 packages to 8 customers or 27 packages to 16 customers:

$$\begin{aligned}(\text{Rs } 2{,}000 \times 26) - (\text{Rs } 1{,}200 \times 26) - (\text{Rs } 100 \times 8) - \text{Rs } 20{,}000 &= \text{Rs } 52{,}000 - \text{Rs } 31{,}200 - \text{Rs } 800 \\ &\quad - \text{Rs } 20{,}000 = \text{Rs } 0 \\ (\text{Rs } 2{,}000 \times 27) - (\text{Rs } 1{,}200 \times 27) - (\text{Rs } 100 \times 16) - \text{Rs } 20{,}000 &= \text{Rs } 54{,}000 - \text{Rs } 32{,}400 - \text{Rs } 1{,}600 \\ &\quad - \text{Rs } 20{,}000 = \text{Rs } 0\end{aligned}$$

Decision Point

How can CVP analysis be applied to a company producing multiple products?

CVP Analysis in Service and Nonprofit Organizations

Thus far, our CVP analysis has focused on a merchandising company. CVP can also be applied to decisions by manufacturing, service, and nonprofit organizations. To apply CVP analysis in service and nonprofit organizations, we need to focus on measuring their output, which is different from the tangible units sold by manufacturing and merchandising companies. Examples of output measures in various service and nonprofit industries are:

Industry	Measure of Output
Airlines	Passenger miles
Hotels/motels	Room-nights occupied
Hospitals	Patient days
Universities	Student credit-hours

Concepts in Action

Fixed Costs, Variable Costs, and the Future of Radio

Building up too much fixed costs can be hazardous to a company's health. Because fixed costs, unlike variable costs, do not automatically decrease as volume declines, companies with too much fixed costs can lose a considerable amount of money during lean times. Sirius XM, the satellite radio broadcaster, learned this lesson the hard way.

To begin broadcasting in 2001, both Sirius Satellite Radio and XM Satellite Radio—the two companies now comprising Sirius XM—spent billions of dollars on broadcasting licenses, space satellites, and other technology infrastructure. Once operational, the companies also spent billions on other fixed items such as programming and content (including Howard Stern and Major League Baseball), satellite transmission, and R&D. In contrast, variable costs were minimal, consisting mainly of artist-royalty fees and customer service and billing. In effect, this created a business model with a high operating leverage—that is, the companies' cost structure had a very significant proportion of fixed costs. As such, profitability could only be achieved by amassing millions of paid subscribers and selling advertising.

The competitive disadvantage of this highly-leveraged business model was nearly disastrous. Despite amassing more than 14 million subscribers, over the years Sirius and XM rang up $3 billion in debt and tallied cumulative operating losses in excess of $10 billion. Operating leverage, and the threat of bankruptcy, forced the merger of Sirius and XM in 2007, and since then the combined entity has struggled to cut costs, refinance its sizable debt, and reap the profits from over 18 million monthly subscribers.

While satellite radio has struggled under the weight of too much fixed cost, Internet radio had the opposite problem—too much variable costs. But "How?" you ask. Don't variable costs only increase as revenues increase? Yes, but if the revenue earned is less than the variable cost, an increase in revenue can lead to bankruptcy. This is almost what happened to Pandora, the Internet radio service.

Pandora launched in 2005 with only $3 million in venture capital. Available free over the Internet, Pandora earned revenue in three ways: advertising on its Web site, subscription fees from users who wanted to opt-out of advertising, and affiliate fees from iTunes and Amazon.com. Pandora had low fixed costs but high variable costs for streaming and performance royalties. Over time, as Pandora's popular service attracted millions of loyal listeners, its costs for performance royalties—set by the Copyright Royalty Board on a per song basis—far exceeded its revenues from advertising and subscriptions. As a result, even though royalty rates were only a fraction of a cent, Pandora lost more and more money each time it played another song!

In 2009, Pandora avoided bankruptcy by renegotiating a lower per-song royalty rate in exchange for at least 25% of its U.S. revenue annually. Further, Pandora began charging its most frequent users a small fee and also started increasing its advertising revenue.

Sources: Birger, Jon. 2009. Mel Karmazian fights to rescue Sirius. *Fortune*, March 16; Clifford, Stephanie. 2007. Pandora's long strange trip. *Inc.*, October 1; Pandora: Royalties kill the web radio star? (A). Harvard Business School Case No. 9-310-026; Satellite radio: An industry case study. Kellogg School of Management, Northwestern University. Case No. 5-206-255; XM satellite radio (A). Harvard Business School Case No. 9-504-009.

Consider an agency of the Delhi Muncipal Corporation's Social Welfare Department with a Rs 90,00,000 budget appropriation (its revenues) for 2008. This nonprofit agency's purpose is to assist handicapped people seeking employment. On average, the agency supplements each person's income by Rs 50,000 annually. The agency's only other costs are fixed costs of rent and administrative salaries equal to Rs 27,00,000. The agency manager wants to know how many people could be assisted in 2008.

We can use CVP analysis here by setting operating income to Rs 0. Let Q be the number of handicapped people to be assisted:

$$\text{Revenues} - \text{Variable costs} - \text{Fixed costs} = 0$$
$$\text{Rs } 90{,}00{,}000 - \text{Rs } 50{,}000\, Q - \text{Rs } 27{,}00{,}000 = 0$$
$$\text{Rs } 50{,}000\, Q = \text{Rs } 90{,}00{,}000 - \text{Rs } 27{,}00{,}000 = \text{Rs } 63{,}00{,}000$$
$$Q = \text{Rs } 63{,}00{,}000 \div \text{Rs } 50{,}000 \text{ per person} = 126 \text{ people}$$

Suppose the manager is concerned that the total budget appropriation for 2009 will be reduced by 15% to Rs 90,00,000 × (1 − 0.15) = Rs 76,50,000. The manager wants to know how many handicapped people could be assisted with this reduced budget. Assume the same amount of monetary assistance per person:

$$\text{Rs } 76{,}50{,}000 - \text{Rs } 50{,}000\, Q - \text{Rs } 27{,}00{,}000 = 0$$
$$\text{Rs } 50{,}000 Q = \text{Rs } 76{,}50{,}000 - \text{Rs } 27{,}00{,}000 = \text{Rs } 49{,}50{,}000$$
$$Q = \text{Rs } 49{,}50{,}000 \div \text{Rs } 50{,}000 \text{ per person} = 126 \text{ people}$$

Note the following two characteristics of the CVP relationships in this nonprofit situation:

1. The percentage drop in the number of people assisted, (126 − 99) ÷ 126, or 21.4%, is greater than the 15% reduction in the budget appropriation. That's because the Rs 27,00,000 in fixed costs still must be paid, leaving a proportionately lower budget to assist people. The percentage drop in service exceeds the percentage drop in budget appropriation.
2. Given the reduced budget appropriation (revenues) of Rs 76,50,000, the manager can adjust operations to stay within this appropriation in one or more of three basic ways: (a) reduce the number of people assisted from the current 126, (b) reduce the variable cost (the extent of assistance per person) from the current Rs 50,000 per person, or (c) reduce the total fixed costs from the current Rs 27,00,000.

Contribution Margin versus Gross Margin

Clearly distinguish contribution margin, which provides information for CVP analysis, from gross margin discussed in Chapter 2.

$$\text{Gross margin} = \text{Revenues} - \text{Cost of goods sold}$$
$$\text{Contribution margin} = \text{Revenues} - \text{All variable costs}$$

Gross margin is a measure of competitiveness—how much a company can charge for its products over and above the cost of acquiring or producing them. Companies, such as branded pharmaceuticals, have high gross margins because their products provide unique and distinctive benefits to consumers. Products such as televisions that operate in competitive markets, have low gross margins. Contribution margin indicates how much of a company's revenues are available to cover fixed costs. It helps in assessing risk of loss. Risk of loss is low (high) if, when sales are low, contribution margin exceeds (is less than) fixed costs. Gross margins and contribution margin are related but give different insights. For example, a company operating in a competitive market with a low gross margin will have a low risk of loss if its fixed costs are small.

Consider the distinction between gross margin and contribution margin in the context of manufacturing companies. In the manufacturing sector, contribution margin and gross margin differ in two respects: fixed manufacturing costs and variable nonmanufacturing costs. The following example (figures assumed) illustrates this difference:

Contribution Income Statement Emphasizing Contribution Margin (in 000s)			Financial Accounting Income Statement Emphasizing Gross Margin (in 000s)	
Revenues		Rs 10,000	Revenues	Rs 10,000
Variable manufacturing costs	Rs 2,500		Cost of goods sold (Rs 2,500 + Rs 1,600)	4,100
Variable nonmanufacturing costs	2,700	5,200		
Contribution margin		4,800	Gross margin	5,900
Fixed manufacturing costs	1,600		Nonmanufacturing costs	
Fixed nonmanufacturing costs	1,380	2,980	(Rs 2,700 + Rs 1,380)	4,080
Operating income		Rs 1,820	Operating income	Rs 1,820

Fixed manufacturing costs of Rs 16,00,000 are not deducted from revenues when computing contribution margin but are deducted when computing gross margin. Cost of goods sold in a manufacturing company includes all variable manufacturing costs and all fixed manufacturing costs (Rs 25,00,000 + Rs 16,00,000). Variable nonmanufacturing costs (such as commissions paid to salespersons) of Rs 27,00,000 are deducted from revenues when computing contribution margin but are not deducted when computing gross margin.

Like contribution margin, gross margin can be expressed as a total, as an amount per unit, or as a percentage. For example, the **gross margin percentage** is the gross margin divided by revenues—59% (Rs 5,900 ÷ Rs 10,000) in our manufacturing-sector example.

One reason why gross margin and contribution margin are confused with each other is that the two are identical in the case of merchandising companies. That's because cost of goods sold equals the variable cost of goods purchased (and subsequently sold).

Problem for Self-Study

National Travel Agency specializes in flights between New Delhi and Dubai. It books passengers on Indian Airlines at Rs 9,000 per round-trip ticket. Until last month, Indian Airlines paid National a commission of 10% of the ticket price paid by each passenger. This commission was National's only source of revenues. National's fixed costs are Rs 1,40,000 per month (for salaries, rent, and so on), and its variable costs are Rs 200 per ticket purchased for a passenger. This Rs 200 includes a Rs 150 per ticket delivery fee paid to Desk-to-Desk Couriers. (To keep the analysis simple, we assume each round-trip ticket purchased is delivered in a separate package. Thus, the Rs 150 delivery fee applies to each ticket.)

Indian Airlines has just announced a revised payment schedule for all travel agents. It will now pay travel agents a 10% commission per ticket up to a maximum of Rs 500. Any ticket costing more than Rs 5,000 generates only a Rs 500 commission, regardless of the ticket price.

Required

1. Under the old 10% commission structure, how many round-trip tickets must National sell each month (a) to break even and (b) to earn an operating income of Rs 70,000?
2. How does Indian's revised payment schedule affect your answers to (a) and (b) in requirement 1?

Solution

1. National receives a 10% commission on each ticket: 10% × Rs 9,000 = Rs 900. Thus,

$$\text{Selling price} = \text{Rs } 900 \text{ per ticket}$$
$$\text{Variable cost per unit} = \text{Rs } 200 \text{ per ticket}$$
$$\text{Contribution margin per unit} = \text{Rs } 900 - \text{Rs } 200 = \text{Rs } 700 \text{ per ticket}$$
$$\text{Fixed costs} = \text{Rs } 1{,}40{,}000 \text{ per month}$$

a. $$\frac{\text{Breakeven number}}{\text{of tickets}} = \frac{\text{Fixed costs}}{\text{Contribution margin per unit}} = \frac{\text{Rs } 1{,}40{,}000}{\text{Rs } 700 \text{ per ticket}} = 200 \text{ tickets}$$

b. When target operating income = Rs 70,000 per month:

$$\text{Quantity of tickets required to be sold} = \frac{\text{Fixed costs} + \text{Target operating income}}{\text{Contribution margin per unit}}$$

$$= \frac{\text{Rs } 1{,}40{,}000 + \text{Rs } 70{,}000}{\text{Rs } 700 \text{ per ticket}} = \frac{\text{Rs } 2{,}10{,}000}{\text{Rs } 700 \text{ per ticket}} = 300 \text{ tickets}$$

2. Under the new system, National would receive only Rs 500 on the Rs 9,000 ticket. Thus,

Selling price = Rs 500 per ticket
Variable cost per unit = Rs 200 per ticket
Contribution margin per unit = Rs 500 − Rs 200 = Rs 300 per ticket
Fixed costs = Rs 1,40,000 per month

a. $$\text{Breakeven number of tickets} = \frac{\text{Rs } 1{,}40{,}000}{\text{Rs } 300 \text{ per ticket}} = 467 \text{ tickets (rounded up)}$$

b. $$\text{Quantity of tickets required to be sold} = \frac{\text{Rs } 2{,}10{,}000}{\text{Rs } 300 \text{ per ticket}} = 700 \text{ tickets}$$

The Rs 500 cap on the commission paid per ticket causes the breakeven point to more than double (from 200 to 467 tickets) and the tickets required to be sold to earn Rs 70,000 per month to also more than double (from 300 to 700 tickets). As would be expected, travel agents reacted very negatively to the Indian Airlines announcement to change commission payments. Unfortunately for travel agents, other airlines also changed their commission structure in similar ways.

Decision Points

The following question-and-answer format summarizes the chapter's learning objectives. Each decision presents a key question related to a learning objective. The guidelines are the answer to that question.

Decision	Guidelines
1. How can CVP analysis assist managers?	CVP analysis assists managers in understanding the behavior of a product's or service's total costs, total revenues, and operating income as changes occur in the output level, selling price, variable costs, or fixed costs.
2. How do companies determine the breakeven point or the output needed to achieve a target operating income?	The breakeven point is the quantity of output at which total revenues equal total costs. The three methods for computing the breakeven point and the quantity of output to achieve target operating income are the equation method, the contribution margin method, and the graph method. Each method is merely a restatement of the others. Managers often select the method they find easiest to use in the specific decision situation.
3. How should companies incorporate income taxes into CVP analysis?	Income taxes can be incorporated into CVP analysis by using target net income rather than target operating income. The breakeven point is unaffected by income taxes because no income taxes are paid when operating income equals zero.
4. How should companies cope with uncertainty or changes in underlying assumptions?	Sensitivity analysis, a "what-if" technique, examines how an outcome will change if the original predicted data are not achieved or if an underlying assumption changes. When making decisions, managers use CVP analysis to compare contribution margins and fixed costs under different assumptions.

5. How should companies choose between different variable-cost/fixed-cost structures?	Choosing the variable-cost/fixed-cost structure is a strategic decision for companies. CVP analysis highlights the risk of losses when revenues are low and the upside profits when revenues are high for different proportions of variable and fixed costs in a company's cost structure.
6. Can CVP analysis be applied to a company producing multiple products?	CVP analysis can be applied to a company producing multiple products by assuming the sales mix of products sold remains constant as the total quantity of units sold changes.
7. Can CVP analysis be applied to a product that has multiple cost drivers?	The basic concepts of CVP analysis can be applied to multiple-cost-driver situations, but there is no unique breakeven point.

APPENDIX: DECISION MODELS AND UNCERTAINTY

This appendix explores the characteristics of uncertainty and describes an approach managers can use to make decisions in a world of uncertainty. We will also illustrate the insights gained when uncertainty is recognized in CVP analysis.

Coping with Uncertainty[2]

In the face of uncertainty, managers rely on decision models to help them make the right choices.

Role of a Decision Model

Uncertainty is the possibility that an actual amount will deviate from an expected amount. In the Do-All example, Neeta might forecast sales at 40 units, but actual sales might turn out to be 30 units or 60 units. A decision model helps managers deal with such uncertainty. It is a formal method for making a choice, commonly involving both quantitative and qualitative analyses. The quantitative analysis usually includes the following steps:

Step 1: Identify a choice criterion. A **choice criterion** is an objective that can be quantified. This objective can take many forms. Most often the choice criterion is to maximize income or to minimize costs. The choice criterion provides a basis for choosing the best alternative action. Neeta's choice criterion is to maximize expected operating income at the New Delhi computer convention.

Step 2: Identify the set of alternative actions to be considered. We use the letter a with subscripts $_1$, $_2$, and $_3$ to distinguish each of Neeta's three possible actions:

a_1 = Pay Rs 20,000 fixed fee

a_2 = Pay Rs 8,000 fixed fee plus 15% of convention revenues

a_3 = Pay 25% of convention revenues with no fixed fee

Step 3: Identify the set of events that can occur. An **event** is a possible relevant occurrence, such as the actual number of software packages Neeta may sell at the convention. The set of events should be mutually exclusive and collectively exhaustive. Events are mutually exclusive if they cannot occur at the same time. Events are collectively exhaustive if, taken together, they make up the entire set of possible relevant occurrences (no other event can occur). Examples of mutually exclusive and collectively exhaustive events are growth, decline, or no change in industry demand, and increase, decrease, or no change in interest rates. Only one event out of the entire set of mutually exclusive and collectively exhaustive events will actually occur.

Suppose Neeta's only uncertainty is the number of units of Do-All Software that she can sell. For simplicity, suppose Neeta estimates that sales will be either 30 or 60 units.

[2] The presentation here draws (in part) from teaching notes prepared by R. Williamson.

We use the letter x with subscripts $_1$ and $_2$ to distinguish the set of mutually exclusive and collectively exhaustive events:

$$x_1 = 30 \text{ units}$$
$$x_2 = 60 \text{ units}$$

Step 4: Assign a probability to each event that can occur. A **probability** is the likelihood or chance that an event will occur. The decision model approach to coping with uncertainty assigns probabilities to events. A **probability distribution** describes the likelihood, or the probability, that each of the mutually exclusive and collectively exhaustive set of events will occur. In some cases, there will be much evidence to guide the assignment of probabilities. For example, the probability of obtaining heads in the toss of a coin is 1/2 and that of drawing a particular playing card from a standard, well-shuffled deck is 1/52. In business, the probability of having a specified percentage of defective units may be assigned with great confidence on the basis of production experience with thousands of units. In other cases, there will be little evidence supporting estimated probabilities—for example, expected sales of a new pharmaceutical product next year.

Suppose that Neeta, on the basis of past experience, assesses a 60% chance, or a 6/10 probability, that she will sell 30 units and a 40% chance, or a 4/10 probability, that she will sell 60 units. Using $P(x)$ as the notation for the probability of an event, the probabilities are:

$$P(x_1) = 6/10 = 0.60$$
$$P(x_2) = 4/10 = 0.40$$

The probabilities of these events add to 1.00 because they are mutually exclusive and collectively exhaustive.

Step 5: Identify the set of possible outcomes. Outcomes specify, in terms of the choice criterion, the predicted economic results of the various possible combinations of actions and events. The outcomes in the Do-All Software example take the form of six possible operating incomes that are displayed in a decision table in Exhibit 3-6. A **decision table** is a summary of the alternative actions, events, outcomes, and probabilities of events.

Distinguish actions from events. Actions are decision choices available to managers—for example, the particular rental alternatives that Neeta can choose. Events are the set of all relevant occurrences that can happen—for example, the different quantities of software packages that may be sold at the convention. The outcome is operating income,

Exhibit 3-6 Table for Do-All Software

File Edit View Insert Format Tools Data Window Help

	A	B	C	D	E	F	G	H	I
1	Selling price =	Rs 2,000		Operating Income					
2	Package cost =	Rs 1,200		Under Each Possible Event					
3			Percentage						
4		Fixed	of Convention	Event x_1: Units Sold = 30			Event x_2: Units Sold = 60		
5	Actions	Fee	Revenues	Probability(x_1) = 0.60			Probability(x_2) = 0.40		
6	a_1: Pay Rs 20,000 fixed fee	Rs 20,000	0%	Rs 4, 000[l]			Rs 28, 000[m]		
7	a_2: Pay Rs 8,000 fixed fee plus 15% of convention revenues	Rs 8,000	15%	Rs 7, 000[n]			Rs 22, 000[p]		
8	a_3: Pay 25% of convention revenues with no fixed fee	Rs 0	25%	Rs 9, 000[q]			Rs 18, 000[r]		
9									
10	[l]Operating Income = (Rs 2,000 - Rs 1,200 (30) - Rs 20,000	=	Rs 4, 000						
11	[m]Operating Income = (Rs 2,000 - Rs 1,200 (60) - Rs 20,000)	=	Rs28, 000						
12	[n]Operating Income = (Rs 2,000 - Rs 1,200-15% x Rs 2,000 (30)-Rs 8,000)	=	Rs 7, 000						
13	[p]Operating Income = (Rs 2,000 - Rs 1,200-15% x Rs 2,000 (60)-Rs 8,000)	=	Rs22, 000						
14	[q]Operating Income = (Rs 2,000 - Rs 1,200-25% x Rs 2,000 (30)	=	Rs 9, 000						
15	[r]Operating Income = (Rs 2,000 - Rs 1,200-25% x Rs 2,000 (60)	=	Rs18, 000						

Exhibit 3-7 A Decision Made and Its Link to Performance Evaluation

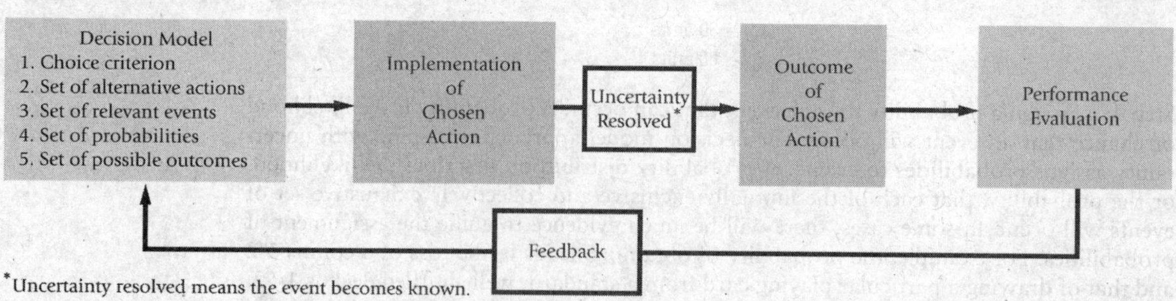

*Uncertainty resolved means the event becomes known.

which depends both on the action the manager selects (rental alternative chosen) and the event that occurs (the quantity of packages sold).

Exhibit 3-7 presents an overview of relationships among a decision model, the implementation of a chosen action, its outcome, and a subsequent performance evaluation. Thoughtful managers step back and evaluate what happened and learn from their experiences. This learning serves as feedback for adapting the decision model for future actions.

Expected Value

An **expected value** is the weighted average of the outcomes, with the probability of each outcome serving as the weight. When the outcomes are measured in monetary terms, expected value is often called **expected monetary value.** Using information in Exhibit 3-6, the expected monetary value of each booth-rental alternative denoted by $E(a_1)$, $E(a_2)$, and $E(a_3)$ is:

Pay Rs 20,000 fixed fee:	$E(a_1)$ = 0.60 (Rs 4,000) + 0.40 (Rs 28,000) = Rs 13,600
Pay Rs 8,000 fixed fee plus 15% of revenues:	$E(a_2)$ = 0.60 (Rs 7,000) + 0.40 (Rs 22,000) = Rs 13,000
Pay 25% of revenues with no fixed fee:	$E(a_3)$ = 0.60 (Rs 9,000) + 0.40 (Rs 18,000) = Rs 12,600

To maximize expected operating income, Neeta should select action a_1—pay Computer Conventions, Ltd. a Rs 20,000 fixed fee.

To interpret the expected value of selecting action a_1, imagine that Neeta attends many conventions, each with the probability distribution of operating incomes given in Exhibit 3-6. For a specific convention, Neeta will earn operating income of either Rs 4,000, if she sells 30 units, or Rs 28,000, if she sells 60 units. But if Neeta attends 100 conventions, she will expect to earn Rs 4,000 operating income 60% of the time (at 60 conventions), and Rs 28,000 operating income 40% of the time (at 40 conventions), for a total operating income of Rs 13,60,000 (Rs 4,000 × 60 + Rs 28,000 × 40). The expected value of Rs 13,600 is the operating income per convention that Neeta will earn when averaged across all conventions (Rs 13,60,000 ÷ 100). Of course, in many real-world situations, managers must make one-time decisions under uncertainty. Even in these cases, expected value is a useful tool for choosing among alternatives.

Consider the effect of uncertainty on the preferred action choice. If Neeta were certain she would sell only 30 units (that is, $P(x_1) = 1$), she would prefer alternative a_3—pay 25% of convention revenues with no fixed fee. To follow this reasoning, examine Exhibit 3-6. When 30 units are sold, alternative a_3 yields the maximum operating income of Rs 9,000. Because fixed costs are Rs 0, booth-rental costs are lower, equal to Rs 15,000 (25% of revenues = 0.25 × Rs 2,000 per unit × 30 units), when sales are low.

However, if Neeta were certain she would sell 60 software packages (that is, $P(x_2) = 1$), she would prefer alternative a_1—pay a Rs 20,000 fixed fee. Exhibit 3-6 indicates that when 60 units are sold, alternative a_1 yields the maximum operating income of Rs 28,000. Rental payments under a_2 and a_3 increase with units sold but are fixed under a_1.

Despite the high probability of selling only 30 units, Neeta still prefers to take action a_1, which is to pay a fixed fee of Rs 20,000. That's because the high risk of low operating income (the 60% probability of selling only 30 units) is more than offset by the high return from selling 60 units, which has a 40% probability. If Neeta were more averse to risk (measured in our example by the difference between operating incomes when 30 versus 60 units are sold), she might have preferred action a_2 or a_3. For example, action a_2 ensures an operating income of at least Rs 7,000, greater than the operating income of Rs 4,000 that she would earn under action a_1 if only 30 units were sold. Of course, choosing a_2 limits the upside potential to Rs 22,000 relative to Rs 28,000 under a_1, if 60 units are sold. If Neeta is very concerned about downside risk, however, she may be willing to forgo some upside benefits to protect against a Rs 4,000 outcome by choosing a_2.[3]

Good Decisions and Good Outcomes

Always distinguish between a good decision and a good outcome. One can exist without the other. Suppose you are offered a one-time-only gamble tossing a coin. You will win Rs 200 if the event is heads, but you will lose Rs 1 if the event is tails. As a decision maker, you proceed through the logical phases: gathering information, assessing outcomes, and making a choice. You accept the bet. Why? Because the expected value is Rs 95 [0.5(Rs 200) + 0.5(− Rs 10)]. The coin is tossed and the event is tails. You lose. From your viewpoint, this was a good decision but a bad outcome.

A decision can be made only on the basis of information that is available at the time of evaluating and making the decision. By definition, uncertainty rules out guaranteeing that the best outcome will always be obtained. As in our example, it is possible that bad luck will produce bad outcomes even when good decisions have been made. A bad outcome does not mean a bad decision was made. The best protection against a bad outcome is a good decision.

TERMS TO LEARN

This chapter and the Glossary at the end of the book contain definitions of the following important terms:

breakeven point (BEP) **(p. 70)**
choice criterion **(p. 86)**
contribution income statement **(p. 67)**
contribution margin **(p. 66)**
contribution margin per unit **(p. 66)**
contribution margin percentage **(p. 67)**
contribution margin ratio **(p. 67)**
cost-volume-profit (CVP) analysis **(p. 65)**
decision table **(p. 87)**
degree of operating leverage **(p. 78)**
event **(p. 86)**
expected monetary value **(p. 88)**
expected value **(p. 88)**
gross margin percentage **(p. 84)**
margin of safety **(p. 76)**
net income **(p. 72)**
operating leverage **(p. 77)**
outcomes **(p. 87)**
probability **(p. 87)**
probability distribution **(p. 87)**
PV graph **(p. 72)**
revenue driver **(p. 69)**
sales mix **(p. 79)**
sensitivity analysis **(p. 75)**
uncertainty **(p. 76)**

ASSIGNMENT MATERIAL

Note: To underscore the basic CVP relationships, the assignment material ignores income taxes unless stated otherwise.

Questions

3-1 Define cost-volume-profit analysis.

3-2 Describe the assumptions underlying CVP analysis.

[3] For more formal approaches, refer to J. Moore and L. Weatherford, *Decision Modeling with Microsoft Excel*, 6th ed. (Upper Saddle River, NJ: Prentice Hall, 2001).

3-3 Distinguish between operating income and net income.

3-4 Define contribution margin, contribution margin per unit, and contribution margin percentage.

3-5 Describe three methods that can be used to express CVP relationships.

3-6 Why is it more accurate to describe the subject matter of this chapter as CVP analysis rather than as breakeven analysis?

3-7 "CVP analysis is both simple and simplistic. If you want realistic analysis to underpin your decisions, look beyond CVP analysis." Do you agree? Explain.

3-8 How does an increase in the income tax rate affect the breakeven point?

3-9 Describe sensitivity analysis. How has the advent of the electronic spreadsheet affected the use of sensitivity analysis?

3-10 Give an example of how a manager can decrease variable costs while increasing fixed costs.

3-11 Give an example of how a manager can increase variable costs while decreasing fixed costs.

3-12 What is operating leverage? How is knowing the degree of operating leverage helpful to managers?

3-13 "There is no such thing as a fixed cost. All costs can be 'unfixed' given sufficient time." Do you agree? What is the implication of your answer for CVP analysis?

3-14 How can a company with multiple products compute its breakeven point?

3-15 "In CVP analysis, gross margin is a less-useful concept than contribution margin." Do you agree? Explain briefly.

Solved Examples

3-16 CVP computations. Fill in the blanks for each of the following independent cases:

Case A

Revenues	Variable Costs	Fixed Costs	Total Costs	Operating Income	Contribution Margin	Contribution Margin Percentage
	Rs 10,000		Rs 15,000	Rs 20,000	25,000	

Solution

Variable cost + Fixed cost = Total costs
Rs 10,000 + Fixed cost = Rs 10,000
Fixed cost = Rs 5,000
Revenue − Variable cost − Fixed cost = Operating income
Revenue − Rs 10,000 − Rs 5,000 = Rs 20,000
Revenue = Rs 20,000 + 10,000 + 5,000
Revenue = Rs 35,000
Contribution margin % = Contribution margin/Revenue
= Rs 25,000/Rs 35,000 = 71.428%

Case B

Revenue	Variable Costs	Fixed Costs	Total Costs	Operating Income	Contribution Margin	Contribution margin Percentage
Rs 15,000		Rs 3,000		Rs 3,000	Rs 6,000	

Solution

Contribution margin % = Contribution margin/Revenue
0.40 = Contribution margin/Rs 15,000
Contribution margin = Rs 6,000
Revenue variable cost = Contribution margin
15,000 Variable cost = Rs 6,000
Variable cost = Rs 9,000
Variable cost + Fixed cost = Total cost
Rs 9,000 + Rs 3,000 = Rs 12,000
Operating income = Revenue Total costs
Rs 15,000 − Rs 12,000 = Rs 3,000

3-17 CVP computations. Jain Manufacturing sold 20,000 units of its product for Rs 100 per unit in the current year. Variable cost per unit is Rs 60 and total fixed costs are Rs 2,00,000.

Required

1. Calculate (a) contribution margin (b) operating income.
2. Jain's current manufacturing process is labour intensive. Rahul, Jain's production manager, has proposed investing in state-of-the-art manufacturing equipment, which will increase the annual fixed costs to Rs 7,00,000. The variable costs are expected to decrease to Rs 30 per unit. Jain expects to maintain the same sales volume and selling price next year. How would acceptance of Rahul's proposal affect your answers to (a) and (b) in requirement (1)?
3. Should Jain accept Rahul's proposal? Explain.

Solution

1. a. Calculation of Contribution Margin
   Sales − Variable costs = Contribution margin
   (20,000 × Rs 100 − (Rs 60 × 20,000) = Contribution margin
   (Rs 20,00,000 − Rs 12,00,000) = Contribution margin
   Rs 8,00,000 = Contribution margin
2. b. Calculation of Operating Income
   Contribution margin − Fixed costs = Operating income
   Rs 8,00,000 − Rs 2,00,000 = Rs 6,00,000 = Operating income
1. a. Impact of Acceptance of Proposal on Contribution Margin
   Fixed costs = Rs 7,00,000 Variable cost per unit = Rs 30 per unit
   Sales Variable costs = Contribution margin
   (20,000 × Rs 100) − (Rs 30 × 20,000)
   Rs 20,00,000 − Rs 6,00,000 = Rs 14,00,000
2. b. Impact of Acceptance of Proposal on Operating Income
   Fixed costs = Rs 7,00,000
   Contribution margin × Fixed costs = Operating income
   = Rs 14,00,000 − Rs 7,00,000
   = Rs 7,00,000 = Operating income
3. Rahul's proposal should be accepted as it is expected to increase operating income by Rs 1,00,000.

3-18 CVP analysis, charging revenues and costs. Cox and Kings Travel Agency specializes in flight between India and Malaysia. It books passengers on Malaysian Air. Cox and Kings fixed costs are Rs 10,00,000 per month. Malaysian Air charges a passenger Rs 20,000 per round trip ticket.

Required

Calculate the number of tickets Cox and Kings must sell each month to (a) breakeven and (b) make a target operating income of Rs 4,00,000 per month in each of the following independent cases.

1. Cox and Kings variable costs are Rs 400 per ticket. Malaysian Air pays Cox and Kings 10 per cent commission on ticket price.
2. Cox and Kings variable costs are Rs 200 per ticket. Malaysian Air pays Cox and Kings 10 per cent commission on ticket price.
3. Cox and Kings variable costs are Rs 200 per ticket. Malaysian Air pays Rs 500 fixed commission per ticket to Cox and Kings. Comment on the results.
4. Cox and Kings variable costs are Rs 200 per ticket. It receives Rs 500 commission per ticket from Malaysian Air. It charges its customer a delivery fee of Rs 50 per ticket. Comment on the results.

Solution

CVP Analysis, changing revenues and costs

(a) Selling commission per ticket = 10% × Rs 20,000 = Rs 2,000 per ticket
    Variable cost per unit = Rs 400
    Contribution margin per unit = Rs 2,000 − Rs 400 = Rs 1,600 per ticket
    Fixed cost = Rs 10,00,000 per month
    Breakeven (Q) = Fixed cost/Contribution margin per unit
    = Rs 10,00,000/Rs 1,600 = 625 tickets
(b) Q = (Fixed cost + Target operating income)/Contribution margin per unit
    Q = (Rs 10,00,000 + Rs 4,00,000)/Rs 1,600 per ticket = Rs 14,00,000 /Rs 1,600
    Q = 875 tickets
    1. Selling price = Rs 2,000 per ticket
       Variable cost per unit = Rs 200 per ticket
       Contribution margin per unit = Rs 2,000 − Rs 200 = Rs 1800 per ticket
       Fixed cost = Rs 10,00,000 per month
       Q = Fixed cost /Contribution margin per unit = Rs 10,00,000/1,800 per ticket
       =556 tickets (rounded up)

2. Q = (Total cost + Target operating income)/Contribution margin per unit
   = (Rs 10,00,000 + Rs 4,00,000)/1800 per ticket
   = 14,00,000/1,800 = 778 tickets (rounded up)
3. a. Selling Price = Rs 500 per ticket
   Variable cost per unit = Rs 200 per ticket
   Contribution margin per unit = Rs 300 per ticket
   Fixed costs = Rs 10,00,000 per month
   Q = Fixed cost/contribution margin per unit = Rs 10,00,000/Rs 300 per ticket
   = 3,334 tickets (rounded up)
3. b. Q = (Fixed cost + Target operating income)/Contribution margin per unit
   = (Rs 10,00,000 + Rs 4,00,000)/Rs 300 per ticket = 4667 tickets (rounded up)

The reduced commission sizably increases the breakeven point and the number of tickets required to yield a target operating income of Rs 4,00,000.

	10 per cent Commission	Fixed Commission of Rs 500
Breakeven point	556	3,334
Attain Operating Income of Rs 4,00,000	778	4,667

4. a. The Rs 50 delivery fee can be treated as either an extra source of revenue or as a cost offset. Both approaches increases CMU by Rs 50.
   Selling price = Rs (500 + 50) = Rs 550 per ticket
   Variable cost per unit = Rs 200 per ticket
   Contribution margin per unit = Rs 350 per ticket
   Fixed cost = Rs 10,00,000 per month
   Q = Fixed cost /Contribution margin per unit = Rs 10,00,000/Rs 350
   = 2,857 tickets (rounded up)
4. b. Q = (Fixed cost + Total operating income)/Contribution margin per unit
   = (Rs 10,00,000 + Rs 4,00,000)/Rs 350 per ticket
   = Rs 14,00,000/Rs 350 = 4,000 tickets

3-19 CVP analysis, income taxes. Borosil Ltd., a manufacturer of quality bowls, has a steady growth in sales for the past four years. However, increasing competition has led Mr. Aashish, the president, to believe that an aggressive market campaign will be necessary next year to maintain the company's present growth. To prepare for next year's marketing campaign, the company's controller has prepared and presented Mr. Aashish with the following data for the current year.

Variable Costs (per bowl)	
Direct material	Rs 6.50
Direct manufacturing labor	16.00
Variable overhead (manufacturing, marketing, distribution, and customer service)	5.00
Total variable costs	Rs 27.5
Fixed costs	
Manufacturing	50,000
Marketing, distribution and customer service	2,20,000
Total fixed costs	2,70,000
Selling price	Rs 50
Expected sales, 20,000 units	10,00,000
Income tax rate	40%

Required

1. What is the projected net income for the current year?
2. What is the breakeven point in units for the current year?
3. Mr. Aashish has set the revenue target for the next year at a level of Rs 11,00,000 (or 22,000 bowls). He believes an additional marketing cost of Rs 22,500 for advertising in the next year, with all other costs remaining constant, will be necessary to attain the revenue target. What will be the net income for the next year if an additional Rs 22,500 is spent and the revenue target is met?
4. What will be the breakeven point in revenues for the next year if an additional Rs 22,500 is spent for advertising?
5. If the additional Rs 22,500 is spent, what are the required next year revenues for net income to equal current year's net income?
6. At a sales level of 22,000 units what maximum amount can be spent on advertising if net income of Rs 1,20,000 is desired, next year?

Solution

1. Operating income = Revenues − Variable costs − Fixed costs
   = Rs 10,00,000 × 5,50,000 × 2,70,000 = Rs 1,80,000
   Income taxes = 0.40 × Rs 1,80,000 = Rs 72,000
   Net income = Operating income − Income taxes
   = Rs 1,80,000 − 72,000 = Rs 1,08,000
2. Breakeven units = Fixed cost/Contribution margin per unit
   Contribution margin per unit = Rs 50 − Rs 27.5 = Rs 22.5
   BEP (units) = Rs 2,70,000/Rs 22.5 = 12,000 units
3. Let net income for next year = χ
   22,000 × Rs 50 − 22,000 − 27.5 — (2,70,000 + 22,500) = χ/(1 − 0.40)
   Rs 11,00,000 6,05,000 2,92,500 = c/0.60
   2,02,500 × 0.60 = χ
   χ = Rs 1,21,500
   Net income for next year will be Rs 1,21,500
4. New fixed costs = Rs 2,70,000 + 22,500 = Rs 2,92,500
   Let Q be the number of units to breakeven
   Rs 50 Q − Rs 27.5Q − Rs 2,92,500 = 0
   22.5Q = Rs 2,92,500
   Q = Rs 2,92,500/22.5 = 13,000 units
   Breakeven revenues = 13,000 × Rs 50 = Rs 6,50,000
5. Let S = Required sales units to equal current year net income.
   Rs 50S − Rs 27.5S − Rs 2,92,500 = Rs 1,08,000/(1-40)
   Rs 22.5S − Rs 2,92,500 = Rs 1,80,000
   Rs 22.5S = Rs 1,80,000 + 2,92,500
   S = Rs 4,72,500/22.5 = 21,000 units
   Revenues = 21,000 units × 50 × Rs 10,50,000
6. Let A = Amount spent on adverting in next year
   22,000 × Rs 50 − 22,000 × Rs 27.5 − (2,70,000 +A) = Rs 1,20,000/(1-.40)
   Rs 11,00,000 − 6,05,000 − 2,70,000 − A = Rs 2,00,000
   Rs 2,25,000 − 2,00,000 × A
   A = Rs 25,000

3-20 CVP analysis, decision making. The Exide Battery Ltd. manufactures a high quality battery. The company's plant has an annual capacity of 25,000 units. Exide currently sells 20,000 units at a price of Rs 1,050. It has the following cost structure:

	Rs
Variable manufacturing cost per unit	450
Fixed manufacturing costs	16,00,000
Variable marketing and distribution cost per unit	100
Fixed marketing and distribution costs	12,00,000

Required

Consider each case separately.

1. The Marketing Department indicates that decreasing the selling price to Rs 990 would increase sales to 25,000 units. This strategy will require Exide to increase its fixed marketing and distribution costs. Calculate the maximum increase in fixed marketing and distribution costs that will allow Exide to reduce the selling price to Rs 990 and maintain its operating income.
2. The Manufacturing Department proposes changes in the manufacturing process to add new features to the product. These changes will increase fixed manufacturing costs by Rs 5,00,000 and variable manufacturing cost by Rs 20 per unit. At its current sales quantity of 20,000 units, compute the minimum selling price that will allow Exide to add these new features and maintain its operating income.

Solution

1. **Current operating income**

Revenues, (20,000 × 1,050)	Rs 2,10,00,000
Variable costs (20,000 × 550)	1,10,00,000
Contribution margin	1,00,00,000
Fixed costs	28,00,000
Operating income	Rs 72,00,000

Let the fixed marketing and distribution costs be F. We calculate F when operating income is Rs 72,00,000 and selling price is Rs 990.

(Rs 990 × 25,000) − (Rs 550 × 25,000) − F = Rs 72,00,000
Rs 2,47,50,000 − Rs 137,50,000 − F = Rs 72,00,000
F = Rs 38,00,000
Hence, the maximum increase in fixed marketing and distribution costs that will allow Exide to reduce the selling price and maintain Rs 72,00,000 in operating income is Rs 10,00,000 (Rs 38,00,000 — 28,00,000).

2. Let the selling price be P
We calculate P for which, after increasing fixed manufacturing costs by Rs 5,00,000 to Rs 21,00,000 and variable manufacturing cost per unit by Rs 20 to Rs 470.
Operating income = Rs 72,00,000
20,000 P − (Rs 470 × 20,000) − (20,000 × Rs 100) − Rs 21,00,000 − Rs 12,00,000 = Rs 72,00,000
= 20,000P − Rs 94,00,000 − 20,00,000 − 21,00,000 − 12,00,000 = Rs 72,00,000
20,000P − Rs 1,47,00,000 = Rs 72,00,000
20,000P = Rs 2,19,00,000
P = Rs 2,19,00,000/20,000 = Rs 1,095

Exide will consider adding the new features provided the selling price is at least Rs 1,095 per unit.

3-21 Sales mix, three products. The Lee Company has three product lines of belts: X, Y and Z with contribution margins of Rs 15, Rs 10 and Rs 5 respectively. The president foresees sales of 1,00,000 units in the coming period, consisting of 10,000 units of X, 50,000 units of Y and 40,000 units of Z. The company's fixed costs for the period are Rs 5,10,000.

Required

1. What is the company's breakeven point in units, assuming that the given sales mix is maintained?
2. If the sales mix is maintained, what is the total contribution when 1,00,000 units are sold? What is the operating income?
3. What would operating income be if 10,000 units of X, 40,000 units of Y and 50,000 units of Z were sold? What is the new breakeven point in units if these relationships persist in the next period?

Solution

1. Sales of X, Y and Z are in the ratio 10,000:50,000:40,000. So for every 1 unit of X, 5 units of Y are sold, and 4 units of Z are sold.
Let Q = Number of units of X to breakeven
5Q = Number of units of Y to breakeven
4Q = Number of units of Z to breakeven
Total Contribution Fixed costs = Zero operating income
Rs 15 × Q + Rs 10 (5Q) + Rs 5 (4Q) − Rs 5,10,000 = 0
85Q − Rs 5,10,000 = 0
Q = 5,10,000/85 = 6,000 units
Q = 6,000 units of X
5Q = 30,000 units of Y
4Q = 24,000 units of Z
Total 60,000 units

2. **Total Contribution and Operating Income**

X: 10,000 × Rs 15	Rs 1,50,000
Y: 50,000 × Rs 10	5,00,000
Z: 40,000 × Rs 5	2,00,000
Total contribution	8,50,000
Fixed costs	5,10,000
Operating income	3,40,000

3. **Operating Income**

X: 10,000 × 15	Rs 1,50,000	
Y: 40,000 × 10	4,00,000	
Z: 50,000 × 5	2,50,000	
Total contribution		Rs 8,00,000
Fixed costs		5,10,000
Operating income		2,90,000

Let Q = Number of units of X to breakeven
4Q = Number of units of Y to breakeven
5Q = Number of units of Z to breakeven
Contribution margin − Fixed costs = Breakeven point
Rs 15 (Q) + Rs 10 (4Q) + Rs 5 (5Q) − Rs 5,10,000 = 0
80 Q = Rs 5,10,000

Q = 6,375 units of X
4Q = 25,500 units of Y
5Q = 31,875 units of Z
Total = 63,750 units

Breakeven point increases because the new mix contains less of the higher contribution margin per unit, product Y, and more of the lower contribution margin per unit, product Z.

3-22 Operating leverage. Harisons Furnishings is holding a two-week carpet sale at Richi Rich, a local warehouse store. Harisons plans to sell carpets for Rs 5,000 each. The company will purchase the carpets from a local distributor for Rs 3,500 each, with the privilege of returning any unsold units for a full refund. Richi Rich has offered Harisons two payment alternatives for the use of space.

Option 1: A fixed payment of Rs 50,000 for the sale period.
Option 2: 10 per cent of total revenues earned during the sale period.

Assume Harrison will incur no other costs.

Required

1. Calculate the breakeven point in units for (a) option 1 and (b) option 2.
2. At what level of revenues will Harison earn the same operating income under either option?
3. a. For what range of unit sales will Harison prefer option 1?
   b. For what range of unit sales will Harison prefer option 2?
4. Calculate the degree of operating leverage at sales of 100 units for the two rental options.
5. Briefly explain and interpret your answer to requirement 4.

Solution

Operating leverage

1. a. Let Q denote the quantity of carpets sold
Breakeven point under option 1
Rs 5,000Q − Rs 3,500Q = Rs 50,000
Rs 1,500Q = Rs 50,000
Q = 50,000/1,500 = 34 carpets (rounded)

1. b. Breakeven point under option 2
Rs 5,000Q 3,500Q (0.10 ´ Rs 5,000Q) = 0
1,000Q = 0
Q = 0

2. Operating income under option 1 = Rs 1,500Q − 50,000
Operating income under option 2 = Rs 1,000Q
Find Q such that Rs 1,500Q 50,000 = Rs 1,000Q
500Q = Rs 50,000
Q = Rs 50,000/500 = 100 carpets
For Q = 100 carpets, operating income under both option 1 and option 2 = Rs 1,00,000

3. a. Let Q > 100, say, 101 carpets,
Option 1 gives operating income = Rs 1,500 × 101 — Rs 50,000 = Rs 1,01,500
Option 2 gives operating income = Rs 1,000 × 101 = Rs 1,01,000
So Harrison's furnishings will prefer option 1.
b. For Q < 100, say, 99 carpets,
Option 1 gives operating income = Rs 1,500 × 99 50,000 = Rs 98,500
Option 2 gives operating income = Rs 1,000 × 99 = Rs 99,000
So Harrison's furnishings will prefer option 2,

4. Degree of operating leverage = Contribution margin/Operating income
Under Option 1, degree of operating leverage = (Rs 1,500 × 100)/Rs 1,00,000 = 1.5
Under Option 2, degree of operating leverage = (Rs 1,000 × 100)/1,00,000 = 1

5. The calculations in requirement 4 indicate that when sales are 100 units, a percentage change in sales and contribution margin will result in 1.5 times that percentage change in operating income for option 1, but there would be the same percentage change in operating income with change in sales for option 2. The degree of operating leverage at a given level of sales helps managers to determine the effect of fluctuations in sales on operating income.

3-23 Uncertainty, CVP analysis. Dara Singh is the promoter for boxer Dharmendra. Dara Singh is promoting a new world championship fight for Dharmendra. The key area of uncertainty is the size of the cable pay-per-view TV market. Dara Singh will pay Dharmendra a fixed fee of Rs 2 million and 25 per cent of net cable pay-per-view revenues. Every cable TV home receiving the event pays Rs 29.95, of which Dara Singh receives Rs 16. Dara Singh pays Dharmendra 25 per cent of Rs 16.

Dara Singh estimates the following probability distribution for homes purchasing the pay-per-view event.

Demand	Probability
1,00,000	0.05
2,00,000	0.10
3,00,000	0.30
4,00,000	0.35
5,00,000	0.15
10,00,000	0.05

Required

1. What is the expected value of the payment Dara Singh will make to Dharmendra?
2. Assume the only uncertainty is about cable TV demand for the fight. Dara Singh wants to know the breakeven point given own fixed costs of Rs 1 million and his own variable costs of Rs 2 per home. (Also include Dara Singh's payments to Dharmendra in calculating your answer).

Solution

1. Dara Singh pays Dharmendra Rs 2 million plus Rs 4 (25% of Rs 16) for every home purchasing the pay-per-view. The expected value of the variable component is:

Demand (1)	Payment (2) = (1) × Rs 4	Probability (3)	Expected Payment (4)
1,00,000	Rs 4,00,000	0.05	Rs 20,000
2,00,000	8,00,000	0.10	80,000
3,00,000	12,00,000	0.30	3,60,000
4,00,000	16,00,000	0.35	5,60,000
5,00,000	20,00,000	0.15	3,00,000
10,00,000	40,00,000	0.05	2,00,000
			Rs 15,20,000

The expected value of Dara Singh's payment is (Rs 20,00,000 fixed fee + Rs 15,20,000) = Rs 35,20,000

2. SP = Rs 16

VCU = Rs 6 (Rs 4 payment to Dara Singh + Rs 2 variable cost)

CMU = Rs 10

FC = Rs 20,00,000 + Rs 10,00,000 = Rs 30,0.0,000

Q = Fixed cost/Contribution margin per unit

= Rs 30,00,000/Rs10

= 3,00,000 homes

If 3,00,000 homes purchase the pay-per-view, Dara Singh will breakeven.

3-24 CVP analysis, multiple cost drivers. Ritu is a distributor of brass picture frames. For current year, she plans to purchase frames for Rs 60 each and sell them for Rs 90 each. Ritu's fixed costs for current year are expected to be Rs 4,80,000. Ritu's only other costs will be variable costs of Rs 120 per shipment for preparing the invoice and delivery documents, organizing the delivery, and following up for collection accounts receivable. The Rs 120 cost will be incurred each time Ritu ships an order of picture frames, regardless of the number of frames in the order.

Required

1. a. Suppose Ritu sells 40,000 picture frames in 1,000 shipments in current year. Calculate Ritu's current year operating income.
   b. Suppose Ritu sells 40,000 picture frames in 800 shipments in current year. Calculate Ritu's current year operating income.
2. Suppose Ritu anticipates making 500 shipments in current year. How many picture frames must Ritu sell to breakeven in current year?
3. Calculate another breakeven point for current year different from the one described in requirement 2. Explain briefly why Ritu has multiple break even points.

Solution

1. a. Operating income = Revenues − (Cost of picture frames × Quantity of picture frames) − (Cost of shipment × Number of shipments) − Fixed costs
   = (Rs 90 × 40,000) − (Rs 60 × 40,000) − (Rs 120 × 1,000) − Rs 4,80,000
   = Rs 36,00,000 − 24,00,000 − 1,20,000 − 4,80,000 = Rs 6,00,000
   b. Operating income = (Rs 90 × 40,000) − (Rs 60 × 40,000) — (Rs 120 × 800) — Rs 4,80,000
   = Rs 36,00,000 − 24,00,000 − 96,000 − Rs 4,80,000 = Rs 6,24,000
2. Denote the number of picture frames sold by Q, then Rs 90Q Rs 60Q 500 × Rs 120 Rs 4,80,000 = 0
   Rs 30Q − Rs 60,000 − Rs 4,80,000 = 0

Rs 30Q = Rs 5,40,000
Q = 5,40,000/30 = 18,000 picture frames

3. Suppose Ritu had 1,000 shipments
Rs 90Q − Rs 60Q − (1,000 × Rs 120) −" Rs 4,80,000 = 0
30Q = 1,20,000 = 4,80,000
Q = 6,00,000/30 = 20,000 picture frames.

There are multiple BEP, as there are two cost drivers quantity of picture frames and number of shipments. Various combinations of the two cost drivers can yield zero operating income.

3-25 Sales mix, new and upgrade customers. Far Point Spread is a top-selling electronic spreadsheet product. Far Point Technologies India is about to release version 5.0. It divides its customer into two groups: new customers and upgrade customers (those who previously purchased Far Point Spread 4.0 or earlier versions) Although the same physical product is provided to each customer group, sizable differences exist in selling prices and variable marketing costs:

Particulars		**New Customers**		**Upgrade Customers**
Selling price		Rs 10,500		Rs 6,000
Variable costs				
Manufacturing	Rs 1,250		Rs 1,250	
Marketing	3,250	4,500	750	2,000
Contribution margin		Rs 6,000		Rs 4,000

The fixed costs of Far Point Spread 5.0 are Rs 1,40,00,000. The planned sales mix in units is 60 per cent new customers and 40 per cent upgrade customers.

Required

1. What is the Far Point Spread 5.0 breakeven point in units, assuming that the planned 60 per cent/40 per cent sales mix is attained?
2. If the sales mix is attained, what is the operating income when 2,00,000 units are sold?
3. Show how the breakeven point in units changes with the following customer mixes:
   a. New 50 per cent/Upgrade 50 per cent
   b. New 90 per cent/Upgrade 10 per cent
   c. Comment on the results

Solution

1.

	New Customers	**Upgrade Customers**
Selling Price	Rs 10,500	Rs 6,000
Variable Cost per unit	4,500	2,000
Contribution Margin per unit	6,000	4,000

Let S = Number of units sold to upgrade customers
1.5S = Number of units sold to new customers
Operating Income = Revenues Variable Costs Fixed Costs
Operating Income = [Rs 10,500 (1.5S) + 6,000S] − [Rs 4,500 (1.5S) + 2000S] − 1,40,00,000
Operating Income = Rs 21,750S − 8,750S − Rs 1,40,00,000
Operating Income = Rs 13,000S − Rs 1,40,00,000
S = Rs 1,40,00,000/13,000 = Rs 1,077 units (rounded up)
S = 1,077 units sold to upgrade customers
1.5S = 1,615 units sold to new customers
Breakeven point is 2,692 units when operating income = 0
We can check the value:

Check

Revenues (Rs 10,500 × 1,615; Rs 6,000 × 1,077)	Rs 2,34,19,500
Variable costs (Rs 4,500 × 1,615; Rs 2,000 × 1,077)	94,21,500
Contribution margin	1,39,98,000
Fixed costs	1,40,00,000
Operating income (subject to rounding)	0

2. When 2,00,000 units are sold, mix is:

Units sold to new customers (60% × 2,00,000)	1,20,000
Units sold to upgrade customers (40% × 2,00,000)	80,000
Revenues (Rs 10,500 × 1,20,000; Rs 6,000 × 80,000)	Rs 1,74,00,00,000
Variable costs (Rs 4,500 × 1,20,000; Rs 2,000 × 80,000)	70,00,00,000
Contribution margin	1,04,00,00,000

Fixed cost	1,40,00,000
Operating income	1,02,60,00,000

3. a. Let S = Number of units sold to upgrade customers
   then S = Number of units sold to new customers
   (Rs 10,500S + 6,000S) — (Rs 4,500S + 2,000S) — Rs 1,40,00,000 = Operating Income
   16,500S — 6,500S — Rs 1,40,00,000 = Operating Income
   10,000S = Rs 1,40,00,000
   S = 1,40,00,000/10,000 = 1,400 units
   S = 1,400 units sold to upgrade customers
   S = 1,400 units sold to new customers
   Total unit = 2800 unit

Check

Revenues (Rs 10,500 × 1,400; Rs 6,000 × 1,400)	Rs 2,31,00,000
Variable costs (Rs 4,500 × 1,400; Rs 2,000 × 1,400)	91,00,000
Contribution margin	1,40,00,000
Fixed costs	1,40,00,000
Operating income	0

3. b. Let S = Number of units sold to upgrade customers
   then 9S = Number of units sold to new customers
   (Rs 10,500 (9S) + 6,000 S) — (Rs 4,500 × (9S) + 2,000 × S) — Rs 1,40,00,000 × Operating income
   1,00,500 S − 42,500 S − Rs 1,40,00,000 = Operating income
   58,000 S = Rs 1,40,00,000
   S = 241 units
   S = 241 units sold to upgrade customers
   9S = 2169 units sold to new customer
   Total units 2410

Check:

Revenues (Rs 10,500 × 2,169; Rs 6,000 × 241)	Rs 2,42,20,500
Variable costs (Rs 4,500 × 2,169; Rs 2,000 × 241)	1,02,42,500
Contribution margin	1,39,78,000
Fixed costs	1,40,00,000
Operating income (subject to rounding)	0

3. c. As Far Point Technologies India increases its percentage of new customers, which have a higher contribution margin per unit than upgrade customers, the number of units required to breakeven decreases.

	New Customers	Upgrade Customers	Breakeven Point
Requirement 3 (a)	50%	50%	2,800 units
Requirement 1	60	40	2,692 units
Requirement 3 (b)	90	10	2,410 units

3-26 Choosing between compensation plans, operating leverage. (CMA, adapted) Ranbaxy Ltd. Manufactures pharmaceutical products that are sold through a network of sales agents. The agents are paid a commission of 18 per cent of revenues. The income statement for the current year ending March 31, is as follows:

Ranbaxy Limited
Income Statement
For the Current Year Ended March 31

Revenues		Rs 2,60,00,000
Cost of goods sold		
Variable	Rs 1,17,00,000	
Fixed	28,70,000	1,45,70,000
Gross margin		1,14,30,000
Marketing costs		
Commissions	46,80,000	
Fixed costs	34,20,000	81,00,000
Operating income		33,30,000

Ranbaxy is considering hiring its own sales staff to replace the network of sales agents. Ranbaxy would pay its salespeople a commission of 10 per cent of revenues and incur additional fixed costs of Rs 20,80,000.

Required

1. Calculate Ranbaxy Ltd's breakeven point in revenues for the current year.
2. Calculate Ranbaxy Ltd's breakeven point in revenues for the current year if the company had hired its own sales force in the current year to replace the network of sales agents.
3. Calculate the degree of operating leverage at revenues of Rs 2,60,00,000 if (a) Ranbaxy uses sales agents and (b) Ranbaxy employs its own sales staff. Describe the advantages and disadvantages of each alternative.
4. If Ranbaxy had hired its own sales staff and increased the commission paid to them to 15 per cent, keeping all other cost behavior patterns the same, how much revenue would Ranbaxy have to generate to earn the same operating income as in the current year?

Solution

1. Variable costs of goods sold as a percentage of revenues = Rs 1,17,00,000/2,60,00,000 = 45 per cent

   Let breakeven revenues be denoted by R, then

   R = Variable manufacturing costs + Fixed manufacturing costs + Variable marketing costs + Fixed marketing costs

   R = 0.45R + Rs 28,70,000 + 0.18R + Rs 34,20,000

   0.37R = Rs 62,90,000

   R = 62,90,000/ 0.37 = Rs 1,70,00,000

2. With its own sales force, Ranbaxy fixed marketing costs would increase to Rs 34,20,000 + Rs 20,80,000 = Rs 55,00,000

   Variable cost of marketing = 10 per cent of revenues

   Let break even revenues be denoted by R, then

   R = 0.45R + Rs 28,70,000 + 0.10R + Rs 55,00,000

   R 0.45R 0.10R = Rs 28,70,000 + 55,00,000

   0.45R = Rs 83,70,000

   R = 83,70,000/0.45 = Rs 1,86,00,000

3. **Calculation of Degree of Operating Leverage Under Both Alternatives**

	Using Sales Agents	Employing Own Sales Staff
Revenues	Rs 2,60,00,000	Rs 2,60,00,000
Variable manufacturing costs (Rs 2,60,00,000 × 0.45)	Rs 1,17,00,000	Rs 1,17,00,000
Variable marketing costs	46,80,000*	26,00,000**
Contribution margin	96,20,000	1,17,00,000
Fixed costs		
Fixed manufacturing costs	28,70,000	28,70,000
Fixed marketing costs	34,20,000	55,00,000
Total fixed costs	62,90,000	83,70,000
Operating income	Rs 33,30,000	Rs 33,30,000
Degree of operating leverage Contribution Margin/Operating Income	= Rs 96,20,000/33,30,000 = 2.89	Rs 1,17,00,000/33,30,000 = 3.51

*(2,60,00,000 × 0.18)
**(2,60,00,000 × 0.10)

The calculations indicate that at sales of Rs 2,60,00,000 a percentage change in sales and contribution margin will result in 2.89 times percentage change in operating income if Ranbaxy Ltd continues to use sales agent and 3.51 times that percentage change in operating income if Ranbaxy Ltd employs its own sales staff. The higher contribution margin per rupee of sales and higher fixed costs gives Ranbaxy more operating leverage, that is greater benefits (increase in operating income) if revenues increase but greater risks (decreases in operating income) if revenues decrease.

4. Variable costs of marketing = 15 per cent of revenues

   Fixed marketing costs = Rs 55,00,000

   Operating income = Revenues − Variable manufacturing costs − Fixed manufacturing costs − Variable marketing costs − Fixed marketing costs

   Denote the revenues required to earn Rs 34,20,000 of operating income by R, then

   R − 0.45R − Rs 28,70,000 0.15R − Rs 55,00,000 = Rs 33,30,000

   R − 0.45 − 0.15R = Rs 33,30,000 + 55,00,000 + 28,70,000

   0.40R = Rs 1,17,00,000

   R = 1,17,00,000/ 0.40 = Rs 2,92,50,000

3-27 Ethics, CVP analysis. Milton Ltd. produces a molded plastic casing, LX 201, for desktop computer. Summary data from its current year income statement are as follows:

Revenues	Rs 50,00,000
Variable costs	30,00,000
Fixed costs	21,60,000
Operating income	Rs (1,60,000)

Kamna, Milton's president, is very concerned about Milton's poor profitability. She asks Amit, production manager, and Sudhir, controller, to see if there are ways to reduce costs.

After two weeks Amit returns with a proposal to reduce variable costs to 52 per cent of revenues by reducing the costs Milton currently incurs for safe disposal of wasted plastic. Sudhir is concerned that this would expose the company to potential environmental liabilities. He tells Amit, We would need to estimate some of these potential environmental costs and include them in our analysis. You can't do that," Amit replies. "We are not violating any laws. There is some possibility that we may have to incur environmental costs in the future, but if we ring it up now, this proposal will not go through because our senior management always assumes these costs to be larger than they turn out to be. The market is very tough, and we are in danger of shutting down the company. We don't want all our colleagues to lose their jobs. The only reason our competitors are making money is because they are doing exactly what I am proposing".

Required

1. Calculate Milton's break even revenues for the current year.
2. Calculate Milton's break even revenues if variable costs are 52 per cent of revenues.
3. Calculate Milton's operating income in current year if variable costs had been 52 per cent of revenues.
4. Given Amit's comments, what should Sudhir do?

Solution

1. Contribution margin percentage = (Revenues − Variable costs)/Revenues
= (Rs 50,00,000 − Rs 30,00,000)/Rs 50,00,000
= Rs 20,00,000/Rs 50,00,000 = 40 per cent
Breakeven revenues = Fixed costs/Contribution margin percentage
= Rs 21,60,000/0.40 = Rs 54,00,000
2. If variable costs are 52 per cent of revenues, contribution margin percentage equals 48 per cent (100% – 52%)
Break even revenues = Fixed costs/Contribution margin percentage
= Rs 21,60,000/0.48 = Rs 45,00,000
3.

Revenues	Rs 50,00,000
Variable costs (0.52 × Rs 50,00,000)	26,00,000
Fixed costs	21,60,000
Operating income	Rs 2,40,000

4. Incorrect reporting of environmental costs with the goal of continuing operations is unethical.

Sudhir should indicate to Kamna that estimates of environmental costs and liabilities should be included in the analysis. If Kamna still insists on modifying the numbers and reporting lower environmental costs, Sudhir should raise the matter with one of Kamna's superiors. If after taking all these steps, there is continued pressure to understate environmental costs, Sudhir should consider resigning from the company and not engage in unethical behavior.

3-28 Deciding where to produce (CMA, adapted) Tata Power produces the same power take off units in two plants, a new plant in Orissa and an older plant in Delhi. The Tata Power is expected to produce and sell 1,92,000 power takeoff units during the coming year. The following data are available for the two plants.

	Orissa		Delhi	
Selling price		Rs 15,000		Rs 15,000
Variable manufacturing cost per unit	Rs 7,200		Rs 8,800	
Fixed manufacturing cost per unit	3,000		1,500	
Variable marketing and distribution cost per unit	1,400		1,400	
Fixed marketing and distribution cost per unit	1,900		1,450	
Total cost per unit		13,500		13,150
Operating income per unit		1,500		1,850
Production rate per day	400 units		320 units	

All fixed costs per unit are calculated based on normal year consisting of 240 working days. When the number of working days exceeds 240, variable manufacturing costs increase by Rs 300 per unit in Orissa and Rs 800 per unit in Delhi. Capacity for each plant is 300 working days per year.

Wishing to take advantage of the higher operating income per unit at Delhi, Tata Power's manager has decided to manufacture 96,000 units at each plant. This production plan results in Delhi operating at capacity (320 units per day × 300 days) and Orissa operating at its normal volume (400 units per day × 240 days).

Required

1. Calculate the breakeven point in units for the Orissa and Delhi plants.
2. Calculate the operating income that would result from the production manager's plan to produce 96,000 units at each plant.
3. Determine how the production of the 1,92,000 units should be allocated between Orissa and Delhi plants to maximize operating income for Tata Power. Show your calculations.

Solution

1. Calculation of breakeven point in units

Contribution Margin per unit calculation

Particulars	Orissa	Delhi
Selling price	15,000	15,000
Less: variable costs		
Manufacturing	7,200	8,800
Marketing and distribution	1,400	1,400
Contribution margin per unit	Rs 6,400	Rs 4,800

Fixed Costs calculation

Total fixed costs = (Fixed manufacturing costs per unit + Fixed marketing and distribution cost per unit) × Production rate per day × Normal working days

Orissa = (Rs 3,000 + 1,900) × 400 × 240 = Rs 47,04,00,000

Delhi = (Rs 1,500 + 1,450) × 320 × 240 = Rs 22,65,60,000

Breakeven calculation:

Breakeven units = Fixed costs/Contribution margin per unit

Orissa = Rs 47,04,00,000/6,400 = 73,500 units

Delhi = Rs 22,65,60,000/4,800 = 47,200 units

2. The operating income that would result from the division production manager's plan to produce 96,000 units at each plant is Rs 36,28,80,000. The normal capacity at the Orissa plant is 96,000 units (400 × 240); however, the normal capacity at the Delhi plant is 76,800 units (320 × 240). Therefore, 19,200 units (96,000–76,800) will be manufactured at Delhi at a reduced contribution margin of Rs 4,000 per unit (4,800 – 800).

Contribution Margin per plant:

Orissa, 96,000 × Rs 6,400	Rs 61,44,00,000
Delhi, 76,800 × Rs 4,800	36,86,40,000
Delhi, 19,200 × Rs 4,000	7,68,00,000
Total contribution margin	1,05,98,40,000
Deduct fixed costs, Rs 47,04,00,000 + 22,65, 60,000	69,69,60,000
Operating income	36,28,80,000

3. The optimal production plant is to produce 1,20,000 units at the Orissa plant and 72,000 units at the Delhi plant. The full capacity of the Orissa plant, 1,20,000 (400 units × 300 days), should be utilized as the contribution from these units is higher at all levels of production than the contribution from units produced at the Delhi plant:

Contribution Margin per plant:

Orissa, 96,000 × Rs 6,400	Rs 61,44,00,000
Orissa, 24,000 × (Rs 6,400 300)	14,64,00,000
Delhi, 72,000 × Rs 4,800	34,56,00,000
Total contribution margin	1,10,64,00,000
Deduct total fixed costs	69,69,60,000
Operating income	Rs 40,94,40,000

The contribution margin is higher when 1,20,000 units are produced at the Orissa plant and 72,000 units at the Delhi plant. As a result, operating income will also be higher in this case since total fixed costs for the division remain unchanged regardless of the quantity produced at each plant.

3-29 Multi product breakeven decision making. Bharat Seat Ltd. manufactures and sells one product—an infant car seat called Babycomfort—at a price of Rs 500. Variable costs equal Rs 200 per car seat. Fixed costs are Rs 49,50,000. Bharat Seats Ltd. manufactures Babycomfort upon the receipt of orders from its customers. In year 1, it sold 30,000 units of Babycomfort. One of Bharat Seats Ltd. customers, Hyundai Motor Co., has asked if in year 2 Bharat Seats will manufacture a different style of car seat called Babyluxury. Hyundai will pay Rs 250 for each unit of Babyluxury. The variable costs for Babyluxury are estimated at Rs 150 per seat. Bharat Seats has enough capacity to manufacture all the units of Babycomfort it can sell as well as the units of Babyluxury that Huyndai wants and will thus incur no additional fixed costs. Bharat Seats estimates that in year 2 it will sell 30,000 units of Babycomfort (assuming the same price and variable costs in year 1) and 20,000 units of Babyluxury.

Siddharth, the president of Bharat Seats, checked the effect of accepting Hyundai's offer on the breakeven revenues for year 2. Using the planned sales mix for year 2, he was surprised to find that the revenues required to break even appeared to increase. He was not sure that his numbers were correct, but if they were, Siddharth felt inclined to reject Hyundai's offer. He asks for your advice.

Required

1. Calculate the breakeven point in units and in revenues for year 1.
2. Calculate the breakeven point in units and in revenues for year 2 at the planned sales mix.
3. Explain why the breakeven point in revenues calculated in requirements 1 and 2 are different.
4. Should Siddharth accept Hyundai's offer? Provide supporting computations.

Solution

1. Breakeven point in year 1 (units) = Fixed costs/Contribution margin per unit
   = Rs 49,50,000/Rs 300 = 16,500 units
   Breakeven point in year 1 (in revenues) = 16,500 × Rs 500 = Rs 82,50,000
2. Breakeven point in year 2 (in units)
   Bharat Seats expects to sell 3 units of Babycomfort for every 2 units of Babyluxury in year 2, so consider a bundle consisting of 3 units of Babycomfort and 2 units of Babyluxury.
   Unit contribution Margin from Babycomfort = Rs 500 − 200 = Rs 300
   Unit contribution Margin from Babyluxury = Rs 250 − 150 = Rs 100

   The contribution margin for the bundle is
   Rs 300 × 3 units of Babycomfort + Rs 100 × 2 units of Babyluxury = Rs 1,100
   So bundles to be sold to breakeven = Rs 49,50,000/1,100 = 4,500 bundles
   Breakeven point in year 2 (in units)
   Babycomfort, 4,500 × 3 = 13,500 units
   Babyluxury, 4,500 × 2 = 9,000 units
   Breakeven point in revenues:

Babycomfort 13,500 units × Rs 500 per unit	67,50,000
Babyluxury 9,000 units × Rs 250 per unit	22,50,000
Total	Rs 90,00,000

3. Contribution margin percentage in year 1 = Contribution margin per unit in year 1/Selling price in year 1
   = Rs 300/Rs 500 = 60 per cent
   Contribution margin percentage in year 2 = Contribution margin of bundle in year 2/Selling price of bundle in year 2
   = Rs 1,100/(3 × Rs 500) + (2 × Rs 250) = 1,100/2,000 = 55 per cent
   The breakeven point in year 2 increases because fixed costs are the same in both years but the contribution margin generated by each rupee of sales revenue at the give product mix decreases in year 2 relative to year 1.
4. Despite the breakeven sales revenue being higher, Bharat Seats should accept Hyundai's offer. The breakeven points are irrelevant because Bharat Seats is already above the breakeven sales volume in year 1. By accepting Hyundai's offer, Bharat Seats has the ability to sell all the 30,000 units of Babycomfort in year 2 and make more sales of Babyluxury to Hyundai without incurring any more fixed costs.

   Operating Income in year 2 with and without Babyluxury are expected to be as follows:

	Without Babyluxury	With Babyluxury	
Sales	Rs 1,50,00,000	Rs 2,00,00,000	(Rs 500 × 30,000 + Rs250 × 20,000)
Variable costs	60,00,000	90,00,000	(Rs200 × 30,000 + Rs150 × 20,000)
Contribution margin	90,00,000	1,10,00,000	
Fixed costs	49,50,000	49,50,000	
Operating income	40,50,000	60,50,000	

Exercises

3-30 The Digital Company has fixed costs of Rs 3,00,000 and a variable cost percentage of 75 per cent. The company earns net income after taxes of Rs 80,000 in current year. The income tax rate is 40 per cent.

Compute (1) Operating income (2) Contribution margin (3) Total revenues (4) Breakeven revenues. **Required**

3-31 CVP exercises. The Reynolds Company manufactures and sells pens. Currently 6,00,000 units are sold per year at Rs 10 per unit. Fixed costs are Rs 15,00,000 per year. Variable costs are Rs 6 per unit.

Consider each case separately: **Required**

1. (a) What is the present operating income for a year?
   (b) What is the present breakeven point in revenues?
   Compute the new operating income for each of the following changes.
2. A Re 0.50 per unit increase in variable costs.
3. A 10 per cent increase in fixed costs and a 10 per cent increase in units sold.
4. A 20 per cent decrease in fixed costs, a 20 per cent decrease in selling price, a 10 per cent decrease in variable cost per unit and a 40 per cent increase in units sold.
   Compute the new breakeven point in units for each of the following changes:
5. A 15 per cent increase in fixed costs.
6. A 10 per cent increase in selling price and a Rs 1,00,000 increase in fixed costs.

3-32 Gross margin and contribution margin, making decision. Big Jos clothing's revenues and cost data for 2011 appear below:

Revenues		Rs 10,00,000
Cost of goods sold (40 per cent of sales)		4,00,000
Gross margin		6,00,000
Operating costs		
Salaries	Rs 3,00,000	
Sales commissions (10 per cent of sales)	1,00,000	
Depreciation of equipment and fixtures	24,000	
Store rent (Rs 8,000 per month)	96,000	
Other operating costs	1,00,000	6,20,000
Operating income (loss)		Rs (20,000)

Mr. Nitin, the owner of the store is unhappy with the operating results. An analysis of other operating costs reveals that it includes Rs 80,000 variable costs, which vary with sales volume, and Rs 20,000 fixed costs.

Required

1. Compute the contribution margin of Big Jos Clothing.
2. Compute the contribution margin percentage.
3. Mr. Nitin estimates he can increase revenues by 20 per cent by incurring additional advertising costs of Rs 20,000. Calculate the impact on operating income.

3-33 CVP analysis, service firm. Thomas Cook India generates average revenue of Rs 20,000 per person on its five-day package tours to Goa. The variable costs per person are as follows:

Airfare	Rs 5,000
Hotel accommodation	2,000
Meals	3,000
Ground transportation	3,000
Park tickets and other costs	1,000
Total	Rs 14,000

Annual fixed costs total Rs 18,00,000

Required

1. Calculate the number of package tours that must be sold to breakeven.
2. Calculate the revenue needed to earn a target operating income of Rs 6,00,000
3. If fixed costs increase by Rs 3,00,000 what decrease in variable costs must be achieved to maintain the breakeven point calculated in requirement 1?

3-34 CVP analysis, income taxes. The Grand Plaza has two restaurants that are open 24 hours a day. Fixed costs for the two restaurants together total Rs 10,00,000 per year. Service varies from a cup of tea to full meals. The average sales revenue per customer is Rs 20. The average cost of food and other variable costs for each customer is Rs 8. The income tax rate is 30 per cent. Target net income is Rs 3,50,000.

Required

1. Compute the revenues needed to obtain the target net income.
2. How many customers are needed to breakeven? To earn net income of Rs 3,50,000?
3. Compute net income if the number of customer is 2,00,000.

3-35 CVP analysis, international cost structure differences. Vardhman Spinning is considering three countries for the sole manufacturing site of its new sweater: Singapore, Thailand and the Unites States. All sweaters are to be sold to retail outlets in the United States at Rs 32 per unit. These retail outlets add their own markup when selling to final customers. The three countries differ in their fixed cost and their variable cost per sweater.

Country	Annual Fixed Costs	Variable Manufacturing Cost per Sweater	Variable Marketing and Distribution Cost per Sweater
Singapore	$ 6.5 million	$ 8.00	$ 11.00
Thailand	4.5 million	5.50	11.50
United States	12.0 million	13.00	9.00

Required

1. Compute the breakeven point of Vardhman Spinning in (a) units sold for each country and (b) revenues for each country.
2. If Vardhman Spinning sells 8,00,000 sweaters in current year, what is the budgeted operating income for each country? Comment on the result.

3-36 Gross margin and contribution margin. Ramesh Fork Pvt. Ltd's. income statement for current year at the level of production and sales of 2,00,000 units is as follows:

Revenues	Rs 26,00,000
Cost of goods sold	16,00,000
Gross margin	10,00,000
Marketing and distribution costs	11,50,000
Operating income (loss)	Rs (1,50,000)

Ramesh's fixed manufacturing costs are Rs 5,00,000 and variable marketing and distribution costs are Rs 4 per unit.

Required

1. a. Calculate Ramesh's variable manufacturing cost per unit in current year.
   b. Calculate Ramesh's fixed marketing and distribution costs in current year.
2. Ramesh's gross margin per unit is Rs 5 (Rs 10,00,000/2,00,000 units). Sudhir, Ramesh's president, believes that if production and sales had been 2,30,000 units, it would have also recovered Rs 1,50,000 of marketing and distribution costs (Rs 11,50,000/5 = 2,30,000) and enabled Ramesh's to breakeven for the year. Calculate Ramesh's operating income if production and sales equal 2,30,000 units, Explain briefly why Sudhir is wrong.
3. Calculate the breakeven point for current year in units and in revenues.

3-37 Athletic scholarships, CVP analysis. Delhi University has an annual budget of Rs 1,00,00,000 for athletic scholarships. Each athletic scholarship is for Rs 40,000 per year. Fixed operating costs of the athletic scholarship program are Rs 12,00,000 and variable operating costs are Rs 4,000 per scholarship offered.

Required

1. Determine the number of athletic scholarships Delhi University can offer each year.
2. Suppose the total budget for next year is reduced by 22 per cent. Fixed costs are to remain the same. Calculate the number of athletic scholarships that Delhi University can offer next year.
3. As in requirement 2, assume a budget reduction of 22 per cent and the same fixed costs. If Delhi University wanted to offer the same number of athletic scholarships as it did in requirement 1, calculate the amount that will be paid to each student who receives a scholarship.

3-38 CVP analysis, income taxes, sensitivity. (CMA, adapted) Birla Company manufactures and sells adjustable canopies that attach to motor homes and trailers. For its current year budget, Birla estimated the following:

Selling price	Rs 20,000
Variable cost per canopy	10,000
Annual fixed costs	50,00,000
Net income	1,20,00,000
Income tax rate	40%

The May financial statements reported that sales were not meeting expectations. For the first five months of the year, only 350 units had been sold at the established price, with variable costs as planned, and it was clear that the net income projection for current year would not be reached unless some actions were taken. A management committee presented the following mutually exclusive alternatives to the president.

Reduce the selling price by Rs 2,000. The sales organization forecasts that at this significantly reduced price, 2,700 units can be sold during the remainder of the year. Total fixed costs and variable cost per unit will stay as budgeted.

Lower variable cost per unit by Rs 500 through the use of less expensive direct materials and slightly modified manufacturing techniques. The selling price will also be reduced by Rs 1,500 and sales of 2,200 units are expected for the remainder of the year.

Reduce fixed costs by Rs 5,00,000 and lower the selling price by 5 per cent. Variable cost per unit will be unchanged. Sales of 2,000 units are expected for the remainder of the year.

Required

1. If no changes are made to the selling price or cost structure, determine the number of units that Birla Company must sell (a) to break even and (b) to achieve its net income objective.
2. Determine which alternative Birla should select to achieve its net income objective. Show your calculations.

3-39 Sales mix, two products. The VIP company retails two products, a standard and a deluxe version of a luggage carrier. The budgeted income statement for next period is as follows:

Particulars	Standard Carrier	Deluxe Carrier	Total
Units sold	1,50,000	5,00,000	2,00,000
Revenues at Rs 1,000 and Rs 1,500 per unit	Rs 15,00,00,000	Rs 7,50,00,000	Rs 22,50,00,000
Variable costs at Rs 700 and Rs 900 per unit	10,50,00,000	4,50,00,000	15,00,00,000
Contribution margins at Rs 300 and Rs 600 per unit	4,50,00,000	30,00,000	7,50,00,000
Fixed costs			6,00,00,000
Operating income			1,50,00,000

Required

1. Compute the breakeven point, in units, assuming that the planned sales mix is attained.
2. Compute the breakeven point in units (a) if only standard carriers are sold and (b) if only deluxe carriers are sold.
3. Suppose 2,00,000 units are sold, but only 20,000 of them are deluxe. Compute the operating income. Compute the breakeven point in units. Compare your answer with the answer to requirement 1. What is the major lesson of this problem?

3-40 CVP analysis under uncertainty. The Jindal Company is considering two new colors for their umbrella products: emerald green and shocking pink. Either can be produced using present facilities. Each product requires an increase in annual fixed costs of Rs 40,00,000. The products have the same Rs 100 selling price and the same Rs 80 variable cost per unit.

Management, after studying past experience with similar products, has prepared the following probability distribution:

Even (Units Demanded)	Probability for Emerald Green Umbrella	Shocking Pink Umbrella
50,000	0.0	0.1
1,00,000	0.1	0.1
2,00,000	0.2	0.1
3,00,000	0.4	0.2
4,00,000	0.2	0.4
5,00,000	0.1	0.1
	1.0	1.0

Required

1. What is the breakeven point units for each product?
2. Which product should be chosen, assuming the objective is to maximize expected operating income? Why? Show your computations.
3. Suppose management is absolutely certain that 3,00,000 units of shocking pink will be sold, but it still faces the same uncertainty about the demand for emerald green as outlined in the problem. Which product should be chosen? Why? What benefits are available to management from having the complete probability distribution instead of just an expected value?

3-41 CVP analysis, shoe stores. The Liberty Shoe Company operates a chain of shoe stores. The stores sell 10 different styles of inexpensive men's shoes with identical unit costs and selling prices. A unit is defined as a pair of shoes. Each store has a store manager who is paid a fixed salary. Individual salespeople receive a fixed salary and a sales commission. Liberty is trying to determine whether to open another store, which is expected to have the following revenue and cost relationships:

Unit variable data (per pair of shoe)		
Selling price	Rs	300
Cost of shoes		195
Sales commissions		15
Variable costs per unit		210
Annual fixed costs		
Rent		1,20,000
Salaries		4,00,000
Advertising		1,60,000
Other fixed costs		40,000
Total fixed costs		7,20,000

Consider each question independently.

Required

1. What is the annual breakeven point in (a) units sold and (b) revenues?
2. If 35,000 units are sold, what will be the store's operating income (loss)?

3. If sales commissions were discontinued for individual salespeople in favor of Rs 1,62,000 increase in fixed salaries, what would be the annual breakeven point in (a) units sold and (b) revenues?
4. Refer to the original data. If the store manager were paid Rs 0.3 per unit sold in addition to his current fixed salary, what would be the annual breakeven point in (a) units sold and (b) revenues?
5. Refer to the original data. If the store manager were paid Rs 0.3 per unit commission on each unit sold in excess of the breakeven point, what would be store's operating income if 50,000 units were sold? (This Rs 0.3 is in addition to both the commission paid to the sales staff and the store manager's fixed salary.)

3-42 **CVP analysis, shoe stores (continuation of 3-41).** Refer to requirement 3 of 3-41.

Required

1. Calculate the number of units sold at which the operating income under the fixed-salary plan and the lower fixed-salary-and-commission plan (for sales people only) would be equal. Above that number of units sold, one plan would be more profitable than the other; below that number of units sold, the reverse would occur.
2. Compute the operating income or loss under each plan in requirement 1 at sales levels of (a) 50,000 units and (b) 60,000 units.
3. Suppose the target operating income is Rs 16,80,000. How many units must be sold to reach the target under (a) the fixed-salary plan and (b) the lower fixed-salary-and-commission plan?

3-43 **Sensitivity and inflation (continuation of previous question).** As president of Liberty shoe Co., you are concerned that inflation may squeeze your profitability. Specifically, you feel committed to the Rs 300 selling price and fear that decreasing the quality of the shoes in the face of rising costs would be an unwise move. You expect the cost of shoes to rise by 10 per cent during the coming year. You are tempted to avoid the cost increase by placing a non-cancelable order with a large supplier that would provide 50,000 units of the specified quality for each store at Rs 195 per units. (to simplify this analysis, assume that all stores will face identical demands.) These shoes could be acquired and paid for as delivered throughout the year. However, all shoes must be delivered to the stores by the end of the year.

As a shrewd merchandiser, you foresee some risks. If sales were less than 50,000 units, you feel that markdowns of the unsold merchandise would be necessary to sell the goods. You predict that the average selling price of the leftover units would be Rs 180. The regular commission of 5 per cent of revenues would be paid to salespeople.

Required

1. Suppose that actual sales for the year are 48,000 units at Rs 300 per unit and that you contracted for 50,000 units, what is the operating income for the Liberty Shoe Company?
2. If you had perfect forecasting ability, you would have contracted for 48,000 units rather than 50,000 units. What would the operating income have been if you had ordered 48,000 units.
3. Given actual sales of 48,000 units, by how much would the average cost per unit have had to rise before the Shoe Company would have been indifferent to having the contract for 50,000 units or not having the contract?

4 Job Costing

Learning Objectives

1. Describe the building-block concepts of costing systems
2. Distinguish job costing from process costing
3. Describe the approaches to evaluating and implementing job-costing systems
4. Outline the seven-step approach to job costing
5. Distinguish actual costing from normal costing
6. Track the flow of costs in a job-costing system
7. Dispose of under or over-allocated manufacturing overhead costs at the end of the fiscal year using alternative methods
8. Apply variations from normal costing

It's fair to say that no one likes to lose money. Whether a company is a new startup venture providing marketing consulting services or an established manufacturer of custom-built motorcycles, knowing how to job cost—how much it costs to produce an individual product—is critical if a profit is to be generated. As the following article shows, Nexamp, a clean-energy company, knows this all too well.

Job Costing and Nexamp's Next Generation Energy and Carbon Solutions[1]

Making a profit on a project depends on pricing it correctly. At Nexamp, a leading renewable-energy systems provider in Massachusetts, a team of managers and employees is responsible for the costing and pricing of its solar, geothermal, wind, and biomass installation jobs for homeowners and businesses.

For each project, account managers carefully examine and verify job costs as part of a competitive bidding process. Using a computer model developed from previous projects, a company executive double-checks all the numbers, watching for costs that could wreak havoc with the net profit on the job. Projects of a certain size, such as a recent $20 million government stimulus contract to install solar panels, require the approval of a company vice president or other high-ranking officer. This type of approval ensures that Nexamp does not approve jobs that could lose money.

Nexamp holds a weekly project management meeting where managers report on the status of each job approved and scheduled. Once a project is underway, on-site project managers provide weekly reports on the progress of each phase of installation. Nexamp project managers are also responsible for identifying any potential problems with each project and determining any alterations necessary to ensure high quality, on-time delivery within the original project budget.

At Nexamp, job costing includes three key elements: direct costs of a job, indirect costs of a job, and general administrative costs. Direct costs are costs traceable to a specific job such as costs of solar panels, electricity converters, mounting systems, and subcontractor payments. All materials are purchased through a formal procurement process, which helps Nexamp carefully manage

[1] *Sources*: Conversations with Nexamp management. June 4, 2010. Noblett, Jackie. 2010. Nexamp lands $20M stimulus contract. *Boston Business Journal*, February 5.

and control material costs. Another key element of direct costs is direct labor. Besides the actual wages paid to employees, direct labor costs include costs of workers' compensation insurance, health insurance, vacations and holidays, sick days, and paid days off.

Indirect costs of a job are allocated to each project. These include cost of supervisory labor, company-owned equipment, construction supplies, and safety equipment. Finally, Nexamp allocates general and administrative costs, such as office rent, utilities, and general insurance to each job.

Just like at Nexamp, managers at Nissan need to know how much it costs to manufacture its new Leaf electric car, and managers at Ernst & Young need to know what it costs to audit Whole Foods, the organic grocer. Knowing the costs and profitability of jobs helps managers pursue their business strategies, develop pricing plans, and meet external reporting requirements. Of course, when making decisions, managers combine cost information with noncost information, such as personal observations of operations, and nonfinancial performance measures, such as quality and customer satisfaction.

Building-Block Concepts of Costing Systems

Before we begin our discussion of costing systems, let's review some terms discussed in Chapter 2 that we'll use to introduce costing systems:

Learning Objective 1

Describe the building-block concepts of costing systems

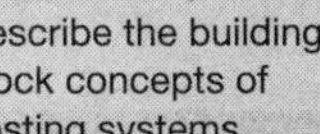

. . . the building blocks are cost object, direct costs, indirect costs, cost pools, and cost-allocation bases

- *Cost object*—anything for which a measurement of costs is desired—for example, a product, such as an iMac computer, or a service, such as the cost of repairing an iMac computer.
- *Direct costs of a cost object*—costs related to a particular cost object that can be traced to that cost object in an economically feasible (cost-effective) way—for example the cost of purchasing the main computer board or the cost of parts used to make an iMac computer.
- *Indirect costs of a cost object*—costs related to a particular cost object that cannot be traced to that cost object in an economically feasible (cost-effective) way—for example, the costs of supervisors who oversee multiple products, one of which is the iMac, or the rent paid for the repair facility that repairs many different Apple computer products besides the iMac. Indirect costs are allocated to the cost object using a cost-allocation method.

Recall that *cost assignment* is a general term for assigning costs, whether direct or indirect, to a cost object. *Cost tracing* is a specific term for assigning direct costs; *cost allocation* refers to assigning indirect costs. The relationship among these three concepts can be graphically represented as

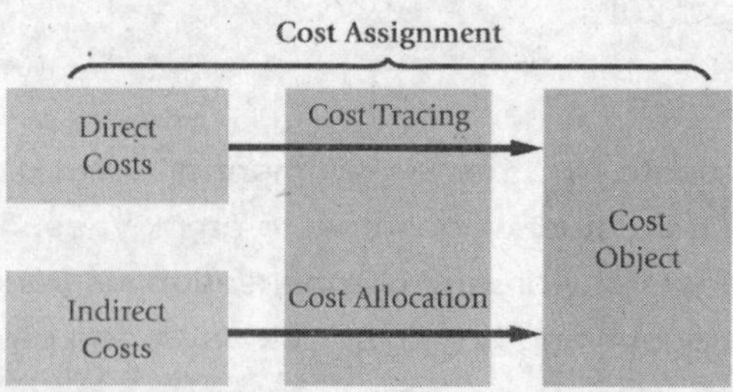

Throughout this chapter, the costs assigned to a cost object, include both variable and fixed costs. Managers use costs of products and services to guide long-run strategic decisions (for example, what mix of products and services to produce and sell and what prices to charge for them). In making these decisions, managers include all costs for two reasons. First, in the long run more costs can be managed and fewer costs are regarded as fixed. Second, also in the long run, a business cannot survive unless the prices of the products and services it chooses to sell cover both variable and fixed costs.

We need to introduce and explain two more terms to discuss costing systems:

1. **Cost pool.** A **cost pool** is a grouping of individual indirect cost items. Cost pools can range from broad, such as all manufacturing-plant costs, to narrow, such as the costs of operating metal-cutting machines. Cost pools are often organized in conjunction with cost-allocation bases.
2. **Cost-allocation base.** How should a company allocate costs to operate metal-cutting machines among different products? One way would be to allocate the costs based on the number of machine-hours used to produce the different products. The **cost-allocation base** (in our example, the number of machine-hours) is a systematic way to link an indirect cost or group of indirect costs (in our example, operating costs of all metal-cutting machines) to a cost object (in our example, different products). For example, if overhead costs of operating metal-cutting machines is Rs 50,00,000 based on running these machines for 10,000 hours, the cost allocation rate is Rs 50,00,000 ÷ 10,000 hours = Rs 500 per machine-hour, where machine-hours is the cost allocation base. If a product uses 800 machine-hours, it will be allocated Rs 4,00,000, Rs 500 per machine-hour × 800 machine hours. Companies often use the cost driver of indirect costs as the cost-allocation base because of the cause-and-effect relationship between changes in the level of the cost driver and changes in indirect costs over the long run. A cost-allocation base can be either financial (such as direct labor costs) or nonfinancial (such as the number of machine-hours). When the cost object is a job, product, or customer, the cost-allocation base is also called a **cost-application base.**

The concepts represented by these five terms constitute the building blocks that we will use to design the costing systems described in this chapter.

Learning Objective 2

Distinguish job costing

. . . job costing is used to cost a distinct product

from process costing

. . . process costing is used to cost masses of identical or similar units

Job-Costing and Process-Costing Systems

Management accountants use two basic types of costing systems to assign costs to products or services:

1. **Job-costing system.** In this system, the cost object is a unit or multiple units of a distinct product or service called a **job**. Each job generally uses different amounts of resources. The product or service is often a single unit, such as a specialized machine made at Hitachi, a construction project managed by Larsen and Toubro, a repair job done at an Honda Service Center, or an advertising campaign produced by Saatchi & Saatchi. Each special machine made by Hitachi is unique and distinct. An advertising campaign for one client at Saatchi and Saatchi is unique and distinct from advertising

campaigns for other clients. Job costing is also used to cost multiple identical units of a distinct product, such as the costs incurred by Hindustan Aeronautics Ltd. to manufacture multiple units of the Agni missile for the ministry of Defense. Because the products and services are distinct, job-costing systems accumulate costs separately for each product or service.

2. **Process-costing system.** In this system, the cost object is masses of identical or similar units of a product or service. For example, Citibank provides the same service to all its customers when processing customer deposits. Intel provides the same product (say, a Pentium 4 chip) to each of its customers. Customers of Reliance Fresh all receive the same frozen orange juice product. In each period, process-costing systems divide the total costs of producing an identical or similar product or service by the total number of units produced to obtain a per-unit cost. This per-unit cost is the average unit cost that applies to each of the identical or similar units produced in that period.

Exhibit 4-1 presents examples of job costing and process costing in the service, merchandising, and manufacturing sectors. These two types of costing systems are best considered as opposite ends of a continuum; in between, one type of system can blur into the other to some degree.

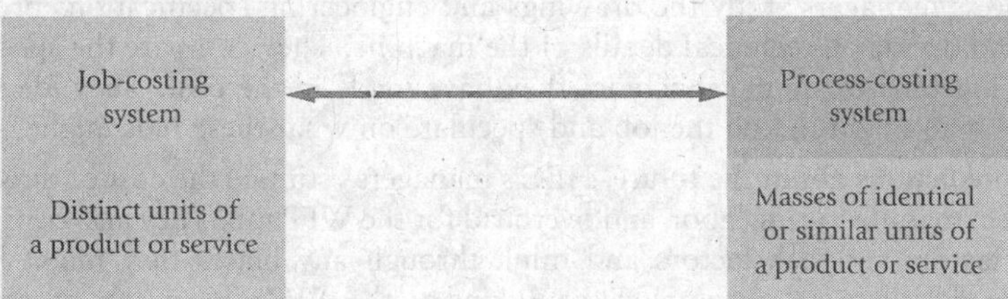

Many companies have costing systems that are neither pure job costing nor pure process costing but have elements of both. Costing systems, therefore, need to be tailored to the underlying operations. For example, Kellogg Corporation uses job costing to calculate the total cost to manufacture each of its different and distinct types of products—such as Corn Flakes, Crispix, and Froot Loops—but process costing to calculate the per-unit cost of producing each identical box of Corn Flakes. In this chapter, we focus on job-costing systems. Chapters 17 and 18 discuss process-costing systems.

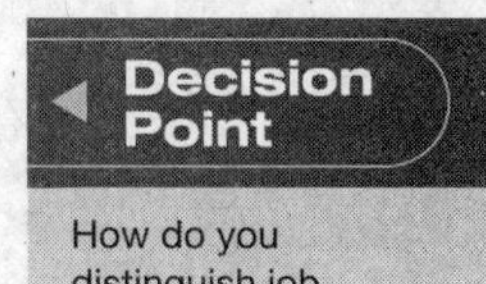

How do you distinguish job costing from process costing?

Exhibit 4-1

Examples of Job Costing and Process Costing in the Service, Merchandising, and Manufacturing Sectors

	Service Sector	Merchandising Sector	Manufacturing Sector
Job Costing Used	• Audit engagements done by Price Waterhouse Coopers • Consulting engagements done by McKinsey & Co. • Advertising-agency campaigns run by Ogilvy and Mather • Individual legal cases argued by Hale & Dorr • Computer-repair jobs done by Intel India • Movies produced by RK Studios	• Sending individual items by mail order • Special promotion of new products by Shoppers' shop	Assembly of individual aircrafts at Boeing • Construction of ships at Mazgaon Dock
Process Costing Used	• Bank-check clearing at Bank of America • Postal delivery (standard items) by Indian Postal Service	• Grain dealing • Lumber dealing	• Oil refining by Indian Oil • Beverage production by PepsiCo

Job Costing: Evaluation and Implementation

Learning Objective 3

Describe the approaches to evaluating and implementing job-costing systems

. . . to determine costs of jobs in a timely manner

We illustrate job costing using the example of Heavy Engineering Corporation (HEC), a company that manufactures and installs specialized machinery for the paper-making industry at its Ranchi plant. In early 2011, HEC receives a request to bid for the manufacturing and installation of a new paper-making machine for the Western Pulp and Paper Company (WPP). HEC's has never made a machine quite like this one, and its managers wonder what to bid for the job. HEC's management works through the five-step decision-making process.

1. **Identify the problems and uncertainties.** The decision of whether and how much to bid for the WPP job depends on how management resolves two critical uncertainties—what it will cost to complete the job and the prices that its competitors are likely to bid.
2. **Obtain information.** HEC's managers first evaluate whether doing the WPP job is consistent with the company's strategy. Are these the kinds of jobs they want to be doing more of? Is this an attractive segment of the market? Will HEC be able to develop a competitive advantage over its competitors? Strategy is as much about what to do as it is about what not to do. HEC's managers conclude that the WPP job fits well with the company's strategy.

   HEC's managers study the drawings and engineering specifications provided by WPP and decide on technical details of the machine. They compare the specifications of this machine to similar machines they have made in the past. They identify competitors who might bid on the job and speculate on what these bids might be.
3. **Make predictions about the future.** HEC's managers estimate the cost of direct materials, direct manufacturing labor, and overhead for the WPP job. They also consider qualitative factors and risk factors and think through any biases they might have. For example, do engineers and employees working on the WPP job have the necessary skills and technical competence? Would they find the experience valuable and challenging. If the project runs into trouble, what effect might it have on employee morale and on other jobs? How accurate are the cost estimates, and what is the likelihood of cost overruns? What biases do HEC's managers have to be careful about? Remember, HEC has not made a machine quite like this one. The predictions about costs are based on other similar machines. HEC's managers need to be careful not to draw inappropriate analogies and to seek the most relevant information when making their judgments.
4. **Make decisions by choosing among alternatives.** HEC bids Rs 1,50,000 for the WPP job. This bid is based on a manufacturing cost estimate of Rs 1,00,000 and a markup of 50% over manufacturing cost. The Rs 1,50,000 price takes into account likely bids by competitors, the technical and business risks, and qualitative factors. HEC's managers are very confident that they have obtained the best possible information in reaching their decision.
5. **Implement the decision, evaluate performance, and learn.** HEC wins the bid for the WPP job. As HEC works on the WPP job, it keeps careful track of all the costs it has incurred (which are detailed later in this chapter). Ultimately, HEC's managers compare the predicted amounts against actual costs to evaluate how well they did on the WPP job.

In its job-costing system, HEC accumulates costs incurred on a job in different parts of the value chain, such as manufacturing, marketing, and customer service. We focus here on HEC's manufacturing function (which also includes product installation). To make a machine, HEC purchases some components from outside suppliers and makes others itself. Each of HEC's jobs also has a service element: installing a machine at a customer's site, integrating it with the customer's other machines and processes, and ensuring the machine meets customer expectations.

One form of a job-costing system that HEC can use is actual costing. **Actual costing** is a costing system that traces direct costs to a cost object by using the actual direct-cost rates times the actual quantities of the direct-cost inputs. It allocates indirect costs based on the actual indirect-cost rates times the actual quantities of the cost-allocation bases. The *actual indirect-cost rate* is calculated by dividing actual total indirect costs by the actual total quantity of the cost-allocation base. As its name suggests, actual costing systems calculate the actual costs of jobs. Yet, actual costing systems are not commonly found in practice because actual costs cannot be computed in a *timely* manner. The problem is not with computing direct-cost rates for direct materials and direct manufacturing labor. For example, HEC records the actual prices paid for materials. As it uses these materials, the prices paid serve as actual direct-cost rates for charging material costs to jobs. As we discuss next, calculating actual indirect-cost rates on a timely basis each week or each month is, however, a problem. HEC can only calculate actual indirect-cost rates at the end of the fiscal year and HEC's managers are unwilling to wait that long to learn the costs of various jobs.

Time Period Used to Compute Indirect-Cost Rates

There are two reasons for using longer periods, such as a year, to calculate indirect-cost rates.

1. **The numerator reason (indirect-cost pool).** The shorter the period, the greater the influence of seasonal patterns on the amount of costs. For example, if indirect-cost rates were calculated each month, costs of heating (included in the numerator) would be charged to production only during the winter months. An annual period incorporates the effects of all four seasons into a single, annual indirect-cost rate.

   Levels of total indirect costs are also affected by nonseasonal erratic costs. Examples of nonseasonal erratic costs include costs incurred in a particular month that benefit operations during future months, such as costs of repairs and maintenance of equipment, and costs of vacation and holiday pay. If monthly indirect-cost rates were calculated, jobs done in a month with high, nonseasonal erratic costs would be charged with these costs. Pooling all indirect costs together over the course of a full year and calculating a single annual indirect-cost rate helps smooth some of the erratic bumps in costs associated with shorter periods.

2. **The denominator reason (quantity of the cost-allocation base).** Another reason for longer periods is to avoid spreading monthly fixed indirect costs over fluctuating levels of monthly output and fluctuating quantities of the cost-allocation base. Consider the following example.

Choksi & Choksi are tax accountants whose work follows a highly seasonal pattern with very busy months during tax season and less busy months at other times. Assume the following mix of variable indirect costs (such as supplies, food, power, and indirect support labor) that vary with the quantity of the cost-allocation base (direct professional labor-hours) and fixed indirect costs (depreciation and general administrative support) that do not vary with short-run fluctuations in the quantity of the cost-allocation base:

	Indirect Costs			Direct	Allocation Rate per Direct
	Variable	Fixed	Total	Professional Labor-Hours	Professional Labor-Hour
	(1)	(2)	(3)	(4)	(5) = (3) ÷ (4)
High-output month	Rs 4,00,000	Rs 6,00,000	Rs 10,00,000	3,200	Rs 312.6
Low-output month	1,00,000	6,00,000	7,00,000	800	875.0

You can see that variable indirect costs change in proportion to changes in direct professional labor-hours. Therefore, the variable indirect-cost rate is the same in both the high-output months and the low-output months (Rs 4,00,000 ÷ 3,200 labor-hours = Rs 125 per labor-hour; Rs 1,00,000 ÷ 800 labor-hours = Rs 125 per labor-hour). Sometimes overtime payments can cause the variable indirect-cost rate to be higher in high-output months. In such cases, variable indirect costs will be allocated at a higher rate to production in high-output months relative to production in low-output months.

Consider now the fixed costs of Rs 6,00,000. The fixed costs cause monthly total indirect-cost rates to vary considerably—from Rs 312.5 per hour to Rs 875.0 per hour. Few managers believe that identical jobs done in different months should be allocated indirect-cost charges per hour that differ so significantly (Rs 875.0 ÷ Rs 312.5 = 2.80, or 280%) because of fixed costs. Furthermore, if fees for preparing tax returns are based on costs, fees would be high in low-output months leading to lost business, when in fact management wants to accept more bids to utilize idle capacity. Choksi & Choksi chose a specific level of capacity based on a time horizon far beyond a mere month. An average, annualized rate based on the relationship of total annual indirect costs to the total annual level of output smoothes the effect of monthly variations in output levels and is more representative of the total costs and total output that management considered when choosing the level of capacity and, hence, fixed costs. Another denominator reason for using annual overhead rates is that the calculation of monthly indirect-cost rates is affected by the number of Monday-to-Friday workdays in a month. The number of workdays per month varies from 20 to 23 during a year. If separate rates are computed each month, jobs in February would bear a greater share of indirect costs (such as depreciation and property taxes) than jobs in other months, because February has the fewest workdays (and consequently labor-hours) in a month. Many managers believe such results to be an unrepresentative and unreasonable way to assign indirect costs to jobs. An annual period reduces the effect that the number of working days per month has on unit costs.

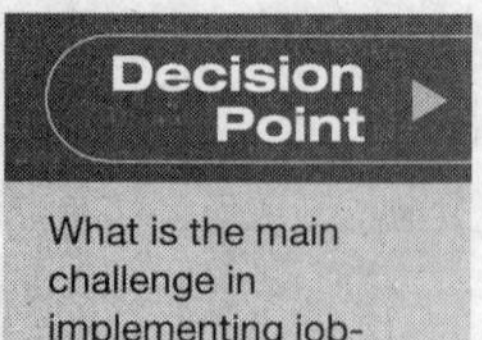

What is the main challenge in implementing job-costing systems?

Normal Costing

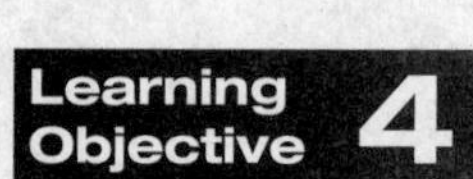

Outline the seven-step approach to job costing

. . . the seven-step approach is used to compute direct and indirect costs of a job

The difficulty of calculating actual indirect-cost rates on a weekly or monthly basis means managers cannot calculate the actual costs of jobs as they are completed. However, managers, including those at HEC, want a close approximation of the costs of various jobs regularly during the year, not just at the end of the fiscal year. Managers want to know manufacturing costs (and other costs, such as marketing costs) for ongoing uses, including pricing jobs, monitoring and managing costs, evaluating the success of the job, learning about what worked and what didn't, bidding on new jobs, and preparing interim financial statements. Because of the need for immediate access to job costs, few companies wait to allocate overhead costs until year-end when the actual manufacturing overhead is finally known. Instead, a *predetermined* or *budgeted* indirect-cost rate is calculated for each cost pool at the beginning of a fiscal year, and overhead costs are allocated to jobs as work progresses. For the numerator and denominator reasons already described, the **budgeted indirect-cost rate** for each cost pool is computed as follows:

$$\text{Budgeted indirect cost rate} = \frac{\text{Budgeted annual indirect costs}}{\text{Budgeted annual quantity of the cost-allocation base}}$$

Using budgeted indirect-cost rates gives rise to normal costing.

Normal costing is a costing system that (1) traces direct costs to a cost object by using the actual direct-cost rates times the actual quantities of the direct-cost inputs and (2) allocates indirect costs based on the *budgeted* indirect-cost rates times the actual quantities of the cost-allocation bases.

We illustrate normal costing for the HEC example using the following seven steps to assign costs to an individual job. This approach is commonly used by companies in the manufacturing, merchandising, and service sectors.

General Approach to Job Costing

Step 1: Identify the Job That Is the Chosen Cost Object. The cost object in the HEC example is Job WPP 298, manufacturing a paper-making machine for the Western Pulp and Paper Company in 2011. HEC's managers and management accountants gather information to cost jobs through source documents. A **source document** is an original record (such as a labor time card on which an employee's work hours are recorded) that supports journal entries in an accounting system. The main source document for Job WPP 298 is a job-cost record. A **job-cost record**, also called a **job-cost sheet,** records and accumulates all the costs assigned to a specific job, starting when work begins. Exhibit 4-2

Exhibit 4-2 Source Documents at HEC Company: Job-Cost Record

File Edit View Insert Format Tools Data Window Help

	A	B	C	D	E	
1			**JOB-COST RECORD**			
2	JOB NO:	WPP 298		CUSTOMER:	Western Pulp and Paper	
3	Date Started:	Feb. 4, 2011		Date Completed	Feb. 28, 2011	
4						
5						
6	**DIRECT MATERIALS**					
7	Date	Materials		Quantity	Unit	Total
8	Received	Requisition No.	Part No.	Used	Cost	Costs
9	Feb. 4, 2011	2011: 198	MB 468-A	8	Rs 140	Rs 1,120
10	Feb. 4, 2011	2011: 199	TB 267-F	12	630	7,560
11						•
12						•
13	Total					Rs 46,060
14						
15	**DIRECT MANUFACTURING LABOR**					
16	Period	Labor Time	Employee	Hours	Hourly	Total
17	Covered	Record No.	No.	Used	Rate	Costs
18	Feb. 4-10, 2011	LT 232	551-87-3076	25	Rs 180	Rs 4,500
19	Feb. 4-10, 2011	LT 247	287-31-4671	5	190	950
20						•
21						•
22	Total					Rs 15,790
23						
24	**MANUFACTURING OVERHEAD***					
25		Cost Pool		Allocation-Base	Allocation-	Total
26	Date	Category	Allocation-Base	Quantity Used	Base Rate	Costs
27	Dec. 31, 2011	Manufacturing	Direct Manufacturing	88 hours	Rs 400	Rs 35,200
28			Labor-Hours			
29						
30	Total					35,200
31	**TOTAL MANUFACTURING COST OF JOB**					Rs 97,050
32						
33						
34	*The HEC uses a single manufacturing-overhead cost pool. The use of multiple overhead cost pools					
35	would mean multiple entries in the "Manufacturing Overhead" section of the job-cost record.					
36						

shows the job-cost record for the paper-making machine ordered by Western Pulp and Paper Company. Follow the various steps in costing Job WPP 298 on the job-cost record in Exhibit 4-2.

Step 2: Identify the Direct Costs of the Job. HEC identifies two direct-manufacturing cost categories: direct materials and direct manufacturing labor.

- **Direct materials:** On the basis of the engineering specifications and drawings provided by WPP, a manufacturing engineer orders materials from the storeroom. The order is placed using a basic source document called a **materials-requisition record,** which contains information about the cost of direct materials used on a specific job and in a specific department. Exhibit 4-3, Panel A, shows a materials-requisition record for the HEC. See how the record specifies the job for which the material is requested (WPP 298), the description of the material (Part Number MB 468-A, metal brackets), the actual quantity (8), the actual unit cost (Rs 140), and the actual total

Exhibit 4-3 Source Documents at HEC: Materials Requisition Record and Labor-Time Record.

PANEL A:

MATERIALS-REQUISITION RECORD

Materials-Requisition Record No. 2008: 198

Job No. WPP 298 Date: FEB. 4, 2008

Part No.	Part Description	Quantity	Unit Cost	Total Cost
MB 468-A	Metal Brackets	8	Rs.140	Rs.1,120

Issued By: B. Clyde Date: Feb. 7, 2011

Received By: L. Daley Date: Feb. 7, 2011

PANEL B:

LABOR-TIME RECORD

Labor-Time Record No: LT 232

Employee Name: Ram Prasad Employee No: 551-87-3076

Employee Classification Code: Grade 3 Machinist

Hourly Rate: Rs 180

Week Start: Feb. 4, 2011 Week End: Feb. 13, 2011

Job. No.	M	T	W	Th	F	S	Su	Total
WPP 298	4	8	3	6	4	0	0	25
JL 256	3	0	4	2	3	0	0	12
Maintenance	1	0	1	0	1	0	0	3
Total	8	8	8	8	8	0	0	40

Supervisor: R. Stuart Date: Feb. 7, 2011

cost (Rs 1,120). The Rs 1,120 actual total cost also appears on the job-cost record in Exhibit 4-2. If we add the cost of all material requisitions, the total actual direct material cost is Rs 46,060, which is shown in the Direct Materials panel of the job-cost record in Exhibit 4-2.

- **Direct manufacturing labor:** The accounting for direct manufacturing labor is similar to the accounting described for direct materials. The source document for direct manufacturing labor is a **labor-time record**, which contains information about the amount of labor time used for a specific job in a specific department. Exhibit 4-3, Panel B, shows a typical weekly labor-time record for a particular employee (Ram Prasad). Each day Prasad records the time spent on individual jobs (in this case WPP 298 and JL 256), as well as the time spent on other tasks, such as maintenance of machines or cleaning, that are not related to a specific job.

  The 25 hours that Prasad spent on Job WPP 298 appears on the job-cost record in Exhibit 4-2 at a cost of Rs 4,500 (25 hours × Rs 180 per hour). Similarly, the job-cost record for Job JL 256 will carry a cost of Rs 2,160 (12 hours × Rs 180 per hour). The three hours of time spent on maintenance and cleaning at Rs 180 per hour equals Rs 540. This cost is part of indirect manufacturing costs because it is not traceable to any particular job. This indirect cost is included as part of the manufacturing-overhead cost pool allocated to jobs. The total direct manufacturing labor costs of Rs 15,790 for the paper-making machine that appears in the Direct Manufacturing Labor panel of the job-cost record in Exhibit 4-2 is the sum of all the direct manufacturing labor costs charged to this job by different employees.

  All costs other than direct materials and direct manufacturing labor are classified as indirect costs.

Step 3: Select the Cost-Allocation Bases to Use for Allocating Indirect Costs to the Job. Indirect manufacturing costs are costs that are necessary to do a job but that cannot be traced to a specific job. It would be impossible to complete a job without incurring indirect costs such as supervision, manufacturing engineering, utilities, and repairs. Because these costs cannot be traced to a specific job, they must be allocated to all jobs in a systematic way. Different jobs require different quantities of indirect resources. The objective is to allocate the costs of indirect resources in a systematic way to their related jobs.

Companies often use multiple cost-allocation bases to allocate indirect costs because different indirect costs have different cost drivers. For example, some indirect costs such as depreciation and repairs of machines are more closely related to machine-hours. Other indirect costs such as supervision and production support are more closely related to direct manufacturing labor-hours. HEC, however, chooses direct manufacturing labor-hours as the sole allocation base for linking all indirect manufacturing costs to jobs. That's because, in its labor-intensive environment, HEC believes that the number of direct manufacturing labor-hours is a good measure of how individual jobs use all the manufacturing overhead resources, such as salaries paid to supervisors, engineers, production support staff, and quality management staff. There is a cause-and-effect relationship between the direct manufacturing labor-hours required by an individual job—the cause—and the indirect manufacturing resources demanded by that job—the effect. (We will see in Chapter 5 that, in many manufacturing environments, we need to broaden the set of cost drivers.) In 2011, HEC records 27,000 actual direct manufacturing labor-hours.

Step 4: Identify the Indirect Costs Associated with Each Cost-Allocation Base. Because HEC believes that a single cost-allocation base—direct manufacturing labor-hours—can be used to allocate indirect manufacturing costs to jobs, HEC creates a single cost pool called manufacturing overhead costs. This pool represents all indirect costs of the Manufacturing Department that are difficult to trace directly to individual jobs. In 2011, actual manufacturing overhead costs total Rs 1,12,00,000.

As we saw in Steps 3 and 4, managers first identify cost-allocation bases and then identify the costs related to each cost-allocation base, not the other way around. That's because managers must first understand the cost driver, the reasons why costs are being incurred (for example, setting up machines, moving materials, or designing jobs), before they can determine the costs associated with each cost driver. The reason for not doing Step 4 before Step 3 is that there is nothing to guide the creation of the cost pools. As a result, the cost pools created may not have cost-allocation bases that are cost drivers of the costs in the cost pool. Of course, Steps 3 and 4 can be done almost simultaneously.

Step 5: Compute the Rate per Unit of Each Cost-Allocation Base Used to Allocate Indirect Costs to the Job. For each cost pool, the **actual indirect-cost rate** is calculated by dividing actual total indirect costs in the pool (determined in Step 4) by the actual total quantity of the cost-allocation base (determined in Step 3). HEC calculates the allocation rate for its single manufacturing overhead cost pool as follows:

$$\text{Actual manufacturing overhead rate} = \frac{\text{Actual manufacturing overhead costs}}{\text{Actual total quantity of cost-allocation base}}$$

$$= \frac{\text{Rs 1,12,00,000}}{\text{28,000 direct manufacturing labor-hours}}$$

$$= \text{Rs 400 per direct manufacturing labor-hour}$$

Step 6: Compute the Indirect Costs Allocated to the Job. The indirect costs of a job are computed by multiplying the actual quantity of each different allocation base (one allocation base for each cost pool) associated with the job by the indirect cost rate of each allocation base (computed in Step 5). Recall that HEC's managers selected direct manufacturing labor-hours as the only cost-allocation base. Out of the 28,000 total direct manufacturing labor-hours for 2011, HEC uses 88 direct manufacturing labor-hours on the WPP 298 job. Manufacturing overhead costs allocated to WPP 298 equal Rs 35,200 (Rs 400 per direct manufacturing labor-hour × 88 hours) and appear in the Manufacturing Overhead panel of the WPP 298 job-cost record in Exhibit 4-2.

Step 7: Compute the Total Cost of the Job by Adding All Direct and Indirect Costs Assigned to the Job. Exhibit 4-2 shows that the total manufacturing costs of the WPP job are Rs 97,050

Direct manufacturing costs		
Direct materials	Rs 46,060	
Direct manufacturing labor	15,790	Rs 61,850
Manufacturing overhead costs		
(Rs 400 per direct manuf. labor-hour × 88 hours)		35,200
Total manufacturing costs of job WPP 298		Rs 97,050

Recall that HEC bid a price of Rs 1,50,000 for the job. At that revenue, the actual-costing system shows a gross margin of Rs 52,950 (Rs 1,50,000 − Rs 97,050) and a gross-margin percentage of 35.3% (Rs 52,950 ÷ Rs 1,50,000 = 0.35).

HEC's manufacturing managers and sales managers can use the gross-margin and gross-margin percentage calculations to compare the profitability of different jobs see the following Concepts in Action to try to understand the reasons why some jobs show low

Exhibit 4-4

Job-Costing Overview for Determining Manufacturing Costs of Jobs at HEC Company

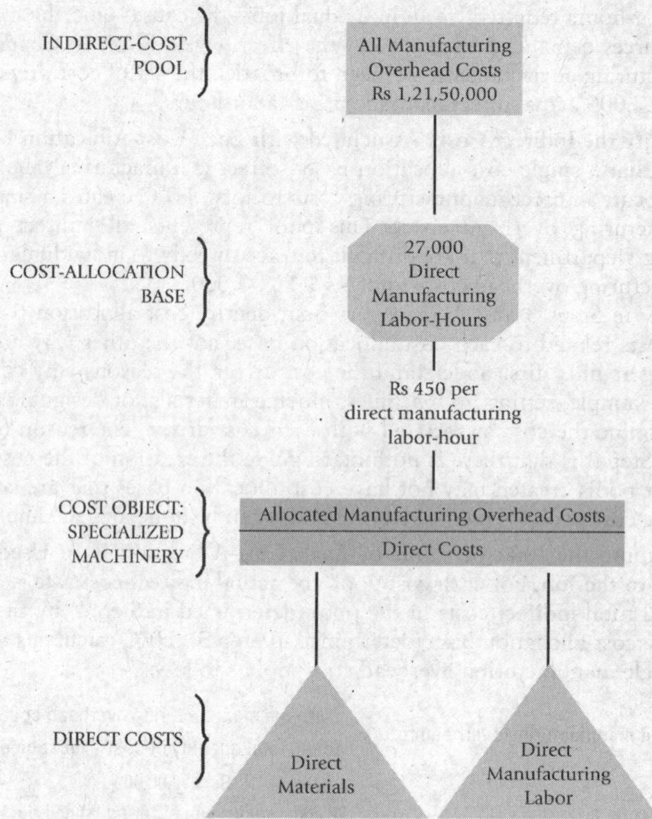

profitability. Have direct materials been wasted? Was direct manufacturing labor too high? Were there ways to improve the efficiency of these jobs? Were these jobs simply underpriced? Job-cost analysis provides the information needed for judging the performance of manufacturing and sales managers and for making future improvements. (see Concepts in Action the following).

Exhibit 4-4 is an overview of HEC's job-costing system. This exhibit represents the concepts comprising the five building blocks—cost object, direct costs of a cost object, indirect costs of a cost object, indirect-cost pool, and cost-allocation base—of job-costing systems that were first introduced at the beginning of this chapter. Costing-system overviews such as Exhibit 4-4 are important learning tools. We urge you to sketch one when you need to understand a costing system in manufacturing, merchandising, or service companies. (The symbols in Exhibit 4-4 are used consistently in the costing-system overviews presented in this book. A triangle always identifies a direct cost; a rectangle represents the indirect-cost pool; and an octagon describes the cost-allocation base.) Note the parallel between the overview diagram and the cost of the WPP 298 job described in Step 7. Exhibit 4-4 shows two direct-cost categories (direct materials and direct manufacturing labor) and one indirect-cost category (manufacturing overhead) used to allocate indirect costs. The costs in Step 7 also have three rupee amounts, each corresponding respectively to the two direct-cost and one indirect-cost categories.

The Role of Technology

To improve the efficiency of their operations, managers use costing information about products and jobs to control materials, labor, and overhead costs. Modern information technology provides managers with quick and accurate product-cost information, making it easier to manage and control jobs. For example, in many costing systems, source documents exist only in the form of computer records. We next describe bar coding and other forms of online information recording that reduce human intervention and improve the accuracy of the records of materials and labor time for individual jobs.

Concepts in Action

Job Costing on Cowboys Stadium

Over the years, fans of the National Football League have identified the Dallas Cowboys as "America's Team." Since 2009, however, the team known for winning five Super Bowls has become just as recognized for its futuristic new home, Cowboys Stadium in Arlington, Texas.

When the Cowboys take the field, understanding each week's game plan is critical for success. But for Manhattan Construction, the company that managed the development of the $1.2 billion Cowboys Stadium project, understanding costs is just as critical for making successful pricing decisions, winning contracts, and ensuring that each project is profitable. Each job is estimated individually because the unique end-products, whether a new stadium or an office building, demand different quantities of Manhattan Construction's resources.

In 2006, the Dallas Cowboys selected Manhattan Construction to lead the construction of its 73,000 seat, 3 million-square-foot stadium. To be completed in three years, the stadium design featured two monumental arches spanning about a quarter-mile in length over the dome, a retractable roof, the largest retractable glass doors in the world (in each end zone), canted glass exterior walls, 325 private suites, and a 600-ton JumboTron hovering 90 feet above the field.

With only 7% of football fans ever setting foot in a professional stadium, "Our main competition is the home media center," Cowboys owner Jerry Jones said in unveiling the stadium design in 2006. "We wanted to offer a real experience that you can't have at home, but to see it with the technology that you do have at home."

Generally speaking, the Cowboys Stadium project had five stages: (1) conceptualization, (2) design and planning, (3) preconstruction, (4) construction, and (5) finalization and delivery. During this 40-month process, Manhattan Construction hired architects and subcontractors, created blueprints, purchased and cleared land, developed the stadium—ranging from excavation to materials testing to construction—built out and finished interiors, and completed last-minute changes before the stadium's grand opening in mid-2009.

While most construction projects have distinct stages, compressed timeframes and scope changes required diligent management by Manhattan Construction. Before the first game was played, Manhattan Construction successfully navigated nearly 3,000 change requests and a constantly evolving budget.

To ensure proper allocation and accounting of resources, Manhattan Construction project managers used a job-costing system. The system first calculated the budgeted cost of more than 500 line items of direct materials and labor costs. It then allocated estimated overhead costs (supervisor salaries, rent, materials handling, and so on) to the job using direct material costs and direct labor-hours as allocation bases. Manhattan Construction's job-costing system allowed managers to track project variances on a weekly basis. Manhattan Construction continually estimated the profitability of the Cowboys Stadium project based on the percentage of work completed, insight gleaned from previous stadium projects, and revenue earned. Managers used the job-costing system to actively manage costs, while the Dallas Cowboys had access to clear, concise, and transparent costing data.

Just like quarterback Tony Romo navigating opposing defenses, Manhattan Construction was able to leverage its job-costing system to ensure the successful construction of a stadium as iconic as the blue star on the Cowboys' helmets.

Sources: Dillon, David. 2009. New Cowboys Stadium has grand design, but discipline isn't compromised *The Dallas Morning News*, June 3. http://www.dallasnews.com/sharedcontent/dws/ent/stories/DN-stadiumarchitecture_03gd.ART.State.Edition2.5125e7c.html; Knudson, Brooke. 2008. Profile: Dallas Cowboys Stadium. *Construction Today*, December 22. http://www.construction-today.com/cms1/content/view/1175/139/1/0/; Lacayo, Richard. 2009. Inside the new Dallas Cowboys stadium. *Time*, September 21. http://www.time.com/time/nation/article/0,8599,1924535,00.html; Penny, Mark, Project Manager, Manhattan Construction Co. 2010. Interview. January 12.

Consider, for example, direct materials charged to jobs for product-costing purposes. Managers control these costs as materials are purchased and used. Using Electronic Data Interchange (EDI) technology, companies like HEC order materials from their suppliers by clicking a few keys on a computer keyboard. EDI, an electronic computer link between a company and its suppliers, ensures that the order is transmitted quickly and accurately with minimum paperwork and costs. A bar code scanner records the receipt of incoming materials. The computer matches the receipt with the order, prints out a cHECk to the supplier, and records the material received. When an operator on the production floor transmits a request for materials via a computer terminal, the computer prepares a materials-requisition record, instantly recording the issue of materials in the materials and job-cost records. Each day, the computer sums the materials-requisition records charged to a particular job or manufacturing department. A performance report is then prepared comparing budgeted costs and actual costs of direct materials. Direct material usage can be reported hourly—if the benefits exceed the cost of such frequent reporting.

Similarly, information about direct manufacturing labor is obtained as employees log into computer terminals and key in the job numbers, their employee numbers, and start and end times of their work on different jobs. The computer automatically prints the labor time record and, using hourly rates stored for each employee, calculates the direct manufacturing labor costs of individual jobs. Information technology also provides managers with instantaneous feedback to help control manufacturing overhead costs, jobs in process, jobs completed, and jobs shipped and installed at customer sites.

Actual Costing

Learning Objective 5

Distinguish actual costing

. . . actual costing uses actual indirect-cost rates

from normal costing

. . . normal costing uses budgeted indirect-cost rates

How would the cost of Job WPP 298 change if HEC had used actual costing rather than normal costing? Both actual costing and normal costing trace direct costs to jobs in the same way because source documents identify the actual quantities and actual rates of direct materials and direct manufacturing labor for a job as the work is being done. The only difference between costing a job with normal costing and actual costing is that normal costing uses *budgeted* indirect-cost rates, whereas actual costing uses *actual* indirect-cost rates calculated annually at the end of the year. Exhibit 4-5 distinguishes actual costing from normal costing.

The following actual data for 2011 are for HEC's manufacturing operations:

	Actual
Total manufacturing overhead costs	Rs 1,21,50,000
Total direct manufacturing labor-hours	2,70,000

Steps 1 and 2 are exactly as before: Step 1 identifies WPP 298 as the cost object; Step 2 calculates actual direct material costs of Rs 46,060, and actual direct manufacturing labor costs of Rs 15,790. Recall from Step 3 that HEC uses a single cost-allocation base, direct manufacturing labor-hours, to allocate all manufacturing overhead costs to jobs. The actual quantity of direct manufacturing labor-hours for 2011 is 27,000 hours. In Step 4, HEC groups all actual indirect manufacturing costs of Rs 1,21,50,000 into a single manufacturing overhead cost pool. In Step 5, the **actual indirect-cost rate** is calculated by dividing actual total indirect costs in the pool (determined in Step 4) by the actual total quantity of the cost-allocation base (determined in Step 3). HEC calculates the actual manufacturing overhead rate in 2011 for its single manufacturing overhead cost pool as follows:

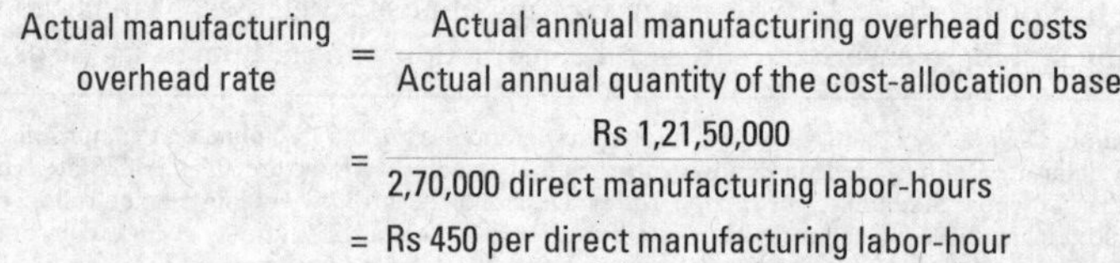

$$\text{Actual manufacturing overhead rate} = \frac{\text{Actual annual manufacturing overhead costs}}{\text{Actual annual quantity of the cost-allocation base}}$$
$$= \frac{\text{Rs } 1{,}21{,}50{,}000}{2{,}70{,}000 \text{ direct manufacturing labor-hours}}$$
$$= \text{Rs } 450 \text{ per direct manufacturing labor-hour}$$

In Step 6, under an actual-costing system,

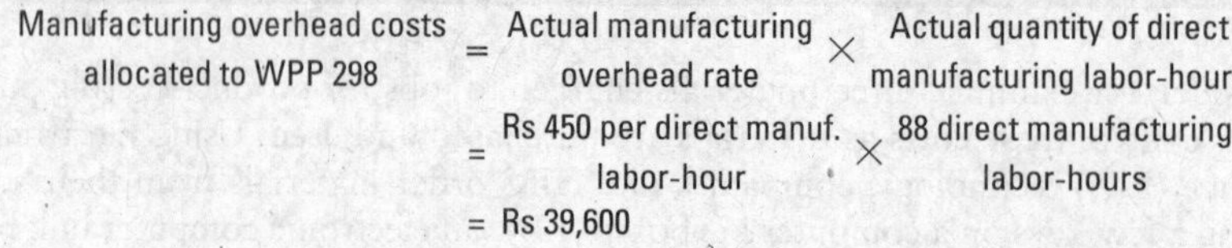

$$\text{Manufacturing overhead costs allocated to WPP 298} = \text{Actual manufacturing overhead rate} \times \text{Actual quantity of direct manufacturing labor-hours}$$
$$= \text{Rs } 450 \text{ per direct manuf. labor-hour} \times 88 \text{ direct manufacturing labor-hours}$$
$$= \text{Rs } 39{,}600$$

Exhibit 4-5

Actual Costing and Normal Costing Methods

	Actual Costing	Normal Costing
Direct Costs	*Actual direct-cost rates* × actual quantities of direct-cost inputs	*Actual direct-cost rates* × actual quantities of direct-cost inputs
Indirect Costs	*Actual indirect-cost rates* × actual quantities of cost-allocation bases	*Budgeted indirect-cost rates* × actual quantities of cost-allocation bases

In Step 7, the cost of the job under actual costing is Rs 1,01,450, calculated as follows:

Direct manufacturing costs		
Direct materials	Rs 46,060	
Direct manufacturing labor	15,790	Rs 61,850
Manufacturing overhead costs		
(Rs 450 per direct manufacturing labor-hour × 88 actual direct manufacturing labor-hours)		39,600
Total manufacturing costs of job		Rs1,01,450

The manufacturing cost of the WPP 298 job is higher by Rs 4,400 under actual costing (Rs 1,01,450) than it is under normal costing (Rs 97,050) because the actual indirect-cost rate is Rs 450 per hour, whereas the budgeted indirect-cost rate is Rs 400 per hour. That is, (Rs 450 – Rs 400) × 88 actual direct manufacturing labor-hours = Rs 4,400.

As we discussed previously, manufacturing costs of a job are available much earlier under a normal-costing system. Consequently, HEC's manufacturing and sales managers can evaluate the profitability of different jobs, the efficiency with which the jobs are done, and the pricing of different jobs as soon as the jobs are completed, while the experience is still fresh in everyone's mind. Another advantage of normal costing is that corrective actions can be implemented much sooner. At the end of the year, though, costs allocated using normal costing will not, in general, equal actual costs incurred. If material, adjustments will need to be made so that the cost of jobs and the costs in various inventory accounts are based on actual rather that normal costing. We describe these adjustments later in the chapter.

Decision Point

How do you distinguish actual costing from normal costing?

A Normal Job-Costing System in Manufacturing

Track the flow of costs in a job-costing system

. . . from purchase of materials to sale of finished goods

We now explain how a normal job-costing system operates in manufacturing. Continuing with the HEC example, the following illustration considers events that occurred in February 2011. Before getting into details, study Exhibit 4-6, which provides a broad framework for understanding the flow of costs in job costing.

The upper part of Exhibit 4-6 shows the flow of inventoriable costs from the purchase of materials and other manufacturing inputs, to their conversion into work-in-process and finished goods, to the sale of finished goods.

Direct materials used and direct manufacturing labor can be easily traced to jobs. They become part of work-in-process inventory on the balance sheet because direct manufacturing labor transforms direct materials into another asset, work-in-process inventory. HEC also incurs manufacturing overhead costs (including indirect materials and indirect manufacturing labor) to convert direct materials into work-in-process inventory. These overhead (indirect) costs, however, cannot be easily traced to individual jobs. Manufacturing overhead costs, therefore, are first accumulated in a manufacturing overhead account and then allocated to individual jobs. As manufacturing overhead costs are allocated, they become part of work-in-process inventory.

As individual jobs are completed, work-in-process inventory becomes another balance sheet asset, finished goods inventory. Only when finished goods are sold is an expense, cost of goods sold, recognized in the income statement and matched against revenues earned.

The lower part of Exhibit 4-6 shows the period costs—marketing and customer-service costs. These costs do not create any assets on the balance sheet because they are not incurred to transform materials into a finished product. Instead, they are expensed in the income statement as they are incurred to best match revenues.

We next describe the entries made in the general ledger.

General Ledger

You know by this point that a job-costing system has a separate job-cost record for each job. A summary of the job-cost record is typically found in a subsidiary ledger. The general ledger account Work-in-Process Control presents the total of these separate job-cost

Exhibit 4-6 Flow of Costs in Job Costing

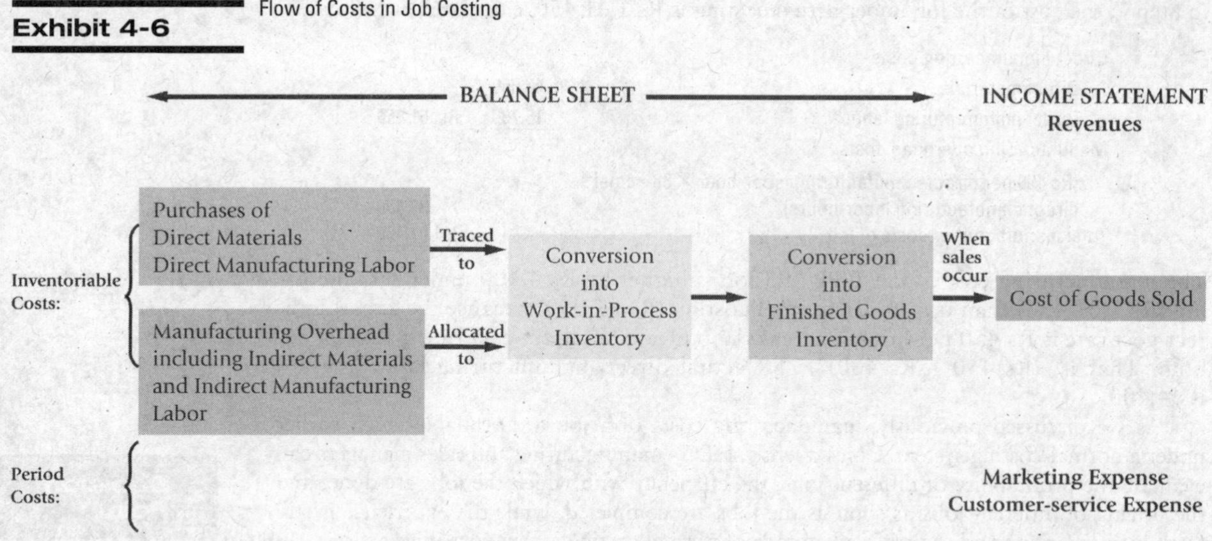

records pertaining to all unfinished jobs. The job-cost records and Work-in-Process Control account track job costs from when jobs start until they are complete.

Exhibit 4-7 shows T-account relationships for HEC's general ledger. The general ledger gives a "bird's-eye view" of the costing system. The amounts shown in Exhibit 4-7

Exhibit 4-7 Manufacturing Job-Costing System Using Normal Costing: Diagram of General Ledger Relationships for February 2011

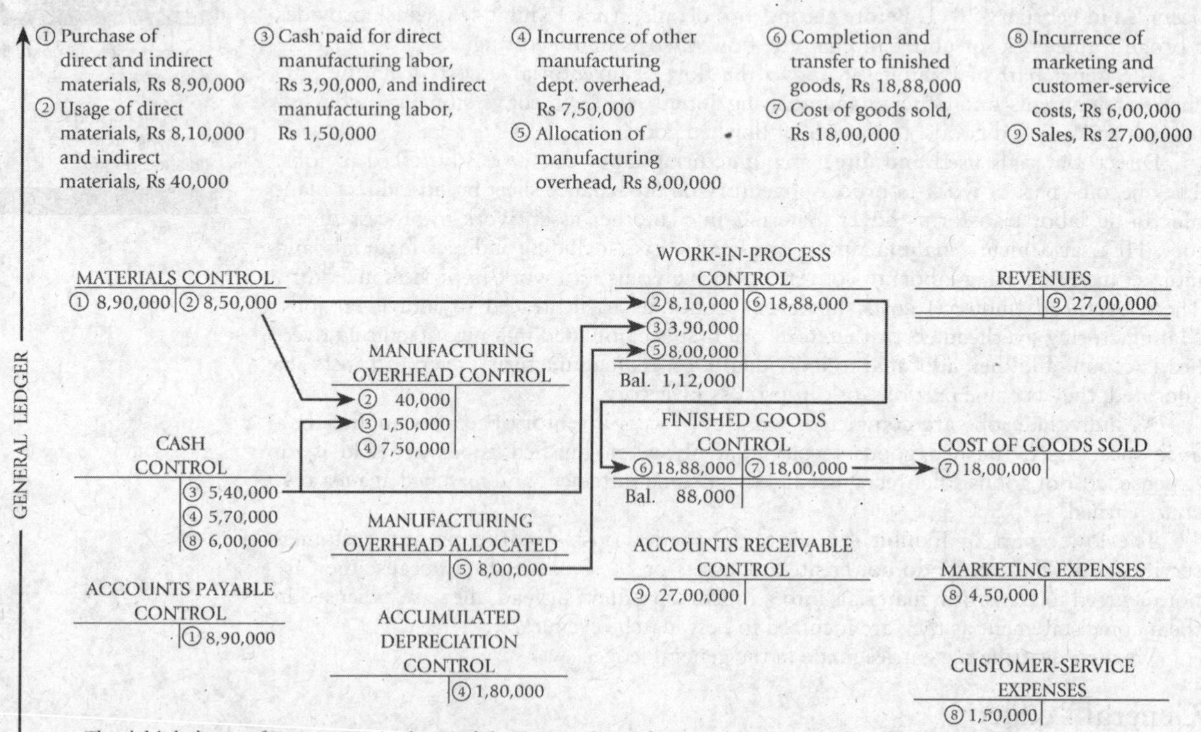

The debit balance of Rs 1,12,000 in the Work-in-Process Control account represents the total cost of all jobs that have not been completed as of the end of February 2008.

The debit balance of Rs 88,000 in the Finished Goods Control account represents the cost of all jobs that have been completed but not sold as of the end of February 2008.

are based on the transactions and journal entries that follow. As you go through each journal entry, use Exhibit 4-7 to see how the various entries being made come together. General ledger accounts with "Control" in the titles (for example, Materials Control and Accounts Payable Control) have underlying subsidiary ledgers that contain additional details, such as each type of material in inventory and individual suppliers that HEC must pay.

Software programs process the transactions in most accounting systems. Some programs make general ledger entries simultaneously with entries in the subsidiary ledger accounts. Other software programs make general ledger entries at, say, weekly or monthly intervals, with entries in the subsidiary ledger accounts made more frequently. The HEC makes entries in its subsidiary ledger when transactions occur and then makes entries in its general ledger on a monthly basis.

A general ledger should be viewed as only one of many tools that assist management in planning and control. To control operations, managers rely on not only the source documents used to record amounts in the subsidiary ledgers, but also nonfinancial information such as the percentage of jobs requiring rework.

Explanations of Transactions

We next look at a summary of HEC's transactions for February 2011 and the corresponding journal entries for those transactions.

1. Purchases of materials (direct and indirect) on credit, Rs 8,90,000

Materials Control	8,90,000	
Accounts Payable Control		8,90,000

2. Usage of direct materials, Rs 8,10,000 and indirect materials, Rs 40,000

Work-in-Process Control	8,10,000	
Manufacturing Overhead Control	40,000	
Materials Control		8,50,000

3. Manufacturing payroll for February: direct labor, Rs 3,90,000 and indirect labor, Rs 1,50,000 paid in cash

Work-in- Process Control	3,90,000	
Manufacturing Overhead Control	1,50,000	
Cash Control		5,40,000

4. Other manufacturing overhead costs incurred during February, Rs 7,50,000, consisting of supervision and engineering salaries, Rs 4,40,000 (paid in cash); plant utilities, repairs, and insurance, Rs 1,30,000 (paid in cash); and plant depreciation, Rs 1,80,000

Manufacturing Overhead Control	7,50,000	
Cash Control		5,70,000
Accumulated Depreciation Control		1,80,000

5. Allocation of manufacturing overhead to jobs, Rs 8,00,000

Work-in-Process Control	8,00,000	
Manufacturing Overhead Allocated		8,00,000

Under normal costing, **manufacturing overhead allocated**—also called **manufacturing overhead applied**—is the amount of manufacturing overhead costs allocated to individual jobs based on the budgeted rate multiplied by actual quantity used of the allocation base. Manufacturing overhead allocated contains all manufacturing overhead costs. They are assigned to jobs using a cost-allocation base because these costs cannot be traced specifically to jobs in an economically feasible way.

Keep in mind the distinct difference between transactions 4 and 5. In transaction 4, actual overhead costs incurred throughout the month are added (debited) to the Manufacturing Overhead Control account. These costs are not debited to Work-in-Process Control. Manufacturing overhead costs are added (debited) to Work-in-Process Control *only when* manufacturing overhead costs are allocated in transaction 5. At the time these costs are allocated, Manufacturing Overhead Control is, *in effect,* decreased (credited) via its contra account, Manufacturing Overhead Allocated. Under the normal-costing system described in our illustration, the budgeted manufacturing overhead rate of Rs 400 per direct manufacturing labor-hour is calculated at the beginning of the year on the basis of predictions of annual manufacturing overhead costs and the annual quantity of the cost-allocation base. Almost certainly, the actual amounts allocated will differ from the predictions. In a later section, we discuss what to do with this difference.

6. Completion and transfer of individual jobs to finished goods, Rs 18,88,000

Finished Goods Control	18,88,000	
Work-in- Process Control		18,88,000

7. Cost of goods sold, Rs 18,00,000

Cost of Goods Sold	18,00,000	
Finished Goods Control		18,00,000

8. Marketing costs for February, Rs 4,50,000 and customer service costs for February Rs 1,50,000, paid in cash

Marketing Expenses	4,50,000	
Customer Service Expenses	1,50,000	
Cash Control		6,00,000

9. Sales revenues, all on credit, Rs 27,00,000

Accounts Receivable Control	27,00,000	
Revenues		27,00,000

Subsidiary Ledgers

Exhibits 4-8 and 4-9 present subsidiary ledgers that contain the underlying details—the "worm's-eye view" as opposed to the "bird's-eye view" of the general ledger—such as each type of materials in inventory and costs accumulated in individual jobs. The sum of

Exhibit 4-8 Subsidiary Ledger for Materials, Labor, and Manufacturing Department Overhead[1]

PANEL A: Materials Records by Type of Materials

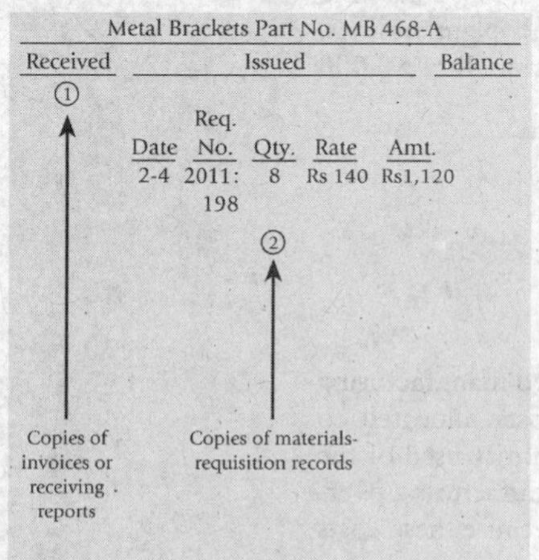

Total cost of all types of materials received in February, Rs 8,90,000

Total cost of all types of materials issued in February, Rs 8,50,000

PANEL B: Labor Records by Employee

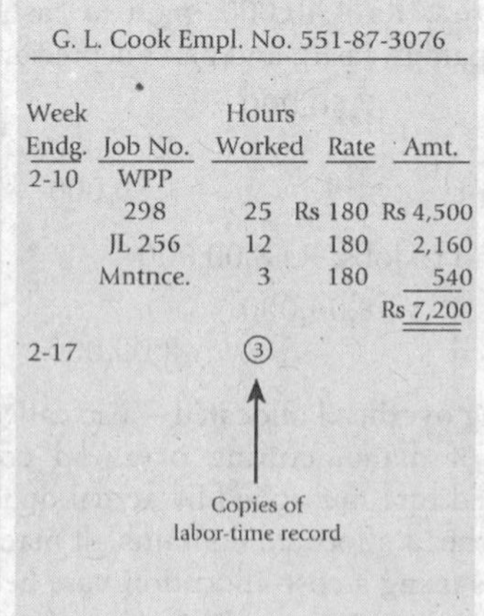

Total cost of all direct and indirect manufacturing labor incurred in February, Rs 5,40,000 (Rs 3,90,000 + Rs 1,50,000)

PANEL C: Manufacturing Department Overhead Records by Month

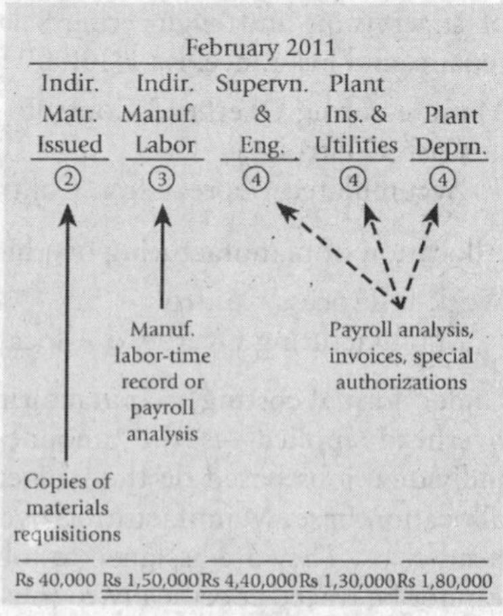

Other manufacturing overhead costs incurred in February, Rs 7,50,000

[1]The arrows show how the supporting documentation (for example, copies of materials requisition records) results in the journal entry number shown in circles (for example, journal entry number 2) that corresponds to the entries in Exhibit 4-7.

Exhibit 4-9 Subsidiary Ledger for Individual Jobs[1]

PANEL A: Work-in-Process Inventory Records by Jobs

Job No. WPP 298

	In-Process				Completed		Balance	
Date	Direct Materials	Direct Manuf. Labor	Allocated Manuf. Overhead	Total Cost	Date	Total Cost	Date	Total Cost
2-4	Rs 1,120			Rs 1,120				
2-10		Rs 4,500		Rs 4,500				
	•	•		•				
2-28	Rs 46,060	Rs 15,790	Rs 35,200	Rs 97,050	2-28	Rs 97,050	2-28	Rs 0
	②	③	⑤			⑥		
	Copies of materials-requisition records	Copies of labor-time records	Budgeted rate × actual direct manuf. labor-hours			Completed job-cost record		

Total cost of direct materials issued to all jobs in Feb., Rs 8,10,000

Total cost of direct manuf. labor used on all jobs in Feb., Rs 3,90,000

Total manuf. overhead allocated to all jobs in Feb., Rs 8,00,000

Total cost of all jobs completed and transferred to finished goods in Feb., Rs 18,88,000

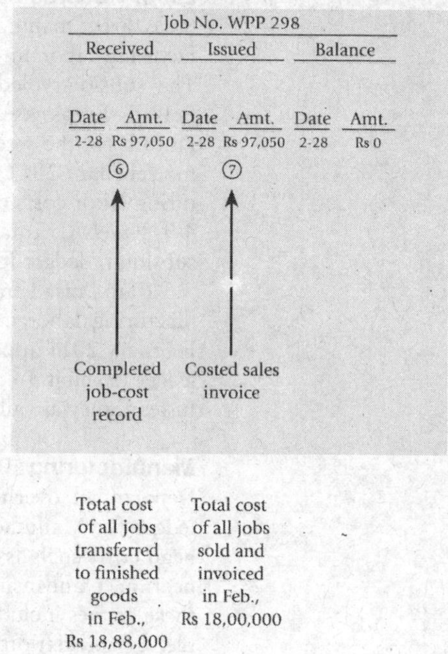

PANEL B: Finished Goods Inventory Records by Job

Job No. WPP 298

Received		Issued		Balance	
Date	Amt.	Date	Amt.	Date	Amt.
2-28	Rs 97,050	2-28	Rs 97,050	2-28	Rs 0
	⑥		⑦		
	Completed job-cost record		Costed sales invoice		

Total cost of all jobs transferred to finished goods in Feb., Rs 18,88,000

Total cost of all jobs sold and invoiced in Feb., Rs 18,00,000

[1]The arrows show how the supporting documentation (for example, copies of materials requisition records) results in the journal entry number shown in circles (for example, journal entry number 2) that corresponds to the entries in Exhibit 4-7.

all entries in underlying subsidiary ledgers equals the total amount in the corresponding general ledger control accounts.

Material Records by Type of Materials The subsidiary ledger for materials at HEC—called *Materials Records*—keeps a continuous record of quantity received, quantity issued to jobs, and inventory balances for each type of material. Panel A of Exhibit 4-8 shows the Materials Record for Metal Brackets (Part No. MB 468-A). In many companies, the source documents supporting the receipt and issue of materials are scanned into a computer. Software programs then automatically update the Materials Records and make all the necessary accounting entries in the subsidiary and general ledgers.

As direct materials are used, they are recorded as issued in the Materials Records (see Exhibit 4-8, Panel A, for a record of the Metal Brackets issued for the Western Pulp and Paper [WPP] machine job). Direct materials are also charged to individual job records, which are the subsidiary ledger accounts for the Work-in-Process Control account in the general ledger. For example, the metal brackets used in the WPP machine job appear as direct material costs of Rs 1,120 in the subsidiary ledger under the job-cost record for WPP 298 (Exhibit 4-9, Panel A). The cost of direct materials used across all job-cost records for February 2008 is Rs 8,10,000 (Exhibit 4-9, Panel A).

As indirect materials (for example, lubricants) are used, they are charged to the Manufacturing Department overhead records (Exhibit 4-8, Panel C), which comprise the subsidiary ledger for Manufacturing Overhead Control. The Manufacturing Department overhead records accumulate actual costs in individual overhead categories by each indirect-cost-pool account in the general ledger. Recall that HEC has only one indirect-cost pool: Manufacturing Overhead. The cost of indirect materials used is not added directly to individual job records. Instead, the cost of these indirect materials is allocated to individual job records as a part of manufacturing overhead.

Labor Records by Employee Labor-time records (see Exhibit 4-8, Panel B) are used to trace direct manufacturing labor to individual jobs and to accumulate the indirect manufacturing labor in Manufacturing Department overhead records (Exhibit 4-8, Panel C). The subsidiary ledger for employee labor records shows the different jobs that Ram Prasad, Employee No. 551-87-3076 worked on and the Rs 7,200 of wages owed to Prasad, for the week ending February 10. The sum of total wages owed to all employees for February 2011 is Rs 40,000. The job-cost record for WPP 298 shows direct manufacturing labor costs of Rs 4,500 for the time Prasad spent on the WPP machine job (Exhibit 4-9, Panel A). Total direct manufacturing labor costs recorded in all job-cost records (the subsidiary ledger for Work-in-Process Control) for February 2011 is Rs 3,90,000.

Ram Prasad employee record shows Rs 540 for maintenance, which is an indirect manufacturing labor cost. The total indirect manufacturing labor costs of Rs 1,50,000 for February 2011 appear in the Manufacturing Department overhead records in the subsidiary ledger (Exhibit 4-8, Panel C). These costs, by definition, are not traced to an individual job. Instead, they are allocated to individual jobs as a part of manufacturing overhead.

Manufacturing Department Overhead Records by Month The Manufacturing Department overhead records (see Exhibit 4-8, Panel C) that make up the subsidiary ledger for Manufacturing Overhead Control show details of different categories of overhead costs such as indirect materials, indirect manufacturing labor, supervision and engineering, plant insurance and utilities, and plant depreciation. The source documents for these entries include invoices (for example, a utility bill) and special schedules (for example, a depreciation schedule) from the responsible accounting officer.

Work-in-Process Inventory Records by Jobs As we have already discussed, the job-cost record for each individual job in the subsidiary ledger will be debited by the cost of direct materials and direct manufacturing labor used by individual jobs. The job-cost record for each individual job in the subsidiary ledger will also be debited for manufacturing overhead allocated for the actual direct manufacturing labor-hours used in that job. For example, the job-cost record for Job WPP 298 (Exhibit 4-9, Panel A) shows Manufacturing Overhead Allocated of Rs 35,200 (budgeted rate of Rs 400 per labor-hour × 88 actual direct manufacturing labor-hours used). We assume 2,000 actual direct manufacturing labor-hours were used for all jobs in February 2008, resulting in a total manufacturing overhead allocation of Rs 400 per labor-hour × 2,000 direct manufacturing labor-hours = Rs 8,00,000.

Finished Goods Inventory Records by Jobs Exhibit 4-9, Panel A, shows that Job WPP 298 was completed at a cost of Rs 97,050 Job WPP 298 also simultaneously appears in the finished goods records of the subsidiary ledger. Given HEC's use of normal costing, cost of goods completed consists of actual direct materials, actual direct manufacturing labor, and manufacturing overhead allocated to each job based on the budgeted manufacturing overhead rate times actual direct manufacturing labor-hours.

Exhibit 4-9, Panel B, indicates that Job WPP 298 was sold and delivered to the customer on February 28, 2011.

Other Subsidiary Records Just as in the case of the manufacturing payroll, HEC maintains employee labor records in subsidiary ledgers for marketing and customer service payroll as well as records for different types of advertising costs (print, television, and radio). An accounts receivable subsidiary ledger is also used to record the February 2011 amounts due from each customer, including the Rs 1,50,000 due from the sale of Job WPP 298.

At this point, pause and review the nine entries in this illustration. Exhibit 4-7 is a handy summary of all nine general-ledger entries presented in T-account form. Be sure to trace each journal entry, step-by-step, to T-accounts in the general ledger presented in Exhibit 4-7.

Revenues		Rs 27,00,000
Cost of goods sold (Rs 18,00,000 + Rs 1,40,000)		19,40,000
Gross margin		7,60,000
Operating costs		
Marketing costs	Rs 4,50,000	
Customer-service costs	1,50,000	
Total operating costs		6,00,000
Operating income		Rs 1,60,000

[1]Cost of goods sold has been increased by Rs 1,40,000 the difference between the Manufacturing overhead control account (Rs 9,40,000) and the Manufacturing overhead allocated (Rs 8,00,000). In a later section of this chapter, we discuss this adjustment, which represents the amount by which actual manufacturing overhead cost exceeds the manufacturing overhead allocated to jobs during February 2011.

Exhibit 4-10

HEC Income Statement for the Month Ending February 2011

Exhibit 4-10 provides HEC's income statement for February 2011 using information from entries 7, 8, and 9. If desired, the cost of goods sold calculations can be further subdivided and presented in the format of Exhibit 2-8.

Nonmanufacturing Costs and Job Costing Chapter 2 pointed out that companies use product costs for different purposes. The product costs reported as inventoriable costs to shareholders may differ from product costs reported for government contracting and may also differ from product costs reported to managers for guiding pricing and product-mix decisions. We emphasize that even though, as described previously, marketing and customer-service costs are expensed when incurred for financial accounting purposes, companies often trace or allocate these costs to individual jobs for pricing, product-mix, and cost-management decisions.

Decision Point

How are transactions recorded in a manufacturing job-costing system?

To identify marketing and customer-service costs of individual jobs, HEC can use the same approach to job costing described earlier in this chapter in the context of manufacturing. HEC can trace the direct marketing costs and customer-service costs to jobs. Assume marketing and customer-service costs have the same cost-allocation base, revenues, and are included in a single cost pool. HEC can then calculate a budgeted indirect-cost rate by dividing budgeted indirect marketing costs plus budgeted indirect customer-service costs by budgeted revenues. HEC can use this rate to allocate these indirect costs to jobs. For example, if this rate were 15% of revenues, HEC would allocate Rs 22,500 to Job WPP 298 (0.15 × Rs 1,50,000, the revenue from the job). By assigning both manufacturing costs and nonmanufacturing costs to jobs, HEC can compare all costs against the revenues that different jobs generate.

Budgeted Indirect Costs and End-of-Accounting-Year Adjustments

Learning Objective 7

Dispose of under- or overallocated manufacturing overhead costs at the end of the fiscal year using alternative methods

. . . for example, writing off this amount to the Cost of Goods Sold account

Using budgeted indirect-cost rates and normal costing instead of actual costing has the advantage that indirect costs can be assigned to individual jobs on an ongoing and timely basis, rather than only at the end of the fiscal year when actual costs are known. However, budgeted rates are unlikely to equal actual rates because they are based on estimates made up to 12 months before actual costs are incurred. We now consider adjustments that are needed when, at the end of the fiscal year, indirect costs allocated differ from actual indirect costs incurred. Recall that for the numerator and denominator reasons discussed earlier, we do *not* expect actual overhead costs incurred each month to equal overhead costs allocated each month.

Underallocated and Overallocated Direct Costs

Underallocated indirect costs occur when the allocated amount of indirect costs in an accounting period is less than the actual (incurred) amount. **Overallocated indirect costs**

occur when the allocated amount of indirect costs in an accounting period is greater than the actual (incurred) amount.

Underallocated (overallocated) indirect costs = Actual indirect costs incurred − Indirect costs allocated

Underallocated (overallocated) indirect costs are also called **underapplied (overapplied) indirect costs** and **underabsorbed (overabsorbed) indirect costs.**

Consider the manufacturing overhead indirect-cost pool at HEC. There are two indirect-cost accounts in the general ledger that have to do with manufacturing overhead:

1. Manufacturing Overhead Control, the record of the actual costs in all the individual overhead categories (such as indirect materials, indirect manufacturing labor, supervision, engineering, utilities, and plant depreciation)
2. Manufacturing Overhead Allocated, the record of the manufacturing overhead allocated to individual jobs on the basis of the budgeted rate multiplied by actual direct manufacturing labor-hours

Assume the following annual data for the HEC Company:

Manufacturing Overhead Control			Manufacturing Overhead Allocated	
Bal. Dec 31, 2011	1,21,50,000		Bal. Dec 31, 2011	1,08,00,000

The Rs 1,08,00,000 credit balance in Manufacturing Overhead Allocated results from multiplying the 27,000 actual direct manufacturing labor-hours worked on all jobs in 2008 by the budgeted rate of Rs 400 per direct manufacturing labor-hour.

The Rs 13,50,000 difference (a net debit) is an underallocated amount because actual manufacturing overhead costs are greater than the allocated amount. This difference arises from two reasons related to the computation of the Rs 400 budgeted hourly rate:

1. **Numerator reason (indirect-cost pool).** Actual manufacturing overhead costs of Rs 1,21,50,000 are greater than the budgeted amount of Rs 1,12,00,000.
2. **Denominator reason (quantity of allocation base).** Actual direct manufacturing labor-hours of 27,000 are fewer than the budgeted 28,000 hours.

There are three main approaches to accounting for the Rs 13,50,000 underallocated manufacturing overhead caused by HEC underestimating manufacturing overhead costs and overestimating the quantity of the cost-allocation base: (1) adjusted allocation-rate approach, (2) proration approach, and (3) write-off to cost of goods sold approach.

Adjusted Allocation-Rate Approach

The **adjusted allocation-rate approach** restates all overhead entries in the general ledger and subsidiary ledgers using actual cost rates rather than budgeted cost rates. First, the actual manufacturing overhead rate is computed at the end of the fiscal year. Then, the manufacturing overhead costs allocated to every job during the year are recomputed using the actual manufacturing overhead rate (rather than the budgeted manufacturing overhead rate). Finally, end-of-year closing entries are made. The result is that at year-end, every job-cost record and finished goods record—as well as the ending Work-in-Process Control, Finished Goods Control, and Cost of Goods Sold accounts—represent actual manufacturing overhead costs incurred.

The widespread adoption of computerized accounting systems has greatly reduced the cost of using the adjusted allocation-rate approach. Consider the HEC example. The actual manufacturing overhead (Rs 1,21,50,000) exceeds the manufacturing overhead allocated (Rs 1,08,00,000) by 12.5% [(Rs 1,21,50,000 − Rs 1,08,00,000) ÷ Rs 1,08,00,000]. At year-end, HEC could increase the manufacturing overhead allocated to each job in 2008 by 12.5% using a single software command. The command would adjust both the subsidiary ledgers and the general ledger.

Consider the Western Pulp and Paper machine job, WPP 298. Under normal costing, the manufacturing overhead allocated to the job is Rs 35,200 (the budgeted rate of Rs 400 per direct manufacturing labor-hour × 88 hours). Increasing the manufacturing overhead allocated by 12.5%, or Rs 4,400 (Rs 35,200 × 0.125), means the adjusted amount of manufacturing overhead allocated to Job WPP 298 equals Rs 39,600 (Rs 35,200 + Rs 4,400). Note from page 117 that using actual costing, manufacturing overhead allocated to this job is also Rs 39,600 (the actual rate of Rs 450 per direct manufacturing labor-hour × 88 hours). Making this adjustment under normal costing for each job in the subsidiary ledgers ensures that all Rs 1,21,50,000 of manufacturing overhead is allocated to jobs.

The adjusted allocation-rate approach yields the benefits of both the *timeliness and convenience of normal costing during the year and the allocation of actual manufacturing overhead costs at year-end.* Each individual job-cost record and the end-of-year account balances for inventories and cost of goods sold are adjusted to actual costs. After-the-fact analysis of actual profitability of individual jobs provides managers with accurate and useful insights for future decisions about job pricing, which jobs to emphasize, and ways to manage job costs.

Proration Approach

Proration spreads underallocated overhead or overallocated overhead among ending work in process inventory, finished goods inventory, and cost of goods sold. Materials inventory is not included in this proration because no manufacturing overhead costs have been allocated to it. In our HEC example, end-of-year proration is made to the ending balances in Work-in-Process Control, Finished Goods Control, and Cost of Goods Sold. Assume the following actual results for HEC in 2011:

	A	B	C
1	Account	Account Balance (Before Proration)	Allocated Manufacturing Overhead Included in Each Account Balance (Before Proration)
2	Work in process control	Rs 5,00,000	Rs 1,62,000
3	Finished goods control	7,50,000	3,13,200
4	Cost of goods sold	2,37,50,000	1,03,24,800
5		Rs 2,50,00,000	Rs 1,08,00,000

How should HEC prorate the underallocated Rs 13,50,000 of manufacturing overhead at the end of 2011?

HEC prorates underallocated or overallocated amounts on the basis of the total amount of manufacturing overhead allocated in 2011 (before proration) in the ending balances of Work-in-Process Control, Finished Goods Control, and Cost of Goods Sold. The Rs 13,50,000 underallocated overhead is prorated over the three affected accounts in proportion to their total amount of manufacturing overhead allocated (before proration) in column 2 of the following table, resulting in the ending balances (after proration) in column 5 at actual costs.

	A	B	C	D	E	F	G
10		Account Balance (Before Proration)	Allocated Manufacturing Overhead Included in Each Account Balance (Before Proration)	Allocated Manufacturing Overhead Included in Each Account Balance as a Percent of Total	Proration of Rs 13,50,000 of Underallocated Manufacturing Overhead		Account Balance (After Proration)
11	Account	(1)	(2)	(3) = (2) / Rs 1,08,00,000	(4) = (3) x Rs 13,50,000		(5) = (1) + (4)
12	Work in process control	Rs 5,00,000	Rs 1,62,000	1.5%	0.015 x Rs 13,50,000 =	Rs 20,250	Rs 5,20,250
13	Finished goods control	7,50,000	3,13,200	2.9%	0.029 x 13,50,000 =	39,150	7,89,150
14	Cost of goods sold	2,37,50,000	1,03,24,800	95.6%	0.956 x 13,50,000 =	12,90,600	2,50,40,600
15	Total	Rs 2,50,00,000	Rs 1,08,00,000	100.0%		Rs 13,50,000	Rs 2,63,50,000

Prorating on the basis of the manufacturing overhead allocated (before proration) results in allocating manufacturing overhead based on actual manufacturing overhead costs. Recall that the actual manufacturing overhead (Rs 1,21,50,000) exceeds the manufacturing overhead allocated (Rs 1,08,00,000) by 12.5%. The proration amounts in column 4 can also be derived by multiplying the balances in column 2 by 0.125. For example, the Rs 39,150 proration to Finished Goods is 0.125 × Rs 3,13,200. Adding these amounts effectively means allocating manufacturing overhead at 112.5% of what had been allocated before. The journal entry to record this proration is:

Work-in-Process Control	20,250	
Finished Goods Control	39,150	
Cost of Goods Sold	12,90,600	
Manufacturing Overhead Allocated	1,08,00,000	
Manufacturing Overhead Control		1,21,50,000

If manufacturing overhead had been overallocated, the Work-in-Process Control, Finished Goods Control, and Cost of Goods Sold accounts would be decreased (credited) instead of increased (debited).

This journal entry closes (brings to zero) the manufacturing overhead-related accounts and restates the 2008 ending balances for Work-in-Process Control, Finished Goods Control, and Cost of Goods Sold to what they would have been if actual manufacturing overhead rates had been used rather than budgeted manufacturing overhead rates. This method reports the same 2008 ending balances in the general ledger as the adjusted allocation-rate approach.

Some companies use the proration approach but base it on the column 1 amounts of the preceding table—that is, the ending balances of Work-in-Process Control, Finished Goods Control, and Cost of Goods Sold before proration. The following table shows that prorations based on ending account balances are not the same as the more-accurate prorations calculated earlier based on the amount of manufacturing overhead allocated to the accounts because the proportions of manufacturing overhead costs to total costs in these accounts are not the same.

However, proration based on ending balances is frequently justified as being an expedient way of approximating the more-accurate results from using indirect costs allocated.

	A	B	C	D	E	F
1		Account Balance (Before Proration)	Account Balance as a Percent of Total	Proration of Rs 13,50,000 of Underallocated Manufacturing Overhead		Account Balance (After Proration)
2	Account	(1)	(2) = (1) / Rs 2,50,00,000	(3) = (2) x Rs 13,50,000		(4) = (1) + (3)
3	Work in process control	Rs 5,00,000	2.0%	0.02 x Rs 13,50,000 =	Rs 27,000	Rs 5,27,000
4	Finished goods control	7,50,000	3.0%	0.03 x 13,50,000 =	40,500	7,90,500
5	Cost of goods sold	2,37,50,000	95.0%	0.95 x 13,50,000 =	12,82,500	2,50,32,500
6	Total	Rs 2,50,00,000	100.0%		Rs 13,50,000	Rs 2,63,50,000

Write-Off to Cost of Goods Sold Approach

Under this approach, the total under- or overallocated manufacturing overhead is included in this year's Cost of Goods Sold. For HEC, the journal entry would be:

Cost of Goods Sold	13,50,000	
Manufacturing Overhead Allocated	1,08,00,000	
Manufacturing Overhead Control		1,21,50,000

HEC two Manufacturing Overhead accounts are closed with the difference between them included in cost of goods sold. The Cost of Goods Sold account after the write-off equals Rs 2,51,00,000, the balance before the write-off of Rs 2,37,50,000 *plus the under-allocated* manufacturing overhead amount of Rs 13,50,000.

Choice Among Approaches

Which of these three approaches is the best one to use? In making this decision, managers should be guided by the causes for underallocation or overallocation and how the information will be used. Many management accountants, industrial engineers, and managers argue that to the extent that the under- or overallocated overhead cost measures inefficiency during the period, it should be written off to Cost of Goods Sold instead of being prorated. This line of reasoning argues for applying a combination of the write-off and proration methods. For example, the portion of the underallocated overhead cost that is due to inefficiency (say, because of excessive spending) and that could have been avoided should be written off to Cost of Goods Sold, whereas the portion that is unavoidable should be prorated. Unlike full proration, this approach avoids carrying the costs of inefficiency as part of inventory assets.

Proration should be based on the manufacturing overhead allocated component in the ending balances of Work-in-Process Control, Finished Goods Control, and Cost of Goods Sold. Prorating to each individual job (as in the adjusted allocation-rate approach) is useful if the goal is to develop the most accurate record of individual job costs for profitability analysis purposes.

For balance sheet and income statement reporting purposes, the write-off to Cost of Goods Sold is the simplest approach for dealing with under- or overallocated overhead. If the amount of under- or overallocated overhead is small—in comparison with total operating income or some other measure of materiality—the write-off to Cost of Goods Sold approach yields a good approximation to more-accurate, but more-complex, approaches. Companies are also becoming increasingly conscious of inventory control, and quantities of inventories are lower than they were in earlier years. As a result, cost of goods sold tends to be higher in relation to the rupee amount of work-in-process and finished goods inventories. Also, the inventory balances of job-costing companies are usually small because goods are often made in response to customer orders. Consequently, as is true in our HEC example, writing off, instead of prorating, under- or overallocated overhead is unlikely to result in significant distortions in financial statements.

The HEC illustration assumed that a single manufacturing overhead cost pool with direct manufacturing labor-hours as the cost-allocation base was appropriate for allocating all manufacturing overhead costs to jobs. Had HEC used multiple cost-allocation bases, such as direct manufacturing labor-hours and machine-hours, it would have created two cost pools and calculated two budgeted overhead rates: one based on direct manufacturing labor-hours and the other based on machine-hours to allocate overhead costs to jobs. The general ledger would contain Manufacturing Overhead Control and Manufacturing Overhead Allocated amounts for each cost pool. End-of-year adjustments for under- or overallocated overhead costs would then be made separately for each cost pool.

Multiple Overhead Cost Pools

The HEC illustration assumed that a single manufacturing overhead cost pool with direct manufacturing labor-hours as the cost-allocation base was appropriate for allocating all manufacturing overhead costs to jobs. HEC could have used multiple cost-allocation bases, say, direct manufacturing labor-hours and machine-hours, to allocate manufacturing overhead costs to jobs. But HEC would use multiple cost-allocation bases only if its managers believed that the benefits of the information generated by adding one or more pools (more-accurate costing and pricing of jobs and better ability to manage costs) exceeded the additional costs of that costing system. (We discuss these issues in Chapter 5.)

To implement a normal-costing system with two overhead cost pools, HEC would determine, say, the budgeted total direct manufacturing labor-hours and the budgeted total machine-hours for 2008, and identify the associated total budgeted overhead costs for each cost pool. It would then calculate two budgeted overhead rates, one based on direct manufacturing labor-hours and the other on machine-hours. Manufacturing overhead costs would be allocated to jobs using these two budgeted overhead rates and the actual direct manufacturing labor-hours and actual machine hours used by various jobs. The general ledger would contain Manufacturing Overhead Control and Manufacturing Overhead Allocated amounts for each cost pool. End-of-year adjustments for under- or overallocated overhead costs would then be made separately for each cost pool.

Variations from Normal Costing: A Service-Sector Example

Learning Objective 8

Apply variations from normal costing

. . . variations from normal costing use budgeted direct-cost rates

Job costing is also very useful in service industries such as accounting and consulting firms, advertising agencies, auto repair shops, and hospitals. In an accounting firm, each audit is a job. The costs of each audit are accumulated in a job-cost record, much like the document used by HEC, based on the seven-step approach described earlier. On the basis of labor-time records, direct labor costs of the professional staff—audit partners, audit managers, and audit staff—are traced to individual jobs. Other direct costs such as travel, out-of-town meals and lodging, phone, fax, and copying are also traced to jobs. The costs of secretarial support, office staff, rent, and depreciation of furniture and equipment are indirect costs because these costs cannot be traced to jobs in an economically feasible way. Indirect costs are allocated to jobs, for example, using a cost-allocation base such as number of professional labor-hours.

In some service organizations, a variation from normal costing is helpful because actual direct-labor costs—the largest component of total costs—can be difficult to trace to jobs as they are completed. For example, in our audit illustration, the actual direct-labor costs may include bonuses that become known only at the end of the year (a numerator reason). Also, the hours worked each period might vary significantly depending on the number of working days each month and the demand from clients (a denominator reason). In situations like these, a company needing timely information during the progress of an audit (and not wanting to wait until the end of the fiscal year) will use budgeted rates for some direct costs and budgeted rates for indirect costs. All budgeted rates are calculated at the start of the fiscal year. In contrast, normal costing uses actual cost rates for all direct costs and budgeted cost rates only for indirect costs.

The mechanics of using budgeted rates for direct costs are similar to the methods employed when using budgeted rates for indirect costs in normal costing. We illustrate this for Batliboi & Co, a public accounting firm. For 2011, Batliboi budgets total direct-labor costs of Rs 14,40,00,000, total indirect costs of Rs 12,96,00,000, and total direct (professional) labor-hours of 288,000. In this case,

$$\text{Budgeted direct-labor cost rate} = \frac{\text{Budgeted total direct-labor costs}}{\text{Budgeted total direct-labor hours}}$$

$$= \frac{\text{Rs } 14{,}40{,}00{,}000}{288{,}000 \text{ direct labor-hours}} = \text{Rs } 500 \text{ per direct labor-hour}$$

Assuming only one indirect-cost pool and total direct-labor costs as the cost-allocation base,

$$\text{Budgeted indirect cost rate} = \frac{\text{Budgeted total costs in indirect cost pool}}{\text{Budgeted total quantity of cost-allocation base (direct-labor costs)}}$$

$$= \frac{\text{Rs } 12{,}96{,}00{,}000}{\text{Rs } 14{,}40{,}00{,}000} = 0.90\text{, or } 90\% \text{ of direct-labor costs}$$

Suppose that in March 2011, an audit of Jaipur Golden Transport, a client of Batliboi, uses 800 direct labor-hours. Batliboi calculates the direct-labor costs of the Jaipur Golden Transport audit by multiplying the budgeted direct-labor cost rate, Rs 500 per direct labor-hour, by 800, the actual quantity of direct labor-hours. The indirect costs allocated to the Jaipur Golden Transport audit are determined by multiplying the budgeted indirect-cost rate (90%) by the direct-labor costs assigned to the job (Rs 4,00,000). Assuming no other direct costs for travel and the like, the cost of the Tracy Transport audit is:

Direct-labor costs, Rs 500 × 800	Rs 4,00,000
Indirect costs allocated, 90% × Rs 4,00,000	3,60,000
Total	Rs 7,60,000

At the end of the fiscal year, the direct costs traced to jobs using budgeted rates will generally not equal actual direct costs because the actual rate and the budgeted rate are developed at different times using different information. End-of-year adjustments for under- or overallocated direct costs would need to be made in the same way that adjustments are made for under- or overallocated indirect costs.

The Batliboi & Co example illustrates that all costing systems do not exactly match either the actual-costing system or the normal-costing system described earlier in the chapter. As another example, engineering consulting firms often have some actual direct costs (cost of making blueprints or fees paid to outside experts), other direct costs (professional labor costs) assigned to jobs using a budgeted rate, and indirect costs (engineering and office-support costs) allocated to jobs using a budgeted rate. Therefore, users of costing systems should be aware of the different systems that they may encounter.

Problem for Self-Study

You are asked to bring the following incomplete accounts of Thomson Press Ltd., up-to-date through January 31, 2012. Consider the data that appear in the T-accounts as well as the following information in items (a) through (j).

Thomson's normal-costing system has two direct-cost categories (direct material costs and direct manufacturing labor costs) and one indirect-cost pool (manufacturing overhead costs, which are allocated using direct manufacturing labor costs).

Materials Control		Wages Payable Control	
12-31-2011 Bal. 1,50,000			1-31-2012 Bal. 30,000
Work-in-Process Control		**Manufacturing Overhead Control**	
		1-31-2012 Bal. 5,70,000	
Finished Goods Control		**Costs of Goods Sold**	
12-31-2011 Bal. 2,00,000			

Additional Information:

a. Manufacturing overhead is allocated using a budgeted rate that is set every December. Management forecasts next year's manufacturing overhead costs and next year's direct manufacturing labor costs. The budget for 2012 is Rs 60,00,000 for manufacturing overhead costs and Rs 40,00,000 for direct manufacturing labor costs.

b. The only job unfinished on January 31, 2012, is No. 419, on which direct manufacturing labor costs are Rs 20,000 (125 direct manufacturing labor-hours) and direct material costs are Rs 80,000.

c. Total direct materials issued to production during January 2012 are Rs 9,00,000.

d. Cost of goods completed during January is Rs 18,00,000.

e. Materials inventory as of January 31, 2012, is Rs 2,00,000.

f. Finished goods inventory as of January 31, 2012, is Rs 1,50,000.

g. All plant workers earn the same wage rate. Direct manufacturing labor-hours used for January total 2,500 hours. Other labor costs total Rs 1,00,000.
h. The gross plant payroll paid in January equals Rs 5,20,000. Ignore withholdings.
i. All "actual" manufacturing overhead incurred during January has already been posted.
j. All materials are direct materials.

Required Calculate:

1. Materials purchased during January
2. Cost of Goods Sold during January
3. Direct manufacturing labor costs incurred during January
4. Manufacturing Overhead Allocated during January
5. Balance, Wages Payable Control, December 31, 2011
6. Balance, Work-in-Process Control, January 31, 2012
7. Balance, Work-in-Process Control, December 31, 2011
8. Manufacturing Overhead Underallocated or Overallocated for January 2012

Solution

Amounts from the T-accounts are labeled "(T)"

1. From Materials Control T-account, Materials purchased: Rs 9,00,000 (c) + Rs 2,00,000 (e) − Rs 1,50,000 (T) = Rs 9,50,000
2. From Finished Goods Control T-account, Cost of Goods Sold: Rs 2,00,000 (T) + Rs 18,00,000 (d) − Rs 1,50,000 (f) = Rs 18,50,000
3. Direct manufacturing wage rate: Rs 20,000 (b) ÷ 125 direct manufacturing labor-hours (b) = Rs 160 per direct manufacturing labor-hour
   Direct manufacturing labor costs: 2,500 direct manufacturing labor-hours (g) × Rs 160 per hour = Rs 4,00,000
4. Manufacturing overhead rate: Rs 60,00,000 (a) × Rs 40,00,000 (a) = 150%

Manufacturing Overhead Allocated: 150% of Rs 4,00,000 = 1.50 × Rs 4,00,000 (see 3) × Rs 6,00,000

5. From Wages Payable Control T-account, Wages Payable Control, December 31, 2011: Rs 5,20,000 (h) + Rs 30,000 (T) − Rs 4,00,000 (see 3) − Rs 1,00,000 (g) = Rs 50,000
6. Work-in-Process Control, January 31, 2012: Rs 80,000 (b) + Rs 20,000 (b) + 150% of Rs 20,000 (b) = Rs 1,30,000 (This answer is used in item 7.)
7. From Work-in-Process Control T-account, Work-in-Process Control, December 31, 2011: Rs 18,00,000 (d) + Rs 1,30,000 (see 6) − Rs 9,00,000 (c) − Rs 4,00,000 (see 3) − Rs 6,00,000 (see 4) = Rs 30,000
8. Manufacturing overhead overallocated: Rs 6,00,000 (see 4) + Rs 5,70,000 (T) = Rs 30,000.

Letters alongside entries in T-accounts correspond to letters in the preceding additional information. Numbers alongside entries in T-accounts correspond to numbers in the requirements above.

Materials Control

December 31,2011 Bal.	(given)	1,50,000		
	(1)	9,50,000[1]	(c)	9,00,000
January 31, 2012 Bal.	(e)	2,00,000		

[1] Can be computed only after all other postings in the account have been found.

Work-in-Process Control

December 31,2011 Bal.	(7) 30,000		(d) 18,00,000
Direct materials	(c) 9,00,000		
Direct manufacturing labor	(b) (g) (3) 4,00,000		
Manufacturing overhead allocated	(3) (a) (4) 6,00,000		
January 31, 2012 Bal.	(b) (6) 1,30,000		

Finished Goods Control

December 31, 2011 Bal.	(given) 2,00,000		(2) 18,50,000
	(d) 18,00,000		
January 31, 2012 Bal.	(f) 1,50,000		

Wages Payable Control

	(h) 5,20,000	December 31,2011 Bal.	(5) 50,000
			(g) (3) 4,00,000
			(g) 1,00,000
		January 31, 2012	(given) 30,000

Manufacturing Overhead Control

Total January charges	(given) 5,70,000		

Manufacturing Overhead Allocated

			(3) (a) (4) 6,00,000

Cost of Goods Sold

	(d) (f) (2) 18,50,000		

Decision Points

The following question-and-answer format summarizes the chapter's learning objectives. Each decision presents a key question related to a learning objective. The guidelines are the answer to that question.

Decision	Guidelines
1. What are the building-block concepts of a costing system?	The building-block concepts of a costing system are cost object, direct costs of a cost object, indirect costs of a cost object, cost pool, and cost-allocation base. Costing-system overview diagrams represent these concepts in a systematic way. Costing systems aim to report cost numbers that reflect the way chosen cost objects (such as products or services) use the resources of an organization.
2. How do you distinguish job costing from process costing?	Job-costing systems assign costs to distinct units of a product or service. Process-costing systems assign costs to masses of identical or similar units and compute unit costs on an average basis. These two costing systems represent opposite ends of a continuum. The costing systems of many companies combine some elements of both job costing and process costing.
3. How do you implement a job-costing system?	A general seven-step approach to job costing requires identifying (1) the job, (2) the direct-cost categories, (3) the cost-allocation bases, (4) the indirect-cost categories, (5) the cost-allocation rates, (6) the allocated indirect costs of a job, and (7) the total direct and indirect costs of a job.

4. How do you distinguish actual costing from normal costing?	Actual costing and normal costing differ in the type of indirect-cost rates used:

	Actual Costing	Normal Costing
Direct-cost rates	Actual rates	Actual rates
Indirect-cost rates	Actual rates	Budgeted rates

Both systems use actual quantities of inputs for tracing direct costs and actual quantities of the allocation bases for allocating indirect costs.

5. When are transactions recorded in a manufacturing job-costing system?	A job-costing system in manufacturing records the flow of inventoriable costs: (a) acquisition of materials and other manufacturing inputs; (b) their conversion into work in process; (c) their conversion into finished goods; and (d) the sale of finished goods. The job costing system also expenses period costs such as marketing costs as these costs are incurred.
6. How should you dispose of under- or overallocated manufacturing overhead costs at the end of the fiscal year?	The two theoretically correct approaches to disposing of under- or overallocated manufacturing overhead costs at the end of the fiscal year are (1) to adjust the allocation rate and (2) to prorate on the basis of the total amount of the allocated manufacturing overhead cost in the ending balances of Work-in-Process Control, Finished Goods Control, and Cost of Goods Sold. Many companies, however, simply write off amounts of under- or overallocated manufacturing overhead to Cost of Goods Sold when amounts are immaterial.
7. What variations from normal costing can be used?	In some variations from normal costing, organizations use budgeted rates to assign direct costs, as well as indirect costs, to jobs.

TERMS TO LEARN

This chapter and the Glossary at the end of the book contain definitions of:

actual costing (**p. 112**)
actual indirect-cost rate (**p. 117**)
adjusted allocation-rate approach (**p. 128**)
budgeted indirect-cost rate (**p. 120**)
cost-allocation base (**p. 110**)
cost-application base (**p. 110**)
cost pool (**p. 110**)
job (**p. 111**)
job-cost record (**p. 114**)
job-cost sheet (**p. 114**)
job-costing system (**p. 110**)
labor-time record (**p. 116**)
manufacturing overhead allocated (**p. 123**)
manufacturing overhead applied (**p. 123**)
materials-requisition record (**p. 115**)
normal costing (**p. 114**)
process-costing system (**p. 111**)
proration (**p. 129**)
source document (**p. 114**)
underabsorbed indirect costs (**p. 128**)
underallocated indirect costs (**p. 128**)
underapplied indirect costs (**p. 128**)

ASSIGNMENT MATERIAL

Questions

4-1 Define cost pool, cost tracing, cost allocation, and cost-allocation base.

4-2 How does a job-costing system differ from a process-costing system?

4-3 Why might an advertising agency use job costing for an advertising campaign by Pepsi, whereas a bank might use process costing to determine the cost of cHECking account deposits?

4-4 Describe the seven steps in job costing.

4-5 What are the two major cost objects that managers focus on in companies using job costing?

4-6 Describe three major source documents used in job-costing systems.

4-7 What is the main concern about source documents used to prepare job-cost records?

4-8 Give two reasons why most organizations use an annual period rather than a weekly or monthly period to compute budgeted indirect-cost rates.

4-9 Distinguish between actual costing and normal costing.

4-10 Describe two ways in which a house construction company may use job-cost information.

4-11 Comment on the following statement: "In a normal-costing system, the amounts in the Manufacturing Overhead Control account will always equal the amounts in the Manufacturing Overhead Allocated account."

4-12 Describe three different debit entries to the Work-in-Process Control T-account under normal costing.

4-13 Describe three alternative ways to dispose of under- or overallocated overhead costs.

4-14 When might a company use budgeted costs rather than actual costs to compute direct-labor rates?

4-15 Describe briefly why modern technology such as Electronic Data Interchange (EDI) is helpful to managers.

Solved Examples

4-16 Job order costing, process costing. In each of the following situations, determine whether job-costing or process costing would be more appropriate.

a. ACA firm
b. An oil refinery
c. A custom furniture manufacturer
d. A tyre manufacturer
e. A textbook publisher
f. A pharmaceutical company
g. An advertising agency
h. An apparel manufacturing plant
i. A flour mill
j. A paint manufacturer
k. A hospital
l. A software company
m. A cola-drink-concentrate producer
n. A movie studio
o. A law firm
p. A commercial aircraft manufacturer
q. A management consulting firm
r. A biscuit manufacturing
s. A catering service
t. A paper mill
u. An auto repair garage

Solution

a. Job Costing
b. Process Costing
c. Job Costing
d. Process Costing
e. Job Costing
f. Process Costing
g. Job Costing
h. Job Costing (but some process costing)
i. Process Costing
j. Process Costing
k. Job Costing
l. Job Costing
m. Process Costing
n. Job Costing
o. Job Costing
p. Job Costing
q. Job Costing
r. Process Costing
s. Job Costing
t. Process Costing
u. Job Costing

4-17 Actual costing, normal costing, accounting for manufacturing overhead. Paras Products uses a job-costing system with two direct-cost categories (direct materials and direct manufacturing labor) and one manufacturing overhead cost pool. Paras allocates manufacturing overhead costs using direct manufacturing labor costs. Paras provides the following information:

	Budget for Year 1	Actual Results for Year 1
Direct materials costs	Rs 7,50,000	Rs 7,25,000
Direct manufacturing labor costs	5,00,000	4,90,000
Direct manufacturing overhead costs	8,75,000	9,31,000

Required

1. Compute the actual and budgeted manufacturing overhead rates for Year 1.
2. During March, the job-cost record for Job 626 contained the following information:
   a. Direct materials used Rs 20,000
   b. Direct manufacturing labor costs Rs 15,000
   Compute the cost of Job 626 using (a) actual costing and (b) normal-costing.
3. At the end of Year 1, compute the under or overallocated manufacturing overhead under normal costing. Why is there no under or overallocated overhead under actual costing?

Solution

1. Actual manufacturing overhead rate = Actual manufacturing overhead costs/Actual direct manufacturing labor costs
   = Rs 9,31,000/Rs 4,90,000 = 1.9 or 190%
   Budgeted manufacturing overhead rate = Budgeted manufacturing overhead costs/Budgeted direct manufacturing labor costs
   = Rs 8,75,000/Rs 5,00,000 = 1.75 or 175%
2. Cost of Job 626 under actual and normal costing below:

Particulars	Actual Costing	Normal Costing
Direct materials	Rs 20,000	Rs 20,000
Direct manufacturing labor costs	15,000	15,000
Manufacturing overhead costs Rs 15,000 × 1.9; 15,000 × 1.75	28,500	26,250
Total manufacturing costs of Job 626	63,500	61,250

3. Total manufacturing overhead allocated under normal costing = Actual manufacturing labor costs × Budgeted overhead rate
   = Rs 4,90,000 × 1.75 = Rs 8,57,500
   Under-allocated manufacturing overhead = Actual manufacturing overhead costs − Manufacturing overhead allocated
   = Rs 9,31,000 − Rs 8,57,500 = Rs 73,500

   There is no under or over allocated overhead under actual costing because overhead is allocated under actual costing by multiplying actual manufacturing labor costs and the actual manufacturing overhead rate. This, of course, equals the actual manufacturing overhead costs. All actual overhead costs are allocated to products. Hence, there is no under or overallocated overhead.

4-18 Job-costing, accounting for manufacturing overhead, budgeted rates. The Maruti Co. uses a job-costing system at its Gurgaon plant. The plant has a Machining Department and an Assembly Department. Its job-costing system has two direct-cost categories (direct materials and direct manufacturing labor) and two manufacturing overhead cost pools (the Machining Department overhead, allocated to jobs based on actual machine-hours, and the Assembly Department overhead, allocated to jobs based on actual direct manufacturing labor cost). The Year 1 budget for the plant is:

Particulars	Machining Department	Assembly Department
Manufacturing overhead	Rs 36,00,000	Rs 72,00,000
Direct manufacturing labor cost	28,00,000	40,00,000
Direct manufacturing labor-hours	2,00,000	4,00,000
Machine-hours	1,00,000	4,00,000

Required

1. Present an overview diagram of Maruti's job-costing system. Compute the budgeted manufacturing overhead rate for each department.
2. During February, the job-cost record for Job 494 contained the following:

Particulars	Machining Department	Assembly Department
Direct materials used	Rs 90,000	Rs 1,40,000
Direct manufacturing labor cost	28,000	30,000
Direct manufacturing labor-hours	2,000	3,000
Machine-hours	4,000	2,000

3. At the end of Year 1, the actual manufacturing overhead costs were Rs 42,00,000 in Machining and Rs 74,00,000 in Assembly. Assume that Rs 1,10,000 actual machine-hours were used in Machining and that actual direct manufacturing labor costs in Assembly were Rs 44,00,000. Compute the over or under allocated manufacturing overhead for each department.

Solution

1. An overview of the product costing system is:

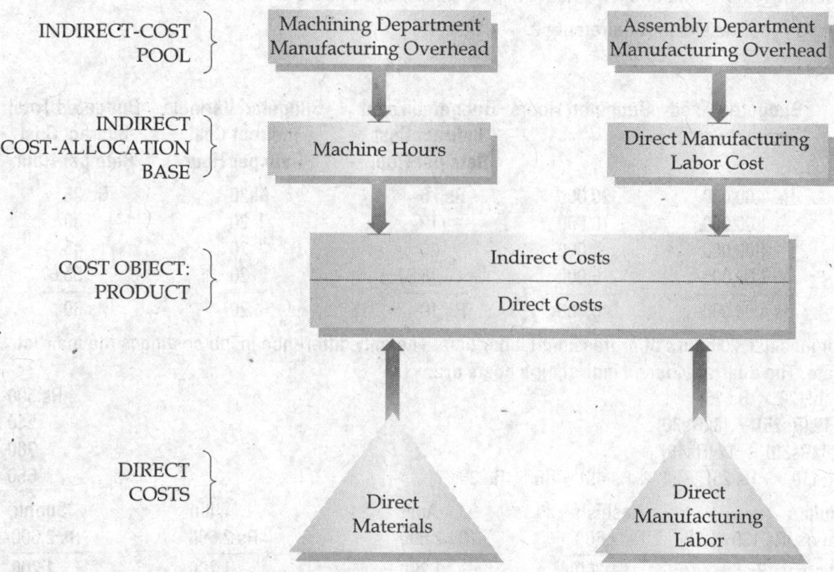

Budgeted manufacturing overhead divided by allocation base:

Machining overhead: Rs 36,00,000/1,00,000 = Rs 36 per machine hour

Assembly overhead: Rs 72,00,000/40,00,000 = 180 % direct manufacturing labor costs

2.

Machining department, 4,000 hours × Rs 36	Rs 1,44,000
Assembly department 180% × 30,000	54,000
Total manufacturing overhead allocated to Job 494	1,98,000

3.

Particulars	Machining	Assembly
Actual manufacturing overhead	42,00,000	74,00,000
Manufacturing overhead allocated, 1,10,000 × Rs 36	39,60,000	79,20,000
180% x Rs 44,00,000		
Underallocated (overallocated)	2,40,000	(Rs 5,20,000)

4-19 Computing indirect-cost rates, job-costing. Sanjay Iyer, the president of Tax Assist, is examining alternative ways to compute indirect-cost rates. He collects the following information from the budget for current Year:

- Budgeted variable indirect costs: Rs 20 per hour of professional labor time
- Budgeted fixed indirect costs: Rs 1,00,000 per quarter

The budgeted billable professional labor-hours per quarter are:

January-March	20,000 hours
April-June	10,000
July-September	4,000
October-December	6,000

Sanjay pays all tax professionals employed by Tax Assist on an hourly basis (Rs 60 per hour, including all fringe benefits).

Tax Assist's job-costing system has a single direct-cost category (professional labor at Rs 60 per hour) and a single indirect-cost pool (office support that is allocated using professional labor-hours).

Tax Assist charges clients Rs 130 per professional labor-hour.

Required

1. Compute the budgeted indirect-cost rate per professional labor-hour using
   a. Quarterly budgeted billable hours as the denominator
   b. Annual budgeted billable hours as the denominator
2. Compute the operating income for the following four customers using
   a. Quarterly indirect-cost rates
   b. An annual indirect-cost rate

- Aashish: 20 hours in February
- Amit: 12 hours in March and 8 hours in April
- Nitin: 8 hours in June and 12 hours in August
- Sudhir: 10 hours in January, 4 hours in September, and 6 hours in November.

3. Comment on your results in requirement 2.

Solution

1. a.	Budgeted Fixed Indirect Costs	Budgeted Hours	Budgeted Fixed Indirect Cost Rate per Hour	Budgeted Variable Indirect Cost Rate per Hour	Budgeted Total Indirect Cost Rate per Hour
Jan-March	Rs 1,00,000	20,000	Rs 5	Rs20	Rs 25
April-June	1,00,000	10,000	10	20	30
July-Sep	1,00,000	4,000	25	20	45
Oct-Dec	1,00,000	6,000	16.67	20	36.67
1. b.	Rs 4,00,000	40,000	Rs 10	Rs20	Rs 30

2. a. All four jobs use 20 hours of professional labor time. The only difference in job costing is the indirect cost rate. The quarterly based indirect job costs are:

Aashish: (20 × Rs 25)	Rs 500
Amit:(12xRs25) + (8xRs30)	540
Nitin:(8xRs30) + 12xRs45)	780
Sudhir: (10 × Rs 25) + (4 × Rs 45) + (6 × Rs 36.67)	650

Particulars	Aashish	Amit	Nitin	Sudhir
Revenues, Rs 130 × 20	Rs 2,600	Rs 2,600	Rs 2,600	Rs 2,600
Direct costs, Rs 60 × 20	1,200	1,200	1,200	1,200
Indirect costs	500	540	780	650
Total costs	1,700	1,740	1,980	1,850
Operating income	Rs 900	860	620	750

2. b. Using annual based indirect job-cost rates, all four customers will have the same operating income:

Revenues, Rs 130 × 20	Rs 2,600
Direct costs, Rs 60 × 20	1,200
Indirect costs, Rs 30 × 20	600
Total costs	1,800
Operating income	Rs 800

3. All four jobs use 20 hours of professional labor time. Using the quarterly-based indirect-cost rates, there are four different operating incomes because the work done on them is completed in different quarters. In contrast, using the annual indirect-cost rate, all four customers show the same operating income. All these different operating income figures for jobs with the same number of professional labor-hours are due to the allocation of fixed indirect costs.

4-20 Accounting for manufacturing overhead. Consider the following selected cost data for the Bharat Forge Co. for the current year

Budgeted manufacturing overhead	Rs 70,00,000
Budgeted machine-hours	2,00,000
Actual manufacturing overhead	Rs 68,00,000
al machine-hours	1,95,000

The company uses normal costing. Its job-costing system has a single manufacturing overhead cost pool. Costs are allocated to jobs using a budgeted machine-hour rate. Any amount of under or overallocation is written off to cost of goods sold

Required

1. Compute the budgeted manufacturing overhead rate.
2. Prepare the journal entries to record the allocation of manufacturing overhead.
3. Compute the amount of under or overallocation of manufacturing overhead. Is the amount significant? Prepare a journal entry to dispose of this amount.

Solution

1. Budgeted manufacturing overhead rate = Rs 70,00,000/2,00,000 = Rs 35 per machine hour
2. Work-in-process control Rs 68,25,000

   To manufacturing overhead allocated Rs 68,25,000

   (1,95,000 machine hours × Rs 35 per machine hour = Rs 68,25,000)

3. Rs 68,25,000 − 68,00,000 = Rs 25,000 overallocated, an insignificant amount

Manufacturing overhead allocated	68,25,000	
Manufacturing department overhead control		68,00,000
Cost of goods sold		25,000

4-21 Job costing, unit cost, ending work in process. Raymond Ltd. worked on only two jobs during May. Information on the jobs is given below:

Particulars	Job M1	Job M2
Direct materials	Rs 75,000	Rs 50,000
Direct manufacturing labor	2,70,000	2,10,000
Direct manufacturing labor-hours	6,000	5,000

Manufacturing overhead costs are allocated at the budgeted rate of Rs 30 per direct manufacturing labor-hour. Job M1 was completed in May.

Required

1. Compute the total cost of Job M1.
2. Calculate per unit cost for Job M1 assuming it has 15,000 units.
3. Prepare the journal entry transferring Job M1 to Finished goods.
4. Determine the ending balance in the Work-in-process account

Solution

1. **Cost of Job M1:**

Direct materials	Rs 75,000
Direct manufacturing labor	2,70,000
Manufacturing overhead allocated	1,80,000
Total cost	Rs 5,25,000

Budgeted rate Rs 30 × 6,000 direct manufacturing labor-hours = Rs 1,80,000

2. Per unit cost = Total cost of the job/Number of units in the job
= Rs 5,25,000/15,000 units = Rs 35 per unit

3.

Finished goods control	Rs 5,25,000	
Work-in-process control		Rs 5,25,000

4. **The work-in-process consists of Job M2 only:**

Direct materials	Rs 50,000
Direct manufacturing labor	2,10,000
Manufacturing overhead allocated	1,50,000
Work-in-process May 31	Rs 4,10,000

Budgeted rate of Rs 30 × 5,000 direct manufacturing labor-hours.

4-22 Job costing, accounting for manufacturing overhead, budgeted rates. The Hero Honda Motors uses a job-costing system at its Gurgaon plant. The plant has a Machining Department and a Finishing Department. Hero Honda uses normal-costing with two direct-cost categories (direct materials and direct machine-hours as the allocation base, and the Finishing Department, with direct manufacturing labor costs as the allocation base). The current year budget for the plant is as follows:

Particulars	Machining Department	Assembly Department
Manufacturing overhead	Rs 1,00,00,000	Rs 80,00,000
Direct manufacturing labor cost	Rs 9,00,000	Rs 10,00,000
Direct manufacturing labor-hours	30,000	1,60,000
Machine-hours	2,00,000	33,000

Required

1. Present an overview diagram of Hero Honda Motor's job-costing system.
2. What is the budgeted overhead rate that should be used in the Machining Department? In the Finishing Department?
3. During the month of January, the job-cost record for Job 431 shows the follows:

Particulars	Machining Department	Assembly Department
Direct materials used	Rs 14,000	Rs 3,000
Direct manufacturing labor costs	Rs 600	Rs 1,250
Direct manufacturing labor-hours	30	50
Machine-hours	130	10

Compute the total manufacturing overhead allocated to Job 431.

4. Assuming that Job 431 consisted of 200 units of product, what is the unit product cost of Job 431?

5. Amounts at the end of current year are as follows:

Particulars	Machining Department	Finishing Department
Manufacturing overhead incurred	Rs 1,12,00,000	Rs 79,00,000
Direct manufacturing labor costs	Rs 9,50,000	Rs 41,00,000
Machine-hours	2,20,000	32,000

Compute the under or allocated manufacturing overhead for each department and for the Gurgaon plant as a whole.

6. Why might Hero Honda use two different manufacturing overhead cost pools in its job-costing system?

Solution

1. An overview of the job-costing system is:

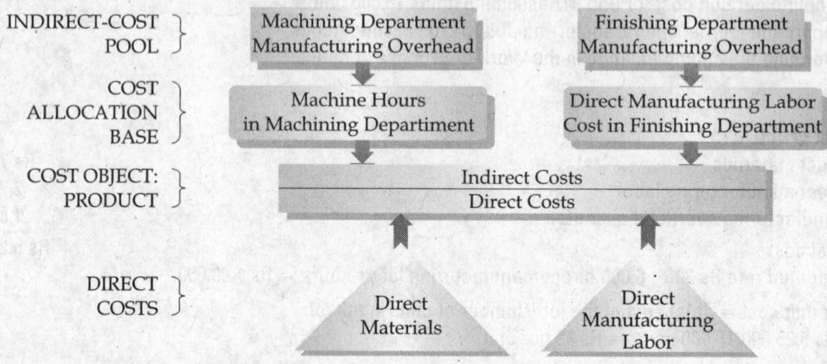

2. Budgeted manufacturing overhead divided by allocation base:
   a. Machining Department:
      Rs 1,00,00,000/2,00,000 = Rs 50 per machine hour
   b. Finishing Department:
      Rs 80,00,000/40,00,000 = 200% of direct manufacturing labor costs
3. Machining Department overhead, Rs 50 × 130 hours = Rs 6,500
   Finishing Department overhead, 200 per cent of Rs 1,250 = 2,500
   Total manufacturing overhead allocated 9,000
4. **Total costs of Job 431:**

Direct costs	
Direct materials - Machining department	Rs 14,000
- Finishing department	3,000
Direct manufacturing labor - Machining department	600
- Finishing department	1,250
	18,850
Indirect costs	
Machining department overhead, Rs 50 × 130	6,500
Finishing department overhead, 200% of Rs 1,250	2,500
	9,000
Total costs	Rs 27,850

The per unit product cost of job 431 is Rs 27,850/200 units = Rs 139.25 per unit

The point of this part is (a) to get the definitions straight multiplying the actual amount of the allocation base by the budgeted rate.

5.

Particulars	Machining	Finishing
Manufacturing overhead incurred (actual)	Rs 1,12,00,000	Rs 79,00,000
Manufacturing overhead allocated		
2,20,000 hours × Rs 50	1,10,00,000	
200% of Rs 41,00,000		82,00,000
Underallocated manufacturing overhead	2,00,000	
Overallocated manufacturing overhead		3,00,000
Total overallocated overhead = (Rs 3,00,000 − Rs 2,00,000)		1,00,000

6. A homogeneous cost pool is one where all costs have the same or a similar cause-and-effect or benefits-received relationship with the cost-allocation base. Hero Honda Motors likely assumes that all its manufacturing overhead cost items are not homogeneous. Specifically, those in the Machining Department have a cause-and-effect relationship with machine-hours, while those in the Finishing Department have a cause-and-effect relationship with direct manufacturing labor costs. Hero Honda Motors believes that the benefits of using two cost pools (more accurate product costs and better ability to manage costs) exceeds the costs of implementing a more complex system.

4-23 Proration of overhead. (Z. Iqbal, adapted). The Ruia Radiator Company uses a normal-costing with a single manufacturing overhead cost pool and machine-hours as the cost-allocation base. The following data are for current year:

Budgeted manufacturing overhead	Rs 24,00,000
Overhead allocation base	Machine-hours
Budgeted machine-hours	40,000
Manufacturing overhead incurred	24,50,000
Actual machine-hours	37,500

Machine-hours data and the ending balances (before proration of under- or overallocated overhead) are as follows:

	Actual Machine-hours	Year-end Balance
Cost of goods sold	30,000	Rs 40,00,000
Finished goods	5,500	6,25,000
Work in process	2,000	3,75,000

Required

1. Compute the budgeted manufacturing overhead rate for current year.
2. Compute under— or overallocated manufacturing overhead of Ruia Radiator in current year. Dispose of this amount using
   a. Write-off to cost of goods sold.
   b. Proration based on ending balances (before proration) in work in process, finished goods, and cost of goods sold.
   c. Proration based on the allocated overhead amount (before proration) in the ending balances of work in process, finished goods, and cost of goods sold.
3. Which method do you prefer in requirement 2? Explain.

Solution

1. Budgeted manufacturing overhead rate is Rs 24,00,000/40,000 = Rs 60 per machine hour.
2. Manufacturing overhead underallocated = Manufacturing overhead incurred − Manufacturing overhead allocated
   = Rs 24,50,000 − Rs 60 × 37,500
   = Rs 24,50,000 − Rs 22,50,000 = Rs 2,00,000

a. Write-off Cost of Goods Sold

Account	Account Balance (before proration)	Write off of Rs 2,00,000 Underallocated Manufacturing Overhead	Account Balance (after proration)
Work in process	Rs 3,75,000	Rs 0	Rs 3,75,000
Finished goods	6,25,000	0	6,25,000
Cost of goods sold	40,00,000	2,00,000	42,00,000
Total	50,00,000	2,00,000	52,00,000

b. Proration based on ending balances (before proration) in Work-in-process, Finished goods and Cost of goods sold,

Account	Account Balance (before proration)	Proration of Rs 2,00,000 Underallocated Manufacturing Overhead	Account Balance (after proration)
Work in process	Rs 3,75,000 (7.5%)	0.075 × Rs 2,00,000 = Rs 15,000	Rs 3,90,000
Finished goods	6,25,000 (12.5%)	0.125 × Rs 2,00,000 = 25,000	6,50,000
Cost of goods sold	40,00,000 (80.0%)	0.800 × 2,00,000 = 1,60,000	41,60,000
Total	50,00,000(100%)	2,00,000	52,00,000

c. **Proration based on the allocated overhead amount (before proration) in the ending balances of Work-in-process, Finished goods and Cost of goods sold.**

Account	Account Balance (before proration)	Allocated Overhead component in the account balance (before proration)	Proration of Rs 2,00,000 Underallocated Manufacturing Overhead		Account Balance (after proration)
Work in process	Rs 3,75,000	Rs 1,20,000[a] (5.33%)	0.0533 × Rs 2,00,000 =	10,660	3,85,660
Finished goods	6,25,000	3,30,000[b] (14.67%)	0.1467 × 2,00,000 =	29,340	6,54,340
Cost of goods sold	40,00,000	18,00,000[c] (80.00%)	0.800 × 2,00,000 =	1,60,000	41,60,000
Total	Rs 50,00,000	22,50,000 (100%)		2,00,000	52,00,000

a. Rs 60 × 2,000 machine hours
b. Rs 60 × 5,500 machine hours
c. Rs 60 × 30,000 machine hours

3. Alternative (c) is preferred over (a) and (b). Alternative (c) yields the same ending balances in work-in process, finished goods and cost of goods sold that would have been reported had actual indirect cost rates been used.

4-24 Proration of overhead, two indirect-cost pools. LG Electronics Ltd. uses two manufacturing overhead cost pools-one for the overhead costs incurred in the Machining Department and another for overhead costs incurred in the Assembly Department. LG Electronics uses normal costing. It allocates overhead costs to jobs from the Machining Department using a budgeted machine-hour (MH) overhead rate, and from the Assembly Department using a budgeted direct manufacturing labor-hour (DLH) rate.

The following data are for current year:

	Machining Department	Assembly Department
Budgeted manufacturing overhead rate	Rs 60 per machine-hour	Rs 40 per direct manufacturing labor-hour
Actual manufacturing overhead costs	Rs 1,24,00,000	Rs 94,00,000

Machine-hours are direct manufacturing labor-hours data and ending balances are as follows:

Particulars	Actual Machine-hours	Actual Direct Manufacturing Labor-hours	Balance Before Proration December 31
Cost of goods sold	1,35,000	1,80,000	Rs 3,20,00,000
Finished goods control	9,000	9,600	15,00,000
Work-in-process	36,000	50,400	65,00,000

Required

1. Compute the underallocated or overallocated overhead in each department in current year. Dispose of the underallocated or overallocated amount in each department using:
   a. write-off to cost of goods sold.
   b. Proration based on ending balances (before proration) in cost of goods sold, finished goods control, and work-in-process control.
   c. Proration based on the allocated overhead amount (before proration) in the ending balances of cost of goods sold, finished goods control, and work-in-process control.
2. Explain which proration method you prefer in requirement 1.

Solution

Machining Department

Total actual machine hours = 1,35,000 + 9,000 + 36,000 = 1,80,000 machine hours

Manufacturing overhead allocated = 1,80,000 × Rs 60 = Rs 1,08,00,000

Manufacturing overhead costs under allocated = Actual manufacturing overhead costs − Manufacturing overhead allocated

Rs 1,24,00,000 − Rs 1,08,00,000 = Rs 16,00,000

Assembly Department

Total actual direct manufacturing labor hours = 1,80,000 + 9,600 + 50,400 = 2,40,000 direct manufacturing labor hours

Manufacturing overhead allocated = 2,40,000 × Rs 40 = Rs 96,00,000

Manufacturing overhead costs overallocated = Manufacturing overhead allocated — Actual manufacturing overhead costs = Rs 96,00,000 — 94,00,000 = Rs 2,00,000

1. **a. Write off to Cost of Goods Sold Leads to**
   i. Higher cost of goods sold of Rs 16,00,000 as a result of underallocation of manufacturing overhead in the Machining Department.
   ii. Lower cost of goods sold of Rs 2,00,000 as a result of overallocation of manufacturing overhead in the Assembly Department, Hence,

Cost of goods sold = Rs 3,20,00,000 + Rs 16,00,000 − Rs 2,00,000 = Rs 3,34,00,000

1. b. Proration Based on Ending Balances (before proration) in Work-in Process, Finished Goods, and Cost of Goods Sold.

Account balance in each account after proration follows:

Account	Account Balance (before proration)	Proration of Rs 16,00,000 Under-allocated Overhead in Manufacturing Department	Proration of Rs 2,00,000 Over-allocated Overhead in Assembly Department	Account Balance (after in proration)
	(1)	(2)	(3)	(4) = (1) + (2) + (3)
Work in process	Rs 65,00,000 (16.25%)	0.1625 × Rs 16,00,000 = 2,60,000	0.1 625 × (Rs 2,00,000) = (32,500)	Rs 67,27,500
Finished goods	15,00,000 (3.75%)	0.0375 × 16,00,000 = 60,000	0.0375 × (2,00,000) = (7,500)	15,52,500
Cost of goods sold	3,20,00,000 (80%)	0.80 × 16,00,000 = 12,80,000	0.80 × (2,00,000) = (1,60,000)	3,31,20,000
Total	4,00,00,000 (100%)	16,00,000	(2,00,000)	Rs 4,14,00,000

1. c. Proration Based on Overhead Allocated (before proration) in the Ending Balances of Cost of Goods Sold, Finished Goods and Work in Process for Each Department Follows.

Machining Department

Account	Overhead Costs Allocated to Each Account in Machining Department Using Budgeted Machine Hour rate x Actual Machine-hours	Proration of Rs 16,00,000 Underallocated Machining Department Overhead
Work in process	Rs 60 × 36,000 = Rs 21,60,000 (20%)	0.20 × Rs 16,00,000 = Rs 3,20,000
Finished goods	Rs 60 × 9,000 = 5,40,000 (5%)	0.05 × 16,00,000 = 80,000
Cost of goods sold	Rs 60 × 1,35,000 = 81,00,000 (75%)	0.75 × 16,00,000 = 12,00,000
Total	1,08,00,000 (100%)	16,00,000

Assembly Department

Account	Overhead Costs Allocated to Each Account in Assembly Department Using Budgeted Direct Manufacturing Labor-hour Rate x Actual Direct Manufacturing Labor-hours	Proration of (Rs 2,00,000) Overallocated Assembly Department Overhead
Work in process	Rs 40 × 50,400 = Rs 20,16,000 (21%)	0.21 × (Rs 2,00,000) = (Rs 42,000)
Finished goods	Rs 40 × 9,600 = 3,84,000 (4%)	0.04 × (2,00,000) = (8,000)
Cost of goods sold	Rs 40 × 1,80,000 = 72,00,000 (75%)	0.75 × (2,00,000) = (1,50,000)
	96,00,000 (100%)	(2,00,000)

Account balances in each account after proration of underallocated Machining Department costs and overallocated Assembly Department costs follow.

Account	Account Balance (before proration)	Proration of Rs 16,00,000 Underallocated Machining Department Overhead	Proration of (Rs 2,00,000) Overallocated Assembly Department Overhead	Account Balance (after proration)
	(1)	(2)	(3)	(4) = (1) + (2) +(3)
Work in process	Rs 65,00,000	Rs 3,20,000	Rs (42,000)	Rs 67,78,000
Finished goods	15,00,000	80,000	(8,000)	15,72,000
Cost of goods sold	3,20,00,000	12,00,000	(1,50,000)	3,30,50,000
	Rs 4,00,00,000	Rs 16,00,000	Rs (2,00,000)	Rs 4,14,00,000

2. If the purpose is to report the most accurate inventory and cost of goods sold figures, the preferred method is to prorate based on the manufacturing overhead allocated amount in the Inventory and cost of goods sold accounts (as in requirement 1c). Note, however, that prorating based on ending balances in work in process, finished goods, and cost of goods sold (as in requirement 1b) yields a close approximation to the more accurate proration in requirement 1c. Also note that the write-off to cost of goods sold method (as in requirement 1a) results in account balances in work in process, finished goods, and cost of goods sold that are not very different from the most accurate method. Furthermore, the write off to cost of goods sold method is simpler than the other methods. Depending on the objectives of proration, a manager may prefer any one of the methods over the other two.

4-25 General ledger relationships, under and overallocation. (S.Sridhar, adapted) Neelam Company uses normal costing in its job-costing system. Partially completed T-accounts and additional information for Neelam for current year are as follows:

Materials Control

Beginning	Rs 30,000	Rs 3,80,000
	4,00,000	

Work-in-process Control

Beginning	Rs 20,000
Direct manufacturing labor	3,60,000

Finished Goods Control

Beginning	Rs 10,000	Rs 9,00,000
	9,40,000	

Manufacturing Overhead Control

Rs 5,40,000

Additional information

a. Direct manufacturing labor wage rate was Rs 30 per hour.
b. Manufacturing overhead was allocated at Rs 40 per direct manufacturing-labor hour.
c. During the year, sales revenues were Rs 10,90,000, and marketing and distribution costs were Rs 1,40,000.

Required

1. what was the amount of direct materials issued to production during current year?
2. What was the amount of manufacturing overhead allocated to jobs during current year?
3. What was the cost of jobs completed during current year?
4. What was the balance of ending work-in-process inventory on December 31, current year?
5. What was the cost of goods sold before proration of under-or overallocated overhead?
6. What was the under-allocated or overallocated manufacturing.overhead in current year?
7. Dispose of the under-allocated or overallocated manufacturing overhead using
   a. Write-off to cost of goods sold.
   b. Proration based on ending balances (before proration) in work-in-process, finished goods, and cost of goods sold.
8. Using each of the approaches in requirement 7, calculate Neelam's operating income for the current year.
9. Which approach in requirement 7 do you recommend Neelam use? Explain your answer briefly.

Solution

The solution assumes all materials used are direct material. A summary of the T-accounts for Neelam Company before adjusting for under- or overallocation of overhead follows:

Direct Materials Control

Beginning	Rs 30,000	Materials used for manufacturing	Rs 3,80,000
Purchases	4,00,000		
Ending	50,000		

Work-in-process Control

Beginning	Rs 20,000	Transferred to finished goods	Rs 9,40,000
Direct materials	3,80,000		
Direct manufacturing labor	3,60,000		
Manufacturing overhead allocated	4,80,000		
Ending	3,00,000		

Finished Goods Control

Beginning	Rs 10,000	Cost of goods sold	Rs 9,00,000
Transferred from work-in-process	9,40,000		
Ending	50,000		

Cost of Goods Sold

Finished goods sold	Rs 9,00,000

Manufacturing Overhead Control

Manufacturing overhead costs	Rs 5,40,000

Manufacturing Overhead Allocated

Manufacturing overhead allocated to work-in-process	Rs 4,80,000

1. From Direct Material Control T-account
   Direct material issued to production = Rs 3,80,000 that appears as a credit.
2. Direct manufacturing labor-hours = Direct manufacturing labor costs/Direct manufacturing wage rate per hour
   = Rs 3,60,000/Rs 30 per hour = 12,000 hours
3. From the debit entry to Finished Goods T-account
   Cost of jobs completed and transferred from Work-in-Process = Rs 9,40,000
4. From Work-in-Process T-account, Work-in-Process inventory
   On 31st December = Rs 20,000 + Rs 3,80,000 + 3,60,000 + 4,80,000 —
   Rs 9,40,000 = Rs 3,00,000

5. From the credit entry to Finished Goods Control T-account, Cost of goods sold (before proration) = Rs 9,00,000
6. Manufacturing overhead underallocated = Debit to Manufacturing Overhead Control — Credit to Manufacturing Overhead Allocated = Rs 5,40,000-Rs 4,80,000 = Rs 60,000 underallocated.
7. **a.** Write-off to Cost of Goods Sold will increase (debit) Cost of Goods Sold by Rs 60,000. Hence, Cost of Goods Sold = Rs 9,00,000 + 60,000 = Rs 9,60,000

   b. Proratioin based on ending balances (before proration) in Work-in-Process, Finished Goods and Cost of Goods Sold.

Account balances in each account after proration follows:

Account	Account Balance (before proration)	Proration of Rs 60,000 Underallocated Manufacturing Overhead	Account Balance (after proration)
(1)	(2)	(3)	(4) = (2) + (3)
Work in process	Rs 3,00,000 (24%)	0.24 × Rs 60,000 = Rs 14,400	Rs 3,14,400
Finished goods	50,000 (4%)	0.04 × 60,000 = 2,400	52,400
Cost of goods sold	9,00,000 (72%)	0.72x60,000 = 43,200	9,43,200
	Rs 12,50,000 (100%)	60,000	13,10,000

8. Neelam's Operating Income under the write off to Cost of Goods Sold and Proration based on ending balances (before proration) follows

Particulars	Write off to Cost of Goods Sold	Proration Based on Ending Balances
Revenues	Rs 10,90,000	Rs 10,90,000
Cost of goods sold	9,60,000	9,43,200
Gross margin	1,30,000	1,46,800
Marketing and distribution costs	1,40,000	1,40,000
Operating income/floss)	Rs (10,000)	Rs 6,800

9. If the purpose is to report the most accurate inventory and cost of goods sold figures, the preferred method is to prorate based on the manufacturing overhead allocated component in the inventory and cost of goods sold accounts. Proration based on the balances in work in process, finished goods, and cost of goods sold will equal the proration based on the manufacturing overhead allocated component if the proportions of direct costs to manufacturing overhead costs are constant in the work in process, finished goods and cost of goods sold accounts. Even if this is not the case, the prorations based on work in process, finished goods, and cost of goods sold will better approximate the results if actual cost rates had been used rather than the write-off to cost of goods sold method.

Another consideration in Neelam's decision about how to dispose of underallocated manufacturing overhead is the effects on operating income. The write-off to cost of goods sold will lead to an operating loss, proration based on the balances in work in process, finished goods, and cost of goods sold will help Neelam avoid the loss and show an operating income.

The main merit of the write-off to cost of goods sold method is its simplicity. However, accuracy and the effect on operating income favor the preferred and recommended proration approach.

4-26 Job costing, contracting, ethics. George is the owner and CEO of Aerospace Comfort, a firm specializing in the manufacture of seats for air transport. He has just received a copy of a letter written to the General Audit Section of the Indian Navy. He believes it is from an ex-employee of Aerospace.

Dear Sir,

Aerospace Comfort manufactured 100 × 7 seats for the Navy in current year. You may be interested to know the following.

1. Direct materials costs billed for the 100 × 7 seats were Rs 25,000.
2. Direct manufacturing labor costs billed for 100 × 7 seats were Rs 6,000. These costs include 16 hours of setup labor at Rs 25 per hour, an amount included in the manufacturing overhead cost pool as well. The Rs 6,000 also includes 12 hours of design time at Rs 50 an hour. Design time was explicitly identified as a cost the Navy would not reimburse.
3. Manufacturing overhead costs billed for 100 × 7 seats were Rs 9,000 (150 per cent of direct manufacturing labor costs). This amount includes the 16 hours of setup labor at Rs 25 per hour that is incorrectly included as part of direct manufacturing labor costs.

You may also want to know that over 40 per cent of the direct materials is purchased from Frontier Technology, a company that is 51 per cent owned by George's brother. For obvious reasons, this letter will not be signed.

Cc: The Times of India.

George, CEO of Aerospace Comfort

Aerospace Comfort's contract states that the Navy reimburses Aerospace at 130 per cent of total manufacturing costs. Assume that the facts in the letter are correct as you answer the following questions.

Required

1. What is the cost amount per × 7 seat that Aerospace Comfort billed the Navy? Assume that the actual direct material costs were Rs 25,000.
2. What is the amount per × 7 seat that Aerospace Comfort should have billed the Navy? Assume that the actual direct materials costs were Rs 25,000.
3. What should the Navy do to tighten its procurement procedures to reduce the likelihood of such situations recurring in the future?

Solution

1.

Direct manufacturing costs		
Direct materials	Rs 25,000	
Direct manufacturing labor	6,000	Rs 31,000
Indirect manufacturing costs,		
150 per cent xRs 6,000		9,000
Total manufacturing costs		40,000

Aerospace bills the Navy Rs 52,000 (Rs 40,000 × 13%) for 100 × 7 Seats or Rs 520 (Rs 52,000/100) per × 7 Seat.

2.

Direct manufacturing costs		
Direct materials	Rs 25,000	
Direct manufacturing labor	5,000[a]	Rs 30,000
Indirect manufacturing costs,		
150 per cent xRs 5,000		7,500
Total manufacturing costs		37,500

(a) Rs 6,000 - Rs 400 (25 × 16) set up - Rs 600 (50 × 12) design = Rs 5,000
Aerospace should have billed the Navy Rs 48,750 (Rs 37,500 × 130%) for 100 × 7 seats or Rs 487.50 (Rs 48,750/100) per × 7 seat.

3. The problems the letter highlights (assuming it is correct) include:
   a. Costs included that should be excluded (design costs).
   b. Costs double-counted (setup included as both a direct cost and in an indirect cost pool).
   c. Possible conflict of interest in Aerospace Comfort purchasing materials from a family-related company.

Steps the Navy Could Undertake Include:

(i) Use only contractors with a reputation for ethical behavior as well as quality products or services.
(ii) Issue guidelines detailing acceptable and unacceptable billing practices by contractors. For example, prohibiting the use of double-counting cost allocation methods by contractors.
(iii) Issue guidelines detailing acceptable and unacceptable procurement practices by contractors. For example, if a contractor purchases from a family-related company, require that the contractor obtain quotes from at least two other bidders.
(iv) Employ auditors who aggressively monitor the bills submitted by contractors.
(v) Ask contractors for details regarding determination of costs.

Exercises

4-27 Job-costing, normal and actual costing. Ansal Construction assembles residential houses. It uses a job-costing system with two direct-cost categories (direct materials and direct labor) and one indirect-cost pool (assembly support). Direct labor-hours is the allocation base for assembly support costs. In December Year 1, Ansal budgets Year 2 assembly-support costs to be Rs 4,000,000 and Year 2 direct labor-hours to be Rs 80,000.

At the end of Year 2, Ansal is comparing the costs of several jobs that were started and completed in Year 2.

Particulars	Gurgaon Model	Noida Model
Construction period	Feb-June 2004	May–Oct. 2004
Direct materials	Rs 2,12,900	Rs 2,55,208
Direct labor	Rs 72,552	Rs 82,820
Direct labor-hours	1,800	2,020

Direct materials and direct labor are paid for on a contract basis. The costs of each are known when direct materials are used or direct labor-hours are worked. The Year 2 actual assembly-support costs were Rs 1,37,76,000, and the actual direct labor-hours were 328,000.

Required

1. Compute the (a) budgeted and (b) actual indirect-cost rates. Why do they differ?
2. What is the job cost of the Gurgaon Model and the Noida Model using (a) normal costing and (b) actual costing?
3. Why might Ansal construction prefer normal costing over actual costing?

4-28 Job-costing, consulting firm. Vaish and Associates, a consulting firm, has the following condensed budget for Year 1.

Revenues		Rs 4,00,00,000
Total costs		
Direct costs		
Professional labor	Rs 1,00,00,000	
Indirect costs		
Consulting support	2,60,00,000	3,60,00,000
Operating income		40,00,000

Vaish has a single direct-cost category (professional labor) and a single indirect-cost pool (client support). Indirect costs are allocated to jobs on the basis of professional labor costs.

Required

1. Present an overview diagram of the job-costing system. Compute the Year 1 budgeted indirect-cost rate of Vaish and Associates.
2. The markup rate for pricing jobs is intended to produce operating income equal to 10 per cent of revenues. Compute the markup rate as a percentage of professional labor costs.
3. Vaish is bidding on a consulting job for Karim's, a fast-food chain. The budgeted breakdown of professional labor on the job is as follows:

Professional labor category	budgeted rate per hour	Budgeted Hours
Director	Rs 2,000	3
Partner	1,000	16
Associate	500	40
Assistant	300	160

Compute the budgeted cost of the Karim's job. How much will Vaish bid for the job if it is to earn its target operating income of 10 per cent of revenues?

4-29 Job costing, journal entries. The University of Delhi Press is wholly owned by the university. It performs the bulk of its work for other university departments, which pay as though the press were an outside business enterprise. The press also publishes and maintains a stock of books for general sale. Ajob-costing system is used to cost each job. There are two direct-cost categories (direct materials and direct manufacturing labor) and one indirect-cost pool (manufacturing overhead, allocated on the basis of direct manufacturing labor costs).

The following data (in thousands) pertain to current year

Direct materials and supplies purchased on account	Rs 8,000
Direct materials used	7,100
Indirect materials issued to various production departments	1,000
Direct manufacturing labor	13,000
Indirect manufacturing labor incurred by various departments	9,000
Depreciation on building and manufacturing equipment	4,000
Miscellaneous manufacturing overhead* incurred by various departments (ordinarily would be detailed as repairs, photocopying, utilities, etc.)	5,500
Manufacturing overhead allocated at 160 per cent of direct manufacturing labor costs	
Cost of goods manufactured	41,200
Revenues	80,000
Cost of goods sold	40,200
Beginning inventories	
Materials control	10,000
Work-in-process control	600
Finished goods control	5,000

*The term manufacturing overhead is not used uniformly. Other terms that are often encountered in printing companies include job overhead and shop overhead.

Required

1. Present an overview diagram of the job-costing system at the University of Delhi Press.
2. Prepare journal entries to summarize current year transactions. As your final entry, dispose of the year-end under or overallocated manufacturing overhead as a write-off to Cost of goods sold. Number your entries. Explanations for each entry may be omitted.
3. Show posted T-accounts for all inventories, Cost of goods sold, Manufacturing overhead control, and Manufacturing overhead allocated.

4-30 Job costing; actual, normal, and variation from normal costing. S R Batliboi and Co. is a Delhi-based public accounting partnership specializing in audit services. Its job-costing system has a single direct-cost category (professional labor) and a single indirect-cost pool (audit support, which contains all the costs in the Audit Support Department). Audit support costs are allocated to individual jobs using actual professional labor-hours. S R Batliboi and Co. employs ten professionals who are involved in their auditing services.

Budgeted and actual amounts for current year are as follows:

Budget for current year	
Professional labor compensation	Rs 9,60,000
Audit Support Department costs	7,20,000
Professional labor-hours billed to clients	6,000 hours
Actual Results for current year	
Audit Support Department costs	Rs 7,44,000
Professional labor-hours billed to clients	5,500 hours
Actual professional labor cost rate	58 per hour

Required

1. Compute the direct-cost rate per professional labor-hour and the indirect-cost rate per professional labor-hour for current year under (a) actual costing, (b) normal costing, and (c) the variation of normal costing that uses budgeted rates for direct costs.
2. The audit of the Gupta Entreprises, done in current year, was budgeted to take 110 hours of professional labor time. The actual professional labor time on the audit was 120 hours. Compute the current year job cost using (a) actual costing, (b) normal costing, and (c) the variation of normal costing that uses budgeted rates for direct costs. Explain any differences in the job cost.

4-31 Service industry, job costing, law firm. Viash & Associates is a law firm specializing in labor relations and employee-related work. It employs 50 professionals (10 partners and 40 associates) who work directly with its clients. The average budgeted total compensation per professional for current year is Rs 2,08,000. Each professional is budgeted to have 3,200 billable hours to clients in current year. Viash & Associates is a highly respected firm; all professional work for clients to their maximum 3,200 billable hours available. All professional labor costs are included in a single direct-cost category and are traced to jobs on a per-hour basis.

All costs of Viash & Associates other than professional labor costs are included in a single indirect-cost pool (legal support) and are allocated to jobs using professional labor-hours as the allocation base. The budgeted level of indirect costs in current year is Rs 44,00,000.

Required

1. Present an overview diagram of Vaish's job-costing system.
2. Compute the current year budgeted direct-cost rate per hour of professional labor.
3. Compute the current year budgeted indirect-cost rate per hour of professional labor.
4. Viash & Associates is considering bidding on two jobs:
   a. Litigation work for Saw Pipes Ltd. which requires 100 budgeted hours of professional labor.
   b. Labor contract work for J K Paper Ltd. which requires 150 budgeted hours of professional labor.
   Prepare a cost estimate for each job.

4-32 Service industry, job costing two direct and two indirect-cost categories, law firm (continuation of 4-31) Vaish has just completed a review of its job-costing system. This review included a detailed analysis of how past jobs used the firm's resources and interviews with personnel about what factors drive the level of indirect costs. Management concluded that a system with two direct-cost categories (professional partner labor and professional associate labor) and two indirect-cost categories (general support and secretarial support) would yield more accurate job costs. Budgeted information for current year related to the two direct-cost categories is as follows:

Particulars	Professional Partner Labor	Professional Associate Labor
Number of professionals	10	40
Hours of billable time per professional	3,200 per year	3,200 per year
Total compensation (average per professional)	Rs 4,00,000	Rs 1,60,000

Budgeted information for current year relating to the two indirect-cost categories is

Particulars	General Support	Secretarial Support
Total costs	Rs 36,00,000	Rs 8,00,000
Cost-allocation base	Professional labor-hours	Partner labor-hours

Required

1. Compute the current year budgeted direct-cost rates for (a) professional partners and (b) professional associates.
2. Compute the current year budgeted indirect-cost rates for (a) general support and (b) secretarial support.

3. Compute the budgeted costs for the Saw Pipes and J K Paper jobs, given the following information:

	Saw Pipes	J.K. Paper
Professional partners	120 hours	60 hours
Professional associates	80 hours	240 hours

4. Comment on the results in requirement 3. Why are the job costs different from those computed in Problem 4-31?

4-33 Normal costing, overhead allocation, working backwards. (M. Rajan, adapted) Tata Company uses normal costing. Its job-costing system has two direct-cost categories (direct materials and direct manufacturing labor) and one indirect-cost category (manufacturing overhead). The following information is obtained from the company's records for current year:

- Total manufacturing costs Rs 1,60,00,000.
- Cost of finished goods manufactured Rs 1,58,40,000.
- Manufacturing overhead allocated Rs 72,00,000.
- Manufacturing overhead was allocated to production at a rate of 200 per cent of direct manufacturing labor costs.
- The rupee amount of work-in-process inventory on January 1, current year was Rs 6,40,000.

Required

1. Compute the total direct manufacturing labor costs in current year.
2. Calculate the total cost of direct materials used in current year.
3. Determine work-in-process inventory on December 31, current year.

4-34 General ledger relationships, under and overallocation, service industry. ICT International Enginneering consulting firm, uses a variation from normal costing in its job-costing system. It charges jobs for fees paid to outside experts at actual costs, professional direct-labor costs at a budgeted direct-labor rate, and engineering support overhead costs at a budgeted indirect-cost rate.

ICT maintains a "Jobs-in-Process Control" account in its general ledger that accumulates all costs of jobs. As a job is completed, ICT immediately bills the client and transfers the cost of the completed job to a "Cost of Jobs Billed" account.

The following data pertain to current year:

1. Direct costs of fees (all cash)	Rs 3,00,000
2. Actual direct professional labor costs (all cash)	30,00,000
3. Direct professional labor allocated at Rs 100 per actual	29,00,000
4. Actual engineering support overhead costs (all cash)	23,60,000
5. Engineering support overhead allocated at 80% of actual direct professional labor costs	24,00,000
6. Cost of jobs billed	50,00,000

Required

1. Prepare summary journal entries for the above transactions using these accounts: Jobs-in-Process control, Cost of jobs billed, Direct professional labor control, Direct professional labor allocated, Engineering support overhead control, Engineering support overhead allocated, and Cash control.
2. As your final entry, dispose of the year-end under or overallocated account balances as direct writeoffs to cost of jobs billed.

4-35 Overview of general ledger relationships. Amitabh Company is a small machine shop that uses normal costing in its job-costing system. The total debits and credits in certain accounts one day before current year-end are as follows:

	December 30	
Particulars	**Total Debits**	**Total Credits**
Materials control	Rs 1,00,000	Rs 70,000
Work-in-process control	3,20,000	3,05,000
Manufacturing department overhead control	85,000	3,00,000
Finished goods control	3,25,000	–
Cost of goods sold	3,00,000	–
Manufacturing overhead allocated	–	90,000

All materials purchased are direct material. Note that "total debits" in the inventory accounts would include beginning inventory balances, if any.

The total debits and total credits above do not include the following:

a. The manufacturing labor costs for the December 31 working day: direct manufacturing labor, Rs 5,000 and indirect manufacturing labor, Rs 1,000
b. Miscellaneous manufacturing overhead incurred on December 31, Rs 1,000.

Additional information

a. Manufacturing overhead has been allocated as a percentage of direct manufacturing labor costs through December 30.

b. Direct materials purchased during the current year were Rs 85,000.
c. No direct materials were returned to suppliers.
d. Direct manufacturing labor costs during the current year totaled Rs 1,50,000, not including the December 31 working day described previously.

Required

1. Compute the inventories (December 31, previous year) of Materials control, Work-in-process control, and Finished goods control. Show T-accounts.
2. Prepare all adjusting and closing journal entries for the preceding accounts. Assume that all under- or overallocated manufacturing overhead is closed directly to cost of goods sold.
3. Compute the ending inventories (December 31), after adjustments and closing of materials control, Work-in-process control, and Finished goods control.

4-36 Service industry, job costing, accounting for overhead costs, budgeted rates. Sinhgama's Company, a painting contractor, uses normal costing to cost each job. Sinhgama's job costing system has two direct-cost categories (direct materials and direct labor) and one indirect-cost pool called overhead costs. Sinhgama's budgeted overhead rate for allocating overhead costs to jobs is 80 per cent of direct labor costs. Sinhgama's provides the following additional information:

1. As of January 31, current year, Job A21 was the only job in process, with direct materials costs of Rs 30,000 and direct labor costs of Rs 50,000.
2. Jobs A22, A23, and A24 were started during February.
3. Direct materials used during February were Rs 50,000.
4. Direct-labor costs for February were Rs 20,000.
5. Actual overhead costs for February were Rs 1,02,000.
6. The only job still in process as of February 29, current year, was job A24, with direct materials costs of Rs 20,000 and direct labor costs of Rs 40,000.

Sinhgama maintains a "Jobs-in-process control" account in its general ledger. When a job is completed, Sinhgama transfers the cost of the completed job to "Cost of jobs billed" account. Each month, Sinhgama closes any underallocated or overallocated overhead to "Cost of jobs billed".

Required

1. Calculate the overhead allocated to Job A21 as of January 31, current year and the overhead allocated to job A24 as of February 29, current year.
2. Calculate the underallocated or overallocated overhead for February current year.
3. Calculate the cost of jobs billed for February current year.

4-37 Allocation and proration of manufacturing overhead. (SMA, heavily adapted) Usha Limited is a company that produces machinery to customer order. Its job-costing system (using normal costing) has two direct-cost categories (direct materials and direct manufacturing labor) and one indirect-cost pool (manufacturing overhead, allocated using a budgeted rate based on direct manufacturing labor costs). The budget for the current year was

Direct manufacturing labor	Rs 8,40,000
Manufacturing overhead	5,04,000

At the end of current year, two jobs were incomplete: No. 1768B (total direct manufacturing labor costs were Rs 22,000) and No. 1819C (total direct manufacturing labor costs were Rs 78,000). Machine time totaled 287 hours for No 1768B and 647 hours for No. 1819C. Direct materials issued to No. 1768B amounted to Rs 44,000. Direct materials for No. 1819C were Rs 84,000.

Total charges to the Manufacturing overhead control account for the year were Rs 3,73,680. Direct manufacturing labor costs of all jobs were Rs 8,00,000, representing 20,000 direct manufacturing labor-hours.

There were no beginning inventories. In addition to the ending work in process, the ending finished goods showed a balance of Rs 3,12,000 (including direct manufacturing labor costs of Rs 80,000). Revenues for current year totaled Rs 54,01,360, cost of goods sold was Rs 32,00,000 and marketing costs were Rs 17,15,740. Usha prices on a cost-plus basis. It currently uses a guideline of cost plus 40 per cent of cost.

Required

1. Prepare a detailed schedule showing the ending balances in the inventories and Cost of Goods Sold (before considering any under- or overallocated manufacturing overhead). Show also the manufacturing overhead allocated in these ending balances.
2. Compute the under- or overallocated manufacturing overhead for current year.
3. Prorate the amount computed in requirement 2 on the basis of:
   a. The ending balances (before proration) of Work-in-Process Control, Finished Goods Control, and Cost of Goods Sold.
   b. The allocated overhead amount (before proration) in the ending balances of Work-in-Process Control, Finished Goods Control, and Cost of Goods Sold.

4. Assume Usha decides to write off to Cost of Goods Sold any under- or overallocated manufacturing overhead. Will operating income be higher or lower than the operating income that would have resulted from the proration in requirements 3a and 3b?
5. Calculate the cost of job No. 1819C if Usha Limited had used the adjusted allocation-rate approach to dispose of under- or overallocated manufacturing overhead in current year.

5 Activity-Based Costing and Activity-Based Management

Learning Objectives

1. Explain how broad averaging undercosts and overcosts products or services
2. Present three guidelines for refining a costing system
3. Distinguish between simple and activity-based costing systems
4. Describe a four-part cost hierarchy
5. Cost products or services using activity-based costing
6. Evaluate the costs and benefits of implementing activity-based costing systems
7. Explain how activity-based costing systems are used in activity-based management
8. Compare activity-based costing systems and department costing systems

A good mystery never fails to capture the imagination. Money is stolen or lost; property disappears or someone meets with foul play. On the surface, what appears unremarkable to the untrained eye can turn out to be quite a revelation once the facts and details are uncovered. Getting to the bottom of the case, understanding what happened and why, and taking action can make the difference between a solved case and an unsolved one. Business and organizations are much the same. Their costing systems are often mysteries, with unresolved questions: Why are we bleeding red ink? Are we pricing our products accurately? Activity-based costing can help unravel the mystery and result in improved operations, as Scotland Yard discovers in the following article.

LG Electronics Reduces Costs and Inefficiencies Through Activity-Based Costing[1]

LG Electronics is one of the world's largest manufacturers of flat-screen televisions and mobile phones. In 2009, the Seoul, South Korea-based company sold 16 million liquid crystal display televisions and 117 million mobile phones worldwide.

To make so many electronic devices, LG Electronics spends nearly $40 billion annually on the procurement of semiconductors, metals, connectors, and other materials. Costs for many of these components have soared in recent years. Until 2008, however, LG Electronics did not have a centralized procurement system to leverage its scale and to control supply costs. Instead, the company had a decentralized system riddled with wasteful spending and inefficiencies.

To respond to these challenges, LG Electronics hired its first chief procurement officer who turned to activity-based costing ("ABC") for answers. ABC analysis of the company's procurement system revealed that most company resources were applied to administrative and not strategic tasks. Furthermore, the administrative tasks were done manually and at a very high cost.

The ABC analysis led LG Electronics to change many of its procurement practices and processes, improve efficiency and focus on the highest-value tasks such as managing costs of commodity

[1] *Sources:* Carbone, James. 2009. LG Electronics centralizes purchasing to save. *Purchasing*, April. http://www.purchasing.com/article/217108-LG_Electronics_centralizes_purchasing_to_save.php; Linton's goals. 2009. Supply Management, May 12. http://www.supplymanagement.com/analysis/features/2009/lintons-goals/; Yoou-chul, Kim. 2009. CPO expects to save $1 billion in procurement. *The Korea Times*, April 1. http://www.koreatimes.co.kr/www/news/biz/2009/04/123_42360.html

products and negotiating with suppliers. Furthermore, the company developed a global procurement strategy for its televisions, mobile phones, computers, and home theatre systems by implementing competitive bidding among suppliers, standardizing parts across product lines, and developing additional buying capacity in China.

The results so far have been staggering. In 2008 alone, LG Electronics reduced its materials costs by 16%, and was expected to further reduce costs by $5 billion by the end of 2011.

Most companies—such as Dell, Oracle, JP Morgan Chase, and Honda—offer more than one product (or service). Dell Computer, for example, produces desktops, laptops, and servers. The three basic activities for manufacturing computers are (a) designing computers, (b) ordering component parts, and (c) assembly. The different products, however, require different quantities of the three activities. For example, a server has a more complex design, many more parts, and a more complex assembly than a desktop.

To measure the cost of producing each product, Dell separately tracks activity costs for each product. In this chapter, we describe activity-based costing systems and how they help companies make better decisions about pricing and product mix. And, just as in the case of LG Electronics, we show how ABC systems assist in cost management decisions by improving product designs, processes, and efficiency.

Broad Averaging and Its Consequences

Historically, companies (for example, television and automobile manufacturers) produced a limited variety of products. Indirect (or overhead) costs were a relatively small percentage of total costs. So, using simple costing systems to allocate costs broadly was easy, inexpensive, and reasonably accurate. However, as product diversity and indirect costs have increased, broad averaging has resulted in greater inaccuracy of product costs. For example, the use of a single, plant-wide manufacturing overhead rate to allocate costs to products often produces unreliable cost data. The term *peanut-butter costing* (yes, that's what it's called) describes a particular costing approach that uses broad averages for assigning (or spreading, as in spreading peanut butter) the cost of resources uniformly to cost objects (such as products or services) when the individual products or services, may in fact, use those resources in nonuniform ways.

Learning Objectives 1

Explain how broad averaging undercosts and overcosts products or services

. . . this problem arises when reported costs of products do not equal their actual costs

Undercosting and Overcosting

The following example illustrates how averaging can provide inaccurate and misleading cost data. Consider the cost of a restaurant bill for four colleagues who meet monthly to discuss business developments. Each diner orders separate entrees, desserts, and drinks. The restaurant bill for the most recent meeting is:

	Anita	Anurag	Ajit	Anshul	Total	Average
Entree	Rs 110	Rs 200	Rs 150	Rs 140	Rs 600	Rs 150
Dessert	0	80	40	40	160	40
Drinks	40	140	80	60	320	80
Total	Rs 150	Rs 420	Rs 270	Rs 240	Rs 1,080	Rs 270

If the Rs 1,080 total restaurant bill is divided evenly, Rs 270 is the average cost per diner. This cost-averaging approach treats each diner the same. Anita would probably object to paying Rs 270 because her actual cost is only Rs 150; she ordered the lowest-cost entree, had no dessert, and had the lowest-cost drink. When costs are averaged across all four diners, both Anita and Anshul are overcosted, Anurag is undercosted, and Ajit is (by coincidence) accurately costed.

Broad averaging can lead to undercosting or overcosting of products or services:

- **Product undercosting**—a product consumes a high level of resources but is reported to have a low cost per unit (Anurag's dinner).
- **Product overcosting**—a product consumes a low level of resources but is reported to have a high cost per unit (Anita's dinner).

What are the strategic consequences of product undercosting and overcosting? Think of a company that uses cost information about its products to guide pricing decisions. Undercosted products will be underpriced, increasing demand for these products but lowering profits. In fact, undercosted products may lead to sales that actually result in losses—the sales bring in less revenue than the cost of resources they use. Overcosted products lead to overpricing, causing these products to lose market share to competitors producing similar products. Worse still, product undercosting and overcosting draws managerial attention to the wrong products, drawing attention to overcosted products whose costs may in fact be perfectly reasonable and ignoring undercosted products that in fact consume large amounts of resources.

Product-Cost Cross-Subsidization

Product-cost cross-subsidization means that if a company undercosts one of its products, then it will overcost at least one of its other products. Similarly, if a company overcosts one of its products, it will undercost at least one of its other products. Product-cost cross-subsidization is very common in situations in which a cost is uniformly spread—meaning it is broadly averaged—across multiple products without recognizing the amount of resources consumed by each product.

In the restaurant-bill example, the amount of cost cross-subsidization of each diner can be readily computed *because all cost items can be traced as direct costs to each diner*. If all diners pay Rs 270, Anita is paying Rs 120 more than her actual cost of Rs 150. She is cross-subsidizing Anurag who is paying Rs 150 less than his actual cost of Rs 420. Calculating the amount of cost cross-subsidization takes more work when there are indirect costs to be considered. Why? Because the resources represented by the indirect costs are used by two or more diners, and we need to find a way to allocate costs to each diner. Consider, for example, a Rs 400 bottle of wine whose cost is shared equally. Each diner would pay Rs 100 (Rs 400 ÷ 4). Suppose Anshul drinks 2 glasses of wine while Anita, Anurag and Ajit drink one glass each for a total of 5 glasses. Allocating the cost of the bottle of wine on the basis of the glasses of wine that each diner drinks would result in Anshul paying Rs 160 (Rs 400) and each of the others Rs 80 (Rs 400 × 1/5). In this case, sharing the cost equally, Anita, Anurag and Ajit are each paying Rs 20 (Rs 100 – Rs 80) more and are cross-subsidizing Anshul who is paying Rs 60 (Rs 160 – Rs 100) less for the wine he consumes.

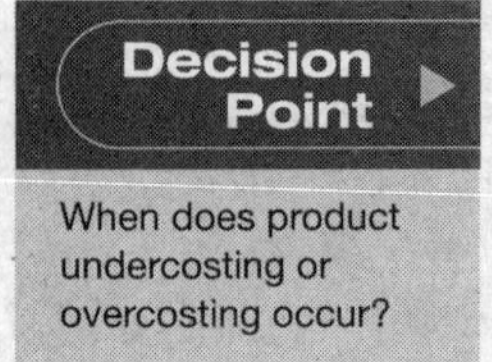

When does product undercosting or overcosting occur?

To see the effects of broad averaging on direct and indirect costs, we consider Plastim Corporation's costing system.

Simple Costing System at Plastim Corporation

Plastim Corporation manufactures lenses for the rear taillights of automobiles. A lens, made from black, red, orange, or white plastic, is the part of the lamp visible on the automobile's exterior. Lenses are made by injecting molten plastic into a mold to give the lamp its desired shape. The mold is cooled to allow the molten plastic to solidify, and the lens is removed.

Under its contract with Tata Motors, a major automobile manufacturer, Plastim makes two types of lenses: a complex lens, CL5, and a simple lens, S3. The complex lens is a large lens with special features, such as multicolor molding (when more than one color is injected into the mold) and a complex shape that wraps around the corner of the car. Manufacturing CL5 lenses is more complex because various parts in the mold must align and fit precisely. The S3 lens is simpler to make because it has a single color and few special features.

Design, Manufacturing, and Distribution Processes

The sequence of steps to design, produce, and distribute lenses, whether simple or complex, is:

- **Design products and processes.** Each year Tata Motors specifies some modifications to the simple and complex lenses. Plastim's Design Department designs the molds from which the lenses will be made and specifies the processes needed (that is, details of the manufacturing operations).
- **Manufacture lenses.** The lenses are molded, finished, cleaned, and inspected.
- **Distribute lenses.** Finished lenses are packed and sent to Tata Motors.

Plastim is operating at capacity and incurs very low marketing costs. Because of its high-quality products, Plastim has minimal customer-service costs. Plastim's business environment is very competitive with respect to simple lenses. At a recent meeting, Tata's purchasing manager indicates that a new supplier, Jain Motors, which makes only simple lenses, is offering to supply the S3 lens to Tata at a price of Rs 530, well below Plastim's Rs 630 price. Unless Plastim can lower its selling price, it will lose the Tata business for the simple lens for the upcoming model year. Fortunately, the same competitive pressures do not exist for the complex lens, which Plastim currently sells to Tata at Rs 1,370 per lens.

Plastim's management has various options available to it.

- Plastim can give up the Tata business in simple lenses if it is unprofitable. Jain Motors makes only simple lenses and perhaps, therefore, uses simpler technology and processes than Plastim, which makes both simple and complex lenses. The simpler operations may give Jain Motors a cost advantage that Plastim cannot match. If so, it is better for Plastim to not supply the S3 lens to Tata.
- Plastim can reduce the price of the simple lens and either accept a lower margin or aggressively seek to reduce costs.

To make these long-run strategic decisions, management needs to first understand the costs to design, make, and distribute the S3 and CL5 lenses.

Jain Motors makes essentially one product, simple lenses. It therefore has a very simple costing environment where the cost of a lens can be calculated fairly accurately by dividing total costs incurred by units produced. Plastim's costing environment is more challenging. The processes to make simple and complex lenses are quite different and Plastim needs to determine what it costs to make each type of lens.

In computing these costs, Plastim assigns both variable costs and costs that are fixed in the short run to the S3 and CL5 lenses. Why? For two reasons. First because, in the long run, almost all costs can be changed and managed including those that are fixed in the short run. Second because, to survive and prosper in the long run, the prices charged for S3 and CL5 must exceed total costs (variable and fixed) to design, make and distribute the lenses. To guide their pricing and cost-management decisions, Plastim's managers assign all costs, both manufacturing and nonmanufacturing, to the S3 and CL5 lenses. Had the purpose been inventory costing to comply with generally accepted accounting principles, Plastim's management accountants would have assigned only manufacturing costs to the lenses. Surveys of company practice across the globe overwhelmingly indicate that the vast majority of companies use costing systems not just for inventory costing but also for strategic purposes such as pricing and product-mix decisions and decisions about cost reduction, process improvement, design, and planning and budgeting. As a result, even merchandising-sector companies (for whom inventory costing is straightforward) and service-sector companies (who have no inventory) expend considerable resources in designing and operating their costing systems. In this chapter, we take this more strategic focus and allocate costs in all functions of the value chain to the S3 and CL5 lenses.

Simple Costing System Using a Single Indirect-Cost Pool

Plastim has historically had a simple costing system that allocates indirect costs using a single indirect-cost rate, the type of system described in Chapter 4. To budget costs for 2010, we first describe Plastim's simple costing system and later contrast it with a different costing system: activity-based costing. (Note that instead of jobs, as in Chapter 4, we now have products as the cost objects.) Exhibit 5-1 shows an overview of Plastim's simple costing system. Use this exhibit as a guide as you study the following steps, each of which is marked in Exhibit 5-1.

Step 1: Identify the Products That Are the Chosen Cost Objects. The cost objects are the 60,000 simple S3 lenses and the 15,000 complex CL5 lenses that Plastim will produce in 2010. Plastim's goal is to first calculate the total costs and then the unit cost of designing, manufacturing, and distributing these lenses.

Step 2: Identify the Direct Costs of the Products. Plastim identifies the direct costs—direct materials and direct manufacturing labor—of the lenses. Exhibit 5-2 shows the direct and indirect costs for the S3 and the CL5 lenses using the simple costing system. The direct cost calculations appear on lines 5, 6, and 7 of Exhibit 5-2. Plastim classifies all other costs as indirect costs.

Step 3: Select the Cost-Allocation Bases to Use for Allocating Indirect (or Overhead) Costs to the Products. A majority of the indirect costs consist of salaries paid to supervisors, engineers, manufacturing support, and maintenance staff, all supporting direct manufacturing labor. Plastim uses direct manufacturing labor-hours as the only allocation base to allocate all manufacturing and nonmanufacturing indirect costs to S3 and CL5. In 2010, Plastim plans to use 39,750 direct manufacturing labor-hours.

Step 4: Identify the Indirect Costs Associated with Each Cost-Allocation Base. Because Plastim uses only a single cost-allocation base, Plastim groups all budgeted indirect costs of Rs 2,38,50,000 for 2010 into a single overhead cost pool.

Step 5: Compute the Rate per Unit of Each Cost-Allocation Base.

$$\text{Budgeted indirect-cost rate} = \frac{\text{Budgeted total costs in indirect-cost pool}}{\text{Budgeted total quantity of cost-allocation base}}$$

$$= \frac{\text{Rs } 2{,}38{,}50{,}000}{39{,}750 \text{ direct manufacturing labour-hours}}$$

$$= \textbf{Rs 600 per direct manufacturing labor-hour}$$

Step 6: Compute the Indirect Costs Allocated to the Products. Plastim expects to use 30,000 total direct manufacturing labor-hours to make the 60,000 S3 lenses and 9,750 total direct manufacturing labor-hours to make the 15,000 CL5 lenses. Exhibit 5-2 shows indirect costs of Rs 1,80,00,000 (Rs 600 per direct manufacturing labor-hour × 30,000 direct manufacturing labor-hours) allocated to the simple lens and Rs 58,50,000 (Rs 600 per direct manufacturing labor-hour × 9,750 direct manufacturing labor-hours) allocated to the complex lens.

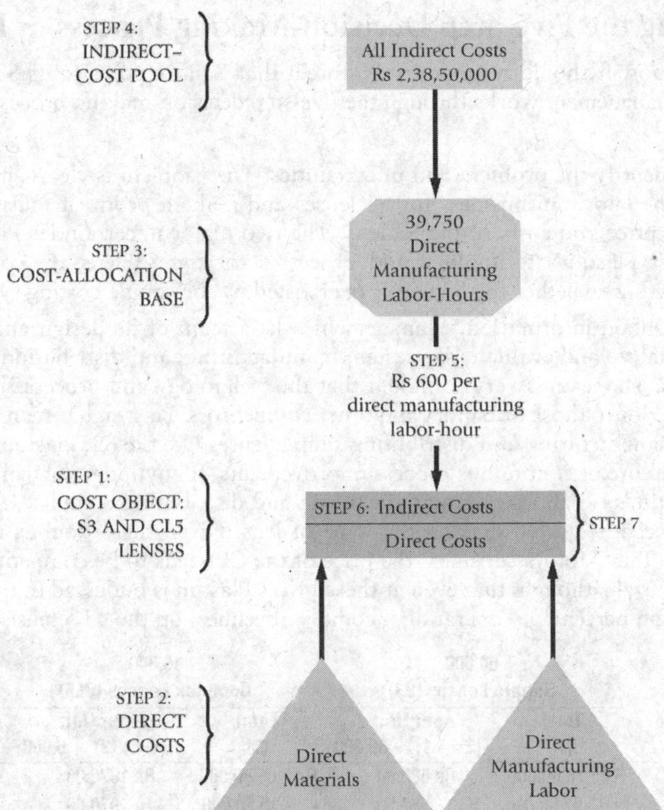

Exhibit 5-1

Overview of Plastim's Simple Costing System

Step 7: Compute the Total Cost of the Products by Adding All Direct and Indirect Costs Assigned to the Products. Exhibit 5-2 presents the product costs for the simple and complex lenses. The direct costs are calculated in step 2 and the indirect costs in step 6. Be sure you see the parallel between the simple costing system overview diagram (Exhibit 5-1) and the costs calculated in step 7. Exhibit 5-1 shows two direct-cost categories and one indirect-cost category. Hence, the budgeted cost of each type of lens in step 7 (Exhibit 5-2) has three line items: two for direct costs and one for allocated indirect costs. The unit cost of the S3 lens will be Rs 587.5, well above the Rs 530 selling price quoted by Jain Motors. The cost per CL5 lens is Rs 970.

Exhibit 5-2

Plastim's Product Costs Using the Simple Costing System

	A	B	C	D	E	F	G
1		60,000			15,000		
2		Simple Lenses (S3)			Complex Lenses (CL5)		
3		Total	per Unit		Total	per Unit	Total
4		(1)	(2) = (1) ÷ 60,000		(3)	(4) = (3) ÷ 15,000	(5) = (1) + (3)
5	Direct materials	Rs.1,12,50,000	Rs. 187.50		Rs.67,50,000	Rs. 450.00	Rs.1,80,00,000
6	Direct manufacturing labor	60,00,000	100.00		19,50,000	130.00	79,50,000
7	Total direct costs (Step 2)	1,72,50,000	287.50		87,00,000	580.00	Rs.2,59,50,000
8	Indirect costs allocated (Step 6)	1,80,00,000	300.00		58,50,000	390.00	2,38,50,000
9	Total costs (Step 7)	Rs. 3,52,50,000	Rs. 587.50		Rs. 1,45,50,000	Rs. 970.00	Rs. 4,98,00,000
10							

Applying the Five-Step Decision-Making Process at Plastim

To decide how it should respond to the threat that Bandix poses to its S3 lens business, Plastim's management works through the five-step decision-making process introduced in Chapter 1.

Step 1: Identify the problem and uncertainties. The problem is clear—if Plastim wants to retain the Giovanni business for S3 lenses and make a profit, it must find a way to reduce the price and costs of the S3 lens. The two major uncertainties Plastim faces are (1) whether Plastim's technology and processes for the S3 lens are competitive with Bandix's and (2) whether the S3 lens is overcosted by the simple costing system.

Step 2: Obtain information. Management asks a team of its design and process engineers to analyze and evaluate the design, manufacturing, and distribution operations for the S3 lens. The team is very confident that the technology and processes for the S3 lens are not inferior to those of Bandix and other competitors. Plastim has many years of experience in manufacturing and distributing simple lenses like the S3. Plastim also has a history and culture of continuous process improvements. If anything, the team is less certain about Plastim's capabilities in manufacturing and distributing complex lenses because it has only recently started making this type of lens. Given these doubts, management is happy that Tata Motors considers the price of the CL5 lens to be competitive. It is somewhat of a puzzle, though, that even at these prices Plastim is budgeted to earn a very large profit margin percentage (operating income ÷ revenues) on the CL5 lenses:

	60,000 Simple Lenses (S3)		15,000 Complex Lenses (CL5)		
	Total (1)	per Unit (2) = 1) ÷ 60,000	Total (3)	per Unit (4) = (3) ÷ 5,000	Total (5) = (1) + (3)
Revenues	Rs 3,78,00,000	Rs 630.00	Rs 2,05,50,000	Rs 1370.00	Rs 5,83,50,000
Total costs	3,52,50,000	587.50	1,45,50,000	970.00	4,98,00,000
Operating income	Rs 25,50,000	42.50	Rs 60,00,000	Rs 400	Rs 85,50,000
Profit margin percentage		6.75%		29.20%	

As it continues to gather information, Plastim's management begins to ponder why the profit margin percentage is low for the S3 lens, where the company has strong capabilities, but high on the newer, less-established CL5 lens. Plastim is not deliberately charging a low price for S3, so management starts to believe that perhaps the problem lies with its costing system. Plastim's simple costing system may be overcosting the simple S3 lens (assigning too much cost to it) and undercosting the complex CL5 lens (assigning too little cost to it).

Step 3: Make predictions about the future. Plastim's key challenge is to get a better estimate of what it will cost to design, make, and distribute the S3 and CL5 lenses. Management is fairly confident about the direct material and direct manufacturing labor costs of each lens because these costs are easily traced to the lenses. But management is quite concerned about how accurately the simple costing system measures the indirect resources used by each type of lens. It believes it can do much better.

At the same time, management wants to ensure that no biases enter its thinking. In particular, it wants to be careful that the desire to be competitive on the S3 lens should not lead to assumptions that bias in favor of lowering costs of the S3 lens.

Step 4: Make decisions by choosing among alternatives. On the basis of predicted costs, and taking into account how Jain Motors might respond, Plastim must decide whether to bid for the Tata Motors' S3 lens business and if it does bid, what price it should offer.

Step 5: Implement the decision, evaluate performance, and learn. If Plastim wins Tata's S3 lens business, it must compare actual costs, as it makes and ships S3 lenses, to predicted costs and learn why actual costs deviate from predicted costs. Such evaluation and learning form the basis for future improvements.

The next few sections focus on Steps 3, 4 and 5—how Plastim improves the allocation of indirect costs to the S3 and CL5 lenses, how it uses these predictions to bid for the S3 lens business, and how it makes product design and process improvements.

Refining a Costing System

Learning Objective 2

Present three guidelines for refining a costing system

. . . classify more costs as direct costs, expand the number of indirect-cost pools, and identify cost drivers

A **refined costing system** reduces the use of broad averages for assigning the cost of resources to cost objects (such as jobs, products, and services) and provides better measurement of the costs of indirect resources used by different cost objects—no matter how differently various cost objects use indirect resources. There are three principal reasons that have accelerated the demand for such refinements.

1. **Increase in product diversity.** The growing demand for customized products has led companies to increase the variety of products and services they offer. Banks, offer many different types of accounts and services: special passbook accounts, ATMs, credit cards, and electronic banking. These products differ in the demands they place on the resources needed to produce them because of differences in volume, process, and complexity. The use of broad averages is likely to lead to distorted and inaccurate cost information.
2. **Increase in indirect costs.** The use of product and process technology such as computer-integrated manufacturing (CIM) and flexible manufacturing systems (FMS), has led to an increase in indirect costs and a decrease in direct costs, particularly direct manufacturing labor costs. In CIM and FMS, computers on the manufacturing floor give instructions to set up and run equipment quickly and automatically. The computers accurately measure hundreds of production parameters and directly control the manufacturing processes to achieve high-quality output. Managing more complex technology and producing very diverse products also requires committing an increasing amount of resources for various support functions, such as production scheduling and product and process design and engineering. Because direct manufacturing labor is not a cost driver of these costs, allocating indirect costs on the basis of direct manufacturing labor (which was the common practice) often does not accurately measure how resources are being used by different products.
3. **Competition in product markets.** As markets have become more competitive, managers have felt the need to obtain more accurate cost information to help them make important strategic decisions, such as how to price products and which products to sell. Making correct pricing and product mix decisions is critical in competitive markets because competitors quickly capitalize on a company's mistakes.

Whereas the above factors point to reasons for the increase in *demand* for refined cost systems, *advances in information technology* have enabled companies to implement these refinements. Costing system refinements require more data gathering and more analysis, and improvements in information technology have drastically reduced the costs to gather, validate, store, and analyze vast quantities of data.

Guidelines for Refining a Costing System

There are three main guidelines for refining a costing system. In the following sections, we delve more deeply into each in the context of the Plastim example.

1. **Direct-cost tracing.** Identify as many direct costs as is economically feasible. This guideline aims to reduce the amount of costs classified as indirect, thereby minimizing the extent to which costs have to be allocated, rather than traced.
2. **Indirect-cost pools.** Expand the number of indirect-cost pools until each of these pools is more homogeneous. In a *homogeneous cost pool,* all of the costs have the same or a similar cause-and-effect (or benefits-received) relationship with a single cost driver that is used as the cost-allocation base. Consider, for example, a single indirect-cost pool containing both indirect machining costs and indirect distribution costs that are allocated to products using machine-hours. This pool is not homogeneous because machine-hours are a cost driver of machining costs but not of distribution costs, which has a different cost driver, number of shipments. If, instead, machining costs and distribution costs are separated into two indirect-cost pools (with machine-hours as the cost-allocation base for the machining cost pool and number of shipments

as the cost-allocation base for the distribution cost pool), each indirect-cost pool would become homogeneous.

3. **Cost-allocation bases.** As we describe later in the chapter, whenever possible, use the cost driver (the cause of indirect costs) as the cost-allocation base for each homogeneous indirect-cost pool (the effect).

Activity-Based Costing Systems

Learning Objective 3

Distinguish between simple and activity-based costing systems

. . . unlike simple systems, ABC systems calculate costs of individual activities to cost products

One of the best tools for refining a costing system is activity-based costing. **Activity-based costing (ABC)** refines a costing system by identifying individual activities as the fundamental cost objects. An **activity** is an event, task, or unit of work with a specified purpose—for example, designing products, setting up machines, operating machines, and distributing products. More informally, activities are verbs; they are things that a firm does. Consistent with their more strategic focus, ABC systems identify activities in all functions of the value chain. ABC systems first calculate the costs of individual activities and then assign costs to cost objects such as products and services on the basis of the mix of activities needed to produce each product or service:[2]

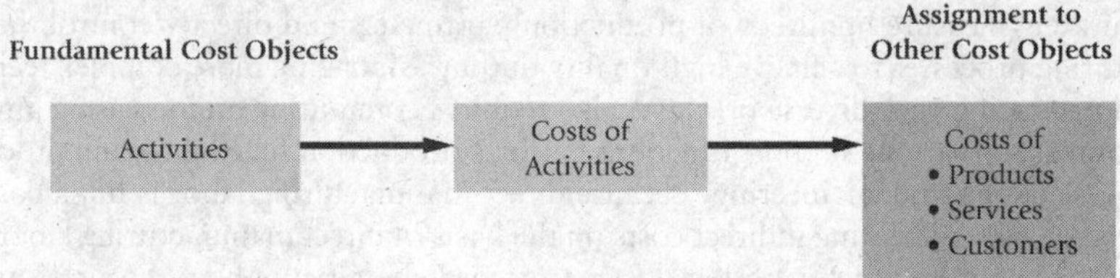

Plastim's ABC System

After reviewing its simple costing system and the potential miscosting of product costs, Plastim decides to implement an ABC system. Direct costs can be traced to products easily, so the ABC system focuses on refining the assignment of indirect costs to departments, processes, products, or other cost objects. Plastim's ABC system identifies various activities that help explain why Plastim incurs the costs it currently classifies as indirect. In other words, it breaks up the current indirect cost pool into finer pools of costs related to various activities. To identify these activities, Plastim organizes a team comprised of managers from design, manufacturing, distribution, accounting, and administration.

Defining activities is not a simple matter. The team evaluates hundreds of tasks performed at Plastim before choosing the activities that form the basis of its ABC system. For example, it decides if maintenance of molding machines, operations of molding machines, process control, and product inspection should each be regarded as a separate activity or should be combined into a single activity. An activity-based costing system with many activities becomes overly detailed and unwieldy to operate. An activity-based costing system with too few activities may not be refined enough to measure cause-and-effect relationships between cost drivers and various indirect costs. In choosing activities, Plastim's team identifies those that account for a sizable fraction of indirect costs and combines activities that have the same cost driver into a single activity. For example, the team decides to combine maintenance of molding machines, operations of molding machines, process control, and product inspection into a single activity—molding machine operations—because all these activities have the same cost driver: molding machine-hours.

---

[2] For more details on ABC systems, see R. Cooper and R. S. Kaplan, *The Design of Cost Management Systems* (Upper Saddle River, NJ: Prentice Hall, 1999); G. Cokins, *Activity-Based Cost Management: An Executive's Guide* (Hoboken, NJ: John Wiley & Sons, 2001); and R. S. Kaplan and S. Anderson, *Time-Driven Activity-Based Costing: A Simpler and More Powerful Path to Higher Profits* (Boston: Harvard Business School Press, 2007).

The team identifies the following seven activities by developing a flowchart of all the steps and processes needed to design, manufacture, and distribute S3 and CL5 lenses.

a. Design products and processes
b. Set up molding machines to ensure that the molds are properly held in place and parts are properly aligned before manufacturing starts
c. Operate molding machines to manufacture lenses
d. Clean and maintain the molds after lenses are manufactured
e. Prepare batches of finished lenses for shipment
f. Distribute lenses to customers
g. Administer and manage all processes at Plastim

These activity descriptions form the basis of the activity-based costing system—sometimes called an *activity list* or an *activity dictionary*. The list of tasks, however, is only the first step in implementing activity-based costing systems. Plastim must also identify the cost of each activity and the related cost driver. To do so, Plastim uses the three guidelines for refining a costing system.

1. **Direct-cost tracing.** Plastim's ABC system subdivides the single indirect cost pool into seven smaller cost pools related to the different activities. Plastim determines that the costs in the cleaning and maintenance activity cost pool (item d) is a direct cost. The costs of cleaning and maintenance consist of salaries and wages paid to workers responsible for cleaning the mold. These costs can be economically traced to the specific mold used to produce the lens.
2. **Indirect-cost pools.** Plastim considers the remaining six activity cost pools as indirect cost pools. Unlike the single indirect cost pool of Plastim's simple costing system, each of the activity-related cost pools is homogeneous. That is, each activity cost pool includes only those narrow and focused set of costs that have the same cost driver. For example, the distribution cost pool includes only those costs (such as wages of truck drivers) that, over time, increase as the cost driver of distribution costs, cubic feet of packages delivered, increases. In the simple costing system, all costs were lumped together and the cost-allocation base, direct manufacturing labor-hours, was not a cost driver of the indirect costs.

   Determining costs of activity pools requires assigning and reassigning costs accumulated in support departments, such as human resources and information systems, to each of the activity cost pools on the basis of how various activities use support department resources. This is commonly referred to as *first-stage allocation*, a topic which we discuss in detail in Chapters 14 and 15. We focus here on the *second-stage allocation*, the allocation of costs of activity cost pools to products.
3. **Cost-allocation bases.** For each activity cost pool, the cost driver is used (whenever possible) as the cost-allocation base. To identify cost drivers, Plastim's managers consider various alternatives and use their knowledge of operations to choose among them. For example, Plastim's managers choose setup-hours rather than the number of setups as the cost driver of setup costs, because Plastim's managers believe that more complex setups take more time and are more costly. Over time, Plastim's managers can use data to test their beliefs. (Chapter 10 discusses several methods to estimate the relationship between a cost driver and costs.)

The logic of ABC systems is twofold. First, structuring activity cost pools more finely with cost drivers for each activity cost pool as the cost-allocation base leads to more accurate costing of activities. Second, allocating these costs to products by measuring the cost-allocation bases of different activities used by different products leads to more accurate product costs. We illustrate this logic by focusing on the setup activity at Plastim.

Setting up molding machines frequently entails trial runs, fine-tuning, and adjustments. Improper setups cause quality problems such as scratches on the surface of the lens. The resources needed for each setup depend on the complexity of the manufacturing operation. Complex lenses require more setup resources per setup than simple lenses.

Furthermore, complex lenses can be produced only in small batches because the molds for complex lenses need to be cleaned more often than molds for simple lenses. Thus, relative to simple lenses, complex lenses not only use more resources per setup, but they also require more frequent setups.

Setup data for the simple S3 lens and the complex CL5 lens are:

		Simple S3 Lens	Complex CL5 Lens	Total
1	Quantity of lenses produced	60,000	15,000	
2	Number of lenses produced per batch	240	50	
3 = (1) ÷ (2)	Number of batches	250	300	
4	Setup time per batch	2 hours	5 hours	
5 = (3) × (4)	Total setup-hours	500 hours	1,500 hours	2,000 hours

Setup hours represents the demand that each product places on setup resources.

Of the Rs 2,38,50,000 in the total indirect-cost pool, Plastim identifies the total costs of setups (consisting mainly of allocated costs of process engineers, quality engineers, supervisors, and depreciation on setup equipment) to be Rs 30,00,000. The following table illustrates the effect of using direct manufacturing labor-hours—the cost-allocation base for all indirect costs in Plastim's pre-ABC costing system—versus setup-hours—the cost-allocation base for setup costs in the ABC system—to allocate setup costs to the simple and complex lenses. Of the Rs 600 total rate per direct manufacturing labor-hour, the setup cost per direct manufacturing labor-hour amounts to Rs 75.4717(Rs 30,00,000 ÷ 39,750 total direct manufacturing labor-hours). The setup cost per setup-hour equals Rs 1,500 (Rs 30,00,000 ÷ 2,000 total setup-hours).

	Simple S3 Lens	Complex CL5 Lens	Total
Setup cost allocated using direct manufacturing labor-hours: Rs 75.4717 × 30,000; Rs 75.4717 × 9,750	Rs 22,64,150	Rs 7,35,850	Rs 30,00,000
Setup cost allocated using setup-hours: Rs 1,500 × 500; Rs 1,500 × 1,500	Rs 7,50,000	Rs 22,50,000	Rs 30,00,000

What is the difference between the design of a simple costing system and an activity-based costing (ABC) system?

As we have already discussed when presenting guidelines 2 and 3, setup hours, not direct manufacturing labor hours, are the cost driver of set-up costs. Setup costs depend on the number of batches and the difficulty of the setups, both of which result in more setup-hours. The CL5 lens uses substantially more setup-hours than the S3 lens (1,500 hours ÷ 2,000 hours = 75% of the total setup hours) because the CL5 requires a greater number of setups (batches) and each setup is more challenging.

The ABC system therefore allocates substantially more setup costs to CL5 than to S3 because of the greater demand that CL5 places on setup resources. When direct manufacturing labor-hours rather than setup-hours are used to allocate setup costs in the simple costing system, it is the S3 lens that is allocated a very large share of the setup costs because the S3 lens uses a larger proportion of direct manufacturing labor-hours (30,000 ÷ 39,750 = 75.47%). As a result, the simple costing system overcosts the S3 lens with regard to setup costs.

Learning Objective 4

Describe a four-part cost hierarchy

. . . a four-part cost hierarchy is used to categorize costs based on different types of cost drivers—for example, costs that vary with each unit of a product versus costs that vary with each batch of products

Note that setup-hours are related to batches (or groups) of lenses made, not the number of individual lenses. Activity-based costing attempts to identify the most relevant cause-and-effect relationship for each activity pool, without restricting the cost driver to only units of output or variables related to units of output (such as direct manufacturing labor-hours). As our discussion of setups illustrates, limiting cost-allocation bases in this manner weakens the cause-and-effect relationship between the cost allocation base and the costs in a cost pool.

Cost Hierarchies

A **cost hierarchy** categorizes various activity cost pools on the basis of the different types of cost drivers, or cost-allocation bases, or different degrees of difficulty in determining cause-and-effect (or benefits-received) relationships. ABC systems commonly use a cost hierarchy having four levels—output unit-level costs, batch-level costs, product-sustaining costs, and facility-sustaining costs—to identify cost-allocation bases that are, whenever possible, drivers of costs in activity cost pools.

Output unit-level costs are the costs of activities performed on each individual unit of a product or service. Machine operations costs (such as the cost of energy, machine depreciation, and repair) related to the activity of running the automated molding machines are output unit-level costs. They are output unit-level costs because, over time, the cost of this activity increases with additional units of output produced (or machine-hours used). Plastim's ABC system uses molding machine-hours—an output-unit level cost-allocation base—to allocate machine operations costs to products.

Batch-level costs are the costs of activities related to a group of units of products or services rather than to each individual unit of product or service. In the Plastim example, setup costs are batch-level costs because, over time, the cost of this setup activity increases with setup-hours needed to produce batches of lenses. The S3 lens requires 500 setup-hours (2 setup-hours per batch × 250 batches). The CL5 lens requires 1,500 setup-hours (5 setup-hours per batch × 300 batches). The total setup costs allocated to S3 and CL5 depend on the total setup-hours required by each type of lens, not on the number of units of S3 and CL5 produced. (Setup costs being a batch-level cost cannot be avoided by producing one less unit of S3 or CL5.) Plastim's ABC system uses setup-hours—a batch-level cost-allocation base—to allocate setup costs to products.

Other examples of batch-level costs are material-handling and quality-inspection costs associated with batches (not the quantities) of products produced, and costs of placing purchase orders, receiving materials, and paying invoices related to the number of purchase orders placed rather than the quantity or value of materials purchased.

Product-sustaining costs (service-sustaining costs) are the costs of activities undertaken to support individual products or services regardless of the number of units or batches in which the units are produced. In the Plastim example, design costs are product-sustaining costs. Over time, design costs depend largely on the time designers spend on designing and modifying the product, the mold, and the process. These design costs are a function of the complexity of the mold, measured by the number of parts in the mold multiplied by the area (in square feet) over which the molten plastic must flow (12 parts × 2.5 square feet, or 30 parts-square feet for the S3 lens, and 14 parts × 5 square feet, or 70 parts-square feet for the CL5 lens). The total design costs allocated to S3 and CL5 depend on the complexity of the mold, regardless of the number of units or batches of production. Design costs cannot be avoided by producing fewer units or running fewer batches. Plastim's ABC system uses parts-square feet—a product-sustaining cost-allocation base—to allocate design costs to products. Other examples of product-sustaining costs are product research and development costs, costs of making engineering changes, and marketing costs to launch new products.

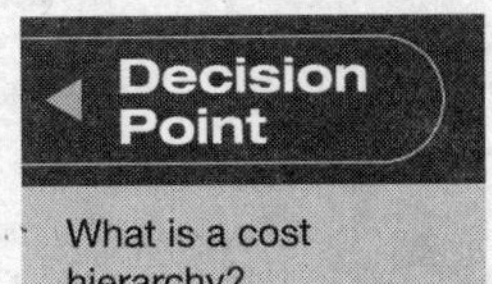

What is a cost hierarchy?

Facility-sustaining costs are the costs of activities that cannot be traced to individual products or services but that support the organization as a whole. In the Plastim example, the general administration costs (including top management compensation, rent, and building security) are facility-sustaining costs. It is usually difficult to find a good cause-and-effect relationship between these costs and the cost-allocation base. This lack of a cause-and-effect relationship causes some companies not to allocate these costs to products and instead to deduct them separately from operating income. Other companies, such as Plastim, allocate facility-sustaining costs to products on some basis—for example, direct manufacturing labor-hours—because management believes all costs should be allocated to products. Allocating all costs to products or services becomes important when management wants to set selling prices on the basis of an amount of cost that includes all costs.

Learning Objective 5

Cost products or services using activity-based costing

. . . use cost rates for different activities to compute indirect costs of a product

Implementing Activity-Based Costing at Plastim

In order to apply ABC to Plastim's costing system, we follow the seven-step approach to costing and the three guidelines for refining costing systems (increasing direct-cost tracing, creating homogeneous indirect-cost pools, and identifying cost-allocation bases that

Exhibit 5-3 Overview of Plastim's Activity-Based Costing System

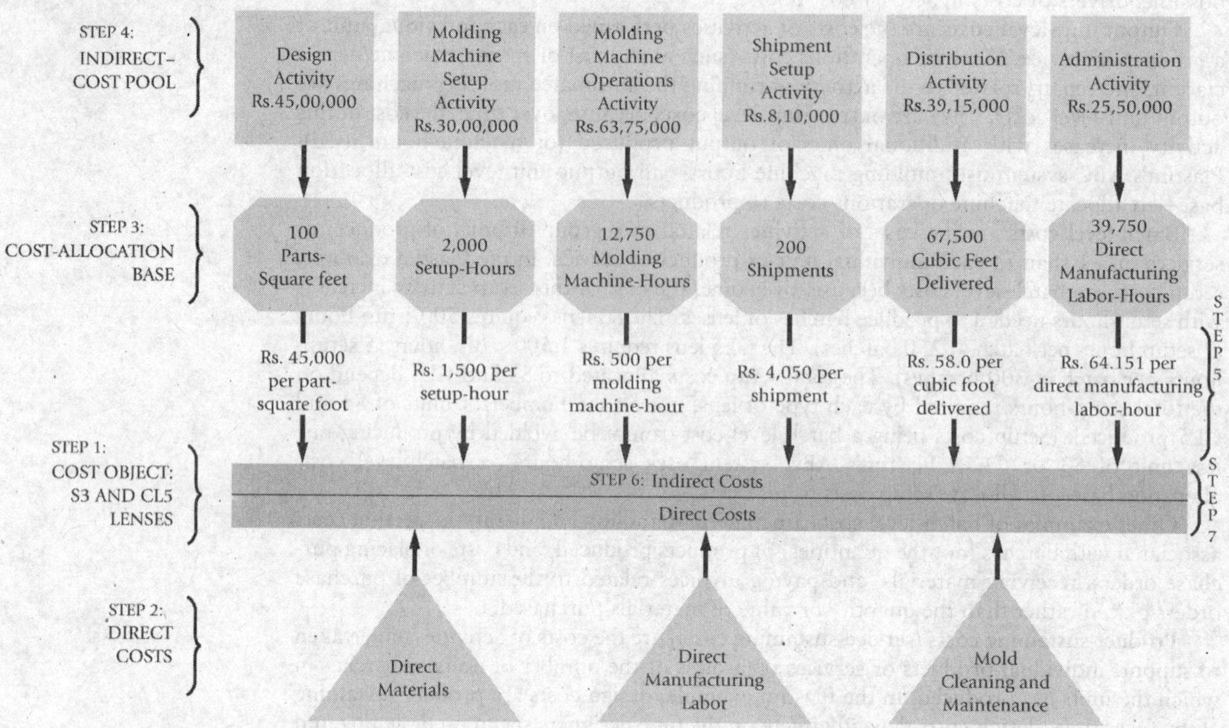

have cause-and-effect relationships with costs in the cost pool). Exhibit 5-3 shows an overview of Plastim's ABC system. Use this exhibit as a guide as you study the following steps, each of which is marked in Exhibit 5-3.

Step 1: Identify the Products That Are the Chosen Cost Objects. The cost objects are the 60,000 S3 and the 15,000 CL5 lenses that Plastim will produce in 2010. Plastim's goal is to first calculate the total costs and then the per-unit cost of designing, manufacturing, and distributing these lenses.

Step 2: Identify the Direct Costs of the Products. Plastim identifies as direct costs of the lenses: direct material costs, direct manufacturing labor costs, and mold cleaning and maintenance costs because these costs can be economically traced to a specific lens or mold.

Exhibit 5-5 shows the direct and indirect costs for the S3 and CL5 lenses using the ABC system. The direct costs calculations appear on lines 6, 7, 8 and 9 of Exhibit 5-5. Plastim classifies all other costs as indirect costs, as we will see in Exhibit 5-4.

Step 3: Select the Activities and Cost-Allocation Bases to Use for Allocating Indirect Costs to the Products. Following guidelines 2 and 3 for refining a costing system, Plastim identifies six activities—(a) design, (b) molding machine setups, (c) machine operations, (d) shipment setup, (e) distribution, and (f) administration—for allocating indirect costs to products. Exhibit 5-4, column 2, shows the cost hierarchy category, and column 4 shows the cost-allocation base and the budgeted quantity of the cost-allocation base for each activity described in column 1.

Identifying the cost-allocation bases defines the number of activity pools into which costs must be grouped in an ABC system. For example, rather than define the design activities of product design, process design, and prototyping as separate activities, Plastim defines these three activities together as a combined "design" activity and forms a homogeneous design cost pool. Why? Because the complexity of the mold is an appropriate cost driver for costs incurred in each of the three separate design activities.

Exhibit 5-4 Activity-Cost Rates for Indirect-Cost Pools

	A	B	C	D	E	F	G	H
1			(Step 4)	(Step 3)		(Step 5)		
2	Activity	Cost Hierarchy Category	Total Budgeted Indirect Costs	Budgeted Quantity of Cost-Allocation Base		Budgeted Indirect Cost Rate		Cause-and-Effect Relationship Between Allocation Base and Activity Cost
3	(1)	(2)	(3)	(4)		(5) = (3) ÷ (4)		(6)
4	Design	Product-sustaining	Rs.45,00,000	100	parts-square feet	Rs. 45,000	per part-square foot	Design Department indirect costs increase with more complex molds (more parts, larger surface area).
5	Setup molding machines	Batch-level	Rs.30,00,000	2,000	setup-hour	Rs. 1,500	per setup-hour	Indirect setup costs increase with setup-hours.
6	Machine operations	Output unit-level	Rs.63,75,000	12,750	molding machine-hours	Rs. 500	per molding machine-hour	Indirect costs of operating molding machines increases with molding machine-hours.
7	Shipment setup	Batch-level	Rs. 8,10,000	200	shipments	Rs. 4,050	per shipment	Shipping costs incurred to prepare batches for shipment increase with the number of shipments.
8	Distribution	Output-unit-level	Rs.39,15,000	67,500	cubic feet delivered	Rs. 58.0	per cubic foot delivered	Distribution costs increase with the cubic feet of packages delivered.
9	Administration	Facility sustaining	Rs.25,50,000	39,750	direct manuf. labor-hours	Rs.64.151	per direct manuf. labor-hour	The demand for Administrative resources increases with direct manufacturing labor-hours.

A second consideration before choosing a cost-allocation base is the availability of reliable data and measures. Consider the problem of determining a cost-allocation base for the design activity. The driver of design cost, which is a product-sustaining cost, is the complexity of the mold; more-complex molds take more time to design. In its ABC system, Plastim measures mold complexity in terms of the number of parts in the mold and the surface area of the mold (parts-square feet). If these data are difficult to obtain or measure, Plastim may be forced to use some other measure of complexity, such as the amount of material flowing through the mold. A potential problem with this measure is that the quantity of material flow may not adequately represent the cost of the design activity.

Step 4: Identify the Indirect Costs Associated with Each Cost-Allocation Base. In this step, Plastim assigns budgeted indirect costs for 2010 to activities (see Exhibit 5-4, column 3), to the extent possible, on the basis of a cause-and-effect relationship between the cost-allocation base for an activity and the costs of the activity. For example, all costs that have a cause-and-effect relationship to cubic feet of packages moved are assigned to the distribution cost pool. Of course, the strength of the cause-and-effect relationship between the cost-allocation base and the respective cost of the activity varies across cost pools. For example, the cause-and-effect relationship between direct manufacturing labor-hours and administration activity costs is not as strong as the relationship between setup-hours and setup activity costs.

Some costs can be directly identified with a particular activity. For example, cost of materials used when designing products, salaries paid to design engineers, and depreciation of equipment used in the design department are directly identified with the design activity. Other costs need to be allocated across activities. For example, on the basis of interviews or time records, manufacturing engineers and supervisors estimate the time they will spend on design, molding machine setup, and machine operations. The time to be spent on these activities serves as a basis for allocating each manufacturing engineer's and supervisor's salary costs to various activities.

Plastim allocates support costs to activity-cost pools using allocation bases that best describe how support costs are used by the different activities. For example, rent costs are allocated to activity cost pools on the basis of square-feet area used by different activities.

Exhibit 5-5 Plastim's Product Costs Using Activity-Based Costing System

File Edit View Insert Format Tools Data Window Help

	A	B	C	D	E	F	G
1		60,000			15,000		
2		Simple Lenses (S3)			Complex Lenses (CL5)		
3		Total	per Unit		Total	per Unit	Total
4	**Cost Description**	(1)	(2) = (1) ÷ 60,000		(3)	(4) = (3) ÷ 15,000	(5) = (1) + (3)
5	Direct costs						
6	Direct materials	Rs 1,12,50,000	Rs 187.50		Rs 67,50,000	Rs 450.00	Rs 1,80,00,000
7	Direct manufacturing labor	60,00,000	100.00		19,50,000	130.00	79,50,000
8	Direct mold cleaning and maintenance costs	12,00,000	20.00		15,00,000	100.00	27,00,000
9	Total direct costs (Step 2)	1,84,50,000	307.50		1,02,00,000	680.00	2,86,50,000
10	Indirect Costs of Activities						
11	Design						
12	S3, 30 parts-sq.ft. x Rs 45,000	13,50,000	22.50				45,00,000
13	CL5, 70 parts-sq.ft. x Rs 45,000				31,50,000	210.00	
14	Setup of molding machines						
15	S3, 500 setup-hours x Rs 1,500	7,50,000	12.50				30,00,000
16	CL5, 1,500 setup-hours x Rs 1,500				22,50,000	150,00	
17	Machine operations						
18	S3, 9,000 molding machine-hours x Rs 500	45,00,000	75.0				63,75,000
19	CL5, 3,750 molding machine-hours x Rs 500				18,75,000	125.00	
20	Shipment setup						
21	S3, 100 shipments x Rs 4,050	4,05,000	6.7				8,10,000
22	CL5, 100 shipments x Rs 4,050				4,05,000	27.00	
23	Distribution						
24	S3, 45,000 cubic feet delivered x Rs 58.0	26,10,000	43.5				39,15,000
25	CL5, 22,500 cubic feet delivered x Rs 58.0				13,05,000	87.00	
26	Administration						
27	S3, 30,000 dir. manuf. labor-hours x Rs 64.151	19,24,530	32.1				25,50,000
28	CL5, 9,750 dir. manuf. labor-hours x Rs 64.151	1,15,39,530	192.3		6,25,470	41.70	
29	Total indirect costs allocated (Step 6)				96,10,470	640.70	2,11,50,000
30	Total Costs (Step 7)	Rs 2,99,89,530	Rs 499.8		Rs 1,98,10,470	Rs 1,320.70	Rs 4,98,00,000
31							

The point here is that all costs do not fit neatly into activity categories. Often, costs may first need to be allocated to activities (Stage 1 of the 2-stage cost-allocation model) before the costs of the activities can be allocated to products (Stage 2).

Step 5: Compute the Rate per Unit of Each Cost-Allocation Base. Exhibit 5-4, column 5, summarizes the calculation of the budgeted indirect cost rates using the budgeted quantity of the cost-allocation base from step 3 and the total budgeted indirect costs of each activity from step 4.

Step 6: Compute the Indirect Costs Allocated to the Products. Exhibit 5-5 shows total budgeted indirect costs of Rs 1,15,39,530 allocated to the simple lens and Rs 96,10,470 allocated to the complex lens. Follow the budgeted indirect cost calculations for each lens in Exhibit 5-5. For each activity, Plastim's operations personnel indicate the total quantity of the cost-allocation base that will be used for each lens (recall that Plastim operates at capacity). For example, lines 15 and 16 of Exhibit 5-5 show that of the 2,000 total setups hours, the S3 lens is budgeted to use 500 hours and the CL5 lens 1,500 hours. The budgeted indirect cost rate is Rs 1,500 per setup hour (Exhibit 5-4, column 5, line 5).

Therefore, total budgeted cost of setup activity allocated to the S3 lens is Rs 7,50,000 (500 setup-hours × Rs 1,500 per setup-hour) and to the CL5 lens is Rs 22,50,000 (1,500 setup-hours × Rs 1,500 per setup-hour). Budgeted setup cost per unit equals Rs 12.50 (Rs 7,50,000 ÷ 60,000 units) for the S3 lens and Rs 1,500 (Rs 22,50,000 ÷ 15,000 units) for the CL5 lens.

Step 7: Compute the Total Cost of the Products by Adding All Direct and Indirect Costs Assigned to the Products. Exhibit 5-5 presents the product costs for the simple and complex lenses. The direct costs are calculated in step 2, and the indirect costs are calculated in step 6. The ABC system overview in Exhibit 5-3 shows three direct-cost categories and six indirect-cost categories. The budgeted cost of each lens type in Exhibit 5-5 has nine line items, three for direct costs and six for indirect costs. The differences between the ABC product costs of S3 and CL5 calculated in Exhibit 5-5 highlight how each of these products uses different amounts of direct and indirect costs in each activity area.

We emphasize two features of ABC systems. First, these systems identify all costs used by products, whether the costs are variable or fixed in the short run. That's because the focus of ABC systems is on long-run decisions when more of the costs can be managed and fewer costs are regarded as fixed. As we saw in Chapter 3, if Plastim's managers were interested in short-run decisions, they would need to focus on only the variable costs of activities used by products and not all costs. Second, recognizing the hierarchy of costs is critical when allocating costs to products. It is easiest to use the cost hierarchy to first calculate the total costs of each product. The per-unit costs can then be derived by dividing total costs by the number of units produced.

Comparing Alternative Costing Systems

Exhibit 5-6 compares the simple costing system using a single indirect-cost pool (Exhibit 5-1 and Exhibit 5-2) Plastim had been using and the ABC system (Exhibit 5-3 and Exhibit 5-5). Note three points in Exhibit 5-6, consistent with the guidelines for refining a costing system: (1) ABC systems trace more costs as direct costs; (2) ABC systems create homogeneous cost pools linked to different activities; and (3) for each activity-cost pool, ABC systems seek a cost-allocation base that has a cause-and-effect relationship with costs in the cost pool.

The homogeneous cost pools and the choice of cost-allocation bases, tied to the cost hierarchy, give Plastim's managers greater confidence in the activity and product cost numbers from the ABC system. The bottom part of Exhibit 5-6 shows that allocating costs to lenses using only an output unit-level allocation base—direct manufacturing labor-hours, as in the single indirect-cost pool system used prior to ABC—overcosts the simple S3 lens by Rs 87.70 per unit and undercosts the complex CL5 lens by Rs 350.7 per unit. The CL5 lens uses a disproportionately larger amount of output unit-level, batch-level, and product-sustaining costs than is represented by the direct manufacturing labor-hour cost-allocation base. The S3 lens uses a disproportionately smaller amount of these costs. The ABC system, by its use of multiple indirect cost pools and activity-specific drivers at various levels of the cost hierarchy, is able to better recognize the resources used by the S3 and CL5 lenses.

The benefit of an ABC system is that it provides information to make better decisions. But this benefit must be weighed against the measurement and implementation costs of an ABC system.

Evaluate the costs and benefits of implementing activity-based costing systems

. . . measurement difficulties versus more accurate costs that aid in decision making

Considerations in Implementing Activity-Based-Costing Systems

Managers choose the level of detail to use in a costing system by evaluating the expected costs of the system against the expected benefits that result from better decisions. There are telltale signs of when an ABC system is likely to provide the most benefits. Here are some of these signs:

- Significant amounts of indirect costs are allocated using only one or two cost pools.
- All or most indirect costs are identified as output unit-level costs (few indirect costs are described as batch-level costs, product-sustaining costs, or facility-sustaining costs).

Exhibit 5-6

Comparing Alternative Costing Systems

	Simple Costing System Using a Single Indirect-Cost Pool (1)	ABC System (2)	Difference (3) = (2) – (1)
Direct-cost categories	2	3	1
	Direct materials Direct manufacturing labor	Direct materials Direct manufacturing labor Direct mold cleaning and maintenance labor	
Total direct costs	Rs 2,59,50,000	Rs 2,86,50,000	Rs 27,00,000
Indirect-cost pools	1	6	5
	Single indirect-cost pool allocated using direct manufacturing labor-hours	Design (parts-square feet)[1] Molding machine setup (setup-hours) Machine operations (molding machine-hours) Shipment setup (number of shipments) Distribution (cubic feet delivered) Administration (direct manufacturing labor-hours)	
Total indirect costs	Rs 2,38,50,000	Rs 2,11,50,000	(Rs 27,00,000)
Total costs assigned to simple (S3) lens	Rs 3,52,50,000	Rs 2,99,89,530	(Rs 52,60,470)
Cost per unit of simple (S3) lens	Rs 587.5	Rs 499.80	(Rs 87.70)
Total costs assigned to complex (CL5) lens	Rs 1,45,50,000	Rs 1,98,10,470	Rs 52,60,470
Cost per unit of complex (CL5) lens	Rs 970.0	Rs 1,320.7	Rs 350.7

[1]Cost drivers for the various indirect-cost pools are shown in parentheses.

- Products make diverse demands on resources because of differences in volume, process steps, batch size, or complexity.
- Products that a company is well-suited to make and sell show small profits; whereas products that a company is less suited to produce and sell show large profits.
- Operations staff has substantial disagreement with the reported costs of manufacturing and marketing products and services.

When a company decides to implement ABC, it must make important choices about the level of detail to use. Should it choose many finely specified activities, cost drivers, and cost pools, or would a few suffice? For example, Plastim could identify a different molding machine-hour rate for each different type of molding machine. In making such choices, managers weigh the benefits against the costs and limitations of implementing a more detailed costing system.

The main costs and limitations of an ABC system are the measurements necessary to implement it. ABC systems require management to estimate costs of activity pools and to identify and measure cost drivers for these pools to serve as cost-allocation bases. Even basic ABC systems require many calculations to determine costs of products and services. These measurements are costly. Activity cost rates also need to be updated regularly.

As ABC systems get very detailed and more cost pools are created, more allocations are necessary to calculate activity costs for each cost pool. This increases the chances of misidentifying the costs of different activity cost pools. For example, supervisors are more prone to incorrectly identify the time they spent on different activities if they have to allocate their time over five activities rather than only two activities.

At times, companies are also forced to use allocation bases for which data are readily available rather than allocation bases they would have liked to use. For example, a company might be forced to use the number of loads moved, instead of the degree of difficulty and distance of different loads moved, as the allocation base for material-handling costs, because data on degree of difficulty and distance of moves are difficult to obtain. When erroneous cost-allocation bases are used, activity-cost information can be misleading. For example, if the cost per load moved decreases, a company may conclude that it has become more efficient in its materials-handling operations. In fact, the lower cost per load move may have resulted solely from moving many lighter loads over shorter distances.

Many companies, such as Kanthal, the Swedish manufacturer of heating elements, have found the strategic and operational benefits of a less-detailed ABC system to be good enough to not warrant incurring the costs and challenges of operating a more-detailed system. Other organizations, such as Hewlett-Packard, implement ABC in chosen divisions or functions. As improvements in information technology and accompanying declines in measurement costs continue, more-detailed ABC systems have become a practical alternative in many companies. As such trends persist, more detailed ABC systems will be better able to pass the cost–benefit test.

Global surveys of company practice suggest that ABC implementation varies among companies. Nevertheless, its framework and ideas provide a standard for judging whether any simple costing system is good enough for a particular management's purposes. Any contemplated changes in a simple costing system will inevitably be improved by ABC thinking. The following Concepts in Action box describes some of the behavioral issues that management accountants must be sensitive to as they seek to immerse an organization in ABC thinking.

Decision Point

What should managers consider when deciding to implement ABC systems?

Using ABC Systems for Improving Cost Management and Profitability

Learning Objective 7

Explain how activity-based costing systems are used in activity-based management

. . . such as pricing decisions, product-mix decisions, and cost reduction

The emphasis of this chapter so far has been on the role of ABC systems in obtaining better product costs. But Plastim's managers must now use this information to make decisions (step 4 of the 5-step decision process) and to implement the decision, evaluate performance, and learn (step 5). **Activity-based management (ABM)** is a method of management decision-making that uses activity-based costing information to improve customer satisfaction and profitability. We define ABM broadly to include decisions about pricing and product mix, how to reduce costs, how to improve processes, and decisions relating to product design.

Pricing and Product-Mix Decisions

An ABC system gives managers information about the costs of making and selling diverse products. With this information, managers can make pricing and product-mix decisions. For example, the ABC system indicates that Plastim can match its competitor's price of Rs 530 for the S3 lens and still make a profit because the ABC cost of S3 is Rs 499.8 (see Exhibit 5-5).

Plastim's managers offer Tata Motors a price of Rs 520 for the S3 lens. Plastim's managers are confident that they can use the deeper understanding of costs that the ABC system provides to improve efficiency and further reduce the cost of the S3 lens. Without information from the ABC system, Plastim managers might have erroneously concluded that they would incur an operating loss on the S3 lens at a price of Rs 530. This incorrect conclusion would have probably caused Plastim to reduce its business in simple lenses and focus instead on complex lenses, where its single indirect-cost-pool system indicated it is very profitable.

Focusing on complex lenses would have been a mistake. The ABC system indicates that the cost of making the complex lens is much higher—Rs 1,320.7 versus Rs 970 under the direct manufacturing labor-hour-based costing system Plastim had been using. As Plastim's operations staff had thought all along, Plastim has no competitive advantage in making CL5 lenses. At a price of Rs 1,370 per lens for CL5, the profit margin is very small (Rs 1,370 − Rs 1,370.7 = Rs 49.3). As Plastim reduces its prices on simple lenses, it would need to negotiate a higher price for complex lenses with Tata Motors.

Cost Reduction and Process Improvement Decisions

Manufacturing and distribution personnel use ABC systems to focus on how and where to reduce costs. Managers set cost reduction targets in terms of reducing the cost per unit of the cost-allocation base in different activity areas. For example, the supervisor of the distribution activity area at Plastim could have a performance target of decreasing distribution cost per cubic foot of products delivered from Rs 58.0 to Rs 54.0 by reducing distribution labor and warehouse rental costs. The goal is to reduce these costs without compromising customer service or the actual or perceived value (usefulness) customers obtain from the product or service. That is, Plastim will attempt to take out only those costs that are *nonvalue added*.

Doing an analysis of the factors that cause costs to be incurred (cost drivers) reveals many opportunities for improving the way work is done. Management can evaluate whether particular nonvalue-added activities can be reduced or eliminated. Each of the cost-allocation bases in Plastim's ABC system is a nonfinancial variable (number of setup-hours, cubic feet delivered, and so on). Controlling physical items such as setup-hours or cubic feet delivered is often the most fundamental way that operating personnel manage costs. For example, Plastim can decrease distribution costs by packing the lenses in a way that reduces the bulkiness of the packages delivered.

The following table shows the reduction in distribution costs of the S3 and CL5 lenses as a result of actions that lower cost per cubic foot delivered (from Rs 58.0 to Rs 54.0) and total cubic feet of deliveries (from 45,000 to 40,000 for S3 and 22,500 to 20,000 for CL5).

	60,000 (S3) Lenses		15,000 (CL5) Lenses	
	Total (1)	per Unit (2) = (1) ÷ 60,000	Total (3)	per Unit (4) = (3) ÷ 15,000
Distribution costs (from Exhibit 5-5)				
S3, 45,000 cubic feet × Rs 58.0/cubic foot	Rs 26,10,000	Rs 43.5		
CL5, 22,500 cubic feet × Rs 58.0/cubic foot			Rs 13,05,000	Rs 87.0
Distribution costs as a result of process improvements				
S3, 40,000 cubic feet × Rs 58.0/cubic foot	Rs 26,10,000	36.0		
CL5, 20,000 cubic feet × Rs 58.0/cubic foot			10,80,000	72.0
Savings in distribution costs from process improvements	Rs 4,50,000	Rs 7.50	Rs 22,50,000	Rs 15.0

In the long-run, total distribution costs will decrease from Rs 39,15,000 (Rs 26,10,000 + Rs 13,05,000) to Rs 32,40,000 (Rs 21,60,000 + Rs 10,80,000). In the short run, however, distribution costs may be fixed and may not decrease. Suppose all Rs 39,15,000 of distribution costs are fixed costs in the short run. The efficiency improvements (using less distribution labor and space) mean that the same Rs 39,15,000 of distribution costs can now be used to distribute 72,500 $\left(\frac{\text{Rs } 39{,}15{,}000}{\text{Rs } 54.0 \text{ per cubic feet}}\right)$ cubic feet of lenses. In this case, how should costs be allocated to the S3 and CL5 lenses?

ABC systems distinguish *costs incurred* from *resources used* to design, manufacture, and deliver products and services. For the distribution activity, after process improvements,

Costs incurred = Rs 39,15,000

Resources used = Rs 21,60,000 (for S3 lens) + Rs 10,80,000 (for CL5 lens) = Rs 32,40,000

On the basis of the resources used by each product, Plastim's ABC system allocates Rs 21,60,000 to S3 and Rs 10,80,000 to CL5 for a total of Rs 32,40,000. The difference of Rs 6,75,000 (Rs 39,15,000 – Rs 32,40,000) is shown as costs of unused but available distribution capacity. Plastim's ABC system does not allocate the costs of unused capacity to products so as not to burden the product costs of S3 and CL5 with the cost of resources not used by these products. Instead, the system highlights the amount of unused capacity as a separate line item to signal to managers the need to reduce these costs, such as by redeploying labor to other uses or laying off workers. Chapter 9 discusses issues related to unused capacity in more detail.

Design Decisions

Management can evaluate how its current product and process designs affect activities and costs as a way of identifying new designs to reduce costs. For example, design decisions that decrease complexity of the mold reduce costs of design, materials, labor, machine setups, machine operations, and mold cleaning and maintenance. Plastim's customers may be willing to give up some features of the lens in exchange for a lower price.

Note that Plastim's previous costing system, which used direct manufacturing labor-hours as the cost-allocation base for all indirect costs, would have mistakenly signaled that Plastim choose those designs that most reduce direct manufacturing labor-hours when, in fact, there is a weak cause-and-effect relationship between direct manufacturing labor-hours and indirect costs.

Planning and Managing Activities

Many companies implementing ABC systems for the first time analyze actual costs to identify activity-cost pools and activity-cost rates. To be useful for planning, making decisions, and managing activities, companies specify budgeted costs for activities and use budgeted cost rates to cost products as we saw in the Plastim example. At year-end, budgeted costs and actual costs are compared to provide feedback on how well activities were managed. As activities and processes are changed, new activity-cost rates are calculated. At the end of the year, adjustments must also be made for underallocated or overallocated indirect costs for each activity area using methods described in Chapter 4.

We will return to activity-based management in later chapters. Management decisions that use activity-based costing information are described in Chapter 6, in which we discuss activity-based budgeting; Chapter 11, in which we discuss outsourcing and adding or dropping business segments; in Chapter 12, in which we evaluate alternative design choices to improve efficiency and reduce nonvalue-added costs; in Chapter 13, in which we cover reengineering and downsizing; in Chapter 14, in which we explore managing customer profitability; in Chapter 19, in which we explain quality improvements; and in Chapter 20, in which we describe how to evaluate suppliers.

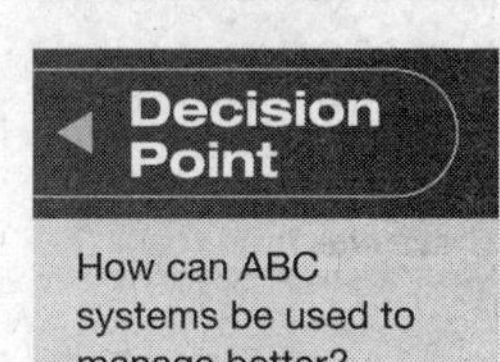

How can ABC systems be used to manage better?

Activity-Based Costing and Department Costing Systems

Learning Objective 

Compare activity-based costing systems and department costing systems

. . . activity-based costing systems are a refinement of department costing systems into more-focused and homogenous cost pools

Companies often use costing systems that have features of ABC systems—such as multiple cost pools and multiple cost-allocation bases—but that do not emphasize individual activities. Many companies have evolved their costing systems from using a single indirect cost rate system to using separate indirect cost rates for each department (for example, design, manufacturing, distribution, and so on) or each subdepartment (for example, machining and assembly departments within manufacturing) that can be thought of as representing broad tasks. ABC systems, with its focus on specific activities, are a further refinement of department costing systems. In this section, we compare ABC systems and department costing systems.

Plastim uses the Design Department indirect cost rate to cost its design activity. Plastim calculates the design activity rate by dividing total Design Department costs by total parts-square feet, a measure of the complexity of the mold and the driver of Design Department costs. Plastim does not find it worthwhile to calculate separate activity rates within the Design Department for the different design activities, such as designing products, making temporary molds, and designing processes. Why? Because complexity of a mold is an appropriate cost-allocation base for costs incurred for all those design activities: The Design Department costs are homogeneous with respect to this cost-allocation base.

In contrast, using ABC, Plastim identifies in the Manufacturing Department, two activity cost pools—a setup cost pool and a machine operations cost pool—instead of using a single Manufacturing Department overhead cost pool. It identifies these activity cost pools for two reasons. First, each of these activities within manufacturing incurs significant costs and has a different cost driver. Second, the S3 and CL5 lenses do not use resources from these two activity areas in the same proportion. For example, CL5 uses 75% (1,500 ÷ 2,000) of the setup-hours but only 29.4% (3,750 ÷ 12,750) of the machine-hours. Using only machine-hours, say, to allocate all Manufacturing Department costs at Plastim would result in CL5 being undercosted because it would not be charged for the significant amounts of setup resources it actually uses.

Based on what we just explained, using department indirect cost rates to allocate costs to products results in similar information as activity cost rates if: (1) a single activity accounts for a sizable proportion of the department's costs; or (2) significant costs are incurred on different activities within a department but each activity has the same cost driver and hence cost-allocation base (as was the case in Plastim's Design Department). From a purely product costing standpoint, department and activity indirect cost rates will also give the same product costs if significant costs are incurred for different activities with different cost-allocation bases within a department but different products use resources from the different activity areas in the same proportions (for example, if CL5 had used 65%, say, of the setup-hours and 65% of the machine-hours). In this case, though, not identifying activities and cost drivers within departments conceals activity cost information that would be valuable for cost management and design and process improvements.

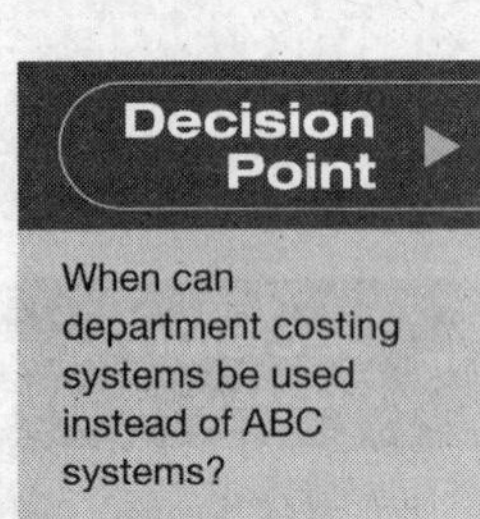

When can department costing systems be used instead of ABC systems?

We close this section with a note of caution. Do not assume that because department costing systems require the creation of multiple indirect cost pools that they properly recognize the drivers of costs within departments as well as how resources are used by products. As we have indicated, in many situations, department costing systems can be refined using ABC. Emphasizing activities leads to more-focused and homogeneous cost pools, aids in identifying cost-allocation bases for activities that have a better cause-and-effect relationship with the costs in activity cost pools, and leads to better design and process decisions. But the benefits of an ABC system must be balanced against its costs and limitations.

ABC in Service and Merchandising Companies

Although many of the early examples of ABC originated in manufacturing, ABC has many applications in service and merchandising companies. In addition to manufacturing activities, the Plastim example includes the application of ABC to a service activity—design—and to a merchandising activity—distribution. The Problem for Self-Study describes an application of ABC in a supermarket. Finally, as we describe in Chapter 14, a large number of financial services companies (as well as other companies) employ variations of ABC systems to analyze and improve the profitability of their customer interactions.

The widespread use of ABC systems in service and merchandising companies reinforces the idea that ABC systems are used by managers for strategic decisions rather than for inventory valuation. (Inventory valuation is fairly straightforward in merchandising companies and not needed in service companies.) Service companies, in particular, find great value from ABC because a vast majority of their cost structure comprises indirect costs. After all, there are few direct costs when a bank makes a loan, or when a representative answers a phone call at a call center. As we have seen, a major benefit of ABC is its ability to assign indirect costs to cost objects by identifying activities and cost drivers. As a result, ABC systems provide greater insight than traditional systems into the management

Concepts in Action

Successfully Championing ABC

Successfully implementing ABC systems requires more than an understanding of the technical details. ABC implementation often represents a significant change in the costing system and, as the chapter indicates, it requires a manager to make major choices with respect to the definition of activities and the level of detail. What then are some of the behavioral issues that the management accountant must be sensitive to?

1. **Gaining support of top management and creating a sense of urgency for the ABC effort.** This requires management accountants to lay out the vision for the ABC project and to clearly communicate its strategic benefits (for example, the resulting improvements in product and process design). It also requires selling the idea to end users, working with members of other departments and as business partners of the managers in the various areas affected by the ABC project. For example, at USAA Federal Savings Bank, project managers demonstrated how the information gained from ABC would provide insights into the efficiency of bank operations, which was previously unavailable. Now the finance area communicates regularly with operations about new reports and proposed changes to the financial reporting package that managers receive.
2. **Creating a guiding coalition of managers throughout the value chain for the ABC effort.** ABC systems measure how the resources of an organization are used. Managers responsible for these resources have the best knowledge about activities and cost drivers. Getting managers to cooperate and take the initiative for implementing ABC is essential for gaining the required expertise, the proper credibility, and the necessary leadership.

   There are several other benefits to gaining wide participation among managers. First, implementing ABC requires a significant time commitment. If managers feel more involved in the process, they are more likely to be willing to commit their time to the ABC effort. Second, there inevitably will be some managers who may be, or may perceive themselves to be, negatively affected by the ABC information. In our Plastim example, the manager of the complex CL5 lens may feel that ABC disadvantages him because it assigns more costs to the CL5 lens. Involving managers who are skeptical of the ABC process and giving them an opportunity to express their concerns reduces the likelihood of these managers negatively affecting the process. Finally, engaging managers throughout the value chain creates greater opportunities for coordination and cooperation across the different functions. For example, an ABC analysis might reveal that a company is incurring high manufacturing costs because of quality problems in its plant. The best way to reduce costs may be to redesign the product. This requires that the design department and the manufacturing department work closely together.
3. **Educating and training employees in ABC as a basis for employee empowerment.** Disseminating information about ABC throughout an organization allows workers in all areas of a business to use their knowledge of ABC to make improvements. For example, WS Industries, an Indian manufacturer of insulators, not only shared ABC information with its workers but also established an incentive plan that gave employees a percentage of the cost savings. The results were dramatic because employees were empowered and motivated to implement numerous cost-saving projects.
4. **Seeking small short-run successes as proof that the ABC implementation is yielding results.** Too often, managers and management accountants seek big results and major changes far too quickly. In many situations, achieving a significant change overnight is difficult. However, showing how ABC information has helped improve a process and save costs, even if only in small ways, motivates the team to stay on course and build momentum. The credibility gained from small victories leads to additional and bigger improvements involving larger numbers of people and different parts of the organization. Eventually ABC and ABM will be rooted in the culture of the organization. Sharing short-term successes may also help motivate employees to be innovative. At USAA Federal Savings Bank, managers created a "process improvement" mailbox in Microsoft Outlook to facilitate the sharing of process improvement ideas.
5. **Recognizing that ABC information is not perfect because it balances the need for better information against the costs of creating a complex system that few managers and employees can understand.** The management accountant must help managers recognize both the value and the limitations of ABC and not oversell it. Open and honest communication about ABC ensures that managers use ABC thoughtfully to make good decisions. Critical judgments can then be made without being adversarial, and tough questions can be asked to help drive better decisions about the system.

Concepts in Action

Time-Driven Activity-Based Costing at Charles Schwab

Time-driven activity-based costing ("TDABC") helps Charles Schwab, the leading stock brokerage, with strategic-analysis, measurement, and management of its stock trading activity across multiple channels such as branches, call centers, and the Internet. Because the costs for each channel are different, TDABC helps answer questions such as the following: What are the total costs of branch transactions versus online transactions? Which channels help reduce overall costs? How can Charles Schwab price its services to drive changes in customer behavior?

TDABC assigns all of the company's resource costs to cost objects using a framework that requires two sets of estimates. TDABC first calculates the cost of supplying resource capacity, such as broker time. The total cost of resources including personnel, management, occupancy, technology, and supplies is divided by the available capacity—the time available for brokers to do the work—to obtain the capacity cost rate. Next, TDABC uses the capacity cost rate to drive resource costs to cost objects, such as stock trades executed through brokers at a branch, by estimating the demand for resource capacity (time) that the cost object requires.

Realizing that trades executed online cost much less than trades completed through brokers, Charles Schwab developed a fee structure for trading of mutual funds to stimulate the use of cheaper channels. Charles Schwab also used TDABC information to lower process costs by several hundred million dollars annually and to better align product pricing and account management to the company's diverse client segments. The company is working on other opportunities, including priority-call routing and email marketing, to further reduce costs while maintaining or enhancing Charles Schwab's already top-rated customer service.

Sources: Kaplan, R. S. and S. R., Anderson. 2007. The innovation of time-driven activity-based costing. *Cost Management,* March–April: 5–15; Kaplan R. S. and S.R. Anderson. 2007. *Time-driven activity-based costing*. Boston, MA: Harvard Business School Press; Martinez-Jerez, F. Asis. 2007. Understanding customer profitability at Charles Schwab. Harvard Business School Case Study No. 9-106-102, January.

of these indirect costs. The general approach to ABC in service and merchandising companies is similar to the ABC approach in manufacturing.

The Cooperative Bank followed the approach described in this chapter when it implemented ABC in its retail baking operations. It calculated the costs of various activities, such as performing ATM transactions, opening and closing accounts, administering mortgages, and processing Visa transactions. It then used the activity cost rates to calculate costs of various products, such as checking accounts, mortgages, and Visa cards and the costs of supporting different customers. ABC information helped The Cooperative Bank to improve its processes and to identify profitable products and customer segments. The Concepts in Action feature above describes how Charles Schwab has similarly benefited from using ABC analysis.

Activity-based costing raises some interesting issues when it is applied to a public service institution such as te U.S. Postal Service. The costs of delivering mail to remote locations are far greater than the costs of delivering mail within urban areas. Howerver, for fairness and community-building reasons, the Postal Service cannot charge customers in remote areas higer prices. In this case, activity-based coosting is valuable for understanding, managing, and reducing costs but not for pricing decisions.

Problem for Self-Study

Family Supermarkets (FS) has decided to increase the size of its NOIDA store. It wants information about the profitability of individual product lines: soft drinks, fresh produce, and packaged food. FS provides the following data for 2012 for each product line:

	Soft Drinks	Fresh Produce	Packaged Food
Revenues	Rs 31,74,000	Rs 84,02,400	Rs 48,39,600
Cost of goods sold	Rs 24,00,000	Rs 60,00,000	36,00,000
Cost of bottles returned	Rs 4,800	Rs 0	Rs 0
Number of purchase orders placed	144	336	144
Number of deliveries received	120	876	264
Hours of shelf-stocking time	216	2,160	1,080
Items sold	50,400	441,600	122,400

FS also provides the following information for 2010:

Activity (1)	Description of Activity (2)	Total Support Costs (3)	Cost-Allocation Base (4)
1. Bottle returns	Returning of empty bottles to store	Rs 48,000	Direct tracing to soft-drink line
2. Ordering	Placing of orders for purchases	Rs 6,24,000	624 purchase orders
3. Delivery	Physical delivery and receipt of merchandise	Rs 10,08,000	1,260 deliveries
4. Shelf-stocking	Stocking of merchandise on store shelves and ongoing restocking	Rs 6,91,200	3,456 hours of shelf-stocking time
5. Customer support	Assistance provided to customers, including checkout and bagging	Rs 12,28,800	614,400 items sold
Total		Rs 36,00,000	

Required

1. Family Supermarkets currently allocates store support costs (all costs other than cost of goods sold) to product lines on the basis of cost of goods sold of each product line. Calculate the operating income and operating income as a percentage of revenues for each product line.
2. If Family Supermarkets allocates store support costs (all costs other than cost of goods sold) to product lines using an ABC system, calculate the operating income and operating income as a percentage of revenues for each product line.
3. Comment on your answers in requirements 1 and 2.

Solution

1. The following table shows the operating income and operating income as a percentage of revenues for each product line. All store support costs (all costs other than cost of goods sold) are allocated to product lines using cost of goods sold of each product line as the cost-allocation base. Total store support costs equal Rs 36,00,000 (cost of bottles returned, Rs 48,000 + cost of purchase orders, Rs 6,24,000 + cost of deliveries, Rs 10,08,000 + cost of shelf-stocking, Rs 6,91,200 + cost of customer support, Rs 12,28,200). The allocation rate for store support costs = Rs 36,00,000 ÷ Rs 1,20,00,000 (soft drinks Rs 24,00,000 + fresh produce Rs 60,00,000 + packaged food, Rs 36,00,000) = 30% of cost of goods sold. To allocate support costs to each product line, FS multiplies the cost of goods sold of each product line by 0.30.

	Soft Drinks	Fresh Produce	Packaged Food	Total
Revenues	Rs 31,74,000	Rs 84,02,400	Rs 48,39,600	Rs 1,64,16,000
Cost of goods sold	24,00,000	60,00,000	36,00,000	1,20,00,000
Store support cost (Rs 24,00,000; Rs 60,00,000; Rs 36,00,000) × 0.30	7,20,000	18,00,000	10,80,000	36,00,000
Total costs	31,20,000	78,00,000	46,80,000	1,56,00,000
Operating income	Rs 54,000	Rs 6,02,400	Rs 1,59,600	Rs 8,16,000
Operating income ÷ Revenues	1.70%	7.17%	3.30%	4.97%

2. Under an ABC system, FS identifies bottle-return costs as a direct cost because these costs can be traced to the soft drink product line. FS then calculates cost-allocation rates for each activity area (as in step 5 of the seven-step costing system, described in the chapter). The activity rates are as follows:

Activity (1)	Cost Hierarchy (2)	Total Costs (3)	Quantity of Cost-Allocation Base (4)	Overhead Allocation Rate (5) = (3) = (4)
Ordering	Batch-level	Rs 6,24,000	624 purchase orders	Rs 1,000 per purchase order
Delivery	Batch-level	Rs 10,08,000	1,260 deliveries	Rs 800 per delivery
Shelf-stocking	Output unit-level	Rs 6,91,200	3,456 shelf-stocking-hours	Rs 200 per stocking-hour
Customer support	Output unit-level	Rs 12,28,800	614,400 items sold	Rs 2.0 per item sold

Store support costs for each product line by activity are obtained by multiplying the total quantity of the cost-allocation base for each product line by the activity cost rate. Operating income and operating income as a percentage of revenues for each product line are as follows:

	Soft Drinks	Fresh Produce	Packaged Food	Total
Revenues	Rs 31,74,000	Rs 84,02,400	Rs 48,39,600	Rs 1,6416,000
Cost of goods sold	24,00,000	60,00,000	36,00,000	1,20,00,000
Bottle-return costs	48,000	0	0	4,800
Ordering costs				
(144; 336; 144) purchase orders × Rs 1,000	1,44,000	3,36,000	1,44,000	6,24,000
Delivery costs				
(120; 876; 264) deliveries × Rs 800	96,000	7,00,800	2,11,200	10,08,000
Shelf-stocking costs				
(216; 2,160; 1,080) stocking-hours × Rs 200	43,200	4,32,000	2,16,000	6,91,200
Customer-support costs				
(50,400; 441,600; 122,400) items sold × Rs 2.0	10,08,000	8,83,200	2,44,800	12,28,800
Total costs	28,32,000	83,52,000	44,16,000	1,56,00,000
Operating income	Rs 3,42,000	Rs 50,400	Rs 4,23,600	Rs 8,16,000
Operating income ÷ Revenues	10.78%	0.60%	8.75%	4.97%

3. Managers believe the ABC system is more credible than the simple costing system. The ABC system distinguishes the different types of activities at FS more precisely. It also tracks more accurately how individual product lines use resources. Rankings of relative profitability—operating income as a percentage of revenues—of the three product lines under the simple costing system and under the ABC system are:

Simple Costing System		ABC System	
1. Fresh produce	7.17%	1. Soft drinks	10.78%
2. Packaged food	3.30%	2. Packaged food	8.75%
3. Soft drinks	1.70%	3. Fresh produce	0.60%

The percentage of revenues, cost of goods sold, and activity costs for each product line are as follows:

	Soft Drinks	Fresh Produce	Packaged Food
Revenues	19.34%	51.18%	29.48%
Cost of goods sold	20.00	50.00	30.00
Bottle returns	100.00	0	0
Activity areas:			
Ordering	23.08	53.84	23.08
Delivery	9.53	69.52	20.95
Shelf-stocking	6.25	62.50	31.25
Customer-support	8.20	71.88	19.92

Soft drinks consume fewer resources than either fresh produce or packaged food. Soft drinks have fewer deliveries and require less shelf-stocking time than required for either fresh produce or packaged food. Most major soft-drink suppliers deliver merchandise to the store shelves and stock the shelves themselves. In contrast, the fresh produce area has the most deliveries and consumes a large percentage of shelf-stocking time. It also has the highest number of individual sales items. The simple costing system assumed that each product line used the resources in each activity area in the same ratio as their respective individual cost of goods sold to total cost of goods sold. Clearly, this assumption is incorrect. The simple costing system is an example of averaging that is too broad.

FS managers can use the ABC information to guide decisions such as how to allocate a planned increase in floor space. An increase in the percentage of space allocated to soft drinks is warranted. Note, however, that ABC information should be but one input into decisions about shelf-space allocation. FS may have minimum limits on the shelf space allocated to fresh produce because of shoppers' expectations that supermarkets will carry products from this product line. In many situations, companies cannot make product decisions in isolation but must consider the effect that dropping a product might have on customer demand for other products.

Pricing decisions can also be made in a more informed way with ABC information. For example, suppose a competitor announces a 5% reduction in soft-drink prices. Given the 10.77% margin FS currently earns on its soft-drink product line, it has flexibility to reduce prices and still make a profit on this product line. In contrast, the simple costing system erroneously implied that soft drinks only had a 1.70% margin, leaving little room to counter a competitor's pricing initiatives.

Decision Points

The following question-and-answer format summarizes the chapter's learning objectives. Each decision presents a key question related to a learning objective. The guidelines are the answer to that question.

Decision	Guidelines
1. When does product undercosting or overcosting occur?	Product undercosting (overcosting) occurs when a product or service consumes a high (low) level of resources but is reported to have a low (high) cost. Broad averaging, or peanut-butter costing, a common cause of undercosting or overcosting, is the result of using broad averages that uniformly assign, or spread, the cost of resources to products when the individual products use those resources in a nonuniform way. Product-cost cross-subsidization exists when one undercosted (overcosted) product results in at least one other product being overcosted (undercosted).
2. How do managers refine a costing system?	Refining a costing system means making changes that result in cost numbers that better measure the way different cost objects, such as products, use different amounts of resources of the company. These changes can require additional direct-cost tracing, the choice of more-homogeneous indirect cost pools, or the use of different cost-allocation bases.
3. What is the difference between the design of a simple costing system and an activity-based costing (ABC) system?	The ABC system differs from the simple system by its fundamental focus on activities. The ABC system typically has more-homogeneous indirect-cost pools than the simple system, and more cost drivers are used as cost-allocation bases.
4. What is a cost hierarchy?	A cost hierarchy categorizes costs into different cost pools on the basis of the different types of cost-allocation bases or different degrees of difficulty in determining cause-and-effect (or benefits-received) relationships. A four-part cost hierarchy consists of output unit-level costs, batch-level costs, product-sustaining or service-sustaining costs, and facility-sustaining costs.

5. How do managers cost products or services using ABC systems?	In ABC, costs of activities are used to assign costs to other cost objects such as products or services based on the activities the products or services consume.
6. How can ABC systems be used to manage better?	Activity-based management (ABM) is a management method of decision-making that uses ABC information to satisfy customers and improve profits. ABC systems are used for such management decisions as pricing, product-mix, cost reduction, process improvement, product and process redesign, and planning and managing activities.
7. When can department costing systems be used instead of ABC systems?	Cost information in department costing systems approximates cost information in ABC systems only when each department has a single activity, or a single cost driver for different activities, or when different products use the different activities of the department in the same proportions.
8. When should managers use ABC systems?	ABC systems are likely to yield the most benefits when indirect costs are a high percentage of total costs or when products and services make diverse demands on indirect resources. The main costs of ABC systems are the difficulties of the measurements necessary to implement and update the systems.

TERMS TO LEARN

This chapter and the Glossary at the end of this book contain definitions of:

activity (**p. 162**)
activity-based costing (ABC) (**p. 162**)
activity-based management (ABM) (**p. 171**)
batch-level costs (**p. 165**)
cost hierarchy (**p. 164**)
facility-sustaining costs (**p. 165**)
output unit-level costs (**p. 165**)
product-cost cross-subsidization (**p. 156**)
product overcosting (**p. 156**)
product-sustaining costs (**p. 165**)
product undercosting (**p. 156**)
refined costing system (**p. 161**)
service-sustaining costs (**p. 165**)

ASSIGNMENT MATERIAL

Questions

5-1 What is broad averaging and what consequences can it have on costs?

5-2 Why should managers worry about product overcosting or undercosting?

5-3 What is costing system refinement? Describe three guidelines for refinement.

5-4 What is an activity-based approach to designing a costing system?

5-5 Describe four levels of a cost hierarchy.

5-6 Why is it important to classify costs into a cost hierarchy?

5-7 What are the key reasons for product cost differences between simple costing systems and ABC systems?

5-8 Describe four decisions for which ABC information is useful.

5-9 "Department indirect-cost rates are never activity-cost rates." Do you agree? Explain.

5-10 Describe four signs that help indicate when ABC systems are likely to provide the most benefits.

5-11 What are the main costs and limitations of implementing ABC systems?

5-12 "ABC systems only apply to manufacturing companies." Do you agree? Explain.

5-13 "Activity-based costing is the wave of the present and the future. All companies should adopt it." Do you agree? Explain.

5-14 "Increasing the number of indirect-cost pools is guaranteed to sizably increase the accuracy of product or service costs." Do you agree? Why?

5-15 The controller of a retail company has just had a Rs 5,00,000 request to implement an ABC system quickly turned down. A senior vice president, in rejecting the request, noted, "Given a choice, I will always prefer a Rs 5,00,000 investment in improving things a customer sees or experiences, such as our shelves or our store layout. How does a customer benefit by our spending Rs 5,00,000 on a supposedly better accounting system?" How should the controller respond?

Solved Examples

5-16 ABC, distribution. (W. Bruns, adapted) Shaw Wallace makes two wines: a regular wine and a premium wine. Shaw Wallace distributes the regular wine and the premium wine through different distribution channels. It distributes 2,40,000 cases of regular wine through 10 general distributors and 1,60,000 cases of the premium wine through 30 specialty distributors. Shaw Wallace incurs Rs 42,60,000 in distribution costs. Under its existing costing system, Shaw Wallace allocates distribution costs to products on the basis of cases shipped.

To understand better the demands on its resources in the distribution area, Shaw Wallace identifies three activities and related activity costs.

a. Promotional costs–Shaw Wallace estimates it incurs Rs 16,000 per distributor.

b. Order handling costs–Shaw Wallace estimates costs of Rs 600 pertaining to each order. Shaw Wallace records show that distributors of regular wine place an average of 10 orders per year, whereas distributors of premium wine place an average of 20 orders per year.

c. Delivery costs–Rs 8 per case.

Required

1. Using Shaw Wallace existing costing system, calculate the total distribution costs and distribution cost per case for the regular wine and the premium wine.

2. Using Shaw Wallace activity-based costing system, calculate the total distribution costs and distribution cost per case for the regular wine and the premium wine.

3. Explain the cost differences and the accuracy of the product costs calculated using the existing costing system and the ABC system. How might Shaw Wallace management use the information from the ABC system to manage its business better?

Solution

1. Total distribution costs (given), Rs 42,60,000

$$\text{Distribution cost per case under existing system} = \frac{\text{Total distribution costs}}{\text{Total cases of premium and regular wine shipped}}$$

$$= \text{Rs } 42,60,000/4,00,000 = \text{Rs } 10.65 \text{ per case}$$

	Regular Per Case		Premium Per Case	
	Total (1)	(2) (1) ÷ 2,40,000	Total (3)	(4) 3 ÷ 1,60,000
Distribution costs Rs 10.65 × 2,40,000 and Rs 10.65 × 1,60,000	Rs 25,56,000	Rs 10.65	Rs 17,04,000	Rs 10.65

2.

	Regular Per Case		Premium Per Case	
Particulars	Total (1)	(2) 1 ÷ 2,40,000	Total (3)	(4) 3 ÷ 1,60,000
Delivery costs				
Rs 8 × 2,40,000 cases Rs 8 × 1,60,000 cases	Rs 19,20,000	Rs 8.00	Rs 12,80,000	Rs 8.00
Ordering costs				
Rs 600 × 10 orders/year × 10 distributors Rs 600 × 20 orders/year × 30 distributors	60,000	0.25	3,60,000	2.25
Promotion costs				
Rs 16,000 × 10 distributors Rs 16,000 × 30 distributors	1,60,000	0.67	4,80,000	3.00
Total costs	21,40,000	8.92	21,20,000	13.25

3. The existing costing system uses cases shipped as the only cost allocation base for distribution costs. As a result, the distribution cost per case is the same for premium and regular wines (Rs 10.65). In fact, premium wine uses distribution resources more intensively than regular wine: (a) Shaw Wallace spends Rs 16,000 on promotional costs at each distributor independent of cases sold. Premium wine distributors sell fewer cases a year than regular wine distributors. As a result the promotional cost per case of wine sold is higher for premium wine than for regular wine. (b) Shaw Wallace's cost per order is Rs 600 regardless of the number of cases sold in each order. Because premium wine distributors order fewer cases per order, the ordering costs per case are higher for premium wines than for regular wines.

The existing costing system undercosts distribution costs per case for premium wine and overcosts distribution costs per case for regular wine.

Shaw Wallace's management can use the information from the ABC system to make better pricing and product mix decisions, to reduce costs by eliminating processes and activities that do not add value, to reduce the costs of doing various activities, and to plan and manage activities.

5-17 ABC, cost hierarchy, service. (CMA, adapted) Apollo Test Laboratories does heat testing (HT) and stress testing (ST) on materials. Under its current costing system, Apollo aggregates all operating costs of Rs 1,20,00,000 into a single overhead cost pool. Apollo calculates a rate per test-hour of Rs 150 (Rs 1,20,00,000/80,000 total test-hours). HT uses 50,000 test-hours, and ST uses 30,000 test-hours. Apollo controller, believes that there is enough variation in test procedures and cost structures to establish separate costing and billing rates for HT and ST. The market for test services is becoming competitive. Without this information, any miscasting and mispricing of its services could cause Apollo to lose business. Vikas divides Apollo's costs into four activity-cost categories.

a. Direct-labor costs, Rs 24,00,000. These costs can be directly traced to HT, Rs 18,00,000 and ST Rs 6,00,000.

b. Equipment-related costs (rent, maintenance, energy, and so on), Rs 40,00,000. These costs are allocated to HT and ST on the basis of test-hours.

c. Setup costs, Rs 35,00,000. These costs are allocated to HT and ST on the basis of the number of setup-hours required. HT requires 13,500 setup-hours, and ST required 4,000 setup-hours.

d. Costs of designing tests, Rs 21,00,000. These costs are allocated to HT and ST on the basis of the time required to design the tests. HT requires 2,800 hours, and ST requires 1,400 hours.

Required

1. Classify each activity cost as output unit-level, batch-level, product or service-sustaining, or facility sustaining. Explain each answer.
2. Calculate the cost per test-hour for HT and ST. Explain briefly the reasons why these numbers differ from Rs 150 per test-hour that Apollo calculated using its existing costing system.
3. Explain the accuracy of the product costs calculated using the existing costing system and the ABC system. How might Apollo's management use the cost hierarchy and ABC information to manage its business better?

Solution

1. Output unit-level costs

Direct-labor costs, Rs 24,00,000

Equipment-related costs (rent, maintenance, energy, and so on), Rs 40,00,000

These costs are output unit-level costs because they are incurred on each unit of materials tested, that is, for every hour of testing.

Batch-level costs

Setup costs, Rs 35,00,000

These costs are batch-level costs because they are incurred each time a batch of materials is set up for either HT or ST, regardless of the number of hours for which the tests are subsequently run.

Service-sustaining costs

Costs of designing tests, Rs 21,00,000.

These costs are service-sustaining costs because they are incurred to design the HT and ST tests, regardless of the number of batches tested or the number of hours of test time.

2.

Particulars	Heat Testing (HT) Total (1)	Heat Testing (HT) Per Hour (2) (1) ÷ 50,000	Stress Testing (ST) Total (3)	Stress Testing (ST) Per Hour (4) =(3) ÷ 30,000
Direct labor costs (given)	Rs 18,00,000	Rs 36	Rs 6,00,000	Rs 20
Equipment-related costs				
Rs 50 per hour × 50,000 hours				
Rs 50 per hour* × 30,000 hours	25,00,000	50	15,00,000	50
*Rs 40,00,000 ÷ (50,000 + 30,000 hours) = Rs 50 per test hour				
Setup costs				
Rs 200 per setup-hour × 13,500 setup-hours				
Rs 200 per setup-hour × 40,000 setup-hours	27,00,000	54	8,00,000	26.67
(Rs 35,00,000) ÷ (13,500 + 4,000) set up hours = Rs 200 per set up hour				

Costs of designing tests				
Rs 500 per hour × 2,800 hours				
Rs 500 per hour × 1,400 hours	14,00,000	28	7,00,000	23.33
*Rs 21,00,000 ÷ (2,800 + 1,400)				
hours = Rs 500 per hour				
Total costs	84,00,000	168	36,00,000	120

At a cost per test-hour of Rs 150, the existing costing system undercosts heat testing (Rs 18) and overcosts stress testing (Rs 30). The reason is that heat testing uses direct labor, setup, and design resources per hour more intensively than stress testing. Heat tests are more complex, take longer to set up, and are more difficult to design. The existing costing system assumes that testing costs per hour are the same for heat testing and stress testing.

3. The ABC system better captures the resources needed for heat testing and stress testing because it identifies all the various activities undertaken when performing the tests and recognizes the levels of the cost hierarchy at which costs vary.

   Apollo's management can use the information from the ABC system to make better pricing and product mix decisions. For example, it might decide to increase the prices charged for the more costly heat testing and consider reducing prices on the less costly stress testing. Apollo should watch if competitors are underbidding Apollo in stress testing, and causing it to lose business. Apollo can also use ABC information to reduce costs by eliminating processes and activities that do not add value, identifying and evaluating new methods to do testing that reduce the activities needed to do the tests, reducing the costs of doing various activities, and planning and managing activities.

5-18 Alternative allocation bases foı a professional services firm. Ernst & Young (E&Y) provides tax advice to multinational firms, E&Y charges clients for (a) direct professional time (at an hourly rate) and (b) support services (at 30 per cent of the direct professional costs billed). The three professionals in E&Y and their rates per professional hour are

Professional	Billing Rate per Hour
Ajay	Rs 5,000
Vijay	1,200
Vinay	800

E&Y has just prepared the May bills for two clients. The hours of professional time spent on each client are as follows?

Hours per Client

Professional	LG Electronics Ltd.	Electrolux Ltd.
Ajay	15	2
Vijay	3	8
Vinay	22	30
Total	40	40

Required

1. What amounts did E&Y bill to LG Electronics Ltd. and Electrolux Ltd. for May?
2. Suppose support services were billed at Rs 500 per professional labor-hour (instead of 30 per cent of professional labor costs). How would this change affect the amounts E&Y billed to the two clients for May? Comment on the differences between the amounts billed in requirements 1 and 2.
3. How would you determine whether professional labor costs or professional labor-hours is the more appropriate allocation base for E&Y support services?

Solution

Alternative allocation bases for a professional services firm.

1.

Client	Direct Professional Time Rate per Hour	Number of Hours	Total	Support Services Rate	Total	Amount Billed to Client
(1)	(2)	(3)	(4) = (2) × (3)	(5)	(6) = (4) × (5)	(7) = (4) + (6)
LG Electronics Ltd.						
Ajay	Rs 5,000	15	Rs 75,000	30%	Rs 22,500	Rs 97,500
Vijay	1,200	3	3,600	30%	1,080	4,680
Vinay	800	22	17,600	30%	5,280	22,880
						1,25,060

Electrolux Ltd.						
Ajay	5,000	2	10,000	30%	3,000	13,000
Vijay	1,200	8	9,600	30%	2,880	12,480
Vinay	800	30	24,000	30%	7,200	31,200
						56,680

2.

	Direct Professional Time			Support Services		
Client (1)	**Rate per Hour** (2)	**Number of Hours** (3)	**Total** (4) = (2) × (3)	**hour** (5)	**Total** (6) = (3) × (5)	**Amount Billed to Client** (7) = (4) + (6)
Ajay	5,0					
Ajay Gupta	Rs 5,000	15	Rs 75,000	Rs 500	Rs 7,500	Rs 82,500
Vijay Gupta	1,200	3	3,600	500	1,500	5,100
Vinay Aggarwal	800	22	17,600	500	11,000	28,600
						1,16,200
Electrolux Ltd.						
Ajay Gupta	5,000	2	10,000	500	1,000	11,000
Vijay Gupta	1,200	8	9,600	500	4,000	13,600
Vinay Aggarwal	800	30	24,000	500	15,000	39,000
						63,600

	Requirement 1	**Requirement 2**
Seattle Dominion	Rs 1,25,060	Rs 1,16,200
Tokyo Enterprises	56,680	63,600
	1,81,740	1,79,800

Both clients use 40 hours of professional labor time. However, LG Electronics Ltd. uses a higher proportion of Ernst & Young's time (15 hours), which is more costly. This attracts the highest support-services charge when allocated on the basis of direct professional labor costs.

3. Assume that the Ernst & Young uses a cause-and-effect criterion when choosing the allocation base for support services. You could use several pieces of evidence to determine whether professional labor costs or hours is the driver of support-service costs:
   a. *Interviews with personnel.* For example, staff in the major cost categories in support services could be interviewed to determine whether Ernst & Young requires more support per hour than, say, Vinay. The professional labor costs allocation base implies that an hour of Ernst & Young's time requires 6.25 (Rs 500 ÷ Rs 80) times more support-service rupees than does an hour of Vinays' time.
   b. *Analysis of tasks undertaken for selected clients.* For example, if computer-related costs are a sizable part of support costs, you could determine if there was a systematic relationship between the percentage involvement of professionals with high billing rates on cases and the computer resources consumed for those cases.

5-19 ABC, process costing. Citizen Company produces mathematical and financial calculators. Data related to the two products is presented below.

	Mathematical	**Financial**
Annual production in units	50,000	1,00,000
Direct materials costs	Rs 1,50,000	Rs 3,00,000
Direct manufacturing labor costs	Rs 50,000	Rs 1,00,000
Direct manufacturing labor-hours	2,500	5,000
Machine-hours	25,000	50,000
Number of production runs	50	50
Inspection hours	1,000	500

Both products pass through Department 1 and Department 2. The departments' combined manufacturing overhead costs are

	Total
Machining costs	Rs 3,75,000
Setup costs	1,20,000
Inspection costs	1,05,000

Required

1. Compute the manufacturing overhead cost per unit for each product.
2. Compute the manufacturing cost per unit for each product.

Solution

Rates per unit cost driver.

Activity	Cost Driver	Rate
Machining	Machine-hours	Rs 3,75,000 ÷ (25,000 + 50,000) = Rs 5 per machine-hour
Set up	Production runs	Rs 1,20,000 ÷ (50 + 50) = Rs 1,200 per production run
Inspection	Inspection-hours	Rs 1,05,000 ÷ (1,000 + 500) = Rs 70 per inspection-hour

Overhead cost per unit:

Particulars	Mathematical	Financial
Machining: Rs 5 × 25,000; 50,000 × Rs 5 Rs 2,50,000	Rs 1,25,000	Rs 1,25,000
Set up: Rs 1,200 × 50; Rs 1,200 × 50	60,000	60,000
Inspection: Rs 70 × 1,000; Rs 70 × 500	70,000	35,000
Total manufacturing overhead costs	2,55,000	3,45,000
Divide by number of units	÷50,000	÷1,00,000
Manufacturing overhead cost per unit	Rs 5.10	Rs 3.45

Particulars	Mathematical	Financial
Manufacturing cost per unit		
Direct materials Rs 1,50,000 ÷ 50,000	Rs 3	
Rs 3,00,000 ÷ 1,00,000		Rs 3
Direct manufacturing labor Rs 50,000 ÷ 50,000	1	
Rs 100,000 ÷ 100,000		1
Manufacturing overhead (from Requirement 1)	5.10	3.45
Manufacturing cost per unit	9.10	7.45

5-20 ABC, retail product-line profitability. Nirula decides to apply ABC analysis to three product lines: Ice creams, Milk shakes and ice-cream, and Food products. It identifies four activities and activity-cost rates for each activity as

Ordering	Rs 1,000 per purchase order
Delivery and receipt of merchandise	Rs 800 per delivery
Shelf-stocking	Rs 200 per hour
Customer support and assistance	Rs 2 per item sold

The revenues, cost of goods sold, store support costs, and activity area usage of the three product lines are

	Ice-Creams	Milk and Ice Cream Shakes	Food Products
Financial data:			
Revenues	Rs 5,70,000	Rs 6,30,000	Rs 5,20,000
Cost of goods sold	3,80,000	4,70,000	3,50,000
Store support	1,14,000	1,41,000	1,05,000
Activity-area usage (cost-allocation base)			
Ordering (purchase orders)	30	25	13
Delivery (deliveries)	98	36	28
Shelf-stocking (hours)	183	166	24
Customer support (items sold)	15,500	20,500	7,900

Under its previous costing system, Nirula allocated support costs to products at the rate of 30 per cent of cost of goods sold.

Required

1. Use the previous costing system to prepare a product-line profitability report for Nirula's.
2. Use the ABC system to prepare a product-line profitability report for Nirula's.
3. What new insights does the ABC system in requirement 2 provide to Nirula's managers?

Solution

1. The previous costing system (Panel A of Solution Exhibit 5-20) reports the following:

Particulars	Ice Creams	Milk & Ice Cream Shakes	Food Products	Total
Revenues	Rs 5,70,000	Rs 6,30,000	Rs 5,20,000	Rs 17,20,000
Costs				
Cost of goods sold	3,80,000	4,70,000	3,50,000	12,00,000
Store support (30% of COGS)	1,14,000	1,41,000	1,05,000	3,60,000
Total costs	4,94,000	6,11,000	4,55,000	15,60,000
Operating income	76,000	19,000	65,000	1,60,000
Operating income ÷ Revenues	13.33%	3.02%	12.50%	9.30%

PANEL A: PREVIOUS COSTING SYSTEM

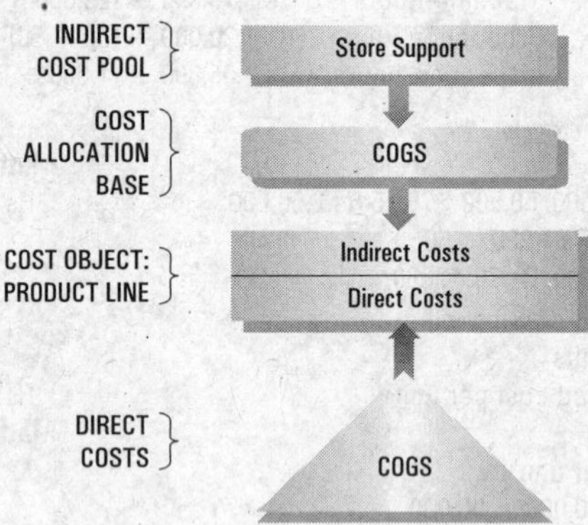

PANEL B: ABC COSTING SYSTEM

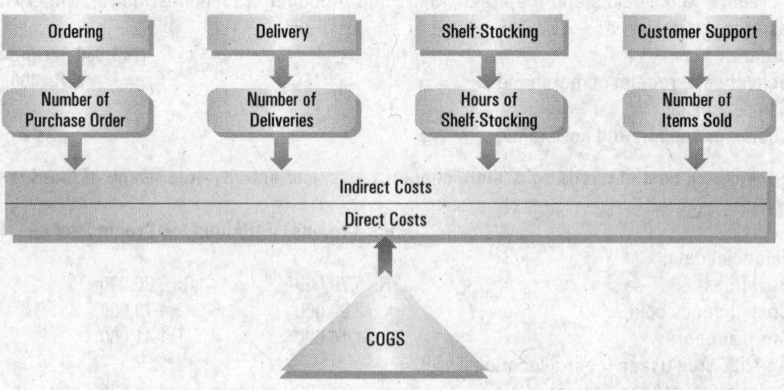

2. **The ABC system reports the following:**

Particulars	**Ice Creams**	**Milk & Ice Cream Shakes**	**Food Products**	**Total**
Revenues	Rs 5,70,000	Rs 6,30,000	Rs 5,20,000	Rs 17,20,000
Costs				
Cost of goods sold	3,80,000	4,70,000	3,50,000	12,00,000
Ordering (Rs1,000 × 30; 25; 13)	30,000	25,000	13,000	68,000
Delivery (Rs 800 × 98; 36; 28)	78,400	28,800	22,400	1,29,600
Shelf-stocking (Rs 200 × 183; 166; 24)	36,600	33,200	4,800	74,600
Customer support (Rs 2 × 15,500; 20,500; 7,900)	31,000	41,000	15,800	87,800
Total costs	5,56,000	5,98,000	4,06,000	15,60,000
Operating income	14,000	32,000	1,14,000	1,60,000
Operating income ÷ Revenues	2.46%	5,08%	21.92%	9.30%

These activity costs are based on the following:

Activity	Cost Allocation Rate	Ice Creams	Milk & Ice Cream Shakes	Food Products
Ordering	Rs 1,000 per purchase order	30	25	13
Delivery	800 per delivery	98	36	28
Shelf-stocking	200 per hour	183	166	24
Customer support	2 per item sold	15,500	20,500	7,900

The rankings of products in terms of relative profitability are:

Previous Costing System		ABC System	
1. **Ice Creams**	13.33%	**Food Products**	21.92%
2. **Food Products**	12.50	**Milk & Ice Cream Shakes**	5.08
3. **Milk & Ice Cream Shakes**	3.02	**Ice Creams**	2.46

The percentage revenue, COGS, and activity costs for each product line are:

	Ice Creams	Milk & Ice Cream Shakes	Food Products	Total
Revenues	33.14	36.63	30.23	100.00
COGS	31.67	39.17	29.16	100.00
Activity areas:				
Ordering	44.12	36.76	19.12	100.00
Delivery	60.49	22.22	17.29	100.00
Shelf-stocking	49.06	44.50	6.44	100.00
Customer support	35.31	46.70	17.99	100.00

3. The Ice Creams line drops sizably in profitability when ABC is used. Although it constitutes 31.67% of COGS, it uses a higher percentage of total resources in each activity area, especially the high cost delivery activity area. In contrast, Food Products draws a much lower percentage of total resources used in each activity area than its percentage of total COGS. Hence, under ABC, Food Products is much more profitable.

Nirula's management may want to explore ways to increase sales of Food Products. It may also want to explore price increases on Ice Creams.

5-21 ABC, wholesale, customer profitability. Delitte Furnitures sells furniture items to four department-store chains. Mr. Vijay commented, "We apply ABC to determine product-line profitability. The same ideas apply to customer profitability, and we should find out our customer profitability as well." Delitte Furnitures send catalogs to the corporate purchasing departments on a monthly basis. The customers are entitled to return unsold merchandise within a six-month period from the purchase data and receive a full purchase price refund. The following data were collected from last year's operations.

	Chain			
Particulars	**1**	**2**	**3**	**4**
Gross sales	Rs 5,00,000	Rs 3,00,000	Rs 10,00,000	Rs 7,00,000
Sales returns				
Number of items	100	26	60	40
Amount	Rs 1,00,000	Rs 50,000	Rs 70,000	Rs 60,000
Number of orders				
Regular	40	150	50	70
Rush	10	50	10	30

Mr. Vijay has calculated the following activity rates.

Activity	Cost driver rate
Regular order processing	Rs 200 per regular order
Rush order processing	1,000 per rush order
Returned items processing	100 per item
Catalogs and customer support	10,000 per customer

Customers pay the transportation costs. The cost of goods sold average 80 per cent of sales.

Required

Determine the contribution to profit from each chain last year. Comment on your solution.

Solution

Particulars	**Chain**			
	1	**2**	**3**	**4**
Gross sales	Rs 5,00,000	Rs 3,00,000	Rs 10,00,000	Rs 7,00,000
Sale returns	1,00,000	50,000	70,000	60,000
Net sales	4,00,000	2,50,000	9,30,000	6,40,000
Cost of goods sold (80%)	3,20,000	2,00,000	7,44,000	5,12,000
Gross margin	80,000	50,000	1,86,000	1,28,000
Customer-related costs:				
Regular orders Rs 200 × 40; 150; 50; 70	8,000	30,000	10,000	14,000
Rush orders Rs 1,000 × 10; 50; 10; 30	10,000	50,000	10,000	30,000
Returned items Rs 100 × 100; 26; 60; 40	10,000	2,600	6,000	4,000
Catalogs and customer support	10,000	10,000	10,000	10,000
Customer related costs	38,000	92,600	36,000	58,000
Contribution (loss) margin	42,000	(42,600)	1,50,000	70,000
Contribution (loss) margin as percentage of gross sales	8.4%	(14.2%)	15.0%	10.0%

The analysis indicates that customers' profitability (loss) contribution varies widely from (14.2%) to 15.0%. Immediate attention to Chain 2 is required which is currently showing a loss contribution. The chain has a disproportionate number of both regular orders and rush orders. Delitte should work with the management of Chain 2 to find ways to reduce the number of orders, while maintaining or increasing the sales volume. If this is not possible, Delitte should consider dropping Chain 2, if it can save the customer-related costs.

Chain 1 has a disproportionate number of the items returned as well as sale returns. The causes of these should be investigated so that the profitability contribution of Chain 1 could be improved.

5-22 Activity-based costing, job-costing system. The HCL Ltd. plant in Noida, assembles and tests printed-circuit (PC) boards. The job-costing system at this plant has two direct-cost categories (direct materials and direct manufacturing labor) and seven indirect-cost pools. These indirect cost pools represent the seven activity areas that operating personnel at the plant determined are sufficiently different (in terms of cost-behavior patterns or individual products being assembled) to warrant separate cost pools. The cost-allocation base chosen for each activity area is the cost driver at that activity area.

Ajay, a newly appointed marketing manager at HCL, is attending a training session that describes how an activity-based costing approach was used to design the Noida plant's job-costing system. He is provided with the following incomplete information for a specific job (an order for a single PC board, No A82):

Direct materials	Rs 7,500	
Direct manufacturing labor	1,500	Rs 9,000
Manufacturing overhead (see below)		?
Total manufacturing		?

Manufacturing Overhead Cost Pool	Cost-allocation Base	Cost-Allocation Rate	Units of Cost-Allocation Base Used on Job No. A82	Manufacturing Overhead Allocated to Job
1. Axial insertion	Axial insertion	8	450	
2. Dip insertion	Dip insertion	25		600
3. Manual insertion	Manual insertion		1,100	550
4. Wave solder	Boards soldered	350		350
5. Backload	Backload insertions		600	420
6. Test	Budgeted time board is in test activity	90	25	
7. Defect analysis	Budgeted time for defect analysis and repair		10	800

Required

1. Present an overview diagram of the activity-based job-costing system at the Noida plant.
2. Fill in the blanks (noted by question marks) in the cost information provided to Ajay for Job No. A82.
3. Why might manufacturing managers and marketing managers favor this ABC job-costing system over the previous costing system, which had the same two direct-cost categories but only a single indirect cost pool (manufacturing overhead allocated using direct manufacturing labor costs)?

Solution

1. **An overview of the activity-based job-costing system is:**

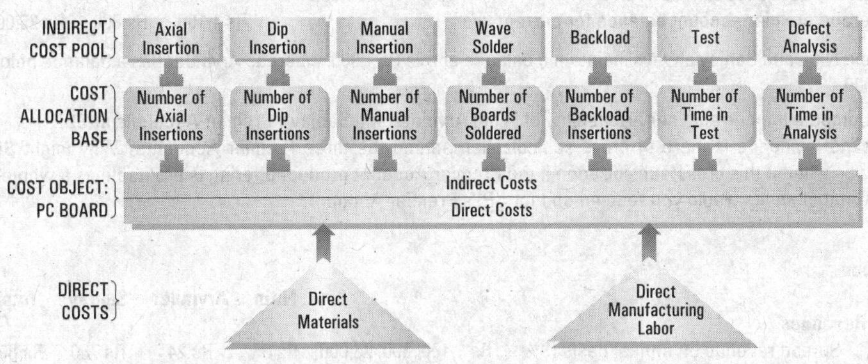

2.

Activity Area	Indirect Manufacturing				Costs Allocated
1. Axial insertion	Rs 8	×	450	=	Rs 3,600
2. Dip insertion	25	×	24	=	600
3. Manual insertion	50	×	1,100	=	550
4. Wave solder	350	×	1	=	350
5. Backload	70	×	600	=	420
6. Test	90	×	25	=	2,250
7. Defect analysis	80	×	10	=	800
Total					Rs 8,570

Direct manufacturing costs		
Direct materials	Rs 7,500	
Direct manufacturing labor	1,500	Rs 9,000
Indirect manufacturing costs		
Manufacturing overhead (see above)		8,570
Total manufacturing costs		17,570

3. The manufacturing manager likely would find the ABC job-costing system useful in cost management. Unlike direct manufacturing labor costs, the seven indirect cost pools are systematically linked to the activity areas at the plant. The result is more accurate product costing. Productivity measures can be developed that directly link to the management accounting system.

   Marketing managers can use ABC information to price jobs as well as to advise customers about how selecting different product features will affect price.

5-23 ABC, product-costing at banks, cross-subsidization. State Bank of India (SBI) is examining the profitability of its Premier Account, a combined savings and checking account. Depositors receive a 7 per cent annual interest rate on their average deposit. SBI earns an interest rate spread of 3 per cent (the difference between the rate at which it lends money and the rate it pays depositors) by lending money for home loan purposes at 10 per cent. Thus, SBI would gain Rs 60 on the interest spread if a depositor has an average Premier Account balance of Rs 2,000, that is, Rs 2,000 × 3% = Rs 60.

The Premier Account allows depositors unlimited use of services such as deposits, withdrawals, checking accounts, and foreign currency drafts. Depositors with Premier Account balances of Rs 1,000 or more receive unlimited free use of services. Depositors with minimum balances of less than Rs 1,000 pay a Rs 20-a-months service fee for their Premier Account.

SBI recently conducted an activity-based costing study of its services. It assessed the following costs for six individual services. The use of theses services in current year by three customers is as follows:

Particulars	Activity-based Cost per Transaction"	Nitin	Arvinder	Sanjay
Deposit/withdrawal with teller	Rs 2.50	40	50	5
Deposit/withdrawal with automatic teller machine (ATM)	0.80	10	20	16
Deposit/withdrawal on prearranged				

monthly basis	0.50	0	12	60
Bank checks written	8.00	9	3	2
Foreign currency drafts	12.00	4	1	6
Inquiries about account balance	1.50	10	18	9
Average premier account balance for current year		Rs 1,100	Rs 800	Rs 25,000

Assume Nitin and Sanjay always maintain a balance above Rs 1,000, whereas Arvinder has a balance below Rs 1,000.

Required

1. Compute the current year profitability of Nitin, Arvinder and Sanjay's Premier Accounts at SBI.
2. What evidence is there of cross-subsidization among the three Premier Accounts? Why might SBI worry about this cross-subsidization if the Premier Account product offering is profitable as a whole?
3. What changes would you recommend for SBI's Premier Account?

Solution

1.

	Nitin	Arvinder	Sanjay	Total
Revenues				
Spread revenue on annual basis (3% ×; Rs 1,100, 800, 25,000)	Rs 33	Rs 24	Rs 750	Rs 807
Monthly fee charges (Rs 20 ×; 0, 12, 0)	0	240	0	240
Total revenues	33	264	750	1,047
Costs				
Deposit/withdrawal with teller Rs 2.50 × 40; 50; 5	100	125	12.5	237.5
Deposit/withdrawal with ATM Rs 0.80 × 10; 20; 16	8	16	12.8	36.8
Deposit/withdrawal on prearranged basis Rs 0.50 × 0; 12; 60	0	6	30.0	36.0
Bank checks written Rs 8 × 9; 3; 2	72	24	16.0	112.0
Foreign currency drafts Rs 12 × 4; 1; 6	48	12	72.0	132.0
Inquiries Rs 1.50 × 10; 18; 9	15	27	13.5	55.5
Total costs	243	210	156.8	609.8
Operating income (loss)	(210)	54	593.2	437.2

The assumption that the Nitin and Sanjay accounts exceed Rs 1,000 every month and the Arvinder account is less than Rs 1,000 each month means the monthly charges apply only to Arvinder.

One student with a banking background noted that in this solution 100% of the spread is attributed to the "depositor side of the bank." He noted that often the spread is divided between the "depositor side" and the "lending side" of the bank.

2. Cross-subsidization across individual Premier Accounts occurs when profits made on some accounts are offset by losses on other accounts. The aggregate profitability on the three customers is Rs 437.20. The Sanjay account is highly profitable (Rs 593.20), while the Nitin account is sizably unprofitable. The Arvinder account shows a small profit but only because of the Rs 240 monthly fees. It is unlikely that Arvinder will keep paying these high fees and that SBI would want Arvinder to pay such high fees from a customer relationship standpoint.

   The facts also suggest that the customers do not use the bank services uniformly. For example, Nitin and Arvinder have a lot of transactions with the teller or ATM, and also inquire about their account balances more often than Sanjay. This suggests cross-subsidization. SBI should be very concerned about the cross-subsidization. Competition likely would "understand" that high-balance low-activity type accounts (such as Sanjay) are highly profitable. Offering free services to these customers is not likely to retain these accounts if other banks offer higher interest rates. Competition likely will reduce the interest rate spread SBI can earn on the high-balance low-activity accounts they are able to retain.

3. **Possible changes SBI could make are:**
   a. Offer higher interest rates on high-balance accounts to increase SBI's competitiveness in attracting and retaining these accounts.
   b. Introduce charges for individual services.

5-24 Planwide, department, and activity-cost rates. (CGA, adapted) The Birla Company manufactures and sells two products, A and B. The manufacturing activity is organized in two departments. Manufacturing overhead costs at its Portland plant are allocated to each product using a plantwide rate of Rs 170 per direct manufacturing labor-hour. This rate is based on budgeted manufacturing overhead of Rs 34,00,000 and 20,000 budgeted direct manufacturing labor-hours.

Manufacturing department	Budgeted manufacturing overhead	Budgeted direct manufacturing labor-hours
1	Rs 24,00,000	10,000
2	10,00,000	10,000
Total	34,00,000	20,000

The number of direct manufacturing labor-hours required to manufacture each product is

Manufacturing department	Product A	Product B
1	4	1
2	1	4
Total	5	5

Per-unit costs for the two categories of direct manufacturing costs are

Direct manufacturing costs	Product A	Product B
Direct materials costs	Rs 1,200	Rs 1,500
Direct manufacturing labor costs	800	800

At the end of the year, there was no work in process. There were 200 finished units of product A and 600 finished units of product B on hand. Assume that the budgeted production level of the Portland plant was exactly attained.

Birla sets the selling price of each product by adding 120 per cent to its unit manufacturing costs; that is, if the unit manufacturing costs are Rs 1,000, the selling price is Rs 2,200 (Rs 1,000 + Rs 1,200). This 120 per cent markup is designed to cover costs upstream to manufacturing (R&D and design) and costs downstream from manufacturing (marketing, distribution, and customer service), as well as to provide a profit.

Required

1. How much manufacturing overhead cost would be included in the inventory of products A and B if Birla used (a) a plantwide overhead rate and (b) department overhead rates?
2. By how much would the selling prices of product A and product B differ if Birla used a plantwide overhead rate instead of department overhead rates?
3. Should Birla Company prefer plantwide or department overhead rates?
4. Under what conditions should Birla Company further subdivide the department cost pools into activity-cost pools?

Solution

1. Budgeted manufacturing overhead rates:
   - i. Plantwide rate:
     Rs 34,00,000/20,000 = Rs 170 per direct manufacturing labor-hour
   - ii. Departmental rates:
     Department 1: Rs 24,00,000 ÷ 10,000 = Rs 240 per direct manufacturing labor-hour
     Department 2: Rs 10,00,000 ÷ 10,000 = Rs 100 per direct manufacturing labor-hour

Manufacturing overhead portion of ending inventories:

i. Using plantwide overhead rate:	
800 units × 5 hours × Rs 170	Rs 6,80,000
ii. Using department overhead rates	
Product A: 200 × [(4 × Rs 240) + (1 × Rs 100)]	2,12,000
Product B: 600 × [(1 × Rs 240) + (4 × Rs 100)]	3,84,000
	5,96,000

The difference in inventory costs due to the different methods of allocating manufacturing overhead is Rs 84,000 (Rs 6,80,000 – Rs 5,96,000).

2. **Product A**	**Plantwide Overhead Rate**	**Department Overhead Rates**
Direct materials	Rs 1,200	Rs 1,200
Direct manufacturing labor	800	800
Manufacturing overhead: Rs 170 × 5	850	
(Rs 240 × 4) + (Rs 100 × 1)		1,060
Total manufacturing costs markup	2,850	3,060
(Rs 2,850 × 120%; Rs 3,060 × 120%)	3,420	3,672
Selling price	6,270	6,732

Product B	**Plantwide Overhead Rate**	**Department Overhead Rate**
Direct materials	Rs 1,500	Rs 1,500
Direct manufacturing labor	800	800
Manufacturing overhead: Rs 170 × 5	850	
(Rs 240 × 1) + (Rs 100 × 4)		640
Total manufacturing costs markup	3,150	2,940
(Rs 3,150 × 120%); Rs 2,940 × 120%)	3,780	3,528
Selling price	6,930	6,468

3. Birla Company should use budgeted department manufacturing overhead rates because:

a. The two manufacturing departments differ sizably in their overhead cost structures, despite having the same budgeted direct manufacturing labor-hours. Department 1 has Rs 24,00,000 budgeted overhead, and Department 2 has Rs 10,00,000 budgeted overhead.

b. The two products use resources in the two manufacturing departments quite differently. The direct manufacturing labor-hours used in each department are:

Department	Product A	Product B
1	4	1
2	1	4

Differences a. and b. mean that more refined product costs will be calculated with budgeted department manufacturing overhead rates.

4. Birla should further subdivide the department cost pools into activity-cost pools if (a) significant costs are incurred on *different* activities within the department, (b) the different activities have different cost-allocation bases, and (c) different products use the different activities in different proportions.

5-25 Activity-based costing, merchandising. Nicholas Pharma Ltd. specializes in the distribution of pharmaceutical products. Nicholas Pharma Ltd. buys from pharmaceutical companies and resells to each of three different markets:

a. General supermarket chains
b. Drugstore chains
c. Ma and Pa single-store pharmacies

Anand, the new controller of Nicholas Pharma, reported the following data for August:

Particulars	General Supermarket	Drugstore Chains Chains	Ma and Pa Single Stores
Average revenue per delivery	Rs 15,450	Rs 5,250	Rs 990
Average cost of goods sold per delivery	15,000	5,000	900
Number of deliveries	120	300	1,000

For many years, Nicholas Pharma has used gross margin percentage [(Revenue – Cost of goods sold) ÷ Revenue] to evaluate the relative profitability of its groups (distribution outlets).

Anand recently attended a seminar on activity-based costing and decides to consider using it at Nicholas Pharma. Anand meets with all the key managers and many staff members. Generally, these individuals agree that there are five key activity areas at Nicholas Pharma:

Activity Area	Cost Driver
1. Customer purchase order processing	Purchase orders by customers
2. Line item ordering	Line items per purchase order
3. Store delivery	Store deliveries
4. Cartons shipped to stores	Cartons shipped to a store per delivery
5. Shelf stocking at customer stores	Hours of shelf stocking

Each customer purchase order consists of one or more line items. A line item represents a single product (such as Extra Strength Tylenol Tablets). Each store delivery entails delivery of one or more cartons of products to a customer. Each product is delivered in one or more separate cartons. Nicholas Pharma staff stack cartons directly onto display shelves in a store. Currently, there is no charge for this service, and not all customers use Nicholas Pharma for this activity.

The August operating costs (other than costs of goods sold) of Nicholas Pharma are Rs 1,50,540. These operating costs are assigned to the five activity areas. The costs in each area and the quantity of the cost-allocation base used in that area for August are as follows:

Activity Area	Total Costs in August	Total Units of Cost-allocation Base Used in August
1. Customer purchase order processing	Rs 40,000	1,000 orders
2. Line item ordering	31,920	10,640 line items
3. Store deliveries	35,500	710 store deliveries
4. Cartons shipped to stores	38,000	38,000 cartons
5. Shelf stocking at customer stores	5,120	320 hours
	1,50,540	

Other data for August include the following:

Total number of orders	70	180	750
Average number of line items per order	14	12	10
Total number of store deliveries	60	150	500

Average number of cartons shipped per store delivery	300	80	16
Average number of hours of shelf stocking per store delivery	3	0.6	0.1

Required

1. Compute the August gross-margin percentage for each of its three distribution markets. What is the operating income of Nicholas Pharma? Also determine its operating income margin.
2. Compute the August rate per unit of the cost-allocation base for each of the five activity areas.
3. Compute the operating income of each distribution market in August using the activity-based costing information. Comment on the results. What new insights are available with the activity-based information?

Solution

1. **Computation of gross margin percentage and operating income:**

Particulars	General Supermarket Chains	Drugstore Chains	Ma and Pa Single Stores	Total
Revenues[a]	Rs 18,54,000	Rs 15,75,000	Rs 9,90,000	Rs 44,19,000
Cost of goods sold[b]	18,00,000	15,00,000	9,00,000	42,00,000
Gross margin	54,000	75,000	90,000	2,19,000
Other operating costs				1,50,540
Operating income				68,460
Gross margin (%)	2.91	4.76	9.09	4.96
Operating income margin (%)	–	–	–	1.55

[a](Rs 15,450 × 120); (Rs 5,250 × 300); (Rs 990 × 1,000)
[b](Rs 15,000 × 120); (Rs 5,000 × 300); (Rs 900 × 1,000)

2. **The per-unit cost driver rates are:**

1. Customer purchase order processing, Rs 40,000/1,000 orders	Rs 40 per order
2. Line item ordering, Rs 31,920/10,640	Rs 3 per line item
3. Store delivery, Rs 35,500/710 deliveries	Rs 50 per delivery
4. Cartons shipped, Rs 38,000/38,000 cartons	Rs 1 per carton
5. Shelf-stocking, Rs 5,120/320 hour	Rs 16 per hour

3. **The activity-based costing of each distribution market for August is:**

Particulars	General Supermarket Chains	Drugstore Chains	Ma and Pa Single Stores
1. Customer purchase order processing, (Rs 40 × 70; 180; 750)	Rs 2,800	Rs 7,200	Rs 30,000
2. Line item ordering, (Rs 3 × (70 × 14; 180 × 12; 750 × 10)	2,940	6,480	22,500
3. Store delivery, (Rs 50 × (60, 150, 500)	3,000	7,500	25,000
4. Cartons shipped, (Rs 1 × (60 × 300; 150 × 80; 500 × 16)	18,000	12,000	8,000
5. Shelf-stocking, (Rs 16 × (60 × 3, 150 × 0.6, 500 × 0.1)	2,880	1,440	800
	29,620	34,620	86,300

The revised operating income statement is:

Particulars	General Supermarket Chains	Drugstore Chains	Ma and Pa Single Stores	Total
Revenues	Rs 18,54,000	Rs 15,75,000	Rs 9,90,000	Rs 44,19,000
Cost of goods sold	18,00,000	15,00,000	9,00,000	42,00,000
Gross margin	54,000	75,000	90,000	2,19,000
Operating costs	29,620	34,620	86,300	1,50,540
Operating income	24,380	40,380	3,700	68,460
Operating income margin	1.31%	2.56%	0.37%	1.55%

The ranking of the three markets are:

Using Gross Margin		Using Operating Income	
1. Ma and Pa Single Stores	9.09%	1. Drugstore Chains	2.56%
2. Drugstore Chains	4.76%	2. General Supermarket Chains	1.31%
3. General Supermarket Chains	2.91%	3. Ma and Pa Single Stores	0.37%

The activity-based analysis of costs highlights how the Ma and Pa Single Stores use a larger amount of Nicholas Pharma resources per revenue rupee than do the other two markets. The ratio of the operating costs to revenues across the three markets is:

General Supermarket Chains	1.60%	(Rs 29,620/Rs 18,54,000)
Drugstore Chains	2.20%	(Rs 36,620/Rs 15,75,000)
Ma and Pa Single Stores	8.72%	(Rs 86,300/Rs 9,90,000)

This is a classic illustration of the maxim that "all revenue rupee are not created equal." The analysis indicates that the Ma and Pa Single Stores are the least profitable market. Nicholas Pharma should work to increase profits in this market through: (1) a possible surcharge, (2) decreasing the number of orders, (3) offering discounts for quantity purchases etc.

5-26 Activity-based job costing. Godrej Ltd. manufactures a variety of prestige boardroom chairs. Its job-costing system uses an activity-based approach. There are two direct-cost categories (direct materials and direct manufacturing labor) and three indirect-cost pools. The cost pools represent three activity areas at the plant.

Manufacturing Activity Area	Budgeted Costs for 2012	Cost Driver Used As Allocation Base	Cost-allocation Rate
Materials handling	Rs 1,00,000	Parts	Rs 0.25
Cutting	10,00,000	Parts	2.50
Assembly	10,00,000	Direct manufacturing labor-hours	25.00

Two styles of chairs were produced in March: the executive chair and the chairman chair. Their quantities, direct material costs, and other data for March are as follows:

	Units Produced	Direct material Costs	Number of Parts Labor-hours	Direct Manufacturing
Executive chair	5,000	Rs 3,00,000	1,00,000	7,500
Chairman chair	100	12,500	3,500	500

The direct manufacturing labor rate is Rs 20 per hour. Assume no beginning or ending inventory.

Required

1. Compute the March total manufacturing costs and unit costs of the executive chair and the chairman chair.
2. The upstream activities to manufacturing (R&D and design) and the downstream activities (marketing, distribution, and customer service) were analyzed, and the unit costs in were budgeted to be as follows:

	Upstream Activities	Downstream Activities
Executive chair	Rs 30	55
Chairman chair	73	118

Compute the full costs per unit of each chair. (Full costs of each chair are the sum of the costs of all business functions.)

3. Compare the per unit cost figures for the executive chair and the chairman chair computed in 1 and 2 above. Why do the costs differ for each chair? Why might these differences be important to Godrej Ltd.?

Solution

1. **Computation of total manufacturing costs and unit costs:**

Particulars	**Executive Chair**	**Chairman Chair**
1. Direct manufacturing costs:		
Direct materials	Rs 3,00,000	Rs 12,500
Direct manufacturing labor, Rs 20 x 7,500; Rs 20 x 500	1,50,000	10,000
Direct manufacturing costs	4,50,000	22,500
Indirect manufacturing costs		
Materials handling, Re 0.25 × 1,00,000; Re 0.25 × 3,500	25,000	875
Cutting, Rs 2.50 × 1,00,000; Rs 2.50 × 3,500	2,50,000	8,750
Assembly, Rs 25 × 7,500; Rs 25 × 500	1,87,500	12,500
Total indirect manufacturing costs	4,62,500	22,125
Total manufacturing costs	9,12,500	44,625

Unit Costs

Executive chair: Rs 9,12,500/5,000 = Rs 182.5

Chairman chair: Rs 44,625/100 = Rs 446.25

2.

Particulars	**Executive Chair**	**Chairman Chair**
Upstream costs	Rs 30.0	Rs 73.00
Manufacturing costs	182.5	446.25
Downstream costs	55.0	118.00
Total costs	267.5	637.25

3. In requirement 1, the costs for each chair include only manufacturing costs. In requirement 2, the costs for each chair include manufacturing costs as well as upstream costs and downstream costs. It is important for Godrej Ltd. to take into account other than manufacturing costs for strategic decisions, especially long-term pricing decisions and product emphasis. When comparing the Executive Chair and the Chairman Chair, the Chairman Chair uses more of the upstream and downstream activities per unit than does the Executive Chair. The Chairman Chair also uses more of the manufacturing activities per unit than the Executive Chair.

5-27 Activity-based job costing, unit-cost comparisons. The GE India Ltd. has a machining facility specializing in jobs for the aircraft-components market. The previous job-costing system had two direct-cost categories (direct materials and direct manufacturing labor) and a single indirect-cost pool (manufacturing overhead, allocated using direct manufacturing labor-hours). The indirect cost-allocation rate of the previous system for current year would have been Rs 230 per direct manufacturing labor-hours.

Recently a team with members from product design, manufacturing, and accounting used an ABC approach to refine its job-costing system. The two direct-cost categories were retained. The team decided to replace the single indirect-cost pool with five indirect-cost pools. The cost pools represent five activity areas at the facility, each with its own supervisor and budget responsibility. Pertinent data are as follows:

Activity Area	Cost-allocation Base	Cost-allocation Rate
Material handling	Parts	Rs 0.80
Lathe work	Lathe turns	0.40
Milling	Machine-hours	40.00
Grinding	Parts	1.60
Testing	Units tested	30.00

Information-gathering technology has advanced to the point at which the data necessary for budgeting in these five activity areas collected automatically.

Two representative jobs processed under the ABC system at the facility in the most recent period had the following characteristics.

Particulars	Job 410	Job 411
Direct materials cost per job	Rs 9,700	Rs 59,900
Direct manufacturing labor cost per job	Rs 750	Rs 11,250
Number of direct manufacturing labor-hours per job	25	375
Parts per job	500	2,000
Lathe turns per job	20,000	60,000
Machine-hours per job	150	1,050
Units per job (all units are tested)	10	200

Required

1. Compute the manufacturing costs per unit for each job under the previous job-costing system.
2. Compute the manufacturing costs per unit for each job under the activity-based costing system.
3. Compare the per unit cost figures for Jobs 410 and 411 computed in requirements 1 and 2. Why do the previous and the activity-based costing systems differ in the manufacturing costs per unit for each job? Why might these differences be important to Tracy Corporation?

Solution

1. **Computation of manufacturing costs per unit for each job**

Particulars	Job Order 410		Job Order 411	
Direct manufacturing costs:				
Direct materials	Rs 9,700		Rs 59,900	
Direct manufacturing labor				
Rs 30 × 25; Rs 30 × 375	750	Rs 10,450	11,250	Rs 71,150
Indirect manufacturing costs				
Rs 230 ×n 25; Rs 230 × 375		5,750		86,250
Total manufacturing costs		16,200		1,57,400
Number of units		÷ 10		÷ 200
Manufacturing costs per unit		1,620		787

2. **Computation of manufacturing costs per unit for each job under activity-based costing**

Particulars	Job Order 410	Job Order 411
Direct materials	Rs 9,700	Rs 59,900
Direct manufacturing costs:		
Direct materials	Rs 9,700	Rs 59,900
Direct manufacturing labor		

Rs 30 × 25; Rs 30 × 375	750	Rs 10,450	11,250	Rs 71,150
Indirect manufacturing costs:				
Materials handling				
Rs 0.80 × 500; Re 0.80 × 2,000	400		1,600	
Lathe work				
Rs 0.40 × 20,000; Re 0.40 × 60,000	8,000		24,000	
Milling				
Rs 40 × 150; Rs 40 × 1,050	6,000		42,000	
Grinding				
Rs 1.60 × 500; Rs 1.60 × 2,000	800		3,200	
Testing				
Rs 30 × 10; Rs 30 × 200	300	15,500	6,000	76,800
Total manufacturing costs		25,950		1,47,950
Number of units per job		÷ 10		÷ 200
Unit manufacturing cost per job		2,595		739.75

3.

	Job Order 410	Job Order 411
Number of units in job	10	200
Costs per unit with prior costing system	Rs 1,620	Rs 787
Costs per unit with activity-based costing	2,595	739.75

Job order 410 has an increase in reported unit cost of 60.18% [(Rs 2,595 − Rs 1,620) ÷ Rs 1,620], while job order 411 has a decrease in reported unit cost of 6% [(Rs 739.75 − Rs 787) ÷ Rs 787].

A common finding when activity-based costing is implemented is that low-volume products have increases in their reported costs while high-volume products have decreases in their reported cost. This result is also found in requirements 1 and 2 of this problem. Costs such as materials-handling costs vary with the number of parts handled (a function of batches and complexity of products) rather than with direct manufacturing labor-hours, an output-unit level cost driver, which was the only cost driver in the previous job-costing system.

The product cost figures computed in requirements 1 and 2 differ because:

a. The job orders differ in the way they use each of five activity areas.

b. The activity areas differ in their indirect cost allocation bases (specifically, each area does not use the direct manufacturing labor-hours indirect cost allocation base).

The following table documents how the two job orders differ in the way they use each of the five activity areas included in indirect manufacturing costs:

	Usage Based on Analysis of Activity Area Cost Drivers		Usage Assumed with Direct Manufacturing Labor-Hours as Application Base	
Activity Area	**Job Order 410**	**Job Order 411**	**Job Order 410**	**Job Order 411**
Materials handling	20.0%	80.0%	6.25%	93.75%
Lathe work	25.0	75.0	6.25	93.75
Milling	12.5	87.5	6.25	93.75
Grinding	20.0	80.0	6.25	93.75
Testing	4.8	95.2	6.25	93.75

The differences in product cost figures might be important to GE Indian Ltd. for product pricing and product emphasis decisions. The activity-based accounting approach indicates that job order 410 is being undercosted while job order 411 is being overcosted. GE Indian Ltd. may erroneously push job order 410 and deemphasize job order 411. Moreover, by its actions, GE Indian Ltd. may encourage a competitor to enter the market for job order 411 and take market share away from it.

5-28 ABC, implementation, ethics. (CMA, adapted) Sony Electronics, a division of Sony Corporation, manufactures two large-screen television models the Flatron, which has been produced since 2005 and sells for Rs 45,000 and the Wega, a newer model introduced in early 2008 that sells for Rs 57,000. Based on the following income statement for the current year ended March 31, senior management at Sony have decided to concentrate Sony's marketing resources on the Wega and to phase out the Flatron model.

Sony Electronics

Income Statement

For the Current Fiscal Year Ended March 31

Particulars	Flatron	Wega	Total
Revenues	Rs 1,98,00,000	Rs 45,60,000	Rs 2,43,60,000
Cost of goods sold	1,25,40,000	31,92,000	1,57,32,000
Gross margin	72,60,000	13,68,000	86,28,000

Selling and administrative expenses	58,30,000	9,78,000	68,08,000
Operating income	14,30,000	3,90,000	18,20,000
Units produced and sold	440	80	
Net income per unit sold	Rs 3,250	Rs 4,875	

Unit Cost for Flatron and Wega are as follows:

Particulars	**Flatron**	**Wega**
Direct materials	Rs 10,400	Rs 29,200
Direct manufacturing labor		
Flatron (1.5 hours × Rs 600)		900
Wega (3.5 hours × Rs 600)		2,100
Machine costs[a]		
Flatron (8 hours × Rs 900)		7,200
Wega (4 hours × Rs 900)		3,600
Manufacturing overhead other than machine costs[b]	10,000	5,000
Total cost	28,500	39,900

[a]Machine costs include lease costs of the machine, repairs, and maintenance.

[b]Manufacturing overhead was allocated to products based on machine-hours at the rate of Rs 1,250 per hour.

Sony's controller, Susan Thomas, is advocating the use of activity-based costing and activity-based management and has gathered the following information about the company's manufacturing overhead costs for the current year ended March 31.

Activity Center (Cost-allocation Base)	**Total Activity Costs**	**Units of the Cost-allocation Base**		
		Flatron	**Wega**	**Total**
Soldering (number of solder points)	Rs 9,42,000	11,85,000	3,85,000	15,70,000
Shipments (number of shipments)	8,60,000	16,200	3,800	20,000
Quality control (number of inspection)	12,40,000	56,200	21,300	77,500
Purchase orders (number of orders)	9,50,400	80,100	1,09,980	1,90,080
Machine power (machine-hours)	57,600	1,76,000	16,000	1,92,000
Machine setups (number of setups)	7,50,000	16,000	14,000	30,000
Total manufacturing overhead	48,00,000			

After completing her analysis Thomas shows the result to Fred Duval, the Sony division president. Duval does not like what he sees. "If you show headquarters this analysis, they are going to ask us to phase out the Wega line which we have just introduced. This whole costing stuff has been a major problem for us. First Flatron was not profitable and now Wega."

"Looking at the ABC analysis, I see two problems. First, we do many more activities than the ones you have listed. If you had included all activities, maybe your conclusions would be different. Second, you used number of setups and number of inspections as allocation bases. The numbers would be different had you used setup-hours and inspection-hours instead. I know that measurement problems precluded you from using these other cost-allocation bases, but I believe you ought to make some adjustments to our current numbers to compensate for these issues. I know you can do better. We can't afford to phase out either product."

Thomas knows her numbers are fairly accurate. On a limited sample, she calculated the profitability of Wega and Flatron using more and different allocation bases. The set of activities and activity rates she had used resulted in numbers that closely approximate those based on more detailed analyses. She is confident that headquarters, knowing that Wega was introduced only recently, will not ask Sony to phase it out. She is also aware that a sizable portion of Duval's bonus is based on division revenues. Phasing out either product would adversely affect his bonus. Still, she feels some pressure from Duval to do something.

Required

1. Using activity-based costing, calculate the profitability of the Wega and Flatron models.
2. Explain briefly why these numbers differ from the profitability of the Wega and Flatron models calculated using Sony's existing costing system.
3. Comment on Duval's concerns about the accuracy and limitations of ABC.

Solution

1. Sony Electronics should not emphasize the Wega model and phase out the Flatron model. Under activity-based costing, the Wega model has an operating income percentage of less than 3%, while the Flatron model has an operating income percentage of nearly 43%.

Cost driver rates for the various activities identified in the activity-based costing (ABC) system are as follows:

Soldering	Rs 942,000	÷	1,570,000	= Rs 0.60 per solder point
Shipments	860,000	÷	20,000	= 43.00 per shipment
Quality control	1,240,000	÷	77,500	= 16.00 per inspection
Purchase orders	950,400	÷	1,90,080	= 5.00 per order
Machine power	57,600	÷	1,92,000	= 0.30 per machine-hour
Machine setups	750,000	÷	30,000	= 25.00 per setup

Sony Electronics
Calculation of costs of each model under activity-based costing

Particulars	**Flatron**	**Wega**
Direct costs		
Direct materials (Rs 10,400 × 440; 80 × Rs 29,200)	Rs 45,76,000	Rs 23,36,000
Direct manufacturing labor (Rs 900 × 440; Rs 2,100 × 80)	3,96,000	1,68,000
Machine costs Rs 7,200 × 440; Rs 3,600 × 80)	31,68,000	2,88,000
Total direct costs	81,40,000	27,92,000
Indirect costs		
Soldering (Re 0.60 × 11,85,000; 0.60 × 3,85,000)	7,11,000	2,31,000
Shipments (Rs 43 × 16,200; 43 × 3,800)	6,96,600	1,63,400
Quality control (16 × 56,200; Rs (6 ×21,300)	8,99,200	3,40,800
Purchase orders (Rs 5 × 80,100; 5 × 1,09,980)	4,00,500	5,49,900
Machine power (Re 0.30 × 1,76,000; 0.30 × 16,000)	52,800	4,800
Machine setups (25 × 16,000; 25 × 14,000)	4,00,000	3,50,000
Total indirect costs	31,60,100	16,39,900
Total costs	1,13,00,100	44,31,900

Profitability analysis

Particulars	**Flatron**	**Wega**	**Total**
Revenues	Rs 1,98,00,000	Rs 45,60,000	Rs 2,43,60,000
Cost of goods sold	1,13,00,100	44,31,900	1,57,32,000
Gross margin	84,99,900	1,28,100	86,28,000
Per-unit calculations:			
Units sold	440	80	
Selling price (Rs 1,98,00,000/440; Rs 45,60,000/80)	45,000	57,000	
Cost of goods sold (Rs 1,13,00,100/440; Rs 44,31,900/80)	25,682	55,399	
Gross margin	19,318	1,601	
Gross margin percentage	42.9%	2.8%	

2. Sony's existing costing system allocates all manufacturing overhead other than machine costs on the basis of machine-hours, an output unit-level cost driver. Consequently, the more machine-hours per unit that a product needs, the greater the manufacturing overhead allocated to it. Because Flatron uses twice the number of machine-hours per unit compared to Wega, a large amount of manufacturing overhead is allocated to Flatron.

   The ABC analysis recognizes several batch-level cost drivers such as purchase orders, shipments, and setups. Wega uses these resources much more intensively than Flatron. The ABC system recognizes Wega's use of these overhead resources. Consider, for example, purchase order costs. The existing system allocates these costs on the basis of machine-hours. As a result, each unit of Flatron is allocated twice the purchase order costs of each unit of Wega. The ABC system allocates Rs 4,00,500 of purchase order costs to Flatron (equal to Rs 910.22 (Rs 400,500 ÷ 440) per unit) and Rs 5,49,900 of purchase order costs to Wega (equal to Rs 6,873.75 (Rs 5,49,900 ÷ 80) per unit). Each unit of Wega uses Rs 7.55 (Rs 6,873.75 ÷ 910.22) times the purchases order costs of each unit of Flatron.

   Recognizing Wega's more intensive use of manufacturing overhead results in Regal showing a much lower profitability under the ABC system. By the same token, the ABC analysis shows that Flatron is quite profitable. The existing costing system overcosted Flatron, and so made it appear less profitable.
3. Duval's comments about ABC implementation are valid. When designing and implementing ABC systems, managers and management accountants need to trade off the costs of the system against its benefits. Adding more activities makes the system harder to understand and more costly to implement but would probably improve the accuracy of cost information, which, in turn, would help Sony make better decisions.
4. Incorrect reporting of ABC costs with goal of retaining both the Flatron and Wega Product lines is unethical.

Thomas should indicate to Duval that the product cost calculations are, indeed, appropriate. If Duval still insists on modifying the product cost numbers, Thomas should raise the matter with one of Duval's superiors. If, after taking all these steps, there is continued pressure to modify product cost numbers, Thomas should consider resigning from the company, rather than engage in unethical behavior.

Exercises

5-29 Cost smoothing or peanut-butter costing, cross-subsidization. For many years five former classmates – Aashish, Amit, Nitin, Ankur and Aakash – have had a reunion dinner at the annual meeting of the College Alumni Association. The details of the bill for the most recent dinner at the Parikrama Restaurant break down as follows:

Diner	Entree	Dessert	Drinks	Total
Aashish	Rs 270	Rs 80	Rs 240	Rs 590
Amit	240	30	0	270
Nitin	210	60	130	400
Ankur	310	60	120	490
Aakash	150	40	60	250

For at least the last 10 dinners, Nitin has put the total restaurant bill on his ICICI Bank card. He then mails the other four bills for the average cost. Nitin continued this practice for the Parikrama dinner. However, just before he sent the bill to the other diners, Aakash phoned him to complain. He was livid at Ankur for ordering the steak and lobster entrée ("he always does that") and at Aashish for having three glasses of imported champagne ("What's wrong with domestic beer?").

Required

1. Why is the average-cost approach in the context of the reunion dinner an example of cost smoothing or peanut-butter costing?
2. Compute the average cost to each of the five diners. Who is undercharged and who is overcharged under the average-cost approach? Is Aakash's complaint justified?
3. Give an example of a dining situation in which Nitin would find it more difficult to compute the amount of under or overcosting. How might the behavior of the diners be affected if each person paid his or her own bill instead of continuing with the average cost approach?

5-30 Cost hierarchy. Telecom Ltd. manufactures boom boxes (music systems with radio, cassette, and compact disc players) for several well-known companies. The boom boxes differ significantly in their complexity and their manufacturing batch sizes. The following costs were incurred in current year.

a. Designing processes, drawing process charts, making engineering process changes for products, Rs 8,00,000.
b. Procurement costs of placing purchase orders, receiving materials, and paying suppliers related to the number of purchase orders placed, Rs 5,00,000.
c. Direct materials costs, Rs 60,00,000.
d. Costs incurred to set up machines each time a different product needs to be manufactured, Rs 6,00,000.
e. Direct manufacturing labor costs, Rs 10,00,000.
f. Machine-related overhead costs such as depreciation, maintenance, production engineering, Rs 11,00,000. (These resources relate to the activity of running the machines.)
g. Plant management, plant rent, and plant insurance, Rs 9,00,000.

Required

1. Classify each of the preceding costs as output unit-level, batch-level, product-sustaining, or facility sustaining. Explain each answer.
2. Consider two types of boom boxes made by Telecom. Ltd. One boom box is complex to make and is produced in many batches. The other boom box is simple to make and is produced in few batches. Suppose that Telecom needs the same number of machine-hours to make each type of boom box and that Telecom allocates all overhead costs using machine-hours as the only allocation base. How, if at all, would the boom boxes be miscosted? Briefly explain why.
3. How is the cost hierarchy helpful to Telecom in managing its business?

5-31 Plant wide indirect-cost rates. Delphi Automotive Systems Ltd. (DASL) designs, manufactures, and sells automotive parts. It has three main operating departments: design, engineering, and production.

- Design-the design of parts, using state of the art, computer aided design (CAD) equipments.
- Engineering- the prototyping of parts and testing of their specifications.
- Production-the manufacture of parts.

For many years, (DASL) had long-term contracts with major automobile assembly companies. These contracts had large production runs DASL's costing system allocates variable manufacturing overhead on the basis of machine-hours. Actual variable manufacturing overhead costs for current year were Rs 6,17,200.

DASL had three contracts in current year, and its machine-hours used in current year were assigned as follows:

Tata Motors	240
Maruti Udyog	5,600
Hyundai Motors	2,160
	8,000

Required

1. Compute the plantwide variable manufacturing overhead rate for current year.
2. Compute the variable manufacturing overhead allocated to each contract in current year.
3. What conditions must hold for machine-hours to provide an accurate estimate of the variable manufacturing overhead incurred on each individual contract at DASL in current year?

5-32 Department indirect-cost rates as activity rates (continuation of 5-31). The controller of Delphi Automotive Systems Ltd decides to interview key managers of the Design, Engineering, and Production departments. Each manager is to indicate the consensus choice among department personnel of the cost driver of variable manufacturing overhead costs for his or her department. Summary data are

Department	Variable Manufacturing Overhead	Cost Driver
Design	Rs 78,000	CAD design-hours
Engineering	59,200	Engineering-hours
Production	4,80,000	Machine-hours
	6,17,200	

Details pertaining to usage of these cost drivers for each of the three contracts are:

Department	Cost Driver	Tata Motors	Maruti Udyog	Hyundai Motors
Design	CAD design-hours	220	400	160
Engineering	Engineering-hours	140	120	480
Production	Machine-hours	240	5,600	2,160

Required

1. What is the variable manufacturing overhead rate for each department in current year?
2. What is the variable manufacturing overhead allocated to each contract in current year using department variable manufacturing overhead rates?
3. Compare your answer in requirement 2 to that in requirement 2 of Exercise 5-31. Comment on the results.

5-33 ABC, activity area cost-driver rates, product cross-subsidization. Lays Potatoes (LP) processes potatoes into potato cuts at its highly automated Noida Plant. It sells potatoes to the retail consumer market and to the institutional market, which includes hospitals, cafeterias, and university dormitories.

LP's existing costing system has a single direct-cost category (direct materials, which are the raw potatoes) and a single indirect-cost pool (production support). Support costs are allocated on the basis of kgs of potato cuts processed. Support costs include packaging materials. The current year total actual costs for producing 10,00,000 kgs of potato cuts (9,00,000 for the retail market and 1,00,000 for the institutional market) are

Direct materials used	Rs 1,50,000
Production support	9,83,000

The existing costing system does not distinguish between potato cuts produced for the retail and the institutional markets.

At the end of current year, LP unsuccessfully bid for a large institutional contract. Its bid was reported to be 30 per cent above the winning bid. This feedback came as a shock because LP included only a minimum profit margin on its bid. Moreover, the Noida plant was acknowledged as the most efficient in the industry.

As a result of its review process of the lost contract bid, LP decided to explore ways to refine its costing system. First, it identified that Rs 88,000 of the Rs 9,83,000 pertaining to packaging materials could be traced to individual jobs Rs 1,80,000 for retail and Rs 8,000 for institutional). These costs will now be classified as direct material. The Rs 1,50,000 of direct materials used were classified as Rs 1,35,000 for retail and Rs 15,000 for institutional. Second, it used ABC to examine how the two products (retail potato cuts and institutional potato cuts) used indirect support resources. The finding was that three activity areas could be distinguished.

- Cleaning Activity Area – LP uses 12,00,000 kgs of raw potatoes to yield 10,00,000 kgs of potato cuts. The cost-allocation base is kgs of raw potatoes cleaned. Costs in the cleaning activity area are Rs 1,20,000.
- Cutting Activity Area – LP processes raw potatoes for the retail market independently of those processed for the institutional market. The production line produces (a) 250 kgs of retail potato cuts

per cutting-hour and (b) 400 kgs of institutional potato cuts per cutting-hour. The cost-allocation base is cutting-hours on the production line. Costs in cutting activity area are Rs 2,31,000.

- Packaging Activity Area – LP packages potato cuts for the retail market independently of those packaged for the institutional market. The packaging line packages (a) 25 kgs of retail potato cuts per packaging-hour and (b) 100 kgs of institutional potato cuts per packaging-hour. The cost-allocation based is packaging-hours on the production line. Costs in the packaging activity area are Rs 4,44,000.

Required

1. Using the existing costing system, what is the cost per kg of potato cuts produced by LP.
2. Calculate the cost rate per unit of the cost driver in the (a) cleaning, (b) cutting, and (c) packaging activity areas.
3. Suppose LP uses information from its activity-cost rates to calculate costs incurred on retail potato cuts and institutional potato cuts. Using the ABC system, what is the cost per kg of (a) retail potato cuts and (b) institutional potato cuts?
4. Comment on the cost differences between the two costing system in 1 and 3. How might LP use the information in 3 to make better decisions?

5-34 Job costing with single direct-cost category, single indirect-cost pool, law firm. Ramesh Associates is a recently formed law partnership. Ramesh, the managing partner of Ramesh Associates, has just finished a tense phone call with Harish, president of Coal India Ltd. Harish strongly complained about the price Ramesh charged for some legal work done for Coal India.

Ramesh also received a phone call from its only other client (Asahi Glass), which was very pleased with both the quality of the work and the price charged on its most recent job.

Ramesh Associates uses a cost-based approach to pricing (billing) each job. Currently it uses a single direct-cost category (professional labor-hours) and a single indirect-cost pool (general support). Indirect costs are allocated to cases on the basis of professional labor-hours per case. The job files show the following:

	Coal India	Asahi Glass
Professional labor	104 hours	96 hours

Professional labor costs at Ramesh Associates are Rs 700 an hour. Indirect costs are allocated to cases at Rs 1,050 an hour. Total indirect costs in the most recent period were Rs 2,10,000.

Required

1. Why is it important for Ramesh Associates to understand the costs associated with individual jobs?
2. Compute the costs of the Coal India and Asahi Glass jobs using Ramesh's existing job-costing system.

5-35 Job costing with multiple direct-cost categories, single indirect-cost pool, law firm (continuation of 5-34). Ramesh asks his assistant, Ratan to collect details on those costs included in the Rs 10,000 indirect-cost pool that can be traced to each individual job. After analysis, Ratan is able to reclassify Rs 1,40,000 of the Rs 10,000 as direct costs:

Other direct costs	Coal India	Asahi Glass
Research support labor	Rs 16,000	Rs 34,000
Computer time	5,000	13,000
Travel and allowances	6,000	44,000
Telephones/faxes	2,000	10,000
Photocopying	2,500	7,500
Total	31,500	1,08,500

Ramesh decides to calculate the costs of each job. Ratan used six direct-cost pools and a single indirect-cost pool. The single indirect-cost pool would have Rs 70,000 of costs and would be allocated to each case using the professional labor-hours base.

Required

1. What is the revised indirect-cost allocation rate per professional labor-hour for Ramesh Associates when total indirect costs are Rs 70,000.
2. Compute the costs of the Coal India and Asahi Glass jobs if the firm in question had used its refined costing system with multiple direct-cost categories and one indirect-cost pool.
3. Compare the costs of Coal India and Asahi Glass jobs in 2 above with those in requirement 2 of Problem 5-34. Comment on the results.

5-36 Job costing with multiple direct-cost categories, multiple indirect-cost pools, law firm (continuation of 5-33 and 5-34). Ramesh has two classifications of professional staff: partners and associates. Ramesh asks his assistant to examine the relative use of partners and associates on the recent Coal India and Asahi Glass jobs. The Coal India job used 24 partner-hours and 80 associate-hours. The Asahi glass job used 56 partner-hours and 40 associates-hours. Therefore, totals of the two jobs together were 80 partner-hours and 120 associate-hours. Ramesh decides to examine how using separate direct-cost rates for part-

ners and associates and using separate indirect-cost pools for partners and associates would have affected the costs of the Coal India and Asahi Glass jobs. Indirect costs in each indirect-cost pool would be allocated on the basis of total hours of that category of professional labor. From the total indirect-cost pool would be allocated on the basis of total hours of that category of professional labor. From the total indirect-cost pool of Rs 70,000, Rs 46,000 is attributable to the activities of partners, and Rs 24,000 is attributable to the activities of associates.
The rates per category of professional labor are as follows:

Category of Professional Labor	Direct Cost Per Hour	Indirect Cost Per Hour
Partner	Rs 1,000	Rs 46,000/80 hours = Rs 575
Associate	500	Rs 24,000/120 hours = Rs 200

Required

1. Compute the costs of the Coal India and Asahi Glass cases using Ramesh's further refined system, with multiple direct-cost categories and multiple indirect-cost pools.
2. For what decisions might Ramesh Associates find it more useful to use this job-costing approach rather than the approaches in problems 5-29 or 5-30?

5-37 Plantwide versus department overhead cost rates. (CMA, adapted) The Samsonite Ltd. manufactures a complete line of fiberglass suitcases. Samsonite has three manufacturing departments (molding, component, and assembly) and two support departments (maintenance and power).

The sides of the cases are manufactured in the Molding Department. The frames, hinges, locks, and so forth are manufactured in the Component Department. The cases are completed in the Assembly Department. Varying amounts of materials, time, and effort are required for each of the various cases. The maintenance Department and Power Department provide services to the three manufacturing departments. Samsonite has always used a plantwide manufacturing overhead rate. Direct manufacturing labor-hours are used to allocate the overhead to each product. The budgeted rate is calculated dividing the company's total budgeted manufacturing overhead cost by the total budgeted direct manufacturing labor-hours to be worked in the three manufacturing departments.

Aditya, manager of Cost Accounting, has recommended that Samsonite use department overhead rates. Aditya has projected operating costs and production levels for the coming year. They are presented (in thousands) by department in the following table:

Particulars	Manufacturing Department		
	Molding	Component	Assembly
Department operating data			
Direct manufacturing labor-hours	500	2,000	1,500
Machine-hours	875	125	–
Department costs			
Direct manufacturing materials	Rs 24,800	60,000	Rs 2,500
Direct manufacturing labor	7,000	40,000	24,000
Manufacturing overhead	42,000	32,400	45,200
Total department costs	73,800	1,32,400	71,700
Uses of support departments			
Estimated usage of maintenance resources in labor-hours for coming year	90	25	10
Estimated usage of power (in kilowatt-hours) for coming year	360	320	120

Estimated costs are Rs 8,000 for the Maintenance Department and Rs 36,800 for the Power Department.

Required

1. Calculate the plantwide overhead rate for Samsonite Ltd. for the coming year using the same method as used in the past.
2. Aditya has been asked to develop department overhead rates for comparison with the plantwide rate. Follow these steps in developing the department rates:
   a. Allocate the Maintenance Department and Power Department costs to the three manufacturing departments.
   b. Calculate department overhead rates for the three manufacturing departments using a machine-hour allocation based for the Molding Department and a direct manufacturing labor-hour allocation base for the Component Department and Assembly Department.
3. Should the Samsonite Ltd. use a plantwide rate or department rates to allocate overhead cost to its products? Explain your answer.
4. Under what conditions should Samsonite Ltd. further subdivide the department cost pools into activity-cost pools?

5-38 Activity-based costing, product-cost cross-subsidization. Ever Bake (EB) has been in the food processing business for three years. For its first two years (year 1 and year 2), its sole product was raisin cake. All cakes were manufactured and packaged in one-kg units. EB used a normal costing system. The two direct-cost categories were direct materials and direct manufacturing labor. The sole indirect manufacturing cost category-manufacturing overhead-was allocated to products using units of production as the allocation base.

In its year 3, EB added a second product-layered carrot cake-which was packaged in one-kg units. This product-differs from raisin cake in several ways:

- More expensive ingredients are used.
- More direct manufacturing labor time is required.
- More-complex manufacturing processing is required.

In year 3, EB continued to use its existing costing system, in which it allocated manufacturing overhead using total units produced of raisin and layered carrot cakes.

Direct materials, costs in year 3 were Rs 120 per kg of raisin cake and Rs 180 per kg of layered carrot cake. Direct manufacturing labor cost in year 3 was Rs 28 per kg of raisin cake and Rs 40 per kg layered carrot cake.

During year 3, EB sales staff reported greater-than-expected sales of layered carrot cake and less-than-expected sales of raisin cake. The budgeted and actual sales volume for year 3 is as follows:

	Budgeted	Actual
Raisin cake	1,60,000 kgs	1,20,000 kgs
Layered carrot cake	40,000 kgs	80,000 kgs

The budgeted manufacturing overhead for year 3 is Rs 42,16,000.

At the end of year 3, Manish, the controller of EB, decided to investigate how an activity-based costing system would affect the product-cost numbers. After consultation with operating personnel the single manufacturing overhead cost pool was subdivided into five activity areas. These activity areas, the cost-allocation base, the budgeted year 3 cost-allocation rate, and the quantity of the cost-allocation base used by the raisin and layered carrot cakes are as follows:

Activity	Cost-allocation Base	Budgeted Year 3 Cost per Unit of Cost-allocation Base	Quantity of Cost-Allocation Base: Raising Cake	Quantity of Cost-Allocation Base: Layered Carrot Cake
Mixing	Labor-hours	Re 0.80	6,00,000	6,40,000
Cooking	Over-hours	2.80	2,40,000	2,40,000
Cooling	Cool room-hours	0.40	3,60,000	4,00,000
Creaming/Icing	Machine-hours	5.00	0	2,40,000
Packaging	Machine-hours	1.60	3,60,000	5,60,000

Required

1. Compute the year 3 unit-product cost of raisin cake and layered carrot cake using the existing costing system used in the year 3 to year 3 period.
2. Compute the year 3 unit-product cost of raisin cake and layered carrot cake using the activity-based costing system.
3. Explain the differences in unit-product costs computed in requirements 1 and 2.
4. Describe three uses Ever Bake might make of the activity-based cost numbers.

5-39 ABC, health care. Max Health Center runs three programs: (1) alcoholic rehabilitation, (2) drug addict rehabilitation, and (3) after care (counseling and support of patients after release from a mental hospital).

The center's budget for current year follows:

Professional salaries		
4 physicians ? Rs 6,00,000	Rs 24,00,000	
18 psychologists ? Rs 3,00,000	54,00,000	
20 nurses ? Rs 1,20,000	24,00,000	Rs 1,02,00,000
Medical supplies		6,00,000
General overhead (administrative salaries, rent, utilities, etc.)		17,60,000
		1,25,60,000

Amitabh, the director of the Center, is keen on determining the cost of each program. Amitabh compiled the following data describing employee allocations to individual programs:

	Alcohol	Drug	Aftercare	Total Employees
Physicians		4		4
Psychologists	6	4	8	18
Nurses	4	6	10	20

Eighty patients are in residence in the alcohol program, each staying about six months. Thus, the clinic provides 40 patient-years of service in the alcohol program. Similarly, 100 patients are involved in the drug program for about six months each. Thus, the clinic provides 50 patient-years of service in the drug program.

Amitabh has recently become aware of activity-based costing as a method to refine costing systems. He asks his accountant, Suresh, how he should apply this new technique. Suresh obtains the following information:

1. Consumption of medical supplies depends on the number of patient-years.
2. **General overhead costs consists of**

Rent and clinic maintenance	Rs 3,60,000
Administrative costs to manage patient charts, food, laundry	12,00,000
Laboratory services	2,00,000
Total	17,60,000

3. **Other information about individual departments:**

	Alcohol	Drug	Aftercare	Total Employees
Square feet of space occupied by each program	9,000	9,000	12,000	30,000
Patient-years of service	40	50	60	150
Number of laboratory tests	400	1,400	70	2,500

Required

1. a. Select cost-allocation bases that you believe are the most appropriate for allocating indirect costs to programs, calculate the indirect-cost rates for medical supplies, rent, and clinic maintenance; administrative costs for patient charts, food, and laundry; and laboratory services.
   b. Using an activity-based costing approach to cost analysis, calculate the cost of each program and the cost per patient-year of the alcohol and drug programs.
   c. What benefits can Max Health Center obtain by implementing the ABC system?
2. What factors, other than cost, do you think Max Health Center should consider in allocating resources to its programs?

5-40 Activity-based costing, cost hierarchy. (CMA, adapted) Basista Coffee Ltd. (BCL) buys coffee beans from around the world and roasts, blends, and packages them for resale. The major cost is direct materials; however, there is substantial manufacturing overhead in the predominantly automated roasting and packing process. The company uses relatively little direct labor.

Some of the coffees are very popular and sell in large volumes, whereas a few of the newer blends sell in very low volumes. BCL prices its coffee at budgeted cost, including allocated overhead, plus a markup on cost of 30 per cent.

Data for the current year budget include manufacturing overhead of Rs 30,00,000, which has been allocated on the basis of each product's budgeted direct-labor cost. The budget direct-labor cost for current year totals Rs 6,00,000. Purchases and use of materials (mostly coffee beans) are budgeted to total Rs 60,00,000.

The budgeted direct costs for one-kg bags of two of the company's products are

	Indian	Malaysian
Direct materials	Rs 42	Rs 32
Direct labor	3	3

BCL's controller believes the existing costing system may be providing misleading cost information. She has developed an activity-based analysis of current year budgeted manufacturing overhead costs shown in the following table.

Activity	Cost Driver	Cost Driver Rate
Purchasing	Purchase orders	Rs 5,000
Materials handling	Setups	4,000
Quality control	Batches	2,400
Roasting	Roasting-hours	100
Blending	Blending-hours	100
Packaging	Packaging-hours	100

Data regarding the current year production of the Indian and Malaysian coffee follow. There will be no beginning or ending materials inventory for either of these coffees.

Particulars	Indian	Malaysian
Expected sales	1,00,000 kg	2,000 kg
Purchase orders	4	4
Batches	10	4
Setups	30	12
Roasting-hours	1,000	20

Blending-hours	500	10
Packaging-hours	100	2

Required

1. Using BCL's existing costing system:
   a. Determine the company's current year budgeted manufacturing overhead rate using direct-labor cost as the single allocation base.
   b. Determine the current year budgeted costs and selling prices of 1 kg of Indian coffee and 1 kg of Malaysian coffee.
2. Use the controller's activity-based approach to estimate the current year budgeted cost for 1 kg of:
   a. Indian coffee
   b. Malaysian coffee
   Allocate all costs to the 1,00,000 kg of Indian and the 2,000 kg of Malaysian coffee. Compare the results with those in requirement 1.
3. Examine the implications of your answers to requirement 2 for BCL's pricing and product-mix strategy.

6 Master Budget and Responsibility Accounting

Learning Objectives

1. Describe the master budget and explain its benefits
2. Describe the advantages of budgets
3. Prepare the operating budget and its supporting schedules
4. Use computer-based financial planning models in sensitivity analysis
5. Describe responsibility centers and responsibility accounting
6. Recognize the human aspects of budgeting
7. Appreciate the special challenges of budgeting in multinational companies

Amid the recent recession, one of the hottest innovations was the growth of Web sites that enable users to get an aggregate picture of their financial data and to set up budgets to manage their spending and other financial decisions online. (Mint.com, a pioneer in this market, was acquired by Intuit for $170 million in September 2009.)

Budgets play a similar crucial role in businesses. Without budgets, it's difficult for managers and their employees to know whether they're on target for their growth and spending goals. You might think a budget is only for companies that are in financial difficulty (such as Citigroup) or whose profit margins are slim—Wal-Mart, for example. As the following article shows, even companies that sell high-dollar value goods and services adhere to budgets.

"Scrimping" at the Ritz: Master Budgets

"Ladies and gentlemen serving ladies and gentlemen." That's the motto of the Ritz-Carlton. With locations ranging from South Beach (Miami) to South Korea, the grand hotel chain is known for its indulgent luxury and sumptuous surroundings. However, the aura of the chain's old-world elegance stands in contrast to its rather heavy emphasis—behind the scenes, of course—on cost control and budgets. It is this very approach, however, that makes it possible for the Ritz to offer the legendary grandeur its guests expect during their stay.

A Ritz hotel's performance is the responsibility of its general manager and controller at each location worldwide. Local forecasts and budgets are prepared annually and are the basis of subsequent performance evaluations for the hotel and people who work there.

The preparation of a hotel's budget begins with the hotel's sales director, who is responsible for all hotel revenues. Sources of revenue include hotel rooms, conventions, weddings, meeting facilities, merchandise, and food and beverage. The controller then seeks input about costs. Standard costs, based on cost per occupied room, are used to build the budget for guest room stays. Other standard costs are used to calculate costs for meeting rooms and food and beverages. The completed sales budget and annual operating budget are sent to corporate headquarters. From there, the hotel's actual monthly performance is monitored against the approved budget.

The managers of each hotel meet daily to review the hotel's performance to date relative to plan. They have the ability to adjust

prices in the reservation system if they so choose. Adjusting prices can be particularly important if a hotel experiences unanticipated changes in occupancy rates.

Each month, the hotel's actual performance is monitored against the approved budget. The controller of each hotel receives a report from corporate headquarters that shows how the hotel performed against budget, as well as against the actual performance of other Ritz hotels. Any ideas for boosting revenues and reducing costs are regularly shared among hotel controllers.

Why does a successful company feel the need to watch its spending so closely? In many profitable companies, a strict budget is actually a key to their success. As the Ritz-Carlton example illustrates, budgeting is a critical function in organizations. Southwest Airlines, for example, uses budgets to monitor and manage fuel costs. Wal-Mart depends on its budget to maintain razor-thin margins as it competes with Target. Gillette uses budgets to plan marketing campaigns for its razors and blades.

Budgeting is a common accounting tool that companies use for implementing strategy. Management uses budgets to communicate directions and goals throughout a company. Budgets turn managers' perspectives forward and aid in planning and controlling the actions managers must undertake to satisfy their customers and succeed in the marketplace. Budgets provide measures of the financial results a company expects from its planned activities and help define objectives and timelines against which progress can be measured. Through budgeting, managers learn to anticipate and avoid potential problems. Interestingly, even when it comes to entrepreneurial activities, business planning has been shown to increase a new venture's probability of survival, as well as its product development and venture organizing activities.[1] As the old adage goes: "If you fail to plan, you plan to fail."

[1] For more details, take a look at F. Delmar and S. Shane, "Does Business Planning Facilitate the Development of New Ventures?" *Strategic Management Journal*, December 2003.

Budgets and the Budgeting Cycle

A *budget* is (a) the quantitative expression of a proposed plan of action by management for a specified period and (b) an aid to coordinate what needs to be done to implement that plan. A budget generally includes both financial and non-financial aspects of the plan, and it serves as a blueprint for the company to follow in an upcoming period. A financial budget quantifies management's expectations regarding income, cash flows, and financial position. Just as financial statements are prepared for past periods, financial statements can be prepared for future periods—for example, a budgeted income statement, a budgeted statement of cash flows, and a budgeted balance sheet. Underlying these financial budgets are nonfinancial budgets for, say, units manufactured or sold, number of employees, and number of new products being introduced to the marketplace.

Strategic Plans and Operating Plans

Budgeting is most useful when it is integrated with a company's strategy. *Strategy* specifies how an organization matches its own capabilities with the opportunities in the marketplace to accomplish its objectives. In developing successful strategies, managers consider questions such as:

- What are our objectives?
- How do we create value for our customers while distinguishing ourselves from our competitors?
- Are the markets for our products local, regional, national, or global? What trends affect our markets? How are we affected by the economy, our industry, and our competitors?
- What organizational and financial structures serve us best?
- What are the risks and opportunities of alternative strategies, and what are our contingency plans if our preferred plan fails?

A company, such as Reliance Retail, can have a strategy of providing quality products or services at a low price. Another company, such as Pfizer or Porsche, can have a strategy of providing a unique product or service that is priced higher than the products or services of competitors. Exhibit 6-1 shows that strategic plans are expressed through long-run budgets and operating plans are expressed via short-run budgets. But there is more to the story! The exhibit shows arrows pointing backward as well as forward. The backward arrows are a way of graphically indicating that budgets can lead to changes in plans and strategies. Budgets help managers assess strategic risks and opportunities by providing them with feedback about the likely effects of their strategies and plans. And sometimes the feedback signals to managers that they need to revise their plans and possibly their strategies.

Boeing's experience with the 747-8 program illustrates how budgets can help managers rework their operating plans. Boeing viewed updating its 747 jumbo jet by sharing design synergies with the ongoing 787 Dreamliner program as a relatively inexpensive way to take sales from Airbus' A380 superjumbo jet. However, continued cost overruns and delays have undermined that strategy: The 747-8 program is already Rs 2,000 crore over budget and a year behind schedule. The company recently revealed that it expects to earn no profit on virtually any of the 105 747-8 planes on its order books. With the budget for 2010 revealing higher-than-expected costs in design, rework, and production, Boeing has postponed plans to accelerate the jumbo's production to 2013. Some aerospace experts are urging Boeing to consider more dramatic steps, including discontinuing the passenger aircraft version of the 747-8 program.

Exhibit 6-1

Strategy, Planning, and Budgets

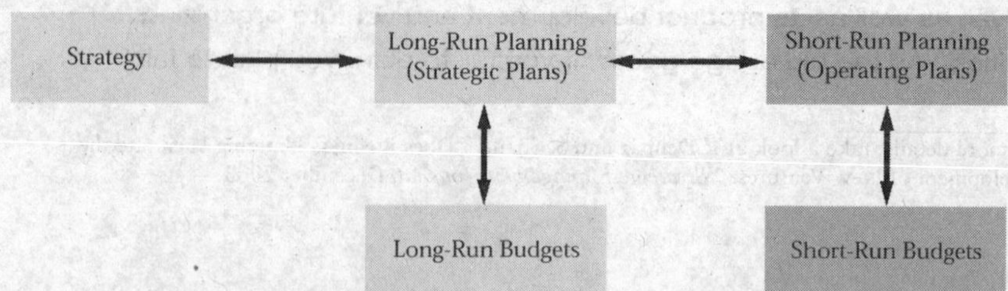

Budgeting Cycle and Master Budget

Well-managed companies usually cycle through the following budgeting steps during the course of the fiscal year:

1. Working together, managers and management accountants plan the performance of the company as a whole and the performance of its subunits (such as departments or divisions). Taking into account past performance and anticipated changes in the future, managers at all levels reach a common understanding on what is expected.
2. Senior managers give subordinate managers a frame of reference, a set of specific financial or nonfinancial expectations against which actual results will be compared.
3. Management accountants help managers investigate variations from plans, such as an unexpected decline in sales. If necessary, corrective action follows, such as a reduction in price to boost sales or cutting of costs to maintain profitability.
4. Managers and management accountants take into account market feedback, changed conditions, and their own experiences as they begin to make plans for the next period. For example, a decline in sales may cause managers to make changes in product features for the next period.

Learning Objective 

Describe the master budget

. . . The master budget is the initial budget prepared before the start of a period

and explain its benefits

. . . benefits include planning, coordination, and control

The preceding four steps describe the ongoing budget process. The working document at the core of this process is called the master budget. The **master budget** expresses management's operating and financial plans for a specified period (usually a fiscal year), and it includes a set of budgeted financial statements. The master budget is the initial plan of what the company intends to accomplish in the budget period. The master budget evolves from both operating and financing decisions made by managers.

- Operating decisions deal with how to best use the limited resources of an organization.
- Financing decisions deal with how to obtain the funds to acquire those resources.

The terminology used to describe budgets varies among companies. For example, budgeted financial statements are sometimes called **pro forma statements**. Some companies, such as Hewlett-Packard, refer to budgeting as *targeting*. And many companies refer to the budget as a *profit plan*. Microsoft refers to goals as *commitments* and distributes firm-level goals across the company, connecting them to organizational, team, and ultimately individual commitments.

The focus of this book is how management accounting helps managers make operating decisions. That's why this chapter emphasizes operating budgets. Managers spend a significant part of their time preparing and analyzing budgets. The many advantages of budgeting make spending time on budgeting a worthwhile investment of managers' energies.

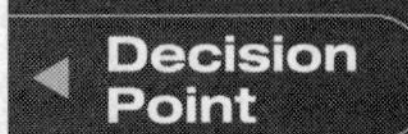

What is the master budget and why is it useful?

Advantages of Budgets

Budgets are an integral part of management control systems. When administered thoughtfully by managers, budgets:

- Promote coordination and communication among subunits within the company
- Provide a framework for judging performance and facilitating learning
- Motivate managers and other employees

Learning Objective 

Describe the advantages of budgets

. . . advantages include coordination, communication, performance evaluation, and managerial motivation

Coordination and Communication

Coordination is meshing and balancing all aspects of production or service and all departments in a company in the best way for the company to meet its goals. *Communication* is making sure those goals are understood by all employees.

Coordination forces executives to think of relationships among individual departments and the company as a whole, and across companies. Consider budgeting at Samsung, a South Korea–based manufacturer of electronic products. A key product is Samsung's decoder boxes for cable television. The production manager can achieve more timely production by coordinating and communicating with the company's marketing team to understand when decoder boxes will be needed. In turn, the marketing team can make better predictions of future demand for decoder boxes by coordinating and communicating with Samsung's customers.

Suppose BSKYB, one of Samsung's largest customers, is planning to launch a new digital satellite service nine months from now. If Samsung's marketing group is able to obtain information about the launch date for the satellite service, it can share this information with Samsung's manufacturing group. The manufacturing group must then coordinate and communicate with Samsung's materials-procurement group, and so on. The point to understand is that Samsung is more likely to have satisfied customers (by having decoder boxes in the demanded quantities at the times demanded) if Samsung coordinates and communicates both within its business functions and with its suppliers and customers during the budgeting process as well as during the production process.

Framework for Judging Performance and Facilitating Learning

Budgets enable a company's managers to measure actual performance against predicted performance. Budgets can overcome two limitations of using past performance as a basis for judging actual results. One limitation is that past results often incorporate past miscues and substandard performance. Consider a cellular telephone company (Airtel Communications) examining the current-year (2012) performance of its sales force. Suppose the performance for 2011 incorporated the efforts of many salespeople who have since left Airtel because they did not have a good understanding of the marketplace. (The president of Airtel said, "They could not sell ice cream in a heat wave.") Using the sales record of those departed employees would set the performance bar for 2012 much too low.

The other limitation of using past performance is that future conditions can be expected to differ from the past. Consider again Airtel Communications. Suppose, in 2012, Airtel had a 20% revenue increase, compared with a 10% revenue increase in 2011. Does this increase indicate outstanding sales performance? Before you say yes, consider the following facts. In November 2011, an industry trade association forecast that the 2012 growth rate in industry revenues would be 40%, which also turned out to be the actual growth rate. As a result, Airtel's 20% actual revenue gain in 2012 takes on a negative connotation, even though it exceeded the 2011 actual growth rate of 10%. Using the 40% budgeted sales growth rate provides a better measure of the 2012 sales performance than using the 2011 actual growth rate of 10%.

It is important to remember that a company's budget should not be the only benchmark used to evaluate performance. Many companies also consider performance relative to peers as well as improvement over prior years. The problem with evaluating performance relative only to a budget is it creates an incentive for subordinates to set a target that is relatively easy to achieve.[2] Of course, managers at all levels recognize this incentive, and therefore they work to make the budget more challenging to achieve for the individuals who report to them. Negotiations occur among managers at each of these levels to understand what is possible and what is not. The budget is the end product of these negotiations.

One of the most valuable benefits of budgeting is that it helps managers learn. When actual performance falls short of budgeted or planned performance, it prompts thoughtful senior managers to ask questions about what happened and why, and how performance can be improved in the future. This probing and learning is one of the most important reasons why budgeting helps improve performance.

Motivating Managers and Other Employees[3]

Research shows that challenging budgets improve employee performance. That's because employees view falling short of budgeted numbers as a failure. Most employees

[2] See J. Hope and R. Fraser, *Beyond Budgeting* (Boston, MA: Harvard Business School Press, 2003) for several examples.

[3] For a more-detailed discussion, see R. Larnick, G. Wu, and C. Heath, "Raising the Bar on Goals," Graduate School of Business Publication, University of Chicago, Spring 1999.

are motivated to work more intensely to avoid failure than to achieve success. As employees get closer to a goal, they work harder to achieve it. Therefore, many executives like to set demanding but achievable goals for their subordinate managers and employees. Creating a little anxiety improves performance, but overly ambitious and unachievable budgets increase anxiety without motivation—that's because employees see little chance of avoiding failure. General Electric's former CEO, Jack Welch, describes challenging, yet achievable, budgets as energizing, motivating, and satisfying for managers and other employees, and capable of unleashing out-of-the-box and creative thinking.

Challenges in Administering Budgets

Budgeting is a time-consuming process that involves all levels of management. Top managers want lower-level managers to participate in the budgeting process because lower-level managers have more specialized knowledge and first-hand experience with day-to-day aspects of running the business. Participation creates greater commitment and accountability toward the budget among lower-level managers. This is the bottom-up aspect of the budgeting process.

The budgeting process, however, is a time-consuming one. It has been estimated that senior managers spend about 10% to 20% of their time on budgeting, and finance planning departments spend as much as 50% of their time on it.[4] For most organizations, the annual budget process is a months-long exercise that consumes a tremendous amount of resources. Despite his admiration for setting challenging targets, Jack Welch has also referred to the budgeting process as "the most ineffective process in management," and as "the bane of corporate America."

The widespread prevalence of budgets in companies ranging from major multinational corporations to small local businesses indicates that the advantages of budgeting systems outweigh the costs. To gain the benefits of budgeting, management at all levels of a company should understand and support the budget and all aspects of the management control system. This is critical for obtaining lower-level management's participation in the formulation of budgets and for successful administration of budgets. Lower-level managers who feel that top management does not "believe" in a budget are unlikely to be active participants in a budget process.

Budgets should not be administered rigidly. Attaining the budget is not an end in itself, especially when conditions change dramatically. A manager may commit to a budget, but if a situation arises in which some unplanned repairs or an unplanned advertising program would serve the long-run interests of the company, the manager should undertake the additional spending. On the flip side, the dramatic decline in consumer demand during the recent recession led designers such as Gucci to slash their ad budgets and put on hold planned new boutiques. Macy's and other retailers, stuck with shelves of merchandise ordered before the financial crisis, had no recourse but to slash prices and cut their workforce. JCPenney eventually missed its sales projections. However, its aggressive actions during the year enabled it to survive the recession and emerge with sophisticated new inventory management plans to profit from the next holiday season.

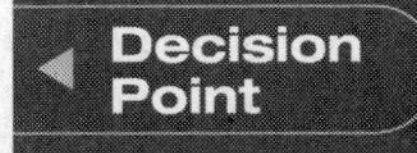

When should a company prepare budgets? What are the advantages of preparing budgets?

Prepare the operating budget

. . . the budgeted income statement

and its supporting schedules

. . . such as cost of goods sold and nonmanufacturing costs

Developing an Operating Budget

Budgets are typically developed for a set period, such as a month, quarter, year, and so on. The set period can itself be broken into subperiods. For example, a 12-month cash budget may be broken into 12 monthly periods so that cash inflows and outflows can be better coordinated.

[4] See P. Horvath and R. Sauter, "Why Budgeting Fails: One Management System is Not Enough," Balanced Scorecard Report, (September 2004).

Time Coverage of Budgets

The motive for creating a budget should guide a manager in choosing the period for the budget. For example, consider budgeting for a new Bajaj 500-cc motorcycle. If the purpose is to budget for the total profitability of this new model, a five-year period (or more) may be suitable and long enough to cover the product from design through to manufacture, sales, and after-sales support. In contrast, consider budgeting for a school play. If the purpose is to estimate all cash outlays, a six-month period from the planning stage to the final performance may suffice.

The most frequently used budget period is one year, which is often subdivided into months and quarters. The budgeted data for a year are frequently revised as the year goes on. At the end of the second quarter, management may change the budget for the next two quarters in light of new information obtained during the first six months. For example, Amerigroup, a health insurance firm, had to make substantial revisions to its third-quarter and annual cost projections for 2011 because of higher-than-expected costs related to the H1N1 virus.

Businesses are increasingly using rolling budgets. A **rolling budget**, also called a **continuous budget**, is a budget that is always available for a specified future period. It is created by continually adding a month, quarter, or year to the period that just ended. Consider Electrolux, the global appliance company, which has a three- to five-year strategic plan and a four-quarter rolling budget. A four-quarter rolling budget for the April 2011 to March 2012 period is superseded in the next quarter—that is in June 2009—by a four-quarter rolling budget for July 2011 to June 2012, and so on. There is always a 12-month budget (for the next year) in place. Rolling budgets constantly force Electrolux's management to think about the forthcoming 12 months, regardless of the quarter at hand. Some companies prepare rolling financial forecasts that look ahead five quarters. Examples are Borealis, Europe's leading polyolefin plastics manufacturer; Millipore, a life sciences research and manufacturing firm headquartered in Massachusetts; and Nordea, the largest financial services group in the Nordic and Baltic Sea region. Others, such as EMC Corporation, the information infrastructure giant, employ a six-quarter rolling-forecast process so that budget allocations can be constantly adjusted to meet changing market conditions.

Steps in Developing an Operating Budget

The best way to explain how to prepare an operating budget is with an example. Consider Stylistic Furniture, a company that makes two types of granite-top coffee tables—Casual and Deluxe. It is late 2011 and Stylistic's CEO, Usha Thorat, is very concerned about how he is going to respond to the Board of Directors' mandate to increase profits by 10% in the coming year. Usha goes through the five-step decision-making process introduced in Chapter 1.

1. **Identify the problem and uncertainties.** The problem is to identify a strategy and to build a budget to achieve a 10% profit growth. There are several uncertainties. Can Stylistic dramatically increase sales for its more profitable Deluxe tables? What price pressures is Stylistic likely to face? Will the cost of materials increase? Can costs be reduced through efficiency improvements?
2. **Obtain information.** Stylistic's managers gather information about sales of Deluxe tables in the current year. They are delighted to learn that sales have been stronger than expected. Moreover, one of Stylistic's key competitors in its line of Casual tables has had quality problems that are unlikely to be resolved until early 2012. Unfortunately, they also discover that the prices of direct materials have increased slightly during 2011.
3. **Make predictions about the future.** Stylistic's managers feel confident that with a little more marketing, they will be able to grow the Deluxe tables business and even increase prices slightly relative to 2011. They also do not expect significant

price pressures on Casual tables in the early part of the year because of the quality problems faced by a key competitor. They are concerned, however, that when the competitor does start selling again, pressure on prices could increase.

The purchasing manager anticipates that prices of materials will be about the same as in 2011. The manufacturing manager believes that efficiency improvements would allow costs of manufacturing tables to be maintained at 2011 costs despite an increase in the volume of production. Achieving these efficiency improvements is important if Stylistic is to maintain its 12% operating margin (that is, operating income ÷ sales = 12%).

4. **Make decisions by choosing among alternatives.** Usha and his managers feel confident in their strategy of pushing sales of Deluxe tables. This decision has some risks but is easily the best option available for Stylistic to increase profits by 10%.
5. **Implement the decision, evaluate performance, and learn.** As we will discuss in Chapters 7 and 8, managers compare actual to predicted performance to learn about why things turned out the way they did and how to do things better. Stylistic's managers would want to know whether their predictions about prices of Casual and Deluxe tables were correct. Did prices of direct materials increase more or less than anticipated? Did efficiency improvements occur? Such learning would be very helpful as Stylistic plans its budgets in subsequent years.

Learning Objective 4

Prepare the operating budget

. . . the budgeted income statement

and its supporting schedules

. . . such as cost of goods sold and nonmanufacturing costs

Stylistic's managers begin their work toward the 2012 budget. Exhibit 6-2 shows a diagram of the various parts of the *master budget*. The master budget comprises the financial projections of all the individual budgets for a company for a specified period, usually a fiscal year. The light, medium and dark purple boxes in Exhibit 6-2 represent the budgeted income statement and its supporting budget schedules—together called the **operating budget.**

We show the revenues budget box in a light purple color to indicate that it is often the starting point of the operating budget. The supporting schedules—shown in medium purple—quantify the budgets for various business functions of the value chain, from research and development to distribution costs. These schedules build up to the budgeted income statement—the key summary statement in the operating budget—shown in dark purple.

The light and dark blue boxes in the exhibit are the **financial budget,** which is that part of the master budget made up of the capital expenditures budget, the cash budget, the budgeted balance sheet, and the budgeted statement of cash flows. A financial budget focuses on how operations and planned capital outlays affect cash—shown in light blue.

The cash budget and the budgeted income statement can then be used to prepare two other summary financial statements—the budgeted balance sheet and the budgeted statement of cash flows—shown in dark blue. The master budget is finalized only after several rounds of discussions between top management and managers responsible for various business functions in the value chain.

We next present the steps in preparing an operating budget for Stylistic Furniture for 2012. Use Exhibit 6-2 as a guide for the steps that follow. The appendix to this chapter presents Stylistic's cash budget, which is another key component of the master budget. Details needed to prepare the budget follow:

- Stylistic sells two models of granite-top coffee tables—Casual and Deluxe. Nonsales-related revenue, such as interest income, is zero.
- Work-in-process inventory is negligible and is ignored.
- Direct materials inventory and finished goods inventory are costed using the first-in, first-out (FIFO) method. Unit costs of direct materials purchased and unit costs of finished goods sold remain unchanged throughout each budget year but can change from year to year.
- There are two types of direct materials: red oak (RO) and granite slabs (GS). Direct material costs are variable with respect to units of output—coffee tables.

Exhibit 6-2

Overview of the Master Budget for Stylistic Furniture

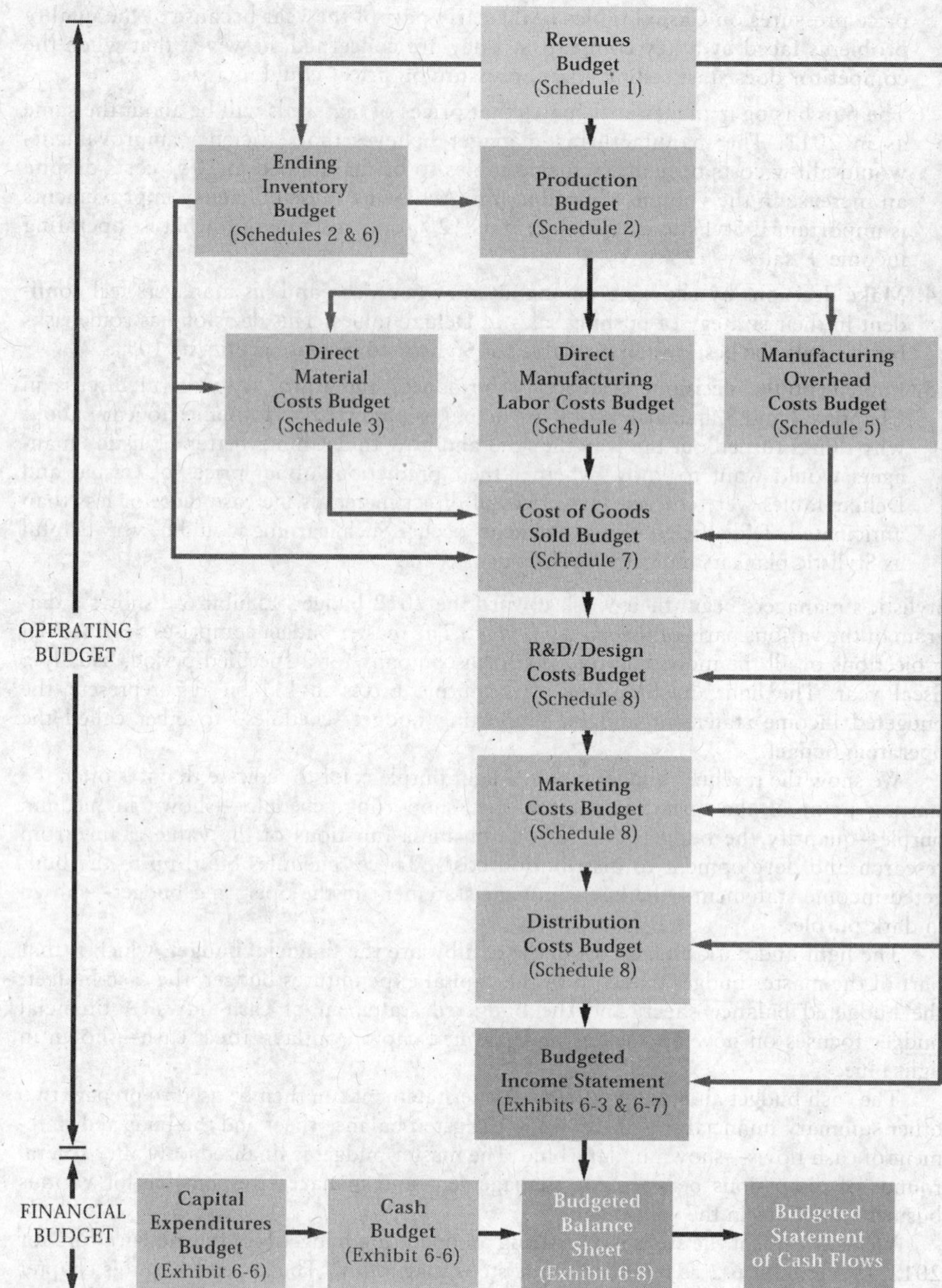

- Direct manufacturing labor workers are hired on an hourly basis; no overtime is worked.
- There are two cost drivers for manufacturing overhead costs—direct manufacturing labor-hours and setup labor-hours.
- Direct manufacturing labor-hours is the cost driver for the variable portion of manufacturing operations overhead. The fixed component of manufacturing operations overhead is tied to the manufacturing capacity of 300,000 direct manufacturing labor-hours that Stylistic has planned for 2012.

- Setup labor-hours is the cost driver for the variable portion of machine setup overhead. The fixed component of machine setup overhead is tied to the setup capacity of 15,000 setup labor-hours that Stylistic has planned for 2012.
- For computing inventoriable costs, Stylistic allocates all (variable and fixed) manufacturing operations overhead costs using direct manufacturing labor-hours and machine setup overhead costs using setup labor-hours.
- Nonmanufacturing costs consist of product design, marketing and distribution costs. All product design costs are fixed costs for 2012. The variable component of marketing costs equals the 6.5% sales commission on revenues paid to salespeople. The variable portion of distribution costs varies with cubic feet of tables moved.

The following data are available for the 2012 budget:

Direct materials	
Red Oak	Rs 70 per board foot (b.f.) (same as in 2011)
Granite	Rs 100 per square foot (s.f.) (same as in 2011)
Direct manufacturing labor	Rs 200 per hour

Content of Each Product Unit

	Product	
	Casual Granite Table	**Deluxe Granite Table**
Red Oak	12 board feet	12 board feet
Granite	6 square feet	8 square feet
Direct manufacturing labor	4 hours	6 hours

	Product	
	Casual Granite Table	**Deluxe Granite Table**
Expected sales in units	50,000	10,000
Selling price	Rs 6,000	Rs 8,000
Target ending inventory in units	11,000	500
Beginning inventory in units	1,000	500
Beginning inventory in rupees	Rs 38,40,000	Rs 26,20,000

	Direct Materials	
	Red Oak	**Granite**
Beginning inventory	70,000 b.f.	60,000 s.f.
Target ending inventory	80,000 b.f.	20,000 s.f.

Stylistic bases its budgeted cost information on the costs it predicts it will incur to support its revenue budget, taking into account the efficiency improvements it expects to make in 2012. Recall from step 3 in the decision-making process that efficiency improvements are critical to offset anticipated increases in direct materials prices and to maintain Stylistic's 12% operating margin. Some companies rely heavily on past results when developing budgeted amounts; others rely on detailed engineering studies. Companies differ in how they compute their budgeted amounts.

Most companies have a budget manual that contains a company's particular instructions and relevant information for preparing its budgets. Although the details differ among companies, the following basic steps are common for developing the operating budget for a manufacturing company. Beginning with the revenues budget, each of the other budgets follows step-by-step in logical fashion.

Step 1: Prepare the Revenues Budget. A revenues budget, calculated in Schedule 1, is the usual starting point for the operating budget. That's because the production level and the inventory level—and therefore manufacturing costs—as well as nonmanufacturing costs, generally depend on the forecasted level of unit sales or revenues. Many factors influence the sales forecast, including the sales volume in recent periods, general economic and industry conditions, market research studies, pricing policies, advertising and sales promotions, competition, and regulatory policies. In Stylistic's case, the revenues budget for

2012 reflects Stylistic's strategy to grow revenues by increasing sales of Deluxe tables from 8,000 tables in 2011 to 10,000 tables in 2012.

Schedule 1: Revenues Budget
For the Year Ending December 31, 2012

	Units	Selling Price	Total Revenues
Casual	50,000	Rs 6,000	Rs 30,00,00,000
Deluxe	10,000	8,000	8,00,00,000
Total			Rs 38,00,00,000

The Rs 38,00,00,000 is the amount of revenues in the budgeted income statement. The revenues budget is often the result of elaborate information gathering and discussions among sales managers and sales representatives who have a detailed understanding of customer needs, market potential, and competitors' products. This information is often gathered through a customer response management (CRM) or sales management system. Statistical approaches such as regression and trend analysis can also help in sales forecasting. These techniques use indicators of economic activity and past sales data to forecast future sales. Managers should use statistical analysis only as one input to forecast sales. In the final analysis, the sales forecast should represent the collective experience and judgment of managers.

The usual starting point for step 1 is to base revenues on expected demand. Occasionally, a factor other than demand limits budgeted revenues. For example, when demand is greater than available production capacity or a manufacturing input is in short supply, the revenues budget would be based on the maximum units that could be produced. Why? Because sales would be limited by the amount produced.

Step 2: Prepare the Production Budget (in Units). After revenues are budgeted, the manufacturing manager prepares the production budget, which is calculated in Schedule 2. The total finished goods units to be produced depends on budgeted unit sales and expected changes in units of inventory levels:

$$\text{Budget production (units)} = \text{Budget sales (units)} + \text{Target ending finished goods inventory (units)} - \text{Beginning finished goods inventory (units)}$$

Schedule 2: Production Budget (in Units)
For the Year Ending December 31, 2012

	Product	
	Casual	Deluxe
Budgeted unit sales (Schedule 1)	50,000	10,000
Add target ending finished goods inventory	11,000	500
Total required units	61,000	10,500
Deduct beginning finished goods inventory	1,000	500
Units of finished goods to be produced	60,000	10,000

Step 3: Prepare the Direct Material Usage Budget and Direct Material Purchases Budget. The number of units to be produced, calculated in Schedule 2, is the key to computing the usage of direct materials in quantities and in rupees. The direct material quantities used depend on the efficiency with which materials are consumed to produce a table. In determining budgets, managers are constantly anticipating ways to make process improvements that increase quality and reduce waste, thereby reducing direct material usage and costs.

Like many companies, Stylistic has a *bill of materials*, stored and updated in its computer systems. This document identifies how each product is manufactured, specifying all materials (and components), the sequence in which the materials are used, the quantity of materials in each finished unit, and the work centers where the operations are performed. For example, the bill of materials would indicate that 12 board feet of red oak and 6 square feet of granite are needed to produce each Casual coffee table, and 12 board feet of red oak and 8 square feet of granite to produce each Deluxe coffee table. This information is then used to calculate the amounts in Schedule 3A.

Schedule 3A: Direct Material Usage Budget in Quantity and Rupees
For the Year Ending December 31, 2012

	Material		
	Red Oak	**Granite**	**Total**
Physical Units Budget			
Direct materials required for			
Casual tables (60,000 units × 12 b.f. and 6 s.f.)	720,000 b.f.	360,000 s.f.	
Direct materials required for			
Deluxe tables (10,000 units × 12 b.f. and 8 s.f.)	120,000 b.f.	80,000 s.f.	
Total quantity of direct materials to be used	840,000 b.f.	440,000 s.f.	
Cost Budget			
Available from beginning direct materials inventory			
(under a FIFO cost-flow assumption)			
Red Oak: 70,000 b.f. × Rs 70 per b.f.	Rs 49,00,000		
Granite: 60,000 s.f. × Rs 100 per s.f.		Rs 60,00,000	
To be purchased this period			
Red Oak: (840,000 − 70,000) b.f. × Rs 70 per b.f.	5,39,00,000		
Granite: (440,000 − 60,000) s.f. × Rs 100 per s.f.		3,80,00,000	
Direct materials to be used this period	Rs 5,88,00,000	Rs 4,40,00,000	Rs 10,28,00,000

The purchasing manager prepares the budget for direct material purchases, calculated in Schedule 3B, based on the budgeted direct materials to be used, the beginning inventory of direct materials, and the target ending inventory of direct materials:

$$\text{Purchases of direct materials} = \text{Direct materials used in production} + \text{Target ending inventory of direct materials} - \text{Beginning inventory of direct material}$$

Schedule 3B: Direct Material Purchases Budget
For the Year Ending December 31, 2012

	Material		
	Red Oak	**Granite**	**Total**
Physical Units Budget			
To be used in production (from Schedule 3A)	840,000 b.f.	440,000 s.f.	
Add target ending inventory	80,000 b.f.	20,000 s.f.	
Total requirements	920,000 b.f.	460,000 s.f.	
Deduct beginning inventory	70,000 b.f.	60,000 s.f.	
Purchases to be made	850,000 b.f.	400,000 s.f.	
Cost Budget			
Red Oak: 850,000 b.f. × Rs 70 per b.f.	Rs 5,95,00,000		
Granite: 400,000 s.f × Rs 100 per s.f.		Rs 4,00,00,000	
Purchases	Rs 5,95,00,000	Rs 4,00,00,000	Rs 9,95,00,000

Step 4: **Prepare the Direct Manufacturing Labor Costs Budget.** In this step, manufacturing managers use *labor standards,* the time allowed per unit of output, to calculate the direct manufacturing labor costs budget in Schedule 4. These costs depend on wage rates, production methods, process and efficiency improvements and hiring plans.

Schedule 4: Direct Manufacturing Labor Costs Budget
For the Year Ending December 31, 2012

	Output Units Produced (Schedule 2)	Direct Manufacturing Labor-Hours per Unit	Total Hours	Hourly Wage Rate	Total
Casual	60,000	4	240,000	Rs 200	Rs 4,80,00,000
Deluxe	10,000	6	60,000	200	1,20,00,000
Total			300,000		Rs 6,00,00,000

Step 5: Prepare the Manufacturing Overhead Costs Budget. As we described earlier, direct manufacturing labor-hours is the cost driver for the variable portion of manufacturing operations overhead and setup labor-hours is the cost driver for the variable portion of machine setup overhead costs. The use of activity-based cost drivers such as these gives rise to *activity-based budgeting*. **Activity-based budgeting (ABB)** focuses on the budgeted cost of the activities necessary to produce and sell products and services.

For the 300,000 direct manufacturing labor-hours, Stylistic's manufacturing managers estimate various line items of overhead costs that constitute manufacturing operations overhead (that is, all costs for which direct manufacturing labor-hours is the cost driver). Managers identify opportunities for process improvements and determine budgeted manufacturing operations overhead costs in the operating department. They also determine the resources that they will need from the two support departments—kilowatt hours of energy from the power department and hours of maintenance service from the maintenance department. The support department managers, in turn, plan the costs of personnel and supplies that they will need to provide the operating department with the support services it requires. The costs of the support departments are then allocated (first-stage cost allocation) as part of manufacturing operations overhead. Chapter 15 describes how the allocation of support department costs to operating departments is done when support departments provide services to each other and to operating departments. The upper half of Schedule 5 shows the various line items of costs that constitute manufacturing operations overhead costs—that is, all overhead costs that are caused by the 300,000 direct manufacturing labor-hours (the cost driver).

Stylistic's managers determine how setups should be done for the Casual and Deluxe line of tables, taking into account past experiences and potential improvements in setup efficiency.

For example, managers consider:

- Increasing the length of the production run per batch so that fewer batches (and therefore fewer setups) are needed for the budgeted production of tables.
- Decreasing the setup time per batch.
- Reducing the supervisory time needed, for instance by increasing the skill base of workers.

Stylistic's managers forecast the following setup information for the Casual and Deluxe tables:

	Casual Tables	Deluxe Tables	Total
1. Quantity of tables to be produced	60,000 tables	10,000 tables	
2. Number of tables to be produced per batch	50 tables/batch	40 tables/batch	
3. Number of batches (1) ÷ (2)	1,200 batches	250 batches	
4. Setup time per batch	10 hours/batch	12 hours/batch	
5. Total setup-hours (3) ÷ (4)	12,000 hours	3,000 hours	15,000 hours
6. Setup-hour per table (5) × (1)	0.2 hour	0.3 hour	

Using an approach similar to the one described for manufacturing operations overhead costs, Stylistic's managers estimate various line items of costs that comprise machine setup overhead costs—that is, all costs that are caused by the 15,000 setup labor-hours (the cost driver). Note how using activity-based cost drivers provides more-detailed information that improves decision making compared with budgeting based solely on output-based cost drivers. Of course, managers must always evaluate whether the expected benefit of adding more cost drivers exceeds the expected cost.[5] The bottom half of Schedule 5 summarizes these costs.

[5] The Stylistic example illustrates ABB using setup costs included in Stylistic's manufacturing overhead costs budget. ABB implementations in practice include costs in many parts of the value chain. For an example, see S. Borjesson, "A Case Study on Activity-Based Budgeting," *Journal of Cost Management*, Vol. 10, No. 4, pp. 7–18.

Schedule 5: Manufacturing Overhead Costs Budget
For the Year Ending December 31, 2012
Manufacturing Operations Overhead Costs

Variable costs		
Supplies	Rs 1,50,00,000	
Indirect manufacturing labor	1,68,00,000	
Power (support department costs)	2,10,00,000	
Maintenance (support department costs)	1,20,00,000	Rs 6,48,00,000
Fixed costs (to support capacity of 300,000 direct manufacturing labor-hours)		
Depreciation	1,02,00,000	
Supervision	39,00,000	
Power (support department costs)	63,00,000	
Maintenance (support department costs)	48,00,000	2,52,00,000
Total manufacturing operations overhead costs		Rs 9,00,00,000

Machine Setup Overhead Costs

Variable costs		
Supplies	Rs 39,00,000	
Indirect manufacturing labor	84,00,000	
Power (support department costs)	9,00,000	Rs 1,32,00,000
Fixed costs (to support capacity of 15,000 setup labor-hours)		
Depreciation	60,30,000	
Supervision	1,05,00,000	
Power (support department costs)	2,70,000	1,68,00,000
Total machine setup overhead costs		Rs 3,00,00,000
Total manufacturing operations overhead costs		Rs 12,00,00,000

Step 6: Prepare the Ending Inventories Budget. The management accountant prepares the ending inventories budget, calculated in Schedules 6A and 6B. In accordance with generally accepted accounting principles, Stylistic treats both variable and fixed manufacturing overhead as inventoriable (product) costs. Stylistic is budgeted to operate at capacity. Manufacturing operations overhead costs are allocated to finished goods inventory at the budgeted rate of Rs 300 per direct manufacturing labor-hour (total budgeted manufacturing operations overhead, Rs 9,00,00,000 ÷ 300,000 budgeted direct manufacturing labor-hours). Machine setup overhead costs are allocated to finished goods inventory at the budgeted rate of Rs 2,000 per setup-hour (total budgeted machine setup overhead, Rs 3,00,00,000 ÷ 15,000 budgeted setup labor-hours). Schedule 6A shows the computation of the unit cost of coffee tables started and completed in 2012.

Schedule 6A: Unit Costs of Ending Finished Goods Inventory
December 31, 2012

		Product			
		Casual Tables		Deluxe Tables	
	Cost per Unit of Input	Input per Unit of Output	Total	Input per Unit of Output	Total
Red Oak	Rs 70	12 b.f.	Rs 840	12 b.f.	Rs 840
Granite	100	6 s.f.	600	8 s.f.	800
Direct manufacturing labor	200	4 hrs.	800	6 hrs.	1,200
Manufacturing overhead	300	4 hrs.	1,200	6 hrs.	1,800
Machine setup overhead	2,000	0.2 hrs.	400	0.3 hrs	600
Total			Rs 3,840		Rs 5,240

Under the FIFO method, this unit cost is used to calculate the cost of target ending inventories of finished goods in Schedule 6B.

Schedule 6B: Ending Inventories Budget
December 31, 2012

	Quantity	Cost per Unit	Total	
Direct Materials				
Red Oak	80,000*	Rs 70	Rs 56,00,000	
Granite	20,000*	100	20,00,000	Rs 76,00,000
Finished Goods				
Casual	11,000**	Rs 3,840***	Rs 4,22,40,000	
Deluxe	500**	5,240***	26,20,000	4,48,60,000
Total ending inventory				Rs 5,24,60,000

*Data are from p. 214. ***From Schedule 6A, this is based on 2012 costs of manufacturing finished goods because under the FIFO costing method, the units in finished goods ending inventory consists of units that are produced during 2012.

Step 7: Prepare the Cost of Goods Sold Budget. The manufacturing and purchase managers, together with the management accountant, use information from Schedules 3 through 6 to prepare Schedule 7.

Schedule 7: Cost of Goods Sold Budget
For the Year Ending December 31, 2012

	From Schedule		Total
Beginning finished goods inventory, January 1, 2012	Given*		Rs 64,60,000
Direct materials used	3A	Rs 10,28,00,000	
Direct manufacturing labor	4	6,00,00,000	
Manufacturing overhead	5	12,00,00,000	
Cost of goods manufactured			28,28,00,000
Cost of goods available for sale			28,92,60,000
Deduct ending finished goods inventory, December 31, 2012	6B		4,48,60,000
Cost of Goods Sold			Rs 24,44,00,000

*Given in the description of basic data and requirements (Casual, Rs 38,40,000, Deluxe Rs 26,20,000).

Step 8: Prepare the Nonmanufacturing Costs Budget. Schedules 2 through 7 cover budgeting for Stylistic's production function of the value chain. For brevity, other parts of the value chain—product design, marketing and distribution—are combined into a single schedule. Just as in the case of manufacturing costs, managers in other functions of the value chain build in process and efficiency improvements and prepare nonmanufacturing cost budgets on the basis of the quantities of cost drivers planned for 2012.

Product design costs are fixed costs, determined on the basis of the product design work anticipated for 2012. The variable component of budgeted marketing costs is the commissions paid to sales people equal to 6.5% of revenues. The fixed component of budgeted marketing costs equal to Rs 1,33,00,000 is tied to the marketing capacity for 2012. The cost driver of the variable component of budgeted distribution costs is cubic feet of tables moved (Casual: 18 cubic feet × 50,000 tables + Deluxe: 24 cubic feet × 10,000 tables = 1,140,000 cubic feet). Variable distribution costs equal Rs 20 per cubic foot. The fixed component of budgeted distribution costs equals Rs 1,59,60,000 and is tied to the distribution capacity for 2012. Schedule 8 shows the product design, marketing, and distribution costs budget for 2012.

Schedule 8: Nonmanufacturing Costs Budget
For the Year Ending December 31, 2012

Business Function	Variable Costs	Fixed Costs	Total Costs
Product Design	—	Rs 1,02,40,000	Rs 1,02,40,000
Marketing (Variable cost: Rs 38,00,00,000 × 0.065)	Rs 2,47,00,000	1,33,00,000	3,80,00,000
Distribution (Variable cost: Rs 20 × 1,140,000 cu. ft.)	2,28,00,000	1,59,60,000	3,87,60,000
	Rs 4,75,00,000	Rs 3,95,00,000	Rs 8,70,00,000

	A	B	C	D
1	**Budgeted Income Statement for Stylistic Furniture**			
2	**For the Year Ending December 31, 2012**			
3	Revenues	Schedule 1		Rs 38,00,00,000
4	Cost of goods sold	Schedule 7		24,44,00,000
5	Gross margin			13,56,00,000
6	Operating costs			
7	Product design costs	Schedule 8	Rs 1,02,40,000	
8	Marketing costs	Schedule 8	3,80,00,000	
9	Distribution costs	Schedule 8	3,87,60,000	8,70,00,000
10	Operating income			Rs 4,86,00,000

Exhibit 6-3

Budgeted Income Statement for Stylistic Furniture

Step 9: Prepare the Budgeted Income Statement. The CEO and managers of various business functions, with help from the management accountant, use information in Schedules 1, 7, and 8 to finalize the budgeted income statement, shown in Exhibit 6-3. The style used in Exhibit 6-3 is typical, but more details could be included in the income statement; the more details that are put in the income statement, the fewer supporting schedules that are needed for the income statement.

Budgeting is a cross-functional activity. Top management's strategies for achieving revenue and operating income goals influence the costs planned for the different business functions of the value chain. For example, a budgeted increase in sales based on spending more for marketing must be matched with higher production costs to ensure that there is an adequate supply of tables and with higher distribution costs to ensure timely delivery of tables to customers.

Usha Thorat, the CEO of Stylistic Furniture, is very pleased with the 2012 budget. It calls for a 10% increase in operating income compared with 2011. The keys to achieving a higher operating income are a significant increase in sales of Deluxe tables, and process improvements and efficiency gains throughout the value chain. As Usha studies the budget more carefully, however, she is struck by two comments appended to the budget: First, to achieve the budgeted number of tables sold, Stylistic may need to reduce its selling prices by 3% to Rs 5,820 for Casual tables and to Rs 7,760 for Deluxe tables. Second, a supply shortage in direct materials may result in a 5% increase in the prices of direct materials (red oak and granite) above the material prices anticipated in the 2012 budget. If direct materials prices increase, however, no reduction in selling prices is anticipated. She asks Tina Muneem, the management accountant, to use Stylistic's financial planning model to evaluate how these outcomes will affect budgeted operating income.

Decision Point

What is the operating budget and what are its components?

Financial Planning Models and Sensitivity Analysis

Learning Objective 5

Use computer-based financial planning models in sensitivity analysis

. . . for example, understand the effects of changes in selling prices and direct material prices on budgeted income

Financial planning models are mathematical representations of the relationships among operating activities, financing activities, and other factors that affect the master budget. Companies can use computer-based systems, such as Enterprise Resource Planning (ERP) systems, to perform calculations for these planning models. Companies that use ERP systems, and other such budgeting tools, find that these systems simplify budgeting and reduce the computational burden and time required to prepare budgets. The following Concepts in Action box provides an example of one such company. ERP systems store vast quantities of information about the materials, machines and equipment, labor, power, maintenance, and setups needed to manufacture different products. Once sales quantities for different products have been identified, the software can quickly compute the budgeted costs for manufacturing these products. The software packages have a module on sensitivity analysis to assist managers in their planning and budgeting activities. *Sensitivity analysis* is a "what-if" technique that examines how a result will change if the original predicted data are not achieved or if an underlying assumption changes.

Exhibit 6-4 Effect of Changes in Budget Assumptions on Budgeted Operating Income for Stylistic Furniture

	A	B	C	D	E	F	G	H	I
1	Key Assumptions								
2		Units Sold		Selling Price		Direct Material Cost		Budgeted Operating Income	
3	What-If Scenario	Casual	Deluxe	Casual	Deluxe	Red Oak	Granite	Amount	Change from Master Budget
4	Master budget	50,000	10,000	Rs 6,000	Rs 8,000	Rs 70.0	Rs 100	Rs 4,86,00,000	
5	Scenario 1	50,000	10,000	5,820	7,760	Rs 70.0	Rs 100	3,79,41,000	22% decrease
6	Scenario 2	50,000	10,000	6,000	8,000	Rs 73.5	Rs 105	4,48,38,000	8% decrease

To see how sensitivity analysis works, we consider two scenarios identified as possibly affecting Stylistic Furniture's budget model for 2012.

Scenario 1: A 3% decrease in the selling price of the Casual table and a 3% decrease in the selling price of the Deluxe table.

Scenario 2: A 5% increase in the price per board foot of red oak and a 5% increase in the price per square foot of granite.

Exhibit 6-4 presents the budgeted operating income for the two scenarios.

Note that under Scenario 1, a change in selling prices per table affects revenues (Schedule 1) as well as variable marketing costs (sales commissions, Schedule 8). The Problem for Self-Study at the end of the chapter shows the revised schedules for Scenario 1. Similarly, a change in the price of direct materials affects the direct material usage budget (Schedule 3A), the unit cost of ending finished goods inventory (Schedule 6A), the ending finished goods inventories budget (in Schedule 6B) and the cost of goods sold budget (Schedule 7). Sensitivity analysis is especially useful in incorporating such interrelationships into budgeting decisions by managers.

Exhibit 6-4 shows a substantial decrease in operating income as a result of decreases in selling prices but a smaller decline in operating income if direct material prices increase by 5%. The sensitivity analysis prompts Stylistic's managers to put in place contingency plans. For example, should selling prices decline in 2012, Stylistic may choose to postpone some product development programs that it had included in its 2012 budget but that could be deferred to a later year. More generally, when the success or viability of a venture is highly dependent on attaining one or more targets, managers should frequently update their budgets as uncertainty is resolved. These updated budgets can help managers to adjust expenditure levels as circumstances change.

Instructors and students who, at this point, want to explore the cash budget and the budgeted balance sheet for the Stylistic Furniture example can skip ahead to the appendix: The cash budget.

Learning Objective 6

Describe responsibility centers

. . . a part of an organization that a manager is accountable for

and responsibility accounting

. . . measurement of plans and actual results that a manager is accountable for

Budgeting and Responsibility Accounting

To attain the goals described in the master budget, a company must coordinate the efforts of all its employees—from the top executive through all levels of management to every supervised worker. Coordinating the company's efforts means assigning responsibility to managers who are accountable for their actions in planning and controlling human and other resources. How each company structures its own organization significantly shapes how the company's efforts will be coordinated.

Concepts in Action

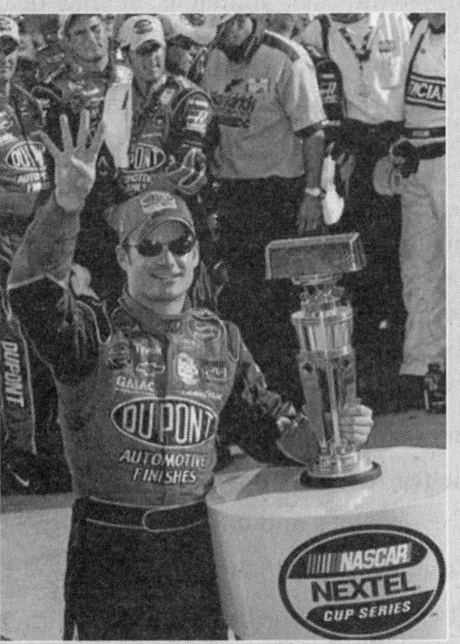

Web-Enabled Budgeting and Hendrick Motorsports

In recent years, an increasing number of companies have implemented comprehensive software packages that manage budgeting and forecasting functions across the organization. One such option is Microsoft Corporation's Forecaster package, which is designed for businesses looking to gain control over their budgeting and forecasting process within a fully integrated Web-based environment.

Among the more unique companies implementing Web-enabled budgeting is Hendrick Motorsports. Featuring champion drivers Jeff Gordon and Jimmie Johnson, Hendrick is the premier NASCAR Sprint Cup (formerly NEXTEL Cup) stock car racing organization. Headquartered on a 12 building, 600,000-square-foot campus near Charlotte, North Carolina, Hendrick operates four full-time teams in the Sprint Cup series, which runs annually from February through November and features 36 races at 23 speedways across the United States. The Hendrick organization has annual operating costs of $100 million and 550 employees, with tasks ranging from accounting and marketing to engine building and racecar driving. Such an environment features multiple functional areas and units, varied worksites, and ever-changing circumstances. Patrick Perkins, director of marketing, noted, "Racing is a fast business. It's just as fast off the track as it is on it. With the work that we put into development of our teams and technologies, and having to respond to change as well as anticipate change, I like to think of us in this business as change experts."

Microsoft Forecaster, Hendrick's Web-enabled budgeting package, has allowed Hendrick's financial managers to seamlessly manage the planning and budgeting process. Authorized users from each functional area or team sign on to the application through the corporate intranet. Security on the system is tight: Access is limited to only the accounts that a manager is authorized to budget. That way, for example, Jeff Gordon's crew chief can't see what Jimmie Johnson's team members are doing. Forecaster also allows users at the racetrack to access the application remotely, which allows mangers to receive or update real-time "actuals" from the system. This way, team managers know their allotted expenses for each race. Forecaster also provides users with additional features, including seamless links with general ledger accounts and the option to perform what-if (sensitivity) analyses. Scott Lampe, chief financial officer, said, "Forecaster allows us to change our forecasts to respond to changes, either rule changes [such as changes in the series' points system] or technology changes [such as pilot testing NASCAR's new, safer "Car of Tomorrow"] throughout the racing season."

Hendrick's Web-enabled budgeting system frees the finance department so it can work on strategy, analysis, and decision-making. It also allows Hendrick to complete its annual budgeting process in only six weeks, a 50 percent reduction in the time spent budgeting and planning, which is critical given NASCAR's extremely short off-season. Patrick Pearson from Hendrick Motorsports believes the system gives the organization a competitive advantage, "In racing, the team that wins is not only the team with the fastest car, but the team that is the most disciplined and prepared week in and week out. Forecaster allows us to respond to that changing landscape."

Source: Ryan, Nate, "Hendrick Empire Strikes Back with Three Contenders in Chase for Nextel Cup," *USA Today,* September 17, 2006; Hendrick Motorsports, "About Hendrick Motorsports," Hendrick Motorsports Web site www.hendrickmotorsports.com (April 12, 2007); Microsoft Corporation, "Microsoft Forecaster: Hendrick Motorsports Customer Video," Microsoft Corporation Web site www.microsoft.com (April 12, 2007); Goff, John, "In the Fast Lane," *CFO Magazine,* December 1, 2004; Lampe, Scott, "NASCAR Racing Team Stays on Track with FRx Software's Comprehensive Budget Planning Solution," *DM Review,* July 1, 2003.

Organization Structure and Responsibility

Organization structure is an arrangement of lines of responsibility within the organization. A company such as Bharat Petroleum may be organized primarily by business function—exploration, refining, and marketing—with each manager having decision-making authority over her function. Another company, such as Procter & Gamble, the household-products giant, may be organized by product line or brand. The managers of the individual divisions (toothpaste, soap, and so on) would each have decision-making authority concerning all the business functions (manufacturing, marketing, and so on) within that division.

Each manager, regardless of level, is in charge of a responsibility center. A **responsibility center** is a part, segment, or subunit of an organization whose manager is accountable for a specified set of activities. The higher the manager's level, the broader the responsibility center and, generally, the larger the number of his or her subordinates. **Responsibility accounting** is a system that measures the plans, budgets, actions, and actual results of each responsibility center. Four types of responsibility centers are:

1. **Cost center**—the manager is accountable for costs only.
2. **Revenue center**—the manager is accountable for revenues only.
3. **Profit center**—the manager is accountable for revenues and costs.
4. **Investment center**—the manager is accountable for investments, revenues, and costs.

The Maintenance Department of a Oberoi hotel is a cost center because the maintenance manager is responsible only for costs, so this budget is based on costs. The Sales Department is a revenue center because the sales manager is responsible primarily for revenues, so this budget is based on revenues. The hotel manager is in charge of a profit center because the manager is accountable for both revenues and costs, so this budget is based on revenues and costs. The regional manager responsible for determining the amount to be invested in new hotel projects and for revenues and costs generated from these investments is in charge of an investment center, so this budget is based on revenues, costs, and the investment base.

A responsibility center can be structured to promote better alignment of individual and company goals. For example, until recently, Godrej, an office products distributor, operated its Sales Department as a revenue center. Each salesperson received a commission of 3% of the revenues per order, regardless of its size, the cost of processing it, or the cost of delivering the office products. An analysis of customer profitability at Godrej found that many customers were unprofitable. The main reason was the high ordering and delivery costs of small orders. Godrej's managers decided to make the Sales Department a profit center, accountable for revenues and costs, and to change the incentive system for salespeople to 15% of the monthly profits per customer. The costs for each customer included the ordering and delivery costs. The effect of this change was immediate. The Sales Department began charging customers for ordering and delivery, and salespeople at Godrej actively encouraged customers to consolidate their purchases into fewer orders. As a result, each order began producing larger revenues. Customer profitability increased because of a 40% reduction in ordering and delivery costs in one year.

Feedback

Budgets coupled with responsibility accounting provide feedback to top management about the performance relative to the budget of different responsibility center managers.

Differences between actual results and budgeted amounts—called *variances*—if properly used, can help managers implement and evaluate strategies in three ways:

1. *Early warning.* Variances alert managers early to events not easily nor immediately evident. Managers can then take corrective actions or exploit the available opportunities. For example, after observing a small decline in sales this period, managers may want to investigate if this is an indication of an even steeper decline to follow later in the year.

2. ***Performance evaluation.*** Variances prompt managers to probe how well the company has performed in implementing its strategies. Were materials and labor used efficiently? Was R&D spending increased as planned? Did product warranty costs decrease as planned?
3. ***Evaluating strategy.*** Variances sometimes signal to managers that their strategies are ineffective. For example, a company seeking to compete by reducing costs and improving quality may find that it is achieving these goals but that it is having little effect on sales and profits. Top management may then want to re-evaluate the strategy.

Responsibility and Controllability

Controllability is the degree of influence that a specific manager has over costs, revenues, or related items for which he or she is responsible. A **controllable cost** is any cost that is primarily subject to the influence of a given *responsibility center manager* for a given *period*. A responsibility accounting system could either exclude all uncontrollable costs from a manager's performance report or segregate such costs from the controllable costs. For example, a machining supervisor's performance report might be confined to direct materials, direct manufacturing labor, power, and machine maintenance costs and might exclude costs such as rent and taxes paid on the plant.

In practice, controllability is difficult to pinpoint for at least two reasons:

1. Few costs are clearly under the sole influence of one manager. For example, prices of direct materials may be influenced by a purchasing manager, but these prices also depend on market conditions beyond the manager's control. Quantities used may be influenced by a production manager, but quantities used also depend on the quality of materials purchased. Moreover, managers often work in teams. Think about how difficult it is to evaluate individual responsibility in a team situation.
2. With a long enough time span, all costs will come under somebody's control. However, most performance reports focus on periods of a year or less. A current manager may benefit from a predecessor's accomplishments or may inherit a predecessor's problems and inefficiencies. For example, present managers may have to work under undesirable contracts with suppliers or labor unions that were negotiated by their predecessors. How can we separate what the current manager actually controls from the results of decisions made by others? Exactly what is the current manager accountable for? Answers may not be clear-cut.

Executives differ in how they embrace the controllability notion when evaluating those reporting to them. Some CEOs regard the budget as a firm commitment that subordinates must meet. Failure to meet the budget is viewed unfavorably. Other CEOs believe a more risk-sharing approach with managers is preferable, in which noncontrollable factors and performance relative to competitors are taken into account when judging the performance of managers who fail to meet their budgets.

Managers should avoid overemphasizing controllability. Responsibility accounting is more far-reaching. It focuses on gaining *information and knowledge*, not only on control. *Responsibility accounting helps managers to first focus on whom they should ask to obtain information and not on whom they should blame.* For example, if actual revenues at a Oberoi hotel are less than budgeted revenues, the managers of the hotel may be tempted to blame the sales manager for the poor performance. The fundamental purpose of responsibility accounting, however, is not to fix blame but to gather information to enable future improvement.

The question is, Who can tell us the most about the specific item in question, regardless of that person's ability to exert personal control over that item? For instance, purchasing managers may be held accountable for total purchase costs, not because of their ability to control market prices, but because of their ability to predict uncontrollable prices and to explain uncontrollable price changes. Similarly, managers at a Pizza Hut unit may be held responsible for operating income of their units, even though they (a) do not fully control selling prices nor the costs of many food items and (b) have minimal flexibility about what items to sell or the ingredients in the items they sell. They are, however, in the best position to explain differences between their actual operating incomes and their budgeted operating incomes.

Performance reports for responsibility centers are sometimes designed to change managers' behavior in the direction top management desires. A cost-center manager may emphasize efficiency and deemphasize the pleas of sales personnel for faster service and rush orders. When evaluated as a profit center, the manager will more likely consider ways to influence activities that affect sales and weigh the impact of decisions on costs and revenues rather than on costs alone. To induce that change, some companies have changed the accountability of a cost center to a profit center. Call centers are an interesting example of this trend. As firms continue to differentiate on customer service while attempting to control operating expenses, driving efficiency wherever possible in the call centers has become a critical issue—as has driving revenue through this unique channel. There is increasing pressure for customer service representatives to promote new offers through upsell and cross-sell tactics. Microsoft, Oracle, and others offer software platforms that seek to evolve the call center from cost center to profit center. The new adage is, "Every service call is a sales call."

Decision Point

How do companies use responsibility centers? Should performance reports of responsibility center managers include only costs the manager can control?

Human Aspects of Budgeting

Learning Objective 7

Recognize the human aspects of budgeting

. . . to engage subordinate managers in the budgeting process

Why did we discuss the two major topics, the master budget and responsibility accounting, in the same chapter? Primarily to emphasize that human factors are crucial in budgeting. Too often, budgeting is thought of as a mechanical tool. The budgeting techniques themselves are free of emotion. However, the administration of budgeting requires education, persuasion, and intelligent interpretation.

Budgetary Slack

As we discussed earlier in this chapter, budgeting is most effective when lower-level managers actively participate and meaningfully engage in the budgeting process. Participation adds credibility to the budgeting process and creates greater commitment and accountability toward the budget. But participation requires "honest" communication about the business from subordinates and lower-level managers to their bosses.

At times, subordinates may try to "play games" and build in *budgetary slack*. **Budgetary slack** describes the practice of underestimating budgeted revenues, or overestimating budgeted costs, to make budgeted targets more easily achievable. It frequently occurs when budget variances (the differences between actual results and budgeted amounts) are used to evaluate performance. Line managers are also unlikely to be fully honest in their budget communications if top management mechanically institutes across-the-board cost reductions (say, a 10% reduction in all areas) in the face of projected revenue reductions.

Budgetary slack provides managers with a hedge against unexpected adverse circumstances. But budgetary slack also misleads top management about the true profit potential of the company, which leads to inefficient resource planning and allocation and poor coordination of activities across different parts of the company.

To avoid problems of budgetary slack, some companies use budgets primarily for planning purposes. They evaluate managerial performance using multiple indicators that take into account various factors such as the prevailing business environment and performance relative to competitors. But evaluating performance in this way takes time and requires careful exercise of judgment. Other companies use budgets for both planning and performance evaluation and use different approaches to obtain accurate information.

To explain one approach, let's consider the plant manager of a beverage bottler who is suspected by top management of understating the productivity potential of the bottling lines in his forecasts for the coming year. His presumed motivation is to increase the likelihood of meeting next year's production bonus targets. Suppose top management could purchase a consulting firm's study that reports productivity levels—such as the number of bottles filled per hour—at a number of comparable plants owned by other bottling companies. This report shows that its own plant manager's productivity forecasts are well below actual productivity levels being achieved at other comparable plants.

Top management could share this independent information source with the plant manager and ask him to explain why his productivity differs from that at other similar plants. They could also base part of the plant manager's compensation on his plant's productivity in comparison with other "benchmark" plants rather than on the forecasts he provided. Using external benchmark performance measures reduces a manager's ability to set budget levels that are easy to achieve.[6]

Another approach to reducing budgetary slack is for managers to involve themselves regularly in understanding what their subordinates are doing. Such involvement should not result in managers dictating the decisions and actions of subordinates. Rather, a manager's involvement should take the form of providing support, challenging in a motivational way the assumptions subordinates make, and enhancing mutual learning about the operations. Regular interaction with subordinates allows managers to become knowledgeable about the operations and diminishes the ability of subordinates to create slack in their budgets.

Part of top management's responsibility is to promote commitment among the employees to a set of core values and norms. These values and norms describe what constitutes acceptable and unacceptable behavior. For example, Johnson & Johnson (J&J) has a credo that describes its responsibilities to doctors, patients, employees, communities, and shareholders. Employees are trained in the credo to help them understand the behavior that is expected of them. Managers are often promoted from within and are therefore very familiar with the work of the employees reporting to them. Managers also have the responsibility to interact with and mentor their subordinates. These values and practices create a culture at J&J that discourages budgetary slack.

Some companies, such as IBM and Kodak, have designed innovative performance evaluation measures that reward managers based on the subsequent accuracy of the forecasts used in preparing budgets. For example, the *higher and more accurate* the budgeted profit forecasts of division managers, the higher their incentive bonuses.

Many of the best performing companies, such as General Electric, Microsoft, and Novartis, set "stretch" targets. Stretch targets are challenging but achievable levels of expected performance, intended to create a little discomfort and to motivate employees to exert extra effort and attain better performance.

Many managers regard budgets negatively. To them, the word budget is about as popular as, say, *downsizing*, *layoff*, or *strike*. Top managers must convince their subordinates that the budget is a tool designed to help them set and reach goals. But whatever the manager's perspective on budgets—pro or con—budgets are not remedies for weak management talent, faulty organization, or a poor accounting system.

The management style of executives is a factor in how budgets are perceived in companies. Some CEOs argue that "numbers always tell the story." An executive once noted, "You can miss your plan once, but you wouldn't want to miss it twice." Other CEOs believe "too much focus on making the numbers in a budget" can lead to poor decision-making and unethical practices.

Kaizen Budgeting

Chapter 1 noted the importance of continuous improvement, or *kaizen* in Japanese. **Kaizen budgeting** explicitly incorporates continuous improvement anticipated during the budget period into the budget numbers. Many companies that have cost reduction as a strategic focus, including General Electric in the United States and Citizens Watch and

[6] For an excellent discussion of these issues, see Chapter 14 ("Formal Models in Budgeting and Incentive Contracts") of R. S. Kaplan and A. A. Atkinson, *Advanced Management Accounting*, 3rd ed. (Upper Saddle River, NJ: Prentice Hall, 1998).

Toyota in Japan, use kaizen budgeting to continuously reduce costs. Much of the cost reduction associated with kaizen budgeting arises from many small improvements rather than "quantum leaps."

A significant aspect of kaizen budgeting is employee suggestions. Companies implementing kaizen budgeting believe that employees who actually do the job, whether in manufacturing, sales, or distribution, have the best information and knowledge of how the job can be done better. These companies create a culture in which employee suggestions are valued, recognized, and rewarded.

As an example, throughout our nine budgeting steps for Stylistic Furniture, we assumed four hours of direct labor time to manufacture each Casual coffee table. A kaizen budgeting approach would incorporate continuous improvement resulting from, for example, employee suggestions for doing the work faster or reducing idle time. The kaizen budget might then prescribe 4.00 direct manufacturing labor-hours per table for the first quarter of 2012, 3.95 hours for the second quarter, 3.90 hours for the third quarter, and so on. The implications of these reductions would be lower direct manufacturing labor costs, as well as lower variable manufacturing overhead costs, because direct manufacturing labor is the driver of these costs. If these continuous improvement goals are not met, Stylistic's managers will explore the reasons behind it and either adjust the targets or implement process changes that will accelerate continuous improvement.

Why are human factors crucial in budgeting?

Kaizen budgeting can also be applied to activities such as setups with the goal of reducing setup time and setup costs, or distribution with the goal of reducing the cost of moving each cubic foot of table. Kaizen budgeting and budgeting for specific activities are key building blocks of the master budget. Interestingly, companies are not the only ones interested in kaizen techniques. A growing number of cash-strapped states in the United States are bringing together government workers, regulators, and end users of government processes to identify ways to attack inefficiencies arising from bureaucratic procedures. Environmental regulators, whose cumbersome processes have long been the targets of business developers, have taken particular interest in kaizen. By the end of 2008, 29 state environmental agencies had conducted a kaizen session or were planning one.[7] How successful these efforts will be depends heavily on human factors such as the commitment and engagement of the individuals involved.

Budgeting in Multinational Companies

Learning Objective 8

Appreciate the special challenges of budgeting in multinational companies

. . . exposure to currency fluctuations and to different legal, political, and economic environments

Multinational companies, such as Federal Express, Kraft, and Pfizer, have operations in many countries. An international presence carries with it positives—access to new markets and resources—and negatives—operating in less-familiar business environments and exposure to currency fluctuations. For example, multinational companies earn revenues and incur expenses in many different currencies, and they must translate their operating performance into a single currency (say, U.S. dollars) for reporting results to their shareholders each quarter. This translation is based on the average exchange rates that prevail during the quarter. That is, in addition to budgeting in different currencies, management accountants in multinational companies also need to budget for foreign exchange rates. This is difficult because management accountants need to anticipate potential changes that might take place during the year. Exchange rates are constantly fluctuating, so to reduce the possible negative impact on performance caused by unfavorable exchange rate movements, finance managers will frequently use sophisticated techniques such as forward, future, and option contracts to minimize exposure to foreign currency fluctuations. Besides currency issues, multinational companies need to understand the political, legal, and, in particular, economic environments of the different countries in which they operate. For example, in countries

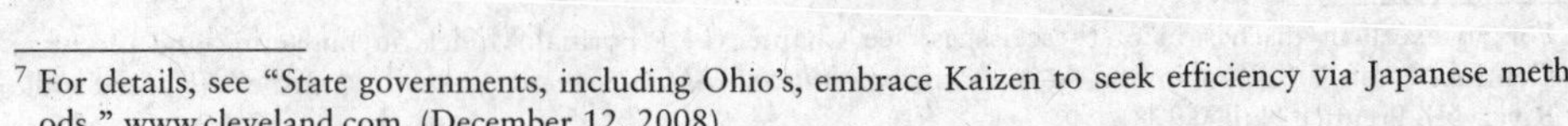

[7] For details, see "State governments, including Ohio's, embrace Kaizen to seek efficiency via Japanese methods," www.cleveland.com, (December 12, 2008).

such as Zimbabwe, Iraq, and Guinea, annual inflation rates are very high, resulting in sharp declines in the value of the local currency. Issues related to differences in tax regimes are also critical, especially when the company transfers goods or services across the many countries in which it operates.

Multinational companies find budgeting to be a valuable tool when operating in very uncertain environments. As circumstances and conditions change, companies revise their budgets. The purpose of budgeting in such environments is not to evaluate performance relative to budgets, which is a meaningless comparison when conditions are so volatile, but to help managers throughout the organization to learn and to adapt their plans to the changing conditions and to communicate and coordinate the actions that need to be taken throughout the company. Senior managers evaluate performance more subjectively, based on how well subordinate managers have managed in these uncertain environments.

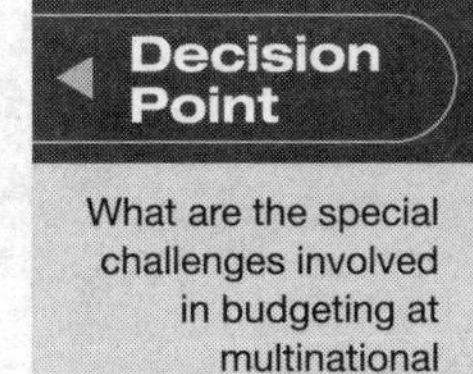

What are the special challenges involved in budgeting at multinational companies?

Problem for Self-Study

Consider the Stylistic Furniture example described earlier. Suppose that to maintain its sales quantities, Stylistic needs to decrease selling prices to Rs 5,820 per Casual table and Rs 7,760 per Deluxe table, a 3% decrease in the selling prices used in the chapter illustration. All other data are unchanged.

Required

Prepare a budgeted income statement, including all necessary detailed supporting budget schedules that are different from the schedules presented in the chapter. Indicate those schedules that will remain unchanged.

Solution

Schedules 1 and 8 will change. Schedule 1 changes because a change in selling price affects revenues. Schedule 8 changes because revenues are a cost driver of marketing costs (sales commissions). The remaining schedules will not change because a change in selling price has no effect on manufacturing costs. The revised schedules and the new budgeted income statement follow.

Schedule 1: Revenue Budget
For the Year Ending December 31, 2012

	Selling Price	Units	Total Revenues
Casual tables	Rs 5,820	50,000	Rs 29,10,00,000
Deluxe tables	7,760	10,000	7,76,00,000
Total			Rs 36,86,00,000

Schedule 8: Nonmanufacturing Costs Budget
For the Year Ending December 31, 2012

Business Function	Variable Costs	Fixed Costs (as in Schedule 8)	Total Costs
Product Design		Rs 1,02,40,000	Rs 1,02,40,000
Marketing			
(Variable cost: Rs 36,86,00,000 × 0.065)	Rs 2,39,59,000	1,33,00,000	3,72,59,000
Distribution			
(Variable cost: Rs 20 × 1,140,000 cu. ft.)	2,28,00,000	1,59,60,000	3,87,60,000
	Rs 4,67,59,000	Rs 3,95,00,000	Rs 8,62,59,000

Stylistic Furniture
Budgeted Income Statement
For the Year Ending December 31, 2012

Revenues	Schedule 1		Rs 36,86,00,000
Cost of goods sold	Schedule 7		24,44,00,000
Gross margin			12,42,00,000
Operating costs			
Product design	Schedule 8	Rs 1,02,40,000	
Marketing costs	Schedule 8	3,72,59,000	
Distribution costs	Schedule 8	3,87,60,000	8,62,59,000
Operating income			Rs 3,79,41,000

Decision Points

The following question-and-answer format summarizes the chapter's learning objectives. Each decision presents a key question related to a learning objective. The guidelines are the answer to that question.

Decision	Guidelines
1. What is the master budget and why is it useful?	The master budget summarizes the financial projections of all the company's budgets. It expresses management's operating and financing plans—the formalized outline of the company's financial objectives and how they will be attained. Budgets are tools that, by themselves, are neither good nor bad. Budgets are useful when administered skillfully.
2. When should a company prepare budgets? What are the advantages of preparing budgets?	Budgets should be prepared when their expected benefits exceed their expected costs. The advantages of budgets include: (a) they compel strategic analysis and planning, (b) they promote coordination and communication among subunits of the company, (c) they provide a framework for judging performance and facilitating learning, and (d) they motivate managers and other employees.
3. What is the operating budget and why is it useful?	The operating budget is the budgeted income statement and its supporting budget schedules. The starting point for the operating budget is generally the revenues budget. The following supporting schedules are derived from the revenues budget and the activities needed to support the revenues budget: production budget, direct material usage budget, direct material purchases budget, direct manufacturing labor cost budget, manufacturing overhead costs budget, ending inventories budget, cost of goods sold budget, R&D/product design cost budget, marketing cost budget, distribution cost budget, and customer-service cost budget.
4. How can managers plan for changes in the underlying budget assumptions?	Managers can use financial planning models—mathematical statements of the relationships among operating activities, financing activities, and other factors that affect the budget. These models make it possible for management to conduct what-if (sensitivity) analysis of the effects that changes in the original predicted data or changes in underlying assumptions would have on the master budget and to develop plans to respond to changed conditions.
5. How can budgets include the effects of future improvements?	Kaizen budgeting is based on the idea that it is possible to continuously reduce costs over time. Costs in kaizen budgeting are based on improvements that are yet to be implemented rather than on current practices or methods.

6. How do companies use responsibility centers and responsibility accounting?	A responsibility center is a part, segment, or subunit of an organization whose manager is accountable for a specified set of activities. Four types of responsibility centers are cost centers, revenue centers, profit centers, and investment centers. Responsibility accounting systems are useful because they measure the plans, budgets, actions, and actual results of each responsibility center.
7. Should performance reports of responsibility center managers include only costs the manager can control?	No. Controllable costs are costs primarily subject to the influence of a given responsibility center manager for a given time period. Performance reports of responsibility center managers often include costs, revenues, and investments that the managers cannot control. Responsibility accounting associates financial items with managers on the basis of which manager has the most knowledge and information about the specific items, regardless of the manager's ability to exercise full control.
8. Why are human factors crucial in budgeting?	The administration of budgets requires education, participation, persuasion, and intelligent interpretation. When wisely administered, budgets create commitment, accountability and honest communication. When badly managed, budgeting can lead to game-playing and budgetary slack—the practice of making budget targets more easily achievable.

APPENDIX: THE CASH BUDGET

The chapter illustrated the operating budget, which is one part of the master budget. The other part is the financial budget, which comprises the capital expenditures budget, the cash budget, the budgeted balance sheet, and the budgeted statement of cash flows. This appendix focuses on the cash budget and the budgeted balance sheet. Capital budgeting is discussed in Chapter 21. The budgeted statement of cash flows is beyond the scope of this book, and generally is covered in financial accounting and corporate finance courses.

Suppose Stylistic Furniture had the balance sheet for the year ended December 31, 2011, shown in Exhibit 6-5. The budgeted cash flows for 2012 are:

	Quarters			
	1	2	3	4
Collections from customers	Rs 9,13,66,000	Rs 10,12,20,000	Rs 10,26,32,000	Rs 8,56,12,000
Disbursements				
Direct materials	2,94,76,050	2,71,46,120	2,15,79,630	2,15,53,560
Payroll	3,60,45,120	2,67,17,420	2,32,09,460	2,56,28,000
Manufacturing overhead costs	2,10,90,180	1,53,09,640	1,31,35,680	1,46,34,500
Nonmanufacturing costs	1,84,77,500	1,97,90,000	1,96,82,500	1,70,50,000
Machinery purchase	—	—	75,80,000	—
Income taxes	72,50,000	40,00,000	40,00,000	40,00,000

The quarterly data are based on the budgeted cash effects of the operations formulated in Schedules 1 through 8 in the chapter, but the details of that formulation are not shown here to keep this illustration as brief and as focused as possible.

The company wants to maintain a Rs 35,00,000 minimum cash balance at the end of each quarter. The company can borrow or repay money at an interest rate of 12% per year. Management does not want to borrow any more short-term cash than is necessary. By special arrangement, interest is computed and paid when the principal is repaid. Assume, for simplicity, that borrowing takes place at the beginning and repayment at the end of the quarter under consideration (in multiples of Rs 10,000). Interest is computed to the nearest rupee.

Exhibit 6-5

Balance Sheet for Stylistic Furniture, December 31, 2011

	A	B	C	D
1	Stylistic Furniture Balance Sheet			
2	December 31, 2011			
3	Assets			
4	Current Assets			
5	Cash		Rs 30,00,000	
6	Accounts receivable		1,71,10,000	
7	Direct materials inventory		1,09,00,000	
8	Finished goods inventory		64,60,000	Rs 3,74,70,000
9	Property, plant, and equipment:			
10	Land		2,00,00,000	
11	Building and equipment	Rs 22,00,00,000		
12	Accumulated depreciation	(6,90,00,000)	15,10,00,000	17,10,00,000
13	Total			Rs 20,84,70,000
14	Liabilities and Stockholders' Equity			
15	Current Liabilities			
16	Accounts payable		Rs 90,40,000	
17	Income taxes payable		Rs 32,50,000	Rs 1,22,90,000
18	Stockholders' equity			
19	Common stock, no-par,			
20	25,000 shares outstanding		3,50,00,000	
21	Retained earnings		16,11,80,000	19,61,80,000
22	Total			Rs 20,84,70,000

Suppose the management accountant at Stylistic is given the preceding data and the other data contained in the budgets in the chapter. She is instructed as follows:

1. Prepare a cash budget for 2012 by quarter. That is, prepare a statement of cash receipts and disbursements by quarter, including details of borrowing, repayment, and interest.
2. Prepare a budgeted income statement for the year ending December 31, 2012. This statement should include interest expense and income taxes (at a rate of 40% of operating income).
3. Prepare a budgeted balance sheet on December 31, 2012.

Preparation of Budgets

1. The **cash budget** (Exhibit 6-6) is a schedule of expected cash receipts and disbursements. It predicts the effects on the cash position at the given level of operations. Exhibit 6-6 presents the cash budget by quarters to show the impact of cash flow timing on bank loans and their repayment. In practice, monthly—and sometimes weekly or even daily—cash budgets are critical for cash planning and control. Cash budgets help avoid unnecessary idle cash and unexpected cash deficiencies. They thus keep cash balances in line with needs. Ordinarily, the cash budget has these main sections:
   a. **Cash available for needs (before any financing)**. The beginning cash balance plus cash receipts equals the total cash available for needs before any financing. Cash receipts depend on collections of accounts receivable, cash sales, and miscellaneous recurring sources, such as rental or royalty receipts. Information on the expected collectibility of accounts receivable is needed for accurate predictions. Key factors include bad-debt (uncollectible accounts) experience (not an issue in the Stylistic case because Stylistic sells to only a few large wholesalers) and average time lag between sales and collections.

Exhibit 6-6 Cash Budget for Stylistic Furniture for the Year Ending December 31, 2012

File Edit View Insert Format Tools Data Window Help

	A	B	C	D	E	F
1				**Stylistic Furniture**		
2				**Cash Budget**		
3				**For Year Ending December 31, 2012**		
4				**Quarters**		**Year as a**
5		**1**	**2**	**3**	**4**	**Whole**
6	Cash balance, beginning	Rs 30,00,000	Rs 35,07,150	Rs 35,06,570	Rs 35,00,700	Rs 30,00,000
7	Add receipts					
8	Collections from customers	9,13,66,000	10,12,20,000	10,26,32,000	8,56,12,000	38,08,30,000
9	Total cash available for needs (x)	9,43,66,000	10,47,27,150	10,61,38,570	8,91,12,700	38,38,30,000
10	Deduct disbursements					
11	Direct materials	2,94,76,050	2,71,46,120	2,15,79,630	2,15,53,560	9,97,55,360
12	Payroll	3,60,45,120	2,67,17,420	2,32,09,460	2,56,28,000	11,16,00,000
13	Manufacturing overhead costs	2,10,90,180	1,53,09,640	1,31,35,680	1,46,34,500	6,41,70,000
14	Nonmanufacturing costs	1,84,77,500	1,97,90,000	1,96,82,500	1,70,50,000	7,50,00,000
15	Machinery purchase			75,80,000		75,80,000
16	Income taxes	72,50,000	40,00,000	40,00,000	40,00,000	1,92,50,000
17	Total disbursements (y)	11,23,38,850	9,29,63,180	8,91,87,270	8,28,66,060	37,73,55,360
18	Minimum cash balance desired	35,00,000	35,00,000	35,00,000	35,00,000	35,00,000
19	Total cash needed	11,58,38,850	9,64,63,180	9,26,87,270	8,63,66,060	38,08,55,360
20	Cash excess (deficiency)*	Rs(2,14,72,850)	Rs 82,63,970	Rs 1,34,51,300	Rs 27,46,640	Rs 29,74,460
21	Financing					
22	Borrowing (at beginning)	Rs 2,14,80,000	Rs 0	Rs 0	Rs 0	Rs 2,14,80,000
23	Repayment (at end)	0	(77,90,000)	(1,23,40,000)	(13,50,000)	(2,14,80,000)
24	Interest (at 12% per year)**	0	(4,67,400)	(11,10,600)	(1,62,000)	(17,40,000)
25	Total effects of financing (z)	Rs 2,14,80,000	Rs(82,57,400)	Rs(1,34,50,600)	Rs(15,12,000)	Rs (17,40,000)
26	Cash balance, ending***	Rs 35,07,150	Rs 35,06,570	Rs 35,00,700	Rs 47,34,640	Rs 47,34,640
27	*Excess of total cash available for needs − Total cash needed before financing.					
28	**Note that the short-term interest payments pertain only to the amount of principal being repaid at the end of a quarter. The specific computations regarding interest are Rs 77,90,000 x 0.12 x 0.5 = Rs 4,67,400; Rs 1,23,40,000 x 0.12 x 0.75 = Rs 11,10,600; Rs 13,50,000 x 0.12 = Rs 1,62,000. Also note that *depreciation does not require a cash outlay.*					
29	***Ending cash balance = Total cash available for needs (x) − Total disbursements (y) + Total effects of financing (z)					

b. **Cash disbursements.** Cash disbursements by Stylistic Furniture include:

i. *Direct material purchases.* Suppliers are paid in full three weeks after the goods are delivered.

ii. *Direct labor and other wage and salary outlays.* All payroll-related costs are paid in the month in which the labor effort occurs.

iii. *Other costs.* These depend on timing and credit terms. (In the Stylistic case, all other costs are paid in the month in which the cost is incurred.) *Note, depreciation does not require a cash outlay.*

iv. *Other disbursements.* These include outlays for property, plant, equipment, and other long-term investments.

v. Income tax payments.

c. **Financing effects.** Short-term financing requirements depend on how the total cash available for needs (keyed as (x) in Exhibit 6-6) compares with the total cash disbursements (keyed as (y)), plus the minimum ending cash balance desired. The financing plans will depend on the relationship between total cash available for needs and total cash needed. If there is a deficiency of cash, loans will be obtained. If there is excess cash, any outstanding loans will be repaid.

Exhibit 6-7

Budgeted Income Statement for Stylistic Furniture for the Year Ending December 31, 2012

	A	B	C	D
1	**Stylistic Furniture Budgeted Income Statement**			
2	For the Year Ending December 31, 2012			
3	Revenues	Schedule 1		Rs 38,00,00,000
4	Cost of goods sold	Schedule 7		24,44,00,000
5	Gross margin			13,56,00,000
6	Operating costs			
7	Product design costs	Schedule 8	Rs 1,02,40,000	
8	Marketing costs	Schedule 8	3,80,00,000	
9	Distribution costs	Schedule 8	3,87,60,000	8,70,00,000
10	Operating income			4,86,00,000
11	Interest expense	Exhibit 6-6		17,40,000
12	Income before income taxes			4,68,60,000
13	Income taxes (at 40%)			1,87,44,000
14	Net income			Rs 2,81,16,000

d. **Ending cash balance.** The cash budget in Exhibit 6-6 shows the pattern of short-term "self-liquidating" cash loans. In quarter 1, Stylistic budgets a Rs 2,14,72,850 cash deficiency. Hence, it undertakes short-term borrowing of Rs 2,14,80,000 that it pays off over the course of the year. Seasonal peaks of production or sales often result in heavy cash disbursements for purchases, payroll, and other operating outlays as the products are produced and sold. Cash receipts from customers typically lag behind sales. The loan is *self-liquidating* in the sense that the borrowed money is used to acquire resources that are used to produce and sell finished goods, and the proceeds from sales are used to repay the loan. This self-liquidating cycle is the movement from cash to inventories to receivables and back to cash.

2. The budgeted income statement is presented in Exhibit 6-7. It is merely the budgeted operating income statement in Exhibit 6-3 expanded to include interest expense and income taxes.
3. The budgeted balance sheet is presented in Exhibit 6-8. Each item is projected in light of the details of the business plan as expressed in all the previous budget schedules. For example, the ending balance of accounts receivable of Rs 1,62,80,000 is computed by adding the budgeted revenues of Rs 38,00,00,000 (from Schedule 1) to the beginning balance of accounts receivable of Rs 1,71,10,000 (from Exhibit 6-5) and subtracting cash receipts of Rs 38,08,30,000 (from Exhibit 6-6).

For simplicity, the cash receipts and disbursements were given explicitly in this illustration. Usually, the receipts and disbursements are calculated based on the lags between the items reported on the accrual basis of accounting in an income statement and balance sheet and their related cash receipts and disbursements. Consider accounts receivable. In the first three quarters, Stylistic estimates that 80% of all sales made in a quarter are collected in the same quarter and 20% are collected in the following quarter. Estimated collections from customers each quarter are calculated in the following table (assuming sales by quarter of Rs 9,28,20,000, Rs 10,33,20,000, Rs 10,24,60,000, and Rs 8,14,00,000 that equal 2010 budgeted sales of Rs 38,00,00,000).

Exhibit 6-8 Budgeted Balance Sheet for Stylistic Furniture, December 31, 2012

File Edit View Insert Format Tools Data Window Help

	A	B	C	D
1	**Stylistic Furniture**			
2	**Budgeted Balance Sheet**			
3	December 31, 2012			
4	**Assets**			
5	Current Assets			
6	Cash (from Exhibit 6-6)		Rs 47,34,640	
7	Accounts receivable (1)		1,62,80,000	
8	Direct materials inventory (2)		76,00,000	
9	Finished goods inventory (2)		4,48,60,000	Rs 7,34,74,640
10	Property, plant, and equipment			
11	Land (3)		2,00,00,000	
12	Building and equipment (4)	Rs 22,75,80,000		
13	Accumulated depreciation (5)	Rs (8,52,30,000)	14,23,50,000	16,23,50,000
14	Total			Rs 23,58,24,640
15	**Liabilities and Stockholders' Equity**			
16	Current Liabilities			
17	Accounts payable (6)		Rs 87,84,640	
18	Income taxes payable (7)		27,44,000	Rs 1,15,28,640
19	Stockholders' equity			
20	Common stock, no-par, 25,000 shares outstanding (8)		3,50,00,000	
21	Retained earnings (9)		18,92,96,000	22,42,96,000
22	Total			Rs 23,58,24,640
23				
24	Notes:			
25	Beginning balances are used as the starting point for most of the following computations:			
26	(1) Rs 1,71,10,000 + Rs 38,00,00,000 revenues − Rs 38,08,30,000 receipts (Exhibit 6-6) = Rs 1,62,80,000			
27	(2) From Schedule 6B, p. 193			
28	(3) From beginning balance sheet, p. 204			
29	(4) Rs 22,00,00,000 + Rs 75,80,000 purchases = Rs 22,75,80,000			
30	(5) Rs 6,90,00,000 + Rs 1,02,00,000 + Rs 60,30,000 depreciation from Schedule 5, p.192			
31	(6) Rs 90,40,000 + Rs 9,95,00,000 (Schedule 3B) − Rs 9,97,55,360 (Exhibit 6-6) = Rs 87,84,640			
32	There are no other current liabilities. Cash flows for payroll, manufacturing overhead and nonmanufacturing costs totaling Rs 25,07,70,000 on the cash budget (Exhibit 6-6) consists of direct manufacturing labor costs of Rs 6,00,00,000 from Schedule 4 + cash manufacturing overhead costs of Rs 10,37,70,000 (Rs 12,00,00,000 − depreciation of Rs 1,62,30,000) from Schedule 5 + cash nonmanufacturing costs of Rs 8,70,00,000 from Schedule 8.			
33	(7) Rs 32,50,000 + Rs 1,87,44,000 current year − Rs 19,25,00,000 payment = Rs 2,74,40,000.			
34	(8) From beginning balance sheet.			
35	(9) Rs 16,11,80,000 + Rs 2,81,16,000 net income per Exhibit 6-7 = Rs 18,92,96,000			

Note that the quarterly cash collections from customers calculated in this schedule equal the cash collections by quarter. Furthermore, the difference between fourth-quarter sales and the cash collected from fourth-quarter sales, Rs 8,14,00,000 − Rs 6,51,20,000 = Rs 1,62,80,000 appears as accounts receivable in the budgeted balance sheet as of December 31, 2012 (see Exhibit 6-8).

Schedule of Cash Collections

	Quarters			
	1	2	3	4
Accounts receivable balance on 1-1-2012 (Fourth quarter sales from prior year collected in first quarter of 2012)	Rs 1,71,10,000			
From first-quarter 2012 sales (9,28,20,000 × 0.80; 9,28,20,000 × 0.20)	7,42,56,000	Rs 1,85,64,000		
From second-quarter 2012 sales (10,33,20,000 × 0.80; 10,33,20,000 × 0.20)		8,26,56,000	Rs 2,06,64,000	
From third-quarter 2012 sales (10,24,60,000 × 0.80; 10,24,60,000 × 0.20)			8,19,68,000	Rs 2,04,92,000
From fourth-quarter 2012 sales (8,14,00,000 × 0.80)				6,51,20,000
Total collections	Rs 9,13,66,000	Rs 10,12,20,000	Rs 10,26,32,000	Rs 8,56,12,000

Sensitivity Analysis and Cash Flows

Exhibit 6-4 shows how differing assumptions about selling prices of coffee tables and direct material prices led to differing amounts for budgeted operating income for Stylistic Furniture. A key use of sensitivity analysis is to budget cash flow. Exhibit 6-9 outlines the short-term borrowing implications of the two combinations examined in Exhibit 6-4. Scenario 1, with the lower selling prices per table (Rs 5,820 for the Casual table and Rs 7,760 for the Deluxe table), requires Rs 2,35,20,000 of short-term borrowing in quarter 1 that cannot be fully repaid as of December 31, 2012. Scenario 2, with the 5% higher direct material costs, requires Rs 2,25,00,000 borrowing by Stylistic Furniture, that also cannot be repaid by December 31, 2012. Sensitivity analysis helps managers anticipate such outcomes and take steps to minimize the effects of expected reductions in cash flows from operations.

Exhibit 6-9 Sensitivity Analysis: Effects of Key Budget Assumptions in Exhibit 6-4 on 2012 Short-Term Borrowing for Stylistic Furniture

File Edit View Insert Format Tools Data Window Help

	A	B	C	D	E	F	G	H	I	J
1				Direct Material			Short-Term Borrowing and Repayment by Quarter			
2		Selling Price		Purchase Costs		Budgeted	Quarters			
3	Scenario	Casual	Deluxe	Red Oak	Granite	Operating Income	1	2	3	4
4	1	Rs 5,820	Rs 7,760	Rs 70.00	Rs 100.00	Rs 3,79,41,000	Rs 2,35,20,000	(Rs 51,10,000)	(Rs 96,90,000)	(Rs 3,00,000)
5	2	Rs 6,000	Rs 8,000	73.50	105.00	4,48,38,000	2,25,00,000	(65,10,000)	(1,13,40,000)	(14,90,000)

TERMS TO LEARN

The chapter and the Glossary at the end of the book contain definitions of:

activity-based budgeting (ABB) (**p. 218**)
budgetary slack (**p. 226**)
cash budget (**p. 232**)
continuous budget (**p. 212**)
controllability (**p. 225**)
controllable cost (**p. 225**)
cost center (**p. 224**)
financial budget (**p. 213**)
financial planning models (**p. 221**)
investment center (**p. 224**)
kaizen budgeting (**p. 227**)
master budget (**p. 209**)
operating budget (**p. 213**)
organization structure (**p. 224**)
pro forma statements (**p. 209**)
profit center (**p. 224**)
responsibility accounting (**p. 224**)
responsibility center (**p. 224**)
revenue center (**p. 224**)
rolling budget (**p. 212**)

ASSIGNMENT MATERIAL

Questions

6-1 What are the four elements of the budgeting cycle?

6-2 Define master budget.

6-3 "Strategy, plans, and budgets are unrelated to one another." Do you agree? Explain.

6-4 "Budgeted performance is a better criterion than past performance for judging managers." Do you agree? Explain.

6-5 "Production managers and marketing managers are like oil and water. They just don't mix." How can a budget assist in reducing battles between these two areas?

6-6 "Budgets meet the cost-benefit test. They force managers to act differently." Do you agree? Explain.

6-7 Define rolling budget. Give an example.

6-8 Outline the steps in preparing an operating budget.

6-9 "The sales forecast is the cornerstone for budgeting." Why?

6-10 How can sensitivity analysis be used to increase the benefits of budgeting?

6-11 Define kaizen budgeting.

6-12 Describe how nonoutput-based cost drivers can be incorporated into budgeting.

6-13 Explain how the choice of the type of responsibility center (cost, revenue, profit, or investment) affects behavior.

6-14 What are some additional considerations that arise when budgeting in multinational companies?

6-15 "Cash budgets must be prepared before the operating income budget." Do you agree? Explain.

Solved Examples

6-16 Sales and production budget. The Royal Industries expects sales in current year of 1,00,000 units of serving trays. Royal's beginning inventory for current year is 7,000 trays, target ending inventory, 11,000 trays. Compute the number of trays budgeted for production in current year.

Solution

Production Budget	
Budgeted sales in units	1,00,000
Add target ending finished goods inventory	11,000
Total requirements	1,11,000
Deduct beginning finished goods inventory	7,000
Units to be produced	1,04,000

6-17 Revenues and production budget. Pearlpet Company, bottles and distributes mineral water from the company's natural springs in Shimla. Pearlpet markets two products: 12-ounce disposable plastic bottles and 4-gallon reusable plastic containers.

1. For 2012 Pearlpet marketing managers project monthly sales of 2,00,000 twelve-ounce units and 50,000 four-gallon units. Average selling prices are estimated at Rs 2.50 per twelve-ounce unit and Rs 15 four-gallon unit. Prepare a revenues budget for Pearlpet Company, for the year ending December 31, 2012.
2. Pearlpet begins 2012 with 4,50,000 twelve-ounce units in inventory. The vice president of operations requests that twelve-ounce ending inventory on December 31, 2011, be no less than 3,00,000 units. Based on sales projections as budgeted above, what is the minimum number of twelve-ounce units Pearlpet must produce during 2012?
3. The VP of operations requests that ending inventory of four-gallon units on December 31, 2012, be 1,00,000 units. If the production budget calls for Pearlpet to produce 6,50,000 four-gallon units during 2012, what is the beginning inventory of four-gallon units on January 1, 2012?

Solution

Sales (revenues) budget

1.	Selling Price	Units Sold	Total Revenues
12-ounce bottles	Rs 2.50	24,00,000[a]	60,00,000
4-gallon units	15	6,00,000[b]	90,00,000
			Rs 1,50,00,000

[a]2,00,000 × 12 months = 24,00,000
[b]50,000 × 12 months = 6,00,000

2. Production budget

Budgeted unit sales (12-ounce bottles)	24,00,000
Add target ending finished goods inventory	3,00,000
Total requirements	27,00,000
Deduct beginning finished goods inventory	4,50,000
Units to be produced	22,50,000

3. Beginning inventory = Budgeted sales + Target ending inventory − Budgeted production
= 6,00,000 + 1,00,000 − 6,50,000
= 50,000 4-gallon units

6-18 Direct materials usage, unit costs, and gross margins (continuation of previous question). Pearlpet Company, bottles and distributes mineral water from the company's natural springs in Shimla. Pearlpet markets two products: 12-ounce disposable plastic bottles and 4-gallon reusable plastic containers. The 12-ounce bottles are purchased from Plastico, a plastics manufacturer, at a cost of 60 paise per unit. The 4-gallon containers are sterilized and put back into service at a cost of Rs 3 per container. Spring water is extracted at a direct labor cost of 10 paise per 8 ounces (there are 128 ounces in a gallon). Manufacturing overhead is allocated at the rate of Rs 1.5 per unit. (Note: A unit can be a 12-ounce bottle or a 4-gallon container). In 2012, the production budget calls for the production of 22,50,000 twelve-ounce units and 6,50,000 four-gallon units.

Required

1. Assume four-gallon containers are fully depreciated, so that the only cost incurred is that of sterilization. Beginning and ending inventories for four-gallon containers are zero. There are 2,50,000 empty twelve-ounce bottles in beginning inventory on January 1, 2013. The vice president of operations would like to end 2013 with 1,50,000 empty twelve-ounce bottles in inventory. Accounting for sterilization as the only cost of the four-gallon containers, prepare a direct materials usage budget (relating to both bottles and container) in both units and rupees.
2. The cost of direct manufacturing labor is captured through the extraction cost as detailed above. Based on the data given, prepare a direct manufacturing labor budget for 2013.
3. Calculate the manufacturing cost per unit for each product.
4. Assuming average selling prices as in previous question, what is the expected average gross margin per unit for each product?
5. Consider Pearlpet's choice of a cost allocation base for manufacturing overhead. Can you suggest alternative cost allocation bases?

Solution

Direct materials usage, unit costs and gross margins

1. Direct Materials Usage Budget

	12-ounce Units	4-gallon Units
Physical Units Budget		
To be used in production:		
12-ounce units	22,50,000	
4-gallon units		6,50,000
Cost Budget		
Available from beginning inventory:		
12-ounce units[a]	Rs 1,50,000	
4-gallon units		
To be used from purchases of this period:		
12-ounce: Re 0.60 × (22,50,000 − 2,50,000)	12,00,000	
4-gallon: Rs 3 × (6,50,000 − 0)		Rs 19,50,000
Direct materials to be used	Rs 13,50,000	Rs 19,50,000

[a]2,50,000 × Re 0.60 = Rs 1,50,000

2. Direct manufacturing labour budget

	12-ounce Bottles	4-gallon Units
1. Output units produced	22,50,000	4,50,000
2. Number of ounces	2,70,00,000[a]	33,28,00,000[b]
3. Equivalent 8-ounce units (line 2 × 8)	33,75,000	4,16,00,000
4. Direct labor cost per 8 ounces	Re 0.10	Re 0.10
5. Total direct labor cost (line 3 × line 4)	3,37,500	41,60,000

[a]22,50,000 × 12 ounces per unit = 2,70,00,000

[b]6,50,000 × 128 ounces per gallon × 4 gallons per unit = 33,28,00,000

Total direct labor cost is:

12-ounce bottles	Rs 3,37,500
4-gallon units	41,60,000
	44,97,500

3. Manufacturing cost per unit

	12-ounce bottle Cost per Unit of Input	Inputs	Total	4-gallon container Cost per Unit of Input	Inputs	Total
Direct materials						
12-ounce bottles	Rs 0.60	1	Rs 0.60			
4-gallon containers				Rs 3	1	Rs 3
Direct labor (per 8 ounce)	Rs 0.10	1.5	0.15	0.10	64	6.40
Manufacturing overhead	Rs 1.5	1	1.50	1.50	1	1.50
Unit manufacturing cost			2.25			10.9

4. Gross margin per unit

	12-ounce Bottles	4-gallon Container
Selling price	Rs 2.50	Rs 15
Unit manufacturing cost	2.25	10.90
Gross margin	Re 0.25	Rs 4.10
Gross margin percentage	10%	27.3%

5. The chosen cost allocation base is units of production, with different products (12-ounce bottles and 4-gallon containers) being given the same weight.

A key issue here is whether there is a cause-and-effect relationship between units produced and manufacturing overhead. Alternative allocation bases include direct material costs, direct manufacturing labor costs, direct manufacturing labor hours, and time on the production line.

6-19 Activity-based budgeting. Big Bazaar (BB) is preparing its activity-based budget for January 2013. Its current concern is with its four activities (which are also indirect-cost categories in its product profitability reporting system):

1. Ordering – covers purchasing activities. The cost driver is number of purchase orders.
2. Delivery – covers the physical delivery and receipt of merchandise. The cost driver is number of deliveries.
3. Shelf-stocking – covers the stocking of merchandise on store shelves and the ongoing restocking before sale. The cost drivers is hours of stocking time.
4. Customer support – covers assistance provided to customers, including checkout and bagging. The cost driver is number of items sold.

Assume BB has only three product types: soft drinks, fresh produce, and packaged food. The budgeted usage of each cost driver in these three product types and the January 2013 budgeted cost-driver rates are:

	Cost-Driver Rates		January 2013 Budgeted Amount of Driver Used		
Activity and Driver	2012 Actual Rate	January 2013 Budgeted Rate	Soft Drinks	Fresh Drinks	Packaged Food
Ordering (per purchase order)	Rs 10,000	Rs 9,000	14	24	14
Delivery (per delivery)	8,000	8,200	12	62	19
Shelf-stocking (per hour)	2,000	2,100	16	172	94
Customer support (per item sold)	20	18	4,600	34,200	10,750

Required

1. What is the total budgeted cost for each activity in January 2013.
2. What advantages might BB gain by using an activity-based budgeting approach over, say, an approach that allocates the cost of these activities to products as a percentage of the cost of goods sold?

Solution

1. Calculation of total budgeted cost for each activity

Activity	Cost Hierarchy	Soft Drinks	Fresh Produce	Packaged Food	Total
Ordering Rs 9,000 × 14; 24; 14	Batch-level	Rs 1,26,000	Rs 2,16,000	Rs 1,26,000	Rs 4,68,000
Delivery Rs 8,200 × 12; 62; 19	Batch-level	98,400	5,08,400	1,55,800	7,62,600
Shelf-stocking Rs 2,100 × 16; 172; 94	Output-unit level	33,600	3,61,200	1,97,400	5,92,200
Customer support Rs 18 × 4,600; 34,200; 10,750	Output-unit level	82,800	6,15,600	1,93,500	8,91,900
Total budgeted costs		3,40,800	17,01,200	6,72,700	27,14,700

2. An ABB approach recognizes how different products require different mixes of support activities. The relative percentage of how each product area uses the cost driver at each activity area is:

Activity	Cost Hierarchy	Soft Drinks	Fresh Produce	Packaged Food	Total
Ordering	Batch-level	26.9	46.2	26.9	100.0%
Delivery	Batch-level	12.9	66.7	20.4	100.0
Shelf-stocking	Output-unit-level	5.7	61.0	33.3	100.0
Customer support	Output-unit-level	9.3	69.0	21.7	100.0

By recognizing these differences, (BB) managers are better able to budget for different unit sales levels and different mixes of individual product-line items sold. Using a single cost driver (such as COGS) assumes homogeneity in the use of indirect costs (support activities) across product lines which does not occur at (BB). Other benefits cited by managers include: (1) better identification of resource needs, (2) clearer linking of costs with staff responsibilities, and (3) identification of budgetary slack.

6-20 Kaizen approach to activity-based budgeting (continuation 6-19). Big Bazaar (BB) has a kaizen (continuous improvement) approach to budgeting monthly activity costs for each month of 2013. February's budgeted cost-driver rate is 0.998 times the budgeted January 2013 rate. March's budgeted cost-driver rate is 0.998 times the budgeted February 2013 rate and so on. Assume that March 2013 has the same budgeted amount of cost-driver usage as January 2013.

Required

1. What is the total budgeted cost for each activity in March 2013?
2. What are the benefits of BB adopting a kaizen budgeting approach? What are the limitations?

Solution

1. March 2013 rates

Activity	Cost Hierarchy	January	February	March
Ordering	Batch-level	Rs 9,000	Rs 8,982	Rs 8,964
Delivery	Batch-level	8,200	8,183.6	8,167
Shelf-stocking	Output-unit-level	2,100	2,095.8	2,092
Customer support	Output-unit-level	18	17.964	1,792

These March 2013 rates can be used to compute the total budgeted cost for each activity area:

Activity	Cost Hierarchy	Soft Drinks	Fresh Produce	Packaged Food	Total
Ordering Rs 8,964 × 14; 24; 14	Batch-level	Rs 1,25,496	Rs 2,15,136	Rs 1,25,496	Rs 4,66,128
Delivery Rs 8,167 × 12; 62; 19	Batch-level	98,004	5,06,354	1,55,173	7,59,531
Shelf-stocking Rs 2,092 × 16; 172; 94	Output-unit-level	33,472	3,59,824	1,96,648	5,89,944
Customer support Rs 17.92 × 4,600; 34,200; 10,750	Output-unit-level	82,432	6,12,864	1,92,640	8,87,936
		3,39,404	16,94,178	6,69,957	27,03,539

2. A kaizen budgeting approach signals management's commitment to systematic cost reduction. Compare the budgeted costs from previous question and this question.

	Ordering	Delivery	Shelf-Stocking	Customer Support
Previous Question	Rs 4,68,000	Rs 7,62,600	Rs 5,92,200	Rs 8,91,900
This Question	4,66,128	7,59,531	5,89,944	8,87,936

The kaizen budget number will show unfavorable variances for managers whose activities do not meet the required monthly cost reductions. This likely will put more pressure on managers to creatively seek out cost reductions by working "better" within BB or by having "better" interactions with suppliers or customers.

One limitation of kaizen budgeting, as illustrated in this question, is that it assumes small incremental improvements each month. It is possible that some cost improvements arise from large discontinuous changes in operating processes, supplier networks, or customer interactions. Companies need to highlight the importance of seeking these large discontinuous improvements as well as the small incremental improvements.

6-21 Responsibility and controllability. Consider each of the following independent situations.

1. A purchasing agent forgot to order a part. A rush order had to be placed for the part, resulting in extra costs.
2. A supplier has increased prices of the materials ordered by a purchasing agent, resulting in higher costs of the materials purchased.
3. A higher-than-budgeted quantity of direct materials was used for the output. The supervisor of the production department correctly pointed out that it was due to the substandard quality of materials purchased by the purchasing department.
4. A higher-than-budgeted quantity of direct materials was used for the output. The cause was traced to abnormal spoilage resulting from a faulty machine setting by the machine operator.
5. A higher-than-budgeted quantity of direct materials was used for the output. This happened because of the spoilage occurring from the machine breakdown. The machine was to undergo regular maintenance last month. However, maintenance was not performed because the maintenance department is behind schedule due to heavy labor turnover.
6. A newly appointed division manager has high labor costs as a result of the unfavorable terms of a labor contract negotiated by her predecessor. Her predecessor, who was retiring, according to one observer, "gave the store away during labor contract negotiations."
7. A production department operated only at 80% of its capacity during a month. This was done at the instructions of the plant superintendent, who commented that increasing the department output will only build up inventory in the next production department, which is a bottleneck department.

Determine for each situation where (a) responsibility and (b) controllability lie.

Solution

Responsibility and controllability.

1. (a) Purchasing agent
   (b) Purchasing agent
2. (a) Purchasing agent
   (b) Supplier
3. (a) Production department supervisor
   (b) Purchasing agent
4. (a) Production department supervisor
   (b) Production department supervisor
5. (a) Production department supervisor
   (b) Maintenance department supervisor
6. (a) New division manager
   (b) Former division manager
7. (a) *Production department supervisor
   (b) Plant superintendent/Bottleneck department supervisor

*The production department here refers to the one operating below capacity, and not the next, bottleneck, production department.

6-22 Cash flow analysis. (CMA, adapted) HCL Computers Ltd. is a retail distributor for MZB-33 computer hardware and related software and support services. HCL computers prepares annual sales forecasts of which the first six months for 2012 are presented below.

Cash sales account for 25% of HCL Computers total sales, 30% of the total sales are paid by bank credit card and the remaining 45% are on open account (HCL computers own charge accounts). The cash sales and cash from bank credit-card sales are received in the month of the sale. Bank credit-card sales are subject to a 4% discount deducted at the time of the daily deposit. The cash receipts for sales on open account are 70% in the month following the sale and 28% in the second month following the sale. The remaining accounts receivable are estimated to be uncollectible.

HCL Computers month-end inventory requirements for computer hardware units are 30% of the next month's sales. A one-month lead time is required for delivery from the manufacturer. Thus, orders for computer hardware units are placed on the 25th of each month to assure that they will be in the store by the first day of the month needed. The computer hardware units are purchased under terms of n/45 (payment in full with 45 days of invoice), measure from the time the units are delivered to HCL Computer. HCL Computer's purchase price for the computer units is 60% of the selling price.

HCL Computer Ltd. – Sales Forecast First Six Months of 2012

	Hardware Sales			
	Units	**Rupees**	**Software Sales and Support**	**Total Revenues**
January	1,300	Rs 39,00,000	Rs 16,00,000	Rs 55,00,000
February	1,200	36,00,000	14,00,000	50,00,000
March	1,100	33,00,000	15,00,000	48,00,000
April	900	27,00,000	13,00,000	40,00,000

May	1,000	30,00,000	12,50,000	42,50,000
June	1,250	37,50,000	22,50,000	60,00,000
Total	6,750	2,02,50,000	93,00,000	2,95,50,000

Required

1. Calculate the cash that HCL Computers Ltd., can expect to collect during April 2012. Be sure to show all of your calculations.
2. HCL Computer Ltd., is determining how many MZB-33 computer hardware units to order on January 25, 2012.
   a. Determine the projected number of computer hardware units that will be ordered.
   b. Calculate the rupees amount of the order that HCL Computers will place for these computer hardware units.
3. As part of the annual budget process, HCL Computers prepares a cash budget by month for the entire year. Explain why a company such as HCL Computer prepares a cash budget by month for the entire year.

Solution

Cash flow analysis

1. The cash that HCL Computers Ltd. can expect to collect during April 2012 is calculated below.

April cash receipts:	
April cash sales (Rs 40,00,000 × .25)	Rs 10,00,000
April credit card sales (Rs 40,00,000 × .30 3 .96)	11,52,000
Collections on account:	
March (Rs 48,00,000 × .45 3 .70)	15,12,000
February (Rs 50,00,000 × .45 3 .28)	6,30,000
January (uncollectible-not relevant)	0
Total collections	Rs 42,94,000

2. (a) The projected number of the MZB-33 computer hardware units that HCL Computers Ltd. will order on January 25, 2012, is calculated as follows.

MZB-33 Units	
March sales	1,100
Plus: Ending inventory[a]	270
Total needed	1,370
Less: Beginning inventory[b]	330
Projected purchases in units	1,040

[a] 0.30 × 900 unit sales in April

[b] 0.30 × 1,100 unit sales in March

(b) Purchase price =	
Selling price per unit[c]	
× 60%	Rs 1,800
× Projected unit purchases	1,040
Total MZB-33 purchases	Rs 18,72,000

[c] Selling price = Rs 2,02,50,000 ÷ 6750 units, or for March, Rs 33,00,000 ÷ 1,100 units = Rs 3,000 per unit

3. Monthly cash budgets are prepared by companies such as HCL Computers Ltd. in order to plan for their cash needs. This means identifying when both excess cash and cash shortages may occur. A company needs to know when cash shortages will occur so that prior arrangements can be made with lending institutions in order to have cash available for borrowing when the company needs it. At the same time, a company should be aware of when there is excess cash available for investment or for repaying loans.

6-23 Sensitivity analysis, changing budget assumptions, and kaizen approach. Choco Chips produces two brands of chocolate chip cookies: Chippo and Choco. Choco Chips's cookies are produced from two ingredients: chocolate chips and cookie dough. Chippo is 50% chips and 50% dough, whereas Choco is 25% chips and 75% dough.

Package of either brand weigh 1 kg. Choco Chips's master budget projects sales of 5,00,000 packages of each product in 2013. According to the master budget, estimated selling prices are Rs 30 per package for each product. Forecasted 2013 ingredients costs are as follows: 1 kg of chocolate will cost Rs 20, and 1 kg of cookie dough will cost Rs 10. A total of 5,000 direct manufacturing labor-hours – 2,000 hours for Chippo and 3,000 hours for Choco – are budgeted at the hourly rate of Rs 20 per hour. Indirect manufacturing costs are expected to be Rs 16,00,000. The indirect manufacturing costs are allocated equally between Chips and Choco on the basis of packages produced in 2013.

Required

1. Use the preceding information to calculate Choco Chip's budgeted gross margins for 2013.
2. By working with suppliers, Choco Chip was able to reduce the purchase cost of ingredients by 3%. Calculate Choco Chips's revised gross margin for 2013.

3. Assume that in addition to the 3% reduction in the purchase cost of ingredients mentioned in requirement 2, Choco Chips plans a 1% cost reduction in direct manufacturing labor-hours and a 2% cost reduction in the indirect manufacturing costs from the original data. These revisions to the original budget resulted from an analysis of all activities by a cross-functional team as a part of Choco Chips's efforts toward continuous improvement. Compute Choco Chips's revised gross margin for 2013 under these assumptions.

Solution

Computation of budgeted gross margin for 2013:

1.

	Chippo	Choco	Total
Revenues	Rs 1,50,00,000		Rs 1,50,00,000
Chippo, Rs 30 × 5,00,000	–	Rs 1,50,00,000	1,50,00,000
Choco, Rs 30 × 5,00,000	Rs 1,50,00,000	Rs 1,50,00,000	Rs 3,00,00,000
Cost of goods sold Chocolate chips			
(Rs 20 × 2,50,000[a]; Rs 20 × 1,25,000[b])	50,00,000	25,00,000	75,00,000
Cookie dough (Rs 10 × 2,50,000[a]; Rs 10 × 3,75,000[b])	25,00,000	37,50,000	62,50,000
Direct manufacturing labor (Rs 20 × 20,000; Rs 20 × 30,000)	4,00,000	6,00,000	10,00,000
Indirect manufacturing costs (50% × Rs 16,00,000; 50% × Rs 16,00,000)	8,00,000	8,00,000	16,00,000
Cost of goods sold	87,00,000	76,50,000	1,63,50,000
Gross margin	Rs 63,00,000	Rs 73,50,000	Rs 1,36,50,000

[a]Chippo: 5,00,000 × 0.50 = 2,50,000 kgs chocolate chips; 5,00,000 × 0.50 = 2,50,000 kgs cookie dough

[b]Choco: 5,00,000 × 0.25 = 1,25,000 kgs chocolate chips; 5,00,000 × 0.75 = 3,75,000 kgs cookie dough

2. **Computation of revised gross margin for 2013:**

	Chippo	Choco	Total
Revenues	Rs 1,50,00,000		Rs 1,50,00,000
Chippo, Rs 30 × 5,00,000	–	Rs 1,50,00,000	1,50,00,000
Choco, Rs 30 × 5,00,000	Rs 1,50,00,000	Rs 1,50,00,000	Rs 3,00,00,000
Cost of goods sold			
Chocolate chips (Rs 19.40 × 2,50,000; Rs 19.40 × 1,25,000)	48,50,000	24,25,500	72,75,000
Cookie dough (Rs 9.70 × 2,50,000; Rs 9.70 × 3,75,000)	24,25,000	36,37,500	60,62,500
Direct manufacturing labor (Rs 20 × 20,000; Rs 20 × 30,000)	4,00,000	6,00,000	10,00,000
Indirect manufacturing costs (50% × Rs 16,00,000; 50% × Rs 16,00,000)	8,00,000	8,00,000	16,00,000
	84,75,000	74,62,500	1,59,37,500
Gross margin	65,25,000	75,37,500	1,40,62,500

3. **Computation of revised gross margin**

	Chippo	Choco	Total
Revenues	Rs 1,50,00,000		Rs 1,50,00,000
Chippo, Rs 30 × 5,00,000		– Rs 1,50,00,000	1,50,00,000
Choco, Rs 30 × 5,00,000	Rs 1,50,00,000	Rs 1,50,00,000	Rs 3,00,00,000
Cost of goods sold			
Chocolate chips (Rs 19.40 × 2,50,000; Rs 19.40 × 1,25,000)	48,50,000	24,25,500	72,75,000
Cookie dough (Rs 9.70 × 2,50,000; Rs 9.70 × 3,75,000)	24,25,000	36,37,500	60,62,500
Direct manufacturing labor (Rs 20 × 19,800; Rs 20 × 29,700)	3,96,000	5,94,000	9,90,000
Indirect manufacturing costs (50% × Rs 15,68,000; 50% × Rs 15,68,000)	7,84,000	7,84,000	15,68,000
	84,55,000	74,40,500	1,58,95,500
Gross margin	Rs 65,45,000	Rs 75,59,500	Rs 1,41,04,500

6-24 Revenue and production budgets. (CPA, adapted) The Lakshmi Corporation manufactures and sells two products, Royal Bucket and Royal Drum. In July 2012, Lakshmi's Budget Department gathered the following data to prepare budgets for 2013:

2013-14 Projected Sales

Product	Units	Price
Royal Bucket	60,000	Rs 165
Royal Drum	40,000	Rs 250

2013-14 Inventories (in Units)

	Expected	Target
Product	**April 1, 2013**	**March 31, 2014**
Royal Bucket	20,000	25,000
Royal Drum	8,000	9,000

The following direct materials are used in the two products:

Amount Used per Unit

Direct Materials	Unit	Royal Bucket	Royal Drum
A	kg	4	5
B	kg	2	3
C	kg	0	1

Projected data for 2013-14 with respect to direct materials are as follows:

Direct Materials	Anticipated Purchase Price	Expected Inventories April 1, 2013	Target Inventories March 31, 2014
A	Rs 12	32,000 kg	36,000 kg
B	5	29,000 kg	32,000 kg
C	3	6,000 units	7,000 units

Projected direct manufacturing labor requirements and rates for 2013-14 are as follows:

Product	Hours per Unit	Rate per Hour
Royal Bucket	2	Rs 12
Royal Drum	3	Rs 16

Manufacturing overhead is allocated at the rate of Rs 20 per direct manufacturing labor hour.

Based on the preceding projections and budget requirements for Royal Bucket and Royal Drum, prepare the following budgets for 2013-14:

Required

1. Revenues budget (in rupees)
2. Production budget (in units)
3. Direct materials purchases budget (in quantities)
4. Direct materials purchases budget (in rupees)
5. Direct manufacturing labor budget (in rupees)
6. Budgeted finished goods inventory at March 31, 2013-14 (in rupees)

Solution

The key to its solution is to compute the correct *quantities* of finished goods and direct materials. Use the following general formula:

$$\begin{pmatrix}\text{Budgeted}\\ \text{production}\\ \text{or pruchases}\end{pmatrix} = \begin{pmatrix}\text{Target}\\ \text{ending}\\ \text{inventory}\end{pmatrix} + \begin{pmatrix}\text{Budgeted}\\ \text{sales or}\\ \text{materials used}\end{pmatrix} - \begin{pmatrix}\text{Beginning}\\ \text{inventory}\end{pmatrix}$$

1.

Lakshmi Corporation
Revenue Budget for 2013-14

	Units	Price	Total
Royal bucket	60,000	Rs 165	Rs 99,00,000
Royal drum	40,000	250	1,00,00,000
Budgeted revenues			Rs 1,99,00,000

2. Production Budget (in units) for 2013-14

	Royal Bucket	Royal Drum
Budgeted sales in units	60,000	40,000
Add target finished goods inventories, March 31, 2014	25,000	9,000
Total requirements	85,000	49,000
Deduct finished goods inventories, April 1, 2013	20,000	8,000
Units to be produced	65,000	41,000

3. Direct Materials Purchases Budget (in quantities) for 2013-14

	Direct Materials A	B	C
Direct materials to be used in production			
• Royal Bucket (budgeted production of 65,000 units times 4 kg of A, 2 kg of B)	2,60,000	1,30,000	–
• Royal Drum (budgeted production of 41,000 units times 5 kg of A, 3 kg of B, 1 kg of C)	2,05,000	1,23,000	41,000
Total	4,65,000	2,53,000	41,000
Add target ending inventories, March 31, 2014	36,000	32,000	7,000
Total requirements in units	5,01,000	2,85,000	48,000
Deduct beginning inventories, April 1, 2013	32,000	29,000	6,000
Direct materials to be purchased (units)	4,69,000	2,56,000	42,000

4. Direct Materials Purchases Budget (in rupees) for 2013-14

	Budgeted Purchases (kgs)	Expected Purchases Price per kg	Total
Direct material A	4,69,000	Rs 12	Rs 56,28,000
Direct material B	2,56,000	5	12,80,000
Direct material C	42,000	3	1,26,000
Budgeted purchases			Rs 70,34,000

5. Direct Manufacturing Labor Budget (in rupees) for 2013-14

	Budgeted Production (Units)	Direct Manufacturing Labor-Hours per Unit	Total Hours	Rate perHour	Total
Royal Bucket	65,000	2	1,30,000	Rs 12	Rs 15,60,000
Royal Drum	41,000	3	1,23,000	16	19,68,000
Total					Rs 35,28,000

6. **Budgeted Finished Goods Inventory At March 31, 2014**

Royal Bucket:			
Direct materials costs:			
A, 4 kg × Rs 12	Rs 48		
B, 2 kg × Rs 5	10	Rs 58	
Direct manufacturing labor costs, 2 hours × Rs 12		24	
Manufacturing overhead costs at Rs 20 per direct manufacturing labor-hour (2 hours × Rs 20)		40	
Budgeted manufacturing costs per unit		Rs 122	
Finished goods inventory (Rs 122 × 25,000 units)		Rs 30,50,000	
Royal Drum:			
Direct materials costs:			
A, 5 kg × Rs 12	Rs 60		
B, 3 kg × Rs 5	15		
C, 1 kg × Rs 3	3	Rs 78	
Direct manufacturing labor costs 3 hours ? Rs 16		48	
Manufacturing overhead costs at Rs 20 per direct manufacturing labor-hour (3 hours × Rs 20)		60	
Budgeted manufacturing costs per unit		Rs 186	
Finished goods inventory of (Rs 186 × 9,000 units)		16,74,000	
Budgeted finished goods inventory, March 31, 2014		Rs 47,24,000	

6-25 Budgeted income statement. (CMA, adapted) Polycom Company is a manufacturer of video-conferencing products. Regular units are manufactured to meet marketing projections, and specialized units are made after an order is received. Maintaining the video-conferencing equipment is an important area of customer satisfaction. With the recent downturn in the computer industry, the video-conferencing equipment segment has suffered, leading to a decline in Polycom's financial performance. The following income statement shows results for 2012.

Polycom Company
Income Statement
For the Year Ended December 31, 2012 (in thousands)

Revenues		
Equipment	Rs 6,00,000	
Maintenance contracts	1,80,000	
Total revenues		Rs 7,80,000
Cost of goods sold		4,60,000
Gross margin		3,20,000
Operating costs		
Marketing	60,000	
Distribution	15,000	
Customer maintenance	1,00,000	
Administration	90,000	
Total operating costs		2,65,000
Operating income		55,000

Polycom's management team is in the process of preparing the 2013 budget and is studying the following information:

1. Selling prices of equipment are expected to increase by 10% as the economic recovery begins. The selling price of each maintenance contract is unchanged from 2012.
2. Equipment sales in unit are expected to increase by 6%, with a corresponding 6% growth in units of maintenance contracts.
3. Cost of each units sold is expected to increase by 3% to pay for the necessary technology and quality improvements.
4. Marketing costs are expected to increase by Rs 2,50,00,000, but administration costs are expected to remain at 2012 levels.
5. Distribution costs vary in proportion to the number of units of equipment sold.
6. Two maintenance technicians are to be added at a total cost of Rs 1,30,00,000, which covers wages and related travel costs. The objective is to improve customer service and shorten response time.
7. There is no beginning or ending inventory of equipment.

Prepare a budgeted income statement for 2013.

Solution

Polycom Company
Budgeted Income Statement for 2013
(in thousands)

Revenues		
Equipment (Rs 6,00,000 × 1.06 × 1.10)	Rs 6,99,600	
Maintenance contracts (Rs 1,80,000 × 1.06)	1,90,800	
Total revenues		Rs 8,90,400
Cost of goods sold (Rs 4,60,000 × 1.03 × 1.06)		5,02,228
Gross margin		3,88,172
Operating costs:		
Marketing costs (Rs 60,000 + Rs 25,000)	85,000	
Distribution costs (Rs 15,000 × 1.06)	15,900	
Customer maintenance costs (Rs 1,00,000 + Rs 13,000)	1,13,000	
Administrative costs	90,000	
Total operating costs		3,03,900
Operating income		Rs 84,272

6-26 Cash budgeting. Retail outlets purchase snowboards from J. K. Wood Company throughout the year. However, in anticipation of late summer and early fall purchase, outlets ramp up inventories from May through August. Outlets are billed when boards are ordered. Invoices are payable within 60 days. From past experience, J. K's accountant projects 20% of invoices are paid in the month invoiced, 50% are paid in the following month, and 30% of invoices are paid two months after the month of invoice. The average selling price per snowboard is Rs 1,000.

To meet demand, J. K. increases production from April through July, because the snowboards are produced a month prior to their projected sale. Direct materials are purchased in the month of production and paid for during the following month (terms are payment in full within 30 days of the invoice data). During this period there is no production for inventory, and no materials are purchased for inventory.

Direct manufacturing labor and manufacturing overhead are paid monthly. It may be noted that the firm has annual fixed manufacturing overhead costs of Rs 1,32,000. Variable manufacturing overhead is incurred at the rate of Rs 14 per direct manufacturing labor-hour. Variable marketing costs are driven by the number of sales visits. However, there are no sales visits during the months studied. J. K. also incurs fixed manufacturing overhead costs of 11,000 per month and fixed nonmanufacturing overhead costs of Rs 5,000 per month.

Projected Sales

May	80 units	August	100 units
June	120 units	September	60 units
July	200 units	October	40 units

Direct Materials and Direct Manufacturing Labor Utilization and Cost

	Units per Board	Price per Unit	Unit
Wood	5	Rs 60	Board feet
Fiberglass	6	10	Yard
Direct manufacturing labor	5	25	Hour

On September 1, 2011, J. K. had a cash crunch and borrowed Rs 1,00,000 on a 10% one-year note with interest payable monthly. The note is due October 1, 2012.

Required

1. Prepared a cash budget for the months of July through September, 2012. Show supporting schedules for the calculation of receivables and payables. Assume the beginning cash balance for July 1, 2012, is Rs 10,000.
2. Will J. K. be in a position to pay off Rs 1,00,000 one-year note on October 1, 2012? If not, what actions would you recommend to its management?

Solution

Cash Budget

1. Projected Sales

	May	June	July	August	September	October
Sales in Units	80	120	200	100	60	40
Revenues	Rs 80,000	Rs 1,20,000	Rs 2,00,000	Rs 1,00,000	Rs 60,000	

Collections of Receivables

	May	June	July	August	September	October
From sales in:						
May (30% × Rs 80,000)			Rs 24,000			
June (50%; 30% × Rs 1,20,000)			60,000	Rs 36,000		
July (20%; 50%; 30% × Rs 2,00,000)			40,000	1,00,000	Rs 60,000	
August (20%; 50% × Rs 1,00,000)				20,000	50,000	
September (20% × Rs 60,000)					12,000	
Total			Rs 1,24,000	Rs 1,56,000	1,22,000	

Calculation of Payables

	May	June	July	August	September	October
Material and Labor Use, Units						
Budgeted production		200	100	60	40	
Direct materials						
Wood (board feet)		1,000	500	300	200	
Fiberglass (yards)		1,200	600	360	240	
Direct manufacturing labor (hours)		1,000	500	300	200	
Disbursement of Payments						
Direct materials						
Wood (1,000; 500; 300 × Rs 60)			Rs 60,000	Rs 30,000	Rs 18,000	
Fiberglass (1,200; 600; 360 × Rs 10)				12,000	6,000	3,600
Direct manufacturing labor (500; 300; 200 × Rs 25)			12,500	7,500	5,000	
Interest payment (10% × Rs 1,00,000 ÷ 12)			1,000	1,000	1,000	
Variable OHD Calculation						
Variable OHD rate			Rs 14	Rs 14	Rs 14	
OHD driver			500	300	200	
Variable OHD expense			Rs 7,000	Rs 4,200	Rs 2,800	

Cash Budget for the months of July, August, September 2011

	July	August	September
Beginning cash balance	Rs 10,000	Rs 25,500	Rs 79,000
Add receipts:			
Collection of receivables	1,24,000	1,56,000	1,22,000
Total cash available	1,34,000	1,81,500	2,01,000
Deduct disbursements:			
Material purchases	72,000	36,000	21,600
Direct manufacturing labor	12,500	7,500	5,000
Variable costs	7,000	4,200	2,800
Fixed costs	16,000	16,000	16,000
Interest payments	1,000	1,000	1,000
Total disbursements	1,08,500	1,02,500	46,400
Ending cash balance	25,500	79,000	1,54,600

2. Yes, J. K. has a budgeted cash balance of Rs 1,54,600 on 10/1/2011 and so will be in a position to pay off the Rs 1,00,000 1-year note on October 1, 2012.

6-27 Cash budgeting. On December 1, 2012, Sadar Wholesale Co. is attempting to project cash receipts and disbursements through January 31, 2013. On this later date, a note will be payable in the amount of Rs 10 lakh. This amount was borrowed in September to carry the company through the seasonal peak in November and December.

Selected general ledger balances on December 1 are

Cash	Rs 1,00,000	
Accounts receivable	28,00,000	
Allowance for bad debts		1,58,000
Inventory	8,75,000	
Accounts payable		9,20,000

Sales terms call for a 2% discount if payment is made within the first 10 days of the month after purchase, with the balance due by the end of the month after purchase. Experience has shown that 70% of the billings will be collected within the discount period, 20% by the end of the month after purchase, and 8% in the following month. The remaining 2% will be uncollectible. There are no cash sales.

The average selling price of the company's products is Rs 100 per unit. Actual and projected sales are

October actual	Rs 18 lakh
November actual	25 lakh
December estimated	30 lakh
January estimated	15 lakh
February estimated	12 lakh
Total estimated for year ended June 30, 2013	150 lakh

All purchases are payable within 15 days. Thus, approximately 50% of the purchases in a month are due and payable in the next month. The average unit purchase cost is Rs 70. Target ending inventories are 5,000 units plus 25% of the next month's unit sales.

Total budgeted marketing, distribution, and customer-service costs for the year are Rs 40 lakh. Of this amount, Rs 15 lakh are considered fixed (and includes depreciation of Rs 3 lakh). The remainder vary with sales. Both fixed and variable marketing, distribution, and customer-service costs are paid as incurred.

Required Prepare a cash budget for December and January. Supply supporting schedules for collections of receivables; payments for merchandise; and marketing, distribution, and customer-service costs.

Solution

Cash Budget

Sadar Wholesale Co.
Statement of Budgeted Cash Receipts and Disbursements
For the Months of December 2012 and January 2013

	December, 2012	January, 2013
Cash balance, beginning	Rs 1,00,000	Rs 20,250
Add receipts:		
Collections of receivables (Schedule 1)	23,59,000	28,58,000
(a) Total cash available for needs	24,59,000	28,78,250
Deduct disbursements:		
For merchandise purchases (Schedule 2)	18,38,750	14,17,500
For variable costs (Schedule 3)	5,00,000	2,50,000
For fixed costs (Schedule 3)	1,00,000	1,00,000
(b) Total disbursements	24,38,750	17,67,500
Cash balance, end of month (a – b)	Rs 20,250	Rs 11,10,750

Enough cash (Rs 11,10,750) should be available for repayment of the note on January 31, 2013.

Schedule 1: Collections of Receivables

Collections in	October	November	December	Total
December	Rs 1,44,000[a]	Rs 5,00,000[b] + 17,15,000[c]		Rs 23,59,000
January		2,00,000[d]	Rs 6,00,000[e] + 20,58,000[f]	28,58,000

[a]0.08 × Rs 18,00,000 [b]0.20 × Rs 25,00,000 [c]0.70 × Rs 25,00,000 × .98
[d]0.08 × Rs 25,00,000 [e]0.20 × Rs 30,00,000 [f]0.70 × Rs 30,00,000 × .98

Schedule 2: Payments for Merchandise

	December	January
Target ending inventory (in units)	8,750[a]	8,000[c]
Add units sold (sales ¸ Rs 100)	30,000	15,000
Total requirements	38,750	23,000
Deduct beginning inventory (in units)	12,500[b]	8,750
Purchases (in units)	26,250	14,250
Purchases in rupees (units ´ Rs 70)	Rs 18,37,500	Rs 9,97,500

	December	January
Cash disbursements:		
For previous month's purchases at 50%	Rs 9,20,000	Rs 9,18,750
For current month's purchases at 50%	9,18,750	4,98,750
	Rs 18,38,750	Rs 14,17,500

[a]5,000 units + 0.25 (Rs 15,00,000 ÷ Rs 100)
[b]Rs 8,75,000 ÷ Rs 70
[c]5,000 units + 0.25 (Rs 12,00,000 ÷ Rs 100)
[d]Accounts payable at beginning

Schedule 3: Marketing, Distribution, and Customer-Service Costs

Total annual fixed costs, Rs 15,00,000, minus Rs 3,00,000 depreciation	Rs 12,00,000
Monthly fixed cost requiring cash outlay	Rs 1,00,000
Variable cost ratio to sales	$= \dfrac{\text{Rs } 40{,}00{,}000 - \text{Rs } 15{,}00{,}000}{\text{Rs } 2{,}50{,}000} = 1/6$
December variable costs: 1/6 ´ Rs 30,00,000 sales	= Rs 5,00,000
January variable costs: 1/6 ´ Rs 15,00,000 sales	= Rs 2,50,000

Exercises

6-28 Direct materials budget. Shaw Walace Company produces liquor. The company expects to produce 15,00,000 two-liter bottles of Royal Challenge in 2013. Shaw Walace purchases empty glass bottles from an outside vendor. Its target ending inventory of such bottles is 50,000; its beginning inventory is 20,000. For simplicity, ignore breakage. Compute the number of bottles to be purchased in 2013.

6-29 Budgeting material purchases. The Sunrise Company has prepared a sales budget of 4,20,000 finished units for a three-month period. The company has an inventory of 2,20,000 units of finished goods on hand at December 31 and has a target finished goods inventory of 2,40,000 units at the end of the succeeding quarter.

It takes 3 gallons of direct materials to make one unit of finished product. The company has an inventory of 9,00,000 gallons of direct materials at December 31 and has a target ending inventory of 11,00,000 gallons at the end of the succeeding quarter. How many gallons of direct materials should be purchased during the three months ending March 31?

6-30 Revenue, production, and purchases budgets. The Honda Co. in India has a division that manufactures two-wheel motorcycles. Its budgeted sales for Model G in 2013 are 80,00,000 units. Honda's target ending inventory is 10,00,000 units, and its beginning inventory is 12,00,000 units. The company's budgeted selling price to its distributors and dealers is Rs 40,000 per motorcycle.

Honda buys all its wheels from an outside supplier. No defective wheels are accepted. Honda's needs for extra wheels for replacement parts are ordered by a separate division of the company. The company's target ending inventory is 3,00,000 wheels, and its beginning inventory is 2,00,000 wheels. The budgeted purchase price is Rs 1,600 per wheel.

Required

1. Compute the budgeted revenues in rupees.
2. Compute the number of motorcycles to be produced.
3. Compute the budgeted purchases of wheels in units and in rupees.

6-31 Budgets for production and direct manufacturing labor. (CMA, adapted) Archies Company makes and sells artistic frames for pictures of weddings, graduations, and other special events. Rahul, the controller, is responsible for preparing Archies master budget and has accumulated the following information for 2012.

Particulars	January	February	March	April	May
Estimated sales in units	1,00,000	1,20,000	80,000	90,000	90,000
Selling price	Rs 540	Rs 515	Rs 515	Rs 515	Rs 515
Direct manufacturing labor-hours per unit	2	2	1.5	1.5	1.5
Wage per direct manufacturing labor-hour	Rs 10	Rs 10	Rs 10	Rs 11	Rs 11

Besides wages, direct manufacturing labor-related costs include pension contributions of Re 0.50 per hour, worker's compensation insurance of Re 0.15 per hour, employee medical insurance of Rs 0.40 per hour, and social security taxes. Assume that as of January 1, 2012, the social security tax rates are 7.5% for employers and 7.5% for employees. The cost of employee benefits paid by Archies on its employees is treated as a direct manufacturing labor cost.

Archies has a labor contract that calls for a wage increase to Rs 11 per hour on April 1, 2012. New labor-saving machinery has been installed and will be fully operational by March 1, 2012. Archies expects to have 1,60,000 frames on hand at December 31, 2011, and it has a policy of carrying an end-of-month inventory of 100% of the following month's sales plus 50% of the second following month's sales.

Prepare a production budget and a direct manufacturing labor budget for Archies Company by month and for the first quarter of 2012. Both budgets may be combined in one schedule. The direct manufacturing labor budget should include labor-hours and show the details for each labor cost category.

6-32 Budget schedules for a manufacturer. Delite Furniture is an elite desk manufacturer. It makes two products:

- Executive desks – 3 × 5 oak desks
- Chairman desks – 6 × 4 red oak desks

The budgeted direct-cost inputs for each product in 2012 are

	Executive Line	Chairman Line
Oak top	16 square feet	0
Red oak top	0	25 square feet
Oak legs	4	0
Red oak legs	0	4
Direct manufacturing labor	3 hours	5 hours

Unit data pertaining to the direct materials for March 2012 are

Actual-beginning Direct Materials Inventory (3/1/2012)

	Executive Line	Chairman Line
Oak top (square feet)	320	0
Red oak top (square feet)	0	150
Oak legs	100	0
Red oak legs	0	40

Target Ending Direct Materials Inventory (3/31/2012)

	Executive Line	Chairman Line
Oak top (square feet)	192	0
Red oak top (square feet)	0	200
Oak legs	80	0
Red oak legs	0	44

Unit cost data for direct-cost inputs pertaining to February 2012 and March 2012 are

	February (actual)	March 2005 (budgeted)
Oak top (per square feet)	Rs 18	Rs 20
Red oak top (per square feet)	23	25
Oak legs (per leg)	11	12
Red oak legs (per leg)	17	18
Manufacturing labor cost per hour	30	30

Manufacturing overhead (both variable and fixed) is allocated to each desk on the basis of budgeted direct manufacturing labor-hours per desk. The budgeted variable manufacturing overhead rate for March 2012 is Rs 35 per direct manufacturing labor-hour. The budgeted fixed manufacturing overhead for March 2012 is Rs 42,500. Both variable and fixed manufacturing overhead cost are allocated to each unit of finished goods.

Data relating to finished goods inventory for March 2012 are

	Executive Line	Chairman Line
Beginning inventory in units	20	5
Beginning inventory in rupees (cost)	Rs 10,480	Rs 4,850
Target ending inventory in units	30	15

Budgeted sales for March 2012 are 740 units of the executive line and 390 units of the chairman line. The budgeted selling prices per unit in March 2012 are Rs 1,020 for the executive line desk and Rs 1,600 for the chairman line desk. Assume the following in your answer:

- Work-in-process inventories are negligible and ignored.
- Direct materials inventory and finished goods inventory are costed using the first-in-first-out (FIFO) method.
- Unit costs of direct materials purchased and finished goods are constant in March 2006.

Required

1. Prepare the following budgets for March 2012:
   a. Revenues budget
   b. Production budget in units
   c. Direct materials usage budget and direct materials purchases budget
   d. Direct manufacturing labor budget
   e. Manufacturing overhead budget
   f. Ending inventory budget
   g. Cost of goods sold budget
2. Suppose Delite Furniture decides to incorporate continuous improvement into its budgeting process. Describe two areas where Delite could incorporate continuous improvement into the budget schedules in requirement 1.

6-33 Responsibility of purchasing agent. (Adapted from a description by R. Villers) Aashish Jain is the purchasing agent for the Birla Manufacturing Company, Sanjay Gupta is head of the Production Planning and Control Department. Every six months, Sanjay gives Aashish a general purchasing program. Aashish gets specifications from the Engineering Department. He then selects suppliers and negotiates prices. When he took this job, Aashish was informed very clearly that he bore responsibility for meeting the general purchasing program once he accepted it from Sanjay.

During week 24, Aashish is advised that Part No. 1234 – a critical part – Would be needed for assembly on Tuesday morning of week 32. He found that the regular supplier could not deliver. He called everywhere and finally found a supplier in Bombay who accepted the commitment.

He followed up by e-mail. Yes, the supplier assured him the part would be ready. The matter was so important that on Thursday of week 31, Aashish checked by phone. Yes, the shipment had left in time. Aashish was reassured and did not check further. But on Tuesday of week 32, the part had not arrived. Inquiry revealed that the shipment had been misdirected by the railroad and was still in Bombay.

What department should bear the costs of time lost in the plant due to the delayed shipment? Why? As purchasing agent, do you think it fair that such costs be charged to your department?

Required

6-34 Activity-based budgeting. Anderson Manufacturing, Inc, uses activity-based costing and activity-based budgeting. Budgetary information for selected activities for 2012 is provided below.

Activity	Cost Driver	Items Cost Pool (fixed cost + cost per unit of cost driver)
Machining	Machine hours	Indirect materials Rs 0 + Rs 10 per hour
		Indirect labor Rs 20,000 + Rs 15 per hour
		Utilities Rs 0 + Rs 5 per hour
Setups and quality assurance	Production runs	Indirect materials Rs 0 + Rs 1,000 per run
		Indirect labor Rs 0 + Rs 1,200 per run
		Inspection Rs 80,000 + Rs 2,000 per run
Procurement	Purchase orders	Indirect materials Rs 0 + Rs 4 per order
		Indirect labor Rs 45,000 + Rs 0 per order
Design Material handling	Design hours	Engineering Rs 75,000 + Rs 50 per hour
	Square feet of materials handled	Indirect materials Rs 0 + Rs 2 per square feet
		Indirect labor Rs 30,000 + Rs 0 per square feet

Additional budget for 2012

Activity	Cost Driver Budgeted Volume
a. Machining	10,000 machine hours
b. Setups and quality assurance	40 production runs
c. Procurement	15,000 purchase orders
d. Design	100 engineering hours
e. Material handling	1,00,000 square feet

Calculate the budgeted amount for each activity in 2012

6-35 Comprehensive operating budget, budgeted balance sheet. J. K. Wood Company is promoted by an entrepreneur. It manufactures and sells snowboards. In the summer of 2011 its accountant gathered the following data to prepare budgets for 2012:

Materials and labor requirements

Direct materials	
Wood	5 board feet per snowboard
Fiberglass	6 yards per snowboard
Direct manufacturing labor	5 hours per snowboard

J.K.'s CEO expects to sell 1,000 snowboards during 2012 at an estimated retail price of Rs 1,000 per board. Further, he expects 2012 beginning inventory of 100 boards and would like to end 2012 with 200 snowboards in stock.

Direct materials inventories

	Beginning Inventory 1/1/2012	Ending Inventory 12/31/2012
Wood	2,000	1,500
Fiberglass	1,000	2,000

Variable manufacturing overhead is allocated at the rate of Rs 14 per direct manufacturing labor-hour. There are also Rs 1,32,000 in fixed manufacturing overhead costs budgeted for 2012. J. K. combines both variable and fixed manufacturing overhead into a single rate based on direct manufacturing labor-hours. Variable marketing costs are allocated at the rate of Rs 2,500 per sales visit. The marketing plan calls for 30 sales visits during 2012. Finally, there are Rs 60,000 in fixed nonmanufacturing costs budgeted for 2012.

Other data includes:

	2011 Unit Price	2012 Unit Price
Wood	Rs 56 per b.f.	60 per b.f.
Fiberglass	9.60 per yard	10 per yard
Direct manufacturing labor	24.00 per hour	25.00 per hour

The inventoriable unit cost for ending finished goods inventory on December 31, 2011, is Rs 647.60. Assume J. K. uses a FIFO inventory method for both direct materials and finished goods. Ignore work in process in your calculations.

Required

1. Prepare the 2012 revenues budget (in Rupees).
2. Prepare the 2012 production budget (in units).
3. Prepare the direct materials usage and purchases budgets.
4. Prepare a direct manufacturing labor budget.
5. Prepare a manufacturing overhead budget.
6. What is the budgeted manufacturing overhead rate?
7. What is the budgeted manufacturing overhead cost per output unit?
8. Calculate the cost of a snowboard manufactured in 2012.
9. Prepare an ending inventory budget for both direct materials and finished goods.
10. Prepare a cost of goods sold budget.
11. Prepare the budgeted income statement for J. K. for 2012.

6-36 Comprehensive budget; fill in schedules. The following information is for Retail Stationery Store:

1. **Balance sheet information as of December 31, 2011**

Current assets	
Cash	Rs 12,000
Accounts receivable	10,000
Inventory	63,600
Equipment – net	1,00,000
Liabilities as of December 31, 2011	None

2. **Recent and anticipated sales:**

December	Rs 40,000
January	48,000
February	60,000
March	80,000
April	36,000

3. Credit sales: Sales are 75% cash and 25% on credit. Assume that credit accounts are all collected within 30 days from sale. The accounts receivable on December 31 are the result of the credit sales for December (25% of Rs 40,000).
4. Gross margin averages 30% of revenues. Store treats cash discounts on purchases in the income statement as "other income."
5. Operating costs: Salaries and wages average 15% of monthly revenues; rent, 5%; other operating costs, excluding depreciation, 4%. Assume that these costs are disbursed each month. Depreciation is Rs 1,000 per month.
6. Purchases: Store keeps a minimum inventory of Rs 30,000. The policy is to purchase each month additional inventory in the amount necessary to provide for the following month's sales. Terms on purchases are 2/10, net/30. (payments on purchases are to be made in 30 days; a 2% discount is available if the payment is made within 10 days after purchase.) Assume that payments are made in the month of purchase and that all discounts are taken.
7. Light fixtures: in January, Rs 600 is spent for light fixtures, and in February, Rs 400 is to be expended for this purpose. These amounts are to be capitalized.

Assume that a minimum cash balance of Rs 8,000 must be maintained. Assume also that all borrowing is effective at the beginning of the month and all repayments are made at the end of the month of repayment. Loans are repaid when sufficient cash is available. Interest is paid only at the time of repaying principal. The interest rate is 18% per year. The owner of store does not want to borrow any more cash than is necessary and wants to repay as soon as cash is available.

On the basis of the preceding facts

Required

1. Complete Schedule A.

Schedule A: Budgeted Monthly Cash Receipts

Item	December	January	February	March
Total sales	Rs 40,000	Rs 48,000	Rs 60,000	Rs 80,000.
Credit sales (25%)	10,000	12,000		
Cash sales (75%)	_____	_____	_____	_____
Receipts:	_____	_____	_____	_____

Cash sales	Rs 36,000			
Collections on accounts receivable	10,000			
Total	46,000			

2. Complete Schedule B. Note that purchases are 70% of next month's sales.

Schedule B: Budgeted Monthly Cash Disbursements for Purchases

Item	January	February	March	4th Quarter
Purchases	Rs 42,000			
Deduct 2% cash discount	840			
Disbursements	Rs 41,160			

3. Complete Schedule C.

Schedule C: Budgeted Monthly Cash Disbursements for Operating Costs

Item	January	February	March	4th Quarter
Salaries and wages	Rs 7,200			
Rent	2,400			
Other cash operating costs	1,920			
Total	11,520			

4. Complete Schedule D.

Schedule D: Budgeted Total Monthly Cash Disbursements

Item	January	February	March	4th Quarter
Purchases	Rs 41,160			
Cash operating costs	11,520			
Light fixtures	600			
Total	Rs 53,280			

5. Complete Schedule E.

Schedule E: Budgeted Cash Receipts and Disbursements

Item	January	February	March	4th Quarter
Receipts	Rs 46,000			
Disbursements	53,280			
Net cash increase				
Net cash decrease	Rs 7,280			

6. Complete Schedule F (assume that borrowings must be made in multiples of Rs 1,000).

Schedule F: Financing Required

Item	January	February	March	4th Quarter
Beginning cash balance	Rs 12,000			
Net cash increase				
Net cash decrease	7,280			
Cash position before borrowing (a)	4,720			
Minimum cash balance required	8,000			
Excess (Deficiency)	(3,280)			
Borrowing required (b)	4,000			
Interest payments (c)				
Borrowing repaid (d)				
Ending cash balance	8,720			

7. What do you think is the most logical type of loan needed by Retail Stationery Store?
8. Prepare a budgeted income statement for the fourth quarter and a budgeted balance sheet as of December 31. Ignore income taxes.
9. Some simplifications have been included in this problem. What complicating factors might arise in a typical business situation?

7 Flexible Budgets, Direct-Cost Variances, and Management Control

Learning Objectives

1. Understand static budgets and static-budget variances
2. Examine the concept of a flexible budget and learn how to develop it
3. Calculate flexible-budget variances and sales-volume variances
4. Explain why standard costs are often used in variance analysis
5. Compute price variances and efficiency variances for direct-cost categories
6. Understand how managers use variances
7. Describe benchmarking and explain its role in cost management

Professional sports leagues thrive on providing excitement for their fans. It seems that no expense is spared to entertain spectators and keep them occupied before, during, and after games. Professional basketball has been at the forefront of this trend, popularizing such crowd-pleasing distractions as pregame pyrotechnics, pumped-in noise, fire-shooting scoreboards, and T-shirt-shooting cheerleaders carrying air guns. What is the goal of investing millions in such "game presentation" activities? Such showcasing attracts and maintains the loyalty of younger fans. But eventually, every organization, regardless of its growth, has to step back and take a hard look at the wisdom of its spending choices. And when customers are affected by a recession, the need for an organization to employ budgeting and variance analysis tools for cost control becomes especially critical, as the following article shows.

The NBA: Where Frugal Happens[1]

For more than 20 years, the National Basketball Association (NBA) flew nearly as high as one of LeBron James's slam dunks. The league expanded from 24 to 30 teams, negotiated lucrative TV contracts, and made star players like Kobe Bryant and Dwayne Wade household names and multimillionaires. The NBA was even advertised as "where amazing happens." While costs for brand new arenas and player contracts increased, fans continued to pay escalating ticket prices to see their favorite team. But when the economy nosedived in 2008, the situation changed dramatically.

In the season that followed (2008–2009), more than half of the NBA's franchises lost money. Fans stopped buying tickets and many companies could no longer afford pricy luxury suites. NBA commissioner David Stern announced that overall league revenue for the 2009–2010 season was expected to fall by an additional 5% over the previous disappointing campaign. With revenues dwindling and operating profits tougher to achieve, NBA teams began to heavily emphasize cost control and operating-variance reduction for the first time since the 1980s.

Some of the changes were merely cosmetic. The Charlotte Bobcats stopped paying for halftime entertainment, which cost up to $15,000 per game, while the Cleveland Cavaliers saved $40,000 by switching from paper holiday cards to electronic ones. Many other

[1] *Sources:* Arnold, Gregory. 2009. NBA teams cut rosters, assistants, scouts to reduce costs. *The Oregonian,* October 26; Biderman, David. 2009. The NBA: Where frugal happens. *Wall Street Journal*, October 27.

teams—including the Dallas Mavericks, Indiana Pacers, and Miami Heat—reduced labor costs by laying off front-office staff.

Other changes, however, affected play on the court. While NBA teams were allowed to have 15 players on their respective rosters, 10 teams chose to save money by employing fewer players. For example, the Memphis Grizzlies eliminated its entire scouting department, which provided important information on upcoming opponents and potential future players, while the New Jersey Nets traded away most of its high-priced superstars and chose to play with lower-salaried younger players. Each team cutting costs experienced different results. The Grizzlies were a playoff contender, but the Nets were on pace for one of the worst seasons in NBA history.

Just as companies like General Electric and Bank of America have to manage costs and analyze variances for long-term sustainability, so, too, do sports teams. "The NBA is a business just like any other business," Sacramento Kings co-owner Joe Maloof said. "We have to watch our costs and expenses, especially during this trying economic period. It's better to be safe and watch your expenses and make sure you keep your franchise financially strong."

In Chapter 6, you saw how budgets help managers with their planning function. We now explain how budgets, specifically flexible budgets, are used to compute variances, which assist managers in their control function. Flexible budgets and variances enable managers to make meaningful comparisons of actual results with planned performance, and to obtain insights into why actual results differ from planned performance. They form the critical final function in the five-step decision-making process, by making it possible for managers to *evaluate performance and learn* after decisions are implemented. In this chapter and the next, we explain how.

Learning Objective 1

Understand static budgets

. . . the master budget based on output planned at start of period

and static-budget variances

. . . the difference between the actual result and the corresponding budgeted amount in the static budget

Static Budgets and Variances

A variance is the difference between actual results and expected performance. The expected performance is also called budgeted performance, which is a point of reference for making comparisons.

The Use of Variances

Variances lie at the point where the planning and control functions of management come together. They assist managers in implementing their strategies by enabling management by exception. This is the practice of focusing management attention on areas that are not operating as expected (such as a large shortfall in sales of a product) and devoting less time to areas operating as expected. In other words, by highlighting the areas that have deviated most from expectations, variances enable managers to focus their efforts on the most critical areas. Consider scrap and rework costs at a NOIDA appliances plant. If actual costs are much higher than budgeted, the variances will guide managers to seek explanations and to take early corrective action, ensuring that future operations result in less scrap and rework. Sometimes a large positive variance may occur, such as a significant decrease in manufacturing costs of a product. Managers will try to understand the reasons for this decrease, for example, better operator training or changes in manufacturing methods, so these practices can be appropriately continued and transferred to other divisions within the organization.

Variances are also used in performance evaluation and to motivate managers. Production-line managers at NOIDA plant may have quarterly efficiency incentives linked to achieving a budgeted amount of operating costs.

Sometimes variances suggest that the company should consider a change in strategy. For example, large negative variances caused by excessive defect rates for a new product may suggest a flawed product design. Managers may then want to investigate the product design and potentially change the mix of products being offered.

Variance analysis contributes in many ways to making the five-step decision process more effective. It allows managers to evaluate performance and learn by providing a framework for correctly assessing current performance. In turn, managers take corrective actions to ensure that decisions are implemented correctly and that previously budgeted results are in fact attained. Variances also enable managers to generate more informed predictions about the future, and thereby improve the quality of the five-step decision-making process.

The benefits of variance analysis are not restricted to companies. In today's difficult economic environment, public officials have realized that the ability to make timely tactical alterations based on variance information guards against having to make more draconian adjustments later. For example, the city of Scottsdale, Arizona, monitors its tax and fee performance against expenditures monthly. Why? One of the city's goals is to keep its water usage rates stable. By monitoring the extent to which water revenues are meeting current expenses and obligations, while simultaneously building up funds for future infrastructure projects, the city can avoid rate spikes and achieve long-run rate stability.[2]

How important is variance analysis? A survey by the United Kingdom's Chartered Institute of Management Accountants in July 2009 found that variance analysis was easily the most popular costing tool in practice, and retained that distinction across organizations of all sizes.

Static Budgets and Static-Budget Variances

We will take a closer look at variances by examining one company's accounting system. Note as you study the exhibits in this chapter that "level" followed by a number denotes the amount of detail shown by a variance analysis. Level 1 reports the least detail, level 2 offers more information, and so on.

Consider Color Plus Company, a firm that manufactures and sells jackets. The jackets require tailoring and many hand operations. Color Plus sells exclusively to distributors, who in turn sell to independent clothing stores and retail chains. For simplicity, we assume that Color Plus's only costs are in the manufacturing function; Color Plus incurs no costs in other value-chain functions, such as marketing and distribution. We also assume that all units manufactured in April 2008 are sold in April 2008. Therefore, all direct materials are

[2] For an excellent discussion and other related examples from governmental settings, see S. Kavanagh and C. Swanson, "Tactical Financial Management: Cash Flow and Budgetary Variance Analysis," *Government Finance Review* (October 1, 2009).

purchased and used in the same budget period, and there is no direct materials inventory at either the beginning or the end of the period. No work-in-process or finished goods inventories exist at either the beginning or the end of the period. The Problem for Self-Study at the end of this chapter relaxes some of these assumptions. Color Plus has three variable-cost categories. The budgeted variable cost per jacket for each category is:

Cost Category	Variable Cost per Jacket
Direct material costs	Rs 600
Direct manufacturing labor costs	160
Variable manufacturing overhead costs	120
Total variable costs	Rs 880

The number of units manufactured is the cost driver for direct materials, direct manufacturing labor, and variable manufacturing overhead. The relevant range for the cost driver is from 0 to 12,000 jackets. Budgeted and actual data for April 2011 follow:

Budgeted fixed costs for production between 0 and 12,000 jackets	Rs 27,60,000
Budgeted selling price	Rs 1,200 per jacket
Budgeted production and sales	12,000 jackets
Actual production and sales	10,000 jackets

The **static budget**, or master budget, is based on the level of output planned at the start of the budget period. The master budget is called a static budget because the budget for the period is developed around a single (static) planned output level. Exhibit 7-1, column 3, presents the static budget for Color Plus Company for April 2011 that was prepared at the end of 2010. For each line item in the income statement, Exhibit 7-1, column 1, displays data for the actual April results. For example, actual revenues are Rs 1,25,00,000, and the actual selling price is Rs 1,25,00,000 ÷ 10,000 jackets = Rs 1,250 per jacket—compared with the budgeted selling price of Rs 1,200 per jacket. Similarly, actual direct material costs are Rs 62,16,000, and the direct material cost per jacket is Rs 621.6 ÷ 10,000 = Rs 621.6 per jacket—compared with the budgeted direct material cost per jacket of Rs 600. We describe potential reasons and explanations for these differences as we discuss different variances throughout the chapter.

The **static-budget variance** (see Exhibit 7-1, column 2) is the difference between the actual result and the corresponding budgeted amount in the static budget.

A **favorable variance**—denoted F in this book—has the effect, when considered in isolation, of increasing operating income relative to the budgeted amount. For revenue

Exhibit 7-1

Static-Budget-Based Variance Analysis for Color Plus Company for April 2011[a]

Level 1 Analysis

	Actual Results (1)	Static-Budget Variances (2) = (1) – (3)	Static Budget (3)
Units sold	10,000	2,000 U	12,000
Revenues	Rs1,25,00,000	Rs19,00,000 U	Rs1,44,00,000
Variable costs			
Direct materials	62,16,000	9,84,000 F	72,00,000
Direct manufacturing labor	19,80,000	60,000 U	19,20,000
Variable manufacturing overhead	13,05,000	1,35,000 F	14,40,000
Total variable costs	95,01,000	10,59,000 F	1,05,60,000
Contribution margin	29,99,000[b]	8,41,000 U	38,40,000[c]
Fixed costs	28,50,000	90,000 U	27,60,000
Operating income	Rs 1,49,000	Rs 9,31,000 U	Rs 10,80,000

Rs 9,31,000 U

Static-budget variance

[a]F = favorable effect on operating income; U = unfavorable effect on operating income.

[b]Contribution margin percentage = Rs 29,99,000 ÷ Rs 1,25,00,000 = 24.0%.

[c]Contribution margin percentage = Rs 38,40,000 ÷ Rs 1,44,00,000 = 26.7%.

items, F means actual revenues exceed budgeted revenues. For cost items, F means actual costs are less than budgeted costs. An *unfavorable variance*—denoted U in this book—has the effect, when viewed in isolation, of decreasing operating income relative to the budgeted amount. Unfavorable variances are also called *adverse variances* in some countries.

The unfavorable static-budget variance for operating income of Rs 9,31,000 in Exhibit 7-1 is calculated by subtracting static-budget operating income of Rs 10,80,000 from actual operating income of Rs 1,49,000:

$$\text{Static-budget variance for operating income} = \text{Actual result} - \text{Static-budget amount}$$

$$= \text{Rs } 1{,}49{,}000 - \text{Rs } 10{,}80{,}000$$

$$= \text{Rs } 9{,}31{,}000 \text{ U.}$$

The analysis in Exhibit 7-1 provides managers with additional information on the static-budget variance for operating income of Rs 9,31,000 U. The more detailed breakdown indicates how the line items that comprise operating income—revenues, individual variable costs, and fixed costs—add up to the static-budget variance of Rs 9,31,000.

Decision Point

What are static budgets and static-budget variances?

Remember, Color Plus produced and sold only 10,000 jackets, although managers anticipated an output of 12,000 jackets in the static budget. *Managers want to know how much of the static-budget variance is because of inaccurate forecasting of output units sold and how much is due to Color Plus's performance in manufacturing and selling 10,000 jackets.* Managers, therefore, create a flexible budget, which enables a more in-depth understanding of deviations from the static budget.

Flexible Budgets

Learning Objective 2

Examine the concept of a flexible budget

. . . the budget that is adjusted (flexed) to recognize the actual output level

and learn how to develop it

. . . proportionately increase variable costs; keep fixed costs the same

A **flexible budget** calculates budgeted revenues and budgeted costs based on *the actual output in the budget period.* The flexible budget is prepared at the end of the period (April 2011), after the actual output of 10,000 jackets is known. The flexible budget is the *hypothetical* budget that Color Plus would have prepared at the start of the budget period if it had correctly forecast the actual output of 10,000 jackets. In preparing the flexible budget:

- The budgeted selling price is the same Rs 1,200 per jacket used in preparing the static budget.
- The budgeted variable costs are the same Rs 880 per jacket used in the static budget.
- The budgeted fixed costs are the same static-budget amount of Rs 27,60,000. Why? Because the 10,000 jackets produced falls within the relevant range of 0 to 12,000 jackets. Therefore, Color Plus would have budgeted the same amount of fixed costs, Rs 27,60,000, whether it anticipated making 10,000 or 12,000 jackets.

The *only* difference between the static budget and the flexible budget is that the static budget is prepared for the planned output of 12,000 jackets, whereas the flexible budget is based on the actual output of 10,000 jackets. The static budget is being "flexed," or adjusted, from 12,000 jackets to 10,000 jackets.[3] The flexible budget for 10,000 jackets assumes that all costs are either completely variable or completely fixed with respect to the number of jackets produced.

Color Plus develops its flexible budget in three steps.

Step 1: Identify the Actual Quantity of Output. In April 2011, Color Plus produced and sold 10,000 jackets.

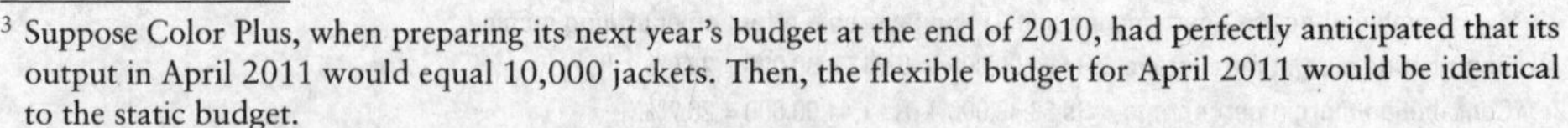

[3] Suppose Color Plus, when preparing its next year's budget at the end of 2010, had perfectly anticipated that its output in April 2011 would equal 10,000 jackets. Then, the flexible budget for April 2011 would be identical to the static budget.

Step 2: Calculate the Flexible Budget for Revenues Based on Budgeted Selling Price and Actual Quantity of Output.

Flexible-budget variable = Rs 1,200 per jacket × 10,000 jackets
= Rs 1,20,00,000

Step 3: Calculate the Flexible Budget for Costs Based on Budgeted Variable Cost per Output Unit, Actual Quantity of Output, and Budgeted Fixed Costs.

Flexible-budget variable costs	
Direct materials, Rs 600 per jacket × 10,000 jackets	Rs 60,00,000
Direct manufacturing labor, Rs 160 per jacket × 10,000 jackets	16,00,000
Variable manufacturing overhead, Rs 120 per jacket × 10,000 jackets	12,00,000
Total flexible-budget variable costs	88,00,000
Flexible-budget fixed costs	27,60,000
Flexible-budget total costs	Rs 1,15,60,000

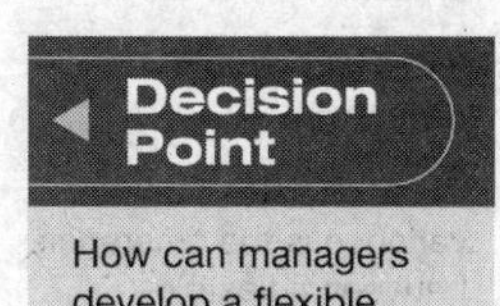

How can managers develop a flexible budget and why is it useful to do so?

These three steps enable Color Plus to prepare a flexible budget, as shown in Exhibit 7-2, column 3. The flexible budget allows for a more detailed analysis of the Rs 9,31,000 unfavorable static-budget variance for operating income.

Flexible-Budget Variances and Sales-Volume Variances

Exhibit 7-2 shows the flexible-budget-based variance analysis for Color Plus, which subdivides the Rs 9,31,000 unfavorable static-budget variance for operating income into two parts: a flexible-budget variance of Rs 2,91,000 U and a sales-volume variance of Rs 6,40,000 U. The **sales-volume variance** is the difference between a flexible-budget amount and the corresponding static-budget amount. The **flexible-budget variance** is the difference between an actual result and the corresponding flexible-budget amount.

Exhibit 7-2 Level 2 Flexible-Budget-Based Variance Analysis for Color Plus Company for April 2011[a]

Level 2 Analysis

	Actual Results (1)	Flexible-Budget Variances (2) = (1) − (3)	Flexible Budget (3)	Sales-Volume Variances (4) = (3) − (5)	Static Budget (5)
Units sold	10,000	0	10,000	2,000 U	12,000
Revenues	Rs 1,25,00,000	Rs 5,00,000 F	Rs 1,20,00,000	Rs 24,00,000 U	Rs 1,44,00,000
Variable costs					
Direct materials	62,16,000	2,16,000 U	60,00,000	12,00,000 F	72,00,000
Direct manufacturing labor	19,80,000	3,80,000 U	16,00,000	3,20,000 F	19,20,000
Variable manufacturing overhead	13,05,000	1,05,000 U	12,00,000	2,40,000 F	14,40,000
Total variable costs	95,01,000	7,01,000 U	88,00,000	17,60,000 F	1,05,60,000
Contribution margin	29,99,000	2,01,000 U	32,00,000	6,40,000 U	38,40,000
Fixed manufacturing costs	28,50,000	90,000 U	27,60,000	0	27,60,000
Operating income	Rs 1,49,000	Rs 2,91,000 U	Rs 4,40,000	Rs 6,40,000 U	Rs 10,80,000

Level 2: Rs 2,91,000 U — Flexible-budget variance; Rs 6,40,000 U — Sales-volume variance

Level 1: Rs 9,31,000 U — Static-budget variance

[a]F = favorable effect on operating income; U = unfavorable effect on operating income.

Sales-Volume Variances

Learning Objective 3

Calculate flexible-budget variances

. . . each flexible-budget variance is the difference between an actual result and a flexible-budget amount

and sales-volume variances

. . . each sales-volume variance is the difference between a flexible-budget amount and a static-budget amount

Keep in mind that the flexible-budget amounts in column 3 of Exhibit 7-2 and the static-budget amounts in column 5 are both computed using budgeted selling prices, budgeted variable cost per jacket, and budgeted fixed costs. The difference between the static-budget and the flexible-budget amounts is called the sales-volume variance because it arises *solely* from the difference between the 10,000 actual quantity (or volume) of jackets sold and the 12,000 quantity of jackets expected to be sold in the static budget.

$$\text{Sales-budget variance for operating income} = \text{Flexible-budget amount} - \text{Static-budget amount}$$

$$= \text{Rs } 4,40,000 - \text{Rs } 10,80,000$$

$$= \text{Rs } 6,40,000 \text{ U}$$

The sales-volume variance in operating income for Color Plus measures the change in budgeted contribution margin because Color Plus sold only 10,000 jackets rather than the budgeted 12,000.

$$\text{Sales-volume variance for operating income} = \left(\text{Budgeted contribution margin per unit}\right) \times \left(\text{Actual units sold} - \text{Static-budget units sold}\right)$$

$$= \left(\text{Budgeted selling price} - \text{Budgeted variable cost per unit}\right) \times \left(\text{Actual units sold} - \text{Static-budget units sold}\right)$$

$$= (\text{Rs}1,200 \text{ per jacket} - \text{Rs } 880 \text{ per jacket}) \times (10,000 \text{ jackets} - 12,000 \text{ jackets})$$

$$= \text{Rs } 320 \text{ per jacket} \times (-2,000 \text{ jackets})$$

$$= \text{Rs } 6,40,000 \text{ U}$$

Exhibit 7-2, column 4, shows the components of this overall variance by identifying the sales-volume variance for each of the line items in the income statement. Color Plus's managers determine that the unfavorable sales-volume variance in operating income could be because of one or more of the following reasons:

1. The overall demand for jackets is not growing at the rate that was anticipated.
2. Competitors are taking away market share from Color Plus.
3. Color Plus did not adapt quickly to changes in customer preferences and tastes.
4. Budgeted sales targets were set without careful analysis of market conditions.
5. Quality problems developed that led to customer dissatisfaction with Color Plus's jackets.

How Color Plus responds to the unfavorable sales-volume variance will be influenced by what management believes to be the cause of the variance. For example, if Color Plus's managers believe the unfavorable sales-volume variance was caused by market-related reasons (reasons 1, 2, 3, or 4), the sales manager would be in the best position to explain what happened and to suggest corrective actions, such as sales promotions, that may be needed. If, however, managers believe the unfavorable sales-volume variance was caused by quality problems (reason 5), the production manager would be in the best position to analyze the causes and to suggest strategies for improvement, such as changes in the manufacturing process or investments in new machines.

The static-budget variances compared actual revenues and costs for 10,000 jackets against budgeted revenues and costs for 12,000 jackets. Separating the sales-volume variance—which reflects the effects of inaccurate forecasting of output units sold—from the static-budget variance enables managers to compare actual revenues earned and costs incurred for April 2011 against the revenues and costs Color Plus would have budgeted for the 10,000 jackets actually produced and sold—the flexible budget. *These flexible-budget variances are a better measure of operating performance than static-budget variances because they compare actual revenues to budgeted revenues and actual costs to budgeted costs for the same 10,000 jackets of output.*

Flexible-Budget Variances

The first three columns of Exhibit 7-2 compare actual results with flexible-budget amounts. Flexible-budget variances are in column 2 for each line item in the income statement:

$$\text{Flexible-budget variance} = \text{Actual result} - \text{Flexible-budget amount}$$

The operating income line in Exhibit 7-2 shows the flexible-budget variance is Rs 2,91,000 U (Rs 1,49,000 − Rs 4,40,000). The Rs 2,91,000 U arises because actual selling price, actual variable cost per unit, and actual fixed costs differ from their budgeted amounts. The actual results and budgeted amounts for the selling price and variable cost per unit are:

	Actual Result	Budgeted Amount
Selling price	Rs 1,250 (Rs 1,25,00,000 ÷ 10,000 jackets)	Rs 1,200 (Rs 1,20,00,000 ÷ 10,000 jackets)
Variable cost per jacket	Rs 950.1 (Rs 95,01,000 ÷ 10,000 jackets)	Rs 880 (Rs 88,00,000 ÷ 10,000 jackets)

The flexible-budget variance for revenues is called the **selling-price variance** because it arises solely from the difference between the actual selling price and the budgeted selling price:

$$\text{Selling-price variance} = \left(\text{Actual selling price} - \text{Budgeted selling price}\right) \times \text{Actual units sold}$$

$$= (\text{Rs } 1{,}250 \text{ per jacket} - \text{Rs } 1{,}250 \text{ per jacket}) \times 10{,}000 \text{ jackets}$$

$$= \text{Rs } 5{,}00{,}000$$

Color Plus has a favorable selling-price variance because the Rs 1,250 actual selling price exceeds the Rs 1,200 budgeted amount, which increases operating income. Marketing managers are generally in the best position to understand and explain the reason for this selling price difference. For example, was the difference due to better quality? Or was it due to an overall increase in market prices? Color's managers concluded it was due to a general increase in prices.

The flexible-budget variance for total variable costs is unfavorable (Rs 7,01,000 U) for the actual output of 10,000 jackets. It's unfavorable because of one or both of the following:

- Color Plus used greater quantities of inputs (such as direct manufacturing labor-hours) compared to the budgeted quantities of inputs.
- Color Plus incurred higher prices per unit for the inputs (such as the wage rate per direct manufacturing labor-hour) compared to the budgeted prices per unit of the inputs.

Higher input quantities and/or higher input prices relative to the budgeted amounts could be the result of Color Plus's deciding to produce a better product than what was planned or the result of inefficiencies in Color Plus's manufacturing and purchasing, or both. *You should always think of variance analysis as providing suggestions for further investigation rather than as establishing conclusive evidence of good or bad performance.*

The actual fixed costs of Rs 28,50,000 are Rs 90,000 more than the budgeted amount of Rs 27,60,000. This unfavorable flexible-budget variance reflects unexpected increases in the cost of fixed indirect resources, such as factory rent or supervisory salaries.

In the rest of this chapter, we will focus on variable direct-cost input variances. Chapter 8 emphasizes indirect (overhead) cost variances.

Price Variances and Efficiency Variances for Direct-Cost Inputs

To gain further insight, almost all companies subdivide the flexible-budget variance for direct-cost inputs into two more-detailed variances:

1. A price variance that reflects the difference between an actual input price and a budgeted input price

2. An efficiency variance that reflects the difference between an actual input quantity and a budgeted input quantity

The information available from these variances (which we call level 3 variances) helps managers to better understand past performance and take corrective actions to implement superior strategies in the future. Managers generally have more control over efficiency variances than price variances. That's because the quantity of inputs used is primarily affected by factors inside the company, but price changes are primarily due to market forces outside the company.

Obtaining Budgeted Input Prices and Budgeted Input Quantities

Learning Objective 4

Explain why standard costs are often used in variance analysis

. . . standard costs exclude past inefficiencies and take into account expected future changes

To calculate price and efficiency variances, Color Plus needs to obtain budgeted input prices and budgeted input quantities. Color's three main sources for this information are:

1. **Actual input data from past periods.** Most companies have past data on actual input prices and actual input quantities. These past prices and quantities could be used as the budgeted prices and quantities in a flexible budget. The advantage of past data is that they represent quantities and prices that are "real" rather than hypothetical and can serve as benchmarks for continuous improvement. Another advantage is that past data are typically available at low cost. However, there are limitations to using past data. Past data can include inefficiencies such as wastage of direct materials. Past data also do not incorporate any changes expected for the budget period.
2. **Data from other companies that have similar processes.** The benefit of using this data is that the budget numbers represent competitive benchmarks from other companies. For example, Baptist Healthcare System in Louisville, Kentucky, maintains detailed flexible budgets and benchmarks its labor performance against hospitals that provide similar types of services and volumes and are in the upper quartile of a national benchmark. The main difficulty of using this source is that input-price and input quantity data from other companies are often not available or may not be comparable to a particular company's situation. Consider American Apparel, which makes over 1 million articles of clothing a week. At its sole factory, in Los Angeles, workers receive hourly wages, piece rates, and medical benefits well in excess of those paid by its competitors, virtually all of whom are offshore. Moreover, because sourcing organic cotton from overseas results in too high of a carbon footprint, American Apparel purchases more expensive domestic cotton in keeping with its sustainability programs.
3. **Standards developed by Color Plus.** A **standard** is a carefully determined price, cost, or quantity that is used as a benchmark for judging performance. A standard is usually expressed on a per-unit basis. Consider how Color Plus determines its direct manufacturing labor standards. Color Plus conducts engineering studies to obtain a detailed breakdown of the steps required to make a jacket. Each step is assigned a standard time based on work performed by a *skilled* worker using equipment operating in an *efficient* manner. There are two advantages of using standard times: (i) they aim to exclude past inefficiencies and (ii) they aim to take into account changes expected to occur in the budget period. An example of (ii) is the decision by Color Plus, for strategic reasons, to lease new sewing machines that operate at a faster speed and enable output to be produced with lower defect rates. Similarly, Color Plus determines the standard quantity of square yards of cloth required by a skilled operator to make each jacket.

The term "standard" refers to many different things. Always clarify its meaning and how it is being used. A **standard input** is a carefully determined quantity of input—such as square yards of cloth or direct manufacturing labor-hours—required for one unit of output, such as a jacket. A **standard price** is a carefully determined price that a company expects to pay for a unit of input. In the Color Plus example, the standard wage rate that Color Plus expects to pay its operators is an example of a standard price of a direct manufacturing labor-hour. A **standard cost** is a carefully determined cost of a unit of output—for example, the standard direct manufacturing labor cost of a jacket at Color Plus.

$$\text{Standard cost per output unit for each variable direct-cost input} = \text{Standard input allowed for one output unit} \times \text{Standard price per input unit}$$

Standard direct material cost per jacket: 2 square yards of cloth input allowed per output unit (jacket) manufactured, at Rs 300 standard price per square yard

Standard direct material cost per jacket = 2 Square yards square yard × Rs 300 per square yard = Rs 600

Standard direct manufacturing labor cost per jacket: 0.8 manufacturing labor-hour of input allowed per output unit manufactured, at Rs 200 standard price per hour

Standard direct manufacturing labor cost per jacket = 0.8 labor-hours × Rs 160 per labor-hour = Rs 160

How are the words "budget" and "standard" related? Budget is the broader term. To clarify: Budgeted input prices, budgeted input quantities, and budgeted costs need *not* be based on standards. However, when standards *are* used to obtain budgeted input quantities and budgeted input prices, the terms "standard" and "budget" are used interchangeably. The standard cost of each input required for one unit of output is determined by the standard quantity of each input required for one unit of output and the standard price per input unit. See how the standard-cost computations for direct materials and direct manufacturing labor equal the budgeted direct material cost per jacket of Rs 600 and the budgeted direct manufacturing labor cost of Rs 160.

In its standard costing system, Color Plus uses standards that are attainable through efficient operations but that allow for normal disruptions. An alternative is to set more-challenging standards that are more difficult to attain. As we discussed in Chapter 6, setting challenging standards can increase motivation and performance. If, however, standards are regarded by workers as essentially unachievable, it can increase frustration and hurt performance.

Decision Point

What is a standard cost and what are its purposes?

Data for Calculating Color Plus's Price Variances and Efficiency Variances

Learning Objective 5

Compute price variances

... each price variance is the difference between an actual input price and a budgeted input price

and efficiency variances

... each efficiency variance is the difference between an actual input quantity and a budgeted input quantity for actual output

for direct-cost categories

Consider Color's two direct-cost categories. The actual cost for each of these categories for the 10,000 jackets manufactured and sold in April 2011 is:

Direct materials purchased and used[4]	
1. Square yards of cloth input purchased and used	22,200
2. Actual price incurred per square yard	Rs 280
3. Direct material costs (22,200 × Rs 280) [shown in Exhibit 7-2, column 1]	Rs 62,16,000
Direct manufacturing labor	
1. Direct manufacturing labor-hours	9,000
2. Actual price incurred per direct manufacturing labor-hour	Rs 220
3. Direct manufacturing labor costs (9,000 × Rs 220) [shown in Exhibit 7-2, column 1]	Rs 19,80,000

Let's use the Color Company data to illustrate the price variance and the efficiency variance for direct-cost inputs.

A **price variance** is the difference between actual price and budgeted price multiplied by actual input quantity, such as direct materials purchased or used. A price variance is

[4] The Problem for Self-Study later in this chapter relaxes the assumption that the quantity of direct materials used equals the quantity of direct materials purchased.

sometimes called an **input-price variance** or **rate variance,** especially when referring to a price variance for direct manufacturing labor. An **efficiency variance** is the difference between actual input quantity used—such as square yards of cloth of direct materials—and budgeted input quantity allowed for actual output, multiplied by budgeted price. An efficiency variance is sometimes called a **usage variance**. Let's explore price and efficiency variances in greater detail so we can see how managers use these variances to improve their future performance.

Price Variances

The formula for computing the price variance is:

$$\text{Price variance} = \left(\text{Actual price of input} - \text{Budgeted price of input}\right) \times \text{Actual quanity of input}$$

Price variances for Color Plus's two direct-cost categories are:

Direct-Cost Category	(Actual price of input − Budgeted price of input)	×	Actual quantity of input	=	Price Variance
Direct materials	(Rs 280 per sq. yard − Rs 300 per sq. yard)	×	22,200 square yards	=	Rs 4,44,000 F
Direct manufacturing labor	(Rs 220 per hour − Rs 200 per hour)	×	9,000 hours	=	Rs 1,80,000 U

The direct materials price variance is favorable because actual price of cloth is less than budgeted price, resulting in an increase in operating income. The direct manufacturing labor price variance is unfavorable because actual wage rate paid to labor is more than the budgeted rate, resulting in a decrease in operating income.

Always consider a broad range of possible causes for a price variance. For example, Color Plus's favorable direct materials price variance could be due to one or more of the following:

- Color's purchasing manager negotiated the direct materials prices more skillfully than was planned for in the budget.
- The purchasing manager changed to a lower-price supplier.
- Color purchasing manager ordered larger quantities than the quantities budgeted, thereby obtaining quantity discounts.
- Direct material prices decreased unexpectedly because of, say, industry oversupply.
- Budgeted purchase prices of direct materials were set too high without careful analysis of market conditions.
- The purchasing manager received favorable prices because he was willing to accept unfavorable terms on factors other than prices (such as lower-quality material).

Color's response to a direct materials price variance depends on what is believed to be the cause of the variance. Assume Color's managers attribute the favorable price variance to the purchasing manager ordering in larger quantities than budgeted, thereby receiving quantity discounts. Color could examine if purchasing in these larger quantities resulted in higher storage costs. If the increase in storage and inventory holding costs exceeds the quantity discounts, purchasing in larger quantities is not beneficial. Some companies have reduced their materials storage areas to prevent their purchasing managers from ordering in larger quantities.

Efficiency Variance

For any actual level of output, the efficiency variance is the difference between actual quantity of input used and the budgeted quantity of input allowed to produce actual output, multiplied by budgeted price:

$$\text{Efficiency Variance} = \left(\text{Actual quantity of input used} - \text{Budgeted quantity of unput allowed for actual output}\right) \times \text{Budgeted price of input}$$

The idea here is that a company is inefficient if it uses a larger quantity of input than the budgeted quantity for its actual level of output; the company is efficient if it uses a smaller quantity of inputs than was budgeted for that output level.

The efficiency variances for each of Color's direct-cost categories are:

Direct-Cost Category	(Actual quantity of input used − Budgeted quantity of input allowed for actual output)	× Budgeted price of input	=	Efficiency Variance
Direct materials	[22,200 sq. yds. − (10,000 units × 2 sq. yds./unit)]	× Rs 300 per sq. yard		
	= (22,200 sq. yds − 20,000 sq. yds.)	× Rs 300 per sq. yard	=	Rs 6,60,000 U
Direct manufacturing	[9,000 hours − (10,000 units × 0.8 hour/unit)]	× Rs 200 per hour		
labor	= (9,000 hours − 8,000 hours) × Rs 200 per hour	× Rs 200 per hour	=	2,00,000 U

The two manufacturing efficiency variances—direct materials efficiency variance and direct manufacturing labor efficiency variance—are each unfavorable because more input was used than was budgeted for the actual output, resulting in a decrease in operating income.

As with price variances, there is a broad range of possible causes for these efficiency variances. For example, Color Plus's unfavorable efficiency variance for direct manufacturing labor could be because of one or more of the following:

- Color's personnel manager hired underskilled workers.
- Color's production scheduler inefficiently scheduled work, resulting in more manufacturing labor time than budgeted being used per jacket.
- Color maintenance department did not properly maintain machines, resulting in more manufacturing labor time than budgeted being used per jacket.
- Budgeted time standards were set too tight without careful analysis of the operating conditions and the employees' skills.

Suppose Color's managers determine that the unfavorable variance is due to poor machine maintenance. Color may then establish a team consisting of plant engineers and machine operators to develop a maintenance schedule that will reduce future breakdowns and thereby prevent adverse effects on labor time and product quality.

Exhibit 7-3 provides an alternative way to calculate price and efficiency variances. It also illustrates how the price variance and the efficiency variance subdivide the flexible-budget variance. Consider direct materials. The direct materials flexible-budget variance of Rs 2,16,000 U is the difference between actual costs incurred (actual input quantity × actual price) of Rs 62,16,000 shown in column 1 and the flexible budget (budgeted input quantity allowed for actual output × budgeted price) of Rs 60,00,000 shown in column 3. Column 2 (actual input quantity × budgeted price) is inserted between column 1 and column 3. The difference between columns 1 and 2 is the price variance of Rs 4,44,000 F. This price variance occurs because the same actual input quantity (22,200 sq. yds.) is multiplied by *actual price* (Rs 280) in column 1 and *budgeted price* (Rs 300) in column 2. The difference between columns 2 and 3 is the efficiency variance of Rs 6,60,000 U because the same budgeted price (Rs 300) is multiplied by *actual input quantity* (22,200 sq. yds) in column 2 and *budgeted input quantity allowed for actual output* (20,000 sq. yds.) in column 3. The sum of the direct materials price variance, Rs 4,44,000 F, and the direct materials efficiency variance, Rs 6,60,000 U, equals the direct materials flexible budget variance, Rs 2,16,000 U.

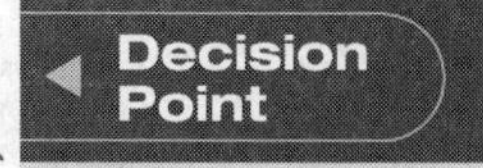

Why should a company calculate price and efficiency variances?

Summary of Variances

Exhibit 7-4 provides a summary of the different variances. Note how the variances at each higher level provide disaggregated and more detailed information for evaluating performance.

The following computations show why actual operating income is Rs 1,49,000 when the static budget operating income is Rs 10,80,000. The numbers in the computations can be found in Exhibits 7-2 and 7-3.

Exhibit 7-3 Columnar Presentation of Variance Analysis: Direct Costs for Color Plus Company for April 2011[a]

Level 3 Analysis

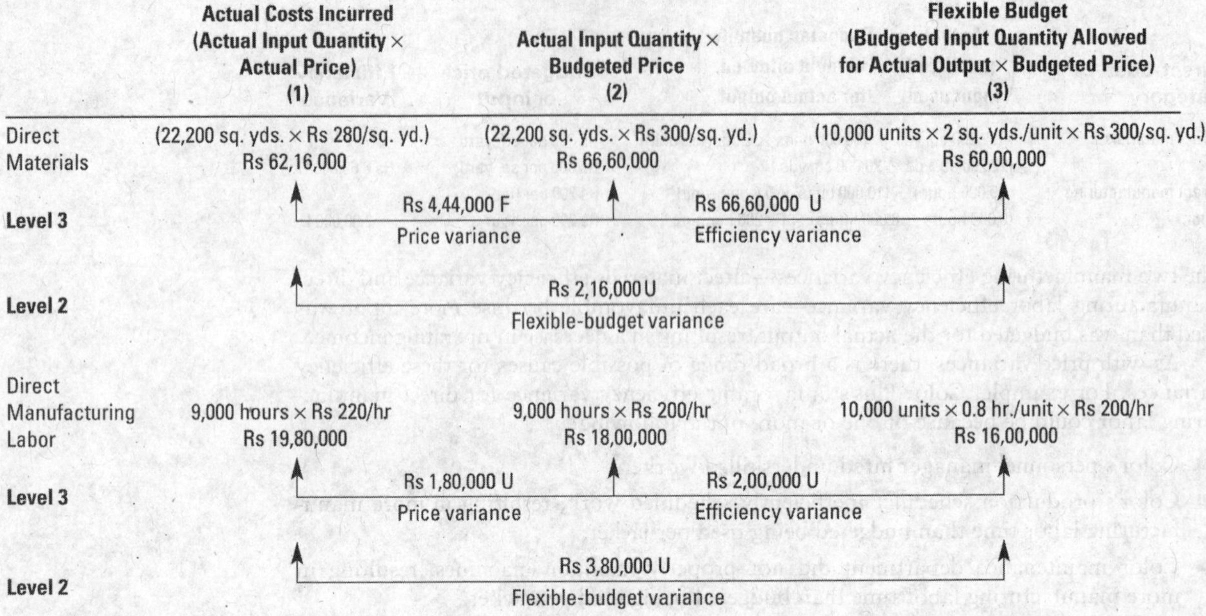

[a]F = favorable effect on operating income; U = unfavorable effect on operating income.

Static budget operating income			Rs 10,80,000
Unfavorable sales-volume variance for operating income			(6,40,000)
Flexible-budget operating income			4,40,000
Flexible-budget variances for operating income:			
Favorable selling-price variance		Rs 5,00,000	
Direct materials variances:			
Favorable direct materials price variance	Rs 4,44,000		
Unfavorable direct materials efficiency variance	(6,60,000)		
Unfavorable direct materials variance		(2,16,000)	
Direct manufacturing labor variances:			
Unfavorable direct manufacturing labor price variance	(1,80,000)		
Unfavorable direct manufacturing labor efficiency variance	(2,00,000)		
Unfavorable direct manufacturing labor variance		(3,80,000)	
Unfavorable variable manufacturing overhead variance		(1,05,000)	
Unfavorable fixed manufacturing overhead variance		(90,000)	
Unfavorable flexible-budget variance for operating income			(2,91,000)
Actual operating income			Rs 1,49,000

The summary of variances highlights three main effects.

1. Color Plus sold 2,000 fewer units than budgeted, resulting in an unfavorable sales volume variance of Rs 6,40,000. Sales declined because of quality problems and new styles of jackets introduced by Color's competitors.
2. Color Plus sold units at a higher price than budgeted, resulting in a favorable selling-price variance of Rs 5,00,000. Color's prices, however, were lower than the prices charged by Color's competitors.

Exhibit 7-4 Summary of Levels 1, 2, and 3 Variance Analysis

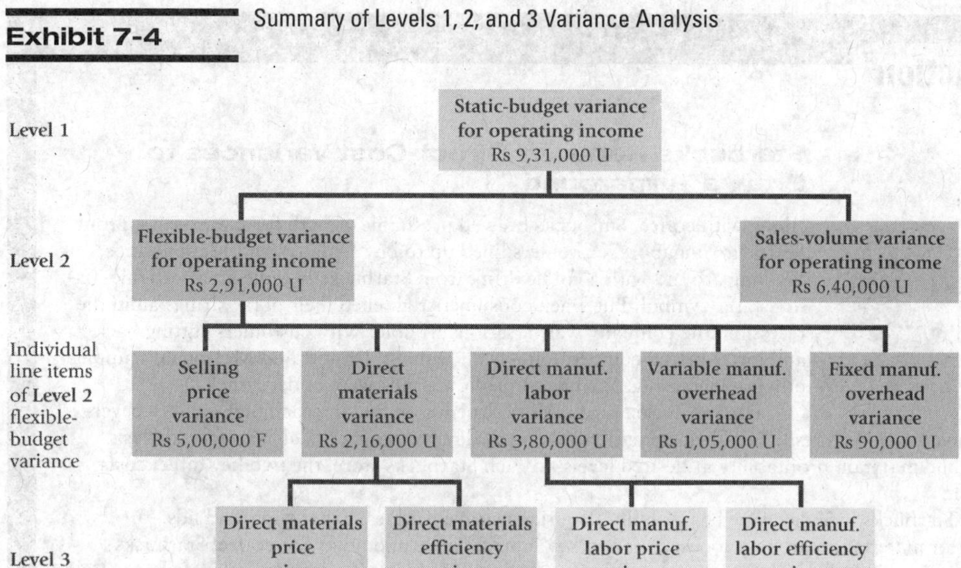

3. Manufacturing costs for the actual output produced were higher than budgeted—direct materials by Rs 2,16,000; direct manufacturing labor by Rs 3,80,000; variable manufacturing overhead by Rs 1,05,000; and fixed overhead by Rs 90,000—because of poor quality of cloth, poor maintenance of machines, and underskilled workers.

We now present Color Plus's journal entries under its standard costing system.

Journal Entries Using Standard Costs

Chapter 4 illustrated journal entries when normal costing is used. We will now illustrate journal entries for Color's Company using standard costs. Our focus is on direct materials and direct manufacturing labor. All the numbers included in the following journal entries are found in Exhibit 7-3.

Note: In each of the following entries, unfavorable variances are always debits (they decrease operating income), and favorable variances are always credits (they increase operating income).

JOURNAL ENTRY 1A: Isolate the direct materials price variance at the time of purchase by increasing (debiting) Direct Materials Control at standard prices. This is the earliest time possible to isolate this variance.

1a. Direct Materials Control		
(22,200 square yards × Rs 300 per square yard)	66,60,000	
Direct Materials Price Variance		
(22,200 square yards × Rs 20 per square yard)		4,44,000
Accounts Payable Control		
(22,200 square yards × Rs 280 per square yard)		62,16,000
To record direct materials purchased.		

JOURNAL ENTRY 1B: Isolate the direct materials efficiency variance at the time the direct materials are used by increasing (debiting) Work-in-Process Control at standard quantities allowed for actual output units manufactured times standard prices.

Concepts in Action

Starbucks Reduces Direct-Cost Variances to Brew a Turnaround

Along with coffee, Starbucks brewed profitable growth for many years. From Seattle to Singapore, customers lined up to buy $4 lattes and Frappuccinos. Walking around with a coffee drink from Starbucks became an affordable-luxury status symbol. But when consumers tightened their purse strings amid the recession, the company was in serious trouble. With customers cutting back and lower-priced competition—from Dunkin' Donuts and McDonald's among others—increasing, Starbucks' profit margins were under attack.

For Starbucks, profitability depends on making each high-quality beverage at the lowest possible costs. As a result, an intricate understanding of direct costs is critical. Variance analysis helps managers assess and maintain profitability at desired levels. In each Starbucks store, the two key direct costs are materials and labor.

Materials costs at Starbucks include coffee beans, milk, flavoring syrups, pastries, paper cups, and lids. To reduce budgeted costs for materials, Starbucks focused on two key inputs: coffee and milk. For coffee, Starbucks sought to avoid waste and spoilage by no longer brewing decaffeinated and darker coffee blends in the afternoon and evening, when store traffic is slower. Instead, baristas were instructed to brew a pot only when a customer ordered it. With milk prices rising (and making up around 10% of Starbucks' cost of sales), the company switched to 2% milk, which is healthier and costs less, and redoubled efforts to reduce milk-related spoilage.

Labor costs at Starbucks, which cost 24% of company revenue annually, were another area of variance focus. Many stores employed fewer baristas. In other stores, Starbucks adopted many "lean" production techniques. With 30% of baristas' time involved in walking around behind the counter, reaching for items, and blending drinks, Starbucks sought to make its drink-making processes more efficient. While the changes seem small—keeping bins of coffee beans on top of the counter so baristas don't have to bend over, moving bottles of flavored syrups closer to where drinks are made, and using colored tape to quickly differentiate between pitchers of soy, nonfat, and low-fat milk—some stores experienced a 10% increase in transactions using the same number of workers or fewer.

The company took additional steps to align labor costs with its pricing. Starbucks cut prices on easier-to-make drinks like drip coffee, while lifting prices by as much as 30 cents for larger and more complex drinks, such as a venti caramel macchiato.

Starbucks' focus on reducing year-over-year variances paid off. In fiscal year 2009, the company reduced its store operating expenses by $320 million, or 8.5%. Continued focus on direct-cost variances will be critical to the company's future success in any economic climate.

Sources: Adamy, Janet. 2009. Starbucks brews up new cost cuts by putting lid on afternoon decaf. *Wall Street Journal,* January 28; Adamy, Janet. 2008. New Starbucks brew attracts customers, flak. *Wall Street Journal,* July 1; Harris, Craig. 2007. Starbucks slips; lattes rise. *Seattle Post Intelligencer,* July 23; Jargon, Julie. 2010. Starbucks growth revives, perked by Via. *Wall Street Journal,* January 21; Jargon, Julie. 2009. Latest Starbucks buzzword: 'Lean' Japanese techniques. *Wall Street Journal,* August 4; Kesmodel, David. 2009. Starbucks sees demand stirring again. *Wall Street Journal,* November 6.

1b. Work-in-Process Control		
(10,000 jackets × 2 yards per jacket × Rs 300 per square yard)	60,00,000	
Direct Materials Efficiency Variance		
(2,200 square yards × Rs 300 per square yard)	6,60,000	
Direct Materials Control		
(22,200 square yards × Rs 300 per square yard)		66,60,000
To record direct materials used.		

JOURNAL ENTRY 2: Isolate the direct manufacturing labor price variance and efficiency variance at the time this labor is used by increasing (debiting) Work-in-Process Control at standard quantities allowed for actual output units manufactured at standard prices. Note that Wages Payable Control measures the actual amounts payable to workers based on actual hours worked and actual wage rates.

2. Work-in-Process Control		
(10,000 jackets × 0.80 hour per jacket × Rs 200 per hour)	16,00,000	
Direct Manufacturing Labor Price Variance		
(9,000 hours × Rs 20 per hour)	1,80,000	
Direct Manufacturing Labor Efficiency Variance		
(1,000 hours × Rs 200 per hour)	2,00,000	
Wages Payable Control		
(9,000 hours × Rs 220 per hour)		19,80,000
To record liability for direct manufacturing labor costs.		

We have seen how standard costing and variance analysis help to focus management attention on areas not operating as expected. The journal entries here point to another advantage of standard costing systems—that is, standard costs simplify product costing. As each unit is manufactured, costs are assigned to it using the standard cost of direct materials, the standard cost of direct manufacturing labor and, as you will see in Chapter 8, standard manufacturing overhead cost.

From the perspective of control, all variances are isolated at the earliest possible time. For example, by isolating the direct materials price variance at the time of purchase, corrective actions—such as seeking cost reductions from the current supplier or obtaining price quotes from other potential suppliers—can be taken immediately when a large unfavorable variance is first known rather than waiting until after the materials are used in production.

At the end of the fiscal year, the variance accounts are written off to cost of goods sold if they are immaterial in amount. For simplicity, we assume that the balances in the different direct cost variance accounts as of April 2011 are also the balances at the end of 2011 and therefore immaterial in total. Color Plus would record the following journal entry to write off the direct cost variance accounts to Cost of Goods Sold.

Cost of Goods Sold	5,96,000	
Direct Materials Price Variance	4,44,000	
Direct Materials Efficiency Variance		6,60,000
Direct Manufacturing Labor Price Variance		1,80,000
Direct Manufacturing Labor Efficiency Variance		2,00,000

Alternatively, assuming Color Plus has inventories at the end of the fiscal year, and the variances are material in their amounts, the variance accounts are prorated between cost of goods sold and various inventory accounts using the methods described in Chapter 4. For example, Direct Materials Price Variance is prorated among Materials Control, Work-in-Process Control, Finished Goods Control and Cost of Goods Sold on the basis of the standard costs of direct materials in each account's ending balance. Direct Materials Efficiency Variance is prorated among Work-in-Process Control, Finished Goods Control and Cost of Goods Sold on the basis of the direct material costs in each account's ending balance (after proration of the direct materials price variance).

Many accountants, industrial engineers, and managers maintain that to the extent that variances measure inefficiency or abnormal efficiency during the year, they should be written off instead of being prorated among inventories and cost of goods sold. This reasoning argues for applying a combination of the write-off and proration methods for each individual variance. Consider the efficiency variance. The portion of the efficiency variance that is due to inefficiency and could have been avoided should be written off to cost of goods sold while the portion that is unavoidable should be prorated. If another variance, such as the direct materials price variance, is considered unavoidable because it is entirely caused by general market conditions, it should be prorated. Unlike full proration, this approach avoids carrying the costs of inefficiency as part of inventoriable costs.

Implementing Standard Costing

Standard costing provides valuable information for the management and control of materials, labor, and other activities related to production.

Standard Costing and Information Technology

Modern information technology promotes the increased use of standard costing systems for product costing and control. Companies such as Dell and Sandoz (the manufacturer of generic pharmaceuticals) store standard prices and standard quantities in their computer systems. A bar code scanner records the receipt of materials, immediately costing each material using its stored standard price. The receipt of materials is then matched with the purchase order to record accounts payable and to isolate the direct materials price variance.

The direct materials efficiency variance is calculated as output is completed by comparing the standard quantity of direct materials that should have been used with the computerized request for direct materials submitted by an operator on the production floor. Labor variances are calculated as employees log into production-floor terminals and punch in their employee numbers, start and end times, and the quantity of product they helped produce. Managers use this instantaneous feedback from variances to initiate immediate corrective action, as needed.

Wide Applicability of Standard Costing

Companies that have implemented total quality management and computer-integrated manufacturing (CIM) systems, as well as companies in the service sector, find standard costing to be a useful tool. Companies implementing total quality management programs use standard costing to control materials costs. Service-sector companies such as McDonald's are labor intensive and use standard costs to control labor costs. Companies that have implemented CIM, such as Toyota, use flexible budgeting and standard costing to manage activities such as materials handling and setups. The growing use of Enterprise Resource Planning (ERP) systems, as described in Chapter 6, has made it easy for firms to keep track of standard, average, and actual costs for inventory items and to make real-time assessments of variances. Managers use variance information to identify areas of the firm's manufacturing or purchasing process that most need attention.

Management Uses of Variances

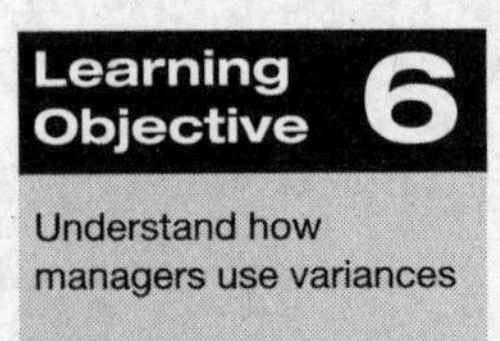

Understand how managers use variances

. . . managers use variances to improve future performance

Managers and management accountants use variances to evaluate performance after decisions are implemented, to trigger organization learning, and to make continuous improvements. Variances serve as an early warning system to alert managers to existing problems or to prospective opportunities. Variance analysis enables managers to evaluate the effectiveness of the actions and performance of personnel in the current period, as well as to fine-tune strategies for achieving improved performance in the future. To make sure that managers interpret variances correctly and make appropriate decisions based on them, managers need to recognize that variances can have multiple causes.

Multiple Causes of Variances

Managers must not interpret variances in isolation of each other. The causes of variances in one part of the value chain can be the result of decisions made in another part of the value chain. Consider an unfavorable direct materials efficiency variance on Color's production line. Possible operational causes of this variance across the value chain of the company are:

1. Poor design of products or processes
2. Poor work on the production line because of underskilled workers or faulty machines
3. Inappropriate assignment of labor or machines to specific jobs

4. Congestion due to scheduling a large number of rush orders from Color's sales representatives
5. Color's suppliers not manufacturing cloth materials of uniformly high quality

Item 5 offers an even broader reason for the cause of the unfavorable direct materials efficiency variance by considering inefficiencies in the supply chain of companies—in this case, by the cloth suppliers for Color's jackets. Whenever possible, managers must attempt to understand the root causes of the variances.

When to Investigate Variances

Managers realize that a standard is not a single measure but rather a range of possible acceptable input quantities, costs, output quantities, or prices. Consequently, they expect small variances to arise. A variance within an acceptable range is considered to be an "in control occurrence" and calls for no investigation or action by managers. So when would managers need to investigate variances?

Frequently, managers investigate variances based on subjective judgments or rules of thumb. For critical items, such as product defects, even a small variance may prompt investigations and actions. For other items, such as direct material costs, labor costs, and repair costs, companies generally have rules such as "investigate all variances exceeding Rs 50,000 or 25% of budgeted cost, whichever is lower." The idea is that a 4% variance in direct material costs of Rs 1,00,00,000—a Rs 4,00,000 variance—deserves more attention than a 20% variance in repair costs of Rs 1,00,000—a Rs 20,000 variance. Variance analysis is subject to the same cost-benefit test as all other phases of a management control system.

Performance Measurement Using Variances

Managers often use variance analysis when evaluating the performance of their subordinates. Two attributes of performance are commonly evaluated:

1. **Effectiveness:** the degree to which a predetermined objective or target is met—for example, sales, customer satisfaction, and quality of Nokia's new line of cell phones.
2. **Efficiency:** the relative amount of inputs used to achieve a given output level—the smaller the quantity of inputs used to make a given number of cell phones or the greater the number of cell phones made from a given quantity of input, the greater the efficiency.

As we discussed earlier, managers must be sure they understand the causes of a variance before using it for performance evaluation. Suppose a Color Plus purchasing manager has just negotiated a deal that results in a favorable price variance for direct materials. The deal could have achieved a favorable variance for any or all of the following reasons:

1. The purchasing manager bargained effectively with suppliers.
2. The purchasing manager secured a discount for buying in bulk with fewer purchase orders. However, buying larger quantities than necessary for the short run resulted in excessive inventory.
3. The purchasing manager accepted a bid from the lowest-priced supplier after only minimal effort to check quality amid concerns about the supplier's materials.

If the purchasing manager's performance is evaluated solely on price variances, then the evaluation will be positive. Reason 1 would support this favorable conclusion: The purchasing manager bargained effectively. Reasons 2 and 3 have short-run gains, buying in bulk or making only minimal effort to check the supplier's quality-monitoring procedures. However, these short-run gains could be offset by higher inventory storage costs or higher inspection costs and defect rates on Color's production line, leading to unfavorable direct manufacturing labor and direct materials efficiency variances.

Color Plus may ultimately lose more money because of reasons 2 and 3 than it gains from the favorable price variance.

Bottom line: Managers should not automatically interpret a favorable variance as "good news."

Managers benefit from variance analysis because it highlights individual aspects of performance. However, if any single performance measure (for example, a labor efficiency variance or a consumer rating report) receives excessive emphasis, managers will tend to make decisions that will cause the particular performance measure to look good. These actions may conflict with the company's overall goals, inhibiting the goals from being achieved. This faulty perspective on performance usually arises when top management designs a performance evaluation and reward system that does not emphasize total company objectives.

Organization Learning

The goal of variance analysis is for managers to understand why variances arise, to learn, and to improve future performance. For instance, to reduce the unfavorable direct materials efficiency variance, Color's managers may seek improvements in product design, in the commitment of workers to do the job right the first time, and in the quality of supplied materials, among other improvements. Sometimes an unfavorable direct materials efficiency variance may signal a need to change product strategy, perhaps because the product cannot be made at a low enough cost. Variance analysis should not be a tool to "play the blame game" (that is, seeking a person to blame for every unfavorable variance). Rather, it should help the company learn about what happened and how to perform better in the future.

Managers need to strike a delicate balance between the two uses of variances we have discussed: performance evaluation and organization learning. Variance analysis is helpful for performance evaluation, but an overemphasis on performance evaluation and meeting individual variance targets can undermine learning and continuous improvement. Why? Because achieving the standard becomes an end in and of itself. As a result, managers will seek targets that are easy to attain rather than targets that are challenging and that require creativity and resourcefulness. For example, if performance evaluation is overemphasized, Color's manufacturing manager will prefer an easy standard that allows workers ample time to manufacture a jacket; he will then have little incentive to improve processes and methods to reduce manufacturing time and cost.

An overemphasis on performance evaluation may also cause managers to take actions to achieve the budget and avoid an unfavorable variance, even if such actions could hurt the company in the long run. For example, the manufacturing manager may push workers to produce jackets within the time allowed, even if this action could lead to poorer quality jackets being produced, which could later hurt revenues. Such negative impacts are less likely to occur if variance analysis is seen as a way of promoting organization learning.

Continuous Improvement

Managers can also use variance analysis to create a virtuous cycle of continuous improvement. How? By repeatedly identifying causes of variances, initiating corrective actions, and evaluating results of actions. Improvement opportunities are often easier to identify when products are first produced. Once the easy opportunities have been identified ("the low-hanging fruit picked"), much more ingenuity may be required to identify successive improvement opportunities.

Financial and Nonfinancial Performance Measures

Almost all companies use a combination of financial and nonfinancial performance measures for planning and control rather than relying exclusively on either type of measure. To control a production process, supervisors cannot wait for an accounting report with variances reported in rupees. Instead, timely nonfinancial performance measures are frequently used for control purposes in such situations. For example, a Honda plant compiles data such as defect rates and production-schedule attainment and broadcasts them in ticker-tape fashion on screens throughout the plant.

In Color's cutting room, cloth is laid out and cut into pieces, which are then matched and assembled. Managers exercise control in the cutting room by observing workers and by focusing on *nonfinancial measures,* such as number of square yards of cloth used to produce 1,000 jackets or percentage of jackets started and completed without requiring any rework. Color Plus production workers find these nonfinancial measures easy to understand. At the same time, Color Plus production managers will also use *financial measures* to evaluate the overall cost efficiency with which operations are being run and to help guide decisions about, say, changing the mix of inputs used in manufacturing jackets. Financial measures are often critical in a company because they indicate the economic impact of diverse physical activities. This knowledge allows managers to make trade-offs—increase the costs of one physical activity (say, cutting) to reduce the costs of another physical measure (say, defects).

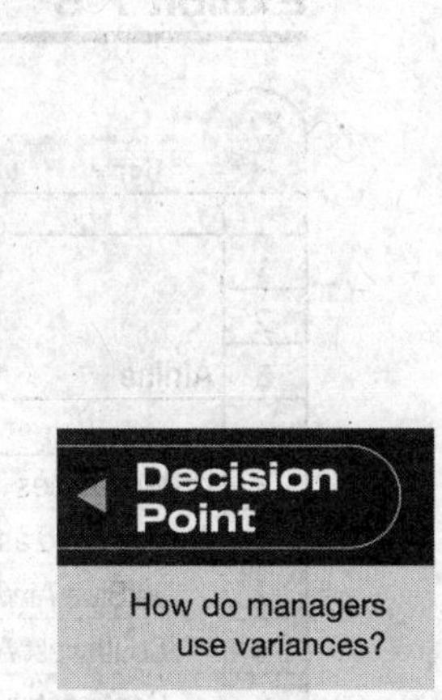
Decision Point
How do managers use variances?

Benchmarking and Variance Analysis

Learning Objective 7

Describe benchmarking and explain its role in cost management

. . . benchmarking compares actual performance against the best levels of performance

The budgeted amounts in the Color Plus Company illustration are based on analysis of operations within their own respective companies. We now turn to the situation in which companies develop standards based on an analysis of operations at other companies. **Benchmarking** is the continuous process of comparing the levels of performance in producing products and services and executing activities against the best levels of performance in competing companies or in companies having similar processes. When benchmarks are used as standards, managers and management accountants know that the company will be competitive in the marketplace if it can attain the standards.

Companies develop benchmarks and calculate variances on items that are the most important to their businesses. Consider the cost per available seat mile (ASM) for United Airlines; ASMs equal the total seats in a plane multiplied by the distance traveled, and are a measure of airline size. Assume United uses data from each of seven competing U.S. airlines in its benchmark cost comparisons. Summary data are in Exhibit 7-5. The benchmark companies are ranked from lowest to highest operating cost per ASM in column 1. Also reported in Exhibit 7-5 are operating revenue per ASM, operating income per ASM, labor cost per ASM, fuel cost per ASM, and total available seat miles. The impact of the recession on the travel industry is evident in the fact that only two airlines—JetBlue and Southwest—have positive levels of operating income.

How well did United manage its costs? The answer depends on which specific benchmark is being used for comparison. United's actual operating cost of Re. 1.574 per ASM is above the average operating cost of Re 1.356 per ASM of the seven other airlines. Moreover, United's operating cost per ASM is 55.7% higher than JetBlue Airways, the lowest-cost competitor at Re 1.011 per ASM [(1.574 – 1.011) ÷ 1.011 = 55.7%]. So why is United's operating cost per ASM so high? Columns E and F suggest that both fuel cost and labor cost are possible reasons. These benchmarking data alert management at United that it needs to become more efficient in its use of both material and labor inputs to become more cost competitive.

Using benchmarks such as those in Exhibit 7-5 is not without problems. Finding appropriate benchmarks is a major issue in implementing benchmarking. Many companies purchase benchmark data from consulting firms. Another problem is ensuring the benchmark numbers are comparable. In other words, there needs to be an "apples to apples" comparison. Differences can exist across companies in their strategies, inventory costing methods, depreciation methods, and so on. For example, JetBlue serves fewer cities and has mostly long-haul flights compared with United, which

Exhibit 7-5 Available Seat Mile (ASM) Benchmark Comparison of United Airlines with Seven Other Airlines

	A	B	C	D	E	F	G
1		Operating Cost	Operating Revenue	Operating Income	Fuel Cost	Labor Cost	Total ASMs
2		per ASM	per ASM	per ASM	per ASM	per ASM	(Millions)
3	Airline	(1)	(2)	(3) = (2) – (1)	(4)	(5)	(6)
4							
5	United Airlines	Rs 1.574	Rs 1.258	–Rs 0.315	Rs 0.568	Rs 0.317	13,58,610
6	Airlines used as benchmarks:						
7	JetBlue Airways	Rs 1.011	Rs 1.045	Rs 0.034	Rs 0.417	Rs 0.214	3,24,220
8	Southwest Airlines	Rs 1.024	Rs 1.067	Rs 0.043	Rs 0.360	Rs 0.323	10,32,710
9	Continental Airlines	Rs 1.347	Rs 1.319	–Rs 0.027	Rs 0.425	Rs 0.258	11,55,110
10	Alaska Airlines	Rs 1.383	Rs 1.330	–Rs 0.053	Rs 0.480	Rs 0.319	2,42,180
11	American Airlines	Rs 1.387	Rs 1.301	–Rs 0.086	Rs 0.551	Rs 0.407	16,35,320
12	U.S. Airways	Rs 1.466	Rs 1.263	–Rs 0.203	Rs 0.488	Rs 0.301	7,41,510
13	Delta/Northwest Airlines	Rs 1.872	Rs 1.370	–Rs 0.502	Rs 0.443	Rs 0.290	16,56,390
14	Average of airlines						
15	used as benchmarks	Rs 1.356	Rs 1.242	–Rs 0.113	Rs 0.452	Rs 0.302	9,69,630
16							
17							
18	*Source:* Individual companies' 10-K reports for the year ending December 31, 2008						

serves almost all major U.S. cities and several international cities and has both long-haul and short-haul flights. Southwest Airlines differs from United because it specializes in short-haul direct flights and offers fewer services on board its planes. Because United's strategy is different from the strategies of JetBlue and Southwest, one might expect its cost per ASM to be different too. United's strategy is more comparable to the strategies of American, Continental, Delta, and U.S. Airways. Note that its costs per ASM are relatively more competitive with these airlines. But United competes head-to-head with JetBlue and Southwest in several cities and markets, so it still needs to benchmark against these carriers as well.

United's management accountants can use benchmarking data to address several questions. How do factors such as plane size and type, or the duration of flights, affect the cost per ASM? Do airlines differ in their fixed cost/variable cost structures? Can performance be improved by rerouting flights, using different types of aircraft on different routes, or changing the frequency or timing of specific flights? What explains revenue differences per ASM across airlines? Is it differences in perceived quality of service or differences in competitive power at specific airports? Management accountants are more valuable to managers when they use benchmarking data to provide insight into *why* costs or revenues differ across companies, or within plants of the same company, as distinguished from simply reporting the magnitude of such differences.

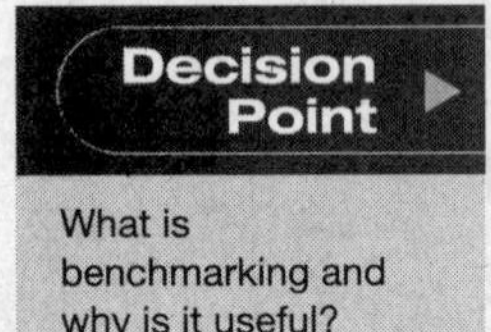

What is benchmarking and why is it useful?

Problem for Self-Study

Somani Pilkingston Company manufactures ceramic vases. It uses its standard costing system when developing its flexible-budget amounts. In April 2012, 2,000 finished units were produced. The following information relates to its two direct manufacturing cost categories: direct materials and direct manufacturing labor.

Direct materials used were 4,400 kilograms (kg). The standard direct materials input allowed for one output unit is 2 kilograms at Rs 150 per kilogram. Somani purchased 5,000 kilograms of materials at Rs 165.0 per kilogram, a total of Rs 8,25,000. (This Problem for Self-Study illustrates how to calculate direct materials variances when the quantity of materials *purchased* in a period differs from the quantity of materials *used* in that period.)

Actual direct manufacturing labor-hours were 3,250, at a total cost of Rs 6,63,000. Standard manufacturing labor time allowed is 1.5 hours per output unit, and the standard direct manufacturing labor cost is Rs 200 per hour.

Required

1. Calculate the direct materials price variance and efficiency variance, and the direct manufacturing labor price variance and efficiency variance. Base the direct materials price variance on a flexible budget for *actual quantity purchased,* but base the direct materials efficiency variance on a flexible budget for *actual quantity used.*
2. Prepare journal entries for a standard costing system that isolates variances at the earliest possible time.

Solution

1. Exhibit 7-6 shows how the columnar presentation of variances introduced in Exhibit 7-3 can be adjusted for the difference in timing between purchase and use of materials. Note, in particular, the two sets of computations in column 2 for direct materials—the Rs 7,50,000 for direct materials purchased and the Rs 6,60,000 for direct materials used. The direct materials price variance is calculated on purchases so that managers responsible for the purchase can immediately identify and isolate reasons for the variance and initiate any desired corrective action. The efficiency variance is the responsibility of the production manager, so this variance is identified only at the time materials are used.
2.

Materials Control (5,000 kg × Rs 150 per kg)	7,50,000	
Direct Materials Price Variance (5,000 kg × Rs 15 per kg)	75,000	
Accounts Payable Control (5,000 kg × Rs 165 per kg)		8,25,000
Work in Process Control (2,000 units × 2 kg per uni × Rs 150 per kg)	6,00,000	
Direct Materials Efficiency Variance (400 kg × Rs 150 per kg)	60,000	
Materials Control (4,400 kg × Rs 150 per kg)		6,60,000
Work in Process Control (2,000 units × 1.5 hours per unit × Rs 200 per hour)	6,00,000	
Direct Manufacturing Labor Price Variance (3,250 hours × Rs 4 per hour)	13,000	
Direct Manufacturing Labor Efficiency Variance (250 hours × Rs 200 per hour)	50,000	
Wages Payable Control (3,250 hours × Rs 204 per hour)		6,63,000

Note: All the variances are debits because they are unfavorable and therefore reduce operating income.

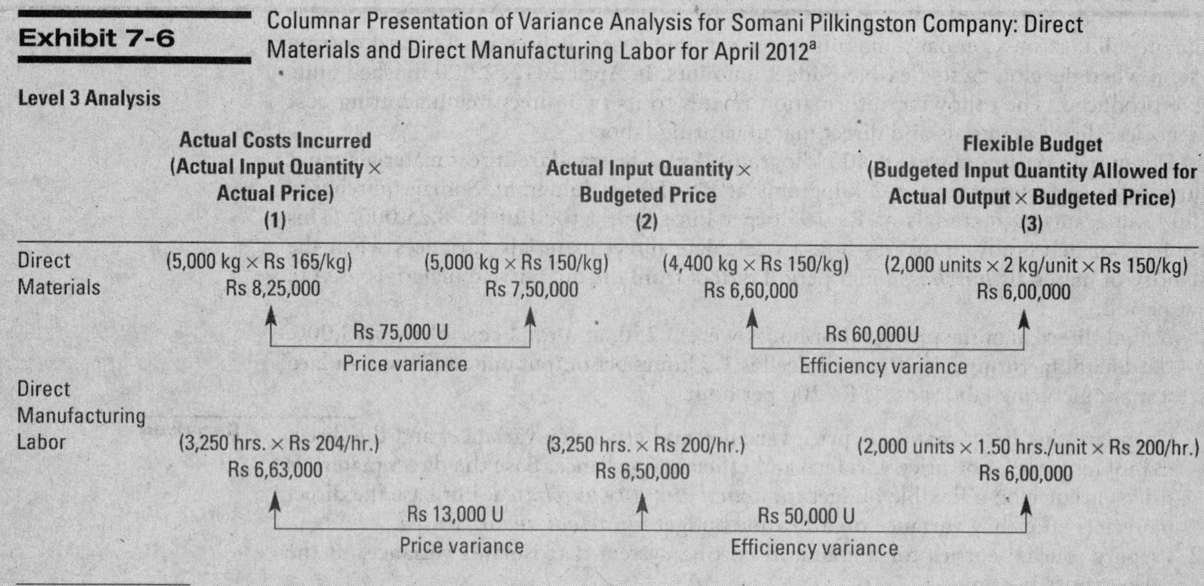

Exhibit 7-6 Columnar Presentation of Variance Analysis for Somani Pilkingston Company: Direct Materials and Direct Manufacturing Labor for April 2012[a]

Level 3 Analysis

	Actual Costs Incurred (Actual Input Quantity × Actual Price) (1)		Actual Input Quantity × Budgeted Price (2)		Flexible Budget (Budgeted Input Quantity Allowed for Actual Output × Budgeted Price) (3)
Direct Materials	(5,000 kg × Rs 165/kg) Rs 8,25,000	(5,000 kg × Rs 150/kg) Rs 7,50,000	(4,400 kg × Rs 150/kg) Rs 6,60,000		(2,000 units × 2 kg/unit × Rs 150/kg) Rs 6,00,000
	Rs 75,000 U Price variance			Rs 60,000U Efficiency variance	
Direct Manufacturing Labor	(3,250 hrs. × Rs 204/hr.) Rs 6,63,000		(3,250 hrs. × Rs 200/hr.) Rs 6,50,000		(2,000 units × 1.50 hrs./unit × Rs 200/hr.) Rs 6,00,000
	Rs 13,000 U Price variance			Rs 50,000 U Efficiency variance	

[a]F = favorable effect on operating income; U = unfavorable effect on operating income.

Decision Points

The following question-and-answer format summarizes the chapter's learning objectives. Each decision presents a key question related to a learning objective. The guidelines are the answer to that question.

Decision	Guidelines
1. How does a flexible budget differ from a static budget, and why should companies use flexible budgets?	A static budget is based on the level of output planned at the start of the budget period. A flexible budget is adjusted (flexed) to recognize the actual output level of the budget period. Flexible budgets help managers gain more insight into the causes of variances than is available from static budgets.
2. How can managers develop a flexible budget and compute the flexible-budget variance and the sales-volume variance?	Managers use a three-step procedure to develop a flexible budget. When all costs are either variable with respect to output units or fixed, these three steps require only information about budgeted selling price, budgeted variable cost per output unit, budgeted fixed costs, and actual quantity of output units. The static-budget variance can be subdivided into a flexible-budget variance (the difference between an actual result and the corresponding flexible-budget amount) and a sales-volume variance (the difference between the flexible-budget amount and the corresponding static-budget amount).
3. What is a standard cost and what are its purposes?	A standard cost is a carefully determined cost used as a benchmark for judging performance. The purposes of a standard cost are to exclude past inefficiencies and to take into account changes expected to occur in the budget period.
4. Why should a company calculate price and efficiency variables?	The computation of price and efficiency variances helps managers gain insight into two different—but not independent—aspects of performance. The price variance focuses on the difference between actual input price and budgeted input price. The efficiency variance focuses on the difference between actual quantity of input and budgeted quantity of input allowed for actual output.

5. How do managers use variances?	Managers use variances for control, decision implementation, performance evaluation, organization learning, and continuous improvement. When using variances for these purposes, managers consider several variances together rather than focusing only on an individual variance.
6. Can variance analysis be used with an activity-based costing system?	Variance analysis can be applied to activity costs (such as setup costs) to gain insight into why actual activity costs differ from activity costs in the static budget or in the flexible budget. Interpreting cost variances for different activities requires understanding whether the costs are output unit-level, batch-level, product-sustaining, or facility-sustaining costs.
7. What is benchmarking and why is it useful?	Benchmarking is the process of comparing the level of performance in producing products and services and executing activities against the best levels of performance in competing companies or companies with similar processes. Benchmarking measures how well a company and its managers are doing in comparison to other organizations.

TERMS TO LEARN

This chapter and the Glossary at the end of the book contain definitions of:

benchmarking **(p. 273)**
budgeted performance **(p. 255)**
effectiveness **(p. 271)**
efficiency **(p. 271)**
efficiency variance **(p. 264)**
favorable variance **(p. 257)**
flexible budget **(p. 258)**
flexible-budget variance **(p. 259)**
input-price variance **(p. 264)**
management by exception **(p. 255)**
price variance **(p. 263)**
rate variance **(p. 264)**
sales-volume variance **(p. 259)**
selling-price variance **(p. 261)**
standard **(p. 262)**
standard cost **(p. 263)**
standard input **(p. 262)**
standard price **(p. 262)**
static budget **(p. 257)**
static-budget variance **(p. 257)**
unfavorable variance **(p. 258)**
usage variance **(p. 264)**
variance **(p. 255)**

ASSIGNMENT MATERIAL

Questions

7-1 What is the relationship between management by exception and variance analysis?

7-2 What are two possible sources of information a company might use to compute the budgeted amount in variance analysis?

7-3 Distinguish between a favorable variance and an unfavorable variance.

7-4 What is the key difference between a static budget and a flexible budget?

7-5 Why might managers find a flexible-budget analysis more informative than a static-budget analysis?

7-6 Describe the steps in developing a flexible budget.

7-7 List four reasons for using standard costs.

7-8 How might a manager gain insight into the causes of a flexible-budget variance for direct materials?

7-9 List three causes of a favorable direct materials price variance.

7-10 Describe three reasons for an unfavorable direct manufacturing labor efficiency variance.

7-11 How does variance analysis help in continuous improvement?

7-12 Why might an analyst examining variances in the production area look beyond that business function for explanations of those variances?

7-13 Comment on the following statement made by a plant manager: "Meetings with my plant accountant are frustrating. All he wants to do is pin the blame on someone for the many variances he reports."

7-14 How can variances be used to analyze costs in individual activity areas?

7-15 "Benchmarking against other companies enables a company to identify the lowest-cost producer. This amount should become the performance measure for next year." Do you agree?

Solved Examples

7-16 Flexible budget. Bridgestone Limited manufactures tires. For August 2012, it budgeted to manufacture and sell 3,000 tires at a variable cost of Rs 740 per tire and total fixed costs for Rs 5,40,000. The budgeted selling price was Rs 1,100 per tire. Actual results in August 2012 were 2,800 tires manufactured and sold at a selling price of Rs 1,120 per tire. The actual total variable costs were Rs 22,96,000, and the actual total fixed costs were Rs 5,00,000.

Required

1. Prepare a performance report that uses a flexible budget and a static budget.
2. Comment on the results in requirement 1.

Solution

1. **Flexible budget.**

	Actual Results (1)	Flexible-Budget Variances (2) = (1) — (3)	Flexible Budget (3)	Sales-Volume Variances (4) = (3) — (5)	Static Budget (5)
Units sold	2,800[G]	0	2,800	200 U	3,000[G]
Revenues	Rs 31,36,000[a]	Rs 56,000 F	Rs 30,80,000[b]	Rs 2,20,000 U	Rs 33,00,000[c]
Variable costs	22,96,000[d]	2,24,000 U	20,72,000[e]	1,48,000 F	22,20,000[f]
Contribution margin	8,40,000	1,68,000 U	10,08,000	72,000 U	10,80,000
Fixed costs	5,00,000[G]	40,000 F	5,40,000[G]	0	5,40,000[G]
Operating income	Rs 3,40,000	Rs 1,28,000 U	Rs 4,68,000	Rs 72,000 U	Rs 5,40,000

Rs 1,28,000 U — Total flexible-budget variance

Rs 72,000 U — Total sales-volume variance

Rs 20,0000 U — Total static-budget variance

[a]Rs 1,120 × 2,800 = Rs 31,36,000
[b]Rs 1,100 × 2,800 = Rs 30,80,000
[c]Rs 1,100 × 3,000 = Rs 33,00,000
[d]Given. Unit variable cost = Rs 22,96,000 ÷ 2,800 = Rs 820 per tire
eRs 740 × 2,800 = Rs 20,72,000
[f]Rs 740 × 3,000 = Rs 22,20,000
[G]Given

2. The total static-budget variance in operating income is Rs 2,00,000 U. There is both an unfavorable total flexible-budget variance (Rs 1,28,000) and an unfavorable sales-volume variance (Rs 72,000).

The unfavorable sales-volume variance arises solely because actual units manufactured and sold were 200 less than the budgeted 3,000 units. The unfavorable flexible-budget variance of Rs 1,28,000 in operating income is due primarily to the Rs 80 increase in unit variable costs. This increase in unit variable costs is only partially offset by the Rs 20 increase in unit selling price and Rs 40,000 decrease in fixed costs.

7-17 Flexible budget. VIP Company's budgeted prices for direct materials, direct manufacturing labor, and direct marketing (distribution) cost per attaché case are Rs 400, Rs 80, and Rs 120, respectively. The president is pleased with the following performance report:

	Actual Costs	Static Budget	Variance
Direct materials	Rs 36,40,000	Rs 40,00,000	Rs 3,60,000 F
Direct manufacturing labor	7,80,000	8,00,000	20,000 F
Direct marketing (distribution) cost	11,00,000	12,00,000	1,00,000 F

Required

Actual output was 8,800 attache' cases. Is the president's pleasure justified? Prepare a revised performance report that uses a flexible budget and a static budget. Assume all three direct-cost items above are variable costs.

Solution

Flexible budget.

The existing performance report is a Level 1 analysis, based on a static budget. It makes no adjustment for changes in output levels. The budgeted output level is 10,000 units—direct materials of Rs 40,00,000 in the static budget ÷ budgeted direct materials cost per attaché case of Rs 400.

The following is a Level 2 analysis that presents a flexible-budget variance and a sales-volume variance of each direct cost category:

	Actual Results (1)	Flexible-Budget Variances (2) = (1) — (3)	Flexible Budget (3)	Sales-Volume Variances (4) = (3) — (5)	Static Budget (5)
Output units	8,800	0	8,800	-1,200 U	10,000
Direct materials	Rs 36,40,000	Rs 1,20,000 U	Rs 35,20,000	Rs 4,80,000 F	Rs 40,00,000
Direct manufacturing labor	7,80,000	76,000 U	7,04,000	96,000 F	8,00,000

Direct marketing cost	11,00,000	44,000 U	10,56,000	1,44,000 F	12,00,000
Total direct costs	Rs 55,20,000	Rs 2,40,000 U	Rs 52,80,000	Rs 7,20,000 F	Rs 60,00,000

Rs 2,40,000 U | Rs 7,20,000 F

Flexible-budget variance | Sales-volume variance

Rs 4,80,000 F

Static-budget variance

The Level 1 analysis shows total direct costs have a Rs 4,80,000 favorable variance. However, the Level 2 analysis reveals that this favorable variance is due to the reduction in output of 1,200 units from the budgeted 10,000 units. Once this reduction in output is taken into account (via a flexible budget), the flexible-budget variance shows each direct cost category to have an unfavorable variance indicating less efficient use of each direct cost item than was budgeted, or the use of more costly direct cost items than was budgeted, or both.

	Actual	Budgeted
Units	8,800	10,000
Direct materials	Rs 413.60	Rs 400
Direct manufacturing labor	Rs 88.60	Rs 80
Direct marketing labor	Rs 125.00	Rs 120

7-18 Price and efficiency variances. Bikaner Foods makes milk cake. For January it budgeted to purchase and use 15,000 kg of milk at Rs 17.80 a kg. Actual purchase and usage for January was 16,000 kg at Rs 16.40 a kg. It budgets for 3,750 kg milk cake. Actual output was 3,800 kg milk cake. Ignore, other ingredients inputs used to make milk-cake.

Required

1. Compute the 1 flexible-budged variance and (2) price and efficiency variances.
2. Comment on the results in requirements 1 and 2.

Solution

Price and efficiency variances.

1. The key information items are:

	Actual	Budgeted
Output units (scones)	3,800	3,750
Input units (kg of pumpkin)	16,000	15,000
Cost per input unit	Rs 16.40	Rs 17.80

Bikaner budgets to obtain one-four kg of milk-cake from each kg of milk used.

2.

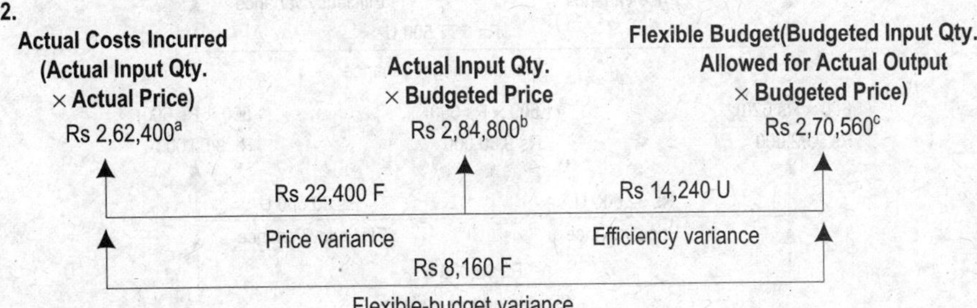

[a]16,000 × Rs 16.40 = Rs 2,62,400
[b]16,000 × Rs 17.80 = Rs 2,84,800
[c]3,800 × 4 × Rs 17.80 = Rs 2,70,560

2. The favorable flexible-budget variance of Rs 8,160 has two offsetting components:

(a) favorable price variance of Rs 22,400—reflects the Rs 16.40 actual purchase cost being lower than the Rs 17.80 budgeted purchase cost per kg.

(b) unfavorable efficiency variance of Rs 14,240—reflects the actual materials yield of 0.2375 per kg of milk (3,800 ÷ 16,000 = 0.2375) being less than the budgeted yield of 0.25 (3,750 ÷ 15,000 = 0.25). (The company used more milk to make the milk-cake than was budgeted.)

One explanation may be that Bikaner Foods purchased lower quality milk at a lower cost per kg.

7-19 Price and efficiency variances. Idea is a cellular phone service reseller. Idea contracts with major cellular operators for airtime in bulk and then resells service to retail customers. Idea budgeted to sell, 78,00,000 minutes in the month ended March 31, 2012. Actual minutes sold totaled only 75,00,000. Due to fluctuations in hourly usage, Idea "overbuys" airtime from cellular operators. Idea plans to buy 10% more airtime than it plans to sell. For example, Idea's budgets called for the purchase of 85,80,000 minutes, based on the plan to sell 78,00,000 minutes. In what follows, think of purchased airtime as direct materials.

Idea budgets purchased airtime to cost 45 paise per minute. Actual purchased airtime in 2012 averaged 50 paise per minute. Idea incurs direct labor costs due to the employment of technicians. One hour of technical support is required for every 5,000 minutes of airtime sold. In practice, only 1,600 hours of technical support were used. Technical support was planned at Rs 600 per hour. Actual technical support costs averaged Rs 620 per hour.

Required

1. Calculate the flexible-budget variance for direct materials and direct labor costs. (Use 82,50,000 (75,00,000 × 1.10) minutes in the flexible budget).
2. Calculate the price and efficiency variances for direct materials and labor costs.

Solution

Flexible budget variance.

1.

	Actual Results (1)	Flexible-Budget Variances (2) = (1) − (3)	Flexible-Budget (3)
Direct materials	Rs 42,90,000	Rs 5,77,500 U	Rs 37,12,500[a]
Direct labor	9,92,000	92,000 U	9,00,000[c]

Actual Results

Direct materials: 85,80,000[b] minutes × Rs 0.50 per minute = Rs 42,90,000

Direct labor: 1,600 hours × Rs 620 per hour = Rs 9,92,000

[a]75,00,000 minutes sold × 110% purchase × Re 0.45 = Rs 37,12,500

[b]78,00,000 minutes × 110% purchase = 85,80,000

[c]75,00,000 minutes sold ÷ 5,000 minutes per hour = 1,500 hours × Rs 600 = Rs 9,00,000

Idea commits to purchase 110% of the budgeted amount of time. Due to the forward commitment of time purchase, the actual time purchased will be the same as the budgeted amount of time to be purchased.

2. Price and Efficiency Variance

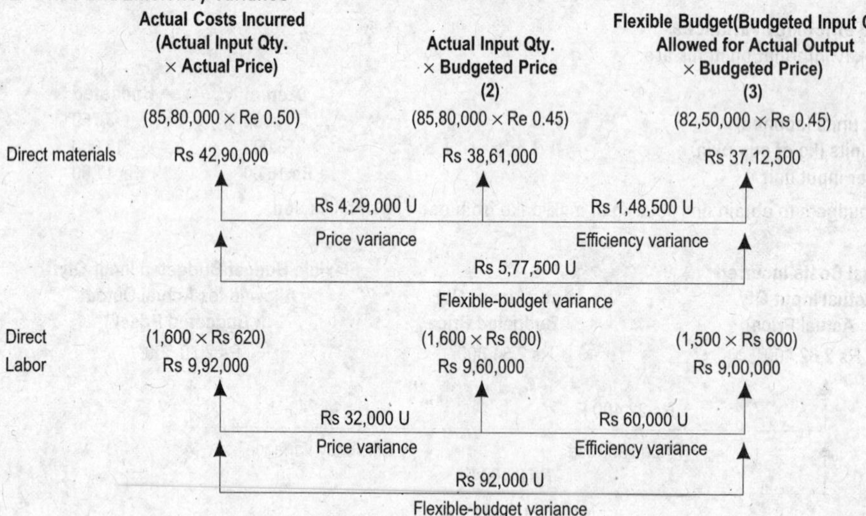

	Actual Costs Incurred (Actual Input Qty. × Actual Price) (1)	Actual Input Qty. × Budgeted Price (2)	Flexible Budget(Budgeted Input Qty. Allowed for Actual Output × Budgeted Price) (3)
	(85,80,000 × Re 0.50)	(85,80,000 × Re 0.45)	(82,50,000 × Rs 0.45)
Direct materials	Rs 42,90,000	Rs 38,61,000	Rs 37,12,500
	Price variance: Rs 4,29,000 U	Efficiency variance: Rs 1,48,500 U	
	Flexible-budget variance: Rs 5,77,500 U		
Direct Labor	(1,600 × Rs 620) Rs 9,92,000	(1,600 × Rs 600) Rs 9,60,000	(1,500 × Rs 600) Rs 9,00,000
	Price variance: Rs 32,000 U	Efficiency variance: Rs 60,000 U	
	Flexible-budget variance: Rs 92,000 U		

7-20 Price and efficiency variances, journal entries. Asian Paints Ltd. has set up the following standards per finished unit for direct materials and direct manufacturing labor:

Direct materials: 10 kg, at Rs 30 per kg.	Rs 300
Direct manufacturing labor: 1 hour at Rs 40 per hour	40

The number of finished units budgeted for March was 10,000; 9,810 units were actually produced. Actual results in March were

Direct materials: 98,073 kg used	
Direct manufacturing labor: 9,800 hours @ Rs 42 per hour	Rs 4,11,600

Assume that there was no beginning inventory of either direct materials or finished units.

During the month, materials purchases amounted to 100,00 kg, at a total cost of Rs 31,00,000. Input-price variances are isolated upon purchase. Input-efficiency variances are isolated at the time of usage.

Required

1. Compute the March price and efficiency variances of direct materials and direct manufacturing labor.
2. Prepare journal entries to record the variances in requirement 1.
3. Comment on the March price and efficiency variances.
4. Why might Asian Paints Ltd. calculate materials price variances and materials efficiency variances separately?

Solution

Price and efficiency variances, journal entries.

1. Direct materials and direct manufacturing labor are analyzed in turn:

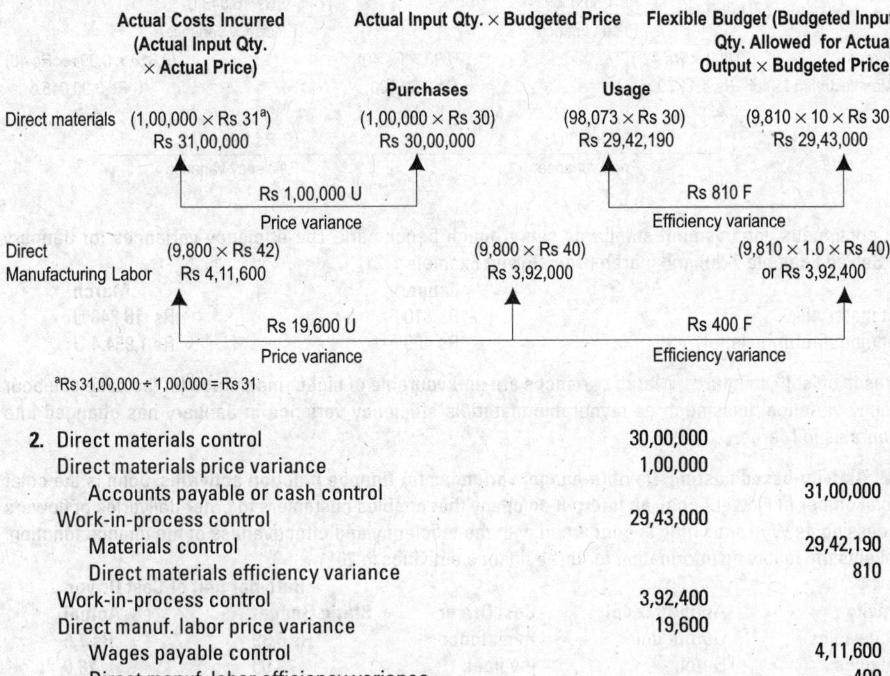

[a]Rs 31,00,000 ÷ 1,00,000 = Rs 31

2.

Direct materials control	30,00,000	
Direct materials price variance	1,00,000	
Accounts payable or cash control		31,00,000
Work-in-process control	29,43,000	
Materials control		29,42,190
Direct materials efficiency variance		810
Work-in-process control	3,92,400	
Direct manuf. labor price variance	19,600	
Wages payable control		4,11,600
Direct manuf. labor efficiency variance		400

3. A possibility is that approximately the same labor force, paid somewhat more, is taking slightly less time with better materials and causing less waste and spoilage.
   A key point in this problem is that all of these efficiency variances are likely to be insignificant. They are so small as to be nearly meaningless. Fluctuations about standards are bound to occur in a random fashion. Practically, from a control viewpoint, a standard is a band or range of acceptable performance rather than a single-figure measure.
4. Asian Paints Ltd. will assign responsibility to two different responsible managers. While the purchase manager is responsible for material price variance, the production manager will be accountable for materials efficiency variance. Therefore, there is need to compute these variances separately.

7-21 Continuous improvement (continuation of 7-20). Asian Paints Ltd., adopts a continuous improvement approach to setting monthly standards costs. Assume the direct materials standard costs of Rs 300 per unit and the direct manufacturing labor cost of Rs 40 per unit pertain to January. The standard amounts for February are 0.997 of the January standard amount. The standard amounts for March are 0.997 of the February standard amount. Assume the same information for March as in Solved Example 7-20, except for these revised standard amounts.

Required

1. Compute March standard amounts for direct materials and direct manufacturing labor.
2. Compute the March price and efficiency variances for direct materials and direct manufacturing labor.

Solution

Continuous improvement. (continuation of 7-20)

1. Standard quantity input amounts per output unit are:

	Direct Materials(kg)	Direct Manufacturing Labor(hours)
January	10.0000	0.1000
February (Jan. × 0.997)	9.9700	0.997
March (Feb. × 0.997)	9.9400	0.994

2. The answer to requirement 1 of Question 7-20 is identical except for the flexible-budget amount.

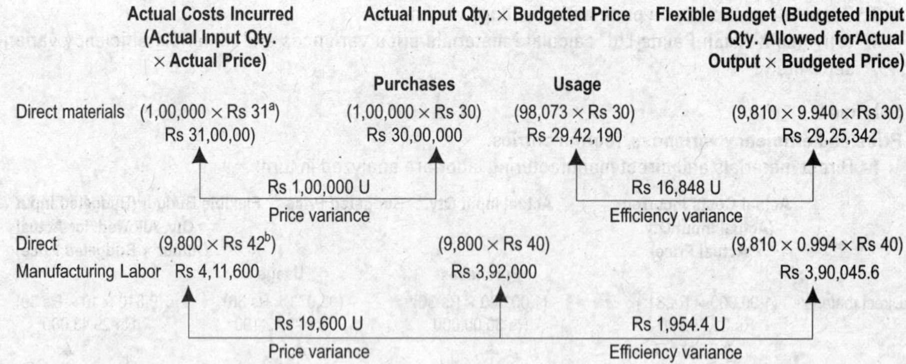

Using continuous imporvement standards sets a tough benchmark. The effciency variances for Jaunary (from Solved Example 7-20) and march (from Solved Example 7-21)

	January	March
Direct materials	Rs 810 F	Rs 16,848 U
Direct manufacturing labor	Rs 400 F	Rs 1,954.4 U

As a result of 'stiff' standards, March variances are unfavourable of higher magnitude (in the case of labour efficiency variance); inasmuch as favourable materials efficiency variance in January has changed into unfarourable in March.

7-22 Activity-based costing, flexible-budget variances for finance function activities. John is the chief financial officer of Flowers.com, an Internet company that enables customers to order deliveries of flowers by accessing its Web site. John is concerned with the efficiency and effectiveness of the finance function. He collects the following information for three finance activities in 2011.

			Rate per unit of Cost Driver	
Activity	**Activity Level**	**Cost Driver**	**Static Budget**	**Actual**
Receivables	Output unit	Remittances	Rs 6.39	Rs 7.5
Payables	Batch	Invoices	29.00	28.0
Travel expenses	Batch	Travel claims	76.00	74.0

The output measure is the number of deliveries, which is the same as the number of remittances. The following is additional information.

	Static-Budget Amounts	Actual Amounts
Number of deliveries	10,00,000	9,48,000
Batch size in terms of deliveries:		
Payables	5	4.468
Travel expenses	500	501.587

Required

1. Calculate the flexible-budget variance for each activity in 2011.
2. Calculate the price and efficiency variances for each activity in 2011.

Solution

Activity-based costing, flexible-budget variances for finance function activities.

1. Receivables

Receivables is an output unit level activity. Its flexible-budget variance can be calculated as follows:

$$\text{Flexible - budget variance} = \text{Actual costs} - \text{Flexible - budget costs}$$
$$= (\text{Rs } 7.5 \times 9{,}48{,}000) - (\text{Rs } 6.39 \times 9{,}48{,}000)$$
$$= \text{Rs } 71{,}10{,}000 - \text{Rs } 60{,}57{,}720$$
$$= \text{Rs } 10{,}52{,}280 \text{ U}$$

Payables

Payables is a batch level activity.

	Static-Budget Amounts	Actual Amounts
a. Number of deliveries	10,00,000	9,48,000
b. Batch size (units per batch)	5	4.468
c. Number of batches (a ÷ b)	2,00,000	2,12,175
d. Cost per batch	Rs 29	Rs 28
e. Total payables activity cost (c × d)	Rs 58,00,000	Rs 59,40,900

Step 1: The number of batches in which payables should have been processed = 9,48,000 actual units × 5 budgeted units per batch = 189,600 batches

Step 2: The flexible-budget amount for payables
= 1,89,600 batches × Rs 29 budgeted cost per batch = Rs 54,98,400

The flexible-budget variance can be computed as follows:

Flexible-budget variance = Actual costs – Flexible-budget costs
= (2,12,175 × Rs 28) – (1,89,600 × Rs 29)
= Rs 59,40,900 – Rs 54,98,400 = Rs 4,42,500 U

Travel expenses

Travel expenses is a batch level activity.

	Static-Budget Amounts	Actual Amounts
a. Number of deliveries	10,00,000	9,48,000
b. Batch size (units per batch)	500	501.587
c. Number of batches (a ÷ b)	2,000	1,890
d. Cost per batch	Rs 76	Rs 74
e. Total travel expenses activity cost (c × d)	Rs 1,52,000	Rs 1,39,860

Step 1: The number of batches in which the travel expense should have been processed = 948,000 actual units ÷ 500 budgeted units per batch = 1,896 batches

Step 2: The flexible-budget amount for travel expenses
= 1,896 batches × Rs 76 budgeted cost per batch = Rs 1,44,096

The flexible budget variance can be calculated as follows:

Flexible budget variance = Actual costs – Flexible-budget costs
= (1,890 × Rs 74) – (1,896 × Rs 76)
= Rs 1,39,860 – Rs 1,44,096 = Rs 4,236 F

$$\text{Price variance} = \left[\begin{array}{c}\text{Actual price}\\ \text{of input}\end{array} - \begin{array}{c}\text{Budgeted price}\\ \text{of input}\end{array}\right] \times \begin{array}{c}\text{Actual quantity}\\ \text{of input}\end{array}$$

$$\text{Efficiency variance} = \left[\begin{array}{c}\text{Actual quantity}\\ \text{of input used}\end{array} - \begin{array}{c}\text{Budgeted quantity of}\\ \text{input allowed for}\\ \text{actual output}\end{array}\right] \times \begin{array}{c}\text{Budgeted price}\\ \text{of input}\end{array}$$

2. The flexible budget variances can be subdivided into price and efficiency variances.

Receivables
Price Variance = (Rs 7.50 – Rs 6.39) × 9,48,000 = Rs 10,52,280 U
Efficiency variance = (9,48,000 – 9,48,000) × Rs 6.39 = Zero

Payables
Price variance = (Rs 28 – Rs 29) × 2,12,175 = Rs 2,12,175 F
Efficiency variance = (2,12,175 – 1,89,600) × Rs 29 = Rs 6,54,675 U

Travel expenses
Price variance = (Rs 74 – Rs 76) × 1,890 = Rs 3,780 F
Efficiency variance = (1,890 – 1,896) × Rs 76 = Rs 456 F

7-23 Finance function activities, benchmarking (continuation of 7-22) John, CFO of Flowers.com, engages the BCG Group, a consulting firm specializing in benchmarking. He asks BCG to provide benchmark data of the finance function at "world-class" retail companies (both traditional retail and Internet-based retail). BCG's cost benchmarks for Flowers.com's three finance activities are

Finance Activity	"World-Class" Cost Performance
Payables	Rs 7.1 per invoice
Receivables	Rs 1.0 per remittance
Travel expenses	Rs 15.80 per travel claim

Required

1. What new insight might arise with the BCG benchmark data using the amounts in Solved Example 7-22?
2. Assume you are in charge of travel-claim processing. What concerns might you have with John using the BCG benchmark of Rs 15.80 per travel claim as the key to evaluate your performance next period?

Solution

Finance function fctivities, benchmarking.

1. The key new insight is how Flowers.com compares with "world-class" organizations. At face value, there is much room for improvement. The per unit cost differences are dramatic:

	Flowers.com		
	Budgeted	Actual	"World-Class" Cost Performance
Receivables	Rs 6.39	Rs 7.50	Rs 1.0 per remittance
Payables	Rs 29.00	Rs 28.0	Rs 7.1 per invoice
Travel	Rs 76.00	Rs 74.0	Rs 15.8 per travel claim

2. For any meaningful comparison, the figures being compared must be comparable. John should first determine whether there is an "apples to apples" comparison with these figures. Are costs of the finance department activities measured the same across Flowers.com and the company with "world-class" cost performance? Suppose Flowers.com allocates other costs into the finance area (such as the President's salary), while the Rs 15.80 per travel claim figure is for finance department costs only.

John should consider whether the benchmark company also obtains information on why the large cost differences occur. For example, is it because the "world-class" performer is using new technologies in the finance area? If this is the case, then is John willing to invest in new technologies in the same way that "world-class" finance function organizations do? If not, then the Rs 15.80 benchmark could be unattainable, no matter how hard and smart the travel claim processing group performs.

In addition, John should consider whether the benchmark company provides a valid comparison point. The benchmark company is a world-class retail company that has traditional retail and Internet-based retail functions. Flowers.com is an Internet company. Costs and activities of Internet companies are going to differ from those of traditional retailers.

7-24 Static budget, flexible budget, service sector, professional labor efficiency and effectiveness. LIC Housing Finance helps prospective homeowners find low-cost financing and assists existing homeowners in refinancing their current loans at lower interest rates.

LIC Housing charges clients 0.5% of the loan amount it arranges. In its 2011 static budget, LIC Housing assumes the average loan amount will be Rs 20,00,000. Budgeted cost data per loan application for 2012 are

- Professional labor: 6 hours at a rate of Rs 400 per hour
- Loan filing fees: Rs 1,000
- Credit-worthiness checks: Rs 1,200
- Courier mailings: Rs 500

Office support is budgeted to be Rs 3,10,000 per month. LIC Housing Finance views this amount as a fixed cost.

Required

1. Prepare a static budget for November 2012 assuming 90 loan applications.
2. Prepare a Level 2 variance analysis identifying sales-volume and flexible-budget variances for LIC Housing Finance for November 2012. Actual loan applications in November 2012 were 120, and the average loan amount was Rs 2,24,000. Other actual data for November 2012 were
   - Revenue: Rs 13,44,000
   - Professional labor: 7.2 hours per loan application at Rs 420 per hour; total cost Rs 3,62,880
   - Loan filing fees: Rs 1,000 per loan application; total cost Rs 1,20,000
   - Credit-worthiness checks: Rs 1,250 per loan application; total cost Rs 1,50,000
   - Courier mailings: Rs 540 per loan application; total cost Rs 64,800
   - Office support costs: Rs 33,500
3. Compute professional labor price and efficiency variances for November 2012. (Compute labor price on a per-hour basis).
4. What factors would you consider in evaluation the effectiveness of professional labor in November 2012?

Solution

Static budget, flexible budget, service sector, professional labor efficiency and effectiveness.

		Static Budget
1.	Revenue (90 × 0.5 per cent × Rs 20,00,000)	Rs 9,00,000
	Variable costs:	
	Professional labor (6 × Rs 400 × 90)	2,16,000
	Loan filing fees (Rs 1,000 × 90)	90,000
	Credit-worthiness checks (Rs 1,200 × 90)	1,08,000
	Courier mailings (Rs 500 × 90)	45,000
	Total variable costs	4,59,000
	Contribution margin	4,41,000
	Fixed costs	3,10,000
	Operating income	1,31,000
2.	Flexible budget for November 2007:	
	Revenue (120 × 0.5 per cent × Rs 20,00,000)	Rs 12,00,000
	Variable costs:	
	Professional labor (6 × Rs 400 × 120)	2,88,000
	Loan filing fees (Rs 1,000 × 120)	1,20,000
	Credit-worthiness checks (Rs 1,200 × 120)	1,44,000
	Courier mailings (Rs 500 × 120)	60,000
	Total variable costs	6,12,000
	Contribution margin	5,88,000
	Fixed costs	3,10,000
	Operating income	Rs 2,78,000

Level 2 Analysis

	Actual Results (1)	Flexible-Budget Variances (1) − (3)	Flexible Budget (3)	Sales-Volume Variances (3) − (5)	Static Budget (5)
Loans	120	0	120	30 F	90
Revenue	Rs 13,44,000	Rs 1,44,000 F	Rs 12,00,000	Rs 3,00,000	Rs 9,00,000
Variable costs:					
Professional labor	3,62,880	74,880 U	2,88,000	72,000 U	2,16,000
Loan filing fees	1,20,000	0	1,20,000	30,000 U	90,000
Credit-worthiness checks	1,50,000	6,000 U	1,44,000	36,000 U	1,08,000
Courier mailings	64,800	4,800 U	60,000	15,000 U	45,000
Total variable costs	6,97,680	85,680 U	6,12,000	1,53,000 U	4,59,000
Contribution margin	6,46,320	58,320 F	5,88,000	1,47,000 F	4,41,000
Fixed costs	3,35,000	25,000 U	3,10,000	0	3,10,000
Operating income	Rs 3,11,320	Rs 33,320 F	Rs 2,78,000	Rs 1,47,000	Rs 1,31,000

Rs 33,320 F — Total flexible-budget variance
Rs 1,47,000 F — Total sales-volume variance
Rs 1,80,320 F — Total static-budget variance

3.

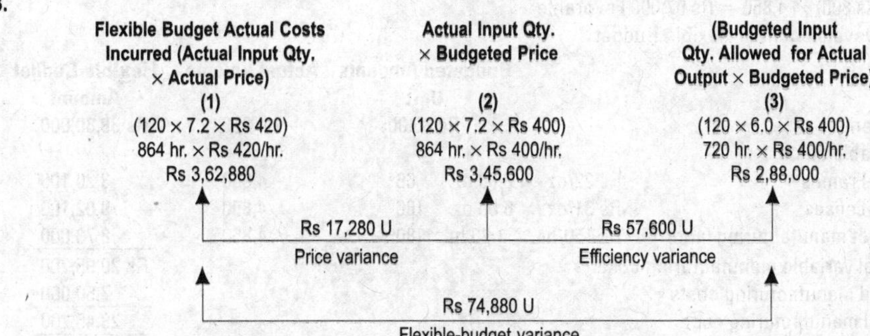

4. Effectiveness refers to the degree to which a predetermined objective is accomplished. One objective of LIC Housing Finance professional labor is to maximize loan-based revenue (0.5 per cent of loan amount × number of loans). The professional staff has increased loans from a budgeted 90 to 120, a significant increase. Additionally, the average loan amount increased from a budgeted Rs 20,00,000 to Rs 22,40,000. The result is an increase in revenue from the budgeted Rs 9,00,000 to actual Rs 13,44,000. With both a higher number of loans and a higher average amount per loan, there was an increase in the effectiveness of professional labor in November 2012.

7-25 Comprehensive variance analysis, responsibility issue (CMA, adapted). Rayban manufactures a full line of well-known sunglasses frames and lenses. Rayban uses a standard-costing system to set attainable standards for direct materials, labor and overhead costs. Standards have been reviewed and revised annually, as necessary. Departmental managers, whose evaluations and bonuses are affected by their department's performance, have been held responsible to explain variances in their department performance reports.

Recently, the manufacturing variances in the Visionaire prestige line of sunglasses have caused some concern. For no apparent reason, unfavorable material and labor variance have occurred. At the monthly staff meeting, Ravi, manager of the Visionaire line, will be expected to explain his variances and suggest ways of improving performance. Ravi will be asked to explain the following performance report for 2011:

	Actual Results	Static-Budget Amounts
Units sold	4,850	5,000
Revenues	Rs 39,77,000	Rs 40,00,000
Variable manufacturing costs	23,46,430	21,60,000
Fixed manufacturing costs	7,22,650	7,50,000
Gross margin	9,07,920	10,90,000

Ravi collected the following information:

a. The standard variable manufacturing costs in 2011 comprised three items:

- Direct materials: Frames. Static budget cost of Rs 3,30,000. The standard input for 2011 is 3.00 ounces per unit.
- Direct materials: Lenses. Static budget costs of Rs 9,30,000. The standard input for 2011 is 6.00 ounces per unit.
- Direct manufacturing labor. Static budget costs of Rs 9,00,000. The standard input for 2011 is 1.20 hours per unit.

Assume there are no indirect variable manufacturing costs in 2011 were

b. The actual variable manufacturing costs in 2011 were

- Direct materials: Frames. Actual costs of Rs 3,72,480. Actual ounces used per frame were 3.20 ounces per unit.
- Direct materials: Lenses. Actual costs of Rs 10,04,920. Actual ounces used per frame were 7.00 ounces per unit.
- Direct manufacturing labor. Actual costs of Rs 9,69,030. The actual labor rate was Rs 148 per hour.

Required

1. Prepare a report that includes:
   a. Selling-price variance
   b. Sales-volume variance and flexible-budget variance in the format of the Level 2 analysis in Exhibit 7-2.
   c. Price and efficiency variances for (i) Direct materials: frames, (ii) Direct materials: lenses, (iii) Direct manufacturing labor
2. Give three possible explanations for each of the three price and efficiency variances at Rayban in requirement 1c.

Solution

Comprehensive variance analysis, responsibility issues.

1a. Actual selling price = Rs 820 = (Rs 39,77,000/4,850)
Budgeted selling price = Rs 800 = (Rs 40,00,000/5,000)
Actual sales volume = 4,850 units
Selling price variance = (Actual sales price − Budgeted sales price) × Actual units = (Rs 820 − Rs 800) × 4,850 = Rs 97,000 Favorable

1b. Development of Flexible Budget

		Budgeted Amounts Unit	Actual Volume	Flexible Budget Amount
Revenues		Rs 80.00	4,850	Rs 38,80,000
Variable costs				
DM-Frames	Rs 22/oz. × 3.00 oz.	66[a]	4,850	3,20,100
DM-Lenses	Rs 31/oz. × 6.00 oz.	186[b]	4,850	9,02,100
Direct manufacturing labor	Rs 150/hr. × 1.20 hr.	180[c]	4,850	8,73,000
Total variable manufacturing costs				Rs 20,95,200
Fixed manufacturing costs				7,50,000
Total manufacturing cost				28,45,200
Gross margin				Rs 10,34,800

[a]Rs 3,30,000 ÷ 5,000 units; [b]Rs 9,30,000 ÷ 5,000 units; [c]Rs 9,00,000 ÷ 5,000 units

	Actual Results (1)	Flexible-Budget Variances (2) = (1) − (3)	Flexible Budget (3)	Sales-Volume Variance (4) = (3) − (5)	Static Budget (5)
Units sold	4,850	0	4,850	150 U	5,000
Revenues	Rs 39,77,000	Rs 97,000 F	Rs 38,80,000	Rs 1,20,000 U	Rs 40,00,000
Variable costs:					
DM-frames	3,72,480	52,380 U	3,20,100	9,900 F	3,30,000
DM-lens	10,04,920	1,02,820 U	9,02,100	27,900 F	9,30,000
Direct labor	9,69,030	96,030 U	8,73,000	27,000 F	9,00,000
Total variable costs	23,46,430	2,51,230 U	20,95,200	64,800 F	21,60,000
Fixed manufacturing costs	7,22,650	27,350 F	7,50,000	0	7,50,000
Total costs	30,69,080	2,23,880 U	28,45,200	64,800 F	29,10,000
Gross margin	Rs 9,07,920	Rs 1,26,880 U	Rs 10,34,800	Rs 55,200 U	Rs 10,90,000

1c. Price and Efficiency Variances

DM-Frames-Actual ounces used = 3.20 per unit × 4,850 units = 15,520 oz.
Price per oz = Rs 3,72,480/15,520 = Rs 24
DM-Lenses-Actual ounces used = 7.00 per unit × 4,850 units = 33,950 oz.
Price per oz = Rs 10,04,920/33,950 = Rs 29.6
Direct Labor-Actual labor hours = Rs 9,69,030/148 = 6,547.5 hours
Labor hours per unit = 6,547.5/4,850 units = 1.35 hours per unit

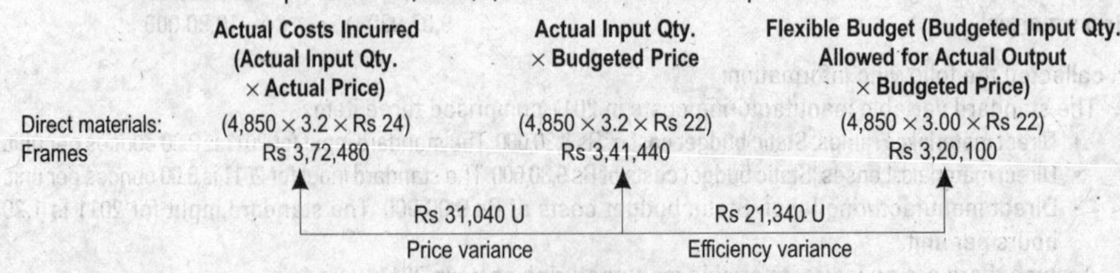

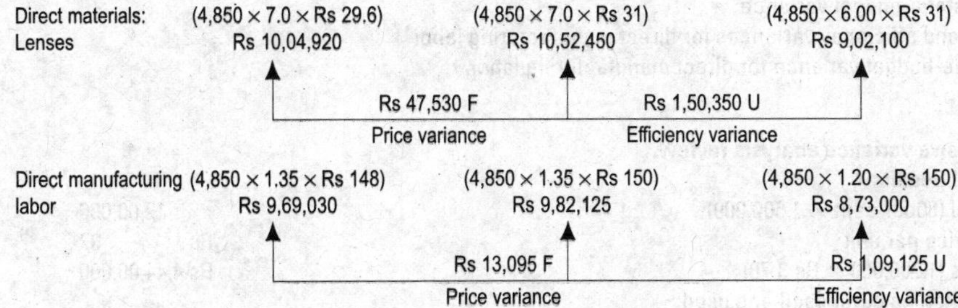

Possible explanations for price variances are: (a) Purchasing and labor negotiations. (b) Quality of frames and lenses purchased. (c) Standards set incorrectly.

Possible explanations for efficiency variance are: (a) Higher materials usage due to lower quality frames and lenses purchased at lower price. (b) Lesser trained workers hired at lower rates result in higher materials usage and lower labor efficiency. (c) Standards set incorrectly.

7-26 Continuous improvement (continuation 7-25). Rayban receives a suggestion that continuous improvement standard costs be used that are updated monthly. Consider monthly revisions in 2012 for the three variable manufacturing cost items.

Required

The January 2012 standard input usage is 0.99 times the December 2011 standard. The February 2012 standard input usage is 0.995 times the January 2012 standard. Using the data from Problem 7-25, what is the standard for the direct materials usage for each variable cost item in January and February 2012?

Solution

Continuous improvement.

1. Monthly Standards

	December 2011	January 2012	February 2012
Frames	3.00 oz	2.985 (3.00 × 0.995)	2.970075
Lenses	6.00 oz	5.97 (6.00 × 0.995)	5.94015

These are expressed in physical terms, assuming a constant standard price (Rs 22 for frames and Rs 31 for lenses), we can express these in rupees:

	December 2011	January 2012	February 2012
Frames	Rs 66	Rs 65.67	Rs 65.34165
Lenses	186	185.07	184.14465

7-27 Comprehensive variance analysis review. Royal Industries manufactures diskettes. The CFO has provided you with the following budgeted standards for the month of February 2012:

Average selling price per diskette	Rs 40.00
Total direct material cost per diskette	Rs 8.50
Direct manufacturing labor	
Direct manufacturing labor cost per hour	Rs 150.00
Average labor productivity rate (diskettes per hour)	300
Direct marketing cost per unit	Rs 3.00
Fixed overhead	Rs 90,00,000

Sales of 15,00,000 units are budgeted for February. Actual February results are as follows:

- Units sales totaled 80% of plan.
- Actual average selling price declined to Rs 37.
- Productivity dropped to 250 diskettes per hour.
- Actual direct manufacturing labor cost is Rs 150 per hour.
- Actual total direct material cost per unit dropped to Rs 8.0.
- Actual direct marketing costs were Rs 3 per unit.
- Fixed costs were Rs 3,00,000 below plan.

Required

Calculate the following

1. Static-budget and actual operating income
2. Total static-budget variance
3. Flexible-budget operating income
4. Total flexible-budget variance
5. Total sales-volume variance

6. Total static-budget variance
7. Price and efficiency variances for direct manufacturing labor
8. Flexible-budget variance for direct manufacturing labor.

Solution

Comprehensive variance analysis review.

1. Actual Results	
Units sold (80per cent × 1,500,000)	12,00,000
Selling price per unit	Rs 37
Revenues (1,200,000 × Rs 3.70)	Rs 4,44,00,000
Direct materials purchased and used:	
Direct materials per unit	Rs 8
Total direct materials cost (1,200,000 × Rs 8)	Rs 96,00,000
Direct manufacturing labor:	
Actual manufacturing rate per hour	Rs 15
Labor productivity per hour in units	250
Manufacturing labor-hours of input (1,200,000 ÷ 250)	4,800
Total direct manufacturing labor costs (4,800 × Rs 150)	Rs 7,20,000
Direct marketing costs:	
Direct marketing cost per unit	Rs 3
Total direct marketing costs (1,200,000 × Rs 3)	Rs 36,00,000
Fixed costs (Rs 90,00,000 – Rs 3,00,000)	Rs 87,00,000
Static Budgeted Amounts	
Units sold	15,00,000
Selling price per unit	Rs 40
Revenues (1,500,000 × 40)	Rs 6,00,00,000
Direct materials purchased and used:	
Direct materials per unit	*Rs 8.5*
Total direct materials costs (1,500,000 × Rs 8.5)	Rs 1,27,50,000
Direct manufacturing labor:	
Direct manufacturing rate per hour	*Rs 150*
Labor productivity per hour in units	300
Manufacturing labor-hours of input (1,500,000 × 300)	5,000
Total direct manufacturing labor cost (5,000 × Rs 150)	Rs 7,50,000
Direct marketing costs:	
Direct marketing cost per unit	Rs 3
Total direct marketing cost (1,500,000 × Rs 3)	Rs 45,00,000
Fixed costs	*Rs 90,00,000*

	Actual Results	**Static-Budgeted Amounts**
Revenues		
Variable costs	Rs 4,44,00,000	Rs 6,00,00,000
Direct materials	96,00,000	1,27,50,000
Direct manufacturing labor	7,20,000	7,50,000
Direct marketing costs	36,00,000	45,00,000
Total variable costs	1,39,20,000	1,80,00,000
Contribution margin	3,04,80,000	4,20,00,000
Fixed costs	87,00,000	90,00,000
Operating income	Rs 2,17,80,000	Rs 3,30,00,000

2.	
Actual operating income	Rs 2,17,80,000
Static-budget operating income	3,30,00,000
Total static-budget variance	Rs 1,12,20,000 U

3., **4.**, **5.** and **6.**

	Actual Results	Flexible-Budget Variances	Flexible Budget	Sales-Volume Variances	Static Budget
Units sold	12,00,000	0	12,00,000	3,00,000	15,00,000
Revenues	Rs 4,44,00,000	Rs 36,00,000 U	Rs 4,80,00,000	Rs 1,20,00,000 U	Rs 6,00,00,000
Variable costs					
Direct materials	96,00,000	6,00,000 F	1,02,00,000	25,50,000 F	1,27,50,000
Direct manufacturing labor	7,20,000	1,20,000 U	6,00,000	1,50,000 F	7,50,000
Direct marketing costs	36,00,000	0	36,00,000	9,00,000 F	45,00,000
Total variable costs	1,39,20,000	4,80,000 F	1,44,00,000	36,00,000 F	1,80,00,000

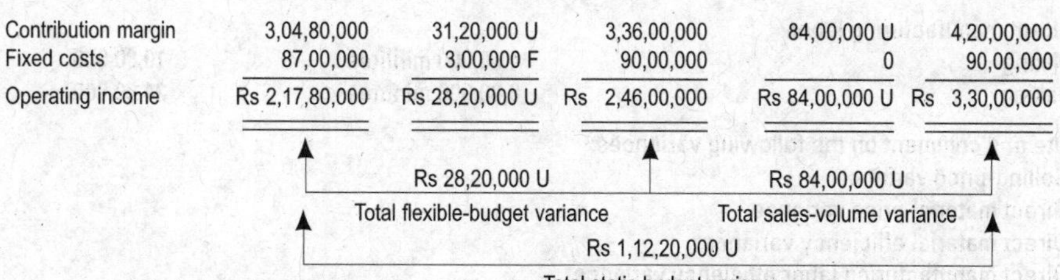

Contribution margin	3,04,80,000	31,20,000 U	3,36,00,000	84,00,000 U	4,20,00,000
Fixed costs	87,00,000	3,00,000 F	90,00,000	0	90,00,000
Operating income	Rs 2,17,80,000	Rs 28,20,000 U	Rs 2,46,00,000	Rs 84,00,000 U	Rs 3,30,00,000

7. and **8.**

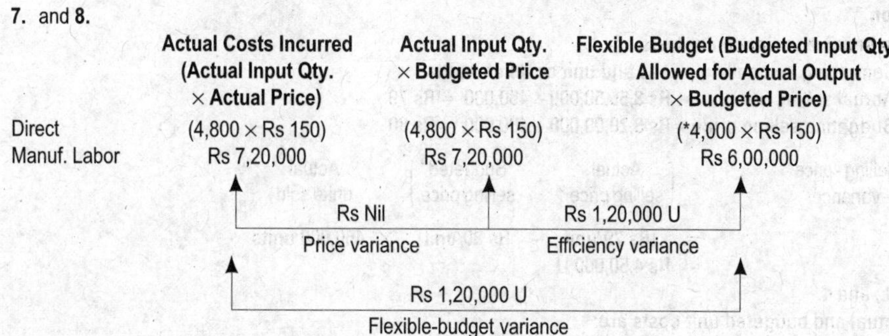

	Actual Costs Incurred (Actual Input Qty. × Actual Price)	Actual Input Qty. × Budgeted Price	Flexible Budget (Budgeted Input Qty. Allowed for Actual Output × Budgeted Price)
Direct Manuf. Labor	(4,800 × Rs 150) Rs 7,20,000	(4,800 × Rs 150) Rs 7,20,000	(*4,000 × Rs 150) Rs 6,00,000

*1,200,000 units ÷ 300 direct manufacturing labor standard productivity rate per hour.

7-28 Comprehensive variance analysis. (CMA) Meghraj Cookies bakes cookies for retail stores. The Company's best-selling cookie is Chocolate Nut Supreme, which is marketed as a gourmet cookie and regularly sells for Rs 80 per kg. The standard cost per kg of Chocolate Nut Supreme, based on Meghraj's normal monthly production of 400,000 kg, follows:

Cost Item	**Quantity**	**Standard Unit Costs**	**Total Standard Cost**
Direct materials			
Cookie mix	10 oz.	Rs 0.2/oz.	Rs 2.0
Milk chocolate	5 oz.	1.5/oz.	7.5
Almonds	1 oz.	5.0/oz.	5.0
			14.5
Direct manufacturing labor[a]			
Mixing	1 min.	144/hr.	2.4
Baking	2 min.	180/hr.	6.0
			8.4
Variable Overhead[b]	3 min.	324/hr.	16.2
Total standard cost per kg			Rs 39.1

[a]Direct manufacturing labor rates include employee benefits.
[b]Allocated on the basis of direct labor-hours.

Meghraj's management accountant, Zaheer, prepares monthly budget reports based on these standard costs. Presented below is April-June report.

Performance Report, April-June 2012

	Actual	**Budget**	**Variance**
Units (in kg)	4,50,000	4,00,000	50,000 F
Revenues	Rs 3,55,50,000	Rs 3,20,00,000	Rs 35,50,000 F
Direct materials	86,50,000	58,00,000	28,50,000 U
Direct manufacturing labor	34,80,000	33,60,000	1,20,000 U

Abbas, president of the company, is disappointed with the results. Despite a sizable increase in the number of cookies sold, the product's expected contribution to the overall profitability of the company decreased. Abbas has asked Zaheer to identify the reasons why the contribution margin decreased. Zaheer has gathered the following information to help in his analysis of the decrease.

Usage Report, April–June 2012

Cost Item	**Quantity**	**Actual Cost**
Direct materials:		
Cookie mix	46,50,000 ounces	Rs 9,30,000
Milk chocolate	26,60,000 ounces	53,20,000
Almonds	4,80,000 ounces	24,00,000

Direct manufacturing labor		
Mixing	4,50,000 minutes	10,80,000
Baking	8,00,000 minutes	24,00,000

Required Compute and comment on the following variances:

1. Selling-price variance.
2. Direct material price variance.
3. Direct material efficiency variance.
4. Direct manufacturing labor efficiency variance

Solution

Comprehensive variance analysis.

1. Computing unit selling prices and unit costs of inputs:
   Actual selling price = Rs 3,55,50,000 ÷ 450,000 = Rs 79
   Budgeting selling price = Rs 3,20,00,000 ÷ 400,000 = Rs 80

$$\text{Selling-price variance} = \left(\text{Actual selling price} - \text{Budgeted selling price}\right) \times \text{Actual units sold}$$

$$= (\text{Rs } 79/\text{unit} - \text{Rs } 80/\text{unit}) \times 450{,}000 \text{ units}$$

$$= \text{Rs } 4{,}50{,}000 \text{ U}$$

2., 3., and 4.

The actual and budgeted unit costs are:

	Actual	Budgeted
Direct materials		
Cookie mix	Rs 0.20 (Rs 9,30,000 ÷ 46,50,000)	Rs 0.20
Milk chocolate	2.0 (Rs 53,20,000 ÷ 26,60,000)	1.50
Almonds	5.0 (Rs 24,00,000 ÷ 4,80,000)	5.00
Direct manufacturing labor		
Mixing	144 (Rs 10,80,000 ÷ 4,50,000 × 60)	144.00
Baking	180 (Rs 24,00,000 ÷ 8,00,000 × 60)	180.00

The actual output achieved is 450,000 kg of chocolate Nut Supreme.

The direct cost price and efficiency variances are:

	Actual Costs Incurred (Actual Input Qty. × Actual Price)	Price Variance	Actual Input Qty. × Budgeted Price	Efficiency Variance	Flexible Budget (Budgeted Input Qty. Allowed for Actual Output × Budgeted Price)
	(1)	(2) = (1) – (3)	(3)	(4) = (3) – (5)	(5)
Direct materials					
Cookie mix	Rs 9,30,000	Re 0	Rs 9,30,000[a]	Rs 30,000 U	Rs 9,00,000[f]
Milk chocolate	53,20,000	13,30,000 U	39,90,000[b]	6,15,000 U	33,75,000[g]
Almonds	24,00,000	0	24,00,000[c]	1,50,000 U	22,50,000[h]
	Rs 86,50,000	Rs 13,30,000 U	Rs 73,20,000	Rs 7,95,000 U	Rs 65,25,000
Direct manufacturing labor costs					
Mixing	Rs 10,80,000	Re 0	Rs 10,80,000[d]	Rs 0	Rs 10,80,000[i]
Baking	24,00,000	0	24,00,000[e]	3,00,000 F	27,00,000[j]
	Rs 34,80,000	Rs 0	Rs 34,80,000	Rs 3,00,000 F	Rs 37,80,000

[a]Rs 0.20 × 46,50,000 = Rs 9,30,000
[b]Rs 1.50 × 26,60,000 = Rs 39,90,000
[c]Rs 5.0 × 4,80,000 = Rs 24,00,000
[d]Rs 144 × (4,50,000 ÷ 60) = Rs 10,80,000
[e]Rs 180 × (8,00,000 ÷ 60) = Rs 24,00,000
[f]Rs 0.20 × 10 × 4,50,000 = Rs 9,00,000
[g]Rs 1.50 × 5 × 4,50,000 = Rs 33,75,000
[h]Rs 5.0 × 1 × 4,50,000 = Rs 22,50,000
[i]Rs 144 × (4,50,000 ÷ 60) = Rs 10,80,000
[j]Rs 180 × (4,50,000 ÷ 30) = Rs 27,00,000

Comments on the variances include:

- Selling price variance. This may arise from a proactive decision to reduce price to expand market share or from a reaction to a price reduction by a competitor.
- Material price variance. The Rs 0.50 increase in the price per ounce of milk chocolate could arise from uncontrollable market factors or from poor contract negotiations.

- Material efficiency variance. For all three material inputs, usage is greater than budgeted. Possible reasons include lower quality inputs, use of lower quality workers, and the mixing and baking equipment not being maintained in a fully operational mode.
- Labor efficiency variance. The favorable efficiency variance for baking could be due to workers eliminating nonvalue-added steps in production.

7-29 Flexible budgeting, activity-based costing, variance analysis. Britania is a manufacturer of fruitcakes. One of its plants produces five different cake products. Each cake product differs in terms of material inputs. They are identical in terms of the cooking and changeover processes.

The changeover process entails switching the production line from the manufacturing of one product to another product. The costs of a changeover are a batch cost. They comprise the labor cost of the workers who clean the equipment so that the contents of each different product are not mixed together. The following information pertains to March 2012:

	Static-Budget Amounts	Actual Amounts
Units of cakes produced and sold	240,000	330,000
Average batch size (cakes per batch)	6,000	10,000
Changeover labor-hours per batch	20	24
Changeover labor cost per hour	Rs 200	Rs 210

Required

1. Compute the flexible-budget variance for total changeover labor costs in March 2012. Comment on the results.
2. Compute the price and efficiency variances for total changeover labor costs in March 2012. Comment on the results.
3. Provide two explanations for each of the price and efficiency variances in requirement 2.

Solution

Flexible budgeting, activity-based costing, variance analysis.

		Static-Budget Amounts	Actual Amounts
1.a	Units of cakes produced and sold	240,000	330,000
b.	Average batch size (cakes per batch)	6,000	10,000
c.	Number of batches (a ÷ b)	40	33
d.	Changeover labor-hours per batch	20	24
e.	Total changeover labor-hours (c × d)	800	792
f.	Cost per changeover labor-hours	Rs 200	Rs 210
g.	Total changeover labor cost (e × f)	Rs 1,60,000	Rs 1,66,320

Step 1: The number of batches in which the actual output units should have been produced:
3,30,000 actual units of output ÷ 6,000 budgeted batch size = 55 batches

Step 2: The number of changeover labor-hours that should have been used:
20 budgeted changeover-hours × 55 batches = 1,100 changeover-hours.

Step 3: The flexible-budget amount for changeover hours:
1,100 changeover-hours × Rs 200 budgeted cost per changeover-hour = Rs 2,20,000.

Flexible-budget variance = Actual costs – Flexible-budget costs
= (792 × Rs 210) – (1,100 × Rs 200)
= Rs 1,66,320 – Rs 2,20,000 = Rs 53,680 F

2. Price variance $= \left[\text{Actual price of input} - \text{Budgeted price of input}\right] \times \text{Actual quantity of input}$

= (Rs 210 — Rs 200) × 792 = Rs 10 × 792 = Rs 7,920 U

Efficiency variance $= \left[\text{Actual quantity of input used} - \text{Budget quantity of input allowed for actual output}\right] \times \text{Budgeted price of input}$

= (792 — 1,100) × Rs 200 = 308 × Rs 200 = Rs 61,600 F

The favorable flexible-budget variance of Rs 53,680 is comprised of two offsetting amounts:

- Price variance of Rs 7,920 U due to actual changeover labor cost of Rs 210 per hour exceeding the Rs 200 budgeted rate.
- Efficiency variance of Rs 61,600 F due to the actual batch size of 10,000 being sizably above the budgeted batch size of 6,000. Efficiency variance is favorable because less batches were required to produce 3,30,000 cakes even though actual changeover labor-hours of 24 per batch were higher than the budgeted changeover-hours per batch of 20 hours.

3. Explanations for the price variance of Rs 7,920 U include:
   - More highly trained workers hired to make changeovers.
   - Change in labor market required unexpected increase in labor rates to retain workers.

- Budgeted amounts were set without adequate analysis.

Explanations for the efficiency variance of Rs 61,600 F include:

- More highly trained workers were able to produce larger batch sizes.
- More automated machinery was acquired.
- Budgeted amounts were set without adequate analysis.

7-30 Procurement costs, variance analysis, ethics. Vijay is the manager of the athletic shoe division of Action Shoes. Action Shoes is a company that has just purchased Relaxo, a leading shoe company. Relaxo has long-term production contracts with suppliers in two States, Uttar Pradesh and Bihar. Vijay receives a request from Anil, president of Action Shoes. Vijay and his controller, Mohan, are to make a presentation to the next Board of Directors meeting on the cost competitiveness of the Relaxo. This report should include budgeted and actual procurement costs for 2011 at its Uttar Pradesh and Bihar supply sources.

Mohan decides to visit the two supply operations. The budgeted average procurement cost for 2011 was Rs 120 per pair of shoes. This cost includes payments to the shoe manufacturer and all other payments to conduct business in each state. Mohan reports the following to Vijay:

- Uttar Pradesh. Total 2011 procurement costs for 2,50,000 pairs of shoes were Rs 3,32,50,000. Payment to the shoe manufacturer was Rs 2,65,00,000. Very few receipts existed for the remaining Rs 67,50,000. Kickback payments are viewed as common in Uttar Pradesh.
- Bihar. Total 2011 procurement costs for 9,00,000 pairs of shoes were Rs 10,48,50,000. Payment to the shoe manufacturer was Rs 8,64,00,000. Receipts existed for Rs 70,50,000 of the other costs, but Mohan said he is skeptical of their validity. Kickback payments are a "way of business" at Bihar.

At both Uttar Pradesh and Bihar plants, Mohan was disturbed by the employment of young children (many of them younger than 15 years). He was told that all major shoe-producing companies had similar low-cost employment practices in both states.

Vijay is uncomfortable about the upcoming presentation to the board. He was a leading advocate of the acquisition. A recent business magazine reported that Relaxo acquisition would make Action Shoes the global low-cost producer in its market lines. The stock price of Action Shoes jumped 21% the day Relaxo acquisition was announced. Mohan likewise is widely identified as a proponent of the acquisition. He is seen as a "rising star" due for a promotion to a division manager in the near future.

Required

1. What summary procurement cost variances could be reported to the Board of Directors of Action Shoes?
2. What ethical issues do (a) Vijay and (b) Mohan face when preparing and making a report to the Board of Directors?
3. How should Mohan address the issues you identify in requirement 2?

Solution

Procurement costs, variance analysis, ethics.

1. Purchase price variances can be computed for each country.

$$\text{Purchase price variance} = \left[\begin{array}{c}\text{Actual price}\\ \text{of input}\end{array} - \begin{array}{c}\text{Budgeted price}\\ \text{of input}\end{array}\right] \times \begin{array}{c}\text{Actual quantity}\\ \text{of input}\end{array}$$

Uttar Pradesh

= (Rs 133[a] – Rs 120) × 2,50,000 = Rs 32,50,000 U

[a]Rs 3,32,50,000 ÷ 250,000 = Rs 133

On a per-unit basis, there is a Rs 106 payment to the shoe manufacturer and a Rs 27 payment for "other costs."

Bihar

= (Rs 116.5[a] – Rs 120) × 9,00,000 = Rs 31,50,000 F

[a]Rs 10,48,50,000 ÷ 9,00,000 = Rs 116.50

On a per-unit basis, there is a Rs 96 payment to the shoe manufacturer and a Rs 20.5 payment for "other costs."

Vijay and Mohan face many ethical issues:

(a) Reliability of cost information to be presented to the board of directors. There are minimal or questionable receipts for Rs 67,50,000 in Uttar Pradesh and Rs 1,84,50,000 in Bihar.

(b) Potential existence of kickback payments in both Uttar Pradesh and Bihar.

(c) Employment of young children (many of them under 15 years).

Should Vijay and Mohan be forthright and present all their concerns on (a), (b), and (c)?

Both Vijay and Mohan face the dilemma that any discussion of (a), (b), or (c) will raise questions about their own behavior at the time the acquisitions were made. Board members may ask "When did they first know about (a), (b), and (c)?," and "Why did they not undertake examination of these issues at the time they supported the acquisitions?"

3. Mohan has very high standards of ethical conduct to meet. He should not make presentations to the Board based on information he has strong doubts about. If he decides to make the presentation, all his concerns and caveats should be presented.

He should require detailed documentation for all payments. No future payments should be made without adequate documentation. Investigation of kickback allegations should be made, however difficult that may be. Mohan should be able to make a good-faith effort to ensure kickback payments are not an ongoing practice in Uttar Pradesh or Bihar.

Exercises

7-31 Flexible budget. Haldiram Company sells sweets. Its budgeted operating income for the year ended December 31, 2011, was Rs 31,50,000. As a result of continued explosive growth in its sales, actual operating income totaled Rs 65,56,000.

Required

1. Calculate the total static-budget variances.
2. Flexible-budget operating income was Rs 69,30,000. Calculate the total flexible-budget and total sales-volume variances.
3. Comment on the total flexible-budget variance in light of the explosive growth in its sales.

7-32 Materials and manufacturing labor variances. Consider the following data collected (for March) for Alps Industries Limited.

Required

Particulars	Direct Materials	Direct Manufacturing Labor
Cost incurred: actual inputs × actual prices	Rs 2,00,000	Rs 90,000
Actual inputs × standard prices	2,14,000	86,000
Standard inputs allowed for actual outputs × standard prices	2,25,000	80,000

Compute the price, efficiency, and flexible-budget variances for direct materials and direct manufacturing labor.

7-33 Flexible budgets, variance analysis. You have been hired as a consultant by Sandeep, the president of a small manufacturing company that makes automobile parts. Sandeep is an excellent engineer, but he has been frustrated by working with inadequate cost data..

You helped install flexible budgeting and standard costs. Sandeep has asked you to consider the following May data and recommend how variances might be computed and presented in performance reports:

Static budget in output units	20,000
Actual output units produced and sold	23,000
Budgeted selling price per output unit	Rs 40
Budgeted variable costs per output unit	Rs 25
Budgeted total fixed costs per month	Rs 2,00,000
Actual revenue	Rs 8,74,000
Actual variable costs	Rs 6,30,000
Favorable variance in fixed costs	Rs 5,000

Sandeep was disappointed. Although output units sold exceeded expectations, operating income did not. Assume that there was no beginning or ending inventory.

Required

1. You decide to present Sandeep with alternative ways to analyze variances so that he can decide what level of detail he prefers. The reporting system can then be designed accordingly. Prepare an analysis similar to Levels 0, 1, and 2 in Exhibit 7-1 and Exhibit 7-2.
2. What are some likely causes for the variances you report in requirement 1?

7-34 Flexible-budget preparation and analysis. Bank Printers Limited, produces luxury check-books with three checks and stubs per page. Each checkbook is designed for an individual customer and is ordered through the customer's bank.

The company's operating budget for September included these data:

Number of checkbooks	15,000
Selling price per book	Rs 20
Variable cost per book	Rs 8
Fixed costs for the month	Rs 1,45,000
The actual results for September were:	
Number of checkbooks produced and sold	12,000
Average selling price per book	Rs 21
Variable cost per book	Rs 7
Fixed costs for the month	Rs 1,50,000

The executive Vice-president of the company observed that the operating income for September was much less than anticipated, despite a higher-than-budgeted selling price and a lower-than-budgeted variable cost per unit. You have been asked to provide explanations for the disappointing September results.

Bank Printer Limited develops its flexible budget on the basis of budgeted per-output-unit revenue and per-output-unit variable costs without detailed analysis of budgeted inputs.

1. Prepare a Level 1 analysis of the September performance.
2. Prepare a Level 2 analysis of the September performance.
3. Why might Bank Printer find the Level 2 analysis more informative than the Level 1 analysis? Explain your answer.

7-35 Materials and manufacturing labor variances, standard costs. Consider the following selected data regarding the manufacture of a line of upholstered chairs:

	Standards per Chair
Direct materials	2 square yards of input at Rs 100 per square yard
Direct manufacturing labor	0.5 hour of input at 40 per hour

The following data were compiled regarding actual performance:

Actual output units (chairs) produced, 20,000; square yards of input purchased and used, 37,000; price per square yard, Rs 102; direct manufacturing labor costs, Rs 3,52,800; actual hours of input 9,000; labor price per hour, Rs 39.20.

Required

Show computations of price and efficiency variances for direct materials and direct manufacturing labor. Give a plausible explanation of why the variances occurred.

7-36 Flexible budget. (Refer to Exercise 7-35) Suppose the static budget was for 24,000 units of output. The general manager is thrilled about the following report:

	Actual Results	Static Budget	Variance
Direct materials	Rs 37,74,000	Rs 48,00,000	Rs 10,26,000 F
Direct manufacturing labor	Rs 3,52,800	Rs 4,80,000	Rs 1,27,200 F

Required

Is the manager's glee warranted? Prepare a report that provides a more detailed explanation of why the static budget was not achieved. Actual output was 20,000 units.

7-37 Flexible budget, direct materials and direct manufacturing labor variances. TNT manufactures bust statues of famous historical figures. All statues are the same size. Each unit requires the same amount of resources. The following information is from the static budget for 2012:

Expected production and sales	5,000 units
Direct materials	50,000 kgs
Direct manufacturing labor	20,000 hours
Total fixed costs	Rs 10,00,000

Standard quantities, standard prices, and standard unit costs follow for direct materials and direct manufacturing labor.

	Standard Quantity	Standard Price	Standard Unit Cost
Direct material	10 kgs	Rs 100 per kg	Rs 1,000
Direct manufacturing labor	4 hours	Rs 40 per hour	Rs 160

During 2011, actual number of units produced and sold was 6,000. Actual cost of direct materials used was Rs 59,40,000, based on 54,000 kgs purchased at Rs 110 per kg. Direct manufacturing labor-hours actually used were 25,000, at the rate of Rs 38 per hour. This resulted in actual direct manufacturing labor cost of Rs 9,50,000. Actual fixed costs were Rs 10,05,000. There were no beginning or ending inventories.

Required

1. Calculate sales-volume variance and flexible-budget variance.
2. Compute price and efficiency variances for direct materials and direct manufacturing labor.

7-38 Level 2 variance analysis, solve for unknowns. Home Sports manufactures and distributes baseball caps to ballparks and other sports venues. Home's plan for 2012 forecast sales of 6,00,000 caps. However, only 5,00,000 caps were sold. Based on the following data, calculate the missing numbers and complete the analysis.

	Actual Results (1)	Flexible-Budget Variances (2) = (1) — (3)	Flexible Budget (3)	Sales-Volume Variance (4) = (3) — (5)	Static Budget (5)
Units sold	5,00,000	______	______	______	6,00,000
Revenues (sales)	Rs 5,00,00,000				Rs 4,80,00,000
Variable costs	1,40,00,000	______	______		1,80,00,000
Contribution margin	3,60,00,000	Rs 1,10,00,000 F		Rs 50,00,000 U	3,00,00,000
Fixed costs	1,15,00,000	______	Rs 1,00,00,000		1,00,00,000
Operating income	______		______		______

Total sales-volume variance — Total flexible-budget variance

Total static-budget variance

Required

1. Calculate the budgeted and actual selling prices.
2. Assuming that the driver for variable costs is units sold, what are the budgeted and actual variable costs per unit?

3. Calculate the flexible-budget operating income.
4. Calculate the total flexible-budget variance.
5. Calculate the total sales-volume variance.
6. Calculate the total static-budget variance.

7-39 Direct labor and direct materials variances, missing data (CMA, heavily adapted). Amit Surfboards manufactures fiberglass surfboards. The standard cost of direct materials and direct manufacturing labor is Rs 500 per board. This includes 20 kg of direct materials, at the budgeted price of Rs 10 per kg, and five hours of direct manufacturing labor, at the budgeted rate of Rs 60 per hour. Following are the data for the month of July:

Units completed	6,000 units
Direct material purchases	1,50,000 kgs
Cost of direct material purchases	Rs 14,62,500
Actual direct manufacturing labor-hours	32,000 hours
Actual direct-labor cost	Rs 18,40,000
Direct materials efficiency variance	Rs 62,500 U

There were no beginning inventories.

Required

1. Compute direct manufacturing labor variances for July.
2. Compute the actual kg of direct materials used in production in July.
3. Calculate the actual price per kg of direct materials purchased.
4. Calculate direct materials price variance.

7-40 Direct materials and manufacturing labor variances, solving unknowns. (CPA, adapted) On May 1, 2012, First Call Company began the manufacture of a new product. The company installed a standard-costing system to account for manufacturing costs. The standard costs per unit is:

Direct materials (3 kg. at Rs 5 per kg.)	Rs	15.00
Direct manufacturing labor (1/2 hour at Rs 20 per hour)		10.00
Manufacturing overhead (75 per cent of direct manufacturing labor costs)		7.50
	Rs	32.50

The following data were obtained from the records for the month of May:

Particulars	Debit	Credit
Revenues		Rs 125,000
Accounts payable control (for May's purchases of direct materials)		68,250
Direct materials price variance	Rs 3,250	
Direct materials efficiency variance	2,500	
Direct manufacturing labor price variance	1,900	
Direct manufacturing labor efficiency variance		2,000

Actual production in May was 4,000 units and actual sales in May were 2,500 units.

The amount shown earlier for direct materials price variance applies to materials purchased during May. There was no beginning inventory of materials on May 1, 2012.

Required

Compute each of the following items for First Call for the month of May. Show your computations.

1. Standard direct manufacturing labor-hours allowed for actual output produced.
2. Actual direct manufacturing labor-hours worked.
3. Actual direct manufacturing labor wage rate.
4. Standard quantity of direct materials allowed (in kg).
5. Actual quantity of direct materials used (in kg).
6. Actual quantity of direct materials purchased (in kg).
7. Actual direct materials price per kg.

7-41 Flexible budgeting, activity-based costing, variance analysis. Toymaster Limited produces a toy car, TGC, in batches. After each batch of TGC is run, the molds are cleaned. The labor costs of cleaning the molds can be traced to TGC because TGC can only be produced for a specific mold. The following information pertains to June 2012:

Particulars	Static-Budget Amounts	Actual Amounts
Units of TGC produced and sold	30,000	22,500
Batch size (units per batch)	250	225
Cleaning labor-hours per batch	3	3.5
Cleaning labor cost per hour	Rs 140	Rs 125

Required

1. Calculate the flexible-budget variance for total cleaning labor costs in June 2012.
2. Calculate the price and efficiency variances for total cleaning labor costs in June 2012. Comment on the results.

8 Flexible Budgets, Overhead Cost Variances, and Management Control

Learning Objectives

1. Explain the similarities and differences in planning variable overhead costs and fixed overhead costs
2. Develop budgeted variable overhead cost rates and budgeted fixed overhead cost rates
3. Compute the variable overhead flexible-budget variance, the variable overhead efficiency variance, and the variable overhead spending variance
4. Compute the fixed overhead flexible-budget variance, the fixed overhead spending variance, and the fixed overhead production-volume variance
5. Show how the 4-variance analysis approach reconciles the actual overhead incurred with the overhead amounts allocated during the period
6. Explain the relationship between the sales-volume variance and the production-volume variance
7. Calculate overhead variances in activity-based costing
8. Examine the use of overhead variances in nonmanufacturing settings

What do this week's weather forecast, courtroom witness testimony, and organization performance have in common? Most of the time, reality doesn't match expectations: It doesn't rain when forecast, and the witness swears the defendant was at the scene of the crime even though a solid alibi exists. The organization discovers at the end of the month that its skyrocketing costs have significantly reduced its profits, or perhaps that dramatically lower costs have improved its profits tremendously. Differences, or variances, are all around us.

For organizations, variances can have unpleasant consequences. This is especially true when executives and employees don't tell the truth about why and how the variances occurred, as the following article shows.

Overhead Cost Variances Force Macy's to Shop for Changes in Strategy[1]

Managers frequently review the differences, or variances, in overhead costs and make changes in the operations of a business. Sometimes staffing levels are increased or decreased, while at other times managers identify ways to use fewer resources like, say, office supplies and travel for business meetings that don't add value to the products and services that customers buy.

At the department-store chain Macy's, however, managers analyzed overhead cost variances and changed the way the company purchased the products it sells. In 2005, when Federated Department Stores and the May Department Store Company merged, Macy's operated seven buying offices across the United States. Each of these offices was responsible for purchasing some of the clothes, cosmetics, jewelry, and many other items Macy's sells. But overlapping responsibilities, seasonal buying patterns (clothes are generally purchased in the spring and fall) and regional differences in costs and salaries (for example, it costs more for employees and rent in San Francisco than Cincinnati) led to frequent and significant variances in overhead costs.

These overhead costs weighed on the company as the retailer struggled with disappointing sales after the merger. As a result, Macy's leaders felt pressured to reduce its costs that were not directly related to selling merchandise in stores and online.

[1] *Sources*: Boyle, Matthew. 2009. A leaner Macy's tries to cater to local tastes. *BusinessWeek.com*, September 3; Kapner, Suzanne. 2009. Macy's looking to cut costs. *Fortune*, January 14. http://money.cnn.com/2009/01/14/news/companies/macys_consolidation.fortune/; *Macy's 2009 Corporate Fact Book*. 2009. Cincinnati: Macy's, Inc., 7.

In early 2009, the company announced plans to consolidate its network of seven buying offices into one location in New York. With all centralized buying and merchandise planning in one location, Macy's buying structure and overhead costs were in line with how many other large chains operate, including JCPenney and Kohl's. All told, the move to centralized buying would generate $100 billion in annualized cost savings for the company.

While centralized buying was applauded by industry experts and shareholders, Macy's CEO Terry Lundgren was concerned about keeping a "localized flavor" in his stores. To ensure that nationwide buying accommodated local tastes, a new team of merchants was formed in each Macy's market to gauge local buying habits. That way, the company could reduce its overhead costs while ensuring that Macy's stores near water parks had extra swimsuits.

Companies such as DuPont, International Paper, and U.S. Steel, which invest heavily in capital equipment, or Amazon.com and Yahoo!, which invest large amounts in software, have high overhead costs. As the Macy's example suggests, understanding the behavior of overhead costs, planning for them, performing variance analysis, and acting appropriately on the results are critical for a company.

In this chapter, we will examine how flexible budgets and variance analysis can help managers plan and control overhead costs. Chapter 7 emphasized the direct-cost categories of direct materials and direct manufacturing labor. In this chapter, we focus on the indirect-cost categories of variable manufacturing overhead and fixed manufacturing overhead. Finally, we explain why managers should be careful when interpreting variances based on overhead-cost concepts developed primarily for financial reporting purposes.

Planning of Variable and Fixed Overhead Costs

Learning Objective 1

Explain the similarities and differences in planning variable overhead costs and fixed overhead costs

. . . for both, plan only essential activities and be efficient; fixed overhead costs are usually determined well before the budget period begins

We'll use the Color Plus Company example again to illustrate the planning and control of variable and fixed overhead costs. Recall that Color Plus manufactures jackets that are sold to distributors, who in turn sell to independent clothing stores and retail chains. For simplicity, we assume Color Plus's only costs are *manufacturing* costs. For ease of exposition, we use the term overhead costs instead of manufacturing overhead costs. Variable (manufacturing) overhead costs for Color include energy, machine maintenance, engineering support, and indirect materials. Fixed (manufacturing) overhead costs include plant leasing costs, depreciation on plant equipment, and the salaries of the plant managers.

Planning Variable Overhead Costs

To effectively plan variable overhead costs for a product or service, managers must eliminate the activities that do not add value to the product or service. By doing this, managers can focus their attention on the activities that create a superior product or service for their customers. Color's managers examine how each of their variable overhead costs relates to delivering a superior product or service to customers. For example, customers expect Color Plus's jackets to last. So managers at Color Plus consider sewing to be an essential activity. Therefore, maintenance activities for sewing machines—included in Color's variable overhead costs—are also essential activities for which management must plan. In addition, such maintenance should be done in a cost-effective way. This means, for example, scheduling periodic equipment maintenance rather than waiting for sewing machines to break down. For many companies today, it is critical to plan for ways to become more efficient in the use of energy, a rapidly growing component of variable overhead costs. Color Plus installs smart meters in order to monitor energy use in real time and steer production operations away from peak consumption periods.

Planning Fixed Overhead Costs

Effective planning of fixed overhead costs is similar to effective planning for variable overhead costs—planning to undertake only essential activities and then planning to be efficient in that undertaking. But in planning fixed overhead costs, there is one more strategic issue that managers must take into consideration: choosing the appropriate level of capacity or investment that will benefit the company in the long run. Consider Color's leasing of sewing machines, each having a fixed cost per year. Leasing insufficient machine capacity—say, because Color Plus underestimates demand or because of limited space in the plant—will result in an inability to meet demand, lost sales of jackets, and unhappy customers. Consider the example of AT&T, which did not foresee the iPhone's appeal or the proliferation of "apps" and did not upgrade its network sufficiently to handle the resulting data traffic. AT&T has since had to impose limits on how customers can use the iPhone (such as by curtailing tethering and the streaming of Webcasts). In December 2009, AT&T had the lowest customer satisfaction ratings among all major carriers.

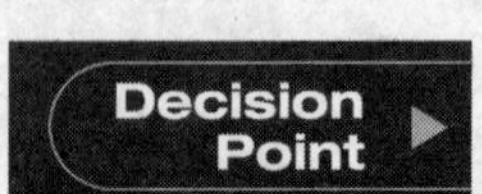

How do managers plan variable overhead costs and fixed overhead costs?

The planning of fixed overhead costs differs from the planning of variable overhead costs in one important respect: timing. At the start of a budget period, management will have made most of the decisions that determine the level of fixed overhead costs to be incurred. But, it's the day-to-day, ongoing operating decisions that mainly determine the level of variable overhead costs incurred in that period. In health care settings, for example, variable overhead, which includes disposable supplies, unit doses of medication, suture packets, and medical waste disposal costs, is a function of the number and nature of procedures carried out, as well as the practice patterns of the physicians. However, the majority of the cost of providing hospital service is related to buildings, equipment, and salaried labor, which are fixed overhead items, unrelated to the volume of activity.[2]

Learning Objective 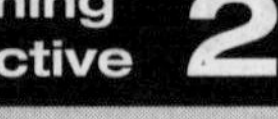

Develop budgeted variable overhead cost rates

. . . budgeted variable costs divided by quantity of cost-allocation base

and budgeted fixed overhead cost rates

. . . budgeted fixed costs divided by quantity of cost-allocation base

Standard Costing at Color Plus Company

Color Plus uses standard costing. The development of standards for Color's direct manufacturing costs was described in Chapter 7. This chapter discusses the development of standards for Color's manufacturing overhead costs. **Standard costing** is a costing sys-

[2] Related to this, free-standing surgery centers have thrived because they have an economic advantage of lower fixed overhead when compared to a traditional hospital. For an enlightening summary of costing issues in health care, see A. Macario, "What Does One Minute of Operating Room Time Cost?" Stanford University School of Medicine (2009).

tem that (a) traces direct costs to output produced by multiplying the standard prices or rates by the standard quantities of inputs allowed for actual outputs produced and (b) allocates overhead costs on the basis of the standard overhead-cost rates times the standard quantities of the allocation bases allowed for the actual outputs produced.

The standard cost of Color's jackets can be computed at the start of the budget period. This feature of standard costing simplifies record keeping. That is because no record is needed of the actual overhead costs or of the actual quantities of the cost-allocation bases used for making the jackets. What is needed are the standard overhead cost rates for variable and fixed overhead. Color's management accountants calculate these cost rates based on the planned amounts of variable and fixed overhead and the standard quantities of the allocation bases. We describe these computations in the following sections. Note that once standards have been set, the costs of using standard costing are low relative to the costs of using actual costing or normal costing.

Developing Budgeted Variable Overhead Cost Rates

Budgeted variable overhead cost-allocation rates can be developed in four steps. We use the Color Plus example to illustrate these steps. Throughout the chapter, we use the broader term "budgeted rate" rather than "standard rate" to be consistent with the term used in describing normal costing in earlier chapters. In standard costing, the budgeted rates are standard rates.

Step 1: Choose the Period to Be Used for the Budget. Color Plus uses a 12-month budget period to help smooth out seasonal effects.

Step 2: Select the Cost-Allocation Bases to Use in Allocating Variable Overhead Costs to Output Produced. Color's operating managers select machine-hours as the cost-allocation base because they believe that machine-hours is the only cost driver of variable overhead. Based on an engineering study, Color Plus estimates it will take 0.40 of a machine-hour per actual output unit. For its budgeted output of 144,000 jackets in 2008, Color Plus budgets 57,600 (0.40 × 144,000) machine-hours.

Step 3: Identify the Variable Overhead Costs Associated with Each Cost-Allocation Base. Color Plus groups all of its variable overhead costs, including costs of energy, machine maintenance, engineering support, indirect materials, and indirect manufacturing labor in a single cost pool. Color's total budgeted variable overhead costs for 2008 are Rs 1,72,80,000.

Step 4: Compute the Rate per Unit of Each Cost-Allocation Base Used to Allocate Variable Overhead Costs to Output Produced. Dividing the amount in step 3 (Rs 1,72,80,000.) by the amount in step 2 (57,600 machine-hours), Color Plus estimates a rate of Rs 300 per standard machine-hour for allocating its variable overhead costs.

In standard costing, the variable overhead rate per unit of the cost-allocation base (Rs 300 per machine-hour for Color Plus) is generally expressed as a standard rate per output unit. Color Plus calculates the budgeted variable overhead cost rate per output unit as:

$$\begin{aligned}\text{Budgeted variable overhead cost rate per output unit} &= \text{Budgeted input allowed per output unit} \times \text{Budgeted variable overhead cost rate per input unit}\\ &= 0.40 \text{ hour per jacket} \times \text{Rs } 300 \text{ per hour}\\ &= \text{Rs. } 120 \text{ per jacket}\end{aligned}$$

Color Plus uses Rs 120 per jacket as the budgeted variable overhead cost rate in both its static budget for 2008 and in the monthly performance reports it prepares during 2008.

The Rs 120 per jacket represents the amount by which Color's variable overhead costs are expected to change with respect to output units (jackets) for the planning and control (budgeting) purpose and also for the inventory costing purpose. As the number of jackets manufactured increases, budgeted variable overhead costs (for the planning and control purpose of cost accounting) and variable overhead costs allocated to output units (for the inventory costing purpose) both increase at the rate of Rs 120 per jacket. Of course, this presents an overall picture of total variable overhead costs, which in reality consist of many items, including energy, repairs, indirect labor, and so on. Managers help control variable overhead costs by budgeting each line item and then investigating possible causes for any significant variances.

Developing Budgeted Fixed Overhead Rates

Fixed overhead costs are, by definition, a lump sum of costs that remains unchanged in total for a given period, despite wide changes in the level of total activity or volume related to those overhead costs. Fixed costs are included in flexible budgets, but they remain the same total amount within the relevant range of activity regardless of the output level chosen to "flex" the variable costs and revenues. Recall from Exhibit 7-2 and the steps in developing a flexible budget, that the fixed-cost amount is the same Rs 27,60,000 in the static budget and in the flexible budget. Do not assume, however, that fixed overhead costs can never be changed. Managers can reduce fixed overhead costs by selling equipment or by laying off employees. But they are fixed in the sense that, unlike variable costs such as direct material costs, fixed costs do not *automatically* increase or decrease with the level of activity within the relevant range.

The process of developing the budgeted fixed overhead rate is the same as that detailed earlier for calculating the budgeted variable overhead rate. The four steps are as follows:

Step 1: Choose the Period to Use for the Budget. As with variable overhead costs, the budget period for fixed overhead costs is typically 12 months to help smooth out seasonal effects.

Step 2: Select the Cost-Allocation Bases to Use in Allocating Fixed Overhead Costs to Output Produced. Color Plus uses machine-hours as the only cost-allocation base for fixed overhead costs. Why? Because Color Plus's managers believe that, in the long run, fixed overhead costs will increase or decrease to the levels needed to support the amount of machine-hours. Therefore, in the long run, the amount of machine-hours used is the only cost driver of fixed overhead costs. The number of machine-hours is the denominator in the budgeted fixed overhead rate computation and is called the **denominator level** or, in manufacturing settings, the **production-denominator level.** For simplicity, we assume Color Plus expects to operate at capacity in fiscal year 2011—with a budgeted usage of 57,600 machine-hours for a budgeted output of 144,000 jackets.[3]

Step 3: Identify the Fixed Overhead Costs Associated with Each Cost-Allocation Base. Because Color Plus identifies only a single cost-allocation base—machine-hours—to allocate fixed overhead costs, it groups all such costs into a single cost pool. Costs in this pool include depreciation on plant and equipment, plant and equipment leasing costs, and the plant manager's salary. Color Plus's fixed overhead budget for 2011 is Rs 3,31,20,000.

Step 4: Compute the Rate per Unit of Each Cost-Allocation Base Used to Allocate Fixed Overhead Costs to Output Produced. Dividing the Rs 3,31,20,000 from Step 3 by the 57,600 machine-hours from Step 2, Color Plus estimates a fixed overhead cost rate of Rs 575.0 per machine-hour:

$$\begin{array}{c}\text{Budgeted fixed}\\\text{overhead cost per}\\\text{unit of cost-allocation}\\\text{base}\end{array} = \frac{\text{Budgeted total costs in fixed overhead cost pool}}{\text{Budgeted total quantity of cost-allocation base}} = \frac{\text{Rs } 3{,}31{,}20{,}000}{57{,}600} = \text{Rs } 575.0 \text{ per machine-hour}$$

In standard costing, the Rs 575.0 fixed overhead cost per machine-hour is usually expressed as a standard cost per output unit. Recall that Color Plus's engineering study

[3] Because Color Plus plans its capacity over multiple periods, anticipated demand in 2011 could be such that budgeted output for 2011 is less than capacity. Companies vary in the denominator levels they choose; some may choose budgeted output and others may choose capacity. In either case, the basic approach and analysis presented in this chapter is unchanged. Chapter 9 discusses choosing a denominator level and its implications in more detail.

estimates that it will take 0.40 machine-hour per output unit. Color Plus can now calculate the budgeted fixed overhead cost per output unit as follows:

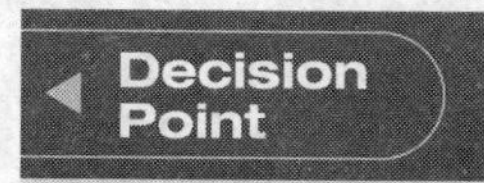

How are budgeted variable overhead and fixed overhead cost rates calculated?

$$\text{Budgeted fixed overhead cost per output unit} = \text{Budgeted quantity of cost-allocation base allowed per output unit} \times \text{Budgeted fixed overhead cost per unit of cost-allocation base}$$

$$= 0.40 \text{ of a machine-hour per jacket} \times \text{Rs } 575.0 \text{ per machine-hour}$$

$$= \text{Rs } 230.0 \text{ per jacket}$$

When preparing monthly budgets for 2011, Color Plus divides the Rs 3,31,20,000 annual total fixed costs into 12 equal monthly amounts of Rs 27,60,000.

Variable Overhead Cost Variances

We now illustrate how the budgeted variable overhead rate is used in computing Color's variable overhead cost variances. The following data are for April 2008, when Color Plus produced and sold 10,000 jackets:

	Actual Result	Flexible-Budget Amount
1. Output units (jackets)	10,000	10,000
2. Machine-hours per output unit	0.45	0.40
3. Machine-hours (1 × 2)	4,500	4,000
4. Variable overhead costs	Rs 13,05,000	Rs 12,00,000
5. Variable overhead costs per machine-hour (4 ÷ 3)	Rs 90	Rs 300
6. Variable overhead costs per output unit (4 ÷ 1)	Rs 130.5	Rs 120

Learning Objective 3

Compute the variable overhead flexible-budget variance,

. . . difference between actual variable overhead costs and flexible-budget variable overhead amounts the variable overhead efficiency variance,

. . . difference between actual quantity of cost-allocation base and budgeted quantity of cost-allocation base and the variable overhead spending variance

. . . difference between actual variable overhead cost rate and budgeted variable overhead cost rate

As we saw in Chapter 7, the flexible budget enables Color Plus to highlight the differences between actual costs and actual quantities versus budgeted costs and budgeted quantities for the actual output level of 10,000 jackets.

Flexible-Budget Analysis

The **variable overhead flexible-budget variance** measures the difference between actual variable overhead costs incurred and flexible-budget variable overhead amounts.

$$\text{Variable overhead flexible-budget variance} = \text{Actual costs incurred} - \text{Flexible-budget amount}$$

$$= \text{Rs } 13{,}05{,}000 - \text{Rs } 12{,}00{,}000$$

$$= \text{Rs } 1{,}05{,}000 \text{ U}$$

This Rs 1,05,000 unfavorable flexible-budget variance means Color's actual variable overhead exceeded the flexible-budget amount by Rs 1,05,000 for the 10,000 jackets actually produced and sold. Color's managers would want to know the reasons why actual costs exceeded the flexible-budget amount. Did Color Plus use more machine-hours than planned to produce the 10,000 jackets? If so, was it because workers were less skilled than expected in using machines? Or did Color Plus spend more on variable overhead costs, such as maintenance?

Just as we illustrated in Chapter 7 with the flexible-budget variance for direct-cost items, Color's managers can get further insight into the reason for the Rs 1,05,000 unfavorable variance by subdividing it into the efficiency variance and spending variance.

Variable Overhead Efficiency Variance

The **variable overhead efficiency variance** is the difference between actual quantity of the cost-allocation base used and budgeted quantity of the cost-allocation base that should have been used to produce actual output, multiplied by budgeted variable overhead cost per unit of the cost-allocation base.

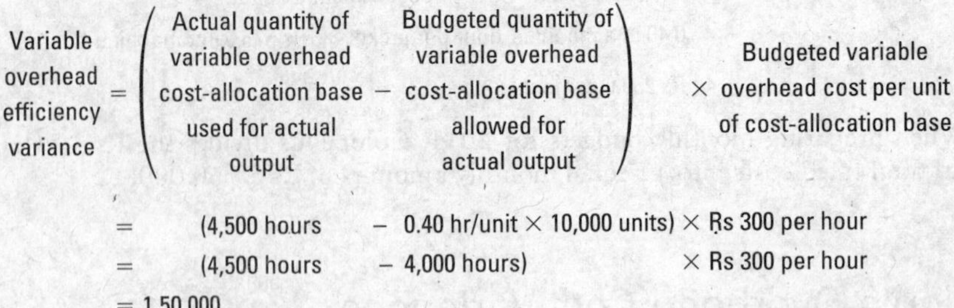

= (4,500 hours − 0.40 hr/unit × 10,000 units) × Rs 300 per hour
= (4,500 hours − 4,000 hours) × Rs 300 per hour
= 1,50,000

Columns 2 and 3 of Exhibit 8-1 depict the variable overhead efficiency variance. Note the variance arises solely because of the difference between actual quantity (4,500 hours) and budgeted quantity (4,000 hours) of the cost-allocation base. The variable overhead efficiency variance is computed the same way as the efficiency variance for direct-cost items (Chapter 7). But the interpretation of the variable overhead efficiency variance differs from the interpretation of direct-cost efficiency variances. In Chapter 7, efficiency variances for direct-cost items are based on differences between actual inputs used and budgeted inputs allowed for actual output produced. For example, an efficiency variance for direct manufacturing labor for Color Plus will indicate whether more or fewer direct labor-hours are used per jacket than were budgeted for actual output produced. In contrast, the efficiency variance for variable overhead cost is based on the efficiency with which *the cost-allocation base* is used. Color's unfavorable variable overhead efficiency variance of Rs 1,50,000 means that the actual machine-hours (the cost-allocation base) of 4,500 hours turned out to be higher than the budgeted machine-hours of 4,000 hours allowed to manufacture 10,000 jackets.

Exhibit 8-1 Columnar Presentation of Variable Overhead Variance Analysis: Color Plus Company for April 2011[a]

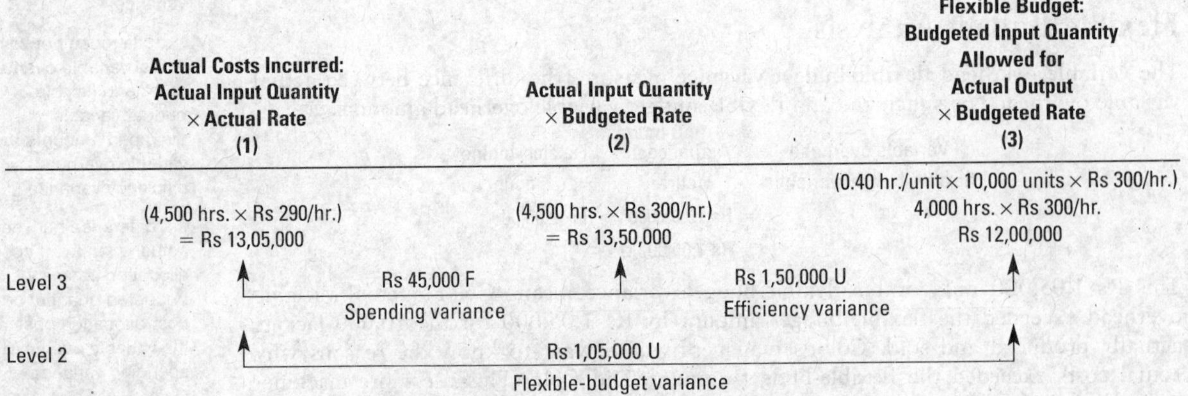

[a]F = favorable effect on operating income; U = unfavorable effect on operating income.

The following table shows possible causes for Color's actual machine-hours exceeding budgeted machine-hours and management's potential responses to each of these causes.

Possible Causes for Exceeding Budget	Potential Management Responses
1. Workers were less skilled than expected in using machines.	1. Encourage the human resources department to implement better employee-hiring practices and training procedures.
2. Production scheduler inefficiently scheduled jobs, resulting in more machine-hours used than budgeted.	2. Improve plant operations by installing production scheduling software.
3. Machines were not maintained in good operating condition.	3. Ensure preventive maintenance is done on all machines.
4. Color's sales staff promised a distributor a rush delivery, which resulted in more machine-hours used than budgeted.	4. Coordinate production schedules with sales staff and distributors and share information with them.
5. Budgeted machine time standards were set too tight.	5. Commit more resources to develop appropriate standards.

Management's response to this Rs 1,50,000 U variance would be guided by which cause(s) best describes the April 2008 results. Note how, depending on the cause(s) of the variance, corrective actions may need to be taken not just in manufacturing but also in other business functions of the value chain, such as sales and distribution.

Color's managers discovered that one reason the machines operated below budgeted efficiency levels in April 2008 was insufficient maintenance performed in the prior two months. A former plant manager delayed maintenance in a presumed attempt to meet monthly budget cost targets. As we discussed in Chapter 6, managers should not be focused on meeting short-run budget targets if it is likely to result in harmful long-run consequences. Color Plus is now strengthening its internal maintenance procedures so that failure to do monthly maintenance as needed will raise a "red flag" that must be immediately explained to management. Another reason for actual machine-hours exceeding budgeted machine-hours was the use of underskilled workers. As a result, Color Plus is initiating steps to improve hiring and training practices.

Variable Overhead Spending Variance

The **variable overhead spending variance** is the difference between actual variable overhead cost per unit of the cost-allocation base and budgeted variable overhead cost per unit of the cost-allocation base, multiplied by the actual quantity of variable overhead cost-allocation base used for actual output.

$$\begin{array}{l}\text{Variable overhead spending variance} = \left(\begin{array}{c}\text{Actual variable overhead cost per unit}\\\text{of cost-allocation base}\end{array} - \begin{array}{c}\text{Budgeted variable overhead cost per unit}\\\text{of cost-allocation base}\end{array}\right) \times \begin{array}{c}\text{Actual quantity of variable overhead}\\\text{cost-allocation base used for actual output}\end{array}\\ = \text{Rs }(290 \text{ per machine-hour} - \text{Rs } 300 \text{ per machine-hour}) \times 4{,}500 \text{ machine-hour}\\ = (-\text{Rs } 10 \text{ per machine-hour}) \times 4{,}500 \text{ machine-hour}\\ = \text{Rs } 45{,}000 \text{ F}\end{array}$$

Color Plus operated in April 2008 with a lower-than-budgeted variable overhead cost per machine-hour. Hence, there is a favorable variable overhead spending variance. Columns 1 and 2 in Exhibit 8-1 depict this variance.

To understand the favorable variable overhead spending variance and its implications, Color's managers need to recognize why *actual* variable overhead cost per unit of the cost-allocation base (Rs 290 per machine-hour) is *lower* than *budgeted* variable overhead cost per unit of the cost-allocation base (Rs 300 per machine-hour). Overall, Color Plus used 4,500 machine-hours, which is 12.5% greater than the flexible-budget amount of 4,000 machine hours. However, actual variable overhead costs of Rs 13,05,000 are only 8.75% greater than the flexible-budget amount of Rs 12,00,000. Thus, relative to the flexible budget, the percentage increase in actual variable overhead costs is *less* than the percentage increase in machine-hours. Consequently, actual variable overhead cost per machine-hour is lower than the budgeted amount, resulting in a favorable variable overhead spending variance.

Recall that variable overhead costs include costs of energy, machine maintenance, indirect materials, and indirect labor. Two reasons why the percentage increase in actual variable overhead costs is less than the percentage increase in machine-hours are:

1. Actual prices of individual inputs included in variable overhead costs, such as the price of energy, indirect materials, or indirect labor, are lower than budgeted prices of these inputs. For example, the actual price of electricity may only be Rs 0.90 per kilowatt-hour, compared with a price of Rs 1.0 per kilowatt-hour in the flexible budget.
2. Relative to the flexible budget, the percentage increase in the actual quantity usage of individual items in the variable overhead-cost pool is less than the percentage increase in machine-hours. Suppose actual energy used is 32,400 kilowatt-hours, compared with the flexible-budget amount of 30,000 kilowatt-hours. The 8% [(32,400 − 30,000) ÷ 30,000] increase in energy usage compared with the 12.5% [(4,500 − 4,000) ÷ 4,000] increase in machine-hours will lead to a favorable variable overhead spending variance. The favorable spending variance can be partially or completely traced to the efficient use of energy and other variable overhead items.

As part of the last stage of the five-step decision-making process, Color's managers will need to examine the signals provided by the variable overhead variances to *evaluate performance and learn*. By understanding the reasons for these variances, Color Plus can take appropriate actions and make more precise predictions in order to achieve improved results in future periods.

For example, Color's managers must examine why actual prices of variable overhead cost items are different from budgeted prices. The price effects could be the result of skillful negotiation on the part of the purchasing manager, oversupply in the market, or lower quality of inputs such as indirect materials. Color's response depends on what is believed to be the cause of the variance. If the concerns are about quality, for instance, Color Plus may want to put in place new quality management systems.

Similarly, Color's managers should understand the possible causes for the efficiency with which variable overhead resources are used. These causes include skill levels of workers, maintenance of machines and the efficiency of the manufacturing process. Color's managers discovered that Color Plus used fewer supervision resources per machine hour because of manufacturing process improvements. As a result, they began organizing cross-functional teams to see if more process improvements could be achieved.

We emphasize that a favorable variable overhead spending variance is not always desirable. For example, the variable overhead spending variance is not would be favorable if Color's managers purchased lower-priced, poor-quality indirect materials, hired less-talented supervisors, or performed less machine maintenance. These decisions, however, are likely to hurt product quality and harm the long-run prospects of the business.

To clarify the concepts of variable overhead efficiency variance and variable overhead spending variance, consider the following example, assuming that (a) energy is the only item of variable overhead cost and machine-hours is the cost-allocation base, (b) actual machine-hours used to produce actual output equals budgeted machine-hours, and (c) actual price of energy equals budgeted price. Under those assumptions, there would be no efficiency variance, but there could be a spending variance. The company has been efficient with respect to the number of machine-hours used to produce the actual output. But it could be using too much energy—not because of excessive machine-hours but because of waste (using more energy per machine-hour). The cost of this higher energy usage is reflected in the spending variance.

Journal Entries for Variable Overhead Costs and Variances

We now prepare journal entries for Variable Overhead Control and the contra account Variable Overhead Allocated.

Entries for variable overhead for April 2011 (data from Exhibit 8-1) are:

1.	Variable Overhead Control	13,05,000	
	Accounts Payable and various other accounts		13,05,000
	To record actual variable overhead costs incurred.		

		Debit	Credit
2.	Work-in-Process Control	12,00,000	
	Variable Overhead Allocated		12,00,000
	To record variable overhead cost allocated (0.40 machine-hour/unit × 10,000 units × Rs 300/machine-hour). (The costs accumulated in Work-in-Process Control are transferred to Finished Goods Control when production is completed and to Cost of Goods Sold when the products are sold.)		
3.	Variable Overhead Allocated	12,00,000	
	Variable Overhead Efficiency Variance	15,000	
	Variable Overhead Control		13,05,000
	Variable Overhead Spending Variance		45,000
	To record variances for the accounting period.		

These variances are the underallocated or overallocated variable overhead costs. At the end of the fiscal year, the variance accounts are written off to cost of goods sold if immaterial in amount. If the variances are material in amount, they are prorated among Work-in-Process Control, Finished Goods Control, and Cost of Goods Sold on the basis of the variable overhead allocated to these accounts, as described in Chapter 4. As we discussed in Chapter 7, only unavoidable costs are prorated. Any part of the variances attributable to avoidable inefficiency are written off in the period. Assume that the balances in the variable overhead variance accounts as of April 2011 are also the balances at the end of the 2011 fiscal year and are immaterial in amount. The following journal entry records the write-off of the variance accounts to cost of goods sold.

	Debit	Credit
Cost of Goods Sold	1,05,000	
Variable Overhead Spending Variance	45,000	
Variable Overhead Efficiency Variance		1,50,000

We next consider fixed overhead costs.

Decision Point

What variances can be calculated for variable overhead costs?

Fixed Overhead Cost Variances

Learning Objective 4

Compute the fixed overhead flexible-budget variance,

. . . difference between actual fixed overhead costs and flexible-budget fixed overhead amounts

the fixed overhead spending variance,

. . . same as the preceding explanation

and the fixed overhead production-volume variance

. . . difference between budgeted fixed overhead and fixed overhead allocated on the basis of actual output produced

The flexible-budget amount for a fixed-cost item is also the amount included in the static budget prepared at the start of the period. No adjustment is required for differences between actual output and budgeted output for fixed costs. That's because fixed costs are unaffected by changes in the output level within the relevant range. At the start of 2011, Color Plus budgeted fixed overhead costs to be Rs 27,60,000 per month. The actual amount for April 2011 turned out to be Rs 28,50,000. The **fixed overhead flexible-budget variance** is the difference between actual fixed overhead costs and fixed overhead costs in the flexible budget:

$$\text{Fixed overhead flexible-budget variance} = \text{Actual costs incurred} - \text{Flexible-budget amount}$$
$$= \text{Rs } 28{,}50{,}000 - \text{Rs } 27{,}60{,}000$$
$$= \text{Rs } 90{,}000 \text{ U}$$

The variance is unfavorable because Rs 28,50,000 actual fixed overhead costs exceed the Rs 27,60,000 budgeted for April 2011, which decreases that month's operating income by Rs 90,000.

The variable overhead flexible-budget variance described earlier in this chapter was subdivided into a spending variance and an efficiency variance. There is not an efficiency variance for fixed overhead costs. That's because a given lump sum of fixed overhead costs will be unaffected by how efficiently machine-hours are used to produce output in a given budget period. As we will see later on, this does not mean that a company cannot be efficient or inefficient in its use of fixed-overhead-cost resources. As Exhibit 8-2 shows,

Exhibit 8-2

Columnar Presentation of Fixed Overhead Variance Analysis: Color Plus Company for April 2011[a]

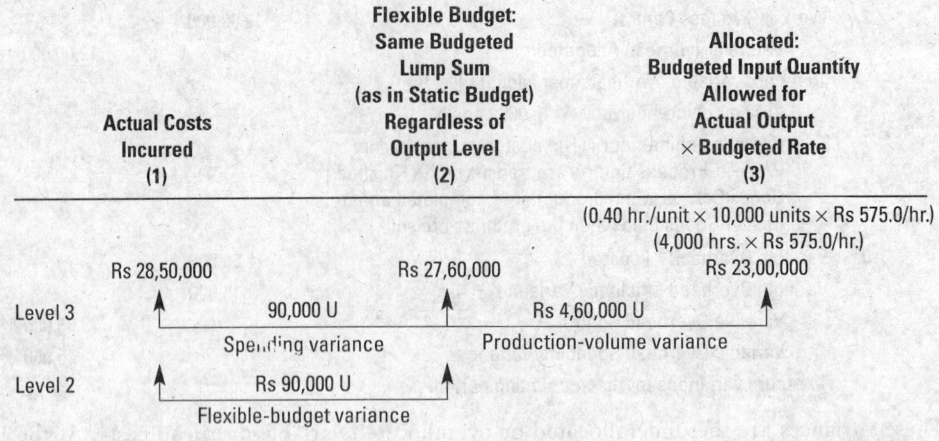

[a]F = favorable effect on operating income; U = unfavorable effect on operating income.

because there is no efficiency variance, the **fixed overhead spending variance** is the same amount as the fixed overhead flexible-budget variance:

$$\text{Fixed overhead spending variance} = \text{Actual costs incurred} - \text{Flexible-budget amount}$$
$$= \text{Rs } 28{,}50{,}000 - \text{Rs } 27{,}60{,}000$$
$$= \text{Rs } 90{,}000 \text{ U}$$

Reasons for the unfavorable spending variance could be higher plant-leasing costs, higher depreciation on plant and equipment, and higher administrative costs such as a higher-than-budgeted salary paid to the plant manager. Color Plus investigated this variance and found that there was a Rs 90,000 per month unexpected increase in its equipment-leasing costs. However, management concluded that the new lease rates were competitive with lease rates available elsewhere. If this were not the case, management would look to lease equipment from other suppliers.

Production-Volume Variance

We now examine a variance—the production-volume variance—that arises only for fixed costs. Recall that at the start of the year, Color Plus calculated a budgeted fixed overhead rate of Rs 575.0 per standard machine-hour or Rs 230 per jacket (0.40 machine-hour per jacket × Rs 575.0 per machine-hour). So, if Color Plus produces 1,000 jackets, Rs 2,30,000 (Rs 230 per jacket × 1,000 jackets) out of April's budgeted fixed overhead costs of Rs 27,60,000 will be allocated to the jackets. If Color Plus produces 10,000 jackets, Rs 23,00,000 (Rs 230 per jacket × 10,000 jackets) will be allocated. Only if Color Plus produces 12,000 jackets (that is, operates at capacity), will all Rs 27,60,000 (Rs 230 per jacket × 12,000 jackets) of the budgeted fixed overhead cost be allocated to the jacket output. The key point here is that even though Color Plus budgets fixed overhead costs to be Rs 27,60,000 it does not necessarily allocate all these costs to output. The reason is that Color Plus budgets Rs 27,60,000 of fixed costs to support its planned production of 12,000 jackets. If Color Plus produces fewer than 12,000 jackets, it only allocates the budgeted cost of capacity actually needed and used to produce the jackets.

The **production-volume variance**, also referred to as the **denominator-level variance,** is the difference between budgeted fixed overhead and fixed overhead allocated on the basis of actual output produced. The allocated fixed overhead can be expressed in terms of allocation-base units (machine-hours for Color Plus) or in terms of the budgeted fixed cost per unit:

Production volume variance	=	Budgeted fixed overhead	−	Fixed overhead allocated for actual output units produced
	=	Rs 27,60,000	−	(0.40 hour per jacket × Rs 575.0 per hour × 10,000 jackets)
	=	Rs 27,60,000	−	Rs 230 per jacket × 10,000 jackets)
	=	Rs 27,60,000	−	Rs 23,00,000
	=	Rs 4,60,000 U		

As shown in Exhibit 8-2, the budgeted fixed overhead (Rs 27,60,000) will be the lump sum shown in the static budget and also in any flexible budget within the relevant range. Fixed overhead allocated (Rs 23,00,000) is the amount of fixed overhead costs allocated; it is calculated by multiplying the number of output units produced during the budget period (10,000 units) by the budgeted cost per output unit (Rs 230). The Rs 4,60,000 U production-volume variance can also be thought of as Rs 230 per jacket × 2,000 jackets that were *not* produced (12,000 jackets planned – 10,000 jackets produced). We will explore possible causes for the unfavorable production-volume variance and its management implications in the following section.

Exhibit 8-3 is a graphical presentation of the production-volume variance. Exhibit 8-3 shows that for planning and control purposes, fixed (manufacturing) overhead costs do not change in the 0- to 12,000-unit relevant range. Contrast this behavior of fixed costs with how these costs are depicted for the inventory costing purpose in Exhibit 8-3. Under generally accepted accounting principles, fixed (manufacturing) overhead costs are allocated as an inventoriable cost to the output units produced. Every output unit that Color Plus manufactures will increase the fixed overhead allocated to products by Rs 230. That is, for purposes of allocating fixed overhead costs to jackets, these costs are viewed *as if* they had a variable-cost behavior pattern. As the graph in Exhibit 8-3 shows, the difference between the fixed overhead costs budgeted of Rs 27,60,000 and the Rs 23,00,000 of costs allocated is the Rs 4,60,000 unfavorable production-volume variance.

Managers should always be careful to distinguish the behavior of fixed costs from how fixed costs are allocated to products. In particular, managers should not use the unitization of fixed overhead costs for planning and control decisions, where it is important to understand how fixed costs behave. When forecasting fixed costs, managers should concentrate on total lump-sum costs. Similarly, when managers are looking to assign costs for control purposes or identify the best way to use capacity resources that are fixed in the short run, we will see in Chapter 9 and Chapter 11 that the use of unitized fixed costs often leads to incorrect decisions.

Interpreting the Production-Volume Variance

Lump-sum fixed costs represent costs of acquiring capacity, such as plant and equipment leases, that do not decrease automatically if the resources needed turn out to be less than

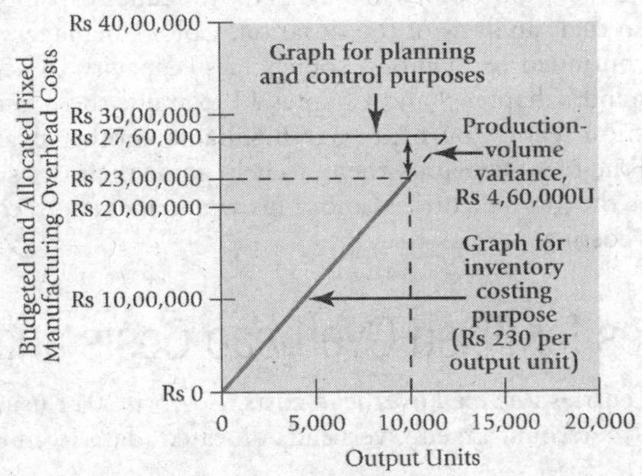

Exhibit 8-3

Behavior of Fixed Manufacturing Overhead Costs: Budgeted for Planning and Control Purposes and Allocated for Inventory Costing Purposes for Color Plus Company for April 2011

the resources acquired. Sometimes costs are fixed for contractual reasons such as a lease contract; at other times, costs are fixed because of lumpiness in acquiring and disposing of capacity—for example, Color Plus may be able to add capacity to produce jackets only in increments of say 1,000 jackets. If this is the case, Color Plus may choose capacity levels of 10,000, 11,000, or 12,000 jackets but nothing in between.

Color's management would want to analyze why this overcapacity occurred. Is demand weak? Should Color Plus reevaluate its product and marketing strategies? Is there a quality problem? Or did Color Plus make a strategic mistake by acquiring too much capacity? The causes of the Rs 4,60,000 unfavorable production-volume variance will drive the actions Color's managers will take in response to this variance.

In contrast, a favorable production-volume variance indicates an overallocation of fixed overhead costs. That is, the overhead costs allocated to the actual output produced exceed the budgeted fixed overhead costs of Rs 27,60,000. The favorable production-volume variance comprises the fixed costs recorded in excess of Rs 27,60,000.

Be careful when drawing conclusions regarding a company's decisions about capacity planning and usage from the type (that is, favorable, F, or unfavorable, U) or the magnitude associated with a production-volume variance. To interpret the Rs 4,60,000 unfavorable variance, Color Plus should consider why it sold only 10,000 jackets in April. Suppose a new competitor had gained market share by pricing below Color's selling price. To sell the budgeted 12,000 jackets, Color Plus might have had to reduce its own selling price on all 12,000 jackets. Suppose it decided that selling 10,000 jackets at a higher price yielded higher operating income than selling 12,000 jackets at a lower price. The production-volume variance does not take into account such information. That's why Color Plus should not interpret the Rs 4,60,000 U amount as the total economic cost of selling 2,000 jackets fewer than the 12,000 jackets budgeted. If, however, Color's managers anticipate they will not need capacity beyond 10,000 jackets, they may reduce the excess capacity, say, by canceling the lease on some of the machines.

Companies plan their plant capacity strategically on the basis of market information about how much capacity will be needed over some future time horizon. For 2008, Color's budgeted quantity of output is equal to the maximum capacity of the plant for that budget period. Actual demand (and quantity produced) turned out to be below the budgeted quantity of output, so Color Plus reports an unfavorable production-volume variance for April 2008. However, it would be incorrect to conclude that Color's management made a poor planning decision regarding plant capacity. Demand for Color's jackets might be highly uncertain. Given this uncertainty and the cost of not having sufficient capacity to meet sudden demand surges (for example, lost contribution margins and reduced follow-on business), Color's management may have made a wise choice in planning 2008 plant capacity. Of course, if demand is unlikely to pick up again, Color's managers may look to cancel the lease on some of the machines or to sublease the machines to other parties with the goal of reducing the unfavorable production-volume variance.

Managers must always explore the why of a variance before concluding that the label unfavorable or favorable necessarily indicates, respectively, poor or good management performance. Understanding the reasons for a variance also helps managers decide on future courses of action. Should Color's managers try to reduce capacity, increase sales, or do nothing? Based on their analysis of the situation, Color's managers decided to reduce some capacity but continued to maintain some excess capacity to accommodate unexpected surges in demand. Chapter 9 and Chapter 13 examine these issues in more detail. The Concepts in Action feature on next page highlights another example of managers using variances, and the reasons behind them, to help guide their decisions.

Next we describe the journal entries Color Plus would make to record fixed overhead costs using standard costing.

Journal Entries for Fixed Overhead Costs and Variances

We illustrate journal entries for fixed overhead costs for April 2011 using Fixed Overhead Control and the contra account Fixed Overhead Allocated (data from Exhibit 8-2).

Concepts in Action

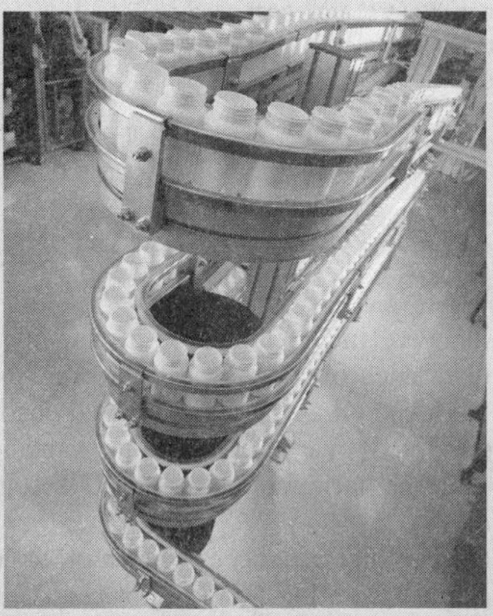

Variance Analysis and Standard Costing Help Sandoz Manage Its Overhead Costs

In the United States, the importance of generic pharmaceuticals is growing dramatically. In recent years, Wal-Mart has been selling hundreds of generic drugs for $4 per prescription, a price many competitors have since matched. Moreover, with recent legislation extending health insurance coverage to 32 million previously uninsured Americans, the growing use of generic drugs is certain to accelerate, a trend rooted both in demographics—the aging U.S. population takes more drugs each year—and in the push to cut health care costs.

Sandoz US, a $7.5 billion subsidiary of Swiss-based Novartis AG, is one of the largest developers of generic pharmaceutical substitutes for market-leading therapeutic drugs. Market pricing pressure means that Sandoz, Teva Pharmaceutical, and other generic manufacturers operate on razor-thin margins. As a result, along with an intricate analysis of direct-cost variances, firms like Sandoz must also tackle the challenge of accounting for overhead costs. Sandoz uses standard costing and variance analysis to manage its overhead costs.

Each year, Sandoz prepares an overhead budget based on a detailed production plan, planned overhead spending, and other factors, including inflation, efficiency initiatives, and anticipated capital expenditures and depreciation. Sandoz then uses activity-based costing techniques to assign budgeted overhead costs to different work centers (for example, mixing, blending, tableting, testing, and packaging). Finally, overhead costs are assigned to products based on the activity levels required by each product at each work center. The resulting standard product cost is used in product profitability analysis and as a basis for making pricing decisions. The two main focal points in Sandoz's performance analyses are overhead absorption analysis and manufacturing overhead variance analysis.

Each month, Sandoz uses absorption analysis to compare actual production and actual costs to the standard costs of processed inventory. The monthly analysis evaluates two key trends:

1. Are costs in line with the budget? If not, the reasons are examined and the accountable managers are notified.
2. Are production volume and product mix conforming to plan? If not, Sandoz reviews and adjusts machine capacities and the absorption trend is deemed to be permanent. Plant management uses absorption analysis as a compass to determine if it is on budget and has an appropriate capacity level to efficiently satisfy the needs of its customers.

Manufacturing overhead variances are examined at the work center level. These variances help determine when equipment is not running as expected, which leads to repair or replacement. Variances also help in identifying inefficiencies in processing and setup and cleaning times, which leads to more efficient ways to use equipment. Sometimes, manufacturing overhead variance analysis leads to the review and improvement of the standards themselves—a critical element in planning the level of plant capacity. Management reviews current and future capacity use on a monthly basis, using standard hours entered into the plan's enterprise resource planning system. The standards are a useful tool in identifying capacity constraints and future capital needs.

As the plant controller remarked, "Standard costing at Sandoz produces costs that are not only understood by management accountants and industrial engineers, but by decision makers in marketing and on the production floor. Management accountants at Sandoz achieve this by having a high degree of process understanding and involvement. The result is better pricing and product mix decisions, lower waste, process improvements, and efficient capacity choices—all contributing to overall profitability."

Source: Booming US Generic Drug Market. Delhi, India: RNCOS Ltd, 2010; Conversations with, and documents prepared by, Eric Evans and Erich Erchr (of Sandoz US), 2004; Day, Kathleen. 2006. Wal-Mart sets $4 price for many generic drugs. *Washington Post,* September 22; Halpern, Steven. 2010. Teva: Generic gains from health care reform. *AOL Inc.* "Blogging Stocks" blog, May 13. http://www.bloggingstocks.com/2010/05/13/teva-teva-generic-gains-from-healthcare-reform/

		Debit	Credit
1.	Fixed Overhead Control	28,50,000	
	Salaries Payable, Accumulated Depreciation, and various other accounts		28,50,000
	To record actual fixed overhead costs incurred.		

2.	Work-in-Process Control	23,00,000	
	Fixed Overhead Allocated		23,00,000
	To record fixed overhead costs allocated, (0.40 machine-hour/unit × 10,000 units × Rs 575.0/machine-hour). (The costs accumulated in Work-in-Process Control are transferred to Finished Goods Control when production is completed and to Cost of Goods Sold when the products are sold.)		
3.	Fixed Overhead Allocated	23,00,000	
	Fixed Overhead Spending Variance	90,000	
	Fixed Overhead Production-Volume Variance	4,60,000	
	Fixed Overhead Control		28,50,000
	To record variances for the accounting period.		

Overall, Rs 28,50,000 of fixed overhead costs were incurred during April, but only Rs 23,00,000 were allocated to jackets. The difference of Rs 5,50,000 is precisely the underallocated fixed overhead costs that we introduced when studying normal costing in Chapter 4. The third entry illustrates how the fixed overhead spending variance of Rs 90,000 and the fixed overhead production-volume variance of Rs 4,60,000 together record this amount in a standard costing system.

At the end of the fiscal year, the fixed overhead spending variance is written off to cost of goods sold if it is immaterial in amount, or prorated among Work-in-Process Control, Finished Goods Control and Cost of Goods Sold on the basis of the fixed overhead allocated to these accounts as described in Chapter 4. Some companies combine the write-off and proration methods—that is, they write off the portion of the variance that is due to inefficiency and could have been avoided and prorate the portion of the variance that is unavoidable. Assume that the balance in the Fixed Overhead Spending Variance account as of April 2011 is also the balance at the end of 2011 and is immaterial in amount. The following journal entry records the write-off to Cost of Goods Sold.

Cost of Goods Sold	90,000	
Fixed Overhead Spending Variance		90,000

We now consider the production-volume variance. Assume that the balance in Fixed Overhead Production-Volume Variance as of April 2011 is also the balance at the end of 2011. Also assume that some of the jackets manufactured during 2011 are in work-in-process and finished goods inventory at the end of the year. Many management accountants make a strong argument for writing off to Cost of Goods Sold and not prorating an unfavorable production-volume variance. Proponents of this argument contend that the unfavorable production-volume variance of Rs 4,60,000 measures the cost of resources expended for 2,000 jackets that were not produced (Rs 230 per jacket × 2,000 jackets = Rs 4,60,000). Prorating these costs would inappropriately allocate fixed overhead costs incurred for the 2,000 jackets that were not produced to the jackets that were produced. The jackets produced already bear their representative share of fixed overhead costs of Rs 230 per jacket. Therefore, this argument favors charging the unfavorable production-volume variance against the year's revenues so that fixed costs of unused capacity are not carried in work-in-process inventory and finished goods inventory.

There is, however, an alternative view. This view regards the denominator level chosen as a "soft" rather than a "hard" measure of the fixed resources required and needed to produce each jacket. Suppose that either because of the design of the jacket or the functioning of the machines, it took more machine-hours than previously thought to manufacture each jacket. Consequently, Color Plus could make only 10,000 jackets rather than the planned 12,000 in April. In this case, the Rs 27,60,000 of budgeted fixed overhead costs support the production of the 10,000 jackets manufactured. Under this reasoning, prorating the fixed overhead production-volume variance would appropriately spread fixed overhead costs among Work-in-Process Control, Finished Goods Control, and Cost of Goods Sold.

What about a favorable production-volume variance? Suppose Color Plus manufactured 13,800 jackets in April 2011.

		Budgeted fixed overhead		Fixed overhead allocated using budgeted cost per output unit overhead allowed for actual output produced
Production-volume variance	=	Budgeted fixed overhead	−	Fixed overhead allocated using budgeted cost per output unit overhead allowed for actual output produced

= Rs 27,60,000 – (Rs 230 per jacket × 13,800 jackets)

= Rs 27,60,000 – Rs 31,74,000 = Rs 4,14,000 F

Because actual production exceeded the planned capacity level, clearly the fixed overhead costs of Rs 27,60,000 supported production of, and so should be allocated to, all 13,800 jackets. Prorating the favorable production-volume variance achieves this outcome and reduces the amounts in Work-in-Process Control, Finished Goods Control, and Cost of Goods Sold. Proration is also the more conservative approach in the sense that it results in a lower operating income than if the entire favorable production-volume variance were credited to Cost of Goods Sold.

One more point is relevant to the discussion of whether to prorate the production-volume variance or to write it off to cost of goods sold. If variances are always written off to cost of goods sold, a company could set its standards to either increase (for financial reporting purposes) or decrease (for tax purposes) operating income. In other words, always writing off variances invites gaming behavior. For example, Color Plus could generate a favorable (unfavorable) production-volume variance by setting the denominator level used to allocate fixed overhead costs low (high) and thereby increase (decrease) operating income. The proration method has the effect of approximating the allocation of fixed costs based on actual costs and actual output so it is not susceptible to the manipulation of operating income via the choice of the denominator level.

There is no clear-cut or preferred approach for closing out the production-volume variance. The appropriate accounting procedure is a matter of judgment and depends on the circumstances of each case. Variations of the proration method may be desirable. For example, a company may choose to write off a portion of the production-volume variance and prorate the rest. The goal is to write off that part of the production-volume variance that represents the cost of capacity not used to support the production of output during the period. The rest of the production-volume variance is prorated to Work-in-Process Control, Finished Goods Control, and Cost of Goods Sold.

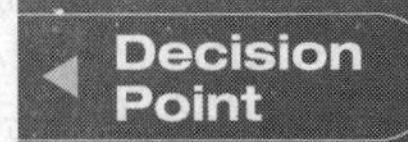

What variances can be calculated for fixed overhead costs?

If Color Plus were to write off the production-volume variance to cost of goods sold, it would make the following journal entry.

Cost of Goods Sold	4,60,000	
Fixed Overhead Production-Volume Variance		4,60,000

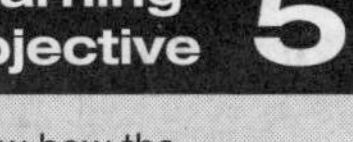

Show how the 4-variance analysis approach reconciles the actual overhead incurred with the overhead amounts allocated during the period

. . . the 4-variance analysis approach identifies spending and efficiency variances for variable overhead costs and spending and production-volume variances for fixed overhead costs

Integrated Analysis of Overhead Cost Variances

As our discussion indicates, the variance calculations for variable overhead and fixed overhead differ.

- Variable overhead has no production-volume variance.
- Fixed overhead has no efficiency variance.

Exhibit 8-4 presents an integrated summary of the variable overhead variances and the fixed overhead variances computed using standard costs for April 2008. Panel A shows the variances for variable overhead, while Panel B contains the fixed overhead variances. As you study Exhibit 8-4, note how the columns in Panels A and B are aligned to measure the different variances. In both Panels A and B,

- The difference between columns 1 and 2 measures the spending variance.
- The difference between columns 2 and 3 measures the efficiency variance (if applicable).
- The difference between columns 3 and 4 measures the production-volume variance (if applicable).

Exhibit 8-4 Columnar Presentation of Integrated Variance Analysis: Color Plus Company for April 2011[a]

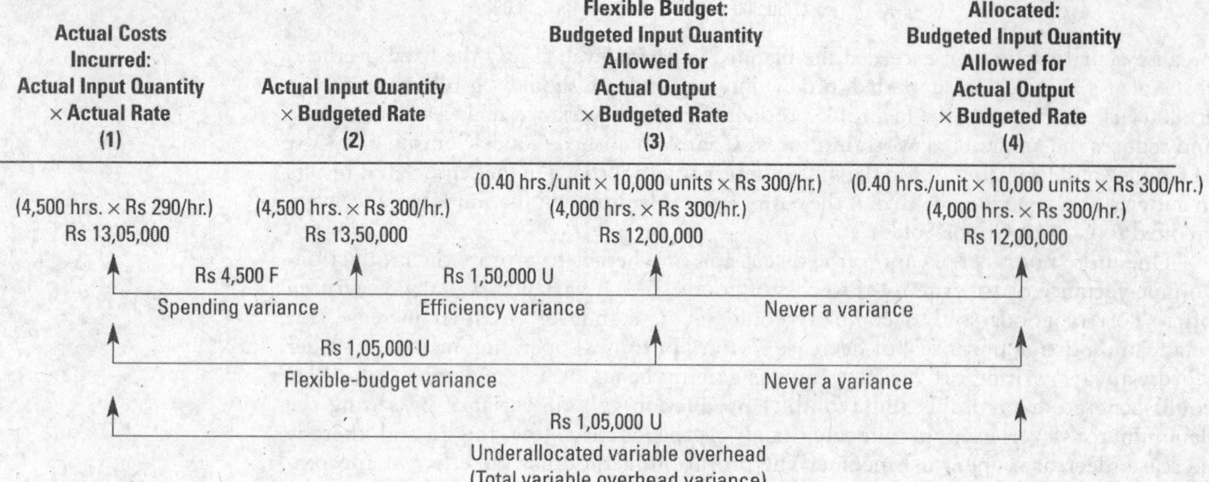

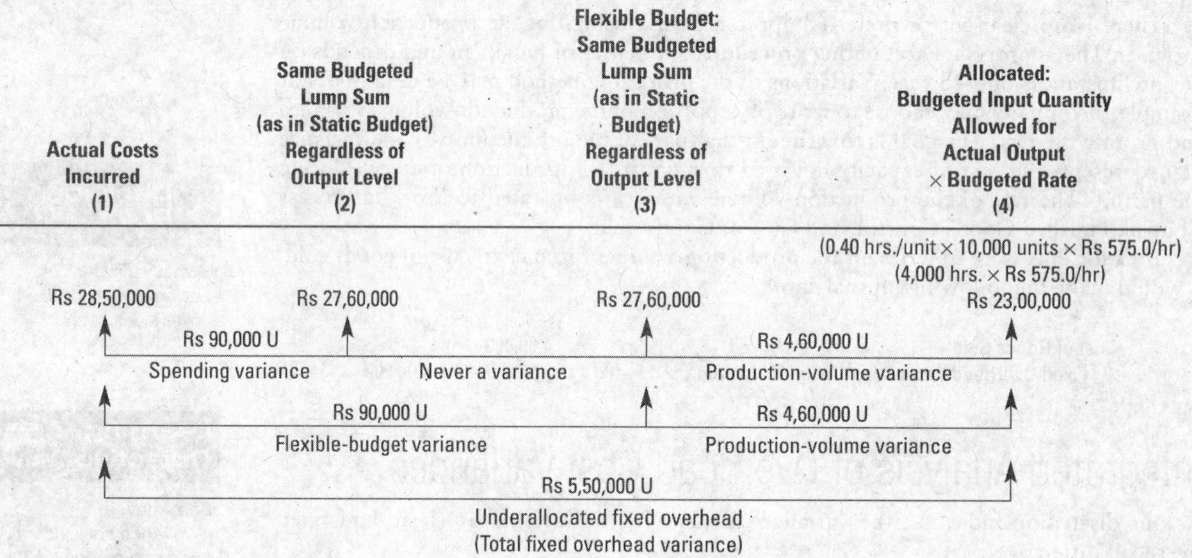

[a]F = favorable effect on operating income; U = unfavorable effect on operating income.

Panel A contains an efficiency variance; Panel B has no efficiency variance for fixed overhead. As discussed earlier, a lump-sum amount of fixed costs will be unaffected by the degree of operating efficiency in a given budget period.

Panel A does not have a production-volume variance. That's because the amount of variable overhead allocated is always the same as the flexible-budget amount. Variable costs never have any unused capacity. When production and sales decline from 12,000 jackets to 10,000 jackets, budgeted variable overhead costs proportionately decline. Fixed costs are different. Panel B has a production-volume variance (see Exhibit 8-3) because Color Plus had to acquire the fixed manufacturing overhead resources it had committed to when it planned production of 12,000 jackets, even though it produced only 10,000 jackets and did not use some of its capacity.

4-Variance Analysis

When all of the overhead variances are presented together as in Exhibit 8-4, we refer to it as a 4-variance analysis:

4-Variance Analysis

	Spending Variance	Efficiency Variance	Production-Volume Variance
Variable overhead	Rs 45,000 F	Rs 1,50,000 U	Never a variance
Fixed overhead	Rs 90,000 U	Never a variance	Rs 4,60,000 U

Note that the 4-variance analysis provides the same level of information as the variance analysis carried out earlier for variable overhead and fixed overhead separately (in Exhibits 8-1 and 8-2, respectively), but it does so in a unified presentation that also indicates those variances that are never present.

As you have seen in the case of other variances, the variances in Color's 4-variance analysis are not necessarily independent of each other. For example, Color Plus may purchase lower-quality machine fluids (leading to a favorable variable overhead spending variance), which results in the machines taking longer to operate than budgeted (causing an unfavorable variable overhead efficiency variance), and producing less than budgeted output (causing an unfavorable production-volume variance).

Combined Variance Analysis

Detailed 4-variance analyses are most common in large, complex businesses. That's because it is impossible for managers at a company such as General Electric to keep track of all that is happening within their areas of responsibility. The detailed analyses help managers identify and focus attention on the areas not operating as expected. Managers of small businesses understand their operations better based on personal observations and nonfinancial measures. They find less value in doing the additional measurements required for 4-variance analyses. For example, to simplify their costing systems, small companies may not distinguish variable overhead incurred from fixed overhead incurred because making this distinction is often not clear-cut. As we saw in Chapter 2 and will see in Chapter 10, many costs such as supervision, quality control, and materials handling have both variable- and fixed-cost components that may not be easy to separate. Managers may therefore use a less detailed analysis that *combines* the variable overhead and fixed overhead into a single total overhead.

When a single total overhead cost category is used, it can still be analyzed at varying levels of detail. For each level of detail, the variances are the sums of the variable overhead and fixed overhead variances for that level, as computed in Exhibit 8-4. At its most detailed level of analysis, the combined variance analysis looks as follows.

Combined 3-Variance Analysis

	Spending Variance	Efficiency Variance	Production-Volume Variance
Total overhead	Rs 45,000 U	Rs 1,50,000 U	Rs 4,60,000 U

The accounting for 3-variance analysis is simpler than for 4-variance analysis, but some information is lost. In particular, the 3-variance analysis combines the variable and fixed overhead spending variances into a single total overhead spending variance.

A 2-variance analysis aggregates the spending and efficiency variances from the 3-variance analysis.

Combined 2-Variance Analysis

	Flexible-Budget Variance	Production-Volume Variance
Total overhead	Rs 1,95,000 U	Rs 4,60,000 U

The accounting for 3-variance analysis is simpler than for 4-variance analysis, but some information is lost. In particular, the 3-variance analysis combines the variable and fixed overhead spending variances into a single total overhead spending variance.

Decision Point

What is the most detailed way for a company to reconcile actual overhead incurred with the amount allocated during a period?

Finally, the overall **total-overhead variance** is given by the sum of the preceding variances. In the Color Plus example, this equals Rs 6,55,000 U. Note that this amount, which aggregates the flexible-budget and production-volume variances, equals the total amount of underallocated (or underapplied) overhead costs. Using figures from Exhibit 8-4, the Rs 6,55,000 U total-overhead variance is the difference between (a) the total actual overhead incurred (Rs 13,05,000 + Rs 28,50,000 = Rs 41,55,000) and (b) the overhead allocated (Rs 12,00,000 + Rs 23,00,000 = Rs 35,00,000) to the actual output produced. If the total-overhead variance were favorable, it would have corresponded instead to the amount of overapplied overhead costs.

Production-Volume Variance and Sales-Volume Variance

Learning Objective 6

Explain the relationship between the sales-volume variance and the production-volume variance

. . . the production-volume and operating-income volume variances together comprise the sales-volume variance

As we complete our study of variance analysis for Color Plus Company, it is helpful to step back to see the "big picture" and to link the accounting and performance evaluation functions of standard costing. Exhibit 7-2 subdivided the static-budget variance of Rs 9,31,000 U into a flexible-budget variance of Rs 2,91,000 U and a sales-volume variance of Rs 6,40,000 U. In both Chapter 7 and this chapter, we presented more detailed variances that subdivided, whenever possible, individual flexible-budget variances for selling price, direct materials, direct manufacturing labor, variable overhead, and fixed overhead. Here is a summary:

Selling price	Rs 5,00,000 F
Direct materials (Price, Rs 4,44,000 F + Efficiency, Rs 6,60,000 U)	Rs 2,16,000 U
Direct labor (Price, Rs 1,80,000 U + Efficiency, Rs 200,000 U)	Rs 3,80,000 U
Variable overhead (Spending, Rs 45,000 F + Efficiency, Rs 1,50,000 U)	Rs 1,05,000 U
Fixed overhead (Spending, Rs 90,000 U)	Rs 90,000 U
Total flexible budget variance	Rs 2,91,000 U

We also calculated one other variance in this chapter, the production-volume variance, which is not part of the flexible-budget variance. The natural question that arises is: where does the production-volume variance fit into the "big picture?" As we shall see, the production-volume variance is a component of the sales-volume variance.

Under our assumption of actual production and sales of 10,000 jackets, Color's costing system debits to Work-in-Process Control the standard costs of the 10,000 jackets produced, which are then transferred to Finished Goods and finally to Cost of Goods Sold:

Direct materials (Chapter 7, Entry 1b)	
(Rs 600 per jacket × 10,000 jackets)	Rs 60,00,000
Direct manufacturing labor (Chapter 7, Entry 2)	
(Rs 160 per jacket × 10,000 jackets)	16,00,000
Variable overhead (Chapter 8, Entry 2)	
(Rs 120 per jacket × 10,000 jackets)	12,00,000
Fixed overhead (Chapter 8, Entry 2)	
(Rs 230 per jacket × 10,000 jackets)	23,00,000
Cost of goods sold at standard cost	
(Rs 1,110 per jacket × 10,000 jackets)	Rs 1,11,00,000

Color's costing system also records the revenues from the 10,000 jackets sold at the budgeted selling price of Rs 1,200 per jacket. The net effect of these entries on Color's budgeted operating income is as follows:

Revenues at budgeted selling price	
(Rs 1,200 per jacket × 10,000 jackets)	Rs 1,20,00,000
Cost of goods sold at standard cost	
(Rs 1,110 per jacket × 10,000 jackets)	1,11,00,000
Operating income based on budgeted profit per jacket	
(Rs 90 per jacket × 10,000 jackets)	Rs 9,00,000

A crucial point to keep in mind is that in standard costing, fixed overhead cost is treated as if it is a variable cost. That is, in determining the budgeted operating income of Rs 9,00,000 only Rs 23,00,000 (Rs 230 per jacket × 10,000 jackets) of fixed overhead is considered, whereas the budgeted fixed overhead costs are Rs 27,60,000. Color's accountants then record the Rs 4,60,000 unfavorable production-volume variance (the difference between budgeted fixed overhead costs, Rs 27,60,000, and allocated fixed overhead costs, Rs 23,00,000, Entry 2), as well as the various flexible-budget variances (including the fixed overhead spending variance) that total Rs 2,91,000 unfavorable (see Exhibit 7-2). This results in actual operating income of Rs 1,49,000 as follows:

Operating income based on budgeted profit per jacket (Rs 90 per jacket × 10,000 jackets)	Rs 9,00,000
Unfavorable production-volume variance	(4,60,000)
Flexible-budget operating income (Exhibit 7-2)	4,40,000
Unfavorable flexible-budget variance for operating income (Exhibit 7-2)	(2,91,000)
Actual operating income (Exhibit 7-2)	Rs 1,49,000

In contrast, the static-budget operating income of Rs 10,80,000 is not entered in Color's costing system. The reason is that standard costing records budgeted revenues, standard costs, and variances only for the 10,000 jackets actually produced and sold, not for the 12,000 jackets that were *planned* to be produced and sold. It follows that the sales-volume variance of Rs 6,40,000 U, which is the difference between static-budget operating income, Rs 10,80,000, and flexible-budget operating income, Rs 4,40,000 (Exhibit 7-2), is never actually recorded in standard costing. Nevertheless, the sales-volume variance is useful because it helps managers understand the lost contribution margin from selling 2,000 fewer jackets (the sales-volume variance assumes fixed costs remain at the budgeted level of Rs 27,60,000).

The sales-volume variance has two components. They are as follows:

1. A difference between the static-budget operating income of Rs 10,80,000 for 12,000 jackets and budgeted income of Rs 9,00,000 for 10,000 jackets. This is the **operating-income volume variance** of Rs 1,80,000 U (Rs 10,80,000 – Rs 9,00,000), and reflects the fact that Color Plus produced and sold 2,000 fewer units than budgeted.
2. A difference between the budgeted operating income of Rs 9,00,000 and the flexible budget operating income of Rs 4,40,000 (Exhibit 7-2) for the 10,000 actual units. This difference arises because Color Plus's costing system treats fixed costs as if they behave in a variable manner and so assumes fixed costs equal the allocated amount of Rs 23,00,000, rather than the budgeted fixed costs of Rs 27,60,000. Of course, the difference between the allocated and budgeted fixed costs is precisely the production-volume variance of Rs 4,60,000 U.

In summary, we have the following:

	Operating-income volume variance	Rs 1,80,000 U
(+)	Production-volume variance	4,60,000 U
Equals	Sales-volume variance	Rs 6,40,000 U

That is, the sales-volume variance is comprised of production volume and operating-income volume variances.

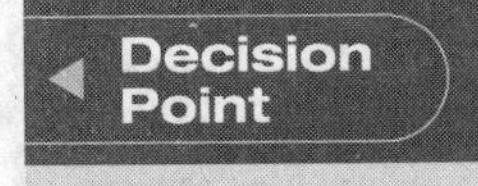

What is the relationship between the sales-volume variance and the production-volume variance?

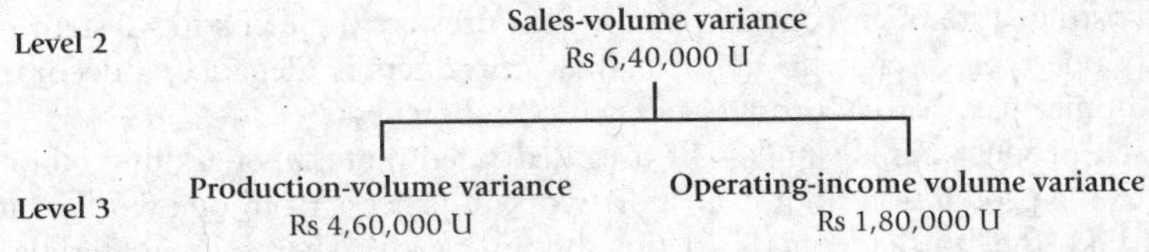

Variance Analysis and Activity-Based Costing

Learning Objective 7

Calculate overhead variance in activity-based costing

. . . compare budgeted and actual overhead costs of activities

ABC systems classify costs of various activities into a cost hierarchy: output unit-level, batch-level, product-sustaining, and facility-sustaining. The basic principles and concepts for variable overhead costs and fixed overhead costs presented earlier in the chapter can be applied to ABC systems. In this section, we illustrate variance analysis for variable batch-level setup overhead costs and fixed batch-level setup overhead costs. Batch-level costs are costs of activities that are related to a group of units of products or services rather than to each individual unit.

We continue the Chapter 7 example of Nanak Brass Works, which manufactures Elegance, a line of decorative brass faucets for home spas. Nanak produces Elegance in batches. To manufacture a batch of Elegance, Nanak must set up the machines and molds. Setting up the machines and molds requires highly trained skills. Hence, a separate Setup Department is responsible for setting up machines and molds for different batches of products. Setup costs are overhead costs of products.

Setup costs consist of some costs that are variable and some that are fixed with respect to the number of setup-hours. Variable setup costs consist of wages paid to direct setup labor and indirect support labor, costs of maintenance of setup equipment, and costs of indirect materials and energy used during setups. Fixed setup costs consist of salaries paid to engineers and supervisors and costs of leasing setup equipment.

Information regarding Elegance for 2012 follows:

	Static-Budget Amount	Actual Amount
1. Units of Elegance produced and sold	180,000	151,200
2. Batch size (units per batch)	150	140
3. Number of batches (Line 1 ÷ Line 2)	1,200	1,080
4. Setup-hours per batch	6	6.25
5. Total setup-hours (Line 3 × Line 4)	7,200	6,750
6. Variable overhead cost per setup-hour	Rs 200	Rs 210
7. Variable setup overhead costs (Line 5 × Line 6)	Rs 14,40,000	Rs 14,17,500
8. Total fixed setup overhead costs	Rs 21,60,000	Rs 22,00,000

Flexible Budget and Variance Analysis for Variable Setup Overhead Costs

To prepare the flexible budget for variable setup overhead costs, Nanak starts with the actual units of output produced, 151,200 units, and proceeds using the following steps.

Activity-based costing (ABC) systems focus on individual activities as the fundamental cost objects. ABC systems classify the costs of various activities into a cost hierarchy—output unit-level costs, batch-level costs, product-sustaining costs, and facility-sustaining costs. In this section, we show how a company that has an ABC system and batch-level costs can benefit from variance analysis. Batch-level costs are the costs of activities related to a group of units of products or services rather than to each individual unit of product or service. We illustrate variance analysis for variable batch-level direct costs and fixed batch-level setup overhead costs.[4]

Consider Nanak Brass Works, which manufactures many different types of faucets and brass fittings. Because of the wide range of products it produces, Nanak uses an activity-based costing system. In contrast, Color Plus uses a simple costing system because it makes only one type of jacket. One of Nanak's products is Elegance, a decorative brass faucet for home spas. Nanak produces Elegance in batches.

For each product Nanak makes, it uses dedicated materials-handling labor to bring materials to the production floor, transport work in process from one work center to the next, and take the finished goods to the shipping area. Therefore, materials-handling

[4] The techniques we demonstrate can be applied to analyze variable batch-level overhead costs as well.

labor costs for Elegance are direct costs of Elegance. Because the materials for a batch are moved together, materials-handling labor costs vary with number of batches rather than with number of units in a batch. Materials-handling labor costs are variable direct batch-level costs.

To manufacture a batch of Elegance, Nanak must set up the machines and molds. Setting up the machines and molds requires highly trained skills. Hence, a separate setup department is responsible for setting up machines and molds for different batches of products. Setup costs are overhead costs of products. For simplicity, assume that setup costs are fixed with respect to the number of setup-hours. They consist of salaries paid to engineers and supervisors and costs of leasing setup equipment.

To prepare the flexible budget for materials-handling labor costs, Nanak starts with the actual units of output produced, 151,200 units, and proceeds with the following steps.

Step 1: Using Budgeted Batch Size, Calculate the Number of Batches that Should Have Been Used to Produce Actual Output. At the budgeted batch size of 150 units per batch, Nanak should have produced 151,200 units of output in 1,008 batches (151,200 units ÷ 150 units per batch).

Step 2: Using Budgeted Materials-Handling Labor-Hours per Batch, Calculate the Number of Materials-Handling Labor-Hours that Should Have Been Used. At the budgeted quantity of 5 hours per batch, 1,008 batches should have required 5,040 materials-handling labor-hours (1,008 batches × 5 hours per batch).

Step 3: Using Budgeted Cost per Materials-Handling Labor-Hour, Calculate the Flexible-Budget Amount for Materials-Handling Labor-Hours. The flexible-budget amount is 5,040 materials-handling labor-hours × Rs 140 budgeted cost per materials-handling labor-hour = Rs 7,05,600.

Note how the flexible-budget calculations for materials-handling labor costs focus on batch-level quantities (materials-handling labor-hours per batch rather than per unit). Flexible-budget quantity computations focus at the appropriate level of the cost hierarchy. For example, because materials handling is a batch-level cost, the flexible-budget quantity calculations are made at the batch level—the quantity of materials-handling labor-hours that Nanak should have used based on the number of batches it should have used to produce the actual quantity of 151,200 units. If a cost had been a product-sustaining cost—such as product design cost—the flexible-budget quantity computations would focus at the product-sustaining level, for example, by evaluating the actual complexity of product design relative to the budget.

The flexible-budget variance for materials-handling labor costs can now be calculated as follows:

$$
\begin{aligned}
\text{Flexible-budget variance} &= \text{Actual costs} - \text{Flexible-budget costs} \\
&= (5{,}670 \text{ hours} \times \text{Rs } 145.0 \text{ per hour}) - (5{,}040 \text{ hours} \times \text{Rs } 140 \text{ per hour}) \\
&= \text{Rs } 8{,}22{,}150 - \text{Rs } 7{,}05{,}600 \\
&= \text{Rs } 1{,}16{,}550 \text{ U}
\end{aligned}
$$

The unfavorable variance indicates that materials-handling labor costs were Rs 1,16,550 higher than the flexible-budget target. We can get some insight into the possible reasons for this unfavorable outcome by examining the price and efficiency components of the flexible-budget variance. Exhibit 8-5 presents the variances in columnar form.

$$
\begin{aligned}
\text{Price variance} &= \left(\text{Actual price of input} - \text{Budgeted price of input}\right) \times \text{Actual quantity of input} \\
&= (\text{Rs } 145.0 \text{ per hour} - \text{Rs } 140 \text{ per hour}) \times 5{,}670 \text{ hours} \\
&= \text{Rs } 5.0 \text{ per hour} \times 5{,}670 \text{ hours} \\
&= \text{Rs } 28{,}350 \text{ U}
\end{aligned}
$$

Exhibit 8-5

Columnar Presentation of Variance Analysis for Direct Materials-Handling Labor Costs: Nanak Brass Works for 2012[a]

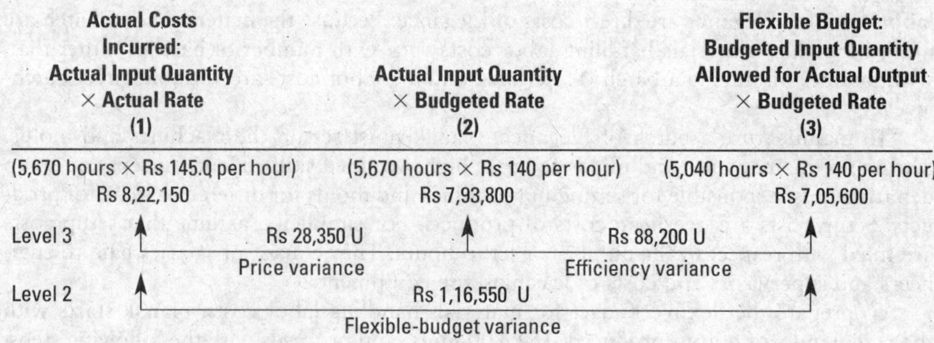

[a]F = favorable effect on operating income; U = unfavorable effect on operating income.

The unfavorable price variance for materials-handling labor indicates that the Rs 145.0 actual cost per materials-handling labor-hour exceeds the Rs 140.0 budgeted cost per materials-handling labor-hour. This variance could be the result of Nanak's human resources manager negotiating wage rates less skillfully or of wage rates increasing unexpectedly due to scarcity of labor.

$$\text{Efficiency variance} = \left(\begin{array}{c}\text{Actual}\\ \text{quantity of}\\ \text{input used}\end{array} - \begin{array}{c}\text{Budgeted quantity}\\ \text{of input allowed}\\ \text{for actual output}\end{array}\right) \times \begin{array}{c}\text{Budgeted price}\\ \text{of input}\end{array}$$

$$= (5{,}670 \text{ hours} - 5{,}040 \text{ hours}) \times \text{Rs } 140 \text{ per hour}$$

$$= 630 \text{ hours} \times \text{Rs } 140 \text{ per hour}$$

$$= \text{Rs } 88{,}200 \text{ U}$$

The unfavorable efficiency variance indicates that the 5,670 actual materials-handling labor-hours exceeded the 5,040 budgeted materials-handling labor-hours for actual output. Possible reasons for the unfavorable efficiency variance are as follows:

- Smaller actual batch sizes of 140 units, instead of the budgeted batch sizes of 150 units, resulting in Nanak producing the 151,200 units in 1,080 batches instead of 1,008 (151,200 ÷ 150) batches
- Higher actual materials-handling labor-hours per batch of 5.25 hours instead of budgeted materials-handling labor-hours of 5 hours

Reasons for smaller-than-budgeted batch sizes could include quality problems when batch sizes exceed 140 faucets and high costs of carrying inventory.

Possible reasons for larger actual materials-handling labor-hours per batch are as follows:

- Inefficient layout of the Elegance production line
- Materials-handling labor having to wait at work centers before picking up or delivering materials
- Unmotivated, inexperienced, and underskilled employees
- Very tight standards for materials-handling time

Identifying the reasons for the efficiency variance helps Nanak's managers develop a plan for improving materials-handling labor efficiency and to take corrective action that will be incorporated into future budgets.

We now consider fixed setup overhead costs.

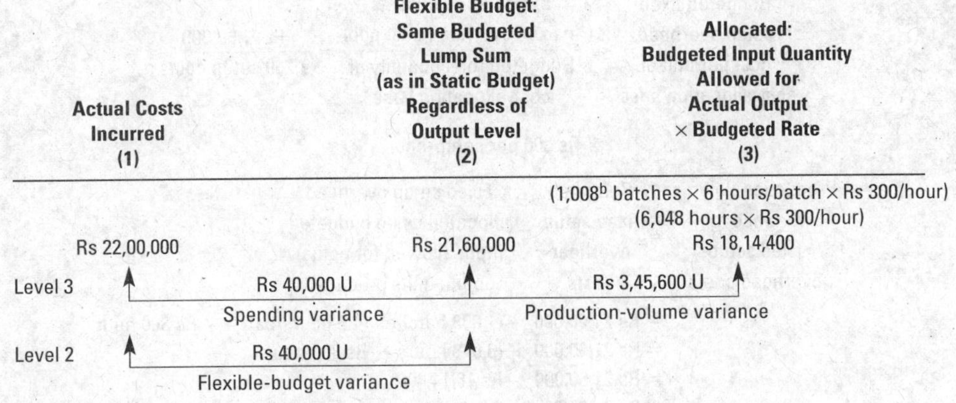

[a]F = favorable effect on operating income; U = unfavorable effect on operating income.

[b]1,008 batches = 151,200 units ÷ 150 units per batch.

Exhibit 8-6

Columnar Presentation of Fixed Setup Overhead Variance Analysis: Nanak Brass Works for 2012[a]

Flexible Budget and Variance Analysis for Fixed Setup Overhead Costs

Exhibit 8-6 presents the variances for fixed setup overhead costs in columnar form.

Nanak's fixed setup overhead flexible-budget variance is calculated as follows:

$$\begin{aligned}\text{Fixed-setup overhead flexible-budget variance} &= \text{Actual costs incurred} - \text{Flexible-budget costs}\\ &= \text{Rs } 22{,}00{,}000 - \text{Rs } 21{,}60{,}000\\ &= \text{Rs } 40{,}000\end{aligned}$$

Note that the flexible-budget amount for fixed setup overhead costs equals the static-budget amount of Rs 21,60,000. That's because there is no "flexing" of fixed costs. Moreover, because fixed overhead costs have no efficiency variance, the fixed setup overhead spending variance is the same as the fixed overhead flexible-budget variance. The spending variance could be unfavorable because of higher leasing costs of new setup equipment or higher salaries paid to engineers and supervisors. Nanak may have incurred these costs to alleviate some of the difficulties it was having in setting up machines.

To calculate the production-volume variance, Nanak first computes the budgeted cost-allocation rate for fixed setup overhead costs using the same four-step approach described under 'Developing Budgeted Variable Overhead cost Rates' earlier in this chapter.

Step 1: Choose the Period to Use for the Budget. Nanak uses a period of 12 months (the year 2012).

Step 2: Select the Cost-Allocation Base to Use in Allocating Fixed Overhead Costs to Output Produced. Nanak uses budgeted setup-hours as the cost-allocation base for fixed setup overhead costs. Budgeted setup-hours in the static budget for 2012 are 7,200 hours.

Step 3: Identify the Fixed Overhead Costs Associated with the Cost-Allocation Base. Nanak's fixed setup overhead cost budget for 2012 is Rs 21,60,000.

Step 4: Compute the Rate per Unit of the Cost-Allocation Base Used to Allocate Fixed Overhead Costs to Output Produced. Dividing the Rs 21,60,000 from step 3 by the 7,200 setup-hours from step 2, Nanak estimates a fixed setup overhead cost rate of Rs 300 per setup-hour:

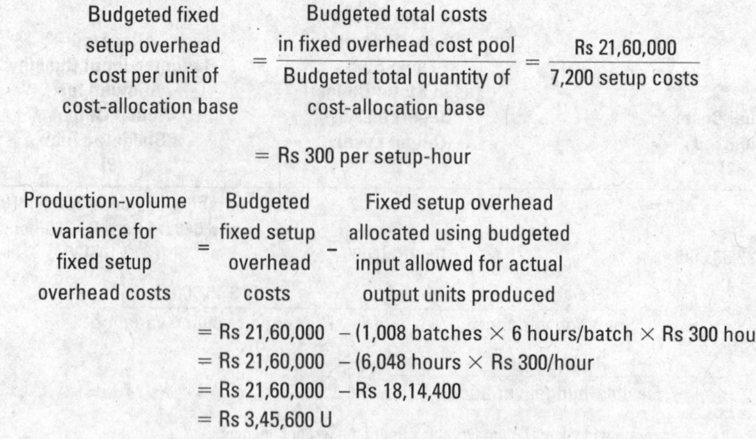

$$\text{Budgeted fixed setup overhead cost per unit of cost-allocation base} = \frac{\text{Budgeted total costs in fixed overhead cost pool}}{\text{Budgeted total quantity of cost-allocation base}} = \frac{\text{Rs } 21{,}60{,}000}{7{,}200 \text{ setup costs}}$$

$$= \text{Rs } 300 \text{ per setup-hour}$$

$$\text{Production-volume variance for fixed setup overhead costs} = \text{Budgeted fixed setup overhead costs} - \text{Fixed setup overhead allocated using budgeted input allowed for actual output units produced}$$

$$= \text{Rs } 21{,}60{,}000 - (1{,}008 \text{ batches} \times 6 \text{ hours/batch} \times \text{Rs } 300 \text{ hour}$$
$$= \text{Rs } 21{,}60{,}000 - (6{,}048 \text{ hours} \times \text{Rs } 300/\text{hour}$$
$$= \text{Rs } 21{,}60{,}000 - \text{Rs } 18{,}14{,}400$$
$$= \text{Rs } 3{,}45{,}600 \text{ U}$$

Decision Point

How can variance analysis be used in an activity-based costing system?

During 2012, Nanak planned to produce 180,000 units of Elegance but actually produced 1,51,200 units. The unfavorable production-volume variance measures the amount of extra fixed setup costs that Nanak incurred for setup capacity it had but did not use. One interpretation is that the unfavorable Rs 3,45,600 production-volume variance represents inefficient use of setup capacity. However, Nanak may have earned higher operating income by selling 1,51,200 units at a higher price than 1,80,000 units at a lower price. As a result, Nanak's managers should interpret the production-volume variance cautiously because it does not consider effects on selling prices and operating income.

Overhead Variances in Nonmanufacturing Settings

Learning Objective 8

Examine the use of overhead variances in nonmanufacturing settings

. . . analyze nonmanufacturing variable overhead costs for decision making and cost management; fixed overhead variances are especially important in service settings

Our Color Plus Company example examines variable manufacturing overhead costs and fixed manufacturing overhead costs. Should the overhead costs of the nonmanufacturing areas of the company be examined using the variance analysis framework discussed in this chapter? Companies often use variable-cost information pertaining to nonmanufacturing, as well as manufacturing, costs in pricing and product mix decisions. Managers consider variance analysis of all variable overhead costs when making such decisions and when managing costs. For example, managers in industries in which distribution costs are high, such as automobiles, consumer durables, and cement and steel, may use standard costing to give reliable and timely information on variable distribution overhead spending variances and efficiency variances.

Consider service-sector companies such as airlines, hospitals, hotels, and railroads. The measures of output commonly used in these companies are passenger-miles flown, patient days provided, room-days occupied, and ton-miles of freight hauled, respectively. Few costs can be traced to these outputs in a cost-effective way. The majority of costs are fixed overhead costs, such as the costs of equipment, buildings, and staff. Using capacity effectively is the key to profitability, and fixed overhead variances can help managers in this task. Retail businesses, such as Kmart, also have high capacity-related fixed costs (lease and occupancy costs). In the case of Kmart, sales declines resulted in unused capacity and unfavorable fixed-cost variances. Kmart reduced fixed costs by closing some of its stores, but it also had to file for Chapter 11 bankruptcy in January 2002.

Consider the following data for the mainline operations of United Airlines for selected years from the past decade. Available seat miles (ASMs) are the actual seats in an airplane multiplied by the distance traveled.

Year	Total ASMs (Millions) (1)	Operating Revenue per ASM (2)	Operating Cost per ASM (3)	Operating Income per ASM (4) = (2) − (3)
2000	175,485	Rs 11.0	Rs 10.6	Rs 0.4
2003	136,630	Rs 9.6	Rs 10.5	Rs −0.9
2006	143,095	Rs 11.5	Rs 11.2	Rs 0.3
2008	135,861	Rs 12.6	Rs 15.7	Rs −3.1

After September 11, 2001, as air travel declined, United's revenues decreased but a majority of its costs comprising fixed costs of airport facilities, equipment, and personnel did not. United had a large unfavorable production-volume variance as its capacity was underutilized. As column 1 of the table indicates, United responded by reducing its capacity substantially over the next few years. Available seat miles declined from 175,485 million in 2000 to 136,630 million in 2003. Yet, United was unable to fill even the planes it had retained, so revenue per ASM declined (column 2) and cost per ASM stayed roughly the same (column 3). United filed for Chapter 11 bankruptcy in December 2002 and began seeking government guarantees to obtain the loans it needed. Subsequently, strong demand for airline travel, as well as yield improvements gained by more efficient use of resources and networks, led to increased traffic and higher average ticket prices. By maintaining a disciplined approach to capacity and tight control over growth, United saw close to a 20% increase in its revenue per ASM between 2003 and 2006. The improvement in performance allowed United to come out of bankruptcy on February 1, 2006. In the past year, however, the severe global recession and soaring jet fuel prices have had a significant negative impact on United's performance (and that of its competitor airlines), as reflected in the negative operating income for 2008.

Financial and Nonfinancial Performance Measures

The overhead variances discussed in this chapter are examples of financial performance measures. As the preceding examples illustrate, nonfinancial measures such as those related to capacity utilization and physical measures of input usage also provide useful information. Returning to the Color Plus example one final time, we can see that nonfinancial measures that managers of Color Plus would likely find helpful in planning and controlling its overhead costs include the following:

1. Quantity of actual indirect materials used per machine-hour, relative to quantity of budgeted indirect materials used per machine-hour
2. Actual energy used per machine-hour, relative to budgeted energy used per machine-hour
3. Actual machine-hours per jacket, relative to budgeted machine-hours per jacket

These performance measures, like the financial variances discussed in this chapter and Chapter 7, can be described as signals to direct managers' attention to problems. These nonfinancial performance measures probably would be reported daily or hourly on the production floor. The overhead variances we discussed in this chapter capture the financial effects of items such as the three factors listed, hich in many cases first appear as nonfinancial performance measures. An especially interesting example along these lines comes from Japan, where some companies have introduced budgeted-to-actual variance analysis and internal trading systems among group units as a means to rein in their CO_2 emissions. The goal is to raise employee awareness of emissions reduction in preparation for the anticipated future costs of greenhouse-gas reduction plans being drawn up by the new Japanese government.

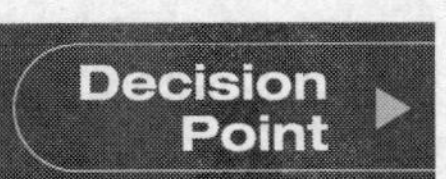

How are overhead variances useful in nonmanufacturing settings?

Finally, both financial and nonfinancial performance measures are used to evaluate the performance of managers. Exclusive reliance on either is always too simplistic because each gives a different perspective on performance. Nonfinancial measures (such as those described previously) provide feedback on individual aspects of a manager's performance, whereas financial measures evaluate the overall effect of and the tradeoffs among different nonfinancial performance measures. We provide further discussion of these issues in Chapters 13, 19, and 23.

Problem for Self-Study

Nina Ganotra is the newly appointed president of Laser Products. She is examining the May 2011 results for the Aerospace Products Division. This division manufactures wing parts for satellites. Nina's current concern is with manufacturing overhead costs at the Aerospace Products Division. Both variable and fixed overhead costs are allocated to the wing parts on the basis of laser-cutting-hours. The following budget information is available:

Budgeted variable overhead rate	Rs 2,000 per hour
Budgeted fixed overhead rate	Rs 2,400 per hour
Budgeted laser-cutting time per wing part	1.5 hours
Budgeted production and sales for May 2009	5,000 wing parts
Budgeted fixed overhead costs for May 2009	Rs 1,80,00,000

Actual results for May 2011 are:

Wing parts produced and sold	4,800 units
Laser-cutting-hours used	8,400 hours
Variable overhead costs	Rs 1,47,84,000
Fixed overhead costs	Rs 1,83,22,000

Required

1. Compute the spending variance and the efficiency variance for variable overhead.
2. Compute the spending variance and the production-volume variance for fixed overhead.
3. Give two explanations for each of the variances calculated in requirements 1 and 2.

Solution

1. and 2. See Exhibit 8-7.

3. *a.* Variable overhead spending variance, Rs 20,16,000 F. One possible reason for this variance is that the actual prices of individual items included in variable overhead (such as cutting fluids) are lower than budgeted prices. A second possible reason is that the percentage increase in the actual quantity usage of individual items in the variable overhead cost pool is less than the percentage increase in laser-cutting-hours compared to the flexible budget.

   b. Variable overhead efficiency variance, Rs 24,00,000 U. One possible reason for this variance is inadequate maintenance of laser machines, causing them to take more laser-cutting time per wing part. A second possible reason is use of undermotivated, inexperienced, or underskilled workers with the laser-cutting machines, resulting in more laser-cutting time per wing part.

   c. Fixed overhead spending variance,Rs 3,22,000 U. One possible reason for this variance is that the actual prices of individual items in the fixed-cost pool unexpectedly increased from the prices budgeted (such as an unexpected increase in machine leasing costs). A second possible reason is misclassification of items as fixed that are in fact variable.

d. Production-volume variance, Rs 7,20,000 U. Actual production of wing parts is 4,800 units, compared with 5,000 units budgeted. One possible reason for this variance is demand factors, such as a decline in an aerospace program that led to a decline in demand for aircraft parts. A second possible reason is supply factors, such as a production stoppage due to labor problems or machine breakdowns.

Exhibit 8-7 Columnar Presentation of Integrated Variance Analysis: Laser Products for May 2011[a]

PANEL A: Variable (Manufacturing) Overhead

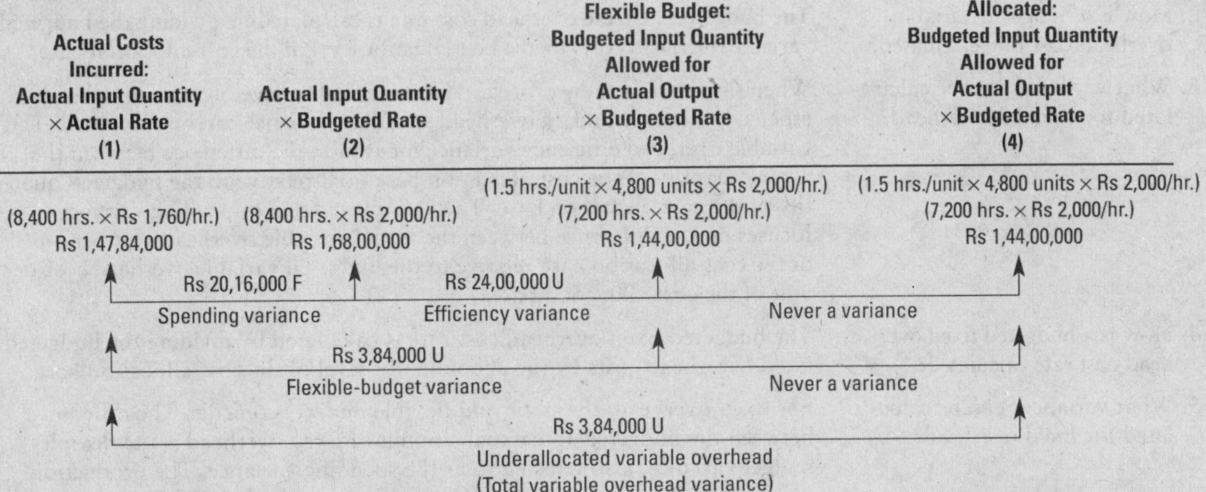

PANEL B: Fixed (Manufacturing) Overhead

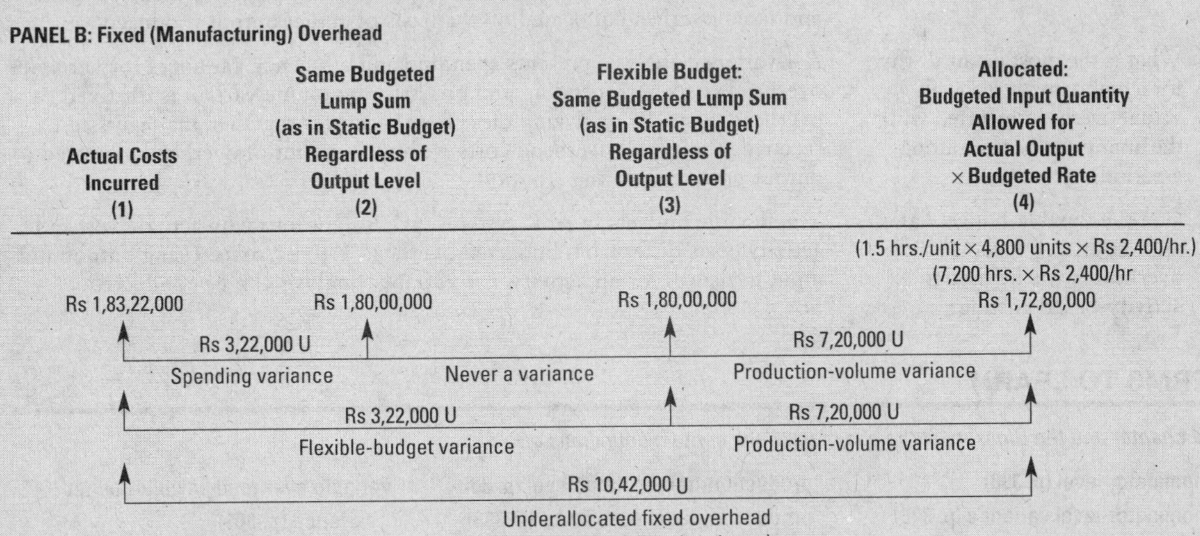

[a]F = favorable effect on operating income; U = unfavorable effect on operating income.

Source: From "The Case for Management Accounting" by Paul Sherman. Used with permission from STRATEGIC FINANCE, October 2003, published by the Institute of Management Accountants, Montvale, NJ, www.imanet.org.

Decision Points

The following question-and-answer format summarizes the chapter's learning objectives. Each decision presents a key question related to a learning objective. The guidelines are the answer to that question.

Decision	Guidelines
1. How do managers plan variable overhead costs and fixed overhead costs?	Planning of both variable and fixed overhead costs involves undertaking only activities that add value and then being efficient in that undertaking. The key difference is that for variable-cost planning, ongoing decisions during the budget period play a much larger role; whereas for fixed-cost planning, most key decisions are made before the start of the period.
2. How is a budgeted variable overhead cost rate calculated?	The budgeted variable overhead cost rate is calculated by dividing the budgeted variable overhead costs by the denominator level of the cost-allocation base.
3. What variances can be calculated for variable overhead?	When the flexible budget for variable overhead is developed, an overhead efficiency variance and an overhead spending variance can be computed. The variable overhead efficiency variance focuses on the difference between the actual quantity of the cost-allocation base used relative to the budgeted quantity of the cost-allocation base. The variable overhead spending variance focuses on the difference between the actual variable overhead cost per unit of the cost-allocation base relative to the budgeted variable overhead cost per unit of the cost-allocation base.
4. How is a budgeted fixed overhead cost rate calculated?	The budgeted fixed overhead cost rate is calculated by dividing the budgeted fixed ovzerhead costs by the denominator level of the cost-allocation base.
5. What variances can be calculated for fixed overhead?	For fixed overhead, the static and flexible budgets coincide. The difference between the budgeted and actual amount of fixed overhead is the flexible-budget variance, also referred to as the spending variance. The production-volume variance measures the difference between budgeted fixed overhead and fixed overhead allocated on the basis of actual output produced.
6. What is the most detailed way for a company to reconcile actual overhead incurred with the amount allocated during a period?	A 4-variance analysis presents spending and efficiency variances for variable overhead costs and spending and production-volume variances for fixed overhead costs. By analyzing these four variances together, managers can reconcile the actual overhead costs with the amount of overhead allocated to output produced during a period.
7. Can the flexible-budget variance approach for analyzing overhead costs be used in activity-based costing?	Yes, flexible budgets in ABC systems give insight into why actual overhead activity costs differ from budgeted overhead activity costs. Using output and input measures for an activity, a 4-variance analysis can be conducted.

TERMS TO LEARN

The chapter and the Glossary at the end of the book contain definitions of:

denominator level (**p. 300**)
denominator-level variance (**p. 306**)
fixed overhead flexible-budget variance (**p. 305**)
fixed overhead spending variance (**p. 306**)
production-denominator level (**p. 300**)
production-volume variance (**p. 306**)
standard costing (**p. 298**)
total-overhead variance (**p. 314**)
variable overhead efficiency variance (**p. 302**)
variable overhead flexible-budget variance (**p. 301**)
variable overhead spending variance (**p. 303**)

ASSIGNMENT MATERIAL

Questions

8-1 How do managers plan for variable overhead costs?

8-2 How does the planning of fixed overhead costs differ from the planning of variable overhead costs?

8-3 How does standard costing differ from actual costing?

8-4 What are the steps in developing a budgeted variable overhead cost-allocation rate?

8-5 What are the factors that affect the spending variance for variable manufacturing overhead?

8-6 Assume variable manufacturing overhead is allocated using machine-hours. Give three possible reasons for a favorable variable overhead efficiency variance.

8-7 Describe the difference between a direct materials efficiency variance and a variable manufacturing overhead efficiency variance.

8-8 What are the steps in developing a budgeted fixed overhead rate?

8-9 Why is the flexible-budget variance the same amount as the spending variance for fixed manufacturing overhead?

8-10 Explain how the analysis of fixed manufacturing overhead costs differs for (a) planning and control on the one hand and (b) inventory costing for financial reporting on the other hand.

8-11 Provide one caveat that will affect whether a production-volume variance is a good measure of the economic cost of unused capacity.

8-12 "The production-volume variance should always be written off to Cost of Goods Sold." Do you agree? Explain.

8-13 What are the variances in a 4-variance analysis?

8-14 "Overhead variances should be viewed as interdependent rather than independent." Give an example.

8-15 Describe how flexible-budget variance analysis can be used in the control of costs of activity areas.

Solved Examples

8-16 Variable manufacturing overhead, variance analysis. Standard Clothing is a manufacturer of designer suits. The cost of each suit is the sum of three variable costs (direct materials costs, direct manufacturing labor costs and manufacturing overhead costs) and one fixed-cost category (manufacturing overhead costs). Variable manufacturing overhead cost is allocated to each suit on the basis of budgeted direct manufacturing labor-hours per suit. For the month of June, each suit is budgeted to take four labor-hours. Budgeted variable manufacturing overhead cost per labor-hour is Rs 60. The budgeted number of suits to be manufactured in June is 1,040.

Actual variable manufacturing costs in June was Rs 2,60,820 for 1,080 suits started and completed. There were no beginning or ending inventories of suits. Actual direct manufacturing labor-hours for June were 4,536.

Required

1. Compute the flexible-budget variance, the spending variance, and the efficiency variance for variable manufacturing overhead.
2. Comment on the results.

Solution

Variable manufacturing overhead, variance analysis.

1.

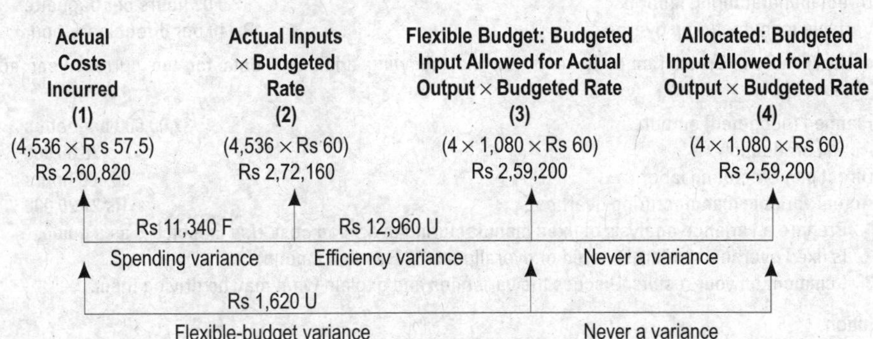

2. Standard had a favorable spending variance of Rs 11,340 because the actual variable overhead rate of Rs 57.50 per direct manufacturing labor-hour was lower than Rs 60 budgeted. It had an unfavorable efficiency variance of Rs 12,960 because each suit averaged 4.2 labor-hours (4,536 hours ÷ 1,080 suits) versus 4.0 budgeted.

8-17 Fixed manufacturing overhead, variance analysis. (continuation of 8-16) Standard Clothing allocates fixed manufacturing overhead to each suit using budgeted direct manufacturing labor-hours per suit. Data pertaining to fixed manufacturing overhead costs for June 2012 are budgeted, Rs 6,24,000 and actual, Rs 6,39,160.

Required

1. Compute the spending variance for fixed manufacturing overhead. Comment on the results.
2. Compute the production-volume variance for June 2012. What inferences can Standard Clothing draw from this variance?

Solution

Fixed-manufacturing overhead, variance analysis.

1 and 2. Budgeted fixed overhead rate per unit of = Rs 6,24,000/(1,040 × 4) = 6,24,000/4,160

= Rs 150 per hour

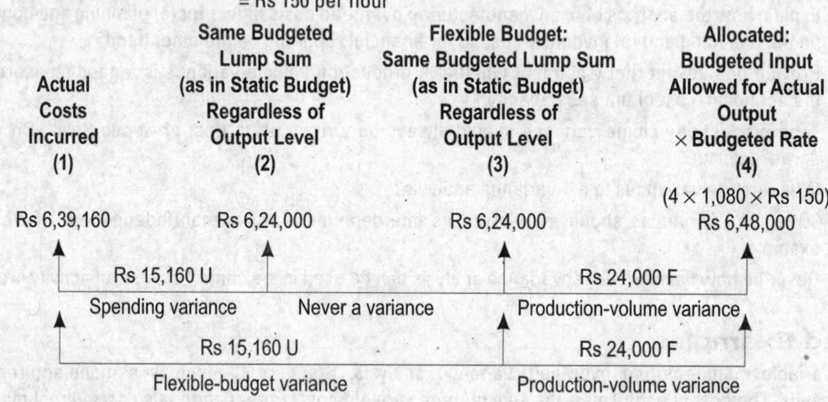

The fixed manufacturing overhead spending variance and the fixed manufacturing flexible budget variance are the same—Rs 15,160 U. Standard Clothing spent Rs 15,160 above Rs 6,24,000 budgeted amount for June.

The production-volume variance is Rs 24,000 F. This arises because Standard Clothing utilized its capacity more intensively than budgeted (the actual production of 1,080 suits exceeds the budgeted 1,040 suits). This results in overallocated fixed manufacturing overhead of Rs 24,000 (4 × 40 × Rs 150). Standard Clothing would want to understand the reasons for a favorable production-volume variance. Is the market growing? Is Standard Clothing gaining market share? Will Standard Clothing need to add capacity?

8-18 Fixed manufacturing overhead variance analysis. The Harvest Gold Bread Company bakes baguettes for distribution to upscale grocery stores. The company has two direct-cost categories, direct materials and direct manufacturing labor. Fixed manufacturing overhead is allocated to products on the basis of standard direct manufacturing labor-hours. Following is some pertinent budgeted data for the Harvest Gold Bread Company:

Direct manufacturing labor use	0.02 hours per baguette
Variable manufacturing overhead	Rs 40 per direct labor-hour

The Harvest Gold Bread Company recorded the following additional data for the current year ended December 31:

Planned (budgeted) output	32,00,000 baguettes
Actual production	28,00,000
Direct manufacturing labor	50,400 hours
Actual variable manufacturing overhead	Rs 27,20,000

Required

1. Prepare a variance analysis of fixed manufacturing overhead cost. Use Exhibit 8-3 as a guide.
2. Is fixed overhead underallocated or overallocated? By what amount?
3. Comment on your results. Discuss the variances and explain what may be driving them.

Solution

Fixed manufacturing overhead variance analysis.

1. Budgeted standard direct manufacturing labor used = 0.02 hours per baguette
Budgeted output = 32,00,000 baguettes
Budgeted standard direct manufacturing labor-hours: = 32,00,000 × 0.02 = 64,000 hours

Budgeted fixed manufacturing overhead costs: = 64,000 × Rs 40 per hour = Rs 25,60,000
Actual output = 28,00,000 baguettes
Allocated fixed manufacturing overhead
= 28,00,000 × 0.02 × Rs 40 = Rs 22,40,000

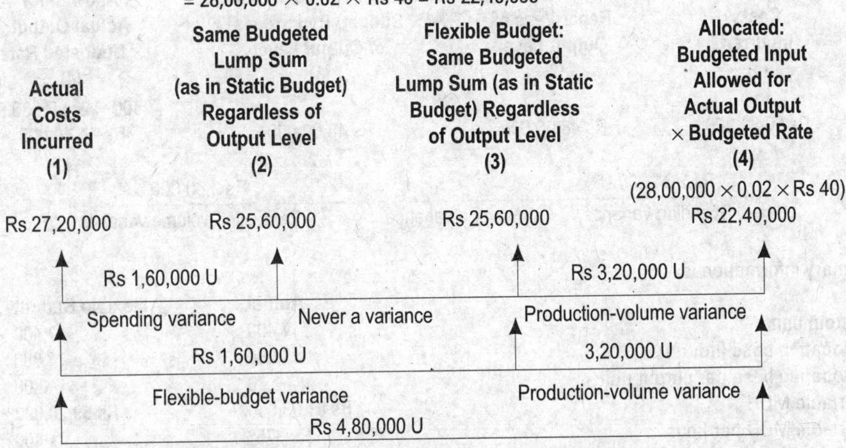

2. The fixed manufacturing overhead is underallocated by Rs 4,80,000.
3. The production-volume variance captures the difference between the budgeted 32,00,0000 baguettes and the actual 28,00,000 baguettes. The spending variance of Rs 1,60,000 unfavorable means that the actual aggregate of fixed costs (Rs 27,20,000) exceeds the budget amount (Rs 25,60,000). For example, monthly leasing rates for baguette-making machines may have increased above those in the budget for current year.

8-19 Manufacturing overhead, variance analysis. BPL Ltd. assembles its CTV product at its Noida plant. Manufacturing overhead (both variable and fixed) is allocated to each CTV unit using budgeted assembly-hours. Budgeted assembly time per CTV product is two hours. The budgeted variable manufacturing overhead cost per assembly-hour is Rs 400. The budgeted number of CTV units to be assembled in March is 8,000. Budgeted fixed manufacturing overhead costs are Rs 48,00,000.

Actual variable manufacturing overhead costs for March were Rs 61,05,000 for 7400 units actually assembled. Actual assembly-hours were 16,280. Actual fixed manufacturing overhead costs were Rs 50,34,200.

Required

1. Prepare a 4-variance analysis for BPL's Noida plant.
2. Comment on the results in requirement 1.

Solution

Manufacturing overhead, variance analysis.

1. The summary analysis is:

	Spending Variance	Efficiency Variance	Production-Volume Variance
Variable manufacturing overhead	Rs 4,07,000 F	Rs 5,92,000 U	Never a variance
Fixed manufacturing overhead	Rs 2,34,200 U	Never a variance	Rs 3,60,000 U

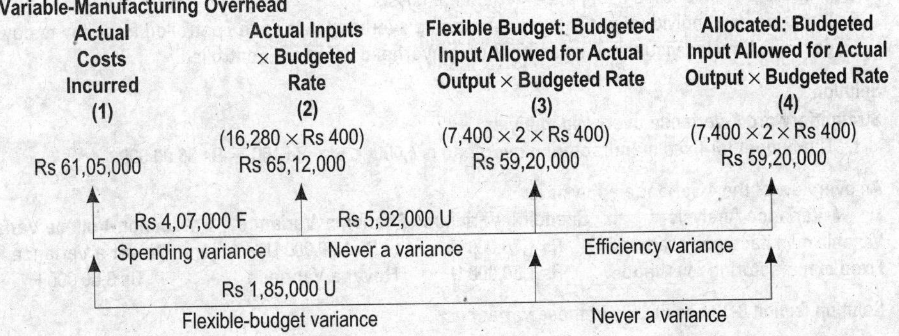

Fixed-Manufacturing Overhead

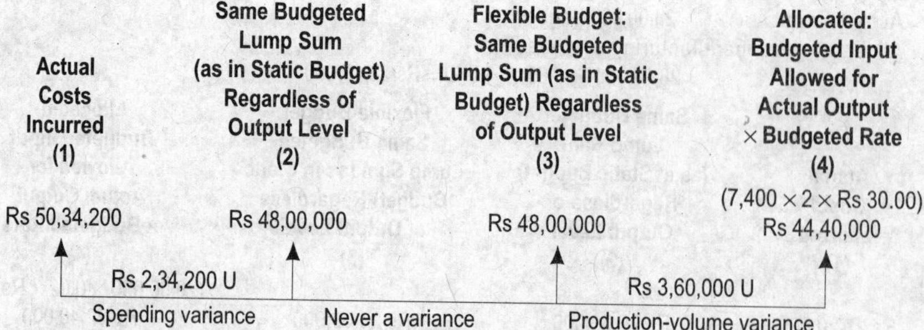

Summary information is:

	Actual	Flexible Budget
Output units	7,400	7,400
Allocation base (hours)	16,280	14,800[a]
Allocation base per output unit	2.20	2.00
Variable MOH	Rs 61,05,000	Rs 59,20,000[b]
Variable MOH per hour	Rs 375[c]	Rs 400
Fixed MOH	Rs 50,34,200	Rs 48,00,000
Fixed MOH per hour	Rs 309.22[d]	—

a7,400 × 2.00 = 14,800 c Rs 61,05,000 ÷ 16,280 hours = Rs 375 per hour

b7,400 × Rs 400 = Rs 59,20,000 d Rs 50,34,200 ÷ 16,280 hours = Rs 309.22 per hour

The budgeted fixed manufacturing overhead rate is Rs 300 for assembly by hour:

$$\frac{\text{Rs } 48{,}00{,}000}{8{,}000 \times 2 \text{ hours}} = \text{Rs } 300 \text{ per assembly-hour}$$

2. BPL Ltd. produced 600 less CTV units than were budgeted. The variable manufacturing overhead cost efficiency variance of Rs 5,92,000 U arises because more assembly-time-hours per output unit (16,280 ÷ 7,400 = 2.2 hours) were used than the budgeted 2.0 hours per unit. The variable manufacturing overhead cost spending variance of Rs 4,07,000 F indicates one or more of the following probably occurred–(i) actual prices of individual items included in variable overhead differ from their budgeted prices, or (ii) actual usage of individual items included in variable overhead differs from their budgeted usage.

   The fixed manufacturing overhead cost spending variance of Rs 2,34,200 U means fixed overhead was above that budgeted. For example, it could be due to an unexpected increase in plant leasing costs. The unfavorable production-volume variance of Rs 3,60,000 arises because actual output of 7,400 units is below the 8,000 units used in determining Rs 300 per assembly-hour budgeted rate.

8-20 Straightforward 4-variance overhead analysis. The Omax Auto Company uses a standard-costing system in its manufacturing plant for auto parts. Its standard cost of an auto part, based on a denominator level of 4,000 output units per year, included 6 machine-hours of variable manufacturing overhead at Rs 80 per hour and 6 machine-hours of fixed manufacturing overhead at Rs 150 per hour. Actual output produced was 4,400 units. Variable manufacturing overhead incurred was Rs 24,50,000. Fixed manufacturing overhead incurred was Rs 37,30,000. Actual machine-hours were 28,400.

Required

1. Prepare an analysis of all variable manufacturing overhead variances, using the 4-variance analysis in Exhibit 8-3.
2. Prepare journal entries using the 4-variance analysis.
3. Describe how individual variable manufacturing overhead items are controlled from day to day. Also, describe how individual fixed manufacturing overhead items are controlled.

Solution

Straightforward 4-variance overhead analysis.

1. The budget for fixed manufacturing overhead is 4,000 × 6 × Rs 150 = Rs 36,00,000.

An overview of the 4-variance analysis is:

4-Variance Analysis	Spending Variance	Efficiency Variance	Production-Volume Variance
Variable manufacturing overhead	Rs 1,78,000 U	Rs 1,60,000 U	Never a Variance
Fixed manufacturing overhead	Rs 1,30,000 U	Never a Variance	Rs 3,60,000 F

Solution Exhibit 8-20 has details of these variances.

A detailed comparison of actual and flexible budgeted amounts is:

	Actual	Flexible Budget
Output units (auto parts)	4,400	4,400
Allocation base (machine-hours)	28,400	26,400[a]
Allocation base per output unit	6.45[b]	6.00
Variable MOH	Rs 24,50,000	Rs 21,12,000[c]
Variable MOH per hour	Rs 86.30[d]	Rs 80
Fixed MOH	Rs 37,30,000	Rs 36,00,000[e]
Fixed MOH per hour	Rs 131.30[f]	–

[a]4,400 units × 6.00 machine-hours/unit = 26,400 machine-hours

[b]28,400 ÷ 4,400 = 6.45 machine-hours per unit

[c]4,400 units × 6.00 machine-hours per unit × Rs 80 per machine-hour = Rs 21,12,000

[d]Rs 24,50,000 ÷ 28,400 = Rs 86.30

[e]4,000 units × 6.00 machine-hours per unit × Rs 150 per machine-hour = Rs 36,00,000

[f]Rs 37,30,000 ÷ 28,400 = Rs 131.30

2.

Variable Manufacturing Overhead Control	Rs 24,50,000	
Accounts payable control and other accounts		Rs 24,50,000
Work-in-process control	21,12,000	
Variable manufacturing overhead allocated		21,12,000
Variable manufacturing overhead allocated	21,12,000	
Variable manufacturing Overhead spending variance	1,78,000	
Variable manufacturing overhead efficiency variance	1,60,000	
Variable manufacturing overhead control		24,50,000
Fixed manufacturing overhead control	37,30,000	
Wages payable control, accumulated depreciation control, etc.		37,30,000
Work-in-process control	39,60,000	
Fixed manufacturing overhead allocated		39,60,000
Fixed manufacturing overhead allocated	39,60,000	
Fixed manufacturing overhead spending variance	1,30,000	
Fixed manufacturing overhead production-volume variance		3,60,000
Fixed manufacturing overhead control		37,30,000

3. The control of variable manufacturing overhead requires the identification of the cost drivers for such items as energy, supplies, and repairs. Control often entails monitoring nonfinancial measures that affect each cost item, one by one. Examples are kilowatt used, quantities of lubricants used, and repair parts and hour used. The most convincing way to discover why overhead performance did not agree with a budget is to investigate possible causes, line item by line item.
Individual fixed manufacturing overhead items are not usually affected very much by day-to-day control. Instead, they are controlled periodically through planning decisions and budgeting procedures that may sometimes have horizons covering six months or a year (for example, management salaries) and sometimes covering many years (for example, long-term leases and depreciation on plant and equipment).

Solution Exhibit 8-20

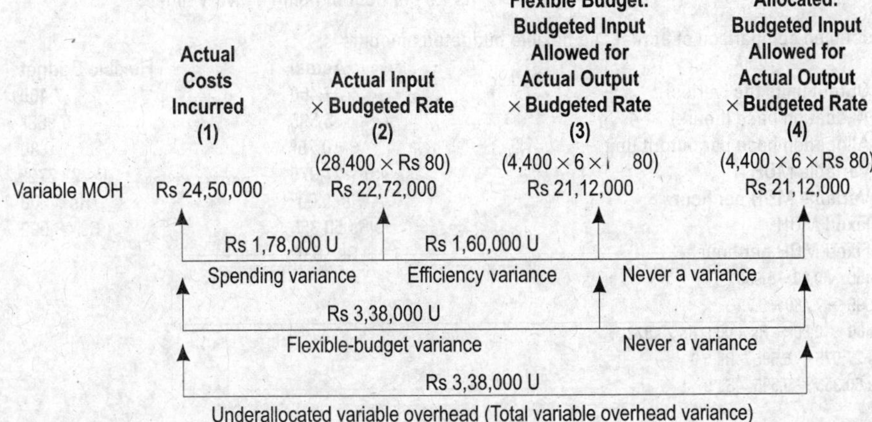

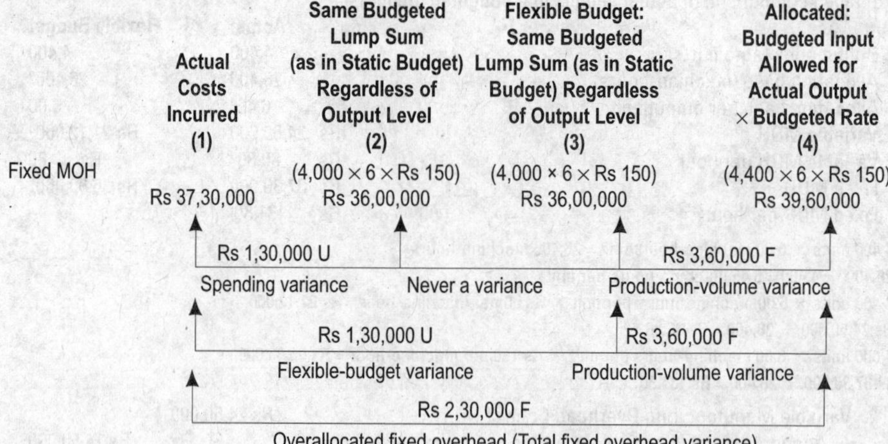

8-21 Spending and efficiency overhead variances, service sector. Meals on Wheels (MOW) operates a home meal delivery service. It has agreements with 20 restaurants to pick up and deliver meals to customers who phone or fax orders to MOW. MOW is currently examining its overhead costs for May.

Variable overhead costs for May were budgeted at Rs 4 per hour of home delivery time. Fixed overhead costs were budgeted at Rs 48,000. The budgeted number of home deliveries (MOW's output measure) were 8,000. Delivery time, the allocation base for variable and fixed overhead costs, is budgeted to be 0.80 hour per delivery.

Actual results for May were:

Variable overhead	Rs 27,975
Fixed overhead	Rs 50,355
Number of home deliveries	7,460
Hours of delivery time	5,595

Customers are charged Rs 24 per delivery. The delivery driver is paid Rs 14 per delivery.

MOW receives a 10 per cent commission on the meal costs that the restaurants charge the customer who use MOW.

Required

1. Compute spending and efficiency variances for MOW's variable overhead in May. Comment on the results.
2. Compute the spending variance for MOW's variable overhead in May. Comment on the results.

Solution

Spending and efficiency overhead variances, service sector.

1. and 2. Budgeted variable overhead rate = Rs 4 per hour of home delivery time

$$\text{Budgeted fixed overhead rate} = \frac{\text{Rs } 48{,}00{,}000}{8{,}000 \times 0.80} = \frac{\text{Rs } 48{,}00{,}000}{6{,}400 \text{ hours}}$$

$$= \text{Rs 7.5 per hour of home delivery time}$$

A detailed comparison of actual and flexible budgeted amounts is:

	Actual	Flexible Budget
Output units (deliveries)	7,460	7,460
Allocation base (hours)	5,595	5,968[a]
Allocation base per output unit	0.75[b]	0.80
Variable MOH	Rs 27,975	Rs 23,872[c]
Variable MOH per hour	Rs 5.00[d]	Rs 4.00
Fixed MOH	Rs 50,355	Rs 48,000
Fixed MOH per hour	Rs 9.0[e]	-

[a]7,460 × 0.80 = 5,968
[b]5,595 ÷ 7,460 = 0.75
[c]7,460 × 0.80 × Rs 4.00 = Rs 23,872
[d]Rs 27,975 ÷ 5,595 = Rs 5.0
[e]Rs 50,355 ÷ 5,595 = Rs 9

The required variances are:

	Spending Variance	Efficiency Variance
Variable overhead	Rs 5,595 U	Rs 1,492 F
Fixed overhead	Rs 2,355 U	—

These variances are computed as follows:

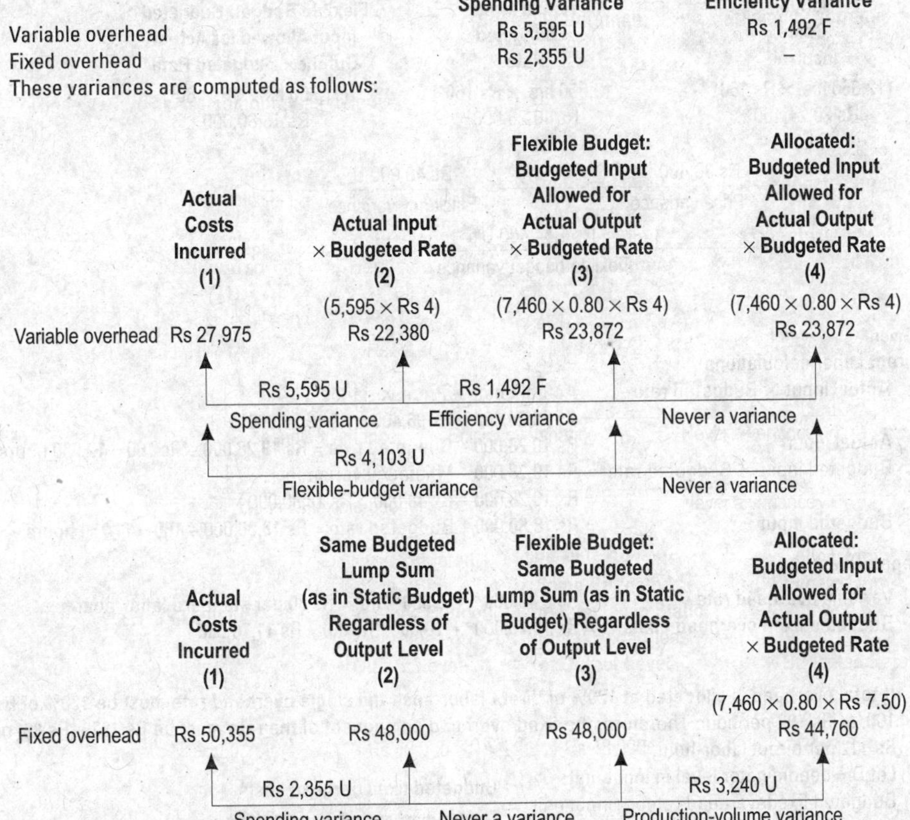

The spending variances for variable and fixed overhead are both unfavorable. This means that MOW had increases over budget in either or both the cost of individual items (such as telephone calls and gasoline) in the overhead cost pools, or the usage of these individual items per unit of the allocation base (delivery time). The favorable efficiency variance for variable overhead costs results from more efficient use of the cost allocation base—each delivery takes 0.75 hours versus a budgeted 0.80 hours.

8-22 Total overhead, 3-variance analysis. Delhi Cantt Air Force Base has an extensive repair facility for jet engines. It developed standard costing and flexible budgets to account for this activity. Budgeted variable overhead at a level of 8,000 standard monthly direct labor-hours was Rs 6,40,000; budgeted total overhead at 10,000 standard direct labor-hours was Rs 19,76,000. The standard cost allocated to repair output included a total overhead rate of 120 per cent of standard direct labor costs. Total overhead incurred for October was Rs 24,90,000. Direct labor costs incurred were Rs 20,24,400. The direct labor price variance was Rs 96,400 unfavorable. The direct labor flexible-budget variance was Rs 1,44,400 unfavorable. The standard labor price was Rs 160 per hour. The production-volume variance was Rs 1,40,000 favorable.

Required

1. Compute the direct labor efficiency variance and the spending, efficiency, and production-volume variances for overhead. Also, compute the denominator level.
2. Describe how individual variable manufacturing overhead items are controlled from day to day. Also, describe how individual fixed manufacturing overhead items are controlled.

Solution

Total overhead, 3-variance analysis.

1. An analysis of direct manufacturing labor will provide the data for actual hours of input and standard hours allowed. One approach is to plug the known figures (designated by asterisks) into the analytical framework and solve for the unknowns. The direct manufacturing labor efficiency variance can be computed by subtracting Rs 96,400 from Rs 1,44,400.

The complete picture is:

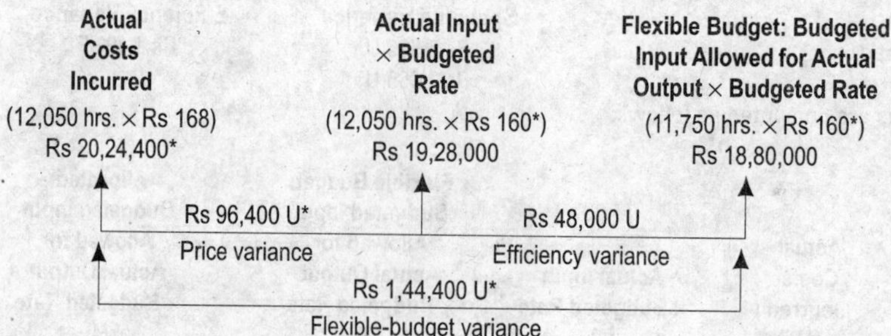

*Given

Direct Labor calculations

Actual input × Budgeted rate = Actual costs – Price variance
= Rs 20,24,400 – Rs 96,400 = Rs 19,28,000

Actual input = Rs 19,28,000 ÷ Budgeted rate = Rs 19,28,000 ÷ Rs 160 = 12,050 hours

Budgeted input × Budgeted rate = Rs 19,28,000 – Efficiency variance
= Rs 19,28,000 – Rs 48,000 = Rs 18,80,000

Budgeted input = Rs 18,80,000 ÷ Budgeted rate = Rs 18,80,000 ÷ 160 = 11,750 hours

Repair Overhead

Variable overhead rate = Rs 6,40,000* ÷ 8,000* hrs. = Rs 80 per standard labor-hour

Budgeted fixed overhead costs = Rs 19,76,000* – 10,000*(Rs 80) = Rs 11,76,000

If total overhead is allocated at 120% of direct labor-cost, the single overhead rate must be 120% of Rs 160, or Rs 192 per hour. Therefore, the fixed overhead component of the rate must be Rs 192 – Rs 80, or Rs 112 per direct labor-hour.

Let D = denominator level in input units

$$\text{Budgeted fixedoverhead rateper input unit} = \frac{\text{Budgeted fixed oerhead costs}}{\text{Denominator level in input units}}$$

$$\text{Rs } 112 = \text{Rs } 11{,}76{,}000/D$$

$$D = 10{,}500 \text{ direct labor-hours}$$

A summary 3-variance analysis for October follows:

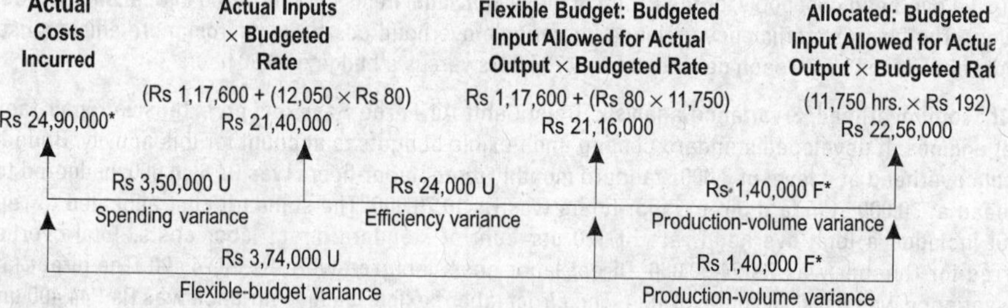

*Known figure

An overview of the 3-variance analysis using the block format in the text is:

3-Variance Analysis	Spending Variance	Efficiency Variance	Production-Volume Variance
Total Overhead	Rs 3,50,000 U	Rs 24,000 U	Rs 1,40,000 F

2. The control of variable manufacturing overhead requires the identification of the cost drivers for such items as energy, supplies, equipment, and maintenance. Control often entails monitoring nonfinancial measures that affect each cost item, one by one. Examples are kilowatt used, quantities of lubricants used, and equipment parts and hours used. The most convincing way to discover why overhead performance did not agree with a budget is to investigate possible causes, line item by line item.

   Individual fixed manufacturing overhead items are not usually affected very much by day-to-day control. Instead, they are controlled periodically through planning decisions and budgeting that may sometimes have horizons covering six months or a year (for example, management salaries) and sometimes covering many years (for example, long-term leases and depreciation on plant and equipment).

8-23 4-variance analysis, working backwards. Lookmeup.com is striving to become a Web portal. The site allows surfers to find anything they wish to lookup-be it a person, a site, a company, or a news article – through one interactive and easy-to-use interface. Most of Lookmeup.com's operating overhead is due to Internet connection costs. Lookmeup.com faces fixed as well as variable Internet connection charges. Following is the 4-variance analysis of Lookmeup.com's operating overhead for June:

	Spending Variance	Efficiency Variance	Production-VolumeVariance
Variable operating overhead	Rs 37,000 F	Rs 24,000 F	Never a variance
Fixed operating overhead	Rs 14,000 U	Never a variance	Rs 17,000 U

Required

1. For total operating overhead, compute the following:
   a. Spending variance
   b. Efficiency variance
   c. Production-volume variance
   d. Flexible-budget variance
   e. Total-overhead variance
   Arrange your results in a suitable format for presenting 3-variance, 2-variance, and 1-variance analyses.
2. If Lookmeup.com's total actual operating overhead were Rs 420,000, what was the operating overhead allocated to actual output units provided?
3. Can you say whether fixed operating overhead was underallocated or overallocated? If so, by what amount?
4. Are Lookmeup.com's different variances in the 4-variance analysis given necessarily independent? Explain and provide an example.

Solution

4-Variance analysis, working backwards.

1. To arrive at the 3-variance analysis amounts, simply sum the numbers in each column of the table provided in the question:

4-Variance Analysis	Spending Variance	Efficiency Variance	Production-VolumeVariance
Total operating overhead	Rs 23,000 F	Rs 24,000 F	Rs 17,000 U

2-Variance Analysis

The 2-variance analysis includes numbers for the flexible-budget and production-volume (PVV) variances. The PVV is as above. The flexible-budget variance is the sum of the spending and efficiency variances:

	Flexible-Budget Variance	Production-Volume Variance
Total Operating Overhead	Rs 47,000 F	Rs 17,000 U

1-Variance Analysis

The total overhead variance is simply the sum of the flexible-budget and the production-volume variances:

	Total Overhead Variance
Total Operating Overhead	Rs 30,000 F

2. The total overhead variance is Rs 30,000 F. The total overhead variance is equal to the difference between the total actual operating overhead incurred and the operating overhead allocated to the actual output units. Therefore, if the actual operating overhead was Rs 4,20,000, this must be Rs 30,000 less than budgeted for, that is, the operating overhead allocated to actual output units provided is Rs 4,50,000.
3. Flexible-budget variance for fixed overhead is equal to the spending variance since the flexible-budget variance is equal to the sum of the spending and efficiency variances, and there is never an efficiency variance for fixed overhead. Therefore, fixed operating overhead flexible budget variance is Rs 14,000 U. The production volume variance is Rs 17,000 U. The under or overallocation of fixed operating overhead is determined as the sum of the flexible-budget variance and the production volume variance. So, summing Rs 14,000 U and Rs 17,000 U, the total fixed overhead variance is Rs 31,000 U—actual fixed operating overhead was higher than budgeted for, that is, fixed operating overhead was underallocated.
4. Variances in the 4-variance analysis are not necessarily independent. The cause of one variance may affect another. For example, consider the case where Lookmeup.com acquires less expensive Internet access for its servers. This may give rise to a favorable spending variance. However, cheaper Internet access may be of lower quality and require longer connection times and congestion, resulting in an unfavorable efficiency variance.

8-24 Comprehensive variance analysis. Santel Color manufactures flat-panel LCD displays. The displays are sold to major PC manufacturers. Following is some manufacturing overhead data for Santel for the year ended December 31,2011:

Manufacturing Overhead	Actual	Flexible Budget	Allocated Amount
Variable	Rs 15,32,160	Rs 15,36,000	Rs 15,36,000
Fixed	70,04,160	69,61,920	75,26,400

Santel's budget was based on the assumption that 17,760 units (panels) will be manufactured during 2011. The planned allocation rate was 2 machine-hours per unit. Actual number of machine-hours used during 2011 was 36,480. The static-budget variable manufacturing overhead costs equal Rs 1,420,800.

Required Compute the following quantities (you should be able to do so in the prescribed order):

1. Budgeted number of machine-hours planned
2. Budgeted fixed manufacturing overhead costs per machine-hour
3. Budgeted variable manufacturing overhead costs per machine-hour
4. Budgeted number of machine-hours allowed for actual output produced
5. Actual number of output units
6. Actual number of machine-hours used per panel

Solution

Comprehensive variance analysis.

(a) Budgeted number of machine-hours planned can be calculated multiplying the number of units planned (budgeted) by the number of machine-hours allocated per unit:
17,760 units × 2 machine-hours per unit = 35,520 machine-hours.

(b) Budgeted fixed MOH costs per machine-hour can be computed dividing the flexible budget amount for fixed MOH (which is the same as the static budget) by the number of machine-hours planned. [(calculated in (a)]:
Rs 6,961,920 ÷ 35,520 machine-hours = Rs 196.00 per machine-hour.

(c) Budgeted variable MOH costs per machine-hour are calculated as budgeted variable MOH costs divided by the budgeted number of machine-hours planned:
Rs 1,420,800 ÷ 35,520 machine-hours = Rs 40.00 per machine-hour.

(d) Budgeted number of machine-hours allowed for actual output achieved can be calculated dividing the flexible-budget amount for variable MOH by budgeted variable MOH costs per machine-hour:
Rs 1,536,000 ÷ Rs 40.00 per machine-hour = 38,400 machine-hours allowed.

(e) The actual number of output units is the budgeted number of machine-hours allowed for actual output achieved divided by the planned allocation rate of machine hours per unit:
38,400 machine-hours ÷ 2 machine-hours per unit = 19,200 units.

(f) The actual number of machine-hours used per panel is the actual number of machine hours used (given) divided by the actual number of units manufactured:
36,480 machine-hours ÷ 19,200 units = 1.9 machine-hours used per panel.

8-25 Journal entries. (continuation of 8-24)

Required

1. Prepare journal entries for variable and fixed manufacturing overhead (you will need to calculate the various variances to accomplish this).
2. Overhead variances are written off to Cost of Goods Sold (COGS) account at the end of the fiscal year. COGS is then entered in the income statement. Show how COGS is adjusted through journal entries.

Solution

Journal entries. (continuation of 8-24).

1. Key information underlying the computation of variances is:

	Actual Results	Flexible Amount Budget	Static-Budget Amount
Output units (panels)	19,200	19,200	17,760
Machine-hours	36,480	38,400	35,520
Machine-hours per panel	1.90	2.00	2.00
Variable MOH costs	Rs 1,532,160	Rs 1,536,000	Rs 1,420,800
Variable MOH costs per machine-hour (Row 4 ÷ Row 2)	Rs 42.00	Rs 40.00	Rs 40.00
Variable MOH costs per unit (Row 4 ÷ Row 1)	Rs 79.80	Rs 80.00	Rs 80.00
Fixed MOH costs	Rs 7,004,160	Rs 6,961,920	Rs 6,961,920
Fixed MOH costs per machine-hour (Row 7 ÷ Row 2)	Rs 192.00	Rs 181.30	Rs 196.00
Fixed MOH costs per unit (7 ÷ 1)	Rs 364.80	Rs 362.60	Rs 392.00

Solution Exhibit 8-25 shows the computation of the variances.

Journal entries for variable MOH, year ended December 31, 2011:

Variable MOH control	Rs 15,32,160	
Accounts payable control and other accounts		Rs 15,32,160
Work-in-process control		15,36,000
Variable MOH allocated		15,36,000

Variable MOH allocated	15,36,000	
Variable MOH spending variance	72,960	
Variable MOH control		15,32,160
Variable MOH efficiency variance		76,800

Journal entries for fixed MOH, year ended December 31, 2011:

Fixed MOH control	Rs 70,04,160	
Wages payable, accumulated depreciation, etc.		Rs 70,04,160
Work-in-process control	75,26,400	
Fixed MOH allocated		75,26,400
Fixed MOH allocated	75,26,400	
Fixed MOH spending variance	42,240	
Fixed MOH control		70,04,160
Fixed MOH production-volume variance		5,64,480

2. **Adjustment of COGS**

Variable MOH efficiency variance	Rs 76,800	
Fixed MOH production-volume variance	5,64,480	
Variable MOH spending variance		Rs 72,960
Fixed MOH spending variance		42,240
Cost of goods sold		5,26,080

Solution Exhibit 8-25

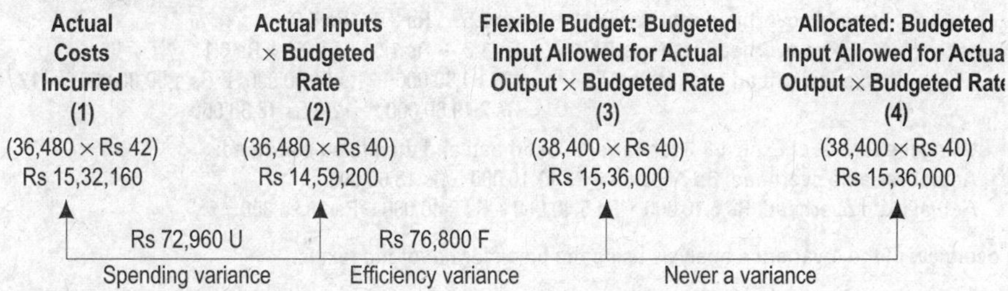

Fixed Manufacturing Overhead

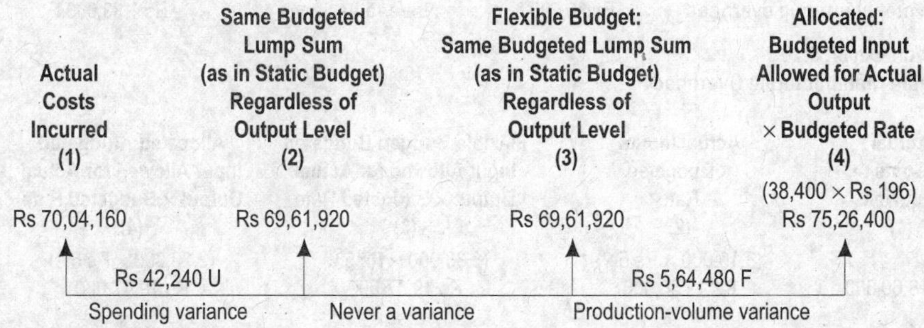

8-26 Flexible budgets, 4-variance analysis. (CMA, adapted) Essel Products use a standard-costing system. It allocates manufacturing overhead (both variable and fixed) to products on the basis of standard direct manufacturing labor-hours (DLH). Essel develops its manufacturing overhead rate from the current annual budget. The manufacturing overhead budget for 2012 is based on budgeted output of 720,000 units, requiring 3,600,000 DLH. The company is able to schedule production uniformly throughout the year.

A total of 66,000 output units requiring 315,000 DLH was produced during May 2012. Manufacturing overhead (MOH) costs incurred for May amounted to Rs 37,50,000. The actual costs, compared with the annual budget and 1/12 of the annual budget are as follows:

Annual Manufacturing Overhead Budget 2012:

	Total Amount	Per Output Unit	Per DLH Input Unit	Monthly MOH Budget May 2012	Actual MOH Costs for May 2012
Variable MOH					
Indirect manufacturing labor	Rs 90,00,000	Rs 12.5	Rs 2.5	Rs 7,50,000	Rs 7,50,000
Supplies	1,22,40,000	17.0	3.4	10,20,000	11,10,000

Fixed MOH					
Supervision	64,80,000	9.0	1.8	5,40,000	5,10,000
Utilities	54,00,000	7.5	1.5	4,50,000	5,40,000
Depreciation	1,00,80,000	14.0	2.8	8,40,000	8,40,000
Total	4,32,00,000	60.0	12	36,00,000	37,50,000

Required Calculate the following amounts for Essel Products for May 2012:

1. Total manufacturing overhead costs allocated.
2. variable manufacturing overhead spending variance.
3. Fixed manufacturing overhead spending variance.
4. variable manufacturing overhead efficiency variance.
5. Production-volume variance.

Be sure to identify each variance as favorable (F) or unfavorable (U).

Solution

Flexible budgets, 4-variance analysis.

1. Budgeted hours allowed per unit of output per unit $= \dfrac{\text{Budgeted DLH}}{\text{Budgeted actual output}}$ = 36,00,000/7,20,000 = 5 hours

Budgeted DLH allowed for May output = 66,000 units × 5 hrs./unit = 3,30,000 hrs.
Allocated total MOH = 3,30,000 × Total MOH rate per hour
= 3,30,000 × Rs 12 = Rs 39,60,000

2, 3, 4, 5. See Solution Exhibit 8-26

Variable overhead rate per DLH = Rs 2.5 + Rs 3.4 = Rs 5.9
Fixed overhead rate per DLH = Rs 1.8 + Rs 1.5 + Rs 2.8 = Rs 6.1
Fixed overhead budget for May = (Rs 64,80,000 + Rs 54,00,000 + Rs 1,00,80,000) ÷ 12
= Rs 2,19,60,000 ÷ 12 = Rs 18,30,000

Using the format of Exhibit 8-3 for variable overhead and then fixed overhead:
Actual variable overhead: Rs 7,50,000 + Rs 11,10,000 = Rs 18,60,000
Actual fixed overhead: Rs 5,10,000 + Rs 5,40,000 + Rs 8,40,000 = Rs 18,90,000

An overview of the 4-variance analysis using the block format of the text is:

4-Variance Analysis	Spending Variance	Efficiency Variance	Production-Volume Variance
Variable manufacturing overhead	Rs 1,500 U	Rs 88,500 F	Never a variance
Fixed manufacturing overhead	Rs 60,000 U	Never a variance	Rs 1,83,000 F

Solution Exhibit 8-26
Variable Manufacturing Overhead

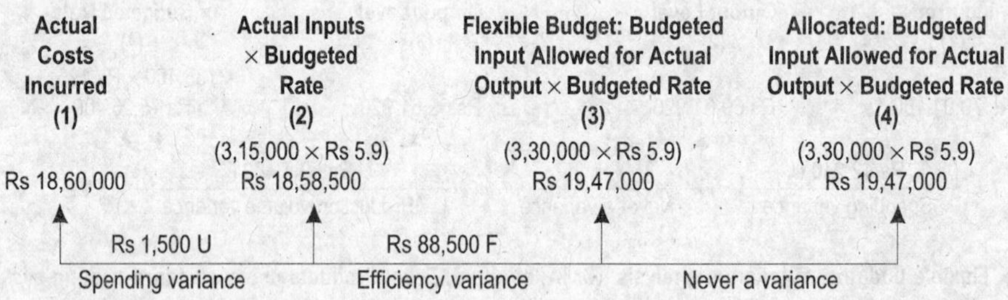

Fixed Manufacturing Overhead

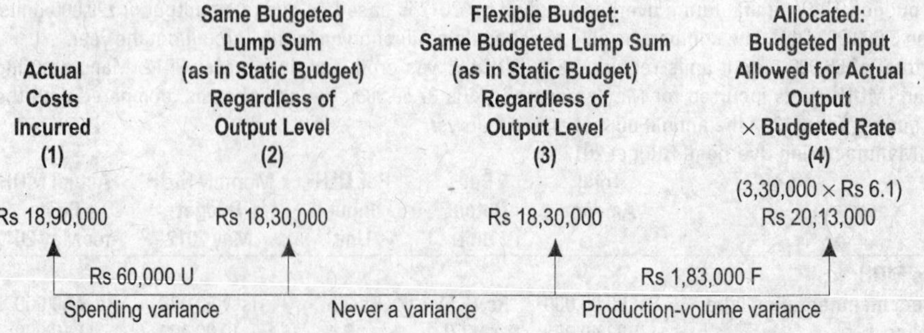

Alternate computation of the production volume variance:

$$= \left[\left(\begin{array}{c}\text{Budgeted hours}\\ \text{allowed for actual}\\ \text{output achieved}\end{array}\right) - \left(\begin{array}{c}\text{Denominator}\\ \text{hours}\end{array}\right)\right] \times \left[\begin{array}{c}\text{Budgeted fixed}\\ \text{overhead}\\ \text{rate}\end{array}\right]$$

= [(3,30,000) — (36,00,000/12) × Rs 6.10

= (3,30,000 — 3,00,000) × Rs 6.10 = Rs 1,83,000 F

8-27 Sales-volume variance, production-volume variance. Apollo Company prepared its budgeted output and sales at its maximum capacity of 20,000 units for 2012. However, due to efficiency improvements, Apollo was able to sell 22,000 units for the year. Other data for 2012 follows as:

Budgeted fixed overhead costs	Rs 5,00,000
Budgeted selling price	100
Budgeted variable cost per unit	40

Required

1. Calculate the budgeted profit per unit, the operating income based on the budgeted profit per unit, and the flexible-budget operating income.
2. Compute sales-volume variance and production-volume variance. What do each of these variance measure?

Solution

Sales-volume variance, production-volume variance.

1.

Budgeted selling price		Rs 100
Budgeted variable cost per unit	Rs 40	
Budgeted fixed cost per unit (Rs 5,000,000 × 20,000)	25	
Budgeted cost per unit		65
Budgeted profit per unit		Rs 35
Operating income based on budgeted profit per unit Rs 35 per unit × 22,000 units		Rs 7,70,000
Flexible-budget operating income is Revenues Rs 100 × 22,000		Rs 22,00,000
Variable costs Rs 40 × 22,000		8,80,000
Fixed costs		5,00,000
Operating income		8,20,000
Static-budget operating income is:		
Revenues Rs 100 × 20,000		Rs 20,00,000
Variable costs Rs 40 × 20,000		8,00,000
Fixed costs		5,00,000
Operating income		Rs 7,00,000

2. The sales-volume variance recognizes that when Appolo sells 22,000 units instead of the budgeted 20,000, only the revenue and the variable costs are affected. Fixed costs remain unchanged.

$$\text{Sales volume variance} = \left[\begin{array}{c}\text{Budgeted}\\ \text{selling price}\end{array} - \begin{array}{c}\text{Budgeted}\\ \text{variable costs}\\ \text{per unit}\end{array}\right] \times \begin{array}{c}\text{Difference in quantity of}\\ \text{units sold relative to the}\\ \text{static budget}\end{array}$$

= (Rs 100 – Rs 40) × 2,000 = Rs 60 × 2,000 = Rs 1,20,000 F

$$\text{Production-volume variance} = \begin{array}{c}\text{Budget fixed}\\ \text{overhead cost}\\ \text{per unit}\end{array} \times \begin{array}{c}\text{Difference in quantity of}\\ \text{units sold relative to the}\\ \text{static budget}\end{array}$$

$$= \frac{\text{Rs } 5,00,000}{20,000} \times 2,000 = \text{Rs } 25 \times 2,000 = \text{Rs } 50,000 \text{ F}$$

Compare the sales-volume variance and the production-volume variance. The Rs 120,000 F sales-volume variance explains the difference between the static-budget operating income and the flexible-budget operating income:

Static-budget operating income	Rs 7,00,000
Sales-volume variance	1,20,000 F
Flexible-budget operating income	8,20,000

The Rs 50,000 F production-volume variance explains the difference between operating income based on the budgeted profit per unit and the flexible-budget operating income:

Operating income based on budgeted profit per unit	Rs 7,70,000
Production-volume variance	50,000 F
Flexible-budget operating income	8,20,000

8-28 Activity-based costing, variance analysis. Toymaster Ltd. Produces a plastic toy car, TGC, in batches. To manufacture a batch of TGCs, Toymaster must set up the machines. Setup costs are batch-level costs. A separate Setup Department is responsible for setting up machines for TGC.

Setup overhead costs consist of some costs that are variable and some that are fixed with respect to the number of setup-hours. The following information pertains to 2012:

	Static-Budget Amounts	Actual Amounts
Units of TGC produced and sold	30,000	22,500
Batch size (number of units per batch)	250	225
Setup-hours per batch	5	5.25
Variable overhead cost per setup-hour	Rs 250	Rs 240
Total fixed setup overhead costs	Rs 1,80,000	Rs 1,75,350

Required

1. For variable setup overhead costs, compute the efficiency and spending variances. Comment on the results.
2. For fixed setup overhead costs, compute the spending and the production-volume variances. Comment on the results.

Solution

Activity-based costing, variance analysis.

1.

	Static-Budget Amounts	Actual Amounts
a. Units of TGC produced and sold	30,000	22,500
b. Batch size	250	225
c. Number of batches (a ÷ b)	120	100
d. Setup-hours per batch	5	5.25
e. Total setup-hours (c × d)	600	525
f. Variable overhead cost per setup-hour	Rs 250	Rs 240
g. Variable setup overhead costs (e × f)	Rs 1,50,000	Rs 1,26,000
h. Total fixed setup overhead costs	Rs 1,80,000	Rs 1,75,350
i. Fixed overhead cost per setup-hour (h ÷ e)	Rs 300	Rs 334

The flexible-budget is based on the budgeted number of setups for the actual output achieved:
22,500 units ÷ 250 units per batch = 90 batches

Computation of variable setup overhead cost variances follows:

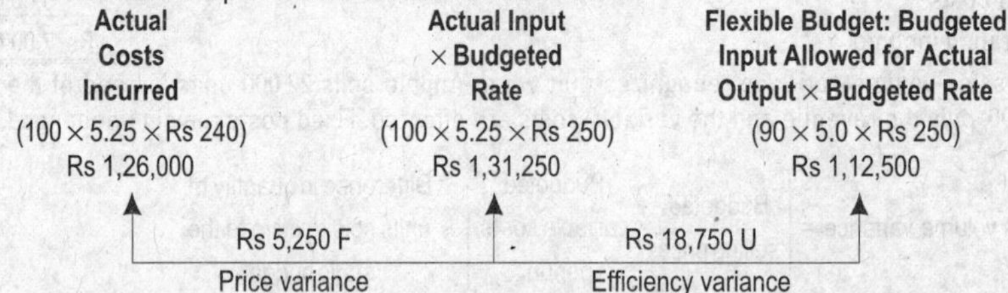

Actual Costs Incurred	Actual Input × Budgeted Rate	Flexible Budget: Budgeted Input Allowed for Actual Output × Budgeted Rate
(100 × 5.25 × Rs 240)	(100 × 5.25 × Rs 250)	(90 × 5.0 × Rs 250)
Rs 1,26,000	Rs 1,31,250	Rs 1,12,500
Rs 5,250 F Price variance	Rs 18,750 U Efficiency variance	

The favorable spending variance is due to the actual variable overhead cost per setup-hour declining from the budgeted Rs 250 per hour to the actual rate of Rs 240 per hour. The unfavorable efficiency variance is due to the actual output of 22,500 units (1) requiring more setups (100) than the budgeted amount (90), and (2) each setup taking longer time (5.25 hours) than the budgeted time (5.0 hours). The flexible-budget variance of Rs 13,500 U reflects the larger unfavorable efficiency variance not being offset by the favorable spending variance.

2. Computation of the fixed setup overhead cost variances follows:

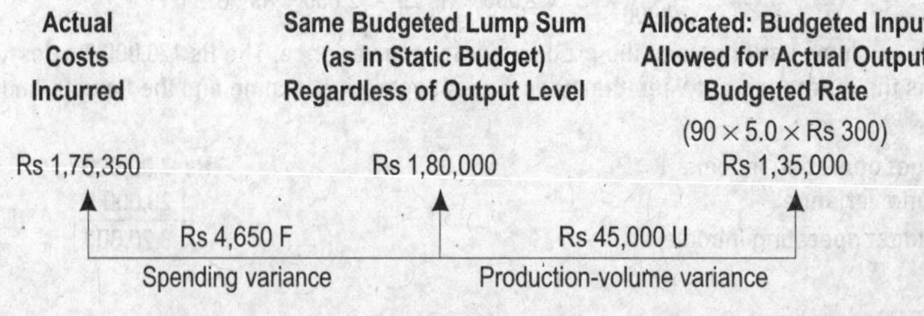

Actual Costs Incurred	Same Budgeted Lump Sum (as in Static Budget) Regardless of Output Level	Allocated: Budgeted Input Allowed for Actual Output Budgeted Rate
		(90 × 5.0 × Rs 300)
Rs 1,75,350	Rs 1,80,000	Rs 1,35,000
Rs 4,650 F Spending variance	Rs 45,000 U Production-volume variance	

The fixed setup overhead cost spending variance is Rs 4,650 F because the amount of actual costs was lower than the budgeted amount of Rs 1,80,000. The production-volume variance is Rs 45,000 U because the actual units of TGC produced and sold require fewer budgeted setup-hours than the budgeted setup-hour capacity available.

8-29 Overhead variances, ethics. New India Company uses a standard-costing system. The company prepared its static budget for 2012 at 1,000,000 machine-hours for the year. Total budgeted overhead cost is Rs 12,50,00,000. The variable overhead rate is Rs 100 per machine-hour (Rs 200 per unit). Actual results for 2012 are as follows:

Machine-hours	9,60,000 hours
Output	4,98,000 hours
Variable overhead	Rs 10,08,00,000
Fixed overhead spending variance	Rs 60,00,000 U

Required

1. Compute for the fixed overhead
   a. Budgeted amount
   b. Budgeted cost per machine-hour
   c. Actual cost
   d. Production-volume variance
2. Compute variable overhead spending variance and variable overhead efficiency variance.
3. James, the controller, prepares the variance analysis. It is common knowledge in the company that he and Manu, the production manager, are not on the best of terms. In a recent executive committee meeting, Manu had complained about the lack of usefulness of the accounting reports he receives. To get back at him James manipulated the actual fixed overhead amount by assigning a greater-than-normal share of allocated costs to the production area. And, he decided to depreciate all of the newly acquired production equipment using the double-declining balance method rather than the straight-line method, contrary to the company practice. As a result, there was a sizable unfavorable fixed overhead spending variance. He boasted to one of his confidants, "I am just returning the favor." Discuss James's actions and their ramifications.

Solution

Overhead variances, ethics.

1. a. Total budgeted overhead — Rs 12,50,00,000
   Budgeted variable overhead
   (Rs 100 budgeted rate per machine-hour × 1,000,000 budgeted machine-hours) — 10,00,00,000
   Budgeted fixed overhead — Rs 2,50,00,000

   b. Budgeted fixed OH rate $= \dfrac{\text{Rs 2,50,00,000 Budgeted amount}}{\text{10,00,000 Budgeted machine - hours}}$
   = Rs 25 per machine-hour

   c. **Fixed overhead spending variance = Actual costs incurred - Budgeted amount.**
   Because fixed overhead spending variance is unfavorable, the amount of actual costs is higher than the budgeted amount.
   Actual cost = Rs 2,50,00,000 + Rs 60,00,000 = Rs 3,10,00,000

   d. Production-volume variance

   $$= [\text{Budgeted fixed overhead}] - \left[\begin{array}{c}\text{Fixed overhead allocated using budgeted}\\ \text{input allowed for actual output units produced}\end{array}\right]$$

   = Rs 2,50,00,000 – (Rs 25 per machine-hour × 2 machine-hours per unit* × 4,98,000 units)
   = Rs 2,50,00,000 – Rs 2,49,00,000
   = Rs 1,00,000 U

   *Budgeted variable overhead per unit = Rs 200
   Budgeted variable overhead rate = Rs 100 per machine-hour
   Therefore, budgeted machine hours allowed per unit $= \dfrac{\text{Rs } 200}{\text{Rs } 100} = 2$ machine-hours

2. Variable overhead spending variance:

$$\left[\begin{array}{c}\text{Actual variable}\\ \text{overhead cost}\\ \text{per unit of cost}\\ \text{actual output}\end{array} - \begin{array}{c}\text{Budgeted variable}\\ \text{overhead cost}\\ \text{cost - allocation base}\\ \text{actual output}\end{array}\right] \times \begin{array}{c}\text{Actual quantity}\\ \text{of variable overhead}\\ \text{cos t-allocation base}\\ \text{used for actual output}\end{array}$$

$$= \left(\frac{\text{Rs 10,08,00,000 Budgeted amount}}{\text{9,60,000 actual machine-hours}} - \text{Rs 100 per machine-hour}\right) \times \text{9,60,000 machine-hours}$$

= (Rs 105 — Rs 100) × 9,60,000 = Rs 48,00,000 U

Variable overhead efficiency variance:

$$\left[\begin{array}{c}\text{Actual units of}\\ \text{variable overhead}\\ \text{cost-allocation}\\ \text{base used for}\\ \text{actual output}\end{array} - \begin{array}{c}\text{Budgeted units of}\\ \text{variable overhead}\\ \text{cost-allocation base}\\ \text{allowed for}\\ \text{actual output}\end{array}\right] \times \begin{array}{c}\text{Budgeted}\\ \text{variable}\\ \text{overhead}\\ \text{rate}\end{array}$$

= (9,60,000 – (2 × 4,98,000)) × Rs 100

= (9,60,000 – 9,96,000) ´ 100 = Rs 36,00,000 F

3. By manipulating, James has created a sizable unfavorable fixed overhead spending variance or, at least, has increased its magnitude. James's action is clearly unethical. Variances draw attention to the areas which need management attention. If the top management relies on James, due to his expertise, to interpret and explain the reasons for the unfavorable variance, it is likely that his report will be biased and misleading to the top management. The top management may erroneously conclude that Manu is not able to manage his fixed overhead costs effectively. Another probable adverse outcome of James's actions will be that Manu will have even less confidence in the usefulness of accounting reports. This, of course, defeats the purpose of preparing the reports. In summary, James's unethical actions will waste top management's time and may lead to wrong decisions.

Exercises

8-30 Variable manufacturing overhead variance analysis. The Harvest Gold Bread Company bakes baguettes for distribution to upscale grocery stores. The company has two direct-cost categories, direct materials and direct manufacturing labor. Variable manufacturing overhead is allocated to products on the basis of standard direct manufacturing labor-hours.

Following is some pertinent data for the Harvest Gold:

Direct manufacturing labor use	0.02 hour per baguette
Variable manufacturing overhead	Rs 100 per direct manufacturing labor-hour

The Harvest Gold Company recorded the following additional data for the current year ended December 31:

Planned (budgeted) output	32,00,000 baguettes
Actual production	28,00,000
Direct manufacturing labor	50,400 hours
Actual variable manufacturing overhead	Rs 68,04,000

Required

1. What is the denominator used for allocating variable manufacturing overhead? (That is, for how many direct manufacturing labor-hour is Harvest Gold Bread budgeting?).
2. Prepare a variance analysis of variable manufacturing overhead. Use Exhibit 8-3 for reference.
3. Discuss the variances you have calculated and give possible explanations for them.

8-31 4-variance analysis, fill in the blanks. Use the following manufacturing overhead data to fill in the following blanks:

	Variable	Fixed
Actual costs incurred	Rs 1,19,000	Rs 60,000
Costs allocated to products	90,000	45,000
Flexible budget: Budgeted input allowed for actual output produced x Budgeted rate	90,000	50,000
Actual input x Budgeted rate	1,00,000	50,000

Use F for favorable and U for unfavorable:

	Variable (Rs)	Fixed (Rs)
1. Spending variance		
2. Efficiency variance		
3. Production-volume variance		
4. Flexible-budget variance		
5. Underallocated (overallocated) manufacturing overhead		

8-32 Straightforward coverage of manufacturing overhead, standard-costing system. The Indian division of a Canadian telecommunications company uses a standard-costing system for its machine-paced production of telephone equipment. Data regarding production during June are as follows:

Variable manufacturing overhead costs incurred	Rs 15,51,000
Variable manufacturing overhead cost rate	Rs 120 per standard machine-hour
Fixed manufacturing overhead costs incurred	Rs 40,10,000
Fixed manufacturing overhead budgeted	Rs 39,00,000
Denominator level in machine-hours	13,000
Standard machine-hour allowed per unit of output	0.30
Units of output	41,000
Actual machine-hours used	13,300
Ending work-in-process inventory	0

Required

1. Prepare an analysis of all manufacturing overhead variances. Use the 4-variance analysis framework illustrated in Exhibit 8-3.
2. Prepare journal entries for manufacturing overhead.
3. Describe how individual variable manufacturing overhead items are controlled from day to day. Also, describe how individual fixed manufacturing overhead items are controlled.

8-33 Overhead variances, missing information. Aasbi Printing prepared its budget at 10,000 machine hours. Aasbi reported a Rs 7,500 unfavorable spending variance for fixed overhead and a Rs 2,500 unfavorable spending variance for variable overhead. The budgeted variable overhead rate is Rs 50 per machine hour. The input allowed for actual output was 9,900 machine hours. Actual machine hours were 9,800, and actual total overhead costs were Rs 8,00,000.

Required

1. Compute variable overhead efficiency variance, flexible-budget variance, and the amount underallocated or overallocated.
2. Calculate fixed overhead production-volume variance, flexible-budget variance, and the amount underallocated or overallocated.

8-34 Flexible-budget variances. The Times of India budgets to produce 3,00,000 copies of its monthly magazine (the output unit) for August. It is budgeted to have 50 print pages per magazine. Actual production was 320,000 copies, with 17,280,000 print pages run. Each magazine had only 50 print pages, but quality problems with paper led to many pages being unusable.

Variable costs are direct materials, direct labor, and variable indirect costs. Variable and fixed indirect costs are allocated to each copy on the basis of good print pages. The driver for all variable costs is the number of print pages.

Data pertaining to August are:

	Budgeted	Actual
Direct materials	Rs 5,40,000	Rs 6,73,920
Direct labor	1,35,000	1,50,336
Variable indirect	1,80,000	1,91,808
Fixed indirect	2,70,000	2,91,000

The actual direct labor rate was Rs 87 per hour. Actual and budgeted pages produced per direct labor-hour were 10,000 print pages. Data pertaining to revenues for Times of India in August are

	Budgeted	Actual
Circulation revenue	Rs 4,20,000	Rs 4,62,000
Advertising revenue	10,80,000	11,83,800

The Magazine sells for Rs 1.50 per copy. Copies produced but not sold have no value. Advertising revenues covers receipts from all advertising sources.

Required

1. Prepare a comprehensive set of flexible-budget variances for the two direct-cost items (using Exhibit 7-3) and the two indirect-cost items (using Exhibit 8-3) for The Times of India.
2. Comment on the results in requirement 1.

8-35 Variance analysis, graphs. Hindalco Industries budgets and allocates overhead costs using machine-hours. Hindalco's budget for 2012 was 10,000 machine-hours. Following is additional information relating to overhead for 2012:

Budgeted fixed overhead	Rs 60,00,000
Actual fixed overhead	59,00,000
Budgeted variable overhead	1,00,00,000
Actual variable overhead	1,10,00,000
Budgeted machine-hours allowed for actual output	9,800
Actual machine-hours used	9,500

Required

1. Compute the variable overhead spending variance and efficiency variance.
2. Compute the fixed overhead spending variance and production-volume variance.
3. Draw graphs similar to those in Exhibit 8-4.

8-36 4-variance analysis, find the unknowns. Consider each of the following situations–cases A, B, and C – independently. Data refers to operations for April. For each situations, assume a standard-costing system. Also assume the use of a flexible budget for control of variable and fixed manufacturing overhead based on machine-hours.

	Cases A	B	C
1. Fixed manufacturing overhead incurred	Rs 1,06,000	—	Rs 1,20,000
2. Variable manufacturing overhead incurred	Rs 70,000	—	—
3. Denominator level in machine-hours	500	—	1,100
4. Standard machine-hours allowed for actual output achieved	—	650	—
Flexible-budget data:			
5. Fixed manufacturing overhead	—	—	—
6. Variable manufacturing overhead (per standard machine-hour)	—	Rs 85	Rs 50
7. Budgeted fixed manufacturing overhead	Rs 1,00,000	—	Rs 1,10,000
8. Budgeted variable manufacturing overhead[a]			
9. Total budgeted manufacturing overhead[a]	—	Rs 1,25,250	—
Additional data:			
10. Standard variable manufacturing overhead allocated	Rs 75,000	—	—
11. Standard Fixed manufacturing overhead allocated	Rs 1,00,000		
12. Production-volume variance	Rs 5,000 U	Rs 5,000 U	
13. Variable manufacturing overhead spending variance	Rs 9,500 F	0	Rs 3,500 U
14. Variable manufacturing overhead efficiency variance	0	Rs 1,000 U	
15. Fixed manufacturing overhead spending variance	Rs 3,000		
16. Actual machine-hours used			

[a]For standard machine-hours allowed for actual output produced.

Required

Fill in the blanks under each case. (Hint: Prepare a worksheet similar to that in Exhibit 8-3. Fill in the knowns and then solve for the unknowns.)

8-37 Overhead analysis. Hyundai Motors`uses standard costing. The following information is for 2012:

Static-budget machine-hours	33,000
Fixed overhead budget costs	Rs 49,50,000
Fixed overhead actual costs	Rs 45,00,000
Variable overhead actual costs	Rs 96,00,000
Variable overhead rate per machine-hour	Rs 300
Actual machine-hours used	30,000
Budgeted machine-hours allowed for actual output	35,000

Required

1. Calculate variable overhead spending variance and efficiency variance.
2. Compute fixed overhead spending variance and production-volume variance.

8-38 Activity-based costing, variance analysis. Precision Surgical Instruments, Ltd. makes a special line of forceps, SFA, in batches. Precision randomly selects forceps from each SFA batch for quality-testing purposes. Quality testing costs consist of some variable and some fixed costs in relation to the quality-testing hours. The following information is for 2012:

	Static-Budget Amounts	Actual Amounts
Units of SFA produced and sold	21,000	22,000
Batch size (number of units per batch)	500	550
Testing-hours per batch	5.5	5.4
Variable overhead cost per testing-hour	Rs 400	Rs 420
Total fixed testing overhead costs	Rs 2,88,750	Rs 2,72,160

Required

1. For variable testing overhead costs, compute the efficiency and spending variances. Comment on the results.
2. For fixed testing overhead costs, compute the spending and the production-volume variances. Comment on the results.

8-39 Comprehensive review, working backward from given variances. Maruti company uses a flexible budget and standard costs to aid planning and control of its machining manufacturing operations. Its normal-costing system for manufacturing has two direct-cost categories (direct materials and direct manufacturing labor-both variable) and two indirect-cost categories (variable manufacturing overhead and fixed manufacturing overhead, both allocated using direct manufacturing labor-hours).

At the 40,000 budgeted direct manufacturing labor-hour level for August, budgeted direct manufacturing labor is Rs 40,00,000, budgeted variable manufacturing overhead is Rs 24,00,000, and budgeted fixed manufacturing overhead is Rs 32,00,000.

The following actual results for August are:

Direct materials price variance (based on purchases)	Rs 8,80,000 F
Direct materials efficiency variance	3,45,000 U
Direct manufacturing labor costs incurred	26,13,750
Variable manufacturing overhead flexible-budget variance	51,750 U
Variable manufacturing overhead efficiency variance	90,000 U
Fixed manufacturing overhead incurred	29,87,300
Fixed manufacturing overhead spending variance	2,12,700 F

The standard cost per kg of direct materials is Rs 57.5. The standard allowance is three kg of direct materials for each unit of product. During August 30,000 units of product were produced. There was no beginning inventory of direct materials. There was no beginning or ending work in process. In August, the direct materials price variance was Rs 5.5 per kg.

In July, labor unrest caused a major slowdown in the pace of production, resulting in an unfavorable direct manufacturing labor efficiency variance of Rs 2,25,000. There was no direct manufacturing labor price variance. Labor unrest persisted into August. Some workers quit. Their replacements had to be hired at higher rates, which had to be extended to all workers. The actual average wage rate in August exceeded the standard average wage rate by Rs 2.50 per hour.

1. Compute the following for August
   a. Total kg of direct materials purchased
   b. Total number of kg of excess direct materials used
   c. Variable manufacturing overhead spending variance
   d. Total number of actual direct manufacturing labor-hours used
   e. Total number of standard direct manufacturing labor-hours allowed for the units produced
   f. Production-volume variance
2. Describe how Maruti's control of variable manufacturing overhead items differs from its control of fixed manufacturing overhead items.

8-40 Review 3-variance analysis. (CPA, adapted) The Ajanta Manufacturing Company's job-costing system has two direct-cost categories: direct materials and direct manufacturing labor. Manufacturing overhead (both variable and fixed) is allocated to products on the basis of standard direct manufacturing labor-hours (DLH). At the beginning of 2013, Ajanta adopted the following standards for its manufacturing costs:

	Input	Cost per Output Unit
Direct materials	3 kgs. At Rs 5 per kg	Rs 15.00
Direct manufacturing labor	5 hrs. at Rs 15 per hr	75.00
Manufacturing overhead:		
Variable	Rs 6 per DLH	30.00
Fixed	Rs 8 per DLH	40.00
Standard manufacturing cost per output unit		Rs 160.00

The denominator level for total manufacturing overhead per month in 2011 is 40,000 direct manufacturing labor-hours. Ajanta's flexible budget for January 2012 was based on this denominator level. The records for January indicated the following:

Direct materials purchased	25,000 kgs. At Rs 5.20 per kg
Direct materials used	23,100 kgs.
Direct manufacturing labor	40,100 hrs. at Rs 14.60 per hr
Total actual manufacturing overhead (variable and fixed)	Rs 6,00,000
Actual production	7,800 output units

Required

1. Prepare a schedule of total standard manufacturing costs for the 7,800 output units in January 2013.
2. For the month of January 2013, compute the following variances, indicating whether each is favorable (F) or unfavorable (U):
   a. Direct materials price variance, based on purchases
   b. Direct materials efficiency variance
   c. Direct manufacturing labor price variance
   d. Direct manufacturing labor efficiency variance
   e. Total manufacturing overhead spending variance
   f. Variable manufacturing overhead efficiency variance
   g. Production-volume variance

Inventory Costing and Capacity Analysis

Learning Objectives

1. Identify what distinguishes variable costing from absorption costing
2. Compute income under absorption costing and variable costing, and explain the difference in income
3. Understand how absorption costing can provide undesirable incentives for managers to build up inventory
4. Differentiate throughput costing from variable costing and absorption costing
5. Describe the various capacity concepts that can be used in absorption costing
6. Examine the key factors in choosing a capacity level to compute the budgeted fixed manufacturing cost rate
7. Understand other issues that play an important role in capacity planning and control

Few numbers capture the attention of managers and shareholders more than operating profits. In industries that require significant upfront investments in capacity, the decisions made regarding the level of such fixed investments, and the extent to which the capacity is eventually utilized to meet customer demand, have a substantial impact on corporate profits. Unfortunately, the choice of compensation and reward systems, as well as the choice of inventory-costing methods, may induce managerial decisions that benefit short-term earnings at the expense of a firm's long-term health. It may take a substantial external shock, like a sharp economic slowdown, to motivate firms to make the right capacity and inventory choices, as the following article illustrates.

Lean Manufacturing Helps Companies Reduce Inventory and Survive the Recession[1]

Can changing the way a mattress is pieced together save a company during an economic downturn? For Sealy, the world's largest mattress manufacturer, the answer is a resounding "yes!"

Sealy is among thousands of manufacturers that have remained profitable during the recession by using lean manufacturing to become more cost-efficient. Lean manufacturing involves producing output in an uninterrupted flow, rather than as part of unfinished batches, and producing only what customers order. Driving this lean movement is an urgent need to pare inventory, which reduces inventory costs.

Before the adoption of lean practices, the company used to manufacture units at peak capacity. That is, it made as many mattresses as its resources allowed. Sealy employees were also paid based on the number of mattresses produced each day. While factories operated at peak capacity, inventory often piled up, which cost the company millions of dollars each year.

While Sealy launched its lean strategy in 2004, its efforts intensified during the recession. Old processes were reconfigured to be more efficient. As a result, each bed is now completed in 4 hours, down from 21. Median delivery times have been cut to 60 hours from 72, and plants have cut their raw-material inventories by 50%.

Additionally, the company now adheres to a precise production schedule that reflects orders from retailers such as Mattress Discounters

[1] *Source*: Paul Davidson. 2009. Lean manufacturing helps companies survive recession. *USA Today*, November 2; Sealy Corporation. 2009. Annual Report. Trinity, NC: Sealy Corporation, 2010. http://ccbn.10kwizard.com/xml/download.php?repo=tenk&ipage=6709696&format=PDF

and Macy's. While factories no longer run at full capacity, no mattress is made now until a customer orders it.

Sealy's manufacturing and inventory strategy has been key to its survival during the recession. While 2009 sales were 14% less than 2008 sales, earnings rose more than $16 million. Moreover, a large part of the earnings increase was due to reductions in inventory costs, which were lower by 12%, or nearly $8 million, in 2009.

Managers in industries with high fixed costs, like manufacturing, must manage capacity levels and make decisions about the use of available capacity. Managers must also decide on a production and inventory policy (as Sealy did). These decisions and the accounting choices managers make affect the operating incomes of manufacturing companies. This chapter focuses on two types of cost accounting choices:

1. *The inventory-costing choice* determines which manufacturing costs are treated as inventoriable costs. Recall from Chapter 2, *inventoriable costs* are all costs of a product that are regarded as assets when they are incurred and expensed as cost of goods sold when the product is sold. There are three types of inventory costing methods: absorption costing, variable costing, and throughput costing.
2. *The denominator-level capacity choice* focuses on the cost allocation base used to set budgeted fixed manufacturing cost rates. There are four possible choices of capacity levels: theoretical capacity, practical capacity, normal capacity utilization, and master-budget capacity utilization.

Variable and Absorption Costing

Learning Objective 1

Identify what distinguishes variable costing

. . . fixed manufacturing costs excluded from inventoriable costs

from absorption costing

. . . fixed manufacturing costs included in inventoriable costs

The two most common methods of costing inventories in manufacturing companies are *variable costing* and *absorption costing*. We describe each next and then discuss them in detail, using a hypothetical lens-manufacturing company as an example.

Variable Costing

Variable costing is a method of inventory costing in which all variable manufacturing costs (direct and indirect) are included as inventoriable costs. All fixed manufacturing costs are excluded from inventoriable costs and are instead treated as costs of the period in which they are incurred. Note that *variable costing* is a less-than-perfect term to describe this inventory-costing method, because only variable manufacturing costs are inventoried; variable nonmanufacturing costs are still treated as period costs and are expensed. Another common term used to describe this method is **direct costing.** This is also a misnomer because variable costing considers variable manufacturing overhead (an indirect cost) as inventoriable, while excluding direct marketing costs, for example.

Absorption Costing

Absorption costing is a method of inventory costing in which all variable manufacturing costs and all fixed manufacturing costs are included as inventoriable costs. That is, inventory "absorbs" all manufacturing costs. The job costing system you studied in Chapter 4 is an example of absorption costing.

Under both variable costing and absorption costing, all variable manufacturing costs are inventoriable costs and all nonmanufacturing costs in the value chain (such as research and development and marketing), whether variable or fixed, are period costs and are recorded as expenses when incurred.

Comparing Variable and Absoption Costing

The easiest way to understand the difference between variable costing and absorption costing is with an example. We will study Stassen Company, an optical consumer-products manufacturer. We focus in particular on its product line of high-end telescopes for aspiring astronomers.

Stassen uses standard costing:

- Direct costs are traced to products using standard prices and standard inputs allowed for actual outputs produced.
- Indirect (overhead) manufacturing costs are allocated using standard indirect rates times standard inputs allowed for actual outputs produced.

Stassen's management wants to prepare an income statement for 2012 (the fiscal year just ended) to evaluate the performance of the telescope product line. The operating information for the year is:

File Edit View Insert Format Tools Data Window Help

	A	B
1		**Units**
2	Beginning Inventory	0
3	Production	8,000
4	Sales	6,000
5	Ending Inventory	2,000

Actual price and cost data for 2012 are:

File Edit View Insert Format Tools Data Window Help

	A	B
10	Selling price	Rs 10,000
11	Variable manufacturing cost per unit	
12	Direct material cost per unit	Rs 1,100
13	Direct manufacturing labor cost per unit	400
14	Manufacturing overhead cost per unit	500
15	Total variable manufacturing cost per unit	Rs 2,000
16	Variable marketing cost per unit sold	Rs 1,850
17	Fixed manufacturing costs (all indirect)	Rs 1,08,00,000
18	Fixed marketing costs (all indirect)	Rs 1,38,00,000

For simplicity and to focus on the main ideas, we assume the following about Stassen:

- Stassen incurs manufacturing and marketing costs only. The cost driver for all variable manufacturing costs is units produced; the cost driver for variable marketing costs is units sold. There are no batch-level costs and no product-sustaining costs.
- There are no price variances, efficiency variances, or spending variances. Therefore, the *budgeted* (standard) price and cost data for 2012 are the same as the *actual* price and cost data.
- Work-in-process inventory is zero.
- Stassen budgeted production of 8,000 units for 2012. This was used to calculate the budgeted fixed manufacturing cost per unit of Rs 1,350 (Rs 1,08,00,000/8,000 units).
- Stassen budgeted sales of 6,000 units for 2012, which is the same as the actual sales for 2012.
- The actual production for 2012 is 8,000 units. As a result, there is no production-volume variance for manufacturing costs in 2012. Later examples, based on data for 2010 and 2011, do include production-volume variances. However, even in those cases, the income statements contain no variances other than the production-volume variance.
- All variances are written off to cost of goods sold in the period (year) in which they occur.

Based on the preceding information, Stassen's inventoriable costs per unit produced in 2012 under the two inventory costing methods are as follows:

	Variable Costing		Absorption Costing	
Variable manufacturing cost per unit produced:				
Direct materials	Rs 1,100		Rs 1,100	
Direct manufacturing labor	400		400	
Manufacturing overhead	500	Rs 2,000	500	Rs 2,000
Fixed manufacturing cost per unit produced		—		Rs 1,350
Total inventoriable cost per unit produced		Rs 2,000		Rs 3,350

To summarize, the main difference between variable costing and absorption costing is the accounting for fixed manufacturing costs:

- Under variable costing, fixed manufacturing costs are not inventoried; they are treated as an expense of the period.
- Under absorption costing, fixed manufacturing costs are inventoriable costs. In our example, the standard fixed manufacturing cost is Rs 1350 per unit (Rs 1,08,00,000 ÷ 8,000 units) produced.

Learning Objective 2

Compute income under absorption costing

. . . using the gross-margin format

and variable costing,

. . . using the contribution-margin format

and explain the difference in income

. . . affected by the unit level of production and sales under absorption costing, but only the unit level of sales under variable costing

Variable vs. Absorption Costing: Operating Income and Income Statements

When comparing variable and absorption costing, we must also take into account whether we are looking at short- or long-term numbers. How does the data for a one-year period differ from that of a three-year period under variable and absorption costing?

Comparing Income Statements for One Year

What will Stassen's operating income be if it uses variable costing or absorption costing? The differences between these methods are apparent in Exhibit 9-1. Panel A shows the variable costing income statement and Panel B the absorption-costing income statement for Stassen's telescope product line for 2012. The variable-costing income statement uses the contribution-margin format introduced in Chapter 3. The absorption-costing income statement uses the gross-margin format introduced in Chapter 2. Why these differences in format? The distinction between variable costs and fixed costs is central to variable costing, and it is highlighted by the contribution-margin format. Similarly, the distinction

Exhibit 9-1 Comparison of Variable Costing and Absorption Costing for Stassen Company: Telescope Product-Line Income Statements for 2012

File Edit View Insert Format Tools Data Window Help

	A	B	C	D	E	F	G
1	**Panel A: VARIABLE COSTING**				**Panel B: ABSORPTION COSTING**		
2	Revenues: Rs 10,000 x 6,000 units		Rs 6,00,00,000		Revenues: Rs 10,000 x 6,000 units		Rs 6,00,00,000
3	Variable cost of goods sold:				Cost of goods sold:		
4	Beginning inventory	Rs 0			Beginning inventory	Rs 0	
5	Variable manufacturing costs: Rs 2,000 x 8,000 units	1,60,00,000			Variable manufacturing costs: Rs 2,000 x 8,000 units	1,60,00,000	
6					Allocated fixed manufacturing costs: Rs 1,350 x 8,000 units	1,08,00,000	
7	Cost of goods available for sale	1,60,00,000			Cost of goods available for sale	2,68,00,000	
8	Deduct ending inventory: Rs 2,000 x 2,000 units	(400,000)			Deduct ending inventory: Rs 3,350 x 2,000 units	(67,00,000)	
9	Variable cost of goods sold		1,20,00,000		Cost of goods sold		2,01,00,000
10	Variable marketing costs: Rs 1,850 x 6,000 units sold		1,11,00,000				
11	Contribution margin		3,69,00,000		Gross Margin		3,99,00,000
12	Fixed manufacturing costs		1,08,00,000		Variable marketing costs: Rs 1,850 x 6,000 units sold		1,11,00,000
13	Fixed marketing cost		1,38,00,000		Fixed marketing costs		13,80,00,000
14	Operating income		Rs 1,23,00,000		Operating Income		Rs 1,50,00,000
15							
16	Manufacturing costs expensed in Panel A:		Rs 1,20,00,000		Manufacturing costs expensed in Panel B:		
17	Variable cost of goods sold		1,08,00,000				
18	Fixed manufacturing costs						
19	Total		Rs 2,28,00,000		Cost of goods sold		Rs 2,01,00,000

between manufacturing and nonmanufacturing costs is central to absorption costing, and it is highlighted by the gross-margin format.

Absorption-costing income statements need not differentiate between variable and fixed costs. However, we will make this distinction between variable and fixed costs in the Stassen example to show how individual line items are classified differently under variable costing and absorption costing. In Exhibit 9-1, Panel B, note that inventoriable cost is Rs 3,350 per unit under absorption costing: allocated fixed manufacturing costs of Rs 1,350 per unit plus variable manufacturing costs of Rs 2,000 per unit.

Notice how the fixed manufacturing costs of Rs 1,08,00,000 are accounted for under variable costing and absorption costing in Exhibit 9-1. The income statement under variable costing deducts the Rs 1,08,00,000 lump sum as an expense for 2012. In contrast, the income statement under absorption costing regards each finished unit as absorbing Rs 1,350 of fixed manufacturing cost. Under absorption costing, the Rs 1,08,00,000 (Rs 1,350 per unit × 8,000 units) is initially treated as an inventoriable cost in 2012. Of this, Rs 81,00,000 (Rs 1,350 per unit × 6,000 units sold) subsequently becomes a part of cost of goods sold in 2012, and Rs 27,00,000 (Rs 1,350 per unit × 2,000 units) remains an asset—part of ending finished goods inventory on December 31, 2012.

Operating income is Rs 27,00,000 higher under absorption costing compared with variable costing, because only Rs 81,00,000 of fixed manufacturing costs are expensed under absorption costing, whereas all Rs 1,08,00,000 of fixed manufacturing costs are expensed under variable costing. Note that the variable manufacturing cost of Rs 2,000 per unit is accounted for the same way in both income statements in Exhibit 9-1.

These points can be summarized as follows:

	Variable Costing	Absorption Costing
Variable manufacturing costs: Rs 2,000 per telescope produced	Inventoriable	Inventoriable
Fixed manufacturing costs: Rs 1,08,00,000 per year	Deducted as an expense of the period	Inventoriable at Rs 1,350 per telescope produced using budgeted denominator level of 8,000 units produced per year (Rs 1,080,00,00 ÷ 8,000 units = Rs 1,350 per unit)

The basis of the difference between variable costing and absorption costing is how fixed manufacturing costs are accounted for. If inventory levels change, operating income will differ between the two methods because of the difference in accounting for fixed manufacturing costs. To see this, let's compare telescope sales of 6,000, 7,000, and 8,000 units by Stassen in 2012, when 8,000 units were produced. Of the Rs 1,08,00,000 total fixed manufacturing costs, the amount expensed in the 2012 income statement under each of these scenarios would be:

	A	B	C	D	E	G	H
1			Variable Costing			Absorption Costing	
2						Fixed Manufacturing Costs	
3	Units	Ending	Fixed Manufacturing Costs			Included in Inventory	Amount Expensed
4	Sold	Inventory	Included in Inventory	Amount Expensed		=Rs 1,350 x Ending Inv.	=Rs 1,350x Units Sold
5	6,000	2,000	Rs 0	Rs 1,08,00,000		Rs 27,00,000	Rs 81,00,000
6	7,000	1,000	Rs 0	Rs 1,08,00,000		Rs 13,50,000	Rs 94,50,000
7	8,000	0	Rs 0	Rs 1,08,00,000		Rs 0	Rs 1,08,00,000

In the last scenario, where 8,000 units are produced and sold, both variable and absorption costing report the same net income because inventory levels are unchanged. This chapter's appendix describes how the choice of variable costing or absorption costing affects the breakeven quantity of sales when inventory levels are allowed to vary.

Comparing Income Statements for Three Years

To get a more-comprehensive view of the effects of variable costing and absorption costing, Stassen's management accountants prepare income statements for three years of operations, starting with 2012.

In both 2013 and 2014, Stassen has a production-volume variance because actual telescope production differs from the budgeted level of production of 8,000 units per year used to calculate budgeted fixed manufacturing cost per unit. The actual quantities sold for 2013 and 2014 are the same as the sales quantities budgeted for these respective years, which are given in units in the following table:

	E	F	G	H
1		**2012**	**2013**	**2014**
2	Beginning inventory	0	2,000	500
3	Production	8,000	5,000	10,000
4	Sales	6,000	6,500	7,500
5	Ending inventory	2,000	500	3,000

All other 2012 data given earlier for Stassen also apply for 2013 and 2014.

Exhibit 9-2 presents the income statement under variable costing in Panel A and the income statement under absorption costing in Panel B for 2012, 2013, and 2014. As you study Exhibit 9-2, note that the 2012 columns in both Panels A and B show the same figures as Exhibit 9-1. The 2013 and 2014 columns are similar to 2012 *except for the production-volume variance line item under absorption costing in Panel B*. Keep in mind the following points about absorption costing as you study Panel B of Exhibit 9-2:

1. The Rs 1,350 fixed manufacturing cost rate is based on the budgeted denominator capacity level of 8,000 units in 2012, 2013, and 2014 (Rs 1,08,00,000 ÷ 8,000 units = Rs 1,350 per unit). Whenever production—that's the quantity produced, not the quantity sold—deviates from the denominator level, there will be a production-volume variance. The amount of Stassen's production-volume variance is determined by multiplying Rs 1,350 per unit by the difference between the actual level of production and the denominator level.

   In 2013, production was 5,000 units, 3,000 lower than the denominator level of 8,000 units. The result is an unfavorable production-volume variance of Rs 40,50,000 (Rs 1,350 per unit × 3,000 units). The year 2014 has a favorable production-volume

Exhibit 9-2 Comparison of Variable Costing and Absorption Costing for Stassen Company: Telescope Product-Line Income Statements for 2012, 2013, and 2014

File Edit View Insert Format Tools Data Window Help

	A	B	C	D	E	F	G
1	**Panel A: VARIABLE COSTING**						
2		**2012**		**2013**		**2014**	
3	Revenues: Rs 10,000 x 6,000; 6,500; 7,500 units		Rs 6,00,00,000		Rs 6,50,00,000		Rs 7,50,00,000
4	Variable cost of goods sold:						
5	Beginning inventory: Rs 2,000 x 0; 2,000; 500 units	Rs 0		Rs 40,00,000		Rs 10,00,000	
6	Variable manufacturing costs: Rs 2,000 x 8,000; 5,000; 10,000 units	1,60,00,000		1,00,00,000		2,00,00,000	
7	Cost of goods available for sale	1,60,00,000		1,40,00,000		2,10,00,000	
8	Deduct ending inventory: Rs 2,000 x 2,000; 500; 3,000 units	(40,00,000)		10,00,000		(60,00,000)	
9	Variable cost of goods sold		1,20,00,000		1,30,00,000		1,50,00,000
10	Variable marketing costs: Rs 1,850 x 6,000; 6,500; 7,500 units		1,11,00,000		1,20,25,000		1,38,75,000
11	Contribution margin		3,69,00,000		3,99,75,000		4,61,25,000
12	Fixed manufacturing costs		1,08,00,000		1,08,00,000		1,08,00,000
13	Fixed marketing costs		1,38,00,000		1,38,00,000		1,38,00,000
14	Operating income		Rs 1,23,00,000		Rs 1,53,75,000		Rs 2,15,25,000
15							
16	**Panel B: ABSORPTION COSTING**						
17		**2012**		**2013**		**2014**	
18	Revenues: Rs 10,000 x 6,000; 6,500; 7,500 units		Rs 6,00,00,000		Rs 6,50,00,000		Rs 7,50,00,000
19	Cost of goods sold:						
20	Beginning inventory: Rs 3,350 x 0; 2,000; 500 units	Rs 0		Rs 67,00,000		Rs 16,75,000	
21	Variable manufacturing costs: Rs 2,000 x 8,000; 5,000; 10,000 units	1,60,00,000		1,00,00,000		2,00,00,000	
22	Allocated fixed manufacturing costs: Rs 1,350 x 8,000; 5,000; 10,000 units	1,08,00,000		67,50,000		1,35,00,000	
23	Cost of goods available for sale	2,68,00,000		2,34,50,000		3,51,75,000	
24	Deduct ending inventory: Rs 3,350 x 2,000; 500; 3,000 units	(67,00,000)		(16,75,000)		(1,00,50,000)	
25	Adjustment for production-volume variance[a]	0		40,50,000	U	(27,00,000)	F
26	Cost of goods sold		2,01,00,000		2,58,25,000		2,24,25,000
27	Gross Margin		3,99,00,000		3,91,75,000		5,25,75,000
28	Variable marketing costs: Rs 1,850 x 6,000; 6,500; 7,500 units		1,11,00,000		1,20,25,000		1,38,75,000
29	Fixed marketing costs		1,38,00,000		1,38,00,000		1,38,00,000
30	Operating Income		Rs 1,50,00,000		Rs 1,33,50,000		Rs 2,49,00,000
31							
32	[a]Production-volume variance = Budgeted fixed manufacturing costs - Fixed manufacturing overhead allocated using budgeted cost per output unit allowed for actual output produced (Panel B, line 22)						
33	2012: Rs 1,08,00,000 – (Rs 1,350 x 8,000) = Rs 1,08,00,000 - Rs 1,08,00,000 = Rs 0						
34	2013: Rs 1,08,00,000 – (Rs 1,350 x 5,000) = Rs 1,08,00,000 - Rs 67,50,000 = Rs 40,50,000 U						
35	2012: Rs 1,08,00,000 – (Rs 1,350 x 10,000) = Rs 1,08,00,000 - Rs 1,35,00,000 = (Rs 27,00,000) F						
36							
37	Production volume variance can also be calculated as:						
38	Fixed manufacturing cost per unit x (Denominator level - Actual output units produced)						
39	2012: Rs 1,350 x (8,000 – 8,000) units = Rs 1,350 x 0 = Rs 0						
40	2013: Rs 1,350 x (8,000 – 5,000) units = Rs 1,350 x 3,000 = Rs 40,50,000 U						
41	2014: Rs 1,350 x (8,000 – 10,000) units = Rs 1,350 x (2,000) = (Rs 27,00,000) F						

variance of Rs 27,00,000 (Rs 1,350 per unit × 2,000 units), due to production of 10,000 units, which exceeds the denominator level of 8,000 units.

Recall how standard costing works under absorption costing. Each time a unit is manufactured, Rs 1,350 of fixed manufacturing costs is included in the cost of goods manufactured and available for sale. In 2013, when 5,000 units are manufactured, Rs 67,50,000 (Rs 1,350 per unit × 5,000 units) of fixed manufacturing costs is included in the cost of goods available for sale (see Exhibit 9-2, Panel B, line 22). Total fixed manufacturing costs for 2013 are Rs 1,08,00,000. The production-volume variance of Rs 40,50,000 U equals the difference between Rs 1,08,00,000 and Rs 67,50,000. In Panel B, note how, for each year, the fixed manufacturing costs included in the cost of goods available for sale plus the production-volume variance always equals Rs 1,08,00,000.

2. The production-volume variance, which relates only to fixed manufacturing overhead, exists under absorption costing but not under variable costing. That's because

under variable costing, fixed manufacturing costs of Rs 1,08,00,000 are always treated as an expense of the period, regardless of the level of production (and sales).

Here's a summary (using information from Exhibit 9-2) of the operating-income differences for Stassen Company during the 2012 to 2014 period:

	2012	2013	2014
1. Absorption-costing operating income	Rs 1,50,00,000	Rs 1,33,50,000	Rs 2,49,00,000
2. Variable-costing operating income	1,23,00,000	1,53,75,000	2,15,25,000
3. Difference: (1) – (2)	27,00,000	(20,25,000)	33,75,000

The sizeable differences in the preceding table illustrate why managers whose performance is measured by reported income are concerned about the choice between variable costing and absorption costing.

Why do variable costing and absorption costing usually report different operating income numbers? In general, if inventory increases during an accounting period, less operating income will be reported under variable costing than absorption costing. Conversely, if inventory decreases, more operating income will be reported under variable costing than absorption costing. The difference in reported operating income is due solely to (a) moving fixed manufacturing costs into inventories as inventories increase and (b) moving fixed manufacturing costs out of inventories as inventories decrease.

The difference between operating income under absorption costing and variable costing can be computed by formula 1, which focuses on fixed manufacturing costs in beginning inventory and ending inventory:

File Edit View Insert Format Tools Data Window Help

	A	B	C	D	E	F	G	H
1	Formula 1							
2						Fixed manufacturing		Fixed manufacturing
3		Absorption-costing	-	Variable-costing	=	costs in ending inventory	-	costs in beginning inventory
4		operating income		operation income		under absorption costing		under absorption costing
5	2009	Rs 1,50,00,000	-	Rs 1,23,00,000	=	(Rs 1350 x 2,000 units)	-	(Rs 1350 x 0 units)
6				Rs 27,00,000	=	Rs 27,00,000		
7								
8	2010	Rs 1,33,50,000	-	Rs 1,53,75,000	=	(Rs 1350 x 500 units)	-	(Rs 1350 x 2,000 units)
9				Rs 20,25,000		(Rs 20,25,000)		
10								
11	2011	Rs 2,49,00,000	-	Rs 2,15,25,000	=	(Rs 1350 x 3,000 units)	-	(Rs 1350 x 500 units)
12				Rs 33,75,000	=	Rs 33,75,000		

Fixed manufacturing costs in ending inventory are deferred to a future period under absorption costing. For example, Rs 27,00,000 of fixed · anufacturing overhead is deferred to 2013 at December 31, 2011. Under variable cos..ng, all Rs 1,08,00,000 of fixed manufacturing costs are treated as an expense of 2012.

Recall that,

$$\text{Beginning inventory} + \text{Cost of goods manufactured} = \text{Cost of goods sold} + \text{Ending Inventory}$$

Therefore, instead of focusing on fixed manufacturing costs in ending and beginning inventory, we could alternatively focus on fixed manufacturing costs in units produced and units sold. This approach highlights how fixed manufacturing costs move between units produced and units sold during the fiscal year.

File Edit View Insert Format Tools Data Window Help

	A	B	C	D	E	F	G	H
16	Formula 2							
17						Fixed manufacturing costs		Fixed manufacturing costs
18		Absorption-costing	-	Variable-costing	=	inventoried in units produced	-	in cost of goods sold
19		operating income		operation income		under absorption costing		under absorption costing
20	**2012**	Rs 1,50,00,000	-	Rs 1,23,00,000	=	(Rs 1,350 x 8,000 units)	-	(Rs 1,350 x 6,000 units)
21				Rs 27,00,000	=	Rs 27,00,000		
22								
23	**2013**	Rs 1,33,50,000	-	Rs 1,53,75,000	=	(Rs1,350 x 5,000 units)	-	(Rs 1,350 x 6,500 units)
24				(Rs 20,25,000)	=	(Rs 20,25,000)		
25								
26	**2014**	Rs 2,49,00,000	-	Rs 2,15,25,000	=	(Rs 1,350 x 10,000 units)	-	(Rs 1,350 x 7,500 units)
27				Rs 33,75,000	=	Rs 33,75,000		

How does income differ under variable and absorption costing?

Managers face increasing pressure to reduce inventory levels. Some companies are achieving steep reductions in inventory levels using policies such as just-in-time production—a production system under which products are manufactured only when needed. Formula 1 illustrates that, as Stassen reduces its inventory levels, operating income differences between absorption costing and variable costing become immaterial. Consider, for example, the formula for 2012. If instead of 2,000 units in ending inventory, Stassen had only 2 units in ending inventory, the difference between absorption-costing operating income and variable-costing operating income would drop from Rs 27,00,000 to Rs 2,700 [(Rs 1,350 per unit × 2) – (Rs 1,350 per unit × 0)].

Variable Costing and the Effect of Sales and Production on Operating Income

Given a constant contribution margin per unit and constant fixed costs, the period-to-period change in operating income under variable costing is *driven solely by changes in the quantity of units actually sold*. Consider the variable-costing operating income of Stassen in (a) 2013 versus 2012 and (b) 2014 versus 2013. Recall that:

$$\text{Contribution margin per unit} = \text{Selling price} - \text{Variable manufacturing cost per unit} - \text{Variable marketing cost per unit}$$

$$= \text{Rs } 10{,}000 \text{ per unit} - \text{Rs } 2{,}000 \text{ per unit} - \text{Rs } 1{,}850 \text{ per unit}$$

$$= \text{Rs } 6{,}150 \text{ per unit}$$

$$\text{Change in variable-costing operating income} = \text{Contribution margin per unit} \times \text{Change in quantity of units sold}$$

(a) 2013 vs. 2012: Rs 1,53,75,000 – Rs 1,23,00,000 = Rs 6,150 per unit × (6,500 units – 6,000 units)
Rs 30,75,000 = Rs 30,75,000

(b) 2014 vs. 2013: Rs 2,15,25,000 – Rs 1,53,75,000 = Rs 6,150 per unit × (7,500 units – 6,500 units)
Rs 61,50,000 = Rs 6,150

Under variable costing, Stassen managers cannot increase operating income by "producing for inventory." Why not? Because, as you can see from the preceding computations, when using variable costing, only the quantity of units sold drives operating income. We'll explain later in this chapter that absorption costing enables managers to increase operating income by increasing the unit level of sales, as well as by producing more units. Before you proceed to the next section, make sure that you examine Exhibit 9-3 for a detailed comparison of the differences between variable costing and absorption costing.

Exhibit 9-3 Comparative Income Effects of Variable Costing and Absorption Costing

Question	Variable Costing	Absorption Costing	Comment
Are fixed manufacturing costs inventoried?	No	Yes	Basic theoretical question of when these costs should be expensed
Is there a production-volume variance?	No	Yes	Choice of denominator level affects measurement of operating income under absorption costing only
Are classifications between variable and fixed costs routinely made?	Yes	Infrequently	Absorption costing can be easily modified to obtain subclassifications for variable and fixed costs, if desired (for example, see Exhibit 9-1, Panel B)
How do changes in unit inventory levels affect operating income?[a]			Differences are attributable to the timing of when fixed manufacturing costs are expensed
Production = sales	Equal	Equal	
Production > sales	Lower[b]	Higher[c]	
Production < sales	Higher	Lower	
What are the effects on cost-volume-profit relationship (for a given level of fixed costs and a given contribution margin per unit)?	Driven by unit level of sales	Driven by (a) unit level of sales, (b) unit level of production, and (c) chosen denominator level	Management control benefit: Effects of changes in production level on operating income are easier to understand under variable costing

[a]Assuming that all manufacturing variances are written off as period costs, that no change occurs in work-in-process inventory, and no change occurs in the budgeted fixed manufacturing cost rate between accounting periods.

[b]That is, lower operating income than under absorption costing.

[c]That is, higher operating income than under variable costing.

Absorption Costing and Performance Measures

Learning Objective 

Understand how absorption costing can provide undesirable incentives for managers to build up inventory

. . . producing more units for inventory absorbs fixed manufacturing costs and increases operating income

Absorption costing is the required inventory method for external reporting in most countries. Many companies use absorption costing for internal accounting as well. Why? Because it is cost-effective and less confusing to managers to use one common method of inventory costing for both external and internal reporting and performance evaluation. A common method of inventory costing can also help prevent managers from taking actions that make their performance measure look good but that hurt the income they report to shareholders. Another advantage of absorption costing is that it measures the cost of all manufacturing resources, whether variable or fixed, necessary to produce inventory. Many companies use inventory costing information for long-run decisions such as pricing and choosing a product mix. For these long-run decisions, inventory costs should include both variable *and* fixed costs.

One problem with absorption costing is that it enables a manager to increase operating income in a specific period by increasing production—even if there is no customer demand for the additional production! The chapter opener illustrated this effect—Intel's margins and income were higher because the firm produced more ending inventory. Stassen's managers may be tempted to do this to get higher bonuses based on absorption-costing operating income. Generally, higher operating income also has a positive effect on stock price, which increases managers' stock-based compensation.

To reduce the undesirable incentives to build up inventories that absorption costing can create, a number of companies use variable costing for internal reporting. Variable costing focuses attention on distinguishing variable manufacturing costs from fixed manufacturing costs. This distinction is important for short-run decision making (as in cost-volume-profit analysis in Chapter 3 and in planning and control in Chapters 6, 7, and 8).

Companies that use both methods for internal reporting—variable costing for short-run decisions and performance evaluation and absorption costing for long-run decisions—benefit from the different advantages of both. In the next section, we explore in more detail the challenges that arise from absorption costing.

Undesirable Buildup of Inventories

Recall that one motivation for an undesirable buildup of inventories could be because a manager's bonus is based on reported absorption-costing operating income. Assume that Stassen's managers have such a bonus plan. Exhibit 9-4 shows how Stassen's absorption-costing operating income for 2013 changes as the production level changes. This exhibit assumes that the production-volume variance is written off to cost of goods sold at the end of each year. Beginning inventory of 2,000 units and sales of 6,500 units for 2010 are unchanged from the case shown in Exhibit 9-2. *As you review Exhibit 9-4, keep in mind that the computations are basically the same as those in Exhibit 9-2.*

Exhibit 9-4 shows that production of 4,500 units meets the 2013 sales budget of 6,500 units (2,000 units from beginning inventory+ 4,500 units produced). Operating income at this production level is Rs 1,26,75,000. By producing more than 4,500 units, commonly referred to as *producing for inventory*, Stassen increases absorption-costing operating income. Each additional unit in 2013 ending inventory will increase operating income by Rs 1,350. For example, if 8,000 units are produced, ending inventory will be 3,500 units and operating income increases to Rs 1,74,00,000. This amount is Rs 47,25,000 more than he operating income with zero ending inventory (Rs 1,74,00,000 – Rs1,26,75,000, or 3,500 units × Rs 1,350 per unit = Rs 47,25,000). Under absorption costing, the company, by producing 3,500 units for inventory, includes Rs 47,25,000 of fixed manufacturing costs in finished goods inventory, so they are not expensed in 2013.

Can top management implement checks and balances that limit managers from producing for inventory under absorption costing? The answer is yes, as we will see in the next section, but producing for inventory cannot be completely prevented. There are many subtle ways a manager can produce for inventory that, if done to a limited extent, may not be easy to detect. For example,

- A plant manager may switch to manufacturing products that absorb the highest amount of fixed manufacturing costs, regardless of the customer demand for these products (called "cherry picking" the production line). Production of items that absorb the least or lower fixed manufacturing costs may be delayed, resulting in failure to meet promised customer delivery dates (which, over time, can result in unhappy customers).

Exhibit 9-4 Effect on Absorption-Costing Operating Income of Different Production Levels for Stassen Company: Telescope Product-Line Income Statement for 2013 at Sales of 6,500 Units

File Edit View Insert Format Tools Data Window Help

	A	B	C	D	E	F	G	H	I	J	K
1	**Unit Data**										
2	Beginning inventory	2,000		2,000		2,000		2,000		2,000	
3	Production	4,500		5,000		6,500		8,000		9,000	
4	Goods available for sale	6,500		7,000		8,500		10,000		11,000	
5	Sales	6,500		6,500		6,500		6,500		6,500	
6	Ending inventory	0		500		2,000		3,500		4,500	
7											
8	**Income Statement**										
9	Revenues	Rs 6,50,00,000		Rs 6,50,00,000		Rs 6,50,00,000		Rs 6,50,00,000		Rs 6,50,00,000	
10	Cost of goods sold:										
11	Beginning inventory (Rs 3,350 x 2,000)	67,00,000		67,00,000		67,00,000		67,00,000		67,00,000	
12	Variable manufacturing costs: Rs 2,000 x production	Rs 90,00,000		Rs 1,00,00,000		Rs 1,30,00,000		Rs 1,60,00,000		Rs 1,80,00,000	
13	Allocated fixed manufacturing costs: Rs 1,350 x production	60,75,000		67,50,000		87,75,000		1,08,00,000		1,21,50,000	
14	Cost of goods available for sale	2,17,75,000		2,34,50,000		2,84,75,000		3,35,00,000		3,68,50,000	
15	Deduct ending inventory: Rs 3,350 x ending inventory	0		(16,75,000)		(67,00,000)		(1,17,25,000)		1,50,75,000	
16	Adjustment for production-volume variance[a]	47,25,000U		40,50,000U		20,25,000U		0		13,50,000F	
17	Cost of goods sold	2,65,00,000		2,58,25,000		2,38,00,000		2,17,75,000		2,04,25,000	
18	Gross Margin	3,85,00,000		3,91,75,000		4,12,00,000		4,32,25,000		4,45,75,000	
19	Marketing costs: (Rs 1,38,00,000 + Rs 1,850 per unit x 6,500 units sold)	2,58,25,000		2,58,25,000		2,58,25,000		2,58,25,000		2,58,25,000	
20	Operating Income	Rs 1,26,75,000		Rs 1,33,50,000		Rs 1,53,75,000		Rs 1,74,00,000		Rs 1,87,50,000	
21											
22	[a]Production-volume variance = Budgeted fixed manufacturing costs - Allocated fixed manufacturing costs (Income Statement, line 13)										
23	At production of 4,500 units: Rs 1,08,00,000 – Rs 60,75,000 = Rs 47,25,000 U										
24	At production of 5,000 units: Rs 1,08,00,000 – Rs 67,50,000 = Rs 40,50,000 U										
25	At production of 6,500 units: Rs 1,08,00,000 – Rs 87,75,000 = Rs 20,25,000 U										
26	At production of 8,000 units: Rs 1,08,00,000 – Rs 1,08,00,000 = Rs 0										
27	At production of 9,000 units: Rs 1,08,00,000 – Rs 1,21,50,000 = (Rs 13,50,000) F										

- A plant manager may accept a particular order to increase production, even though another plant in the same company is better suited to handle that order.
- To increase production, a manager may defer maintenance beyond the current period. Although operating income in this period may increase as a result, future operating income could decrease by a larger amount if repair costs increase and equipment becomes less efficient.

The example in Exhibit 9-4 focuses on only one year (2013). A Stassen manager who built up ending inventories of telescopes to 4,500 units in 2013 would have to further increase ending inventories in 2014 to increase that year's operating income by producing for inventory. There are limits to how much inventory levels can be increased over time (because of physical constraints on storage space and management supervision and controls). Such limits reduce the likelihood of incurring some of absorption costing's undesirable effects.

Proposals for Revising Performance Evaluation

Top management, with help from the controller and management accountants, can take several steps to reduce the undesirable effects of absorption costing.

- Focus on careful budgeting and inventory planning to reduce management's freedom to build up excess inventory. For example, the budgeted monthly balance sheets have estimates of the rupee amount of inventories. If actual inventories exceed these rupee amounts, top management can investigate the inventory buildups.
- Incorporate a carrying charge for inventory in the internal accounting system. For example, the company could assess an inventory carrying charge of 1% per month on the investment tied up in inventory and for spoilage and obsolescence when it evaluates a manager's performance. An increasing number of companies are beginning to adopt this inventory carrying charge.
- Change the period used to evaluate performance. Critics of absorption costing give examples in which managers take actions that maximize quarterly or annual income at the potential expense of long-run income. When their performance is evaluated over a three- to five-year period, managers will be less tempted to produce for inventory.
- Include nonfinancial as well as financial variables in the measures used to evaluate performance (see the Concepts in Action feature later in this chapter). Examples of nonfinancial measures that can be used to monitor the performance of Stassen's managers in 2014 are:

$$\text{(a)}\quad \frac{\text{Ending inventory in units in 2014}}{\text{Beginning inventory in units in 2014}} = \frac{3{,}000}{500} = 6$$

$$\text{(b)}\quad \frac{\text{Units produced in 2014}}{\text{Units sold in 2014}} = \frac{10{,}000}{7{,}500} = 1.33$$

Top management would want to see production equal to sales and relatively stable levels of inventory. Companies that manufacture or sell several products could report these two measures for each of the products they manufacture and sell.

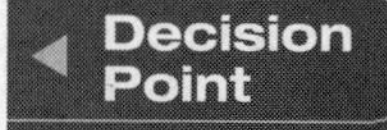

Decision Point

Why might managers build up finished goods inventory if they use absorption costing?

Learning Objective 4

Differentiate throughput costing

. . . direct material costs inventoried from variable costing

. . . variable manufacturing costs inventoried and absorption costing

. . . variable and fixed manufacturing costs inventoried

Comparing Inventory Costing Methods

Before we begin our discussion of capacity, we will look at *throughput costing*, a variation of variable costing, and compare the various costing methods.

Throughput Costing

Some managers maintain that even variable costing promotes an excessive amount of costs being inventoried. They argue that only direct materials are "truly variable." **Throughput costing,** which also is called **super-variable costing** because it is an extreme form of variable

Exhibit 9-5

Throughput Costing for Stassen Company: Telescope Product-Line Income Statements for 2012, 2013, and 2014

	A	B	C	D
1		2012	2013	2014
2	Revenues: Rs 10,000 x 6,000; 6,500; 7,500 units	Rs 6,00,00,000	Rs 6,50,00,000	Rs 7,50,00,000
3	Direct material cost of goods sold			
4	Beginning inventory: Rs 1,100 x 0; 2,000; 500 units	Rs 0	Rs 22,00,000	Rs 5,50,000
5	Direct materials: Rs 1,100 x 8,000; 5,000; 10,000 units	88,00,000	55,00,000	1,10,00,000
6	Cost of goods available for sale	88,00,000	77,00,000	1,15,50,000
7	Deduct ending inventory: Rs 1,100 x 2,000; 500; 3,000 units	(22,00,000)	(5,50,000)	(33,00,000)
8	Direct material cost of goods sold	66,00,000	71,50,000	82,50,000
9	Throughput contribution[a]	5,34,00,000	5,78,50,000	6,67,50,000
10	Manufacturing costs (other than direct materials)[b]	1,80,00,000	1,53,00,000	1,98,00,000
11	Marketing costs[c]	2,49,00,000	2,58,25,000	2,76,75,000
12	Operating income	1,05,00,000	Rs 1,67,25,000	Rs 1,92,75,000
13				
14	[a]Throughput contribution equals revenues minus all direct material cost of goods sold			
15	[b]Fixed manuf. costs + [(variable manuf. labor + variable manuf. overhead) x units produced];			
16	Rs 1,08,00,000 + [(Rs 400 + Rs 500) x 8,000; 5,000; 10,000 units]			
17	[c]Fixed marketing costs + (variable marketing cost per unit x units sold);			
18	Rs 1,38,00,000 + (Rs 1,850 x 6,000; 6,500; 7,500 units)			

costing, is a method of inventory costing in which only direct material costs are included as inventoriable costs. All other costs are costs of the period in which they are incurred. In particular, variable direct manufacturing labor costs and variable manufacturing overhead costs are regarded as period costs and are deducted as expenses of the period.

Exhibit 9-5 is the throughput-costing income statement for Stassen Company for 2012, 2013, and 2014. *Throughput contribution* equals revenues minus all direct material cost of the goods sold. Compare the operating income amounts reported in Exhibit 9-5 with those for absorption costing and variable costing:

	2012	2013	2014
Absorption-costing operating income	Rs 1,50,00,000	Rs 1,33,50,000	Rs 2,49,00,000
Variable-costing operating income	Rs 1,23,00,000	Rs 1,53,75,000	Rs 2,15,25,000
Throughput-costing operating income	Rs 1,05,00,000	Rs 1,67,25,000	Rs 1,92,75,000

Decision Point

How does throughput costing differ from variable costing and absorption costing?

Only the Rs 1,100 direct material cost per unit is inventoriable under throughput costing, compared with Rs 3,350 per unit for absorption costing and Rs 2,000 per unit for variable costing. When the production quantity exceeds sales as in 2012 and 2014, throughput costing results in the largest amount of expenses in the current period's income statement. Advocates of throughput costing say it provides less incentive to produce for inventory than either variable costing or, especially, absorption costing. Throughput costing is a more recent phenomenon in comparison with variable costing and absorption costing and has avid supporters, but so far it has not been widely adopted.[2]

A Comparison of Alternative Inventory-Costing Methods

Variable costing and absorption costing (as well as throughput costing) may be combined with actual, normal, or standard costing. Exhibit 9-6 compares product costing under six alternative inventory-costing systems.

[2] See E. Goldratt, *The Theory of Constraints* (New York: North River Press, 1990); E. Noreen, D. Smith, and J. Mackey, *The Theory of Constraints and Its Implications for Management Accounting* (New York: North River Press, 1995).

Exhibit 9-6 Comparison of Alternative Inventory-Costing Systems

			Actual Costing	Normal Costing	Standard Costing
Absorption Costing	Variable Costing	Variable Direct Manufacturing Cost	Actual prices × Actual quantity of inputs used	Actual prices × Actual quantity of inputs used	Standard prices × Standard quantity of inputs allowed for actual output achieved
		Variable Manufacturing Overhead Costs	Actual variable overhead rates × Actual quantity of cost-allocation bases used	Budgeted variable overhead rates × Actual quantity of cost-allocation bases used	Standard variable overhead rates × Standard quantity of cost-allocation bases allowed for actual output achieved
		Fixed Direct Manufacturing Costs	Actual prices × Actual quantity of inputs used	Actual prices × Ac quantity of inputs used	Standard prices × Standard quantity of inputs allowed for actual output achieved
		Fixed Manufacturing Overhead Costs	Actual fixed overhead rates × Actual quantity of cost-allocation bases used	Budgeted fixed overhead rates × Actual quantity of cost-allocation bases used	Standard fixed overhead rates × Standard quantity of cost-allocation bases allowed for actual output achieved

Variable Costing	Absorption Costing
Actual costing	Actual costing
Standard costing	Standard costing
Normal costing	Normal costing

Variable costing has been controversial among accountants—not because of disagreement about the need to delineate between variable and fixed costs for internal planning and control, but as it pertains to *external reporting*. Accountants who favor variable costing for external reporting maintain that the fixed portion of manufacturing costs is more closely related to the capacity to produce than to the actual production of specific units. Hence, fixed costs should be expensed, not inventoried.

Accountants who support absorption costing for *external reporting* maintain that inventories should carry a fixed-manufacturing-cost component. Why? Because both variable manufacturing costs and fixed manufacturing costs are necessary to produce goods. Therefore, both types of costs should be inventoried in order to match all manufacturing costs to revenues, regardless of their different behavior patterns. For external reporting to shareholders, companies around the globe tend to follow the generally accepted accounting principle that all manufacturing costs are inventoriable.

Similarly, for tax reporting in the United States, direct production costs, as well as fixed and variable indirect production costs, must be taken into account in the computation of inventoriable costs in accordance with the "full absorption" method of inventory costing. Indirect production costs include items such as rent, utilities, maintenance, repair expenses, indirect materials, and indirect labor. For other indirect cost categories (including depreciation, insurance, taxes, officers' salaries, factory administrative expenses, and strike-related costs), the portion of the cost that is "incident to and necessary for production or manufacturing operations or processes" is inventoriable for tax purposes if (and only if) it is treated as inventoriable for the purposes of financial reporting. Accordingly, costs must often be allocated between those portions related to manufacturing activities and those not related to manufacturing.[3]

[3] Details regarding tax rules can be found in Section 1.471-11 of the U.S. Internal Revenue Code: Inventories of Manufacturers (see http://ecfr.gpoaccess.gov). Recall from Chapter 2 that costs not related to production, such as marketing, distribution, or research expenses, are treated as period expenses for financial reporting. Under U.S. tax rules, a firm can still consider these costs as inventoriable for tax purposes provided that it does so consistently.

DENOMINATOR-LEVEL CAPACITY CONCEPTS AND FIXED-COST CAPACITY ANALYSIS

Learning Objective 5

Describe the various capacity concepts that can be used in absorption costing

. . . theoretical capacity, practical capacity, normal capacity utilization, and master-budget capacity utilization

We have seen that the difference between variable and absorption costing methods arises solely from the treatment of fixed manufacturing costs. Spending on fixed manufacturing costs enables firms to obtain the scale or capacity needed to satisfy the expected demand from customers. Determining the "right" level of capacity is one of the most strategic and most difficult decisions managers face. Having too much capacity to produce relative to that needed to meet market demand means incurring some costs of unused capacity. Having too little capacity to produce means that demand from some customers may be unfilled. These customers may go to other sources of supply and never return. Therefore, both managers and accountants should have a clear understanding of the issues that arise with capacity costs.

We start by analysing a key question in absorption costing: Given a level of spending on fixed manufacturing costs, what capacity level should be used to compute the fixed manufacturing cost per unit produced? We then study the broader question of how a firm should decide on its level of capacity investment.

Absorption Costing and Alternative Denominator-Level Capacity Concepts

Earlier chapters, especially Chapters 4, 5, and 8, have highlighted how normal costing and standard costing report costs in an ongoing timely manner throughout a fiscal year. The choice of the capacity level used to allocate budgeted fixed manufacturing costs to products can greatly affect the operating income reported under normal costing or standard costing and the product-cost information available to managers.

Consider the Stassen Company example again. Recall that the annual fixed manufacturing costs of the production facility are Rs 1,08,00,000. Stassen currently uses absorption costing with standard costs for external reporting purposes, and it calculates its budgeted fixed manufacturing rate on a per unit basis. We will now examine four different capacity levels used as the denominator to compute the budgeted fixed manufacturing cost rate: theoretical capacity, practical capacity, normal capacity utilization, and master-budget capacity utilization.

Theoretical Capacity and Practical Capacity

In business and accounting, *capacity* ordinarily means a "constraint," an "upper limit." **Theoretical capacity** is the level of capacity based on producing at full efficiency all the time. Stassen can produce 25 units per shift when the production lines are operating at maximum speed. If we assume 360 days per year, the theoretical annual capacity for two shifts per day is:

25 units per shift × 2 shifts per day × 360 days = 18,000 units

Theoretical capacity is theoretical in the sense that it does not allow for any plant maintenance, shutdown periods, interruptions because of downtime on the assembly lines, or any other factors. Theoretical capacity represents an ideal goal of capacity utilization. Theoretical capacity levels are unattainable in the real world but they provide a target to which a company can aspire.

Practical capacity is the level of capacity that reduces theoretical capacity by considering unavoidable operating interruptions, such as scheduled maintenance time, shutdowns for holidays, and so on. Assume that practical capacity is the practical production rate of 20 units per shift (as opposed to 25 units per shift under theoretical capacity) for two shifts per day for 300 days a year (as distinguished from 360 days a year under theoretical capacity). The practical annual capacity is:

25 units per shift × 2 shifts per day × 300 days = 12,000 units

Engineering and human resource factors are both important when estimating theoretical or practical capacity. Engineers at the Stassen facility can provide input on the technical capabilities of machines for cutting and polishing lenses. Human-safety factors, such as increased injury risk when the line operates at faster speeds, are also necessary considerations in estimating practical capacity. With difficulty, practical capacity is attainable.

Normal Capacity Utilization and Master-Budget Capacity Utilization

Both theoretical capacity and practical capacity measure capacity levels in terms of what a plant can *supply*—available capacity. In contrast, normal capacity utilization and master-budget capacity utilization measure capacity levels in terms of *demand* for the output of the plant—the amount of available capacity that the plant expects to use based on the demand for its products. In many cases, budgeted demand is well below production capacity available.

Normal capacity utilization is the level of capacity utilization that satisfies average customer demand over a period (say, two to three years) that includes seasonal, cyclical, and trend factors. **Master-budget capacity utilization** is the level of capacity utilization that managers expect for the current budget period, which is typically one year. These two capacity-utilization levels can differ—for example, when an industry, such as automobiles or semiconductors, has cyclical periods of high and low demand or when management believes that budgeted production for the coming period is not representative of long-run demand.

Consider Stassen's master budget for 2012, based on production of 8,000 telescopes per year. Despite using this master-budget capacity-utilization level of 8,000 telescopes for 2012, top management believes that over the next three years the normal (average) annual production level will be 10,000 telescopes. They view 2012's budgeted production level of 8,000 telescopes to be "abnormally" low. That's because a major competitor has been sharply reducing its selling price and spending large amounts on advertising. Stassen expects that the competitor's lower price and advertising blitz will not be a long-run phenomenon and that, by 2014 and beyond, Stassen's production and sales will be higher.

Effect on Budgeted Fixed Manufacturing Cost Rate

We now illustrate how each of these four denominator levels affects the budgeted fixed manufacturing cost rate. Stassen has budgeted (standard) fixed manufacturing overhead costs of Rs 1,08,00,000 for 2012. This lump-sum is incurred to provide the capacity to produce telescopes. The amount includes, among other costs, leasing costs for the facility and the compensation of the facility managers. The budgeted fixed manufacturing cost rates for 2012 for each of the four capacity-level concepts are:

	A	B	C	D
1		Budgeted Fixed	Budget	Budgeted Fixed
2	Denominator-Level	Manufacturing	Capacity Level	Manufacturing
3	Capacity Concept	Costs per Year	(in units)	Cost per Unit
4	(1)	(2)	(3)	(4) = (2) / (3)
5	Theoretical capacity	Rs 1,08,00,000	18,000	Rs 600
6	Practical capacity	Rs 1,08,00,000	12,000	Rs 900
7	Normal capacity utilization	Rs 1,08,00,000	10,000	Rs 1,080
8	Master-budget capacity utilization	Rs 1,08,00,000	8,000	Rs 1,350

The significant difference in cost rates (from Rs 600 to Rs 1,350) arises because of large differences in budgeted capacity levels under the different capacity concepts.

Budgeted (standard) variable manufacturing cost is Rs 2,000 per unit. The total budgeted (standard) manufacturing cost per unit for alternative capacity-level concepts is:

	A	B	C	D
1		Budgeted Variable	Budgeted Fixed	Budgeted Total
2	Denominator-Level	Manufacturing	Manufacturing	Manufacturing
3	Capacity Concept	Cost per Unit	Cost per Unit	Cost per Unit
4	(1)	(2)	(3)	(4) = (2) + (3)
5	Theoretical capacity	Rs 2,000	Rs 600	Rs 2,600
6	Practical capacity	Rs 2,000	Rs 900	Rs 2,900
7	Normal capacity utilization	Rs 2,000	Rs 1,080	Rs 3,080
8	Master-budget capacity utilization	Rs 2,000	Rs 1,350	Rs 3,350

Decision Point

What are the various capacity levels a company can use to compute the budgeted fixed manufacturing cost rate?

Because different denominator-level capacity concepts yield different budgeted fixed manufacturing costs per unit, Stassen must decide which capacity level to use. Stassen is not required to use the same capacity-level concept, say, for management planning and control, external reporting to shareholders, and income tax purposes.

Choosing a Capacity Level

Learning Objective 

Examine the key factors in choosing a capacity level to compute the budgeted fixed manufacturing cost rate

. . . managers must consider the effect a capacity level has on product costing, capacity management, pricing decisions, and financial statements

As we just saw, at the start of each fiscal year, managers determine different denominator levels for the different capacity concepts and calculate different budgeted fixed manufacturing costs per unit. We now discuss the problems with and effects of different denominator-level choices for different purposes, including (a) product costing and capacity management, (b) pricing, (c) performance evaluation, (d) external reporting, (e) regulatory requirements, and (f) difficulties in forecasting capacity levels.

Product Costing and Capacity Management

Data from normal costing or standard costing are often used in pricing or product-mix decisions. As the Stassen example illustrates, use of theoretical capacity results in an unrealistically small fixed manufacturing cost per unit because it is based on an idealistic and unattainable level of capacity. Theoretical capacity is rarely used to calculate budgeted fixed manufacturing cost per unit because it departs significantly from the real capacity available to a company.

Many companies favor practical capacity as the denominator to calculate budgeted fixed manufacturing cost per unit. Practical capacity in the Stassen example represents the maximum number of units (12,000) that Stassen can reasonably expect to produce per year for the Rs 1,08,00,000 it will spend annually on capacity. If Stassen had consistently planned to produce fewer units, say 6,000 telescopes each year, it would have built a smaller plant and incurred lower costs.

Stassen budgets Rs 900 in fixed manufacturing cost per unit based on the Rs 1,08,00,000 it costs to acquire the capacity to produce 12,000 units. This level of plant capacity is an important strategic decision that managers make well before Stassen uses the capacity and even before Stassen knows how much of the capacity it will actually use. That is, budgeted fixed manufacturing cost of Rs 900 per unit measures the *cost per unit of supplying the capacity*.

Demand for Stassen's telescopes in 2012 is expected to be 8,000 units, which is 4,000 units lower than the practical capacity of 12,000 units. However, the cost of *supplying* the capacity needed to make 12,000 units is still Rs 900 per unit. That's because it costs Stassen Rs 1,08,00,000 per year to acquire the capacity to make 12,000 units. The capacity and its cost are fixed *in the short run*; unlike variable costs, the capacity supplied does not automatically reduce to match the capacity needed in 2013. As a result, not all of the capacity supplied at Rs 900 per unit will be needed or used in 2013. Using practical capacity as the denominator level, managers can subdivide the cost of resources supplied into used and unused components. At the supply cost of Rs 900 per unit, the manufacturing resources that

Stassen will use equal Rs 72,00,000 (Rs 900 per unit × 8,000 units). Manufacturing resources that Stassen will not use are Rs 36,00,000 [Rs 900 per unit × (12,000 − 8,000) units].

Using practical capacity as the denominator level sets the cost of capacity at the cost of supplying the capacity, regardless of the demand for the capacity. Highlighting the cost of capacity acquired but not used directs managers' attention toward managing unused capacity, perhaps by designing new products to fill unused capacity, by leasing unused capacity to others, or by eliminating unused capacity. In contrast, using either of the capacity levels based on the demand for Stassen's telescopes—master-budget capacity utilization or normal capacity utilization—hides the amount of unused capacity. If Stassen had used master-budget capacity utilization as the capacity level, it would have calculated budgeted fixed manufacturing cost per unit as Rs 1,350 (Rs 1,08,00,000 ÷ 8,000 units). This calculation does not use data about practical capacity, so it does not separately identify the cost of unused capacity. Note, however, that the cost of Rs 1,350 per unit includes a charge for unused capacity: it comprises the Rs 900 fixed manufacturing resource that would be used to produce each unit at practical capacity plus the cost of unused capacity allocated to each unit, Rs 450 per unit (Rs 36,00,000 ÷ 8,000 units).

From the perspective of long-run product costing, which cost of capacity should Stassen use for pricing purposes or for benchmarking its product cost structure against competitors: Rs 900 per unit based on practical capacity or Rs 1,350 per unit based on master-budget capacity utilization? Probably the Rs 900 per unit based on practical capacity. Why? Because Rs 900 per unit represents the budgeted cost per unit of only the capacity used to produce the product, and it explicitly excludes the cost of any unused capacity. Stassen's customers will be willing to pay a price that covers the cost of the capacity actually used but will not want to pay for unused capacity that provides no other benefits to them. Customers expect Stassen to manage its unused capacity or to bear the cost of unused capacity, not pass it along to them. Moreover, if Stassen's competitors manage unused capacity more effectively, the cost of capacity in the competitors' cost structures (which guides competitors' pricing decisions) is likely to approach Rs 900. In the next section we show how the use of normal capacity utilization or master-budget capacity utilization can result in setting selling prices that are not competitive.

Pricing Decisions and the Downward Demand Spiral

Learning Objective 

Describe how attempts to recover fixed costs of capacity may lead to price increases and lower demand

. . . this situation is the downward demand spiral, which explains why customers are unwilling to pay for a company's unused capacity

The **downward demand spiral** for a company is the continuing reduction in the demand for its products that occurs when competitor prices are not met; as demand drops further, higher and higher unit costs result in greater reluctance to meet competitors' prices.

The easiest way to understand the downward demand spiral is via an example. Assume Stassen uses master-budget capacity utilization of 8,000 units for product costing in 2012. The resulting manufacturing cost is Rs 3,350 per unit (Rs 2,000 variable manufacturing cost per unit 1 + Rs 1,350 fixed manufacturing cost per unit). Assume that in December 2011, a competitor offers to supply a major customer of Stassen (a customer who was expected to purchase 2,000 units in 2012) telescopes at Rs 3,000 per unit. The Stassen manager, not wanting to show a loss on the account and wanting to recoup all costs in the long run, declines to match the competitor's price. The account is lost. The loss means budgeted fixed manufacturing costs of Rs 1,08,00,000 will be spread over the remaining master-budget volume of 6,000 units at a rate of Rs1,800 per unit (Rs 1,08,00,000 ÷ 6,000 units).

Suppose yet another Stassen customer—who also accounts for 2,000 units of budgeted volume—receives a bid from a competitor at a price of Rs 3,500 per unit. The Stassen manager compares this bid with his revised unit cost of Rs 3,800 (Rs 2,000 + Rs 1,800), declines to match the competition, and the account is lost. Planned output would shrink further to 4,000 units. Budgeted fixed manufacturing cost per unit for the remaining 4,000 telescopes would now be Rs 2,700 (Rs 1,08,00,000 ÷ 4,000 units). The following table shows the effect of spreading fixed manufacturing costs over a shrinking amount of master-budget capacity utilization:

	A	B	C	D
1	Master-Budget		Budgeted Fixed	
2	Capacity Utilization	Budgeted Variable	Manufacturing	Budgeted Total
3	Denominator Level	Manufacturing Cost	Cost per Unit	Manufacturing
4	(Units)	per Unit	[$1,080,000 ÷ (1)]	Cost per Unit
5	(1)	(2)	(3)	(4) = (2) + (3)
6	8,000	Rs 2,000	Rs 1,350	Rs 3,350
7	6,000	Rs 2,000	Rs 1,800	Rs 3,800
8	4,000	Rs 2,000	Rs 2,700	Rs 4,700
9	3,000	Rs 2,000	Rs 3,600	Rs 5,600

Practical capacity, by contrast, is a stable measure. The use of practical capacity as the denominator to calculate budgeted fixed manufacturing cost per unit avoids the recalculation of unit costs when expected demand levels change. That's because the fixed cost rate would be calculated based on *capacity available* rather than *capacity used to meet demand*. Managers who use reported unit costs in a mechanical way to set prices are less likely to promote a downward demand spiral when they use practical capacity than when they use normal capacity utilization or master-budget capacity utilization.

Using practical capacity as the denominator level also gives the manager a more accurate idea of the resources needed and used to produce a unit by excluding the cost of unused capacity. As discussed earlier, the cost of manufacturing resources supplied to produce a telescope is Rs 2,900 (Rs 2,000 variable manufacturing cost per unit plus Rs 900 fixed manufacturing cost per unit). This cost is lower than the prices offered by Stassen's competitors and would have correctly led the manager to match the prices and retain the accounts (assuming for purposes of this discussion that Stassen has no other costs). If, however, the prices offered by competitors were lower than Rs 2,900 per unit, the Stassen manager would not recover the cost of resources used to supply telescopes. This would signal to the manager that Stassen was noncompetitive even if it had no unused capacity. The only way then for Stassen to be profitable and retain customers in the long run would be to reduce its manufacturing cost per unit. The following Concepts in Action feature highlights the downward spiral currently at work in the traditional landline phone industry.

Performance Evaluation

Consider how the choice among normal capacity utilization, master-budget capacity utilization, and practical capacity affects the evaluation of a marketing manager. Normal capacity utilization is often used as a basis for long-run plans. Normal capacity utilization depends on the time span selected and the forecasts made for each year. *However, normal capacity utilization is an average that provides no meaningful feedback to the marketing manager for a particular year.* Using normal capacity utilization as a reference for judging current performance of a marketing manager is an example of misusing a long-run measure for a short-run purpose. Master-budget capacity utilization, rather than normal capacity utilization or practical capacity, should be used to evaluate a marketing manager's performance in the current year. That's because the master budget is the principal short-run planning and control tool. Managers feel more obligated to reach the levels specified in the master budget, which should have been carefully set in relation to the maximum opportunities for sales in the current year.

When large differences exist between practical capacity and master-budget capacity utilization, several companies (such as Texas Instruments, Polysar, and Sandoz) classify the difference as *planned unused capacity*. One reason for this approach is performance evaluation. Consider our Stassen telescope example. The managers in charge of capacity planning usually do not make pricing decisions. Top management decided to build a production facility with 12,000 units of practical capacity, focusing on demand over the next five years. But Stassen's marketing managers, who are mid-level managers, make the pricing decisions. These marketing managers believe they should be held accountable only for the

Concepts in Action

The "Death Spiral" and the End of Landline Telephone Service

Can you imagine a future without traditional landline telephone service? Verizon and AT&T, the two largest telephone service providers in the United States, are already working to make that future a reality. Recently, both companies announced plans to reduce their focus on providing copper-wire telephone service to homes and businesses. According to AT&T, with the rise of mobile phones and Internet communications such as voice over Internet Protocol (VoIP), less than 20% of Americans now rely exclusively on landlines for voice service and another 25% have abandoned them altogether.

But why would telephone companies abandon landlines if 75% of Americans still use them? Continued reduced service demand is leading to higher unit costs, or a downward demand spiral. As AT&T recently told the U.S. Federal Communications Commission, "The business model for legacy phone services is in a death spiral. With an outdated product, falling revenues, and rising costs, the plain-old telephone service business is unsustainable for the long run."

Marketplace statistics support AT&T's claim. From 2000 to 2008, total long-distance access minutes fell by 42%. As a result, revenue from traditional landline phone service decreased by 27% between 2000 and 2007. In 2008 alone, AT&T lost 12% of its landline customers, while Verizon lost 10%. Industry observers estimate that customers are permanently disconnecting 700,000 landline phones every month.

As all these companies lose landline customers and revenue, the costs of maintaining the phone wires strung on poles and dug through trenches is not falling nearly as quickly. It now costs phone companies an average of $52 per year to maintain a copper phone line, up from $43 in 2003, largely because of the declining number of landlines. These costs do not include other expenses required to maintain landline phone service including local support offices, call centers, and garages.

New competitors are taking advantage of this situation. Vonage, the leading Internet phone company, offers its services for as little as $18 per month. Without relying on wires to transmit calls, its direct costs of providing telephone service come to $6.67 a month for each subscriber. And the largest part of that is not true cost, but subsidies to rural phone carriers for connecting long distance calls. As Vonage attracts more customers, its economies of scale will increase while its costs of providing service will decrease for each additional subscriber.

Hamstrung by increasing unit costs, legacy carriers like Verizon and AT&T are unable to compete with Vonage on price. As such, their traditional landline businesses are in permanent decline. So what are these companies doing about it? Verizon is reducing its landline operations by selling large parts of its copper-wire business to smaller companies at a significant discount. AT&T recently petitioned the U.S. government to waive a requirement that it and other carriers maintain their costly landline networks. As the landline phone service "death spiral" continues, the future of telecommunications will include more wireless, fiber optics, and VoIP with less of Alexander Graham Bell's original vision of telephones connected by copper wires.

Source: *Comments of AT&T Inc. on the Transition from the Legacy Circuit-switched Network to Broadband*. Washington, DC: AT&T Inc., December 21, 2009. http://fjallfoss.fcc.gov/ecfs/document/view?id=7020354032; Hansell, Saul. 2009. Verizon boss hangs up on landline phone business. *New York Times*, September 17; Hansell, Saul. 2009. Will the phone industry need a bailout, too? *New York Times*, May 8.

manufacturing overhead costs related to their potential customer base in 2012. The master-budget capacity utilization suggests a customer base in 2012 of 8,000 units (2/3 of the 12,000 practical capacity). Using responsibility accounting principles (see Chapter 6), only 2/3 of the budgeted total fixed manufacturing costs (Rs 1,08,00,000 × 2/3 = Rs 72,00,000) would be attributed to the fixed capacity costs of meeting 2012 demand. The remaining 1/3 of the numerator (Rs 1,08,00,000 × 1/3 = Rs 36,00,000) would be separately shown as the capacity cost of meeting increases in long-run demand expected to occur beyond 2012.[4]

[4] For further discussion, see T. Klammer, *Capacity Measurement and Improvement* (Chicago: Irwin, 1996). This research was facilitated by CAM-I, an organization promoting innovative cost management practices. CAM-I's research on capacity costs explores ways in which companies can identify types of capacity costs that can be reduced (or eliminated) without affecting the required output to meet customer demand. An example is improving processes to successfully eliminate the costs of capacity held in anticipation of handling difficulties due to imperfect coordination with suppliers and customers.

External Reporting

The magnitude of the favorable/unfavorable production-volume variance under absorption costing is affected by the choice of the denominator level used to calculate the budgeted fixed manufacturing cost per unit. Assume the following actual operating information for Stassen in 2012:

	A	B	C
1	Beginning inventory	0	
2	Production	8,000	units
3	Sales	6,000	units
4	Ending inventory	2,000	units
5	Selling price	Rs 10,000	per unit
6	Variable manufacturing cost	Rs 2,000	per unit
7	Fixed manufacturing costs	Rs 1,08,00,000	
8	Variable marketing cost	Rs 1,850	per unit sold
9	Fixed marketing costs	Rs 1,38,00,000	

Note that this is the same data used to calculate the income under variable and absorption costing for Stassen in Exhibit 9-1. As before, we assume that there are no price, spending, or efficiency variances in manufacturing costs.

Recall from Chapter 8 the equation used to calculate the production-volume variance:

$$\text{Production-volume variance} = \left(\begin{array}{c}\text{Budgeted}\\ \text{fixed}\\ \text{manufacturing}\\ \text{overhead}\end{array}\right) - \left(\begin{array}{c}\text{Fixed manufacturing overhead allocated using}\\ \text{budgeted cost per output unit}\\ \text{allowed for acutal output produced}\end{array}\right)$$

The four different capacity-level concepts result in four different budgeted fixed manufacturing overhead cost rates per unit. The different rates will result in different amounts of fixed manufacturing overhead costs allocated to the 8,000 units actually produced and different amounts of production-volume variance. Using the budgeted fixed manufacturing costs of Rs 1,08,00,000 (equal to actual fixed manufacturing costs) and the rates calculated for different denominator levels, the production-volume variance computations are as follows:

Production-volume variance (theoretical capacity) = Rs 1,08,00,000 − (8,000 unitd × Rs 600 per unit)
= Rs 1,08,00,000 − 48,00,000
= 60,00,000 U

Production-volume variance (practical capacity) = Rs 1,08,00,000 − (8,000 unitd × Rs 900 per unit)
= Rs 1,08,00,000 − 72,00,000
= 36,00,000 U

Production-volume variance (normal capacity) utilization = Rs 1,08,00,000 − (8,000 unitd × Rs 1,080 per unit)
= Rs 1,08,00,000 − 86,40,000
= 21,60,000 U

Production-volume variance (master-budget) capacity utilization) = Rs 1,08,00,000 − (8,000 unitd × Rs 1,350 per unit)
= Rs 1,08,00,000 − 1,08,00,000
= 0

How Stassen disposes of its production-volume variance at the end of the fiscal year will determine the effect this variance has on the company's operating income. We now discuss the three alternative approaches Stassen can use to dispose of the production-volume variance. These approaches were first discussed in Chapter 4.

1. **Adjusted allocation-rate approach.** This approach restates all amounts in the general and subsidiary ledgers by using actual rather than budgeted cost rates. Given that actual fixed manufacturing costs are Rs 1,08,00,000 and actual production is 8,000 units, the recalculated fixed manufacturing cost is Rs 1,350 per unit (Rs 1,08,00,000 ÷ 8,000 actual units). Under the adjusted allocation-rate approach, the choice of the capacity level used to calculate the budgeted fixed manufacturing cost per unit has no effect on year-end financial statements. In effect, actual costing is adopted at the end of the fiscal year.
2. **Proration approach.** The underallocated or overallocated overhead is spread among ending balances in Work-in-Process Control, Finished Goods Control, and Cost of Goods Sold. The proration restates the ending balances in these accounts to what they would have been if actual cost rates had been used rather than budgeted cost rates. The proration approach also results in the choice of the capacity level used to calculate the budgeted fixed manufacturing cost per unit having no effect on year-end financial statements.
3. **Write-off variances to cost of goods sold approach.** Exhibit 9-7 shows how use of this approach affects Stassen's operating income for 2012. Recall that Stassen had no beginning inventory, and it had production of 8,000 units and sales of 6,000 units. Therefore, the ending inventory on December 31, 2012, is 2,000 units. Using master-budget capacity utilization as the denominator level results in assigning the highest amount of fixed manufacturing cost per unit to the 2,000 units in ending inventory (see the line item "deduct ending inventory" in Exhibit 9-7). Accordingly, operating income is highest using master-budget capacity utilization. The differences in operating income for the four denominator-level concepts in Exhibit 9-7 are due to different amounts of fixed manufacturing overhead being inventoried at the end of 2012:

	Fixed Manufacturing Overhead in Dec. 31, 2012 Inventory	
Theoretical capacity	2,000 units × Rs 600 per unit	= Rs 12,00,000
Practical capacity	2,000 units × Rs 900 per unit	= Rs 18,00,000
Normal capacity utilization	2,000 units × Rs 1,080 per unit	= Rs 21,60,000
Master-budget capacity utilization	2,000 units × Rs 1,350 per unit	= Rs 27,00,000

In Exhibit 9-7, for example, the Rs 5,40,000 difference (Rs 1,50,00,000 – Rs 1,44,60,000) in operating income between master-budget capacity utilization and normal capacity utilization is due to the difference in fixed manufacturing overhead inventoried (Rs 27,00,000 – Rs 21,60,000).

What is the common reason and explanation for the increasing operating-income numbers in Exhibit 9-4 and Exhibit 9-7? It is the amount of fixed manufacturing costs incurred that is included in ending inventory at the end of the year. As this amount increases, so does operating income. The amount of fixed manufacturing costs inventoried depends on two factors: the number of units in ending inventory and the rate at which fixed manufacturing costs are allocated to each unit. Exhibit 9-4 shows the effect on operating income of increasing the number of units in ending inventory (by increasing production). Exhibit 9-7 shows the effect on operating income of increasing the fixed manufacturing cost allocated per unit (by decreasing the denominator level used to calculate the rate).

Chapter 8 discusses the various issues managers and management accountants must consider when deciding whether to prorate the production-volume variance among inventories and cost of goods sold or to simply write off the variance to cost of goods sold. The objective is to write off the portion of the production-volume variance that represents the cost of capacity not used to support the production of output during the period. Determining this amount is almost always a matter of judgment.

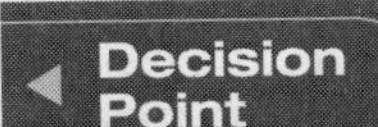

What are the major factors managers consider in choosing the capacity level to compute the budgeted fixed manufacturing cost rate?

Tax Requirements

For tax reporting purposes in the United States, the Internal Revenue Service (IRS) requires companies to assign inventoriable indirect production costs by a "method of allocation which fairly apportions such costs among the various items produced." Approaches that

Exhibit 9-7 Income-Statement Effects of Using Alternative Capacity-Level Concepts: Stassen Company for 2012

	A	B	C	D	E	F	G	H
1		Theoretical Capacity		Practical Capacity		Normal Capacity Utilization		Master-Budget Capacity Utilization
2	Denominator level in cases	18,000		12,000		10,000		8,000
3	Revenues[a]	Rs 6,00,00,000		Rs 6,00,00,000		Rs 6,00,00,000		Rs 6,00,00,000
4	Cost of goods sold							
5	Beginning inventory	Rs 0		Rs 0		Rs 0		Rs 0
6	Variable manufacturing costs[b]	Rs 1,60,00,000		Rs 1,60,00,000		Rs 1,60,00,000		Rs 1,60,00,000
7	Fixed manufacturing costs[c]	Rs 48,00,000		Rs 72,00,000		Rs 86,40,000		Rs 1,08,00,000
8	Cost of goods available for sale	Rs 2,08,00,000		Rs 2,32,00,000		Rs 2,46,40,000		Rs 2,68,00,000
9	Deduct ending inventory[d]	(Rs 52,00,000)		(Rs 58,00,000)		(Rs 61,60,000)		(Rs 67,00,000)
10	Cost of goods sold (at standard cost)	Rs 1,56,00,000		Rs 1,74,00,000		Rs 1,84,80,000		Rs 2,01,00,000
11	Adjustment for production-volume variance	Rs 60,00,000	U	Rs 36,00,000	U	Rs 21,60,000	U	Rs 0
12	Cost of goods sold	Rs 2,16,00,000		Rs 2,10,00,000		Rs 2,06,40,000		Rs 2,01,00,000
13	Gross margin	Rs 3,84,00,000		Rs 3,90,00,000		Rs 3,93,60,000		Rs 3,99,00,000
14	Marketing costs[e]	Rs 2,49,00,000		Rs 2,49,00,000		Rs 2,49,00,000		Rs 2,49,00,000
15	Operating income	Rs 1,35,00,000		Rs 1,41,00,000		Rs 1,44,60,000		Rs 1,50,00,000
16								
17	[a]Rs 10,000 x 6,000 units = Rs 6,00,00,000			[d]Ending inventory costs:				
18	[b]Rs 2,000 x 8,000 units = Rs 1,60,00,000			(Rs 2,000+ Rs 600) x 2,000 units = Rs 52,00,000				
19	[c]Fixed manufacturing overhead costs:			(Rs 2,000 + Rs 900) x 2,000 units = Rs 58,00,000				
20	Rs 600 x 8,000 units = Rs 48,00,000			(Rs 2,000 + Rs 1,080) x 2,000 units = Rs 61,60,000				
21	Rs 900 x 8,000 units = Rs 72,00,000			(Rs 2,000 + Rs 1,350) x 2,000 units = Rs 67,00,000				
22	Rs 1,080 x 8,000 units = Rs 86,40,000			[e]Marketing costs:				
23	Rs 1,350 x 8,000 units = Rs 1,08,00,000			Rs 1,38,00,000 + Rs 1,850 x 6,000 units = Rs 24,90,000				

involve the use of either overhead rates (which the IRS terms the "manufacturing burden rate method") or standard costs are viewed as acceptable. Under either approach, U.S. tax reporting requires end-of-period reconciliation between actual and applied indirect costs using the adjusted allocation-rate method or the proration method.[5] More interestingly, under either approach, the IRS permits the use of practical capacity to calculate budgeted fixed manufacturing cost per unit. Further, the production-volume variance thus generated can be deducted for tax purposes in the year in which the cost is incurred. The tax benefits from this policy are evident from Exhibit 9-7. Note that the operating income when the denominator is set to practical capacity (column D, where the production volume variance of $360,000 is written off to cost of goods sold) is lower than those under normal capacity utilization (column F) or master-budget capacity utilization (column H).

Difficulties in Forecasting Chosen Denominator-Level Concept

Practical capacity measures the available supply of capacity. Managers can usually use engineering studies and human-resource considerations (such as worker safety) to obtain a reliable estimate of this denominator level for the budget period. It is more difficult to

[5] For example, Section 1.471-11 of the U.S. Internal Revenue Code states, "The proper use of the standard cost method . . . requires that a taxpayer must reallocate to the goods in ending inventory a pro rata portion of any net negative or net positive overhead variances." Of course, if the variances are not material in amount, they can be expensed (i.e., written off to cost of goods sold), provided the same treatment is carried out in the firm's financial reports.

obtain reliable estimates of demand-side denominator-level concepts, especially longer-term normal capacity utilization figures. For example, many U.S. steel companies in the 1980s believed they were in the downturn of a demand cycle that would have an upturn within two or three years. After all, steel had been a cyclical business in which upturns followed downturns, making the notion of normal capacity utilization appear reasonable. Unfortunately, the steel cycle in the 1980s did not turn up; some companies and numerous plants closed. More recently, the global economic slowdown has made a mockery of demand projections. Consider that in 2006, the forecast for the Indian automotive market was that annual demand for cars and passenger vehicles would hit 1.92 million in the year 2009–2010. In early 2009, the forecast for the same period was revised downward to 1.37 million vehicles. Even ignoring the vagaries of economic cycles, another problem is that marketing managers of firms are often prone to overestimate their ability to regain lost sales and market share. Their estimate of "normal" demand for their product may consequently reflect an overly optimistic outlook. Master-budget capacity utilization focuses only on the expected demand for the next year. Therefore, master-budget capacity utilization can be more reliably estimated than normal capacity utilization. However, it is still just a forecast, and the true demand realization can be either higher or lower than this estimate.

It is important to understand that costing systems, such as normal costing or standard costing, do not recognize uncertainty the way managers recognize it. A single amount, rather than a range of possible amounts, is used as the denominator level when calculating the budgeted fixed manufacturing cost per unit in absorption costing. Consider Stassen's facility, which has an estimated practical capacity of 12,000 units. The estimated master-budget capacity utilization for 2012 is 8,000 units. However, there is still substantial doubt regarding the actual number of units Stassen will have to manufacture in 2012 and in future years. Managers recognize uncertainty in their capacity-planning decisions. Stassen built its current plant with a 12,000 unit practical capacity in part to provide the capability to meet possible demand surges. Even if such surges do not occur in a given period, do not conclude that capacity unused in a given period is wasted resources. The gains from meeting sudden demand surges may well require having unused capacity in some periods.

Difficulties in Forecasting Fixed Manufacturing Costs

The fixed manufacturing cost rate is based on a numerator (budgeted fixed manufacturing costs) and a denominator (some measure of capacity or capacity utilization). Our discussion so far has emphasized issues concerning the choice of the denominator. Challenging issues also arise in measuring the numerator. For example, deregulation of the U.S. electric utility industry has resulted in many electric utilities becoming unprofitable. This situation has led to write-downs in the values of the utilities' plants and equipment. The write-downs reduce the numerator because there is less depreciation expense included in the calculation of fixed capacity cost per kilowatt-hour of electricity produced. The difficulty that managers face in this situation is that the amount of write-downs is not clear-cut but, rather, a matter of judgment.

Nonmanufacturing Costs

Capacity costs also arise in nonmanufacturing parts of the value chain. Stassen may acquire a fleet of vehicles capable of distributing the practical capacity of its production facility. When actual production is below practical capacity, there will be unused-capacity cost issues with the distribution function, as well as with the manufacturing function.

As you saw in Chapter 8, capacity cost issues are prominent in many service-sector companies, such as airlines, hospitals, and railroads—even though these companies carry no inventory and so have no inventory costing problems. For example, in calculating the fixed overhead cost per patient-day in its obstetrics and gynecology department, a hospital must decide which denominator level to use: practical capacity, normal capacity utilization, or master-budget capacity utilization. Its decision may have implications for capacity management, as well as pricing and performance evaluation.

Activity-Based Costing

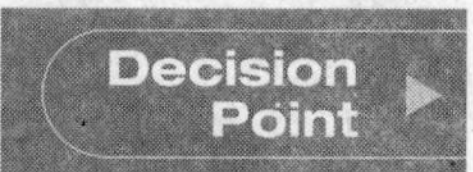

What issues must managers take into account when planning capacity levels and for assigning capacity costs?

To maintain simplicity and the focus on choosing a denominator to calculate a budgeted fixed manufacturing cost rate, our Stassen example assumed that all fixed manufacturing costs had a single cost driver: telescope units produced. As you saw in Chapter 5, activity-based costing systems have multiple overhead cost pools at the output-unit, batch, product-sustaining, and facility-sustaining levels—each with its own cost driver. In calculating activity cost rates (for fixed costs of setups and material handling, say), management must choose a capacity level for the quantity of the cost driver (setup-hours or loads moved). Should management use practical capacity, normal capacity utilization, or master-budget capacity utilization? For all the reasons described in this chapter (such as pricing and capacity management), most proponents of activity-based costing argue that practical capacity should be used as the denominator level to calculate activity cost rates.

Problem for Self-Study

Assume Stassen Company on January 1, 2012, decides to contract with another company to preassemble a large percentage of the components of its telescopes. The revised manufacturing cost structure during the 2012–2014 period is as follows:

Variable manufacturing cost per unit produced		
Direct materials	Rs	2,500
Direct manufacturing labor		200
Manufacturing overhead		50
Total variable manufacturing cost per unit produced	Rs	2,750
Fixed manufacturing costs		Rs 48,00,000

Under the revised cost structure, a larger percentage of Stassen's manufacturing costs are variable with respect to units produced. The denominator level of production used to calculate budgeted fixed manufacturing cost per unit in 2012, 2013, and 2014 is 8,000 units. Assume no other change from the data underlying Exhibits 9-1 and 9-2. Summary information pertaining to absorption-costing operating income and variable-costing operating income with this revised cost structure is as follows:

	2012	2013	2014
Absorption-costing operating income	Rs1,50,00,000	Rs 1,56,00,000	Rs 2,34,00,000
Variable-costing operating income	1,38,00,000	1,65,00,000	2,19,00,000
Difference	Rs 12,00,000	Rs (9,00,000)	Rs 15,00,000

Required

1. Compute the budgeted fixed manufacturing cost per unit in 2012, 2013, and 2014.
2. Explain the difference between absorption-costing operating income and variable-costing operating income in 2012, 2013, and 2014, focusing on fixed manufacturing costs in beginning and ending inventory.
3. Why are these differences smaller than the differences in Exhibit 9-2?
4. Assume the same preceding information, except that for 2012, the master-budget capacity utilization is 10,000 units instead of 8,000. How would Stassen's absorption-costing income for 2012 differ from the Rs 1,50,00,000 shown previously? Show your computations.

Solution

1. $$\text{Budgeted fixed manufacturing cost per unit} = \frac{\text{Budgeted fixed manufacturing costs}}{\text{Budgeted production units}}$$

$$= \frac{\text{Rs } 48{,}00{,}000}{8{,}000 \text{ units}}$$

= Rs 600 per unit

2.

Absorption-costing operating income	–	Variable-costing operating income	=	Fixed manufacturing costs in ending inventory under absorption costing	–	Fixed manufacturing costs in beginning inventory under absorption costing
2012: Rs 1,50,00,000	–	Rs 1,38,00,000	=	(Rs 60 per unit × 20,000 units)	–	(Rs 6,000 per unit × 0 units)
		Rs 12,00,000	=	Rs 12,00,000		
2013: Rs 1,56,00,000	–	Rs 1,65,00,000	=	(Rs 600 per unit × 500 units)	–	(Rs 600 per unit × 2,000 units)
		– Rs 9,00,000	=	– Rs 9,00,000		
2014: Rs 2,34,00,000	–	Rs 2,19,00,000	=	(Rs 600 per unit × 3,000 units)	–	(Rs 600 per unit × 500 units)
		Rs 15,00,000	=	Rs 15,00,000		

3. Subcontracting a large part of manufacturing has greatly reduced the magnitude of fixed manufacturing costs. This reduction, in turn, means differences between absorption costing and variable costing are much smaller than in Exhibit 9-2.
4. Given the higher master-budget capacity utilization level of 10,000 units, the budgeted fixed manufacturing cost rate for 2012 is now as follows:

$$\frac{\text{Rs } 48{,}00{,}000}{10{,}000 \text{ units}} = \text{Rs } 480 \text{ per unit}$$

The manufacturing cost per unit is Rs 3,230 (Rs 2,750 + Rs 480). So, the production-volume variance for 2012 is

(10,000 units – 8,000 units) × Rs 480 per unit = Rs 9,60,000 U

The absorption-costing income statement for 2012 is as follows:

Revenues: Rs 10,000 per unit × 6,000 units	Rs 6,00,00,000
Cost of goods sold:	
Beginning inventory	0
Variable manufacturing costs: Rs 2,750 per unit × 8,000 units	2,20,00,000
Fixed manufacturing costs: Rs 480 per unit × 8,000 units	38,40,000
Cost of goods available for sale	2,58,40,000
Deduct ending inventory: Rs 3,230 per unit × 2,000 units	(64,60,000)
Cost of goods sold (at standard costs)	1,93,80,000
Adjustment for production-volume variance	9,60,000 U
Cost of goods sold	20,34,000
Gross margin	2,03,40,000
Marketing costs: Rs 1,38,00,000 fixed + (Rs 1,850 per unit) × (6,000 units sold)	2,49,00,000
Operating income	Rs 1,47,60,000

The higher denominator level used to calculate the budgeted fixed manufacturing cost per unit means that fewer fixed manufacturing costs are inventoried (Rs 480 per unit × 2,000 units = Rs 9,60,000) than when the master-budget capacity utilization was 8,000 units (Rs 600 per unit × 2,000 units = Rs 12,00,000). This difference of Rs 2,40,000 (Rs 12,00,000 – Rs 9,60,000) results in operating income being lower by Rs 2,40,000 relative to the prior calculated income level of Rs 1,50,00,000.

Decision Points

The following question-and-answer format summarizes the chapter's learning objectives. Each decision presents a key question related to a learning objective. The guidelines are the answer to that question.

Decision	Guidelines
1. How does variable costing differ from absorption costing?	Variable costing and absorption costing differ in only one respect: how to account for fixed manufacturing costs. Under variable costing, fixed manufacturing costs are excluded from inventoriable costs and are a cost of the period in which they are incurred. Under absorption costing, fixed manufacturing costs are inventoriable and become a part of cost of goods sold in the period when sales occur.
2. How does income differ under variable and absorption costing?	The variable-costing income statement is based on the contribution-margin format. Under it, operating income is driven by the unit level of sales. Under absorption costing, the income statement follows the gross-margin format. Operating income is driven by the unit level of production, the unit level of sales, and the denominator level used for assigning fixed costs.
3. Why might managers build up finished goods inventory if they use absorption costing?	When absorption costing is used, managers can increase current operating income by producing more units for inventory. Producing for inventory absorbs more fixed manufacturing costs into inventory and reduces costs expensed in the period. Critics of absorption costing label this manipulation of income as the major negative consequence of treating fixed manufacturing costs as inventoriable costs.
4. How does throughput costing differ from variable costing and absorption costing?	Throughput costing treats all costs except direct materials as costs of the period in which they are incurred. Throughput costing results in a lower amount of manufacturing costs being inventoried than either variable or absorption costing.
5. What are the various capacity levels a company can use to compute the budgeted fixed manufacturing cost rate?	Capacity levels can be measured in terms of capacity supplied—theoretical capacity or practical capacity. Capacity can also be measured in terms of output demanded—normal capacity utilization or master-budget capacity utilization.
6. What are the major factors managers consider in choosing the capacity level to compute the budgeted fixed manufacturing cost rate?	The major factors managers consider in choosing the capacity level to compute the budgeted fixed manufacturing cost rate are (a) effect on product costing and capacity management, (b) effect on pricing decisions, (c) effect on performance evaluation, (d) effect on financial statements, (e) regulatory requirements, and (f) difficulties in forecasting chosen capacity-level concepts.
7. Should a company with high fixed costs and unused capacity raise selling prices to try to fully recoup its costs?	No, companies with high fixed costs and unused capacity may encounter ongoing and increasingly greater reductions in demand if they continue to raise selling prices to try to fully recoup variable and fixed costs from a declining sales base. This phenomenon is called the downward demand spiral.

APPENDIX: BREAKEVEN POINTS IN VARIABLE COSTING AND ABSORPTION COSTING

Chapter 3 introduced cost-volume-profit analysis. If variable costing is used, the breakeven point (that's where operating income is Re 0) is computed in the usual manner. There is only one breakeven point in this case, and it depends on (1) fixed (manufacturing and operating) costs and (2) contribution margin per unit.

The formula for computing breakeven point under variable costing is a special case of the more-general target operating income formula from Chapter 3:

$$\text{Let } Q = \text{Number of units sold to earn the target operating income}$$

$$\text{Then } Q = \frac{\text{Total fixed costs} + \text{Target operating income}}{\text{Contribution margin per unit}}$$

Breakeven occurs when the target operating income is Rs 0. In our Stassen illustration for 2009 (see Exhibit 9-1):

$$Q = \frac{(\text{Rs } 1{,}08{,}00{,}000 + \text{Rs } 1{,}38{,}00{,}000) + \text{Rs } 0}{(\text{Rs } 10{,}000 + (\text{Rs } 2{,}000 + \text{Rs } 1{,}850))} = \frac{\text{Rs } 2{,}46{,}00{,}000}{\text{Rs } 6{,}150}$$
$$= 4{,}000 \text{ units}$$

Proof of breakeven point:

Revenues, Rs 10,000 × 4,000 units	Rs 4,00,00,000
Variable costs, Rs 3,850 × 4,000 units	1,54,00,000
Contribution margin, Rs 6,150 × 4,000 units	2,46,00,000
Fixed costs	2,46,00,000
Operating income	Rs 0

If absorption costing is used, the required number of units to be sold to earn a specific target operating income is not unique because of the number of variables involved. The following formula shows the factors that will affect the target operating income under absorption costing:

$$Q = \frac{\begin{matrix}\text{Total}\\ \text{fixed}\\ \text{costs}\end{matrix} + \begin{matrix}\text{Target}\\ \text{operating}\\ \text{income}\end{matrix} + \left[\begin{matrix}\text{Fixed}\\ \text{manufacturing}\\ \text{cost rate}\end{matrix} \times \left(\begin{matrix}\text{Breakeven}\\ \text{sales}\\ \text{in units}\end{matrix} - \begin{matrix}\text{Units}\\ \text{produced}\end{matrix}\right)\right]}{\text{Contribution margin per unit}}$$

In this formula, the numerator is the sum of three terms (from the perspective of the two "+" signs), compared with two terms in the numerator of the variable-costing formula stated earlier. The additional term in the numerator under absorption costing is:

$$\left[\begin{matrix}\text{Fixed manufacturing}\\ \text{cost rate}\end{matrix} \times \left(\begin{matrix}\text{Breakeven sales}\\ \text{in units}\end{matrix} - \begin{matrix}\text{Units}\\ \text{produced}\end{matrix}\right)\right]$$

This term reduces the fixed costs that need to be recovered when units produced exceed the breakeven sales quantity. When production exceeds the breakeven sales quantity, some of the fixed manufacturing costs that are expensed under variable costing are not expensed under absorption costing; they are instead included in finished goods inventory.

For Stassen Company in 2009, suppose that actual production is 5,280 units. Then, one breakeven point, Q, under absorption costing is:

$$Q = \frac{(\text{Rs } 1{,}08{,}00{,}000 + \text{Rs } 1{,}38{,}00{,}000) + \text{Rs } 0 + [\text{Rs } 1{,}350\ 3\ (Q - 5{,}280)]}{(\text{Rs } 10{,}000 - (\text{Rs } 2{,}000 + \text{Rs } 1{,}850))}$$

$$= \frac{(\text{Rs } 2{,}46{,}00{,}000 + \text{Rs } 1{,}350\ Q - \text{Rs } 71{,}28{,}000)}{\text{Rs } 6{,}150}$$

$$\text{Rs } 6{,}150\ Q = \text{Rs } 1{,}74{,}72{,}000 + \text{Rs } 1{,}350\ Q$$
$$\text{Rs } 4{,}800\ Q = \text{Rs } 1{,}74{,}72{,}000$$
$$Q = 36{,}400$$

Proof of breakeven point:

Revenues, Rs 10,000 × 3,640 units		Rs 3,64,00,000
Cost of goods sold:		
Cost of goods sold at standard cost, Rs 3,350 × 3,640 units	Rs 1,21,94,000	
Production-volume variance, Rs 1,350 × (8,000 − 5,280) units	36,72,000 U	1,58,66,000
Gross margin		2,05,34,000
Marketing costs:		
Variable marketing costs, Rs 1,850 × 3,640 units	67,34,000	
Fixed marketing costs	1,38,00,000	2,05,34,500
Operating income		Rs 0

The breakeven point under absorption costing depends on (1) fixed manufacturing costs, (2) fixed operating (marketing) costs, (3) contribution margin per unit, (4) unit level of production, and (5) the capacity level chosen as the denominator to set the fixed manufacturing cost rate. For Stassen in 2009, a combination of 3,640 units sold, fixed manufacturing costs of Rs 1,08,00,000, fixed marketing costs of Rs 1,38,00,000, contribution margin per unit of Rs 6,150, an 8,000-unit denominator level, and production of 5,280 units would result in an operating income of Rs 0. *Note, however, that there are many combinations of these five factors that would give an operating income of Rs 0.* For example, holding all other factors constant, a combination of 6,240 units produced and 3,370 units sold also results in an operating income of Rs 0 under absorption costing.

Proof of breakeven point:

Revenues, Rs 10,000 × 3,370 units		Rs 3,37,00,000
Cost of goods sold:		
Cost of goods sold at standard cost, Rs 3,350 × 3,370 units	Rs 1,12,89,500	
Production-volume variance, Rs 1,350 × (8,000 − 6,240) units	23,76,000 U	1,36,65,500
Gross margin		2,00,34,500
Marketing costs:		
Variable marketing costs, Rs 1,850 × 3,370 units	62,34,500	
Fixed marketing costs	1,38,00,000	2,00,34,500
Operating income		Rs 0

Suppose actual production in 2009 was equal to the denominator level, 8,000 units, and there were no units sold and no fixed marketing costs. All the units produced would be placed in inventory, so all the fixed manufacturing costs would be included in inventory. There would be no production-volume variance. Under these conditions, the company could break even with no sales whatsoever! In contrast, under variable costing, the operating loss would be equal to the fixed manufacturing costs of Rs 1,08,00,000.

TERMS TO LEARN

This chapter and the Glossary at the end of the book contain definitions of:

absorption costing (**p. 346**)
direct costing (**p. 346**)
downward demand spiral (**p. 361**)
master-budget capacity utilization (**p. 359**)
normal capacity utilization (**p. 359**)
practical capacity (**p. 358**)
super-variable costing (**p. 355**)
theoretical capacity (**p. 358**)
throughput costing (**p. 355**)
variable costing (**p. 345**)

ASSIGNMENT MATERIAL

Questions

9-1 Differences in operating income between variable costing and absorption costing are due solely to accounting for fixed costs. Do you agree? Explain.

9-2 Why is the term *direct costing* a misnomer?

9-3 Do companies in either the service sector or the merchandising sector make choices about absorption costing versus variable costing?

9-4 Explain the main conceptual issue under variable costing and absorption costing regarding the timing for the release of fixed manufacturing overhead as expense.

9-5 "Companies that make no variable-cost/fixed-cost distinctions must use absorption costing, and those that do make variable-cost/fixed-cost distinctions must use variable costing." Do you agree? Explain.

9-6 The main trouble with variable costing is that it ignores the increasing importance of fixed costs in manufacturing companies. Do you agree? Why?

9-7 Give an example of how, under absorption costing, operating income could fall even though the unit sales level rises.

9-8 What are the factors that affect the breakeven point under (a) variable costing and (b) absorption costing?

9-9 Critics of absorption costing have increasingly emphasized its potential for leading to undesirable incentives for managers. Give an example.

9-10 What are two ways of reducing the negative aspects associated with using absorption costing to evaluate the performance of a plant manager?

9-11 What denominator-level capacity concepts emphasize the output a plant can supply? What denominator-level capacity concepts emphasize the output customers demand for products produced by a plant?

9-12 Describe the downward demand spiral and its implications for pricing decisions.

9-13 Will the financial statements of a company always differ when different choices at the start of the accounting period are made regarding the denominator-level capacity concept?

9-14 What is the IRS's requirement for tax reporting regarding the choice of a denominator-level capacity concept?

9-15 "The difference between practical capacity and master-budget capacity utilization is the best measure of management's ability to balance the costs of having too much capacity and having too little capacity." Do you agree? Explain.

Solved Examples

9-16 Variable and absorption costing, explaining operating income differences. Saya Motors assembles and sells motor vehicles. Data relating to April and May of current year are:

	April	May
Unit data		
Beginning inventory	0	150
Production	500	400
Sales	350	520
Variable costs		
Manufacturing cost per unit produced	Rs 1,00,000	1,00,000
Operating cost per unit sold	30,000	30,000
Fixed costs		
Manufacturing costs	Rs 2,00,00,000	Rs 2,00,00,000
Operating costs	60,00,000	60,00,000

The selling price per motor vehicle (excluding government taxes) is Rs 2,40,000.

Required

1. Present income statements for Saya Motors in April and May under (a) variable costing and (b) absorption costing.
2. Prepare a numerical reconciliation and explanation of the difference between operating income for each month under absorption costing and variable costing.

Solution

Variable and absorption costing, explaining operating income differences.

1. Key inputs for income statement computations are:

	April	May
Beginning inventory	0	150
Production	500	400
Goods available for sale	500	550
Units sold	350	520
Ending inventory	150	30

The fixed cost per unit and total manufacturing costs per unit under absorption costing are:

		April	May
(a)	Fixed manufacturing costs	Rs 2,00,00,000	Rs 2,00,00,000
(b)	Units produced	500	400

(c) = (a) ÷ (b) Fixed manufacturing costs per unit	Rs	40,000	Rs	50,000
(d) Variable manufacturing costs per unit	Rs	1,00,000	Rs	1,00,000
(e) = (c) + (d) Total manufacturing costs per unit	Rs	1,40,000	Rs	1,50,000

(a) Variable costing

	April		May	
Revenues[a]		Rs 8,40,00,000		Rs 12,48,00,000
Variable costs:				
Beginning inventory	Rs 0		Rs 1,50,00,000	
Variable manufacturing costs[b]	5,00,00,000		4,00,00,000	
Cost of goods available for sale	5,00,00,000		5,50,00,000	
Deduct ending inventory[c]	1,50,00,000		30,00,000	
Variable cost of goods sold	3,50,00,000		5,20,00,000	
Variable operating costs[d]	1,05,00,000		1,56,00,000	
Total variable costs		4,55,00,000		6,76,00,000
Contribution margin		3,85,00,000		5,72,00,000
Fixed costs				
Fixed manufacturing costs	2,00,00,000		2,00,00,000	
Fixed operating costs	60,00,000		60,00,000	
Total fixed costs		2,60,00,000		2,60,00,000
Operating income		Rs 1,25,00,000		Rs 3,12,00,000

[a]Rs 2,40,000 × 350; Rs 2,40,000 × 520 [c]Rs 1,00,000 × 150; Rs 1,00,000 × 30
[b]Rs 1,00,000 × 500; Rs 1,00,000 × 400 [d]Rs 30,000 × 350; Rs 30,000 × 520

(b) Absorption costing

	April		May	
Revenues[a]		Rs 8,40,00,000		Rs 12,48,00,000
Cost of goods sold				
Beginning inventory	Rs 0		Rs 2,10,00,000	
Variable manufacturing costs[b]	5,00,00,000		4,00,00,000	
Fixed manufacturing costs[c]	2,00,00,000		2,00,00,000	
Cost of goods available for sale	7,00,00,000		8,10,00,000	
Deduct ending inventory[d]	2,10,00,000		45,00,000	
Cost of goods sold		4,90,00,000		7,65,00,000
Gross margin		3,50,00,000		4,83,00,000
Operating costs				
Variable operating costse	1,05,00,000		1,56,00,000	
Fixed operating costs	60,00,000		60,00,000	
Total operating costs		1,65,00,000		2,16,00,000
Operating income		Rs 1,85,00,000		Rs 2,67,00,000

[a]Rs 2,40,000 × 350; Rs 2,40,000 × 520 [d](Rs 1,40,000 × 150; Rs 1,50,000 × 30)
[b]Rs 1,00,000 × 500; Rs 1,00,000 × 400 [e](Rs 30,000 × 350; Rs 30,000 × 520)
[c](Rs 40,000 × 500); (Rs 50,000 × 400)

2. $$\begin{pmatrix}\text{Absorption-costing}\\ \text{operating income}\end{pmatrix} - \begin{pmatrix}\text{Variable-costing}\\ \text{operating income}\end{pmatrix} = \begin{pmatrix}\text{Fixed manufacturing}\\ \text{costs in}\\ \text{ending inventory}\end{pmatrix} - \begin{pmatrix}\text{Fixed manufacturing}\\ \text{costs in}\\ \text{beginning inventory}\end{pmatrix}$$

April:

Rs 1,85,00,000 – Rs 1,25,00,000 = (Rs 40,000 × 150) – (Rs 0)
Rs 60,00,000 = Rs 60,00,000

May:

Rs 2,67,00,000 – Rs 3,12,00,000 = (Rs 50,000 × 30) – (Rs 40,000 × 150)
– Rs 45,00,000 = Rs 15,00,000 – Rs 60,00,000
– Rs 45,00,000 = – Rs 45,00,000

The difference between absorption and variable costing is due solely to moving fixed manufacturing costs into inventories as inventories increase (as in April) and out of inventories as they decrease (as in May).

9-17 Throughput costing (continuation of 9-16). The variable manufacturing costs per unit of Saya Motors are

	April	May
Direct materials	Rs 67,000	Rs 67,000
Direct manufacturing labor	15,000	15,000
Manufacturing overhead	18,000	18,000

Required

1. Present income statements for Saya Motors in April and May under throughput costing.
2. Contrast the results in requirement 1 with those in requirement 1 of 9-16.
3. Give one motivation for Saya Motors to adopt throughput costing.

Solution

Throughput costing (continuation of 9-16).

1.

	April		May	
Revenues[a]		Rs 8,40,00,000		Rs 12,48,00,000
Direct material cost of goods sold				
Beginning inventory				
Direct materials in goods manufactured[b]	Rs 0		Rs 1,00,50,000	
	3,35,00,000		2,68,00,000	
Cost of goods available for sale	3,35,00,000		3,68,50,000	
Deduct ending inventory[c]	1,00,50,000		20,10,000	
Total direct material cost of goods sold		2,34,50,000		3,48,40,000
Throughput contribution		6,05,50,000		8,99,60,000
Other costs				
Manufacturing costs	3,65,00,000[d]		3,32,00,000[e]	
Other operating costs	1,65,00,000[f]		2,16,00,000[g]	
Total other costs		5,30,00,000		5,48,00,000
Operating income		Rs 75,50,000		Rs 3,51,60,000

[a]Rs 2,40,000 × 350; Rs 2,40,000 × 520
[b]Rs 67,000 × 500; Rs 67,000 × 400
[c]Rs 67,000 × 150; Rs 67,000 × 30
[d](Rs 33,000 × 500) + Rs 2,00,00,000
[e](Rs 33,000 × 400) + Rs 2,00,00,000
[f](Rs 30,000 × 350) + Rs 60,00,000
[g](Rs 30,000 × 520) + Rs 60,00,000

2. Operating income under:

	April	May
Absorption costing	Rs 1,85,00,000	Rs 2,67,00,000
Variable costing	1,25,00,000	3,12,00,000
Throughput costing	75,50,000	3,51,60,000

In April, throughput costing has the lowest operating income, whereas in May throughput costing has the highest operating income. Throughput costing puts greater emphasis on sales as the source of operating income than does either absorption or variable costing.

3. Throughput costing puts a penalty on producing without a corresponding sale in the same period. Costs other than direct materials that are variable with respect to production are expensed in the period of incurrence, whereas under variable costing they would be capitalized. As a result, throughput costing provides less incentive to produce for inventory than either variable costing or absorption costing.

9-18 Variable versus absorption costing. The Timex Company manufactures trendy, high-quality moderately priced watches. As Timex's senior financial analyst, you are asked to recommend a method of inventory costing. The CFO will use your recommendation to construct Timex's current year income statement. The following data are for the current year ended December 31:

Beginning inventory, January 1	85,000 units
Ending inventory, December 31	34,500 units
Current year sales	3,45,400 units
Selling price (to distributor)	Rs 200 per unit
Variable manufacturing cost per unit, including direct materials	Rs 51 per unit
Variable operating cost per unit sold	Rs 11 per unit
Fixed manufacturing overhead	Rs 1,44,00,000
Denominator-level machine-hours	6,000
Standard production rate	50 units per machine-hour
Fixed operating costs	Rs 1,08,00,000

Assume standard costs per unit are the same for units in beginning inventory and units produced during the year. Also, assume no price, spending, or efficiency variances.

Required

1. Prepare income statements under variable and absorption costing for the current year ended December 31.
2. What is Timex's operating income under each costing method (in percentage terms)?
3. Explain the difference in operating income between the two methods.
4. Which costing method would you recommend to the CFO? Why ?

Solution

Variable vs absorption costing.

1.

Income Statement for Timex Company, Variable Costing
For the Current Year Ended December 31

Revenues: Rs 220 × 3,45,400		Rs 7,59,88,000
Variable costs		
Beginning inventory: Rs 51 × 85,000	Rs 43,35,000	
Variable manufacturing costs: Rs 51 × 2,94,900	1,50,39,900	
Cost of goods available for sale	1,93,74,900	
Deduct ending inventory: Rs 51 × 34,500	17,59,500	
Variable cost of goods sold	1,76,15,400	
Variable operating costs: Rs 11 × 3,45,400	37,99,400	
Total variable costs (at standard costs)	2,14,14,800	
Adjustment for variances	0	
Total variable costs		2,14,14,800
Contribution margin		5,45,73,200
Fixed costs		
Fixed manufacturing overhead costs	1,44,00,000	
Fixed operating costs	1,08,00,000	
Adjustment for fixed cost variances	0	
Total fixed costs		2,52,00,000
Operating income		2,93,73,200

Absorption Costing Data

Fixed manufacturing overhead allocation rate =

Fixed manufacturing overhead/Denominator level machine-hours = Rs 1,44,00,000/6,000
= Rs 2,400 per machine-hour

Fixed manufacturing overhead allocation rate per unit =

Fixed manufacturing overhead allocation rate/standard production rate = Rs 2,400/50
= Rs 48 per unit

Income Statement for Timex Company, Absorption Costing
For the Year Ended December 31

Revenues: Rs 220 × 3,45,400		Rs 7,59,88,000
Cost of goods sold		
Beginning inventory: (Rs 51 + Rs 48) × 85,000	Rs 84,15,000	
Variable manufacturing costs: Rs 51 × 2,94,900	1,50,39,900	
Fixed manufacturing costs: Rs 48 × 2,94,900	1,41,55,200	
Cost of goods available for sale	Rs 3,76,10,100	
Deduct ending inventory: (Rs 51 + Rs 48) × 34,500	(34,15,500)	
Adjust for manufacturing variances (Rs 48 × 5,100)[a]	2,44,800	
Cost of goods sold		3,44,39,400
Gross margin		4,15,48,600
Operating costs		
Variable operating costs: Rs 110 × 345,400	Rs 37,99,400	
Fixed operating costs	1,08,00,000	
Adjust for operating cost variances	0	
Total operating costs		1,45,99,400
Operating income		Rs 2,69,49,200

[a] Production volume variance .
= [(6,000 hours × 50) – 2,94,900) × Rs 48
= (3,00,000 – 2,94,900) × Rs 48
= Rs 2,44,800

2. Timex's pre-tax profit margins

Under variable costing:

Revenues	Rs 7,59,88,000
Operating income	2,93,73,200
Pre-tax profit margin	38.7%

Under absorption costing:

Revenues	Rs 7,59,88,000
Operating income	2,69,49,200
Pre-tax profit margin	35.5%

3. Operating income using variable costing is about 9% higher than operating income calculated using absorption costing.
   Variable costing operating income – Absorption costing operating income
   = Rs 2,93,73,200 – Rs 2,69,49,200 = Rs 24,24,000

Fixed manufacturing costs in beginning inventory under absorption costing– Fixed manufacturing costs in ending inventory under absorption costing = (Rs 48 × 85,000) – (Rs 48 × 34,500) = Rs 24,24,000

4. The factors the CFO should consider include:
   a. Effect on managerial behavior, and
   b. Effect on external users of financial statements.

   Absorption costing has many critics. However, the dysfunctional aspects associated with absorption costing can be reduced by:
   - Careful budgeting and inventory planning,
   - Adding a capital charge to reduce the incentives to build up inventory, and
   - Monitoring nonfinancial performance measures.

9-19 Absorption versus variable costing. Ranbaxy produces a single drug-Mimic™-for the treatment of hair loss in men. It began commercial production of Mimic™ on January 1, 2012. Patients use three pills per day (365 days a year). Ranbaxy marketing analysts estimate 50,000 patients will use Mimic™ in 2012. Production in 2012 is 5,47,50,000 units (pills). However, only 44,800 patients are prescribed Mimic™ during 2012. Each patient used three pills per day for 365 days a year. The average wholesale selling price (the price Ranbaxy receives from distributors) is Rs 12 per pill. Ranbaxy's actual costs are as follows:

Variable cost per unit	
Manufacturing cost per pill produced	
Direct materials	Rs 0.50
Direct manufacturing labor	0.40
Manufacturing overhead	1.10
Marketing cost per pill sold	0.70
Fixed costs	
Manufacturing costs	Rs 7,35,84,000
R&D	4,90,56,000
Marketing	19,62,24,000

Required

1. What is the number of Mimic™ pills actually sold in 2012, assuming all patients began using the drug on January 1 and used it through December 31? What is ending inventory on December 31, 2012?
2. Calculate operating income under variable costing and absorption costing for Ranbaxy for the year ended December 31, 2012. The allocation base for fixed manufacturing costs under absorption costing is Rs 1.50 per unit (pill) produced. All under or overabsorbed fixed costs are written off to cost of goods sold.
3. Explain differences in operating income in requirement 2.

Solution

Absorption variable costing.

1. The number of Mimic™ pills sold in 2012 is
   44,800 × 365 × 3 = 4,90,56,000 pills

   Ending inventory on December 31, 2012, is 56,94,000 pills

Unit data	
Beginning inventory	0
Production	5,47,50,000
Sales	4,90,56,000
Ending inventory	56,94,000
Variable cost data	
Manufacturing costs per pill produced	
Direct materials	Rs 0.50
Direct manufacturing labor	0.40
Manufacturing overhead	1.10
Total variable manufacturing costs	Rs 2.00
Fixed cost data	
Manufacturing costs	Rs 7,35,84,000
R&D	4,90,56,000
Marketing	19,62,24,000
Wholesale selling price per pill	Rs 12
Fixed manufacturing costs allocation rate per pill	Rs 1.50 (Given)

2. Variable costing

Revenues: Rs 12 × 4,90,56,000	Rs 58,86,72,000

Variable costs		
Beginning inventory	Rs 0	
Variable manufacturing cost: Rs 2.00 × 54,750,000	10,95,00,000	
Cost of goods available for sale	10,95,00,000	
Deduct ending inventory: Rs 2.00 × 56,94,000	1,13,88,000	
Variable cost of goods sold	9,81,12,000	
Variable marketing costs: Rs 0.70 × 4,90,56,000	3,43,39,200	
Adjust for variable-cost variance	0	
Total variable costs		13,24,51,200
Contribution margin		45,62,20,800
Fixed costs		
Fixed manufacturing costs	7,35,84,000	
Fixed R&D	4,90,56,000	
Fixed marketing	19,62,24,000	
Total fixed costs		31,88,64,000
Operating income		Rs 13,73,56,800
Absorption costing		
Revenues: Rs 12 × 4,90,56,000		Rs 58,86,72,000
Costs of goods sold		
Beginning inventory	Rs 0	
Variable manufacturing cost: Rs 2.0 × 5,47,50,000	10,95,00,000	
Fixed manufacturing costs: Rs 1.5 × 5,47,50,000	8,21,25,000	
Cost of goods available for sale	19,16,25,000	
Deduct ending inventory: Rs 3.5 × 56,94,000	(1,99,29,000)	
Adjust for manufacturing variances a	(85,41,000)	
Cost of goods sold		16,31,55,000
Gross margin		42,55,17,000
Operating costs		
Variable marketing costs: Rs 0.70 × 4,90,56,000	3,43,39,200	
Fixed R&D	4,90,56,000	
Fixed marketing	19,62,24,000	
Adjustment for operating cost variances	0	
Total operating costs		27,96,19,200
Operating income		Rs 14,58,97,800

[a]Production-volume variance = (1.50 × 5,47,50,000 units) – Rs 73,58,40,000 = Rs 85,41,000 F

3. The difference of Rs 85,41,000 is due to:

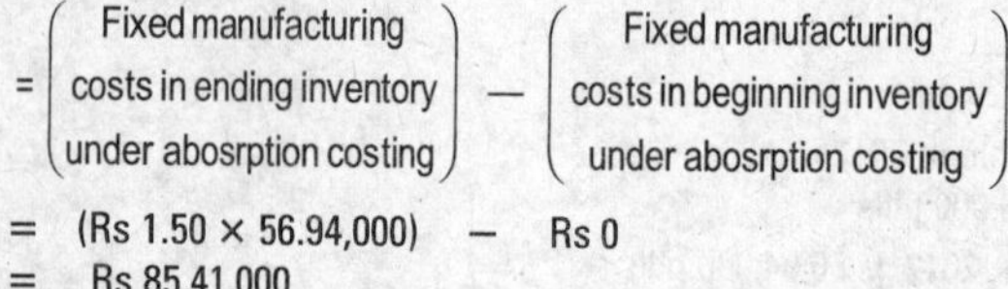

$$= \begin{pmatrix}\text{Fixed manufacturing}\\ \text{costs in ending inventory}\\ \text{under abosrption costing}\end{pmatrix} - \begin{pmatrix}\text{Fixed manufacturing}\\ \text{costs in beginning inventory}\\ \text{under abosrption costing}\end{pmatrix}$$

= (Rs 1.50 × 56.94,000) – Rs 0

= Rs 85,41,000

9-20 Capacity management, denominator-level capacity concepts. Each of the following items is identified by a number

1. Should be used for performance evaluation
2. Measures the denominator level in terms of demand for the output of the plant
3. Represents the expected level of capacity utilization for the next budget period
4. Is based on producing at full efficiency all the time
5. Takes into account seasonal, cyclical, and trend factors
6. Measures the denominator level in terms of what a plant can supply
7. Represents an ideal benchmark
8. Highlights the cost of capacity acquired but not used
9. Hides the cost of capacity acquired but not used
10. Should be used for long-term pricing purposes.
11. If used as the denominator-level concept, would avoid the restatement of unit costs when expected demand levels change

Required Match each of the items with one or more of the following denominator-level capacity concepts by putting appropriate letter(s) by each number:

a. Theoretical capacity
b. Practical capacity

c. Normal capacity utilization
d. Master-budget capacity utilization

Solution

Capacity management, denominator-level capacity concepts.

1. d
2. c, d
3. d
4. a
5. c
6. a, b
7. a
8. b
9. c, d
10. b
11. a, b

9-21 Denominator-level problem. The Goa Sails company produces the Goa 26, a very popular 26-foot recreational yacht. Goa Sails takes pride in the high quality they build into their affordable yachts. The company has been in business for 35 years. Management has recently adopted absorption costing and is debating which denominator-level concept to use. The Goa 26 sells for an average price of Rs 1,50,000. Budgeted fixed manufacturing overhead for 2012 is estimated at Rs 3,80,00,000. Goa Sails uses sub-assembly operators that provide component parts. Assume for simplicity that each yacht can be started and completed in a single shift. The following are the denominator-level options that management has been considering:

a. Theoretical capacity-based on two shifts, completion of four boats per shift, and a 360-day year 2 × 4 × 360 = 2,880.
b. Practical capacity-theoretical capacity adjusted for unavoidable interruptions, breakdowns, and so forth-2 × 3 × 300 = 1,800.
c. Normal capacity utilization-based on the Marketing Department's estimate of 1,000 units.
d. Master budget capacity utilization-the booming stock market and a record number of baby boomers retiring over the coming year has prompted the Marketing Department to issue a special estimate for 2007 of 1,200 units.

Required

1. Calculate the budgeted fixed manufacturing overhead cost rates under the four denominator-level concepts.
2. Why compute fixed costs at the individual product level? Why is this only done under absorption costing?
3. Why would Goa Sails prefer to use either theoretical or practical capacity?
4. Under a cost-based pricing system, what is the negative aspect of a master-budget denominator level? What may be the positive aspect?

Denominator-level problem.

1. Budgeted fixed manufacturing overhead costs rates:

Denominator Level Capacity Concept	Budgeted Fixed Manufacturing Overhead per Period	Budgeted Capacity Level Overhead Cost Rate	Budgeted Fixed Manufacturing
Theoretical	Rs 3,80,00,000	2,880	Rs 13,194.4
Practical	3,80,00,000	1,800	21,111.1
Normal	3,80,00,000	1,000	38,000
Master budget	3,80,00,000	1,200	31,666.7

The rates are different because of varying denominator-level concepts. Theoretical and practical capacity levels are driven by supply-side concepts, that is, "how much can I produce?" Normal and master budget capacity levels are driven by demand-side concepts, that is, "how much can I sell?" (or "how much should I produce?")

2. In order to incorporate fixed manufacturing costs into unit product costs, fixed manufacturing costs have to be unitized for inventory costing. Absorption costing is the method used for tax reporting and for financial reporting using generally accepted accounting principles. The choice of a denominator level becomes relevant under absorption costing because fixed costs are accounted for along with variable costs at the individual product level. Variable and throughput costing account for fixed costs as a lump sum, expensed in the period incurred.
3. The variances that arise from use of the theoretical or practical level concepts will signal that there is a divergence between the supply of capacity and demand for capacity. This is useful input to managers. As a general rule, however, it is important not to place undue reliance on the production-volume variance as a measure of the economic costs of unused capacity.

4. Under a cost-based pricing system, the choice of a master-budget level denominator will lead to high prices when demand is low (more fixed costs allocated to the individual product level), further eroding demand; conversely it will lead to low prices when demand is high, forgoing profits. This has been referred to as the downward demand spiral—the continuing reduction in demand that occurs when the prices of competitors are not met and demand drops, resulting in even higher unit costs and even more reluctance to meet the prices of competitors. The positive aspect of the master-budget denominator level is that it indicates the price at which all costs per unit would be recovered to enable the company to make a profit. Master-budget denominator level is also a good benchmark against which to evaluate performance.

9-22 Variable and absorption costing and breakeven points (chapter appendix). Radico Khaitan a distillery in northern India manufactures a premium liquor and sells primarily to distributors. Liquor is sold in cases of one dozen bottles. In the year ended December 31, 2012, Radico Khaitan sold 242,400 cases at an average selling price of Rs 940 per case. The following additional data are Radico Khaitan for the year ended December 31, 2012 (assume constant unit costs and no price, spending, or efficiency variances):

Beginning inventory, January 1, 2012	32,600 cases
Ending inventory, December 31,2012	24,800 cases
Fixed manufacturing overhead	Rs 3,75,36,000
Fixed operating costs Variable costs	Rs 6,56,88,000
Variable costs:	
Direct materials	
Grapes	Rs 160 per case
Bottles, corks, and crates	Rs 100 per case
Direct labor:	
Bottling	Rs 60 per case
Fermenting	Rs 140 per case
packing	Rs 20 per case

On December 31, 2011, the cost per case for ending inventory is Rs 460 for variable costing and Rs 610 for absorption costing.

Required

1. Calculate cases of production for Radico Khaitan in 2012.
2. Find the breakeven point (number cases) in 2012
   a. under variable costing
   b. under absorption costing

Solution

Variable and absorption costing and breakeven points.

1. Production = Sales + Ending inventory – Beginning inventory
   = 242,400 + 24,800 – 32,600
   = 234,600 cases
2. Breakeven point in cases:
   a. Variable costing:
   46 QT – 16 QT = Rs 6,56,88,000

$$QT = \frac{\text{Total fixed costs} + \text{Target operating income}}{\text{Contribution margin per unit}}$$

$$QT = \frac{(\text{Rs } 3{,}75{,}36{,}000 + \text{Rs } 6{,}56{,}88{,}000) + \text{Rs } 0}{\text{Rs } 940 - (\text{Rs } 160 + \text{Rs } 100 + \text{Rs } 60 + \text{Rs } 140 + \text{Rs } 20)}$$

$$QT = \frac{\text{Rs } 10{,}32{,}24{,}000}{\text{Rs } 460} = 2{,}24{,}400 \text{ cases}$$

B. Absorption costing:
Fixed manufacting cost rate + Rs 3,75,36,000 ÷ Rs 234,600 = Rs 160 per case

$$QT = \frac{\text{Total fixed cost} + \text{Target OI} + \left[\text{Fixed manufacturing cost rate} \times \left(\text{Breakeven sales in units} - \text{Units produced}\right)\right]}{\text{Contribution margin per unit}}$$

$$QT = \frac{\text{Rs } 10{,}32{,}24{,}000 + [\text{Rs } 160(QT - 234{,}600)]}{\text{Rs } 460}$$

$$QT = \frac{\text{Rs } 10{,}32{,}24{,}000 + 16\,QT - 3{,}753{,}600}{\text{Rs } 460}$$

$$QT = \frac{\text{Rs } 6{,}56{,}88{,}000 + 16QT}{\text{Rs } 460}$$

30 QT = Rs 6,56,88,000
QT = 218,960 cases.

9-23 ABC and capacity usage. The controller of Dabur Ltd. has collected the following data for two activities. Harris calculates activity cost rates based on cost driver capacity.

Activity	Cost Driver	Capacity	Cost
Power	Kilowatt hours	50,000 kilowatt hours	Rs 20,00,000
Quality inspection	Number of inspections	10,000 inspections	30,00,000

The company makes two products: Hajmola and Ambla oil. For the year just ended, the following consumption of cost drivers was reported:

Product	Kilowatt hour	Quality Inspections
Hajmola	10,000	5,000
Amla oil	35,000	4,000

Required

1. Compute the costs allocated to each product from each activity.
2. Calculate the cost of unused capacity for each activity.

Solution

ABC and capacity usage.

1. Activity	Rate per Unit of Cost Driver
Power	Rs 20,00,000 activity costs ÷ 50,000 kilowatt hours = Rs 40 per kilowatt hour
Quality inspection	Rs 30,00,000 activity costs ÷ 10,000 inspections = Rs 300 per inspection

Cost allocation:

Power	
Hajmola (10,000 kilowatt hours × Rs 40)	Rs 4,00,000
Amla oil (35,000 kilowatt hours × Rs 40)	14,00,000
Total power costs allocation	Rs 18,00,000
Quality inspection	
Hajmola (5,000 inspections ´ Rs 300)	Rs 15,00,000
Amla oil (4,000 inspections ´ Rs 300)	12,00,000
Total quality inspection costs allocation	Rs 27,00,000

2. Cost of unused capacity:

Power (Rs 20,00,000 – Rs 18,00,000)	Rs 2,00,000
Quality inspection (Rs 30,00,000 – Rs 27,00,000)	3,00,000
Total cost of unused capacity	Rs 5,00,000

9-24 Comparison of variable costing and absorption costing. Consider the following data

Hindustan Company

Income Statement for the Year Ended December 31, 2011

	Variable Costing	Absorption Costing
Revenues	Rs 70,00,000	Rs 70,00,000
Cost of goods sold (at standard)	36,60,000	45,75,000
Fixed manufacturing overhead	10,00,000	–
Manufacturing variances (all unfavorable):		
Direct materials price and efficiency	50,000	50,000
Direct manufacturing labor price and efficiency	60,000	60,000
Variable manufacturing overhead spending and efficiency	30,000	30,000
Fixed manufacturing overhead:		
Spending	1,00,000	1,00,000
Production volume	–	4,00,000
Total marketing costs (all fixed)	10,00,000	10,00,000
Total administrative costs (all fixed)	5,00,000	5,00,000
Total costs	64,00,000	67,15,000
Operating income	6,00,000	2,85,000

The inventories, carried at standard costs, were:

	Variable Costing	Absorption Costing
December 31, 2010	Rs 13,20,000	Rs 16,50,000
December 31, 2011	60,000	75,000

Required

1. Ahmed president of Hindustan Company, has asked you to explain why the operating income for 2011 is less than for 2010, even though sales have increased 40% over last year. What will you tell him?
2. At what percentage of denominator level was the plant operating during 2011?
3. Prepare a numerical reconciliation and explanation of the difference between operating income under absorption costing and variable costing.

Solution

Comparison of variable costing and absorption costing.

i. Operating income is a function of both sales and production under absorption costing, whereas it is a function only of sales under variable costing. Therefore, inventory changes can have dramatic effects on operating income under absorption costing. In this case, the severe decline in inventory has resulted in enormous fixed costs from beginning inventory being charged against 2011 operations.

ii. The income statement deliberately contains an ambiguity about whether the fixed manufacturing overhead of Rs 10,00,000 is the budgeted or actual amount. Of course, it must be the budgeted amount because the spending variance and the output level variance are shown separately. Therefore,

$$\text{Production-volume variance} = \text{Budgeted fixed manufacturing overhead} - \text{Fixed manufacturing overhead allocated}$$

Rs 400,000 = Rs 10,00,000 – Allocated

Allocated = Rs 6,00,000, which is 60% of denominator level

iii. Note that the answer to (3) is independent of (2). The difference in operating income of Rs 315,000 (Rs 600,000 – Rs 285,000) is explained by the release of Rs 315,000 of fixed manufacturing costs when the inventories were decreased during 2011:

	Absorption Costing	Variable Costing	Fixed Manufacturing Overhead in Inventory
Inventories:			
December 31, 2010	Rs 16,50,000	Rs 13,20,000	Rs 3,30,000
December 31, 2011	75,000	60,000	15,000
Release of fixed manufacturing costs			Rs 3,15,000

The above schedule in this requirement is a formal presentation of the equation:

$$\begin{pmatrix}\text{Absorption-costing operating income} - \text{Variable-costing operating income}\end{pmatrix} = \begin{pmatrix}\text{Fixed manufacturing costs in ending inventory} - \text{Fixed manufacturing costs in beginning inventory}\end{pmatrix}$$

$$(\text{Rs } 2{,}85{,}000 - \text{Rs } 6{,}00{,}000) = (\text{Rs } 15{,}000 - \text{Rs } 3{,}30{,}000)$$
$$= -\text{Rs } 3{,}15{,}000$$

Alternatively, the presence of fixed manufacturing overhead costs in each income statement can be analyzed:

Absorption costing,	
Fixed manufacturing costs in cost of goods sold (Rs 4,575,000 " Rs 3,660,000)	Rs 9,15,000
Production-volume variance	4,00,000
	13,15,000
Variable costing, fixed manufacturing costs charged to expense	10,00,000
Difference in operating income explained	Rs 3,15,000

Although it is not required, the following supplementary analysis may clarify the relationships (all amounts are at standard costs):

	Variable Costing	Absorption Costing
Inventory, December 31, 2010	Rs 16,50,000	Rs 13,20,000
Cost of goods manufactured*	30,00,000	24,00,000
Available for sale	46,50,000	37,20,000
Inventory, December 31, 2011	75,000	60,000
Cost of goods sold	Rs 45,75,000	Rs 36,60,000

*Computed from the other data, which are given.

9-25 Effects of denominator-level choice. The TCL Ltd. installed standard costs and a flexible budget on January 1, 2012. The President has been pondering how fixed manufacturing overhead should be allocated to products. Machine-hours has been chosen as the allocation base. His remaining uncertainty is the denominator-level for machine-hours. He decides to wait for the first month's results before making a final choice of what denominator-level should be used from that day forward.

In January 2012, the actual units of output had a standard of 70,000 machine-hours allowed. If the company used practical capacity as the denominator-level, the fixed manufacturing overhead spending variance would be Rs 1,00,000, unfavorable, and the production-volume variance would be Rs 3,60,000, unfavorable. If the company used normal capacity utilization as the denominator-level, the production-volume variance would be Rs 2,00,000, favorable.

Budgeted fixed manufacturing overhead was Rs 12,00,000 for the month.

Required

1. Compute the denominator level, assuming that the normal capacity utilization concept is chosen.
2. Compute the denominator level, assuming that the practical capacity concept is chosen.
3. Suppose you are the executive Vice-President. You want to maximize your 2012 bonus, which depends on 2012 operating income. Assume that the production-volume variance is added or deducted from operating income at year-end. Which denominator-level would you favor? Why?

Solution

Effects of denominator-level concept choice.

1. Normal capacity utilization. Givens denoted*

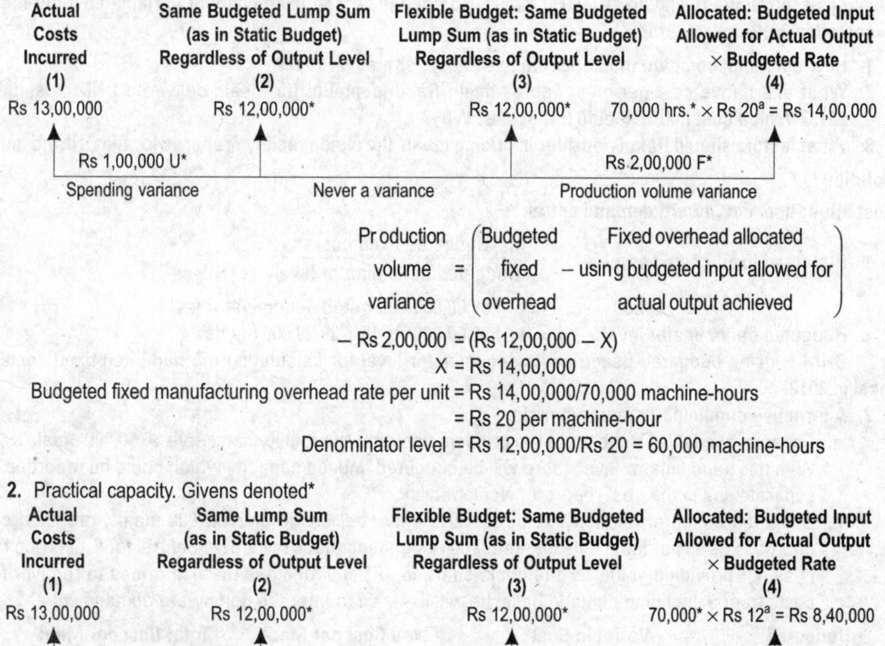

$$\text{Production volume variance} = \left(\text{Budgeted fixed overhead} - \text{Fixed overhead allocated using budgeted input allowed for actual output achieved}\right)$$

$$-\text{Rs } 2{,}00{,}000 = (\text{Rs } 12{,}00{,}000 - X)$$

$$X = \text{Rs } 14{,}00{,}000$$

Budgeted fixed manufacturing overhead rate per unit = Rs 14,00,000/70,000 machine-hours
= Rs 20 per machine-hour

Denominator level = Rs 12,00,000/Rs 20 = 60,000 machine-hours

2. Practical capacity. Givens denoted*

$$\text{Production volume variance} = \left(\text{Budgeted fixed overhead} - \text{Fixed overhead allocated using budgeted input allowed for actual output achieved}\right)$$

$$\text{Rs } 3{,}60{,}000 = (\text{Rs } 12{,}00{,}000 - X)$$

$$X = \text{Rs } 8{,}40{,}000$$

Budgeted manufacturing overhead rate per unit = Rs 8,40,000/70,000 machine-hours
= Rs 12 per machine-hour

Denominator level = Rs 12,00,000/Rs 12 = 1,00,000 machine-hours

3. To maximize operating income, the executive Vice-President would favor using normal capacity utilization rather than practical capacity. Why? Because normal capacity utilization is a smaller base than practical capacity, resulting in any year-end inventory having a higher unit cost. Thus, less fixed manufacturing overhead would become a 2012 expense as part of the production-volume variance if normal capacity utilization were used as the denominator level.

9-26 Cost allocation, downward demand spiral. Delhi Health maintenance operates a chain of 10 hospitals in the Delhi. For many years, it has operated a central food-catering facility in Noida, which delivers meals to the hospitals. The Noida facility has the capacity to serve 36,50,000 meals a year (10,000 meals a day). In 2012 it budgeted for 29,20,000 meals (8,000 meals a day), based on demand estimates from each hospital controller. The budgeted variable cost per meal in 2012 is Rs 38, which includes delivery to the hospital. Budgeted fixed costs for 2012 are Rs 4,38,00,000.

In July 2012, the new DHM resident announces that each hospital is to be a profit centre. In addition, the head of each hospital can purchase services from outside DHM, provided those services meet the DHM quality requirements. The President gives catering as an example. Rahul, the head of the Noida Monica catering facility, is less than pleased. This facility will also become a profit center (it has been cost centre for many years) under the reorganization.

Rahul charged each hospital Rs 53 per meal in 2012-comprising Rs 38 variable cost plus Rs 15 allocation of budgeted fixed costs. Several hospitals complained about the Rs 53 cost, as well as the quality of the food. Moreover, the cost rose from Rs 49 in 2011 to Rs 53 in 2012. Rahul defended the increase, claiming he needed to spread the same fixed costs over a smaller number of patient-days in 2012. DHM experienced negative press on a local TV station in 2011 and early 2012, and local doctors are referring fewer patients to the DHM hospitals.

In October 2012, Rahul started to prepare the 2013 budget, including the new cost to be charged per meal. He estimated that the total annual demand for meals at all DMH hospitals would be 25,50,000. Then he learned that 3 of the 10 hospitals will use an outside canteen service, which reduces the 2013 budgeted demand at the Noida facility to 20,00,000 meals. No change in total fixed costs or variable cost per meal is expected in 2012.

Required

1. How did Rahul compute the budgeted fixed cost per meal in 2012?
2. What alternative cost-per-meal figures might Rahul compute for meals delivered DHM hospitals in 2013? Which cost figure should Rahul use? Why?
3. What factors should Rahul consider in pricing meals the Noida facility prepares for the DHMhospitals?

Solution

Cost allocation, downward demand spiral.

1. Budgeted fixed costs per meal $= \dfrac{\text{Budgeted fixed costs}}{\text{Budgeted denominator level}}$

Rs 1.50 = Rs 4,38,00,000/Budgeted denominator level

Budgeted denominator level = Rs 4,38,00,000/Rs 15 = 29,20,000 meals

DHM is using budgeted usage as its denominator level for calculating the budgeted fixed costs per meal in 2012.

2. Alternative denominator levels include:
   a. Capacity available. The data in the problem note that the facility can serve 36,50,000 meals a year. With this denominator level, there will be budgeted unused capacity which could be recorded as a separate line in the cost report for Noida facility.
   b. Budgeted usage of capacity. With the 2012 budgeted usage of 29,20,000 meals, the fixed costs charge is Rs 15 per meal. The marketplace is signaling that DHM's own central food-catering facility is not providing value for the costs charged. If Rahul decides to raise prices to recover fixed costs from a declining demand base, he will likely encounter the downward demand spiral:

Budgeted Denominator (1)	Variable Cost per Meal (2)	Fixed Cost per Meal Rs 4,38,00,000 ÷ (1) (3)	Total Cost per Meal (4)
36,50,000	Rs 38	Rs 12	Rs 50
29,20,000	38	15	53
25,50,000	38	17.2	55.2
20,00,000	38	21.9	59.9

Rahul might adopt a contribution margin approach, which means viewing the Rs 38 variable cost as the only per-unit cost and the Rs 4,38,00,000 as a fixed cost. Alternatively, Rahul could use practical capacity to cost the meals and work to reduce costs of unused capacity.

3. Three factors managers should consider in pricing decisions:
   a. Customers. Rahul is facing customers who are dissatisfied with both the cost and quality of the meal service. Three of the 10 hospitals have already elected to use an outside canteen service.
   b. Competitors. For the three hospitals terminating use of Noida facility, at least one competitor is more cost-effective. The seven remaining hospitals likely will be very interested in how this competitor performs at the three hospitals.
   c. Costs. Rahul should consider ways to reduce both the variable costs per meal and the fixed costs.

9-27 Cost allocation, budgeted rates, ethics (continuation of 9-26). The actual meal counts used in 2012 by all of DHM's hospitals were less than the budgeted amounts each hospital controller provided Rahul at the start of 2012. Rahul suspects collusion on the part of the hospital controllers. He is concerned that the 2013 budgeted meal counts from the individual hospital will likewise turn out to be way too optimistic about actual demand.

Required

1. Why might the individual hospital administrators deliberately overestimate the 2012 budgeted meal-count demand?
2. Rahul decides to approach the DHM corporate controller to discuss his concerns about the indivuual hospital controllers colluding on budgeted meal-count demand. What evidence should the corporate controller seek to investigate Rahul's concern.
3. What steps should the corporate controller take to reduce any incentives individual hospital controllers have to deliberately overestimate meal demand for 2013?

Solution

Cost allocation, budgeted rates, ethics (continuation of 9-26).

1. Hospitals are charged a budgeted variable cost rate and an allocation of budgeted fixed costs. By overestimating budgeted meal counts, the denominator of the budgeted fixed cost rate is larger, and hence the amount charged to individual hospitals is lower. Consider 2012 where the budgeted fixed cost rate of Rs 15 is computed as follows:

   Rs 4,38,00,000/29,20,000 meals = Rs 15 per meal

   Suppose in 2006, hospital administrators "inflated" their budgeted meal count by 20%. The budgeted fixed cost rate for 2012 rate would have been Rs 4,38,00,000/35,04,000 meals = Rs 12.5 per meal

   Hence, by deliberately overstating budgeted meal count demand, they could reduce the costs charged per meal in 2012. The use of budgeted meals as the denominator means the central food-catering facility bears the risk of demand overestimates.

2. Evidence that could be collected include:
   a. Budgeted meal-count estimates and actual meal-count figures each year for each hospital controller. Over an extended time period, there should be a sizable number of both underestimates and overestimates. Controllers could be ranked on both their percentage of overestimation and the frequency of their overestimation.
   b. Look at the underlying demand estimates by patients at individual hospitals. Each hospital controller has other factors (such as hiring of nurses) that gives insight into their expectations of future meal-count demands. If these factors are inconsistent with the meal-count demand figures provided to the central food-catering facility, explanations should be sought.

3. a. Highlight the importance of a corporate culture of honesty and openness. DHM could institute a Code of Ethics that highlights the upside of individual hospitals providing honest estimates of demand (and the penalties for those who do not).
   b. Have individual hospitals contract in advance for their budgeted meal count. Unused amounts would be charged to each hospital at the end of the accounting period. This approach puts a penalty on hospital administrators who overestimate demand.
   c. Use an incentive scheme that has an explicit component for meal-count forecasting accuracy. Each meal-count "forecasting error" would reduce the bonus by Re 0.50. Thus, if a hospital bids for 2,92,000 meals and actually uses 200,000 meals, its bonus would be reduced by

   Rs 0.50 × (292,000 – 200, 000) = Rs 46,000.

9-28 Absorption, variable and throughput costing. The Gurgaon plant of Maruti Udyog Ltd. assembles the Wagon R motor vehicle. The standard unit manufacturing cost per vehicle in 2011 is:

Direct materials	Rs 60,000
Direct manufacturing labor	18,000
Variable manufacturing overhead	20,000
Fixed manufacturing overhead	?

The Gurgaon plant is highly automated. Maximum productive capacity per month is 4,000 vehicles. Variable manufacturing overhead is allocated to vehicles on the basis of assembly time. The standard assembly time per vehicle is 20 hours. Fixed manufacturing overhead in 2011 is allocated on the basis of the standard assembly time for the budgeted normal capacity utilization of the plant. In 2011, the budgeted normal capacity utilization is 3,000 vehicles per month. The budgeted monthly fixed manufacturing overhead is Rs 7,50,00,000.

On January 1, 2011, there is zero beginning inventory of Wagon R vehicles. The actual unit production and sales figures for the first three months of 2011 are:

	January	February	March
Production	3,200	2,400	3,800
Sales	2,000	2,900	3,200

Assume no direct materials variances, no direct manufacturing labor variances, and no manufacturing overhead spending or efficiency variances in the first three months of 2011.

Anil, Vice-President of Maruti Udyog Ltd., is the manager of the Gurgaon plant. His compensations includes a bonus that is 0.5% of quarterly operating income. Operating income is calculated using absorption costing. Maruti Udyog Ltd. prepares absorption-costing income statements monthly, which includes an adjustment to cost of goods sold for the total manufacturing variances occurring in that month.

The Gurgaon plant "sells" each Wagon R at Rs 1,60,000 per vehicle (net of government taxes). No marketing costs are incurred by the Gurgaon plant.

Required

1. Compute (a) the fixed manufacturing overhead cost per unit and (b) the total manufacturing cost per unit.
2. Compute the monthly operating income for January, February, and March under absorption-costing. What bonus is paid each month to Anil?

3. How much would use of variable costing change Anil's bonus each month if the same 0.5% figure were applied to variable-costing operating income?
4. Explain the differences in Anil's bonuses in requirements 2 and 3.
5. How much would the use of throughput costing change Anil's bonus if the same 0.5% figure were applied to throughput-costing operating income?
6. Outline different approaches Maruti Udyog Ltd. could use to reduce possible undesirable behavior associated with the use of absorption costing at its Gurgaon plant.

Solution

Absorption, variable, and throughput costing.

1.
   a. Unit fixed manufacturing overhead cost = Rs 7,50,00,000/3,000 vehicles x 20 standard hours
      = Rs 7,50,00,000/60,000
      = Rs 1,250 per standard assembly hour or Rs 25,000 per vehicle

   b.

Direct materials per unit	Rs 60,000
Direct manufacturing labor per unit	18,000
Variable manufacturing overhead per unit	20,000
Fixed manufacturing overhead per unit	25,000
Total manufacturing cost per unit	Rs 1,23,000

2. Amounts in thousands.

	Absorption Costing		
	January	**February**	**March**
Revenues (Rs 1,60,000 ´ 2,000; 2,900; 3200)	Rs 3,20,000	Rs 4,64,000	Rs 5,12,000
Cost of goods sold			
Beginning inventory	0	1,47,600	86,100
Variable manufacturing costs (Rs 98 ´ 3,200; 2,400; 3800)	3,13,600	2,35,200	3,72,400
Fixed manufacturing costs (Rs 25 ´ 3,200; 2,400; 3,800)	80,000	60,000	95,000
Cost of goods available for sale	3,93,600	4,42,800	5,53,500
Deduct ending inventory (Rs 123 ´ 1,200; 700; 1,300)	1,47,600	86,100	1,59,900
Cost of goods sold (at standard cost)	2,46,000	3,56,700	3,93,600
Adjustment for manufacturing variances[a]	5,000 F	5,000 U	20,000 F
Total cost of goods sold	2,41,000	3,71,700	3,73,600
Gross margin	79,000	92,300	1,38,400
Marketing costs	0	0	0
Operating income	Rs 79,0000	Rs 92,300	Rs 1,38,400
Inventory Details (Units)			
Beginning inventory	0	1,200	700
Production	3,200	2,400	3,800
Goods available for sale	3,200	3,600	4,500
Sales	2,000	2,900	3,200
Ending inventory	1,200	700	1,300
Inventory Details (Rs 1,23,000 per unit)			
Beginning inventory (Rs 1,23,000 per unit)	Rs 0	Rs 1,47,600	Rs 86,100
Ending inventory (Rs 10,000s)	Rs 1,47,600	Rs 86,100	Rs 1,59,900

Computation of Bonus	**January**	**February**	**March**
Operating income × 0.5%	Rs 7,90,00,000	Rs 9,23,00,000	Rs 13,84,00,000
	Rs 3,95,000	Rs 4,61,500	Rs 6,92,000

[a]Production–volume variances = (Denomination level – Production) × Budgeted rate
January: (3,000 – 3,200) × Rs 25,000 per vehicle = Rs 50,00,000 F
February: (3,000 – 2,400) × Rs 25,000 per vehicle = Rs 1,50,00,000 U
March: (3,000 – 3,800) × Rs 25,000 per vehicle = Rs 2,00,00,000 F

3. Amounts in thousands.

	Variable Costing		
	January	**February**	**March**
Revenues	Rs 3,20,000	Rs 4,64,000	Rs 5,12,000
Variable costs:			
Beginning inventory	0	1,17,600	68,600
Variable manufacturing costs (Rs 98 × 3,200; 2,400, 3,800)	3,13,600	2,35,200	3,72,400
Cost of goods available for sale	3,13,600	3,52,800	4,41,000
Deduct ending inventory (Rs 98 × 1,200; 700, 1,300)	1,17,600	68,600	1,27,400
Variable COGS	1,96,000	2,84,200	3,13,600
Variable marketing costs	0	0	0

Variable costs (at standard cost)	1,96,000	2,84,200	3,13,600
Adjustment for variances	0	0	0
Total variable costs	1,96,000	2,84,200	3,13,600
Contribution margin	1,24,000	1,79,800	1,98,400
Fixed costs			
Fixed manufacturing overhead costs	75,000	75,000	75,000
Fixed marketing costs	0	0	0
Fixed costs (at standard cost)	75,000	75,000	75,000
Adjustment for variances	0	0	0
Total fixed costs	75,000	75,000	75,000
Operating income	Rs 49,000	Rs 1,04,800	Rs 1,23,400
Inventory Details (Rs 9,800 per unit)			
Beginning inventory (units)	0	1,200	700
Ending inventory (units)	1,200	700	1,300
Beginning inventory (Rs 000's)	Rs 0	Rs 1,17,600	Rs [illegible],600
Ending inventory (Rs 000's)	Rs 1,17,600	Rs 68,600	Rs 1,[illegible]

Computation of Bonus	**January**	**February**	**March**
Operating income ´ 0.5%	Rs 4,90,00,000	Rs 10,48,00,000	Rs 12,34,00,000
	Rs 2,45,000	Rs 5,24,000	Rs 6,17,000

4.

	January	**February**	**March**	**Total**
Absorption-costing Bonus	Rs 3,95,000	Rs 4,61,500	Rs 6,92,000	Rs 15,48,500
Variable-costing Bonus	2,45,000	5,24,000	6,17,000	13,86,000
Difference	Rs 1,50,000	Rs (62,500)	Rs 75,000	Rs 1,62,500

The difference between absorption and variable costing arises because of differences in production and sales:

	January	**February**	**March**	**Total**
Production	3,200	2,400	3,800	9,400
Sales	2,000	2,900	3,200	8,100
Increase (decrease) in inventory	1,200	(500)	600	1,300

With absorption costing, by building for inventory, Anil can capitalize Rs 25,000 of fixed manufacturing overhead costs per unit. This will provide a bonus payment of Rs 125 (0.5% × Rs 25,000) per unit. Operating income under absorption costing will exceed that under variable costing when production is greater than sales. Over the three-month period, the inventory buildup is 1,300 units giving a difference of Rs 1,62,500 (Rs 125 × 1,300) in bonus payments.

5. Amounts in thousands.

	Throughput Costing		
	January	**February**	**March**
Revenues	Rs 3,20,000	Rs 4,64,000	Rs 5,12,000
Direct material cost of goods sold			
Beginning inventory (Rs 60 × 0;1,200; 700)	0	72,000	42,000
Direct materials (Rs 60 × 3,200; 2,400; 3,800)	1,92,000	1,44,000	2,28,000
Cost of goods available for sale	1,92,000	2,16,000	2,70,000
Deduct ending inventory (Rs 60 × 1,200; 700;1,300)	72,000	42,000	78,000
Total direct material cost of good sold	1,20,000	1,74,000	1,92,000
Throughput contribution	2,00,000	2,90,000	3,20,000
Other costs			
Manufacturing[a]	1,96,600	1,66,200	2,19,400
Marketing	0	0	0
Total other costs	1,96,600	1,66,200	2,19,400
Operating income	Rs 3,400	Rs 1,23,800	Rs 1,00,600

[a](Rs 38,000 × 3,200) + Rs 7,50,00,000
(Rs 38,000 × 2,400) + Rs 7,50,00,000
(Rs 38,000 × 3,800) + Rs 7,50,00,000

Computation of Bonus	**January**	**February**	**March**
Operating income × 0.5%	Rs 34,00,000	Rs 12,38,00,000	Rs 10,06,00,000
	Rs 17,000	Rs 6,19,000	Rs 5,03,000

A summary of the bonuses paid is:

	January	**February**	**March**	**Total**
Absorption costing	Rs 3,95,000	Rs 4,61,500	Rs 6,92,000	Rs 15,48,500
Variable costing	2,45,000	5,24,000	6,17,000	13,86,000
Throughput costing	17,000	6,19,000	5,03,000	11,39,000

6. Alternative approaches include:
   a. Careful budgeting and inventory planning,
   b. Use an alternative income computation approach to absorption-costing (such as variable costing or throughput costing),
   c. Use a financial charge for inventory buildup,
   d. Change the compensation package to have a longer-term focus using either an external variable (e.g., stock options) or an internal variable (e.g., five-year average income), and
   e. Adopt non-financial performance targets—e.g., attaining but not exceeding present inventory levels.

Exercises

9-29 Variable and absorption costing, explaining operating income differences. Sony Corporation manufactures and sells 50-inch television sets. Data relating to January, February, and March are:

	January	February	March
Unit data			
Beginning inventory	0	300	300
Production	1,000	800	1,250
Sales	700	800	1,500
Variable costs			
Manufacturing cost per unit produced	Rs 9,000	Rs 9,000	Rs 9,000
Operating cost per unit sold	6,000	6,000	6,000
Fixed costs			
Manufacturing costs	Rs 40,00,000	Rs 40,00,000	Rs 40,00,000
Operating costs	14,00,000	14,00,000	14,00,000

The selling price per unit is Rs 25,000.

Required

1. 1. Present income statements Sony in January, February, and March under (a) variable costing and (b) absorption costing.
2. 2. Explain differences between (a) and (b) for January, February, and March.

9-30 Throughput costing (continuation of 9-29). The variable manufacturing costs per unit of Sony Corporation are:

	January	February	March
Direct materials	Rs 5,000	Rs 5,000	Rs 5,000
Direct manufacturing labor	1,000	1,000	1,000
Manufacturing overhead	3,000	3,000	3,000
	9,000	9,000	9,000

Required

1. Present income statements for Sony in January, February, and March under throughput costing.
2. Contrast the results in requirement 1 with those in requirement 1 of 9-29.
3. Give one motivation for Sony to adopt throughput costing.

9-31 Absorption and variable costing. (CMA) Ashoka Ltd. planned and actually manufactured 200,000 units of its single product in 2011, its first year of operation. Variable manufacturing cost was Rs 20 per unit produced. Variable operating cost was Rs 10 per unit sold. Planned and actual fixed manufacturing costs were Rs 600,000. Planned and actual fixed operating costs totaled Rs 400,000 in 2011. Ashoka sold 120,000 units of product in 2011 at Rs 40 per unit.

Required

1. Ashoka's 2011 operating income using absorption costing is (a) Rs 440,000, (b) Rs 200,000, (c) Rs 600,000, (d) Rs 840,000, (e) none of these.
2. Ashoka's 2011 operating income using variable costing is (a) Rs 800,000, (b) Rs 440,000, (c) Rs 200,000, (d) Rs 600,000, (e) none of these.

9-32 Comparison of actual-costing methods. The Razor India sells its razors at Rs 30 per unit. The company uses a first-in, first-out actual-costing system. A new fixed manufacturing overhead rate is computed each year dividing the actual fixed manufacturing overhead cost by the actual production units. The following simplified data are related to its first two years of operation:

	2011	2012
Sales	1,000 units	1,200 units
Production	1,400 units	1,000 units
Costs:		
Variable manufacturing	Rs 7,000	Rs 5,000
Fixed manufacturing	7,000	7,000
Variable operating	10,000	12,000
Fixed operating	4,000	4,000

Required

1. Prepare income statements based on variable costing for each of the two years.
2. Prepare income statements based on absorption costing for each of the two years.
3. Prepare a numerical reconciliation and explanation of the difference between operating income for each year under absorption-costing and variable costing.
4. Critics have claimed that a widely used accounting system has led to undesirable buildups of inventory levels. (a) Is variable costing or absorption costing more likely to lead to such buildups? Why? (b) What can be done to counteract undesirable inventory buildups?

9-33 ABC and capacity usage. Engineering Company has identified the following activities and cost drivers for its manufacturing overhead. The company calculates activity cost rates based on cost driver capacity.

Machine setup	Rs 50,00,000	5,000 setup-hours
Material handling	20,00,000	1,00,000 kg of material

The Company makes only two products:.A and B. During 2011, A required 3,000 machine setup-hours and handling of 40,000 kgs of materials. B production required 1,500 setup-hours and handling of 50,000 kg of materials.

Required

1. Calculate the costs allocated to each product from each activity.
2. Compute the cost of unused capacity for each activity.

9-34 Cost behavior, activity-based costing, capacity usage. John & Charles Company employs five individuals for its bill processing activity. Each of the employees is paid fixed annual salary of Rs 3,00,000. The budgeted annual activity output of bill processing is 6,000 bills per employee. All other costs in the bill processing activity are variable and are budgeted at Rs 2,25,000 for the year. During the year, 26,000 bills were actually processed. There are no price, efficiency, or spending variances for variable costs and there is no spending variance for fixed costs.

Required

1. Calculate the budgeted fixed rate, budgeted variable rate, and the budgeted total rate for bill processing activity.
2. Compute the total capacity available in bill processing activity in units.
3. Compute the unused capacity in bill processing activity in units.
4. For (a) fixed costs and (b) variable costs, calculate the cost of bill processing activity supplied, the cost of capacity used for the bill processing activity, and the cost of unused capacity, if any, for the bill processing activity. Are there any differences between fixed costs and variable costs with respect to unused capacity. Explain.

9-35 Variable costing versus absorption costing. The Neelkamal Plastics Company uses an absorption-costing system based on standard costs. Total variable manufacturing cost, including direct material cost, is Rs 30 per unit; the standard production rate is 10 units per machine-hour. Total budgeted and actual fixed manufacturing overhead costs are Rs 42,00,000. Fixed manufacturing overhead is allocated at Rs 70 per machine-hour (Rs 42,00,000 ÷ 60,000 machine-hours of denominator level). Selling price is Rs 50 per unit. Variable operating cost, which is driven by units sold, is Rs 10 per unit. Fixed operating costs are Rs 12,00,000. Beginning inventory in 2011 is 30,000 units; ending inventory is 40,000 units. Sales in 2012 are 5,40,000 units. The same standard unit costs persisted throughout 2011 and 2012. For simplicity, assume that there are no price, spending, or efficiency variances.

Required

1. Prepare an income statement for 2012 assuming that all underallocated or overallocated overhead is written off at year-end as an adjustment to Cost of Goods Sold.
2. The President has heard about variable costing. He asks you to recast the 2012 statement as it would appear under variable costing.
3. Explain the difference in operating income as calculated in requirements (1) and (2).
4. Critics have claimed that a widely used accounting system has led to undesirable buildups of inventory levels. (a) Is variable costing or absorption costing more likely to lead to such buildups? Why? (b) What can be done to counteract undesirable inventory buildups?

9-36 Breakeven under absorption costing (chapter appendix). Refer to Solved Example 9-35.

Required

1. Compute the breakeven point (in units) under variable costing.
2. Compute the breakeven point (in units) under absorption costing.
3. Suppose that production is exactly equal to the denominator level, but no units are sold. Fixed manufacturing costs are unaffected. Assume, however, that all operating costs are avoided. Compute operating income under (a) variable costing and (b) absorption costing. Explain the difference between your answers.

9-37 The All-Fixed Company. (R. Marple, adapted) It is the end of 2011. The All-Fixed Company began operations in January 2010. The company is so named because it has no variable costs. All its costs are fixed; they do not vary with output.

The All-Fixed Company is located on the bank of a river and has its own hydroelectric plant to supply power, light, and heat. The company manufactures a synthetic fertilizer from air and river water and sells its product at a price that is not expected to change. It has a small staff of employees all hired on a fixed annual salary. The output of the plant can be increased or decreased by adjusting a few dials on a control panel. The following data are for the operations of the All-Fixed Company:

	2010	2011[a]
Sales	10,000 tons	10,000 tons
Production	20,000 tons	—
Selling price	Rs 300 per ton	Rs 300 per ton
Costs (all fixed):		
Manufacturing	Rs 28,00,000	Rs 28,00,000
Operating	Rs 4,00,000	Rs 4,00,000

[a]Management adopted the policy, effective January 1, 2011, of producing only as much product as needed to fill sales orders. During 2011, sales were the same as for 2011 and were filled entirely from inventory at the start of 2011.

Required

1. Prepare income statements with one column for 2010, one column for 2011, and one column for the two years together, using (a) variable costing and (b) absorption costing.
2. What is the breakeven point under (a) variable costing and (b) absorption costing?
3. What inventory costs would be carried on the balance sheet on December 31, 2010 and 2011, under each method?
4. Assume that the performance of the top manager of the company is evaluated and rewarded largely on the basis of reported operating income. Which costing method would the manager prefer? Why?

9-38 Alternative denominator-level concepts. Lucky Ali recently purchased a brewing plant from a bankrupt company. The brewery is in Warangal, Andhar Pradesh. It was constructed only two years ago. The plant has budgeted fixed manufacturing overhead of Rs 4,200 lakh (Rs 350 lakh each month) in 2012. Amitabh, the controller of the brewery, must decide on the denominator-level concept to use in its absorption costing system for 2012. The options available to him are

a. Theoretical capacity for 2012: 600 barrels an hour for 24 hours per day × 365 days = 5,256,000 barrels
b. Practical capacity for 2012: 500 barrels an hour for 20 hours per day × 350 days = 3,500,000 barrels
c. Normal capacity utilization for 2012: 400 barrels an hour for 20 hours per day × 350 days = 2,800,000 barrels
d. Master-budget capacity utilization for 2012 (separate rates computed for each half-year)
   - January-June 2012 budget: 320 barrels an hour for 20 hours a day × 175 days = 1,120,000 barrels
   - July- December 2012 budget: 480 barrels an hour for 20 hours a day × 175 days = 1,680,000 barrels

Variable standard manufacturing costs per barrel are Rs 450 (variable direct materials, Rs 320; variable manufacturing labor, Rs 60; and variable manufacturing overhead, Rs 70). The Warangal brewery "sells" its output to the sales division of Lucky Ali at a budgeted price of Rs 680 per barrel.

Required

1. Compute the budgeted fixed manufacturing overhead rate using each of the four denominator-level concepts for (a) beer produced in March 2012 and (b) beer produced in September 2012. Explain why any differences arise.
2. Explain why the theoretical capacity and practical capacity concepts are different.
3. Which denominator-level concept would the plant manager of the Warangal brewery prefer when senior management of Lucky Ali is judging plant manager performance during 2012? Explain.

9-39 Operating income effects of alternative denominator-level concepts (continuation of Problem 9-38). In 2012, the Warangal brewery of Lucky Ali showed these results:

Beginning inventory, January 1, 2012	0 barrels
Production	26,00,000 barrels
Ending inventory, December 31, 2012	2,00,000 barrels

The Warangal brewery had actual costs of:

Variable manufacturing costs	Rs 1,20,38,00,000
Fixed manufacturing overhead costs	40,63,20,000

The sales division of Lucky Ali purchased 2,400,000 barrels in 2012 at the Rs 680 per barrel rate. All manufacturing variances are written off to cost of goods sold in the period in which they are incurred.

Required

1. Compute the operating income of the Warangal brewery using the denominator-level concepts of (a) theoretical capacity, (b) practical capacity, and (c) normal capacity utilization. Explain any differences among (a), (b), and (c).
2. What denominator-level concept would Lucky Ali prefer for income tax reporting, assuming he has the choice? Explain.

9-40 Downward demand spiral. Moser beer Company manufactures 1 terabyte optical mini-disk systems. The current year's monthly production and sales are budgeted at 10,000 units. Moser beer's variable manufacturing cost per unit is Rs 2,000, and its monthly fixed manufacturing overhead costs total Rs 1,00,00,000. Moser beer sets the selling price of its product by adding a 100% markup to the full product cost per unit. The full product cost per unit includes variable manufacturing cost per unit plus the fixed manufacturing overhead cost per unit based on fully allocating total fixed manufacturing overhead costs to the units produced.

Required

1. Compute Moser beer's Company's budgeted selling price.
2. Due to intense competition, Moser beer had to revise its budgeted monthly production and sales downward to 8,000 units. Compute Moser beer Company's revised budgeted selling price.
3. Comment on your results in (1) and (2) above.

9-41 Denominator level, production-volume variance. Mirc Electronics Ltd. acquired plant assets based on forecasts of long-range demand for its products. Its budgeted manufacturing overhead costs for 2012 are Rs 10,50,00,000. For each of the four alternative denominator-level capacities, Mirc's capacity is:

Denominator-Level Capacity	Denominator-Level (in machine-hours)
Theoretical capacity	21,00,000
Practical capacity	15,00,000
Normal capacity utilization	13,12,500
Master-budget capacity utilization	10,00,000

Required

1. Calculate budgeted fixed manufacturing overhead rate per machine-hour for each denominator-level capacity.
2. For 2012 actual output, 11,00,000 budgeted machine-hours were allowed. Compute production-volume variance under each of the denominator-level capacity assumptions.

10 Determining How Costs Behave

Learning Objectives

1. Describe linear cost functions and three common ways in which they behave
2. Explain the importance of causality in estimating cost functions
3. Understand various methods of cost estimation
4. Outline six steps in estimating a cost function using quantitative analysis
5. Describe three criteria used to evaluate and choose cost drivers
6. Explain nonlinear cost functions, in particular those arising from learning curve effects
7. Be aware of data problems encountered in estimating cost functions

What is the value of looking at the past? Perhaps it is to recall fond memories you've had or help you understand historical events. Or, maybe your return to the past enables you to better understand and predict the future. When an organization looks at the past, it typically does so to analyze its results, so that the best decisions can be made for the company's future. This activity requires gathering information about costs and how they behave so that managers can predict what they will be "down the road." But sometimes looking at the past isn't enough—especially when the firm is undertaking new opportunities, as the following article shows.

Management Accountants at Cisco Embrace Opportunities, Enhance Sustainability[1]

Understanding how costs behave is a valuable technical skill. Managers look to management accountants to help them identify cost drivers, estimate cost relationships, and determine the fixed and variable components of costs. To be effective, management accountants must have a clear understanding of the business's strategy and operations to identify new opportunities to reduce costs and increase profitability. At Cisco Systems, management accountants' in-depth understanding of the company's costs and operations led to reduced costs, while also helping the environment.

Cisco, makers of computer networking equipment including routers and wireless switches, traditionally regarded the used equipment it received back from its business customers as scrap and recycled it at a cost of about $8 million a year. As managers looked at the accumulated costs and realized that they may literally be "throwing away money," they decided to reassess their treatment of scrap material. In 2005, managers at Cisco began trying to find uses for the equipment, mainly because 80% of the returns were in working condition. A value recovery team at Cisco identified groups within the company that could use the returned equipment. These included its customer service group, which supports warranty claims and service contracts, and the labs that provide technical support, training, and product demonstrations.

[1] *Source:* Nidumolu, R., C. Prahalad, and M. Rangaswami. 2009. Why sustainability is now the key driver of innovation. *Harvard Business Review,* September 2009; Cisco Systems, Inc. 2009. *2009 corporate social responsibility report.* San Jose, CA: Cisco Systems, Inc.

Based on the initial success of the value recovery team, in 2005, Cisco designated its recycling group as a company business unit, set clear objectives for it, and assigned the group its own income statement. As a result, the reuse of equipment rose from 5% in 2004 to 45% in 2008, and Cisco's recycling costs fell by 40%. The unit has become a profit center that contributed $153 million to Cisco's bottom line in 2008.

With product returns reducing corporate profitability by an average of about 4% a year, companies like Cisco can leverage management accountants' insight to reduce the cost of these returns while decreasing its environmental footprint. Not only can this turn a cost center into a profitable business, but sustainability efforts like these signals that the company is concerned about preventing environmental damage by reducing waste.

As the Cisco example illustrates, managers must understand how costs behave to make strategic and operating decisions that have a positive environmental impact. Consider several other examples. Managers at FedEx decided to replace old planes with new Boeing 757s that reduced fuel consumption by 36%, while increasing capacity by 20%. At Clorox, managers decided to create a new line of non-synthetic cleaning products that were better for the environment and helped create a new category of 'green' cleaning products worth about $200 million annually.

In each situation, knowledge of cost behavior was needed to answer key questions. This chapter will focus on how managers determine cost-behavior patterns—that is, how costs change in relation to changes in activity levels, in the quantity of products produced, and so on.

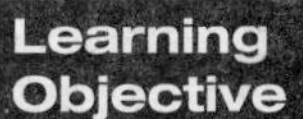

Learning Objective 1

Describe linear cost functions

. . . graph of cost function is a straight line

and three common ways in which they behave

. . . variable, fixed, and mixed

Basic Assumptions and Examples of Cost Functions

Managers are able to understand cost behavior through cost functions. A **cost function** is a mathematical description of how a cost changes with changes in the level of an activity relating to that cost. Examples of activities are preparing setups for production runs and operating machines. Cost functions can be plotted on a graph by measuring the level of an activity, such as number of batches produced or number of machine-hours used, on the horizontal axis (called the *x*-axis) and the amount of total costs corresponding to—or, preferably, dependent on—the levels of that activity on the vertical axis (called the *y*-axis).

Basic Assumptions

Managers often estimate cost functions based on two assumptions:

1. Variations in the level of a single activity (the cost driver) explain the variations in the related total costs.
2. Cost behavior is approximated by a linear cost function within the relevant range. Recall that a relevant range is the range of the activity in which there is a relationship between total cost and the level of activity. For a **linear cost function** represented graphically, total cost versus the level of a single activity related to that cost is a straight line within the relevant range.

We use these two assumptions throughout most, but not all, of this chapter. Not all cost functions are linear and can be explained by a single activity. Later sections will discuss cost functions that do not rely on these assumptions.

Linear Cost Functions

To understand three basic types of linear cost functions and to see the role of cost functions in business decisions, consider the negotiations between Cannon Services and World Wide Communications (WWC) for exclusive use of a telephone line between New Delhi and Paris.

- **Alternative 1:** Rs 10 per phone-minute used. Total cost to Cannon changes in proportion to the number of phone-minutes used. The number of phone-minutes used is the only factor whose change causes a change in total cost.

  Panel A in Exhibit 10-1 presents this *variable cost* for Cannon Services. Under alternative 1, there is no fixed cost. We write the cost function in Panel A of Exhibit 10-1 as

  $$Y = \text{Rs } 10X$$

  where X measures the actual number of phone-minutes used (on the x-axis), and y measures the total cost of the phone-minutes used (on the y-axis) calculated using the cost function. Panel A illustrates the Rs 10 **slope coefficient**, the amount by which total cost changes when a one-unit change occurs in the level of activity (one phone-minute in the Cannon example). *Throughout the chapter, uppercase letters, such as X, refer to the actual observations, and lowercase letters, such as y, represent estimates or calculations made using a cost function.*
- **Alternative 2:** Total cost will be fixed at Rs 1,00,000 per month, regardless of the number of phone-minutes used. (We use the same activity measure, number of phone-minutes used, to compare cost-behavior patterns under the three alternatives.)

Exhibit 10-1 Examples of Linear Cost Functions

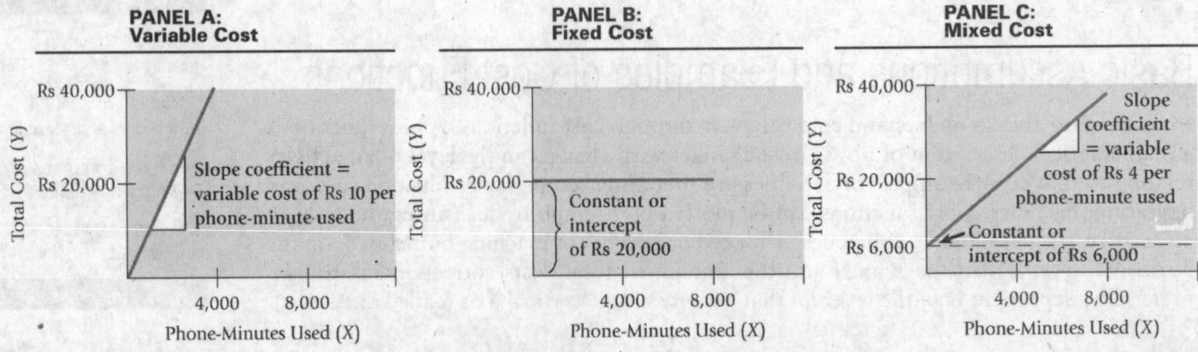

Panel B in Exhibit 10-1 presents this *fixed cost* for Cannon Services. We write the cost function in Panel B as

$$Y = \text{Rs } 20{,}000$$

The fixed cost of Rs 20,000 is called a **constant**; it is the component of total cost that does not vary with changes in the level of the activity. Under alternative 2, the constant accounts for all the cost because there is no variable cost. Graphically, the slope coefficient of the cost function is zero; this cost function intersects the *y*-axis at the constant value, and therefore the *constant* is also called the **intercept**.

- **Alternative 3:** Rs 6,000 per month plus Rs 4 per phone-minute used. This is an example of a mixed cost. A **mixed cost**—also called a **semivariable cost**—is a cost that has both fixed and variable elements.

Panel C in Exhibit 10-1 presents this *mixed cost* for Cannon Services. We write the cost function in Panel C of Exhibit 10-1 as

$$Y = \text{Rs } 6{,}000 + \text{Rs } 4X$$

Unlike the graphs for alternatives 1 and 2, Panel C has both a constant, or intercept, value of Rs 6,000 and a slope coefficient of Rs 4. In the case of a mixed cost, total cost in the relevant range increases as the number of phone-minutes used increases. Note, total cost does not vary strictly in proportion to the number of phone-minutes used within the relevant range. For example, when 4,000 phone-minutes are used, the total cost equals Rs 22,000 [Rs 6,000 + (Rs 4 per phone-minute × 4,000 phone-minutes)], but when 8,000 phone-minutes are used, total cost equals Rs 38,000 [Rs 6,000 + (Rs 4 per phone-minute × 8,000 phone-minutes)]. Although the number of phone-minutes used has doubled, total cost has increased by only about 73% [(Rs 38,000 − Rs 22,000) ÷ Rs 22,000].

Cannon's managers must understand the cost-behavior patterns in the three alternatives to choose the best deal with WWC. Suppose Cannon expects to use at least 4,000 phone-minutes per month. Its cost for 4,000 phone-minutes under the three alternatives would be as follows:

- **Alternative 1:** Rs 40,000 (Rs 10 per phone-minute × 4,000 phone-minutes)
- **Alternative 2:** Rs 20,000
- **Alternative 3:** Rs 22,000 [Rs 6,000 × (Rs 4 per phone-minute × 4,000 phone-minutes)]

Alternative 2 is the least costly. Moreover, if Cannon were to use more than 4,000 phone-minutes, as is likely to be the case, alternatives 1 and 3 would be even more costly. Cannon's managers, therefore, should choose alternative 2.

Note that the graphs in Exhibit 10-1 are linear. That is, they appear as straight lines. We simply need to know the constant, or intercept, amount (commonly designated *a*) and the slope coefficient (commonly designated *b*). For any linear cost function based on a single activity (recall our two assumptions discussed at the start of the chapter), knowing *a* and *b* is sufficient to describe and graphically plot all the values within the relevant range of number of phone-minutes used. We write a general form of this linear cost function as

$$Y = a + bX$$

Under alternative 1, a = Rs 0 and b = Rs 10 per phone-minute used; under alternative 2, a = Rs 20,000 and b = Rs 0 per phone-minute used; and under alternative 3, a = Rs 6,000 and b = Rs 4 per phone-minute used. To plot the mixed-cost function in Panel C, we draw a line starting from the point marked Rs 6,000 on the *y*-axis and increasing at a rate of Rs 4 per phone-minute used, so that at 1,000 phone-minutes, total costs increase by Rs 4,000 (Rs 4 per phone-minute × 1,000 phone-minutes) to Rs 10,000 (Rs 6,000 + Rs 4,000) and at 2,000 phone-minutes, total costs increase by Rs 8,000 (Rs 4 per phone-minute × 2,000 phone-minutes) to Rs 14,000 (Rs 6,000 + Rs 8,000) and so on.

Review of Cost Classification

Before we discuss issues related to the estimation of cost functions, we briefly review the three criteria laid out in Chapter 2 for classifying a cost into its variable and fixed components.

Choice of Cost Object A particular cost item could be variable with respect to one cost object and fixed with respect to another cost object. Consider Super Shuttle, an airport transportation company. If the fleet of vans it owns is the cost object, then the annual van registration and license costs would be variable costs with respect to the number of vans owned. But if a particular van is the cost object, then the registration and license costs for that van are fixed costs with respect to the miles driven during a year.

Time Horizon Whether a cost is variable or fixed with respect to a particular activity depends on the time horizon being considered in the decision situation. The longer the time horizon, all other things being equal, the more likely that the cost will be variable. For example, inspection costs at Boeing Company are typically fixed in the short run with respect to inspection-hours used because inspectors earn a fixed salary in a given year regardless of the number of inspection-hours of work done. But, in the long run, Boeing's total inspection costs will vary with the inspection-hours required: More inspectors will be hired if more inspection-hours are needed, and some inspectors will be reassigned to other tasks or laid off if fewer inspection-hours are needed.

Decision Point

What is a linear cost function and what types of cost behavior can it represent?

Relevant Range Managers should never forget that variable and fixed cost-behavior patterns are valid for linear cost functions only within the given relevant range. Outside the relevant range, variable and fixed cost-behavior patterns change, causing costs to become nonlinear (nonlinear means the plot of the relationship on a graph is not a straight line). For example, Exhibit 10-2 plots the relationship (over several years) between total direct manufacturing labor costs and the number of snowboards produced each year by Ski Authority. In this case, the nonlinearities outside the relevant range occur because of labor and other inefficiencies (first because workers are learning to produce snowboards and later because capacity limits are being stretched). Knowing the relevant range is essential to properly classify costs.

Identifying Cost Drivers

Learning Objective 2

Explain the importance of causality in estimating cost functions

. . . only a cause-and-effect relationship establishes an economically plausible relationship between an activity and its costs

The Cannon Services/WWC example illustrates variable-, fixed-, and mixed-cost functions using information about *future* cost structures proposed to Cannon by WWC. Often, however, cost functions are estimated from *past* cost data. Managers use **cost estimation** to measure a relationship based on data from past costs and the related level of an activity. For example, marketing managers at Volkswagen could use cost estimation to understand what causes their marketing costs to change from year to year (for example, the number of cars sold or the number of new car models introduced) and the fixed and variable components of these costs. Managers are interested in estimating past cost-behavior functions primarily because these estimates can help them make more-accurate **cost predictions**, or forecasts, about future costs. Better cost predictions help managers make more-informed planning and control decisions, such as preparing next year's marketing budget. But better management decisions, cost predictions, and estimation of cost functions can be achieved only if managers correctly identify the factors that affect costs.

Exhibit 10-2

Linearity Within Relevant Range for Ski Authority, Inc. Ltd

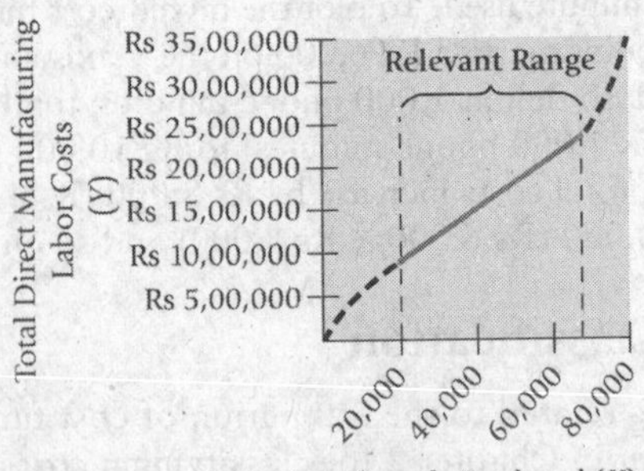

The Cause-and-Effect Criterion

The most important issue in estimating a cost function is determining whether a cause-and-effect relationship exists between the level of an activity and the costs related to that level of activity. Without a cause-and-effect relationship, managers will be less confident about their ability to estimate or predict costs. Recall from Chapter 2 that when a cause-and-effect relationship exists between a change in the level of an activity and a change in the level of total costs, we refer to the activity measure as a *cost driver*. We use the terms *level of activity* and *level of cost driver* interchangeably when estimating cost functions. Understanding the drivers of costs is crucially important for managing costs. The cause-and-effect relationship might arise as a result of:

- **A physical relationship between the level of activity and costs.** An example is when units of production is used as the activity that affects direct material costs. Producing more units requires more direct materials, which results in higher total direct material costs.
- **A contractual arrangement.** In alternative 1 of the Cannon Services example described earlier, number of phone-minutes used is specified in the contract as the level of activity that affects the telephone line costs.
- **Knowledge of operations.** An example is when number of parts is used as the activity measure of ordering costs. A product with many parts will incur higher ordering costs than a product with few parts.

Managers must be careful not to interpret a high correlation, or connection, in the relationship between two variables to mean that either variable causes the other. Consider direct material costs and labor costs. For a given product mix, producing more units generally results in higher material costs and higher labor costs. Material costs and labor costs are highly correlated, but neither causes the other. Using labor costs to predict material costs is problematic. Some products require more labor costs relative to material costs, while other products require more material costs relative to labor costs. If the product mix changes toward more labor-intensive products, say, labor costs will increase while material costs will decrease. Labor costs are a poor predictor of material costs. By contrast, factors that drive material costs such as product mix, product designs, and manufacturing processes, would have more accurately predicted the changes in material costs.

Only a cause-and-effect relationship—not merely correlation—establishes an economically plausible relationship between the level of an activity and its costs. Economic plausibility is critical because it gives analysts and managers confidence that the estimated relationship will appear again and again in other sets of data from the same situation. Identifying cost drivers also gives managers insights into ways to reduce costs and the confidence that reducing the quantity of the cost drivers will lead to a decrease in costs.

To identify cost drivers on the basis of data gathered over time, always use a long time horizon. Why? Because, as our example of inspection costs at Boeing Company illustrates costs may be fixed in the short run (during which time they have no cost driver), but they are usually variable and have a cost driver in the long run.

Cost Drivers and the Decision-Making Process

Consider Elegant Rugs, which uses state-of-the-art automated weaving machines to produce carpets for homes and offices. Management has made many changes in manufacturing processes and wants to introduce new styles of carpets. It would like to evaluate how these changes have affected costs and what styles of carpets it should introduce. It follows the five-step decision-making process outlined in Chapter 1.

Step 1: Identify the problem and uncertainties. The changes in the manufacturing process were specifically targeted at reducing indirect manufacturing labor costs, and management wants to know whether costs such as supervision, maintenance, and quality control did, in fact, decrease. One option is to simply compare indirect manufacturing labor costs before and after the process change. The problem with this approach is that the volume of activity before and after the process change was very different so costs need to be compared after taking into account the change in activity volume.

Managers were fairly confident about the direct material and direct manufacturing labor costs of the new styles of carpets. They were less certain about the impact that the choice of different styles would have on indirect manufacturing costs.

Step 2: Obtain information. Managers gathered information about potential cost drivers—factors such as machine-hours or direct manufacturing labor-hours that cause indirect manufacturing labor costs to be incurred. They also began considering different techniques (discussed in the next section) such as the industrial engineering method, the conference method, the account analysis method, the high-low method, and the regression method for estimating the magnitude of the effect of the cost driver on indirect manufacturing labor costs. Their goal was to identify the best possible single cost driver.

Step 3: Make predictions about the future. Managers used past data to estimate the relationship between cost drivers and costs and used this relationship to predict future costs.

Step 4: Make decisions by choosing among alternatives. As we will describe later, Elegant Rugs chose machine-hours as the cost driver of indirect manufacturing labor costs. Using the regression analysis estimate of indirect manufacturing labor cost per machine-hour, managers estimated the costs of alternative styles of carpets and chose to introduce the most profitable styles.

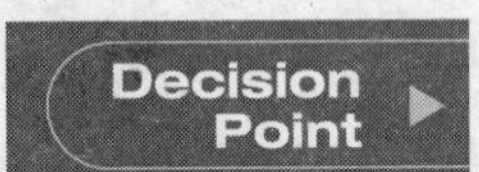

What is the most important issue in estimating a cost function?

Step 5: Implement the decision, evaluate performance, and learn. After the managers at Elegant Rugs introduced the new carpet styles, they focused on evaluating the results of their decision. Comparing predicted to actual costs helped managers to learn how accurate the estimates were, to set targets for continuous improvement, and to constantly seek ways to improve efficiency and effectiveness.

Cost Estimation Methods

Understand various methods of cost estimation

. . . for example, the regression analysis method determines the line that best fits past data

As we mentioned in Step 2, four methods of cost estimation are the industrial engineering method, the conference method, the account analysis method, and the quantitative analysis method (which takes different forms). These methods differ with respect to how expensive they are to implement, the assumptions they make, and the information they provide about the accuracy of the estimated cost function. They are not mutually exclusive, and many organizations use a combination of these methods.

Industrial Engineering Method

The **industrial engineering method**, also called the **work-measurement method**, estimates cost functions by analyzing the relationship between inputs and outputs in physical terms. Consider Elegant Rugs. It uses inputs of cotton, wool, dyes, direct manufacturing labor, machine time, and power. Production output is square yards of carpet. Time-and-motion studies analyze the time required to perform the various operations to produce the carpet. For example, a time-and-motion study may conclude that to produce 10 square yards of carpet requires one hour of direct manufacturing labor. Standards and budgets transform these physical input measures into costs. The result is an estimated cost function relating direct manufacturing labor costs to the cost driver, square yards of carpet produced.

The industrial engineering method is a very thorough and detailed way to estimate a cost function when there is a physical relationship between inputs and outputs, but it can be very time-consuming. Some government contracts mandate its use. Many organizations, such as Bose and Nokia, use it to estimate direct manufacturing costs but find it too costly or impractical for analyzing their entire cost structure. For example, physical relationships between inputs and outputs are difficult to specify for some items, such as indirect manufacturing costs, R&D costs and advertising costs.

Conference Method

The **conference method** estimates cost functions on the basis of analysis and opinions about costs and their drivers gathered from various departments of a company (purchasing, process engineering, manufacturing, employee relations, and so on). The Cooperative Bank in the United Kingdom has a Cost-Estimating Department that develops cost functions for its retail banking products (checking accounts, VISA cards, mortgages, and so on) based on the consensus of estimates from personnel of the particular departments. Elegant Rugs gathers opinions from supervisors and production engineers about how indirect manufacturing labor costs vary with machine-hours and direct manufacturing labor-hours.

The conference method encourages interdepartmental cooperation. The pooling of expert knowledge from different business functions of the value chain gives the conference method credibility. Because the conference method does not require detailed analysis of data, cost functions and cost estimates can be developed quickly. However, the emphasis on opinions rather than systematic éstimation means that the accuracy of the cost estimates depends largely on the care and skill of the people providing the inputs.

Account Analysis Method

The **account analysis method** estimates cost functions by classifying various cost accounts as variable, fixed, or mixed with respect to the identified level of activity. Typically, managers use qualitative rather than quantitative analysis when making these cost-classification decisions. The account analysis approach is widely used because it is reasonably accurate, cost-effective, and easy to use.

Consider indirect manufacturing labor costs for a small production area (or cell) at Elegant Rugs. Indirect manufacturing labor costs include wages paid for supervision, maintenance, quality control, and setups. During the most recent 12-week period, Elegant Rugs ran the machines in the cell for a total of 862 hours and incurred total indirect manufacturing labor costs of Rs 1,25,010. Using qualitative analysis, the manager and the cost analyst determine that over this 12-week period indirect manufacturing labor costs are mixed costs with only one cost driver—machine hours. As machine-hours vary, one component of the cost (such as supervision cost) is fixed, whereas another component (such as maintenance cost) is variable. The goal is to use account analysis to estimate a linear cost function for indirect manufacturing labor costs with number of machine-hours as the cost driver. The cost analyst uses experience and judgment to separate total indirect manufacturing labor costs (Rs 1,25,010) into costs that are fixed (Rs 21,570, based on 950 hours of machine capacity for the cell over a 12-week period) and costs that are variable (Rs 1,03,440) with respect to the number of machine-hours used. Variable cost per machine-hour is Rs 1,03,440 ÷ 862 machine-hours = Rs 120 per machine-hour. The linear cost equation, $y = a + bX$, in this example is:

Indirect manufacturing labor cost = Rs 21,570 +(Rs 120 per machine-hour × Number of machine-

The indirect manufacturing labor cost per machine-hour is Rs 1,25,010 ÷ 862 machine-hours = Rs 145.0 per machine-hour. Management at Elegant Rugs can use the cost function to estimate the indirect manufacturing labor costs of using, say, 950 machine-hours to produce carpet in the next 12-week period. Estimated costs equal Rs 21,570 + (950 machine-hours × Rs 120 per machine-hour) = Rs 1,35,570. The indirect manufacturing labor cost per machine-hour decreases to Rs 1,35,570 ÷ 950 machine-hours = Rs 142.7 per machine-hour, as fixed costs of Rs 21,570 are spread over a greater number of machine-hours.

To obtain reliable estimates of the fixed and variable components of cost, organizations such as Target take care to ensure that individuals thoroughly knowledgeable about the operations make the cost-classification decisions. Supplementing the account analysis method with the conference method improves credibility.

Exhibit 10-3

Weekly Indirect Manufacturing Labor Costs and Machine-Hours for Elegant Rugs

	A	B	C
1	Week	Cost Driver: Machine-Hours	Indirect Manufacturing Labor Costs
2		(X)	(Y)
3	1	68	Rs 11,900
4	2	88	12,110
5	3	62	10,040
6	4	72	9,170
7	5	60	7,700
8	6	96	14,560
9	7	78	11,800
10	8	46	7,100
11	9	82	13,160
12	10	94	10,320
13	11	68	7,520
14	12	48	9,630
15	Total	862	Rs 1,25,010
16			

Quantitative Analysis Method

Quantitative analysis uses a formal mathematical method to fit cost functions to past data observations. Excel is a useful tool for performing quantitative analysis. Columns B and C of Exhibit 10-3 show the breakdown of Elegant Rugs's total machine-hours (862) and total indirect manufacturing labor costs (Rs 1,25,010) into weekly data for the most recent 12-week period. Note that the data are paired—for each week there is data for the number of machine-hours and corresponding indirect manufacturing labor costs. For example, week 12 shows 48 machine-hours and indirect manufacturing labor costs of Rs 9,630. The next section uses the data in Exhibit 10-3 to illustrate how to estimate a cost function using quantitative analysis.

Steps in Estimating a Cost Function Using Quantitative Analysis

Outline six steps in estimating a cost function using quantitative analysis

. . . the end result (step 6) is to evaluate the cost driver of the estimated cost function

There are six steps in estimating a cost function using a quantitative analysis of a past cost relationship. We illustrate the steps as follows using the Elegant Rugs example.

Step 1: Choose the dependent variable. Choice of the **dependent variable** (the cost to be predicted and managed) will depend on the cost function being estimated. In the Elegant Rugs example, the dependent variable is indirect manufacturing labor costs.

Step 2: Identify the independent variable, or cost driver. The **independent variable** (level of activity or cost driver) is the factor used to predict the dependent variable (costs). When the cost is an indirect cost, as with Elegant Rugs, the independent variable is also called a cost-allocation base. Although these terms are sometimes used interchangeably, we use the term *cost driver* to describe the independent variable. Frequently, the cost analyst, working with the management team, will cycle through the six steps several times, trying alternative economically plausible cost drivers to identify a cost driver that best fits the data.

A cost driver should have an *economically plausible* relationship with the dependent variable and be measurable. Economic plausibility means that the relationship (describing how changes in the cost driver lead to changes in the costs being considered) is based on a physical relationship, a contract, or knowledge of operations and makes economic sense to the operating manager and the management accountant. As we saw in

Chapter 5, all the individual items of costs included in the dependent variable should have the same cost driver, that is, the cost pool should be homogenous. When all items of costs in the dependent variable do not have the same cost driver, the cost analyst should investigate the possibility of creating homogenous cost pools and estimating more than one cost function, one for each cost item/cost driver pair.

As an example, consider several types of fringe benefits paid to employees and the cost drivers of the benefits:

Fringe Benefit	**Cost Driver**
Health benefits	Number of employees
Cafeteria meals	Number of employees
Pension benefits	Salaries of employees
Life insurance	Salaries of employees

The costs of health benefits and cafeteria meals can be combined into one homogenous cost pool because they have the same cost driver—the number of employees. Pension benefits and life insurance costs have a different cost driver—the salaries of employees—and, therefore, should not be combined with health benefits and cafeteria meals. Instead, pension benefits and life insurance costs should be combined into a separate homogenous cost pool. The cost pool comprising pension benefits and life insurance costs can be estimated using salaries of employees receiving these benefits as the cost driver.

Step 3: Collect data on the dependent variable and the cost driver. This is usually the most difficult step in cost analysis. Cost analysts obtain data from company documents, from interviews with managers, and through special studies. These data may be time-series data or cross-sectional data.

Time-series data pertain to the same entity (organization, plant, activity, and so on) over successive past periods. Weekly observations of indirect manufacturing labor costs and number of machine-hours at Elegant Rugs are examples of time-series data. The ideal time-series database would contain numerous observations for a company whose operations have not been affected by economic or technological change. A stable economy and technology ensure that data collected during the estimation period represent the same underlying relationship between the cost driver and the dependent variable. Moreover, the periods (for example, daily, weekly, or monthly) used to measure the dependent variable and the cost driver should be consistent throughout the observations.

Cross-sectional data pertain to different entities during the same period. For example, studies of loans processed and the related personnel costs at 50 individual, yet similar branches of a bank during March 2009 would produce cross-sectional data for that month. The cross-sectional data should be drawn from entities that, within each entity, have a similar relationship between the cost driver and costs. Later in this chapter, we describe the problems that arise in data collection.

Step 4: Plot the data. The general relationship between the cost driver and costs can be readily observed in a graphical representation of the data, which is commonly called a plot of the data. Moreover, the plot highlights extreme observations (observations outside the general pattern) that analysts should check. Was there an error in recording the data or an unusual event, such as a work stoppage, that makes these observations unrepresentative of the normal relationship between the cost driver and the costs? Plotting the data also provides insight into whether the relationship is approximately linear and what the relevant range of the cost function is.

Exhibit 10-4 is a plot of the weekly data from columns B and C of the Excel spreadsheet in Exhibit 10-3. This graph provides strong visual evidence of a positive linear relationship between number of machine-hours and indirect manufacturing labor costs (that is, when machine-hours go up, so do indirect manufacturing labor costs). There do not appear to be any extreme observations in Exhibit 10-4. The relevant range is from 46 to 96 machine-hours per week (weeks 8 and 6, respectively).

Step 5: Estimate the cost function. We will show two ways to estimate the cost function for our Elegant Rugs data. One uses the high-low method, and the other uses regression analysis, the two most frequently described forms of quantitative analysis. The widespread

Exhibit 10-4

Plot of Weekly Indirect Manufacturing Labor Costs and Machine-Hours for Elegant Rugs

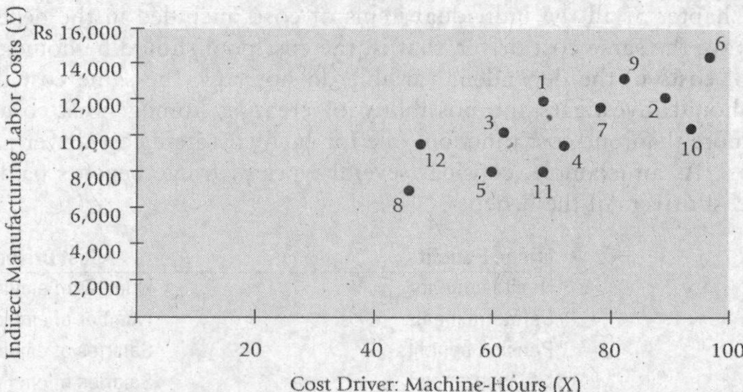

availability of computer packages such as Excel makes regression analysis much more easy to use. Still, we describe the high-low method to provide some basic intuition for the idea of drawing a line to "fit" a number of data points. We present these methods after Step 6.

Step 6: Evaluate the cost driver of the estimated cost function. In this step, we describe criteria for evaluating the cost driver of the estimated cost function. We do this after illustrating the high-low method and regression analysis.

High-Low Method

The simplest form of quantitative analysis to "fit" a line to data points is the **high-low method.** It uses only the highest and lowest observed values of the cost driver within the relevant range and their respective costs to estimate the slope coefficient and the constant of the cost function. It provides a first cut at understanding the relationship between a cost driver and costs. We illustrate the high-low method using data from Exhibit 10-3.

	Cost Driver: Machine-Hours (X)	Indirect Manufacturing Labor Costs (Y)
Highest observation of cost driver (week 6)	96	Rs 14,560
Lowest observation of cost driver (week 8)	46	7,100
Difference	50	Rs 7,460

The slope coefficient, *b*, is calculated as:

$$\text{Slope coefficient} = \frac{\text{Difference between costs associated with highest and lowest observations of the cost driver}}{\text{Difference between highest and lowest observations of the cost driver}}$$

$$= \text{Rs } 7{,}460 \div 50 \text{ machine-hours} = \text{Rs } 149.2 \text{ per machine-hour}$$

To compute the constant, we can use either the highest or the lowest observation of the cost driver. Both calculations yield the same answer because the solution technique solves two linear equations with two unknowns, the slope coefficient and the constant. Because

$$Y = a + bX$$
$$a = y - bX$$

At the highest observation of the cost driver, the constant, *a*, is calculated as:

$$\text{Constant} = \text{Rs } 14{,}560 - \text{Rs } 149.2 \text{ per machine-hours} \times 96 \text{ machine-hours} = \text{Rs } 236.8$$

And at the lowest observation of the cost driver,

$$\text{Constant} = \text{Rs } 7{,}100 - \text{Rs } 149.2 \text{ per machine-hours} \times 46 \text{ machine-hours} = \text{Rs } 236.8$$

Thus, the high-low estimate of the cost function is:

$$a = y + bX$$
$$Y = \text{Rs } 236.8 + (\text{Rs } 149.2 \text{ per machine-hours} \times \text{Number of machine-hours})$$

The black line in Exhibit 10-5 shows the estimated cost function using the high-low method (based on the data in Exhibit 10-3). The estimated cost function is a straight line joining the observations with the highest and lowest values of the cost driver (number of machine-hours). Note how this simple high-low line falls "in-between" the data points with three observations on the line, four above it and five below it. The intercept (a = Rs 236.8), the point where the dashed extension of the maroon line meets the y-axis, is the constant component of the equation that provides the best linear approximation of how a cost behaves *within the relevant range* of 46 to 96 machine-hours. The intercept should *not* be interpreted as an estimate of the fixed costs of Elegant Rugs if no machines were run. That's because running no machines and shutting down the plant—that is, using zero machine-hours—is *outside the relevant range*.

Suppose indirect manufacturing labor costs in week 6 were Rs 12,800, instead of Rs 14,560, while 96 machine-hours were used. In this case, the highest observation of the cost driver (96 machine-hours in week 6) will not coincide with the newer highest observation of the costs (Rs 13,160 in week 9). How would this change affect our high-low calculation? Given that the cause-and-effect relationship runs *from* the cost driver *to* the costs in a cost function, we choose the highest and lowest observations of the cost driver (the factor that causes the costs to change). The high-low method would still estimate the new cost function using data from weeks 6 (high) and 8 (low).

There is a danger of relying on only two observations to estimate a cost function. Suppose that because a labor contract guarantees certain minimum payments in week 8, indirect manufacturing labor costs in week 8 were Rs 10,000, instead of Rs 7,100, when only 46 machine-hours were used. The gray line in Exhibit 10-5 shows the cost function that would be estimated by the high-low method using this revised cost. Other than the two points used to draw the line, all other data lie on or below the line! In this case, choosing the highest and lowest observations for machine-hours would result in an estimated cost function that poorly describes the underlying linear cost relationship between number of machine-hours and indirect manufacturing labor costs. In this case, the high-low method can be modified so that the two observations chosen are a *representative high* and a *representative low*. Managers use this modification to avoid having extreme observations, which arise from abnormal events, affect the cost function. The modification allows managers to estimate a cost function that is representative of the relationship between the cost driver and costs and, therefore, is more useful for making decisions (such as pricing and performance evaluation).

The advantage of the high-low method is that it is simple to compute and easy to understand; it gives a quick, initial insight into how the cost driver—number of machine hours—affects indirect manufacturing labor costs. The disadvantage is that it ignores information from all but two observations when estimating the cost function. We next describe the regression analysis method of quantitative analysis that uses all available data to estimate the cost function.

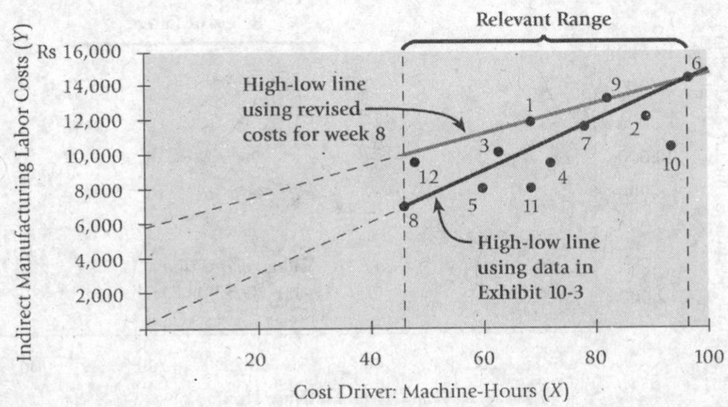

Exhibit 10-5

High-Low Method for Weekly Indirect Manufacturing Labor Costs and Machine-Hours for Elegant Rugs

Regression Analysis Method

Regression analysis is a statistical method that measures the average amount of change in the dependent variable associated with a unit change in one or more independent variables. In the Elegant Rugs example, the dependent variable is total indirect manufacturing labor costs. The independent variable, or cost driver, is number of machine-hours. **Simple regression** analysis estimates the relationship between the dependent variable and *one* independent variable. **Multiple regression** analysis estimates the relationship between the dependent variable and *two or more* independent variables. Multiple regression analysis for Elegant Rugs might use as the independent variables, or cost drivers, number of machine-hours and number of batches. The appendix to this chapter will explore simple regression and multiple regression in more detail.

In later sections, we will illustrate how Excel performs the calculations associated with regression analysis. The following discussion emphasizes how managers interpret and use the output from Excel to make critical strategic decisions. Exhibit 10-6 shows the line developed using regression analysis that best fits the data in columns B and C of Exhibit 10-3. Excel estimates the cost function to be

$$Y = \text{Rs } 3{,}009.8 + \text{Rs } 103.1X$$

The regression line in Exhibit 10-6 is derived using the least-squares technique. The least-squares technique determines the regression line by minimizing the sum of the squared vertical differences from the data points (the various points in the graph) to the regression line. The vertical difference, called **residual term**, measures the distance between actual cost and estimated cost for each observation. Exhibit 10-6 shows the residual term for the week 1 data. The line from the observation to the regression line is drawn perpendicular to the horizontal axis, or x-axis. The smaller the residual terms, the better the fit between actual cost observations and estimated costs. *Goodness of fit* indicates the strength of the relationship between the cost driver and costs. The regression line in Exhibit 10-6 rises from left to right. The positive slope of this line and small residual terms indicate that, on average, indirect manufacturing labor costs increase as the number of machine-hours increases. The vertical dashed lines in Exhibit 10-6 indicate the relevant range, the range within which the cost function applies.

The estimate of the slope coefficient, b, indicates that indirect manufacturing labor costs vary at the average amount of Rs 103.1 for every machine-hour used within the relevant range. Management can use the regression equation when budgeting for future indirect manufacturing labor costs. For instance, if 90 machine-hours are budgeted for the upcoming week, the predicted indirect manufacturing labor costs would be

$$Y = \text{Rs } 3{,}009.8 + (\text{Rs } 103.1 \text{ per machine-hours} \times \text{Number of machine-hours}) = \text{Rs } 12{,}288.8$$

Exhibit 10-6

Regression Model for Weekly Indirect Manufacturing Labor Costs and Machine-Hours for Elegant Rugs

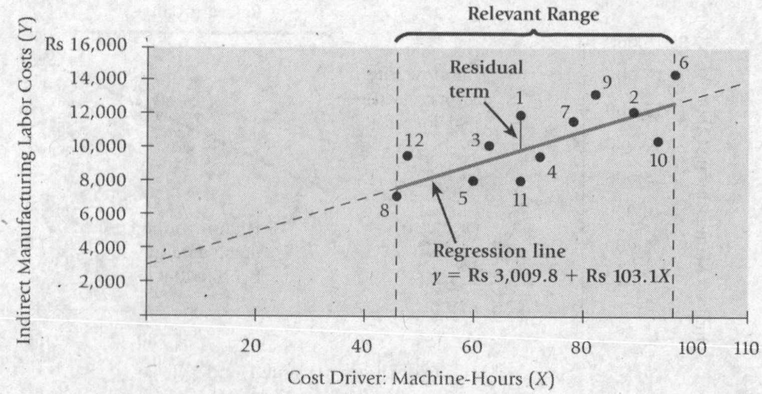

As we have already mentioned, the regression method is more accurate than the high-low method because the regression equation estimates costs using information from all observations, whereas the high-low equation uses information from only two observations. The inaccuracies of the high-low method can mislead managers. Consider the high-low method equation in the preceding section, y = Rs 236.8 + Rs 149.2 per machine-hour × Number of machine-hours. For 90 machine-hours, the predicted weekly cost based on the high-low method equation is Rs 236.8 + (Rs 149.2 per machine-hour × 90 machine-hours) = Rs 13,664.8. Suppose that for 7 weeks over the next 12-week period, Elegant Rugs runs its machines for 90 hours each week. Assume average indirect manufacturing labor costs for those 7 weeks are RS 13,000. Based on the high-low method prediction of Rs Rs 13,664.8, Elegant Rugs would conclude it has performed well because actual costs are less than predicted costs. But comparing the Rs 13,000 performance with the more-accurate Rs 12,288.8 prediction of the regression model tells a much different story and would probably prompt Elegant Rugs to search for ways to improve its cost performance.

Accurate cost estimation helps managers predict future costs and evaluate the success of cost-reduction initiatives. Suppose the manager at Elegant Rugs is interested in evaluating whether recent strategic decisions that led to changes in the production process and resulted in the data in Exhibit 10-3 have reduced indirect manufacturing labor costs, such as supervision, maintenance, and quality control. Using data on number of machine-hours used and indirect manufacturing labor costs of the previous process (not shown here), the manager estimates the regression equation,

Y = Rs 5,452.6 + (Rs 158.6 per machine-hours × Number of machine-hours)

The constant (Rs 3,009.8 versus Rs 5,452.6) and the slope coefficient (Rs 103.1 versus Rs 158.6) are both smaller for the new process relative to the old process. It appears that the new process has decreased indirect manufacturing labor costs.

What are the steps to estimate a cost function using quantitative analysis?

Evaluating Cost Drivers of the Estimated Cost Function

Learning Objective 5

Describe three criteria used to evaluate and choose cost drivers

. . . economically plausible relationships, goodness of fit, and significant effect of the cost driver on costs

How does a company determine the best cost driver when estimating a cost function? In many cases, the choice of a cost driver is aided substantially by understanding both operations and cost accounting.

To see why understanding operations is needed, consider the costs to maintain and repair metal-cutting machines at Helix Company Ltd., a manufacturer of treadmills. Helix schedules repairs and maintenance at a time when production is at a low level to avoid having to take machines out of service when they are needed most. An analysis of the monthly data will then show high repair costs in months of low production and low repair costs in months of high production. Someone unfamiliar with operations might conclude that there is an inverse relationship between production and repair costs. The engineering link between units produced and repair costs, however, is usually clear-cut. Over time, there is a cause-and-effect relationship: the higher the level of production, the higher the repair costs. To estimate the relationship correctly, operating managers and analysts will recognize that repair costs will tend to lag behind periods of high production, and hence, they will use production of prior periods as the cost driver.

In other cases, choosing a cost driver is more subtle and difficult. Consider again indirect manufacturing labor costs at Elegant Rugs. Management believes that both the number of machine-hours and the number of direct manufacturing labor-hours are plausible cost drivers of indirect manufacturing labor costs. However, management is not sure which is the better cost driver. Exhibit 10-7 presents weekly data (in Excel) on indirect manufacturing labor costs and number of machine-hours for the most recent 12-week period from Exhibit 10-3, together with data on the number of direct manufacturing labor-hours for the same period.

Exhibit 10-7

Weekly Indirect Manufacturing Labor Costs, Machine-Hours, and Direct Manufacturing Labor-Hours for Elegant Rugs

	A	B	C	D
1	Week	Original Cost Driver: Machine-Hours	Alternate Cost Driver: Direct Manufacturing Labor-Hours (X)	Indirect Manufacturing Labor Costs (Y)
2	1	68	30	Rs 11,900
3	2	88	35	12,110
4	3	62	36	10,040
5	4	72	20	9,170
6	5	60	47	7,700
7	6	96	45	14,560
8	7	78	44	11,800
9	8	46	38	7,100
10	9	82	70	13,160
11	10	94	30	10,320
12	11	68	29	7,520
13	12	48	38	9,630
14	Total	862	462	Rs 1,25,010
15				

Choosing Among Cost Drivers

What guidance do the different cost-estimation methods provide for choosing among cost drivers? The industrial engineering method relies on analyzing physical relationships between cost drivers and costs, relationships that are difficult to specify in this case. The conference method and the account analysis method use subjective assessments to choose a cost driver and to estimate the fixed and variable components of the cost function. In these cases, managers must rely on their best judgment. Managers cannot use these methods to test and try alternative cost drivers. The major advantages of quantitative methods are that they are objective—a given data set and estimation method result in a unique estimated cost function—and managers can use them to evaluate different cost drivers. We use the regression analysis approach to illustrate how to evaluate different cost drivers.

First, the cost analyst at Elegant Rugs enters data in columns C and D of Exhibit 10-7 in Excel and estimates the following regression equation of indirect manufacturing labor costs based on number of direct manufacturing labor-hours:

$$Y = \text{Rs } 7{,}446.7 + \text{Rs } 77.2X$$

Exhibit 10-8 shows the plot of the data points for number of direct manufacturing labor-hours and indirect manufacturing labor costs, and the regression line that best fits the data. Exhibit 10-6 shows the corresponding graph when number of machine-hours is the cost driver. To decide which of the two cost drivers Elegant Rugs should choose, the analyst compares the machine-hour regression equation and the direct manufacturing labor-hour regression equation. There are three criteria used to make this evaluation.

1. **Economic plausibility.** Both cost drivers are economically plausible. However, in the state-of-the-art, highly automated production environment at Elegant Rugs, managers familiar with the operations believe that costs such as machine maintenance are likely to be more closely related to number of machine-hours used than to number of direct manufacturing labor-hours used.
2. **Goodness of fit.** Compare Exhibits 10-6 and 10-8. The vertical differences between actual costs and predicted costs are much smaller for the machine-hours regression than for the direct manufacturing labor-hours regression. Number of machine-hours

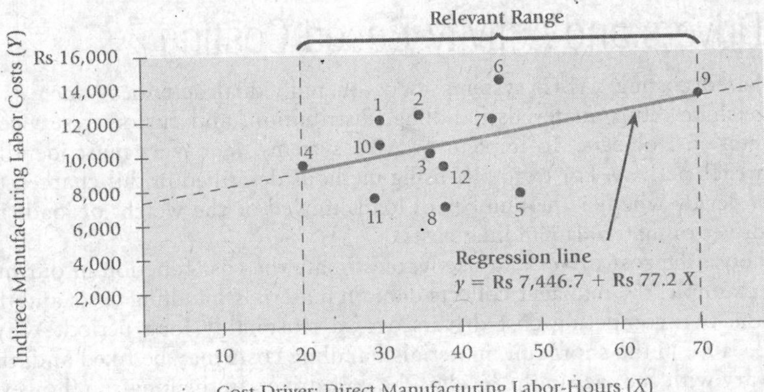

Exhibit 10-8

Regression Model for Weekly Indirect Manufacturing Labor Costs and Direct Manufacturing Labor-Hours for Elegant Rugs

used, therefore, has a stronger relationship—or goodness of fit—with indirect manufacturing labor costs.

3. **Significance of independent variable.** Again compare Exhibits 10-6 and 10-8 (both of which have been drawn to roughly the same scale). The machine-hours regression line has a steep slope relative to the slope of the direct manufacturing labor-hours regression line. *For the same (or more) scatter of observations about the line (goodness of fit)*, a flat, or slightly sloped regression line indicates a weak relationship between the cost driver and costs. In our example, changes in direct manufacturing labor-hours appear to have a small influence or effect on indirect manufacturing labor costs.

Based on this evaluation, managers at Elegant Rugs select number of machine-hours as the cost driver and use the cost function y = Rs 3009.8 + (Rs 10.31 per machine-hour × Number of machine-hours) to predict future indirect manufacturing labor costs.

Why is choosing the correct cost driver to estimate indirect manufacturing labor costs important? Consider the following strategic decision that management at Elegant Rugs must make. The company is thinking of introducing a new style of carpet that, from a manufacturing standpoint, is similar to the carpets it has manufactured in the past. Prices are set by the market and sales of 650 square yards of this carpet are expected each week. Management estimates 72 machine-hours and 21 direct manufacturing labor-hours would be required per week to produce the 650 square yards of carpet needed. Using the machine-hour regression equation, Elegant Rugs would predict indirect manufacturing labor costs of y = Rs 3,009.8 + (Rs 103.1 per machine-hour × 72 machine-hours) = Rs 10,433.0. If it used direct manufacturing labor-hours as the cost driver, it would incorrectly predict costs of Rs 7,446.7 + (Rs 77.2 per labor-hour × 21 labor-hours) = Rs 9,067.9. If Elegant Rugs chose similarly incorrect cost drivers for other indirect costs as well and systematically underestimated costs, it would conclude that the costs of manufacturing the new style of carpet would be low and basically fixed (fixed because the regression line is nearly flat). But the actual costs driven by number of machine-hours used and other correct cost drivers would be higher. By failing to identify the proper cost drivers, management would be misled into believing the new style of carpet would be more profitable than it actually is. It might decide to introduce the new style of carpet, whereas if Elegant identifies the correct cost driver it might decide not to introduce the new carpet.

Incorrectly estimating the cost function would also have repercussions for cost management and cost control. Suppose number of direct manufacturing labor-hours were used as the cost driver, and actual indirect manufacturing labor costs for the new carpet were Rs 9,700. Actual costs would then be higher than the predicted costs of Rs 9,067.9. Management would feel compelled to find ways to cut costs. In fact, on the basis of the preferred machine-hour cost driver, the plant would have actual costs lower than the Rs 10,433 predicted costs—a performance that management should seek to replicate, not change!

Cost Drivers and Activity-Based Costing

Activity-based costing (ABC) systems focus on individual activities—such as product design, machine setup, materials handling, distribution, and customer service—as the fundamental cost objects. To implement ABC systems, managers must identify a cost driver for each activity. For example, using methods described in this chapter, the manager must decide whether the number of loads moved or the weight of loads moved is the cost driver of materials-handling costs.

To choose the cost driver and use it to estimate the cost function in our materials-handling example, the manager collects data on materials-handling costs and the quantities of the two competing cost drivers over a reasonably long period. Why a long period? Because in the short run, materials-handling costs may be fixed and, therefore, will not vary with changes in the level of the cost driver. In the long run, however, there is a clear cause-and-effect relationship between materials-handling costs and the cost driver. Suppose number of loads moved is the cost driver of materials-handling costs. Increases in the number of loads moved will require more materials-handling labor and equipment; decreases will result in equipment being sold and labor being reassigned to other tasks.

ABC systems have a great number and variety of cost drivers and cost pools. That means ABC systems require many cost relationships to be estimated. In estimating the cost function for each cost pool, the manager must pay careful attention to the cost hierarchy. For example, if a cost is a batch-level cost such as setup cost, the manager must only consider batch-level cost drivers like number of setup-hours. In some cases, the costs in a cost pool may have more than one cost driver from different levels of the cost hierarchy. In the Elegant Rugs example, the cost drivers for indirect manufacturing labor costs could be machine-hours and number of production batches of carpet manufactured. Furthermore, it may be difficult to subdivide the indirect manufacturing labor costs into two cost pools and to measure the costs associated with each cost driver. In these cases, companies use multiple regression to estimate costs based on more than one independent variable. The appendix to this chapter discusses multiple regression in more detail.

As the Concepts in Action feature illustrates, managers implementing ABC systems use a variety of methods—industrial engineering, conference, and regression analysis—to estimate slope coefficients. In making these choices, managers trade off level of detail, accuracy, feasibility, and costs of estimating cost functions.

Learning Objective 6

Explain nonlinear cost functions

. . . graph of cost function is not a straight line, for example, because of quantity discounts or costs changing in steps

in particular those arising from learning curve effects

. . . either cumulative average-time learning, where cumulative average time per unit declines by a constant percentage, as units produced double

. . . or incremental unit-time learning, in which incremental time to produce last unit declines by constant percentage, as units produced double

Nonlinearity and Cost Functions

In practice, cost functions are not always linear. A **nonlinear cost function** is a cost function for which the graph of total costs (based on the level of a single activity) is not a straight line within the relevant range. To see what a nonlinear cost function looks like, return to Exhibit 10-2, but now let's expand the relevant range from 0 to 80,000 snowboards produced from the original relevant range of 20,000 to 65,000. You can see that the cost function over this expanded range is graphically represented by a line that is not a straight line.

Consider another example. Economies of scale in advertising may enable an advertising agency to produce double the number of advertisements for less than double the costs. Even direct material costs are not always linear variable costs because of quantity discounts on direct material purchases. As shown in Exhibit 10-9, Panel A, total direct material costs rise as the units of direct materials purchased increase. But, because of quantity discounts, these costs rise more slowly (as indicated by the slope coefficient) as the units of direct materials purchased increase. This cost function has b = Rs 250 per unit for 1 to 1,000 units purchased, b = Rs 150 per unit for 1,001 to 2,000 units purchased, and b = Rs 100 per unit for 2,001 to 3,000 units purchased. The direct material cost per unit falls at each price break—that is, the cost per unit decreases with larger purchase orders. If managers are interested in understanding cost behavior over the relevant range from 1 to 3,000 units, the cost function is nonlinear—not a straight line. If, however, managers are only interested in understanding cost behavior over a more narrow relevant range (for example, from 1 to 1,000 units), the cost function is linear.

Exhibit 10-9 Examples of Nonlinear Cost Functions

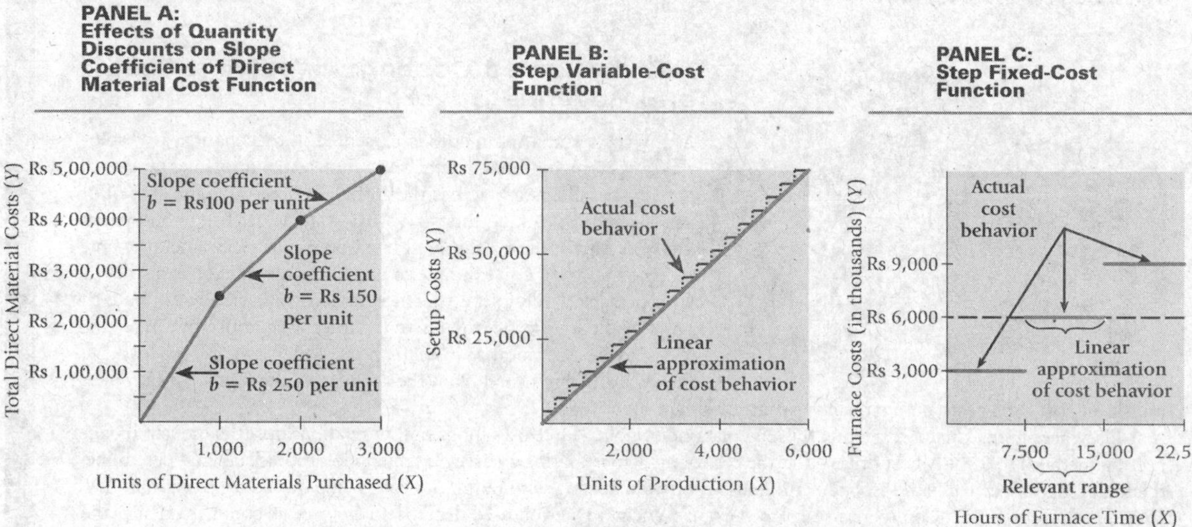

Step cost functions are also examples of nonlinear cost functions. A **step cost function** is a cost function in which the cost remains the same over various ranges of the level of activity, but the cost increases by discrete amounts—that is, increases in steps—as the level of activity increases from one range to the next. Panel B in Exhibit 10-9 shows a *step variable-cost function*, a step cost function in which cost remains the same over *narrow* ranges of the level of activity in each relevant range. Panel B presents the relationship between units of production and setup costs. The pattern is a step cost function because, as we described in Chapter 5 on activity-based costing, setup costs are related to each production batch started. If the relevant range is considered to be from 0 to 6,000 production units, the cost function is nonlinear. However, as shown by the gray line in Panel B, managers often approximate step variable costs with a continuously-variable cost function. This type of step cost pattern also occurs when production inputs such as materials-handling labor, supervision, and process engineering labor are acquired in discrete quantities but used in fractional quantities.

Panel C in Exhibit 10-9 shows a *step fixed-cost function* for Crofton Steel, a company that operates large heat-treatment furnaces to harden steel parts. Looking at Panel C and Panel B, you can see that the main difference between a step variable-cost function and a step fixed-cost function is that the cost in a step fixed-cost function remains the same over *wide* ranges of the activity in each relevant range. The ranges indicate the number of furnaces being used (each furnace costs Rs 30,00,000). The cost increases from one range to the next higher range when the hours of furnace time needed require the use of another furnace. The relevant range of 7,500 to 15,000 hours of furnace time indicates that the company expects to operate with two furnaces at a cost of Rs 60,00,000. Management considers the cost of operating furnaces as a fixed cost within this relevant range of operation. However, if the relevant range is considered to be from 0 to 22,500 hours, the cost function is nonlinear: The graph in Panel C is not a single straight line; it is three broken lines.

Learning Curves

Nonlinear cost functions also result from learning curves. A **learning curve** is a function that measures how labor-hours per unit decline as units of production increase because workers are learning and becoming better at their jobs. Managers use learning curves to predict how labor-hours, or labor costs, will increase as more units are produced.

Concepts in Action

Activity-Based Costing: Identifying Cost and Revenue Drivers

Many cost estimation methods presented in this chapter are essential to service, manufacturing, and retail-sector implementations of activity-based costing across the globe. To determine the cost of an activity in the banking industry, ABC systems often rely on expert analyses and opinions gathered from operating personnel (the conference method). For example, the loan department staff at the Co-operative Bank in the United Kingdom subjectively estimate the costs of the loan processing activity and the quantity of the related cost driver—the number of loans processed, a batch-level cost driver, as distinguished from the amount of the loans, an output unit-level cost driver—to derive the cost of processing a loan.

Elsewhere in the United Kingdom, the City of London police force uses input-output relationships (the industrial engineering method) to identify cost drivers and the cost of an activity. Using a surveying methodology, officials can determine the total costs associated with responding to house robberies, dealing with burglaries, and filling out police reports. In the United States, the Boeing Commercial Airplane Group's Wichita Division used detailed analyses of its commercial airplane-manufacturing methods to support make/buy decisions for complex parts required in airplane assembly. The industrial engineering method is also used by U.S. government agencies such as the U.S. Postal Service to determine the cost of each post office transaction and the U.S. Patent and Trademark Office to identify the costs of each patent examination.

Regression analysis is another helpful tool for determining the cost drivers of activities. Consider how fuel service retailers (that is, gas stations with convenience stores) identify the principal cost driver for labor within their operations. Two possible cost drivers are gasoline sales and convenience store sales. Gasoline sales are batch-level activities because payment transactions occur only once for each gasoline purchase, regardless of the volume of gasoline purchased; whereas convenience store sales are output unit-level activities that vary based on the amount of food, drink, and other products sold. Fuel service retailers generally use convenience store sales as the basis for assigning labor costs because multiple regression analyses confirm that convenience store sales, not gasoline sales, are the major cost driver of labor within their operations.

While popular, these are not the only methods used to evaluate cost drivers. If you recall from chapter five, Charles Schwab is one of the growing number of companies using time-driven activity based costing, which uses time as the cost driver. At Citigroup, the company's internal technology infrastructure group uses time to better manage the labor capacity required to provide reliable, secure, and cost effective technology services to about 60 Citigroup business units around the world.

The trend of using activity-based costing to identify cost and revenue drivers also extends into emerging areas. For example, the U.S. government allocated $19 billion in 2009 to support the adoption of electronic health records. Using the input-output method, many health clinics and doctor's offices are leveraging activity-based costing to identify the cost of adopting this new health information technology tool.

Sources: Barton, T., and J. MacArthur. 2003. Activity-based costing and predatory pricing: The case of the retail industry. *Management Accounting Quarterly* (Spring); Carter, T., A. Sedaghat, and T. Williams. 1998. How ABC changed the post office. *Management Accounting,* (February); The Cooperative Bank. Harvard Business School. Case No. N9-195-196; Federowicz, M., M. Grossman, B. Hayes, and J. Riggs. 2010. A tutorial on activity-based costing of electronic health records. *Quality Management in Health Care* (January–March); Kaplan, Robert, and Steven Anderson. 2008. *Time-driven activity-based costing: A simpler and more powerful path to higher profits.* Boston: Harvard Business School Publishing; Leapman, B. 2006. Police spend £500m filling in forms. *The Daily Telegraph,* January 22; Paduano, Rocco, and Joel Cutcher-Gershenfeld. 2001. Boeing Commercial Airplane Group Wichita Division (Boeing Co.). MIT Labor Aerospace Research Agenda Case Study. Cambridge, MA: MIT; Peckenpaugh, J. 2002. Teaching the ABCs. *Government Executive,* April 1; The United Kingdom Home Office. 2007. *The police service national ABC model: Manual of guidance.* London: Her Majesty's Stationary Office.

The aircraft-assembly industry first documented the effect that learning has on efficiency. In general, as workers become more familiar with their tasks, their efficiency improves. Managers learn how to improve the scheduling of work shifts and how to operate the plant better. As a result of improved efficiency, unit costs decrease as productivity increases, and the unit-cost function behaves nonlinearly. These nonlinearities must be considered when estimating and predicting unit costs.

Managers have extended the learning-curve notion to other business functions in the value chain, such as marketing, distribution, and customer service, and to costs other than labor costs. The term *experience curve* describes this broader application of the learning curve. An **experience curve** is a function that measures the decline in cost per unit in various business functions of the value chain—marketing, distribution, and so on—as the amount of these activities increases. For companies such as Dell Computer, Wal-Mart, and McDonald's, learning curves and experience curves are key elements of their strategies. These companies use learning curves and experience curves to reduce costs and increase customer satisfaction, market share, and profitability.

We now describe two learning-curve models: the cumulative average-time learning model and the incremental unit-time learning model.

Cumulative Average-Time Learning Model

In the **cumulative average-time learning model**, cumulative average time per unit declines by a constant percentage each time the cumulative quantity of units produced doubles. Consider Rayburn Company, a radar systems manufacturer. Rayburn has an 80% learning curve. The 80% means that when the quantity of units produced is doubled from X to $2X$, cumulative average time *per unit* for $2X$ units is 80% of cumulative average time *per unit* for X units. Average time per unit has dropped by 20% (100% − 80%). Exhibit 10-10 is an Excel spreadsheet showing the calculations for the cumulative average-time learning model for Rayburn Company. Note that as the number of units produced doubles from 1 to 2 in column A, cumulative average time per unit declines from 100 hours to 80% of 100 hours (0.80 × 100 hours = 80 hours) in column B. As the number of units doubles from 2 to 4, cumulative average time per unit declines to 80% of 80 hours − 64 hours, and so on. To obtain the cumulative total time in column D, multiply cumulative average time per unit by the cumulative number of units produced. For example, to produce 4 cumulative units would require 256 labor-hours (4 units × 64 cumulative average labor-hours per unit).

Incremental Unit-Time Learning Model

In the **incremental unit-time learning model**, incremental time needed to produce the last unit declines by a constant percentage each time the cumulative quantity of units produced doubles. Again, consider Rayburn Company and an 80% learning curve. The 80% here means that when the quantity of units produced is doubled from X to $2X$, the time needed to produce the last unit when $2X$ total units are produced is 80% of the time needed to produce the last unit when X total units are produced. Exhibit 10-11 is an Excel spreadsheet showing the calculations for the incremental unit-time learning model for Rayburn Company based on an 80% learning curve. Note how when units produced double from 2 to 4 in column A, the time to produce unit 4 (the last unit when 4 units are produced) is 64 hours in column B, which is 80% of the 80 hours needed to produce unit 2 (the last unit when 2 units are produced). We obtain the cumulative total time in column D by summing individual unit times in column B. For example, to produce 4 cumulative units would require 314.21 labor-hours (100.00 + 80.00 + 70.21 + 64.00).

Exhibit 10-12 presents graphs using Excel for the cumulative average-time learning model (using data from Exhibit 10-10) and the incremental unit-time learning model (using data from Exhibit 10-11). Panel A graphically illustrates cumulative average time per unit as a function of cumulative units produced for each model. The curve for the cumulative average-time learning model is plotted using the data from Exhibit 10-10, column B, versus column A. The curve for the incremental unit-time learning model is plotted using the data from Exhibit 10-11, column E, versus column A. Panel B graphically illustrates cumulative total labor-hours as a function of cumulative units produced for each model. The curve for the cumulative average-time learning model is plotted using the data from Exhibit 10-10, column D, versus column A. The curve for the incremental unit-time learning model is plotted using the data from Exhibit 10-11, column D, versus column A.

The incremental unit-time learning model predicts a higher cumulative total time to produce two or more units than the cumulative average-time learning model, assuming the same learning rate for both models. That is, in Exhibit 10-12, Panel B, the graph for the 80% incremental unit-time learning model lies above the graph for the 80% cumulative average-time learning model. If we compare the results in Exhibit 10-10 (column D) with the results in Exhibit 10-11 (column D), to produce 4 cumulative units, the 80%

Exhibit 10-10 Cumulative Average-Time Learning Model for Rayburn Company

File Edit View Insert Format Tools Data Window Help

	A	B	C	D	E	F	G	H	I
1	Cumulative Average-Time Learning Model for Rayburn Company								
2									
3		80% Learning Curve							
4									
5	Cumulative	Cumulative		Cumulative	Individual Unit				
6	Number	Average Time		Total Time:	Time for *X*th				
7	of Units (*X*)	per Unit (*y*)*: Labor Hours		Labor-Hours	Unit: Labor Hours				
8									
9				D = Col A x Col B					
10						E13 = D13 - D12 = 210.63 - 160.00			
11	1	100.00		100.00	100.00				
12	2	80.00	=(100x0.8)	160.00	60.00				
13	3	70.21		210.63	50.63				
14	4	64.00	=(80x0.8)	256.00	45.37				
15	5	59.56		297.82	41.82				
16	6	56.17		337.01	39.19				
17	7	53.45		374.14	37.13				
18	8	51.20	=(64x0.8)	409.60	35.46				
19	9	49.29		443.65	34.05				
20	10	47.65		476.51	32.86				
21	11	46.21		508.32	31.81				
22	12	44.93		539.22	30.89				
23	13	43.79		569.29	30.07				
24	14	42.76		598.63	29.34				
25	15	41.82		627.30	28.67				
26	16	40.96	=(51.2x0.8)	655.36	28.06				
27									

*The mathematical relationship underlying the cumulative average-time learning model is:

$$y = aX^b$$

where y = Cumulative average time (labor-hours) per unit
X = Cumulative number of units produced
a = Time (labor-hours) required to produce the first unit
b = Factor used to calculate cumulative average time to produce units

The value of b is calculated as

$$\frac{\ln\text{(learning-curve \% in decimal form)}}{\ln 2}$$

For an 80% learning curve, $b = \ln 0.8/\ln 2 = -0.2231/0.6931 = -0.3219$
when $X = 3$, $a = 100$, $b = -0.3219$,

$$y = 100 \times 3^{-0.3219} = 70.21 \text{ labor hours}$$

Numbers in table may not be exact because of rounding.

incremental unit-time learning model predicts 314.21 labor-hours versus 256.00 labor-hours predicted by the 80% cumulative average-time learning model. That's because under the cumulative average-time learning model *average labor-hours needed to produce all 4 units* is 64 hours; the labor-hour amount needed to produce unit 4 is much less than 64 hours—it is 45.37 hours (see Exhibit 10-10). Under the incremental unit-time learning model, the labor-hour amount needed to produce unit 4 is 64 hours, and the labor-hours needed to produce the first 3 units are more than 64 hours, so average time needed to produce all 4 units is more than 64 hours.

How do managers choose which 5 model and what percent learning curve to use? They make their choices on a case-by-case basis. For example, if the behavior of manufacturing labor-hour usage as production levels increase follows a pattern like the one predicted by the 80% learning curve cumulative average-time learning model, then the 80% learning curve cumulative average-time learning model should be used. Engineers, plant managers, and workers are good sources of information on the amount and type of learning actually occurring as production increases. Plotting this information and estimating the model that best fits the data is helpful in selecting the appropriate model.[2]

Incorporating Learning-Curve Effects into Prices and Standards

How do companies use learning curves? Consider the data in Exhibit 10-10 for the cumulative average-time learning model at Rayburn Company. Suppose variable costs

[2] For details, see C. Bailey, "Learning Curve Estimation of Production Costs and Labor-Hours Using a Free Excel Add-In," *Management Accounting Quarterly,* Summer 2000: 25–31. Free software for estimating learning curves is available at Dr. Bailey's Web site (www.profbailey.com).

Exhibit 10-11 Incremental Unit-Time Learning Model for Rayburn Company

Incremental Unit-Time Learning Model for Rayburn Company

80% Learning Curve

Cumulative Number of Units (X)	Individual Unit Time for Xth Unit (y)*: Labor Hours		Cumulative Total Time: Labor-Hours	Cumulative Average Time per Unit: Labor-Hours
				E = Col D ÷ Col A
1	100.00		100.00	100.00
2	80.00	=(100x0.8)	180.00	90.00
3	70.21		250.21	83.40
4	64.00	=(80x0.8)	314.21	78.55
5	59.56		373.77	74.75
6	56.17		429.94	71.66
7	53.45		483.39	69.06
8	51.20	=(64x0.8)	534.59	66.82
9	49.29		583.89	64.88
10	47.65		631.54	63.15
11	46.21		677.75	61.61
12	44.93		722.68	60.22
13	43.79		766.47	58.96
14	42.76		809.23	57.80
15	41.82		851.05	56.74
16	40.96	=(51.2x0.8)	892.01	55.75

D14 = D13 + D14
= 180.00 + 70.21

*The mathematical relationship underlying the incremental unit-time learning model is:

$$y = aX^b$$

where y = Time (labor-hours) taken to produce the last single unit
X = Cumulative number of units produced
a = Time (labor-hours) required to produce the first unit
b = Factor used to calculate incremental unit time to produce units

$$= \frac{\ln (\text{learning-curve \% in decimal form})}{\ln 2}$$

For an 80% learning curve, $b = \ln 0.8 \div \ln 2 = -0.2231 \div 0.6931 = -0.3219$
Where $X = 3$, $a = 100$, $b = -0.3219$,
$y = 100 \times 3^{-0.3219} = 70.21$ labor hours
The cumulative total time when $X = 3$ is 100+80+70.21=250.21 labor-hours.
Numbers in the table may not be exact because of rounding.

subject to learning effects consist of direct manufacturing labor, at Rs 200 per hour, and related overhead, at Rs 300 per direct manufacturing labor-hour. Managers should predict the costs shown in Exhibit 10-13.

These data show that the effects of the learning curve could have a major influence on decisions. For example, managers at Rayburn Company might set an extremely low

Exhibit 10-12 Plots for Cumulative Average-Time Learning Model and Incremental Unit-Time Learning Model for Rayburn Company

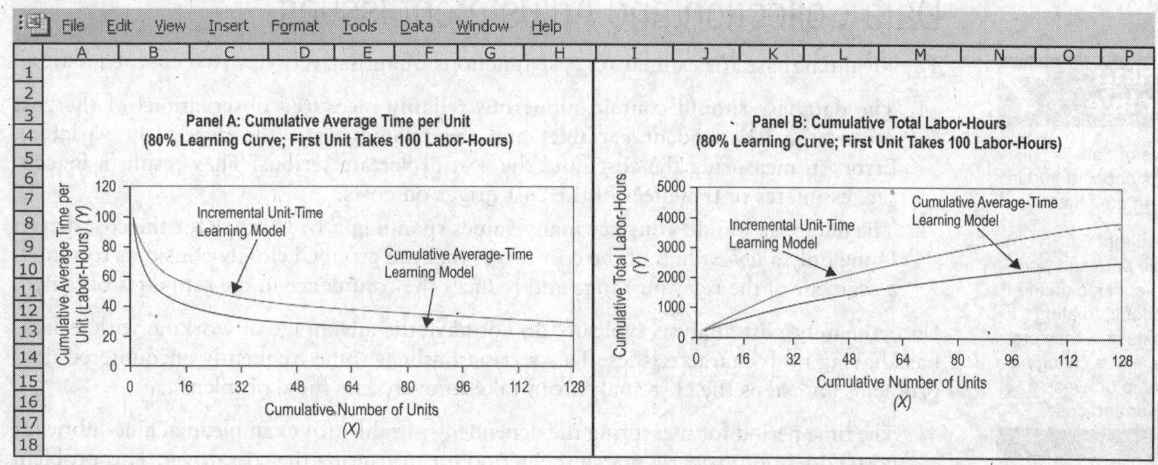

Exhibit 10-13

Predicting Costs Using Learning Curves at Rayburn Company

	A	B	C	D	E	F
1		Cumulative				
2	Cumulative	Average Time	Cumulative	Cumulative Costs		Additions to
3	Number of	per Unit:	Total Time:	at Rs 500 per		Cumulative
4	Units	Labor-Hours[a]	Labor-Hours[a]	Labor-Hour		Costs
5	1	100.00	100.00	Rs 50,000	(100.00 x Rs 500)	Rs 50,000
6	2	80.00	160.00	80,000	(160.00 x Rs 500)	30,000
7	4	64.00	256.00	1,28,000	(256.00 x Rs 500)	48,000
8	8	51.20	409.60	2,04,800	(409.60 x Rs 500)	76,800
9	16	40.96	655.36	3,27,680	(655.36 x Rs 500)	1,22,880
10						
11	[a]Based on the cumulative average-time learning model. See Exhibit 10-10 for the computations					
12	of these amounts.					

selling price on its radar systems to generate high demand. As its production increases to meet this growing demand, cost per unit drops. Rayburn "rides the product down the learning curve" as it establishes a larger market share. Although it may have earned little operating income on its first unit sold—it may actually have lost money on that unit—Rayburn earns more operating income per unit as output increases.

Alternatively, subject to legal and other considerations, Rayburn's managers might set a low price on just the final 8 units. After all, the total labor and related overhead costs per unit for these final 8 units are predicted to be only Rs 1,22,880 (Rs 3,27,680 − Rs 2,04,800). On these final 8 units, the Rs 15,360 cost per unit (Rs 1,22,880 ÷ 8 units) is much lower than the Rs 50,000 cost per unit of the first unit produced.

Many companies, such as Pizza Hut and Home Depot, incorporate learning-curve effects when evaluating performance. The Nissan Motor Company expects its workers to learn and improve on the job and evaluates performance accordingly. It sets assembly-labor efficiency standards for new models of cars after taking into account the learning that will occur as more units are produced.

Decision Point

What is a nonlinear cost function and in what ways do learning curves give rise to nonlinearities?

The learning-curve models examined in Exhibits 10-10 to 10-13 assume that learning is driven by a single variable (production output). Other models of learning have been developed (by companies such as Analog Devices and Yokogawa Hewlett-Packard) that focus on how quality—rather than manufacturing labor-hours—will change over time, regardless of whether more units are produced. Studies indicate that factors other than production output, such as job rotation and organizing workers into teams, contribute to learning that improves quality.

Data Collection and Adjustment Issues

Learning Objective 7

Be aware of data problems encountered in estimating cost functions

. . . for example, unreliable data and poor recordkeeping, extreme observations, treating fixed costs as if they are variable, and a changing relationship between a cost driver and cost

The ideal database for estimating cost functions quantitatively has two characteristics:

1. **The database should contain numerous reliably measured observations of the cost driver (the independent variable) and the related costs (the dependent variable).** Errors in measuring the costs and the cost driver are serious. They result in inaccurate estimates of the effect of the cost driver on costs.
2. **The database should consider many values spanning a wide range for the cost driver.** Using only a few values of the cost driver that are grouped closely considers too small a segment of the relevant range and reduces the confidence in the estimates obtained.

Unfortunately, cost analysts typically do not have the advantage of working with a database having both characteristics. This section outlines some frequently encountered data problems and steps the cost analyst can take to overcome these problems.

1. The time period for measuring the dependent variable (for example, machine-lubricant costs) does not properly match the period for measuring the cost driver. This problem

often arises when accounting records are not kept on the accrual basis. Consider a cost function with machine-lubricant costs as the dependent variable and number of machine-hours as the cost driver. Assume that the lubricant is purchased sporadically and stored for later use. Records maintained on the basis of lubricants purchased will indicate little lubricant costs in many months and large lubricant costs in other months. These records present an obviously inaccurate picture of what is actually taking place. The analyst should use accrual accounting to measure cost of lubricants consumed to better match costs with the machine-hours cost driver in this example.

2. Fixed costs are allocated as if they are variable. For example, costs such as depreciation, insurance, or rent may be allocated to products to calculate cost per unit of output. *The danger is to regard these costs as variable rather than as fixed. They seem to be variable because of the allocation methods used.* To avoid this problem, the analyst should distinguish carefully fixed costs from variable costs and not treat allocated fixed cost per unit as a variable cost.
3. Data are either not available for all observations or are not uniformly reliable. Missing cost observations often arise from a failure to record a cost or from classifying a cost incorrectly. For example, marketing costs may be understated because costs of sales visits to customers may be incorrectly recorded as customer-service costs. Recording data manually rather than electronically tends to result in a higher percentage of missing observations and erroneously entered observations. Errors also arise when data on cost drivers originate outside the internal accounting system. For example, the Accounting Department may obtain data on testing-hours for medical instruments from the company's Manufacturing Department and data on number of items shipped to customers from the Distribution Department. One or both of these departments might not keep accurate records. To minimize these problems, the cost analyst should design data collection reports that regularly and routinely obtain the required data and should follow up immediately whenever data are missing.
4. Extreme values of observations occur from errors in recording costs (for example, a misplaced decimal point), from nonrepresentative periods (for example, from a period in which a major machine breakdown occurred or from a period in which a delay in delivery of materials from an international supplier curtailed production), or from observations outside the relevant range. Analysts should adjust or eliminate unusual observations before estimating a cost relationship.
5. There is no homogeneous relationship between the cost driver and the individual cost items in the dependent variable-cost pool. A homogeneous relationship exists when each activity whose costs are included in the dependent variable has the same cost driver. In this case, a single cost function can be estimated. As discussed in step 2 for estimating a cost function using quantitative analysis when the cost driver for each activity is different, separate cost functions, each with its own cost driver, should be estimated for each activity. Alternatively, as discussed the cost function should be estimated with more than one independent variable using multiple regression.
6. The relationship between the cost driver and the cost is not stationary. That is, the underlying process that generated the observations has not remained stable over time. For example, the relationship between number of machine-hours and manufacturing overhead costs is unlikely to be stationary when the data cover a period in which new technology was introduced. One way to see if the relationship is stationary is to split the sample into two parts and estimate separate cost relationships—one for the period before the technology was introduced and one for the period after the technology was introduced. Then, if the estimated coefficients for the two periods are similar, the analyst can pool the data to estimate a single cost relationship. When feasible, pooling data provides a larger data set for the estimation, which increases confidence in the cost predictions being made.
7. Inflation has affected costs, the cost driver, or both. For example, inflation may cause costs to change even when there is no change in the level of the cost driver. To study the underlying cause-and-effect relationship between the level of the cost driver and costs, the analyst should remove purely inflationary price effects from the data by dividing each cost by the price index on the date the cost was incurred.

In many cases, a cost analyst must expend considerable effort to reduce the effect of these problems before estimating a cost function on the basis of past data.

Problem for Self-Study

The Helicopter Division of GLD, Ltd. is examining helicopter assembly costs at its Indiana plant. It has received an initial order for eight of its new land-surveying helicopters. GLD can adopt one of two methods of assembling the helicopters:

File Edit View Insert Format Tools Data Window Help

	A	B	C	D	E
1		Labor-Intensive Assembly Method		Machine-Intensive Assembly Method	
2	Direct material cost per helicopter	Rs 4,00,000		Rs 3,60,000	
3	Direct-assembly labor time for first helicopter	2,000	labor-hours	800	labor-hours
4	Learning curve for assembly labor time per helicopter	85%	cumulative average time*	90%	incremental unit time**
5	Direct-assembly labor cost	Rs 300	per hour	Rs 300	per hour
6	Equipment-related indirect manufacturing cost	Rs 120	per direct-assembly labor-hour	Rs 450	per direct-assembly labor-hour
7	Material-handling-related indirect manufacturing cost	50%	of direct material cost	50%	of direct material cost
8					
9					
10	*Using the formula (p. 000), for an 85% learning curve, $b = \frac{\ln 0.85}{\ln 2} = \frac{-0.162519}{0.693147} = -0.234465$				
11					
12					
13					
14					
15	**Using the formula (p. 000), for a 90% learning curve, $b = \frac{\ln 0.90}{\ln 2} = \frac{-0.105361}{0.693147} = -0.152004$				
16					
17					

Required

1. How many direct-assembly labor-hours are required to assemble the first eight helicopters under (a) the labor-intensive method and (b) the machine-intensive method?
2. What is the total cost of assembling the first eight helicopters under (a) the labor-intensive method and (b) the machine-intensive method?

Solution

1. a. The following calculations show the labor-intensive assembly method based on an 85% cumulative average-time learning model (using Excel):

File Edit View Insert Format Tools Data Window Help

	G	H	I	J	K
1–4	Cumulative Number of Units	Cumulative Average Time per Unit (y): Labor Hours		Cumulative Total Time: Labor-Hours	Individual time for Xth unit: Labor-Hours
5				Col J = Col G x Col H	
6	1	2,000		2,000	2,000
7	2	1,700	(2,000 x 0.85)	3,400	1,400
8	3	1,546		4,637	1,237
9	4	1,445	(1,700 x 0.85)	5,780	1,143
10	5	1,371		6,857	1,077
11	6	1,314		7,884	1,027
12	7	1,267		8,871	987
13	8	1,228.25	(1,445 x 0.85)	9,826	955
14					

Cumulative average-time per unit for the Xth unit in column H is calculated as $y = aX^b$; see Exhibit 10-10. For example, when $X = 3$, $y = 2{,}000 \times 3^{-0.234465} = 1{,}546$ labor-hours.

b. The following calculations show the machine-intensive assembly method based on a 90% incremental unit-time learning model:

File Edit View Insert Format Tools Data Window Help

	G	H	I	J	K
1	Cumulative	Individual		Cumulative	Cumulative
2	Number	Unit Time		Total Time:	Average Time
3	of Units	for Xth Unit (y):		Labor-Hours	Per Unit:
4		Labor Hours			Labor-Hours
5					Col K = Col J ÷ Col G
6	1	800		800	800
7	2	720	(800 x 0.9)	1,520	760
8	3	677		2,197	732
9	4	648	(720 x 0.9)	2,845	711
10	5	626		3,471	694
11	6	609		4,081	680
12	7	595		4,676	668
13	8	583	(648 x 0.9)	5,258	657

Individual unit time for the Xth unit in column H is calculated as $y = aX^b$; see Exhibit 10-11. For example, when $X = 3$, $y = 800 \times 3^{-0.152004} = 677$ labor-hours.

2. Total costs of assembling the first eight helicopters are:

File Edit View Insert Format Tools Data Window Help

	O	P	Q
1		Labor-Intensive	Machine-Intensive
2		Assembly Method	Assembly Method
3		(using data from part 1a)	(using data from part 1b)
4	Direct materials:		
5	8 helicopters x Rs 4,00,000; Rs 3,60,000 per helicopte	Rs 32,00,000	Rs 28,80,000
6	Direct-assembly labor:		
7	9,826 hrs.; 5,258 hrs. x Rs 300/hr.	Rs 29,47,800	15,77,400
8	Indirect manufacturing costs		
9	Equipment related		
10	9,826 hrs. x Rs 120/hr.; 5,258 hrs. x Rs 450/hr.	Rs 11,79,120	23,66,100
11	Materials-handling related		
12	0.50 x Rs 32,00,000; Rs 28,80,000	Rs 16,00,000	14,40,000
13	Total assembly costs	Rs [illegible],26,920	Rs 82,63,500

The machine-intensive method's assembly costs are Rs 6,63,420 lower than the labor-intensive method (Rs 89,26,920 – Rs 82,63,500).

Decision Points

The following question-and-answer format summarizes the chapter's learning objectives. Each decision presents a key question related to a learning objective. The guidelines are the answer to that question.

Decision	Guidelines
1. What assumptions are usually made when estimating a cost function?	The two assumptions frequently made in cost-behavior estimation are (a) changes in the level of a single activity explain changes in total costs and (b) cost behavior can adequately be approximated by a linear function of the activity level within the relevant range.
2. What is a linear cost function and what types of cost behavior can it represent?	A linear cost function is a cost function in which, within the relevant range, the graph of total costs based on the level of a single activity is a straight line. Linear cost functions can be described by a constant, *a*, which represents the estimate of the total cost component that, within the relevant range, does not vary with changes in the level of the activity; and a slope coefficient, *b*, which represents the estimate of the amount by which total costs change for each unit change in the level of the activity within the relevant range. Three types of linear cost functions are variable, fixed, and mixed (or semivariable).
3. What are the different methods that can be used to estimate a cost function?	Four methods for estimating cost functions are the industrial engineering method, the conference method, the account analysis method, and the quantitative analysis method (which includes the high-low method and the regression analysis method). If possible, the cost analyst should apply more than one method. Each method is a check on the others.
4. What are the steps to estimate a cost function using quantitative analysis?	There are six steps to estimate a cost function using quantitative analysis: (a) Choose the dependent variable; (b) identify the cost driver; (c) collect data on the dependent variable and the cost driver; (d) plot the data; (e) estimate the cost function; and (f) evaluate the cost driver of the estimated cost function. In most situations, working closely with operations managers, the cost analyst will cycle through these steps several times before identifying an acceptable cost function.
5. How should a company evaluate and choose cost drivers?	Three criteria for evaluating and choosing cost drivers are (a) economic plausibility, (b) goodness of fit, and (c) significance of independent variable.
6. What is a nonlinear cost function and how does it arise?	A nonlinear cost function is a cost function in which the graph of total costs based on the level of a single activity is not a straight line within the relevant range. Nonlinear costs can arise because of quantity discounts, step cost functions, and learning-curve effects.
7. What are two types of learning curve models that a company can use?	The learning curve is an example of a nonlinear cost function. Labor-hours per unit decline as units of production increase. In the cumulative average-time learning model, cumulative average-time per unit declines by a constant percentage each time the cumulative quantity of units produced doubles. In the incremental unit-time learning model, incremental unit time (the time needed to produce the last unit) declines by a constant percentage each time the cumulative quantity of units produced doubles. A company should use the model that better fits its observed labor-hour usage.
8. What are the common data problems a company must watch for when estimating costs?	The most difficult task in cost estimation is collecting high-quality, reliably measured data on the costs and the cost driver. Common problems include missing data, extreme values of observations, changes in technology, and distortions resulting from inflation.

APPENDIX: REGRESSION ANALYSIS

This appendix describes estimation of the regression equation, several commonly used regression statistics, and how to choose among cost functions that have been estimated by regression analysis. We use the data for Elegant Rugs presented in Exhibit 10-3 and displayed here again for easy reference.

Week	Cost Driver: Machine-Hours (X)	Indirect Manufacturing Labor Costs (Y)
1	68	Rs 11,900
2	88	12,110
3	62	10,040
4	72	9,170
5	60	7,700
6	96	14,560
7	78	11,800
8	46	7,100
9	82	13,160
10	94	10,320
11	68	7,520
12	48	9,630
Total	862	Rs 1,25,010

Estimating the Regression Line

The least-squares technique for estimating the regression line minimizes the sum of the squares of the vertical deviations from the data points to the estimated regression line (also called *residual term* in Exhibit 10-6). The objective is to find the values of a and b in the linear cost function $y = a + bX$, where y is the *predicted* cost value as distinguished from the *observed* cost value, which we denote by Y. We wish to find the numerical values of a and b that minimize $\Sigma(Y - y)^2$, the sum of the squares of the vertical deviations between Y and y. Generally, these computations are done using software packages such as Excel. For the data in our example,[3] a = Rs 3,009.80 and b = Rs 103.10, so that the equation of the regression line is y = Rs 3,009.80 + Rs 103.10X.

[3] The formulae for a and b are:

$$a = \frac{(\Sigma Y)(\Sigma X^2) - (\Sigma X)(\Sigma XY)}{n(\Sigma X^2) - (\Sigma X)(\Sigma X)} \text{ and } b = \frac{n(\Sigma XY) - (\Sigma X)(\Sigma Y)}{n(\Sigma X^2) - (\Sigma X)(\Sigma X)}$$

where for the Elegant Rugs data in Exhibit 10-3,

n = number of data points = 12

ΣX = sum of the given X values = 68 + 88 + ... + 48 = 862

ΣX^2 = sum of squares of the X values = $(68)^2 + (88)^2 + ... + (48)^2$ = 4,624 + 7,744 + ... + 2,304 = 64,900

ΣY = sum of given Y values = 1,190 + 1,211 + ... + 963 = 12,501

ΣXY = sum of the amounts obtained by multiplying each of the given X values by the associated observed Y value = (68) (11,900) + (88)(12,110) + ... + (48) (9,630) = 8,09,200 + 10,65,680 + ... + 4,62,240 = 92,87,160

$$a = \frac{(\text{Rs } 1{,}25{,}010)(64{,}900) - (862)(2{,}87{,}160)}{12(64{,}900) - (862)(862)\ 20{,}580} = \text{Rs } 3{,}009.80$$

$$b = \frac{12(\text{Rs } 2{,}87{,}160) - (862)(1{,}25{,}010)}{12(64{,}900) - (862)(862)} = \text{Rs } 103.10$$

Goodness of Fit

Goodness of fit measures how well the predicted values, y, based on the cost driver, X, match actual cost observations, Y. The regression analysis method computes a measure of goodness of fit, called the coefficient of determination. The **coefficient of determination, r^2**, measures the percentage of variation in Y explained by X (the independent variable). That is, the coefficient of determination indicates the proportion of the variance of Y that is explained by the independent variable X. It is more convenient to express the coefficient of determination as 1 minus the proportion of total variance that is *not* explained by the independent variable—that is, 1 minus the ratio of unexplained variation to total variation. The unexplained variance arises because of differences between the actual values, Y, and the predicted values, y, which in the Elegant Rugs example is given by[4]

$$r^2 = 1 - \frac{\text{Unexplained variation}}{\text{Total variation}} = 1 - \frac{\Sigma(Y - y)^2}{\Sigma(Y - \bar{Y})^2} = 1 - \frac{29{,}08{,}240}{60{,}76{,}990} = 0.52$$

The calculations indicate that r^2 increases as the predicted values, y, more closely approximate the actual observations, Y. The range of r^2 is from 0 (implying no explanatory power) to 1 (implying perfect explanatory power). Generally, an r^2 of 0.30 or higher passes the goodness-of-fit test. However, do not rely exclusively on goodness of fit. It can lead to the indiscriminate inclusion of independent variables that increase r^2 but have no economic plausibility as cost drivers. *Goodness of fit has meaning only if the relationship between the cost drivers and costs is economically plausible.*

An alternative and related way to evaluate goodness of fit is to calculate the *standard error of the regression*. The **standard error of the regression** is the variance of the residuals. It is equal to

$$S = \sqrt{\frac{\Sigma(Y - y)^2}{\text{Degrees of freedom}}} = \sqrt{\frac{\Sigma(Y - y)^2}{n - 2}} = \sqrt{\frac{29{,}08{,}240}{12 - 2}} = \text{Rs } 1{,}705.40$$

Degrees of freedom equal the number of observations, 12, *minus* the number of coefficients estimated in the regression (in this case two, a and b). On average, actual Y and the predicted value, y, differ by Rs 1,705.40. For comparison, the average value of $Y = \bar{Y}$ is Rs 10,417.50. The smaller the standard error of the regression, the better the fit and the better the predictions for different values of X.

Significance of Independent Variables

Do changes in the economically plausible independent variable result in significant changes in the dependent variable? Or alternatively stated, is the slope coefficient, b = Rs 103.10, of the regression line statistically significant (that is, different from Re 0)? Recall, for example, that in the regression of number of machine-hours and indirect manufacturing labor costs in the Elegant Rugs illustration, b is estimated from a sample of 12 weekly observations. The estimate, b, is subject to random factors, as are all sample statistics. That is, a different sample of 12 data points would undoubtedly give a different estimate of b. The **standard error of the estimated coefficient** indicates how much the estimated value, b, is likely to be affected by random factors. The t-value of the b coefficient measures how large the value of the estimated coefficient is relative to its standard error.

The cutoff t-value for making inferences about the b coefficient is a function of the number of degrees of freedom, the significance level and whether it is a one-sided or two-

[4] From footnote 3, $\Sigma Y = 1{,}25{,}010$ and $\bar{Y} = 1{,}25{,}010 \div 12 = 10{,}417.50$

$$\Sigma(Y - \bar{Y})^2 = (11{,}900 - 10{,}417.50)^2 + (12{,}110 - 10{,}417.50)^2 + \ldots + (9{,}630 - 10{,}417.50)^2 = 60{,}76{,}990$$

Each value of X generates a predicted value of y. For example, in week 1, y = Rs 3,009.80 + (Rs 103.10 × 68) = Rs 10,020.60; in week 2, y = Rs 3,009.80 + (Rs 103.10 × 88) = Rs 12,082.60; and in week 12, y = Rs 3,009.80 + (Rs 103.10 × 48) = Rs 7,958.60.

$$\Sigma(Y - Y)^2 = (11{,}900 - 10{,}020.60)^2 + (12{,}110 - 12{,}082.60)^2 + \ldots + (9{,}630 - 7{,}958.60)^2 = 29{,}08{,}240$$

sided test. A 5% level of significance indicates that there is less than a 5% probability that random factors could have affected the coefficient. A two-sided test assumes that random factors could have caused the coefficient to be either greater than Rs 103.10 or less than Rs 103.10 with equal probability. At a 5% level of significance, this means that there is less than a 2.5% (5% ÷ 2) probability that random factors could have caused the coefficient to be greater than Rs 103.10 and less than 2.5% probability that random factors could have caused the coefficient to be less than Rs 103.10. Under the expectation that the coefficient of *b* is positive, a one-sided test at the 5% level of significance assumes that there is less than 5% probability that random factors would have caused the coefficient to be less than Rs 103.10. The cutoff *t*-value at the 5% significance level and 10 degrees of freedom for a two-sided test is 2.228. If there were more observations and 60 degrees of freedom, the cutoff *t*-value would be 2.00 at a 5% significance level for a two-sided test.

The *t*-value (called *t* Stat in the Excel output) for the slope coefficient *b* is the value of the estimated coefficient, Rs 103.10 ÷ the standard error of the estimated coefficient Rs 31.20 = 3.30, which exceeds the cutoff *t*-value of 2.228. In other words, a relationship exists between the independent variable, machine-hours, and the dependent variable that cannot be attributed to random chance alone. Exhibit 10-14 shows a convenient format (in Excel) for summarizing the regression results for number of machine-hours and indirect manufacturing labor costs.

An alternative way to test that the coefficient *b* is significantly different from zero is in terms of a *confidence interval*: There is less than a 5% chance that the true value of the machine-hours coefficient lies outside the range Rs 103.10 ± (2.228 × Rs 31.20), or Rs 103.10 ± Rs 69.50, or from Rs 33.60 to Rs 172.60. Because 0 does not appear in the confidence interval, we can conclude that changes in the number of machine-hours do affect indirect manufacturing labor costs. Similarly, using data from Exhibit 10-14, the *t*-value for the constant term *a* is Rs 3,009.80 ÷ Rs 2,297.50 = 1.31, which is less than 2.228. This *t*-value indicates that, within the relevant range, the constant term is *not* significantly different from zero. The Durbin-Watson statistic in Exhibit 10-14 will be discussed in the following section.

Specification Analysis of Estimation Assumptions

Specification analysis is the testing of the assumptions of regression analysis. If the assumptions of (1) linearity within the relevant range, (2) constant variance of residuals, (3) independence of residuals, and (4) normality of residuals all hold, then the simple regression procedures give reliable estimates of coefficient values. This section provides a brief overview of specification analysis. When these assumptions are not satisfied, more-complex regression procedures are necessary to obtain the best estimates.[5]

Exhibit 10-14 Simple Regression Results with Indirect Manufacturing Labor Costs as Dependent Variable and Machine-Hours as Independent Variable (Cost Driver) for Elegant Rugs

File Edit View Insert Format Tools Data Window Help

	A	B	C	D	E	F
1		**Coefficients**	**Standard Error**	***t* Stat**		= Coefficient/Standard Error
2		**(1)**	**(2)**	**(3) = (1) ÷ (2)**		= B3/C3
3	Intercept	Rs 3,009.80	Rs 2,297.50	1.31	→	= 3,009.80/2,297.50
4	Independent Variable: Machine-Hours (*X*)	Rs 103.10	Rs 31.20	3.30		
5						
6	**Regression Statistics**					
7	R Square	0.52				
8	Durbin-Watson Statistic	2.05				

[5] For details see, for example, W. H. Greene, *Econometric Analysis*, 4th ed. (Upper Saddle River, NJ: Prentice Hall, 2000).

1. **Linearity within the relevant range.** A common assumption—and one that appears to be reasonable in many business applications—is that a linear relationship exists between the independent variable X and the dependent variable Y within the relevant range. If a linear regression model is used to estimate a nonlinear relationship, however, the coefficient estimates obtained will be inaccurate.

   When there is only one independent variable, the easiest way to check for linearity is to study the data plotted in a scatter diagram, a step that often is unwisely skipped. Exhibit 10-6 presents a scatter diagram for the indirect manufacturing labor costs and machine-hours variables of Elegant Rugs shown in Exhibit 10-3. The scatter diagram reveals that linearity appears to be a reasonable assumption for these data.

   The learning-curve models discussed in this chapter are examples of nonlinear cost functions. Costs increase when the level of production increases, but by lesser amounts than would occur with a linear cost function. In this case, the analyst should estimate a nonlinear cost function that incorporates learning effects.

2. **Constant variance of residuals.** The vertical deviation of the observed value Y from the regression line estimate y is called the *residual term, disturbance term*, or *error term*, $u = Y - y$. The assumption of constant variance implies that the residual terms are unaffected by the level of the cost driver. The assumption also implies that there is a uniform scatter, or dispersion, of the data points about the regression line as in Exhibit 10-15, Panel A. This assumption is likely to be violated, for example, in cross-sectional estimation of costs in operations of different sizes. For example, suppose Elegant Rugs has production areas of varying sizes. The company collects data from these different production areas to estimate the relationship between machine-hours and indirect manufacturing labor costs. It is very possible that the residual terms in this regression will be larger for the larger production areas that have higher machine-hours and higher indirect manufacturing labor costs. There would not be a uniform scatter of data points about the regression line (see Exhibit 10-15, Panel B). Constant variance is also known as *homoscedasticity.* Violation of this assumption is called *heteroscedasticity*.

   Heteroscedasticity does not affect the accuracy of the regression estimates a and b. It does, however, reduce the reliability of the estimates of the standard errors and thus affects the precision with which inferences about the population parameters can be drawn from the regression estimates.

3. **Independence of residuals.** The assumption of independence of residuals is that the residual term for any one observation is not related to the residual term for any other observation. The problem of *serial correlation* (also called *autocorrelation*) in the residuals arises when there is a systematic pattern in the sequence of residuals such that the residual in observation n conveys information about the residuals in observations $n + 1$, $n + 2$, and so on. Consider another production cell at Elegant Rugs that has, over a 20-week period, seen an increase in production and hence machine-hours. Exhibit 10-16 Panel B is a scatter diagram of machine-hours and indirect manufacturing labor costs. Observe the systematic pattern of the residuals in Panel B—positive residuals for extreme (high and low) quantities of machine-hours and negative residuals for moderate quantities of machine-hours. One reason for this observed pattern at low values of the cost driver is the "stickiness" of costs. When machine hours are below 50 hours, indirect manufacturing labor costs do not decline. When machine-hours increase over time as production is ramped up, indirect manufacturing labor costs increase more as managers at Elegant Rugs struggle to manage the higher volume. How would the plot of residuals look if there were no auto-correlation? Like the plot in Exhibit 10-16, Panel A that shows no pattern in the residuals.

   Like nonconstant variance of residuals, serial correlation does not affect the accuracy of the regression estimates a and b. It does, however, affect the standard errors of the coefficients, which in turn affect the precision with which inferences about the population parameters can be drawn from the regression estimates.

   The Durbin-Watson statistic is one measure of serial correlation in the estimated residuals. For samples of 10 to 20 observations, a Durbin-Watson statistic in the

Exhibit 10-15 Constant Variance of Residuals Assumption

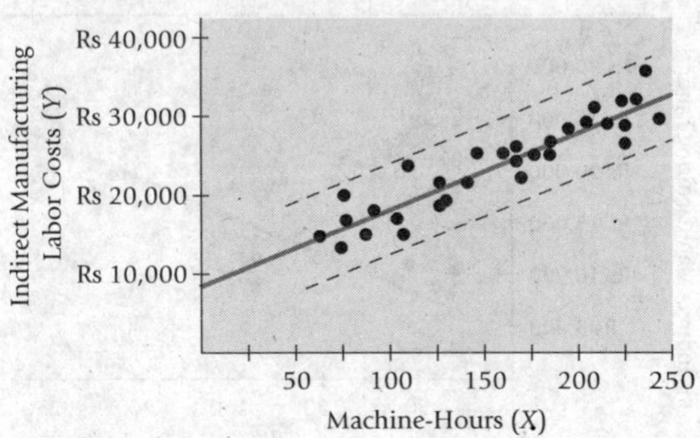

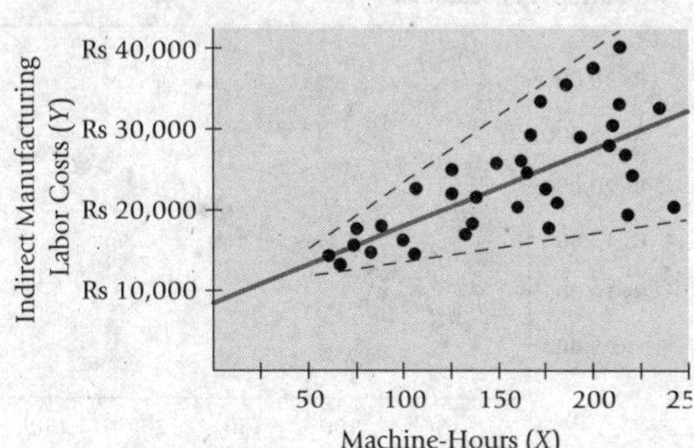

1.10-to-2.90 range indicates that the residuals are independent. The Durbin-Watson statistic for the regression results of Elegant Rugs in Exhibit 10-14 is 2.05. Therefore, an assumption of independence in the estimated residuals is reasonable for this regression model.

4. **Normality of residuals.** The normality of residuals assumption means that the residuals are distributed normally around the regression line. The normality of residuals assumption is frequently satisfied when using regression analysis on real cost data. Even when the assumption does not hold, accountants can still generate accurate estimates based on the regression equation, but the resulting confidence interval around these estimates is likely to be inaccurate.

Using Regression Output to Choose Cost Drivers of Cost Functions

Consider the two choices of cost drivers we described earlier in this chapter for indirect manufacturing labor costs (y):

$$Y = a + (b \times \text{Number of machine-hours})$$
$$Y = a + (b \times \text{Number of direct manufacturing labour-hours})$$

Exhibits 10-6 and 10-8 show plots of the data for the two regressions. Exhibit 10-14 reports regression results for the cost function using number of machine-hours as the independent variable. Exhibit 10-17 presents comparable regression results (in Excel) for the cost function using number of direct manufacturing labor-hours as the independent variable.

On the basis of the material presented in this appendix, which regression is better? Exhibit 10-18 compares these two cost functions in a systematic way. For several criteria, the cost function based on machine-hours is preferable to the cost function based on direct manufacturing labor-hours. The economic plausibility criterion is especially important.

Do not always assume that any one cost function will perfectly satisfy all the criteria in Exhibit 10-18. A cost analyst must often make a choice among "imperfect" cost functions, in the sense that the data of any particular cost function will not perfectly meet one or more of the assumptions underlying regression analysis. For example, both of the cost functions

Exhibit 10-16 Independence of Residuals Assumption

PANEL A:
Independence of Residuals
(No Pattern in Residuals)

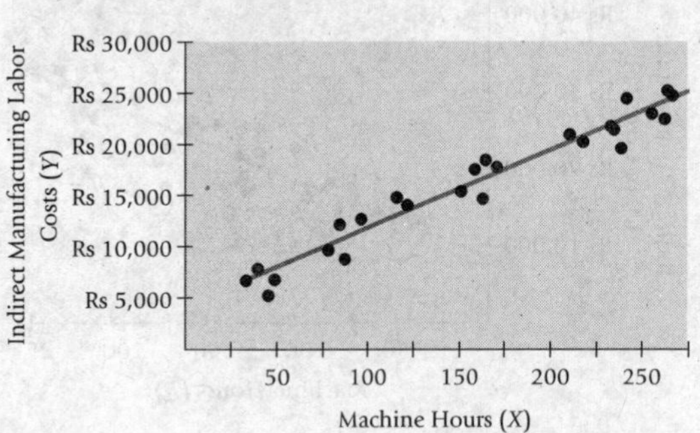

PANEL B:
Serial Correlation in Residuals
(A Pattern of Positive Residuals for Extreme Machine Hours Used; Negative Residuals for Moderate Machine Hours Used)

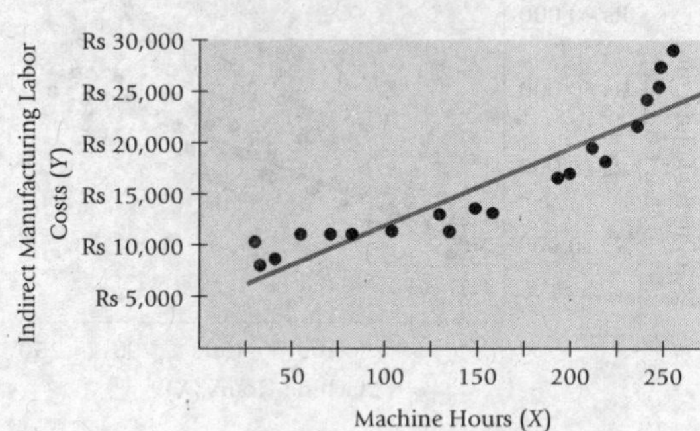

Exhibit 10-17 Simple Regression Results with Indirect Manufacturing Labor Costs as Dependent Variable and Direct Manufacturing Labor-Hours as Independent Variable (Cost Driver) for Elegant Rugs

File Edit View Insert Format Tools Data Window Help

	A	B	C	D	E	F	G	H
1		**Coefficients**	**Standard Error**	***t* Stat**				
2		**(1)**	**(2)**	**(3) = (1) ÷ (2)**				
3	Intercept	Rs 7,446.70	Rs 2,176.10	3.42				
4	Independent Variable: Direct Manufacturing Labor-Hours (*X*)	Rs 77.20	Rs 54.00	1.43 →		= Coefficient/Standard Error = B4/C4 = 77.20/54.00		
5								
6	**Regression Statistics**							
7	R Square	0.17						
8	Durbin-Watson Statistic	2.26						

in Exhibit 10-18 are imperfect because, as stated in the section on specification analysis of estimation assumptions, inferences drawn from only 12 observations are not reliable.

Multiple Regression and Cost Hierarchies

In some cases, a satisfactory estimation of a cost function may be based on only one independent variable, such as number of machine-hours. In many cases, however, basing the estimation on more than one independent variable (that is, *multiple regression*) is more economically plausible and improves accuracy. The most widely used equations to express relationships between two or more independent variables and a dependent variable are linear in the form

$$y = a + b_1X_1 + b_2X_2 + \dots + U$$

where,

Exhibit 10-18

Comparison of Alternative Cost Functions for Indirect Manufacturing Labor Costs Estimated with Simple Regression for Elegant Rugs

Criterion	Cost Function 1: Machine-Hours as Independent Variable	Cost Function 2: Direct Manufacturing Labor-Hours as Independent Variable
Economic plausibility	A positive relationship between indirect manufacturing labor costs (technical support labor) and machine-hours is economically plausible in Elegant Rugs's highly automated plant	A positive relationship between indirect manufacturing labor costs and direct manufacturing labor-hours is economically plausible, but less so than machine-hours in Elegant Rugs's highly automated plant on a week-to-week basis.
Goodness of fit [a]	r^2 = 0.52; standard error of regression = Rs 1,705.0. Excellent goodness of fit.	r^2 = 0.17; standard error of regression = Rs 2,246.0. Poor goodness of fit.
Significance of independent variable(s)	The *t*-value of 3.30 is significant at the 0.05 level.	The *t*-value of 1.43 is not significant at the 0.05 level.
Specification analysis of estimation assumptions	Plot of the data indicates that assumptions of linearity, constant variance, independence of residuals, (Durbin-Watson statistic = 2.05), and normality of residuals hold, but inferences drawn from only 12 observations are not reliable.	Plot of the data indicates that assumptions of linearity, constant variance, independence of residuals (Durbin-Watson statistic = 2.26) and normality of residuals hold, but inferences drawn from only 12 observations are not reliable.

[a]If the number of observations available to estimate the machine-hours regression differs from the number of observations available to estimate the direct manufacturing labor-hours regression, an *adjusted* r^2 can be calculated to take this difference (in degrees of freedom) into account. Programs such as Excel calculate and present *adjusted* r^2.

y = Cost to be predicted
$X_1, X_2, \ldots$ = Independent variables on which the prediction is to be based
$a, b_1, b_2, \ldots$ = Estimated coefficients of the regression model
u = Residual term that includes the net effect of other factors not in the model as well as measurement errors in the dependent and independent variables

Example Consider the Elegant Rugs data in Exhibit 10-19. The company's ABC analysis indicates that indirect manufacturing labor costs include large amounts incurred for setup and changeover costs when a new batch of carpets is started. Management believes that in addition to number of machine-hours (an output unit-level cost driver), indirect manufacturing labor costs are also affected by the number of batches of carpet produced during each week (a batch-level driver). Elegant Rugs estimates the relationship between two independent variables, number of machine-hours and number of production batches of carpet manufactured during the week, and indirect manufacturing labor costs.

Exhibit 10-20 presents results (in Excel) for the following multiple regression model, using data in columns B, C, and E of Exhibit 10-19:

$$y = \text{Rs } 425.80 + \text{Rs } 76.0\, X_1 + \text{Rs } 377.70\, X_2$$

where X_1 is the number of machine-hours and X_2 is the number of production batches. It is economically plausible that both number of machine-hours and number of production batches would help explain variations in indirect manufacturing labor costs at Elegant Rugs. The r^2 of 0.52 for the simple regression using number of machine-hours (Exhibit 10-14) increases to 0.72 with the multiple regression in Exhibit 10-20. The *t*-values suggest that the independent variable coefficients of both number of machine-hours (Rs 76.0) and number of production batches (Rs 377.70)

Exhibit 10-19

Weekly Indirect Manufacturing Labor Costs, Machine-Hours, Direct Manufacturing Labor-Hours, and Number of Production Batches for Elegant Rugs

File Edit View Insert Format Tools Data Window Help

	A	B	C	D	E
1	Week	Machine-Hours (X_1)	Number of Production Batches (X_2)	Direct Manufacturing Labor-Hours	Indirect Manufacturing Labor Costs (Y)
2	1	68	12	30	Rs 11,900
3	2	88	15	35	12,110
4	3	62	13	36	10,040
5	4	72	11	20	9,170
6	5	60	10	47	7,700
7	6	96	12	45	14,560
8	7	78	17	44	11,800
9	8	46	7	38	7,100
10	9	82	14	70	13,160
11	10	94	12	30	10,320
12	11	68	7	29	7,520
13	12	48	14	38	9,630
14	Total	862	144	462	RS 1,25,010
15					

are significantly different from zero ($t = 2.74$ is the t-value for number of machine-hours, and $t = 2.48$ is the t-value for number of production batches compared to the cut-off t-value of 2.26). The multiple regression model in Exhibit 10-20 satisfies both economic plausibility and statistical criteria, and it explains much greater variation (that is, r^2 of 0.72 versus r^2 of 0.52) in indirect manufacturing labor costs than the simple regression model using only number of machine-hours as the independent variable.[6] The standard error of the regression equation that includes number of batches as an independent variable is

$$\sqrt{\frac{\Sigma(Y-y)^2}{n-3}} = \sqrt{\frac{17{,}01{,}560}{9}} = \text{Rs } 1{,}375.0$$

which is lower than the standard error of the regression with only machine-hours as the independent variable, Rs 1,705.0. That is, even though adding a variable reduces the degrees of freedom in the denominator, it substantially improves fit so that the numerator, $\Sigma(Y - y)^2$, decreases even more. Number of machine-hours and number of production batches are both important cost drivers of indirect manufacturing labor costs at Elegant Rugs.

In Exhibit 10-20, the slope coefficients—Rs 76.0 for number of machine-hours and Rs 377.70 for number of production batches—measure the change in indirect manufacturing labor costs associated with a unit change in an independent variable (assuming that

[6] Adding another variable always increases r^2. The question is whether adding another variable increases r^2 sufficiently. One way to get insight into this question is to calculate an adjusted r^2 as follows:

Adjusted $r^2 = 1 - (1 - r^2)\frac{n-1}{n-p-1}$, where n is the number of observations and p is the number of coefficients estimated. In the model with only machine-hours as the independent variable, Adjusted $r^2 = 1 - (1 - 0.52)\frac{12-1}{12-2-1} = 0.41$. In the model with both machine-hours and number of batches as independent variables, Adjusted $r^2 = 1-(1-0.72)\frac{12-1}{12-3-1} = 0.62$. Adjusted r^2 does not have the same interpretation as r^2 but the increase in adjusted r^2 when number of batches is added as an independent variable suggests that adding this variable significantly improves the fit of the model in a way that more than compensates for the degree of freedom lost by estimating another coefficient.

Exhibit 10-20 Multiple Regression Results with Indirect Manufacturing Labor Costs and Two Independent Variables of Cost Drivers (Machine-Hours and Production Batches) for Elegant Rugs

File Edit View Insert Format Tools Data Window Help

	A	B	C	D	E	F
1		Coefficients	Standard Error	t Stat		
2		(1)	(2)	(3) = (1) ÷ (2)		
3	Intercept	Rs 425.80	Rs 2,139.10	0.20		
4	Independent variable 1: Machine-Hours (*X1*)	Rs 76.00	Rs 27.70	2.74 →	= Coefficient/Standard Error = B4/C4 = 76.0/27.70	
5	Independent variable 2: Number of production batches (*X2*)	Rs 377.70	Rs 152.50	2.48		
6						
7	Regression Statistics					
8	R Square	0.72				
9	Durbin-Watson Statistic	2.49				

the other independent variable is held constant). For example, indirect manufacturing labor costs increase by Rs 377.70 when one more production batch is added, assuming that the number of machine-hours is held constant.

An alternative approach would create two separate cost pools for indirect manufacturing labor costs: one for costs related to number of machine-hours and another for costs related to number of production batches. Elegant Rugs would then estimate the relationship between the cost driver and the costs in each cost pool. The difficult task under this approach is to properly subdivide the indirect manufacturing labor costs into the two cost pools.

Multicollinearity

A major concern that arises with multiple regression is multicollinearity. **Multicollinearity** exists when two or more independent variables are highly correlated with each other. Generally, users of regression analysis believe that a *coefficient of correlation* between independent variables greater than 0.70 indicates multicollinearity. Multicollinearity increases the standard errors of the coefficients of the individual variables. That is, variables that are economically and statistically significant will appear not to be significantly different from zero.

The matrix of correlation coefficients of the different variables described in Exhibit 10-19 are:

	Indirect manufacturing labor costs	Machine-hours	Number of production batches	Direct manufacturing labor-hours
Indirect manufacturing labor costs	1			
Machine-hours	0.72	1		
Number of production batches	0.69	0.4	1	
Direct manufacturing labor-hours	0.41	0.12	0.31	1

These results indicate that multiple regressions using any pair of the independent variables in Exhibit 10-19 are not likely to encounter multicollinearity problems.

When multicollinearity exists, try to obtain new data that do not suffer from multicollinearity problems. Do not drop an independent variable (cost driver) that should be included in a model because it is correlated with another independent variable. Omitting such a variable will cause the estimated coefficient of the independent variable included in the model to be biased away from its true value.

TERMS TO LEARN

This chapter and the Glossary at the end of this book contain definitions of:

conference method (**p. 399**)
constant (**p. 395**)
cost estimation (**p. 396**)
cost function (**p. 393**)
cost predictions (**p. 396**)
industrial engineering method (**p. 398**)
intercept (**p. 395**)
learning curve (**p. 409**)
linear cost function (**p. 394**)
mixed cost (**p. 395**)
semivariable cost (**p. 395**)
slope coefficient (**p. 394**)
work-measurement method (**p. 398**)

ASSIGNMENT MATERIAL

Questions

10-1 What two assumptions are frequently made when estimating a cost function?

10-2 Describe three alternative linear cost functions.

10-3 What is the difference between a linear and a nonlinear cost function? Give an example of each type of cost function.

10-4 "High correlation between two variables means that one is the cause and the other is the effect." Do you agree? Explain.

10-5 Name four approaches to estimating a cost function.

10-6 Describe the conference method for estimating a cost function. What are two advantages of this method?

10-7 Describe the account analysis method for estimating a cost function.

10-8 List the six steps in estimating a cost function on the basis of an analysis of a past cost relationship. Which step is typically the most difficult for the cost analyst?

10-9 When using the high-low method, should you base the high and low observations on the dependent variable or on the cost driver?

10-10 Describe three criteria for evaluating cost functions and choosing cost drivers.

10-11 Define learning curve. Outline two models that can be used when incorporating learning into the estimation of cost functions.

10-12 Discuss four frequently encountered problems when collecting cost data on variables included in a cost function.

10-13 What are the four key assumptions examined in specification analysis in the case of simple regression?

10-14 "All the independent variables in a cost function estimated with regression analysis are cost drivers." Do you agree? Explain.

10-15 "Multicollinearity exists when the dependent variable and the independent variable are highly correlated." Do you agree? Explain.

Solved Examples

10-16 Estimating a cost function. The CFO of the Colgate Co. wants you to estimate a cost function from the following two observations in a general ledger account called maintenance:

Month	Machine-Hours	Maintenance Costs Incurred
January	4,000	Rs 3,00,000
February	7,000	3,90,000

Required

1. Estimate the cost function for maintenance.
2. Can the constant in the cost function be used as an estimate of fixed maintenance cost per month? Explain.

Solution

Estimating a cost function.

1. Slope coefficient = $\dfrac{\text{Difference in costs}}{\text{Difference in machine-hours}}$

   = (Rs 3,90,000 – Rs 3,00,000)/(7,000 – 4,000)

   Rs 90,000/3,000 = Rs 30 per machine-hour

   Constant = Total cost – (Slope coefficient × Quantity of cost driver)

   = Rs 3,90,000 – (Rs 30 × 7,000) = Rs 1,80,000

   = Rs 3,00,000 – (Rs 30 × 4,000) = Rs 1,80,000

   The cost function based on the two observations is

   Maintenance costs = Rs 1,80,000 + (Rs 30 × Machine-hours)

2. The cost function in requirement 1 is an estimate of how costs behave within the relevant range, not at cost levels outside the relevant range. If there are no months with zero machine-hours represented in the maintenance account, data in that account cannot be used to estimate the fixed costs at the zero machine-hours level. Rather, the constant component of the cost function provides the best available starting point for a straight line that approximates how a cost behaves within the relevant range.

10-17 Identifying variable, fixed, and mixed-cost functions. The Avis Ltd. operates car rental agencies at more than 20 airports. Customers can choose from one of three contracts for car rentals of one day or less:

1. Contract 1: Rs 600 for the day
2. Contract 2: Rs 300 for the day plus Rs 6 per mile traveled
3. Contract 3: Rs 10 per mile traveled

Required

1. Express each contract as a linear cost function of the form $y = a + bX$.
2. Identify each contract as a variable, fixed, or mixed-cost function.

Solution

Identifying variable, fixed, and mixed-cost functions.

1. Contract 1: y = Rs 600

   Contract 2: y = Rs 300 + Rs 6X

   Contract 3: y = Rs 10X

   where X is the number of miles traveled in the day.

2.

Contract	Cost Function
1	Fixed
2	Mixed
3	Variable

10-18 Matching graphs with descriptions of cost and revenue behavior. (D. Green. Adapted) Given below are a number of graphs.

If the horizontal axis represents the units produced over the year and the vertical axis represents total cost or revenue, indicate by number which graph best fits the situation or item described. Some graphs may be used more than once; some may not apply to any of the situations.

(a) Direct materials costs

(b) Supervisors' salaries for one shift and two shifts

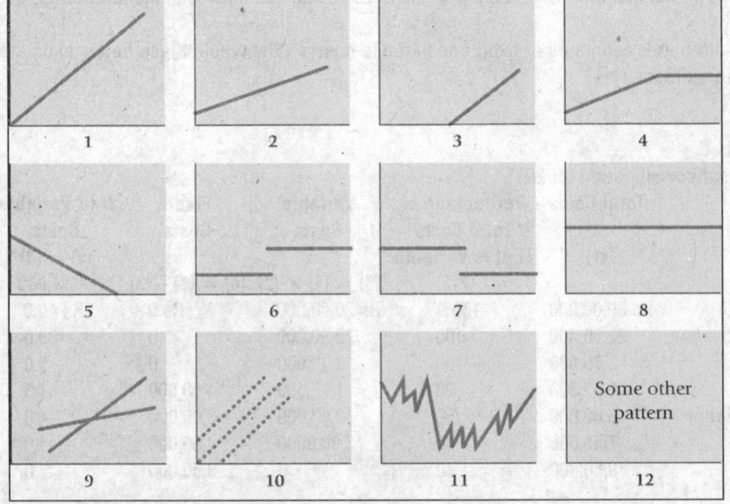

(c) A cost-volume-profit graph
(d) Mixed costs-for example, car rental fixed charge plus variable rate for miles driven
(e) Depreciation of plant, computed on a straight-line basis
(f) Data supporting the use of a variable-cost rate, such as manufacturing labor cost of Rs 14 per unit produced
(g) Incentive bonus plan that pays manages Re 1for every unit produced above some level of production
(h) Interest expense on Rs 20 lakh borrowed at a fixed rate of interest

Solution

Matching graphs with descriptions of cost and revenue behavior.

a. (1)
b. (6) A step-cost function.
c. (9)
d. (2)
e. (8)
f. (10) It is data plotted on a scatter diagram showing a linear variable cost function with constant variance of residuals. The constant variance of residuals implies that there is a uniform dispersion of the data points about the regression line.
g. (3)
h. (8)

10-19 Account analysis method. Supreme Industries, a manufacturer of plastic products, reports the following manufacturing costs and account analysis classification for the current year ended December 31, 2011:

Account	Classification	Amount
Direct materials	All variable	Rs 30,00,000
Direct manufacturing labor	All variable	22,50,000
Power	All variable	3,75,000
Supervision labor	20% variable	5,62,500
Materials-handling labor	50% variable	6,00,000
Maintenance labor	40% variable	7,50,000
Depreciation	0% variable	9,50,000
Rent, property taxes, and administration	0% variable	10,00,000

Supreme Industries produced 75,000 units of product in 2011. Supreme's management is estimating costs for 2012 on the basis of 2011 numbers. The following additional information is available for 2012.

a. Direct materials prices in 2012 are expected to increase by 5% compared with 2011.
b. Under the terms of the labor contract, direct manufacturing labor wage rates are expected to increase by 10% in 2012 compared with 2011.
c. Power rates and wage rates for supervision, materials handling, and maintenance are not expected to change from 2011 to 2012.
d. Depreciation costs are expected to increase by 5% and rent, property taxes, and administration costs are expected to increase by 7%.
e. Supreme Industries expects to manufacture and sell 80,000 units in 2012.

Required

1. Prepare a schedule of variable, fixed, and total manufacturing costs for each account category in 2012. Estimate total manufacturing costs for 2012.
2. Calculate Supreme's total manufacturing cost per unit in 2011, and estimate total manufacturing cost per unit in 2012.
3. How can you obtain better estimates of fixed and variable costs? Why would these better estimates be useful to Supreme Industries?

Solution

Account analysis method.

1. Manufacturing cost classification for 2011

Account	Total Costs (1)	Percentage of Total Costs That Is Variable (2)	Variable Costs (3) = (1) × (2)	Fixed Costs (4) = (1) – (3)	Unit Variable Costs (5) = (3) ÷ 75,000
Direct materials	Rs 30,00,000	100%	Rs 30,00,000	Rs 0	Rs 40.0
Direct manufacturing labor	22,50,000	100	22,50,000	0	30.0
Power	3,75,000	100	3,75,000	0	5.0
Supervision labor	5,62,500	20	1,12,500	4,50,000	1.5
Materials-handling labor	6,00,000	50	3,00,000	3,00,000	4.0
Maintenance labor	7,50,000	40	3,00,0000	4,50,000	4.0
Depreciation	9,50,000	0	0	9,50,000	0

Rent, property taxes, and administration	10,00,000	0	0	10,00,000	0
Total	Rs 94,87,500		Rs 63,37,500	Rs 31,50,000	Rs 84.5

Total manufacturing cost for 2011 = Rs 94,87,500

Variable costs in 2012

Account	Unit Variable Cost for 2011 (6)	Percentage Increase (7)	Increase in Variable Costs per Unit (8) = (6) × (7)	Unit Variable Cost for 2012 (9) = (6) + (8)	Total Variable Costs for 2012 (10) = (9) × 80,000
Direct materials	Rs 40.0	5%	Rs 2.0	Rs 42.0	Rs 33,60,000
Direct manufacturing labor	30.0	10	3.0	33.0	26,40,000
Power	5.0	0	0	5.0	4,00,000
Supervision labor	1.5	0	0	1.5	1,20,000
Materials-handling labor	4.0	0	0	4.0	3,20,000
Maintenance labor	4.0	0	0	4.00	3,20,0000
Depreciation	0	0	0	0	0
Rent, property taxes, administration	0	0	0	0	0
Total	Rs 84.5		Rs 5.0	Rs 89.5	Rs 71,60,000

Fixed and total costs in 2012

Account	Fixed Costs for 2011 (11)	Percentage Increase (12)	Rupee Increase in Fixed Costs (13) = (11) × (12)	Fixed Costs for 2012 (14) = (11) + (13)	Variable Costs for 2012 (15)	Total Costs (16) = (14) + (15)
Direct materials	Rs 0	0%	Rs 0	Rs 0	Rs 33,60,000	Rs 33,60,000
Direct manufacturing labor	0	0	0	0	26,40,000	26,40,000
Power	0	0	0	0	4,00,000	4,00,000
Supervision labor	4,50,000	0	0	4,50,000	1,20,000	5,70,000
Materials-handling labor	3,00,000	0	0	3,00,000	3,20,000	6,20,000
Maintenance labor	4,50,000	0	0	4,50,000	3,20,000	7,70,000
Depreciation	9,50,000	5	47,500	9,97,500	0	9,97,500
Rent, property taxes, administration	10,00,000	7	70,000	10,70,000	0	10,70,000
Total	31,50,000		1,17,500	32,67,500	71,60,000	1,04,27,500

Total manufacturing costs for 2012 = Rs 1,04,27,500

2. Total cost per unit, 2011 = $\frac{\text{Rs } 94,87,500}{75,000}$ = Rs 126.5

Total cost per unit, 2012 = $\frac{\text{Rs } 1,04,27,500}{80,000}$ = Rs 130.3

3. Cost classification into variable and fixed costs is based on qualitative, rather than quantitative, analysis. How good the classifications are depends on the knowledge of individual managers who classify the costs. Supreme Industries may want to undertake quantitative analysis of costs, using regression analysis on time-series or cross-sectional data to better estimate the fixed and variable components of costs. Better knowledge of fixed and variable costs will help Supreme Industries to better price its products, know when he is getting a positive contribution margin, and to better manage costs.

10-20 Estimating a cost function, high-low method. Fardeen is examining customer-service costs in the Southern Region of Crompton Greaves. Crompton Greaves has more than 200 separate electrical products that are sold with a 6-month guarantee of full repair or replacement with a new product includes details of the problem and the time and cost of resolving the problem. Weekly data for the most recent 10-week period is

Week	Customer-Service Department Costs	Number of Service Reports
1	Rs 13,845	201
2	20,624	276
3	12,941	122
4	18,452	386
5	14,843	274
6	21,890	436

7	16,831	321
8	21,429	328
9	18,267	243
10	16,832	161

Required

1. Plot the relationship between customer-service costs and number of service reports. Is the relationship economically plausible?
2. Use the high-low method to compute the cost function, relating customer-service costs to the number of service reports.
3. What variables, in addition to number of service reports, might be cost drivers of monthly customer service costs of Crompton Products?

Solution

Estimating a cost function, high-low method.

1. See Solution Exhibit 10-20. There is a positive relationship between the number of service reports (a cost driver) and the customer-service department costs. This relationship is economically plausible.
2.

	Number of Service Reports	Customer-Service Department Costs
Highest observation of cost driver	436	Rs 21,890
Lowest observation of cost driver	122	12,941
Difference	314	Rs 8,949

Customer-service department costs $= a + b$ (number of service reports)

$$\text{Slope coefficient } (b) = \frac{\text{Rs } 8{,}949}{314} = \text{Rs } 28.50 \text{ per service report}$$

$$\text{Constant (a)} = \text{Rs } 21{,}890 - \text{Rs } 28.50\ (436) = \text{Rs } 9{,}464$$
$$= \text{Rs } 12{,}941 - \text{Rs } 28.50\ (122) = \text{Rs } 9{,}464$$

Customer-service department costs = Rs 9,464 + Rs 28.50 (number of service reports)

3. Other possible cost drivers of customer-service department costs are:
   a. Number of products replaced with a new product (and the rupee value of the new products charged to the customer-service department).
   b. Number of products repaired and the time and cost of repairs.

Solution Exhibit 10-20

Plot of Number of Service Reports versus Customer-Service Department Costs for Crompton Products

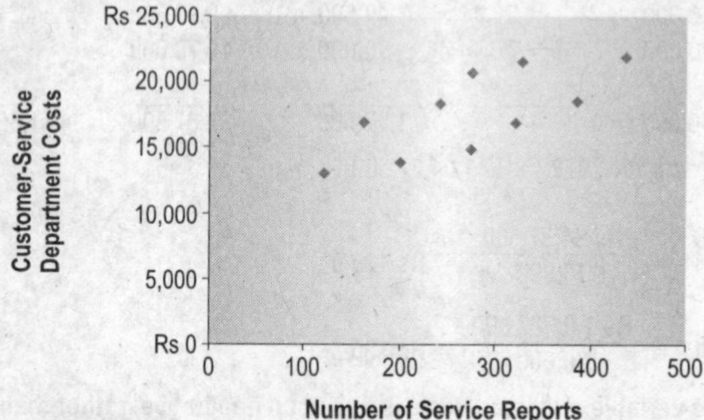

10-21 Cost-volume-profit and regression analysis. Hero Cycles manufactures a children's bicycle, Model C18. Hero Cycles currently manufactures the bicycle frame. During 2011, Hero Cycles made 30,000 frames at a total cost of Rs 90,00,000. Rehman Ltd. has offered to supply as many frames as Hero Cycle wants at a cost of Rs 285 per frame. Hero Cycles anticipates needing 36,000 frames each year for the next few years.

Required

1. (a) What is the average cost of manufacturing a bicycle frame in 2011? How does it compare to Rehman's offer. (b) Can Hero Cycles use the answer in requirement (a) to determine the cost of manufacturing 36,000 bicycle/frames? Explain.
2. Hero Cycles cost analyst uses annual data from past years to estimate the following regression equation with total manufacturing costs of the bicycle frame as the dependent variable and bicycle frames produced as the independent variable

$$y = \text{Rs } 43{,}20{,}000 + \text{Rs } 150X$$

During the years used to estimate the regression equation, the production of bicycle frames had varied from 28,000 to 36,000. Using this equation, estimate how much it would cost Hero Cycles to manufacture 36,000 bicycle frames. How much more or less costly is it to manufacture the frames rather than to acquire them from Rehman. (3) What other information would you need in order to be confident that the equation in requirement 2 accurately predicts the cost of manufacturing bicycle frames?

Solution

Cost-volume-profit and regression analysis.

1a. Average cost of manufacturing $= \dfrac{\text{Total manufacturing costs}}{\text{Number of bicycle frames}}$

$= \dfrac{\text{Rs } 90,00,000}{30,000} = \text{Rs } 300 \text{ per frame}$

This cost is greater than the Rs 285 per frame that Rehman has quoted.

1b. Hero Cycles cannot take the average manufacturing cost in 2011 of Rs 300 per frame and multiply it by 36,000 bicycle frames to determine the total cost of manufacturing 36,000 bicycle frames. The reason is that some of the Rs 90,00,000 (or equivalently the Rs 300 cost per frame) are fixed costs and some are variable costs. Without distinguishing fixed from variable costs, Hero Cycles cannot determine the cost of manufacturing 36,000 frames. For example, if all costs are fixed, the manufacturing costs of 36,000 frames will continue to be Rs 90,00,000. If, however, all costs are variable, the cost of manufacturing 36,000 frames would be Rs 300 × 36,000 = Rs 1,08,00,000. If some costs are fixed and some are variable, the cost of manufacturing 36,000 frames will be somewhere between Rs 90,00,000 and Rs 1,08,00,000.

Some students could argue that another reason for not being able to determine the cost of manufacturing 36,000 bicycle frames is that not all costs are output unit-level costs. If some costs are, for example, batch-level costs, more information would be needed on the number of batches in which the 36,000 bicycle frames would be produced, in order to determine the cost of manufacturing 36,000 bicycle frames.

2. Expected cost to make 36,000 bicycle frames = Rs 43,20,000 + Rs 150 × 36,000
= Rs 43,20,000 + Rs 54,00,000 = Rs 97,20,000

Purchasing bicycle frames from Ryan will cost Rs 285 × 36,000 = Rs 1,02,60,000. Hence it will cost Hero Cycles Rs 1,02,60,000 – Rs 97,20,000 = Rs 5,40,000 more to purchase the frames from Hero Cycles rather than manufacture them in-house.

3. Hero Cycles would need to consider several factors before being confident that the equation in requirement 2 accurately predicts the cost of manufacturing bicycle frames.

a. Is the relationship between total manufacturing costs and quantity of bicycle frames economically plausible? For example, is the quantity of bicycles made the only cost driver or are there other cost-drivers (for example batch-level costs of setups, production-orders or material handling) that affect manufacturing costs?

b. How good is the goodness of fit? That is, how well does the estimated line fit the data?

c. Is the relationship between the number of bicycle frames produced and total manufacturing costs linear?

d. Does the slope of the regression line indicate that a strong relationship exists between manufacturing costs and the number of bicycle frames produced?

e. Are there any data problems such as, for example, errors in measuring costs, trends in prices of materials, labor or overheads that might affect variable or fixed costs over time, extreme values of observations, or a nonstationary relationship over time between total manufacturing costs and the quantity of bicycles produced?

f. How is inflation expected to affect costs?

g. Will Rehman supply high-quality bicycle frames on time?

10-22 Regression analysis, service company. (CMA, adapted) Paul owns a catering company that prepares banquets and parties. For a standard cocktail party the cost on a per-person basis is:

Food and beverages	Rs 150
Labor (0.5 hour × Rs 100 per hour)	50
Overhead (0.5 hour × Rs 140 per hour)	70
Total cost per person	Rs 270

Paul is quite certain about his estimates of the food, beverages, and labor costs but is not as, comfortable with the overhead estimate. The overhead estimate was based on the actual data for the past 12 months presented below. These data indicate that overhead costs vary with the direct labor-hours used. The Rs 140 estimate was determined dividing total overhead costs for the 12 months by total labor-hours.

Month	Labor-Hours	Overhead Costs
January	2,500	Rs 5,50,000
February	2,700	5,90,000
March	3,000	6,00,000
April	4,200	6,40,000
May	7,500	7,70,000
June	5,500	7,10,000
July	6,500	7,40,000
August	4,500	6,70,000

September	7,000	7,50,000
October	4,500	6,80,000
November	3,100	6,20,000
December	6,500	7,30,000
Total	57,500	Rs 80,50,000

Paul has recently become aware of regression analysis. He estimated the following regression equation with overhead costs as the dependent variable and labor-hours as the independent variable.

$$y = \text{Rs } 4{,}82{,}710 + \text{Rs } 39.40X$$

Required

1. Plot the relationship between overhead costs and labor-hours. Draw the regression line and evaluate it using the criteria of economic plausibility, goodness of fit, and slope of the regression line.
2. Using data from the regression analysis, what is the variable cost per person for a cocktail party?
3. Paul has been asked to prepare a bid for a 200-person cocktail party to be given next month. Determine the minimum bid price that Paul would be willing to submit to recoup variable costs.

Solution

Regression analysis, service company.

1. Solution Exhibit 10-22 plots the relationship between labor-hours and overhead costs and shows the regression line.

$$y = \text{Rs } 4{,}82{,}710 + \text{Rs } 39.40\ X$$

Economic plausibility. Labor-hours appears to be an economically plausible driver of overhead costs for a catering company. Overhead costs such as scheduling, hiring and training of workers, and managing the workforce are largely incurred to support labor.

Goodness of fit. The vertical differences between actual and predicted costs are extremely small, indicating a very good fit. The good fit indicates a strong relationship between the labor-hour cost driver and overhead costs.

Slope of regression line. The regression line has a reasonably steep slope from left to right. Given the small scatter of the observations around the line, the positive slope indicates that, on average, overhead costs increases as labor-hours increase.

2. The regression analysis indicates that, within the relevant range of 2,500 to 7,500 labor-hours, the variable cost per person for a cocktail party equals:

Food and beverages	Rs 150.0
Labor (0.5 hr. × Rs 100 per hour)	50.0
Variable overhead (0.5 hr × Rs 39.40 per labor-hour)	19.7
Total variable cost per person	Rs 219.7

3. To earn a positive contribution margin, the minimum bid for a 200-person cocktail party would be any amount greater than Rs 43,940. This amount is calculated multiplying the variable cost per person of Rs 219.70 by the 200 people. At a price above the variable costs of Rs 43,940, Paul will be earning a contribution margin towards coverage of his fixed costs.

Of course, Paul will consider other factors in developing his bid including (a) an analysis of the competition—vigorous competition will limit Paul's ability to obtain a higher price (b) a determination of whether or not his bid will set a precedent for lower prices—overall, the prices Paul charges should generate enough contribution to cover fixed costs and earn a reasonable profit, and (c) a judgment of how representative past historical data (used in the regression analysis) is about future costs.

Solution Exhibit 10-22

Regression Line of Labor-Hours on Overhead Costs for Paul's Catering Company

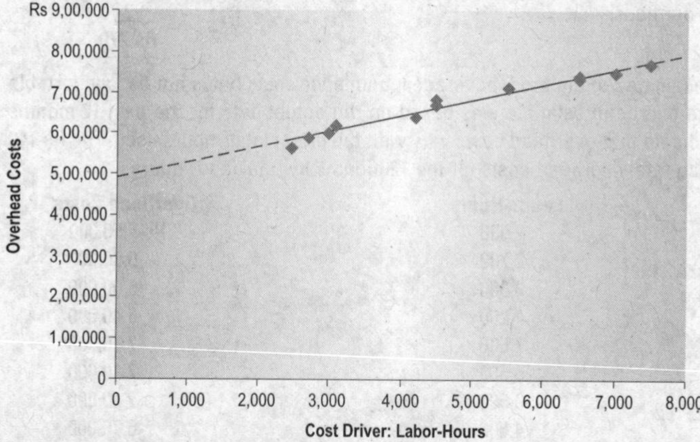

10-23 Learning curve, cumulative average-time learning model. Global Defense manufactures radar systems. It has just completed the manufacture of its first newly designed system, RS-32. It took 3,000 direct manufacturing labor-hours (DMLH) to produce this one unit. Global believes that a 90% cumulative average-time learning model for direct manufacturing labor-hours applies to RS-32. (A 90% learning curve means $b = -0.1520$). The variable costs of producing RS-32 are

Direct material costs	Rs 8,00,000 per unit of RS-32
Variable manufacturing overhead costs	Rs 250 per DMLH
Direct manufacturing labor costs	Rs 150 per DMLH

Required

Calculate the total variable costs of producing 2,4, and 8 units.

Solution

Learning curve, cumulative average-time learning model.

The direct manufacturing labor-hours (DMLH) required to produce the first 2, 4, and 8 units given the assumption of a cumulative average-time learning curve of 90%, is as follows:

Cumulative Number of Units (1)	Cumulative Average-Time per Unit (2)	Cumulative Total Time (3) = (1) × (2)
1	3,000	3,000
2	2,700 (3,000 × 0.90)	5,400
4	2,430 (2,700 × 0.90)	9,720
8	2,187 (2,430 × 0.90)	17,496

Alternatively, to compute the values in column (2) we should use the formula

$y = aX^b$

where $a = 3{,}000$, $X = 2, 4$, or 8, and $b = -0.1520$, which gives

when $X = 2$, $y = 3{,}000 \times 2^{-0.1520} = 2{,}700$

when $X = 4$, $y = 3{,}000 \times 4^{-0.1520} = 2{,}430$

when $X = 8$, $y = 3{,}000 \times 8^{-0.1520} = 2{,}187$

	Variable Costs of Producing		
	2 Units	4 Units	8 Units
Direct materials Rs 8,00,000 × 2; 4; 8	Rs 16,00,000	Rs 32,00,000	Rs 64,00,000
Direct manufacturing labor Rs 250 × 5,400; 9,720; 17,496	13,50,000	24,30,000	43,74,000
Variable manufacturing overhead Rs 150 × 5,400; 9,720; 17,496	8,10,000	14,58,000	26,24,400
Total variable costs	Rs 37,60,000	Rs 70,88,000	Rs 1,33,98,400

10-24 Learning curve, incremental unit-time learning model. Assume the same information for Global Defense as in Exercise 10-23, except that Global Defense uses a 90% incremental unit-time learning model as a basis for predicting direct manufacturing labor-hours. (A 90% learning curve means $b = -0.1520$.)

Required

1. Calculate the total variable costs of producing 2,3, and 4 units.
2. If you having solved Exercise 10-23, compare your cost predictions in the two exercises for 2 and 4 units. Why are the predictions different?

Solution

Learning curve, incremental unit-time learning model.

1. The direct manufacturing labor-hours (DMLH) required to produce the first 2, 3, and 4 units, given the assumption of an incremental unit-time learning curve of 90%, is as follows:

Cumulative Number of Units (1)	Individual Unit Time for Xth Unit (2)	Cumulative Total Time (3)
1	3,000	3,000
2	2,700 (3,000 × 0.90)	5,700
3	2,539	8,239
4	2,430 (2,700 × 0.90)	10,669

Values in column 2 are calculated using the formula $y = aX^b$

where $a = 3{,}000$, $X = 2, 3$, or 4, and $b = -0.1520$, which gives

when $X = 2$, $y = 3{,}000 \times 2 - 0.1520 = 2{,}700$

when $X = 3$, $y = 3{,}000 \times 3 - 0.1520 = 2{,}539$

when $X = 4$, $y = 3{,}000 \times 4 - 0.1520 = 2{,}430$

	Variable Costs of Producing		
	2 Units	4 Units	8 Units
Direct materials Rs 8,00,000 × 2; 3; 4	Rs 16,00,000	Rs 24,00,000	Rs 32,00,000
Direct manufacturing labor Rs 250 × 5,700; 8,239; 10,669	14,25,000	20,59,750	26,67,250
Variable manufacturing overhead Rs 150 × 5,700; 8,239;10669	8,55,000	12,35,850	16,00,350
Total variable costs	Rs 38,80,000	Rs 56,95,600	Rs 74,67,600

2.

	Variable Costs of Producing	
	2 Units	4 Units
Incremental unit-time learning model (from requirement 1)	Rs 38,80,000	Rs 74,67,600
Cumulative average-time learning model (from Exercise 10-23)	37,60,000	70,88,000
Difference	1,20,000	Rs 3,79,600

Total variable costs for manufacturing 2 and 4 units are lower under the cumulative average-time learning curve relative to the incremental unit-time learning curve. Direct manufacturing labor-hours required to make additional units decline more slowly in the incremental unit-time learning curve relative to the cumulative average-time learning curve when the same 90% factor is used for both curves. The reason is that, in the incremental unit-time learning curve, as the number of units double, only the last unit produced has a cost of 90% of the initial cost. In the cumulative average-time learning model, doubling the number of units causes the average cost of all the additional units produced (not just the last unit) to be 90% of the initial cost.

10-25 Regression analysis, activity-based costing, choosing cost drivers. Amitabh, the plant controller at Rohan Plastics, wants to identify cost drivers for support overhead costs. Indirect support consists of skilled staff responsible for the efficient functioning of all aspects (setup, production, maintenance, and quality control) of the plastic injection molding facility. In talking to the support staff, Amitabh has the impression that the staff spends a sizable portion of their time ensuring that the equipment is set up correctly and checking that the first units of production in each batch are of good quality.

Amitabh has collected the following data for the past 12 months:

Month	Support Overhead	Machine-Hours	Number of Batches
January	Rs 8,40,000	2,250	309
February	4,10,000	2,400	128
March	6,30,000	2,850	249
April	4,40,000	2,100	159
May	4,40,000	2,700	216
June	4,80,000	2,250	174
July	6,60,000	3,800	264
August	4,60,000	3,600	162
September	3,30,000	1,850	147
October	6,60,000	3,300	219
November	8,10,000	3,750	303
December	5,70,000	2,000	106
Total	Rs 67,30,000	32,850	2,436

Amitabh estimates the following two regression equations:

y = Rs 2,80,890 + (Rs 102.3 × Machine-hours)

y = Rs 1,60,310 + (Rs 1,973 × Number of batches)

Where *y is* the monthly support overhead.

Required

1. Plot the monthly data and the regression lines for each of the following cost functions: a. Support overhead costs = *a* + *(b* × Machine-hours). b. Support overhead costs = a + *(b* × Number of batches). Which cost driver for support overhead costs would you choose? Explain.
2. Amitabh anticipates 2,600 machine-hours and 300 batches for next month Using the cost driver you chose in requirement 1, what amount of support overhead costs Should Amitabh budget?
3. Amitabh adds 20% to costs to determine target revenues (and hence prices). Costs other than support overhead are expected to equal Rs 12,50,000 next month. Compare the target revenue numbers obtained if the cost driver is (i) machine-hours or (ii) number of batches. What would happen if Amitabh picked the cost driver you did not choose in requirement 1 to set target revenues and prices. Describe any other implications of choosing the "other" cost driver and cost function.

Solution

Regression analysis, activity-based costing, choosing cost drivers.

1. Solution Exhibit 10-25a presents the plots and regression line of machine–hours on support overhead. Solution Exhibit 10-25b presents the plots and regression line of number of batches on support overhead. As described below, using the three criteria of economic plausibility, goodness of fit, and slope of regression line, Amitabh should choose number of batches as the cost driver of support overhead costs.

   Economic plausibility. Number of batches appears to be a more plausible cost driver of support overhead costs than machine-hours. Support staff indicates that they spend a good portion of their time at the start of each batch ensuring that the equipment is set up correctly and checking that the first units of production in each batch are of good quality. Once the machine is working properly, support staff are not needed to supervise the actual running of the machines. Consequently, support staff resources are more likely to vary with the number of batches rather than the total number of machine-hours worked.

   Goodness of fit. Compare Solution Exhibits 10-25a and 10-25b. The vertical differences between actual and predicted costs are much smaller for number of batches than for machine-hours. This indicates that number of batches have a better fit and a stronger relationship with support overhead costs.

   Slope of regression line. Again, compare Solution Exhibits 10-25a and 10-25b. The slope of the regression line of number of batches on support overhead is relatively steep with less scatter of observations about the regression line while the regression line of machine-hours on support overhead is relatively flat (small slope) with more scatter of observations about the regression line. A relatively steep regression line with less scatter for number of batches indicates that, on average, support overhead costs increases as number of batches increase. On the other hand, the relatively flat regression line for machine-hours with more scatter indicates a weak or no relationship between support overhead costs and machine hours—on average, changes in machine-hours appear to have a minimal effect on support overhead costs.

2. As described in requirement 1, number of batches is the preferred cost driver. Using this cost driver and the regression equation

   y = Rs 1,60,310 + Rs 1973 × number of batches, Amitabh should budget the following support overhead costs for the 300 batches that will be run next month:

   y = Rs 1,60,310 + Rs 1,973 × 300 = Rs 1,60,310 + Rs 5,91,900 = Rs 7,52,210.

3a. Using machine-hours as the cost driver and the regression equation y = Rs 2,80,890 + Rs 102.3 × machine-hours, Amitabh would budget support overhead costs for the 2,600 machine-hours that will be worked next month as:

y = Rs 2,80,890 + Rs 102.3 × 2,600 = Rs 2,80,890 + Rs 2,65,980 = Rs 5,46,870

	Budgeted Revenues and Costs for Next Month Using	
	Number of Batches as the Cost Driver	**Machine-Hours as the Cost Driver**
Costs other than support overhead	Rs 12,50,000	Rs 12,50,000
Support overhead costs	7,52,210	5,46,870
Total costs	20,02,210	17,96,870
Add margin of 20% of total costs	4,00,440	3,59,370
Target revenues	Rs 24,02,650	21,56,240

Picking machine-hours rather than the number of batches as the cost driver will cause Amitabh to underestimate costs and choose lower target revenues and prices. Support overhead costs, however, will vary with number of batches rather than machine-hours. Using information from the preceding table, actual costs will be closer to Rs 20,02,210 against target revenues of Rs 21,56,240. Target profitability is unlikely to be met. With better cost driver information, Amitabh would probably have priced products higher and earned greater revenues, assuming, of course, that customers are willing to pay the higher prices.

Choosing the "wrong" cost driver and estimating the incorrect cost function will also have repercussions for cost management and cost control. Suppose Rohan Plastics budgets support overhead costs of Rs 5,46,870 for next month using the machine-hour regression. Suppose actual support overhead costs, driven by number of batches, are Rs 7,40,000 next month. Management of Rohan Plastics would regard this as unsatisfactory performance and begin to explore ways to cut costs to bring them more in line with budgeted support overhead costs. In fact, on the basis of the preferred cost driver, number of batches, the plant's actual costs are lower than the predicted amount, Rs 7,52,210—a performance that management should seek to replicate rather than change. Using "wrong" cost drivers misleads management in cost planning, cost management, and cost control besides contributing to inappropriate product pricing decisions.

Solution Exhibit 10-25a

Regression Line of Machine-Hours on Support Overhead Costs for Rohan Plastics

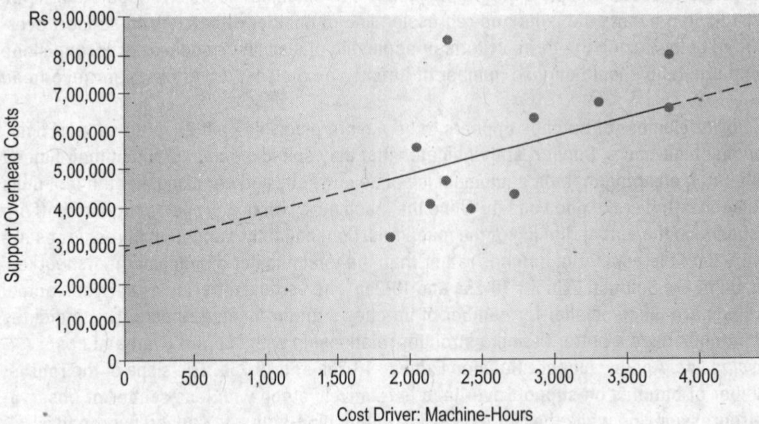

Solution Exhibit 10-25b

Regression Line of Number of Batches on Support Overhead Costs for Rohan Plastics

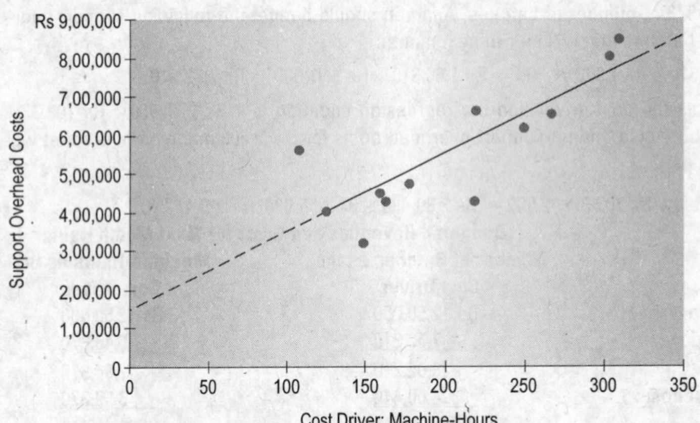

10-26 Time lag consideration in interpreting regression results. Lily Put Company manufactures apparel for young adults. It has four peak-load periods, one each for manufacturing the clothing suitable for spring, summer, fall, and winter. Each of these periods lasts for two months. In off-peak period, Lily Put schedules equipment maintenance and runs advertising campaigns to introduce new lines of clothing.

Lily Put wanted to study the cost-behavior pattern of its equipment maintenance costs and the relationship between its sales and advertising costs. Using monthly data and linear regression analysis, the following results were obtained:

Maintenance costs = Rs 3,80,000 – (Rs 12 per Machine-hour × Number of Machine - hours)

Sales revenue = Rs 2,50,000 – (2.10 × Advertising costs)

Required Interpret the regression results.

Solution

Time lag consideration in interpreting regression results. The relationship between machine-hours and maintenance costs is negative because Lily Put Company schedules maintenance during slow production periods. There is a time lag between heavy machine usage during peak production months, and maintenance in later months when the production volume is low. To correctly understand the relationship between machine-hours and maintenance costs, Lily Put should estimate the regression equation of maintenance costs on lagged machine-hours (that is, machine-hours in prior months).

The explanation for the relationship between sales revenue and advertising costs is that the result of advertising is often not instantaneous. Generally advertising generates increased sales revenue in subsequent month(s), so Lily Put should estimate the relationship between advertising costs in a particular period and sales in future periods. Another explanation is that Lily Put increases its advertising costs during periods of declining sales in an attempt to increase sales volume of the clothing lines that will soon be out of season. For example, Lily Put may increase its advertising on winter clothing during late winter before the customers start purchasing spring clothes.

10-27 Cost estimation, incremental unit-time learning model. Assume the same information for the Bharat Company as in Solved Example 10-34 with one exception. This exception is that Bharat uses an 85% incremental unit-time learning model as a basis for predicting direct manufacturing labor-hours on its assembling operations. (An 85% learning curve means $b = -0.2345$.)

Required

1. Prepare a prediction of the total costs for producing the seven PT109s for the Navy.
2. If you solved requirement 1 of Solved Example 10-26, compare your cost prediction there with the one you made here. Why are the predictions different?

Solution

Cost estimation, incremental unit-time learning model.

1. Cost to produce the second through the eighth boats:

Direct materials, 7 × Rs 3,00,000	Rs 21,00,000
Direct manufacturing labor, 49,356* × Rs 90	44,42,040
Variable overhead, 49,356 × Rs 60	29,61,360
Other overhead, 25% of Rs 44,42,040	11,10,510
Total costs	Rs 1,06,13,910

*The direct labor hours to produce the second through the eighth boats can be calculated via a table format, given the assumption of an incremental unit-time learning curve of 85%:

Cumulative Numberof Units	Individual Unit Timefor *X*th Unit (*m*)*	Cumulative Total Time
1	10,000	10,000
2	8,500	18,500
3	7,729	26,229
4	7,225	33,454
5	6,856	40,310
6	6,569	46,879
7	6,336	53,215
8	6,141	59,356

*Calculated as $m = pX^q$ where $p = 10{,}000$, $q = -0.2345$, and $X = 1, 2, 3, ..., 8$.

The direct manufacturing labor-hours to produce the second through the eighth boat is 59,356 – 10,000 = 49,356 hours.

2. Difference in total costs to manufacture the second through the eighth boat under the incremental unit-time learning model and the cumulative average-time learning model is Rs 1,06,13,910 (calculated in requirement 1 of this problem) – Rs 88,49,925 (from requirement 1 of Problem 10-26) = Rs 17,63,985.

   The incremental unit-time learning curve has a slower decline in the reduction in time required to produce successive units than does the cumulative average-time learning curve (see Problem 10-26, requirement 1). Assuming the same 85% factor is used for both curves:

	Estimated Cumulative Direct Manufacturing Labor-Hours	
Cumulative Number of Units	Cumulative Average-Time Learning Model	Incremental Unit-Time Learning Model
1	10,000	10,000
2	17,000	18,500
4	28,900	33,454
8	49,130	59,356

The reason is that, in the incremental unit-time learning model, as the number of units double, only the last unit produced has a cost of 85% of the initial cost. In the cumulative average-time learning model, doubling the number of units causes the average cost of all the additional units produced (not just the last unit) to be 85% of the initial cost.

Nautilus should examine its own internal records on past jobs and seek information from engineers, plant managers, and workers when deciding which learning curve better describes the behavior of direct manufacturing labor-hours on the production of the PT109 boats.

Exercises

10-28 Various cost-behavior patterns. (CPA, adapted) Select the graph that matches the numbered manufacturing cost data. Indicate by letter which graph best fits the situation or item described.

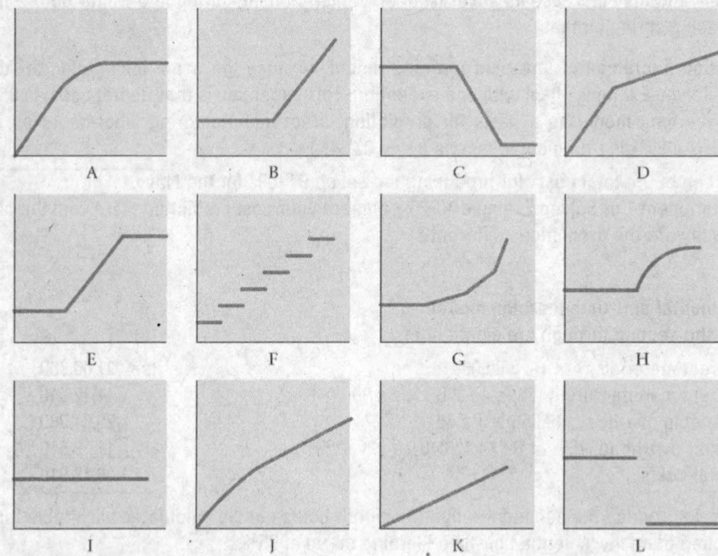

The vertical axes of the graphs represent total cost, and the horizontal axes represent units produced during a calendar year. In each case, the zero point of rupees and production is at the intersection of the two axes. The graphs may be used more than once.

a. Annual depreciation of equipment, where the amount of depreciation charged is computed by the machine-hours method.

b. Electricity bill – a flat fixed charge, plus a variable cost after a certain number of kilowatt-hours are used, in which the quantity of kilowatt-hours used varies proportionately with quantity of units produced.

c. City water bill, which is computed as follows:

First 1,00,000 gallons or less	Rs	10,000 flat fee
Next 10,000 gallons	Rs	3 per gallon used
Next 10,000 gallons	Rs	6 per gallon used
Next 10,000 gallons and so on	Rs 9 per gallon used and so on	

The gallons of water used vary proportionately with the quantity of production output.

d. Cost of direct materials, where direct material cost per unit produced decreases with each kg of material used (for example, if 1 kg is used, the cost is Rs 10; if 2 kg are used, the cost is Rs 19.98; if 3 kg are used, the cost is Rs 29.94), with a minimum cost per unit of Rs 9.20.

e. Annual depreciation of equipment, where the amount is computed by the straight-line method. When the depreciation schedule was prepared, it was anticipated that the obsolescence factor would be greater than the wear-and-tear factor.

f. Rent on a manufacturing plant donated by the city, where the agreement calls for a fixed-fee payment unless 200,000 labor-hours are worked, in which case no rent is paid.

g. Salaries of repair personnel, where one person is needed for every 1,000 machine-hours or less (that is, 0-1,000 hours requires one person, 1,001-2,000 hours requires two people, and so on).

h. Cost of direct materials used (assume no quantity discounts).

i. Rent on a manufacturing plant donated by the county, where the agreement calls for rent of Rs 10,00,000 to be reduced by Rs 10 for each direct manufacturing labor-hour worked in excess of 20,00,000 hours, but a minimum rental fee of Rs 2,00,000 must be paid.

10-29 Account analysis method. Johnson operates a car wash. Incoming cars are put on an automatic conveyor belt. Cars are washed as the conveyor belt carries the car from the start station to the finish station. After the car moves off the conveyor belt, the car is dried manually. Workers then clean and vacuum the inside of the car. Johnson serviced 80,000 cars in 2011. Johnson reports the following costs for 2011:

Account Description	Costs
Car wash labor	Rs 24,00,000
Soap, cloth, and supplies	3,20,000
Water	2,80,000
Electric power to move conveyor belt	7,20,000
Depreciation	6,40,000
Salaries	4,60,000

Required

1. Classify each account as variable or fixed with respect to the number of cars washed. Explain.
2. Johnson expects to wash 90,000 cars in 2012. Use the cost classification You developed in requirement 1 to estimate Johnson's total costs in 2012. Depreciation is computed on a straight-line basis.

10-30 Linear cost approximation. Rajeev Menon, managing director of the Ernst & Young Consulting is examining how overhead costs behave with changes in monthly professional labor-hours billed to clients. Assume the following historical data:

Total Overhead Costs	Professional Labor-Hours Billed to Clients
Rs 34,00,000	3,000
40,00,000	4,000
43,50,000	5,000
47,70,000	6,000
52,90,000	7,000
58,70,000	8,000

Required

1. Compute the linear cost function, relating total overhead cost to professional labor-hours, using the representative observations of 4,000 and 7,000 hours. Plot the linear cost function. Does the constant component of the cost function represent the fixed overhead costs of the Ernst & Young Consulting? Why?
2. What would be the predicted total overhead costs for (a) 5,000 hours and (b) 8,000 hours using the cost function estimated in requirement 1? Plot the predicted costs and actual costs for 5,000 and 8,000 hours.
3. Rajeev had a chance to accept a special job that would have boosted professional labor-hours from 4,000 to 5,000 hours. Suppose Rajeev guided by the linear cost function, rejected this job because it would have brought a total increase in contribution margin of Rs 3,80,000, before deducting the predicted increase in total overhead cost, Rs 4,30,000. What is the total contribution margin actually forgone?

10-31 Regression analysis, activity-based costing, choosing cost drivers. Akshita collects the following data to identify cost drivers of distribution costs at Container Corporation. Distribution costs includes the costs of organizing shipments and moving packaged units. Akshita thinks that because the product is heavy, the number of units moved will affect distribution costs significantly, but she is uncertain.

Month	Distribution Costs	Number of Packaged Units Moved	Number of Shipments Made
January	Rs 2,80,000	51,000	200
February	2,00,000	43,000	210
March	1,70,000	28,000	185
April	3,20,000	67,000	315
May	4,00,000	73,000	335
June	2,40,000	54,000	225
July	2,20,000	37,000	190
August	3,50,000	72.000	390
September	4,20,000	71,000	280
October	2,30,000	56,000	360
November	3,30,000	52,000	380
December	2,20,000	45,000	270
Total	Rs 33,80,000	6,49,000	3,340

Akshita estimates the following regression equations:

y = Rs 13,490 + (Rs 4.96 × Number of packaged units moved)
y = Rs 1,04,170 + (Rs 637.7 × Number of shipments made)

Required

1. Plot the monthly data and the regression lines for each of the following cost functions:
   a. Distribution costs = a + (b × Number of packaged units moved)
   b. Distribution costs = a + (b × Number of shipments made)
   Which cost driver for distribution costs would you choose? Explain briefly.
2. Akshita anticipates moving 40,000 units in 220 shipments next month. Using the preferable cost function, what amount of distribution costs should Akshita budget?

10-32 High-low method. Faraz, financial analyst at J B Chemicals (JVC) is examining the behavior of quarterly maintenance costs for budgeting purposes. Faraz collects the following data on machine-hours worked and maintenance costs for the past 12 quarters:

Quarter	Machine-Hours	Maintenance Costs
1	90,000	Rs 18,50,000
2	110,000	22,00,000
3	100,000	20,00,000
4	120,000	24,00,000
5	85,000	17,00,000
6	105,000	21,50,000
7	95,000	19,50,000
8	115,000	23,50,000
9	95,000	19,00,000
10	115,000	22,50,000
11	105,000	18,00,000
12	125,000	25,00,000

Required

1. Estimate the cost function for the quarterly data using the high-low method.
2. Plot and comment on the estimated cost function.
3. Faraz anticipates that JVC will operate machines for 90,000 hours in quarter 13. Calculate the predicted maintenance costs in quarter 13 using the cost function estimated in requirement 1.

10-33 High-low method; regression analysis. (CIMA, adapted) Ruha the financial manager at the Casa restaurant, is checking if there is any relationship between newspaper advertising and sales revenue at the restaurant. She obtains the following monthly data for the past 10 months.

Month	Revenues	Advertising Costs
March	Rs 5,00,000	Rs 20,000
April	7,00,000	30,000
May	5,50,000	15,000
June	6,50,000	35,000
July	5,50,000	10,000
August	6,50,000	20,000
September	4,50,000	15,000
October	8,00,000	40,000
November	5,50,000	25,000
December	6,00,000	25,000

They estimate the following regression equation:

Monthly revenues = Rs 3,95,020 + (8.723 × Advertising costs)

Required

1. Plot the relationship between advertising costs and revenues.
2. Draw the regression line and evaluate it using the criteria of economic plausibility, goodness of fit, and slope of the regression line.
3. Use the high-low method to compute the cost function, relating advertising costs and revenues.
4. Using (a) the regression equation and (b) the high-low equation, what is the increase in revenues for each Rs 1,000 spent on advertising within the relevant range? Which method should Ruha use to predict the effect of advertising costs on revenues? Explain briefly.

10-34 Cost estimation, cumulative average-time learning curve. The Bharat Company, which is under contract to the Indian Navy, assembles troop deployment boats. As part of its research program, it completes the assembly of the first of a new model (PT109) of deployment boats. The Navy is impressed with the PT109. It requests that Bharat submit a proposal on the cost of producing another seven PT109s.
Bharat reports the following cost information for the first PT109 assembled by Bharat:

Direct materials	Rs 3,00,000
Direct manufacturing labor (10,000 labor-hours × Rs 90)	9,00,000
Tooling cost[a]	1,50,000
Variable manufacturing overhead[b]	6,00,000
Other manufacturing overhead[c]	2,25,000
	Rs 21,75,000

[a]Tooling can be reused at no extra cost, because all of its cost has been assigned to the first deployment boat.
[b]Variable manufacturing overhead is proportional to direct manufacturing labor-hours; a rate of Rs 60 per hour is used for purposes of bidding on contracts.
[c]Other manufacturing overhead is allocated at a flat rate of 25% of direct manufacturing labor costs for purposes of bidding on contracts.

Bharat uses an 85% cumulative average-time learning model as a basis for forecasting direct manufacturing labor-hours on its assembling operations. (An 85% learning curve means $b = -0.2345$.)

Required

1. Calculate predicted total costs of producing seven PT109s for the Navy. (Bharat will keep the first deployment boat assembled, costed at Rs 21,75,000, as a demonstration model for potential customers.)
2. What is the rupee amount of difference between (a) the predicted total costs for producing the seven PT109s in requirement 1, and (b) the predicted total costs for producing the seven PT109s assuming that there is no learning curve for direct manufacturing labor? That is, for (b) assume a linear function for units produced and direct manufacturing labor-hours.

11 Decision Making and Relevant Information

Learning Objectives

1. Use the five-step decision-making process to make decisions
2. Distinguish relevant from irrelevant information in decision situations
3. Explain the opportunity-cost concept and why it is used in decision making
4. Know how to choose which products to produce when there are capacity constraints
5. Discuss factors managers must consider when adding or dropping customers or segments
6. Explain why book value of equipment is irrelevant in equipment-replacement decisions
7. Explain how conflicts can arise between the decision model used by a manager and the performance-evaluation model used to evaluate the manager

How many decisions have you made today? Maybe you made a big one, such as accepting a job offer. Or maybe your decision was as simple as settling on your plans for the weekend or choosing a restaurant for dinner. Regardless of whether decisions are big or routine, most people follow a simple, logical process of making them. This process involves gathering information, making predictions, making a choice, acting on the choice, and evaluating results. It also includes deciding what costs and benefits each choice affords. Some costs are irrelevant. They are what they are. For example, they were incurred in the past, and the money is spent and can't be recouped. This chapter will explain which costs and benefits are relevant and which are not—and how you should think of them when choosing among alternatives.

Relevant Costs, JetBlue, and Twitter[1]

What does it cost JetBlue to fly a customer on a round-trip flight from New York City to Nantucket? The incremental cost is very small, around $5 for beverages, because the other costs (the plane, pilots, ticket agents, fuel, airport landing fees, and baggage handlers) are fixed. Because most costs are fixed, would it be worthwhile for JetBlue to fill a seat provided it earns at least $5 for that seat? The answer depends on whether the flight is full.

Suppose JetBlue normally charges $330 for this round-trip ticket. If the flight is full, JetBlue would not sell the ticket for anything less than $330, because there are still customers willing to pay this fare for the flight. What if there are empty seats? Selling a ticket for something more than $5 is better than leaving the seat empty and earning nothing.

If a customer uses the Internet to purchase the ticket a month in advance, JetBlue will likely quote $330 because it expects the flight to be full. If, on the Monday before the scheduled Friday departure, JetBlue finds that the plane will not be full, the airline may be willing to lower its prices dramatically in hopes of attracting more customers and earning a profit on the unfilled seats.

Enter Twitter. Like the e-mails that Jet Blue has sent out to customers for years, the widespread messaging service allows JetBlue to quickly connect with customers and fill seats on flights that might otherwise take off less than full. When JetBlue began promoting last-minute fare sales on

[1] *Source*: Jones, Charisse. 2009. JetBlue and United give twitter a try to sell airline seats fast. *USA Today*, August 2. www.usatoday.com/travel/flights/2009-08-02-jetblue-united-twitter-airfares_N.htm

Twitter in 2009 and Twitter-recipients learned that $330 round-trip tickets from New York City to Nantucket were available for just $18, the flights filled up quickly. JetBlue's Twitter fare sales usually last only eight hours, or until all available seats are sold. To use such a pricing strategy requires a deep understanding of costs in different decision situations.

Just like JetBlue, managers in corporations around the world use a decision process to help them make decisions. Managers at JPMorgan Chase gather information about financial markets, consumer preferences, and economic trends before determining whether to offer new services to customers. Macy's managers examine all the relevant information related to domestic and international clothing manufacturing before selecting vendors. Managers at Porsche gather cost information to decide whether to manufacture a component part or purchase it from a supplier. The decision process may not always be easy, but as Napoleon Bonaparte said, "Nothing is more difficult, and therefore more precious, than to be able to decide."

Information and the Decision Process

Learning Objective  1

Use the five-step decision-making process to make decisions

. . . the five steps are identify the problem and uncertainties, obtain information, make predictions about the future, make decisions by choosing among alternatives, and implement the decision, evaluate performance, and learn

Managers usually follow a *decision model* for choosing among different courses of action. A **decision model** is a formal method of making a choice, and it often involves both quantitative and qualitative analyses. Management accountants work with managers by analyzing and presenting relevant data to guide decisions.

Consider a strategic decision facing management at Precision Sporting Goods, a manufacturer of golf clubs: Should it reorganize its manufacturing operations to reduce manufacturing labor costs? Assume that there are only two alternatives: do not reorganize or reorganize.

The reorganization will eliminate all manual handling of materials. The current manufacturing labor consists of 20 workers—15 workers operate machines, and 5 workers handle materials. The 5 materials-handling workers have been hired on contracts that permit layoffs without additional payments. Each worker works 2,000 hours annually. The cost of reorganization (consisting mostly of new equipment leases) is predicted to be Rs 9,00,000 each year. The predicted production output of 25,000 units will be unaffected by the decision. Also unaffected will be the predicted selling price of Rs 2,500, the direct material cost per unit of Rs 500, manufacturing overhead of Rs 75,00,000, and marketing costs of Rs 2,00,00,000.

Managers use the five-step decision-making process presented in Exhibit 11-1 and first introduced in Chapter 1 to make decisions such as whether to reorganize. In this exhibit, study the sequence of the steps and note how step 5 evaluates performance to provide feedback about actions taken in the previous steps. This feedback might affect future predictions, the prediction methods used, the way choices are made, or the implementation of the decision.

Decision Point

What is the five-step process that managers can use to make decisions?

Exhibit 11-1

Five-Step Decision-Making Process for Precision Sporting Goods

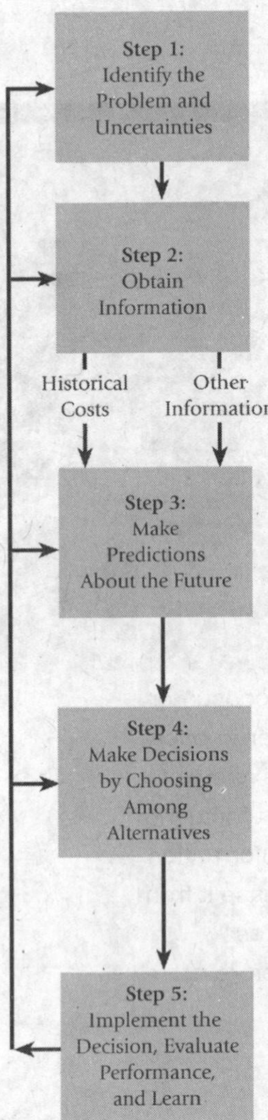

Should Precision Sporting Goods reorganize its manufacturing operations to reduce manufacturing labor costs? An important uncertainty is how the reorganization will affect employee morale.

Historical hourly wage rates are Rs140 per hour. However, a recently negotiated increase in employee benefits of Rs 20 per hour will increase wages to Rs160 per hour. The reorganization of manufacturing operations is expected to reduce the number of workers from 20 to 15 by eliminating all 5 workers who handle materials. The reorganization is likely to have negative effects on employee morale.

Managers use information from step 2 together with an assessment of probability as a basis for predicting future manufacturing labor costs. Under the existing do-not-reorganize alternative, costs are predicted to be Rs 64,00,000 (20 workers × 2,000 hours per worker per year × Rs160 per hour), and under the reorganize alternative, costs are predicted to be Rs 48,00,000 (15 workers × 2,000 hours per worker per year ×Rs 160 per hour). Recall, the reorganization is predicted to cost Rs 9,00,000 per year.

Managers compare the predicted benefits calculated in step 3 (Rs 64,00,000 − Rs 48,00,000 = Rs 16,00,000—that is, savings from eliminating materials-handling labor costs, 5 workers × 2,000 hours per worker per year × Rs 160 per hour = Rs 16,00,000) against the cost of the reorganization (Rs 9,00,000) along with other considerations (such as likely negative effects on employee morale). Management chooses the reorganize alternative because the financial benefits are significant and the effects on employee morale are expected to be temporary and relatively small.

Evaluating performance after the decision is implemented provides critical feedback for managers, and the five-step sequence is then repeated in whole or in part. Managers learn from actual results that the new manufacturing labor, costs are Rs 54,00,000, rather than the predicted Rs 48,00,000, because of lower-than-expected manufacturing labor productivity. This (now) historical information can help managers make better subsequent predictions that allow for more learning time. Alternatively, managers may improve implementation via employee training and better supervision.

The Concept of Relevance

Learning Objective 

Distinguish relevant from irrelevant information in decision situations

. . . only costs and revenues that are expected to occur in the future and differ among alternative courses of action are relevant

Much of this chapter focuses on step 4 in Exhibit 11-1 and on the concepts of relevant costs and relevant revenues when choosing among alternatives.

Relevant Costs and Relevant Revenues

Relevant costs are *expected future costs* and **relevant revenues** are *expected future revenues* that differ among the alternative courses of action being considered. Revenues and costs that are *not relevant* are said to be *irrelevant*. Be sure you understand that to be relevant costs and relevant revenues they *must*

- **Occur in the future**—every decision deals with selecting a course of action based on its expected future results—and
- **Differ among the alternative courses of action**—costs and revenues that do not differ will not matter and, hence, will have no bearing on the decision being made.

The question is always, "What difference will an action make?"

Exhibit 11-2 presents the financial data underlying the choice between the do-not-reorganize and reorganize alternatives for Precision Sporting Goods. There are two ways to do the analysis. The first considers "All revenues and costs," whereas the second considers only "Relevant revenues and costs."

The first two columns describe the first way and present *all data*. The last two columns describe the second way and present *only relevant costs*—the Rs 64,00,000 and Rs 48,00,000 expected future manufacturing labor costs and the Rs 9,00,000 expected future reorganization costs that differ between the two alternatives. The revenues, direct materials, manufacturing overhead, and marketing items can be ignored because they will remain the same whether or not Precision Sporting Goods reorganizes. They do not differ between the alternatives and, therefore, are irrelevant.

Note, the past (historical) manufacturing hourly wage rate of Rs 140 and total past (historical) manufacturing labor costs of Rs 56,00,000 (20 workers × 2,000 hours per worker per year × Rs 140 per hour) do not appear in Exhibit 11-2. *Although they may be a useful basis for making informed predictions of the expected future manufacturing labor costs of Rs 64,00,000 and Rs 48,00,000, historical costs themselves are past costs that, therefore, are irrelevant to decision making.* Past costs are also called **sunk costs** because they are unavoidable and cannot be changed no matter what action is taken.

The analysis in Exhibit 11-2 indicates that reorganizing the manufacturing operations will increase predicted operating income by Rs 7,00,000 each year. Note that the managers at Precision Sporting Goods reach the same conclusion whether they use all data or include only relevant data in the analysis. By confining the analysis to only the relevant data, managers can clear away the clutter of potentially confusing irrelevant data. Focusing on the relevant data is especially helpful when all the information needed to prepare a detailed income statement is unavailable. Understanding which costs are relevant and which are irrelevant helps the decision maker concentrate on obtaining only the pertinent data and is more efficient.

Qualitative and Quantitative Relevant Information

Managers divide the outcomes of decisions into two broad categories: *quantitative* and *qualitative*. **Quantitative factors** are outcomes that are measured in numerical terms. Some quantitative factors are financial; they can be expressed in monetary terms. Examples include the cost of direct materials, direct manufacturing labor, and marketing. Other quantitative factors are nonfinancial; they can be measured numerically, but they are not expressed in monetary terms. Reduction in new product-development time for a manufacturing company and the percentage of on-time flight arrivals for an airline company are examples of quantitative nonfinancial factors. **Qualitative factors** are outcomes that are difficult to measure accurately in numerical terms. Employee morale is an example.

Exhibit 11-2

Determining Relevant Revenues and Relevant Costs for Precision Sporting Goods

	All Revenues and Costs		Relevant Revenues and Costs	
	Alternative 1: Do Not Reorganize	Alternative 2: Reorganize	Alternative 1: Do Not Reorganize	Alternative 2: Reorganize
Revenues[a]	Rs 6,25,00,000	Rs 6,25,00,000	—	—
Costs:				
Direct materials[b]	Rs 1,25,00,000	Rs 1,25,00,000	—	—
Manufacturing labor	Rs 64,00,000[c]	Rs 48,00,000[d]	Rs 64,00,000[c]	Rs 48,00,000[d]
Manufacturing overhead	Rs 75,00,000	Rs 75,00,000	—	—
Marketing	Rs 2,00,00,000	Rs 2,00,00,000	—	—
Reorganization costs	—	Rs 9,00,000	—	Rs 9,00,000
Total costs	Rs 4,64,00,000	Rs 4,57,00,000	Rs 64,00,000	Rs 57,00,000
Operating income	Rs 1,61,00,000	Rs 1,68,00,000	Rs (64,00,000)	Rs (57,00,000)
	Rs 7,00,000 Difference		Rs 7,00,000 Difference	

[a]25,000 units × Rs 2,500 per unit = Rs 6,25,00,000 [c]20 workers × 2,000 hours per worker × Rs 160 per hour = Rs 64,00,000

[b]25,000 units × Rs 500 per unit = Rs 1,25,00,000 [d]15 workers × 2,000 hours per worker × Rs 160 per hour = Rs 48,00,000

Relevant-cost analysis generally emphasizes quantitative factors that can be expressed in financial terms. *But just because qualitative factors and quantitative nonfinancial factors cannot be measured easily in financial terms does not make them unimportant.* In fact, managers must at times give more weight to these factors. For example, managers at Precision Sporting Goods carefully considered the negative effect on employee morale of laying off materials-handling workers, a qualitative factor, before choosing the reorganize alternative. Comparing and trading off nonfinancial and financial considerations is seldom easy.

Exhibit 11-3 summarizes the key features of relevant information.

An Illustration of Relevance: Choosing Output Levels

The concept of relevance applies to all decision situations. In this and the following several sections of this chapter, we present some of these decision situations. Later chapters describe other decision situations that require application of the relevance concept, such as Chapter 12 on pricing, Chapter 16 on joint costs, Chapter 19 on quality and timeliness, Chapter 20 on inventory management and supplier evaluation, Chapter 21 on capital investment, and Chapter 22 on transfer pricing. We start by considering decisions that affect output levels such as whether to introduce a new product or to try to sell more units of an existing product.

One-Time-Only Special Orders

One type of decision that affects output levels is accepting or rejecting special orders when there is idle production capacity and the special orders have no long-run implications. We use the term **one-time-only special order** to describe these conditions.

Example 1: Surf Gear manufactures quality beach towels. The plant has a production capacity of 48,000 towels each month. Current monthly production is 30,000 towels. Retail department stores account for all existing sales. Expected results for the coming month (August) are shown in Exhibit 11-4. (These amounts are predictions based on past costs.) We assume all costs can be classified as either fixed or variable with respect to a single cost driver (units of output).

As a result of a strike at its existing towel supplier, a luxury hotel chain has offered to buy 5,000 towels from Surf Gear in August at Rs 110 per towel. No subsequent sales to this hotel chain are anticipated. Fixed manufacturing costs are tied to the 48,000-towel production capacity. That is, fixed manufacturing costs relate to the production capacity available, regardless of the capacity used. If Surf Gear accepts the special order, it will use existing idle capacity to produce the 5,000 towels, and fixed manufacturing costs will not change. No marketing costs will be necessary for the 5,000-unit one-time-only special order. Accepting this special order is not expected to affect the selling price or the quantity of towels sold to regular customers. Should Surf Gear accept the hotel chain's offer?

Exhibit 11-4 presents data for this example on an absorption-costing basis (that is, both variable and fixed manufacturing costs are included in inventoriable costs and cost of goods sold). In this exhibit, the manufacturing cost of Rs 120 per unit and the marketing cost of Rs 70 per unit include both variable and fixed costs. The sum of all costs (variable and fixed)

Exhibit 11-3

Key Features of Relevant Information

- Past (historical) costs may be helpful as a basis for making *predictions.* However, past costs themselves are always irrelevant when making *decisions.*
- Different alternatives can be compared by examining differences in expected total future revenues and expected total future costs.
- Not all expected future revenues and expected future costs are relevant. Expected future revenues and expected future costs that do not differ among alternatives are irrelevant and, hence, can be eliminated from the analysis. The key question is always, What difference will an action make?
- Appropriate weight must be given to qualitative factors and quantitative nonfinancial factors.

Exhibit 11-4

Budgeted Income Statement for August, Absorption-Costing Format for Surf Gear[a]

	A	B	C	D
1		**Total**	**Per Unit**	
2	Units sold	30,000		
3				
4	Revenues	Rs 60,00,000	Rs 200.0	
5	Cost of goods sold (manufacturing costs)			
6	Variable manufacturing costs	22,50,000	75.0[b]	
7	Fixed manufacturing costs	13,50,000	45.0[c]	
8	Total cost of goods sold	36,00,000	120.0	
9	Marketing costs			
10	Variable marketing costs	15,00,000	50.0	
11	Fixed marketing costs	6,00,000	20.0	
12	Total marketing costs	21,00,000	70.0	
13	Full costs of the product	57,00,000	190.0	
14	Operating income	Rs 3,00,000	Rs 10.0	
15				
16	[a]Surf Gear incurs no R&D, product-design, distribution or customer-service costs			
17	[b]Variable manufacturing cost per unit = Direct material cost per unit + Direct manufacturing labor cost per unit + Variable manufacturing overhead cost per unit			
18				
19	= Rs 60.0 + Rs 5.0 + Rs10.0 = Rs 75.0			
20	[c]Fixed manufacturing cost per unit = Fixed direct manufacturing labor cost per unit + Fixed manufacturing overhead cost per unit			
21				
22	= Rs 15.0 + Rs 30.0 = Rs 45.0			

in a particular business function of the value chain, such as manufacturing costs or marketing costs, are called **business function costs. Full costs of the product,** in this case Rs 190 per unit, are the sum of all variable and fixed costs in all business functions of the value chain (R&D, design, production, marketing, distribution, and customer service). For Surf Gear, full costs of the product consist of costs in manufacturing and marketing because these are the only business functions. No marketing costs are necessary for the special order, so the manager of Surf Gear will focus only on manufacturing costs. Based on the manufacturing cost per unit of Rs 120—which is greater than the Rs 110-per-unit price offered by the hotel chain—the manager might decide to reject the offer.

Exhibit 11-5 separates manufacturing and marketing costs into their variable- and fixed-cost components and presents data in the format of a contribution income statement. The relevant revenues and costs are the expected future revenues and costs that differ as a result of accepting the special offer—revenues of Rs 5,50,000 (Rs 110 per unit × 5,000 units) and variable manufacturing costs of Rs 3,75,000 (Rs 75.0 per unit × 5,000 units). The fixed manufacturing costs and all marketing costs (*including variable marketing costs*) are irrelevant in this case. That's because these costs will not change in total whether the special order is accepted or rejected. Surf Gear would gain an additional Rs 1,75,000 (relevant revenues, Rs 5,50,000—relevant costs, Rs 3,75,000) in operating income by accepting the special order. In this example, comparing total amounts for 30,000 units versus 35,000 units or focusing only on the relevant amounts in the difference column in Exhibit 11-5 avoids a misleading implication—the implication that would result from comparing the Rs 110.-per-unit selling price against the manufacturing ost per unit of Rs 120 (Exhibit 11-4), which includes both variable and fixed manufacturing costs.

The assumption of no long-run or strategic implications is crucial to management's analysis of the one-time-only special-order decision. Suppose Surf Gear concludes that the retail department stores (its regular customers) will demand a lower price if it sells towels at Rs 110 apiece to the luxury hotel chain. In this case, revenues from regular customers will be relevant. Why? Because the future revenues from regular customers will differ depending on whether the special order is accepted or rejected. The relevant-revenue and relevant-cost analysis of the hotel-chain order would have to be modified to consider both the short-run benefits from accepting the order and the long-run consequences on profitability if prices were lowered to all regular customers.

Exhibit 11-5

One-Time-Only Special-Order Decision for Surf Gear: Comparative Contribution Income Statements

	A	B	C	D	E	F	G	H
1		Without the Special Order				With the Special Order		Difference: Relevant Amounts
2		30,000				35,000		for the
3		Units to be Sold				Units to be Sold		5,000
4		Per Unit		Total		Total		Units Special Order
5		(1)		(2) = (1) x 30,000		(3)		(4) = (3) – (2)
6	Revenues	Rs 200.0		Rs 60,00,000		Rs 65,50,000		Rs 5,50,000[a]
7	Variable costs:							
8	Manufacturing	Rs 75.0		22,50,000		26,25,000		3,75,000[b]
9	Marketing	Rs 50.0		15,00,000		15,00,000		0[c]
10	Total variable costs	Rs 125.0		37,50,000		41,25,000		3,75,000
11	Contribution margin	Rs 75.0		22,50,000		24,25,000		1,75,000
12	Fixed costs:							
13	Manufacturing	Rs 45.0		13,50,000		13,50,000		0[d]
14	Marketing	Rs 20.0		6,00,000		6,00,000		0[d]
15	Total fixed costs	Rs 65.0		19,50,000		19,50,000		0
16	Operating income	Rs 10.0		Rs 3,00,000		Rs 4,75,000		Rs 1,75,000
17								
18	[a]5,000 units x Rs 110 per unit = Rs 5,50,000.							
19	[b]5,000 units x Rs 75 per unit = Rs 3,75,000.							
20	[c]No variable marketing costs would be incurred for the 5,000-unit one-time-only special order.							
21	[d]Fixed manufacturing costs and fixed marketing costs would be unaffected by the special order.							

Potential Problems in Relevant-Cost Analysis

Managers should avoid two potential problems in relevant-cost analysis. First, they must watch for incorrect general assumptions, such as all variable costs are relevant and all fixed costs are irrelevant. In the Surf Gear example, the variable marketing cost of Rs 50 per unit is irrelevant because Surf Gear will incur no extra marketing costs by accepting the special order. But fixed manufacturing costs could be relevant. The extra production of 5,000 towels per month does not affect fixed manufacturing costs because we assumed that the relevant range is from 30,000 to 48,000 towels per month. In some cases, however, producing the extra 5,000 towels might increase fixed manufacturing costs. Suppose Surf Gear would need to run three shifts of 16,000 towels per shift to achieve full capacity of 48,000 towels per month. Increasing the monthly production from 30,000 to 35,000 would require a partial third shift because two shifts could produce only 32,000 towels. The extra shift would increase fixed manufacturing costs, thereby making these additional fixed manufacturing costs relevant for this decision.

Second, unit-cost data can potentially mislead decision makers in two ways:

1. **When irrelevant costs are included.** Consider the Rs 45 of fixed manufacturing cost per unit (direct manufacturing labor, Rs 15 per unit, plus manufacturing overhead, Rs 30 per unit) included in the Rs 120-per-unit manufacturing cost in the one-time-only special-order decision (see Exhibits 11-4 and 11-5). This Rs 45-per-unit cost is irrelevant, given the assumptions in our example, so it should be excluded.
2. **When the same unit costs are used at different output levels.** Generally, managers use total costs rather than unit costs because total costs are easier to work with and reduce the chance for erroneous conclusions. Then, if desired, the total costs can be unitized. In the Surf Gear example, total fixed manufacturing costs remain at Rs 13,50,000 even if Surf Gear accepts the special order and produces 35,000 towels.

Including the fixed manufacturing cost per unit of Rs 45 as a cost of the special order would lead to the erroneous conclusion that total fixed manufacturing costs would increase to Rs 15,75,000 (Rs 45 per towel × 35,000 towels).

The best way for managers to avoid these two potential problems is to keep focusing on (1) total revenues and total costs (rather than unit revenue and unit cost) and (2) the relevance concept. Managers should always require all items included in an analysis to be expected total future revenues and expected total future costs that differ among the alternatives.

Decision Point

When is a revenue or cost item relevant for a particular decision and what potential problems should be avoided in relevant cost analysis?

Insourcing-versus-Outsourcing and Make-versus-Buy Decisions

We now apply the concept of relevance to another strategic decision: whether a company should make a component part or buy it from a supplier. We again assume idle capacity.

Learning Objective 

Explain the opportunity-cost concept and why it is used in decision making

. . . in all decisions, it is important to consider the contribution to income forgone by choosing a particular alternative and rejecting others

Outsourcing and Idle Facilities

Outsourcing is purchasing goods and services from outside vendors rather than **insourcing**, which is producing the same goods or providing the same services within the organization. For example, Kodak prefers to manufacture its own film (insourcing), but it has IBM do its data processing (outsourcing). Toyota relies on outside vendors to supply some component parts but chooses to manufacture other parts internally.

Decisions about whether a producer of goods or services will insource or outsource are also called **make-or-buy decisions.** Surveys of companies indicate that managers consider quality, dependability of suppliers, and costs as the most important factors in the make-or-buy decision. Sometimes, however, qualitative factors dominate management's make-or-buy decision. For example, Dell Computer buys the Pentium chip for its personal computers from Intel because Dell does not have the know-how and technology to make the chip itself. To maintain the secrecy of its formula, Coca-Cola does not outsource the manufacture of its concentrate.

Example 2: The Soho Company manufactures a two-in-one video system consisting of a DVD player and a digital media receiver (that downloads movies and video from internet sites such as NetFlix). Columns 1 and 2 of the following table show the expected total and per-unit costs for manufacturing the DVD-player of the video system. Soho plans to manufacture the 250,000 units

	Expected Total Costs of Producing 250,000 Units in 2,000 Batches Next Year (1)	Expected Cost per Unit (2) = (1) ÷ 250,000
Direct materials (Rs 360 per unit × 250,000 units)	Rs 9,00,00,000	Rs 360.00
Direct manufacturing labor (Rs 100 per unit × 250,000 units)	2,50,00,000	100.00
Variable manufacturing overhead costs of power and utilities (Rs 60 per unit × 250,000 units)	1,50,00,000	60.00
Mixed (variable and fixed) batch-level manufacturing overhead costs of materials handling and setup [Rs 75,00,000 + (Rs 6,250 per batch × 2,000 batches)]	2,00,00,000	80.00
Fixed manufacturing overhead costs of plant lease, insurance, and administration	3,00,00,000	120.00
Total manufacturing cost	Rs18,00,00,000	Rs720.00

in 2,000 batches of 125 units each. Variable batch-level costs of Rs 6,250 per batch vary with the number of batches, not the total number of units produced.

Broadfield, Inc., a manufacturer of DVD players, offers to sell Soho 250,000 DVD players next year for Rs 640 per unit on Soho's preferred delivery schedule. Assume that financial factors will be the basis of this make-or-buy decision. Should Soho make or buy the DVD player?

Columns 1 and 2 of the preceding table indicate the expected total costs and expected cost per unit of producing 250,000 DVD players next year. The expected manufacturing cost per unit for next year is Rs 720. At first glance, it appears that the company should buy DVD players because the expected Rs 720-per-unit cost of making the DVD player is more than the Rs 640 per unit to buy it. But a make-or-buy decision is rarely obvious. To make a decision, management needs to answer the question, "What is the difference in relevant costs between the alternatives?"

For the moment, suppose (a) the capacity now used to make the DVD players will become idle next year if the DVD players are purchased and (b) the Rs 3,00,00,000 of fixed manufacturing overhead will continue to be incurred next year regardless of the decision made. Assume the Rs 75,00,000 in fixed salaries to support materials handling and setup will not be incurred if the manufacture of DVD players is completely shut down.

Exhibit 11-6 presents the relevant-cost computations. Note that Soho will *save* Rs 1,00,00,000 by making DVD players rather than buying them from Broadfield. Making DVD players is the preferred alternative.

Note how the key concepts of relevance presented in Exhibit 11-3 apply here:

- Exhibit 11-6 compares differences in expected total future revenues and expected total future costs. Past costs are always irrelevant when making decisions.
- Exhibit 11-6 shows Rs 2,00,00,000 of future materials-handling and setup costs under the make alternative but not under the buy alternative. Why? Because buying DVD players and not manufacturing them will save Rs 2,00,00,000 in future variable costs per batch and avoidable fixed costs. The Rs 2,00,00,000 represents future costs that differ between the alternatives and so is relevant to the make-or-buy decision.
- Exhibit 11-6 excludes the Rs 3,00,00,000 of plant-lease, insurance, and administration costs under both alternatives. Why? Because these future costs will not differ between the alternatives, so they are irrelevant.

A common term in decision making is *incremental cost*. An **incremental cost** is the additional total cost incurred for an activity. In Exhibit 11-6, the incremental cost of making DVD players is the additional total cost of Rs 15,00,00,000 that Soho will incur if it decides to

Exhibit 11-6

Relevant (Incremental) Items for Make-or-Buy Decision for DVD Players at Soho Company

Relevant Items	Total Relevant Costs: Make	Total Relevant Costs: Buy	Relevant Cost Per Unit: Make	Relevant Cost Per Unit: Buy
Outside purchase of parts (Rs 640 × 250,000 units)		Rs16,00,00,000		Rs 640
Direct materials	Rs 9,00,00,000		Rs360	
Direct manufacturing labor	2,50,00,000		100	
Variable manufacturing overhead	1,50,00,000		60	
Mixed (variable and fixed) materials-handling and setup overhead	2,00,00,000		80	
Total relevant costs[a]	Rs15,00,00,000	Rs16,00,00,000	Rs580	Rs640
Difference in favor of making DVD players	Rs1,00,00,000		Rs40	

[a]The Rs 3,00,00,000 of plant-lease, plant-insurance, and plant-administration costs could be included under both alternatives. Conceptually, they do not belong in a listing of relevant costs because these costs are irrelevant to the decision. Practically, some managers may want to include them in order to list all costs that will be incurred under each alternative.

make DVD players. The Rs 3,00,00,000 of fixed manufacturing overhead is not an incremental cost because Soho will incur these costs whether or not it makes DVD players. Similarly, the incremental cost of buying DVD players from Broadfield is the additional total cost of Rs 16,00,00,000 that Soho will incur if it decides to buy DVD players. A **differential cost** is the difference in total cost between two alternatives. In Exhibit 11-6, the differential cost between the make-DVD-players and buy-DVD-players alternatives is Rs 1,00,00,000 (Rs 16,00,00,000 – Rs 15,00,00,000). Note that *incremental cost* and *differential cost* are sometimes used interchangeably in practice. When faced with these terms, always be sure to clarify what they mean.

We define *incremental revenue* and *differential revenue* similarly to incremental cost and differential cost. **Incremental revenue** is the additional total revenue from an activity. **Differential revenue** is the difference in total revenue between two alternatives.

Strategic and Qualitative Factors

Strategic and qualitative factors affect outsourcing decisions. For example, Soho ... prefer to manufacture CD players in-house to retain control over the design, quality, reliability, and delivery schedules of the CD players it uses in its stereos. Conversely, despite the cost advantages documented in Exhibit 11-6, Soho may prefer to outsource, become a leaner organization, and focus on areas of its core competencies—the manufacture and sale of stereos. As an example of focus, advertising companies, such as J. Walter Thompson, only do the creative and planning aspects of advertising (their core competencies), and they outsource production activities, such as film, photographs, and illustrations.

Outsourcing is not without risks. As a company's dependence on its suppliers increases, suppliers could increase prices and let quality and delivery performance slip. To minimize these risks, companies generally enter into long-run contracts specifying costs, quality, and delivery schedules with their suppliers. Intelligent managers build close partnerships or alliances with a few key suppliers. Toyota goes so far as to send its own engineers to improve suppliers' processes. Suppliers of companies such as Ford, Hyundai, Panasonic, and Sony have researched and developed innovative products, met demands for increased quantities, maintained quality and on-time delivery, and lowered costs—actions that the companies themselves would not have had the competencies to achieve.

Outsourcing decisions invariably have a long-run horizon in which the financial costs and benefits of outsourcing become more uncertain. Almost always, strategic and qualitative factors such as those described here become important determinants of the outsourcing decision. Weighing all these factors requires the exercise of considerable management judgment and care.

International Outsourcing

What additional factors would Soho have to consider if the supplier of DVD players was based in India? The most important would be exchange-rate risk. Suppose the Indian supplier offers to sell Soho 250,000 DVD players for Rs 192,000,000. Should Soho make or buy? The answer depends on the exchange rate that Soho expects next year. If Soho forecasts an exchange rate of Rs 48 per $1, Soho's expected purchase cost equals Rs 16,00,00,000 (Rs 192,000,000/Rs 48 per $) greater than the relevant costs for making the DVD players in Exhibit 11-6, so Soho would prefer to make DVD players rather than buy them.

Another option is for Soho to enter into a forward contract to purchase Rs 192,000,000. A forward contract allows Soho to contract today to purchase pesos next year at a predetermined, fixed cost, thereby protecting itself against exchange rate risk. If Soho decides to go this route, it would make (buy) DVD players if the cost of the contract is greater (less) than Rs 1,50,00,000. International outsourcing requires companies to evaluate exchange rate risks and to implement strategies and costs for managing them. The following Concepts in Action feature describes *offshoring*—the practice of outsourcing services to lower-cost countries.

Opportunity Costs and Outsourcing

In the simple make-or-buy decision in Exhibit 11-6, we assumed that the capacity currently used to make DVD players will remain idle if Soho purchases the parts from the outside manufacturer. Often, however, the released capacity can be used for other, more-profitable purposes. Then, the choice Soho's managers are faced with is not whether to make or buy. It is how best to use available production capacity.

Example 3: Suppose that if Soho decides to buy DVD players for its stereos from the outside supplier, then Soho's best use of the capacity that becomes available is to produce 1,00,000 digitals, a portable, stand-alone DVD player. From a manufacturing standpoint, digitals are similar to stereo DVD players. With help from operating managers, Soho's management accountant, estimates the following future revenues and costs if Soho decides to manufacture and sell digitals:

Incremental future revenues		Rs 8,00,00,000
Incremental future costs		
Direct materials	Rs 3,40,00,000	
Direct manufacturing labor	1,00,00,000	
Variable overhead (such as power, utilities)	60,00,000	
Materials-handling and setup overheads	50,00,000	
Total incremental future costs		5,50,00,000
Incremental future operating income		Rs 2,50,00,000

Because of capacity constraints, Soho can make either DVD players for its stereo unit or digitals, but not both. Which of the following three alternatives should Soho choose?

1. Make video system DVD and do not make digitals
2. Buy video system DVD and make digitals

Exhibit 11-7, Panel A, summarizes the "total-alternatives" approach—the future costs and revenues for *all* alternatives. Alternative 2, buying video-system DVD and using the available capacity to make and sell digitals, is the preferred alternative. The future incremental costs of buying video-system DVD players from an outside supplier (Rs 16,00,00,000) are more than the future incremental costs of making video-system DVD players in-house (Rs 15,00,00,000). But Soho can use the capacity freed up by buying video-system DVD players to gain Rs 2,50,00,000 in operating income (incremental future revenues of Rs 8,00,00,000 minus total incremental future costs of Rs 5,50,00,000) by making and selling digitals. The *net relevant* costs of buying video-system DVD players and making and selling digitals are Rs 16,00,00,000 − Rs 2,50,00,000 = Rs 13,50,00,000.

The Opportunity-Cost Approach

Deciding to use a resource in a particular way causes a manager to forgo the opportunity to use the resource in alternative ways. This lost opportunity is a cost that the manager must consider when making a decision. **Opportunity cost** is the contribution to operating income that is forgone by not using a limited resource in its next-best alternative use. For example, the (relevant) cost of going to school for an MBA degree is not only the cost of tuition, books, lodging, and food, but also the income sacrificed (opportunity cost) by not working. Presumably the estimated future benefits of obtaining an MBA (for example, a higher-paying career) will exceed these costs.

Exhibit 11-7, Panel B, displays the opportunity-cost approach for analyzing the alternatives faced by Soho. *Note that the alternatives are defined differently in the total alternatives approach (1. Make Video-System DVD Players and Do Not Make Digitals and 2. Buy Video-System DVD Players and Make Digitals) and the opportunity cost*

Exhibit 11-7

Total-Alternatives Approach and Opportunity-Cost Approach to Make-or-Buy Decisions for Soho Company

Relevant Items	Alternatives for Soho: 1. Make video-system DVD Players and Do Not Make Digitals	2. Buy video-system DVD Players and Make Digitals
PANEL A Total-Alternatives Approach to Make-or-Buy Decisions		
Total incremental future costs of making/buying stereo CD players (from Exhibit 11-6)	Rs15,00,00,000	Rs16,00,00,000
Deduct excess of future revenues over future costs from Discmans	0	(2,50,00,000)
Total relevant costs under total-alternatives approach	Rs 15,00,00,000	Rs13,50,00,000
PANEL B Opportunity-Cost Approach to Make-or-Buy Decisions		
Total incremental future costs of making/buying stereo CD players (from Exhibit 11-6)	Rs15,00,00,000	Rs16,00,00,000
Opportunity cost: Profit contribution forgone because capacity will not be used to make Discmans, the next-best alternative	2,50,00,000	0
Total relevant costs under opportunity-cost approach	Rs17,50,00,000	Rs16,00,00,000

Note that the differences in costs across the columns in Panels A and B are the same: The cost of alternative 3 is Rs1,50,00,000 less than the cost of alternative 1, and Rs 2,50,00,000 less than the cost of alternative 2.

approach (1. Make Video-System DVD Players and 2. Buy Video-System DVD Players), which does not reference Digitals. Under the opportunity-cost approach, the cost of each alternative includes (1) the incremental costs and (2) the opportunity cost, the profit forgone from not making Digitals. This opportunity cost arises because Digitals is excluded from formal consideration in the alternatives.

Consider alternative 1, make video-system DVD players what are all the costs of making video-system DVD players? Certainly Soho will incur Rs 15,00,00,000 of incremental costs to make video-system DVD players. But is this the entire cost? No, because by deciding to use limited manufacturing resources to make video-system DVD players, Soho will give up the opportunity to earn Rs 2,50,00,000 by not using these resources to make digitals. Therefore, the relevant costs of making video-system DVD players are the incremental costs of Rs 15,00,00,000 plus the opportunity cost of Rs 2,50,00,000.

Next consider alternative 2, buy video-system DVD players and make digitals. The incremental cost of buying video-system DVD players will be Rs 16,00,00,000. The opportunity cost is zero. Why? Because by choosing this alternative, Soho will not forgo the profit it can earn from making and selling digitals.

Panel B leads management to the same conclusion as Panel A: buying video-system DVD players and making digitals is the preferred alternative.

Panels A and B of Exhibit 11-7 describe two consistent approaches to decision making with capacity constraints. The total-alternatives approach in Panel A includes all future incremental costs and revenues. For example, under alternative 3, the additional future operating income from *using capacity to make and sell digitals* (Rs 2,50,00,000) is subtracted from the future incremental cost of buying stereo DVD (Rs 16,00,00,000). The opportunity-cost analysis in Panel B takes the opposite approach. It focuses on stereo DVD players. *Whenever capacity is not going to be used to make and sell digitals*, the future forgone operating income is added as an opportunity cost of making or buying stereo DVD players, as in alternatives 1 and 2. (Note that when digitals are made, as in alternative 3, there is no "opportunity cost of not making digitals.") Therefore, whereas Panel A *subtracts* Rs 2,50,00,000 under alternative 3, Panel B *adds* Rs 2,50,00,000 under alternative 1 and also under alternative 2. *Panel B*

Concepts in Action

Pringles Prints and the Offshoring of Innovation

According to a recent survey, 67% of U.S. companies are engaged in the rapidly-evolving process of "offshoring," which is the outsourcing of business processes and jobs to other countries. Offshoring was initially popular with companies because it yielded immediate labor-cost savings for activities such as software development, call centers, and technical support.

While the practice remains popular today, offshoring has transformed from lowering costs on back-office processes to accessing global talent for innovation. With global markets expanding and domestic talent scarce, companies are now hiring qualified engineers, scientists, inventors, and analysts all over the world for research and development (R&D), new product development (NPD), engineering, and knowledge services.

Innovation Offshoring Services

R&D	NPD	Engineering	Knowledge Services
■ Programming	■ Prototype design	■ Testing	■ Market analysis
■ Code development	■ Product development	■ Reengineering	■ Credit analysis
■ New technologies	■ Systems design	■ Drafting/modeling	■ Data mining
■ New materials/ process research	■ Support services	■ Embedded systems development	■ Forecasting
			■ Risk management

By utilizing offshoring innovation, companies not only continue to reduce labor costs, but cut back-office costs as well. Companies also obtain local market knowledge and access to global best practices in many important areas.

Some companies are leveraging offshore resources by creating global innovation networks. Procter & Gamble (P&G), for instance, established "Connect and Develop," a multinational effort to create and leverage innovative ideas for product development. When the company wanted to create a new line of Pringles potato chips with pictures and words—trivia questions, animal facts, and jokes—printed on each chip, the company turned to offshore innovation.

Rather than trying to invent the technology required to print images on potato chips in-house, Procter & Gamble created a technology brief that defined the problems it needed to solve, and circulated it throughout the company's global innovation network for possible solutions. As a result, P&G discovered a small bakery in Bologna, Italy, run by a university professor who also manufactured baking equipment. He had invented an ink-jet method for printing edible images on cakes and cookies, which the company quickly adapted for potato chips.

As a result, Pringles Prints were developed in less than a year—as opposed to a more traditional two year process—and immediately led to double-digit product growth.

Sources: Cuoto, Vinay, Mahadeva Mani, Vikas Sehgal, Arie Lewin, Stephan Manning, and Jeff Russell. 2007. *Offshoring 2.0: Contracting knowledge and innovation to expand global capabilities*. Duke University Offshoring Research Network: Durham, NC. Heijmen, Ton, Arie Lewin, Stephan Manning, Nidthida Prem-Ajchariyawong, and Jeff Russell. 2008. *Offshoring reaches the c-suite*. Duke University Offshoring Research Network: Durham, NC. Huston, Larry and Nabil Sakkab. 2006. Connect and develop: Inside Procter & Gamble's new model for innovation. *Harvard Business Review*, March.

highlights the idea that when capacity is constrained, the relevant revenues and costs of any alternative equal the incremental future revenues and costs plus the opportunity cost. However, when more than two alternatives are being considered simultaneously, it is generally easier to use the total-alternatives approach.

Opportunity costs are not incorporated into formal financial accounting records. Why? Because historical record keeping is limited to transactions involving alternatives that were *actually selected*, rather than alternatives that were rejected. Rejected alternatives do not produce transactions and so they are not recorded. If Soho makes stereo DVD players, it will not make Digitals, and it will not record any accounting entries for Digitals. Yet the opportunity cost of making stereo DVD players, which equals the operating income that Soho forgoes by not making Digitals, is a crucial input into the make-or-buy decision. Consider again Exhibit 11-7, Panel B. On the basis of only the incremental costs systematically recorded in the accounting system, it is less costly for Soho to make rather than buy stereo DVD players. Recognizing the opportunity cost of Rs 2,50,00,000 leads to the different conclusion: buying stereo DVD players is preferable.

Suppose Soho has sufficient capacity to make Digitals even if it makes stereo DVD players. In this case, Soho has a fourth alternative: make stereo DVD players and make Digital. For this alternative, the opportunity cost of making stereo DVD players is Rs 0 because Soho does not give up the Rs 2,50,00,000 operating income from making Digitals even if it chooses to make stereo DVD players. The relevant costs are Rs 15,00,00,000 (incremental costs of Rs 15,00,00,000 plus opportunity cost of Rs 0). Under these conditions, Soho would prefer to make stereo DVD players, rather than buy them, and also make Digitals.

Besides quantitative considerations, the make-or-buy decision should also consider strategic and qualitative factors. If Soho decides to buy stereo DVD players from an outside supplier, it should consider factors such as the supplier's reputation for quality and timely delivery. Soho would also want to consider the strategic consequences of selling Digitals. For example, will selling Digitals take Soho's focus away from its stereo business?

Carrying Costs of Inventory

To see another example of an opportunity cost, consider the following data for Soho:

Annual estimated stereo DVD player requirements for next year	1,000,000 units
Cost per unit when each purchase is equal to 10,000 units	Rs 160.0
Cost per unit when each purchase is equal to or greater than 500,000 units; Rs 160 minus 1% discount	Rs 158.4
Cost of a purchase order	Rs 5,000
Alternatives under consideration:	
A. Make 100 purchases of 10,000 units each during next year	
B. Make 2 purchases of 500,000 units during the year	
Average investment in inventory:	
A. (10,000 units × Rs 160.0 per unit) ÷ 2[a]	Rs 8,00,000
B. (500,000 units × Rs 158.4 per unit) ÷ 2[a]	Rs 3,96,00,000
Annual rate of return if cash is invested elsewhere (for example, bonds or stocks) at the same level of risk as investment in inventory)	9%

[a] The example assumes that DVD-player purchases will be used uniformly throughout the year. The average investment in inventory during the year is the cost of the inventory when a purchase is received plus the cost of inventory just before the next purchase is delivered (in our example, zero) divided by 2.

Soho will pay cash for the video-system DVD players it buys. Which purchasing alternative is more economical for Soho?

The following table presents the analysis using the total alternatives approach recognizing that Soho has, on average, Rs 3,96,00,000 of cash available to invest. If Soho invests only Rs 8,00,000 in inventory as in alternative A, it will have Rs 3,88.00,000 (Rs 3,96,00,000 – Rs 8,00,000) of cash available to invest elsewhere, which at a 9% rate of return will yield a total return of Rs 34,92,000. This income is subtracted from the ordering and purchasing costs incurred under alternative A. If Soho invests all Rs 3,96,00,000 in inventory as in alternative B, it will have Re 0 (Rs 3,96,00,000 – Rs 3,96,00,000) available to invest elsewhere and will earn no return on the cash.

Consistent with the trends toward holding smaller inventories, purchasing smaller quantities of 10,000 units 100 times a year is preferred to purchasing 5,00,000 units twice a year by Rs 14,02,000.

	Alternative A: Make 100 Purchases of 10,000 Units Each During the Year and Invest Any Excess Cash (1)	Alternative B: Make 2 Purchases of 5,00,000 Units Each During the Year and Invest Any Excess Cash (2)	Difference (3) = (1) – (2)
Annual purchase-order costs (100 purch. orders × Rs 5,000/purch. order; 2 purch. orders × Rs 5,000/purch. order)	Rs 5,00,000	Rs 10,000	Rs 4,90,000
Annual purchase costs (10,00,000 units × Rs 640.00/unit; 10,00,000 units × Rs 633.6/unit)	16,00,00,000	15,84,00,000	16,00,000
Deduct annual rate of return earned by investing cash not tied up in inventory elsewhere at the same level of risk [0.09 × (Rs 3,96,00,000 – Rs 8,00,000); 0.09 × (Rs 3,96,00,000 – Rs 3,96,00,000)	(34,92,000)	0	(34,92,000)
Relevant costs	Rs 15,70,08,000	Rs 15,84,10,00,000	Rs (14,02,000)

The following table presents the two alternatives using the opportunity cost approach. Each alternative is defined only in terms of the two purchasing choices with no explicit reference to investing the excess cash.

	Alternative A: Make 100 Purchases of 10,000 Units Each During the Year (1)	Alternative B: Make 2 Purchases of 500,000 Units Each During the Year (2)	Difference (3)× (1)– (2)
Annual purchase-order costs (100 purch. orders × Rs 5,000/purch. order; 2 purch. orders × Rs 5,000/purch. order)	Rs 5,00,000	Rs 10,000	Rs 4,90,000
Annual purchase costs (1,000,000 units × Rs 160.0/unit; 1,000,000 units × Rs 158.4/unit)	16,00,00,000	15,84,00,000	16,00,000
Opportunity cost: Annual rate of return that could be earned if investment in inventory were invested elsewhere at the same level of risk (0.09 × Rs 8,00,000; 0.09 × Rs 3,96,00,000)	72,000	35,64,000	(34,92,000)
Relevant costs	Rs 16,05,72,000	Rs 16,19,74,000	Rs (14,02,000)

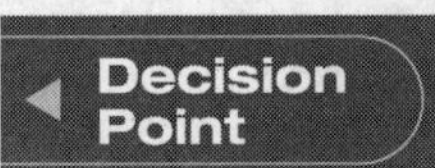

What is an opportunity cost and why should it be included when making decisions?

Recall that under the opportunity cost approach, the relevant cost of any alternative is (1) the incremental cost of the alternative plus (2) the opportunity cost of the profit forgone from choosing that alternative. The opportunity cost of holding inventory is the income forgone by tying up money in inventory and not investing it elsewhere. The opportunity cost would not be recorded in the accounting system because, once the alternative of investing money elsewhere is rejected, there are no transactions related to this alternative to record. On the basis of the costs recorded in the accounting system (purchase-order costs and purchase costs), Soho would erroneously conclude that making two purchases of 5,00,000 units each is the less costly alternative. Column 3, however, indicates that, consistent with the trends toward holding smaller inventories, purchasing smaller quantities of 10,000 units 100 times a year is preferred to purchasing 5,00,000 units twice during the year. Why? Because the lower opportunity cost of holding smaller inventory exceeds the higher purchase and ordering costs. If the opportunity cost of money tied up in inventory were greater than 9% per year, or if other incremental benefits of holding lower inventory were considered—such as lower insurance, materials-handling, storage, obsolescence, and breakage costs—making 100 purchases would be even more economical.

Product-Mix Decisions with Capacity Constraints

Learning Objective 4

Know how to choose which products to produce when there are capacity constraints

. . . select the product with the highest contribution margin per unit of the limiting resource

We now examine how the concept of relevance applies to **product-mix decisions**—the decisions made by a company about which products to sell and in what quantities. These decisions usually have only a short-run focus because the level of capacity can be expanded in the long run. For example, BMW, the German car manufacturer, must continually adapt the mix of its different models of cars (for example, 325i, 525i, and 740i) to short-run fluctuations in selling prices and demand. To determine product mix, a company maximizes operating income, given constraints such as capacity and demand. Throughout this section, we assume that as short-run changes in product mix occur, the only costs that change are costs that are variable with respect to the number of units produced (and sold). Under this assumption, the analysis of individual product contribution margins provides insight into the product mix that maximizes operating income.

Example 4: Power Recreation assembles two engines—a snowmobile engine and a boat engine

	Snowmobile Engine	Boat Engine
Selling price	Rs 8,000	Rs 10,000
Variable cost per unit	5,600	6,250
Contribution margin per unit	Rs 2,400	Rs 3,750
Contribution margin percentage		
(Rs 2,400 ÷ Rs 8,000 Rs 3,750 ÷ Rs 10,000)	30%	37.5%

Assume that only 600 machine-hours are available daily for assembling engines. Additional capacity cannot be obtained in the short run. Power Recreation can sell as many engines as it produces. The constraining resource, then, is machine-hours. It takes two machine-hours to produce one snowmobile engine and five machine-hours to produce one boat engine. What product mix should Power Recreation's managers choose to maximize its operating income?

In terms of contribution margin per unit and contribution margin percentage, boat engines are more profitable than snowmobile engines. The product that Power Recreation should produce and sell, however, is not necessarily the product with the higher individual contribution margin per unit or contribution margin percentage. Managers should choose the product with *the highest contribution margin per unit of the constraining resource (factor)*. That's the resource that restricts or limits the production or sale of products.

	Snowmobile Engine	Boat Engine
Contribution margin per unit	Rs 2,400	Rs 3,750
Machine-hours required to produce one unit	2 machine-hours	5 machine-hours
Contribution margin per machine-hour		
Rs 2,400 per unit ÷ 2 machine-hours/unit	Rs 1,200/machine-hour	
Rs 3,750 per unit ÷ 5 machine-hours/unit		Rs 750/machine-hour
Total contribution margin for 600 machine-hours		
Rs 1,200/machine-hour × 600 machine-hours	Rs 7,20,000	
Rs 750/machine-hour × 600 machine-hours		Rs 4,50,000

Producing snowmobile engines earns more contribution margin per machine-hour, which is the constraining resource in this example. Therefore, choosing to produce and sell snowmobile engines maximizes *total* contribution margin and operating income. Other constraints in manufacturing settings can be the availability of direct materials, components, or skilled labor, as well as financial and sales factors. In a retail department store, the constraining resource may be linear feet of display space. Regardless of the specific constraining resource, managers should always focus on maximizing *total* contribution margin by choosing products that give the highest contribution margin per unit of the constraining resource.

In many cases, a manufacturer or retailer has the challenge of trying to maximize total operating income for a variety of products, each with more than one constraining resource. Some constraints may require a manufacturer or retailer to stock minimum quantities of products even if these products are not very profitable. For example, supermarkets must stock less-profitable products because customers will be willing to shop at a supermarket only if it carries a wide range of products that customers desire. To determine the most profitable production schedule and the most profitable product mix, the manufacturer or retailer needs to determine the maximum total contribution margin in the face of many constraints. Optimization techniques, such as linear programming discussed in the appendix to this chapter, help solve these more-complex problems.

When resources are constrained, how should managers choose which of multiple products to produce and sell?

Finally, there is the question of managing the bottleneck constraint to increase output and, therefore, contribution margin. Can the available machine-hours for assembling engines be increased beyond 600, for example, by reducing idle time? Can the time needed to assemble each snowmobile engine (two machine-hours) and each boat engine (five machine-hours) be reduced, for example, by reducing setup time and processing time of assembly? Can quality be improved so that constrained capacity is used to produce only good units rather than some good and some defective units? Can some of the assembly operations be outsourced to allow more engines to be built? Implementing any of these options will likely require Power Recreation to incur incremental costs. Power Recreation will implement only those options where the increase in contribution margins exceeds the increase in costs. *Instructors and students who, at this point, want to explore these issues in more detail can go to the section in Chapter 19.*

Customer Profitability, Activity-Based Costing, and Relevant Costs

Learning Objective 5

Discuss factors managers must consider when adding or dropping customers or segments

. . . managers should focus on how total costs differ among alternatives and ignore allocated overhead costs

Not only must companies make choices regarding which products and how much of each product to produce, they must often make decisions about adding or dropping a product line or a business segment. Similarly, if the cost object is a customer, companies must make decisions about adding or dropping customers (analogous to a product line) or a branch office (analogous to a business segment). We illustrate relevant-revenue and relevant-cost analysis for these kinds of decisions using customers rather than products as the cost object.

Example 5: Allied West, the West Coast sales office of Allied Furniture, a wholesaler of specialized furniture, supplies furniture to three local retailers: Vogel, Brenner, and Wisk. Exhibit 11-8 presents expected revenues and costs of Allied West by customer for the upcoming year using its activity-based costing system. Allied West assigns costs to customers based on the activities needed to support each customer. Information on Allied West's costs for different activities at various levels of the cost hierarchy follows:

- Furniture-handling labor costs vary with the number of units of furniture shipped to customers.
- Allied West reserves different areas of the warehouse to stock furniture for different customers. For simplicity, assume that furniture-handling equipment in an area and depreciation costs on the equipment are identified with individual customers (customer-level costs). Any unused equipment remains idle. The equipment has a one-year useful life and zero disposal value.

	Customer			
	Vogel	Brenner	Wisk	Total
Revenues	Rs 50,00,000	Rs 30,00,000	Rs 40,00,000	Rs1,20,00,000
Cost of goods sold	37,00,000	22,00,000	33,00,000	92,00,000
Furniture-handling labor	4,10,000	1,80,000	3,30,000	9,20,000
Furniture-handling equipment cost written off as depreciation	1,20,000	40,000	90,000	2,50,000
Rent	1,40,000	80,000	1,40,000	3,60,000
Marketing support	1,10,000	90,000	1,00,000	3,00,000
Sales-order and delivery processing	1,30,000	70,000	1,20,000	3,20,000
General administration	2,00,000	1,20,000	1,60,000	4,80,000
Allocated corporate-office costs	1,00,000	60,000	80,000	2,40,000
Total costs	49,10,000	28,40,000	43,20,000	1,20,70,000
Operating income	Rs 90,000	Rs1,60,000	Rs (3,20,000)	Rs (70,000)

Exhibit 11-8

Customer Profitability Analysis for Allied West

- Allied West allocates rent to each customer on the basis of the amount of warehouse space reserved for that customer.
- Marketing costs vary with the number of sales visits made to customers.
- Sales-order costs are batch-level costs that vary with the number of sales orders received from customers; delivery-processing costs are batch-level costs that vary with the number of shipments made.
- Allied West allocates fixed general-administration costs (facility-level costs) to customers on the basis of customer revenues.
- Allied Furniture allocates its fixed corporate-office costs to sales offices on the basis of the square feet area of each sales office. Allied West then allocates these costs to customers on the basis of customer revenues.

In the following sections, we consider several decisions that Allied West's managers face: Should Allied West drop the Wisk account? Should it add a fourth customer, Loral? Should Allied Furniture close down Allied West? Should it open another sales office, Allied South, whose revenues and costs are identical to those of Allied West?

Relevant-Revenue and Relevant-Cost Analysis of Dropping a Customer

Exhibit 11-8 indicates a loss of Rs 3,20,000 on the Wisk account. Allied West's managers believe the reason for the loss is that Wisk places low-margin orders with Allied, and has relatively high sales-order, delivery-processing, furniture-handling, and marketing costs. Allied West is considering several possible actions with respect to the Wisk account: reducing its own costs of supporting Wisk by becoming more efficient, cutting back on some of the services it offers Wisk, asking Wisk to place larger, less frequent orders, charging Wisk higher prices, or dropping the Wisk account. The following analysis focuses on the operating-income effect of dropping the Wisk account.

To determine what to do, Allied West's managers must answer the question, What are the relevant revenues and relevant costs? Information about the effect of dropping the Wisk account follows.

- Dropping the Wisk account will save cost of goods sold, furniture-handling labor, marketing support, sales-order, and delivery-processing costs incurred on the account.

- Dropping the Wisk account will leave idle the warehouse space and furniture-handling equipment currently used to supply products to Wisk.
- Dropping the Wisk account will have no effect on fixed general-administration costs or corporate-office costs.

Exhibit 11-9, column 1, presents the relevant-revenue and relevant-cost analysis using data from the Wisk column in Exhibit 11-8. Allied West's operating income will be Rs 1,50,000 lower if it drops the Wisk account—the cost savings from dropping the Wisk account, Rs 38,50,000, will not be enough to offset the loss of Rs 40,00,000 in revenues—so Allied West's managers decide to keep the account. Note that there is no opportunity cost of using warehouse space for Wisk because without Wisk, the space and equipment will remain idle.

Depreciation is a past cost, therefore it is irrelevant; rent, general-administration, and corporate-office costs are irrelevant because they are future costs that will not change if Allied West drops the Wisk account. For purposes of this decision, Allied West's managers should be particularly mindful of allocated overhead costs such as corporate-office costs. They should ignore amounts allocated to the sales office and individual customers. The question Allied West's managers must ask when deciding whether corporate-office costs are relevant is, will expected total corporate-office costs decrease as a result of dropping the Wisk account? In our example, they will not, so these costs are irrelevant. *If expected total corporate-office costs* decreased by dropping the Wisk account, those savings would be relevant even if *the amount allocated to Allied West did not change.*

Now suppose that if Allied West drops the Wisk account, it could lease the extra warehouse space to Sanchez Corporation for Rs 2,00,000 per year. Then Rs 2,00,000 would be Allied's opportunity cost of continuing to use the warehouse to service Wisk. Allied West would gain Rs 50,000 by dropping the Wisk account (Rs 2,00,000 from lease revenue minus lost operating income of Rs 1,50,000). Before reaching a decision, Allied West's managers must examine whether Wisk can be made more profitable so that supplying products to Wisk earns more than the Rs 2,00,000 from leasing to Sanchez. The managers must also consider strategic factors such as the effect of the decision on Allied West's reputation for developing stable, long-run business relationships with its customers.

Relevant-Revenue and Relevant-Cost Analysis of Adding a Customer

Suppose that in addition to Vogel, Brenner, and Wisk, Allied West's managers are evaluating the profitability of adding a customer, Loral. Allied West is already incurring annual costs of Rs 3,60,000 for warehouse rent and Rs 4,80,000 for general-administration costs. These costs together with *actual total* corporate-office costs will not change if Loral is added as a customer. Loral has a customer profile much like Wisk's. Suppose Allied West's

Exhibit 11-9

Relevant-Revenue and Relevant-Cost Analysis for Dropping the Wisk Account and Adding the Loral Account

	(Loss in Revenues) and Savings in Costs from Dropping Wisk Account (1)	Incremental Revenues and (Incremental Costs) from Adding Loral Account (2)
Revenues	Rs(40,00,000)	Rs 40,00,000
Cost of goods sold	33,00,000	(33,00,000)
Furniture-handling labor	3,30,000	(3,30,000)
Furniture-handling equipment cost written off as depreciation	0	(90,000)
Rent	0	0
Marketing support	1,00,000	(1,00,000)
Sales-order and delivery processing	1,20,000	(1,20,000)
General administration	0	0
Corporate-office costs	0	0
Total costs	38,50,000	(39,40,000)
Effect on operating income (loss)	Rs(1,50,000)	Rs 60,000

managers predict revenues and costs of doing business with Loral to be the same as the revenues and costs described under the Wisk column of Exhibit 11-8. In particular, Allied West would have to acquire furniture-handling equipment for the Loral account costing Rs 90,000, with a one-year useful life and zero disposal value. Should Allied West add Loral as a customer?

Exhibit 11-9, column 2, shows incremental revenues exceed incremental costs by Rs 60,000. On the basis of this analysis, Allied West's managers would recommend adding Loral as a customer. Rent, general-administration, and corporate-office costs are irrelevant because these costs will not change if Loral is added as a customer. However, the cost of new equipment to support the Loral order (written off as depreciation of Rs 90,000 in Exhibit 11-9, column 2) is relevant. That's because this cost can be avoided if Allied West decides not to add Loral as a customer. Note the critical distinction here: *Depreciation cost is irrelevant in deciding whether to drop Wisk as a customer because depreciation is a past cost, but the cost of purchasing new equipment that will then be written off as depreciation in the future is relevant in deciding whether to add Loral as a customer.*

Relevant-Revenue and Relevant-Cost Analysis of Closing or Adding Branch Offices or Segments

Companies periodically confront decisions about closing or adding branch offices or business segments. For example, given Allied West's expected loss of Rs 70,000 (see Exhibit 11-8), should it be closed? Assume that closing Allied West will have no effect on total corporate-office costs.

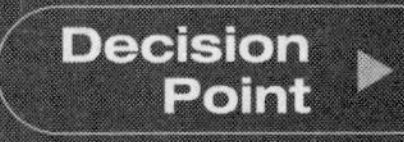

In deciding to add or drop customers or to add or discontinue branch offices or segments, what should managers focus on and how should they take into account allocated overhead costs?

Exhibit 11-10, column 1, presents the relevant-revenue and relevant-cost analysis using data from the Total column in Exhibit 11-8. The revenue losses of Rs 1,20,00,000 will exceed the cost savings of Rs 1,15,80,000, leading to a decrease in operating income of Rs 4,20,000. Allied West should not be closed. The key reasons are that closing Allied West will not save depreciation cost of Rs 2,50,000, which is a past or sunk cost, or actual total corporate-office costs. Corporate-office costs allocated to various sales offices will change *but the total amount of these costs will not decline*. The Rs 2,40,000 no longer allocated to Allied West will be allocated to other sales offices. Therefore, the Rs 2,40,000 of allocated corporate-office costs should not be included as expected cost savings from closing Allied West.

Now suppose Allied Furniture has the opportunity to open another sales office, Allied South, whose revenues and costs would be identical to Allied West's costs, including a cost of Rs 2,50,000 to acquire furniture-handling equipment with a one-year useful life and zero disposal value. Opening this office will have no effect on total corporate-office costs. Should Allied Furniture open Allied South? Exhibit 11-10, column 2, indicates that it should do so because opening Allied South will increase operating income by Rs 1,70,000.

Exhibit 11-10

Relevant-Revenue and Relevant-Cost Analysis for Closing Allied West and Opening Allied South

	(Loss in Revenues) and Savings in Costs from Closing Allied West (1)	Incremental Revenues and (Incremental Costs) from Opening Allied South (2)
Revenues	Rs (1,20,00,000)	Rs 1,20,00,000
Cost of goods sold	92,00,000	(92,00,000)
Furniture-handling labor	9,20,000	(9,20,000)
Furniture-handling equipment cost written off as depreciation	0	(2,50,000)
Rent	3,60,000	(3,60,000)
Marketing support	3,00,000	(3,00,000)
Sales-order and delivery processing	3,20,000	(3,20,000)
General administration	4,80,000	(4,80,000)
Corporate-office costs	0	0
Total costs	1,15,80,000	(1,18,30,000)
Effect on operating income (loss)	Rs (4,20,000)	Rs 1,70,000

As before, the cost of new equipment (written off as depreciation) is relevant. But the point here is to ignore *allocated* corporate-office costs and focus on *total* corporate-office costs. Total corporate-office costs will not change if Allied South is opened, therefore these costs are irrelevant.

Irrelevance of Past Costs and Equipment-Replacement Decisions

Learning Objective 

Explain why book value of equipment is irrelevant in equipment-replacement decisions

. . . it is a past cost

At several points in this chapter, when discussing the concept of relevance, we reasoned that past (historical or sunk) costs are irrelevant to decision making. That's because a decision cannot change something that has already happened. We now apply this concept to decisions about replacing equipment. We stress the idea that **book value**—original cost minus accumulated depreciation—of existing equipment is a past cost that is irrelevant.

Example 6: Toledo Company is considering replacing a metal-cutting machine with a newer model. The new machine is more efficient than the old machine, but it has a shorter life. Revenues from aircraft parts (Rs 1,10,00,000 million per year) will be unaffected by the replacement decision. Here are the data the management accountant prepares for the existing (old) machine and the replacement (new) machine:

	Old Machine	New Machine
Original cost	Rs 1,00,00,000	Rs 60,00,000
Useful life	5 years	2 years
Current age	3 years	0 years
Remaining useful life	2 years	2 years
Accumulated depreciation	Rs 60,00,000	Not acquired yet
Book value	Rs 40,00,000	Not acquired yet
Current disposal value (in cash)	Rs 4,00,000	Not acquired yet
Terminal disposal value (in cash 2 years from now)	Rs 0	Rs 0
Annual operating costs (maintenance, energy, repairs, coolants, and so on)	Rs 80,00,000	Rs 46,00,000

Toledo Corporation uses straight-line depreciation. To focus on relevance, we ignore the time value of money and income taxes.[2] Should Toledo replace its old machine?

Exhibit 11-11 presents a cost comparison of the two machines. Consider why each of the four items in Toledo's equipment-replacement decision is relevant or irrelevant:

1. **Book value of old machine, Rs 40,00,000.** Irrelevant, because it is a past or sunk cost. All past costs are "down the drain." Nothing can change what has already been spent or what has already happened.
2. **Current disposal value of old machine, Rs 4,00,000.** Relevant, because it is an expected future benefit that will only occur if the machine is replaced.
3. **Loss on disposal, Rs 36,00,000.** This is the difference between amounts in items 1 and 2. It is a meaningless combination blurring the distinction between the irrelevant book value and the relevant disposal value. Each should be considered separately, as was done in items 1 and 2.
4. **Cost of new machine, Rs 60,00,000.** Relevant, because it is an expected future cost that will only occur if the machine is purchased.

[2] See Chapter 21 for a discussion of time-value-of-money and income-tax considerations in capital investment decisions.

Exhibit 11-11

Operating Income Comparison: Replacement of Machine, Relevant and Irrelevant Items for Toledo Company

	Two Years Together		
	Keep (1)	**Replace (2)**	**Difference (3) = (1) – (2)**
Revenues	Rs 2,20,00,000	Rs 2,20,00,000	—
Operating costs			
Cash operating costs (Rs 80,00,000/yr. × 2 years; Rs 46,00,000/yr. × 2 years)	1,60,00,000	92,00,000	Rs 68,00,000
Book value of old machine			
Periodic write-off as depreciation or	40,00,000	—	—
Lump-sum write-off	—	40,00,000[a]	
Current disposal value of old machine	—	(4,00,000)[a]	4,00,000
New machine cost, written off periodically as depreciation	—	60,00,000	(60,00,000)
Total operating costs	2,00,00,000	1,88,00,000	12,00,000
Operating income	Rs 20,00,000	Rs 32,00,000	Rs (12,00,000)

[a]In a formal income statement, these two items would be combined as "loss on disposal of machine" of Rs 36,00,000.

Exhibit 11-11 should clarify these four assertions. Column 3 in Exhibit 11-11 shows that the book value of the old machine does not differ between the alternatives and could be ignored for decision-making purposes. No matter what the timing of the write-off—whether a lump-sum charge in the current year or depreciation charges over the next two years—the total amount is still Rs 40,00,000 because it is a past (historical) cost. In contrast, the Rs 60,00,000 cost of the new machine and the current disposal value of Rs 4,00,000 for the old machine are relevant because they would not arise if Toledo's managers decided not to replace the machine. Note that the operating income from replacing is Rs 12,00,000 higher for the two years together.

To provide focus, Exhibit 11-12 concentrates only on relevant items. Note that the same answer—higher operating income as a result of lower costs of Rs 12,00,000 by replacing the machine—is obtained even though the book value is omitted from the calculations. The only relevant items are the cash operating costs, the disposal value of the old machine, and the cost of the new machine, which is represented as depreciation in Exhibit 11-12.

Learning Objective 

Explain how conflicts can arise between the decision model used by a manager and the performance-evaluation model used to evaluate the manager

. . . tell managers to take a multiple-year view in decision making but judge their performance only on the basis of the current year's operating income

Decisions and Performance Evaluation

Consider our equipment-replacement example in light of the five-step sequence in Exhibit 11-1.

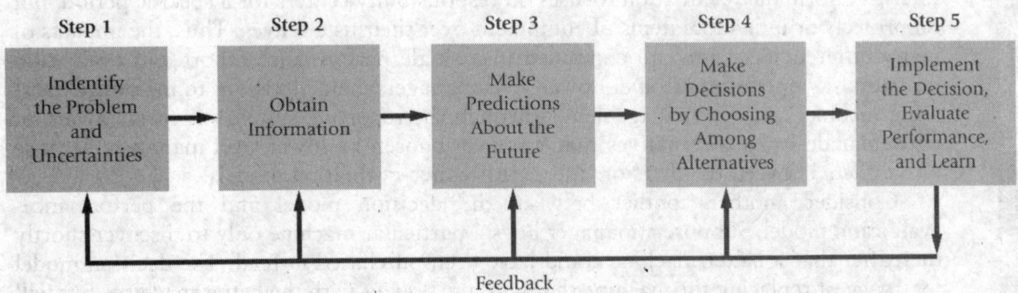

The decision model analysis (step 4), which is presented in Exhibits 11-11 and 11-12, dictates replacing the machine rather than keeping it. In the real world, however, would the manager replace? An important factor in replacement decisions is the manager's perception of whether the decision model is consistent with how the manager's performance will be judged after the decision is implemented (the performance-evaluation model in step 5).

Exhibit 11-12

Cost Comparison: Replacement of Machine, Relevant Items Only, for Toledo Company

	Two Years Together		
	Keep (1)	Replace (2)	Difference (3) = (1) – (2)
Cash operating costs	Rs 1,60,00,000	Rs 92,00,000	Rs 68,00,000
Current disposal value of old machine	—	(4,00,000)	4,00,000
New machine, written off periodically as depreciation	—	60,00,000	(60,00,000)
Total relevant costs	Rs 1,60,00,000	Rs 1,48,00,000	Rs 12,00,000

From the perspective of their own careers, it is no surprise that managers tend to favor the alternative that makes their performance look better. If the performance-evaluation model conflicts with the decision model, the performance-evaluation model often prevails in influencing managers' decisions. For example, if the promotion or bonus of the manager at Toledo hinges on his or her first year's operating income performance under accrual accounting, the manager's temptation *not* to replace will be overwhelming. Why? Because the accrual accounting model for measuring performance will show a higher first-year operating income if the old machine is kept rather than replaced (as the following table shows):

First-Year Results: Accrual Accounting

	Keep		Replace	
Revenues		Rs 1,10,00,000		Rs 1,10,00,000
Operating costs				
Cash-operating costs	Rs 80,00,000		46,00,000	
Depreciation	20,00,000		30,00,000	
Loss on disposal	—		36,00,000	
Total operating costs		1,00,00,000		1,12,00,000
Operating income (loss)		Rs 10,00,000		Rs (2,00,000)

Even though top management's goals encompass the two-year period (consistent with the decision model), the manager will focus on first-year results if his or her evaluation is based on short-run measures such as the first-year's operating income.

Resolving the conflict between the decision model and the performance-evaluation model is frequently a baffling problem in practice. In theory, resolving the difficulty seems obvious: Design models that are consistent. Consider our replacement example. Year-by-year effects on operating income of replacement can be budgeted for the two-year planning horizon. The manager then would be evaluated on the expectation that the first year would be poor and the next year would be much better. Doing this for every decision, however, makes the performance evaluation model very cumbersome. As a result of these practical difficulties, accounting systems rarely track each decision separately. Performance evaluation focuses on responsibility centers for a specific period, not on projects or individual items of equipment over their useful lives. Thus, the impacts of many different decisions are combined in a single performance report and evaluation measure, say operating income. Lower-level managers make decisions to maximize operating income, and top management—through the reporting system—is rarely aware of particular desirable alternatives that were *not* chosen by lower-level managers because of conflicts between the decision and performance-evaluation models.

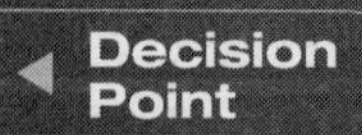

How can conflicts arise between the decision model used by a manager and the performance-evaluation model used to evaluate that manager?

Consider another conflict between the decision model and the performance-evaluation model. Suppose a manager buys a particular machine only to discover shortly thereafter that a better machine could have been purchased instead. The decision model may suggest replacing the machine that was just bought with the better machine, but will the manager do so? Probably not. Why? Because replacing the machine so soon after its purchase will reflect badly on the manager's capabilities and performance. If the manager's bosses have no knowledge of the better machine, the manager may prefer to keep the recently purchased machine rather than alert them to the better machine.

Chapter 23 discusses performance evalution models in more detail and ways to reduce conflict between the decision model and the performance evaluation model.

Problem for Self-Study

Praveen Singh is manager of the engineering development division of Goldcoast Products. Praveen has just received a proposal signed by all 15 of his engineers to replace the workstations with networked personal computers (networked PCs). Praveen is not enthusiastic about the proposal.

Data on workstations and networked PCs are:

	Workstations	Networked PCs
Original cost	Rs 30,00,000	Rs 13,50,000
Useful life	5 years	3 years
Current age	2 years	0 years
Remaining useful life	3 years.	3 years
Accumulated depreciation	Rs 12,00,000	Not acquired yet
Current book value	Rs 18,00,000	Not acquired yet
Current disposal value (in cash)	Rs 9,50,000	Not acquired yet
Terminal disposal value (in cash 3 years from now)	Rs 0	Rs 0
Annual computer-related cash operating costs	Rs 4,00,000	Rs 1,00,000
Annual revenues	Rs 1,00,00,000	Rs 1,00,00,000
Annual noncomputer-related operating costs	Rs 88,00,000	Rs 88,00,000

Praveen's annual bonus includes a component based on division operating income. He has a promotion possibility next year that would make him a group vice president of Goldcoast Products.

Required

1. Compare the costs of workstations and networked PCs. Consider the cumulative results for the three years together, ignoring the time value of money and income taxes.
2. Why might Praveen be reluctant to purchase the networked PCs?

Solution

1. The following table considers all cost items when comparing future costs of workstations and networked PCs:

	Three Years Together		
All Items	**Workstations (1)**	**Networked PCs (2)**	**Difference (3) = (1) − (2)**
Revenues	Rs 3,00,00,000	Rs 3,00,00,000	—
Operating costs			
Noncomputer-related operating costs	2,64,00,000	2,64,00,000	—
Computer-related cash operating costs	12,00,000	3,00,000	Rs 9,00,000
Workstations' book value			
Periodic write-off as depreciation or	18,00,000		} —
Lump-sum write-off	—	18,00,000	
Current disposal value of workstations	—	(9,50,000)	9,50,000
Networked PCs, written off periodically as depreciation	—	13,50,000	(13,50,000)
Total operating costs	2,94,00,000	2,89,00,000	5,00,000
Operating income	Rs 6,00,000	Rs 11,00,000	Rs (5,00,000)

Alternatively, the analysis could focus on only those items in the preceding table that differ between the alternatives.

	Three Years Together		
Relevant Items	**Workstations**	**Networked PCs**	**Difference**
Computer-related cash operating costs	Rs 12,00,000	Rs 3,00,000	Rs 9,00,000
Current disposal value of workstations	—	(9,50,000)	9,50,000
Networked PCs, written off periodically as depreciation	—	13,50,000	(13,50,000)
Total relevant costs	Rs 12,00,000	Rs 7,00,000	Rs 5,00,000

The analysis suggests that it is cost-effective to replace the workstations with the networked PCs.

2. The accrual-accounting operating incomes *for the first year* under the keep-workstations versus the buy-networked-PCs alternatives are:

	Keep Workstations		Buy Networked PCs	
Revenues		Rs 1,00,00,000		Rs 1,00,00,000
Operating costs				
Noncomputer-related operating costs	Rs 88,00,000		Rs 88,00,000	
Computer-related cash operating costs	4,00,000		1,00,000	
Depreciation	6,00,000		4,50,000	
Loss on disposal of workstations	—		8,50,000[a]	
Total operating costs		98,00,000		1,02,00,000
Operating income (loss)		Rs 2,00,000		Rs (2,00,000)

[a] Rs 8,50,000 = Book value of workstations, Rs 18,00,000 − Current disposal value, Rs 9,50,000.

Praveen would be less happy with the expected operating loss of Rs 2,00,000 if the networked PCs are purchased than he would be with the expected operating income of Rs 2,00,000 if the workstations are kept. Buying the networked PCs would eliminate the component of his bonus based on operating income. He might also perceive the Rs 2,00,000 operating loss as reducing his chances of being promoted to a group vice president.

Decision Points

The following question-and-answer format summarizes the chapter's learning objectives. Each decision presents a key question related to a learning objective. The guidelines are the answer to that question.

Decision	Guidelines
1. What is the five-step process that can be used to make decisions?	The five-step decision-making process is (a) identify the problem and uncertainties, (b) obtain information, (c) make predictions about the future, (d) make decisions by choosing among alternatives, and (e) implement the decision, evaluate performance, and learn.
2. When is a revenue or cost item relevant for a particular decision and what potential problems should be avoided in relevant-cost analysis?	To be relevant for a particular decision, a revenue or cost item must meet two criteria: (a) it must be an expected future revenue or expected future cost, and (b) it must differ among alternative courses of action. The outcomes of alternative actions can be quantitative and qualitative. Quantitative outcomes are measured in numerical terms. Some quantitative outcomes can be expressed in financial terms, others cannot. Qualitative factors, such as employee morale, are difficult to measure accurately in numerical terms. Consideration must be given to relevant quantitative and qualitative factors in making decisions. Two potential problems to avoid in relevant-cost analysis are (a) making incorrect general assumptions—such as all variable costs are relevant and all fixed costs are irrelevant—and (b) losing sight of total amounts, focusing instead on unit amounts.
3. What is an opportunity cost and why should it be included when making decisions?	Opportunity cost is the contribution to income that is forgone by not using a limited resource in its next-best alternative use. Opportunity cost is included in decision making because it represents the best alternative way in which an organization may have used its resources had it not made the decision it did.

4. When resources are constrained, how should managers choose which of multiple products to produce and sell?	Under these conditions, managers should select the product that yields the highest contribution margin per unit of the constraining or limiting resource (factor). In this way, total contribution margin will be maximized.
5. In deciding to add or drop customers or to add or discontinue branch offices or segments, what should managers focus on and how should they take into account allocated overhead costs?	Managers should focus on what costs will change when making decisions about adding or dropping customers or adding or discontinuing branch offices and segments. Managers should ignore allocated overhead costs.
6. Is book value of existing equipment relevant in equipment-replacement decisions?	Book value of existing equipment is a past (historical or sunk) cost and, therefore, is irrelevant in equipment-replacement decisions.
7. How can conflicts arise between the decision model used by a manager and the performance-evaluation model used to evaluate that manager?	Top management faces a persistent challenge: making sure that the performance-evaluation model of lower-level managers is consistent with the decision model. A common inconsistency is to tell these managers to take a multiple-year view in their decision making but then to judge their performance only on the basis of the current year's operating income.

APPENDIX: LINEAR PROGRAMMING

In this chapter's Power Recreation example, suppose both the snowmobile and boat engines must be tested on a very expensive machine before they are shipped to customers. The available machine-hours for testing are limited. Production data are:

Department	Available Daily Capacity in Hours	Use of Capacity in Hours per Unit of Product: Snowmobile Engine	Boat Engine	Daily Maximum Production in Units: Snowmobile Engine	Boat Engine
Assembly	600 machine-hours	2.0 machine-hours	5.0 machine-hours	300[a] snow engines	120 boat engines
Testing	120 testing-hours	1.0 machine-hour	0.5 machine-hour	120 snow engines	240 boat engines

[a] For example, 600 machine-hours ÷ 2.0 machine-hours per snowmobile engine = 300, the maximum number of snowmobile engines that the Assembly Department can make if it works exclusively on snowmobile engines.

Exhibit 11-13 summarizes these and other relevant data. In addition, as a result of material shortages for boat engines, Power Recreation cannot produce more than 110 boat engines per day. How many engines of each type should Power Recreation produce and sell daily to maximize operating income?

Exhibit 11-13

Operating Data for Power Recreation

	Department Capacity (per Day) In Product Units: Assembly	Testing	Selling Price	Variable Cost per Unit	Contribution Margin per Unit
Only snowmobile engines	300	120	Rs 8,000	Rs 5,600	Rs 2,400
Only boat engines	120	240	Rs10,000	Rs 6,250	Rs 3,750

Because there are multiple constraints, a technique called *linear programming* or *LP* can be used to determine the number of each type of engine Power Recreation should produce. LP models typically assume that all costs are either variable or fixed with respect to a single cost driver (units of output). As we shall see, LP models also require certain other linear assumptions to hold. When these assumptions fail, other decision models should be considered.[3]

Steps in Solving an LP Problem

We use the data in Exhibit 11-13 to illustrate the three steps in solving an LP problem. Throughout this discussion, S equals the number of units of snowmobile engines produced and sold, and B equals the number of units of boat engines produced and sold.

Step 1: Determine the objective function. The **objective function** of a linear program expresses the objective or goal to be maximized (say, operating income) or minimized (say, operating costs). In our example, the objective is to find the combination of snowmobile engines and boat engines that maximizes total contribution margin. Fixed costs remain the same regardless of the product-mix decision and are irrelevant. The linear function expressing the objective for the total contribution margin (TCM) is:

$$TCM = \text{Rs } 2{,}400S + \text{Rs } 3{,}750B$$

Step 2: Specify the constraints. A **constraint** is a mathematical inequality or equality that must be satisfied by the variables in a mathematical model. The following linear inequalities express the relationships in our example:

Assembly Department constraint	$2S + 5B \leq 600$
Testing Department constraint	$1S + 0.5B \leq 120$
Materials-shortage constraint for boat engines	$B \leq 110$
Negative production is impossible	$S \geq 0$ and $B \geq 0$

The three solid lines on the graph in Exhibit 11-14 show the existing constraints for Assembly and Testing and the materials-shortage constraint.[4] The feasible or technically possible alternatives are those combinations of quantities of snowmobile engines and boat engines that satisfy all the constraining resources or factors. The shaded "area of feasible solutions" in Exhibit 11-14 shows the boundaries of those product combinations that are feasible.

Step 3: Compute the optimal solution. Linear programming (LP) is an optimization technique used to maximize the *objective function* when there are multiple *constraints*. We present two approaches for finding the optimal solution using LP: trial-and-error approach and graphic approach. These approaches are easy to use in our example because there are only two variables in the objective function and a small number of constraints. Understanding these approaches provides insight into LP. In most real-world LP applications, managers use computer software packages to calculate the optimal solution.[5]

[3] Other decision models are described in J. Moore and L. Weatherford, *Decision Modeling with Microsoft Excel*, 7th ed. (Upper Saddle River, NJ: Prentice Hall, 2005); and S. Nahmias, *Production and Operations Analysis*, 5th ed. (New York: McGraw-Hill/Irwin, 2006).

[4] As an example of how the lines are plotted in Exhibit 11-14, use equal signs instead of inequality signs and assume for the Assembly Department that $B = 0$; then $S = 300$ (600 machine-hours ÷ 2 machine-hours per snowmobile engine). Assume that $S = 0$; then $B = 120$ (600 machine-hours ÷ 5 machine-hours per boat engine). Connect those two points with a straight line.

[5] Standard computer software packages rely on the simplex method. The *simplex method* is an iterative step-by-step procedure for determining the optimal solution to an LP problem. It starts with a specific feasible solution and then tests it by substitution to see whether the result can be improved. These substitutions continue until no further improvement is possible and the optimal solution is obtained.

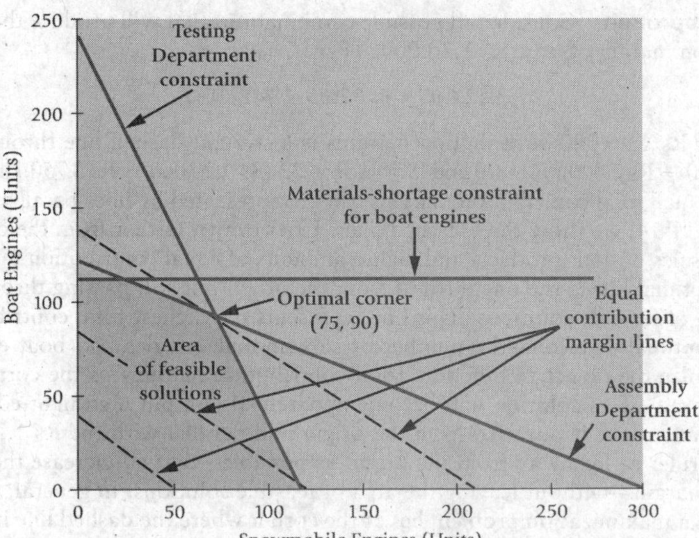

Exhibit 11-14

Linear Programming: Graphic Solution for Power Recreation

Trial-and-error approach The optimal solution can be found by trial and error, by working with coordinates of the corners of the area of feasible solutions.

First, select any set of corner points and compute the total contribution margin. Five corner points appear in Exhibit 11-14. It is helpful to use simultaneous equations to obtain the exact coordinates in the graph. To illustrate, the corner point (S = 75, B = 90) can be derived by solving the two pertinent constraint inequalities as simultaneous equations:

$$2S + 5B = 600 \quad (1)$$
$$1S + 0.5B = 120 \quad (2)$$

Multiplying (2) by 2: $2S + B = 240 \quad (3)$

Subtracting (3) from (1): $4B = 360$

Therefore, $B = 360 \div 4 = 90$

Substituting for B in (2): $1S + 0.5(90) = 120$

$$S = 120 - 45 = 75$$

Given S = 75 snowmobile engines and B = 90 boat engines, TCM = (Rs 2,400 per snowmobile engine × 75 snowmobile engines) + (Rs 3,750 per boat engine × 90 boat engines) = Rs 5,17,500.

Second, move from corner point to corner point and compute the total contribution margin at each corner point.

Trial	Corner Point (*S, B*)	Snowmobile Engines (*S*)	Boat Engines (*B*)	Total Contribution Margin
1	(0, 0)	0	0	Rs 2,400(0) + Rs 3,750(0) = Rs 0
2	(0, 110)	0	110	Rs 2,400(0) + Rs 3,750(110) = Rs 4,12,500
3	(25,110)	25	110	Rs 2,400(25) + Rs 3,750(110) = Rs 4,72,500
4	(75, 90)	75	90	Rs 2,400(75) + Rs 3,750(90) = Rs 5,17,500[a]
5	(120, 0)	120	0	Rs 2,400(120) + Rs 3,750(0) = Rs 2,88,000

[a]The optimal solution.

The optimal product mix is the mix that yields the highest total contribution: 75 snowmobile engines and 90 boat engines. To understand the solution, consider what happens when moving from the point (25,110) to (75,90). Power Recreation gives up Rs 75,000 [Rs 3,750 × (110 − 90)] in contribution margin from boat engines while gaining Rs 1,20,000 [Rs 2,400 × (75 − 25)] in contribution margin from snowmobile engines. This results in a net increase in contribution margin of Rs 45,000 (Rs 1,20,000 − Rs 75,000), from Rs 4,72,500 to Rs 5,17,500.

Graphic approach Consider all possible combinations that will produce the same total contribution margin of, say, Rs 1,20,000. That is,

$$\text{Rs } 2{,}400S + \text{Rs } 3{,}750B = \text{Rs } 1{,}20{,}000$$

This set of Rs 1,20,000 contribution margins is a straight dashed line through [S = 50 (Rs 1,20,000 ÷ Rs 2,400); B = 0)] and [S = 0, B = 32 (Rs 1,20,000 ÷ Rs 3,750)] in Exhibit 11-14. Other equal total contribution margins can be represented by lines parallel to this one. In Exhibit 11-14, we show three dashed lines. Lines drawn farther from the origin represent more sales of both products and higher amounts of equal contribution margins.

The optimal line is the one farthest from the origin but still passing through a point in the area of feasible solutions. This line represents the highest total contribution margin. The optimal solution—the number of snowmobile engines and boat engines that will maximize the objective function, total contribution margin—is the corner point (S = 75, B = 90). This solution will become apparent if you put a straight-edge ruler on the graph and move it outward from the origin and parallel with the Rs 1,20,000 line. Move the ruler as far away from the origin as possible—that is, increase the total contribution margin—without leaving the area of feasible solutions. In general, the optimal solution in a maximization problem lies at the corner where the dashed line intersects an extreme point of the area of feasible solutions. Moving the ruler out any farther puts it outside the area of feasible solutions.

Sensitivity Analysis

What are the implications of uncertainty about the accounting or technical coefficients used in the objective function (such as the contribution margin per unit of snowmobile engines or boat engines) or the constraints (such as the number of machine-hours it takes to make a snowmobile engine or a boat engine)? Consider how a change in the contribution margin of snowmobile engines from Rs 2,400 to Rs 3,000 per unit would affect the optimal solution. Assume the contribution margin for boat engines remains unchanged at Rs 3,750 per unit. The revised objective function will be:

$$TCM = \text{Rs } 3{,}000S + \text{Rs } 3{,}750B$$

Using the trial-and-error approach to calculate the total contribution margin for each of the five corner points described in the previous table, the optimal solution is still (S = 75, B = 90). What if the contribution margin of snowmobile engines falls to Rs 1,600 per unit? The optimal solution remains the same (S = 75, B = 90). Thus, big changes in the contribution margin per unit of snowmobile engines have no effect on the optimal solution in this case. That's because, although the slopes of the equal contribution margin lines in Exhibit 11-14 change as the contribution margin of snowmobile engines changes from Rs 2,400 to Rs 3,000 to Rs 1,600 per unit, the farthest point at which the equal contribution margin lines intersect the area of feasible solutions is still (S = 75, B = 90).

TERMS TO LEARN

This chapter and the Glossary at the end of the book contain definitions of:

book value (**p. 464**)
business function costs (**p. 449**)
constraint (**p. 470**)
decision model (**p. 445**)
differential cost (**p. 453**)
differential revenue (**p. 453**)
full costs of the product (**p. 449**)
incremental cost (**p. 452**)
incremental revenue (**p. 453**)
insourcing (**p. 451**)
linear programming (LP) (**p. 470**)
make-or-buy decisions (**p. 451**)
objective function (**p. 470**)
one-time-only special order (**p. 448**)
opportunity cost (**p. 454**)
outsourcing (**p. 451**)
product-mix decisions (**p. 459**)
qualitative factors (**p. 447**)
quantitative factors (**p. 447**)
relevant costs (**p. 446**)
relevant revenues (**p. 446**)
sunk costs (**p. 447**)

ASSIGNMENT MATERIAL

Questions

11-1 Outline the five-step sequence in a decision process.

11-2 Define relevant costs. Why are historical costs irrelevant?

11-3 "All future costs are relevant." Do you agree? Why?

11-4 Distinguish between quantitative and qualitative factors in decision making.

11-5 Describe two potential problems that should be avoided in relevant-cost analysis.

11-6 "Variable costs are always relevant, and fixed costs are always irrelevant." Do you agree? Why?

11-7 "A component part should be purchased whenever the purchase price is less than its total manufacturing cost per unit." Do you agree? Why?

11-8 Define opportunity cost.

11-9 "Managers should always buy inventory in quantities that result in the lowest purchase cost per unit." Do you agree? Why?

11-10 "Management should always maximize sales of the product with the highest contribution margin per unit." Do you agree? Why?

11-11 "A branch office or business segment that shows negative operating income should be shut down." Do you agree? Explain briefly.

11-12 "Cost written off as depreciation on equipment already purchased is always irrelevant." Do you agree? Why?

11-13 "Managers will always choose the alternative that maximizes operating income or minimizes costs in the decision model." Do you agree? Why?

11-14 Describe the three steps in solving a linear programming problem.

11-15 How might the optimal solution of a linear programming problem be determined?

Solved Examples

11-16 Disposal of assets.

1. A company has an inventory of 100 assorted parts for a line of missiles that has been discontinued. The inventory cost is Rs 80,000. The parts can be either (a) remachined at total additional costs of Rs 30,000 and then sold for Rs 35,000 or (b) sold as scrap for Rs 2,000. Which action is more profitable? Show your calculations.
2. A motor, costing Rs 1,00,000 and uninsured, is wrecked its first day in use. It can be either (a) disposed of for Rs 10,000 cash and replaced with a similar motor costing Rs 1,02,000 or (b) rebuilt for Rs 85,000, and thus be brand new as far as operating characteristics and looks are concerned. Which action is less costly? Show your calculations.

Solution

Disposal of assets.

1. This is a situation in which the Rs 80,000 costs are irrelevant regarding the decision to re-machine or scrap. The only relevant factors are the future revenues and future costs. By ignoring the accumulated costs and deciding on the basis of expected future costs, operating income will be maximized (or losses minimized). The difference in favor of re-machining is Rs 3,000.

	(a) Re-machine	(b) Scrap
Future revenues	Rs 35,000	Rs 2,000
Deduct future costs	30,000	–
Operating income	Rs 5,000	Rs 2,000
Difference in favor of remachining	Rs 3,000	

2. In this situation too, the Rs 1,00,000 original cost is irrelevant to this decision. The difference in relevant costs in favor of rebuilding is Rs 7,000 as follows:

	(a) Replace	(b) Rebuild
New motor	Rs 1,02,000	–
Deduct current disposal price of existing motor	10,000	–
Rebuild existing motor	–	Rs 85,000
	Rs 92,000	Rs 85,000
Difference in favor of rebuilding	Rs 7,000	

Note, here, that the current disposal price of Rs 10,000 is relevant, but the original cost (or book value, if the motor were not brand new) is irrelevant.

11-17 The careening personal computer. (W. A. Paton) An employee in the accounting Department of a company was moving a personal computer from one room to another. As he came alongside an open stairway, he slipped and the computer got away from him. It careened down the stairs with a great racket and wound up at the bottom, completely destroyed. Hearing the crash, the office manager came rushing out and turned rather pale when he saw what had happened. "Someone tell me quickly," the manager yelled, "if that is one of our fully depreciated items." A check of the accounting records showed that the smashed computer was, indeed, one of those items that had been written off. "Thank God!" exclaimed the manager.

Required Explain and comment on the point of this anecdote.

Solution

The careening personal computer.

Considered alone, book value is irrelevant as a measure of loss when equipment is destroyed. The measure of the loss is replacement cost or some computation of the present value of future services lost because of equipment loss or damage. In the specific case described, the following observations may be appropriate:

1. A fully depreciated item probably is relatively old. Chances are that the loss from this equipment is less than the loss for a partially depreciated item because the replacement cost of an old item would be far less than that for a nearly new item.
2. The loss of an old item, assuming replacement is necessary, automatically accelerates the timing of replacement. Thus, if the old item were to be junked and replaced tomorrow, no economic loss would be evident. However, if the old item were supposed to last five more years, replacement is accelerated five years. The best practical measure of such a loss probably would be the cost of comparable used equipment that had five years of remaining useful life.

The fact that the computer was fully depreciated also means the accounting reports will not be affected by the accident. If accounting reports are used to evaluate the office manager's performance, the manager will prefer any accidents to be on fully depreciated units.

11-18 Special order, activity-based costing. (CMA, adapted) The Tanisque Company manufactures medals for winners of athletic events and other contests. Its manufacturing plant has the capacity to produce 10,000 medals each month. Current production and sales are 7,500 medals per month. The company normally charges Rs 150 per medal. Cost information for the current activity level is as follows:

Variable costs that vary with number of units produced	
Direct materials	Rs 2,62,500
Direct manufacturing labor	3,00,000
Variable costs (for setup materials handling quality control and so on) that vary with number of batches 150 batches x Rs 500 per batch	75,000
Fixed manufacturing costs	2,75,000
Fixed marketing costs	1,75,000
Total costs	10,87,500

Tanisque has just received a special one-time-only order for 2,500 medals at Rs 100 per medal. Accepting the special order would not affect the company's regular business. Tanisque makes medals for its existing customers in batch sizes of 50 medals (150 batches × 50 medals per batch = 7,500 medals). The special order requires Tanisque to make medals in 25 batches of 100 each.

Required

1. Should Tanisque accept this special order? Show your calculations.
2. Suppose plant capacity were only 9,000 medals instead of 10,000 medals each month. The special order must either be taken in full or rejected completely. Should Tanisque accept the special order? Show your calculations.
3. As in requirement (1), assume that monthly capacity is 10,000 medals. Tanisque is concerned that if it accepts the special order, its existing customers will immediately demand a price discount of Rs 10 in the month in which the special order is being filled. They would argue that Tanisque's capacity costs are now being spread over more units and that existing customers should get the benefit of these lower costs should Tanisque accept the special order under these conditions? Show your calculations.

Solution

Special order, activity-based costing (CMA, adapted).

1. Tanisque's operating income under the alternatives of accepting/rejecting the special order are:

	Without One-Time Only Special Order 7,500 Units	With One-Time Only Special Order 10,000 Units	Difference 2,500 Units
Revenues	Rs 11,25,000	Rs 13,75,000	Rs 2,50,000
Variable costs:			
Direct materials	2,62,500	35,00,00[1]	87,500

Direct manufacturing labor	3,00,000	40,00,00²	1,00,000
Batch manufacturing costs	75,000	8,75,00³	12,500
Fixed costs:			
Fixed manufacturing costs	2,75,000	2,75,000	–
Fixed marketing costs	1,75,000	1,75,000	–
Total costs	10,87,500	12,87,500	2,00,000
Operating income	Rs 37,500	Rs 87,500	Rs 50,000

$^1\frac{\text{Rs } 2,62,500}{7,500} \times 10,000$ $^2\frac{\text{Rs } 3,00,000}{7,500} \times 10,000$ ^{3}Rs 75,000 + (25 × Rs 500)

Alternatively, we can calculate the incremental revenue and the incremental costs of the additional 2,500 units as follows:

Incremental revenue Rs 100 × 2,500	Rs 2,50,000
Incremental direct manufacturing costs (Rs 2,62,500/7,500) × 2,500	87,500
Incremental direct manufacturing costs (Rs 3,00,000/7,500) × 2,500	1,00,000
Incremental batch manufacturing costs Rs 500 × 25	12,500
Total incremental costs	2,00,000
Total incremental operating income from accepting the special order	Rs 50,000

Tanisque should accept the one-time-only special order if it has no long-term implications because accepting the order increases Tanisque's operating income by Rs 50,000.

If, however, accepting the special order would cause the regular customers to be dissatisfied or to demand lower prices, then Tanisque will have to trade off the Rs 50,000 gain from accepting the special order against the operating income it might lose from regular customers.

2. Tanisque has a capacity of 9,000 medals. Therefore, if it accepts the special one-time order of 2,500 medals, it can sell only 6,500 medals instead of the 7,500 medals that it currently sells to existing customers. That is, by accepting the special order, Tanisque must forgo sales of 1,000 medals to its regular customers. Alternatively, Tanisque can reject the special order and continue to sell 7,500 medals to its regular customers.

Tanisque's operating income from selling 6,500 medals to regular customers and 2,500 medals under one-time special order follows:

Revenues (6,500 × Rs 150) + (2,500 × Rs 100)	Rs 12,25,000
Direct materials (6,500 × Rs 35¹) + (2,500 × Rs 35¹)	3,15,000
Direct manufacturing labor (6,500 × Rs 40²) + (2,500 × Rs 40²)	3,60,000
Batch manufacturing costs (130³ × Rs 500) + (25 × Rs 500)	77,500
Fixed manufacturing costs	2,75,000
Fixed marketing costs	1,75,000
Total costs	12,02,500
Operating income	Rs 22,500

$^1\text{Rs } 35 = \frac{\text{Rs } 2,62,500}{7,500}$ $^2\text{Rs } 40 = \frac{\text{Rs } 3,00,000}{7,500}$

³Tanisque makes regular medals in batch sizes of 50. To produce 6,500 medals requires 130 (6,500 ÷ 50) batches.

Accepting the special order will result in a decrease in operating income of Rs 15,000 (Rs 37,500 – Rs 22,500). The special order should, therefore, be rejected.

A more direct approach would be to focus on the incremental effects—the benefits of accepting the special order of 2,500 units versus the costs of selling 1,000 fewer units to regular customers. Increase in operating income from the 2,500-unit special order equals Rs 50,000 (requirement 1). The loss in operating income from selling 1,000 fewer units to regular customers equals:

Lost revenue Rs 150 × 1,000	Rs (1,50,000)
Savings in direct materials costs Rs 35 × 1,000	35,000
Savings in direct manufacturing labor costs Rs 40 × 1,000	40,000
Savings in batch manufacturing costs Rs 500 × 20	10,000
Operating income lost	Rs (65,000)

Accepting the special order will result in a decrease in operating income of Rs 15,000 (Rs 50,000 – Rs 65,000). The special order should, therefore, be rejected.

3. Tanisque should not accept the special order.

Increase in operating income by selling 2,500 units under the special order (requirement 1)	Rs 50,000
Operating income lost from existing customers (Rs 10 × 7,500)	(75,000)
Net effect on operating income of accepting special order	Rs (25,000)

The special order should, therefore, be rejected.

11-19 Make versus buy, activity-based costing. The Bharti Televentures manufactures cellular modems. It manufactures its own cellular modem circuit boards (CMCB), an important part of the cellular modem. It reports the following cost information about the costs of making CMCBs in 2011 and the expected costs in 2012:

	Current Costs in 2011	Expected Costs in 2012
Variable manufacturing costs		
Direct material cost per CMCB	Rs 1,800	Rs 1,700
Direct manufacturing labor cost per CMCB	500	450
Variable manufacturing cost per batch for setups, material handling, and quality control	16,000	15,000
Fixed manufacturing cost		
Fixed manufacturing overhead costs that can be avoided if CMCBs are not made	32,00,000	32,00,000
Fixed manufacturing overhead costs of plant depreciation, insurance, and administration that cannot be avoided even if CMCBs are not made	80,00,000	80,00,000

Bharti manufactured 8,000 CMCBs in 2006 in 40 batches of 200 each. In 2012, Bharti anticipates a requirement of 10,000 CMCBs. The CMCBs would be needed in 80 batches of 125 each.

The Reliance Infocom has approached Bharti about supplying CMCBs to Bharti in 2012 at Rs 3,000 per CMCB on whatever delivery schedule Bharti wants.

Required

1. Calculate the total expected manufacturing cost per unit of making CMCBs in 2012.
2. Suppose the capacity currently used to make CMCBs will become idle if Bharti purchases CMCBs from Reliance. On the basis of financial considerations alone, should Bharti make CMCBs or buy them from Reliance? Show your calculations.
3. Now suppose that if Bharti purchases CMCBs from Reliance, its best alternative use of the capacity currently used for CMCBs is to make and sell special circuit boards (CB3s) to the Airtel Corporation. Bharti estimates the following incremental revenues and costs from CB3s:

Total expected incremental future revenues	Rs 2,00,00,000
Total expected incremental future costs	Rs 2,15,00,000

On the basis of financial considerations alone, should Bharti make CMCBs or buy them from Reliance? Show your calculations.

Solution

Make versus buy, activity-based costing.

1. The expected manufacturing cost per unit of CMCBs in 2012 is as follows:

	Total Manufacturing Costs of CMCB (1)	Manufacturing Cost per Unit (2) = (1) ÷ 10,000
Direct materials Rs 1,700 × 10,000	Rs 1,70,00,000	Rs 1,700
Direct manufacturing labor Rs 450 × 10,000	45,00,000	450
Variable batch manufacturing costs Rs 15,000 × 80	12,00,000	120
Fixed manufacturing costs		
Avoidable fixed manufacturing costs	32,00,000	320
Unavoidable fixed manufacturing costs	80,00,000	800
Total manufacturing costs	Rs 3,39,00,000	Rs 3,390

2. The following table identifies the incremental costs in 2012 if Bharti (a) made CMCBs and (b) purchased CMCBs from Reliance.

Incremental Items	Total Incremental Costs Make	Total Incremental Costs Buy	Per-Unit Incremental Costs Make	Per-Unit Incremental Costs Buy
Cost of purchasing CMCBs from Reliance		Rs 3,00,00,000		Rs 3,000
Direct materials	Rs 1,70,00,000		Rs 1,700	
Direct manufacturing labor	45,00,000		450	
Variable batch manufacturing costs	12,00,000		120	
Avoidable fixed manufacturing costs	32,00,000		320	
Total incremental costs	Rs 2,59,00,000	Rs 3,00,00,000	Rs 2,590	Rs 3,000
Difference in favor of making	↑ Rs 41,00,000 ↑		↑ Rs 410 ↑	

Note that the opportunity cost of using capacity to make CMCBs is zero since Bharti would keep this capacity idle if it purchases CMCBs from Reliance.

Bharti should continue to manufacture the CMCBs internally since the incremental costs to manufacture are Rs 2,590 per unit compared to the Rs 3,000 per unit that Reliance has quoted. Note that the unavoidable fixed manufacturing costs of Rs 80,00,000 (Rs 800 per unit) will continue to be incurred whether Bharti makes or buys CMCBs. These are not incremental costs under either the make or the buy alternative and are, hence, irrelevant.

3. Bharti should continue to make CMCBs. The simplest way to analyze this problem is to recognize that Bharti would prefer to keep any excess capacity idle rather than use it to make CB3s. Why? Because expected incremental future revenues from CB3s, Rs 2,00,00,000 are less than expected incremental future costs, Rs 2,15,00,000. If Bharti keeps its capacity idle, we know from requirement 2 that it should make CMCBs rather than buy them.

An important point to note is that, because Bharti forgoes no contribution by not being able to make and sell CB3s, the opportunity cost of using its facilities to make CMCBs is zero. It is, therefore, not forgoing any profits by using the capacity to manufacture CMCBs. If it does not manufacture CMCBs, rather than lose money on CB3s, Bharti will keep capacity idle.

A longer and more detailed approach is to use the total alternatives or opportunity cost analyses shown in Exhibit 11-7 of the chapter.

	Choices for Bharti		
Relevant Items	**Make CMCBs and Do Not Make CB3s**	**Buy CMCBs and Do Not Make CB3s**	**Buy CMCBs and Make CB3s**
Total-alternatives approach to make-or-buy decisions			
Total incremental costs of making/buying CMCBs (from requirement 2)	Rs 2,59,00,000	Rs 3,00,00,000	Rs 3,00,00,000
Excess of future costs over future revenues from CB3s	0	0	15,00,000
Total relevant costs	Rs 2,59,00,000	Rs 3,00,00,000	Rs 3,15,00,000
Bharti will minimize manufacturing costs by making CMCBs.			
Opportunity-cost approach to make-or-buy decisions			
Total incremental costs of making/buying CMCBs (from requirement 2)	Rs 2,59,00,000	Rs 3,00,00,000	Rs 3,00,00,000
Opportunity cost: profit contribution forgone because capacity will not be used to make CB3s	0*	0*	0
Total relevant costs	2,59,00,000	3,00,00,000	3,00,00,000

*Opportunity cost is 0 because Bharti does not give up anything by not making CB3s. Bharti is best off leaving the capacity idle (rather than manufacturing and selling CB3s).

11-20 Selection of most profitable product. Children Toy Company produces two models of toy Car, Deluxe and Super. Pertinent data are as follows:

	Per Unit	
	Deluxe	**Super**
Selling price	Rs 100.00	Rs 70.00
Costs		
Direct material	28.00	13.00
Direct manufacturing labor	15.00	25.00
Variable manufacturing overhead*	25.00	12.50
Fixed manufacturing overhead*	10.00	5.00
Marketing (all variable)	14.00	10.00
Total cost	92.00	65.50
Operating income	8.00	4.50

* Allocated on the basis of machine-hours.

The car craze is such that enough of either Deluxe or Super can be sold to keep the plant operating at full capacity. Both products are processed through the same production departments.

Which products should be produced? Briefly explain your answer. **Required**

Solution

Selection of most profitable product.

Only Super model should be produced. The key to this problem is the relationship of manufacturing overhead to each product. Note that it takes twice as long to produce Deluxe; machine-hours for Deluxe model are twice that for Super model. Management should choose the product mix that maximizes operating income for a given production capacity (the scarce resource in this situation). In this case, Super model will yield a Rs 9.50 contribution to fixed costs per machine hour, and Deluxe model will yield Rs 9.00:

	Deluxe	Super
Selling price	Rs 100.00	Rs 70.00
Variable costs per unit	82.00	60.50
Contribution margin per unit	Rs 18.00	Rs 9.50
Relative use of machine-hours per unit of product	÷ 2	÷ 1
Contribution margin per machine hour	Rs 9.00	Rs 9.50

11-21 Which base to close, relevant-cost analysis, opportunity costs. The Indian Defense Department has the difficult decision of deciding which military bases to shut down. Military and political factors obviously matter, but cost savings are also an important factor. Consider two naval bases one located on the West Coast and the other on South Coast. The Navy has decided that it needs only one of those two bases permanently, so one must be shut down. The decision regarding which base to shut down will be made on cost considerations alone. The following information is available:

a. The West Coast base was built at a cost of Rs 100 crore. The operating costs of the base are Rs 400 crore per year. The base is built on land owned by the Navy, so the Navy pays nothing for the use of the property. If the base is closed, the land will be sold to developers for Rs 500 crore.

b. The South Coast base was built at a cost of Rs 150 crore on land leased by the Navy from private citizens. The Navy can choose to lease the land permanently for a lease payment of Rs 3 crore per year. If it decides to keep the South Coast base open, the Navy plans to invest Rs 60 crore in a fixed income note, which at 5% interest will earn the Rs 3 crore the government needs for the lease payments. The land and buildings will immediately revert back to the owner if the base is closed. The operating costs of the base, excluding lease payments, are Rs 300 crore per year.

c. If the West Coast base is shut down, the Navy will have to transfer some personnel to the South Coast facility. As a result, the yearly operating costs at South Coast will increase by Rs 100 crore per year. If the South Coast facility is closed down, no extra costs will be incurred to operate the West Coast facility.

Required The Defense Department argues that it is cheaper to shut down the South Coast base for two reasons:

1. It would save Rs 100 crore per year in additional costs required to operate the South Coast base, and

2. it would save the lease payment of Rs 3 crore per year. (Recall that he West Coast base requires no cash payments for use of the land because the land is owned by the Navy). Do you agree with the Defense Department's arguments and conclusions? In your answer, identify and explain all costs that you consider relevant and all costs that you consider irrelevant for the base-closing decision.

Solution

Which base to close, relevant-cost analysis, opportunity costs.

The future outlay operating costs will be Rs 400 crore regardless of which base is closed, given the additional Rs 100 crore in costs at South Coast if West Coast is closed. Further, one of the bases will permanently remain open while the other will be shut down. The only relevant revenue and cost comparisons are:

a. Rs 500 crore from sale of the West Coast base. Note that the historical cost of building the West Coast base (Rs 100 crore) is irrelevant. Note, also, that future increases in the value of the land at the West Coast base is also irrelevant. One of the bases must be kept open, so if it is decided to keep the West Coast base open, the Defense Department will not be able to sell this land at a future date.

b. Rs 60 crore in savings in fixed income note if the South Coast base is closed. Again, the historical cost of building the South Coast base (Rs 150 crore) is irrelevant.

The relevant costs and benefits analysis favors closing the West Coast base despite the objections raised by the Defense Department. The net benefit equals Rs 440 (Rs 500 – Rs 60) crore.

11-22 Closing and opening stores. Ravi, an entrepreneur runs two convenience stores, one in Gurgaon and the other in Noida. Operating income for each store in 2011 is as follows:

	Gurgaon Store	Noida Store
Revenues	Rs 1,07,00,000	Rs 86,00,000
Operating costs.		
Cost of goods sold	75,00,000	66,00,000
lease rent (renewable each year)	9,00,000	7,50,000
labor costs (paid on an hourly basis)	4,20,000	4,20,000
Depreciation of equipment	2,50,000	2,20,000
Utilities (electricity heating)	4,30,000	4,60,000
Allocated corporate overhead	5,00,000	4,00,000
Total operating costs	1,00,00,000	88,50,000
Operating income (loss)	7,00,000	(2,50,000)

The equipment has a zero disposal value. Mohan the accountant makes the following comment, "Ravi can increase his profitability by closing down the Noida store or by adding another store like it."

Required

1. By closing down the Noida store, Ravi can reduce overall corporate overhead costs by Rs 4,40,000. Calculate Ravi's operating income if it closes the Noida store. Is Mohan's statement about the effect of closing the Noida store correct? Explain.
2. Calculate Ravi's operating income if it keeps the Noida store open and opens another store with revenues and costs identical to the Noida store (including a cost of Rs 2,20,000 to acquire equipment with a one-year useful life and zero disposal value). Opening this store will increase corporate overhead costs by Rs 40,000. Is Mohan's statement about the effect of adding another store like the Noida store correct? Explain.

Solution

Closing and opening stores.

1. Solution Exhibit 11-22, Column 1, presents the relevant loss in revenues and the relevant savings in costs from closing the Noida store. Mohan is correct that Ravi Corporation's operating income would increase by Rs 70,000 if it closes down the Noida store. Closing down the Noida store results in a loss of revenues of Rs 86,00,000 but cost savings of Rs 86,70,000 (from cost of goods sold, rent, labor, utilities, and corporate costs). Note that by closing down the Noida store, Ravi will save none of the equipment-related costs because this is a past cost. Also note that the relevant corporate overhead costs are the actual corporate overhead costs Rs 4,40,000 that Ravi expects to save by closing the Noida store. The corporate overhead of Rs 4,00,000 allocated to the Noida store is irrelevant to the analysis.
2. Solution Exhibit 11-22, Column 2, presents the relevant revenues and relevant costs of opening another store like the Noida store. Mohan is correct that opening such a store would increase Ravi Corporation's operating income by Rs 1,10,000. Incremental revenues of Rs 86,00,000 exceeds the incremental costs of Rs 84,90,000 (from higher cost of goods sold, rent, labor, utilities, and some additional corporate costs). Note that the cost of equipment written off as depreciation is relevant because it is an expected future cost that Ravi will incur only if it opens the new store. Also note that the relevant corporate overhead costs are the Rs 40,000 of actual corporate overhead costs that Ravi expects to incur as a result of opening the new store. Ravi may, in fact, allocate more than Rs 40,000 of corporate overhead to the new store but this allocation is irrelevant to the analysis.

The key reason that Ravi's operating income increases either if he closes down the Noida store or if it opens another store like it is the behavior of corporate overhead costs. By closing down the Noida store, Ravi can significantly reduce corporate overhead costs presumably by reducing the corporate staff that oversees the Noida operation. On the other hand, adding another store like Noida does not increase actual corporate costs by much, presumably because the existing corporate staff will be able to oversee the new store as well.

Solution Exhibit 11-22

Relevant-Revenue and Relevant-Cost Analysis of Closing Noida Store and Opening Another Store Like It.

	(Loss in Revenues) and Savings in Costs from Closing Noida Store (1)	**Incremental Revenues and (Incremental Costs) of Opening New Store Like Noida Store (2)**
Revenues	Rs (86,00,000)	Rs 86,00,000
Cost of goods sold	66,00,000	(66,00,000)
Lease rent	7,50,000	(7,50,000)
Labor costs	4,20,000	(4,20,000)
Depreciation of equipment	0	(2,20,000)
Utilities (electricity heating)	4,60,000	(4,60,000)
Corporate overhead costs	4,40,000	(40,000)
Total costs	86,70,000	(84,90,000)
Effect on operating income (loss)	Rs 70,000	Rs 1,10,000

11-23 Relevance of equipment costs. The Auto Wash Company has just today paid for and installed a special machine for polishing cars at one of its several outlets. It is the first day of the company's fiscal year. The machine costs Rs 2,00,000. Its annual cash operating costs total Rs 1,50,000. The machine will have a four year useful life and a zero terminal disposal value.

After the machine has been used for only one day, a salesperson offers a different machine that promises to do the same job at annual cash operating costs of Rs 90,000. The new machine will cost Rs 2,40,000 cash, installed. The "old" machine is unique and can be sold outright for only Rs 1,00,000, minus Rs 20,000 removal cost The new machine, like the old one, will have a four-year useful life and zero terminal disposal value. Revenues, all in cash, will be Rs 15,00,000 annually, and other cash costs will be Rs 11,00,000 annually, regardless of this decision.

For simplicity, ignore income taxes and the time value of money

Required

1. (a) Prepare a statement of cash receipts and disbursement for each of the four years under each alternative. What is the cumulative difference in cash flow for the four years taken together? (b) Prepare income statements for each of the four years under each alternative. Assume straight-line depreciation. What is the cumulative difference in operating income for the four years taken together? (c) What are the irrelevant items in your presentations in requirements (a) and (b)? Why are they irrelevant?
2. Suppose the cost of the "old" machine was Rs 10 lakh rather than Rs 20,000. Nevertheless, the old machine can be sold outright for only Rs 10,000, minus Rs 2,000 removal cost. Would the net differences in requirements 1(a) and 1(b) change? Explain.
3. Is there any conflict between the decision model and the incentives of the manager who has just purchased the "old" machine and is considering replacing it a day later?

Solution

Relevance of equipment costs.

1. (a) Statements of Cash Receipts and Disbursements

	Keep			Buy New Machine		
	Year 1	Year 2, 3, 4	Four Years Together	Year 1	Year 2, 3, 4	Four Years Together
Receipts from operations						
Revenues	Rs 15,00,000	Rs 15,00,000	Rs 60,00,000	Rs 15,00,000	Rs 15,00,000	Rs 60,00,000
Deduct disbursements						
Other operating costs	(11,00,000)	(11,00,000)	(44,00,000)	(11,00,000)	(11,00,000)	(44,00,000)
Operation of machine	(1,50,000)	(1,50,000)	(6,00,000)	(90,000)	(90,000)	(3,60,000)
Purchase of "old" machine	(2,00,000)*		(2,00,000)	(2,00,000)		(2,00,000)
Purchase of "new" equipment				(2,40,000)		(2,40,000)
Cash inflow from sale of old equipment				80,000		80,000
Net cash inflow	50,000	2,50,000	8,00,000	(50,000)	3,10,000	8,80,000

**Prima-facie*, it appears that Rs 2,00,000 on buying a machine should be ignored because it is the same for each alternative. However, note that a statement for the *entire year* has been required. Obviously, the Rs 2,00,000 would affect Year 1 only under both the "keep" and "buy" alternatives.

The difference is Rs 80,000 for four years taken together. In particular, note that the Rs 2,00,000 book value can be omitted from the comparison. Merely cross out the entire line; although the column totals are affected, the net difference is still Rs 80,000.

1. (b) Again, the difference is Rs 80,000

Income Statements

	Keep		Buy New Machine		
	Year 1, 2, 3, 4	Four Years Together	Year 1	Year 2, 3, 4	Four Years Together
Revenues	Rs 15,00,000	Rs 60,00,000	Rs 15,00,000	Rs 15,00,000	Rs 60,00,000
Costs (excluding disposal)					
Other operating costs	11,00,000	44,00,000	11,00,000	11,00,000	44,00,000
Depreciation	50,000	2,00,000	60,000	60,000	2,40,000
Operating costs of machine	1,50,000	6,00,000	90,000	90,000	3,60,000
Total costs (excluding disposal)	13,00,000	52,00,000	12,50,000	12,50,000	50,00,000
Loss on disposal					
Book value ("cost")			2,00,000		2,00,000*
Proceeds ("revenue")			(80,000)		(80,000)
Loss on disposal			1,20,000		1,20,000
Total costs	13,00,000	52,00,000	13,70,000	12,50,000	51,20,000
Operating income	Rs 2,00,000	Rs 8,00,000	Rs 1,30,000	Rs 2,50,000	Rs 8,80,000

*As in part (1), the Rs 2,00,000 book value may be omitted from the comparison without changing the Rs 80,000 difference. This adjustment would mean excluding the depreciation item of Rs 50,000 per year (a cumulative effect of Rs 2,00,000) under the "keep" alternative and excluding the book value item of Rs 2,00,000 in the loss on disposal computation under the "buy" alternative.

1. **(c)** The Rs 2,00,000 purchase cost of the old equipment, the revenues, and the other costs are irrelevant because their amounts are common to both alternatives.

2. The net difference would be unaffected. Any number may be substituted for the original Rs 2,00,000 figure without changing the final answer. Of course, the net cash outflows under both alternatives would be high. The Auto Wash manager really blundered. However, keeping the old equipment will increase the cost of the blunder to the cumulative tune of Rs 80,000 over the next four years.
3. Book value is irrelevant in decisions about the replacement of equipment, because it is a past (historical) cost. All past costs are sunk costs/down the drain. Nothing can change what has already been spent or what has already happened. The Rs 2,00,000 has been spent. How it is subsequently accounted for is irrelevant. The analysis in requirement (1) clearly shows that we may completely ignore the Rs 2,00,000 and still have a correct analysis. The only relevant items are those expected future items that will differ among alternatives.

Despite the economic analysis shown here, many managers would keep the old machine rather than replace it. Why? Because, in many organizations, the income statements of part (2) would be a principal means of evaluating performance. Note that the first-year operating income would be higher under the "keep" alternative. The conventional accrual accounting model might motivate managers toward maximizing their first-year reported operating income at the expense of long-run cumulative betterment for the organization as a whole. This criticism is often made of the accrual accounting model. That is, the action favored by the "correct" or "best" economic decision model may not be taken because the performance-evaluation model is either inconsistent with the decision model or because the focus is on only the short-run part of the performance-evaluation model.

There is yet another potential conflict between the decision model and the performance-evaluation model. Replacing the machine so soon after it is purchased may reflect badly on the manager's capabilities and performance. Why didn't the manager search and find the new machine before buying the old machine? Replacing the old machine one day later at a loss may make the manager appear incompetent to his or her superiors. If the manager's bosses have no knowledge of the better machine, the manager may prefer to keep the existing machine rather than alert his or her bosses about the better machine.

11-24 Contribution approach, relevant costs. Jet Airways has leased a single jet aircraft that it operates between Delhi and Bangalore. Only economy class seats are available on this plane. An analyst has collected the following information:

Seating capacity per plane	360 passengers
Average number of passengers per flight	200 passengers
Average one-way fare	Rs 5,000
Variable fuel costs	Rs 1,40,000 per flight
Food and beverage service costs (no charge to passenger)	Rs 200 per passenger
Commission to travel agents paid by Air India(all tickets are booked by travel agents)	8 % of fare
Fixed annual lease costs allocated to each flight	Rs 5,30,000 per flight
Fixed ground-services (maintenance, check in, baggage handling) costs allocated to each flight	Rs 70,000 per flight
Fixed flight-crew salaries allocated to each flight	Rs 40,000 per flight

For simplicity, assume that fuel costs are unaffected by the actual number of passengers on a flight.

Required

1. Calculate the total contribution margin from passenger that Jet Airways earns on each one-way flight between Delhi and Bangalore.
2. The Market Research Department of Jet Airways indicates that lowering the average one-way fare to Rs 4,800 will increase the average number of passenger per flight to 212. On the basis of financial considerations alone, should Jet Airways lower its fare? Show your calculations.
3. Travel International, a tour operator, approaches Jet Airways on the possibility of chartering its aircraft. The terms of charter are as follows: (a) For each one-way flight, Travel International will pay Jet Airways Rs 7,45,000 to charter the plane and to use its flight crew and ground-service staff; (b) Travel International will pay for fuel costs; and (c) Travel International will pay for all food costs. On the basis of financial considerations alone, should Jet Airways accept Travel International offer? Show your calculations. What other factors should Jet Airways consider in deciding whether to charter its plane to Travel International?

Solution

Contribution approach, relevant costs.

1.

Average one-way fare per passenger	Rs 5,000
Commission at 8% of Rs 5,000	400
Net cash to Jet Airways per ticket	Rs 4,600
Average number of passengers per flight	× 200
Revenues per flight (Rs 4,600 × 200)	Rs 9,20,000
Food and beverage cost per flight (Rs 200 × 200)	40,000
Total contribution margin from passengers per flight	Rs 8,80,000

2. If fare is

If fare is	Rs	4,800
Commission at 8% of Rs 4,800		384
Net cash per ticket		4,416
Food and beverage cost per ticket		200
Contribution margin per passenger	Rs	4,216
Total contribution margin from passengers per flight (Rs 4,216 × 212)	Rs	8,93,792

All other costs are irrelevant.

On the basis of quantitative factors alone, Jet Airways should decrease its fare to Rs 4,800 because reducing the fare gives Jet Airways a higher contribution margin from passengers (Rs 8,93,792 versus Rs 8,80,000).

3. In evaluating whether Jet Airways should charter its plane to Travel International, we compare the charter alternative to the solution in requirement 2 because requirement 2 is preferred to requirement 1.

Under requirement 2, contribution from passengers	Rs 8,93,792
Deduct fuel costs	1,40,000
Total contribution per flight	Rs 7,53,792

Jet Airways gets Rs 7,45,000 per flight from chartering the plane to Travel International. On the basis of quantitative financial factors, Jet Airways is better off not chartering the plane and, instead, lowering its own fares.

Other qualitative factors that Jet Airways should consider in coming to a decision are:

a. The lower risk from chartering its plane relative to the uncertainties regarding the number of passengers it might get on its scheduled flights.

b. The stability of the relationship between Jet Airways and Travel International. If this is not a long-term arrangement, Jet Airways may lose current market share and not benefit from sustained charter revenues.

11-25 Relevant costs, opportunity costs. Rizwan, the general manager of Infosys, is to decide when to release the new version of Infosys's spreadsheet package, Easyspread 2.0. Development of Easyspread 2.0 is complete. However, the diskettes, compact discs, and user manuals have not yet been produced. The product can be shipped starting 2012.

The key problem is that Infosys has overstocked the previous version of its spreadsheet package, Easyspread 1.0. Rizwan knows that once Easyspread 2.0 is introduced, Infosys will not be able to sell any more units of Easyspread 1.0. Rather than just throwing away the inventory of Easyspread 1.0, Rizwan is wondering if it might be better to continue to sell Easyspread 1.0 for next three months and introduce Easyspread 2.0 on April 1, 2012, when the inventory of Easyspread 1.0 will be sold out.

The following information is available:

	Easyspread 1.0	Easyspread 2.0
Selling price	Rs 1,500	Rs 1,850
Variable cost per unit of diskettes, compact discs, user manuals	200	250
Development cost per unit	650	950
Marketing and administrative cost per unit	350	400
Total cost per unit	1,200	1,600
Operating income per unit	300	250

Development cost per unit for each product equals the total costs of developing the software product divided by the anticipated unit sales over the life of the product. Marketing and administrative costs are fixed costs in 2012, incurred to support all marketing and administrative activities of Infosys. Marketing and administrative costs are allocated to products on the basis of the budgeted revenues of each product. The preceding unit costs assume Easyspread 2.0 will be introduced on April 1, 2012.

Required

1. On the basis of financial considerations alone, should Rizwan introduce Easyspread 2.0 on 2012, or wait until April 1, 2012? Show your calculations, clearly identifying relevant and irrelevant revenues and costs.
2. What other factors might Rizwan consider in making a decision?

Solution

Relevant costs, opportunity costs.

1. Easyspread 2.0 has a higher relevant operating income than Easyspread 1.0. Based on this analysis, Easyspread 2.0 should be introduced immediately.

	Easyspread 1.0	Easyspread 2.0
Relevant revenues	Rs 1,500	Rs 1,850

Relevant costs:		
Manuals, diskettes, compact discs	Re 0	Rs 250
Total relevant costs	0	250
Relevant operating income	Rs 1,500	Rs 1,600

Reasons for other cost items being irrelevant are:

Easyspread 1.0

- Manuals, diskettes-already incurred
- Development costs-already incurred
- Marketing and administrative-fixed costs of period

Easyspread 2.0

- Development costs-already incurred
- Marketing and administration-fixed costs of period

Note that total marketing and administration costs will not change whether Easyspread 2.0 is introduced on January 1, 2012, or on April 1, 2012.

2. Other factors to be considered:
   a. **Customer satisfaction.** If 2.0 is significantly better than 1.0 for its customers, a customer driven organization would immediately introduce it unless other factors offset this bias towards "do what is best for the customer."
   b. **Quality level of Easyspread 2.0.** It is critical for new software products to be fully debugged. Easyspread 2.0 must be error-free. Consider an immediate release only if 2.0 passes all quality tests and can be fully supported by the salesforce.
   c. **Importance of being perceived to be a market leader.** Being first in the market with a new product can give Infosys a "first-mover advantage," e.g., capturing an initial large share of the market that, in itself, causes future potential customers to lean towards purchasing Easyspread 2.0. Moreover, by introducing 2.0 earlier, Infosys can get quick feedback from users about ways to further refine the software while its competitors are still working on their own first versions. Moreover, by locking in early customers, Infosys may increase the likelihood of these customers also buying future upgrades of Easyspread 2.0.
   d. **Morale of developers.** These are key people at Infosys. Delaying introduction of a new product can hurt their morale, especially if a competitor then preempts Infosys from being viewed as a market leader.

11-26 Product mix, relevant costs. Hindustan Machine Tools (HMT) makes cutting tools for metalworking operations. It makes two types of tools: R3, a regular cutting tool, and HP6, a high-precision cutting tool. R3 is manufactured on a regular machine, but HP6 must be manufactured on both the regular machine and a high-precision machine. The following information is available:

	R3	HP6
Selling price	Rs 1,000	Rs 1,500
Variable manufacturing cost per unit	600	1,000
Variable marketing cost per unit	150	350
Budgeted total fixed overhead costs	35,00,000	55,00,000
Hours required to produce 1 unit on the regular machine	1.0	0.5

Additional information includes:

a. HMT faces a capacity constraint on the regular machine of 50,000 hours per year.
b. The capacity of the high-precision machine is not a constraint
c. Of the Rs 55,00,000 budgeted fixed overhead costs of HP6, Rs 30,00,000 are lease payments for the high-precision machine. This cost is charged entirely to HP6 because HMT uses the machine exclusively to produce HP6. The lease agreement for the high-precision machine can be canceled at any time with out penalties.
d. All other overhead costs are fixed and cannot be changed.

Required

1. What product mix-that is, how many units of R3 and HP6-will maximize HMT's operating income?
2. Suppose HMT can increase the annual capacity of regular machines by 15,000 machine-hours at a cost of Rs 15,00,000. Should HMT increase the capacity of regular machines by 15,000 machine hours? By how much will HMT's operating income increase? Show your calculations.
3. Suppose that the capacity of the regular machines has been increased to 65,000 hours. HMT has been approached by Titan to supply 20,000 units of another cutting tool, S3, for Rs 1,200 per unit. HMT must either accept the order for all 20,000 units or reject it totally. S3 is exactly like R3 except that its variable manufacturing costs are Rs 700 per unit (It takes one hour to produce one unit of S3 on the regular machine, and variable marketing costs equal Rs 150 per unit) What product mix should HMT choose to maximize operating income? Show your calculations.

Solution

Product mix, relevant costs

1.

	R3	HP6
Selling price	Rs 1,000	Rs 1,500
Variable manufacturing cost per unit	600	1,000
Variable marketing cost per unit	150	350
Total variable costs per unit	750	1,350
Contribution margin per unit	Rs 250	Rs 150

Contribution margin per hour of the constrained resource (the regular machine)

$$\frac{\text{Rs } 250}{1} = \text{Rs } 250 \qquad \frac{\text{Rs } 15}{1} = \text{Rs } 300$$

Total contribution margin from selling only R3 or only HP6 R3: Rs 250 × 50,000; HP6: Rs 300 × 50,000	Rs 1,25,00,000	Rs 1,50,00,000
Less Lease costs of high-precision machine to produce and sell HP6	–	30,00,000
Net relevant benefit	Rs 1,25,00,000	Rs 1,20,00,000

Even though HP6 has the higher contribution margin per unit of the constrained resource, the fact that HMT must incur additional costs of Rs 30,00,000 to achieve this higher contribution margin means that HMT is better off using its entire 50,000-hour capacity on the regular machine to produce and sell 50,000 units (50,000 hours ÷ 1 hour per unit) of R3. The additional contribution from selling HP6 rather than R3 is Rs 25,00,000 (Rs 1,50,00,000 – Rs 1,25,00,000), which is not enough to cover the additional costs of leasing the high-precision machine. Note that, because all other overhead costs are fixed and cannot be changed, they are irrelevant for the decision.

2. If capacity of the regular machines is increased by 15,000 machine-hours to 65,000 machine-hours (50,000 originally + 15,000 new), the net relevant benefit from producing R3 and HP6 is as follows:

	R3	HP6
Total contribution margin from selling only R3 or only HP6 R3: Rs 250 × 65,000; HP6: Rs 300 × 65,000	Rs 1,62,50,000	Rs 1,95,00,000
Less Lease costs of high-precision machine that would be incurred if HP6 is produced and sold	–	30,00,000
Less Cost of increasing capacity by 15,000 hours on regular machine	15,00,000	15,00,000
Net relevant benefit	Rs 1,47,50,000	Rs 1,50,00,000

Investing in the additional capacity increases HMT's operating income by Rs 25,00,000 (Rs 1,50,00,000 calculated in requirement 2 *minus* Rs 1,25,00,000 calculated in requirement 1), so HMT should add 15,000 hours to the regular machine. With the extra capacity available to it, HMT should use its entire capacity to produce HP6. Using all 65,000 hours of capacity to produce HP6 rather than to produce R3 generates additional contribution margin of Rs 32,50,000 (Rs 1,95,00,000 – Rs 1,62,50,000) which is more than the additional cost of Rs 30,00,000 to lease the high-precision machine. HMT should therefore produce and sell 1,30,000 units of HP6 (65,000 hours ÷ 0.5 hours per unit of HP6) and zero units of R3.

3.

	R3	HP	S3
Selling price	Rs 1,000	Rs 1,500	Rs 1,200
Variable manufacturing costs per unit	600	1,000	700
Variable marketing costs per unit	150	350	150
Total variable costs per unit	750	1,350	850
Contribution margin per unit	Rs 250	Rs 150	Rs 350

Contribution margin per hour of the constraned resource (the regular machine)

$$\frac{\text{Rs } 250}{1} = \text{Rs } 250 \qquad \frac{\text{Rs } 15}{0.5} = \text{Rs } 300 \qquad \frac{\text{Rs } 350}{1} = \text{Rs } 350$$

The first step is to compare the operating profits that HMT could earn if it accepted the Titan Corporation offer for 20,000 units with the operating profits HMT is currently earning. S3 has the highest contribution margin per hour on the regular machine and requires no additional investment such as leasing a high-precision machine. To produce the 20,000 units of S3 requested by Titan Corporation, HMT would require 20,000 hours on the regular machine resulting in contribution margin of Rs 350 × 20,000 = Rs 70,00,000.

HMT now has 45,000 hours available on the regular machine to produce R3 or HP6.

	R3	HP6
Total contribution margin from only selling R3 or only HP6		
R3: Rs 250 × 45,000; HP6: Rs 300 × 45,000	Rs 1,12,50,000	Rs 1,35,00,000
Less Lease costs of high-precision machine to produce and sell HP 6	–	30,00,000
Net relevant benefit	Rs 1,12,50,000	Rs 1,05,00,000

HMT should use all the 45,000 hours of available capacity to produce 45,000 units of R3. Thus, the product mix that maximizes operating income is 20,000 units of S3, 45,000 units of R3, and zero units of HP6. This optimal mix results in a contribution margin of Rs 1,82,50,000 (Rs 70,00,000 from S3 and Rs 1,12,50,000 from R3). Relative to requirement 2, operating income increases by Rs 32,50,000 (Rs 1,82,50,000 minus Rs 1,50,00,000 calculated in requirement 2). Hence, HMT should accept the Titan business and supply 20,000 units of S3.

11-27 Discontinuing a product line, selling more units. The Northern Division of Steel Craft and Furnishings makes and sells tables and beds. The following estimated revenue and cost information from the division's activity-based costing system is available for 2011.

	4,000 Tables	5,000 Beds	Total
Revenues (Rs 1,250 × 4,000; Rs 2,000 × 5,000)	Rs 50,00,000	Rs 1,00,00,000	Rs 1,50,00,000
Variable direct materials and direct manufacturing labor costs (Rs 750 × 4,000; Rs 1,050 × 5,000)	30,00,000	52,50,000	82,50,000
Depreciation on equipment used exclusively by each product line	4,20,000	5,80,000	10,00,000
Marketing and distribution costs Rs 4,00,000 (fixed) + Rs 7,500 per consignment × 40 consignments Rs 6,00,000 (fixed) + Rs 7,500 per consignment × 100 consignments	7,00,000	13,50,000	20,50,000
Fixed general administration costs of the division allocated to product lines on the basis of revenues	11,00,000	22,00,000	33,00,000
Allocated corporate-office costs allocated to product lines on the basis of revenues	5,00,000	10,00,000	15,00,000
Total costs	57,20,000	1,03,80,000	1,61,00,000
Operating income (loss)	Rs (7,20,000)	Rs (3,80,000)	Rs (11,00,000)

Additional information includes:

a. On January I, 2011, the equipment has a book value of Rs 10,00,000 and zero disposal value. Any equipment not used will remain idle.

b. Fixed marketing and distribution costs of a product line can be avoided if the line is discontinued.

c. Fixed general administration costs of the division and corporate-office costs will not change if sales of individual product lines are increased or decreased or if product lines are added or dropped.

Required

1. On the basis of financial considerations alone, should the Northern Division discontinue the tables product line, assuming the released facilities remain idle? Show your calculations.
2. What would be the effect on Northern Division's operating income if it were to sell 4,000 more tables? Assume that to do so the division would have to acquire additional equipment costing Rs 4,20,000 with a one-year useful life and zero terminal disposal value. Assume further that the fixed marketing and distribution costs would not change but that the number of consignments would double. Show your calculations.

Solution

Discontinuing a product line, selling more units.

1. The incremental revenue losses and incremental savings in cost by discontinuing the Tables product line follows:

	Difference: Incremental(Loss in Revenues) and Savings in Costs from Dropping Tables Line
Revenues	Rs (50,00,000)
Direct materials and direct manufacturing labor	30,00,000
Depreciation on equipment	0
Marketing and distribution	7,00,000
General administration	0
Corporate office costs	0
Total costs	37,00,000
Operating income (loss)	Rs (13,00,000)

Dropping the Tables product line results in revenue losses of Rs 50,00,000 and cost savings of Rs 37,00,000. Hence, Steel Craft's and Furnishing's operating income will be Rs 13,00,000 higher if it does not drop the Tables line.

Note that, by dropping the Tables product line, Steel Craft and Furnishings will save none of the depreciation on equipment, general administration costs, and corporate office costs, but it will save variable manufacturing costs and all marketing and distribution costs on the Tables product line.

2. Steel Craft's will generate incremental operating income of Rs 12,80,000 from selling 4,000 additional tables and, hence, should try to increase table sales. The calculations follow:

	Incremental Revenues (Costs) and Operating Income
Revenues	Rs 50,00,000
Direct materials and direct manufacturing labor	(30,00,000)
Cost of equipment written off as depreciation	(4,20,000)*
Marketing and distribution costs	(3,00,000)†
General administration costs	0**
Corporate office costs	0**
Operating income	Rs 12,80,000

*Note that the additional costs of equipment are relevant future costs for the "selling more tables decision" because they represent incremental future costs that differ between the alternatives of selling and not selling additional tables.

†Current marketing and distribution costs which varies with number of consignments = Rs 7,00,000 – Rs 4,00,000 = Rs 3,00,000. As the sales of tables double, the number of consignments will double, resulting in incremental marketing and distribution costs of (2 × Rs 3,00,000) – Rs 3,00,000 = Rs 3,00,000.

**General administration and corporate office costs will be unaffected if Steel Craft and Furnishings decides to sell more tables. Hence, these costs are irrelevant for the decision.

11-28 Discontinuing or adding division (continuation of 11-27). Refer to the information presented in Solved Example 11-27.

Required

1. Given the Northern Division's expected operating loss of Rs 11,00,000, should Steel Craft and Furnishings shut it down? Assume that shutting down the Northern Division will have no effect on corporate-office costs but will lead to savings of all general administration costs of the division. Show your calculations.
2. Suppose the manager at corporate headquarters responsible for making the decision of whether to shut down the Northern Division will be evaluated in 2011 on the Northern Division's operating income after allocating' corporate-office costs. Will the manager prefer to shut down the division? Show your calculations. Is the decision model consistent with the performance evaluation model? Explain.
3. Suppose Steel Craft has the opportunity to open another division, the Southern Division, whose revenues and costs are expected to be identical to the Northern Division's revenues and costs (including a cost of Rs 10,00,000 to acquire equipment with a one-year useful life and zero terminal disposal value). Opening the new division will have no effect on corporate office costs. Should Steel Craft open the Southern Division? Show your calculations.

Solution

Discontinuing or adding another division (continuation of 11-27).

1. Solution Exhibit 11-28, Column 1, presents the relevant loss of revenues and the relevant savings in costs from closing the Northern Division. As the calculations show, Steel Craft's operating income would decrease by Rs 14,00,000 if it shuts down the Northern Division (loss in revenues of Rs 1,50,00,000 versus savings in costs of Rs 1,36,00,000).

   Steel Craft will save variable manufacturing costs, marketing and distribution costs, and division general administration costs by closing the Northern Division but equipment related depreciation and corporate office allocations are irrelevant to the decision. Equipment related costs are irrelevant because they are past costs (and the equipment has zero disposal price). Corporate office costs are irrelevant because Steel Craft will not save any actual corporate office costs by closing the Northern Division. The corporate office costs that used to be allocated to the Northern Division will be allocated to other divisions.
2. The manager at corporate headquarters responsible for making the decision is evaluated on Northern Division's operating income after allocating corporate office costs. The manager will evaluate the options as follows: If the manager does not close the Northern Division in 2011, the division is expected to show an operating loss of Rs 11,00,000 after allocating all corporate office costs. If the manager closes the Northern Division, the division would show an operating loss of Rs 10,00,000 from the write off of equipment. It would show no revenues and, hence, would not attract any corporate office costs. It would also not incur any manufacturing, marketing and distribution, and general administration costs.

From the viewpoint of maximizing the operating income against which the manager is evaluated, the manager would prefer to shut down Northern Division (and show an operating loss of Rs 10,00,000 instead of an operating loss of Rs 11,00,000 by operating it). In fact, the manager might argue that even the Rs 10,00,000 operating loss is more a consequence of accounting write offs rather than a "real" operating loss.

Recall from requirement 1 that the decision model favored keeping the Northern Division open. The performance evaluation model of the manager making the decision suggests that the Northern Division be closed. Hence, the performance evaluation model is inconsistent with the decision model.

3. Solution Exhibit 11-28, Column 2, presents the relevant revenues and relevant costs of opening the Southern Division (a division whose revenues and costs are expected to be identical to the revenues and costs of the Northern Division). Steel Craft should open the Southern Division because it would increase operating income by Rs 4,00,000 (increase in relevant revenues of Rs 1,50,00,000 and increase in relevant costs of Rs 1,46,00,000). The relevant costs include direct materials, direct manufacturing labor, marketing and distribution, equipment, and division general administration costs but not corporate office costs. Note, in particular, that the cost of equipment written off as depreciation is relevant because it is an expected future cost that Steel Craft will incur only if it opens the Southern Division. Corporate office costs are irrelevant because actual corporate office costs will not change if Steel opens the Southern Division. The current corporate staff will be able to oversee the Southern Division's operations. Steel Craft will allocate some corporate office costs to the Southern Division but this allocation represents corporate office costs that are already currently being allocated to some other division. Because actual total corporate office costs do not change, they are irrelevant to the division.

Solution Exhibit 11-28

Relevant-Revenue and Relevant-Cost Analysis for Closing Northern Division and Opening Southern Division

	(Loss in Revenues) and Savings in Costs from Closing Northern Division (1)	Incremental Revenues and (Incremental Costs) from Opening Southern Division (2)
Revenues	Rs (1,50,00,000)	Rs 1,50,00,000
Variable direct materials and direct manufacturing labor costs	82,50,000	(82,50,000)
Equipment cost written off as depreciation	0	(10,00,000)
Marketing and distribution costs	20,50,000	(20,50,000)
Division general administration costs	33,00,000	(33,00,000)
Corporate office costs	0	0
Total costs	1,36,00,000	(1,46,00,000)
Effect on operating income (loss)	Rs (14,00,000)	Rs 4,00,000

11-29 Make versus buy, ethics. (CMA, adapted) Harish Aggarwal, a management accountant with the Maruti Udyog, is evaluating whether a component MTR.2000 should continue to manufactured by Maruti or purchased from Outside Vendor Company. Outside Vendor has submitted a bid to manufacture and supply the 32,000 units of MTR.2000 that Maruti Udyog will need for 2012 at a selling price of Rs 173.

Harish has gathered the following information regarding Maruti's costs to manufacture 30,000 units of MTR-2000 in 2011:

Direct materials	Rs 19,50,000
Direct manufacturing labor	12,00,000
Plant space rental	8,40,000
Equipment leasing	3,60,000
Other manufacturing overhead	22,50,000
Total manufacturing costs	66,00,000

Harish has also collected the following information related to manufacturing MTR 2000:

- Prices of direct materials used in the production of MTR.2000 are expected to increase by 8% in 2012.
- Maruti Udyog's direct manufacturing labor contract calls for a 5% increase in 2012.
- Maruti Udyog can withdraw from the plant space rental agreement without any penalty. Maruti Udyog will have no need for this space if MTR.2000 is not manufactured.
- The equipment lease can be terminated by paying Rs 60,000.
- 40% of the other manufacturing overhead is considered variable. Variable overhead changes proportionately with the number of units produced. The fixed component of other manufacturing overhead costs is expected to remain the same whether or not MTR.2000 is manufactured.

Pradeep, plant manager at Maruti Udyog, indicates to Harish that the current performance of the plant can be significantly improved and that the cost increases he is assuming are unlikely to occur. Hence, the analysis should be done assuming costs will be considerably below current levels, Harish knows that Pradeep is concerned about outsourcing MTR.2000 because it will mean that some of his close friends will be laid off.

Harish believes that it is unlikely that the plant will achieve the lower costs as Pradeep describes. He is very confident about the accuracy of the information he has collected, but he is also unhappy about laying off employees.

Required

1. On the basis of the financial information Harish has obtained, should Maruti Udyog make MTR.2000 or buy it in 2012? Show your calculations.
2. What other factors should Maruti Udyog consider before making a decision?
3. What should Harish do in response to Pradeep's comments?

Solution

Make versus buy, ethics (CMA, adapted).

1. An analysis of relevant costs that shows whether Maruti Udyog should make MTR.2000 or purchase it from Outside Vendor Company for 2012 follows:

	Total Costs for 32,000 Units
Cost to purchase MTR.2000 from Outside Vendor	
Bid price from Outside Vendor, Rs 173 × 32,000	Rs 55,36,000
Equipment lease penalty	60,000
Total incremental cost to purchase	55,96,000
Cost for Maruti Udyog to make MTR.2,000 in 2012	
Direct materials (Rs 19,50,000 × 1.08) × 32,000/32,000	22,46,400
Direct manufacturing labor (Rs 12,00,000 × 1.05) × 32,000/32,000	13,44,000
Factory space rental	8,40,000
Equipment leasing costs	3,60,000
Variable manufacturing overhead (Rs 22,50,000 × 40%) × $\frac{32,000}{30,000}$	9,60,000
Fixed manufacturing overhead (not relevant)	–
Total incremental cost to make MTR.2000	57,50,400
Savings if purchased from Outside Vendor	Rs 1,54,400

2. Based solely on the financial results, the 32,000 units of MTR.2000 for 2012 should be purchased from Outside Vendor. The total cost from Outside Vendor would be Rs 55,96,000, or Rs 1,54,400 less than if the units were made by Maruti.

   At least three other factors that Maruti Udyog should consider before agreeing to purchase MTR.2000 from Outside Vendor Company include the following:

   - The quality of the Outside Vendor component should be equal to, or better than, the quality of the internally made component. Otherwise, the quality of the final product might be compromised and Maruti Udyog's reputation affected.
   - Outside Vendor's reliability as an on-time supplier is important, since late deliveries could hamper Maruti Udyog's production schedule and delivery dates for the final product.
   - Layoffs may result if the component is outsourced to Outside Vendor. This could impact Maruti Udyog's other employees and cause labor problems or affect the company's position in the community. In addition, there may be termination costs, which have not been factored into the analysis.

Exercises

11-30 Multiple choice. (CPA) Choose the best answer.

1. The Bata Company manufactures slippers and sells them at Rs 100 a pair. Variable manufacturing cost is Rs 45 a pair, and allocated fixed manufacturing cost is Rs 15 a pair. It has enough idle capacity available to accept a one-time-only special order of 20,000 pairs of slippers at Rs 60 a pair. Bata will not incur any marketing costs as a result of the special order. What would the effect on operating income be if the special order could be accepted without affecting normal sales? (a) Rs 0, (b) Rs 3,00,000 increase, (c) Rs 9,00,000 increase, or (d) Rs 12,00,000 increase.
2. The Sona Steering manufactures Part No. 498 for use in its production line. The manufacturing cost per unit for 20,000 units of Part No. 498 is as follows:

Direct material	Rs 6
Direct manufacturing labor	30
Variable manufacturing overhead	12
Fixed manufacturing overhead allocated	16
Total manufacturing cost per unit	64

The Sundaram Fastners Company has offered to sell 20,000 units of Part No. 498 to Sona Steering for Rs 60 per unit. Sona Steering will make the decision to buy the part from Sundaram Fastners if there is an overall savings of at least Rs 25,000 for Sona Steering. If Sona Steering accepts Sundaram Fastners's offer, Rs 9 per unit of the fixed overhead allocated would be eliminated. Furthermore, Sona Steering has determined that the released facilities could be used to save relevant costs in the manufacture of Part No. 575. For Sona Steering to achieve an overall savings of Rs 25,000, the amount of relevant costs that would have to be saved by using the released facilities in the manufacture of Part No. 575 would be (a) Rs 80,000 (b) Rs 85,000 (c) Rs 1,25,000 or (d) Rs 1,40,000.

11-31 Inventory decision, opportunity costs. Maharaja, a manufacturer of lawn mowers, predicts that 2,40,000 spark plugs will have to be purchased next year. Maharaja estimates that 20,000 spark plugs will be required each month. A supplier quotes a price of Rs 80 per spark plug. The supplier also offers a special discount option: If all 2,40,000 spark plugs are purchased at the start of the year, a discount of 5% off the Rs 80 price will be given. Maharaja can invest its cash at 8% per year. It costs Maharaja Rs 2,000 to place each purchase order.

Required

1. What is the opportunity cost of interest forgone from purchasing all 2,40,000 units at the start of the year instead of in 12 monthly purchases of 20,000 units per order?
2. Would this opportunity cost ordinarily be recorded in the accounting system? Why?
3. Should Maharaja purchase 2,40,000 units at the start of the year or 20,000 units each month? Show your calculations.

11-32 Relevant costs, contribution margin, product emphasis. The Rainbows is a take-out food store, at a popular beach resort. Sudhir, owner of the Rainbows, is deciding how much refrigerator space to devote to four different drinks. Pertinent data on these four drinks are as follows:

	Cola	Lemonade	Punch	Natural Orange Juice
Selling price per case	Rs 180	Rs 192	Rs 264	Rs 384
Variable cost per case	135	152	201	302
Cases sold per foot of shelf space per day	25	24	4	5

Sudhir has a maximum front shelf-space of 12 feet to devote to the four drinks. He wants a minimum of 1 foot and a maximum of 6 feet of front shelf-space for each drink.

Required

1. Compute the contribution margin per case of each type of drink?
2. A co-worker of Sudhir's recommends that he maximize the shelf space devoted to those drinks with the highest contribution margin per case. Evaluate this recommendation.
3. What shelf-space allocation for the four drinks would you recommend for the Rainbows? Show your calculations.

11-33 Choosing customers. Sharma Printers operates a printing press with a monthly capacity of 2,000 machine-hours. Sharma has two main customers, Hyundai and Maruti. Data on each customer for January follows:

			Hyundai
Maruti	**Total**		
Revenues	Rs 12,00,000	Rs 8,00,000	Rs 20,00,000
Variable costs	4,20,000	4,80,000	9,00,000
Contribution margin	7,80,000	3,20,000	11,00,000
Fixed costs (allocated)	6,00,000	4,00,000	10,00,000
Operating income	Rs 1,80,000	Rs (80,000)	Rs 1,00,000
Machine-hours required	1,500 hours	500 hours	2,000 hours

Maruti indicates that it wants Sharma to do an additional Rs 8,00,000 worth of printing jobs during February. These jobs are identical to the existing business Sharma did for Maruti in January in terms of variable costs and machine-hours required. Sharma anticipates that the business from Hyundai in February would be the same as that in January. Sharma can choose to accept as much of the Hyundai and Maruti business for February as its capacity allows. Assume that total machine-hours and fixed costs for February will be the same as in January.

Required

What action should Sharma take to maximize its operating income? Show your calculations.

11-34 Equipment upgrade versus replacement (A. Spero, adapted) The Steel Authority of India (SAIL) makes steel table lamps. It is considering either upgrading its existing production line or replacing it The production equipment was purchased two years ago for Rs 60,00,000. It has an expected useful life of five years, a terminal disposal value of Rs 0, and is depreciated on a straight-line basis at the rate of Rs 12,00,000 per year. The equipment has a current book value of Rs 36,00,000 and a current disposal value of Rs 9,00,000. The following table presents expected costs under the upgrade and replace alternatives:

	Upgrade	Replace
Expected one-time-only equipment costs	Rs 30,00,000	Rs 75,00,000
Variable manufacturing cost per lamp	Rs 120	Rs 90
Expected production and sales of lamps per year	60,000 units	60,000 units
Selling price of lamps	Rs 250	Rs 250

The expected useful life after the machine is upgraded or replaced is three years, and the expected terminal disposal value is Re 0. If the machine is upgraded, the Rs 30,00,000 would be added to the current book value of Rs 36,00,000 and depreciated on a straight-line basis. The new equipment, if purchased, will also be depreciated on a straight-line basis.

For simplicity, ignore income taxes and the time value of money.

Required

1. Should SAIL upgrade its production line or replace it? Show your calculations.
2. Now suppose the capital expenditure needed to replace the production line is not known. All other data are as given previously. What is the maximum price that SAIL would be willing to pay for the new line to prefer replacing the existing line to upgrading it?
3. Consider again the basic information given in this exercise. Suppose Rohan, the manager of the SAIL, is evaluated on operating income. The coming year's operating income is crucial to Rohan's bonus. What alternative would Rohan choose? Explain.

11-35 Opportunity costs. (H. Schaefer) The Bajaj is working at full production capacity producing 10,000 units of a unique product, Rosebo. Manufacturing cost per unit for Rosebo is as follows:

Direct material	Rs 20
Direct manufacturing labor	30
Manufacturing overhead	50
Total manufacturing cost	100

Manufacturing overhead cost per unit is based on variable cost per unit of Rs 20 and fixed costs of Rs 3,00,000 (at full capacity of 10,000 units). Marketing cost, all variable, is Rs 40 per unit, and the selling price is Rs 200.

A customer, the Royal Company, has asked Bajaj to produce 2,000 units of Orangebo, a modification of Rosebo. Orangebo would require the same manufacturing processes as Rosebo. Royal has offered to pay Bajaj Rs 150 for a unit of Orangebo and half the marketing cost per unit.

Required

1. What is the opportunity Cost to Bajaj of producing the 2,000 units of Orangebo? (Assume that no overtime is worked.)
2. The Reliable Corporation has offered to produce 2,000 units of Roseba for Bajaj so that Bajaj may accept the Royal offer. That is, if Bajaj accepts the Reliable offer, Bajaj would manufacture 8,000 units of Rosebo and 2,000 units of Orangebo and purchase 2,000 units of Rosebo from Reliable. Reliable would charge Bajaj Rs 140 per unit to manufacture Rosebo. On the basis of financial considerations alone, should Bajaj accept the Reliable offer? Show your calculations.
3. Suppose Bajaj had been working at less than full capacity, producing 8,000 units of Rosebo at the time the Royal offer was made. Calculate the minimum price Bajaj should accept far Orangebo under these conditions. (Ignore the previous Rs 150 selling price.)

11-36 Make or buy, unknown level of volume. (A. Atkinson) Hindustan Motors manufactures small engines. The engines are sold to manufacturers who install them in such products as lawn mowers. The company currently manufactures all the parts used in these engines but is considering a proposal from an external supplier who wishes to supply the starter assemblies used in these engines.

The starter assemblies are currently manufactured in Division 3 of Hindustan Motors. The costs relating to the starter assemblies for the past 12 months were as follows:

Direct materials	Rs 20,00,000
Direct manufacturing labor	15,00,000
Manufacturing overhead	40,00,000
Total	75,00,000

Over the past year, Division 3 manufactured 1,50,000 starter assemblies. The average cost for each starter assembly is Rs 50 (Rs 75,00,000 ÷ 1,50,000).

Further analysis of manufacturing overhead revealed the following information. Of the total manufacturing overhead, only 25% is considered variable. Of the fixed portion, Rs 15,00,000 is an allocation of general overhead that would remain unchanged for the company as a whole if production of the starter assemblies is discontinued. A further Rs 10,00,000 of the fixed overhead is avoidable if production of the starter assemblies is discontinued. The balance of the current fixed overhead, Rs 5,00,000, is the division manager's salary. If production of the starter assemblies is discontinued, the manager of Division 3 will be transferred to Division 2 at the same salary. This move will allow the company to save the Rs 4,00,000 salary that would otherwise be paid to attract an outsider to this position.

Required

1. Bharat Electronics, a reliable supplier, has offered to supply starter assembly units at Rs 40 per unit. Since this price is less than the current average cost of Rs 50 per unit, the vice-president of manufacturing is eager to accept this offer. On the basis of financial considerations alone, should the outside offer be accepted? Show your calculations. (Hint: Production output in the coming year may be different from production output in the last year.)
2. How, if at all, would your response to requirement 1 change if the company could use the vacated plant space for storage and, in so doing, avoid Rs 5,00,000 of outside storage charges currently incurred? Why is this information relevant or irrelevant?

11-37 Make versus buy, activity-based costing, opportunity costs. (N. Melumad and S. Reichelstein, adapted) The Atlas Company produces bicycles. This year's expected production is 10,000 units. Currently, Atlas makes the chains for its bicycles. Atlas's management accountant reports the following costs for making the 10,000 bicycle chains:

	Cost per Unit	Costs for 10,000 Units
Direct materials	Rs 40	Rs 4,00,000
Direct manufacturing labor	20	2,00,000
Variable manufacturing overhead (power and utilities)	15	1,50,000
Inspection setup materials handling'		20,000
Machine rent		30,000
Allocated fixed costs of plant administration taxes and insurance		3,00,000
Total costs		11,00,000

Atlas has received an offer from an outside vendor to supply any number of chains. Atlas requires Rs 82 per chain. The following additional information is available:

a. Inspection, setup, and materials handling costs vary with the number of batches in which the chains, are produced. Atlas produces chains in batch sizes of 1,000 units. Atlas estimates that it will produce the 10,000 units in 10 batches.
b. Atlas rents the machine used to make the chains. If Atlas buys all of its chains from the outside vendor, it does not need to pay rent on this machine.

Required

1. Assume that if Atlas purchases the chains from the outside supplier, the facility where the chains are currently made will remain idle. On the basis of financial considerations alone, should Atlas accept the outside supplier's offer at the anticipated production (and sales) volume of 10,000 units? Show your calculations.
2. For this question, assume that if the chains are purchased outside, the facilities where the chains are currently made will be used to upgrade the bicycles by adding mud flaps and reflectors. As a consequence, the selling price of bicycles will be raised by Rs 200. The variable cost per unit of the upgrade would be Rs 180, and additional tooling costs of Rs 1,60,000 would be incurred. On the basis of financial considerations alone, should Atlas make or buy the chains, assuming that 10,000 units are produced (and sold)? Show your calculations.
3. The sales manager at Atlas is concerned that the estimate of 10,000 units may be high and believes that only 6,200 units will be sold. Production will be cut back, freeing up work space. This space can be used to add the mud flaps and reflectors whether Atlas goes outside for the chains or makes them in-house. At this lower output, Atlas will produce the chains in eight batches of 775 units each. On the basis of financial considerations alone, should Atlas purchase the chains from the outside vendor? Show your calculations.

11-38 Multiple choice, comprehensive problem on relevant costs. The following are the Parkar Company's unit cost of manufacturing and marketing a high-style pen at an output level of 20,000 units per month:

Manufacturing cost	
Direct material	Rs 10
Direct manufacturing labor	12
Variable manufacturing indirect cost	8
Fixed manufacturing indirect cost	5
Marketing cost	
Variable	15
Fixed	9

The following situations refer only to the preceding data; there is no connection between the situations. Unless stated otherwise, assume a regular selling price of Rs 60 per unit. Choose the best answer to each question. Show your calculations.

Required

1. In an inventory of 10,000 units of the high-style pen presented in the balance sheet, the appropriate unit cost to use is (a) Rs 30, (b) Rs 35, (c) Rs 50, (d) Rs 22, or (e) Rs 59.
2. The pen is usually produced and sold at the rate of 2,40,000 units per year (an average of 20,000 per month). The selling price is Rs 60 per unit, which yields total annual revenues of Rs 1,44,00,000. Total

costs are Rs 1,41,60,000, and operating income is Rs 2,40,000, or Re 1 per unit. Market research estimates that unit sales could be increased by 10% if prices were cut to Rs 58. Assuming the implied cost-behavior patterns continue, this action, if taken, would

a. Decrease operating income by Rs 72,000.

b. Decrease operating income by Rs 2 per unit (Rs 4,80,000) but increase operating income by 10% of revenues (Rs 14,40,000), for a net increase of Rs 9,60,000.

c. Decrease fixed cost per unit by 10%, or Rs 1.4, per unit, and thus decrease operating income by Rs 0.6 (Rs 2.0 – Rs 1.4) per unit.

d. Increase unit sales to 2,64,000 units, which at the Rs 58 price would give total revenues of Rs 1,53,12,000 and lead to costs of Rs 59 per unit for 2,64,000 units, which would equal Rs 1,55,76,000, and result in an operating loss of Rs 2,64,000.

e. None of these.

3. A contract with the government for 5,000 units of the pens calls for the reimbursement of all manufacturing costs plus a fixed fee of Rs 10,000. No variable marketing costs are incurred on the government contract. You are asked to compare the following two alternatives:

Sales Each Month to	Alternative A	Alternative B
Regular customers	15,000 units	15,000 units
Government	0 units	5,000 units

Operating income under alternative B is greater than that under alternative A by (a) Rs 10,000, (b) Rs 25,000, (c) Rs 35,000, (d) Rs 3,000, or (e) none of these.

4. Assume the same data with respect to the government contract as in requirement 3 except that the two alternatives to be compared are

Sales Each Month to	Alternative A	Alternative B
Regular customers	20,000 units	15,000 units
Government	0 units	5,000 units

Operating income under alternative B relative to that under alternative A is (a) Rs 40,000 less, (b) Rs 30,000 greater, (c) Rs 65,000 less, (d) Rs 5,000 greater, or (e) none of these.

5. The company wants to enter a foreign market in which price competition is keen. The company seeks a one-time-only special order for 10,000 units on a minimum-unit-price basis. It expects that shipping costs for this order will amount to only Rs 7.5 per unit, but the fixed costs of obtaining the contract will be Rs 40,000. The company incurs no variable marketing costs other than shipping costs. Domestic business will be unaffected. The selling to break-even is (a) Rs 35, (b) Rs 41.5, (c) Rs 42.5, (d) Rs 30 or (e) Rs 50.

6. The company has an inventory of 1,000 units of pens that must be sold immediately at reduced prices. Otherwise, the inventory will be worthless. The unit cost that is relevant for establishing the minimum selling price is (a) Rs 45, (b) Rs 40, (c) Rs 30, (d) Rs 59, or (e) Rs 15.

7. A proposal is received from an outside supplier who will make and transport these high-style pens directly to the Parkar Company's customers as sales orders are forwarded from Parkar's sales staff. Parkar's fixed marketing costs will be unaffected, but its variable marketing costs will be slashed by 20%. Parkar's plant will be idle, but its fixed manufacturing overhead will continue at 50% of present levels. How much per unit would the company be able to pay the supplier without decreasing operating income?
(a) Rs 47.5, (b) Rs 39.5, (c) Rs 29.5, (d) Rs 53.5, or (e) none of these.

11-39 Make or buy (continuation of 11-38). Assume that, as in requirement 7 of Exercise 11-38, a proposal is received from an outside supplier who will make and transport high-style pens directly to the Parkar Company's customers as sales orders are forwarded from Parkar's sales staff. If the supplier's offer is accepted, the present plant facilities will be used to make a new pen whose unit costs will be

Variable manufacturing cost	Rs 50
Fixed manufacturing cost	10
Variable marketing cost	20
Fixed marketing cost	5

Total fixed manufacturing overhead will be unchanged from the original level given at the beginning of Problem 11-37. Fixed marketing costs for the new pens are over and above the fixed marketing costs incurred for marketing the high-style pens at the beginning of Problem 11 -37. The new pen will sell for Rs 90. The minimum desired operating income on the two pens taken together is Rs 5,00,000 per year.

Required What is the maximum purchase cost per unit that the Parkar Company would be willing to pay for subcontracting the production of the high-style pens?

11-40 Optimal product mix. (CMA, adapted) Royal Sport's Plastics Department is currently manufacturing 5,000 pairs of skates annually, making full use of its machine capacity. The selling price and total cost per unit associated with Royal Sport's skates are

Selling price per pair of skates		Rs 980
Cost per pair of skates		
Direct material,	Rs 200	
Variable machine operating cost (Rs 160 per machine-hour)	240	
Manufacturing overhead cost	180	
Marketing and administrative cost	210	830
Operating income per pair of skates		150

Royal Sport believes it could sell 8,000 pairs of skates annually if it had sufficient manufacturing capacity. Outside vendor has offered to provide up to 6,000 pairs of skates per year at a price of Rs 750 per pair delivered at Royal place.

Krishna, Royal Sport product manager, has suggested that the company can make better use of its Plastics Department by manufacturing snowboard bindings. Krishna believes that Royal Sport could expect to sell up to 12,000 snowboard bindings annually. Krishna's estimate of the selling price and total cost per unit to manufacture 12,000 snowboard bindings are:

Selling price per snowboard binding		Rs 600
Cost per snowboard binding		
Direct material	Rs 200	
Variable machine operating cost (Rs 160 per machine-hour)	80	
Manufacturing overhead cost	60	
Marketing and administrative cost	100	440
Operating income per snowboard binding		160

Other information pertinent to Royal Sport's operations includes the following:

- In the Plastics Department, Royal Sport uses machine-hours as the allocation base for manufacturing overhead costs. The fixed manufacturing overhead component of these costs for the current year is the Rs 3,00,000 of fixed plantwide manufacturing overhead that has been allocated to the Plastics Department. These costs will not be affected by the product-mix decision.
- Variable marketing and administrative cost per unit for the various products are as follows:

Manufactured in-line skates	Rs 90
Purchased in-line skates	40
Manufactured snowboard bindings	80

Fixed marketing and administrative costs of Rs 6,00,000 are not affected by the product-mix decision.

Required

Calculate the quantity of each product that Royal Sport should manufacture and/or purchase to maximize operating income. Show your calculations.

Pricing Decisions and Cost Management

Learning Objectives

1. Discuss the three major influences on pricing decisions
2. Understand how companies make short-run pricing decisions
3. Understand how companies make long-run pricing decisions
4. Price products using the target-costing approach
5. Apply the concepts of cost incurrence and locked-in costs
6. Price products using the cost-plus approach
7. Use life-cycle budgeting and costing when making pricing decisions
8. Describe two pricing practices in which noncost factors are important when setting prices

Most companies make a tremendous effort to analyze their costs and prices. They know if the price is too high, customers will look elsewhere, too low, and the firm won't be able to cover the cost of making the product. Some companies, however, understand that it is possible to charge a low price to stimulate demand and meet customer needs while relentlessly managing costs to earn a profit. Tata Motors is one such company.

Target Pricing and Tata Motors' $2,500 Car[1]

Despite India's rapid economic growth and growing market for consumer goods, transportation options in the world's most populous country remain limited. Historically, Indians relied on public transportation, bicycles, and motorcycles to get around. Less than 1% owned cars, with most foreign models ill-suited to India's unique traffic conditions. Most cars had unnecessary product features and were priced too high for the vast majority of Indians.

But Ratan Tata, chairman of India's Tata Motors, saw India's dearth of cars as an opportunity. In 2003, after seeing a family riding dangerously on a two-wheel scooter, Mr. Tata set a challenge for his company to build a 'people's car' for the Indian market with three requirements: It should (1) adhere to existing regulatory requirements, (2) achieve certain performance targets for fuel efficiency and acceleration, and (3) cost only $2,500, about the price of the optional DVD player in a new Lexus sport utility vehicle sold in the United States.

The task was daunting: $2,500 was about half the price of the cheapest Indian car. One of Tata's suppliers said, "It's basically throwing out everything the auto industry has thought about cost structures in the past and taking a clean sheet of paper and asking, 'What's possible?'" Mr. Tata and his managers responded with what some analysts have described as "Gandhian engineering" principles: deep frugality with a willingness to challenge conventional wisdom.

At a fundamental level, Tata Motors' engineers created a new category of car by doing more with less. Extracting costs from

[1] *Sources*: Giridharadas, Anand. 2008. Four wheels for the masses: The $2,500 car. *New York Times*, January 8. http://www.nytimes.com/2008/01/08/business/worldbusiness/08indiacar.html Kripalani, Manjeet. 2008. Inside the Tata Nano Factory. *BusinessWeek*, May 9. http://www.businessweek.com/print/innovate/content/may2008/id2008059_312111.htm

traditional car development, Tata eschewed traditional long-term supplier relationships, and instead forced suppliers to compete for its business using Internet-based auctions. Engineering innovations led to a hollowed-out steering-wheel shaft, a smaller diameter drive shaft, a trunk with space for a briefcase, one windshield wiper instead of two, and a rear-mounted engine not much more powerful than a high-end riding lawnmower. Moreover, Tata's car has no radio, no power steering, no power windows, and no air conditioning—features standard on most vehicles.

But when Tata Motors introduced the "Nano" in 2008, the company had successfully built a $2,500 entry-level car that is fuel efficient, 50 miles to the gallon; reaches 65 miles per hour; and meets all current Indian emission, pollution, and safety standards. While revolutionizing the Indian automotive marketplace, the "Nano" is also changing staid global automakers. Already, the French-Japanese alliance Renault-Nissan and the Indian-Japanese joint venture Maruti Suzuki are trying to make ultra-cheap cars for India, while Ford recently made India the manufacturing hub for all of its low-cost cars.

Just like Ratan Tata, managers at many innovative companies are taking a fresh look at their strategic pricing decisions. This chapter describes how managers evaluate demand at different prices and manage costs across the value chain and over a product's life cycle to achieve profitability.

Major Influences on Pricing Decisions

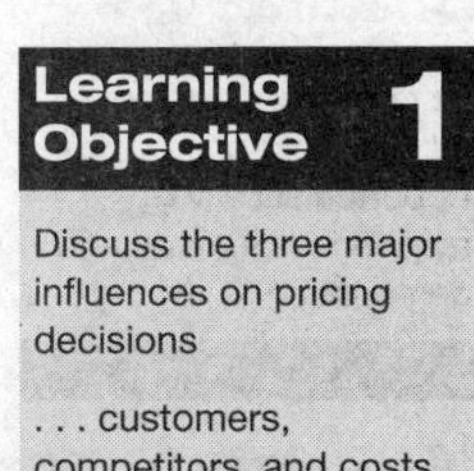

Consider for a moment how managers at Adidas might price their newest line of sneakers, or how decision makers at Microsoft would determine how much to charge for a monthly subscription of MSN Internet service. How companies price a product or a service ultimately depends on the demand and supply for it. Three influences on demand and supply are customers, competitors, and costs.

Customers, Competitors, and Costs

Customers Customers influence price through their effect on the demand for a product or service, based on factors such as the features of a product and its quality. As the Tata Motors example illustrates, companies must always examine pricing decisions through the eyes of their customers and then manage costs to earn a profit.

Competitors No business operates in a vacuum. Companies must always be aware of the actions of their competitors. At one extreme, alternative or substitute products of competitors can affect demand and force a company to lower its prices. At the other extreme, a company without a competitor can set higher prices. When there are competitors, knowledge of rivals' technology, plant capacity, and operating strategies enables a company to estimate its competitors' costs—valuable information in setting its own prices.

Because competition spans international borders, costs and pricing decisions are also affected by fluctuations in the exchange rates between different countries' currencies. For example, if the yen weakens against the U.S. dollar, Japanese products become cheaper for American consumers and, consequently, more competitive in U.S. markets.

Costs Costs influence prices because they affect supply. The lower the cost of producing a product, the greater the quantity of product the company is willing to supply. Generally, as companies increase supply, the cost of producing an additional unit initially declines but eventually increases. Companies supply products as long as the revenue from selling additional units exceeds the cost of producing them. Managers who understand the cost of producing products set prices that make the products attractive to customers while maximizing operating income.

Weighing Customers, Competitors, and Costs Surveys of how managers make pricing decisions reveal that companies weigh customers, competitors, and costs differently. At one extreme, companies operating in a perfectly competitive market sell very similar commodity-type products, such as wheat, rice, steel, and aluminum. These companies have no control over setting prices and must accept the price determined by a market consisting of many participants. Cost information helps a company decide only on the output level that maximizes its operating income.

In less-competitive markets, such as those for cameras, televisions, and cellular phones, products are differentiated, and all three factors affect prices: The value customers place on a product and the prices charged for competing products affect demand, and the costs of producing and delivering the product influence supply.

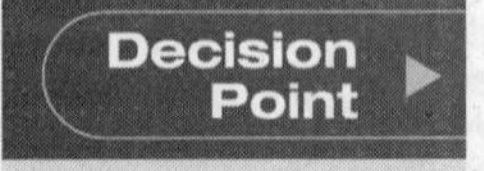

What are the three major influences on pricing decisions?

As competition lessens even more, the key factor affecting pricing decisions is the customer's willingness to pay based on the value that customers place on the product or service, not costs or competitors. In the extreme, there are monopolies. A monopolist has no competitors and has much more leeway to set high prices. Nevertheless, there are limits. The higher the price a monopolist sets, the lower the demand for the monopolist's product as customers seek substitute products.

Costing and Pricing for the Short Run

Learning Objective 2

Understand how companies make short-run pricing decisions

. . . consider only incremental costs as relevant and price opportunistically to respond to demand and competition

Short-run pricing decisions typically have a time horizon of less than a year and include decisions such as (a) pricing a *one-time-only special order* with no long-run implications and (b) adjusting product mix and output volume in a competitive market. Long-run pricing decisions have a time horizon of a year or longer and include pricing a product in a major market in which there is some leeway in setting price.

Consider a short-run pricing decision facing the management team at Astel Computers. Astel manufactures two brands of personal computers (PCs)—Deskpoint, Astel's top-of-the-line product, and Provalue, a less-powerful Pentium chip-based machine. Datatech Corporation has asked Astel to bid on supplying 5,000 Provalue computers over the last three months of 2008. After this three-month period, Datatech is unlikely to place any future sales orders with Astel. Datatech will sell Provalue computers under its own brand name in regions and markets where Astel does not sell Provalue. Whether Astel accepts or rejects this order will not affect Astel's revenues—neither the units sold nor the selling price—from existing sales channels.

Relevant Costs for Short-Run Pricing Decisions

Before Astel can bid on Datatech's offer, Astel's managers must estimate how much it will cost to supply the 5,000 computers. Similar to the Surf Gear example in Chapter 11, the relevant costs Astel's managers must focus on include all direct and indirect costs throughout the value chain that will change in total by accepting the one-time-only special order from Datatech. Astel's managers outline the relevant costs in the following table:

Direct materials (Rs 4,600 per computer × 5,000 computers)	Rs 2,30,00,000
Direct manufacturing labor (Rs 640 per computer × 5,000 computers)	32,00,000
Fixed costs of additional capacity to manufacture Provalue	25,00,000
Total costs	Rs 2,87,00,000*

*No additional costs will be required for R&D, design, marketing, distribution, or customer service.

The relevant cost per computer is Rs 5,740 (Rs 2,87,00,000 ÷ 5,000). Therefore, any selling price above Rs 5,740 will improve Astel's profitability in the short run. What price should Astel's managers bid for the 5,000-computer order?

Strategic and Other Factors in Short-Run Pricing

Based on its market intelligence, Astel believes that competing bids will be between Rs 5,960 and Rs 6,100 per computer, Astel makes a bid of Rs 5,950 per computer. If it wins this bid, operating income will increase by Rs 10,50,000 (relevant revenues, Rs 5,950 × 5,000 = Rs 2,97,50,000 minus relevant costs, Rs 2,87,00,000). Management's strategy is to bid as high above Rs 5,740 as possible while remaining lower than competitors' bids.

What if Astel were the only supplier and Datatech could undercut Astel's selling price in Astel's current markets? The relevant cost of the bidding decision would then include the contribution margin lost on sales to existing customers. What if there were many parties eager to bid and win the Datatech contract? In this case, the contribution margin lost on sales to existing customers would be irrelevant to the decision because the existing business would be undercut by Datatech regardless of whether Astel wins the contract.

In contrast to the Astel case, in some short-run situations, a company may experience strong demand for its products or have limited capacity. In these circumstances, a company will strategically increase prices in the short run to as much as the market will bear. We observe high short-run prices in the case of new products or new models of older products, such as microprocessors, computer chips, cellular telephones, and software.

Effect of Time Horizon on Short-Run Pricing Decisions

Two key factors affect short-run pricing.

1. Many costs are irrelevant in short-run pricing decisions. In the Astel example, most of Astel's costs in R&D, design, manufacturing, marketing, distribution, and customer service are irrelevant for the short-run pricing decision, because these costs will not change whether Astel wins or does not win the Datatech business. These costs will change in the long run and therefore will be relevant.
2. Short-run pricing is opportunistic. Prices are decreased when demand is weak and competition is strong and increased when demand is strong and competition is weak. As we will see, long-run prices need to be set to earn a reasonable return on investment.

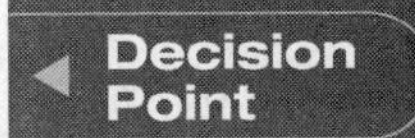

What do companies consider when making short-run pricing decisions?

Costing and Pricing for the Long Run

Learning Objective

Understand how companies make long-run pricing decisions

Consider all future variable and fixed costs as relevant and earn a target return on investment

Long-run pricing is a strategic decision designed to build long-run relationships with customers based on stable and predictable prices. A stable price reduces the need for continuous monitoring of prices, improves planning, and builds long-run buyer–seller relationships. But to charge a stable price and earn the target long-run return, a company must, over the long run, know and manage its costs of supplying product to customers. As we will see, relevant costs for long-run pricing decisions include *all* future fixed and variable costs.

Calculating Product Costs for Long-Run Pricing Decisions

Let's return to the Astel example. However, this time we consider the long-run pricing decision for Provalue.

We start by reviewing data for the year just ended, 2011. Astel has no beginning or ending inventory of Provalue and manufactures and sells 150,000 units during the year. Astel uses activity-based costing (ABC) to calculate the manufacturing cost of Provalue. Astel has three direct manufacturing costs, direct materials, direct manufacturing labor, and direct machining costs, and three manufacturing overhead cost pools, ordering and receiving components, testing and inspection of final products, and rework (correcting and fixing errors and defects), in its accounting system. Astel treats machining costs as a direct cost of Provalue because Provalue is manufactured on machines that only make Provalue.[2]

Astel uses a long-run time horizon to price Provalue. Over this horizon, Astel's management observes the following:

- Direct material costs vary with number of units of Provalue produced.
- Direct manufacturing labor costs vary with number of direct manufacturing labor-hours used.
- Direct machining costs, such as rental and lease charges, do not vary with number of machine-hours used over this time horizon. They are fixed in the long run based on Astel's capacity of 3,00,000 machine-hours. Each unit of Provalue requires 2 machine-hours. Therefore, the entire machining capacity is used to manufacture Provalue (2 machine-hours per unit × 1,50,000 units ÷ 3,00,000 machine-hours).
- Ordering and receiving, testing and inspection, and rework costs vary with the quantity of their respective cost driver. For example, ordering and receiving costs vary with the number of orders. Staff members responsible for placing orders can be reassigned or laid off in the long run if fewer orders need to be placed, or the number of staff members can be increased in the long run to process more orders.

The following Excel spreadsheet summarizes manufacturing cost information to produce 1,50,000 units of Provalue in 2011.

	A	B	C	D	E	F	G	H
1			Manufacturing cost information					
2			to produce 150,000 units of Provalue					
3	Cost Category	Cost Driver	Details of Cost Driver Quantities				Total Quantity of Cost Driver	Cost per Unit of Cost Driver
4	(1)	(2)	(3)		(4)		(5)=(3)x(4)	(6)
5	Direct Manufacturing Costs							
6	Direct materials	No. of kits	1	kit per unit	1,50,000	units	1,50,000	Rs 4,600
7	Direct manufacturing labor (DML)	DML hours	3.2	DML hours per unit	1,50,000	units	4,80,000	Rs 200
8	Direct machining (fixed)	Machine-hours					3,00,000	Rs 380
9	Manufacturing Overhead Costs							
10	Ordering and receiving	No. of orders	50	orders per component	450	components	22,500	Rs 800
11	Testing and inspection	Testing-hours	30	testing-hours per unit	1,50,000	units	45,00,000	Rs 20
12	Rework				8%	defect rate		
13		Rework-hours	2.5	rework-hours per defective unit	12,000[a]	defective units	30,000	Rs 400
14								
15	[a]8% defect rate x 150,000 units = 12,000 defective units							

[2] Recall that Astel makes two types of PCs: Deskpoint and Provalue. If Deskpoint and Provalue had shared the same machines, Astel would have allocated machining costs on the basis of the budgeted machine-hours used to manufacture the two products and would have treated these costs as fixed overhead costs.

Exhibit 12-1 indicates that the total cost of manufacturing Provalue is Rs 1,020 million, and the manufacturing cost per unit is Rs 6,800. Manufacturing, however, is just one business function in the value chain. To set long-run prices, Astel's managers must calculate the *full cost* of producing and selling Provalue.

For its nonmanufacturing business functions in the value chain, Astel's managers identify direct costs and choose cost drivers and cost pools for indirect costs that measure cause-and-effect relationships. Astel's managers allocate costs to Provalue based on the quantity of cost-driver units that Provalue uses. Exhibit 12-2 summarizes the operating income for Provalue for 2009 based on an activity-based analysis of costs in all business functions. (For brevity, supporting calculations for nonmanufacturing business functions are not given.) Astel earns Rs 150 million from Provalue, or Rs 1,000 per unit sold in 2011.

Alternative Long-Run Pricing Approaches

How do companies use product cost information to make long-run pricing decisions? Two different approaches for pricing decisions are:

1. Market-based
2. Cost-based, which is also called cost-plus

The market-based approach to pricing starts by management asking, "Given what our customers want and how our competitors will react to what we do, what price should we charge?" The cost-based approach to pricing starts by management asking, "Given what it costs us to make this product, what price should we charge that will recoup our costs and achieve a target return on investment?"

Companies operating in *competitive* markets (for example, commodities such as steel, oil, and natural gas) use the market-based approach. The items produced or services provided by one company are very similar to items produced or services provided by others. Companies in these markets must accept the prices set by the market.

Companies operating in *less competitive* markets offering products or services that differ from each other (for example, automobiles, computers, management consulting, and

File Edit View Insert Format Tools Data Window Help

	A	B	C
1		Total Manufacturing	
2		Costs for	Manufacturing
3		1,50,000 Units	Cost per Unit
4		(1)	(2) = (1) ÷ 1,50,000
5	Direct manufacturing costs		
6	Direct material costs		
7	(1,50,000 kits x Rs 4,600 per kit)	Rs 69,00,00,000	Rs 4,600
8	Direct manufacturing labor costs		
9	(4,80,000 DML-hours x Rs 200 per hour)	9,60,00,000	640
10	Direct machining costs		
11	(3,00,000 machine-hours x Rs 380 per machine-hour)	11,40,00,000	760
12	Direct manufacturing costs	90,00,00,000	6,000
13			
14	Manufacturing overhead costs		
15	Ordering and receiving costs		
16	(22,500 orders x Rs 800 per order)	1,80,00,000	120
17	Testing and inspection costs		
18	(45,00,000 testing-hours x Rs 20 per hour)	9,00,00,000	600
19	Rework costs		
20	(30,000 rework-hours x Rs 400 per hour)	1,20,00,000	80
21	Manufacturing overhead cost	12,00,00,000	800
22	Total manufacturing costs	Rs 1,02,00,00,000	Rs 6,800

Exhibit 12-1

Manufacturing Costs of Provalue for 2011 Using Activity-Based Costing

Exhibit 12-2

Product Profitability of Provalue for 2011 Using Value-Chain Activity-Based Costing

	A	B	C
1		Total Amounts	
2		for 1,50,000 Units	Per Unit
3		(1)	(2) = (1) ÷ 1,50,000
4	Revenues	Rs 1,50,00,00,000	Rs 10,000
5	Costs of goods sold[a] (from Exhibit 12-1)	1,02,00,00,000	6,800
6	Operating costs[b]		
7	R&D costs	5,40,00,000	360
8	Design cost of product and process	6,00,00,000	400
9	Marketing costs	15,00,00,000	1,000
10	Distribution costs	3,60,00,000	240
11	Customer-service costs	3,00,00,000	200
12	Operating costs	33,00,00,000	2,200
13	Full cost of the product	1,35,00,00,000	9,000
14	Operating income	Rs 15,00,00,000	Rs 1,000
15			
16	[a]Cost of goods sold = Total manufacturing costs because there is no beginning or ending inventory		
17	of Provalue in 2011		
18	[b]Numbers for operating cost line-items are assumed without supporting calculations		

legal services), can use either the market-based or cost-based approach as the starting point for pricing decisions. Some companies first look at costs because cost information is more easily available and then consider customers or competitors—the cost-based approach. Others start by considering customers and competitors and then look at costs—the market-based approach. Both approaches consider customers, competitors, and costs. Only their starting points differ. Management must always keep in mind market forces, regardless of which pricing approach is used. For example, building contractors often bid on a cost-plus basis but then reduce their prices during negotiations to respond to other lower-cost bids.

How do companies make long-run pricing decisions?

Companies operating in markets that are *not competitive* favor cost-based approaches. That's because these companies do not need to respond or react to competitors' prices. The margin they add to costs to determine price depends on the value customers place on the product or service.

We consider first the market-based approach.

Target Costing for Target Pricing

Learning Objective 4

Price products using the target-costing approach

. . . target costing identifies an estimated price customers are willing to pay and then computes a target cost to earn the desired profit

Market-based pricing starts with a target price. A **target price** is the estimated price for a product or service that potential customers will pay. This estimate is based on an understanding of customers' perceived value for a product or service and how competitors will price competing products or services. Having this understanding of customers and competitors has become important for three reasons:

1. Competition from lower-cost producers has meant that prices cannot be increased.
2. Products are on the market for shorter periods of time, leaving less time and opportunity to recover from pricing mistakes, loss of market share, and loss of profitability.
3. Customers have become more knowledgeable and demand quality products at reasonable prices.

Understanding Customers' Perceived Value

A company's sales and marketing organization, through close contact and interaction with customers, is usually in the best position to identify customers' needs and their perceptions of the value of a product or service. Companies such as Apple also conduct market research on features that customers want and the prices they are willing to pay for those features for products such as the iPhone and the Macintosh computer.

Doing Competitor Analysis

To gauge how competitors might react to a prospective price, a company must understand competitors' technologies, products or services, costs, and financial conditions. For example, knowing competitors' technologies and products helps a company (a) to evaluate how distinctive its own products or services will be in the market and (b) to determine the prices it might be able to charge as a result of being distinctive. Where does a company obtain information about its competitors? Usually from former customers, suppliers, and employees of competitors. Another source of information is *reverse engineering*—that's disassembling and analyzing competitors' products to determine product designs and materials and to become acquainted with the technologies competitors use. Many companies, including Ford, General Motors, and PPG Industries, have departments whose sole purpose is to analyze competitors with respect to these considerations. At no time should a company resort to illegal or unethical means to obtain information from competitors. For example, a company should never pay off current employees or pose as a supplier or customer in order to obtain competitor information.

Implementing Target Pricing and Target Costing

There are five steps in developing target prices and target costs. We illustrate these steps using our Provalue example.

Step 1: Develop a product that satisfies the needs of potential customers. Based on an understanding of customer requirements and an analysis of competitors' products, Astel plans the product features and design modifications for Provalue for 2010. Astel's market research indicates that customers do not value Provalue's extra features, such as special audio features and designs that accommodate upgrades that can make the PC run faster. They want Astel to redesign Provalue into a no-frills but reliable PC and to sell it at a much lower price.

Step 2: Choose a target price. Based on Astel's research of its competitors' products and technologies, Astel expects its competitors to lower the prices of PCs that compete with Provalue to Rs 8,500. Astel's management wants to respond aggressively by reducing Provalue's price by 20%, from Rs 10,000 to Rs 8,000 per unit. At this lower price, Astel's marketing manager forecasts an increase in annual sales from 1,50,000 to 2,00,000 units.

Step 3: Derive a target cost per unit by subtracting target operating income per unit from the target price. The target price is the basis for calculating target cost per unit. *Target cost per unit* is the target price minus *target operating income per unit.* **Target operating income per unit** is the operating income that a company aims to earn per unit of a product or service sold. **Target cost per unit** is the estimated long-run cost per unit of a product or service that enables the company to achieve its target operating income per unit when selling at the target price.[3] Target cost per unit is often lower than the existing *full cost per unit of the product.* Target cost per unit is really just that—a target—something the company must commit to achieve.

To attain the target return on the capital invested in the business, Astel's management needs a 10% target operating income on target revenues.

Total target revenues	= Rs 8,000 per unit × 2,00,000 = Rs 160,00,00,000
Total target operating income	= 10% × Rs 160,00,00,000 = Rs 16,00,00,000
Total operating income per unit	= Rs 16,00,00,000 ÷ 2,00,000 units = Rs 800 per unit
Total cost per unit	= Traget price − Target operating income per unit
	= Rs 8,000 per unit − Rs 800 per unit = Rs 7,200 per unit
Total current full cost of provalue	= Rs 135,00,00,000 (from Exhibit 12-2)
Current full cost per unit of provalue	= Rs 135,00,00,000 ÷ 1,50,000 units = Rs 9,000 per unit
	Exhibit 12-2

[3] For a more-detailed discussion of target costing, see S. Ansari, J. Bell and The CAM-I Target Cost Core Group, *Target Costing: The Next Frontier in Strategic Cost Management* (Homewood, IL: Irwin McGraw-Hill, 1997). For implementation information, see S. Ansari, L. D. Swenson, and J. Bell, "A Template for Implementing Target Costing," *Cost Management* (September–October 2006): 20–27.

Provalue's Rs 7,200 target cost per unit is well below its existing Rs 9,000 unit cost. Astel must reduce its unit cost by Rs 1,800 to reach its goal. Cost-reduction efforts need to extend to all parts of the value chain—from R&D to customer service—including seeking lower prices from suppliers for materials and components, while maintaining quality.

Target costs include *all* future costs, variable costs and costs that are fixed in the short run, because in the long run, a company's prices and revenues must recover all its costs if it is to remain in business. Contrast relevant costs for long-run pricing decisions (all variable and fixed costs) with relevant costs for short-run pricing decisions (costs that change in the short run, mostly but not exclusively variable costs).

Step 4: Perform cost analysis. This step analyzes which aspects of a product or service to target for cost reduction. For Provalue, Astel's managers consider the following:

- The functions performed by different component parts such as the motherboard, disc drives, and the graphics and video cards.
- The importance that customers place on different product features. For example, Astel's targeted customers place greater emphasis on the reliability of the computer than on video quality.
- The relationship and tradeoffs across product features and component parts. For example, choosing a simpler mother board enhances reliability but is unable to support the top-of-the-line video card.

How do companies determine target costs?

Step 5: Perform value engineering to achieve target cost. Value engineering is a systematic evaluation of all aspects of the value chain; its objective is to reduce costs and achieve a quality level that satisfies customers. As we describe next, value engineering encompasses improvements in product designs, changes in materials specifications, and modifications in process methods. (See the Concepts in Action feature to learn about IKEA's approach to target pricing and target costing.)

Value Engineering, Cost Incurrence, and Locked-In Costs

Learning Objective 5

Apply the concepts of cost incurrence

. . . when resources are consumed and locked-in costs

. . . when resources are committed to be incurred in the future

To implement value engineering, managers distinguish value-added activities and costs from nonvalue-added activities and costs. A **value-added cost** is a cost that, if eliminated, would reduce the actual or perceived value or utility (usefulness) customers obtain from using the product or service. Examples are costs of specific product features and attributes desired by customers. For Provalue, these features and attributes are a reliable PC, adequate memory, desired preloaded software, clear images on the monitor, and prompt customer service. A **nonvalue-added cost** is a cost that, if eliminated, would not reduce the actual or perceived value or utility (usefulness) customers obtain from using the product or service. It is a cost that the customer is unwilling to pay for. Examples of nonvalue-added costs are costs of producing defective products and machine breakdowns. Successful companies keep nonvalue-added costs to a minimum.

Activities and their costs do not always fall neatly into value-added or nonvalue-added categories. Some costs, such as supervision and production control, fall in a gray area because they include mostly value-added but also some nonvalue-added aspects. Despite these troublesome gray areas, attempts to distinguish value-added from nonvalue-added costs provide a useful overall framework for value engineering.

In the Provalue example, direct materials, direct manufacturing labor, and direct machining costs are value-added costs. Ordering, receiving, testing, and inspection costs fall in the gray area. Rework costs are nonvalue-added costs.

Through value engineering, Astel's managers plan to reduce, and possibly eliminate, nonvalue-added costs and increase the efficiency of value-added activities. To do value engineering, Astel's managers must distinguish when costs are incurred from when costs are locked in. **Cost incurrence** describes when a resource is consumed (or benefit forgone) to meet a specific objective. Costing systems emphasize cost incurrence. For example,

Concepts in Action

Extreme Target Pricing and Cost Management at IKEA

Around the world, IKEA has exploded into a furniture-retailing-industry phenomenon. Known for products named after small Swedish towns, modern design, flat packaging, and do-it-yourself instructions, IKEA has grown from humble beginnings to become the world's largest furniture retailer with 301 stores in 38 countries. How did this happen? Through aggressive target pricing, coupled with relentless cost management. IKEA's prices typically run 30%–50% below its competitors' prices. Moreover, while the prices of other companies' products rise over time, IKEA says it has reduced its retail prices by about 20% over the last four years.

During the conceptualization phase, product developers identify gaps in IKEA's current product portfolio. For example, they might identify the need to create a new flat-screen-television stand. "When we decide about a product, we always start with the consumer need" IKEA Product Developer June Deboehmler said. Second, product developers and their teams survey competitors to determine how much they charge for similar items, if offered, and then select a target price that is 30%–50% less than the competitor's price. With a product and price established, product developers then determine what materials will be used and what manufacturer will do the assembly work—all before the new item is fully designed. For example, a brief describing a new couch's target cost and basic specifications like color and style is submitted for bidding among IKEA's over 1,800 suppliers in more than 50 countries. Suppliers vie to offer the most attractive bid based on price, function, and materials to be used. This value-engineering process promotes volume-based cost efficiencies throughout the design and production process.

Aggressive cost management does not stop there. All IKEA products are designed to be shipped unassembled in flat packages. The company estimates that shipping costs would be at least six times greater if all products were assembled before shipping. To ensure that shipping costs remain low, packaging and shipping technicians work with product developers throughout the product development process. When IKEA recently designed its Lillberg chair, a packaging technician made a small tweak in the angle of the chair's arm. This change allowed more chairs to fit into a single shipping container, which meant a lower cost to the consumer.

What about products that have already been developed? IKEA applies the same cost management techniques to those products, too. For example, one of IKEA's best selling products is the Lack bedside table, which has retailed for the same low price since 1981. How is this possible, you may ask. Since hitting store shelves, more than 100 technical development projects have been performed on the Lack table. Despite the steady increase in the cost of raw materials and wages, IKEA has aggressively sought to reduce product and distribution costs to maintain the Lack table's initial retail price without jeopardizing the company's profit on the product.

As founder Ingvar Kamprad once summarized, "Waste of resources is a mortal sin at IKEA. Expensive solutions are a sign of mediocrity, and an idea without a price tag is never acceptable."

Sources: Baraldi, Enrico and Torkel Strömsten. 2009. Managing product development the IKEA way. Using target costing in inter-organizational networks. Working Paper, December. Margonelli, Lisa. 2002. How IKEA designs its sexy price tags. *Business 2.0,* October. Terdiman, Daniel. 2008. Anatomy of an IKEA product. CNET News.com, April 19.

Astel's costing system recognizes direct material costs of Provalue as each unit of Provalue is assembled and sold. But Provalue's direct material cost per unit is *locked in*, or *designed in*, much earlier, when product designers choose the components that will go into Provalue. **Locked-in costs—designed-in costs**—are costs that have not yet been incurred but, based on decisions that have already been made, will be incurred in the future.

To manage costs well, a company must identify how design choices lock in costs, *before* the costs are incurred. For example, scrap and rework costs incurred during

Exhibit 12-3

Pattern of Cost Incurrence and Locked-In Costs for Provalue

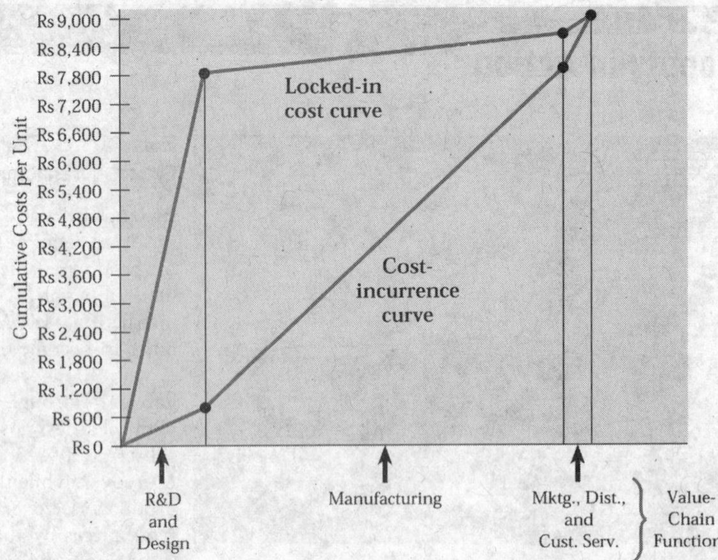

manufacturing are often locked in much earlier by faulty design. Similarly, in the software industry. Costly and difficult-to-fix errors during coding and testing are frequently locked in by bad software designs an analysis.

Exhibit 12-3 illustrates the locked-in cost curve and the cost-incurrence curve for Provalue. The bottom curve, graphically representing cost incurrence, uses information from Exhibit 12-2 to plot the cumulative cost per unit incurred in different business functions of the value chain. The top curve plots how cumulative costs are locked in. (The specific numbers underlying this curve are not presented.) Total cumulative cost per unit for both curves is Rs 9,000. *However, the graph emphasizes the wide divergence between the time when costs are locked in and when they are incurred.* For example, once the product is designed and the operations to manufacture, market, distribute, and support the product are determined, more than 86% (Rs 7,800 ÷ Rs 9,000) of the unit cost of Provalue (for example, direct materials, ordering, testing and rework) is locked in, when only about 8% (Rs 760 ÷ Rs 9,000) of the unit cost is actually incurred!

Value-Chain Analysis and Cross-Functional Teams

A cross-functional value-engineering team consisting of marketing managers, product designers, manufacturing engineers, purchasing managers, suppliers, dealers, and management accountants redesign Provalue to reduce costs while retaining features that customers value. Some of the team's ideas are as follows:

- Use a simpler, more-reliable motherboard without complex features to reduce manufacturing and repair costs..
- Snap-fit rather than solder parts together to decrease direct manufacturing labor-hours and related costs.
- Use fewer components to decrease ordering, receiving, testing, and inspection costs.
- Make Provalue lighter and smaller to reduce distribution and packaging costs.

Management accountants use their understanding of the value chain to estimate cost savings.

Not all costs are locked in at the design stage. Managers always have opportunities to reduce costs by improving operating efficiency and productivity. Many companies combine value engineering with *kaizen*, or *continuous improvement* methods that seek to reduce the time it takes to do a task and to eliminate waste during production and delivery of products.

In summary, the key steps in value-engineering are as follows:

1. Understanding customer requirements, value-added and nonvalue-added costs
2. Anticipating how costs are locked in before they are incurred
3. Using cross-functional teams to redesign products and processes to reduce costs while meeting customer needs

Achieving the Target Cost per Unit for Provalue

Exhibit 12-4 uses an activity-based approach to compare cost-driver quantities and rates for the 1,50,000 units of Provalue manufactured and sold in 2011 and the 2,00,000 units of Provalue II budgeted for 2012. Value engineering reduces both value-added costs (by designing Provalue II to need fewer and less costly direct materials and components in each

Exhibit 12-4 Cost-Driver Quantities and Rates for Provalue in 2011 and Provalue II for 2012 Using Activity-Based Costing

File Edit View Insert Format Tools Data Window Help

	A	B	C	D	E	F	G	H	I	J	K	L	M	N
1														
2			Manufacturing cost information for 150,000 units of Provalue in 2011						Manufacturing cost information for 200,000 units of Provalue II for 2012					
3	**Cost Category**	**Cost Driver**	**Details of Actual Cost Driver Quantities**				**Actual Total Quantity of Cost Driver**	**Actual Cost per Unit of Cost Driver (p. 000)**	**Details of Budgeted Cost Driver Quantities**				**Budgeted Total Quantity of Cost Driver**	**Budgeted Cost per Unit of Cost Driver (Given)**
4	**(1)**	**(2)**	**(3)**		**(4)**		**(5)=(3)x(4)**	**(6)**	**(7)**		**(8)**		**(9)=(7)x(8)**	**(10)**
5	**Direct Manufacturing Costs**													
6	Direct materials	No. of kits	1	kit per unit	1,50,000	units	1,50,000	Rs 4,600	1	kit per unit	2,00,000	units	2,00,000	Rs 3,850
7	Direct manuf. labor (DML)	DML hours	3.2	DML hours per unit	1,50,000	units	4,80,000	Rs200	2.65	DML hours per unit	2,00,000	units	5,30,000	Rs 200
8	Direct machining (fixed)	Machine-hours					3,00,000	Rs 380					3,00,000	Rs 380
9	**Manufacturing Overhead Costs**													
10	Ordering and receiving	No. of orders	50	orders per component	450	compo-nents	22,500	Rs 800	50	orders per compo-nent	425	compo-nents	21,250	Rs 800
11	Testing and inspection	Testing-hours	30	testing-hours per unit	1,50,000	units	45,00,000	Rs 20	15	testing hours per unit	2,00,000	units	30,00,000	Rs 20
12	Rework				8%	defect rate					6.5%	defect rate		
13		Rework-hours	2.5	rework-hours per defective unit	12,000[a]	defective units	30,000	Rs 400	2.5	rework-hours per defective unit	13,000[b]	defective units	32,500	Rs 400
14														
15	[a]8% defect rate x 150,000 units = 12,000 defective units													
16	[b]6.5% defect rate x 200,000 units = 13,000 defective units													

Exhibit 12-5 Target Manufacturing Costs of Provalue II for 2012

	A	B	C	D	E	F
1		PROVALUE II				PROVALUE
2		Budgeted		Budgeted		Actual Manufacturing
3		Manufacturing Costs		Manufacturing		Cost per Unit
4		for 2,00,000 Units		Cost per Unit		(Exhibit 12-1)
5		(1)		(2) = (1) ÷ 2,00,000		(3)
6	Direct manufacturing costs					
7	Direct material costs					
8	(2,00,000 kits x Rs 3,850 per kit)	Rs 77,00,00,000		Rs 3,850.0		Rs 4,600.0
9	Direct manufacturing labor costs					
10	(5,30,000 DML-hours x Rs 200 per hour)	10,60,00,000		530.0		640.0
11	Direct machining costs					
12	(3,00,000 machine-hours x Rs 380 per machine-hour)	11,40,00,000		570.0		760.0
13	Direct manufacturing costs	99,00,00,000		4,950.0		6,000.0
14	Manufacturing overhead costs					
15	Ordering and receiving costs					
16	(21,250 orders x Rs 800 per order)	1,70,00,000		85.0		120.0
17	Testing and inspection costs					
18	(30,00,000 testing-hours x Rs 20 per hour)	6,00,00,000		300.0		600.0
19	Rework costs					
20	(32,500 rework-hours x Rs 400 per hour)	1,30,00,000		65.0		80.0
21	Manufacturing overhead costs	9,00,00,000		450.0		800.0
22	Total manufaturing costs	Rs 1,08,00,00,000		Rs 5,400.0		6,800.0

kit, and fewer direct manufacturing labor-hours and testing-hours per unit) and nonvalue-added costs (by simplifying Provalue II's design to reduce the percentage of units that require rework). Astel maintains 3,00,000 machine-hours of capacity but through value engineering reduces the machine-hours required to make Provalue II to 1.5 hours per unit. This reduction allows Astel to use the 3,00,000 machine-hours of capacity to make and sell more units of Provalue II (2,00,000 units versus 1,50,000 units for Provalue), thereby reducing machining cost per unit. For simplicity, we assume that value engineering will not reduce the Rs 200 cost per direct manufacturing labor-hour, the Rs 800 cost per order, the Rs 20 cost per testing-hour, or the Rs 400 cost per rework-hour. By making these activities more efficient, value engineering can also reduce costs by reducing these cost-driver rates (see the Problem for Self-Study).

Exhibit 12-5 presents the target manufacturing costs of Provalue II, using data for the quantity of the cost driver and the cost-driver rate from the Provalue II columns in Exhibit 12-4. For comparison, Exhibit 12-5 also shows the actual 2009 manufacturing cost per unit of Provalue from Exhibit 12-1. The new design is budgeted to reduce total manufacturing cost per unit by Rs 1,400 (from Rs 6,800 to Rs 5,400) at the budgeted sales quantity of 2,00,000 units. Astel's managers also expect the new design to reduce costs in other business functions from Rs 2,200 (Exhibit 12-2) to Rs 1,800 (calculations not shown). The budgeted full unit cost of Provalue II is Rs 7,200—the target cost per unit. At the end of 2010, Astel's managers will compare actual costs and target costs to gain insight about improvements that can be made in subsequent target-costing efforts.

Unless managed properly, value engineering and target costing can have undesirable effects:

- Employees may feel frustrated if they fail to attain targets.
- The cross-functional team may add too many features just to accommodate the different wishes of team members.
- A product may be in development for a long time as alternative designs are evaluated repeatedly.

- Organizational conflicts may develop as the burden of cutting costs falls unequally on different business functions in the company's value chain, for example, more on manufacturing than on marketing.

To avoid these pitfalls, target-costing efforts should always (a) encourage employee participation and celebrate small improvements toward achieving the target, (b) focus on the customer, (c) pay attention to schedules, and (d) set cost-cutting targets for all value-chain functions to encourage a culture of teamwork and cooperation.

Cost-Plus Pricing

Learning Objective 

Price products using the cost-plus approach

. . . cost-plus pricing is based on some measure of cost plus a markup

Instead of using the market-based approach for their long-run pricing decisions, managers sometimes use a cost-based approach. The general formula for setting a cost-based price adds a markup component to the cost base to determine a prospective selling price. Because a markup is added, cost-based pricing is often called cost-plus pricing, with the plus referring to the markup component. Managers use the cost-plus pricing formula only as a starting point for pricing decisions. Therefore, the markup component is rarely a rigid number. Instead, it is flexible, depending on the behavior of customers and competitors. The markup component is ultimately determined by the market.[4]

Cost-Plus Target Rate of Return on Investment

We illustrate a cost-plus pricing formula for our Astel example. Assume Astel's engineers have redesigned Provalue into Provalue II and that Astel uses a 12% markup on the full unit cost of the product in developing the prospective selling price.

Cost base (full unit cost of Provalue II)	Rs 7,200
Markup component of 12% (0.12 × Rs 7,200)	864
Prospective selling price	Rs 8064

How is the markup percentage of 12% determined? One way is to choose a markup to earn a *target rate of return on investment*. The **target rate of return on investment** is the target annual operating income that an organization aims to achieve divided by invested capital. Invested capital can be defined in many ways. In this chapter, we define invested capital as total assets—that is, long-term assets plus current assets. Suppose Astel's (pretax) target rate of return on investment is 18% and Provalue II's capital investment is Rs 96,00,00,000. The target annual operating income for Provalue II is:

Invested capital	Rs 96,00,00,000
Target rate of return on investment	18%
Target annual operating income (0.18 × 96,00,00,000)	Rs 17,28,00,000
Target operating income per unit of Provalue II (Rs 17,28,00,000 ÷ 2,00,000 units)	Rs 864.0

This calculation indicates that Astel needs to earn a target operating income of Rs 864 on each unit of Provalue II. The markup of Rs 864 expressed as a percentage of the full product cost per unit of Rs 7,200 equals 12% (Rs 864 ÷ Rs 7,200).

Do not confuse the 18% target rate of return on investment with the 12% markup percentage.

- The 18% target rate of return on investment expresses Astel's expected annual operating income as a percentage of investment.
- The 12% markup expresses operating income per unit as a percentage of the full product cost per unit.

[4] Exceptions are pricing of electricity and natural gas in many countries, where prices are set by the government on the basis of costs plus a return on invested capital. Chapter 15 discusses the use of costs to set prices in the defense-contracting industry. In these situations, products are not subject to competitive forces and cost accounting techniques substitute for markets as the basis for setting prices.

Astel first calculates target rate of return on investment and then determines markup percentage.

Alternative Cost-Plus Methods

Companies sometimes find it difficult to determine the specific amount of capital they invested to support a specific product. That's because computing the specific amount of invested capital requires knowing, for example, the allocations of investments in equipment and buildings to produce individual products—a difficult and somewhat arbitrary task. Some companies prefer to use alternative cost bases and markup percentages that still earn a return on invested capital but do not require explicit calculations of invested capital to set prices.

The following table presents some alternative cost bases for Provalue II without providing details of the calculations and using assumed markup percentages.

Cost Base	Estimated Cost per Unit (1)	Markup Percentage (2)	Markup Component (3) ÷ (1) × (2)	Prospective Selling Price (4)= (1) + (3)
Variable manufacturing cost	Rs 4,750.00	65%	Rs 3,087.5	Rs 7,837.5
Variable cost of the product	5,470.00	45	2,461.5	7,931.5
Manufacturing cost	5,400.00	50	2,700.0	8,100.0
Full cost of the product	7,200.00	12	864.0	8,064.0

The different cost bases and markup percentages give four prospective selling prices that are close to each other. In practice, a company will choose a cost base that it regards as reliable and a markup percentage that is based on its experience in pricing products to recover its costs and earn a target return on investment. For example, a company may choose the full cost of the product as a base if it is unsure about distinguishing variable costs from fixed costs.

The markup percentages in the preceding table vary a great deal, from a high of 65% on variable manufacturing cost to a low of 12% on full cost of the product. Why the wide variation? When determining a prospective selling price, a cost base such as variable manufacturing cost (that includes fewer costs) requires a higher markup percentage because the price needs to be set to earn a profit margin *and* to recover costs that have been excluded from the base.

Surveys indicate that most managers use the full cost of the product for their cost-based pricing decisions—that is, they include both fixed and variable costs when calculating the cost per unit. Managers cite the following advantages for including fixed cost per unit in the cost base for pricing decisions:

1. **Full recovery of all costs of the product.** For long-run pricing decisions, full cost of the product informs managers of the minimum cost they need to recover to continue in business. Using just the variable cost as a base does not give managers this information. There is then a temptation, as has happened in the airline industry, to engage in excessive long-run price cutting as long as prices provide a positive contribution margin. Long-run price cutting, however, will result in losses if long-run revenues are less than the long-run full cost of the product.
2. **Price stability.** Managers believe that basing prices on the full cost of the product promotes price stability, because it limits the ability and temptations of salespersons to cut prices. Managers prefer price stability because it facilitates more-accurate forecasting and planning.
3. **Simplicity.** A full-cost formula for pricing does not require a detailed analysis of cost-behavior patterns to separate costs into fixed and variable components. Variable and fixed cost components are difficult to identify for many costs such as testing, inspection, and setups.

Including fixed cost per unit in the cost base for pricing is not without problems. Allocating fixed costs to products can be arbitrary. Also, calculating fixed cost per unit requires a denominator level that is likely only an estimate of capacity or expected units of future sales. Errors in these estimates will cause actual full cost per unit of the product to differ from the estimated amount.

Cost-Plus Pricing and Target Pricing

The selling prices computed under cost-plus pricing are *prospective* prices. Suppose Astel's initial product design results in a Rs 7,500 full cost for Provalue II. Assuming a 12% markup, Astel sets a prospective price of Rs 8,400 [Rs 7,500 + (0.12 × Rs 7,500)]. In the competitive personal computer market, customer and competitor reactions to this price may force Astel to reduce the markup percentage and lower the price to, say, Rs 8,000. Astel may then want to redesign Provalue II to reduce the full cost to Rs 7,200 per unit, as in our example, and achieve a markup close to 12% while keeping the price at Rs 8,000. The eventual design and cost-plus price chosen must balance the trade-offs among costs, markup, and customer reactions.

The target-pricing approach reduces the need to go back and forth among prospective cost-plus prices, customer reactions, and design modifications. Relative to cost-plus pricing, target pricing first determines product characteristics and target price on the basis of customer preferences and expected competitor responses, and then a target cost.

Suppliers who provide unique products and services—accountants and management consultants, for example—usually use cost-plus pricing. Professional service firms set prices based on hourly cost-plus billing rates of partners, managers, and associates. These prices are, however, reduced in competitive situations. Professional service firms also take a multiple-year client perspective when deciding prices. Certified public accountants, for example, sometimes charge a client a low price initially and a higher price later.

Service companies such as home repair services, automobile repair services, and architectural firms use a cost-plus pricing method called the *time-and-materials method*. Individual jobs are priced based on materials and labor time. The price charged for materials equals the cost of materials plus a markup. The price charged for labor represents the cost of labor plus a markup. That is, the price charged for each direct cost item includes its own markup. The markups are chosen to recover overhead costs and earn a profit.

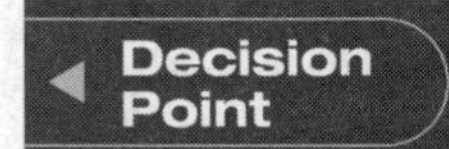

How do companies price products using the cost-plus approach?

Life-Cycle Product Budgeting and Costing

Learning Objective 7

Use life-cycle budgeting and costing when making pricing decisions

. . . accumulate all costs of a product from initial R&D to final customer service for each year of its life

Companies sometimes need to consider target prices and target costs for a product over a multiple-year product life cycle. The **product life cycle** spans the time from initial R&D on a product to when customer service and support is no longer offered for that product. For automobile companies such as DaimlerChrysler, Ford, and Nissan, the product life cycle for different car models ranges from 12 to 15 years to design, introduce, and sell different car models. For pharmaceutical products, the life cycle at companies such as Pfizer, Merck, and Glaxo Smith Kline may be 15 to 20 years. For banks such as Wachovia and Chase Manhattan Bank, a product such as a newly designed savings account with specific privileges can have a life cycle of 10 to 20 years. Personal computers have a shorter life-cycle of 3 to 5 years, because rapid innovations in the computing power and speed of microprocessors that run the computers makes older models obsolete.

In **life-cycle budgeting**, managers estimate the revenues and business function costs of the value chain attributable to each product from its initial R&D to its final customer service and support. **Life-cycle costing** tracks and accumulates business function costs of the value chain attributable to each product from initial R&D to final customer service and support. Life-cycle budgeting and life-cycle costing span several years.

Life-Cycle Budgeting and Pricing Decisions

Budgeted life-cycle costs can provide useful information for strategically evaluating pricing decisions. Consider Insight, Inc., a computer software company, which is developing a new accounting package, "General Ledger." Assume the following budgeted amounts for General Ledger over a six-year product life cycle:

Years 1 and 2

	Total Fixed Costs
R&D costs	Rs 24,00,000
Design costs	16,00,000

Years 3 to 6

	Total Fixed Costs	Variable Cost per Package
Production costs	Rs 10,00,000	Rs 250
Marketing costs	7,00,000	240
Distribution costs	5,00,000	160
Customer-service costs	8,00,000	300

Exhibit 12-6 presents the life-cycle budget for General Ledger for three alternative selling-price/sales-quantity combinations.

Several features make life-cycle budgeting particularly important:

1. **The development period for R&D and design is long and costly.** In the General Ledger example, R&D and design span two years and constitute more than 30% of total costs for each of the three combinations of selling price and predicted sales quantity. When a high percentage of total life-cycle costs are incurred before any production begins and before any revenues are received, the company especially needs to consider revenues and costs over the life-cycle of the product. It uses this information to decide whether to begin the costly R&D and design activities.
2. **Many costs are locked in at R&D and design stages—even if R&D and design costs themselves are small.** In our General Ledger example, a poorly designed accounting software package that is difficult to install and use would result in higher marketing, distribution, and customer-service costs in several subsequent years. These costs would be even higher if the product failed to meet promised quality-performance levels. A life-cycle revenue-and-cost budget prevents these relationships among business-function costs across years from being overlooked in decision making. Life-cycle budgeting highlights costs throughout the product's life cycle and so facilitates target pricing, target costing, and value engineering at the design stage before costs are locked in. The amounts presented in Exhibit 12-6 are the outcome of value engineering.

Insight decides to sell the General Ledger package for Rs 4,800 per package because this price maximizes life-cycle operating income. Insight's managers will eventually compare actual costs incurred to life-cycle budgets to obtain feedback and learn about how to estimate costs for subsequent products. Exhibit 12-6 assumes that the selling price per package is the same over the entire life cycle. For strategic reasons, however, Insight may decide to skim the market—charging higher prices to customers eager to try General Ledger when it is first introduced and lowering prices later as the product matures. In these later stages, Insight may even add new features to differentiate the product to maintain prices and sales. The life-cycle budget must then incorporate these strategies.

Management of environmental costs provides another example of life-cycle costing and value engineering. Environmental laws—have introduced tougher environmental standards, imposed stringent cleanup requirements, and introduced severe penalties for polluting the air and contaminating subsurface soil and groundwater. Environmental costs that are incurred over several years of the product's life-cycle are often locked in at the product- and process-design stage. To avoid environmental liabilities, companies in industries such as oil refining, chemical processing, and automobiles do value engineering; they design products and processes to prevent and reduce pollution over the product's life cycle. For example, laptop computer manufacturers like Hewlett Packard and Apple have introduced costly recycling programs to ensure that chemicals from nickel-cadmium batteries do not leak hazardous chemicals into the soil.

Exhibit 12-6

Budgeting Life-Cycle Revenues and Costs for "General Ledger" Software Package of Insight, Inc.[a]

	Alternative Selling-Price/ Sales-Quantity Combinations		
	A	**B**	**C**
Selling price per package	Rs 4,000	Rs 4,800	Rs 6,000
Sales quantity in units	5,000	4,000	2,500
Life-cycle revenues (Rs 4,000 × 5,000; Rs 4,800 × 4,000; Rs 6,000 × 2,500)	Rs 2,00,00,000	Rs 1,92,00,000	Rs 1,50,00,000
Life-cycle costs			
R&D costs	24,00,000	24,00,000	24,00,000
Design costs of product/process	16,00,000	16,00,000	16,00,000
Production costs Rs 10,00,000 + (Rs 250 × 5,000); Rs 10,00,000 + (Rs 250 × 4,000); Rs 10,00,000 + (Rs 250 × 2,500)	22,50,000	20,00,000	16,25,000
Marketing costs Rs 7,00,000 + (Rs 240 × 5,000); Rs 7,00,000+ (Rs 240× 4,000); Rs 7,00,000 + (Rs 240 × 2,500)	19,00,000	16,60,000	13,00,000
Distribution costs Rs 5,00,000 + (Rs 160 × 5,000); Rs 5,00,000+ (Rs 160 ×4,000); Rs 5,00,000 + (Rs 160×2,500)	13,00,000	11,40,000	9,00,000
Customer-service costs Rs 8,00,000 + (Rs 300× 5,000); Rs 8,00,000 + (Rs 300× 4,000); Rs 8,00,000 + (Rs 300 × 2,500)	23,00,000	20,00,000	15,50,000
Total life-cycle costs	1,17,50,000	1,08,00,000	93,75,000
Life-cycle operating income	Rs 82,50,000	Rs 84,00,000	Rs 56,25,000

[a]This exhibit does not take into consideration the time value of money when computing life-cycle revenues or life-cycle costs. Chapter 21 outlines how this important factor can be incorporated into such calculations.

Customer Life-Cycle Costing

A different notion of life-cycle costs is *customer life-cycle costs*. **Customer life-cycle costs** focus on the total costs incurred by a customer to acquire, use, maintain, and dispose of a product or service. Customer life-cycle costs influence the prices a company can charge for its products. For example, Ford can charge a higher price and/or gain market share if its cars require minimal maintenance for 100,000 miles. Similarly, Maytag charges higher prices for appliances that save electricity and have low maintenance costs. Boeing Corporation justifies a higher price for the Boeing 777 because the plane's design allows mechanics easier access to different areas of the plane to perform routine maintenance, reduces the time and cost of maintenance, and significantly decreases the life-cycle cost of owning the plane.

Decision Point

Describe life-cycle budgeting and life-cycle costing and when companies should use these techniques.

Additional Considerations for Pricing Decisions

Learning Objective 8

Describe two pricing practices in which noncost factors are important when setting prices

. . . price discrimination—charging different customers different prices for the same product; and peak-load pricing—charging higher prices when demand approaches capacity

In some cases, cost is *not* a major factor in setting prices. We explore some of the ways that market structures and laws and regulations influence price setting outside of cost.

Price Discrimination

Consider the prices airlines charge for a round-trip flight from New Delhi to Bombay. A coach-class ticket for a flight with 21-day advance purchase is Rs 4,000 if the passenger stays in Bombay over a Saturday night. It is Rs 18,000 if the passenger returns without staying over a Saturday night. Can this price difference be explained by the difference in the cost to the airline of these round-trip flights? No; it costs the same amount to transport the passenger from New Delhi to Bombay and back, regardless of whether the passenger stays in Bombay over a Saturday night. To explain this difference in price, we must recognize the potential for *price discrimination*.

Price discrimination is the practice of charging different customers different prices for the same product or service. How does price discrimination work in our airline example? The demand for airline tickets comes from two main sources: business travelers and pleasure travelers. Business travelers must travel to conduct business for their organizations, so their demand for air travel is relatively insensitive to price and airlines can earn higher operating incomes by charging business travelers higher prices. Insensitivity of demand to price changes is called *demand inelasticity*. Also, business travelers generally go to their destinations, complete their work, and return home without staying over a Saturday night. Pleasure travelers, however, usually don't need to return home during the week, and they prefer to spend weekends at their destinations. Because they pay for their tickets themselves, pleasure travelers' demand is more price-elastic, lowering prices stimulates demand. Airlines can earn higher operating incomes by charging pleasure travelers lower prices.

How can airlines keep fares high for business travelers while, at the same time, keeping fares low for pleasure travelers? Requiring a Saturday night stay discriminates between the two customer segments. The airlines price-discriminate to take advantage of different sensitivities to prices exhibited by business travelers and pleasure travelers. Price differences exist even though there is no cost difference in serving the two segments of customers.

What if economic conditions weaken such that business travelers become more sensitive to price? The airlines may then need to lower the prices charged to business travelers. Following the events of September 11, 2001, airlines started offering discounted fares on certain routes without requiring a Saturday night stay to stimulate business travel. Business travel picked up and airlines started filling more seats than they otherwise would have. Unfortunately, travel did not pick up enough, and the airline industry as a whole suffered severe losses over the next few years.

Peak-Load Pricing

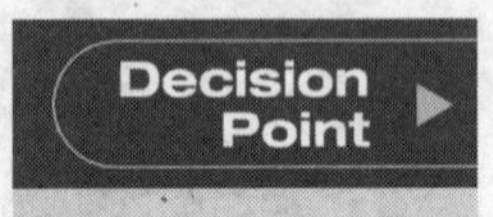

Describe price discrimination and peak-load pricing.

In addition to price discrimination, pricing decisions also consider other noncost factors such as capacity constraints. **Peak-load pricing** is the practice of charging a higher price for the same product or service when the demand for it approaches the physical limit of the capacity to produce that product or service. Prices charged during periods when demand on the production capacity is high represent what customers are willing to pay for the product or service. These prices are greater than the prices charged when slack or excess capacity is available when the goal is to utilize capacity by lowering prices to stimulate demand. Peak-load pricing occurs in the telephone, telecommunications, hotel, car rental, and electric-utility industries. For the 2004 Summer Olympics in Athens, hotels charged very high rates and required multiple-night stays. Airlines charged high fares for flights into and out of many cities in the region for roughly a month around the time of the games. Given that demand far exceeded capacity, the hospitality industry and airlines employed peak-load pricing to increase their profits.

International Considerations

Another example of considerations other than costs affecting prices occurs when the same product is sold in different countries. Consider software, books, and medicines produced in one country and sold globally. The prices charged in each country vary much more than the costs of delivering the product to each country. These price differences arise because of differences in the purchasing power of consumers in different countries (a form of price discrimination) and government restrictions that may limit the prices that can be charged.

Problem for Self-Study

Reconsider the Astel Computer example. Astel's marketing manager realizes that a further reduction in price is necessary to sell 2,00,000 units of Provalue II. To maintain a target profitability of Rs 16,00,00,000 or Rs 800 per unit, Astel will need to reduce costs of Provalue II by Rs 6,00,00,000 or Rs 300 per unit. Astel targets a reduction of Rs 4,00,00,000, or Rs 200 per unit, in manufacturing costs, and Rs 2,00,00,000 or Rs 100 per unit, in marketing, distribution, and customer-service costs. The cross-functional team assigned to this task proposes the following changes to manufacture a different version of Provalue, called Provalue III:

1. Reduce direct materials and ordering costs by purchasing subassembled components rather than individual components.
2. Reengineer ordering and receiving to reduce ordering and receiving costs per order.
3. Reduce testing time and the labor and power required per hour of testing.
4. Develop new rework procedures to reduce rework costs per hour.

No changes are proposed in direct manufacturing labor cost per unit and in total machining costs.

The following table summarizes the cost-driver quantities and the cost per unit of each cost driver for Provalue III compared with Provalue II.

File Edit View Insert Format Tools Data Window Help

	A	B	C	D	E	F	G	H	I	J	K	L	M	N
1				Manufacturing cost information						Manufacturing cost information				
2				for 200,000 units of Provalue II for 2010						for 200,000 units of Provalue III for 2010				
3	Cost Category	Cost Driver	Details of Budgeted Cost Driver Quantities				Budgeted Total Quantity of Cost Driver	Budgeted Cost per Unit of Cost Driver	Details of Budgeted Cost Driver Quantities				Budgeted Total Quantity of Cost Driver	Budgeted Cost per Unit of Cost Driver
4	(1)	(2)	(3)		(4)		(5)=(3)x(4)	(6)	(7)		(8)		(9)=(7)x(8)	(10)
5	Direct materials	No. of kits	1	kit per unit	2,00,000	units	2,00,000	Rs 3,850	1	kit per unit	2,00,000	units	2,00,000	Rs 3,750
6	Direct manuf. labor (DML)	DML hours	2.65	DML hours per unit	2,00,000	units	5,30,000	Rs 200	2.65	DML hours per unit	2,00,000	units	5,30,000	Rs 200
7	Direct machining (fixed)	Machine-hours					3,00,000	Rs 380					3,00,000	Rs 380
8	Ordering and receiving	No. of orders	50	orders per component	425	components	21,250	Rs 800	50	orders per component	400	components	20,000	Rs 600
9	Test and inspection	Testing-hours	15	testing-hours per unit	2,00,000	units	30,00,000	Rs 20	14	testing-hours per unit	2,00,000	units	28,00,000	Rs 17
10	Rework				6.5%	defect rate					6.5%	defect rate		
11		Rework-hours	2.5	rework-hours per defective unit	13,000[a]	defective units	32,500	Rs 400	2.5	rework-hours per defective unit	13,000[a]	defective units	32,500	Rs 320
12														
13	[a]6.5% defect rate x 200,000 units = 13,000 defective units													

Will the proposed changes achieve Astel's targeted reduction of Rs 4,00,00,000, or Rs 200 per unit, in manufacturing costs for Provalue III? Show your computations. **Required**

Solution

Exhibit 12-7 presents the manufacturing costs for Provalue III based on the proposed changes. Manufacturing costs will decline from Rs 108,00,00,000, or Rs 5,400 per unit (Exhibit 12-5), to Rs 104,00,00,000, or Rs 5,200 per unit (Exhibit 12-7), and will achieve the target reduction of Rs 4,00,00,000, or Rs 200 per unit.

Exhibit 12-7

Target Manufacturing Costs of Provalue III for 2010 Based on Proposed Changes

	A	B	C	D
1		Budgeted		Budgeted
2		Manufacturing Costs		Manufacturing
3		for, 200,000 Units		Cost per Unit
4		(1)		(2) = (1) ÷ 2,00,000
5	Direct manufacturing costs			
6	Direct material costs			
7	(2,00,000 kits x Rs 3,750 per kit)	Rs 75,00,00,000		Rs 3,750
8	Direct manufacturing labor costs			
9	(5,30,000 DML-hours x Rs 200 per hour)	10,60,00,000		530
10	Direct machining costs			
11	(3,00,000 machine-hours x Rs 380 per machine-hour)	11,40,00,000		570
12	Direct manufacturing costs	97,00,00,000		4,850
13				
14	Manufacturing overhead costs			
15	Ordering and receiving costs			
16	(20,000 orders x Rs 600 per order)	1,20,00,000		60
17	Testing and inspection costs			
18	(28,00,000 testing-hours x Rs 17 per hour)	4,76,00,000		238
19	Rework costs			
20	(32,500 rework-hours x Rs 320 per hour)	1,04,00,000		52
21	Manufacturing overhead costs	7,00,00,000		350
22	Total manufacturing costs	Rs 104,00,00,000		Rs 5,200

Decision Points

The following question-and-answer format summarizes the chapter's learning objectives. Each decision presents a key question related to a learning objective. The guidelines are the answers to that question.

Decision	Guidelines
1. What are the three major influences on pricing decisions?	Customers, competitors, and costs influence prices through their effects on demand and supply; customers and competitors affect demand, and costs affect supply.
2. How do short-run pricing decisions differ from long-run pricing decisions?	Short-run pricing decisions focus on a time horizon of less than a year and have no long-run implications. Long-run pricing decisions focus on a time horizon of a year or longer. The time horizon appropriate to a decision on pricing dictates which costs are relevant, how costs are managed, and the profit that must be earned.
3. How do companies determine target costs?	One approach to long-run pricing is to use a target price. Target price is the estimated price that potential customers are willing to pay for a product or service. Target operating income per unit is subtracted from the target price to determine target cost per unit. Target cost per unit is the estimated long-run cost of a product or service that when sold enables the company to achieve target operating income per unit. The challenge for the company is to make the cost improvements necessary through value-engineering methods to achieve the target cost.

4. Why is it important to distinguish cost incurrence from locked-in costs?	Cost incurrence describes when a resource is sacrificed. Locked-in costs are costs not yet incurred but which, based on decisions that have already been made, will be incurred in the future. To reduce costs, techniques such as value engineering are most effective *before* costs are locked in.
5. How do companies price products using the cost-plus approach?	The cost-plus approach to pricing adds a markup component to a cost base as the starting point for pricing decisions. Many different costs, such as full cost of the product or manufacturing cost, can serve as the cost base in applying the cost-plus formula. Prices are then modified on the basis of customers' reactions and competitors' responses. Therefore, the size of the "plus" is determined by the marketplace.
6. What are life-cycle budgeting and life-cycle costing, and when should companies use these techniques?	Life-cycle budgeting estimates and life-cycle costing tracks and accumulates the costs (and revenues) attributable to a product from its initial R&D to its final customer service and support. These life-cycle techniques are particularly important when (a) a high percentage of total life-cycle costs are incurred before production begins and revenues are earned over several years, and (b) a high fraction of the life-cycle costs are locked in at the R&D and design stages.
7. What are price discrimination and peak-load pricing?	Price discrimination is charging some customers a higher price for a given product or service than other customers. Peak-load pricing is charging a higher price for the same product or service when demand approaches physical-capacity limits. Under price discrimination and peak-load pricing, prices differ among market segments even though the cost of providing the product or service is approximately the same.
8. How do antitrust laws affect pricing?	To comply with antitrust laws, a company must not engage in predatory pricing, dumping, or collusive pricing, which lessen competition; put another company at a competitive disadvantage; or harm consumers.

TERMS TO LEARN

The chapter and the Glossary at the end of the book contain definitions of:

collusive pricing (**p. 515**)
cost incurrence (**p. 502**)
customer life-cycle costs (**p. 511**)
designed-in costs (**p. 503**)
dumping (**p. 515**)
life-cycle budgeting (**p. 509**)
life-cycle costing (**p. 509**)
locked-in costs (**p. 503**)
nonvalue-added cost (**p. 502**)
peak-load pricing (**p. 512**)
predatory pricing (**p. 515**)
price discrimination (**p. 512**)
product life cycle (**p. 509**)
target cost per unit (**p. 501**)
target operating income per unit (**p. 501**)
target price (**p. 500**)
target rate of return on investment (**p. 507**)
value-added cost (**p. 502**)
value engineering (**p. 502**)

ASSIGNMENT MATERIAL

Questions

12-1 What are the three major influences on pricing decisions?

12-2 "Relevant costs for pricing decisions are full costs of the product." Do you agree? Explain.

12-3 Give two examples of pricing decisions with a short-run focus.

12-4 How is activity-based costing useful for pricing decisions?

12-5 Describe two alternative approaches to long-run pricing decisions.

12-6 What is a target cost per unit?

12-7 Describe value engineering and its role in target costing.

12-8 Give two examples of a value-added cost and two examples of a nonvalue-added cost.

12-9 "It is not important for a company to distinguish between cost incurrence and locked-in costs." Do you agree? Explain.

12-10 What is cost-plus pricing?

12-11 Describe three alternative cost-plus pricing methods.

12-12 Give two examples in which the difference in the costs of two products or services is much smaller than the difference in their prices.

12-13 What is life-cycle budgeting?

12-14 What are three benefits of using a product life-cycle reporting format?

12-15 Define predatory pricing, dumping, and collusive pricing.

Solved Examples

12-16 **Relevant-cost approach to short-run pricing decisions.** The Videocon Company is an electronics business with eight product lines. Income data for one of the products (XT-I07) for June are:

Revenues, 200,000 units at average price of Rs 1,000		Rs 20,00,00,000
Variable costs		
Direct materials at Rs 350 per unit	Rs 7,00,00,000	
Direct manufacturing labor at Rs 100 per unit	2,00,00,000	
Variable manufacturing overhead at Rs 50 per unit	1,00,00,000	
Sales commissions at 15 % of revenues	3,00,00,000	
Other variable costs at Rs 50 per unit	1,00,00,000	
Total variable costs		14,00,00,000
Contribution margin		6,00,00,000
Fixed costs		5,00,00,000
Operating income		Rs 1,00,00,000

Delhi Electronics an instruments company, has a problem with its preferred supplier of XT-I07 components. This supplier has had a three-week labor strike. Delhi Electronics approaches the sales representative, Sachin, of the Videocon Company about providing 3,000 units of XT-I07 at a price of Rs 800 per unit. Sachin informs the XT-I07 product manager, that he would accept a flat commission of Rs 60,000 rather than the usual 15% of revenues if this special order were accepted. Videocon has the capacity to produce 3,00,000 units of XT-107 each month, but demand has not exceeded 2,00,000 units in any month in the past year.

Required

1. If the 3,000-unit order from Delhi Electronics is accepted, how much will operating income increase or decrease? (Assume the same cost structure as in June.)
2. Production Manager ponders whether to accept the 3,000-unit special order. He is afraid of the precedent that might be set by cutting the price. He says, "The price is below our full cost of Rs 950 per unit. I think we should quote a full price, or Delhi Electronics will expect favored treatment again and again if we continue to do business with them." Do you agree with Production Manager? Explain.

Solution

Relevant-cost approach to short-run pricing decisions.

1. Analysis of special order:

Sales, 3,000 units × Rs 800		Rs 24,00,000
Variable costs		
Direct materials, 3,000 units × Rs 350	Rs 10,50,000	
Direct manufacturing labor, 3,000 units × Rs 100	3,00,000	
Variable manufacturing overhead, 3,000 units × Rs 50	1,50,000	
Other variable costs, 3,000 units × Rs 50	1,50,000	
Sales commission	60,000	
Total variable costs		17,10,000
Contribution margin		Rs 6,90,000

Note that the variable costs, except for commissions, are affected by production volume, not sales rupees. If the special order is accepted, operating income would be Rs 1,00,00,000 = Rs 6,90,000 = Rs 1,06,90,000.

2. Whether Production Manager is making a correct decision depends on many factors. He is incorrect if the capacity would otherwise be idle and if his objective is to increase operating income in the short run. If the offer is rejected, Videocon, in effect, is willing to invest Rs 6,90,000 in immediate gains forgone (an opportunity cost) to preserve the long-run selling-price structure. Production Manager is correct if he thinks future competition or future price concessions to customers will hurt Videocon's operating income by more than Rs 6,90,000.

There is also the possibility that Delhi Electronics could become a long-term customer. In this case, is it a price that covers only short-run variable costs adequate? Would Sachin be willing to accept a Rs 60,000 sales commission (as distinguished from his regular Rs 3,60,000 = 15% × Rs 24,00,000) for every Delhi Electronics order of this size if Delhi Electronics becomes a long-term customer?

12-17 Short-run pricing, capacity constraints. Tata Chemicals makes a specialized chemical product, Bolzene, from a specially imported material, Pyrone. To make 1 kilogram of Bolzene requires 1.5 kilogram of Pyrone. Bolzene has a contribution margin of Rs 60 per kilogram. Tata has just received a request to manufacture 3,000 kilograms of Seltium, which also requires Pyrone as the material input. An analyst at Tata calculates the following costs of making 1 kilogram of Seltium:

Pyrone (2 kilograms x Rs 40 per kilogram)	Rs 80
Direct manufacturing labor	40
Variable manufacturing overhead cost	30
Fixed manufacturing overhead cost allocated	50
Total manufacturing cost	200

Tata has adequate unused plant capacity to make Seltium.

Required

1. Suppose Tata has adequate Pyrone available to make Seltium. What is the minimum price per kilogram that Tata should charge to manufacture Seltium?
2. Now suppose Pyrone is in short supply. The Pyrone used to make Seltium will reduce the Bolzene that Tata can make and sell. What is the minimum price per kilogram that Tata should charge to manufacture Seltium?

Solution

Short-run pricing, capacity constraints.

1. With no constraints on availability of Pyrone or on plant capacity, Tata would want to charge a minimum price for Seltium that would cover its incremental costs to manufacture Seltium. (Because there is excess capacity, there is no opportunity cost.) In this case, the incremental costs are the variable costs to manufacture a kilogram of Seltium:

Pyrone (2 kilograms × Rs 40 per kilogram)	Rs 80
Direct manufacturing labor	40
Variable manufacturing overhead costs	30
Total variable manufacturing costs	Rs 150

Hence, the minimum price that Tata should charge to manufacture Seltium is Rs 150 per kilogram. For 3,000 kilograms of Seltium, it should charge a minimum of Rs 4,50,000 (Rs 150 × 3,000).

2. Now Pyrone is in short supply. Using it to make Seltium reduces the Bolzene that Tata can make and sell. There is, therefore, an opportunity cost of manufacturing Seltium, the lost contribution from using the Pyrone to manufacture Bolzene. To make 3,000 kilograms of Seltium requires 6,000 (2 × 3,000) kilograms of Pyrone.
   The 6,000 kilograms of Pyrone can be used to manufacture 4,000 (6,000 ÷ 1.5) kilograms of Bolzene, since each kilogram of Bolzene requires 1.5 kilograms of Pyrone.
   The contribution margin from 4,000 kilograms of Bolzene is Rs 2,40,000 (Rs 60 per kilogram × 4,000 kilograms). This is the opportunity cost of using Pyrone to manufacture Seltium. The minimum price that Tata should charge to manufacture Seltium should cover not only the incremental (variable) costs of manufacturing Seltium but also the opportunity cost:

Relevant Costs	Costs of Manufacturing Seltium Total for 3,000 Kilograms (1)	Per Kilogram (2) = (1) ÷ 3,000
Incremental (variable) costs of manufacturing Seltium	Rs 4,50,000	Rs 150
Opportunity cost of forgoing manufacture and sale of Bolzene	2,40,000	80
Minimum cost of order	Rs 6,90,000	Rs 230

For 3,000 kilograms of Seltium, Tata should charge a minimum of Rs 6,90,000. The minimum price per kilogram that Tata should charge for Seltium is Rs 230 per kilogram (Rs 6,90,000 ÷ 3,000 kilograms).

12-18 Value-added, nonvalue-added costs. The Laxmi Repair Shop repairs and services machine tools. A summary of its costs (by activity) for April–June is as follows:

a. Materials and labor for servicing machine tools	Rs 8,00,000
b. Rework costs	75,000
c. Expediting costs caused by work delays	60,000
d. Materials-handling costs	50,000
e. Materials procurement and inspection costs	35,000
f. Preventive maintenance of equipment	15,000
g. Breakdown maintenance of equipment	55,000

Required

1. Classify each cost as value-added, nonvalue-added, or in the gray area in between.
2. For any cost classified in the gray area, assume 65 % of it is value-added and 35 % is nonvalue-added. How much of the total of all seven costs is value-added and how much is nonvalue-added?

3. Laxmi is considering the following changes: (a) introducing quality improvement programs whose net effect will be to reduce rework and expediting costs by 75 % and materials and labor costs for servicing machine tools by 5 %; (b) working with suppliers to reduce materials procurement and inspection costs by 20 % and materials-handling costs by 25 %; and (c) increasing preventive maintenance costs by 50 % to reduce breakdown maintenance costs by 40 %. Calculate the effect of programs (a), (b), and (c) on value-added costs, nonvalue-added costs, and total costs? Comment briefly.

Solution

Value-added, nonvalue-added costs.

1.

Category	**Examples**	
Value-added costs	a. Materials and labor for servicing machine tools	Rs 8,00,000
Nonvalue-added costs	b. Rework costs	Rs 75,000
	c. Expediting costs caused by work delays	60,000
	g. Breakdown maintenance of equipment	55,000
	Total	Rs 1,90,000
Gray area	d. Materials handling costs	Rs 50,000
	e. Materials procurement and inspection costs	35,000
	f. Preventive maintenance of equipment	15,000
	Total	Rs 1,00,000

Classifications of value-added, nonvalue-added, and gray area costs are often not clear-cut. Other classifications of some of the cost categories are also plausible. For example, some students may include materials handling, materials procurement, and inspection costs and preventive maintenance as value-added costs (costs that customers perceive as adding value and as being necessary for good repair service) rather than as in the gray area. Preventive maintenance, for instance, might be regarded as value-added because it helps prevent nonvalue-adding breakdown maintenance.

2. Total costs in the gray area are Rs 1,00,000. Of this, we assume 65%, or Rs 65,000, are value-added and 35%, or Rs 35,000, are nonvalue-added

Total value-added costs: Rs 8,00,000 + Rs 65,000	Rs 8,65,000
Total nonvalue-added costs: Rs 1,90,000 + Rs 35,000	2,25,000
Total costs	Rs 10,90,000

Nonvalue-added costs are Rs 2,25,000 ÷ Rs 10,90,000 = 20.64% of total costs.
Value-added costs are Rs 8,65,000 ÷ Rs 10,90,000 = 79.36% of total costs.

3.

Program	**Effect on Costs Classified as** Value-Added	Nonvalue-Added	Gray Area
(a) Quality improvement programs to			
• reduce rework costs by 75% (0.75 × Rs 75,000)		– Rs 56,250	
• reduce expediting costs by 75% (0.75 × Rs 60,000)		– 45,000	
• reduce materials and labor costs by 5% (0.05 × Rs 8,00,000)	– Rs 40,000		
Total effect	– Rs 40,000	– Rs 1,01,250	
(b) Working with suppliers to			
• reduce materials procurement and inspection costs by 20% (0.20 × Rs 35,000)			– Rs 7,000
• reduce materials handling costs by 25% (0.25 × Rs 50,000)			– 12,500
Total effect			–19,500
Transferring 65% of gray area costs (0.65 × Rs 19,500 = Rs 12,675) as value-added and 35% (0.35 × Rs 19,500 = Rs 6,825) as nonvalue-added	– Rs 12,675	– Rs 6,825	+ 19,500
Effect on value-added and nonvalue-added costs	– Rs 12,675	– Rs 6,825	Rs 0
(c) Maintenance programs to			
•increase preventive maintenance costs by 50% (0.50 × Rs 15,000)			+ Rs 7,500
•decrease breakdown maintenance costs by 40% (0.40 × Rs 55,000)		– Rs 22,000	
Total effect		– 22,000	
Transferring 65% of gray area costs (0.65 × Rs 7,500 = Rs 4,875)			+ Rs 7,500

as value-added and 35% (0.35 × Rs 7,500 = Rs 2,625) as nonvalue-added	+Rs 4,875	+ 2,625	− 7,500
Effect on value-added and nonvalue-added costs	+Rs 4,875	− Rs 19,375	Rs 0
Total effect of all programs	− Rs 47,800	−Rs 1,27,450	
Value-added and nonvalue-added costs calculated 2 in requirement	8,65,000	2,25,000	
Expected value-added and nonvalue-added costs as a result of implementing these programs	Rs 8,17,200	Rs 97,550	

If these programs had been implemented in remaining months of current year, total costs would decrease from Rs 10,90,000 (requirement 2) to Rs 8,17,200 + Rs 97,550 = Rs 9,14,750, and the percentage of nonvalue-added costs would decrease from 20.64% (requirement 2) to Rs 97,550 ÷ 9,14,750 = 10.66%. These are significant improvements in Laxmi's performance.

12-19 Target prices, target costs, activity-based costing. Kajaria Tiles is a small distributor of marble tiles. Kajaria identifies its three major activities and cost pools as ordering, receiving and storage, and transporting, and reports the following details for 2011:

Activity	Cost Driver	Quantity of Driver Cost	Cost per Unit of Cost Driver
1. Placing and paying for orders of marble tiles	Number of orders	500	Rs 500 per order
2. Receiving and storage	Loads moved	4,000	Rs 300 per load
3. Transporting of marble tiles to retailers	Number of consignments	1,500	Rs 400 per consignment

Kajaria buys 250,000 marble tiles at an average cost of Rs 30 per tile and sells them to retailers at an average price of Rs 40 per tile. Assume Kajaria has no fixed costs.

Required

1. Calculate Kajaria's operating income for 2011.
2. For 2011, retailers are demanding a 5 % discount off the 2011 price. Kajaria's suppliers are only willing to give a 4 % discount. Kajaria expects to sell the same quantity of marble tiles in 2012 as in 2011. If all other costs and cost-driver information remain the same, calculate Kajaria's operating income for 2012.
3. Suppose further that Kajaria decides to make changes in its ordering and receiving and storing practices. By placing long-run orders with its key suppliers, Kajaria expects to reduce the number of orders to 200 and the cost per order to Rs 250 per order. By redesigning the layout of the warehouse and reconfiguring the crates in which the marble tiles are moved, Kajaria expects to reduce the number of loads moved to 3,125 and the cost per load moved to Rs 280. Will Kajaria achieve its target operating income of Rs 3 per tile in 2012 Show your calculations.

Solution

Target prices, target costs, activity-based costing.

1. Kajaria's operating income in 2011 is as follows:

	Total for 2,50,000 Tiles (1)	Per Unit (2) = (1) ÷ 2,50,000
Revenues (Rs 40 × 2,50,000)	Rs 1,00,00,000	Rs 40
Purchase cost of tiles (Rs 30 × 2,50,000)	75,00,000	30
Ordering costs (Rs 500 × 500)	2,50,000	1
Receiving and storage (Rs 300 × 4,000)	12,00,000	4.8
Transporting costs (Rs 400 × 1,500)	6,00,000	2.4
Total costs	95,50,000	38.2
Operating income	Rs 4,50,000	Rs 1.8

2. Price to retailers in 2012 is 95% of 2011's price = 0.95 × Rs 40 = Rs 38; cost per tile in 2012 is 96% of 2006's cost = 0.96 × Rs 30 = Rs 28.8.

Kajaria's operating income in 2012 is as follows:

	Total for 2,50,000 Tiles (1)	Per Unit (2) = (1) ÷ 2,50,000
Revenues (Rs 38 × 250,000)	Rs 95,00,000	Rs 38.0
Purchase cost of tiles (Rs 28.8 × 2,50,000)	72,00,000	28.8
Ordering costs (Rs 500 × 500)	2,50,000	1.0
Receiving and storage (Rs 300 × 4,000)	12,00,000	4.8
Transporting costs (Rs 400 × 1,500)	6,00,000	2.4
Total costs	92,50,000	37.0
Operating income	Rs 2,50,000	Rs 1.0

3. Kajaria's operating income in 2012, if it makes changes in ordering and material handling, will be as follows:

	Total for 250,000 Tiles (1)	Per Unit (2) = (1) ÷ 250,000
Revenues (Rs 38 × 250,000)	Rs 95,00,000	Rs 38.0
Purchase cost of tiles (Rs 28.8 × 250,000)	72,00,000	28.8
Ordering costs (Rs 250 × 200)	50,000	0.2
Receiving and storage (Rs 280 × 3,125)	8,75,000	3.5
Transporting costs (Rs 400 × 1,500)	6,00,000	2.4
Total costs	87,25,000	34.9
Operating income	Rs 7,75,000	Rs 3.1

Through better cost management, Kajaria will be able to achieve its target operating income of Rs 3 per tile despite the fact that its revenue per tile has decreased by Rs 2 (Rs 40 – Rs 38), while its purchase cost per tile has decreased by only Rs 1.2 (Rs 30 – Rs 28.8)

12-20 Target costs, effect of product-design changes on product costs. Medical Instruments uses a manufacturing costing system with one direct-cost category (direct materials) and three indirect-cost categories:

a. Setup, production order, and materials-handling costs that vary with the number of batches
b. Manufacturing operations costs that vary with machine-hours
c. Costs of engineering changes that vary with the number of engineering changes made

In response to competitive pressures at the end of 2011, Medical Instruments employed value engineering techniques to reduce manufacturing costs. Actual information for 2011 and 2012 are:

	2011	2012
Setup, production-order, and materials-handling cost per batch	Rs 8,000	Rs 7,500
Total manufacturing operating cost per machine-hour	55	50
Cost per engineering change	12,000	10,000

The management of Medical Instruments wants to evaluate whether value engineering has succeeded in reducing the target manufacturing cost per unit of one of its products, HJ6, by 10 %. Actual results for 2011 and 2012 for HJ6 are

	Actual Results for 2011	Actual Results for 2012
Units of HJ6 produced	3,500	4,000
Direct material cost per unit of HJ6	Rs 1,200	Rs 1,100
Total number of batches required to produce HJ6	70	80
Total machine-hours required to produce HJ6	21,000	22,000
Number of engineering changes made	14	10

Required

1. Calculate the manufacturing cost per unit of HJ6 in 2011.
2. Calculate the manufacturing cost per unit of HJ6 in 2012.
3. Did Medical Instruments achieve the target manufacturing cost per unit for HJ6 in 2012 Explain.
4. Explain how Medical Instruments reduced the manufacturing cost per unit of HJ6 in 2012.

Solution

Target costs, effect of product-design changes on product costs.

1. and 2. Manufacturing costs of HJ6 in 2011 and 2012 are as follows:

	2011 Total (1)	2011 Per Unit (2) = (1) ÷ 3,500	2012 Total (3)	2012 Per Unit (4) = (3) ÷ 4,000
Direct materials, Rs 1,200 × 3,500; Rs 1,100 × 4,000	Rs 42,00,000	Rs 1,200	Rs 44,00,000	Rs 1,100
Batch-level costs, Rs 8,000 × 70; Rs 7,500 × 80	5,60,000	160	6,00,000	150
Manufacturing operations costs, Rs 55 × 21,000; Rs 50 × 22,000	11,55,000	330	11,00,000	275
Engineering change costs, Rs 12,000 × 14; Rs 10,000 × 10	1,68,000	48	1,00,000	25
Total	Rs 60,83,000	Rs 1,738	Rs 62,00,000	Rs 1,550

3. Target manufacturing cost per unit of HJ6 in 2012 = Manufacturing costs per unit in 2011 × 90% = Rs 1,738 × 0.90 = Rs 1,564.20
   Actual manufacturing cost per unit of HJ6 in 2012 was Rs 1,550. Hence, Medical Instruments did achieve its target manufacturing cost per unit of Rs 1,564.20
4. To reduce the manufacturing cost per unit in 2012, Medical Instruments reduces the cost per unit of activity in each of the four cost categories—direct materials costs, batch-level costs, manufacturing operations costs, and engineering change costs. It also reduced machine-hours and number of engineering changes made—the quantities of the cost drivers. In 2011, Medical Instruments used 6

machine-hours per unit of HJ6 (21,000 machine-hours ÷ 3,500 units). In 2012, Medical Instruments used 5.5 machine-hours per unit of HJ6 (22,000 machine-hours ÷ 4,000 units). Medical Instruments reduced engineering changes from 14 in 2011 to 10 in 2012. Medical Instruments achieved these gains through value engineering activities that retained only those product features that customers wanted while eliminating activities and their costs.

12-21 Cost-plus target return on investment pricing. John is the managing partner of a business that has just finished building a 60-room motel. John anticipates that he will rent these rooms for 16,000 nights next year (or 16,000 room-nights). All rooms are similar and will rent for the same price. John estimates the following operating costs for next year:

Variable operating costs	Rs 30 per room-night
Fixed costs	
Salaries and wages	Rs 17,50,000
Maintenance of building and pool	3,70,000
Other operating and administration costs	14,00,000
Total fixed costs	Rs 35,20,000

The capital invested in the motel is Rs 96,00,000. The partnership's target return on investment is 25 %. John expects demand for rooms to be uniform throughout the year. He plans to price the rooms at full cost plus a markup on full cost to earn the target return on investment.

Required

1. What price should John charge for a room-night? What is the markup as a percentage of the full cost of a room-night?
2. John's market research indicates that if the price of a room-night determined in requirement 1 is reduced by 10 %, the expected number of room-nights John could rent would increase by 10 %. Should John reduce prices by 10 %? Show your calculations.

Solution

Cost-plus target return on investment pricing.

1. Target operating income = Target return on investment × Invested capital

Target operating income (25% × Rs 96,00,000)	Rs 24,00,000	
Total fixed costs	35,20,000	
Target contribution margin	Rs 59,20,000	
Target contribution margin per room, (Rs 59,20,000 ÷ 16,000)	Rs 370	
Add variable costs per room	30	
Price to be charged per room	Rs 400	
Proof		
Total room revenues (Rs 400 × 16,000 rooms)		Rs 64,00,000
Total costs		
Variable costs (Rs 30 × 16,000)	Rs 4,80,000	
Fixed costs	35,20,000	
Total costs		40,00,000
Operating income		Rs 24,00,000

The full cost of a room = variable cost per room + fixed cost per room
The full cost of a room = Rs 30 + (Rs 35,20,000 ÷ 16,000) = Rs 30 + Rs 220 = Rs 250
Markup per room = Rental price per room – Full cost of a room
= Rs 400 – Rs 250 = Rs 150
Markup percentage as a fraction of full cost = Rs 150 ÷ Rs 250 = 60%

2. If price is reduced by 10%, the number of rooms John could rent would increase by 10%.

The new price per room would be 90% × Rs 400	Rs 360
The number of rooms John expects to rent is 110% of 16,000	17,600
The contribution margin per room would be Rs 360 – Rs 30	Rs 330
Contribution margin (Rs 330 × 17,600)	Rs 58,08,000

Because the contribution margin of Rs 58,08,000 at the reduced price of Rs 360 is less than the contribution margin of Rs 59,20,000 at a price of Rs 400, John should not reduce the price of the rooms. Note that the fixed costs of Rs 35,20,000 will be the same under the Rs 400 and the Rs 360 price alternatives and are, hence, irrelevant to the analysis.

12-22 Life-cycle product costing, activity-based costing. Timex makes digital watches. Timex is preparing a product life-cycle budget for a new watch, MX3. Development on the new watch is to start shortly. Estimates for MX3 are as follows:

Life-cycle units manufactured and sold	4,00,000
Selling price per watch	Rs 400

Life-cycle costs		
R&D and design costs		1,00,00,000
Manufacturing		
Variable cost per watch	Rs	150
Variable cost per batch	Rs	6,000
Watches per batch		500
Fixed costs		Rs 1,80,00,000
Marketing		
Variable cost per watch	Rs	32
Fixed costs	Rs	10,00,000
Distribution		
Variable cost per batch	Rs	280
Watches per batch		160
Fixed costs	Rs	72,00,000
Customer-service cost per watch	Rs	15

Ignore the time value of money.

Required

1. Calculate the budgeted life-cycle operating income for the new watch.
2. What percentage of the budgeted total product life-cycle costs will be incurred by the end of the R&D and design stages?
3. An analysis reveals that 80 % of the budgeted total product life-cycle costs of the new watch will be locked in at the R&D and design stage. What are the implications for managing MX3's costs?
4. Timex's Market Research Department estimates that reducing MX3's price by Rs 30 will increase life-cycle unit sales by 10 %. If unit sales increase by 10 %, Timex plans to increase manufacturing and distribution batch sizes by 10 % as well. Assume that all variable costs per watch, variable costs per batch, and fixed costs will remain the same. Should Timex reduce MX3's price by Rs 30? Show your calculations.

Solution

Life-cycle product costing, activity-based costing.

1. The budgeted life-cycle operating income for the new watch MX3 is Rs 2,42,00,000, as shown below.

	Life-Cycle Revenues and Costs
Revenues, Rs 400 × 400,000	Rs 16,00,00,000
R&D and design costs	1,00,00,000
Manufacturing costs:	
Variable, Rs 150 × 400,000	6,00,00,000
Batch, Rs 6,000 × 800[1] batches	48,00,000
Fixed	1,80,00,000
Marketing costs:	
Variable, Rs 32 × 400,000	1,28,00,000
Fixed	1,00,00,000
Distribution costs:	
Batch, Rs 2,800 × 2,500[2] batches	70,00,000
Fixed	72,00,000
Customer-service costs:	
Variable, Rs 15 × 400,000	60,00,000
Total costs	13,58,00,000
Operating income	Rs 2,42,00,000

[1]4,00,000 watches ÷ 500 watches per batch = 800 batches
[2]4,00,000 watches ÷ 160 watches per batch = 2,500 batches

2. Budgeted product life-cycle costs for R&D and design Rs 1,00,00,000
Total budgeted product life-cycle costs Rs 13,58,00,000

Percentage of budgeted product life-cycle costs incurred till the R&D and design stages

$$= \frac{\text{Rs } 1,00,00,000}{\text{Rs } 13,58,00,000} \, 7.36\%$$

3. An analysis reveals that 80% of the total product life-cycle costs of the new watch will be locked in at the end of the R&D and design stages when only 7.36% of the costs are incurred (requirement 2). The implication is that it will be difficult to alter or reduce the costs of MX3 once Timex finalizes the design of MX3. To reduce and manage total costs, Timex must act to modify the design before costs get locked in.

4. The budgeted life-cycle operating income for MX3 if Timex reduces its price by Rs 30 is Rs 1,91,20,000, as shown next. This is less than the operating income of Rs 2,42,00,000 calculated in requirement 1. Therefore, Timex should not reduce MX3's price by Rs 30.

	Life-Cycle Revenues And Costs
Revenues, Rs 370 × 4,40,000	Rs 16,28,00,000
R&D and design costs	1,00,00,000
Manufacturing costs:	
Variable, Rs 150 × 4,40,000	6,60,00,000
Batch, Rs 6,000 × 800[3] batches	48,00,000
Fixed	1,80,00,000
Marketing costs:	
Variable, Rs 32 × 4,40,000	1,40,80,000
Fixed	1,00,00,000
Distribution costs:	
Batch, Rs 2,800 × 2,500[4] batches	70,00,000
Fixed	72,00,000
Customer-service costs:	
Variable, Rs 15 × 4,40,000	66,00,000
Total costs	14,36,80,000
Operating income	Rs 1,91,20,000

[3]4,40,000 watches ÷ 550 watches per batch = 800 batches
[4]4,40,000 watches ÷ 176 watches per batch = 2,500 batches

12-23 Considerations other than cost in pricing. Examples of prices charged per minute by BSNL for long-distance state-to-state telephone calls within the country at different times of the day and week are:

Peak period (8 a.m. to 7 p.m., Monday through Friday)	Rs 3.0
Evenings (7 p.m. to 11 p.m., Monday through Friday)	2.5
Nights and weekends	1.6

Required

1. Are there differences in incremental costs per minute to BSNL for telephone calls made during peak hours compared with telephone calls made at other times of the day?
2. Why do you think BSNL charges different prices per minute for telephone calls made during peak hours compared with telephone calls made at other times of the day?

Solution

Considerations other than cost in pricing.

1. No. We would expect the incremental costs of providing telephone services to be no different in peak versus off-peak hours. Most costs of maintaining and operating the telephone network are fixed costs that are the same in peak and off-peak periods. In fact, the unit cost per telephone call is likely to be higher during off-peak hours when fewer calls are made. Yet the prices charged for telephone calls during peak periods are higher than the prices charged for off-peak evenings, nights, and weekends.
2. Charging higher prices for peak period calls is an example of price discrimination. Price discrimination occurs because calls made between 8 a.m. and 7 p.m. on working days are generally made by businesses that are relatively more price insensitive—they must make telephone calls to conduct their regular day-to-day business activities. Charging a higher price for calls during business hours maximizes the telephone company's operating income. Charging higher prices during business hours is also an example of peak-load pricing. Because the number of telephone calls that can be put through at any one time is limited, the telephone company raises prices to levels that the market will bear when demand is high.

   Calls during evenings, nights, and weekends are generally made by individuals for personal or pleasure reasons. Because they pay for the calls themselves, individuals are much more sensitive to price than business callers—that is, their demand is more price-elastic. It is profitable for BSNL to charge low rates to stimulate demand for personal and pleasure calls.

12-24 Cost-plus and market-based pricing. (CMA, adapted) Best Test laboratories evaluates the reaction of materials to extreme increases in temperature. Much of the company's early growth was attributable to government contracts. Recent growth has come from diversification and expansion into commercial markets. Environmental testing at Best Test now includes:

Heat testing	(HTT)	Arctic condition testing	(ACT)
Air turbulence testing	(ATT)	Aquatic testing	(AQT)
Stress testing	(SST)		

Currently, all of the budgeted operating costs are collected in a single overhead pool. All of the estimated testing hours are also collected in a single pool. One rate per test-hour is used for all five types of testing. This hourly rate is marked up by 45% to recover administrative costs, taxes, and profit in the selling price.

Wise Shaw, Best Test's controller, believes that there is enough variation in the test procedures and cost structure to establish separate costing and billing rates. He also believes that the inflexible rate structure currently being used is inadequate in today's competitive environment. After analyzing the following data, he has recommended new rates for Best Test's upcoming fiscal year.

The budgeted total test laboratory costs for the coming year are:

Test pool labor (10 employees)	Rs 42,00,000
Supervision	7,20,000
Equipment depreciation	17,84,600
Heat	17,00,000
Electricity	12,40,000
Water	7,40,000
Setup	5,80,000
Indirect materials	10,40,000
Operating supplies	6,20,000
Total test lab costs	Rs 1,26,24,600
Total estimated test-hours	1,06,000

Shaw has determined the resource usage by test type in the following table:

	HTT	SST	AQT	ATT	ACT
Test pool labor employees	3	2	2	1	2
Supervision	40 %	15 %	15 %	15 %	15 %
Depreciation	Rs 4,82,300	Rs 2,20,000	Rs 3,92,300	Rs 3,20,000	Rs 3,70,000
Heat	50 %	5 %	5 %	30 %	10 %
Electricity	30 %	10 %	10 %	40 %	10 %
Water	-	-	20 %	20 %	60 %
Setup	20 %	15 %	30 %	15 %	20 %
Indirect materials	15 %	15 %	30 %	20 %	20 %
Operating supplies	10 %	10 %	25 %	20 %	35 %
Test-hours	29,680	12,720	27,560	22,260	13,780
Competitors' hourly billing rates	Rs 175	Rs 190	Rs 155	Rs 160	Rs 200

Required

1. Compute the single pool hourly cost and hourly billing rate for Best Test Laboratories.
2. Compute the five separate hourly billing rates for Best Test Laboratories.
3. Discuss what effect the new cost-plus method will have on the pricing structure for each of the five test types. Given the competitors' hourly billing rates, how might Best Test modify its pricing?
4. In general, identify at least three other internal or external factors that influence pricing structure.

Solution

Cost-plus and market-based pricing.

1. Single pool:

$$\text{Cost Rate} = \frac{\text{Rs}1{,}26{,}24{,}600}{1{,}06{,}000 \text{ hours}} = \text{Rs } 119.1 \text{ per testing-hour}$$

$$\text{Hourly billing rate} = \text{Rs } 119.1 \times 1.45$$
$$= \text{Rs } 172.7 \text{ per billing-hour}$$

2. See Solution Exhibit 12-24.

Solution Exhibit 12-24

	HTT (Rs)	ATT (Rs)	SST (Rs)	ACT (Rs)	AQT (Rs)	Total (Rs)
Test pool labor (.3, .2, .2, .1, .2)	12,60,000	8,40,000	8,40,000	4,20,000	8,40,000	42,00,000
Supervision (.40, .15, .15, .15, .15)	2,88,000	1,08,000	1,08,000	1,08,000	1,08,000	7,20,000
Equipment depreciation	4,82,300	2,20,000	3,92,300	3,20,000	3,70,000	17,84,600
Heat (.50, .05, .05, .30, .10)	8,50,000	85,000	85,000	5,10,000	1,70,000	17,00,000
Electricity (.30, .10, .10, .40, .10)	3,72,000	1,24,000	1,24,000	4,96,000	1,24,000	12,40,000
Water (.00, .00, .20, .20, .60)	0	0	1,48,000	1,48,000	4,44,000	7,40,000
Set-up (.20, .15, .30, .15, .20)	1,16,000	87,000	1,74,000	87,000	1,16,000	5,80,000
Indirect materials (.15, .15, .30, .20, .20)	1,56,000	1,56,000	3,12,000	2,08,000	2,08,000	10,40,000
Operating supplies (.10, .10, .25, .20, .35)	62,000	62,000	1,55,000	1,24,000	2,17,000	6,20,000
Total costs (in rupees)	35,86,300	16,82,000	23,38,300	24,21,000	25,97,000	1,26,24,600

Total test-hours	29,680	12,720	27,560	22,260	13,780
Hourly test-cost	Rs 120.8	Rs 132.2	Rs 84.8	Rs 108.8	Rs 188.5
Hourly billing rate (hourly test-cost × 1.45)	Rs 175.2	Rs 191.7	Rs 123.0	Rs 157.8	Rs 273.3

3. The new costing method will have the following effects on the pricing structure for each of the five test types given the competitors' hourly billing rates.

	HTT	ATT	SST	ACT	AQT
New hourly billing rate (hourly test-cost × 1.45)	Rs 175.2	Rs 191.7	Rs 123.0	Rs 157.8	Rs 273.3
Competitor rate	Rs 175	Rs 190	Rs 155	Rs 160	Rs 200
New rate over/(under) market	Rs .2	Rs 1.7	Rs (32)	Rs (2.2)	Rs 73.3
Percent over/(under) market	0.1%	0.9%	(20.6)%	(1.4)%	36.7%
Common pool hourly billing-rate	Rs 172.7	Rs 172.7	Rs 72.7	Rs 172.7	Rs 172.7
New rate over/(under) old rate	Rs 2.5	Rs 19	Rs (49.7)	Rs 14.9)	Rs 100.6
Percent over/(under) old rate	1.4%	11.0%	(28.8)%	(8.7)%	58.3%

- Best Test will now be pricing all its laboratory tests more competitively in the market.
- For Heat Testing (HTT), there is minimal variance between the common pool rate, the new separate rate, and the competitors' rates. The HTT rate could either be left at the old rate, or nominally raised to the competitors' rates or new pool rate without much impact, depending on how Best Test wanted to position the test compared to the competition.
- For Air Turbulence Testing (ATT), the new separate computed billing rate is significantly different than the common pool rate as well as close to the competitors' rates. The same is true of Arctic Condition Testing (ACT). In both cases, Best Test would probably want to adjust billing rates (raise ATT rate and lower ACT rate) to the newly computed rates or competitors' rates to better reflect resources consumed by the tests.
- For Stress Testing (SST), the newly computed rate is dramatically less than both the common pool rate and the competitors' rates. Best Test would want to significantly reduce the price to at least meet the competitors' price or reduce it further to the newly computed price, depending upon how aggressively it wanted to market this test.
- For Aquatic Testing (AQT), the newly computed rate is significantly higher than both the common pool rate and the competitors' rates. Best Test would want to raise the billing rate at least to the competitors' rates to recover its cost plus some contribution towards administrative costs. Its current common billing rate of Rs 172.7 is below the Rs 188.5 cost to perform the AQT test.
- Because the newly computed billing prices for both SST and AQT are significantly different than competitors' prices, the cost assumptions should be further analyzed to verify accuracy and identify opportunities.

4. In general, at least three other internal or external factors that influence pricing structure include:

- number and nature of competitors for additional tests and their quality and timeliness of service.
- company's overall capacity and its ability to react to volume and mix changes for tests if the demand changes due to the new pricing structure.
- number of potential customers, overall demand for the tests, and price elasticity of demand for the tests.
- strategic focus, such as desire to gain or defend market share, long-term support for entry into or exit from a market, or stage in the test's product life cycle (introduction, growth, mature, or dying).

12-25 Life-cycle product costing, product mix. Polaris, a company engaged in Decision Support System (DSS) is examining the profitability and pricing policies of three of its recent engineering software packages:

- EE-46: package for electrical engineers
- ME-83: package for mechanical engineers
- IE-17: package for industrial engineers

Summary details on each package over their two-year "infancy-to-grave" product lives are as follows:

		Number of Units Sold	
Package	**Selling Price**	**Year 1**	**Year 2**
EE-46	Rs 2,500	2,000	8,000
ME-83	3,000	2,000	3,000
IE-17	2,000	5,000	3,000

Assume that no inventory remains on hand at the end of Year 2.

Polaris is deciding which product lines to emphasize. In the past two years, profitability has been mediocre. Polaris is particularly concerned with the increase in R&D costs. An analyst pointed out that for one of its most recent packages (IE-17), major efforts had been made to reduce R&D costs.

Praveen, the engineering software manager, decides to collect the following life-cycle revenue and cost information for the EE-46, ME-83, and IE-17 packages:

	EE-46		ME-83		IE-17	
	Year 1	Year 2	Year 1	Year 2	Year 1	Year 2
Revenues (Rs 000s)	Rs 5,000	Rs 20,000	Rs 6,000	Rs 9,000	Rs 10,000	Rs 6,000
Costs (Rs 000s)						
R&D	7,000	0	4,500	0	2,400	0
Design of product	1,850	150	1,100	100	800	160
Manufacturing	750	2,250	1,050	1,050	1,430	650
Marketing	1,400	3,600	1,200	1,500	2,400	2,080
Distribution	150	600	240	360	600	360
Customer service	500	3,250	450	1,050	2,200	3,880

Required

1. How does a product life-cycle income statement differ from a conventional income statement? What are the benefits of using a product life-cycle reporting format?
2. Present a product life-cycle income statement for each software package. Which package is the most profitable and which is the least profitable? Ignore the time value of money.
3. How do the three software packages differ in their cost structure (the percentage of total costs in each cost category)?

Solution

Life-cycle product costing, product mix.

1. A life-cycle income statement traces revenue and costs of each individual software package from its initial research and development to its final customer servicing and support. The two main differences from a conventional income statement are:
   a. Costs incurred in different calendar periods are included in the same statement.
   b. Costs and revenue of each package are reported separately rather than aggregated into companywide categories.

   The benefits of using a product life-cycle report are:
   a. The full set of revenues and costs associated with each product becomes visible.
   b. Differences among products in the percentage of total costs committed at early stages in the life cycle are highlighted.
   c. Interrelationships among business function cost categories are highlighted. What is the effect, for example, of cutting back on R&D and product-design cost categories on customer-service costs in subsequent years?

2.

	EE-46		ME-83		IE-17	
Revenue (Rs 000s)		Rs 25,000		Rs 15,000		Rs 16,000
Costs (Rs 000s)						
Research & development	Rs 7,000		Rs 4,500		Rs 2,400	
Design	2,000		1,200		960	
Production	3,000		2,100		2,080	
Marketing	5,000		2,700		4,480	
Distribution	750		600		960	
Customer service	3,750	21,500	1,500	12,600	6,080	16,960
Operating income (Rs 0,000s)		Rs 3,500		Rs 2,400		Rs (960)

As emphasized in this chapter, the time value of money is not taken into account when summing life-cycle revenue or life-cycle costs. Chapter 19 discusses this topic in detail.

Rankings of the three packages on profitability (and relative profitability) are:

Operating income	Operating income / Revenues
1. EE-46 : Rs 35,00,000	1. ME-83: 16.0%
2. ME-83: Rs 24,00,000	2. EE-46 : 14.0%
3. IE-17 : Rs (9,60,000)	3. IE-17 : (6.0%)

The EE-46 and ME-83 packages should be emphasized, and the IE-17 package should be de-emphasized. It is interesting that IE-17 had the lowest R&D costs but was the least profitable. Polaris should evaluate whether reducing R&D costs contributed in any way to IE-17's poor performance.

3. The cost structures of the three software packages are:

	EE-46	ME-83	IE-17
Research & development	32.5%	35.7%	14.1%
Design	9.3	9.5	5.7
Production	14.0	16.7	12.3
Marketing	23.3	21.4	26.4
Distribution	3.5	4.8	5.7
Customer service	17.4	11.9	35.8
	100.0%	100.0%	100.0%

The major differences are:

a. EE-46 and ME-83 have over 30% of their costs in the R&D/product design categories, compared to less than 15% (14.1%) for IE-17.

b. IE-17 has 35.8% of its costs in the customer-service category, compared to 17.4% for EE-46 and 11.9% for ME-83.

There are several explanations for these differences:

a. EE-46 and ME-83 differ sizably from IE-17 in their R&D/product design intensity. For example, EE-46 and ME-83 may require considerably (a) more interaction with users, and (b) more experimentation with software algorithms than does IE-17.

b. The software division should have invested more in the R&D/product design categories for IE-17. The high percentage for customer service costs could reflect the correcting of problems that should have been corrected prior to manufacture. Life-cycle reports highlight possible causal relationships among cost categories.

12-26 Ethics and pricing. Supreme Industries, is preparing to submit a bid for a ball-bearings order. Sandeep, controller of the Bearings Division of Supreme, has asked Rohan, the cost analyst, to prepare the bid. To determine price, Supreme's policy is to mark up the full costs of the product by 10 %. Sandeep tells Rohan that he is keen on winning the bid and that the price he calculates should be competitive.

Rohan prepares the following costs for the bid:

Direct materials		Rs 4,00,000
Direct manufacturing labor Overhead costs		1,00,000
Design and parts administration	Rs 40,000	
Production-order	50,000	
Setup	55,000	
Materials-handling	65,000	
General and administration	90,000	
Total overhead costs		3,00,000
Full product costs		Rs 8,00,000

All direct costs and 30 % of overhead costs are incremental costs of the order.

Sandeep reviews the numbers and says, "Your costs are way too high. You have allocated too much overhead costs to this job. You know our fixed overhead is not going to change if we win this order and manufacture the bearings. Rework your numbers. You have got to make the costs lower."

Rohan verifies his numbers are correct. He knows that Sandeep wants this order because the additional revenues from the order would lead to a big bonus for Sandeep and the senior division managers. Rohan knows that if he does not come up with a lower bid, Sandeep will be very upset.

Required

1. Using Supreme's pricing policy and based on Rohan's estimates, calculate the price Supreme should bid for the ball-bearings order.
2. Calculate the incremental costs of the ball-bearing order. Why do you think Supreme uses full costs of the product rather than incremental costs in its pricing decisions?
3. Evaluate whether Sandeep's suggestion to Rohan to use lower cost numbers is unethical. Would it be unethical for Rohan to change his analysis so that a lower cost can be calculated? What steps should Rohan take to resolve this situation?

Solution
Ethics and pricing.

1. Supreme prices at full product costs plus a mark-up of 10% = Rs 8,00,000 + 10% of Rs 8,00,000 = Rs 8,00,000 + Rs 80,000 = Rs 8,80,000.
2. The incremental costs of the order are as follows:

Direct materials	Rs 4,00,000
Direct manufacturing labor	1,00,000
30% of overhead costs 30% × Rs 3,00,000	90,000
Incremental costs	Rs 5,90,000

Any bid above Rs 5,90,000 will generate a positive contribution margin for Supreme. Supreme may prefer to use full product costs because it regards the new ball-bearings order as a long-term business relationship rather than a special order. For long-run pricing decisions, managers prefer to use full product costs because it indicates the bare minimum costs they need to recover to continue in business rather than shut down. For a business to be profitable in the long run, it needs to recover both its variable and its fixed product costs. Using only variable costs may tempt the manager to engage in excessive long-run price cutting as long as prices give a positive contribution margin. Using full product costs for pricing thereby prompts price stability.

3. Not using full product costs (including an allocation of fixed overhead) to price the order, particularly if it is in direct contradiction of company policy, may be unethical.

Rohan should indicate to Sandeep that the costs were correctly computed and that determining prices on the basis of full product costs plus a mark-up of 10% are required by company policy. If Sandeep still insists on making the changes and reducing the costs of the order, Rohan should raise the matter with Sandeep's superior. If, after taking all these steps, there is continued pressure to understate the costs, Rohan should consider resigning from the company, rather than engage in unethical behavior.

Exercises

12-27 Relevant-cost approach to pricing decisions, special order. The following financial data apply to the videotape production plant of the HMV for October:

Budgeted Manufacturing Cost per Video Tape	
Direct material	Rs 15
Direct manufacturing labor	8
Variable manufacturing overhead	7
Fixed manufacturing overhead	10
Total manufacturing cost	Rs 40

Variable manufacturing overhead varies with the number of units produced. Fixed manufacturing overhead of Rs 10 per tape is based on budgeted fixed manufacturing overhead of Rs 15,00,000 per month and budgeted production of 1,50,000 tapes per month. The HMV sells each tape for Rs 50.
Marketing costs have two components:

- Variable marketing costs (sales commissions) of 5 % of revenues
- Fixed monthly costs of Rs 6,50,000

During October, Ravi, a HMV salesperson, asked the president for permission to sell 1,000 tapes at Rs 38 per tape to a customer not in HMV's normal marketing channels. The president refused this special order because the selling price was below the total budgeted manufacturing cost.

Required

1. What would have been the effect on monthly operating income of accepting the special order?
2. Comment on the president's "below manufacturing costs" reasoning for rejecting the special order.
3. What other factors should the president consider before accepting or rejecting the special order?

12-28 Target operating income, value-added costs, service company. Architecture Associates prepares architectural drawings to conform to local structural safety codes. Its income statement for April-June is:

Revenues	Rs 6,80,000
Salaries of professional staff (8,000 hours x Rs 50 per hour)	4,00,000
Travel	18,000
Administrative and support costs	1,60,000
Total costs	5,78,000
Operating income	Rs 1,02,000

Following is the percentage of time spent by professional staff on various activities:

Doing calculations and preparing drawings for clients	75 %
Checking calculations and drawings	4

Correcting errors found in drawings (not billed to clients)	7
Making changes in response to client requests (billed to clients)	6
Correcting own errors regarding building codes (not billed to clients)	8
Total	100 %

Assume administrative and support costs vary with professional labor costs.

Required

Consider each requirement independently.

1. How much of the total costs in April-June are value-added, nonvalue-added, or in the gray area in between? Explain your answers briefly. What actions can Architecture Associates take to reduce its costs?
2. Suppose Architecture Associates could eliminate all errors so that it did not have any need to spend time making corrections and, as a result, could proportionately reduce professional labor costs. Calculate Architecture Associates's operating income.
3. Now suppose Architecture Associates could take on as much business as it could get done, but it could not add more professional staff. Assume that Architecture Associates could eliminate all errors so that it does not need to spend any time correcting errors. Assume Architecture Associates could use the time saved to increase revenues proportionately. Assume travel costs will remain at Rs 18,000. Calculate Architecture Associates's operating income.

12-29 Cost-plus and target pricing. (S. Sridhar, adapted) Babloo Toys, manufactures and sells 15,000 units of Teddy Bear toy (TB), in 2011. The full cost per unit is Rs 200. Babloo Toys earns a 20 % return on an investment of Rs 18,00,000 in 2011.

Required

1. Calculate the selling price and the markup percentage on the full cost per unit of TB toy in 2011.
2. If the selling price in requirement 1 represents a markup percentage of 40 % on variable cost per unit, calculate the variable cost per unit of TB toy in 2011.
3. Calculate Babloo Toys's operating income if it had increased the selling price to Rs 230. At this price Babloo Toys would have sold 13,500 units of TB toy. Assume no change in total fixed costs. Should Babloo Toys increase the selling price of TB toy to Rs 230?
4. In response to competitive pressures, Babloo Toys must reduce the price of TB toy to Rs 210 in 2012, in order to achieve sales of 15,000 units. Babloo Toys plans to reduce its investment to Rs 1,650,000. If Babloo Toys wants to maintain a 20% return on investment, what is the target cost per unit in 2012?

12-30 Relevant-cost approach to pricing decisions. Best Foods Bakery sells biscuits to food distributors. All costs are classified as either manufacturing or marketing. Best prepares monthly budgets. The March budgeted absorption-costing income statement is as follows:

Revenues (1,000 packets × Rs 100 a packet)	Rs 1,00,000
Cost of goods sold	60,000
Gross margin	40,000
Marketing costs	30,000
Operating income	Rs 10,000

Normal markup percentage:
Rs 40,000.; – Rs 60,000 = 66.7% of absorption cost

Monthly costs are classified as fixed or variable (with respect to the number of packets produced for manufacturing costs and with respect to the number of packets sold for marketing costs):

	Fixed	Variable
Manufacturing	Rs 20,000	Rs 40,000
Marketing	16,000	14,000

Best has the capacity to produce 1,500 packets per month. The relevant range in which monthly fixed manufacturing costs will be "fixed" is from 500 to 1,500 packets per month.

Required

1. Calculate the markup percentage based on total variable costs.
2. Assume that a new customer approaches Best to buy 200 packets at Rs 55 per packet for cash. The customer does not require additional marketing effort. Additional manufacturing costs of Rs 2,000 (for special packaging) will be required. Best believes that this is a one-time only special order because the customer is discontinuing business in six weeks' time. Best is reluctant to accept this 200-packet special order because the Rs 55 per packet price is below the Rs 60 per packet absorption cost. Do you agree with this reasoning? Explain.
3. Assume that the new customer decides to remain in business. How would this longevity affect your willingness to accept the Rs 55 per packet offer? Explain.

12-31 Cost-plus and market-based pricing. Reliable Labour Supplying Company, supplies contract labor to building construction companies. For October, Reliable Labour Supplying Company has budgeted to supply 80,000 hours of contract labor. Its variable costs are Rs 12 per hour, and its fixed costs per month are Rs 2,40,000. Anwar, the general manager, has proposed a cost-plus approach for pricing labor at full cost plus 20 %.

Required

1. Calculate the price per hour that Reliable Labour Supplying Company should charge based on Anwar's proposal.
2. The marketing manager supplies the following information on demand levels at different prices:

Price per Hour	Demand (Hours)
Rs 16	1,20,000
17	1,00,000
18	80,000
19	70,000
20	60,000

Reliable Labour Supplying Company can meet any of these demand levels. Fixed costs will remain unchanged for all the demand levels. On the basis of this additional information, calculate the price per hour that Reliable Labour Supplying Company should charge.

3. Comment on your answers to requirements 1 and 2. Why are they the same or different?

12-32 Product costs, activity-based costing. IBM manufactures and sells computers and computer peripherals to several nationwide retail chains. Vishal is the manager of the printer division. Its two best-selling printers are P-41 and P-63.

The manufacturing cost of each printer is calculated using IBM's activity-based costing system. IBM has one direct-manufacturing cost category (direct materials) and the following five indirect-manufacturing cost pools:

Indirect-Manufacturing Cost Pool	Quantity of Allocation Base	Allocation Rate
1. Materials handling	Number of parts	Rs 12 per part
2. Assembly management	Hours of assembly time	Rs 400 per hour of assembly time
3. Machine insertion of parts	Number of machine-inserted parts	Rs 7 per machine-inserted part
4. Manual insertion of parts	Number of manually inserted parts	Rs 21 per manually inserted part
5. Quality testing	Hours of quality testing time	Rs 250 per testing-hour

Product characteristics of P-41 and P-63 are as follows:

	P-41	P-63
Direct material costs	Rs 4075	Rs 2921
Number of parts	85 parts	46 parts
Hours of assembly time	3.2 hours	1.9 hours
Number of machine-inserted parts	49 parts	31 parts
Number of manually inserted parts	36 parts	15 parts
Hours of quality testing	1.4 hours	1.1 hours

Required

What is the manufacturing cost of P-41 and P-63?

12-33 Target cost, activity-based costing (continuation of 12-32). Assume all the information in Exercise 12-32. A foreign competitor has introduced products very similar to P-41 and P-63. Given their announced selling prices, Vishal estimates the P-41 clone to have a manufacturing cost of approximately Rs 6,800 and the P-63 clone to have a manufacturing cost of approximately Rs 3,900. He calls a meeting of product designers and manufacturing personnel. They all agree to use the Rs 6,800 and Rs 3,900 figures as target costs for redesigned versions of EP's P-41 and P-63, respectively. Product designers examine alternative ways of designing printers with comparable performance but lower cost. They come up with the following revised designs for P-41 and P-63 (called P-41 REV and P-63 REV, respectively):

	P-41 REV	P-63 REV
Direct material costs	Rs 3,812	Rs 2,631
Number of parts	71 parts	39 parts
Hours of assembly time	2.1 hours	1.6 hours
Number of machine-inserted parts	59 parts	29 parts
Number of manually inserted parts	12 parts	10 parts
Hours of quality testing	1.2 hours	0.9 hours

Required

1. What is a target cost per unit?
2. Using the activity-based costing system outlined in Problem 12-32, compute the manufacturing costs of P-41 REV and P-63 REV. How do these costs compare with the Rs 6,800 and Rs 3,900 target costs per unit?
3. Explain the differences between P-41 and P-41 REV and between P-63 and P-63 REV.
4. Assume now that Vishal has achieved major cost reductions in one activity. As a result, the allocation rate in the assembly-management activity will be reduced from Rs 400 to Rs 280 per assembly-hour. How will this activity-cost reduction affect the manufacturing costs of P-41 REV and P-63 REV? Comment on the results.

12-34 Target prices, target costs, value engineering, cost incurrence, locked-in costs, activity-based costing. Videocon makes a radio-cassette player. CE100, which has 80 components. Videocon sells 7,000 units each month for Rs 700 each. The costs of manufacturing CE100 are Rs 450 per unit, or Rs 31,50,000 per month. Monthly manufacturing costs incurred are:

Direct material costs	Rs 18,20,000
Direct manufacturing labor costs	2,80,000
Machining costs (fixed)	3,15,000
Testing costs	3,50,000
Rework costs	1,40,000
Ordering costs	33,600
Engineering costs (fixed)	2,11,400
Total manufacturing costs	Rs 31,50,000

Videocon's management identifies the activity cost pools, the cost drivers for each activity, and the cost per unit of the cost driver for each overhead cost pool as follows:

Manufacturing Activity	Description of Activity	Cost Driver	Cost per Unit of Cost Driver
1. Machining costs	Machining components	Machine-hours of capacity	Rs 45 per machine-hour
2. Testing costs	Testing components and final product (Each unit of CE100 is tested individually.)	Testing-hours.	Rs 20 per testing-hour
3. Rework costs	Correcting and fixing errors and defects	Units of CE100 reworked	Rs 200 per unit
4. Ordering costs	Ordering of components	Number of orders	Rs 210 per order
5. Engineering costs	Designing and managing of products and processes	Capacity of engineering-hours	Rs 350 per engineering hour

Videocon's management views direct material costs and direct manufacturing labor costs as variable with respect to the units of CE100 manufactured. Over a long-run horizon, each of the overhead costs described in the preceding table varies, as described, with the chosen cost drivers.

The following additional information describes the existing design:

a. Testing and inspection time per unit is 2.5 hours.
b. 10 % of the CE100s manufactured are reworked.
c. Videocon places two orders with each component supplier each month. Each component is supplied by a different supplier.
d. It currently takes 1 hour to manufacture each unit of CE100.

In response to competitive pressures, Videocon must reduce its price to Rs 620 per unit and its costs by Rs 80 per unit. No additional sales are anticipated at this lower price. However, Videocon stands to lose significant sales if it does not reduce its price. Manufacturing has been asked to reduce its costs by Rs 60 per unit. Improvements in manufacturing efficiency are expected to yield a net savings of Rs 15 per radio-cassette player, but that is not enough. The chief engineer has proposed a new modular design that reduces the number of components to 50 and also simplifies testing. The newly designed radio-cassette player, called "New CE100" will replace CE100. The expected effects of the new design are as follows:

a. Direct material costs for the New CEl00 are expected to be lower by Rs 22 per unit.
b. Direct manufacturing labor costs for the New CE100 are expected to be lower by Rs 5 per unit.
c. Machining time required to manufacture the New CE100 is expected to be 20 % less, but machine-hour capacity will not be reduced.
d. Time required for testing the New CE100 is expected to be lower by 20 %.
e. Rework is expected to decline to 4 % of New CE100s manufactured.
f. Engineering-hours capacity will remain the same.

Assume that the cost per unit of each cost driver for CE100 continues to apply to New CEl00.

Required

1. Calculate Videocon's manufacturing cost per unit of New CE100.
2. Will the new design achieve the per unit cost reduction targets that have been set for the manufacturing costs of New CE100? Show your calculations.
3. The problem describes two strategies to reduce costs: (a) improving manufacturing efficiency and (b) modifying the design. Which strategy has a bigger impact on Videocon's costs? Why? Explain briefly.

12-35 Cost-plus pricing. (CMA, adapted) Dr. Reddy specializes in packaging bulk drugs. Batra Hospital has asked Dr. Reddy to bid on the packaging of one million doses of medication at full cost plus a return on full cost of no more than 9 % after income taxes. Batra defines cost as including all variable costs of performing the service, a reasonable amount of fixed overhead, and incremental administrative costs. The hospital will supply all packaging materials and ingredients. Batra has indicated that any bid over Re 0.70 per dose will be rejected.

Director of cost accounting at the Dr. Reddy, has accumulated the following information prior to the preparation of the bid:

Variable direct manufacturing labor cost	Rs 160/direct manufacturing labor-hour
Variable overhead cost	Rs 90/direct manufacturing labor-hour
Fixed overhead cost	Rs 300/direct manufacturing labor-hour
Incremental administrative costs	Rs 50,000 for the order
Production rate	1,000 doses/direct manufacturing labor-hour

Dr. Reddy is subject to an income tax rate of 40 %.

Required

1. Calculate the minimum price per dose that Dr. Reddy could bid for the Batra job without changing Dr. Reddy's net income.
2. Calculate Dr. Reddy's bid price per dose using the full-cost criterion and the maximum allowable return specified by Batra.
3. Without considering your answer to requirement 2, assume that the price per dose that Dr. Reddy calculated using the cost-plus criterion specified by Batra is greater than the maximum bid of Re 0.70 per dose allowed by Batra. Discuss the factors that Dr. Reddy should consider before deciding whether to submit a bid at the maximum price of Re 0.70 per dose.

12-36 Considerations other than cost in pricing. In an advertisement in a Times of India newspaper, three hotel chains published their weekend and weekday daily room rates for various cities in India.

Daily Rate

Hotel	City	Weekend	Weekday
Holiday Inn	New Delhi	Rs 149	Rs 319
Taj Palace	Agra	89	239
Sheraton	Bangalore (airport)	109	219
Sheraton	Jaipur	89	209
Meridean	Udaipur	75	169
Meridean	Baroda	89	209

Weekend rates required Friday and/or Saturday night stay.

Required

Explain the reason(s) why the hotels charge lower rates for Friday and Saturday nights.

12-37 Target prices, target costs, value engineering. Sona Koya, manufactures component parts. One component part, P-100, has annual sales of 50,000 units and sells for Rs 406 per unit. Sona includes all R&D and design costs in engineering costs. Sona has no marketing, distribution, or customer-service costs.

Direct costs of P-100 including long-run fixed cost of machine capacity dedicated to P-100 are:

Direct material costs (variable)	Rs 85,00,000
Direct manufacturing labor costs (variable)	30,00,000
Direct machining costs (fixed, 50,000 hr × Rs 30/hr)	15,00,000

Sona's management identifies the following activity cost pools, cost drivers for each activity, and the cost per unit of each cost driver:

Activity	Cost Driver	Cost per Unit of Cost Driver
Setup	Setup-hours	Rs 250 per setup-hour
Testing	Testing-hours	Rs 20 per testing-hour
Engineering	Complexity of product and process	Costs assigned to products by special study

Over a long-run horizon, management views indirect costs as variable with respect to their chosen cost drivers. For example, setup costs vary with the number of setup-hours. Additional data for P-100 are

Production batch size	500 units
Setup time per batch	12 hours
Testing and inspection time per unit of product produced	2.5 hours
Engineering costs incurred on P-100	Rs 17,00,000

Facing competitive pressures, Sona wants to reduce the price of P-100 to Rs 348, well below its current price of Rs 406. The reduction in price will allow Sona to maintain its current unit sales. If Sona does not reduce price, it will lose sales. The challenge for Sona is to reduce the cost of P-100. Sona's engineers have proposed product design and process improvements for the "New P-100" to replace P-100.

The expected effects of the new design relative to P-100 are as follows:

a. Direct material costs for New P-100 are expected to decrease by Rs 30 per unit.
b. Direct manufacturing labor costs for New P-100 are expected to decrease by Rs 7.5 per unit.
c. New P-100 will take 6 setup-hours for each setup.
d. Time required for testing each unit of New P-100 is expected to be reduced by 0.5 hour.
e. Engineering costs will be unchanged.

Assume that the batch sizes are the same for New P-100 as for P-100. If Sona requires additional resources to implement the new design, it can acquire these resources in the quantities needed. Further assume the cost per unit of each cost driver for the New P-100 is the same as for P-100.

Required

1. Calculate the full cost per unit for P-100 using activity-based costing.
2. What is the markup percentage on the full cost per unit for P-100?
3. What is Sona's target cost per unit for New P-100 if it is to maintain the same markup perçentage on the full cost per unit as for P-100?
4. Will the New P-100 design achieve the target cost calculated in requirement 3? Explain.
5. What price will Sona charge for New P-100 if it uses the same markup percentage on the full cost per unit for New P-100 as for P-100?

13 Strategy, Balanced Scorecard, and Strategic Profitability Analysis

Learning Objectives

1. Recognize which of two generic strategies a company is using
2. Understand what comprises reengineering
3. Understand the four perspectives of the balanced scorecard
4. Analyze changes in operating income to evaluate strategy
5. Identify unused capacity and how to manage it

Olive Garden wants to know. So do Barnes and Noble, PepsiCo, and L.L. Bean. Even your local car dealer and transit authority are curious. They all want to know how well they are doing and how they score against the measures they strive to meet. The balanced scorecard can help them answer this question by evaluating key performance measures. Many companies have successfully used the balanced scorecard approach. KeyCorp, a Cleveland-based bank, is one of them.

Balanced Scorecard Helps Infosys Transform into a Leading Consultancy[1]

In the early 2000s, Infosys Technologies was a company in transition. The Bangalore-based company was a market leader in information technology outsourcing, but needed to expand to meet increased client demand. Infosys invested in many new areas including business process outsourcing, project management, and management consulting. This put Infosys in direct competition with established consulting firms, such as IBM and Accenture.

Led by CEO Kris Gopalakrishnan, the company developed an integrated management structure that would help align these new, diverse initiatives. Infosys turned to the balanced scorecard to provide a framework the company could use to formulate and monitor its strategy. The balanced scorecard measures corporate performance along four dimensions—financial, customer, internal business process, and learning and growth.

The balanced scorecard immediately played a role in the transformation of Infosys. The executive team used the scorecard to guide discussion during its meetings. The continual process of adaptation, execution, and management that the scorecard fostered helped the team respond to, and even anticipate, its clients' evolving needs. Eventually, use of the scorecard for performance measurement spread to the rest of the organization, with monetary incentives linked to the company's performance along the different dimensions.

Over time, the balanced scorecard became part of the Infosys culture. In recent years, Infosys has begun using the balanced scorecard concept to create "relationship scorecards" for many of its largest clients. Using the scorecard framework, Infosys began measuring its performance for key clients not only on project

---

[1] *Source*: Asis Martinez-Jerez, F., Robert S. Kaplan, and Katherine Miller. 2011. Infosys's relationship scorecard: Measuring transformational partnerships. Harvard Business School Case No. 9-109-006. Boston: Harvard Business School Publishing.

management and client satisfaction, but also on repeat business and anticipating clients' future strategic needs.

The balanced scorecard helped successfully steer the transformation of Infosys from a technology outsourcer to a leading business consultancy. From 1999 to 2007, the company had a compound annual growth rate of 50%, with sales growing from $120 million in 1999 to more than $3 billion in 2007. Infosys was recognized for its achievements by making the *Wired* 40, *BusinessWeek* IT 100, and *BusinessWeek* Most Innovative Companies lists.

This chapter focuses on how management accounting information helps companies such as Infosys, Merck, Verizon, and Volkswagen implement and evaluate their strategies. Strategy drives the operations of a company and guides managers' short-run and long-run decisions. We describe the balanced scorecard approach to implementing strategy and methods to analyze operating income to evaluate the success of a strategy. We also show how management accounting information helps strategic initiatives, such as productivity improvement, reengineering, and downsizing.

What Is Strategy?

Strategy specifies how an organization matches its own capabilities with the opportunities in the marketplace to accomplish its objectives. In other words, strategy describes how an organization can create value for its customers while differentiating itself from its competitors. For example, Wal-Mart, the retail giant, creates value for its customers by locating stores in suburban and rural areas, and by offering low prices, a wide range of product categories, and few choices within each product category. Consistent with its strategy, Wal-Mart has developed the capability to keep costs down by aggressively negotiating low prices with its suppliers in exchange for high volumes and by maintaining a no-frills, cost-conscious environment.

In formulating its strategy, an organization must first thoroughly understand its industry. Industry analysis focuses on five forces: (1) competitors, (2) potential entrants into the market, (3) equivalent products, (4) bargaining power of customers, and (5) bargaining power of input suppliers.[2] The collective effect of these forces shapes an organization's profit potential. In general, profit potential decreases with greater competition, stronger potential entrants, products that are similar, and more-demanding customers and suppliers. We illustrate these five forces for Chipset, Inc., maker of linear integrated circuit devices (LICDs) used in modems and communication networks. Chipset produces a single specialized product, CX1. This standard, high-performance microchip can be used in multiple applications. Chipset designed CX1 with extensive input from customers.

[2] M. Porter, *Competitive Strategy* (New York: Free Press, 1980); M. Porter, *Competitive Advantage* (New York: Free Press, 1985); and M. Porter, "What Is Strategy?" *Harvard Business Review* (November–December 1996): 61–78.

1. **Competitors.** The CX1 model faces severe competition with respect to price, timely delivery, and quality. Companies in the industry have high fixed costs, and persistent pressures to reduce selling prices and utilize capacity fully. Price reductions spur growth because it makes LICDs a cost-effective option in new applications such as digital subscriber lines (DSLs).
2. **Potential entrants into the market.** The small profit margins and high capital costs discourage new entrants. Moreover, incumbent companies such as Chipset are further down the learning curve with respect to lowering costs and building close relationships with customers and suppliers.
3. **Equivalent products.** Chipset tailors CX1 to customer needs and lowers prices by continuously improving CX1's design and processes to reduce production costs. This reduces the risk of equivalent products or new technologies replacing CX1.
4. **Bargaining power of customers.** Customers, such as EarthLink and Verizon, negotiate aggressively with Chipset and its competitors to keep prices down because they buy large quantities of product.
5. **Bargaining power of input suppliers.** To produce CX1, Chipset requires high-quality materials (such as silicon wafers, pins for connectivity, and plastic or ceramic packaging) and skilled engineers, technicians, and manufacturing labor. The skill-sets suppliers and employees bring gives them bargaining power to demand higher prices and wages.

Recognize which of two generic strategies a company is using

. . . product differentiation or cost leadership

In summary, strong competition and the bargaining powers of customers and suppliers put significant pressure on Chipset's selling prices. To respond to these challenges, Chipset must choose one of two basic strategies: *differentiating its product* or *achieving cost leadership*.

Product differentiation is an organization's ability to offer products or services perceived by its customers to be superior and unique relative to the products or services of its competitors. Hewlett-Packard has successfully differentiated its products in the electronics industry, as have Johnson & Johnson in the pharmaceutical industry and Coca-Cola in the soft drink industry. These companies have achieved differentiation through innovative product R&D, careful development and promotion of their brands, and the rapid push of products to market. Differentiation increases brand loyalty and the willingness of customers to pay higher prices.

Cost leadership is an organization's ability to achieve lower costs relative to competitors through productivity and efficiency improvements, elimination of waste, and tight cost control. Cost leaders in their respective industries include Wal-Mart (consumer retailing), Home Depot and Lowe's (building products), Texas Instruments (consumer electronics), and Emerson Electric (electric motors). These companies all provide products and services that are similar to—not differentiated from—those of their competitors, but they are provided at a lower cost to the customer. Lower selling prices, rather than unique products or services, provide a competitive advantage for these cost leaders.

What strategy should Chipset follow? To help it decide, Chipset develops the customer preference map shown in Exhibit 13-1. The *y*-axis describes various attributes of the product desired by customers. The *x*-axis describes how well Chipset and Visilog, a competitor of Chipset that follows a product-differentiation strategy, do along the various attributes desired by customers from 1 (poor) to 5 (very good). The map highlights the trade-offs in any strategy. Chipset's CX1 chip has an advantage in terms of price, scalability (the CX1 technology allows Chispet's customer to achieve different performance levels by simply altering the number of CX1 units in their product), and customer service. Visilog's chips are faster and more powerful and are customized for various applications such as different types of modems and communication networks.

CX1 is already somewhat differentiated from competing products. Differentiating CX1 further would be costly, but Chipset may be able to charge a higher price. Conversely, reducing the cost of manufacturing CX1 would allow the Chipset to lower price, spur growth, and increase market share. The scalability of CX1 makes it an

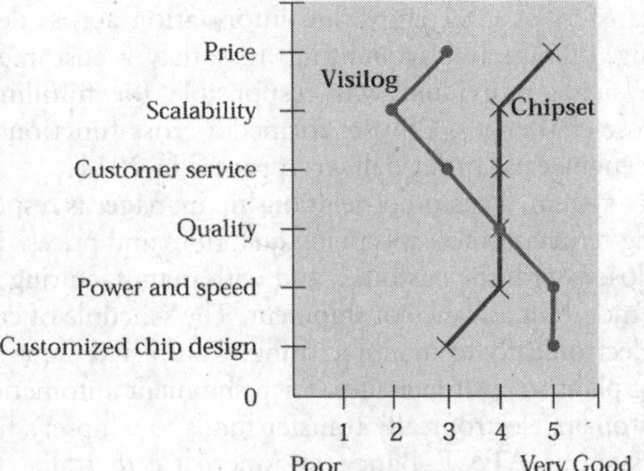

Exhibit 13-1

Customer Preference Map for LICDs

effective solution for meeting varying customer needs. Also, Chipset's current engineering staff is more skilled at making product and process improvements than at creatively designing new products and technologies. Chipset decides to follow a cost-leadership strategy.

To achieve its cost-leadership strategy, Chipset must improve its own internal capabilities. It must enhance quality and reengineer processes to downsize and eliminate excess capacity. At the same time, Chipset's management team does not want to make cuts in personnel that would hurt company morale and hinder future growth.

Decision Point

What are two generic strategies a company can use?

Building Internal Capabilities: Quality Improvement and Reengineering at Chipset

Learning Objective 2

Understand what comprises reengineering

. . . redesigning business processes to improve performance by reducing cost and improving quality

To improve product quality—that is, reduce defect rates and improve yields in its manufacturing process—Chipset must maintain process parameters within tight ranges. To achieve this goal, Chipset needs real-time data about manufacturing-process parameters, such as temperature and pressure, and more-effective process-control methods. Chipset must also train its workers in quality-management techniques to help them identify the causes of defects and ways to prevent them. Following this training, Chipset needs to empower its workers to make decisions and take actions that will improve quality.

A second element of Chipset's strategy is reengineering its order-delivery process. Some of Chipset's customers have complained about the time span between ordering products and receiving them. **Reengineering** is the fundamental rethinking and redesign of business processes to achieve improvements in critical measures of performance, such as cost, quality, service, speed, and customer satisfaction.[3] To illustrate reengineering, consider the order-delivery system at Chipset in 2008. When Chipset received an order from a customer, a copy was sent to manufacturing, where a production scheduler began planning the manufacturing of the ordered products. Frequently, a considerable amount of time elapsed before production began on the ordered product. After manufacturing was complete, CX1 chips moved to the Shipping Department, which matched the quantities of CX1 to be shipped against customer orders. Often, completed CX1 chips stayed in inventory until a truck became available for shipment. If the quantity to be shipped was less than the number of chips requested by the customer, a special shipment was made for the balance of the chips. Shipping documents moved to the Billing Department for issuing invoices. Special staff in the Accounting Department followed up with customers for payments.

[3] See M. Hammer and J. Champy, *Reengineering the Corporation: A Manifesto for Business Revolution* (New York: Harper, 1993); E. Ruhli, C. Treichler, and S. Schmidt, "From Business Reengineering to Management Reengineering—A European Study," *Management International Review* (1995): 361–371; and K. Sandberg, "Reengineering Tries a Comeback—This Time for Growth, Not Just for Cost Savings," *Harvard Management Update* (November 2001).

The many transfers of CX1 chips and information across departments (sales, manufacturing, shipping, billing, and accounting) to satisfy a customer's order created delays. Furthermore, no single individual was responsible for fulfilling each customer order. To respond to these challenges, Chipset formed a cross-functional team in late 2010 and implemented a reengineered order-delivery process in 2011.

Under the new system, a customer-relationship manager is responsible for each customer and negotiates long-term contracts specifying quantities and prices. The customer-relationship manager works closely with the customer and with manufacturing to specify delivery schedules for CX1 one month in advance of shipment. The schedule of customer orders and delivery dates is sent electronically to manufacturing. Completed chips are shipped directly from the manufacturing plant to customer sites. Each shipment automatically triggers an electronic invoice and customers electronically transfer funds to Chipset's bank.

Companies, such as AT&T, Banca di America e di Italia, Cigna Insurance, Cisco, PepsiCo, and Siemens Nixdorf, have realized significant benefits by reengineering their processes across design, production, and marketing (just as in the Chipset example). Reengineering has only limited benefits when reengineering efforts focus on only a single activity such as shipping or invoicing rather than the entire order-delivery process. To be successful, reengineering efforts must focus on changing roles and responsibilities, eliminating unnecessary activities and tasks, using information technology, and developing employee skills.

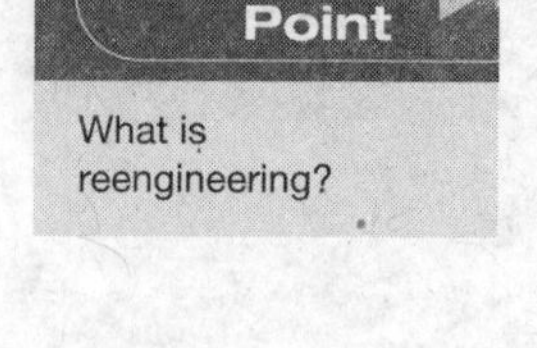
Decision Point
What is reengineering?

Take another look at Exhibit 13-1 and note the interrelatedness and consistency in Chipset's strategy. To help meet customer preferences for price, quality, and customer service, Chipset decides on a cost-leadership strategy. And to achieve cost leadership, Chipset builds internal capabilities by reengineering its processes. Chipset's next challenge is to effectively implement its strategy.

Strategy Implementation and the Balanced Scorecard

Many organizations, such as Allstate Insurance, Bank of Montreal, BP, and Dow Chemical, have introduced a *balanced scorecard* approach to manage the implementation of their strategies.

The Balanced Scorecard

The **balanced scorecard** translates an organization's mission and strategy into a set of performance measures that provides the framework for implementing its strategy.[4] The balanced scorecard does not focus solely on achieving financial objectives. It also highlights the nonfinancial objectives that an organization must achieve to meet and sustain its financial objectives. The scorecard measures an organization's performance from four perspectives: (1) financial, (2) customer, (3) internal business processes, and (4) learning and growth, the people and system capabilities that support operations. A company's strategy influences the measures it uses to track performance in each of these perspectives.

Why is this tool called a balanced scorecard? Because it balances the use of financial and nonfinancial performance measures to evaluate short-run and long-run performance in a single report. The balanced scorecard reduces managers' emphasis on short-run financial performance, such as quarterly earnings, because the key strategic nonfinancial and operational indicators, such as product quality and customer satisfaction, measure changes that a company is making for the long run. The financial benefits of these long-run changes may not appear immediately in short-run earnings; however, strong improvement in non-

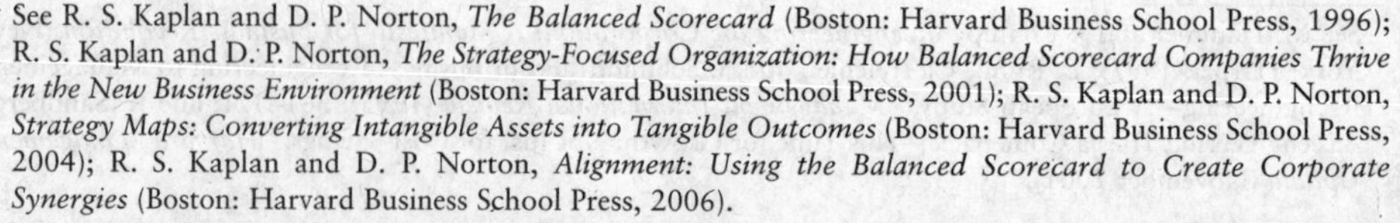

4 See R. S. Kaplan and D. P. Norton, *The Balanced Scorecard* (Boston: Harvard Business School Press, 1996); R. S. Kaplan and D. P. Norton, *The Strategy-Focused Organization: How Balanced Scorecard Companies Thrive in the New Business Environment* (Boston: Harvard Business School Press, 2001); R. S. Kaplan and D. P. Norton, *Strategy Maps: Converting Intangible Assets into Tangible Outcomes* (Boston: Harvard Business School Press, 2004); R. S. Kaplan and D. P. Norton, *Alignment: Using the Balanced Scorecard to Create Corporate Synergies* (Boston: Harvard Business School Press, 2006).

financial measures usually indicates the creation of future economic value. For example, an increase in customer satisfaction, as measured by customer surveys and repeat purchases, signals a strong likelihood of higher sales and income in the future. By balancing the mix of financial and nonfinancial measures, the balanced scorecard broadens management's attention to short-run *and* long-run performance. Never lose sight of the key point. In for-profit companies, the goal of the balanced scorecard is to improve a company's overall financial performance. Nonfinancial measures simply serve as leading indicators for the hard-to-measure long-run financial performance.

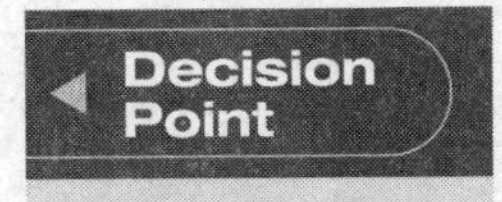

What is reengineering?

Strategy Maps and the Balanced Scorecard

Learning Objective 3

Understand the four perspectives of the balanced scorecard

. . . financial, customer, internal business process, learning and growth

We use the Chipset example to develop strategy maps and the four perspectives of the balanced scorecard. The objectives and measures Chipset's managers choose for each perspective relates to the action plans for furthering Chipset's cost leadership strategy: *improving quality* and *reengineering processes*.

Strategy Maps

A useful first step in designing a balanced scorecard is a *strategy map*. A **strategy map** is a diagram that describes how an organization creates value by connecting strategic objectives in explicit cause-and-effect relationships with each other in the financial, customer, internal business process, and learning and growth perspectives. Exhibit 13-2 presents Chipset's strategy map. Follow the arrows to see how a strategic objective affects other

Exhibit 13-2 Strategy Map for Chipset, Inc., for 2011

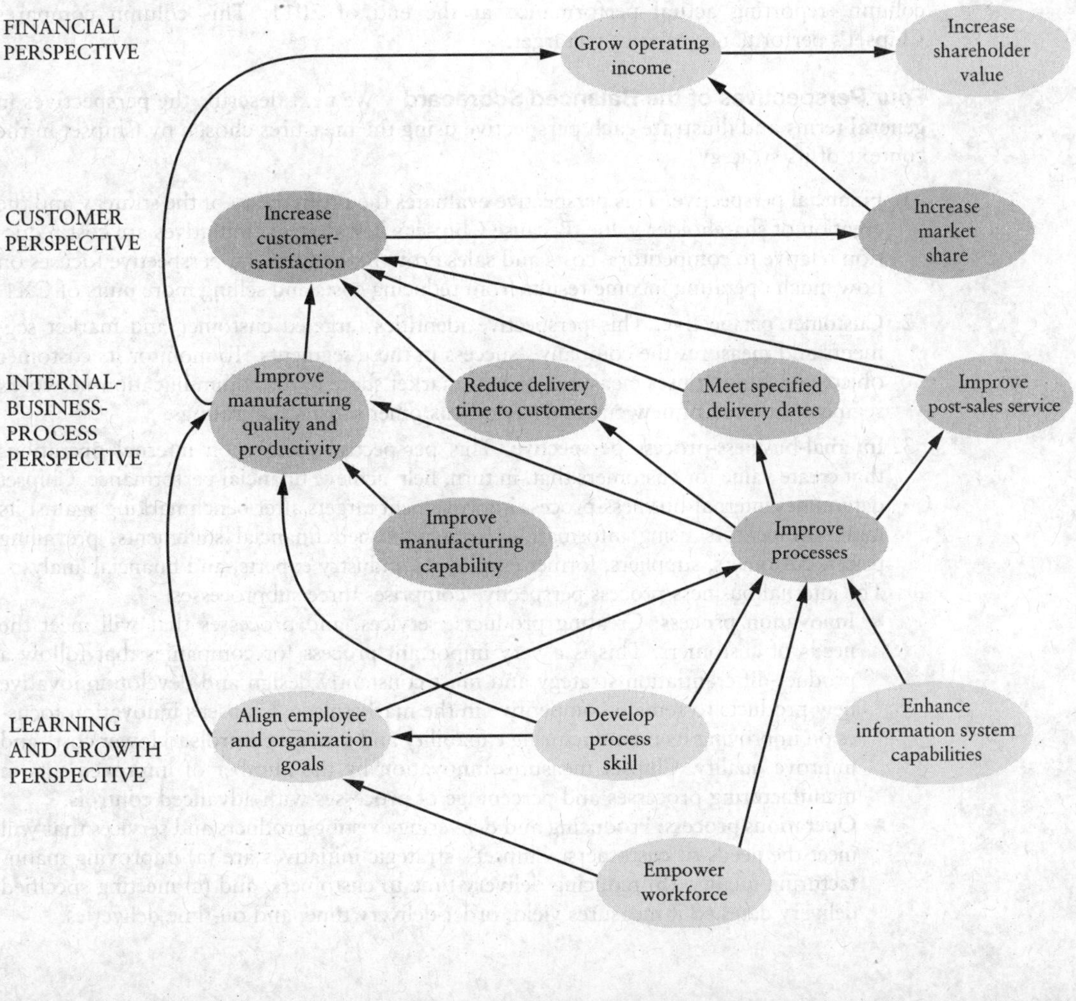

FINANCIAL PERSPECTIVE
Grow operating income
Increase shareholder value
CUSTOMER PERSPECTIVE
Increase customer-satisfaction
Increase market share
INTERNAL-BUSINESS-PROCESS PERSPECTIVE
Improve manufacturing quality and productivity
Reduce delivery time to customers
Meet specified delivery dates
Improve post-sales service
Improve manufacturing capability
Improve processes
LEARNING AND GROWTH PERSPECTIVE
Align employee and organization goals
Develop process skill
Enhance information system capabilities
Empower workforce

strategic objectives. For example, empowering the workforce helps align employee and organization goals and improves processes. Employee and organizational alignment also helps improve processes that improve manufacturing quality and productivity, reduce customer delivery time, meet specified delivery dates, and improve post-sales service, all of which increase customer satisfaction. Improving manufacturing quality and productivity grows operating income and increases customer satisfaction that, in turn, increases market share, operating income, and shareholder value.

Chipset operates in a knowledge-intensive business. To compete successfully, Chipset invests in its employees, implements new technology and process controls, improves quality, and reengineers processes. Doing these activities well enables Chipset to build capabilities and intangible assets, which are not recorded as assets in its financial books. The strategy map helps Chipset evaluate whether these intangible assets are generating financial returns.

Chipset could include many other cause-and-effect relationships in the strategy map in Exhibit 13-2. But, Chipset, like other companies implementing the balanced scorecard, focuses on only those relationships that it believes to be the most significant.

Chipset uses the strategy map from Exhibit 13-2 to build the balanced scorecard presented in Exhibit 13-3. The scorecard highlights the four perspectives of performance: financial, customer, internal business process, and learning and growth. The first column presents the strategic objectives from the strategy map in Exhibit 13-2. At the beginning of 2011, the company's managers specify the strategic objectives, measures, initiatives (the actions necessary to achieve the objectives), and target performance (the first four columns of Exhibit 13-3).

Chipset wants to use the balanced scorecard targets to drive the organization to higher levels of performance. Managers therefore set targets at a level of performance that is achievable, yet distinctly better than competitors. Chipset's managers complete the fifth column, reporting actual performance at the end of 2011. This column compares Chipset's performance relative to target.

Four Perspectives of the Balanced Scorecard We next describe the perspectives in general terms and illustrate each perspective using the measures chosen by Chipset in the context of its strategy.

1. **Financial perspective.** This perspective evaluates the profitability of the strategy and the creation of shareholder value. Because Chipset's key strategic initiatives are cost reduction relative to competitors' costs and sales growth, the financial perspective focuses on how much operating income results from reducing costs and selling more units of CX1.
2. **Customer perspective.** This perspective identifies targeted customer and market segments and measures the company's success in these segments. To monitor its customer objectives, Chipset uses measures such as market share in the communication-networks segment, number of new customers, and customer-satisfaction ratings.
3. **Internal-business-process perspective.** This perspective focuses on internal operations that create value for customers that, in turn, help achieve financial performance. Chipset determines internal-business-process improvement targets after benchmarking against its main competitors using information from published financial statements, prevailing prices, customers, suppliers, former employees, industry experts, and financial analysts. The internal-business-process perspective comprises three subprocesses:
   - **Innovation process:** Creating products, services, and processes that will meet the needs of customers. This is a very important process for companies that follow a product-differentiation strategy and must constantly design and develop innovative new products to remain competitive in the marketplace. Chipset's innovation focuses on improving its manufacturing capability and process controls to lower costs and improve quality. Chipset measures innovation by the number of improvements in manufacturing processes and percentage of processes with advanced controls.
   - **Operations process:** Producing and delivering existing products and services that will meet the needs of customers. Chipset's strategic initiatives are (a) improving manufacturing quality, (b) reducing delivery time to customers, and (c) meeting specified delivery dates so it measures yield, order-delivery time, and on-time deliveries.

Exhibit 13-3 The Balanced Scorecard for Chipset, Inc., for 2011

Strategic Objectives	Measures	Initiatives	Target Performance	Actual Performance
Financial Perspective				
Grow operating income	Operating income from productivity gain	Manage costs and unused capacity	Rs 1,85,00,000	Rs 1,91,25,000
Increase shareholder value	Operating income from growth	Build strong customer relationships	Rs 2,50,00,000	Rs 2,82,00,000
	Revenue growth		9%	10%[a]
Customer Perspective				
Increase market share	Market share in communication-networks segment	Identify future needs of customers	6%	7%
Increase customer satisfaction	Number of new customers	Identify new target-customer segments	1	1[b]
	Customer-satisfaction ratings	Increase customer focus of sales organization	90% of customers give top two ratings	87% of customers give top two ratings
Internal-Business-Process Perspective				
Improve postsales service	Service response time	Improve customer-service process	Within 4 hours	Within 3 hours
Improve manufacturing quality and productivity	Yield	Identify root causes of problems and improve quality	78%	79.3%
Reduce delivery time to customers	Order-delivery time	Reengineer order-delivery process	30 days	30 days
Meet specified delivery dates	On-time delivery	Reengineer order-delivery process	92%	90%
Improve processes	Number of major improvements in manufacturing and business processes	Organize teams from manufacturing and sales to modify processes	5	5
Improve manufacturing capability	Percentage of processes with advanced controls	Organize R&D/manufact-uring teams to implement advanced controls	75%	75%
Learning-and-Growth Perspective				
Align employee and organization goals	Employee-satisfaction ratings	Employee participation and suggestions program to build teamwork	80% of employees give top two ratings	88% of employees give top two ratings
Empower workforce	Percentage of line workers empowered to manage processes	Have supervisors act as coaches rather than decision makers	85%	90%
Develop process skill	Percentage of employees trained in process and quality management	Employee training programs	90%	92%
Enhance information-system capabilities	Percentage of manufacturing processes with real-time feedback	Improve online and offline data gathering	80%	80%

[a](Revenues in 2011 + Revenues in 2010) ÷ Revenues in 2010 = (Rs 25,30,00,000 + Rs 23,00,00,000) ÷ Rs 23,00,00,000 = 10%.

[b]Number of customers increased from seven to eight in 2011.

- **Postsales-service process:** Providing service and support to the customer after the sale of a product or service. Chipset monitors how quickly and accurately it is responding to customer-service requests.

4. **Learning-and-growth perspective.** This perspective identifies the capabilities the organization must excel at to achieve superior internal processes that in turn create value for customers and shareholders. Chipset's learning and growth perspective emphasizes three capabilities: (1) information-system capabilities, measured by the percentage of manufacturing processes with real-time feedback; (2) employee capabilities, measured by the percentage of employees trained in process and quality management; and (3) motivation, measured by employee satisfaction and the percentage of manufacturing and sales employees (line employees) empowered to manage processes.

The arrows in Exhibit 13-3 indicate the *broad* cause-and-effect linkages: how gains in the learning-and-growth perspective lead to improvements in internal business processes, which lead to higher customer satisfaction and market share, and finally lead to superior financial performance. Note how the scorecard describes elements of Chipset's strategy implementation. Worker training and empowerment improve employee satisfaction and lead to manufacturing and business-process improvements that improve quality and reduce delivery time. The result is increased customer satisfaction and higher market share. These initiatives have been successful from a financial perspective. Chipset has earned significant operating income from its cost leadership strategy, and that strategy has also led to growth.

A major benefit of the balanced scorecard is that it promotes causal thinking. Think of the balanced scorecard as a *linked scorecard* or a *causal scorecard*. Managers must search for empirical evidence (rather than rely on faith alone) to test the validity and strength of the various connections. A causal scorecard enables a company to focus on the key drivers that steer the implementation of the strategy. Without convincing links, the scorecard loses much of its value.

Implementing a Balanced Scorecard

To successfully implement a balanced scorecard requires commitment and leadership from top management. At Chipset, the team building the balanced scorecard (headed by the vice president of strategic planning) conducted interviews with senior managers, probed executives about customers, competitors, and technological developments, and sought proposals for balanced scorecard objectives across the four perspectives. The team then met to discuss the responses and to build a prioritized list of objectives.

In a meeting with all senior managers, the team sought to achieve consensus on the scorecard objectives. Senior management was then divided into four groups, with each group responsible for one of the perspectives. In addition, each group broadened the base of inputs by including representatives from the next-lower levels of management and key functional managers. The groups identified measures for each objective and the sources of information for each measure. The groups then met to finalize scorecard objectives, measures, targets, and the initiatives to achieve the targets. Management accountants played an important role in the design and implementation of the balanced scorecard, particularly in determining measures to represent the realities of the business. This required management accountants to understand the economic environment of the industry, Chipset's customers and competitors, and internal business issues such as human resources, operations, and distribution.

Managers made sure that employees understood the scorecard and the scorecard process. The final balanced scorecard was communicated to all employees. Sharing the scorecard allowed engineers and operating personnel, for example, to understand the reasons for customer satisfaction and dissatisfaction and to make suggestions for improving internal processes directly aimed at satisfying customers and implementing Chipset's strategy. Too often, scorecards are seen by only a select group of managers. By limiting the scorecard's exposure, an organization loses the opportunity for widespread organization engagement and alignment.

Chipset, like Cigna Property and Casualty Insurance and Wells Fargo, also encourages each department to develop its own scorecard that ties into Chipset's main scorecard described in Exhibit 13-2. For example, the quality control department's scorecard has measures that its department managers use to improve quality—number of quality circles, statistical process control charts, Pareto diagrams, and root-cause analyses implemented (see Chapter 19 for more deatails). Department scorecards help align actions that each department needs to perform to implement Chipset's strategy.

Companies frequently use balanced scorecards to evaluate and reward managerial performance and to thereby influence a manager's behavior. This use of the balanced scorecard motivates managers to give stronger consideration to nonfinancial drivers of performance and to thereby widen the performance management lens. Surveys indicate, however, that companies continue to assign more weight to the financial perspective (55%) than to the other perspectives—customer (19%), internal business process (12%), and learning and growth (14%). Companies cite several reasons for this—difficulty evaluating the relative importance of different measures, challenges in measuring and quantifying qualitative, nonfinancial data, and problems in compensating managers despite poor financial performance (see Chapter 23 for a more detailed discussion of performance evaluation). For the balanced scorecard to be effective, managers must view it as fairly assessing and rewarding all important aspects of a manager's performance and promotion prospects.

Aligning the Balanced Scorecard to Strategy

Different strategies call for different scorecards. Recall Chipset's competitor Visilog, which follows a product-differentiation strategy by designing custom chips for modems and communication networks. Visilog designs its balanced scorecard to fit its strategy. For example, in the financial perspective, Visilog evaluates how much of its operating income comes from charging premium prices for its products. In the customer perspective, Visilog measures the percentage of its revenues from new products and new customers. In the internal-business-process perspective, Visilog measures the number of new products introduced and new product development time. In the learning-and-growth perspective, Visilog measures the development of advanced manufacturing capabilities to produce custom chips. Visilog also uses some of the measures described in Chipset's balanced scorecard in Exhibit 13-2. For example, revenue growth, customer satisfaction ratings, order-delivery time, on-time delivery, percentage of frontline workers empowered to manage processes, and employee-satisfaction ratings are also important measures under the product-differentiation strategy. The point is to align the balanced scorecard with company strategy.[5] Exhibit 13-4 presents some common measures found on company scorecards in the service, retail, and manufacturing sectors.

Features of a Good Balanced Scorecard

A well-designed balanced scorecard has several features:

1. It tells the story of a company's strategy, articulating a sequence of cause-and-effect relationships—the links among the various perspectives that align implementation of the strategy. In for-profit companies, each measure in the scorecard is part of a cause-and-effect chain leading to financial outcomes. Not-for-profit organizations design the cause-and-effect chain to achieve their strategic service objectives—for example, number of people no longer in poverty, or number of children still in school.
2. The balanced scorecard helps to communicate the strategy to all members of the organization by translating the strategy into a coherent and linked set of understandable and measurable operational targets. Guided by the scorecard, managers and employees take actions and make decisions to achieve the company's strategy. Companies that have distinct strategic business units (SBUs)—such as consumer products and pharmaceuticals at Johnson & Johnson—develop their balanced scorecards at the SBU level. Each SBU has its own unique strategy and implementation

[5] For simplicity, we have presented the balanced scorecard in the context of companies that have followed either a cost-leadership or a product-differentiation strategy. Of course, a company may have some products for which cost leadership is critical and other products for which product differentiation is important. The company will then develop separate scorecards to implement the different product strategies. In still other contexts, product differentiation may be of primary importance, but some cost leadership must also be achieved. The balanced scorecard measures would then be linked in a cause-and-effect way to this strategy.

Exhibit 13-4

Frequently Cited Balanced Scorecard Measures

Financial Perspective
Income measures: Operating income, gross margin percentage
Revenue and cost measures: Revenue growth, revenues from new products, cost reductions in key areas
Income and investment measures: Return on investment
Customer Perspective
Market share, customer satisfaction, customer-retention percentage, time taken to fulfill customers' requests, number of customer complaints
Internal-Business-Process Perspective
Innovation Process: Operating capabilities, number of new products or services, new-product development times, and number of new patents
Operations Process: Yield, defect rates, time taken to deliver product to customers, percentage of on-time deliveries, average time taken to respond to orders, setup time, manufacturing downtime
Postsales Service Process: Time taken to replace or repair defective products, hours of customer training for using the product
Learning-and-Growth Perspective
Employee measures: Employee education and skill levels, employee-satisfaction ratings, employee turnover rates, percentage of employee suggestions implemented, percentage of compensation based on individual and team incentives
Technology measures: Information system availability, percentage of processes with advanced controls

goals; building separate scorecards allows each SBU to choose measures that help implement its distinctive strategy.

3. In for-profit companies, the balanced scorecard must motivate managers to take actions that eventually result in improvements in financial performance. Managers sometimes tend to focus too much on innovation, quality, and customer satisfaction as ends in themselves. For example, Xerox spent heavily to increase customer satisfaction without a resulting financial payoff. The company later discovered that a measure of customer loyalty, not general customer satisfaction, was a leading indicator of future financial performance. When financial and nonfinancial performance measures are properly linked, most, if not all, of the nonfinancial measures serve as leading indicators of lagging future financial performance. Some companies use statistical methods, such as regression analysis, to test the anticipated cause-and-effect relationships among various nonfinancial measures and financial measures. The data for this analysis can come from either time series data (collected over time) or cross-sectional data (collected, for example, across multiple stores of a retail chain). In the Chipset example, improvements in nonfinancial factors have, in fact, already led to improvements in financial factors.
4. The balanced scorecard limits the number of measures, identifying only the most critical ones. Chipset's scorecard, for example, has 16 measures, between 3 and 5 measures for each perspective. Limiting the number of measures focuses managers' attention on those that most affect strategy implementation. Using too many measures makes it difficult for managers to process relevant information.
5. The balanced scorecard highlights less-than-optimal trade-offs that managers may make when they fail to consider operational and financial measures together. For example, a company whose strategy is innovation and product differentiation could achieve superior short-run financial performance by reducing spending on R&D. A good balanced scorecard would signal that the short-run financial performance might have been achieved by taking actions that hurt future financial performance because a leading indicator of that performance, R&D spending and R&D output, has declined.

Pitfalls in Implementing a Balanced Scorecard

Pitfalls to avoid in implementing a balanced scorecard include the following:

1. Managers should not assume the cause-and-effect linkages are precise. They are merely hypotheses. Over time, a company must gather evidence of the strength and

timing of the linkages among the nonfinancial and financial measures. With experience, organizations should alter their scorecards to include those nonfinancial objectives and measures that are the best leading indicators (the causes) of financial performance (a lagging indicator or effect). Understanding that the scorecard evolves over time helps managers to avoid unproductively spending time and money trying to design the "perfect" scorecard at the outset. Furthermore, as the business environment and strategy change over time, the measures in the scorecard will also need to change.

2. Managers should not seek improvements across all of the measures all of the time. For example, strive for quality and on-time performance but not beyond a point at which further improvement in these objectives is so costly that it is inconsistent with long-run profit maximization. Cost-benefit considerations should always be a central element when designing a balanced scorecard.
3. Managers should not use only objective measures in the balanced scorecard. Chipset's balanced scorecard includes both objective measures (such as operating income from cost leadership, market share, and manufacturing yield) and subjective measures (such as customer- and employee-satisfaction ratings). When using subjective measures, though, management must be careful that the benefits of this potentially rich information are not lost by using measures that are inaccurate or that can be easily manipulated.
4. Despite challenges of measurement, top management should not ignore nonfinancial measures when evaluating managers and other employees. Managers tend to focus on what their performance is measured by. Excluding nonfinancial measures when evaluating performance will reduce the significance and importance that managers give to nonfinancial measures.

Decision Point

How can an organization translate its strategy into a set of performance measures?

Evaluating the Success of Strategy and Implementation

To evaluate how successful Chipset's strategy and its implementation have been, its management compares the target- and actual-performance columns in the balanced scorecard (Exhibit 13-2). Chipset met most targets set on the basis of competitor benchmarks in 2009 itself. That's because, in the Chipset context, improvements in the learning and growth perspective quickly ripple through to the financial perspective. Chipset will continue to seek improvements on the targets it did not achieve, but meeting most targets suggests that the strategic initiatives that Chipset identified and measured for learning and growth resulted in improvements in internal business processes, customer measures, and financial performance.

How would Chipset know if it had problems in strategy implementation? If it did not meet its targets on the two perspectives that are more internally focused: learning and growth and internal business processes.

What if Chipset performed well on learning and growth and internal business processes, but customer measures and financial performance in this year and the next did not improve? Chipset's managers would then conclude that Chipset did a good job of implementation (the various internal nonfinancial measures it targeted improved) but that its strategy was faulty (there was no effect on customers or on long-run financial performance and value creation). Management failed to identify the correct causal links. It implemented the wrong strategy well! Management would then reevaluate the strategy and the factors that drive it.

Now what if Chipset performed well on its various nonfinancial measures, and operating income over this year and the next also increased? Chipset's managers might be tempted to declare the strategy a success because operating income increased. Unfortunately, management still cannot conclude with any confidence that Chipset successfully formulated and implemented its strategy. Why? Because operating income can increase simply because entire markets are expanding, not because a company's strategy has been successful. Also, changes in operating income might occur because of factors outside the strategy. For example, a company such as Chipset that has chosen a cost-leadership strategy may find that its operating-income increase instead resulted incidentally from, say, some degree of product differentiation. *Managers and management accountants need to evaluate the success of a strategy by linking the sources of operating-income increases to the strategy.*

For Chipset to conclude that it was successful in implementing its strategy, it must demonstrate that improvements in its financial performance and operating income over time resulted from achieving targeted cost savings and growth in market share. Fortunately, the top two rows of Chipset's balanced scorecard in Exhibit 13-2 show that operating-income gains from productivity (Rs 2,01,25,000) and growth (Rs 3,42,00,000) exceeded targets. The next section of this chapter describes how these numbers were calculated. To be sure that the strategy has been successful, Chipset's management would like to see similar gains in subsequent years.

Chipset's management accountants subdivide changes in operating income into components that can be identified with product differentiation, cost leadership, and growth. Why growth? Because successful cost leadership or product differentiation generally increases market share and helps a company to grow. Subdividing the change in operating income to evaluate the success of a strategy is conceptually similar to the variance analysis discussed in Chapters 7 and 8. One difference, however, is that management accountants compare actual operating performance over two different periods, not actual to budgeted numbers in the same time period as in variance analysis.[6]

Strategic Analysis of Operating Income

Learning Objective 4

Analyze changes in operating income to evaluate strategy

. . . growth, price recovery, and productivity

The following illustration explains how to subdivide the change in operating income from one period to *any* future period. The individual components describe company performance with regard to cost leadership, product differentiation, and growth.[7] We illustrate the analysis using data from 2010 and 2011 because Chipset implemented key elements of its strategy in late 2010 and early 2011 and expects the financial consequences of these strategies to appear in 2011. Suppose the financial consequences of these strategies had been expected to affect operating income in, say, 2012 only. Then we could just as easily have compared 2010 to 2012. If necessary, we could also have compared 2010 to 2011 and 2012 taken together.

Chipset's data for 2010 and 2011 follow.

	2010	2011
1. Units of CX1 produced and sold	1,000,000	1,150,000
2. Selling price	Rs 270	Rs 250
3. Direct materials (square centimeters of silicon wafers)	3,000,000	2,900,000
4. Direct material cost per square centimeter	Rs 14	Rs 15
5. Manufacturing processing capacity (in square centimeters of silicon wafer)	3,750,000	3,500,000
6. Conversion costs (all manufacturing costs other than direct material costs)	Rs 16,05,00,000	Rs 15,22,50,000
7. Conversion cost per unit of capacity (Row 6 ÷ Row 5)	Rs 42.8	Rs 43.5

Chipset provides the following additional information.

1. Conversion costs for each year depend on production capacity defined in terms of the quantity of square centimeters of silicon wafers that can be processed. Such costs do not vary with the actual quantity of silicon wafers processed.

[6] Other examples of focusing on actual performance over two periods rather than comparisons of actuals with budgets can be found in J. Hope and R. Fraser, *Beyond Budgeting* (Boston, MA: Harvard Business School Press, 2003).

[7] For other details, see R. Banker, S. Datar, and R. Kaplan, "Productivity Measurement and Management Accounting," *Journal of Accounting, Auditing and Finance* (1989): 528–554; and A. Hayzen and J. Reeve, "Examining the Relationships in Productivity Accounting," *Management Accounting Quarterly* (2000): 32–39.

2. Chipset incurs no R&D costs. Its marketing, sales, and customer-service costs are small relative to the other costs. Chipset has fewer than 10 customers, each purchasing roughly the same quantities of CX1. Because of the highly technical nature of the product, Chipset uses a cross-functional team for its marketing, sales, and customer-service activities. This cross-functional approach ensures that, although marketing, sales, and customer-service costs are small, the entire Chipset organization, including manufacturing engineers, remains focused on increasing customer satisfaction and market share. (The Problem for Self-Study at the end of this chapter describes a situation in which marketing, sales, and customer-service costs are significant.)
3. Chipset's asset structure is very similar in 2010 and 2011.
4. Operating income for each year is as follows:

	2010	2011
Revenues		
(Rs 230 per unit × 1,000,000 units; Rs 220 per unit × 1,150,000 units)	Rs 23,00,00,000	Rs 25,30,00,000
Costs		
Direct material costs		
(Rs 14/sq. cm. × 3,000,000 sq. cm.; Rs 15/sq. cm. × 2,900,000 sq. cm.)	4,20,00,000	4,35,00,000
Conversion costs		
(Rs 42.8/sq. cm. × 3,750,000 sq. cm.; Rs 43.5/sq. cm. × 3,500,000 sq. cm.)	16,05,00,000	15,22,50,000
R&D costs (Rs 10,00,000 × 40 employees; Rs 10,00,000 × 39 employees)	4,00,00,000	3,90,00,000
Total costs	20,25,00,000	19,57,50,000
Operating income	Rs 2,75,00,000	Rs 5,72,50,000
Change in operating income	Rs 2,97,50,000 F	

The goal of Chipset's managers is to evaluate how much of the Rs 2,52,50,000 increase in operating income was caused by the successful implementation of the company's cost-leadership strategy. To do this, management accountants analyze three main factors: growth, price recovery, and productivity.

The **growth component** measures the change in operating income attributable solely to the change in the quantity of output sold between 2010 and 2011.

The **price-recovery component** measures the change in operating income attributable solely to changes in Chipset's prices of inputs and outputs between 2010 and 2011. The price-recovery component measures change in output price compared with changes in input prices. A company that has successfully pursued a strategy of product differentiation will be able to increase its output price faster than the increase in its input prices, boosting profit margins and operating income: It will show a large positive price-recovery component.

The **productivity component** measures the change in costs attributable to a change in the quantity of inputs used in 2011 relative to the quantity of inputs that would have been used in 2010 to produce the 2011 output. The productivity component measures the amount by which operating income increases by using inputs efficiently to lower costs. A company that has successfully pursued a strategy of cost leadership will be able to produce a given quantity of output with a lower cost of inputs: It will show a large positive productivity component. Given Chipset's strategy of cost leadership, we expect the increase in operating income to be attributable to the productivity and growth components, not to price recovery. We now examine these three components in detail.

Growth Component of Change in Operating Income

The growth component of the change in operating income measures the increase in revenues minus the increase in costs from selling more units of CX1 in 2011 (1,150,000 units) than in 2010 (1,000,000 units), *assuming nothing else has changed*. That is, the growth-component calculations use 2010 output prices, input prices, efficiencies, and capacity relationships.

Revenue effect of growth

$$\text{Revenue effect of growth} = \left(\begin{matrix}\text{Actual units of}\\\text{output sold}\\\text{in 2011}\end{matrix} - \begin{matrix}\text{Actual units of}\\\text{output sold}\\\text{in 2010}\end{matrix}\right) \times \begin{matrix}\text{Selling}\\\text{price}\\\text{in 2010}\end{matrix}$$

$$= (11{,}50{,}000 \text{ units} - 10{,}00{,}000 \text{ units}) \times \text{Rs } 230 \text{ per unit}$$

$$= \text{Rs } 34{,}50{,}000 \text{ F}$$

This component is favorable (F) because the increase in output sold in 2011 increases operating income. Components that decrease operating income are unfavorable (U).

Note that Chipset uses the 2010 price of CX1 here and focuses only on the increase in units sold between 2010 and 2011, because the objective of the revenue effect of the growth component measures how much revenues would have changed in 2010 if Chipset had sold 1,150,000 units instead of 1,000,000 units.

Cost effect of growth The cost effect of growth measures how much costs would have changed in 2010 if Chipset had produced 11,50,000 units of CX1 instead of 10,00,000 units. To measure the cost effect of growth, Chipset's managers distinguish variable costs such as direct material costs from fixed costs such as conversion costs and R&D costs. That's because as units produced (and sold) increase, variable costs increase proportionately but fixed costs, generally, do not change.

$$\begin{matrix}\text{Cost effect of}\\\text{growth for}\\\text{variable costs}\end{matrix} = \left(\begin{matrix}\text{Units of input}\\\text{required to}\\\text{produce 2011}\\\text{output in 2010}\end{matrix} - \begin{matrix}\text{Actual units of}\\\text{input used}\\\text{to produce}\\\text{2010 output}\end{matrix}\right) \times \begin{matrix}\text{Input}\\\text{price}\\\text{in 2010}\end{matrix}$$

$$\begin{matrix}\text{Cost effect of}\\\text{growth for}\\\text{direct materials}\end{matrix} = \left(30{,}00{,}000 \text{ sq.cm.} \times \frac{11{,}50{,}000 \text{ units}}{10{,}00{,}000 \text{ units}} - 30{,}00{,}000 \text{ sq.cm.}\right) \times \text{Rs } 14 \text{ per sq.cm.}$$

$$= (34{,}50{,}000 \text{ sq. cm.} - 30{,}00{,}000 \text{ sq.cm.}) \times \text{Rs } 14 \text{ per sq.cm.} = \text{Rs } 63{,}00{,}000 \text{ U}$$

The units of input required to produce 2011 output in 2010 can also be calculated as follows:

$$\text{Units of input per unit of output in 2010} = \frac{3{,}000{,}000 \text{ sq. cm.}}{1{,}000{,}000 \text{ units}} = 3 \text{ sq. cm./unit}$$

Units of input required to produce 2011 output of 1,150,000 units in 2010 = 3 sq. cm. per unit × 1,150,000 units = 3,450,000 sq. cm.

$$\begin{matrix}\text{Cost effect of}\\\text{growth for}\\\text{fixed costs}\end{matrix} = \left(\begin{matrix}\text{Actual units of capacity in}\\\text{2010 because adequate capacity}\\\text{exists to produce 2011 output in 2010}\end{matrix} - \begin{matrix}\text{Actual units}\\\text{of capacity}\\\text{in 2010}\end{matrix}\right) \times \begin{matrix}\text{Price per}\\\text{unit of}\\\text{capacity}\\\text{in 2010}\end{matrix}$$

$$\begin{matrix}\text{Cost effect of}\\\text{growth for}\\\text{conversion costs}\end{matrix} = (37{,}50{,}000 \text{ sq. cm.} - 37{,}50{,}000 \text{ sq. cm.}) \times \text{Rs } 42.8 \text{ per sq. cm.} = \text{Re } 0$$

Conversion costs are fixed costs at a given level of capacity. Chipset has manufacturing capacity to process 37,50,000 square centimeters of silicon wafers in 2010 at a cost of Rs 16,05,00,000, or Rs 42.8 per square centimeter. To produce 11,50,000 units of output in 2010, Chipset would have needed to process 34,50,000 square centimeters of direct materials. which is less than the available capacity of 3,750,000 sq. cm. Throughout this chapter, we assume adequate capacity exists in the current year (2010) to produce next year's (2011) output. Under this assumption, the cost effect of growth for capacity-related fixed costs is, by definition, Rs 0. Had 2010 capacity been inadequate to produce 2011 output in 2010, we would need to calculate the additional capacity required to produce 2011 output in 2010. These calculations are beyond the scope of the book.

In summary, the net increase in operating income attributable to growth equals:

Revenue effect of growth		Rs 3,45,00,000 F
Cost effect of growth		
Direct material costs	Rs 63,00,000 U	
Conversion costs	0	
R&D costs	0	63,00,000 U
Change in operating income due to growth		Rs 2,82,00,000 F

Price-Recovery Component of Change in Operating Income

Assuming that the 2010 relationship between inputs and outputs continued in 2011, the price-recovery component of the change in operating income measures solely the effect of price changes on revenues and costs to produce and sell the 11,50,000 units of CX1 in 2011.

Revenue effect of price recovery

$$\text{Revenue effect of price recovery} = \left(\text{Selling price in 2011} - \text{Selling price in 2010}\right) \times \text{Actual units of output sold in 2011}$$

$$= (\text{Rs } 220 \text{ per unit} - \text{Rs } 230 \text{ per unit}) \times 11{,}50{,}000 \text{ units}$$

$$= \text{Rs } 115{,}00{,}000 \text{ U}$$

Note that the calculation focuses on revenue changes caused by changes in the selling price of CX1 between 2010 and 2011.

Cost effect of price recovery Chipset's management accountants calculate the cost effects of price recovery separately for variable costs and for fixed costs, just as they did when calculating the cost effect of growth.

$$\text{Cost effect of price recovery for variable costs} = \left(\text{Input price in 2011} - \text{Input price in 2010}\right) \times \text{Units of input required to produce 2011 output in 2010}$$

$$\text{Cost effect of price recovery for direct materials} = (\text{Rs } 15 \text{ per sq.cm.} - \text{Rs } 14 \text{ per sq.cm.}) \times 34{,}50{,}000 \text{ sq.} = \text{Rs } 34{,}50{,}000 \text{ U}$$

Recall that the direct materials of 34,50,000 square centimeters required to produce 2011 output in 2010 had already been calculated when computing the cost effect of growth.

$$\text{Cost effect of price recovery for fixed costs} = \left(\text{Price per unit of capacity in 2011} - \text{Price per unit of capacity in 2010}\right) \times \text{Actual units of capacity in 2010, if adequate to produce 2011 output in 2010}$$

Cost effects of price recovery for fixed costs are:

Conversion costs: (Rs 43.5 per sq. cm. – Rs 42.8 per sq. cm.) × 37,50,000 sq. cm. = Rs 26,25,000 U

Note that the detailed analyses of capacities were presented on the previous page when computing the cost effect of growth.

In summary, the net decrease in operating income attributable to price recovery equals:

Revenue effect of price recovery		Rs 1,15,00,000 U
Cost effect of price recovery		
Direct material costs	Rs 34,50,000 U	
Conversion costs	26,25,000 U	
R&D costs	0	60,75,000 U
Change in operating income due to price recovery		Rs 1,75,75,000 U

The price-recovery analysis indicates that, even as the prices of its inputs increased, the selling prices of CX1 decreased and Chipset could not pass on input-price increases to its customers.

Productivity Component of Change in Operating Income

The productivity component of the change in operating income uses 2011 input prices to measure how costs have decreased as a result of using fewer inputs, a better mix of inputs, and/or less capacity to produce 2011 output, compared with the inputs and capacity that would have been used in 2010.

The productivity-component calculations use 2011 prices and output. That's because the productivity component isolates the change in costs between 2010 and 2011 caused solely by the change in the quantities, mix, and/or capacities of inputs.[8]

$$\text{Cost effect of productivity for variable costs} = \left(\begin{array}{c}\text{Actual units of input used to produce 2011 output}\end{array} - \begin{array}{c}\text{Units of input required to produce 2011 output in 2010}\end{array}\right) \times \begin{array}{c}\text{Input price in 2011}\end{array}$$

Using the 2011 data and the calculation of units of input required to produce 2011 output in 2010 when discussing the cost effects of growth,

$$\begin{aligned}\text{Cost effect of productivity for direct materials} &= (29{,}00{,}000 \text{ sq. cm.} - 34{,}50{,}000 \text{ sq. cm.}) \times \text{Rs } 15 \text{ per sq. cm} \\ &= 5{,}50{,}000 \text{ sq. cm.} \times \text{Rs } 15 \text{ per sq. cm.} = \text{Rs } 82{,}50{,}000 \text{ F}\end{aligned}$$

Chipset's quality and yield improvements reduced the quantity of direct materials needed to produce output in 2011 relative to 2010.

$$\text{Cost effect of productivity for fixed costs} = \left(\begin{array}{c}\text{Actual units of capacity in 2011}\end{array} - \begin{array}{c}\text{Actual units of capacity in 2010, if adequate to produce 2011 output in 2010}\end{array}\right) \times \begin{array}{c}\text{Price per unit of capacity in 2011}\end{array}$$

Using the 2011 data, and the analyses of capacity required to produce 2011 output in 2010 when discussing the cost effect of growth,

Cost effects of productivity for fixed costs are

Conversion costs: (35,00,000 sq. cm. – 37,50,000 sq. cm. × Rs 43.5 per sq. cm. = Rs 1,08,75,000 F

Chipset's managers decreased manufacturing capacity in 2011 to 35,00,000 square centimeters by selling off old equipment and laying off workers.

In summary, the net increase in operating income attributable to productivity equals

Cost effect of productivity	
Direct material costs	Rs 82,50,000 F
Conversion costs	1,08,75,000 F
Change in operating income due to productivity	1,91,25,000 F

[8] Note that the productivity-component calculation uses actual 2009 input prices, whereas its counterpart, the efficiency variance in Chapters 7 and 8, uses budgeted prices. (In effect, the budgeted prices correspond to 2008 prices). Year 2009 prices are used in the productivity calculation because Chipset wants its managers to choose input quantities to minimize costs in 2009 based on currently prevailing prices. If 2008 prices had been used in the productivity calculation, managers would choose input quantities based on irrelevant input prices that prevailed a year ago! Why does using budgeted prices in Chapters 7 and 8 not pose a similar problem? Because, unlike 2008 prices that describe what happened a year ago, budgeted prices represent prices that are expected to prevail in the current period. Moreover, budgeted prices can be changed, if necessary, to bring them in line with actual current-period prices.

Exhibit 13-5 Strategic Analysis of Profitability

	Income Statement Amounts in 2010 (1)	Revenue and Cost Effects of Growth Component in 2011 (2)	Revenue and Cost Effects of Price-Recovery Component in 2011 (3)	Cost Effect of Productivity Component in 2011 (4)	Income Statement Amounts in 2011 (5) = (1) + (2) + (3) + (4)
Revenues	Rs 23,00,00,000	Rs 3,45,00,000 F	Rs 1,15,00,000 U	—	Rs 25,30,00,000
Costs	20,25,00,000	63,00,000 U	60,75,000 U	Rs 1,91,25,000 F	19,57,50,000
Operating income	Rs 2,75,00,000	Rs 2,82,00,000 F	Rs 1,75,75,000 U	Rs 1,91,25,000 F	Rs 5,72,50,000
			Rs 2,97,50,000 F		
			Change in operating income		

The productivity component indicates that Chipset was able to increase operating income by improving quality and productivity, eliminating capacity, and reducing costs. The appendix to this chapter examines partial and total factor productivity changes between 2010 and 2011 and describes how the management accountant can obtain a deeper understanding of Chipset's cost-leadership strategy. Note that the productivity component focuses exclusively on costs, so there is no revenue effect for this component.

Exhibit 13-5 summarizes the growth, price-recovery, and productivity components of the changes in operating income. Generally, companies that have been successful at cost leadership will show favorable productivity and growth components. Companies that have successfully differentiated their products will show favorable price-recovery and growth components. In Chipset's case, consistent with its strategy and its implementation, productivity contributed Rs 1,91,25,000 to the increase in operating income, and growth contributed Rs 2,82,00,000. Price-recovery contributed a Rs 1,75,75,000 decrease in operating income, however, because, even as input prices increased, the selling price of CX1 decreased. Had Chipset been able to differentiate its product and charge a higher price, the price-recovery effects might have been less unfavorable or perhaps even favorable. As a result, Chipset's managers plan to evaluate some modest changes in product features that might help differentiate CX1 somewhat from competing products.

Further Analysis of Growth, Price-Recovery, and Productivity Components

As in all variance and profit analysis, Chipset's managers want to more closely analyze the change in operating income. Chipset's growth might have been helped, for example, by an increase in industry market size. Therefore, at least part of the increase in operating income may be attributable to favorable economic conditions in the industry rather than to any successful implementation of strategy. Some of the growth might also have come as a result of a management decision to decrease selling price, made possible by the productivity gains. In this case, the increase in operating income from cost leadership must include operating income from productivity-related growth in market share in addition to the productivity gain.

We illustrate these ideas, using the Chipset example and the following additional information. *Instructors who do not wish to cover these detailed calculations can go to the next section on "Applying the Five-Step Decision-Making Framework to Strategy" without any loss of continuity.*

- The market growth rate in the industry is 10% in 2011. Of the 1,50,000 (11,50,000 – 10,00,000) units of increased sales of CX1 between 2010 and 2011, 10,00,000 (0.10 × 10,00,000) units are due to an increase in industry market size (which Chipset should have benefited from regardless of its productivity gains), and the remaining 50,000 units are due to an increase in market share.

- During 2011, Chipset could have maintained the price of CX1 at the 2010 price of Rs 230 per unit. But management decided to take advantage of the productivity gains to reduce the price of CX1 by Rs 10 to grow market share leading to the 70,000-unit increase in sales.

The effect of the industry-market-size factor on operating income (rather than any specific strategic actions) is:

Change in operating income due to growth in industry market size

$$\text{Rs } 2{,}82{,}00{,}000 \text{ (Exhibit 13-5, column 2)} \times \frac{80{,}000 \text{ units}}{1{,}50{,}000 \text{ units}} = \text{Rs } 1{,}50{,}40{,}000 \text{ F}$$

Lacking a differentiated product, Chipset could have maintained the price of CX1 at Rs 230 per unit even while the prices of its inputs increased.

The effect of product differentiation on operating income is:

Change in prices of inputs (cost effect of price recovery)	60,75,000 U
Change in operating income due to product differentiation	Rs 60,75,000 U

To exercise cost and price leadership, Chipset made the strategic decision to cut the price of CX1 by Rs 10. This decision resulted in an increase in market share and 70,000 units of additional sales.

The effect of cost leadership on operating income is:

Productivity component	Rs 1,91,25,000 F
Effect of strategic decision to reduce price (Rs 10/unit × 11,50,000 units)	11,50,000 U
Growth in market share due to productivity improvement and strategic decision to reduce prices Rs 2,82,00,000 (Exhibit 13-5, column 2) × 70,000 units / 1,50,000 units	1,31,60,000 F
Change in operating income due to cost leadership	Rs 2,07,85,000

A summary of the change in operating income between 2010 and 2011 follows.

Change due to industry market size	Rs 1,50,40,000 F
Change due to product differentiation	60,75,000 U
Change due to cost leadership	2,07,85,000 F
Change in operating income	Rs 2,97,50,000 F

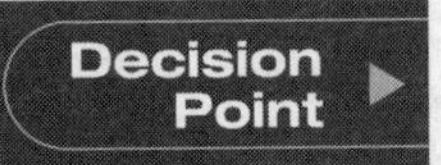

How can a company analyze changes in operating income to evaluate the success of its strategy?

Consistent with its cost-leadership strategy, the productivity gains of Rs 1,91,25,000 in 2011 were a big part of the increase in operating income from 2010 to 2011. Chipset took advantage of these productivity gains to decrease price by Rs 10 per unit at a cost of Rs 1,15,00,000 to gain Rs 1,31,60,000 in operating income by selling 70,000 additional units. The Problem for Self-Study later in this chapter describes the analysis of the growth, price-recovery, and productivity components for a company following a product-differentiation strategy. The following Concepts in Action feature describes the unique challenges that dot-com companies face in choosing a profitable strategy.

Under different assumptions about the change in selling price, the analysis will attribute different amounts to the different strategies.

Applying the Five-Step Decision-Making Framework to Strategy

We next briefly describe how the five-step decision-making framework, introduced in Chapter 1, is also useful in making decisions about strategy.

1. *Identify the problem and uncertainties.* The decision about what strategy Chipset must choose depends on resolving two uncertainties—whether Chipset can add value to its customers that its competitors cannot emulate, and whether Chipset can develop the necessary internal capabilities to add this value.
2. *Obtain information.* Chipset's managers develop customer preference maps to identify various product attributes desired by customers and the competitive advantage or disadvantage it has on each attribute relative to competitors. The managers also gather data on Chipset's internal capabilities. How good is Chipset's R&D capability in designing and developing innovative new products? How good are its process and marketing capabilities?
3. *Make predictions about the future.* Chipset's managers conclude that they will not be able to develop innovative new products in a cost-effective way. They believe that Chipset's strength lies in improving quality, reengineering processes, reducing costs, and delivering products faster to customers.
4. *Make decisions by choosing among alternatives.* Chipset's management decides to follow a cost leadership rather than a product differentiation strategy. It decides to introduce a balanced scorecard to align and measure its quality improvement and process reengineering efforts.
5. *Implement the decision, evaluate performance, and learn.* On its balanced scorecard, Chipset's managers compare actual and targeted performance and evaluate possible cause-and-effect relationships. They learn, for example, that increasing the percentage of processes with advanced controls improves yield. As a result, just as they had anticipated, productivity and growth initiatives result in increases in operating income in 2009. The one change Chipset's managers plan for 2010 is to make modest changes in product features that might help differentiate CX1 somewhat from competing products. In this way, feedback and learning help in the development of future strategies and implementation plans.

Downsizing and the Management of Capacity

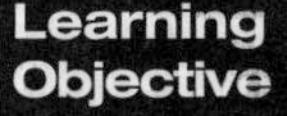

Learning Objective 5

Identify unused capacity

. . . capacity available minus capacity used for engineered costs but difficult to determine for discretionary costs

and how to manage it

. . . downsize to reduce capacity

As we saw in our discussion of the productivity component, fixed costs are tied to capacity. Unlike variable costs, fixed costs do not change automatically with changes in activity level (for example, fixed conversion costs do not change with changes in the quantity of silicon wafers started into production). How then can managers reduce capacity-based fixed costs? By measuring and managing unused capacity. **Unused capacity** is the amount of productive capacity available over and above the productive capacity employed to meet consumer demand in the current period. To understand unused capacity, it is necessary to distinguish *engineered costs* from *discretionary costs*.

Engineered and Discretionary Costs

Engineered costs result from a cause-and-effect relationship between the cost driver—output—and the (direct or indirect) resources used to produce that output. In the Chipset example, direct material costs are *direct engineered costs*. Conversion costs are an example of *indirect engineered costs*. Consider 2011. The output of 11,50,000 units of CX1 and the efficiency with which inputs are converted into outputs result in 29,00,000 square centimeters of silicon wafers being started into production. Manufacturing-conversion-cost resources used to produce 11,50,000 units of CX1 equal Rs 12,61,50,000 (Rs 43.5 per sq. cm. × 29,00,000 sq. cm.). Conversion costs (Rs 15,22,50,000) are higher because these costs relate to the manufacturing capacity to process 35,00,000 square centimeters of silicon wafer (Rs 43.5 per sq. cm. × 35,00,000 sq. cm. = 15,22,50,000). Although these costs are fixed in the short run, over the long run there is a cause-and-effect relationship between output and manufacturing capacity required (and conversion costs needed). Chipset will try to match its capacity to its needs.

Discretionary costs have two important features: (1) They arise from periodic (usually annual) decisions regarding the maximum amount to be incurred; and (2) they have no measurable cause-and-effect relationship between output and resources used. There is often a delay between when a resource is acquired and when it is used. Examples of discretionary costs include advertising, executive training, R&D, and corporate-staff department costs such as legal, human resources, and public relations. Unlike engineered costs, a noteworthy aspect of discretionary costs is that managers are seldom confident that the "correct" amounts are being spent. The founder of Lever Brothers, an international consumer-products company, once noted, "Half the money I spend on advertising is wasted; the trouble is, I don't know which half!".

Identifying Unused Capacity for Engineered and Discretionary Overhead Costs

Identifying unused capacity is very different for engineered costs compared to discretionary costs. Consider engineered conversion costs.

At the start of 2011, Chipset had capacity to process 37,50,000 square centimeters of silicon wafers. Quality and productivity improvements made during 2011 enabled Chipset to produce 11,50,000 units of CX1 by processing 29,00,000 square centimeters of silicon wafers. Unused manufacturing capacity as 8,50,000 (37,50,000 − 29,00,000) square centimeters of silicon-wafer processing capacity at the beginning of 2011. At the 2011 conversion cost of Rs 43.5 per square centimeter,

$$\text{Cost of unused capacity} = \text{Cost of capacity at the beginning of the year} - \text{Manufacturing resources used during the year}$$

$$= (37{,}50{,}000 \text{ sq. cm.} \times \text{Rs } 43.5 \text{ per sq. cm.}) - (29{,}00{,}000 \text{ sq. cm.} \times \text{Rs } 43.5 \text{ per sq. cm.})$$

$$= \text{Rs } 16{,}31{,}25{,}000 - \text{Rs } 12{,}61{,}50{,}000 = \text{Rs } 3{,}69{,}75{,}000$$

The absence of a cause-and-effect relationship makes identifying unused capacity for discretionary costs difficult. Management cannot determine the R&D resources used for the actual output produced to compare to R&D capacity. And without a measure of capacity used, it is not possible to compute unused capacity.

Managing Unused Capacity

What actions can Chipset management take when it identifies unused capacity? In general, it has two alternatives: Chipset can attempt to eliminate the unused capacity, or it can attempt to grow output to utilize the unused capacity.

In recent years, many companies have *downsized* in an attempt to eliminate their unused capacity. **Downsizing** (also called **rightsizing**) is an integrated approach of configuring processes, products, and people to match costs to the activities that need to be performed to operate effectively and efficiently in the present and future. Companies such as AT&T, Delta Airlines, General Motors, IBM, and Scott Paper have downsized to focus on their core businesses and have instituted organization changes to increase efficiency, reduce costs, and improve quality. However, downsizing often means eliminating jobs, which can adversely affect employee morale and the culture of a company.

Consider Chipset's alternatives with respect to its unused manufacturing capacity. Because it needed to process 29,00,000 square centimeters of silicon wafers in 2011, it could have reduced capacity to 30,00,000 square centimeters (Chipset can add or reduce manufacturing capacity in increments of 2,50,000 sq. cm.), resulting in cost savings of Rs 3,26,25,000 [(37,50,000 sq. cm. – 30,00,000 sq. cm.) × Rs 43.5 per sq. cm.]. Chipset's strategy, however, was not only to reduce costs but also to grow its business. So early in 2011, Chipset reduced its manufacturing capacity by

Concepts in Action

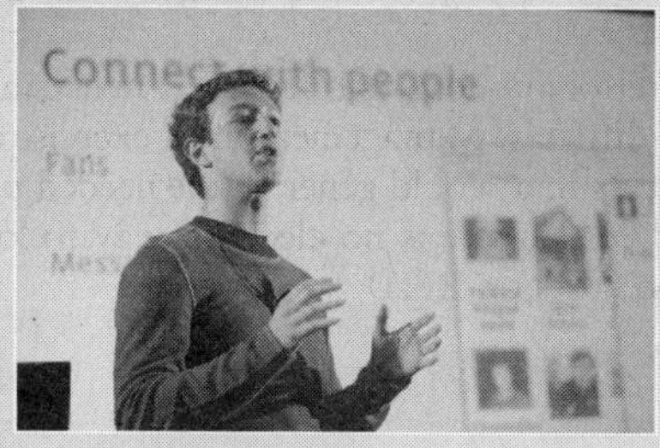

The Growth Versus Profitability Choice at Facebook

Competitive advantage comes from product differentiation or cost leadership. Successful implementation of these strategies helps a company to be profitable and to grow. Many Internet start-ups pursue a strategy of short-run growth to build a customer base, with the goal of later benefiting from such growth by either charging user fees or sustaining a free service for users supported by advertisers. However, during the 1990s dot-com boom (and subsequent bust), the most spectacular failures occurred in dot-com companies that followed the "get big fast" model but then failed to differentiate their products or reduce their costs.

Today, many social networking companies (Web-based communities that connect friends, colleagues, and groups with shared interests) face this same challenge. At Facebook, the most notable of the social networking sites, users can create personal profiles that allow them to interact with friends through messaging, chat, sharing Web site links, video clips, and more. Additionally, Facebook encourages other companies to build third-party programs, including games and surveys, for its Web site and mobile applications on the iPhone and BlackBerry devices. From 2007 to 2010, Facebook grew from 12 million users to more than 400 million users uploading photos, sharing updates, planning events, and playing games in the Facebook ecosystem.

During this phenomenal growth, the company wrestled with one key question: How could Facebook become profitable? In 2009, experts estimate that Facebook had revenues of $635 million, mostly through advertising and the sale of virtual gifts (as a private company, Facebook does not publicly disclose its financial information). But the company still did not turn a profit. Why not? To keep its global Web site and mobile applications operating, Facebook requires a massive amount of electricity, Internet bandwidth, and storage servers for digital files. In 2009, the company earmarked $100 million to buy 50,000 new servers, along with a new $2 million network storage system per week.

The cost structure of Facebook means that the company must generate tens of millions a month in revenue to sustain its operations over the long term. But how? Facebook has implemented the following popular methods of online revenue generation:

- Additional advertising: To grow its already significant advertising revenue, Facebook recently introduced "Fan Pages" for brands and companies seeking to communicate directly with its users. The company is also working on a tool that will let users share information about their physical whereabouts via the site, which will allow Facebook to sell targeted advertisements for nearby businesses.
- Transactions: Facebook is also testing a feature that would expand Facebook Credits, its transactions platform that allows users to purchase games and gifts, into an Internet-wide "virtual currency," that could be accepted by any Web site integrating the Facebook Connect online identity management platform. Facebook currently gets a 30% cut of all transactions conducted through Facebook Credits.

Despite rampant rumors, Facebook has rejected the idea of charging monthly subscription fees for access to its Web site or for advanced features and premium content.

With increased growth around the world, Facebook anticipates 2010 revenues to exceed Rs 10 billion. Despite the opportunity to become the "world's richest twenty-something," Facebook's 25-year-old CEO Mark Zuckerberg has thus far resisted taking the company public through an initial public offering (IPO). "A lot of companies can go off course because of corporate pressures," says Mr. Zuckerberg. "I don't know what we are going to be building five years from now." With his company's focus on facilitating people's ability to share almost any- and everything with anyone, at any time, via the Internet, mobile phones, and even videogames, Facebook expects to offer users a highly personal and differentiated online experience in the years ahead and expects that this product differentiation will drive its future growth and profitability.

Sources: Vascellaro, Jessica E. 2010. Facebook CEO in no rush to 'friend' wall street. *Wall Street Journal*, March 3. http://online.wsj.com/article/SB10001424052748703787304575075942803630712.html; Eldon, Eric. 2010. Facebook revenues up to $700 million in 2009, on track towards $1.1 billion in 2010. *Inside Facebook*. Blog, March 2. http://www.insidefacebook.com/2010/03/02/facebook-made-up-to-700-million-in-2009-on-track-towards-1-1-billion-in-2010/; Arrington, Michael. 2010. Facebook may be growing too fast. And hitting the capital markets again. *Tech Crunch*. Blog, October 31. http://techcrunch.com/2010/10/31/facebooks-growing-problem/

only 2,50,000 square centimeters—from 37,50,000 square centimeters to 35,00,000 square centimeters—saving Rs 1,08,75,000 (Rs 43.5 per sq. cm. × 2,50,000 sq. cm.). It retained some unused capacity for future growth. By avoiding greater reductions in capacity, it also maintained the morale of its skilled and capable workforce. The success of this strategy will depend on Chipset achieving the future growth it has projected.

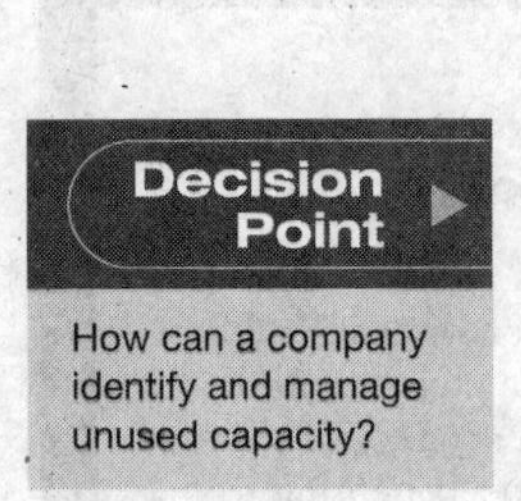

Decision Point
How can a company identify and manage unused capacity?

Because identifying unused capacity for discretionary costs is difficult, downsizing or otherwise, managing this unused capacity is also difficult. Management must exercise considerable judgment in deciding the level of R&D costs that would generate the needed product and process improvements. Unlike engineered costs, there is no clear-cut way to know whether management is spending too much (or too little) on R&D.

Problem for Self-Study

Following a strategy of product differentiation, Westwood Company makes a high-end kitchen range hood, KE8. Westwood's data for 2008 and 2009 follow:

	2008	2009
1. Units of KE8 produced and sold	40,000	42,000
2. Selling price	Rs 1,000	Rs 1,100
3. Direct materials (square feet)	1,20,000	1,23,000
4. Direct material cost per square foot	Rs 100	Rs 110
5. Manufacturing capacity for KE8	50,000 units	50,000 units
6. Conversion costs	Rs 1,00,00,000	Rs 1,10,00,000
7. Conversion cost per unit of capacity (Row 6 ÷ Row 5)	Rs 200	Rs 220
8. Selling and customer-service capacity	30 customers	29 customers
9. Selling and customer-service costs	Rs 72,00,000	Rs 72,50,000
10. Cost per customer of selling and customer-service capacity (Row 9 ÷ Row 8)	Rs 2,40,000	Rs 2,50,000

Westwood produced no defective units and reduced direct material usage per unit of KE8 in 2009. Conversion costs in each year are tied to manufacturing capacity. Selling and customer service costs are related to the number of customers that the selling and service functions are designed to support. Westwood has 23 customers (wholesalers) in 2008 and 25 customers in 2009.

Required

1. Describe briefly the elements you would include in Westwood's balanced scorecard.
2. Calculate the growth, price-recovery, and productivity components that explain the change in operating income from 2008 to 2009.
3. Suppose during 2009, the market size for high-end kitchen range hoods grew 3% in terms of number of units and all increases in market share (that is, increases in the number of units sold greater than 3%) are due to Westwood's product-differentiation strategy. Calculate how much of the change in operating income from 2008 to 2009 is due to the industry-market-size factor, cost leadership, and product differentiation.
4. How successful has Westwood been in implementing its strategy? Explain.

Solution

1. The balanced scorecard should describe Westwood's product-differentiation strategy. Elements that should be included in its balanced scorecard are:
   - **Financial perspective** Increase in operating income from higher margins on KE8 and from growth

- **Customer perspective** Market share in the high-end market and customer satisfaction
- **Internal business process perspective** Manufacturing quality, order-delivery time, on-time delivery, new product features added, development time for new products, and improvements in manufacturing processes
- **Learning-and-growth perspective** Percentage of employees trained in process and quality management and employee satisfaction ratings

2. Operating income for each year is:

	2008	2009
Revenues		
(Rs 1,000 per unit × 40,000 units; Rs 1,100 per unit × 42,000 units)	Rs 4,00,00,000	Rs 4,62,00,000
Costs		
Direct material costs		
(Rs 100 per sq. ft. × 1,20,000 sq. ft.; Rs 110 per sq. ft. × 1,23,000 sq. ft.)	1,20,00,000	1,35,30,000
Conversion costs		
(Rs 200 per unit × 50,000 units; Rs 220 per unit × 50,000 units)	1,00,00,000	1,10,00,000
Selling and customer-service cost		
(Rs 2,40,000 per customer × 30 customers; Rs 2,50,000 per customer × 29 customers)	72,00,000	72,50,000
Total costs	2,92,00,000	3,17,80,000
Operating income	Rs1,08,00,000	Rs1,44,20,000
Change in operating income	Rs 36,20,000 F	

Growth Component of Operating Income Change

$$\text{Revenue effect of growth} = \left(\begin{array}{c}\text{Actual units of}\\ \text{output sold}\\ \text{in 2009}\end{array} - \begin{array}{c}\text{Actual units of}\\ \text{output sold}\\ \text{in 2008}\end{array}\right) \times \begin{array}{c}\text{Selling}\\ \text{price}\\ \text{in 2008}\end{array}$$

$$= (42{,}000 \text{ units} - 40{,}000 \text{ units}) \times \text{Rs } 1{,}000 \text{ per unit} = \text{Rs } 20{,}00{,}000 \text{ F}$$

$$\begin{array}{c}\text{Cost effect}\\ \text{of growth for}\\ \text{variable costs}\end{array} = \left(\begin{array}{c}\text{Units of input}\\ \text{required to produce}\\ \text{2009 output in 2008}\end{array} - \begin{array}{c}\text{Actual units of input}\\ \text{used to produce}\\ \text{2008 output}\end{array}\right) \times \begin{array}{c}\text{Input}\\ \text{price}\\ \text{in 2008}\end{array}$$

$$\begin{array}{c}\text{Cost effect}\\ \text{of growth for}\\ \text{direct meterials}\end{array} = \left(1{,}20{,}000 \text{ sq. ft} \times \frac{42{,}000 \text{ units}}{40{,}000 \text{ units}} - 1{,}20{,}000\text{sq. ft.}\right) \text{Rs } 100\text{per sq. ft.}$$

$$= (1{,}26{,}000\text{sq. ft.} - 1{,}20{,}000\text{sq. ft.}) \times \text{Rs } 100\text{per sq. ft.} = \text{Rs } 6{,}00{,}000 \text{ U}$$

$$\begin{array}{c}\text{Cost effect}\\ \text{of growth for}\\ \text{fixed costs}\end{array} = \left(\begin{array}{c}\text{Actual units of capacity in}\\ \text{2008, because adequate capacity}\\ \text{exists to produce 2009 output in 2008}\end{array} - \begin{array}{c}\text{Actual units}\\ \text{of capacity}\\ \text{in 2008}\end{array}\right) \times \begin{array}{c}\text{Price per}\\ \text{unit of}\\ \text{capacity}\\ \text{in 2008}\end{array}$$

Cost effects of growth for fixed costs are:

Conversion costs: (50,000 units – 50,000 units) × Rs 200 per unit = Re 0

Selling and customer-service costs: (30 costomers – 30 customers) × Rs 2,40,000 per customer = Re 0

In summary, the net increase in operating income attributable to growth equals:

Revenue effect of growth		Rs 20,00,000 F
Cost effect of growth		
Direct material costs	Rs 6,00,000 U	
Conversion costs	0	
Selling and customer-service costs	0	6,00,000 U
Change in operating income due to growth		Rs 14,00,000 F

Price-Recovery Component of Operating-Income Change

$$\text{Revenue effect of price recovery} = \left(\text{Selling price in 2009} - \text{Selling price in 2008}\right) \times \text{Actual units of output sold in 2009}$$

$$= (\text{Rs } 1{,}110 \text{ per unit} - \text{Rs } 1{,}000 \text{ per unit}) \times 42{,}000 \text{ units} = \text{Rs } 42{,}00{,}000 \text{ F}$$

$$\text{Cost effect of price recovery for variable costs} = \left(\text{Input price in 2009} - \text{Input price in 2008}\right) \times \text{Units of input required to produce 2009 output in 2008}$$

Direct material costs: (Rs 110 per sq. ft. – Rs 100 per sq. ft.) × 1,26,000 sq. ft. = Rs 12,60,000 U

$$\text{Cost effect of price recovery for fixed costs} = \left(\text{Price per unit of capacity in 2009} - \text{Price per unit of capacity in 2008}\right) \times \text{Actual units of capacity in 2008, because adequate capacity exists to produce 2009 output in 2008}$$

Cost effects of price recovery for fixed costs are:

Conversion cots: (Rs 220 per unit – Rs 200 per unit) × 50,000 units = Rs 10,00,000 U
Selling and cust. - service costs: (Rs 2,50,000 per cust – Rs 2,40,000 per cust.) × 30 customers × Rs 3,00,000 U

In summary, the net increase in operating income attributable to price recovery equals:

Revenue effect of price recovery		Rs 42,00,000 F
Cost effect of price recovery		
Direct material costs	Rs 12,60,000 U	
Conversion costs	10,00,000 U	
Selling and customer-service costs	3,00,000 U	25,60,000 U
Change in operating income due to price recovery		Rs 16,40,000 F

Productivity Component of Operating-Income Change

$$\text{Cost effect of productivity for variable costs} = \left(\text{Actual units of input used to produce 2009 output} - \text{Units of input required to produce 2009 output in 2008}\right) \times \text{Input price in 2009}$$

$$\text{Cost effect of productiity for direct materials} = (1{,}23{,}000 \text{ sq. ft.} - 1{,}26{,}000 \text{ sq. ft.}) \times \text{Rs } 110 \text{ per sq. ft.} = \text{Rs } 3{,}30{,}000\text{F}$$

$$\text{Cost effect of productivity for fixed costs} = \left(\text{Actual units of capacity in 2009} - \text{Actual units of capacity in 2008, because adequate capacity exists to produce 2009 output in 2008}\right) \times \text{Price per unit of capacity in 2009}$$

Cost effects of productivity for fixed costs are:

Conversion cots: (50,000 unit – 50,000 unit) × Rs 220 per unit = Re 0
Selling and customer - service costs: (29 customers – 30 customers) × Rs 2,50,000/customer = Rs 2,50,000 F

In summary, the net increase in operating income attributable to productivity equals:

Cost effect of productivity:	
Direct material costs	Rs 3,30,000 F
Conversion costs	0
Selling and customer-service costs	2,50,000 F
Change in operating income due to productivity	Rs 5,80,000 F

A summary of the change in operating income between 2008 and 2009 follows:

	Income Statement Amounts in 2008 (1)	Revenue and Cost Effects of Growth Component in 2009 (2)	Revenue and Cost Effects of Price-Recovery Component in 2009 (3)	Cost Effect of Productivity Component in 2009 (4)	Income Statement Amounts in 2009 (5) = (1) + (2) + (3) + (4)
Revenue	Rs 4,00,00,000	Rs 20,00,000 F	Rs 42,00,000 F	—	Rs 4,62,00,000
Costs	2,92,00,000	6,00,000 U	25,60,000 U	Rs 5,80,000 F	3,17,80,000
Operating income	Rs 1,08,00,000	Rs 14,00,000 F	Rs 16,40,000 F	Rs 5,80,000 F	Rs 1,44,20,000
			36,20,000 F		

Change in operating income

3. *Effect of the industry-market-size factor on operating income* Of the increase in sales from 40,000 to 42,000 units, 3%, or 1,200 units (0.03 × 40,000), is due to growth in market size, and 800 units (2,000 – 1,200) are due to an increase in market share. The change in Westwood's operating income from the industry-market-size factor rather than specific strategic actions is:

Rs 14,00,000 (column 2 of precedig table) $\times \dfrac{1{,}200 \text{ units}}{2{,}000 \text{ units}}$ Rs 8,40,000 F

Effect of product differentiation on operating income

Increase in the selling price of KE8 (revenue effect of the price-recovery component)	Rs 42,00,000 F
Increase in prices of inputs (cost effect of the price-recovery component)	25,60,000 U
Growth in market share due to product differentiation	
Rs 14,00,000 (column 2 of precedig table) $\times \dfrac{800 \text{ units}}{2{,}000 \text{ units}}$	5,60,000 F
Change in operating income due to product differentiation	Rs 22,00,000 F

Effect of cost leadership on operating income

Productivity component	Rs 5,80,000 F

A summary of the net increase in operating income from 2008 to 2009 follows:

Change due to the industry-market-size factor	Rs 8,40,000 F
Change due to product differentiation	22,00,000 F
Change due to cost leadership	5,80,000 F
Change in operating income	Rs 36,20,000 F

4. The analysis of operating income indicates that a significant amount of the increase in operating income resulted from Westwood's successful implementation of its product-differentiation strategy. The company was able to continue to charge a premium price for KE8 while increasing market share. Westwood was also able to earn additional operating income from improving its productivity.

Decision Points

The following question-and-answer format summarizes the chapter's learning objectives. Each decision presents a key question related to a learning objective. The guidelines are the answer to that question.

Decision	Guidelines
1. What are two generic strategies a company can use?	Two generic strategies are product differentiation and cost leadership. Product differentiation is offering products and services that are perceived by customers as being superior and unique. Cost leadership is achieving low costs relative to competitors. A company chooses its strategy based on an understanding of customer preferences and its own internal capabilities, while differentiating itself from its competitors.
2. What is reengineering?	Reengineering is the rethinking of business processes, such as the order-delivery process, to improve critical performance measures such as cost, quality, and customer satisfaction.
3. How can an organization translate its strategy into a set of performance measures?	An organization can develop a balanced scorecard that provides the framework for a strategic measurement and management system. The balanced scorecard measures performance from four perspectives: (1) financial, (2) customer, (3) internal business processes, and (4) learning and growth. Organizations sometimes implement strategy maps to represent more detailed cause-and-effect relationships across various scorecard measures.
4. How can a company analyze changes in operating income to evaluate the success of its strategy?	To evaluate the success of its strategy, a company can subdivide the change in operating income into growth, price-recovery, and productivity components. The growth component measures the change in revenues and costs from selling more or less units, assuming no changes in prices of outputs and inputs or efficiencies. The price-recovery component measures changes in revenues and costs solely as a result of changes in the prices of outputs and inputs. The productivity component measures the decrease in costs from using fewer inputs, a better mix of inputs, and reducing capacity. A company is considered successful in implementing its strategy when changes in operating income align closely with its strategy.
5. How can a company distinguish engineered costs from discretionary costs?	Engineered costs result from a cause-and-effect relationship between output and the resources needed to produce that output. Discretionary costs arise from periodic (usually annual) management decisions regarding the amount to be incurred. Discretionary costs are not tied to a cause-and-effect relationship between inputs and outputs.
6. How can a company identify unused capacity, and if it is present, how can unused capacity be managed?	Identifying unused capacity is easier for engineered costs and more difficult for discretionary costs. Downsizing is an approach to managing unused capacity that matches costs to the activities that need to be performed to operate effectively.

APPENDIX: PRODUCTIVITY MEASUREMENT

Productivity measures the relationship between actual inputs used (both quantities and costs) and actual outputs produced. The lower the inputs for a given quantity of outputs or the higher the outputs for a given quantity of inputs, the higher the productivity. Measuring productivity improvements over time highlights the specific input-output relationships that contribute to cost leadership.

Partial Productivity Measures

Partial productivity, the most frequently used productivity measure, compares the quantity of output produced with the quantity of an individual input used. In its most common form, partial productivity is expressed as a ratio:

$$\text{Partial productivity} = \frac{\text{Quantity of output produced}}{\text{Quantity of input used}}$$

The higher the ratio, the greater the productivity.

Consider direct materials productivity at Chipset in 2009.

$$\begin{aligned}\text{Direct materials partial productivity} &= \frac{\text{Quantity of CX1 units produced during 2009}}{\text{Quantity of direct materials used to produce CX1 in 2009}}\\ &= \frac{\text{11,50,000 units of CX1}}{\text{29,00,000 sq. cm. of direct materials}}\\ &= \text{0.397 units of CX1 per sq. cm. of direct materials}\end{aligned}$$

Note direct materials partial productivity ignores Chipset's other inputs, manufacturing conversion capacity, and R&D. Partial-productivity measures become more meaningful when comparisons are made that examine productivity changes over time, either across different facilities or relative to a benchmark. Exhibit 13-6 presents partial-productivity measures for Chipset's inputs for 2009 and the comparable 2008 inputs that would have been used to produce 2009 output, using information from the productivity-component calculations on pages 000–000. These measures compare actual inputs used in 2009 to produce 11,50,000 units of CX1 with inputs that would have been used in 2009 had the input–output relationship from 2008 continued in 2009.

Evaluating Changes in Partial Productivities

Note how the partial-productivity measures differ for variable-cost and fixed-cost components. For variable-cost elements, such as direct materials, productivity improvements measure the reduction in input resources used to produce output (34,50,000 square centimeters of silicon wafers to 29,00,000 square centimeters). For fixed-cost elements such as manufacturing conversion capacity, partial productivity measures the reduction in overall capacity from 2008 to 2009 (37,50,000 square centimeters of silicon wafers to 35,00,000 square centimeters) regardless of the amount of capacity actually used in each period.

An advantage of partial-productivity measures is that they focus on a single input. As a result, they are simple to calculate and easily understood by operations personnel. Managers and operators examine these numbers to understand the reasons underlying productivity changes—better training of workers, lower labor turnover, better incentives, improved methods, or substitution of materials for labor. Isolating the relevant factors helps Chipset implement and sustain these practices in the future.

For all their advantages, partial-productivity measures also have serious drawbacks. Because partial productivity focuses on only one input at a time rather than on all inputs

Exhibit 13-6

Comparing Chipset's Partial Productivities in 2008 and 2009

Input (1)	Partial Productivity in 2009 (2)	Comparable Partial Productivity Based on 2008 Input–Output Relationships (3)	Percentage Change from 2008 to 2009 (4)
Direct materials	$\frac{11,50,000}{29,00,000} = 0.397$	$\frac{11,50,000}{34,50,000} = 0.333$	$\frac{0.397 - 0.333}{0.333} = 19.2\%$
Manufacturing conversion capacity	$\frac{11,50,000}{35,00,000} = 0.329$	$\frac{11,50,000}{37,50,000} = 0.307$	$\frac{0.329 - 0.307}{0.307} = 7.2\%$
R&D	$\frac{11,50,000}{39} = 29,487$	$\frac{11,50,000}{40} = 28,750$	$\frac{29,487 - 28,750}{28,750} = 2.6\%$

simultaneously, managers cannot evaluate the effect on overall productivity, if (say) manufacturing-conversion-capacity partial productivity increases while direct materials partial productivity decreases. Total factor productivity (TFP), or total productivity, is a measure of productivity that considers all inputs simultaneously.

Total Factor Productivity

Total factor productivity (TFP) is the ratio of the quantity of output produced to the costs of all inputs used based on current-period prices.

$$\text{Total factor productivity} = \frac{\text{Quantity of output produced}}{\text{Costs of all inputs used}}$$

TFP considers all inputs simultaneously and the trade-offs across inputs based on current input prices. Do not think of all productivity measures as physical measures lacking financial content—how many units of output are produced per unit of input. TFP is intricately tied to minimizing total cost—a financial objective.

Calculating and Comparing Total Factor Productivity

We first calculate Chipset's TFP in 2009, using 2009 prices and 11,50,000 units of output produced (based on information from the first part of the productivity-component calculations).

$$\begin{aligned}
\begin{array}{c}\text{Total factor productivity}\\ \text{for 2009 using 2009 prices}\end{array} &= \frac{\text{Quantity of output produced in 2009}}{\text{Costs of inputs used in 2009 based on 2009 prices}}\\
&= \frac{11{,}50{,}000}{(29{,}00{,}000 \times \text{Rs } 15) + (35{,}00{,}000 \times \text{Rs } 43.5) + (39 \times \text{Rs } 10{,}00{,}000)}\\
&= \frac{11{,}50{,}000}{\text{Rs } 23{,}47{,}50{,}000}\\
&= 0.48988 \text{ units of output per dollar of input cost}
\end{aligned}$$

By itself, the 2009 TFP of 0.48988 units of CX1 per rupee of input costs is not particularly helpful. We need something to compare the 2009 TFP against. One alternative is to compare TFPs of other similar companies in 2009. However, finding similar companies and obtaining accurate comparable data are often difficult. Companies, therefore, usually compare their own TFPs over time. In the Chipset example, we use as a benchmark TFP calculated using the inputs that Chipset would have used in 2008 to produce 11,50,000 units of CX1 at 2009 prices (that is, we use the costs calculated from the second part of the productivity-component calculations). Why do we use 2009 prices? Because using the current year's prices in both calculations controls for input-price differences and focuses the analysis on adjustments the manager made in quantities of inputs in response to changes in prices.

$$\begin{aligned}
\begin{array}{c}\text{Benchmark}\\ \text{TFP}\end{array} &= \frac{\text{Quantity of output produced in 2009}}{\begin{array}{c}\text{Costs of inputs that would have been used in 2008}\\ \text{to produce 2009 output}\end{array}}\\
&= \frac{11{,}50{,}000}{(34{,}50{,}000 \times \text{Rs } 15) + (37{,}50{,}000 \times \text{Rs } 43.5) + (40 \times \text{Rs } 10{,}00{,}000}\\
&= \frac{11{,}50{,}000}{\text{Rs } 25{,}48{,}75{,}000}\\
&= 0.45120 \text{ units of output per dollar of input cost}
\end{aligned}$$

Using 2009 prices, TFP increased 8.6% [(0.48988 − 0.45120) ÷ 0.45120 = 0.086, or 8.6%] from 2008 to 2009. Note that the 8.6% increase in TFP also equals the Rs 2,01,25,000 gain (Exhibit 13-5, column 4) divided by the Rs 23,47,50,000 of actual costs incurred in

2009 (Exhibit 13-5, column 5). Total factor productivity increased because Chipset produced more output per rupee of input cost in 2009 relative to 2008, measured in both years using 2009 prices. The gain in TFP occurs because Chipset increases the partial productivities of individual inputs and, consistent with its strategy, seeks a combination of inputs to produce CX1 to lower its costs. Note that increases in TFP cannot be due to differences in input prices because we used 2009 prices to evaluate both the inputs that Chipset would have used in 2008 to produce 11,50,000 units of CX1 and the inputs actually used in 2009.

Using Partial and Total Factor Productivity Measures

A major advantage of TFP is that it measures the combined productivity of all inputs used to produce output and explicitly considers gains from using fewer physical inputs as well as substitution among inputs. Managers can analyze these numbers to understand the reasons for changes in TFP—for example, better human resource management practices, higher quality of materials, or improved manufacturing methods.

Although TFP measures are comprehensive, operations personnel find financial TFP measures more difficult to understand and less useful than physical partial-productivity measures. For example, companies that are more labor intensive than Chipset use manufacturing-labor partial-productivity measures. However, if productivity-based bonuses depend on gains in manufacturing-labor partial productivity alone, workers have incentives to substitute materials (and capital) for labor. This substitution improves their own productivity measure, while possibly decreasing the overall productivity of the company as measured by TFP. To overcome these incentive problems, some companies—for example, TRW, Eaton, and Whirlpool—explicitly adjust bonuses based on manufacturing-labor partial productivity for the effects of other factors such as investments in new equipment and higher levels of scrap. That is, they combine partial productivity with TFP-like measures.

Many companies such as Behlen Manufacturing, a steel fabricator, and Dell Computers use both partial productivity and total factor productivity to evaluate performance. *Partial productivity and TFP measures work best together because the strengths of one offset the weaknesses of the other.*

TERMS TO LEARN

This chapter and the Glossary at the end of the book contain definitions of:

balanced scorecard (**p. 538**)
cost leadership (**p. 536**)
discretionary costs (**p. 554**)
downsizing (**p. 554**)
engineered costs (**p. 553**)
growth component (**p. 547**)
partial productivity (**p. 561**)
price-recovery component (**p. 547**)
product differentiation (**p. 536**)
productivity (**p. 560**)
productivity component (**p. 547**)
reengineering (**p. 537**)
rightsizing (**p. 554**)
total factor productivity (TFP) (**p. 562**)
unused capacity (**p. 553**)

ASSIGNMENT MATERIAL

Questions

13-1 Define strategy.

13-2 Describe the five key forces to consider when analyzing an industry.

13-3 Describe two generic strategies.

13-4 What is a customer preference map and why is it useful?

13-5 What is reengineering?

13-6 What are four key perspectives in the balanced scorecard?

13-7 What is a strategy map?

13-8 Describe three features of a good balanced scorecard.

13-9 What are three important pitfalls to avoid when implementing a balanced scorecard?

13-10 Describe three key components in doing a strategic analysis of operating income.

13-11 Why might an analyst incorporate the industry-market-size factor and the interrelationships among the growth, price-recovery, and productivity components into a strategic analysis of operating income?

13-12 How does an engineered cost differ from a discretionary cost?

13-13 What is downsizing?

13-14 What is a partial-productivity measure?

13-15 "We are already measuring total factor productivity. Measuring partial productivities would be of no value." Do you agree? Comment briefly.

Solved Examples

13-16 **Strategy, balanced scorecard, merchandizing operation.** Octave buys T-shirts in bulk, applies its own trendsetting silk-screen designs, and then sells the T-shirts to a number of retailers. Octave wants to be known for its trendsetting designs, and it wants every teenager to be seen in a distinctive Octave T-shirt. Octave presents the following data for its first two years of operations, 2011 and 2012.

	A	B 2011	C 2012
1	Number of T-shirts purchased	2,00,000	2,50,000
2	Number of T-shirts discarded	2,000	3,300
3	Number of T-shirts sold	1,98,000	2,46,700
4	Average selling price	Rs 250	Rs 260
5	Average cost per T-shirt	Rs 100	Rs 85
6	Administrative capacity (number of customers)	4,000	3,750
7	Administrative cost	Rs 1,20,00,000	Rs 1,16,25,000
8	Administrative cost per customer	Rs 3,000	Rs 3,100
9	Design staff	5	5
10	Total design costs	Rs 25,00,000	Rs 27,50,000
11	Design cost per employee	Rs 5,00,000	Rs 5,50,000

Administrative costs depend on the number of customers that Octave has created as capacity to support, not on the actual number of customers served. Octave had 3,600 customers in 2011 and 3,500 customers in 2012. At the start of each year, the management uses its discretion to determine the number of employees on the design staff for the year. The design staff and its costs have no direct relationship with the number of T-shirts purchased and sold, or the number of customers to whom T-shirts are sold.

Required

1. Is Octave's strategy one of product differentiation or cost leadership? Explain briefly.
2. Describe briefly the key elements Octave should include in its balanced scorecard and the reasons it should do so.

Solution

Strategy, balanced scorecard, merchandizing operation.

1. Octave follows a product differentiation strategy. Octave's designs are "trendsetting" and its T-shirts are distinctive, and it aims to make its T-shirts a "must have" for each and every teenager. These are all clear signs of a product differentiation strategy, and, to succeed, Octave must continue to innovate and be able to charge a premium price for its product.
2. Possible key elements of Octave's balance scorecard, given its product differentiation strategy are:

Financial Perspective

(1) Increase in operating income from charging higher margins and (2) price premium earned on products. These measures will indicate whether Octave has been able to charge premium prices and achieve operating-income increases through product differentiation.

Customer Perspective

(1) Market share in distinctive, name-brand T-shirts, (2) customer satisfaction, (3) new customers, (4) number of mentions of Octave's T-shirts in the leading fashion magazines.

Octave's strategy should result in improvements in these customer measures that help evaluate whether Octave's product differentiation strategy is succeeding with its customers. These measures are, in turn, leading indicators of superior financial performance.

Internal-Business-Process Perspective

(1) Quality of silk-screening (number of colors, use of glitter, durability of the design),
(2) frequency of new designs, and (3) time between concept and delivery of design.

Improvements in these measures are expected to result in more distinctive and trendsetting designs delivered to its customers and in turn, superior financial performance.

Learning-and-Growth Perspective

(1) Ability to attract and retain talented designers (2) improvements in silk-screening processes, (3) continuous education and skill levels of marketing and sales staff, and (4) employee satisfaction.

Improvements in these measures are expected to improve Octave's capabilities to produce distinctive designs that have a cause-and-effect relationship with improvements in internal business processes, which in turn lead to customer satisfaction and financial performance.

13-17 Strategic analysis of operating income (continuation of 13-16). Refer to Exercise 13-16. If you want to use Excel to solve this exercise, go to the Excel Lab at **www.prenhall.com/horngren/cost13e** and download the template for Exercise 13-16.

Required

1. Calculate Octave's operating income in both 2011 and 2012.
2. Calculate the growth, price-recovery, and productivity components that explain the change in operating income from 2011 to 2012.
3. Comment on your answers in requirement 2. What do each of these components indicate?

Solution

Strategic analysis of operating income (continuation of 13-16).

1. Operating–Income Statement

	2011	2012
Revenues (Rs 250 × 1,98,000; Rs 260 × 2,46,700)	Rs 4,95,00,000	Rs 6,41,42,000
Costs		
T-shirts purchased (Rs 100 × 2,00,000; Rs 85 × 2,50,000)	2,00,00,000	2,12,50,000
Administrative costs	1,20,00,000	1,16,25,000
Design costs	25,00,000	27,50,000
Total costs	3,45,00,000	3,56,25,000
Operating income	Rs 1,50,00,000	Rs 2,85,17,000
Change in operating income	Rs 1,35,17,000 F	

2. The Growth Component

Revenue effect of grwoth = (Actual units of output sold in 2012 − Actual units of oupput sold in 2011) × Selling price in 2011

= (20,46,700 − 1,98,000) × Rs 250 = Rs 1,21,75,000 F

Cost effect of growth for variable costs = (Units of input required to produc 2012 output in 2011 − Actual units of input used to produce 2011 output) × Input price in 2011

Cost effect of growth for fixed costs = (Actual units of capacity in 2011 if adequate to produce 2012 output in 2011 OR In 2011 capacity inadequate to produce 2012 output in 2011, units of capacity required to produce 2012 output in 2011 − Actual units of capacity in 2011) × Price per unit of capacity in 2011

Direct materials (purchased T-shirts) costs that would be required in 2012 to sell 2,46,700 T-shirts instead of the 1,98,000 sold in 2011, assuming the 2011 input–output relationship continued into 2012, would equal 2,49,192 purchased T-shirts ($\frac{2,46,700}{1,98,000}$ × 2,00,000).

Administrative costs will not change as adequate capacity exists in 2011 to support year 2012 output and customers. Design capacity is discretionary and adequate to support output in year 2012.

The cost effects of growth component are

Direct materials costs	(2,49,192 – 2,00,000)	×	Rs 100	=	Rs 49,19,200 U
Administrative costs	(4,000 – 4,000)	×	Rs 3,000	=	0
Design costs	(5 – 5)	×	Rs 5,00,000	=	0
Cost effect of growth					Rs 49,19,200 U

In summary, the net increase in operating income as a result of the growth component equals:

Revenue effect of growth	Rs 1,21,75,000 F
Cost effect of growth	49,19,200 U
Change in operating income due to growth	Rs 72,55,800 F

The Price-Recovery Component

Revenue effect of price-recovery = (Selling price in 2012 − Selling price in 2011) × Actual units of output sold in 2012

= (Rs 260 − Rs 250) × 2,46,700 = Rs 24,67,000 F

Cost effect of price-recovery for variable costs = (Input price in 2012 − Input price in 2011) × Units of input required to produce 2012 output in 2011

Cost effect of price-recovery for fixed costs = (Price per unit of capacity in 2012 − Price per unit of capacity in 2011) × Actual units of capacity in 2011, if adequate to produce 2012 output in 2011 OR If 2011 capacity inadequate to produce 2012 output in 2011, then units of capacity required to produce 2012 output in 2011

Direct materials costs	(Rs 85 – Rs 100)	×	2,49,192	=	Rs 37,37,880 F
Administrative costs	(Rs 3,100 – Rs 3,000)	×	4,000	=	4,00,000 U
Design costs	(Rs 5,50,000 – Rs 5,00,000)	×	5	=	2,50,000 U
Total cost effect of price-recovery component					Rs 30,87,880 F

In summary, the net increase in operating income as a result of the price-recovery component equals:

Revenue effect of price-recovery	Rs 24,67,000 F
Cost effect of price-recovery	30,87,880 F
Change in operating income due to price-recovery	Rs 55,54,880 F

The Productivity Component

Cost effect of productivity for variable costs = (Actual units of input used to produce 2012 output − Units of input required to produce 2012 output in 2011) × Input price in 2012

Cost effect of productivity for fixed costs = (Actual units of capacity in 2012 − Actual units of capacity in 2011, if adequate to produce 2012 output in 2011 OR If 2011 capacity inadequate to produce 2012 output in 2011, than units of capacity required to produce 2012 output in 2011) × Price per unit of capacity in 2012

The productivity component of cost changes are

Direct materials costs	(2,50,000 – 2,49,192)	×	Rs 85	=	Rs 68,680 U
Administrative costs	(4,000 – 3,750)	×	Rs 3,100	=	7,75,000 F
Design costs	(5 – 5)	×	Rs 5,50,000	=	0
Change in operating income due to productivity					Rs 7,06,320 F

The change in operating income between 2011 and 2012 can be analyzed as follows:

	Income Statement Amounts in 2011 (1)	Revenue-and-Cost Effects of Growth in 2012 (2)	Revenue-and-Cost Effects of Price-Recovery in 2012 (3)	Cost Effect of Productivity in 2012 (4)	Income Statement Amounts in 2012 (5) = (1) + (2) + (3) + + (4)
Revenues	Rs 4,95,00,000	Rs 1,21,75,000 F	Rs 24,67,000 F	–	Rs 6,41,42,000
Costs	3,45,00,000	49,19,200 U	30,87,880 F	Rs 7,06,320 F	3,56,25,000

Operating income	Rs 1,50,00,000	Rs 72,55,800 F	Rs 55,54,880 F	Rs 7,06,320 F	Rs 2,85,17,000

Rs 1,35,17,000 F
Change in operating income

3. The analysis of operating income indicates that growth, price-recovery, and productivity, all resulted in favorable changes in operating income in 2012. Further, a significant amount of the increase in operating income resulted from Octave's product differentiation strategy. The company was able to continue to charge a premium price while growing sales. It was also able to earn an additional operating income by improving its productivity.

13-18 Analysis of growth, price-recovery, and productivity components (continuation of 13-17). Refer to Exercise 13-17. Suppose that the market for silk-screened T-shirts grew by 10% during 2012. All other increases in Octave's sales were the result of its own strategic actions.

If you want to use Excel to solve this exercise, go to the Excel Lab at **www.prenhall.com/horngren/cost13e** and download the template for Exercise 13-16.

Required

Calculate the change in operating income from 2011 to 2012, due to growth in market size, cost leadership, and product differentiation. How successful has Octave been in implementing its strategy? Explain.

Solution

Analysis of growth, price-recovery, and productivity components (continuation of 13-17).

Effect of the industry-market-size factor on operating income

Of the 48,700-unit (2,46,700 – 1,98,000) increase in sales between 2011 and 2012, 19,800 (10% × 1,98,000) units are due to the growth in market size, and 28,900 units are due to an increase in market share.

The change in Octave's operating income from the industry-market-size factor rather than from specific strategic actions is:

Rs 72,55,800 (the growth component in Exercise 13-17) $\times \frac{19,800}{48,700}$ Rs 29,50,000 F

Effect of product differentiation on operating income

The change in operating income due to:

Increase in the selling price (revenue effect of price-recovery)	Rs 24,67,000 F
Increase in price of inputs (cost effect of price-recovery)	30,87,880 F
Growth in market share due to product differentiation	
Rs 72,55,800 (the growth component in Exercise 13-17) $\times \frac{28,900}{48,700}$	43,05,800 F
Change in operating income due to product differentiation	Rs 98,60,680 F

Effect of cost leadership on operating income

The change in operating income from cost leadership is:

Productivity component Rs 7,06,320 F

The change in operating income between 2011 and 2012 can be summarized as follows:

Change due to industry-market size	Rs 29,50,000 F
Change due to product differentiation	98,60,680 F
Change due to cost leadership	7,06,320 F
Change in operating income	Rs 1,35,17,000 F

Octave has been very successful in implementing its product differentiation strategy. Nearly 73% (Rs 98,60,680 ÷ Rs 1,35,17,000) of the increase in operating income during 2012 was due to product differentiation, that is, the distinctiveness of its T-shirts. It was able to raise prices of its products despite a decline in the cost of the T-shirts purchased. Octave's operating-income increase in 2012 was also helped by a growth in the overall market and a small productivity improvement, which it did not pass on to its customers in the form of lower prices.

13-19 Identifying and managing unused capacity (continuation of 13-16). Refer to Exercise 13-16.

Required

1. Calculate the amount and cost of (a) unused administrative capacity and (b) unused design capacity at the beginning of 2012, based on the information for 2012. If you are unable to calculate the amount and cost of a particular unused capacity, then indicate why not.
2. Suppose Octave can only add or reduce administrative capacity in increments of 200 customers. What is the maximum amount of costs that Octave can save in 2012 by downsizing administrative capacity?
3. What factors, other than cost, should Octave consider before it downsizes the administrative capacity?

Solution

Identifying and managing unused capacity (continuation of 13-16).

1. The amount and cost of unused capacity at the beginning of year 2012 based on year 2012 production follows:

	Amount of Unused Capacity	Cost of Unused Capacity
Administrative, 4,000 – 3,500; (4,000 – 3,500) × Rs 3,100	500	Rs 15,50,000
Design	Discretionary cost, so cannot determine unused capacity*	Discretionary cost so cannot be calculated*

*The absence of a cause-and-effect relationship makes identifying the unused capacity for discretionary costs difficult. Management cannot determine the design resources used for the actual output produced against which to compare design capacity.

2. Octave can at most reduce the administrative capacity by another 200 customers (3,750 – 200 = 3,550 × 3,500 = actual customers; but 3,750 – 400 = 3,350 × 3,500 = actual customers). Octave will save another 200 × Rs 3,100 = Rs 6,20,000. This is the maximum amount of costs Octave can save in 2012.
3. Before Octave downsizes the administrative capacity, it should consider whether sales increases in future would lead to a greater demand for and utilization of capacity as new customers are drawn to Octave's distinctive products—at that point, customer service may be the key to new customer retention and further growth. Also, the market feedback often provided by customer service staff is probably a key to Octave's cutting-edge fashion strategy; some of this may be lost if the administrative capacity is cut back. Additionally, significant reductions in capacity usually mean laying off people which can hurt employee morale.

13-20 Strategy, balanced scorecard. Laxmi Machine makes a special-purpose small machine, D4H, used in the textile industry. Laxmi Machine has designed the D4H machine for 2012 to be distinct from its competitors. It has been generally regarded as a superior machine. Laxmi Machine presents the following data for 2011 and 2012.

	2011	2012
1. Units of D4H produced and sold	200	210
2. Selling price	Rs 40,000	Rs 42,000
3. Direct materials (kilograms)	3,00,000	3,10,000
4. Direct material cost per kilogram	Rs 8	Rs 8.50
5. Manufacturing capacity in units of D4H	250	250
6. Total conversion costs	Rs 20,00,000	Rs 20,25,000
7. Conversion cost per unit of capacity	Rs 8,000	Rs 8,100
8. Selling and customer-service capacity	100 customers	95 customers
9. Total selling and customer-service costs	Rs 10,00,000	Rs 9,40,500
10. Selling and customer-service capacity cost per customer	Rs 10,000	Rs 9,900
11. Design staff	12	12
12. Total design costs	Rs 12,00,000	Rs 12,12,000
13. Design cost per employee	Rs 1,00,000	Rs 1,01,000

Laxmi Machine produces no defective machines, but it wants to reduce direct materials usage per D4H machine in 2012. Conversion costs in each year depend on production capacity defined in terms of D4H units that can be produced, not the actual units produced. Selling and customer-service costs depend on the number of customers that Laxmi Machine can support, not the actual number of customers it serves. Laxmi Machine has 75 customers in 2011 and 80 customers in 2012. At the start of each year, the management uses its discretion to determine the number of design staff for the year. The design staff and its costs have no direct relationship with the quantity of D4H produced or the number of customers to whom D4H is sold.

Required

1. Is Laxmi Machine's strategy one of product differentiation or cost leadership? Explain briefly.
2. Describe briefly the key elements that you would include in Laxmi Machine's balanced scorecard and the reasons for doing so?

Solution

Strategy, balanced scorecard.

1. Laxmi Machine follows a product differentiation strategy in 2012. Laxmi Machine's D4H machine is distinct from its competitors and generally regarded as superior to competitors' products. To succeed, Laxmi Machine must continue to differentiate its product and charge a premium price.
2. Balanced Scorecard Measures for 2012 follow:

Financial Perspective

(1) Increase in operating income from charging higher margins and (2) price premium earned on products.

These measures indicate whether Laxmi Machine has been able to charge premium prices and achieve operating-income increases through product differentiation.

Customer Perspective

(1) Market share in high-end special-purpose textile machines, (2) customer satisfaction, and (3) new customers.

Laxmi Machine's strategy should result in improvements in these customer measures that help evaluate whether Laxmi Machine's product differentiation strategy is succeeding with its customers. These measures are leading indicators of superior financial performance.

Internal-Business-Process Perspective

(1) Manufacturing quality, (2) new product features added, and (3) order delivery time.

Improvements in these measures are expected to result in more distinctive products delivered to its customers and in turn, superior financial performance.

Learning-and-Growth Perspective

(1) Development time for designing new machines, (2) improvements in manufacturing processes, (3) employee education and skill levels, and (4) employee satisfaction.

Improvements in these measures are likely to improve Laxmi Machine's capabilities to produce distinctive products that have a cause-and-effect relationship with improvements in internal business processes, which in turn lead to customer satisfaction and financial performance.

13-21 Strategic analysis of operating income (continuation of 13-20). Refer to Exercise 13-20.

Required

1. Calculate the operating income of Laxmi Machine in 2011 and 2012.
2. Calculate the growth, price-recovery, and productivity components that explain the change in operating income from 2011 to 2012.
3. Comment on your answer in requirement 2. What do these components indicate?

Solution

Strategic analysis of operating income (continuation of 13-20).

1. Operating income for each year is as follows:

	2011	2012
Revenue (Rs 40,000 × 200; Rs 42,000 × 210)	Rs 80,00,000	Rs 88,20,000
Costs		
Direct materials costs (Rs 8 ×3,00,000; Rs 8.50 × 3,10,000)	24,00,000	26,35,000
Manufacturing conversion costs (Rs 8,000 × 250; 8,100 × 250)	20,00,000	20,25,000
Selling and customer service costs (Rs 10,000 × 100; Rs 9,900 × 95)	10,00,000	9,40,500
Design costs (Rs 1,00,000 × 12; Rs 1,01,000 × 12)	12,00,000	12,12,000
Total costs	66,00,000	68,12,500
Operating income	Rs 14,00,000	Rs 20,07,500
Change in operating income	Rs 6,07,500 F	

2. The Growth Component

Revenue effect of grwoth = (Actual units of output sold in 2012 − Actual units of oupput sold in 2011) × Selling rice in 2011

= (210 − 200) × Rs 40,000 = Rs 4,00,000 F

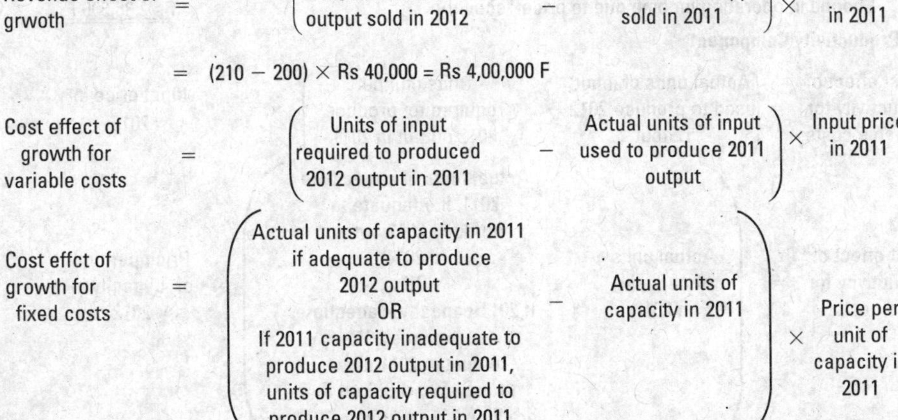

Cost effect of growth for variable costs = (Units of input required to produced 2012 output in 2011 − Actual units of input used to produce 2011 output) × Input price in 2011

Cost effct of growth for fixed costs = (Actual units of capacity in 2011 if adequate to produce 2012 output OR If 2011 capacity inadequate to produce 2012 output in 2011, units of capacity required to produce 2012 output in 2011 − Actual units of capacity in 2011) × Price per unit of capacity in 2011

Direct materials costs that would be required in 2012 to produce 210 units instead of the 200 units produced in 2011, assuming that the 2011 input–output relationship continued into 2012, equal 3,15,000 kilograms $\left(\frac{3,00,000}{200} \times 210\right)$. Manufacturing conversion costs and selling, and customer-service costs will not change as adequate capacity exists in 2011 to support year 2012 output and customers. R&D costs are discretionary costs and would not change in 2011 if Laxmi Machine had to produce and sell the higher 2012 volume in 2011. The cost effects of growth component are:

Direct materials costs	(3,15,000 – 3,00,000) × Rs 8	=	Rs 1,20,000 U
Manufacturing conversion costs	(250 – 250) × Rs 8,000	=	0
Selling and customerservice costs	(100 – 100) × Rs 25,000	=	0
Design costs	(12 – 12) × Rs 1,00,000	=	0
Cost effect of growth			Rs 1,20,000 U

In summary, the net increase in operating income as a result of the growth component equals:

Revenue effect of growth	Rs 4,00,000 F
Cost effect of growth	1,20,000 U
Change in operating income due to growth	Rs 2,80,000 F

The Price-Recovery Component

$$\text{Revenue effect of price-recovery} = \left(\text{Selling price in 2012} - \text{Selling price in 2011}\right) \times \text{Actual units of output sold in 2012}$$

$$= (\text{Rs } 42,000 - \text{Rs } 40,000) \times 210 = \text{Rs } 4,20,000 \text{ F}$$

$$\text{Cost effect of price-recovery for variable costs} = \left(\text{Input price in 2012} - \text{Input price in 2011}\right) \times \text{Units of input required to produce 2012 output in 2011}$$

$$\text{Cost effect of price-recovery for fixed costs} = \left(\text{Price per unit of capacity in 2012} - \text{Price per unit of capacity in 2011}\right) \times \left(\begin{array}{c}\text{Actual units of capacity in 2011, if adequate}\\ \text{to produce 2012 output in 2011}\\ \text{OR}\\ \text{If 2011 capacity inadequate to produce 2012}\\ \text{output in 2011, then units of capacity required to}\\ \text{produce 2012 output in 2011}\end{array}\right)$$

Direct materials costs	(Rs 8.50 – Rs 8)	×	3,15,000	=	Rs 1,57,500 U
Manufacturing conversion costs	(Rs 8,100 – Rs 8,000)	×	250	=	25,000 U
Selling and customer-service costs	(Rs 9,900 – Rs 10,000)	×	100	=	10,000 F
Design costs	(Rs 1,01,000 – Rs 1,00,000)	×	12	=	12,000 U
Cost effect of price-recovery					Rs 1,84,500 U

In summary, the net increase in operating income as a result of the price-recovery component equals:

Revenue effect of price-recovery	Rs 4,20,000 F
Cost effect of price-recovery	1,84,500 U
Change in operating income due to price-recovery	Rs 2,35,500 F

The Productivity Component

$$\text{Cost effect of productivity for variable costs} = \left(\text{Actual units of input used to produce 2012 output} - \text{Units of input required to produce 2012 output in 2011}\right) \times \text{Input price in 2012}$$

$$\text{Cost effect of productivity for fixed costs} = \left(\text{Actual units of capacity in 2012} - \begin{array}{c}\text{Actual units of capacity in 2011, if adequate to}\\ \text{produce 2012 output in 2011}\\ \text{OR}\\ \text{If 2011 capacity inadequate to produce 2012}\\ \text{output in 2011 units of capacity required to}\\ \text{produce 2012 output in 2011}\end{array}\right) \times \text{Price per unit of capacity in 2012}$$

The productivity component of cost changes are

Direct materials costs	(3,10,000 – 3,15,000)	×	Rs 8.50	=	Rs 42,500 F
Manufacturing conversion costs	(250 – 250)	×	Rs 8,100	=	0
Selling and customer-service costs	(95 – 100)	×	Rs 9,900	=	49,500 F
Design costs	(12 – 12)	×	Rs 1,01,000	=	0
Change in operating income due to productivity					Rs 92,000 F

The change in operating income between 2011 and 2012 can be analyzed as follows:

	Income Statement Amounts in 2011 (1)	Revenue and Cost Effects of Growth Component in 2012 (2)	Revenue and Cost Effects of Price-Recovery Component in 2012 (3)	Cost Effect of Productivity Component in 2012 (4)	Income Statement Amounts in 2012 (5) = (1) + (2) + (3) + (4)
Revenues	Rs 80,00,000	Rs 4,00,000 F	Rs 4,20,000 F	–	Rs 88,20,000
Costs	66,00,000	1,20,000 U	1,84,500 U	Rs 92,000 F	68,12,500
Operating in come	Rs 14,00,000	Rs 2,80,000 F	Rs 2,35,500 F	Rs 92,000 F	Rs 20,07,500

Rs 6,07,500 F
Change in operating income

The analysis of operating income indicates that a significant amount of the increase in operating income resulted from Laxmi Machine's product differentiation strategy. The company was able to continue to charge a premium price even while growing its sales. Laxmi Machine was also able to earn additional operating income by improving its productivity.

13-22 Analysis of growth, price-recovery, and productivity components (continuation of 13-21). Suppose that during 2012, the market for Laxmi Machine's special-purpose machines grew by 3%. All increases in market share (i.e., sales increases greater than 3%) are the result of Laxmi Machine's strategic actions.

Required

Calculate how much of the change in operating income from 2011 to 2012 is due to the industry-market-size factor, cost leadership, and product differentiation. How successful has Laxmi Machine been in implementing its strategy? Explain.

Solution

Analysis of growth, price-recovery, and productivity components (continuation of 13-21).

Effect of the industry-market-size factor on operating income

If the 10-unit increase in sales from 200 to 210 units is 3%, or 6 (3% ×200) units are due to growth in market size, and 4 (10 - 6) units are due to an increase in market share,

The change in Laxmi Machine's operating income from the industry-market-size factor rather than from specific strategic actions is:

Rs 2,80,000 (the growth component in Exercise 13-21) × $\frac{6}{10}$ = Rs 1,68,000 F

Effect of product differentiation on operating income

The change in operating income due to:

Increase in the selling price of D4H (revenue effect of price recovery)	Rs 4,20,000 F
Increase in price of inputs (cost effect of price recovery)	1,84,500 U
Growth in market share due to product differentiation	
Rs 2,80,000 (the growth component in Exercise 13-21) × $\frac{4}{10}$	1,12,000 F
Change in operating income due to product differentiation	Rs 3,47,500 F

Effect of cost leadership on operating income

The change in operating income from cost leadership is:

Productivity component	Rs 92,000 F

The change in operating income between 2011 and 2012 can be summarized as follows:

Change due to industry-market size	Rs 1,68,000 F
Change due to product differentiation	3,47,500 F
Change due to cost leadership	92,000 F
Change in operating income	Rs 6,07,500 F

Laxmi Machine has been successful in implementing its product differentiation strategy. More than 57% (Rs 3,47,500 ÷ Rs 6,07,500) of the increase in operating income during 2012 was due to product differentiation, that is the distinctiveness of its machines. It was able to raise the prices of its machines faster than the costs of its inputs and still, grow the market share. Laxmi Machine's operating-income increase in 2012 was also helped by a growth in the overall market and some productivity improvements.

13-23 Identifying and managing unused capacity (continuation of 13-20). Refer to Exercise 13-20.

Required

1. Where possible, calculate the amount and cost of (a) unused manufacturing capacity, (b) unused selling and customer-service capacity, and (c) unused design capacity at the beginning of 2012, based on 2012 production. If you are unable to calculate the amount and cost of unused capacity, then indicate why not.
2. Suppose Laxmi Machine can add or reduce its manufacturing capacity in increments of 30 units. What is the maximum amount of costs that Laxmi Machine could save in 2012 by downsizing the manufacturing capacity?
3. Laxmi Machine, in fact, does not eliminate any of its unused manufacturing capacity. Why might Laxmi Machine not downsize?

Solution

Identifying and managing unused capacity (continuation of 13-20).

1. The amount and cost of unused capacity at the beginning of year 2012 based on the year 2012 production follows:

	Amount of Unused Capacity	Cost of Unused Capacity
Manufacturing, 250 – 210; (250 – 210) × Rs 8,100	40	Rs 3,24,000
Selling and customer service, 100 – 80; (100 – 80) × Rs 9,900	20	1,98,000
Design	Discretionary cost, so cannot determine unused capacity*	Discretionary cost so cannot be calculated*

*The absence of a cause-and-effect relationship makes identifying unused capacity for discretionary costs difficult. Management cannot determine the R&D resources used for the actual output produced to compare R&D capacity against.

2. Laxmi Machine can reduce manufacturing capacity from 250 units to 220 (250 – 30) units. Laxmi Machine will save 30 × Rs 8,100 = Rs 2,43,000. This is the maximum amount of costs Laxmi Machine can save in 2012. It cannot reduce capacity further (by another 30 units to 190 units) because it would then not have enough capacity to manufacture 210 units in 2012 (units that contribute significantly to operating income).
3. Laxmi Machine may choose not to downsize because it projects sales increases that would lead to a greater demand for and utilization of capacity. Laxmi Machine may have also decided not to downsize because downsizing requires a significant reduction in capacity. For example, Laxmi Machine may have chosen to downsize some more manufacturing capacity if it could do so in increments of say, 10, rather than 30 units. Also, Laxmi Machine may be focused on product differentiation, which is the key to its strategy, rather than on cost reduction. Not reducing the significant capacity also helps to boost and maintain employee morale.

13-24 Balanced scorecard. Following is a random-order listing of perspectives, strategic objectives, and performance measures for the balanced scorecard.

Perspectives
Internal business process
Customer
Learning-and-growth
Financial

Strategic Objectives
Acquire new customers
Increase shareholder value
Retain customers
Improve manufacturing quality
Develop profitable customers
Increase proprietary products
Increase information-system capabilities
Enhance employee skills
On-time delivery by suppliers
Increase profit generated by each salesperson
Introduce new products
Minimize invoice-error rate

Performance Measures
Percentage of defective-product units
Return on assets
Number of patents
Employee turnover rate
Net income
Customer profitability
Percentage of processes with real-time feedback
Return on sales
Average job-related training hours per employee
Return on equity
Percentage of on-time deliveries by suppliers
Product cost per unit
Profit per salesperson
Percentage of error-free invoices
Customer cost per unit
Earnings per share
Number of new customers
Percentage of customers retained

Required

For each perspective, select those strategic objectives from the list that best relate to it. For each strategic objective, select the most appropriate performance measure(s) from the list.

Solution

Balanced scorecard.

Perspectives	Strategic Objectives	Performance Measures
• Financial	• Increase shareholder value	• Earnings per share • Net income • Return on assets • Return on sales • Return on equity • Product cost per unit • Customer cost per unit
	• Increase profit generated by each salesperson	• Profit per salesperson
• Customer	• Acquire new customers Retain customers Develop profitable customers	• Number of new customers • Percentage of customers retained • Customer profitability
• Internal Business Process	• Improve manufacturing quality Introduce new products	• Percentage of defective • product units
	• Minimize invoice-error rate On-time delivery by suppliers	• Percentage of error-free invoices • Percentage of on-time deliveries by suppliers
	• Increase proprietary products	• Number of patents
• Learning and Growth	• Increase information system capabilities	• Percentage of processes with real-time feedback
	• Enhance employee skills	• Employee turnover rate • Average job-related training hours per employee

13-25 Balanced scorecard. (R. Kaplan, adapted) Bharat Petroleum Corporation Limited (BPCL) refines gasoline and sells it through its own BPCL Gas Stations. On the basis of market research, BPCL determines that 60% of the overall gasoline market consists of "service-oriented customers," medium- to high-income individuals who are willing to pay a higher price for gas if the gas stations can provide excellent customer service, such as a clean facility, a convenience store, friendly employees, a quick turnaround, the ability to pay by credit card, and high-octane premium gasoline. The remaining 40% of the overall market are "price shoppers" who look to buy the cheapest gasoline available. BPCL's strategy is to focus on that 60% of service-oriented customers. BPCL's Balanced Scorecard for 2012 follows. For brevity, the initiatives taken under each objective are omitted.

Objectives	Measures	Target Performance	Actual Performance
Financial Perspective			
Increase shareholder value	Operating-income changes from price-recovery	Rs 90,00,00,000	Rs 95,00,00,000
	Operating-income changes from growth	Rs 65,00,00,000	Rs 67,00,00,000
Customer Perspective			
Increase market share	Market share of overall gasoline market	10%	9.8%
Internal-Business-Process Perspective			
Improve gasoline quality	Quality index	94 points	95 points
Improve refinery performance	Refinery-reliability index	91%	91%
Ensure gasoline availability	Product-availability index	99%	100%
Learning-and-Growth Perspective			
Increase refinery-process capability	Percentage of refinery processes with advanced controls	88%	90%

Required

1. Was BPCL successful in implementing its strategy in 2012? Explain your answer.
2. Would you have included some measure of employee satisfaction and employee training in the learning-and-growth perspective? Are these objectives critical to BPCL for implementing its strategy? Why or why not? Explain briefly.

3. Explain how BPCL did not achieve its target market share in the total gasoline market but still exceeded its financial targets. Is "market share of overall gasoline market" the correct measure of market share? Explain briefly.
4. Is there a cause-and-effect linkage between improvements in the measures in the internal business-process perspective and the measure in the customer perspective? That is, would you add other measures to the internal-business-process perspective or the customer perspective? Why or why not? Explain briefly.
5. Do you agree with BPCL's decision of not to include measures of changes in operating income from productivity improvements under the financial perspective of the balanced scorecard? Explain briefly.

Solution

Balanced scorecard.

1. BPCL's strategy is to focus on "service-oriented customers" who are willing to pay a higher price for services. Even though gasoline is largely a commodity product, BPCL wants to differentiate itself through the service it provides at its retailing stations.

Does the scorecard represent BPCL's strategy? By and large it does. The focus of the scorecard is on measures of process improvement, quality, market share, and financial success from product differentiation, and charging higher prices for customer service. There are some deficiencies that the subsequent assignment questions raise but, abstracting from these concerns for the moment, the scorecard does focus on implementing a product differentiation strategy.

Having concluded that the scorecard has been reasonably well designed, how has BPCL performed relative to its strategy in 2012? It appears from the scorecard that BPCL was successful in implementing its strategy in 2012. It achieved all targets in the financial, internal business, and learning-and-growth perspectives. The only target it missed was the market-share target in the customer perspective. At this stage, students may raise some questions about whether this is a good scorecard measure. Requirement 3 gets at this issue in more detail. The bottom line is that measuring market share in the "overall gasoline market" rather than measuring that in the "service-oriented customer segment" is not a good scorecard measure, so not achieving this target may not be as big an issue as it may seem at first.

2. Yes, BPCL should include some measure of employee satisfaction and employee training in the learning-and-growth perspective. BPCL's differentiation strategy and ability to charge a premium price is based on customer service. The key to good, fast, and friendly customer service is well-trained and satisfied employees. Untrained and dissatisfied employees will have poor interactions with customers and cause the strategy to fail. Hence, training and employee satisfaction are very important to BPCL for implementing its strategy. These measures are leading indicators of whether BPCL will be able to successfully implement its strategy and should be measured on the balanced scorecard.
3. BPCL's strategy is to focus on the 60% of gasoline consumers who are service-oriented, not on the 40% price-shopper segment. To evaluate if it has been successful in implementing its strategy, BPCL needs to measure its market share in its targeted market segment, "service-oriented customer," not its market share in the overall market. Given BPCL's strategy, it should not be concerned if its market share in the price-shopper segment declines. In fact, charging premium prices will probably cause its market share in this segment to decline. BPCL should replace "market share in the overall gasoline market" with "market share in the service-oriented customer segment" in its balanced scorecard customer measure. BPCL may also want to consider putting a customer-satisfaction measure on the scorecard. This measure should capture an overall evaluation of customer reactions to the facility, the convenience store, employee interactions, and quick turnaround. The customer-satisfaction measure would serve as a leading indicator of market share in the service-oriented customer segment.
4. Although there is a cause-and-effect link between internal-business-process measures and customer measures on the current scorecard, BPCL should add more measures to tighten this linkage. In particular, the current scorecard measures focus exclusively on refinery operations and not on gas station operations. BPCL should add measures of gas station performance such as cleanliness of the facility, turnaround time at the gas pumps, the shopping experience at the convenience store, and the service provided by employees. Many companies do random audits of their facilities to evaluate how well their branches and retail outlets are performing. These measures would serve as leading indicators of customer satisfaction and market share in BPCL's targeted segments.
5. BPCL is correct in not measuring changes in operating income from productivity improvements on its scorecard under the financial perspective. BPCL's strategy is to grow by charging premium prices for customer service. The scorecard measures focus on BPCL's success in implementing this strategy. Productivity gains *per se* are not critical to BPCL's strategy and therefore, should not be measured on the scorecard.

13-26 Engineered and discretionary overhead costs, unused capacity, customer help desk. Wire & Wireless Ltd., a large cable television operator, had 7,50,000 subscribers in 2011. Wire & Wireless Ltd. employs five customer-help-desk representatives to respond to customer questions and problems. During 2011, each customer-help-desk representative worked 8 hours per day for 250 days at a fixed annual salary of Rs 3,60,000. Wire & Wireless Ltd. received 45,000 telephone calls from its customers in 2011. Each call took an average of 10 minutes.

Required

1. Do you think customer-help-desk costs at Wire & Wireless Ltd. are engineered costs or discretionary costs? Explain your answer.
2. Where possible, calculate the cost of unused customer-help-desk capacity in 2011 under each of the following assumptions: (a) customer-help-desk costs are engineered costs and (b) customer-help-desk costs are discretionary costs. If you are unable to calculate the amount and cost of unused capacity, then indicate why not.
3. Assume that Wire & Wireless Ltd. had 9,00,000 subscribers in 2012 and that the 2011 percentage of telephone calls received to total subscribers continued in 2012. Customer-help-desk capacity in 2012 was the same as it was in 2011. Where possible, calculate the cost of unused customer-help-desk capacity in 2012 under each of the following assumptions: (a) customer-service costs are engineered costs and (b) customer-service costs are discretionary costs. If you are unable to calculate the amount and cost of unused capacity, then indicate why not.

Solution

Engineered and discretionary overhead costs, unused capacity, customer help-desk.

1. Wire & Wireless Ltd.'s customer-help-desk costs are indirect engineered costs. Over time, there is a clear cause-and-effect relationship among the output (number of subscribers or customers) and customer-help-desk representatives needed and customer-help-desk costs. The more the number of homes serviced, the greater the number of customer-service calls expected, and therefore greater is the number of customer-help-desk representatives needed.

2a. Assume customer-help-desk costs are engineered costs.

(1) Available customer-help-desk capacity 8 hours per day × 250 days × 5 representatives	10,000 hours
(2) Customer-help-desk services actually used 45,000 calls × $\frac{1}{6}$ hour per call	7,500 hours
(3) = (1) – (2) Hours of unused customer-help-desk capacity	2,500 hours
(4) Cost per hour, Rs 3,60,000 ÷ 2,000 hours (8 hours/day × 250 days)	Rs 180 per hour
(5) = (3) × (4) Cost of unused customer-help-desk capacity in 2011	Rs 4,50,000

2b. Assume customer-help-desk costs are discretionary costs. In this case, cost of unused capacity in 2011 cannot be determined. The absence of a cause-and-effect relationship between homes serviced and customer-service calls means that Wire & Wireless Ltd. cannot determine the customer-help-desk resources used and, hence, the amount of unused capacity.

3. $$\frac{\text{Telephone calls received in 2011}}{\text{Total subscribers in 2011}} = \frac{45{,}000}{7{,}50{,}000} = 6\%$$

Applying this 6% to the 9,00,000 subscribers in 2012 means that Wire & Wireless Ltd. received 54,000 (6% × 9,00,000) calls in 2012.

a. Assume customer-help-desk costs are engineered costs.

(1) Available customer-help-desk capacity in 2012	10,000 hours
(2) Customer-help-desk services actually used 54,000 calls × $\frac{1}{6}$ hour per call	9,000 hours
(3) = (1) – (2) Hours of unused customer-help-desk capacity	1,000 hours
(4) Cost per hour	Rs 180 per hour
(5) = (3) ×(4) Cost of unused customer-help-desk capacity in 2012	Rs 1,80,000

b. Assume customer-help-desk costs are discretionary costs. For the reasons described in 2b, the cost of unused capacity in 2012 cannot be determined.

13-27 Balanced scorecard, ethics. Ravi, division manager of the Household Products Division, a maker of kitchen dishwashers, has just seen the balanced scorecard for his division for 2012. He immediately calls Raj, the division's management accountant, into his office for a meeting. "I think the employee-satisfaction and customer-satisfaction numbers are way too low. These numbers are based on a random sample of subjective assessments made by individual managers and customer representatives. My own experience indicates that we are doing well on both these dimensions. Until we do a formal survey of employees and customers sometime next year, I think we are doing a disservice to ourselves and this company by reporting such low scores for employee and customer satisfaction. These scores will be an embarrassment for us at the division managers' meeting next month. We need to get these numbers up."

Raj knows that the employee- and customer-satisfaction scores are subjective, but the procedure he used this year is identical to the procedures he has used in the past. He knows from the comments he had asked for that the scores represent the unhappiness of employees with the latest work rules and the unhappiness of customers with late deliveries. He also knows that these problems will be corrected in time.

Required

1. Do you think that the Household Products Division should include subjective measures of employee satisfaction and customer satisfaction in its balanced scorecard? Explain.
2. What should Raj do?

Solution

Balanced scorecard, ethics.

1. Yes, the Household Products Division (HPD) should include measures of employee satisfaction and customer satisfaction even if these measures are subjective. For a maker of kitchen dishwashers, employee- and customer satisfaction are leading indicators of future financial performance. There is a cause-and-effect linkage between these measures and future financial performance. If HPD's strategy is correct and if the scorecard has been properly designed, employee- and customer-satisfaction information is very important in evaluating the implementation of HPD's strategy.

HPD should use employee- and customer-satisfaction measures even though these measures are subjective. One of the pitfalls to avoid when implementing a balanced scorecard is not to use only objective measures in the scorecard. Of course, HPD should guard against imprecision and potential for manipulation. Raj appears to be aware of this. He has tried to understand the reasons for the poor scores, and has been able to relate these scores to other objective evidence such as employee dissatisfaction, with the new work rules and customer unhappiness with missed delivery dates.

2. Incorrect reporting of employee- and customer-satisfaction ratings to make a division's performance look good is unethical. In assessing the situation, the specific "Standards of Ethical Conduct for Management Accountants," which the management account should consider are listed below.

Competence

Clear reports using relevant and reliable information should be prepared. Preparing reports on the basis of incorrect employee- and customer-satisfaction ratings to make the division's performance look better than it is, violates competence standards. It is unethical for Raj to change the employee- and customer-satisfaction ratings to make the division's performance look good.

Integrity

The management accountant has a responsibility to avoid actual or apparent conflicts of interest and advice all appropriate parties of any potential conflict. Raj may be tempted to report better employee- and customer-satisfaction ratings to please Ravi. This action, however, violates the responsibility for integrity. The Standards of Ethical Conduct require the management accountant to communicate favorable as well as unfavorable information.

Objectivity

The management accountant's standards of ethical conduct require that information should be fairly and objectively communicated and that all relevant information should be disclosed. From a management accountant's standpoint, modifying employee- and customer-satisfaction ratings to make division performance look good would violate the standard of objectivity.

Raj should indicate to Ravi that the employee- and customer-satisfaction ratings are, indeed, appropriate. If Ravi still insists on reporting better employee- and customer-satisfaction numbers, Raj should raise the matter with one of Ravi's superiors. If, after taking all these steps, there is a continued pressure to overstate employee- and customer-satisfaction ratings, Raj should consider resigning from the company and not engage in unethical behavior.

13-28 Strategic analysis of operating income. Van Heusen Company sells women's clothing. Van Heusen's strategy is to offer a wide selection of clothes and excellent customer service, and to charge a premium price. Van Heusen presents the following data for 2011 and 2012. For simplicity, assume that each customer purchases one piece of clothing.

	2011	2012
1. Pieces of clothing purchased and sold	40,000	40,000
2. Average selling price	Rs 600	Rs 590
3. Average cost per piece of clothing	Rs 400	Rs 410
4. Selling and customer-service capacity	51,000 customers	43,000 customers
5. Selling and customer-service costs	Rs 35,70,000	Rs 29,67,000
6. Selling and customer-service capacity cost per customer (Line 5 , Line 4)	Rs 70 per customer	Rs 69 per customer
7. Purchasing and administrative capacity	980 designs	850 designs

8. Purchasing and administrative costs	Rs 24,50,000	Rs 20,40,000
9. Purchasing and administrative capacity cost per distinct design	Rs 2,500 per design	Rs 2,400 per design

Total selling and customer-service costs depend on the number of customers that Van Heusen has created capacity to support, not the actual number of customers that Van Heusen serves. Total purchasing and administrative costs depend on purchasing and administrative capacity that Van Heusen has created (defined in terms of the number of distinct clothing designs that Van Heusen can purchase and administer). Purchasing and administrative costs do not depend on the actual number of distinct clothing designs purchased. Van Heusen purchased 930 distinct designs in 2011 and 820 distinct designs in 2012.

At the start of 2012, Van Heusen planned to increase the operating income by 10% over the operating income in 2011.

Required

1. Is Van Heusen's strategy one of product differentiation or cost leadership? Explain.
2. Calculate Van Heusen's operating income in 2011 and 2012.
3. Calculate the growth, price-recovery, and productivity components of changes in operating income between 2011 and 2012.
4. Does the strategic analysis of operating income indicate that Van Heusen was successful in implementing its strategy in 2012? Explain.

Solution

Strategic analysis of operating income.

1. Van Heusen is following a product differentiation strategy. Van Heusen offers a wide selection of clothes and excellent customer service. Van Heusen's strategy is to distinguish itself from its competitors and to charge a premium price.
2. Operating income for each year is as follows:

	2011	2012
Revenues (Rs 600 × 40,000; Rs 590 × 40,000)	Rs 2,40,00,000	Rs 2,36,00,000
Costs		
Costs of goods sold (Rs 400 × 40,000; Rs 410 × 40,000)	1,60,00,000	1,64,00,000
Selling and customer service costs (Rs 70 × 51,000); Rs 69 × 43,000)	35,70,000	29,67,000
Purchasing and administrative costs (Rs 2,500 × 980; Rs 2,400 × 850)	24,50,000	20,40,000
Total costs	2,20,20,000	2,14,07,000
Operating income	Rs 19,80,000	Rs 21,93,000
Change in operating income	Rs 2,13,000 F	

2. The Growth Component

$$\text{Revenue effect of grwoth} = \left(\text{Actual units of output sold in 2012} - \text{Actual units of output sold in 2011}\right) \times \text{Selling rice in 2011}$$

$$= (40{,}000 - 40{,}000) \times \text{Rs } 600 = \text{Rs } 0$$

$$\text{Cost effect of growth for variable costs} = \left(\text{Units of input required to produced 2012 output in 2011} - \text{Actual units of inputs used to produce 2011 output}\right) \times \text{Input price in 2011}$$

$$\text{Cost effct of growth for fixed costs} = \left(\begin{array}{c}\text{Actual units of capacity in 2011 if adequate to produce 2012 output in 2011}\\ \text{OR}\\ \text{In 2011 capacity inadequate to produce 2012 output in 2011, units of capacity required to produce 2012 output in 2011}\end{array} - \text{Actual units of capacity in 2011}\right) \times \text{Price per unit of capacity in 2011}$$

Pieces of clothing that would be required to be purchased in 2012 would be the same as that required in 2011 because output is the same between 2011 and 2012. Purchasing and administrative costs and selling and customer-service costs will not change as adequate capacity exists in 2011 to support year 2012 output and customers.

The cost effects of growth component are:

Costs of goods sold	(40,000 – 40,000)	×	Rs 400	=	Re 0
Selling and customer-service costs	(51,000 – 51,000)	×	Rs 70	=	0
Purchase and administrative costs	(980 – 980)	×	Rs 2,500	=	0
Cost effect of growth					Re 0

In summary, the net effect on operating income as a result of the growth component equals:

Revenue effect of growth	Rs 0
Cost effect of growth	0
Change in operating income due to growth	Rs 0

The Price-Recovery Component

Revenue effect of price-recovery = (Selling price in 2012 − Selling price in 2011) × Actual units of output sold in 2012

= (Rs 590 − Rs 600) × 40,000 = Rs 4,00,000 U

Cost effect of price-recovery for variable costs = (Input price in 2012 − Input price in 2011) × Units of input required to produce 2012 output in 2011

Cost effect of price-recovery for fixed costs = (Price per unit of capacity in 2012 − Price per unit of capacity in 2011) × Actual units of capacity in 2011, if adequate to produce 2012 output in 2011 OR If 2011 capacity inadequate to produce 2012 output in 2011, units of capacity required to produce 2012 output in 2011

Costs of goods sold	(Rs 410 – Rs 400)	×	40,000	=	Rs 4,00,000 U
Selling and customer-service costs	(Rs 69 – Rs 70)	×	51,000	=	51,000 F
Purchase and administrative costs	(Rs 2,400 – Rs 2,500)	×	980	=	98,000 F
Cost effect of price-recovery					Rs 2,51,000 U

In summary, the net decrease in operating income as a result of the price-recovery component equals:

Revenue effect of price-recovery	Rs 4,00,000 U
Cost effect of price-recovery	2,51,000 U
Change in operating income due to price-recovery	Rs 6,51,000 U

The Productivity Component

The productivity component of cost changes are:

Cost effect of productivity for variable costs = (Actual units of input used to produce 2012 output − Units of input required to produce 2012 output in 2011) × Input price in 2011

Cost effect of productivity for fixed costs = (Actual units of capacity in 2012 − Actual units of capacity in 2010, if adequate to produce 2012 output in 2011 OR If 2011 capacity inadequate to produce 2011 output in 2011, than units of capacity required to produce 2012 output in 2011) × Price per unit of capacity in 2012

Costs of goods sold	(40,000 – 40,000)	× Rs 410	=	0
Selling and customer-service costs	(43,000 – 51,000)	× Rs 69	=	Rs 5,52,000 F
Purchasing and administrative costs	(850 – 980)	× Rs 2,400	=	3,12,000 F
Change in operating income due to productivity				Rs 8,64,000 F

The change in operating income between 2011 and 2012 can be analyzed as follows:

	Income Statement Amounts in 2011 (1)	Revenue and Cost Effects of Growth Component in 2012 (2)	Revenue and Cost Effects of Price-Recovery Component in 2012 (3)	Cost Effect of Productivity Component in 2012 (4)	Income Statement Amounts in 2011 (5) = (1) + (2) + (3) + (4)
Revenues	Rs 2,40,00,000	Rs 0	Rs 4,00,000 U	—	Rs 2,36,00,000
Costs	2,20,20,000	0	2,51,000 U	Rs 8,64,000 F	2,14,07,000
Operating income	Rs 19,80,000	Rs 0	Rs 6,51,000 U	Rs 8,64,000 F	Rs 21,93,000
			Rs 2,13,000 F		

Change in operating income

4. The analysis of operating income indicates that a significant amount of the increase in operating income resulted from productivity gains rather than product differentiation. The company was unable to charge a premium price for its clothes. Thus, the strategic analysis of operating income indicates that Van Heusen has not been successful at implementing its premium price, product differentiation strategy, despite the fact that operating income increased by more than 10% between 2011 and 2012. Van Heusen could not pass on increases in purchase costs to its customers via higher prices. Van Heusen must either reconsider its product-differentiation strategy or focus managers on increasing margins and growing market share by offering better product variety and superb customer service.

Exercises

13-29 Balanced scorecard. Ballarpur Industries manufactures corrugated cardboard boxes. It competes and plans to grow by producing high-quality boxes at a low cost and by delivering them to customers quickly after receiving customers' orders. There are many other manufacturers who produce similar boxes. Ballarpur Industries believes that continuously improving its manufacturing processes and having satisfied employees are critical to implementing its strategy in 2011.

Required

1. Is Ballarpur Industries's 2011 strategy one of product differentiation or cost leadership? Explain briefly.
2. AP Paper, a competitor of Ballarpur Industries, manufactures corrugated boxes with more designs and color combinations than Ballarpur Industries at a higher price. AP Paper's boxes are of high quality but require more time to produce and so have longer delivery times. Draw a simple customer preference map as in Exhibit 13-1 for Ballarpur Industries, and AP Paper using the attributes of price, delivery time, quality, and design.

13-30 Analysis of growth, price-recovery, and productivity components (continuation of 13-29). An analysis of Ballarpur Industries's operating-income changes between 2010 and 2011 shows the following:

Operating income for 2010	Rs 17,00,000
Add growth component	70,000
Deduct price-recovery component	(60,000)
Add productivity component	1,40,000
Operating income for 2011	Rs 18,50,000

The industry-market size for corrugated cardboard boxes did not grow in 2011, input prices did not change, and Ballarpur Industries reduced the prices of its boxes.

Required

1. Was Ballarpur Industries's gain in operating income in 2011 consistent with the strategy you identified in requirement 1 of Exercise 13-29?
2. Explain the productivity component. In general, does it represent savings in only variable costs, only fixed costs, or both variable and fixed costs?

13-31 Strategy, balanced scorecard, service company. Heritage Systems is a small information-systems consulting firm that specializes in helping companies implement sales-management software. The market for Heritage's products is very competitive. To compete, Heritage must deliver quality service at a low cost. Heritage bills clients in terms of units of work performed, which depends on the size and complexity of the sales-management system. Heritage presents the following data for 2011 and 2012.

		2011	2012
1	Units of work performed	60	70
2	Selling price	Rs 5,00,000	Rs 4,80,000
3	Software-implementation labor hours	30,000	32,000
4	Cost per software-implementation labor hour	Rs 600	Rs 630
5	Software-implementation support capacity (in units of work)	90	90
6	Total cost of software-implementation support	Rs 36,00,000	Rs 36,90,000
7	Software-implementation support-capacity cost per unit of work	Rs 40,000	Rs 41,000
8	Number of employees doing software development	3	3
9	Total software-development costs	Rs 37,50,000	Rs 39,00,000
10	Software-development cost per employee	Rs 12,50,000	Rs 13,00,000

Software-implementation labor-hour costs are variable costs. Software-implementation support costs for each year depend on the software-implementation support capacity (defined in terms of units of work) that Heritage chooses to maintain each year. It does not vary with the actual units of work performed that year. At the start of each year, the management uses its discretion to determine the number of software-development employees. The software-development staff and costs have no direct relationship with the number of units of work performed.

Required

1. Is Heritage Systems's strategy one of product differentiation or cost leadership? Explain briefly.
2. Describe the key elements you would include in Heritage's balanced scorecard and your reasons for doing so.

13-32 Strategic analysis of operating income (continuation of 13-31). Refer to Exercise 13-31.

Required

1. Calculate the operating income of Heritage Systems in 2011 and 2012.
2. Calculate the growth, price-recovery, and productivity components that explain the change in operating income from 2011 to 2012.
3. Comment on your answer in requirement 2. What do these components indicate?

13-33 Analysis of growth, price-recovery, and productivity components (continuation of 13-32). Suppose that during 2012 the market for implementing sales-management software increases by 5% and that Heritage experiences a 1% decline in selling prices. Assume that any further decreases in selling price and increases in market share are strategic choices by Heritage's management to implement their strategy.

Required

Calculate how much of the change in operating income from 2011 to 2012 is due to the industry-market-size factor, cost leadership, and product differentiation. How successful has Heritage been in implementing its strategy? Explain.

13-34 Identifying and managing unused capacity (continuation of 13-31). Refer to Exercise 13-31.

Required

1. Where possible, calculate the amount and cost of (a) unused software-implementation support capacity and (b) unused software-development capacity at the beginning of 2012, based on units of work performed in 2012. If you are unable to calculate the amount and cost of unused capacity, then indicate why not.
2. Suppose Heritage can add or reduce its software-implementation support capacity in increments of 15 units. What is the maximum amount of costs that Heritage could save in 2012 by downsizing software-implementation support capacity?
3. Heritage, in fact, does not eliminate any of its unused software-implementation support capacity. Why might Heritage not downsize?

13-35 Balanced scorecard. Hewlett Packard (HP) manufactures various types of color laser printers in a highly automated facility with high fixed costs. The market for laser printers is competitive. The various color laser printers on the market are comparable in terms of features and price. HP believes that satisfying customers with products of high quality at low costs is key to achieving its target profitability. For 2012, HP plans to achieve higher quality and lower costs by improving yields and reducing defects in its manufacturing operations. HP will train workers, and encourage and empower them to take the necessary actions. Currently, a significant amount of HP's capacity is used to produce products that are defective and cannot be sold. HP expects that higher yields will reduce the capacity that HP needs to manufacture products. HP does not anticipate that improving manufacturing will automatically lead to lower costs because HP has high fixed costs. To reduce fixed costs per unit, HP could lay off employees and sell equipment, or it could use the capacity to produce and sell more of its current products or improved models of its current products.

HP's balanced scorecard (initiatives omitted) for the just-completed fiscal year 2012 follows:

Objectives	Measures	Target Performance	Actual Performance
Financial Perspective			
Increase shareholder value	Operating-income changes from productive improvements	Rs 1,00,00,000	Rs 40,00,000
	Operating-income changes from growth	Rs 1,50,00,000	Rs 60,00,000
Customer Perspective			
Increase market share	Market share in color laser printers	5%	4.6%
Internal-Business-Process Perspective			
Improve manufacturing quality	Yield	82%	85%
Reduce delivery time to customers	Order-delivery time	25 days	22 days
Learning-and-Growth Perspective			
Develop process skills	Percentage of employees trained in process and quality management	90%	92%
Enhance information-system capabilities	Percentage of manufacturing processes with real-time feedback	85%	87%

Required

1. Was HP successful in implementing its strategy in 2012? Explain.
2. Is HP's balanced scorecard useful in helping the company understand why it did not reach its target market share in 2012? If it is, explain why. If it is not, explain what other measures you might want to add under the customer perspective and why.

3. Would you have included some measure of employee satisfaction in the learning-and-growth perspective and new-product development in the internal-business-process perspective? That is, do you think employee satisfaction and development of new products are critical for HP to implement its strategy? Why or why not? Explain briefly.
4. What problems, if any, do you see in HP improving quality and significantly downsizing to eliminate unused capacity?

14 Cost Allocation, Customer-Profitability Analysis, and Sales-Variance Analysis

Learning Objectives

1. Identify four purposes for allocating costs to cost objects
2. Understand criteria to guide cost-allocation decisions
3. Discuss decisions faced when collecting costs in indirect-cost pools
4. Discuss why a company's revenues can differ across customers purchasing the same product
5. Identify the importance of customer-profitability profiles
6. Subdivide the sales-volume variance into the sales-mix variance and the sales-quantity variance

Companies desperately want to make their customers happy. But how far should they go to please them, and at what price? At what point are you better off not to do business with some customers at all? The following article explains why it's so important for managers to be able to figure out how profitable each of their customers is.

Minding the Store: Analyzing Customers, Best Buy Decides Not All Are Welcome[1]

As the former CEO of Best Buy, Brad Anderson decided to implement a rather unorthodox approach to retail: to separate his 1.5 million daily customers into "angels" and "devils."

The angels, customers who increase profits by purchasing high-definition televisions, portable electronics, and newly released DVDs without waiting for markdowns or rebates, are favored over the devils, who buy products, apply for rebates, return the purchases, and then buy them back at returned-merchandise discounts. These devils focus their spending on "loss leaders," discounted merchandise designed to encourage store traffic, but then flip the goods at a profit on sites like eBay.com.

Best Buy found that its most desirable customers fell into five distinct groups: upper-income men, suburban mothers, small-business owners, young family men, and technology enthusiasts. Male technology enthusiasts, nicknamed Buzzes, are early adopters, interested in buying and showing off the latest gadgets. Each store analyzes the demographics of its local market, and then focuses on two of these groups. For example, at stores popular with Buzzes, Best Buy sets up videogame areas with leather chairs and game players hooked to mammoth, plasma-screen televisions.

Best Buy also began working on ways to deter customers who drove profits down. It couldn't bar them from its stores. Starting in 2004, however, it began taking steps to put a stop to their most damaging practices by enforcing a restocking fee of 15% of the purchase price on returned merchandise. To discourage customers who return items with the intention of repurchasing them at an

[1] *Source:* Excerpted from, "Minding the Store: Analyzing Customers, Best Buy Decides Not All Are Welcome," *The Wall Street Journal*, November 8, 2004; "Best Buy Investor and Analyst Day: Customer Growth," Best Buy Inc; www.bestbuy.com Webcast Presentation August 9, 2007.

"open-box" discount, Best Buy started reselling the returned items over the Internet, so the goods didn't reappear in the store where they were originally purchased.

This strategy stimulated growth for several years at Best Buy and helped the company survive the economic downturn while Circuit City, its leading competitor, went bankrupt. But Best Buy's angels and devils strategy now must confront a new competitor, Walmart. With Walmart's focus on consumers seeking no-frills bargains, Best Buy intends to match its new competitor's prices while leveraging its tech-savvy sales force to help consumers navigate increasingly complicated technology.

To determine which product, customer, program, or department is profitable, organizations must decide how to allocate costs. Best Buy analyzed its operations and chose to allocate costs towards serving its most profitable customers. In this chapter and the next, we provide insight into cost allocation. The emphasis in this chapter is on macro issues in cost allocation: allocation of costs into divisions, plants, and customers. Chapter 15 describes micro issues in cost allocation—allocating support-department costs to operating departments and allocating costs to various cost objects—as well as revenue allocations.

Purposes of Cost Allocation

Learning Objectives 1

Identify four purposes for allocating costs to cost objects

. . . to provide information for decisions, motivate managers, justify costs, and measure income

Recall that *indirect costs* of a particular cost object are costs that are related to that cost object but cannot be traced to it in an economically feasible (cost-effective) way. These costs often comprise a large percentage of the overall costs assigned to such cost objects as products, customers, and distribution channels. Why do managers allocate indirect costs to these cost objects? Exhibit 14-1 illustrates four purposes of cost allocation.

Different costs are appropriate for different purposes. Consider costs of a product in terms of the business functions in the value chain.

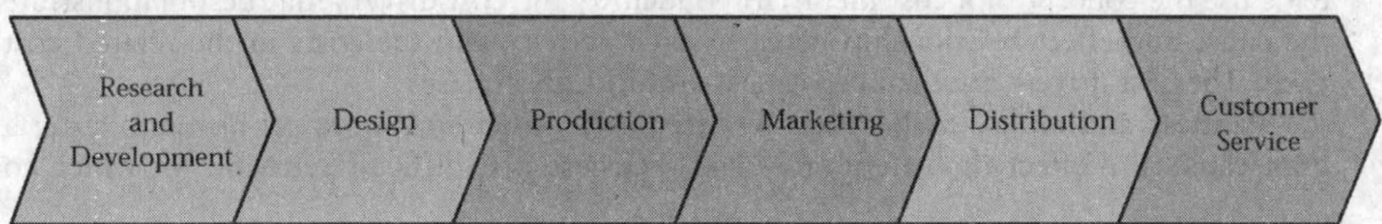

For some decisions related to the economic-decision purpose (for example, long-run product pricing), the costs in all six functions are relevant. For other decisions, particularly

Exhibit 14-1

Purposes of Cost Allocation

Purpose	Examples
1. To provide information for economic decisions	To decide whether to add a new airline flight To decide whether to manufacture a component part of a television set or to purchase it from another manufacturer To decide on the selling price for a customized product or service To evaluate the cost of available capacity used to support different products
2. To motivate managers and other employees	To encourage the design of products that are simpler to manufacture or less costly to service To encourage sales representatives to emphasize high-margin products or services
3. To justify costs or compute reimbursement amounts	To cost products at a "fair" price, often required by law and government defense contracts To compute reimbursement for a consulting firm based on a percentage of the cost savings resulting from the implementation of its recommendations
4. To measure income and assets	To cost inventories for reporting to external parties To cost inventories for reporting to tax authorities

short-run economic decisions (for example, make or buy decisions), costs from only one or two functions (for example, design and manufacturing) might be relevant.

For the motivation purpose, costs from more than one but not all business functions are often included to emphasize to decision makers how costs in different functions are related to one another. For example, to estimate product costs, product designers at companies such as Hitachi and Toshiba include costs of production, distribution, and customer service. The goal: to focus designers' attention on how different product-design choices affect total costs.

Decision Point

What are four purposes for allocating costs to cost objects?

For the cost-reimbursement purpose, a particular contract will often stipulate what costs will be reimbursed.

For the purpose of income and asset measurement for reporting to external parties under GAAP, only manufacturing costs (and product-design costs in some cases) are inventoriable and allocated to products.

Criteria to Guide Cost-Allocation Decisions

After identifying the purposes of cost allocation, managers and management accountants must decide how to allocate costs. This section describes the different criteria companies use to allocate costs.

Understand criteria to guide cost-allocation decisions

. . . such as identifying factors that cause resources to be consumed

Exhibit 14-2 presents four criteria used to guide cost-allocation decisions. These decisions affect both the number of indirect-cost pools and the cost-allocation base for each indirect-cost pool. We emphasize the superiority of the cause-and-effect and the benefits-received criteria, especially when the purpose of cost allocation is to provide information for economic decisions or to motivate managers and employees.[2] Cause and effect is the primary criterion used in activity-based costing (ABC) applications. ABC systems use the concept of a cost hierarchy to identify the cost drivers that best demonstrate the cause-and-effect relationship between each activity and the costs in the related cost pool. The cost drivers are then chosen as cost-allocation bases.

Fairness and ability to bear are less-frequently-used and more problematic criteria than cause and effect or benefits received. Fairness is a difficult criterion on which to

[2] The Federal Accounting Standards Advisory Board (which sets standards for management accounting for U.S.-government departments and agencies) recommends: "Cost assignments should be performed by: (a) directly tracing costs whenever feasible and economically practicable, (b) assigning costs on a cause-and-effect basis, and (c) allocating costs on a reasonable and consistent basis." (*FASAB*, 1995, p. 12)

Exhibit 14-2

Criteria for Cost-Allocation Decisions

1. Cause and Effect. Using this criterion, managers identify the variables that cause resources to be consumed. For example, managers may use hours of testing as the variable when allocating the costs of a quality-testing area to products. Cost allocations based on the cause-and-effect criterion are likely to be the most credible to operating personnel.

2. Benefits Received. Using this criterion, managers identify the beneficiaries of the outputs of the cost object. The costs of the cost object are allocated among the beneficiaries in proportion to the benefits each receives. Consider a corporatewide advertising program that promotes the general image of the corporation rather than any individual product. The costs of this program may be allocated on the basis of division revenues; the higher the revenues, the higher the division's allocated cost of the advertising program. The rationale behind this allocation is that divisions with higher revenues apparently benefited from the advertising more than divisions with lower revenues and, therefore, ought to be allocated more of the advertising costs.

3. Fairness or Equity. This criterion is often cited in government contracts when cost allocations are the basis for establishing a price satisfactory to the government and its suppliers. Cost allocation here is viewed as a "reasonable" or "fair" means of establishing a selling price in the minds of the contracting parties. For most allocation decisions, fairness is a matter of judgment rather than an operational criterion.

4. Ability to Bear. This criterion advocates allocating costs in proportion to the cost object's ability to bear costs allocated to it. An example is the allocation of corporate executive salaries on the basis of division operating income. The presumption is that the more-profitable divisions have a greater ability to absorb corporate headquarters' costs.

obtain agreement. What one party views as fair, another party may view as unfair.[3] For example, a university may view allocating a share of general administrative costs to government contracts as fair because general administrative costs are incurred to support all activities of the university. The government may view the allocation of such costs as unfair because the general administrative costs would have been incurred by the university regardless of whether the government contract existed. Perhaps the fairest way to resolve this issue is to understand, as well as possible, the cause-and-effect relationship between the government contract activity and general administrative costs. In other words, fairness is more a matter of judgment than an easily implementable choice criterion.

To get a sense of the issues that arise when using the ability-to-bear criterion, consider a product that consumes a large amount of indirect costs but whose selling price is currently below its direct costs. This product has no ability to bear any of the indirect costs it uses. If the indirect costs it consumes are allocated to other products, these other products are subsidizing the product that is losing money. An integrated airline, for example, might allocate fewer costs to its activities in a highly contested market such as freight transportation, thereby subsidizing it via passenger transport. Some airports cross-subsidize costs associated with serving airline passengers through sales of duty-free goods. Such practices provide a distorted view of relative product and service profitability, and have the potential to invite both regulatory scrutiny as well as competitors attempting to undercut artificially higher-priced services.

Most importantly, companies must weigh the costs and benefits when designing and implementing their cost allocations. Companies incur costs not only in collecting data but also in taking the time to educate managers about cost allocations. In general, the more complex the cost allocations, the higher these education costs.

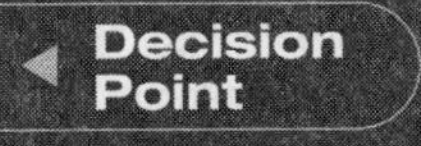

What criteria should managers use to guide cost-allocation decisions?

The costs of designing and implementing complex cost allocations are highly visible. Unfortunately, the benefits from using well-designed cost allocations—enabling managers to make better-informed sourcing decisions, pricing decisions, cost-control decisions, and so on—are difficult to measure. Still, when making cost allocations, managers should consider the benefits as well as the costs. As costs of collecting and processing information decrease, companies are building more-detailed cost allocations.

[3] Kaplow and Shavell, for example, in a review of the legal literature, note that "notions of fairness are many and varied. They are analyzed and rationalized by different writers in different way, and they also typically depend upon the circumstances under consideration. Accordingly, it is not possible to identify and consensus view on these notions ..." See L. Kaplow and S. Shavell, "Fairness Versus Welfare," *Harvard Law Review* (February 2001): 961-1388; and L. Kaplow and S. Shavell, *Fairness Versus Welfare* (Boston: Harvard University Press, 2002).

Cost Allocation Decisions

Learning Objectives 3

Discuss decisions faced when collecting costs in indirect-cost pools

. . . determining the number of cost pools and the costs to be included in each cost pool

In this section, we focus on the first purpose of cost allocation: to provide information for economic decisions, such as pricing, by measuring the full costs of delivering products based on an ABC system.

Chapter 5 described how ABC systems define indirect-cost pools for different activities and use cost drivers as allocation bases to assign costs of indirect-cost pools to products—the second stage of cost allocation. In this section, we focus on the first stage of cost allocation—how costs are assigned to indirect-cost pools.

We will use Consumer Appliances, Inc. (CAI), to illustrate how costs incurred in different parts of a company can be assigned, and then reassigned, for costing products, services, customers, or contracts. CAI has two divisions; each has its own manufacturing plant. The Refrigerator Division has a plant in Minneapolis, and the Clothes Dryer Division has a plant in St. Paul. CAI's headquarters is in a separate location in Minneapolis. Each division manufactures and sells multiple products that differ in size and complexity.

CAI's management team collects costs at the following levels:

- **Corporate costs**—there are three major categories of corporate costs:
  1. **Treasury costs**—Rs 90,00,000 of costs incurred for financing the construction of new assembly equipment in the two divisions. The cost of new assembly equipment is Rs 5,20,00,000 in the Refrigerator Division and Rs 3,80,00,000 in the Clothes Dryer Division.
  2. **Human-resource-management costs**—recruitment and ongoing employee training and development, Rs 1,60,00,000.
  3. **Corporate-administration costs**—executive salaries, rent, and general administration costs, Rs 5,40,00,000.
- Division cost— Each division has two direct-cost categories (direct materials and direct manufacturing labor) and seven indirect-cost pools—one cost pool each for the five activities (design, setup, manufacturing, distribution, and administration), one cost pool to accumulate facility costs, and one cost pool for the allocated corporate treasury costs. Exhibit 14-3 presents data for six of the division indirect-cost pools and cost-allocation bases. (In a later section, we describe how corporate treasury costs are

Exhibit 14-3 Division Indirect-Cost Pools and Cost-Allocation Bases, CAI, Inc., for Refrigerator Division (R) and Clothes Dryer Division (CD)

Division Indirect-Cost Pools	Example of Costs		Total Indirect Costs	Cost Hierarchy Category	Cost-Allocation Base	Cause-and-Effect Relationship That Motivates Management's Choice of Allocation Base
Design	Design engineering salaries	(R) (CD)	Rs 6,00,00,000 4,25,00,000	Product sustaining	Parts times cubic feet	Complex products (more parts and larger size) require greater design resources.
Setups of machines	Setup labor and equipment cost	(R) (CD)	Rs 3,00,00,000 2,40,00,000	Batch level	Setup-hours	Overhead costs of the setup activity increase as setup-hours increase.
Manufacturing operations	Plant and equipment, energy	(R) (CD)	Rs 25,00,00,000 18,75,00,000	Output unit level	Machine-hours	Manufacturing-operations overhead costs support machines and, hence, increase with machine usage.
Distribution	Shipping labor and equipment	(R) (CD)	Rs 8,00,00,000 5,50,00,000	Output unit level	Cubic feet	Distribution-overhead costs increase with cubic feet of product shipped.
Administration	Division executive salaries	(R) (CD)	Rs 1,00,00,000 80,00,000	Facility sustaining	Revenues	Weak relationship between division executive salaries and revenues, but justified by CAI on a benefits-received basis.
Facility	Annual building and space costs	(R) (CD)	Rs 4,50,00,000 3,50,00,000	All	Square feet	Facility costs increase with square feet of space.

allocated to each division to create the seventh division indirect-cost pool.) CAI identifies the cost hierarchy category for each cost pool— output-unit level, batch level, product sustaining level, and facility- sustaining level (as described in Chapter 5).

Exhibit 14-4 presents an overview diagram of the allocation of corporate and division indirect costs to products of the Refrigerator Division. Note: The Clothes Dryer Division has its own seven indirect-cost pools used to allocate costs to products. These cost pools and cost-allocation bases parallel the indirect-cost pools and allocation bases for the Refrigerator Division.

Look first at the middle row of the exhibit, where you see "Division Indirect-Cost Pools," and scan the lower half. It is similar to Exhibit 5-3, which illustrates ABC systems using indirect-cost pools and cost drivers for different activities. A major difference in the lower half of Exhibit 14-4 is the cost pool called Facility Costs (far right, middle row), which accumulates all annual costs of buildings and furnishings (such as depreciation) incurred in the division. The arrows in Exhibit 14-4 indicate that CAI allocates facility costs to the five activity-cost pools. Recall from Exhibit 14-3 that CAI uses square feet area required for various activities (design, setup, manufacturing, distribution, and administration) to allocate these facility costs. These activity-cost pools then include the costs of the building and facilities needed to perform the various activities.

The costs in the six remaining indirect-cost pools (that is, after costs of the facility cost pool have been allocated to other cost pools) are allocated to products on the basis of cost drivers described in Exhibit 14-3 (We later describe how corporate treasury costs that have been allocated to divisions are further allocated to products.). These cost drivers are chosen as the cost-allocation bases because there is a cause-and-effect relationship between the cost drivers and the costs in the indirect-cost pool. A cost rate per unit is calculated for each cost-allocation base. Indirect costs are allocated to products on the basis of the total quantity of the cost allocation base for each activity used by the product.

Next focus on the upper half of Exhibit 14-4: how corporate costs are allocated to divisions and then to indirect-cost pools. Before getting into the details of the allocations, let's first consider some broader choices that CAI faces regarding the allocation of corporate costs.

Allocating Corporate Costs to Divisions and Products

CAI's management team has several choices to make when accumulating and allocating corporate costs to divisions.

1. Which corporate-cost categories should CAI allocate as indirect costs of the divisions? Should CAI allocate all corporate costs or only some of them?
   - Some companies allocate all corporate costs to divisions because corporate costs are incurred to support division activities. Allocating all corporate costs motivates division managers to examine how corporate costs are planned and controlled. Also, companies that want to calculate the full cost of products must allocate all corporate costs to indirect-cost pools of divisions.
   - Other companies do not allocate corporate costs to divisions because these costs are not controllable by division managers.
   - Still other companies allocate only those corporate costs, such as corporate human resources, that are widely perceived as causally related to division activities or that provide explicit benefits to divisions. These companies exclude corporate costs such as corporate donations to charitable foundations because division managers often have no say in making these decisions and because the benefits to the divisions are less evident or too remote. If a company decides not to allocate some or all corporate costs, this results in total company profitability being less than the sum of individual division or product profitabilities.

   For some decision purposes, allocating some but not all corporate costs to divisions may be the preferred alternative. Consider the performance evaluation of division managers. The controllability notion is frequently used to justify excluding

Exhibit 14-4 Overview Diagram of Allocation of Corporate and Division Indirect Costs to Products of the Refrigerator Division, CAI, Inc.

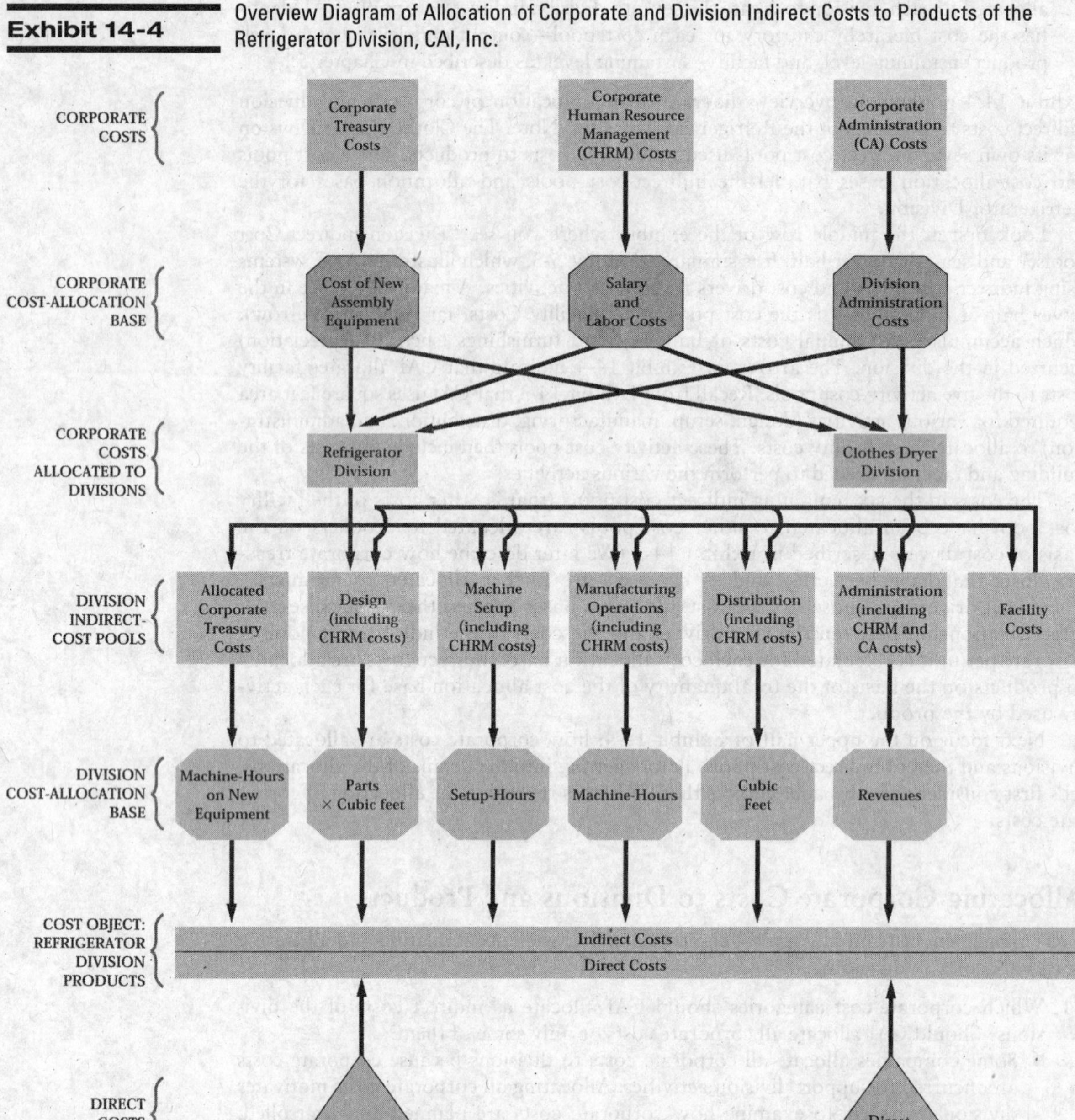

some corporate costs from division reports. For example, salaries of the top management at corporate headquarters are often excluded from responsibility accounting reports of division managers. Although divisions tend to benefit from these corporate costs, division managers argue they have no say in ("are not responsible for") how much of these corporate resources they use or how much they cost. The contrary argument is that full allocation is justified because the divisions receive benefits from all corporate costs.

2. When allocating corporate costs to divisions, should CAI allocate only costs that vary with division activity or fixed costs as well? Companies allocate both variable and fixed costs to divisions and then to products because they use these product costs to make long-run strategic decisions, such as which products they should sell and at

what price. To make good long-run decisions, managers need to know the cost of all resources (whether variable or fixed) needed to produce products. Why? Because in the long run, firms can manage the levels of virtually all of their costs; very few costs are truly fixed. Moreover, to survive and prosper in the long run, firms must ensure that the prices charged for products exceed the total resources consumed to produce them, regardless of whether these costs are variable or fixed in the short run.

Companies that allocate corporate costs to divisions must carefully identify relevant costs for specific decisions. Suppose a division is profitable before any corporate costs are allocated but "unprofitable" after allocation of corporate costs. Should the division be closed down? The relevant corporate costs in this case are not the allocated corporate costs but those corporate costs that will be saved if the division is closed. If division profits exceed the relevant corporate costs, the division should not be closed.

3. If CAI allocates corporate costs to divisions, how many cost pools should it use? One extreme is to aggregate all corporate costs into a single cost pool. The other extreme is to have numerous individual corporate cost pools. As discussed in Chapter 5, a major consideration is to construct **homogeneous cost pools** so that all of the costs in the cost pool have the same or a similar cause-and-effect or benefits-received relationship with the cost-allocation base.

   For example, when allocating corporate costs to divisions, CAI can combine corporate administration costs and corporate human-resource-management costs into a single cost pool if both cost categories have the same or similar cause-and-effect relationship with the same cost-allocation base (say, number of employees in each division). If, however, each cost category has a cause-and-effect relationship with a different cost-allocation base (for example, number of employees in each division affects corporate human-resource-management costs, whereas revenues of each division affect corporate administration costs), CAI will prefer to maintain separate cost pools for each of these costs. Determining homogeneous cost pools requires judgment and should be revisited on a regular basis.

   The benefit of using a multiple cost-pool system must be balanced against the costs of implementing it. Advances in information-gathering technology make it more likely that multiple cost-pool systems will pass the cost-benefit test.

Implementing Corporate Cost Allocations

After much discussion and debate, CAI's management team chooses to allocate all corporate costs to divisions. We now illustrate the allocation of corporate costs to divisions in CAI's ABC system.

The demands for corporate resources by the Refrigerator Division and the Clothes Dryer Division depend on the demands that each division's products place on these resources. The top half of Exhibit 14-4 graphically represents the allocations.

1. CAI allocates treasury costs to each division on the basis of the cost of new assembly equipment installed in each division (the cost driver of treasury costs). It allocates the Rs 90,00,000 of treasury costs as follows:

$$\text{Refrigerator Division: Rs } 90{,}00{,}000 \times \frac{\text{Rs } 5{,}20{,}00{,}000}{\text{Rs } 5{,}20{,}00{,}000 + \text{Rs } 3{,}80{,}00{,}000} = \text{Rs } 52{,}00{,}000$$

$$\text{Clothes Dryer Division: Rs } 90{,}00{,}000 \times \frac{\text{Rs } 3{,}80{,}00{,}000}{\text{Rs } 5{,}20{,}00{,}000 + \text{Rs } 3{,}80{,}00{,}000} = \text{Rs } 38{,}00{,}000$$

Each division then creates a separate cost pool consisting of the allocated corporate treasury costs and reallocates these costs to products on the basis of machine-hours used on the new equipment. Treasury costs are an output unit-level cost because they represent resources used on activities performed on each individual unit of a product.

2. CAI's analysis indicates that the demand for corporate human-resource-management (CHRM) costs for recruitment and training varies with total salary and labor costs in each division. Suppose salary and labor costs are Rs 44,00,00,000 in the Refrigerator

Division and Rs 36,00,00,000 in the Clothes Dryer Division. Then CHRM costs are allocated to the divisions as follows:

$$\text{Refrigerator Division: Rs } 1{,}60{,}00{,}000 \times \frac{\text{Rs } 44{,}00{,}00{,}000}{\text{Rs } 44{,}00{,}00{,}000 + \text{Rs } 36{,}00{,}00{,}000} = \text{Rs } 88{,}00{,}000$$

$$\text{Clothes Dryer Division: Rs } 1{,}60{,}00{,}000 \times \frac{\text{Rs } 44{,}00{,}00{,}000}{\text{Rs } 44{,}00{,}00{,}000 + \text{Rs } 36{,}00{,}00{,}000} = \text{Rs } 72{,}00{,}000$$

Each division reallocates the CHRM costs allocated to it to the indirect-cost pools—design, machine setup, manufacturing operations, distribution, and division administration (the allocated-corporate-treasury cost pool and the facility costs pool have no salary and labor costs, so no CHRM costs are allocated to them)—on the basis of total salary and labor costs of each indirect-cost pool. CHRM costs that are added to division indirect-cost pools are then allocated to products using the cost driver for the respective cost pool. Therefore, CHRM costs are product-sustaining costs (for the portion of CHRM costs allocated to the design cost pool), batch-level costs (for the portion of CHRM costs allocated to the machine-setup cost pool), output unit-level costs (for the portions of CHRM costs allocated to the manufacturing-operations and distribution cost pools), and facility-sustaining costs (for the portion of CHRM costs allocated to the division-administration cost pool).

3. CAI allocates corporate administration costs to each division on the basis of division administration costs (see Exhibit 14-3 shows the amounts of division administration costs) because corporate administration's main role is to support division administration.

$$\text{Refrigerator Division: Rs } 5{,}40{,}00{,}000 \times \frac{\text{Rs } 1{,}00{,}00{,}000}{\text{Rs } 1{,}00{,}00{,}000 + \text{Rs } 80{,}00{,}000} = \text{Rs } 3{,}00{,}00{,}000$$

$$\text{Clothes Dryer Division: Rs } 5{,}40{,}00{,}000 \times \frac{\text{Rs } 80{,}00{,}000}{\text{Rs } 1{,}00{,}00{,}000 + \text{Rs } 80{,}00{,}000} = \text{Rs } 2{,}40{,}00{,}000$$

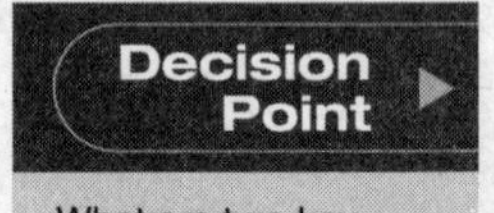

What are two key decisions managers must make when collecting costs in indirect-cost pools?

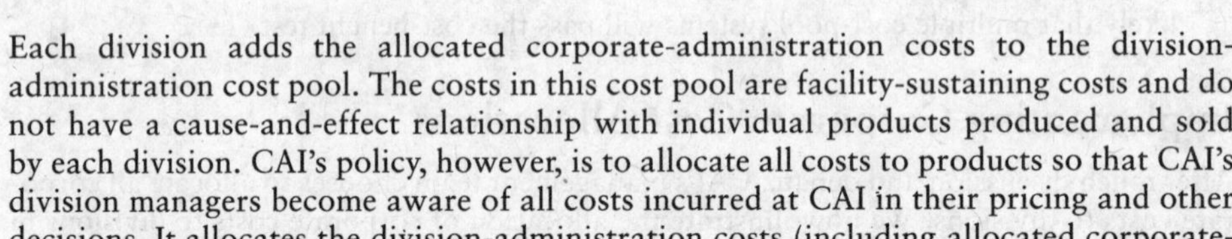

Each division adds the allocated corporate-administration costs to the division-administration cost pool. The costs in this cost pool are facility-sustaining costs and do not have a cause-and-effect relationship with individual products produced and sold by each division. CAI's policy, however, is to allocate all costs to products so that CAI's division managers become aware of all costs incurred at CAI in their pricing and other decisions. It allocates the division-administration costs (including allocated corporate-administration costs) to products on the basis of product revenues (a benefits-received criterion).

The issues discussed in this section regarding divisions and products apply nearly identically to customers, as we shall show next. *Instructors and students who, at this point, want to explore more-detailed issues in cost allocation rather than focusing on how activity-based costing extends to customer profitability can skip ahead to Chapter 15.*

Customer Revenues and Customer Costs

Customer-Profitability analysis is the reporting and analysis of revenues earned from customers and the costs incurred to earn those revenues. An analysis of customer differences in revenues and costs can provide insight into why differences exist in the operating income earned from different customers. Managers use this information to ensure that customers making large contributions to the operating income of a company receive a high level of attention from the company.

Consider Oasis Bottling Company, which sells bottled water. It has two distribution channels: (1) a wholesale distribution channel, in which the wholesaler sells to supermarkets, drugstores, and other stores, and (2) a retail distribution channel for a small number of business customers. We focus mainly on customer-profitability analysis in Oasis's retail distribution channel. The list selling price in this channel is Rs 144 per case (24 bottles). The full cost to Oasis is Rs 120 per case. If every case is sold at list price in this distribution channel, Oasis would earn a gross margin of Rs 24 per case.

Customer-Revenue Analysis

Consider revenues from 4 of Oasis's 10 retail customers in June 2012:

	A	B	C	D	E
1			CUSTOMER		
2		A	B	G	J
3	Cases sold	42,000	33,000	2,900	2,500
4	List selling price	Rs 144.0	Rs 144.0	Rs 144.0	Rs 144.0
5	Price discount	Rs 9.6	Rs 2.4	Rs 12.0	Rs 0
6	Invoice price	Rs 134.4	Rs 141.6	Rs 132.0	Rs 144.0
7	Revenues (Row 3 x Row 6)	Rs 56,44,880	Rs 46,72,280	Rs 3,82,800	Rs 3,60,000

Learning Objectives 4

Discuss why a company's revenues can differ across customers purchasing the same product

. . . revenues can differ because of differences in the quantity purchased and the price discounts given

Two variables explain revenue differences across these four customers: (1) the number of cases they purchased and (2) the magnitude of price discounting. A **price discount** is the reduction in selling price below list selling price to encourage customers to purchase more. Companies that record only the final invoice price in their information system cannot readily track the magnitude of their price discounting.[4]

Price discounts are a function of multiple factors, including the volume of product purchased (higher-volume customers receive higher discounts) and the desire to sell to a customer who might help promote sales to other customers. Discounts could also be because of poor negotiating by a salesperson or the unwanted effect of an incentive plan based only on revenues. At no time should price discounts run afoul of the law by way of price discrimination, predatory pricing, or collusive pricing.

Tracking price discounts by customer and by salesperson helps improve customer profitability. For example, Oasis Bottling Company may decide to strictly enforce its volume-based price discounting policy. It may also require its salespeople to obtain approval for giving large discounts to customers who do not normally qualify for such discounts. In addition, Oasis could track the future sales of customers who its salespeople have given sizable price discounts to because of their "high growth potential." For example, Oasis should track future sales to customer G to see if the Rs 12-per-case discount translates into higher future sales.

Customer revenues are one element of customer profitability. The other element that is equally important to understand is the cost of acquiring, serving, and retaining customers. We study this topic next.

Customer-Cost Analysis

We apply to customers the cost hierarchy discussed in the previous section and in Chapter 5. A **customer-cost hierarchy** categorizes costs related to customers into different cost pools on the basis of different types of cost drivers, or cost-allocation bases, or different degrees of difficulty in determining cause-and-effect or benefits-received relationships. Oasis's ABC system focuses on customers rather than products. It has one direct cost—the cost of bottled water—and multiple indirect-cost pools. Oasis identifies five categories of indirect costs in its customer cost hierarchy:

1. **Customer output unit-level costs**—costs of activities to sell each unit (case) to a customer. An example is product-handling costs of each case sold.
2. **Customer batch-level costs**—costs of activities related to a group of units (cases) sold to a customer. Examples are costs incurred to process orders or to make deliveries.

[4] Further analysis of customer revenues could distinguish gross revenues from net revenues. This approach highlights differences across customers in sales returns. Additional discussion of ways to analyze revenue differences across customers is in R. S. Kaplan and R. Cooper, *Cost and Effect* (Boston, MA: Harvard Business School Press, 1998, Chapter 10); and G. Cokins, *Activity-Based Cost Management: An Executive's Guide* (New York: John Wiley & Sons, 2001, Chapter 3).

3. **Customer-sustaining costs**—costs of activities to support individual customers, regardless of the number of units or batches of product delivered to the customer. Examples are costs of visits to customers or costs of displays at customer sites.
4. **Distribution-channel costs**—costs of activities related to a particular distribution channel rather than to each unit of product, each batch of product, or specific customers. An example is the salary of the manager of Oasis's retail distribution channel.
5. **Corporate-sustaining costs**—costs of activities that cannot be traced to individual customers or distribution channels. Examples are top-management and general-administration costs.

Note from these descriptions that four of the five levels of Oasis's cost hierarchy closely parallel the cost hierarchy described in Chapter 5, except that Oasis focuses on customers whereas the cost hierarchy in Chapter 5 focused on products. Oasis has one additional cost hierarchy category—distribution-channel costs—for the costs it incurs to support its wholesale and retail distribution channels.

Customer-Level Costs

Oasis is particularly interested in analyzing *customer-level indirect costs*—costs incurred in the first three categories of the customer-cost hierarchy: customer output-unit-level costs, customer batch-level costs, and customer-sustaining costs. Oasis wants to work with customers to reduce these costs. It believes customer actions will have less impact on distribution-channel and corporate-sustaining costs. The following table shows five activities (in addition to cost of goods sold) that Oasis identifies as resulting in customer-level costs. The table indicates the cost drivers and cost-driver rates for each activity, as well as the cost-hierarchy category for each activity.

	G	H	I	J
1	**Activity Area**	**Cost Driver and Rate**		**Cost-Hierarchy Category**
2	Product handling	Rs 5.0	per case sold	Customer output-unit-level costs
3	Order taking	Rs 1,000.0	per purchase order	Customer batch-level costs
4	Delivery vehicles	Rs 20.0	per delivery mile traveled	Customer batch-level costs
5	Rush deliveries	Rs 3,000.0	per expedited delivery	Customer batch-level costs
6	Visits to customers	Rs 800.0	per sales visit	Customer-sustaining costs

Information on the quantity of cost drivers used by each of four customers is:

	A	B	C	D	E
10		**CUSTOMER**			
11		**A**	**B**	**G**	**J**
12	Number of purchase orders	30	25	15	10
13	Number of deliveries	60	30	20	15
14	Miles traveled per delivery	5	12	20	6
15	Number of rush deliveries	1	0	2	0
16	Number of visits to customers	6	5	4	3

Exhibit 14-5 shows a customer-profitability analysis for the four retail customers using information on customer revenues previously presented and customer-level costs from the ABC system.

Oasis Bottling can use the information in Exhibit 14-5 to work with customers to reduce the quantity of activities needed to support them. Consider a comparison of Customer G and Customer A. Customer G purchases only 7% of the cases that customer A purchases (2,900 versus 42,000). Yet, compared with Customer A, Customer G uses one-half as many purchase orders, two-thirds as many visits to customers, one-third as many deliveries, and twice as many rush deliveries. By implementing charges for each of these services, Oasis might be able to induce Customer G to make fewer but larger purchase orders, and require fewer customer visits, deliveries and rush deliveries while looking to increase sales in the future.

Consider Owens and Minor, a distributor of medical supplies to hospitals. It strategically prices each of its services separately. For example, if a hospital wants a rush delivery or special packaging, Owens and Minor charges the hospital an additional price for each particular service. How have Owens and Minor's customers reacted? Hospitals that value these services continue to demand them and pay for them while hospitals that do not value these services drop them, saving Owens and Minor some costs. Owens and Minor's pricing strategy influences customer behavior in a way that increases its revenues or decreases its costs.

The ABC system also highlights a second opportunity for cost reduction: Spring can seek to reduce costs of each activity. For example, improving the efficiency of the ordering process (such as by having customers order electronically) can reduce costs even if customers place the same number of orders.

Exhibit 14-6 shows a monthly operating income statement for Oasis Bottling Company. The customer-level operating income of customers A and B in Exhibit 14-5 are shown in columns 8 and 9 of Exhibit 14-6. The format of Exhibit 14-6 is based on Oasis's cost hierarchy. All costs incurred to serve customers are not included in customer-level costs and therefore are not allocated to customers in Exhibit 14-6. For example, distribution-channel costs such as the salary of the manager of the retail distribution channel are not included in customer-level costs and are not allocated to customers. Instead, these costs are identified as costs of the retail channel as a whole. That's because Oasis's management believes that changes in customer behavior will not affect distribution-channel costs. These costs will be affected only by decisions pertaining to the whole channel, such as a decision to discontinue retail distribution. Another reason Oasis does not allocate distribution-channel costs to customers is motivation. Oasis's managers contend that salespersons responsible for managing individual customer accounts would lose motivation if their bonuses were affected by the allocation to customers of distribution-channel costs over which they had minimal influence.

Next, consider corporate-sustaining costs such as top-management and general-administration costs. Oasis's managers have concluded that there is no cause-and-effect or benefits-received relationship between any cost-allocation base and corporate-sustaining costs. Consequently, allocation of corporate-sustaining costs serves no useful purpose in deci-

Exhibit 14-5 Customer-Profitability Analysis for Four Retail Channel Customers of Oasis Bottling Company for June 2011

	A	B	C	D	E
1		CUSTOMER			
2		A	B	G	J
3	Revenues at list price: Rs144.0 x 42,000; 33,000; 2,900; 2,500	Rs 60,48,000	Rs 47,52,000	Rs 4,17,600	Rs 3,60,000
4	Price discount: Rs 96.6 x 42,000; Rs 2.4 x 33,000; Rs12.0 x 2,900; Rs 0 x 2,500	4,03,200	79,200	34,800	0
5	Revenues (at actual price)	56,44,800	46,72,800	3,82,800	3,60,000
6	Cost of goods sold: Rs 120.0 x 42,000; 33,000; 2,900; 2,500	50,40,000	39,60,000	3,48,000	3,00,000
7	Gross margin	6,04,800	7,12,800	34,800	60,000
8	Customer-level operating costs				
9	Product handling Rs 5.0 x 42,000; 33,000; 2,900; 2,500	2,10,000	1,65,000	14,500	12,500
10	Order taking Rs 1,000 x 30; 25; 15; 10	30,000	25,000	15,000	10,000
11	Delivery vehicles Rs 20 x (5 x 60); (12 x 30); (20 x 20); (6 x 15)	6,000	7,200	8,000	1,800
12	Rush deliveries Rs 3,000 x 1; 0; 2; 0	3,000	0	6,000	0
13	Visits to customers Rs 800 x 6; 5; 4; 3	4,800	4,000	3,200	2,400
14	Total customer-level operating costs	2,53,800	2,01,200	46,700	26,700
15	Customer-level operating income	Rs 3,51,000	Rs 5,11,600	Rs (11,900)	Rs 33,300

Exhibit 14-6 Income Statement of Oasis Bottling Company for June 2011

	A	B	C	D	E	F	G	H	I	J	K	L	M
1					CUSTOMER DISTRIBUTION CHANNELS								
2				Wholesale Customers						Retail Customers			
3		Total	Total	A1	A2	A3	▪		Total	A[a]	B[a]	C	▪
4		(1) = (2) + (7)	(2)	(3)	(4)	(5)	(6)		(7)	(8)	(9)	(10)	(.:.)
5	Revenues (at actual prices)	Rs 12,13,81,200	Rs 10,10,77,200	Rs 1,94,60,000	Rs1,47,60,000	▪	▪		Rs2,03,04,000	Rs 56,44,800	Rs 46,72,800	▪	▪
6	Customer-level costs	11,63,37,600	9,73,72,800	1,86,80,000	1,41,60,000	▪	▪		1,89,64,800	52,93,800[b]	41,61,200[b]	▪	▪
7	Customer-level operating income	50,43,600	37,04,400	Rs 7,80,000	Rs 6,00,000	▪	▪		13,39,200	Rs 3,51,000	Rs 5,11,600	▪	▪
8	Distribution-channel costs	16,05,000	10,25,000						5,80,000				
9	Distribution-channel-level operating income	34,38,600	Rs 26,79,400						Rs 7,59,200				
10	Corporate-sustaining costs	26,30,000											
11	Operating income	Rs 8,08,600											
12													
13	[a]Full details are presented in Exhibit 14-5												
14	[b]Cost of goods sold + Total customer-level operating costs from Exhibit 14-5.												

sion making, performance evaluation, or motivation. For example, suppose Oasis allocated the Rs 26,30,000 of corporate-sustaining costs to its distribution channels: Rs 17,30,000 to the wholesale channel and Rs 9,00,000 to the retail channel. Using information from Exhibit 14-6, the retail channel would then show a loss of Rs 1,40,800 (Rs 7,59,200 – Rs 9,00,000).

If this same situation persisted in subsequent months, should Oasis shut down the retail distribution channel? No, because if retail distribution were discontinued, corporate-sustaining costs would be unaffected. Allocating corporate-sustaining costs to distribution channels could give the misleading impression that the potential cost savings from discontinuing a distribution channel would be greater than the likely amount.

Some managers and management accountants advocate fully allocating all costs to customers and distribution channels so that (1) the sum of operating incomes of all customers in a distribution channel (segment) equals the operating income of the distribution channel and (2) the sum of the distribution-channel operating incomes equals companywide operating income. These managers and management accountants argue that customers and products must eventually be profitable on a full-cost basis. In the previous example, CAI allocated all corporate and division-level costs to its refrigerator and clothes dryer products. For some decisions, such as pricing, allocating all costs ensures that long-run prices are set at a level to cover the cost of all resources used to produce and sell products. Nevertheless, the value of the hierarchical format in Exhibit 14-6 is that it distinguishes among various degrees of objectivity when allocating costs, and it dovetails with the different levels at which decisions are made and performance is evaluated. The issue of when and what costs to allocate is another example of the "different costs for different purposes" theme emphasized throughout this book.

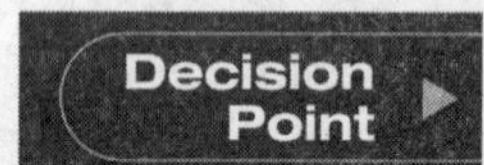

How can a company's revenues and costs differ across customers?

Customer-Profitability Profiles

Learning Objectives 5

Identify the importance of customer-profitability profiles

. . . highlight that a small percentage of customers contributes a large percentage of operating income.

Customer-profitability profiles provide a useful tool for managers. Exhibit 14-7 ranks Oasis's 10 retail customers based on customer-level operating income. (Four of these customers are analyzed in Exhibit 14-5.)

Column 4, computed by adding the individual amounts in column 1, shows the cumulative customer-level operating income. For example, customer C has a cumulative income of Rs 10,73,300 in column 4. This Rs 10,73,300 is the sum of Rs 5,11,600 for customer B, Rs 3,51,000 for customer A, and Rs 2,10,700 for customer C.

Column 5 shows what percentage the Rs 10,73,300 *cumulative* total for customers B, A, and C is of the total customer-level operating income of Rs 13,39,200 earned in the retail distribution channel from all 10 customers. The three most profitable customers contribute 80% of total customer-level operating income. These customers deserve the highest service and priority. In many companies, it is common for a small number of customers to contribute a high percentage of operating income. Microsoft uses the phrase "not all revenue dollars are endowed equally in profitability" to stress this point.

Exhibit 14-7 Customer-Profitability Analysis for Retail Channel Customers: Oasis Bottling Company, June 2011

	A	B	C	D	E	F
1	**Customers Ranked on Customer-Level Operating Income**					
2						**Cumulative**
3						**Customer-Level**
4		**Customer-**				**Operating Income**
5		**Level**		**Customer-Level**	**Cumulative**	**as a % of Total**
6		**Operating**	**Customer**	**Operating Income**	**Customer-Level**	**Customer-Level**
7	**Customer**	**Income**	**Revenue**	**Divided by Revenue**	**Operating Income**	**Operating Income**
8	**Code**	**(1)**	**(2)**	**(3) = (1) ÷ (2)**	**(4)**	**(5) = (4) ÷ Rs 13,39,200**
9	B	Rs 5,11,600	Rs 46,72,800	10.9%	Rs 5,11,600	38%
10	A	3,51,000	56,44,800	6.2%	8,62,600	64%
11	C	2,10,700	25,56,400	8.2%	10,73,330	80%
12	D	1,75,800	27,70,000	6.3%	12,49,100	93%
13	F	75,040	12,35,000	6.1%	13,24,140	99%
14	J	33,300	3,60,000	9.3%	13,57,440	101%
15	E	31,760	19,30,000	1.6%	13,89,200	104%
16	G	-11,900	3,82,800	-3.1%	13,77,300	103%
17	H	-16,900	3,82,200	-4.4%	13,60,400	102%
18	I	-21,200	3,70,000	-5.7%	13,39,200	100%
19		Rs 13,39,200	Rs2,03,04,000			
20						

Column 3 shows the profitability per rupee of revenue by customer. This measure of customer profitability indicates that, although customer A contributes the second-highest operating income, the profitability per rupee of revenue is lower because of high price discounts. Oasis's goal is to increase profit margins for Customer A by decreasing the price discounts or saving customer-level costs while maintaining or increasing sales. Customer J has a higher profit margin percentage but has lower total sales. Oasis's challenge with Customer J is to maintain margins while increasing sales.

Presenting Profitability Analysis

There are two common ways of presenting the results of customer-profitability analysis. Managers often find the bar chart presentation in Exhibit 14-8 to be the most intuitive way to visualize customer profitability. The highly profitable customers clearly stand out. Moreover, the number of "unprofitable" customers and the magnitude of their losses are apparent. A popular alternative way to express customer profitability is by plotting the contents of column 5 of Exhibit 14-7. This chart is called the **whale curve** since it is backward bending at the point where customers start to become unprofitable, and thus resembles a humpback whale.[5] Oasis's managers must explore ways to make unprofitable customers profitable. Exhibits 14-5 to 14-8 emphasize short-run customer profitability. Other factors managers should consider in deciding how to allocate resources among customers include:

- **Likelihood of customer retention.** The more likely a customer will continue to do business with a company, the more valuable the customer. Customers differ in their loyalty and their willingness to frequently "shop their business."
- **Potential for sales growth.** The higher the likely growth of the customer's industry and the customer's sales, the more valuable the customer. Customers to whom a company can cross-sell other products are more desirable.

[5] In practice, the curve of the chart can be quite steep. The whale curve for cumulative profitability usually reveals that the most profitable 20% of customers generate between 150% and 300% of total profits, the middle 70% of customers break even, and the least profitable 10% of customers lose from 50% to 200% of total profits (see Robert Kaplan and V.G. Narayanan, Measuring and Managing Customer Profitability, Journal of Cost Management, Sept/Oct 2001, pp. 1–11).

Exhibit 14-8

Bar Chart of Customer-Level Operating Income for Oasis Bottling Company's Retail Channel Customers in June 2009

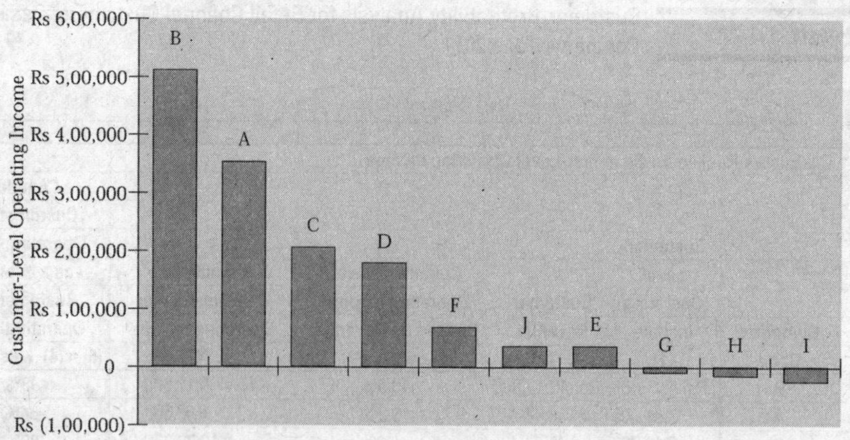

The Whale Curve of Cumulative Profitability for Oasis Bottling Company's Customers in June 2012

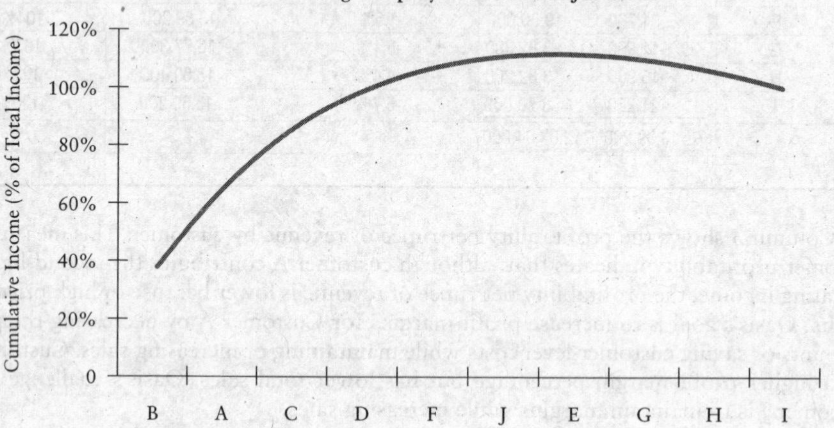

- **Long-run customer profitability.** This factor will be influenced by the first two factors specified and the cost of customer-support staff and special services required to retain customer accounts.
- **Increases in overall demand from having well-known customers.** Customers with established reputations help generate sales from other customers through product endorsements.
- **Ability to learn from customers.** Customers who provide ideas about new products or ways to improve existing products are especially valuable.

Managers should be cautious when deciding to discontinue customers. In Exhibit 14-7, the current unprofitability of customer G, for example, may provide misleading signals about G's profitability in the long-run. Moreover, as in any ABC-based system, the costs assigned to customer G are not all variable. In the short run, it may well have been efficient for Spring to use its spare capacity to serve G on a contribution-margin basis. Discontinuing customer G will not eliminate all the costs assigned to that customer, and will leave the firm worse off than before.

Of course, particular customers might be chronically unprofitable and hold limited future prospects. Or they might fall outside a firm's target market or require unsustainably high levels of service relative to the firm's strategies and capabilities. In such cases, organizations are becoming increasingly aggressive in severing customer relationships. For example, ING Direct, the largest direct lender and fastest growing financial services organization in the United States, asks 10,000 "high maintenance" customers to close their accounts each month.[6] The following Concepts in Action feature provides an example of a company that is struggling with the question of how to manage its resources and profitability without affecting the satisfaction of its customers.

Using the Five-Step Decision-Making Process to Manage Customer Profitability

The different types of customer analyses that we have just covered provide companies with key information to guide the allocation of resources across customers. Use the five-step decision-making process, introduced in Chapter 1, to think about how managers use these analyses to make customer-management decisions.

1. *Identify the problem and uncertainties.* The problem is how to manage and allocate resources across customers.
2. *Obtain information.* Managers identify past revenues generated by each customer and customer-level costs incurred in the past to support each customer.
3. *Make predictions about the future.* Managers estimate the revenues they expect from each customer and the customer-level costs they will incur in the future. In making these predictions, managers consider the effects that future price discounts will have on revenues, the effect that pricing for different services (such as rush deliveries) will have on the demand for these services by customers, and ways to reduce the cost of providing services.
4. *Make decisions by choosing among alternatives.* Managers use the customer-profitability profiles to identify the small set of customers who deserve the highest service and priority. They also identify ways to make less-profitable customers (for example, Oasis's Customer G) more profitable. In making resource-allocation decisions, managers also consider long-term effects, such as the potential for future sales growth and the opportunity to leverage a particular customer account to make sales to other customers.
5. *Implement the decision, evaluate performance, and learn.* After the decision is implemented, managers compare actual results to predicted outcomes to evaluate the decision they made, its implementation, and ways in which they might improve profitability.

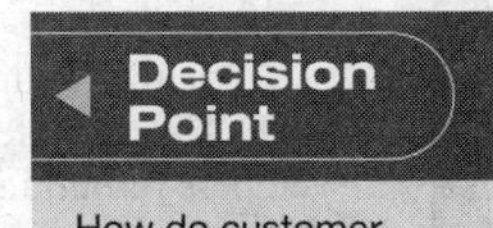

How do customer-profitability profiles help managers?

Sales Variances

The customer-profitability analysis in the previous section focused on the actual profitability of individual customers within a distribution channel (retail, for example) and their effect on Oasis Bottling's profitability for June 2012. At a more-strategic level, however, recall that Oasis operates in two different markets: wholesale and retail. The operating margins in the retail market are much higher than the operating margins in the wholesale market. In June 2012, Oasis had budgeted to sell 80% of its cases to wholesalers and 20% to retailers. It actually sold more cases in total than it had budgeted, but its actual sales mix (in cases) was 84% to wholesalers and 16% to retailers. Regardless of the profitability of sales to individual customers within each of the retail and wholesale channels, Oasis's actual operating income, relative to the master budget, is likely to be positively affected by the higher sales of cases and negatively affected by the shift in mix away from the more-profitable retail customers. Sales-quantity and sales-mix variances can identify the effect of each of these factors on Oasis's profitability. Companies such as Cisco, GE, and Hewlett-Packard perform similar analyses because they sell their products through multiple distribution channels, for example, via the Internet, over the telephone, or in retail stores.

Oasis classifies all customer-level costs as variable costs and distribution-channel and corporate-sustaining costs as fixed costs. To simplify the sales-variances analysis and calcu-

Concepts in Action

iPhone "Apps" Challenge Customer Profitability at AT&T

AT&T is the second largest wireless provider in the United States. The company provides mobile telephone and data access to more than 85 million individuals, businesses, and government agencies. AT&T uses cost accounting to price its various wireless service plans and calculate overall profitability for its customers, including more than 10 million owners of Apple's iPhone. AT&T is the exclusive wireless provider for the popular iPhone smart phone.

Traditionally, the cost of serving different wireless customers varied. Most business customers, for example, required reliable service during business hours and large amounts of data bandwidth for e-mail and Internet access. In contrast, many individuals use their wireless devices extensively on nights and weekends and use features such as text messages and music ringtones. Accordingly, wireless providers considered the costs for these services when developing pricing plans and calculating customer profitability. Therefore, individuals using their phone service sparingly could select a less-expensive plan with fewer minutes, for use mostly at night and on weekends, whereas more-demanding individuals and lucrative business customers chose plans with more telephone minutes, large amounts of wireless data bandwidth, and guaranteed reliability . . . for a higher price.

When AT&T began selling the iPhone in mid-2007, cost accountants projected the profitability for its new customers, and new plans were designed accordingly. Similar to traditional wireless plans, iPhone buyers were offered subscription options with different amounts of telephone minutes at different price points. For example, 450 telephone minutes cost $59.99, while 1,350 minutes were $99.99. However, to showcase the iPhone's wireless and Internet capabilities, Apple insisted that AT&T offer only one data package, an unlimited plan.

While the unlimited data package proved initially lucrative, technology developments added significant costs to AT&T. When Apple introduced the iPhone 3G in 2008, the third-generation data capabilities encouraged software developers to build new programs for the iPhone platform. Within two years, nearly 140,000 applications, ranging from Pandora's mobile music player to Mint's on-the-go budgeting program, were downloaded more than 3 billion times by iPhone users. Each of the applications, however, uses a lot of data bandwidth.

Recall that AT&T does not charge iPhone subscribers for marginal bandwidth use. As a result, subscribers who download and use many iPhone applications quickly became unprofitable for the company. With each 100MB of bandwidth costing AT&T $1, the company is currently considering cost-reducing options, such as limiting data access and changing its all-you-can-eat data subscription plan, but it is very concerned about alienating its customers.

iPhone application usage has also created a bigger cost problem for the company. With data bandwidth on the AT&T wireless network increasing by 5,000% between 2006 and 2009, the company's network is showing signs of strain and poor performance. To act on these concerns, AT&T will spend $18–19 billion making improvements to its data network in 2010, and more in the years to come. As a result, AT&T will need to balance customer satisfaction with ensuring that its iPhone customers remain profitable for the carrier.

Sources: AT&T Inc. and Apple Inc. 2007. AT&T and Apple announce simple, affordable service plans for iPhone. AT&T Inc. and Apple Inc. Press Release, June 26. http://www.apple.com/pr/library/2007/06/26plans.html; Fazard, Roben. 2010. AT&T's iPhone mess. *BusinessWeek*, February 3; Sheth, Niraj. 2010. AT&T, boosted and stressed by iPhone, lays out network plans. *Wall Street Journal*, January 29; Sheth, Niraj. 2010. For wireless carriers, iPad signals further loss of clout. *Wall Street Journal*, January 28.

lations, we assume that all these variable costs are variable with respect to units (cases) sold. (This means, for example, that average batch sizes remain the same as the total cases sold vary.) Without this assumption, the analysis would become more complex and would have to be done using the ABC-variance analysis approach described in Chapter 8. The basic insights, however, would not change.

Budgeted and actual operating data for June 2012 are:

Budget Data for June 2012

	Selling Price (1)	Variable Cost per Unit (2)	Contribution Margin per Unit (3) = (1) – (2)	Sales Volume in Units (4)	Sales Mix (Based on Units) (5)	Contribution Margin (6) = (3) × (4)
Wholesale channel	Rs 133.7	Rs 128.8	Rs 4.9	7,12,000	80%[a]	Rs 34,88,800
Retail channel	Rs 141.0	Rs 131.2	9.8	1,78,000	20	17,44,400
Total				8,90,000	100%	Rs 52,33,200

[a] Percentage of unit sales to wholesale channel = 7,12,000 units ÷ 8,90,000 total unit = 80%.

Actual Results for June 2012

	Selling Price (1)	Variable Cost per Unit (2)	Contribution Margin per Unit (3) = (1) – (2)	Sales Volume in Units (4)	Sales Mix (Based on Units) (5)	Contribution Margin (6) = (3) × 4)
Wholesale channel	Rs 133.7	Rs 128.8	Rs 4.9	7,56,000	84%	Rs 37,04,400
Retail channel	141.0	131.7	9.3	1,44,000	16	13,39,200
Total				9,00,000	100%	Rs 50,43,600

The budgeted and actual fixed distribution-channel costs and corporate-sustaining costs are Rs 16,05,000 and Rs 26,30,000, respectively (see Exhibit 14-6).

Recall that the levels of detail introduced in Chapter 7 included the static-budget variance (level 1), the flexible-budget variance (level 2), and the sales-volume variance (level 2). The sales-quantity and sales-mix variances are level 3 variances that subdivide the sales-volume variance.[6]

Static-Budget Variance

The *static-budget variance* is the difference between an actual result and the corresponding budgeted amount in the static budget. Our analysis focuses on the difference between actual and budgeted contribution margins (column 6 in the preceding tables). The total static-budget variance is Rs 1,89,600 U (actual contribution margin of Rs 50,43,600 – budgeted contribution margin of Rs 52,33,200). Exhibit 14-9 (columns 1 and 3) uses the columnar format introduced in Chapter 7 to show detailed calculations of the static-budget variance. Managers can gain more insight about the static-budget variance by subdividing it into the flexible-budget variance and the sales-volume variance.

Flexible-Budget Variance and Sales-Volume Variance

The *flexible-budget variance* is the difference between an actual result and the corresponding flexible-budget amount based on actual output level in the budget period. The flexible budget contribution margin is equal to budgeted contribution margin per unit times actual units sold of each product. Exhibit 14-9, column 2, shows the flexible-budget calculations. The flexible budget measures the contribution margin that Oasis would have budgeted for the actual quantities of cases sold. The flexible-budget variance is the difference between columns 1 and 2 in Exhibit 14-9. The only difference between columns 1 and 2 is that actual units sold of each product is multiplied by actual contribution margin per unit in column 1 and budgeted contribution margin per unit in column 2. The Rs 72,000 U flexible-budget variance arises because actual contribution margin on retail sales of Rs 9.3 per case

[6] The presentation of the variances in this chapter and the appendix draws on teaching notes prepared by J. K. Harris.

Exhibit 14-9 Flexible-Budget and Sales-Volume Variance Analysis of Oasis Bottling Company for June 2012

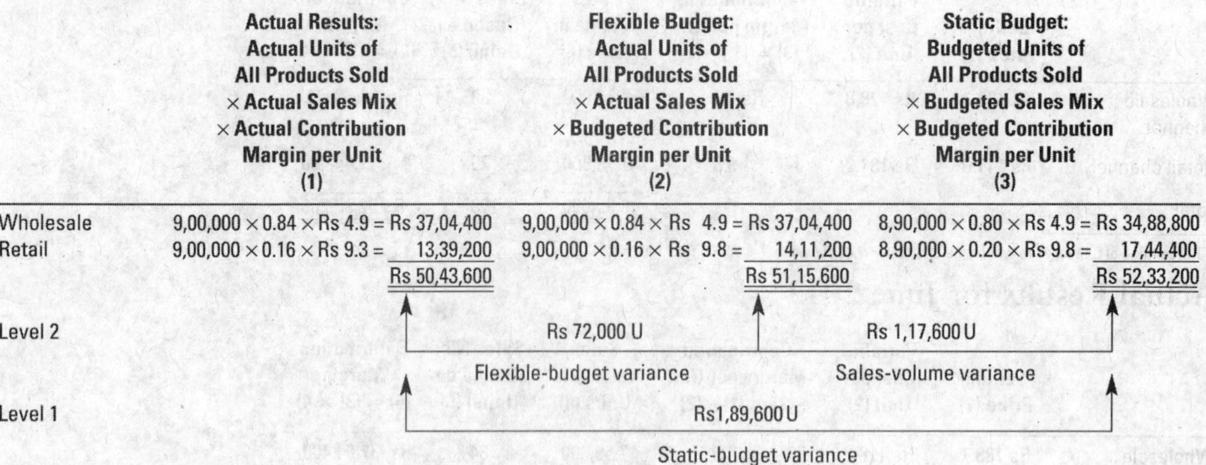

	Actual Results: Actual Units of All Products Sold × Actual Sales Mix × Actual Contribution Margin per Unit (1)	Flexible Budget: Actual Units of All Products Sold × Actual Sales Mix × Budgeted Contribution Margin per Unit (2)	Static Budget: Budgeted Units of All Products Sold × Budgeted Sales Mix × Budgeted Contribution Margin per Unit (3)
Wholesale	9,00,000 × 0.84 × Rs 4.9 = Rs 37,04,400	9,00,000 × 0.84 × Rs 4.9 = Rs 37,04,400	8,90,000 × 0.80 × Rs 4.9 = Rs 34,88,800
Retail	9,00,000 × 0.16 × Rs 9.3 = 13,39,200	9,00,000 × 0.16 × Rs 9.8 = 14,11,200	8,90,000 × 0.20 × Rs 9.8 = 17,44,400
	Rs 50,43,600	Rs 51,15,600	Rs 52,33,200

F = favorable effect on operating income; U = unfavorable effect on operating income.

is lower than the budgeted amount of Rs 9.8 per case. Oasis's management is aware that this difference of Rs 0.5 per case resulted from excessive price discounts, and they have put in place action plans to reduce discounts in the future.

The *sales-volume variance* is the difference between a flexible-budget amount and the corresponding static-budget amount. In Exhibit 14-9, the sales-volume variance shows the effect on budgeted contribution margin of the difference between actual quantity of units sold and budgeted quantity of units sold. The sales-volume variance of Rs 1,17,600 U is the difference between columns 2 and 3 in Exhibit 14-9. Oasis's managers can gain substantial insight into the sales-volume variance by subdividing it into the sales-mix variance and the sales-quantity variance.

Sales-Mix Variance

The sales-mix variance is the difference between (1) budgeted contribution margin for the *actual sales mix* and (2) budgeted contribution margin for the *budgeted sales mix*. The formula and computations are:

	Actual Units of All Products Sold	×	(Actual Sales-Mix Percentage − Budgeted Sales-Mix Percentage)	×	Budgeted Contribution Margin per Unit	=	Sales-Mix Variance
Wholesale	9,00,000 units	×	(0.84 − 0.80)	×	Rs 4.9 per unit	=	Rs 1,76,400 F
Retail	9,00,000 units	×	(0.16 − 0.20)	×	Rs 9.8 per unit	=	Rs 3,52,800 U
Total sales-mix variance							Rs 1,76,400 U

A favorable sales-mix variance arises for the wholesale channel because the 84% actual sales-mix percentage exceeds the 80% budgeted sales-mix percentage. In contrast, the retail channel has an unfavorable variance because the 16% actual sales-mix percentage is less than the 20% budgeted sales-mix percentage. The total sales-mix variance is unfavorable because actual sales mix shifted toward the less-profitable wholesale channel relative to budgeted sales mix.

The concept underlying the sales-mix variance is best explained in terms of composite unit. A **composite unit** is a hypothetical unit with weights based on the mix of individual units. Given the budgeted sales for June 2012, the composite unit consists of 0.80 units of sales to the wholesale channel and 0.20 units of sales to the retail channel. Therefore, the

Exhibit 14-10 Sales-Mix and Sales-Quantity Variance Analysis of Oasis Bottling Company for June 2009

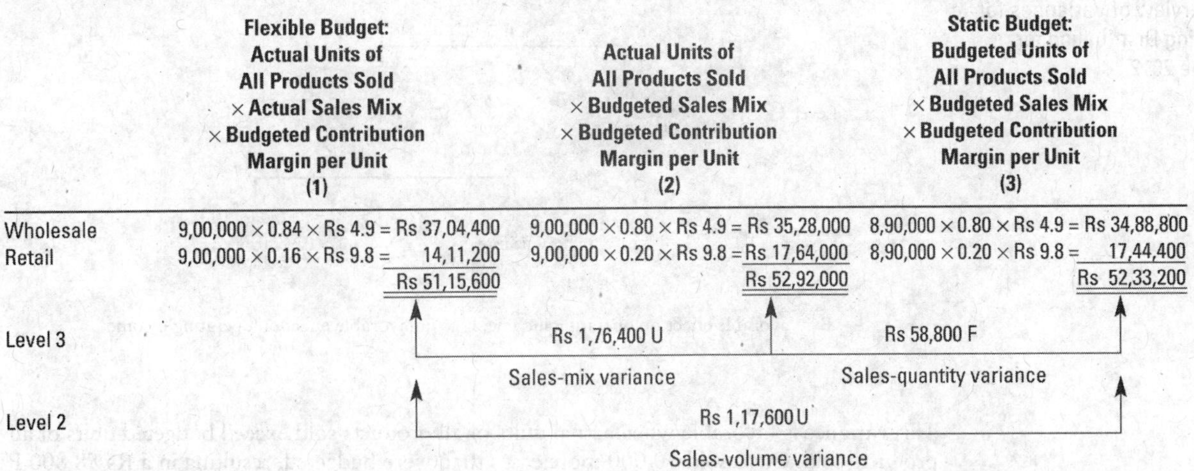

	Flexible Budget: Actual Units of All Products Sold × Actual Sales Mix × Budgeted Contribution Margin per Unit (1)	Actual Units of All Products Sold × Budgeted Sales Mix × Budgeted Contribution Margin per Unit (2)	Static Budget: Budgeted Units of All Products Sold × Budgeted Sales Mix × Budgeted Contribution Margin per Unit (3)
Wholesale	9,00,000 × 0.84 × Rs 4.9 = Rs 37,04,400	9,00,000 × 0.80 × Rs 4.9 = Rs 35,28,000	8,90,000 × 0.80 × Rs 4.9 = Rs 34,88,800
Retail	9,00,000 × 0.16 × Rs 9.8 = 14,11,200	9,00,000 × 0.20 × Rs 9.8 = Rs 17,64,000	8,90,000 × 0.20 × Rs 9.8 = 17,44,400
	Rs 51,15,600	Rs 52,92,000	Rs 52,33,200

Level 3: Rs 1,76,400 U Sales-mix variance; Rs 58,800 F Sales-quantity variance

Level 2: Rs 1,17,600 U Sales-volume variance

F = favorable effect on operating income; U = unfavorable effect on operating income.

budgeted contribution margin per composite unit for the budgeted sales mix is as follows:

$$(0.80) \times (\text{Rs } 4.9) + (0.20) \times (\text{Rs } 9.8) = \text{Rs } 5.880.^{7}$$

Similarly, for the actual sales mix, the composite unit consists of 0.84 units of sales to the wholesale channel and 0.16 units of sales to the retail channel. The budgeted contribution margin per composite unit for the actual sales mix is therefore as follows:

$$(0.84) \times (\text{Rs } 4.9) + (0.16) \times (\text{Rs } 9.8) = \text{Rs } 5.684.$$

The impact of the shift in sales mix is now evident. Spring obtains a lower budgeted contribution margin per composite unit of Rs 0.196 (Rs 5.880 – Rs 5.684). For the 900,000 units actually sold, this decrease translates to a Rs 1,76,400 U sales-mix variance (Rs 0.196 per unit × 900,000 units).

Managers should probe why the Rs 1,76,400 U sales-mix variance occurred in June 2012. Is the shift in sales mix because, as the analysis in the previous section showed, profitable retail customers proved to be more difficult to find? Is it because of a competitor in the retail channel providing better service at a lower price? Or is it because the initial sales-volume estimates were made without adequate analysis of the potential market?

Exhibit 14-10 uses the columnar format to calculate the sales-mix variance and the sales-quantity variances.

Sales-Quantity Variance

The **sales-quantity variance** is the difference between (1) budgeted contribution margin based on *actual units sold of all products* at the budgeted mix and (2) contribution margin in the static budget (which is based on *budgeted units of all products to be sold* at budgeted mix). The formula and computations are:

	(Actual Units of All Products Sold − Budgeted Units of All Products Sold)	×	Budgeted Sales-Mix Percentages	×	Budgeted Contribution Margin per Unit	=	Sales-Quantity Variance
Wholesale	(9,00,000 units – 8,90,000 units)	×	0.80	×	Rs 4.9 per unit	=	Rs 39,200 F
Retail	(9,00,000 units – 8,90,000 units)	×	0.20	×	Rs 9.8 per unit	=	Rs19,600 F
Total sales-quantity variance							Rs 58,800 F

[7] Budgeted contribution margin per composite unit can be computed in another way by dividing total budgeted contribution margin of Rs 52,33,200 by total budgeted units of 89,00,000: Rs 52,33,200 ÷ 8,90,000 units = Rs 5.880 per unit.

Exhibit 14-11

Overview of Variances for Spring Distribution for June 2012

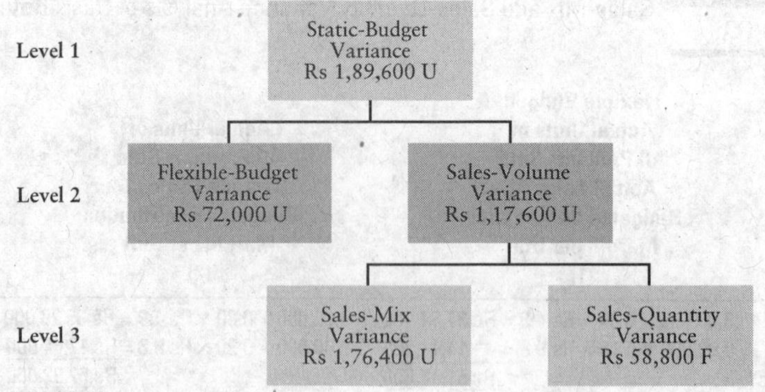

F = favorable effect on operating income; U = unfavorable effect on operating income

This variance is favorable when actual units of all products sold exceed budgeted units of all products sold. Oasis sold 10,000 more cases than were budgeted, resulting in a Rs 58,800 F sales-quantity variance (also equal to budgeted contribution margin per composite unit for the budgeted sales mix times additional cases sold, Rs 5.880 × 10,000). Managers would want to probe the reasons for the increase in sales. Did higher sales come as a result of a competitor's distribution problems? Better customer service? Or growth in the overall market? Further insight into the causes of the sales-quantity variance can be gained by analyzing changes in Oasis's share of the total industry market and in the size of that market. The sales-quantity variance can be de composed into market-share and market-size variances.

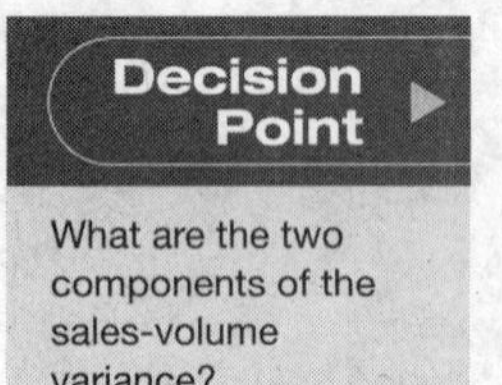

What are the two components of the sales-volume variance?

Exhibit 14-11 presents an overview of the sales-mix and sales-quantity variances for the Spring example. The sales-mix variance and sales-quantity variance can also be calculated in a multiproduct company, in which each individual product has a different contribution margin per unit. The Problem for Self-Study takes you through such a setting, and also demonstrates the link between these sales variances and the market-share and market-size variances studied earlier. The appendix to this chapter describes mix and quantity variances for production inputs.

Problem for Self-Study

The SB Enterprise manufactures two types of vinyl flooring. Budgeted and actual operating data for 2012 are:

	Static Budget			Actual Results		
	Commercial	**Residential**	**Total**	**Commercial**	**Residential**	**Total**
Unit sales in rolls	20,000	60,000	80,000	25,200	58,800	84,000
Contribution margin	Rs 10,00,00,000	Rs 24,00,00,000	Rs 34,00,00,000	Rs 11,97,00,000	Rs 24,69,60,000	Rs 36,66,60,000

In late 2011, a marketing research firm estimated industry volume for commercial and residential vinyl flooring for 2012 at 8,00,000 rolls. Actual industry volume for 2012 was 7,00,000 rolls.

Required

1. Compute the sales-mix variance and the sales-quantity variance by type of vinyl flooring and in total. (Compute all variances in terms of contribution margins.)

2. Compute the market-share variance and the market-size variance.
3. What insights do the variances calculated in 1 and 2 provide about SB Enterprise's performance in 2012?

Solution

1. Actual sales-mix percentage:

Commercial = 25,200 ÷ 84,000 = 0.30, or 30%

Residential = 58,800 ÷ 84,000 = 0.70, or 70%

Budgeted sales-mix percentage:

Commercial = 20,000 ÷ 80,000 = 0.25, or 25%

Residential = 60,000 ÷ 80,000 = 0.75, or 75%

Budgeted contribution margin per unit:

Commercial = Rs 10,00,00,000 ÷ 20,000 units = Rs 5,000 per unit

Residential = Rs 24,00,00,000 ÷ 60,000 units = Rs 4,000 per unit

	Actual units of All Products Sold	×	(Actual Sales-Mix Percentage − Budgeted Sales-Mix Percentage)	×	Budgeted Contribution Margin per Unit	=	Sales-Mix Variance
Commercial	84,000 units	×	(0.30 – 0.25)	×	Rs 5,000 per unit	=	Rs 2,10,00,000 F
Residential	84,000 units	×	(0.70 – 0.75)	×	Rs 4,000 per unit	=	1,68,00,000 U
Total sales-mix variance							Rs 42,00,000 F

	(Actual Units of All Products Sold − Budgeted Units of All Products Sold)	×	Budgeted Sales-Mix Percentage	×	Budgeted Contribution Margin per Unit	=	Sales-Quantity Variance
Commercial	(84,000 units – 80,000 units)	×	0.25	×	Rs 5,000 per unit	=	Rs 50,00,000 F
Residential	(84,000 units – 80,000 units)	×	0.75	×	Rs 4,000 per unit	=	1,20,00,000 F
Total sales-quantity variance							Rs 17,00,000 F

2. Actual market share = 84,000 ÷ 700,000 = 0.12, or 12%
Budgeted market share = 80,000 ÷ 800,000 units = 0.10, or 10%
Budgeted contribution margin per composite unit of budgeted mix = Rs 34,00,00,000 ÷ 80,000 units Rs 4,250 per units

Budgeted contribution margin per composite unit of budgeted mix can also be calculated as:

Commercial: Rs 5,000 per unit × 0.25	= Rs	1,250
Residential: Rs 4,000 per unit × 0.75	=	3,000
Budgeted contribution margin per composite unit	Rs	4,250

$$\text{Market-share variance} = \text{Actual market size in units} \times \left(\text{Actual market share} - \text{Budgeted market share}\right) \times \text{Budgeted contribution margin per composite unit for budgeted mix}$$

= 7,00,000 units × (0.12 – 0.10) × Rs 4,250 per unit

= Rs 5,95,00,000 F

$$\text{Market-size variance} = \left(\begin{array}{c}\text{Actual} \\ \text{market size} \\ \text{in units}\end{array} - \begin{array}{c}\text{Budgeted} \\ \text{market size} \\ \text{in units}\end{array}\right) \times \begin{array}{c}\text{Budgeted} \\ \text{market} \\ \text{share}\end{array} \times \begin{array}{c}\text{Budgeted} \\ \text{contribution margin} \\ \text{per composite unit} \\ \text{for budgeted mix}\end{array}$$

$$= (7{,}00{,}00 \text{ units} - 8{,}00{,}000 \text{ units}) \times 0.10 \times \text{Rs } 4{,}250 \text{ per unit}$$

$$= \text{Rs } 4{,}25{,}00{,}000 \text{ U}$$

Note that the algebraic sum of the market-share variance and the market-size variance is equal to the sales-quantity variance: Rs 5,95,00,000 F + Rs 4,25,00,000 U = Rs 1,70,00,000 F.

3. Both the total sales-mix variance and the total sales-quantity variance are favorable. The favorable total sales-mix variançe occurred because the actual mix comprised more of the higher-margin commercial vinyl flooring. The favorable total sales-quantity variance occurred because the actual total quantity of rolls sold exceeded the budgeted amount.

   The company's large favorable market-share variance is due to a 12% actual market share compared with a 10% budgeted market share. The market-size variance is unfavorable because the actual market size was 1,00,000 rolls less than the budgeted market size. SB's performance in 2012 appears to be very good. Although overall market size declined, the company sold more units than budgeted by gaining market share.

Decision Points

The following question-and-answer format summarizes the chapter's learning objectives. Each decision presents a key question related to a learning objective. The guidelines are the answer to that question.

Decision	Guidelines
1. What are four purposes for allocating costs to cost objects?	Four purposes of cost allocation are (a) to provide information for economic decisions, (b) to motivate managers and other employees, (c) to justify costs or compute reimbursement amounts, and (d) to measure income and assets for reporting to external parties. Different cost allocations are appropriate for different purposes.
2. What criteria should managers use to guide cost-allocation decisions?	Managers should use the cause-and-effect and the benefits-received criteria to guide most cost-allocation decisions. Other criteria are fairness or equity and ability to bear.
3. What are two key decisions managers must make when collecting costs in indirect-cost pools?	Two key decisions related to indirect-cost pools are the number of indirect-cost pools to form and the individual cost items to be included in each cost pool to make homogeneous cost pools.
4. Why can revenues differ across customers purchasing the same product?	Revenues can differ because of differences in the quantity purchased and price discounts given from the list selling price.
5. What is the advantage of using a customer-cost hierarchy?	Customer-cost hierarchies highlight how different cost pools have different types of cost drivers and how some costs can be reliably assigned to individual customers whereas other costs can be reliably assigned only to distribution channels or to companywide activities.

6. Why do customer-level costs differ across customers?	Different customers place different demands on a company's resources in terms of processing purchase orders, making deliveries, and customer support. Companies should be aware of and devote sufficient resources to maintaining and expanding relationships with customers who contribute significantly to profitability. Customer-profitability reports often highlight that a small percentage of customers contributes a large percentage of operating income.
7. What are the two components of the sales-volume variance?	The two components are (a) the difference between actual sales mix and budgeted sales mix (the sales-mix variance) and (b) the difference between actual unit sales and budgeted unit sales (the sales-quantity variance).
8. What are the two components of the sales-quantity variance?	The two components are (a) the difference between actual share of the market attained and budgeted share (the market-share variance) and (b) the difference between actual market size in units and budgeted market size in units (the market-size variance).

APPENDIX: MIX AND YIELD VARIANCES FOR SUBSTITUTABLE INPUTS

The framework for calculating the sales-mix variance and the sales-quantity variance can also be used to analyze production-input variances in cases in which managers have some leeway in combining and substituting inputs. For example, Del Monte can combine material inputs (such as pineapples, cherries, and grapes) in varying proportions for its cans of fruit cocktail. Within limits, these individual fruits are *substitutable inputs* in making the fruit cocktail.

We illustrate how the efficiency variance discussed in Chapter 7 can be subdivided into variances that highlight the financial impact of input mix and input yield when inputs are substitutable. Consider Delpino Corporation, which makes tomato ketchup. Our example focuses on direct material inputs and substitution among three of these inputs. The same approach can also be used to examine substitutable direct manufacturing labor inputs.

To produce ketchup of a specified consistency, color, and taste, Delpino mixes three types of tomatoes grown in different regions: Latin American tomatoes (Latoms), California tomatoes (Caltoms), and Florida tomatoes (Flotoms). Delpino's production standards require 1.60 tons of tomatoes to produce 1 ton of ketchup; 50% of the tomatoes are budgeted to be Latoms, 30% Caltoms, and 20% Flotoms. The direct material inputs budgeted to produce 1 ton of ketchup are:

0.80 (50% of 1.6) ton of Latoms at Rs 700 per ton	Rs 560
0.48 (30% of 1.6) ton of Caltoms at Rs 800 per ton	384
0.32 (20% of 1.6) ton of Flotoms at Rs 900 per ton	288
Total budgeted cost of 1.6 tons of tomatoes	Rs 1,232

Budgeted average cost per ton of tomatoes is Rs 1,232 ÷ 1.60 tons = Rs 770 per ton.

Because Delpino uses fresh tomatoes to make ketchup, no inventories of tomatoes are kept. Purchases are made as needed, so all price variances relate to tomatoes purchased and used. Actual results for June 2009 show that a total of 6,500 tons of tomatoes were used to produce 4,000 tons of ketchup:

3,250	tons of Latoms at actual cost of Rs 700 per ton	Rs 22,75,000
2,275	tons of Caltoms at actual cost of Rs 820 per ton	18,65,500
975	tons of Flotoms at actual cost of Rs 960 per ton	9,36,000
6,500	tons of tomatoes	50,76,500
Budgeted cost of 4,000 tons of ketchup at Rs 1,232 per ton		49,28,000
Flexible-budget variance for direct materials		Rs 1,48,500 U

Given the standard ratio of 1.60 tons of tomatoes to 1 ton of ketchup, 6,400 tons of tomatoes should be used to produce 4,000 tons of ketchup. At standard mix, quantities of each type of tomato required are:

Latoms:	$0.50 \times 6{,}400 = 3{,}200$ tons
Caltoms:	$0.30 \times 6{,}400 = 1{,}920$ tons
Flotoms:	$0.20 \times 6{,}400 = 1{,}280$ tons

Direct Materials Price and Efficiency Variances

Exhibit 14-12 presents in columnar format the analysis of the flexible-budget variance for direct materials discussed in Chapter 7. The materials price and efficiency variances are calculated separately for each input material and then added together. The variance analysis prompts Delpino to investigate the unfavorable price and efficiency variances. Why did it pay more for tomatoes and use greater quantities than they had budgeted? Were actual market prices of tomatoes higher, in general, or could the Purchasing Department have negotiated lower prices? Did the inefficiencies result from inferior tomatoes or from problems in processing?

Direct Materials Mix and Direct Materials Yield Variances

Managers sometimes have discretion to substitute one material for another. The manager of Delpino's ketchup plant has some leeway in combining Latoms, Caltoms, and Flotoms without affecting the ketchup's quality. We will assume that to maintain quality, mix percentages of each type of tomato can only vary up to 5% from standard mix. For example, the percentage of Caltoms in the mix can vary between 25% and 35% (30% ± 5%). When inputs are substitutable, direct materials efficiency improvement relative to budgeted costs can come from two sources: (1) using a cheaper mix to produce a given quantity of output, measured by the direct materials mix variance, and (2) using less input to achieve a given quantity of output, measured by the direct materials yield variance.

Holding actual total quantity of all direct materials inputs used constant, the total **direct materials mix** variance is the difference between (1) budgeted cost for actual mix of actual total quantity of direct materials used and (2) budgeted cost of budgeted mix of actual total quantity of direct materials used. Holding budgeted input mix constant, the **direct materials yield variance** is the difference between (1) budgeted cost of direct materials based on actual total quantity of direct materials used and (2) flexible-budget cost of direct materials based on budgeted total quantity of direct materials

Exhibit 14-12 Direct Materials Price and Efficiency Variances for the Delpino Corporation June 2012

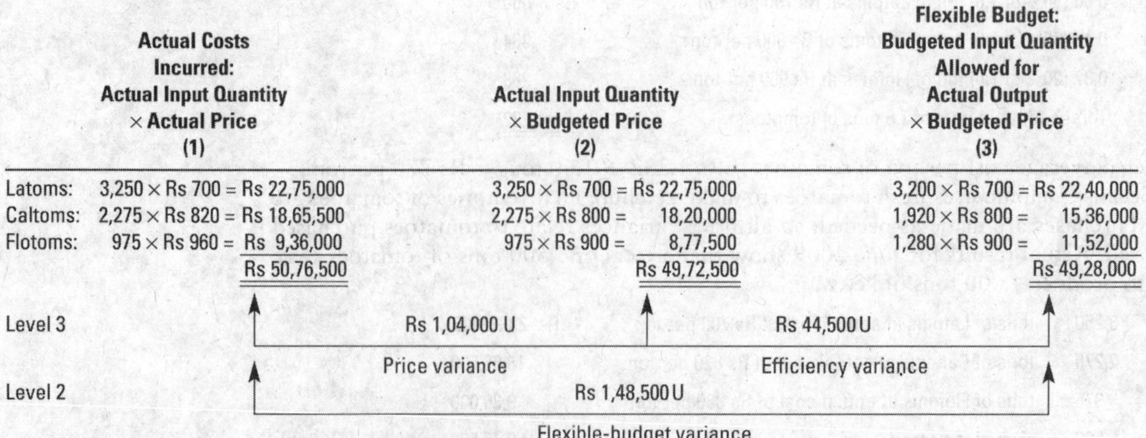

	Actual Costs Incurred: Actual Input Quantity × Actual Price (1)	Actual Input Quantity × Budgeted Price (2)	Flexible Budget: Budgeted Input Quantity Allowed for Actual Output × Budgeted Price (3)
Latoms:	3,250 × Rs 700 = Rs 22,75,000	3,250 × Rs 700 = Rs 22,75,000	3,200 × Rs 700 = Rs 22,40,000
Caltoms:	2,275 × Rs 820 = Rs 18,65,500	2,275 × Rs 800 = 18,20,000	1,920 × Rs 800 = 15,36,000
Flotoms:	975 × Rs 960 = Rs 9,36,000	975 × Rs 900 = 8,77,500	1,280 × Rs 900 = 11,52,000
	Rs 50,76,500	Rs 49,72,500	Rs 49,28,000

Level 3: Rs 1,04,000 U Price variance; Rs 44,500 U Efficiency variance

Level 2: Rs 1,48,500 U Flexible-budget variance

F = favorable effect on operating income; U = unfavorable effect on operating income.

Direct materials mix variance The direct materials mix variance is the sum of the direct materials mix variances for each input:

The direct materials mix variances are:

$$\begin{matrix}\text{Direct}\\ \text{materials}\\ \text{mix variance}\\ \text{for each input}\end{matrix} = \begin{matrix}\text{Actual total}\\ \text{quantity of all}\\ \text{direct materials}\\ \text{inputs used}\end{matrix} \times \left(\begin{matrix}\text{Actual}\\ \text{direct materials}\\ \text{input mix}\\ \text{percentage}\end{matrix} - \begin{matrix}\text{Budgeted}\\ \text{direct materials}\\ \text{input mix}\\ \text{percentage}\end{matrix}\right) \times \begin{matrix}\text{Budgeted}\\ \text{price of}\\ \text{direct materials}\\ \text{input}\end{matrix}$$

Latoms:	6,500 tons × (0.50 − 0.50) × Rs 700 per ton = 6,500 × 0.00 × Rs 700	=	Rs 0
Caltoms:	6,500 tons × (0.35 − 0.30) × Rs 800 per ton = 6,500 × 0.05 × Rs 800	=	2,60,000 U
Flotoms:	6,500 tons × (0.15 − 0.20) × Rs 900 per ton = 6,500 × 0.05 × Rs 900	=	2,92,500 F
Total direct materials mix variance			Rs 32,500 F

The direct materials mix variance is favorable because relative to the budgeted mix, Delpino substitutes 5% of the cheaper Caltoms for 5% of the more-expensive Flotoms.

Direct Materials Yield Variance The direct materials yield variance is the sum of the direct materials yield variances for each input:

$$\begin{matrix}\text{Direct}\\ \text{materials}\\ \text{yield variance}\\ \text{for each input}\end{matrix} = \left(\begin{matrix}\text{Actual total}\\ \text{quantity of}\\ \text{all direct}\\ \text{materials}\\ \text{inputs used}\end{matrix} - \begin{matrix}\text{Budgeted total}\\ \text{quantity of all}\\ \text{direct materials}\\ \text{inputs allowed}\\ \text{for actual output}\end{matrix}\right) \times \begin{matrix}\text{Budgeted}\\ \text{direct materials}\\ \text{input mix}\\ \text{percentage}\end{matrix} \times \begin{matrix}\text{Budgeted}\\ \text{price of}\\ \text{direct materials}\\ \text{input}\end{matrix}$$

The direct materials yield variances are:

Latoms:	(6,500 − 6,400) tons × 0.50 × Rs 700 per ton = 100 × 0.50 = Rs 700 =	Rs 35,000 U
Caltoms:	(6,500 − 6,400) tons × 0.30 × Rs 800 per ton = 100 × 0.30 = Rs 800 =	24,000 U
Flotoms:	(6,500 − 6,400) tons × 0.20 × Rs 900 per ton = 100 = 0.20 = Rs 900 =	18,000 U
Total direct materials yield variance		Rs 77,000 U

The direct materials yield variance is unfavorable because Delpino used 6,500 tons of tomatoes rather than the 6,400 tons that it should have used to produce 4,000 tons of

Exhibit 14-13 Total Direct Materials Yield and Mix Variances for the Delpino Corporation for June 2012

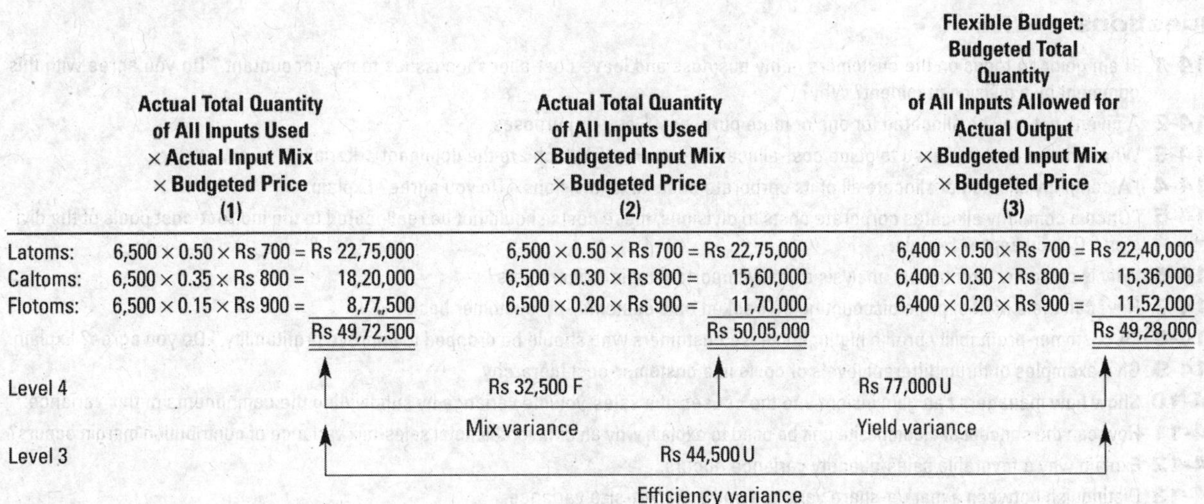

	Actual Total Quantity of All Inputs Used × Actual Input Mix × Budgeted Price (1)	Actual Total Quantity of All Inputs Used × Budgeted Input Mix × Budgeted Price (2)	Flexible Budget: Budgeted Total Quantity of All Inputs Allowed for Actual Output × Budgeted Input Mix × Budgeted Price (3)
Latoms:	6,500 × 0.50 × Rs 700 = Rs 22,75,000	6,500 × 0.50 × Rs 700 = Rs 22,75,000	6,400 × 0.50 × Rs 700 = Rs 22,40,000
Caltoms:	6,500 × 0.35 × Rs 800 = 18,20,000	6,500 × 0.30 × Rs 800 = 15,60,000	6,400 × 0.30 × Rs 800 = 15,36,000
Flotoms:	6,500 × 0.15 × Rs 900 = 8,77,500	6,500 × 0.20 × Rs 900 = 11,70,000	6,400 × 0.20 × Rs 900 = 11,52,000
	Rs 49,72,500	Rs 50,05,000	Rs 49,28,000

F = favorable effect on operating income; U = unfavorable effect on operating income.

ketchup. Holding the budgeted mix and budgeted prices of tomatoes constant, the budgeted cost per ton of tomatoes in the budgeted mix is Rs 770 per ton. The unfavorable yield variance represents the budgeted cost of using 100 more tons of tomatoes, (6,500 – 6,400) tons × Rs 770 per ton = Rs 77,000 U. Delpino would want to investigate reasons for this unfavorable yield variance. For example, did the substitution of the cheaper Caltoms for Flotoms that resulted in the favorable mix variance also cause the unfavorable yield variance?

The direct materials variances computed in Exhibits 14-12 and 14-13 can be summarized as follows:

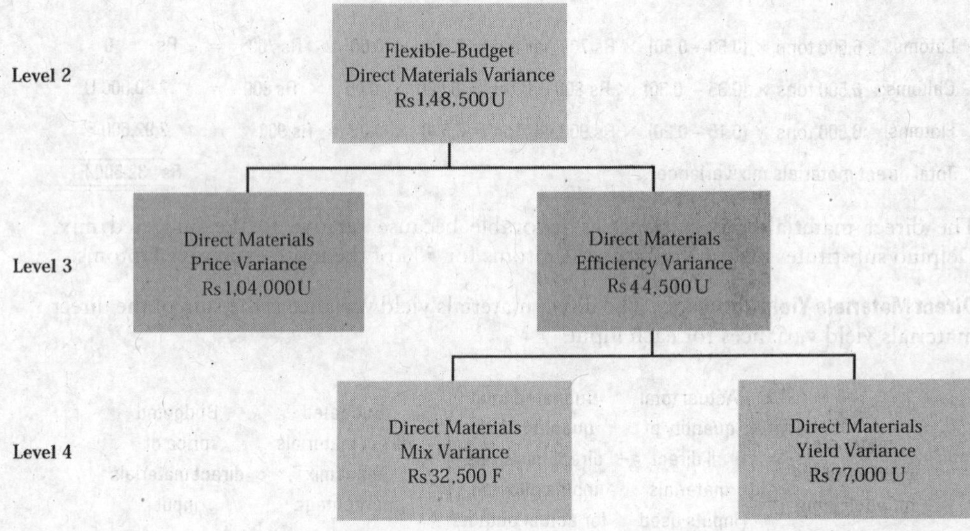

TERMS TO LEARN

This chapter and the Glossary at the end of the book contain definitions of:

composite unit (**p. 600**)
customer-cost hierarchy (**p. 591**)
customer-profitability analysis (**p. 590**)
direct materials mix variance (**p. 606**)
direct materials yield variance (**p. 606**)
homogeneous cost pool (**p. 589**)
market-share variance (**p. 603**)
market-size variance (**p. 603**)
price discount (**p. 591**)
sales-mix variance (**p. 600**)
sales-quantity variance (**p. 601**)

ASSIGNMENT MATERIAL

Questions

14-1 "I am going to focus on the customers of my business and leave cost-allocation issues to my accountant." Do you agree with this comment by a division president? Why?

14-2 A given cost may be allocated for one or more purposes. List four purposes.

14-3 What criteria might be used to guide cost-allocation decisions? Which are the dominant criteria?

14-4 "A company should not allocate all of its corporate costs to its divisions." Do you agree? Explain.

14-5 "Once a company allocates corporate costs to divisions, these costs should not be reallocated to the indirect-cost pools of the division." Do you agree? Explain.

14-6 Why is customer-profitability analysis a vitally important topic to managers?

14-7 How can the extent of price discounting be tracked on a customer-by-customer basis?

14-8 "A customer-profitability profile highlights those customers who should be dropped to improve profitability." Do you agree? Explain.

14-9 Give examples of three different levels of costs in a customer-cost hierarchy.

14-10 Show how managers can gain insight into the causes of a sales-volume variance by subdividing the components of this variance.

14-11 How can the concept of a composite unit be used to explain why an unfavorable total sales-mix variance of contribution margin occurs?

14-12 Explain why a favorable sales-quantity variance occurs.

14-13 Distinguish between a market-share variance and a market-size variance.

14-14 Why might some companies not compute market-size and market-share variances?

14-15 Explain how the direct materials mix and yield variances provide additional information about the direct materials efficiency variance.

Solved Examples

14-16 Cost allocation and motivation. Reliance Petroleum Company is engaged in all phases of exploring, refining, and marketing of oil and petrochemical products. To ensure full compliance with all applicable laws, the company has a legal department staffed by lawyers who have expertise in a variety of legal areas. The top management of Reliance wants to motivate all operating managers to seek legal counsel from the in-house lawyers whenever necessary to avoid violation of any laws during the course of its operations.

Currently, users of the legal Department are allocated cost at a Rs 400 standard hourly rate based on actual usage. The chief financial officer has suggested that department managers would make more use of the Legal Department services, and thus avoid potential legal pitfalls, if the service was provided free of cost to their departments.

Comment on the proposal of the chief financial officer. Do you have any alternative suggestion(s)?

Solution

Cost allocation and motivation.

Because corporate policy encourages line managers to seek legal counsel on pertinent issues from the Legal Department, any step in the direction of reducing costs of legal department services would be consistent with the corporate policy.

Currently a user department is charged a standard fee of Rs 400 per hour based on actual usage. It is possible that some managers may not be motivated to seek the legal counsel they need due to the high allocated cost of the service. It is also possible that those managers whose departments are currently experiencing budgetary cost overruns may be disinclined to make use of the service; it would save them from the Legal Department's cost allocation. However, it could potentially result in much costlier penalties for Reliance later if the corporation inadvertently engaged in some activities that violated one or more laws.

It is quite likely that the line managers would seek legal counsel, whenever there were any pertinent legal issues, if the service were free. Making the service of the Legal Department free, however, might induce some managers to make excessive use of the service. To avoid any potential abuse, Reliance may want to adjust the rate downward considerably, perhaps at a level lower than what it would cost if outside legal services were sought, but not eliminate it altogether. As long as the managers know that their respective departments would be charged for using the service, they would be disinclined to make use of it unnecessarily. However, they would be motivated to use it when necessary because it would be considered a "good value" if the standard hourly rate was low enough.

14-17 Cost allocation to divisions. Taj Palace is situated near sea shore in Mumbai. The complex includes a 300-room hotel, a shopping centre, and a restaurant. As Taj's new controller, you are asked to recommend the basis to be used for allocating fixed overhead costs to the three divisions in 2012. You are presented with the following income statement information for 2011:

	Hotel	Restaurant	Shopping Centre
Revenues	Rs 16,42,50,000	Rs 5,25,60,000	Rs 12,34,00,000
Direct costs	9,81,92,600	3,74,91,720	4,24,87,680
Segment margin	Rs 6,60,57,400	Rs 1,50,68,280	Rs 8,09,12,320

You are also given the following data on the three segments:

	Hotel	Restaurant	Shopping Centre
Floor space (square feet)	80,000	16,000	64,000
Number of employees	200	50	250

You may choose to allocate indirect costs based on direct costs, square feet, or the number of employees. Total fixed overhead for 2011 was Rs 14,55,00,000.

Required

1. Calculate segment margins in percentage terms prior to allocating fixed overhead costs.
2. Allocate indirect costs to the three divisions using each of the three allocation bases suggested. Calculate segment margins in rupees and percentage terms with each allocation base.
3. Discuss the results. How would you decide how to allocate indirect costs to the divisions? Why?
4. Would you recommend closing any of the three divisions (and possibly reallocating resources to other divisions) as a result of your analysis? If so, which division would you close and why?

Solution

Cost allocation to divisions.

1.

	Hotel	Restaurant	Shopping Centre	Total
Revenue	Rs 16,42,50,000	Rs 5,25,60,000	Rs 12,34,00,000	Rs 34,02,10,000
Direct costs	9,81,92,600	3,74,91,720	4,24,87,680	17,81,72,000
Segment margin	Rs 6,60,57,400	Rs 1,50,68,280	Rs 8,09,12,320	16,20,38,000
Indirect costs				14,55,00,000
Income before taxes				Rs 1,65,38,000
Segment margin %	40.22%	28.67%	65.57%	

2.

	Hotel	Restaurant	Shopping Centre	Total
Direct costs	Rs 9,81,92,600	Rs 3,74,91,720	Rs 4,24,87,680	Rs 17,81,72,000
Direct cost %	55.11%	21.04%	23.85%	100.00%
Square footage	80,000	16,000	64,000	160,000
Square footage %	50.00%	10.00%	40.00%	100.00%
# of Employees	200	50	250	500
# of Employees %	40.00%	10.00%	50.00%	100.00%

A: Cost allocation based on direct costs:

	Hotel	Restaurant	Shopping Centre	Total
Revenue	Rs 16,42,50,000	Rs 5,25,60,000	Rs 12,34,00,000	Rs 34,02,10,000
Direct costs	9,81,92,600	3,74,91,720	4,24,87,680	17,81,72,000
Segment margin	6,60,57,400	1,50,68,280	8,09,12,320	16,20,38,000
Allocated indirect costs	8,01,85,050	3,06,13,200	3,47,01,750	14,55,00,000
Segment pre-tax income	Rs (1,41,27,650)	Rs (1,55,44,920)	Rs 4,62,10,570	Rs 1,65,38,000
Segment pre-tax income %	–8.60%	–29.58%	37.45%	

B: Cost allocation based on floor space:

	Hotel	Restaurant	Shopping Centre	Total
Allocated indirect costs	Rs 7,27,50,000	Rs 1,45,50,000	Rs 5,82,00,000	Rs 14,55,00,000
Segment pre-tax income	Rs (66,92,600)	Rs 5,18,280	Rs 2,27,12,320	Rs 1,65,38,000
Segment pre-tax income %	–4.07%	0.99%	18.41%	

C: Cost allocation based on # of employees

	Hotel	Restaurant	Shopping Centre	Total
Allocated indirect costs	Rs 5,82,00,000	Rs 1,45,50,000	Rs 7,27,50,000	Rs 14,55,00,000
Segment pre-tax income	Rs 78,57,400	Rs 5,18,280	Rs 81,62,320	Rs 1,65,38,000
Segment pre-tax income %	4.78%	0.99%	6.61%	

3. The segment pre-tax income percentages show the dramatic effect of choice of the cost allocation base on reported numbers:

Denominator	Hotel	Restaurant	Shopping Centre
Direct costs	– 8.60%	– 29.58%	37.45%
Floor space	– 4.07	0.99	18.41
# of employees	4.78	0.99	6.61

The decision context should guide (a) whether costs should be allocated, and (b) the preferred cost allocation base. Decisions about, say, performance measurement may be made on a combination of financial and nonfinancial measures. It may well be that Taj Palace may prefer to exclude allocated costs from the financial measures to reduce areas of dispute.

Where cost allocation is required, the cause-and-effect and benefits-received criteria are recommended in Chapter 13. The Rs 14,55,00,000 is a fixed overhead cost. This means that on a short-run basis, the cause-and-effect criterion is not appropriate but Taj Palace could attempt to identify the cost drivers for these costs in the long run when these costs are likely to be more variable. Taj should look at how the Rs 14,55,00,000 cost benefits the three divisions. This will help guide the choice of an allocation base in the short run.

4. The analysis in requirement 2 should not guide the decision on whether to shut down any of the divisions. The overhead costs are fixed costs in the short run. It is not clear how these costs would be affected in the long run if Taj Palace shut down one of the divisions. Also, each division is not independent of the other two. A decision to shut down, say, the restaurant likely would negatively affect the attendance at the shopping centre and possibly the hotel. Taj Palace should examine the future revenue and future cost implications of different resource investments in the three divisions. This is a future-oriented exercise, whereas the analysis in requirement 2 is an analysis of past costs.

14-18 Cost allocation to divisions. J. K. Paper Corporation has three divisions: Fibers, Paper, and Pulp. As J. K. Paper's new controller, you are reviewing the basis to be used for allocating fixed overhead costs to the three divisions in 2012. The following information is available for 2011:

	Pulp	Paper	Fibers
Revenue	Rs 85,00,000	Rs 1,75,00,000	Rs 2,40,00,000
Administrative costs	Rs 12,00,000	Rs 18,00,000	Rs 30,00,000
Number of employees	300	250	450
Floor space (square feet)	30,000	24,000	66,000
Segment margin	Rs 32,00,000	Rs 71,00,000	Rs 97,00,000

In the past, J. K. Paper has allocated fixed overhead costs to the division using segment margin percentages. A review of the fixed overhead costs indicates that they consist of the following:

Human resource management	Rs 18,00,000
Facility	27,00,000
Corporate administration	45,00,000
Total	Rs 90,00,000

After considering the nature of the fixed-cost items, you decide to make the allocations in 2012 using the following bases:

Human resource management	Number of employees
Facility	Floor space
Corporate administration	Divisional administrative costs

Required

1. Allocate 2011 indirect costs to the three divisions using segment margin percentages.
2. Allocate 2011 indirect costs to the three divisions using the bases you have selected.
3. Discuss the reason(s) why your approach is preferable.

Solution

Cost allocation to divisions.

1.	Pulp	Paper	Fibers
Segment margin	Rs 32,00,000	Rs 71,00,000	Rs 97,00,000
Percentages	16.0%	35.5%	48.5%
Allocation (Rs 9,000,000 × 16.0%, 35.5%, 48.5%)	Rs 14,40,000	Rs 31,95,000	Rs 43,65,000

2. Percentages for new bases of allocation

	Pulp	Paper	Fibers
Number of employees	300	250	450
Percentages	30%	25%	45%
Floor space (square feet)	30,000	24,000	66,000
Percentages	25%	20%	55%
Divisional administrative	Rs 12,00,000	Rs 18,00,000	Rs 30,00,000
Percentages	20%	30%	50%

Allocation of indirect costs

	Pulp	Paper	Fibers
Human resource management (Rs 1,800,000 × 30%, 25%, 45%)	Rs 5,40,000	Rs 4,50,000	Rs 8,10,000
Facility (Rs 2,700,000 × 25%, 20%, 55%)	6,75,000	5,40,000	14,85,000
Corporate administration (Rs 4,500,000 × 20%, 30%, 50%)	9,00,000	13,50,000	22,50,000
Total	Rs 21,15,000	Rs 23,40,000	Rs 45,45,000

3. The new approach is preferable because it is based on cause-and-effect relationships between costs and their respective cost drivers in the long run.

Human resource management costs are allocated using the number of employees in each division because the costs for recruitment, training, etc., are mostly related to the number of employees in each division. Facility costs are mostly incurred on the basis of space occupied by each division. Corporate administration costs are allocated on the basis of divisional administrative costs because these costs are incurred to provide support to divisional administrations.

14-19 Customer profitability, distribution. Reliable Medicines Supplier (RMS) is a distributor of pharmaceutical products. Its ABC system has five activities:

Activity Area	Cost Driver Rate in 2011
1. Order processing	Rs 400 per order
2. Line-item ordering	Rs 30 per line item
3. Store deliveries	Rs 500 per store delivery
4. Carton deliveries	Rs 10 per carton
5. Shelf-stocking	Rs 160 per stocking-hour

The controller of RMS wants to use ABC system to examine individual customer profitability within each distribution market. He focuses first on the Ma and Pa single-store distribution market. Two customers are used to exemplify the insights available with the ABC approach. Data pertaining to these two customers in August 2011 are as follows:

	Chemist Pharmacy	Patent Pharmacy
Total orders	12	10
Average line items per order	10	18
Total store deliveries	6	10
Average cartons sent per store delivery	24	20
Average hours of shelf stocking per store delivery	0	0.5

Average revenue per delivery	Rs 24,000	Rs 18,000
Average cost of goods sold per delivery	Rs 21,000	Rs 16,500

Required

1. Use the ABC information to compute the operating income of each customer in August 2010. Comment on the results.
2. The Controller ranks the individual customers in the Ma and Pa single-store distribution market on the basis of monthly operating income. The cumulative operating income of the top 20% of customers is Rs 5,56,800. RMS reports negative operating income of Rs 2,12,470 for the bottom 40% of its customers. Make four recommendations that you think RMS should consider in light of this new customer profitability information.

Solution

Customer profitability, distribution.

1. The activity-based costing for each customer is:

	Chemist Pharmacy	Patent Pharmacy
1. Order processing, Rs 400 × 12; Rs 400 × 10	Rs 4,800	Rs 4,000
2. Line-item ordering, Rs 30 × (12 × 10;10 × 18)	3,600	5,400
3. Store deliveries, Rs 500 × 6; Rs 500 × 10	3,000	5,000
4. Carton deliveries, Rs 10 × (6 × 24; 10 × 20)	1,440	2,000
5. Shelf-stocking, Rs 160 × (6 × 0; 10 × 0.5)	0	800
Operating costs	Rs 12,840	Rs 17,200

The operating income of each customer is:

	Chemist Pharmacy	Patent Pharmacy
Revenues, Rs 24,000 × 6; Rs 18,000 × 10	Rs 1,44,000	Rs 1,80,000
Cost of goods sold, Rs 21,000 × 6; Rs 16,500 × 10	1,26,000	1,65,000
Gross margin	18,000	15,000
Operating costs	12,840	17,200
Operating income	Rs 5,160	Rs (2,200)

Patent Pharmacy has a lower gross margin percentage than Chemist (8.33% vs. 12.50%) and consumes more resources to obtain this lower margin.

2. Ways RMS could use this information include:
   a. Pay increased attention to the top 20% of the customers. This could entail asking them for ways to improve service. Alternatively, RMS may want to highlight to its own personnel the importance of these customers; e.g., it could entail stressing to delivery people the importance of never missing delivery dates for these customers.
   b. Work out ways internally at RMS to reduce the rate per cost driver; e.g., reduce the cost per order by having better order placement linkages with customers. This cost reduction by RMS will improve the profitability of all customers.
   c. Work with customers so that their behavior reduces the total "system-wide" costs. At a minimum, this approach could entail having customers make fewer orders and fewer line items. The rationale is that a reduction in the number of line items (diversity of products) carried by Ma and Pa stores may reduce the diversity of products RMS carries.
   There are several options here:
   - Simple verbal persuasion by showing customers cost drivers at RMS.
   - Explicitly pricing out activities like cartons delivered and shelf-stocking so that customers pay for the costs they cause.
   - Restricting options available to certain customers, e.g., customers with low revenues could be restricted to one free delivery per week.

   An even more extreme example is working with customers so that deliveries are easier to make and shelf-stocking can be done faster.
   d. Offer salespeople bonuses based on the operating income of each customer rather than the gross margin of each customer.

14-20 Variance analysis, multiple products. Coca Cola manufactures and sells three soft drinks: Kola, Soda, and Limca. Budgeted and actual results for 2011 (all in rupees) are as follows:

	Budget for 2011			Actual for 2011		
Product	Selling Price per Carton	Variable Cost per Carton	Cartons Sold	Selling Price per Carton	Variable Cost per Carton	Cartons Sold
Kola	Rs 60	Rs 40	4,00,000	Rs 62	Rs 45	4,80,000
Soda	Rs 40	Rs 28	6,00,000	Rs 42.5	Rs 27.5	9,00,000
Limca	Rs 70	Rs 45	15,00,000	Rs 68	Rs 46	16,20,000

Required

1. Compute the total sales-volume variance, the total sales-mix variance, and the total sales-quantity variance. (Calculate all variances in terms of contribution margin). Show results for each product in your computations.
2. What inferences can you draw from the variances computed in requirement 1?

Solution

Variance analysis, multiple products.

1. **Budget for 2011**

	Selling Price (1)	Variable Cost per Unit (2)	Contribution Margin per Unit (3) = (1) – (2)	Units Sold (4)	Sales Mix (5)	Contribution Margin (6) = (3) × (4)
Kola	Rs 60	Rs 40	Rs 20	4,00,000	16%	Rs 80,00,000
Soda	40	28	12	6,00,000	24	72,00,000
Limca	70	45	25	15,00,000	60	3,75,00,000
Total				25,00,000	100%	Rs 5,27,00,000

Actual for 2011

	Selling Price (1)	Variable Cost per Unit (2)	Contribution Margin per Unit (3) = (1) – (2)	Units Sold (4)	Sales Mix (5)	Contribution Margin (6) = (3) × (4)
Kola	Rs 62	Rs 45	Rs 17	4,80,000	16%	Rs 81,60,000
Soda	42.5	27.5	15	9,00,000	30	1,35,00,000
Limca	68	46	22	16,20,000	54	3,56,40,000
Total				30,00,000	100%	Rs 5,73,00,000

Solution Exhibit 14-20 presents the sales-volume, sales-quantity, and sales-mix variances for each product and in total for 2011.

$$\text{Sales-volume variance} = \left(\text{Actual sales quantity in units} - \text{Budgeted sales quantity in units}\right) \times \text{Budgeted contribution margin per unit}$$

Kola	= (4,80,000 – 4,00,000) × Rs 20	=	Rs 16,00,000 F
Soda	= (9,00,000 – 6,00,000) × Rs 12	=	36,00,000 F
Limca	= (16,20,000 – 15,00,000) × Rs 25	=	30,00,000 F
Total			Rs 82,00,000 F

$$\text{Sales-quantity variance} = \left(\text{Actual units of all product sold} - \text{Budgeted units of all products sold}\right) \times \text{Budgeted sales-mix percentage} \times \text{Budgeted contribution margin per unit}$$

Kola	= (30,00,000 – 25,00,000) × 0.16 × Rs 20	=	Rs 16,00,000 F
Soda	= (30,00,000 – 25,00,000) × 0.24 × Rs 12	=	14,40,000 F
Limca	= (30,00,000 – 25,00,000) × 0.60 × Rs 25	=	75,00,000 F
Total			Rs 1,05,40,00 F

$$\text{Sales-mix} = \text{Actual units of all products sold} \times \left(\text{Actual sales-mix percentage} - \text{Budgeted sales-mix percentage}\right) \times \text{Budged contribution margin per unit}$$

Kola	= 30,00,000 × (0.16 – 0.16) × Rs 20	=	Rs 0
Soda	= 30,00,000 × (0.30 – 0.24) × Rs 12	=	21,60,000 F
Limca	= 30,00,000 × (0.54 – 0.60) × Rs 25	=	45,00,000 U
Total			Rs 23,40,000 U

2. The breakdown of the favorable sales-volume variance of Rs 82,00,000 shows that the biggest contributor is the 5,00,000 unit increase in sales resulting in a favorable sales-quantity variance of Rs 1,05,40,000. There is a partially offsetting unfavorable sales-mix variance of Rs 23,40,000 in contribution margin.

F = favorable effect on operating income; U = unfavorable effect on operating income

SOLUTION EXHIBIT 14-20

Sales-Mix and Sales-Quantity Variance Analysis of Coca cola for 2011

	Flexible Budget: Actual Units of All Products Sold × Actual Sales-Mix × Budgeted Contribution Margin Per Unit	Actual Units of All Products Sold × Budgeted Sales-Mix × Budgeted Contribution Margin Per Unit	Static Budget: Budgeted Units of All Products Sold × Budgeted Sales-Mix × Budgeted Contribution Margin Per Unit
Kola	30,00,000 × 0.16 × Rs 20 = Rs 96,00,000	30,00,000 × 0.16 × Rs 20 = Rs 96,00,000	25,00,000 × 0.16 × Rs 20 = Rs 80,00,000
Soda	30,00,000 × 0.30 × Rs 12 = Rs 1,08,00,000	30,00,000 × 0.24 × Rs 12 = Rs 86,40,000	25,00,000 × 0.24 × Rs 12 = Rs 72,00,000
Limca	30,00,000 × 0.54 × Rs 25 = Rs 4,05,00,000	30,00,000 × 0.60 × Rs 25 = Rs 4,50,00,000	25,00,000 × 0.60 × Rs 25 = Rs 3,75,00,000
	Rs 6,09,00,000	Rs 6,32,40,000	Rs 5,27,00,000

Rs 23,40,000 U — Sales-mix variance

Rs 1,05,40,000 F — Sales-quantity variance

Rs 82,00,000 F — Sales-volume variance

14-21 Market-share and market-size variances (continuation of 14-20). Coca Cola prepared the budget for 2006 assuming a 10 per cent market share based on total sales in the Western region of India. The total soft drinks market was estimated to reach sales of 250 lakh cartons in the region. However, actual total sales volume in the Western region was 240 lakh cartons.

Required Calculate the market-share and market-size variances for Coca Cola in 2011. (Report all variances in terms of contribution margin.) Comment on the results.

Solution

Market-share and market-size variances (continuation of 14-20).

	Actual	Budgeted
Western region	240 lakh	250 lakh
Coca cola	30 lakh	25 lakh
Market share	12.5%	10%

Average budgeted contribution margin per unit = Rs 21.08 (Rs 5,27,00,000 × 25,00,000)

Solution Exhibit 14-21 presents the sales-quantity variance, market-size variance, and market-share variance for 2011.

$$\text{Market-share variance} = \text{Actual market size in units} \times \left(\text{Actual market share} - \text{Budgeted market share}\right) \times \text{Budgeted contribution margin per composite unit for budgeted mix}$$

$$= 2{,}40{,}00{,}000 \times (0.125 - 0.10) \times \text{Rs } 21.08$$
$$= 2{,}40{,}00{,}000 \times .025 \times \text{Rs } 21.08$$
$$= \text{Rs } 1{,}26{,}48{,}000 \text{ F}$$

$$\text{Market-size variance} = \left(\text{Actual market size in units} - \text{Budgeted market size in units}\right) \times \text{Budgeted market share} \times \text{Budgeted contribution margin per composite unit for budgeted mix}$$

$$= (2{,}40{,}00{,}000 - 2{,}50{,}00{,}000) \times 0.10 \times \text{Rs } 21.08$$
$$= -10{,}00{,}000 \times 0.10 \times \text{Rs } 21.08$$
$$= \text{Rs } 21{,}08{,}000 \text{ U}$$

The market share variance is favorable because the actual 12.5% market share was higher than the budgeted 10% market share. The market size variance is unfavorable because the market size decreased 4% [(25,000,000 - 24,000,000) ÷ 25,000,000].

While the overall total market size declined (from 250 lakh to 240 lakh), the increase in market share meant a favorable sales-quantity variance.

Sales-quantity Variance
Rs 1,05,40,000 F

Market-share variance
Rs 1,26,48,000 F

Market-size variance
Rs 21,08,000 U

Solution Exhibit 14-21

Market-Share and Market-Size Variance Analysis for 2011

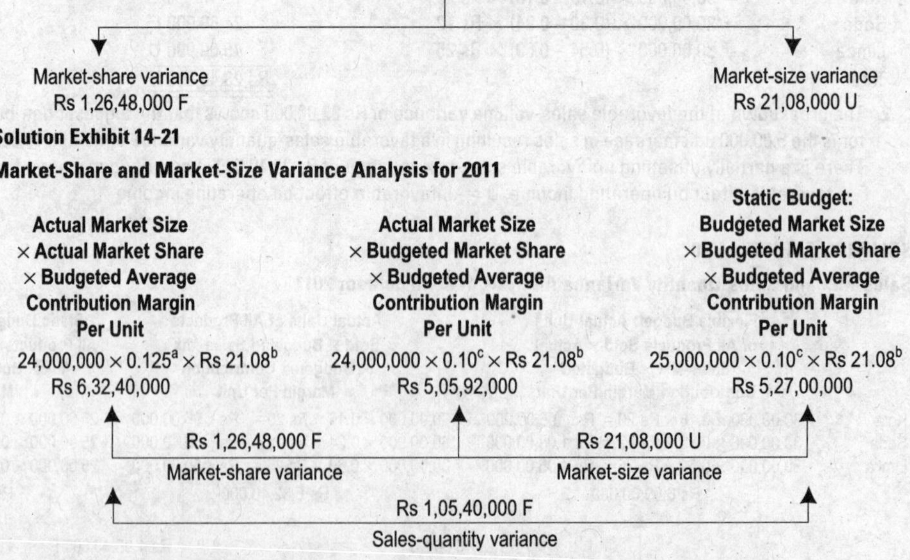

F = favorable effect on operating income; U = unfavorable effect on operating income

[a]Actual market share: 30,00,000 units × 2,40,00,000 units = 0.125, or 12.5%

[b]Budgeted average contribution margin per unit Rs 5,27,00,000 × 25,00,000 units = Rs 21.08 per unit

[c]Budgeted market share: 25,00,000 units × 2,50,00,000 units = 0.10, or 10%

14-22 Allocation of central corporate costs to divisions. Vijay, the corporate controller of Indian Oil Corporation (IOCL), is about to make a presentation to the senior corporate executives and the top managers of its four divisions. These divisions are

- Oil & Gas Upstream (the exploration, production, and transportation of oil and gas)
- Oil & Gas Downstream (the refining and marketing of oil and gas)
- Chemical Products
- Copper Mining

Under the existing internal accounting system, costs incurred at central corporate headquarters are collected in a single pool and allocated to each division on the basis of its actual revenues. The central corporate costs (in lakh) for the most recent year are:

Interest on debt	Rs 20,000
Corporate salaries	1,000
Accounting and control	1,000
General marketing	1,000
Legal	1,000
Research and development	2,000
Public affairs	2,080
Personnel and payroll	1,920
	30,000

Public affairs includes the public relations staff, the lobbyists, and the sizable donations IOCL makes to numerous charities and nonprofit institutions.

Summary data (rupee amounts in lakhs) related to the four divisions for the most recent year are:

	Oil & Gas Upstream	Oil & Gas Downstream	Chemical Products	Copper Mining	Total
Revenues	Rs 70,000	Rs 1,60,000	Rs 40,000	Rs 30,000	Rs 3,00,000
Operating costs	Rs 30,000	Rs 1,50,000	Rs 38,000	Rs 32,000	Rs 2,50,000
Operating income	Rs 40,000	Rs 10,000	Rs 2,000	Rs (2,000)	Rs 50,000
Identifiable assets	Rs 1,40,000	Rs 60,000	Rs 30,000	Rs 20,000	Rs 2,50,000
Number of employees	9,000	12,000	6,000	3,000	30,000

The top managers of each division share in a divisional-income bonus pool. Divisional income is defined as operating income less allocated central corporate costs.

Vijay is about to propose a change in the method used to allocate central corporate costs. He favors collecting these costs in four separate pools:

- Cost Pool1-Interest on debt. Allocated using identifiable assets of divisions
- Cost Pool2-Corporate salaries accounting and control, general marketing, legal, and research and development. Allocated using revenues of divisions
- Cost Pool3-Public affairs. Allocated using operating income (if positive) of divisions, with only divisions with positive operating income included in the allocation base
- Cost Pool4-Personnel and payroll. Allocated using number of employees in divisions

Required

1. What purposes might be served by the allocation of central corporate costs to each division at IOCL?
2. Compute the operating income of each division when all central corporate costs are allocated using revenues of each division.
3. Compute the operating income of each division when central corporate costs are allocated using the four cost pools.
4. What are the strengths and weaknesses of Vijay' proposal relative to the existing single cost-pool method

Solution

Allocation of central corporate costs to divisions.

1. The purposes for allocating central corporate costs to each division include:
   a. **To provide information for economic decisions.** Allocations can signal to division managers that decisions to expand (contract) activities will likely require increases (decreases) in corporate costs that should be considered in the initial decision about expansion (contraction). When top management is allocating resources to divisions, analysis of relative division profitability should consider differential use of corporate services by divisions. Some allocation schemes can encourage the use of central services that would otherwise be underutilized. A common rationale related to this purpose is "to remind profit center managers that central corporate costs exist and that division earnings must be adequate to cover some share of those costs."
   b. **Motivation.** Creates an incentive for division managers to control costs; for example, by reducing the number of employees at a division, a manager will save direct labor costs as well as central personnel and payroll costs allocated on the basis of number of employees. Allocation also creates incentives for division managers to monitor the effectiveness and efficiency with which central corporate costs are spent.
   c. **Cost justification or reimbursement.** Some lines of business of IOCL may be regulated with cost data used in determining "fair prices"; allocations of central corporate costs will result in higher prices being set by a regulator.

d. Income measurement for external parties. IOCL may include allocations of central corporate costs in its external line-of-business reporting.

2. Total costs in single pool = Rs 30,000
   Allocation base = Rs 3,00,000 revenue
   Allocation rate = Rs 30,000 × Rs 3,00,000 = Rs 1 per Rs 10 of revenue

See Solution Exhibit 14-22 for additional answers.

3. See Solution Exhibit 14-22 for answer.

SOLUTION EXHIBIT 14-22
(in lakh)

	Oil & Gas Upstream	Oil & Gas Downstream	Chemical Products	Copper Mining	Total
Revenues	Rs 70,000	Rs 1,60,000	Rs 40,000	Rs 30,000	Rs 3,00,000
Operating costs	30,000	1,50,000	38,000	32,000	2,50,000
Allocated costs, Re 1 per Rs 10 revenue	7,000	16,000	4,000	3,000	30,000
Division income	Rs 33,000	Rs (6,000)	Rs (2,000)	Rs (5,000)	Rs 20,000

Allocation Base	Oil & Gas Upstream	Oil & Gas Downstream	Chemical Products	Copper Mining
1. Allocated on basis of identifiable assets	14/25	6/25	3/25	2/25
Total costs = Rs 20,000	Rs 11,200	Rs 4,800	Rs 2,400	Rs 1,600
2. Allocated on basis of revenues	7/30	16/30	4/30	3/30
Total costs = Rs 6,000	Rs 1,400	Rs 3,200	Rs 800	Rs 600
3. Allocated on basis of operating income (if positive)	40/52	10/52	2/52	—
Total costs = Rs 2,080	Rs 1,600	Rs 400	Rs 80	Rs 0
4. Allocated on basis of number of employees	9/30	12/30	6/30	3/30
Total costs = Rs 1,920	Rs 576	Rs 768	Rs 384	Rs 192

	Oil & Gas Upstream	Oil & Gas Downstream	Chemical Products	Copper Mining	Total
Revenues	Rs 70,000	Rs 1,60,000	Rs 40,000	Rs 30,000	Rs 3,00,000
Operating costs	30,000	1,50,000	38,000	32,000	2,50,000
Cost Pool 1 Allocation	11,200	4,800	2,400	1,600	20,000
Cost Pool 2 Allocation	1,400	3,200	800	600	6,000
Cost Pool 3 Allocation	1,600	400	80	0	2,080
Cost Pool 4 Allocation	576	768	384	192	1,920
Division income	Rs 25,224	Rs 832	Rs (1,664)	Rs (4,392)	Rs 20,000

4. Strengths of Vijay's proposal relative to existing single-cost pool method:
   a. Better able to capture cause-and-effect relationships. Interest on debt is more likely caused by the financing of assets than by revenues. Personnel and payroll costs are more likely caused by the number of employees than by revenues.
   b. Relatively simple. No extra information need be collected beyond that already available. (Some students will list the extra costs of Vijay's proposal as a weakness. However, for a company with Rs 30 billion in revenues, those extra costs are minimal.)

   Weaknesses of Vijay's proposal relative to existing single-cost pool method:
   a. May promote dysfunctional decision making. May encourage division managers to lease or rent assets rather than to purchase assets, even where it is economical for IOCL to purchase them. This off-balance sheet financing will reduce the "identifiable assets" of the division and thus will reduce the interest on debt costs allocated to the division. (IOCL could counteract this problem by incorporating leased and rented assets in the "identifiable assets" base.)

   It may be noted that Vijay's proposal may be subject to criticism. These criticisms include:
   a. Proposal does not adequately capture cause-and-effect relationships for the legal and research and development cost pools. For these cost pools, specific identification of individual projects with an individual division can better capture cause-and-effect relationships.
   b. Proposal may give rise to disputes over the definition and valuation of "identifiable assets."
   c. Use of actual rather than budgeted amounts in the allocation bases creates interdependencies between divisions. Moreover, use of actual amounts means that division managers do not know cost allocation consequences of their decisions until the end of each reporting period.
   d. Separate allocation of fixed and variable costs would result in more refined cost allocations.
   e. Questionable that 100% of central corporate costs should be allocated. It may be argued that public affairs should not be allocated to any division, based on the notion that division managers may not control many of the individual expenditures in this cost pool.

14-23 Customer-profitability analysis, customer-cost hierarchy. Pantaloon's Suits is a ready-to-wear suit manufacturer. Pantaloon's has four customers: two wholesale-channel customers and two retail-channel customers:

- Suit Wholesalers
- Match Wholesale Company
- Suitors Men's Store
- Design Clothing Store

Pantaloon's owner and CEO, Siddarth, has developed the following ABC system:

Activity	Cost Driver	Rate in 2011
Order Processing	Number of purchase orders	Rs 2,450 per order
Sales Visits	Number of customer visits	Rs 14,300 per visit
Delivery-Regular	Number of regular deliveries	Rs 3,000 per delivery
Delivery-Rushed	Number of rushed deliveries	Rs 8,500 per delivery

List selling price per suit is Rs 2,000, and average cost per suit is Rs 1,100. Siddarth wants to evaluate the profitability of each of the four customers in 2011 to explore opportunities for increasing the profitability of his company in 2012. The following data are available for 2011:

	Wholesale Customers		Retail Customers	
Item	Suit	Match	Suitors	Design
Total number of orders	44	62	212	250
Total number of sale visits	8	12	22	20
Regular deliveries	41	48	166	190
Rush deliveries	3	14	46	60
Average number of suits per order	400	200	30	25
Average selling price per suit	Rs 1,400	Rs 1,600	Rs 1,700	Rs 1,800

Required

1. Calculate the customer-level operating income in 2011 using the format in Exhibit 14-5.
2. What do you recommend Siddarth to do to increase the company's operating income in 2012?
3. Assume Pantaloon's distribution-channel costs are Rs 35,00,000 for its wholesale customers and Rs 21,00,000 for the retail customers. Also assume that its corporate-sustaining costs are Rs 25,00,000 Prepare a customer cost hierarchy report for Pantaloon's using the format in Exhibit 14-6.

Solution

Customer-profitability analysis, customer cost hierarchy.

1.

Item	Suit	Match	Suitors	Design
Revenues at list prices 17,600[a] × Rs 2,000; 12,400[b] × Rs 2,000; 6,360[c] × Rs 2,000; 6,250[d] × Rs 2,000	Rs 3,52,00,000	Rs 2,48,00,000	Rs 1,27,20,000	Rs 1,25,00,000
Discount 17,600 × Rs 600[e]; 12,400 × Rs 400[f]; 6,360 × Rs 300[g]; 6,250 × Rs 200[h]	1,05,60,000	49,60,000	19,08,000	12,50,000
Revenues (at actual prices)	2,46,40,000	1,98,40,000	1,08,12,000	1,12,50,000
Cost of goods sold 17,600 × Rs 1,100; 12,400 × Rs 1,100; 6,360 × Rs 1,100; 6,250 × Rs 1,100	1,93,60,000	1,36,40,000	69,96,000	68,75,000
Gross Margin	52,80,000	62,00,000	38,16,000	43,75,000
Customer-level operating costs				
Order processing 44, 62, 212, 250 × Rs 2,450	1,07,800	1,51,900	5,19,400	6,12,500
Sales visits 8, 12, 22, 20 × Rs 14,300	1,14,400	1,71,600	3,14,600	2,86,000
Delivery – regular 41, 48, 166, 190 × Rs 3,000	1,23,000	1,44,000	4,98,000	5,70,000
Delivery – rushed 3, 14, 46, 60 × Rs 8,500	25,500	1,19,000	3,91,000	5,10,000
Total customer-level operating costs	3,70,700	5,86,500	17,23,000	19,78,500
Customer-level operating income	Rs 49,09,300	Rs 56,13,500	Rs 20,93,000	Rs 23,96,500

[a] 44 × 400 = 17,600
[b] 62 × 200 = 12,400
[c] 212 × 30 = 6,360
[d] 250 × 25 = 6,250
[e] Rs 2,000 – Rs 1,400 = Rs 600
[f] Rs 2,000 – Rs 1,600 = Rs 400
[g] Rs 2,000 – Rs 1,700 = Rs 300
[h] Rs 2,000 – Rs 1,800 = Rs 200

2. Key challenges facing Siddarth are:
   a. Reduce level of price discounting, especially by Suit
   b. Reduce level of customer-level costs, especially by Suitors and Design

   The ABC cost system highlights areas where the Suitors and Design accounts are troublesome. They have:
   - A high number of orders,
   - A high number of customer visits, and
   - A high number of rushed deliveries.

   Siddarth needs to consider whether this high level of activity can be reduced without reducing customer revenues.
3. Solution Exhibit 14-23 presents a customer cost hierarchy report for Pantaloon's Suits,

SOLUTION EXHIBIT 14-23
Income statement of pantaloon's suits for 2011

	Customer Distribution Channels						
		Wholesale customers			Retail customers		
	Total (1)	Total (2)	Suit (3)	Match (4)	Total (5)	Suitors (6)	Design (7)
Revenues (at actual prices)	Rs 66,54,200	Rs 44,48,000	Rs 24,64,000	Rs 19,84,0000	Rs 22,06,200	Rs 10,81,200	Rs 11,25,000
Customer-level expand costs	51,52,970	33,95,720	19,73,070	14,22,650	17,57,250	8,71,900	8,85,350
Customer-level operating income	15,01,230	10,52,280	Rs 4,90,930	Rs 5,61,350	4,48,950	Rs 2,09,300	Rs 2,39,650
Distribution-channel costs	5,60,000	3,50,000			2,10,000		
Distribution-channel-level operating income	9,41,230	Rs 7,02,280			Rs 2,38,950		
Corporate-sustaining costs	2,50,000						
Operating income	Rs 6,91,230						

14-24 Customer loyalty clubs and profitability analysis. The Taj Group of Hotels chain embarked on a new customer loyalty program in 2011. The 2011 year-end data have been collected, and it is now time for you to determine whether the loyalty program should be continued, discontinued, or perhaps altered to improve loyalty and profitability levels at Taj.

Taj's loyalty program consists of three different customer loyalty levels. All new customers can sign up for the Taj Bronze Card. This card provides guests with a complimentary bottle of beer per night (cost to the chain is Rs 50 per bottle) and Rs 200 in restaurant coupons each night (cost to the chain is Rs 100). Bronze customers also receive a 10 per cent discount off the nightly rate. The program enables the chain to track a member's stays and activities. Once customers have stayed and paid for 20 nights at any of the chain's locations worldwide, they are upgraded to Silver Customer status. Silver benefits include the bottle of beer (cost to the chain is Rs 50 per bottle per night), Rs 300 in restaurant coupons per night (cost to the chain is Rs 150), and a 20 per cent off every night from the 21st night on. A customer who reaches the 50.night level is upgraded to Gold Customer status. Gold status increases the nightly discount to 30 per cent and replaces the Rs 50 bottle of beer with a bottle of champagne per night (cost to the chain is Rs 200 per bottle). As well, Rs 400 in restaurant coupons per night are granted (cost to the chain is Rs 200). Assume all bottles and coupons offered are used.

The average full price for one night's stay is Rs 2,000. The chain incurs variable costs of Rs 650 per night, exclusive of loyalty program costs. Total fixed costs for the chain are Rs 1,40,58,00,000. Taj operates 10 hotels, with, on average, 500 rooms each. All hotels are open for business 365 days a year, and approximate average occupancy rates are around 80 per cent. Following are some loyalty program characteristics:

Loyalty Program	Number of Customers	Average Number of Nights per Customer
Gold	2,430	60
Silver	8,340	35
Bronze	80,300	10
No program	219,000	1

Note that a Gold Customer would have received the 10 per cent discount for his or her first 20 stays, received the 20 per cent discount for the next 30 stays, and the 30 per cent discount only for the last 10 nights. Assume that all program members signed on to the program the first time they stayed with one of the chain's hotels. Also, assume the restaurants are managed by a 100 per cent-owned subsidiary of Taj.

Required

1. Calculate the program contribution margin for each of the three programs, as well as for the customers not subscribing to the loyalty program. Which of the programs is the most profitable? Which is the least profitable? Do not allocate fixed costs to individual rooms or specific loyalty programs.
2. Prepare an income statement for Taj for the year ended December 31, 2011.

3. What is the average room rate per night? What are average variable costs per night inclusive of the loyalty program?

4. Explain what drives the profitability (or lack thereof) of Taj's loyalty program.

Solution

Customer loyalty clubs and profitability analysis.

1.

Gold Program	
Revenues	
2,430 × 20 × (Rs 2,000 × 0.90)	Rs 8,74,80,000
2,430 × 30 × (Rs 2,000 × 0.80)	11,66,40,000
2,430 × 10 × (Rs 2,000 × 0.70)	3,40,20,000
Total revenues	23,81,40,000
Variable Costs	
Hotel variable costs, 2,430 × 60 × Rs 650	9,47,70,000
Beer Costs	
2,430 × 50 × Rs 50	60,75,000
2,430 × 10 × Rs 200	48,60,000
Restaurant costs	
2,430 × 20 × Rs 100	48,60,000
2,430 × 30 × Rs 150	1,09,35,000
2,430 × 10 × Rs 200	48,60,000
Total variable costs	12,63,60,000
Contribution margin	Rs 11,17,80,000
Silver Program	
Revenues	
8,340 × 20 × (Rs 2,000 × 0.90)	Rs 30,02,40,000
8,340 × 15 × (Rs 2,000 × 0.80)	20,01,60,000
Total revenues	50,04,00,000
Variable Costs	
Hotel variable costs, 8,340 × 35 × Rs 650	18,97,35,000
Beer costs, 8,340 × 35 × Rs 50	1,45,95,000
Restaurant Costs	
8,340 × 20 × Rs 100	1,66,80,000
8,340 × 15 × Rs 150	1,87,65,000
Total variable costs	23,97,75,000
Contribution margin	Rs 26,06,25,000
Bronze Program	
Revenues, 80,300 × 10 × (Rs 2,000 × 0.90)	Rs 1,44,54,00,000
Variable costs	
Hotel variable costs, 80,300 × 10 × Rs 650	52,19,50,000
Beer costs 80,300 × 10 × Rs 50	4,01,50,000
Restaurant costs 80,300 × 10 × Rs 100	8,03,00,000
Total variable costs	64,24,00,000
Contribution margin	Rs 80,30,00,000
No Program	
Revenues, 219,000 × 1 × Rs 2,000	Rs 43,80,00,000
Variable costs, 219,000 × 1 × Rs 650	14,23,50,000
Contribution margin	Rs 29,56,50,000

Loyalty Program	Total Revenues	Variable Costs	Contribution Margin	Contribution Margin Total Revenues
Gold	Rs 23,81,40,000	Rs 12,63,60,000	Rs 11,17,80,000	46.94%
Silver	50,04,00,000	23,97,75,000	26,06,25,000	52.08
Bronze	1,44,54,00,000	64,24,00,000	80,30,00,000	55.56
No program	43,80,00,000	14,23,50,000	29,56,50,000	67.50
Total	Rs 2,62,19,40,000	Rs 1,15,08,85,000	Rs 1,47,10,55,000	

The no-program group of customers has the highest contribution margin per revenue rupee. However, it comprises only 16.71% (Rs 43,80,00,000 × Rs 2,62,19,40,000) of total revenues. The gold program has the lowest contribution margin per revenue rupee. However, it is misleading to evaluate each program in isolation. A key aim of loyalty programs is to promote a high frequency of return business. The contribution margin to total revenue ratio of each program in isolation does not address this issue.

2.

Revenues	Rs 2,62,19,40,000
Variable costs	1,15,08,85,000
Contribution margin	1,47,10,55,000
Fixed costs	1,40,58,00,000
Operating income	Rs 6,52,55,000

3. Number of room nights

Gold, 2,430 × 60	1,45,800
Silver, 8,340 × 35	2,91,900
Bronze, 80,300 × 10	8,03,000
No program, 219,000 × 1	2,19,000
	14,59,700

Average room rate per night: $\frac{\text{Rs } 2,62,19,40,000}{14,59,700} = \text{Rs } 796.22$

Average variable cost per night: $\frac{\text{Rs } 1,15,08,85,000}{14,59,700} = \text{Rs } 788.44$

4. Taj Group of Hotels has fixed costs of Rs 1,40,58,00,000. A key challenge is to attract a high number of repeat business customers. Loyalty programs aim to have customers return to Taj multiple times. Their aim is increasing the revenues beyond what they would be without the program. It is to be expected that the higher the level of nights stayed, the greater the inducements necessary to keep attracting the customer to return. However, given the low level of variable costs to room rates, there is considerable cushion available for Taj Group of Hotels to offer high inducements for frequent stayers.

Taj Group of Hotels could adopt a net present value analysis of customers who are in the different loyalty clubs. It would be informative for Taj Group of Hotels to have information on how much of each customer's total lodging industry expenditures it captures. It may well want to give higher levels of inducements to frequent stayers if the current program attracts only, say, 30% of each of its frequent customer's total business in cities where it has lodging properties available.

14-25 Variance analysis, multiple products. Parle, operates a chain of cookie stores. Budgeted and actual operating data of its three stores for August are as follows:

Budget for August

	Selling Price per Pound	Variable Cost per Pound	Contribution Margin per Pound	Sales Volume in Pounds
Chocolate chip	Rs 45.0	Rs 25.0	Rs 20.0	45,000
Oatmeal raisin	50.0	27.0	23.0	25,000
Coconut	55.0	29.0	26.0	10,000

Budget for August (continued)

	Selling Price per Pound	Variable Cost per Pound	Contribution Margin per Pound	Sales Volume in Pounds
White chocolate	60.0	30.0	30.0	5,000
Macadamia nut	65.0	34.0	31.0	15,000
				1,00,000

Actual for August

	Selling Price per Pound	Variable Cost per Pound	Contribution Margin per Pound	Sales Volume in Pounds
Chocolate chip	Rs 45.0	Rs 26.0	Rs 19.0	57,600
Oatmeal raisin	52.0	29.0	23.0	18,000
Coconut	55.0	28.0	27.0	9,600
White chocolate	60.0	34.0	26.0	13,200
Macadamia nut	70.0	40.0	30.0	21,600
				1,20,000

Required Parle's focuses on contribution margin in its variance analysis.

1. Compute the total sales-volume variance for August.
2. Compute the total sales-mix variance for August.

3. Compute the total sales-quantity variance for August.
4. Comment on your results in requirements 1,2, and 3.

Solution

Variance analysis, multiple products.

1, 2, and **3.** Solution Exhibit 14-25 presents the sales-volume, sales-quantity, and sales-mix variances for each type of cookie and in total for Parle in August.

The sales-volume variances can also be computed as:

$$\text{Sales - volume variance} = \left(\begin{matrix}\text{Actual sales}\\ \text{quantity in punds}\end{matrix} - \begin{matrix}\text{Budgeted sales}\\ \text{quantity in pounds}\end{matrix}\right) \times \begin{matrix}\text{Budgeted contribution}\\ \text{margin per pound}\end{matrix}$$

The sales-volume variances are:

Chocolate chip	= (57,600 – 45,000) × Rs 20	=	Rs 2,52,000 F
Oatmeal raisin	= (18,000 – 25,000) × Rs 23	=	1,61,000 U
Coconut	= (9,600 – 10,000) × Rs 26	=	10,400 U
White chocolate	= (13,200 – 5,000) × Rs 30	=	2,46,000 F
Macadamia nut	= (21,600 – 15,000) × Rs 31	=	2,04,600 F
All cookies			Rs 5,31,200 F

The sales-quantity variance can also be computed as:

$$\text{Sales-quantity variance} = \left(\begin{matrix}\text{Actual pounds of all}\\ \text{cookies sold}\end{matrix} - \begin{matrix}\text{Budgeted pounds of all}\\ \text{cookies sold}\end{matrix}\right) \times \begin{matrix}\text{Budgeted sales-}\\ \text{mix percentage}\end{matrix} \times \begin{matrix}\text{Budgeted contribution}\\ \text{margin per pound}\end{matrix}$$

The sales-quantity variances are:

Chocolate chip	= (120,000 – 100,000) × 0.45 × Rs 20	=	Rs 1,80,000 F
Oatmeal raisin	= (120,000 – 100,000) × 0.25 × Rs 23	=	1,15,000 F
Coconut	= (120,000 – 100,000) × 0.10 × Rs 26	=	52,000 F
White chocolate	= (120,000 – 100,000) × 0.05 × Rs 30	=	30,000 F
Macadamia nut	= (120,000 – 100,000) × 0.15 × Rs 31	=	93,000 F
All cookies			Rs 4,70,000 F

The sales-mix variance can also be computed as:

$$\text{Sales-mix variance} = \left(\begin{matrix}\text{Actual sales-}\\ \text{mix percentage}\end{matrix} - \begin{matrix}\text{Budgeted sales-}\\ \text{mix percentage}\end{matrix}\right) \times \begin{matrix}\text{Actual pounds of all}\\ \text{cookies sold}\end{matrix} \times \begin{matrix}\text{Budgeted contribution}\\ \text{margin per pound}\end{matrix}$$

The sales-mix variances are:

Chocolate chip	= (0.48 – 0.45) × 120,000 × Rs 20	=	Rs 72,000 F
Oatmeal raisin	= (0.15 – 0.25) × 120,000 × Rs 23	=	2,76,000 U
Coconut	= (0.08 – 0.10) × 120,000 × Rs 26	=	62,400 U
White chocolate	= (0.11 – 0.05) – 120,000 × Rs 30	=	2,16,000 F
Macadamia nut	= (0.18 – 0.15) × 120,000 × Rs 31	=	1,11,600 F
All cookies			Rs 61,200 F

A summary of the variances is:

Sales-Volume Variance

Chocolate chip	Rs 2,52,000 F
Oatmeal raisin	1,61,000 U
Coconut	10,400 U
White chocolate	2,46,000 F
Macadamia nut	2,04,600 F
All cookies	Rs 5,31,200 F

Sales-Mix Variance

Chocolate chip	Rs 72,000 F
Oatmeal raisin	2,76,000 U
Coconut	62,400 U
White chocolate	2,16,000 F
Macadamia nut	1,11,600 F
All cookies	Rs 61,200 F

Sales-Quantity Variance

Chocolate chip	Rs 1,80,000F
Oatmeal raisin	1,15,000F
Coconut	52,000F
White chocolate	30,000F
Macadamia nut	93,000F
All cookies	Rs 4,70,000F

4. Parle shows a favorable sales-quantity variance because it sold more cookies in total than was budgeted. Together with the higher quantities, Parle also sold more of the high-contribution margin white chocolate and macadamia nut cookies relative to the budgeted mix–hence, Parle also showed a favorable total sales-mix variance.

Solution Exhibit 14-25

Columnar Presentation of Sales-Volume, Sales-Quantity, and Sales-Mix Variances: for Parle

	Flexible Budget: Actual Kg of All Cookies Sold × Actual Sales-Mix × Budgeted Contribution Margin per Kg (1)	Actual Kg of All Cookies Sold × Budgeted Sales-Mix × Budgeted Contribution Margin per Kg (2)	Static Budget: Budgeted Kg of All Cookies Sold × Budgeted Sales-Mix × Budgeted Contribution Margin per Kg (3)
Panel A: Chocolate Chip	(1,20,000 × 0.48[a]) × Rs 20	(1,20,000 × 0.45[b]) × Rs 20	(1,00,000 × 0.45[b]) × Rs 20
	57,600 × Rs 20	54,000 × Rs 20	45,000 × Rs 20
	Rs 11,52,000	Rs 10,80,000	Rs 9,00,000
	Rs 72,000 F Sales-mix	Rs 1,80,000 F Sales-quantity	
	Rs 2,52,000 F Sales-volume variance		
Panel B: Oatmeal Raisin	(1,20,000 × 0.15[c]) × Rs 23	(1,20,000 × 0.25[d]) × Rs 23	(1,00,000 × 0.25[d]) × Rs 23
	18,000 × Rs 23	30,000 × Rs 23	25,000 × Rs 23
	Rs 4,14,000	Rs 6,90,000	Rs 5,75,000
	Rs 2,76,000 U Sales-mix	Rs 1,15,000 F Sales-quantity	
	Rs 1,61,000 U Sales-volume variance		
Panel C: Coconut	(1,20,000 × 0.08[e]) × Rs 26	(1,20,000 × 0.10[f]) × Rs 26	(1,00,000 × 0.10[f]) × Rs 26
	9,600 × Rs 26	12,000 × Rs 26	10,000 × Rs 26
	Rs 2,49,600	Rs 3,12,000	Rs 2,60,000
	Rs 62,400 U Sales-mix variance	Rs 52,000 F Sales-quantity variance	
	Rs 10,400 U Sales-volume variance		

F = favorable effect on operating income; U = unfavorable effect on operating income.

Actual Sales Mix:	Budgeted Sales Mix:
[a]Chocolate Chip = 57,600 ÷ 120,000 = 48%	[b]Chocolate Chip = 45,000 ÷ 100,000 = 45%
[c]Oatmeal Raisin = 18,000 ÷ 120,000 = 15%	[d]Oatmeal Raisin = 25,000 ÷ 100,000 = 25%
[e]Coconut = 9,600 ÷ 120,000 = 8%	[f]Coconut = 10,000 ÷ 100,000 = 10%

SOLUTION EXHIBIT 14-25

Columnar Presentation of Sales-Volume, Sales-Quantity, and Sales-Mix Variances for Parle:

	Flexible Budget: Actual Kg of All Cookies Sold × Actual Sales-Mix × Budgeted Contribution Margin per Kg (1)	**Actual Kg of All Cookies Sold × Budgeted Sales-Mix × Budgeted Contribution Margin per Kg (2)**	**Static Budget: Budgeted Kg of All Cookies Sold × Budgeted Sales-Mix × Budgeted Contribution Margin per Kg (3)**
Panel D: White Chocolate	(1,20,000 × 0.11[g]) × Rs 30	(1,20,000 × 0.05[h]) × Rs 30	(1,00,000 × 0.05[h]) × Rs 30
	13,200 × Rs 30	6,000 × Rs 30	5,000 × Rs 30
	Rs 3,96,000	Rs 1,80,000	Rs 1,50,000
	Rs 2,16,000 F Sales-mix	Rs 30,000 F Sales-quantity	
	Rs 2,46,000 F Sales-volume variance		

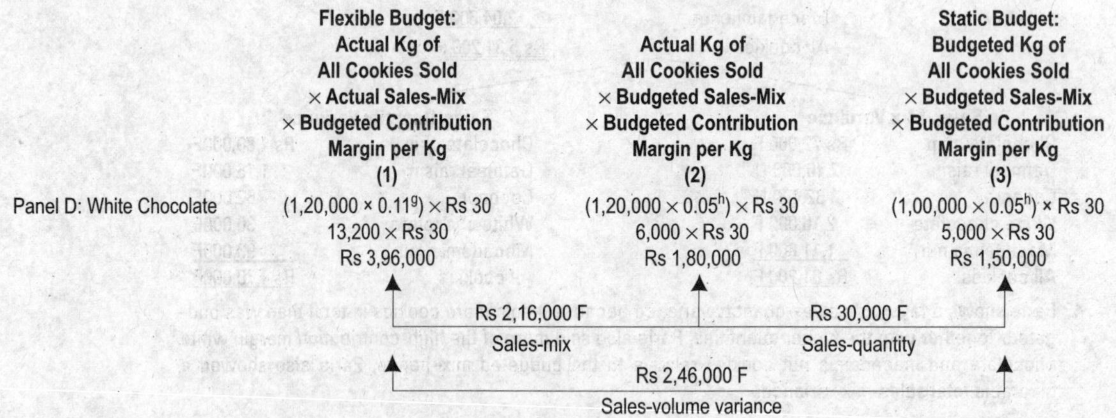

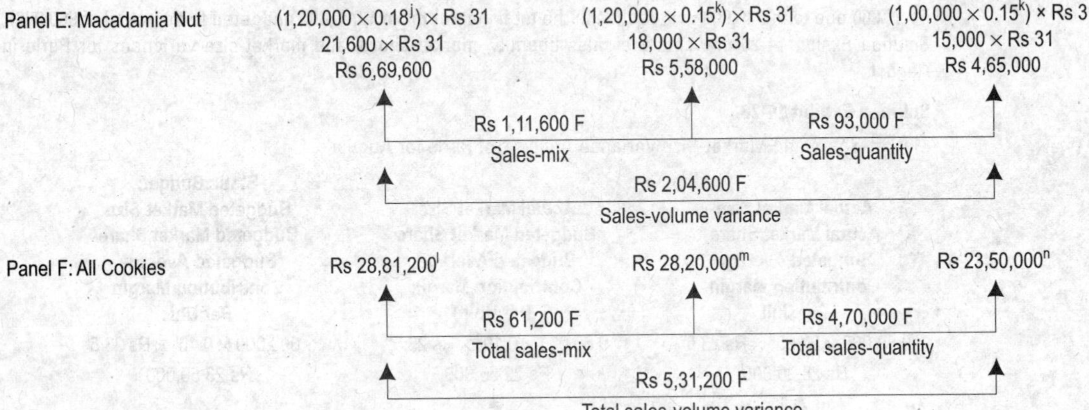

F = favorable effect on operating income; U = unfavorable effect on operating income.

Actual Sales Mix:
[g]White Chocolate = 13,200 ÷ 120,000 = 11%
[j]Macadamia Nut = 21,600 ÷ 120,000 = 18%
[l]Rs 11,52,000 + Rs 4,14,000 + Rs 2,49,600 + Rs 3,96,000 + Rs 6,69,600 = Rs 28,81,200

Budgeted Sales Mix:
[h]White Chocolate = 5,000 ÷ 100,000 = 5%
[k]Macadamia Nut = 15,000 ÷ 100,000 = 15%
[m]Rs 10,80,000 + Rs 6,90,000 + Rs 3,12,000 + Rs 1,80,000 + Rs 5,58,000 = Rs 28,20,000
[n]Rs 9,00,000 + Rs 5,75,000 + Rs 2,60,000 + Rs 1,50,000 + Rs 4,65,000 = Rs 23,50,000

14-26 Market-share and market-size variances (continuation of 14-25). Parle attains a 10 per cent market share based on total sales of the market. The total market is expected to be 10,00,000 pounds in sales volume for August. The actual total market for August was 9,60,000 pounds in sales volume.

Required

Compute the market-share and market-size variances for Parle in August. Report all variances in contribution-margin terms. Comment on the results.

Solution

Market-share and market-size variances (continuation of 14-25).

1.

	Actual	**Budgeted**
Market size	9,60,000	1,000,000
Parle's share	1,20,000	1,00,000
Market share	0.125	0.100

The budgeted average contribution margin per unit (also called budgeted contribution margin per composite unit for budgeted mix) is Rs 23.5:

	Budgeted Contribution Margin per Pound	**Budgeted Sales Volume in Pounds**	**Budgeted Contribution Margin**
Chocolate chip	Rs 20	45,000	Rs 9,00,000
Oatmeal raisin	23	25,000	5,75,000
Coconut	26	10,000	2,60,000
White chocolate	30	5,000	1,50,000
Macadamia nut	31	15,000	4,65,000
All cookies		1,00,000	Rs 23,50,000

$$\text{Budgeted average contribution margin per unit} = \frac{\text{Rs } 23{,}50{,}000}{1{,}00{,}000} = \text{Rs } 23.5$$

$$\text{Market-size variance in contribution margin} = \left(\text{Actual market size in units} - \text{Budgeted market size in units}\right) \times \text{Budgeted market share} \times \text{Budgeted average contribution margin per unit}$$

$$= (9{,}60{,}000 \times 10{,}00{,}000) \times 0.100 \times \text{Rs } 23.5$$

$$= \text{Rs } 94{,}000 \text{ U}$$

$$\text{Market-size variance in contribution margin} = \text{Actual market size in units} \times \left(\text{Atual market share} - \text{Budgeted market share}\right) \times \text{Budgeted average contribution margin per unit}$$

$$= 9{,}60{,}000 \times (0.125 - 0.100) \times \text{Rs } 23.5$$

$$= \text{Rs } 5{,}64{,}000 \text{ F}$$

By increasing its actual market share from the 10% budgeted to the actual 12.50%, Parle has a favorable market-share variance of Rs 5,64,000. There is a smaller offsetting unfavorable market-size variance of

Rs 94,000 due to the 40,000 unit decline in the total market (from 1,000,000 budgeted to an actual of 960,000). Solution Exhibit 14-26 presents the sales-quantity, market-share, and market-size variances for Parle in August.

Solution Exhibit 14-26

Market-Share and Market-Size Variance Analysis of Parle for August

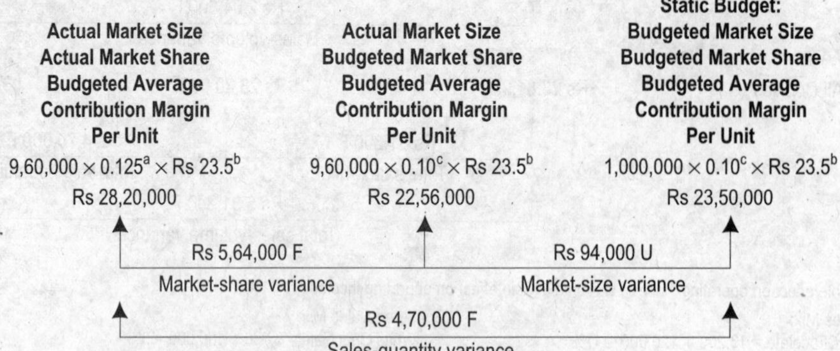

F = favorable effect on operating income; U = unfavorable effect on operating income

[a] Actual market share: 1,20,000 units ÷ 9,60,000 units = 0.125, or 12.5%

[b] Budgeted average contribution margin per unit: Rs 23,50,000 ÷ 10,00,000 units = Rs 23.5 per unit

[c] Budgeted market share: 1,00,000 units ÷ 10,00,000 units = 0.10, or 10%

An overview of Solved Problems 13-25 and 13-26 is:

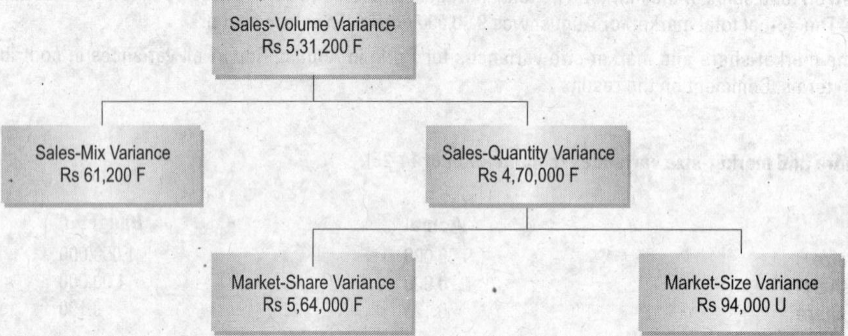

14-27 Direct materials price, efficiency, mix and yield variances. Himachal Foods, manufactures apple products such as apple jelly and applesauce. It makes applesauce by blending Tolman, Golden Delicious, and Ribston apples. Budgeted costs to produce 100,000 kg of applesauce in November are as follows:

45,000 kg of Tolman apples at Rs 30 per kg	Rs 13,50,000
180,000 kg of Golden Delicious apples at Rs 26 per kg	46,80,000
75,000 kg of Ribston apples at Rs 22 per kg	16,50,000

Actual costs in November are

62,000 kg of Tolman apples at Rs 28 per kg	Rs 17,36,000
155,000 kg of Golden Delicious apples at Rs 26 per kg	40,30,000
93,000 kg of Ribston apples at Rs 20 per kg	18,60,000

Required

1. Calculate the total direct materials price and efficiency variances for November.
2. Calculate the total direct materials mix and yield variances for November.
3. Comment on your results in requirements 1 and 2.

Solution

Direct Materials Price, Efficiency, Mix and Yield Variances

1. Solution Exhibit 14-27A presents the total price variance (Rs 3,10,000F), the total efficiency variance (Rs 2,56,000U), and the total flexible-budget variance (Rs 54,000F).

   Total direct materials price variance can also be computed as:

$$\text{Direct materials price variance for each input} = \left(\text{Actual price} - \text{Budgeted price}\right) \times \text{Actual Inputs}$$

Tolman	= (Rs 28 – Rs 30) × 62,000	=	Rs 1,24,000 F
Golden Delicious	= (Rs 26 – Rs 26) × 155,000	=	0

Ribston	= (Rs 20 – Rs 22) × 93,000 =	1,86,000 F
Total direct materials price variance		Rs 3,10,000 F

Total direct materials efficiency variance can also be computed as:

$$\text{Direct materials price variance for each input} = \left(\text{Actual inputs} - \text{Budgeted inputs allowed for actual outputs achieved}\right) \times \text{Budged prices}$$

Tolman	= (62,000 – 45,000) × Rs 30 =	Rs 5,10,000 U
Golden Delicious	= (155,000 – 180,000) × Rs 26 =	6,50,000 F
Ribston	= (93,000 – 75,000) × Rs 22 =	3,96,000 U
Total direct materials efficiency variance		Rs 2,56,000 U

SOLUTION EXHIBIT 14-27A

Columnar Presentation of Direct Materials Price and Efficiency Variances for Himachal Foods for November:

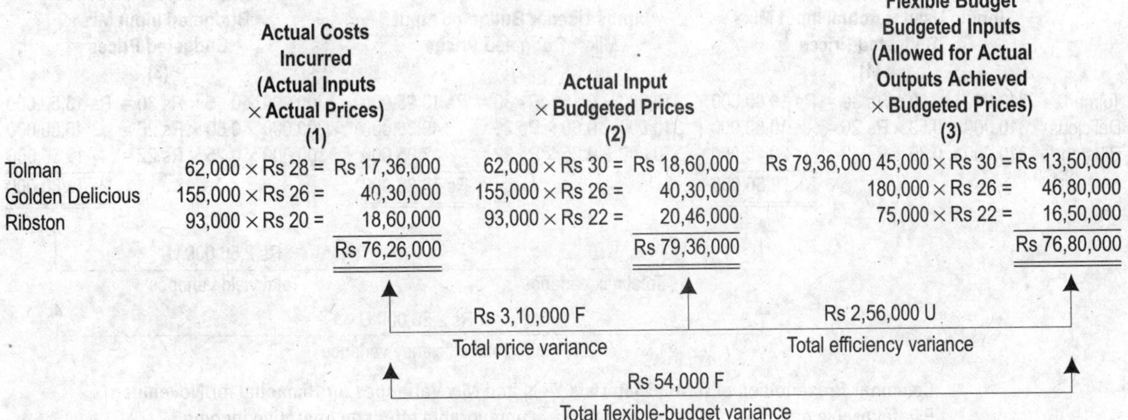

	Actual Costs Incurred (Actual Inputs × Actual Prices) (1)		Actual Input × Budgeted Prices (2)		Flexible Budget Budgeted Inputs (Allowed for Actual Outputs Achieved × Budgeted Prices) (3)	
Tolman	62,000 × Rs 28 =	Rs 17,36,000	62,000 × Rs 30 =	Rs 18,60,000	Rs 79,36,000 45,000 × Rs 30 =	Rs 13,50,000
Golden Delicious	155,000 × Rs 26 =	40,30,000	155,000 × Rs 26 =	40,30,000	180,000 × Rs 26 =	46,80,000
Ribston	93,000 × Rs 20 =	18,60,000	93,000 × Rs 22 =	20,46,000	75,000 × Rs 22 =	16,50,000
		Rs 76,26,000		Rs 79,36,000		Rs 76,80,000

Rs 3,10,000 F — Total price variance

Rs 2,56,000 U — Total efficiency variance

Rs 54,000 F — Total flexible-budget variance

F = favorable effect on operating income; U = unfavorable effect on operating income

2. Solution Exhibit 14-27B presents the total direct materials yield and mix variances for Himachal Foods for November.

The total direct materials yield variance can also be computed as the sum of the direct materials yield variances for each input:

$$\text{Direct materials yield variance for each input} = \left(\text{Actual total quantity of all direct materials inputs used} - \text{Budgeted total quantity of all direct materials inputs allowed for acutal output achieved}\right) \times \text{Budgeted direct materials input mix percentage} \times \text{Budgeted price of direct materials inputs}$$

Tolman	= (3,10,000 – 3,00,000) × 0.15 × Rs 30 = 10,000 × 0.15 × Rs 30 =	Rs 45,000U
Golden Delicious	= (3,10,000 – 3,00,000) × 0.60 × Rs 26 = 10,000 × 0.60 × Rs 26 =	1,56,000U
Ribston	= (3,10,000 – 3,00,000) × 0.25 × Rs 22 = 10,000 × 0.25 × Rs 22 =	55,000U
Total direct materials yield variance		Rs 2,56,000U

The total direct materials mix variance can also be computed as the sum of the direct materials mix variances for each input:

$$\text{Direct materials mix variance for each input} = \left(\text{Actual direct materials input mix percentange} - \text{Budgeted direct materials input mix percentage}\right) \times \text{Actual total quantity of all direct materials inputs}$$

Tolman	= (0.20 – 0.15) × 3,10,000 × Rs 30 = 0.05 × 3,10,000 × Rs 30 =	Rs 4,65,000 U
Golden Delicious	= (0.50 – 0.60) × 3,10,000 × Rs 26 = –0.10 × 3,10,000 × Rs 26 =	8,06,000 F
Ribston	= (0.30 – 0.25) × 3,10,000 × Rs 22 = 0.05 × 3,10,000 × Rs 22 =	3,41,000 U
Total direct materials mix variance		Re 0 U

3. Himachal Foods paid less for Tolman and Ribston apples and, so, had a favorable direct materials price variance of Rs 3,10,000. It also had an unfavorable efficiency variance of Rs 2,56,000. Himachal Foods would need to evaluate if these were unrelated events or if the lower price resulted from the purchase of apples of poorer quality that affected efficiency. The net effect in this case from the cost standpoint was favorable–the savings in price being greater than the loss in efficiency. Of course, if the applesauce is of poorer quality, Himachal Foods must also evaluate the potential effects on current and future revenues that have not been considered in the variances described in requirements 1 and 2. The unfavorable efficiency variance is entirely attributable to an unfavorable yield. The actual mix does deviate from the budgeted mix but at the budgeted prices, the greater quantity of Tolman and Ribston apples used in the actual mix exactly offsets the fewer Golden Delicious apples used. Again, management should evaluate the reasons for the unfavorable yield variance. Is it due to poor quality Tolman and Ribston apples (recall from requirement 1 that these apples were acquired at a price lower than the standard price) × Is it due to the change in mix (recall that the mix used is different from the budgeted mix, even though the mix variance is Rs 0) × Isolating the reasons can lead management to take the necessary corrective actions.

Solution Exhibit 14-27B

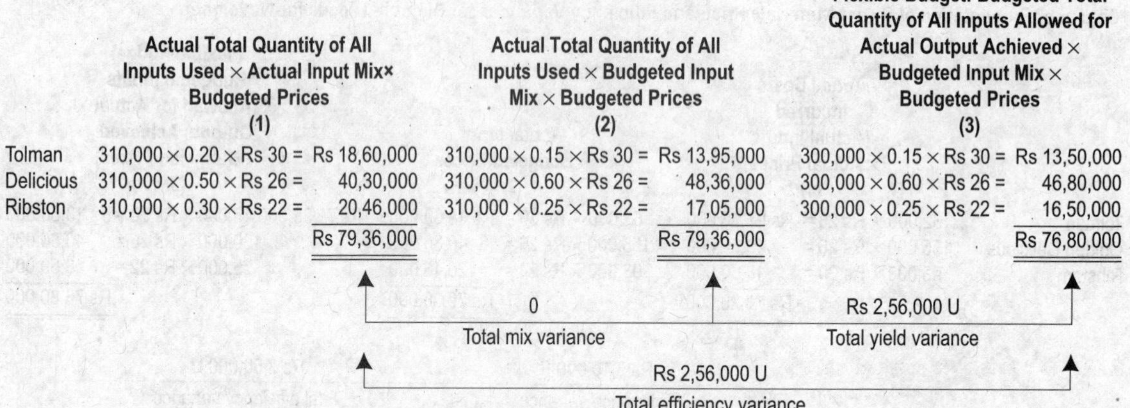

	Actual Total Quantity of All Inputs Used × Actual Input Mix× Budgeted Prices (1)		Actual Total Quantity of All Inputs Used × Budgeted Input Mix × Budgeted Prices (2)		Flexible Budget: Budgeted Total Quantity of All Inputs Allowed for Actual Output Achieved × Budgeted Input Mix × Budgeted Prices (3)	
Tolman	310,000 × 0.20 × Rs 30 =	Rs 18,60,000	310,000 × 0.15 × Rs 30 =	Rs 13,95,000	300,000 × 0.15 × Rs 30 =	Rs 13,50,000
Delicious	310,000 × 0.50 × Rs 26 =	40,30,000	310,000 × 0.60 × Rs 26 =	48,36,000	300,000 × 0.60 × Rs 26 =	46,80,000
Ribston	310,000 × 0.30 × Rs 22 =	20,46,000	310,000 × 0.25 × Rs 22 =	17,05,000	300,000 × 0.25 × Rs 22 =	16,50,000
		Rs 79,36,000		Rs 79,36,000		Rs 76,80,000

0 — Total mix variance

Rs 2,56,000 U — Total yield variance

Rs 2,56,000 U — Total efficiency variance

Columnar Presentation of Direct Materials Yield and Mix Variances for Himachal for November:
F = favorable effect on operating income; U = unfavorable effect on operating income.

14-28 Customer profitability, responsibility for environmental cleanup, ethics. Industrial Fluids (IF). manufactures and sells fluids used by metal-cutting plants. These fluids enable metal cutting to be done more accurately and more safely.

IF has more than 1,000 customers. It is currently undertaking a customer-profitability analysis. Nidhi, a newly hired MBA, is put in charge of the project. One issue in this analysis is IF's liability for its customers' fluid disposal.

Nidhi discovers that IF may have a responsibility under India environmental legislation for the disposal of toxic waste by its customers. Moreover, she visits 10 customer sites and finds dramatic differences in their toxic-waste-handling procedures. She describes one site owned by Wazirpur Metal as an "Environmental nightmare about to become a reality." She tells the IF controller that even if they have only one-half of the responsibility for the cleanup at Wazirpur's site, they will still be facing very high damages. IF Controller is displeased that Wazirpur metal has not paid its account to IF for the past three months and has formally sought protection from its creditors. He cautions Nidhi to be careful in her written report. He notes that, "IF does not want any smoking guns in its files in case of subsequent litigation."

Required

1. As Nidhi prepares IF's customer-profitability analysis, how should she handle any estimates of litigation and cleanup costs that IF may be held responsible for ?
2. How should Nidhi handle the Wazirpur metal situation when she prepares a profitability report for that customer?

Solution

Customer Profitability, Responsibility for Environmental Clean-Up, Ethics.

1. Customer-profitability analysis examines how individual customers differ in their profitability. The revenues and costs of each customer can be estimated with varying degrees of accuracy. Revenues of IF typically would be known at the time of sale. Many costs also would be known, e.g., the cost of materials used to manufacture the fluids sold to each customer. A major area of uncertainty is future costs associated with obligations arising from the sale. There are several issues here:
   a. Uncertainty as to the existence and extent of legal liability. Each customer has primary responsibility to dispose its own toxic waste. However, Nidhi is to determine whether under some India laws suppliers to a company may be partially liable for disposal of toxic material. Nidhi also needs to determine the extent of IF's liability. It would be necessary to seek legal guidance on this issue.

b. Uncertainty as to when the liability will occur. The further in the future, the lower the amount of the liability (assuming discounting for the time-value of money occurs.)

c. Uncertainty as to the amount of the liability, given that the liability exists and the date of the liability can be identified. Nidhi faces major difficulties here–see the answer to requirement 2.

Many companies argue that uncertainties related to (a), (b), and (c) make the inclusion of "hard-rupee estimates meaningless." However, at a minimum, a contingent liability should be recognized and included in the internal customer-profitability reports.

2. Nidhi's controller may believe that if estimates of future possible legal exposure are sufficiently uncertain, then they should not be recorded. His concern about "smoking guns" may have a very genuine basis, that is, if litigation arises, third parties may misrepresent Nidhi's concerns to the detriment of IF. Any written comments that she makes may surface 5 or 10 years later and be interpreted as "wide-spread knowledge" within IF that they have responsibility for large amounts of Environmental clean-up.

Given this background, Nidhi still has the responsibility to prepare a report in an objective and competent way. Moreover, she has visited 10 customer sites and has details as to their toxic-waste handling procedures. If Wazirpur goes bankrupt and has no liability insurance, one of the "deep pockets" available to meet toxic waste handling costs is likely to be IF. At a minimum, she should report the likely bankruptcy and the existence of IF's contingent liability for toxic-waste clean-up in her report. Whether she quantifies this contingent liability is a more difficult question. Nidhi has limited information available to make a meaningful quantification. She is not an employee of Wazirpur Metal and has no information about Wazirpur's liability insurance. Moreover, she does not know what other parties (such as other suppliers) are also jointly liable to pay Wazirpur's clean-up costs.

The appropriate course appears to highlight the contingent liability but to not attempt to quantify it.

Exercises

14-29 Customer profitability, service company. Instant Service (IS) is a repair-service company specializing in the rapid repair of photocopying machines. Each of its 10 clients pays a fixed monthly service fee (based on the type of photocopying machines owned by that client and the number of employees at that site). IS keeps records of the time technicians spend at each client's location and the cost of the equipment used to repair each photocopying machine. IS recently decided to compute the profitability of each customer. The following data (in thousands) pertain to May:

	Customer Revenues	Customer Costs
Avery Group	Rs 2,600	Rs 1,820
Duran Systems	1,800	1,840
Retail Systems	1,630	1,780
Ernst & Young	3,220	2,250
IIT Delhi	2,350	3,080
Grainger Services	800	740
Software Partners	1,740	1,000
Problem Solvers	760	1,080
Business Systems	1,370	1,100
Consultancy Enterprises	3,730	2,310

Required

1. Compute the operating income of each customer. Prepare exhibits for Instant Service that are Patterned after Exhibits 14-7 and 14-8. Comment on the results.
2. What options regarding individual customers should Instant Service consider in light of your customer profitability analysis in requirement 1?
3. What problems might Instant Service encounter in accurately estimating the operating costs of each customer

14-30 Variance analysis, multiple products. The Shimla Penguins play in the Indian Ice Hockey League. The Penguins play in Downtown Arena, (owned and managed by the City of Shimla, which has a capacity of 15,000 seats (5,000 lower-tier seats and 10,000 upper-tier seats). The Downtown Arena charges the Penguins per ticket charge for use of their facility. All tickets are sold by the Reservation Network, which charges the Penguin's a reservation fee per ticket. The Penguins' budgeted contribution margin for each type of ticket in 2011 is computed as follows:

	Lower-Tier Tickets	Upper-Tier Tickets
Selling price	Rs 350	Rs 140
Downtown Arena fee	100	60
Reservation Network fee	50	30
Contribution margin per ticket	200	50

The budgeted and actual average attendance figures per game in the 2010 season are

	Budgeted Seats Sold	Actual Seats Sold
Lower tier	4,000	3,300
Upper tier	6,000	7,700
Total	10,000	11,000

There was no difference between the budgeted and actual contribution margin for lower-tier or upper-tier seats.

The manager of the Penguins was delighted that actual attendance was 10 per cent above budgeted attendance per game.

Required

1. Compute the sales-volume variance for each type of ticket and in total for the Shimla Penguins in 2011 (Calculate all variances in terms of contribution margins.)
2. Compute the sales-quantity and sales-mix variances for each type of ticket and in total in 2011.
3. Present a summary of the variances in requirements 1 and 2. Comment on the results.

14-31 Variance analysis, working backward. The Yera Glasses sells two brands of wine glasses: Plain and Chic. Yera provides the following information for sales in the month of June:

Static-budget total contribution margin	Rs 56,000
Budgeted units to be sold of all glasses in June	2,000 units
Budgeted contribution margin per unit of Plain	Rs 20 per unit
Budgeted contribution margin per unit of Chic	Rs 60 per unit
Total sales-quantity variance	Rs 14,000 U
Actual sales-mix percentage of Plain	60 per cent

All variances are to be computed in contribution-margin terms.

Required

1. Calculate the sales-quantity variances for each product for June.
2. Calculate the individual product and total sales-mix variances for June. Calculate the individual product and total sales-volume variances for June.
3. Briefly describe the conclusions you would draw from the variances.

14-32 Allocation of central corporate costs to divisions. Times Group has four geographically dispersed divisions:

- Book publishing
- Broadcasting
- Print Media
- Multimedia

Under the current allocation system, costs incurred at Times Group corporate headquarters are collected in a single pool and allocated to eacl1 division on the basis of its revenues. The central corporate costs for 2011 are:

Interest on debt	Rs 1,00,00,000
Human resource management	15,00,00,000
Corporate administration	5,00,00,000
Research and development	10,00,00,000
Advertising	20,00,00,000
	Rs 51,00,00,000

Summary data (in lakh of rupees) related to the divisions for 2011 are:

	Multimedia	Broadcasting	Print Media	Book Publishing
Revenues	Rs 14,000	Rs 45,000	Rs 25,000	Rs 16,000
Direct costs	7,500	35,000	20,000	10,000
Segment margin	Rs 6,500	Rs 10,000	Rs 5,000	6,000

The following information on the four divisions is also available.

	Multimedia	Broadcasting	Print Media	Book Publishing
Floor space (square feet)	40,000	160,000	200,000	1,00,000
Number of employees	1,000	3,000	2,500	1,500
Divisional administrative costs (in lakh of rupees)	Rs 1,500	Rs 4,000	Rs 2,500	Rs 2,000

A review of the central corporate costs for divisions reveals the following:

- Out of the total Rs 100 lakh interest on debt, Rs 65 lakh is for the debt to purchase a building for the Broadcasting division. The remaining Rs 35 lakh interest cost is on the borrowings for the purchase of equipment for the Multimedia division.
- No research and development work is done for the Print Media division. The director of research and development estimates that 40 per cent of the work in his responsibility area is done for the Multimedia division, and the remaining 60 per cent is done equally for the Broadcasting and Book Publishing divisions.

- Advertising campaigns sponsored at the central corporate level are to boost the overall corporate image. It is assumed that the benefits to the divisions are in proportion to their revenues.
- The resources expended by human resource management on recruiting, training, and so forth for the divisions are approximately in proportion to the number of employees.
- To support divisional managers, the corporate management works very closely with them. The divisional administrative costs are a good indicator of the relative size of each division's management team.

Required

Allocate the central corporate costs to divisions that are consistent with cause-and-effect or benefits-received criteria.

14-33 Customer profitability, distribution. Efficient Distribution has decided to analyze the profitability of five new customers. It buys bottled water at Rs 12 per unit and sells to retail customers at a list price of Rs 14.40 per unit. Data pertaining to five customers for the recent quarter are:

	Customer				
	P	Q	R	S	T
Bottels sold	2,080	8,750	60,800	31,800	3,900
List selling price	Rs 14.40	Rs 14.40	Rs 14.40	Rs 14.40	Rs 14.40
Actual selling price	Rs 14.40	Rs 14.16	Rs 13.20	Rs 13.92	12.96
Number of purchase orders	15	25	30	25	30
Number of customer visits	2	3	6	2	3
Number of deliveries	10	30	60	40	20
Miles traveled per delivery	14	4	3	8	40
Number of expedited deliveries	0	0	0	0	1

Its five activities and their cost drivers are:

Activity	Cost Driver Rate
Order taking	Rs 100 per purchase order
Customer visits	Rs 80 per customer visit
Deliveries	Rs 2 per delivery mile traveled
Product handling	Rs 0.50 per bottle sold
Expedited deliveries	Rs 300 per expedited delivery

Required

1. Compute the customer-level operating income of each of the five retail customers now being examined (P, Q, R, S, and T). Comment on the results.
2. What insights are gained by reporting both the list selling price and the actual selling price for each customer?
3. What factors should Efficient Distribution consider in deciding whether to drop one or more of the five customers?

14-34 Customer profitability, customer cost hierarchy. Surya Electronics has two retail customers and two wholesale customers. Pertinent information relating to each customer for 2011 follows (all amounts are in thousands of rupees):

	Wholesale		Retail	
	North India Wholesaler	South India Wholesaler	Ramesh Electronics	Shyam Electricals
Cost of goods sold	Rs 325,000	Rs 490,000	Rs 112,000	Rs 92,000
Delivery costs				
Regular	300	450	150	80
Expedited	120	200	10	5
Order processing	800	1,000	200	130
Product handling	5,000	6,000	800	900
Sales visits	480	550	240	165
Revenues at list prices	400,000	600,000	130,000	100,000
Discounts from list prices	30,000	50,000	7,000	0

Surya's distribution-channel costs are Rs 300 lakh for wholesale customers and Rs 100 lakh for retail customers. Its corporate-sustaining costs are Rs 600 lakh.

Required

1. Calculate customer-level operating income using the format in Exhibit 14-5.
2. Prepare a customer cost hierarchy report, using the format in Exhibit 14-6.

14-35 Variance analysis, sales-mix and sales-quantity variances. ABC company adopts a standard costing system. It produces three products (A,B and C). You are Company's senior vice-president of marketing. The CEO has discovered that the total contribution margin came in lower than budget, and it is your responsibility to explain to him why actual results are different from the budget. Budgeted and actual operating data for the company's third quarter (2011) are as follows:

Budgeted Operating Data, Third Quarter 2011

	Selling Price	Variable Cost per Unit	Contribution Margin per Unit	Sales Volume in Units
A	Rs 379	Rs 182	Rs 197	12,500
B	269	98	171	37,500
C	149	65	84	50,000
				1,00,000

Actual Operating Data, Third Quarter 2011

	SellingPrice	Variable Costper Unit	Contribution Margin per Unit	Sales Volumein Units
A	Rs 349	Rs 178	Rs 171	11,000
B	285	92	193	44,000
C	102	73	29	55,000
				1,10,000

Required

1. Compute the actual and budgeted contribution margins in rupees for each product and in total.
2. Calculate the actual and budgeted sales mixes for the three products.
3. Calculate total sales-volume, sales-mix, and sales-quantity variances for the third quarter of 2011.
4. Write a brief note explaining why actual results were not as good as the budgeted amounts.

14-36 Market-share and market-size variances (continuation of 14-35). ABC senior vice-president of marketing prepared his budget at the beginning of the third quarter assuming a 25 per cent market share based on total sales. The total market was estimated by Market Research unit of the Company to reach sales of 400,000 units worldwide in the third quarter. However, actual sales were 500,000 units.

Required

1. Calculate the market-share and market-size variances for ABC in the third quarter of 2011 (report all variances in terms of contribution margins).
2. Explain what happened based on the market-share and market-size variances.
3. Calculate the actual market size, in units, that would have led to no market-size variance (again using budgeted contribution margin per unit). Use this market-size figure to find the actual market share that would have led to a zero market-share variance.

14-37 Direct materials efficiency, mix, and yield variances. (CMA adapted) The Energy Products Company produces a gasoline additive, Gas Gain, that increases engine efficiency and improves gasoline mileage. The actual and budgeted quantities (in gallons) of materials required to produce Gas Gain and the budgeted prices of materials in August are as follows:

Chemical	Actual Quantity	Budgeted Quantity	Budgeted Price
Echol	24,080	25,200	Rs 2.0
Protex	15,480	16,800	4.5
Benz	36,120	33,600	1.5
CT-40	10,320	8,400	3.0

Required

1. Calculate the total direct materials efficiency variance for August.
2. Calculate the total direct materials mix and yield variances for August.
3. What conclusions would you draw from the variance analysis?

14-38 Customer profitability, credit-card operations. The Freedom Card is a credit card that competes with national credit cards such as Visa and Master Card. Freedom Card is marketed by the City Bank. Anwar is manager of the Freedom Card division. He is seeking to develop a customer-profitability reporting system. He collects the following information on four users of the Freedom Card during 2011:

	A	B	C	D
Annual purchases at retail merchants	Rs 80,000	Rs 26,000	Rs 34,000	Rs 8,000
Customer transactions at retail merchant	800	520	272	200
Annual fee	50	0	50	0
Average annual outstanding balance on credit card on which interest is paid to City Bank	6,000	0	2,000	100
Inquiries to City Bank	6	12	8	2
Credit-card replacement due to loss or theft	0	2	1	0

Customer B pays no membership fee because his card was issued under a special "lifetime promotion program," in which annual fees are waived as long as the card is used at least once a year. Customer D is a student. City Bank does not charge an annual fee to student credit-card holders at select universities.

City Bank has an ABC system that Anwar can use in his analysis. The following data apply to 2011:

a. Each customer transaction with a retail merchant costs City Bank Rs 0.50 to process.
b. Each customer inquiry to City Bank costs Rs 5.
c. Replacing a lost card costs Rs 120.
d. Annual cost to City Bank of maintaining a credit-card account is Rs 108 (includes sending out monthly statements).

City Bank receives 2.0 per cent of the purchase amount from retail merchants when the Freedom Card is used. Bad debts of the Freedom Card in 2011 were 0.5 per cent of the total purchases at retail merchants. Thus, City Bank nets 1.5 per cent of the total purchases made using the Freedom Card.

City Bank had an interest spread of 9 per cent in 2011 on the average outstanding balances on which interest is paid by its credit-card holders. An interest spread is the difference between what City Bank receives from card holders on outstanding balances and what it pays to obtain the funds so used. Thus, on a Rs 500 average annual outstanding balance in 2011, City Bank would receive Rs 45 in interest revenues (9 per cent x Rs 500).

Required

1. Compute the customer profitability of the four representative credit-card users of the Freedom Card for 2011.
2. Develop profiles of (a) profitable card holders and (b) unprofitable card holders for City Bank.
3. Should City Bank charge its card holders for making inquiries (such as outstanding balances or disputed charges) or for replacing lost or stolen cards?
4. Anwar has an internal proposal that City Bank discontinue a sizable number of the low-volume credit-card customers. What factors should he consider in evaluating and responding to this proposal?
5. Anwar seeks your group's advice on an ethical issue he is facing. A chain of gambling Shopping Centres (Lucky Roller) has offered to provide Freedom Card holders with money advances of up to Rs 500 at its Shopping Centres. Anwar observes that from a strictly financial perspective, providing money advances to its customers would be highly profitable. Should Freedom Card holders be able to obtain money advances at Lucky Roller gambling Shopping Centres? Explain.

15 Allocation of Support-Department Costs, Common Costs, and Revenues

Learning Objectives

1. Distinguish the single-rate method from the dual-rate method
2. Understand how divisional incentives are affected by the choice between allocation based on budgeted and actual rates, and budgeted and actual usage
3. Allocate multiple support-department costs using the direct method, the step-down method, and the reciprocal method
4. Allocate common costs using the stand-alone method and the incremental method
5. Understand how bundling of products gives rise to revenue-allocation issues

How a company allocates its overhead and internal support costs—costs related to marketing, advertising, and other internal services—among its various production departments or projects, can have a big impact on how profitable those departments or projects are.

While the allocation won't affect the firm's profit as a whole, if the allocation isn't done properly, it can make some departments and projects (and their managers) look better or worse than they should profit-wise. As the following article shows, the method of allocating costs for a project affects not just the firm but also the consumer. Based on the method used, consumers may spend more, or less, for the same service.

Cost Allocation and the Future of "Smart Grid" Energy Infrastructure[1]

Across the globe, countries are adopting alternative methods of generating and distributing energy. In the United States, government leaders and companies ranging from GE to Google are advocating the movement towards a "Smart Grid"—that is, making transmission and power lines operate and communicate in a more effective and efficient manner using technology, computers, and software. This proposed system would also integrate with emerging clean energy sources, such as solar farms and geothermal systems, to help create a more sustainable electricity supply that reduces carbon emissions.

According to the Electric Power Resource Institute, the cost of developing the "Smart Grid" is $165 billion over the next two decades. These costs include new infrastructure and technology improvements—mostly to power lines—as well as traditional indirect costs for the organizations upgrading the power system, which include traditional support-department costs and common costs. Private utilities and the U.S. government will pay for the upfront costs of "Smart Grid" development, but those costs will be recouped over time by charging energy consumers. But one question remains: How should those costs be allocated for reimbursement?

A controversy has emerged as two cost allocation methods are being debated by the U.S. government. One method is interconnection-wide cost allocation. Under this system, everybody in the region where a new technology is deployed would have to help pay for it. For example, if new power lines and "smart" energy

[1] *Sources*: Garthwaite, Josie. 2009. The $160B question: Who should foot the bill for transmission buildout?" Salon.com, March 12; Jaffe, Mark. 2010. Cost of Smart-Grid projects shocks consumer advocates. *The Denver Post*, February 14.

meters are deployed in Denver, everybody in Colorado would help pay for them. Supporters argue that this method would help lessen the costs consumers would be charged by utilities for the significant investments in new technology.

Another competing proposal would only allocate costs to utility ratepayers that actually benefit from the new "Smart Grid" system. Using the previous example, only utility customers in Denver would be charged for the new power lines and energy meters (likely through additional monthly utility costs). Supporters of this method believe that customers with new "Smart Grid" systems should not be subsidized by those not receiving any of the benefits.

Regardless of the method selected, cost allocation is going to play a key role in the future of the U.S. energy generation and distribution system. The same allocation dilemmas apply to the costs of corporate support departments and the apportionment of revenues when products are sold in bundles. These concerns are common to managers at manufacturing companies such as Nestle, service companies such as Comcast, merchandising companies such as Trader Joe's, and academic institutions such as Auburn University. This chapter focuses on several challenges that arise with regard to cost and revenue allocations.

Allocating Support Department Costs Using the Single-Rate and Dual-Rate Methods

Learning Objective 

Distinguish the single-rate method

. . . one rate for allocating costs in a cost pool from the dual-rate method

. . . two rates for allocating costs in a cost pool—one for variable costs and one for fixed costs

Companies distinguish operating departments (and operating divisions) from support departments. An **operating department**, which is also called a **production department**, directly adds value to a product or service. A **support department**, which is also called a **service department**, provides the services that assist other internal departments (operating departments and other support departments) in the company. Examples of support departments are information systems and plant maintenance. Managers face two questions when allocating the costs of a support department to operating departments or divisions: (1) Should fixed costs of support departments be allocated to operating divisions? (2) If fixed costs are allocated, should variable and fixed costs be allocated in the same way? With regard to the first question, most companies believe that fixed costs of support departments should be allocated because the support department needs to incur fixed costs to provide operating divisions with the services they require. Depending on the answer to the second question, there are two approaches to allocating support-department costs: the *single-rate cost-allocation method* and the *dual-rate cost-allocation method*.

Single-Rate and Dual-Rate Methods

The **single-rate method** makes no distinction between fixed and variable costs. It allocates costs in each cost pool (support department in this section) to cost objects (operating divisions in this section) using the same rate per unit of a single allocation base. By contrast, the **dual-rate method** partitions the cost of each support department into two pools—a variable-cost pool and a fixed-cost pool—and allocates each using a different cost-allocation base. When using either the single-rate method or the dual-rate method, managers can allocate support-department costs to operating divisions based on either a *budgeted* rate or the eventual *actual* cost rate. The latter approach is neither conceptually preferred nor widely used in practice (we explain why in the next section). Accordingly, we illustrate the single-rate and dual-rate methods next based on the use of *budgeted* rates.

Consider the Central Computer Department of Sand Hill Company (SHC). This support department has two users, both operating divisions: the Microcomputer Division and the Peripheral Equipment Division. The following data relate to the 2012 budget:

Practical capacity	18,750 hours
Fixed costs of operating the computer facility in the 6,000-hour to 18,750-hour relevant range	Rs 3,00,00,000
Budgeted long-run usage (quantity) in hours:	
Microcomputer Division	8,000 hours
Peripheral Equipment Division	4,000 hours
Total	12,000 hours
Budgeted variable cost per hour in the 6,000-hour to 18,750-hour relevant range	Rs 2,000 per hour used
Actual usage in 2009 in hours:	
Microcomputer Division	9,000 hours
Peripheral Equipment Division	3,000 hours
Total	12,000 hours

The budgeted rates for Central Computer Department costs can be computed based on either the demand for computer services or the supply of computer services. We consider the allocation of Central Computer Department costs based first on the demand for (or usage of) computer services and then on the supply of computer services.

Allocation Based on the Demand for (or Usage of) Computer Services

We present the single-rate method followed by the dual-rate method.

Single-rate method In this method, a combined budgeted rate is used for fixed and variable costs. The rate is calculated as follows.

Budgeted usage	12,000 hours
Budgeted total cost pool: Rs 3,00,00,000 + (12,000 hours × Rs 2,000/hour)	Rs 5,40,00,000
Budgeted total rate per hour: Rs 5,40,00,000 ÷ 12,000 hours	Rs 4,500 per hour used
Allocation rate for Microcomputer Division	Rs 4,500 per hour used
Allocation rate for Peripheral Equipment Division	Rs 4,500 per hour used

Note that the budgeted rate of Rs 4,500 per hour is substantially higher than the Rs 2,000 budgeted *variable* cost per hour. That's because the Rs 4,500 rate includes an allocated amount of Rs 2,500 per hour (budgeted fixed costs, Rs 3,00,00,000, ÷ budgeted usage, 12,000 hours) for the *fixed* costs of operating the facility.

Under the single-rate method, divisions are charged the budgeted rate for each hour of *actual* use of the central facility. Applying this to our example, SHC allocates central computer department costs based on the Rs 4,500 per hour budgeted rate and actual hours used by the operating divisions. The support costs allocated to the two divisions under this method are as follows:

Microcomputer Division: 9,000 hours × Rs 4,500 per hour	Rs 4,05,00,000
Peripheral Equipment Division: 3,000 hours × Rs 4,500 per hour	Rs 1,35,00,000

Dual-rate method When the dual-rate method is used, allocation bases must be chosen for both the variable and fixed cost pools of the Central Computer Department. As in the single-rate method, variable costs are assigned based on the *budgeted* variable cost per hour of Rs 2,000 for *actual* hours used by each division. However, fixed costs are assigned based on *budgeted* fixed costs per hour and the *budgeted* number of hours for each division. Given the budgeted usage of 8,000 hours for the microcomputer division and 4,000 hours for the peripheral equipment division, the budgeted fixed-cost rate is Rs 2,500 per hour (Rs 3,00,00,000 ÷ 12,000 hours), as before. Since this rate is charged on the basis of the *budgeted* usage, however, the fixed costs are effectively allocated in advance as a lump-sum based on the relative proportions of the central computing facilities expected to be used by the operating divisions.

The costs allocated to the microcomputer division in 2012 under the dual-rate method would be as follows:

Fixed costs: Rs 2,500 per hour × 8,000 (budgeted) hours	Rs 2,00,00,000
Variable costs: Rs 2,000 per hour × 9,000 (actual) hours	1,80,00,000
Total costs	Rs 3,80,00,000

The costs allocated to the Peripheral Equipment Division in 2012 would be:

Fixed costs: Rs 2,500 per hour × 4,000 (budgeted) hours	Rs 1,00,00,000
Variable costs: Rs 2,000 per hour × 3,000 (actual) hours	60,00,000
Total costs	Rs 1,60,00,000

Note that each operating division is charged the same amount for variable costs under the single-rate and dual-rate methods (Rs 2,000 per hour multiplied by the actual hours of use). However, the overall assignment of costs differs under the two methods because the single-rate method allocates fixed costs of the support department based on actual usage of computer resources by the operating divisions, whereas the dual-rate method allocates fixed costs based on budgeted usage.

We next consider the alternative approach of allocating Central Computer Department costs based on the capacity of computer services supplied.

Allocation Based on the Supply of Capacity

We illustrate this approach using the 18,750 hours of practical capacity of the Central Computer Department. The budgeted rate is then determined as follows:

Budgeted fixed-cost rate per hour, Rs 3,00,00,000 ÷ 18,750 hours	Rs 1,600 per hour
Budgeted variable-cost rate per hour	2,000 per hour
Budgeted total-cost rate per hour	Rs 3,600 per hour

Using the same options for the single-rate and dual-rate methods as in the previous section, the support cost allocations to the operating divisions are as follows:

Single-rate method

Microcomputer Division: Rs 3,600 per hour × 9,000 (actual) hours	Rs 3,24,00,000
Peripheral Equipment Division: Rs 3,600 per hour × 3,000 (actual) hours	1,08,00,000
Fixed costs of unused computer capacity:	
Rs 1,600 per hour × 6,750 hours[a]	1,08,00,000

[a] 6,750 hours = Practical capacity of 18,750 – (9,000 hours used by Microcomputer Division + 3,000 hours used by Peripheral Equipment Division).

Dual-rate method

Microcomputer Division	
Fixed costs: Rs 1,600 per hour × 8,000 (budgeted) hours	Rs 1,28,00,000
Variable costs: Rs 2,000 per hour × 9,000 (actual) hours	1,80,00,000
Total costs	Rs 3,08,00,000

Peripheral Equipment Division		
Fixed costs: Rs 1,600 per hour × 4,000 (budgeted) hours		Rs 64,00,000
Variable costs: Rs 2,000 per hour × 3,000 (actual) hours		60,00,000
Total costs	Rs 1,24,00,000	
Fixed costs of unused computer capacity:		
Rs 1,600 per hour × 6,750 hours[b]		Rs 1,08,00,000

[b] 6,750 hours = Practical capacity of 18,750 hours – (8,000 hours budgeted to be used by Microcomputer Division + 4,000 hours budgeted to be used by Peripheral Equipment Division).

When practical capacity is used to allocate costs, the single-rate method allocates only the actual fixed-cost resources used by the microcomputer and peripheral equipment divisions, while the dual-rate method allocates the budgeted fixed-cost resources to be used by the operating divisions. Unused central computer department resources are highlighted but usually not allocated to the divisions.[2]

The advantage of using practical capacity to allocate costs is that it focuses management's attention on managing unused capacity (described in Chapter 9 and Chapter 13). Using practical capacity also avoids burdening the user divisions with the cost of unused capacity of the Central Computer Department. In contrast, when costs are allocated on the basis of the demand for computer services (either budgeted or actual usage), all Rs 3,00,00,000 of fixed costs, including the cost of unused capacity, are allocated to user divisions. If costs are used as a basis for pricing, then charging user divisions for unused capacity could result in the downward demand spiral.

Single-Rate Versus Dual-Rate Method

There are benefits and costs of both the single-rate and dual-rate methods. One benefit of the single-rate method is the low cost to implement it. The single-rate method avoids the often-expensive analysis necessary to classify the individual cost items of a department into fixed and variable categories. Also, by conditioning the final allocations on the actual usage of central facilities, rather than basing them solely on uncertain forecasts of expected demand, it offers the user divisions some operational control over the charges they bear.

A problem with the single-rate method is that it makes the allocated fixed costs of the support department appear as variable costs to the operating divisions. Consequently, the single-rate method may lead division managers to make outsourcing decisions that are in their own best interest but that may be inefficient from the standpoint of the organization as a whole. Consider the setting where allocations are made on the basis of the demand for computer services. In this case, each user division is charged Rs 4,500 per hour under the single-rate method (recall that Rs 2,500 of this charge relates to the allocated fixed costs of the central computer department). Suppose an external vendor offers the microcomputer division computer services at a rate of Rs 3,400 per hour, at a time when the central computer department has unused capacity. The microcomputer division's managers would be tempted to use this vendor because it would lower the division's costs (Rs 3,400 per hour instead of the Rs 4,500 per hour internal charge for computer services). In the short run, however, the fixed costs of the central computer department remain unchanged in the relevant range (between 6,000 hours of usage and the practical capacity of 18,750 hours). SHC will therefore incur an additional cost of Rs 1,400 per hour if the managers were to take this offer—the difference between the Rs 3,400 external purchase price and the true internal variable cost of Rs 2,000 of using the central computer department.

The divergence created under the single-rate method between SHC's interests and those of its division managers is lessened when allocation is done on the basis of practical

[2] In our example, the cost of unused capacity under the single-rate and the dual-rate methods coincide (each equals Rs 1,08,00,000). This occurs because the total actual usage of the facility matches the total expected usage of 12,000 hours. The budgeted cost of unused capacity (in the dual-rate method) can be either greater or lower than the actual cost (in the single-rate method), depending on whether the total actual usage is lower or higher than the budgeted usage.

capacity. The variable cost per hour perceived by the operating division managers is now Rs 3,600 (rather than the Rs 4,500 rate when allocation is based on budgeted usage). However, any external offer above Rs 2,000 (SHC's true variable cost) and below Rs 3,600 (the single-rate charge per hour) will still result in the user manager preferring to outsource the service at the expense of SHC's overall profits.

A benefit of the dual-rate method is that it signals to division managers how variable costs and fixed costs behave differently. This information guides division managers to make decisions that benefit the organization as a whole, as well as each division. For example, using a third-party computer provider that charges more than Rs 2,000 per hour would result in SHC's being worse off than if its own central computer department were used, because the latter has a variable cost of Rs 2,000 per hour. Under the dual-rate method, neither division manager has an incentive to pay more than Rs 2,000 per hour for an external provider because the internal charge for computer services is precisely that amount. By charging the fixed costs of resources budgeted to be used by the divisions as a lump sum, the dual-rate method succeeds in removing fixed costs from the division managers' consideration when making marginal decisions regarding the outsourcing of services. It thus avoids the potential conflict of interest that can arise under the single-rate method.

Recently, the dual-rate method has been receiving more attention. Resource Consumption Accounting (RCA), an emerging management accounting system, employs an allocation procedure akin to a dual-rate system. For each cost/resource pool, cost assignment rates for fixed costs are based on practical capacity supplied, while rates for proportional costs (i.e., costs that vary with regard to the output of the resource pool) are based on planned quantities.[3]

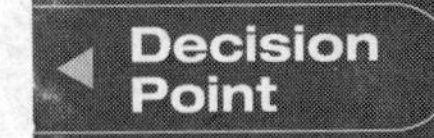

When should managers use the dual-rate method over the single-rate method?

Budgeted Versus Actual Costs, and the Choice of Allocation Base

Learning Objective

Understand how divisional incentives are affected by the choice between allocation based on budgeted and actual rates,

. . . budgeted rates provide certainty to users about charges and motivate the support division to engage in cost control

and budgeted and actual usage

. . . budgeted usage helps in planning and efficient utilization of fixed resources, actual usage controls consumption of variable resources

The allocation methods previously outlined follow specific procedures in terms of the support department costs that are considered as well as the manner in which costs are assigned to the operating departments. In this section, we examine these choices in greater detail and consider the impact of alternative approaches. We show that the decision whether to use actual or budgeted costs, as well as the choice between actual and budgeted usage as allocation base, has a significant impact on the cost allocated to each division and the incentives of the division managers.

Budgeted Versus Actual Rates

In both the single-rate and dual-rate methods, we use budgeted rates to assign support department costs (fixed as well as variable costs). An alternative approach would involve using the actual rates based on the support costs realized during the period. This method is much less common because of the level of uncertainty it imposes on user divisions. When allocations are made using budgeted rates, managers of divisions to which costs are allocated know with certainty the rates to be used in that budget period. Users can then determine the amount of the service to request and—if company policy allows—whether to use the internal source or an external vendor. In contrast, when actual rates are used for cost allocation, user divisions are kept unaware of their charges until the end of the budget period.

[3] Other salient features of Resource Consumption Accounting (RCA) include the selective use of activity-based costing, the nonassignment of fixed costs when causal relationships cannot be established, and the depreciation of assets based on their replacement cost. RCA has its roots in the nearly fifty-year-old German cost accounting system called Grenzplankostenrechnung (GPK), which is used by organizations such as Mercedes-Benz, Porsche, and Stihl. For further details, as well as illustrations of the use of RCA and GPK in organizations, see S. Webber and B. Clinton, "Resource Consumption Accounting Applied: The Clopay Case," *Management Accounting Quarterly* (Fall 2004) and B. Mackie, "Merging GPK and ABC on the Road to RCA," *Strategic Finance* (November 2006).

Budgeted rates also help motivate the manager of the support (or supplier) department (for example, the central computer department) to improve efficiency. During the budget period, the support department, not the user divisions, bears the risk of any unfavorable cost variances. That's because user divisions do not pay for any costs or inefficiencies of the supplier department that cause actual rates to exceed budgeted rates.

The manager of the supplier department would likely view the budgeted rates negatively if unfavorable cost variances occur due to price increases outside of his or her control. Some organizations try to identify these uncontrollable factors and relieve the support department manager of responsibility for these variances. In other organizations, the supplier department and the user division agree to share the risk (through an explicit formula) of a large, uncontrollable increase in the prices of inputs used by the supplier department. This procedure avoids imposing the risk completely on either the supplier department (as when budgeted rates are used) or the user division (as in the case of actual rates).

For the rest of this chapter, we will continue to consider only allocation methods that are based on the budgeted cost of support services.

Budgeted Versus Actual Usage

In both the single-rate and dual-rate methods, the variable costs are assigned on the basis of budgeted rates and actual usage. Since the variable costs are directly and causally linked to usage, charging them as a function of the actual usage is appropriate. Moreover, allocating variable costs on the basis of budgeted usage would provide the user departments with no incentive to control their consumption of support services.

What about the fixed costs? Consider the budget of Rs 3,00,00,000 fixed costs at the central computer department of SHC. Recall that budgeted usage is 8,000 hours for the microcomputer division and 4,000 hours for the peripheral equipment division. Assume that actual usage by the microcomputer division is always equal to budgeted usage. We consider three cases: when actual usage by the peripheral equipment division equals (Case 1), is greater than (Case 2), and is less than (Case 3) budgeted usage.

Fixed Cost Allocation Based on Budgeted Rates and Budgeted Usage This is the dual-rate procedure outlined in the previous section. When budgeted usage is the allocation base, regardless of the actual usage of facilities (i.e., whether Case 1, 2, or 3 occurs), user divisions receive a preset lump-sum fixed cost charge. If rates are based on expected demand (Rs 2,500 per hour), the microcomputer division is assigned Rs 2,00,00,000 and the peripheral equipment division, Rs 1,00,00,000. If rates are set using practical capacity (Rs 1,600 per hour), the microcomputer division is charged Rs 1,28,00,000, the peripheral equipment division is allocated Rs 64,00,000, and the remaining Rs 1,08,00,000 is the unallocated cost of excess capacity.

The advantage of knowing the allocations in advance is that it helps the user divisions with both short-run and long-run planning. Companies commit to infrastructure costs (such as the fixed costs of a support department) on the basis of a long-run planning horizon; budgeted usage measures the long-run demands of the user divisions for support-department services.

Allocating fixed costs on the basis of budgeted long-run usage may tempt some managers to underestimate their planned usage. Underestimating will result in their divisions bearing a lower percentage of fixed costs (assuming all other managers do not similarly underestimate their usage). To discourage such underestimates, some companies offer bonuses or other rewards—the "carrot" approach—to managers who make accurate forecasts of long-run usage. Other companies impose cost penalties—the "stick" approach—for underestimating long-run usage. For instance, a higher cost rate is charged after a division exceeds its budgeted usage.

Fixed Cost Allocation Based on Budgeted Rates and Actual Usage Column 2 of Exhibit 15-1 provides the allocations when the budgeted rate is based on expected demand (Rs 2,500 per hour), while column 3 shows the allocations when practical capacity is used to derive the rate (Rs 1,600 per hour). Note that each operating division's fixed

Exhibit 15-1 Effect of Variations in Actual Usage on Fixed Cost Allocation to Operating Divisions

	(1) Actual Usage		(2) Budgeted Rate Based on Expected Demand[a]		(3) Budgeted Rate Based on Practical Capacity[b]		(4) Allocation of Budgeted Total Fixed Cost	
Case	Micro. Div.	Periph. Div.	Micro. Div.	Periph. Div.	Micro. Div.	Periph. Div.	Micro. Div.	Periph. Div.
1	8,000 hours	4,000 hours	Rs 2,00,00,000	Rs 1,00,00,000	Rs 1,28,00,000	Rs 64,00,000	Rs 2,00,00,000[c]	Rs 1,00,00,000[d]
2	8,000 hours	7,000 hours	Rs 2,00,00,000	Rs 1,75,00,000	Rs 1,28,00,000	Rs 1,12,00,000	Rs 1,60,00,000[e]	Rs 1,40,00,000[f]
3	8,000 hours	2,000 hours	Rs 2,00,00,000	Rs 50,00,000	Rs 1,28,00,000	Rs 32,00,000	Rs 2,40,00,000[g]	Rs 60,00,000[h]

a $\frac{\text{Rs } 3{,}00{,}00{,}000}{(8{,}000 + 4{,}000) \text{ hours}} = \text{Rs } 2500 \text{ per hour}$ b $\frac{\text{Rs } 3{,}00{,}00{,}000}{18{,}750 \text{ hours}} = \text{Rs } 1{,}600 \text{ per hour}$ c $\frac{8{,}000}{(8{,}000 + 4{,}000)} \times \text{Rs } 3{,}00{,}00{,}000$ d $\frac{4{,}000}{(8{,}000 + 4{,}000)} \times \text{Rs } 3{,}00{,}00{,}000$

e $\frac{8{,}000}{(8{,}000 + 7{,}000)} \times \text{Rs } 3{,}00{,}00{,}000$ f $\frac{7{,}000}{(8{,}000 + 7{,}000)} \times \text{Rs } 3{,}00{,}00{,}000$ g $\frac{8{,}000}{(8{,}000 + 2{,}000)} \times \text{Rs } 3{,}00{,}00{,}000$ h $\frac{2{,}000}{(8{,}000 + 2{,}000)} \times \text{Rs } 3{,}00{,}00{,}000$

cost allocation varies based on its actual usage of support facilities. However, variations in actual usage in one division do not affect the costs allocated to the other division. The microcomputer division is allocated either Rs 2,00,00,000 or Rs 1,28,00,000, depending on the budgeted rate chosen, independent of the peripheral equipment division's actual usage. Therefore, combining actual usage as the allocation base with budgeted rates provides user divisions with advanced knowledge of rates, as well as control over the costs charged to them.[4]

Note, however, that this allocation procedure for fixed costs is exactly the same as that under the single-rate method. As such, the procedure shares the disadvantages of the single-rate method discussed in the previous section, such as charging excessively high costs, including the cost of unused capacity, when rates are based on expected usage. Moreover, even when rates are based on practical capacity, recall that allocating fixed cost rates based on actual usage induces conflicts of interest between the user divisions and the firm when evaluating outsourcing possibilities.

Allocating Budgeted Fixed Costs Based on Actual Usage Finally, consider the impact of having actual usage as the allocation base when the firm assigns total budgeted fixed costs to operating divisions (rather than specifying budgeted fixed cost rates, as we have thus far). If the budgeted fixed costs of Rs 3,00,00,000 are allocated using budgeted usage, we are back in the familiar dual-rate setting. On the other hand, if the actual usage of the facility is the basis for allocation, the charges would equal the amounts in Exhibit 15-1, column 4. In Case 1, the fixed-cost allocation equals the budgeted amount (which is also the same as the charge under the dual-rate method). In Case 2, the fixed-cost allocation is Rs 40,00,000 less to the microcomputer division than the amount based on budgeted usage (Rs 1,60,00,000 versus Rs 2,00,00,000). In Case 3, the fixed-cost allocation is Rs 40,00,000 more to the microcomputer division than the amount based on budgeted usage (Rs 2,40,00,000 versus Rs 2,00,00,000). Why does the microcomputer division receive Rs 40,00,000 more in costs in Case 3, even though its actual usage equals its budgeted usage? Because the total fixed costs of Rs 3,00,00,000 are now spread over 2,000 fewer hours of actual total usage. In other words, the lower usage by the peripheral equipment division leads to an increase in the fixed costs allocated to the microcomputer division. When budgeted fixed costs are allocated based on actual usage, user divisions will not know their fixed cost allocations until the end of the budget period. This method therefore shares the same flaw as those that rely on the use of actual cost realizations rather than budgeted cost rates.

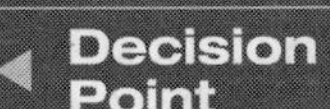

What factors should managers consider when deciding between allocation based on budgeted and actual rates, and budgeted and actual usage?

To summarize, there are excellent economic and motivational reasons to justify the precise forms of the single-rate and dual-rate methods considered in the previous section, and in particular, to recommend the dual-rate allocation procedure.

[4] The total amount of fixed costs allocated to divisions will in general not equal the actual realized costs. Adjustments for overallocations and underallocations would then be made using the methods discussed previously in chapters 4, 7 and 8.

Allocating Costs of Multiple Support Departments

Learning Objective 3

Allocate multiple support-department costs using the direct method,

. . . allocate support-department costs directly to operating departments the step-down method,

. . . partially allocates support-department costs to other support departments and the reciprocal method

. . . fully allocates support-department costs to other support departments

We just examined general issues that arise when allocating costs from one support department to operating divisions. In this section, we examine the special cost-allocation problems that arise when two or more of the support departments whose costs are being allocated provide reciprocal support to each other as well as to operating departments. An example of reciprocal support is a Corporate Human Resource (HR) Department providing services to a Corporate Legal Department (such as advice about hiring attorneys) while the Corporate Legal Department provides services to the HR department (such as advice on compliance with labor laws). More-accurate support-department cost allocations result in more-accurate product, service, and customer costs.

Consider Castleford Engineering, which operates at practical capacity to manufacture engines used in electric-power generating plants. Castleford has two support departments and two operating departments in its manufacturing facility:

Support Departments	Operating Departments
Plant (and equipment) maintenance	Machining
Information systems	Assembly

The two support departments at Castleford provide reciprocal support to each other as well as support to the two operating departments. Costs are accumulated in each department for planning and control purposes. Exhibit 15-2 displays the data for this example. To understand the percentages in this exhibit, consider the Plant Maintenance Department. This support department provides a total of 20,000 hours of support work: 20% (4,000 ÷ 20,000 = 0.20) for the Information Systems Department, 30% (6,000 ÷ 20,000 = 0.30) for the Machining Department, and 50% (10,000 ÷ 20,000 = 0.50) for the Assembly Department.

We now examine three methods of allocating the costs of reciprocal support departments: *direct*, *step-down*, and *reciprocal*. To simplify the explanation and to focus on concepts, we use the single-rate method to allocate the costs of each support department using budgeted rates and budgeted hours used by the other departments. (The Problem for Self-Study illustrates the dual-rate method for allocating reciprocal support-department costs.)

Direct Method

The **direct method** allocates each support department's costs to operating departments only. The direct method does not allocate support-department costs to other support departments. Exhibit 15-3 illustrates this method using the data in Exhibit 15-2. The

Exhibit 15-2 Data for Allocating Support-Department Costs at Castleford Engineering for 2011

File Edit View Insert Format Tools Data Window Help

	A	B	C	D	E	F	G
1		SUPPORT DEPARTMENTS			OPERATING DEPARTMENTS		
2		Plant Maintenance	Information Systems		Machining	Assembly	Total
3	Budgeted overhead costs						
4	before any interdepartment cost allocations	Rs 6,30,00,000	Rs 1,45,21,500		Rs 4,00,00,000	Rs 2,00,00,000	Rs 13,75,21,500
5	Support work furnished:						
6	By Plant Maintenance						
7	Budgeted labor-hours	—	4,000		6,000	10,000	20,000
8	Percentage	—	20%		30%	50%	100%
9	By Information Systems						
10	Budgeted computer hours	500	—		4,000	500	5,000
11	Percentage	10%	—		80%	10%	100%

Exhibit 15-3 Direct Method of Allocating Support-Department Costs at Castleford Engineering for 2011

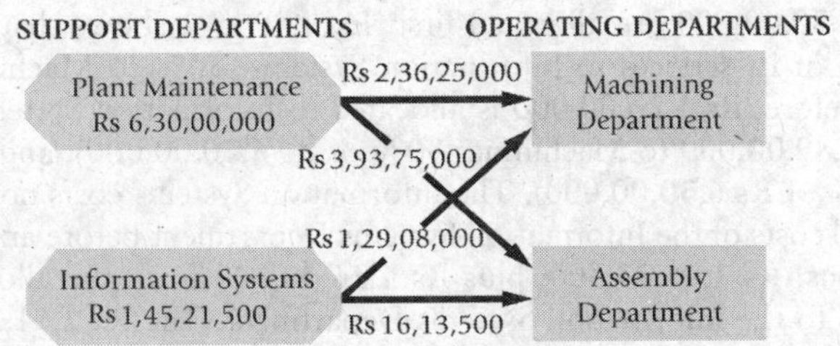

	A	B	C	D	E	F	G
1		SUPPORT DEPARTMENTS			OPERATING DEPARTMENTS		
2		Plant Maintenance	Information Systems		Machining	Assembly	Total
3	Budgeted overhead costs						
4	before any interdepartment cost allocations	Rs 6,30,00,000	Rs 1,45,21,500		Rs 4,00,00,000	Rs 2,00,00,000	Rs 13,75,21,500
5	Allocation of Plant Maintenance (3/8, 5/8)[a]	(6,30,00,000)			2,36,25,000	3,93,75,000	
6	Allocation of Information Systems (8/9, 1/9)[b]		(1,45,21,500)		1,29,08,000	16,13,500	
7							
8	Total budgeted overhead of operating departments	Rs 0	Rs 0		Rs 7,65, 33,000	Rs 6,09,88,500	Rs 13,75,21,500
9							
10	[a] Base is (6,000 + 10,000), or 16,000 hours; 6,000 ÷ 16,000 = 3/8; 10,000 ÷ 16,000 = 5/8.						
11	[b] Base is (4,000 + 500), or 4,500 hours; 4,000 ÷ 4,500 = 8/9; 500 ÷ 4,500 = 1/9.						

base used to allocate Plant Maintenance costs to the operating departments is the budgeted total maintenance labor-hours worked in the operating departments: 6,000 + 10,000 = 16,000 hours. This amount excludes the 4,000 hours of budgeted support time provided by Plant Maintenance to Information Systems. Similarly, the base used for allocation of Information Systems costs to the operating departments is 4,000 + 500 = 4,500 budgeted hours of computer time, which excludes the 500 hours of budgeted support time provided by Information Systems to Plant Maintenance.

An equivalent approach to implementing the direct method involves calculating a budgeted rate for each support department's costs. For example, the rate for Plant Maintenance Department costs is Rs 6,30,00,000 ÷ 16,000 hours, or Rs 3,937.5 per hour. The Machining Department is then allocated Rs 2,36,25,000 (Rs 3,937.5 per hour ÷ 6,000 hours) while the Assembly Department is assigned Rs 3,93,75,000 (Rs 3,937.5 per hour × 10,000 hours). For ease of explanation throughout this section, we will use the fraction of the support-department services used by other departments, rather than calculate budgeted rates, to allocate support-department costs.

The direct method is widely practiced because of its ease of use. The benefit of the direct method is simplicity. There is no need to predict the usage of support-department services by other support departments. A disadvantage of the direct method is that it ignores information about reciprocal services provided among support departments and can therefore lead to inaccurate estimates of the cost of operating departments. We now examine a second approach, which partially recognizes the services provided among support departments.

Step-Down Method

Some organizations use the **step-down method**—also called the **sequential allocation method**—which allocates support-department costs to other support departments and to operating departments in a sequential manner that partially recognizes the mutual services provided among all support departments.

Exhibit 15-4 shows the step-down method. The Plant Maintenance costs of Rs 6,30,00,000 are allocated first. Exhibit 15-2 shows that Plant Maintenance provides 20% of its services to Information Systems, 30% to Machining, and 50% to Assembly. Therefore, Rs 1,26,00,000 is allocated to Information Systems (20% of Rs 6,30,00,000), Rs 1,89,00,000 to Machining (30% of Rs 6,30,00,000), and Rs 3,15,00,000 to Assembly (50% of Rs 6,30,00,000). The Information Systems costs now total Rs 2,71,21,500: budgeted costs of the Information Systems Department before any interdepartmental cost allocations, Rs 1,45,21,500, plus Rs 1,26,00,000 from the allocation of Plant Maintenance costs to the Information Systems Department. The Rs 2,71,21,500 is then only allocated between the two operating departments based on the proportion of the Information Systems Department services provided to Machining and Assembly. From Exhibit 15-2, the Information Systems Department provides 80% of its services to Machining and 10% to Assembly, so Rs 2,41,08,000 (8/9 × Rs 2,71,21,500) is allocated to Machining and Rs 30,13,500 (1/9 × Rs 2,71,21,500) is allocated to Assembly.

Note that this method requires the support departments to be ranked (sequenced) in the order that the step-down allocation is to proceed. In our example, the costs of the Plant Maintenance Department were allocated first to all other departments, including the Information Systems Department. The costs of the Information Systems support department were allocated second, but only to the two operating departments. Different sequences will result in different allocations of support-department costs to operating departments—for example, if the Information Systems Department costs had been allocated first and the Plant Maintenance Department costs second. A popular step-down sequence begins with the support department that renders the highest percentage of its total services to *other support departments*. The sequence continues with the department

Exhibit 15-4 Step-Down Method of Allocating Support-Department Costs at Castleford Engineering for 2011

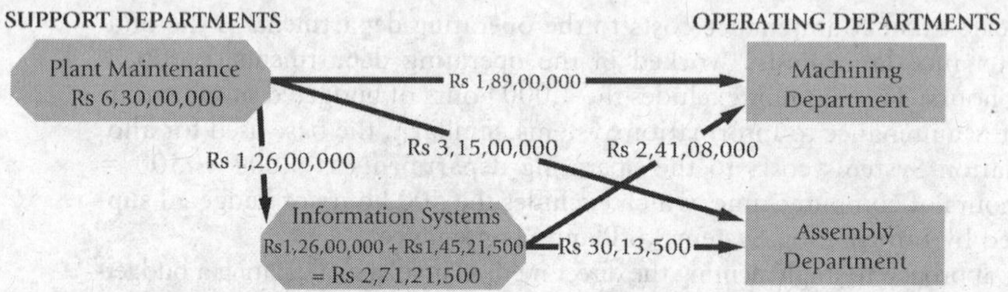

	A	B	C	D	E	F	G
1		SUPPORT DEPARTMENTS			OPERATING DEPARTMENTS		
2		Plant Maintenance	Information Systems		Machining	Assembly	Total
3	Budgeted overhead costs before any						
4	interdepartment cost allocations	Rs 6,30,00,000	Rs1,45,21,500		Rs 4,00,00,000	Rs 2,00,00,000	Rs 13,75,21,500
5	Allocation of Plant Maintenance (2/10, 3/10, 5/10)[a]	(6,30,00,000)	1,26,00,000		1,89,00,000	3,15,00,000	
6			2,71,21,500				
7	Allocation of Information Systems (8/9, 1/9)[b]		(2,71,21,500)		2,41,00,000	30,13,500	
8							
9	Total budgeted overhead of operating departments	Rs 0	Rs 0		Rs 8,30,00,000	Rs 5,45,13,500	Rs 13,75,21,500
10							
11	[a] Base is (4,000 + 6,000 + 10,000), or 20,000 hours; 4,000 ÷ 20,000 = 2/10; 6,000 ÷ 20,000 = 3/10; 10,000 ÷ 20,000 = 5/10.						
12	[b] Base is (4,000 + 500), or 4,500 hours; 4,000 ÷ 4,500 = 8/9; 500 ÷ 4,500 = 1/9.						

that renders the next-highest percentage, and so on, ending with the support department that renders the lowest percentage.[5] In our example, costs of the Plant Maintenance Department were allocated first because it provides 20% of its services to the Information Systems Department, whereas the Information Systems Department provides only 10% of its services to the Plant Maintenance Department (see Exhibit 15-2).

Under the step-down method, once a support department's costs have been allocated, no subsequent support-department costs are allocated back to it. Once the Plant Maintenance Department costs are allocated, it receives no further allocation from other (lower-ranked) support departments. The result is that the step-down method does not recognize the total services that support departments provide to one another. The reciprocal method fully recognizes all such services, as you will see next.

Reciprocal Method

The **reciprocal method** allocates support-department costs to operating departments by fully recognizing the mutual services provided among all support departments. For example, the Plant Maintenance Department maintains all the computer equipment in the Information Systems Department. Similarly, Information Systems provides database support for Plant Maintenance. The reciprocal method fully incorporates interdepartmental relationships into the support-department cost allocations.

Exhibit 15-5 presents one way to understand the reciprocal method. First, Plant Maintenance costs are allocated to all other departments, including the Information Systems support department (Information Systems, 20%; Machining, 30%; Assembly, 50%). The costs in the Information Systems Department then total Rs 2,71,21,500 (Rs 1,45,21,500 + Rs 1,26,00,000 from the first-round allocation), as in Exhibit 15-4. The Rs 2,71,21,500 is then allocated to all other departments that the Information Systems Department supports, including the Plant Maintenance support department—Plant Maintenance, 10%; Machining, 80%; and Assembly, 10% (see Exhibit 15-2). The Plant Maintenance costs that had been brought down to Rs 0 now have Rs 27,12,150 from the Information Systems Department allocation. These costs are again reallocated to all other departments, including Information Systems, in the same ratio that the Plant Maintenance costs were previously assigned. Now the Information Systems Department costs that had been brought down to Rs 0 have Rs 5,42,430 from the Plant Maintenance Department allocations. These costs are again allocated in the same ratio that the Information Systems Department costs were previously assigned. Successive rounds result in smaller and smaller amounts being allocated to and reallocated from the support departments until eventually all support-department costs are allocated to the operating departments under the reciprocal method are given by the amounts in line 16 of Exhibit 15-5.

An alternative way to implement the reciprocal method is to formulate and solve linear equations. This process requires three steps.

Step 1: Express Support Department Costs and Reciprocal Relationships in the Form of Linear Equations. Let *PM* be the *complete reciprocated costs* of Plant Maintenance and *IS* be the *complete reciprocated costs* of Information Systems. By **complete reciprocated costs,** we mean the support department's own costs plus any interdepartmental cost allocations. We then express the data in Exhibit 15-2 as follows:

$$PM = \text{Rs } 6{,}30{,}00{,}000 + 0.1IS \quad (1)$$
$$IS = \text{Rs } 1{,}45{,}21{,}500 + 0.2PM \quad (2)$$

The 0.1*IS* term in equation (1) is the percentage of the Information Systems services *used by* Plant Maintenance. The 0.2*PM* term in equation (2) is the percentage of Plant Maintenance services *used by* Information Systems.

[5] An alternative approach to selecting the sequence of allocations is to begin with the support department that renders the highest rupee amount of services to other support departments. The sequence ends with the allocation of the costs of the department that renders the lowest rupee amount of services to other support departments.

Exhibit 15-5 Reciprocal Method of Allocating Support-Department Costs Using Repeated Iterations at Castleford Engineering for 2011

	A	B	C	D	E	F	G
1		SUPPORT DEPARTMENTS			OPERATING DEPARTMENTS		
2		Plant Maintenance	Information Systems		Machining	Assembly	Total
3	Budgeted overhead costs before any						
4	interdepartment cost allocations	Rs6,30,00,000	Rs1,45,21,500		Rs 4,00,00,000	Rs 2,00,00,000	Rs 13,75,21,500
5	1st Allocation of Plant Maintenance (2/10, 3/10, 5/10)[a]	(6,30,00,000)	1,26,00,000		1,89,00,000	3,15,00,000	
6			2,71,21,500				
7	1st Allocation of Information Systems (1/10, 8/10, 1/10)[b]	27,12,150	(2,71,21,500)		2,16,97,200	27,12,150	
8	2nd Allocation of Plant Maintenance (2/10, 3/10, 5/10)[a]	(27,12,150)	5,42,430		8,13,640	13,56,080	
9	2nd Allocation of Information Systems (1/10, 8/10, 1/10)[b]	54,240	(5,42,430)		4,33,950	54,240	
10	3rd Allocation of Plant Maintenance (2/10, 3/10, 5/10)[a]	(54,240)	10,850		16,270	27,120	
11	3rd Allocation of Information Systems (1/10, 8/10, 1/10)[b]	1,090	(10,850)		8,670	1,090	
12	4th Allocation of Plant Maintenance (2/10, 3/10, 5/10)[a]	(1,090)	220		330	540	
13	4th Allocation of Information Systems (1/10, 8/10, 1/10)[b]	20	(220)		180	20	
14	4th Allocation of Plant Maintenance (2/10, 3/10, 5/10)[a]	(20)	0		10	10	
15							
16	Total budgeted overhead of operating departments	Rs 0	Rs 0		Rs 8,18,70,250	Rs5,56,51,250	Rs 13,75,21,500
17							
18	Total support department amounts allocated and reallocated (the numbers in parentheses in the first two columns):						
19	Plant Maintenance: Rs 6,30,00,000 + Rs 27,12,150 + Rs 54,240 + Rs 1,090 + Rs 20 = Rs 6,57,67,500						
20	Information Systems: Rs 2,71,21,500 + Rs 5,42,430 + Rs10,850 + Rs 220 = Rs 2,76,75,000						
21							
22	[a] Base is (4,000 + 6,000 + 10,000), or 20,000 hours; 4,000 ÷ 20,000 = 2/10; 6,000 ÷ 20,000 = 3/10; 10,000 ÷ 20,000 = 5/10.						
23	[b] Base is (500 + 4,000 + 500), or 5,000 hours; 500 ÷ 5,000 = 1/10; 4,000 ÷ 5,000 = 8/10; 500 ÷ 5,000 = 1/10.						

Step 2: Solve the Set of Linear Equations to Obtain the Complete Reciprocated Costs of Each Support Department. Substituting equation (1) into (2):

$$IS = \text{Rs}1{,}45{,}21{,}500 + [0.2(6{,}30{,}00{,}000 + 0.1IS)]$$
$$IS = \text{Rs } 1{,}45{,}21{,}500 + \text{Rs } 1{,}26{,}00{,}000 + 0.02IS$$
$$0.98IS = \text{Rs } 2{,}71{,}21{,}500$$
$$IS = \text{Rs } 2{,}76{,}75{,}000$$

Substituting this into equation (1):

$$PM = \text{Rs } 6{,}30{,}00{,}000 + 0.1\ (\text{Rs } 2{,}76{,}75{,}000)$$
$$PM = \text{Rs } 6{,}30{,}00{,}000 + \text{Rs } 2{,}76{,}75{,}000 = \text{Rs } 6{,}57{,}67{,}500$$

The complete reciprocated costs or artificial costs for plant maintenance and information systems are Rs 6,57,67,500 and Rs 2,76,75,000, respectively. Note that these are the same amounts that appear at the bottom of Exhibit 15-5 (lines 19 and 20) as the total support department costs allocated and reallocated during the iterative process. By setting up the system of simultaneous equations, we are able to solve for these amounts directly. When there are more than two support departments with reciprocal relationships, software such as Excel or Matlab is required to compute the complete reciprocated costs of each support department. Since the calculations involve finding the inverse of a matrix, the reciprocal method is also sometimes referred to as the **matrix method.**[6]

[6] If there are n support departments, then Step 1 will yield n linear equations. Solving the equations to calculate the complete reciprocated costs then requires finding the inverse of an n-by-n matrix.

Step 3: Allocate the Complete Reciprocated Costs of Each Support Department to All Other Departments (Both Support Departments and Operating Departments) on the Basis of the Usage Percentages (Based on Total Units of Service Provided to All Departments). Consider the Information Systems Department. The complete reciprocated costs of Rs 2,76,75,000 are allocated as follows:

To Plant Maintenance (1/10) × Rs 2,76,75,000	= Rs 27,67,500
To Machining (8/10) × Rs 2,76,75,000	= 2,21,40,000
To Assembly (1/10) × Rs 2,76,75,000	= 27,67,500
Total	Rs 2,76,75,000

Exhibit 15-6 presents summary data pertaining to the reciprocal method.

Castleford's Rs 9,34,42,500 complete reciprocated costs of the support departments exceeds the budgeted amount of Rs 7,75,21,500.

Support Department	Complete Reciprocated Costs	Budgeted Costs	Difference
Plant Maintenance	Rs 6,57,67,500	Rs 6,30,00,000	Rs 27,67,500
Information Systems	2,76,75,000	1,45,21,500	1,31,53,500
Total	Rs 9,34,42,500	Rs 7,75,21,500	Rs 1,59,21,000

Exhibit 15-6 Reciprocal Method of Allocating Support-Department Costs Using Linear Equations at Castleford Engineering for 2009

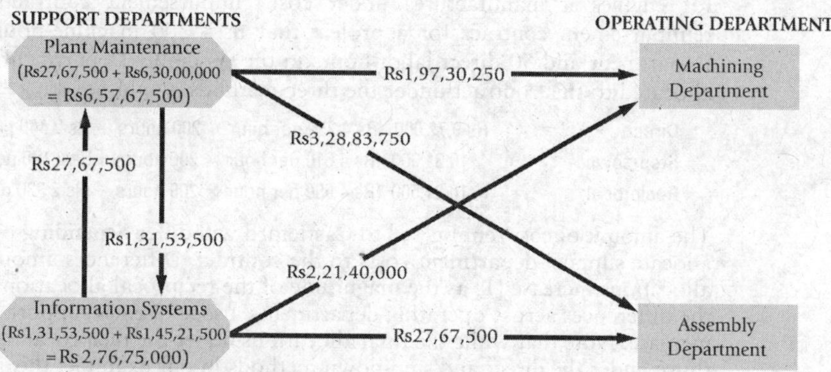

	A	B	C	D	E	F	G
1		SUPPORT DEPARTMENTS			OPERATING DEPARTMENTS		
2		Plant Maintenance	Information Systems		Machining	Assembly	Total
3	Budgeted overhead costs before any						
4	interdepartment cost allocations	Rs6,30,00,000	Rs1,45,21,500		Rs4,00,00,000	Rs2,00,00,000	Rs13,75,21,500
5	Allocation of Plant Maintenance (2/10, 3/10, 5/10)[a]	(6,57,67,500)	1,31,53,500		1,97,30,250	3,28,83,750	
6	Allocation of Information Systems (1/10, 8/10, 1/10)[b]	27,67,500	(2,76,75,000)		2,21,40,000	27,67,500	
7							
8	Total budgeted overhead of operating departments	Rs 0	Rs 0		Rs8,18,70,250	Rs5,56,51,250	Rs13,75,21,500
9							
10	[a] Base is (4,000 + 6,000 + 10,000), or 20,000 hours; 4,000 ÷ 20,000 = 2/10; 6,000 ÷ 20,000 = 3/10; 10,000 ÷ 20,000 = 5/10.						
11	[b] Base is (500 + 4,000 + 500), or 5,000 hours; 500 ÷ 5,000 = 1/10; 4,000 ÷ 5,000 = 8/10; 500 ÷ 5,000 = 1/10.						

Each support department's complete reciprocated cost is greater than the budgeted amount to take into account that the allocation of support costs will be made to all departments using its services and not just to operating departments. This step ensures that the reciprocal method fully recognizes all interrelationships among support departments, as well as relationships between support and operating departments. The difference between complete reciprocated costs and budgeted costs for each support department reflects the costs allocated among support departments. The total costs allocated to the operating departments under the reciprocal method are still only Rs 7,75,21,500.

Overview of Methods

Assume that Castleford reallocates the total budgeted overhead costs of each operating department in Exhibits 15-3 through 15-6 to individual products on the basis of budgeted machine-hours for the Machining Department (18,000 hours) and budgeted direct labor-hours for the Assembly Department (25,000 hours). The budgeted overhead allocation rates (to the nearest rupee) for each operating department by allocation method are:

Support Department Cost-Allocation Method	Total Budgeted Overhead Costs After Allocation of All Support-Department Costs		Budgeted Overhead Rate per Hour for Product-Costing Purposes	
	Machining	Assembly	Machining (18,000 machine-hours)	Assembly (25,000 labor hours)
Direct	Rs 7,65,33,000	Rs 6,09,88,500	Rs 4,250	Rs 2,440
Step-down	8,30,08,000	5,45,13,500	4,610	2,180
Reciprocal	8,18,70,250	5,56,51,250	4,550	2,230

These differences in budgeted overhead rates under the three support-department cost-allocation methods can, for example, affect the amount of costs Castleford is reimbursed for engines it manufactures under cost-reimbursement contracts. Consider a cost-reimbursement contract for a project that uses 200 machine-hours in the Machining Department and 50 direct labor-hours in the Assembly Department. The overhead costs allocated to this contract under the three methods would be:

Direct:	Rs 9,72,000	(Rs 4,250 per hour × 200 hours + Rs 2,440 per hour × 50 hours)
Step-down:	10,31,000	(Rs 4,610 per hour × 200 hours +Rs 2,180 per hour × 50 hours)
Reciprocal:	10,21,500	(Rs 4,550 per hour × 200 hours + Rs 2,230 per hour × 50 hours)

The amount of cost reimbursed to Castleford will differ depending on the method used to allocate support-department costs to the contract. Differences among the three methods' allocations increase (1) as the magnitude of the reciprocal allocations increases and (2) as the differences across operating departments' usage of each support department's services increase. Note that while the final allocations under the reciprocal method are in between those under the direct and step-down methods in our example, this is not true in general. To avoid disputes in cost-reimbursement contracts that require allocation of support-department costs, managers should always clarify the method to be used for allocation. For example, Medicare reimbursements and federal contracts with universities that pay for the recovery of indirect costs typically mandate use of the step-down method, with explicit requirements about the costs that can be included in the indirect cost pools.

The reciprocal method is conceptually the most precise method because it considers the mutual services provided among all support departments. The advantage of the direct and step-down methods is that they are simple to compute and understand relative to the reciprocal method. However, as computing power to perform repeated iterations (as in Exhibit 15-5) or to solve sets of simultaneous equations increases, more companies find the reciprocal method easier to implement.

Another advantage of the reciprocal method is that it highlights the complete reciprocated costs of support departments and how these costs differ from budgeted or actual costs of the departments. Knowing the complete reciprocated costs of a support department is a key input for decisions about whether to outsource all the services that the support department provides.

Suppose all of Castleford's support-department costs are variable over the period of a possible outsourcing contract. Consider a third party's bid to provide, say, all the information systems services currently provided by Castleford's Information Systems Department. Do not compare the bid to the Rs 1,45,21,500 costs reported for the Information Systems Department. The complete reciprocated costs of the Information Systems Department, which include the services the Plant Maintenance Department provides the Information Systems Department, are Rs 2,76,75,000 to deliver 5,000 hours of computer time to all other departments at Castleford. The complete reciprocated costs for computer time are Rs 5,535 per hour (Rs 2,76,75,000 ÷ 5,000 hours). Other things being equal, a third party's bid to provide the same information services as Castleford's internal department at less than Rs 2,76,75,000, or Rs 5,535 per hour (even if much greater than Rs 1,45,21,500) would improve Castleford's operating income.

To see this point, note that the relevant savings from shutting down the Information Systems Department are Rs 1,45,21,500 of Information Systems Department costs *plus* Rs 1,31,53,500 of Plant Maintenance Department costs. By closing down the Information Systems Department, Castleford will no longer incur the 20% of reciprocated Plant Maintenance Department costs (equal to Rs 1,31,53,500) that were incurred to support the Information Systems Department. Therefore, the total cost savings are Rs 2,76,75,000 (Rs 1,45,21,500 + Rs 1,31,53,500).[7] Neither the direct nor the step-down methods can provide this relevant information for outsourcing decisions.

We now consider common costs, another special class of costs for which management accountants have developed specific allocation methods.

Decision Point

What methods can managers use to allocate costs of multiple support departments to operating departments?

Allocating Common Costs

A **common cost** is a cost of operating a facility, activity, or like cost object that is shared by two or more users. Common costs exist because each user obtains a lower cost by sharing than the separate cost that would result if such user were an independent entity.

Learning Objective 4

Allocate common costs using the stand-alone method

. . . uses cost information of each user as a separate entity to allocate common costs and the incremental method

. . . allocates common costs primarily to one user and the remainder to other users

The goal is to allocate common costs to each user in a reasonable way. Consider Jagan Sharma, a graduating senior in Mumbai who has been invited to a job interview with an employer in New Delhi. The round-trip Mumbai–New Delhi airfare costs Rs 12,000. A week later, Jagan is also invited to an interview with an employer in Bangalore. The Mumbai–Bangalore round-trip airfare costs Rs 8,000. Stevens decides to combine the two recruiting trips into a Mumbai–New Delhi–Bangalore–Mumbai trip that will cost Rs 15,000 in airfare. The Rs 15,000 is a common cost that benefits both prospective employers. Two methods of allocating this common cost between the two prospective employers are the stand-alone method and the incremental method.

Stand-Alone Cost-Allocation Method

The **stand-alone cost-allocation method** determines the weights for cost allocation by considering each user of the cost as a separate entity. For the common-cost airfare of Rs 15,000, information about the separate (stand-alone) round-trip airfares (Rs 12,000 and Rs 8,000) is used to determine the allocation weights:

$$\text{New Delhi employer: } \frac{\text{Rs }12{,}000}{\text{Rs }12{,}000 + \text{Rs }8{,}000} \times \text{Rs }15{,}000 = 0.60 \times \text{Rs }15{,}000 = \text{Rs }9{,}000$$

$$\text{Bangalore employer: } \frac{\text{Rs }8{,}000}{\text{Rs }8{,}000 + \text{Rs }12{,}000} \times \text{Rs }15{,}000 = 0.40 \times \text{Rs }15{,}000 = \text{Rs }6{,}000$$

Advocates of this method often emphasize the fairness or equity criterion described in Exhibit 14-2. The method is viewed as reasonable because each employer bears a proportionate share of total costs in relation to the individual stand-alone costs.

Incremental Cost-Allocation Method

The **incremental cost-allocation method** ranks the individual users of a cost object in the order of users most responsible for the common cost and then uses this ranking to allocate cost among those users. The first-ranked user of the cost object is the *primary user* (also called the *primary party*) and is allocated costs up to the costs of the primary user as a

[7] Technical issues when using the reciprocal method in outsourcing decisions are discussed in R. S. Kaplan and A. A. Atkinson, *Advanced Management Accounting*, 3rd ed. (Upper Saddle River, NJ: Prentice Hall, 1998, pp. 73–81).

stand-alone user. The second-ranked user is the *first incremental user* (*first incremental party*) and is allocated the additional cost that arises from two users instead of only the primary user. The third-ranked user is the *second incremental user* (*second incremental party*) and is allocated the additional cost that arises from three users instead of two users, and so on.

To see how this method works, consider again Jagan Sharma and his Rs 15,000 airfare cost. Assume the New Delhi employer is viewed as the primary party. Jagan's rationale is that he had already committed to go to New Delhi before accepting the invitation to interview in Bangalore. The cost allocations would be:

Party	Costs Allocated	Cumulative Costs Allocated
New Delhi (primary)	Rs 12,000	Rs 12,000
Bangalore (incremental)	3,000 (Rs 15,000 – Rs 12,000)	Rs 15,000
Total	Rs 15,000	

The New Delhi employer is allocated the full Mumbai–New Delhi airfare. The unallocated part of the total airfare is then allocated to the Bangalore employer. If the Bangalore employer had been chosen as the primary party, the cost allocations would have been Bangalore Rs 8,000 (the stand-alone round-trip Mumbai–Bangalore airfare) and New Delhi Rs 7,000 (Rs 15,000 – Rs 8,000). When there are more than two parties, this method requires them to be ranked from first to last (say, based on the date on which each employer invited the candidate to interview).

Under the incremental method, the primary party typically receives the highest allocation of the common costs. If the incremental users are newly formed companies or subunits, such as a new product line or a new sales territory, the incremental method may enhance their chances for short-run survival by assigning them a low allocation of the common costs. The difficulty with the method is that, particularly if a large common cost is involved, every user would prefer to be viewed as the incremental party!

One approach to sidestep disputes in such situations is to use the stand-alone cost-allocation method. Another approach is to use the *Shapley value*, which considers each party as first the primary party and then the incremental party. From the calculations shown earlier, the New Delhi employer is allocated Rs 12,000 as the primary party and Rs 7,000 as the incremental party, for an average of Rs 9,500 [(Rs 12,000 + Rs 7,000) ÷ 2]. The Bangalore employer is allocated Rs 8,000 as the primary party and Rs 3,000 as the incremental party, for an average of Rs 5,500 [(Rs 8,000 + Rs 3,000) ÷ 2]. The Shapley value method allocates, to each employer, the average of the costs allocated as the primary party and as the incremental party—that is, Rs 9,500 to the New Delhi employer and Rs 5,500 to the Bangalore employer.[8]

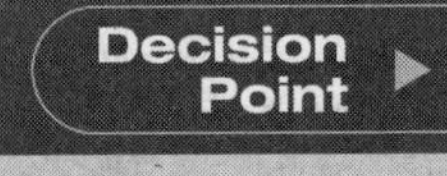

What methods can managers use to allocate common costs to two or more users?

As our discussion suggests, allocating common costs is not clear-cut and can generate disputes. Whenever feasible, the rules for such allocations should be agreed on in advance. If this is not done, then, rather than blindly follow one method or another, managers should exercise judgment when allocating common costs. For instance, Jagan must choose an allocation method for his airfare cost that is acceptable to each prospective employer. He cannot, for example, exceed the maximum reimbursable amount of airfare for either firm. The next section discusses the role of cost data in various types of contracts, another area where disputes about cost allocation frequently arise.

Bundled Products and Revenue Allocation Methods

Allocation issues can also arise when revenues from multiple products (for example, different software programs) are bundled together and sold at a single price. The methods for revenue allocation parallel those described for common-cost allocations.

Bundling and Revenue Allocation

Revenues are inflows of assets (almost always cash or accounts receivable) received for products or services provided to customers. Similar to cost allocation, **revenue allocation** occurs when revenues are related to a particular *revenue object* but cannot be traced to it in

[8] For further discussion of the Shapley value, see J. Demski, "Cost Allocation Games," in S. Moriarity (Ed.), *Joint Cost Allocations* (University of Oklahoma Center for Economic and Management Research, 1981); L. Kruz and P. Bronisz, "Cooperative Game Solution Concepts to a Cost Allocation Problem," *European Journal of Operations Research* (vol. 122: 2000, 258–271).

an economically feasible (cost-effective) way. A **revenue object** is anything for which a separate measurement of revenue is desired. Examples of revenue objects include products, customers, and divisions. We illustrate revenue-allocation issues for Supersoft Corporation, which develops, sells, and supports three software programs:

Learning Objective 5

Understand how bundling of products

. . . two or more products sold for a single-price

gives rise to revenue-allocation issues

. . . allocating revenues to each product in the bundle to evaluate managers of individual products

1. WordMaster, a word-processing program—current version is WordMaster 5.0, released 36 months ago (January 2007).
2. SpreadMaster, a spreadsheet program—current version is SpreadMaster 3.0, released 18 months ago (July 2008).
3. FinanceMaster, a budgeting and cash-management program—current version is FinanceMaster 1.0, released six months ago (July 2011) with a lot of favorable media attention.

Supersoft sells these three products individually as well as together as bundled products.

A **bundled product** is a package of two or more products (or services) that is sold for a single price but whose individual components may be sold as separate items at their own "stand-alone" prices. The price of a bundled product is typically less than the sum of the prices of the individual products sold separately. For example, banks often provide individual customers with a bundle of services from different departments (checking, safety-deposit box, and investment advisory) for a single fee. A resort hotel may offer, for a single amount per customer, a weekend package that includes services from its Lodging (the room), Food (the restaurant), and Recreational (golf and tennis) departments. When department managers have revenue or profit responsibilities for individual products, the bundled revenue must be allocated among the individual products in the bundle.[9]

Supersoft allocates revenues from its bundled product sales (called "suite sales") to individual products. Individual-product profitability is used to compensate software engineers, outside developers, and product managers responsible for developing and managing each product.

How should Supersoft allocate suite revenues to individual products? Consider information pertaining to the three "stand-alone" and "suite" products in 2011:

	Selling Price	Manufacturing Cost per Unit
Stand-alone		
WordMaster	Rs 1,250	Rs 180
SpreadMaster	1,500	Rs 200
FinanceMaster	2,250	Rs 250
Suite		
Word + Spread	Rs 2,200	
Word + Finance	2,800	
Finance + Spread	3,050	
Word + Finance + Spread	3,800	

Just as we saw in the section on common-cost allocations, the two main revenue-allocation methods are the stand-alone method and the incremental method.

Stand-Alone Revenue-Allocation Method

The **stand-alone revenue-allocation method** uses product-specific information on the products in the bundle as weights for allocating the bundled revenues to the individual products. The term *stand-alone* refers to the product as a separate (nonsuite) item. Consider the Word + Finance suite, which sells for Rs 2,800. Three types of weights for the stand-alone method are as follows:

1. **Selling prices.** Using the individual selling prices of Rs 1,250 for WordMaster and Rs 2,250 for FinanceMaster, the weights for allocating the Rs 2,800 suite revenues between the products are:

[9] Revenue-allocation issues also arise in external reporting. Statement of Position 97-2 (Software Revenue Recognition) states that with bundled products, revenue allocation "based on vendor-specific objective evidence of fair value" is required. The "price charged when the element is sold separately" is said to be "objective evidence of fair value." See American Institute of Certified Public Accountants, "Statement of Position 97-2" (Jersey City, NJ: AICPA, 1998).

$$\text{WordMaster: } \frac{\text{Rs } 1{,}250}{\text{Rs } 1{,}250 + \text{Rs } 2{,}250} \times \text{Rs } 2{,}800 = 0.357 \times \text{Rs } 2{,}800 = \text{Rs } 1{,}000$$

$$\text{FinanceMaster: } \frac{\text{Rs } 2{,}250}{\text{Rs } 1{,}250 + \text{Rs } 2{,}250} \times \text{Rs } 2{,}800 = 0.643 \times \text{Rs } 2{,}800 = \text{Rs } 1{,}800$$

2. **Unit costs.** This method uses the costs of the individual products (in this case, manufacturing cost per unit) to determine the weights for the revenue allocations.

$$\text{WordMaster: } \frac{\text{Rs } 180}{\text{Rs } 180 + \text{Rs } 250} \times \text{Rs } 2{,}800 = 0.419 \times \text{Rs } 2{,}800 = \text{Rs } 1{,}170$$

$$\text{FinanceMaster: } \frac{\text{Rs } 250}{\text{Rs } 180 + \text{Rs } 250} \times \text{Rs } 2{,}800 = 0.581 \times \text{Rs } 2{,}800 = \text{Rs } 1{,}630$$

3. **Physical units.** This method gives each product unit in the suite the same weight when allocating suite revenue to individual products. Therefore, with two products in the Word + Finance suite, each product is allocated 50% of the suite revenues.

$$\text{WordMaster: } \frac{1}{1+1} \times \text{Rs } 2{,}800 = 0.50 \times \text{Rs } 2{,}800 = \text{Rs } 1{,}400$$

$$\text{FinanceMaster: } \frac{1}{1+1} \times \text{Rs } 2{,}800 = 0.50 \times \text{Rs } 2{,}800 = \text{Rs } 1{,}400$$

These three approaches to determining weights for the stand-alone method result in very different revenue allocations to the individual products:

Revenue-Allocation Weights	WordMaster	FinanceMaster
Selling prices	Rs 1,000	Rs 1,800
Unit costs	1,170	1,630
Physical units	1,400	1,400

Which method is preferred? The selling prices method is best, because the weights explicitly consider the prices customers are willing to pay for the individual products. Weighting approaches that use revenue information better capture "benefits received" by customers than unit costs or physical units. The physical-units revenue-allocation method is used when any of the other methods cannot be used (such as when selling prices are unstable or unit costs are difficult to calculate for individual products).

Incremental Revenue-Allocation Method

The **incremental revenue-allocation method** ranks individual products in a bundle according to criteria determined by management—such as the product in the bundle with the most sales—and then uses this ranking to allocate bundled revenues to individual products. The first-ranked product is the *primary product* in the bundle. The second-ranked product is the *first incremental product*, the third-ranked product is the *second incremental product*, and so on.

How do companies decide on product rankings under the incremental revenue-allocation method? Some organizations survey customers about the importance of each of the individual products to their purchase decision. Others use data on the recent stand-alone sales performance of the individual products in the bundle. A third approach is for top managers to use their knowledge or intuition to decide the rankings.

Consider again the Word + Finance suite. Assume WordMaster is designated as the primary product. If the suite selling price exceeds the stand-alone price of the primary product, the primary product is allocated 100% of its *stand-alone* revenue. Because the suite price of Rs 2,800 exceeds the stand-alone price of Rs 1,250 for WordMaster, WordMaster is allocated revenues of Rs 1,250, with the remaining revenue of Rs 1,550 (Rs 2,800 – Rs 1,250) allocated to FinanceMaster:

Product	Revenue Allocated	Cumulative Revenue Allocated
WordMaster	Rs 1,250	Rs 1,250
FinanceMaster	1,550 (Rs 2,800 – Rs 1,250)	Rs 2,800
Total	Rs 2,800	

If the suite price is less than or equal to the stand-alone price of the primary product, the primary product is allocated 100% of the *suite* revenue. All other products in the suite receive no allocation of revenue.

Now suppose FinanceMaster is designated as the primary product and WordMaster as the first incremental product. Then, the incremental revenue-allocation method allocates revenues of the Word + Finance suite as:

Product	Revenue Allocated	Cumulative Revenue Allocated
FinanceMaster	Rs 2,250	Rs 2,250
WordMaster	550 (Rs 2,800 – Rs 2,250)	Rs 2,800
Total	Rs 2,800	

If Supersoft sells equal quantities of WordMaster and FinanceMaster, then the Shapley value method allocates to each product the average of the revenues allocated as the primary and first incremental products:

WordMaster:	(Rs 1,250 + Rs 550) ÷ 2 = Rs 1,800 ÷ 2 =	Rs 900
FinanceMaster:	(Rs 2,250 + Rs 1,550) ÷ 2 = Rs 3,800 ÷ 2 =	1900
Total		Rs 2800

But what if, in the most recent quarter, Supersoft sells 80,000 units of WordMaster and 20,000 units of FinanceMaster. Because Supersoft sells four times as many units of WordMaster, its managers believe that the sales of the Word + Finance suite are four times more likely to be driven by WordMaster as the primary product. The *weighted Shapley value method* takes this fact into account by weighting the revenue allocations when WordMaster is the primary product four times as much as when FinanceMaster is the primary product:

WordMaster:	(Rs 1,250 × 4 + Rs 550 × 1) ÷ (4 + 1) = Rs 5,550 ÷ 5 =	Rs 1,110
FinanceMaster:	(Rs 2,250 × 1 + Rs 1,550 × 4) ÷ (4 + 1) = Rs 8,450 ÷ 5 =	1,690
Total		Rs 2,800

When there are more than two products in the suite, the incremental revenue-allocation method allocates suite revenues sequentially. Assume WordMaster is the primary product in Supersoft's three-product suite (Word + Finance + Spread). FinanceMaster is the first incremental product, and SpreadMaster is the second incremental product. This suite sells for Rs 3,800. The allocation of the Rs 3,800 suite revenues proceeds as follows:

Product	Revenue Allocated	Cumulative Revenue Allocated
WordMaster	Rs 1,250	Rs 1,250
FinanceMaster	Rs 1,550 (Rs 2,800 – Rs 1,250)	Rs 2,800 (price of Word + Finance suite)
SpreadMaster	1,000 (Rs 3,800 – Rs 2,800)	Rs 3,800 (price of Word + Finance + Spread suite)
Total	Rs 3,800	

Now suppose WordMaster is the primary product, SpreadMaster is the first incremental product, and FinanceMaster is the second incremental product.

Product	Revenue Allocated	Cumulative Revenue Allocated
WordMaster	Rs 1,250	Rs 1,250
SpreadMaster	Rs 950 (Rs 2,200 – Rs 1,250)	Rs 2,200 (price of Word + Spread suite)
FinanceMaster	1,600 (Rs 3,800 – Rs 2,200)	Rs 3,800 (price of Word + Spread + Finance suite)
Total	Rs 3,800	

The ranking of the individual products in the suite determines the revenues allocated to them. Product managers at Supersoft likely would differ on how they believe their individual products contribute to sales of the suite products. In fact, each product manager would claim to be responsible for the primary product in the Word + Finance + Spread suite![10] Because the stand-alone revenue-allocation method does not require rankings of individual products in the suite, this method is less likely to cause debates among product managers.

[10] Calculating the Shapley value mitigates this problem because each product is considered as a primary, first-incremental, and second-incremental product. Assuming equal weights on all products, the revenue allocated to each product is an average of the revenues calculated for the product under these different assumptions. In the above example, the interested reader can verify that this will result in the following revenue assignments: FinanceMaster, Rs 1,800; WordMaster, Rs 875; and SpreadMaster, Rs 1,125.

Problem for Self-Study

This problem illustrates how costs of two corporate support departments are allocated to operating divisions using the dual-rate method. Fixed costs are allocated using budgeted costs and budgeted hours used by other departments. Variable costs are allocated using actual costs and actual hours used by other departments.

Computer Horizons budgets the following amounts for its two central corporate support departments (legal and personnel) in supporting each other and the two manufacturing divisions, the Laptop Division (LTD) and the Work Station Division (WSD):

	A	B	C	D	E	F	G
1		SUPPORT			OPERATING		
2		Legal Department	Personnel Department		LTD	WSD	Total
3	**BUDGETED USAGE**						
4	Legal (hours)	—	250		1,500	750	2,500
5	(Percentages)	—	10%		60%	30%	100%
6	Personnel (hours)	2,500	—		22,500	25,000	50,000
7	(Percentages)	5%	—		45%	50%	100%
8							
9	**ACTUAL USAGE**						
10	Legal (hours)	—	400		400	1,200	2,000
11	(Percentages)	—	20%		20%	60%	100%
12	Personnel (hours)	2,000	—		26,600	11,400	40,000
13	(Percentages)	5%	—		66.50%	28.5%	100%
14	Budgeted fixed overhead costs before any						
15	interdepartment cost allocations	Rs 36,00,000	Rs 47,50,000		—	—	Rs 83,50,000
16	Actual variable overhead costs before any						
17	interdepartment cost allocations	Rs 20,00,000	Rs 60,00,000		—	—	Rs 80,00,000

What amount of support-department costs for legal and personnel will be allocated to LTD and WSD using (a) the direct method, (b) the step-down method (allocating the Legal Department costs first), and (c) the reciprocal method using linear equations?

Solution

Exhibit 15-7 presents the computations for allocating the fixed and variable support-department costs. A summary of these costs follows:

	Laptop Division (LTD)	Work Station Division (WSD)
(a) Direct Method		
Fixed costs	Rs 46,50,000	Rs 37,00,000
Variable costs	47,00,000	33,00,000
	Rs 93,50,000	Rs 70,00,000
(b) Step-Down Method		
Fixed costs	Rs 45,80,530	Rs 37,69,470
Variable costs	48,80,000	31,20,000
	Rs 94,60,530	Rs 68,89,470
(c) Reciprocal Method		
Fixed costs	Rs 46,25,130	Rs 37,24,870
Variable costs	47,63,640	32,36,360
	Rs 93,88,770	Rs 69,61,230

Exhibit 15-7 Alternative Methods of Allocating Corporate Support-Department Costs to Operating Divisions of Computer Horizons: Dual-Rate Method

File Edit View Insert Format Tools Data Window Help

	A	B	C	D	E	F	G
20		CORPORATE SUPPORT DEPARTMENTS			OPERATING DIVISIONS		
21	Allocation Method	Legal Department	Personnel Department		LTD	WSD	Total
22	**A. DIRECT METHOD**						
23	Fixed Costs	Rs 36,00,000	Rs 47,50,000				
24	Legal (1,500 ÷ 2,250; 750 ÷ 2,250)	(36,00,000)			Rs 24,00,000	Rs 12,00,000	
25	Personnel (22,500 ÷ 47,500; 25,000 ÷ 47,500)		(47,50,000)		22,50,000	25,00,000	
26	Fixed support dept. cost allocated to operating divisions	Rs 0	Rs 0		Rs 46,50,000	Rs 37,00,000	Rs 83,50,000
27	Variable Costs	Rs 20,00,000	Rs 60,00,000				
28	Legal (400 ÷ 1,600; 1,200 ÷ 1,600)	(20,00,000)			Rs 5,00,000	Rs 15,00,000	
29	Personnel (26,600 ÷ 38,000; 11,400 ÷ 38,000)		(60,00,000)		42,00,000	18,00,000	
30	Variable support dept. cost allocated to operating divisions	Rs 0	Rs 0		Rs 47,00,000	Rs 33,00,000	Rs 80,00,000
31	**B. STEP-DOWN METHOD**						
32	(Legal Department First)						
33	Fixed Costs	Rs 36,00,000	Rs 47,50,000				
34	Legal (250 ÷ 2,500; 1,500 ÷ 2,500; 750 ÷ 2,500)	(36,00,000)	3,60,000		Rs 21,60,000	Rs 10,80,000	
35	Personnel (22,500 ÷ 47,500; 25,000 ÷ 47,500)		(51,10,000)		24,20,530	26,89,470	
36	Fixed support dept. cost allocated to operating divisions	Rs 0	Rs 0		Rs 45,80,530	Rs 37,69,470	Rs 83,50,000
37	Variable Costs	Rs 20,00,000	Rs 60,00,000				
38	Legal (400 ÷ 2,000; 400 ÷ 2,000; 1,200 ÷ 2,000)	(20,00,000)	4,00,000		Rs 4,00,000	Rs 12,00,000	
39	Personnel (26,600 ÷ 38,000; 11,400 ÷ 38,000)		(64,00,000)		44,80,000	19,20,000	
40	Variable support dept. cost allocated to operating divisions	Rs 0	Rs 0		Rs 48,80,000	Rs 31,20,000	Rs 80,00,000
41	**C. RECIPROCAL METHOD**						
42	Fixed Costs	Rs 36,00,000	Rs 47,50,000				
43	Legal (250 ÷ 2,500; 1,500 ÷ 2,500; 750 ÷ 2,500)	(38,56,780)[a]	3,85,680		Rs 23,14,070	Rs 11,57,030	
44	Personnel (2,500 ÷ 50,000; 22,500 ÷ 50,000; 25,000 ÷ 50,000)	2,56,780	(51,35,680)[a]		23,11,060	25,67,840	
45	Fixed support dept. cost allocated to operating divisions	Rs 0	Rs 0		Rs 46,25,130	Rs 37,24,870	Rs 83,50,000
46	Variable Costs	Rs 20,00,000	Rs 60,00,000				
47	Legal (400 ÷ 2,000; 400 ÷ 2,000; 1,200 ÷ 2,000)	(23,23,230)[b]	4,64,650		Rs 4,64,650	Rs 13,93,930	
48	Personnel (2,000 ÷ 40,000; 26,600 ÷ 40,000; 11,400 ÷ 40,000)	3,23,230	(64,64,650)[b]		42,98,990	18,42,430	
49	Variable support dept. cost allocated to operating divisions	Rs 0	Rs 0		Rs 47,63,640	Rs 32,36,360	Rs 80,00,000
50							
51	[a] FIXED COSTS	[b] VARIABLE COSTS					
52	Letting *LF* = Legal Department Fixed Costs, and *PF* = Personnel Department Fixed Costs, the simultaneous equations for the reciprocal method for fixed costs are	Letting *LF* = Legal Department Variable Costs, and *PV* = Personnel Department Variable Costs, the simultaneous equations for the reciprocal method for variable costs are					
53	*LF* = Rs 36,00,000 + 0.05 *PF*	*LV* = Rs 20,00,000 + 0.05 *PV*					
54	*PF* = Rs 47,50,000 + 0.10 *LF*	*PV* = Rs 60,00,000 + 0.20 *LV*					
55	*LF* = Rs 36,00,000 + 0.05 (Rs 47,50,000 + 0.10 *LF*)	*LV* = Rs 20,00,000 + 0.05 (Rs 60,00,000 + 0.20 *LV*)					
56	*LF* = Rs 38,56,780	*LV* = Rs 23,23,230					
57	*PF* = Rs 47,50,000 + 0.10 (Rs 38,56,780) = Rs 51,35,680	*PV* = Rs 60,00,000 + 0.20 (Rs 23,23,230) = Rs 64,64,650					

Decision Points

The following question-and-answer format summarizes the chapter's learning objectives. Each decision presents a key question related to a learning objective. The guidelines are the answer to that question.

Decision	Guidelines
1. Should managers use the single-rate or the dual-rate method?	The single-rate method aggregates fixed and variable costs and allocates them to objects using a single allocation base and rate. Under the dual-rate method, costs are grouped into separate variable cost and fixed cost pools; each pool uses a different cost-allocation base and rate. If costs can be easily separated into variable and fixed costs, the dual-rate method should be used because it provides better information for making decisions.
2. What factors should managers consider when deciding whether to use budgeted or actual cost allocation rates?	When cost allocations are made using budgeted rates, managers of divisions to which costs are allocated face no uncertainty about the rates to be used in that budget period. In contrast, when actual rates are used for cost allocation, managers do not know the rates until the end of the budget period. If actual rates are used, the efficiency of the supplier department affects the costs allocated to the user departments.
3. What methods can managers use to allocate costs of multiple support departments to operating departments?	The three methods managers can use are the direct, the step-down, and the reciprocal methods. The direct method allocates each support department's costs to operating departments without allocating a support department's costs to other support departments. The step-down method allocates support-department costs to other support departments and to operating departments in a sequential manner that partially recognizes the mutual services provided among all support departments. The reciprocal method fully recognizes mutual services provided among all support departments.
4. What methods can managers use to allocate common costs to two or more users?	Common costs are the costs of a cost object (such as operating a facility or performing an activity) that are shared by two or more users. The stand-alone cost-allocation method uses information pertaining to each user of the cost object to determine cost-allocation weights. The incremental cost-allocation method ranks individual users of the cost object and allocates common costs first to the primary user and then to the other incremental users. The Shapley value method considers each user, in turn, as the primary and the incremental user.
5. How can contract disputes over reimbursement amounts based on costs be reduced?	Disputes can be reduced by making the cost-allocation rules as explicit as possible and in writing at the time the contract is signed. These rules should include details such as the allowable cost items, the acceptable cost-allocation bases, and how differences between budgeted and actual costs are to be accounted for.
6. What is product bundling and why does it give rise to revenue-allocation issues?	Bundling occurs when a package of two or more products (or services) is sold for a single price. Revenue allocation of the bundled price is required when managers of the individual products in the bundle are evaluated on product revenue or product operating income.
7. What methods can managers use to allocate revenues of a bundled product to individual products in the package?	Revenues can be allocated for a bundled product using the stand-alone method, the incremental method, the Shapley value method, or management judgment.

TERMS TO LEARN

This chapter and the Glossary at the end of the book contain definitions of:

bundled product (**p. 649**)
common cost (**p. 647**)
complete reciprocated costs (**p. 643**)
direct method (**p. 640**)
dual-rate method (**p. 634**)
incremental cost-allocation method (**p. 647**)

incremental revenue-allocation method (**p. 650**)
operating department (**p. 633**)
production department (**p. 633**)
reciprocal method (**p. 643**)
revenue allocation (**p. 648**)
revenue object (**p. 649**)
service department (**p. 633**)
single-rate method (**p. 634**)
sequential allocation method (**p. 641**)
stand-alone cost-allocation method (**p. 647**)
stand-alone revenue-allocation method (**p. 649**)
step-down method (**p. 641**)
support department (**p. 633**)

ASSIGNMENT MATERIAL

Questions

15-1 Distinguish between the single-rate and the dual-rate methods.

15-2 Describe how the dual-rate method is useful to division managers in decision making.

15-3 How do budgeted cost rates motivate the support-department manager to improve efficiency?

15-4 Give examples of allocation bases used to allocate support-department cost pools to operating departments.

15-5 Why might a manager prefer that budgeted rather than actual cost-allocation rates be used for costs being allocated to his or her department from another department?

15-6 "To ensure unbiased cost allocations, fixed costs should be allocated on the basis of estimated long-run use by user-department managers." Do you agree? Why?

15-7 Distinguish among the three methods of allocating the costs of support departments to operating departments.

15-8 What is conceptually the most defensible method for allocating support-department costs? Why?

15-9 Distinguish between two methods of allocating common costs.

15-10 What role does the Cost Accounting Standards Board play when companies contract with the U.S. government?

15-11 What is one key way to reduce cost-allocation disputes that arise with government contracts?

15-12 Describe how companies are increasingly facing revenue-allocation decisions.

15-13 Distinguish between the stand-alone and the incremental revenue-allocation methods.

15-14 Identify and discuss arguments that individual product managers may put forward to support their preferred revenue-allocation method.

15-15 How might a dispute over the allocation of revenues of a bundled product be resolved?

Solved Examples

15-16 Single-rate versus dual-rate allocation methods, support department. The Indian Engineering Company which owns epower plant that services all manufacturing departments of the Company has a budget for the coming year. This budget has been expressed in the following terms on a monthly basis:

Manufacturing Department	Needed at Practical Capacity Production Level (Kilowatt-Hours)	Average Expected Monthly Usage (Kilowatt-Hours)
A	10,000	8,000
B	20,000	9,000
C	12,000	7,000
D	8,000	6,000
Totals	50,000	30,000

The expected monthly costs for operating the power plant during the budget year are Rs 15,00,000: Rs 6,00,000 variable and Rs 9,00,000 fixed.

Required

1. Assume that a single cost pool is used for the power plant costs. What amounts will be allocated to each manufacturing department if (a) the rate is calculated based on practical capacity and costs are allocated based on practical capacity and (b) the rate is calculated based on expected monthly usage and costs are allocated based on expected monthly usage.
2. Assume that dual-rate method is used with separate cost pools for the variable and fixed costs. Variable costs are allocated on the basis of expected monthly usage. Fixed costs are allocated on the basis of practical capacity. What amount in rupee will be allocated to each manufacturing department? Why might you prefer the dual-rate method?

Solution

Single-rate versus dual-rate allocation methods, support department.

Bases available (kilowatt hours):

	A	B	C	D	Total
Practical capacity	10,000	20,000	12,000	8,000	50,000
Expected monthly usage	8,000	9,000	7,000	6,000	30,000

1a. Single-rate method based on practical capacity:

Total costs in pool = Rs 6,00,000 + Rs 9,00,000 = Rs 15,00,000
Practical capacity = 50,000 kilowatt hours
Allocation rate = Rs 15,00,000 ÷ 50,000 = Rs 30 per hour of capacity

	A	B	C	D	Total
Practical capacity in hours	10,000	20,000	12,000	8,000	50,000
Costs allocated at Rs 30 per hour	Rs 3,00,000	Rs 6,00,000	Rs 3,60,000	Rs 2,40,000	Rs 15,00,000

1b. Single-rate method based on expected monthly usage:

Total costs in pool = Rs 6,00,000 + Rs 9,00,000= Rs 15,00,000
Expected usage = 30,000 kilowatt hours
Allocation rate = Rs 15,00,000 ÷ 30,000 = Rs 50 per hour of expected usage

	A	B	C	D	Total
Expected monthly usage in hours	8,000	9,000	7,000	6,000	30,000
Costs allocated at Rs 50 per hour	Rs 4,00,000	Rs 4,50,000	Rs 3,50,000	Rs 3,00,000	Rs 15,00,000

2. Variable-Cost Pool:

Total costs in pool = Rs 6,00,000
Expected usage = 30,000 kilowatt hours
Allocation rate = Rs 20 per hour of expected usage

Fixed-Cost Pool:

Total costs in pool = Rs 9,00,000
Practical capacity = 50,000 kilowatt hours
Allocation rate = Rs 18 per hour of capacity

	A	B	C	D	Total
Variable-cost pool					
Rs 20 × 8,000; 9,000; 7,000, 6,000	Rs 1,60,000	Rs 1,80,000	Rs 1,40,000	Rs 1,20,000	Rs 6,00,000
Fixed-cost pool					
Rs 18 × 10,000; 20,000; 12,000, 8,000	1,80,000	3,60,000	2,16,000	1,44,000	9,00,000
Total	Rs 3,40,000	Rs 5,40,000	Rs 3,56,000	Rs 2,64,000	Rs 15,00,000

The dual-rate method permits a more refined allocation of the power department costs; it permits the use of different allocation bases for different cost pools. The fixed costs result from decisions most likely associated with the practical capacity level. The variable costs result from decisions most likely associated with monthly usage.

15-17 Single-rate cost-allocation method, budgeted versus actual costs and quantities. Dabur Food Company, processes orange juice at its Orange Juice Division and grapefruit juice at its Grapefruit Juice Division. It purchases oranges and grapefruit from growers' cooperatives at Nagpur. It owns its own trucking fleet. Each plant is the same distance from Nagpur. The trucking fleet is operated as a cost center. Each plant is billed for the direct and indirect costs of each round-trip.

The trucking fleet costs include direct costs (labor costs of drivers, fuel, and toll charges) and indirect costs. Indirect costs include depreciation on tires and the vehicle, insurance, and state registration fees.

At the start of 2011, the Orange Juice Division budgeted for 150 round-trips and the Grapefruit Juice Division budgeted for 100 round-trips. Based on these 250 budgeted trips (equal to the practical capacity of the trucking fleet), the budgeted indirect costs of the trucking fleet were Rs 28,75,000. The following actual results occurred:

Trucking fleet indirect costs	Rs 24,18,750
Number of round-trips,	150
Number of round-trips	75

The trucking fleet division uses the single-rate method when allocating indirect trucking costs.

Required

1. What is the indirect cost rate per round-trip when (a) budgeted costs and budgeted round-trips are used and (b) when actual costs and actual round-trips are used?
2. What are the effects of using the rate based on budgeted costs/budgeted round-trips rather than the rate based on actual costs/actual round-trips to allocate costs to the Orange Juice Division using the actual number of round trips.

Solution

Single-rate cost allocation method, budgeted versus actual costs and ouantities.

1.a. Budgeted indirect costs = Rs 28,75,000 ÷ Rs 11,500 per round-trip

Budgeted trips = 250 trips

b. Actual indirect costs = Rs 24,18,750 ÷ Rs 10,750 per round-trip

Actual trips = 225 trips

2. When budgeted costs/budgeted quantities are used, the Orange Juice Division knows at the start of 2011 that it will be charged a rate of Rs 11,500 per trip. This enables it to make operating decisions knowing the rate it will have to pay for transportation. In contrast, when actual costs/actual quantities are used, the Orange Juice Division must wait until year-end to know its transportation charges.

The use of actual costs/actual quantities makes the costs allocated to one user a function of the actual demand of other users. In 2010, the actual usage was 225 trips, which is 25 trips below the 250 trips budgeted. The Orange Juice Division used all the 150 trips it had budgeted. The Grapefruit Juice Division used only 75 of the 100 trips budgeted. When costs are allocated based on actual costs and actual quantities, the same fixed costs are spread over fewer trips resulting in a higher rate than if the Grapefruit Division had used 100 trips. The Orange Juice Division then bears a proportionately higher share of the fixed costs.

Using actual costs/actual rates also means then any efficiencies or inefficiencies of the trucking division gets passed along to the user divisions. In general, this will have the effect of making the trucking division less sensitive about its costs, although in 2011, the trucking division appears to have managed its costs well leading to a lower cost per roundtrip relative to the budgeted cost per round trip.

15-18 Dual-rate cost-allocation method, budgeted versus actual costs, and practical capacity versus actual quantities (continuation of 15-17). Dabur Food Company decides to examine the effect of using the dual-rate method for allocating indirect trucking costs to each round-trip. At the start of 2011, the budgeted indirect costs were:

Variable indirect cost per round-trip	Rs 7,500
Fixed indirect costs	Rs 10,00,000

The actual results for the 225 round-trips made in 2011 were:

Variable indirect costs	Rs 15,18,750
Fixed indirect costs	9,00,000
	Rs 24,18,750

Assume all other information to be the same as in example 15-17.

Required

1. What is the indirect cost rate per round-trip with the dual-rate method when budgeted costs and budgeted round-trips are used? Total costs are computed using budgeted rate times actual usage (trips) for variable costs and budgeted rate times practical capacity usage for fixed costs.
2. From the viewpoint of the Orange Juice Division, what are the effects of using the dual-rate method rather than the single-rate methods?

Solution

Dual-rate cost-allocation method, budgeted versus actual costs, and practical capacity vs actual quantities (continuation of 15-17).

1. Charges with dual rate method

Variable indirect cost rate = Rs 7,500 per trip

Fixed indirect cost rate $= \dfrac{\text{Rs 10,00,000 budgeted costs}}{\text{250 trips at practical capacity}}$

= Rs 4,000 per trip at practical capacity

Orange Juice Division	
Variable indirect costs, Rs 7,500 × 150	Rs 11,25,000
Fixed indirect costs, Rs 4,000 × 150	6,00,000
	Rs 17,25,000

Grapefruit Juice Division	
Variable indirect costs, Rs 7,500 × 75	Rs 5,62,500
Fixed indirect costs, Rs 4,000 × 100	4,00,000
	Rs 9,62,500

2. The dual-rate changes according to the fixed indirect cost component treatement. By using budgeted trips made, the Orange Juice Division is unaffected by changes from its own budgeted usage or that of other divisions.

15-19 Direct and step-down allocation. e-books is an online book retailer. The company has four departments. The two revenue-producing departments are Corporate Sales and Consumer Sales. The two support departments are Administrative (human resources, accounting, and so on), and Information Systems. Each of the sales departments conducts merchandising and marketing operations independently.

The following data are available for September:

Departments	Revenues	Number of Employees	Processing Time Used (in minutes)
Corporate Sales	Rs 13,34,200	42	1,920
Consumer Sales	6,67,100	28	1,600
Administrative	–	14	320
Information Systems	–	21	1,120

Costs incurred in each of the four departments for September are as follows:

Corporate Sales	Rs 9,98,270
Consumer Sales	4,89,860
Administrative	72,700
Information Systems	2,34,400

Use number of employees to allocate Administrative costs and processing time used to allocate Information Systems costs.

Required

1. Allocate the support department costs to the revenue-producing departments using the direct method.
2. Rank the support departments based on the percentage of their services rendered to other support departments. Use this ranking to allocate support costs based on the step-down allocation method.
3. How could you have ranked the support departments differently?

Solution

Direct and step-down allocation.

1.

	Support Depts		Operating Depts		Total
	Administration	Info. Systems	Corporate	Consumer	
Costs Incurred	Rs 72,700	Rs 2,34,400	Rs 9,98,270	Rs 4,89,860	Rs 17,95,230
Allocation of Administration (42/70, 28/70)	(72,700)		43,620	29,080	
Allocation of Info. Syst. (1,920/3,520, 1,600/3,520)		(2,34,400)	127,855	106,545	
	Rs 0	Rs 0	Rs 1,169,745	Rs 625,485	Rs 1,795,230

2. Rank on percentage of services rendered to other support departments.

Step 1: Administrative provides 23.077% of its services to information systems:

$$\frac{21}{42 + 28 + 21} = \frac{21}{91} = 23.077\%$$

This 23.077% of Rs 72,700 administrative department costs is Rs 16,777.

Step 2: Information systems provides 8.333% of its services to administrative:

$$\frac{320}{1{,}920 + 1{,}600 + 320} = \frac{320}{3{,}840} = 8.333\%$$

This 8.333% of Rs 234,400 information systems department costs is Rs 19,533.

	Support Departments		Operating Departments		Total
	Administration	Info. Systems	Corporate	Consumer	
Costs Incurred	Rs 72,700	Rs 2,34,400	Rs 9,98,270	Rs 489,860	Rs 17,95,230
Allocation of Administration (21/91, 42/91, 28/91)	(72,700)	16,777	33,554	22,369	
	Re 0	2,51,177			
Allocation of Info. System (1,920/3,520, 1600/3,520)		(2,51,177)	1,37,006	114,171	
		Re 0	11,68,830	6,26,400	Rs 17,95,230

3. An alternative ranking is based on the rupee amount of services rendered to other support departments. Using numbers from requirement 2, this approach would use the following sequence:

Step 1: Allocate information systems first (Rs 19,533 provided to administrative).

Step 2: Allocate administrative second (Rs 16,777 provided to information systems).

15-20 Reciprocal cost allocation (continuation 15-19). Consider e-books again. The controller of e-books reads a widely used text that states that "the reciprocal method is conceptually the most defensible." He seeks your assistance.

Required

1. Allocate the support department costs (Administrative and Information Systems) to the two revenue-producing departments using the reciprocal allocation method.
2. Under what condition is the reciprocal method more accurate than the direct and step-down methods? In the case presented in this exercise, which method would you recommend? Why?

Solution

Reciprocal cost allocation (continuation of 15-19).

1. The reciprocal allocation method explicitly includes the mutual services provided among all support departments. Interdepartmental relationships are fully incorporated into the support department cost allocations.
2.

$$\begin{aligned} AD &= \text{Rs } 72{,}700 + .08333IS \\ IS &= \text{Rs } 2{,}34{,}400 + .23077AD \\ AD &= \text{Rs } 72{,}700 + [.08333(\text{Rs } 234{,}400 + .23077AD)] \\ &= \text{Rs } 72{,}700 + [\text{Rs } 19{,}532.55 + 0.01923AD] \\ 0.98077AD &= \text{Rs } 92{,}232.55 \\ AD &= \text{Rs } 92{,}232.55 \div 0.98077 \\ &= \text{Rs } 94{,}041 \\ IS &= \text{Rs } 2{,}34{,}400 + (0.23077 \times \text{Rs } 94{,}041) \\ &= \text{Rs } 2{,}56{,}102 \end{aligned}$$

	Support Departments		Operating Departments		
	Administration	Info. Systems	Corporate	Consumer	Total
Costs Incurred	Rs 72,700	Rs 2,34,400	Rs 9,98,270	Rs 4,89,860	Rs 17,95,230
Allocation of Administration (21/91, 42/91, 28/91)	(94,041)	21,702	43,404	28,935	
Allocation of Info. System (320/3,840, 1,920/3,840, 1,600/3,840)	21,341	(2,56,102)	1,28,051	1,06,710	
	Re 0	Re 0	Rs 11,69,725	Rs 6,25,505	Rs 17,95,230

Solution Exhibit 15-21 presents the reciprocal method using repeated iterations.

Solution Exhibit 15-20

Reciprocal Method of Allocating Support Department Costs for September at e-books Using Repeated Iterations

	Support Departments		Operating Departments		
	Administration	Information Systems	Corporate Sales	Consumer Sales	Total
Budgeted manufacturing overhead costs before any interdepartmental cost allocation	Rs 72,700	Rs 2,34,400	Rs 9,98,270	Rs 4,89,860	Rs 17,95,230
1st Allocation of Administrative (21/91, 42/91, 28/91)[a]	(72,700)	16,777 2,51,177	33,554	22,369	
1st Allocation of Information Systems (320/3,840, 1920/3840, 1,600/3,840)[b]	20,931	(2,51,777)	1,25,589	1,04,657	
2nd Allocation of Administrative (21/91, 42/91, 28/91)[a]	(20,931)	4,830	9,661	6,440	
2nd Allocation of Information Systems (320/3,840, 1,920/3,840, 1,600/3,840)[b]	402	(4,830)	2,415	2,013	
3rd Allocation of Administrative (21/91, 42/91, 28/91)[a]	(402)	93	185	124	
3rd Allocation of Information Systems (320/3,840, 1,920/3,840, 1,600/3,840)[b]	8	(93)	46	39	
4th Allocation of Administrative (21/91, 42/91, 28/91)[a]	(8)	2	4	2	
4th Allocation of Information Systems: (320/3,840, 1,920/3,840, 1,600/3,840)[b]	0	(2)	1	1	
Total budgeted manufacturing overhead of operating departments	Re 0	Re 0	Rs 11,69,725	Rs 6,25,505	Rs 17,95,230

Total accounts allocated and reallocated (the numbers in parentheses in first two columns)

Administrative	Rs 72,700 + Rs 20,931 + Rs 402 + Rs 8 = Rs 94,041
Information Systems	Rs 2,51,177 + Rs 4,830 + Rs 93 + Rs 2 = Rs 2,56,102

[a]Base is (21 + 42 + 28) or 91 employees
[b]Base is (320 + 1,920 + 1,600) or 3,840 minutes

3. The reciprocal method is more accurate than the direct and step-down methods when there is reciprocal relationships among support departments.
A summary of the alternatives is:

	Corporate Sales	Consumer Sales
Direct method	Rs 11,69,745	Rs 6,25,485
Step-down method (Administration first)	11,68,830	6,26,400
Reciprocal method	11,69,725	6,25,505

The reciprocal method is the preferred method, although for September the numbers do not appear materially different across the alternatives.

15-21 Single-rate, dual-rate, and practical capacity allocation. Shopper's Stop has a free gift-wrapping service for the customers who want to get their purchases gift wrapped. It has a monthly practical capacity to gift wrap 8,000 items that it allocates among its different departments. Monthly fixed practical capacity costs of the gift-wrapping service are Rs 60,000. Average budgeted variable cost to gift wrap an item is Rs 6. Though the service is free to the customers, the department where the customer made the purchase is allocated gift-wrapping service costs.
Various departments' actual use of the gift-wrapping service during the current month and their respective needs at practical capacity follows:

Department	Actual Number of Gifts Wrapped	Number of Gifts That Can Be Wrapped at Practical Capacity
Gifts	2,200	2,800
Men's Wear	750	1,000
Women's Wear	1,600	2,100
Footwear	450	700
China	650	900
Linen	350	500

Required

1. Allocate the costs for the gift-wrapping service to each department using a single-rate method based on actual number of gifts wrapped.
2. Compute the amount allocated to each department using the dual-rate method when fixed costs are allocated based on practical capacity and variable costs are allocated using actual usage.
3. Comment on your results in requirements 1 and 2.

Solution

Single-rate, dual-rate, and practical capacity allocation.

1. Actual number of gifts wrapped = 6,000
Practical capacity fixed costs = Rs 60,000
Average fixed capacity cost per item = Rs 60,000 ÷ 6,000 = Rs 10
Average budgeted variable cost per item = 6
Total cost per item Rs 16

Allocation:

Gifts (2,200 × Rs 16)	Rs 35,200
Men's Wear (750 × Rs 16)	12,000
Women's Wear (1,600 × Rs 16)	25,600
Footwear (450 × Rs 16)	7,200
China (650 × Rs 16)	10,400
Linen (350 × Rs 16)	5,600
Total	Rs 96,000

2. Rate for fixed costs $= \dfrac{\text{Fixed Costs}}{\text{Practical Capacity}}$

$$= \frac{\text{Rs } 60{,}000}{8{,}0000} = \text{Rs } 7.5 \text{ per item}$$

Rate for variable costs = Rs 6 per item

Allocation:

Department	Variable Costs	Fixed Costs	Total
Gifts	2,200 × Rs 6 = Rs 13,200	2,800 × Rs 7.5 = Rs 21,000	Rs 34,200
Men's Wear	750 × Rs 6 = 4,500	1,000 × Rs 7.5 = 7,500	12,000
Women's Wear	1,600 × Rs 6 = 9,600	2,100 × Rs 7.5 = 15,750	25,350
Footwear	450 × Rs 6 = 2,700	700 × Rs 7.5 = 5,250	7,950
China	650 × Rs 6 = 3,900	900 × Rs 7.5 = 6,750	10,650
Linen	350 × Rs 6 = 2,100	500 × Rs 7.5 = 3,750	5,850
Total	Rs 36,000	Rs 60,000	Rs 96,000

3. The dual-rate method has two major advantages over the single-rate method:
   a. Fixed costs are allocated proportionately to the departments causing the incurrence of those costs based on the capacity of each department.
   b. The costs allocated to a department are not affected by the usage by other departments.

   Note: If capacity costs are the result of a long-term decision by top management, it may be desirable to allocate to each department the cost of capacity used based on actual usage. The users are then not allocated the costs of unused capacity.

15-22 Cost allocation, actual versus budgeted usage. (CMA, revised) Reliance Industries, is a large manufacturing company that runs its own electrical power plant from the excess steam produced in its manufacturing process. Power is provided to two production departments: Department A and Department B. The capacity of the power plant was originally determined by the expected peak demands of the two production departments. The expected normal usages are, respectively, 60% and 6,00,00,000 kilowatt-hours (kwh) for Department A, and 40% and 4,00,00,000 kwh for Department B.

The budgeted monthly costs of producing power, based on normal usage of 10,00,00,000 kwh, are Rs 3,00,00,000 in fixed costs and Rs 7,50,00,000 in variable costs. For November, the actual kilowatt-hours used were 6,00,00,000 by Department A and 2,00,00,000 by Department B. Actual fixed costs were Rs 30,00,00,000, and actual variable costs were Rs 7,50,00,000.

The Finance Controller of Reliance Industries prepared the following monthly report:

Reliance Industries Monthly Allocation Report November

Power plant usage	8,00,00,000 kwh
Actual costs:	
Variable	Rs 7,50,00,000
Fixed	30,00,00,000
Total	Rs 37,50,00,000
Rate per kwh (Rs 37,50,00,000 ÷ 8,00,00,000 kwh)	Rs 4.6875
Allocations:	
To Department A (6,00,00,000 kwh × Rs 4.6875)	Rs 28,12,50,000
To Department B (2,00,00,000 kwh × Rs 4.6875)	9,37,50,000
Total allocated	Rs 37,50,00,000

Finance Controller fully allocated all power plant costs on the basis of actual kilowatt-hours used by each production department. This report will be submitted to the two production-department operating managers.

Required

1. Discuss at least two problems with the monthly allocation report prepared by Finance Controller for November.
2. Prepare a revised monthly allocation report for November using a flexible-budget approach. Use budgeted rates times actual usage for variable costs and budgeted rates assuming budgeted (normal) usage for fixed costs.
3. Discuss the behavioral implication of Finance Controller's monthly allocation report for November on the production manager of Department B.

Solution

Cost allocation, actual versus budgeted usage

1. Problems with the monthly allocation report include:
   a. The single-rate method used does not distinguish between fixed vs variable costs.
   b. Actual costs and actual quantities are used. This results in managers not knowing cost rates until year-end.
   c. Monthly time periods are used to determine cost rates. The use of a monthly time period can result in highly variable cost rates depending on seasonality, days in a month, demand surges and so on.
2. Budgeted variable cost (based on normal usage):

Monthly Allocation Report November

Allocations of Variable Costs (based on budgeted rate × actual usage)*	
To Department A: 6,00,00,000 × Rs 0.75	Rs 4,50,00,000
To Department B: 2,00,00,000 × Rs 0.75	1,50,00,000
	Rs 6,00,00,000

*There will be Rs 1,50,00,000 of unallocated variable costs for November.

Allocation of fixed costs (Based on budgeted usage 3 budgeted amount)	
To Department A: 60% × Rs 30,00,00,000	Rs 1,80,00,0000
To Department B: 40% × Rs 30,00,00,000	1,20,00,0000
Total	Rs 3,00,00,0000

Or alternatively,

$$\text{Budgeted fixed cost rate} = \frac{\text{Budgeted fixed costs}}{\text{Budgeted kwh}} = \frac{\text{Rs } 30{,}00{,}00{,}000}{6{,}00{,}00{,}000 + 4{,}00{,}00{,}000}$$

$$= \text{Rs 3 per kwh}$$

Allocation of fixed costs (based on budgeted usage)	
To Department A: Rs 3 × 6,00,00,000 kwh =	Rs 18,00,00,000
To Department B: Rs 3 × 4,00,00,000 kwh =	12,00,00,000
Total	Rs 30,00,00,000
Department A allocation of costs	
Variable costs	Rs 4,50,00,000
Fixed costs	18,00,00,000
Total	Rs 22,50,00,000
Department B allocation of costs	
Variable costs	Rs 1,50,00,000
Fixed costs	12,00,00,000
Total	Rs 13,50,00,000

3. Under Finance Controller's allocation report, the production manager has both risk-exposure and uncertainty concerns:
   Risk-exposure–Changes in the demand for energy by Department A affects the costs Finance Controller will report for Department B. Increase in demand by A will reduce B's cost per kwh and vice-versa. Department B's production manager may seek to curtail production in periods when Departments A's production declines. This could create an ever-diminishing cycle of production. Alternatively, Department B may subcontract outside to avoid a higher energy rate, even if it is not in Reliance Industries's best interest to subcontract.
   Uncertainty–When actual costs are used, managers cannot plan costs with certainty. Managers typically have less ability to bear uncertainty than do companies. The result is that managers may reject alternatives that are good risks from Reliance Industries's perspective but not attractive risks for themselves.

15-23 Support department cost allocations; single-department cost pools; direct, step-down, and reciprocal methods. The BPL Company has two products. Product 1 is manufactured entirely in Department X. Product 2 is manufactured entirely in Department Y. To produce these two products, the BPL Company has two support departments: A (a materials-handling department) and B (a power-generating department).

An analysis of the work done by departments A and B in a typical period follows:

	Used By			
Supplied By	**A**	**B**	**X**	**Y**
A	—	100	250	150
B	500	—	100	400

The work done in Department A is measured by the direct labor-hours of materials-handling time. The work done in Department B is measured by the kilowatt-hours of power.

The budgeted costs of the support departments for the coming year are:

	Department A	Department B
Variable indirect labor and indirect materials costs	Rs 70,000	Rs 10,000
Supervision	10,000	10,000
Depreciation	20,000	20,000
	Rs 100,000	Rs 40,000
	+ Power costs	+ Materials-handling costs

The budgeted costs of the operating departments for the coming quarter are Rs 1,500,000 for Department X and Rs 800,000 for Department Y.

Supervisory costs are salary costs. Depreciation in B is the straight-line depreciation of power-generation equipment in its nineteenth year of an estimated 25-year useful life; it is old but well-maintained equipment.

Required

1. What are the allocations of costs of support departments A and B to operating departments X and Y using (a) the direct method, (b) the step-down method (allocate Department A first), (c) the step-down method (allocate Department B first), and (d) the reciprocal method?
2. The power company has offered to supply all the power needed by the BPL Company and to provide all the services of the present power department. The cost of this service will be Rs 40 per kilowatt-hour of power. Should BPL accept? Explain.

Solution

Support department cost allocations; single-department cost pools; direct, step-down, and reciprocal methods.

All the following computations are in rupees.

1.

Direct method:

	To X		To Y	
A	250/400 × Rs 100,000	= Rs 62,500	150/400 × Rs 100,000 =	Rs 37,500
B	100/500 × Rs 40,000	= 8,000	400/500 × Rs 40,000 =	32,000
Total		Rs 70,500		Rs 69,500

Step-down method, allocating A first:

	A	B	X	Y
Costs to be allocated	Rs 1,00,000	Rs 40,000	–	–
Allocate A: (100; 250; 150 × 500)	(1,00,000)	20,000	Rs 50,000	Rs 30,000
Allocate B: (100; 400 × 500)	–	(60,000)	12,000	48,000
Total	Re 0	Re 0	Rs 62,000	Rs 78,000

Step-down method, allocating B first:

	A	B	X	Y
Costs to be allocated	Rs 1,00,000	Rs 40,000	–	–
Allocate B: (500; 100; 400 ÷ 1,000)	20,000	(40,000)	Rs 4,000	Rs 16,000
Allocate A: (250/400, 150/400)	(1,20,000)	–	75,000	45,000
Total	Re 0	Re 0	Rs 79,000	Rs 61,000

Note that these methods produce significantly different results, so the choice of method may frequently make a difference in the budgeted department overhead rates.

Reciprocal method:

Stage 1: Let A = total costs of materials-handling department

B = total costs of power-generating department

(1) A = Rs 100,000 + 0.5B

(2) B = Rs 40,000 + 0.2A

Stage 2: Substituting in (1): A = Rs 1,00,000 + 0.5(Rs 40,000 + 0.2A)

A = Rs 1,00,000 + Rs 20,000 + 0.1A

0.9A = Rs 1,20,000

A = Rs 1,33,333

Substituting in (2): B = Rs 40,000 + 0.2(Rs 1,33,333)

B = Rs 66,666

Stage 3:

	A	B	X	Y
Original amounts	1,00,000	40,000	–	–
Allocation of A (30%)	(1,33,333)	26,666 (20%)	66,667 (50%)	40,000
Allocation of B (40%)	33,333 (50%)	(66,666)	6,667 (10%)	26,666
Totals accounted for	–	–	73,334	66,666

Solution Exhibit 15-23

Reciprocal Method of Allocating Support Department Costs for BPL Company Using Repeated Iterations.

	Support Departments		Operating Departments	
	A	B	X	Y
Budgeted manufacturing overhead costsbefore any interdepartmental cost allocations	Rs 1,00,000	Rs 40,000		
1st Allocation of Dept. A: (2/10, 5/10, 3/10)[a]	(1,00,000)	20,000	Rs 50,000	Rs 30,000
1st Allocation of Dept. B(5/10, 1/10, 4/10)[b]	30,000	(60,000)	6,000	24,000

2nd Allocation of Dept. A(2/10, 5/10, 3/10)[a]	(30,000)	6,000	15,000	9,000
2nd Allocation of Dept B: (5/10, 1/10, 4/10)[b]	3,000	(6,000)	600	2,400
3rd Allocation of Dept A: (2/10, 5/10, 3/10)[a]	(3,000)	600	1,500	900
3rd Allocation of Dept. B:(5/10, 1/10, 4/10)[b]	300	(600)	60	240
4th Allocation of Dept. A (2/10, 5/10, 3/10)[a]	(300)	60	150	90
4th Allocation of Dept. B (5/10, 1/10, 4/10)[b]	30	(60)	6	24
5th Allocation of Dept A(2/10, 5/10, 3/10)	(30)	6	15	9
5th Allocation of Dept B(5/10, 1/10, 4/10)	3	(6)	1	2
6th Allocation of Dept A(2/10, 5/10, 3/10)	(3)	0	2	1
Total budgeted manufacturingoverhead of operating departments	Re 0	Re 0	Rs 73,334	Rs 66,666

Total accounts allocated and reallocated (the numbers in parentheses in first two columns)
Plant Maintenance: Rs 1,00,000 + Rs 30,000 + Rs 3,000 + Rs 300 + Rs 30 + Rs 3 = Rs 133,333
Information Systems: Rs 60,000 + Rs 6,000 + Rs 600 + Rs 60 + Rs 6 = Rs 66,666

[a]Base is (100 + 250 +150) or 500 labor-hours; 100 ÷ 500 = 2/10, 250 ÷ 500 = 5/10, 150 ÷ 500 = 3/10.
[b]Base is (500 + 100 + 400) or 1,000 kwhours ; 500 ÷ 1,000 = 5/10, 100 ÷ 1,000 = 1/10, 400 ÷ 1,000 = 4/10.

Comparison of methods:

Method of Allocation	X	Y
Direct method	Rs 70,500	Rs 69,500
Step-down: A first	62,000	8,000
Step-down: B first	79,000	61,000
Reciprocal method	73,334	66,666

Note that in this case the direct method produces answers that are the closest to the "correct" answers (that is, those from the reciprocal method), step-down allocating B first is next, and step-down allocating A first is least accurate.

2. At first glance, it appears that the cost of power is Rs 40 per unit plus the material handling costs. If so, BPL would be better off by purchasing from the power company. However, the decision should be influenced by the effects of the interdependencies and the fixed costs. Note that the power needs would be less if they were purchased from the outside:

	Outside Power Units Needed
X	100
Y	400
A (500 units minus 20% of 500 units, because there is no need to service the nonexistent power department)	400
Total units	900

Total costs, 900 × Rs 40 = Rs 36,000

In contrast, the total costs that would be saved by not producing the power inside would depend on the effects of the decision on various costs:

	Avoidable Costs of 1000 Units of Power Produced Inside
Variable indirect labor and indirect material costs	Rs 10,000
Supervision in power department	10,000
Materials handling, 20% of Rs 70,000*	14,000
Probable minimum cost savings	Rs 34,000
Possible additional savings:	
a. Can any supervision in materials handling be saved because of overseeing less volume? Minimum savings is probably zero; the maximum is probably 20% of Rs 10,000 or Rs 2,000.	?
b. Is any depreciation a truly variable, wear-and-tear type of cost?	?
Total savings by not producing 1000 units of power	Rs 34,000 + ?

*Materials handling costs are higher because the power department uses 20% of materials handling. Therefore, materials-handling costs will decrease by 20%

In the short run (at least until a capital investment in equipment is necessary), the data suggest continuing to produce internally because the costs eliminated would probably be less than the comparable purchase costs.

15-24 Allocating costs of support departments; dual rates; direct, step-down, and reciprocal methods. Airtight Security, specializes in the assembly and installation of high-quality security systems for the home and business segments of the market. The four departments at its highly automated state-of-the-art assembly plant are:

Service Departments	**Assembly Departments**
Engineering Support (ES)	Home Security Systems
Information Systems Support (IS)	Business Security Systems

The budgeted level of service relationships, which is at practical capacity, for 2011 is:

	Used By			
Supplied By	**Engineering Support**	**Information Systems Support**	**Home Security Systems**	**Business Security Systems**
Engineering Support	—	0.10	0.40	0.50
Information Systems Support	0.20	—	0.30	0.50

The actual level of service relationships for 2011 is:

	Used By			
Supplied By	**Engineering Support**	**Information Systems Support**	**Home Security Systems**	**Business Security Systems**
Engineering Support	—	0.15	0.30	0.55
Information Systems Support	0.25	—	0.15	0.60

Airtight collects fixed costs and variable costs for each department in separate cost pools. The actual costs in each pool for 2011 are:

	Fixed-Cost Pool	**Variable-Cost Pool**
Engineering Support	Rs 27,00,000	Rs 85,00,000
Information Systems Support	80,00,000	37,50,000

Fixed costs are allocated on the basis of budgeted level of service. Variable costs are allocated on the basis of the actual level of service.

The support department costs allocated to each assembly department are allocated to products on the basis of units assembled. The units assembled in each department during 2011 are

Home Security Systems	7,950 units
Business Security Systems	3,750 units

Required

1. Allocate the support department costs to the assembly departments using the dual-rate method and (a) the direct method, (b) the step-down method (allocate Information Systems Support first), (c) the step-down method (allocate Engineering Support first), (d) the reciprocal method (use linear equations), and (e) the reciprocal method (use repeated iterations). Present results in a format similar to Exhibit 15-7.
2. Compare the support department costs allocated to each Home Security Systems unit assembled and each Business Security Systems unit assembled under (a), (b), (c), (d), and (e) in requirement 1.
3. What factors might explain why the reciprocal method is not more widely used in practice?
4. Refer to the results obtained in requirements 1 and 2. Which alternative would be preferred by the manager of Home Security Systems? Explain.

Solution

Allocating costs of support departments; dual rates; direct, step-Down, and reciprocal methods.

1. Solution Exhibit 15-24 presents the costs allocated to each assembly department under the four service department cost allocation methods.

   The linear equations underlying the complete reciprocated costs reported in Solution Exhibit 15-24 (in 000s) are:

   Fixed-Cost Pool:

$$
\begin{aligned}
ES &= \text{Rs } 2{,}700 + 0.20IS \\
IS &= \text{Rs } 8{,}000 + 0.10ES \\
ES &= \text{Rs } 2{,}700 + 0.20\,(\text{Rs } 8{,}000 + 0.10ES) \\
ES &= \text{Rs } 4{,}300 + 0.02ES \\
0.98ES &= \text{Rs } 4{,}300 \\
ES &= \text{Rs } 4{,}300 \div 0.98 = \text{Rs } 4{,}387.76 \\
IS &= \text{Rs } 8{,}000 + 0.10\,(\text{Rs } 4{,}387.76) \\
&= \text{Rs } 8{,}438.78
\end{aligned}
$$

   Variable-Cost Pool:

$$
\begin{aligned}
ES &= \text{Rs } 8{,}500 + 0.25IS \\
IS &= \text{Rs } 3{,}750 + 0.15ES \\
ES &= \text{Rs } 8{,}500 + 0.25\,(\text{Rs } 3{,}750 + 0.15ES) \\
ES &= \text{Rs } 9{,}437.5 + 0.0375ES \\
0.9625ES &= \text{Rs } 9{,}437.5 \\
ES &= \text{Rs } 9{,}437.5 \div 0.9625 = \text{Rs } 9{,}805.19
\end{aligned}
$$

IS = Rs 3,750 + 0.15 (Rs 9,805.19)
= Rs 3,750 + Rs 1,470.78 = Rs 5,220.78

The repeated iterations underlying the complete reciprocated costs reported in Fixed-Cost Pool:

	Support Departments		Operating Departments	
	ES	IS	Home Security Systems	Business Security Systems
Costs	Rs 2,700.00	Rs 8,000.00		
1st Allocation of ES (.1, .4, .5)	(2,700.00)	270.00	Rs 1,080.00	Rs 1,350.00
		8,270.00		
1st Allocation of IS (.2, .3, .5)	1,654.00	(8,270.00)	2,481.00	4,135.00
2nd Allocation of ES (.1, .4, .5)	(1,654.00)	165.40	661.60	827.00
2nd Allocation of IS (.2, 3, .5)	33.08	(165.40)	49.62	82.70
3rd Allocation of ES (.1, .4, .5)	(33.08)	3.31	13.23	16.54
3rd Allocation of IS (.2, .3, .5)	0.66	(3.31)	0.99	1.66
4th Allocation of ES (.1, .4, .5)	(0.66)	0.07	0.26	0.33
4th Allocation of IS (.2, .3, .5)	0.01	(0.07)	0.02	0.04
5th Allocation of ES (.1, .4, .5)	(0.01)	0	0.01	0
Fixed-costs allocation	Re 0	Re 0	Rs 4,286.73	Rs 6,413.27

The reported iterations underlying the complete reciprocated costs reported in Variable-Cost Pool:

	Support Departments		Operating Departments	
	ES	IS	Home Security Systems	Business Security Systems
Costs	Rs 8,500.00	Rs 3,750.00		
1st Allocation of ES (.15, .30, .55)	(8,500.00)	1, 275.00	Rs 2,550.00	Rs 4,675.00
		5,025.00		
1st Allocation of IS (.25, .15, .60)	1,256.25	(5,025.00)	753.75	3,015.00
2nd Allocation of ES (.15, .30, .55)	(1,256.25)	188.44	376.87	690.94
2nd Allocation of IS (.25, .15, .60)	47.11	(188.44)	28.27	113.06
3rd Allocation of ES(.15, .30, .55)	(47.11)	7.07	14.13	25.91
3rd Allocation of IS (.25, .15, .60)	1.77	(7.07)	1.06	4.24
4th Allocation of ES (.15, .30, .55)	(1.77)	0.27	0.53	0.97
4th Allocation of IS (.25, .15, .60)	0.07	(0.27)	0.04	0.16
5th Allocation of ES (.15, .30, .55)	(0.07)	0	0.03	0.04
Variable-cost allocation	Re 0	Re 0	Rs 3,724.68	Rs 8,525.32

Solution Exhibit 15-24
(in thousands)

	Engineering Support	Information Systems Support	Home Security Systems	Business Security Systems
a. Direct Method				
Fixed-Cost Pool	Rs 2,700	Rs 8,000		
Engineering Support (4/9, 5/9)	(2,700)		Rs 1,200.00	Rs 1,500.00
Information Support (3/8, 5/8)		(8,000)	3,000.00	5,000.00
			Rs 4,200.00	Rs 6,500.00
Variable-Cost Pool:	Rs 8,500	Rs 3,750		
Engineering Support (30/85, 55/85)	(8,500)		Rs 3,000.00	Rs 5,500.00
Information Support (15/75,60/75)		(3,750)	750.00	3,000.00
			Rs 3,750.00	Rs 8,500.00
b. Step-down (Information First)				
Fixed-Cost Pool:	Rs 2,700	Rs 8,000		
Information Support (.2, .3, .5)	1,600	(8,000)	Rs 2,400.00	Rs 4,000.00
Engineering Support (4/9, 5/9)	(4,300)	–	1,911.11	2,388.89
			Rs 4,311.11	Rs 6,388.89
Variable-Cost Pool:	Rs 8,500	Rs 3,750		
Information Support (.25, .15, .60)	937.5	(3,750)	Rs 562.50	Rs 2,250.00
Engineering Support (30/85, 55/85)	(9,437.5)	–	3,330.88	6,106.62
			Rs 3,893.38	Rs 8,356.62

c. Step-down (Engineering First):				
Fixed-Cost Pool:	Rs 2,700	Rs 8,000		
Engineering Support (.1, .4, .5)	(2,700)	270	Rs 1,080.00	Rs 1,350.00
Information Support (3/8, 5/8)		(8,270)	3,101.25	5,168.75
			Rs 4,181.25	Rs 6,518.75
Variable-Cost Pool:	Rs 8,500	Rs 3,750		
Engineering Support (.15, .30, .55)	(8,500)	1,275	Rs 2,550.00	Rs 4,675.00
Information Support (.2, .8)		(5,025)	1,005.00	4,020.00
			Rs 3,555.00	Rs 8,695.00
d. Reciprocal Method				
Fixed-Cost Pool:	Rs 2,700	Rs 8,000.00		
Engineering Support (.1, .4, .5)	(4,387.76)	438.78	Rs 1,755.10	Rs 2,193.88
Information Support (.2, .3, .5)	1,687.76	(8,438.78)	2,531.63	4,219.39
			Rs 4,286.73	Rs 6,413.27
Variable-Cost Pool:	Rs 8,500.00	Rs 3,750.00		
Engineering Support (.15, .30, .55)	(9,805.19)	1,470.78	Rs 2,941.56	Rs 5,392.85
Information Support (.25, .15, .60)	1,305.19	(5,220.78)	783.12	3,132.47
			Rs 3,724.68	Rs 8,525.32

A summary of the costs allocated under each method from Solution Exhibit 15-24 is:

(In Thousands)	**Home Security Systems**	**Business Security Systems**
a. Direct Method:		
Fixed-cost pool	Rs 4,200.00	Rs 6,500.00
Variable-cost pool	3,750.00	8,500.00
	Rs 7,950.00	Rs 15,000.00
b. Step-down (Information First):		
Fixed-cost pool	Rs 4,311.11	Rs 6,388.89
Variable-cost pool	3,893.38	8,356.62
	Rs 8,204.49	Rs 14,745.51
c. Step-down (Engineering First):		
Fixed-cost pool	Rs 4,181.25	Rs 6,518.75
Variable-cost pool	3,555.00	8,695.00
	Rs 7,736.25	Rs 15,213.75
d. & e. Reciprocal Method:		
Fixed-cost pool	Rs 4,286.73	Rs 6,413.27
Variable-cost pool	3,724.68	8,525.32
	Rs 8,011.41	Rs 14,938.59

2. Support department costs allocated per unit:

	Home Security Systems Allocation Costs ÷ Rs 7,950 units	**Business Security Systems Allocation Costs ÷ Rs 3,750 units**
a. Direct method	Rs 1,000	Rs 4,000
b. Step-down (Information first)	1,032	3,932
c. Step-down (Engineering first)	973	4,057
d. & e. Reciprocal method	1,008	3,984

3. Factors that might explain why the reciprocal method is not more widely used in practice include:

a. Managers find the reciprocal method difficult to understand, especially where there are many support departments.

b. The final cost allocations yielded by using the reciprocal method differ little in some cases from those yielded by using the direct or step-down methods. As illustrated in requirement 2, the differences among the four methods in this problem appear small.

c. It is costly to maintain records of the use of the support departments by other support departments.

4. The manager of the Home Security Department would prefer the step-down method with the sequence starting with Engineering Support. This alternative results in the lowest amount of support departments' costs allocated to Home Security Systems

Exercises

15-25 Support department cost allocation; direct and step-down methods. Avalon Consulting provides outsourcing services and advice to both government and corporate clients. For costing purposes, Avalon classifies its departments into two support departments (Administrative/Human Resources and Information Systems) and two operating departments (Government Consulting and Corporate Consulting). For the first quarter of current year, Avalon incurs the following costs in its four departments:

Administrative/Human Resources (A/H)	Rs 6,00,000

Information Systems (IS)	24,00,000
Government Clients (GOVT)	87,56,000
Corporate Clients (CORP)	1,24,52,000

The actual level of support relationships among the four departments for the first quarter was:

	Used By			
Supplied By	**A/H**	**IS**	**GOVT**	**CORP**
A/H	—	25%	40%	35%
IS	10%	—	30%	60%

The Administrative/Human Resources support percentages are based on head count. The Information Systems support percentages are based on actual computer time used.

Required

1. Allocate the two support department costs to the two operating departments using the following methods:
   a. Direct method
   b. Step-down method (allocate A/H first)
   c. Step-down method (allocate IS first)
2. Compare and explain differences in the support department costs allocated to each operating department.
3. What approaches might be used to decide the sequence in which to allocate support departments when using the step-down method? What approach would you recommend Avalon 1 to 3 use if, on government consulting jobs, it is required to use the step-down method?

15-26 Support department cost allocation, reciprocal method (continuation of 15-25). Refer to the data given in Exercise 15-25.

Required

1. Allocate the two support department costs to the two operating departments using the reciprocal method. Use (a) linear equations and (b) repeated iterations.
2. Compare and explain differences in requirement 1 with those in requirement 1 of Exercise 15-25. Which method do you prefer? Why?

15-27 Revenue allocation, bundled products. Taj Group operates a five-star hotel with a world-recognized championship golf course. It has a decentralized management structure. These are three divisions:

- Lodging (rooms, conference facilities)
- Food (restaurants and in-room service)
- Recreation (golf course, tennis courts, and so on)

Starting next month, Taj will offer a two-day, two-person "getaway package" deal for Rs 7,000. This deal includes:

- Two nights' stay for two in an ocean-view room–separately priced at Rs 6,400 (Rs 3,200 per night for two).
- Two rounds of golf separately priced at Rs 3,000 (Rs 1,500 per round). One person can do two rounds, or two people can do one round each.
- Candlelight dinner for two at the exclusive Taj Restaurant–separately priced at Rs 800 per person.

Sudhir, president of the Recreation Division, recently asked the CEO of Taj Group how his division would share in the Rs 7,000 revenue from the package. The golf course was operating at 100% capacity (and then some). Under the "getaway package" rules, participants who booked one week in advance were guaranteed access to the golf course. Sudhir noted that every "getaway" booking would displace a Rs 1,500 booking. He stressed that the high demand reflected the devotion of his team to keeping the golf course rated in the "Best 10 Courses in the World" listings in Golf Monthly. As an aside, he also noted that the Lodging and Food divisions only had to turn away customers on "peak-season events such as the New Year's period."

Required

1. With selling prices as the weights, allocate the Rs 7,000 "getaway package" revenue to the three divisions using:
   a. The stand-alone revenue-allocation method
   b. The incremental revenue-allocation method (with Recreation first, then Lodging, and then Food)
2. What are the pros and cons of a and b in requirement 1?

15-28 Revenue allocation, bundled products, additional complexities (continuation of 15-27). The individual items in the "getaway package" deal at Taj Group are not fully used by each guest. Assume that 10% of the "getaway package" users in its first month do not use the golfing option, and 5% do not use the food option. The lodging option has a 100% usage rate.

Required

How should Taj Group recognize this nonuse factor in its revenue sharing of the Rs 7,000 package across the Lodging, Food, and Recreation divisions? Explain.

15-29 Single-rate, dual-rate, and practical capacity allocations. Raymond, has its own power plant, which has two users, Cutting Department and Welding Department. When the plans were prepared for the

power plant, top management decided that its practical capacity should be 1,50,000 machine-hours (MH). Annual budgeted practical capacity fixed costs are Rs 45,00,000, and budgeted variable costs are Rs 20 per machine-hour. The following data are available:

	Cutting Department	Welding Department	Total
Actual usage in 2011 (MH)	60,000	40,000	1,00,000
Practical capacity for each department (MH)	90,000	60,000	1,50,000

Required

1. **Allocate the power plant's costs to the Cutting and the Welding departments using a single-rate method in which the budgeted rate is calculated using practical capacity and costs are allocated based on actual usage.**
2. **Allocate the power plant's costs to the Cutting and Welding departments using the dual-rate method in which the fixed costs are allocated based on practical capacity and variable costs are allocated based on actual usage.**
3. **Allocate the power plant's costs to the Cutting and Welding departments using the dual-rate method in which the fixed-cost rate is calculated using practical capacity but fixed costs are allocated to the Cutting and Welding departments based on actual usage. Variable costs are allocated based on act...**
4. **Comment on your results in requirements 1, 2, and 3.**

15-30 Allocating costs of support departments; step-down and direct methods. The Central Valley Compa... has prepared department overhead budgets for April for normal-volume levels before allocations as follows:

Support departments:		
Building and grounds	**Rs 10,000**	
Personnel	**1,000**	
General factory administration	**26,090**	
Cafeteria operating loss	**1,640**	
Storeroom	**2,670**	
Total		**Rs 41,400**
Operating departments:		
Machining	**Rs 34,700**	
Assembly	**48,900**	
Total		**83,600**
Total for support and operating departments		**Rs 125,000**

Management has decided that the most appropriate inventory costs are achieved by using individual department overhead rates. These rates are developed after support department costs are allocated to operating departments.

Bases for allocation are to be selected from the following:

Department	Direct Manufacturing Labor-Hours	Number of Employees	Square Feet of Floor Space Occupied	Manufacturing Labor-Hours	Number of Requisitions
Building and grounds	0	0	0	0	0
Personnel[a]	0	0	2,000	0	0
General plant administration	0	35	7,000	0	0
Cafeteria operating loss	0	10	4,000	1,000	0
Storeroom	0	5	7,000	1,000	0
Machining	5,000	50	30,000	8,000	2,000
Assembly	15,000	100	50,000	17,000	1,000
Total	20,000	200	1,00,000	27,000	3,000

[a]Basis used is number of employees.

Required

1. **Using a worksheet, allocate support department costs by the step-down method. Develop overhead rates per direct manufacturing labor-hour for machining and assembly. Allocate the costs of the support departments in the order given in this problem. Use the allocation base for each support department you think is most appropriate.**
2. **Using the direct method, rework requirement 1.**
3. **Based on the following information about two jobs, determine the total overhead costs for each job by using rates developed in (a) requirement 1 and (b) requirement 2.**

	Direct Manufacturing Labor-Hours	
	Machining	**Assembly**
Job 88	**18**	**2**
Job 89	**3**	**17**

4. The company evaluates performance of operating departments' managers on the basis of how well they managed their total costs, including allocated costs. As the manager of the Machining Department, which allocation method would you prefer from the results obtained in requirements 1 and 2? Explain.

15-31 Common costs. Mohan and Sohan would like to lease an office building to open their separate audit offices. The building has a total of 1,500 square feet of office space. They need 900 square feet and 600 square feet, respectively. If each rents the space on his own, the rent will be Rs 100 per square foot. If they rent the space together, the rent will decrease to Rs 80 per square foot.

Required

1. Calculate their respective share of the rent under the stand-alone cost-allocation method.
2. Do requirement 1 using the incremental cost-allocation method. Assume Mohan to be the primary party.
3. What method would you recommend Mohan and Sohan use to share the rent?

15-32 Revenue allocation, bundled products. Indian Sandal Company (IS) manufactures and sells upscale perfumes. In recent months, IS has started selling its products in bundled form, as well as in individual form. Sales in 2011 of three products that have been sold individually are as follows:

	Retail Price	Units Sold
Stand-alone		
Axe	Rs 100	20,000
Rexona	80	37,500
Sandal	250	20,000
Suite		
Axe + Rexona	150	
Axe + Sandal	280	

Each of the products is manufactured by a separate division.

Required

1. Compute the weights for allocating revenues to each division for each of the bundled products using:
   a. The stand-alone revenue-allocation method based on total revenues of individual products
   b. The incremental revenue-allocation method, with Sandal ranked 1; Rexona, 2; and Axe, 3; based on retail prices of individual products. According to this ranking, the primary product in a suite has the highest rank, and so on.
2. What method would you recommend for allocating revenues to each division for each of the bundled products?

15-33 Overhead disputes. (Suggested by Howard Wright) The Essar Shipping Company works on Indian Navy vessels and commercial vessels. General yard overhead (for example, the cost of the Purchasing Department) is allocated to the jobs on the basis of direct labor costs.

In 2011, Essar Shipping's total Rs 15 crore of direct labor costs consisted of Rs 5 crore Navy and Rs 10 crore commercial. The general yard overhead was Rs 3 crore.

Navy auditors periodically examine the records of defense contractors. The auditors investigated a nuclear submarine contract, which was based on cost-plus-fixed-fee pricing. The auditors claimed that the Navy was entitled to a refund because of double-counting of overhead in 2011.

The government contract included the following provision related to direct costs:

A direct cost is any cost that can be identified specifically with a particular cost object. Direct costs are not limited to items that are incorporated in the end product such as material or labor. Costs identified specifically with the contract are direct costs of the contract and are to be charged directly thereto. Costs identified specifically with other work of the contractor are direct costs of that work and are not to be charged to the contract directly or indirectly. When items ordinarily chargeable as indirect costs are charged to the contract as direct costs, the cost of like items applicable to other work must be eliminated from indirect costs allocated to the contract.

Essar Shipping formed a special expediting purchasing group, the ES group, to join with the central purchasing group to obtain materials solely for the nuclear submarine. Their direct costs, Rs 50 lakh, were included as direct labor of the nuclear work. Accordingly, overhead was allocated to the contracts in the usual manner. The ES cost of Rs 50 lakh was not included in the general yard overhead. The auditors claimed that no overhead should have been allocated to these ES costs.

Required

1. Compute the amount of the refund that the Navy would claim.
2. Suppose the Navy also discovered that Rs 40 lakh of general yard overhead was devoted exclusively to commercial engine-room purchasing activities. Compute the additional refund that the Navy would claim. (Note: This Rs 40 lakh was never classified as direct labor. Furthermore, the Navy would claim that it should be reclassified as a direct cost but not as direct labor.)

16 Cost Allocation: Joint Products and Byproducts

Learning Objectives

1. Identify the splitoff point in a joint-cost situation and distinguish joint products from byproducts
2. Explain why joint costs are allocated to individual products
3. Allocate joint costs using four methods
4. Explain when the sales value at splitoff method is preferred when allocating joint costs
5. Explain why joint costs are irrelevant in a sell-or-process-further decision
6. Account for byproducts using two methods

Many companies, such as petroleum refiners, produce and sell two or more products simultaneously.

Similarly, some companies, such as health care providers, sell or provide multiple services. The question is, "How should these companies allocate costs to 'joint' products and services?" Knowing how to allocate joint product costs isn't something that only companies need to understand. It's something that farmers have to deal with, too, especially when it comes to the lucrative production of corn to make billions of gallons of ethanol fuel.

Joint Cost Allocation and the Production of Ethanol Fuel[1]

The increased global demand for oil has driven prices higher and forced countries to look for environmentally-sustainable alternatives. In the United States, the largest source of alternative fuel comes from corn-based ethanol. In 2009, the U.S. produced 10.75 billion gallons of ethanol, or 55% of the world's production, up from 1.7 billion gallons per year in 2001.

Producing ethanol requires a significant amount of corn. In 2011, the U.S. Department of Agriculture predicts that more than one-third of U.S. domestic corn production will be used to create ethanol fuel. But not all of that corn winds up in the ethanol that gets blended into gasoline and sold at service station.

Most biotechnology operations, such as making ethanol, produce two or more products. While distilling corn into ethanol, cell mass from the process—such as antibiotic and yeast fermentations—separates from the liquid and becomes a separate product, which is often sold as animal feed. This separation point, where outputs become distinctly identifiable, is called the splitoff point. Similarly, the residues from corn processing plants create secondary products including distillers' dried grains and gluten.

Accountants refer to these secondary products as byproducts. Ethanol byproducts like animal feed and gluten are accounted for by deducting the income from selling these products from the cost of ethanol fuel, the major product. With ethanol production costing

[1] *Sources:* Hacking, Andrew. 1987. *Economic aspects of biotechnology*. Cambridge, United Kingdom: Cambridge University Press; Leber, Jessica. 2010. Economics improve for first commercial cellulosic ethanol plants. *New York Times*, February 16; *USDA Agricultural Predictions to 2019*. 2010. Washington, DC: Government Printing Office; PBS. 2006. Glut of ethanol byproducts coming. *The Environmental Report*, Spring; *Entrepreneur*. 2007. Edible ethanol byproduct is source of novel foods. August.

around $2 per gallon and byproducts selling for a few cents per pound, most of the costs of production are allocated to the ethanol fuel itself, the main product. Since manufacturers would otherwise have to pay to dispose of their ethanol byproducts, most just try to "break even" on byproduct revenue.

In the coming years, however, this may change. With ethanol production growing, corn-based animal feed byproducts are becoming more plentiful. Some ethanol manufacturers are working together to create a market for ethanol feed, which is cheaper and higher in protein than plain corn. This allows ranchers' animals to gain weight faster and at a lower cost per pound. Additionally, scientists are trying to create an edible byproduct from distillers' dry grains, which could become a low-calorie, low-carbohydrate substitute in foods like breads and pastas.

Accounting concerns similar to those in the ethanol example also arise when traditional energy companies like ExxonMobil simultaneously produce crude oil, natural gas, and raw liquefied petroleum gas (LPS) from petroleum, in a single process. This chapter examines methods for allocating costs to joint products. We also examine how cost numbers appropriate for one purpose, such as external reporting, may not be appropriate for other purposes, such as decisions about the further processing of joint products.

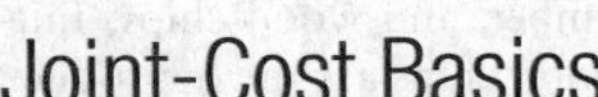

Joint-Cost Basics

Joint costs are the costs of a production process that yields multiple products simultaneously. Consider the distillation of coal, which yields coke, natural gas, and other products. The costs of this distillation are joint costs. The **splitoff point** is the juncture in a joint production process when two or more products become separately identifiable. An example is the point at which coal becomes coke, natural gas, and other products. **Separable costs** are all costs—manufacturing, marketing, distribution, and so on—incurred beyond the splitoff point that are assignable to each of the specific products identified at the splitoff point. At or beyond the splitoff point, decisions relating to the sale or further processing of each identifiable product can be made independently of decisions about the other products.

Industries abound in which a production process simultaneously yields two or more products, either at the splitoff point or after further processing. Exhibit 16-1 presents examples of joint-cost situations in diverse industries. In each of these examples, no individual product can be produced without the accompanying products appearing, although in some cases the proportions can be varied. The focus of joint costing is on allocating costs to individual products at the splitoff point.

Learning Objective 1

Identify the splitoff point in a joint-cost situation

. . . the point at which two or more products become separately identifiable

and distinguish joint products

. . . products with high sales values

from byproducts

. . . products with low sales values

Exhibit 16-1

Examples of Joint-Cost Situations

Industry	Separable Products at the Splitoff Point
Agriculture and Food Processing Industries	
Cocoa beans	Cocoa butter, cocoa powder, cocoa drink mix, tanning cream
Lambs	Lamb cuts, tripe, hides, bones, fat
Hogs	Bacon, ham, spare ribs, pork roast
Raw milk	Cream, liquid skim
Lumber	Lumber of varying grades and shapes
Turkeys	Breast, wings, thighs, drumsticks, digest, feather meal, and poultry meal
Extractive Industries	
Coal	Coke, gas, benzol, tar, ammonia
Copper ore	Copper, silver, lead, zinc
Petroleum	Crude oil, natural gas
Salt	Hydrogen, chlorine, caustic soda
Chemical Industries	
Raw LPG (liquefied petroleum gas)	Butane, ethane, propane
Crude oil	Gasoline, kerosene, benzene, naphtha
Semiconductor Industry	
Fabrication of silicon-wafer chips	Memory chips of different quality (as to capacity), speed, life expectancy, and temperature tolerance

The outputs of a joint production process can be classified into two general categories: outputs with a positive sales value and outputs with a zero sales value.[2] For example, offshore processing of hydrocarbons yields oil and natural gas, which have positive sales value, and it also yields water, which has zero sales value and is recycled back into the ocean. The term **product** describes any output that has a positive total sales value (or an output that enables a company to avoid incurring costs, such as an intermediate chemical product used as input in another process). The total sales value can be high or low.

When a joint production process yields one product with a high total sales value, compared with total sales values of other products of the process, that product is called a **main product**. When a joint production process yields two or more products with high total sales values compared with the total sales values of other products, if any, those products are called **joint products**. The products of a joint production process that have low total sales values compared with the total sales value of the main product or of joint products are called **byproducts**.

Consider some examples. If timber (logs) is processed into standard lumber and wood chips, standard lumber is a main product and wood chips are the byproduct. That's because standard lumber has a high total sales value compared with wood chips. If, however, logs are processed into fine-grade lumber, standard lumber, and wood chips, fine-grade lumber and standard lumber are joint products, and wood chips are the byproduct. That's because both fine-grade lumber and standard lumber have high total sales values when compared with wood chips.

What do the terms joint cost and splitoff point mean, and how do joint products differ from byproducts?

Distinctions among main products, joint products, and byproducts are not so definite in practice. For example, some companies may classify kerosene obtained when refining crude oil as a byproduct because they believe kerosene has a low total sales value relative to the total sales values of gasoline and other products. Other companies may classify kerosene as a joint product because they believe kerosene has a high total sales value relative to the total sales values of gasoline and other products. Moreover, the classification of products—main, joint, or byproduct—can change over time, especially for products such as lower-grade semiconductor chips, whose market prices can increase or decrease by, say, 30% or more in a year. When prices of lower-grade chips are high, they are considered joint products together with higher-grade chips; when prices of lower-grade chips fall considerably, they are considered byproducts. In practice, it is important to understand how a specific company classifies products.

[2] Some outputs of a joint production process have "negative" revenue when their disposal costs (such as the costs of handling nonsalable toxic substances that require special disposal procedures) are considered. These disposal costs should be added to the joint production costs that are allocated to joint or main products.

Allocating Joint Costs

Learning Objective 2

Explain why joint costs are allocated to individual products

. . . to calculate cost of goods sold and inventory, and for reimbursements under cost-plus contracts and other types of claims

Before a manager is able to allocate joint costs, she must first look at the context for doing so. There are several contexts in which joint costs are required to be allocated to individual products or services. These include the following:

- Computation of inventoriable costs and cost of goods sold. Recall from Chapter 9 that absorption costing is required for financial accounting and tax reporting purposes. This necessitates the allocation of joint manufacturing or processing costs to products for calculating ending inventory values.
- Computation of inventoriable costs and cost of goods sold for internal reporting purposes. Many firms use internal accounting data based on joint cost allocations for the purpose of analyzing divisional profitability and in order to evaluate division managers' performance.
- Cost reimbursement for companies that have a few, but not all, of their products or services reimbursed under cost-plus contracts with, say, a government agency. In this case, stringent rules typically specify the manner in which joint costs are assigned to the products or services covered by the cost-plus agreement. That said, fraud in defense contracting, which is often done via cost-plus contracts, remains one of the most active areas of false claim litigation under the Federal False Claims Act. A common practice is "cross-charging," where a contractor shifts joint costs from "fixed-price" defense contracts to those that are done on a cost-plus basis. Defense contractors have also attempted to secure contracts from private businesses or foreign governments by allocating an improper share of joint costs onto the cost-plus agreements they have with the United States government.[3]
- Rate or price regulation for one or more of the jointly produced products or services. This issue is conceptually related to the previous point, and is of great importance in the extractive and energy industries where output prices are regulated to yield a fixed return on a cost basis that includes joint cost allocations. In telecommunications, for example, it is often the case that a firm with significant market power has some products subject to price regulation (e.g., interconnection) and other activities that are unregulated (such as end-user equipment rentals). In this case, it is critical in allocating joint costs to ensure that costs are not transferred from unregulated services to regulated ones.[4]
- Insurance-settlement computations for damage claims made on the basis of cost information of jointly produced products. In this case, the joint cost allocations are essential in order to provide a cost-based analysis of the loss in value.
- More generally, any commercial litigation situation in which costs of joint products or services are key inputs requires the allocation of joint costs.

Decision Point

Why are joint costs allocated to individual products?

Approaches to Allocating Joint Costs

Learning Objective 3

Allocate joint costs using four methods

. . . sales value at splitoff, physical measure, net realizable value (NRV), and constant gross-margin percentage NRV

Two approaches are used to allocate joint costs.

- **Approach 1.** Allocate joint costs using *market-based* data such as revenues. This chapter illustrates three methods that use this approach:
  1. Sales value at splitoff method
  2. Net realizable value (NRV) method
  3. Constant gross-margin percentage NRV method
- **Approach 2.** Allocate joint costs using *physical measures*, such as the weight (say, kilograms), quantity (say, physical units) or volume (say, cubic feet) of the joint products.

In preceding chapters, we used the cause-and-effect and benefits-received criteria for guiding cost-allocation decisions (see Exhibit 14-2). Joint costs do not have a cause-and-effect

[3] See, for example, www.dodig.mil/iginformation/IGInformationReleases/3eSettlementPR.pdf

[4] For details, see the International Telecommunication Union's ICT Regulation Toolkit at www.ictregulationtoolkit.org/en/Section.3497.html.

relationship with individual products because the production process simultaneously yields multiple products. Using the benefits-received criterion leads to a preference for methods under approach 1 because revenues are, in general, a better indicator of benefits received than physical measures. Mining companies, for example, receive more benefits from 1 ton of gold than they do from 10 tons of coal.

In the simplest joint production process, the joint products are sold at the splitoff point without further processing. Example 1, which follows, illustrates the two methods that apply in this case: the sales value at splitoff method and the physical-measure method. Then we introduce joint production processes that yield products that require further processing beyond the splitoff point. Example 2 illustrates the NRV method and the constant-gross margin percentage NRV method. To help you focus on key concepts, we use numbers and amounts in all examples in this chapter that are much smaller than the numbers that are typically found in practice.

The exhibits in this chapter use the following symbols to distinguish a joint or main product from a byproduct:

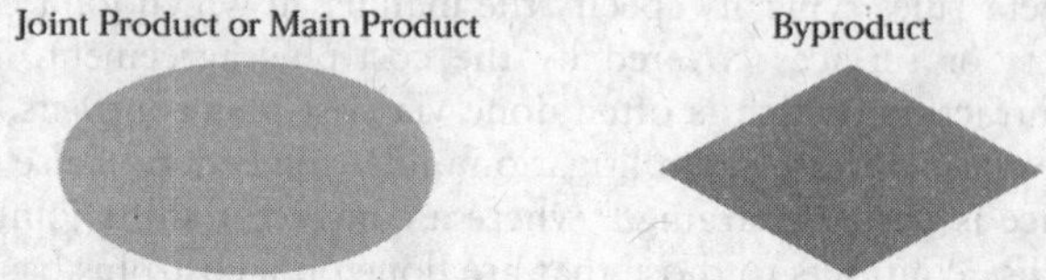

To compare methods, we report gross-margin percentages for individual products under each method.

Example 1: Mother Dairy purchases raw milk from individual farms and processes it until the splitoff point, when two products—cream and liquid skim—emerge. These two products are sold to an independent company, which markets and distributes them to supermarkets and other retail outlets.

In May 2012, Mother Dairy processes 1,10,000 litres of raw milk. During processing, 10,000 litres are lost due to evaporation and spillage, yielding 25,000 litres of cream and 75,000 litres of liquid skim. Summary data follow.

	A	B	C
1		**Joint Costs**	
2	Joint costs (costs of 1,10,000 litres raw milk and processing to splitoff point)	Rs 40,00,000	
3			
4		**Cream**	**Liquid Skim**
5	Beginnning inventory (litres)	0	0
6	Production (litres)	25,000	75,000
7	Sales (litres)	20,000	30,000
8	Ending inventory (litres)	5,000	45,000
9	Selling price per litres	Rs 80	Rs 40

Exhibit 16-2 depicts the basic relationships in this example.

How much of the Rs 40,00,000 joint costs should be allocated to the cost of goods sold of 20,000 litres of cream and 30,000 litres of liquid skim, and how much should be allocated to the ending inventory of 5,000 litres of cream and 45,000 litres of liquid skim? We begin by illustrating the two methods that use the properties of the products at the splitoff point, the sales value at splitoff method and the physical-measure method.

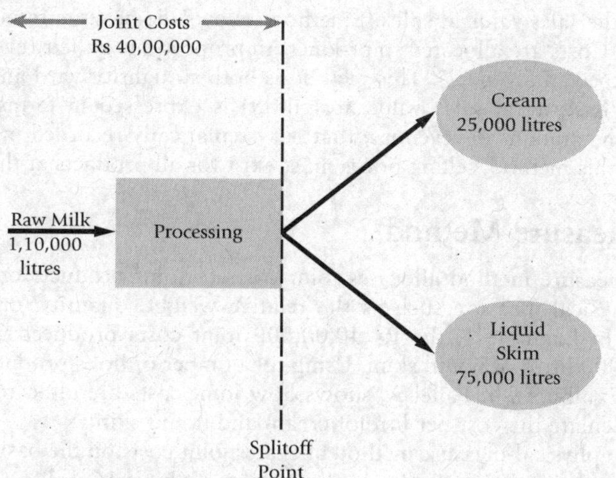

Exhibit 16-2

Example 1: Overview of Mother Dairy

Sales Value at Splitoff Method

The **sales value at splitoff method** allocates joint costs to joint products on the basis of the relative total sales value at the splitoff point. Using this method for Example 1, Exhibit 16-3, Panel A, shows how joint costs are allocated to individual products to calculate cost per litre of cream and liquid skim for valuing ending inventory. This method uses the sales value of the *entire production of the accounting period* (25,000 litres of cream and 75,000 litres of liquid skim), not just the quantity sold (20,000 litres of cream and 30,000 litres of liquid skim). The reason is that the joint costs were incurred on all units produced, not just the portion sold during the current period. Exhibit 16-3, Panel B, presents the product-line income statement using the sales value at splitoff method. Note that the sales value at splitoff method allocates joint costs to each product in proportion to sales value of total production (cream: Rs 16,00,000 ÷ Rs 20,00,000 = 80%; liquid skim: Rs 24,00,000 ÷ Rs 30,00,000 = 80%). Therefore, the gross-margin percentage for each product manufactured in May 2012 is the same: 20%.[5]

Exhibit 16-3 Joint-Cost Allocation and Product-Line Income Statement Using Sales Value at Splitoff Method: Mother Dairy for May 2012

	A	B	C	D
1	**PANEL A: Allocation of Joint Costs Using Sales Value at Splitoff Method**	**Cream**	**Liquid Skim**	**Total**
2	Sales value of total production at splitoff point			
3	(25,000 gallons x Rs 80 per litre ; 75,000 litres x Rs 40 per litre)	Rs 20,00,000	Rs 30,00,000	Rs 50,00,000
4	Weighting (Rs 20,00,000 ÷ Rs 50,00,000; Rs 30,00,000 ÷ 55,00,000	4.0	0.60	
5	Joint costs allocated (0.40 x Rs 40,00,000; 0.60 x Rs 40,00,000)	Rs 16,00,000	Rs 24,00,000	Rs 40,00,000
6	Joint production cost per litre			
7	(Rs 16,00,000 ÷ 25,000 litres; Rs 24,00,000 ÷ 75,000 litres)	Rs 64	Rs 32	
8				
9	**PANEL B: Product-Line Income Statement Using Sales Value at Splitoff Method for May 2012**	**Cream**	**Liquid Skim**	**Total**
10	Revenues (20,000 litres x Rs 80 per litre; 30,000 litres x Rs 40 per litre)	Rs 16,00,000	Rs 12,00,000	Rs 28,00,000
11	Cost of goods sold (joint costs)			
12	Production costs (0.40 x Rs 40,00,000; 0.60 x Rs 40,00,000)	16,00,000	24,00,000	40,00,000
13	Deduct ending inventory (5,000 litres x Rs 64.0 per litre; 45,000 litres x Rs 32.0 per litre)	3,20,000	14,40,000	17,60,000
14	Cost of goods sold (joint costs)	12,80,000	9,60,000	22,40,000
15	Gross margin	Rs 3,20,000	Rs 2,40,000	Rs 5,60,000
16	Gross margin percentage (Rs 3,20,000 ÷ Rs 16,00,000; Rs 2,40,000 ÷ Rs 12,00,000; Rs 5,60,000 ÷ Rs 28,00,000)	20%	20%	20%

[5] Suppose Mother Dairy has beginning inventory of cream and liquid milk in May 2012. Suppose further that when this inventory is sold, Mother Dairy earns a gross margin different from 20%. Then the gross-margin percentage for cream and liquid skim will not be the same. The gross-margin percentage will depend on how much of the sales of each product came from beginning inventory and how much came from current-period production.

Note how the sales value at splitoff method follows the benefits-received criterion of cost allocation: Costs are allocated to products in proportion to their revenue-generating power (their expected revenues). This method is both straightforward and intuitive. The cost-allocation base (total sales value at splitoff) is expressed in terms of a common denominator (the amount of revenues) that is systematically recorded in the accounting system. To use this method, selling prices must exist for all products at the splitoff point.

Physical-Measure Method

The **physical-measure method** allocates joint costs to joint products on the basis of a *comparable* physical measure such as the relative weight, quantity, or volume at the splitoff point. In Example 1, the Rs 40,00,000 joint costs produced 25,000 litres of cream and 75,000 litres of liquid skim. Using the number of litres produced as the physical measure, Exhibit 16-4, Panel A, shows how joint costs are allocated to individual products to calculate the cost per litre of cream and liquid skim.

Because the physical-measure method allocates joint costs on the basis of the number of litres, cost per litre is the same for both products. Exhibit 16-4, Panel B, presents the product-line income statement using the physical-measure method. The gross-margin percentages are 50% for cream and 0% for liquid skim.

Under the benefits-received criterion, the physical-measure method is much less desirable than the sales value at splitoff method. This is because the physical measure of the individual products may have no relationship to their respective revenue-generating abilities. Consider a gold mine that extracts ore containing gold, silver, and lead. Use of a common physical measure (tons) would result in almost all costs being allocated to lead—the product that weighs the most but has the lowest revenue-generating power. In this case, the method of cost allocation is inconsistent with the main reason that the mining company is incurring mining costs—to earn revenues from gold and silver, not lead. When a company uses the physical-measure method in a product-line income statement, products that have a high sales value per ton—for example, gold and silver—would show a large "profit," and products that have a low sales value per ton—for example, lead—would show sizable losses.

Obtaining comparable physical measures for all products is not always straightforward. Consider the joint costs of producing oil and natural gas; oil is a liquid and gas is a vapor. To use a physical measure, the oil and gas need to be converted to the energy equivalent for oil and gas, British thermal units (BTUs). Using some physical measures to allocate joint costs may require assistance from technical personnel outside of accounting.

Determining which products of a joint process to include in a physical-measure computation can greatly affect the allocations to those products. Outputs with no sales value (such as dirt in gold mining) are always excluded. Although many more tons of dirt than

Exhibit 16-4 Joint-Cost Allocation and Product-Line Income Statement Using Physical-Measure Method: Mother Dairy for May 2012

	A	B	C	D
1	**PANEL A: Allocation of Joint Costs Using Physical-Measure Method**	**Cream**	**Liquid Skim**	**Total**
2	Physical measure of total production (litres)	2,50,000	7,50,000	10,00,000
3	Weighting (25,000 litres ÷ 100,000 litres; 75,000 litres ÷ 100,000 litres)	2.5	7.5	
4	Joint costs allocated (0.25 x Rs 40,00,000; 0.75 x Rs 40,00,000)	Rs 10,00,000	Rs 30,00,000	Rs 40,00,000
5	Joint production cost per litre (Rs10,00,000 ÷ 25,000 litres; Rs 30,00,000 ÷ 75,000 litres)	Rs 40	Rs 40	
6				
7	**PANEL B: Product-Line Income Statement Using Physical-Measure Method for May 2012**	**Cream**	**Liquid Skim**	**Total**
8	Revenues (20,000 litres x Rs 80 per litre; 30,000 litres x Rs 40 per litre)	Rs 16,00,000	Rs 12,00,000	Rs 28,00,000
9	Cost of goods sold (joint costs)			
10	Production costs (0.25 x Rs 40,00,000; 0.75 x Rs 40,00,000)	10,00,000	30,00,000	40,00,000
11	Deduct ending inventory (5,000 litres x Rs 40 per litre; 45,000 litres xRs 40 per litre)	2,00,000	18,00,000	20,00,000
12	Cost of goods sold (joint costs)	8,00,000	12,00,000	20,00,000
13	Gross margin	Rs 8,00,000	Rs 0	Rs 8,00,000
14	Gross margin percentage (Rs 8,00,000 ÷ Rs 16,00,000; Rs0 ÷ Rs 12,00,000; Rs 8,00,000 ÷ Rs 28,00,000)	50%	0	28.6%

gold are produced, costs are not incurred to produce outputs that have zero sales value. Byproducts are also often excluded from the denominator used in the physical-measure method because of their low sales values relative to the joint products or the main product. The general guideline for the physical-measure method is to include only the joint-product outputs in the weighting computations.

Net Realizable Value (NRV) Method

In many cases, products are processed beyond the splitoff point to bring them to a marketable form or to increase their value above their selling price at the splitoff point. For example, when crude oil is refined, the gasoline, kerosene, benzene, and naphtha must be processed further before they can be sold. To illustrate, let's extend the Mother Dairy example.

Example 2: Assume the same data as in Example 1 except that both cream and liquid skim can be processed further:

- Cream → Buttercream: 25,000 litres of cream are further processed to yield 20,000 litres of buttercream at additional processing costs of Rs 28,00,000. Buttercream, which sells for Rs 250 per litre, is used in the manufacture of butter-based products.
- Liquid Skim → Condensed Milk: 75,000 litres of liquid skim are further processed to yield 50,000 litres of condensed milk at additional processing costs of Rs 52,00,000. Condensed milk sells for Rs 220 per litre.
- Sales during May 2012 were 12,000 litres of buttercream and 45,000 litres of condensed milk.

Exhibit 16-5, Panel A, depicts how (a) raw milk is converted into cream and liquid skim in the joint production process, and (b) how cream is separately processed into buttercream and liquid skim is separately processed into condensed milk. Panel B shows the data for Example 2.

The **net realizable value (NRV) method** allocates joint costs to joint products on the basis of relative NRV—final sales value minus separable costs. The NRV method is typically used in preference to the sales value at splitoff method only when selling prices for one or more products at splitoff do not exist. Using this method for Example 2, Exhibit 16-6, Panel A, shows how joint costs are allocated to individual products to calculate cost per litre of buttercream and condensed milk.

Exhibit 16-6, Panel B presents the product-line income statement using the NRV method. Gross-margin percentages are 22.0% for buttercream and 26.4% for condensed milk.

The NRV method is often implemented using simplifying assumptions. For example, even though companies may frequently change the number of processing steps beyond the splitoff point, they assume a specific set of such steps when implementing the NRV method. Also, even when selling prices of joint products vary frequently, companies implement the NRV method using a given set of selling prices throughout the accounting period. Similarly, even though companies may occasionally change the number or sequence of processing steps beyond the splitoff point in order to adjust to variations in input quality or local conditions, they assume a specific constant set of such steps when implementing the NRV method.

Constant Gross-Margin Percentage NRV Method

The **constant gross-margin percentage NRV method** allocates joint costs to joint products in such a way that each individual product achieves an identical gross-margin percentage. The method works backward in that the overall gross margin is computed first. Then, for each product, this gross-margin percentage and any separable costs are deducted from the final sales value of production in order to back into the joint cost allocation for that product. The method can be broken down into three discrete steps. Exhibit 16-7, Panel A, shows these steps for allocating the Rs 40,00,000 joint costs between buttercream and condensed milk in the Mother Dairy example. As we describe each step, refer to Exhibit 16-7, Panel A, for an illustration of the step.

Exhibit 16-5 Example 2: Overview of Mother Dairy

PANEL A: Graphical Presentation of Process for Example 2

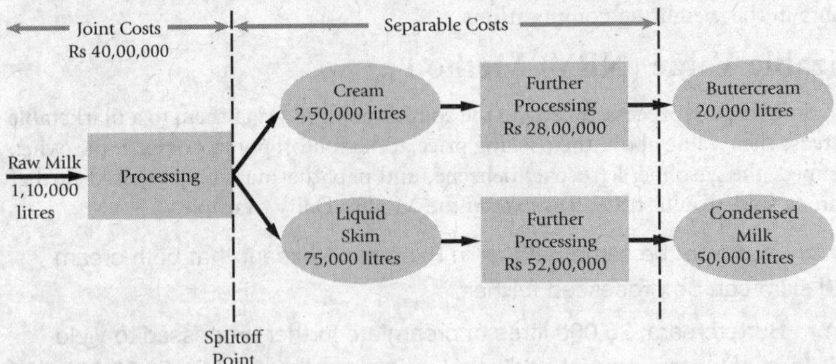

PANEL B: Data for Example 2

	A	B	C	D	E
1		Joint Costs		Buttercream	Condensed Milk
2	Joint costs (costs of 1,10,000 litres raw milk and processing to splitoff point)	Rs 4,000,000			
3	Separable cost of processing 25,000 litres cream into 20,000 litres buttercream			Rs 28,00,000	
4	Separable cost of processing 75,000 litres liquid skim into 50,000 litres condensed milk				Rs 52,00,000
5					
6		Cream	Liquid Skim	Buttercream	Condensed Milk
7	Beginning inventory (litres)	0	0	0	0
8	Production (litres)	25,000	75,000	20,000	50,000
9	Transfer for further processing (litres)	25,000	75,000		
10	Sales (litres)			12,000	45,000
11	Ending inventory (litres)	0	0	8,000	5,000
12	Selling price per litre	Rs 80	Rs 40	Rs 250	Rs 220

Exhibit 16-6 Joint-Cost Allocation and Product-Line Income Statement Using NRV Method: Mother Dairy for May 2012

	A	B	C	D
1	**PANEL A: Allocation of Joint Costs Using Net Realizable Value Method**	Buttercream	Condensed Milk	Total
2	Final sales value of total production during accounting period			
3	(20,000 litres x Rs 250 per litre; 50,000 litres x Rs 220 per litre)	Rs 50,00,000	Rs 1,10,00,000	Rs 1,60,00,000
4	Deduct separable costs	28,00,000	52,00,000	80,00,000
5	Net realizable value at splitoff point	Rs 22,00,000	Rs 58,00,000	Rs 80,00,000
6	Weighting (Rs 22,00,000 ÷ Rs 80,00,000; Rs 58,00,000 ÷ Rs 80,00,000)	.275	0.725	
7	Joint costs allocated (0.275 x Rs 40,00,000; 0.725 x Rs 40,00,000)	Rs 11,00,000	Rs 29,00,000	Rs 40,00,000
8	Production cost per litre			
9	([Rs 11,00,000 + Rs 28,00,000] ÷ 20,000 litres; [Rs 29,00,000 + Rs 52,00,000] ÷ 50,000 litres)	Rs 195	Rs 162	
10				
11	**PANEL B: Product-Line Income Statement Using Net Realizable Value Method for May 2012**	Buttercream	Condensed Milk	Total
12	Revenues (12,000 litres x Rs 250 per litre; 45,000 litres x Rs 220 per litre)	Rs 30,00,000	Rs 99,00,000	Rs 1,29,00,000
13	Cost of goods sold			
14	Joint costs (0.275 x Rs 40,00,000; 0.725 x Rs 40,00,000)	11,00,000	29,00,000	40,00,000
15	Separable costs	28,00,000	52,00,000	80,00,000
16	Production costs	39,00,000	81,00,000	1,20,00,000
17	Deduct ending inventory (8,000 litres x Rs 195.0 per litre; 5,000 litres x Rs 162.0 per litre)	15,60,000	8,10,000	23,70,000
18	Cost of goods sold	23,40,000	72,90,000	96,30,000
19	Gross margin	Rs 6,60,000	Rs 26,10,000	Rs 32,70,000
20	Gross margin percentage (Rs6,60,000 ÷ Rs30,00,000; Rs26,10,000 ÷ Rs99,00,000; Rs32,70,000 ÷ Rs1,29,00,000)	22.0%	26.4%	25.3%

Exhibit 16-7 Joint-Cost Allocation and Product-Line Income Statement Using Constant Gross-Margin Percentage NRV Method: Mother Dairy for May 2012

	A	B	C	D
1	**PANEL A: Allocation of Joint Costs Using Constant Gross-Margin Percentage NRV Method**			
2	**Step 1**			
3	Final sales value of total production during accounting period: (20,000 litres x Rs 250 per litre) + (50,000 litres x Rs 220 per litre)	Rs 1,60,00,000		
4	Deduct joint and separable costs (Rs 40,00,000 + Rs 28,00,000 + Rs 52,00,000)	1,20,00,000		
5	Gross margin	Rs 40,00,000		
6	Gross margin percentage (Rs 40,00,000 ÷ Rs 1,60,00,000)	25%		
7		**Buttercream**	**Condensed Milk**	**Total**
8	**Step 2**			
9	Final sales value of total production during accounting period: (20,000 litres x Rs 250 per litre; 50,000 litres x Rs 220 per litre)	Rs 50,00,000	Rs 1,10,00,000	Rs 1,60,00,000
10	Deduct gross margin, using overall gross-margin percentage (25% x Rs 50,00,000; 25% x Rs 1,10,00,000)	12,50,000	27,50,000	40,00,000
11	Total production costs	37,50,000	82,50,000	1,20,00,000
12	**Step 3**			
13	Deduct separable costs	28,00,000	52,00,000	80,00,000
14	Joint costs allocated	Rs 9,50,000	Rs 30,50,000	Rs 40,00,000
15				
16	**PANEL B: Product-Line Income Statement Using Constant Gross-Margin Percentage NRV Method for May 2012**	**Buttercream**	**Condensed Milk**	**Total**
17	Revenues (12,000 litres x Rs 250 per litre; 45,000 litres x Rs 220 per litre)	Rs 30,00,000	Rs 99,00,000	Rs 1,29,00,000
18	Cost of goods sold			
19	Joint costs (from Panel A)	9,50,000	30,50,000	40,00,000
20	Separable costs	28,00,000	52,00,000	80,00,000
21	Production costs	37,50,000	82,50,000	1,20,00,000
22	Deduct ending inventory			
23	(8,000 litres x Rs 187.5 per litre[a]; 5,000 litres x Rs 165 per litre)[b]	15,00,000	82,50,000	23,25,000
24	Cost of goods sold	22,50,000	74,25,000	96,75,000
25	Gross margin	Rs 7,50,000	Rs 24,75,000	Rs 32,25,000
26	Gross margin percentage (Rs 7,50,000 ÷ 300,000; Rs 24,75,000 ÷ Rs 99,00,000; Rs 32,50,000 ÷ Rs 1,29,00,000)	25%	25%	25%
27				
28	[a]Total production costs of buttercream ÷ Total production of buttercream = Rs 37,50,000 ÷ 20,000 litres = Rs 187.5 per litre.			
29	[b]Total production costs of condensed milk ÷ Total production of condensed milk = Rs 82,50,000 ÷ 50,000 litres = Rs 165 per litre.			

Step 1: Compute overall gross margin percentage. The overall gross-margin percentage for all joint products together is first calculated. This is based on the final sales value of *total production* during the accounting period, not the *total revenues* of the period. Note, Exhibit 16-7, Panel A, uses Rs 1,60,00,000, the final expected sales value of the entire output of buttercream and condensed milk, not the Rs 1,29,00,000 in actual sales revenue for the month of May.

Step 2: Compute total production costs for each product. The gross margin (in rupees) for each product is computed by multiplying the overall gross-margin percentage by the product's final sales value of total production. The difference between the final sales value of total production and the gross margin then yields the total production costs that the product must bear.

Step 3: Compute allocated joint costs. As the final step, the separable costs for each product are deducted from the total production costs that the product must bear to obtain the joint-cost allocation for that product.

Exhibit 16-7, Panel B, presents the product-line income statement for the constant gross-margin percentage NRV method.

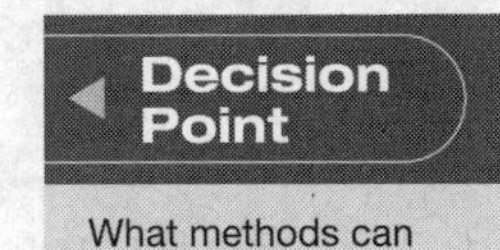

What methods can be used to allocate joint costs to individual products?

The constant gross-margin percentage NRV method is the only method of allocating joint costs under which products may receive negative allocations. This may be required in order to bring the gross-margin percentages of relatively unprofitable products up to the overall average. The constant gross-margin percentage NRV method also differs from the other two market-based joint-cost-allocation methods described earlier in another fundamental way. Neither the sales value at splitoff method nor the NRV method takes account of profits earned either before or after the splitoff point when allocating the joint costs. In contrast, the constant gross-margin percentage NRV method allocates both joint costs and profits: gross margin is allocated to the joint products in order to determine the joint-cost allocations so that the resulting gross-margin percentage for each product is the same.

Choosing a Method

Learning Objective 4

Explain why the sales value at splitoff method is preferred when allocating joint costs

. . . because it objectively measures the benefits received by each product

Which method of allocating joint costs should be used? The sales value at splitoff method is preferable when selling-price data exist at splitoff (even if further processing is done). Reasons for using the sales value at splitoff method include:

1. **Measurement of the value of the joint products at the splitoff point.** Sales value at splitoff is the best measure of the benefits received as a result of joint processing relative to all other methods of allocating joint costs. It is a meaningful basis for allocating joint costs because generating revenues is the reason why a company incurs joint costs in the first place. It is also sometimes possible to vary the physical mix of final output and thereby produce more or less market value by incurring more joint costs. In such cases, there is a clear causal link between total cost and total output value, thereby further validating the use of the sales value at splitoff method.[6]
2. **No anticipation of subsequent management decisions.** The sales value at splitoff method does not require information on the processing steps after splitoff, if there is further processing. In contrast, the NRV and constant gross-margin percentage NRV methods require information on (a) the specific sequence of further processing decisions, (b) the separable costs of further processing, and (c) the point at which individual products will be sold.
3. **Availability of a common basis to allocate joint costs to products.** The sales value at splitoff method (as well as other market-based methods) has a common basis to allocate joint costs to products, which is revenue. In contrast, the physical-measure at splitoff method may lack an easily identifiable common basis to allocate joint costs to individual products.
4. **Simplicity.** The sales value at splitoff method is simple. In contrast, the NRV and constant gross-margin percentage NRV methods can be complex for processing operations having multiple products and multiple splitoff points. This complexity increases when management makes frequent changes in the specific sequence of post-splitoff processing decisions or in the point at which individual products are sold.

When selling prices of all products at the splitoff point are unavailable, the NRV method is commonly used because it attempts to approximate sales value at splitoff by subtracting from selling prices separable costs incurred after the splitoff point. The NRV method assumes that all the markup or profit margin is attributable to the joint process and none of the markup is attributable to the separable costs. Profit, however, is attributable to all phases of production and marketing, not just the joint process. More of the profit may be attributable to the joint process if the separable process is relatively routine, whereas more of the profit may be attributable to the separable process if the separable process uses a special patented technology. Despite its complexities, the NRV method is used when selling prices at splitoff are not available as it provides a better measure of benefits received compared with the constant gross-margin percentage NRV method or the physical-measure method.

The constant gross-margin percentage NRV method makes the simplifying assumption of treating the joint products as though they comprise a single product. This method calculates the aggregate gross-margin percentage, applies this gross-margin percentage to each product, and views the residual after separable costs are accounted for as the

[6] In the semiconductor industry, for example, the use of cleaner facilities, higher quality silicon wafers, and more sophisticated equipment (all of which require higher joint costs) shifts the distribution of output to higher-quality memory devices with more market value. For details, see J. F. Gatti and D. J. Grinnell, "Joint Cost Allocations: Measuring and Promoting Productivity and Quality Improvements," *Journal of Cost Management* (2000). The authors also demonstrate that joint cost allocations based on market value are preferable for promoting quality and productivity improvements.

implicit amount of joint costs assigned to each product. An advantage of this method is that it avoids the complexities inherent in the NRV method to measure the benefits received by each of the joint products at the splitoff point. The main issue with the constant gross-margin percentage NRV method is the assumption that all products have the same ratio of cost to sales value. Recall from our discussion of activity-based costing (ABC) in Chapter 5 that such a situation is very uncommon when companies offer a diverse set of products.

Although there are difficulties in using the physical-measure method—such as lack of congruence with the benefits-received criterion—there are instances when it may be preferred. Consider rate or price regulation. Market-based measures are difficult to use in this context because using selling prices as a basis for setting prices (rates) and at the same time using selling prices to allocate the costs on which prices (rates) are based leads to circular reasoning. To avoid this dilemma, the physical-measure method is useful in rate regulation.

Not Allocating Joint Costs

Some companies choose to not allocate joint costs to products. The usual rationale given by these firms is the complexity of their production or extraction processes and the difficulty of gathering sufficient data for carrying out the allocations correctly. For example, a recent survey of nine sawmills in Norway revealed that none of them allocated joint costs. The study's authors noted that the "interviewed sawmills considered the joint cost problem very interesting, but pointed out that the problem is not easily solved. For example, there is clearly a shortcoming in management systems designed for handling joint cost allocation."[7]

In the absence of joint cost allocation, some firms simply subtract the joint costs directly from total revenues in the management accounts. If substantial inventories exist, then firms that do not allocate joint costs often carry their product inventories at NRV. Industries that use variations of this approach include meatpacking, canning, and mining. Accountants do not ordinarily record inventories at NRV because this practice results in recognizing income on each product at the time production is completed and *before* sales are made. In response, some companies using this no-allocation approach carry their inventories at NRV minus an estimated operating income margin. When any end-of-period inventories are sold in the next period, the cost of goods sold then equals this carrying value. This approach is akin to the "production method" of accounting for byproducts, which we describe in detail later in this chapter.

Decision Point

When is the sales value at splitoff method considered preferable for allocating joint costs to individual products and why?

Irrelevance of Joint Costs for Decision Making

Learning Objective 5

Explain why joint costs are irrelevant in a sell-or-process-further decision

. . . because joint costs are the same whether or not further processing occurs

Chapter 11 introduced the concepts of *relevant revenues*—expected future revenues that differ among alternative courses of action—and *relevant costs*—expected future costs that differ among alternative courses of action. These concepts can be applied to decisions on whether a joint product or main product should be sold at the splitoff point or processed further.

Sell-or-Process-Further Decisions

Consider Mother' Dairy's decision to either sell the joint products, cream and liquid skim, at the splitoff point or to further process them into buttercream and condensed milk. The decision to incur additional costs for further processing should be based on the incremental operating income attainable beyond the splitoff point. Example 2 assumed it was profitable

[7] For further details, see T. Tunes, A. Nyrud, and B. Eikenes, "Cost and Performance Management in the Sawmill Industry," *Scandinavian Forest Economics* (2006).

for both cream and liquid skim to be further processed into buttercream and condensed milk, respectively. The incremental analysis for the decision to process further is:

Further Processing Cream into Buttercream	
Incremental revenues	
(Rs 250/litre × 20,000 litres) – (Rs 80/litre × 25,000 litres)	Rs 30,00,000
Deduct incremental processing costs	28,00,000
Increase in operating income from buttercream	Rs 2,00,000
Further Processing Liquid Skim into Condensed Milk	
Incremental revenues	
(Rs 220/litre × 50,000 litres) – (Rs 40/litre × 75,000 litres)	Rs 80,00,000
Deduct incremental processing costs	52,00,000
Increase in operating income from condensed milk	Rs 28,00,000

In this example, operating income increases for both products, so the manager decides to process cream into buttercream and liquid skim into condensed milk. *The 40,00,000 joint costs incurred before the splitoff point are irrelevant in deciding whether to process further.* Why? Because the joint costs of 40,00,000 are the same whether the products are sold at the splitoff point or processed further.

Incremental costs are the additional costs incurred for an activity, such as further processing. *Do not assume all separable costs in joint-cost allocations are always incremental costs.* Some separable costs may be fixed costs, such as lease costs on buildings where the further processing is done; some separable costs may be sunk costs, such as depreciation on the equipment that converts cream into buttercream; and some separable costs may be allocated costs, such as corporate costs allocated to the condensed milk operations. None of these costs will differ between the alternatives of selling products at the splitoff point or processing further; therefore, they are irrelevant.

Joint-Cost Allocation and Performance Evaluation

The potential conflict between cost concepts used for decision making and cost concepts used for evaluating the performance of managers could also arise in sell-or-process-further decisions. To see how, let us continue with Example 2. Suppose *allocated* fixed corporate and administrative costs of further processing cream into buttercream equal Rs 3,00,000 and that these costs will be allocated only to buttercream and to the manager's product-line income statement if buttercream is produced. How might this policy affect the decision to process further?

As we have seen, on the basis of incremental revenues and incremental costs, Mother Dairy's operating income will increase by Rs 2,00,000 if it processes cream into buttercream. However, producing the buttercream also results in an additional charge for allocated fixed costs of Rs 3,00,000. If the manager is evaluated on a full-cost basis (that is, after allocating all costs), processing cream into buttercream will lower the manager's performance-evaluation measure by Rs 1,00,000 (incremental operating income, Rs 2,00,000 – allocated fixed costs, Rs 3,00,000). Therefore, the manager may be tempted to sell cream at splitoff and not process it into buttercream.

A similar conflict can also arise with respect to production of joint products. Consider again Example 1. Suppose Mother Dairy has the option of selling raw milk at a profit of Rs 2,00,000. From a decision-making standpoint, Mother Dairy would maximize operating income by processing raw milk into cream and liquid skim because the total revenues from selling both joint products (Rs 50,00,000) exceed the joint costs (Rs 40,00,000) by Rs 10,00,000. (This amount is greater than the Rs 2,00,000 Mother Dairy would make if it sold the raw milk instead of processing it.) Suppose, however, the cream and liquid-skim product lines are managed by different managers, each of whom is evaluated based on a product-line income statement. If the physical-measure method of joint-cost allocation is used and the selling price per litre of liquid skim falls below Rs 40 per litre, the liquid-skim product line will show a loss (from Exhibit 16-4, revenues will be less than Rs 12,00,000, but cost of goods sold will be unchanged at Rs 12,00,000). The manager of the liquid-skim line will prefer, from his performance-evaluation standpoint, to not produce liquid skim but rather to sell the raw milk.

This conflict between decision making and performance evaluation is less severe if Mother Dairy uses any of the market-based methods of joint-cost allocations—sales value at splitoff, NRV, or constant gross-margin percentage NRV. That's because each of these methods allocates costs using revenues, which generally leads to a positive income for each joint product.

Pricing Decisions

Firms should be wary of using the full cost of a joint product (that is, the cost after joint costs are allocated) as the basis for making pricing decisions. Why? Because in many situations, there is no direct cause-and-effect relationship that identifies the resources demanded by each joint product that can then be used as a basis for pricing. In fact, the use of the sales value at splitoff or the net realizable value method to allocate joint costs results in a reverse effect—selling prices of joint products drive joint-cost allocations, rather than cost allocations serving as the basis for the pricing of joint products! Of course, the principles of pricing covered in Chapter 12 apply to the joint process taken as a whole. Even if the firm cannot alter the mix of products generated by the joint process, it must ensure that the joint products generate sufficient combined revenue in the long run to cover the joint costs of processing.

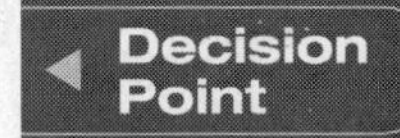

Are joint costs relevant in a sell-or-process-further decision?

Accounting for Byproducts

Learning Objective

Account for byproducts using two methods

. . . recognize in financial statements at time of production or at time of sale

Joint production processes may yield not only joint products and main products but also byproducts. Although byproducts have low total sales values compared with total sales values of joint or main products, the presence of byproducts in a joint production process can affect the allocation of joint costs. Let's consider a two-product example consisting of a main product and a byproduct (also see the following Concepts in Action feature).

Example 3: The Westlake Corporation processes timber into fine-grade lumber and wood chips that are used as mulch in gardens and lawns. Information about these products follows:

- Fine-grade lumber (the main product)—sells for Rs 60 per board foot (b.f.)
- Wood chips (the byproduct)—sells for Rs 10 per cubic foot (c.f.)

Data for July 2012 are:

	Beginning Inventory	Production	Sales	Ending Inventory
Fine-grade lumber (b.f.)	0	50,000	40,000	10,000
Wood chips (c.f.)	0	4,000	1,200	2,800

Joint manufacturing costs for these products in July 2012 were Rs 25,00,000, comprising Rs 15,00,000 for direct materials and Rs 10,00,000 for conversion costs. Both products are sold at the splitoff point without further processing, as Exhibit 16-8 shows.

We present two byproduct accounting methods: the production method and the sales method. The production method recognizes byproducts in the financial statements at the time production is completed. The sales method delays recognition of byproducts until the time of sale.[8] Exhibit 16-9 presents the income statement of Westlake Corporation under both methods.

[8] For a discussion of joint cost allocation and byproduct accounting methods, see P. D. Marshall and R. F. Dombrowski, "A Small Business Review of Accounting for Primary Products, Byproducts and Scrap," *The National Public Accountant* (February/March 2003): 10–13.

Exhibit 16-8

Example 3: Overview of Westlake Corporation

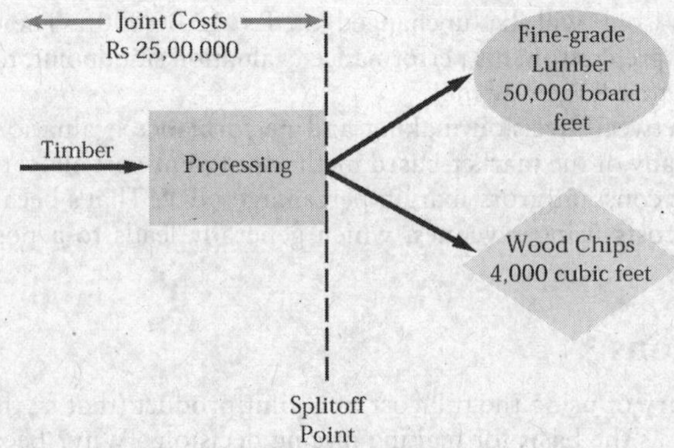

Production Method: Byproducts Recognized at Time Production Is Completed

This method recognizes the byproduct in the financial statements—the 4,000 cubic feet of wood chips—in the month it is produced, July 2012. The NRV from the byproduct produced is offset against the costs of the main product (see Concepts in Action). The following journal entries illustrate the production method:

		Dr	Cr
1.	Work in Process	15,00,000	
	Accounts Payable		15,00,000
	To record direct materials purchased and used in production during July.		
2.	Work in Process	10,00,000	
	Various accounts such as Wages Payable and Accumulated Depreciation		10,00,000
	To record conversion costs in the production process during July; examples include energy, manufacturing supplies, all manufacturing labor, and plant depreciation.		
3.	Byproduct Inventory—Wood Chips (4,000 c.f. × Rs 10 per c.f.)	40,000	
	Finished Goods—Fine-grade Lumber (Rs 25,00,000 – Rs 40,000)	24,60,000	
	Work in Process (Rs 15,00,000 + Rs 10,00,000)		25,00,000
	To record cost of goods completed during July.		

Exhibit 16-9

Income Statements of Westlake Corporation for July 2012 Using the Production and Sales Methods for Byproduct Accounting

	Production Method	Sales Method
Revenues		
Main product: Fine-grade lumber (40,000 b.f. × Rs 60 per b.f.)	Rs 24,00,000	Rs 24,00,000
Byproduct: Wood chips (1,200 c.f. × Rs 10 per c.f.)	–	12,000
Total revenues	Rs 24,00,000	24,12,000
Cost of goods sold		
Total manufacturing costs	Rs 25,00,000	25,00,000
Deduct byproduct revenue (4,000 c.f. × Rs 10 per c.f.)	(40,000)	–
Net manufacturing costs	24,60,000	25,00,000
Deduct main-product inventory	(4,92,000)[a]	(5,00,000)[b]
Cost of goods sold	19,68,000	20,00,000
Gross margin	Rs 4,32,000	Rs 4,12,000
Gross-margin percentage (Rs 4,32,000 ÷ Rs 24,00,000; Rs 4,12,000 ÷ Rs 24,12,000)	18.00%	17.08%
Inventoriable costs (end of period):		
Main product: Fine-grade lumber	Rs 4,92,000	Rs 5,00,000
Byproduct: Wood chips (2,800 c.f. × Rs 10 per c.f.)[c]	28,000	0

[a](10,000 ÷ 5 0,000) × net manufacturing cost = (10,000 ÷ 50,000) × Rs 24,60,000 = Rs 4,92,000.

[b](10,000 ÷ 5 0,000) × total manufacturing cost = (10,000 ÷ 50,000) × Rs 25,00,000 = Rs 5,00,000.

[c]Recorded at selling prices.

		Debit	Credit
4a.	Cost of Goods Sold [(40,000 b.f. ÷ 50,000 b.f.) × Rs 24,60,000]	19,68,000	
	Finished Goods—Fine-grade Lumber		19,68,000
	To record the cost of the main product sold during July.		
4b.	Cash or Accounts Receivable (40,000 b.f. × Rs 60 per b.f.)	24,00,000	
	Revenues—Fine-grade Lumber		24,00,000
	To record the sales of the main product during July.		
5.	Cash or Accounts Receivable (1,200 c.f. × Rs 10 per c.f.)	12,000	
	Byproduct Inventory—Wood Chips		12,000
	To record the sales of the byproduct during July.		

The production method reports the byproduct inventory of wood chips in the balance sheet at its Rs 10 per cubic foot selling price [(4,000 cubic feet – 1,200 cubic feet) × Rs 10 per cubic foot = Rs 28,000].

One variation of this method would be to report byproduct inventory at its NRV reduced by a normal profit margin (Rs 28,000 – 20% × Rs 28,000 = Rs 22,400, assuming a normal profit margin of 20%).[9] When byproduct inventory is sold in a subsequent period, the income statement will match the selling price, Rs 28,000, with the "cost" reported for the byproduct inventory, Rs 22,400, resulting in a byproduct operating income of Rs 5,600 (Rs 28,000 – Rs 22,400).

Sales Method: Byproducts Recognized at Time of Sale

This method makes no journal entries for byproducts until they are sold. Revenues of the byproduct are reported as a revenue item in the income statement at the time of sale. These revenues are either grouped with other sales, included as other income, or are deducted from cost of goods sold. In the Westlake Corporation example, byproduct revenues in July 2009 are Rs 12,000 (1,200 cubic feet × Rs 10 per cubic foot) because only 1,200 cubic feet of wood chips are sold in July (of the 4,000 cubic feet produced). The journal entries are:

		Debit	Credit
1. and 2.	*Same as for the production method.*		
	Work in Process	15,00,000	
	Accounts Payable		15,00,000
	Work in Process	10,00,000	
	Various accounts such as Wages Payable and Accumulated Depreciation		10,00,000
3.	Finished Goods—Fine-grade Lumber	25,00,000	
	Work in Process		25,00,000
	To record cost of main product completed during July.		
4a.	Cost of Goods Sold [(40,000 b.f. ÷ 50,000 b.f.) × 25,00,000]	20,00,000	
	Finished Goods—Fine-grade Lumber		20,00,000
	To record the cost of the main product sold during July.		
4b.	Same as for the production method.		
	Cash or Accounts Receivable (40,000 b.f. × Rs 60 per b.f.)	24,00,000	
	Revenues—Fine-grade Lumber		24,00,000
5.	Cash or Accounts Receivable	12,000	
	Revenues—Wood Chips		12,000
	To record the sales of the byproduct during July.		

Which method should a company use? The production method is conceptually correct in that it is consistent with the matching principle. This method recognizes byproduct inventory in the accounting period in which it is produced and simultaneously reduces the cost of manufacturing the main or joint products, thereby better matching the revenues and expenses from selling the main product. However, the sales method is simpler and is often used in practice, primarily on the grounds that the rupee amounts of byproducts are immaterial. Then again, the sales method permits managers to "manage" reported earnings by timing when they sell

[9] One way to make this calculation is to assume all products have the same "normal" profit margin like the constant gross-margin percentage NRV method. Alternatively, the company might allow products to have different profit margins based on an analysis of the margins earned by other companies that sell these products individually.

Concepts in Action

Byproduct Costing Keeps Wendy's Chili Profitable . . . and on the Menu

There are many examples in which joint and byproduct costing issues arise, including coal mining, semiconductor manufacturing, and Wendy's chili. You may be asking yourself, "chili from Wendy's?" Yes! The primary ingredient in chili at Wendy's, one of the largest fast-food chains in the United States, is a byproduct of overcooked, unsellable hamburger patties.

The most important product that Wendy's offers its customers is an "old-fashioned" hamburger, which is a hamburger served from the grill in accordance with individual customer orders. Operationally, the only way to serve hamburgers this way is to anticipate customer demand and have a sufficient supply of hamburgers already cooking when the customers arrive at the restaurant. The problem with this approach, however, is the fate of the extra hamburgers that become too well done whenever the cooks overestimate customer demand. Throwing them away would be too costly and wasteful, but serving them as "old-fashioned" hamburgers would likely result in considerable customer dissatisfaction.

For Wendy's, the solution to this dilemma involved finding a product that was unique to the fast-food industry and required ground beef as one of the major ingredients. Thus, Wendy's "rich and meaty" chili became one of its original menu items. For each batch of chili, which is prepared daily in each restaurant, Wendy's needs 48 quarter-pound cooked ground-beef patties along with crushed tomatoes, tomato juice, red beans, and seasoning. Only 10% of the time is it necessary for Wendy's to cook meat specifically for use in making chili.

Several years ago, Wendy's management considered eliminating some of its traditional menu items. Chili, composing only about 5% of total restaurant sales, was targeted for possible elimination, and at $0.99 for an eight-ounce serving, it brought in far less revenue than a product like a single hamburger, which sold for $1.89. When Wendy's compared the cost of making chili to its sale price, however, the product remained on the menu. How? The beef in Wendy's chili recipe was a byproduct of hamburger patties, its main product, which affected the allocation of joint costs.

Excluding ground beef, the costs to produce Wendy's chili are around $0.37 per eight-ounce serving, which includes labor. When Wendy's has to cook meat for its chili, again only 10% of the time, the recipe calls for ground beef that costs around $0.73 per serving. Under those circumstances, the chili costs Wendy's $1.10 to make, and each $0.99 serving sells at a $0.11 loss. However, the 90% of the time Wendy's uses precooked ground beef for its chili, most of those costs have already been allocated to hamburgers, the primary product. As a result, each eight-ounce serving of chili Wendy's sells using precooked ground beef is sold at a significant profit. With a lucrative profit margin for each serving sold, customers are likely to find chili on the Wendy's menu for a long time to come.

Source: Brownlee, E. Richard. 2005. Wendy's chili: A costing conundrum. The University of Virginia Darden School of Business Case No. UVA-C-2206. Charlottesville, VA: Darden Business Publishing.

byproducts. Managers may store byproducts for several periods and give revenues and income a "small boost" by selling byproducts accumulated over several periods when revenues and profits from the main product or joint products are low.

Problem for Self-Study

Inorganic Chemicals (IC) processes salt into various industrial products. In July 2012, IC incurred joint costs of Rs 10,00,000 to purchase salt and convert it into two products: caustic soda and chlorine. Although there is an active outside market for chlorine, IC processes all 800 tons of chlorine it produces into 500 tons of PVC (polyvinyl chloride), which is then sold. There were no beginning or ending inventories of salt, caustic soda, chlorine, or PVC in July. Information for July 2012 production and sales follows:

	A	B	C	D
1		Joint Costs		PVC
2	Joint costs (costs of salt and processing to splitoff point)	Rs 10,00,000		
3	Separable cost of processing 800 tons chlorine into 500 tons PVC			Rs 2,00,000
4				
5		Caustic Soda	Chlorine	PVC
6	Beginning inventory (tons)	0	0	0
7	Production (tons)	1,200	800	500
8	Transfer for further processing (tons)		800	
9	Sales (tons)	1,200		500
10	Ending inventory (tons)	0	0	0
11	Selling price per ton in active outside market (for products not actually sold)		Rs 750	
12	Selling price per ton for products sold	Rs 500		Rs 2,000

Required

1. Allocate the joint costs of Rs 10,00,000 between caustic soda and PVC under (a) the sales value at splitoff method and (b) the physical-measure method.
2. Allocate the joint costs of Rs 10,00,000 between caustic soda and PVC under the NRV method.
3. Under the three allocation methods in requirements 1 and 2, what is the gross-margin percentage of (a) caustic soda and (b) PVC?
4. Lifetime Swimming Pool Products offers to purchase 800 tons of chlorine in August 2009 at Rs 750 per ton. Assume all other production and sales data are the same for August as they were for July. This sale of chlorine to Lifetime would mean that no PVC would be produced by IC in August. How would accepting this offer affect IC's August 2009 operating income?

Solution

The following picture provides a visual illustration of the main facts in this problem.

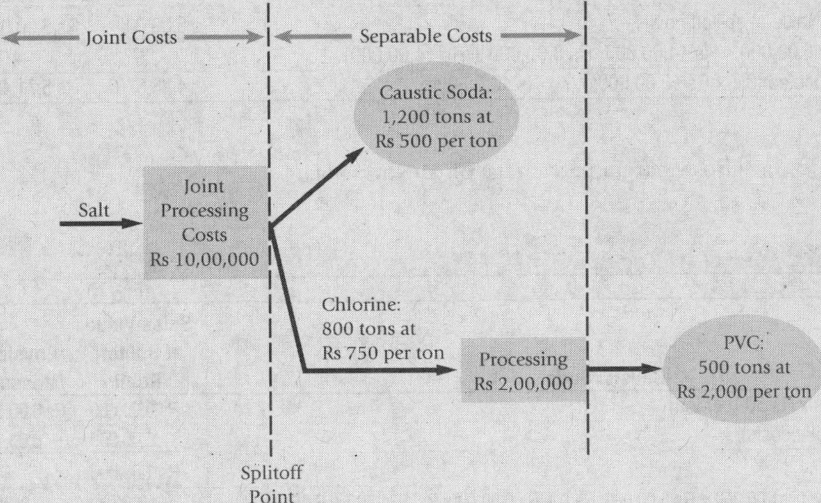

Note that caustic soda is sold as is while chlorine, despite having a market value at splitoff, is sold only in processed form as PVC. The goal is to allocate the joint costs of Rs 10,00,000 to the final products—caustic soda and PVC. However, since PVC exists only in the form of chlorine at the splitoff point, we use chlorine's sales value and physical measure as the basis for allocating joint costs to PVC under the sales value at splitoff and physical measure at splitoff methods. Detailed calculations are shown below.

1a. Sales value at splitoff method

	A	B	C	D
1	**Allocation of Joint costs using Sales Value at Splitoff Method**	**Caustic Soda**	**PVC / Chlorine**	**Total**
2	Sales value of total production at splitoff point			
3	(1,200 tons x Rs 500 per ton; 800 x Rs 750 per ton)	Rs 6,00,000	Rs 6,00,000	Rs 12,00,000
4	Weighting (Rs 6,00,000 ÷ Rs 12,00,000; Rs 6,00,000 ÷ Rs 12,00,000)	0.50	0.50	
5	Joint costs allocated (0.50 x Rs 10,00,000; 0.50 x Rs 10,00,000)	Rs 5,00,000	Rs 5,00,000	Rs 10,00,000

1b. Physical-measure method

	A	B	C	D
8	**Allocation of Joint Costs using Physical-Measure Method**	**Caustic Soda**	**PVC / Chlorine**	**Total**
9	Physical measure of total production (tons)	1,200	800	2,000
10	Weighting (1,200 tons ÷ 2,000 tons; 800 tons ÷ 2,000 tons)	0.60	0.40	
11	Joint cost allocated (0.60 x Rs 10,00,000; 0.40 x Rs 10,00,000)	Rs 6,00,000	Rs 4,00,000	Rs10,00,000

2. Net realizable value (NRV) method

	A	B	C	D
14	**Allocation of Joint Costs using Net Realizable Value Method**	**Caustic Soda**	**PVC**	**Total**
15	Final sales value of total production during accounting period			
16	(1,200 tons x Rs 500 per ton; 500 tons x Rs 2,000 per ton)	Rs 6,00,000	Rs 10,00,000	Rs 16,00,000
17	Deduct separable costs to complete and sell	0	2,00,000	2,00,000
18	Net realizable value at splitoff point	Rs 6,00,000	Rs 8,00,000	Rs 14,00,000
19	Weighting (Rs 6,00,000 ÷ Rs 14,00,000; Rs 8,00,000 ÷ Rs 14,00,000)	3/7	4/7	
20	Joint costs allocated (3/7 x Rs 10,00,000; 4/7 x Rs 10,00,000)	Rs 4,28,570	Rs 5,71,430	Rs 10,00,000

3a. Gross-margin percentage of caustic soda

	A	B	C	D
23	**Caustic Soda**	**Sales Value at Splitoff Point**	**Physical Measure**	**NRV**
24	Revenues (1,200 tons x Rs 500 per ton)	Rs 6,00,000	Rs 6,00,000	Rs 6,00,000
25	Cost of goods sold (joint costs)	5,00,000	6,00,000	4,28,570
26	Gross margin	Rs 1,00,000	Rs 0	Rs 1,71,430
27	Gross margin percentage (Rs1,00,000 ÷ Rs 6,00,000; Rs 0 ÷ Rs 6,00,000; Rs 1,71,430 ÷ Rs 6,00,000)	16.67%	0.00%	28.57%

3b. Gross-margin percentage of PVC

	A	B	C	D
30	PVC	Sales Value at Splitoff Point	Physical Measure	NRV
31	Revenues (500 tons x Rs 2,000 per ton)	Rs 10,00,000	Rs 10,00,000	Rs 10,00,000
32	Cost of goods sold			
33	Joint costs	5,00,000	4,00,000	5,71,430
34	Separable costs	2,00,000	2,00,000	2,00,000
35	Cost of goods sold	7,00,000	6,00,000	7,71,430
36	Gross margin	Rs 3,00,000	Rs 4,00,000	Rs 2,28,570
37	Gross margin percentage (Rs 3,00,000 ÷ Rs 10,00,000; Rs 4,00,000 ÷ Rs 10,00,000; Rs 2,28,570 ÷ Rs 10,00,000)	30.00%	40.00%	22.86%

4.

A	B
Incremental revenue from processing 800 tons of chlorine into 500 tons of PVC (500 tons x Rs 2,000 per ton) – (800 tons x Rs 750 per ton)	Rs 4,00,000
Incremental cost of processing 800 tons of chlorine into 500 tons of PVC	2,00,000
ncremental operating income from further processing	Rs 2,00,000

If IC sells 800 tons of chlorine to Lifetime Swimming Pool Products instead of further processing it into PVC, its August 2012 operating income will be reduced by Rs 2,00,000.

Decision Points

The following question-and-answer format summarizes the chapter's learning objectives. Each decision presents a key question related to a learning objective. The guidelines are the answer to that question.

Decision	Guidelines
1. What are a joint cost and a splitoff point?	A joint cost is the cost of a single production process that yields multiple products simultaneously. The splitoff point is the juncture in a joint production process when the products become separately identifiable.
2. How do joint products differ from byproducts?	Joint products have high total sales values at the splitoff point. A byproduct has a low total sales value at the splitoff point compared with the total sales value of a joint or main product. Products can change from byproducts to joint products when their total sales values significantly increase or change from joint products to byproducts when their total sales values significantly decrease.
3. Why are joint costs allocated to individual products?	The purposes for allocating joint costs to products include inventory costing for financial accounting and internal reporting, cost reimbursement, insurance settlements, rate regulation, and product-cost litigation.
4. What methods can be used to allocate joint costs to individual products?	The methods to allocate joint costs to products are the sales value at splitoff, NRV, constant gross-margin percentage NRV, and physical-measure methods.

5. When is the sales value at splitoff method used for allocating joint costs to individual products and why?	The sales value at splitoff method is used when market prices exist at splitoff because using revenues is consistent with the benefits-received criterion, it does not anticipate subsequent management decisions on further processing, and it is simple.
6. Are joint costs relevant in a sell-or-process-further decision?	No, joint costs and how they are allocated are irrelevant in deciding whether to process further because joint costs are the same regardless of whether further processing occurs.
7. What methods can be used to account for byproducts and which of them is preferable?	The production method recognizes byproducts in financial statements at the time of production, whereas the sales method recognizes byproducts in financial statements at the time of sale. The production method is conceptually superior, but the sales method is often used in practice because rupee amounts of byproducts are immaterial.

TERMS TO LEARN

This chapter and the Glossary at the end of the book contain definitions of:

byproducts **(p. 674)**
constant gross-margin percentage NRV method **(p. 679)**
joint costs **(p. 673)**
joint products **(p. 674)**
main product **(p. 674)**
net realizable value (NRV) method **(p. 679)**
physical-measure method **(p. 678)**
product **(p. 674)**
sales value at splitoff method **(p. 677)**
separable costs **(p. 673)**
splitoff point **(p. 673)**

ASSIGNMENT MATERIAL

Questions

16-1 Give two examples of industries in which joint costs are found. For each example, what are the individual products at the splitoff point?

16-2 What is a joint cost? What is a separable cost?

16-3 Distinguish between a joint product and a byproduct.

16-4 Why might the number of products in a joint-cost situation differ from the number of outputs? Give an example.

16-5 Provide three reasons for allocating joint costs to individual products or services.

16-6 Why does the sales value at splitoff method use the sales value of the total production in the accounting period and not just the revenues from the products sold?

16-7 Describe a situation in which the sales value at splitoff method cannot be used but the NRV method can be used for joint-cost allocation.

16-8 Distinguish between the sales value at splitoff method and the NRV method.

16-9 Give two limitations of the physical-measure method of joint-cost allocation.

16-10 How might a company simplify its use of the NRV method when final selling prices can vary sizably in an accounting period and management frequently changes the point at which it sells individual products?

16-11 Why is the constant gross-margin percentage NRV method sometimes called a "joint-cost-allocation and a profit-allocation" method?

16-12 "Managers must decide whether a product should be sold at splitoff or processed further. The sales value at splitoff method of joint-cost allocation is the best method for generating the information managers need for this decision." Do you agree? Explain.

16-13 "Managers should consider only additional revenues and separable costs when making decisions about selling at splitoff or processing further." Do you agree? Explain.

16-14 Describe two major methods to account for byproducts.

16-15 Why might managers seeking a monthly bonus based on attaining a target operating income prefer the sales method of accounting for byproducts rather than the production method?

Solved Examples

16-16 Net realizable value method. Hindustan Oil produces two joint products, cooking oil and soap oil, from a single vegetable-oil refining process. In July, the joint costs of this process were Rs 2,40,00,000. Separable processing costs beyond the splitoff point were cooking oil, Rs 3,00,00,000, and soap oil, Rs 75,00,000. Cooking oil sells for Rs 50 per litre. Soap oil sells for Rs 25 per litre. Hindustan Oil produced and sold 10,00,000 litres of cooking oil and 5,00,000 litres of soap oil. There are no beginning or ending inventories of cooking oil or soap oil.

Required

Allocate the Rs 2,40,00,000 joint costs using the NRV method.

Solution

Net realizable value method.

A diagram of the situation is in Solution Exhibit 16-16 (all numbers are in thousands).

	Cooking Oil (CO)	Soap Oil (SO)	Total
Final sales value of total production, CO, 1,000 × Rs 50; SO, 500 × Rs 25	Rs 50,000	Rs 12,500	Rs 62,500
Deduct separable costs to complete and sell	30,000	7,500	37,500
Net realizable value at splitoff point	Rs 20,000	Rs 5,000	Rs 25,000
Weighting	$\frac{\text{Rs } 20{,}000}{\text{Rs } 25{,}000} = 0.8$	$\frac{\text{Rs } 5{,}000}{\text{Rs } 25{,}000} = 0.2$	
Joint costs allocated, CO, 0.8 × Rs 24,000; SO, 0.2 × Rs 24,000	Rs 19,200	Rs 4,800	Rs 24,000

Solution Exhibit 16-16 (all numbers are in thousands)

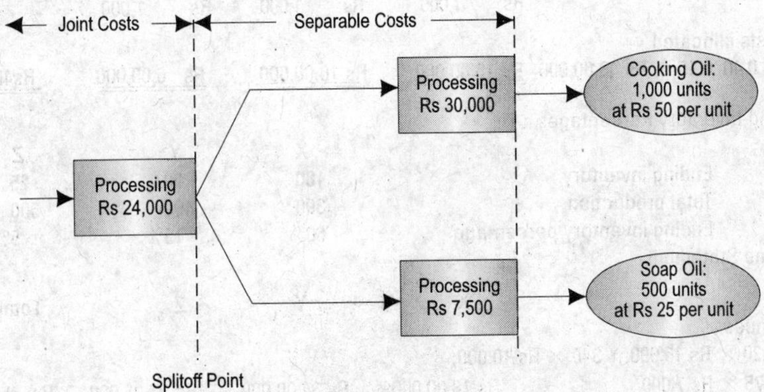

16-17 Alternative methods of joint-cost allocation, ending inventories. The Indraprastha Chemicals operates a simple chemical process to convert a single material into three separate items, referred to here as X, Y, and Z. All three end products are separated simultaneously at a single splitoff point.

Products X and Y are ready for sale immediately upon splitoff without further processing or any other additional costs. Product Z, however, is processed further before being sold. There is no available market price for Z at the splitoff point.

The selling prices quoted here are expected to remain the same in the coming year. During 2005, the selling prices of the items and the total amounts sold were:

- X—120 tons sold for Rs 15,000 per ton
- Y—340 tons sold for Rs 10,000 per ton
- Z—475 tons sold for Rs 7,000 per ton

The total joint manufacturing costs for the year were Rs 40,00,000. An additional Rs 20,00,000 was spent to finish product Z.

There were no beginning inventories of X, Y, or Z. At the end of the year, the following inventories of completed units were on hand: X, 180 tons; Y, 60 tons; Z, 25 tons. There was no beginning or ending work in process.

Required

1. Compute the cost of inventories of X, Y, and Z for balance sheet purposes and the cost of goods sold for income statement purposes as of December 31, 2011, using
   a. NRV method of joint-cost allocation
   b. Constant gross-margin percentage NRV method of joint-cost allocation
2. Compare the gross-margin percentages for X, Y, and Z using the two methods given in requirement 1.

Solution

Alternative methods of joint-cost allocation, ending inventories.

Total production for the year was:

	Sold	Ending Inventories	Total Production
X	120	180	300
Y	340	60	400
Z	475	25	500

A diagram of the situation is in Solution Exhibit 16-17.

1. a. Net realizable value (NRV) method:

	X	Y	Z	Total
Final sales value of total production X 300 × Rs 15,000; Y 400 × Rs 10,000; Z 500 × Rs 7,000	Rs 45,00,000	Rs 40,00,000	Rs 35,00,000	Rs 1,20,00,000
Deduct separable costs	–	–	20,00,000	20,00,000
Net realizable value at splitoff point	Rs 45,00,000	Rs 40,00,000	Rs 15,00,000	Rs 1,00,00,000
Weighting	Rs 450 / Rs 1,000 = 0.45	Rs 400 / Rs 1,000 = 0.40	Rs 150 / Rs 1,000 = 0.15	
Joint costs allocated 0.45; 0.40; 0.15 × Rs 40,00,000	Rs 18,00,000	Rs 16,00,000	Rs 6,00,000	Rs40,00,000

Ending Inventory Percentages

	X	Y	Z
Ending inventory	180	60	25
Total production	300	400	500
Ending inventory percentage	60%	15%	5%

Income Statement

	X	Y	Z	Total
Revenues X 120 × Rs 15,000; Y 340 × Rs 10,000; Z 475 × Rs 7,000	Rs 18,00,000	Rs 34,00,000	Rs 33,25,000	Rs 85,25,000
Cost of goods sold				
Joint costs allocated	18,00,000	16,00,000	6,00,000	40,00,000
Separable costs	–		20,00,000	20,00,000
Cost of goods available for sale	18,00,000	16,00,000	26,00,000	60,00,000
Deduct ending inventory X 60%; Y 15%; Z 5%	10,80,000	2,40,000	1,30,000	14,50,000
Cost of goods sold	7,20,000	13,60,000	24,70,000	45,50,000
Gross margin	Rs 10,80,000	Rs 20,40,000	Rs 8,55,000	Rs 39,75,000
Gross-margin percentage	60%	60%	25.71%	

b. Constant gross-margin percentage NRV method:

Step 1:

Final sales value of prodn. (300 × Rs 15,000) + (400 × Rs 10,000) + (500 × Rs 7,000)	Rs 1,20,00,000
Deduct joint and separable costs Rs 40,00,000 + Rs 20,00,000	60,00,000
Gross margin	Rs 60,00,000
Gross-margin percentage Rs 60,00,000 ÷ Rs 1,20,00,000	50%

	X	Y	Z	Total
Final sales value of total production X 300 × Rs 15,000; Y 400 × Rs 10,000; Z 500 × Rs 7,000	Rs 45,00,000	Rs 40,00,000	Rs 35,00,000	Rs 1,20,00,000
Step 2: Deduct gross margin using overall gross-margin percentage of sales 50%	22,50,000	20,00,000	17,50,000	60,00,000
Step 3: Deduct separable costs	–	–	20,00,000	20,00,000
Joint costs allocated	Rs 22,50,000	Rs 20,00,000	Rs (2,50,000)	Rs 40,00,000

The negative joint-cost allocation to Product Z illustrates one "unusual" feature of the constant gross-margin percentage NRV method. Some products may receive negative cost allocations in order that all individual products have the same gross-margin percentage.

Income Statement

	X	Y	Z	Total
Revenues X 120 × Rs 15,000; Y 340 × Rs 10,000; Z 475 × Rs 7,000	Rs 18,00,000	Rs 34,00,000	Rs 33,25,000	Rs 85,25,000
Cost of goods sold:				
Joint costs allocated	22,50,000	20,00,000	(2,50,000)	40,00,000
Separable costs	–	–	20,00,000	20,00,000
Cost of goods available for sale	22,50,000	20,00,000	17,50,000	60,00,000
Deduct ending inventory X 60%; Y 15%; Z 5%	13,50,000	3,00,000	87,500	17,37,500
Cost of goods sold	9,00,000	17,00,000	16,62,500	42,62,500
Gross margin	Rs 9,00,000	Rs 17,00,000	Rs 16,62,500	Rs 42,62,500
Gross-margin percentage	50%	50%	50%	50%

Summary

	X	Y	Z	Total
a. Estimated NRV method:				
Inventories on balance sheet	Rs 10,80,000	Rs 2,40,000	Rs 1,30,000	Rs 14,50,000
Cost of goods sold on income statement	7,20,000	13,60,000	24,70,000	45,50,000
				Rs 60,00,000
b. Constant gross-margin percentage NRV method				
Inventories on balance sheet	Rs 13,50,000	Rs 3,00,000	Rs 87,500	Rs 17,37,500
Cost of goods sold on income statement	9,00,000	17,00,000	16,62,500	42,62,500
				Rs 60,00,000

2. Gross-margin percentages:

	X	Y	Z
Estimated NRV method	60%	60%	25.71%
Constant gross-margin percentage NRV	50%	50%	50.00%

Solution Exhibit 16-17

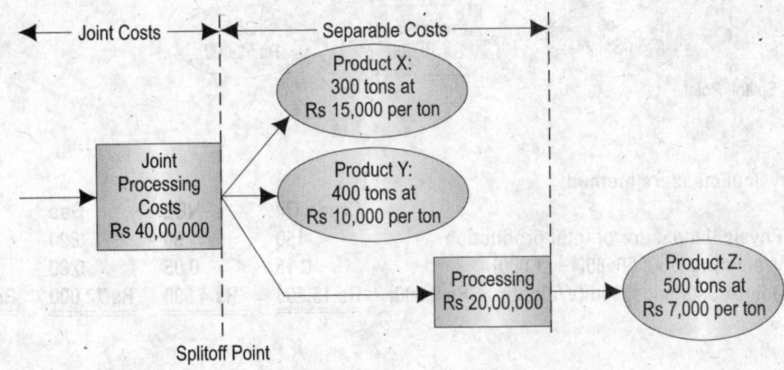

16-18 Joint-cost allocation, process further. Mangalore Refining Petroleum Ltd. (MRPL) is a 100%-owned subsidiary of Oil Natural Gas Corp. (ONGC). MRPL operates a refinery that processes hydrocarbons. MRPL's refinery has three outputs from its processing of hydrocarbons: crude oil, natural gas liquids, and gas. The first two outputs are liquids, whereas gas is a vapor. However, gas can be converted into a liquid equivalent using a standard industry conversion factor. For costing purposes, MRPL assumes all three outputs are jointly produced until a single splitoff point, at which each output appears separately and is then further processed individually.

For April 2011, the following data apply (the numbers are small to keep the focus on key concepts):

- Crude oil—150 barrels produced and sold at Rs 900 per barrel. Separable costs beyond the splitoff point are Rs 8,750.
- Natural gas liquids—50 barrels produced and sold at Rs 7,500 per barrel. Separable costs beyond the splitoff point are Rs 5,250.
- Gas—800 equivalent barrels produced and sold at Rs 65 per equivalent barrel. Separable costs beyond the splitoff point are Rs 10,500.

MRPL paid ONGC Rs 70,000 for hydrocarbons delivered to it from its offshore platform in April 2011. The cost of operating the refinery in August up to the splitoff point was Rs 20,000, including Rs 5,000 of gas charges from Mangalore Utilities, an independent utility company. Mangalore Utilities signed a long-term contract with MRPL several years ago when gas prices were much lower than now.
A new income-tax law has recently been passed that taxes crude oil at 30% of operating income. No new tax is to be paid on natural gas liquid or natural gas. Starting April 2011, MRPL must report a separate product-line income statement for crude oil. One challenge facing MRPL is how to allocate the joint-cost of producing the three separate salable outputs. Assume no beginning or ending inventory.

Required

1. Draw a diagram showing the joint-cost situation for MRPL.
2. Allocate the April 2011 joint cost among the three salable products using
   a. Physical-measures method
   b. NRV method
3. Show the operating income for each product using the methods in requirement 2.
4. Discuss the pros and cons of the two methods to MRPL for product emphasis decisions.
5. Draft a letter to the taxation authorities on behalf of MRPL that justifies the joint-cost allocation method you recommend MRPL use.

Solution

Joint-cost allocation, process further.

1.

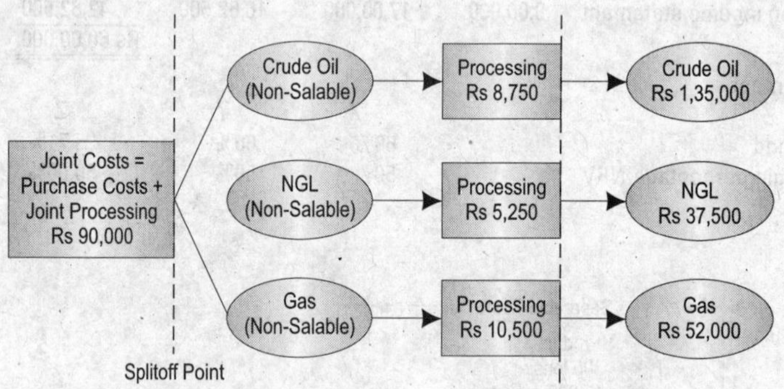

2. a. Physical measure method:

	Crude Oil	NGL	Gas	Total
1. Physical measure of total production	150	50	800	1,000
2. Weighting (150; 50; 800 ÷ 1,000)	0.15	0.05	0.80	1.00
3. Joint-costs allocated (Weights × Rs 9,000)	Rs 13,500	Rs 4,500	Rs 72,000	Rs 90,000

2 b. Estimated NRV method:

	Crude Oil	NGL	Gas	Total
1. Final sales value of total production	Rs 1,35,000	Rs 37,500	Rs 52,000	Rs 2,24,500
2. Deduct separable costs	8,570	5,250	10,500	24,500
3. NRV at splitoff	Rs 1,26,250	Rs 32,250	Rs 41,500	Rs 2,00,000
4. Weighting (in proportion of NRV)	0.63125	0.16125	0.20750	
5. Joint-costs allocated (Weights × Rs 90,000)	Rs 56,812.50	Rs 14,512.50	Rs 18,675	Rs 90,000

3. The operating-income amounts for each product using each method is:

a. Physical measures method:

	Crude Oil	NGL	Gas	Total
Revenues	Rs 1,35,000	Rs 37,500	Rs 52,000	Rs 2,24,500
Costs of goods sold				
Joint costs	13,500	4,500	72,000	90,000
Separable costs	8,750	5,250	10,500	24,500
Total cost of goods sold	22,250	9,750	82,500	1,14,500
Gross margin	1,12,750	27,750	(30,500)	1,10,000

b. NRV method:

	Crude Oil	NGL	Gas	Total
Revenues	Rs 1,35,000	Rs 37,500	Rs 52,000	Rs 2,24,500
Cost of goods sold				
Joint costs	56,812.50	14,512	18,675	90,000
Separable costs	8,750	5,250	10,500	24,500
Total cost of goods sold	65,562.50	19,762.50	29,175	1,14,500
Gross margin	69,437.50	17,737.50	22,825	1,10,000

4. Neither method should be used for product emphasis decisions. It is inappropriate to use joint-cost-allocated data to decide dropping individual products, or pushing individual products, as they are joint by definition. Product-emphasis decisions should be made based on relevant revenues and relevant costs. Each method can lead to product emphasis decisions that do not lead to maximization of operating income.
5. A letter to the taxation authorities would stress the conceptual superiority of the NRV method. Chapter 15 argues that, using a benefits-received cost allocation criterion, market-based joint-cost allocation methods are preferable to physical-measure methods. A meaningful common denominator (revenues) is available when the sales value at splitoff point method or NRV method is used. The physical-measures method requires nonhomogeneous products (liquids and gases) to be converted to a common denominator.

16-19 Joint-cost allocation, physical-measures method (continuation of 16-18). Assume that MRPL is not able to sell its gas output. The refinery is located in a remote area, and a terrorist group has just destroyed major sections of the gas pipeline used to transport the gas to market. The pipeline that carries the crude oil and natural gas liquid is still operational. ONGC must now reinject the gas into the offshore field. The costs of the hydrocarbons to MRPL will not be reduced, but ONGC (not MRPL) will bear the cost of gas reinjection. No separable costs of gas production beyond the splitoff point will now be incurred.

Required

1. Assume the same data for all three outputs for April 2011 apply to the new set of facts. Show the operating income for each salable product using the NRV method of joint-cost allocation.
2. Assume the taxation authorities argue that for crude oil income tax determination the physical-measures method should be used to allocate joint costs and that all outputs (including gas, whether sold or reinjected) should be used in deciding the cost-allocation weights. Draft a letter to the taxation authorities on behalf of ONGC. Be specific when possible.

Solution

Joint-cost allocation, physical-measures method (continuation of 16-18).

1.

	Crude Oil	NGL	Total
1. Final sales value of total production	Rs 1,35,000	Rs 37,500	Rs 1,72,500
2. Deduct separable costs	8,750	5,250	14,000
3. NRV at splitoff	1,26,250	32,250	1,58,500

	Crude Oil	NGL	Total
4. Weighting (in proportion of NPV)	0.7965	0.2035	
5. Joint costs allocated (Weights × Rs 90,000)	71,685	18,315	90,000

	Crude Oil	NGL	Total
Revenues	Rs 1,35,000	Rs 37,500	Rs 1,72,500
Cost of good sold			
Joint costs	71,685	18,315	90,000
Separable costs	8,750	5,250	14,000
Total cost of goods sold	80,435	23,565	1,04,000
Gross margin	54,565	13,935	68,500

2. The State's proposed method results in large profits on crude oil and large losses on gas:

	Crude Oil	NGL	Gas	Total
Revenues	Rs 1,35,000	Rs 37,500	Rs 0	Rs 1,72,500
Cost of goods sold				
Joint costs	13,500	4,500	72,000	90,000
Separable costs	8,750	5,250	0	14,000
Total cost of goods sold	22,250	9,750	72,000	1,04,000
Gross margin	1,12,750	27,750	(72,000)	68,500

The main points to note are:

a. Gas is not a salable product. It is simply a recycled output that adds no revenues. Indeed, costs are incurred to recycle the gas.

b. The physical measure method has all the problems alluded to in the literature—e.g., it ignores the revenue earning potential of products, and it may not have a consistent denominator.

16-20 Accounting for a main product and a byproduct. (Cheatham and Green, adapted) Ahmed is the owner and operator of Parle Bottling, a soft-drink producer. A single production process yields two soft drinks: Rainbow Dew (the main product) and Resi-Dew (the byproduct). Both products are fully processed at the splitoff point, and there are no separable costs.

For September, the cost of the soft-drink operations is Rs 120,000. Production and sales data are as follows:

	Production (in litres)	Sales (in litres)	Selling Price per litre
Main product: Rainbow Dew	10,000	8,000	Rs 20
Byproduct: Resi-Dew	2,000	1,400	2

There were no beginning inventories on September 1.

Required

1. What is the gross margin for Parle Bottling under methods A and B of byproduct accounting described in this chapter?
2. What are the inventory costs reported in the balance sheet on September 30, for Rainbow Dew and Resi-Dew under the two methods of byproduct accounting in requirement 1?

Solution

Accounting for a main product and a byproduct.

	Method A, Recognized at Production	Method B, Recognized at Sale
1. Revenues:		
Main product	Rs 1,60,000[a]	Rs 1,60,000
Byproduct	–	2,800[d]
Total revenues	1,60,000	1,62,800
Cost of goods sold		
Total manufacturing costs	120,000	120,000
Deduct byproduct revenue	4,000[b]	0
Net manufacturing costs	16,000	120,000
Deduct main product inventory	23,200[c]	24,000[e]
Cost of goods sold	92,800	96,000
Gross margin	Rs 67,200	Rs 66,800

[a]8,000 × Rs 20.00

[b]2,000 × Rs 2.00

c $\left(\frac{2,000}{10,0000} \times \text{Rs } 116,000\right)$ = Rs 23,200

[d]1,400 × Rs 2.00

e $\left(\frac{2,000}{10,000} \times \text{Rs } 120,000\right)$ = Rs 24,000

	Method A, Recognized at Production	Method B, Recognized at Sale
2. Rainbow Dew:	Rs 23,200	Rs 24,000
Resi-Dew	1,200[a]	0

[a]Ending inventory shown at unrealized selling price.
BI + Production – Sales = EI
0 + 2,000 – 1,400 = 600 litres
Ending inventory = 600 litres × Rs 2 per litre = Rs 1,200

16-21 Joint costs and byproducts. Sterlite Industries processes an ore in Department 1, from which comes three products, L, W, and X. Product L is processed further in Department 2. Product W is sold without further processing. Product X is considered a byproduct and is processed further in Department 3. Costs in Department 1 are Rs 800,000, Department 2 costs are Rs 100,000, and Department 3 costs are Rs 50,000. Processing 600,000 kg in Department 1 results in 50,000 kg of product L, 300,000 kg of product W, and 100,000 kg of product X.

Product L sells for Rs 10 per kg. Product W sells for Rs 2 per kg. Product X sells for Rs 3 per kg. The company wants to make a gross margin of 10% of revenues on product X and needs to allow 25% of revenues for marketing costs on product X.

Required

1. Compute unit costs per kg for products L, W, and X, treating X as a byproduct. Use the NRV method for allocating joint costs. Deduct the NRV of the byproduct produced from the joint cost of products L and W.
2. Compute unit costs per kg for products L, W, and X, treating all three as joint products and allocating costs by the NRV method.

Solution
Joint costs and byproducts.

A diagram of the situation is in Solution Exhibit 16-21.

1. Computing byproduct deduction to joint costs:

Revenues from X, 1,00,000 × Rs 3	Rs 3,00,000
Deduct: Gross margin, 10% of revenues	30,000
Marketing costs, 25% of revenues	75,000
Department 3 separable costs	50,000
Net realizable value (less gross margin) of X	Rs 1,45,000
Joint costs	Rs 8,00,000
Deduct byproduct contribution	1,45,000
Net joint costs to be allocated	Rs 6,55,000

	Quantity	Unit Sales Price	Final Sales Value	Deduct Separable Processing Cost	Net Realizable Value at Splitoff	Weighting	Allocation of Rs 6,55,000 Joint Costs
L	50,000	Rs 10	Rs 5,00,000	Rs 1,00,000	Rs 4,00,000	40%	Rs 2,62,000
W	300,000	2	6,00,000	–	6,00,000	60%	3,93,000
Totals			Rs 11,00,000	Rs 1,00,000	Rs 10,00,000		Rs 6,55,000

	Joint Costs Allocation	Add Separable Processing Costs	Total Costs	Units	Unit Cost
L	Rs 2,62,000	Rs 1,00,000	Rs 3,62,000	50,000	Rs 7.24
W	3,93,000	–	3,93,000	3,00,000	1.31
Totals	Rs 6,55,000	Rs 1,00,000	Rs 7,55,000	3,50,000	

Unit cost for X: Rs 1.45 (Rs 1,45,000¸ 1,00,000) + Rs 0.50 (Rs 50,000 ÷ 1,00,000) = Rs 1.95, or Rs 3.00 – Rs 0.30 (10% × Rs 3) – Rs 0.75 (25% × Rs 3) = Rs 1.95.

2. If all three products are treated as joint products:

	Quantity	Unit Sales Price	Deduct Final Sales Value	Net Separable Processing Cost	Realizable Value at Splitoff	Weighting	Allocation of Rs 8,00,000 Join Costs
L	50,000	Rs 10	Rs 5,00,000	Rs 1,00,000	Rs 4,00,000	400/1,175	Rs 2,72,340
W	3,00,000	2	6,00,000	–	6,00,000	600/1,175	4,08,511
X	1,00,000	3	3,00,000	1,25,000	1,75,000	175/1,175	1,19,149
Total			Rs 14,00,000	Rs 2,25,000	Rs 11,75,000		Rs 8,00,000

	Joint Costs Allocation	Add Separable Processing Costs	Total Costs	Units	Unit Cost
L	Rs 2,72,340	Rs 1,00,000	Rs 3,72,340	50,000	Rs 7.45
W	4,08,511	–	4,08,511	3,00,000	1.36
X	1,19,149	50,000	1,69,149	1,00,000	1.69
Total	Rs 8,00,000	Rs 1,50,000	Rs 9,50,000	4,50,000	

It is important to note that there are different unit "costs" resulting from the two assumptions about the relative importance of Product X. The point is that costs of individual products depend heavily on which assumptions are made and which accounting methods and techniques are used.

Solution Exhibit 16-21

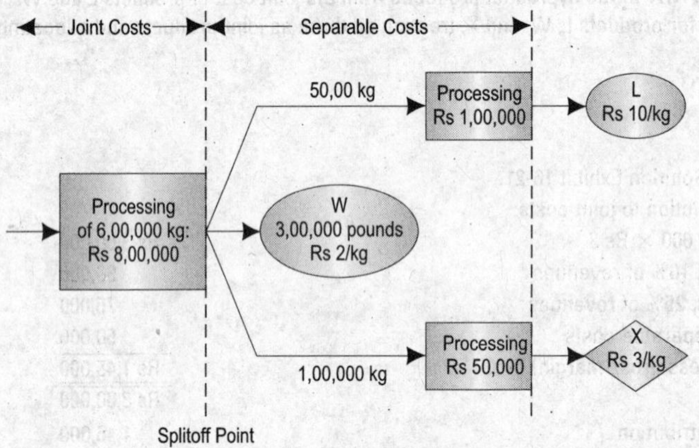

16-22 Comparison of alternative joint-cost-allocation methods, further-processing decision, chocolate products. Nestle manufactures chocolates and distributes chocolate products. It purchases cocoa beans and processes them into two intermediate products:

- Chocolate-powder liquor base
- Milk-chocolate liquor base

These two intermediate products become separately identifiable at a single splitoff point. Every 500 kg of cocoa beans yields 50 litres of chocolate-powder liquor base and 75 litres of milk-chocolate liquor base.

The chocolate-powder liquor base is further processed into chocolate powder. Every 50 litres of chocolate-powder liquor base yield 200 kg of chocolate powder. The milk-chocolate liquor base is further processed into milk chocolate. Every 75 litres of milk-chocolate liquor base yield 340 kg of milk chocolate. An overview of the manufacturing operations at Nestle Chocolates follows:

Production and sales data for August are:

- Cocoa beans processed, 5,000 kg
- Costs of processing cocoa beans to splitoff point (including purchase of beans) = Rs 5,00,000

	Production	Sales	Selling Price
Chocolate powder	2,000 kg	2,000 kg	Rs 200 per kg
Milk chocolate	3,400 kg	3,400 kg	Rs 250 per kg

The August separable costs of processing chocolate-powder liquor base into chocolate powder are Rs 2,12,500. The August separable costs of processing milk-chocolate liquor base into milk chocolate are Rs 4,37,500.

Nestle fully processes both of its intermediate products into chocolate powder or milk chocolate. There is an active market for these intermediate products. In August, Nestle could have sold the chocolate-powder liquor base for Rs 420 a litre and the milk-chocolate liquor base for Rs 520 a litre.

Required

1. Calculate how the joint costs of Rs 5,00,000 would be allocated between the chocolate-powder and milk-chocolate liquor bases under the following methods:
   a. Sales value at splitoff
   b. Physical measure (litres)
   c. NRV
   d. Constant gross-margin percentage NRV
2. What are the gross-margin percentages of the chocolate-powder and milk-chocolate liquor bases under each of the methods in requirement 1?

Solution

Comparison of alternative joint-cost allocation methods,further-process decision, chocolate products.

1 a. Sales value at splitoff method:

	Chocolate-Powder Liquor Base	Milk-Chocolate Liquor Base	Total
Sales value of prodn. at splitoff, 500[a] × Rs 420; 750[b] × Rs 520	Rs 2,10,000	Rs 3,90,000	Rs 6,00,000
Weighting (in proportion of sales value at splitoff)	Rs 2,10,000 / Rs 6,00,000 = 0.35	Rs 3,90,000 / Rs 6,00,000 = 0.65	
Joint costs allocated, 0.35 × Rs 5,00,000; 0.65 × Rs 5,00,000	Rs 1,75,000	Rs 3,25,000	Rs 5,00,000

[a](50/500) × 5,000 [b](75/500) × 5,000

1. b. Physical-measure method:

	500 litres	750 litres	1,250 litres
Weighting	500/1250 = 0.40	750/1250 = 0.60	
Joint costs allocated, 0.40 × Rs 5,00,000; 0.60 × Rs 5,00,000	Rs 2,00,000	Rs 3,00,000	Rs 5,00,000

1. c. Net realizable value (NRV) method:

	Chocolate-Powder Liquor Base	Milk-Chocolate Liquor Base	Total
Final sales value of total production, 2,000 × Rs 200; 3,400 × Rs 250	Rs 4,00,000	Rs 8,50,000	Rs 12,50,000
Deduct separable costs to complete and sell	2,12,500	4,37,500	6,50,000
Net realizable value at splitoff point	Rs 1,87,500	Rs 4,12,500	Rs 6,00,000
Weighting (in proportion of NRV at splitoff point)	Rs 1,87,500 / Rs 6,00,000 = 0.3125	Rs 4,12,500 / Rs 6,00,000 = 0.6875	
Joint costs allocated, 0.3125 × Rs 5,00,000; 0.6875 × Rs 5,00,000	Rs 1,56,250	Rs 3,43,750	Rs 5,00,000

d. Constant gross-margin percentage NRV method:

Step 1:

Final sales value of total production, (2,000 × Rs 200) + (3,400 × Rs 250)	Rs 12,50,000
Deduct joint and separable costs, (Rs 5,00,000 + Rs 2,12,500 + Rs 4,37,500)	11,50,000
Gross margin	Rs 1,00,000
Gross-margin percentage (Rs 1,00,000 ÷ Rs 12,50,000)	8%

Step 2:

	Chocolate-Powder Liquor Base	Milk-Chocolate Liquor Base	Total
Final sales value of total production 2000 × Rs 200); (3,400 × Rs 250)	Rs 4,00,000	Rs 8,50,000	Rs 12,50,000
Deduct gross margin, using overall gross-margin percentage of sales (8%)	32,000	68,000	1,00,000
Cost of goods available for sale	3,68,000	7,82,000	11,50,000
Step 3:			
Deduct separable costs to complete and sell	2,12,500	4,37,500	6,50,000
Joint costs allocated	Rs 1,55,500	Rs 3,44,500	Rs 5,00,000

2.

	Chocolate-Powder Liquor Base	Milk-Chocolate Liquor Base	Total
a. Revenues	Rs 4,00,000	Rs 8,50,000	Rs 12,50,000
Joint costs	1,75,000	3,25,000	5,00,000
Separable costs	2,12,500	4,37,500	6,50,000
Total costs	3,87,500	7,62,500	11,50,000
Gross margin	Rs 12,500	Rs 87,500	Rs 1,00,000
Gross-margin percentage	3.125%	10.294%	8%
b. Revenues	Rs 4,00,000	Rs 8,50,000	Rs 12,50,000
Joint costs	2,00,000	3,00,000	5,00,000
Separable costs	2,12,500	4,37,500	6,50,000
Total costs	4,12,500	7,37,500	11,50,000
Gross margin	(12,500)	1,12,500	1,00,000
Gross-margin percentage	(3.125%)	13.235%	8%
c. Revenues	Rs 4,00,000	Rs 8,50,000	Rs 12,50,000
Joint costs	1,56,250	3,43,750	5,00,000
Separable costs	2,12,500	4,37,500	6,50,000
Total costs	3,68,750	7,81,250	11,50,000
Gross margin	31,250	68,750	1,00,000
Gross-margin percentage	7.812%	8.088%	8%
d. Revenues	Rs 4,00,000	8,50,000	12,50,000
Joint costs	1,55,500	3,44,500	5,00,000
Separable costs	2,12,500	4,37,500	6,50,000
Total costs	3,68,000	7,82,000	11,50,000
Gross margin	32,000	68,000	1,00,000
Gross-margin percentage	8%	8%	8%

16-23 Joint-cost allocation, process further or sell. (CMA, adapted) Assam Sawmill, Limited (ASL), purchases logs from independent timber contractors and processes the logs into three types of lumber products:

- Studs for residential building (walls, ceilings)
- Decorative pieces (fireplace mantels, beams for cathedral ceilings)
- Posts used as support braces (mine support braces, braces for exterior fences around ranch properties)

These products are the result of a joint sawmill process that involves removal of bark from the logs, cutting the logs into a workable size (ranging from 8 to 16 feet in length), and then cutting the individual products from the logs, depending on the type of wood (pine, oak, walnut, or maple) and the size (diameter) of the log. The joint process results in the following costs and outputs of products for a typical quarter:

Direct materials (rough timber logs)	Rs 50,00,000
Debarking (labor and overhead)	5,00,000
Sizing (labor and overhead)	20,00,000
Product cutting (labor and overhead)	25,00,000
Total joint costs	Rs 1,00,00,000

Product yields and average sales values on a per unit basis from the joint process are as follows:

Product	Monthly Output of Materials at Splitoff Point	Fully Processed Selling Price
Studs	75,000 units	Rs 80
Decorative pieces	5,000 units	1,000
Posts	20,000 units	200

The studs are sold as rough-cut lumber after emerging from the sawmill operation without further processing by ASL. Also, the posts require no further processing beyond the splitoff point. The decorative pieces must be planed and further sized after emerging from the sawmill. This additional processing costs Rs 10,00,000 per month and normally results in a loss of 10% of the units entering the process. Without this laning and sizing process, there is still an active intermediate market for the unfinished decorative pieces in which the selling price averages Rs 600 per unit.

Required

1. Based on the information given for Assam Sawmill Limited, allocate the joint processing costs of Rs 1,00,00,000 to each of the three product lines using:
   a. Sales value at splitoff method
   b. Physical-measures method (volume in units)
   c. NRV method
2. Preapre an analysis for Assam Sawmill Limited, that compares processing the decorative pieces further, as they currently do, with selling them as a rough-cut product immediately at splitoff.
3. Assume Assam Sawmill Limited, announced that in six months it will sell the rough-cut product at spiltoff due to increasing competitive pressure. Identify at least three types of likely behavior that will be demonstrated by the skilled labor in the planning and sizing process as a result of this announcement. Include in your discussion how this behavior could be improved by management.

Solution

Joint-cost allocation, process further or sell (CMA, adapted).

1.

a. Sales value at splitoff method:

	Monthly Unit Output	Selling Price Per Unit	Sales Value at Splitoff	% of Sales	Joint Costs Allocated
Studs (Building)	75,000	Rs 80	Rs 60,00,000	46.1539%	Rs 46,15,390
Decorative Pieces	5,000	600	30,00,000	23.0769	23,07,690
Posts	20,000	200	40,00,000	30.7692	30,76,920
Total			1,30,00,000	100.0000%	1,00,00,000

b. Physical measure method at splitoff:

	Physical Unit Volume	% of Total Unit Volume	Joint Costs Allocated
Studs (Building)	75,000	75.00%	Rs 75,00,000
Decorative Pieces	5,000	5.00	5,00,000
Posts	20,000	20.00	20,00,000
Total	1,00,000	100.00%	1,00,00,000

c. Net realizable value method:

	Monthly Unit Output	Fully Processed Selling Price per Unit	Estimated Net Realizable Value	% of Sales	Joint Costs Allocated
Studs (Building)	75,000	Rs 80	Rs 60,00,000	44.4445%	Rs 44,44,450
Decorative Pieces	4,500[a]	100	35,00,000[b]	25.9259	25,92,590
Posts	20,000	20	40,00,000	29.6296	29,62,960
Total			1,35,00,000	1,00.0000%	1,00,00,000

Notes:
[a]5,000 monthly units of output – 10% normal spoilage = 4,500 good units.
[b]4,500 good units × Rs 1,000 = Rs 45,00,000 – Further processing costs of Rs 10,00,000 = Rs 35,00,000

2. Presented below is an analysis for Assam Sawmill Limited comparing the processing of decorative pieces further versus selling the rough-cut product immediately at split-off.

	Units	Amount
Monthly unit output	5,000	
Less: Normal further processing shrinkage	500	
Units available for sale	4,500	
Final sales value (4,500 units × Rs 1,000 per unit)		Rs 45,00,000
Less: Sales value at splitoff		30,00,000
Incremental revenue		15,00,000
Less: Further processing costs		10,00,000
Additional contribution from further processing		Rs 5,00,000

3. Assuming Assam Sawmill Limited announces that in six months it will sell the rough-cut product at split-off, due to increasing competitive pressure, at least three types of likely behavior that will be demonstrated by the skilled labor in the planing and sizing process includes the following.
   - Poorer quality.
   - Reduced motivation and morale.
   - Job insecurity, leading to nonproductive employee time looking for jobs elsewhere.

   Management actions that could improve this behavior include the following.
   - Improve communication by giving the workers a more comprehensive explanation as to the reason for the change so they can better understand the situation and bring out a plan for future operation of the rest of the plant.
   - The company can offer incentive bonuses to maintain quality and production and align rewards with goals.
   - The company could provide job relocation and internal job transfers.

Solution Exhibit 16-23

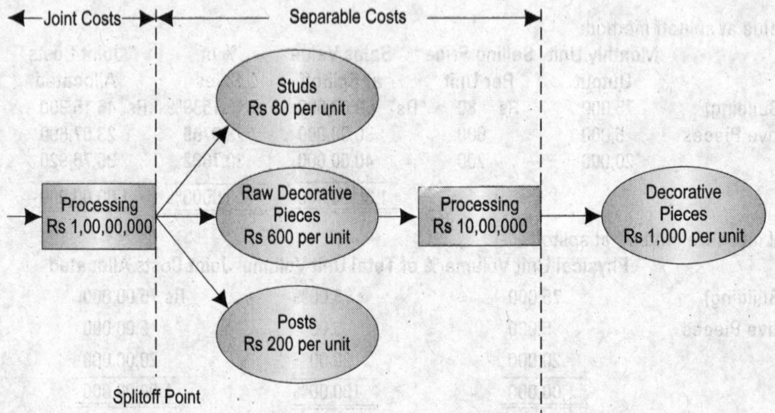

16-24 NRV method, byproducts. (CMA, adapted) Himachal Apples Ltd. (HAL) grows, processes, packages, and sells three joint apple products: (a) sliced apples that are used in frozen pies, (b) applesauce, and (c) apple juice. The outside skin of the apple, processed as animal feed, is treated as a byproduct. HAL uses the NRV method to allocate costs of the joint process to its joint products. The byproduct is inventoried at its estimated selling price when produced. The NRV of the byproduct is used to reduce the joint production costs before the splitoff point. The following details of HAL production process are available:

- The apples are washed and the outside skin is removed in the Cutting Department. The apples are then cored and trimmed for slicing. The three joint products and the byproduct are recognizable after processing in the Cutting Department. Each product is then transferred to a separate department for final processing.

- **The trimmed apples are moved to the Slicing Department, where they are sliced and frozen. Any juice generated during the slicing operation is frozen with the slices.**
- **The pieces of apple trimmed from the fruit are processed into applesauce in the Crushing Department. The juice generated during this operation is used in the applesauce.**
- **The core and any surplus apple pieces generated from the Cutting Department are pulverized into a liquid in the Juicing Department. There is a loss equal to 8% of the weight of the good output produced in this department.**
- **The outside skin is chopped into animal feed and packaged in the Feed Department. It can be kept in cold storage until needed.**

A total of 270,000 kg of apples were processed in the Cutting Department during November. The following schedule shows the costs incurred in each department, the proportion by weight transferred to the four final-processing departments, and the selling price of each end product:

Processing Data and Costs for November:

Department	Costs Incurred	Proportion of Product by Weight Transferred to	Selling Price per Kg of Final Product
Cutting	Rs 60,00,000		
Slicing	11,28,000	33%	Rs 80
Crushing	8,55,000	30	55
Juicing	3,00,000	27	40
Feed	70,000	10	10
Total	Rs 83,53,000	100%	

Required

For the month of November, calculate:

1. **The output of apple slices, applesauce, apple juice, and animal feed, in kg**
2. **The NRV at the splitoff point of each joint product**
3. **The amount of Cutting Department costs assigned to each joint product and the amount assigned to the byproduct following HAL' cost-allocation method described above**
4. **The gross margin in rupees for each joint product**

Solution

NRV method, byproducts (CMA, adapted).

1. For the month of November, HAL output was:

• apple slices	89,100
• apple sauce	81,000
• apple juice	67,500
• animal feed	27,000

These amounts were calculated as follows:

Product	Input	Proportion	Total Kg	Kg Lost	Net Kg
Slices	2,70,000 kg	0.33	89,100	–	89,100
Sauce	2,70,000	0.30	81,000	–	81,000
Juice	2,70,000	0.27	72,900	5,400	67,500[a]
Feed	2,70,000	0.10	27,000	–	27,000
		1.00	2,70,000	5,400	2,64,600

[a]Net kg: = 72,900 – (0.08 × net kg)
1.08 net kg = 72,900
Net kg = 67,500

2. The net realizable value for each of the three main products is calculated below:

Product	Net Kg	Price	Revenue Costs	Separable Value	Net Realizable
Slices	89,100	Rs 80	Rs 71,28,000	Rs 11,28,000	Rs 60,00,000
Sauce	81,000	55	44,55,000	8,55,000	36,00,000
Juice	67,500	40	27,00,000	3,00,000	24,00,000
			Rs 1,42,83,000	Rs 22,83,000	Rs 1,20,00,000

3. and 4.

The net realizable value of the byproduct is deducted from the production costs prior to allocation to the joint products, as presented below:

Allocation of Cutting Department Costs to Joint Products and Byproducts

Net realizable value (NRV) of byproduct = Byproduct revenue – Separable costs
= Rs10 (27,000 kg) – Rs 70,000
= Rs 2,70,000 – Rs 70,000
= Rs 2,00,000

Costs to be allocated = Joint costs – NRV of byproduct
= Rs 60,00,000 – Rs 2,00,000
= Rs 58,00,000

Product	Revenue	Separable Costs	Joint Costs[a]	Gross Margin
Slices	Rs 71,28,000	Rs 11,28,000	Rs 29,00,000	Rs 31,00,000
Sauce	44,55,000	8,55,000	17,40,000	18,60,000
Juice	27,00,000	3,00,000	11,60,000	12,40,000
	Rs 1,42,83,000	Rs 22,83,000	Rs 58,00,000	Rs 62,00,000

[a]Allocated using NRV of the three joint products from requirement b:
Slices (Rs 60,00,000 ÷ Rs 1,20,00,000) × Rs 58,00,000 = Rs 29,00,000
Sauce (Rs 36,00,000 ÷ Rs 1,20,00,000) × Rs 58,00,000 = 17,40,000
Juice (Rs 24,00,000 ÷ Rs 1,20,00,000) × Rs 58,00,000 = 11,60,000

16-25 Byproduct, disposal costs, ethics. Imperial Chemicals, Inc., is a multinational company. One of its subsidiaries is located in India. The country has only a few environmental protection laws, and even those are not enforced so as "to encourage rapid industrialization." The subsidiary's three major products emerge at splitoff point from a common input. The joint costs are allocated to each product using the sales values at splitoff method. In addition to the three joint products, another product that emerges at splitoff point is a hazardous material. The hazardous material can be dumped into the Gulf at zero cost to the company. Alternatively, it can be processed further and sold as a cleaning liquid.

The cost accountant responsible for joint-cost allocation presented the following comparative analysis to you, the controller:

	Alternatives	
	Dump into the Gulf	Process Further
Revenue	Re 0	Rs 5,00,000
Costs:		
Further processing	0	3,00,000
Allocated joint costs	0	2,50,000
Marketing and distribution	0	50,000
Total costs	0	6,00,000
Net realizable value	Re 0	Rs (1,00,000)

Required

1. Comment on the comparative analysis prepared by the cost accountant purely from a financial perspective. Show any supporting computations.
2. Assume, regardless of your conclusions in requirement 1, that adopting the process-further alternative would lead to a decrease in the company's operating income. Disposal of the hazardous waste in a manner different than dumping it into the Gulf would also be costly. Discuss the legal and ethical implications of dumping the hazardous material into the Gulf.

Solution

Byproduct, disposal costs, ethics.

1. The comparative analysis prepared by the cost accountant is flawed. In the process further alternative, he has erroneously included the Rs 2,50,000 allocated joint costs. Allocated joint costs are irrelevant because they are not incremental costs of the alternative being considered. If the joint costs allocated are taken out, it becomes clear that financially it would be to the advantage of the company to process further the product as it would increase the operating income by Rs 1,50,000 [Rs 5,00,000 – (Rs 3,00,000 + Rs 50,000)]. Furthermore, the dumping alternative does not consider potential future costs that may arise from environmental liabilities.

2. It appears that there would be no legal ramifications if the company decided to dump the hazardous product into the Gulf. The country either may have no laws against such dumping, or even if they exist, they are not enforced in accordance with the government policy. A more important consideration, however, is the ethical implications. To knowingly dump a hazardous material into the Gulf would certainly result in water pollution. This is an unacceptable action from a societal standpoint. It is important to remember that an act that does not violate any laws is not necessarily an ethical act. Ethical considerations go beyond legal considerations. In different parts of the world, legal systems are imperfect and not comprehensive. It is the responsibility of top management to take a broader, societal view when making decisions. In other words, a business should take its social responsibility seriously, by making it an integral part of the decision making process. In the long run it is in the best interest of all stakeholders as well as the business itself.

Exercises

16-26 Joint-cost allocation, insurance settlement. Indian Small Manufacturing company produces a product. Each product can be disassembled into five main parts. The Company's management wants to assess profitability if parts are sold instead of full product. Information pertaining to production (in parts) for the month of July is:

Parts	Number of Parts	Wholesale Selling Price per Part When Production is Complete
A	1,000	Rs 11
B	200	4.0
C	400	7.0
D	800	2.0
E	100	1.0

Joint cost of production in July was Rs 10,000.

A special consignment of 200 parts of A and 100 parts of B has been destroyed in a fire. The Company's insurance policy provides for reimbursement for the cost of the parts destroyed. The insurance company permits the Company to use a joint-cost-allocation method. The splitoff point is assumed to be at the end of the production line.

Required

1. Compute the cost of the special consignment destroyed using
   a. Sales value at splitoff method
   b. Physical-measure method (parts of finished parts)
2. Determine the profitability of each part under both the methods.

16-27 Joint products and byproducts (continuation of 16-26). The small Manufacturing company is computing the ending inventory values for its July 31, balance sheet. Ending inventory amounts on July 31 are 100 parts of A, 40 parts of B, 30 parts of C, 50 parts of D, and 20 parts of E.

The Company wants to use the sales value at splitoff point method. However, they want you to explore the effect on ending inventory values of classifying one or more products as a byproduct rather than a joint product.

Required

1. Assume the Company classifies all five products as joint products. What are the ending inventory values of each product on July 31,?
2. Assume the Company uses a byproduct method that recognizes byproducts in the financial statements at the time production is completed. The total revenues to be received from the sale of byproducts produced dueing that period are offset against the joint cost of production of the joint products. What are the ending inventory values for each joint products on July 31, assuming A and C are the joint products and B, D, and E are byproducts?
3. Comment on differences in the results in requirements 1 and 2.

16-28 Alternative joint-cost-allocation methods, further-process decision. The Wood Spirits Company produces two products, turpentine and methanol (wood alcohol), by a joint process. Joint costs amount to Rs 12,00,000 per batch of output. Each batch totals 10,000 litres: 25% methanol and 75% turpentine. Both products are processed further without gain or loss in volume. Separable processing costs are methanol, Rs 30 per litre; turpentine, Rs 20 per litre. Methanol sells for Rs 210 per litre. Turpentine sells for Rs 140 per litre.

Required

1. How much joint costs per batch should be allocated to turpentine and methanol, assuming that joint costs are allocated on a physical-measure (number of litres at splitoff point) basis?
2. If joint costs are to be assigned on an NRV basis, how much joint cost should be assigned to turpentine and methanol?
3. Prepare product-line income statements per batch for requirements 1 and 2. Assume no beginning or ending inventories.

4. The company has discovered an additional process by which the methanol (wood alcohol) can be made into a pleasant-tasting alcoholic beverage. The selling price of this beverage would be Rs 600 a litre. Additional processing would increase separable costs Rs 90 per litre (in addition to the Rs 30 per litre separable cost required to yield methanol). The company would have to pay excise taxes of 20% on the selling price of the beverage. Assuming no other changes in cost, what is the joint cost applicable to the wood alcohol (using the NRV method)? Should the company produce the alcoholic beverage? Show your computations.

16-29 Process further or sell. (R. Capettini, adapted) HLL produces joint products A, B, and C, from a single joint process with a fixed cost of Rs 50,000 and a variable cost of Rs 20 per input unit. Each product can be either processed further or, at the splitoff point, it can be sold or disposed of at a cost. Out of each input unit, HLL produces one unit of product A, three units of product B, and two units of product C.

Required

1. Use the following data to decide whether HLL should process each product further or dispose of it (or sell it) at the splitoff point if HLL inputs 5,000 units. For each product, show how much better off HLL would be if it followed your advice versus making the alternative decision. Assume that if HLL does not further process a product, it does not incur any of the further processing costs.

Product	Selling Price per Unit at Splitoff Point	Cost per Unit to Dispose of Product at Splitoff Point	Further Processing Costs Fixed per unit	Further Processing Costs Variable	Selling Price per Unit After Further Processing
A	–	Rs 2.0	Rs 60,000	Rs 9.0	Rs 15
B	Rs 5	–	10,000	10.0	15
C	–	9.0	1,00,000	11.0	54

2. What is HLL's gross margin at the 5,000-unit input level?

16-30 Alternative methods of joint-cost allocation, product-mix decision. Indigo Lumber processes lumber products for sale to lumber wholesalers. Its most popular line is oak products. Oak tree growers sell Indigo Lumber whole trees. These trees are jointly processed up to the splitoff point at which raw select oak, raw white oak, and raw knotty oak become separable products. Each raw product is then separately further processed by Indigo Lumber into finished products (select oak, white oak, and knotty oak) that are sold to lumber wholesalers. Data for August are:

a. Joint processing costs (including cost of oak trees)–Rs 30,00,000.
b. Separable product at splitoff point
   - Raw select oak, 30,000 board-feet
   - Raw white oak, 50,000 board-feet
   - Raw knotty oak, 20,000 board-feet
c. Final product produced and sold
   - Select oak, 25,000 board feet at Rs 160 per board-foot
   - White oak, 40,000 board feet at Rs 90 per board-foot
   - Knotty oak, 15,000 board feet at Rs 70 per board-foot
d. Separable processing costs
   - For select oak, Rs 6,00,000
   - For white oak, Rs 9,00,000
   - For knotty oak, Rs 1,50,000

There is an active market for raw oak products. Selling prices available in August were raw select oak, Rs 80 per board-foot; raw white oak, Rs 40 per board-foot; and raw knotty oak, Rs 30 per board-foot.

There were no beginning or ending inventories for August.

Required

1. Allocate the joint costs to the three products using
   a. Sales value at splitoff method
   b. Physical-measures method
   c. NRV method
2. Assume that not all final products produced in August were sold. Ending inventory for August was select oak, 1,000 board-feet; white oak, 2,000 board-feet; and knotty oak, 500 board-feet. What would be the ending inventory values in the August 31 balance sheet under each product for the three methods in requirement 1?
3. Is Indigo Lumber maximizing its total August operating income by fully processing each raw oak product into its finished product form? Show your computations.

16-31 Alternative methods of joint-cost allocation, product-mix decisions. The Sunshine Oil Company buys crude vegetable oil. Refining this oil results in four products at the splitoff point: A, B, C, and D. Product C is fully processed at the splitoff point. Products A, B, and D can individually be further refined into Super A, Super B, and Super D. In the most recent month (December), the output at the splitoff point was:

- Product A, 3,000 litres
- Product B, 1,000 litres
- Product C, 500 litres
- Product D, 500 litres

The joint costs of purchasing and processing the crude vegetable oil were Rs 100,000. Sunshine had no beginning or ending inventories. Sales of product C in December were Rs 50,000. Products A, B, and D were further refined and then sold. Data related to December are:

	Separable Processing Costs to Make Super Products	Revenues
Super A	Rs 2,00,000	Rs 3,00,000
Super B	80,000	1,00,000

Sunshine had the option of selling products A, B, and D at the splitoff point. This alternative would have yielded the following revenues for the December production:

- Product A, Rs 50,000
- Product B, Rs 30,000
- Product D, Rs 70,000

Required

1. Compute the gross-margin percentage for each product sold in December, using the following methods for allocating the Rs 1,00,000 joint costs:
   a. Sales value at splitoff
   b. Physical measure
   c. NRV
2. Could Sunshine have increased its December operating income by making different decisions about the further processing of products A, B, or D? Show the effect on operating income of any changes you recommend.

16-32 Joint and byproducts, NRV method. (CPA) The Harrison Limited produces three products: Alpha, Beta, and Gamma. Alpha and Gamma are joint products, and Beta is a byproduct of Alpha. No joint costs are to be allocated to the byproduct. The production processes for a typical month are as follows:

a. In Department 1, 110,000 kg of direct material, are processed at a total cost of Rs 12,00,000. After processing in Department 1, 60% of the units are transferred to Department 2, and 40% of the units (now Gamma) are transferred to Department 3.
b. In Department 2, the material is further processed at a total additional cost of Rs 3,80,000. Then 70% of the units (now Alpha) are transferred to Department 4; and 30% emerge as Beta, the byproduct, to be sold at Rs 12 per kg. Separable marketing costs for Beta are Rs 81,000.
c. In Department 4, Alpha is processed at a total additional cost of Rs 2,36,600. After this processing, Alpha is ready for sale at Rs 50 per kg.
d. In Department 3, Gamma is processed at a total additional cost of Rs 16,50,000. In this department, a normal loss of units of Gamma occurs, which equals 10% of the good units of output. The remaining good units of output are then sold for Rs 120 per kg.

Required

1. Prepare a schedule showing the allocation of the Rs 12,00,000 joint costs between Alpha and Gamma using the NRV method. The NRV of Beta should be treated as an addition to the sales value of Alpha.
2. Independent of your answer to requirement 1, assume that Rs 10,20,000 of total joint costs were appropriately allocated to Alpha. Assume, also that there were 48,000 kg of Alpha and 20,000 kg of Beta available to sell. Prepare an income statement through the gross-margin line item for Alpha using the following facts:
   a. During the year, sales of Alpha were 80% of the kg available for sale. There was no beginning inventory.
   b. The NRV of Beta available for sale is to be deducted from the cost of producing Alpha. The ending inventory of Alpha is to be based on the net costs of production.
   c. All other cost and selling-price data are listed in **(a)** through **(d)** above.

16-33 Process further or sell, byproduct. (CMA, adapted) Coal India Limited (CIL) produces and sells bulk raw coal to other coal companies and exporters. CIL mines and stockpiles the coal. The coal is then passed through a one-step crushing process before being loaded onto river barges for shipment to customers. The annual output of 10 million quintals, which is expected to remain stable, has an average cost of Rs 200 per quintal with an average selling price of Rs 270 per quintal.

Management is currently evaluating the possibility of further processing the coal by sizing and cleaning to expand markets and enhance product revenues. Management has rejected the possibility of constructing a large sizing and cleaning plant because of the significant long-term capital investment required.

Ahmed, controller of CIL, asks Karim, mining engineer (with finance background), to develop cost and revenue projections for further processing the coal using a variety of contractual arrangements. After extensive discussions with vendors and contractors, Karim prepares the following projections of incremental costs of sizing and cleaning CIL's annual output:

Coal India Limited Sizing and Cleaning Processes

Incremental Costs	
Direct labor	Rs 60,00,000 per year
Supervisory personnel	Rs 10,00,000 per year
Heavy equipment rental, operating, and maintenance costs	Rs 2,50,000 per month
Contract sizing and cleaning	Rs 35per quintal
Outbound rail freight (per 600-quintals rail car)	Rs 2,400 per car

In addition to the preceding cost information, market samples obtained by Karim show that electrical utilities enter into contracts for sized and cleaned coal at an expected average price of Rs 360 per quintal.

Karim has learned that 5% of the raw bulk output that enters the sizing and cleaning process will be lost as a primary product. Normally, 75% of this product loss can be salvaged as coal fines, which are small pieces ranging from dustlike particles up to pieces two inches in diameter. Coal fines are too small for use by electrical utilities but are frequently sold to steel manufacturers for use in blast furnaces.

Unfortunately, the price for coal fines frequently fluctuates between Rs 140 and Rs 240 per quintal (F.O.B.), and the timing of market volume is erratic. Although companies generally sell all their coal fines during a year, it is not unusual to stockpile this product for several months before making any significant sales.

Required

1. Prepare an analysis that shows whether it is more profitable for Coal India Limited (CIL) to continue to sell the raw bulk coal or to process it further through sizing and cleaning. (Note: Ignore any value related to the coal fines in your analysis.)
2. Now consider the potential value of the coal fines and prepare an addendum that shows how their value affects the results of your analysis prepared in requirement 1.
3. What other factors should be considered in evaluating a sell-or-process-further decision?

16-34 Joint-cost allocation, process further or sell. (CMA, adapted) Ranbaxy Pharmaceutical Company manufactures three joint products from a joint process: Altox, Lorex, and Hycol. Data regarding these products for the typical fiscal year ended March 31, are as follows:

	Altox	Lorex	Hycol
Units produced	1,70,000	5,00,000	3,30,000
Selling price per unit at splitoff	Rs 3.50	–	Rs 2.00
Separable costs	–	Rs 14,00,000	–
Final selling price per unit	–	Rs 5.00	–

The joint production cost up to the splitoff point at which Altox, Lorex, and Hycol become separable products is Rs 18,00,000.

The president of Ranbaxy is reviewing an opportunity to change the way in which these three products are processed and sold. Proposed changes for each product are as follows:

- Altox is currently sold at the splitoff point to a manufacturer of vitamins. Altox can also be processed into a blood pressure medication. However, this additional processing causes a loss of 20,000 units of Altox. The separable costs to further process Altox are estimated to be Rs 2,50,000 annually. The blood pressure medication sells for Rs 5.50 per unit.
- Lorex is currently processed further after the splitoff point and is sold by Ranbaxy as a cold remedy. The company has received an offer from another pharmaceutical company to purchase Lorex at the splitoff point for Rs 2.25 per unit.
- Hycol is an oil produced from the joint process and is currently sold at the splitoff point to a cosmetics manufacturer. Ranbaxy's Research Department has suggested that the company process this product further and sell it as an ointment to relieve muscle pain. The additional processing would cost Rs 75,000 annually and would result in 25% more units of product. The ointment sells for Rs 1.80 per unit.

Required

1. Allocate the Rs 18,00,000 joint production cost to Altox, Lorex, and Hycol using the NRV method.
2. Identify which of the three joint products Ranbaxy Pharmaceutical Company should sell at the splitoff point in the future and which of the three the company should process further to maximize operating income. Support your decisions with appropriate computations.

17 Process Costing

Learning Objectives

1. Identify the situations in which process-costing systems are appropriate
2. Understand the basic concepts of process-costing and compute average unit costs
3. Describe the five steps in process costing and calculate equivalent units
4. Use the weighted-average method and first-in, first-out (FIFO) method of process costing
5. Apply process-costing methods to situations with transferred-in costs
6. Understand the need for hybrid-costing systems such as operation-costing

Companies that produce identical or similar units of a product or service (for example, an oil-refining company) often use process costing.

A key part of process costing is valuing inventory, which entails determining how many units of the product the firm has on hand at the end of an accounting reporting period, evaluating the units' stages of completion, and assigning costs to the units. There are different methods for doing this, each of which can result in different profits. At times, variations in international rules and customs make it difficult to compare inventory costs across competitors. In the case of ExxonMobil, differences in accounting rules between the United States and Europe also reduce the company's profits and tax liability.

ExxonMobil and Accounting Differences in the Oil Patch[1]

In 2010, ExxonMobil was number two on the *Fortune* 500 annual ranking of the largest U.S. companies. In 2009, the company had $284 billion dollars in revenue with more than $19 billion in profits. Believe it or not, however, by one measure ExxonMobil's profits are *understated*.

ExxonMobil, like most U.S. energy companies, uses last-in, first-out (LIFO) accounting. Under this treatment, ExxonMobil records its cost of inventory at the latest price paid for crude oil in the open market, even though it is often selling oil produced at a much lower cost. This increases the company's cost of goods sold, which in turn reduces profit. The benefit of using LIFO accounting for financial reporting is that ExxonMobil is then permitted to use LIFO for tax purposes as well, thereby lowering its payments to the tax authorities.

In contrast, International Financial Reporting Standards (IFRS) do not permit the use of LIFO accounting. European oil companies such as Royal Dutch Shell and British Petroleum use the first-in, first-out (FIFO) methodology instead when accounting for inventory. Under FIFO, oil companies use the cost of the oldest crude in their inventory to calculate the cost of barrels of oil sold. This reduces costs on the income statement, therefore increasing gross margins.

Assigning costs to inventory is a critical part of process costing, and a company's choice of method can result in substantially different profits. For instance, ExxonMobil's 2009 net income would have been

[1] *Source:* Exxon Mobil Corporation. 2010. 2009 Annual Report. Irving, TX: Exxon Mobil Corporation; Kaminska, Izabella. 2010. Shell, BP, and the increasing cost of inventory. *Financial Times*. "FT Alphaville" blog, April 29; Reilly, David. 2006. Big oil's accounting methods fuel criticism. *Wall Street Journal*, August 8.

$7.1 billion higher under FIFO. Moreover, at the end of fiscal 2009, the cumulative difference—or "LIFO Reserve"—between the value of inventory ExxonMobil was carrying on its balance sheet based on the initial cost versus the current replacement cost of that inventory was $17.1 billion. This number takes on special relevance in the context of current efforts to achieve convergence between U.S. GAAP and IFRS. Should that happen, and if U.S. firms are forced to adopt FIFO for financial and tax reporting, they would have to pay additional taxes on the cumulative savings to date from showing a higher cost of goods sold in LIFO. As an approximation, applying a marginal tax rate of 35% to ExxonMobil's LIFO Reserve of $17.1 billion suggests an incremental tax burden of almost $6 billion.

Companies such as ExxonMobil, Coca-Cola, and Novartis produce many identical or similar units of a product using mass-production techniques. The focus of these companies on individual production processes gives rise to process costing. This chapter describes how companies use process costing methods to determine the costs of products or services and to value inventory and cost of goods sold (using methods like FIFO).

Illustrating Process Costing

Learning Objective 1

Identify the situations in which process-costing systems are appropriate

. . . when masses of identical or similar units are produced

Before we examine process costing in more detail, let's briefly compare job costing and process costing. Job-costing and process-costing systems are best viewed as ends of a continuum:

Job-costing system	Process-costing system
Distinct, identifiable units of a product or service (for example, custom-made machines and houses)	Masses of identical or similar units of a product or service (for example, food or chemical processing)

In a *process-costing system*, the unit cost of a product or service is obtained by assigning total costs to many identical or similar units. In other words, unit costs are calculated by dividing total costs incurred by the number of units of output from the production process. In a manufacturing process-costing setting, each unit receives the same or similar amounts of direct material costs, direct manufacturing labor costs, and indirect manufacturing costs (manufacturing overhead).

The main difference between process costing and job cos g is the *extent of averaging* used to compute unit costs of products or services. In a job-costing system, individual jobs use different quantities of production resources, so it would be incorrect to cost each job at the same average production cost. In contrast, when identical or similar units of products or services are mass-produced, not processed as individual jobs, process costing is used to calculate an average production cost for all units produced. Some processes such as clothes manufacturing have aspects of both process costing (cost per unit of each operation, such as cutting or sewing, is identical) and job costing (different materials are used in different batches of clothing, say, wool versus cotton). The appendix to this chapter describes "hybrid" costing systems that combine elements of both job and process costing.

Consider the following illustration of process costing: Suppose that Pacific Electronics manufactures a variety of cell phone models. These models are assembled in the Assembly Department. Upon completion, units are transferred to the Testing Department. We focus on the Assembly Department process for one model, SG-40. All units of SG-40 are identical and must meet a set of demanding performance specifications. The process-costing system for SG-40 in the Assembly Department has a single direct-cost category—direct materials—and a single indirect-cost category—conversion costs. Conversion costs are all manufacturing costs other than direct material costs, including manufacturing labor, energy, plant depreciation, and so on. Direct materials are added at the beginning of the Assembly process. Conversion costs are added evenly during assembly.

The following graphic represents these facts:

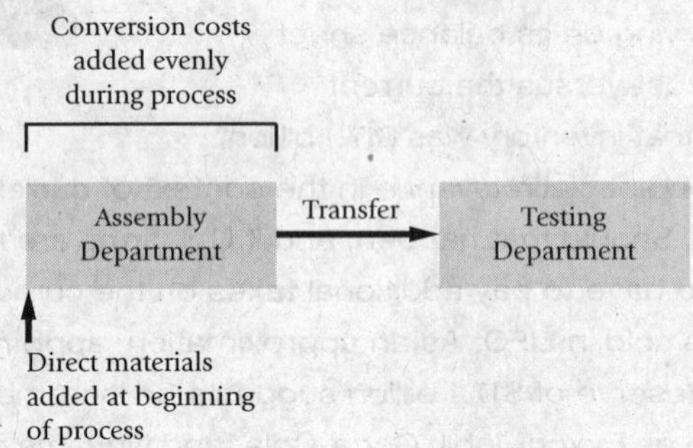

Process-costing systems separate costs into cost categories according to *when costs are introduced into the process*. Often, as in our Pacific Electronics example, only two cost classifications—direct materials and conversion costs—are necessary to assign costs to products. Why only two? Because *all* direct materials are added to the process at one time and all conversion costs generally are added to the process evenly through time. If, however, two different direct materials were added to the process at different times, two different direct-materials categories would be needed to assign these costs to products. Similarly, if manufacturing labor costs were added to the process at a different time from when the other conversion costs were added, an additional cost category—direct manufacturing labor costs—would be needed to separately assign these costs to products.

We will use the production of the SG-40 component in the Assembly Department to illustrate process costing in three cases, starting with the simplest case and introducing additional complexities in subsequent cases:

- Case 1—Process costing with zero beginning and zero ending work-in-process inventory of SG-40 (that is, all units are started and fully completed within the accounting period). *This case presents the most basic concepts of process costing and illustrates the feature of averaging of costs.*
- Case 2—Process costing with zero beginning work-in-process inventory but some ending work-in-process inventory of SG-40 (that is, some units of SG-40 started during the accounting period are incomplete at the end of the period). *This case introduces the concept of equivalent units and the five steps of process costing and the concept of equivalent units.*
- Case 3—Process costing with both some beginning and some ending work-in-process inventory of SG-40. *This case adds more complexity and illustrates the effect of weighted-average and first-in, first-out (FIFO) cost flow assumptions on cost of units completed and cost of work-in-process inventory.*

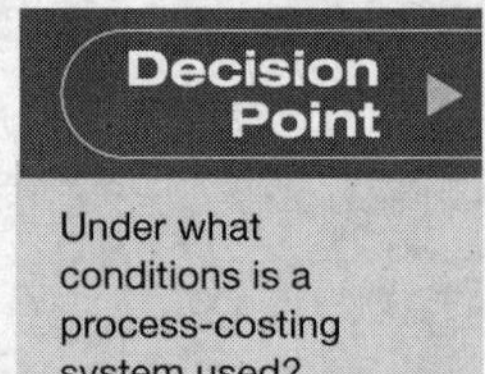

Under what conditions is a process-costing system used?

Case 1: Process Costing with No Beginning or Ending Work-in-Process Inventory

On January 1, 2012, there was no beginning inventory of SG-40 units in the Assembly Department. During January, Pacific Electronics started, completely assembled, and transferred out to the Testing Department 400 units.

Learning Objective 2

Understand the basic concepts of process-costing and compute average unit costs

. . . divide total costs by total units in a given accounting period

Data for the Assembly Department for January 2012 are:

Physical Units for January 2012	
Work in process, beginning inventory (January 1)	0 units
Started during January	400 units
Completed and transferred out during January	400 units
Work in process, ending inventory (January 31)	0 units

Physical units refer to the number of output units, whether complete or incomplete. In January 2012, all 400 physical units started were completed.

Total Costs for January 2012	
Direct material costs added during January	Rs 3,20,000
Conversion costs added during January	2,40,000
Total Assembly Department costs added during January	Rs 5,60,000

Pacific Electronics records direct material costs and conversion costs in the Assembly Department as these costs are incurred. By averaging, assembly cost of SG-40 is Rs 5,60,000 ÷ 400 units = Rs 1,400 per unit, itemized as follows:

Direct material cost per unit (Rs 3,20,000 ÷ 400 units)	Rs 800
Conversion cost per unit (Rs 2,40,000 ÷ 400 units)	600
Assembly Department cost per unit	Rs 1,400

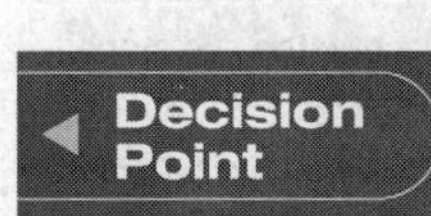

Decision Point

How are average unit costs computed when no inventories are present?

Case 1 shows that in a process-costing system, average unit costs are calculated by dividing total costs in a given accounting period by total units produced in that period. Because each unit is identical, we assume all units receive the same amount of direct material costs and conversion costs. Case 1 applies whenever a company produces a homogeneous product or service but has no incomplete units when each accounting period ends, which is a common situation in service-sector organizations. For example, a bank can adopt this process-costing approach to compute the unit cost of processing 1,00,000 customer deposits, each similar to the other, made in a month.

Case 2: Process Costing with Zero Beginning but Some Ending Work-in-Process Inventory

In February 2012, Pacific Electronics places another 400 units of SG-40 into production. Because all units placed into production in January were completely assembled, there is no beginning inventory of partially completed units in the Assembly Department on February 1. Some customers order late, so not all units started in February are completed by the end of the month. Only 175 units are completed and transferred to the Testing Department.

Data for the Assembly Department for February 2012 are:

	A	B	C	D	E
1		Physical Units (SG-40s) (1)	Direct Materials (2)	Conversion Costs (3)	Total Costs (4) = (2) + (3)
2	Work in process, beginning inventory (February 1)	0			
3	Started during February	400			
4	Completed and transferred out during February	175			
5	Work in process, ending inventory (February 28)	225			
6	Degree of completion of ending work in process		100%	60%	
7	Total costs added during February		Rs 3,20,000	Rs 1,86,000	Rs 5,06,000

The 225 partially assembled units as of February 28, 2012, are fully processed with respect to direct materials. That's because all direct materials in the Assembly Department are added at the beginning of the assembly process. Conversion costs, however, are added evenly during assembly. Based on the work completed relative to the total work required to complete the SG-40 units still in process at the end of February, an Assembly Department supervisor estimates that the partially assembled units are, on average, 60% complete with respect to conversion costs.

The accuracy of the completion estimate of conversion costs depends on the care, skill, and experience of the estimator and the nature of the conversion process. Estimating the degree of completion is usually easier for direct material costs than for conversion costs. That's because the quantity of direct materials needed for a completed unit and the quantity of direct materials in a partially completed unit can be measured more accurately. In contrast, the conversion sequence usually consists of a number of basic operations for a specified number of hours, days, or weeks for various steps in the production process.[2] The degree of completion for conversion costs depends on the proportion of the total conversion costs needed to complete one unit or one batch of production that has already been incurred on the units still in process. It is a challenge for management accountants to make this estimate accurately. Because of these uncertainties, department supervisors and line managers—individuals most familiar with the process—often make conversion cost estimates. Still, in some industries, such as semiconductor manufacturing, no exact estimate is possible or, as in the textile industry, vast quantities in process make the task of estimation costly. In these cases, it is necessary to assume that all work in process in a department is complete to some degree with respect to conversion costs (for example, one-third, one-half, or two-thirds complete).

Learning Objective 3

Describe the five steps in process costing

. . . to assign total costs to units completed and to units in work in process

The point to understand here is that a partially assembled unit is not the same as a fully assembled unit. Faced with some fully assembled units and some partially assembled units, we require a common metric that will enable us to compare the work done in each category and, more important, obtain a total measure of work done. The concept we will use in this regard is that of *equivalent units*. We will explain this notion in greater detail next as part of the set of five steps required to calculate (1) the cost of fully assembled units in February 2012 and (2) the cost of partially assembled units still in process at the end of that month, for Pacific Electronics. The five steps of process costing are:

Step 1: Summarize the flow of physical units (of output).

Step 2: Compute output in terms of equivalent units.

Step 3: Summarize total costs to account for.

Step 4: Compute cost per equivalent unit.

Step 5: Assign total costs to units completed and to units in ending work in process.

Physical Units and Equivalent Units (Steps 1 and 2)

Step 1 tracks physical units of output. Recall that physical units are the number of output units, whether complete or incomplete. Where did physical units come from? Where did they go? The physical-units column of Exhibit 17-1 tracks where the physical units came from (400 units started) and where they went (175 units completed and transferred out, and 225 units in ending inventory).

Because not all 400 physical units are fully completed, output in step 2 is computed in *equivalent units*, not in *physical units*. To see what we mean by equivalent units, let's say that during a month, 50 physical units were started but not completed by the end of the month. These 50 units in ending inventory are estimated to be 70% complete with respect to conversion costs. Let's examine those units from the perspective of the conversion costs already incurred to get the units to be 70% complete. Suppose we put all the conversion costs represented in the 70% into making fully completed units. How many units could have been 100% complete by the end of the month? The answer: 35 units. Why? Because 70% of conversion costs incurred on 50 incomplete units could have been incurred to make 35 (0.70 × 50) complete units by the end of the month. That is, if all the conversion-cost input in the 50 units in inventory had been used to make completed output units, the company would have produced 35 completed units (also called *equivalent units*) of output.

Equivalent units is a derived amount of output units that (1) takes the quantity of each input (factor of production) in units completed and in incomplete units of work in process and (2) converts the quantity of input into the amount of completed output units that could

[2] For example, consider the conventional tanning process for converting hide to leather. Obtaining 250–300 kg of leather requires putting one metric ton of raw hide through as many as 15 steps: from soaking, liming, and pickling to tanning, dyeing, and fatliquoring, the step in which oils are introduced into the skin before the leather is dried.

Exhibit 17-1

Steps 1 and 2: Summarize Output in Physical Units and Compute Output in Equivalent Units for Assembly Department of Pacific Electronics for February 2012

	A	B	C	D
1		(Step 1)	(Step 2)	
2			Equivalent Units	
3	Flow of Production	Physical Units	Direct Materials	Conversion Costs
4	Work in process, beginning	0		
5	Started during current period	400		
6	To account for	400		
7	Completed and transferred out during current period	175	175	175
8	Work in process, ending[a]	225		
9	(225 x 100%; 225 x 60%)		225	135
10	Accounted for	400		
11	Work done in current period only		400	310
12				
13	[a]Degree of completion in this department; direct materials, 100%; conversion costs, 60%.			

be produced with that quantity of input. Note that equivalent units are calculated separately for each input (such as direct materials and conversion costs). Moreover, every completed unit, by definition, is comprised of one equivalent unit of each input required to make it. This chapter focuses on equivalent-unit calculations in manufacturing settings. But, equivalent-unit concepts are also found in nonmanufacturing settings. For example, universities convert their part-time student enrollments into "full-time student equivalents."

When calculating equivalent units in step 2, focus on quantities. Disregard rupee amounts until after equivalent units are computed. In the Pacific Electronics example, all 400 physical units—the 175 fully assembled units and the 225 partially assembled units—are 100% complete with respect to direct materials because all direct materials are added in the Assembly Department at the start of the process. Therefore, Exhibit 17-1 shows output as 400 *equivalent units* for direct materials: 175 equivalent units for the 175 physical units assembled and transferred out, and 225 equivalent units for the 225 physical units in ending work-in-process inventory.

The 175 fully assembled units are also completely processed with respect to conversion costs. The partially assembled units in ending work in process are 60% complete (on average). Therefore, conversion costs in the 225 partially assembled units are *equivalent* to conversion costs in 135 (60% of 225) fully assembled units. Hence, Exhibit 17-1 shows output as 310 *equivalent units* with respect to conversion costs: 175 equivalent units for the 175 physical units assembled and transferred out and 135 equivalent units for the 225 physical units in ending work-in-process inventory.

Calculation of Product Costs (Steps 3, 4, and 5)

Exhibit 17-2 shows steps 3, 4, and 5. Together, they are called the *production cost worksheet.* Step 3 summarizes total costs to account for. Because the beginning balance of work-in-process inventory is zero on February 1, total costs to account for (that is, the total charges or debits to the Work in Process—Assembly account) consist only of costs added during February: direct materials of Rs 3,20,000 and conversion costs of Rs 1,86,000, for a total of Rs 5,06,000.

Step 4 in Exhibit 17-2 calculates cost per equivalent unit separately for direct materials and for conversion costs by dividing direct material costs and conversion costs added during February by the related quantity of equivalent units of work done in February (as calculated in Exhibit 17-1).

To see the importance of using equivalent units in unit-cost calculations, compare conversion costs for January and February 2012. Total conversion costs of Rs 1,86,000 for the 400 units worked on during February are lower than the conversion costs of Rs 2,40,000 for the 400 units worked on in January. However, in this example, the conversion costs to fully assemble a unit are Rs 600 in both January and February. Total conversion costs are lower in February because fewer equivalent units of conversion-costs work were completed in February (310) than in January (400). Using physical units instead

Exhibit 17-2 Steps 3, 4, and 5: Summarize Total Costs to Account For, Compute Cost per Equivalent Unit, and Assign Total Costs to Units Completed and to Units in Ending Work in Process for Assembly Department of Pacific Electronics for February 2012

	A	B	C	D	E
1			Total Production Costs	Direct Materials	Conversion Costs
2	(Step 3)	Costs added during February	Rs 5,06,000	Rs 3,20,000	Rs 1,86,000
3		Total costs to account for	Rs 5,06,000	Rs 3,20,000	Rs 1,86,000
4					
5	(Step 4)	Costs added in current period	Rs 5,06,000	Rs 3,20,000	Rs 1,86,000
6		Divide by equivalent units of work done in current period (Exhibit 17-1)		÷ 400	÷ 310
7		Cost per equivalent unit		Rs 800	Rs 600
8					
9	(Step 5)	Assignment of costs:			
10		Completed and transferred out (175 units)	Rs 2,45,000	(175[a] x Rs800)+	(175[a] x Rs600)
11		Work in process, ending (225 units):	2,61,000	(225[b] x Rs800)+	(135[b] x Rs600)
12		Total costs accounted for	Rs 5,06,000	Rs 3,20,000 +	Rs 1,86,000
13					
14	[a]Equivalent units completed and transferred out from Exhibit 17-1, step 2.				
15	[b]Equivalent units in ending work in process from Exhibit 17-1, step 2.				

of equivalent units in the per-unit calculation would have led to the erroneous conclusion that conversion costs per unit declined from Rs 600 in January to Rs 465 (Rs 1,86,000 ÷ 400 units) in February. This incorrect costing might have prompted Pacific Electronics to presume that greater efficiencies in processing had been achieved and to lower the price of SG-40, for example, when in fact costs had not declined.

Step 5 in Exhibit 17-2 assigns these costs to units completed and transferred out and to units still in process at the end of February 2009. The idea is to attach rupee amounts to the equivalent output units for direct materials and conversion costs of (a) units completed and (b) ending work in process, as calculated in Exhibit 17-1, step 2. *Equivalent output units for each input are multiplied by cost per equivalent unit, as calculated in step 4 of Exhibit 17-2.* For example, costs assigned to the 225 physical units in ending work-in-process inventory are:

Direct material costs of 225 equivalent units (Exhibit 17-1, step 2) × Rs 800 cost per equivalent unit of direct materials calculated in step 4	Rs 1,80,000
Conversion costs of 135 equivalent units (Exhibit 17-1, step 2) × Rs 600 cost per equivalent unit of conversion costs calculated in step 4	81,000
Total cost of ending work-in-process inventory	Rs 2,61,000

Note that total costs to account for in step 3 (Rs 5,06,000) equal total costs accounted for in step 5.

Journal Entries

Journal entries in process-costing systems are similar to the entries made in job-costing systems with respect to direct materials and conversion costs. The main difference is that, in process costing, there is one Work-in-Process account for each process—in our example, Work in Process—Assembly and Work in Process—Testing. Pacific Electronics purchases direct materials as needed. These materials are delivered directly to the Assembly Department. Using amounts from Exhibit 17-2, summary journal entries for February are:

1. Work in Process—Assembly	3,20,000	
Accounts Payable Control		3,20,000
To record direct materials purchased and used in production during February.		
2. Work in Process—Assembly	1,86,000	
Various accounts such as Wages Payable Control and Accumulated Depreciation		1,86,000
To record conversion costs for February; examples include energy, manufacturing supplies, all manufacturing labor, and plant depreciation.		
3. Work in Process—Testing	2,45,000	
Work in Process—Assembly		2,45,000
To record cost of goods completed and transferred from Assembly to Testing during February.		

Exhibit 17-3 shows a general framework for the flow of costs through T-accounts. Notice how entry 3 for Rs 2,45,000 follows the physical transfer of goods from the Assembly to the Testing Department. The T-account Work in Process—Assembly shows February 2012's ending balance of Rs 2,61,000, which is the beginning balance of Work in Process—Assembly in March 2012.

Case 3: Process Costing with Some Beginning and Some Ending Work-in-Process Inventory

At the beginning of March 2012, Pacific Electronics had 225 partially assembled SG-40 units in the Assembly Department. It started production of another 275 units in March. Data for the Assembly Department for March are:

File Edit View Insert Format Tools Data Window Help

	A	B	C	D	E
1		Physical Units (SG-40s) (1)	Direct Materials (2)	Conversion Costs (3)	Total Costs (4) = (2) + (3)
2	Work in process, beginning inventory (March 1)	225	Rs 1,80,000[a]	Rs 81,000[a]	Rs 2,61,000
3	Degree of completion of beginning work in process		100%	60%	
4	Started during March	275			
5	Completed and transferred out during March	400			
6	Work in process, ending inventory (March 31)	100			
7	Degree of completion of ending work in process		100%	50%	
8	Total costs added during March		Rs 1,98,000	Rs 1,63,800	Rs 3,61,800
9					
10					
11	[a]Work in process, beginning inventory (equals work in process, ending inventory for February)				
12	Direct materials: 225 physical units x 100% completed x Rs 800 per unit = Rs 1,80,000				
13	Conversion costs: 225 physical units x 60% completed x Rs 600 per unit = Rs 81,000				

Pacific Electronics now has incomplete units in both beginning work-in-process inventory and ending work-in-process inventory for March 2012. We can still use the five steps described earlier to calculate (1) cost of units completed and transferred out and (2) cost of ending work in process. To assign costs to each of these categories, however, we first need to choose an inventory-valuation method. We next describe the five-step approach for two important methods—the weighted-average method and the first-in, first-out method. These different valuation methods produce different amounts for cost of units completed and for ending work in process when the unit cost of inputs changes from one period to the next.

Exhibit 17-3

Flow of Costs in a Process-Costing System for Assembly Department of Pacific Electronics for February 2012

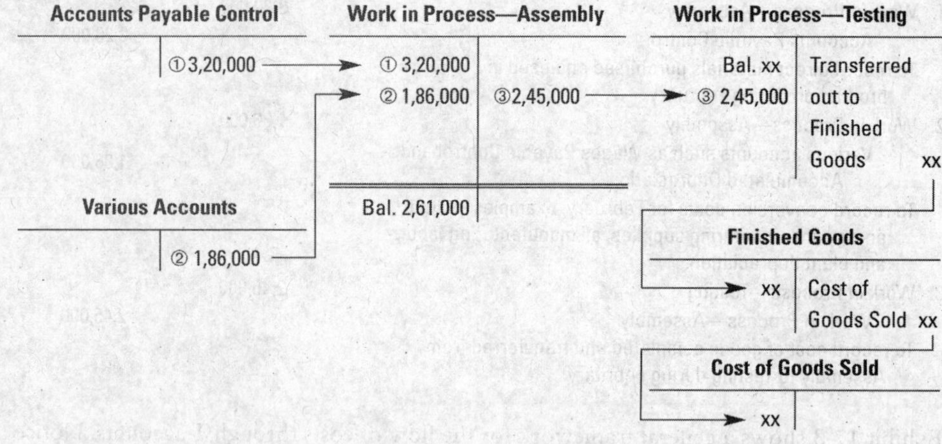

Weighted-Average Method

Learning Objective 4

Use the weighted-average method of process costing

. . . assigns costs based on total costs and equivalent units completed to date

and the first-in, first-out (FIFO) method of process costing

. . . to assign costs based on costs and equivalent units of work done in the current period

The **weighted-average process-costing method** calculates cost per equivalent unit of all *work done to date* (regardless of the accounting period in which it was done) and assigns this cost to equivalent units completed and transferred out of the process and to equivalent units in ending work-in-process inventory. The weighted-average cost is the total of all costs entering the Work in Process account (whether they are from beginning work in process or from work started during the current period) divided by total equivalent units of work done to date. We now describe the weighted-average method using the five-step procedure.

Step 1: Summarize the Flow of Physical Units. The physical-units column of Exhibit 17-4 shows where the units came from—225 units from beginning inventory and 275 units started during the current period—and where they went—400 units completed and transferred out and 100 units in ending inventory.

Step 2: Compute Output in Terms of Equivalent Units. The weighted-average cost of inventory is calculated by merging together the costs of beginning inventory and the manufacturing costs of a period and dividing by the total number of units in beginning inventory and units produced during the accounting period. We apply the same concept here except that calculating the units—in this case equivalent units—is done differently. We use the relationship shown in the equation below.

Equivalent units in beginning work in process	+	Equivalent units of work done in current period	=	Equivalent units completed and transferred out in current period	+	Equivalent units in ending work in process

Although we are interested in calculating the sum of equivalent units in beginning work in process and equivalent units of work done in the current period, it is easier to calculate this sum using the right-hand side of the preceding equation: (1) equivalent units completed and transferred out in the current period plus (2) equivalent units in ending work in process. *Note that the stage of completion of the current-period beginning work in process is not used in this computation.*

The equivalent-units columns in Exhibit 17-4 show equivalent units of work done to date: 500 equivalent units of direct materials and 450 equivalent units of conversion costs. All completed and transferred-out units are 100% complete as to both direct materials and conversion costs. Partially completed units in ending work in process are 100% complete as to direct materials, because direct materials are introduced at the beginning of the process, and 50% complete as to conversion costs, based on estimates made by the Assembly Department manager.

Step 3: Summarize Total Costs to Account For. Exhibit 17-5 presents step 3. Total costs to account for in March 2012 are described in the example data on the next page: beginning work in process, Rs 2,61,000 (direct materials, Rs 1,80,000, plus conversion costs, Rs 81,000),

Exhibit 17-4

Steps 1 and 2: Summarize Output in Physical Units and Compute Output in Equivalent Units Using Weighted-Average Method of Process Costing for Assembly Department of Pacific Electronics for March 2012

	A	B	C	D
1		(Step 1)	(Step 2)	
2			Equivalent Units	
3	Flow of Production	Physical Units	Direct Materials	Conversion Costs
4	Work in process, beginning	225		
5	Started during current period	275		
6	To account for	500		
7	Completed and transferred out during current period	400	400	400
8	Work in process, ending[a]	100		
9	(100 x 100%; 100 x 50%)		100	50
10	Accounted for	500		
11	Work done to date		500	450
12				
13	[a]Degree of completion in this department; direct materials, 100%; conversion costs, 50%.			

plus costs added during March, Rs 3,61,800 (direct materials, Rs 1,98,000, plus conversion costs, Rs 1,63,800). The total of these costs is Rs 6,22,800.

Step 4: Compute Cost per Equivalent Unit. Exhibit 17-5, step 4, shows the computation of weighted-average cost per equivalent unit for direct materials and conversion costs. Weighted-average cost per equivalent unit is obtained by dividing the sum of costs for beginning work in process plus costs for work done in the current period by total equivalent units of work done to date. When calculating weighted-average conversion cost per equivalent unit in Exhibit 17-5, for example, we divide total conversion costs, Rs 2,44,800 (beginning work in process, Rs 81,000, plus work done in current period, Rs 1,63,800), by total equivalent units of work done to date, 450 (equivalent units of conversion costs

Exhibit 17-5

Steps 3, 4 and 5: Summarize Total Costs to Account For, Compute Cost per Equivalent Unit, and Assign Total Costs to Units Completed and to Units in Ending Work in Process Using Weighted-Average Method of Process Costing for Assembly Department of Pacific Electronics for March 2012

	A	B	C	D		E
1			Total Production Costs	Direct Materials		Conversion Costs
2	(Step 3)	Work in process, beginning	Rs 2,61,000	Rs 1,80,000		Rs 81,000
3		Costs added in current period	3,61,800	1,98,000		1,63,800
4		Total costs to account for	Rs 6,22,800	Rs 3,78,000		Rs 2,44,800
5						
6	(Step 4)	Costs incurred to date		Rs 3,78,000		Rs 2,44,800
7		Divide by equivalent units of work done to date (Exhibit 17-4)		÷ 500		÷ 450
8		Cost per equivalent unit of work done to date		Rs 756.0		Rs 544.0
9						
10	(Step 5)	Assignment of costs:				
11		Completed and transferred out (400 units)	Rs 5,20,000	(400[a] x Rs756.0)	+	(400[a] x Rs 544.0)
12		Work in process, ending (100 units):	1,02,800	(100[b] x Rs756.0)	+	(50[a] x Rs 544.0)
13		Total costs accounted for	Rs 6,22,800	Rs 3,78,000	+	Rs 2,44,800
14						
15	[a]Equivalent units completed and transferred out from Exhibit 17-4, step 2.					
16	[b]Equivalent units in ending work in process from Exhibit 17-4, step 2.					

in beginning work in process and in work done in current period), to obtain weighted-average cost per equivalent unit of Rs 544.

Step 5: Assign Total Costs to Units Completed and to Units in Ending Work in Process. Step 5 in Exhibit 17-5 takes the equivalent units completed and transferred out and equivalent units in ending work in process calculated in Exhibit 17-4, step 2, and assigns rupee amounts to them using the weighted-average cost per equivalent unit for direct materials and conversion costs calculated in step 4. For example, total costs of the 100 physical units in ending work in process are:

Direct materials:	
100 equivalent units × weighted-average cost per equivalent unit of Rs 756	Rs 75,600
Conversion costs:	
50 equivalent units × weighted-average cost per equivalent unit of Rs 544	27,200
Total costs of ending work in process	Rs 1,02,800

The following table summarizes total costs to account for (Rs 6,22,800) and how they are accounted for in Exhibit 17-5. The arrows indicate that the costs of units completed and transferred out and units in ending work in process are calculated using weighted-average total costs obtained after merging costs of beginning work in process and costs added in the current period.

Costs to Account For			Costs Accounted for Calculated on a Weighted-Average Basis	
Beginning work in process	Rs 2,61,000	→	Completed and transferred out	Rs 5,20,000
Costs added in current period	3,61,800	→	Ending work in process	1,02,800
Total costs to account for	Rs 6,22,800		Total costs accounted for	Rs 6,22,800

Before proceeding, review Exhibits 17-4 and 17-5 to check your understanding of the weighted-average method. Note: Exhibit 17-4 deals with only physical and equivalent units, not costs. Exhibit 17-5 shows the cost amounts.

Using amounts from Exhibit 17-5, the summary journal entries under the weighted-average method for March 2012 at Pacific Electronics are:

1. Work in Process—Assembly	1,98,000	
Accounts Payable Control		1,98,000
To record direct materials purchased and used in production during March.		
2. Work in Process—Assembly	1,63,800	
Various accounts such as Wages Payable Control and Accumulated Depreciation		1,63,800
To record conversion costs for March; examples include energy, manufacturing supplies, all manufacturing labor, and plant depreciation.		
3. Work in Process—Testing	5,20,000	
Work in Process—Assembly		5,20,000
To record cost of goods completed and transferred from Assembly to Testing during March.		

The T-account Work in Process—Assembly, under the weighted-average method, shows:

Work in Process—Assembly

Beginning inventory, March 1	2,61,000	③ Completed and transferred out to Work in Process—Testing	5,20,000
① Direct materials	1,98,000		
② Conversion costs	1,63,800		
Ending inventory, March 31	1,02,800		

First-In, First-Out Method

The **first-in, first-out (FIFO) process-costing method** (1) assigns the cost of the previous accounting period's equivalent units in beginning work-in-process inventory to the first units completed and transferred out of the process; and (2) assigns the cost of equivalent units worked on during the *current* period first to complete beginning inventory, next to start and complete new units, and finally to units in ending work-in-process inventory. The FIFO method assumes that the earliest equivalent units in work in process are completed first.

A distinctive feature of the FIFO process-costing method is that work done on beginning inventory before the current period is kept separate from work done in the current period. Costs incurred and units produced in the current period are used to calculate cost per equivalent unit of work done in the current period. In contrast, equivalent-unit and cost-per-equivalent-unit calculations under the weighted-average method *merge* units and costs in beginning inventory with units and costs of work done in the current period.

We now describe the FIFO method using the five-step procedure.

Step 1: Summarize the Flow of Physical Units. Exhibit 17-6, step 1, traces the flow of physical units of production. The following observations help explain the calculation of physical units under the FIFO method for Pacific Electronics.

- The first physical units assumed to be completed and transferred out during the period are 225 units from beginning work-in-process inventory.
- The March data on page 607 indicate that 400 physical units were completed during March. The FIFO method assumes that of these 400 units, 175 units (400 units − 225 units from beginning work-in-process inventory) must have been started and completed during March.
- Ending work-in-process inventory consists of 100 physical units—the 275 physical units started minus the 175 units that were started and completed.
- The physical units "to account for" equal the physical units "accounted for" (500 units).

Step 2: Compute Output in Terms of Equivalent Units. Exhibit 17-6 also presents the computations for step 2 under the FIFO method. *The equivalent-unit calculations for each cost category focus on equivalent units of work done in the current period (March) only.*

Under the FIFO method, equivalent units of work done in March on the beginning work-in-process inventory equal 225 physical units times *the percentage of work remaining to be done in March to complete these units*: 0% for direct materials, because beginning work in process is 100% complete with respect to direct materials, and 40% for conversion costs, because beginning work in process is 60% complete with respect to conversion costs. The results are 0 (0% × 225) equivalent units of work for direct materials and 90 (40% × 225) equivalent units of work for conversion costs.

The equivalent units of work done on the 175 physical units started and completed equals 175 units times 100% for both direct materials and conversion costs, because all work on these units is done in the current period.

The equivalent units of work done on the 100 units of ending work in process equal 100 physical units times 100% for direct materials (because all direct materials for these units are added in the current period) and 50% for conversion costs (because 50% of conversion-costs work on these units is done in the current period).

Step 3: Summarize Total Costs to Account For. Exhibit 17-7 presents step 3 and summarizes total costs to account for in March 2012 (beginning work in process and costs added in the current period) of Rs 6,22,800, as described in the example data.

Step 4: Compute Cost per Equivalent Unit. Exhibit 17-7 shows the step 4 computation of cost per equivalent unit for *work done in the current period only* for direct materials and conversion costs. For example, conversion cost per equivalent unit of Rs 520 is obtained by dividing current-period conversion costs of Rs 1,63,800 by current-period conversion-costs equivalent units of 315.

Step 5: Assign Total Costs to Units Completed and to Units in Ending Work in Process. Exhibit 17-7 shows the assignment of costs under the FIFO method. Costs of work done in the current period are assigned (1) first to the additional work done to complete the beginning work in process, then (2) to work done on units started and completed during the current period, and finally (3) to ending work in process. *Step 5 takes each quantity of equivalent units calculated in Exhibit 17-6, step 2, and assigns rupee amounts to them (using the cost-per-equivalent-unit calculations in step 4).* The goal is to use the cost of work done in the current period to determine total costs of all units completed from beginning inventory and from work started and completed in the current period, and costs of ending work in process.

Exhibit 17-6

Steps 1 and 2: Summarize Output in Physical Units and Compute Output in Equivalent Units Using FIFO Method of Process Costing for Assembly Department of Pacific Electronics for March 2012

	A	B	C	D
1		(Step 1)	(Step 2)	
2			Equivalent Units	
3	Flow of Production	Physical Units	Direct Materials	Conversion Costs
4	Work in process, beginning	225	(work done before current period)	
5	Started during current period	275		
6	To account for	500		
7	Completed and transferred out during current period:			
8	From beginning work in process[a]	225		
9	[225 x (100% - 100%); 225 x (100%-60%)]		0	90
10	Started and completed	175[b]		
11	(175 x 100%; 175 x 100%)		175	175
12	Work in process, ending[c]	100		
13	(100 x 100%; 100 x 50%)		100	50
14	Accounted for	500		
15	Work done in current period only		275	315
16				
17	[a]Degree of completion in this department; direct materials, 100%; conversion costs, 60%.			
18	[b]400 physical units completed and transferred out minus 225 physical units completed and			
19	transferred out from beginning work-in-process inventory.			
20	[c]Degree of completion in this department: direct materials, 100%; conversion costs, 50%.			

Of the 400 completed units, 225 units are from beginning inventory and 175 units are started and completed during March. The FIFO method starts by assigning the costs of beginning work-in-process inventory of Rs 2,61,000 to the first units completed and transferred out. As we saw in step 2, an additional 90 equivalent units of conversion costs are needed to complete these units in the current period. Current-period conversion cost per equivalent unit is Rs 520, so Rs 46,800 (90 equivalent units × Rs 520 per equivalent unit) of additional costs are incurred to complete beginning inventory. Total production costs for units in beginning inventory are Rs 2,61,000 + Rs 46,800 = Rs 3,07,800. The 175 units started and completed in the current period consist of 175 equivalent units of direct materials and 175 equivalent units of conversion costs. These units are costed at the cost per equivalent unit in the current period (direct materials, Rs 720, and conversion costs, Rs 520) for a total production cost of Rs 2,17,000 [175 × (Rs 720 + Rs 520)].

Under FIFO, ending work-in-process inventory comes from units that were started but not fully completed during the current period. Total costs of the 100 partially assembled physical units in ending work in process are:

Direct materials:	
100 equivalent units × Rs 720 cost per equivalent unit in March	Rs 72,000
Conversion costs:	
50 equivalent units × Rs 520 cost per equivalent unit in March	26,000
Total cost of work in process on March 31	Rs 98,000

The following table summarizes total costs to account for and costs accounted for of Rs 6,22,800 in Exhibit 17-7. Notice how under the FIFO method, the layers of beginning work in process and costs added in the current period are kept separate. The arrows indicate where the costs in each layer go—that is, to units completed and transferred out or to ending work in process. Be sure to include costs of beginning work in process (Rs 2,61,000) when calculating costs of units completed from beginning inventory.

Exhibit 17-7 Steps 3, 4 and 5: Summarize Total Costs to Account For, Compute Cost per Equivalent Unit, and Assign Total Costs to Units Completed and to Units in Ending Work in Process Using FIFO Method of Process Costing for Assembly Department of Pacific Electronics for March 2012

	A	B	C	D	E
1			**Total Production Costs**	**Direct Material**	**Conversion Costs**
2	**(Step 3)**	Work in process, beginning	Rs 2,61,000	Rs 1,80,000	Rs 81,000
3		Costs added in current period	3,61,800	1,98,000	1,63,800
4		Total costs to account for	Rs 6,22,800	Rs 3,78,000	Rs 2,44,800
5					
6	**(Step 4)**	Costs added in current period		Rs 1,98,000	Rs 1,63,800
7		Divide by equivalent units of work done in current period (Exhibit 17-6)		÷ 275	÷ 315
8		Cost per equivalent unit of work done in current period		Rs 720	Rs 520
9					
10	**(Step 5)**	Assignment of costs:			
11		Completed and transferred out (400 units):			
12		Work in process, beginning (225 units)	Rs 2,61,000	Rs 1,80,000 +	Rs 81,000
13		Costs added to beginning work in process in current period	46,800	(0[a] x Rs 720) +	(90[a] x Rs 520)
14		Total from beginning inventory	3,07,800		
15		Started and completed (175 units)	2,17,000	(175[b] x Rs 720) +	(175[b] x Rs 520)
16		Total costs of units completed and transferred out	5,24,800		
17		Work in process, ending (100 units):	98,000	(100[c] x Rs 720) +	(50[c] x Rs 520)
18		Total costs accounted for	Rs 6,22,800	Rs 3,78,000 +	Rs 2,44,800
19					
20	[a]Equivalent units used to complete beginning work in process from Exhibit 17-6, step 2.				
21	[b]Equivalent units started and completed from Exhibit 17-6, step 2.				
22	[c]Equivalent units in ending work in process from Exhibit 17-6, step 2.				

Costs to Account for		Costs Accounted for Calculated on a FIFO Basis	
		Completed and transferred out	
Beginning work in process	Rs 2,61,000	Beginning work in process	Rs 2,61,000
Costs added in current period	3,61,800	Used to complete beginning work in process	46,800
		Started and completed	2,17,000
		Completed and transferred out	5,24,800
		Ending work in process	98,000
Total costs to account for	Rs 6,22,800	Total costs accounted for	Rs 6,22,800

Before proceeding, review Exhibits 17-6 and 17-7 to check your understanding of the FIFO method. Note: Exhibit 17-6 deals with only physical and equivalent units, not costs. Exhibit 17-7 shows the cost amounts.

The journal entries under the FIFO method are identical to the journal entries under the weighted-average method except for one difference. The entry to record the cost of goods completed and transferred out would be Rs 5,24,800 under the FIFO method instead of Rs 5,20,000 under the weighted-average method.

Keep in mind that FIFO is applied within a department to compile the cost of units *transferred out*, but as a practical matter, units *transferred in* during a given period usually are carried at a single average unit cost. For example, the average cost of units transferred out of the Assembly Department is Rs 5,24,800 ÷ 400 units = Rs 1,312 per SG-40 unit. The Assembly Department uses FIFO to distinguish between monthly batches of production. The succeeding department, Testing, however, costs these units (which consist of costs incurred in both February and March) at one average unit cost (Rs 1,312 in this illustration). If this averaging were not done, the attempt to track costs on a pure FIFO basis throughout a series of processes would be cumbersome. As a result, the FIFO method should really be called a *modified* or *department* FIFO method.

Comparison of Weighted-Average and FIFO Methods

Consider the summary of the costs assigned to units completed and to units still in process under the weighted-average and FIFO process-costing methods in our example for March 2012:

	Weighted Average (from Exhibit 17-5)	**FIFO (from Exhibit 17-7)**	**Difference**
Cost of units completed and transferred out	Rs 5,20,000	Rs 5,24,800	+Rs 4,800
Work in process, ending	1,02,800	Rs 98,000	−Rs 4,800
Total costs accounted for	Rs 6,22,800	Rs 6,22,800	

The weighted-average ending inventory is higher than the FIFO ending inventory by Rs 4,800, or 4.9% (Rs 4,800 ÷ Rs 98,000 = 0.049, or 4.9%). This would be a significant difference when aggregated over the many thousands of products that Pacific Electronics makes. When completed units are sold, the weighted-average method in our example leads to a lower cost of goods sold and, therefore, higher operating income and higher income taxes than the FIFO method. To see why the weighted-average method yields a lower cost of units completed, recall the data on page 720. Direct material cost per equivalent unit in beginning work-in-process inventory is Rs 800, and conversion cost per equivalent unit in beginning work-in-process inventory is Rs 600. These costs are greater, respectively, than the Rs 720 direct materials cost and the Rs 520 conversion cost per equivalent unit of work done during the current period. The current-period costs could be lower due to a decline in the prices of direct materials and conversion-cost inputs, or as a result of Pacific Electronics becoming more efficient in its processes by using smaller quantities of inputs per unit of output, or both.

For the Assembly Department, FIFO assumes that (1) all the higher-cost units from the previous period in beginning work in process are the first to be completed and transferred out of the process and (2) ending work in process consists of only the lower-cost current-period units. The weighted-average method, however, smooths out cost per equivalent unit by assuming that (1) more of the lower-cost units are completed and transferred out and (2) some of the higher-cost units are placed in ending work in process. The decline in the current-period cost per equivalent unit results in a lower cost of units completed and transferred out and a higher ending work-in-process inventory under the weighted-average method compared with FIFO.

Cost of units completed and, hence, operating income, can differ materially between the weighted-average and FIFO methods when (1) direct material or conversion cost per equivalent unit varies significantly from period to period and (2) physical-inventory levels of work in process are large in relation to the total number of units transferred out of the process. As companies move toward long-term procurement contracts that reduce differences in unit costs from period to period and reduce inventory levels, the difference in cost of units completed under the weighted-average and FIFO methods will decrease.[2]

[2] For example, suppose beginning work-in-process inventory for March were 125 physical units (instead of 225), and suppose costs per equivalent unit of work done in the current period (March) were direct materials, Rs 750, and conversion costs, Rs 550. Assume that all other data for March are the same as in our example. In this case, the cost of units completed and transferred out would be Rs 5,88,330 under the weighted-average method and Rs 5,30,000 under the FIFO method. The work-in-process ending inventory would be Rs 1,04,170 under the weighted-average method and Rs 1,02,500 under the FIFO method (calculations not shown). These differences are much smaller than in the chapter example. The weighted-average ending inventory is higher than the FIFO ending inventory by only Rs 1,670 (Rs 1,04,170 − Rs 1,02,500), or 1.6% (Rs 1,670 ÷ Rs 1,02,500 = 0.016, or 1.6%), compared with 4.9% higher in the chapter example.

Managers use information from process-costing systems to aid them in pricing and product-mix decisions and to provide them with feedback about their performance. FIFO provides managers with information about changes in costs per unit from one period to the next. Managers can use this information to adjust selling prices based on current conditions (for example, based on the Rs 720 direct material cost and Rs 520 conversion cost in March). They can also more easily evaluate performance in the current period compared with a budget or relative to performance in the previous period (for example, recognizing the decline in both unit direct material and conversion costs relative to the prior period). By focusing on work done and costs of work done during the current period, the FIFO method provides useful information for these planning and control purposes.

The weighted-average method merges unit costs from different accounting periods, obscuring period-to-period comparisons. For example, the weighted-average method would lead managers at Pacific Electronics to make decisions based on the Rs 756 direct materials and Rs 544 conversion costs, rather than the costs of Rs 720 and Rs 520 prevailing in the current period. Advantages of the weighted-average method, however, are its relative computational simplicity and its reporting of a more-representative average unit cost when input prices fluctuate markedly from month to month.

Activity-based costing plays a significant role in our study of job costing, but how is activity-based costing related to process costing? Each process—assembly, testing, and so on—can be considered a different (production) activity. However, no additional activities need to be identified within each process. That's because products are homogeneous and use resources of each process in a uniform way. The bottom line: activity-based costing has less applicability in process-costing environments. *The appendix illustrates the use of the standard costing method for the assembly department.*

Decision Point

What are the weighted-average and first-in, first-out (FIFO) methods of process costing? Under what conditions will they yield different levels of operating income?

Transferred-In Costs in Process Costing

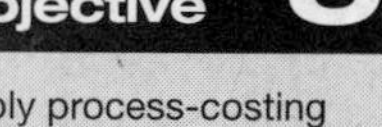

Learning Objective 5

Apply process-costing methods to situations with transferred-in costs

. . . using weighed-average and FIFO methods

Many process-costing systems have two or more departments or processes in the production cycle. As units move from department to department, the related costs are also transferred by monthly journal entries. **Transferred-in costs** (also called **previous-department costs**) are costs incurred in previous departments that are carried forward as the product's cost when it moves to a subsequent process in the production cycle.

We now extend our Pacific Electronics example to the Testing Department. As the assembly process is completed, the Assembly Department of Pacific Electronics immediately transfers SG-40 units to the Testing Department. In Testing, units receive additional direct materials at the *end* of the process, crating and other packing materials to prepare units for shipment. Conversion costs are added evenly during the Testing Department's process. As units are completed in Testing, they are immediately transferred to Finished Goods. Computation of Testing Department costs consists of transferred-in costs, as well as direct materials and conversion costs that are added in Testing.

The following diagram represents these facts:

Conversion costs added evenly during process

Assembly Department → Transfer → Testing Department → Finished Goods

Direct materials added at end of process

Data for the Testing Department for March 2012 are:

	A	B	C	D	E
1		Physical Units (SG-40s)	Transferred-in Costs	Direct Materials	Conversion Costs
2	Work in process, beginning inventory (March 1)	240	Rs 3,36,000	Rs 0	Rs 1,80,000
3	Degree of completion of beginning work in process		100%	0%	62.5%
4	Transferred in during March	400			
5	Completed and transferred out during March	440			
6	Work in process, ending inventory (March 31)	200			
7	Degree of completion of ending work in process		100%	0%	80 %
8	Total costs added during March				
9	Direct materials and conversion costs			Rs 1,32,000	Rs 4,86,000
10	Transferred in (Weighted-average from Exhibit 17-5)[a]		Rs 5,20,000		
11	Transferred in (FIFO from Exhibit 17-7)[a]		Rs 5,24,800		
12					
13	[a]The transferred-in costs during March are different under the weighted-average method (Exhibit 17-5) and the FIFO method (Exhibit 17-7). In our example, beginning work-in-process inventory, Rs 5,16,000 (Rs 3,36,000 + Rs 0 + Rs 1,80,000) is the same under both the weighted-average and FIFO inventory methods because we assume costs per equivalent unit to be the same in both January and February. If costs per equivalent unit had been different in the two months, work-in-process inventory at the end of February (beginning of March) would be costed differently under the weighted-average and FIFO methods. The basic approach to process costing with transferred-in costs, however, would still be the same as what we describe in this section.				

Transferred-in costs are treated as if they are a separate type of direct material added at the beginning of the process. When successive departments are involved, transferred units from one department become all or a part of the direct materials of the next department; however, they are called transferred-in costs, not direct material costs.

Transferred-In Costs and the Weighted-Average Method

To examine the weighted-average process-costing method with transferred-in costs, we use the five-step procedure described earlier to assign costs of the Testing Department to units completed and transferred out and to units in ending work in process.

Exhibit 17-8 shows steps 1 and 2. The computations are similar to the calculations of equivalent units under the weighted-average method for the Assembly Department in Exhibit 17-4, but here we also have transferred-in costs as an additional input. All units,

Exhibit 17-8 Steps 1 and 2: Summarize Output in Physical Units and Compute Output in Equivalent Units Using Weighted-Average Method of Process Costing for Testing Department of Pacific Electronics for March 2012

	A	B	C	D	E
1		(Step 1)		(Step 2)	
2				Equivalent Units	
3	Flow of Production	Physical Units	Transferred-in Costs	Direct Materials	Conversion Costs
4	Work in process, beginning	240			
5	Transferred in during current period	400			
6	To account for	640			
7	Completed and transferred out during current period	440	440	440	440
8	Work in process, ending[a]	200			
9	(200 x 100%; 200 x 0%; 200 x 80%)		200	0	160
10	Accounted for	640			
11	Work done to date		640	440	600
12					
13	[a]Degree of completion in this department; transferred-in costs, 100%; direct materials, 0%; conversion costs, 80%.				

Exhibit 17-9 Steps 3, 4, and 5: Summarize Total Costs to Account For, Compute Cost per Equivalent Unit, and Assign Total Costs to Units Completed and to Units in Ending Work in Process Using Weighted-Average Method of Process Costing for Testing Department of Pacific Electronics for March 2012

File Edit View Insert Format Tools Data Window Help

	A	B	C	D	E	F
1			**Total Production Costs**	**Transferred-in Costs**	**Direct Materials**	**Conversion Costs**
2	**(Step 3)**	Work in process, beginning	Rs 5,16,000	Rs 3,36,000	Rs 0	Rs1,80,000
3		Costs added in current period	11,38,000	5,20,000	1,32,000	4,86,000
4		Total costs to account for	Rs16,54,000	Rs8,56,000	Rs1,32,000	Rs 6,66,000
5						
6	**(Step 4)**	Costs incurred to date		Rs 8,56,000	Rs 1,32,000	Rs 6,66,000
7		Divide by equivalent units of work done to date (Exhibit 17-11)		÷ 640	÷ 440	÷ 600
8		Cost per equivalent unit of work done to date		Rs 1,337.5	Rs 300.0	Rs 1,110.0
9						
10	**(Step [illegible])**	Assignment of costs:				
11		Completed and transferred out (440 units)	Rs12,08,900	(440[a] x Rs1,337.5) +	(440[a] x Rs 300) +	(440[a] x Rs1,110)
12		Work in process, ending (200 units):	4,45,100	(200[b] x Rs1,337.5) +	(0[b] x Rs 300) +	(160[b] x Rs1,110)
13		Total costs accounted for	Rs16,54,000	Rs 8,56,000 +	Rs1,32,000 +	Rs 6,66,000
14						
15	[a]Equivalent units completed and transferred out from Exhibit 17-11, step 2.					
16	[b]Equivalent units in ending work in process from Exhibit 17-11, step 2.					

whether completed and transferred out during the period or in ending work in process, are fully completed as to transferred-in costs carried forward from the previous process. But direct material costs have a zero degree of completion in both beginning and ending work-in-process inventories because, in Testing, direct materials are introduced at the *end* of the process.

Exhibit 17-9 describes steps 3, 4, and 5 for the weighted-average method. Beginning work in process and work done in the current period are combined for purposes of computing cost per equivalent unit for transferred-in costs, direct material costs, and conversion costs.

The journal entry for the transfer from Testing to Finished Goods (see Exhibit 17-9) is:

Finished Goods Control	12,08,900	
Work in Process—Testing		12,08,900
To record cost of goods completed and transferred from Testing to Finished Goods.		

Entries in the Work in Process—Testing account (see Exhibit 17-9) are:

Work in Process—Testing

Beginning inventory, March 1	5,16,000	Transferred out	12,08,900
Transferred-in costs	5,20,000		
Direct materials	1,32,000		
Conversion costs	4,86,000		
Ending inventory, March 31	4,45,100		

Transferred-In Costs and the FIFO Method

To examine the FIFO process-costing method with transferred-in costs, we again use the five-step procedure. Exhibit 17-10 shows steps 1 and 2. Other than considering transferred-in costs, computations of equivalent units are the same as under the FIFO method for the Assembly Department shown in Exhibit 17-6.

Exhibit 17-11 describes steps 3, 4, and 5. In step 3, total costs to account for of Rs 16,58,800 under the FIFO method differs from the corresponding amount under the weighted-average method of Rs16,54,000. That's because of different costs of completed

Exhibit 17-10 Steps 1 and 2: Summarize Output in Physical Units and Compute Output in Equivalent Units Using FIFO Method of Process Costing for Testing Department of Pacific Electronics for March 2012

	A	B	C	D	E
1		(Step 1)		(Step 2)	
2				Equivalent Units	
3	Flow of Production	Physical Units	Transferred-in Costs	Direct Materials	Conversion Costs
4	Work in process, beginning	240		(work done before current period)	
5	Transferred in during current period	400			
6	To account for	640			
7	Completed and transferred out during current period:				
8	From beginning work in process[a]	240			
9	[240 x (100% – 100%); 240 x (100% – 0%); 240 x (100% – 62.5%)]		0	240	90
10	Started and completed	200[b]			
11	(200 x 100%; 200 x 100%; 200 x 100%)		200	200	200
12	Work in process, ending[c]	200			
13	(200 x 100%; 200 x 0%; 200 x 80%)		200	0	160
14	Accounted for	640			
15	Work done in current period only		400	440	450
16					
17	[a]Degree of completion in this department: Transferred-in costs, 100%; direct materials, 0%; conversion costs, 62.5%.				
18	[b]440 physical units completed and transferred out minus 240 physical units completed and transferred out from beginning				
19	work-in-process inventory.				
20	[c]Degree of completion in this department: Transferred-in costs, 100%; direct materials, 0%; conversion costs, 80%.				

units transferred in from the Assembly Department under the two methods—Rs 5,24,800 under FIFO and Rs 5,20,000 under weighted average. Cost per equivalent unit for the current period in step 4 is calculated on the basis of costs transferred in and work done in the current period only. Step 5 then accounts for the total costs of Rs 16,55,800 by assigning them to the units transferred out and those in ending work in process. Again, other than considering transferred-in costs, the calculations mirror those under the FIFO method for the Assembly Department shown in Exhibit 17-7.

Remember that in a series of interdepartmental transfers, each department is regarded as separate and distinct for accounting purposes. The journal entry for the transfer from Testing to Finished Goods (see Exhibit 17-11) is:

Finished Goods Control	12,23,600	
Work in Process—Testing		12,23,600
To record cost of goods completed and transferred from Testing to Finished Goods.		

Entries in the Work in Process—Testing account (see Exhibit 17-11) are:

Work in Process—Testing

Beginning inventory, March 1	5,16,000	Transferred out	12,23,600
Transferred-in costs	5,24,800		
Direct materials	1,32,000		
Conversion costs	4,86,000		
Ending inventory, March 31	4,35,200		

Points to Remember About Transferred-In Costs

Some points to remember when accounting for transferred-in costs are:

1. Be sure to include transferred-in costs from previous departments in your calculations.
2. In calculating costs to be transferred on a FIFO basis, do not overlook costs assigned in the previous period to units that were in process at the beginning of the current

Exhibit 17-11 Steps 3, 4, and 5: Summarize Total Costs to Account For, Compute Cost per Equivalent Unit, and Assign Total Costs to Units Completed and to Units in Ending Work in Process Using FIFO Method of Process Costing for Testing Department of Pacific Electronics for March 2009

	A	B	C	D	E	F
1			Total Production Costs	Transferred-in Cost	Direct Material	Conversion Costs
2	(Step 3)	Work in process, beginning	Rs5,16,000	Rs3,36,000	Rs 0	Rs 1,80,000
3		Costs added in current period	11,42,800	5,24,800	1,32,000	4,86,000
4		Total costs to account for	Rs 16,58,800	Rs 8,60,800	Rs 1,32,000	Rs 6,66,000
5						
6	(Step 4)	Costs added in current period		Rs 5,24,800	Rs 1,32,000	Rs 4,86,000
7		Divide by equivalent units of work done in current period (Exhibit 17-13)		÷ 400	÷ 440	÷ 450
8		Cost per equivalent unit of work done in current period		Rs1,312.0	Rs 300	Rs 1,080
9						
10	(Step 5)	Assignment of costs:				
11		Completed and transferred out (440 units)				
12		Work in process, beginning (240 units)	Rs 5,16,000	Rs 3,36,000 +	Rs 0 +	Rs 1,80,000
13		Costs added to beginning work in process in current period	1,69,200	(0[a] x Rs1,312.0) +	(240[a] x Rs 300)+	(90[a] x Rs 1,080)
14		Total from beginning inventory	6,85,200			
15		Started and completed (200 units)	5,38,400	(200[b] x Rs1,312.0) +	(200[b] x Rs 300)+	(200[b] x Rs 1,080)
16		Total costs of units completed and transferred out	12,23,600			
17		Work in process, ending (200 units):	4,35,200	(200[c] x Rs 1,312.0)+	(0[c] x Rs 300)+	(160[c] x Rs 1,080)
18		Total costs accounted for	Rs 16,58,800	Rs 8,60,800 +	Rs 1,32,000 +	Rs 6,66,000
19						
20	[a]Equivalent units used to complete beginning work in process from Exhibit 17-13, step 2.					
21	[b]Equivalent units started and completed from Exhibit 17-13, step 2.					
22	[c]Equivalent units in ending work in process from Exhibit 17-13, step 2.					

period but are now included in the units transferred. For example, do not overlook the Rs 5,16,000 in Exhibit 17-11.

3. Unit costs may fluctuate between periods. Therefore, transferred units may contain batches accumulated at different unit costs. For example, the 400 units transferred in at Rs 5,24,800 in Exhibit 17-11 using the FIFO method consist of units that have different unit costs of direct materials and conversion costs when these units were worked on in the Assembly Department (see Exhibit 17-7). Remember, however, that when these units are transferred to the Testing Department, they are costed at *one average unit cost* of Rs 1,312 (Rs 5,24,800 ÷ 400 units), as in Exhibit 17-11.
4. Units may be measured in different denominations in different departments. Consider each department separately. For example, unit costs could be based on kilograms in the first department and litres in the second department. Accordingly, as units are received in the second department, their measurements must be converted to litres.

How are the weighted-average and FIFO process-costing methods applied to transferred-in costs?

Hybrid Costing Systems

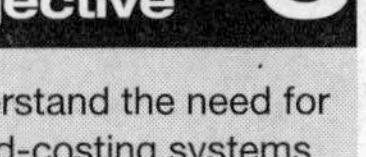

Understand the need for hybrid-costing systems such as operation-costing

. . . when product-costing does not fall into job-costing or process-costing categories

Product-costing systems do not always fall neatly into either job-costing or process-costing categories. Consider Ford Motor Company. Automobiles may be manufactured in a continuous flow (suited to process costing), but individual units may be customized with a special combination of engine size, transmission, music system, and so on (which requires job costing). A **hybrid-costing system** blends characteristics from both job-costing and process-costing systems. Product-costing systems often must be designed to fit the particular characteristics of different production systems. Many production systems are a hybrid: They have some features of custom-order manufacturing and other features of mass-production manufacturing. Manufacturers of a relatively wide variety of closely related standardized products (for example, televisions, dishwashers, and washing machines) tend to use hybrid-costing systems. The following Concepts in Action feature describes a hybrid-costing system at Adidas. The next section explains *operation costing*, a common type of hybrid-costing system.

Concepts in Action

Hybrid Costing for Customized Shoes at Adidas

Adidas has been designing and manufacturing athletic footwear for nearly 90 years. Although shoemakers have long individually crafted shoes for professional athletes like Reggie Bush of the New Orleans Saints, Adidas took this concept a step further when it initiated the *mi adidas* program. *Mi adidas* gives customers the opportunity to create shoes to their exact personal specifications for function, fit, and aesthetics. *Mi adidas* is available in retail stores around the world, and in special *mi adidas* "Performance Stores" in cities such as New York, Chicago, and San Francisco.

The process works as follows: The customer goes to a *mi adidas* station, where a salesperson develops an in-depth customer profile, a 3-D computer scanner develops a scan of the customer's feet, and the customer selects from among 90 to 100 different styles and colors for his or her modularly designed shoe. During the three-step, 30-minute high-tech process, *mi adidas* experts take customers through the "mi fit," "mi performance," and "mi design" phases, resulting in a customized shoe to fit their needs. The resulting data are transferred to an Adidas plant, where small, multiskilled teams produce the customized shoe. The measuring and fitting process is free, but purchasing your own specially made shoes costs between $40 and $65 on top of the normal retail price, depending on the style.

Historically, costs associated with individually customized products have fallen into the domain of job costing. Adidas, however, uses a hybrid-costing system—job costing for the material and customizable components that customers choose and process costing to account for the conversion costs of production. The cost of making each pair of shoes is calculated by accumulating all production costs and dividing by the number of shoes made. In other words, even though each pair of shoes is different, the conversion cost of each pair is assumed to be the same.

The combination of customization with certain features of mass production is called mass customization. It is the consequence of being able to digitize information that individual customers indicate is important to them. Various products that companies are now able to customize within a mass-production setting (for example, personal computers, blue jeans, bicycles) still require job costing of materials and considerable human intervention. However, as manufacturing systems become flexible, companies are also using process costing to account for the standardized conversion costs.

Sources: Adidas. 2010. New Orleans Saints running back Reggie Bush designs custom Adidas shoes to aid in Haiti relief efforts. AG press release. Portland, OR: February 5; Kamenev, Marina. 2006. Adidas' high tech footwear. *BusinessWeek.com*, November 3; Seifert, Ralf. 2003. The "mi adidas" mass customization initiative. IMD No. 159. Lausanne, Switzerland: International Institute for Management Development.

Overview of Operation-Costing Systems

An **operation** is a standardized method or technique that is performed repetitively, often on different materials, resulting in different finished goods. Multiple operations are usually conducted within a department. For instance, a suit maker may have a cutting operation and a hemming operation within a single department. The term *operation*, however, is often used loosely. It may be a synonym for a department or process. For example, some companies may call their finishing department a finishing process or a finishing operation.

An **operation-costing system** is a hybrid-costing system applied to batches of similar, but not identical, products. Each batch of products is often a variation of a single design, and it proceeds through a sequence of operations. Within each operation, all product units are treated exactly alike, using identical amounts of the operation's resources. A key point in the operation system is that each batch does not necessarily move through the same operations as other batches. Batches are also called production runs.

In a company that makes suits, management may select a single basic design for every suit to be made, but depending on specifications, each batch of suits varies somewhat from other batches. Batches may vary with respect to the material used or the type of stitching. Semiconductors, textiles, and shoes are also manufactured in batches and may have similar variations from batch to batch.

An operation-costing system uses work orders that specify the needed direct materials and step-by-step operations. Product costs are compiled for each work order. Direct materials that are unique to different work orders are specifically identified with the appropriate work order, as in job costing. However, each unit is assumed to use an identical amount of conversion costs for a given operation, as in process costing. A single average conversion cost per unit is calculated for each operation, by dividing total conversion costs for that operation by the number of units that pass through it. This average cost is then assigned to each unit passing through the operation. Units that do not pass through an operation are not allocated any costs of that operation. Our examples assume only two cost categories—direct materials and conversion costs—but operation costing can have more than two cost categories. Costs in each category are identified with specific work orders using job-costing or process-costing methods as appropriate.

Managers find operation costing useful in cost management because operation costing focuses on control of physical processes, or operations, of a given production system. For example, in clothing manufacturing, managers are concerned with fabric waste, how many fabric layers that can be cut at one time, and so on. Operation costing measures, in financial terms, how well managers have controlled physical processes.

Illustration of an Operation-Costing System

The Baltimore Clothing Company, a clothing manufacturer, produces two lines of blazers for department stores: those made of wool and those made of polyester. Wool blazers use better-quality materials and undergo more operations than polyester blazers do. Operations information on work order 423 for 50 wool blazers and work order 424 for 100 polyester blazers is as follows:

	Work Order 423	Work Order 424
Direct materials	Wool	Polyester
	Satin full lining	Rayon partial lining
	Bone buttons	Plastic buttons
Operations		
1. Cutting cloth	Use	Use
2. Checking edges	Use	Do not use
3. Sewing body	Use	Use
4. Checking seams	Use	Do not use
5. Machine sewing of collars and lapels	Do not use	Use
6. Hand sewing of collars and lapels	Use	Do not use

Cost data for these work orders, started and completed in March 2012, are as follows:

	Work Order 423	Work Order 424
Number of blazers	50	100
Direct material costs	Rs 60,000	Rs 30,000
Conversion costs allocated:		
Operation 1	5,800	11,600
Operation 2	4,000	—
Operation 3	19,000	38,000
Operation 4	5,000	—
Operation 5	—	8,750
Operation 6	7,000	—
Total manufacturing costs	Rs1,00,800	Rs 88,350

As in process costing, all product units in any work order are assumed to consume identical amounts of conversion costs of a particular operation. Baltimore's operation-costing system uses a budgeted rate to calculate the conversion costs of each operation. The budgeted rate for Operation 1 (amounts assumed) is as follows:

$$\text{Operation 1 budgeted conversion-cost rate for 2012} = \frac{\text{Operation 1 budgeted conversion costs for 2012}}{\text{Operation 1 budgeted product units for 2012}}$$

$$= \frac{\text{Rs } 23{,}20{,}000}{20{,}000 \text{ units}}$$

$$= \text{Rs } 116 \text{ per unit}$$

Budgeted conversion costs of Operation 1 include labor, power, repairs, supplies, depreciation, and other overhead of this operation. If some units have not been completed (so all units in Operation 1 have not received the same amounts of conversion costs), the conversion-cost rate is computed by dividing budgeted conversion costs by *equivalent units* of conversion costs, as in process costing.

As goods are manufactured, conversion costs are allocated to the work orders processed in Operation 1 by multiplying the Rs 116 conversion cost per unit by the number of units processed. Conversion costs of Operation 1 for 50 wool blazers (work order 423) are Rs 116 per blazer × 50 blazers = Rs 5,800, and for 100 polyester blazers (work order 424) are Rs 116 per blazer × 100 blazers = Rs 11,600. When equivalent units are used to calculate the conversion-cost rate, costs are allocated to work orders by multiplying conversion cost per equivalent unit by number of equivalent units in the work order. Direct material costs of Rs 60,000 for the 50 wool blazers (work order 423) and Rs 30,000 for the 100 polyester blazers (work order 424) are specifically identified with each order, as in job costing. Remember the basic point in operation costing: Operation unit costs are assumed to be the same regardless of the work order, but direct material costs vary across orders when the materials for each work order vary.

Journal Entries

Actual conversion costs for Operation 1 in March 2012—assumed to be Rs 2,44,000, including actual costs incurred for work order 423 and work order 424—are entered into a Conversion Costs Control account:

1. Conversion Costs Control	2,44,000	
Various accounts (such as Wages Payable Control and Accumulated Depreciation)		2,44,000

Summary journal entries for assigning costs to polyester blazers (work order 424) follow. Entries for wool blazers would be similar. Of the Rs 30,000 of direct materials for work order 424, Rs 29,750 are used in Operation 1, and the remaining Rs 250 of materials are used in another operation. The journal entry to record direct materials used for the 100 polyester blazers in March 2012 is as follows:

2. Work in Process, Operation 1	29,750	
Materials Inventory Control		29,750

The journal entry to record the allocation of conversion costs to products uses the budgeted rate of Rs 116 per blazer times the 100 polyester blazers processed, or Rs 11,600:

3. Work in Process, Operation 1	11,600	
Conversion Costs Allocated		11,600

The journal entry to record the transfer of the 100 polyester blazers (at a cost of Rs 29,750 + Rs 11,600) from Operation 1 to Operation 3 (polyester blazers do not go through Operation 2) is as follows:

4. Work in Process, Operation 3	41,350	
Work in Process, Operation 1		41,350

After posting these entries, the Work in Process, Operation 1, account appears as follows:

Work in Process, Operation 1

(2) Direct materials	29,750	(4) Transferred to Operation 3	41,350
(3) Conversion costs allocated	11,600		
Ending inventory, March 31	0		

Costs of the blazers are transferred through the operations in which blazers are worked on and then to finished goods in the usual manner. Costs are added throughout the fiscal year in the Conversion Costs Control account and the Conversion Costs Allocated account. Any overallocation or underallocation of conversion costs is disposed of in the same way as overallocated or underallocated manufacturing overhead in a job-costing system.

Problem for Self-Study

Allied Chemicals operates a thermo-assembly process as the second of three processes at its plastics plant. Direct materials in thermo-assembly are added at the end of the process. Conversion costs are added evenly during the process. The following data pertain to the Thermo-Assembly Department for June 2012:

	A	B	C	D	E
1		Physical Units	Transferred-in Costs	Direct Materials	Conversion Costs
2	Work in process, beginning inventory	50,000			
3	Degree of completion of beginning work in process		100%	0%	80%
4	Transferred in during current period	2,00,000			
5	Completed and transferred out during current period	2,10,000			
6	Work in process, ending inventory	?			
7	Degree of completion of ending work in process		100%	0%	40%

Compute equivalent units under (1) the weighted-average method and (2) the FIFO method. **Required**

Solution

1. The weighted-average method uses equivalent units of work done to date to compute cost per equivalent unit. The calculations of equivalent units follow:

	A	B	C	D	E
1		(Step 1)		(Step 2)	
2				Equivalent Units	
3	Flow of Production	Physical Units	Transferred-in Costs	Direct Materials	Conversion Costs
4	Work in process, beginning (given)	50,000			
5	Transferred in during current period (given)	2,00,000			
6	To account for	2,50,000			
7	Completed and transferred out during current period	2,10,000	2,10,000	2,10,000	2,10,000
8	Work in process, ending[a]	40,000[b]			
9	(40,000 x 100%; 40,000 x 0%; 40,000 x 40%)		40,000	0	16,000
10	Accounted for	2,50,000			
11	Work done to date		2,50,000	2,10,000	2,26,000
12					
13	[a]Degree of completion in this department: Transferred-in costs, 100%; direct materials, 0%; conversion costs, 40%.				
14	[b]2,50,000 physical units to account for minus 2,10,000 physical units completed and transferred out				

2. The FIFO method uses equivalent units of work done in the current period only to compute cost per equivalent unit. The calculations of equivalent units follow:

File Edit View Insert Format Tools Data Window Help

	A	B	C	D	E
1		(Step 1)		(Step 2)	
2				Equivalent Units	
3	Flow of Production	Physical Units	Transferred-in Costs	Direct Materials	Conversion Costs
4	Work in process, beginning (given)	50,000			
5	Transferred in during current period (given)	2,00,000			
6	To account for	2,50,000			
7	Completed and transferred out during current period:				
8	From beginning work in process[a]	50,000			
9	[50,000 x (100% - 100%); 50,000 x (100% - 0%); 50,000 x (100% - 80%)]		0	50,000	10,000
10	Started and completed	1,60,000[b]			
11	(1,60,000 x 100%; 1,60,000 x 100%; 1,60,000 x 100%)		1,60,000	1,60,000	1,60,000
12	Work in process, ending[c]	40,000[d]			
13	(40,000 x 100%; 40,000 x 0%; 40,000 x 40%)		40,000	0	16,000
14	Accounted for	2,50,000			
15	Work done in current period only		2,00,000	2,10,000	1,86,000
16					
17	[a]Degree of completion in this department: Transferred-in costs, 100%; direct materials, 0%; conversion costs, 80%.				
18	[b]2,10,000 physical units completed and transferred out minus 50,000 physical units completed and transferred out from beginning work-in-process inventory.				
19	[c]Degree of completion in this department: Transferred-in costs, 100%; direct materials, 0%; conversion costs, 40%.				
20	[d]2,50,000 physical units to account for minus 2,10,000 physical units completed and transferred out.				

Decision Points

The following question-and-answer format summarizes the chapter's learning objectives. Each decision presents a key question related to a learning objective. The guidelines are the answer to that question.

Decision	Guidelines
1. Under what conditions is a process-costing system used?	A process-costing system is used to determine cost of a product or service when masses of identical or similar units are produced. Industries using process-costing systems include food, textiles, and oil refining.
2. What are the five steps in a process-costing system to assign costs to units completed and to units in ending work in process?	The five steps in a process-costing system are (1) summarize the flow of physical units of output, (2) compute output in terms of equivalent units, (3) summarize total costs to account for, (4) compute cost per equivalent unit, and (5) assign total costs to units completed and to units in ending work in process.
3. What are equivalent units and what role do they play in the process-costing sequence?	Equivalent units is a derived amount of output units that (a) takes the quantity of each input (factor of production) in units completed or in incomplete units in work in process and (b) converts the quantity of input into the amount of completed output units that could be made with that quantity of input. Equivalent-unit calculations are necessary when all physical units of output are not uniformly completed during an accounting period.
4. What is the weighted-average method of process costing?	The weighted-average method computes unit costs by dividing total costs in the work-in-process account (whether from beginning work in process or from work started during the period) by total equivalent units completed to date, and it assigns this average cost to units completed and to units in ending work-in-process inventory.

5. What is the first-in, first-out method of process costing?

   The first-in, first-out (FIFO) method computes unit costs based on costs incurred during the current period and equivalent units of work done in the current period. It assigns the costs of beginning work-in-process inventory to the first units completed, and it assigns costs of the equivalent units worked on during the current period first to complete beginning inventory, next to start and complete new units, and finally to units in ending work-in-process inventory.

6. How does the standard-costing method simplify process costing?

   Under this method, standard costs serve as the cost per equivalent unit for assigning cost to units completed and to units in ending work-in-process inventory.

7. How are the weighted-average and FIFO process-costing methods applied to transferred-in costs?

   The weighted-average method computes transferred-in costs per unit by dividing total transferred-in costs to date by total equivalent transferred-in units completed to date, and it assigns this average cost to units completed and to units in ending work-in-process inventory. The FIFO method computes transferred-in costs per unit based on costs transferred in during the current period and equivalent units of transferred-in costs of work done in the current period. The FIFO method assigns transferred-in costs in beginning work in process to units completed and costs transferred in during the current period first to complete beginning inventory, next to start and complete new units, and finally to units in ending work-in-process inventory.

APPENDIX: STANDARD-COSTING METHOD OF PROCESS COSTING

Chapter 7 described accounting in a standard-costing system. Recall that this involves making entries using standard costs and then isolating variances from these standards in order to support management control. This appendix describes how the principles of standard costing can be employed in process-costing systems.

Benefits of Standard Costing

Companies that use process-costing systems produce masses of identical or similar units of output. In such companies, it is fairly easy to set standards for quantities of inputs needed to produce output. Standard cost per input unit can then be multiplied by input quantity standards to develop standard cost per output unit.

The weighted-average and FIFO methods become very complicated when used in process industries that produce a wide variety of similar products. For example, a steel-rolling mill uses various steel alloys and produces sheets of various sizes and finishes. The different types of direct materials used and the operations performed are few, but used in various combinations, they yield a wide variety of products. Similarly, complex conditions are frequently found, for example, in plants that manufacture rubber products, textiles, ceramics, paints, and packaged food products. In each of these cases, if the broad averaging procedure of *actual* process costing were used, the result would be inaccurate costs for each product. Therefore, the standard-costing method of process costing is widely used in these industries.

Under the standard-costing method, teams of design and process engineers, operations personnel, and management accountants work together to determine *separate* standard costs per equivalent unit on the basis of different technical processing specifications for each product. Identifying standard costs for each product overcomes the disadvantage of costing all products at a single average amount, as under actual costing.

Computations Under Standard Costing

We return to the assembly department of Pacific Electronics, but this time we use standard costs. Assume the same standard costs apply in February and March of 2012. Data for the assembly department are as follows:

	A	B	C	D	E
1		Physical Units (SG-40s) (1)	Direct Materials (2)	Conversion Costs (3)	Total Costs (4) = (2) + (3)
2	Standard cost per unit		Rs 740	Rs 540	
3	Work in process, beginning inventory (March 1)	225			
4	Degree of completion of beginning work in process		100%	60%	
5	Beginning work in process inventory at standard costs		Rs 1,66,500[a]	Rs 72,900[a]	Rs 2,39,400
6	Started during March	275			
7	Completed and transferred out during March	400			
8	Work in process, ending inventory (March 31)	100			
9	Degree of completion of ending work in process		100%	50%	
10	Actual total costs added during March		Rs 1,98,000	Rs 1,63,800	Rs 3,61,800
11					
12	[a]Work in process, beginning inventory at standard costs				
13	Direct materials: 225 physical units × 100% completed × Rs 740 per unit = Rs 1,66,500				
14	Conversion costs: 225 physical units × 60% completed × Rs 540 per unit = Rs 72,900				

We illustrate the standard-costing method of process costing using the five-step procedure introduced earlier.

Exhibit 17-12 presents Steps 1 and 2. These steps are identical to the steps described for the FIFO method in Exhibit 17-6 because, as in FIFO, the standard-costing method also assumes that the earliest equivalent units in beginning work in process are completed first. Work done in the current period for direct materials is 275 equivalent units. Work done in the current period for conversion costs is 315 equivalent units.

Exhibit 17-13 describes Steps 3, 4, and 5. In Step 3, total costs to account for (that is, the total debits to Work in Process—Assembly) differ from total debits to Work in Process—Assembly under the actual-cost-based weighted-average and FIFO methods. That's because, as in all standard-costing systems, the debits to the Work in Process account are at standard costs, rather than actual costs. These standard costs total Rs 6,13,000 in Exhibit 17-13. In Step 4, costs per equivalent unit are standard costs: direct materials, Rs 740, and conversion

Exhibit 17-12

Steps 1 and 2: Summarize Output in Physical Units and Compute Output in Equivalent Units Using Standard-Costing Method of Process Costing for Assembly Department of Pacific Electronics for March 2012

	A	B	C	D
1		(Step 1)	(Step 2)	
2			Equivalent Units	
3	Flow of Production	Physical Units	Direct Materials	Conversion Costs
4	Work in process, beginning	225		
5	Started during current period	275		
6	To account for	500		
7	Completed and transferred out during current period:			
8	From beginning work in process[a]	225		
9	[225 × (100% – 100%); 225 × (100% – 60%)]		0	90
10	Started and completed	175[b]		
11	(175 × 100%; 175 × 100%)		175	175
12	Work in process, ending[c]	100		
13	(100 × 100%; 100 × 50%)		100	50
14	Accounted for	500		
15	Equivalent units of work done in current period		275	315
16				
17	[a]Degree of completion in this department: direct materials, 100%; conversion costs, 60%.			
18	[b]400 physical units completed and transferred out minus 225 physical units completed and transferred out from beginning work-in-process inventory.			
19	[c]Degree of completion in this department: direct materials, 100%; conversion costs, 50%.			

Exhibit 17-13 Steps 3, 4, and 5: Summarize Total Costs to Account For, Compute Cost per Equivalent Unit, and Assign Total Costs to Units Completed and to Units in Ending Work in Process Using Standard-Costing Method of Process Costing for Assembly Department of Pacific Electronics for March 2012

	A	B	C	D	E	F	G
1			Total Production Costs	Direct Materials		Conversion Costs	
2	(Step 3)	Work in process, beginning					
3		Direct materials, 225 × Rs 740; Conversion costs, 135 × Rs 540	Rs 2,39,400	Rs 1,66,500		Rs 72,900	
4		Costs added in current period at standard costs					
5		Direct materials, 275 × Rs 740; Conversion costs, 315 × Rs 540	3,73,600	2,03,500		1,70,100	
6		Total costs to account for	Rs 6,13,000	Rs 3,70,000		Rs 2,43,000	
7							
8	(Step 4)	Standard cost per equivalent unit		Rs 740		Rs 540	
9							
10	(Step 5)	Assignment of costs at standard costs:					
11		Completed and transferred out (400 units):					
12		Work in process, beginning (225 units)	Rs 2,39,400	Rs 1,66,500	+	Rs 72,900	
13		Costs added to beginning work in process in current period	48,600	(0[a] × Rs 740)	+	(90[a] × Rs 540)	
14		Total from beginning inventory	2,88,000				
15		Started and completed (175 units)	2,24,000	(175[b] × Rs 740)	+	(175[b] × Rs 540)	
16		Total costs of units completed and transferred out	5,12,000				
17		Work in process, ending (100 units):	1,01,000	(100[c] × Rs 740)	+	(50[c] × Rs 540)	
18		Total costs accounted for	Rs 6,13,000	Rs 3,70,000	+	Rs 2,43,000	
19							
20	Summary of variances for current performance:						
21	Costs added in current period at standard costs (see step 3)			Rs 2,03,500		Rs 1,70,100	
22	Actual costs incurred			Rs 1,98,000		Rs 1,63,800	
23	Variance			Rs 5,500	F	Rs 6,300	F
24							
25	[a]Equivalent units used to complete beginning work in process from Exhibit 17-12, Step 2.						
26	[b]Equivalent units started and completed from Exhibit 17-12, Step 2.						
27	[c]Equivalent units in ending work in process from Exhibit 17-12, Step 2.						

costs, Rs 540. *Therefore, costs per equivalent unit do not have to be computed as they were for the weighted-average and FIFO methods.*

Exhibit 17-13, Step 5, assigns total costs to units completed and transferred out and to units in ending work-in-process inventory, as in the FIFO method. Step 5 assigns amounts of standard costs to equivalent units calculated in Exhibit 17-12. These costs are assigned (1) first to complete beginning work-in-process inventory, (2) next to start and complete new units, and (3) finally to start new units that are in ending work-in-process inventory. Note how the Rs 6,13,000 total costs accounted for in Step 5 of Exhibit 17-13 equal total costs to account for.

Accounting for Variances

Process-costing systems using standard costs record actual direct material costs in Direct Materials Control and actual conversion costs in Conversion Costs Control (similar to Variable and Fixed Overhead Control in Chapter 8). In the journal entries that follow, the first two record these *actual costs*. In entries 3 and 4a, the Work-in-Process—Assembly account accumulates direct material costs and conversion costs at *standard costs*. Entries 3 and 4b isolate total variances. The final entry transfers out completed goods at standard costs.

		Debit	Credit
1.	Assembly Department Direct Materials Control (at actual costs)	1,98,000	
	Accounts Payable Control		1,98,000
	To record direct materials purchased and used in production during March. This cost control account is debited with actual costs.		

2. Assembly Department Conversion Costs Control (at actual costs)	1,63,800	
Various accounts such as Wages Payable Control and Accumulated Depreciation		1,63,800
To record assembly department conversion costs for March. This cost control account is debited with actual costs.		
Entries 3, 4, and 5 use standard cost amounts from Exhibit 17-13.		
3. Work in Process—Assembly (at standard costs)	2,03,500	
Direct Materials Variances		5,500
Assembly Department Direct Materials Control		1,98,000
To record standard costs of direct materials assigned to units worked on and total direct materials variances.		
4a. Work in Process—Assembly (at standard costs)	1,70,100	
Assembly Department Conversion Costs Allocated		1,70,100
To record conversion costs allocated at standard rates to the units worked on during March.		
4b. Assembly Department Conversion Costs Allocated	1,70,100	
Conversion Costs Variances		6,300
Assembly Department Conversion Costs Control		1,63,800
To record total conversion costs variances.		
5. Work in Process—Testing (at standard costs)	5,12,000	
Work in Process—Assembly (at standard costs)		5,12,000
To record standard costs of units completed and transferred out from assembly to testing.		

Variances arise under standard costing, as in entries 3 and 4b. That's because the standard costs assigned to products on the basis of work done in the current period do not equal actual costs incurred in the current period. Recall that variances that result in higher income than expected are termed favorable, while those that reduce income are unfavorable. From an accounting standpoint, favorable cost variances are credit entries, while unfavorable ones are debits. In the preceding example, both direct materials and conversion cost variances are favorable. This is also reflected in the "F" designations for both variances in Exhibit 17-13.

Variances can be analyzed in little or great detail for planning and control purposes, as described in Chapters 7 and 8. Sometimes direct materials price variances are isolated at the time direct materials are purchased and only efficiency variances are computed in entry 3. Exhibit 17-14 shows how the costs flow through the general-ledger accounts under standard costing.

Exhibit 17-14

Flow of Standard Costs in a Process-Costing System for Assembly Department of Pacific Electronics for March 2012

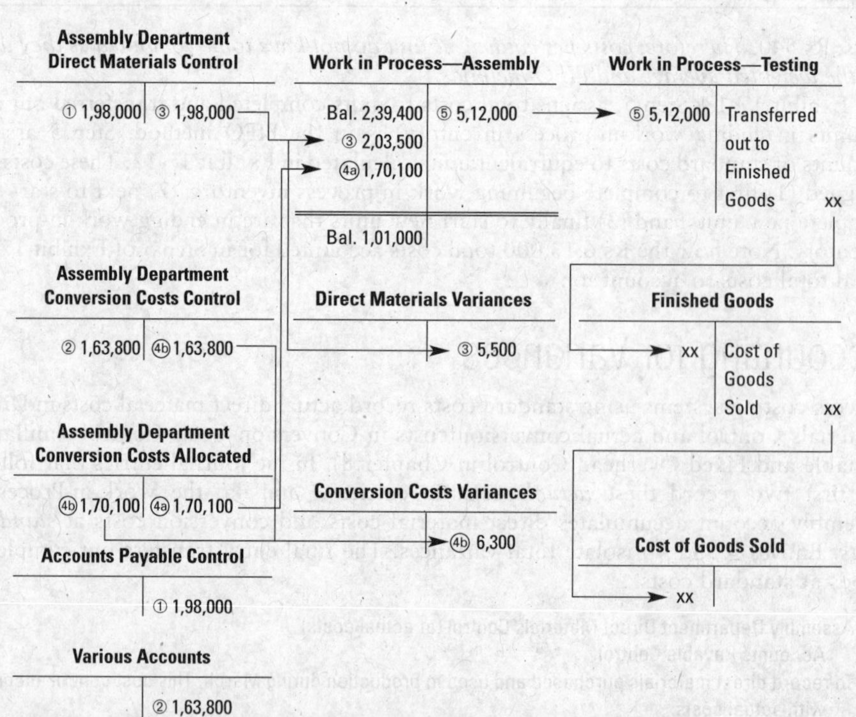

TERMS TO LEARN

This chapter and the Glossary at the end of the book contain definitions of:

equivalent units (**p. 716**)
first-in, first-out (FIFO) process-costing method (**p. 722**)
hybrid-costing system (**p. 731**)
operation (**p. 732**)
operation-costing system (**p. 732**)
previous-department costs (**p. 727**)
transferred-in costs (**p. 727**)
weighted-average process-costing method (**p. 720**)

ASSIGNMENT MATERIAL

Questions

17-1 Give three examples of industries that use process-costing systems.

17-2 In process costing, why are costs often divided into two main classifications?

17-3 Explain equivalent units. Why are equivalent-unit calculations necessary in process costing?

17-4 What problems might arise in estimating the degree of completion of semiconductor chips in a semiconductor plant?

17-5 Name the five steps in process costing when equivalent units are computed.

17-6 Name the three inventory methods commonly associated with process costing.

17-7 Describe the distinctive characteristic of weighted-average computations in assigning costs to units completed and to units in ending work in process.

17-8 Describe the distinctive characteristic of FIFO computations in assigning costs to units completed and to units in ending work in process.

17-9 Why should the FIFO method be called a modified or department FIFO method?

17-10 Identify a major advantage of the FIFO method for purposes of planning and control.

17-11 Identify the main difference between journal entries in process costing and job costing.

17-12 "The standard-costing method is particularly applicable to process-costing situations." Do you agree? Why?

17-13 Why should the accountant distinguish between transferred-in costs and additional direct material costs for each subsequent department in a process-costing system?

17-14 "Transferred-in costs are those costs incurred in the preceding accounting period." Do you agree? Explain.

17-15 "There's no reason for me to get excited about the choice between the weighted-average and FIFO methods in my process-costing system. I have long-term contracts with my materials suppliers at fixed prices." Do you agree with this statement made by a plant controller? Explain.

Solved Examples

17-16 Equivalent units, zero beginning inventory. Indian Electronics manufactures microchips in large quantities. Each microchip undergoes assembly and testing. The total assembly costs during the typical month of January were:

Direct materials used	Rs 72,00,000
Conversion costs	76,00,000
Total manufacturing costs	Rs 1,48,00,000

Required

1. Assume there was no beginning inventory on January 1. During January, 10,000 microchips were placed into production and all 10,000 were fully completed at the end of the month. What is the unit cost of an assembled microchip in January?
2. Assume that during February 10,000 microchips are placed into production. Further assume the same total assembly costs for January are also incurred in February, but only 9,000 microchips are fully completed at the end of the month. All direct materials have been added to the remaining 1,000 microchips. However, on average, these remaining 1,000 microchips are only 50% complete as to conversion costs. (a) What are the equivalent units for direct materials and conversion costs and their respective equivalent-unit costs for February? (b) What is the unit cost of an assembled microchip in the following month, February?
3. Explain the difference in your answers to requirements 1 and 2.

Solution

Equivalent units, zero beginning inventory.

1.	Direct materials cost per unit (Rs 72,00,000 ÷ 10,000)	Rs 720
	Conversion cost per unit (Rs 76,00,000 ÷ 10,000)	760
	Assembly Department cost per unit	Rs 1,480

2. a. Solution Exhibit 17-16A calculates the equivalent units of direct materials and conversion costs in the Assembly Department of International Electronics in February.
Solution Exhibit 17-16B computes equivalent units costs.

2. b.	Direct materials cost per unit	Rs 720
	Conversion cost per unit	800
	Assembly Department cost per unit	Rs 1,520

3. The difference in the Assembly Department cost per unit calculated in requirements 1 and 2 arises because the costs incurred in January and February are the same but fewer equivalent units of work are done in February relative to January. In January, all 10,000 units introduced are fully completed resulting in 10,000 equivalent units of work done with respect to direct materials and conversion costs. In February, of the 10,000 units introduced, 10,000 equivalent units of work is done with respect to direct materials but only 9,500 equivalent units of work is done with respect to conversion costs. The Assembly Department cost per unit is, therefore, higher.

Solution Exhibit 17-16A

Steps 1 and 2: Summarize Output in Physical Units and Compute Equivalent units: Assembly Department of Indian Electronics for February:

	(Step 1) Physical Units	(Step 2) Equivalent Units Direct Materials	Conversion Costs
Flow of Production			
Work in process, beginning	0		
Started during current period	10,000		
To account for	10,000		
Completed and transferred out during current period	9,000	9,000	9,000
Work in process, ending*	1,000		
1,000 × 100%; 1,000 × 50%		1,000	500
Accounted for	10,000		
Work done in current period only		10,000	9,500

*Degree of completion in this department: direct materials, 100%; conversion costs, 50%.

Solution Exhibit 17-16B

Compute Equivalent Unit Costs, Assembly Department of Indian Electronics for February:

		Total Production Costs	Direct Materials	Conversion Costs
Step 3	Costs added during February	Rs 1,48,00,000	Rs 72,00,000	Rs 76,00,000
	Divide by equivalent units of work done in current period (Solution Exhibit 17-16A)		÷ 10,000	÷ 9,500
	Cost per equivalent unit		Rs 720	Rs 800

17-17 Journal entries (continuation of 17-16). Refer to requirement 2 of Example 17-16.

Required Prepare summary journal entries for the use of direct materials and incurrence of conversion costs. Also prepare a journal entry to transfer out the cost of goods completed. Show the postings to the Work-in-Process account.

Solution

Journal entries (continuation of 17-16).

	Rs	Rs
1. Work in Process—*Assembly*	72,00,000	
Accounts Payable		72,00,000
To record Rs 72,00,000 of direct materials purchased and used in production during February		
2. Work in Process—*Assembly*	76,00,000	
Various accounts		76,00,000
To record Rs 76,00,000 of conversion costs for February; examples include energy, manufacturing supplies, all manufacturing labor, and plant depreciation		

3. Work in Process—Testing 1,36,80,000
   Work in Process—*Assembly* 1,36,80,000
   To record 9,000 units completed and transferred from Assembly to Testing during February at Rs 1,520 × 9,000 units = Rs 1,36,80,000

Postings to the Work in Process—Assembly account follow.

Work in Process — Assembly Department

Beginning inventory, Feb. 10		***3. Transferred out to***	
1. Direct materials	Rs 72,00,000	Work in Process—Testing	Rs 1,36,80,000
2. Conversion costs	76,00,000		
Ending inventory, Feb.	11,20,000		

17-18 Weighted-average method, equivalent units. Consider the following data for the Satellite Assembly Division of Aerospatiale:

The Satellite Assembly Division uses the weighted-average method of process costing.

	Physical Units (Satellites)	Direct Materials	Conversion Costs
Beginning work in process (May 1)[a]	8	Rs 49,33,600	Rs 9,10,400
Started in May	50		
Completed during May	46		
Continued			

	Physical Units (Satellites)	Direct Materials	Conversion Costs
Ending work in process (May 31)[b]	12		
Costs added during May		Rs 3,22,00,000	Rs 1,39,20,000

[a]Degree of completion: direct materials, 90%; conversion costs, 40%.
[b]Degree of completion: direct materials, 60%; conversion costs, 30%.

Required

Compute equivalent units for direct materials and conversion costs. Show physical units in the first column of your schedule.

Solution

Weighted-average method, equivalent units.

Under the weighted-average method, equivalent units are calculated as the equivalent units of work done to date. Solution Exhibit 17-18 shows equivalent units of work done to date for the Satellite Assembly Division of Aerospatiale for direct materials and conversion costs.

Solution Exhibit 17-18

Steps 1 and 2: Summarize Output in Physical Units and Compute Equivalent Units
Weighted-Average Method of Process Costing, Satellite Assembly Division of Aerospatiale for May:

	(Step 1)	(Step 2) Equivalent Units	
Flow of Production	Physical Units (given)	Direct Materials	Conversion Costs
Work in process beginning	8		
Started during current period	50		
To account for	58		
Completed and transferred out during current period	46	46.0	46.0
Work in process, ending* (12 × 60%; 12 × 30%)	12	7.2	3.6
Accounted for	58		
Work done to date		53.2	49.6

*Degree of completion in this department: direct materials, 60%; conversion costs, 30%.

17-19 Weighted-average method, assigning costs (continuation of 17-18).

Required

For the data in Solved example 17-18, calculate cost per equivalent unit for direct materials and conversion costs, summarize total costs to account for, and assign these costs to units completed and transferred out and to units in ending work in process.

Solution

Weighted-average method, assigning costs (continuation of 17-18).

Solution Exhibit 17-19 calculates cost per equivalent unit of work done to date in the Assembly Department of Aerospatiale, summarizes total costs to account for, and assigns costs to units completed and to units in ending work-in-process inventory.

Solution Exhibit 17-19

Steps 3, 4, and 5: Compute Equivalent Unit Costs, Summarize Total Costs to Account For, and Assign Costs to Units Completed and to Units in Ending Work in Process

Weighted-Average Method of Process Costing, Satellite Assembly Department of Aerospatiale for May:

		Total Production Costs	Direct Materials	Conversion Costs
(Step 3)	Work in process, beginning (given)	Rs 58,44,000	Rs 49,33,600	Rs 9,10,400
	Costs added in current period (given)	4,61,20,000	3,22,00,000	1,39,20,000
	Costs incurred to date		Rs 3,71,33,600	Rs 1,48,30,400
	Divide by equivalent units of work done to date (Solution Exhibit 17-18)		÷ 53.2	÷ 49.6
	Cost per equivalent unit of work done to date		Rs 6,98,000	Rs 2,99,000
(Step 4)	Total costs to account for	5,19,64,000		
(Step 5)	Assignment of costs:			
	Completed and transferred out (46 units)	4,58,62,000	(46* × Rs 6,98,000) + (46* × Rs 2,99,000)	
	Work in process, ending (12 units)			
	Direct materials	50,25,600	7.2† × Rs 6,98,000	
	Conversion costs	10,76,400	3.6† × Rs 2,99,000	
	Total work in process	61,02,000		
	Total costs accounted for	Rs 5,19,64,000		

*Equivalent units completed and transferred out from Solution Exhibit 17-18, Step 2.
?Equivalent units in work in process, ending from Solution Exhibit 17-18, Step 2.

17-20 FIFO method, equivalent units. Refer to the information in Solved example 17-18. Suppose the Satellite Assembly Division uses the FIFO method of process costing instead of the weighted-average method.

Required Compute equivalent units for direct materials and conversion costs. Show physical units in the first column of your schedule.

Solution

FIFO method, equivalent units.

Under the FIFO method, equivalent units are calculated as the equivalent units of work done in the current period only. Solution Exhibit 17-20 shows equivalent units of work done in May in the Assembly Department of Aerospatiale for direct materials and conversion costs.

Solution Exhibit 17-20

Steps 1 and 2: Summarize Output in Physical Units and Compute Equivalent Units
FIFO Method of Process Costing, Satellite Assembly Division of Aerospatiale for May:

Flow of Production	(Step 1) Physical Units	(Step 2) Equivalent Units Direct Materials	Conversion Costs
Work in process, beginning (given)	8	(work done before current period)	
Started during current period (given)	50		
To account for	58		
Completed and transferred out during current period:			
From beginning work in process§ 8(100% – 90%); 8(100% – 40%)	8	0.8	4.8
Started and completed 38 100%, 38 100%	38†	38.0	38.0
Work in process, ending* (given) 12 60%; 12 30%	12	7.2	3.6
Accounted for	58		
Work done in current period only		46.0	46.4

§Degree of completion in this department: direct materials, 90%; conversion costs, 40%.
†46 physical units completed and transferred out minus 8 physical units completed and transferred out from beginning work-in-process inventory.
*Degree of completion in this department: direct materials, 60%; conversion costs, 30%.

17-21 FIFO method, assigning costs (continuation of 17-20).

Required For the data in Example 17-18, use the FIFO method to calculate cost per equivalent unit for direct materials and conversion costs, summarize total costs to account for, and assign these costs to units completed and transferred out and to units in ending work in process.

Solution

FIFO method, assigning costs (continuation of 17-20).

Solution Exhibit 17-21 calculates cost per equivalent unit of work done in May in the Assembly Department of Aerospatiale, summarizes total costs to account for, and assigns costs to units completed and to units in ending work-in-process inventory.

Solution Exhibit 17-21

Steps 3, 4, and 5: Compute Equivalent Unit Costs, Summarize Total Costs to Account For, and Assign Costs to Units Completed and to Units in Ending Work in Process
FIFO Method of Process Costing, Satellite Assembly Division of Aerospatiale for May:

		Total Production Costs	Direct Materials	Conversion Costs
	Work in process beginning (Rs 49,33,600 + Rs 9,10,400)	Rs 58,44,000	(costs of work done before current period)	
(Step 3)	Costs added in current period (given)	4,61,20,000	Rs 3,22,00,000	Rs 1,39,20,000
	Divide by equivalent units of work done in current period (Solution Exhibit 17-21)		÷ 46	÷ 46.4
	Cost per equivalent unit of work done in current period		Rs 7,00,000	Rs 3,00,000
(Step 4)	Total costs to account for	Rs 5,19,64,000		
(Step 5)	Assignment of costs:			
	Completed and transferred out (46 units):			
	Work in process beginning (8 units)	Rs 58,44,000		
	Direct materials added in current period	5,60,000	0.8* × Rs 7,00,000	
	Conversion costs added in current period	14,40,000		4.8* × Rs 3,00,000
	Total from beginning inventory	78,44,000		
	Started and completed (38 units)	3,80,00,000	(38† × Rs 7,00,000) +	(38† × Rs 3,00,000)
	Total costs of units completed & transf. out	4,58,44,000		
	Work in process ending (12 units)			
	Direct materials	50,40,000	7.2# × Rs 7,00,000	
	Conversion costs	10,80,000		3.6# × Rs 3,00,000
	Total work in process ending	61,20,000		
	Total costs accounted for	Rs 5,19,64,000		

*Equivalent units used to complete beginning work in process from Solution Exhibit 17-20, Step 2.
†Equivalent units started and completed from Solution Exhibit 17-20, Step 2.
#Equivalent units in work in process, ending from Solution Exhibit 17-20, Step 2.

17-22 Standard-costing method, assigning costs. Refer to the information in Example 17-18. Suppose the Satellite Assembly Division uses the standard-costing method of process costing. Suppose further that the Satellite Assembly Division determines standard costs of Rs 6,95,000 per equivalent unit for direct materials and Rs 2,95,000 per equivalent unit for conversion costs for both beginning work in process and work done in the current period.

Required

1. Compute equivalent units for direct materials and conversion costs. Show physical units in the first column of your schedule.
2. Summarize total costs to account for, and assign these costs to units completed and transferred out and to units in ending work in process.
3. Compute the total direct materials and conversion costs variances for May.

Solution

Standard-costing method, assigning costs (Refer to the information in Exercise 17-18).

1. The calculations of equivalent units for direct materials and conversion costs are identical to the calculations of equivalent units under the FIFO method. Solution Exhibit 17-20 shows the equivalent unit calculations under standard costing given by the equivalent units of work done in May in the Assembly Department.
2. Solution Exhibit 17-22 summarizes the total costs to account for, and assigns these costs to units completed and transferred out and to units in ending work in process.
3. Solution Exhibit 17-22 shows the direct materials and conversion cost variances for

Direct materials	Rs 2,30,000 U
Conversion costs	Rs 2,32,000 U

Solution Exhibit 17-22

Steps 3, 4, and 5: Compute Equivalent Unit Costs, Summarize Total Costs to Account For, and Assign Costs to Units Completed and to Units in Ending Work in Process Use of Standard Costs in Process Costing, Satellite Assembly Division of Aerospatiale for May:

		Total Production Costs	Direct Materials	Conversion Costs
(Step 3)	Standard cost per equivalent unit (given)		Rs 6,95,000	Rs 2,95,000
	Work in process, beginning (given)			
	Direct materials, 7.2 Rs 6,95,000;			
	Conversion costs, 3.2Rs 2,95,000	Rs 59,48,000		

	Costs added in current period at standard costs			
	Direct materials, 46.0 × Rs 6,95,000;			
	Conversion costs, 46.4 × Rs 2,95,000	4,56,58,000	Rs 3,19,70,000	Rs 1,36,88,000
(Step 4)	Costs to account for	Rs 5,16,06,000		
(Step 5)	Assignment of costs at standard costs:			
	Completed and transferred out (46 units):			
	Work in process, beginning (8 units)	Rs 59,48,000		
	Direct materials added in current period	5,56,000	0.8* × Rs 6,95,000	
	Conversion costs added in current period	14,16,000	4.8* × Rs 2,95,000	
	Total from beginning inventory	79,20,000		
	Started and completed (38 units)	3,76,20,000	38† × Rs 6,95,000 + 38 × Rs 2,95,000	
	Total costs of units transferred out	4,55,40,000		
	Work in process, ending (12 units)			
	Direct materials	50,04,000	7.2# × Rs 6,95,000	
	Conversion costs	10,62,000	3.6# × Rs 2,95,000	
	Total work in process, ending	60,66,000		
	Total costs accounted for	Rs 5,16,06,000		
	Summary of variances for current performance:			
	Costs added in current period at standard prices (see above)		Rs 3,19,70,000	Rs 1,36,88,000
	Actual costs incurred (given)		3,22,00,000	1,39,20,000
	Variance		Rs 2,30,000 U	Rs 2,32,000 U

*Equivalent units to complete beginning work in process from Solution Exhibit 17-20, Step 2.
†Equivalent units started and completed from Solution Exhibit 17-20, Step 2.
#Equivalent units in work in process, ending from Solution Exhibit 17-20, Step 2.

17-23 Transferred-in costs, weighted-average method. Tata Chemicals manufactures an industrial solvent in two departments: mixing and cooking. This question focuses on the Cooking Department. During June of the recent year, 90 tons of solvent were completed and transferred out from the Cooking Department. Direct materials are added at the end of the process. Conversion costs are added evenly during the process. Tata Chemicals uses the weighted-average method of process costing. The following information is available for June:

	Physical Units (Tons)	Equivalent Units (Tons) Transferred-In Costs	Direct Materials	Conversion Costs
Work in process, June 1a	40	40	0	30
Transferred in during June	80			
Completed and transferred out during June	90	90	90	90
Work in process, June 30b	30	30	0	15

aDegree of completion: transferred-in costs, 100%; direct materials, 0%; conversion costs, 75%.
bDegree of completion: transferred-in costs, 100%; direct materials, 0%; conversion costs, 50%.

Total Costs for June		
Work in process, beginning		
Transferred-in costs	Rs 4,00,000	
Direct materials	0	
Conversion costs	1,80,000	Rs 5,80,000
Transferred-in costs added during June		8,72,000
Direct materials added during June		3,60,000
Conversion costs added during June		4,97,250
Total costs to account for		Rs 23,09,250

Required

1. Calculate cost per equivalent unit for transferred-in costs, direct materials, and conversion costs.
2. Summarize total costs to account for, and assign these costs to units completed (and transferred out) and to units in ending work in process.

Solution

Transferred-in costs, weighted-average method.

1. & 2. Solution Exhibit 17-23A calculates the equivalent units of work done to date. Solution Exhibit 17-23B calculates the cost per equivalent unit of work done to date for transferred-in costs, direct materials, and conversion costs, summarizes total costs to account for, and assigns these costs to units completed and transferred out and to units in ending work-in-process inventory.

Solution Exhibit 17-23A

Steps 1 and 2: Summarize Output in Physical Units and Compute Equivalent Units
Weighted-Average Method of Process Costing Cooking Department of Tata Chemicals for June:

(Step 2) Equivalent Units

Flow of Production	Physical Units (given)	(Step 1) Transferred-in Costs	Direct Materials	Conversion Costs
Work in process, beginning	40			
Transferred in during current period	80			
To account for	120			
Completed and transferred out during current period	90	90	90	90
Work in process, ending*	30			
30 × 100%; 30 × 0%; 30 × 50%		30	0	15
Accounted for	120			
Work done to date		120	90	105

*Degree of completion in this department: transferred-in costs, 100%; direct materials, 0%; conversion costs, 50%.

Solution Exhibit 17-23B

Steps 3, 4, and 5: Compute Equivalent Unit Costs, Summarize Total Costs to Account For, and Assign Costs to Units Completed and to Units in Ending Work in Process
Weighted-Average Method of Process Costing Cooking Department of Tata Chemicals for June:

	Total Production Costs	Transferred-in Costs	Direct Materials	Conversion Costs
(Step 3) Work in process beginning (given)	Rs 5,80,000	Rs 4,00,000	Rs 0	Rs 1,80,000
Costs added in current period (given)	17,29,250	8,72,000	3,60,000	4,97,250
Costs incurred to date		Rs 12,72,000	Rs 3,60,000	Rs 6,77,250
Divide by equivalent units of work done to date (Solution Exhibit 17-23A)		÷ 120	÷ 90	÷ 105
Equivalent unit costs of work done to date		Rs 10,600	Rs 4,000	Rs 6,450
(Step 4) Total costs to account for	Rs 23,09,250			
(Step 5) Assignment of costs:				
Completed and transferred out (90 units)	Rs 18,94,500	(90* × Rs 10,600)	+(90* × Rs 4,000)	+(90* × Rs 6,450)
Work in process, ending (30 units)				
Transferred-in costs	3,18,000	30† × Rs 10,600		
Direct materials	0		0† × Rs 4,000	
Conversion costs	96,750			15† × Rs 6,450
Total work in process, ending	4,14,750			
Total costs accounted for	Rs 23,09,250			

*Equivalent units completed and transferred out from Solution Exhibit 17-23A, Step 2.
†Equivalent units in work in process, ending from Solution Exhibit 17-23A, Step 2.

17-24 Transferred-in costs, FIFO method. Refer to the information in Exercise 17-23. Suppose that Tata uses the FIFO method instead of the weighted-average method in all its departments. The only changes under the FIFO method are that the total transferred-in costs of beginning work in process are Rs 3,92,000 and that the transferred-in costs added during June are Rs 8,56,000.

Required

Do Exercise 17-23 using the FIFO method. Note that you first need to calculate equivalent units of work done in the current period (for transferred-in costs, direct materials, and conversion costs) to complete beginning work in process, to start and complete new units, and to produce ending work in process.

Solution

Transferred-in costs, FIFO method.

1. & 2. Solution Exhibit 17-24A calculates the equivalent units of work done in the current period (for transferred-in costs, direct-materials, and conversion costs) to complete beginning work-in-process inventory, to start and complete new units, and to produce ending work in process. Solution Exhibit 17-24B calculates the cost per equivalent unit of work done in the current period for transferred-in costs, direct materials, and conversion costs, summarizes total costs to account for, and assigns these costs to units completed and transferred out and to units in ending work-in-process inventory.

Solution Exhibit 17-24A

Steps 1 and 2: Summarize Output in Physical Units and Compute Equivalent Units
FIFO Method of Process Costing
Cooking Department of Tata Chemicals for June:

Flow of Production	(Step 1) Physical Units	(Step 2) Equivalent Units Transferred-in Costs	Direct Materials	Conversion Costs
Work in process, beginning (given)	40	(work done before current period)		
Transferred in during current period (given)	80			
To account for	120			
Completed and transferred out during current period:				
From beginning work in process§	40			
40 × (100% – 100%); 40 × (100% – 0%); 40 × (100% – 75%)		0	40	10
Started and completed	50†			
50 × 100%; 50 × 100%; 50 × 100%		50	50	50
Work in process, ending* (given)	30			
30 × 100%; 30 × 0%; 30 × 50%		30	0	15
Accounted for	120			
Work done in current period only		80	90	75

§Degree of completion in this department: Transferred-in costs, 100%; direct materials, 0%; conversion costs, 75%.
†90 physical units completed and transferred out minus 40 physical units completed and transferred out from beginning work-in-process inventory.
*Degree of completion in this department: transferred-in costs, 100%; direct materials, 0%; conversion costs, 50%.

Solution Exhibit 17-24B

Steps 3, 4, and 5: Compute Equivalent Unit Costs, Summarize Total Costs to Account For, and Assign Costs to Units Completed and to Units in Ending Work in Process
FIFO Method of Process Costing
Cooking Department of Tata Chemicals for June

		Total Production Costs	Transferred-in Costs	Direct Materials	Conversion Costs
	Work in process beginning (Rs 3,92,000 + Rs 0 + Rs 1,80,000)	Rs 5,72,000	(Costs of work done before current period)		
(Step 3)	Costs added in current period (given)	17,13,250	Rs 8,56,000	Rs 3,60,000	Rs 4,97,250
	Divide by equivalent units of work done in current period (Solution Exhibit 17-24A)		÷ 80	÷ 90	÷ 75
	Cost per equiv. unit of work done in current period		Rs 10,700	Rs 4,000	Rs 6,630
(Step 4)	Total costs to account for	Rs 22,85,250			
(Step 5)	Assignment of costs:				
	Completed and transferred out (90 units):				
	Work in process beginning (40 units)	Rs 5,72,000			
	Transferred-in costs added in current period	0	0* × Rs 10,700		
	Direct materials added in current period	1,60,000		40* × Rs 4,000	
	Conversion costs added in current period	66,300			10* × Rs 6,630
	Total from beginning inventory	7,98,300			
	Started and completed (50 units)	10,66,500	(50† × Rs 10,700) +	(50† × Rs 4,000) +	(50† × Rs 6,630)
	Total costs of units completed & tfd. out	18,64,800			
	Work in process ending (30 units)				
	Transferred-in costs	3,21,000	30# × Rs 10,700	0# × Rs 4,000	15# × Rs 6,630
	Direct materials	0			
	Conversion costs	99,450			
	Total work in process ending	4,20,450			
	Total costs accounted for	Rs 22,85,250			

*Equivalent units used to complete beginning work in process from Solution Exhibit 17-23A, Step 2.
†Equivalent units started and completed from Solution Exhibit 17-23A, Step 2.
#Equivalent units in work in process, ending from Solution Exhibit 17-23A, Step 2.

17-25 Weighted-average method. Star Toys manufactures one type of wooden toy figure. It buys wood as its direct material for the Forming Department of its Ludhiana plant. The toys are transferred to the Finishing Department, where they are hand-shaped and metal is added to them. The process-costing system at Star Toys has a single direct-cost category (direct materials) and a single indirect-cost category (conversion costs). Direct materials are added when the Forming Department process is 10% complete. Conversion costs are added evenly during the Forming Department's process.

Star Toys uses the weighted-average method of process costing. Consider the following data for the Forming Department in April of the recent year:

	Physical Units (Toys)	Direct Materials	Conversion Costs
Work in process, April 1[a]	300	Rs 75,000	Rs 21,250
Started during April	2,200		
Completed during April	2,000		
Work in process, April 30[b]	500		
Costs added during April		Rs 7,00,000	Rs 4,25,000

[a]Degree of completion: direct materials, 100%; conversion costs, 40%.
[b]Degree of completion: direct materials, 100%; conversion costs, 25%.

Summarize total Forming Department costs for April, and assign these costs to units completed (and transferred out) and to units in ending work in process. **Required**

Solution

Weighted-average method.

Solution Exhibit 17-25A shows equivalent units of work done to date of

Direct materials	2,500 equivalent units
Conversion costs	2,125 equivalent units

Note that direct materials are added when the Forming Department process is 10% complete. Both the beginning and ending work in process are more than 10% complete and hence are 100% complete with respect to direct materials.

Solution Exhibit 17-25B calculates cost per equivalent unit of work done to date for direct materials and conversion costs, summarizes the total Forming Department costs for April, and assigns these costs to units completed (and transferred out), and to units in ending work in process using the weighted-average method.

Solution Exhibit 17-25A

Steps 1 and 2: Summarize Output in Physical Units and Compute Equivalent Units Weighted-Average Method of Process Costing, Forming Department of Star Toys for April:

	(Step 1)	(Step 2) Equivalent Units	
Flow of Production	Physical Units (given)	Direct Materials	Conversion Costs
Work in process, beginning	300		
Started during current period	2,200		
To account for	2,500		
Completed and transferred out during current period	2,000	2,000	2,000
Work in process, ending*	500		
500 × 100%; 500 × 25%		500	125
Accounted for	2,500		
Work done to date		2,500	2,125

*Degree of completion in this department: direct materials, 100%; conversion costs, 25%.

Solution Exhibit 17-25B

Steps 3, 4, and 5: Compute Equivalent Unit Costs, Summarize Total Costs to Account For, and Assign Costs to Units Completed and to Units in Ending Work in Process Weighted-Average Method of Process Costing, Forming Department of Star Toys for April:

		Total Production Costs	Direct Materials	Conversion Costs
(Step 3)	Work in process, beginning (given)	Rs 96,250	Rs 75,000	Rs 21,250
	Costs added in current period (given)	11,25,000	7,00,000	4,25,000
	Costs incurred to date		Rs 7,75,000	Rs 4,46,250
	Divide by equivalent units of work done to date (Solution Exhibit 17-35A)		÷ 2,500	÷ 2,125
	Cost per equivalent unit of work done to date		Rs 310	Rs 210
(Step 4)	Total costs to account for	Rs 12,21,250		
(Step 5)	Assignment of costs:			
	Completed and transferred out (2,000 units)	Rs 10,40,000	2,000* × Rs 310 +	2,000* × Rs 210
	Work in process, ending (500 units)			
	Direct materials	1,55,000	500† × Rs 310	
	Conversion costs	26,250		125† × Rs 210
	Total work in process, ending	1,81,250		
	Total costs accounted for	Rs 12,21,250		

*Equivalent units completed and transferred out from Solution Exhibit 17-25A, Step 2.
†Equivalent units in work in process, ending from Solution Exhibit 17-25A, Step 2.

17-26 Journal entries (continuation of 17-25).

Required Prepare a set of summarized journal entries for all April transactions affecting Work in Process—Forming. Set up a T-account for Work in Process—Forming, and post your entries to it.

Solution

Journal entries (continuation of 17-25).	Rs	Rs
1. Work in Process—Forming Department	7,00,000	
Accounts Payable		7,00,000
To record direct materials purchased and used in production during April		
2. Work in Process—Forming Department	4,25,000	
Various Accounts		4,25,000
To record Forming Department conversion costs for April		
3. Work in Process—Finishing Department	10,40,000	
Work in Process—Forming Department		10,40,000
To record cost of goods completed and transferred out in April from the Forming Department to the Finishing Department		

Work in Process—Forming Department

Beginning inventory, April 1	Rs 96,250	3. Transferred out to	
1. Direct materials	7,00,000	Work in Process—Finishing	Rs 10,40,000
2. Conversion costs	4,25,000		
Ending inventory, April 30	1,81,250		

17-27 FIFO method (continuation of 17-25).

Required Do Example 17-25 using FIFO and two decimal places for unit costs. If you did (the original) Example 17-25, explain any difference between the cost of work completed and transferred out and the cost of ending work in process in the Forming Department under the weighted-average method and the FIFO method.

Solution

FIFO method (continuation of 17-25).

The equivalent units of work done in April in the Forming Department for direct materials and conversion costs are shown in Solution Exhibit 17-27A.

Solution Exhibit 17-27B calculates the cost per equivalent unit of work done in April in the Forming Department for direct materials and conversion costs, summarizes the total Forming Department costs for April, and assigns these costs to units completed (and transferred out) and to units in ending work in process under the FIFO method.

The equivalent units of work done in beginning inventory is: direct materials, 300 × 100% = 300; and conversion costs 300 × 40% = 120. The cost per equivalent unit of beginning inventory and of work done in the current period are:

	Beginning Inventory	Work Done in Current Period (Calculated Under FIFO Method)
Direct materials	Rs 250 (Rs 75,000 ÷ 300)	Rs 318.18
Conversion costs	Rs 177.08 (Rs 21,250 ÷ 120)	Rs 211.97

The following table summarizes the costs assigned to units completed and those still in process under the weighted-average and FIFO process-costing methods for our example.

	Weighted Average (Solution Exhibit 17-25B)	FIFO (Solution Exhibit 17-27B)	Difference
Cost of units completed and transferred out	Rs 10,40,000	Rs 10,35,660	– Rs 4,340
Work in process, ending	1,81,250	1,85,590	+ Rs 4,340
Total costs accounted for	Rs 12,21,250	Rs 12,21,250	

The FIFO ending inventory is higher than the weighted-average ending inventory by Rs 4,340. This is because FIFO assumes that all the lower-cost prior-period units in work in process are the first to be completed and transferred out while ending work in process consists of only the higher-cost current-period units. The weighted-average method, however, smoothes out cost per equivalent unit by assuming that more of the higher-cost units are completed and transferred out, while some of the lower-cost units in beginning work in process are placed in ending work in process. Hence, in this case, the weighted-average method results in a higher cost of units completed and transferred out and a lower ending work-in-process inventory relative to FIFO.

Solution Exhibit 17-27A

Steps 1 and 2: Summarize Output in Physical Units and Compute Equivalent Units FIFO Method of Process Costing, Forming Department of Star Toys for April:

Flow of Production	(Step 1) Physical Units	(Step 2) Equivalent Units Direct Materials	Conversion Costs
Work in process, beginning (given)	300	(work done before current period)	
Started during current period (given)	2,200		
To account for	2,500		
Completed and transferred out during current period:			
From beginning work in process[§]	300		
300 × (100% − 100%); 300 × (100% − 40%)		0	180
Started and completed	1,700[†]		
1,700 × 100%; 1,700 × 100%		1,700	1,700
Work in process, ending* (given)	500		
500 × 100%; 500 × 25%		500	125
Accounted for	2,500		
Work done in current period only		2,200	2,005

[§]Degree of completion in this department: direct materials, 100%; conversion costs, 40%.

[†]2,000 physical units completed and transferred out minus 300 physical units completed and transferred out from beginning work-in-process inventory.

*Degree of completion in this department: direct materials, 100%; conversion costs, 25%.

Solution Exhibit 17-27B

Steps 3, 4, and 5: Compute Equivalent Unit Costs, Summarize Total Costs to Account For, and Assign Costs to Units Completed and to Units in Ending Work in Process FIFO Method of Process Costing, Forming Department of Star Toys for April:

		Total Production Costs	Direct Materials	Conversion Costs
	Work in process beginning (given: Rs 75,000 + Rs 21,250)	Rs 96,250	(work done before current period)	
(Step 3)	Costs added in current period (given)	11,25,000	Rs 7,00,000	Rs 4,25,000
	Divide by equivalent units of work done in current period (Exhibit 17-37A)		÷ 2,200	÷ 2,005
	Cost per equivalent unit of work done in current period		Rs 318.18	Rs 211.97
(Step 4)	Total costs to account for	Rs 12,21,250		
(Step 5)	Assignment of costs:			
	Completed and transferred out (2,000 units):			
	Work in process beginning (300 units)	Rs 96,250		
	Direct materials added in current period	0	0* × Rs 318.18	
	Conversion costs added in current period	38,150	180* × Rs 211.97	
	Total from beginning inventory	1,34,400		
	Started and completed (1,700 units)	9,01,260	(1,700[†] × Rs 318.18) +	(1,700[†] × Rs 211.97)
	Total costs of units completed & tsfd. out	10,35,660		
	Work in process ending (100 units)			
	Direct materials	1,59,090	500[#] × Rs 318.18	
	Conversion costs	26,500	125[#] × Rs 211.97	
	Total work in process ending	1,85,590		
	Total costs accounted for	Rs 12,21,250		

*Equivalent units used to complete beginning work in process from Solution Exhibit 17-27A, Step 2.

[†]Equivelant units started and completed from Solution Exhibit 17-27A, Step 2.

[#]Equivalent units in work in process, ending from Solution Exhibit 17-27A, Step 2.

17-28 Transferred-in costs, weighted-average method (related to 17-25 through 17-27). Star Toys, as you know, manufactures one type of wooden toy figure at its Ludhiana plant. It has two departments: a Forming Department and a Finishing Department. (Examples 17-25 through 17-27 focused on the Forming Department.) Consider now the Finishing Department, which processes the formed toys through hand-shaping and the addition of metal. All additional direct materials are added when the Finishing Department process is 80% complete. Conversion costs are added evenly during finishing operations. When the Finishing Department completes work on each toy, it is immediately transferred to Finished Goods.

Star Toys uses the weighted-average method of process costing. The following is a summary of the April operations in the Finishing Department:

	Physical Units (Toys)	Transferred-InCosts	Direct Materials	Conversion Costs
Work in process, April 1[a]	500	Rs 1,77,500	Rs 0	Rs 72,500
Transferred in during April	2,000			
Completed during April	2,100			
Work in process, April 30[b]	400			
Costs added during April		Rs 10,40,000	Rs 2,31,000	Rs 3,84,000

[a]Degree of completion: transferred-in costs, 100%; direct materials, 0%; conversion costs, 60%.
[b]Degree of completion: transferred-in costs, 100%; direct materials, 0%; conversion costs, 30%.

Required

1. Summarize total Finishing Department costs for April, and assign these costs to units completed (and transferred out) and to units in ending work in process.
2. Prepare journal entries for April transfers from the Forming Department to the Finishing Department and from the Finishing Department to Finished Goods.

Solution

Transferred-in costs, weighted average (related to 17-25 through 17-27).

1. Solution Exhibit 17-28A computes the equivalent units of work done to date in the Finishing Department for transferred-in costs, direct materials, and conversion costs.
   Solution Exhibit 17-28B calculates the cost per equivalent unit of work done to date in the Finishing Department for transferred-in costs, direct materials, and conversion costs, summarizes total Finishing Department costs for April, and assigns these costs to units completed and transferred out and to units in ending work in process using the weighted-average method.
2. Journal entries:

	Rs	Rs
a. Work in Process—Finishing Department	10,40,000	
Work in Process—Forming Department		10,40,000
Cost of goods completed and transferred out during April from the Forming Department to the Finishing Department		
b. Finished Goods	16,85,520	
Work in Process—Finishing Department		16,85,520
Cost of goods completed and transferred out during April from the Finishing Department to Finished Goods inventory		

Solution Exhibit 17-28A

Steps 1 and 2: Summarize Output in Physical Units and Compute Equivalent Units Weighted-Average Method of Process Costing Finishing Department of Star Toys for April:

Flow of Production	(Step 1) Physical Units (given)	(Step 2) Equivalent Units Transferred-in Costs	Direct Materials	Conversion Costs
Work in process, beginning	500			
Transferred in during current period	2,000			
To account for	2,500			
Completed and transferred out during current period	2,100	2,100	2,100	2,100
Work in process, ending*	400			
400 × 100%; 400 × 0%; 400 × 30%		400	0	120
Accounted for	2,500			
Work done to date		2,500	2,100	2,220

*Degree of completion in this department: transferred-in costs, 100%; direct materials, 0%; conversion costs, 30%.

Solution Exhibit 17-28B

Steps 3, 4, and 5: Compute Equivalent Unit Costs, Summarize Total Costs to Account For, and Assign Costs to Units Completed and to Units in Ending Work in Process Weighted-Average Method of Process Costing Finishing Department of Star Toys for April:

		Total Production Costs	Transferred-in Costs	Direct Materials	Conversion Costs
(Step 3)	Work in process beginning (given)	Rs 2,50,000	Rs 1,77,500	Rs 0	Rs 72,500
	Costs added in current period (given)	16,55,000	10,40,000	2,31,000	3,84,000
	Costs incurred to date		Rs 12,17,500	Rs 2,31,000	Rs 4,56,500
	Divide by equivalent units of work done to date (Solution Exhibit 17-38A)		÷ 2,500	÷ 2,100	÷ 2,220
	Equivalent unit costs of work done to date		Rs 487	Rs 110	Rs 205.63
(Step 4)	Total costs to account for	Rs 19,05,000			

(Step 5) Assignment of costs:

Completed and transferred out (2,100 units)	Rs 16,85,520	(2,100* × Rs 487)+	(2,100* × Rs 110)+	(2,100* × Rs 205.63)
Work in process ending (400 units)				
Transferred-in costs	1,94,800	400† × Rs 487		
Direct materials	0		0† × Rs 110	
Conversion costs	24,680	120† × Rs 205.63		
Total work in process ending	2,19,480			
Total costs accounted for	Rs 19,05,000			

*Equivalent units completed and transferred out from Solution Exhibit 17-28A, Step 2.

†Equivalent units in work in process, ending from Solution Exhibit 17-38A, Step 2.

17-29 Transferred-in costs, FIFO method (continuation of 17-28).

Required

1. Using the FIFO process-costing method, do Example 17-28. Under FIFO, the transferred-in costs for the beginning work in process in the Finishing Department on April 1 are Rs 1,75,200, and the costs transferred in during April are Rs 10,35,660. All other data are unchanged.
2. If you did Example 17-28, explain any difference between the cost of work completed and transferred out and the cost of ending work in process in the Finishing Department under the weighted-average method and the FIFO method.

Solution

Transferred-in costs, FIFO method (continuation of 17-28).

1. Solution Exhibit 17-29A calculates the equivalent units of work done in April in the Finishing Department for transferred-in costs, direct materials, and conversion costs.
   Solution Exhibit 17-29B calculates the cost per equivalent unit of work done in April in the Finishing Department for transferred-in costs, direct materials, and conversion costs, summarizes total Finishing Department costs for April, and assigns these costs to units completed and transferred out and to units in ending work in process using the FIFO method.
   Journal entries:

	Rs	Rs
a. Work in Process—Finishing Department	10,35,660	
Work in Process—Forming Department		10,35,660
Cost of goods completed and transferred out during April from the Forming Dept. to the Finishing Dept.		
b. Finished Goods	16,67,230	
Work in Process—Finishing Department		16,67,230
Cost of goods completed and transferred out during April from the Finishing Department to Finished Goods inventory.		

2. The equivalent units of work done in beginning inventory is: Transferred-in costs, 500 × 100% = 500; direct materials, 500 × 0% = 0; and conversion costs, 500 × 60% = 300. The cost per equivalent unit of beginning inventory and of work done in the current period are:

	Beginning Inventory	Work Done in Current Period
Transferred-in costs (weighted average)	Rs 355 (Rs 1,77,500 ÷ 500)	Rs 520 (Rs 10,40,000 ÷ 2,000)
Transferred-in costs (FIFO)	Rs 350.4 (Rs 1,75,200 ÷ 500)	Rs 517.83 (Rs 10,35,660 ÷ 2,000)
Direct materials	–	Rs 110
Conversion costs	Rs 241.67 (Rs 72,500 × 300)	Rs 200

The following table summarizes the costs assigned to units completed and those still in process under the weighted-average and FIFO process-costing methods for our example.

	Weighted Average (Solution Exhibit 17-38B)	FIFO (Solution Exhibit 17-39B)	Difference
Cost of units completed and transferred out	Rs 16,85,520	Rs 16,67,230	– Rs 18,290
Work in process ending	2,19,480	2,31,130	+ Rs 11,650
Total costs accounted for	Rs 19,05,000	Rs 18,98,360	

The FIFO ending inventory is higher than the weighted-average ending inventory by Rs 11,650. This is because FIFO assumes that all the lower-cost prior-period units in work in process (resulting from the lower transferred-in costs in beginning inventory) are the first to be completed and transferred out while ending work in process consists of only the higher-cost current-period units. The weighted-average method, however, smoothes out cost per equivalent unit by assuming that more of the higher-cost units are completed and transferred out, while some of the lower-cost units in beginning work in process are placed in ending work in process. Hence, in this case, the weighted-average method results in a higher cost of units completed and transferred out and a lower ending work-in-process inventory relative to FIFO. Note that the difference in cost of units completed and transferred out (–Rs 18,290) does not fully offset the difference in ending work-in-process inventory (+Rs 11,650). This is because the FIFO and weighted-average methods result in different values for transferred-in costs with respect to both beginning inventory and costs transferred in during the period.

Solution Exhibit 17-29A

Steps 1 and 2: Summarize Output in Physical Units and Compute Equivalent Units FIFO Method of Process Costing Finishing Department of Star Toys for April:

Flow of Production	(Step 1) Physical Units (given)	(Step 2) Equivalent Units Transferred-in Costs	Direct Materials	Conversion Costs
Work in process, beginning (given)	500	(work done before current period)		
Transferred-in during current period (given)	2,000			
To account for	2,500			
Completed and transferred out during current period:				
From beginning work in process[§]	500			
500 × (100% – 100%); 500 × (100% – 0%); 500(100% – 60%)		0	500	200
Started and completed	1,600[†]			
1,600 × 100%; 1,600 × 100%; 1,600 × 100%		1,600	1,600	1,600
Work in process, ending* (given)	400			
400 × 100%; 400 × 0%; 400 × 30%		400	0	120
Accounted for	2,500			
Work done in current period only		2,000	2,100	1,920

[§]Degree of completion in this department: Transferred-in costs, 100%; direct materials, 0%; conversion costs, 60%.
[†]2,100 physical units completed and transferred out minus 500 physical units completed and transferred out from beginning work-in-process inventory.
*Degree of completion in this department: transferred-in costs, 100%; direct materials, 0%; conversion costs, 30%.

Solution Exhibit 17-29B

Steps 3, 4, and 5: Compute Equivalent Unit Costs, Summarize Total Costs to Account For, and Assign Costs to Units Completed and to Units in Ending Work in Process FIFO Method of Process Costing Finishing Department of Star Toys for April:

		Total Production Costs	Transferred-in Costs	Direct Materials	Conversion Costs
	Work in process beginning (given) (Rs 1,75,200 + Rs 0 + Rs 72,500)	Rs 2,47,700	(Costs of work done before current period)		
(Step 3)	Costs added in current period (given)	16,50,660	Rs 10,35,660	Rs 2,31,000	Rs 3,84,000
	Divide by equivalent units of work done in current period (Solution Exhibit 17-39A)		÷ 2,000	÷ 2,100	÷ 1,920
	Cost per equivalent unit of work done in current period		Rs 517.83	Rs 110	Rs 200
(Step 4)	Total costs to account for	Rs 18,98,360			
(Step 5)	Assignment of costs:				
	Completed and transferred out (2100 units):				
	Work in process beginning (500 units)	Rs 2,47,700			
	Transferred-in costs added in current period	0	0* × Rs 517.83		
	Direct materials added in current period	55,000		500* × Rs 110	
	Conversion costs added in current period	40,000			200* × Rs 200
	Total from beginning inventory	3,42,700			
	Started and completed (1600 units)	13,24,530	(1,600[†] × Rs 517.83)+	(1,600[†] × Rs 110)+	(1,600[†] × Rs 200)
	Total costs of units completed & tfd. out	16,67,230			
	Work in process ending (400 units)				
	Transferred-in costs	2,07,130	400[#] × Rs 517.83		
	Direct materials	0		0[#] × Rs 110	
	Conversion costs	24,000			120[#] × Rs 200
	Total work in process ending	2,31,130			
	Total costs accounted for	Rs 18,98,360			

*Equivalent units used to complete beginning work in process from Solution Exhibit 17-29A, Step 2.
[†]Equivalent units started and completed from Solution Exhibit 17-29A, Step 2.
[#]Equivalent units in work in process, ending from Solution Exhibit 17-29A, Step 2.

17-30 Operation costing, equivalent units. (Chapter Appendix, CMA, adapted) Supreme Industries manufactures plastic molded chairs. The three models of molded chairs, all variations of the same design, are Standard, Deluxe, and Executive. The company uses an operation-costing system.

Supreme has extrusion, form, trim, and finish operations. Plastic sheets are produced by the extrusion operation. During the forming operation, the plastic sheets are molded into chair seats and the legs are added. The Standard model is sold after this operation. During the trim operation, the arms are added to the Deluxe and Executive models and the chair edges are smoothed. Only the Executive model enters the finish operation, in which padding is added. All of the units produced receive the same steps within each operation. The May units of production and direct materials costs incurred are as follows:

	Units Produced	Extrusion Materials	Form Materials	Trim Materials	Finish Materials
Standard model	6,000	Rs 7,20,000	Rs 2,40,000	Rs 0	Rs 0
Deluxe model	3,000	3,60,000	1,20,000	90,000	0
Executive model	2,000	2,40,000	80,000	60,000	1,20,000
	11,000	Rs 13,20,000	Rs 4,40,000	Rs 1,50,000	Rs 1,20,000

The total conversion costs for the month of May are:

	Extrusion Operation	Form Operation	Trim Operation	Finish Operation
Total conversion costs	Rs 26,95,000	Rs 13,20,000	Rs 6,90,000	Rs 4,20,000

Required

1. For each product produced by Supreme Industries during May, determine (a) the unit cost and (b) the total cost. Support your answer with appropriate calculations.
2. Now consider the following information for June. All unit costs in June are identical to the May unit costs calculated in 1(a). At the end of June, 1,000 units of the Deluxe model remained in work in process. These units were 100% complete as to materials costs and 60% complete in the trim operation. Determine the cost of the Deluxe model work-in-process inventory at the end of June.

Solution

Operation costing, equivalent units.

1. Materials and conversion costs of each operation, the total units produced, and the material and conversion cost per unit for the month of May are as follows:

	Extrusion	Form	Trim	Finish
1. Units produced	11,000	11,000	5,000	2,000
2. Materials costs	Rs 13,20,000	Rs 4,40,000	Rs 1,50,000	Rs 1,20,000
3. Materials cost per unit (2 ÷ 1)	120	40	30	60
4. Conversion costs	26,95,000	13,20,000	6,90,000	4,20,000
5. Conversion cost per unit (4 ÷ 1)	245	120	138	210

The unit cost and total costs in May for each product are as follows:

Cost Elements	Standard	Deluxe Model	Executive Model
Extrusion materials	Rs 120	Rs 120	Rs 120
Form materials	40	40	40
Trim materials	—	30	30
Finish materials			60
Extrusion conversion	245	245	245
Form conversion	120	120	120
Trim conversion	—	138	138
Finish conversion		—	210
Total unit cost	Rs 525	Rs 693	Rs 963
Multiply by units produced	× 6,000	× 3,000	× 2,000
Total product costs	Rs 31,50,000	Rs 20,79,000	Rs 19,26,000

2.

	Unit Cost	Equivalent Units	Total Costs
Deluxe model work-in process costs at the trim operation			
Extrusion material (100% complete when transferred in)	Rs 120	1,000	Rs 1,20,000
Extrusion conversion (100% complete when transferred in)	245	1,000	2,45,000
Form material (100% complete when transferred in)	40	1,000	40,000
Form conversion (100% complete when transferred in)	120	1,000	1,20,000
Trim material (100% complete)	30	1,000	30,000
Trim conversion (60% complete)	138	600*	82,800
Work-in-process costs			Rs 6,37,800

*1,000 units × 60% complete

17-31 Equivalent-unit computations, benchmarking, ethics. Singhania is the corporate controller of Leisure Suits. Leisure Suits has 20 plants that manufacture suits for retail stores. Each plant uses a process-costing system. At the end of each month, each plant manager submits a production report and a production-cost report. The production report includes the plant manager's estimate of the percentage of completion of the ending work in process as to direct materials and conversion costs. Singhania uses these estimates to compute the equivalent units of work done in each plant and the cost per equivalent unit of work done for both direct materials and conversion costs in each month. Plants are ranked from 1 to 20 in terms of (a) cost per equivalent unit of direct materials and (b) cost per equivalent unit of conversion costs. The three top-ranked plants in each category receive a bonus and are written up as the best in their class in the company newsletter.

Singhania has been pleased with the success of her benchmarking program. However, she has just received some unsigned letters stating that two plant managers have been manipulating their monthly estimates of percentage of completion in an attempt to obtain best-in-class status.

Required

1. How and why might plant managers "manipulate" their monthly estimates of percentage of completion?
2. Singhania's first reaction is to contact each plant controller and discuss the problem raised by the unsigned letters. Is that a good idea?
3. Assume that the plant controller's primary reporting responsibility is to the plant manager and that each plant controller receives the phone call from Singhania mentioned in 2. What is the ethical responsibility of each plant controller (a) to Singhania and (b) to Leisure Suits in relation to the equivalent-unit information each plant provides?
4. How might Singhania gain some insight into whether the equivalent-unit figures provided by particular plants are being manipulated?

Solution

Equivalent-unit computations, benchmarking, ethics.

1. The reported monthly cost per equivalent unit of either direct materials or conversion costs is lower when the plant manager overestimates the percentage of completion of ending work in process; the overestimate increases the denominator and, thus, decreases the cost per equivalent unit. The plant manager has two motivations to report lower cost per equivalent unit numbers: (1) to get a bonus and (2) to be recognized in the company newsletter.
2. While the plant controller has responsibility for preparing the accounting reports for the plant, in most cases, the plant controller reports directly to the plant manager. If this reporting relationship exists, Singhania may create a conflict of interest situation for the plant controller. Only if the plant controller reports directly to the corporate controller, and indirectly to the plant manager, should Singhania show the letters to the plant controller without simultaneously showing them to the plant manager.
3. The plant controller's ethical responsibilities to Singhania and to Leisure Suits are the same. These include:
   - Competence: The plant controller is expected to have the competence to make equivalent unit computations. This competence does not always extend to making estimates of the percentage of completion of a product. In Leisure Suits's case, however, the products are probably easy to understand and observe. Hence, a plant controller could obtain reasonably reliable evidence on percentage of completion at a plant.
   - Objectivity: The plant controller should not allow the possibility of the plant being written up favorably in the company newsletter to influence the way equivalent unit costs are computed. The plant controller has a responsibility to communicate information fairly and objectively.
4. Singhania could seek evidence on possible manipulations as follows:
   a. Have plant controllers report detailed breakdowns on the stages of production and then conduct end-of-month audits to verify the actual stages completed for ending work in process.
   b. Examine trends in ending work in process. Divisions that report low amounts of ending work in process relative to total production are not likely to be able to greatly affect equivalent unit cost amounts by manipulating percentage of completion estimates. Divisions that show sizable quantities of total production in ending work in process are more likely to be able to manipulate equivalent cost computations by manipulating percentage of completion estimates.

Exercises

17-32 Zero beginning inventory, materials introduced in middle of process. Vaasa Chemicals has a Mixing Department and a Refining Department. Its process-costing system in the Mixing Department has two direct materials cost categories (Chemical P and Chemical Q) and one conversion costs pool. The following data pertain to the Mixing Department for July of the current year:

Units	
Work in process, July 1	0
Units started	50,000
Completed and transferred to Refining Department	35,000
Costs	
Chemical P	Rs 25,00,000
Chemical Q	7,00,000
Conversion costs	13,50,000

Chemical P is introduced at the start of operations in the Mixing Department, and chemical Q is added when the product is three-fourths completed in the Mixing Department. Conversion costs are added evenly during the process. The ending work in process in the Mixing Department is two-thirds complete.

Required

1. Compute the equivalent units in the Mixing Department for July for each cost category.
2. Compute (a) the cost of goods completed and transferred to the Refining Department during July and (b) the cost of work in process as of July 31.

17-33 Weighted-average method, assigning costs. The Asian Chemicals Company makes a water-treatment chemical in a single processing department. Direct materials are added at the start of the process. Conversion costs are added evenly during the process. Asian Chemicals uses the weighted-average method of process costing. The following information for July related to current year is available:

		Equivalent Units	
	Physical Units	Direct Materials	Conversion Costs
Work in process, July 1	10,000[a]	10,000	7,000
Started during July	40,000		
Completed and transferred out during July	34,000	34,000	34,000
Work in process, July 31	16,000[b]	16,000	8,000

[a]Degree of completion: direct materials, 100%; conversion costs, 70%.
[b]Degree of completion: direct materials, 100%; conversion costs, 50%.

Total Costs for July		
Work in process, beginning		
Direct materials	Rs 6,00,000	
Conversion costs	7,00,000	Rs 13,00,000
Direct materials added during July		28,00,000
Conversion costs added during July		37,10,000
Total costs to account for		Rs 78,10,000

Required

1. Calculate cost per equivalent unit for direct materials and conversion costs.
2. Summarize total costs to account for, and assign these costs to units completed (and transferred out) and to units in ending work in process.

17-34 FIFO method, assigning costs.

Required

Do Exercise 17-33 using the FIFO method. Note that you first need to calculate the equivalent units of work done in the current period (for direct materials and conversion costs) to complete beginning work-in process, to start and complete new units, and to produce ending work in process.

17-35 Standard-costing method, assigning costs. Refer to the information in Exercise 17-33. Suppose Asian Chemicals determines standard costs of Rs 65 per equivalent unit for direct materials and Rs 103 per equivalent unit for conversion costs for both beginning work in process and work done in the current period.

Required

1. Do Exercise 17-33 using the standard-costing method. Note that you first need to calculate the equivalent units of work done in the current period (for direct materials and conversion costs) to complete beginning work in process, to start and complete new units, and to produce ending work in process.
2. Compute the total direct materials and conversion costs variances for July.

17-36 Operation Costing (Chapter Appendix). Feather Light Shoe Company manufactures two styles of men's shoes: Designer and Regular. Designer style is made from leather, and Regular style uses synthetic materials. Three operations—cutting, sewing and packing—are common to both styles, but only Designer style passes through a lining operation. The conversion cost rates for 2011 are:

	Cutting	Sewing	Lining	Packing
Rate per unit (pair)	Rs 100	Rs 150	Rs 80	Rs 20

Details of two work orders processed in August are:

	Work Order 815	Work Order 831
Number of units (pairs)	1,000	5,000
Direct materials costs	Rs 3,00,000	Rs 5,00,000
Style	Designer	Regular

Required

Calculate the total costs and the total cost per unit of work order 815 and work order 831.

17-37 Weighted-average method. Indian Defence, Limited is a manufacturer of military equipment. Its Orissa plant manufactures the Interceptor Missile under contract to the U.S. government and friendly countries. All Interceptors go through an identical manufacturing process. Every effort is made to ensure that all Interceptors are identical and meet many demanding performance specifications. The process-costing system at the Orissa plant has a single direct-cost category (direct materials) and a single indirect-cost category (conversion costs). Each Interceptor passes through two departments: the Assembly Department and the Testing Department. Direct materials are added at the beginning of the process in Assembly. Conversion costs are added evenly during the Assembly Department's process. When the Assembly Department finishes work on each Interceptor, it is immediately transferred to Testing.

Indian Defence uses the weighted-average method of process costing. Data for the Assembly Department for October of the recent year are:

	Physical Units (Missiles)	Direct Materials	Conversion Costs
Work in process, October 1[a]	20	Rs 46,00,000	Rs 12,00,000
Started during October	80		
Completed during October	90		
Work in process, October 31[b]	10		
Costs added during October		Rs 2,00,00,000	Rs 93,50,000

[a]Degree of completion: direct materials, ?%; conversion costs, 60%.
[b]Degree of completion: direct materials, ?%; conversion costs, 70%.

Required

1. For each cost element, compute equivalent units in the Assembly Department. Show physical units in the first column of your schedule.
2. For each cost element, calculate costs per equivalent unit.
3. Summarize total Assembly Department costs for October and assign these costs to units completed and transferred out and to units in ending work in process.

17-38 Journal entries (continuation of 17-37).

Required Prepare a set of summarized journal entries for all October transactions affecting Work in Process–Assembly. Set up a T-account for Work in Process –Assembly, and post your entries to it.

17-39 FIFO method (continuation of 17-37 and 17-38).

Required Do Exercise 17-37 using the FIFO method of process costing. Explain any difference between the costs per equivalent unit in the Assembly Department under the weighted-average method and the FIFO method.

17-40 Transferred-in costs, weighted average method (related to 17-37 to 17-39). Indian Defence, Limited, as you know, manufactures the Interceptor Missile at its Orissa plant. It has two departments: Assembly Department and Testing Department. This problem focuses on the Testing Department. (Problems 17-37 to 17-39 focused on the Assembly Department.) Direct materials are added when the Testing Department process is 90% complete. Conversion costs are added evenly during the Testing Department's process. As work in Assembly is completed, each unit is immediately transferred to Testing. As each unit is completed in Testing, it is immediately transferred to Finished Goods.

Indian Defence uses the weighted-average method of process costing. Data for the Testing Department for October are

	Physical Units (Missiles)	Transferred-InCosts	Direct Materials	Conversion Costs
Work in process October 1[a]	30	Rs 98,58,000	Rs 0	Rs 33,18,000
Transferred-in during October	?			
Completed during October	105			
Work in process October 31[b]	15			
Costs added during October		Rs 3,19,28,660	Rs 3,88,50,000	Rs 1,58,10,000

[a]Degree of completion: transferred-in costs, ?%; direct materials, ?%; conversion costs, 70%.
[b]Degree of completion: transferred-in costs, ?%; direct materials, ?%; conversion costs, 60%.

Required

1. What is the percentage of completion for (a) transferred-in costs and direct materials in beginning work-in-process inventory, and (b) transferred-in costs and direct materials in ending work-in-process inventory?
2. For each cost category, compute equivalent units in the Testing Department. Show physical units in the first column of your schedule.
3. For each cost category, calculate the cost per equivalent unit, summarize total Testing Department costs for October, and assign these costs to units completed (and transferred out) and to units in ending work in process.
4. Prepare journal entries for October transfers from the Assembly Department to the Testing Department and from the Testing Department to Finished Goods.

17-41 Transferred-in costs, FIFO method (continuation of 17-40).

Required Using the FIFO process-costing method, do the requirements of Exercise 17-40. Under the FIFO method, the transferred-in costs for the beginning work in process in the Testing Department on October 1 are Rs 98,00,600, and costs transferred in during October to the Testing Department are Rs 3,18,80,000. All other data are unchanged.

17-42 Transferred-in costs, weighted-average and FIFO methods. Frito-Lay, Limited manufactures convenience foods, including potato chips and corn chips. Production of corn chips occurs in four departments: cleaning, mixing, cooking, and drying and packaging. Consider the Drying and Packaging Department, where direct materials (packaging) are added at the end of the process. Conversion costs are added evenly during the process. The accounting records of a Frito-Lay plant provides the following information for corn chips in its Drying and Packaging Department during a weekly period (week 37):

	Physical Units (Cases)	Transferred-In Costs	Direct Materials	Conversion Costs
Beginning work in process[a]	1,250	Rs 29,000	Re 0	Rs 9,060
Transferred-in during week 37 from Cooking Department	5,000			
Completed during week 37	5,250			
Ending work in process, week 37[b]	1,000			
Costs added during week 37		Rs 96,000	Rs 25,200	Rs 38,400

[a]Degree of completion: transferred-in costs, 100%; direct materials, ?%; conversion costs, 80%.
[b]Degree of completion: transferred-in costs, 100%; direct materials, ?%; conversion costs, 40%.

Required

1. Using the weighted-average method, summarize the total Drying and Packaging Department costs for week 37, and assign these costs to units completed (and transferred out) and to units in ending work in process.
2. Assume that the FIFO method is used for the Drying and Packaging Department. Under FIFO, the transferred-in costs for work-in-process beginning inventory in week 37 are Rs 28,920, and the transferred-in costs during week 37 from the Cooking Department are Rs 94,000. All other data are unchanged. Summarize the total Drying and Packaging Department costs for week 37, and assign these costs to units completed and transferred out and to units in ending work in process using the FIFO method.

17-43 Standard costing with beginning and ending work in process. The Agrotech Food Limited uses the standard-costing method for its process-costing system. Standard costs for the Cooking Process are Rs 60 per equivalent unit for direct materials and Rs 30 per equivalent unit for conversion costs. All direct materials are introduced at the beginning of the process, and conversion costs are added evenly during the process. The operating summary for the month of May include the following data for the Cooking Process:

Work-in-process inventories:
  May 1, 3,000 units[a]
    (direct materials, Rs 18,000; conversion costs, Rs 54,000)
  May 31, 5,000 units[b]
  Units started in May, 20,000
Units completed and transferred out of cooking in May: 18,000
Additional actual costs incurred for cooking during May:
  Direct materials, Rs 12,50,000
  Conversion costs, Rs 5,70,000

aDegree of completion: direct materials, 100%; conversion costs, 60%.
bDegree of completion: direct materials, 100%; conversion costs, 50%.

Required

1. Compute the total standard costs of units transferred out in May and the total standard costs of the May 31 inventory of work in process.
2. Compute the total May variances for direct materials and conversion costs.

17-44 Transferred-in costs, equivalent-unit costs, working backward. Nilkamal Plastics has two processes: extrusion and thermo-assembly. Consider the June data for physical units in the thermo-assembly process: beginning work in process, 15,000 units; transferred in from the Extruding Department during June, 9,000; ending work in process, 5,000. Direct materials are added when the process in the Thermo-assembly Department is 80% complete. Conversion costs are added evenly during the process. Nilkamal Plastics uses the FIFO method of process costing. The following information is available:

	Transferred-In Costs	Direct Materials	Conversion Costs
Beginning work in process	Rs 9,00,000	–	Rs 4,50,000
Percentage completion of beginning work in process	100%	–	60%
Costs added in current period	Rs 5,85,000	Rs 5,70,000	Rs 5,72,000
Cost per equivalent unit of work done in current period	Rs 65	Rs 30	Rs 52

Required

1. For each cost category, compute equivalent units of work done in the current period.
2. For each cost category, compute separately the equivalent units of work done to complete beginning work-in-process inventory, to start and complete new units, and to produce ending work in process.
3. For each cost category, calculate the percentage of completion of ending work-in-process inventory.
4. Summarize total costs to account for, and assign these costs to units completed (and transferred out) and to units in ending work in process.

Spoilage, Rework, and Scrap

Learning Objectives

1. Understand the definitions of spoilage, rework, and scrap
2. Account for spoilage in process costing using the weighted-average method
3. Account for spoilage in process costing using the first-in, first-out (FIFO) method
4. Account for spoilage in process costing using the standard-costing method
5. Account for spoilage in job costing
6. Account for rework in job costing
7. Account for scrap

When a product doesn't meet specifications but is subsequently repaired and sold, it is called rework. Firms try to minimize rework, and similarly, spoilage and scrap during production. Why? Because higher-than-normal levels of spoilage and scrap can have a significant negative effect on a company's profits. And rework can cause substantial production delays, as the following article shows.

Rework Delays the Boeing Dreamliner by Three Years[1]

In 2007, Boeing was scheduled to introduce its newest airplane, the Dreamliner 787. Engineered to be the most fuel-efficient commercial plane, the Dreamliner received nearly 600 customer orders, making it the fastest selling commercial airplane in history.

By 2010, however, the first Dreamliner still had not rolled off the production line. The design and assembly process was riddled with production snafus, parts shortages, and supply-chain bottlenecks. The Dreamliner was Boeing's first major attempt at giving suppliers and partners far-ranging responsibility for designing and building the wings, fuselage, and other critical components to be shipped to Boeing for final assembly. The approach did not work as planned, with many of the 787's components delivered unfinished, with flaws, and lacking parts.

As a result, the Boeing Dreamliner aircraft required significant rework. The company's engineers had to redesign structural flaws in the airplane's wings, repair cracks in the composite materials used to construct the airplane, and fix faulty software among many other problems. In 2009, one of Boeing's unions calculated that half of its members' time was spent doing rework.

This rework led to costly delays for Boeing. Many of its customers, including Virgin Atlantic and Japan's All Nippon Airways, asked the company to compensate them for keeping less fuel-efficient planes in the air. Other customers cancelled their orders. Australia's Quantas Airways and a Dubai-based aircraft leasing firm each cancelled its orders for 15 airplanes, which cost Boeing at least $4.5 billion. The company

---

[1] *Sources:* Lunsford, J. Lynn. 2009. Dubai firm cancels 16 of Boeing's Dreamliners. *Wall Street Journal*, February 5; Matlack, Carol. 2009. More Boeing 787 woes as Quantas drops order. *BusinessWeek*, June 26; Sanders, Peter. 2009. At Boeing, Dreamliner fix turns up new glitch. *Wall Street Journal*, November 13; West, Karen. 2009. Boeing has much to prove with 787. *MSNBC.com*, December 16; Wilhelm, Steve. 2009. Boeing engineers seek credit for fixing goofs. *Puget Sound Business Journal*, August 17.

also took a $2.5 billion charge in 2009 related to development costs on the Dreamliner program.

Like Boeing, companies are increasingly focused on improving the quality of, and reducing defects in, their products, services, and activities. A rate of defects regarded as normal in the past is no longer tolerable. In this chapter, we focus on three types of costs that arise as a result of defects—spoilage, rework, and scrap—and ways to account for them. We also describe how to determine (1) cost of products, (2) cost of goods sold, and (3) inventory values when spoilage, rework, and scrap occur.

Defining Spoilage, Rework and Scrap

Learning Objective 1

Understand the definitions of spoilage,

. . . unacceptable units of production

rework,

. . . unacceptable units of production subsequently repaired

and scrap

. . . leftover material

While the terms used in this chapter may seem familiar, be sure you understand them in the context of management accounting.

Spoilage is units of production—whether fully or partially completed—that do not meet the specifications required by customers for good units and that are discarded or sold at reduced prices. Some examples of spoilage are defective shirts, jeans, shoes, and carpeting sold as "seconds," or defective aluminum cans sold to aluminum manufacturers for remelting to produce other aluminum products.

Rework is units of production that do not meet the specifications required by customers but which are subsequently repaired and sold as good finished units. For example, defective units of products (such as pagers, computers, and telephones) detected during or after the production process but before units are shipped to customers can sometimes be reworked and sold as good products.

Scrap is residual material that results from manufacturing a product. It has low sales value compared with the total sales value of the product. Examples are short lengths from woodworking operations, edges from plastic molding operations, and frayed cloth and end cuts from suit-making operations. Scrap can sometimes be sold for relatively small amounts. In that sense, scrap is similar to byproducts, which we studied in Chapter 16. The difference is that scrap arises as a residual from the manufacturing process, and is not a product targeted for manufacture or sale by the firm.

Some amounts of spoilage, rework, or scrap are inherent in many production processes. For example, semiconductor manufacturing is so complex and delicate that some spoiled units are commonly produced; usually, the spoiled units cannot be reworked. In the manufacture of high-precision machine tools, spoiled units can be reworked to meet standards, but only at a considerable cost. And in the mining industry, companies process ore that contains varying amounts of valuable metals and rock. Some amount of rock, which is scrap, is inevitable.

Two Types of Spoilage

Accounting for spoilage aims to determine the magnitude of spoilage costs and to distinguish between costs of normal and abnormal spoilage.[2] To manage, control, and reduce

[2] The helpful suggestions of Samuel Laimon, University of Saskatchewan, are gratefully acknowledged.

Learning Objective 2

Identify the differences between normal spoilage

. . . spoilage inherent in an efficient production process

and abnormal spoilage

. . . spoilage that would not arise under efficient operation

spoilage costs, companies need to highlight them, not bury them as an unidentified part of the costs of good units manufactured.

To illustrate normal and abnormal spoilage, consider Mendonza Plastics, which makes plastic casings for the iMac computer using plastic injection molding. In October 2009, Mendonza incurs costs of Rs 61,50,000 to produce 20,500 units. Of these 20,500 units, 20,000 are good units and 500 are spoiled units. Mendonza has no beginning inventory and no ending inventory that month. Of the 500 spoiled units, 400 units are spoiled because the injection molding machines are unable to manufacture good casings 100% of the time. That is, these units are spoiled even though the machines were run carefully and efficiently. The remaining 100 units are spoiled because of machine breakdowns and operator errors.

Normal Spoilage

Normal spoilage is spoilage inherent in a particular production process. In particular, it arises even when the process is operated in an efficient manner. The costs of normal spoilage are typically included as a component of the costs of good units manufactured because good units cannot be made without also making some units that are spoiled. There is a tradeoff between the speed of production and the normal spoilage rate. Management makes a conscious decision about how many units to produce per hour with the understanding that at the rate decided on, a certain level of spoilage is almost unavoidable. This justifies including the cost of normal spoilage in the cost of the good units completed. At Mendonza Plastics, the 400 units spoiled because of the limitations of injection molding machines and despite efficient operating conditions are considered normal spoilage. The calculations are as follows:

Manufacturing cost per unit, Rs 61,50,000 ÷ 20,500 units = Rs 300	
Manufacturing costs of good units alone, Rs 300 per unit × 20,000 units	Rs 60,00,000
Normal spoilage costs, Rs 300 per unit × 400 units	1,20,000
Manufacturing costs of good units completed (includes normal spoilage)	Rs 61,20,000

$$\text{Manufacturing cost per goods unit} = \frac{\text{Rs } 61{,}20{,}000}{20{,}000 \text{ units}} = \text{Rs } 306$$

Because normal spoilage is the spoilage related to the good units produced, normal spoilage rates are computed by dividing units of normal spoilage by total *good units completed*, not total *actual units started* in production. At Mendonza Plastics, the normal spoilage rate is therefore computed as 400 ÷ 20,000 = 2%.

Abnormal Spoilage

Abnormal spoilage is spoilage that is not inherent in a particular production process and would not arise under efficient operating conditions. At Mendonza, the 100 units spoiled because of machine breakdowns and operator errors are abnormal spoilage. Abnormal spoilage is usually regarded as avoidable and controllable. Line operators and other plant personnel generally can decrease or eliminate abnormal spoilage by identifying the reasons for machine breakdowns, operator errors, and the like, and by taking steps to prevent their recurrence. To highlight the effect of abnormal spoilage costs, companies calculate the units of abnormal spoilage and record the cost in the Loss from Abnormal Spoilage account, which appears as a separate line item in the income statement. At Mendonza, the loss from abnormal spoilage is Rs 30,000 (Rs 300 per unit × 100 units).

Decision Point

What is the distinction between normal and abnormal spoilage?

Issues about accounting for spoilage arise in both process-costing and job-costing systems. We discuss both instances next, beginning with spoilage in process-costing.

Spoilage in Process Costing Using Weighted-Average and FIFO

How do process-costing systems account for spoiled units? We have already said that units of abnormal spoilage should be counted and recorded separately in a Loss from Abnormal Spoilage account. But what about units of normal spoilage? The correct method is to count these units when computing output units—physical or equivalent—in a process-costing system. The following example and discussion illustrate this approach.

Learning Objective 3

Account for spoilage in process costing using the weighted-average method

. . . spoilage cost based on total costs and equivalent units completed to date

and the first-in, first-out (FIFO) method

. . . spoilage cost based on costs of current period and equivalent units of work done in current period

Count All Spoilage

Example 1: Chipmakers, Ltd., manufactures computer chips for television sets. All direct materials are added at the beginning of the production process. To highlight issues that arise with normal spoilage, we assume no beginning inventory and focus only on direct material costs. The following data are available for May 2012.

	A	B	C
1		Physical Units	Direct Materials
2	Work in process, beginning inventory (May 1)	0	
3	Started during May	10,000	
4	Good units completed and transferred out during May	5,000	
5	Units spoiled (all normal spoilage)	1,000	
6	Work in process, ending inventory (May 31)	4,000	
7	Degree of completion of ending work in process		100%
8	Direct material costs added in May		Rs 27,00,000

Spoilage is detected upon completion of the process and has zero net disposal value.

An **inspection point** is the stage of the production process at which products are examined to determine whether they are acceptable or unacceptable units. Spoilage is typically assumed to occur at the stage of completion where inspection takes place. As a result, the spoiled units in our example are assumed to be 100% complete with respect to direct materials.

Exhibit 18-1 calculates and assigns cost per unit of direct materials. Overall, Chipmakers generated 10,000 equivalent units of output: 5,000 equivalent units in good units completed (5,000 physical units × 100%), 4,000 units in ending work in process (4,000 physical units × 100%), and 1,000 equivalent units in normal spoilage (1,000 physical units × 100%). Given total direct material costs of Rs 27,00,000 in May, this yields an equivalent-unit cost of Rs 270. The total cost of good units completed and transferred out, which includes the cost of normal spoilage, is then Rs 16,20,000 (6,000 equivalent units × Rs 270), while the ending work in process is assigned a cost of Rs 10,80,000 (4,000 equivalent units × Rs 270).

Exhibit 18-1

Effect of Recognizing Equivalent Units in Spoilage for Direct Material Costs Chipmakers, Inc., for May 2012

	A	B
1		Approach Counting Spoiled Units When Computing Output in Equivalent Units
2	Costs to account for	Rs 27,00,000
3	Divide by equivalent units of output	÷ 10,000
4	Cost per equivalent unit of output	Rs 270
5	Assignment of costs:	
6	Good units completed (5,000 units x Rs 270 per unit)	Rs 13,50,000
7	Add normal spoilage (1,000 units x Rs 270 per unit)	2,70,000
8	Total costs of good units completed and transferred out	16,20,000
9	Work in process, ending (4,000 units x Rs 270 per unit)	10,80,000
10	Costs accounted for	Rs 27,00,000

There are two noteworthy features of this approach. First, the 4,000 units in ending work in process are not assigned any of the costs of normal spoilage. This is appropriate because the units have not yet been inspected. While the units in ending work in process undoubtedly include some that will be detected as spoiled when inspected, these units will only be identified when the units are completed in the subsequent accounting period. At that time, costs of normal spoilage will be assigned to the good units completed in that period. Second, the approach used in Exhibit 18-1 delineates the cost of normal spoilage as Rs 2,70,000. By highlighting the magnitude of this cost, the approach helps to focus management's attention on the potential economic benefits of reducing spoilage.

Five-Step Procedure for Process Costing with Spoilage

Example 2: Anzio Company manufactures a recycling container in its Forming Department. Direct materials are added at the beginning of the production process. Conversion costs are added evenly during the production process. Some units of this product are spoiled as a result of defects, which are detectable only upon inspection of finished units. Normally, spoiled units are 10% of the finished output of good units. That is, for every 10 good units produced, there is 1 unit of normal spoilage. Summary data for July 2012 are:

File Edit View Insert Format Tools Data Window Help

	A	B	C	D	E
1		Physical Units (1)	Direct Materials (2)	Conversion Costs (3)	Total Costs (4) = (2) + (3)
2	Work in process, beginning inventory (July 1)	1,500	Rs 1,20,000	Rs 90,000	Rs 2,10,000
3	Degree of completion of beginning work in process		100%	60%	
4	Started during July	8,500			
5	Good units completed and transferred out during July	7,000			
6	Work in process, ending inventory (July 31)	2,000			
7	Degree of completion of ending work in process		100%	50%	
8	Total costs added during July		Rs 7,65,000	Rs 8,91,000	Rs 16,56,000
9	Normal spoilage as a percentage of good units	10%			
10	Degree of completion of normal spoilage		100%	100%	
11	Degree of completion of abnormal spoilage		100%	100%	

The five-step procedure for process costing used in Chapter 17 needs only slight modification to accommodate spoilage.

Step 1: Summarize the Flow of Physical Units. Identify the number of units of both normal and abnormal spoilage.

$$\text{Total Spoilage} = \left(\text{Units in beginning work-in-process inventory} + \text{Units started}\right) - \left(\text{Good units completed and transferred out} + \text{Units in ending work-in-process inventory}\right)$$

$$= (1{,}500 + 8{,}500) - (7{,}000 + 2{,}000)$$
$$= 10{,}000 - 9{,}000$$
$$= 1{,}000 \text{ units}$$

Recall that normal spoilage is 10% of good output at Anzio Company. Therefore, normal spoilage = 10% of the 7,000 units of *good* output = 700 units.

$$\text{Abnormal spoilage} = \text{Total spoilage}$$
$$= 1{,}000 \text{ units} - 700 \text{ units}$$
$$= 300 \text{ units}$$

Step 2: Compute Output in Terms of Equivalent Units. Compute equivalent units for spoilage in the same way we compute equivalent units for good units. As illustrated above, all spoiled units are included in the computation of output units. Because Anzio's inspection point is at the completion of production, the same amount of work will have been done on each spoiled and each completed good unit.

Step 3: Summarize Total Costs to Account For. The total costs to account for are all the costs debited to Work in Process. The details for this step are similar to step 3 in Chapter 17.

Step 4: Compute Cost per Equivalent Unit. This step is similar to step 4 in Chapter 17.

Step 5: Assign Total Costs to Units Completed, to Spoiled Units, and to Units in Ending Work in Process. This step now includes computation of the cost of spoiled units and the cost of good units.

We illustrate these five steps of process costing for the weighted-average and FIFO methods next. *The standard-costing method is illustrated in the appendix to this chapter.*

Weighted-Average Method and Spoilage

Exhibit 18-2, Panel A, presents steps 1 and 2 to calculate equivalent units of work done to date and includes calculations of equivalent units of normal and abnormal spoilage. Exhibit 18-2, Panel B, presents steps 3, 4, and 5 (together called the production-cost worksheet).

Step 3 summarizes total costs to account for. Step 4 presents cost-per-equivalent-unit calculations using the weighted-average method. Note how, for each cost category, costs of beginning work in process and costs of work done in the current period are totaled and divided by equivalent units of all work done to date to calculate the weighted-average cost per equivalent unit. Step 5 assigns total costs to completed units, normal and abnormal spoiled units, and ending inventory by multiplying the equivalent units calculated in step 2 by the cost per equivalent unit calculated in step 4. Also note that the Rs 1,38,250 costs of normal spoilage are added to the costs of the related good units completed and transferred out.

$$\text{Cost per good units completed and transferred out of the process} = \frac{\text{Total cost transferred out (including normal spoilage)}}{\text{Number of good units produced}}$$

$$= \text{Rs } 15{,}20{,}750 \div 7{,}000 \text{ good units} \times \text{Rs } 217.25 \text{ per good unit}$$

This amount is not equal to Rs 197.5 per good unit, the sum of the Rs 88.5 cost per equivalent unit of direct materials plus the Rs 109 cost per equivalent unit of conversion costs. That's because the cost per good unit equals the sum of the direct material and conversion costs per equivalent unit, Rs 197.5, plus a share of normal spoilage, Rs 19.75 (Rs 1,38,250 ÷ 7,000 good units), for a total of Rs 217.25 per good unit. The Rs 59,250 costs of abnormal spoilage are charged to the Loss from Abnormal Spoilage account and do not appear in the costs of good units.[3]

FIFO Method and Spoilage

Exhibit 18-3, Panel A, presents steps 1 and 2 using the FIFO method, which focuses on equivalent units of work done in the current period. Exhibit 18-3, Panel B, presents steps 3, 4, and 5. Note how when assigning costs, the FIFO method keeps the costs of the beginning work in process separate and distinct from the costs of work done in the current period. All spoilage costs are assumed to be related to units completed during this period, using the unit costs of the current period.[4]

---

[3] The actual costs of spoilage (and rework) are often greater than the costs recorded in the accounting system because the opportunity costs of disruption of the production line, storage, and lost contribution margins are not recorded in accounting systems. Chapter 19 discusses these opportunity costs from the perspective of cost management.

[4] To simplify calculations under FIFO, spoiled units are accounted for as if they were started in the current period. Although some of the beginning work in process probably did spoil, all spoilage is treated as if it came from current production.

Exhibit 18-2 Weighted-Average Method of Process Costing with Spoilage Forming Department of the Anzio Company for July 2012

PANEL A: Steps 1 and 2—Summarize Output in Physical Units and Compute Equivalent Units

File Edit View Insert Format Tools Data Window Help

	A	B	C	D	E
1			(Step 1)	(Step 2)	
2				Equivalent Units	
3		Flow of Production	Physical Units	Direct Materials	Conversion Costs
4		Work in process, beginning	1,500		
5		Started during current period	8,500		
6		To account for	10,000		
7		Good units completed and transferred out during current period	7,000	7,000	7,000
8		Normal spoilage[a]	700		
9		(700 x 100%; 700 x 100%)		700	700
10		Abnormal spoilage[b]	300		
11		(300 x 100%; 300 x 100%)		300	300
12		Work in process, ending[c]	2,000		
13		(2,000 x 100%; 2,000 x 50%)		2,000	1,000
14		Accounted for	10,000		
15		Work done to date		10,000	9,000
16					
17	[a]Normal spoilage is 10% of good units transferred out: 10% x 7,000 = 700 units. Degree of completion of normal spoilage				
18	in this department: direct materials, 100%; conversion costs, 100%.				
19	[b]Abnormal spoilage = Total spoilage – Normal spoilage = 1,000 – 700 = 300 units. Degree of completion of abnormal spoilage				
20	in this department: direct materials, 100%; conversion costs, 100%.				
21	[c]Degree of completion in this department: direct materials, 100%; conversion costs, 50%.				

PANEL B: Steps 3, 4, and 5—Summarize Total Costs to Account For, Compute Cost per Equivalent Unit, and Assign Total Costs to Units Completed, to Spoiled Units, and to Units in Ending Work in Process

			Total Production Costs	Direct Materials	Conversion Costs
23					
24	(Step 3)	Work in process, beginning	Rs 2,10,000	Rs 1,20,000	Rs 90,000
25		Costs added in current period	16,56,000	7,65,000	8,91,000
26		Total costs to account for	Rs 18,66,000	Rs 8,85,000	Rs 9,81,000
27	(Step 4)	Costs incurred to date		8,85,000	Rs 9,81,000
28		Divided by equivalent units of work done to date		÷10,000	÷ 9,000
29		Cost per equivalent unit		Rs 88.5	Rs 109.0
30	(Step 5)	Assignment of costs:			
31		Good units completed and transferred out (7,000 units)			
32		Costs before adding normal spoilage	Rs 13,82,500	(7,000[d] x Rs 88.5)+	(7,000[d] x Rs 109.0)
33		Normal spoilage (700 units)	1,38,250	(700[d] x Rs 88.5) +	(700[d] x Rs 109.0)
34	(A)	Total costs of good units completed and transferred out	15,20,750		
35	(B)	Abnormal spoilage (300 units)	59,250	(300[d] x Rs 88.5) +	(300[d] x Rs 109.0)
36	(C)	Work in process, ending (2,000 units)	2,86,000	(2,000[d] x Rs 88.5)+	1000[d] x Rs 109.0)
37	(A)+(B)+(C)	Total costs accounted for	Rs 18,66,000	Rs 8,85,000 +	Rs 9,81,000
38					
39	[d]Equivalent units of direct materials and conversion costs calculated in step 2 in Panel A.				

Exhibit 18-3 First-In, First-Out (FIFO) Method of Process Costing with Spoilage Forming Department of the Anzio Company for July 2012

PANEL A: Steps 1 and 2—Summarize Output in Physical Units and Compute Equivalent Units

File Edit View Insert Format Tools Data Window Help

	A	B	C	D	E
1			(Step 1)	(Step 2)	
2				Equivalent Units	
3		Flow of Production	Physical Units	Direct Materials	Conversion Costs
4		Work in process, beginning	1,500		
5		Started during current period	8,500		
6		To account for	10,000		
7		Good units completed and transferred out during current period:			
8		From beginning work in process[a]	1,500		
9		[1,500 x (100% − 100%); 1,500 x (100% − 60%)]		0	600
10		Started and completed	5,500[b]		
11		(5,500 x 100%; 5,500 x 100%)		5,500	5,500
12		Normal spoilage[c]	700		
13		(700 x 100%; 700 x 100%)		700	700
14		Abnormal spoilage[d]	300		
15		(300 x 100%; 300 x 100%)		300	300
16		Work in process, ending[e]	2,000		
17		(2,000 x 100%; 2,000 x 50%)		2,000	1,000
18		Accounted for	10,000		
19		Work done in current period only		8,500	8,100
20					
21	[a]Degree of completion in this department: direct materials, 100%; conversion costs, 60%.				
22	[b]7,000 physical units completed and transferred out minus 1,500 physical units completed and transferred out from beginning				
23	work-in-process inventory.				
24	[c]Normal spoilage is 10% of good units transferred out: 10% x 7,000 = 700 units. Degree of completion of normal spoilage				
25	in this department: direct materials, 100%; conversion costs, 100%.				
26	[d]Abnormal spoilage = Actual spoilage − Normal spoilage = 1,000 − 700 = 300 units. Degree of completion of abnormal spoilage				
27	in this department: direct materials, 100%; conversion costs, 100%.				
28	[e]Degree of completion in this department: direct materials, 100%; conversion costs, 50%.				

PANEL B: Steps 3, 4, and 5—Summarize Total Costs to Account For, Compute Cost per Equivalent Unit, and Assign Total Costs to Units Completed, to Spoiled Units, and to Units in Ending Work in

	A	B	C	D	E
30			Total Production Costs	Direct Materials	Conversion Costs
31	(Step 3)	Work in process, beginning	Rs 2,10,000	Rs 1,20,000	Rs 90,000
32		Costs added in current period	16,56,000	7,65,000	8,91,000
33		Total costs to account for	Rs 18,66,000	Rs 8,85,000	Rs 9,81,000
34	(Step 4)	Costs added in current period		Rs 7,65,000	Rs 8,91,000
35		Divided by equivalent units of work done in current period		÷ 8,500	÷ 8,100
36		Cost per equivalent unit		Rs 90.0	Rs 110.0
37	(Step 5)	Assignment of costs:			
38		Good units completed and transferred out (7,000 units)			
39		Work in process, beginning (1,500 units)	Rs 2,10,000	Rs 1,20,000 +	Rs 90,000
40		Costs added to beginning work in process in current period	66,000	(0[f] x Rs 90) +	(600[f] x Rs 110)
41		Total from beginning inventory before normal spoilage	2,76,000		
42		Started and completed before normal spoilage (5,500 units)	11,00,000	(5,500[f] x Rs 90) +	(5,500[f] x Rs 110)
43		Normal spoilage (700 units)	1,40,000	(700[f] x Rs 90) +	(700[f] x Rs 110)
44	(A)	Total costs of good units completed and transferred out	15,16,000		
45	(B)	Abnormal spoilage (300 units)	60,000	(300[f] x Rs 90) +	(300[f] x Rs 110)
46	(C)	Work in process, ending (2,000 units)	2,90,000	(2,000[f] x Rs 90) +	(2,000[f] x Rs 110)
47	(A)+(B)+(C)	Total costs accounted for	Rs 18,66,000	Rs 8,85,000 +	Rs 9,81,000
48					
49					
50					
51	[f]Equivalent units of direct materials and conversion costs calculated in step 2 in Panel A.				

Decision Point

How do the weighted-average and FIFO methods of process costing calculate the costs of good units and spoilage?

Journal Entries

The information from Panel B in Exhibits 18-2 and 18-3 supports the following journal entries to transfer good units completed to finished goods and to recognize the loss from abnormal spoilage.

	Weighted Average		FIFO	
Finished Goods	152,075		151,600	
Work in Process—Forming		152,075		151,600
To record transfer of good units completed in July.				
Loss from Abnormal Spoilage	5,925		6,000	
Work in Process—Forming		5,925		6,000
To record abnormal spoilage detected in July.				

Inspection Points and Allocating Costs of Normal Spoilage

Learning Objective 4

Account for spoilage at various stages of completion in process costing

. . . spoilage costs vary based on the point at which inspection is carried out

Our Anzio Company example assumes inspection occurs upon completion of the units. However, spoilage might actually occur at various stages of the production process, although it is typically detected only at one or more inspection points. The cost of spoiled units is assumed to equal all costs incurred in producing spoiled units up to the point of inspection. When spoiled goods have a disposal value (for example, carpeting sold as "seconds"), the net cost of spoilage is computed by deducting the disposal value from the costs of the spoiled goods that have been accumulated up to the inspection point. The unit costs of normal and abnormal spoilage are the same when the two are detected at the same inspection point. However, situations may arise when abnormal spoilage is detected at a different point from normal spoilage. Consider shirt manufacturing. Normal spoilage in the form of defective shirts is identified upon inspection at the end of the production process. Now suppose a faulty machine causes many defective shirts to be produced at the halfway point of the production process. These defective shirts are abnormal spoilage and occur at a different point in the production process from normal spoilage. In such cases, the unit cost of abnormal spoilage, which is based on costs incurred up to the halfway point of the production process, differs from the unit cost of normal spoilage, which is based on costs incurred through the end of the production process.

Costs of abnormal spoilage are separately accounted for as losses of the accounting period in which they are detected. However, recall that normal spoilage costs are added to the costs of good units, which raises an additional issue: Should normal spoilage costs be allocated between completed units and ending work-in-process inventory? *The common approach is to presume that normal spoilage occurs at the inspection point in the production cycle and to allocate its cost over all units that have passed that point during the accounting period.*

In the Anzio Company example, spoilage is assumed to occur when units are inspected at the end of the production process, so no costs of normal spoilage are allocated to ending work in process. If the units in ending work in process have passed the inspection point, however, the costs of normal spoilage are allocated to units in ending work in process as well as to completed units. For example, if the inspection point is at the halfway point of production, then any ending work in process that is at least 50% complete would be allocated a full measure of normal spoilage costs, and those spoilage costs would be calculated on the basis of all costs incurred up to the inspection point. If ending work in process is less than 50% complete, however, no normal spoilage costs would be allocated to it.

To better understand these issues, let us now assume that inspection at Anzio Company occurs at various stages in the production process. How does this affect the amount of normal and abnormal spoilage? As before, consider the forming department, and recall that direct materials are added at the start of production, while conversion costs are added evenly during the process.

Consider three different cases: Inspection occurs at (1) the 20%, (2) the 55%, or (3) the 100% completion stage. The last option is the one we have analyzed so far (see Exhibit 18-2). Assume that normal spoilage is 10% of the good units passing inspection. A total of 1,000 units are spoiled in all three cases. Normal spoilage is computed on the basis of the number of *good units* that pass the inspection point *during the current period*. The following data are for July 2012. Note how the number of units of normal and abnormal spoilage changes, depending on when inspection occurs.

	A	B	C	D
1		Physical Units: Stage of Completion at Which Inspection Occurs		
2	**Flow of Production**	**20%**	**55%**	**100%**
3	Work in process, beginning[a]	1,500	1,500	1,500
4	Started during July	8,500	8,500	8,500
5	To account for	10,000	10,000	10,000
6	Good units completed and transferred out			
7	(10,000 – 1,000 spoiled – 2,000 ending)	7,000	7,000	7,000
8	Normal spoilage	750[c]	550[d]	700[e]
9	Abnormal spoilage (1,000 – normal spoilage)	250	450	300
10	Work in process, ending[b]	2,000	2,000	2,000
11	Accounted for	10,000	10,000	10,000
12				
13	[a]Degree of completion in this department: direct materials, 100%; conversion costs, 60%.			
14	[b]Degree of completion in this department: direct materials, 100%; conversion costs, 50%.			
15	[c]10% × (8,500 units started – 1,000 units spoiled), because only the units started passed the 20% completion			
16	inspection point in the current period. Beginning work in process is excluded from this calculation because,			
17	being 60% complete at the start of the period, it passed the inspection point in the previous period.			
18	[d]10% × (8,500 units started – 1,000 units spoiled – 2,000 units in ending work in process). Both beginning and			
19	ending work in process are excluded since neither was inspected this period.			
20	[e]10% × 7,000, because 7,000 units are fully completed and inspected in the current period.			

The following diagram shows the flow of physical units for July and illustrates the normal spoilage numbers in the table. Note that 7,000 good units are completed and transferred out—1,500 from beginning work in process and 5,500 started and completed during the period—while 2,000 units are in ending work in process.

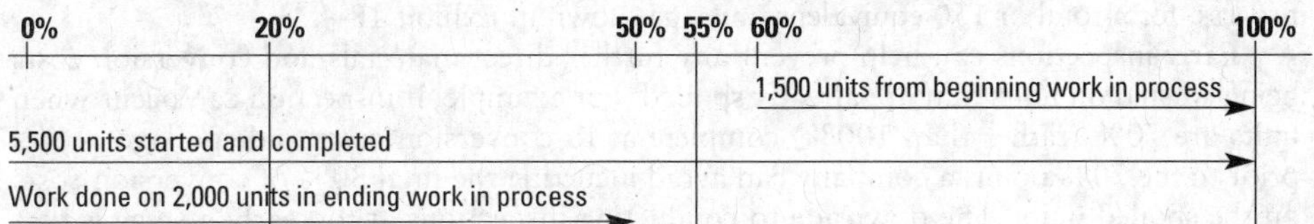

To see the number of units passing each inspection point, consider in the diagram the vertical lines at the 20%, 55%, and 100% inspection points. Note that the vertical line at 20% crosses two horizontal lines—5,500 good units started and completed and 2,000 units in ending work in process—for a total of 7,500 good units. (The 20% vertical line does not cross the line representing work done on the 1,500 good units completed from beginning work in process, because these units are already 60% complete at the start of the period and, hence, are not inspected this period.) Normal spoilage equals 10% of 7,500 = 750 units. On the other hand, the vertical line at the 55% point crosses just the second horizontal line, indicating that only 5,500 good units pass this point. Normal spoilage in this case is 10% of 5,500 = 550 units. At the 100% point, normal spoilage = 10% of 7,000 (1,500 + 5,500) good units = 700 units.

Exhibit 18-4 shows the computation of equivalent units under the weighted-average method, assuming inspection at the 20% completion stage. The calculations depend on the direct materials and conversion costs incurred to get the units to this inspection point. The spoiled units have a full measure of direct materials and a 20% measure of conversion costs. Calculations of costs per equivalent unit and the assignment of total costs to units completed and to ending work in process are similar to calculations in previous illustrations in this chapter. Because ending work in process has passed the inspection point, these units bear normal spoilage costs, just like the units that have been completed and transferred out. For example, conversion costs for units completed and transferred out include conversion costs for 7,000 good units produced plus 20% × (10% × 5,500) = 110 equivalent units of

Exhibit 18-4

Computing Equivalent Units with Spoilage Using Weighted-Average Method of Process Costing with Inspection at 20% of Completion for Forming Department of Anzio Company for July 2012

	A	B	C	D
1		(Step 1)	(Step 2)	
2			Equivalent Units	
3	Flow of Production	Physical Units	Direct Materials	Conversion Costs
4	Work in process, beginning[a]	1,500		
5	Started during current period	8,500		
6	To account for	10,000		
7	Good units completed and transferred out:	7,000	7,000	7,000
8	Normal spoilage	750		
9	(750 × 100%; 750 × 20%)		750	150
10	Abnormal spoilage	250		
11	(250 × 100%; 250 × 20%)		250	50
12	Work in process, ending[b]	2,000		
13	(2,000 × 100%; 2,000 × 50%)		2,000	1,000
14	Accounted for	10,000		
15	Equivalent units of work done to date		10,000	8,200
16				
17	[a]Degree of completion: direct materials, 100%; conversion costs, 60%.			
18	[b]Degree of completion: direct materials, 100%; conversion costs, 50%.			

normal spoilage. *We multiply by 20% to obtain equivalent units of normal spoilage because conversion costs are only 20% complete at the inspection point.* Conversion costs of ending work in process include conversion costs of 50% of 2,000 = 1,000 equivalent good units plus 20% × (10% × 2,000) = 40 equivalent units of normal spoilage. Thus, the equivalent units of normal spoilage accounted for are 110 equivalent units related to units completed and transferred out plus 40 equivalent units related to units in ending work in process, for a total of 150 equivalent units, as shown in Exhibit 18-4.

Decision Point

How does inspection at various stages of completion affect the amount of normal and abnormal spoilage?

Early inspections can help prevent any further direct materials and conversion costs being wasted on units that are already spoiled. For example, if inspection can occur when units are 70% (rather than 100%) complete as to conversion costs and spoilage occurs prior to the 70% point, a company can avoid incurring the final 30% of conversion costs on the spoiled units. The downside to conducting inspections at too early a stage is that spoilage that happens at later stages of the process may go undetected. It is for these reasons that firms often conduct multiple inspections and also empower workers to identify and resolve defects on a timely basis.

Job Costing and Spoilage

Learning Objective 5

Account for spoilage in job costing

. . . normal spoilage assigned directly or indirectly to job; abnormal spoilage written off as a loss of the period

The concepts of normal and abnormal spoilage also apply to job-costing systems. Abnormal spoilage is separately identified so companies can work to eliminate it altogether. Costs of abnormal spoilage are not considered to be inventoriable costs and are written off as costs of the accounting period in which the abnormal spoilage is detected. Normal spoilage costs in job-costing systems—as in process-costing systems—are inventoriable costs, although increasingly companies are tolerating only small amounts of spoilage as normal. When assigning costs, job-costing systems generally distinguish *normal spoilage attributable to a specific job from normal spoilage common to all jobs.*

We describe accounting for spoilage in job costing using the following example.

Example 3: In the Harshad Machine Shop, 5 aircraft parts out of a job lot of 50 aircraft parts are spoiled. Costs assigned prior to the inspection point are Rs 20,000 per part. Our presentation here and in subsequent sections focuses on how the Rs 20,000 cost per part is accounted for. When the spoilage is detected, the spoiled goods are inventoried at Rs 6,000 per part, the net disposal value.

Our presentation here and in subsequent sections focuses on how the Rs 20,000 cost per part is accounted for.

Normal spoilage attributable to a specific job When normal spoilage occurs because of the specifications of a particular job, that job bears the cost of the spoilage minus the disposal value of the spoilage. The journal entry to recognize disposal value (items in parentheses indicate subsidiary ledger postings) is:

Materials Control (spoiled goods at current net disposal value):		
5 units × Rs 6,000 per unit	30,000	
Work-in-Process Control (specific job): 5 units × Rs 6,000 per unit		30,000

Note, the Work-in-Process Control (specific job) has already been debited (charged) Rs 1,00,000 for the spoiled parts (5 spoiled parts × Rs 20,000 per part). The net cost of normal spoilage = Rs 70,000 (Rs 1,00,000 – Rs 30,000), which is an additional cost of the 45 (50 – 5) good units produced. Therefore, total cost of the 45 good units is Rs 9,70,000: Rs 9,00,000 (45 units × Rs 20,000 per unit) incurred to produce the good units plus the Rs 70,000 net cost of normal spoilage. Cost per good unit is Rs 21,555.6 (Rs 9,70,000 ÷ 45 good units).

Normal spoilage common to all jobs In some cases, spoilage may be considered a normal characteristic of the production process. The spoilage inherent in production will, of course, occur when a specific job is being worked on. But the spoilage is not attributable to, and hence is not charged directly to, the specific job. Instead, the spoilage is allocated indirectly to the job as manufacturing overhead because the spoilage is common to all jobs. The journal entry is:

Materials Control (spoiled goods at current disposal value):		
5 units × Rs 6,000 per unit	30,000	
Manufacturing Overhead Control (normal spoilage):		
(Rs 1,00,000 – Rs 30,000)	70,000	
Work-in-Process Control (specific job): 5 units × Rs 20,000 per unit		1,00,000

When normal spoilage is common to all jobs, the budgeted manufacturing overhead rate includes a provision for normal spoilage cost. Normal spoilage cost is spread, through overhead allocation, over all jobs rather than allocated to a specific job.[5] For example, if Harshad produced 140 good units from all jobs in a given month, the Rs 70,000 of normal spoilage overhead costs would be allocated at the rate of Rs 500 per good unit (Rs 70,000 ÷ 140 good units). Normal spoilage overhead costs allocated to the 45 good units in the job would be Rs 22,500 (Rs 500 × 45 good units). Total cost of the 45 good units is Rs 9,22,500: Rs 9,00,000 (45 units × Rs 20,000 per unit) incurred to produce the good units plus Rs 22,500 of normal spoilage overhead costs. Cost per good unit is Rs 20,500 (Rs 9,22,500 ÷ 45 good units).

Abnormal spoilage If the spoilage is abnormal, the net loss is charged to the Loss from Abnormal Spoilage account. Unlike normal spoilage costs, abnormal spoilage costs are not included as a part of the cost of good units produced. Total cost of the 45 good units is Rs 9,00,000 (45 units × Rs 20,000 per unit). Cost per good unit is Rs 20,000 (Rs 9,00,000 ÷ 45 good units).

Materials Control (spoiled goods at current disposal value):		
5 units × Rs 6,000 per unit	30,000	
Loss from Abnormal Spoilage (Rs 1,00,000 – Rs 30,000)	70,000	
Work-in-Process Control (specific job): 5 units × Rs 20,000 per unit		1,00,000

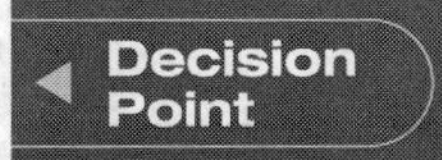

How do job-costing systems account for spoilage?

Even though, for external reporting purposes, abnormal spoilage costs are written off in the accounting period and are not linked to specific jobs or units, companies often identify the particular reasons for abnormal spoilage, and, when appropriate, link abnormal spoilage with specific jobs or units for cost management purposes.

[5] Note that costs already assigned to products are charged back to Manufacturing Overhead Control, which generally accumulates only costs incurred, not both costs incurred and costs already assigned.

Job Costing and Rework

Account for rework in job costing

. . . normal rework assigned directly or indirectly to job; abnormal rework written off as a loss of the period

Rework is units of production that are inspected, determined to be unacceptable, repaired, and sold as acceptable finished goods. We again distinguish (1) normal rework attributable to a specific job, (2) normal rework common to all jobs, and (3) abnormal rework.

Consider the Harshad Machine Shop data in Example 3 on p. 770. Assume the five spoiled parts are reworked. The journal entry for the Rs 1,00,000 of total costs (the details of these costs are assumed) assigned to the five spoiled units before considering rework costs is:

Work-in-Process Control (specific job)	1,00,000	
Materials Control		40,000
Wages Payable Control		40,000
Manufacturing Overhead Allocated		20,000

Assume the rework costs equal Rs 38,000 (comprising Rs 8,000 direct materials, Rs 20,000 direct manufacturing labor, and Rs 10,000 manufacturing overhead).

Normal rework attributable to a specific job If the rework is normal but occurs because of the requirements of a specific job, the rework costs are charged to that job. The journal entry is:

Work-in-Process Control (specific job)	38,000	
Materials Control		8,000
Wages Payable Control		20,000
Manufacturing Overhead Allocated		10,000

Normal rework common to all jobs When rework is normal and not attributable to a specific job, the costs of rework are charged to manufacturing overhead and are spread, through overhead allocation, over all jobs.

Manufacturing Overhead Control (rework costs)	38,000	
Materials Control		8,000
Wages Payable Control		20,000
Manufacturing Overhead Allocated		10,000

Abnormal rework If the rework is abnormal, it is recorded by charging abnormal rework to a loss account.

Loss from Abnormal Rework	38,000	
Materials Control		8,000
Wages Payable Control		20,000
Manufacturing Overhead Allocated		10,000

Accounting for rework in a process-costing system also requires abnormal rework to be distinguished from normal rework. Process costing accounts for abnormal rework in the same way as job costing. Accounting for normal rework follows the accounting described for normal rework common to all jobs (units) because masses of identical or similar units are being manufactured.

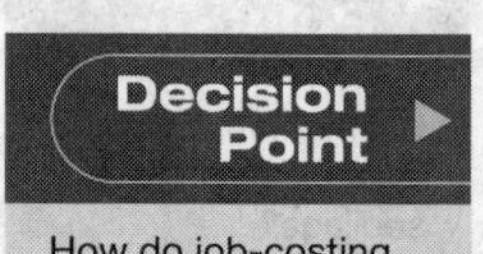

How do job-costing systems account for rework?

Costing rework focuses managers' attention on the resources wasted on activities that would not have to be undertaken if the product had been made correctly. The cost of rework prompts managers to seek ways to reduce rework, for example, by designing new products or processes, training workers, or investing in new machines. To eliminate rework and to simplify the accounting, some companies set a standard of zero rework. All rework is then treated as abnormal and is written off as a cost of the current period.

Accounting for Scrap

Learning Objective 7

Account for scrap

. . . reduces cost of job either at time of sale or at time of production

Scrap is residual material that results from manufacturing a product; it has low total sales value compared with the total sales value of the product. No distinction is made between normal and abnormal scrap because no cost is assigned to scrap. The only distinction made is between scrap attributable to a specific job and scrap common to all jobs.

There are two aspects of accounting for scrap:

1. Planning and control, including physical tracking
2. Inventory costing, including when and how scrap affects operating income

Initial entries to scrap records are commonly in physical terms. In various industries, companies quantify items such as stamped-out metal sheets or edges of molded plastic parts by weighing, counting, or some other measure. Scrap records not only help m[illegible]fficiency, but also help keep track of scrap, and so reduce the chances of theft. Companies use scrap records to prepare periodic summaries of the amounts of actual scrap compared with budgeted or standard amounts. Scrap is either sold or disposed of quickly or it is stored for later sale, disposal, or reuse.

Careful tracking of scrap often extends into the accounting records. Many companies maintain a distinct account for scrap costs somewhere in their accounting system. The issues here are similar to the issues in Chapter 16 regarding the accounting for byproducts:

- When should the value of scrap be recognized in the accounting records—at the time scrap is produced or at the time scrap is sold?
- How should revenues from scrap be accounted for?

To illustrate, we extend our Harshad example. Assume the manufacture of aircraft parts generates scrap and that the scrap from a job has a net sales value of Rs 9,000.

Recognizing Scrap at the Time of Its Sale

When the rupee amount of scrap is immaterial, the simplest accounting is to record the physical quantity of scrap returned to the storeroom and to regard scrap sales as a separate line item in the income statement. In this case, the only journal entry is:

Sale of scrap:	Cash or Accounts Receivable	9,000	
	Scrap Revenues		9,000

When the rupee amount of scrap is material and the scrap is sold quickly after it is produced, the accounting depends on whether the scrap is attributable to a specific job or is common to all jobs.

Scrap attributable to a specific job Job-costing systems sometimes trace scrap revenues to the jobs that yielded the scrap. This method is used only when the tracing can be done in an economically feasible way. For example, the Harshad Machine Shop and its customers, may reach an agreement that provides for charging specific jobs with all rework or spoilage costs and then crediting these jobs with all scrap revenues that arise from the jobs. The journal entry is:

Scrap returned to storeroom:	No journal entry.		
	[Notation of quantity received and related job entered in the inventory record]		
Sale of scrap:	Cash or Accounts Receivable	9,000	
	Work-in-Process Control		9,000
	Posting made to specific job cost record.		

Unlike spoilage and rework, there is no cost assigned to the scrap, so no distinction is made between normal and abnormal scrap. All scrap revenues, whatever the amount, are credited to the specific job. Scrap revenues reduce the costs of the job.

Scrap common to all jobs The journal entry in this case is:

Scrap returned to storeroom:	No journal entry. [Notation of quantity received and related job entered in the inventory record]		
Sale of scrap:	Cash or Accounts Receivable	9,000	
	Manufacturing Overhead Control		9,000
	Posting made to subsidiary ledger—"Sales of Scrap" column on department cost record.		

Scrap is not linked with any particular job or product. Instead, all products bear production costs without any credit for scrap revenues except in an indirect manner: Expected scrap revenues are considered when setting the budgeted manufacturing overhead rate. Thus, the budgeted overhead rate is lower than it would be if the overhead budget had not been reduced by expected scrap revenues. This method of accounting for scrap is also used in process costing when the rupee amount of scrap is immaterial. That's because the scrap in process costing is common to the manufacture of all the identical or similar units produced (and cannot be identified with specific units).

Recognizing Scrap at the Time of Its Production

Our preceding illustrations assume that scrap returned to the storeroom is sold quickly, so it is not assigned an inventory cost figure. Sometimes, as in the case with edges of molded plastic parts, the value of scrap is not immaterial, and the time between storing it and selling or reusing it can be long. In these situations, the company assigns an inventory cost to scrap at a conservative estimate of its net realizable value so that production costs and related scrap revenues are recognized in the same accounting period. Some companies tend to delay sales of scrap until its market price is considered attractive. Volatile price fluctuations are typical for scrap metal. In these cases, it's not easy to determine some "reasonable inventory value."

Scrap attributable to a specific job The journal entry in the Harshad example is:

Scrap returned to storeroom:	Materials Control	9,000	
	Work-in-Process Control		9,000

Scrap common to all jobs The journal entry in this case is:

Scrap returned to storeroom:	Materials Control	9,000	
	Manufacturing Overhead Control		9,000

Observe that the Materials Control account is debited in place of Cash or Accounts Receivable. When the scrap is sold, the journal entry is:

Sale of scrap:	Cash or Accounts Receivable	9,000	
	Materials Control		9,000

Scrap is sometimes reused as direct material rather than sold as scrap. In this case, Materials Control is debited at its estimated net realizable value and then credited when the scrap is reused. For example, the entries when the scrap is common to all jobs are:

Concepts in Action

Managing Waste and Environmental Costs at KB Home

KB Home is one of the largest home builders in the United States. In recent years, public awareness of environmental issues and interest in environmentally-friendly products and services has led to increased demand for sustainable home construction. KB Home has responded by increasing the sustainability of its homebuilding operations, which includes reducing its waste and environmental costs.

Through its "My Home. My Earth." program, launched in 2007, KB Home has established environmental sustainability as top-priority management issue. It developed core principles to guide its efforts including using "innovation and our process-driven approach to reduce waste and natural resource usage throughout our organization." Much of that focus involves reducing scrap, the residual materials that result from its homebuilding processes. These materials pose additional problems for companies like KB Home, because many federal and state environmental laws dictate that scrap materials be deposed of in an environmentally friendly way; therefore, they add to the cost of generating waste.

To reduce these costs during the homebuilding process, all new homes are built with pre-engineered roof trusses, while 90% also use preconstructed panels. These preconstructed materials are cut offsite for greater precision, which reduces wood waste. Further, these precut materials are made of engineered wood products, which reduce the use of long solid boards that require larger trees to be cut. Beyond scrap reduction, these trusses and panels also eliminate the need for costly job-site rework, or the repair of defective materials during construction.

Similarly, all new homes use oriented strand board, which is made from wood chip rather than plywood. Wood chip is both cheaper and more environmentally sustainable than traditional construction materials. These sustainable practices helped KB Home reduce the cost, exclusive of land, of each home manufactured in 2009 by nearly 39% over the previous year, while increasing profit margins by 13% despite the broader U.S. housing market collapse.

Beyond the construction process, KB Home also includes earth-friendly standard features in all of its homes, at no cost to homebuyers, including energy-efficient windows, recyclable carpets, programmable thermostats, and faucets that reduce water usage. Beyond cutting costs, KB Home's efforts to effectively manage waste and environmental costs have helped the company partially stabilize revenues in a difficult real-estate market. Chief executive Jeffrey Mazger said, "Less than 2% of customers a few years ago were asking about energy-efficient options. Since we introduced 'My Home. My Earth.' in April 2007, it's gone up to 75%." This has helped KB Home differentiate itself within a very competitive market for homebuilders.

Sources: KB Home. 2010. 2009 annual report. Los Angeles: KB Home; KB Home. 2010. 2009 sustainability report. Los Angeles: KB Home; Tischler, Linda. 2008. The green housing boom. *Fast Company*, June 23.

Scrap returned to storeroom:	Materials Control	9,000	
	Manufacturing Overhead Control		9,000
Reuse of scrap:	Work-in-Process Control	9,000	
	Materials Control		9,000

Accounting for scrap under process costing is like the accounting under job costing when scrap is common to all jobs. That's because the scrap in process costing is common to the manufacture of masses of identical or similar units.

Managers focus their attention on ways to reduce scrap and to use it more profitably, especially when the cost of scrap is high (see Concepts in Action). For example, General Motors has redesigned its plastic injection molding processes to reduce the scrap plastic that must be broken away from its molded products. General Motors also regrinds and reuses the plastic scrap as direct material, saving substantial input costs.

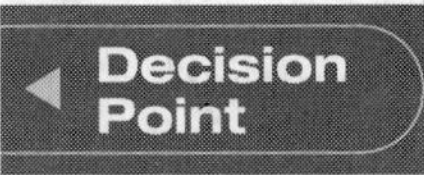

How is scrap accounted for?

Problem for Self-Study

Bhilwara Textiles has some spoiled goods that had an assigned cost of Rs 4,00,000 and zero net disposal value.

Required Prepare a journal entry for each of the following conditions under (a) process costing (Department A) and (b) job costing:

1. Abnormal spoilage of Rs 4,00,000
2. Normal spoilage of Rs 4,00,000 regarded as common to all operations
3. Normal spoilage of Rs 4,00,000 regarded as attributable to specifications of a particular job

Solution

(a) Process Costing			(b) Job Costing		
1. Loss from Abnormal Spoilage	4,00,000		Loss from Abnormal Spoilage	4,00,000	
Work in Process—Dept. A		4,00,000	Work-in-Process Control (specific job)		4,00,000
2. No entry until units are completed and transferred out. Then the normal spoilage costs are transferred as part of the cost of good units.			Manufacturing Overhead Control	4,00,000	
			Work-in-Process Control (specific job)		4,00,000
Work in Process—Dept. B	4,00,000				
Work in Process—Dept. A		4,00,000			
3. Not applicable			No entry. Normal spoilage cost remains in Work-in-Process Control (specific job)		

Decision Points

The following question-and-answer format summarizes the chapter's learning objectives. Each decision presents a key question related to a learning objective. The guidelines are the answer to that question.

Decision	Guidelines
1. What are spoilage, rework, and scrap?	Spoilage is units of production that do not meet the specifications required by customers for good units and that are discarded or sold at reduced prices. Spoilage is generally divided into normal spoilage, which is inherent to a particular production process, and abnormal spoilage, which arises because of inefficiency in operations. Rework is unacceptable units that are subsequently repaired and sold as acceptable finished goods. Scrap is residual material that results from manufacturing a product; it has low total sales value compared with the total sales value of the product.
2. How does the weighted-average method of process costing calculate the costs of good units and spoilage?	The weighted-average method combines costs in beginning inventory with costs of the current period when determining the costs of good units (which include normal spoilage) and the costs of abnormal spoilage, which are written off as a loss of the accounting period.
3. How does the FIFO method of process costing calculate the costs of good units and spoilage?	The FIFO method keeps separate the costs in beginning inventory from the costs of the current period when determining the costs of good units (which include normal spoilage) and the costs of abnormal spoilage, which are written off as a loss of the accounting period.

4. How does the standard-costing method of process costing calculate the costs of good units and spoilage?

   The standard-costing method uses standard costs to determine the costs of good units (which include a normal spoilage amount) and the costs of abnormal spoilage, which are written off as a loss of the accounting period.

5. How do job-costing systems account for spoilage?

   Normal spoilage specific to a job is assigned to that job, or when common to all jobs, is allocated as part of manufacturing overhead. Cost of abnormal spoilage is written off as a loss of the accounting period.

6. How do job-costing systems account for rework?

   Completed reworked units should be indistinguishable from non-reworked good units. Normal rework specific to a job is assigned to that job, or when common to all jobs, is allocated as part of manufacturing overhead. Cost of abnormal rework is written off as a loss of the accounting period.

7. How is scrap accounted for?

   Scrap is recognized in the accounting records either at the time of its sale or at the time of its production. Sale of scrap, if immaterial, is often recognized as other revenue. If not immaterial, sale of scrap or its net realizable value reduces the cost of a specific job or, when common to all jobs, reduces Manufacturing Overhead Control.

APPENDIX: STANDARD-COSTING METHOD AND SPOILAGE

The standard-costing method simplifies the computations for normal and abnormal spoilage. To illustrate, we return to the Anzio Company example in the chapter. Suppose Anzio develops the following standard costs per unit for work done in the forming department in July 2012:

Direct materials	Rs 85
Conversion costs	105
Total manufacturing cost	Rs 190

Assume the same standard costs per unit also apply to the beginning inventory: 1,500 (1,500 × 100%) equivalent units of direct materials and 900 (1,500 × 60%) equivalent units of conversion costs. Hence, the beginning inventory at standard costs is as follows:

Direct materials, 1,500 units × Rs 85 per unit	Rs 1,27,500
Conversion costs, 900 units × Rs 105 per unit	94,500
Total manufacturing costs	Rs 2,22,000

Exhibit 18-5, Panel A, presents Steps 1 and 2 for calculating physical and equivalent units. These steps are the same as for the FIFO method described in Exhibit 18-3. Exhibit 18-5, Panel B, presents Steps 3, 4, and 5.

The costs to account for in Step 3 are at standard costs and, hence, they differ from the costs to account for under the weighted-average and FIFO methods, which are at actual costs. In Step 4, cost per equivalent unit is simply the standard cost: Rs 85 per unit for direct materials and Rs 105 per unit for conversion costs. The standard-costing method makes calculating equivalent-unit costs unnecessary, so it simplifies process costing. Step 5 assigns standard costs to units completed (including normal spoilage), to abnormal spoilage, and to ending work-in-process inventory by multiplying the equivalent units calculated in Step 2 by the standard costs per equivalent unit presented in Step 4. Variances can then be measured and analyzed in the manner described in the appendix to Chapter 17.[6]

[6] For example, from Exhibit 18-5, Panel B, the standard costs for July are direct materials used, 8,500 × Rs 85 = Rs 7,22,500, and conversion costs, 8,100 × Rs 105 = Rs 8,50,500. The actual costs added during July are direct materials, Rs 7,65,000, and conversion costs, Rs 8,91,000, resulting in a direct materials variance of Rs 7,22,500 – Rs 7,65,000 = Rs 42,500 U and a conversion costs variance of Rs 8,50,500 – Rs 8,91,000 = Rs 40,500 U. These variances could then be subdivided further as in Chapters 7 and 8; the abnormal spoilage would be part of the efficiency variance.

Exhibit 18-5 Standard-Costing Method of Process Costing with Spoilage for Forming Department of the Anzio Company for July 2012

PANEL A: Steps 1 and 2 — Summarize Output in Physical Units and Compute Equivalent Units

Home | Insert | Page Layout | Formulas | Data | Review | View

	A	B	C	D	E
1			(Step 1)	(Step 2)	
2				Equivalent Units	
3		Flow of Production	Physical Units	Direct Materials	Conversion Costs
4		Work in process, beginning	1,500		
5		Started during current period	8,500		
6		To account for	10,000		
7		Good units completed and transferred out during current period:			
8		From beginning work in process[a]	1,500		
9		[1,500 × (100% – 100%); 1,500 × (100% – 60%)]		0	600
10		Started and completed	5,500[b]		
11		(5,500 × 100%; 5,500 × 100%)		5,500	5,500
12		Normal spoilage[c]	700		
13		(700 × 100%; 700 × 100%)		700	700
14		Abnormal spoilage[d]	300		
15		(300 × 100%; 300 × 100%)		300	300
16		Work in process, ending[e]	2,000		
17		(2,000 × 100%; 2,000 × 50%)		2,000	1,000
18		Accounted for	10,000		
19		Equivalent units of work done in current period		8,500	8,100
20					

21 [a]Degree of completion in this department: direct materials, 100%; conversion costs, 60%.

22 [b]7,000 physical units completed and transferred out minus 1,500 physical units completed and transferred out from beginning
23 work-in-process inventory.

24 [c]Normal spoilage is 10% of good units transferred out: 10% × 7,000 = 700 units. Degree of completion of normal spoilage in this
25 department: direct materials, 100%; conversion costs, 100%.

26 [d]Abnormal spoilage = Actual spoilage – Normal spoilage = 1,000 – 700 = 300 units. Degree of completion of abnormal spoilage in this
27 department: direct materials, 100%; conversion costs, 100%.

28 [e]Degree of completion in this department: direct materials, 100%; conversion costs, 50%.

PANEL B: Steps 3, 4, and 5 — Summarize Total Costs to Account for, Compute Cost per Equivalent Unit, and Assign Total Costs to Units Completed, to Spoiled Units, and to Units in Ending Work in Process

	A	B	C	D		E
30			Total Production Costs	Direct Materials		Conversion Costs
31	(Step 3)	Work in process, beginning (given, p. 777)	Rs 2,22,000	(1,500 × Rs 85)		(900 × Rs 105)
32		Costs added in current period at standard prices	15,73,000	(8,500 × Rs 85)		(8,100 × Rs 105)
33		Total costs to account for	Rs 17,95,000	Rs 8,50,000		Rs 9,45,000
34	(Step 4)	Standard costs per equivalent unit (given, p. 777)	Rs 190	Rs 85		Rs 105
35	(Step 5)	Assignment of costs at standard costs:				
36		Good units completed and transferred out (7,000 units)				
37		Work in process, beginning (1,500 units)	Rs 2,22,000	(1,500 × Rs 85)	+	(900 × Rs 105)
38		Costs added to beginning work in process in current period	63,000	(0[f] × Rs 85)	+	(600[f] × Rs 105)
39		Total from beginning inventory before normal spoilage	2,85,000			
40		Started and completed before normal spoilage (5,500 units)	10,45,000	(5,500[f] × Rs 85)	+	(5,500[f] × Rs 105)
41		Normal spoilage (700 units)	1,33,000	(700[f] × Rs 85)	+	(700[f] × Rs 105)
42	(A)	Total costs of good units completed and transferred out	14,63,000			
43	(B)	Abnormal spoilage (300 units)	57,000	(300[f] × Rs 85)	+	(300[f] × Rs 105)
44	(C)	Work in process, ending (2,000 units)	2,75,000	(2,000[f] × Rs 85)	+	(1,000[f] × Rs 105)
45	(A)+(B)+(C)	Total costs accounted for	Rs 17,95,000	Rs 8,50,000	+	Rs 9,45,000
46						

47 [f]Equivalent units of direct materials and conversion costs calculated in Step 2 in Panel A.

Finally, note that the journal entries corresponding to the amounts calculated in Step 5 are as follows:

Finished Goods	14,63,000	
Work in Process—Forming		14,63,000
To record transfer of good units completed in July.		
Loss from Abnormal Spoilage	57,000	
Work in Process—Forming		57,000
To record abnormal spoilage detected in July.		

TERMS TO LEARN

This chapter and the Glossary at the end of the book contain definitions of:

abnormal spoilage (**p. 762**)
inspection point (**p. 763**)
normal spoilage (**p. 762**)
rework (**p. 761**)
scrap (**p. 761**)
spoilage (**p. 761**)

ASSIGNMENT MATERIAL

Questions

18-1 Why is there an unmistakable trend in manufacturing to improve quality?

18-2 Distinguish among spoilage, rework, and scrap.

18-3 "Normal spoilage is planned spoilage." Discuss.

18-4 "Costs of abnormal spoilage are losses." Explain.

18-5 "What has been regarded as normal spoilage in the past is not necessarily acceptable as normal spoilage in the present or future." Explain.

18-6 "Units of abnormal spoilage are inferred rather than identified." Explain.

18-7 "In accounting for spoiled units, we are dealing with cost assignment rather than cost incurrence." Explain.

18-8 "Total input includes abnormal as well as normal spoilage and is, therefore, inappropriate as a basis for computing normal spoilage." Do you agree? Explain.

18-9 "The inspection point is the key to the allocation of spoilage costs." Do you agree? Explain.

18-10 "The unit cost of normal spoilage is the same as the unit cost of abnormal spoilage." Do you agree? Explain.

18-11 "In job costing, the costs of normal spoilage that occur while a specific job is being done are charged to the specific job." Do you agree? Explain.

18-12 "The costs of rework are always charged to the specific jobs in which the defects were originally discovered." Do you agree? Explain.

18-13 "Abnormal rework costs should be charged to a loss account, not to manufacturing overhead." Do you agree? Explain.

18-14 When is a company justified in inventorying scrap?

18-15 How do managers use information about scrap?

Solved Examples

18-16 Weighted-average method, spoilage, equivalent units. (CMA, adapted) Consider the following data for November from Eastern Silk Limited, which makes silk pennants and uses a process-costing system. All direct materials are added at the beginning of the process, and conversion costs are added evenly during the process. Spoilage is detected upon inspection at the completion of the process. Spoiled units are disposed of at zero net disposal value. Eastern Silk Limited uses the weighted-average method of process costing.

	Physical Units (Pennants)	Direct Materials	Conversion Costs
Work in process, November 1[a]	1,000	Rs 14,230	Rs 11,100
Started in November	?		
Good units completed and transferred out during November	9,000		
Normal spoilage	100		
Abnormal spoilage	50		
Work in process, November 30[b]	2,000		
Costs added during November		Rs 1,21,800	Rs 2,77,500

[a]Degree of completion: direct materials, 100%; conversion costs, 50%.
[b]Degree of completion: direct materials, 100%; conversion costs, 30%.

Required Compute equivalent units for direct materials and conversion costs. Show physical units in the first column of your schedule.

Solution

Weighted-average method, spoilage, equivalent units (CMA, adapted).

Solution Exhibit 18-16 calculates equivalent units of work done to date for direct materials and conversion costs.

Solution Exhibit 18-16

Summarize Output in Physical Units and Compute Equivalent Units Weighted-Average Method of Process Costing with Spoilage Eastern Silk Limited for November:

Flow of Production	(Step 1) Physical Units (given)	(Step 2) Equivalent Units Direct Materials	Conversion Costs
Work in process, beginning	1,000		
Started during current period	10,150		
To account for	11,150		
Good units completed and transferred out during current period:	9,000	9,000	9,000
Normal spoilage* 100 × 100%; 100 × 100%	100	100	100
Abnormal spoilage† 50 × 100%; 50 × 100%	50	50	50
Work in process, ending‡ 2,000 × 100%; 2,000 × 30%	2,000	2,000	600
Accounted forWork done to date	11,150	11,150	9,750

*Degree of completion of normal spoilage in this department: direct materials, 100%; conversion costs, 100%.

†Degree of completion of abnormal spoilage in this department: direct materials, 100%; conversion costs, 100%.

‡Degree of completion in this department: direct materials, 100%; conversion costs, 30%.

18-17 Weighted-average method, assigning costs (continuation of 18-16).

For the data in Exercise 18-16, calculate the cost per equivalent unit for direct materials and conversion costs, summarize total costs to account for, and assign these costs to units completed and transferred out (including normal spoilage), to abnormal spoilage, and to units in ending work in process.

Weighted-average method, assigning costs (continuation of 18-16).

Solution Exhibit 18-17 calculates the costs per equivalent unit for direct materials and conversion costs, summarizes total costs to account for, and assigns these costs to units completed and transferred out (including normal spoilage), to abnormal spoilage, and to units in ending work in process.

Solution Exhibit 18-17

Compute Equivalent Unit Costs, Summarize Total Costs to Account For, and Assign Costs to Units Completed, to Spoilage Units, and to Units in Ending Work in Process Weighted-Average Method of Process Costing Eastern Silk Limited, November:

		Total Production Costs	Direct Materials	Conversion Costs
(Step 3)	Work in process, beginning (given)	Rs 25,330	Rs 14,230	Rs 11,100
	Costs added in current period (given)	3,99,300	1,21,800	2,77,500
	Costs incurred to date		1,36,030	2,88,600
	Divided by equivalent units of work done to date		÷ 11,150	÷ 9,750
	Equivalent unit costs of work done to date		Rs 12.2	Rs 29.6
(Step 4)	Total costs to account for	Rs 4,24,630		
(Step 5)	Assignment of costs			
	Good units completed and transferred out (9,000 units)			
	Costs before adding normal spoilage	Rs 3,76,200	(9,000# × Rs 12.2) +	(9,000# × Rs 29.6)
	Normal spoilage (100 units)	4,180	(100# × Rs12.2) +	(100# × Rs 29..6)
(A)	Total cost of good units completed & transf. out	3,80,380		
(B)	Abnormal spoilage (50 units)	2,090	(50# × Rs 12.2) +	(50# × Rs 29..6)
	Work in process, ending (2,000 units)			

	Direct materials	24,400	2,000# × Rs 12.2
	Conversion costs	17,760	600# × Rs 29.6
(C)	Total work in process, ending	42,160	
(A) + (B) + (C)	Total costs accounted for	Rs 4,24,630	

#Equivalent units of direct materials and conversion costs calculated in Step 2 in Solution Exhibit 18-16.

18-18 FIFO method, spoilage, equivalent units. Refer to the information in Exercise 18-16. Suppose Eastern Silk Limited uses the FIFO method of process costing instead of the weighted-average method.

Required

Compute equivalent units for direct materials and conversion costs. Show physical units in the first column of your schedule.

Solution

FIFO method, spoilage, equivalent units.

Solution Exhibit 18-18 calculates equivalent units of work done in the current period for direct materials and conversion costs.

Solution Exhibit 18-18

Summarize Output in Physical Units and Compute Equivalent Units. First-in, First-out (FIFO) Method of Process Costing with Spoilage Eastern Silk Limited for November:

Flow of Production	(Step 1) Physical Units	(Step 2) Equivalent Units Direct Materials	Conversion Costs
Work in process, beginning (given)	1,000		
Started during current period (given)	10,150		
To account for	11,150		
Good units completed and transferred out during current period:			
From beginning work in process‖	1,000		
1,000 × (100% − 100%); 1,000 × (100% − 50%)		0	500
Started and completed	8,000#		
8,000 × 100%; 8,000 × 100%		8,000	8,000
Normal spoilage*	100		
100 × 100%; 100 × 100%		100	100
Abnormal spoilage†	50		
50 × 100%; 50 × 100%		50	50
Work in process, ending‡	2,000		
2,000 × 100%; 2,000 × 30%		2,000	600
Accounted for	11,150		
Work done in current period only		10,150	9,250

‖Degree of completion in this department: direct materials, 100%; conversion costs, 50%.

#9,000 physical units completed and transferred out minus 1,000 physical units completed and transferred out from beginning work-in-process inventory.

*Degree of completion of normal spoilage in this department: direct materials, 100%; conversion costs, 100%.

†Degree of completion of abnormal spoilage in this department: direct materials, 100%; conversion costs, 100%.

‡Degree of completion in this department: direct materials, 100%; conversion costs, 30%.

18-19 FIFO method, assigning costs (continuation of 18-18).

Required

For the data in Exercise 18-16, use the FIFO method to calculate the cost per equivalent unit for direct materials and conversion costs, summarize total costs to account for, and assign these costs to units completed and transferred out (including normal spoilage), to abnormal spoilage, and to units in ending work in process.

Solution

FIFO method, assigning costs (continuation of 18-18).

Solution Exhibit 18-19 calculates the costs per equivalent unit for direct materials and conversion costs, summarizes total costs to account for, and assigns these costs to units completed and transferred out (including normal spoilage), to abnormal spoilage, and to units in ending work in process.

Solution Exhibit 18-19

Compute Equivalent Unit Costs, Summarize Total Costs to Account For, and Assign Costs to Units Completed, to Spoilage Units, and to Units in Ending Work in Process FIFO Method of Process Costing Eastern Silk Limited, November:

		Total Production Costs	Direct Materials	Conversion Costs
(Step 3)	Work in process, beginning (given: Rs 14,230 + Rs 11,100)	Rs 25,330		
	Costs added in current period (given)	3,99,300	Rs 1,21,800	Rs 2,77,500
	Divided by equivalent units of work done in current period		÷10,150	÷9,250
	Equivalent unit costs of work done in current period		Rs 12	Rs 30
(Step 4)	Total costs to account for	Rs 4,24,630		
(Step 5)	Assignment of costs:			
	Good units completed and transferred out (9,000 units)			
	Work in process, beginning (1,000 units)			
	Direct materials added in current period	Rs 25,330		
	Conversion costs added in current period	0	0[§] × Rs 12	
	Total from beginning inventory before normal spoilage	15,000		500[§] × Rs 30
	Started and completed before normal spoilage (8,000 units)	40,330		
	Normal spoilage (100 units)	3,36,000	(8,000[§] × Rs 12) +	(8,000[§] × Rs 30)
(A)	Total cost of good units transferred out	4,200	(100[§] × Rs 12) +	(100[§] × Rs 30)
(B)	Abnormal spoilage (50 units)	3,80,530		
	Work in process, ending (2,000 units)	2,100	(50[§] × Rs 12) +	(50[§] × Rs 30)
	Direct materials	24,000	2,000[§] × Rs 12	
	Conversion costs	18,000		600[§] × Rs 30
(C)	Total work in process, ending	42,000		
(A) + (B) + (C)	Total costs accounted for	Rs 4,24,630		

[§]Equivalent units of direct materials and conversion costs calculated in Step 2 in Solution Exhibit 18-18.

18-20 Spoilage and job costing. (L. Bamber) Vegetarian Kitchens produces a variety of items in accordance with special job orders from hospitals, plant cafeterias, and university dormitories. An order for 2,500 cases of mixed vegetables costs Rs 60 per case: direct materials, Rs 30; direct manufacturing labor, Rs 20; and manufacturing overhead allocated, Rs 10. The manufacturing overhead rate includes a provision for normal spoilage. Consider each requirement independently.

Required

1. Assume that a laborer dropped 200 cases. Suppose part of the 200 cases could be sold to a nearby prison for Rs 2,000 cash. Prepare a journal entry to record this event. Calculate and explain briefly the unit cost of the remaining 2,300 cases.
2. Refer to the original data. Tasters at the company reject 200 of the 2,500 cases. The 200 cases are disposed of for Rs 4,000. Assume that this rejection rate is considered normal. Prepare a journal entry to record this event, and calculate the unit cost if
   a. The rejection is attributable to exacting specifications of this particular job.
   b. The rejection is characteristic of the production process and is not attributable to this specific job.
   c. Are unit costs the same in requirements 2a and 2b? Explain your reasoning briefly.
3. Refer to the original data. Tasters rejected 200 cases that had insufficient salt. The product can be placed in a vat, salt can be added, and the product can be reprocessed into jars. This operation, which is considered normal, will cost Rs 200. Prepare a journal entry to record this event and calculate the unit cost of all the cases if
   a. This additional cost was incurred because of the exacting specifications of this particular job.
   b. This additional cost occurs regularly because of difficulty in seasoning.
   c. Are unit costs the same in requirements 3a and 3b? Explain your reasoning briefly.

Solution

Spoilage and job costing

		Rs	Rs
1.	Cash	2,000	
	Loss from Abnormal Spoilage	10,000	
	Work-in-Process Control		12,000

Loss = (Rs 60 × 200) − Rs 2,000 = Rs 10,000

Remaining cases cost = Rs 60 per case. The cost of these cases is unaffected by the loss from abnormal spoilage.

		Rs	Rs
2. a.	Cash	4,000	
	Work-in-Process Control		4,000

The cost of the remaining good cases = [(Rs 60 × 2,500) − Rs 4,000] = Rs 1,46,000
The unit cost of a good case now becomes Rs 1,46,000 ÷ 2,300 = Rs 63.478

b. Cash	4,000	
Manufacturing Department Overhead Control	8,000	
Work-in-Process Control		12,000

The unit cost of a good case remains at Rs 60.

c. The unit cost in the cases 2a and 2b is different because in case 2a, the normal spoilage cost, due to the exacting specifications of this particular job, is charged as a cost of this job. In case 2b, the normal spoilage is due to the production process (not the particular attributes of this specific job). These costs are, therefore, charged as part of manufacturing overhead. The manufacturing overhead cost of Rs 10 per case already includes a provision for normal spoilage.

3. a. Work-in-Process Control	2,000	
Materials Control, Wages Payable Control, Manufacturing Overhead Allocated		2,000

The cost of the good cases = [(Rs 60 × 2,500) + Rs 2,000] = Rs 1,52,000
The unit cost of a good case is Rs 1,52,000 ÷ 2,500 = Rs 60.8

b. Manufacturing Department Overhead Control	2,000	
Materials Control, Wages Payable Control, Manufacturing Overhead Allocated		2,000

The unit cost of a good case = Rs 60 per case

c. The unit cost in the cases 3a and 3b is different because in case 3a, the normal rework cost, due to the exacting specifications of this particular job, is charged as a cost of this job. In case 3b, the normal rework is due to the production process (not the particular attributes of this specific job). These costs are, therefore, charged as part of manufacturing overhead. The manufacturing overhead cost of Rs 10 per case already includes a provision for this normal rework.

18-21 Reworked units, costs of rework. Whirpool India Limited assembles washing machines at its Auburn plant. In December 2006, 60 tumbler units that cost Rs 44 each (from a new supplier who subsequently went bankrupt) were defective and had to be disposed of at zero disposal value. Whirpool India Limited was able to rework all 60 washing machines by substituting new tumbler units purchased from one of its existing suppliers. Each replacement tumbler cost Rs 50.

Required

1. What alternative approaches are there to account for the material costs of reworked units?
2. Should Whirpool India Limited use the Rs 44 tumbler or Rs 50 tumbler to calculate the costs of materials reworked? Explain.
3. What other costs might Whirpool India Limited include in its analysis of the total costs of rework due to the tumbler units purchased from the (now) bankrupt supplier?

Solution

Reworked units, costs of rework.

1. The two alternative approaches to account for the materials costs of reworked units are:
   a. To charge the costs of rework to the current period as a separate expense item as abnormal rework. This approach would highlight to Whirpool India Limited the costs of the supplier problem.
   b. To charge the costs of the rework to manufacturing overhead as normal rework.
2. The Rs 50 tumbler cost is the cost of the actual tumblers included in the washing machines. The Rs 44 tumbler units from the new supplier were eventually never used in any washing machine and that supplier is now bankrupt. The units must now be disposed of at zero disposal value.
3. The total costs of rework due to the defective tumbler units include:
   a. The labor and other conversion costs spent on substituting the new tumbler units.
   b. The costs of any extra negotiations to obtain the replacement tumbler units.
   c. Any higher price the existing supplier may have charged to do a rush order for the replacement tumbler units.
   d. Ordering costs for the replacement tumbler units.

18-22 Weighted-average method, spoilage. The Essar Company operates under the weighted-average method of process costing. It has two departments, Cleaning and Milling. For both departments, conversion costs are added evenly during the processes. Direct materials are added at the beginning of the process in the Cleaning Department, and additional direct materials are added at the end of the milling process. The costs and unit-production statistics for May follow. All unfinished work at the end of May is 25% complete as to conversion costs. The beginning inventory (May 1) was 80% complete as to conversion costs as of May 1. All completed work is transferred to the next department.

	Cleaning	Milling
Beginning Inventories		
Cleaning: Rs 1,000 direct materials, Rs 800 conversion costs	Rs 18,000	
Milling: Rs 6,450 transferred-in costs and Rs 2,450 conversion costs		Rs 89,000
Costs Added During Current Period		
Direct materials	Rs 90,000	Rs 6,400
Conversion costs	Rs 80,000	Rs 49,500
Physical Units		
Units in beginning inventory	1,000	3,000
Units started this month	9,000	7,400
Good units completed and transferred out	7,400	6,000
Normal spoilage	740[a]	300[b]
Abnormal spoilage	260	100

[a]Normal spoilage in Cleaning Department is 10% of good units completed and transferred out.

[b]Normal spoilage in Milling Department is 5% of good units completed and transferred out.

1. Spoilage is assumed to occur at the end of each of the two processes, when the units are inspected. Spoiled units are disposed of at zero net disposal value.
2. Assume that there is no shrinkage, evaporation, or abnormal spoilage other than that indicated in the information given.
3. Carry unit-cost calculations to four decimal places when necessary. Calculate final totals to the nearest rupee.

Required

For the Cleaning Department, summarize total costs to account for, and assign these costs to units completed and transferred out (including normal spoilage), to abnormal spoilage, and to units in ending work in process. (Problem 18-24 explores additional facets of this problem.)

Solution

Weighted-average method, spoilage.

Solution Exhibit 18-22 calculates the equivalent units of work done to date for each cost category, presents computations of the costs per equivalent unit for each cost category, summarizes total costs to account for, and assigns these costs to units completed (including normal spoilage), to abnormal spoilage, and to units in ending work in process using the weighted-average method.

Solution Exhibit 18-22

Weighted-Average Method of Process Costing with Spoilage Cleaning Department of the Essar Company for May:

PANEL A: Steps 1 and 2—Summarize Output in Physical Units and Compute Equivalent Units

Flow of Production	(Step 1) Physical Units (given)	(Step 2) Direct Materials	Equivalent Units Conversion Costs
Work in process, beginning	1,000		
Started during current period	9,000		
To account for	10,000		
Good units completed and transferred out during current period:	7,400	7,400	7,400
Normal spoilage*	740		
740 × 100%; 740 × 100%		740	740
Abnormal spoilage†	260		
260 × 100%; 260 × 100%		260	260
Work in process, ending‡	1,600		
1,600 × 100%; 1,600 × 25%		1,600	400
Accounted for	10,000		
Work done to date		10,000	8,800

*Normal spoilage is 10% of good units transferred out: 10% 7,400 = 740 units. Degree of completion of normal spoilage in this department: direct materials, 100%; conversion costs, 100%.

†Abnormal spoilage = 260 units. Degree of completion of abnormal spoilage in this department: direct materials, 100%; conversion costs, 100%.

‡Degree of completion in this department: direct materials, 100%; conversion costs, 25%.

PANEL B: Steps 3, 4, and 5—Compute Equivalent Unit Costs, Summarize Total Costs to Account For, and Assign Costs to Units Completed, to Spoilage Units, and to Units in Ending Work in Process

		Total Production Costs	Direct Materials	Conversion Costs
(Step 3)	Work in process, beginning (given)	Rs 18,000	Rs 10,000	Rs 8,000
	Costs added in current period (given)	1,70,000	90,000	80,000
	Costs incurred to date		1,00,000	88,000
	Divided by equivalent units of work done to date		÷ 10,000	÷ 8,800
	Equivalent unit costs of work done to date		Rs 10	Rs 10
(Step 4)	Total costs to account for	Rs 1,88,000		
(Step 5)	Assignment of costs			
	Good units completed and transferred out (7,400 units)			
	Costs before adding normal spoilage	Rs 1,48,000	(7,400# × Rs 10) +	(7,400# × Rs 10)
	Normal spoilage (740 units)	14,800	740# × Rs 10) +	740# × Rs 10
(A)	Total cost of good units completed & transferred out	1,62,800		
(B)	Abnormal spoilage (260 units)	5,200	260# × Rs 10 +	260# × Rs 10
	Work in process, ending (1,600 units)			
	Direct materials	16,000	1,600# × Rs 10	
	Conversion costs	4,000		400# × Rs 10
(C)	Total work in process, ending	20,000		
(A) + (B) + (C)	Total costs accounted for	Rs 1,88,000		

#Equivalent units of direct materials and conversion costs calculated in Step 2 in Panel A above.

18-23 FIFO method, spoilage. Refer to the information in Problem 18-22.

Required

Do Problem 18-22 using the FIFO method of process costing. (Problem 18-25 explores additional facets of this problem.)

Solution

FIFO method, spoilage.

For the Cleaning Department, Solution Exhibit 18-23 calculates the equivalent units of work done in the current period for direct materials and conversion costs, presents the costs per equivalent unit for direct materials and conversion costs, summarizes the total costs for May, and assigns these costs to units completed and transferred out (including normal spoilage), to abnormal spoilage, and to units in ending work in process under the FIFO method.

Solution Exhibit 18-23

First-in, First-out (FIFO) Method of Process Costing with Spoilage Cleaning Department of the Essar Company for May:

PANEL A: Steps 1 and 2—Summarize Output in Physical Units and Compute Equivalent Units

Flow of Production	(Step 1) Physical Units	(Step 2) Equivalent Units Direct Materials	Conversion Costs
Work in process, beginning (given)	1,000		
Started during current period (given)	9,000		
To account for	10,000		
Good units completed and transferred out during current period:			
From beginning work in process‖	1,000		
1,000 × (100% − 100%); 1,000 × (100% − 80%)		0	200
Started and completed	6,400#		
6,400 × 100%; 6,400 × 100%		6,400	6,400
Normal spoilage*	740		
740 × 100%; 740% × 100%		740	740
Abnormal spoilage†	260		
260 × 100%; 260 × 100%		260	260
Work in process, ending‡	1,600		
1,600 × 100%; 1,600 × 25%		1,600	400
Accounted for	10,000		
Work done in current period only		9,000	8,000

‖ Degree of completion in this department: direct materials, 100%; conversion costs, 80%.
#7,400 physical units completed and transferred out minus 1,000 physical units completed and transferred out from beginning work-in-process inventory.

*Normal spoilage is 10% of good units transferred out: 10% × 7,400 = 740 units. Degree of completion of normal spoilage in this department: direct materials, 100%; conversion costs, 100%.

†Abnormal spoilage = 260 units. Degree of completion of abnormal spoilage in this department: direct materials, 100%; conversion costs, 100%.

‡Degree of completion in this department: direct materials, 100%; conversion costs, 25%.

PANEL B: Steps 3, 4, and 5—Compute Equivalent Unit Costs, Summarize Total Costs to Account For, and Assign Costs to Units Completed, to Spoilage Units, and to Units in Ending Work in Process

		Total Production Costs	Direct Materials	Conversion Costs
(Step 3)	Work in process, beginning (given: Rs 10,000 + Rs 8,000)	Rs 18,000		
	Costs added in current period (given)	1,70,000	Rs 90,000	Rs 80,000
	Divided by equivalent units of work done in current period		÷ 9,000	÷ 8,000
	Equivalent unit costs of work done in current period		Rs 10	Rs 10
(Step 4)	Total costs to account for	Rs 1,88,000		
(Step 5)	Assignment of costs:			
	Good units completed and transferred out (7,400 units)			
	Work in process, beginning (1,000 units)	Rs 18,000		
	Direct materials added in current period	0	0§ × Rs 10	
	Conversion costs added in current period	2,000		200§ × Rs 10
	Total from beginning inventory before normal spoilage	20,000		
	Started and completed before normal spoilage (6,400 units)	1,28,000	6,400§ × Rs 10	+ 6,400§ × Rs 10
	Normal spoilage (740 units)	14,800	740§ × Rs 10	+ 740§ × Rs 10
(A)	Total cost of good units transferred out	1,62,800		
(B)	Abnormal spoilage (260 units)	5,200	260§ × Rs 10	+ 260 × Rs 10
	Work in process, ending (1,600 units)			
	Direct materials	16,000	1,600§ × Rs 10	
	Conversion costs	4,000		400§ × Rs 10
(C)	Total work in process, ending	20,000		
(A) + (B) + (C)	Total costs accounted for	Rs 1,88,000		

§Equivalent units of direct materials and conversion costs calculated in Step 2 in Panel A.

18-24 Weighted-average method, Milling Department (continuation of 18-22). Refer to the information in Problem 18-22.

Required

For the Milling Department, summarize total costs to account for, and assign these costs to units completed and transferred out (including normal spoilage), to abnormal spoilage, and to units in ending work in process.

Solution

Weighted-average method, Milling Department (continuation of 18-22).

For the Milling Department, Solution Exhibit 18-24 calculates the equivalent units of work done to date for each cost category, presents computations of the costs per equivalent unit for each cost category, summarizes total costs to account for, and assigns these costs to units completed (including normal spoilage), to abnormal spoilage, and to units in ending work in process using the weighted-average method.

Solution Exhibit 18-24

Weighted-Average Method of Process Costing with Spoilage Milling Department of the Essar Company for May:

PANEL A: Steps 1 and 2—Summarize Output in Physical Units and Compute Equivalent Units

Flow of Production	(Step 1) Physical Units (given)	(Step 2) Equivalent Units Transferred-in Costs	Direct Materials	Conversion Costs
Work in process, beginning	3,000			
Started during current period	7,400			
To account for	10,400			
Good units completed and transferred out during current period:	6,000	6,000	6,000	6,000
Normal spoilage*	300			

300 × 100%; 300 × 100%; 300 × 100%		300	300	300
Abnormal spoilage†	100			
100 × 100%; 100 × 100%, 100 × 100%		100	100	100
Work in process, ending‡	4,000			
4,000 × 100%; 4,000 × 0%; 4,000 × 25%		4,000	0	1,000
Accounted for	10,400			
Work done to date		10,400	6,400	7,400

*Normal spoilage is 5% of good units transferred out: 5% × 6,000 = 300 units. Degree of completion of normal spoilage in this department: transferred-in costs, 100%; direct materials, 100%; conversion costs, 100%.
†Abnormal spoilage = 100 units. Degree of completion of abnormal spoilage in this department: transferred-in costs, 100%; direct materials, 100%; conversion costs, 100%.
‡Degree of completion in this department: transferred-in costs, 100%; direct materials, 0%; conversion costs, 25%.

PANEL B: Steps 3, 4, and 5—Compute Equivalent Unit Costs, Summarize Total Costs to Account For, and Assign Costs to Units Completed, to Spoilage Units, and to Units in Ending Work in Process

		Total Production Costs	Transferred-in costs	Direct Materials	Conversion Costs
(Step 3)	Work in process, beginning (given)	Rs 89,000	Rs 64,500	Rs 0	Rs 24,500
	Costs added in current period (given)	2,18,700	1,62,800*	6,400	49,500
	Costs incurred to date		2,27,300	6,400	74,000
	Divided by equivalent units of work done to date		÷10,400	÷6400	÷7400
	Equivalent unit costs of work done to date		Rs 21.856	Rs 1.0	Rs 10
(Step 4)	Total costs to account for	Rs 3,07,700			
(Step 5)	Assignment of costs				
	Good units completed and transferred out (6,000 units)				
	Costs before adding normal spoilage	Rs 1,97,130	6,000# × (Rs 21.856 + Rs 1.0 + Rs 10)		
	Normal spoilage (300 units)	9,860	300# × (Rs 21.856 + Rs 1.0 + Rs 10)		
(A)	Total cost of good units completed & transferred out	2,06,990			
(B)	Abnormal spoilage (100 units)	3,290	100# × (Rs 21.856 + Rs 1.0 + Rs 10)		
	Work in process, ending (4,000 units)				
	Transferred-in costs	87,420	4,000# × Rs 21.856		
	Direct materials	0		0# × Rs 1.0	
	Conversion costs	10,000			1,000# × Rs 10
(C)	Rs Total work in process, ending	97,420			
	(A) + (B) + (C) Total costs accounted for	Rs 3,07,700			

#Equivalent units of direct materials and conversion costs calculated in Step 2 in Panel A above.
*Total costs of good units completed and transferred out in Step 5 Panel B of Solution Exhibit 18-22.

18-25 FIFO method, Milling Department (continuation of 18-23). Refer to the information in Problem 18-22.

Required

For the Milling Department, use the FIFO method to summarize total costs to account for, and assign these costs to units completed and transferred out (including normal spoilage), to abnormal spoilage, and to units in ending work in process.

Solution

FIFO method, Milling Department (continuation of 18-23).

Solution Exhibit 18-25 shows the equivalent units of work done in the Milling Department in the current period for transferred-in costs, direct materials, and conversion costs, presents the costs per equivalent unit for transferred-in costs, direct materials, and conversion costs, summarizes the total Milling Department costs for May, and assigns these costs to units completed and transferred out (including normal spoilage), to abnormal spoilage, and to units in ending work-in-process under the FIFO method.

Solution Exhibit 18-25

First-in, First-out (FIFO) Method of Process Costing with Spoilage Milling Department of the Essar Company for May:

PANEL A: Steps 1 and 2—Summarize Output in Physical Units and Compute Equivalent Units

Flow of Production	(Step 1) Physical Units (given)	(Step 2) Equivalent Units Transferred-in Costs	Direct Materials	Conversion Costs
Work in process, beginning (given)	3,000			
Started during current period (given)	7,400			
To account for	10,400			
Good units completed and transferred out during current period:				
From beginning work in process[‖]	3,000			
3,000 × (100% − 100%); 3,000 × (100% − 0%); 3,000 × (100% − 80%)		0	3,000	600
Started and completed	3,000[#]			
3,000 × 100%; 3,000 × 100%; 3,000 × 100%		3,000	3,000	3,000
Normal spoilage*	300			
300 × 100%; 300% × 100%; 300 × 100%		300	300	300
Abnormal spoilage[†]	100			
100 × 100%; 100 × 100%; 100 × 100%		100	100	100
Work in process, ending[‡]	4,000			
4,000 × 100%; 4,000 × 0%; 4,000 × 25%		4,000	0	1,000
Accounted for	10,400			
Work done in current period only		7,400	6,400	5,000

‖Degree of completion in this department: transferred-in costs, 100%; direct materials, 0%; conversion costs, 80%.

#6,000 physical units completed and transferred out minus 3,000 physical units completed and transferred out from beginning work-in-process inventory.

*Normal spoilage is 5% of good units transferred out: 5% × 6,000 = 300 units. Degree of completion of normal spoilage in this department: transferred-in costs, 100%; direct materials, 100%; conversion costs, 100%.

†Abnormal spoilage = 100 units. Degree of completion of abnormal spoilage in this department: transferred-in costs, 100%; direct materials, 100%; conversion costs, 100%.

‡Degree of completion in this department: transferred-in costs, 100%; direct materials, 0%; conversion costs, 25%.

PANEL B: Steps 3, 4, and 5—Compute Equivalent Unit Costs, Summarize Total Costs to Account For, and Assign Costs to Units Completed, to Spoilage Units, and to Units in Ending Work in Process

		Total Production Costs	Transferred-in costs	Direct Materials	Conversion Costs
(Step 3)	Work in process, begining (given: Rs 64,500 + Rs 0 + Rs 24,500)	Rs 89,000			
	Costs added in current period (given)	2,18,700	Rs 1,62,800*	Rs 6,400	Rs 49,500
	Divided by equivalent units of work done in current period		÷ 7,400	÷ 6,400	÷ 5,000
	Equivalent unit costs of work done in current period		Rs 22	Rs 1.0	Rs 9.9
(Step 4)	Total costs to account for	Rs 3,07,700			
(Step 5)	Assignment of costs:				
	Good units completed and transferred out (6,000 units)				
	Work in process, beginning (3,000 units)	Rs 89,000			
	Transferred-in costs added in current period	0	0 × Rs 22		
	Direct materials added in current period	3,000		3,000[§] × 1	
	Conversion costs added in current period	5,940			600[§] × Rs 9.9
	Total from beginning inventory before normal spoilage	97,940			
	Started and completed before normal spoilage (3,000 units)	98,700	3,000[§] × (Rs 22 + Rs 1 + Rs 9.9)		
	Normal spoilage (300 units)	9,870	300[§] × (Rs 22 + Rs 1 + Rs 9.9)		
(A)	Total cost of good units transferred out	2,06,510			
(B)	Abnormal spoilage (100 units)	3,290	100[§] × (Rs 22 + Rs 1 + Rs 9.9)		
	Work in process, ending (4,000 units)				

	Transferred-in costs	88,000	4,000[§] × Rs 22	
	Direct materials	0	0[§] × Rs 1	
	Conversion costs	9,900		1,000[§] × Rs 9.9
(C)	Total work in process, ending	97,900		
(A) + (B) + (C)	Total costs accounted for	Rs 3,07,700		

[§]Equivalent units of direct materials and conversion costs calculated in Step 2 in Panel A.
*Total costs of good units completed and transferred out in Step 5 Panel B of Solution Exhibit 18-23.

18-26 Job costing, rework. Crompton Greaves manufactures two brands of motors, CG-5 and CG-8. The costs of manufacturing each CG-5 motor, excluding rework costs, are direct materials, Rs 3,000; direct manufacturing labor, Rs 600; and manufacturing overhead, Rs 1,900. Defective units are sent to a separate rework area. Rework costs per CG-5 motor are direct materials, Rs 600; direct manufacturing labor, Rs 450; and manufacturing overhead, Rs 750.

In February, Crompton manufactured 1,000 CG-5 and 500 CG-8 motors. Eighty of the CG-5 motors and none of the CG-8 motors required rework. Crompton classifies 50 of the CG-5 motors reworked as normal rework caused by inherent problems in its production process that only coincidentally occurred during the production of CG-5. Hence the rework costs for these 50 CG-5 motors are normal rework costs not specifically attributable to the CG-5 product. Crompton classifies the remaining 30 units of CG-5 motors reworked as abnormal rework. Crompton allocates manufacturing overhead on the basis of machine-hours required to manufacture CG-5 and CG-8. Each CG-5 and CG-8 motor requires the same number of machine-hours.

Required

1. Prepare journal entries to record the accounting for the cost of the spoiled motors and for rework.
2. What were the total rework costs charged to CG-5 motors in February?

Solution

Job costing, rework.

	Rs	Rs
1. Work-in-Process Control (CG-5 motors) (Rs 5,500 × 80)	4,40,000	
Materials Control (Rs 3,000 × 80)		2,40,000
Wages Payable (Rs 600 × 80)		48,000
Manufacturing Overhead Allocated (Rs 1,900 × 80)		1,52,000
Total costs assigned to 80 spoiled units of CG-5 Motors before considering rework costs.		
Manufacturing Department Overhead Control (rework)	90,000	
Materials Control (Rs 600 × 50)		30,000
Wages Payable (Rs 450 × 50)		22,500
Manufacturing Overhead Allocated (Rs 750 × 50)		37,500
Normal rework on 50 units but not attributable specifically to the CG-5 motor batches or jobs.		
Loss from Abnormal Rework (Rs 1,800 × 30)	54,000	
Materials Control (Rs 600 × 30)		18,000
Wages Payable (Rs 450 × 30)		13,500
Manufacturing Overhead Allocated (Rs 750 × 30)		22,500
Total costs of abnormal rework on 30 units (Abnormal rework = Actual rework – Normal rework = 80 – 50 = 30 units) of CG-5 Motors.		
Work-in-Process Control (CG-5 motors)	60,000	
Work-in-Process Control (CG-8 motors)	30,000	
Manufacturing Department Overhead Allocated (rework)		90,000
(Allocating manufacturing department rework costs to CG-5 and CG-8 in the proportion 1,000:500 since each motor requires the same number of machine-hours.)		

2. Total rework costs for CG-5 motors in February are as follows:

Normal rework costs allocated to CG-5	Rs 60,000
Abnormal rework costs for CG-5	54,000
Total rework costs	Rs 1,14,000

We emphasize two points:

a. Only Rs 6,000 of the normal rework costs are allocated to CG-5 even though the normal rework costs of the 50 CG-5 motors reworked equal Rs 90,000. The reason is that the normal rework costs are not specifically attributable to CG-5. For example, the machines happened to malfunction when CG-5 was being made, but the rework was not caused by the specific requirements of CG-5. If it were, then all Rs 90,000 would be charged to CG-5.

b. Abnormal rework costs of Rs 54,000 are linked to CG-5 in the management control system, even though for financial reporting purposes, the abnormal rework costs are written off to the income statement.

18-27 Job costing, scrap. Indian Auto makes two different types of hubcaps for cars: models HM3 and JB4. Circular pieces of metal are stamped out of steel sheets (leaving the edges as scrap), formed, and finished. The stamping operation is identical for both types of hubcaps. During March, Indian Auto manufactured 20,000 units of HM3 and 10,000 units of JB4. In March, manufacturing costs per unit of HM3 and JB4 before accounting for the scrap were as follows:

	HM3	JB4
Direct materials	Rs 100	Rs 150
Direct manufacturing labor	30	40
Materials-related manufacturing overhead (materials handling, storage, etc.)	20	30
Other manufacturing overhead	60	80
Manufacturing costs per unit	Rs 210	Rs 300

Material-related manufacturing costs are allocated to products at 20% of direct materials costs. Other manufacturing overhead is allocated to products at 200% of direct manufacturing labor costs. Because the same metal sheets are used to make both types of hubcaps, Indian Auto maintains no records of the scrap generated by individual products. Scrap generated during manufacturing is accounted for at the time it is returned to the storeroom as an offset to materials-related manufacturing overhead. The value of scrap generated during March and returned to the storeroom was Rs 70,000.

Required

1. Prepare a journal entry to summarize the accounting for scrap during March.
2. Suppose the scrap generated in March is sold in April for Rs 70,000. Prepare a journal entry to account for this transaction.
3. Do you agree with the manufacturing costs per unit of Rs 210 for HM3 and Rs 30 for JB4? What adjustments, if any, would you make? Explain your answer briefly.

Solution

Job costing, scrap.

	Rs	Rs
1. Materials Control	70,000	
Rs Materials-Related Manufacturing Overhead Control		70,000
(To record scrap common to all jobs at the time it is returned to the storeroom)		
2. Cash or Accounts Receivable	70,000	
Rs Materials Control		70,000
(To record sale of scrap from the storeroom)		

3. A summary of the manufacturing costs for HM3 and JB4 before considering the value of scrap are as follows:

	HM3		JB4		Total Costs
	Cost perUnit (1)	Total Costs (2) = (1) × 20,000	Cost perUnit (3)	TotalCosts (4) = (3) × 10,000	(5) = (2) + (4)
Direct materials	Rs 100	Rs 20,00,000	Rs 150	Rs 15,00,000	Rs 35,00,000
Direct manufacturing labor	30	6,00,000	40	4,00,000	10,00,000
Materials-related manufacturing overhead (20% of direct materials)	20	4,00,000	30	3,00,000	7,00,000
Other manufacturing overhead (200% of direct manufacturing labor)	60	12,00,000	80	8,00,000	20,00,000
Total	Rs 210	Rs 42,00,000	Rs 300	Rs 30,00,000	Rs 72,00,000

The value of scrap of Rs 70,000 generated during March will reduce material-related manufacturing overhead costs by Rs 70,000 from Rs 7,00,000 to Rs 6,30,000. Materials-related manufacturing overhead will then be allocated at 18% of direct materials costs (Rs 6,30,000 ÷ Rs 35,00,000 = 0.18)

The revised manufacturing cost per unit would then be:

	HM3		JB4		Total Costs
	Cost perUnit	Total Costs	Cost perUnit	TotalCosts	
	(1)	(2) = (1) × 20,000	(3)	(4) = (3) × 10,000	(5) = (2) + (4)
Direct materials	Rs 100	Rs 20,00,000	Rs 150	Rs 15,00,000	Rs 35,00,000
Direct manufacturing labor	30	6,00,000	40	4,00,000	10,00,000
Materials-related manufacturing overhead					
(18% of direct materials)	18	3,60,000	27	2,70,000	6,30,000
Other manufacturing overhead					
200% of direct manufacturing labor)	60	12,00,000	80	8,00,000	20,00,000
Total	Rs 208	Rs 41,60,000	Rs 297	Rs 29,70,000	Rs 71,30,000

18-28 Physical units, inspection at various stages of completion. (Chapter Appendix) Normal spoilage is 6% of the good units passing inspection in a forging process. In March, a total of 10,000 units were spoiled. Other data include units started during March, 1,20,000; work in process, beginning, 14,000 units (20% completed for conversion costs); and work in process, ending, 11,000 units (70% completed for conversion costs).

Required

In columnar form, compute the normal and abnormal spoilage in units, assuming the inspection point is at (a) 15% stage of completion, (b) 40% stage of completion, and (c) 100% of stage of completion.

Solution

Physical units, inspection at various stages of completion.

	Inspection at 15%	Inspection at 40%	Inspection at 100%
Work in process, beginning (20%)*	14,000	14,000	14,000
Started during March	1,20,000	1,20,000	1,20,000
To account for	1,34,000	1,34,000	1,34,000
Good units completed and transferred out	1,13,000[a]	1,13,000[a]	1,13,000[a]
Normal spoilage	6,600[b]	7,440[c]	6,780[d]
Abnormal spoilage (10,000 – normal spoilage)	3,400	2,560	3,220
Work in process, ending (70%)*	11,000	11,000	11,000
Accounted for	1,34,000	1,34,000	1,34,000

*Degree of completion for conversion costs of the forging process at the dates of the work-in-process inventories

[a] 14,000 beginning inventory + 1,20,000 – 10,000 spoiled – 11,000 ending inventory = 1,13,000

[b] 6% × (1,13,000 – 14,000 + 11,000) = 6% × 1,10,000 = 6,600

[c] 6% × (1,13,000 + 11,000) = 6% × 1,24,000 = 7,440

[d] 6% × 1,13,000 = 6,780

18-29 Job costing, spoilage, ethics. (CMA, adapted) Jindal Company manufactures products that often require specification changes or modifications to meet its customers' needs. Still, Jindal has been able to establish a normal spoilage rate of 2.5% of normal input. Normal spoilage is recognized during the budgeting process and classified as a component of manufacturing overhead when determining the overhead rate.

Peter, one of Jindal's inspection managers, obtains the following information for Job No. N1192-122, which was recently completed, just before the end of Jindal's current accounting year. The units will be delivered early in the next accounting year. A total of 1,22,000 units were started, and 5,000 spoiled units were rejected at final inspection, yielding 1,17,000 good units. Rejected units were sold at Rs 7 per unit. Peter indicates that all rejects were related to this specific job.

The total costs for all 1,22,000 units of Job No. N1192-122 follow. The job has been completed, but the costs are yet to be transferred to Finished Goods.

Direct materials	Rs 21,96,000
Direct manufacturing labor	18,30,000
Manufacturing overhead	29,28,000
Total manufacturing costs	Rs 69,54,000

Required

1. Calculate the unit quantities of normal and abnormal spoilage.
2. Prepare the journal entry (or entries) to account for Job No. N1192-122, including spoilage, disposal of spoiled units, and transfer of costs to the Finished Goods account.

3. Jindal Company has small profit margins and is anticipating very low operating income for the year. The controller, tells the management accountant responsible for Job No. N1192-122, the following, "This was an unusual job. I think all 5,000 spoiled units should be considered normal." The management accountant knows that Jindal's normal spoilage rate has been a good measure of normal spoilage levels on similar jobs in the past and that the spoilage levels for Job N1192-122 were much greater. He feels the controller made these comments because he wants to show higher operating income for the year.
   a. Prepare the journal entry (or entries), similar to the journal entry (or entries) prepared in requirement 2, to account for Job No. N1192-122 if all spoilage were considered normal. By how much will Jindal's operating income be affected if all spoilage is considered normal?
   b. What should the management accountant do?

Solution

Job costing, spoilage, ethics

1. Analysis of the 5,000 units rejected by Jindal Company for Job No. N1192-122 yields the following breakdown between normal and abnormal spoilage:

	Units
Normal spoilage*	3,000
Abnormal spoilage (5,000 – 3,000)	2,000
Total units rejected	5,000

*Normal spoilage = 0.025 of normal input
When output equals 1,17,000 units,
Normal input = 1,17,000 ÷ (1 – 0.025)
= 1,20,000 units
Normal spoilage = 1,20,000 × 0.025
= 3,000 units

2. The journal entries required to properly account for Job No. N1192-122 are presented below and use an average cost per unit of Rs 57 (Rs 69,54,000 ÷ 1,22,000):

	Rs	Rs
Accounts Receivable or Cash[1]	35,000	
Abnormal loss[2]	1,00,000	
WIP Control[3]		1,35,000
To account for 5,000 units rejected.		
Finished Good Control	68,19,000	
WIP Control		68,19,000

To transfer 1,17,000 units to finished goods inventory (costs incurred on job and debited to WIP Control, Rs 69,54,000, minus Rs 1,35,000 credited to WIP control).

[1]Units sold 5,000 units sold at Rs 7 each.

[2]Loss from abnormal spoilage: 2,000 units at Rs 57	Rs 1,14,000
Cost recovery (2,000 × Rs 7)	(14,000)
	Rs 1,00,000

[3]WIP control:	
2,000 abnormal spoilage units at Rs 57	Rs 1,14,000
3,000 normal spoilage units at Rs 7	21,000
	Rs 1,35,000

3. a. If all spoilage were considered normal, the journal entries to account for Job No. N1192-122 would be as follows:

Accounts Receivable or Cash	35,000	
WIP Control		35,000

To account for 5,000 units of normal spoilage, credited to WIP Control at Rs 35,000 (5,000 units × Rs 7).

Finished Goods Control	69,19,000	
WIP Control		69,19,000

To transfer 1,17,000 units to finished-goods inventory (costs incurred on job and debited to WIP Control, Rs 69,54,000, minus Rs 35,000 credited to WIP Control).

By considering all spoilage as normal, Jindal will show no abnormal loss of Rs 1,00,000 (see requirement 2) but instead will add Rs 1,00,000 to the finished-goods inventory [Rs 69,19,000 (in requirement 3a) minus Rs 68,19,000 (in requirement 2)]. Hence, showing all spoilage as normal will increase Jindal's operating income by Rs 1,00,000.

3. b. Incorrect reporting of spoilage as normal instead of abnormal with the goal of increasing operating income is unethical.

The management accountant should indicate to the controller that the classification of normal and abnormal spoilage established by Jindal Company is, indeed, appropriate. If the controller still insists on modifying the spoilage classification for this job to report higher operating income figures, The management accountant should raise the matter with one of the controller's superiors. If, after taking all these steps, there is continued pressure to overstate operating income, The management accountant should consider resigning from the company, and not engage in unethical behavior.

Exercises

18-30 Weighted-average method, spoilage. Godrej Manufacturing Company uses the weighted-average method of process costing. All direct materials are added at the beginning of the process, and conversion costs are added evenly during the process. Spoiled units are detected upon inspection at the end of the process and are disposed of at zero net disposal value. Summary data for March are:

	Physical Units	Direct Materials	Conversion Costs
Work in process, March 1[a]	30,000	Rs 24,00,000	Rs 18,00,000
Started in March	50,000		
Good units completed and transferred out during March	40,000		
Normal spoilage	6,000		
Abnormal spoilage	2,000		
Work in process, March 31[b]	32,000		
Costs added during March		Rs 42,00,000	Rs 58,32,000

[a]Degree of completion: direct materials, 100%; conversion costs, 60%.
[b]Degree of completion: direct materials, 100%; conversion costs, 75%.

Required

1. For each cost category, compute equivalent units. Show physical units in the first column of your schedule.
2. For each cost category, calculate cost per equivalent unit.
3. Summarize total costs to account for, and assign these costs to units completed and transferred out (including normal spoilage), to abnormal spoilage, and to units in ending work in process.

18-31 FIFO method, spoilage. Refer to the information in 18-30.

Required

Do Exercise 18-30 using the FIFO method. Note that you first need to calculate the equivalent units of work done in the current period (for direct materials and conversion costs) to complete beginning work in process, to start and complete new units, for normal and abnormal spoilage units, and to produce ending work in process.

18-32 Standard-costing method, spoilage. Refer to the information in Exercise 18-30. Suppose Godrej determines standard costs of Rs 80 per equivalent unit for direct materials and Rs 100 per equivalent unit for conversion costs for both beginning work in process and work done in the current period.

Required

Do Exercise 18-30 using the standard-costing method. Note that you first need to calculate the equivalent units of work done in the current period (for direct materials and conversion costs) to complete beginning work in process, to start and complete new units, for normal and abnormal spoilage units, and to produce ending work in process.

18-33 Weighted-average method, spoilage. Superchip specializes in the manufacture of microchips for aircraft. Direct materials are added at the start of the production process. Conversion costs are added evenly during the process. Some units of this product are spoiled as a result of defects not detectable before inspection of finished goods. Normally, the spoiled units are 15% of the good units transferred out. Spoiled units are disposed of at zero net disposal value. Superchip uses the weighted-average method of process costing.
Summary data for September are:

	Physical Units (Microchips)	Direct Materials	Conversion Costs
Work in process, September 1[a]	400	Rs 6,40,000	Rs 1,02,000
Started in September	1,700		
Good units completed and transferred out during September	1,400		
Work in process, September 30[b]	300		
Costs added during September		Rs 37,80,000	Rs 15,36,000

[a]Degree of completion: direct materials, 100%; conversion costs, 30%.
[b]Degree of completion: direct materials, 100%; conversion costs, 40%.

Required

1. For each cost category, compute equivalent units. Show physical units in the first column of your schedule.
2. For each cost category, calculate cost per equivalent unit.
3. Summarize total costs to account for, and assign these costs to units completed and transferred out (including normal spoilage), to abnormal spoilage, and to units in ending work in process.

18-34 FIFO method, spoilage. Refer to the information in Exercise 18-33.

Required

Do Exercise 18-33 using the FIFO method of process costing.

18-35 Standard-costing method, spoilage. Refer to the information in Exercise 18-34. Suppose Superchip determines standard costs of Rs 2,050 per equivalent unit for direct materials and Rs 80 per (equivalent) unit for conversion costs for both beginning work in process and work done in the current period.

Required

Do Exercise 18-36 using the standard-costing method.

18-36 Scrap, job costing. The Jindal Company has an extensive job-costing facility that uses a variety of metals. Consider each requirement independently.

Required

1. Job 372 uses a particular metal alloy that is not used for any other job. Assume that scrap is material in amount and sold quickly after it is produced. The scrap is sold for Rs 490. Prepare the journal entry.
2. The scrap from Job 372 consists of a metal used by many other jobs. No record is maintained of the scrap generated by individual jobs. Assume that scrap is accounted for at the time of sale of scrap. Scrap totaling Rs 4,000 is sold. Prepare two alternative journal entries that could be used to account for the sale of scrap.
3. Suppose the scrap generated in requirement 2 is returned to the storeroom for future use and a journal entry is made to record the scrap. A month later, the scrap is reused as direct material on a subsequent job. Prepare the journal entries to record these transactions.

18-37 Job-costing, spoilage and scrap. (F. Mayne) Mahalaxmi Metal Fabricators Limited, has a large job, No. 2734, that calls for producing various ore bins, chutes, and metal boxes for enlarging a copper concentrator. The following charges were made to the job in November:

Direct materials	Rs 2,69,510
Direct manufacturing labor	1,50,760
Manufacturing overhead	75,380

The contract with the customer called for the total price to be based on a cost-plus approach. The contract defined cost to include direct materials, direct manufacturing labor costs, and manufacturing overhead to be allocated at 50% of direct manufacturing labor costs. The contract also provided that the total costs of all work spoiled were to be removed from the billable cost of the job and that the benefits from scrap sales were to reduce the billable cost of the job.

Required

1. In accordance with the stated terms of the contract, prepare journal entries for the following two items:
   a. A cutting error was made in production. The up-to-date job cost record for this batch of work showed materials of Rs 6,500, direct manufacturing labor of Rs 5,000, and allocated overhead of Rs 2,500. Because fairly large pieces of metal were recoverable, the company believed that the scrap value was Rs 6,000 and that the materials recovered could be used on other jobs. The spoiled work was sent to the warehouse.
   b. Small pieces of metal cuttings and scrap in November amounted to Rs 12,500, which was the price quoted by a scrap dealer. No journal entries were made with regard to the scrap until the price was quoted by the scrap dealer. The scrap dealer's offer was immediately accepted.
2. Consider normal and abnormal spoilage. Suppose the contract described above had contained the clause "a normal spoilage allowance of 1% of the job costs will be included in the billable costs of the job."
   a. Is this clause specific enough to define exactly how much spoilage is normal and how much is abnormal? Explain.
   b. Repeat requirement 1a with this "normal spoilage of 1%" clause in mind. You should be able to provide two slightly different journal entries.

18-38 Weighted-average method, inspection at 80% completion. (A. Atkinson) (Chapter Appendix) Delhi Manufacturing produces a plastic toy in a two-stage molding and finishing operation. The company uses the weighted-average method of process costing. During June, the following data were recorded for the Finishing Department:

Units of beginning inventory	10,000
Percentage completion of beginning units	25%

Cost of direct materials in beginning work in process	Rs 0
Units started	70,000
Units completed	50,000
Units in ending inventory	20,000
Percentage completion of ending units	95%
Spoiled units	10,000
Costs added during current period:	
Direct materials	Rs 6,55,200
Direct manufacturing labor	Rs 6,35,600
Manufacturing overhead	Rs 6,16,000
Work in process, beginning:	
Transferred-in costs	Rs 82,900
Conversion costs	Rs 42,000
Cost of units transferred in during current period	Rs 6,47,500

Conversion costs are incurred evenly during the process. Direct materials costs are incurred when production is 90% complete. The inspection point is at the 80% stage of production. Normal spoilage is 10% of all good units that pass inspection. Spoiled units are disposed of at zero net disposal value.

Required

For June, summarize total costs to account for, and assign these costs to units completed and transferred out (including normal spoilage), to abnormal spoilage, and to units in ending work in process.

18-39 FIFO method, spoilage, working backward. The Cooking Department of Haldiram Foods, uses a process-costing system. Direct materials are added at the beginning of the cooking process. Conversion costs are added evenly during the cooking process. Consider the following data for the Cooking Department for January:

	Physical Units	Direct Materials	Conversion Costs
Work in process, January 1[a]	10,000	Rs 2,20,000	Rs 30,000
Started in January	74,000		
Good units completed and transferred out during January	61,000		
Spoiled units	8,000		
Work in process, January 31	15,000		
Costs added during January		Rs 14,80,000	Rs 9,42,000
Cost per equivalent unit of work done in January		Rs 20	Rs 12

[a]Degree of completion: direct materials, 100%; conversion costs, 25%.

Haldiram Foods uses the FIFO method of process costing. Inspection occurs when production is 100% complete. Normal spoilage is 11% of good units completed and transferred out during the current period.

Required

1. For each cost category, compute equivalent units of work done in the current period (January).
2. For each cost category, compute separately the equivalent units of work done to complete beginning work-in-process inventory, to start and complete new units, for normal and abnormal spoilage, and to produce ending work-in-process inventory.
3. For each cost category, calculate the percentage of completion of ending work-in-process inventory.
4. Summarize total costs to account for, and assign these costs to units completed and transferred out (including normal spoilage), to abnormal spoilage, and to units in ending work in process.

19 Balanced Scorecard: Quality, Time, and the Theory of Constraints

Learning Objectives

1. Explain the four cost categories in a costs-of-quality program
2. Develop nonfinancial measures and methods to improve quality
3. Combine financial and nonfinancial measures to make decisions and evaluate quality performance
4. Describe customer-response time and explain why delays happen and their costs
5. Explain how to manage bottlenecks

To satisfy ever-increasing customer expectations, managers need to find cost-effective ways to continuously improve the quality of their products and services and shorten response times. This requires trading off the costs of achieving these improvements and the benefits from higher performance on these dimensions. When companies do not meet customer expectations, the losses can be substantial, as the following article about Toyota Motor Corporation shows.

Toyota Plans Changes After Millions of Defective Cars Are Recalled[1]

Toyota Motor Corporation, the Japanese automaker, built its reputation on manufacturing reliable cars. In 2002, Toyota executives set an ambitious goal to gain 15% of the global auto industry by 2010, meaning it would surpass General Motors as the world's largest carmaker. In the subsequent years, Toyota grew sales by 50% and managed to win bragging rights as the world's biggest car company. But the company's focus on rapid growth appears to have come at a cost to its reputation for quality.

Between November 2009 and January 2010, Toyota was forced to recall 9 million vehicles worldwide because gas pedals began to stick and were causing unwanted acceleration on eight Toyota models. After months of disagreements with government safety officials, the company ultimately recalled 12 models and suspended the production and sales of eight new Toyota and Lexus models, including its popular Camry and Corolla sedans. While most cars were quickly returned to the sales floor, some industry analysts estimated that the loss of revenue to Toyota could have been as much as $500 million each week.

Beyond lost revenue, Toyota's once-vaunted image took a serious hit. As the crisis unfolded, Toyota was slow to take responsibility for manufacturing problems. The company then faced

[1] *Sources*: Kaufman, Wendy. 2010. Can Toyota recover its reputation for quality? Morning Edition, National Public Radio, February 9. http://www.npr.org/templates/story/story.php?storyId=123519027&ps=rs; Linebaugh, Kate and Norihiko Shirouzu. 2010. Toyota heir faces crisis at the wheel. *Wall Street Journal*, January 27. http://online.wsj.com/article/SB10001424052748704094304575029493222357402.html; Maynard, Micheline and Hiroko Tabuchi. 2010. Rapid growth has its perils, Toyota learns. *New York Times*, January 27. http://www.nytimes.com/2010/01/28/business/28toyota.html; Kageyama, Yuri. 2010. Toyota holds quality meeting to help repair reputation; promises quicker complaint response. *Associated Press*, March 29. http://abcnews.go.com/International/wireStory?id=10238266

the long and difficult task of restoring its credibility and assuring owners and new-car shoppers that it had fixed the problems.

It established a quality committee led by Akio Toyoda, the company's chief executive; announced plans to add a brake override system to all new models; added four new quality training facilities; and promised faster decisions on future recall situations. "Listening to consumer voices is most important in regaining credibility from our customers," Mr. Toyoda said.

The Toyota example vividly illustrates the importance of quality. But improving quality is hard work. This chapter describes how a balanced scorecard approach helps managers and management accountants improve quality, customer-response time, and throughput.

This chapter covers three topics. The first topic addresses quality as a competitive tool, looking at quality from the financial perspective, the customer perspective, the internal business process perspective, and the learning-and-growth perspective before discussing the evaluation of quality performance. The second topic addresses time as a competitive tool and focuses on customer response time, on-time performance, time drivers, and the cost of time. The third topic looks closely at the theory of constraints and throughput-margin analysis, covering the management of bottlenecks and nonfinancial measures of time. The presentation is modular so you can omit a topic or explore it in any order.

QUALITY AS A COMPETITIVE TOOL

The American Society for Quality defines **quality** as the total features and characteristics of a product or a service made or performed according to specifications to satisfy customers at the time of purchase and during use. Many companies throughout the world—for example, Cisco Systems and Motorola in the United States and Canada, British Telecom in the United Kingdom, Fujitsu and Toyota in Japan, Crysel in Mexico, and Samsung in South Korea—have emphasized quality as an important strategic initiative. Service quality has also become increasingly important in nonprofit sectors such as health care and government. For example, Kaiser Permanente, a leading nonprofit health insurer, pays bonuses to its doctors based on patient satisfaction. That's because a quality focus reduces costs and increases customer satisfaction. Several high-profile awards—

the Malcolm Baldrige National Quality Award in the United States, the Deming Prize in Japan, and the Premio Nacional de Calidad in Mexico—are given to companies that have produced high-quality products and services.

International quality standards have also emerged. ISO 9000, developed by the International Organization for Standardization, is a set of five international standards for quality management adopted by more than 85 countries. ISO 9000 enables companies to effectively document and certify the elements of their production processes that lead to quality. To ensure that their suppliers deliver high-quality products at competitive costs, companies such as DuPont and General Electric require their suppliers to obtain ISO 9000 certification. Documenting evidence of quality through ISO 9000 has become a necessary condition for competing in the global marketplace.

As corporations' responsibilities toward the environment grow, managers are applying the quality management and measurement practices discussed in this chapter to find cost-effective ways to reduce the environmental and economic costs of air pollution, wastewater, oil spills, and hazardous waste disposal. An environmental management standard, ISO 14000, encourages organizations to pursue environmental goals vigorously by developing (1) environmental management systems to reduce environmental costs and (2) environmental auditing and performance-evaluation systems to review and provide feedback on environmental goals. Nowhere has the issue of quality and the environment come together in a bigger way than at the British Petroleum (BP) Deepwater Horizon oil rig in the Gulf of Mexico. An explosion on the oil-drilling platform in April of 2010 resulted in millions of gallons of oil spilling out in the Gulf, causing environmental damage over thousands of square miles and resulting in billions of dollars of clean up costs for BP.

We focus on two basic aspects of quality: design quality and conformance quality. **Design quality** refers to how closely the characteristics of a product or service meet the needs and wants of customers. **Conformance quality** is the performance of a product or service relative to its design and product specifications. Apple Inc. has built a reputation for design quality by developing many innovative products such as the iPod, iPhone, and iPad that have uniquely met customers' music, telephone, entertainment, and business needs. Apple's products have also had excellent conformance quality; the products did what they were supposed to do. In the case of the iPhone 4, however, many customers complained about very weak signal receptions on their phones. The enthusiastic customer response to the iPhone 4 when it was launched in the summer of 2010 indicates good design quality, as customers liked what the iPhone 4 had to offer. The problem with its antenna that caused signals not to be received is a problem of conformance quality, because the phone did not do what it was designed to do. The following diagram illustrates that actual performance can fall short of customer satisfaction because of design-quality failure and because of conformance-quality failure.

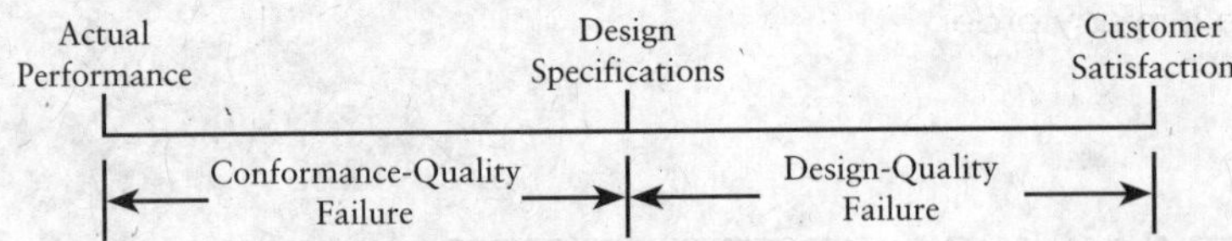

We illustrate the issues in managing quality—computing the costs of quality, identifying quality problems, and taking actions to improve quality—using Photon Corporation. While Photon makes many products, we will focus only on Photon's photocopying machines, which earned an operating income of Rs 240 million on revenues of Rs 3,000 million (from sales of 20,000 copiers) in 2011.

Quality has both financial and nonfinancial components relating to customer satisfaction, improving internal quality processes, reducing defects, and the training and empowering of workers. To provide some structure, we discuss quality from the four perspectives of the balanced scorecard: financial, customer, internal business process, and learning and growth.

The Financial Perspective: Costs of Quality

Learning Objective 1

Explain the four cost categories in a costs-of-quality program

. . . prevention, appraisal, internal failure, and external failure costs

The financial perspective of Photon's balanced scorecard includes measures such as revenue growth and operating income—financial measures that are likely to be affected by quality improvement programs. In addition, Photon measures costs of quality. **Costs of quality** (COQ) are the costs incurred to prevent, or the costs arising as a result of, the production of a low-quality product. Costs of quality are classified into four categories; examples for each category are listed in Exhibit 19-1.

1. **Prevention costs**—costs incurred to preclude the production of products that do not conform to specifications.
2. **Appraisal costs**—costs incurred to detect which of the individual units of products do not conform to specifications.
3. **Internal failure costs**—costs incurred on defective products before they are shipped to customers.
4. **External failure costs**—costs incurred on defective products after they are shipped to customers.

The items in Exhibit 19-1 come from all business functions of the value chain, and they are broader than the internal failure costs of spoilage, rework, and scrap described in Chapter 18.

An important role for management accountants is preparing costs-of-quality reports for managers. Photon determines the costs of quality of its photocopying machines by adapting the seven-step activity-based costing approach described in Chapter 5.

Step 1: Identify the Product That Is the Chosen Cost Object. The cost object is the photocopying machine that Photon made and sold in 2011. Photon's goal is to calculate the total costs of quality of these 20,000 machines.

Step 2: Identify the Direct Costs of Quality of the Product. Direct costs include employees such as inspectors and workers in repair areas who are dedicated to a product line. The photocopying machines have no direct costs of quality because no inspection or repair workers are dedicated to the photocopying machines.

Step 3: Select the Activities and Cost-Allocation Bases to Use for Allocating Indirect Costs of Quality to the Product. Column 1 of Exhibit 19-2, Panel A, classifies the activities that result in prevention, appraisal, and internal and external failure costs, and it indicates in parentheses the business functions of the value chain in which these costs occur. For example, the inspection activity results in appraisal costs and occurs in the manufacturing function. Photon identifies the number of inspection-hours as the cost-allocation base for the inspection activity. (To avoid details not needed to explain the concepts here, we do not provide information on the total quantities of each cost-allocation base.)

Step 4: Identify the Indirect Costs of Quality Associated with Each Cost-Allocation Base. These are the total costs (variable and fixed) incurred for each of the costs-of-quality activities, such as inspections, in all of Photon's operations. (To avoid details not needed to understand the points described here, we do not provide information about these total costs.)

Prevention Costs	Appraisal Costs	Internal Failure Costs	External Failure Costs
Design engineering	Inspection	Spoilage	Customer support
Process engineering	Online products manufacturing and process inspection	Rework	Manufacturing/ process engineering for external failures
Supplier evaluations	Product testing	Scrap	Warranty repair costs
Preventive equipment maintenance		Machine repairs	Liability claims
Quality training		Manufacturing/ process engineering on internal failures	
Testing of new materials			

Exhibit 19-1

Items Pertaining to Costs-of-Quality Reports

Exhibit 19-2 Analysis of Activity-Based Costs of Quality (COQ) for Photocopying Machines at Photon Corporation

File Edit View Insert Format Tools Data Window Help

	A	B	C	D	E	F	G
1	**PANEL A: COQ REPORT**						**Percentage of**
2		**Cost Allocation**		**Quantity of Cost**		**Total**	**Revenues**
3	**Cost of Quality and Value-Chain Category**	**Rate[a]**		**Allocation Base**		**Costs**	**(5) = (4) ÷**
4	**(1)**	**(2)**		**(3)**		**(4) = (2) x (3)**	**Rs 3,00,00,00,000**
5	*Prevention costs*						
6	Design engineering (R&D/Design)	Rs 800	per hour	40,000	hours	Rs 3,20,00,000	1.1%
7	Process engineering (R&D/Design)	Rs 600	per hour	45,000	hours	2,70,00,000	0.9%
8	Total prevention costs					5,90,00,000	2.0%
9	*Appraisal costs*						
10	Inspection (Manufacturing)	Rs 400	per hour	2,40,000	hours	9,60,00,000	3.2%
11	Total appraisal costs					9,60,00,000	3.2%
12	*Internal failure costs*						
13	Rework (Manufacturing)	Rs 1,000	per hour	1,00,000	hours	10,00,00,000	3.3%
14	Total internal failure costs					10,00,00,000	3.3%
15	*External failure costs*						
16	Customer support (Marketing)	Rs 500	per hour	12,000	hours	60,00,000	0.2%
17	Transportation (Distribution)	Rs 2,400	per load	3,000	loads	72,00,000	0.2%
18	Warranty repair (Customer service)	Rs 1,100	per hour	1,20,000	hours	13,20,00,000	4.4%
19	Total external failure costs					14,52,00,000	4.8%
20	Total costs of quality					Rs 40,02,00,000	13.3%
21							
22	[a]Amounts assumed.						
23							
24	**PANEL B: OPPORTUNITY COST ANALYSIS**						
25						**Total Estimated**	**Percentage**
26						**Contribution**	**of Revenues**
27	**Cost of Quality Category**					**Margin Lost**	**(3) = (2) ÷**
28	**(1)**					**(2)**	**Rs 300,00,00,000**
29	*External failure costs*						
30	Estimated forgone contribution margin						
31	and income on lost sales					Rs 12,00,00,000[b]	4.0%
32	Total external failure costs					Rs 12,00,00,000	4.0%
33							
34	[b]Calculated as total revenues minus all variable costs (whether output-unit, batch, product-sustaining, or facility-sustaining) on						
35	lost sales in 2008. If poor quality causes Photon to lose sales in subsequent years as well, the opportunity costs will be						
36	even greater.						

Step 5: Compute the Rate per Unit of Each Cost-Allocation Base. For each activity, total costs (identified in step 4) are divided by total quantity of the cost-allocation base (calculated in step 3) to compute rate per unit of each cost-allocation base. Column 2 of Exhibit 19-2, Panel A, shows these rates (without supporting calculations).

Step 6: Compute the Indirect Costs of Quality Allocated to the Product. Photon first determines the quantity of each cost-allocation base used by the photocopying machines (column 3 of Panel A). For example, photocopying machines use 240,000 inspection-hours. The indirect costs of quality of the photocopying machines, shown in column 4, Panel A, equal the total quantity of the cost-allocation base used by the photocopying machines for each activity (column 3) multiplied by the cost-allocation rate from step 5 (column 2). For example, quality-related inspection costs for the photocopying machines are Rs 9,60,00,000 (Rs 400 per hour × 2,40,000 inspection-hours).

Step 7: Compute the Total Costs of Quality by Adding All Direct and Indirect Costs of Quality Assigned to the Product. Photon's total costs of quality in the COQ report for photocopying machines is Rs 400.2 million (bottom of column 4, Panel A), or 13.3% of current revenues (bottom of column 5).

As we have seen in Chapter 11, opportunity costs are not recorded in financial accounting systems. Yet, a very significant component of costs of quality is the opportunity cost of the contribution margin and income forgone from lost sales, lost production, and lower prices resulting from poor design and conformance quality. Photon's market research department estimates that design and conformance quality problems experienced by some customers resulted in lost sales of 2,000 photocopying machines in 2011 and forgone contribution margin and operating income of Rs 120 million (Exhibit 19-2, Panel B). Total costs of quality, including opportunity costs, equal Rs 520.2 million (Rs 400.2 million recorded in the accounting system and shown in Panel A + Rs 120 million of opportunity costs shown in Panel B), or 17.3% of current revenues. Opportunity costs account for 23.1% (Rs 120 million ÷ Rs 520.2 million) of Photon's total costs of quality.

We turn next to the leading indicators of the costs of quality, the nonfinancial measures of customer satisfaction about the quality of Photon's photocopiers.

Decision Point

What are the four cost categories of a costs-of-quality program?

The Customer Perspective: Nonfinancial Measures of Customer Satisfaction

Learning Objective 2

Develop nonfinancial measures

... customer satisfaction measures such as number of customer complaints, internal-business process measures such as percentage of defective and reworked products, and learning and growth measures such as employee empowerment and training

and methods to improve quality

... control charts, Pareto diagrams, and cause-and-effect diagrams

Similar to Unilever, Federal Express, and TiVo, Photon measures customer satisfaction over time. Some measures are:

- Market research information on customer preferences for and customer satisfaction with specific product features (to measure design quality)
- Market share
- Percentage of customers that give high ratings for customer satisfaction
- Number of defective units shipped to customers as a percentage of total units shipped
- Number of customer complaints (Companies estimate that for every customer who actually complains, there are 10 to 20 others who have had bad experiences with the product or service but did not complain.)
- Percentage of products that fail soon after delivery
- Delivery delays (difference between the scheduled delivery date and the date requested by the customer)
- On-time delivery rate (percentage of shipments made on or before the scheduled delivery date)

Photon's management monitors whether these numbers improve or deteriorate over time. Higher customer satisfaction should lead to lower costs of quality and higher future revenues from greater customer retention, loyalty, and positive word-of-mouth advertising. Lower customer-satisfaction indicates that costs of quality ill likely increase in the future. We next turn to the driver of customer satisfaction, th internal business processes to identify and analyze quality problems and to improve quality.

The Internal-Business-Process Perspective: Analyzing Quality Problems and Improving Quality

We present three techniques for identifying and analyzing quality problems: control charts, Pareto diagrams, and cause-and-effect diagrams.

Control Charts

Statistical quality control (SQC), which is also called statistical process control (SPC), is a formal means of distinguishing between random and nonrandom variations in an operating process. Random variations occur, for example, when power surges or chance fluctuations in temperature cause defective products to be produced in a chemical process. Nonrandom variations occur when defective products are produced as a result of a systematic problem such as inaccurate temperature readings. A **control chart**, one of the tools in SQC, is a graph of a series of successive observations of a particular step, procedure, or operation taken at regular intervals of time. Each observation is plotted relative to specified ranges that represent the limits within which observations are expected to fall. Only those observations outside the control limits are ordinarily regarded as nonrandom and worth investigating.

Exhibit 19-3 presents control charts for the daily defect rates observed at Photon's three photocopying-machine production lines. Defect rates in the prior 60 days for each production line were assumed to provide a good basis from which to calculate the distribution of daily defect rates. The arithmetic mean (μ, read mu) and standard deviation (σ, read sigma) are the two parameters of the distribution that are used in the control charts in Exhibit 19-3. On the basis of experience, the company decides that any observation outside the $\mu \pm 2\sigma$ range should be investigated.

For production line A, all observations are within the range of $\mu \pm 2\sigma$, so management believes no investigation is necessary. For production line B, the last two observations signal that an out-of-control occurrence is highly likely. Given the $\pm 2\sigma$ rule, both observations would be investigated. Production line C illustrates a process that would not prompt an investigation under the $\pm 2\sigma$ rule but that may well be out of control. That's because the last eight observations show a clear direction, and the last six are getting further and further away from the mean. This could be due to the tooling on a machine beginning to wear out. As the tooling deteriorates further, the trend is likely to persist until the production line is no longer in statistical control. Statistical procedures have been developed using the trend as well as the variation to evaluate whether a process is out of control.

Pareto Diagrams

Observations outside control limits serve as inputs for Pareto diagrams. A **Pareto diagram** is a chart that indicates how frequently each type of defect occurs, ordered from the most frequent to the least frequent. Exhibit 19-4 presents a Pareto diagram of quality problems with respect to Photon's photocopying machines. Fuzzy and unclear copies are the most frequently recurring problem. Fuzzy and unclear copies result in high rework costs. Sometimes fuzzy and unclear copies occur at customer sites and result in high warranty and repair costs and low customer satisfaction.

Exhibit 19-3 Statistical Quality Control Charts: Daily Defect Rate for Photocopying Machines at Photon Corporation

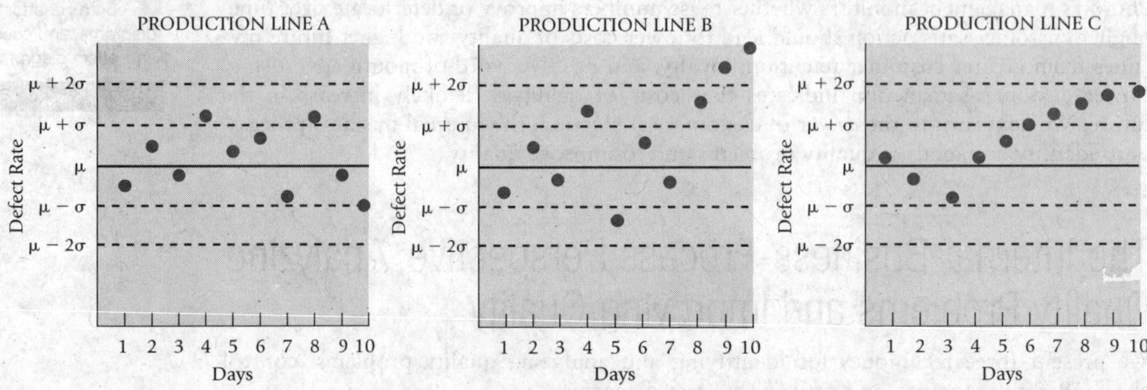

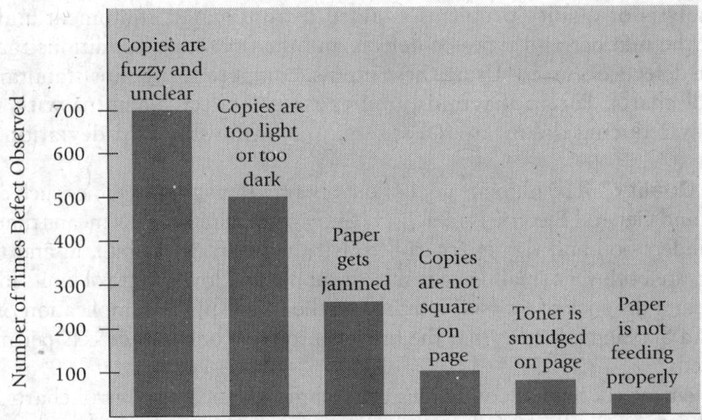

Exhibit 19-4

Pareto Diagram for Photocopying Machines at Photon Corporation

Cause-and-Effect Diagrams

The most frequently recurring and costly problems identified by the Pareto diagram are analyzed using cause-and-effect diagrams. A **cause-and-effect diagram** identifies potential causes of defects using a diagram that resembles the bone structure of a fish (hence, cause-and-effect diagrams are also called *fishbone diagrams*).[2] Exhibit 19-5 presents the cause-and-effect diagram describing potential reasons why fuzzy and unclear copies occur. The "backbone" of the diagram represents the problem being examined. The large "bones" coming off the backbone represent the main categories of potential causes of failure. The exhibit identifies four of these: human factors, methods and design factors, machine-related factors, and materials and components factors. Additional arrows or bones are added to provide more-detailed reasons for each higher-level cause. For example, the two potential causes of material and component problems are variation in purchased components and incorrect component specification. They quickly settle on variation in purchased components as the likely cause and focus on the use of multiple suppliers and mishandling of purchased parts as the root causes of variation in purchased components. Further analysis leads them to conclude that mishandling of the steel frame that holds in place various components of the copier such as drums, mirrors, and lenses results in the misalignment of these components, causing fuzzy and unclear copies.

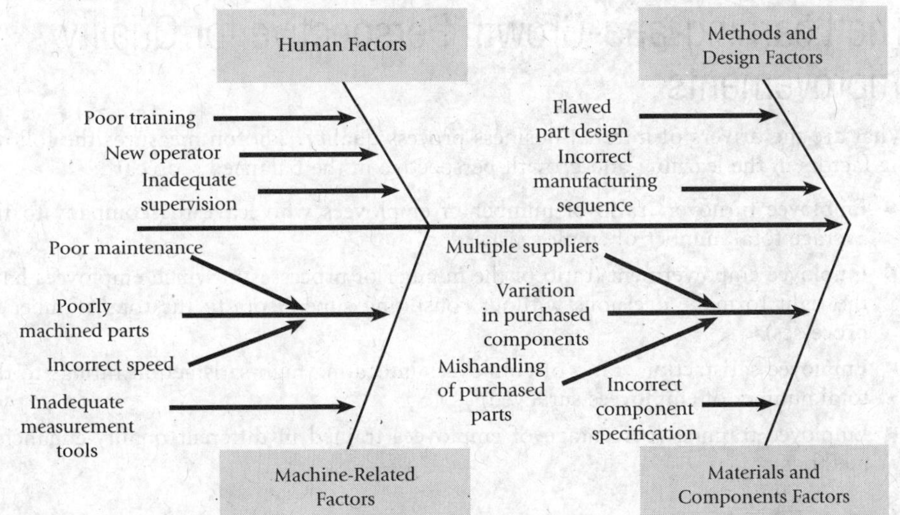

Exhibit 19-5

Cause-and-Effect Diagram for Fuzzy and Unclear Photocopies at Photon Corporation

[2] See P. Clark, "Getting the Most from Cause-and-Effect Diagrams," *Quality Progress* (June 2000).

The analysis of quality problems is aided by automated equipment and computers that record the number and types of defects and the operating conditions that existed at the time the defects occurred. Using these inputs, computer programs simultaneously prepare control charts, Pareto diagrams, and cause-and-effect diagrams with the goal of continuously reducing the mean defect rate, μ, and the standard deviation, σ.

Six Sigma Quality The ultimate goal of quality programs at companies such as Motorola, Honeywell, and General Electric is to achieve Six Sigma quality.[3] This means that the process is so well-understood and tightly controlled that the mean defect rate, μ, and the standard deviation, σ, are both very small. As a result, the upper and lower control limits in Exhibit 19-3 can be set at a distance of 6σ (six sigma) from the mean (μ). The implication of controlling a process at a Six Sigma level is that the process produces only 3.4 defects per million products produced.

To implement Six Sigma, companies use techniques such as control charts, Pareto diagrams, and cause-and-effect diagrams to define, measure, analyze, improve, and control processes to minimize variability in manufacturing and achieve almost zero defects. Critics of Six Sigma argue that it emphasizes incremental rather than dramatic or disruptive innovation. Nevertheless, companies report substantial benefits from Six Sigma initiatives.

Companies routinely use nonfinancial measures to track the quality improvements they are making.

Nonfinancial Measures of Internal-Business-Process Quality

Photon measures internal-business-process quality using the following nonfinancial measures:

- Percentage of defective products
- Average time taken to repair photocopying machines at customer sites
- Percentage of reworked products
- Number of different types of defects analyzed using control charts, Pareto diagrams, and cause-and-effect diagrams
- Number of design and process changes made to improve design quality or reduce costs of quality

Photon's managers believe that improving these measures will lead to greater customer satisfaction, lower costs of quality, and better financial performance.

The Learning-and-Growth Perspective for Quality Improvements

What are the drivers of internal-business-process quality? Photon measures the following factors in the learning-and-growth perspective in the balanced scorecard:

- Employee turnover (ratio of number of employees who leave the company to the average total number of employees)
- Employee empowerment (ratio of the number of processes in which employees have the right to make decisions without consulting supervisors to the total number of processes)
- Employee satisfaction (ratio of employees indicating high satisfaction ratings to the total number of employees surveyed)
- Employee training (percentage of employees trained in different quality-enhancing methods)

Decision Point

What nonfinancial measures and methods can managers use to improve quality?

[3] Six Sigma is a registered trademark of Motorola Inc.

Making Decisions and Evaluating Quality Performance

Learning Objective 

Combine financial and nonfinancial measures to make decisions and evaluate quality performance

. . . Identify relevant incremental and opportunity costs to evaluate tradeoffs across costs of quality and nonfinancial measures to identify problem areas and to highlight leading indicators of future performance

Relevant Costs and Benefits of Quality Improvement When making decisions and evaluating performance, companies combine financial and nonfinancial information. We use the Photon example to illustrate relevant revenues and relevant costs in the context of decisions to improve quality.

Recall that Photon's cause-and-effect diagram reveals that the steel frame (or chassis) of the copier is often mishandled as it travels from a supplier's warehouse to Photon's plant. The frame must meet very precise specifications or else copier components (such as drums, mirrors, and lenses) will not fit exactly on the frame. Mishandling frames during transport causes misalignment and results in fuzzy and unclear copies.

A team of engineers offers two solutions: (1) inspect the frames immediately on delivery or (2) redesign and strengthen the frames and their shipping containers to withstand mishandling during transportation. The cost structure for 2012 is expected to be the same as the cost structure for 2011 presented in Exhibit 19-2.

To evaluate each alternative versus the status quo, management identifies the relevant costs and benefits for each solution by focusing on *how total costs and total revenues will change under each alternative*. As explained in Chapter 11, relevant-cost and relevant-revenue analysis ignores allocated amounts.

Photon uses only a one-year time horizon (2012) for the analysis because it plans to introduce a completely new line of copiers at the end of 2012. The new line is so different that the choice of either the inspection or the redesign alternative will have no effect on the sales of copiers in future years.

Exhibit 19-6 shows the relevant costs and benefits for each alternative.

1. **Estimated incremental costs:** Rs 40,00,000 for the inspection alternative; Rs 46,00,000 for the redesign alternative.
2. **Cost savings from less rework, customer support, and repairs:** Exhibit 19-6, line 10, shows that reducing rework results in savings of Rs 400 per hour. Exhibit 19-2, Panel A, column 2, line 13, shows total rework cost per hour of Rs 1,000. Why the difference? Because as it improves quality, Photon will only save the Rs 400 variable cost per rework-hour, not the Rs 600 fixed cost per rework-hour. Exhibit 19-6, line 10, shows total savings of Rs 96,00,000 (Rs 400 per hour × 24,000 rework-hours saved) if it inspects the frames and Rs 1,28,00,000 (Rs 400 per rework-hour × 32,000

Exhibit 19-6 Estimated Effects of Quality-Improvement Actions on Costs of Quality for Photocopying Machines at Photon Corporation

Home | Insert | Page Layout | Formulas | Data | Review | View

	A	B	C	D	E	F	G	H	I	J
1						Relevant Costs and Benefits of				
2				Further Inspecting Incoming Frames				Redesigning Frames		
3	Relevant Items	Relevant Benefit per Unit		Quantity		Total Benefits		Quantity		Total Benefits
4	(1)	(2)		(3)		(4)		(5)		(6)
5	Additional inspection and testing costs					Rs 40,00,000				
6	Additional process engineering costs									Rs(30,00,000)
7	Additional design engineering costs									(16,00,000)
8										
9						(2) × (3)				(2) × (5)
10	Savings in rework costs	Rs 400	per hour	24,000	hours	Rs 96,00,000		32,000	hours	Rs1,28,00,000
11	Savings in customer-support costs	Rs 200	per hour	2,000	hours	4,00,000		2,800	hours	5,60,000
12	Savings in transportation costs for repair parts	Rs 1,800	per load	500	loads	9,00,000		700	loads	12,60,000
13	Savings in warranty repair costs	Rs 450	per hour	20,000	hours	90,00,000		28,000	hours	1,26,00,000
14	Total contribution margin from additional sales	Rs 60,000	per copier	250	copiers	1,50,00,000		300	copiers	1,80,00,000
15										
16	Net cost savings and additional contribution margin					Rs 3,09,00,000				Rs 4,06,20,000
17										
18	Difference in favor of redesigning frames (J16) – (F16)						Rs97,20,000			

rework-hours saved) if it redesigns the frames. Exhibit 19-6 also shows expected variable-cost savings in customer support, transportation, and warranty repair for the two alternatives.

3. **Increased contribution margin from higher sales as a result of building a reputation for quality and performance (Exhibit 19-6, line 14):** Rs 1,50,00,000 for 250 copiers under the inspection alternative and Rs 1,80,00,000 for 300 copiers under the redesign alternative. Management should always look for opportunities to generate higher revenues, not just cost reductions, from quality improvements.

Exhibit 19-6 shows that both the inspection and the redesign alternatives yield net benefits relative to the status quo. However, the net benefits from the redesign alternative are expected to be Rs 97,20,000 greater.

Note how making improvements in internal business processes affects the COQ numbers reported in the financial perspective. In our example, redesigning the frame increases prevention costs (design and process engineering), decreases internal failure costs (rework), and decreases external failure costs (customer support and warranty repairs). COQ reports provide more insight about quality improvements when managers compare trends over time. In successful quality programs, companies decrease costs of quality and, in particular, internal and external failure costs, as a percentage of revenues. Many companies, such as Hewlett-Packard, go further and believe they should eliminate all failure costs and have zero defects.

How should Photon use financial and nonfinancial measures to evaluate quality performance? They should utilize both types of measures because financial (COQ) and nonfinancial measures of quality have different advantages.

Advantages of COQ Measures

- Consistent with the attention-directing role of management accounting, COQ measures focus managers' attention on the costs of poor quality.
- Total COQ provides a measure of quality performance for evaluating trade-offs among prevention costs, appraisal costs, internal failure costs, and external failure costs.
- COQ measures assist in problem solving by comparing costs and benefits of different quality-improvement programs and setting priorities for cost reduction.

Advantages of Nonfinancial Measures of Quality

- Nonfinancial measures of quality are often easy to quantify and understand.
- Nonfinancial measures direct attention to physical processes and hence help managers identify the precise problem areas that need improvement.
- Nonfinancial measures, such as number of defects, provide immediate short-run feedback on whether quality-improvement efforts are succeeding.
- Nonfinancial measures such as measures of customer satisfaction and employee satisfaction are useful indicators of long-run future performance.

COQ measures and nonfinancial measures complement each other. Without financial quality measures, companies could be spending more money on improving nonfinancial quality measures than it is worth. Without nonfinancial quality measures, quality problems might not be identified until it is too late. As a result, most organizations use both types of measures to gauge quality performance. McDonald's, for example, evaluates employees and individual franchisees on multiple measures of quality and customer satisfaction. A mystery shopper—an outside party contracted by McDonald's to evaluate restaurant performance—scores individual restaurants on quality, cleanliness, service, and value. A restaurant's performance on these dimensions is evaluated over time and against other restaurants. In its balanced scorecard, Photon evaluates whether improvements in various nonfinancial quality measures eventually lead to improvements in financial measures. By doing this, the company ensures that its quality improvement efforts are achieving success and improving profits.

Decision Point

How do managers identify the relevant costs and benefits of quality improvement programs and use financial and nonfinancial measures to evaluate quality?

TIME AS A COMPETITIVE TOOL

Companies increasingly view time as a driver of strategy.[4] Conducting business correctly and quickly helps increase revenues and decrease costs. For example, CapitalOne has increased business on its Web site by promising home-loan approval decisions in thirty minutes or less. Companies such as AT&T, General Electric, and Wal-Mart attribute not only higher revenues but also lower costs to doing things faster and on time. They cite, for example, the need to carry less inventory because of their ability to respond rapidly to customer demands.

Companies need to measure time to manage it properly. In this section, we focus on *operational measures of time*, which reveal how quickly companies respond to customers' demands for their products and services and their reliability in meeting scheduled delivery dates. Two common operational measures of time are customer-response time and on-time performance. We will also show how companies can measure the causes and costs of delays.

Customer-Response Time and On-Time Performance

Learning Objective 4

Describe customer-response time

. . . time between receipt of customer order and product delivery

and explain why delays happen and their costs

. . . uncertainty about the timing of customer orders and limited capacity lead to lower revenues and higher inventory carrying costs

Customer-response time is how long it takes from the time a customer places an order for a product or service to the time the product or service is delivered to the customer. Fast responses to customers are of strategic importance in industries such as construction, banking, car rental, and fast food. Some companies, such as Airbus, have to pay penalties to compensate their customers for lost revenues and profits (such as from being unable to operate flights) as a result of delays in delivering products to them.

Exhibit 19-7 describes the components of customer-response time. In the case of Airbus, *receipt time* is how long it takes the Marketing Department to specify to the Manufacturing Department the exact requirements in the customer's order. **Manufacturing cycle time** (also called **manufacturing lead time**) is how long it takes from the time an order is received by Manufacturing to the time a finished good is produced. Manufacturing cycle time is the sum of waiting time and manufacturing time for an order. An aircraft order received by Airbus may need to wait because the required equipment is busy processing earlier orders. *Delivery time* is how long it takes to deliver a completed order to a customer.

Some companies evaluate their response time improvement efforts using a measure called **manufacturing cycle efficiency (MCE)**:

$$\text{MCE} = (\text{Value-Added manufacturing time} \div \text{Total manufacturing})$$

As discussed in Chapter 12, value-added manufacturing activities are activities that customers perceive as adding value or utility to a product. The time actually spent assembling the product is value-added manufacturing time. The rest of manufacturing cycle time, such as the time the product spends waiting for parts or for the next stage in the production process, and being repaired, represents nonvalue-added manufacturing time.

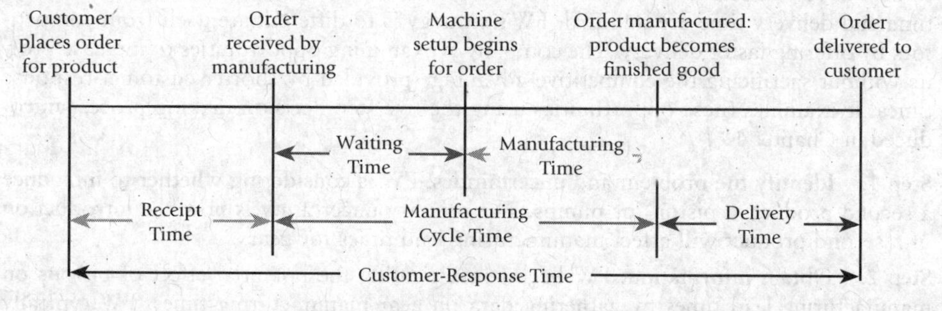

Exhibit 19-7

Components of Customer-Response Time

[4] See K. Eisenhardt and S. Brown, "Time Pacing: Competing in Strategic Markets That Won't Stand Still," *Harvard Business Review* (March–April 1998); and T. Willis and A. Jurkus, "Product Development: An Essential Ingredient of Time-Based Competition," *Review of Business* (2001).

Identifying and minimizing the sources of nonvalue-added manufacturing time increases customer responsiveness and reduces costs.

Similar measures apply to service industries as well. Consider a 40-minute doctor's office visit, of which 9 minutes is spent on administrative tasks such as filling out forms, 20 minutes is spent waiting in the reception area and examination room, and 11 minutes is spent with a nurse or doctor. The service cycle efficiency for this visit equals 11 ÷ 40, or 0.275. In other words, only 27.5% of the time in the office added value to the customer. Minimizing nonvalue-added cycle time in their medical delivery processes has allowed hospitals such as Kailash Medical Center in Noida to treat more patients in less time.

On-time performance is delivery of a product or service by the time it is scheduled to be delivered. Consider Federal Express, which specifies a price per package and a next-day delivery time of 10:30 A.M. for its overnight courier service. Federal Express measures on-time performance by how often it meets its stated delivery time of 10:30 A.M. On-time performance increases customer satisfaction. Commercial airlines gain loyal passengers as a result of consistent on-time service. But there is a trade-off between customer-response time and on-time performance. Deliberately scheduling longer customer-response times, such as airlines lengthening scheduled arrival times, makes achieving on-time performance easier—but it could displease customers!

Bottlenecks and Time Drivers

Managing customer-response time and on-time performance requires understanding the causes and costs of delays that occur, for example, at a machine in a manufacturing plant or at a checkout counter in a store.

A **time driver** is any factor that causes a change in the speed of an activity when the factor changes. Two time drivers we consider are:

1. **Uncertainty about when customers will order products or services.** For example, the more randomly Airbus receives orders for its airplanes, the more likely queues will form and delays will occur.
2. **Bottlenecks due to limited capacity.** A **bottleneck** occurs in an operation when the work to be performed approaches or exceeds the capacity available to do it. For example, a bottleneck results and causes delays when products that must be processed at a particular machine arrive while the machine is being used to process other products. Bottlenecks can also occur on the Internet, for example, when many users try to operate wireless mobile devices at the same time (see the following Concepts in Action). Many banks, such as Bank of China; grocery stores, such as Krogers; and entertainment parks, such as Disneyland, actively work to reduce queues and delays to better serve their customers.

Consider Falcon Works (FW), which uses one turning machine to convert steel bars into a special gear for planes. FW makes this gear, which is its only product, only after customers have ordered it. To focus on manufacturing lead time, we assume FW's receipt time and delivery time are minimal. FW's strategy is to differentiate itself from competitors by offering faster delivery. The company is examining opportunities to increase profits without sacrificing the competitive advantage provided by shorter customer-response times. It examines these opportunities using the five-step decision-making process introduced in Chapter 1.

Step 1. Identify the problem and uncertainties. FW is considering whether to introduce a second product, a piston for pumps. The primary uncertainty is how the introduction of a second product will affect manufacturing lead times for gears.

Step 2. Obtain information. FW begins investigating the potential effect of pistons on manufacturing lead times by gathering data on gear manufacturing times. FW typically receives 30 orders for gears, but it could receive 10, 30, or 50 orders. Each order is for 1,000 units and takes 100 hours of manufacturing time (8 hours of setup time to clean and prepare the machine, and 92 hours of processing time). Annual capacity of the machine is 4,000 hours. If FW receives the 30 orders it expects, the total amount of manufacturing time required on the machine is 3,000 hours (100 hours per order × 30 orders), which is within the available machine capacity of 4,000 hours. Even though capacity utilization is not strained, queues and delays can still occur. That's because uncertainty about when FW's customers will place their orders can cause an order to be received while the machine is processing an earlier order.

Average waiting time, the average amount of time that an order waits in line before the machine is set up and the order is processed, equals,[5]

$$\frac{\text{Annual average number of orders for gears} \times \left(\text{Manufacturing time per order for gears}\right)^2}{2 \times \left[\text{Annual machine capacity} - \left(\text{Annual average number of orders for gears} \times \text{Manufacturing time per order for gears}\right)\right]}$$

$$= \frac{30 \times (100)^2}{2 \times [4{,}000 - (30 \times 100)]} = \frac{30 \times 10{,}000}{2 \times (4{,}000 - 3{,}000)} = \frac{300{,}000}{2 \times 1{,}000} = \frac{300{,}000}{2{,}000} = 150 \text{ hours per order (for gears)}$$

Therefore, the average manufacturing cycle time for an order is 250 hours (150 hours of average waiting time + 100 hours of manufacturing time). Note that manufacturing time per order is a squared term in the numerator. It indicates the disproportionately large impact manufacturing time has on waiting time. As the manufacturing time lengthens, there is a much greater chance that the machine will be in use when an order arrives, leading to longer delays. The denominator in this formula is a measure of the unused capacity, or cushion. As the unused capacity becomes smaller, the chance that the machine is processing an earlier order becomes more likely, leading to greater delays.

The formula describes only the *average* waiting time. A particular order might arrive when the machine is free, in which case manufacturing will start immediately. In another situation, FW may receive an order while two other orders are waiting to be processed, which means the delay will be longer than 150 hours.

Step 3. Make predictions about the future. The manager makes the following predictions about pistons: FW expects to receive 10 orders for pistons, each order for 800 units, in the coming year. Each order will take 50 hours of manufacturing time, comprising 3 hours for setup and 47 hours of processing. Expected demand for FW's gears will be unaffected by whether FW introduces pistons.

Average waiting time *before* machine setup begins is expected to be (the formula is an extension of the preceding formula for the single-product case) as follows:

$$\frac{\left[\text{Annual average number of orders for gears} \times \left(\text{Manufacturing time per order for gears}\right)^2\right] + \left[\text{Annual average number of orders for pistons} \times \left(\text{Manufacturing time per order for pistons}\right)^2\right]}{2 \times \left[\text{Annual machine capacity} - \left(\text{Annual average number of orders for gears} \times \text{Manufacturing time per order for gears}\right) - \left(\text{Annual average number of orders for pistons} \times \text{Manufacturing time per order for pistons}\right)\right]}$$

$$= \frac{[30 \times (100)^2] + [10 \times (50)^2]}{2 \times [4{,}000 - (30 \times 100) - (10 \times 50)]} = \frac{(30 \times 10{,}000) + (10 \times 2{,}500)}{2 \times (4{,}000 - 3{,}000 - 500)}$$

$$= \frac{300{,}000 + 25{,}000}{2 \times 500} = \frac{325{,}000}{1{,}000} = 325 \text{ hours per order (for gears } \textit{and} \text{ pistons)}$$

[5] The technical assumptions are (a) that customer orders for the product follow a Poisson distribution with a mean equal to the expected number of orders (30 in our example), and (b) that orders are processed on a first-in, first-out (FIFO) basis. The Poisson arrival pattern for customer orders has been found to be reasonable in many real-world settings. The FIFO assumption can be modified. Under the modified assumptions, the basic queuing and delay effects will still occur, but the precise formulas will be different.

Concepts in Action

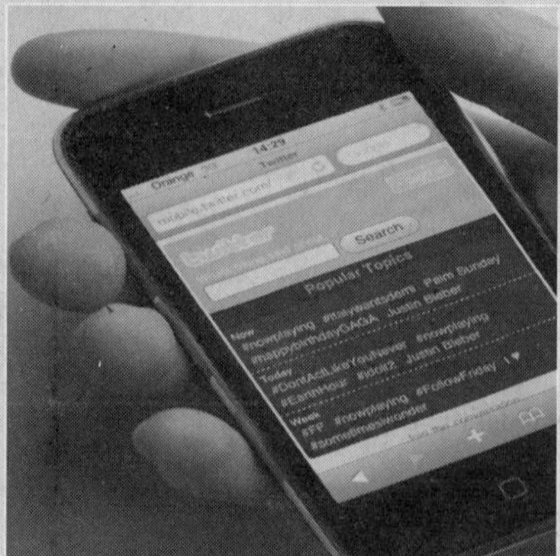

Overcoming Wireless Data Bottlenecks

The wired world is quickly going wireless. In 2010, sales of smartphones—such as the Apple iPhone and BlackBerry—in the United States were predicted to be 53 million units. In addition to the smartphone boom, emerging devices including e-book readers and machine-to-machine appliances (the so-called "Internet of things") will add to rapidly growing data traffic.

With every new device that lets users browse the Internet, and every new business that taps into the convenience and speed of the wireless world, the invisible information superhighway gets a little more crowded. Cisco recently forecast that data traffic will grow at a compound rate of 108% from 90,000 terabytes per month in 2009 to 3.6 million terabytes per month by 2014.

This astronomical growth already causes many users to suffer from mobile bottlenecks caused by too many users trying to transfer mobile data at the same time in a given area. These bottlenecks are most harmful to companies buying and selling products and services over the mobile Internet. Without access, Amazon.com Kindle owners cannot download new e-books and mobile brokerage users cannot buy and sell stocks "on the go."

To relieve mobile bottlenecks, wireless providers and other high-tech companies are working on more efficient mobile broadband networks, such as LTE, that make use of complementary technologies to automatically choose the best available wireless network to increase capacity. Technology providers are also deploying Wi-Fi direct, which allows mobile users to freely transfer video, digital music, and photos between mobile devices without choking up valuable bandwidth. Companies and government agencies around the world are also trying to increase the wireless broadband spectrum. In the United States, for example, current holders of spectrum—such as radio stations—are being encouraged to sell their excess capacity to wireless providers in exchange for a share of the profits.

Sources: Edwards, Cliff. 2010. Wi-fi direct seen as way to alleviate network congestion. *BusinessWeek*, January 7. www.businessweek.com/technology/content/jan2010/tc2010017_884186.htm; Morris, John. 2010. CTIA: More spectrum, and other ways to break the wireless data bottleneck. *ZDNet.* "Laptops & Desktops," blog March 24. http://www.zdnet.com/blog/computers/ctia-more-spectrum-and-other-ways-to-break-the-wireless-data-bottleneck/1877; Pyle, George. 2010. Wireless growth leading to bottlenecks. *Buffalo News*, May 9. www.buffalonews.com/2010/05/09/1044893/wireless-growth-leading-to-bottlenecks.html.

Introducing pistons will cause average waiting time for an order to more than double, from 150 hours to 325 hours. Waiting time increases because introducing pistons will cause unused capacity to shrink, increasing the probability that new orders will arrive while current orders are being manufactured or waiting to be manufactured. Average waiting time is very sensitive to the shrinking of unused capacity.

If the manager decides to make pistons, average manufacturing cycle time will be 425 hours for a gear order (325 hours of average waiting time + 100 hours of manufacturing time), and 375 hours for a piston order (325 hours of average waiting time + 50 hours of manufacturing time). A gear order will spend 76.5% (325 hours ÷ 425 hours) of its manufacturing cycle time just waiting for manufacturing to start!

Step 4. Make decisions by choosing among alternatives. Given the anticipated effects on manufacturing lead time of adding pistons, should FW introduce pistons? To help the manager make a decision, the management accountant identifies and analyzes the relevant revenues and relevant costs of adding the piston product and, in particular, the cost of delays on all products. The rest of this section continues to focus on Step 4. While we do not cover Step 5 in this particular example, we discuss using the balanced scorecard to evaluate and learn from time-based performance.

Relevant Revenues and Relevant Costs of Time

To determine the relevant revenues and costs of adding pistons under Step 4, consider the following additional information:

Product	Annual Average Number of Orders	Average Selling Price per Order If Average Manufacturing Lead Time per Order Is: Less Than 300 Hours	More Than 300 Hours	Direct Material Cost per Order	Inventory Carrying Cost per Order per Hour
Gears	30	Rs 2,20,000	Rs 2,15,000	Rs 1,60,000	Rs 10.0
Pistons	10	1,00,000	96,000	80,000	5.0

Manufacturing cycle times affect both revenues and costs. Revenues are affected because customers are willing to pay a higher price for faster delivery. On the cost side, direct material costs and inventory carrying costs are the only relevant costs of introducing pistons (all other costs are unaffected, and hence irrelevant). Inventory carrying costs consist of the opportunity costs of investment tied up in inventory (see Chapter 11) and the relevant costs of storage, such as space rental, spoilage, deterioration, and materials handling. Usually companies calculate inventory carrying costs on a per-unit, per-year basis. To simplify calculations, the management accountant calculates inventory carrying costs on a per-order, per-hour basis. Also, FW acquires direct materials at the time the order is received by manufacturing, and, therefore, incurs inventory carrying costs for the duration of the manufacturing cycle time.

Exhibit 19-8 presents relevant revenues and relevant costs for the "introduce pistons" and "do not introduce pistons" alternatives. Interestingly, the decision is to not introduce pistons, even though pistons have a positive contribution margin of Rs 16,000 (Rs 96,000 – Rs 80,000) per order. Also, FW has the capacity to process pistons (even if it produces pistons, FW will, on average, use only 3,500 of the available 4,000 machine-hours). So why is FW better off to not introduce pistons? *Because of the negative effects that producing pistons will have on the existing product, gears.* The following table presents the *costs of time*—that is, the expected loss in revenues and expected increase in carrying costs as a result of delays caused by using machine capacity to manufacture pistons.

Exhibit 19-8

Determining Expected Relevant Revenues and Relevant Costs for Falcon Works' Decision to Introduce Pistons

Relevant Items	Alternative 1: Introduce Pistons (1)	Alternative 2: Do Not Introduce Pistons (2)	Difference (3) = (1) – (2)
Expected revenues	Rs 74,10,000[a]	Rs 66,00,000[b]	Rs 8,10,000
Expected variable costs	Rs 56,00,000[c]	48,00,000[d]	(8,00,000)
Expected inventory carrying costs	Rs 1,46,250[e]	75,000[f]	(71,250)
Expected total costs	Rs 57,46,250	48,75,000	8,71,250
Expected revenues minus expected costs	Rs 16,63,750	Rs 17,25,000	Rs (61,250)

[a](Rs 2,15,000 × 30) + (Rs 96,000 × 10) = Rs 74,10,000; average manufacturing lead time will be more than 300 hours.

[b](Rs 2,20,000 × 30) = Rs 66,00,000; average manufacturing lead time will be less than 300 hours.

[c](Rs 1,60,000 × 30) + (Rs 80,000 × 10) = Rs 56,00,000.

[d](Rs 1,60,000 × 30 = Rs 48,00,000.

[e](Average manufacturing lead time for gears × Unit carrying cost per order for gears × Expected number of orders for gears) + (Average manufacturing lead time for pistons × Unit carrying cost per order for pistons × Expected number of orders for pistons) = (425 × Rs 10 × 30) + (375+Rs 5 × 10) Rs 1,27,500 + Rs 18, 750 + Rs 1,46,250

[f]Average manufacturing lead time for gears × Unit carrying cost per order for gears × Expected number of orders for gears = 250 × Rs 10 × 30 = Rs 75,000.

	Effect of Increasing Average Manufacturing Lead Time		Expected Loss in Revenues Plus Expected Increase in Carrying Costs of Introducing Pistons
Product	Expected Loss in Revenues for Gears (1)	Expected Increase in Carrying Costs for All Products (2)	(3) = (1) + (2)
Gears	Rs 1,50,000[a]	Rs 52,500[b]	Rs 2,02,500
Pistons	—	18,750[c]	18,750
Total	Rs 1,50,000	Rs 71,250	Rs 2,21,250

[a](Rs 2,20,000 − Rs 2,15,000) per order × 30 expected orders = Rs 1,50,000.
[b](425−250) hours per order × Rs 10 per hour × 30 expected orders = Rs 52,500.
[c](375−0) hours per order × Rs 5 per hour × 10 expected orders = Rs 18,750.

Introducing pistons causes the average manufacturing lead time of gears to increase from 250 hours to 425 hours. The cost of longer manufacturing lead times is an increase in inventory carrying costs of gears and a decrease in gear revenues (caused by average manufacturing lead time for gears exceeding 300 hours). The expected costs of longer lead times from introducing pistons, Rs 2,21,250, exceeds the expected contribution margin of Rs 1,60,000 (Rs 16,000 per order × 10 expected orders) from selling pistons by Rs 61,250 (the difference calculated in Exhibit 19-8).

Decision Point

What is customer-response time? What are the reasons for and the costs of delays?

This simple setting illustrates that when demand uncertainty is high, some unused capacity is desirable.[6] Increasing the capacity of a bottleneck resource reduces manufacturing lead times and delays. One way to increase capacity is to reduce the time required for setups and processing via more-efficient setups and processing. Another way to increase capacity is to invest in new equipment, such as flexible manufacturing systems that can be programmed to switch quickly from producing one product to producing another. Delays can also be reduced through careful scheduling of orders on machines—for example, by batching similar jobs together for processing.

THEORY OF CONSTRAINTS AND THROUGHPUT-CONTRIBUTION ANALYSIS

In this section, we consider products that are made from multiple parts and processed on multiple machines. With multiple parts and machines, dependencies arise among operations—that is, some operations cannot be started until parts from the preceding operation are available. Furthermore, some operations are bottlenecks (have limited capacity), and others are not.

Managing Bottlenecks

Learning Objective 5

Explain how to manage bottlenecks

. . . keep bottlenecks busy and increase their efficiency and capacity

The **theory of constraints (TOC)** describes methods to maximize operating income when faced with some bottleneck and some nonbottleneck operations.[7] The TOC defines three measures:

1. **Throughput contribution** equals revenues minus the direct material costs of the goods sold.
2. *Investments* equal the sum of materials costs in direct materials, work-in-process, and finished goods inventories; R&D costs; and costs of equipment and buildings.

[6] Other complexities, such as analyzing a network of machines, priority scheduling, and allowing for uncertainty in processing times, are beyond the scope of this book. In these cases, the basic queuing and delay effects persist, but the precise formulas are more complex.

[7] See E. Goldratt and J. Cox, *The Goal* (New York: North River Press, 1986); E. Goldratt, *The Theory of Constraints* (New York: North River Press, 1990); E. Noreen, D. Smith, and J. Mackey, *The Theory of Constraints and Its Implications for Management Accounting* (New York: North River Press, 1995); and M. Woeppel, *Manufacturers' Guide to Implementing the Theory of Constraints* (Boca Raton, FL: Lewis Publishing, 2000).

3. *Operating costs* equal all costs of operations (other than direct materials) incurred to earn throughput contribution. Operating costs include salaries and wages, rent, utilities, depreciation, and the like.

The objective of TOC is to increase throughput contribution while decreasing investments and operating costs. *TOC considers a short-run time horizon and assumes that operating costs are fixed costs.* The steps in managing bottleneck operations are:

Step 1: Recognize that the bottleneck operation determines throughput contribution of the entire system.

Step 2: Identify the bottleneck operation by identifying operations with large quantities of inventory waiting to be worked on.

Step 3: Keep the bottleneck operation busy and subordinate all nonbottleneck operations to the bottleneck operation. That is, the needs of the bottleneck operation determine the production schedule of the nonbottleneck operations.

Step 3 represents one of the concepts described in Chapter 11: To maximize operating income, the manager must maximize contribution margin (in this case, throughput margin) of the constrained or bottleneck resource. The bottleneck machine must always be kept running; it should not be waiting for jobs. To achieve this objective, companies often maintain a small buffer inventory of jobs at the bottleneck machine. The bottleneck machine sets the pace for all nonbottleneck machines. Workers at nonbottleneck machines do not produce more output than can be processed by the bottleneck machine, because producing more nonbottleneck output only creates excess inventory; it does not increase throughput margin.

Step 4: Take actions to increase the efficiency and capacity of the bottleneck operation as long as throughput margin exceeds the incremental costs of increasing efficiency and capacity.

We illustrate step 4 using data from Cardinal Industries (CI). CI manufactures car doors in two operations: stamping and pressing.

	Stamping	Pressing
Capacity per hour	20 units	15 units
Annual capacity (6,000 hours of capacity available in each operation)		
6,000 hours × 20 units/hour; 6,000 hours × 15 units/hour)	120,000 units	90,000 units
Annual production and sales	90,000 units	90,000 units
Other fixed operating costs (excluding direct materials)	Rs 72,00,000	Rs 1,08,00,000
Other fixed operating costs per unit produced		
(Rs 72,00,000 ÷ 90,000 units; Rs 1,08,00,000 ÷ 90,000 units)	Rs 80 per unit	Rs 120 per unit

Each door sells for Rs 1,000 and has a direct material cost of Rs 400. Variable costs in other functions of the value chain—R&D, design of products and processes, marketing, distribution, and customer service—are negligible. CI's output is constrained by the capacity of 90,000 units in the pressing operation. What can CI do to relieve the bottleneck constraint of the pressing operation? Desirable actions include:

1. **Eliminate idle time at the bottleneck operation (time when the pressing machine is neither being set up to process products nor actually processing products).** CI is considering permanently positioning two workers at the pressing operation to unload finished units as soon as one batch of units is processed and to set up the machine to process the next batch. Suppose the annual cost of this action is Rs 4,80,000 and the effect is to increase bottleneck output by 1,000 doors per year. Should CI incur the additional costs? Yes, because CI's throughput contribution increases by Rs 6,00,000 [(selling price per door, Rs 1,000 − direct material cost per door, Rs 400) × 1,000 doors], which exceeds the additional cost of Rs 4,80,000. All other costs are irrelevant.

2. **Process only those parts or products that increase throughput contribution, not parts or products that will remain in finished goods or spare parts inventories.** Making products that remain in inventory does not increase throughput margin.

3. **Shift products that do not have to be made on the bottleneck machine to nonbottleneck machines or to outside processing facilities.** Suppose Spartan Corporation, an outside contractor, offers to press 1,500 doors at Rs 150 per door from stamped parts that CI supplies. Spartan's quoted price is greater than CI's own operating costs in the Pressing Department of Rs 120 per door. Should CI accept the offer? Yes, because pressing is the bottleneck operation. Getting additional doors pressed by Spartan increases throughput contribution by Rs 9,00,000 [(Rs 1,000 − Rs 400) per door × 1,500 doors], while relevant costs increase by Rs 2,25,000 (Rs 150 per door × 1,500 doors). The fact that CI's unit cost is less than Spartan's quoted price is irrelevant.

   Suppose Gemini Industries, another outside contractor, offers to stamp 2,000 doors from direct materials that CI supplies at Rs 60 per door. Gemini's price is lower than CI's operating cost of Rs 80 per door in the Stamping Department. Should CI accept the offer? No, because other operating costs are fixed costs. CI will not save any costs by subcontracting the stamping operations. Total costs will be greater by Rs 1,20,000 (Rs 60 per door × 2,000 doors) under the subcontracting alternative. Stamping more doors will not increase throughput contribution, which is constrained by pressing capacity.
4. **Reduce setup time and processing time at bottleneck operations (for example, by simplifying the design or reducing the number of parts in the product).** Suppose CI can reduce setup time at the pressing operation by incurring additional costs of Rs 5,50,000 a year. Suppose further that reducing setup time enables CI to press 2,500 more doors a year. Should CI incur the costs to reduce setup time? Yes, because throughput contribution increases by Rs 15,00,000 [(Rs 1,000 − Rs 400) per door × 2,500 doors], which exceeds the additional costs incurred of Rs 5,50,000. Will CI find it worthwhile to incur costs to reduce machining time at the nonbottleneck stamping operation? No. Other operating costs will increase, but throughput margin will remain unchanged because bottleneck capacity will not increase.
5. **Improve the quality of parts or products manufactured at the bottleneck operation.** Poor quality is often more costly at a bottleneck operation than it is at a nonbottleneck operation. The cost of poor quality at a nonbottleneck operation is the cost of materials wasted. If CI produces 1,000 defective doors at the stamping operation, the cost of poor quality is Rs 4,00,000 (direct material cost per door, Rs 400, × 1,000 doors). No throughput contribution is forgone because stamping has unused capacity. Despite the defective production, stamping can produce and transfer 90,000 good-quality doors to the pressing operation. At a bottleneck operation, the cost of poor quality is the cost of materials wasted *plus* the opportunity cost of lost throughput contribution. Bottleneck capacity not wasted in producing defective units could be used to generate additional throughput contribution. If CI produces 1,000 defective units at the pressing operation, the cost of poor quality is the lost revenue of Rs 10,00,000, or alternatively stated, direct material costs of Rs 4,00,000 (direct material cost per door, Rs 400, × 1,000 doors) plus forgone throughput contribution of Rs 6,00,000 [(Rs 1,000 − Rs 400) per door × 1,000 doors].

   The high cost of poor quality at the bottleneck operation means that bottleneck time should not be wasted processing units that are defective. That is, inspection should be done before processing parts at the bottleneck operation to ensure that only good-quality units are transferred to the bottleneck operation. Furthermore, quality-improvement programs should place special emphasis on minimizing defects at bottleneck machines.

If successful, the actions in Step 4 will increase the capacity of the pressing operation until it eventually exceeds the capacity of the stamping operation. The bottleneck will then shift to the stamping operation. CI would then focus continuous-improvement actions on increasing stamping efficiency and capacity. For example, the contract with Gemini Industries to stamp 2,000 doors at Rs 60 per door from direct material supplied by CI becomes attractive then. That's because throughput contribution will increase by (Rs 1,000 − Rs 400) per door × 2,000 doors = Rs 12,00,000, while costs will increase by Rs 1,20,000 (Rs 60 per door × 2,000 doors).

The theory of constraints emphasizes management of bottleneck operations as the key to improving performance of production operations as a whole. It focuses on short-run maximization of throughput contribution—revenues minus direct material costs of goods sold. Because TOC regards operating costs as difficult to change in the short run, it does not identify individual activities and drivers of costs. TOC is, therefore, less useful for the long-run management of costs. Activity-based costing (ABC) systems, however, take a longer-run perspective when more costs can be managed; the focus is on improving processes by eliminating nonvalue-added activities and reducing the costs of performing value-added activities. ABC systems, therefore, are more useful for long-run pricing, long-run cost control and profit planning, and capacity management. The short-run TOC emphasis on maximizing throughput contribution by managing bottlenecks complements the long-run strategic-cost-management focus of ABC.[8]

Balanced Scorecard and Time-Related Measures

In this section, we focus on the final step of the five-step decision-making process by tracking changes in time-based measures, evaluating and learning whether these changes affect financial performance, and modifying decisions and plans to achieve the company's goals. We use the structure of the balanced scorecard perspectives—financial, customer, internal business processes, and learning and growth—to summarize how financial and nonfinancial measures of time relate to one another, reduce delays, and increase output of bottleneck operations.

Financial measures
- Revenue losses or price discounts attributable to delays
- Carrying cost of inventories
- Throughput margin minus operating costs

Customer margin
- Customer-response time (the time it takes to fulfill a customer order)
- On-time performance (delivering a product or service by the scheduled time)

Internal-business-process measures
- Average manufacturing time for key products
- Manufacturing cycle efficiency for key processes
- Idle time at bottleneck operations
- Defective units produced at bottleneck operations
- Average reduction in setup time and processing time at bottleneck operations

Learning-and-growth measures
- Employee satisfaction
- Number of employees trained in managing bottleneck operations

To see the cause-and-effect linkages across these balanced scorecard perspectives, consider the example of the Bell Group, a designer and manufacturer of equipment for the jewelry industry. Based on TOC analysis, the company determined that a key financial measure was improving throughput margin by 18% for a specific product line. In the customer perspective, the company set a goal of a two-day turn-around time on all orders for the product. To achieve this goal, the internal-business-process measure was the amount of time a bottleneck machine operated, with a goal of running 22 hours per day, six days a week. Finally, in the learning perspective, the company focused on training new employees to carry out nonbottleneck operations in order to free experienced employees to operate the bottleneck machine. The Bell Group's emphasis on time-related measures in its balanced scorecard has allowed the company to substantially increase manufacturing throughput and slash response times, leading to higher revenues and increased profits.[9]

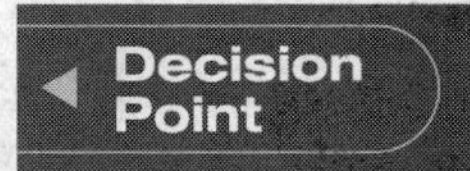

What are the steps managers can take to manage bottlenecks?

[8] For an excellent evaluation of TOC, operations management, cost accounting, and the relationship between TOC and activity-based costing, see A. Atkinson, *"Cost Accounting, the Theory of Constraints, and Costing,"* (Issue Paper, CMA Canada, December 2000).

[9] Management Roundtable, "The Bell Group Uses the Balanced Scorecard with the Theory of Constraints to Keep Strategic Focus," FastTrack.roundtable.com, fasttrack.roundtable.com/app/content/knowledgesource/item/197 (accessed May 15, 2007).

Problem for Self-Study

The Motika Roadlines transports household goods from one city to another within the North India. It measures quality of service in terms of (a) time required to transport goods, (b) on-time delivery (within two days of agreed-upon delivery date), and (c) number of lost or damaged shipments. Motika is considering investing in a new scheduling-and-tracking system costing Rs 16,00,000 per year, which should help it improve performance with respect to items (b) and (c). The following information describes Motika's current performance and the expected performance if the new system is implemented:

	Current Performance	Expected Future Performance
On-time delivery performance	85%	95%
Variable cost per carton lost or damaged	Rs 600	Rs 600
Fixed cost per carton lost or damaged	Rs 400	Rs 400
Number of cartons lost or damaged per year	3,000 cartons	1,000 cartons

Motika expects each percentage point increase in on-time performance to increase revenue by Rs 2,00,000 per year. Motika's contribution margin percentage is 45%.

Required

1. Should Motika acquire the new system? Show your calculations.
2. Motika is very confident about the cost savings from fewer lost or damaged cartons as a result of introducing the new system. Calculate the minimum amount of increase in revenues needed for Motika to invest in the new system.

Solution

1. Additional costs of the new scheduling-and-tracking system are Rs 16,00,000 per year. Additional annual benefits of the new scheduling-and-tracking system are:

Additional annual revenues from a 10% improvement in on-time performance, from 85% to 95%, Rs 2,00,000 per 1% × 10 percentage points	Rs 20,00,000
45% contribution margin from additional annual revenues (0.45 × Rs 20,00,000)	Rs 9,00,000
Decrease in costs per year from fewer cartons lost or damaged (only variable costs are relevant) [Rs 600 per carton × (3,000 − 1,000) cartons]	12,00,000
Total additional benefits	Rs 21,00,000

Because the benefits of Rs 21,00,000 exceed the costs of Rs 16,00,000, Motika should invest in the new system.

2. As long as Motika earns a contribution margin of Rs 4,00,000 (to cover incremental costs of Rs 16,00,000 minus relevant variable-cost savings of Rs 12,00,000) from additional annual revenues, investing in the new system is beneficial. This contribution margin corresponds to additional revenues of Rs 4,00,000 ÷ 0.45 = Rs 8,88,890.

Decision Points

The following question-and-answer format summarizes the chapter's learning objectives. Each decision presents a key question related to a learning objective. The guidelines are the answer to that question.

Decision	Guidelines
1. What are the four cost categories of a costs-of-quality program?	Four cost categories in a costs-of-quality program are prevention costs (costs incurred to preclude the production of products that do not conform to specifications), appraisal costs (costs incurred to detect which of the individual units of products do not conform to specifications), internal failure costs (costs incurred on defective products before they are shipped to customers), and external failure costs (costs incurred on defective products after they are shipped to customers).
2. What nonfinancial quality measures of customer satisfaction can managers use in their balanced scorecards?	Nonfinancial quality measures of customer satisfaction that managers can use in their balanced scorecards include number of customer complaints and percentage of defective units shipped to customers.
3. What methods can managers use to identify quality problems and improve quality?	Three methods to identify quality problems and to improve quality are (a) control charts, to distinguish random from nonrandom variations in an operating process; (b) Pareto diagrams, to indicate how frequently each type of failure occurs; and (c) cause-and-effect diagrams, to identify potential causes of failure.
4. How do managers identify the relevant costs and benefits of quality improvement programs?	The relevant costs of quality improvement programs are the incremental costs to implement the quality program. The relevant benefits are the cost savings and the estimated increase in contribution margin from the higher revenues that result from quality improvements.
5. Why should managers use both financial and nonfinancial measures of quality?	Financial measures are helpful to evaluate trade-offs among prevention costs, appraisal costs, and failure costs. Nonfinancial measures identify problem areas that need improvement and serve as indicators of future long-run performance.
6. What is customer-response time? What are the reasons for and the costs of delays?	Customer-response time is how long it takes from the time a customer places an order for a product or service to the time the product or service is delivered to the customer. Delays occur because of (a) uncertainty about when customers will order products or services and (b) bottlenecks due to limited capacity. Bottlenecks are operations at which the work to be performed approaches or exceeds available capacity. Costs of delays include lower revenues and increased inventory carrying costs.
7. What three measures do managers need to implement the theory of constraints?	The three measures in the theory of constraints are (1) throughput contribution (equal to revenues minus direct material costs of the goods sold); (2) investments (equal to the sum of materials costs in direct materials, work-in-process, and finished goods inventories along with R&D costs and costs of equipment and buildings); and (3) operating costs (equal to all operating costs, other than direct material costs, incurred to earn throughput contribution).
8. What are the steps managers can take to manage bottlenecks?	The four steps in managing bottlenecks are (1) recognize that the bottleneck operation determines throughput contribution, (2) identify the bottleneck, (3) keep the bottleneck busy and subordinate all nonbottleneck operations to the bottleneck operation, and (4) increase bottleneck efficiency and capacity.

TERMS TO LEARN

This chapter and the Glossary at the end of the book contain definitions of:

appraisal costs (**p. 799**)
average waiting time (**p. 809**)
bottleneck (**p. 808**)
cause-and-effect diagram (**p. 803**)
conformance quality (**p. 798**)
control chart (**p. 802**)
costs of quality (COQ) (**p. 799**)
customer-response time (**p. 807**)
design quality (**p. 798**)
external failure costs (**p. 799**)
internal failure costs (**p. 799**)
manufacturing cycle efficiency (MCE) (**p. 807**)
manufacturing cycle time (**p. 807**)
manufacturing lead time (**p. 807**)
on-time performance (**p. 808**)
Pareto diagram (**p. 802**)
prevention costs (**p. 799**)
quality (**p. 797**)
theory of constraints (TOC) (**p. 812**)
throughput contribution (**p. 812**)
time driver (**p. 808**)

ASSIGNMENT MATERIAL

Questions

19-1 Describe two benefits of improving quality.

19-2 How does conformance quality differ from design quality? Explain.

19-3 Name two items classified as prevention costs.

19-4 Distinguish between internal failure costs and external failure costs.

19-5 Describe three methods that companies use to identify quality problems.

19-6 "Companies should focus on financial measures of quality because these are the only measures of quality that can be linked to bottom-line performance." Do you agree? Explain.

19-7 Give two examples of nonfinancial measures of customer satisfaction relating to quality in a balanced scorecard.

19-8 Give two examples of nonfinancial measures of internal-business-process quality in a balanced scorecard.

19-9 Distinguish between customer-response time and manufacturing lead time.

19-10 "There is no trade-off between customer-response time and on-time performance." Do you agree? Explain.

19-11 Give two reasons why delays occur.

19-12 "Companies should always make and sell all products whose selling prices exceed variable costs." Assuming fixed costs are irrelevant, do you agree? Explain.

19-13 Describe the three main measures used in the theory of constraints.

19-14 Describe the four key steps in managing bottleneck operations.

19-15 Describe three ways to improve the performance of a bottleneck operation.

Solved Examples

19-16 Costs of quality analysis. Amron India produces car seats for children from newborn to 2 years old. The company is worried because one of its competitors has recently come under public scrutiny because of product failure. Historically, Amron's only problem with its car seats was stitching in the straps. The problem can usually be detected and repaired during an internal inspection. The per unit cost of the inspection is Rs 50, and the repair cost is Rs 10. All 1,00,000 car seats were inspected last year and 5% were found to have problems with the stitching in the straps during the internal inspection. Another 2% of the 1,00,000 car seats had problems with the stitching, but the internal inspection did not discover them. Defective units that were sold and transported to customers needed to be transported back to Amron and repaired. Transporting costs per unit are Rs 100, and repair costs are Rs 10. However, the out-of-pocket costs (transporting and repair) are not the only costs of defects not discovered in the internal inspection. For 20% of the external failures, negative word of mouth will result in a loss of sales, lowering the following year's sales by Rs 5,000 for each of the 20% of units with external failures.

Required

1. Calculate appraisal cost.
2. Calculate internal failure cost.
3. Calculate out-of-pocket external failure cost.
4. Determine the opportunity cost associated with the external failures.

5. What are the total costs of quality?
6. Amron is concerned with the high up-front cost of inspecting all 1,00,000 units. It is considering an alternative internal inspection plan that will cost only Rs 15 per car seat inspected. During the internal inspection, the alternative technique will detect only 2.5% of the 1,00,000 car seats that have stitching problems. The other 4.5% will be detected after the car seats are sold and shipped. What are the total costs of quality for the alternative technique?
7. What factors other than cost should Amron consider before changing inspection techniques?

Solution

Costs of quality analysis.

1. Appraisal cost = Inspection cost
   = Rs 50 × 1,00,000 car seats
   = Rs 50,00,000
2. Internal failure cost = Rework cost
   = 5% × 1,00,000 × Rs 10
   = 5,000 × Rs 10 = Rs 50,000
3. Out of pocket external failure cost = Transportation cost + Repair cost
   = (2% × 1,00,000) × (Rs 100 + Rs 10)
   = 2,000 × Rs 110 = Rs 2,20,000
4. Opportunity cost of external failure = Lost future sales
   = (2% × 1,00,000) × 20% × Rs 5,000
   = 400 car seats × Rs 5,000 = Rs 20,00,000
5. Total cost of quality control = Rs 50,00,000 + 50,000 + 2,20,000 + 20,00,000
   = Rs 72,70,000
6. Quality control costs under the alternative inspection technique:
   Appraisal cost = Rs 15 × 1,00,000 = Rs 15,00,000
   Internal failure cost = 2.5% × 1,00,000 × Rs 10 = Rs 25,000
   Out of pocket external failure cost = 4.5% × 1,00,000 × (Rs 100 + 10)
   = 4,500 × Rs 110 = Rs 4,95,000
   Opportunity cost of external failure = 4, 500 car seats × 20% × Rs 5,000
   = 900 car seats × Rs 5,000 = Rs 45,00,000

   Total cost of quality control = Rs 15,00,000 + 25,000 + 4,95,000 + 45,00,000
   = Rs 65,20,000
7. In addition to the lower costs under the alternative inspection plan, Amron should consider a number of other factors:

   a. There could easily be serious reputation effects if the percentage of external failures increases by 225% (from 2% to 4.5%). This rise in external failures may lead to costs greater than Rs 5,000 per failure due to lost sales.

   b. Higher external failure rates may increase the probability of lawsuits.

   c. Government intervention is a concern, with the chances of government regulation increasing with the number of external failures.

19-17 Costs of quality, ethical considerations. Refer to information in Exercise 19-16 in answering this question. Amron has discovered a more serious problem with the plastic core of its car seats. An accident can cause the plastic in some of the seats to crack and break, resulting in serious injuries to the occupant. It is estimated that this problem will affect about 200 car seats in the next year. This problem could be corrected by using a higher quality of plastic that would increase the cost of every car seat produced by Rs 100. If this problem is not corrected, Amron India's estimates that out of the 200 accidents, customers will realize that the problem is due to a defect in the seats in only four cases. Amron India's legal team has estimated that each of these accidents would result in a lawsuit that could be settled for about Rs 10,00,000. All lawsuits settled would include a confidentiality clause, so Amron's reputation would not be affected.

Required

1. Assuming that Amron expects to sell 1,00,000 car seats next year, what would be the cost of increasing the quality of all 1,00,000 car seats?
2. What will be the total cost of the lawsuits next year if the problem is not corrected?
3. Amron has decided not to increase the quality of the plastic because the cost of increasing the quality exceeds the benefits (saving the cost of lawsuits). What do you think of this decision? (Note: Because of the confidentiality clause, the decision will have no effect on Amron's reputation.)
4. Are there any other costs or benefits that Amron should consider?

Solution

Cost of quality analysis, ethical considerations

1. Cost of improving quality of plastic = Rs 100 × 1,00,000 = Rs 1,00,00,000
2. Total cost of lawsuits = 4 × Rs 10,00,000 = Rs 40,00,000
3. While economically this may seem like a good decision, qualitative factors should be more important than quantitative factors when it comes to protecting customers from harm and injury. If a product can cause a customer serious harm and injury, an ethical and moral company should take steps to prevent that harm and injury, The company's code of ethics should guide this decision.
4. In addition to ethical considerations, the company should consider the societal cost of this decision, reputation effects if word of these problems leaks out at a later date, and governmental intervention and regulation.

19-18 Quality improvement, relevant costs, relevant revenues. TechnoPrint manufactures and sells 20,000 high-technology printing presses each year. The variable and fixed costs of rework and repair are as follows:

	A	B	C	D
1		Variable Cost	Fixed Cost	Total Cost
2	Rework cost per hour	Rs 80	Rs 120	Rs 200
3	Repair costs			
4	Customer support cost per hour	40	60	100
5	Transportation cost per load	360	120	480
6	Warranty repair cost per hour	90	130	220

TechnoPrint's current presses have a quality problem that causes variations in the shade of some colors. Its engineers suggest changing a key component in each press. The new component will cost Rs 55 more than the old one. In the next year, however, TechnoPrint expects that with the new component it will (1) save 12,875 hours of rework, (2) save 900 hours of customer support, (3) move 200 fewer loads, (4) save 7,000 hours of warranty repairs, and (5) sell an additional 150 printing presses, for a total contribution margin of Rs 18,00,000. TechnoPrint believes that even as it improves quality, it will not be able to save any of the fixed costs of rework or repair. TechnoPrint uses a one-year time horizon for this decision, because it plans to introduce a new press at the end of the year.

Required

1. Should TechnoPrint change to the new component? Show your calculations.
2. Suppose the estimate of 150 additional printing presses sold is uncertain. What is the minimum number of additional printing presses that TechnoPrint needs to sell to justify adopting the new component?

Solution

Quality improvement, relevant costs, and relevant revenues.

1. Relevant costs over the next year of choosing the new component = Rs 55 × 20,000 copiers = Rs 11,00,000

	Relevant Benefits over the Next year of Choosing the New Component
Costs of quality items	
Savings in rework costs	
Rs 80 × 12,875 rework hours	Rs 10,30,000
Savings in customer-support costs	
Rs 40 × 900 customer-support-hours	36,000
Savings in transportation costs for parts	
Rs 360 × 200 fewer loads	72,000
Savings in warranty repair costs	
Rs 90 × 7,000 repair-hours	6,30,000
Opportunity costs	
Contribution margin form increased sales	18,00,000
Cost savings and additional contribution margin	Rs 35,68,000

Because the expected relevant benefits of Rs 35,68,000 exceed the expected relevant costs of the new component of Rs 11,00,000, TechnoPrint should introduce the new component. Note that the opportunity cost benefits in the form of higher contribution margin from increase sales is an important component for justifying the investment in the new component.

2. The incremental cost of the new component of Rs 11,00,000 is less than the incremental savings in rework and repair costs of Rs 17,68,000 (Rs 10,30,000 + Rs 36, 000 + Rs 72, 000 + Rs 6,30,000). Thus, it is beneficial for TechnoPrint to invest in the new component even without making any additional sales.

19-19 Theory of constraints, throughput contribution, relevant costs. The Delite India manufactures filing small cabinets in two operations: machining and finishing. It provides the following information:

	Machining	Finishing
Annual capacity	100,000 units	80,000 units
Annual production	80,000 units	80,000 units
Fixed operating costs (excluding direct materials)	Rs 64,00,000	Rs 40,00,000
Fixed operating costs per unit produce (Rs 64,00,000 ÷ 80,000; Rs 40,00,000 ÷ 80,000)	Rs 80 per unit	Rs 50 per unit

Each cabinet sells for Rs 720 and has direct material costs of Rs 320 incurred at the start of the machining operation. Delite has no other variable costs. Delite can sell whatever output it produces. The following requirements refer only to the preceding data. There is no connection between the requirements.

Required

1. Delite is considering using some modern jigs and tools in the finishing operation that would increase annual finishing output by 1,000 units. The annual cost of these jigs and tools is Rs 3,00,000. Should Delite acquire these tools? Show your calculations.
2. The production manager of the Machining Department has submitted a proposal to do faster setups that would increase the annual capacity of the Machining Department by 10,000 units and would cost Rs 50,000 per year. Should Delite implement the change? Show your calculations.
3. An outside contractor offers to do the finishing operation for 12,000 units at Rs 100 per unit, double the Rs 50 per unit that it costs Delite to do the finishing in-house. Should Delite accept the subcontractor's offer? Show your calculations.
4. The Indian Corporation offers to machine 4,000 units at Rs 40 per unit, half the Rs 80 per unit that it costs Delite to do the machining in-house. Should Delite accept Indian corporation offer? Show your calculations.

Solution

Theory of constraints, throughput contribution, relevant costs.

1. Finishing is a bottleneck operation. Therefore, producing 1,000 more units will generate additional throughput contribution and operating income.

Increase in throughput contribution (Rs 720 − Rs 320) × 1,000	Rs 4,00,000
Incremental costs of the jigs and tools	Rs 3,00,000
Net benefit of investing in jigs and tools	Rs 1,00,000

Delite should invest in the modern jigs and tools because the benefit of higher throughput contribution of Rs 4,00,000 exceeds the cost of Rs 3,00,000.

2. The Machining Department has excess capacity and is not a bottleneck operation. Increasing its capacity further will not increase throughput contribution. There is, therefore, no benefit from spending Rs 50,000 to increase the Machining Department's capacity by 10,000 units. Delite should not implement the change to do setups faster.
3. Finishing is a bottleneck operation. Therefore, getting an outside contractor to produce 12.000 units will increase throughout contribution:

Increase in throughput contribution (Rs 720 − Rs 320) × 12,000	Rs 48,00,000
Incremental contracting costs Rs 100 × 12,000	12,00,000
Net benefit of contracting 12,000 units of finishing	Rs 36,00,000

Delite should contract with an outside contractor to do 12,000 units of finishing at Rs 100 per unit because the benefit of higher throughput contribution of Rs 48,00,000 exceeds the cost of Rs 12,00,000. The fact that the cost of Rs 100 per unit is double Delite's finishing cost of Rs 50 per unit is irrelevant.

4. Operating costs in the Machining Department of Rs 64,00,000, or Rs 80 per unit, are fixed costs. Delite will not save any of these costs by subcontracting machining of 4,000 units to Indian Corporation. Total costs will be greater by Rs 1,60,000 (Rs 40 per unit × 4,000 units) under the subcontracting alternative. Machining more filing cabinets will not increase throughput contribution, which is constrained by the finishing capacity. Delite should not accept Indian's offer. The fact that Indian Corporation's costs of machining per unit are half of what it costs Delite in-house is irrelevant.

19-20 Theory of constraints, throughput contribution, quality. Refer to the information in Exercise 19-19 in answering the following requirements. There is no connection between the requirements.

Required

1. Delite produces 2,000 defective units at the machining operation. What is the cost to Delite of the defective items produced? Explain your answer briefly.

2. Delite produces 2,000 defective units at the finishing operation. What is the cost to Delite of the defective items produced? Explain your answer briefly.

Solution

Theory of constraints, throughput contribution, quality.

1. Cost of defective unit at machining operation which is not a bottleneck operation is the loss in direct materials (variable costs) of Rs 320 per unit. Producing 2,000 units of defectives doe not result in loss of throughput contribution. Despite the defective production, machining can produce and transfer 80.000 units to finishing. Therefore, cost of 2,000 defective units at the machining operation is Rs 320 × 2,000 = Rs 6,40,000.
2. A defective unit produced at the bottleneck finishing operation costs Delite materials costs plus the opportunity cost of lost throughput contribution. Bottleneck capacity not wasted in producing defective units could be used to generate additional sales and throughput contribution. Cost of 2,000 defective units at the finishing operation is:

Loss of direct materials Rs 320 × 2,000	Rs 6,40,000
Forgone throughput contribution (Rs 720 − Rs 320) × 2,000	8,00,000
Total cost of 2,000 defective units	Rs 14,40,000

Alternatively, the cost of 2,000 defective units at the finishing operation can be calculated as the lost revenue of Rs 720 × 2,000 = Rs 14,40,000. This line of reasoning takes the position that direct materials costs of Rs 320 × 2,000 = Rs 6,40,000 and all fixed operating costs in the machining and finishing operations would be incurred anyway whether a defective or good unit is produced. The cost of producing a defective unit is the revenue lost Rs 14,40,000.

19-21 Quality improvement, relevant costs, and relevant revenues. The Puralator Corporation sells 3,00,000 V262 valves to the automobile and truck industry. Thomas has a capacity of 1,10,000 machine-hours and can produce 3 valves per machine-hour. V262's contribution margin per unit is Rs 80. Thomas sells only 3,00,000 valves because 30,000 valves (10% of the good valves) need to be reworked. It takes 1 machine-hour to rework 3 valves, so 10,000 hours of capacity are used in the rework process. Puralator's rework costs are Rs 21,00,000. Rework costs consist of:

- Direct materials and direct rework labor (variable costs): Rs 30 per unit
- Fixed costs of equipment, rent, and overhead allocation: Rs 40 per unit

Puralator's process designers have developed a modification that would maintain the speed of the process and ensure 100% quality and no rework. The new process would cost Rs 31,50,000 per year. The following additional information is available:

- The demand for Puralator's V262 valves is 3,70,000 per year.
- The Jackson Corporation has asked Puralator to supply 22,000 T971 valves (another product) if Puralator implements the new design. The contribution margin per T971 valve is Rs 100. Puralator can make two T971 valves per machine-hour with 100% quality and no rework.

Required

1. Suppose Puralator's designers implement the new design. Should Puralator accept Jackson's order for 22,000 T971 valves? Show your calculations.
2. Should Puralator implement the new design? Show your calculations.
3. What nonfinancial and qualitative factors should Puralator consider in deciding whether to implement the new design?

Solution

Quality improvement, relevant costs, and relevant revenues.

One way to present the alternatives is via a decision tree, as shown, below.

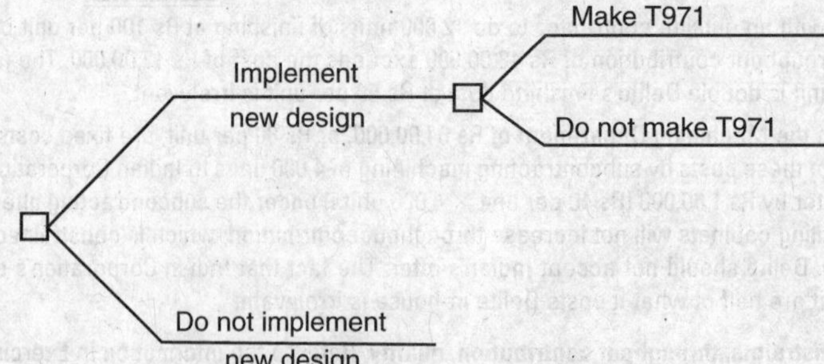

The idea is first evaluate the best action that Puralator should take if it implements the new design (that is, make or not make T971). Puralator can then compare the best mix of products to produce if it implements the new design against the status quo of not implementing the new design.

1. Puralator has capacity constraints. Demand for V262 valves (370,000 valves) exceeds production capacity of 330,000 valves (3 valves per hour × 110,000 machine-hours). Since capacity is constrained, Puralator will choose to sell the product that maximizes contribution margin per machine-hour (the constrained resource).

Contribution margin per machine-hour for V262	= Rs 80 per valve × 3 valves per hour = Rs 240
Contribution margin per machine-hour for T971	= Rs 100 per valve × 2 valves per hour = Rs 200.

Puralator should reject Jackson Corporation's offer and continue to manufacture only V262 valves.

2. Now compare the alternatives of (a) not implementing the new design versus (b) implementing the new design. By implementing the new design, Puralator will save 10,000 machine-hours of rework time. This time can then be used to make and sell 30,000 (3 valves per hour × 10,000 hours) additional V262 valves. The relevant costs and benefits of implementing the new design follow:

The relevant costs of implementing the new design	Rs 31,50,000
Relevant benefits:	
a. Savings in rework costs (Rs 30[a] per V262 valve × 30,000 valves)	9,00,000
b. Additional contribution margin from selling another 30,000 V262 valves (3 valves per hour × 10,000 hours) because capacity previously used for rework is freed up Rs 80 per valve × 30,000 units)	24,00,000
Net relevant benefit	Rs 1,50,000

[a]Note that the fixed rework costs of equipment rent and allocated overhead are irrelevant, because these costs will be incurred whether Puralator implements or does not implement the new design.

Puralator should implement the new design since the relevant benefits exceed the relevant costs by Rs 1,50,000.

3. Puralator Corporation should also consider other benefits of improving quality. For example, the process of quality improvement will help Puralator's managers and workers gain expertise about the product and the manufacturing process that may lead to further cost reductions in the future. Improving quality within the plant is also likely to translate into delivering better quality products to customers. The increased reputation and customer goodwill may well lead to higher future revenues through greater unit sales and higher sales prices.

19-22 Compensation linked with profitability, waiting time, and quality measures. Max Healthcare operates two medical groups, one in Delhi and one in Mumbai. The semi-annual bonus plan for each medical group's president has three components:

a. Profitability performance. Add 1% of operating income.
b. Average patient waiting time. Add Rs 50,000 if the average waiting time for a patient to see a doctor after the scheduled appointment time is less than 15 minutes. If average patient waiting time is more than 15 minutes, add nothing.
c. Patient satisfaction performance. Deduct Rs 50,000 if patient satisfaction (measured using a survey asking patients about their satisfaction with their doctor and their overall satisfaction with Max Healthcare) falls below 70 on a scale from 0 (lowest) to 100 (highest). No additional bonus is awarded for satisfaction scores of 70 or more.

Semi-annual data for 2011 for Delhi and Mumbai groups are as follows:

	A	B	C
1		January-June	July-December
2	Delhi		
3	Operating income	Rs 1,06,50,000	Rs 1,06,00,000
4	Average waiting time	14 minutes	16 minutes
5	Patient satisfaction	79	82
6			
7	Mumbai		
8	Operating income	Rs 90,00,000	Rs 9,50,000
9	Average waiting time	17 minutes	14.5 minutes
10	Patient satisfacation	66	70

Required

1. Compute the bonuses paid in each half year of 2011 to the Delhi and Mumbai medical group presidents.
2. Discuss the validity of the components of the bonus plan as measures of profitability, waiting time performance, and patient satisfaction. Suggest one shortcoming of each measure and how it might be overcome (by redesign of the plan or by another measure).
3. Why do you think Max Healthcare includes measures of both operating income and waiting time in its bonus plan for group presidents? Give one example of what might happen if waiting time was dropped as a performance measure.

Solution

Compensation linked with profitability, on-time delivery, and external quality-performance measures.

1.

	Jan.-June	July-Dec.
Delhi		
Add: Profitability		
1% of operating income	Rs 1,06,500	Rs 1,06,000
Add: Average waiting time		
Rs 50,000 if < 15 minutes	50,000	0
Deduct: Patient satisfaction		
Rs 50,000 if < 70	0	0
Total: Bonus paid	Rs 1,56,500	Rs 1,06,000
Mumbai		
Add: Profitability		
1% of operating income	Rs 90,000	Rs 9,500
Add: Average waiting time		
Rs 50,000 if < 15 minutes	0	50,000
Deduct: Patient satisfaction		
Rs 50,000 if < 70	(50,000)	0
Total: Bonus paid	Rs 40,000	Rs 59,500

2. **Operating income as a measure of profitability**

Operating income captures revenue and cost-related factors. However, there is no recognition of investment differences between the two groups. If one group is substantially bigger than the other, differences in size alone give the president of the larger group the opportunity to earn a bigger bonus. An alternative approach would be to use return on investment (perhaps relative to the budgeted ROI).

15 minute benchmark as a measure of patient response time

This measure reflects the ability of Max Healthcare to meet a benchmark for patient response time. Several concerns arise with this specific measure:

a. It is a yes-or-no cut-off. A 16 minute waiting time earns no bonus, but neither does a two hour wait. Moreover, no extra bonus is paid for additional waiting time reductions below 15 minutes. An alternative is to have the bonus that increases with greater waiting time improvements.
b. It can be manipulated. Doctors might quickly make initial contact with a patient to meet the benchmark, but then leave the patient sitting in the examination room for a more detailed examination or procedure to take place.
c. It reflects performance relative only to the initial waiting time. It does not consider other time-related issues such as the wait for an appointment or the time needed to fill out forms.

Problems in (b) and (c) can be overcome by measuring total patient response time (such as how long it takes from the time a patient makes an appointment to the time the actual appointment is concluded), in addition to average waiting time to meet the doctor.

Patient satisfaction as a measure of quality

This measure represents a common method for assessing quality. However, there are several concerns with its use:

a. Patient satisfaction is likely to be influenced by a number of factors that are outside the groups' control, such as how sick the patients are when coming in or the extent to which they follow doctors' orders,
b. It is influenced by the questions asked in the survey and the survey methodology. As a result, is likely to be "noisy" or very sensitive to assumptions.

c. Patient satisfaction is not the same as patient health outcomes, an important measure of healthcare quality. A combination of measures may work well as a composite measure of quality.

3. Most companies use both financial and nonfinancial measures to evaluate performance, sometimes presented in a single report such as a balanced scorecard. Using multiple measures of performance enables top management to evaluate whether lower-level managers have improved one area at the expense of others. For example, did the better average waiting time (and patient satisfaction) between July and December in the Mumbai group result from significantly higher expenditures that contributed to the dramatic reduction m operating income?
An important issue is the relative importance to place on the different measures. If waiting time is not used for performance evaluation, managers will concentrate on increasing operating income and give less attention to waiting time, even if waiting time has a significant influence on whether customers choose Max Healthcare or another healthcare provider when given the choice. However, the president of the Mumbai group received a larger bonus in the second half of the year due in part to lower average waiting time, even though operating profits dropped by nearly 90%. Companies must understand the relative importance of different financial and nonfinancial objectives when using multiple measures for performance evaluation.

19-23 Manufacturing lead times, relevant revenues, and relevant costs. The GE India makes wire harnesses for the aircraft industry. GE is uncertain about when and how many customer orders will be received. The company makes harnesses only after receiving firm orders from its customers. GE has recently purchased a new machine to make two types of wire harnesses, one for Boeing airplanes (B7) and the other for Airbus Industries airplanes (A3). The annual capacity of the new machine is 6,000 hours. The following information is available for next year:

Customer	Annual Average Number of Orders	Manufacturing Time Required	Selling Price per Order If Average Manufacturing Lead Time per Order Is: Less Than 200 Hours	More Than 200 Hours	Variable Cost per Order	Inventory Carrying Cost per Order per Hour
B7	125	40 hours	Rs 1,50,000	Rs 1,44,000	Rs 1,00,000	Rs 5
A3	10	50 hours	1,35,000	1,29,600	90,000	4.5

Required

1. Calculate the average manufacturing lead times per order (a) if GE manufactures only B7 and (b) if Brandt manufactures both B7 and A3.
2. Even though A3 has a positive contribution margin, GE's managers are evaluating whether GE should (a) make and sell only B7 or (b) make and sell both B7 and A3. Which alternative will maximize GE's operating income? Show your calculations.
3. What other factors should GE consider in choosing between the alternatives in requirement 2?

Solution

Manufacturing lead times, relevant revenues, and relevant costs

1 a. Average waiting time for an order of B7 if GE manufactures only B7

$$= \frac{\left(\text{Average number of order or B7}\right) \times \left(\text{Manufacturing time for B7}\right)^2}{2 \times \left[\text{Annual machine capacity} - \left(\text{Average number of orders of B7} \times \text{Manufacturing time for B7}\right)\right]}$$

$$= \frac{\left[125 \times (40)^2\right]}{2 \times \left[6{,}000 - (125 \times 40)\right]} = \frac{(125 \times 1{,}600)}{2 \times (6{,}000 - 5{,}000)} = \frac{200{,}000}{(2 \times 1{,}000)} = 100 \text{ hour}$$

$$\text{Average manufacturing lead time for B7} = \text{Average order waiting time for B7} + \text{Order manufacturing time for B7}$$

$$= 100 \text{ hours} + 40 \text{ hours} = 140 \text{ hours}$$

1 b. Average waiting time for an order of B7 and A3 if GE manufactures both B7 and A3.

$$\frac{\left[\left(\begin{array}{c}\text{Average number}\\ \text{of orders of B7}\end{array}\right)\times\left(\begin{array}{c}\text{Manufacturing}\\ \text{time for B7}\end{array}\right)^2\right]+\left[\left(\begin{array}{c}\text{Average number}\\ \text{or orders A3}\end{array}\right)\times\left(\begin{array}{c}\text{Manufacturing}\\ \text{time for A3}\end{array}\right)^2\right]}{2\times\left[\begin{array}{c}\text{Annual machine}\\ \text{capacity}\end{array}-\left(\begin{array}{c}\text{Average number}\\ \text{or orders of B7}\end{array}\times\begin{array}{c}\text{Manufacturing}\\ \text{time for B7}\end{array}\right)-\left(\begin{array}{c}\text{Average number}\\ \text{of order of A3}\end{array}\times\begin{array}{c}\text{Manufacturing}\\ \text{time for A3}\end{array}\right)\right]}$$

$$=\frac{\left[125\times(40)^2\right]+\left[10\times(50)^2\right]}{2\times\left[6{,}000-(125\times 40)-(10\times 50)\right]}$$

$$=\frac{\left[(125\times 1{,}600)+(10\times 2{,}500)\right]}{2\times\left[6{,}000-5{,}000-500\right]}=\frac{(200{,}000+25{,}000)}{2\times 500}$$

$$=\frac{225{,}000}{1{,}000}=225\text{ hours}$$

Average manufacturing lead time for B7 = Average order waiting time + Order manufacturing time for B7
= 225 hours + 40 hours = 265 hours

Average manufacturing lead time for A3 = Average order waiting time + Order manufacturing time for A3
= 225 hours + 50 hours = 275 hours

2. The direct approach is to look at incremental revenues and incremental costs of manufacturing and selling A3.

Selling price per order for A3, which has average operating throughput time of 275 hours	1,29,600
Variable cost per order	90,000
Additional contribution per order from A3	39,600
Multiply by expected number of orders	×10
Increase in expected contribution from A3	Rs 3,96,000

Expected loss in revenues and increase in costs from introducing A3:

Product (1)	Expected Loss in Revenues from Increasing Average Manufacturing Lead Times for All Products (2)	Expected Increase in Carrying Costs from Increasing Average Manufacturing Lead Times for All Products (3)	Expected Loss in Revenues Plus Expected Increases in Carrying Costs of Introducing A3 (4) = (2) + (3)
B7	Rs 7,50,000[a]	Rs 78,125[b]	Rs 8,28,125
A3	–	12,375[c]	12,375
Total	Rs 7,50,000	Rs 90,500	Rs 8,40,500

[a] 125 orders × (Rs 1,50,000 – Rs 1,44,000)
[b] (265 hours – 140 hours) × Rs 5 × 125 orders
[c] (275 hours – 0) × Rs 4.5 × 10 orders

Increase in expected contribution from A3 of Rs 3,96,000 is less than increase in expected costs of Rs 8,40,500 by Rs 4,44,500. Therefore, GE should not introduce A3; instead, it should sell only B7.

Alternative calculations of incremental revenues and incremental costs of introducing A3 follow.

	Alternative 1: Introduce A3 (1)	Alternative 2: Do Not Introduce A3 (2)	Relevant Revenues and Relevant Costs (3) = (1) − (2)
Expected revenues	Rs 1,92,96,000[a]	Rs 1,87,50,000[b]	Rs 5,46,000
Expected variable costs	1,34,00,000[c]	1,25,00,000[d]	9,00,000
Expected inventory carrying costs	1,78,000[e]	87,500[f]	90,500
Expected total costs	1,35,78,000	1,25,87,500	9,90,500
Expected revenues minus expected costs	Rs 57,18,000	Rs 61,62,500	(4,44,500)

[a] (125 × Rs 1,44,000) + (10 × Rs 1,29,600)
[b] 125 × Rs 1,50,000
[c] (125 × Rs 1,00,000) + (10 × Rs 90,000)
[d] 125 × Rs 1,00,000
[e] (125 × Re. 5.0 × 265) + (10 × Re. 4.5 ×275)
[f] 125 × Rs 5.0 × 140

3. Delays occur in the processing of B7 and A3 because of (a) uncertainty about how many orders GE will actually receive (GE expects to receive 125 orders of B7 and 10 orders of A3), and (b) uncertainty about the actual dates when GE will receive the orders. The uncertainty (randomness) about the quantity and timing of customer orders means that GE may receive customer orders while another order is still being processed, Orders received while the machine is actually processing another order must wait in queue for the machine to be free. As average capacity utilization of the machine increases, there is less slack and a greater chance that a machine will be busy when another order arrives. Delays can be reduced if the uncertainties facing the firm can be reduced, perhaps by negotiating fixed schedules with customers in advance. GE should explore these alternatives before deciding on whether to manufacture and sell A3.

A3 may be a strategically important product for GE in the future. For example, it may help GE to develop a customer relationship with Airbus Industries that could be helpful in the future. Even though manufacturing A3 is costly in the short run, it may be beneficial to GE in the long term.

If GE could reduce manufacturing time for A3 (and B7), it could find it profitable to manufacture both harnesses. GE may also want to try to negotiate a higher price for A3 that would make manufacturing both B7 and A3 profitable.

19-24 Theory of constraints, throughput contribution, relevant costs. Ericsson India manufactures electronic testing equipment. Ericsson also installs the equipment at customers' sites and ensures that it functions smoothly. Additional information on the Manufacturing and Installation Departments is as follows (capacities are expressed in terms of the number of units of electronic testing equipment):

	Equipment Manufactured	Equipment Installed
Annual capacity	400 units per year	300 units per year
Equipment manufactured and installed	300 units per year	300 units per year

Ericsson manufactures only 300 units per year because the Installation Department has only enough capacity to install 300 units. The equipment sells for Rs 40,000 per unit (installed) and has direct material costs of Rs 15,000. All costs other than direct material costs are fixed. The following requirements refer only to the preceding data. There is no connection between the requirements.

Required

1. Ericsson's engineers have found a way to reduce equipment manufacturing time. The new method would cost an additional Rs 50 per unit and would allow Ericsson to manufacture 20 additional units a year. Should Ericsson implement the new method? Show your calculations.
2. Ericsson's designers have proposed a change in direct materials that would increase direct material costs by Rs 2,000 per unit. This change would enable Ericsson to install 320 units of equipment each year. If Ericsson makes the change, it will implement the new design on all equipment sold. Should Ericsson use the new design? Show your calculations.
3. A new installation technique has been developed that will enable Ericsson's engineers to install 10 additional units of equipment a year. The new method will increase installation costs by Rs 50,000 each year. Should Ericsson implement the new technique? Show your calculations.

Solution

Theory of constraints, throughput contribution, relevant costs.

1. It will cost Ericsson India Rs 50 per unit to reduce manufacturing time. But manufacturing is not a bottleneck operation; installation is. Therefore, manufacturing more equipment will not increase sales and throughput contribution Ericsson India should not implement the new manufacturing method.

2. Additional relevant costs of new direct materials, Rs 2,000 × 320 units, Rs 6,40,000
   Increase in throughput contribution, Rs 25,000 × 20 units, Rs 5,00,000

The additional incremental costs exceed the benefits from higher throughput contribution by Rs 1,40,000, so Ericsson India should not implement the new design.

Alternatively, compare throughput contribution under each alternative.
Current throughput contribution is Rs 25,000 × 300 Rs 75,00,000
With the modification, throughput contribution is Rs 23,000 × 320 Rs 73,60,000

The current throughput contribution is greater than the throughput contribution resulting from the proposed change in direct materials. Therefore, Ericsson India should not implement the new design.

3. Increase in throughput contribution, Rs 25,000 × 10 units Rs 2,50,000
   Increase in relevant costs Rs 50,000

The additional throughput contribution exceeds incremental costs by Rs 2,00,000, so Ericsson India should implement the new installation technique.

4. Motivating installation workers to increase productivity is worthwhile because installation is a bottleneck operation, and any increase in productivity at the bottleneck will increase throughput contribution. On the other hand, motivating workers in the manufacturing department to increase productivity is not worthwhile. Manufacturing is not a bottleneck operation, so any increase in output will result only in extra inventory of equipment. Ericsson India should encourage manufacturing to produce only as much equipment as the installation department needs, not to produce as much as it can. Under these circumstances, it would not be a good idea to evaluate and compensate manufacturing workers on the basis of their productivity.

19-25 Theory of constraints, contribution margin, sensitivity analysis. Barbic Toys (BT) produces dolls in two processes: molding and assembly. Barbic Toys is currently producing two models: Chatty Akshita and Talking Ayera. Production in the Molding Department is limited by the amount of materials available. Production in the Assembly Department is limited by the amount of trained labor available. The only variable costs are materials in the Molding Department and labor in the Assembly Department. Following are the requirements and limitations by doll model and department.

	Molding Materials	Assembly Time	Selling Price
Chatty Akshita	1.5 pounds per doll	20 minutes per doll	Rs 350 per doll
Talking Ayera	2 pounds per doll	30 minutes per doll	Rs 450 per doll
Materials/Labor Available	30,000 pounds	8,400 hours	
Cost	Rs 100 per pound	Rs 120 per hour	

Required

1. If Barbic Toys sold only one type of doll, which doll would it produce? How many of these dolls would it make and sell?
2. If Barbic Toys can sell two Chatty Akshitas for each Talking Ayera, how many dolls of each type would it produce and sell? What would be the total contribution margin?
3. How much would production and contribution margin increase if the Molding Department could buy 10 more pounds of materials for Rs 100 per pound?
4. How much would production and contribution margin increase if the Assembly Department could get 10 more labor hours at Rs 120 per hour?
5. Using the production level in requirement 2, how many pounds of materials are left? How many labor hours are left?

Solution

Theory of constraints, contribution margin, sensitivity analysis

1. Assuming only one type of doll is produced, the maximum production in each department given their resource constraints is:

	Molding Department	Assembly Department	Contribution Margin
Chatty Akshita	$\frac{30{,}000 \text{ lbs}}{1.5 \text{ lbs}} = 20{,}000$	$\frac{8{,}400 \text{ hours}}{1/3 \text{ hours}} = 25{,}200$	Rs 350 – 1.5 × Rs 100 – 1/3 × 120 = Rs 160
Talking Ayera	$\frac{30{,}000 \text{ lbs}}{2 \text{ lbs}} = 15{,}000$	$\frac{8{,}400 \text{ hours}}{1/2 \text{ hours}} = 16{,}800$	Rs 450 – 2 × Rs 100 – 1/2 × 120 = Rs 190

For both types of dolls, the constraining resource is the availability of material since this constraint causes the lowest maximum production.

If only Chatty Akshita is produced, BT can produce 20,000 dolls with a contribution margin of 20,000 × Rs 160 = Rs 32,00,000

If only Talking Ayera is produced, BT can produce 15,000 dolls with a contribution margin of 15,000 × Rs 190 = Rs 28,50,000

BT should produce Chatty Akshitas

2. As shown in Requirement 1, available material in the Molding department is the limiting constraint.

If BT sells two Chatty Akshitas for each Talking Ayera, then the maximum number of Talking Ayera dolls the Molding Department can produce (where the number of Talking Ayera dolls is denoted as T) is:

$$(T \times 2 \text{ lbs.}) + ([2 \times T] \times 1.2 \text{ lbs.}) = 30{,}000 \text{ lbs.}$$
$$2T + 3T = 30{,}000$$
$$5T = 30{,}000$$
$$T = 6{,}000$$

The Molding Department can produce 6,000 Talking Ayera dolls, and 2 × 6,000 (or 12,000) Chatty Akshita dolls.

Since BT can only produce 6,000 Talking Ayera and 12,000 Chatty Akshitas before it runs out of ingredients, the maximum contribution margin (CM) is:

$$CM = 12{,}000 \times \text{Rs } 160 + 6{,}000 + \text{Rs } 190$$
$$= \text{Rs } 30{,}60{,}000$$

3. With 10 more pounds of materials, BT would produce more dolls. Using the same technique as in Requirement 2, the increase in production is:

$$(T \times 2 \text{ lbs.}) + ([2 \times T] \times 1.5 \text{ lbs.}) = 10 \text{ lbs.}$$
$$2T + 3T = 10$$
$$T = 2$$

LTT would produce 2 extra Talking Ayera dolls and 4 extra Chatty Akshita dolls.

Contribution margin would increase by

$$4 \times \text{Rs } 160 + 2 \times \text{Rs } 190 = \text{Rs } 1{,}020$$

4. With 10 more labor hours, production would not change. The limiting constraint is pounds of material, not labor hours. BT already has more labor hours available than it needs.

19-26 Quality improvement, theory of constraints. The Bhilwara Industries makes printed cloth in two departments: Weaving and Printing. Direct material costs are Bhilwara's only variable costs. The demand for Bhilwara's cloth is very strong. Bhilwara Industries can sell whatever output quantities it produces at Rs 12,500 per roll to a distributor who markets, distributes, and provides customer service for the product. Bhilwara provides the following information.

	Weaving	Printing
Monthly capacity	10,000 rolls	15,000 rolls
Monthly production	9,500 rolls	8,550 rolls
Direct material cost per roll of cloth processed at each operation	Rs 5,000	Rs 1,000
Fixed operating costs	Rs 2,85,00,000	Rs 42,75,000
Fixed operating cost per roll		
Rs 2,85,00,000 ÷ 9,500 rolls; Rs 42,75,000 ÷ 8,550 rolls)	Rs 3,000 per roll	Rs 500 per roll

Bhilwara can start only 10,000 rolls of cloth in the Weaving Department because of capacity constraints of the weaving machines. If the Weaving Department produces defective cloth, the cloth must be scrapped and yields zero net disposal value. Of the 10,000 rolls of cloth started in the Weaving Department, 500 (5%) defective rolls are produced. The cost of a defective roll, based on total (fixed and variable) manufacturing cost per roll incurred up to the end of the weaving operation, equals Rs 7,850 per roll, as follows:

Direct material cost per roll (variable)	Rs 5,000
Fixed operating cost per roll Rs 2,85,00,000 ÷ 10,000 rolls)	2,850
Total manufacturing cost per roll in Weaving Department	Rs 7,850

The good rolls from the Weaving Department (called gray cloth) are sent to the Printing Department. Of the 9,500 good rolls started at the printing operation, 950 (10%) defective rolls are produced and scrapped at zero net disposal value. The cost of a defective roll based on total (fixed and variable) manufacturing cost per unit incurred up to the end of the printing operation, equals Rs 9,300 per roll, calculated as follows:

Total manufacturing cost per roll in Weaving Department		Rs 7,850
Printing Department manufacturing cost per roll		
Direct material cost per roll (variable)	Rs 1000	
Fixed operating cost per roll (Rs 42,75,000 ÷ 9,500 rolls)	450	
Total manufacturing cost per roll in Printing Department		1,450
Total manufacturing cost per roll		Rs 9,300

The Bhilwara Industries total monthly sales of printed cloth equal the Printing Department's output.

Each requirement refers only to the preceding data. There is no connection between the requirements.

Required

1. The Printing Department is considering buying 5,000 additional rolls of gray cloth from an outside supplier at Rs 9,000 per roll. The Printing Department manager is concerned that the cost of purchasing the gray cloth is much higher than Bhilwara's cost of manufacturing it. The quality of the gray cloth acquired from the outside supplier is very similar to that manufactured in-house. The Printing Department expects that 10% of the rolls obtained from the outside supplier will result in defective products. Should the Printing Department buy the gray cloth from the outside supplier? Show your calculations.
2. Bhilwara's engineers have developed a method that would lower the Printing Department's rate of defective products to 6% at the printing operation. Implementing the new method would cost Rs 35,00,000 per month. Should Bhilwara implement the change? Show your calculations.
3. The design engineering team has proposed a modification that would lower the Weaving Department's rate of defective products to 3%. The modification would cost the company Rs 17,50,000 per month. Should Bhilwara implement the change? Show your calculations.

Solution

Quality improvement, theory of constraints

1. Consider the incremental revenues and incremental costs to Bhilwara Industries of purchasing additional grey cloth from outside suppliers.

Incremental revenues, Rs 12,500 × (5,000 rolls × 0.90)	Rs 5,62,50,000
Incremental cost:	
Cost of grey cloth, Rs 9,000 × 5,000 rolls	Rs 4,50,00,000
Direct materials variable costs at printing Operation, Rs1,000 × 5,000 rolls	50,00,000
Incremental costs	5,00,00,000
Excess of incremental revenues over incremental costs	Rs 62,50,000

Note that because the printing department has surplus capacity equal to 5,500 (15,000–9,500) rolls per months, purchasing grey from outside entails zero opportunity costs. Yes, the printing Department should buy the grey cloth from the outside supplier.

2. By producing a defective roll in the weaving Department, Bhilwara Industries is worse off by the entire amount of revenue forgone of Rs12,500 per roll. Note that, since the weaving operation is a constraint, any rolls received by the Printing Department that are defective and disposed of at zero net disposal value result in lost revenue to the firm.

An alternative approach to analyzing the problem is to focus on the costs of defective units and the benefits of reducing defective units.

The relevant costs of defective units in the Printing Department are:

a. Direct materials variable costs in the Weaving Department	Rs 5,000
b. Direct materials variable cost in the Printing Department	1,000
c. Contribution margin forgone from not selling one roll Rs 12,500 – Rs 5,000 – Rs 1,000	6,500
Amount by which Bhilwara is worse off as a Result of a defective unit in the Printing Department	Rs 12,500

Note that only the variable costs of defective units of Rs 6,000 per roll (direct materials in the Weaving Department Rs 5,000 per roll: direct materials in the Printing Department, Rs 1,000) are relevant because improving quality will save these costs. Fixed costs of producing defective units, attributable to other operating costs, are irrelevant because these costs will be incurred whether Bhilwara Industries reduces defective units in the Printing Department or not.

Bhilwara Industries should make the proposed modifications in the Printing Department because the incremental benefits exceed the incremental costs by Rs 12,50,000 per month:

Incremental benefits of reducing defective units in the Printing Department by 4% (from 10% to 6%)

4% × 9,500 rolls × Rs 12,500 per roll (computed above)	Rs 47,50,000
Incremental costs of the modification	35,00,000
Excess of incremental benefits over incremental costs	12,50,000

3. To determine how much Bhilwara Industries is worse off by producing a defective roll in the Weaving Department, consider the payoff to Bhilwara from not having a defective roll produced in the Weaving Department. The good roll produced in the Weaving Department will be sent futher processing in the Printing Department. The relevant costs and benefits of printing and selling this roll follow:

Additional direct materials variable costs incurred in the Printing Department	(Rs 1,000)
Expected revenue from selling the finished product, Rs 12,500 × 0.9 (since 10% of the Printing Department output will be defective and will earn zero revenue)	11,250
Net expected benefit of producing a good roll in the Weaving Department	Rs 10,250

By producing a defective roll in the Weaving Department, Bhilwara Industries is worse off by Rs 10,250 per roll. Note that, sine the weaving operation is a constraint, any rolls that are defective will result in lost revenue to the firm.

An alternative approach to analyzing the problem is to focus on the costs and benefits of reducing defective units.

The relevant costs of defective units in the Weaving Department are:

a. Direct materials variable costs in the Weaving Department	Rs 5,000
b. Expected unit contribution margin forgone from not selling one roll, (Rs 12,500 × 0.9) − Rs 5,000 − Rs 1,000	Rs 5,250
Amount by which, Bhilwara Industries is worse off as a result of producing a defective unit in the Weaving Department	Rs 10,250

Note that only the variable scrap costs of Rs 5,000 per roll (direct materials in the Weaving Department) are relevant because improving quality will save these costs. All fixed costs of producing defective units attributable to other operating costs are irrelevant because these costs will be incurred whether Bhilwara Industries reduces defective units in the Weaving Department or not.

Bhilwara Industries should make the improvements proposed by the design engineering team because the incremental benefits exceed the incremental costs by Rs 3,00,000 per month:

Incremental benefits of reducing defective units in the Weaving Department by 2% (from 5% to 3%) 2% × 10,000 rolls × Rs 10,250 per roll (computed above)	Rs 20,50,000
Incremental costs of improvements	17,50,000
Excess of incremental benefits over incremental costs	Rs 3,00,000

Exercises

19-27 Costs of quality. (CMA, adapted) Siemen India produces cell phone equipment. Abhinav Kumar, Siemen's president, decided to devote more resources to the improvement of product quality after learning that her company had been ranked fourth in product quality in a 2011 survey of cell phone users. Siemen's quality-improvement program has now been in operation for two years, and the cost report shown here has recently been issued.

	A	B	C	D	E
1	Semi-annual COQ report, Siemen India				
2	(In thousands)				
3		30/6/2011	31/12/2011	30/6/2012	31/12/2012
4	Prevention costs				
5	Machine maintenance	Rs 440	Rs 440	Rs 390	Rs 330
6	Supplier training	20	100	50	40
7	Design reviews	50	214	210	200
8	Total prevention costs	510	754	650	570
9	Appraisal costs				
10	Incoming inspections	108	123	90	63
11	Final testing	332	332	293	203
12	Total appraisal costs	440	455	383	266
13	Internal failure costs				
14	Rework	231	202	165	112
15	Scrap	124	116	71	67
16	Total internal failure costs	355	318	236	179
17	External failure costs				
18	Warranty repairs	165	85	72	68
19	Customer returns	570	547	264	188
20	Total external failure costs	735	632	336	256
21	Total quality costs	Rs 2,040	Rs 2,159	Rs 1,605	Rs 1,271
22					
23	Total revenues	Rs 8,240	Rs 9,080	Rs 9,300	Rs 9,020

If you want to use Excel to solve this exercise, go to the Excel Lab at **www.prenhall.com/horngren/cost13e** and download the template for Exercise 19-16.

Required

1. For each period, calculate the ratio of each COQ category to revenues and to total quality costs.
2. Based on the results of requirement 1, would you conclude that Siemen's quality program has been successful? Prepare a short report to present your case.
3. Based on the 2011 survey, Abhinav Kumar believed that Siemen had to improve product quality. In making his case to Siemen management, how might Abhinav have estimated the opportunity cost of not implementing the quality-improvement program?

19-28 Nonfinancial measures of quality and time. Nokia has developed a cell phone that can be used anywhere in the world (even countries like Japan that have a relatively unique cell phone system). Nokia has been receiving complaints about the phone. For the past two years, Nokia has been test marketing the phones and gathering nonfinancial information related to actual and perceived aspects of the phone's quality. They expect that, given the lack of competition in this market, increasing the quality of the phone will result in higher sales and thereby higher profits.

Quality data for 2011 and 2012 include the following:

	2011	2012
Cell phones produced and shipped	2,000	10,000
Number of defective units shipped	100	400
Number of customer complaints	150	250
Units reworked before shipping	120	700
Manufacturing lead time	15 days	16 days
Average customer response time	30 days	28 days

Required

1. For each year, 2011 and 2012, calculate:
   a. Percentage of defective units shipped.
   b. Customer complaints as a percentage of units shipped.
   c. Percentage of units reworked during production.
   d. Manufacturing lead time as a percentage of total time from order to delivery.
2. Referring to the information computed in requirement 1, explain whether Nokia's quality and timeliness have improved.
3. Why would manufacturing lead time have increased while customer response time decreased?

19-29 Nonfinancial quality measures, on-time delivery. Domino's Pizza promises to deliver pizzas in twenty-five minutes or less. If pizzas are not delivered on time, then the customer receives Rs 100 off the price of the order. Some store managers, who receive bonuses based on store profits, believe that the guarantee is a win-win situation for Domino's. Because the average pizza sells for Rs 180 but has a marginal cost of Rs 45, the store makes a profit no matter what the delivery time. If a pizza is delivered on time, then the store earns Rs 135 (Rs 180–Rs 45) per pizza. If a pizza is delivered late, then the store still earns Rs 35 (Rs 180–Rs 100–Rs 45) per pizza. If more than one pizza is ordered, then Domino's makes even more money because it only gives one Rs 100 discount per order.

The head of the Domino's chain is worried that this perceived win-win situation may encourage a complacent attitude in store managers with respect to on-time deliveries. While short-run profits are still earned with late deliveries, repeated late deliveries could lead to annoyance on the part of customers and eventually to a loss of customers. Therefore, the Domino's corporate headquarters has decided to gather information about late deliveries and customer satisfaction. It has developed a survey that asks delivery customers to rate their satisfaction based on three attributes: delivery service, value for money, and overall satisfaction with Domino's. Responses can range from 1 to 5, where 1 is "Awful" and 5 is "Excellent." The following responses were gathered from stores in a single city.

	Store 1	Store 2	Store 3	Store 4
Percentage of deliveries that were late	10%	5%	12%	25%
Average rating of delivery service	4	4.5	3.8	2
Average rating of value received	3.5	4.1	3.5	1.5
Average overall satisfaction	3.6	4	3	2

Required

1. Examine the relationship between the percentage of deliveries that were late and average responses to the three survey questions. Do the data provide any support for Domino's headquarters' concerns?
2. Using the high-low method estimate the effect of changes in the late delivery percentage on average overall satisfaction with Domino's. Use the customer satisfaction score as the dependent variable. Based on this analysis, compute the impact of a change from 5% late deliveries to 7% late deliveries on overall customer satisfaction.
3. What factors would Domino's need to consider when determining whether the delivery guarantee is actually beneficial for the company?

19-30 Manufacturing cycle time, manufacturing cycle efficiency. (CMA, adapted) Torrance Manufacturing evaluates the performance of its production managers based on a variety of factors, including cost, quality, and cycle time. The following information relates to the average amount of time needed to complete an order for its one product:

- Wait time:
  - From order being placed to start of production — 8 days
  - From start of production to completion — 6 days
- Inspection time — 2 days
- Process time — 4 days
- Move time — 2 days

Required

1. Compute the manufacturing cycle efficiency for an order.
2. Compute the manufacturing cycle time (or lead time) for an order.

19-31 Quality improvement, relevant costs, and relevant revenues. The Surya India uses multicolor molding to make plastic lamps. The molding operation has a capacity of 2,00,000 units per year. The demand for lamps is very strong. Surya will be able to sell whatever output quantities it can produce at Rs 400 per lamp.

Surya can start only 2,00,000 units into production in the Molding Department because of capacity constraints on the molding machines. If a defective unit is produced at the molding operation, it must be scrapped at a net disposal value of zero. Of the 2,00,000 units started at the molding operation, 30,000 defective units (15%) are produced. The cost of a defective unit, based on total (fixed and variable) manufacturing costs incurred up to the molding operation, equals Rs 250 per unit, as follows:

Direct materials (variable)	Rs 160 per unit
Direct manufacturing labor, setup labor, and materials-handling labor (variable)	30 per unit
Equipment, rent, and other allocated overhead, including inspection and testing costs on scrapped parts (fixed)	60 per unit
Total	Rs 250 per unit

Surya's designers have determined that adding a different type of material to the existing direct materials would result in no defective units being produced, but it would increase the variable costs by Rs 40 per lamp in the Molding Department.

Required

1. Should Surya use the new material? Show your calculations.
2. What nonfinancial and qualitative factors should Surya consider in making the decision?

19-32 Waiting times, manufacturing lead times. The Neelkamal Plastics Limited (NPL) uses an injection molding machine to make a plastic product, Z39. NPL makes products only after receiving firm orders from its customers. NPL estimates that it will receive 50 orders for Z39 (each order is for 1,000 units) during the coming year. Each order of Z39 will take 80 hours of machine time. The annual capacity of the machine is 5,000 hours.

Required

1. Calculate (a) the average amount of time that an order for Z39 will wait in line before it is processed and (b) the average manufacturing lead time per order for Z39.
2. NPL is considering introducing a new product, Y28. NPL expects it will receive 25 orders of Y28 (each order for 200 units) in the coming year. Each order of Y28 will take 20 hours of machine time. The average demand for Z39 will be unaffected by the introduction of Y28. Calculate (a) the average waiting time for an order received and (b) the average manufacturing lead time per order for each product, if NPL introduces Y28.

19-33 Waiting times, relevant revenues, and relevant costs (continuation of 19-32). NPL is still deciding whether it should introduce Y28. The following table provides information on selling prices, variable costs, and inventory carrying costs for Z39 and Y28. NPL will incur additional variable costs and inventory carrying costs for Y28 only if it introduces Y28. Fixed costs equal to 40% of variable costs are allocated to all products produced and sold during the year.

Product	Annual Average Number of Orders	Selling Price per Order If Average Manufacturing Lead Time per Order Is Less Than 320 Hours	More Than 320 Hours	Variable Cost per Order	Inventory Carrying Cost per Order per Hour
Z39	50	Rs 27,000	Rs 26,500	Rs 15,000	Rs 0.75
Y28	25	8,400	8,000	5,000	0.25

Required

1. Should NPL manufacture and sell Y28? Show your calculations.
2. Should NPL manufacture and sell Y28 if the data in Problem 19-32 are changed as follows: Selling price per order is Rs 6,400, instead of Rs 8,400, if average manufacturing lead time per order is less than 320 hours; and Rs 6,000, instead of Rs 8,000, if average manufacturing lead time per order is more than 320 hours? All other data for Y28 are the same.

19-34 Theory of constraints, throughput contribution, quality, relevant costs. Sun Pharmaceuticals manufactures pharmaceutical products in two departments: Mixing and Tablet-Making. Additional information on the two departments follows. Each tablet contains 0.5 gram of direct materials.

	Mixing	Tablet Making
Capacity per hour	150 grams	200 tablets
Monthly capacity		
(2,000 hours available in each department)	3,00,000 grams	4,00,000 tablets
Monthly production	2,00,000 grams	3,90,000 tablets
Fixed operating costs (excluding direct materials)	Rs 1,60,000	Rs 3,90,000
Fixed operating cost per tablet		
(Rs 1,60,000 ÷ 2,00,000 grams; Rs 3,90,000÷3,90,000 tablets)	Re 0.8 per gram	Rs 1.0 per tablet

The Mixing Department makes 2,00,000 grams of direct materials mixture (enough to make 400,000 tablets) because the Tablet-Making Department has only enough capacity to process 4,00,000 tablets. All direct material costs are incurred in the Mixing Department. Sun incurs Rs 156,000 in direct material costs. The Tablet-Making Department manufactures only 3,90,000 tablets from the 2,00,000 grams of mixture processed; 2.5% of the direct materials mixture is lost in the tablet-making process. Each tablet sells for Rs 10. All costs other than direct material costs are fixed costs. The following requirements refer only to the preceding data. There is no connection between the requirements.

Required

1. An outside contractor makes the following offer: If Sun will supply the contractor with 10,000 grams of mixture, the contractor will manufacture 19,500 tablets for Sun (allowing for the normal 2.5% loss of the mixture during the tablet-making process) at Re 0.12 per tablet. Should Sun accept the contractor's offer? Show your calculations.
2. Another company offers to prepare 20,000 grams of mixture a month from direct materials Sun supplies. The company will charge Rs 0.70 per gram of mixture. Should Sun accept the company's offer? Show your calculations.
3. Sun's engineers have devised a method that would improve quality in the Tablet-Making Department. They estimate that the 10,000 tablets currently being lost would be saved. The modification would cost Rs 7,000 a month. Should Sun implement the new method? Show your calculations.
4. Suppose that Sun also loses 10,000 grams of mixture in its Mixing Department. These losses can be reduced to zero if the company is willing to spend Rs 9,000 per month in quality-improvement methods. Should Sun adopt the quality-improvement method? Show your calculations.
5. What are the benefits of improving quality in the Mixing Department compared with improving quality in the Tablet-Making Department?

19-35 Quality improvement, Pareto diagram, cause-and-effect diagram. The Xerox India manufactures, sells, and installs photocopying machines. Xerox India has placed heavy emphasis on reducing defects and failures in its production operations. Xerox India wants to apply the same total quality management principles to manage its accounts receivable.

Required

1. On the basis of your knowledge and experience, what would you classify as failures in accounts receivable?
2. Give examples of prevention activities that could reduce failures in accounts receivable.
3. Draw a Pareto diagram of the types of failures in accounts receivable and a cause-and-effect diagram of possible causes of one type of failure in accounts receivable.

19-36 Ethics and quality. Information from a quality report for 2011 prepared by Nitin Gupta, assistant controller of Crompton Greaves a manufacturer of electric motors, is as follows:

Revenues	Rs 1,00,00,000
Inspection of production	Rs 90,000
Warranty liability	Rs 2,60,000
Product testing	Rs 2,10,000
Scrap	Rs 2,30,000
Design engineering	Rs 2,00,000
Percentage of customer complaints	5%
On-time delivery rate	93%

Salman Khan, the plant manager of Crompton, is eligible for a bonus if the total costs of quality as a percentage of revenues are less than 10%, the percentage of customer complaints is less than 4%, and the on-time delivery rate exceeds 92%. Salman is unhappy about the customer complaints of 5% because, when preparing her report, Arun actually surveyed customers regarding customer satisfaction. Salman khan expected Arun to be less proactive and to wait for customers to complain. Salman Khan concern with Arun's approach is that it introduces subjectivity into the results and also fails to capture the seriousness of customers' concerns. "When you wait for a customer to complain, you know he is complaining because it is something important. When you do customer surveys, customers mention whatever is on their mind, even if it is not terribly important."

Aamir Khan, the controller, asks Arun to see him. He tells him about Salman's concerns. "I think Salman has a point. See what you can do." Arun is confident that the customer complaints are genuine and that customers are concerned about quality and service. He believes it is important for Crompton to be proactive and obtain systematic and timely customer feedback, and then to use this information to make improvements. He is also well aware that Crompton has not done customer surveys in the past, and that, except for his surveys, Salman would probably be eligible for the bonus. He is confused about how to handle Aamir's request.

Required

1. Calculate the ratio of each cost-of-quality category (prevention, appraisal, internal failure, and external failure) to revenues in 2011. Are the total costs of quality as a percentage of revenues less than 10%?
2. Would it be unethical for Arun to modify his analysis? What steps should Arun take to resolve this situation?

20 Inventory Management, Just-in-Time, and Simplified Costing Methods

Learning Objectives

1. Identify six categories of costs associated with goods for sale
2. Balance ordering costs with carrying costs using the economic-order-quantity (EOQ) decision model
3. Identify the effect of errors that can arise when using the EOQ decision model and ways to reduce conflicts between the EOQ model and models used for performance evaluation
4. Describe why companies are using just-in-time purchasing
5. Distinguish materials requirements planning (MRP) systems from just-in-time (JIT) systems for manufacturing
6. Identify the features of a just-in-time production system
7. Describe different ways backflush costing can simplify traditional inventory-costing systems
8. Understand the principles of lean accounting

Suppose you could receive a large quantity discount for a product that you regularly use, but the discount requires you to buy a year's supply and necessitates a large up-front expenditure.

Would you take the quantity discount? Companies face similar decisions because firms pay a price for tying up money in inventory sitting on their shelves or elsewhere. Money tied up in inventory is a particularly serious problem when times are tough. When faced with these circumstances, companies like Costco work very hard to better manage their inventories.

Costco Aggressively Manages Inventory to Thrive in Tough Times[1]

When consumers reduced their spending in 2008, traditional stalwarts like Circuit City and Linens 'n Things wilted under the weight of their own massive inventories. They could not turn their inventories quickly enough to pay suppliers and were forced to close their doors when cash ran out.

At the same time, Costco continued to thrive! How? By intentionally stocking *fewer* items than its competitors—and employing inventory management practices that successfully reduced costs throughout its operations. While the average grocery store carries around 40,000 items, Costco limits its offerings to about 4,000 products, or 90% less! Limiting the number of products on its shelves reduces Costco's costs of carrying inventory.

Costco also employs a just-in-time inventory management system, which includes sharing data directly with many of its largest suppliers. Companies like Kimberly-Clark calculate re-order points in real time and send new inventory, as needed, to replenish store shelves. Costco also works to redesign product packaging to squeeze more bulky goods onto trucks and shelves, reducing the number of orders Costco needs to place with suppliers.

Occasionally, the company leverages its 75 million square feet of warehouse space to reduce purchasing costs. For example, when Procter & Gamble recently announced a 6% price increase for its paper goods, Costco bought 258 truckloads of paper towels at the old rate and stored them using available capacity in its distribution centers and warehouses.

[1] *Source*: McGregor, Jena. 2008. Costco's artful discounts. *BusinessWeek*, October 20.

These inventory management techniques have allowed Costco to succeed in tough times while others have failed. Costco turns its inventory nearly 12 times a year, far more often than other retailers. With many suppliers agreeing to be paid 30 days after delivery, Costco often sells many of its goods before it even has to pay for them!

Inventory management is important because materials costs often account for more than 40% of total costs of manufacturing companies and more than 70% of total costs in merchandising companies. In this chapter, we describe the components of inventory costs, relevant costs for different inventory-related decisions, and planning and control systems for managing inventory.

Inventory Management in Retail Organizations

Inventory management includes planning, coordinating, and controlling activities related to the flow of inventory into, through, and out of an organization. Consider this breakdown of operations for three major retailers for which cost of goods sold constitutes their largest cost item.

	Kroger	Costco	Wal-Mart
Revenues	100.0%	100.0%	100.0%
Deduct costs:			
Cost of goods sold	75.8%	87.7%	75.8%
Selling and administration costs	18.9%	9.5%	18.4%
Other costs, interest, and taxes	3.6%	1.0%	2.2%
Total costs	98.3%	98.2%	96.4%
Net income	1.7%	1.8%	3.6%

The percentages of net income to revenues are very low. This means that improving the purchase and management of goods for sale can cause dramatic percentage increases in net income.

Costs Associated with Goods for Sale

Managing inventories to increase net income requires companies to effectively manage costs that fall into the following six categories:

Learning Objective 1

Identify six categories of costs associated with goods for sale

. . . purchasing, ordering, carrying, stockout, quality, and shrinkage

1. **Purchasing costs**—the cost of goods acquired from suppliers, including incoming freight costs. These costs usually make up the largest cost category of goods for sale. Discounts for various purchase-order sizes and supplier credit terms affect purchasing costs.
2. **Ordering costs**—the costs of preparing and issuing purchase orders, receiving and inspecting the items included in the orders, and matching invoices received, purchase orders, and delivery records to make payments. Ordering costs include the cost of obtaining purchase approvals, as well as other special processing costs.
3. **Carrying costs**—the costs that arise while holding an inventory of goods for sale. Carrying costs include the opportunity cost of the investment tied up in inventory (see Chapter 11) and the costs associated with storage, such as space rental, insurance, obsolescence, and spoilage.
4. **Stockout costs**—the costs that result when a company runs out of a particular item for which there is customer demand—a *stockout*—and the company must act quickly to meet that demand or suffer the costs of not meeting it. A company may respond to a stockout by expediting an order from a supplier, which can be expensive because of additional ordering costs plus any associated transportation costs. Or the company may lose sales due to the stockout. In this case, the opportunity cost of the stockout includes lost contribution margin on the sale not made plus any contribution margin lost on future sales due to customer ill will.
5. **Costs of Quality**—the costs that result when features and characteristics of a product or service are not in conformance with customer specifications. There are four categories of quality costs—prevention costs, appraisal costs, internal failure costs, and external failure costs (described in Chapter 19).
6. **Shrinkage costs**—the costs that result from theft by outsiders, embezzlement by employees, misclassifications, and clerical errors. Shrinkage is measured by the difference between (a) the cost of the inventory recorded on the books in the absence of theft and other incidents just mentioned, and (b) the cost of inventory when physically counted. Shrinkage can often be an important measure of management performance. Consider, for example, the grocery business, where operating income percentages hover around two percent. With such small margins, it is easy to see why one of a store manager's prime responsibilities is controlling inventory shrinkage. A Rs 10,000 increase in shrinkage will erase the operating income from sales of Rs 5,00,000 (2% × Rs 5,00,000 = Rs 10,000).

Note that not all inventory costs are available in financial accounting systems. For example, opportunity costs are seldom recorded in these systems and are a significant component in several of these cost categories.

Decision Point

What are the six categories of costs associated with goods for sale?

Information-gathering technology increases the reliability and timeliness of inventory information and reduces costs in the six cost categories. For example, bar-coding technology allows a scanner to record purchases and sales of individual units. As soon as a unit is scanned, an instantaneous record of inventory movements is created that helps in the management of purchasing, carrying, and stockout costs. In the next several sections, we consider how relevant costs are computed for different inventory-related decisions in merchandising companies.

Learning Objective 2

Balance ordering costs with carrying costs using the economic-order-quantity (EOQ) decision model

. . . choose the inventory quantity per order to minimize costs

Economic-Order-Quantity Decision Model

The first decision in managing goods for sale is *how much to order* of a given product. The **economic order quantity** (EOQ) is a decision model that, under a given set of assumptions, calculates the optimal quantity of inventory to order.

- The simplest version of an EOQ model assumes there are only ordering and carrying costs.
- The same quantity is ordered at each reorder point.
- Demand, ordering costs, and carrying costs are known with certainty. The **purchase-order lead time**—the time between placing an order and its delivery—is also known with certainty.

- Purchasing cost per unit is unaffected by the quantity ordered. This assumption makes purchasing costs irrelevant to determining EOQ because purchasing price is the same, whatever the order size.
- No stockouts occur. The basis for this assumption is that the costs of stockouts are so high that managers maintain adequate inventory to prevent them.
- In deciding on the size of a purchase order, managers consider costs of quality and shrinkage costs only to the extent that these costs affect ordering or carrying costs.

Given these assumptions, EOQ analysis ignores purchasing costs, stockout costs, quality costs, and shrinkage costs. EOQ is the order quantity that minimizes the relevant ordering and carrying costs (that is, the ordering and carrying costs affected by the quantity of inventory ordered):

$$\text{Relevent total costs} = \text{Relevants ordeing costs} + \text{Relevents carrying costs}$$

We use the following notations:

D = Demand in units for a specified period (one year in this example)

Q = Size of each order (order quantity)

$$\text{Number of purchase orders per period (one year)} = \frac{\text{Demand in units for a period (one year)}}{\text{Size of each order (order quantity)}} = \frac{D}{Q}$$

Average inventory in units = $\frac{Q}{2}$, because each time the inventory goes down to 0, an order for Q units is received. The inventory varies from Q to 0 so the average inventory is $\frac{0 + Q}{2}$.

P = Relevant ordering cost per purchase order

C = Relevant carrying cost of one unit in stock for the time period used for D (one year)

For any order quantity, Q,

$$\text{Annual relevant ordering costs} = \left(\begin{array}{c}\text{Number of}\\ \text{purchase orders}\\ \text{per year}\end{array} \times \begin{array}{c}\text{Relevant ordering}\\ \text{cost per}\\ \text{purchase order}\end{array}\right) = \left(\frac{D}{Q} \times P\right)$$

$$\text{Annual relevant carrying costs} = \left(\begin{array}{c}\text{Average inventory}\\ \text{in units}\end{array} \times \begin{array}{c}\text{Annual}\\ \text{relevant carrying}\\ \text{cost per unit}\end{array}\right) = \left(\frac{Q}{2} \times C\right)$$

$$\text{Annual relevant total costs} = \begin{array}{c}\text{Annual}\\ \text{relevant ordering}\\ \text{costs}\end{array} + \begin{array}{c}\text{Annual}\\ \text{relevant carrying}\\ \text{costs}\end{array} = \left(\frac{D}{Q} \times P\right) + \left(\frac{Q}{2} \times C\right)$$

The order quantity that minimizes annual relevant total costs is

$$EOQ = \sqrt{\frac{2DP}{C}}$$

The EOQ model is solved using calculus but the key intuition is that relevant total costs are minimized when relevant ordering costs equal relevant carrying costs. If carrying costs are less (greater) than ordering costs, total costs can be reduced by increasing (decreasing) the order quantity. To solve for EOQ, we set

$$\left(\frac{Q}{2} \times C\right) = \left(\frac{D}{Q} \times P\right)$$

$$\text{Multiplying both sides by } \frac{2Q}{C}\text{, we get } Q^2 = \frac{2DP}{C}$$

$$Q = \sqrt{\frac{2DP}{C}}$$

The formula indicates that EOQ increases with higher demand and/or higher ordering costs and decreases with higher carrying costs.

Let's consider an example to see how EOQ analysis works. CD World is an independent electronics store that sells blank compact disks. CD World purchases the CDs from Sontek at Rs 140 a package (each package contains 10 disks). Sontek pays for all incoming freight. No inspection is necessary at CD World because Sontek supplies quality merchandise. CD World's annual demand is 13,000 packages, at a rate of 250 packages per week. CD World requires a 15% annual rate of return on investment. The purchase-order lead time is two weeks. Relevant ordering cost per purchase order is Rs 2,000.

Relevant carrying cost per package per year is:

Required annual return on investment, 0.15 × Rs 140	Rs 21
Relevant insurance, materials handling, breakage, shrinkage, and so on, per year	31
Total	Rs 52

What is the EOQ of packages of disks? The formula for the EOQ model is:

$$EDO = \sqrt{\frac{2DP}{C}}$$

where

D = Demand in units for a specified period (one year in this example)
P = Relevant ordering cost per purchase order
C = Relevant carrying cost of one unit in stock for the time period used for D (one year)

The formula indicates that EOQ increases with higher demand and/or higher ordering costs and decreases with higher carrying costs.

For CD World:

$$EDO = \sqrt{\frac{2 \times 13{,}000 \times \text{Rs}\,2{,}000}{\text{Rs}\,52}} = \sqrt{\text{Rs}\,10{,}00{,}000} = 1{,}000 \text{ packages}$$

Purchasing 1,000 packages per order minimizes total relevant ordering and carrying costs. Therefore, the number of deliveries each period (one year in this example) is:

$$\frac{D}{EDO} = \frac{13{,}000}{1{,}000} = 13 \text{ deliveries}$$

Recall the annual relevant total costs (RTC) = $\left(\frac{D}{Q} \times P\right) + \left(\frac{Q}{2} \times C\right)$

For Q = 1,000 units,

$$RTC = \frac{13{,}000 \times \text{Rs}\,2{,}000}{1{,}000} + \frac{1{,}000 \times \text{Rs}\,52}{2}$$

$$= \text{Rs}\,26{,}000 + \text{Rs}\,26{,}000 = \text{Rs}\,52{,}000$$

Exhibit 20-1 graphs the annual relevant total costs of ordering (DP/Q) and carrying inventory ($QC/2$) under various order sizes (Q), and it illustrates the trade-off between these two types of costs. The larger the order quantity, the lower the annual relevant ordering costs, but the higher the annual relevant carrying costs. *Annual relevant total costs are at a minimum at the EOQ at which the relevant ordering and carrying costs are equal.*

When to Order, Assuming Certainty

The second decision in managing goods for sale is *when to order* a given product. The **reorder point** is the quantity level of inventory on hand that triggers a new purchase

Exhibit 20-1 Graphic Analysis of Ordering Costs and Carrying Costs for Compact Disks at CD World

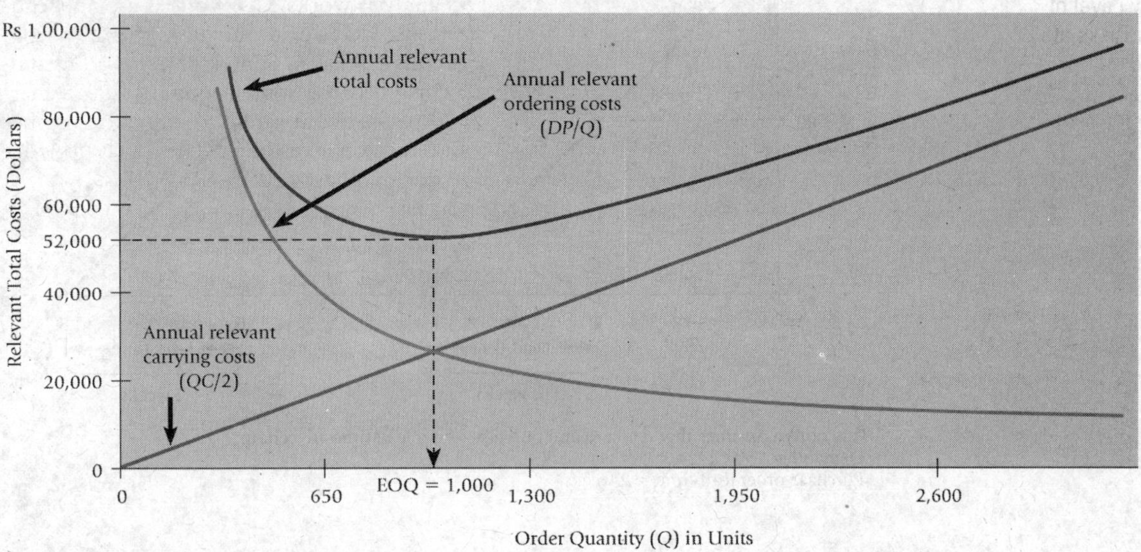

order. The reorder point is simplest to compute when both demand and purchase-order lead time are known with certainty:

$$\text{Reorder point} = \frac{\text{Number of units sold}}{\text{per units of time}} \times \frac{\text{Purchase-order}}{\text{lead time}}$$

In our CD World example, we choose one week as the unit of time in the reorder-point formula:

Economic order quantity	1,000 packages
Number of units sold per week	250 packages per week
Purchase-order lead time	2 weeks

Reorder point = 250 packages per week × 2 week = 500 packages

CD World will order 1,000 packages each time inventory stock falls to 500 packages.[2] The graph in Exhibit 20-2 shows the behavior of the inventory level of compact disk packages, assuming demand occurs uniformly during each week. If purchase-order lead time is two weeks, a new order will be placed when the inventory level falls to 500 packages, so the 1,000 packages ordered will be received at the precise time that inventory reaches zero.

Safety Stock

We have assumed that demand and purchase-order lead time are known with certainty. Retailers who are uncertain about demand, lead time, or the quantity that suppliers can provide, hold safety stock. **Safety stock** is inventory held at all t es regardless of the quantity of inventory ordered using the EOQ model. Safety stock .. used as a buffer against unexpected increases in demand, uncertainty about lead time, and unavailability of stock from suppliers. Suppose that in the CD World example, the only uncertainty is about demand. CD World's managers expect demand to be 250 packages per week, but they feel that a maximum demand of 400 packages per week may occur. If CD World's managers decide costs of stockouts are prohibitively high, they may decide to hold a safety stock of

[2] This handy but special formula does not apply when receipt of the order fails to increase inventory to the reorder-point quantity (for example, when lead time is three weeks and the order is a one-week supply). In these cases, orders will overlap.

Exhibit 20-2

Inventory Level of Compact Disks at CD World[a]

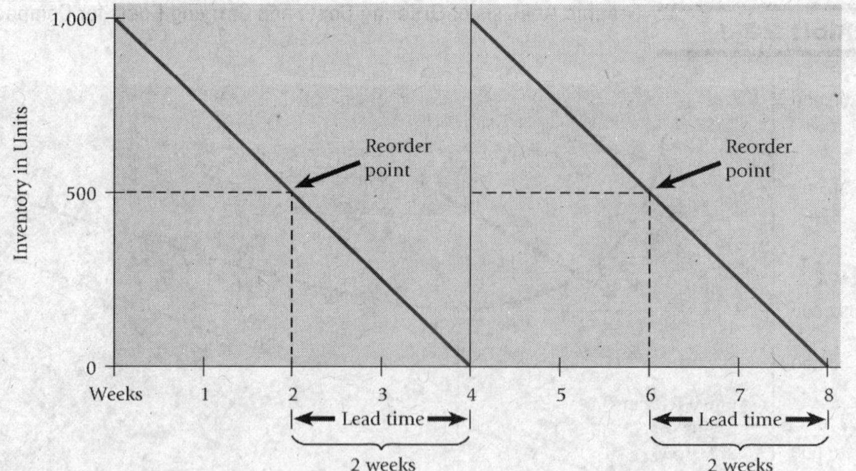

[a] This exhibit assumes that demand and purchase-order lead time are certain:
Demand = 250 CD packages per week
Purchase-order lead time = 2 weeks

300 packages. The 300 packages equal the maximum excess demand of 150 (400 − 250) packages per week times the two weeks of purchase-order lead time. If stockout costs are minimal, CD World will hold no safety stocks and avoid incurring the additional carrying costs.

A frequency distribution based on prior daily or weekly levels of demand forms the basis for computing safety-stock levels. Assume that one of the following levels of demand will occur over the two-week purchase-order lead time at CD World.

Total Demand for 2 Weeks	200 Units	300 Units	400 Units	500 Units	600 Units	700 Units	800 Units
Probability (sums to 1.00)	0.06	0.09	0.20	0.30	0.20	0.09	0.06

We see that 500 units is the most likely level of demand for two weeks because it has the highest probability of occurrence. We see also a 0.35 probability that demand will be 600, 700, or 800 packages (0.20 + 0.09 + 0.06 = 0.35).

If a customer wants to buy compact disks and the store has none in stock, CD World can "rush" them to the customer at an additional cost to CD World of Rs 40 per package. The relevant stockout costs in this case are Rs 40 per package. The optimal safety-stock level is the quantity of safety stock that minimizes the sum of annual relevant stockout and carrying costs. Note that CD World will place 13 orders per year and will incur the same ordering costs whatever level of safety stock it chooses. Therefore, ordering costs are irrelevant for the safety-stock decision. Recall that the relevant carrying cost for CD World is Rs 52 per unit per year.

Decision Point

What does the EOQ decision model help managers do and how do managers decide on the level of safety stocks?

Exhibit 20-3 tabulates annual relevant total stockout and carrying costs when the reorder point is 500 units. We need only consider safety-stock levels of 0, 100, 200, and 300 units, because demand will exceed the 500 units of stock available at reordering by 0 if demand is 500, by 100 if demand is 600, by 200 if demand is 700, and by 300 if demand is 800. As Exhibit 20-3 shows, annual relevant total stockout and carrying costs would be the lowest (Rs 13,520) when a safety stock of 200 packages is maintained. Therefore, 200 units is the optimal safety-stock level. Consider the 200 units of safety stock as extra stock that CD World maintains. For example, CD World's total inventory of compact disks at the time of reordering its EOQ of 1,000 units would be 700 units (the reorder point of 500 units plus safety stock of 200 units).

Exhibit 20-3 Computation of Safety Stock for CD World When Reorder Point Is 500 Units

File Edit View Insert Format Tools Data Window Help

	A	B	C	D	E	F	G	H	I
1–5	Safety Stock Level in Units (1)	Demand Levels Resulting in Stockouts (2)	Stockout in Units[a] (3) = (2) – 500 – (1)	Probability of Stockout (4)	Relevant Stockout Costs[b] (5) = (3) x Rs 40	Number of Orders per Year[c] (6)	Expected Stockout Costs[d] (7) = (4) x (5) x (6)	Relevant Carrying Costs[e] (80) = (1) x Rs 52	Relevant Total Costs (9) = (7) + (8)
6	0	600	100	0.20	Rs 4,000	13	Rs 10,400		
7		700	200	0.09	8,000	13	9,360		
8		800	300	0.06	12,000	13	9,360		
9							Rs 29,120	Rs 0	Rs 29,120
10	100	700	100	0.09	4,000	13	Rs 4,680		
11		800	200	0.06	8,000	13	6,240		
12							Rs 10,920	Rs 5,200	Rs 16,120
13	200	800	100	0.06	4,000	13	Rs 3,120	Rs 10,400	Rs 13,520
14	300	–	–	–	–	–	Rs 0[f]	Rs 15,600	Rs 15,600

[a]Demand level resulting in stockouts – Inventory available during lead time (excluding safety stock), 500 units – Safety stock.

[b]Stockout in units x Relevant stockout costs of Rs 40 per unit.

[c]Annual demand, 13,000 ÷ 1,000 EOQ = 13 orders per year.

[d]Probability of stockout x Relevant stockout costs x Number of orders per year.

[e]Safety stock x Annual relevant carrying costs of Rs 52 per unit (assumes that safety stock is on hand at all times and that there is no overstocking caused by decreases in expected usage).

[f]At a safety stock level of 300 units, no stockout will occur and, hence, expected stockout costs = Rs 0.

Estimating Inventory-Related Relevant Costs and Their Effects

Learning Objective 

Identify the effect of errors that can arise when using the EOQ decision model

. . . errors in predicting parameters have a small effect on costs

and ways to reduce conflicts between the EOQ model and models used for performance evaluation

. . . by making the two models congruent

As in earlier chapters, we need to determine which costs are relevant when making and evaluating inventory-management decisions. We next describe the estimates that need to be made to calculate the annual relevant carrying costs of inventory, stockout costs, and ordering costs.

Considerations in Obtaining Estimates of Relevant Costs

Relevant inventory carrying costs consist of the *relevant incremental costs* plus the *relevant opportunity cost of capital*.

What are the *relevant incremental costs* of carrying inventory? Only those costs of the purchasing company—for example, warehouse rent, warehouse workers' salaries, costs of obsolescence, costs of shrinkage, and costs of breakage—that change with the quantity of inventory held. Salaries paid to clerks, stockkeepers, and materials handlers are irrelevant if they are unaffected by changes in inventory levels. Suppose, however, that as inventories increase (decrease), total salary costs increase (decrease) as clerks, stockkeepers, and materials handlers are added (transferred to other activities or laid off). In this case, salaries paid are relevant costs of carrying inventory. Similarly, costs of storage space owned that cannot be used for other profitable purposes when inventories decrease are irrelevant. But if the space has other profitable uses, or if total rental cost is tied to the amount of space occupied, storage costs are relevant costs of carrying inventory.

What is the *relevant opportunity cost of capital*? It is the return forgone by investing capital in inventory rather than elsewhere. It is calculated as the required rate of return multiplied by the per-unit costs that (a) vary with the number of units purchased and

(b) are incurred at the time the units are received. (Examples of these per-unit costs are the price of units purchased, incoming freight, and incoming inspection.) Opportunity costs are not computed on investments (say, in buildings) if these investments are unaffected by changes in inventory levels.

In the case of stockouts, the relevant incremental cost is the cost of expediting an order from a supplier. The relevant opportunity cost is (1) the lost contribution margin on sales forgone because of the stockout and (2) lost contribution margin on future sales forgone as a result of customer ill will.

Relevant ordering costs are only those ordering costs that change with the number of orders placed (for example, costs of preparing and issuing purchase orders and receiving and inspecting materials).

Cost of a Prediction Error

Predicting relevant costs is difficult and seldom flawless, which raises the question, What is the cost when actual relevant costs differ from the estimated relevant costs used for decision making?

Let's revisit the CD World example. Suppose relevant ordering costs per purchase order are Rs 1,000, instead of the Rs 2,000 estimate we used earlier. We can calculate the cost of this "prediction" error using a three-step approach.

Step 1: Compute the Monetary Outcome from the Best Action That Could Be Taken, Given the *Actual* Amount of the Cost Input (Cost per Purchase Order). This is the benchmark, the decision the manager would have made if the manager had known the correct ordering cost against which actual performance can be measured. Using D = 13,000 packages per year, P = Rs 1,000, and C = Rs 52.0 per package per year,

$$EOQ = \sqrt{\frac{2DP}{C}}$$

$$= \sqrt{\frac{2 \times 13{,}000 \times \text{Rs } 1{,}000}{\text{Rs } 52}} = \sqrt{500{,}000}$$

$$= 707 \text{ packages (rounded)}$$

Annual relevant total costs when EOQ = 707 packages are:

$$RTC = \frac{DP}{Q} + \frac{QC}{2}$$

$$= \frac{13{,}000 \times \text{Rs } 1{,}000}{707} + \frac{707 \times \text{Rs } 52}{2}$$

$$= \text{Rs } 18{,}390 + \text{Rs } 18{,}380 = \text{Rs } 36{,}770$$

Step 2: Compute the Monetary Outcome from the Best Action Based on the Incorrect *Predicted* Amount of the Cost Input (Cost per Purchase Order). When the relevant ordering cost per purchase order is predicted to be Rs 2,000, the best action is to purchase 1,000 packages in each order. Annual relevant total costs using this order quantity when D = 13,000 packages, P = Rs 1,000, and C = Rs 52 are:

$$RTC = \frac{13{,}000 \times \text{Rs } 1{,}000}{1{,}000} + \frac{1{,}000 \times \text{Rs } 52}{2}$$

$$= \text{Rs } 13{,}000 + \text{Rs } 26{,}000$$

$$= 39{,}000$$

Step 3: Compute the Difference Between the Monetary Outcomes from step 1 and step 2.

	Monetary Outcome
Step 1	Rs 36,770
Step 2	39,000
Difference	Rs 2,230

The cost of the prediction error, Rs 2,230, is less than 7% of the relevant total costs of Rs 36,770. Note that the annual relevant-total-costs curve in Exhibit 20-1 is somewhat flat over the range of order quantities from 650 to 1,300 units. *The square root in the EOQ model reduces the sensitivity of the ordering decision to errors in predicting its parameters.*

In the next section, we consider a planning-and-control and performance-evaluation issue that frequently arises when managing inventory.

Decision Point

What is the effect on costs of errors in predicting parameters of the EOQ model? How can companies reduce the conflict between the EOQ decision model and models used for performance evaluation?

Conflict Between the EOQ Decision Model and Managers' Performance Evaluation

What happens if the order quantity calculated based on the EOQ decision model differs from the order quantity that managers making inventory-management decisions would choose to make their own performance look best? For example, because there are no opportunity costs recorded in financial accounting systems, conflicts may arise between the EOQ model's optimal order quantity and the order quantity that purchasing managers (who are evaluated on financial accounting numbers) will regard as optimal. As a result of ignoring some carrying costs (the opportunity costs), managers will be inclined to purchase larger lot sizes of materials than the lot sizes calculated according to the EOQ model. To achieve congruence between the EOQ decision model and managers' performance evaluations, companies such as Wal-Mart design performance-evaluation models that charge managers responsible for managing inventory levels with carrying costs that include a required return on investment.

Just-in-Time Purchasing

Learning Objective 4

Describe why companies are using just-in-time purchasing

. . . high carrying costs, low ordering costs, high-quality suppliers, and reliable supply chains

Just-in-time (JIT) purchasing is the purchase of materials (or goods) so that they are delivered just as needed for production (or sales). Consider JIT purchasing for Hewlett-Packard's (HP's) manufacture of computer printers. HP has long-term agreements with suppliers for the major components of its printers. Each supplier is required to make frequent deliveries of small orders directly to the production floor, based on the production schedule that HP gives its suppliers. Suppliers work hard to keep their commitments because failure to deliver components on time, or to meet agreed-upon quality standards, can cause an HP assembly plant not to meet its own scheduled deliveries for printers.

JIT Purchasing and EOQ Model Parameters

Companies moving toward JIT purchasing to reduce their costs of carrying inventories (parameter C in the EOQ model) say that, in the past, carrying costs have actually been much greater than estimated because costs of warehousing, handling, shrinkage, and capital have not been fully identified. At the same time, the cost of placing a purchase order (parameter *P* in the EOQ model) is decreasing because:

- Companies are establishing long-term purchasing agreements that define price and quality terms over an extended period. Individual purchase orders covered by those agreements require no additional negotiation regarding price or quality.
- Companies are using electronic links to place purchase orders at a cost that is estimated to be a small fraction of the cost of placing orders by telephone or by mail.
- Companies are using purchase-order cards (similar to consumer credit cards such as VISA and MasterCard). As long as purchasing personnel stay within preset total and individual-transaction rupee limits, traditional labor-intensive procurement-approval procedures are not required.

Exhibit 20-4 tabulates the sensitivity of CD World's EOQ to changes in carrying and ordering costs. Exhibit 20-4 supports JIT purchasing because, as relevant carrying costs increase and relevant ordering costs per purchase order decrease, EOQ decreases and ordering frequency increases.

Exhibit 20-4

Sensitivity of EOQ to Variations in Relevant Ordering and Carrying Costs for CD World

	A	B	C	D	E	F	G
1				Economic Order Quantity in Units			
2				At Different Ordering and Carrying Costs			
3	Annual Demand (D) =	13,000	units				
4							
5	Relevant Carrying Costs			Relevant Ordering Costs per Purchase Order (P)			
6	Per Package per Year (C)			Rs 2,000	Rs 1,500	Rs 1,000	Rs 300
7	Rs 52			10,000	8,660	7,070	3,870
8	70			8,620	7,460	6,090	3,340
9	100			7,210	6,240	5,100	2,790
10	150			5,890	5,100	4,160	2,280

Relevant Costs of JIT Purchasing

JIT purchasing is not guided solely by the EOQ model. The EOQ model is designed only to emphasize the trade-off between relevant carrying and ordering costs. However, inventory management also includes purchasing costs, stockout costs, costs of quality, and shrinkage costs. We next present the calculation of relevant costs in a JIT purchasing decision.

CD World has recently established an Internet business-to-business purchase-order link with Sontek. CD World triggers a purchase order for compact disks by a single computer entry. Payments are made electronically for batches of deliveries, rather than for each individual delivery. These changes reduce the ordering cost from Rs 2,000 to only Rs 20 per purchase order! CD World will use the Internet purchase-order link whether or not it shifts to JIT purchasing. CD World is negotiating to have Sontek deliver 100 packages of disks 130 times per year (5 times every 2 weeks), instead of delivering 1,000 packages 13 times per year, as shown in Exhibit 20-1. Sontek is willing to make these frequent deliveries, but it would add Rs 0.20 to the price per compact disk. CD World's required rate of return on investment remains at 15%. Assume the annual relevant carrying cost of insurance, materials handling, shrinkage, breakage, and the like remains at Rs 31 per package per year.

Also assume that CD World incurs no stockout costs under its *current* purchasing policy, because demand and purchase-order lead times during each four-week period are known with certainty. CD World is concerned that lower inventory levels from implementing JIT purchasing will lead to more stockouts. That's because demand variations and delays in supplying disks are more likely in the short time intervals between orders delivered under JIT purchasing. Sontek has flexible manufacturing processes that enable it to respond rapidly to changing demand patterns. Nevertheless, CD World expects to incur stockout costs on 150 compact disk packages per year under the JIT purchasing policy. When a stockout occurs, CD World must rush-order compact disk packages from another supplier at an additional cost of Rs 40 per package. Should CD World implement the JIT purchasing option of 130 deliveries per year? Exhibit 20-5 compares CD World's relevant costs under the current purchasing policy and the JIT policy, and it shows net cost savings of per year by shifting to a JIT purchasing policy.

Supplier Evaluation and Relevant Costs of Quality and Timely Deliveries

Companies that implement JIT purchasing choose their suppliers carefully and develop long-term supplier relationships. Some suppliers are better positioned than others to support JIT purchasing. For example, Frito-Lay, a supplier of potato chips and other snack foods, has a corporate strategy that emphasizes service, consistency, freshness, and quality of the delivered products. As a result, the company makes more-frequent deliveries to retail outlets than many of its competitors.

What are the relevant costs when choosing suppliers? Consider again CD World. Denton Corporation, another supplier of disks, offers to supply all of CD World's compact disk needs at a price of Rs 138 per package—less than Sontek's price of Rs 140.2—under the same JIT delivery terms that Sontek offers. Denton proposes an Internet

Exhibit 20-5 Annual Relevant Costs of Current Purchasing Policy and JIT Purchasing Policy for CD World

File Edit View Insert Format Tools Data Window Help

	A	B	C	D	E	F	G	H	I	J
1		Relevant Costs Under								
2		Current Purchasing Policy					JIT Purchasing Policy			
3	Relevant Items	Relevant Cost Per Unit		Quantity Per Year	Total Costs		Relevant Cost Per Unit		Quantity Per Year	Total Costs
4	(1)	(2)		(3)	(4) = (2) x (3)		(5)		(6)	(7) = (5) x (6)
5	Purchasing costs	Rs 140	per unit	13,000	Rs18,20,000		Rs140.2	per unit	13,000	Rs18,22,600
6	Ordering costs	20	per order	13	260		20.0	per order	130	2,600
7	Opportunity carrying costs	21[a]	per unit of average inventory per year	500[b]	10,500		21.0[a]	per unit of average inventory per year	50[c]	1,050
8	Other carrying costs (insurance, materials handling, and so on)	31	per unit of average inventory per year	500[b]	15,500		31.0	per unit of average inventory per year	50[c]	1,550
9	Stockout costs	40	per unit	0	0		40.0	per unit	150	6,000
10	Total annual relevant costs				Rs18,46,260					Rs18,33,800
11	Annual difference in favor of JIT purchasing					Rs 12,460				
12										
13	[a]Purchasing cost per unit x 0.15 per year									
14	[b]Order quantity ÷ 2 = 1,000 ÷ 2 = 500 units									
15	[c]Order quantity ÷ 2 = 100 ÷ 2 = 50 units									

purchase-order link identical to Sontek's link, making CD World's ordering cost Rs 20 per purchase order. CD World's relevant cost of insurance, materials handling, breakage, and the like would be Rs 30 per package per year if it purchases from Denton, versus Rs 31 if it purchases from Sontek. Should CD World buy from Denton? To answer, we need to consider the relevant costs of quality and delivery performance.

CD World has used Sontek in the past and knows that Sontek will deliver quality disks on time. In fact, CD World does not even inspect the compact disk packages that Sontek supplies and therefore incurs zero inspection costs. Denton, however, does not enjoy such a sterling reputation for quality. CD World anticipates the following negative aspects of using Denton:

- Inspection cost of Rs 0.50 per package.
- Average stockouts of 360 packages per year requiring rush orders at an additional cost of Rs 40 per package.
- Product returns of 2.5% of all packages sold due to poor compact disk quality. CD World estimates an additional cost of Rs100 to handle each returned package.

Exhibit 20-6 shows the relevant costs of purchasing from Sontek and Denton. Even though Denton is offering a lower price per package, there is a net cost savings of Rs 18,730 per year by purchasing disks from Sontek. Selling Sontek's high-quality compact disks also enhances CD World's reputation and increases customer goodwill, which could lead to higher sales and profitability in the future.

JIT Purchasing, Planning and Control, and Supply-Chain Analysis

The levels of inventories held by retailers are influenced by the demand patterns of their customers and supply relationships with their distributors and manufacturers, the suppliers to their manufacturers, and so on. *Supply chain* describes the flow of goods, services, and information from the initial sources of materials and services to the delivery of products to consumers, regardless of whether those activities occur in the same organization or in other organizations. Retailers should purchase inventories on a JIT basis only if activities throughout the supply chain are properly planned, coordinated, and controlled.

Exhibit 20-6 Annual Relevant Costs of Purchasing From Sontek and Denton

File Edit View Insert Format Tools Data Window Help

	A	B	C	D	E	F	G	H	I	J
1		Relevant Cost of Purchasing From								
2		Sontek					Denton			
3	Relevant Items	Relevant Cost Per Unit		Quantity Per Year	Total Costs		Relevant Cost Per Unit		Quantity Per Year	Total Costs
4	(1)	(2)		(3)	(4) = (2) x (3)		(5)		(6)	(7) = (5) x (6)
5	Purchasing costs	Rs140.2	per unit	13,000	Rs 18,22,600		Rs138.0	per unit	13,000	Rs17,94,000
6	Ordering costs	20.0	per order	130	2,600		20.0	per order	130	2,600
7	Inspection costs	0.5	per unit	0	0		0.5	per unit	13,000	6,500
8	Opportunity carrying costs	21.0[a]	per unit of average inventory per year	50[b]	1,050		20.7[a]	per unit of average inventory per year	50[b]	1,030
9	Other carrying costs (insurance, materials handling, and so on)	30.0	per unit of average inventory per year	50[b]	1,550		30.0	per unit of average inventory per year	50[b]	1,500
10	Customer return costs	100.0	per unit returned	0	0		100.0	per unit returned	325[c]	32,500
11	Stockout costs	40.0	per unit	150	6,000		40.0	per unit	360	14,400
12	Total annual relevant costs				Rs 18,33,800					Rs18,52,530
13	Annual difference in favor of Sontek					Rs 18,730				
14										
15	[a]Purchasing cost per unit x 0.15 per year									
16	[b]Order quantity ÷ 2 = 100 ÷ 2 = 50 units									
17	[c]2.5% of units returned x 13,000 units									

Procter and Gamble's (P&G's) experience with its Pampers product illustrates the gains from supply-chain coordination. Retailers selling Pampers encountered variability in weekly demand because families purchased disposable diapers randomly. Anticipating even more demand variability and lacking information about available inventory with P&G, retailers' orders to P&G became more variable. Trade promotions made the situation worse because retailers took advantage of lower prices to stock up for the future. Similarly, the high variability of orders at P&G translated into more variability of orders at P&G's suppliers. This resulted in high levels of inventory at all stages in the supply chain.

How did P&G respond to these problems? By sharing information and planning and coordinating activities throughout the supply chain. The retailers began to share daily sales information about Pampers with P&G and P&G's suppliers. Sharing sales information reduced the level of uncertainty that P&G and its suppliers had about retail demand for Pampers. This reduction in demand uncertainty, combined with the sharing of inventory data throughout the supply chain, led to (1) fewer stockouts at the retail level, (2) reduced manufacture of Pampers not immediately needed by retailers, (3) fewer manufacturing orders that had to be "rushed" or "expedited," and (4) lower inventories held by each company in the supply chain. The benefits of supply chain coordination at P&G have been so great that retailers such as Wal-Mart have contracted with P&G to manage Wal-Mart's retail inventories on a just-in-time basis. This practice is called *supplier- or vendor-managed inventory*. Supply-chain management, however, is not without its challenges such as sharing accurate, timely, and relevant information about sales, inventory, and sales forecasts. These challenges arise because of problems of communication, trust, incompatible information systems and limited people and financial resources.

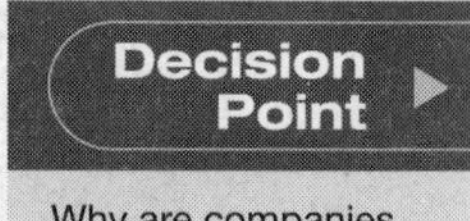

Why are companies using just-in-time purchasing?

We now turn our attention to inventory management in manufacturing companies. Managers at manufacturing companies have also developed numerous systems to plan and implement production and inventory activities within their plants. We consider two widely used types of systems: materials requirements planning (MRP) and just-in-time (JIT) production.

Inventory Management and MRP

We now turn our attention away from purchasing to managing production inventories in manufacturing companies. Managers at manufacturing companies have developed numerous systems to plan and implement inventory activities within their plants. We consider two widely used types of systems: materials requirements planning (MRP) and just-in-time (JIT) production.

Learning Objective 

Distinguish materials requirements planning (MRP) systems

. . . manufacturing products based on demand forecasts

from just-in-time (JIT) systems for manufacturing

. . . manufacturing products only upon receiving customer orders

Materials Requirements Planning

Materials requirements planning (MRP) is a "push-through" system that manufactures finished goods for inventory on the basis of demand forecasts. MRP uses (1) demand forecasts for final products; (2) a bill of materials detailing the materials, components, and subassemblies for each final product; and (3) the quantities of materials, components, and product inventories to determine the necessary outputs at each stage of production. Taking into account the lead time required to purchase materials and to manufacture components and finished products, a master production schedule specifies the quantity and timing of each item to be produced. Once production starts as scheduled, the output of each department is pushed through the production line whether or not it is needed. This "push through" can sometimes result in an accumulation of inventory when workstations receive work they are not yet ready to process.

Inventory management is a challenge in an MRP system. One reason for unsuccessful attempts to implement MRP systems has been a failure to collect and update inventory records. The management accountant aids in MRP by maintaining accurate records of inventory and its costs. For example, after becoming aware of the full costs of carrying finished goods inventory in its MRP system, National Semiconductor contracted with Federal Express to airfreight its microchips from a central location in Singapore to customer sites worldwide, instead of storing products at geographically dispersed warehouses. The change enabled National to move products from plant to customer in 4 days rather than 45 days and to reduce distribution costs from 2.6% to 1.9% of revenues. These benefits subsequently led National to outsource all its shipping activities to Federal Express.

MRP is a push-through approach. We now consider JIT production, a "demand-pull" approach, which is used by companies such as Toyota in the automobile industry, Dell in the computer industry, and Braun in the appliance industry.

JIT Production

Learning Objective 

Identify the features of a just-in-time production system

. . . for example, organizing work in manufacturing cells, improving quality, reducing manufacturing lead time

Just-in-time (JIT) production, which is also called **lean production**, is a "demand-pull" manufacturing system that manufactures each component in a production line as soon as, and only when, needed by the next step in the production line. In a JIT production line, manufacturing activity at any particular workstation is prompted by the need for that workstation's output at the following workstation. Demand triggers each step of the production process, starting with customer demand for a finished product at the end of the process and working all the way back to the demand for direct materials at the beginning of the process. In this way, demand pulls an order through the production line. The demand-pull feature of JIT production systems achieves close coordination among workstations. It smooths the flow of goods, despite low quantities of inventory. JIT production systems aim to simultaneously (1) meet customer demand in a timely manner (2) with high-quality products and (3) at the lowest possible total cost.

Decision Point

How do materials requirements planning (MRP) systems differ from just-in-time (JIT) production systems?

Features of JIT Production Systems

A JIT production system has these features:

- Production is organized in **manufacturing cells**, a grouping of all the different types of equipment used to make a given product. Materials move from one machine to another, and various operations are performed in sequence, minimizing materials-handling costs.

- Workers are hired and trained to be multiskilled and capable of performing a variety of operations and tasks, including minor repairs and routine equipment maintenance.
- Defects are aggressively eliminated. Because of the tight links between workstations in the production line and the minimal inventories at each workstation, defects arising at one workstation quickly affect other workstations in the line. JIT creates an urgency for solving problems immediately and eliminating the root causes of defects as quickly as possible. Low levels of inventories allow workers to trace problems to and solve problems at earlier workstations in the production process, where the problems likely originated.
- *Setup time*—the time required to get equipment, tools, and materials ready to start the production of a component or product—is reduced. Simultaneously, *manufacturing lead time*—the time from when an order is received by manufacturing until it becomes a finished good—is also reduced. Reducing setup time makes production in smaller batches economical, which in turn reduces inventory levels. Reducing manufacturing lead time enables a company to respond faster to changes in customer demand (see Concepts in Action).
- Suppliers are selected on the basis of their ability to deliver quality materials in a timely manner. Most companies implementing *JIT production* also implement *JIT purchasing*. JIT plants expect JIT suppliers to make timely deliveries of high-quality goods directly to the production floor.

We next present a relevant-cost analysis for deciding whether to implement a JIT production system.

Financial Benefits of JIT and Relevant Costs

Early advocates saw the benefit of JIT production as lower carrying costs of inventory. But there are other benefits of lower inventories: heightened emphasis on improving quality by eliminating the specific causes of rework, scrap, and waste, and lower manufacturing lead times. In computing the relevant benefits and costs of reducing inventories in JIT production systems, the cost analyst should take into account all benefits and all costs.

Consider Naman Metal Works, a manufacturer of brass fittings. Naman is considering implementing a JIT production system. To implement JIT production, Naman must incur Rs 10,00,000 in annual tooling costs to reduce setup times. Naman expects that JIT will reduce average inventory by Rs 50,00,000 and that relevant costs of insurance, storage, materials handling, and setup will decline by Rs 3,00,000 per year. The company's required rate of return on inventory investments is 10% per year. Should Naman implement a JIT production system? On the basis of the information provided, we would be tempted to say no. That's because annual relevant cost savings in carrying costs amount to Rs 8,00,000 [(10% of Rs 50,00,000) + Rs 3,00,000)], which is less than the additional annual tooling costs of Rs 10,00,000.

Our analysis, however, is incomplete. We have not considered the other benefits of lower inventories in JIT production. Naman estimates that implementing JIT will improve quality and reduce rework on 500 units each year, resulting in savings of Rs 500 per unit. Also, better quality and faster delivery will allow Naman to charge Rs 20 more per unit on the 20,000 units that it sells each year.

Incremental savings in insurance, storage, materials handling, and set up	Rs 3,00,000
Incremental savings in inventory carrying costs (10% × Rs 50,00,000)	5,00,000
Incremental savings from reduced rework (Rs 500 per unit × 500 units)	2,50,000
Additional contribution margin from better quality and faster delivery (Rs 20 per unit × 20,000 units)	4,00,000
Incremental annual tooling costs	(10,00,000)
Net incremental benefit	Rs 4,50,000

Concepts in Action

After the Encore: Just-in-Time Live Concert Recordings

Each year, millions of music fans flock to concerts to see artists ranging from Lady Gaga to rock-band O.A.R. Although many of them stop by the merchandise stand to pick up a t-shirt or poster after the show ends, they increasingly have another option: buying a professional recording of the concert they just saw! Just-in-time production, enabled by recent advances in audio and computer technology, now allows fans to relive the live concert experience just a few minutes after the final chord is played.

Live concert recordings have long been hampered by production and distribution difficulties. Traditionally, fans could only hear these recordings via unofficial "bootleg" cassettes or CDs. Occasionally, artists would release official live albums between studio releases. Further, live albums typically sold few copies, and retail outlets that profit from volume-driven merchandise turnover, like Best Buy, were somewhat reluctant to carry them.

Enter instant concert recordings. Organizations such as Adreea, Concert Live, and Live Nation employ microphones, recording and audio mixing hardware and software, and an army of high-speed computers to produce concert recordings during the show. As soon as each song is complete, engineers burn that track onto hundreds of CDs or USB drives. At the end of the show, they have to burn only one last song. Once completed, the CDs or USB drives are packaged and rushed to merchandise stands throughout the venue for instant sale.

There are, of course, some limitations to this technology. With such a quick turnaround time, engineers cannot edit or remaster any aspect of the show. Also, although just-in-time live recordings work successfully in smaller venues, the logistics for arenas, amphitheatres, and stadiums are much more difficult. Despite these concerns, the benefits of this new technology include sound-quality assurance, near-immediate production turnaround, and low finished-goods carrying costs. These recordings can also be distributed through Apple's iTunes platform and artist Web sites, making live recordings more accessible than ever. With such opportunities, it's no wonder that bands like O.A.R. augment their existing CD sales with just-in-time recordings.

Sources: Buskirk, Eliot Van. 2009. Apple unveils 'live music' in iTunes. *Wired*. "Epicenter," blog November 24. www.wired.com/epicenter/2009/11/apple-unveils-live-music-in-itunes/ Chartrand, Sabra. 2004. How to take the concert home. *New York Times*, May 3. www.nytimes.com/2004/05/03/technology/03patent.html *Daily Telegraph*. 2009. Online exclusive: How Concert Live co-founders overcame barriers. February 3. www.telegraph.co.uk/sponsored/business/businesstruth/diary_of_a/4448290/Online-Exclusive-How-Concert-Live-co-founders-overcame-barriers.html Humphries, Stephen. 2003. Get your official 'bootleg' here. *Christian Science Monitor*, November 21. www.csmonitor.com/2003/1121/p16s01-almp.html *Websites*: Live O.A.R. http://liveoar.com/store/first_index.php Aderra. www.aderra.net/ Concert Live. www.concertlive.co.uk/

JIT in Service Industries

JIT purchasing and production methods can be applied in service industries as well. For example, inventories and supplies, and the associated labor costs to manage them, represent more than a third of the costs in most hospitals. As a result, inventory cost reductions have been a primary target for cost reduction. By implementing a JIT purchasing and distribution system, Eisenhower Memorial Hospital, reduced its inventories and supplies by 90 percent in 18 months. McDonald's has adapted JIT production practices to making hamburgers.[3] Before, McDonald's precooked a batch of hamburgers that were placed under heat lamps to stay warm until ordered. If the hamburgers didn't sell within a specified period of time, they were thrown out. This had several consequences. First, inventory holding costs were high because each batch included safety stock to make sure

[3] Charles Atkinson, "McDonald's, A Guide to the Benefits of JIT," *Inventory Management Review*, inventorymanagementreview.org/2005/11/mcdonalds_a_gui.html, accessed May 2, 2007.

McDonald's didn't run out of hamburgers and force customers to wait. Second, spoilage costs were high because many unsold hamburgers were thrown out. Third, the quality of hamburgers deteriorated the longer they sat under the heat lamps. Finally, customers placing a special order for a hamburger had to wait a long time for the hamburger to be cooked. Today, the use of new technology (including an innovative bun toaster) and JIT production practices allow McDonald's to cook hamburgers only when they are ordered, significantly reducing inventory holding and spoilage costs. More importantly, JIT has improved customer satisfaction by increasing the quality of hamburgers and reducing the time needed for special orders.

We next turn our attention to planning and control in JIT production systems.

Enterprise Resource Planning (ERP) Systems[4]

The success of a JIT production system hinges on the speed of information flows from customers to manufacturers to suppliers. Information flows are a problem for large companies that have fragmented information systems spread over dozens of unlinked computer systems, making planning and control more difficult. Many companies are implementing Enterprise Resource Planning (ERP) systems to improve these information flows. An ERP system is an integrated set of software modules covering accounting, distribution, manufacturing, purchasing, human resources, and other functions. Instead of concentrating on specific functions separately, ERP uses a single database that collects data and feeds it into all of these software applications, thereby allowing integrated, real-time information sharing and providing visibility to the company's business processes as a whole. For example, using an ERP system, a salesperson can generate a contract for a customer in Germany, verify the customer's credit limits, and place a production order. The system then uses this same information to schedule manufacturing in, say, Brazil, requisition materials from inventory, order components from suppliers, and schedule shipments. At the same time, it credits sales commissions to the salesperson and records all the costing and financial accounting information.

ERP systems give lower-level managers, workers, customers, and suppliers access to detailed and timely operating information. This benefit, coupled with tight coordination across business functions of the value chain, enables ERP systems to shift manufacturing and distribution plans rapidly in response to changes in supply and demand. Companies believe that an ERP system is essential to support JIT initiatives because of the effect it has on lead times. Using an ERP system, Autodesk, a maker of computer-aided design software, reduced order lead time from 2 weeks to 1 day; Fujitsu reduced lead time from 18 to 1.5 days.

ERP systems are large and unwieldy. Because of its complexity, suppliers of ERP systems such as SAP and Oracle provide software packages that are standard, but that can be customized, although at considerable cost. Without some customization, unique and distinctive features that confer strategic advantage will not be available. The challenge when implementing ERP systems is to strike the right balance between the lower cost of standardized systems and the strategic benefits that accrue from customization.

Performance Measures and Control in JIT Production

In addition to personal observation, managers use financial and nonfinancial measures to evaluate and control JIT production. We describe these measures and indicate the effect that JIT systems are expected to have on these measures.

1. Financial performance measures, such as inventory turnover ratio (Cost of goods sold ÷ Average inventory), which is expected to increase

[4] For an excellent discussion, see T. H. Davenport, "Putting the Enterprise into the Enterprise System," *Harvard Business Review*, July–August 1998; also see A. Cagilo, "Enterprise Resource Planning Systems and Accountants: Towards Hybridization?" *European Accounting Review*, May 2003.

2. Nonfinancial performance measures of time, inventory, and quality, such as:
   - Manufacturing lead time, expected to decrease
   - Units produced per hour, expected to increase
   - Number of days of inventory on hand, expected to decrease

$$\frac{\text{Total setup time for machines}}{\text{Total manufacturing time}}\text{, expected to decrease}$$

$$\frac{\text{Number of units requiring rework or scrap}}{\text{Total number of units started and completed}}\text{, expected to decrease}$$

Personal observation and nonfinancial performance measures provide the most timely, intuitive, and easy to understand measures of manufacturing performance. Rapid, meaningful feedback is critical because the lack of inventories in a demand-pull system makes it urgent to detect and solve problems quickly. JIT measures can also be incorporated into the balanced scorecard. As discussed in Chapters 13 and 19, a balanced scorecard contains four perspectives: financial, customer, internal business process, and learning and growth. A key component of JIT production is employees who are multiskilled and well-trained in a variety of tasks. Improvements in these learning and growth measures should lead to improvements in internal business process measures such as the time, inventory, and quality measures above. As JIT improves operational performance, customer satisfaction should also improve due to greater flexibility, responsiveness, and quality. Finally, improvements in all these measures should lead to better financial performance as a result of lower purchasing, inventory holding, and quality costs, and higher revenues.

Effect of JIT Systems on Product Costing

By reducing materials handling, warehousing, and inspection, JIT systems reduce overhead costs. JIT systems also aid in direct tracing of some costs usually classified as indirect. For example, the use of manufacturing cells makes it cost-effective to trace materials handling and machine operating costs to specific products or product families made in these cells. These costs then become direct costs of those products. Also, the use of multiskilled workers in these cells allows the costs of setup, maintenance, and quality inspection to be traced as direct costs. These changes have prompted some companies using JIT to adopt simplified product costing methods that dovetail with JIT production and that are less costly to operate than the traditional costing systems described in Chapters 4, 7, 8, and 17. We examine two of these methods: backflush costing and lean accounting.

Decision Point

What are the features and benefits of a JIT production system?

Backflush Costing

Learning Objective 7

Describe different ways backflush costing can simplify traditional inventory-costing systems

. . . for example, by not recording journal entries for work in process, purchase of materials, or production of finished goods

Organizing manufacturing in cells, reducing defects and manufacturing lead time, and ensuring timely delivery of materials, enables purchasing, production, and sales to occur in quick succession with minimal inventories. The absence of inventories makes choices about cost-flow assumptions (such as weighted-average or first-in, first-out) or inventory-costing methods (such as absorption or variable costing) unimportant: All manufacturing costs of the accounting period flow directly into cost of goods sold. The rapid conversion of direct materials into finished goods that are immediately sold greatly simplifies the costing system.

Simplified Normal or Standard Costing

Traditional normal and standard-costing systems (Chapters 4, 7, 8, and 17) use **sequential tracking**, which is a costing system in which recording of the journal entries occurs in the same order as actual purchases and progress in production. Costs are tracked sequentially as products pass through each of the following four stages:

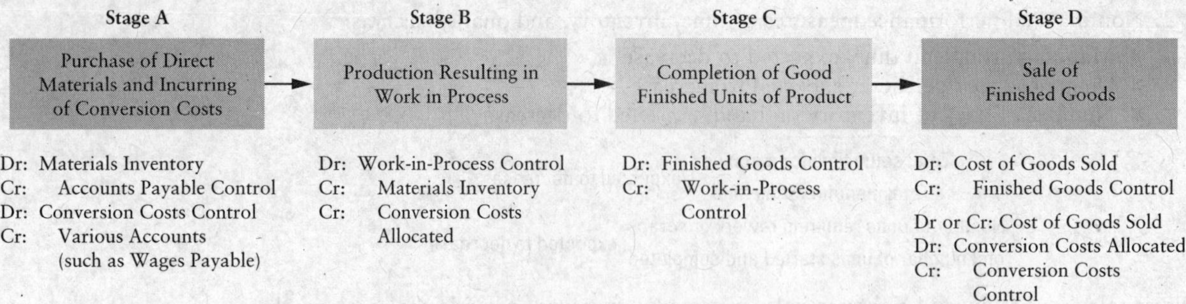

A sequential-tracking costing system has four *trigger points*, corresponding to stages A, B, C, and D. A **trigger point** is a stage in the cycle from purchase of direct materials (stage A) to sale of finished goods (stage D) at which journal entries are made in the accounting system. The journal entries (with Dr. representing debits and Cr. representing credits) for each stage are displayed below the box for that stage (as described in Chapter 4).

An alternative approach to sequential tracking is backflush costing. **Backflush costing** is a costing system that omits recording some of the journal entries relating to the stages from purchase of direct materials to the sale of finished goods. When journal entries for one or more stages are omitted, the journal entries for a subsequent stage use normal or standard costs to work backward to "flush out" the costs in the cycle for which journal entries were *not* made. When inventories are minimal, as in JIT production systems, backflush costing simplifies the costing system without losing much information.

Consider the following data for the month of April for Silicon Valley Computer (SVC), which produces keyboards for personal computers.

- There are no beginning inventories of direct materials and no beginning or ending work-in-process inventories.
- SVC has only one direct manufacturing cost category (direct materials) and one indirect manufacturing cost category (conversion costs). All manufacturing labor costs are included in conversion costs.
- From its bill of materials and an operations list (description of operations to be undergone), SVC determines that the standard direct material cost per keyboard unit is Rs 190 and the standard conversion cost is Rs 120.
- SVC purchases Rs 1,95,00,000 of direct materials. To focus on the basic concepts, we assume SVC has no direct materials variances. Actual conversion costs equal Rs 1,26,00,000. SVC produces 1,00,000 good keyboard units and sells 99,000 units.
- Any underallocated or overallocated conversion costs are written off to cost of goods sold at the end of April.

We use three examples to illustrate backflush costing. *They differ in the number and placement of trigger points.*

Example 1: The three trigger points for journal entries are Purchase of direct materials and incurring of conversion costs (Stage A), Completion of good finished units of product (Stage C), and Sale of finished goods (Stage D).

Note that there is no journal entry for Production resulting in work in process (Stage B) because JIT production has minimal work in process.

SVC records two inventory accounts:

Type	Account Title
Combined materials inventory and materials in work in process	Materials and In-Process Inventory Control
Finished goods	Finished Goods Control

Exhibit 20-7, Panel A, summarizes the journal entries for Example 1 with three trigger points: Purchase of direct materials and incurring of conversion costs, Completion of

Exhibit 20-7 Journal Entries and General Ledger Overview for Backflush Costing and Journal Entries for Sequential Tracking with Three Trigger Points: Purchase of Direct Materials and Incurring of Conversion Costs, Completion of Good Finished Units of Product, and Sale of Finished Goods

PANEL A: Journal Entries

	Backflush Costing			Sequential Tracking		
Stage A: Record Purchase of Direct Materials and Incurring of Conversion Costs						
1. Record Direct Materials Purchased.						
Entry (A1)	Materials and In-Process Inventory Control	1,95,00,000		Materials Inventory Control	1,95,00,000	
	Accounts Payable Control		1,95,00,000	Accounts Payable Control		1,95,00,000
2. Record Conversion Costs Incurred.						
Entry (A2)	Conversion Costs Control	1,26,00,000		Conversion Costs Control	1,26,00,000	
	Various accounts (such as Wages Payable Control)		1,26,00,000	Various accounts (such as Wages Payable Control)		1,26,00,000
Stage B: Record Production Resulting in Work in Process.						
Entry (B1)	No Entry Recorded			Work-in-Process Control	Rs 3,10,00,000	
				Materials Inventory Control		1,90,00,000
				Conversion Costs Allocated		1,20,00,000
Stage C: Record Cost of Good Finished Units Completed.						
Entry (C1)	Finished Goods Control	Rs 3,10,00,000		Finished Goods Control	Rs 3,10,00,000	
	Materials and In-Process Inventory Control		1,90,00,000	Work-in-Process Control		Rs 3,10,00,000
	Conversion Costs Allocated		1,20,00,000			
Stage D: Record Cost of Finished Goods Sold (and Under- or Overallocated Conversion Costs).						
1. Record Cost of Finished Goods Sold.						
Entry (D1)	Cost of Goods Sold	Rs 3,06,90,000		Cost of Goods Sold	Rs 3,06,90,000	
	Finished Goods Control		Rs 3,06,90,000	Finished Goods Control		Rs 3,06,90,000
2. Record Underallocated or Overallocated Conversion Costs.						
Entry (D2)	Conversion Costs Allocated	Rs 1,20,00,000		Conversion Costs Allocated	Rs 1,20,00,000	
	Cost of Goods Sold	6,00,000		Cost of Goods Sold	6,00,000	
	Conversion Costs Control		1,26,00,000	Conversion Costs Control		1,26,00,000

PANEL B: General Ledger Overview for Backflush Costing

Direct Materials

Materials and In-Process Inventory Control	
(A1) 1,95,00,000	(C1) 1,90,00,000 →
Bal. 5,00,000	

Finished Goods Control	
(C1) 3,10,00,000	(D1) 3,06,90,000 →
Bal. 3,10,000	

Cost of Goods Sold	
(D1) 3,06,90,000	
(D2) 6,00,000	
3,12,90,000	

Conversion Costs

Conversion Costs Allocated	
(D2) 1,20,00,000	(C1) 1,20,00,000

Conversion Costs Control	
(A2) 1,26,00,000	(D2) 1,26,00,000

The coding that appears in parentheses for each entry indicates the stage in the production process that the entry relates to as presented in the text.

good finished units of product, and Sale of finished goods (and recognizing under- or overallocated costs). For each stage, the backflush costing entries for SVC are shown on the left. The comparable entries under sequential tracking (costing) are shown on the right.

Consider first the entries for purchase of direct materials and incurring of conversion costs (Stage A). As described earlier, the inventory account under backflush costing combines direct materials and work in process. When materials are purchased, these costs increase (are debited to) Materials and In-Process Inventory Control. Under the sequential tracking approach, the direct materials and work in process accounts are separate, so the purchase of direct materials is debited to Materials Inventory Control. Actual conversion costs are recorded as incurred under backflush costing, just as in sequential tracking, and they increase (are debited to) Conversion Costs Control.

Next consider the entries for production resulting in work in process (Stage B). Recall that 100,000 units were started into production in April and that the standard cost for the units produced is Rs 310 (Rs 190 direct materials + Rs 120 conversion costs) per unit. Under backflush costing, no entry is recorded in Stage B because work-in-process inventory is minimal and all units are quickly converted to finished goods. Under sequential tracking, work-in-process inventory is increased as manufacturing occurs and later decreased as manufacturing is completed and the product becomes a finished good.

The entries to record completion of good finished units of product (Stage C) gives backflush costing its name. Costs have not been recorded sequentially with the flow of product along its production route through work in process and finished goods. Instead, the output trigger point reaches *back* and pulls ("*flushes*") the standard direct material costs from Materials and In-Process Inventory Control and the standard conversion costs for manufacturing the finished goods. Under the sequential tracking approach, Finished Goods Control is debited (increased) and Work-in-Process Control is credited (decreased) as manufacturing is completed and finished goods are produced. The net effect of Stages B and C under sequential tracking is the same as the effect under backflush costing (except for the name of the inventory account).

Finally consider entries to record the sale of finished goods (and under- or overallocated conversion costs) (Stage D). The standard cost of 99,000 units sold in April equals Rs 3,06,90,000 (99,000 units × Rs 310 per unit). The entries to record the cost of finished goods sold are exactly the same under backflush costing and sequential tracking.

Actual conversion costs may be underallocated or overallocated in an accounting period. Chapter 4 discussed various ways to dispose of underallocated or overallocated manufacturing overhead costs. Companies that use backflush costing typically have low inventories, so proration of underallocated or overallocated conversion costs between work in process, finished goods, and cost of goods sold is seldom necessary. Many companies write off underallocated or overallocated conversion costs to cost of goods sold only at the end of the fiscal year. Other companies, like SVC, record the write-off monthly. The journal entry to dispose of the difference between actual conversion costs incurred and standard conversion costs allocated is exactly the same under backflush costing and sequential tracking.

The April 30 ending inventory balances under backflush costing are as follows:

Materials and In-Process Inventory Control (Rs 1,95,00,000 – Rs 1,90,00,000)	Rs 5,00,000
Finished Goods Control, 1,000 units × Rs 310/unit (Rs 3,10,00,000 – Rs 3,06,90,000)	3,10,000
Total	Rs 8,10,000

The April 30 ending inventory balances under sequential tracking would be exactly the same except that the inventory account would be Materials Inventory Control. Exhibit 20-7, Panel B, provides a general-ledger overview of this version of backflush costing.

The elimination of the typical Work-in-Process Control account reduces the amount of detail in the accounting system. Units on the production line may still be tracked in physical terms, but there is "no assignment of costs" to specific work orders while they are in the production cycle. In fact, there are no work orders or labor-time records in the accounting system.

The three trigger points to make journal entries in Example 1 will lead SVC's backflush costing system to report costs that are similar to the costs reported under sequential tracking when SVC has minimal work-in-process inventory. In Example 1, any inventories of direct materials or finished goods are recognized in SVC's backflush costing system when they first appear (as would be done in a costing system using sequential tracking). International Paper Company uses a method similar to Example 1 in its specialty papers plant.

Accounting for Variances Accounting for variances between actual and standard costs is basically the same under all standard-costing systems. The procedures are described in Chapters 7 and 8. Suppose that in Example 1, SVC had an unfavorable direct materials price variance of Rs 4,20,000. Then the journal entry would be as follows:

Materials and In-Process Inventory Control	Rs 1,95,00,000	
Direct Materials Price Variance	4,20,000	
Accounts Payable Control		1,99,20,000

Direct material costs are often a large proportion of total manufacturing costs, sometimes well over 60%. Consequently, many companies will at least measure the direct materials efficiency variance in total by physically comparing what remains in direct materials inventory against what should remain based on the output of finished goods for the accounting period. In our example, suppose that such a comparison showed an unfavorable materials efficiency variance of Rs 3,00,000. The journal entry would be as follows:

Direct Materials Efficiency Variance	Rs 3,00,000	
Materials and In-Process Inventory Control		Rs 3,00,000

The underallocated or overallocated conversion costs are split into various overhead variances (spending variance, efficiency variance, and production-volume variance), as explained in Chapter 8. Each variance is closed to cost of goods sold, if it is immaterial in amount.

Example 2: The two trigger points are Purchase of direct materials and incurring of conversion costs (Stage A) and Sale of finished goods (Stage D).

This example uses the SVC data to illustrate a backflush costing that differs more from sequential tracking than the backflush costing in Example 1. This example and Example 1 have the same first trigger point, purchase of direct materials and incurring of conversion costs. But the second trigger point in Example 2 is the sale, not the completion, of finished goods. *Note that in this example, there is no journal entry for Production resulting in work in progress (Stage B) and Completion of good finished units of product (Stage C) because there are minimal work in process and finished goods inventories.*

In this example, there is only one inventory account: direct materials, whether they are in storerooms, in process, or in finished goods.

Type	Account Title
Combines direct materials inventory and any direct materials in work-in-process and finished goods inventories	Inventory Control

Exhibit 20-8, Panel A, summarizes the journal entries for Example 2 with two trigger points: Purchase of direct materials and incurring of conversion costs, and Sale of finished goods (and recognizing under- or overallocated costs). As in Example 1, for each stage, the backflush costing entries for SVC are shown on the left. The comparable entries under sequential tracking are shown on the right.

The entries for direct materials purchased and conversion costs incurred (Stage A) are the same as in Example 1, except that the inventory account is called Inventory Control. As in Example 1, no entry is made to record production of work-in-process inventory (Stage B) because work-in-process inventory is minimal. When finished goods are completed (Stage C), no entry is recorded because the completed units are expected to be sold quickly and finished goods inventory is expected to be minimal. As finished goods are sold (Stage D), the cost of goods sold is calculated as 99,000 units sold × Rs 310 per unit = Rs 3,06,90,000, which is composed of direct material costs (99,000 units × Rs 190 per unit = Rs 1,88,10,000) and conversion costs allocated (99,000 units × Rs 120 per unit = Rs 1,18,80,000). This is the same Cost of Goods Sold calculated under sequential tracking as described in Example 1.

Under this method of backflush costing, conversion costs are not inventoried because no entries are recorded when finished goods are produced in Stage C. That is, compared with sequential tracking, Example 2 does not assign Rs 1,20,000 (Rs 120 per unit × 1,000 units) of conversion costs to finished goods inventory produced but not sold. Of the Rs 1,26,00,000 in conversion costs, Rs 1,18,80,000 is allocated at standard cost to the units sold. The remaining Rs 7,20,000 (Rs 1,26,00,000 – Rs 1,18,80,000) of conversion costs is underallocated. Entry (D2) presents the journal entry if SVC, like many companies, writes off these underallocated costs monthly as additions to cost of goods sold.

Exhibit 20-8

Journal Entries and General Ledger Overview for Backflush Costing and Journal Entries for Sequential Tracking with Two Trigger Points: Purchase of Direct Materials and Incurring of Conversion Costs and Sale of Finished Goods

PANEL A: Journal Entries

	Backflush Costing			Sequential Tracking		
Stage A: Record Purchase of Direct Materials and Incurring of Conversion Costs						
1. Record Direct Materials Purchased.						
Entry (A1)	Inventory: Control	1,95,00,000		Materials Inventory Control	1,95,00,000	
	Accounts Payable Control		1,95,00,000	Accounts Payable Control		1,95,00,000
2. Record Conversion Costs Incurred.						
Entry (A2)	Conversion Costs Control	1,26,00,000		Conversion Costs Control	1,26,00,000	
	Various accounts (such as Wages Payable Control)		1,26,00,000	Various accounts (such as Wages Payable Control)		1,26,00,000
Stage B: Record Production Resulting in Work in Process.						
Entry (B1)	No Entry Recorded			Work-in-Process Control	3,10,00,000	
				Materials Inventory Control		1,90,00,000
				Conversion Costs Allocated		1,20,00,000
Stage C: Record Cost of Good Finished Units Completed.						
Entry (C1)	No Entry Recorded			Finished Goods Control	3,10,00,000	
				Work-in-Process Control		3,10,00,000
Stage D: Record Cost of Finished Goods Sold (and Under- or Overallocated Conversion Costs).						
1. Record Cost of Finished Goods Sold.						
Entry (D1)	Cost of Goods Sold	3,06,90,000		Cost of Goods Sold	3,06,90,000	
	Inventory Control		1,88,10,000	Finished Goods Control		3,06,90,000
	Conversion Costs Allocated		1,18,80,000			
2. Record Underallocated or Overallocated Conversion Costs.						
Entry (D2)	Conversion Costs Allocated	1,18,80,000		Conversion Costs Allocated	1,20,00,000	
	Cost of Goods Sold	7,20,000		Cost of Goods Sold	6,00,000	
	Conversion Costs Control		1,26,00,000	Conversion Costs Control		1,26,00,000

PANEL B: General Ledger Overview for Backflush Costing

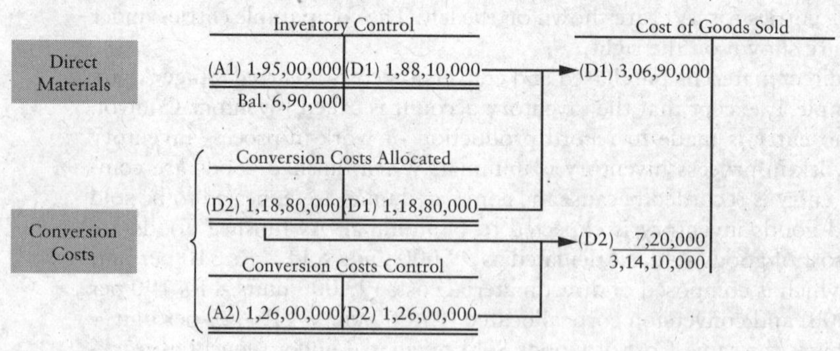

The coding that appears in parentheses for each entry indicates the stage in the production process that the entry relates to as presented in the text.

The April 30 ending balance of Inventory Control is Rs 6,90,000 (Rs 1,95,00,000 – Rs 1,18,80,000). This balance represents the Rs 5,00,000 direct materials still on hand + Rs 1,90,000 direct materials embodied in the 1,000 good finished units manufactured but not sold during the period. Exhibit 20-8, Panel B, provides a general-ledger overview of Example 2. The approach described in Example 2 closely approximates the costs computed using sequential tracking when a company holds minimal work-in-process and finished goods inventories.

Toyota's cost accounting system at its Kentucky plant is similar to this example. Two advantages of this system are (1) it removes the incentive for managers to produce for inventory because conversion costs are recorded as period costs instead of inventoriable costs and (2) it focuses managers on sales.

Example 3: The two trigger points are Completion of good finished units of product (Stage C) and Sale of finished goods (Stage D).

This example has two trigger points. In contrast to Example 2, the first trigger point in Example 3 is delayed until Stage C, SVC's completion of good finished units of product. *Note that in this example, there are no journal entries for Purchase of direct materials and incurring of conversion costs (Stage A) and Production resulting in work in process (Stage B) because there are minimal direct materials and work-in-process inventories.*

Exhibit 20-9, Panel A, summarizes the journal entries for Example 3 with two trigger points: Completion of good finished units of product and Sale of finished goods (and recognizing under- or overallocated costs). As in Examples 1 and 2, for each stage, the backflush costing entries for SVC are shown on the left. The comparable entries under sequential tracking are shown on the right.

No entry is made for direct materials purchases of Rs 1,95,00,000 (Stage A) because the acquisition of direct materials is not a trigger point in this form of backflush costing. As in Examples 1 and 2, actual conversion costs are recorded as incurred and no entry is made to record production resulting in work-in-process inventory (Stage B). The cost of 100,000 good finished units completed (Stage C) is recorded at standard cost of Rs 310 (Rs 190 direct materials + Rs 120 conversion costs) per unit as in Example 1 except that Accounts Payable Control is credited (instead of Materials and In-Process Inventory Control) because no entry had been made when direct materials were purchased in Stage A. Note that at the end of April, Rs 5,00,000 of direct materials purchased have not yet been placed into production (Rs 1,95,00,000 – Rs 1,90,00,000 = Rs 5,00,000), nor have the cost of those direct materials been entered into the inventory-costing system. The Example 3 version of backflush costing is suitable for a JIT production system in which both direct materials inventory and work-in-process inventory are minimal. As finished goods are sold (Stage D), the cost of goods sold is calculated as 99,000 units sold × Rs 310 per unit = Rs 3,06,90,000. This is the same Cost of Goods sold calculated under sequential tracking. Finished Goods Control has a balance of Rs 3,10,000 under both this form of backflush costing and sequential tracking. The journal entry to dispose of the difference between actual conversion costs incurred and standard conversion costs allocated is the same under backflush costing and sequential tracking. The only difference between this form of backflush costing and sequential tracking is that direct materials inventory of Rs 5,00,000 (and the corresponding Accounts Payable Control) is not recorded, which is no problem if direct materials inventories are minimal. Exhibit 20-9, Panel B, provides a general-ledger overview of Example 3.

Extending Example 3, backflush costing systems could use the sale of finished goods as the only trigger point. This version of backflush costing is most suitable for a JIT production system with minimal direct materials, work-in-process, and finished goods inventories. That's because this backflush costing system maintains no inventory accounts.

Special Considerations in Backflush Costing

The accounting procedures illustrated in Examples 1, 2, and 3 do not strictly adhere to generally accepted accounting principles (GAAP). For example, work in process inventory, which is an asset, exists although it is not recognized in the financial statements. Advocates of backflush costing, however, cite the generally accepted accounting principle of materiality in support of the various versions of backflush costing. As the three examples illustrate, backflush costing can approximate the costs that would be reported under sequential tracking by varying the number of trigger points and where they are located. If significant amounts of direct materials inventory or finished goods inventory exist, adjusting entries can be incorporated into backflush costing (as explained next).

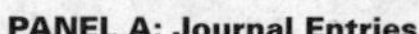

Exhibit 20-9 Journal Entries and General Ledger Overview for Backflush Costing and Journal Entries for Sequential Tracking with Two Trigger Points: Completion of Good Finished Units of Product and Sale of Finished Goods

PANEL A: Journal Entries

	Backflush Costing			Sequential Tracking		
Stage A: Record Purchase of Direct Materials and Incurring of Conversion Costs.						
1. Record Direct Materials Purchased.						
Entry (A1)	No Entry Recorded			Materials Inventory Control	1,95,00,000	
				Accounts Payable Control		1,95,00,000
2. Record Conversion Costs Incurred.						
Entry (A2)	Conversion Costs Control	1,26,00,000		Conversion Costs Control	1,26,00,000	
	Various accounts (such as Wages Payable Control)		1,26,00,000	Various accounts (such as Wages Payable Control)		1,26,00,000
Stage B: Record Production Resulting in Work in Process.						
Entry (B1)	No Entry Recorded			Work-in-Process Control	3,10,00,000	
				Materials Inventory Control		1,90,00,000
				Conversion Costs Allocated		1,20,00,000
Stage C: Record Cost of Good Finished Units Completed.						
Entry (C1)	Finished Goods Control	3,10,00,000		Finished Goods Control	3,10,00,000	
	Accounts Payable Control		1,90,00,000	Work-in-Process Control		3,10,00,000
	Conversion Costs Allocated		1,20,00,000			
Stage D: Record Cost of Finished Goods Sold (and Under- or Overallocated Conversion Costs).						
1. Record Cost of Finished Goods Sold.						
Entry (D1)	Cost of Goods Sold	3,06,90,000		Cost of Goods Sold	3,06,90,000	
	Finished Goods Control		3,06,90,000	Finished Goods Control		3,06,90,000
2. Record Underallocated or Overallocated Conversion Costs.						
Entry (D2)	Conversion Costs Allocated	1,20,00,000		Conversion Costs Allocated	1,20,00,000	
	Cost of Goods Sold	6,00,000		Cost of Goods Sold	6,00,000	
	Conversion Costs Control		1,26,00,000	Conversion Costs Control		1,26,00,000

PANEL B: General Ledger Overview for Backflush Costing

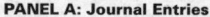

Direct Materials → Finished Goods Control → Cost of Goods Sold

Finished Goods Control	
(C1) 3,10,00,000	(D1) 3,06,90,000
Bal. 3,10,000	

Cost of Goods Sold	
(D1) 3,06,90,000	
(D2) 6,00,000	
3,12,90,000	

Conversion Costs

Conversion Costs Allocated	
(D2) 1,20,00,000	(C1) 1,20,00,000

Conversion Costs Control	
(A2) 1,26,00,000	(D2) 1,26,00,000

The coding that appears in parentheses for each entry indicates the stage in the production process that the entry relates to as presented in the text.

Suppose there are material differences in operating income and inventories based on a backflush costing system and a conventional standard-costing system. A journal entry can be recorded to adjust the backflush number satisfy GAAP. For example, the backflush entries in Example 2 would result in expensing all conversion costs to Cost of Goods Sold (Rs 1,18,80,000 at standard costs + Rs 7,20,000 write-off of underallocated conversion costs = Rs 1,26,00,000). But suppose conversion costs were regarded as sufficiently material in amount to be included in Inventory Control. Then entry (D2) in Example 2, closing the Conversion Costs accounts, would change as follows:

Original entry (e) Conversion Costs Allocated	1,18,80,000	
Cost of Goods Sold	7,20,000	
Conversion Costs Control		1,26,00,000
Revised entry (e) Conversion Costs Allocated	1,18,80,000	
Inventory Control (1,000 units × Rs 12)	1,20,000	
Cost of Goods Sold	6,00,000	
Conversion Costs Control		1,26,00,000

Critics say backflush costing leaves no audit trails—the ability of the accounting system to pinpoint the uses of resources at each step of the production process. However, the absence of large amounts of materials inventory and work-in-process inventory means managers can keep track of operations by personal observations, computer monitoring, and nonfinancial measures.

What are the implications of JIT and backflush costing systems for activity-based costing (ABC) systems? Simplifying the production process, as in a JIT system, makes more of the costs direct and reduces the extent of overhead cost allocations. Simple ABC systems are often adequate for companies implementing JIT. These simple ABC systems work well with backflush costing. Costs from ABC systems yield more-accurate budgeted conversion cost per unit for different products in the backflush costing system. The activity-based cost information is also useful for product costing, decision making, and cost management.

Decision Point

How does backflush costing simplify traditional inventory costing?

Lean Accounting

Learning Objective 8

Understand the principles of lean accounting

. . . focus on costing value streams rather than products, and limit arbitrary allocations

Another approach for simplified product costing in JIT (or lean production) systems is *lean accounting*. Successful JIT production requires companies to focus on the entire value chain from suppliers to manufacturers to customers in order to reduce inventories, lead times, and waste. The emphasis on improvements throughout the value chain has led some JIT companies to develop organizational structures and costing systems that focus on **value streams**, which represent all the value-added activities needed to design, manufacture, and deliver a given product or product line to customers. For example, a value stream can include the activities needed to develop and engineer products, advertise and market these products, process orders, purchase and receive materials, manufacture and ship orders, bill customers, and collect payments. The focus on value streams is aided by the use of manufacturing cells in JIT systems that group together the operations needed to make a given product or product line.

Lean accounting is a costing method that supports creating value for the customer by costing the value stream, not individual products or departments, thereby eliminating waste in the accounting process.[5] If multiple, related products are made in a single value stream, product costs for the individual products are not computed. Actual costs are directly traced to the value stream and standard costs and variances are not computed. Direct tracing of costs is easy because companies using lean accounting dedicate resources to individual value streams.

Consider the following product costs for Allston Company that makes two models of designer purses in one manufacturing cell and two models of designer wallets in another manufacturing cell.

	Purses		Wallets	
	Model A	**Model B**	**Model C**	**Model D**
Revenues	Rs 60,00,000	Rs 70,00,000	Rs 80,00,000	Rs 55,00,000
Direct materials	34,00,000	40,00,000	41,00,000	27,00,000
Direct manufacturing labor	7,00,000	7,80,000	10,50,000	8,20,000
Manufacturing overhead costs (e.g., equipment lease, supervision, and unused facility costs)	11,20,000	13,00,000	12,80,000	10,30,000
Rework costs	1,50,000	1,70,000	1,40,000	1,00,000
Design costs	2,00,000	2,10,000	2,40,000	1,80,000
Marketing and sales costs	3,00,000	3,30,000	4,00,000	2,80,000
Total costs	58,70,000	67,90,000	72,10,000	51,10,000

[5] See B. Baggaley, "Costing by Value Stream," *Journal of Cost Management* (May–June 2003).

Operating income	Rs 1,30,000	Rs 2,10,000	Rs 7,90,000	Rs 3,90,000
Direct materials purchased	Rs 35,00,000	Rs 42,00,000	Rs 43,00,000	Rs 28,50,000
Unused facility costs	Rs 2,20,000	Rs 3,80,000	Rs 1,80,000	Rs 1,50,000

Using lean accounting principles, Allston calculates value-stream operating costs and operating income for purses and wallets, not individual models, as follows:

	Purses	Wallets
Revenues (Rs 60,00,000 + Rs 70,00,000; Rs 80,00,000 + Rs 55,00,000)	Rs 1,30,00,000	Rs 1,35,00,000
Direct material purchases (Rs 35,00,000 + Rs 42,00,000; Rs 43,00,000 + Rs 28,50,000)	77,00,000	71,50,000
Direct manufacturing labor (7,00,000 + Rs 7,80,000; Rs 10,50,000 + Rs 8,20,000)	14,80,000	18,70,000
Manufacturing overhead (after deducting unused facility costs) (Rs 11,20,000 – Rs 2,20,000) + (Rs 13,00,000 – Rs 3,80,000); (Rs 12,80,000 – Rs 1,80,000) + Rs 10,30,000 – Rs 1,50,000)	18,20,000	19,80,000
Design costs (Rs 2,00,000 + Rs 2,10,000; Rs 2,40,000 + Rs 1,80,000)	4,10,000	4,20,000
Marketing and sales costs (Rs 3,00,000 + Rs 3,30,000; Rs 4,00,000 + Rs 2,80,000)	6,30,000	6,80,000
Total value stream operating costs	1,20,40,000	1,21,00,000
Value stream operating income	Rs 9,60,000	Rs 14,00,000

Allston Company, like many lean accounting systems, expenses the costs of all purchased materials in the period in which they are bought to signal that direct material and work-in-process inventory need to be reduced. In our example, the cost of direct material purchases under lean accounting exceeds the cost of direct materials used in the operating income statement.

Facility costs (such as depreciation, property taxes, and leases) are allocated to value streams based on the square footage used by each value stream to encourage managers to use less space for holding and moving inventory. Note that unused facility costs are subtracted when calculating manufacturing overhead costs of value streams. These costs are instead treated as plant or business unit expenses. Excluding unused facility costs from value stream costs means that only those costs that add value are included in value-stream costs. Moreover, increasing the visibility of unused capacity costs creates incentives to reduce these costs or to find alternative uses for capacity. Allston Company excludes rework costs when calculating value-stream costs and operating income because these costs are nonvalue-added costs. Companies also exclude from value stream costs common costs such as corporate or support department costs that cannot reasonably be assigned to value streams.

The analysis indicates that while total cost for purses is Rs 1,26,60,000 (Rs 5,87,00,000 + Rs 67,90,000), the value stream cost using lean accounting is Rs 1,20,40,000 (95.1% of Rs 1,26,60,000), indicating significant opportunities for improving profitability by reducing unused facility and rework costs, and by purchasing direct materials only as needed for production. Wallets portray a different picture. Total cost for wallets is Rs 1,23,20,000 (Rs 72,10,000 + Rs 51,10,000) while the value-stream cost using lean accounting is Rs 1,21,00,000 (98.2% of Rs 1,23,20,000). The wallets value stream has low unused facility and rework costs and is more efficient.

Lean accounting is much simpler than traditional product costing. Why? Because it requires little overhead allocation when computing actual product costs by value stream. Compared to traditional product costing methods, the focus on value streams and costs is consistent with the emphasis of JIT and lean production on improvements in the value chain from suppliers to customers. Moreover, the practices that lean accounting encourages, such as reducing direct material and work-in-process inventories, using less space and eliminating unused capacity support the goals of JIT production.

A potential limitation of lean accounting is that it does not compute costs for individual products. Critics charge that this limits its usefulness for decision making. Proponents of lean accounting argue that the lack of individual product costs is not a problem because most decisions are made at the product line level rather than the individual product level, and that pricing decisions are based on the value created for the customer and not product costs. Another criticism is that lean accounting excludes certain support costs and unused capacity costs. As a result, the decisions based on only value stream costs will look profitable because they do not consider all costs. Supporters argue that lean accounting overcomes this problem by adding a large markup on value stream costs to compensate for these excluded costs. Moreover, in a competitive market, prices will eventually settle at a level that represents a reasonable markup above value stream costs because customers will be unwilling to pay for nonvalue-added costs. The goal must therefore be to eliminate nonvalue-added costs. A final criticism is that lean accounting, like backflush costing, does not correctly account for inventories under generally accepted accounting principles (GAAP). However, proponents are quick to point out that in lean accounting environments, work in process and finished goods inventories are immaterial from an accounting perspective.

Problems for Self-Study

Problem 1

Lee Company has a Mumbai plant that manufactures MP3 players. One component is an XT chip. Expected demand is for 5,200 of these chips in March 2009. Lee estimates the ordering cost per purchase order to be Rs 2,500. The monthly carrying cost for one unit of XT in stock is Rs 50.

Required

1. Compute the EOQ for the XT chip.
2. Compute the number of deliveries of XT in March 2009.

Solution

$$EOQ = \sqrt{\frac{2 \times 5{,}200 \times \text{Rs } 2{,}500}{\text{Rs } 50}}$$

$$= 721 \text{ chips (rounded)}$$

$$\text{Number of deliveriess} = \frac{5{,}200}{721}$$

$$= 8 \text{ (rounded)}$$

Problem 2

Littlefield Company uses a backflush costing system with three trigger points:

- Purchase of direct materials
- Completion of good finished units of product
- Sale of finished goods

There are no beginning inventories. Information for April 2011 is:

Direct materials purchased	Rs 88,00,000	Conversion costs allocated	Rs 40,00,000
Direct materials used	Rs 85,00,000	Costs transferred to finished goods	Rs 1,25,00,000
Conversion costs incurred	Rs 42,20,000	Cost of goods sold	Rs 1,19,00,000

Required

1. Prepare journal entries for April (without disposing of underallocated or overallocated conversion costs). Assume there are no direct materials variances.
2. Under an ideal JIT production system, how would the amounts in your journal entries differ from the journal entries in requirement 1?

Solution

1. Journal entries for April are:

Entry (a)	Inventory: Materials and In-Process Control	88,00,000	
	Accounts Payable Control		88,00,000
	(direct materials purchased)		
Entry (b)	Conversion Costs Control	42,20,000	
	Various accounts (such as Wages Payable Control)		42,20,000
	(conversion costs incurred)		
Entry (c)	Finished Goods Control	1,25,00,000	
	Inventory: Materials and In-Process Control		85,00,000
	Conversion Costs Allocated		40,00,000
	(standard cost of finished goods completed)		
Entry (d)	Cost of Goods Sold	1,19,00,000	
	Finished Goods Control		1,19,00,000
	(standard costs of finished goods sold)		

2. Under an ideal JIT production system, if the manufacturing lead time per unit is very short, there could be zero inventories at the end of each day. Entry (C_1) would be Rs 1,19,00,000 finished goods production [to match finished goods sold in entry (D_1)], not Rs 1,25,00,000. If the Marketing Department could only sell goods costing Rs 1,19,00,000, the JIT production system would call for direct materials purchases and conversion costs of lower than Rs 88,00,000 and Rs 42,20,000, respectively, in entries (A_1) and (A_2).

Decision Points

The following question-and-answer format summarizes the chapter's learning objectives. Each decision presents a key question related to a learning objective. The guidelines are the answer to that question.

Decision	Guidelines
1. What are the six categories of costs associated with goods for sale?	The six categories are purchasing costs (costs of goods acquired from suppliers), ordering costs (costs of preparing a purchase order and receiving goods), carrying costs (costs of holding inventory of goods for sale), stockout costs (costs arising when a customer demands a unit of product and that unit is not on hand), costs of quality (prevention, appraisal, internal failure, and external failure costs), and shrinkage costs (the costs resulting from theft by outsiders, embezzlement by employees, misclassifications, and clerical errors).
2. How do managers use the EOQ decision model?	The economic-order-quantity (EOQ) decision model calculates the optimal quantity of inventory to order by balancing ordering costs and carrying costs. The larger the order quantity, the higher the annual carrying costs and the lower the annual ordering costs. The EOQ model includes costs recorded in the financial accounting system as well as opportunity costs not recorded in the financial accounting system.
3. How can companies reduce the conflict between the EOQ decision model and models used for performance evaluation?	The opportunity cost of investment tied up in inventory is a key input in the EOQ decision model. Many companies include opportunity costs when evaluating managers so that the EOQ decision model is consistent with the performance-evaluation model.

4. What is a supply chain, and what is the benefit of supply-chain analysis?	The supply chain describes the flow of goods, services, and information from the initial sources of materials and services to the delivery of products to consumers, regardless of whether those activities occur in the same organization or in other organizations. Using supply-chain analysis allows companies to coordinate their activities and reduce inventories throughout the supply chain.
5. How do materials requirements planning (MRP) systems differ from just-in-time (JIT) production systems?	Materials requirements planning (MRP) systems use a "push-through" approach that manufactures finished goods for inventory on the basis of demand forecasts. Just-in-time (JIT) production systems use a "demand-pull" approach in which goods are manufactured only to satisfy customer orders.
6. What are the features of a JIT production system?	Five features of a JIT production system are (a) organizing production in manufacturing cells, (b) hiring and training multiskilled workers, (c) emphasizing total quality management, (d) reducing manufacturing lead time and setup time, and (e) building strong supplier relationships.
7. What is backflush costing?	Backflush costing delays recording some of the journal entries (and omits others) relating to the cycle from purchase of direct materials to the sale of finished goods.
8. How does backflush costing simplify inventory costing?	Traditional inventory-costing systems use sequential tracking, in which recording of the journal entries occurs in the same order as actual purchases and progress in production. Most backflush costing systems do not record journal entries for the work-in-process stage of production. Some backflush costing systems also do not record entries for either the purchase of direct materials or the completion of finished goods.
9. How is lean accounting different from traditional costing methods?	Lean accounting costs value streams rather than products. Unused capacity costs and costs that cannot be easily traced to value streams are not allocated.

TERMS TO LEARN

This chapter and the Glossary at the end of the book contain definitions of:

backflush costing (**p. 854**)
carrying costs (**p. 838**)
economic order quantity (EOQ) (**p. 838**)
inventory management (**p. 837**)
just-in-time (JIT) production (**p. 849**)
just-in-time (JIT) purchasing (**p. 845**)
lean accounting (**p. 861**)
lean production (**p. 849**)
manufacturing cells (**p. 849**)
materials requirements planning (MRP) (**p. 849**)
ordering costs (**p. 838**)
purchasing costs (**p. 838**)
purchase-order lead time (**p. 840**)
reorder point (**p. 840**)
safety stock (**p. 841**)
sequential tracking (**p. 853**)
shrinkage costs (**p. 838**)
stockout costs (**p. 838**)
trigger point (**p. 854**)
value stream (**p. 861**)

ASSIGNMENT MATERIAL

Questions

20-1 Why do better decisions regarding the purchasing and managing of goods for sale frequently cause dramatic percentage increases in net income?

20-2 Name six cost categories that are important in managing goods for sale in a retail company.

20-3 What assumptions are made when using the simplest version of the economic-order-quantity (EOQ) decision model?

20-4 Give examples of costs included in annual carrying costs of inventory when using the EOQ decision model.

20-5 Give three examples of opportunity costs that typically are not recorded in accounting systems, although they are relevant when using the EOQ model.

20-6 What are the steps in computing the cost of a prediction error when using the EOQ decision model?

20-7 Why might goal-congruence issues arise when an EOQ model is used to guide decisions on how much to order?

20-8 Describe JIT purchasing and its benefits.

20-9 What are three factors causing reductions in the cost to place purchase orders for materials?

20-10 "You should always choose the supplier who offers the lowest price per unit." Do you agree? Explain.

20-11 What is supply-chain analysis, and how can it benefit manufacturers and retailers?

20-12 What are the main features of JIT production?

20-13 Distinguish inventory-costing systems using sequential tracking from those using backflush costing.

20-14 Describe three different versions of backflush costing.

20-15 Discuss the differences between lean accounting and traditional cost accounting.

Solved Examples

20-16 Economic order quantity for retailer. Delhi Sports (DS) operates a megastore featuring sports merchandise. It uses an EOQ decision model to make inventory decisions. It is now considering inventory decisions for its new Vest product line. This is a highly popular item. Data for 2011 are:

- Expected annual demand for Vests: 10,000
- Ordering costs for purchase order: Rs 225
- Carrying costs per year: Rs 10 per Vest

Each Vest costs DS Rs 40 and sells for Rs 75. The Rs 10 carrying cost per Vest per year comprises the required return on investment of Rs 4.80 (12% × Rs 40 purchase price) plus Rs 5.20 in relevant insurance, handling, and theft-related costs. The purchasing lead time is 7 days. DS is open 365 days a year.

Required

1. Calculate the EOQ.
2. Calculate the number of orders that will be placed each year.
3. Calculate the reorder point.

Solution

Economic order quantity for retailer.

1. D = 10,000, P = Rs 225, C = Rs 10

$$EPQ = \sqrt{\frac{2DP}{C}} = \sqrt{\frac{2 \times 10{,}000 \times \text{Rs } 225}{10}}$$

$$= 670.82 \cong 671 \text{ Vests.}$$

2. Number of orders per year $= \dfrac{D}{EOQ} = \dfrac{10{,}000}{671}$

$$= 14.90 \cong 15 \text{ orders.}$$

3. = Demand each working day $= \dfrac{D}{\textit{Number of working days}}$

$$= \frac{10{,}000}{365}$$

$$= 27.40 \text{ Vests per day}$$

Purchase lead time = 7 days

Reorder point = 27.40 × 7

= 191.80 ≅ 192 Vests.

20-17 Economic order quantity, effect of parameter changes (continuation of 20-16). Athletic Products (AP) manufactures the Vests that Delhi Sports (DS) sells to its customers. AP has recently installed computer software that enables its customers to conduct "one-stop" purchasing using state-of-the-art web site technology. DS's ordering cost per purchase order will be Rs 20 using this new technology.

Required

1. Calculate the EOQ for the Vests using the revised ordering cost of Rs 20 per purchase order. Assume all other data from Exercise 20-16 are the same. Comment on the result.
2. Suppose AP proposes to "assist" DS. AP will allow DS's customers to order directly from the AP web site. AP would transport directly to these customers. AP would pay Rs 10 to DS for every Vest purchased by one of DS's customers. How would this offer affect inventory management at DS? Should DS accept AP's proposal? Explain.

Solution

Economic order quantity, effect of parameter changes (continuation of 20-16).

1. D = 10,000, P = Rs 20, C = Rs 10

$$EOQ = \sqrt{\frac{2DP}{C}} = \sqrt{\frac{2 \times 10{,}000 \times \text{Rs } 20}{10}}$$

$$= 200 \text{ Vests}$$

The sizable reduction in ordering cost (from Rs 225 to Rs 20 per purchase order) has reduced the EOQ from 671 to 200.

2. The AP proposal has both upsides and downsides. The upside is potentially higher sales. DS customers may purchase more online than if they have to physically visit a store. DS would also have lower administrative costs and lower inventory holding costs with the proposal.

   The downside is that AP could capture DS's customers. Repeat customers to the AP Web site need not be classified as DS customers. DS would have to establish enforceable rules to make sure it captures ongoing revenues from customers it directs to the AP Web site.

   There is insufficient information to determine whether DS should accept AP's proposal. Much depends on whether DS views AP as a credible, "honest" partner.

20-18 EOQ for manufacturer. CG Electronics makes air conditioners. It purchases 12,000 units of a particular type of compressor part, LG29, each year at a cost of Rs 500 per unit. CG Electronics requires a 12% rate of return on investment. In addition, relevant carrying costs (for insurance, materials handling, breakage, and so on) are Rs 20 per unit per year. Relevant costs per purchase order are Rs 1,200.

Required

1. Calculate CG Electronics's EOQ for LG29.
2. Calculate CG Electronics's total relevant ordering and carrying costs.
3. Assume that demand is uniform throughout the year and is known with certainty. The purchasing lead time is half a month. Calculate CG Electronics's reorder point for LG29.

Solution

EOQ for manufacturer.

1. Relevant carrying costs per part per year:

Required annual return on investment 12% × 500 =	Rs 60
Relevant insurance, materials handling, breakage, etc. costs per year	20
Relevant carrying costs per part per year	Rs 80

With D = 12,000; P = Rs 1,200; C = Rs 80, EOQ for manufacturer is:

$$\sqrt{\frac{2DP}{C}} = \sqrt{2 \times 12{,}000 \times \text{Rs } 1{,}200)/\text{Rs } 80} = 600 \text{ units}$$

2. Total relevant ordering and carrying costs

$$= \left(\frac{D}{Q} \times P\right) + \left(\frac{Q}{2} \times C\right)$$

$$= \left(\frac{12{,}000}{600} \times \text{Rs } 1{,}200\right) + \left(\frac{600}{2} \times \text{Rs } 80\right)$$

$$= \text{Rs } 24{,}000 + \text{Rs } 24{,}000 = \text{Rs } 48{,}000$$

where Q = 600 units, the quantity ordered.

3. Purchase order lead time is half a month

   Monthly demand is 12,000 units ÷ 12 months = 1,000 units per month.

   Demand in half a month is $\frac{1}{2}$ × 1,000 units or 500 units.

Hence, CG Electronics should reorder when inventory of LG29 falls to 500 units.

20-19 Sensitivity of EOQ to changes in relevant ordering and carrying costs. Bhushan Company's annual demand for Model X253 is 10,000 units. Bhushan is unsure about the relevant carrying cost per unit per year and the relevant ordering cost per purchase order. This table presents six possible combinations of carrying and ordering costs:

Relevant Carrying Cost per Unit per Year	Relevant Ordering Cost per Purchase Order
Rs 10	Rs 300
10	200

15	300
15	200
20	300
20	200

Required

1. Determine EOQ for Bhushan for each of the relevant ordering and carrying-cost alternatives.
2. How does your answer to requirement 1 give insight into the impact on EOQ of changes in relevant ordering and carrying costs.

Solution

Sensitivity of EOQ to changes in relevant ordering and carrying costs.

1. A straightforward approach to the requirement is to construct the following table for EOQ at relevant carrying and ordering costs. Annual demand is 10,000 units. The formula for the EOQ model is:

$$EOQ = \sqrt{\frac{2DP}{C}}$$

where D = demand in units for a specified period of time
P = relevant ordering costs per purchase order
C = relevant carrying costs of one unit in stock for the time period used for D (one year in this problem.

Relevant Carrying Costs Per Unit Per Year	Relevant Ordering Costs Per Purchase Order Rs 300	Rs 200
Rs 10	$\sqrt{\frac{2\times 10{,}0000 \times \text{Rs } 300}{\text{Rs } 10}} = 775$	$\sqrt{\frac{2\times 10{,}0000 \times \text{Rs } 200}{\text{Rs } 10}} = 632$
15	$\sqrt{\frac{2\times 10{,}0000 \times \text{Rs } 300}{\text{Rs } 15}} = 632$	$\sqrt{\frac{2\times 10{,}0000 \times \text{Rs } 200}{\text{Rs } 15}} = 516$
20	$\sqrt{\frac{2\times 10{,}0000 \times \text{Rs } 300}{\text{Rs } 20}} = 548$	$\sqrt{\frac{2\times 10{,}0000 \times \text{Rs } 200}{\text{Rs } 20}} = 447$

2. For a given demand level, as relevant carrying costs increase, EOQ becomes smaller. For a given demand level, as relevant order costs increase, EOQ increases.

20-20 Purchase-order size for retailer, EOQ, just-in-time purchasing. The 24-Hour Mart operates a chain of supermarkets. Its best-selling soft drink is Frooti. Demand (D) in April for Frooti at its Gurgaon supermarket is estimated to be 6,000 cases (24 cans in each case). In March, the Gurgaon supermarket estimated the ordering costs per purchase order (P) for Frooti to be Rs 150. The carrying costs (C) of each case of Frooti in inventory for a month were estimated to be Rs 5. At the end of March, the Gurgaon 24-Hour Mart reestimated its carrying costs to be Rs 7.5 per case per month to take into account an increase in warehouse-related costs.

During March, 24-Hour Mart restructured its relationship with suppliers. It reduced the number of suppliers from 600 to 180. Long-term contracts were signed only with those suppliers that agreed to make product-quality checks before supplying. Each purchase order will now be made by linking into the suppliers' computer network. The Gurgaon 24-Hour Mart estimated that these changes will reduce the ordering costs per purchase order to Rs 25. The 24-Hour Mart is open 30 days in April.

Required

1. Calculate the EOQ in April for Frooti. Assume in turn:
   a. D = 6,000; P = Rs 150; C = Rs 5
   b. D = 6,000; P = Rs150; C = Rs 7.5
   c. D = 6,000; P = Rs 25; C = Rs 7.5
2. How does your answer to requirement 1 give insight into the retailer's movement toward JIT purchasing policies?

Solution

Purchase-order size for retailer, EOQ, just-in-time purchasing.

1. $EOQ = \sqrt{\frac{2DP}{C}}$

   a. D = 6,000; P = Rs 150; C = Rs 5

$$EOQ = \sqrt{(2 \times 6{,}000 \times \text{Rs } 150)/\text{Rs } 5} \times \sqrt{3{,}60{,}000} = 600 \text{ cases.}$$

   b. D = 6,000; P = Rs 150; C = Rs 7.5

$$EOQ = \sqrt{(2 \times 6{,}000 \times \text{Rs } 150)/\text{Rs } 7.5} = \sqrt{2{,}40{,}000} = 489.9 \text{ cases} \cong 490 \text{ cases.}$$

c. D = 6,000; P = Rs 25; C = Rs 7.5

$$EOQ = \sqrt{(2 \times 6{,}000 \times \text{Rs } 25)/\text{Rs } 7.5} = \sqrt{40{,}000} = 200 \text{ cases.}$$

2. A just-in-time purchasing policy involves the purchase of goods or materials such that their delivery immediately precedes their demand or use. Given the purchase order sizes calculated in requirement 1, the number of purchase orders placed each month is:

(D ÷ EOQ):

a. $\frac{D}{EOQ} = \frac{6{,}000}{600} = 10$ orders per month or ≅ 1 every 3 days.

b. $\frac{D}{EOQ} = \frac{6{,}000}{490} = 12.25$ orders per month or ≅ 1 every 2.45 days.

c. $\frac{D}{EOQ} = \frac{6{,}000}{200} = 30$ orders per month or ≅ 1 every day.

An increase in C and a decrease in P lead to increase in the optimal frequency of orders. The 24-Hour Mart has increased the frequency of delivery from every third day (1a: P = Rs 150; C = Rs 5) to a delivery every day (1c: P = Rs.25; C = Rs 7.5). There is a reduction of 200 cases in the average inventory level: (600 – 200) ÷ 2 = 200.

20-21 JIT production, relevant benefits, relevant costs. Motorola manufactures wireless telephones. Motorola is deciding whether to implement a JIT production system, which would require annual tooling costs of Rs 15,00,000. Motorola estimates that the following annual benefits would arise from JIT production:

a. Average inventory would decline by Rs 70,00,000, from Rs 90,00,000 to Rs 20,00,000.
b. Insurance, space, materials-handling, and setup costs, which currently total Rs 20,00,000, would decline by 30%.
c. The emphasis on quality inherent in JIT systems would reduce rework costs by 20%. Motorola currently incurs Rs 35,00,000 on rework.
d. Better quality would enable Motorola to raise the selling prices of its products by Rs 30 per unit. Motorola sells 30,000 units each year.

Motorola's required rate of return on inventory investment is 12% per year.

Required

1. Calculate the net benefit or cost to the Motorola from implementing a JIT production system.
2. What other nonfinancial and qualitative factors should Motorola consider before deciding whether it should implement a JIT system?
3. Suppose Motorola implements JIT production. (a) Give examples of performance measures Motorola could use to evaluate and control JIT production. (b) What is the benefit to Motorola of implementing an enterprise resource planning (ERP) system?

Solution

JIT production, relevant benefits, relevant costs.

1. Solution Exhibit 20-21 presents the annual net benefit of Rs 15,40,000 to Motorola of implementing a JIT production system.
2. Other nonfinancial and qualitative factors that Motorola should consider in deciding whether it should implement a JIT system include:
   a. The possibility of developing and implementing a detailed system for integrating the sequential operations of the manufacturing process. Direct materials must arrive when needed for each subassembly so that the production process functions smoothly.
   b. The ability to design products that use standardized parts and reduce manufacturing time.
   c. The ease of obtaining reliable vendors who can deliver quality direct materials on time with minimum lead time.
   d. Willingness of suppliers to deliver smaller and more frequent orders.
   e. The confidence of being able to deliver quality products on time. Failure to do so would result in customer dissatisfaction.
   f. The skill levels of workers to perform multiple tasks such as minor repairs, maintenance, quality testing and inspection.

Solution Exhibit 20-21

Annual Relevant Costs of Current Production System and JIT Production System for Motorola:

Relevant Items	Relevant Costs under Current Production System	Relevant Costs under JIT Production System
Annual tooling costs	–	Rs 15,00,000
Required return on investment:		
12% per year × Rs 90,00,000 of average inventory per year	Rs 10,80,000	
12% per year × Rs 20,00,000 of average inventory per year		2,40,000
Insurance, space, materials handling, and setup costs	20,00,000	14,00,000 [a]
Rework costs	35,00,000	28,00,000 [b]
Incremental revenues from higher selling prices	–	(9,00,000) [c]
Total net incremental costs	Rs 65,80,000	Rs 50,40,000
Annual difference in favor of JIT production	Rs 15,40,000	

[a]Rs 20,00,000 (1 – 0.30) = Rs 14,00,000
[b]Rs 35,00,000 (1 – 0.20) = Rs 28,00,000
[c]Rs 30 × 30,000 units = Rs 9,00,000

3. a. Personal observation by production line workers and managers is more effective in JIT plants than in traditional plants. A JIT plant's production process layout is streamlined. Operations are not obscured by piles of inventory or rework. As a result, such plants are easier to evaluate by personal observation than cluttered plants where the flow of production is not logically laid out.

Besides personal observation, nonfinancial performance measures are the dominant methods of control. Nonfinancial performance measures provide most timely and easy to understand measures of plant performance. Examples of nonfinancial performance measures of time, inventory, and quality include:
- Manufacturing lead time
- Units produced per hour
- Machine setup time ÷ manufacturing time
- Number of defective units ÷ number of units completed

In addition to personal observation and nonfinancial performance measures, financial performance measures are also used. Examples of financial performance measures include:
- Cost of rework
- Ordering costs
- Stockout costs
- Inventory turnover

3. b. The success of a JIT system depends on the speed of information flows from customers to manufacturers to suppliers. The Enterprise Resource Planning (ERP) system has a single database, and gives lower-level managers, workers, customers, and suppliers access to operating information. This benefit, accompanied by tight coordination across business functions, enables the ERP system to rapidly transmit information in response to changes in supply and demand so that manufacturing and distribution plans may be revised accordingly.

20-22 Effect of different order quantities on ordering costs and carrying costs, EOQ. Jagdish Stores retails a broad line of Indian merchandise at its Preet Vihar store. It sells 26,000 ABC linen bedroom packages (two sheets and two pillow cases) each year. Jagdish Stores pays ABC Limited, Rs 1,040 per package. Its ordering costs per purchase order are Rs 720. The carrying costs per package are Rs 104 per year.

Hans, manager of the Preet Vihar store, seeks your advice on how ordering and carrying costs vary with different order quantities. ABC Merchandise guarantees the Rs 1,040 purchase cost per package for the 26,000 units budgeted to be purchased in the coming year.

Required

1. Compute the annual ordering costs, the annual carrying costs, and their sum for purchase-order quantities of 300, 500, 600, 700, and 900. What is the EOQ? Comment on your results.
2. Assume that ABC Merchandise introduces a computerized ordering network for its customers. Hans estimates that Jagdish Stores's ordering costs will be reduced to Rs 400 per purchase order. How will this reduction in ordering costs affect the EOQ for Jagdish Stores on their linen bedroom packages?

Solution

Effect of different order quantities on ordering costs and carrying costs, EOQ.

1. A straightforward approach to this requirement is to construct the following table for different purchase-order quantities:

D: Demand	26,000	26,000	26,000	26,000	26,000
Q: Order quantity	300	500	600	700	900
Q/2: Average inventory in units	150	250	300	350	450
D/Q: Number of purchase orders	86.67	52	43.33	37.14	28.89

(D/Q) × P: Annual ordering costs	Rs 62,400	Rs 37,440	Rs 31,200	Rs 26,740	Rs 20,800
(Q/2) × C: Annual carrying costs	15,600	26,000	31,200	36,400	46,800
Total relevant costs of ordering and carrying inventory	Rs 78,000	Rs 63,440	Rs 62,400	Rs 63,140	Rs 67,600
			≠ Minimum Cost		

D = 26,000 units
Q = order quantity
P = Rs 720
C = Rs 104

$$EOQ = \sqrt{\frac{2DP}{C}} = \sqrt{\frac{2 \times 26,000 \times \text{Rs } 720}{\text{Rs } 104}} = \sqrt{3,60,000} = 600 \text{ packages}$$

The shape of the total relevant cost function for Jagdish Stores is relatively flat from order quantities 500 to 700.

2. When the ordering cost per purchase order is reduced to Rs 400:

$$EOQ = \sqrt{\frac{2 \times 26,000 \times \text{Rs } 400}{\text{Rs } 104}} = \sqrt{2,00,000} = 447.2 \text{ packages or 447 packages (rounded)}$$

The EOQ drops from 600 packages to 447 packages when Jagdish Stores's ordering cost per purchase order drops from Rs 720 to Rs 400.

20-23 EOQ, uncertainty, safety stock, reorder point. (CMA adapted) The Usha Electronics distributes a wide range of electrical products. One of its best-selling items is a standard small electric motor. The management of the Usha Electronics uses the EOQ decision model to determine the optimal number of motors to order. Management now wants to determine how much safety stock to hold.

The Usha Electronics estimates annual demand (300 working days) to be 30,000 electric motors. Using the EOQ decision model, the company orders 3,000 motors at a time. The lead time for an order is 5 days. The annual carrying costs of one motor in safety stock are Rs 10. Management has also estimated that the additional stockout costs are Rs 20 for each motor they are short.

The Usha Electronics has analyzed the demand during 200 past reorder periods. The records indicate the following patterns:

Demand During Lead Time	Number of Times Quantity Was Demanded
440	6
460	12
480	16
500	130
520	20
540	10
560	6
	200

Required

1. Determine the level of safety stock for electric motors that the Usha Electronics should maintain in order to minimize expected stockout costs and carrying costs. When computing carrying costs, assume that the safety stock is on hand at all times and that there is no overstocking caused by decrease in expected demand. (Consider safety stock levels of 0, 20, 40, and 60 units.)
2. What would be the Usha Electronics's new reorder point?
3. What factors should the Usha Electronics have considered in estimating the stockout costs?

Solution

EOQ, uncertainty, safety stock, reorder point (CMA, adapted).

1. The Usha Electronics is searching for the safety stock level that will minimize the expected total of the costs of carrying additional inventory and the costs associated with insufficient inventories (stockout costs). The present reorder point, alternative safety stock levels, and probability of usage during lead time have to be computed before this level can be determined.

The present reorder point is calculated as follows:

$$\text{Average daily usage} = \frac{\text{Annual demand}}{\text{Number of working days}}$$

$$= \frac{3000 \text{ units}}{300 \text{ days}} = 100 \text{ units per day}$$

Reorder point = Average daily usage × Lead time
= (100 units per day) × 5 days = 500 units

Alternative safety stock levels would be the number of units needed to cover possible demand levels during lead time. These safety levels can be determined as follows:
Possible safety stock levels = Possible demand − Reorder point
The alternative safety stock levels are 0, 20, 40, and 60 units. The probability of demand during lead time is:

Demand During Lead Time	Number of Times Quantity Was Demanded	Probability
440	6	0.03
460	12	0.06
480	16	0.08
500	130	0.65
520	20	0.10
540	10	0.05
560	6	0.03
	200	1.00

Safety Stock Level in Units (1)	Demand Realizations Resulting in Stockouts (2)	Stockout in Units[a] (3) = (2) − 500 − (1)	Probability of Stockout (4)	Relevant Stockout Costs[b] (5) = (3) 3 Rs 20	Number of Orders Per Year[c] (6)	Expected Stockout Costs[d] (7) = (4) 3 (5) × (6)	Relevant Carrying Costs[e] (8) = (1) × Rs 10	Total Relevant Costs (9) = (7) + (8)
0	520	20	0.10	Rs 400	10	Rs 400		
	540	40	0.05	800	10	400		
	560	60	0.03	1,200	10	360		
						Rs 1,160	Rs 0	Rs 1,160
20	540	20	0.05	400	10	Rs 200		
	560	40	0.03	800	10	240		
						Rs 440	Rs 200	Rs 640
40	560	20	0.03	400	10	Rs 120	Rs 400	Rs 520
60	–	–	–	–	–	Rs 0[f]	Rs 600	Re 600

[a]Realized demand − inventory available during lead time (excluding safety stock), 500 units − safety stock.
[b]Stockout units × relevant stockout costs of Rs 20 per motor.
[c]Annual demand 30,000 ÷ 3,000 EOQ = 10 orders per year.
[d]Probability of stockout × relevant stockout costs × number of orders per year.
[e]Safety stock × annual relevant carrying costs of Rs 10 per motor (assumes that safety stock is on hand at all times and that there is no overstocking caused by decreases in expected usage).
[f]At a safety stock level of 60 motors, no stockouts will occur and, hence, expected stockout costs = Rs 0.

Safety stock of 40 units would minimize Usha Electronics's total expected stockout and carrying costs.

2. The new reorder point would be:

Present reorder point (demand during lead time: 100 × 5)	500 units
Safety stock	40 units
New reorder point	540 units

3. The factors Usha Electronics should have considered when estimating the stockout costs include:
   a. Possible lost contribution margin on motors not sold.
   b. Costs associated with disruption or idle time.
   c. Forgone contribution margin on future sales from possible loss of customers and customer goodwill.
   d. Additional clerical costs involved in keeping records of back orders.
   e. How valid is the past empirical distribution of demand when predicting the future demand distribution?
   f. Additional order costs and transportation costs.

20-24 Supplier evaluation and relevant costs of quality and timely deliveries. Jullandhar Sports Store is evaluating two suppliers of footballs, Big Red and Quality Sports. Pertinent information about each potential supplier follows:

Relevant Item	Big Red	Quality Sports
Purchase price per unit (case)	Rs 500	Rs 510
Ordering costs per order	Rs 60	Rs 60
Inspection costs per unit	Rs 0.20	0
Insurance, material handling, and so on per unit per year	Rs 40	Rs 45
Annual demand	12,000 units	12,000 units
Average quantity of inventory held during the year	100 units	100 units
Required return on investment	15 %	15 %

Stockout costs per unit	Rs 200	Rs 100
Stockouts per year	350 units	60 units
Customer returns	300 units	25 units
Customer-return costs per unit	Rs 250	Rs 250

Required

Calculate the relevant costs of purchasing (1) from Big Red and (2) from Quality Sports. From whom should Jullandhar Sports Store buy footballs?

Solution

Supplier evaluation and relevant costs of quality and timely deliveries.

Solution Exhibit 20-24 presents the Rs 14,500 annual relevant costs difference in favor of purchasing from Quality Sports. Jullandhar Sports Store should buy the footballs from Quality Sports.

Solution Exhibit 20-24

Annual Relevant Costs of Purchasing from Big Red and Quality Sports:

	Relevant Costs of Purchasing from	
Relevant Item	Big Red	Quality Sports
Purchasing costs		
Rs 500 per unit × 12,000 units per year	Rs 60,00,000	
Rs 510 per unit × 12,000 units per year		Rs 61,20,000
Ordering costs		
Rs 60 per order × 60[a] orders per year	3,600	
Rs 60 per order × 60[a] orders per year		3,600
Inspection costs		
Rs 0.20 per unit × 12,000 units	2,400	
No inspection necessary		0
Opportunity carrying costs, required return on investment,		
15% per year × Rs 500 cost per unit × 100 units of average inventory per year;	7,500	
15% per year × Rs 510 cost per unit × 100 units of average inventory per year		7,650
Other carrying costs (insurance, material handling, and so on)		
Rs 40 per unit × 100 units of average inventory per year	4,000	
Rs 45 per unit × 100 units of average inventory per year		4,500
Stockout costs		
Rs 200 per unit × 350 units per year	70,000	
Rs 100 per unit × 60 units per year		6,000
Customer returns costs		
Rs 250 per unit × 300 units	75,000	
Rs 250 per unit × 25 units		6,250
Total annual relevant costs	Rs 61,62,500	Rs 61,48,000
Annual difference in favor of Quality Sports	Rs 14,500	

[a]Number of orders placed:
Average inventory per year 100 units
Average order size = 100 × 2 = 200 units
Annual demand = 12,000 units
Number of orders placed = 12,000 units/200 units per order = 60 orders

20-25 Backflush costing, income manipulation, ethics. BV Rajesh, the chief financial officer of Bangalore Computer (BC) is an enthusiastic advocate of JIT production. The BC's Keyboard Division, which produces keyboards for personal computers, has made dramatic improvements in its operations with a highly successful JIT implementation. The Keyboard Division president now wants adopt backflush costing.

Rajesh discusses the backflush costing proposal with Harish, the troller of BC's. Harish is totally opposed to backflush costing. He argues that it will open up "Pandora's box," by allowing division managers to manipulate reported division operating income. A member of Harish's group outlines the three possible variations of backflush costing. Harish notes that none of these three methods tracks work in process. He asserts that this omission would allow managers to "artificially change" reported operating income by manipulating work-in-process levels. He is especially scathing about the backflush costing in which no entries are made until a sale occurs.

"Suppose the division has already met its target operating income and wants to shift some of this year's income to next year," he says. "Under backflush costing with sale of finished goods as the trigger point, the division will have an incentive to not make sales this year of goods produced this year. This is a bizzare incentive. I rest my case about why we should stay with a job-costing system using sequential tracking."

Harish concludes that as long as reported accounting numbers are central to BC's performance and bonus reviews, backflush costing should never be adopted.

Required

1. What factors should BC's consider in deciding whether to adopt a version of backflush costing?
2. Are Harish's concerns about income manipulation sufficiently important for BC's to not adopt backflush costing?
3. What other ways does BC's have to motivate managers to not "artificially change" reported income?

Solution

Backflush costing, income manipulation, ethics.

1. Factors BC's should consider in deciding whether to adopt a version of backflush costing include:
   a. Effects on decision making by managers. There is a loss of information with backflushing. Supporters of backflushing maintain, however, that nonfinancial information and observation of production provide sufficient inputs to monitor production and management costs at the shop-floor level.
   b. Costs of maintaining sequential tracking vis-à-vis backflush costing.
   c. Materiality of the differences. If the production lead time is short (say, less than one day) and inventory levels are minimal (as one would anticipate with JIT), the differences between sequential tracking and backflush may be minimal.
   d. Opportunity for managers to manipulate reported numbers.
2. Harish's concerns certainly warrant consideration. Much depends on the corporate culture at BC's. If the culture is that quarterly or monthly reported numbers are pivotal to evaluations, and that managers "push the accounting system to facilitate meeting the numbers," Harish should raise these issues with Rajesh. Adopting an accounting system with an obvious opportunity for manipulation (backflush with sale as the trigger point) may well send managers the wrong message.
   Harish's concerns, however are not by themselves sufficient to cause BC's to not adopt backflush costing. The factors mentioned in requirement 1 may well be compelling enough to support adoption of backflush costing. Rajesh has alternative ways to address Harish's quite legitimate concerns (see requirement 3).
3. Ways to motivate managers to not "artificially change" reported income include:
   a. Adopting long-term measures that reduce the importance of short-run financial targets.
   b. Increasing the weight on nonaccounting-based variables-e.g., more use of stock options or customer-satisfaction measures.
   c. Penalize heavily (the "stick approach") managers who are found out to have "artificially changed" reported income. This can include withdrawal of bonuses or even termination of employment.

20-26 Backflushing. The following conversation occurred between Vijay, plant manager at Indian Engineering (IE) Company, and Mohan, plant controller. The IE Company manufactures automotive component parts, such as gears and crankshafts, for automobile manufacturers. Vijay has been very enthusiastic about implementing JIT and about simplifying and streamlining production and other business processes.

"Mohan," Vijay began, "I would like to substantially simplify our accounting in the new JIT environment. Can't we just record one accounting entry at the time we send products to our customers? I don't want to have our staff spending time tracking inventory from one stage to the next, when we have as little inventory as we do."

"Vijay," Mohan said, "I think you are right about simplifying the accounting, but we still have a fair amount of direct materials and finished goods inventory that varies from period to period, depending on the demand for specific products. Doing away with all inventory accounting may be a problem."

"Well," Vijay replied, "you know my desire to simplify, simplify, simplify. I know that there are some costs of oversimplifying, but I believe that, in the long run, simplification pays dividends. Why don't you and your staff study the issues involved, and I will put it on the agenda for our next senior plant management meeting."

Required

1. What version of backflush costing would you recommend that Mohan adopt? Remember Vijay's desire to simplify the accounting as much as possible. Develop support for your recommendation.
2. Think about the three examples of backflush costing. These examples differ with respect to the number and types of trigger points used. Suppose your goal of implementing backflush costing is to simplify the accounting, but only if it closely matches the sequential tracking approach. Which version of backflush costing would you propose if:
   a. IE Company had no direct materials and no work-in-process inventories but did have finished goods inventory?
   b. IE Company had no work in process and no finished goods inventories but did have direct materials inventory?
   c. IE Company had no direct materials, no work in process, and no finished goods inventories?

Solution

Backflushing.

1. The IE Company has successfully implemented JIT in its production operations and, hence, minimized work-in-process inventory. It still has a fair amount of raw material and finished goods inventory. The IE Company should, therefore, adopt a backflush costing system with two trigger points, as follows:
   a. Direct materials purchases charged to Inventory: Materials and In-Process Control
   b. Completion of finished goods recorded as Finished Goods Control

   The backflush approach described closely approximates the costs computed using sequential tracking. There is no work in process so there is no need for a Work in Process inventory account.

   Further, by maintaining a Materials and In-Process Inventory Control and Finished Goods Control account, the IE Company can keep track of and control the inventories of direct materials and finished goods in its plant.
2. a. The IE Company should adopt a backflush costing system with trigger points at completion of finished goods and at the sale of finished goods. This would approximate the sequential tracking approach since the question assumes the IE Company has no direct materials or work-in-process inventories. There is, therefore, no need for these inventory accounts.
   b. A backflush costing system with two trigger points-when purchases of direct materials are made (debited to Inventory Control), and when finished goods are sold-would approximate sequential tracking, since the question assumes the IE Company has no work-in-process or finished goods inventories.
   c. A backflush costing system with a single trigger point when finished goods are sold would approximate sequential tracking, since the question assumes the IE Company has no direct material, work-in-process or finished goods inventories. This is a further simplification of the three examples in the text.

The principle here is that backflushing of costs should be triggered at the finished goods inventory stage if the IE Company plans to hold finished goods inventory. If the IE Company plans to hold no finished goods inventory, backflushing can be postponed till the finished goods are sold. In other words, the trigger points for backflushing relate to the points where inventory is being accumulated. As a result, backflushing matches the sequential tracking approach and also maintains a record for the monitoring and control of the inventory.

Exercises

20-27 EOQ for a retailer. The Cloth Center buys and sells fabrics to a wide range of industrial and consumer users. One of the products it carries is denim cloth used in the manufacture of jeans and carrying bags. The supplier for the denim cloth pays all incoming freight. No incoming inspection of the denim is necessary because the supplier has a track record of delivering high-quality merchandise. The purchasing officer of the Cloth Center has collected the following information:

Annual demand for denim cloth	20,000 yards
Ordering costs per purchase order	Rs 200
Carrying costs per year	10% of purchase costs
Safety stock requirements	None
Cost of denim cloth	Rs 80 per yard

The purchasing lead time is 2 weeks. The Cloth Center is open 250 days a year (50 weeks for 5 days a week).

Required

1. Calculate the EOQ for denim cloth.
2. Calculate the number of orders that will be placed each year.
3. Calculate the reorder point for denim cloth.

20-28 Backflush costing and JIT production. HCL Limited assembles handheld computers that have scaled-down capabilities of laptop computers. Each handheld computer takes 6 hours to assemble. HCL Limited uses a JIT production system and a backflush costing system with three trigger points:

- Purchase of direct (raw) materials
- Sale of finished goods
- Completion of good finished units of product

There are no beginning inventories of materials or finished goods. The following data are for August:

Direct (raw) materials purchased	Rs 2,75,40,000	Conversion costs incurred	Rs 72,36,000
Direct (raw) materials used	2,73,36,000	Conversion costs allocated	75,04,000

HCL Limited records direct materials purchased and conversion costs incurred at actual costs. When finished goods are sold, the backflush costing system "pulls through" standard direct materials costs (Rs 1,020 per unit) and standard conversion costs (Rs 280 per unit). HCL Limited produced 26,800 finished units in August and sold 26,400 units. The actual direct materials cost per unit in August was Rs 1,020, and the actual conversion cost per unit was Rs 270.

Required

1. Prepare summary journal entries for August (without disposing of under- or overallocated conversion costs).
2. Post the entries in requirement 1 to T-accounts for applicable Inventory: Direct and In-Process, Conversion Costs Control, Conversion Costs Allocated, and Cost of Goods Sold.
3. Under an ideal JIT production system, how would the amounts in your journal entries differ from those in requirement 1?

20-29 Backflush costing, two trigger points, materials purchase and sale (continuation of 20-28). Assume the same facts as in Exercise 20-28, except that HCL Limited now uses a backflush costing system with the following two trigger points:

- Purchase of direct (raw) materials
- Sale of finished goods

The Inventory Control account will include direct materials purchased but not yet in production, materials in work in process, and materials in finished goods but not sold. No conversion costs are inventoried. Any under/or overallocated conversion costs are written off monthly to cost of goods sold.

Required

1. Prepare summary journal entries for August, including the disposition of under/or overallocated conversion costs.
2. Post the entries in requirement 1 to T-accounts for Inventory Control, Conversion Costs Control, Conversion Costs Allocated, and Cost of Goods Sold.

20-30 Backflush costing, two trigger points, completion of production and sale (continuation of 20-28). Assume the same facts as in Exercise 20-28, except now HCL Limited uses only two trigger points, the completion of good finished units of product and the sale of finished goods. Any under- or overallocated conversion costs are written off monthly to Cost of Goods Sold.

Required

1. Prepare summary journal entries for August, including the disposition of under/or overallocated conversion costs.
2. Post the entries in requirement 1 to T-accounts for Finished Goods Control, Conversion Cost Control, Conversion Costs Allocated, and Cost of Goods Sold.

20-31 EOQ, cost of prediction error. Harvinder is the owner of a truck repair shop. He uses an EOQ model for each of his truck parts. He initially predicts the annual demand for heavy-duty tires to be 2,000. Each tire has a purchase price of Rs 1,000. The incremental ordering costs per purchase order are Rs 800. The incremental carrying costs per year are Rs 80 per tire plus 10% of the supplier's purchase price per tire.

Required

1. Calculate the EOQ for tires, along with the sum of annual relevant ordering costs and relevant carrying costs.
2. Suppose Harvinder is correct in all his predictions except the purchase price. If he had been a faultless predictor, he would have foreseen that the purchase price would drop to Rs 600. What is the cost of the prediction error?

20-32 JIT purchasing, relevant benefits, relevant costs. (CMA adapted) The Omax Auto is an automotive supplier that uses automatic turning machines to manufacture precision parts from steel bars. Omax's inventory of raw steel averages Rs 60,00,000. The president of Omax, and Omax's Controller, are concerned about the costs of carrying inventory. The steel supplier is willing to supply steel in smaller lots at no additional charge. The Controller identified the following effects of adopting a JIT inventory program to virtually eliminate steel inventory:

- Without scheduling any overtime, lost sales due to stockouts would increase by 35,000 units per year. However, by incurring overtime premiums of Rs 4,00,000 per year, the increase in lost sales could be reduced to 20,000 units. This would be the maximum amount of overtime that would be feasible for Omax.
- Two warehouses currently used for steel bar storage would no longer be needed. Omax rents one warehouse from another company under a cancelable leasing arrangement at an annual cost of Rs 6,00,000. The other warehouse is owned by Omax and contains 12,000 square feet. Three-fourths of the space in the owned warehouse could be rented for Rs 15 per square foot per year. Insurance and property tax costs totaling Rs 1,40,000 per year would be eliminated.

Long-term capital investments by Omax are expected to produce an annual rate of return of 20%. Omax Auto Budgeted Income Statement for the Year Ending December 31, 2011, (in thousands) is as follows:

Revenues (9,00,000 units)		Rs 1,08,000
Cost of goods sold		
Variable costs	Rs 40,500	
Fixed costs	14,500	
Total costs of goods sold		55,000
Gross margin		53,000

Marketing and distribution costs		
Variable costs	Rs 9,000	
Fixed costs	15,000	
Total marketing and distribution costs		24,000
Operating income		Rs 29,000

Required

1. Calculate the estimated savings (loss) for the Omax Auto that would result in 2011 from the adoption of the JIT inventory-control method.
2. Identify and explain other factors that Omax should consider before deciding whether to install a JIT system.

20-33 Relevant benefits and costs of JIT purchasing. Maharishi Medical Instruments is considering JIT implementation in 2012. Maharishi's annual demand for product XJ-200, a surgical scalpel, is 20,000 units. If Maharishi implements JIT, the purchase price of the scalpel is expected to increase from Rs 100 to Rs 100.5 because of frequent deliveries by Apollo Manufacturing, Limited. Apollo enjoys a sterling reputation for quality and reliability. Ordering costs will remain at Rs 50 per order. However, the annual number of orders placed will be 200 instead of the current 20. As a result of frequent ordering, Maharishi's order size will decrease proportionally. Maharishi's required rate of return on investment is 20%. Other carrying costs (insurance, materials handling, and so on) will remain at Rs 45 per unit. Currently Maharishi has no stock-out costs. Lower inventory levels from implementing JIT will lead to Rs 30 per unit stockout costs on 100 units during the year.

Required

1. Calculate the estimated savings (loss) for Maharishi Medical Instruments from the adoption of JIT purchasing using the format of Exhibit 20-5.
2. Under what conditions would it be beneficial for Maharishi to have Apollo manage all inventories in the supply chain?

20-34 Supplier evaluation and relevant costs of quality and timely deliveries (continuation of 20-33) Maharishi Medical Instruments installed a JIT purchasing system in 2012 and selected Apollo Manufacturing, Limited, as its supplier. Batra Manufacturing Company also manufactures XJ-200. It offers to supply all of Maharishi's XJ-200 needs at a price of Rs 97.5 per unit (less than Apollo's price of Rs 100.5) under the same JIT delivery terms that Apollo offers. Maharishi's relevant carrying costs of insurance, material handling, and so on would be Rs 44 per unit per year if it purchases from Batra. Due to the lower quality of Batra's product, Maharishi anticipates the following negative consequences of purchasing from Batra:

- Maharishi would incur inspection costs of Rs 0.80 per unit.
- Average stockouts of 800 units per year would occur from late deliveries, requiring rush orders at a cost of Rs 30 per unit.
- Customers would likely return 10% of all units sold due to poor quality of the product. Maharishi estimates its additional costs to handle each returned unit are Rs 60.

Required

Calculate the relevant costs of purchasing (1) from Apollo and (2) from Batra. From whom should Maharishi buy XJ-200?

20-35 Backflush costing and JIT production. National Electric Appliances Company (NEA) manufactures electrical meters. For August, there were no beginning inventories of direct materials and no beginning or ending work in process. NEA uses a JIT production system and backflush costing with three trigger points for making entries in the accounting system:

- Purchase of direct materials-debited to Inventory: Direct and In-Process Control
- Completion of good finished units of product-debited to Finished Goods Control
- Sale of finished goods

NEA's August standard cost per meter is direct materials, Rs 250; and conversion costs, Rs 200. The following data apply to August manufacturing:

Direct materials purchased	Rs 55,00,000	Number of finished units manufactured	21,000
Conversion costs incurred	Rs 44,00,000	Number of finished units sold	20,000

Required

1. Prepare summary journal entries for August (without disposing of under- or overallocated conversion costs). Assume no direct materials variances.
2. Post the entries in requirement 1 to T-accounts for Inventory: Direct and In-Process Control, Conversion Costs Control, Conversion Costs Allocated, and Cost of Goods Sold.

20-36 Backflush, two trigger points, materials purchase and sale (continuation of 20-35). Assume that the second trigger point for NEA company is the sale-rather than the production-of finished goods. Also, the inventory account is confined solely to direct materials, whether these materials are in a storeroom, in work in process, or in finished goods. No conversion costs are inventoried. They are allocated to the units sold at standard costs. Any under/or overallocated conversion costs are written off monthly to Cost of Goods Sold.

Required

1. Prepare summary journal entries for August, including the disposition of under- or overallocated conversion costs. Assume no direct materials variances.
2. Post the entries in requirement 1 to T-accounts for Inventory Control, Conversion Costs Control, Conversion Costs Allocated, and Cost of Goods Sold.

20-37 Backflush, two trigger points, completion of production and sale (continuation of 20-35). Assume the same facts as in Problem 20-35 except now there are only two trigger points: the completion of good finished units of product and the sale of finished goods.

Required

1. Prepare summary journal entries for August, including the disposition of under- or overallocated conversion costs. Assume no direct materials variances.
2. Post the entries in requirement 1 to T-accounts for Finished Goods Control, Conversion Costs Control, Conversion Costs Allocated, and Cost of Goods Sold.

21 Capital Budgeting and Cost Analysis

Learning Objectives

1. Understand the five stages of capital budgeting for a project
2. Use and evaluate the two main discounted cash flow (DCF) methods: the net present value (NPV) method and the internal rate-of-return (IRR) method
3. Use and evaluate the payback and discounted payback methods
4. Use and evaluate the accrual accounting rate-of-return (AARR) method
5. Identify relevant cash inflows and outflows for capital budgeting decisions
6. Understand issues involved in implementing capital budgeting decisions and evaluating managerial performance
7. Identify strategic considerations in capital budgeting decisions

A firm's accountants play an important role when it comes to deciding the major expenditures, or investments, a company should make.

Accountants, along with top executives, have to figure out how and when to best allocate the firm's financial resources among alternative opportunities to create future value for the company. Because it's hard to know what the future holds and what projects will ultimately cost, this can be a challenging task, one that companies like Target constantly confront. To meet this challenge, Target has developed a special group to make project-related capital budgeting decisions. This chapter explains the different methods managers use to get the "biggest bang" for the firm's "buck" in terms of the projects they undertake.

Target's Capital Budgeting Hits the Bull's-Eye[1]

In 2010, Target Corporation, one of the largest retailers in the United States, will spend more than $2 billion on opening new stores, remodeling and expanding existing stores, and investing in information technology and distribution infrastructure.

With intense competition from Wal-Mart, which focuses on low-prices, Target's strategy is to consider the shopping experience as a whole. With the slogan, "Expect more. Pay less." the company is focused on creating a shopping experience that appeals to the profile of its core customer: a college-educated woman with children at home who is more affluent than the typical Wal-Mart customer. This shopping experience is created by emphasizing store décor that gives just the right shopping ambiance.

As a result, investments in the shopping experience are critical to Target. To manage these complex capital investments, Target has a Capital Expenditure Committee (CEC), composed of a team of top executives, that reviews and approves all capital project requests in excess of $100,000. Project proposals that are reviewed by the CEC vary widely and include remodeling, relocating, rebuilding, and closing an existing store to build a new store.

Target's CEC considers several factors in determining whether to accept or reject a project. An overarching objective is to meet the corporate goals of adding a certain number of stores each year

[1] *Sources:* David Ding and Saul Yeaton. 2008. Target Corporation. University of Virginia Darden School of Business No. UV1057, Charlottesville, VA: Darden Business Publishing; Target Corporation. 2010. 2009 annual report. Minneapolis, MN: Target Corporation.

(for 2010, 13 stores) while maintaining a positive brand image. Projects also need to meet a variety of financial objectives, starting with providing a suitable return as measured by discounted cash flow metrics net present value (NPV) and internal rate of return (IRR). Other financial considerations include projected profit and earnings per share impacts, total investment size, impact on sales of other nearby Target stores, and sensitivity of the NPV and IRR to sales variations, like the recent global economic recession.

Managers at companies such as Target, Honda, Sony, and Gap face challenging investment decisions. In this chapter, we introduce several capital budgeting methods used to evaluate long-term investment projects. These methods help managers choose the projects that will contribute the most value to their organizations.

Stages of Capital Budgeting

Capital budgeting is the process of making long-run planning decisions for investments in projects. In much of accounting, income is calculated on a period-by-period basis. In choosing investments, however, managers make a selection from among a group of multiple projects, each of which may span several periods. Exhibit 21-1 illustrates these two different, yet intersecting, dimensions of cost analysis: (1) horizontally across, as the *project dimension*, and (2) vertically upward, as the *accounting-period dimension*. Each project is represented as a horizontal rectangle starting and ending at different times and stretching over time spans longer than one year. The vertical rectangle for the 2012 accounting period, for example, represents the dimensions of income determination and routine annual planning and control that cuts across all projects that are ongoing that year.

Learning Objective 

Understand the five stages of capital budgeting for a project

. . . identify projects, obtain information, make predictions, make decisions, and implement the decision, evaluate performance, and learn

Capital budgeting analyzes each project by considering all the lifespan cash flows from its initial investment through its termination and is analogous to life-cycle budgeting and costing. For example, when Honda considers a new line of automobiles, it begins by estimating all potential revenues from the new line as well as any costs that will be incurred along its life cycle, which may be as long as 10 years. Only after examining the potential costs and benefits across all of the business functions in the value chain, from research and development (R&D) to customer service, across the entire lifespan of the new-car project, does Honda decide whether the new model is a wise investment.

Exhibit 21-1

The Project and Time Dimensions of Capital Budgeting

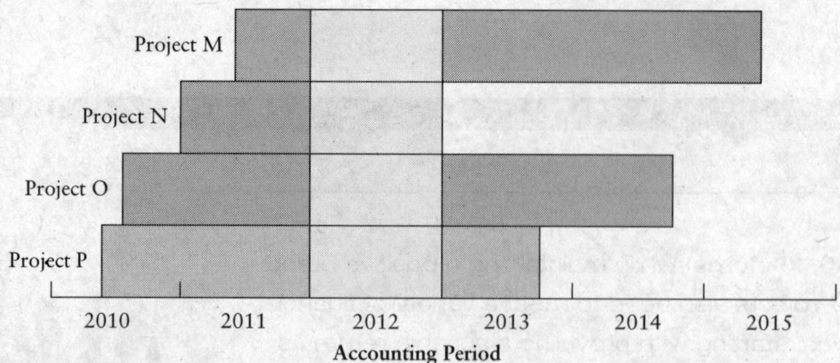

Capital budgeting is both a decision-making and a control tool. Like the five-step decision process that we have emphasized throughout this book, there are five stages to the capital budgeting process:

Stage 1: Identify Projects *Identify potential capital investments that agree with the organization's strategy.* For example, when the Microsoft Office group sought a strategy of product differentiation, it listed possible upgraded and downgraded versions of its present offering. Alternatively, a strategy of cost leadership could be promoted by projects that improve productivity and efficiency. In the case of a manufacturer of computer hardware, such a project could include the outsourcing of certain components to lower-cost contract manufacturing facilities located overseas. Identifying which types of capital projects to invest in is largely the responsibility of senior line managers.

Stage 2: Obtain Information *Gather information from all parts of the value chain to evaluate alternative projects.* Returning to the new car example at Volvo, in this stage, marketing is queried for potential revenue numbers, the plant manager is asked about assembly time, and suppliers are asked about prices and the availability of key components. Some projects may even be rejected at this stage. For example, suppose Volvo learns that the car simply cannot be built using existing plants. It may then opt to cancel the project altogether.

Stage 3: Make Predictions *Forecast all potential cash flows attributable to the alternative projects.* Capital investment projects generally involve substantial initial outlays, which are recouped over time through annual cash inflows and the disposal values from the termination of the project. As a result, they require the firm to make forecasts of cash flows several years into the future. BMW, for example, estimates yearly cash flows and sets its investment budgets accordingly using a 12-year planning horizon. Because of the greater uncertainty associated with these predictions, firms typically analyze a wide range of possible scenarios. In the case of BMW, the marketing group is asked to estimate a band of possible sales figures within a 90% confidence interval.

Stage 4: Make Decisions by Choosing Among Alternatives *Determine which investment yields the greatest benefit and the least cost to the organization.* Using the quantitative information obtained in stage 3, the firm uses any one of several capital budgeting methodologies to determine which project best meets organizational goals. While capital budgeting calculations are typically limited to financial information, managers use their judgment and intuition to factor in qualitative information and strategic considerations as well. For example, even if a proposed new line of cars meets its financial targets on a stand-alone basis, Honda might decide not to pursue it further if it feels that the new model will lessen Honda's perceived quality among consumers and affect the value of the firm's brand.

Stage 5: Implement the Decision, Evaluate Performance, and Learn Given the complexities of capital investment decisions and the longer time horizon they span, this stage can be separated into two phases:

- *Obtain funding and make the investments selected in stage 4.* Sources of funding include internally generated cash flow as well as equity and debt securities sold in capital markets. Making capital investments is often an arduous task, laden with the purchase of many different goods and services. If Volvo opts to build a new car, it must order steel, aluminum, paint, and so on. If some of the supplies are not available according to plan, managers must revisit and determine the economic feasibility of substituting the missing material with alternative inputs.

- *Track realized cash flows, compare against estimated numbers, and revise plans if necessary.* As the cash outflows and inflows begin to accumulate, managers can verify whether the predictions made in stage 3 agree with the actual flows of cash in the organization. When the BMW group initially released the new Mini, realized sales were substantially higher than the original demand estimates. BMW responded by manufacturing more cars to meet the higher demand. It also decided to expand the Mini line to include convertibles and the larger Clubman model.

To illustrate capital budgeting, We consider as an example Top-Spin tennis racquets. Top-Spin was one of the first major tennis-racquet producers to introduce fiberglass in its racquets. This allowed Top-Spin to produce some of the lightest and stiffest racquets in the market. However, new carbon-fiber impregnated racquets are even lighter and stiffer than their fiberglass counterparts. The first step in capital budgeting is identifying projects: Top-Spin has always been a leader in innovation in the tennis-racquet industry, and wants to stay that way by moving quickly to the use of carbon-fiber. The second step in capital budgeting is gathering information. The firm learns that it could feasibly begin using carbon-fiber in its racquets as early as 2011 if it replaces one of its graphite forming machines with a carbon-fiber weaving machine. After collecting additional data, Top-Spin moves to the third stage of capital budgeting-making forecasts of future cash flows. Top-Spin estimates that it can purchase a carbon-fiber weaving machine with a useful life of 5 years for a net after-tax initial investment of Rs 37,91,000, which is calculated as follows:

Cost of new machine	Rs 39,00,000
Investment in working capital (supplies and spare parts for new machine)	90,000
Cash flow from disposing of existing machine (after-tax)	(1,99,000)
Net initial investment for new machine	Rs 37,91,000

Working capital refers to the difference between current assets and current liabilities. New projects often necessitate additional investments in current assets such as inventories and receivables. In the case of Top-Spin, the purchase of the new machine is accompanied by an outlay of Rs 90,000 for supplies and spare parts inventory. At the end of the project, the Rs 90,000 in supplies and spare parts inventory is liquidated, resulting in a cash inflow. However, the machine itself is believed to have no terminal disposal value after five years.

Managers estimate that by introducing carbon-fiber impregnated racquets, their revenues will grow by Rs 10,00,000 (after tax) in the first four years and Rs 9,10,000 in year 5. To simplify the analysis, suppose that all cash flows occur at the end of each year. Note that cash flow at the end of the fifth year also increases by Rs 10,00,000, Rs 9,10,000 in operating cash inflows and Rs 90,000 in working capital. Management next calculates the costs and benefits of the proposed project (stage 4). This chapter discusses four capital budgeting methods to analyze financial information:

1. Net present value (NPV)
2. Internal rate of return (IRR)
3. Payback
4. Accrual accounting rate of return (AARR)

Both the NPV and IRR methods use discounted cash flows.

Learning Objective 2

Use and evaluate the two main discounted cash flow (DCF) methods: the net present value (NPV) method and the internal rate-of-return (IRR) method

. . . to explicitly consider all project cash flows and the time value of money

Discounted Cash Flow

Discounted cash flow (DCF) methods measure all expected future *cash* inflows and outflows of a project discounted back to the present period. The key feature of DCF methods is the **time value of money,** which means that a rupee (or any other monetary unit) received today is worth more than a rupee received at any future time. The reason is that Rs 10 received today can be invested at, say, 10% per year so that it grows to Rs 11 at the end of one year.

The time value of money is the opportunity cost (the return of Re 1 forgone per year) from not having the money today. In this example, Rs 10 received one year from now is worth Rs 10 ÷ 11 = Rs 0.9091 today. In this way, discounted cash flow methods explicitly weigh cash flows by the time value of money. So in our example, Rs 100 received one year from now will be weighted by 0.9091 to yield a discounted cash flow of Rs 90.91, which is today's value of that Rs 100 next year. Note that DCF focuses exclusively on *cash* inflows and outflows rather than on operating income as determined by accrual accounting.

The compound interest tables and formulas used in DCF analysis are in Appendix B. If you are unfamiliar with compound interest, do not proceed until you have studied Appendix B. The tables in Appendix B will be used frequently in this chapter.

The two DCF methods we describe are the **net present value (NPV) method** and the **internal rate-of-return (IRR)** method. Both DCF methods use what is called the **required rate of return (RRR)**, the minimum acceptable annual rate of return on an investment. The RRR is internally set, usually by upper management, and typically reflects the return that an organization could expect to receive elsewhere for an investment of comparable risk. The RRR is also called the **discount rate, hurdle rate, cost of capital**, or **opportunity cost of capital**. Suppose the CFO at Top-Spin has set the required rate of return for the firm's investments at 8% per year.

Net Present Value Method

The **net present value (NPV) method** calculates the expected monetary gain or loss from a project by discounting all expected future cash inflows and outflows back to the present point in time using the required rate of return. To use the NPV method, apply the following three steps:

Step 1: Draw a Sketch of Relevant Cash Inflows and Outflows. The right side of Exhibit 21-2 shows arrows that depict the cash flows of the new carbon-fiber machine. *Note that parentheses denote relevant cash outflows throughout all exhibits in Chapter 20.* The sketch helps the decision maker visualize and organize the data in a systematic way. Note, Exhibit 21-2 includes the outflow for the acquisition of the new machine at the start of year 1 (also referred to as end of year 0). The NPV method specifies cash flows regardless of the source of the cash flows, such as from operations, purchase or sale of equipment, or investment in or recovery of working capital. *Do not* inject accrual-accounting concepts such as sales made on credit or noncash expenses into the determination of cash inflows and outflows.

Step 2: Discount the Cash Flows Using the Correct Compound Interest Table from Appendix B and Sum Them. In our example, we can discount each year's cash flow separately using Table 2, or we can compute the present value of an annuity, a series of equal cash flows at equal time intervals, using Table 4. Both tables are in Appendix B. If we use Table 2, we find the discount factors for periods 1 through 5 under the 8% column. Approach 1 in Exhibit 21-2 uses the five discount factors. To obtain the present value amount, multiply each discount factor by the corresponding amount represented by the arrow on the right in Exhibit 21-2 (– Rs 37,91,000 × 1.000; Rs 10,00,000 × 0.926; and so on to Rs 10,00,000 × 0.681). Because the investment in the new machine produces an annuity, we may also use Table 4. Under Approach 2, we find that the annuity factor for five periods under the 8% column is 3.993, which is the sum of the five discount factors used in Approach 1. We multiply the uniform annual cash inflow by this factor to obtain the present value of the inflows (Rs 39,93,000 = Rs 10,00,000 × 3.993). Subtracting the initial investment then reveals the NPV of the project as Rs 2,02,000 (Rs 2,02,000 = Rs 39,93,000 – Rs 37,91,000).

Step 3: Make the Project Decision on the Basis of the Calculated NPV. If NPV is zero or positive, financial considerations suggest that the project should be accepted; its expected rate of return equals or exceeds the required rate of return. If NPV is negative, the project should be rejected; its expected rate of return is below the required rate of return.

Exhibit 21-2 calculates an NPV of Rs 2,02,000 at the required rate of return of 8% per year. The project is acceptable based on financial information. The cash flows from the project are adequate (1) to recover the net initial investment in the project and (2) to earn a return greater than 8% per year on the investment tied up in the project over its useful life.

Exhibit 21-2 Net Present Value Method: Top-Spin's Carbon-Fiber Machine

	A	B	C	D	E	F	G	H	I
1			Net initial investmen	Rs 37,91,000					
2			Useful life	5 years					
3			Annual cash inflo	Rs 10,00,000					
4			Required rate of return	8%					
5									
6		Present Value	Present Value of		Sketch of Relevant Cash Flows at End of Each Year				
7		of Cash Flow	Rs 10 Discounted at 8%	0	1	2	3	4	5
8	Approach 1: Discounting Each Year's Cash Flow Separately[a]								
9	Net initial investment	Rs (37,91,000)	1.000	Rs (37,91,000)					
10		9,26,000	0.926		Rs 10,00,000				
11		8,57,000	0.857			Rs 10,00,000			
12	Annual cash inflow	7,94,000	0.794				Rs 10,00,000		
13		7,35,000	0.735					Rs 10,00,000	
14		6,81,000	0.681						Rs 10,00,000
15	NPV if new machine purchased	Rs 2,02,000							
16									
17	Approach 2: Using Annuity Table[b]								
18	Net initial investment	Rs (37,91,000)	1.000	Rs (37,91,000)					
19					Rs 10,00,000	Rs 10,00,000	Rs 10,00,000	Rs 10,00,000	Rs 10,00,000
20									
21	Annual cash inflow	39,93,000	3.993						
22	NPV if new machine purchased	Rs 2,02,000							
23									
24	*Note:* Parentheses denote relevant cash outflows throughout all exhibits in Chapter 21.								
25	[a] Present values from Table 2, Appendix B at the end of the book. For example, $0.857 = 1 \div (1.08)^2$.								
26	[b] Annuity present value from Table 4, Appendix B. The annuity table value of 3.993 is the sum of the individual discount rates								
27	0.926 + 0.857 + 0.794 + 0.735 + 0.681, subject to rounding.								

Managers must also weigh nonfinancial factors such as their brand strength. For instance, had the NPV of adding carbon fiber to Top-Spin's line of racquets been negative, management may still have argued for the project because it would make the Top-Spin brand appear to be more technologically advanced, and could possibly help sell other Top-Spin products.

Pause here. Do not proceed until you understand what you see in Exhibit 21-2. Compare approach 1 with approach 2 in Exhibit 21-2 to see how Table 4 in Appendix B merely aggregates the present value factors of Table 2. That is, the fundamental table is Table 2. Table 4 simply reduces calculations when there is an annuity.

Internal Rate-of-Return Method

The **internal rate-of-return (IRR) method** calculates the discount rate at which an investment's present value of all expected cash inflows equals the present value of its expected cash outflows. That is, the IRR is the discount rate that makes NPV = Re 0. Exhibit 21-3 presents the cash flows and shows the calculation of NPV using a 10% annual discount rate for Top-Spin's carbon-fiber project. At a 10% discount rate, the NPV of the project is Re 0. Therefore, IRR is 10% per year.

How do managers determine the discount rate that yields NPV = Re 0? In most cases, managers or analysts solving capital budgeting problems use a calculator or computer program to provide the internal rate of return. The following trial-and-error approach can also provide the answer.

Step 1: Use a discount rate and calculate the project's NPV.

Step 2: If the calculated NPV is less than zero, use a lower discount rate. (A *lower* discount rate will *increase* NPV. Remember that we are trying to find a discount rate for

Exhibit 21-3

Internal Rate-of-Return Method: Top-Spin's Carbon-Fiber Machine[a]

File Edit View Insert Format Tools Data Window Help

	A	B	C	D	E	F	G	H	I
1			Net initial investment	Rs 37,91,000					
2			Useful life	5 years					
3			Annual cash inflow	Rs 10,00,000					
4			Annual discount rate	10%					
5									
6		Present Value	Present Value of		Sketch of Relevant Cash Flows at End of Each Year				
7		of Cash Flow	Rs 10 Discounted at 10%	0	1	2	3	4	5
8	**Approach 1: Discounting Each Year's Cash Flow Separately**[b]								
9	Net initial investment	Rs (37,91,000)	1.000	Rs (37,91,000)					
10		9,09,000	0.909		Rs 10,00,000				
11		8,26,000	0.826			Rs 10,00,000			
12	Annual cash inflow	7,51,000	0.751				Rs 10,00,000		
13		6,83,000	0.683					Rs 10,00,000	
14		6,21,000	0.621						Rs 10,00,000
15	NPV if new machine purchased	Re 0							
16	(the zero difference proves that								
17	the internal rate of return is 10%)								
18									
19	**Approach 2: Using Annuity Table**								
20	Net initial investment	Rs (37,91,000)	1.000	Rs (37,91,000)					
21					Rs 10,00,000	Rs 10,00,000	Rs 10,00,000	Rs 10,00,000	Rs 10,00,000
22									
23	Annual cash inflow	37,91,000	3.791[c]						
24	NPV if new machine purchased	Re 0							
25									
26	*Note: Parentheses denote relevant cash outflows throughout all exhibits in Chapter 21.*								
27	[a]The internal rate of return is computed by methods explained earlier.								
28	[b]Present values from Table 2, Appendix B at the end of the book.								
29	[c]Annuity present value from Table 4, Appendix B. The annuity table value of 3.791 is the sum of the individual discount rates								
30	0.909 + 0.826 + 0.751 + 0.683 + 0.621, subject to rounding.								

which NPV = Re 0.) If NPV is greater than zero, use a higher discount rate to lower NPV. Keep adjusting the discount rate until NPV = Re 0. In the Top-Spin example, a discount rate of 8% yields an NPV of + Rs 2,02,000 (see Exhibit 21-2). A discount rate of 12% yields an NPV of − Rs 1,86,000 (3.605, the present value annuity factor from Table 4, × Rs 10,00,000 minus Rs 37,91,000). Therefore, the discount rate that makes NPV = Re 0 must lie between 8% and 12%. We use 10% and get NPV = Re 0. Hence, the IRR is 10% per year.

The step-by-step computations of internal rate of return are easier when the cash inflows are constant, as in our example. Information from Exhibit 21-3 can be expressed by:

$$\text{Rs } 37{,}91{,}000 = \text{Present value of annuity of Rs } 10{,}00{,}000 \text{ at } X\% \text{ per year for 5 years}$$

Or, what factor F in Table 4 (Appendix B) will satisfy this equation?

$$\text{Rs } 37{,}91{,}000 = \text{Rs } 10{,}00{,}000 F$$
$$F = \text{Rs } 37{,}91{,}000 \div \text{Rs } 10{,}00{,}000 = 3.791$$

On the five-period line of Table 4, find the percentage column that is closest to 3.791. It is exactly 10%. If the factor (F) falls between the factors in two columns, straight-line interpolation is used to approximate IRR. This interpolation is illustrated in the Problem for Self-Study.

A project is accepted only if IRR equals or exceeds required rate of return (RRR). In the Top-Spin example, the carbon-fiber machine has an IRR of 10%, which is greater than the RRR of 8%. On the basis of financial factors, Top-Spin should invest in the new machine. In general, the NPV and IRR decision rules result in consistent project acceptance or rejection decisions. If IRR exceeds RRR, then the project has a positive NPV (favoring acceptance). If IRR equals RRR, NPV = Rs 0, so project acceptance and rejection yield the same value. If IRR is less than RRR, NPV is negative (favoring rejection). Obviously, managers prefer projects with higher IRRs to projects with lower IRRs, if all other things are equal. The IRR of 10% means the cash inflows from the project are adequate to (1) recover the net initial investment in the project and (2) earn a return of exactly 10% on the investment tied up in the project over its useful life.

Comparison of Net Present Value and Internal Rate-of-Return Methods

The NPV method is generally regarded as the preferred method for project selection decisions. The reason is that choosing projects using the NPV criterion leads to shareholder value maximization. At an intuitive level, this occurs because the NPV measure for a project captures the value, in today's dollars, of the surplus the project generates for the firm's shareholders, over and above the required rate of return.[2] Next, we highlight some of the limitations of the IRR method relative to the NPV technique.

One advantage of the NPV method is that it expresses computations in amount, not in percentages. Therefore, we can sum NPVs of individual projects to calculate an NPV of a combination or portfolio of projects. In contrast, IRRs of individual projects cannot be added or averaged to represent the IRR of a combination of projects.

A second advantage is that the NPV of a project can always be computed and expressed as a unique number. From the sign and magnitude of this number, the firm can then make an accurate assessment of the financial consequences of accepting or rejecting the project. Under the IRR method, however, it is possible that more than one IRR may exist for a given project. In other words, there may be multiple discount rates that equate the NPV of a set of cash flows to zero. This is especially true when the signs of the cash flows switch over time, that is, when there are outflows, followed by inflows, followed by additional outflows and so forth. In such cases, it is difficult to know which of the IRR estimates should be compared to the firm's required rate of return.

A third advantage of the NPV method is that it can be used when the RRR varies over the life of a project. Suppose Top-Spin's management sets an RRR of 9% per year in years 1 and 2 and 12% per year in years 3, 4, and 5. Total present value of the cash inflows can be calculated as Rs 37,81,000 (computations not shown). It is not possible to use the IRR method in this case. That's because different RRRs in different years (9% annually for years 1 and 2 versus 12% annually for years 3, 4, and 5) mean there is no single RRR that the IRR (a single figure) can be compared against to decide if the project should be accepted or rejected.

Finally, there are specific settings in which the IRR method is prone to indicating erroneous decisions, such as when comparing mutually exclusive projects with unequal lives or unequal levels of initial investment. The reason is that the IRR method implicitly assumes that project cash flows can be reinvested at the *project's* rate of return. The NPV method, in contrast, accurately assumes that funds obtainable from competing project can be reinvested at the *company's* required rate of return.

Despite its limitations, surveys report widespread use of the IRR method.[3] Why? Probably because managers find the percentage return computed under the IRR method easy to understand and compare. Moreover, in most instances where a single project is being evaluated, their decisions would likely be unaffected by using IRR or NPV.

Sensitivity Analysis

To present the basics of the NPV and IRR methods, we have assumed that the expected values of cash flows will occur *for certain*. In reality, there is substantial uncertainty associated with the prediction of future cash flows. To examine how a result will change if the predicted financial outcomes are not achieved or if an underlying assumption changes, managers can use *sensitivity analysis*, a "what-if" technique introduced in Chapter 3.

[2] More detailed explanations of the preeminence of the NPV criterion can be found in corporate finance texts.

[3] In a recent survey, John Graham and Campbell Harvey found that 75.7% of CFOs always or almost always used IRR for capital budgeting decisions, while a slightly smaller number, 74.9%, always or almost always used the NPV criterion.

Exhibit 21-4

Net Present Value Calculations for Top-Spin's Carbon-Fiber Machine under Different Assumptions of Annual Cash Flows and Required Rates of Return[a]

	Required	Annual Cash Flows				
2	Rate of Return	Rs8,00,000	Rs9,00,000	Rs10,00,000	Rs11,00,000	RS12,00,000
3	6%	Rs(4,21,400)	Rs (200)	Rs4,21,000	Rs8,42,200	Rs12,63,400
4	8%	Rs(5,96,600)	Rs(1,97,300)	Rs2,02,000	Rs6,01,300	Rs10,00,600
5	10%	Rs(7,58,200)	Rs(3,79,100)	Re 0	Rs3,79,100	Rs7,58,200
6						
7	[a]All calculated amounts assume the project's useful life is five years.					

A common way to apply sensitivity analysis in capital budgeting decisions is to vary each of the inputs to the NPV calculation by a certain percentage and assess the effect of the change on the project's NPV. Sensitivity analysis can take various forms. Suppose the manager at Top-Spin believes forecasted savings are difficult to predict. She asks, "What are the minimum annual cash inflows that make the investment in a new carbon-fiber machine acceptable—that is, what inflows lead to an NPV = Re 0?" For the data in Exhibit 21-2, let A = Annual cash flow and let NPV = Re 0. Net initial investment is Rs 37,91,000, and the present value factor at the 8% required annual rate of return for a five-year annuity of Rs 1 is 3.993. Then:

$$\begin{aligned} \text{NPV} &= \text{Re } 0 \\ 3.993A - \text{Rs } 37{,}91{,}000 &= \text{Re } 0 \\ 3.993A &= \text{Rs } 37{,}91{,}000 \\ A &= \text{Rs } 9{,}49{,}410 \end{aligned}$$

Decision Point

What are the two primary discounted cash flow (DCF) methods for project evaluation?

At the discount rate of 8% per year, the annual (after tax) revenue growth can decrease to Rs 9,49,410 (a decline of Rs 10,00,000 − Rs 9,49,410 = Rs 50,590) before the NPV falls to Re 0. If the manager believes she can attain annual revenue growth of at least Rs 9,49,410, she can justify investing in the carbon-fiber machine on financial grounds.

Exhibit 21-4 shows that variations in the annual cash inflows or RRR significantly affect the NPV of the carbon-fiber machine project. NPVs can also vary with different useful lives of a project. Sensitivity analysis helps managers to focus on decisions that are most sensitive to different assumptions and to worry less about decisions that are not so sensitive.

Payback Method

Learning Objective 3

Use and evaluate the payback method

. . . to calculate the time it takes to recoup the investment

We now consider the third method for analyzing the financial aspects of projects. The **payback method** measures the time it will take to recoup, in the form of expected future cash flows, the net initial investment in a project. As in NPV and IRR, payback (also called payback period) does not distinguish among the sources of cash flows, such as from operations, purchase or sale of equipment, or investment or recovery of working capital. Payback is simplest to calculate when a project has uniform cash flows. We consider this case first.

Uniform Cash Flows

In the Top-Spin example, the carbon-fiber machine costs Rs 37,90,000, has a five-year expected useful life. Suppose that the machine is expected to raise revenues (cash inflows) by Rs 10,00,000 *uniformly* each year. The payback period is:

$$\text{Payback period} = \frac{\text{Net initial investment}}{\text{Uniform increase in annual future cash flows}}$$

$$= \frac{\text{Rs } 37{,}91{,}000}{\text{Rs } 10{,}00{,}000} = 3.8 \text{ years}^4$$

[4] Revenues from the new carbon-fiber machine occur uniformly *throughout* the year, but for simplicity in calculating NPV and IRR, we assume they occur at the *end* of each year. A literal interpretation of this assumption would imply a payback of 4 years because Top-Spin will only recover its investment when cash inflows occur at the end of year 4. The calculations shown in the chapter, however, better approximate Top-Spin's payback on the basis of uniform cash flows throughout the year.

The payback method highlights liquidity, a factor that often plays a role in capital budgeting decisions, particularly when the investments are large. Managers prefer projects with shorter payback periods (projects that are more liquid) to projects with longer payback periods, if all other things are equal. Projects with shorter payback periods give an organization more flexibility because funds for other projects become available sooner. Also, managers are less confident about cash flow predictions that stretch far into the future, again favoring shorter payback periods.

Unlike the NPV and IRR methods where management selected a RRR, under the payback method, management chooses a cutoff period for a project. Projects with a payback period that is less than the cutoff period are considered acceptable, and those with a payback period that is longer than the cutoff period are rejected. Japanese companies favor the payback method over other methods and use cutoff periods ranging from three to five years depending on the risks involved with the project. In general, modern risk management calls for using shorter cutoff periods, the riskier the project. If Top-Spin's cutoff period under the payback method is three years, it will reject the new machine.

The payback method is easy to understand. As in DCF methods, the payback method is not affected by accrual accounting conventions such as depreciation. Payback is a useful measure when (1) preliminary screening of many proposals is necessary, (2) interest rates are high, and (3) the expected cash flows in later years of a project are highly uncertain. Under these conditions, companies give much more weight to cash flows in early periods of a capital budgeting project and to recovering the investments they have made, thereby making the payback criterion especially relevant.

Two weaknesses of the payback method are that (1) it fails to explicitly incorporate the time value of money and (2) it does not consider a project's cash flows after the payback period. Consider an alternative to the Rs 37,91,000 carbon-fiber machine. Another carbon-fiber machine, with a three-year useful life and no terminal disposal value, requires only a Rs 30,00,000 net initial investment and will also result in cash inflows of Rs 10,00,000 per year. First, compare the payback periods:

$$\text{Machine 1} = \frac{\text{Rs } 37{,}91{,}000}{\text{Rs } 10{,}00{,}000} = 3.8 \text{ years}$$

$$\text{Machine 2} = \frac{\text{Rs } 30{,}00{,}000}{\text{Rs } 10{,}00{,}000} = 3.0 \text{ years}$$

The payback criterion favors machine 2, with the shorter payback. If the cutoff period were three years, machine 1 would fail to meet the payback criterion.

Consider next the NPV of the two investment options using Top-Spin's 8% required rate of return for the carbon-fiber machine investment. At a discount rate of 8%, the NPV of machine 2 is – Rs 4,22,900 (2.577, the present value annuity factor for three years at 8% per year from Table 4, times Rs 10,00,000 = Rs 25,77,000 minus net initial investment of Rs 30,00,000). Machine 1, as we know, has a positive NPV of Rs 2,02,000 (from Exhibit 21-2). The NPV criterion suggests Top-Spin should acquire machine 1. Machine 2, with a negative NPV, would fail to meet the NPV criterion.

The payback method gives a different answer from the NPV method in this example because the payback method ignores cash flows after the payback period and ignores the time value of money. Another problem with the payback method is that choosing too short a cutoff period for project acceptance may promote the selection of only short-lived projects. An organization will tend to reject long-run, positive-NPV projects. Despite these differences, companies find it useful to look at both NPV and payback when making capital investment decisions.

Nonuniform Cash Flows

When cash flows are not uniform, as is most often the case, the payback computation takes a cumulative form: The cash flows over successive years are accumulated until the amount of net initial investment is recovered. Assume that Venture Law Group is considering the purchase of videoconferencing equipment for Rs 15,00,000. The equipment is expected to provide a total cash savings of Rs 38,00,000 over the next five years, due to reduced travel costs and more effective use of associates' time. The cash savings occur uniformly throughout each year, but nonuniformly across years.

Year	Cash Savings	Cumulative Cash Savings	Net Initial Investment Unrecovered at End of Year
0	—	—	Rs 15,00,000
1	Rs 5,00,000	Rs 5,00,000	10,00,000
2	5,50,000	10,50,000	4,50,000
3	6,00,000	16,50,000	—
4	8,50,000	25,00,000	—
5	9,00,000	34,00,000	—

It is clear from the chart that payback occurs during the third year. Straight-line interpolation within the third year reveals that the final Rs 4,50,000 needed to recover the Rs 15,00,000 investment (that is, Rs 15,00,000 − Rs 10,50,000 recovered by the end of year 2) will be achieved halfway through year 3 (in which Rs 6,00,000 of cash savings occur):

$$\text{Payback period} = 2 \text{ years} + \left(\frac{\text{Rs } 4{,}50{,}000}{\text{Rs } 8{,}00{,}000} \times 1 \text{ year}\right) = 2.75 \text{ years}$$

It is relatively simple to adjust the payback method to incorporate the time value of money by using a similar cumulative approach. The **discounted payback method** calculates the amount of time required for the discounted expected future cash flows to recoup the net initial investment in a project. For the videoconferencing example, we can modify the preceding chart by discounting the cash flows at the 8% required rate of return.

Year (1)	Cash Savings (2)	Present Value of Rs 10 Discounted at 8% (3)	Discounted Cash Savings (4) = (2) × (3)	Cumulative Discounted Cash Savings (5)	Net Initial Investment Unrecovered at End of Year (6)
0	—	1.000	—	—	Rs 15,00,000
1	Rs 5,00,000	0.926	Rs 4,63,000	Rs 4,63,000	10,37,000
2	5,50,000	0.857	4,71,350	9,34,350	5,65,650
3	6,00,000	0.794	4,76,400	14,10,750	89,250
4	8,50,000	0.735	6,24,750	20,35,500	—
5	9,00,000	0.681	6,12,900	28,48,400	—

The fourth column represents the present values of the future cash savings. It is evident from the chart that discounted payback occurs between years 3 and 4. At the end of the third year, Rs 89,250 of the initial investment is still unrecovered. Comparing this to the Rs 6,24,750 in present value of savings achieved in the fourth year, straight-line interpolation then reveals that the discounted payback period is exactly one-seventh of the way into the fourth year:

$$\text{Discounted payback period} = 3 \text{ years} + \left(\frac{\text{Rs } 89{,}250}{\text{Rs } 6{,}24{,}750} \times 1 \text{ year}\right) = 3.14 \text{ years}$$

While discounted payback does incorporate the time value of money, it is still subject to the other criticism of the payback method—cash flows beyond the discounted payback period are ignored, resulting in a bias toward shorter-term projects. Companies such as Hewlett-Packard value the discounted payback method (HP refers to it as "breakeven time") because they view longer-term cash flows as inherently unpredictable in high-growth industries.

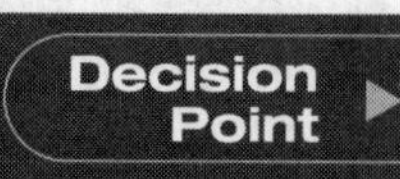

What are the payback and discounted payback methods? What are their main weaknesses?

Finally, the videoconferencing example has a single cash outflow of Rs 15,00,000 in year 0. When a project has multiple cash outflows occurring at different points in time, these outflows are first aggregated to obtain a total cash-outflow figure for the project. For computing the payback period, the cash flows are simply added, with no adjustment for the time value of money. For calculating the discounted payback period, the present values of the outflows are added instead.

Accrual Accounting Rate-of-Return Method

Learning Objective 4

Use and evaluate the accrual accounting rate-of-return (AARR) method

. . . after-tax operating income divided by investment

We now consider a fourth method for analyzing the financial aspects of capital budgeting projects. The **accrual accounting rate of return (AARR)** method divides the average annual (accrual accounting) income of a project by a measure of the investment in it. The ratio is also called the **accounting rate of return.** We illustrate AARR for the Top-Spin example using the project's net initial investment as the amount in the denominator:

$$\text{Accrual accounting rate of return} = \frac{\text{Increase in expected average annual after-tax operating income}}{\text{Net initial investment}}$$

If Top-Spin purchases the new carbon-fiber machine, its net initial investment is Rs 37,91,000. The increase in expected average annual after-tax operating cash inflows is Rs 9,82,000. This amount is the expected after-tax total operating cash inflows of Rs 49,10,000 (Rs 10,00,000 for four years and Rs 9,10,000 in year 5), divided by the time horizon of five years. Suppose that the new machine results in additional depreciation deductions of Rs 7,00,000 per year (Rs 7,80,000 in annual depreciation for the new machine, relative to Rs 80,000 per year on the existing machine).[5] The increase in expected average annual after-tax income is therefore Rs 2,82,000 (the difference between the cash flow increase of Rs 9,82,000 and the depreciation increase of Rs 7,00,000). The AARR on net initial investment is computed as follows:

$$AARR = \frac{\text{Rs } 9{,}82{,}000 - \text{Rs } 7{,}00{,}000}{\text{Rs } 37{,}91{,}000} = \frac{\text{Rs } 2{,}82{,}000 \text{ per year}}{\text{Rs } 37{,}91{,}000} = 0.074, \text{ or } 7.4\% \text{ per year}$$

The 7.4% figure for AARR indicates the average rate at which a dollar of investment generates after-tax operating income. The new carbon-fiber machine has a low AARR for two reasons: (1) the use of net initial investment as the denominator, and (2) the use of income as the numerator, which necessitates deducting depreciation charges from the annual operating cash flows. To mitigate the first issue, many companies calculate AARR using an average level of investment. This alternative procedure recognizes that the book value of the investment declines over time. In its simplest form, average investment for Top-Spin (with terminal disposal value of machine equal to Re 0 and terminal recovery of working capital equal to Rs 90,000) is

$$\text{Average investment over five years} = \frac{\text{Net initial investment} + \text{returned working capital}}{2}$$

$$= \frac{\text{Rs } 37{,}91{,}000 + \text{Rs } 90{,}000}{2} = \text{Rs } 19{,}40{,}500$$

$$AARR = \frac{\text{Rs } 2{,}82{,}000}{\text{Rs } 19{,}40{,}500} = 0.145, \text{ or } 14.5\% \text{ per year}$$

Our point here is that companies vary in how they calculate AARR. There is no uniformly preferred approach. Be sure you understand how AARR is defined in each individual situation. Projects whose AARR exceeds a specified hurdle required rate of return are regarded as acceptable (the higher the AARR, the better the project is considered to be).

The AARR method is similar to the IRR method in that both methods calculate a rate-of-return percentage. The AARR method calculates return using operating-income numbers after considering accruals and taxes, whereas the IRR method calculates return on the basis of after-tax cash flows and the time value of money. Because cash flows and time value of money are central to capital budgeting decisions, the IRR method is regarded as better than the AARR method.

AARR computations are easy to understand, and they use numbers reported in the financial statements. AARR gives managers an idea of how the accounting numbers they will report in the future will be affected if a project is accepted. Unlike the payback method, which ignores cash flows after the payback period, the AARR method considers income

[5] We provide further details on these numbers in the next section; see next page.

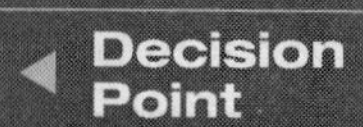

Decision Point

What are the strengths and weaknesses of the accrual accounting rate-of-return (AARR) method for evaluating long-term projects?

earned *throughout* a project's expected useful life. Unlike the NPV method, the AARR method uses accrual accounting income numbers, it does not track cash flows, and it ignores the time value of money. Critics cite these arguments as drawbacks of the AARR method.

Overall, keep in mind that companies frequently use multiple methods for evaluating capital investment decisions. When different methods lead to different rankings of projects, finance theory suggests that more weight be given to the NPV method because the assumptions made by the NPV method are most consistent with making decisions that maximize company value.

Relevant Cash Flows in Discounted Cash Flow Analysis

Learning Objective 5

Identify relevant cash inflows and outflows for capital budgeting decisions

. . . the differences in expected future cash flows resulting from the investment

So far, we have so far examined methods for evaluating long-term projects in settings where the expected future cash flows of interest were assumed to be known. But one of the biggest challenges in capital budgeting, particularly DCF analysis, is determining which cash flows are relevant in making an investment selection. Relevant cash flows are the differences in expected future cash flows as a result of making the investment. In the Top-Spin example, the relevant cash flows are the differences in expected future cash flows between continuing to use the old technology or updating its technology with the purchase of a new machine. *When reading this section, focus on identifying expected future cash flows and the differences in expected future cash flows.*

To illustrate relevant cash flow analysis, consider a more complex version of the Top-Spin example with these additional assumptions:

- Top-Spin is a profitable company. The income tax rate is 40% of operating income each year.
- The before-tax additional revenues from the carbon-fiber machine are Rs 12,00,000 in years 1 through 4 and Rs 10,50,000 in year 5.
- For tax purposes, Top-Spin uses the straight-line depreciation method and assumes no terminal disposal value.
- Gains or losses on the sale of depreciable assets are taxed at the same rate as ordinary income.
- The tax effects of cash inflows and outflows occur at the same time that the cash inflows and outflows occur.
- Top-Spin uses an 8% required rate of return for discounting after-tax cash flows.

Summary data for the machines are:

	Old Graphite Machine	New Carbon-Fiber Machine
Purchase price	–	Rs 39,00,000
Current book value	Rs 4,00,000	–
Current disposal value	65,000	Not applicable
Terminal disposal value 5 years from now	0	0
Annual depreciation	80,000[a]	7,80,000[b]
Working capital required	60,000	1,50,000

[a] Rs 4,00,000 ÷ 5 years = Rs 80,000 annual depreciation.
[b] Rs 39,00,000 ÷ 5 years = Rs 7,80,000 annual depreciation.

Relevant After-Tax Flows

We use the concepts of differential cost and differential revenue introduced in Chapter 11. We compare (1) the after-tax cash outflows as a result of replacing the old machine with (2) the additional after-tax cash inflows generated from using the new machine rather than the old machine.

As Benjamin Franklin said, "Two things in life are certain: death and taxes." Income taxes are a fact of life for most corporations and individuals. It is important first to understand how income taxes affect cash flows in each year. Exhibit 21-5 shows how investing in the new machine will affect Top-Spin's cash flow from operations and its income taxes in year 1. Recall that Top-Spin will generate Rs 12,00,000 in before-tax revenues by

Exhibit 21-5

Effect on Cash Flow from Operations, Net of Income Taxes, in Year 1 for Top-Spin's Investment in the New Carbon-Fiber Machine

PANEL A: Two Methods Based on the Income Statement

R	Revenues from investment in machine	Rs12,00,000
D	Additional depreciation deduction	7,00,000
OI	Increase in operating income	5,00,000
T	Income taxes (Income tax rate $t \times OI$) = 40% × Rs5,00,000	2,00,000
NI	Increase in net income	Rs 3,00,000
	Increase in cash flow from operations, net of income taxes	
	Method 1: $R - T$ = Rs12,00,000 – Rs2,00,000 = Rs10,00,000 or	
	Method 2: $NI + D$ = Rs3,00,000 + Rs7,00,000 = Rs10,00,000	

PANEL B: Item-by-Item Method

	Effect of cash operating flows	
R	Operating cash inflows from investment in machine	Rs12,00,000
$t \times R$	Deduct income tax cash outflow at 40%	4,80,000
$R - (t \times R) = (1 - t) \times R$	After-tax cash flow from operations (excluding the depreciation effect)	7,20,000
	Effect of depreciation	
D	Additional depreciation deduction, Rs7,00,000	
$t \times D$	Income tax cash savings from additional depreciation deduction at 40% × Rs7,00,000	2,80,000
$(1 - t) \times R + (t \times D) = R - (t \times R) + (t \times D)$	Cash flow from operations, net of income taxes	Rs10,00,000

investing in the new machine but will record additional depreciation of Rs 7,00,000 (Rs 7,80,000 – Rs 80,000) for tax purposes.

Panel A shows that the year 1 cash flow from operations, net of income taxes, equals Rs 10,00,000, using two methods based on the income statement. The first method focuses on cash items only, the Rs 12,00,000 cash revenues minus income taxes of Rs 2,00,000. The second method starts with the Rs 3,00,000 increase in net income (calculated after subtracting the Rs 7,00,000 additional depreciation deductions for income tax purposes) and adds back that Rs 7,00,000, because depreciation is an operating cost that reduces net income but is a noncash item itself.

Panel B of Exhibit 21-5 describes a third method that we will use frequently to compute cash flow from operations, net of income taxes. The easiest way to interpret the third method is to think of the government as a 40% (equal to the tax rate) partner in Top-Spin. Each time Top-Spin obtains cost revenues, R, (or cash saving in excess of cash cost), its income is higher by R, so it will pay 40% of the cash revenues ($0.40R$) in taxes. This results in additional after-tax cash operating flows of $R - 0.40R$, which in this example is Rs 12,00,000 – (0.40 × Rs 12,00,000) = Rs 7,20,000, or Rs 12,00,000 × (1 – 0.40) = Rs 7,20,000.

To achieve the higher revenues, R, Top-Spin incurs higher depreciation charges, D, from investing in the new machine. Depreciation costs do not directly affect cash flows because depreciation is a noncash cost, but higher depreciation cost *lowers* Top-Spin's taxable income by D, saving income tax cash outflows of $0.40D$, which in this example is 0.40 × Rs 7,00,000 = Rs 2,80,000.

Letting t = tax rate, cash flow from operations, net of income taxes, in this example equals the revenues R, minus the tax payments on these savings, $t \times R$, plus the tax savings on depreciation deductions, $t \times D$: Rs 12,00,000 – (0.40 × Rs 12,00,000) + (0.40 × Rs 7,00,000) = Rs 12,00,000 – Rs 4,80,000 + Rs 2,80,000 = Rs 10,00,000.

By the same logic, each time Top-Spin has a gain on the sale of assets, G, it will show tax outflows, $t \times G$; and each time Top-Spin has a loss on the sale of assets, L, it will show tax benefits or savings, $t \times L$.

Categories of Cash Flows

A capital investment project typically has three categories of cash flows: (1) net initial investment in the project, which includes the acquisition of assets and any associated additions to working capital, minus the after-tax cash flow from the disposal of existing assets; (2) after-tax cash flow from operations (including income tax cash savings from annual depreciation deductions); and (3) after-tax cash flow from terminal disposal of an asset and recovery of working capital. We use the Top-Spin example to discuss these three categories.

As you work through the cash flows in each category, refer to Exhibit 21-6. This exhibit sketches the relevant cash flows for Top-Spin's decision to purchase the new machine as described in items 1 through 3 here. Note that the total relevant cash flows for each year equal the relevant cash flows used in Exhibits 21-2 and 21-3 to illustrate the NPV and IRR methods.

1. Net Initial Investment Three components of net-initial-investment cash flows are (a) cash outflow to purchase the machine, (b) cash outflow for working capital, and (c) after-tax cash inflow from current disposal of the old machine.

1a. *Initial machine investment.* These outflows, made for purchasing plant and equipment, occur at the beginning of the project's life and include cash outflows for transporting and installing the equipment. In the Top-Spin example, the Rs 39,00,000 cost (including transportation and installation) of the carbon-fiber machine is an outflow in year 0. These cash flows are relevant to the capital budgeting decision because they will be incurred only if Top-Spin decides to purchase the new machine.

1b. *Initial working-capital investment.* Initial investments in plant and equipment are usually accompanied by additional investments in working capital. These additional investments take the form of current assets, such as accounts receivable and inventories, minus current liabilities, such as accounts payable. Working-capital investments are similar to plant and equipment investments in that they require cash. The magnitude of the investment generally increases as a function of the level of additional sales generated by the project. However, the exact relationship varies based on the nature of the project and the operating cycle of the industry. For a given rupee of sales, a maker of heavy equipment, for example, would require more working capital support than Top-Spin, which in turn has to invest more in working capital than a retail grocery store.

The Top-Spin example assumes a Rs 90,000 additional investment in working capital (for supplies and spare-parts inventory) if the new machine is acquired. The additional working-capital investment is the difference between working capital

Exhibit 21-6 Relevant Cash Inflows and Outflows for Top-Spin's Carbon-Fiber Machine

File Edit View Insert Format Tools Data Window Help

	A	B	C	D	E	F	G	H
1				Sketch of Relevant Cash Flows at End of Year				
2			0	1	2	3	4	5
3	1a.	Initial machine investment	Rs (39,00,000)					
4	1b.	Initial working-capital investment	(90,000)					
5	1c.	After-tax cash flow from current disposal						
6		of old machine	1,99,000					
7	Net initial investment		(37,91,000)					
8	2a.	Annual after-tax cash flow from operations						
9		(excluding the depreciation effect)		Rs 7,20,000	Rs 7,20,000	Rs 7,20,000	Rs 7,20,000	6,30,000
10	2b.	Income tax cash savings from annual						
11		depreciation deductions		2,80,000	2,80,000	2,80,000	2,80,000	2,80,000
12	3a.	After-tax cash flow from terminal disposal						
13		of machine						0
14	3b.	After-tax cash flow from recovery of						
15		working capital						90,000
16	Total relevant cash flows,							
17	as shown in Exhibits 21-2 and 21-3		Rs (37,91,000)	Rs 10,00,000	Rs 10,00,000	Rs 10,00,000	Rs 10,00,000	Rs 10,00,000
18								

required to operate the new machine (Rs 1,50,000) and working capital required to operate the old machine (Rs 60,000). The Rs 90,000 additional investment in working capital is a cash outflow in year 0 and is returned at the end of year 5.

1c. *After-tax cash flow from current disposal of old machine.* Any cash received from disposal of the old machine is a relevant cash inflow (in year 0). That's because it is an expected future cash flow that differs between the alternatives of investing and not investing in the new machine. Only if Top-Spin invests in the new carbon-fiber machine, will it dispose of the old machine for Rs 65,000. Recall that the book value (which is original cost minus accumulated depreciation) of the old equipment is irrelevant to the decision (Chapter 11). It is a past, or sunk, cost. Nothing can change what was originally paid.

To calculate the tax consequences of disposing of the old machine, we compute the gain or loss on disposal:

Current disposal value of old machine	Rs 65,000
Deduct current book value of old machine	4,00,000
Loss on disposal of machine	**Rs (3,35,000)**

Any loss on the sale of assets lowers taxable income and results in tax savings. The after-tax cash flow from disposal of the old machine equals:

Current disposal value of old machine	Rs 65,000
Tax savings on loss (0.40 × Rs 3,35,000)	1,34,000
After-tax cash inflow from current disposal of old machine	Rs 1,99,000

The sum of items **1a**, **1b**, and **1c** appears in Exhibit 21-6 as the year 0 net initial investment for the new carbon-fiber machine equal to Rs 37,91,000 (initial machine investment, Rs 39,00,000, plus additional working-capital investment, Rs 90,000, minus after-tax cash inflow from current disposal of the old machine, Rs 1,99,000).[6]

2. Cash Flow from Operations This category includes the difference between each year's cash flow from operations under the two alternatives. Organizations make capital investments to generate future cash inflows. These inflows may result from savings in operating costs, or, as for Top-Spin, from producing and selling additional goods. Annual cash flow from operations can be net outflows in some years. BP makes periodic upgrades to its oil extraction equipment, and in years of upgrades, cash flow from operations tends to be negative for the site being upgraded, albeit in the long-run such upgrades are NPV positive. Always focus on cash flow from operations, not on revenues and expenses under accrual accounting.

Top-Spin's additional revenues—Rs 12,00,000 in each of the first four years and Rs 10,50,000 in the fifth year—are relevant because they are expected future cash flows that will differ between the alternatives of investing and not investing in the new machine. The after-tax effects of these cash flows follow.

2a. *Annual after-tax cash flow from operations (excluding the depreciation effect).* The 40% tax rate reduces the benefit of the Rs 12,00,000 additional revenue for years 1 through 4 with the new carbon-fiber machine. After-tax cash flow (excluding the depreciation effect) is:

Annual cash flow from operations with new machine	Rs 12,00,000
Deduct income tax payments (0.40 × Rs 12,00,000)	4,80,000
Annual after-tax cash flow from operations	Rs 7,20,000

For year 5, the after-tax cash flow (excluding the depreciation effect) is:

Annual cash flow from operations with new machine	Rs 10,50,000
Deduct income tax payments (0.40 × Rs 10,50,000)	4,20,000
Annual after-tax cash flow from operations	Rs 6,30,000

[6] To illustrate the case when there is a gain on disposal, suppose that the old machine could be sold now for Rs 5,00,000 instead. Then, the firm would record a gain on disposal of Rs 1,00,000 (Rs 5,00,000 less the book value of Rs 4,00,000), resulting in additional tax payments of Rs 40,000 (0.40 tax rate × Rs 1,00,000 gain). The after-tax cash inflow from current disposal would therefore equal Rs 4,60,000 (the disposal value of Rs 5,00,000, less the tax payment of Rs 40,000).

Exhibit 21-6, item **2a**, shows the Rs 7,20,000 amounts for each of the years 1 through 4 and Rs 6,30,000 for year 5.

To reinforce the idea about focusing on cash flows, consider the following additional fact about the Top-Spin example. Suppose the total plant overhead costs will not change whether the new machine is purchased or the old machine is kept. The production plant's overhead costs are allocated to individual machines—Top-Spin has several—on the basis of the labor costs for operating each machine. Because the new carbon-fiber machine would have lower labor costs, overhead costs allocated to it would be Rs 3,00,000 less than the amount allocated to the machine it would replace. How should Top-Spin incorporate the decrease in allocated overhead costs of Rs 3,00,000 in the relevant cash flow analysis?

To answer that question, we need to ask, "Do *total* overhead costs decrease at Top-Spin's production plant as a result of acquiring the new machine?" In our example, they do not. Total overhead costs of the production plant remain the same whether or not the new machine is acquired. *Only the overhead costs allocated to individual machines change.* The overhead costs allocated to the new machine are Rs 3,00,000 less than the amount allocated to the machine it would replace. This Rs 3,00,000 difference in overhead would be allocated to *other* machines in the department. That is, no cash flow savings in total overhead would occur. Therefore, the Rs 3,00,000 should not be included as part of annual cash savings from operations.

Next consider the effects of depreciation. *The depreciation line item is itself irrelevant in DCF analysis.* That's because it's a noncash allocation of costs, whereas DCF is based on inflows and outflows of *cash*. In DCF methods, the initial cost of equipment is regarded as a *lump-sum* outflow of cash in year 0. Deducting depreciation expenses from operating cash inflows would result in counting the lump-sum amount twice. *However, depreciation results in income tax cash savings. These tax savings are a relevant cash flow.*

2b. *Income tax cash savings from annual depreciation deductions.* Tax deductions for depreciation, in effect, partially offset the cost of acquiring the new carbon-fiber machine. The additional annual depreciation deduction of Rs 7,00,000 results in incremental income tax cash savings of Rs 7,00,000 × 0.4, or Rs 2,80,000 annually. Exhibit 21-6, item **2b**, shows these Rs 2,80,000 amounts for years 1 through 5.[7]

For economic-policy reasons, usually to encourage (or in some cases, discourage) investments, tax laws specify which depreciation methods and which depreciable lives are permitted. Suppose the government permitted accelerated depreciation to be used, allowing for higher depreciation deductions in earlier years. If allowable, should Top-Spin use accelerated depreciation? Yes, because there is a general rule in tax planning for profitable companies such as Top-Spin: When there is a legal choice, take the depreciation (or any other deduction) sooner rather than later. Doing so causes the (cash) income tax savings to occur earlier, which increases the project's NPV.

3. Terminal Disposal of Investment The disposal of the new investment generally increases cash inflow when the project terminates. Errors in forecasting terminal disposal value are seldom critical for long-duration projects because the present value of amounts to be received in the distant future is usually small. Two components of the terminal disposal value of an investment are (a) after-tax cash flow from terminal disposal of machines and (b) after-tax cash flow from recovery of working capital.

3a. *After-tax cash flow from terminal disposal of machines.* At the end of the useful life of the project, the machine's terminal disposal value may be Rs 0 or an amount considerably less than the net initial investment. The relevant cash inflow is the difference in expected after-tax cash inflow from terminal disposal at the end of five years under the two alternatives of purchasing the new machine or keeping the old machinc.

---

[7] If Top-Spin were a nonprofit foundation not subject to income taxes, cash flow from operations would equal Rs 12,00,000 in years 1 through 4 and Rs 10,50,000 in year 5. The revenues would not be reduced by 40%, nor would there be income tax cash savings from the depreciation deduction.

Although the old machine has a positive terminal disposal value today (year 0), in year 5, it will have a zero terminal value. As such, both the existing and the new machines have zero after-tax cash inflow from terminal disposal in year 5. Hence, the difference in after-tax cash inflow from terminal disposal is also Re 0.

In this example, there are no tax effects at the terminal point because both the existing and new machine have disposal values that equal their book values at the time of disposal (in each case, this value is Re 0). What if either the existing or the new machine had a terminal value that differed from its book value at the time of disposal? In that case, the approach for computing the terminal inflow is identical to that for calculating the after-tax cash flow from current disposal illustrated earlier in part 1c.

3b. *After-tax cash flow from terminal recovery of working-capital investment.* The initial investment in working capital is usually fully recouped when the project is terminated. At that time, inventories and accounts receivable necessary to support the project are no longer needed. Top-Spin receives cash equal to the book value of its working capital. Thus, there is no gain or loss on working capital and, hence, no tax consequences. The relevant cash inflow is the difference in the expected working capital recovered under the two alternatives. At the end of year 5, Top-Spin recovers Rs 1,50,000 cash from working capital if it invests in the new carbon-fiber machine versus Rs 60,000 if it continues to use the old machine. The relevant cash inflow at the end of year 5 if Top-Spin invests in the new machine is thus Rs 90,000 (Rs 1,50,000 − Rs 60,000).

Some capital investment projects *reduce* working capital. Assume that a computer-integrated manufacturing (CIM) project with a seven-year life will reduce inventories and, hence, working capital by Rs 20 crore from, say, Rs 50 crore to Rs 30 crore. This reduction will be represented as a Rs 20 crore cash *inflow* for the project in year 0. At the end of seven years, the recovery of working capital will show a relevant incremental cash *outflow* of Rs 20 crore. That's because, at the end of year 7, the company recovers only Rs 30 crore of working capital under CIM, rather than the Rs 50 crore of working capital it would have recovered had it not implemented CIM.

Exhibit 21-6 shows items **3a** and **3b** in the year 5 column. The relevant cash flows in Exhibit 21-6 serve as inputs for the four capital budgeting methods described earlier in the chapter.

Decision Point

What are the relevant cash inflows and outflows for capital budgeting decisions? How should accrual accounting concepts be considered?

Project Management and Performance Evaluation

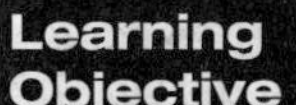

Learning Objective 6

Understand issues involved in implementing capital budgeting decisions and evaluating managerial performance

. . . the importance of post-investment audits and the correct choice of performance measures

We have so far looked at ways to identify relevant cash flows and appropriate techniques for analyzing them. The final stage (stage 5) of capital budgeting begins with implementing the decision, or managing the project.[8] This includes management control of the investment activity itself, as well as management control of the project as a whole.

Capital budgeting projects, such as purchasing a carbon-fiber machine or videoconferencing equipment, are easier to implement than projects that involve building shopping malls or manufacturing plants. The building projects are more complex, so monitoring and controlling the investment schedules and budgets are critical to successfully completing the investment activity. This leads to the second dimension of stage 5 in the capital budgeting process: *evaluate performance and learn.*

Post-Investment Audits

A post-investment audit provides management with feedback about the performance of a project, so management can compare actual results to the costs and benefits expected at the time the project was selected. Suppose actual outcomes (such as additional revenues from the new carbon-fiber machine in the Top-Spin example) are much lower than expected. Management must then investigate to determine if this result occurred because

[8] In this section, we do not consider the different options for financing a project (refer to a text on corporate finance for details).

the original estimates were overly optimistic or because of implementation problems. Either of these explanations is a concern.

Optimistic estimates may result in the acceptance of a project that should have been rejected. To discourage optimistic estimates, companies such as DuPont maintain records comparing actual results to the estimates made by individual managers when seeking approval for capital investments. Post-investment audits punish inaccurate estimates, and therefore discourage unrealistic forecasts. This prevents managers from overstating project cash inflows and accepting projects that should never have been undertaken. Implementation problems, such as weak project management, poor quality control, or inadequate marketing are also a concern. Post-investment audits help to alert senior management to these problems so that they can be quickly corrected.

However, post-investment audits require thoughtfulness and care. They should be done only after project outcomes have stabilized because performing audits too early may yield misleading feedback. Obtaining actual results to compare against estimates is often not easy. For example, additional revenues from the new carbon-fiber technology may not be comparable to the estimated revenues because in any particular season, the rise or decline of a tennis star can greatly affect the popularity of the sport and the subsequent demand for racquets. A better evaluation would look at the average revenues across multiple of seasons.

Performance Evaluation

As the preceding discussion suggests, ideally one should evaluate managers on a project-by-project basis and look at how well managers achieve the amounts and timing of forecasted cash flows. In practice, however, managers are often evaluated based on aggregate information, especially when multiple projects are underway at any point in time. It is important then to ensure that the method of evaluation does not conflict with the use of the NPV method for making capital budgeting decisions. For example, suppose that Top-Spin uses the accrual accounting rate of return generated in each period to assess managerial performance. We know from the NPV method that the manager of the racquet production plant should purchase the carbon-fiber machine because it has a positive NPV of Rs 2,02,000. Despite that, the project may be rejected if the AARR of 7.4% on the net initial investment is lower than the minimum accounting rate of return the manager is required to achieve.

There is an inconsistency between using the NPV method as best for capital budgeting decisions and then using a different method to evaluate performance. This inconsistency means managers are tempted to make capital budgeting decisions on the basis of the method by which they are being evaluated. Such temptations become more pronounced if managers are frequently transferred (or promoted), or if their bonuses are affected by the level of year-to-year accrual income.

Other conflicts between decision making and performance evaluation persist even if a company uses similar measures for both purposes. If the AARR on the carbon-fiber machine exceeds the minimum required AARR but is below the current AARR of the production plant, the manager may still be tempted to reject purchase of the carbon-fiber machine because the lower AARR of the carbon-fiber machine will reduce the AARR of the entire plant and hurt the manager's reported performance. Or, consider an example where the cash inflows from the carbon-fiber machine occur mostly in the later years of the project. Then, even if the AARR on the project exceeds the current AARR of the plant (as well as the minimum required return), the manager may still reject the purchase since it will have a negative effect on the realized accrual accounting rate of return for the first few years. In Chapter 23, we study these conflicts in greater depth and describe how performance evaluation models such as economic value added (EVA®) help achieve greater congruency with decision-making models.

What conflicts can arise between using DCF methods for capital budgeting decisions and accrual accounting for performance evaluation? How can these conflicts be reduced?

Strategic Considerations in Capital Budgeting

A company's strategy is the source of its strategic capital budgeting decisions. Strategic decisions by United Airlines, Westin Hotels, Federal Express, and Pizza Hut to expand in Europe and Asia required capital investments to be made in several countries (see also

Concepts in Action

International Capital Budgeting at Disney

The Walt Disney Company, one of the world's leading entertainment producers, had more than $36 billion in 2009 revenue through movies, television networks, branded products, and theme parks and resorts. Within its theme park business, Disney spends around $1 billion annually in capital investments for new theme parks, rides and attractions, and other park construction and improvements. This money is divided between its domestic properties and international parks in Paris, Hong Kong, and Tokyo.

Years ago, Disney developed a robust capital budgeting approval process. Project approval relied heavily on projected returns on capital investment as measured by net present value (NPV) and internal rate of return (IRR) calculations. While this worked well for Disney's investments in its domestic theme park business, the company experienced challenges when it considered building the DisneySea theme park near Tokyo, Japan.

While capital budgeting in the United States relies on discounted cash flow analysis, Japanese firms frequently use the average accounting return (AAR) method instead. AAR is analogous to an accrual accounting rate of return (AARR) measure based on average investment. However, it focuses on the first few years of a project (five years, in the case of DisneySea) and ignores terminal values.

Disney discovered that the difference in capital budgeting techniques between U.S. and Japanese firms reflected the difference in corporate governance in the two countries. The use of NPV and IRR in the United States underlined the perspective of shareholder-value maximization. On the other hand, the preference for the simple accounting-based measure in Japan reflected the importance of achieving complete consensus among all parties affected by the investment decision.

When the DisneySea project was evaluated, it was found to have a positive NPV, but a negative AAR. To account for the differences in philosophies and capital budgeting techniques, managers at Disney introduced a third calculation method called average cash flow return (ACFR). This hybrid method measured the average cash flow over the first five years, with the asset assumed to be sold for book value at the end of that period as a fraction of the initial investment in the project. The resulting ratio was found to exceed the return on Japanese government bonds, and hence to yield a positive return for DisneySea. As a result, the DisneySea theme park was constructed next to Tokyo Disneyland and has since become a profitable addition to Disney's Japanese operations.

Sources: Misawa, Mitsuru. 2006. Tokyo Disneyland and the DisneySea Park: Corporate governance and differences in capital budgeting concepts and methods between American and Japanese companies. University of Hong Kong No. HKU568, Hong Kong: University of Hong Kong Asia Case Research Center; and The Walt Disney Company. 2010. 2009 annual report. Burbank, CA: The Walt Disney Company.

Concepts in Action feature). The strategic decision by Barnes & Noble to support book sales over the Internet required capital investments creating barnesandnoble.com and an Internet infrastructure. News Corp.'s decision to enlarge its online presence resulted in a large investment to purchase MySpace, and additional supporting investments to integrate MySpace with the firm's pre-existing assets. Pfizer's decision to develop its cholesterol-reducing drug Lipitor led to major investments in R&D and marketing. Toyota's decision to offer a line of hybrids across both its Toyota and Lexus platforms required start-up investments to form a hybrid division and ongoing investments to fund the division's continuing research efforts.

Learning Objective 7

Identify strategic considerations in capital budgeting decisions

. . . critical investments whose benefits are uncertain or difficult to estimate

Capital investment decisions that are strategic in nature require managers to consider a broad range of factors that may be difficult to estimate. Consider some of the difficulties of justifying investments in computer-integrated manufacturing (CIM) technology made by companies such as Mitsubishi, Sony, and Audi. In CIM, computers give instructions that quickly and automatically set up and run equipment to manufacture many different products. Quantifying these benefits requires some notion of long-run future consumer demand changes. CIM tech... 'ogy also increases worker knowledge of, and experience with automation; however, the benefit of this knowledge and experience is difficult to measure. Managers must develop judgment and intuition to make these decisions.

Investment in Research and Development

Companies such as GlaxoSmithKline, in the pharmaceutical industry, and Intel, in the semiconductor industry, regard research and development (R&D) projects as important strategic investments. The distant payoffs from R&D investments, however, are more uncertain than other investments such as new equipment. On the positive side, R&D investments are often staged: As time unfolds, companies can increase or decrease the resources committed to a project based on how successful it has been up to that point. This option feature of R&D investments, called real options, is an important aspect of R&D investments and increases the NPV of these investments, because a company can limit its losses when things are going badly and take advantage of new opportunities when things are going well.

Customer Value and Capital Budgeting

The same framework used to evaluate investment projects can also be used to evaluate customers. Consider Potato Supreme, which makes potato products for sale to retail outlets. It is currently analyzing two of its customers: Shine Stores and Always Open. Potato Supreme predicts the following cash flow from operations, net of income taxes (in thousands), from each customer account for the next five years:

	2011	2012	2013	2014	2015
Shine Stores	Rs 14,500	Rs 13,050	Rs 11,750	Rs 10,580	Rs 9,500
Always Open	6,900	11,600	19,000	29,500	41,600

Which customer is more valuable to Potato Supreme? Looking at only the current period, 2011, Shine Stores provides more than double the cash flow compared to Always Open (Rs 14,500 versus Rs 6,900). A different picture emerges, however, when looking over the entire five-year horizon. Potato Supreme anticipates Always Open's orders to increase; meanwhile, it expects Shine Stores' orders to decline. Using Potato Supreme's 10% RRR, the NPV of the Always Open customer is Rs 76,100, compared to Rs 45,910 for Shine Stores (computations not shown). Note how NPV captures in its estimate of customer value the future growth of Always Open. Potato Supreme uses this information to allocate more resources and salespersons to service the Always Open account. Potato Supreme can also use NPV calculations to examine the effects of alternative ways of increasing customer loyalty and retention, such as introducing frequent-purchaser cards.

A comparison of year-to-year changes in customer NPV estimates highlights whether managers have been successful in maintaining long-run profitable relationships with their customers. Suppose the NPV of Potato Supreme's customer base declines 15% in one year. Management can then examine the reasons for the decline, such as aggressive pricing by competitors, and devise new-product development and marketing strategies for the future.

Capital One, a financial-services company, uses NPV to estimate the value of different credit-card customers. Cellular telephone companies such as Cellular One and Verizon Wireless attempt to sign up customers for multiple years of service. The objective is to prevent "customer churn," customers switching frequently from one company to another. The higher the probability of customer churn, the lower the NPV of the customer.

Decision Point

What strategic considerations arise in the capital budgeting process?

Problem for Self-Study

PART A

Returning to the Top-Spin carbon-fiber machine project, assume that Top-Spin is a *nonprofit organization* and that the expected additional operating cash inflows from the operating cost savings are Rs 13,00,000 in years 1 through 4 and Rs 12,10,000 in year 5. The net initial investment is Rs 39,25,000 (new machine, Rs 39,00,000 plus additional working capital, Rs 90,000 minus terminal disposal value of old machine, Rs 65,000). All other facts are unchanged: a five-year useful life, no terminal disposal value, and an 8% RRR. Year 5 cash inflows are Rs 13,00,000, which includes a Rs 90,000 recovery of working capital.

Required

Calculate the following:

1. Net present value
2. Internal rate of return
3. Payback
4. Accrual accounting rate of return on net initial investment

Solution

1. NPV = Rs 13,00,000 × 3.993) – Rs 39,25,000
   = Rs 51,90,900 × Rs 39,25,000 = Rs 12,65,900

2. There are several approaches to computing IRR. One is to use a calculator with an IRR function. This approach gives an IRR of 19.6%. Another approach is to use Table 4 in Appendix B at the end of the text:

$$\text{Rs } 39{,}25{,}000 = \text{Rs } 13{,}00{,}000$$

$$F = \frac{\text{Rs } 39{,}25{,}000}{\text{Rs } 13{,}00{,}000} = 3.019$$

On the five-period line of Table 4, the column closest to 3.019 is 20%. To obtain a more-accurate number, use straight-line interpolation:

	Present Value Factors	
18%	3.127	3.127
IRR	—	3.019
20%	2.991	—
Difference	0.136	0.108

$$IRR = 18\% + \frac{0.108}{0.136}(2\%) = 19.6\% \text{ per year}$$

3. $$\text{Payback period} = \frac{\text{Net initial investment}}{\text{Uniform increase in annual future cash flows}}$$

$$= \text{Rs } 39{,}25{,}000 \div \text{Rs } 13{,}00{,}000 = 3.0 \text{ years}$$

4. $$AARR = \frac{\text{Increase in expected average annual operating income}}{\text{Net initial investment}}$$

Increase in expected average annual cash operating savings = [(Rs 13,00,000 × 4) + Rs 12,10,000] ÷ 5 years

= Rs 64,10,000 ÷ 5 + Rs 12,82,000

Increase in annual depreciation = Rs 7,00,000 (Rs 7,80,000 – Rs 80,000)

Increase in expected average annual operarating income = Rs 12,82,000 – Rs 7,00,000 = Rs 5,82,000

$$AARR = \frac{\text{Rs } 5{,}82{,}000}{\text{Rs } 39{,}25{,}000} = 14.8\% \text{ per year}$$

PART B

Assume that Top-Spin is subject to income tax at a 40% rate. All other information from Part A is unchanged. Compute the NPV of the new carbon-fiber machine project.

Solution

To save space, Exhibit 21-7 shows the calculations using a format slightly different from the format used in this chapter. Item **2a** is where the new Rs 13,00,000 cash flow assumption affects the NPV analysis (compared to Exhibit 21-6). All other amounts in Exhibit 21-7 are identical to the corresponding amounts in Exhibit 21-6. For years 1 through 4, after-tax cash flow (excluding the depreciation effect) is:

Annual cash flow from operations with new machine	Rs 13,00,000
Deduct income tax payments (0.40 × Rs 13,00,000)	5,20,000
Annual after-tax cash flow from operations	Rs 7,80,000

For year 5, after-tax cash flow (excluding the depreciation effect) is:

Annual cash flow from operations with new machine	Rs 12,10,000
Deduct income tax payments (0.40 × Rs 12,10,000)	4,84,000
Annual after-tax cash flow from operations	Rs 7,26,000

NPV in Exhibit 21-7 is Rs 4,66,100. As computed in Part A, NPV when there are no income taxes is Rs 12,65,900. The difference in these two NPVs illustrates the impact of income taxes in capital budgeting analysis.

Exhibit 21-7 Net Present Value Method Incorporating Income Taxes: Top-Spin's Carbon-Fiber Machine with Revised Annual Cash Flow from Operations

File Edit View Insert Format Tools Data Window Help

	A	B	C	D	E	F	G	H	I	J
1			Present	Present Value of						
2			Value o	Rs1 Discounted at	Sketch of Relevant Cash Flows at End of Year					
3			Cash Flow	8%	0	1	2	3	4	5
4	1a.	Initial machine investment	Rs (39,00,000)	1.000	Rs (39,00,000)					
5										
6	1b.	Initial working-capital investment	(90,000)	1.000	Rs (90,000)					
7	1c.	After-tax cash flow from current								
8		disposal of old machine	1,99,000	1.000	Rs 1,99,000					
9	Net initial investment		(37,91,000)							
10	2a.	Annual after-tax cash flow from								
11		operations (excluding the depreciation effect)								
12		Year 1	7,22,280	0.926		Rs 7,80,000				
13		Year 2	6,68,460	0.857			Rs 7,80,000			
14		Year 3	6,19,320	0.794				Rs 7,80,000		
15		Year 4	5,73,300	0.735					Rs 7,80,000	
16		Year 5	4,94,410	0.681						Rs 7,26,000
17	2b.	Income tax cash savings from annual								
18		depreciation deductions								
19		Year 1	2,59,280	0.926		Rs 2,80,000				
20		Year 2	2,39,960	0.857			Rs 2,80,000			
21		Year 3	2,22,320	0.794				Rs 2,80,000		
22		Year 4	2,05,800	0.735					Rs 2,80,000	
23		Year 5	1,90,680	0.681						Rs 2,80,000
24	3.	After-tax cash flow from								
25		a. Terminal disposal of machine	0	0.681						Re 0
26		b. Recovery of working capital	61,290	0.681						Rs 90,000
27	NPV if new machine purchased		Rs 4,66,100							
28										

Decision Points

The following question-and-answer format summarizes the chapter's learning objectives. Each decision presents a key question related to a learning objective. The guidelines are the answer to that question.

Decision	Guidelines
1. Over what time horizon is capital budgeting done?	Capital budgeting is long-run planning for proposed investment projects. The life of a project is usually longer than one year, so capital budgeting decisions consider cash inflows and outflows over long periods. In contrast, accrual accounting measures income on a year-by-year basis.
2. What are the five stages of capital budgeting?	The five stages of capital budgeting are: 1) Identify projects: identify potential capital investments that agree with the organization's strategy; 2) Obtain information: Gather information from all parts of the value chain to evaluate alternative projects; 3) Make predictions: Forecast all potential cash flows attributable to the alternative projects; 4) Make decisions by Choosing Among Alternatives: Determine which investment yields the greatest benefit and the least cost to the organization; and 5) Implement the Decision, Evaluate Performance, and Learn: Obtain funding and make the investments selected in stage 4; track realized cash flows, compare against estimated numbers, and revise plans if necessary.
3. What are the two main discounted cash flow (DCF) methods? What are their advantages?	The two main DCF methods are the net present value (NPV) method and the internal rate-of-return (IRR) method. The NPV method calculates the expected net monetary gain or loss from a project by discounting to the present all expected future cash inflows and outflows, using the required rate of return. A project is acceptable in financial terms if it has a positive NPV. The IRR method computes the rate of return (also called the discount rate) at which the present value of expected cash inflows from a project equals the present value of expected cash outflows from the project. A project is acceptable in financial terms if its IRR exceeds the required rate of return. DCF is the best approach to capital budgeting. It explicitly includes all project cash flows and recognizes the time value of money. The NPV method is the preferred DCF method.
4. What is the payback method? What are its two main weaknesses?	The payback method measures the time it will take to recoup, in the form of cash inflows, the total cash amount invested in a project. The payback method neglects both cash flows after the payback period and the time value of money.
5. What is the accrual accounting rate-of-return (AARR) method? What is its limitation?	The accrual accounting rate of return (AARR) divides an accrual accounting measure of average annual income from a project by an accrual accounting measure of its investment. AARR considers profitability but does not consider the time value of money.
6. What conflicts can arise between using DCF methods for capital budgeting decisions and accrual accounting for performance evaluation? How can these conflicts be reduced?	Using accrual accounting to evaluate the performance of a manager may create conflicts with using DCF methods for capital budgeting. Frequently, the decision made using a DCF method will not report good "operating income" results in the project's early years under accrual accounting. For this reason, managers are tempted to not use DCF methods even though the decisions based on them would be in the best interests of the company as a whole over the long run. This conflict can be reduced by evaluating managers on a project-by-project basis and by looking at their ability to achieve the amounts and timing of forecasted cash flows.

7. What are the relevant cash inflows and outflows for capital budgeting decisions? How should accrual accounting concepts be considered?	Relevant cash inflows and outflows in DCF analysis are the differences in expected future cash flows as a result of making the investment. Only cash inflows and outflows matter; accrual accounting concepts are irrelevant for DCF methods. For example, the income taxes saved as a result of depreciation deductions are relevant because they decrease cash outflows, but the depreciation itself is a noncash item.

APPENDIX: CAPITAL BUDGETING AND INFLATION

The Top-Spin example (Exhibits 21-2 to 21-6) does not include adjustments for inflation in the relevant revenues and costs. **Inflation** is the decline in the general purchasing power of the monetary unit, such as rupees. An inflation rate of 10% per year means that an item bought for Rs 100 at the beginning of the year will cost Rs 110 at the end of the year.

Why is it important to account for inflation in capital budgeting? Because declines in the general purchasing power of the monetary unit will inflate future cash flows above what they would have been in the absence of inflation. These inflated cash flows will cause the project to look better than it really is unless the analyst recognizes that the inflated cash flows are measured in rupees that have less purchasing power than the rupees that were initially invested. When analyzing inflation, distinguish real rate of return from nominal rate of return:

Real rate of return is the rate of return demanded to cover investment risk if there is no inflation. The real rate is made up of two elements: (a) a risk-free element (that's the pure rate of return on risk-free long-term government bonds when there is no expected inflation) and (b) a business-risk element (that's the risk premium demanded for bearing risk).

Nominal rate of return is the rate of return demanded to cover investment risk and the decline in general purchasing power of the monetary unit as a result of expected inflation. The nominal rate is made up of three elements: (a) a risk-free element when there is no expected inflation, (b) a business-risk element, and (c) an inflation element. Items (a) and (b) make up the real rate of return to cover investment risk. The inflation element is the premium above the real rate. The rates of return earned in the financial markets are nominal rates, because investors want to be compensated both for the investment risks they take and for the expected decline in the general purchasing power, as a result of inflation, of the money they get back.

Assume that the real rate of return for investments in high-risk cellular data-transmission equipment at Network Communications is 20% per year and that the expected inflation rate is 10% per year. Nominal rate of return is:

$$\begin{aligned}\text{Nominal rate} &= (1 + \text{Real rate})(1 + \text{Inflation rate}) - 1\\ &= (1 + 0.20)(1 + 0.10) - 1\\ &= (1.20 \times 1.10) - 1 = (1.32 - 1 = 0.32, \text{ or } 32\%)\end{aligned}$$

Nominal rate of return is related to the real rate of return and the inflation rate:

Real rate of return	0.20
Inflation rate	0.10
Combination (0.20 × 0.10)	0.02
Nominal rate of return	0.32

Note the nominal rate, 0.32, is slightly higher than 0.30, the real rate (0.20) plus the inflation rate (0.10). That's because the nominal rate recognizes that inflation of 10% also decreases the purchasing power of the real rate of return of 20% earned during the year. The combination component represents the additional compensation investors seek for the decrease in the purchasing power of the real return earned during the year because of inflation.[9]

Net Present Value Method and Inflation

When incorporating inflation into the NPV method, the key is *internal consistency*. There are two internally consistent approaches:

1. **Nominal approach**—predicts cash inflows and outflows in nominal monetary units *and* uses a nominal rate as the required rate of return
2. **Real approach**—predicts cash inflows and outflows in real monetary units *and* uses a real rate as the required rate of return

We will limit our discussion to the simpler nominal approach. Consider an investment that is expected to generate sales of 100 units and a net cash inflow of Rs 10,000 (Rs 100 per unit) each year for two years *absent inflation*. Assume cash flows occur at the end of each year. If inflation of 10% is expected each year, net cash inflows from the sale of each unit would be Rs 1,100 (Rs 100 × 1.10) in year 1 and Rs 1,210 (Rs 1,100 × 1.10, or Rs 100 × $(1.10)^2$) in year 2, resulting in net cash inflows of Rs 11,000 in year 1 and Rs 12,100 in year 2. The net cash inflows of Rs 11,000 and Rs 12,100 are nominal cash inflows because they include the effects of inflation. *Nominal cash flows are the cash flows that are recorded in the accounting system.* The cash inflows of Rs 10,000 each year are real cash flows. The accounting system does not record these cash flows. The nominal approach is easier to understand and apply because it uses nominal cash flows from accounting systems and nominal rates of return from financial markets.

Assume that Network Communications can purchase equipment to make and sell a cellular data-transmission product at a net initial investment of Rs 75,00,000. It is expected to have a four-year useful life and no terminal disposal value. An annual inflation rate of 10% is expected over this four-year period. Network Communications requires an after-tax nominal rate of return of 32%. The following table presents the predicted amounts of real (that's assuming no inflation) and nominal (that's after considering cumulative inflation) net cash inflows from the equipment over the next four years (excluding the Rs 75,00,000 investment in the equipment and before any income tax payments):

Year (1)	Before-Tax Cash Inflows in Real Rupees (2)	Cumulative Inflation Rate Factor[a] (3)	Before-Tax Cash Inflows in Nominal Rupees (4) = (2) × (3)
1	Rs 50,00,000	$(1.10)^1 = 1.1000$	Rs 55,00,000
2	60,00,000	$(1.10)^2 = 1.2100$	72,60,000
3	60,00,000	$(1.10)^3 = 1.3310$	79,86,000
4	30,00,000	$(1.10)^4 = 1.4641$	

[a] 1.10 = 1.00 + 0.10 inflation rate.

We continue to make the simplifying assumption that cash flows occur at the end of each year. The income tax rate is 40%. For tax purposes, the cost of the equipment will be depreciated using the straight-line method.

Exhibit 21-8 shows the calculation of NPV using cash flows in nominal rupees and using a nominal discount rate. The calculations in Exhibit 21-8 include the net initial machine investment, annual after-tax cash flows from operations (excluding the depreciation effect), and income tax cash savings from annual depreciation deductions. The NPV is Rs 20,25,130 and, based on financial considerations alone, Network Communications should purchase the equipment.

[9] The real rate of return can be expressed in terms of the nominal rate of return as follows:

$$\text{Real rate} = \frac{1 + \text{Nominal rate}}{1 + \text{Inflation rate}} - 1 = \frac{1 + 0.32}{1 + 0.10} - 1 = 0.20, \text{ or } 20\%$$

Exhibit 21-8 Net Present Value Method Using Nominal Approach to Inflation for Network Communication's New Equipment

File Edit View Insert Format Tools Data Window Help

	A	B	C	D	E	F	G	H	I	J	K	L
1						Present	Present Value					
2						Value of	Discount Factor[a] at	Sketch of Relevant Cash Flows at End of Each Year				
3						Cash Flow	32%	0	1	2	3	4
4	1.	Net initial investment										
5		Year	Investment Outflows									
6		0	Rs (75,00,000)			Rs (75,00,000) ←	1.000 ←	Rs (75,00,000)				
7	2a.	Annual after-tax cash flow from										
8		operations (excluding the depreciation effect)										
9			Annual		Annual							
10			Before-Tax	Income	After-Tax							
11			Cash Flow	Tax	Cash Flow							
12		Year	from Operations	Outflows	from Operations							
13		(1)	(2)	(3) = 0.40 x (2)	(4) = (2) - (3)							
14		1	Rs 55,00,000	Rs 22,00,000	Rs 33,00,000	25,01,400 ←	0.758 ←		Rs 33,00,000			
15		2	72,60,000	29,04,000	43,56,000	25,00,340 ←	0.574 ←			Rs 43,56,000		
16		3	79,86,000	31,94,400	47,91,600	20,84,350 ←	0.435 ←				Rs 47,91,600	
17		4	43,92,300	17,56,920	26,35,380	8,67,040 ←	0.329 ←					Rs 26,35,380
18						79,53,130						
19	2b.	Income tax cash savings from annual										
20		depreciation deductions										
21		Year	Depreciation	Tax Cash Savings								
22		(1)	(2)	(3) = 0.40 x (2)								
23		1	Rs 18,75,000[b]	Rs 7,50,000		5,68,500 ←	0.758 ←		Rs (7,50,000)			
24		2	18,75,000	7,50,000		4,30,500 ←	0.574 ←			Rs (7,50,000)		
25		3	18,75,000	7,50,000		3,26,250 ←	0.435 ←				Rs (7,50,000)	
26		4	18,75,000	7,50,000		2,46,750 ←	0.329 ←					Rs (7,50,000)
27						15,72,000						
28	NPV if new equipment purchased					Rs 20,25,130						
29												
30												
31	[a]The nominal discount rate of 32% is made up of the real rate of return of 20% and the inflation rate of 10% [(1 + 0.20) (1 + 1.10)] – 1 = 0.32.											
32	[b]Rs 75,00,000 ÷ 4 = Rs 18,75,000											

TERMS TO LEARN

This chapter and the Glossary at the end of the book contain definitions of:

accounting rate of return (**p. 891**)
accrual accounting rate of return (AARR) (**p. 891**)
capital budgeting (**p. 881**)
cost of capital (**p. 884**)
discount rate (**p. 884**)
discounted cash flow (DCF) methods (**p. 883**)
hurdle rate (**p. 884**)
inflation (**p. 904**)
internal rate-of-return (IRR) method (**p. 885**)
net present value (NPV) method (**p. 884**)
nominal rate of return (**p. 904**)
opportunity cost of capital (**p. 884**)
payback method (**p. 888**)
real rate of return (**p. 904**)
required rate of return (RRR) (**p. 884**)
time value of money (**p. 883**)

ASSIGNMENT MATERIAL

Questions

21-1 "Capital budgeting has the same focus as accrual accounting." Do you agree? Explain.

21-2 List and briefly describe each of the five stages in capital budgeting.

21-3 What is the essence of the discounted cash flow methods?

21-4 "Only quantitative outcomes are relevant in capital budgeting analyses." Do you agree? Explain.

21-5 How can sensitivity analysis be incorporated in DCF analysis?

21-6 What is the payback method? What are its main strengths and weaknesses?

21-7 Describe the accrual accounting rate-of-return method. What are its main strengths and weaknesses?

21-8 "The trouble with discounted cash flow methods is that they ignore depreciation." Do you agree? Explain.

21-9 "Let's be more practical. DCF is not the gospel. Managers should not become so enchanted with DCF that strategic considerations are overlooked." Do you agree? Explain.

21-10 "All overhead costs are relevant in NPV analysis." Do you agree? Explain.

21-11 Bill Watts, president of Western Publications, accepts a capital budgeting project proposed by Division X. This is the division in which the president spent his first 10 years with the company. On the same day, the president rejects a capital budgeting project proposal from Division Y. The manager of Division Y is incensed. She believes that the Division Y project has an internal rate of return at least 10 percentage points higher than the Division X project. She comments, "What is the point of all our detailed DCF analysis? If Watts is panting over a project, he can arrange to have the proponents of that project massage the numbers so that it looks like a winner." What advice would you give the manager of Division Y?

21-12 Distinguish different categories of cash flows to be considered in an equipment replacement decision by a taxpaying company.

21-13 Describe three ways income taxes can affect the cash inflows or outflows in a motor vehicle-replacement decision by a taxpaying company.

21-14 How can capital budgeting tools assist in evaluating a manager who is responsible for retaining customers of a cellular telephone company?

21-15 Distinguish the nominal rate of return from the real rate of return.

Solved Examples

21-16 Comparison of approaches to capital budgeting, no income taxes. The Children Toy Company is thinking of buying, at a cost of Rs 2,20,000, some new packaging equipment that is expected to save Rs 50,000 in cash-operating costs per year. Its estimated useful life is 10 years, and it will have no terminal disposal value. The required rate of return is 16%. Ignore income tax issues in your answers.

Required

Compute the following:

1. Net present value
2. Payback period
3. Internal rate of return
4. Accrual accounting rate of return based on net initial investment (Assume straight-line depreciation.)

Solution

Comparison of approaches to capital budgeting, no income taxes.

1. The table for the present value of annuities (Appendix B, Table 4) shows:

   10 periods at 16% = 4.833

   Net present value = Rs 50,000 (4.833) − Rs 2,20,000
   = Rs 2,41,650 − Rs 2,20,000 = Rs 21,650.

2. Payback period = Rs 2,20,000 ÷ Rs 50,000 = 4.4 years.

3. Internal rate of return:

   Rs 2,20,000 = Present value of annuity of Rs 50,000 at R% for 10 years, or what factor (F) in the table of present values of an annuity (Appendix B, Table 4) will satisfy the following equation.

   Rs 2,20,000 = Rs 50,000F

   $$F = \frac{\text{Rs } 2{,}20{,}000}{\text{Rs } 50{,}000} = 4.400$$

   On the 10-year line in the table for the present value of annuities (Appendix B, Table 4), find the column closest to 4.400; 4.400 is between a rate of return of 18% and 20%.

   Interpolation is necessary:

	Present Value Factors	
18%	4.494	4.494
IRR rate	–	4.400
20%	4.192	–
Difference	0.302	0.094

$$\text{Internal rate of return} = 18\% + \left[\frac{0.094}{0.302}\right](2\%)$$

$$= 18\% + (0.311)(2\%) = 18.62\%.$$

4. Accrual accounting rate of return based on net initial investment:

Net initial investment = Rs 2,20,000
Estimated useful life = 10 years
Annual straight-line depreciation = Rs 2,20,000 ÷ 10 = Rs 22,000

$$\text{Accrual account rate of return} = \frac{\text{Increase in expected average annual operating income}}{\text{Net initial investment}}$$

$$= \frac{\text{Rs } 50{,}000\text{–Rs } 22{,}000}{\text{Rs } 2{,}20{,}000} = \frac{\text{Rs } 28{,}000}{\text{Rs } 2{,}20{,}000} = 12.73\%$$

Note how the accrual accounting rate of return, whichever way calculated, can produce results that differ markedly from the internal rate of return.

21-17 Capital budgeting methods, no income taxes. City Eye Testing Centre, estimates that it can save Rs 28,000 a year in cash operating costs for the next 10 years if it buys a special-purpose eye-testing machine at a cost of Rs 1,10,000. A no terminal disposal value is expected. City Eye's required rate of return is 14%.

Required

Compute the following:

1. Net present value
2. Payback period
3. Internal rate of return
4. Accrual accounting rate of return based on net initial investment (Assume straight-line depreciation.)

Solution

Capital budgeting methods, no income taxes.

The table for the present value of annuities (Appendix B, Table 4) shows: 10 periods at 14% = 5.216

1. Net present value = Rs 28,000(5.216) − Rs 1,10,000
   = Rs 1,46,048 − Rs 1,10,000 = Rs 36,048.

2. $$\text{Payback period} = \frac{\text{Rs } 1{,}10{,}000}{\text{Rs } 28{,}000} = 3.93 \text{ years.}$$

3. Internal rate of return:

Rs 1,10,000 = Present value of annuity of Rs 28,000 at R% for 10 years, or what factor (F) in the table of present values of an annuity (Appendix B, Table 4) will satisfy the following equation.

Rs 1,10,000 = Rs 28,000F

$$F = \frac{\text{Rs } 1{,}10{,}000}{\text{Rs } 28{,}000} = 3.929$$

On the 10-year line in the table for the present value of annuities (Appendix B, Table 4), find the column closest to 3.929; 3.929 is between a rate of return of 20% and 22%. Interpolation can be used to determine the exact rate:

	Present Value Factors	
20%	4.192	4.192
IRR rate	—	3.929
22%	3.923	
Difference	0.269	0.263

$$\text{Internal rate of return} = 20\% + \left[\frac{0.263}{0.269}\right](2\%)$$

$$= 20\% + (0.978)(2\%) = 21.96\%.$$

4. Accrual accounting rate of return based on net initial investment:

Net initial investment = Rs 1,10,000
Estimated useful life = 10 years
Annual straight-line depreciation = Rs 1,10,000 ÷ 10 = Rs 11,000

$$\text{Accrual accounting rate of return} = \frac{\text{Rs } 28{,}000\text{–Rs } 11{,}000}{\text{Rs } 1{,}10{,}000}$$

$$= \frac{\text{Rs } 17{,}000}{\text{Rs } 1{,}10{,}000} = 15.46\%.$$

21-18 Capital budgeting, income taxes. Assume the same facts as in Example 21-17 except that City Eye Testing Centre is now a taxpaying entity. The income tax rate is 30% for all transactions that affect income taxes.

Required

1. Redo your computations in requirement 1 of Exercise 21-17.
2. How would your computations in requirement 1 be affected if the special-purpose machine has a Rs 10,000 terminal disposal value at the end of 10 years? Assume that depreciation deductions are based on Rs 1,10,000 purchase cost using a straight-line method.

Solution

Capital budgeting, income taxes.

1. a. Net after-tax initial investment = Rs 1,10,000

Annual after-tax cash flow from operations (excluding depreciation effects):

Annual cash flow from operation with new machine	Rs 28,000
Deduct income tax payments (30% of Rs 28,000)	8,400
Annual after-tax cash flow from operations	Rs 19,600
Income tax cash savings from annual depreciation deductions 30% × Rs 11,000	Rs 3,300

These three amounts can be combined to determine the NPV:

Net initial investment	
Rs 1,10,000 × 1.00	Rs (1,10,000)
10-year annuity of annual after-tax cash flows from operations:	
Rs 19,600 × 5.216	1,02,234
10-year annuity of income tax cash savings from annual depreciation deductions	
Rs 3,300 × 5.216	17,213
Net present value	Rs 9,447

b. Payback period

$$= \frac{\text{Rs } 1,10,000}{(\text{Rs } 19,600 + \text{Rs } 3,300)} = \frac{\text{Rs } 1,10,000}{\text{Rs } 22,900} = 4.803 \text{ years.}$$

c. IRR

$$F = \frac{\text{Rs } 1,10,000}{\text{Rs } 22,900} = 4.803$$

Interpolation can be used to determine the exact rate:

	Present Value Factors	
16%	4.833	4.833
IRR		4.803
18%	4.494	
	0.339	0.030

$$\text{IRR} = 16\% + \frac{.030}{.339} \times 2\%$$

$$= 16.18\%$$

d. AARR

$$= \frac{\text{Rs } 22,900 - \text{Rs } 11,000}{\text{Rs } 1,10,000} = \frac{\text{Rs } 11,900}{\text{Rs } 1,10,000}$$

$$= 10.82\%$$

2. a. Increase in NPV. The Rs 10,000 terminal disposal price at the end of 10 years would have an after-tax NPV of:

Rs 10,000 (1 – 0.30) × 0.270 = Rs 1,890.

b. No change in payback as the payback period is 4.803 years. The cash inflow occurs at the end of year10.

c. Increase in internal rate of return.

d. The AARR would increase because accrual accounting income in year 10 would increase by the Rs 7,000 (Rs 10,000 gain from disposal – 30% × Rs 10,000) after-tax gain on disposal of equipment. This increase in year 10 income would result in higher average annual AARR in the numerator of the AARR formula.

21-19 Comparison of projects, no income taxes. (CMA, adapted) The CEO of City Healthcare, has developed a plan to add a new building. He has selected a building contractor, who is ready to start as soon as the contract is signed and will complete the work in two years.

The building contractor has offered City Healthcare a choice of three payment plans, as follows:

- Plan I Payment of Rs 2,00,000 on the signing of the contract and Rs 30,00,000 at the time of completion. The end of the second year is the completion date.
- Plan II Payment of Rs 10,00,000 on the signing of the contract and Rs 10,00,000 at the end of each of the two succeeding years.
- Plan III Payment of Rs 1,00,000 on the signing of the contract and Rs 10,00,000 at the end of each of the three succeeding years.

The CEO has asked the finance manager, for his assessment of the three payment plans. City

Healthcare has a required rate of return of 12%. Assume no taxes.

Required

1. Using the net present value method, calculate the comparative cost of each of the three payment plans being considered by City Healthcare.
2. Which payment plan should the treasurer recommend? Explain.
3. Discuss the financial factors, other than the cost of the plan, and the nonfinancial factors that should be considered in selecting an appropriate payment plan.

Solution

Comparison of projects, no income taxes (CMA adapted).

1.

	Total Present Value	Present Value Discount Factors at 12%	Year 0	1	2	3
Plan I						
	Rs (2,00,000)	1.000	Rs (2,00,000)			
	(23,91,000)	0.797			Rs (30,00,000)	
	Rs (25,91,000)					
Plan II						
	Rs (10,00,000)	1.000	Rs (10,00,000)			
	(8,93,000)	0.893		Rs (10,00,000)		
	(7,97,000)	0.797			Rs (10,00,000)	
	Rs (26,90,000)					
Plan III						
	Rs (1,00,000)	1.000	Rs (1,00,000)			
	(8,93,000)	0.893		Rs (10,00,000)		
	(7,97,000)	0.797			Rs (10,00,000)	
	(7,12,000)	0.712				Rs (10,00,000)
	Rs (25,02,000)					

2. Plan III has the lowest net present value cost. Plan III is the preferred one on financial criteria.
3. Factors to consider, in addition to NPV, are:
   a. Financial factors including:
      - Competing demands for cash.
      - Availability of financing for project.
   b. Nonfinancial factors including:
      - Risk of building contractor not remaining solvent. Plan II exposes City Healthcare most if Contractor becomes bankrupt before completion.
      - Ability to have leverage over Contractor if quality problems arise or delays in construction occur. Plans I and III give City Healthcare more negotiation strength by being able to withhold sizable amounts if, say, quality problems arise in Year 1.
      - Investment alternatives available. If City Healthcare has capital constraints, the new building project will have to compete with other projects for the limited capital available.

21-20 DCF, accrual accounting rate of return, working capital, evaluation of performance, no income taxes. Supreme Manufacturing Company has been offered a special-purpose metal-cutting machine for Rs 11,00,000. The machine is expected to have a useful life of eight years, with a terminal disposal value of Rs 3,00,000. Savings in cash operating costs are expected to be Rs 2,50,000 per year. However, additional working capital is needed to keep the machine running efficiently and without stoppages. Working capital includes such items as filters, lubricants, bearings, abrasives, flexible exhaust pipes, and belts. These items must continually be replaced, so an investment of Rs 80,000 must be maintained in them at all times, but this investment is fully recoverable (will be "cashed in") at the end of the useful life. Supreme's required rate of return is 14%. Ignore income taxes in your analysis.

Required

1. Compute net present value.
2. Compute internal rate of return.
3. Compute accrual accounting rate of return based on net initial investment. Assume straight-line depreciation.
4. You have the authority to make the purchase decision. Why might you be reluctant to base your decision on the DCF methods?

Solution

DCF, accrual accounting rate of return, working capital, evaluation of performance, no income taxes.

1. A summary of cash inflows and outflows (in thousands) are:

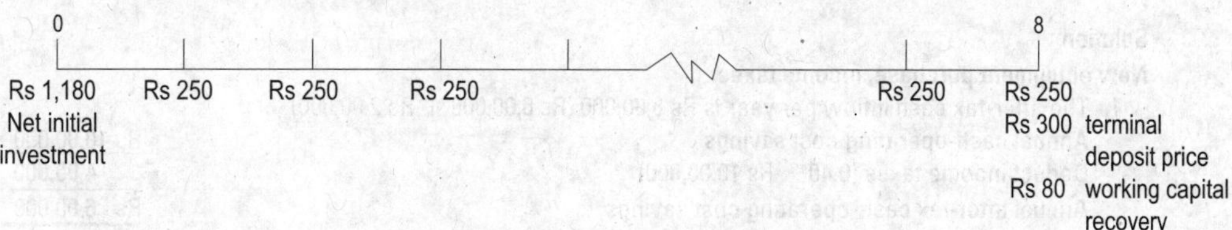

Present value of annuity of savings in cash operating costs (Rs 2,50,000 per year for 8 years at 14%): Rs 2,50,000 × 4.639		Rs 11,59,750
Present value of Rs 3,00,000 terminal disposal price of machine at end of year 8: Rs 3,00,000 × 0.351		1,05,300
Present value of Rs 80,000 recovery of working capital at end of year 8: Rs 80,000 × 0.351		28,080
Gross present value		12,93,130
Deduct net initial investment:		
Special-purpose machine initial investment	Rs 11,00,000	
Additional working capital investment	80,000	11,80,000
Net present value (NPV)		Rs 1,13,130

Since NPV is positive, IRR is to be higher than 14%.

2. Use a trial-and-error approach. First try a 16% discount rate:

Rs 2,50,000 × 4.344	Rs 10,86,000
(Rs 3,00,000 + Rs 80,000) × 0.305	1,15,900
Gross present value	12,01,900
Deduct net initial investment	(11,80,000)
Net present value	Rs 21,900

Second try an 18% discount rate:

Rs 2,50,000 × 4.078	Rs 10,19,500
(Rs 3,00,000 − Rs 80,000) × .266	1,01,080
Gross present value	11,20,580
Deduct net initial investment	(11,80,000)
Net present value	Rs (59,420)

By interpolation:

$$\text{Internal rate of return} = 16\% + \left(\frac{21{,}900}{21{,}900+59{,}420} \times 2\%\right)$$
$$= 16\% + (.2693 \times 2\%)$$
$$= 16.54\%.$$

3. Accrual accounting rate of return based on net initial investment:

Net initial investment = Rs 11,00,000 + Rs 80,000
= Rs 11,80,000

Annual depreciation
(Rs 11,00,000 − Rs 3,00,000) ÷ 8 years = Rs 1,00,000

$$\text{Accrual accounting rate of return} = \frac{\text{Rs } 2{,}50{,}000 - \text{Rs } 1{,}00{,}000}{\text{Rs } 11{,}80{,}000} = 12.71\%.$$

4. If your decision is based on the DCF model, the purchase would be made because the net present value is positive, and the 16.54% internal rate of return exceeds the 14% required rate of return. However, you may believe that your performance may actually be measured using accrual accounting. This approach would show a 12.71% return on the initial investment, which is below the required rate. Your reluctance to make a "buy" decision would be quite natural unless you are assured of reasonable consistency between the decision model and the performance evaluation method.

21-21 New equipment purchase, income taxes. National College Publishing publishes management textbooks. The company estimates it can save Rs 10,00,000 in cash operating costs each year for the next four years if it buys PR2020, a modern printing machine, at a cost of Rs 23,00,000. The printing machine will have Rs 3,00,000 terminal disposal value at the end of year 4. No change in working capital will be required. National has a 12% after-tax required rate of return. Its income tax rate is 40%.

Required

1. Assume that National uses straight-line depreciation on its tax return. Compute (a) net present value, (b) payback period, and (c) internal rate of return.
2. Compare the capital budgeting methods in requirement 1.

Solution

New equipment purchase, income taxes.

1. The after-tax cash inflow per year is Rs 8,00,000 (Rs 6,00,000 + Rs 2,00,000)

Annual cash-operating cost savings	Rs 10,00,000
Deduct income taxes (0.40 × Rs 10,00,000)	4,00,000
Annual after-tax cash-operating cost savings	Rs 6,00,000
Annual depreciation on machine [(Rs 23,00,000 − Rs 3,00,000) ÷ 4]	Rs 5,00,000
Income tax cash savings (0.40 × Rs 5,00,000)	2,00,000

a. Solution Exhibit 19-22A reports the NPV computation. NPV = Rs 3,21,200

b. Payback $= \dfrac{\text{Rs } 23{,}00{,}000}{\text{Rs } 8{,}00{,}000} = 2.88$ years

Solution Exhibits 19-22B and 19-22C report the net present value of the project using 18% and 20%

By interpolation:

$$\text{Internal rate of return} = 18\% + \left[\frac{680}{680 + 8{,}500}\right] \times 2\% = 18.15\%.$$

2. Both the net present value and internal rate of return methods use a discounted cash flow approach in which *all* expected future cash inflows and cash outflows of a project are measured as if they occurred at a single point in time. The payback method considers only cash flows up to the time when the expected future cash inflows recoup the net initial investment in a project. The payback method ignores profitability. However, the payback method is becoming increasingly more important in the global economy. When the local environment in an international location is unstable and, therefore, highly risky for a potential investment, a company would likely pay close attention to the payback period for making its investment decision. In general, the more unstable the environment, the shorter the payback period desired.

Solution Exhibit 21-21A

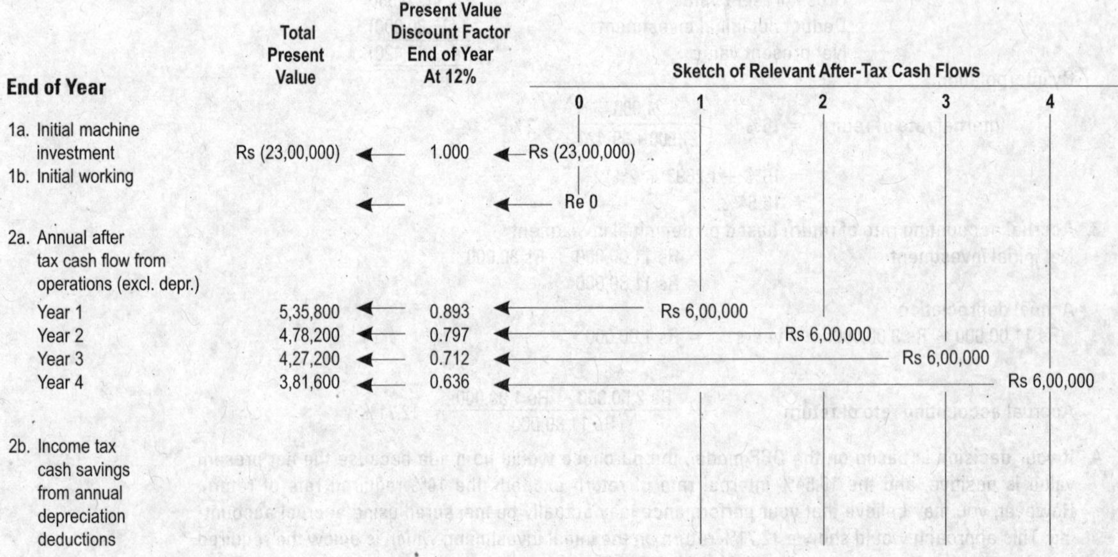

End of Year	Total Present Value	Present Value Discount Factor End of Year At 12%	Sketch of Relevant After-Tax Cash Flows 0	1	2	3	4
1a. Initial machine investment	Rs (23,00,000)	1.000	Rs (23,00,000)				
1b. Initial working			Re 0				
2a. Annual after tax cash flow from operations (excl. depr.)							
Year 1	5,35,800	0.893		Rs 6,00,000			
Year 2	4,78,200	0.797			Rs 6,00,000		
Year 3	4,27,200	0.712				Rs 6,00,000	
Year 4	3,81,600	0.636					Rs 6,00,000
2b. Income tax cash savings from annual depreciation deductions							

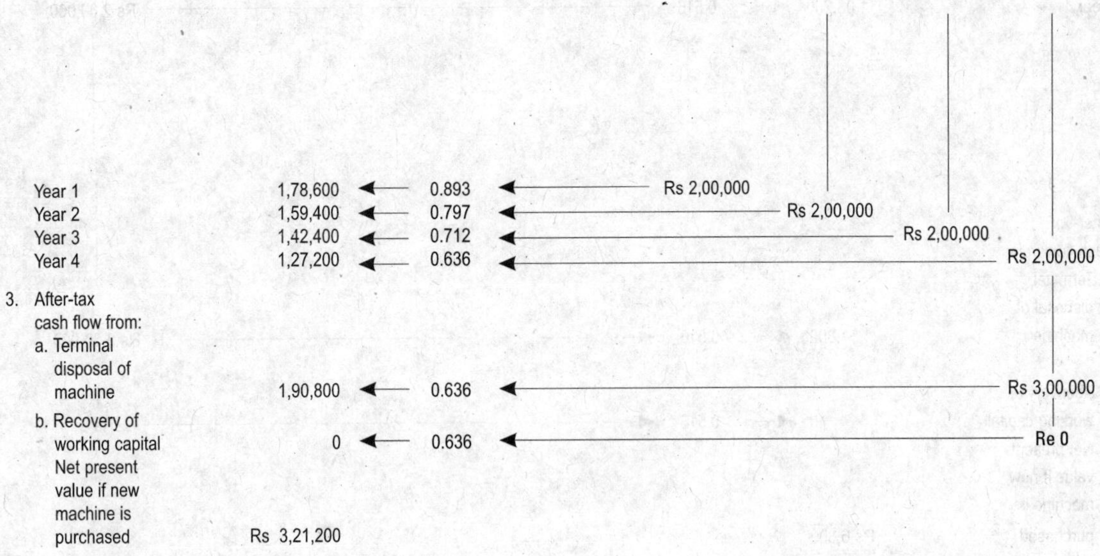

	Total Present Value		Present Value Discount Factor		Sketch of Relevant After-Tax Cash Flows
Year 1	1,78,600	←	0.893	←	Rs 2,00,000 (Year 1)
Year 2	1,59,400	←	0.797	←	Rs 2,00,000 (Year 2)
Year 3	1,42,400	←	0.712	←	Rs 2,00,000 (Year 3)
Year 4	1,27,200	←	0.636	←	Rs 2,00,000 (Year 4)
3. After-tax cash flow from:					
a. Terminal disposal of machine	1,90,800	←	0.636	←	Rs 3,00,000 (Year 4)
b. Recovery of working capital	0	←	0.636	←	Re 0 (Year 4)
Net present value if new machine is purchased	Rs 3,21,200				

Solution Exhibit 21-21B

End of Year	Total Present Value		Present Value Discount Factor At 18%		Sketch of Relevant After-Tax Cash Flows: 0	1	2	3	4
1a. Initial machine investment	Rs (23,00,000)	←	1.000	←	Rs (23,00,000)				
1b. Initial working capital investment	0	←	1.000	←	Re 0				
2a. Annual after tax cash flow from operations (excl. depr.)									
Year 1	5,08,200	←	0.847	←		Rs 6,00,000			
Year 2	4,30,800	←	0.718	←			Rs 6,00,000		
Year 3	3,65,400	←	0.609	←				Rs 6,00,000	
Year 4	3,09,600	←	0.516	←					Rs 6,00,000
2b. Income tax cash savings from annual depreciation deductions									
Year 1	1,69,400	←	0.847	←		Rs 2,00,000			
Year 2	1,43,600	←	0.718	←			Rs 2,00,000		
Year 3	1,21,800	←	0.609	←				Rs 2,00,000	

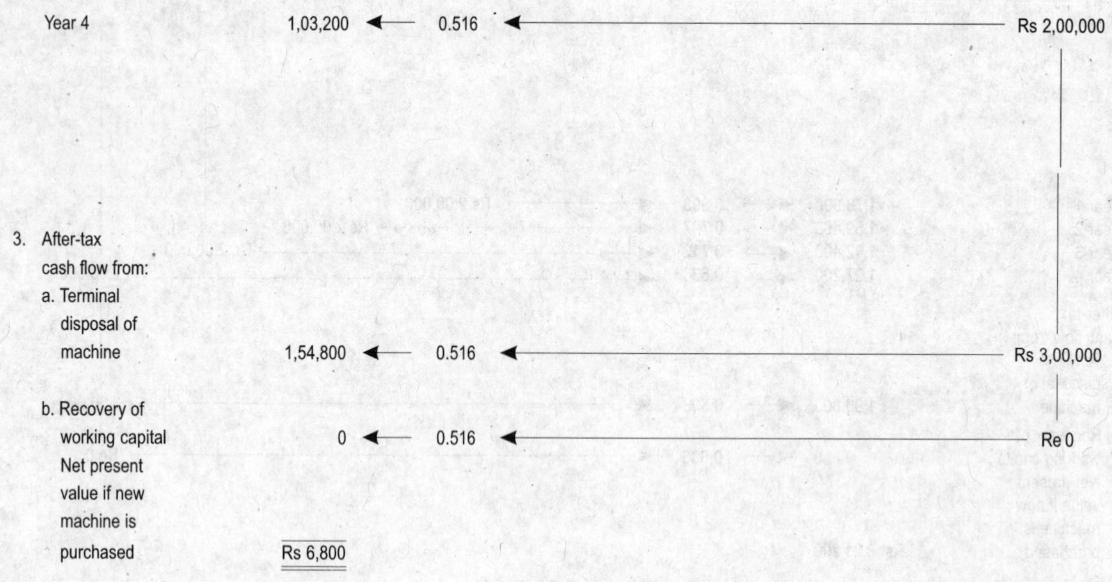

	Total Present Value	Present Value Discount Factor	Sketch of Relevant After-Tax Cash Flows (Year 4)
Year 4	1,03,200	0.516	Rs 2,00,000
3. After-tax cash flow from:			
a. Terminal disposal of machine	1,54,800	0.516	Rs 3,00,000
b. Recovery of working capital	0	0.516	Re 0
Net present value if new machine is purchased	Rs 6,800		

Solution Exhibit 21-21C

End of Year	Total Present Value	Present Value Discount Factor At 20%	0	1	2	3	4
1a. Initial machine investment	Rs (23,00,000)	1.000	Rs (23,00,000)				
1b. Initial working capital investment	0	1.000	Re 0				
2a. Annual after tax cash flow from operations (excl. depr.)							
Year 1	4,99,800	0.833		Rs 6,00,000			
Year 2	4,16,400	0.694			Rs 6,00,000		
Year 3	3,47,400	0.579				Rs 6,00,000	
Year 4	2,89,200	0.482					Rs 6,00,000
2b. Income tax cash savings from annual depreciation deductions							
Year 1	1,66,600	0.833		Rs 2,00,000			
Year 2	1,38,800	0.694			Rs 2,00,000		
Year 3	1,15,800	0.579				Rs 2,00,000	
Year 4	96,400	0.482					Rs 2,00,000
3. After-tax cash flow from:							
a. Terminal disposal of machine	1,44,600	0.482					Rs 3,00,000
b. Recovery of working capital	0	0.482					Re 0
Net present value if new machine is purchased	Rs (85,000)						

21-22 Equipment replacement, no income taxes. Superfast Chips manufactures and delivers prototype chips to customers within 24 hours. The current production facility was set up when the company began operations in 1999. It is outdated and constrains future growth. Next year, in 2012, Superfast expects to deliver 460 prototype chips at an average price of Rs 80,000 per prototype. Superfast's marketing vice president forecasts growth of 50 prototype chips per year through 2018. That is, demand is 460 in 2012, 510 in 2013, 560 in 2014, and so on.

The current facility cannot produce more than 450 prototypes annually. To meet future demand, Superfast must either modernize the current facility or replace it. The old equipment is fully depreciated and can be sold for Rs 30,00,000. If the current facilities are modernized, such costs are to be capitalized and depreciated over the useful life of the updated facility. The old equipment is retained as part of the modernize alternative. Following is some data on the two options available to Superfast:

	Modernize	Replace
Initial investment in 2012	Rs 2,80,00,000	Rs 4,90,00,000
Terminal disposal price in 2018	Rs 50,00,000	Rs 1,20,00,000
Useful life	7 years	7 years
Total annual cash operating costs per prototype	Rs 62,000	Rs 56,000

Superfast uses straight-line depreciation for income reporting, assuming zero terminal disposal value. For simplicity, we assume no change in prices or costs in future years. The investment will be made at the beginning of 2012, and all transactions thereafter occur on the last day of the year. Superfast's required rate of return is 12%.

There is no difference between the modernize and replace alternatives in terms of required working capital. Superfast Chips has a special waiver on income taxes until 2018.

Required

1. Sketch the cash inflows and outflows of the modernize and replace alternatives over the 2007 to 2013 period.
2. Compute payback period for the modernize and replace alternatives.
3 Compute net present value of the modernize and replace alternatives.
4. What factors should Superfast Chips consider in choosing between the alternatives?

Solution

Equipment replacement, no income taxes.

1. Cash flows for modernizing alternative:

Year	Units Sold	Net Cash Contributions	Initial Investments	Sale of Equip. at Termination
(1)	(2)	(3) = (2) × Rs 18,000[a]	(4)	(5)
Jan. 1, 2012	–	–	Rs (2,80,00,000)	–
Dec. 31, 2012	460	82,80,000		
Dec. 31, 2013	510	91,80,000		
Dec. 31, 2014	560	1,00,80,000		
Dec. 31, 2015	610	1,09,80,000		
Dec. 31, 2016	660	1,18,80,000		
Dec. 31, 2017	710	1,27,80,000		
Dec. 31, 2018	760	1,36,80,000		Rs 50,00,000

[a]Rs 80,000 – Rs 62,000 = Rs 18,000 cash contribution per prototype.

Cash flows for replacement alternative:

Year	Units Sold	Net Cash Contributions	Initial Investments	Sale of Equip. at Termination
(1)	(2)	(3) = (2) × Rs 24,000[b]	(4)	(5)
Jan. 1, 2012	–	–	Rs (4,90,00,000)	Rs 30,00,000
Dec. 31, 2012	460	1,10,40,000		
Dec. 31, 2013	510	1,22,40,000		
Dec. 31, 2014	560	1,34,40,000		
Dec. 31, 2015	610	1,46,40,000		
Dec. 31, 2016	660	1,58,40,000		
Dec. 31, 2017	710	1,70,40,000		
Dec. 31, 2018	760	1,82,40,000		Rs 1,20,00,000

[b]Rs 80,000 – Rs 56,000 = Rs 24,000 cash contribution per prototype.

2. Payback period calculations for modernizing alternative:

Year	Cash Inflow	Cumulative Cash Inflow	Net Initial Investment Yet to be Recovered at Year End
(1)	(2)	(3)	(4)
Jan. 1, 2012	–	–	Rs 2,80,00,000
Dec. 31, 2012	Rs 82,80,000	Rs 82,80,000	1,97,20,000
Dec. 31, 2013	91,80,000	1,74,60,000	1,05,40,000
Dec. 31, 2014	1,00,80,000	2,75,40,000	4,60,000
Dec. 31, 2015	1,09,80,000		

$$\text{Payback} = \times + \frac{\text{Rs } 4{,}60{,}000}{\text{Rs } 1{,}09{,}80{,}000} = 3.04 \text{ years}$$

Payback period calculations for replacement alternative:

Year	Cash Inflow	Cumulative Cash Inflow	Net Initial Investment Yet to be Recovered at Year End
(1)	(2)	(3)	(4)
Jan. 1, 2012	—	—	Rs 4,60,00,000
Dec. 31, 2012	Rs 1,10,40,000	Rs 1,10,40,000	3,49,60,000
Dec. 31, 2013	1,22,40,000	2,32,80,000	2,27,20,000
Dec. 31, 2014	1,34,40,000	3,67,20,000	92,80,000
Dec. 31, 2015	1,46,40,000		

$$\text{Payback} = \times + \frac{\text{Rs } 92{,}80{,}000}{\text{Rs } 1{,}46{,}40{,}000} = 3.63 \text{ years}$$

3. Modernizing alternative:

Year	Present Value Discount Factors At 12%	Net Cash Flow	Total Present Value
Jan. 1, 2012	1.000	Rs (2,80,00,000)	Rs (2,80,00,000)
Dec. 31, 2012	0.893	82,80,000	73,94,040
Dec. 31, 2013	0.797	91,80,000	73,16,460
Dec. 31, 2014	0.712	1,00,80,000	71,76,960
Dec. 31, 2015	0.636	1,09,80,000	69,83,280
Dec. 31, 2016	0.567	1,18,80,000	67,35,960
Dec. 31, 2017	0.507	1,27,80,000	64,79,460
Dec. 31, 2018	0.452	1,86,80,000	84,43,360
			Rs 2,25,29,520

Replace Alternative:

Year	Present Value Discount Factors At 12%	Net Cash Flow	Total Present Value
Jan. 1, 2012	1.000	Rs (4,60,00,000)	Rs (4,60,00,000)
Dec. 31, 2012	0.893	1,10,40,000	98,58,720
Dec. 31, 2013	0.797	1,22,40,000	97,55,280
Dec. 31, 2014	0.712	1,34,40,000	95,69,280
Dec. 31, 2015	0.636	1,46,40,000	93,11,040
Dec. 31, 2016	0.567	1,58,40,000	89,81,280
Dec. 31, 2017	0.507	1,70,40,000	86,39,280
Dec. 31, 2018	0.452	3,02,40,000	1,36,68,480
			Rs 2,37,83,360

4. The NPV amounts are based on best estimates. Superfast Chips could examine the sensitivity of the NPV amounts to variations in the estimates.

Nonfinancial qualitative factors could include the quality of the prototypes produced by the modernize and replace alternatives. These alternatives may differ in capacity and their ability to meet surges in demand beyond the estimated amounts. The alternatives may also differ in how workers increase their shop floor-capabilities. Such differences could provide labor force externalities that can be the source of future benefits to Superfast.

21-23 Equipment replacement, income taxes (continuation of 21-23). Assume the same facts as in Example 21-22, except that Superfast has no special waiver on income taxes. It pays a 30% tax rate on all income. Proceeds from sale of equipment above book value are taxed at the same 30% rate.

Required

1. Sketch the after-tax cash inflows and outflows of the modernize and replace alternatives over the 2012 to 2018 period.
2. Compute net present value of the modernize and replace alternatives.

3. Suppose Superfast is planning to build several more plants. It wants to have the most advantageous tax position possible. It has been approached by Spain, Malaysia, and Australia to construct a plant in their country. Use the data in Problem 21-27 and this problem to briefly describe income tax features that would be attractive and advantageous to Superfast. You should discuss the magnitude and timing of cost deductions in your description.

Solution

Equipment replacement, income taxes

1. & 2. Income tax rate = 30%

Modernize Alternative

Annual depreciation:

Rs 2,80,00,000 ÷ 7 years = Rs 40,00,000 a year.

Income tax cash savings from annual depreciation deductions:

Rs 40,00,000 × 0.30 = Rs 12,00,000 a year.

Terminal disposal of equipment = Rs 50,00,000.

After-tax cash flow from terminal disposal:

Rs 50,00,000 × 0.70 = Rs 35,00,000.

The NPV components are:

		NPV
1. Initial investment: Rs (2,80,00,000) × 1.000		Rs (2,80,00,000)
2a. Annual after-tax cash flow from operations (excluding depreciation):		
Dec. 31, 2012	82,80,000 × 0.70 × 0.893	51,75,828
2013	91,80,000 × 0.70 × 0.797	51,21,522
2014	1,00,80,000 × 0.70 × 0.712	50,23,872
2015	1,09,80,000 × 0.70 × 0.636	48,88,296
2016	1,18,80,000 × 0.70 × 0.567	47,15,172
2017	1,27,80,000 × 0.70 × 0.507	45,35,622
2018	1,36,80,000 × 0.70 × 0.452	43,28,352
2b. Income tax cash savings from annual depreciation deductions (annuity of Rs 12,00,000 for 7 years): Rs 12,00,000 × 4.564		54,76,800
3. After-tax cash flow from terminal sale of equipment: Rs 35,00,000 × 0.452		15,82,000
Net present value		Rs 1,28,47,464

Replace alternative

Initial machine replacement = Rs 4,90,00,000

Sale in Jan. 1, 2012, of equipment = Rs 30,00,000

After-tax cash flow from sale:

Rs 30,00,000 × 0.70 = Rs 21,00,000

Net after-tax initial investment

Rs 4,90,00,000 − Rs 21,00,000 = Rs 4,69,00,000

Annual depreciation

Rs 4,90,00,000 ÷ 7 years = Rs 70,00,000 a year

Income-tax cash savings from annual depreciation deductions

Rs 70,00,000 ÷ 0.30 = Rs 21,00,000

Terminal disposal of equipment = Rs 1,20,00,000

After-tax cash flow from terminal disposal

Rs 1,20,00,000 × 0.70 = Rs 84,00,000

The NPV components are:

1. Net after-tax initial investment Rs (4,69,00,000) × 1.000		Rs (4,69,00,000)
2a. Annual after-tax cash flow from operations (excluding depreciation)		
Dec. 31, 2012	Rs 1,10,40,000 × 0.70 × 0.893	69,01,104
2013	1,22,40,000 × 0.70 × 0.797	68,28,696
2014	1,34,40,000 × 0.70 × 0.712	66,98,496
2015	1,46,40,000 × 0.70 × 0.636	65,17,728
2016	1,58,40,000 × 0.70 × 0.567	62,86,896
2017	1,70,40,000 × 0.70 × 0.507	60,47,496
2018	1,82,40,000 × 0.70 × 0.452	57,71,136

2b. Income tax cash savings from annual depreciation deductions (annuity of Rs 21,00,000 for 7 years)

Rs 21,00,000 × 4.564	95,84,400
3. After-tax cash flow from terminal sale of equipment	
Rs 84,00,000 × 0.452	37,96,800
Net present value	Rs 1,15,32,752

3. Superfast would prefer to:
   a. have lower tax rates,
   b. have revenue exempt from taxation,
   c. recognize taxable revenues in later years rather than earlier years,
   d. recognize taxable cost deductions greater than actual outlay costs, and
   e. recognize cost deductions in earlier years rather than later years (including accelerated amounts in earlier years).

21-24 DCF, sensitivity analysis, no income taxes (CMA, adapted). Indian Engineering Company manufactures electronic components. The company has developed a device that management believes could be modified and marketed as an electronic game.

The following information for the new product was developed from the best estimates of the marketing and production managers:

Annual sales volume	1,00,000 units
Selling price	Rs 100 per unit
Cash variable costs	Rs 40 per unit
Cash fixed costs	Rs 20,00,000 per year
Investment required	Rs 1,20,00,000
Project life	5 years

At the end of the five-year useful life, there will be a Rs 0 terminal disposal value. Indian Engineering's required rate of return on this project is 14%.

The electronic game item is a new market for the Company, and management is concerned about the reliability of the estimates. The management accountant has proposed applying sensitivity analysis to selected factors. Ignore income taxes in your computations.

Required

1. What is the net present value of this investment proposal?
2. What is the effect on the net present value of the following two changes in assumptions? (Treat each item independently of the other.) (a) 10% reduction in the selling price (b) 10% increase in the variable cost per unit.
3. Discuss how management would use the data developed in requirements 1 and 2 in its consideration of the proposed capital investment.

Solution

DCF, sensitivity analysis, no income taxes (CMA, adapted).

1. Revenues Rs 100 × 1,00,000	Rs 1,00,00,000
Variable cash costs Rs 40 × 1,00,000	40,00,000
Cash contribution margin	60,00,000
Fixed cash costs	20,00,000
Cash inflow from operations	Rs 40,00,000
Net present value:	
Cash inflow from operations Rs 40,00,000 × 3.433	Rs 1,37,32,000
Cash outflow for initial investment	(1,20,00,000)
Net present value	Rs 17,32,000
2a. 10% Reduction in selling prices:	
Revenues Rs 90 × 1,00,000	Rs 90,00,000
Variable cash costs Rs 40 × 1,00,000	40,00,000
Cash contribution margin	50,00,000
Fixed cash costs	20,00,000
Cash inflow from operations	Rs 30,00,000
Net present value:	
Cash inflow from operations Rs 30,00,000 × 3.433	Rs 1,02,99,000
Cash outflow for initial investment	(1,20,00,000)
Net present value	Rs (17,01,000)
2b. 10% Increase in the variable cost per unit.	
Revenues Rs 100 × 1,00,000	Rs 1,00,00,000

Variable cash costs Rs 44 × 1,00,000	44,00,000
Cash contribution margin	56,00,000
Fixed cash costs	20,00,000
Cash inflow from operations	Rs 36,00,000
Net present value:	
Cash inflow from operations Rs 36,00,000 × 3.433	Rs 1,23,58,800
Cash outflow for initial investment	(1,20,00,000)
Net present value	Rs 3,58,800

3. Sensitivity analysis enables management to see those assumptions for which input variations have sizable impact on NPV. Extra resources could be devoted to getting more informed estimates of those inputs with the greatest impact on NPV.
   Sensitivity analysis also enables management to have contingency plans in place if assumptions are not met. For example, if a 10% reduction in selling price is viewed as occurring with 0.40 probability, management may wish to line up bank loan facilities.

21-25 NPV of JIT, income taxes (CMA, adapted). Robust Furniture Company produces office furniture and sells it wholesale to furniture distributors. Robust's management is reviewing a proposal to purchase a just-in-time inventory (JIT) system to better serve its customers. The JIT system will include a computer system and materials-handling equipment. The decision will be based on whether the new JIT system is cost effective to the organization for the next five years.

The computer system, including hardware and software, will initially cost Rs 12,50,000. Materials-handling equipment will cost Rs 4,50,000. Both groups of equipment will have a five-year useful life for tax reporting of depreciation (straight-line) calculated assuming a Rs 0 terminal disposal value. At the end of the five years, the newly acquired materials-handling equipment is expected to be sold for Rs 1,50,000. The computer system will have a Rs 0 terminal disposal value at the end of five years.
Other factors to be considered over the next five years for this proposal include the following:

- Due to the service improvement resulting from this new JIT system, Robust will realize a Rs 8,00,000 increase in revenues during the first year. Robust expects this initial Rs 8,00,000 revenue increase to continue to grow by 10% per year thereafter.
- The contribution margin is 60%.
- Annual material-ordering costs will increase Rs 50,000 due to a greater level of purchase orders.
- There will be a one-time decrease in working-capital investment of Rs 1,50,000 at the end of the first year.
- There will be a 20% savings in warehouse rent due to less space being needed. The current annual rent is Rs 3,00,000.

Robust uses an after-tax required rate of return of 10% and is subject to an income tax rate of 40%. Assume that all cash flows occur at year-end for tax purposes except for any initial purchase amounts.

Required

1. Prepare an analysis of the after-tax effects for the purchase of the JIT system at Robust using the net present value method for evaluating capital expenditures.
2. Determine whether Robust should purchase the JIT system. Explain your answer.

Solution

NPV of JIT, income taxes (CMA adapted).

1. Initial investment (Year 0):

Computer system	Rs 12,50,000
Materials handling equipment	4,50,000
Total initial investment	Rs 17,00,000

Working-capital investment:

Reduced working capital of	Rs 1,50,000 at end of Year 1.
Increased working capital of	Rs 1,50,000 at end of Year 5.

Depreciation on initial investment:
Rs 17,00,000 ÷ 5 years = Rs 3,40,000 per year
Income tax cash savings from annual depreciation deductions:
Rs 3,40,000 × 0.40 = Rs 1,36,000
After-tax flow from disposal of materials-handling equipment at end of Year 5:
Rs 1,50,000 × 0.60 = Rs 90,000
Annual after tax flow from operations:

	Year 1	Year 2	Year 3	Year 4	Year 5
Revenue	Rs 8,00,000	Rs 8,80,000	Rs 9,68,000	Rs 10,64,800	Rs 11,71,280
Contribution margin, 60%	4,80,000	5,28,000	5,80,800	6,38,880	7,02,768
Rent savings	60,000	60,000	60,000	60,000	60,000

Materials ordering cost	(50,000)	(50,000)	(50,000)	(50,000)	(50,000)
Annual cash inflow from operation	4,90,000	5,38,000	5,90,800	6,48,880	7,12,768
Income tax, 40%	1,96,000	2,15,200	2,36,320	2,59,552	2,85,107
After-tax annual cash inflow from operations	Rs 2,94,000	Rs 3,22,800	Rs 3,54,480	Rs 3,89,328	Rs 4,27,661

Solution Exhibit 21-26 reports the net present value to be Rs 2,46,111.

2. Robust will have a NPV of Rs 2,46,111 with the new JIT system. Based on financial quantitative factors, this is an attractive investment. Qualitative factors could make the JIT system even more attractive. For example, if a competitor adopts JIT but Robust does not, Robust could be at a sizable competitive disadvantage. Not adopting JIT does not mean the status quo will remain. Robust's workers can also gain additional shop-floor expertise when using the JIT system that can be beneficially employed on other Robust projects.

Solution Exhibit 21-25

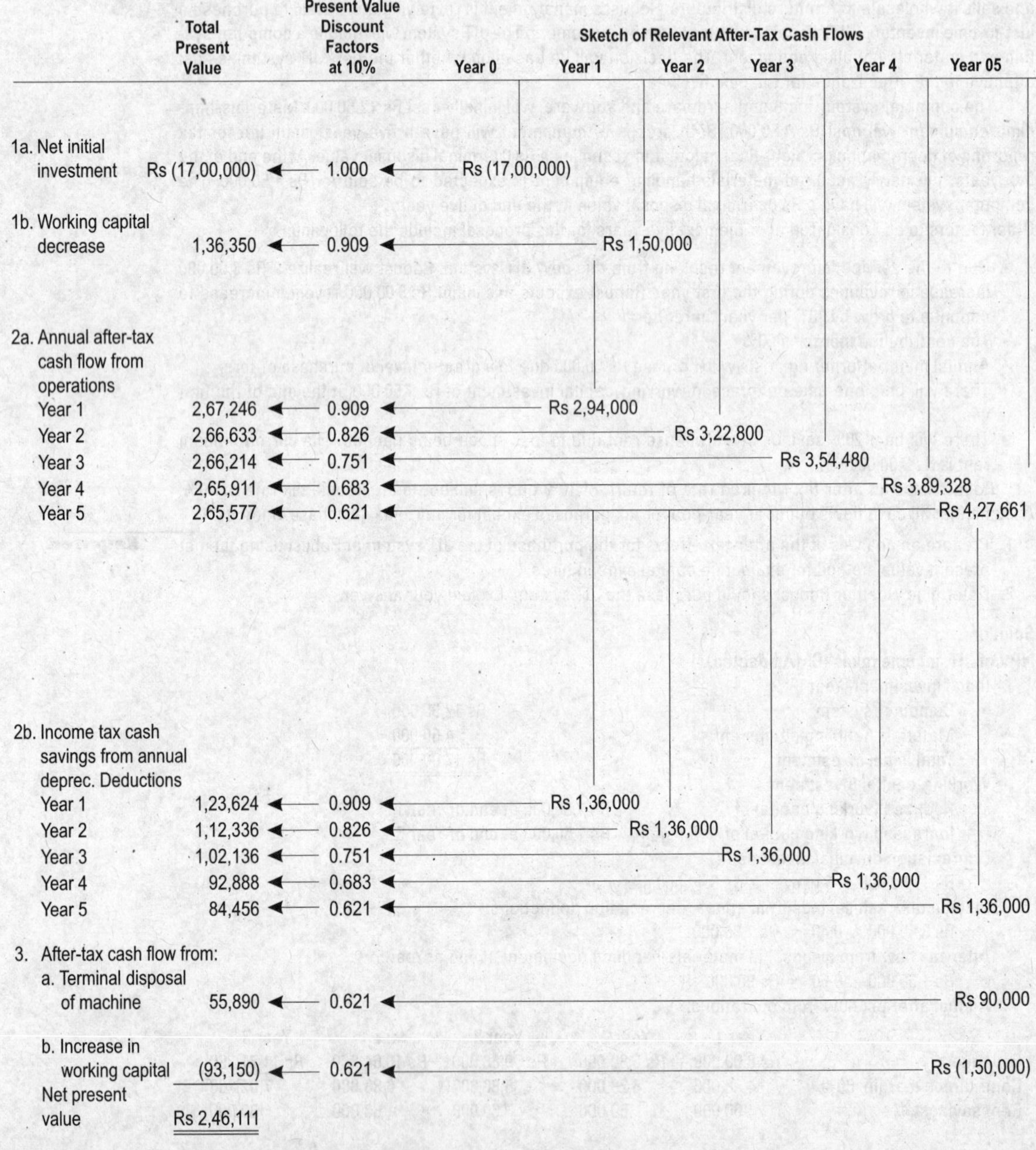

	Total Present Value	Present Value Discount Factors at 10%	Year 0	Year 1	Year 2	Year 3	Year 4	Year 05
1a. Net initial investment	Rs (17,00,000)	1.000	Rs (17,00,000)					
1b. Working capital decrease	1,36,350	0.909		Rs 1,50,000				
2a. Annual after-tax cash flow from operations								
Year 1	2,67,246	0.909		Rs 2,94,000				
Year 2	2,66,633	0.826			Rs 3,22,800			
Year 3	2,66,214	0.751				Rs 3,54,480		
Year 4	2,65,911	0.683					Rs 3,89,328	
Year 5	2,65,577	0.621						Rs 4,27,661
2b. Income tax cash savings from annual deprec. Deductions								
Year 1	1,23,624	0.909		Rs 1,36,000				
Year 2	1,12,336	0.826			Rs 1,36,000			
Year 3	1,02,136	0.751				Rs 1,36,000		
Year 4	92,888	0.683					Rs 1,36,000	
Year 5	84,456	0.621						Rs 1,36,000
3. After-tax cash flow from:								
a. Terminal disposal of machine	55,890	0.621						Rs 90,000
b. Increase in working capital	(93,150)	0.621						Rs (1,50,000)
Net present value	Rs 2,46,111							

21-26 Capital budgeting, inflation, income taxes, appendix (J. Fellingham, adapted). An Electrical Appliance Store is considering buying a repair machine that costs Rs 1,00,000 on December 31, 2011. The machine will last five years. It is estimated that the incremental pre-tax cash savings from using the machine will be Rs 30,000 annually. The Rs 30,000 is measured at current prices and will be received at the end of each year. For tax purposes, the Store will depreciate the machine using the straight-line method, assuming Rs 0 terminal disposal value. The Electric Appliance Store requires a 10% after-tax real rate of return (that is, the rate of return is 10% when all cash flows are denominated in December 31, 2011).

Treat each of the following cases independently.

1. There are no income taxes, but the annual inflation rate is 20%. What is the net present value of the machine? The cash savings each year will be increased by a factor equal to the cumulative inflation rate. Use the nominal discount rate in your computations.
2. The annual inflation rate is 20%, and the income tax rate is 40%. What is the net present value of the machine? Use the same nominal discount rate as in requirement 1 in your computations.

Solution

Capital budgeting, inflation, income taxes, appendix (J. Fellingham, adapted).

1. Nominal rate = (1 + Real rate) (1 + Inflation rate) – 1
   = (1.10) (1.20) – 1
   = 1.32 – 1 = 0.32

Alternatively:

Real rate of interest	0.10
Inflation rate	0.20
Combination (0.10 × 0.20)	0.02
Nominal rate of interest	0.32

Recurring cash-operating savings (nominal rupees and a nominal discount rate):

Year (1)	Cash-Operating Savings in Real rupees (2)	Cumulative Inflation Rate (3)	Cash-Operating Savings In Nominal rupees (4) = (2) × (3)	Nominal rupee Present Value Discount Factor (32%) (5)	Total Present Value (6) = (4) × (5)
2012	Rs 30,000	1.200	Rs 36,000	0.758	Rs 27,290
2013	30,000	1.440	43,200	0.574	24,800
2014	30,000	1.728	51,840	0.435	22,550
2015	30,000	2.074	62,220	0.329	20,470
2016	30,000	2.488	74,640	0.250	18,660
Initial machine investment					(1,00,000)
Net present value					Rs 13,770

2. Recurring after-tax cash-operating savings:

Year (1)	Before-Tax Cash-Operating Savings (Nominal rupees) (2)	Tax Payments (40%) (3) = 0.4 × (2)	After-Tax Cash-Operating Savings (Nominal rupees) (4) = (2) – (3)	Nominal rupee Present Value Discount Factor (32%) (5)	Present Value (6) = (4) × (5)
2012	Rs 36,000	Rs 14,400	Rs 21,600	0.758	Rs 16,370
2013	43,200	17,280	25,920	0.574	14,880
2014	51,840	20,740	31,100	0.435	13,530
2015	62,220	24,890	37,330	0.329	12,280
2016	74,640	29,860	44,780	0.250	11,200
					Rs 68,260

Depreciation Tax Savings:

Year	Income Tax Depreciation Deductions (Straight Line)	Income Tax Cash Savings from Depreciation Deductions at 40%	Nominal rupee Present Value Discount Factor (32%)	Total Present Value
2012	Rs 20,000	Rs 8,000	0.758	Rs 6,060
2013	20,000	8,000	0.574	4,590
2014	20,000	8,000	0.435	3,480
2015	20,000	8,000	0.329	2,630
2016	20,000	8,000	0.250	2,000
				Rs 18,760
Net machine investment				(1,00,000)
Net present value				Rs (12,980)

It may be noted that the depreciation tax deductions are based on the original cost of the asset and equal Rs 2,000 each year, which when discounted at the inflation-adjusted nominal rate of 32% results in a very low present value. This leads to a negative NPV for the project.

Exercises

21-27 Capital budgeting with uneven cash flows, no income taxes. Village Soft Drink Company is considering the purchase of a special purpose bottling machine for Rs 23,000. It is expected to have a useful life of four years with a Rs 0 terminal disposal value. The plant manager estimates the following savings in cash operating costs:

Year	Amount
1	Rs 1,00,000
2	80,000
3	60,000
4	50,000
Total	Rs 2,90,000

Village Soft Drink Company uses a required rate of return of 16% in its capital budgeting decisions. Ignore income taxes in your analysis.

Compute the following:

Required

1. Net present value
2. Payback period
3. Internal rate of return
4. Accrual accounting rate of return based on net initial investment (Assume straight-line depreciation. Use the average annual savings in cash operating costs when computing the numerator of the accrual accounting rate of return.)

21-28 Payback and NPV methods, no income taxes (CMA, adapted). Royal Manufacturing is a small company currently analyzing capital expenditure proposals for the purchase of equipment. The capital budget is limited to Rs 5,00,000, which Royal believes is the maximum capital it can raise.

A consulting company is preparing an analysis of four projects that Royal is considering. The consulting company has projected the future cash flows for each potential purchase. The information concerning the four projects is as follows:

	Project A	Project B	Project C	Project D
Projected cash outflow				
Net initial investment	Rs 2,00,000	Rs 1,90,000	Rs 2,50,000	Rs 2,10,000
Projected cash inflows				
Year 1	Rs 50,000	Rs 40,000	Rs 75,000	Rs 75,000
Year 2	50,000	50,000	75,000	75,000
Year 3	50,000	70,000	60,000	60,000
Year 4	50,000	75,000	80,000	40,000
Year 5	50,000	75,000	1,00,000	20,000

1. Because Royal Manufacturing's cash is limited, its CEO thinks the payback method for calculating investments would be the best method for choosing capital budgeting projects. (a) Explain what the payback method measures and how it is used. Include in your explanation several benefits and limitations of the method. (b) Calculate the payback period for each of the four projects. Ignore income tax considerations.
2. The consulting company would like to compare the projects using the net present value method. The required rate of return for Royal is 12%. All cash flows occur at the end of the year. Calculate the net present value for each project. Ignore income tax considerations.
3. Which projects, if any, would you recommend funding? Briefly state your reasons.

21-29 New equipment purchase, income taxes. Presentation Graphics prepares slides and other aids for individuals making presentations. It estimates it can save Rs 3,50,000 a year in cash operating costs for the next five years if it buys a special-purpose color-slide workstation at a cost of Rs 7,50,000.

The workstation will have a Rs 0 terminal disposal value at the end of year 5. No change in working capital will be required. Presentation Graphics has a 12% after-tax required rate of return. Its income tax rate is 40%.

1. Assume that Presentation Graphics uses straight-line depreciation on its tax return. Compute (a) net present value, (b) payback period, and (c) internal rate of return.
2. Compare and contrast the capital budgeting methods in requirement 1.

21-30 Selling a plant, income taxes (CMA, adapted). Raymond, a clothing manufacturer, has a plant that will become idle on December 31, 2011. The corporate controller, has been asked to look at two options regarding the plant.

- Option 1: The plant, which has been fully depreciated for tax purposes can be sold immediately for Rs 90,00,000.
- Option 2: The plant can be leased to Arvind Mills, one of Raymond's suppliers, for four years. Under the lease terms, Arvind would pay Raymond Rs 24,00,000 rent per year (payable at year-end) and would grant Raymond a Rs 4,74,000 annual discount off the normal price of fabric purchased by Raymond (assume discount received at year-end for each of the four years). Arvind would bear all of the plant's ownership costs. Raymond expects to sell this plant for Rs 20,00,000 at the end of the four-year lease.

Raymond treats all cash flows as if they occur at the end of the year, and it uses an after-tax required rate of return of 12%. Raymond is subject to a 40% income tax rate.

Required

Calculate net present value of each of the options and determine which option Raymond should select using the NPV criterion.

21-31 NPV and customer profitability, no income taxes. National Granite sells granite countertops to the construction industry. National has three customers: X, Y, and Z. Following are National Granite's revenue and cost data by customer for the year ended December 31, 2011:

	X	Y	Z
Revenues	Rs 45,000	Rs 3,25,000	Rs 8,60,000
Cost of goods sold	22,000	1,80,000	5,50,000
Operating costs	10,000	75,000	2,35,000

Jay National, the owner, estimates that revenue and costs will increase as follows on an annual basis:

	X	Y	Z
Revenues	5%	6%	8%
Cost of goods sold	4%	4%	4%
Operating costs	4%	4%	4%

National Granite's required rate of return is 10%. Assume that (a) all transactions occur at year-end, (b) all revenues are cash inflows, and (c) all costs are cash outflows. Ignore income tax considerations.

Required

1. Calculate operating income per customer for 2011 and for each year of the 2012 to 2016 period.
2. National estimates the value of each customer by calculating the customer's projected net present value over the next five years (2012 to 2016). Use the operating incomes calculated in requirement 1 to compute the value of each of its three customers.
3. Recently, customer Y has been threatening to switch suppliers. Y demands a 20% price discount on the revenues for 2012 to 2016 that were estimated for Y in requirement 1 above, if it is to continue using National as a supplier. What is the five-year NPV of Y after incorporating the 20% discount? What other factors should National consider before making its final decision?

21-32 Replacement of a machine, income taxes, sensitivity (CMA, adapted). Rainbow Company operates a snack-food center at the heart of city. On January 1, 2009, Rainbow purchased a special cookie-cutting machine, which has been used for three years. Rainbow is considering purchasing a newer, more-efficient machine. If purchased, the new machine would be acquired today, January 1, 2012. Rainbow expects to sell 3,00,000 cookies in each of the next four years. The selling price of each cookie is expected to average Rs 5.

Rainbow has two options: (1) continue to operate the old machine or (2) sell the old machine and purchase the new machine. The seller of the new machine offered no trade-in. The following information has been assembled to help management decide which option is more desirable:

	Old Machine	New Machine
Initial purchase costs of machine	Rs 8,00,000	Rs 12,00,000
Terminal disposal value at the end of useful life assumed for depreciation purposes	Rs 1,00,000	Rs 2,00,000
Useful life from date of acquisition	7 years	4 years
Expected annual cash operating costs:		
Variable cost per cookie	Rs 2.0	Rs 1.4
Total fixed costs	Rs 1,50,000	Rs 1,40,000
Depreciation method used for tax purposes	Straight-line	Straight-line
Estimated disposal prices of machines:		
January 1, 2012	Rs 4,00,000	Rs 12,00,000
December 31, 2015	Rs 70,000	Rs 2,00,000

Rainbow is subject to a 40% income tax rate. Assume that any gain or loss on the sale of machines is treated as an ordinary tax item and will affect the taxes paid by Rainbow in the year in which it occurs. Rainbow has an after-tax required rate of return of 16%.

Required

1. Use the net present value method to determine whether Rainbow should retain the old machine or acquire the new machine.
2. How much more or less would the recurring after-tax cash operating savings have to be for Rainbow to exactly earn the 16% after-tax required rate of return? Assume all other data about the investment do not change.
3. Assume that the financial differences between the net present values of the two options are so slight that Rainbow is indifferent between the two proposals. Identify and discuss the nonfinancial and qualitative factors that Rainbow should consider.

21-33 Relevant costs, outsourcing, capital budgeting, income taxes. The Indian Electrical appliances (IEA) Company currently makes as many units of Part No. 789 as it needs. David, general manager of the IEA Company, has received a bid from the Philips for supplying Part No. 789. Current plans call for Philips to supply 10,000 units of Part No. 789 per year at Rs 50 a unit. Philips can begin supplying on January 1, 2012, and continue for five years, after which time IEA will not need the part. Philips can accommodate any change in IEA's demand for the part and will supply it for Rs 50 a unit, regardless of quantity.

The management accountant of IEA Company reports the following costs for manufacturing 10,000 units of Part No. 789:

Direct materials	Rs 2,20,000
Direct manufacturing labor	1,10,000
Variable manufacturing overhead	70,000
Depreciation on machine	1,00,000
Product and process engineering	40,000
Rent	20,000
Allocation of general plant overhead costs	50,000
Total costs	Rs 6,10,000

The following additional information is available:

a. Part No. 789 is made on a machine used exclusively for the manufacture of Part No. 789. The machine was acquired on January 1, 2011, at a cost of Rs 6,00,000. The machine has a useful life of six years and Rs 0 terminal disposal value. Depreciation is calculated on the straight-line method.
b. The machine could be sold today for Rs 1,50,000.
c. Product and process engineering costs are incurred to ensure that the manufacturing process for Part No. 789 works smoothly. Although these costs are fixed in the short run with respect to units of Part No. 789 produced, they can be saved in the long run if this part is no longer produced. If Part No. 789 is outsourced, product and process engineering costs of Rs 40,000 will be incurred for 2012 but not thereafter.
d. Rent costs of Rs 20,000 are allocated to products on the basis of the floor space used for manufacturing the product. If Part No. 789 is discontinued, the space currently used to manufacture it would become available. The company could then use the space for storage and save Rs 10,000 currently paid for outside storage.
e. General plant overhead costs are allocated to each department on the basis of direct manufacturing labor costs. These costs will not change in total, but no general plant overhead will be allocated to Part No. 789 if the part is outsourced.

Assume that IEA requires a 12% required rate of return for this project.

Required

Should David outsource Part No. 789? Prepare a quantitative analysis using the net present value method. Assume all cash flows other than disposal of machine occur at the end of each year.

22 Management Control Systems, Transfer Pricing, and Multinational Considerations

Learning Objectives

1. Describe a management control system and its three key properties
2. Describe the benefits and costs of decentralization
3. Explain transfer prices and four criteria used to evaluate alternative transfer-pricing methods
4. Illustrate how market-based transfer prices promote goal congruence in perfectly competitive markets
5. Understand how to avoid making suboptimal decisions when transfer prices are based on full cost plus a markup
6. Describe the range of feasible transfer price when there is unused capacity
7. Apply a general guideline for determining a minimum transfer price
8. Incorporate income tax considerations in multinational transfer pricing

Transfer pricing is the price one subunit of a company charges for the services it provides another subunit of the same company. Top management uses transfer prices (1) to focus managers' attention on the performance of their own subunits and (2) to plan and coordinate the actions of different subunits to maximize the company's income as a whole. But contention can arise because managers of different subunits often have very different preferences about how transfer prices should be set. For example, some managers prefer the prices be based on market prices. Others prefer the prices be based on costs alone. Controversy also arises when multinational corporations seek to reduce their overall income tax burden by charging high transfer prices to units located in countries with high tax rates. Many countries, including the United States, attempt to restrict this practice, as the following article shows.

Symantec Wins $545 million Opinion in Transfer Pricing Dispute with the IRS[1]

Symantec Corp., a large U.S. software company, won a significant court decision in December 2009, potentially saving it $545 million in contested back taxes. The Internal Revenue Service (IRS) had been seeking back taxes it alleged were owed by Veritas Software Corp., a company acquired by Symantec in 2005. The dispute was over the company's formula for "transfer pricing," a complex set of rules determining how companies set prices, fees, and cost-allocation arrangements between their operations in different tax jurisdictions.

At issue were the fees and cost-allocation arrangements between Veritas and its Irish subsidiary. Ireland has emerged as a popular tax haven for U.S. technology companies. Veritas granted rights to Veritas Ireland to conduct research and development on various intangibles (such as computer programs and manufacturing process technologies) related to data storage software and related devices. Under the agreement in effect, Veritas Ireland paid $160 million for this grant of rights from 1999 to 2001. Based on a discounted cash flow analysis, the IRS contended that the true value of the transferred rights was closer to $1.675 billion. As a consequence, it claimed that the transaction artificially increased the income of Veritas Ireland at the expense of income in the U.S. parent corporation, consequently lowering the U.S. tax bills during this period.

[1] *Source*: Chinnis, Cabell et al. 2009. Tax court upends IRS's billion dollar buy-in valuation adjustment in "Veritas." Mondaq Business Briefing, December 17; Letzing, John. 2009. Symantec wins $545M opinion in tax case. *Dow Jones News Service*, December 11.

Veritas, however, maintained that it acted appropriately. The company testified that the $160 million figure was based on royalty rates it had received from seven original equipment manufacturers (OEMs) for rights to incorporate Veritas United States' software and technologies into an operating system, with adjustments made for purposes of comparability. At trial, the United States Tax Court supported this position, and called the IRS's valuation of the intangibles "arbitrary, capricious, and unreasonable." Among other things, the court took issue with the discount and growth rates used in the IRS expert's analysis, and disagreed with his assumption that the transferred intangibles had a perpetual useful life.

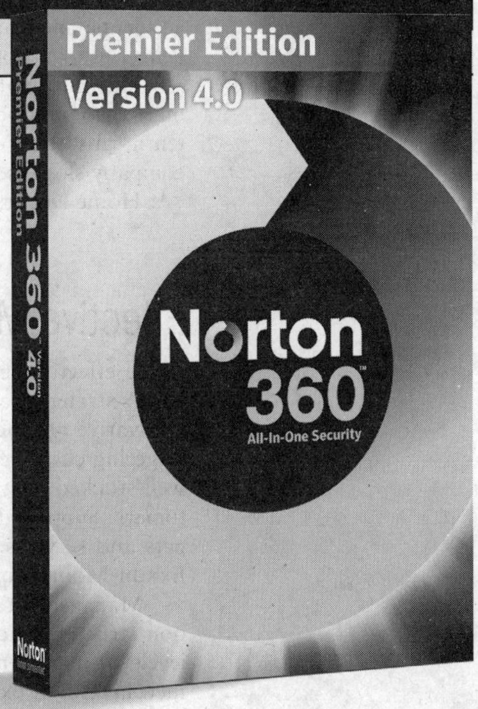

Though not all companies face multinational tax concerns, transfer-pricing issues are common to many companies. In these companies, transfer pricing is part of the larger management control system. This chapter develops the links among strategy, organization structure, management control systems, and accounting information. We'll examine the benefits and costs of centralized and decentralized organization structures, and we'll look at the pricing of products or services transferred between subunits of the same company. We emphasize how accounting information, such as costs, budgets, and prices, helps in planning and coordinating actions of subunits.

Management Control Systems

Learning Objective 1 

Describe a management control system

. . . gathers information for planning and control decisions

and its three key properties

. . . aligns with strategy, supports organizational responsibility of managers, and motivates employees

A **management control system** is a means of gathering and using information to aid and coordinate the planning and control decisions throughout an organization and to guide the behavior of its managers and other employees. Some companies design their management control system around the concept of the balanced scorecard. For example, ExxonMobil's management control system contains financial and nonfinancial information in each of the four perspectives of the balanced scorecard (see Chapter 13 for details). Well-designed management control systems use information both from within the company, such as net income and employee satisfaction, and from outside the company, such as stock price and customer satisfaction.

Formal and Informal Systems

Management control systems consist of formal and informal control systems. The formal management control system of a company includes explicit rules, procedures, performance measures, and incentive plans that guide the behavior of its managers and other employees. The formal control system is comprised of several systems. For example, the management accounting system provides information regarding costs, revenues, and income. The human resources systems provide information on recruiting, training, absenteeism, and accidents; and quality systems provide information on yield, defective products, and late deliveries to customers.

The informal management control system includes shared values, loyalties, and mutual commitments among members of the company, company culture, and the unwritten norms about acceptable behavior for managers and other employees. Examples of company slogans that reinforce values and loyalties are "At Ford, Quality Is Job 1," and "At Home Depot, Low Prices Are Just the Beginning."

Effective Management Control

To be effective, management control systems should be closely aligned with the company's strategies and goals. Two examples of strategies at Exxon-Mobil are (1) providing innovative products and services to increase market share in key customer segments (by targeting customers who are willing to pay more for faster service, better facilities, and well-stocked convenience stores) and (2) reducing costs and targeting price-sensitive customers. Suppose Exxon-Mobil decides, wisely or unwisely, to provide innovative products and services. The management control system must then reinforce this goal, and Exxon-Mobil should tie managers' rewards to achieving the targeted measures.

Management control systems should also be designed to fit the company's organization structure and the decision-making responsibility of individual managers. Different levels of management at Exxon-Mobil need different kinds of information to perform their tasks. For example, top management needs stock-price information to evaluate how much shareholder value the company has created. Stock price, however, is less important for line managers supervising individual refineries. They are more concerned with obtaining information about on-time delivery of gasoline, equipment downtime, product quality, number of days lost to accidents and environmental problems, cost per gallon of gasoline, and employee satisfaction. Similarly, marketing managers are more concerned with information about service at gas stations, customer satisfaction, and market share.

Effective management control systems should also motivate managers and other employees. **Motivation** is the desire to attain a selected goal (the *goal-congruence* aspect) combined with the resulting pursuit of that goal (the *effort* aspect).

Goal congruence exists when individuals and groups work toward achieving the organization's goals—that is, managers working in their own best interest take actions that align with the overall goals of top management. Suppose the goal of Exxon-Mobil's top management is to maximize operating income. If the management control system evaluates the refinery manager *only* on the basis of costs, the manager may be tempted to make decisions that minimize cost but overlook product quality or timely delivery to retail stations, which will likely not maximize operating income of the company as a whole. In this case, the management control system will not achieve goal congruence.

Effort is the extent to which managers strive or endeavor in order to achieve a goal. Effort goes beyond physical exertion, such as a worker producing at a faster rate, to include mental actions as well. For example, effort includes the diligence or acumen with which a manager gathers and analyzes data before authorizing a new investment. It is impossible to directly observe or reward effort. As a result, management control systems motivate employees to exert effort by rewarding them for the achievement of observable goals, such as profit targets or stock returns. This induces managers to exert effort because higher levels of effort increase the likelihood that the goals are achieved. The rewards can be monetary (such as cash, shares of company stock, use of a company car, or membership in a club) or nonmonetary (such as a better title, greater responsibility, or authority over a larger number of employees).

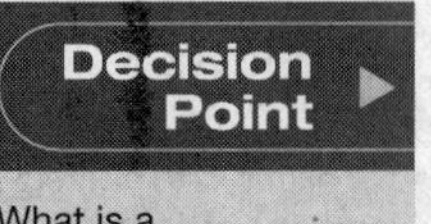

What is a management control system and how should it be designed?

Decentralization

Management control systems must fit an organization's structure. An organization whose structure is decentralized has additional issues to consider for its management control system to be effective.

Learning Objective 2

Describe the benefits of decentralization

. . . responsiveness to customers, faster decision making, management development

and the costs of decentralization

. . . loss of control, duplication of activities

Decentralization is the freedom for managers at lower levels of the organization to make decisions. **Autonomy** is the degree of freedom to make decisions. The greater the freedom, the greater the autonomy. As we discuss the issues of decentralization and autonomy, we use subunit to refer to any part of an organization. A subunit may be a large division, such as the Refining Division of Exxon-Mobil, or a small group, such as a two-person advertising department of a local clothing chain.

Until the mid-twentieth century, many firms were organized in a centralized, hierarchical fashion. Power was concentrated at the top and there was relatively little freedom for managers at the lower levels to make decisions. Perhaps the most famous example of a highly centralized structure is the Soviet Union, prior to its collapse in the late 1980s. Today, organizations are far more decentralized and many companies have pushed decision-making authority down to subunit managers. Examples of firms with decentralized structures include Nucor, the U.S. steel giant, which allows substantial operational autonomy to the general managers of its plants, and Tesco, Britain's largest retailer, which offers great latitude to its store managers. Of course, no firm is completely decentralized. At Nucor headquarters management still retains responsibility for overall strategic planning, company financing, setting base salary levels and bonus targets, purchase of steel scrap, etc. How much decentralization is optimal? Companies try to choose the degree of decentralization that maximizes benefits over costs. From a practical standpoint, top management can seldom quantify either the benefits or the costs of decentralization. Still, the cost-benefit approach helps management focus on the key issues.

Benefits of Decentralization

Supporters of decentralizing decision making and granting responsibilities to managers of subunits advocate the following benefits:

1. **Creates greater responsiveness to local needs.** Good decisions cannot be made without good information. Compared with top managers, subunit managers are better informed about their customers, competitors, suppliers, and employees, as well as about local factors that affect performance, such as ways to decrease costs, improve quality, and be responsive to customers. Eastman Kodak reports that two advantages of decentralization are an "increase in the company's knowledge of the marketplace and improved service to customers."
2. **Leads to gains from faster decision making.** Decentralization speeds decision making, creating a competitive advantage over centralized organizations. Centralization slows decision making as responsibility for decisions creeps upward through layer after layer of management. Interlake, a manufacturer of materials handling equipment, cites this benefit of decentralization: "We have distributed decision-making powers more broadly to the cutting edge of product and market opportunity." Interlake's materials-handling equipment must often be customized to fit customers' needs. Delegating decision making to the sales force allows Interlake to respond faster to changing customer requirements.
3. **Increases motivation of subunit managers.** Subunit managers are more motivated and committed when they can exercise initiative. Johnson & Johnson, a highly decentralized company, maintains that "Decentralization = Creativity = Productivity."
4. **Assists management development and learning.** Giving managers more responsibility helps develop an experienced pool of management talent to fill higher-level management positions. The company also learns which people are not management material. According to Tektronix, an electronics instruments company: "Decentralized units provide a training ground for general managers and a visible field of combat where product champions can fight for their ideas."

5. **Sharpens the focus of subunit managers, broadens the reach of top management.** In a decentralized setting, the manager of a subunit has a concentrated focus. The head of Yahoo Japan, for example, can develop country-specific knowledge and expertise (local advertising trends, cultural norms, payment forms, etc.) and focus attention on maximizing Yahoo's profits in Japan. At the same time, this relieves Yahoo's top management in Sunnyvale, CA from the burden of controlling day-to-day operating decisions in Japan. The American managers can now spend more time and effort on strategic planning for the entire organization.

Costs of Decentralization

Advocates of more-centralized decision making point to the following costs of decentralizing decision making:

1. **Leads to suboptimal decision making.** This cost arises because top management has given up control over decision making. If the subunit managers do not have the necessary expertise or talent to handle this responsibility, the company, as a whole, is worse off.

   Even if subunit managers are sufficiently skilled, **suboptimal decision making**—also called **incongruent decision making** or **dysfunctional decision making**—occurs when a decision's benefit to one subunit is more than offset by the costs to the organization as a whole. This is most prevalent when the subunits in the company are highly interdependent, such as when the end product of one subunit is used or sold by another subunit. For example, suppose that Nintendo's marketing group receives an order for additional Wii consoles in Australia following the release of some unexpectedly popular new games. A manufacturing manager in Japan who is evaluated on the basis of costs may be unwilling to arrange this rush order since altering production schedules invariably increases manufacturing costs. From Nintendo's viewpoint, however, supplying the consoles may be optimal, both because the Australian customers are willing to pay a premium price and because the current shipment is expected to stimulate orders for other Nintendo games and consoles in the future.
2. **Focuses manager's attention on the subunit rather than the company as a whole.** Individual subunit managers may regard themselves as competing with managers of other subunits in the same company as if they were external rivals. This pushes them to view the relative performance of the subunit as more important than the goals of the company. Consequently, managers may be unwilling to assist when another subunit faces an emergency (as in the Nintendo example) or share important information. In the recent Congressional hearings on the recall of Toyota vehicles, it was revealed that it was common for Toyota's Japan unit to not share information about engineering problems or reported defects between its United States, Asian, and European operations. Toyota has since asserted that this dysfunctional behavior will no longer be tolerated.
3. **Results in duplication of output.** If subunits provide similar products or services, their internal competition could lead to failure in the external markets. The reason is that divisions may find it easier to steal market share from one another, by mimicking each other's successful products, rather than from outside firms. Eventually, this leads to confusion in the minds of customers, and the loss of each division's distinctive strengths. The classic example is General Motors, which has had to wind down its Oldsmobile, Pontiac, and Saturn divisions and is now in bankruptcy reorganization. Similarly, Condé Nast Publishing's initially distinct (and separately run) food magazines, *Bon Appétit* and *Gourmet*, eventually ended up chasing the same readers and advertisers, to the detriment of both. *Gourmet* magazine stopped publication in November 2009.[2]
4. **Results in duplication of activities.** Even if the subunits operate in distinct markets, several individual subunits of the company may undertake the same activity

---

[2] For an intriguing comparison of the failure of decentralization in these disparate settings, see Jack Shafer's article, "How Condé Nast is Like General Motors: The Magazine Empire as Car Wreck," Slate, October 5, 2009, www.slate.com/id/2231177/.

separately. In a highly decentralized company, each subunit may have personnel to carry out staff functions such as human resources or information technology. Centralizing these functions helps to streamline and use fewer resources for these activities, and eliminates wasteful duplication. For example, ABB (Switzerland), a global leader in power and automation technology, is decentralized but has generated significant cost savings of late by centralizing its sourcing decisions across business units for parts, such as pipe pumps and fittings, as well as engineering and erection services. The growing popularity of the "shared service center" model, especially for financial transactions and human resources, is predicated on the 30%–40% savings enabled by the consolidation of such functions, rather than allowing them to be controlled by the subunits.[3]

Comparison of Benefits and Costs

To choose an organization structure that will implement a company's strategy, top managers must compare the benefits and costs of decentralization, often on a function-by-function basis. Surveys of companies report that the decisions made most frequently at the decentralized level and least frequently at the corporate level are related to product mix and product advertising. In these areas, subunit managers develop their own operating plans and performance reports and make faster decisions based on local information. Decisions related to the type and source of long-term financing and income taxes are made least frequently at the decentralized level and most frequently at the corporate level. Corporate managers have better information about financing terms in different markets and can obtain the best terms. Centralizing income tax strategies allows the organization to trade off and manage income in a subunit with losses in others. The benefits of decentralization are generally greater when companies face uncertainties in their environments, require detailed local knowledge for performing various jobs, and have few interdependencies among divisions.

Decentralization in Multinational Companies

Multinational companies—companies that operate in multiple countries—are often decentralized because centralized control of a company with subunits around the world is often physically and practically impossible. Also, language, customs, cultures, business practices, rules, laws, and regulations vary significantly across countries. Decentralization enables managers in different countries to make decisions that exploit their knowledge of local business and political conditions and to deal with uncertainties in their individual environments. For example, Philips, a global electronics company headquartered in the Netherlands, delegates marketing and pricing decisions for its television business in the Indian and Singaporean markets to the managers in those countries. Multinational corporations often rotate managers between foreign locations and corporate headquarters. Job rotation combined with decentralization helps develop managers' abilities to operate in the global environment.

There are drawbacks to decentralizing multinational companies. One of the most important is the lack of control and the resulting risks. Barings PLC, a British investment banking firm, went bankrupt and had to be sold when one of its traders in Singapore caused the firm to lose more than Rs 10 crore on unauthorized trades that were not detected until after the trades were made. Similarly, a trader at Sumitomo Corporation racked up Rs 26 crore in copper-trading losses because poor controls failed to detect the magnitude of the trader's activities. Multinational corporations that implement decentralized decision making usually design their management control systems to measure and monitor division performance. Information and communications technology helps the flow of information for reporting and control.

---

[3] For more on this topic, see http://www.sap.com/solutions/business-suite/erp/pdf/BWP_WP_Shared_Services.pdf.

Choices About Responsibility Centers

Recall from Chapter 6 that a responsibility center is a segment or subunit of the organization whose manager is accountable for a specified set of activities. To measure the performance of subunits in centralized or decentralized companies, the management control system uses one or a mix of the four types of responsibility centers:

1. *Cost center*—the manager is accountable for costs only.
2. *Revenue center*—the manager is accountable for revenues only.
3. *Profit center*—the manager is accountable for revenues and costs.
4. *Investment center*—the manager is accountable for investments, revenues, and costs.

Centralization or decentralization is not mentioned in the descriptions of these centers because each type of responsibility center can be found in either centralized or decentralized companies.

What are the benefits and costs of decentralization?

A common misconception is that *profit center*—and, in some cases, *investment center*—is a synonym for a decentralized subunit, and *cost center* is a synonym for a centralized subunit. *Profit centers can be coupled with a highly centralized organization, and cost centers can be coupled with a highly decentralized organization.* For example, managers in a division organized as a profit center may have little freedom in making decisions. They may need to obtain approval from corporate headquarters for every expenditure over, say, Rs 1,00,000 and may be forced to do what the central staff wants. In another company, divisions may be organized as cost centers, but their managers may have great latitude on capital expenditures and on where to purchase materials and services. In short, the labels "profit center" and "cost center" are independent of the degree of centralization or decentralization in a company.

Transfer Pricing

Learning Objective 3

Explain transfer prices

. . . price one subunit charges another for product

and four criteria used to evaluate them

. . . goal congruence, management effort, subunit performance evaluation, and subunit autonomy

In decentralized organizations, much of the decision-making power resides in its individual subunits. In these cases, the management control system often uses *transfer prices* to coordinate the actions of the subunits and to evaluate their performance.

As you may recall from the opener, a **transfer price** is the price one subunit (department or division) charges for a product or service supplied to another subunit of the same organization. If, for example, a car manufacturer has a separate division that manufactures engines, the transfer price is the price the engine division charges when it transfers engines to the car assembly division. The transfer price creates revenues for the selling subunit (the engine division in our example) and purchase costs for the buying subunit (the assembly division in our example), affecting each subunit's operating income. These operating incomes can be used to evaluate subunits' performances and to motivate their managers. The product or service transferred between subunits of an organization is called an **intermediate product.** This product may either be further worked on by the receiving subunit (as in the engine example) or, if transferred from production to marketing, sold to an external customer.

In one sense, transfer pricing is a curious phenomenon. Activities within an organization are clearly nonmarket in nature; products and services are not bought and sold as they are in open-market transactions. Yet, establishing prices for transfers among subunits of a company has a distinctly market flavor. The rationale for transfer prices is that subunit managers (such as the manager of the engine division), when making decisions, need only focus on how their decisions will affect their subunit's performance without evaluating their impact on companywide performance. In this sense, transfer prices ease the subunit managers' information-processing and decision-making tasks. In a well-designed transfer-pricing system, a manager focuses on optimizing subunit performance (the performance of the engine division) and in so doing optimizes the performance of the company as a whole.

Criteria for Evaluating Transfer Prices

As in all management control systems, transfer prices should help achieve a company's strategies and goals and fit its organization structure. In particular, transfer prices should promote goal congruence and a sustained high level of management effort. Subunits selling a product or service should be motivated to hold down their costs; subunits buying the product or service should be motivated to acquire and use inputs efficiently. The transfer price should also help top management evaluate the performance of individual subunits and their managers. If top management favors a high degree of decentralization, transfer prices should also promote a high degree of subunit autonomy in decision making. That is, a subunit manager seeking to maximize the operating income of the subunit should have the freedom to transact with other subunits of the company (on the basis of transfer prices) or to transact with external parties.

Calculating Transfer Prices

There are three methods for determining transfer prices:

1. **Market-based transfer prices.** Top management may choose to use the price of a similar product or service publicly listed in, say, a trade association Web site. Also, top management may select, for the internal price, the external price that a subunit charges to outside customers.
2. **Cost-based transfer prices.** Top management may choose a transfer price based on the cost of producing the product in question. Examples include variable production cost, variable and fixed production costs, and full cost of the product. Full cost of the product includes all production costs plus costs from other business functions (R&D, design, marketing, distribution, and customer service). The cost used in cost-based transfer prices can be actual cost or budgeted cost. Sometimes, the cost-based transfer price includes a markup or profit margin that represents a return on subunit investment.
3. **Hybrid transfer prices.** Hybrid transfer prices take into account both cost and market information. Top management may administer such prices, for example by specifying a transfer price that is an average of the cost of producing and transporting the product internally and the market price for comparable products. At other times, a hybrid transfer price may take the form where the revenue recognized by the selling unit is different from the cost recognized by the buying unit. The most common form of hybrid prices arise via negotiation—the subunits of a company are asked to negotiate the transfer price between them and to decide whether to buy and sell internally or deal with external parties. The eventual transfer price is then the outcome of a bargaining process between selling and buying subunits. Even though there is no requirement that the chosen transfer price bear any specific relationship to cost or market-price data, information regarding costs and prices plays a critical role in the negotiation process. Negotiated transfer prices are often employed when market prices are volatile and change constantly.

To see how each of the three transfer-pricing methods works and to see the differences among them, we examine transfer pricing at Hindustan Petroleum against the four criteria of goal congruence, management effort, subunit performance evaluation, and subunit autonomy (if desired).

An Illustration of Transfer Pricing

Hindustan Petroleum has two divisions, each operating as a profit center. The Transportation Division purchases crude oil in Ankleshwar, Gujarat, and transports it from Ankleshwar to Mathura, U.P. The Refining Division processes crude oil into gasoline. For simplicity, we assume gasoline is the only salable product the Mathura refinery makes and that it takes two barrels of crude oil to yield one barrel of gasoline.

Variable costs in each division are variable with respect to a single cost driver: barrels of crude oil transported by the Transportation Division, and barrels of gasoline produced by the Refining Division. The fixed cost per unit is based on the budgeted annual fixed costs and practical capacity of crude oil that can be transported by Transportation, and the budgeted fixed costs and practical capacity of gasoline that can be produced by Refining division.

- The Transportation Division has obtained rights to certain oil fields in the Ankleshwar area. It has a long-term contract to purchase crude oil produced from these fields at Rs 720 per barrel. The division transports the oil to Mathura and then "sells" it to the Refining Division. The pipeline from Ankleshwar to Mathura has the capacity to carry 40,000 barrels of crude oil per day.
- The Refining Division has been operating at capacity (30,000 barrels of crude oil a day), using oil supplied by Hindustan Petroleum's Transportation Division (an average of 10,000 barrels per day) and oil bought from another producers and delivered to the Mathura refinery (an average of 20,000 barrels per day at Rs 850 per barrel).
- The Refining Division sells the gasoline it produces to outside parties at Rs 1,900 per barrel.

Exhibit 22-1 summarizes Hindustan Petroleum's variable and fixed costs per barrel of crude oil in the Transportation Division and variable and fixed costs per barrel of gasoline in the Refining Division, the external market prices of buying crude oil, and the external market price of selling gasoline. What's missing in the exhibit is the actual transfer price from the Transportation Division to the Refining Division. This transfer price will vary depending on the transfer-pricing method used. Transfer prices from the Transportation Division to the Refining Division under each of the three methods are:

1. Market-based transfer price of Rs 850 per barrel of crude oil based on the competitive market price in Mathura.
2. Cost-based transfer prices at, say, 105% of full cost, where full cost is the cost of the crude oil purchased in Ankleshwar plus the Transportation Division's own variable and fixed costs: 1.05 × (Rs 720 + Rs 10 + Rs 30) = Rs 798.
3. Negotiated transfer price of Rs 820 per barrel of crude oil, which is between the market-based and cost-based transfer prices.

Exhibit 22-2 presents division operating incomes per 100 barrels of crude oil purchased under each transfer-pricing method. Transfer prices create income for the selling division and corresponding costs for the buying division that cancel out when division results are consolidated for the company as a whole. The exhibit assumes all three transfer-pricing

Exhibit 22-1 Operating Data for Hindustan Petroleum

	A	B	C	D	E	F	G	H
1								
2				**Transportation Division**				
3				Variable cost per barrel of crude oi l	Rs10			
4	Contract price per barrel of crude oil supplied in Ankleshwar	=	Rs 720 →	Fixed cost per barrel of crude oil	30			
5				Full cost per barrel of crude oil	Rs40			
6				↓				
7								
8				Barrels of crude oil transferred				
9								
10				↓				
11				**Refining Division**				
12				Variable cost per barrel of gasoline	Rs80			
13	Market price per barrel of crude oil supplied to Mathura refinery	=	Rs 850 →	Fixed cost per barrel of gasoline	60	→	Market price per barrel of gasoline sold to external parties	= Rs 1,900
14				Full cost per barrel of gasoline	Rs140			
15								

Exhibit 22-2 Division Operating Income of Hindustan Petroleum for 100 Barrels of Crude Oil Under Alternative Transfer-Pricing Methods

	A	B	E	G
1	Production and Sales Data			
2	Barrels of crude transferred = 100			
3	Barrels of gasoline sold = 50			
4				
5–8		Internal Transfers at Market Price of Rs 210 per barrel	Internal Transfers at 105% of Full Cost = Rs 798 per barrel	Internal Transfers at Negotiated Price of Rs 820 per barrel
9	**Transportation Division**			
10	Revenues, Rs 210, Rs 176, Rs 192.5 x 100 barrels of crude oil	Rs 85,000	Rs 79,800	Rs 82,000
11	Costs			
12	Crude oil purchase costs,			
13	Rs 120 x 100 barrels of crude oil	72,000	72,000	72,000
14	Division variable costs,			
15	Rs 10 x 100 barrels of crude oil	1,000	1,000	1,000
16	Division fixed costs,			
17	Rs 30 x 100 barrels of crude oil	3,000	3,000	3,000
18	Total division costs	76,000	76,000	76,000
19	Division operating income	Rs 9,000	Rs 3,800	Rs 6,000
20				
21	**Refining Division**			
22	Revenues, Rs 580 x 50 barrels of gasoline	Rs 95,000	Rs 95,000	Rs 95,000
23	Costs			
24	Transferred-in costs, Rs 210, Rs 176, Rs 192.5			
25	x 100 barrels of crude oil	85,000	79,800	82,000
26	Division variable costs,			
27	Rs 80 x 50 barrels of gasoline	4,000	4,000	4,000
28	Division fixed costs,			
29	Rs 60 x 50 barrels of gasoline	3,000	3,000	3,000
30	Total division costs	92,000	86,800	89,000
31	Division operating income	Rs 3,000	Rs 8,200	6,000
32				
33	Operating income of both divisions together	Rs 12,000	Rs 12,000	Rs 12,000

methods yield transfer prices that are in a range that does not cause division managers to change the business relationships shown in Exhibit 22-1. That is, Hindustan Petroleum's total operating income from purchasing, transporting, and refining the 100 barrels of crude oil and selling the 50 barrels of gasoline is the same, Rs 12,000, *regardless of the internal transfer prices used.*

Operating income = Revenues − Cost of crude oil purchases in Matamors − Transportation costs − Refining costs

= (Rs 1,900 × 50 barrels of gasoline − Rs 720 × 100 barrels of crude oil − Rs 40 × 100 barrels of crude oil − Rs 140 × 50 barrels of gasoline
= Rs 95,000 − Rs 72,000 − Rs 4,000 − Rs 7,000 = Rs 12,000

Note further that under all three methods, summing the two division operating incomes equals Hindustan Petroleum's total operating income of Rs 12,000. By keeping total operating income the same, we focus attention on the effects of different transfer-pricing methods on the operating income of each division. Subsequent sections of this chapter show that different transfer-pricing methods can cause managers to take different actions leading to different total operating incomes.

Consider the two methods in the first two columns of Exhibit 22-2. The operating income of the Transportation Division is Rs 5,200 more (Rs 9,000 − Rs 3,800) if transfer prices are based on market prices rather than on 105% of full cost. The operating income of the Refining Division is Rs 5,200 more (Rs 8,200 − Rs 3,000) if transfer prices are based on 105% of full cost rather than market prices. If the Transportation Division's sole criterion were to maximize its own division operating income, it would favor transfer prices at market prices. In contrast, the Refining Division would prefer transfer prices at 105% of full cost to maximize its own division operating income. The transfer price of Rs 820 negotiated by the Transportation and Refining Division managers is between the 105% of full cost and market-based transfer prices and splits the Rs 12,000 of operating income almost equally between the divisions and could arise as a result of negotiations between the transportation and refining division managers. It's not surprising that subunit managers take considerable interest in setting transfer prices, especially those managers whose compensation or promotion directly depends on subunit operating income. To reduce the excessive focus of subunit managers on their own subunits, many companies compensate subunit managers on the basis of both subunit and companywide operating incomes.

Decision Point

What are alternative ways of calculating transfer prices, and what criteria should be used to evaluate them?

We next examine market-based, cost-based, and negotiated transfer prices in more detail. We show how the choice of transfer-pricing method combined with managers' sourcing decisions can determine the size of the companywide operating-income pie itself.

Market-Based Transfer Prices

Learning Objective

Illustrate how market-based transfer prices promote goal congruence in perfectly competitive markets

. . . division managers transacting internally are motivated to take the same actions as if they were transacting externally

Transferring products or services at market prices generally leads to optimal decisions when three conditions are satisfied: (1) The market for the intermediate product is perfectly competitive, (2) interdependencies of subunits are minimal, and (3) there are no additional costs or benefits to the company as a whole from buying or selling in the external market instead of transacting internally.

Perfectly-Competitive-Market Case

A **perfectly competitive market** exists when there is a homogeneous product with buying prices equal to selling prices and no individual buyers or sellers can affect those prices by their own actions. By using market-based transfer prices in perfectly competitive markets, a company can achieve (1) goal congruence, (2) management effort, (3) evaluate subunit performance evaluation, and (4) subunit autonomy.

Consider Hindustan Petroleum again. Assume there is a perfectly competitive market for crude oil in the Mathura area. As a result, the Transportation Division can sell and the Refining Division can buy as much crude oil as each wants at Rs 850 per barrel. Hindustan would prefer its managers to buy or sell crude oil internally. Think about the decisions that Hindustan's division managers would make if each had the autonomy to sell or buy crude oil externally. If the transfer price between Hindustan's Transportation and Refining Divisions is set below Rs 850, the manager of the Transportation Division will be motivated to sell all crude oil to external buyers in the Mathura area at Rs 850 per barrel. If the transfer price is set above Rs 850, the manager of the Refining Division will be motivated to purchase all crude oil requirements from external suppliers. Only a Rs 850 transfer price will motivate the Transportation Division and the Refining Division to buy and sell internally. That's because neither division profits by buying or selling in the external market.

Suppose Hindustan evaluates division managers on the basis of their individual division's operating income. The Transportation Division will sell, either internally or externally, as much crude oil as it can profitably transport, and the Refining Division will buy, either internally or externally, as much crude oil as it can profitably refine. A Rs 850-per-barrel transfer price achieves goal congruence—the actions that maximize each division's operating income are also the actions that maximize operating income of Hindustan Petroleum as a whole. Furthermore, because the transfer price is not based on costs, it motivates each division manager to exert management effort to maximize his or her own

division's operating income. Market prices also serve to evaluate the economic viability and profitability of each division individually. For example, if under market-based transfer prices, the Refining Division consistently shows small or negative profits, Hindustan may decide to shut down the Refining Division and simply transport and sell the oil to other refineries in the Mathura area.

Distress Prices

When supply outstrips demand, market prices may drop well below their historical averages. If the drop in prices is expected to be temporary, these low market prices are sometimes called "distress prices." Deciding whether a current market price is a distress price is often difficult. The market prices of several agricultural commodities, such as wheat and oats, have stayed for many years at what many people initially believed were temporary distress levels!

Which transfer price should be used for judging performance if distress prices prevail? Some companies use the distress prices themselves, but others use long-run average prices, or "normal" market prices. In the short run, the manager of the selling subunit should supply the product or service at the distress price as long as it exceeds the *incremental costs* of supplying the product or service. If the distress price is used as the transfer price, the selling division will show a loss because the distress price will not exceed the *full cost* of the division. If the long-run average market price is used, forcing the manager to buy internally at a price above the current market price will hurt the buying division's short-run operating income. But the long-run average market price will provide a better measure of the long-run profitability and viability of the supplier division. Of course, if the price remains low in the long run, the company should use the low market price as the transfer price. If this price is lower than the variable and fixed costs that can be saved if manufacturing facilities are shut down, the production facilities of the selling subunit should be sold, and the buying subunit should purchase the product from an external supplier.

Imperfect Competition

If markets are not perfectly competitive, selling prices affect the quantity of product sold. If the selling division sells its product in the external market, the selling division manager would choose a price and quantity combination that would maximize the division's operating income. If the transfer price is set at this selling price, the buying division may find that acquiring the product is too costly and results in a loss. It may decide not to purchase the product. Yet, from the point of view of the company as a whole, it may well be that profits are maximized if the selling division transfers the product to the buying division for further processing and sale. For this reason, when the market for the intermediate good is imperfectly competitive, the transfer price must generally be set below the external market price (but above the selling division's variable cost) in order to induce efficient transfers.[4]

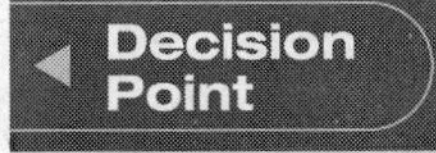

Under what market conditions do market-based transfer prices promote goal congruence?

[4] Consider a firm where division S produces the intermediate product. S has a capacity of 15 units and a variable cost per unit of Rs 20. The imperfect competition is reflected in a downward-sloping demand curve for the intermediate product—if S wants to sell Q units, it has to lower the market price to P = 20 – Q. The division's profit function is therefore given by $Q \times (20 - Q) - 2Q = 18Q - Q^2$. Simple calculus reveals that it is optimal for S to sell 9 units of the intermediate product at a price of Rs 110, thereby making a profit of Rs 810. Now, suppose that division B in the same firm can take the intermediate product, incur an additional variable cost of Rs 40 and sell it in the external market for Rs 120. Since S has surplus capacity (it only uses 9 of its 15 units of capacity), it is clearly in the firm's interest to have S make additional units and transfer them to B. The firm makes an incremental profit of Rs 120 – Rs 20 – Rs 40 = Rs 60 for each transferred unit. However, if the transfer price for the intermediate product were set equal to the market price of Rs 110, B would reject the transaction since it would lose money on it (Rs 120 – Rs 110 – Rs 40 = – Rs 30 per unit).

To resolve this conflict, the transfer price should be set at a suitable *discount* to the external price in order to induce the buying division to seek internal transfers. In our example, the selling price must be greater than S's variable cost of Rs 20, but less than B's contribution margin of Rs 80. That is, the transfer price has to be discounted relative to the market price (Rs 110) by a minimum of Rs 30. We explore the issue of feasible transfer pricing ranges further in the section on hybrid transfer prices.

Learning Objective 5

Understand how to avoid making suboptimal decisions when transfer prices are based on full cost plus a markup

. . . in situations when buying divisions regard the fixed costs and the markup as variable costs

Cost-Based Transfer Prices

Cost-based transfer prices are helpful when market prices are unavailable, inappropriate, or too costly to obtain—for example, when markets are not perfectly competitive, when the product is specialized, or when the internal product is different from the products available externally in terms of quality and customer service.

Full-Cost Bases

In practice, many companies use transfer prices based on full cost. To approximate market prices, cost-based transfer prices are sometimes set at full cost plus a margin. These transfer prices, however, can lead to suboptimal decisions. Suppose Hindustan Petroleum makes internal transfers at 105% of full cost. Recall that the Refining Division purchases, on average, 20,000 barrels of crude oil per day from a local Mathura supplier, who delivers the crude oil to the refinery at a price of Rs 850 per barrel. To reduce crude oil costs, the Refining Division has located an independent producer in Ankleshwar—Reliance Petroleum—that is willing to sell 20,000 barrels of crude oil per day at Rs 790 per barrel, delivered to Hindustan's pipeline in Ankleshwar. Given Hindustan's organization structure, the Transportation Division would purchase the 20,000 barrels of crude oil in Ankleshwar from Reliance Petroleum, transport it to Mathura, and then sell it to the Refining Division. The pipeline has unused capacity and can ship the 20,000 barrels per day at its variable cost of Rs 10 per barrel without affecting the shipment of the 10,000 barrels of crude oil per day acquired under its existing long-term contract arrangement. Will Hindustan Petroleum incur lower costs by purchasing crude oil from Reliance Petroleum in Ankleshwar or by purchasing crude oil from the Mathura supplier? Will the Refining Division show lower crude oil purchasing costs by acquiring oil from Reliance Petroleum or by acquiring oil from its current Mathura supplier?

The following analysis shows that Hindustan Petroleum's operating income would be maximized by purchasing oil from Reliance Petroleum. The analysis compares the incremental costs in both divisions under the two alternatives. The analysis assumes the fixed costs of the Transportation Division will be the same regardless of the alternative chosen. That is, the Transportation Division cannot save any of its fixed costs if it does not transport Reliance's 20,000 barrels of crude oil per day.

- **Alternative 1:** Buy 20,000 barrels from the Mathura supplier at Rs 850 per barrel. Total costs to Hindustan Petroleum are 20,000 barrels × Rs 850 per barrel = Rs 1,70,00,000.
- **Alternative 2:** Buy 20,000 barrels in Ankleshwar at Rs 790 per barrel and transport them to Mathura at a variable cost of Rs 10 per barrel. Total costs to Hindustan Petroleum are 20,000 barrels × (Rs 790 + Rs 10) per barrel = Rs 1,60,00,000.

There is a reduction in total costs to Hindustan Petroleum of Rs 10,00,000 (Rs 1,70,00,000 – Rs 1,60,00,000) by acquiring oil from Reliance.

Suppose the Transportation Division's transfer price to the Refining Division is 110% of full cost. The Refining Division will see its reported division costs increase if the crude oil is purchased from Reliance.

$$\text{Transfer price} = 1.05 \times \left(\begin{array}{c}\text{Purchase price}\\ \text{from}\\ \text{Gulfmex}\end{array} + \begin{array}{c}\text{Variable cost per unit}\\ \text{of Transportation}\\ \text{Division}\end{array} + \begin{array}{c}\text{Fixed cost per unit}\\ \text{of Transportation}\\ \text{Division}\end{array}\right)$$

$$= 1.05 \times (\text{Rs } 790 + \text{Rs } 10 + \text{Rs } 30) = 1.05 \times \text{Rs } 830 = \text{Rs } 871.5 \text{ per barrel}$$

- **Alternative 1:** Buy 20,000 barrels from Mathura supplier at Rs 850 per barrel. Total costs to Refining Division are 20,000 barrels × Rs 850 per barrel = Rs 1,70,00,000.
- **Alternative 2:** Buy 20,000 barrels from the Transportation Division of Hindustan Petroleum that were purchased from Reliance. Total costs to Refining Division are 20,000 barrels × Rs 871.5 per barrel = Rs 1,74,30,000.

As a profit center, the Refining Division can maximize its short-run division operating income by purchasing from the Mathura supplier at Rs 1,70,00,000.

The Refining Division looks at each barrel that it obtains from the Transportation Division as a variable cost of Rs 871.5 per barrel; if 10 barrels are transferred, it costs the Refining Division Rs 8,715; if 100 barrels are transferred, it costs Rs 87,150. In fact, the variable cost per barrel is Rs 800 (Rs 790 to purchase the oil from Reliance plus Rs 10 to transport it to Mathura). The remaining Rs 71.5 (Rs 871.5 − Rs 800) per barrel is the Transportation Division's fixed cost and markup. *The full cost plus a markup transfer-pricing method causes the Refining Division to regard the fixed cost (and the 50% markup) of the Transportation Division as a variable cost and leads to goal incongruence.*

Should Hindustan's top management interfere and force the Refining Division to buy from the Transportation Division? Top management interference would undercut the philosophy of decentralization, so Hindustan's top management would probably view the decision by the Refining Division to purchase crude oil from external suppliers as an inevitable cost of decentralization and not interfere. Of course, some interference may occasionally be necessary to prevent costly blunders. But recurring interference and constraints would simply transform Hindustan Petroleum from a decentralized company into a centralized company.

What transfer price will promote goal congruence for both the Transportation and Refining divisions? The minimum transfer price is Rs 800 per barrel. A transfer price below Rs 800 does not provide the Transportation Division with an incentive to purchase crude oil from Reliance in Ankleshwar. The maximum transfer price is Rs 850 per barrel. A transfer price above Rs 850 will cause the Refining Division to purchase crude oil from the external market rather than from the Transportation Division. A transfer price between the minimum and maximum transfer prices of Rs 800 and Rs 850 will promote goal congruence: Each division will increase its own reported operating income while increasing Hindustan Petroleum's operating income if the Refining Division purchases crude oil from Reliance in Ankleshwar. For example, a transfer price based on the full costs of Rs 800 without a markup will achieve goal congruence; the Transportation Division will show no operating income and will be evaluated as a cost center.

In the absence of a market-based transfer price, senior management at Hindustan Petroleum cannot easily determine the profitability of the investment made in the Transportation Division and hence whether Hindustan should keep or sell the pipeline. Furthermore, if the transfer price had been based on the actual costs of the Transportation Division, it would provide the division with no incentive to control costs. That's because all cost inefficiencies of the Transportation Division would get passed along as part of the actual full-cost transfer price. In fact, every additional dollar of cost arising from wastefulness in the transportation division would generate an additional five cents in profit for the division under the "105% of full cost" rule!

Surveys indicate that, despite the limitations, managers generally prefer to use full-cost-based transfer prices. That's because these transfer prices represent relevant costs for long-run decisions, they facilitate external pricing based on variable and fixed costs, and they are the least costly to administer. However, full-cost transfer pricing does raise many issues. How are each subunit's indirect costs allocated to products? Have the correct activities, cost pools, and cost-allocation bases been identified? Should the chosen fixed-cost rates be actual or budgeted? The issues here are similar to the issues that arise in allocating fixed costs, which were introduced in Chapter 14. Many companies determine the transfer price based on budgeted rates and practical capacity because it overcomes the problem of inefficiencies in actual costs and costs of unused capacity getting passed along to the buying division.

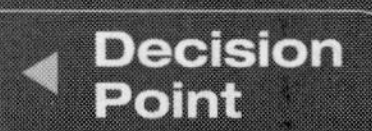

Decision Point

What problems can arise when full cost plus a markup is used as the transfer price?

Variable-Cost Bases

Transferring 20,000 barrels of crude oil from the Transportation Division to the Refining Division at the variable cost of Rs 170 per barrel achieves goal congruence, as shown in the preceding section. The Refining Division would buy from the Transportation Division because the Transportation Division's variable cost is less than the Rs 210 price charged by external suppliers. Setting the transfer price equal to the variable cost has other benefits. Knowledge of the variable cost per barrel of crude oil is very helpful to the Refining Division for many decisions such as the short-run pricing decisions discussed in Chapters 11 and 12. However, at the Rs 170-per-barrel transfer price, the Transportation Division would record an operating loss, and the Refining Division would show large profits because it would be charged only for the variable costs of the Transportation Division. One approach to addressing this problem is to have the Refining Division make a lump-sum transfer payment to cover fixed costs and generate some operating income for the Transportation Division while the Transportation Division continues to make transfers at variable cost. The fixed payment is the price the Refining Division pays for using the capacity of the Transportation Division. The income earned by each division can then be used to evaluate the performance of each division and its manager.

Hybrid Transfer Prices

Learning Objective 6

Describe the range of feasible transfer prices when there is unused capacity

. . . from variable cost to market price of the product transferred

Consider again Hindustan Petroleum. As we saw earlier, the transportation division has unused capacity it can use to transport oil from Ankleshwar to Mathura at an incremental cost of Rs 800 per barrel of crude oil. Hindustan Petroleum, as a whole, maximizes operating income if the refining division purchases crude oil from the transportation division rather than from the Mathura market (incremental cost per barrel of Rs 800 versus price per barrel of Rs 850). Both divisions would be interested in transacting with each other (and the firm achieves goal congruence) if the transfer price is between Rs 800 and Rs 850.

For any internal transaction, there is generally a minimum transfer price the selling division will not go below, based on its cost structure. In the Hindustan Petroleum example, the minimum price acceptable to the transportation division is Rs 800. There is also a maximum price the buying division will not wish to exceed, given by the lower of two quantities—the eventual contribution it generates from an internal transaction and the price of purchasing a comparable intermediate product from an outside party. For the refining division, each barrel of gasoline sold to external parties generates Rs 1,820 in contribution (the Rs 1,900 price less the Rs 80 variable cost of refining). Since it takes two barrels of crude oil to generate a barrel of gasoline, this is equivalent to a contribution of Rs 910 per barrel of crude. For any price higher than Rs 910, the refining division would lose money for each barrel of crude it takes from the transportation division. On the other hand, the refining division can purchase crude oil on the open market for Rs 850 rather than having it transported internally. The maximum feasible transfer price is thus the lower of Rs 910 and Rs 850, or Rs 850 in this instance. We saw previously that a transfer price between the minimum price (Rs 800) and the maximum (Rs 850) would promote goal congruence. We now describe three different ways in which firms attempt to determine the specific transfer price within these bounds.

Prorating the Difference Between Maximum and Minimum Transfer Prices

An approach that Hindustan Petroleum could pursue is to choose a transfer price that splits, on some fair basis, the Rs 50 difference between the Rs 850-per-barrel maximum transfer price the Refining Division is willing to pay and the Rs 800-per-barrel variable cost-based minimum price the transportation division wants to receive. An easy solution is to split the difference equally, resulting in a transfer price of Rs 825. However, this solution ignores the relative costs incurred by the two divisions and might lead to disparate profit margins on the work contributed by each division to the final product. As an alternative approach, Hindustan Petroleum could allocate the Rs 50 difference on the basis of the variable costs of the two divisions. Using the data in Exhibit 22-1 (p. 934), variable costs are as follows:

Transportation Division's variable costs to transport 100 barrels of crude oil (Rs 10 × 100)	Rs 1,000
Refining Division's variable costs to refine 100 barrels of crude oil and produce 50 barrels of gasoline (Rs 80 × 50)	4,000
Total variable costs	Rs 5,000

Of the Rs 50 difference, the Transportation Division gets to keep (Rs 1,000 ÷ Rs 5,000) × Rs 50 = Rs 10 and the Refining Division gets to keep (Rs 4,000 ÷ Rs 5,000) × Rs 50 = Rs 40. That is, the transfer price is Rs 810 per barrel of crude oil (Rs 790 purchase cost + Rs 10 variable cost + Rs 10 that the Transportation Division gets to keep). In effect, this approach results in a budgeted variable-cost-plus transfer price. The "plus" indicates the setting of a transfer price above variable cost.

To decide on the Rs 10 and Rs 40 allocations of the Rs 50 incremental benefit to total company operating income per barrel, the divisions must share information about their variable costs. In effect, each division does not operate (at least for this transaction) in a totally decentralized manner. Furthermore, each division has an incentive to overstate its variable costs to receive a more-favorable transfer price. In the preceding example, suppose the transportation division claims a cost of Rs 20 per barrel to ship crude oil to Mathura. This increased cost raises the variable cost-based minimum price to Rs 790 + Rs 20 = Rs 810 per barrel; the maximum price remains Rs 850. Of the Rs 40 difference between the minimum and maximum, the transportation division now gets to keep (Rs 2,000 ÷ (Rs 2,000 + Rs 4,000)) × Rs 40 = Rs 13.3, resulting in a higher transfer price of Rs 823.3. The refining division similarly benefits from asserting that its variable cost to refine 100 barrels of crude oil is greater than Rs 4,000. As a consequence, proration methods either require a high degree of trust and information exchange among divisions or include provisions for objective audits of cost information in order to be successful.

Negotiated Pricing

This is the most common hybrid method. Under this approach, top management does not administer a specific split of the eventual profits across the transacting divisions. Rather, the eventual transfer price results from a bargaining process between the selling and buying subunits. In the Hindustan Petroleum case, for example, the transportation division and the refining division would be free to negotiate a price that is mutually acceptable to both.

As described earlier, the minimum and maximum feasible transfer prices are Rs 800 and Rs 850, respectively, per barrel of crude oil. Where between Rs 800 and Rs 850 will the transfer price per barrel be set? Under a negotiated transfer price, the answer depends on several things: the bargaining strengths of the two divisions; information the transportation division has about the price minus incremental marketing costs of supplying crude oil to outside refineries; and the information the refining division has about its other available sources of crude oil. Negotiations become particularly sensitive because Hindustan Petroleum can now evaluate each division's performance on the basis of division operating income. The price negotiated by the two divisions will, in general, have no specific relationship to either costs or market price. But cost and price information is often the starting point in the negotiation process.

Consider the following situation: Suppose the refining division receives an order to supply specially processed gasoline. The incremental cost to purchase and supply crude oil is still Rs 800 per barrel. However, suppose the refining division will profit from this order only if the transportation division can supply crude oil at a price not exceeding Rs 820 per barrel.[5] In this case, the transfer price that would benefit both divisions must be greater than Rs 800 but less than Rs 820. Negotiations would allow the two divisions to achieve an acceptable transfer price. By contrast, a rule-based transfer price, such as a market-based price of Rs 850 or a 105% of full-cost-based price of Rs 871.5, would result in Hindustan passing up a profitable opportunity.

A negotiated transfer price strongly preserves division autonomy. It also has the advantage that each division manager is motivated to put forth effort to increase division operating income. Surveys have found that approximately 15%–20% of firms set transfer

[5] For example, suppose a barrel of specially processed gasoline could be sold for Rs 2,000 but also required a higher variable cost of refining of Rs 360 per barrel. In this setting, the incremental contribution to the refining division is Rs 1,640 per barrel of gasoline, which implies that it will pay at most Rs 820 for a barrel of crude oil (since two barrels of crude are required for one barrel of gasoline).

prices based on negotiation among divisions. The key reason cited by firms that do not use negotiated prices is the cost of the bargaining process, that is, the time and energy spent by managers haggling over transfer prices.

Dual Pricing

There is seldom a single cost-based transfer price that simultaneously meets the criteria of goal congruence, management effort, subunit performance evaluation, andsubunit autonomy. As a result, some companies choose **dual pricing**, using two separate transfer-pricing methods to price each transfer from one subunit to another. An example of dual pricing arises when the selling division receives a full-cost-based price and the buying division pays the market price for the internally transferred products. Assume Hindustan Petroleum purchases crude oil from Reliance Petroleum in Ankleshwar at Rs 160 per barrel. One way of recording the journal entry for the transfer between the Transportation Division and the Refining Division is:

1. Debit the Refining Division (the buying division) with the market-based transfer price of Rs 850 per barrel of crude oil.
2. Credit the Transportation Division (the selling division) with the 105%-of-full-cost transfer price of Rs 871.5 per barrel of crude oil.
3. Debit a corporate cost account for the Rs 21.5 (Rs 871.5 − Rs 850) per barrel difference between the two transfer prices.

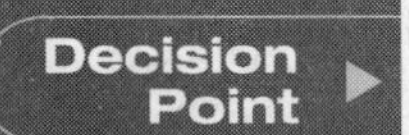

Within a range of feasible transfer prices, what are alternative ways for firms to arrive at the eventual price?

The dual-pricing system promotes goal congruence because it makes the Refining Division no worse off if it purchases the crude oil from the Transportation Division rather than from the external supplier at Rs 850 per barrel. The Transportation Division receives a corporate subsidy. In dual pricing, the operating income for Hindustan Petroleum as a whole is less than the sum of the operating incomes of the divisions.

Dual pricing is not widely used in practice even though it reduces the goal incongruence associated with a pure cost-based transfer-pricing method. One concern with dual pricing is that it leads to problems in computing the taxable income of subunits located in different tax jurisdictions. A second concern is that dual pricing insulates managers from the frictions of the marketplace because costs, not market prices, affect the revenues of the supplying division.

A General Guideline for Transfer-Pricing Situations

Learning Objective 7

Apply a general guideline for determining a minimum transfer price

. . . incremental cost plus opportunity cost of supplying division

Exhibit 22-3 summarizes the properties of the different transfer-pricing methods using the criteria described in this chapter. As the exhibit indicates, there is no transfer-pricing method to meets all criteria. Market conditions, the goal of the transfer-pricing system, and the criteria of goal congruence, management effort, subunit performance evaluation, and subunit autonomy (if desired) must all be considered simultaneously. The transfer price a company will eventually choose depends on the economic circumstances and the decision at hand. Surveys of company practice indicate that the full-cost-based transfer price is generally the most frequently used transfer-pricing method around the world, followed by market-based transfer price and negotiated transfer price.

Our discussion thus far highlight that, barring settings in which a perfectly competitive market exists for the intermediate product, there is generally a range of possible transfer prices that would induce goal congruence. We now provide a general guideline for determining the minimum price in that range. The following formula is a helpful first step in setting the minimum transfer price in many situations:

The following general guideline (formula) is a helpful first step in setting a minimum transfer price in many situations:

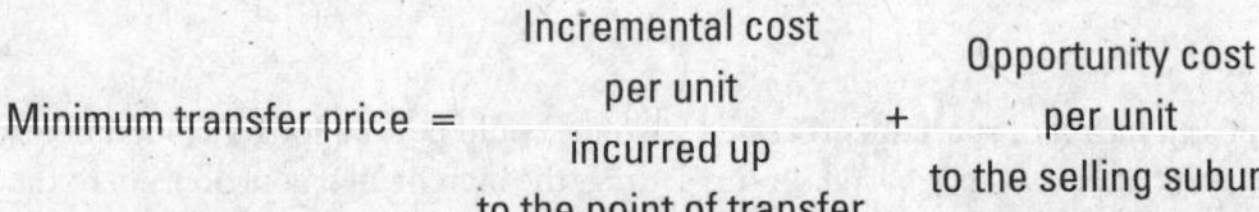

$$\text{Minimum transfer price} = \begin{array}{c}\text{Incremental cost}\\ \text{per unit}\\ \text{incurred up}\\ \text{to the point of transfer}\end{array} + \begin{array}{c}\text{Opportunity cost}\\ \text{per unit}\\ \text{to the selling subunit}\end{array}$$

Incremental cost in this context means the additional cost of producing and transferring the product or service. Opportunity cost here is the maximum contribution margin forgone by the selling subunit if the product or service is transferred internally. For example,

Exhibit 22-3

Comparison of Different Transfer-Pricing Methods

Criteria	Market-Based	Cost-Based	Negotiated
Achieves goal congruence	Yes, when markets are competitive	Often, but not always	Yes
Useful for evaluating subunit performance	Yes, when markets are competitive	Difficult unless transfer price exceeds full cost and even then is somewhat arbitrary	Yes, but transfer prices are affected by bargaining strengths of the buying and selling divisions
Motivates management effort	Yes	Yes, when based on budgeted costs; less incentive to control costs if transfers are based on actual costs	Yes
Preserves subunit autonomy	Yes, when markets are competitive	No, because it is rule-based	Yes, because it is based on negotiations between subunits
Other factors	Market may not exist, or markets may be imperfect or in distress	Useful for determining full cost of products and services; easy to implement	Bargaining and negotiations take time and may need to be reviewed repeatedly as conditions change

if the selling subunit is operating at capacity, the opportunity cost of transferring a unit internally rather than selling it externally is equal to the market price minus variable cost. That's because by transferring a unit internally, the subunit forgoes the contribution margin it could have obtained by selling the unit in the external market. We distinguish incremental cost from opportunity cost because the financial accounting system typically records incremental cost but not opportunity cost. The guideline measures a *minimum* transfer price because it represents the selling unit's cost of transferring the product. We illustrate the general guideline in some specific situations using data from Hindustan Petroleum.

1. **A perfectly competitive market for the intermediate product exists, and the selling division has no unused capacity.** If the market for crude oil in Mathura is perfectly competitive, the Transportation Division can sell all the crude oil it transports to the external market at Rs 850 per barrel, and it will have no unused capacity. The Transportation Division's incremental cost (as shown in Exhibit 22-1) is Rs 730 per barrel (purchase cost of Rs 720 per barrel plus variable transportation cost of Rs 10 per barrel) for oil purchased under the long-term contract or Rs 800 per barrel (purchase cost of Rs 790 plus variable transportation cost of Rs 10) for oil purchased at current market prices from Reliance Petroleum. The Transportation Division's opportunity cost per barrel of transferring the oil internally is the contribution margin per barrel forgone by not selling the crude oil in the external market: Rs 120 for oil purchased under the long-term contract (market price, Rs 850, minus variable cost, Rs 730) and Rs 50 for oil purchased from Reliance (market price, Rs 850, minus variable cost, Rs 800). In either case,

$$\text{Minimum transfer price per barrel} = \text{Incremental cost per barrel} + \text{Opportunity cost per barrel}$$
$$= \text{Rs } 730 + \text{Rs } 120 = \text{Rs } 850$$
or
$$= \text{Rs } 800 + \text{Rs } 50 = \text{Rs } 850$$

2. **An intermediate market exists that is not perfectly competitive, and the selling division has unused capacity.** In markets that are not perfectly competitive, capacity utilization can only be increased by decreasing prices. Unused capacity exists because decreasing prices is often not worthwhile—it decreases operating income.

Concepts in Action

Transfer Pricing Dispute Temporarily Stops the Flow of Fiji Water

Tax authorities and government officials across the globe pay close attention to taxes paid by multinational companies operating within their boundaries. At the heart of the issue are the transfer prices that companies use to transfer products from one country to another. Since 2008, Fiji Water, LLC, a U.S.-based company that markets its famous brand of bottled water in more than a dozen counties, has been engaged in a fierce transfer-pricing dispute with the government of the Fiji Islands, where its water bottling plant is located.

While Fiji Water is produced in the Fiji Islands, all other activities in the company's value chain—importing, distributing, and retailing—occur in the countries where Fiji Water is sold. Over time, the Fiji Islands government became concerned that Fiji Water was engaging in transfer price manipulations, selling the water shipments produced in the Fiji Islands at a very low price to the company headquarters in Los Angeles. It was feared that very little of the wealth generated by Fiji Water, the country's second largest exporter, was coming into the Fiji Islands as foreign reserves from export earnings, which Fiji badly needed to fund its imports. To the Fiji Islands government, Fiji Water was funneling most of its cash to the United States.

As a result of these concerns, the Fiji Islands Revenue and Customs Authority (FIRCA) decided to take action against Fiji Water. FIRCA halted exports in January 2008 at ports in the Fiji Islands by putting 200 containers loaded with Fiji Water bottled under armed guard, and issuing a statement accusing Fiji Water of transfer price manipulations. FIRCA's chief executive, Jitoko Tikolevu, said, "The wholly U.S.-owned Fijian subsidiary sold its water exclusively to its U.S. parent at the declared rate, in Fiji, of $4 a carton. In the U.S., though, the same company then sold it for up to $50 a carton."

Fiji Water immediately filed a lawsuit against FIRCA with the High Court of Fiji. The court issued an interim order, allowing the company to resume shipment of the embargoed containers upon payment of a bond to the court. In the media and subsequent court filings, the company stated that on a global basis it sold each carton of water for $20–28, and it did not make a profit due to "heavy investments in assets, employees, and marketing necessary to aggressively grow a successful branded product."

The dispute between FICRA and Fiji Water remains unresolved in the Fiji Islands court system. In the interim, Fiji Water has maintained its previous transfer price of $4 for water produced at its bottling plant in the Fiji Islands. To pressure the company to change its transfer pricing practices, the Fiji Islands government considered adding a 20-cents-per-litre excise tax on water produced in the country, but the tax was ultimately rejected as too draconian. As this high-profile case demonstrates, transfer pricing formulas and taxation details remain a contentious issue for governments and countries around the globe.

Source: Matau, Robert. 2008. Fiji water explains saga. *Fiji Times*, February 9; McMaster, James and Jan Novak. 2009. Fiji water and corporate social responsibility—Green makeover or 'green-washing'? The University of Western Ontario Richard Ivey School of Business No. 909A08, London, Ontario: Ivey Publishing.

If the Transportation Division has unused capacity, its opportunity cost of transferring the oil internally is zero because the division does not forgo any external sales or contribution margin from internal transfers. In this case,

$$\text{Minimum transfer price per barrel} = \text{Incremental cost per barrel} = \text{Rs 730 per barrel for oil purchased under the long-term contract or Rs 800 per barrel for oil purchased from Reliance Petroleum in Ankleshwar}$$

In general, when markets are not perfectly competitive, the potential to influence demand and operating income through prices complicates the measurement of opportunity costs. The transfer price depends on constantly changing levels of supply and demand. There is not just one transfer price. Rather, the transfer prices for various quantities supplied and demanded depend on the incremental costs and opportunity costs of the units transferred.

3. **No market exists for the intermediate product.** This situation would occur for the Hindustan Petroleum case if the crude oil transported by the Transportation Division could be used only by the Mathura refinery (due to, say, its high tar content) and

would not be wanted by external parties. Here, the opportunity cost of supplying crude oil internally is zero because the inability to sell crude oil externally means no contribution margin is forgone. For the Transportation Division of Hindustan Petroleum, the minimum transfer price under the general guideline is the incremental cost per barrel (either Rs 730 or Rs 800). As in the previous case, any transfer price between the incremental cost and Rs 850 will achieve goal congruence.

Decision Point

What is the general guideline for determining a minimum transfer price?

Multinational Transfer Pricing and Tax Considerations

Learning Objective 8

Incorporate income tax considerations in multinational transfer pricing

. . . set transfer prices to minimize tax payments to the extent permitted by tax authorities

Transfer pricing is an important accounting priority for managers around the world. A 2007 Ernst & Young survey of multinational enterprises in 24 countries found that 74% of parent firms and 81% of subsidiary respondents believed that transfer pricing was "absolutely critical" or "very important" to their organizations. The reason is that parent companies identify transfer pricing as the single most important tax issue they face. The sums of money involved are often staggering. Google, for example, has a 90% market share of UK internet searches and earned £1.6 billion in advertising revenues last year in Britain; yet, Google UK reported a pretax loss of £26 million. The reason is that revenues from customers in Britain are transferred to Google's European headquarters in Dublin. By paying the low Irish corporate tax rate of 12.5%, Google saved £450 million in UK taxes in 2009 alone. Transfer prices affect not just income taxes, but also payroll taxes, customs duties, tariffs, sales taxes, value-added taxes, environment-related taxes, and other government levies. Our aim here is to highlight tax factors, and in particular income taxes, as important considerations in determining transfer prices.

Transfer Pricing for Tax Minimization

Consider the Hindustan Petroleum data in Exhibit 22-2. Assume that the transportation division based in India pays income taxes at 30% of operating income and that the refining division based in the United States pays income taxes at 20% of operating income. Hindustan Petroleum would minimize its total income tax payments with the 105%-of-full-cost transfer-pricing method, as shown in the following table, because this method minimizes income reported in India, where income is taxed at a higher rate than in the United States.

	Operating Income for 100 Barrels of Crude Oil			Income Tax on 100 Barrels of Crude Oil		
Transfer-Pricing Method	Transportation Division (India) (1)	Refining Division (United States) (2)	Total (3) = (1) + (2)	Transportation Division (India) (4) = 0.30 × (1)	Refining Division (United States) (5) = 0.20 × (2)	Total (6) = (4) + (5)
Market price	Rs 9,000	Rs 3,000	Rs 12,000	Rs 2,700	Rs 600	Rs 3,300
105% of full costs	3,800	8,200	12,000	1,140	1,640	2,780
Hybrid price	6,000	6,000	12,000	1,800	1,200	3,000

Income tax considerations raise additional issues. Tax issues may conflict with other objectives of transfer pricing. Suppose the market for crude oil is perfectly competitive. In this case, the market-based transfer price achieves goal congruence, provides incentives for management effort, and helps Hindustan to evaluate the economic profitability of the transportation division. But it is costly from the perspective of income taxes. To minimize income taxes, Hindustan would favor using 105% of full cost for tax reporting. Tax laws however, constrain this option. In particular, the tax authorities, aware of Hindustan's incentives to minimize income taxes by reducing the income reported in India, would challenge any attempts to shift income to the refining division through an unreasonably low transfer price (see also preceding Concepts in Action).

If the market for crude oil is perfectly competitive, Hindustan would be required to calculate taxes using the market price of Rs 850 for transfers from the transportation division to the refining division. Hindustan might successfully argue that the transfer price should be set below the market price because the transportation division incurs no marketing and distribution costs when selling crude oil to the refining division. For example, if marketing and distribution costs equal Rs 20 per barrel, Hindustan could set the transfer price at Rs 830 (Rs 850 – Rs 20) per barrel, the selling price net of marketing and distribution costs. Under the U.S. Internal Revenue Code, Hindustan could obtain advanced approval of the transfer-pricing arrangements from the tax authorities, called an *advanced pricing agreement* (*APA*). The APA is a binding agreement for a specified number of years. The goal of the APA program is to avoid costly transfer-pricing disputes between taxpayers and tax authorities. In 2007, there were 81 APAs executed, of which 54 were bilateral agreements with other tax treaty countries. Included in this was the completion of the first bilateral APA between the United States and China, involving Wal-Mart Stores.

The current global recession has pushed governments around the world to impose tighter trading rules and more aggressively pursue tax revenues. The number of countries that have imposed transfer pricing regulations has approximately quadrupled from 1995 to 2007, according to a 2008 KPMG report. Officials in China, where foreign businesses enjoyed favorable treatment until last year, recently issued new rules requiring multinationals to submit extensive transfer-pricing documentation. Countries such as India, Canada, Turkey, and Greece have brought greater scrutiny to bear on transfer pricing, focusing in particular on intellectual-property values, costs of back-office functions and losses of any type. In the United States, the Obama administration plans to shrink a "tax gap" the IRS estimates may be as high as Rs 3,450 billion by restricting or closing several widely used tax loopholes. While the plan does not directly address transfer pricing practice, the IRS has become even more aggressive with enforcement. The agency added 1,200 people to its international staff in 2009, and the 2010 budget called for hiring another 800.

Transfer Prices Designed for Multiple Objectives

To meet multiple transfer-pricing objectives, such as minimizing income taxes, achieving goal congruence, and motivating management effort, a company may choose to keep one set of accounting records for tax reporting and a second set for internal management reporting. Of course, it is costly to maintain two sets of books and companies such as Case New Holland, a world leader in the agricultural and construction equipment business, also oppose it for conceptual reasons. However, a survey by the AnswerThink Consulting Group of large companies (more than Rs 20 billion in revenues) found that 77% used separate reporting systems to track internal pricing information, compared with about 25% of large companies outside that "best practices" group. Microsoft, for example, believes in "delinking" transfer pricing and employs an internal measurement system (Microsoft Accounting Principles, or MAPs) that uses a separate set of company-designed rules and accounts.[6] A key aspect of management control at Microsoft is the desire to hold local managers accountable for product profitability and to establish appropriate sales and marketing spending levels for every product line. To establish these sales and spending levels, the firm creates a profitability statement for every product in every region, and allocates G&A and R&D costs across sales divisions in ways that aren't necessarily the most tax efficient.

Even if a company does not have such formal separated reporting systems, it can still informally adjust transfer prices to satisfy the tradeoff between tax minimization and incentive provision. Consider a multinational firm that makes semiconductor products that it sells through its sales organization in a higher-tax country. To minimize taxes, the parent sets a high transfer price, thereby lowering the operating income of the foreign sales organization. It would be inappropriate to penalize the country sales manager for this low income since the sales organization has no say in determining the transfer price. As an alternative, the company can evaluate the sales manager on the direct contribution (revenues minus marketing costs) incurred in the country. That is, the transfer price incurred to acquire the semiconductor products is omitted for performance-evaluation purposes. Of course, this is not a perfect solution. By ignoring the cost of acquiring the products, the sales manager is given incentives to overspend on local marketing relative to what would be optimal from the firm's overall perspective. If the dysfunctional effects of this are suitably large, corporate managers must

[6] For further details, see I. Springsteel, "Separate but Unequal," *CFO Magazine*, August 1999.

then step in and dictate specific operational decisions and goals for the manager based on the information available to them. More generally, adoption of a tax-compliant transfer pricing policy creates a need for nonfinancial performance indicators at lower management levels in order to better evaluate and reward performance.[7]

Additional Issues in Transfer Pricing

Additional factors that arise in multinational transfer pricing include tariffs and customs duties levied on imports of products into a country. The issues here are similar to income tax considerations; companies will have incentives to lower transfer prices for products imported into a country to reduce tariffs and customs duties charged on those products.

In addition to the motivations for choosing transfer prices already described, multinational transfer prices are sometimes influenced by restrictions that some countries place on dividend- or income-related payments to parties outside their national borders. By increasing the prices of goods or services transferred into divisions in these countries, companies can seek to increase the cash paid out of these countries without violating dividend- or income-related restrictions.

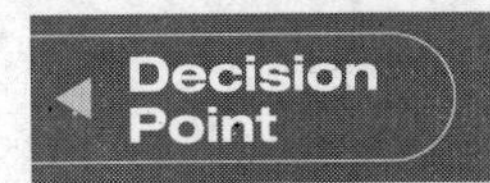

How do income tax considerations affect transfer pricing in multinationals?

Problem for Self-Study

The Pillercat Corporation is a highly decentralized company. Each division manager has full authority for sourcing decisions and selling decisions. The Machining Division of Pillercat has been the major supplier of the 2,000 crankshafts that the Tractor Division needs each year.

The Tractor Division, however, has just announced that it plans to purchase all its crankshafts in the forthcoming year from two external suppliers at Rs 2,000 per crankshaft. The Machining Division of Pillercat recently increased its selling price for the forthcoming year to Rs 2,200 per unit (from Rs 2,000 per unit in the current year).

Juan Gomez, manager of the Machining Division, feels that the 10% price increase is justified. It results from a higher depreciation charge on some new specialized equipment used to manufacture crankshafts and an increase in labor costs. Gomez wants the president of Pillercat Corporation to force the Tractor Division to buy all its crankshafts from the Machining Division at the price of Rs 2,200. The following table summarizes the key data.

File Edit View Insert Format Tools Data Window Help

	A	B
1	Number of crankshafts purchased by Tractor Division	2,000
2	External supplier's market price per crankshaft	Rs 2,000
3	Variable cost per crankshaft in Machining Division	Rs 1,900
4	Fixed cost per crankshaft in Machining Division	Rs 200

Required

1. Compute the advantage or disadvantage in terms of annual operating income to the Pillercat Corporation as a whole if the Tractor Division buys crankshafts internally from the Machining Division under each of the following cases:
   a. The Machining Division has no alternative use for the facilities used to manufacture crankshafts.
   b. The Machining Division can use the facilities for other production operations, which will result in annual cash operating savings of Rs 2,90,000.

[7] Cools et al. "Management control in the transfer pricing tax compliant multinational enterprise," *Accounting, Organizations and Society*, August 2008 provides an illustrative case study of this issue in the context of a semiconductor product division of a multinational firm.

c. The Machining Division has no alternative use for its facilities, and the external supplier drops the price to Rs 1,850 per crankshaft.

2. As the president of Pillercat, how would you respond to Juan Gomez's request that you force the Tractor Division to purchase all of its crankshafts from the Machining Division? Would your response differ according to the three cases described in requirement 1? Explain.

Solution

1. Computations for the Tractor Division buying crankshafts internally for one year under cases **a**, **b**, and **c** are:

	A	B	C	D
1			Case	
2		a	b	c
3	Number of crankshafts purchased by Tractor Division	2,000	2,000	2,000
4	External supplier's market price per crankshaft	Rs 2,000	Rs 2,000	Rs 1,850
5	Variable cost per crankshaft in Machining Division	Rs 1,900	Rs 1,900	Rs 1,900
6	Opportunity costs of the Machining Division supplying crankshafts to the Tractor Division	-	Rs2,90,000	-
7				
8	Total purchase costs if buying from an external supplier			
9	(2,000 shafts x Rs2,000, Rs2,000, Rs1,850 per shaft)	Rs40,00,000	Rs40,00,000	Rs37,00,000
10	Incremental cost of buying from the Machining Division			
11	(2,000 shafts x Rs1,900 per shaft)	38,00,000	38,00,000	38,00,000
12	Total opportunity costs of the Machining Division	-	2,90,000	-
13	Total relevant costs	38,00,000	40,90,000	38,00,000
14	Annual operating income advantage (disadvantage) to			
15	Pillercat of buying from the Machining Division	Rs2,00,000	Rs(90,000)	Rs(1,00,000)

The general guideline that was introduced in the chapter as a first step in setting a transfer price can be used to highlight the alternatives:

	A	B	C	D	E	F	G
1	Case	Incremental Cost per Unit Incurred to Point of Transfer	+	Opportunity Cost per Unit to the Supplying Division	=	Transfer Price	External Market Price
2	a	Rs1,900	+	Re 0	=	Rs1,900	Rs2,000
3	b	Rs1,900	+	Rs 145[a]	=	Rs2,045	Rs2,000
4	c	Rs1,900	+	Re 0	=	Rs1,900	Rs1,850
5							
6	[a]Opportunity cost	÷	Total opportunity	=	Number of		
7	per unit		costs		crankshafts	= Rs2,90,000 ÷ 2,000 = Rs145	

Comparing transfer price to external-market price, the Tractor Division will maximize annual operating income of Pillercat Corporation as a whole by purchasing from the Machining Division in case **a** and by purchasing from the external supplier in cases **b** and **c**.

2. Pillercat Corporation is a highly decentralized company. If no forced transfer were made, the Tractor Division would use an external supplier, a decision that would be in the best interest of the company as a whole in cases **b** and **c** of requirement 1 but not in case **a**.

Suppose in case **a**, the Machining Division refuses to meet the price of Rs 2,000. This decision means that the company will be Rs 2,00,000 worse off in the short run. Should top management interfere and force a transfer at Rs 2,000 This interference would undercut the philosophy of decentralization. Many top managements would not interfere because they would view the Rs 2,00,000 as an inevitable cost of a suboptimal decision that can occur under decentralization. But how high must this cost be before the temptation to interfere would be irresistible? Rs 3,00,000? Rs 4,00,000?

Any top management interference with lower-level decision making weakens decentralization. Of course, Pillercat's management may occasionally interfere to prevent costly mistakes. But recurring interference and constraints would hurt Pillercat's attempts to operate as a decentralized company.

Decision Points

The following question-and-answer format summarizes the chapter's learning objectives. Each decision presents a key question related to a learning objective. The guidelines are the answer to that question.

Decision	Guidelines
1. What is a management control system and how should it be designed?	A management control system is a means of gathering and using information to aid and coordinate the planning and control decisions throughout the organization and to guide the behavior of managers and other employees. Effective management control systems (a) are closely aligned to the organization's strategy, (b) fit the organization's structure, and (c) motivate managers and other employees to give effort to achieve the organization's goals.
2. What are the benefits and costs of decentralization?	The benefits of decentralization include (a) greater responsiveness to local needs, (b) gains from faster decision making, (c) increased motivation of subunit managers, (d) greater management development and learning, and (e) sharpened focus of subunit managers. The costs of decentralization include (a) suboptimal decision making, (b) decreased loyalty toward the organization, (c) increased costs of information gathering, and (d) duplication of activities.
3. What is a transfer price, and what is it intended to achieve?	A transfer price is the price one subunit charges for a product or service supplied to another subunit of the same organization. Transfer prices seek to (a) goal congruence, (b) management effort, (c) subunit performance evaluation, and (d) subunit autonomy (if desired).
4. What methods can be used to calculate transfer prices?	Transfer prices can be (a) market-based, (b) cost-based, or (c) negotiated. Different transfer-pricing methods produce different revenues and costs for individual subunits, and hence, different operating incomes for the subunits.
5. What transfer price should be used if the market for the product to be transferred is perfectly competitive?	In perfectly competitive markets, there is no unused capacity, and division managers can buy and sell as much of a product or service as they want at the market price. Setting the transfer price at the market price motivates division managers to transact internally and to take exactly the same actions as they would if they were transacting in the external market.

6. What problems can arise when full cost plus a markup is used as a transfer price?	A transfer price based on full cost plus a markup may lead to suboptimal decisions because it leads the buying division to regard the fixed costs and the markup of the selling division as a variable cost. The buying division may then purchase products from an external supplier expecting savings in costs that, in fact, will not occur.
7. What is the range over which two divisions will negotiate a transfer price when there is unused capacity?	When there is unused capacity, the transfer-price range for negotiations generally lies between the minimum price at which the selling division is willing to sell (its variable cost per unit) and the maximum price the buying division is willing to pay (the price at which the product is available from external suppliers).
8. What is the general guideline for determining a minimum transfer price?	The general guideline states that the minimum transfer price equals the incremental cost per unit incurred up to the point of transfer plus the opportunity cost per unit to the selling division resulting from transferring products or services internally.
9. What are the income tax considerations when determining transfer prices?	Transfer prices can reduce income tax payments by reporting more income in low-tax-rate countries and less income in high-tax-rate countries. However, tax regulations of different countries restrict the transfer prices that companies can use.

TERMS TO LEARN

This chapter and the Glossary at the end of the book contain definitions of:

autonomy (**p. 929**)
decentralization (**p. 929**)
dual pricing (**p. 942**)
dysfunctional decision making (**p. 930**)
effort (**p. 928**)
goal congruence (**p. 928**)
incongruent decision making (**p. 930**)
intermediate product (**p. 932**)
management control system (**p. 927**)
motivation (**p. 928**)
perfectly competitive market (**p. 936**)
suboptimal decision making (**p. 930**)
transfer price (**p. 932**)

ASSIGNMENT MATERIAL

Questions

22-1 What is a management control system?

22-2 Describe three criteria you would use to evaluate whether a management control system is effective.

22-3 What is the relationship among motivation, goal congruence, and effort?

22-4 Name three benefits and two costs of decentralization.

22-5 "Organizations typically adopt a consistent decentralization or centralization philosophy across all their business functions." Do you agree? Explain.

22-6 "Transfer pricing is confined to profit centers." Do you agree? Explain.

22-7 What are the three methods for determining transfer prices?

22-8 What properties should transfer-pricing systems have?

22-9 "All transfer-pricing methods give the same division operating income." Do you agree? Explain.

22-10 Under what conditions is a market-based transfer price optimal?

22-11 What is one potential limitation of full-cost-based transfer prices?

22-12 Give two reasons why the dual-pricing system of transfer pricing is not widely used.

22-13 "Cost and price information play no role in negotiated transfer prices." Do you agree? Explain.

22-14 "Under the general guideline for transfer pricing, the minimum transfer price will vary depending on whether the supplying division has unused capacity or not." Do you agree? Explain.

22-15 How should managers consider income tax issues when choosing a transfer-pricing method?

Solved Examples

22-16 Decentralization, responsibility centers. Phillips India manufactures and sells lighting products. Phillips's sales and marketing divisions are organized along product lines–wall sconces, recessed lights, track lights, and so on. The Manufacturing Division produces lighting products for all the sales and marketing divisions.

During the planning process, each sales and marketing division specifies the quantity of each style of light to be manufactured. Senior management then assigns the task of manufacturing the lights to different plants in the Manufacturing Division. Because manufacturing capacity is limited, some of the production is also outsourced. Senior management determines the manufacturing schedule on the basis of detailed studies that have been done to measure the time and cost of manufacturing different types of lighting products. Manufacturing managers are evaluated based on achieving target output within budgeted costs.

Required

1. Are the manufacturing plants in the Manufacturing Division cost centers or profit centers? Explain.
2. Phillips India is considering decentralizing its marketing and manufacturing decisions by letting manufacturing and marketing managers directly negotiate the prices for manufacturing various products.
   a. How should Phillips evaluate manufacturing plant managers under this proposal?
   b. Would you recommend that Phillips India decentralize its marketing and manufacturing decisions? Explain.

Solution

Decentralization, responsibility centers.

1. The manufacturing plants in the Manufacturing Division are cost centers. Senior management determines the manufacturing schedule based on the quantity of each type of lighting product specified by the sales and marketing division and detailed studies of the time and cost to manufacture each type of product. Manufacturing managers are accountable only for costs. They are evaluated based on achieving target output within budgeted costs.

2a. If manufacturing and marketing managers were to directly negotiate the prices for manufacturing various products, Phillips should evaluate manufacturing plant managers as profit centers–revenues received from marketing minus the costs incurred to produce and sell output.

2b. Phillips India would be better off decentralizing its marketing and manufacturing decisions and evaluating each division as a profit center. Decentralization would encourage plant managers to increase total output to achieve the greatest profitability, and motivate plant managers to cut their costs to increase margins. Manufacturing managers would be motivated to design their operations according to the criteria that meet the marketing managers' approval, thereby improving cooperation between manufacturing and marketing.

Under Phillips's existing system, manufacturing managers had every incentive not to improve. Manufacturing managers' incentives were to get as high a cost target as possible so that they could produce output within budgeted costs. Any significant improvement could result in the target costs being lowered for the next year, increasing the possibility of not achieving budgeted costs. By the same line of reasoning, manufacturing managers would also try to limit their production so that production quotas would not be increased in the future. Decentralizing manufacturing and marketing decisions overcomes these problems.

22-17 Transfer-pricing methods, goal congruence. Assam Lumber has a Raw Lumber Division and a Finished Lumber Division. The variable costs are

- Raw Lumber Division: Rs 1,000 per 100 board-feet of raw lumber
- Finished Lumber Division: Rs 1,250 per 100 board-feet of finished lumber

Assume that there is no board-feet loss in processing raw lumber into finished lumber. Raw lumber can be sold at Rs 2,000 per 100 board-feet. Finished lumber can be sold at Rs 2,750 per 100 board-feet.

Required

1. Should Assam Lumber process raw lumber into its finished form? Show your computations.
2. Assume that internal transfers are made at 110% of variable costs. Will each division maximize its division operating income contribution by adopting the action that is in the best interest of Assam Lumber? Explain.
3. Assume that internal transfers are made at market prices. Will each division maximize its division operating income contribution by adopting the action that is in the best interest of Assam Lumber? Explain.

Solution

Transfer-pricing methods, goal congruence.

1. Alternative 1: Sell as raw lumber for Rs 2,000 per 100 board feet:

Revenue	Rs 2,000	
Variable costs	1,000	
Contribution margin	Rs 1,000	per 100 board feet

Alternative 2: Sell as finished lumber for Rs 2,750 per 100 board feet:

Revenue		Rs 2,750
Variable costs:		
Raw lumber	Rs 1,000	
Finished lumber	1,250	2,250
Contribution margin		Rs 500 per 100 board feet

Assam Lumber will maximize its total contribution margin by selling lumber in its raw form.

An alternative approach is to examine the incremental revenues and incremental costs in the Finished Lumber Division:

Incremental revenues, Rs 2,750 − Rs 2,000	Rs 750
Incremental costs	1,250
Incremental loss	Rs (500) per 100 board feet

2. Transfer price at 110% of variable costs:
= Rs 1,000 + (Rs 1,000 × 0.10)
= Rs 1,100 per 100 board feet

	Sell as Raw Lumber	Sell as Finished Lumber
Raw Lumber Division		
Division revenues	Rs 2,000	Rs 1,100
Division variable costs	1,000	1,000
Division operating income	Rs 1,000	Rs 100
Finished Lumber Division		
Division revenues	Re 0	Rs 2,750
Transferred-in costs	–	1,100
Division variable costs	–	1,250
Division operating income	Re 0	Rs 400

The Raw Lumber Division will maximize reported division operating income by selling raw lumber, which is the action preferred by the company as a whole. The Finished Lumber Division will maximize division operating income by selling finished lumber, which is contrary to the action preferred by the company as a whole.

3. Transfer price at market price = Rs 2,000 per 100 board feet.

	Sell as Raw Lumber	Sell as Finished Lumber
Raw Lumber Division		
Division revenues	Rs 2,000	Rs 2,000
Division variable costs	1,000	1,000
Division operating income	Rs 1,000	Rs 1,000
Finished Lumber Division		
Division revenues	Re 0	Rs 2,750
Transferred-in costs	–	2,000
Division variable costs		1,250
Division operating income	Re 0	Rs (500)

The Raw Lumber Division will maximize division operating income by selling raw lumber, which is the action preferred by the company as a whole. Finished Lumber Division will maximize division operating income by not further processing raw lumber; not further processing is preferred by the company as a whole.

22-18 Effect of alternative transfer-pricing methods on division operating income (CMA, adapted). Gujarat Mineral Development Corporation (GMDC) has two divisions. The Mining Division makes toldine, which is then transferred to the Metals Division. The toldine is further processed by the Metals Division and is sold to customers at a price of Rs 1,500 per unit. The Mining Division is currently required by GMDC to transfer its total yearly output of 4,00,000 units of toldine to the Metals Division at 110% of full manufacturing cost. Unlimited quantities of toldine can be purchased and sold on the outside market at Rs 900 per unit.

The following table gives the manufacturing costs per unit in the Mining and Metals divisions for 2011:

	Mining Division	Metals Division
Direct materials	Rs 120	Rs 60
Direct manufacturing labor costs	160	200
Manufacturing overhead costs	320[a]	250[b]
Total manufacturing costs per unit	Rs 600	Rs 510

[a]Manufacturing overhead costs in the Mining Division are 25% fixed and 75% variable.
[b]Manufacturing overhead costs in the Metals Division are 60% fixed and 40% variable.

Required

1. Calculate the operating incomes for the Mining and Metals divisions for the 4,00,000 units of toldine transferred under the following transfer-pricing methods: (a) market price and (b) 110% of full manufacturing costs.
2. Suppose GMDC rewards each division manager with a bonus, calculated as 1% of division operating income (if positive). What is the amount of bonus that will be paid to each division manager under the transfer-pricing methods in requirement 1? Which transfer-pricing method will each division manager prefer to use?
3. What arguments would Amit, manager of the Mining Division, make to support the transfer-pricing method that he prefers?

Solution

Effect of alternative transfer-pricing methods on division operating income.

	Internal Transfers at Market Prices Method A	Internal Transfers at 110% of Full Costs Method B
1. Mining Division		
Revenues		
Rs 900, Rs 660[1] × 4,00,000 units	Rs 36,00,00,000	Rs 26,40,00,000
Deduct		
Division variable costs:		
Rs 520[2] × 4,00,000 units	20,80,00,000	20,80,00,000
Division fixed costs		
Rs 80[3] × 4,00,000 units	3,20,00,000	3,20,00,000
Division operating income	Rs 12,00,00,000	Rs 2,40,00,000
Metals Division		
Revenues		
Rs 1,500 × 4,00,000 units	Rs 60,00,00,000	Rs 60,00,00,000
Deduct		
Transferred-in costs		
Rs 900, Rs 660 × 4,00,000 units	36,00,00,000	26,40,00,000
Division variable costs		
Rs 360[4] × 4,00,000 units	14,40,00,000	14,40,00,000
Division fixed costs		
Rs 150[5] × 4,00,000 units	6,00,00,000	6,00,00,000
Division operating income	Rs 3,60,00,000	Rs 13,20,00,000

[1]Rs 660 = Rs 600 × 110%

[2]Variable cost per unit in Mining Division = Direct materials + Direct manufacturing labor + 75% of Manufacturing overhead = Rs 120 + Rs 160 + 75% × Rs 320 = Rs 520

[3]Fixed cost per unit = 25% of Manufacturing overhead = 25% × Rs 320 = Rs 80

[4]Variable cost per unit in Metals Division = Direct materials + Direct manufacturing labor + 40% of Manufacturing overhead = Rs 60 + Rs 200 + 40% × Rs 250 = Rs 360

[5]Fixed cost per unit in Metals Division = 60% of Manufacturing overhead = 60% × Rs 250 = Rs 150

2. Bonus paid to division managers at 1% of division operating income will be as follows:

	Method A Internal Transfers at Market Prices	Method B Internal Transfers at 110% of Full Costs
Mining Division manager's bonus		
(1% × Rs 12,00,00,000; 1% × Rs 2,40,00,000)	Rs 12,00,000	Rs 2,40,000
Metals Division manager's bonus		
(1% × Rs 3,60,00,000; 1% × Rs 13,20,00,000)	3,60,000	13,20,000

The Mining Division manager will prefer Method A (transfer at market prices) because this method gives Rs 12,00,000 of bonus rather than Rs 2,40,000 under Method B (transfers at 110% of full costs). The Metals Division manager will prefer Method B because this method gives Rs 13,20,000 of bonus rather than Rs 3,60,000 under Method A.

3. Amit, the manager of the Mining Division, will appeal to the existence of a competitive market to price transfers at market prices. Using market prices for transfers in these conditions leads to goal congruence. Division managers acting in their own best interests make decisions that are also in the best interests of the company as a whole. Further, setting transfer prices based on cost will cause the Mining Division to pay no attention to controlling costs since all costs incurred will be recovered from the Metals Division at 110% of full costs.

22-19 General guideline, transfer-price range. The BPL Ltd. manufactures and sells television sets. The Assembly Division assembles the television sets. It buys the screens for the television sets from the Screen Division. The Screen Division is operating at capacity. The incremental cost of manufacturing the screens is Rs 700 per unit. The Screen Division can sell as many screens as it wants in the outside market at a price of Rs 1,100 per screen. If it sells screens in the outside market, the Screen Division will incur variable marketing and distribution costs of Rs 40 per unit. Similarly, if the Assembly Division purchases screens from outside suppliers, it will incur variable purchasing costs of Rs 20 per screen.

Required

1. Using the general guideline presented in the chapter, what is the minimum transfer price at which the Screen Division will sell screens to the Assembly Division?
2. Suppose division managers act autonomously to maximize their own division's operating income, either by transacting internally or buying and selling in the market. If the two division managers were to negotiate a transfer price, what is the range of acceptable transfer prices?

Solution

General guideline, transfer price range.

1. If the Screen Division sells screens in the outside market, it will receive, for each screen, the market price of the screen minus variable marketing and distribution costs per screen = Rs 1,100 – Rs 40 = Rs 1,060. The incremental cost of manufacturing each screen is Rs 700. The Screen Division is operating at capacity. Hence, the opportunity cost per screen of selling the screen to the Assembly Division rather than in the outside market is the contribution margin the Screen Division would forgo if it transferred screens internally rather than sold them in the outside market.
   Contribution margin per screen = Rs 1,060 – Rs 700 = Rs 360.
   Using the general guideline,

Minimum transfer price per screen	=	Incremental costs per screen per screen up to the point of transfer	+	Opportunity costs to the selling division

   That is, Minimum transfer price per screen = Rs 700 + Rs 360 = Rs 1,060

2. If the two division managers were to negotiate a transfer price, the range of possible transfer prices is between Rs 1,060 and Rs 1,120 per screen. As calculated in requirement 1, the Screen Division will be willing to supply screens to the Assembly Division only if the transfer price equals or exceeds Rs 1,060 per screen.
   If the Assembly Division were to purchase the screens in the outside market, it will incur a cost of Rs 1,120, the cost of the screen equal to Rs 1,100 plus variable purchasing costs of Rs 20 per screen. Hence, the Assembly Division will be willing to buy screens from the Screen Division only if the price does not exceed Rs 1,120 per screen. Within the price range of Rs 1,060 and Rs 1,120 per screen, each division will be willing to transact with the other. The exact transfer price between Rs 1,060 and Rs 1,120 will depend on the bargaining strengths of the two divisions.

22-20 Transfer-pricing dispute. The Escorts Ltd., manufacturer of tractors and other heavy farm equipment, is organized along decentralized lines, with each manufacturing division operating as a separate profit center. Each division manager has been delegated full authority on all decisions involving the sale of that division's output both to outsiders and to other divisions of Escorts Ltd.. Division C has in the past always purchased its requirement of a particular tractor-engine component from Division A. However, when informed that Division A is increasing its selling price to Rs 1,500, Division C's manager decides to purchase the engine component from outside suppliers.

Division C can purchase the component for Rs 1,350 in the open market. Division A insists that, because of the recent installation of some highly specialized equipment and the resulting high depreciation charges, it will not be able to earn an adequate return on its investment unless it raises its price. Division A's manager appeals to top management of Escorts Ltd. for support in the dispute with Division C and supplies the following operating data:

C's annual purchases of the tractor-engine component	1,000 units
A's variable costs per unit of the tractor-engine component	Rs 1,200
A's fixed costs per unit of the tractor-engine component	Rs 200

Required

1. Assume that there are no alternative uses for internal facilities. Determine whether the company as a whole will benefit if Division C purchases the component from outside suppliers for Rs 1,350 per unit. What should the transfer price for the component be set at so that division managers acting in their own divisions' interests take actions that are in the best interest of the company as a whole?
2. Assume that internal facilities of Division A would not otherwise be idle. By not producing the 1,000 units for Division C, Division A's equipment and other facilities would be used for other production operations that would result in annual cash-operating savings of Rs 1,80,000. Should Division C purchase from outside suppliers? Show your computations.

3. Assume that there are no alternative uses for Division A's internal facilities and that the price from outsiders drops Rs 200. Should Division C purchase from outside suppliers? What should the transfer price for the component be set at so that division managers acting in their own divisions' interests take actions that are in the best interest of the company as a whole?

Solution

Transfer-pricing dispute.

This problem is similar to the Problem for Self-Study in the chapter.

1. Company as a whole will not benefit if Division C buys on the outside market:

Purchase costs from outsider, 1,000 units × Rs 1,350	Rs 13,50,000
Deduct: Savings in variable costs by reducing Division A output, 1,000 units × Rs 1,200	12,00,000
Net cost (benefit) to company as a whole by buying from outside	Rs 1,50,000

Any transfer price between Rs 1,200 to Rs 1,350 per unit will achieve goal congruence. Division managers acting in their own best interests will take actions that are in the best interests of the company as a whole.

2. Company will benefit if C purchases from the outsider supplier:

Purchase costs from outsider, 1,000 units × Rs 1,350		Rs 13,50,000
Deduct: Savings in variable costs, 1,000 units × Rs 1,200	Rs 12,00,000	
Savings due to A's equipment and facilities assigned to other operations	1,80,000	13,80,000
Net cost (benefit) to company as a whole by buying from outside		Rs (30,000)

Division C should purchase from outside suppliers.

3. Company will benefit if C purchases from the outside supplier:

Purchase costs from outsider, 1,000 units × Rs 1,150	Rs 11,50,000
Deduct: Savings in variable costs by reducing Division A output, 1,000 units × Rs 1,200	12,00,000
Net cost (benefit) to company as a whole by buying from outside	Rs (50,000)

The three requirements are summarized below (in thousands):

	(1)	(2)	(3)
Total purchase costs from outsider	Rs 1,350	Rs 1,350	Rs 1,150
Total relevant costs if purchased from Division A			
Total incremental (outlay) costs if purchased from A	1,200	1,200	1,200
Total opportunity costs if purchased from A	–	180	–
Total relevant costs if purchased from A	1,200	1,380	1,200
Operating income advantage (disadvantage) to company as a whole by buying from A	Rs 150	Rs (30)	Rs (50)

Goal congruence would be achieved if the transfer price is set equal to the total relevant costs of purchasing from Division A.

22-21 Transfer-pricing problem (continuation of 22-20). Refer to Example 22-20. Assume that Division A can sell the 1,000 units to other customers at Rs 1,550 per unit, with variable marketing costs of Rs 50 per unit.

Required

Determine whether Escorts Ltd. will benefit if Division C purchases the 1,000 components from outside suppliers at Rs 1,350 per unit. Show your computations.

Solution

Transfer-pricing problem (continuation of 22-20).

The company as a whole would benefit in this situation if C purchased from outside suppliers. The Rs 1,50,000 disadvantage to the company as a whole by purchasing from the outside supplier would be more than offset by the Rs 3,00,000 contribution margin of A's sale of 1,000 units to other customers.

Purchase costs from outside supplier, 1,000 units × Rs 1,350		Rs 13,50,000
Deduct variable cost savings, 1,000 units × Rs 1,200		12,00,000
Net cost to company as a whole by buying units from outside		Rs 1,50,000
A's sales to other customers, 1,000 units × Rs 1,550		Rs 15,50,000
Deduct:		
Variable manufacturing costs, Rs 1,200 × 1,000 units	Rs 12,00,000	

Variable marketing costs, Rs 50 × 1,000 units	50,000	
Total variable costs		12,50,000
Contribution margin from selling units to other customers		Rs 3,00,000

22-22 Pertinent transfer price. Hero Cycles has two divisions, A and B, which manufacture expensive bicycles. Division A produces the bicycle frame, and Division B assembles the rest of the bicycle onto the frame. There is a market for both the subassembly and the final product. Each division has been designated as a profit center. The transfer price for the subassembly has been set at the long-run average market price. The following data are available for each division:

Selling price for final product	Rs 3,000
Long-run average selling price for intermediate product	2,000
Incremental costs for completion in Division B	1,500
Incremental costs in Division A	1,200

The manager of Division B has made the following calculation:

Selling price for final product		Rs 3,000
Transferred-in costs (market)	Rs 2,000	
Incremental costs for completion	1,500	3,500
Contribution (loss) on product		Rs (500)

Required

1. Should transfers be made to Division B if there is no unused capacity in Division A? Is the market price the correct transfer price? Show your computations.
2. Assume that Division A's maximum capacity for this product is 1,000 units per month, and sales to the intermediate market are now 800 units. Should 200 units be transferred to Division B? At what transfer price? Assume that for a variety of reasons, Division A will maintain the Rs 2,000 selling price indefinitely. That is, Division A is not considering lowering the price to outsiders even if idle capacity exists.
3. Suppose Division A quoted a transfer price of Rs 1,500 for up to 200 units. What would be the contribution to the company as a whole if a transfer were made? As manager of Division B, would you be inclined to buy at Rs 1,500? Explain.

Solution

Pertinent transfer price.

This problem explores the "general transfer-pricing guideline" discussed in the chapter.

1. No, transfers should not be made to Division B if there is no excess capacity in Division A.
An incremental (outlay) cost approach shows a positive contribution for the company as a whole.

Selling price of final product		Rs 3,000
Incremental costs in Division A	Rs 1,200	
Incremental costs in Division B	1,500	2,700
Contribution		Rs 300

However, if there is no excess capacity in Division A, any transfer will result in diverting products from the market for the intermediate product. Sales in this market results in a greater contribution for the company as a whole. Division B should not assemble the bicycle since the incremental revenue Hero Cycles can earn, Rs 1,000 per unit (Rs 3,000 from selling the final product – Rs 2,000 from selling the intermediate product) is less than the incremental costs of Rs 1,500 to assemble the bicycle in Division B. Alternatively put, Hero Cycles's contribution margin from selling the intermediate product exceeds Hero Cycles's contribution margin from selling the final product.

Selling price of intermediate product	Rs 2,000
Incrementral (outlay) costs in Division A	1,200
Contribution	Rs 800

The general guideline described in the chapter is

$$\text{Minimum transfer price} = \begin{pmatrix}\text{Additional incremental costs per unit} \\ \text{incurred up to the point of transfer}\end{pmatrix} + \begin{pmatrix}\text{Opportunity costs per unit to the} \\ \text{supplying division}\end{pmatrix}$$

$$= \text{Rs } 1{,}200 + (\text{Rs } 2{,}000 - \text{Rs } 1{,}200)$$

$$= \text{Rs } 2{,}000, \text{ which is the market price}$$

The market price is the transfer price that leads to the correct decision, that is, do not transfer to Division B unless there are extenuating circumstances for continuing to market the final product. Therefore, B must either drop the product or reduce the incremental costs of assembly from Rs 1,500 per bicycle to less than Rs 1,000.

2. If (a) A has excess capacity, (b) there is intermediate external demand for only 800 units at Rs 2,000, and (c) the Rs 2,000 price is to be maintained, then the opportunity costs per unit to the supplying division are Re 0. The general guideline indicates a minimum transfer price of: Rs 1,200 + Re 0 = Rs 1,200,

which is the incremental or outlay costs for the first 200 units. B would buy 200 units from A at a transfer price of Rs 1,200 because B can earn a contribution of Rs 300 per unit [Rs 3,000 – (Rs 1,200 + Rs 1,500)]. In fact, B would be willing to buy units from A at any price up to Rs 1,500 per unit because any transfers at a price of up to Rs 1,500 will still yield B a positive contribution margin.

Note, however, that if B wants more than 200 units, the minimum transfer price will be Rs 2,000 as computed in requirement 1 because A will incur an opportunity cost in the form of lost contribution of Rs 800 (market price, Rs 2,000 – outlay costs of Rs 1,200) for every unit above 200 units that are transferred to B. The following schedule summarizes the transfer prices for units transferred from A to B:

Units	Transfer Price
0–200	Rs 1,200–Rs 1,500
200–1,000	Rs 2,000

3. Division B would show zero contribution, but the company as a whole would generate a contribution of Rs 300 per unit on the 200 units transferred. Any price between Rs 1,200 and Rs 1,500 would induce the transfer that would be desirable for the company as a whole. A motivational problem may arise regarding how to split the Rs 300 contribution between Division A and B. Unless the price is below Rs 1,500, B would have little incentive to buy.

Note: The transfer price that may appear optimal in an economic analysis may, in fact, be totally unacceptable from the viewpoints of (1) preserving autonomy of the managers, and (2) evaluating the performance of the divisions as economic units. For instance, consider the simplest case discussed previously, where there is idle capacity and the Rs 2,000 intermediate price is to be maintained. To direct that A should sell to B at A's variable cost of Rs 1,200 may be desirable from the viewpoint of B and the company as a whole. However, the autonomy (independence) of the manager of A is eroded. Division A will earn nothing, although it could argue that it is contributing to the earning of income on the final product.

If the manager of A wants a portion of the total company contribution of Rs 300 per unit, the question is: How is an appropriate amount determined? This is a difficult question in practice. The price can be negotiated upward to somewhere between Rs 1,200 and Rs 1,500 so that some "equitable" split is achieved. A dual transfer-pricing scheme has also been suggested, whereby the supplier gets credit for the full intermediate market price and the buyer is charged with only variable or incremental costs. In any event, when there is heavy interdependence between divisions, such as in this case, some system of subsidies may be needed to deal with the three problems of goal congruence, management effort, and subunit autonomy. Of course, where heavy subsidies are needed, a question can be raised as to whether the existing degree of decentralization is optimal.

22-23 Pricing in imperfect markets (continuation of 22-22). Refer to Example 22-22.

Required

1. Suppose the manager of Division A has the option of (a) cutting the external price to Rs 1,950, with the certainty that sales will rise to 1,000 units, or (b) maintaining the outside price of Rs 2,000 for the 800 units and transferring the 200 units to Division B at a price that would produce the same operating income for Division A. What transfer price would produce the same operating income for Division A? Is that price consistent with that recommended by the general guideline in the chapter so that the desirable decision for the company as a whole would result?
2. Suppose that if the selling price for the intermediate product is dropped to Rs 1,950, outside sales can be increased to 900 units. Division B wants to acquire as many as 200 units if the transfer price is acceptable. For simplicity, assume that there is no outside market for the final 100 units of Division A's capacity.
   a. Using the general guideline, what is (are) the minimum transfer price(s) that should lead to the correct economic decision? Ignore performance-evaluation considerations.
   b. Compare the total contributions under the alternatives to show why the transfer price(s) recommended lead(s) to the optimal economic decision.

Solution

Pricing in imperfect markets (continuation of 22-22).

An alternative presentation, which contains the same numerical answers, can be found at the end of this solution.

1. Potential contribution from external intermediate sale is:

1,000 × (Rs 1,950 – Rs 1,200)	Rs 7,50,000
Contribution through keeping price at Rs 2,000 is	
800 × Rs 800.	6,40,000
Forgone contribution by transferring 200 units	Rs 1,10,000

Opportunity cost per unit to the supplying division by transferring internally:

$$\frac{\text{Rs } 1{,}10{,}000}{200} = \text{Rs } 550$$

Transfer price = Rs 1,200 + Rs 550 = Rs 1,750

An alternative approach to obtaining the same answer is to recognize that the incremental or outlay cost is the same for all 1,000 units in question. Therefore, the total revenue desired by A would be the same for selling outside or inside.

Let X equal the transfer price at which Division A is indifferent between selling all units outside versus transferring 200 units inside.

$$1{,}000 \times \text{Rs } 1{,}950 = (800 \times \text{Rs } 2{,}000) + 200X$$
$$X = \text{Rs } 1{,}750$$

The Rs 1,750 price will lead to the correct decision. Division B will not buy from Division A because its total costs of Rs 1,750 + Rs 1,500 will exceed its prospective selling price of Rs 3,000. Division A will then sell 1,000 units at Rs 1,950 to the outside; Division A and the company will have a contribution margin of Rs 7,50,000. Otherwise, if 800 units were sold at Rs 2,000 and 200 units were transferred to Division B, the company would have a contribution of Rs 6,40,000 plus Rs 60,000 (200 units of final product × Rs 300), or Rs 7,00,000.

A comparison might be drawn regarding the computation of the appropriate transfer prices between the preceding problem and this problem:

$$\text{Minimum transfer price} = \begin{pmatrix}\text{Additional incremental costs per unit}\\ \text{incurred upto the point of transfer}\end{pmatrix} + \begin{pmatrix}\text{Opportunity costs per unit}\\ \text{to Division A}\end{pmatrix}$$

$$\text{Perfect markets: } = \text{Rs } 1{,}200 + (\text{Selling price} - \text{Outlay costs per unit})$$
$$= \text{Rs } 1{,}200 + (\text{Rs } 2{,}000 - \text{Rs } 1{,}200) = \text{Rs } 2{,}000$$

$$\text{Imperfect markets: } = \text{Rs } 1{,}200 + \frac{\text{Marginal revenues} - \text{Outlay costs}}{\text{Number of units transferred}}$$

$$= \text{Rs } 1{,}200 + \frac{\text{Rs } 3{,}50{,}000^{a} - \text{Rs } 2{,}40{,}000^{b}}{200} = \text{Rs } 1{,}750$$

[a]Marginal revenues of Division A from selling 200 units outside rather than transferring to Division B
= (Rs 1,950 × 1,000) – (Rs 2,000 × 800) = Rs 19,50,000 – Rs 16,00,000 = Rs 3,50,000.

[b]Incremental (outlay) costs incurred by Division A to produce 200 units
= Rs 1,200 × 200 = Rs 2,40,000.

Therefore, selling price (Rs 1,950) and marginal revenues per unit (Rs 1,750 = Rs 3,50,000 ÷ 200) are not the same.

Some students may erroneously say that the "new" market price of Rs 1,950 is the appropriate transfer price. They will claim that the general guideline says that the transfer price should be Rs 1,200 + (Rs 1,950 – Rs 1,200) = Rs 1,950, the market price. This conclusion assumes a perfect market. But, here, there are imperfections in the intermediate market. That is, the market price is *not* a good approximation of alternative revenue. If a division's sales are heavy enough to reduce market prices, marginal revenue will be less than market price.

It is true that *either* Rs 1,950 or Rs 1,750 will lead to the correct decision by B in this case. But suppose that B's variable costs were Rs 1,200 instead of Rs 1,500. Then B would buy at a transfer price of Rs 1,750 (but not at a price of Rs 1,950, because then B would earn a negative contribution of Rs 150 per unit [Rs 3,000 – (Rs 1,950 + Rs 1,200)]. Note that if B's variable costs were Rs 1,200, transfers would be desirable:

Division A contribution is:	
800 × (Rs 2,000 – Rs 1,200) + 200 (Rs 1,750 – Rs 1,200) =	Rs 7,50,000
Division B contribution is:	
200 × [Rs 3,000 – (Rs 1,750 + Rs 1,200)] =	10,000
Total contribution	Rs 7,60,000

Or the same facts can be analyzed for the company as a whole:

Sales of intermediate product,	
800 × (Rs 2,000 – Rs 1,200) =	Rs 6,40,000
Sales of final products,	
200 × [3,000 – (Rs 1,200 + Rs 1,200)] =	1,20,000
Total contribution	Rs 7,60,000

If the transfer price were Rs 1,950, B would not accept the transfer and would not earn any contribution. As shown above, Division A and the company as a whole will earn a total contribution of Rs 7,50,000 instead of Rs 7,60,000.

2a. Division A can sell 900 units at Rs 1,950 to the outside market and 100 units to Division B, or 800 at Rs 2,000 to the outside market and 200 units to Division B. Note that, under both alternatives, 100 units can be transferred to Division B at no opportunity cost to A.

Using the general guideline, the minimum transfer price of the first 100 units [901–1000] is:

$$TP_1 = \text{Rs } 1{,}200 + 0 = \text{Rs } 1{,}200$$

If Division B needs 100 additional units, the opportunity cost to A is not zero, because Division A will then have to sell only 800 units to the outside market for a contribution of 800 × (Rs 2,000 – Rs 1,200) = Rs 6,40,000 instead of 900 units for a contribution of 900 × (Rs 1,950 – Rs 1,200) = Rs 6,75,000. Each unit sold to B in addition to the first 100 units has an opportunity cost to A of (Rs 6,75,000 – Rs 6,40,000) ÷ 100 = Rs 350.

Using the general guideline, the minimum transfer price of the next 100 units [801–900] is:

$$TP_2 = \text{Rs } 1{,}200 + \text{Rs } 350 = \text{Rs } 1{,}550$$

Alternatively, the computation could be:

Increase in contribution from 100 more units, 100 × Rs 750	Rs 75,000	
Loss in contribution on 800 units, 800 × (Rs 800 - Rs 750)	40,000	
Net "marginal revenue"	Rs 35,000 ÷100 units = Rs 350	
(Minimum) transfer price applicable to first 100 units offered by A is Rs 1,200 + Rs 0		= Rs 1,200 per unit
(Minimum) transfer price applicable to next 100 units offered by A is Rs 1,200 + (Rs 35,000 ÷ 100)		= Rs 1,550 per unit
(Minimum) transfer price applicable to next 800 units		= Rs 1,950 per unit

2b. The manager of Division B will not want to purchase more than 100 units because the units at Rs 1,550 would decrease his contribution (Rs 1,550 + Rs 1,500 > Rs 3,000). Because the manager of B does not buy more than 100 units, the manager of A will have 900 units available for sale to the outside market. The manager of A will strive to maximize the contribution by selling them all at Rs 1,950.

This solution maximizes the company's contribution:

900 × (Rs 1,950 – Rs 1,200) =	Rs 6,75,000
100 × (Rs 3,000 – Rs 2,700) =	30,000
	Rs 7,05,000

which compares favorably to:

800 × (Rs 2,000 – Rs 1,200) =	Rs 6,40,000
200 × (Rs 3,000 – Rs 2,700) =	60,000
	Rs 7,00,000

Alternative Presentation

1. Company Viewpoint

a: Sell 1,000 outside at Rs 1,950		b: Sell 800 outside at Rs 2,000, transfer 200	
Price	Rs 1,950	Transfer price	Rs 2,000
Variable costs	1,200	Variable costs	1,200
Contribution	Rs 750 × 1,000 = Rs 7,50,000	Contribution	Rs 800 × 800 = Rs 6,40,000

Total contribution given up if transfer occurs*
= Rs 7,50,000 – Rs 6,40,000 = Rs 1,10,000

On a per-unit basis, the relevant costs are:

Incremental costs topoint of transfer + Opportunity costs to Division A of transfer = Transfer price

$$\text{Rs } 1{,}200 + \frac{\text{Rs } 1{,}10{,}000}{200} = \text{Rs } 1{,}750$$

By formula, costs are:

[Incremental costs to point of transfer] + [Lost opportunity to sell 200 at Rs 1,950, for contribution of Rs 750] – [Gain when 1st 800 sell at Rs 2,000 instead of Rs 1,950]

$$= \text{Rs } 1{,}200 + \frac{200 \times \text{Rs } 750}{200} - \frac{[(\text{Rs } 2{,}000 - \text{Rs } 1{,}950) \times 800]}{200}$$

$$= \text{Rs } 1{,}200 + \text{Rs } 750 - \text{Rs } 200 = \text{Rs } 1{,}750$$

*Contribution of Rs 300 per unit by B is not given up if transfer occurs, so it is not relevant here.

2a. At most, Division A can sell only 900 units and can produce 1,000. Therefore, at least 100 units should be transferred, at a transfer price no less than Rs 1,200. The question is whether or not a second 100 units should be transferred.

Company Viewpoint

a: Sell 900 outside at Rs 1,950		b: Sell 800 outside at Rs 2,000, transfer 100	
Transfer price	Rs 1,950	Transfer price	Rs 2,000
Variable cost	1,200	Variable cost	1,200
Contribution	Rs 750 × 900 = Rs 6,75,000	Contribution	Rs 800 × 800 = Rs 6,40,000

Total contribution forgone if transfer of 100 units occurs

= Rs 6,75,000 – Rs 6,40,000 = Rs 35,000 (or Rs 350 per unit)

Incremental costs to point of transfer	+	Opportunity costs to Division A of transfer	=	Transfer price
Rs 1,200	+	Rs 350	=	Rs 1,550

2b. By formula:

[Incremental costs to point of transfer] + [Lost opportunity to sell 100 at Rs 1,950, for contribution of Rs 750] – [Gain when 1st 800 sell at Rs 2,000 instead of Rs 1,950]

$$= \text{Rs } 1{,}200 + \frac{100 \times \text{Rs } 750}{100} - \frac{[(\text{Rs } 2{,}000 \times \text{Rs } 1{,}950) \times 800]}{100}$$

= Rs 1,200 + Rs 750 – Rs 400 = Rs 1,550

Transfer Price Schedule (minimum acceptable transfer price)

Units	Transfer Price
0–100	Rs 1,200
101–200	Rs 1,550
201–1,000	Rs 1,950

22-24 Transfer pricing, goal congruence. The XYZ Company manufactures and sells 10,000 boom boxes per year. The Assembly Division assembles the boom boxes. It buys the cassette deck for the boom box from the Cassette Deck Division. The Cassette Deck Division can manufacture at most 12,000 cassette decks. The demand for cassette decks is strong. Any cassette deck not sold to the Assembly Division can be sold in the outside market for Rs 350 per unit. The Cassette Deck Division currently sells 10,000 cassette decks to the Assembly Division and 2,000 cassette decks in the outside market. The incremental cost of manufacturing the cassette deck is Rs 250 per unit.

A crucial component for producing high-quality cassette decks is the (cassette) head mechanism. The Cassette Deck Division manufactures the head mechanism for its cassette decks. Many outside suppliers have offered to supply cassette decks to XYZ Company. To ensure quality, XYZ Company requires that any outside supplier wanting to supply cassette decks to XYZ Company must purchase the head mechanism from the Cassette Deck Division. The Cassette Deck Division will charge Rs 180 per unit for the head mechanism. The incremental cost of manufacturing the head mechanism is Rs 120 per unit out of the total incremental costs of Rs 250 per unit to manufacture the cassette deck. The Cassette Deck Division has unused capacity for manufacturing the head mechanism. That is, even if the Cassette Deck Division manufactures the head mechanism for outside suppliers, it will still be able to manufacture 12,000 cassette decks for sale in the outside market at Rs 350 per unit.

An outside supplier is currently negotiating to supply 10,000 cassette decks to the Assembly Division for a price in the range of Rs 370 to Rs 430. If the outside supplier gets the business, it will buy the head mechanism from the Cassette Deck Division for Rs 180 per unit.

Consider each question independently.

Required

1. From the standpoint of XYZ Company as a whole, should the Assembly Division accept outside vendor's offer (a) at a price of Rs 370 per cassette deck? (b) at a price of Rs 430 per cassette deck? Show your computations.
2. What transfer price for cassette decks will result in the Cassette Deck Division and the Assembly Division taking actions that are optimal for XYZ Company as a whole? Explain your answer.

Solution

Transfer pricing, goal congruence.

1a. & b. As the following calculations show, if the outside supplier offers a price of Rs 370 per cassette deck, XYZ Company should purchase the cassette decks from the outside supplier. If the outside supplier Corporation offers a price of Rs 430 per cassette deck, XYZ Company should manufacture the cassette decks in-house.

	Transfer 10000 cassette decks to Assembly. Sell 2000 in outside market (1)	Buy 10000 cassette decks from the outside supplier at Rs 37. Sell 12000 cassette decks in outside market (2)	Buy 10000 cassette decks from the outside supplier at Rs 43. Sell 12000 cassette decks in outside market (3)
Incremental cost of Cassette Deck Division supplying 10,000 cassette decks to Assembly Rs 250 × 10,000; 0; 0	Rs (25,00,000)	Re 0	Re 0
Incremental costs of buying 10,000 cassette decks from the outside supplier Re 0; Rs 370 × 10,000; Rs 430 × 10,000	0	(37,00,000)	(43,00,000)
Revenue from selling cassette decks in outside market Rs 350 × 2,000; 12,000; 12,000	7,00,000	42,00,000	42,00,000
Incremental costs of manufacturing cassette decks for sale in outside market Rs 250 × 2,000; 12,000; 12,000	(5,00,000)	(30,00,000)	(30,00,000)
Revenue from supplying cassette-head mechanism to the outside supplier Rs 180 × 0; 10,000; 10,000	0	18,00,000	18,00,000
Incremental costs of supplying cassette-head mechanism to the outside supplier Rs 120 × 0; 10,000; 10,000	0	(12,00,000)	(12,00,000)
Net costs	Rs (23,00,000)	Rs (19,00,000)	Rs (25,00,000)

At a price of Rs 370 per cassette deck, the net cost of Rs 19,00,000 is less than the net cost of Rs 23,00,000 if XYZ Company made the cassette decks inhouse. Hence, XYZ Company should outsource to the outside vendor.

At a price of Rs 430 per cassette deck, the net cost of Rs 25,00,000 is greater than the net cost of Rs 23,00,000 if XYZ Company made the cassette decks inhouse. Hence, XYZ Company should reject the outside supplier's offer.

2. For the Cassette Deck Division and the Assembly Division to take actions that are optimal for XYZ Company as a whole, the transfer price should be set at Rs 410, calculated as follows:

The Cassette Deck Division can manufacture at most 12,000 cassette decks and is currently operating at capacity. The incremental costs of manufacturing a cassette deck are Rs 250 per deck. The opportunity cost of manufacturing cassette decks for the Assembly Division is (1) the contribution margin of Rs 100 (selling price, Rs 350 minus incremental costs Rs 250) that the Cassette Deck Division would forgo by not selling cassette decks in the outside market and (2) the contribution margin of Rs 60 (selling price, Rs 180 minus incremental costs, Rs 120) that the Cassette Deck Division would forgo by not being able to sell the cassette-head mechanism to outside suppliers of cassette decks (as is the present situation). Thus, the total opportunity cost of the Cassette Deck Division of supplying cassette decks to Assembly is Rs 100 + Rs 60 = Rs 160 per unit.

Using the general guideline,

$$\text{Minimum transfer price per cassette deck} = \begin{matrix}\text{Incremental cost per}\\ \text{cassette deck up to}\\ \text{the point of transfer}\end{matrix} + \begin{matrix}\text{Opportunity costs per}\\ \text{cessette deck to}\\ \text{the selling division}\end{matrix}$$

$$= \text{Rs } 250 + \text{Rs } 160 = \text{Rs } .10$$

Note that, at a price of Rs 410, XYZ Company is indifferent between manufacturing cassette decks inhouse or purchasing them from an outside supplier. Each results in a net cost of Rs 23,00,000. For an outside price per cassette deck below Rs 410, the Assembly Division would prefer to purchase from outside; above it, the Assembly Division would prefer to purchase from the Cassette Deck Division.

When selling prices are uncertain, the transfer price should be set at the minimum acceptable transfer price. For example, if the transfer price were set above the minimum transfer price at Rs 420 per cassette deck, say, and an outside supplier offered to supply the cassette decks at Rs 415 per unit, the Assembly Division would purchase the cassette deck from the outside supplier. In fact, as the following calculations show, XYZ Company, as a whole, would be better off had the Assembly Division purchased the cassette decks from the Cassette Deck Division. The net cost to XYZ Company if the Cassette Deck Division transfers 10,000 cassette decks to the Assembly Division is Rs 230,000 as calculated in Column 1 of the table presented in requirement 1. If an outside supplier supplies cassette decks at Rs 415 each, we simply substitute Rs 415 × 10,000 = Rs 41,50,000 for the incremental costs of buying 10,000 cassette decks in column 2 or 3 and leave everything else unchanged. This gives a higher net cost of Rs 23,50,000 to XYZ Company as a whole.

It is only if the price charged by the outside supplier falls below Rs 410 that XYZ Company as a whole is better off purchasing from the outside market. Setting the transfer price at Rs 410 per unit achieves goal congruence.

22-25 Ethics, transfer pricing. The A Division of Samtel Industries manufactures component R47, which it transfers to the B Division at 200% of variable costs. The variable cost of R47 is Rs 140 per unit. Vikas, the management accountant of the A Division, calls Sonal, his assistant, into his office. Vikas says, "I am not sure about the fixed- and variable-cost distinctions you are making. I think the variable cost is higher than Rs 140 per unit."

Sonal knows that showing higher variable costs will increase the A Division's profits and lead to higher bonuses for the division employees. However, Sonal is uncomfortable about making any changes because he has used the same method to classify costs as either variable or fixed over the last few years. Nevertheless, Sonal recognizes that fixed- and variable-cost distinctions are not always clear-cut.

Required

1. Calculate A Division's contribution margin from transferring 10,000 units of R47 (a) if variable cost is Rs 140 per unit, and (b) if variable cost is Rs 160 per unit.
2. Evaluate whether Vikas's suggestion to Sonal regarding variable costs is ethical. Would it be ethical for Sonal to revise the variable cost per unit? What steps should Sonal take to resolve this situation?

Solution

Ethics, transfer pricing.

1. Contribution margin for 10,000 units of R47 if variable costs are Rs 140 and Rs 160 per unit, respectively, are as follows:

	Variable Costs of Rs 14 per Unit	Variable Costs of Rs 16 per Unit
Transfer price at 200% of variable costs	Rs 280	Rs 320
Variable costs per unit	140	160
Contribution margin per unit	Rs 140	Rs 160
Contribution margin for 10,000 units Rs 140 × 10,000; Rs 160 × 10,000	Rs 14,00,000	Rs 16,00,000

2. Sonal should indicate to Vikas that the variable costs of R47 are indeed appropriate, given that the methods for computing variable costs and fixed costs have been in place for some time. If Vikas still insists on making the changes and increasing the variable costs of making R47, Sonal should raise the matter with Vikas's superior. If, after taking all these steps, there is continued pressure to increase the variable cost component, Sonal should consider resigning from the company and not engage in unethical behavior.

Exercises

22-26 Decentralization, goal congruence, responsibility centers. Jubilant Chemicals consists of seven operating divisions that operate independently. The operating divisions are assisted by a number of support groups, such as R&D, human resources, and environmental management. The environmental management group consists of 20 environmental engineers. These engineers must seek business from the operating divisions that is, the projects they work on must be mutually agreed to and paid for by one of the operating divisions. Under Jubilant's rules, the environmental group is required to charge the operating divisions for environmental services at cost.

Required

1. Is the environmental management group centralized or decentralized?
2. What type of responsibility center is the environmental management group?
3. What benefits and problems do you see in structuring the environmental management group in this way? Does it lead to goal congruence and motivation? Explain.

22-27 Transfer pricing, general guideline, goal congruence (CMA, adapted). Tata, operates as a decentralized multidivision company. The Igo Division of Tata purchases most of its airbags from the Airbag Division. The Airbag Division's incremental costs for manufacturing the airbags are Rs 1,100 per unit. The Airbag Division is currently working at 80% of capacity. The current market price of the airbags is Rs 1,400 per unit.

Required

1. Using the general guideline presented in the chapter, what is the minimum price at which the Airbag Division would sell airbags to the Igo Division?

2. Suppose that Tata requires that whenever divisions with idle capacity sell products internally, they must do so at incremental costs. Evaluate this transfer-pricing policy using the criteria of goal congruence, evaluating division performance, motivating management effort, and preserving division autonomy.
3. If the two divisions were to negotiate a transfer price, what is the range of possible transfer prices? Evaluate this negotiated transfer-pricing policy using the criteria of goal congruence, evaluating division performance, motivating management effort, and preserving division autonomy.
4. Do you prefer the transfer-pricing policy in requirement 2 or requirement 3? Explain your answer briefly.

22-28 Multinational transfer pricing and taxation (Richard Lambert, adapted). Anita Corporation, headquartered in India, manufactures state-of-the-art milling machines in India. It has two marketing subsidiaries, one in Brazil and one in Switzerland, that sell its products. Anita is building one new machine, at a cost of Rs 5,00,000. There is no market for the equipment in India. The equipment can be sold in Brazil for Rs 10,00,000, but the Brazilian subsidiary would incur transportation and modification costs of Rs 2,00,000. Alternatively, the equipment can be sold in Switzerland for Rs 9,50,000, but the Swiss subsidiary would incur transportation and modification costs of Rs 2,50,000. The Indian company can sell the equipment to either its Brazilian or its Swiss subsidiary, but not to both. The Anita Corporation and its subsidiary companies operate in a very decentralized manner. Managers in each company have considerable autonomy, with managers interested in maximizing their own company's income.

Required

1. From the viewpoint of Anita and its subsidiaries taken together, should the Anita Corporation manufacture the equipment? If it does, where should it sell the equipment to maximize total operating income? What would the operating income for Anita and its subsidiaries be from the sale? Ignore any income tax effects.
2. What range of transfer prices will result in achieving the actions determined to be optimal in requirement 1? Explain your answer.
3. The effective income tax rates are as follows: 40% in India, 60% in Brazil, and 15% in Switzerland. The tax authorities in the three countries are uncertain about the cost of the intermediate product and will allow any transfer price between Rs 500,000 and Rs 700,000. If Anita and its subsidiaries want to maximize after-tax operating income, (a) should the equipment be manufactured, and (b) where and at what price should it be transferred and sold? Show your computations.
4. Now suppose managers act autonomously to maximize their own subsidiary's after-tax operating income. The tax authorities will allow transfer prices only between Rs 5,00,000 and Rs 7,00,000. Which subsidiary will get the product and at what price? Is your answer the same as your answer in requirement 3? Explain why or why not.

22-29 Transfer pricing, utilization of capacity (J. Patell, adapted). The Banagalore Instrument Company (BIC) consists of the Semiconductor Division and the Process-Control Division, each of which operates as an independent profit center. The Semiconductor Division employs craftsmen who produce two different electronic components, the new high-performance Super-chip and an older product called Okay-chip. These two products have the following cost characteristics:

	Super-chip	Okay-chip
Direct materials	Rs 20	Rs 10
Direct manufacturing labor 2 hours × Rs 140; 0.5 hour × Rs 140	280	70

Annual overhead in the Semiconductor Division totals Rs 4,00,000, all fixed. Due to the high skill level necessary for the craftsmen, the Semiconductor Division's capacity is set at 50,000 hours per year.

One customer orders a maximum of 15,000 Super-chips per year, at a price of Rs 600 per chip. If BIC cannot meet this entire demand, the customer curtails its own production. The rest of the Semiconductor Division's capacity is devoted to the Okay-chip, for which there is unlimited demand at Rs 120 per chip.

The Process-Control Division produces only one product, a process-control unit, with the following cost structure:

- Direct materials (circuit board): Rs 600
- Direct manufacturing labor (5 hours × Rs 100): Rs 500

Fixed overhead costs of the Process-Control Division are Rs 8,00,000 per year. The current market price for the control unit is Rs 1,320 per unit.

A joint research project has just revealed that a single Super-chip could be substituted for the circuit board currently used to make the process-control unit. Using Super-chip would require an extra one hour of labor per control unit for a new total of six hours per control unit.

Required

1. Calculate the contribution margin per hour of selling Super-chip and Okay-chip. If no transfers of Super-chip were made to the Process-Control Division, how many Super-chips and Okay-chips should the Semiconductor Division sell? Show your computations.

2. The Process-Control Division expects to sell 5,000 control units this year. From the viewpoint of Banagalore Instruments as a whole, should 5,000 Super-chips be transferred to the Process-Control Division to replace circuit boards? Show your computations.
3. If demand for the control unit is certain to be 5,000 units but its price is uncertain, what should the transfer price of Super-chip be to ensure that the division managers' actions maximize operating income for BIC as a whole? (All other data are unchanged.)
4. If demand for the control unit is certain to be 12,000 units, but its price is uncertain, what should the transfer price of Super-chip be to ensure that the division managers' actions maximize operating income for BIC as a whole? (All other data are unchanged.)

22-30 Goal congruence, income taxes, different market conditions. The KSM Pumps makes water pumps. The Engine Division makes the engines and supplies them to the Assembly Division, where the pumps are assembled. KSM Pumps is a successful and profitable company that attributes much of its success to its decentralized operating style. Each division manager is compensated on the basis of division operating income.

The Assembly Division currently acquires all its engines from the Engine Division. The Assembly Division manager could purchase similar engines in the market for Rs 4,000 each.

The Engine Division is currently operating at 80% of its capacity of 4,000 units and has the following costs:

Direct materials (Rs 1,250 per unit × 3,200 units)	Rs 40,00,000
Direct manufacturing labor (Rs 500 per unit × 3,200 units)	16,00,000
Variable manufacturing overhead costs (Rs 250 per unit × 3,200 units)	8,00,000
Fixed manufacturing overhead costs	52,00,000

All the Engine Division's 3,200 units are currently transferred to the Assembly Division. No engines are sold in the outside market.

The Engine Division has just received an order for 2,000 units at Rs 3,750 per engine that would utilize half the capacity of the plant. The order must either be taken in full or rejected. The order is for a slightly different engine than what the Engine Division currently makes, but it takes the same amount of manufacturing time. To produce the new engine would require direct materials per unit of Rs 1,000, direct manufacturing labor per unit of Rs 400, and variable manufacturing overhead costs per unit of Rs 250.

Required

1. From the viewpoint of the KSM Pumps as a whole, should the Engine Division accept the order for the 2,000 units? Show your computations.
2. What range of transfer prices will result in achieving the actions determined to be optimal in requirement 1 if division managers act in a decentralized manner?
3. The manager of the Assembly Division has proposed a transfer price for the engines equal to the full costs of the engines, including an allocation of overhead costs. The Engine Division allocates overhead costs to engines on the basis of the total capacity of the plant used to manufacture the engines.
   a. Calculate the transfer price for the engines transferred to the Assembly Division under this arrangement.
   b. Do you think that the transfer price calculated in requirement 3a will result in achieving the actions determined to be optimal in requirement 1 if division managers act in a decentralized manner?
   c. Comment in general on one advantage and one disadvantage of using full costs of the producing division as the basis for setting transfer prices.
4. Now consider the effect of income taxes.
   a. Suppose the Assembly Division is located in a state that imposes a 10% tax on income earned within its boundaries, and the Engine Division is located in a state that imposes no tax on income earned within its boundaries. What transfer price would be chosen by the KSM Pumps to minimize state income tax payments for the corporation as a whole? Assume that only transfer prices that are greater than or equal to full manufacturing costs and less than or equal to the market price of "substantially similar" engines are acceptable to the tax authorities.
   b. Suppose that the KSM Pumps announces the transfer price computed in requirement 4a to price all transfers between the Engine and Assembly divisions. Each division manager then acts autonomously to maximize division operating income. Will division managers acting in a decentralized manner achieve the actions determined to be optimal in requirement 1? Explain.
5. Consider your responses to requirements 1 through 4 and assume the Engine Division will continue to have opportunities for outside business as described in requirement 1. What transfer-pricing policy would you recommend KSM Pumps use, and why? Would you continue to evaluate division performance on the basis of division operating incomes? Explain.

Performance Measurement, Compensation, and Multinational Considerations

Misalignment Between CEO Compensation and Performance at AIG

23 Performance Measurement, Compensation, and Multinational Considerations

Learning Objectives

1. Select financial and nonfinancial performance measures to use in a balanced scorecard
2. Examine accounting-based measures for evaluating business unit performance, including return on investment (ROI), residual income (RI), and economic value added (EVA®)
3. Analyze the key measurement choices in the design of each performance measure
4. Study the choice of performance targets and design of feedback mechanisms
5. Indicate the difficulties that occur when the performance of divisions operating in different countries is compared
6. Understand the roles of salaries and incentives when rewarding managers
7. Describe the four levers of control and why they are necessary

At the end of this school term, you're going to receive a grade that represents a measure of your performance in this course.

Your grade will likely consist of four elements—homework, quizzes, exams, and class participation. Do some of these elements better reflect your knowledge of the material than others? Would the relative weights placed on the various elements when determining your final grade influence how much effort you expend to improve performance on the different elements? Would it be fair if you received a good grade regardless of your performance? The following article about former AIG chief executive Martin Sullivan examines that very situation in a corporate context. Sullivan continued to receive performance bonuses despite pushing AIG to the brink of bankruptcy. By failing to link pay to performance, the AIG board of directors rewarded behavior that led to a government takeover of the firm.

Misalignment Between CEO Compensation and Performance at AIG[1]

After the September 2008 collapse of AIG, many shareholders and observers focused on the company's executive compensation. Many believed that the incentive structures for executives helped fuel the real estate bubble. Though people were placing long-term bets on mortgage-backed securities, much of their compensation was in the form of short-term bonuses. This encouraged excessive risk without the fear of significant repercussions.

Executive compensation at AIG had been under fire for many years. The Corporate Library, an independent research firm specializing in corporate governance, called the company "a serial offender in the category of outrageous CEO compensation."

Judging solely by company financial measures, AIG's 2007 results were a failure. Driven by the write-down of $11.1 billion in fixed income guarantees, the company's revenue was down 56% from 2006 results. AIG also reported $5 billion in losses in the final quarter of 2007 and warned of possible future losses due to ill-advised investments. Despite this, AIG chief executive Martin Sullivan earned

[1] *Source:* Blair, Nathan. 2009. AIG – Blame for the bailout. Stanford Graduate School of Business No. A-203, Stanford, CA: Stanford Graduate School of Business; Son, Hugh. 2008. AIG chief Sullivan's compensation fell 32 percent. *Bloomberg.com*, April 4; Son, Hugh and Erik Holm. 2008. AIG's former chief Sullivan gets Rs 470 million package. *Bloomberg.com*, July 1.

$14.3 million in salary, bonus, stock options, and other long-term incentives. Sullivan's compensation was in the 90th percentile for CEOs of S&P 500 firms for 2007.

On June 15, 2008, AIG replaced Sullivan as CEO. By then, AIG reported cumulative losses totaling $20 billion. During Sullivan's three-year tenure at the helm, AIG lost 46% of its market value. At the time of his dismissal, the AIG board of directors agreed to give the ousted CEO about $47 million in severance pay, bonus, and long-term compensation.

Two months later, on the verge of bankruptcy, the U.S. government nationalized AIG. At a Congressional hearing in the aftermath of AIG's failure, one witness testified on Sullivan's compensation stating, "I think it is fair to say by any standard of measurement that this pay plan is as uncorrelated to performance as it is possible to be."

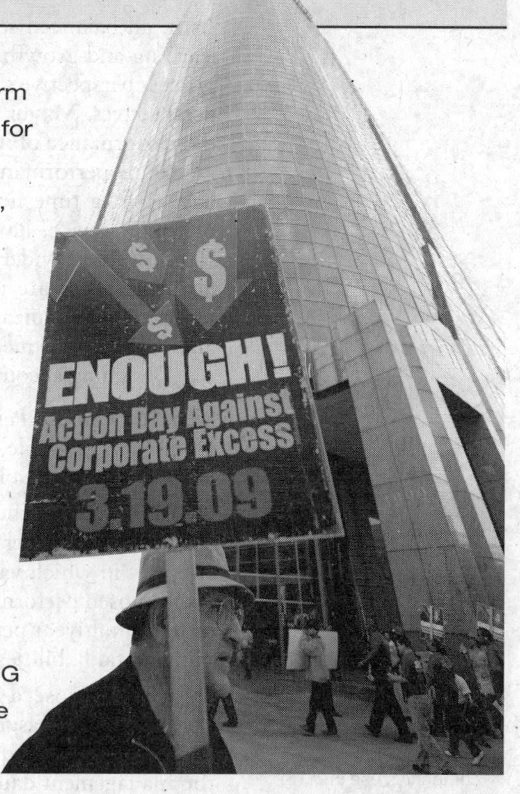

Companies measure reward and performance to motivate managers to achieve company strategies and goals. As the AIG example illustrates, however, if the measures are inappropriate or not connected to sustained performance, managers may improve their performance evaluations and increase compensation without achieving company goals. This chapter discusses the general design, implementation, and uses of performance measures, part of the final step in the decision-making process.

Financial and Nonfinancial Performance Measures

Learning Objective 1

Select financial performance measures

. . . such as return on investment, residual income

and nonfinancial performance measures to use in a balanced scorecard

. . . such as customer-satisfaction, number of defects

Many organizations are increasingly presenting financial and nonfinancial performance measures for their subunits in a single report called the *balanced scorecard* (Chapter 13). Different organizations stress different measures in their scorecards, but the measures are always derived from a company's strategy. Consider the case of Mayur Inns, a chain of hotels. Mayur Inns' strategy is to provide excellent customer service and to charge a higher room rate than its competitors. Mayur Inns uses the following measures in its balanced scorecard:

1. **Financial perspective**—stock price, net income, return on sales, return on investment, economic value added
2. **Customer perspective**—market share in different geographic locations, customer satisfaction, average number of repeat visits
3. **Internal-business-process perspective**—customer-service time for making reservations, for check-in, and in restaurants; cleanliness of hotel and room, quality of room service; time taken to clean rooms; quality of restaurant experience; number of new

services provided to customers (fax, wireless Internet, video games); time taken to plan and build new hotels

4. **Learning-and-growth perspective**—employee education and skill levels, employee satisfaction, employee turnover, hours of employee training, and information-system availability

As in all balanced scorecard implementations, the goal is to make improvements in the learning-and-growth perspective that will lead to improvements in the internal-business-process perspective that, in turn, will result in improvements in the customer and financial perspectives. Mayur Inns also uses balanced scorecard measures to evaluate and reward the performance of its managers.

Some performance measures, such as the time it takes to plan and build new hotels, have a long time horizon. Other measures, such as time taken to check in or quality of room service, have a short time horizon. In this chapter, we focus on *organization subunits'* most widely used performance measures that cover an intermediate-to-long time horizon. These are internal financial measures based on accounting numbers routinely reported by organizations. In later sections, we describe why companies use both financial and nonfinancial measures to evaluate performance.

Designing accounting-based performance measures requires several steps:

Step 1: Choose Performance Measures That Align with Top Management's Financial Goals. For example, is operating income, net income, return on assets, or revenues the best measure of a subunit's financial performance?

Step 2: Choose the Details of Each Performance Measure in Step 1. Once a firm has chosen a specific performance measure, it must make a variety of decisions about the precise way in which various components of the measure are to be calculated. For example, if the chosen performance measure is return on assets, should it be calculated for one year or for a multiyear period? Should assets be defined as total assets or net assets (total assets minus total liabilities)? Should assets be measured at historical cost or current cost?

Step 3: Choose a Target Level of Performance and Feedback Mechanism for Each Performance Measure in Step 1. For example, should all subunits have identical targets, such as the same required rate of return on assets? Should performance reports be sent to top management daily, weekly, or monthly?

Decision Point

What financial and nonfinancial performance measures do companies use in their balanced scorecards?

These steps need not be done sequentially. The issues considered in each step are interdependent, and top management will often proceed through these steps several times before deciding on one or more accounting-based performance measures. The answers to the questions raised at each step depend on top management's beliefs about how well each alternative measure fulfills the behavioral criteria discussed in Chapter 22: promoting goal congruence, motivating management effort, evaluating subunit performance, and preserving subunit autonomy.

Learning Objective 2

Examine accounting-based measures for evaluating business unit performance, including return on investment (ROI),

. . . return on sales times investment turnover

residual income (RI),

. . . income minus a dollar amount for required return on investment

and economic value added (EVA®)

. . . a variation of residual income

Accounting-Based Measures for Business Units

Companies commonly use four measures to evaluate the economic performance of their subunits. We illustrate these measures for Mayur Inns.

Mayur Inns owns and operates three hotels—one each in Mumbai, Kolkata, and New Delhi. Exhibit 23-1 summarizes data for each hotel for 2011. At present, Mayur Inns does not allocate the total long-term debt of the company to the three separate hotels. The exhibit indicates that the New Delhi hotel generates the highest operating income, Rs 51,00,000, compared with Kolkata's Rs 30,00,000 and Mumbai's Rs 24,00,000. But does this comparison mean the New Delhi hotel is the most "successful"? The main weakness of comparing operating incomes alone is that differences in *the size of the investment* in each hotel are ignored. **Investment** refers to the resources or assets used to generate income. The question is not, How large is operating income? Rather, it is, How large is operating income in relation to the investment made to earn it?

Exhibit 23-1

Financial Data for Mayur Inns for 2012 (in Thousands)

File Edit View Insert Format Tools Data Window Help

	A	B	C	D	E
1		Mumbai Hotel	Kolkata Hotel	New Delhi Hotel	Total
2	Hotel revenues	Rs 1,20,00,000	Rs 1,40,00,000	Rs 3,18,50,000	Rs 5,78,50,000
3	Hotel variable costs	31,00,000	37,50,000	99,50,000	1,68,00,000
4	Hotel fixed costs	65,00,000	72,50,000	1,68,00,000	3,05,50,000
5	Hotel operating income	Rs 24,00,000	Rs 30,00,000	Rs 51,00,000	Rs 1,05,00,000
6	Interest costs on long-term debt at 10%				45,00,000
7	Income before income taxes				60,00,000
8	Income taxes at 30%				18,00,000
9	Net income				42,00,000
10	Net book value at the end of 2011:				
11	Current assets	Rs 40,00,000	Rs 50,00,000	Rs 66,00,000	Rs 1,56,00,000
12	Long-term assets	60,00,000	1,50,00,000	2,34,00,000	4,44,00,000
13	Total assets	Rs 1,00,00,000	Rs 2,00,00,000.	Rs 3,00,00,000	Rs 6,00,00,000
14	Current liabilities	Rs 5,00,000	Rs 15,00,000	Rs 30,00,000	Rs 50,00,000
15	Long-term debt				4,50,00,000
16	Stockholders' equity				1,00,00,000
17	Total liabilities and stockholders' equity				Rs 6,00,00,000
18					

Three of the approaches to measuring performance include a measure of investment: return on investment, residual income, and economic value added. A fourth approach, return on sales, does not measure investment.

Return on Investment

Return on investment (ROI) is an accounting measure of income divided by an accounting measure of investment.

$$\text{Return on investment} = \frac{\text{Income}}{\text{Investment}}$$

Return on investment is the most popular approach to measure performance. ROI is popular for two reasons: it blends all the ingredients of profitability—revenues, costs, and investment—into a single percentage; and it can be compared with the rate of return on opportunities elsewhere, inside or outside the company. Like any single performance measure, however, ROI should be used cautiously and in conjunction with other measures.

ROI is also called the *accounting rate of return* or the *accrual accounting rate of return* (Chapter 21). Managers usually use the term ROI when evaluating the performance of an organization subunit such as a division and the term accrual accounting rate of return when using an ROI measure to evaluate a project. Companies vary in the way they define income in the numerator and investment in the denominator of the ROI calculation. Some companies use operating income for the numerator; others prefer to calculate ROI on an after-tax basis and use net income. Some companies use total assets in the denominator; others prefer to focus on only those assets financed by long-term debt and stockholders' equity and use total assets minus current liabilities.

Consider the ROIs of each of the three Mayur hotels in Exhibit 23-1. For our calculations, we use the operating income of each hotel for the numerator and total assets of each hotel for the denominator.

Using these ROI figures, the Mumbai hotel appears to make the best use of its total assets.

Hotel	Operating Income	÷	Total Assets	=	ROI
Mumbai	Rs 24,00,000	÷	Rs 1,00,00,000	=	24%
Kolkata	30,00,000	÷	2,00,00,000	=	15%
New Delhi	51,00,000	÷	3,00,00,000	=	17%

Each hotel manager can increase ROI, for example, by increasing revenues or decreasing costs (each of which increases the numerator), or by decreasing investment (which decreases the denominator). A hotel manager can increase ROI even when operating income decreases by reducing total assets by a greater percentage. Suppose, for example, that operating income of the Kolkata hotel decreases by 4% from Rs 30,00,000 to Rs 28,80,000 [Rs 30,00,000 × (1 − 0.04)] and total assets decrease by 10% from Rs 2,00,00,000 to Rs 1,80,00,000 [Rs 2,00,00,000 × (1 − 0.10)]. The ROI of the Kolkata hotel would then increase from 15% to 16% (Rs 28,80,000 ÷ Rs 1,80,00,000).

ROI can provide more insight into performance when it is represented as two components:

$$\frac{\text{Income}}{\text{Investment}} \times \frac{\text{Income}}{\text{Revenues}} \times \frac{\text{Revenues}}{\text{Investment}}$$

which is also written as,

$$\text{ROI} = \text{Return on sales} \times \text{Investment turnover}$$

This approach is known as the *DuPont method of profitability analysis*. The DuPont method recognizes the two basic ingredients in profit-making: increasing income per rupee of revenues and using assets to generate more revenues. An improvement in either ingredient without changing the other increases ROI.

Assume that top management at Mayur Inns adopts a 30% target ROI for the Mumbai hotel. How can this return be attained? We illustrate the DuPont method for the Mumbai hotel and show how this method can be used to describe three alternative ways in which the Mumbai hotel can increase its ROI from 24% to 30%.

	Operating Income (1)	Revenues (2)	Total Assets (3)	Operating Income / Revenues (4)	×	Revenues / Total Assets (5) = (2) ÷ (3)	=	Operating Income / Total Assets (6) = (4) × (5)
Current ROI	Rs 24,00,000	Rs 1,20,00,000	Rs 1,00,00,000	20%	×	1.2	=	24%
Alternatives								
A. Decrease assets (such as receivables), keeping revenues and operating income per rupee of revenue constant	Rs 24,00,000	Rs 1,20,00,000	Rs 80,00,000	20%	×	1.5	=	30%
B. Increase revenues (via higher occupancy rate), keeping assets and operating income per rupee of revenue constant	Rs 30,00,000	Rs 1,50,00,000	Rs 1,00,00,000	20%	×	1.5	=	30%
C. Decrease costs (via, say, efficient maintenance) to increase operating income per rupee of revenue, keeping revenue and assets constant	Rs 30,00,000	Rs 1,20,00,000	Rs 1,00,00,000	25%	×	1.2	=	30%

Other alternatives, such as increasing the selling price per room, could increase both the revenues per rupee of total assets and the operating income per rupee of revenues. ROI makes clear the benefits that managers can obtain by reducing their investment in current or long-term assets. Some managers know the need to boost revenues or to control costs, but they pay less attention to reducing their investment base. Reducing the investment base means decreasing idle cash, managing credit judiciously, determining proper inventory levels, and spending carefully on long-term assets.

Residual Income

Residual income (RI) is an accounting measure of income minus a rupee amount for required return on an accounting measure of investment.

$$\text{Residual income } (RI) = \text{Income} \times (\text{Required rate of return} \times \text{Investment})$$

Required rate of return multiplied by the investment is the *imputed cost of the investment*. **Imputed costs** are costs recognized in particular situations but not incorporated in financial accounting systems because it is an opportunity cost. In this situation, the imputed cost refers to the return Mayur Inns could have obtained by making an alternative investment with similar risk characteristics.

Assume each hotel faces similar risks. Mayur Inns defines RI for each hotel as operating income minus the required rate of return of 12% of total assets:

Hotel	Operating Income	–	Required Rate of Return	×	Investment	=	Residual Income
Mumbai	Rs 24,00,000	–	(12%	×	Rs 1,00,00,000)	=	Rs 12,00,000
Kolkata	Rs 30,00,000	–	(12%	×	Rs 2,00,00,000)	=	Rs 6,00,000
New Delhi	Rs 51,00,000	–	(12%	×	Rs 3,00,00,000)	=	Rs 15,00,000

Note that the New Delhi hotel has the best RI.

Some companies favor the RI measure because managers will concentrate on maximizing an absolute amount, such as rupees of RI, rather than a percentage, such as ROI. The objective of maximizing RI means that as long as a subunit earns a return in excess of the required return for investments, that subunit should continue to invest.

The objective of maximizing ROI may induce managers of highly profitable subunits to reject projects that, from the viewpoint of the company as a whole, should be accepted. Suppose Mayur Inns is considering upgrading room features and furnishings at the Mumbai hotel. The upgrade will increase operating income of the Mumbai hotel by Rs 7,00,000 and increase its total assets by Rs 40,00,000. The ROI for the expansion is 17.5% (Rs 7,00,000 ÷ Rs 40,00,000), which is attractive to Mayur Inns because it exceeds the required rate of return of 12%. By making this expansion, however, the Mumbai hotel's ROI will decrease:

$$\text{Preupgrade } ROI = \frac{\text{Rs } 24{,}00{,}000}{\text{Rs } 1{,}00{,}00{,}000} = 0.24, \text{ or } 24\%$$

$$\text{Preupgrade } ROI = \frac{\text{Rs } 24{,}00{,}000 + \text{Rs } 7{,}00{,}000}{\text{Rs } 1{,}00{,}00{,}000 + \text{Rs } 40{,}00{,}000} = \frac{\text{Rs } 31{,}00{,}000}{\text{Rs } 1{,}40{,}00{,}000} = 0.221, \text{ or } 22.1\%$$

The annual bonus paid to the Mumbai manager may decrease if ROI affects the bonus calculation and the upgrading option is selected. Consequently, the manager may shun the expansion. In contrast, if the annual bonus is a function of RI, the Mumbai manager will favor the expansion:

$$\text{Preupgrade } RI = \text{Rs } 24{,}00{,}000 - (0.12 \times \text{Rs } 1{,}00{,}00{,}000) = \text{Rs } 12{,}00{,}000$$

$$\text{Preupgrade } RI = \text{Rs } 31{,}00{,}000 - (0.12 \times \text{Rs } 1{,}40{,}00{,}000) = \text{Rs } 14{,}20{,}000$$

Goal congruence (ensuring that subunit managers work toward achieving the company's goals) is more likely using RI rather than ROI as a measure of the subunit manager's performance.

To see that this is a general result, observe that the post-upgrade ROI is a weighted average of the pre-upgrade ROI and the ROI of the project under consideration. Therefore, whenever a new project has a return higher than the required rate of return (12% in our example) but below the current ROI of the division (24% in our example), the division manager is tempted to reject it even though it is a project the shareholders would like to pursue.[2] On the other hand, RI is a measure that aggregates linearly. Therefore, the post-upgrade RI always equals the pre-upgrade RI plus the RI of the project under consideration (in the preceding example, the project's RI is Rs 7,00,000 – 12% × Rs 40,00,000 = Rs 2,20,000, which is the difference between the post-upgrade and pre-upgrade RI amounts). As a result, a manager who is evaluated on residual income will choose a new project if and only if it has a positive RI. But this is exactly the criterion shareholders want the manager to employ; in other words, RI achieves goal congruence.

[2] Analogously, the manager of an underperforming division with an ROI of 7%, say, may wish to accept projects with returns between 7% and 12% even though these opportunities do not meet the shareholders' required rate of return.

Economic Value Added[3]

Economic value added is a specific type of RI calculation that is used by many companies. **Economic value added (EVA®)** equals after-tax operating income *minus* the (after-tax) weighted-average cost of capital *multiplied* by total assets minus current liabilities.

$$\text{Economic value added (EVA)} = \text{After-tax operating income} - \left[\text{Weighted average cost of capital} \times \left(\text{Total assets} - \text{Current liabilities}\right)\right]$$

EVA substitutes the following numbers in the RI calculations: (1) Income equal to after-tax operating income, (2) required rate of return equal to the (after-tax) weighted-average cost of capital, and (3) investment equal to total assets minus current liabilities.[4]

We use the Mayur Inns data in Exhibit 23-1 to illustrate the basic EVA calculations. The weighted-average cost of capital (WACC) equals the *after-tax* average cost of all the long-term funds used by Mayur Inns. The company has two sources of long-term funds: (a) long-term debt with a market value and book value of Rs 45 million issued at an interest rate of 10%, and (b) equity capital that also has a market value of Rs 45 million (but a book value of Rs 10 million).[5] Because interest costs are tax-deductible and the income tax rate is 30%, the after-tax cost of debt financing is 0.10 × (1 − Tax rate) = 0.10 × (1 − 0.30) = 0.10 × 0.70 = 0.07, or 7%. The cost of equity capital is the opportunity cost to investors of not investing their capital in another investment that is similar in risk to Mayur Inns. Mayur Inns' cost of equity capital is 14%.[6] The WACC computation, which uses market values of debt and equity, is:

$$WACC = \frac{(7\% \text{ Market value of debt}) + (14\% \times \text{Market value equity})}{\text{Market value of debt} + \text{Market value of equity}}$$

$$= \frac{(0.07 \times \text{Rs } 4{,}50{,}00{,}000 + (0.14 \times \text{Rs } 4{,}50{,}00{,}000)}{\text{Rs } 4{,}50{,}00{,}000 + \text{Rs } 4{,}50{,}00{,}000}$$

$$= \frac{\text{Rs } 94{,}50{,}000}{\text{Rs } 9{,}00{,}00{,}000} = 0.105, \text{ or } 10.5\%$$

The company applies the same WACC to all its hotels because each hotel faces similar risks.

Total assets minus current liabilities (see Exhibit 23-1) can also be computed as:

$$\text{Total assets} - \text{Current liabilities} = \text{Long-term assets} + \text{Current assets} - \text{Current liabilities}$$
$$= \text{Long-term assets} + \text{Working capital}$$

where

$$\text{Working capital} = \text{Current assets} - \text{Current liabilities}$$

After-tax hotel operating income is:

$$\text{Hotel operating income} \times (1 - \text{Tax rate}) = \text{Hotel operating income} \times (1 - 0.30) = \text{Hotel operating income} \times 0.70$$

---

[3] S. O'Byrne and D. Young, *EVA and Value-Based Management: A Practical Guide to Implementation* (New York: McGraw-Hill, 2000); J. Stein, J. Shiely, and I. Ross, *The EVA Challenge: Implementing Value Added Change in an Organization* (New York: John Wiley and Sons, 2001).

[4] When implementing EVA, companies make several adjustments to the operating income and asset numbers reported under generally accepted accounting principles (GAAP). For example, when calculating EVA, costs such as R&D, restructuring costs, and leases that have long-run benefits are recorded as assets (which are then amortized), rather than as current operating costs. The goal of these adjustments is to obtain a better representation of the economic assets, particularly intangible assets, used to earn income. Of course, the specific adjustments applicable to a company will depend on its individual circumstances.

[5] The market value of Mayur Inns' equity exceeds book value because book value, based on historical cost, does not measure the current value of the company's assets and because various intangible assets, such as the company's brand name, are not shown at current value in the balance sheet under GAAP.

[6] For details on calculating cost of equity capital adjusted for risk, see J. Van Horne, *Financial Management and Policy*, 12th ed. (Upper Saddle River, NJ: Prentice Hall, 2002).

EVA calculations for Mayur Inns are as follows:

Hotel	After-Tax Operating Income	−	[WACC ×	(Total Assets − Current Liabilities)]	=	EVA
Mumbai	Rs 24,00,000 × 0.07	−	[10.50% ×	(Rs 1,00,00,000 − Rs 5,00,000)]	=	Rs 6,82,500
Kolkata	30,00,000 × 0.07	−	[10.50% ×	(2,00,00,000 − 15,00,000)]	=	1,57,500
New Delhi	51,00,000 × 0.07	−	[10.50% ×	(3,00,00,000 − 30,00,000)]	=	7,35,000

The New Delhi hotel has the highest EVA. Economic value added, like residual income, charges managers for the cost of their investments in long-term assets and working capital. Value is created only if after-tax operating income exceeds the cost of investing the capital. To improve EVA, managers can, for example, (a) earn more after-tax operating income with the same capital, (b) use less capital to earn the same after-tax operating income, or (c) invest capital in high-return projects.[7]

Managers in companies such as Briggs and Stratton, Coca-Cola, CSX, Equifax, and FMC use the estimated impact on EVA to guide their decisions. Division managers find EVA helpful because it allows them to incorporate the cost of capital, which is generally only available at the companywide level, into decisions at the division level. Comparing the actual EVA achieved to the estimated EVA is useful for evaluating performance and providing feedback to managers about performance. CSX, a railroad company, credits EVA for decisions such as to run trains with three locomotives instead of four and to schedule arrivals just in time for unloading rather than having trains arrive at their destination several hours in advance. The result? Higher income because of lower fuel costs and lower capital investments in locomotives.

Return on Sales

The income-to-revenues ratio (or sales ratio)—often called *return on sales (ROS)*—is a frequently used financial performance measure. ROS is one component of ROI in the DuPont method of profitability analysis. To calculate ROS for each of Mayur's hotels, we divide operating income by revenues:

Hotel	Operating Income	÷	Revenues (Sales)	=	ROS
Mumbai	Rs 24,00,000	÷	Rs 1,20,00,000	=	20%
Kolkata	Rs 30,00,000	÷	Rs 1,40,00,000	=	21.4%
New Delhi	Rs 51,00,000	÷	Rs 3,18,50,000	=	16.0%

The Kolkata hotel has the highest ROS, but its performance is rated worse than the other hotels using measures such as ROI, RI, and EVA.

Comparing Performance Measures

The following table summarizes the performance of each hotel and ranks it (in parentheses) under each of the four performance measures:

Hotel	ROI	RI	EVA	ROS
Mumbai	24% (1)	Rs 12,00,000 (2)	Rs 6,82,500 (2)	20.0% (2)
Kolkata	15% (3)	Rs 6,00,000 (3)	Rs 1,57,500 (3)	21.4% (1)
New Delhi	17% (2)	Rs 15,00,000 (1)	Rs 7,35,000 (1)	16.0% (3)

The RI and EVA rankings are the same. They differ from the ROI and ROS rankings. Consider the ROI and RI rankings for the Mumbai and New Delhi hotels. The New Delhi hotel has a smaller ROI. Although its operating income is only slightly more than twice the operating income of the Mumbai hotel—Rs 51,00,000 versus Rs 24,00,000—its total assets are three times as large—Rs 30 million versus Rs 10 million. The New Delhi hotel has a higher RI because it earns a higher income after covering the

[7] Observe that the sum of the divisional after-tax operating incomes used in the EVA calculation, (Rs 24,00,000 + Rs 30,00,000 + Rs 51,00,000) × 0.7 = Rs 73,50,000, exceeds the firm's net income of Rs 42,00,000. The difference is due to the firm's after-tax interest expense on its long-term debt, which amounts to Rs 45,00,000 × 0.7 = Rs 31,50,000. Because the EVA measure includes a charge for the weighted average cost of capital, which includes the after-tax cost of debt, the income figure used in computing EVA should reflect the after-tax profit before interest payments on debt are considered. After-tax operating income (often referred to in practice as NOPAT, or net operating profit after taxes) is thus the relevant measure of divisional profit for EVA calculations.

required rate of return on investment of 12%. The high ROI of the Mumbai hotel indicates that its assets are being used efficiently. Even though each rupee invested in the New Delhi hotel does not give the same return as the Mumbai hotel, this large investment creates considerable value because its return exceeds the required rate of return. The Kolkata hotel has the highest ROS but the lowest ROI. The high ROS indicates that the Kolkata hotel has the lowest cost structure per rupee of revenues of all of Mayur Inns' hotels. The reason for Kolkata's low ROI is that it generates very low revenues per rupee of assets invested. Is any one method better than the others for measuring performance? No, because each evaluates a different aspect of performance.

Decision Point

What are the relative merits of return on investment (ROI), residual income (RI), and economic value added (EVA) as performance measures for subunit managers?

ROS measures how effectively costs are managed. To evaluate overall aggregate performance, ROI, RI, or EVA measures are more appropriate than ROS because they consider both income and investment. ROI indicates which investment yields the highest return. RI and EVA measures overcome some of the goal-congruence problems of ROI. Some managers favor EVA because it explicitly considers tax effects while (pretax) RI measures do not. Other managers favor (pretax) RI because it is easier to calculate and because, in most cases, it leads to the same conclusions as EVA. Generally, companies use multiple financial measures to evaluate performance.

Choosing the Details of the Performance Measures

Learning Objective 3

Analyze the key measurement choices in the design of each performance measure

. . . choice of time horizon, alternative definitions, and measurement of assets

It is not sufficient for a company to identify the set of performance measures it wishes to use. The company has to make several choices regarding the specific details of how the measures are computed. These range from decisions regarding the time frame over which the measures are computed, to the definition of key terms such as "investment" and the calculation of particular components of each performance measure.

Alternative Time Horizons

An important element in designing accounting-based performance measures is choosing the time horizon of the performance measures. The ROI, RI, EVA, and ROS calculations represent the results for a single period, one year in our example. Managers could take actions that cause short-run increases in these measures but that conflict with the long-run interest of the company. For example, managers may curtail R&D and plant maintenance in the last three months of a fiscal year to achieve a target level of annual operating income. For this reason, many companies evaluate subunits on the basis of ROI, RI, EVA, and ROS over multiple years.

Another reason to evaluate subunits over multiple years is that the benefits of actions taken in the current period may not show up in short-run performance measures, such as the current year's ROI or RI. For example, an investment in a new hotel may adversely affect ROI and RI in the short run but benefit ROI and RI in the long run.

A multiyear analysis highlights another advantage of the RI measure: Net present value of all cash flows over the life of an investment equals net present value of the RIs.[8]

[8] This equivalence, often referred to as the "Conservation Property" of residual income, was originally articulated by Gabriel Preinreich in 1938. To see the equivalence, suppose the Rs 40,00,000 investment in the Mumbai hotel increases operating income by Rs 7,00,000 per year as follows: Increase in operating cash flows of Rs 15,00,000 each year for five years minus depreciation of Rs 8,00,000 (Rs 40,00,000 ÷ 5) per year, assuming straight-line depreciation and Re 0 terminal disposal value. Depreciation reduces the investment amount by Rs 8,00,000 each year. Assuming a required rate of return of 12%, net present values of cash flows and residual incomes are as follows:

Year	0	1	2	3	4	5	Net Present Value
(1) Cash flow	– Rs 40,00,000	Rs 15,00,000	Rs 15,00,000	Rs 15,00,000	Rs 15,00,000	Rs 15,00,000	Rs 14,07,160
(2) Present value of Rs 1 discounted at 12%	1	0.89286	0.79719	0.71178	0.63552	0.56743	
(3) Present value: (1) × (2)	– Rs 40,00,000	Rs 13,39,290	Rs 11,95,780	Rs 10,67,670	Rs 9,53,820	Rs 8,51,140	
(4) Operating income		Rs 7,00,000	Rs 7,00,000	Rs 7,00,000	Rs 7,00,000	Rs 7,00,000	
(5) Assets at start of year		Rs 40,00,000	Rs 32,00,000	Rs 24,00,000	Rs 16,00,000	Rs 8,00,000	
(6) Capital charge: (5) × 12%		Rs 4,80,000	Rs 3,84,000	Rs 2,88,000	Rs 1,92,000	Rs 96,000	
(7) Residual income: (4) – (6)		Rs 2,20,000	Rs 3,16,000	Rs 4,12,000	Rs 5,08,000	Rs 6,04,000	
(8) Present value of RI: (7) × (2)		Rs 1,96,430	Rs 2,51,910	Rs 2,93,250	Rs 3,22,840	Rs 3,42,730	Rs 14,07,160

This characteristic means that if managers use the net present value method to make investment decisions (as advocated in Chapter 21), then using multiyear RI to evaluate managers' performances achieves goal congruence.

Another way to motivate managers to take a long-run perspective is by compensating them on the basis of changes in the market price of the company's stock. That's because stock prices incorporate the expected future effects of current decisions.

Alternative Definitions of Investment

Companies use a variety of definitions for measuring investment in divisions. Four common alternative definitions used in the construction of accounting-based performance measures are as follows:

1. **Total assets available**—includes all assets, regardless of their intended purpose.
2. **Total assets employed**—total assets available minus the sum of idle assets and assets purchased for future expansion. For example, if the New Delhi hotel in Exhibit 23-1 has unused land set aside for potential expansion, total assets employed by the hotel would exclude the cost of that land.
3. **Total assets employed minus current liabilities**—total assets excluding assets financed by short-term creditors. One negative feature of defining investment in this way is that it may encourage subunit managers to use an excessive amount of short-term debt because short-term debt reduces the amount of investment.
4. **Stockholders' equity**—calculated by assigning liabilities among subunits and deducting these amounts from the total assets of each subunit. One drawback of this method is that it combines operating decisions made by hotel managers with financing decisions made by top management.

Companies that use ROI or RI generally define investment as the total assets available. When top management directs a subunit manager to carry extra or idle assets, total assets employed can be more informative than total assets available. Companies that adopt EVA define investment as total assets employed minus current liabilities. The most common rationale for using total assets employed minus current liabilities is that the subunit manager often influences decisions on current liabilities of the subunit.

Alternative Asset Measurements

To design accounting-based performance measures, we must consider different ways to measure assets included in the investment calculations. Should assets be measured at historical cost or current cost? Should gross book value (that is, original cost) or net book value (original cost minus accumulated depreciation) be used for depreciable assets?

Current Cost

Current cost is the cost of purchasing an asset today identical to the one currently held, or the cost of purchasing an asset that provides services like the one currently held if an identical asset cannot be purchased. Of course, measuring assets at current costs will result in different ROIs than the ROIs calculated on the basis of historical costs.

We illustrate the current-cost ROI calculations using the data for Mayur Inns (Exhibit 23-1) and then compare current-cost-based ROIs and historical-cost-based ROIs. Assume the following information about the long-term assets of each hotel:

	Mumbai	Kolkata	New Delhi
Age of facility in years (at end of 2011)	8	4	2
Gross book value (original cost)	Rs 1,40,00,000	Rs 2,10,00,000	Rs 2,73,00,000
Accumulated depreciation	80,00,000	60,00,000	39,00,000
Net book value (at end of 2011)	60,00,000	1,50,00,000	2,34,00,000
Depreciation for 2011	10,00,000	15,00,000	19,50,000

Mayur Inns assumes a 14-year estimated useful life, zero terminal disposal value for the physical facilities, and straight-line depreciation.

An index of construction costs indicating how the cost of construction has changed over the eight-year period that Mayur Inns has been operating (2003 year-end = 100) is:

Year	2005	2006	2007	2008	2009	2010	2011	2012
Construction cost index	110	122	136	144	152	160	174	180

Earlier in this chapter, we computed an ROI of 24% for Mumbai, 15% for Kolkata, and 17% for New Delhi. One possible explanation of the high ROI for the Mumbai hotel is that its long-term assets are expressed in 2003 construction-price levels—prices that prevailed eight years ago—and the long-term assets for the Kolkata and New Delhi hotels are expressed in terms of higher, more-recent construction-price levels, which depress ROIs for these two hotels.

Exhibit 23-2 illustrates a step-by-step approach for incorporating current-cost estimates of long-term assets and depreciation expense into the ROI calculation. We make these calculations to approximate what it would cost today to obtain assets that would produce the same expected operating income that the subunits currently earn. (Similar adjustments to represent the current costs of capital employed and depreciation expense can also be made in the RI and EVA calculations.) The current-cost adjustment reduces the ROI of the Mumbai hotel by more than half.

	Historical-Cost ROI	Current-Cost ROI
Mumbai	24%	10.8%
Kolkata	15%	11.1%
New Delhi	17%	14.7%

Adjusting assets to recognize current costs negates differences in the investment base caused solely by differences in construction-price levels. Compared with historical-cost ROI, current-cost ROI better measures the current economic returns from the investment. If Mayur Inns were to invest in a new hotel today, investing in one like the New Delhi hotel offers the best ROI.

Current cost estimates may be difficult to obtain for some assets. Why? Because the estimate requires a company to consider, in addition to increases in price levels, technological advances and processes that could reduce the current cost of assets needed to earn today's operating income.

Long-Term Assets: Gross or Net Book Value?

Historical cost of assets is often used to calculate ROI. There has been much discussion about whether gross book value or net book value of assets should be used. Using the data in Exhibit 23-1, we calculate ROI using net and gross book values of plant and equipment as follows:

	Operating Income (from Exhibit 23-1)	Net Book Value of Total Assets (from Exhibit 23-1)	Accumulated Depreciation	Gross Book Value of Total Assets	2011 ROI Using Net Book Value of Total Assets (calculated earlier)	2011 ROI Using Gross Book Value of Total Assets
	(1)	(2)	(3)	(4) = (2) + (3)	(5) = (1) ÷ (2)	(6) = (1) ÷ (4)
Mumbai	Rs 24,00,000	Rs 1,00,00,000	Rs 80,00,000	Rs 1,80,00,000	24%	13.3%
Kolkata	30,00,000	2,00,00,000	60,00,000	2,60,00,000	15%	11.5%
New Delhi	5,10,000	3,00,00,000	39,00,000	3,39,00,000	17%	15.0%

Using gross book value, the 13.3% ROI of the older Mumbai hotel is lower than the 15.0% ROI of the newer New Delhi hotel. Those who favor using gross book value claim it enables more-accurate comparisons of ROI across subunits. For example, using gross-book-value calculations, the return on the original plant-and-equipment investment is higher for the newer New Delhi hotel than for the older Mumbai hotel. This difference probably reflects the decline in earning power of the Mumbai hotel. Using the net book value masks this decline in earning power because the constantly decreasing investment base results in a higher ROI for the Mumbai hotel—24% in this example.

Exhibit 23-2 ROI for Mayur Inns: Computed Using Current-Cost Estimates as of the End of 2011 for Depreciation Expense and Long-Term Assets

File Edit View Insert Format Tools Data Window Help

	A	B	C	D	E	F	G	H	I	J
1	**Step 1:** Restate long-term assets from gross book value at historical cost to gross book value at current cost as of the end of 2011.									
2		Gross book value of long-term assets at historical cost	x	Construction cost index in 2011	÷	Construction cost index in year of construction	=	Gross book value of long-term assets at current cost at end of 2011		
3	Mumbai	Rs 1,40,00,000	x	(180	÷	100)	=	Rs 2,52,00,000		
4	Kolkata	Rs 2,10,00,000	x	(180	÷	144)	=	Rs 2,62,50,000		
5	New Delhi	Rs 2,73,00,000	x	(180	÷	160)	=	Rs 3,07,12,500		
6										
7	**Step 2:** Derive net book value of long-term assets at current cost as of the end of 2011 (Assume estimated useful life of each hotel is 14 years.)									
8		Gross book value of long-term assets at current cost at end of 2011	x	Estimated remaining useful life	÷	Estimated total useful life	=	Net book value of long-term assets at current cost at end of 2011		
9	Mumbai	Rs 2,52,00,000	x	(6	÷	14)	=	Rs 1,08,00,000		
10	Kolkata	Rs 2,62,50,000	x	(10	÷	14)	=	Rs 1,87,50,000		
11	New Delhi	Rs 3,07,12,500	x	(12	÷	14)	=	Rs 2,63,25,000		
12										
13	**Step 3:** Compute current cost of total assets in 2011 (Assume current assets of each hotel are expressed in 2011 rupees.)									
14		Current assets at end of 2011 (from Exhibit 23-1)	+	Long-term assets from Step 2 above	=	Current cost of total assets at end of 2011				
15	Mumbai	Rs 40,00,000	+	Rs 1,08,00,000	=	Rs 1,48,00,000				
16	Kolkata	Rs 50,00,000	+	Rs 1,87,50,000	=	Rs 2,37,50,000				
17	New Delhi	Rs 66,00,000	+	Rs 2,63,25,000	=	Rs 3,29,25,000				
18										
19	**Step 4:** Compute current-cost depreciation expense in 2011 rupees.									
20		Gross book value of long-term assets at current cost at end of 2011 (from Step 1)	÷	Estimated total useful life	=	Current-cost depreciation expense in 2011 rupees				
21	Mumbai	Rs 2,52,00,000	÷	14	=	Rs 18,00,000				
22	Kolkata	Rs 2,62,50,000	÷	14	=	Rs 18,75,000				
23	New Delhi	Rs 3,07,12,500	÷	14	=	Rs 21,93,750				
24										
25	**Step 5:** Compute 2011 operating income using 2011 current-cost depreciation expense.									
26		Historical-cost operating income	–	Current-cost depreciation expense in 2011 rupees (from Step 4)	–	Historical-cost depreciation expense	=	Operating income for 2011 using current-cost depreciation expense in 2011 rupees		
27	Mumbai	Rs 24,00,000	–	(Rs 18,00,000	–	Rs 10,00,000)	=	Rs 16,00,000		
28	Kolkata	Rs 30,00,000	–	(Rs 18,75,000	–	Rs 15,00,000)	=	Rs 26,25,000		
29	New Delhi	Rs 51,00,000	–	(Rs 21,93,750	–	Rs 19,50,000)	=	Rs 48,56,250		
30										
31	**Step 6:** Compute ROI using current-cost estimates for long-term assets and depreciation expense.									
32		Operating income for 2011 using current-cost depreciation expense in 2011 rupees (from Step 5)	÷	Current cost of total assets at end of 2011 (from step 3)	=	ROI using current-cost estimate				
33	Mumbai	Rs 16,00,000	÷	Rs 1,48,00,000	=	10.8%				
34	Kolkata	Rs 26,25,000	÷	Rs 2,37,50,000	=	11.1%				
35	New Delhi	Rs 48,56,250	÷	Rs 3,29,25,000	=	14.7%				

Decision Point

Over what time frame should companies measure performance, and what are the alternative choices for calculating the components of each performance measure?

This higher rate may mislead decision makers into thinking that the earning power of the Mumbai hotel has not decreased.

The proponents of using net book value as an investment base maintain it is less confusing because (1) it is consistent with the amount of total assets shown in the conventional balance sheet, and (2) it is consistent with income computations that include deductions for depreciation expense. Surveys report net book value to be the dominant measure of assets used by companies for internal performance evaluation.

Target Levels of Performance and Feedback

Now that we have covered the different types of measures and how to choose them, let us turn our attention to how mangers set and measure target levels of performance.

Learning Objective 4

Study the choice of performance targets and design of feedback mechanisms

. . . carefully crafted budgets and sufficient feedback for timely corrective action

Choosing Target Levels of Performance

We next consider target-setting for accounting-based measures of performance against which actual performance can be compared. Historical-cost-based accounting measures are usually inadequate for evaluating economic returns on new investments, and in some cases, they create disincentives for expansion. Despite these problems, historical-cost ROIs can be used to evaluate current performance by establishing *target* ROIs. For Mayur Inns, we need to recognize that the hotels were built in different years, which means they were built at different construction-price levels. Top management could adjust the target historical-cost-based ROIs accordingly, say, by setting Mumbai's ROI at 26%, Kolkata's at 18%, and New Delhi's at 19%.

This useful alternative of comparing actual results with target or budgeted performance is frequently overlooked. The budget should be carefully negotiated with full knowledge of historical-cost accounting pitfalls. *Companies should tailor a budget to a particular subunit, a particular accounting system, and a particular performance measure.* For example, many problems of asset valuation and income measurement can be resolved if top management can get subunit managers to focus on what is attainable in the forthcoming budget period—whether ROI, RI, or EVA is used and whether the financial measures are based on historical cost or some other measure, such as current cost.

A popular way to establish targets is to set continuous improvement targets. If a company is using EVA as a performance measure, top management can evaluate operations on year-to-year changes in EVA, rather than on absolute measures of EVA. Evaluating performance on the basis of *improvements* in EVA makes the initial method of calculating EVA less important.

In establishing targets for financial performance measures, companies using the balanced scorecard simultaneously determine targets in the customer, internal-business-process, and learning-and-growth perspectives. For example, Mayur Inns will establish targets for employee training and employee satisfaction, customer-service time for reservations and check-in, quality of room service, and customer satisfaction that each hotel must reach to achieve its ROI and EVA targets.

Choosing the Timing of Feedback: Step 6

A final step in designing accounting-based performance measures is the timing of feedback. Timing of feedback depends largely on (a) how critical the information is for the success of the organization, (b) the specific level of management receiving the feedback, and (c) the sophistication of the organization's information technology. For example, hotel managers responsible for room sales want information on the number of rooms sold (rented) on a daily or weekly basis. That's because a large percentage of hotel costs are fixed costs, so achieving high room sales and taking quick action to reverse any declining sales trends are critical to the financial success of each hotel. Supplying managers with daily information about room sales is much easier if Mayur Inns has a computerized room-reservation and check-in system. Top management, however, may look at information about daily room sales only on a monthly basis. In some instances, for example because of concern about the low sales-to-total-assets ratio of the Kolkata hotel, they may want the information weekly.

The timing of feedback for measures in the balanced scorecard varies. For example, human resources managers at each hotel measure employee satisfaction annually because satisfaction is best measured over a longer horizon. However, housekeeping-department managers measure the quality of room service over much shorter time horizons, such as a week. That's because poor levels of performance in these areas for even a short period of time can harm a hotel's reputation for a long period. Moreover, housekeeping problems can be detected and resolved over a short time period.

Decision Point

What targets should companies use and when should they give feedback to managers regarding their performance relative to these targets?

Performance Measurement in Multinational Companies

Learning Objective 5

Indicate the difficulties that occur when the performance of divisions operating in different countries is compared

. . . adjustments needed for differences in inflation rates and changes in exchange rates

Our discussion so far has focused on performance evaluation of different divisions of a company operating within a single country. We next discuss the additional difficulties created when the performance of divisions of a company operating in different countries is compared. Several issues arise.[9]

- The economic, legal, political, social, and cultural environments differ significantly across countries.
- Governments in some countries may limit selling prices of, and impose controls on, a company's products. For example, some countries in Asia, Latin America, and Eastern Europe impose tariffs and custom duties to restrict imports of certain goods.
- Availability of materials and skilled labor, as well as costs of materials, labor, and infrastructure (power, transportation, and communication), may also differ significantly across countries.
- Divisions operating in different countries account for their performance in different currencies. Issues of inflation and fluctuations in foreign-currency exchange rates affect performance measures.

As a result of these differences, adjustments need to be made to compare performance measures across countries.

Calculating the Foreign Division's ROI in the Foreign Currency

Suppose Mayur Inns invests in a hotel in Mexico City. The investment consists mainly of the costs of buildings and furnishings. Also assume:

- The exchange rate at the time of Mayur's investment on December 31, 2010, was 10 pesos = Rs 10.
- During 2011, the Mexican peso suffered a steady decline in its value. The exchange rate on December 31, 2011, was 15 pesos = Rs 10.
- The average exchange rate during 2011 was [(10 + 15) ÷ 2] = 12.5 pesos = Rs 10.
- The investment (total assets) in the Mexico City hotel was 3,00,00,000 pesos.
- The operating income of the Mexico City hotel in 2011 was 60,00,000 pesos.

What is the historical-cost-based ROI for the Mexico City hotel in 2012?

To answer, Mayur Inns' managers first have to determine: Should they calculate the ROI in pesos or in rupees? If they calculate the ROI in rupees, what exchange rate should

[9] See M. Z. Iqbal, *International Accounting—A Global Perspective* (Cincinnati: South-Western College Publishing, 2002).

they use? The managers may also be interested in how the ROI of Mayur Inns Mexico City (MIMC) compares with the ROI of Mayur Inns New Delhi (MIND), which is also a relatively new hotel of approximately the same size. The answers to these questions yield information that will be helpful when making future investment decisions.

$$\text{MIMC's } ROI \text{ (calculated using pesos)} = \frac{\text{Operating incomes}}{\text{Total assets}} = \frac{60{,}00{,}000 \text{ pesos}}{3{,}00{,}00{,}000 \text{ pesos}} = 0.20, \text{ or } 20\%$$

MIMC's ROI of 20% is higher than MIND's ROI of 17%. Does this mean that MIMC outperformed MIND based on the ROI criterion? Not necessarily. That's because MIMC operates in a very different economic environment than MIND.

Again, assume that the peso has declined in value relative to the rupee in 2011. This decline has led to higher inflation in Mexico than in India. As a result of the higher inflation in Mexico, MIMC will charge higher prices for its hotel rooms, which will increase MIMC's operating income and lead to a higher ROI. Inflation clouds the real economic returns on an asset and makes historical-cost-based ROI higher. Differences in inflation rates between the two countries make a direct comparison of MIMC's peso-denominated ROI with MIND's rupee-denominated ROI misleading.

Calculating the Foreign Division's ROI in Indian Rupees

One way to make a comparison of historical-cost-based ROIs more meaningful is to restate MIMC's performance in Indian rupees. But what exchange rate should be used to make the comparison meaningful? Assume operating income was earned evenly throughout 2011. Mayur Inns' managers should use the average exchange rate of 12.5 pesos = Rs 10 to convert operating income from pesos to rupees: 60,00,000 pesos ÷ 12.5 pesos per rupee = Rs 48,00,000. The effect of dividing the operating income in pesos by the higher pesos-to-rupee exchange rate prevailing during 2011, rather than the 10 pesos = Rs 10 exchange rate prevailing on December 31, 2010, is that any increase in operating income in pesos as a result of inflation during 2011 is eliminated when converting back to rupees.

At what rate should MIMC's total assets of 3,00,00,000 pesos be converted? The 10 pesos = Rs 10 exchange rate prevailing when the assets were acquired on December 31, 2010. That's because MIMC's assets are recorded in pesos at the December 31, 2010, cost, and they are not revalued as a result of inflation in Mexico in 2011. Because the cost of assets in MIMC's financial accounting records is unaffected by subsequent inflation, the exchange rate prevailing when the assets were acquired should be used to convert the assets into rupees. Using exchange rates after December 31, 2010, would be incorrect because these exchange rates incorporate the higher inflation in Mexico in 2011. Total assets are converted to 3,00,00,000 pesos ÷ 10 pesos per rupee = Rs 3,00,00,000.

Then,

$$\text{MIMC's } ROI \text{ (calculated using rupees)} = \frac{\text{Operating income}}{\text{Total assets}} = \frac{\text{Rs } 48{,}00{,}000}{\text{Rs } 3{,}00{,}00{,}000} = 0.16, \text{ or } 16\%$$

As we have discussed, these adjustments make the historical-cost-based ROIs of the Mexico City and New Delhi hotels comparable because they negate the effects of any differences in inflation rates between the two countries. MIMC's ROI of 16% is less than MIND's ROI of 17%.

Residual income calculated in pesos suffers from the same problems as ROI calculated using pesos. Calculating MIMC's RI in rupees adjusts for changes in exchange rates and makes for more-meaningful comparisons with Mayur's other hotels:

Decision Point

How can companies compare the performance of divisions operating in different countries?

$$\begin{aligned}\text{MIMC's } RI &= \text{Rs } 48{,}00{,}000 - (0.12 \times \text{Rs } 3{,}00{,}00{,}000)\\ &= \text{Rs } 48{,}00{,}000 - \text{Rs } 36{,}00{,}000 = \text{Rs } 12{,}00{,}000\end{aligned}$$

which is also less than MIND's RI of Rs 15,00,000. In interpreting MIMC's and MIND's ROI and RI, keep in mind that they are historical-cost-based calculations. They do, however, pertain to relatively new hotels.

Distinction Between Managers and Organization Units[10]

Our focus has been on how to evaluate the performance of a subunit of a company, such as a division. However, is evaluating the performance of a subunit manager the same as evaluating the performance of the subunit? If the subunit performed well, does it mean the manager performed well? In this section, we argue that the performance evaluation of a *manager* should be distinguished from the performance evaluation of that manager's *subunit*. For example, companies often put the most skillful division manager in charge of the division producing the poorest economic return in an attempt to improve it. The division may take years to show improvement. Furthermore, the manager's efforts may result merely in bringing the division up to a minimum acceptable ROI. The division may continue to be a poor performer in comparison with other divisions, but it would be a mistake to conclude from the poor performance of the division that the manager is performing poorly. The division's performance may be adversely affected by economic conditions over which the manager has no control.

As another example, consider again the Mayur Inn Mexico City (MIMC) hotel. Suppose, despite the high inflation in Mexico, MIMC could not increase room prices because of price-control regulations imposed by the government. MIMC's performance in rupee terms would be very poor because of the decline in the value of the peso. But should top management conclude from MIMC's poor performance that the MIMC manager performed poorly? Probably not. That's because most likely the poor performance of MIMC is largely the result of regulatory factors beyond the manager's control.

In the following sections, we show the basic principles for evaluating the performance of an individual subunit manager. These principles apply to managers at all organization levels. Later sections consider examples at the individual-worker level and the top-management level. We illustrate these principles using the RI performance measure.

The Basic Trade-Off: Creating Incentives versus Imposing Risk

Understand the roles of salaries and incentives when rewarding managers

. . . balancing risk and performance-based rewards

How the performance of managers and other employees is measured and evaluated affects their rewards. Compensation arrangements range from a flat salary with no direct performance-based incentive (or bonus), as in the case of many government employees, to rewards based on only performance, as in the case of real estate agents who receive no salary and are compensated via commissions paid on the properties they sell. Most managers' total compensation includes some combination of salary and performance-based incentive. In designing compensation arrangements, we need to consider the *trade-off between creating incentives and imposing risk*. We illustrate this trade-off in the context of our Mayur Inns example.

Sultan Sharma owns the Mayur Inns chain of hotels. Roshan Bhatt manages the Mayur Inns Mumbai (MIM) hotel. Assume Sharma uses RI to measure performance. To improve RI, Sharma would like Bhatt to increase sales, control costs, provide prompt and courteous customer service, and reduce working capital. But even if Bhatt did all those things, high RI is not guaranteed. That's because MIM's RI is affected by many factors beyond Sharma's and Bhatt's control, such as a recession in the Mumbai economy or an earthquake that might negatively affect MIM. Or, there could be other uncontrollable factors, such as road construction near competing hotels, that might have a positive effect on MIM's RI. Uncontrollable factors make MIM's profitability uncertain and, therefore, risky.

As an entrepreneur, Sharma expects to bear risk. But Bhatt does not like being subject to risk. One way of "insuring" Bhatt against risk is to pay Bhatt a flat salary, regardless of the actual amount of RI earned. All the risk would then be borne by Sharma. This arrangement creates a problem, however, because Bhatt's effort is difficult to monitor. The absence of performance-based compensation means that Bhatt has no direct incentive to

[10] The presentations here draw (in part) from teaching notes prepared by S. Huddart, N. Melumad, and S. Reichelstein.

work harder or to undertake extra physical and mental effort beyond what is necessary to retain his job or to uphold his own personal values.

Moral hazard describes a situation in which an employee prefers to exert less effort (or to report distorted information) compared with the effort (or accurate information) desired by the owner because the employee's effort (or validity of the reported information) cannot be accurately monitored and enforced.[11] In some repetitive jobs, such as in electronic assembly, a supervisor can monitor the workers' actions, and the moral-hazard problem may not arise. However, a manager's job is to gather and interpret information and to exercise judgment on the basis of the information obtained. Monitoring a manager's effort is more difficult.

Paying no salary and rewarding Bhatt *only* on the basis of some performance measure—RI in our example—raises different concerns. In this case, Bhatt would be motivated to strive to increase RI because his rewards would increase with increases in RI. But compensating Bhatt on RI also subjects him to risk. That's because MIM's RI depends not only on Bhatt's effort, but also on factors such as local economic conditions over which Bhatt has no control.

Bhatt does not like being subject to risk. To compensate Bhatt for taking risk, Sharma must pay him extra compensation. That is, using performance-based bonuses will cost Fonda more money, *on average*, than paying Bhatt a flat salary. Why "on average"? Because Sharma's compensation payment to Bhatt will vary with RI outcomes. When averaged over these outcomes, the RI-based compensation will cost Sharma more than paying Bhatt a flat salary. The motivation for having some salary and some performance-based bonus in compensation arrangements is to balance the benefit of incentives against the extra cost of imposing risk on the manager.

Intensity of Incentives and Financial and Nonfinancial Measurements

What affects the intensity of incentives? That is, how large should the incentive component of a manager's compensation be relative to the salary component? To answer these questions, we need to understand how much the performance measure is affected by actions the manager takes to further the owner's objectives.

Preferred performance measures are those that are sensitive to or that change significantly with the manager's performance. They do not change much with changes in factors that are beyond the manager's control. Sensitive performance measures motivate the manager as well as limit the manager's exposure to risk, reducing the cost of providing incentives. Less-sensitive performance measures are not affected by the manager's performance and fail to induce the manager to improve. The more that owners have sensitive performance measures available to them, the more they can rely on incentive compensation for their managers.

The salary component of compensation dominates when performance measures that are sensitive to managers' actions are not available. This is the case, for example, for some corporate staff and government employees. A high salary component, however, does not mean incentives are completely absent. Promotions and salary increases do depend on some overall measure of performance, but the incentives are less direct. The incentive component of compensation is high when sensitive performance measures are available and when monitoring the employee's effort is difficult, such as in real estate agencies.

In evaluating Bhatt, Sharma uses measures from multiple perspectives of the balanced scorecard because nonfinancial measures on the balanced scorecard—employee satisfaction and the time taken for check-in, cleaning rooms, and providing room service—are more sensitive to Bhatt's actions. Financial measures such as RI are less sensitive to Bhatt's actions because they are affected by external factors such as local economic conditions beyond Bhatt's control. Residual income may be a very good measure of the economic viability of the hotel, but it is only a partial measure of Bhatt's performance.

---

[11] The term *moral hazard* originated in insurance contracts to represent situations in which insurance coverage caused insured parties to take less care of their properties than they might otherwise. One response to moral hazard in insurance contracts is the system of deductibles (that is, the insured pays for damages below a specified amount).

Another reason for using nonfinancial measures in the balanced scorecard is that these measures follow Mayur Inns' strategy and are drivers of future performance. Evaluating managers on these nonfinancial measures motivates them to take actions that will sustain long-run performance. Therefore, evaluating performance in all four perspectives of the balanced scorecard promotes both short- and long-run actions.

Benchmarks and Relative Performance Evaluation

Owners often use financial and nonfinancial benchmarks to evaluate performance. Benchmarks representing "best practice" may be available inside or outside an organization. For MIM, benchmarks could be from similar hotels, either within or outside the Mayur Inns chain. Suppose Bhatt has responsibility for revenues, costs, and investments. In evaluating Bhatt's performance, Sharma would want to use as a benchmark a hotel of a similar size influenced by the same uncontrollable factors—for example, location, demographic trends, and economic conditions—that affect MIM. If all these factors were the same, *differences* in performances of the two hotels would occur only because of differences in the two managers' performances. Benchmarking, which is also called *relative performance evaluation*, filters out the effects of the common uncontrollable factors.

Can the performance of two managers responsible for running similar operations within a company be benchmarked against each other? Yes, but this approach could create a problem: The use of these benchmarks may reduce incentives for these managers to help one another. That's because a manager's performance-evaluation measure improves either by doing a better job or as a result of the other manager doing poorly. When managers do not cooperate, the company suffers. In this case, using internal benchmarks for performance evaluation may not lead to goal congruence.

Performance Measures at the Individual Activity Level

There are two issues when evaluating performance at the individual-activity level:

1. Designing performance measures for activities that require multiple tasks
2. Designing performance measures for activities done in teams

Performing Multiple Tasks

Most employees perform more than one task as part of their jobs. Marketing representatives sell products, provide customer support, and gather market information. Manufacturing workers are responsible for both the quantity and quality of their output. Employers want employees to allocate their time and effort intelligently among various tasks or aspects of their jobs.

Consider mechanics at an auto repair shop. Their jobs have two distinct aspects: repair work—performing more repair work generates more revenues for the shop—and customer satisfaction—the higher the quality of the job, the more likely the customer will be pleased. If the employer wants an employee to focus on both aspects, then the employer must measure and compensate performance on both aspects.

Suppose that the employer can easily measure the quantity, but not the quality, of auto repairs. If the employer rewards workers on a by-the-job rate, which pays workers only on the basis of the number of repairs actually performed, mechanics will likely increase the number of repairs they make and quality will likely suffer. Sears experienced this problem when it introduced by-the-job rates for its mechanics. To resolve the problem, Sears' managers took three steps to motivate workers to balance both quantity and quality: (1) They dropped the by-the-job rate system and paid mechanics an hourly salary, a step that deemphasized the quantity of repairs. Management determined mechanics' bonuses, promotions, and pay increases on the basis of an assessment of each mechanic's overall performance regarding quantity and quality of repairs. (2) Sears evaluated employees, in part, using data such as customer-satisfaction surveys, the number of dissatisfied customers, and the number of customer complaints. (3) Finally, Sears used staff from an independent outside agency to randomly monitor whether the repairs performed were of high quality.

Team-Based Compensation Arrangements

Many manufacturing, marketing, and design problems can be resolved when employees with multiple skills, knowledge, experiences, and perceptions pool their talents. A team achieves better results than individual employees acting alone.[12] Companies reward individuals on a team based on team performance. Such team-based incentives encourage individuals to help one another as they strive toward a common goal.

The specific forms of team-based compensation vary across companies. Colgate Palmolive rewards teams on the basis of each team's performance. Novartis, the Swiss pharmaceutical company, rewards teams on companywide performance—a certain amount of team-based bonuses are paid only if the company reaches certain goals. To encourage the development of team skills, Tennessee Eastman, a chemical manufacturer, rewards team members using a checklist of team skills, such as communication and willingness to help one another. Whether team-based compensation is desirable depends, to a large extent, on the culture and management style of a particular organization. For example, one criticism of team-based compensation, especially in the United States, is that incentives for individual employees to excel are diminished, harming overall performance. Another problem is how to manage team members who are not productive contributors to the team's success but who, nevertheless, share in the team's rewards.

Executive Performance Measures and Compensation

The principles of performance evaluation described in the previous sections also apply to executive compensation plans. These plans are based on both financial and nonfinancial performance measures and consist of a mix of (1) base salary; (2) annual incentives, such as a cash bonus based on achieving a target annual RI; (3) long-run incentives, such as stock options (described later in this section) based on stock performance over, say, a five-year period; and (4) other benefits, such as medical benefits, pensions plans, and life insurance.

Well-designed plans use a compensation mix that balances risk (the effect of uncontrollable factors on the performance measure and hence compensation) with short-run and long-run incentives to achieve the organization's goals. For example, evaluating performance on the basis of annual EVA sharpens an executive's short-run focus. And using EVA and stock option plans over, say, five years motivates the executive to take a long-run view as well.

Stock options give executives the right to buy company stock at a specified price (called the exercise price) within a specified period. Suppose that on September 16, 2008, Mayur Inns gave its CEO the option to buy 200,000 shares of the company's stock at any time before June 30, 2016, at the September 16, 2008, market price of Rs 490 per share. Let's say Mayur Inns' stock price rises to Rs 690 per share on March 24, 2014, and the CEO exercises his options on all 200,000 shares. The CEO would earn Rs 200 (Rs 690 − Rs 490) per share on 200,000 shares, or Rs 40 million. If Mayur Inns' stock price stays below Rs 490 during the entire period, the CEO will simply forgo his right to buy the shares. By linking CEO compensation to increases in the company's stock price, the stock option plan motivates the CEO to improve the company's long-run performance and stock price. (See also the Concepts in Action feature.)[13]

The Securities and Exchange Commission (SEC) requires detailed disclosures of the compensation arrangements of top-level executives. In complying with these rules in 2007,

[12] *Teams That Click: The Results-Driven Manager Series* (Boston: Harvard Business School Press, 2004).

[13] Although stock options can improve incentives by linking CEO pay to improvements in stock price, they have been criticized for promoting improper or illegal activities by CEOs to increase the options' value. See J. Fox, "Sleazy CEOs Have Even More Options Tricks," www.money.cnn.com/2006/11/13/magazines/fortune/options_scandals.fortune/index.htm, accessed September 5, 2007.

Concepts in Action

Government Bailouts, Record Profits, and the 2009 Wall Street Compensation Dilemma

Wall Street firms paid out near-record bonuses to their employees for 2009 and many in the public were furious, given Wall Street's role in triggering the recent economic crisis. After losing $42.8 billion in 2008 and requiring a government bailout, Wall Street firms recorded $55 billion in 2009 profits, a sum nearly three times greater than the previous record. These results begged a serious question for managers at Goldman Sachs, Morgan Stanley, JPMorgan Chase, and leading financial institutions: After requiring public support just a year earlier, just how big should bankers' paydays be?

Highly paid executives on Wall Street are virtually always investment bankers or the top executives of the firms that employ them. Wall Street firms traditionally paid their investment bankers a share of the total revenue garnered by their unit. While this system worked in previous years, many argued it led to bankers taking the excessive risks that pushed the U.S. financial system to the brink of collapse.

Moreover, 2008 Wall Street bonuses infuriated the public. Just months after government intervention totaling $700 billion, the largest Wall Street banks paid out $56.9 billion in bonuses, or 45.4% of their 2008 revenues. As a result, President Barack Obama laid out strict new regulations on compensation for the 100 highest-paid employees at firms that the government deemed "exceptional assistance recipients" (i.e., firms receiving the largest bailouts). Further, there is little question that without the government intervening to save the financial sector in late 2008, the investment banks would have had a much worse year in 2009. This created a difficult situation for the banks. As one observer noted, "It is fair to say that some of the pay schemes promoted bad behavior and led to excessive risk, but you still need some sort of short-term incentive" for good performance, which Wall Street produced in 2009.

Wall Street firms tried to find some middle ground in 2009 by reducing bonus pools, or the amount of revenues allocated to bonuses, and introducing more long-term compensation into the bonus mix. At Goldman Sachs, for example, top executives received no cash bonuses in 2009, and instead received shares in the company that must be held for five years. For investment bankers and other employees, the company reduced its bonus pool to 36% of company revenue (down from 44% in 2008) and increased the stock-to-cash compensation ratio. Despite these changes, the average Wall Street bonus jumped 25% in 2009 to $123,850. At Goldman Sachs, where profits hit an all-time high, employees made an average of $500,000 each in 2009, including salary and bonus.

While many observers lauded the movement towards having a higher-percentage of bonuses be deferred, the size of 2009 Wall Street bonuses outraged others and ensured that investment banker compensation will remain a hot-button issue on Wall Street, Main Street, and in Washington, DC, for many years to come.

Source: Corkery, Michael. 2009. Goldman bows to pressure, makes changes to compensation. *Wall Street Journal* "Deal Journal," blog December 10; Elliott, Douglas J. 2010. *Wall Street Pay: A Primer*. Washington, DC: The Brookings Institution; Gandel, Stephen. 2009. Wall Street, meet Ken Feinberg, the pay czar. *Time*, November 2; Phillips, Matt. 2010. Goldman: Employees don't mind record low pay ratios. *Wall Street Journal*. "MarketBeat," blog February 3; Shell, Adam. 2010. Despite recession, average Wall Street bonus leaps 25%. *USA*, February 24; *Wall Street Journal*. 2010. The easy guide to Wall Street pay and bonuses. January 20; Weisman, Jonathan and Joanna S. Lublin. 2009. Obama lays out limits on executive pay. *Wall Street Journal*, February 5.

Hilton Hotels, for example, disclosed a compensation table showing the salaries, bonuses, stock options, other stock awards, and other compensation earned by its top five executives during the 2004, 2005, and 2006 fiscal years. Hilton also disclosed the peer companies that it uses to set executive pay and conduct performance comparisons. These include competitors in the hospitality industry, as well as similarly sized companies in other industries with strong brands and multiple locations. Investors use this information to evaluate the relationship between compensation and performance across companies generally, across companies of similar sizes, and across companies operating in similar industries.

The SEC rules also require companies to disclose the principles underlying their executive compensation plans and the performance criteria—such as profitability, revenue growth, and market share—used in determining compensation. In its financial statements, Hilton Hotels described some of these principles as supporting a unified company culture

Decision Point

Why are managers compensated based on a mix of salary and incentives?

and brands across the globe, providing clear communication of performance expectations and reward opportunities, and linking pay to performance that drives stockholder value creation. Hilton uses corporate earnings as one performance criteria to determine annual incentives for all of its executives. In addition, each executive has an individual scorecard of financial and nonfinancial performance measures. The company's board of directors creates the overall strategic direction of the company. Individual and strategic goals for executives are then established to support the overall company goals but are tailored to each executive's area of control.

Strategy and Levers of Control[14]

Learning Objective 7

Describe the four levers of control and why they are necessary

. . . boundary, belief, and interactive control systems counterbalance diagnostic control systems

Given the management accounting focus of this book, this chapter has emphasized the role of quantitative financial and nonfinancial performance-evaluation measures that companies use to implement their strategies. These measures—such as ROI, RI, EVA, customer satisfaction, and employee satisfaction—monitor critical performance variables that help managers track progress toward achieving a company's strategic goals. Because these measures help diagnose whether a company is performing to expectations, they are collectively called **diagnostic control systems**. Companies motivate managers to achieve goals by holding them accountable for and by rewarding them for meeting these goals. The concern, however, is that the pressure to perform may cause managers to cut corners and misreport numbers to make their performance look better than it is, as happened at companies such as Enron, WorldCom, Tyco, and Health South. To prevent unethical behavior, companies need to balance the push for performance resulting from diagnostic control systems, the first of four levers of control, with three other levers: *boundary systems, belief systems,* and *interactive control systems*.

Boundary Systems

Boundary systems describe standards of behavior and codes of conduct expected of all employees, especially actions that are off-limits. Ethical behavior on the part of managers is paramount. In particular, numbers that subunit managers report should not be tainted by "cooking the books." They should be free of, for example, overstated assets, understated liabilities, fictitious revenues, and understated costs.

Codes of business conduct signal appropriate and inappropriate individual behaviors. The following is from Caterpillar Tractor's "Code of Worldwide Business Conduct and Operating Principles":

> *The law is a floor. Ethical business conduct should normally exist at a level well above the minimum required by law. Caterpillar employees shall not accept costly entertainment or gifts (excepting mementos and novelties of nominal value) from dealers, suppliers and others with whom we do business. And we won't tolerate circumstances that produce, or reasonably appear to produce, conflict between personal interests of an employee and interests of the company.*

Division managers often cite enormous pressure from top management "to make the budget" as excuses or rationalizations for not adhering to ethical accounting policies and procedures. A healthy amount of motivational pressure is desirable, as long as the "tone from the top" and the code of conduct simultaneously communicate the absolute need for all managers to behave ethically at all times. Managers should train employees to behave ethically. They should promptly and severely reprimand unethical conduct, regardless of the benefits that might accrue to the company from unethical actions. Some companies, such as Lockheed-Martin, emphasize ethical behavior by routinely evaluating employees against a business code of ethics.

[14] For a more-detailed discussion see R. Simons, *Levers of Control: How Managers Use Innovative Control Systems to Drive Strategic Renewal* (Boston: Harvard Business School Press, 2005).

Many organizations also set explicit boundaries precluding actions that harm the environment. Environmental violations (such as water and air pollution) carry heavy fines and prison terms under the laws of the United States and other countries. But in many companies, environmental responsibilities extend beyond legal requirements.

Socially responsible companies set aggressive environmental goals and measure and report their performance against them. German, Swiss, Dutch, and Scandinavian companies report on environmental performance as part of a larger set of social responsibility disclosures (such as employee welfare and community development activities). Some companies, such as DuPont, make environmental performance a line item on every employee's salary appraisal report. Duke Power Company appraises employees on their performance in reducing solid waste, cutting emissions and discharges, and implementing environmental plans. The result? Duke Power has met all its environmental goals.

Belief Systems

Belief systems articulate the mission, purpose, and core values of a company. They describe the accepted norms and patterns of behavior expected of all managers and other employees with respect to one another, shareholders, customers, and communities. For example, Johnson & Johnson describes its values and norms in a credo statement that is intended to inspire all managers and other employees to do their best.[15] Belief systems play to employees' *intrinsic motivation*, the desire to achieve self-satisfaction from good performance regardless of external rewards such as bonuses or promotion. Intrinsic motivation comes from being given greater responsibility, doing interesting and creative work, having pride in doing that work, establishing commitment to the organization, and developing personal bonds with coworkers. High intrinsic motivation enhances performance because managers and workers have a sense of achievement in doing something important, feel satisfied with their jobs, and see opportunities for personal growth.

Interactive Control Systems

Interactive control systems are formal information systems that managers use to focus organization attention and learning on key strategic issues. Managers use interactive control systems to create an ongoing dialogue around these key issues and to personally involve themselves in subordinates' decision-making activities. An excessive focus on diagnostic control systems and critical performance variables can cause an organization to ignore emerging threats and opportunities—changes in technology, customer preferences, regulations, and industry competition that can undercut a business. Interactive control systems help prevent this problem by highlighting and tracking strategic uncertainties that businesses face, such as the emergence of digital imaging in the case of Kodak and Fujifilm, airline deregulation in the case of American Airlines and Southwest Airlines, and the shift in customer preferences for mini- and microcomputers in the case of IBM. The key to this control lever is frequent face-to-face communications regarding these critical uncertainties. The result is ongoing discussion and debate about assumptions and action plans. New strategies emerge from the dialogue and debate surrounding the interactive process. Interactive control systems force busy managers to step back from the actions needed to manage the business today and to shift their focus forward to positioning the organization for the opportunities and threats of tomorrow.

Measuring and rewarding managers for achieving critical performance variables is an important driver of corporate performance. But these diagnostic control systems must be counterbalanced by the other levers of control—boundary systems, belief systems, and interactive control systems—to ensure that proper business ethics, inspirational values, and attention to future threats and opportunities are not sacrificed while achieving business results.

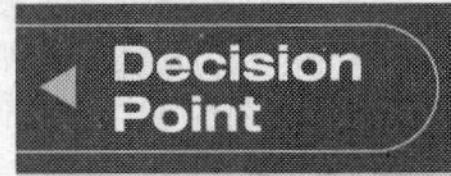

What are the four levers of control, and why does a company need to implement them?

Problem for Self-Study

The Baseball Division of Home Run Sports manufactures and sells baseballs. Assume production equals sales. Budgeted data for February 2011 are:

Current assets	Rs 40,00,000
Long-term assets	60,00,000
Total assets	Rs 1,00,00,000
Production output	2,00,000 baseballs per month
Target ROI (Operating income ÷ Total assets)	30%
Fixed costs	Rs 4[illegible],00,000 per month
Variable cost	Rs 40 per baseball

Required

1. Compute the minimum selling price per baseball necessary to achieve the target ROI of 30%.
2. Using the selling price from requirement 1, separate the target ROI into its two components using the DuPont method.
3. Compute the RI of the Baseball Division for February 2011, using the selling price from requirement 1. Home Run Sports uses a required rate of return of 12% on total division assets when computing division RI.
4. In addition to her salary, Pamela Stephenson, the division manager, receives 3% of the monthly RI of the Baseball Division as a bonus. Compute Stephenson's bonus. Why do you think Stephenson is rewarded using both salary and a performance-based bonus? Stephenson does not like bearing risk.

Solution

1.

Target operating income = 30% of Rs 1,00,00,000 of total assets
= Rs 30,00,000

Let P = Selling price

Revenues − Variable costs − Fixed costs = Operating income

$2,00,000P$ − (2,00,000 × Rs 40) − Rs 40,00,000 = Rs 30,00,000

$2,00,000P$ = Rs 30,00,000 + Rs 80,00,000 + Rs 40,00,000
= Rs 1,50,00,000

P = Rs 75 baseball

Proof:

Revenues, 2,00,000 baseballs × Rs 75 baseball	Rs 1,50,00,000
Variable costs, 2,00,000 baseballs × Rs 40 baseball	Rs 80,00,000
Contribution margin	Rs 70,00,000
Fixed costs	Rs 40,00,000
Operating income	Rs 30,00,000

2. The DuPont method describes ROI as the product of two components: return on sales (income ÷ revenues) and investment turnover (revenues ÷ investment).

$$\frac{\text{Income}}{\text{Revenues}} \times \frac{\text{Revenues}}{\text{Investment}} = \frac{\text{Income}}{\text{Investment}}$$

$$\frac{\text{Rs } 30,00,000}{\text{Rs } 1,50,00,000} \times \frac{\text{Rs } 1,50,00,000}{\text{Rs } 1,00,00,000} = \frac{\text{Rs } 30,00,000}{\text{Rs } 1,00,00,000}$$

$$0.2 \times 1.5 = 0.30, \text{or } 30\%$$

3. RI = Operating income − Requied return on investment
= Rs 30,00,000 − (0.12 × Rs 1,00,00,000)
= Rs 30,00, 000 − Rs 12,00,000
= Rs 18,00,000

4. Stephenson's bonus = 3% of RI
   = 0.03 × Rs 18,00,000 = Rs 54,000

The Baseball Division's RI is affected by many factors, such as general economic conditions, beyond Stephenson's control. These uncontrollable factors make the Baseball Division's profitability uncertain and risky. Because Stephenson does not like bearing risk, paying her a flat salary, regardless of RI, would shield her from this risk. But there is a moral-hazard problem with this compensation arrangement. Because Stephenson's effort is difficult to monitor, the absence of performance-based compensation will provide her with no incentive to undertake extra physical and mental effort beyond what is necessary to retain her job or to uphold her personal values.

Paying no salary and rewarding Stephenson only on the basis of RI provides her with incentives to work hard but also subjects her to excessive risk because of uncontrollable factors that will affect RI and hence Stephenson's compensation. A compensation arrangement based only on RI would be more costly for Home Run Sports because it would have to compensate Stephenson for taking on uncontrollable risk. A compensation arrangement that consists of both a salary and an RI-based performance bonus balances the benefits of incentives against the extra costs of imposing uncontrollable risk

Decision Points

The following question-and-answer format summarizes the chapter's learning objectives. Each decision presents a key question related to a learning objective. The guidelines are the answer to that question.

Decision	Guidelines
1. What financial and nonfinancial performance measures do companies use in their balanced scorecards?	Financial measures such as return on investment and residual income measure aspects of both manager performance and organization-subunit performance. In many cases, financial measures are supplemented with nonfinancial measures of performance from the customer, internal-business-process, and learning-and-growth perspectives of the balanced scorecard—for example, customer-satisfaction, quality of products and services, and employee satisfaction.
2. What are the steps in designing an accounting-based performance measure?	The steps are (1) choose performance measures that align with top management's financial goals, (2) choose the time horizon of each performance measure, (3) choose a definition of the components in each performance measure, (4) choose a measurement alternative for each performance measure, (5) choose a target level of performance, and (6) choose the timing of feedback.
3. How does the DuPont method analyze return on investment?	The DuPont method describes return on investment (ROI) as the product of two components: income divided by revenues (return on sales) and revenues divided by investment (investment turnover). For example, ROI can be increased by increasing revenues, decreasing costs, and decreasing investment.
4. What is residual income and what are its advantages?	Residual income (RI) is income minus a rupee amount of required return on investment. RI is designed to overcome some of the limitations of ROI. For example, RI is more likely than ROI to promote goal congruence. ROI may induce managers of highly profitable divisions to reject projects (because accepting the project reduces ROI) even though the project should be accepted from the perspective of the company as a whole.
5. What is economic value added?	Economic value added (EVA) is a variation of the RI calculation. It equals after-tax operating income minus the product of (after-tax) weighted-average cost of capital and total assets minus current liabilities.

6. Should companies use the current cost or the historical cost of assets to measure performance?	Current cost of an asset is the cost now of purchasing an asset identical to the one currently held. Historical-cost asset-measurement methods generally consider net book value of the assets, which is original cost minus accumulated depreciation. Historical-cost measures are often inadequate for measuring economic returns. Current-cost measures are better. More generally, however, problems in any performance measure can be overcome by emphasizing budgets and targets that stress continuous improvement.
7. How can companies compare the performance of divisions operating in different countries?	Comparing the performance of divisions operating in different countries is difficult because of legal, political, social, economic, and currency differences. ROI and RI calculations for subunits operating in different countries need to be adjusted for differences in inflation between the two countries and changes in exchange rates.
8. Why are managers compensated based on a mix of salary and incentives?	Companies create incentives by rewarding managers on the basis of performance. But managers face risks because factors beyond their control may also affect their performance. Owners choose a mix of salary and incentive compensation to trade off the incentive benefit against the cost of imposing risk.
9. What are the four levers of control, and why does a company need to implement them?	The four levers of control are diagnostic control systems, boundary systems, belief systems, and interactive control systems. Implementing the four levers of control helps a company simultaneously strive for performance, behave ethically, inspire employees, and respond to strategic threats and opportunities.

TERMS TO LEARN

This chapter and the Glossary at the end of the book contain definitions of:

belief systems (**p. 987**)
boundary systems (**p. 986**)
current cost (**p. 975**)
diagnostic control systems (**p. 986**)
economic value added (EVA®) (**p. 972**)
imputed costs (**p. 971**)
interactive control systems (**p. 987**)
investment (**p. 968**)
moral hazard (**p. 982**)
residual income (RI) (**p. 971**)
return on investment (ROI) (**p. 969**)

ASSIGNMENT MATERIAL

Questions

23-1 Give examples of financial and nonfinancial performance measures that can be found in each of the four perspectives of the balanced scorecard.

23-2 What are the six steps in designing accounting-based performance measures?

23-3 What factors affecting ROI does the DuPont method of profitability analysis highlight?

23-4 "RI is not identical to ROI, although both measures incorporate income and investment into their computations." Do you agree? Explain.

23-5 Describe EVA.

23-6 Give three definitions of investment used in practice when computing ROI.

23-7 Distinguish between measuring assets based on current cost and historical cost.

23-8 What special problems arise when evaluating performance in multinational companies?

23-9 Why is it important to distinguish between the performance of a manager and the performance of the organization subunit for which the manager is responsible? Give an example.

23-10 Describe moral hazard.

23-11 "Managers should be rewarded only on the basis of their performance measures. They should be paid no salary." Do you agree? Explain.

23-12 Explain the role of benchmarking in evaluating managers.

23-13 Explain the incentive problems that can arise when employees must perform multiple tasks as part of their jobs.

23-14 Describe two disclosures required by the SEC with respect to executive compensation.

23-15 Describe the four levers of control.

Solved Examples

23-16 Analysis of return on invested assets, comparison of two divisions, DuPont method. Brilliant Classes has two divisions: Test Preparation and Language Arts. Results (in lakh of rupees) for the past three years are partially displayed here:

File Edit View Insert Format Tools Data Window Help

	A	B	C	D	E	F	G
1		Operating Income	Operating Revenues	Total Assets	Operating Income/ Operating Revenues	Operating Revenues/ Total Assets	Operating Income/ Total Assets
2	Test Preparation Division						
3	2009	Rs 680	Rs 7,960	Rs 1920	?	?	?
4	2010	840	?	?	10%	?	42%
5	2011	1,160	?	?	11%	5	?
6	Language Arts Department						
7	2009	Rs 620	Rs 2,360	Rs 1,280	?	?	?
8	2010	?	3,000	1,800	22%	?	?
9	2011	?	?	2,340	?	2	25%
10	Brilliant Classes						
11	2009	Rs 1,300	Rs 10,320	Rs 3,200	?	?	?
12	2010	?	?	?	?	?	?
13	2011	?	?	?	?	?	?

Required

1. Complete the table by filling in the blanks.
2. Use the DuPont method of profitability analysis to explain changes in the operating-income-to-total-assets ratios over the 2009 through 2011 period for each division and for Brilliant Classes as a whole. Comment on the results.

Solution

Analysis of return on invested assets, comparison of two divisions, DuPont method (Amount in Rs lakh)

1.

	Operating Income	Operating Revenues	Total Assets	Operating Income 4 Operating Revenues	Operating Revenues 4 Total Assets	Operating Income 4 Total Assets
Test Preparation Division						
2009	Rs 680	Rs 7,960	Rs 1920	8.5%	4.1	35.4%
2010	840	Rs 840 ÷ 10% = Rs 8,400	Rs 840 ÷ 42% = Rs 2,000	10%	4.2	42%
2011	1,160	Rs 1,160 ÷ 11% = Rs 10,545	Rs 10,545 ÷ 5= Rs 2,109	11%	5	55%
Language Arts Department						
2009	Rs 620	Rs 2,360	Rs 1,280	26.3%	1.8	48.4%
2010	Rs 3,000 × 22% = Rs 660	3,000	1,800	22%	1.7	36.7
2011	Rs 2,340 × 25% = Rs 585	Rs 2,340 × 2 = Rs 4,680	2,340	12.5%	2	25%
Brilliant Classes						
2009	Rs 1,300	Rs 10,320	Rs 3,200	12.6%	3.2	40.6%
2010	Rs 840 + Rs 660 = Rs 1,500	Rs 8,400 + Rs 3,000 = Rs 11,400	Rs 2,000 + Rs 18,00 = Rs 3,800	13.2%	3	39.5%
2011	Rs 1.160 + Rs 585 = Rs 1,745	Rs 19,545 + Rs 4,680 = Rs 15,225	Rs 2,109 + Rs 2,340 = Rs 4,449	11.5%	3.4	39.2%

2. Based on revenues, Test Preparation is about twice as big as Language Arts. The Language Arts Department earns higher margins (operating income as a percent of operating revenues); the Test Preparation Division turns over its assets at more than twice the rate of the Language Arts Department (operating revenues as a multiple of total assets).

The net result is that the ROI of the two divisions was similar (in the 30–50% range). But whereas the ROI of the Test Preparation Division has been increasing from 2009 to 2011, the ROI of the Language Arts Department has been falling. Overall, this has resulted in Brilliant Classes showing stable ROI over the past three years.

23-17 ROI and RI with manufacturing costs. Superior Motor Company makes electric cars and has only two products, the Simplegreen and the Superiorgreen. To produce the Simplegreen, Superior Motor employed assets of Rs 13,50,00,000 at the beginning of the period, and Rs 13,40,00,000 of assets at the end of the period. Other costs to manufacture the Simplegreen include:

Direct materials	Rs 30,000 per unit
Setup	Rs 13,000 per setup hour
Production	Rs 4,150 per machine hour

General administration and selling costs total Rs 7,34,00,000 for the period. In the current period, Superior Motor produced 10,000 Simplegreen cars using 6,000 setup hours and Rs 1,75,200 machine hours. Superior Motor sold these cars for Rs 1,20,000 each.

Required

1. Assuming that Superior Motor defines investment as average assets during the period, what is the return on investment for the Simplegreen division?
2. Calculate the residual income for the Simplegreen if Superior Motor has a required rate of return of 12% on investments.

Solution

ROI and RI with manufacturing costs.

1. The operating income is:

Sales revenue (Rs 1,20,000 × 10,000)		Rs 1,20,00,00,000
Less:		
Direct materials (Rs 30,000 × 10,000)	Rs 30,00,00,000	
Setup (Rs 13,000 × 6,000)	7,80,00,000	
Production (Rs 4,150 × 1,75,200)	72,70,80,000	110,50,80,000
Gross margin		Rs 9,49,20,000
Selling and administration		7,34,00,000
Operating income		Rs 2,15,20,000

Average invested capital is (Rs 13,50,00,000 + Rs 13,40,00,000) ÷ 2 = Rs 13,45,00,000

$$\text{ROI} = \frac{\text{Rs } 2{,}15{,}20{,}000}{\text{Rs } 13{,}45{,}00{,}000} = 16\%$$

2. Residual income = operating income − (12% × Invested capital)
= Rs 2,15,20,000 − (12% × Rs 13,45,00,000)
= Rs 2,15,20,000 − Rs 1,61,40,000
= Rs 53,80,000

23-18 Financial and nonfinancial performance measures, goal congruence. (CMA, adapted) GE Equipment specializes in the manufacture of medical equipment, a field that has become increasingly competitive. Approximately two years ago, Pradeep Goel, president of GE, decided to revise the bonus plan (based, at the time, entirely on operating income) to encourage division managers to focus on areas that were important to customers and that added value without increasing cost. In addition to a profitability incentive, the revised plan includes incentives for reduced rework costs, reduced sales returns, and on-time deliveries. Bonuses are calculated and awarded semiannually on the following basis: A base bonus is calculated at 2% of operating income; this amount is then adjusted as follows:

a. (i) Reduced by excess of rework costs over and above 2% of operating income
(ii) No adjustment if rework costs are less than or equal to 2% of operating income
b. (i) Increased by Rs 50,000 if more than 98% of deliveries are on time, and by Rs 20,000 if 96% to 98% of deliveries are on time
(ii) No adjustment if on-time deliveries are below 96%
c. (i) Increased by Rs 30,000 if sales returns are less than or equal to 1.5% of sales
(ii) Decreased by 50% of excess of sales returns over 1.5% of sales

Note: If the calculation of the bonus results in a negative amount for a particular period, the manager simply receives no bonus, and the negative amount is not carried forward to the next period.

Results for GE's Charter Division and Mesa Division for 2011, the first year under the new bonus plan, follow. In 2010, under the old bonus plan, the Charter Division manager earned a bonus of Rs 2,70,600 and the Mesa Division manager, a bonus of Rs 2,24,400.

	Charter Division		Mesa Division	
	January 1, 2011 to June 30, 2011	July 1, 2011 to Dec. 31, 2011	January 1, 2011 to June 30, 2011	July 1, 2011 to Dec. 31, 2011
Revenues	Rs 4,20,00,000	Rs 4,40,00,000	Rs 2,85,00,000	Rs 2,90,00,000
Operating income	Rs 46,20,000	Rs 44,00,000	Rs 34,20,000	Rs 40,60,000
On-time delivery	95.4%	97.3%	98.2%	94.6%
Rework costs	Rs 1,15,000	Rs 1,10,000	Rs 60,000	Rs 80,000
Sales returns	Rs 8,40,000	Rs 7,00,000	Rs 4,47,500	Rs 4,25,000

Required

1. Why did Pradeep Goel need to introduce these new performance measures? That is, why does Pradeep Goel need to use these performance measures in addition to the operating-income numbers for the period?
2. Calculate the bonus earned by each manager for each six-month period and for 2011.
3. What effect did the change in the bonus plan have on each manager's behavior? Did the new bonus plan achieve what Pradeep Goel desired? What changes, if any, would you make to the new bonus plan?

Solution

Financial and nonfinancial performance measures, goal congruence.

1. Operating income is a good summary measure of short-term financial performance. By itself, however, it does not indicate whether operating income in the short run was earned by taking actions that would lead to long-run competitive advantage, For example, GE's division might be able to increase short-run operating income by producing more product while ignoring quality or rework. Pradeep, however, would like to see division managers increase operating income without sacrificing quality. The new performance measures take a balanced scorecard approach by evaluating and rewarding managers on the basis of direct measures (such as rework costs, on-time delivery performance, and sales returns). This motivates managers to take actions that Pradeep believes will increase operating income now and in the future. The nonoperating income measures serve as surrogate measures of future profitability.
2. The semiannual instalments and total bonus for the Charter Division are calculated as follows:

Charter Division Bonus Calculation
For Year Ended December 31, 2011

January 1, 2011 to June 30, 2011

Profitability	(0.02 × Rs 46,20,000)	Rs 92,400
Rework	(0.02 × Rs 46,20,000) − Rs 1,15,000	(22,600)
On-time delivery	No bonus—under 96%	0
Sales returns	[(0.015 × Rs 4,20,00,000) − Rs 8,40,000] × 50%	(1,05,000)
Semiannual instalment		Rs (35,200)
Semiannual bonus awarded		Re 0

July 1, 2011 to December 31, 2011

Profitability	(0.02 × Rs 44,00,000)	Rs 88,000
Reword	(0.02 × Rs 44,00,000) − Rs 1,10,000	(22,000)
On-time delivery	96% to 98%	20,000
Sales returns	[(0.015 × Rs 4,40,00,000) − Rs 7,00,000] × 50%	(20,000)
Semiannual instalment		Rs 66,000
Semiannual bonus awarded		Rs (66,000)
Total bonus awarded for the year		Rs 66,000

The semiannual instalments and total bonus for the Mesa Divison are calculated as follows:

Mesa Division Bonus Calculation
For Year Ended December 31, 2011

January 1, 2011 to June 30, 2011

Profitability	(0.02 × Rs 34,20,000)	Rs 68,400
Rework	(0.02 × Rs 34,20,000) − Rs 60,000	0

On-time delivery	Over 98%	50,000
Sales returns	[(0.015 × Rs 2,85,00,000) − Rs 4,47,500] × 50%	(10,000)
Semiannual bonus instalment		Rs 1,08,400
Semiannual bonus awarded		Rs 1,08,400

July 1, 2011 to December 31, 2011

Profitability	(0.02 × Rs 40,60,000)	Rs 81,200
Rework	(0.02 × Rs 40,60,000) − Rs 80,000	0
On-time delivery	No bonus—under 96%	0
Sales returns	[(0.015 × Rs 2,90,00,000) − Rs 4,25,000] which is greater than zero, yielding a bonus	30,000
Semiannual bonus instalment		Rs 1,11,200
Semiannual bonus awarded		1,11,200
Total bonus awarded for the year		2,19,600

3. The manager of the Charter Divison is likely to be frustrated by the new plan, as the division bonus has fallen by more than Rs 2,00,000 compared to the bonus of the previous year. However, the new performance measures have begun to have the desired effect—both on-time deliveries and sales returns improved in the second half of the year, while rework costs were relatively even. If the division continues to improve at the same rate, the Charter bonus could approximate or exceed what it was under the old plan.

The manager of the Mesa Division should be as satisfied with the new plan as with the old plan, as the bonus is almost equivalent. On-time deliveries declined considerably in the second half of the year and rework costs increased. However, sales returns decreased slightly. Unless the manager institutes better controls, the bonus situation may not be as favorable in the future. This could motivate the manager to improve in the future but currently, at least, the manager has been able to maintain his bonus with showing improvement in only one area targeted by Pradeep.

Pradeep's revised bonus plan for the Charter Division fostered the following improvements in the second half of the year despite an increase in sales:

- An increase of 1.9% in on-time deliveries.
- A Rs 5,000 reduction in rework costs.
- A Rs 1,40,000 reduction in sales returns.

However, operating income as a percent of sales ahs decreased (11% to 10%).

The Mesa division's bonus has remained at the status quo as a result of the following effects:

- An increase of 2.0% in operating income as a percent of sales (12% to 14%).
- A decrease of 3.6% in on-time deliveries.
- A Rs 20,000 increase in rework costs.
- As Rs 22,500 decrease in sales returns.

This would suggest that revisions to the bonus plan are needed. Possible changes include:

- increasing the weights put on on-time deliveries, rework costs, and sales returns in the performance measures while decreasing the weight put on operating income;
- a reward structure for rework costs that are below 2% of operating income that would encourage managers to drive costs lower;
- reviewing the whole year in total. The bonus plan should carry forward the negative amounts for one six-month period into the next six-month period incorporating the entire year when calculating a bonus; and
- developing benchmarks, and then giving rewards for improvements over prior periods and encouraging continuous improvement.

23-19 ROI, RI, EVA. Performance Auto Company operates a New Car Division (that sells high performance sports cars) and a Performance Parts Division (that sells performance improvement parts for family cars). Some division financial measures for 2011 are as follows:

	A	B	C
1		New Car Division	Performance Parts Division
2	Total assets	Rs 3,30,00,000	Rs 2,85,00,000
3	Current liabilities	Rs 66,00,000	Rs 84,00,000
4	Operating income	Rs 24,75,000	Rs 25,65,000
5	Required rate of return	12%	12%

Required

1. Calculate return on investment (ROI) for each division using operating income as a measure of income and total assets as a measure of investment.
2. Calculate residual income (RI) for each division using operating income as a measure of income and total assets minus current liabilities as a measure of investment.
3. William Abraham, the New Car Division manager, argues that the Performance Parts Division has "loaded up on a lot of short-term debt" to boost its RI. Calculate an alternative RI for each division that is not sensitive to the amount of short-term debt taken on by the Performance Parts Division. Comment on the result.
4. Performance Auto Company, whose tax rate is 40%, has two sources of funds: long-term debt with a market value of Rs 1,80,00,000 at an interest rate of 10%, and equity capital with a market value of Rs 1,20,00,000 and a cost of equity of 15%. Applying the same weighted-average cost of capital (WACC) to each division, calculate EVA for each division.
5. Use your preceding calculations to comment on the relative performance of each division.

Solution

ROI, RI, EVS.

1. The required division ROIs using total assets as a measure of investment is shown in the row labeled (1) in Solution Exhibit 23-19.

Solution Exhibit 23-19

	New Car Division	Performance Parts Division
Total assets	Rs 3,30,00,000	Rs 2,85,00,000
Current liabilities	Rs 66,00,000	Rs 84,00,000
Operating income	Rs 24,75,000	Rs 25,65,000
Required rate of return	12%	12%
Total assets − current liabilities	Rs 2,64,00,000	Rs 2,01,00,000
(1) ROI (basses on total assets) (Rs 24,75,000 ÷ Rs 3, 30,00,000; Rs 25,65,000 ÷ Rs 2,85,00,000)	7.5%	9.0%
(2) RI (based on total assets − current liabilities) (Rs 24,75,000 − (12% × Rs 2,64,00,000); Rs 25,65,000 (12% × Rs 2,01,00,000))	Rs 6,93,000	Rs 1,53,000
(3) RI (based on total assets) (Rs 24,75,000 − (12% × Rs 3,30,00,000); Rs 25,65,000 − (12% × Rs 2,85,00,000)	(Rs 14,85,000)	(Rs 8,55,000)

2. The required division RIs using total assets minus current liabilities as a measure of investment is shown in the row labeled (2) in the table above.
3. The row labeled (3) in the table above shows division RIs using assets as a measure of investment. Even with this new measure that is insensitive to the level of short-term debt, the New Car Division has a relatively worse RI than the Performance Parts Division. Both RIs are negative, indicating that the divisions are not earning the 12% required rate of return on their assets.
4. After-tax cost of debt financing = (1 − 0.4) × 10% = 6%
   After-tax cost of equity financing = 15%

$$\text{Weight average cost of capital} = \frac{(\text{Rs } 1{,}80{,}00{,}000 \times 6\%) + (\text{Rs } 1{,}20{,}00{,}000 \times 15\%)}{\text{Rs } 1{,}80{,}00{,}000 + \text{Rs } 1{,}20{,}00{,}000} = 9.6\%$$

	New Car Division	Performance Parts Division
Operating income after tax		
0.6 × operating income before tax (0.6 × Rs 24,75,000; 0.6 × Rs 25,65,000)	Rs 14,85,000	Rs 15,39,000
Required return for EVA		
9.6% × Investment (9.6% × Rs 2,64,00,000; 9.6% × Rs 2,01,00,000)	25,34,400	19,29,600
EVA (Optg. inc. after tax − reqd. return)	Rs (10,49,400)	(Rs 3,90,600)

5. Both the residual income and the EVA calculations indicate that the Performance Parts Division is performing nominally better than the New Car Division. The Performance Parts Division has a higher residual income. The negative EVA for both divisions indicates that, on an after-tax basis, the divisions are destroying value—the after-tax economic returns from them are less than the required returns.

23-20 ROI, RI, EVA and Performance Evaluation. Provogue India makes fashion products and competes on the basis of quality and leading-edge designs. The company has Rs 30,00,000 invested in assets in its clothing manufacturing division. After-tax operating income from sales of clothing this year is Rs 6,00,000. The cosmetics division has Rs 1,00,00,000 invested in assets and an after-tax operating income this year of Rs 16,00,000. Income for the clothing division has grown steadily over the last few years. The weighted average cost of capital for Provogue is 10% and the previous period's after-tax return on investment for each division was 15%. The CEO of Provogue has told the manager of each division that the division that "performs best" this year will get a bonus.

Required

1. Calculate the ROI and residual income for each division of Provogue India, and briefly explain which manager will get the bonus. What are the advantages and disadvantages of each measure?
2. The CEO of Provogue India has recently heard of another measure similar to residual income called EVA. The CEO has the accountant calculate EVA adjusted incomes of Clothing and Cosmetics, and finds that the adjusted after-tax operating incomes are Rs 7,20,000 and Rs 14,30,000, respectively. Also, the Clothing Division has Rs 4,00,000 of current liabilities, while the Cosmetics Division has only Rs 2,00,000 of current liabilities. Using the above information, calculate EVA, and discuss which division manager will get the bonus.
3. What nonfinancial measures could Provogue use to evaluate divisional performances?

Solution

ROI, RI, EVA and Performance Evaluation.

1. ROI and residual income:

	Clothing	Cosmetics
Operating income after tax	Rs 6,00,000	Rs 16,00,000
Net assets	Rs 30,00,000	Rs 1,00,00,000
ROI (Rs 6,00,000 ÷ Rs 30,00,000; Rs 16,00,000 ÷ Rs 1,00,00,000)	20.00%	16.00%
RI (Rs 6,00,000 − 10% × 30,00,000; Rs 16,00,000 − 10% × Rs 1,00,00,000)	Rs 3,00,000	Rs 6,00,000

Which measure is being used to evaluate performance will determine which division gets the bonus. If the firm uses ROI, then the Clothing Division will get the bonus. However, the Cosmetics Division has much larger absolute and residual income, If the firm evaluates performance based on residual income, then the Cosmetics Division will get the bonus.

The advantages of ROI are that it is easy to calculate and easy to understand. It combines revenue, cost, and investment into a single number, so that managers can clearly see what can be changed to increase returns. But ROI has limitations. Managers who are evaluated based on ROI have incentives to reject investments with ROIs below their divisions' current average ROI, even when the investments have positive net present values.

Residual income has the advantage of goal congruence because any investment that earns more than the required capital charge increases RI, and thereby increases the managers performance evaluations. The measure is not subject to the "cutoff" problems that occur when managers compare a new investment's ROI to the average ROI being earned on existing investments. However, RI is not as easy to measure because it requires the company to determine the amount of capital and the cost of capital for each business unit.

2.

	Clothing	Cosmetics
Adjusted operating income	Rs 7,20,000	Rs 14,30,000
Net assets less current liabilities	Rs 26,00,000	Rs 98,00,000
Revised ROI (Rs 7,20,000 ÷ Rs 26,00,000; Rs 14,30,000 ÷ 98,00,000)	27.69%	14.59%
EVA (Rs 7,20,000 − 10% × Rs 26,00,000; Rs 14,30,000 − 10% is × Rs 98,00,000)	Rs 4,60,000	Rs 4,50,000

Clothing Division will get the bonus because both EVA and ROI (using EVA's definition of operating income and assets) are higher than those of the Cosmetics Division.

3. Since this is a manufacturing firm, there are a variety of non-financial performance measures such as market share, customer satisfaction, defect rates, and response times that can be used to ensure that managers do not increase short-term operating income, residual income, or EVA at the expense of performance categories that are long-term drivers of company value.

23-21 Residual Income and EVA; timing issues. Doorwhistle Company makes doorbells. It has a weighted average cost of capital of 8%, and total assets of Rs 5,69,00,000. Its net income for the year was Rs 64,90,000. Net after tax operating income is the same as net income. However, one of the expenses for accounting purposes was a Rs 10,00,000 advertising campaign. The entire amount was spent this year, although the Doorwhistle CEO believes the effects of this advertising will last four years. Doorwhistle has current liabilities of Rs 70,00,000.

Required

1. Calculate the residual income using the formula from the chapter assuming, Doorwhistle defines investment as total assets.

2. Adjust both the assets and operating income for advertising assuming that for the purposes of economic value added the advertising is capitalized and amortized over four years. Calculate EVA using the formula from the chapter. Ignore taxes.
3. Discuss the difference between the outcomes of requirements 1 and 2 and which measure is preferred.

Solution

Residual income and EVA; timing issues.

1. RI = Operating income − (WACC × Assets)
   = Rs 64,90,000 − (0.08 × Rs 5,69,00,000)
   = Rs 64,90,000 − Rs 45,52,000
   = Rs 19,38,000

2. EVA = Adjusted operating income − (WACC × (Total assets − Current liabilities))

Operating income is adjusted as follows:	
Operating income	Rs 64,90,000
Add back this period's advertising expense	10,00,000
Less amortized advertising (1/4 of year's expense)	(2,50,000)
Adjusted operating income	Rs 72,40,000
Assets are adjusted as follows:	
Total assets	Rs 5,69,00,000
Plus capitalized, unamortized advertising	7,50,000
Adjusted total assets	Rs 5,76,50,000

EVA = Rs 72,40,000 − (0.08 × (Rs 5,76,50,000 − Rs 70,00,000))
= Rs 72,40,000 − Rs 40,52,000
= Rs 31,88,000

3. The differences between the RI and EVA results are due to two factors in this problem: the definition of capital and the treatment of advertising. EVA subtracts current liabilities from total assets when computing capital. Since some types of current liabilities represent sources of "free" short-term funds (e.g., holding off payments to suppliers), they reduce the assets needed to produce income. If short-term liabilities represent a source of funds, EVA more accurately reflects the assets that the company employed to achieve its operating income. Under traditional accounting rules, advertising is a period expense, and the costs and benefits of advertising are not matched if advertising's effects affect revenues over multiple years. Consequently, EVA does a better job matching revenues and costs when the effects of advertising persist over multiple periods and solves the goal incongruence problem that sometimes arises with the RO1 measure.

23-22 ROI performance measures based on historical cost and current cost. Dabur India operates three divisions that process and bottle natural fruit juices. The historical-cost accounting system reports the following information for 2011:

	Orange Division	Pineapple Division	Mango Division
Revenues	Rs 1,00,00,000	Rs 1,40,00,000	Rs 2,20,00,000
Operating costs (excluding plant depreciation)	60,00,000	76,00,000	1,20,00,000
Plant depreciation	14,00,000	20,00,000	24,00,000
Operating income	Rs 26,00,000	Rs 44,00,000	Rs 76,00,000
Current assets	Rs 40,00,000	Rs 50,00,000	Rs 60,00,000
Long-term assets—plant	28,00,000	1,80,00,000	2,64,00,000
Total assets	Rs 68,00,000	Rs 2,30,00,000	Rs 3,24,00,000

Dabur estimates the useful life of each plant to be 12 years, with no terminal disposal value. The straight-line depreciation method is used. At the end of 2010, the Orange plant is 10 years old, the Pineapple plant is 3 years old, and the Mango plant is 1 year old. An index of construction costs over the 10-year period that Dabur has been operating (2000 year-end = 100) is:

2001	2009	2010	2011
100	136	160.	170

Given the high turnover of current assets, management believes that the historical-cost and current-cost measures of current assets are approximately the same.

1. Compute the ROI ratio (operating income to total assets) of each division using historical-cost measures. Comment on the results.

2. Use the approach in Exhibit 23-2 to compute the ROI of each division, incorporating current-cost estimates as of 2010 for depreciation expense and long-term assets. Comment on the results.
3. What advantages might arise from using current-cost asset measures as compared with historical-cost measures for evaluating the performance of the managers of the three divisions?

Solution

ROI performance measures based on historical cost and current cost.

1. ROI using historical cost measures:

Orange Fruit	Rs 26,00,000 ÷ Rs 68,00,000	=	38.24%
Pineapple Fruit	Rs 44,00,000 ÷ Rs 2,30,00,000	=	19.13%
Mango Fruit	Rs 76,00,000 ÷ Rs 3,24,00,000	=	23.46%

The Orange Fruit Division appears to be considerably more efficient than the Pineapple Fruit and Mango Fruit Divisions.

2. The gross book values (i.e., the original costs of the plants) under historical cost are calculated as the useful life of each plant (12 years) × the annual depreciation:

Orange Fruit	12 × Rs 14,00,000	=	Rs 1,68,00,000
Pineapple Fruit	12 × Rs 20,00,000	=	Rs 2,40,00,000
Mango Fruit	12 × Rs 24,00,000	=	Rs 2,88,00,000

Step 1: Restate long-term assets from gross book value at historical cost to gross book value at current cost as of the end of 2011:

(Gross book value of long-term assets at historical cost) × (Construction cost index in 2011 ÷ Construction cost index in year of construction).

Orange Fruit	Rs 1,68,00,000 × (170 ÷ 100)	=	Rs 2,85,60,000
Pineapple Fruit	Rs 2,40,00,000 × (170 ÷ 136)	=	Rs 3,00,00,000
Mango Fruit	Rs 2,88,00,000 × (170 ÷ 160)	=	Rs 3,06,00,000

Step 2: Derive net book value of long-term assets at current cost as of the end of 2011. (Estimated useful life of each plant is 12 years.)

(Gross book value of long-term assets at current cost at the end of 2011) × (Estimated remaining useful life ÷ Estimated total useful life)

Orange Fruit	Rs 2,85,60,000 × (2 ÷ 12)	=	Rs 47,60,000
Pineapple Fruit	Rs 3,00,00,000 × (9 ÷ 12)	=	Rs 2,25,00,000
Mango Fruit	Rs 3,06,00,000 × (11 ÷ 12)	=	Rs 2,80,50,000

Step 3: Compute current cost of total assets at the end of 2011. (Assume current assets of each plant are expressed in 2011 rupees.)

(Current assets at the end of 2011 [given]) + (Net book value of long-term assets at current cost at the end of 2011 [Step 2])

Orange Fruit	Rs 40,00,000 + Rs 47,60,000	=	Rs 87,60,000
Pineapple Fruit	Rs 50,00,000 + Rs 2,25,00,000	=	Rs 2,75,00,000
Mango Fruit	Rs 60,00,000 + Rs 2,80,50,000	=	Rs 3,40,50,000

Step 4: Compute current-cost depreciation expense in 2011 rupees.

Gross book value of long-term assets at current cost at the end of 2011 (from Step 1) ÷ 12

Orange Fruit	Rs 2,85,60,000 ÷ 12 = Rs 23,80,000
Pineapple Fruit	Rs 3,00,00,000 ÷ 12 = Rs 25,00,000
Mango Fruit	Rs 3,06,00,000 ÷ 12 = Rs 25,50,000

Step 5: Compute 2011 operating income using 2011 current-cost depreciation expense.

(Historical-cost operating income – [Current-cost depreciation expense in 2011 rupees (Step 4) – Historical-cost depreciation expense])

Orange Fruit	Rs 26,00,000 − (Rs 23,80,000 − Rs 14,00,000)	=	Rs 16,20,000
Pineapple Fruit	Rs 44,00,000 − (Rs 25,00,000 − Rs 20,00,000)	=	Rs 39,00,000
Mango Fruit	Rs 76,00,000 − (Rs 25,50,000 − Rs 24,00,000)	=	Rs 74,50,000

Step 6: Compute ROI using current-cost estimates for long-term assets and depreciation expense (Step 5 ÷ Step 3).

Orange Fruit	Rs 16,20,000 ÷ Rs 87,60,000	=	18.49%
Pineapple Fruit	Rs 39,00,000 ÷ Rs 2,75,00,000	=	14.18%
Mango Fruit	Rs 74,50,000 ÷ Rs 3,40,50,000	=	21.88%

	ROI: Historical Cost	ROI: Current Cost
Orange Fruit	38.24%	18.49%
Pineapple Fruit	19.13	14.18
Mango Fruit	23.46	21.88

Use of current cost results in the Mango Fruit Division appearing to be the most efficient. The Orange Fruit ROI reduced substantially when the ten-year-old plant is restated for the 70% increase in construction costs over the 2001 to 2011 period.

3. Use of current costs increases the comparability of ROI measures across divisions' operating plants built at different construction cost price levels. Use of current cost also will increase the willingness of managers, evaluated on the basis of ROI, to move between divisions with assets purchased many years ago and divisions with assets purchased in recent years.

Required

23-23 Evaluating managers, ROI, DuPont method, value-chain analysis of cost structure. IBM Computer Corporation is the largest personal computer company in the world. The CEO of IBM is retiring, and the board of directors is considering external candidates to fill the position. The board's top two choices are CEOs Sudhir Goenka (current CEO of Dell) and Kapil Singhania (current CEO of Hewlett Packard (HP)). As a board member on the search committee, you collect the following information (in Rs Crore):

	A	B	C	D	E
1		Dell		Hewlett Packard (HP)	
2		2010	2011	2010	2011
3	Revenues	Rs 600.0	Rs 480.0	Rs 300.0	Rs 525.0
4	Costs				
5	R&D	71.2	40.2	35.9	76.1
6	Production	132.6	145.6	107.6	128.2
7	Marketing and distribution	173.2	193.7	96.4	153.8
8	Customer service	65.5	40.0	30.4	67.6
9	Total costs	442.5	419.5	270.3	425.7
10	Operating income	Rs 157.5	Rs 60.5	Rs 29.7	Rs 99.3
11	Total assets	Rs 540.00	Rs 510.0	Rs 240.0	Rs 360.0

In early 2012, a leading computer magazine gave HP's main product five stars, its highest rating. Dell's main product received three stars, down from five stars a year earlier. In the same article, HP's new products received praise; Dell's new products were judged as "mediocre."

Required

1. Use the DuPont method to calculate Dell's and HP's ROIs in 2010 and 2011. Comment on the results. What can you tell from the DuPont analysis that you might have missed from calculating ROI itself?
2. Compute the percentage of costs in each of the four business-function cost categories for Dell and HP in 2010 and 2011. Comment on the results.
3. Relate the results of requirements 1 and 2 to the comments made by the computer magazine. Of Goenka and Singhania, whom would you suggest to be the new CEO of IBM?

Solution

Evaluating managers, ROI, DuPont method, value-chain analysis of cost structure. (Amount in Rs crore)

1.

		$\frac{\text{Revenues}}{\text{Total Assets}}$	× $\frac{\text{Operating Income}}{\text{Revenues}}$	ROI = $\frac{\text{Operating Income}}{\text{Total Assets}}$
Dell				
	2010	1.11 (Rs 600 ÷ Rs 540)	0.26 (Rs 157.5 ÷ Rs 600)	0.29 (Rs 157.5 ÷ Rs 540)
	2011	0.94 (Rs 480 ÷ Rs 510)	0.13 (Rs 60.5 ÷ Rs 480)	0.12 (Rs 60.5 ÷ Rs 510)
Hewlett packard				
	2010	1.25 (Rs 300 ÷ Rs 240)	0.10 (Rs 29.7 ÷ Rs 300)	0.12 (Rs 29.7 ÷ Rs 240)
	2011	1.46 (Rs 525 ÷ Rs 360)	0.19 (Rs 99.3 ÷ Rs 525)	0.28 (Rs 99.3 ÷ Rs 360)

Dell's ROL has declined sizably from 2010 to 2011 largely because of a decline in operating income to revenues (return on sales or ROS). On point's ROI has more than doubled from 2010 to 2011, in large part due to an increase in operating income to revenues (return on sales or ROS). The DuPont analysis tells us that Dell's ROI decline arises from a serious degradation in its ROS, and not from any significant problem in assets turns, i.e., its management should probably examine and try to fix its eroding margins. This insight would not be available from a direct calculation of ROI.

2.	Dell		Hewlett packard	
Business Function	**2010**	**2011**	**2010**	**2011**
Research and development[a]	16%	10%	13%	18%
Production	30	35	40	30
Marketing & Distribution	39	46	36	36
Customer Service	15	10	11	16
Total costs*	100%	100%	100%	100%

[a] For example, Rs 71.2 ÷ Rs 442.5; Rs 40.2 ÷ Rs 419.5; Rs 35.9 ÷ Rs 270.3; Rs 76.1 ÷ Rs 425.37

* May sum to more than 100% due to rounding.

Business functions with increases/decreases in the percentage of total costs from 2008 to 2009 are:

	Dell	Hewlett Packard
Increases	Production Marketing & Distribution	Research and development Customer service
Decreases	Research and development Customer service	Production

Dell has decreased expenditures in two key business functions that are critical in the computer industry—research and development and customer service. These costs are discretionary and they can be reduced in the short run without any short-run effect on customers, but such action is likely to create serious problems in the long run. Hewlett Packard, on the other hand, increased its percentage of total costs in these two areas.

3. Based on the information provided, Singhania is the better candidate for president of IBM Computer. Both Dell and HP are in the same industry. Singhania has been CEO of HP at a time when it has considerably outperformed Dell:

   a. The ROI of HP has increased from 2010 to 2011, while that of Dell has decreased.
   b. The computer magazine has given the highest ranking to HP's main product, while Dell's received a lower ranking.
   c. HP has received high marks for new products (the lifeblood of a computer company), while Dell's new-product introductions have been described as "mediocre".

It is likely that HP's better rating for its current product is based on customer service and its better rating for its new product is based on research and development spending.

23-24 ROI, RI and Multinational Firms. Konekopf Corporation has a division in the United States, and another in France. The investment in the French assets was made when the exchange rate was $1.2 per euro. The average exchange rate for the year was $1.3 per euro. The exchange rate at the end of the fiscal year was $1.38 per euro. Income and investment for the two divisions are:

	United States	France
Investment in assets	$3,490,000	2,400,000 euros
Income for current year	$ 383,900	266,400 euros

Required

1. The required return for Konekopf is 10%. Calculate ROI and RI for the two divisions. For the French division, calculate these measures using both dollars and euros. Which division is doing better?
2. What are the advantages and disadvantages of translating the French division information from euros to dollars?

Solution

ROI, RI, and multinational firms.

1. Calculation of ROI and RI before currency translation:

	United States	France
Investment in assets	$3,490,000	2,400,000 eu
Income for current year	$ 383,900	266,400 eu
ROI ($383,900 ÷ $3,490,000; 266,400 eu ÷ 2,400,000 eu)	11.0%	11.1%
RI ($383,900 − 0.10 × $3,490,000; 266,400 eu − 0.10 × 2,400,000 eu)	$ 34,900	26, 400 eu

	United States	France
Investment in assets	$ 3,490,000	$2,880,000 (2,400,000 eu × $ 1.20)
Income for current year	$ 383,900	$ 346,320 (266,400 eu × $1.30)
ROI ($383,900 ÷ $3,490,000; $346,320 ÷ $2,880,000)	11.0%	12.0%
RI ($383,900 − 0.10 × $3,490,000; $346,320 − 0.10 × $2,880,000)	$ 34,900	$ 58,320

Without currency translation, the ROIs in the United States and France are similar, but after currency translation the ROI of France is substantially higher. Residual income is not comparable before currency translation given the different currencies used by the units. After translation, RI is higher in France. Together with the higher ROI, the RI results suggest that performance was better in France than in the United States.

2. Adjusting for differences in currency values makes the comparison of performance between foreign countries more meaningful since the accounting measures being examined are more comparable. However, changes in relative currency values can lead to misleading performance evaluations if interdependencies exist across units in different countries.

23-25 ROI, RI, DuPont method, investment decisions, balanced scorecard. Times Group has two major divisions: Print and Internet. Summary financial data (in lakh rupees) for 2010 and 2011 are as follows:

	A	B	C	D	E	F	G	H	I
1		Operating Income			Revenues			Total Assets	
2		2010	2011		2010	2011		2010	2011
3	Print	Rs 3,780	Rs 4,620		Rs18,900	Rs 19,320		Rs 18,480	Rs 20,580
4	Internet	546	672		25,200	26,880		11,340	12,600

The two division managers' annual bonuses are based on division ROI (defined as operating income divided by total assets). If a division reports an increase in ROI from the previous year, its management is automatically eligible for a bonus; however, the management of a division reporting a decline in ROI has to present an explanation to the Times Group board and is unlikely to get any bonus.

Arvind, manager of the Print Division, is considering a proposal to invest Rs 800 lakh in a new computerized news reporting and printing system. It is estimated that the new system's state-of-the-art graphics and ability to quickly incorporate late-breaking news into papers will increase 2010 division operating income by Rs 120 lakh. Times Group uses a 15% required rate of return on investment for each division.

Required

1. Use the DuPont method of profitability analysis to explain differences in 2011 ROIs between the two divisions. Use 2011 total assets as the investment base.
2. Why might Arvind be less than enthusiastic about accepting the investment proposal for the new system, despite her belief in the benefits of the new technology?
3. Ashish, CEO of Times Group, is considering a proposal to base division executive compensation on division RI.
   a. Compute the 2011 RI of each division.
   b. Would adoption of an RI measure reduce Arvind's reluctance to adopt the new computerized system investment proposal?
4. Ashish is concerned that the focus on annual ROI could have an adverse long-run effect on News Times Group's customers. What other measurements, if any, do you recommend that Ashish use? Explain briefly.

Solution

ROI, RI, DuPont method, investment decisions, balanced scorecard. (Amount in Rs Lakh)

1.

2011	Revenues / Total Assets	×	Operating Income / Revenues	=	ROI = Operating Income / Total Assets
Print	0.939 (Rs 19,320 ÷ Rs 20,580)		0.239 (Rs 4,620 ÷ Rs 19,320)		0.224 (Rs 4,620 ÷ Rs 20,580)
Internet	2.133 (Rs 26,880 ÷ Rs 12,600)		0.025 (Rs 672 ÷ Rs 26.880)		0.053 (Rs 672 ÷ Rs 12,600)

The Print Division has a relatively high ROI because of its high income margin relative to Internet. The Internet Division has a low ROI despite a high investment turnover because of its very low income margin.

2. Although the proposed investment is small, relative to the total assets invested, it earns less than the 2011 return on investment (0.224) (Amount in Rs Lakh):

$$\text{2011 ROI (before proposal)} = \frac{\text{Rs } 4{,}620}{\text{Rs } 20{,}580} = 0.224$$

$$\text{Investment proposal ROI Y} = \frac{\text{Rs } 120}{\text{Rs } 800} = 0.150$$

$$\text{2011 ROI (with proposal)} = \frac{\text{Rs } 4{,}620 + \text{Rs } 120}{\text{Rs } 20{,}580 + \text{Rs } 800} = 0.222$$

Given the existing bonus plan, any proposal that reduces the ROI is unattractive.

3a. Residual income for 2011 (before proposal, in Rs lakh):

	Operating Income		Imputed Interest Charge		Division Residual Income
Print	Rs 4,620	–	Rs 2,470 (0.12 × Rs 20,580)	=	Rs 2,150
Internet	672	–	1,512 (0,12 × Rs 12,600)	=	(840)

3b. Residual income for proposal (in Rs lakh):

Operating Income		Imputed Interest Charge		Residual Income
Rs 120	–	Rs 120 (0.15 × Rs 800)	=	Re 0

Investing in the fast-speed printing press will have no effect on the Print Division's residual income. As a result, if Arvind is evaluated using a residual income measure, Arvind would be indifferent to adopting the printing press proposal.

4. As discussed in requirement 3b, Ashish could consider using RI. The use of RI motivates managers to accept any project that makes a positive contribution to net income after the cost of the invested capital is taken into account. Making such investments will have a positive effect on Times Group's customers.

   Ashish may also want to consider nonfinancial measures such as newspaper subscription levels, internet audience size, repeat purchase patterns, and market share. These measures will require managers to invest in areas that have favorable long-run effects on Times Group's customers.

23-26 Division managers' compensation, levers of control (continuation of 23-25). Ashish seeks your advice on revising the existing bonus plan for division managers of Times Group. Assume division managers do not like bearing risk. Ashish is considering three ideas:

- Make each division manager's compensation depend on division RI.
- Make each division manager's compensation depend on companywide RI.
- Use benchmarking, and compensate division managers on the basis of their division's RI minus the RI of the other division.

Required

1. Evaluate the three ideas Ashish has put forth using performance-evaluation concepts described in this chapter. Indicate the positive and negative features of each proposal.
2. Ashish is concerned that the pressure for short-run performance may cause managers to cut corners. What systems might Ashish introduce to avoid this problem? Explain briefly.
3. Ashish is also concerned that the pressure for short-run performance might cause managers to ignore emerging threats and opportunities. What system might Ashish introduce to prevent this problem? Explain briefly.

Solution

Division manager's compensation, levers of control.

1 Consider each of the three proposals that Ashish is considering:

a. *Compensate managers on the basis of division RI.*

The benefit of this arrangement is that managers would be motivated to put in extra effort to increase RI because managers' rewards would increase with increases in RI. But compensating managers largely on the basis of RI subjects the managers to excessive risk, because each division's RI depends not only on the manager's effort but also on random factors over which the manager has no control. A manager may put in a great deal of effort, but the division's RI may be low because of adverse factors (high interest, recession) that the manager cannot control.

To compensate managers for taking on uncontrollable risk, Ashish must pay them additional amounts within the structure of the RI-based arrangement. Thus, using mainly performance-based incentives will cost Ashish more money, on average, than paying a flat salary. The key question is whether the benefits of motivating additional effort justify the higher costs of performance-based rewards. The motivation for having some salary and some performance-based bonus in compensation arrangements is to balance the benefits of incentives against the extra costs of imposing uncontrollable risk on the manager.

Finally, rewarding a manager only on the basis of division RI will induce managers to maximize the division's RI even if taking such actions are not in the best interest of the company as a whole.

b. *Compensate managers on the basis of companywide RI.*

Rewarding managers on the basis of companywide RI will motivate managers to take actions that are in the best interests of the company rather than actions that maximize a division's RI.

A negative feature of this arrangement is that each division manager's compensation will now depend not only on the performance of that division manager but also on the performance of the other division managers. For example, the compensation of Arvind, the manager of the Print Division, will depend on how well the manager of Internet performs, even though Arvind himself may have little influence over the performance of these divisions. Therefore, compensating managers on the basis of companywide RI will impose extra risk on each division manager, and will raise the cost of compensating them, on average.

c. *Compensate managers using the other division's RI as a benchmark,*

The benefit of benchmarking or relative performance evaluation is to cancel out the effects of common noncontrollable factors that affect a performance measure. Taking out the effects of these factors provides better information about a manager's performance. What is critical, however, for benchmarking and relative performance evaluation to be effective is that similar noncontrollable factors affect each division. It is not clear that the same noncontrollable factors that affect the performance of the Print Division (cost of newsprint paper, for example) also affect the performance of the Internet division. If the noncontrollable factors are not the same, then comparing the RI of one division to the RI of the other division will not provide useful information for relative performance evaluation.

A second factor for Ashish to consider is the impact that benchmarking and relative performance evaluation will have on the incentives for the division managers of the Print and Internet Divisions to cooperate with one another. Benchmarking one division against another means that a division manager will look good by improving his or her own performance or by making the performance, of the other division manager look bad.

2. Using measures like RI and ROI—diagnostic levers of control—can cause managers to cut corners and take other actions that boost short-run performance but harm the company in the long run. Ashish can guard against such problems by introducing and upholding strong boundary and belief systems of control within the company. Strict codes of conduct should govern what employees cannot do. Ashish should also foster a culture where employees have a deep belief in the value of the company's journalistic mission.

3. Another potential problem of an excessive focus on diagnostic measures is a myopic disregard for emerging threats and opportunities. Interactive control systems, based on debate and discussion and regular review of strategic uncertainties and the corripetitive landscape can help overcome this problem. Ashish should not only ask for regular reports on ROI, RI, etc., he should meet regularly with division managers, discuss 5- and 10-year strategic plans, and obtain their field-based inputs. Such regular dialogues will help surface emerging threats and opportunities, and the action plans that need to be taken in response.

23-27 Ethics, levers of control. (R. Madison, adapted, *Strategic Finance*, January 2000). Plywood Forest Products (PFP) is a large timber and wood processing plant. PFP's performance-evaluation system pays its managers substantial bonuses if the company achieves annual budgeted profit numbers. In the last quarter of 2011, Amita, PFP's controller, noted a slight increase in output and a significant decrease in the purchase cost of raw timber.

One day when Amita was at the log yard where timber is received and scaled (weighed and checked for quality) to determine what PFP pays for it, she noted that a timber contractor was quite aggravated when he was given the scale report (board feet and quality). When she asked one of the scale employees what was bothering the contractor, he revealed that the scalers had received instructions from their supervisors to deliberately "lowball" evaluations of timber quantity and quality. This reduced the price paid to timber suppliers, which also reduced direct material costs, helping PFP to meet its profit target.

Required

1. What should Amita do? You may want to refer to *Standards of Ethical Conduct for Management Accountants and Resolution of Ethical Conflict.*
2. Which lever of control is PFP emphasizing? What changes, if any, should be made?

Solution

Ethics, levers of control.

1. If Amita "turns a blind eye" toward what she has just observed at the PFP log yard, she will be violating the competence, integrity, and objectivity standards for management accountants.

Competence

- Performs professional duties in accordance with technical standards

Integrity

- Communicate unfavorable as well favorable information and professional judgments or opinions
- Refrain from engaging in or supporting any activity that would discredit the profession

Credibility

- Communicate information fairly and objectively
- Discolse fully all relevant information that could reasonably be expected to influence an intended user's understanding of the reports, comments, and recommendations.

Amita should:

a Try to follow established PFP policies to try to bring the issue to the attention of PFP management through regular channels; then, if necessary,
b Discuss the problem with the immediate superior who is not involved in the understatement of quality and costs.
c Clarify relevant ethical issues with an objective advisor, preferably a professional person outside PFP.
d If all the above channels fail to lead to a correction in the organization, she may have to resign and become a "whistle-blower" to bring PFP to justice.

2. PFP is clearly emphasizing profit, driving managers to find ways to keep profits strong and increasing. This is a diagnostic measure, and over-emphasis on diagnostic measures can cause employees to do whatever is necessary—including unethical actions—to keep the measures in the acceptable range, not attract negative senior management attention and possibly improve compensation and job reviews.

To avoid problems like this in the future, PFP needs to establish some strong boundary systems and codes of conduct. There should be a clear message from upper management that unethical behavior will not be tolerated. Training, role-plays, and case studies can be used to raise awareness about these issues, and strong sanctions should be put in place if the rules are violated. An effective boundary system is needed to keep managers "on the right path."

PFP also needs to articulate a belief system of core values. The goal is to inspire managers and employees to do their best, exercise greater responsibility, take pride in their work, and do things the right way.

23-28 ROI, RI, division manager's compensation, balanced scorecard. Key information for the Peoria Division (PD) of Ballarpur Industries for 2011 follows.

Revenues	Rs 15,00,00,000
Operating income	Rs 1,80,00,000
Total assets	Rs 10,00,00,000

PD's managers are evaluated and rewarded on the basis of ROI defined as operating income divided by total assets. Ballarpur Industries expects its divisions to increase ROI each year.

Next year, 2012, appears to be a difficult year for PD. PD had planned a new investment to improve quality but, in view of poor economic conditions, has postponed the investment. ROI for 2012 was certain to decrease if PD had made the investment.

Management is now considering ways to meet its target ROI of 20% for next year. It anticipates revenues to be steady at Rs 15,00,00,000 in 2012.

Required

1. Calculate PD's return on sales (ROS) and ROI for 2011.
2. **a.** By how much would PD need to cut costs in 2012 to achieve its target ROI of 20%, assuming no change in total assets between 2011 and 2012?
   b. By how much would PD need to decrease total assets in 2012 to achieve its target ROI of 20%, assuming no change in operating income between 2011 and 2012?
3. Calculate PD's RI in 2011 assuming a required rate of return on investment of 15%.
4. PD wants to increase RI by 50% in 2012. Assuming it could cut costs by Rs 4,50,000 in 2012, by how much would PD need to decrease total assets in 2012?
5. Ballarpur Industries is concerned that the focus on cost cutting, asset sales, and no new investments will have an adverse long-run effect on PD's customers. Yet Ballarpur wants PD to meet its financial goals. What other measurements, if any, do you recommend that Ballarpur use? Explain briefly.

Solution

ROI, RI, division manager's compensation, balanced scorecard.

1. $$\text{ROS} = \frac{\text{Operating Income}}{\text{Sales}} = \frac{\text{Rs } 1{,}80{,}00{,}000}{\text{Rs } 15{,}00{,}00{,}000} = 12\%$$

$$\text{ROI} = \frac{\text{Operating Income}}{\text{Total Assets}} = \frac{\text{Rs } 1{,}80{,}00{,}000}{\text{Rs } 10{,}00{,}00{,}000} = 18\%$$

2a. $$\text{ROI} = 20\% = \frac{\text{Operating Income}}{\text{Total Assets}} = \frac{X}{\text{Rs } 10{,}00{,}00{,}000}$$

Hence, operating income = 20% × Rs 10,00,00,000 = Rs 2,00,00,000
Operating income = Revenue − Costs
Therefore, Costs = Rs 15,00,00,000 − Rs 2,00,00,000 = Rs 13,00,00,000
Currently,
Costs = Revenues − Operating income = Rs 15,00,00,000 − Rs 1,80,00,000 = Rs 13,20,00,000
Costs need to be reduced by Rs 20,00,000 (Rs 13,20,00,000 − Rs 13,00,00,000).

2b. $$\text{ROI} = 20\% = \frac{\text{Operating Income}}{\text{Total assets}} = \frac{\text{Rs } 1{,}80{,}00{,}000}{X}$$

Hence X = Rs 1,80,00,000 ÷ 20% = Rs 9,00,00,000
PD would need to decrease total assets in 2012 by Rs 1,00,00,000 (Rs 10,00,00,000 − Rs 9,00,00,000).

3. RI = Income − (Required rate of return × Investment)
= Rs 1,80,00,000 − (0.15 × Rs 10,00,00,000)
= Rs 30,00,000

4. PD wants RI to increase by 50% × Rs 30,00,000 = Rs 15,00,000
That is, PD wants RI in 2012 to be Rs 30,00,000 + Rs 15,00,000 = Rs 45,00,000
If PD cuts costs by Rs 4,50,000 its operating income will increase to
Rs 1,80,00,000 + Rs 4,50,000 = Rs 1,84,50,000
RI_{2012} = Rs 45,00,000 = Rs 1,84,50,000 − (0.15 × Assets)
Rs 1,39,50,000 = 0.15 × Assets
Assets = Rs 1,39,50,000 ÷ 0.15 = Rs 9,30,00,000

PD would need to decrease total assets by Rs 70,00,000 (Rs 10,00,00,000 − Rs 9,30,00,000).

Ballarpur could focus more on revenues and ROS. Then, it will focus less on cutting costs and reducing assets and put more emphasis on customers, actual revenues, and how they translate into operating income.

Ballarpur may also want to consider nonfinancial measures such as customer satisfaction and market share, quality, yield, and on-time performance as well as monitor employee satisfaction and the development of employee skills. Maintaining high performance along these measures will have a favorable long-run effect on PD's customers.

Exercises

23-29 ROI, comparisons of three companies. (CMA, adapted) Return on investment (ROI) is often expressed as follows:

$$\frac{\text{Income}}{\text{Investment}} = \frac{\text{Income}}{\text{Revenues}} \times \frac{\text{Revenues}}{\text{Investment}}$$

Required

1. What advantages are there in the breakdown of the computation into two separate components?
2. Fill in the following blanks:

	Companies in Same Industry		
	A	**B**	**C**
Revenues	Rs 10,00,000	Rs 5,00,000	?
Income	Rs 1,00,000	Rs 50,000	?
Investment	Rs 5,00,000	?	Rs 50,00,000
Income as a percentage of revenues	?	?	0.5%
Investment turnover	?	?	2
ROI	?	1%	?

After filling in the blanks, comment on the relative performance of these companies as thoroughly as the data permit.

23-30 ROI and RI. (D. Kleespie, adapted) The Outdoor Sports Company produces a wide variety of outdoor sports equipment. Its newest division, Golf Technology, manufactures and sells a single product: AccuDriver, a golf club that uses global positioning satellite technology to improve the accuracy of golfers' shots. The demand for AccuDriver is relatively insensitive to price changes. The following data are available for Golf Technology, which is an investment center for Outdoor Sports:

Total annual fixed costs	Rs 3,00,00,000
Variable cost per AccuDriver	Rs 500
Number of AccuDrivers sold each year	1,50,000
Average operating assets invested in the division	Rs 4,80,00,000

Required

1. Compute Golf Technology's ROI if the selling price of AccuDrivers is Rs 720 per club.
2. If management requires an ROI of at least 25% from the division, what is the minimum selling price that the Golf Technology Division should charge per AccuDriver club?
3. Assume that Outdoor Sports judges the performance of its investment centers on the basis of RI rather than ROI. What is the minimum selling price that Golf Technology should charge per AccuDriver if the company's required rate of return is 20%?

23-31 Goal incongruence and ROI. Godrej Industries manufactures furniture in several divisions, including the Patio Furniture division. The manager of the Patio Furniture division plans to retire in two years. The manager receives a bonus based on the division's ROI, which is currently 11%. Godrej Industry's weighted average cost of capital is 6%.

One of the machines that the Patio Furniture division uses to manufacture the furniture is rather old, and the manager must decide whether to replace it. The new machine would cost Rs 3,00,000 and would last 10 years. It would have no salvage value. The old machine is fully depreciated and has no trade-in value. Godrej uses straight-line depreciation for all assets. The new machine, being new and more efficient, would save the company Rs 50,000 per year in cash operating costs. The only difference between cash flow and net income is depreciation. The internal rate of return of the project is 11%.

Required

1. Should Godrej Industries replace the machine? Why or why not?
2. Assume that "investment" is defined as average net long-term assets after depreciation. Compute the project's ROI for each of its first five years. If the Patio Furniture manager is interested in maximizing his bonus, would he replace the machine before he retires? Why or why not?
3. What can Godrej do to entice the manager to replace the machine before retiring?

23-32 ROI, RI, measurement of assets. (CMA, adapted) Royal Plastics recently announced a bonus plan to be awarded to the manager of the most profitable division. The three division managers are to choose whether ROI or RI will be used to measure profitability. In addition, they must decide whether investment will be measured using gross book value or net book value of assets. Royal Plastics defines income as operating income and investment as total assets. The following information is available for the year just ended:

Division	Gross Book Value of Assets	Accumulated Depreciation	Operating Income
Drums	Rs 12,00,000	Rs 6,45,000	Rs 1,42,050
Buckets	Rs 11,40,000	Rs 6,15,000	Rs 1,37,550
Trays	Rs 7,50,000	Rs 4,20,000	Rs 92,100

Royal uses a required rate of return of 12% on investment to calculate RI.

Required

Each division manager has selected a method of bonus calculation that ranks his or her division Number 1. Identify the method for calculating profitability that each manager selected, supporting your answer with appropriate calculations. Comment on the strengths and weaknesses of the methods chosen by each manager.

23-33 Risk sharing, incentives, benchmarking, multiple tasks. The Battery Division of Exide Industries sells car batteries. Exide's corporate management gives Battery management considerable operating and investment autonomy in running the division. Exide Industries is considering how it should compensate Praveen Tiwari, the general manager of the Battery Division. Proposal 1 calls for paying Praveen a fixed salary. Proposal 2 calls for paying Praveen no salary and compensating him only on the basis of the division's ROI, calculated based on operating income before any bonus payments. Proposal 3 calls for paying Praveen some salary and some bonus based on ROI. Assume that Praveen does not like bearing risk.

Required

1. Evaluate the three proposals, specifying the advantages and disadvantages of each.
2. Suppose that Exide' competes against Supreme Batteries in the car battery business. Supreme is approximately the same size as the Battery Division and operates in a business environment that is similar to Battery's. The top management of Exide is considering evaluating Praveen on the basis of

Exide's ROI minus Supreme's ROI. Praveen complains that this approach is unfair because the performance of another company, over which he has no control, is included in his performance-evaluation measure. Is Praveen's complaint valid? Why or why not?

3. Now suppose that Praveen has no authority for making capital-investment decisions. Corporate management makes these decisions. Is ROI a good performance measure to use to evaluate Praveen? Is ROI a good measure to evaluate the economic viability of the Battery Division? Explain.
4. Battery's salespersons are responsible for selling and providing customer service and support. Sales are easy to measure. Although customer service is important to Battery in the long run, it has not yet implemented customer-service measures. Praveen wants to compensate his sales force only on the basis of sales commissions paid for each unit of product sold. He cites two advantages to this plan: (a) It creates strong incentives for the sales force to work hard, and (b) the company pays salespersons only when the company itself is earning revenues. Do you like his plan? Why or why not?

23-34 Multinational firms, differing risk, comparison of profit, ROI and RI. Suzlon Energy has divisions in the United States, Germany, and New Zealand. The U.S. division is the oldest and most established of the three, and has a cost of capital of 6%. The German division was started three years ago when the exchange rate for euros was 1 euro = $1.25. Although it is a large and powerful division of Suzlon Energy its cost of capital is 10%. The New Zealand division was started this year, when the exchange rate was 1 New Zealand Dollar (NZD) = $$0.64. Its cost of capital is 13%. Average exchange rates for the current year are 1 euro=$1.32 and 1 New Zealand dollar = $0.67. Other information for the three divisions includes:

	United States	Germany	New Zealand
Long term assets	$14,845,000	9,856,000 euros	9,072,917 NZD
Operating revenues	$10,479,000	5,200,000 euros	4,800,000 NZD
Operating expenses	$ 7,210,000	3,400,000 euros	3,400,000 NZD
Income expense	$ 300,000	200,000 euros	100,000 NZD
Income tax rate	40%	30%	20%

Required

1. Translate the German and New Zealand information into dollars. Find the net income for each division and compare the profits.
2. Calculate ROI using net income. Compare among divisions.
3. Use the individual cost of capital of each division to calculate residual income and compare.
4. Redo requirement 2 using pretax operating income instead of net income. Why is there a big difference, and what does it mean for performance evaluation?

23-35 Executive compensation, balanced scorecard. HDFC Bank recently introduced a new bonus plan for its business unit executives. The company believes that current profitability and customer satisfaction levels are equally important to the bank's long-term success. As a result, the new plan awards a bonus equal to 1% of salary for each 1% increase in net income or 1% increase in the company's customer satisfaction index. For example, increasing net income from Rs 3 crore to Rs 3.3 crore (or 10% from its initial value) leads to a bonus of 10% of salary, while increasing the bank's customer satisfaction index from 70 to 73.5 (or 5% from its initial value) leads to a bonus of 5% of salary. There is no bonus penalty when net income or customer satisfaction declines. In 2010 and 2011, HDFC Bank's three business units reported the following performance results:

	Retail Banking		Business Banking		Credit Cards	
	2010	2011	2010	2011	2010	2011
Net income	Rs 2,80,00,000	Rs 3,22,00,000	Rs 2,90,00,000	Rs 3,01,60,000	Rs 2,75,00,000	Rs 2,72,25,000
Customer satisfaction	73	73	70	75.6	69	79.35

Required

1. Compute the bonus as a percent of salary earned by each business unit executive in 2011.
2. What factors might explain the different improvement rates for net income and customer satisfaction in the three units?
3. HDFC Bank's board of directors is concerned that the 2011 bonus awards may not actually reflect the executives' overall performance. In particular, it is concerned that executives can earn large bonuses by doing well on one performance dimension but underperforming on the other. What changes can it make to the bonus plan to prevent this from happening in the future? Explain briefly.

23-36 Ethics, manager's performance evaluation. (A. Spero, adapted) Tarla Semiconductors manufactures specialized chips that sell for Rs 200 each. Tarla's manufacturing costs consist of variable cost of Rs 20 per chip and fixed costs of Rs 9,00,00,000. Tarla also incurs Rs 40,00,000 in fixed marketing costs each year.

Tarla calculates operating income using absorption costing—that is, Tarla calculates manufacturing cost per unit by dividing total manufacturing costs by actual production. Tarla costs all units in inventory at this rate and expenses the costs in the income statement at the time when the units in inventory are sold. Next year, 2012, appears to be a difficult year for Tarla. It expects to sell only 5,00,000 units. The demand for these chips fluctuates considerably, so Tarla usually holds minimal inventory.

Required

1. Calculate Tarla's operating income in 2012 (a) if Tarla manufactures 5,00,000 units and (b) if Tarla manufactures 6,00,000 units.
2. Would it be unethical for Sunil Jalan, the general manager of Tarla Semiconductors, to produce more units than can be sold in order to show better operating results? Jalan's compensation has a bonus component based on operating income. Explain your answer.
3. Would it be unethical for Jalan to ask distributors to buy more product than they need? Tarla follows the industry practice of booking sales when products are transported to distributors. Explain your answer.

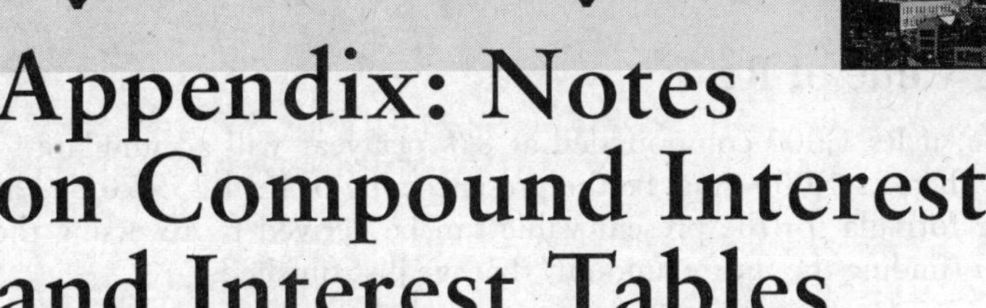

Appendix: Notes on Compound Interest and Interest Tables

Interest is the cost of using money. It is the rental charge for funds, just as renting a building and equipment entails a rental charge. When the funds are used for a period of time, it is necessary to recognize interest as a cost of using the borrowed ("rented") funds. This requirement applies even if the funds represent ownership capital and if interest does not entail an outlay of cash. Why must interest be considered? Because the selection of one alternative automatically commits a given amount of funds that could otherwise be invested in some other alternative.

Interest is generally important, even when short-term projects are under consideration. Interest looms correspondingly larger when long-run plans are studied. The rate of interest has significant enough impact to influence decisions regarding borrowing and investing funds. For example, Rs 1,00,000 invested now and compounded annually for 10 years at 8% will accumulate to Rs 2,15,900; at 20%, the Rs 1,00,000 will accumulate to Rs 6,19,200.

Interest Tables

Many computer programs and pocket calculators are available that handle computations involving the time value of money. You may also turn to the following four basic tables to compute interest.

Table 1—Future Amount of Re 1

Table 1 shows how much Re 1 invested now will accumulate in a given number of periods at a given compounded interest rate per period. Consider investing Rs 1,000 now for three years at 8% compound interest. A tabular presentation of how this Rs 1,000 would accumulate to Rs 1,259.70 follows:

Year	Interest per Year	Cumulative Interest Called Compound Interest	Total at End of Year
0	Rs —	Rs —	Rs 1,000.00
1	80.00 (0.08 × Rs 1,000)	80.00	1,080.00
2	86.40 (0.08 × Rs 1,080)	166.40	1,166.40
3	93.30 (0.08 × Rs 1,166.40)	259.70	1,259.70

This tabular presentation is a series of computations that could appear as follows, where S is the future amount and the subscripts 1, 2, and 3 indicate the number of time periods.

$$S_1 = \text{Rs } 1{,}000(1.08)^1 = \text{Rs } 1.080$$
$$S_2 = \text{Rs } 1{,}080(1.08) = \text{Rs } 1{,}000(1.08)^2 = \text{Rs } 1{,}166.40$$
$$S_3 = \text{Rs } 1{,}166.40 \times (1.08) = \text{Rs } 1{,}000(1.08)^3 = \text{Rs } 1{,}259.70$$

The formula for the "amount of 1," often called the "future value of Re 1" or "future amount of Re 1," can be written

$$S = P(1 + r)^n$$
$$S = \text{Rs } 1{,}000(1 + .08)^3 = \text{Rs } 1{,}259.70$$

S is the future value amount; P is the present value, Rs 1,000 in this case; r is the rate of interest; and n is the number of time periods.

Fortunately, tables make key computations readily available. A facility in selecting the *proper* table will minimize computations. Check the accuracy of the preceding answer using Table 1.

Table 2—Present Value of Re 1

In the previous example, if Rs 1,000 compounded at 8% per year will accumulate to Rs 1,259.70 in 3 years, then Rs 1,000 must be the present value of Rs 1,259.70 due at the end of 3 years. The formula for the present value can be derived by reversing the process of *accumulation* (finding the future amount) that we just finished.

If
$$S = P(1 + r)^n$$

then
$$P = \frac{S}{(1 + r)^n}$$

$$P = \frac{\text{Rs } 1,259.70}{(1.08)^3} = \text{Rs } 1,000$$

Use Table 2 to check this calculation.

When accumulating, we advance or roll forward in time. The difference between our original amount and our accumulated amount is called *compound interest.* When discounting, we retreat or roll back in time. The difference between the future amount and the present value is called *compound discount*. Note the following formulas (where P = Rs 1,000):

$$\text{Compound interest} = P[(1 + r)^n - 1] = \text{Rs } 259.70$$

$$\text{Compound discount} = S\left[1 - \frac{1}{(1 + r)^n}\right] = \text{Rs } 259.70$$

Table 3—Amount of Annuity of Re 1

An (ordinary) *annuity* is a series of equal payments (receipts) to be paid (or received) at the end of successive periods of equal length. Assume that Rs 1,000 is invested at the end of each of 3 years at 8%:

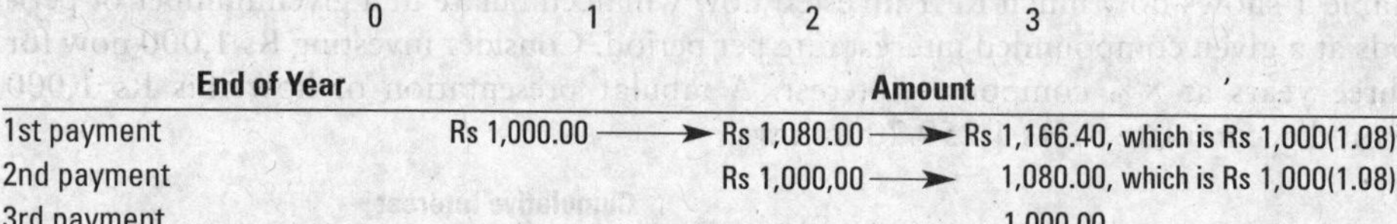

End of Year		Amount	
1st payment	Rs 1,000.00 ⟶	Rs 1,080.00 ⟶	Rs 1,166.40, which is Rs 1,000(1.08)^2
2nd payment		Rs 1,000,00 ⟶	1,080.00, which is Rs 1,000(1.08)^1
3rd payment			1,000.00
Accumulation (future amount)			Rs 3,246.40

The preceding arithmetic may be expressed algebraically as the amount of an ordinary annuity of Rs 1,000 for 3 years = Rs $1,000(1 + r)^2$ + Rs $1,000(1 + r)^1$ + Rs 1,000.

We can develop the general formula for S_n, the amount of an ordinary annuity of Re 1, by using the example above as a basis:

1. $S_n = 1 + (1 + r)^1 + (1 + r)^2$
2. Substitute: $S_n = 1 + (1.08)^1 + (1.08)^2$
3. Multiply (2) by $(1 + r)$: $(1.08)S_n = (1.08)^1 + (1.08)^2 + (1.08)^3$
4. Subtract (2) from (3): $(1.08)S_n - S_n = (1.08)^3 - 1$
   Note that all terms on the right-hand side are removed except $(1.08)^3$ in equation (3) and 1 in equation (2).

5. Factor (4): $S_n(1.08 - 1) = (1.08)^3 - 1$

6. Divide (5) by (1.08 − 1): $S_n = \frac{(1.08)^3 - 1}{1.08 - 1} = \frac{(1.08)^3 - 1}{.08}$

7. The general formula for the amount of an ordinary annuity of Re 1 becomes: $S_n = \frac{(1 + r)^n - 1}{r}$ or $\frac{\text{Compound interest}}{\text{Rate}}$

This formula is the basis for Table 3. Look at Table 3 or use the formula itself to check the calculations.

Table 4—Present Value of an Ordinary Annuity of Re 1

Using the same example as for Table 3, we can show how the formula of P_n, *the present value of an ordinary annuity*, is developed.

End of Year			0	1	2	3
1st payment	$\frac{1,000}{(1.08)^1}$ =	Rs 926.14 ←		Rs 1,000		
2nd payment	$\frac{1,000}{(1.08)^2}$ =	Rs 857.52 ←			Rs 1,000	
3rd payment	$\frac{1,000}{(1.08)^3}$ =	Rs 794.00 ←				Rs 1,000
Total present value		Rs 2,577.66				

For the general case, the present value of an ordinary annuity of Re 1 may be expressed as:

1. $P_n = \frac{1}{1 + r} + \frac{1}{(1 + r)^2} + \frac{1}{(1 + r)^3}$

2. Substitute $P_n = \frac{1}{1.08} + \frac{1}{(1.08)^2} + \frac{1}{(1.08)^3}$

3. Multiply by $P_n = \frac{1}{1.08} = \frac{1}{(1.08)^2} + \frac{1}{(1.08)^3} + \frac{1}{(1.08)^4}$

4. Subtract (3) from (2): $P_n - P_n\frac{1}{1.08} = \frac{1}{1.08} - \frac{1}{(1.08)^4}$

5. Factor: $P_n\left(1 - \frac{1}{(1.08)}\right) = \frac{1}{1.08}\left[1 - \frac{1}{(1.08)^3}\right]$

6. or $P_n\left(\frac{.08}{1.08}\right) = \frac{1}{1.08}\left[1 - \frac{1}{(1.08)^3}\right]$

7. Multiply by $\frac{1.08}{.08}$ $P_n = \frac{1}{.08}\left[1 - \frac{1}{(1.08)^3}\right]$

The general formula for the present value of an annuity of Rs 1.00 is:

$$P_n = \frac{1}{r}\left[1 - \frac{1}{(1 + r)^n}\right] = \frac{\text{Compound discount}}{\text{Rate}}$$

Solving, $P_n = \frac{.2062}{.08} = 2.577$

The formula is the basis for Table 4. Check the answer in the table. The present value tables, Tables 2 and 4, are used most frequently in capital budgeting.

The tables for annuities are not essential. With Tables 1 and 2, compound interest and compound discount can readily be computed. It is simply a matter of dividing either of these by the rate to get values equivalent to those shown in Tables 3 and 4.

Table 1

Compound Amount of Re 1.00 (The Future Value of Re 1.00)

$S = P(1 + r)^n$. In this table $P =$ Re 1.00

Periods	2%	4%	6%	8%	10%	12%	14%	16%	18%	20%	22%	24%	26%	28%	30%	32%	40%	Periods
1	1.020	1.040	1.060	1.080	1.100	1.120	1.140	1.160	1.180	1.200	1.220	1.240	1.260	1.280	1.300	1.320	1.400	1
2	1.040	1.082	1.124	1.166	1.210	1.254	1.300	1.346	1.392	1.440	1.488	1.538	1.588	1.638	1.690	1.742	1.960	2
3	1.061	1.125	1.191	1.260	1.331	1.405	1.482	1.561	1.643	1.728	1.816	1.907	2.000	2.097	2.197	2.300	2.744	3
4	1.082	1.170	1.262	1.360	1.464	1.574	1.689	1.811	1.939	2.074	2.215	2.364	2.520	2.684	2.856	3.036	3.842	4
5	1.104	1.217	1.338	1.469	1.611	1.762	1.925	2.100	2.288	2.488	2.703	2.932	3.176	3.436	3.713	4.007	5.378	5
6	1.126	1.265	1.419	1.587	1.772	1.974	2.195	2.436	2.700	2.986	3.297	3.635	4.002	4.398	4.827	5.290	7.530	6
7	1.149	1.316	1.504	1.714	1.949	2.211	2.502	2.826	3.185	3.583	4.023	4.508	5.042	5.629	6.275	6.983	10.541	7
8	1.172	1.369	1.594	1.851	2.144	2.476	2.853	3.278	3.759	4.300	4.908	5.590	6.353	7.206	8.157	9.217	14.758	8
9	1.195	1.423	1.689	1.999	2.358	2.773	3.252	3.803	4.435	5.160	5.987	6.931	8.005	9.223	10.604	12.166	20.661	9
10	1.219	1.480	1.791	2.159	2.594	3.106	3.707	4.411	5.234	6.192	7.305	8.594	10.086	11.806	13.786	16.060	28.925	10
11	1.243	1.539	1.898	2.332	2.853	3.479	4.226	5.117	6.176	7.430	8.912	10.657	12.708	15.112	17.922	21.199	40.496	11
12	1.268	1.601	2.012	2.518	3.138	3.896	4.818	5.936	7.288	8.916	10.872	13.215	16.012	19.343	23.298	27.983	56.694	12
13	1.294	1.665	2.133	2.720	3.452	4.363	5.492	6.886	8.599	10.699	13.264	16.386	20.175	24.759	30.288	36.937	79.371	13
14	1.319	1.732	2.261	2.937	3.797	4.887	6.261	7.988	10.147	12.839	16.182	20.319	25.421	31.691	39.374	48.757	111.120	14
15	1.346	1.801	2.397	3.172	4.177	5.474	7.138	9.266	11.974	15.407	19.742	25.196	32.030	40.565	51.186	64.359	155.568	15
16	1.373	1.873	2.540	3.426	4.595	6.130	8.137	10.748	14.129	18.488	24.086	31.243	40.358	51.923	66.542	84.954	217.795	16
17	1.400	1.948	2.693	3.700	5.054	6.866	9.276	12.468	16.672	22.186	29.384	38.741	50.851	66.461	86.504	112.139	304.913	17
18	1.428	2.026	2.854	3.996	5.560	7.690	10.575	14.463	19.673	26.623	35.849	48.039	64.072	85.071	112.455	148.024	426.879	18
19	1.457	2.107	3.026	4.316	6.116	8.613	12.056	16.777	23.214	31.948	43.736	59.568	80.731	108.890	146.192	195.391	597.630	19
20	1.486	2.191	3.207	4.661	6.727	9.646	13.743	19.461	27.393	38.338	53.358	73.864	101.721	139.380	190.050	257.916	836.683	20
21	1.516	2.279	3.400	5.034	7.400	10.804	15.668	22.574	32.324	46.005	65.096	91.592	128.169	178.406	247.065	340.449	1171.356	21
22	1.546	2.370	3.604	5.437	8.140	12.100	17.861	26.186	38.142	55.206	79.418	113.574	161.492	228.360	321.184	449.393	1639.898	22
23	1.577	2.465	3.820	5.871	8.954	13.552	20.362	30.376	45.008	66.247	96.889	140.831	203.480	292.300	417.539	593.199	2295.857	23
24	1.608	2.563	4.049	6.341	9.850	15.179	23.212	35.236	53.109	79.497	118.205	174.631	256.385	374.144	542.801	783.023	3214.200	24
25	1.641	2.666	4.292	6.848	10.835	17.000	26.462	40.874	62.669	95.396	144.210	216.542	323.045	478.905	705.641	1033.590	4499.880	25
26	1.673	2.772	4.549	7.396	11.918	19.040	30.167	47.414	73.949	114.475	175.936	268.512	407.037	612.998	917.333	1364.339	6299.831	26
27	1.707	2.883	4.822	7.988	13.110	21.325	34.390	55.000	87.260	137.371	214.642	332.955	512.867	784.638	1192.533	1800.927	8819.764	27
28	1.741	2.999	5.112	8.627	14.421	23.884	39.204	63.800	102.967	164.845	261.864	412.864	646.212	1004.336	1550.293	2377.224	12347.670	28
29	1.776	3.119	5.418	9.317	15.863	26.750	44.693	74.009	121.501	197.814	319.474	511.952	814.228	1285.550	2015.381	3137.935	17286.737	29
30	1.811	3.243	5.743	10.063	17.449	29.960	50.950	85.850	143.371	237.376	389.758	634.820	1025.927	1645.505	2619.996	4142.075	24201.432	30
35	2.000	3.946	7.686	14.785	28.102	52.800	98.100	180.314	327.997	590.668	1053.402	1861.054	3258.135	5653.911	9727.860	16599.217	130161.112	35
40	2.208	4.801	10.286	21.725	45.259	93.051	188.884	378.721	750.378	1469.772	2847.038	5455.913	10347.175	19426.689	36118.865	66520.767	700037.697	40

Table 2 (*Place a clip on this page for easy reference.*)

Present Value of Re 1.00

$P = \frac{S}{(1+r)^n}$. In this table S = Re 1.00

Periods	2%	4%	6%	8%	10%	12%	14%	16%	18%	20%	22%	24%	26%	28%	30%	32%	40%	Periods
1	0.980	0.962	0.943	0.926	0.909	0.893	0.877	0.862	0.847	0.833	0.820	0.806	0.794	0.781	0.769	0.758	0.714	1
2	0.961	0.925	0.890	0.857	0.826	0.797	0.769	0.743	0.718	0.694	0.672	0.650	0.630	0.610	0.592	0.574	0.510	2
3	0.942	0.889	0.840	0.794	0.751	0.712	0.675	0.641	0.609	0.579	0.551	0.524	0.500	0.477	0.455	0.435	0.364	3
4	0.924	0.855	0.792	0.735	0.683	0.636	0.592	0.552	0.516	0.482	0.451	0.423	0.397	0.373	0.350	0.329	0.260	4
5	0.906	0.822	0.747	0.681	0.621	0.567	0.519	0.476	0.437	0.402	0.370	0.341	0.315	0.291	0.269	0.250	0.186	5
6	0.888	0.790	0.705	0.630	0.564	0.507	0.456	0.410	0.370	0.335	0.303	0.275	0.250	0.227	0.207	0.189	0.133	6
7	0.871	0.760	0.665	0.583	0.513	0.452	0.400	0.354	0.314	0.279	0.249	0.222	0.198	0.178	0.159	0.143	0.095	7
8	0.853	0.731	0.627	0.540	0.467	0.404	0.351	0.305	0.266	0.233	0.204	0.179	0.157	0.139	0.123	0.108	0.068	8
9	0.837	0.703	0.592	0.500	0.424	0.361	0.308	0.263	0.225	0.194	0.167	0.144	0.125	0.108	0.094	0.082	0.048	9
10	0.820	0.676	0.558	0.463	0.386	0.322	0.270	0.227	0.191	0.162	0.137	0.116	0.099	0.085	0.073	0.062	0.035	10
11	0.804	0.650	0.527	0.429	0.350	0.287	0.237	0.195	0.162	0.135	0.112	0.094	0.079	0.066	0.056	0.047	0.025	11
12	0.788	0.625	0.497	0.397	0.319	0.257	0.208	0.168	0.137	0.112	0.092	0.076	0.062	0.052	0.043	0.036	0.018	12
13	0.773	0.601	0.469	0.368	0.290	0.229	0.182	0.145	0.116	0.093	0.075	0.061	0.050	0.040	0.033	0.027	0.013	13
14	0.758	0.577	0.442	0.340	0.263	0.205	0.160	0.125	0.099	0.078	0.062	0.049	0.039	0.032	0.025	0.021	0.009	14
15	0.743	0.555	0.417	0.315	0.239	0.183	0.140	0.108	0.084	0.065	0.051	0.040	0.031	0.025	0.020	0.016	0.006	15
16	0.728	0.534	0.394	0.292	0.218	0.163	0.123	0.093	0.071	0.054	0.042	0.032	0.025	0.019	0.015	0.012	0.005	16
17	0.714	0.513	0.371	0.270	0.198	0.146	0.108	0.080	0.060	0.045	0.034	0.026	0.020	0.015	0.012	0.009	0.003	17
18	0.700	0.494	0.350	0.250	0.180	0.130	0.095	0.069	0.051	0.038	0.028	0.021	0.016	0.012	0.009	0.007	0.002	18
19	0.686	0.475	0.331	0.232	0.164	0.116	0.083	0.060	0.043	0.031	0.023	0.017	0.012	0.009	0.007	0.005	0.002	19
20	0.673	0.456	0.312	0.215	0.149	0.104	0.073	0.051	0.037	0.026	0.019	0.014	0.010	0.007	0.005	0.004	0.001	20
21	0.660	0.439	0.294	0.199	0.135	0.093	0.064	0.044	0.031	0.022	0.015	0.011	0.008	0.006	0.004	0.003	0.001	21
22	0.647	0.422	0.278	0.184	0.123	0.083	0.056	0.038	0.026	0.018	0.013	0.009	0.006	0.004	0.003	0.002	0.001	22
23	0.634	0.406	0.262	0.170	0.112	0.074	0.049	0.033	0.022	0.015	0.010	0.007	0.005	0.003	0.002	0.002	0.000	23
24	0.622	0.390	0.247	0.158	0.102	0.066	0.043	0.028	0.019	0.013	0.008	0.006	0.004	0.003	0.002	0.001	0.000	24
25	0.610	0.375	0.233	0.146	0.092	0.059	0.038	0.024	0.016	0.010	0.007	0.005	0.003	0.002	0.001	0.001	0.000	25
26	0.598	0.361	0.220	0.135	0.084	0.053	0.033	0.021	0.014	0.009	0.006	0.004	0.002	0.002	0.001	0.001	0.000	26
27	0.586	0.347	0.207	0.125	0.076	0.047	0.029	0.018	0.011	0.007	0.005	0.003	0.002	0.001	0.001	0.001	0.000	27
28	0.574	0.333	0.196	0.116	0.069	0.042	0.026	0.016	0.010	0.006	0.004	0.002	0.002	0.001	0.001	0.000	0.000	28
29	0.563	0.321	0.185	0.107	0.063	0.037	0.022	0.014	0.008	0.005	0.003	0.002	0.001	0.001	0.000	0.000	0.000	29
30	0.552	0.308	0.174	0.099	0.057	0.033	0.020	0.012	0.007	0.004	0.003	0.002	0.001	0.001	0.000	0.000	0.000	30
35	0.500	0.253	0.130	0.068	0.036	0.019	0.010	0.006	0.003	0.002	0.001	0.001	0.000	0.000	0.000	0.000	0.000	35
40	0.453	0.208	0.097	0.046	0.022	0.011	0.005	0.003	0.001	0.001	0.000	0.000	0.000	0.000	0.000	0.000	0.000	40

Table 3

Compound Amount of Annuity of Re 1.00 in Arrears* (Future Value of Annuity)

$$S_n = \frac{(1 + r)^n - 1}{r}$$

Periods	2%	4%	6%	8%	10%	12%	14%	16%	18%	20%	22%	24%	26%	28%	30%	32%	40%	Periods
1	1.000	1.000	1.000	1.000	1.000	1.000	1.000	1.000	1.000	1.000	1.000	1.000	1.000	1.000	1.000	1.000	1.000	1
2	2.020	2.040	2.060	2.080	2.100	2.120	2.140	2.160	2.180	2.200	2.220	2.240	2.260	2.280	2.300	2.320	2.400	2
3	3.060	3.122	3.184	3.246	3.310	3.374	3.440	3.506	3.572	3.640	3.708	3.778	3.848	3.918	3.990	4.062	4.360	3
4	4.122	4.246	4.375	4.506	4.641	4.779	4.921	5.066	5.215	5.368	5.524	5.684	5.848	6.016	6.187	6.362	7.104	4
5	5.204	5.416	5.637	5.867	6.105	6.353	6.610	6.877	7.154	7.442	7.740	8.048	8.368	8.700	9.043	9.398	10.946	5
6	6.308	6.633	6.975	7.336	7.716	8.115	8.536	8.977	9.442	9.930	10.442	10.980	11.544	12.136	12.756	13.406	16.324	6
7	7.434	7.898	8.394	8.923	9.487	10.089	10.730	11.414	12.142	12.916	13.740	14.615	15.546	16.534	17.583	18.696	23.853	7
8	8.583	9.214	9.897	10.637	11.436	12.300	13.233	14.240	15.327	16.499	17.762	19.123	20.588	22.163	23.858	25.678	34.395	8
9	9.755	10.583	11.491	12.488	13.579	14.776	16.085	17.519	19.086	20.799	22.670	24.712	26.940	29.369	32.015	34.895	49.153	9
10	10.950	12.006	13.181	14.487	15.937	17.549	19.337	21.321	23.521	25.959	28.657	31.643	34.945	38.593	42.619	47.062	69.814	10
11	12.169	13.486	14.972	16.645	18.531	20.655	23.045	25.733	28.755	32.150	35.962	40.238	45.031	50.398	56.405	63.122	98.739	11
12	13.412	15.026	16.870	18.977	21.384	24.133	27.271	30.850	34.931	39.581	44.874	50.895	57.739	65.510	74.327	84.320	139.235	12
13	14.680	16.627	18.882	21.495	24.523	28.029	32.089	36.786	42.219	48.497	55.746	64.110	73.751	84.853	97.625	112.303	195.929	13
14	15.974	18.292	21.015	24.215	27.975	32.393	37.581	43.672	50.818	59.196	69.010	80.496	93.926	109.612	127.913	149.240	275.300	14
15	17.293	20.024	23.276	27.152	31.772	37.280	43.842	51.660	60.965	72.035	85.192	100.815	119.347	141.303	167.286	197.997	386.420	15
16	18.639	21.825	25.673	30.324	35.950	42.753	50.980	60.925	72.939	87.442	104.935	126.011	151.377	181.868	218.472	262.356	541.988	16
17	20.012	23.698	28.213	33.750	40.545	48.884	59.118	71.673	87.068	105.931	129.020	157.253	191.735	233.791	285.014	347.309	759.784	17
18	21.412	25.645	30.906	37.450	45.599	55.750	68.394	84.141	103.740	128.117	158.405	195.994	242.585	300.252	371.518	459.449	1064.697	18
19	22.841	27.671	33.760	41.446	51.159	63.440	78.969	98.603	123.414	154.740	194.254	244.033	306.658	385.323	483.973	607.472	1491.576	19
20	24.297	29.778	36.786	45.762	57.275	72.052	91.025	115.380	146.628	186.688	237.989	303.601	387.389	494.213	630.165	802.863	2089.206	20
21	25.783	31.969	39.993	50.423	64.002	81.699	104.768	134.841	174.021	225.026	291.347	377.465	489.110	633.593	820.215	1060.779	2925.889	21
22	27.299	34.248	43.392	55.457	71.403	92.503	120.436	157.415	206.345	271.031	356.443	469.056	617.278	811.999	1067.280	1401.229	4097.245	22
23	28.845	36.618	46.996	60.893	79.543	104.603	138.297	183.601	244.487	326.237	435.861	582.630	778.771	1040.358	1388.464	1850.622	5737.142	23
24	30.422	39.083	50.816	66.765	88.497	118.155	158.659	213.978	289.494	392.484	532.750	723.461	982.251	1332.659	1806.003	2443.821	8032.999	24
25	32.030	41.646	54.865	73.106	98.347	133.334	181.871	249.214	342.603	471.981	650.955	898.092	1238.636	1706.803	2348.803	3226.844	11247.199	25
26	33.671	44.312	59.156	79.954	109.182	150.334	208.333	290.088	405.272	567.377	795.165	1114.634	1561.682	2185.708	3054.444	4260.434	15747.079	26
27	35.344	47.084	63.706	87.351	121.100	169.374	238.499	337.502	479.221	681.853	971.102	1383.146	1968.719	2798.706	3971.778	5624.772	22046.910	27
28	37.051	49.968	68.528	95.339	134.210	190.699	272.889	392.503	566.481	819.223	1185.744	1716.101	2481.586	3583.344	5164.311	7425.699	30866.674	28
29	38.792	52.966	73.640	103.966	148.631	214.583	312.094	456.303	669.447	984.068	1447.608	2128.965	3127.798	4587.680	6714.604	9802.923	43214.343	29
30	40.568	56.085	79.058	113.263	164.494	241.333	356.787	530.312	790.948	1181.882	1767.081	2640.916	3942.026	5873.231	8729.985	12940.859	60501.081	30
35	49.994	73.652	111.435	172.317	271.024	431.663	693.573	1120.713	1816.652	2948.341	4783.645	7750.225	12527.442	20188.966	32422.868	51869.427	325400.279	35
40	60.402	95.026	154.762	259.057	442.593	767.091	1342.025	2360.757	4163.213	7343.858	12936.535	22728.803	39792.982	69377.460	120392.883	207874.272	1750091.741	40

*Payments (or receipts) at the end of each period.

Table 4 (*Place a clip on this page for easy reference.*)

Present Value of Annuity Re 1.00 in Arrears*

$$P_n = \frac{1}{r}\left[1 - \frac{1}{(1+r)^n}\right]$$

Periods	2%	4%	6%	8%	10%	12%	14%	16%	18%	20%	22%	24%	26%	28%	30%	32%	40%	Periods
1	0.980	0.962	0.943	0.926	0.909	0.893	0.877	0.862	0.847	0.833	0.820	0.806	0.794	0.781	0.769	0.758	0.714	1
2	1.942	1.886	1.833	1.783	1.736	1.690	1.647	1.605	1.566	1.528	1.492	1.457	1.424	1.392	1.361	1.331	1.224	2
3	2.884	2.775	2.673	2.577	2.487	2.402	2.322	2.246	2.174	2.106	2.042	1.981	1.923	1.868	1.816	1.766	1.589	3
4	3.808	3.630	3.465	3.312	3.170	3.037	2.914	2.798	2.690	2.589	2.494	2.404	2.320	2.241	2.166	2.096	1.849	4
5	4.713	4.452	4.212	3.993	3.791	3.605	3.433	3.274	3.127	2.991	2.864	2.745	2.635	2.532	2.436	2.345	2.035	5
6	5.601	5.242	4.917	4.623	4.355	4.111	3.889	3.685	3.498	3.326	3.167	3.020	2.885	2.759	2.643	2.534	2.168	6
7	6.472	6.002	5.582	5.206	4.868	4.564	4.288	4.039	3.812	3.605	3.416	3.242	3.083	2.937	2.802	2.677	2.263	7
8	7.325	6.733	6.210	5.747	5.335	4.968	4.639	4.344	4.078	3.837	3.619	3.421	3.241	3.076	2.925	2.786	2.331	8
9	8.162	7.435	6.802	6.247	5.759	5.328	4.946	4.607	4.303	4.031	3.786	3.566	3.366	3.184	3.019	2.868	2.379	9
10	8.983	8.111	7.360	6.710	6.145	5.650	5.216	4.833	4.494	4.192	3.923	3.682	3.465	3.269	3.092	2.930	2.414	10
11	9.787	8.760	7.887	7.139	6.495	5.938	5.453	5.029	4.656	4.327	4.035	3.776	3.543	3.335	3.147	2.978	2.438	11
12	10.575	9.385	8.384	7.536	6.814	6.194	5.660	5.197	4.793	4.439	4.127	3.851	3.606	3.387	3.190	3.013	2.456	12
13	11.348	9.986	8.853	7.904	7.103	6.424	5.842	5.342	4.910	4.533	4.203	3.912	3.656	3.427	3.223	3.040	2.469	13
14	12.106	10.563	9.295	8.244	7.367	6.628	6.002	5.468	5.008	4.611	4.265	3.962	3.695	3.459	3.249	3.061	2.478	14
15	12.849	11.118	9.712	8.559	7.606	6.811	6.142	5.575	5.092	4.675	4.315	4.001	3.726	3.483	3.268	3.076	2.484	15
16	13.578	11.652	10.106	8.851	7.824	6.974	6.265	5.668	5.162	4.730	4.357	4.033	3.751	3.503	3.283	3.088	2.489	16
17	14.292	12.166	10.477	9.122	8.022	7.120	6.373	5.749	5.222	4.775	4.391	4.059	3.771	3.518	3.295	3.097	2.492	17
18	14.992	12.659	10.828	9.372	8.201	7.250	6.467	5.818	5.273	4.812	4.419	4.080	3.786	3.529	3.304	3.104	2.494	18
19	15.678	13.134	11.158	9.604	8.365	7.366	6.550	5.877	5.316	4.843	4.442	4.097	3.799	3.539	3.311	3.109	2.496	19
20	16.351	13.590	11.470	9.818	8.514	7.469	6.623	5.929	5.353	4.870	4.460	4.110	3.808	3.546	3.316	3.113	2.497	20
21	17.011	14.029	11.764	10.017	8.649	7.562	6.687	5.973	5.384	4.891	4.476	4.121	3.816	3.551	3.320	3.116	2.498	21
22	17.658	14.451	12.042	10.201	8.772	7.645	6.743	6.011	5.410	4.909	4.488	4.130	3.822	3.556	3.323	3.118	2.498	22
23	18.292	14.857	12.303	10.371	8.883	7.718	6.792	6.044	5.432	4.925	4.499	4.137	3.827	3.559	3.325	3.120	2.499	23
24	18.914	15.247	12.550	10.529	8.985	7.784	6.835	6.073	5.451	4.937	4.507	4.143	3.831	3.562	3.327	3.121	2.499	24
25	19.523	15.622	12.783	10.675	9.077	7.843	6.873	6.097	5.467	4.948	4.514	4.147	3.834	3.564	3.329	3.122	2.499	25
26	20.121	15.983	13.003	10.810	9.161	7.896	6.906	6.118	5.480	4.956	4.520	4.151	3.837	3.566	3.330	3.123	2.500	26
27	20.707	16.330	13.211	10.935	9.237	7.943	6.935	6.136	5.492	4.964	4.524	4.154	3.839	3.567	3.331	3.123	2.500	27
28	21.281	16.663	13.406	11.051	9.307	7.984	6.961	6.152	5.502	4.970	4.528	4.157	3.840	3.568	3.331	3.124	2.500	28
29	21.844	16.984	13.591	11.158	9.370	8.022	6.983	6.166	5.510	4.975	4.531	4.159	3.841	3.569	3.332	3.124	2.500	29
30	22.396	17.292	13.765	11.258	9.427	8.055	7.003	6.177	5.517	4.979	4.534	4.160	3.842	3.569	3.332	3.124	2.500	30
35	24.999	18.665	14.498	11.655	9.644	8.176	7.070	6.215	5.539	4.992	4.541	4.164	3.845	3.571	3.333	3.125	2.500	35
40	27.355	19.793	15.046	11.925	9.779	8.244	7.105	6.233	5.548	4.997	4.544	4.166	3.846	3.571	3.333	3.125	2.500	40

*Payments (or receipts) at the end of each period.

Glossary

Abnormal spoilage. Spoilage that would not arise under efficient operating conditions; it is not inherent in a particular production process.

Absorption costing. Method of inventory costing in which all variable manufacturing costs and all fixed manufacturing costs are included as inventoriable costs.

Account analysis method. Approach to cost function estimation that classifies various cost accounts as variable, fixed, or mixed with respect to the identified level of activity. Typically, qualitative rather than quantitative analysis is used when making these cost-classification decisions.

Accrual accounting rate of return (AARR) method. Capital budgeting method that divides an accrual accounting measure of average annual income of a project by an accrual accounting measure of its investment. See also *return on investment (ROI)*.

Activity. An event, task, or unit of work with a specified purpose.

Activity-based budgeting (ABB). Budgeting approach that focuses on the budgeted cost of the activities necessary to produce and sell products and services.

Activity-based costing (ABC). Approach to costing that focuses on individual activities as the fundamental cost objects. It uses the costs of these activities as the basis for assigning costs to other cost objects such as products or services.

Activity-based management (ABM). Method of management decision-making that uses activity-based costing information to improve customer satisfaction and profitability.

Actual cost. Cost incurred (a historical or past cost), as distinguished from a budgeted or forecasted cost.

Actual costing. A costing system that traces direct costs to a cost object by using the actual direct-cost rates times the actual quantities of the direct-cost inputs and allocates indirect costs based on the actual indirect-cost rates times the actual quantities of the cost allocation bases. (102)

Actual indirect-cost rate. Actual total indirect costs in a cost pool divided by the actual total quantity of the cost-allocation base for that cost pool. (110)

Adjusted allocation-rate approach. Restates all overhead entries in the general ledger and subsidiary ledgers using actual cost rates rather than budgeted cost rates.

Allowable cost. Cost that the contract parties agree to include in the costs to be reimbursed.

Appraisal costs. Costs incurred to detect which of the individual units of products do not conform to specifications.

Artificial costs. See *complete reciprocated costs*.

Autonomy. The degree of freedom to make decisions.

Average cost. See *unit cost*.

Average waiting time. The average amount of time that an order will wait in line before the machine is set up and the order is processed.

Backflush costing. Costing system that omits recording some of the journal entries relating to the stages from purchase of direct material to the sale of finished goods.

Balanced scorecard. A framework for implementing strategy that translates an organization's mission and strategy into a set of performance measures.

Batch-level costs. The costs of activities related to a group of units of products or services rather than to each individual unit of product or service.

Belief systems. Lever of control that articulates the mission, purpose, norms of behaviors, and core values of a company intended to inspire managers and other employees to do their best.

Benchmarking. The continuous process of comparing the levels of performance in producing products and services and executing activities against the best levels of performance in competing companies or in companies having similar processes.

Book value. The original cost minus accumulated depreciation of an asset.

Bottleneck. An operation where the work to be performed approaches or exceeds the capacity available to do it.

Boundary systems. Lever of control that describes standards of behavior and codes of conduct expected of all employees, especially actions that are off-limits.

Breakeven point (BEP). Quantity of output sold at which total revenues equal total costs, that is where the operating income is zero.

Budget. Quantitative expression of a proposed plan of action by management for a specified period and an aid to coordinating what needs to be done to implement that plan.

Budgetary slack. The practice of underestimating budgeted revenues, or overestimating budgeted costs, to make budgeted targets more easily achievable.

Budgeted cost. Predicted or forecasted cost (future cost) as distinguished from an actual or historical cost.

Budgeted indirect-cost rate. Budgeted annual indirect costs in a cost pool divided by the budgeted annual quantity of the cost allocation base.

Budgeted performance. Expected performance or a point of reference to compare actual results.

Bundled product. A package of two or more products (or services) that is sold for a single price, but whose individual components may be sold as separate items at their own "standalone" prices.

Business function costs. The sum of all costs (variable and fixed) in a particular business function of the value chain.

Byproducts. Products from a joint production process that have low total sales values compared with the total sales value of the main product or of joint products.

Capital budgeting. The making of long-run planning decisions for investments in projects.

Carrying costs. Costs that arise while holding inventory of goods for sale.

Cash budget. Schedule of expected cash receipts and disbursements.

Cause-and-effect diagram. Diagram that identifies potential causes of defects. Four categories of potential causes of failure are human factors, methods and design factors, machine-related factors, and materials and components factors. Also called a *fishbone diagram.*

Chief financial officer (CFO). Executive responsible for overseeing the financial operations of an organization. Also called *finance director.*

Choice criterion. Objective that can be quantified in a decision model.

Coefficient of determination (r^2). Measures the percentage of variation in a dependent variable explained by one or more independent variables.

Collusive pricing. Companies in an industry conspire in their pricing and production decisions to achieve a price above the competitive price and so restrain trade.

Common cost. Cost of operating a facility, activity, or like cost object that is shared by two or more users.

Complete reciprocated costs. The support department's own costs plus any interdepartmental cost allocations. Also called the *artificial costs* of the support department.

Composite unit. Hypothetical unit with weights based on the mix of individual units.

Conference method. Approach to cost function estimation on the basis of analysis and opinions about costs and their drivers gathered from various departments of a company (purchasing, process engineering, manufacturing, employee relations, and so on).

Conformance quality. Refers to the performance of a product or service relative to its design and product specifications.

Constant. The component of total cost that, within the relevant range, does not vary with changes in the level of the activity. Also called *intercept.*

Constant gross-margin percentage NRV method. Method that allocates joint costs to joint products in such a way that the overall gross-margin percentage is identical for the individual products.

Constraint. A mathematical inequality or equality that must be satisfied by the variables in a mathematical model.

Continuous budget. See *rolling budget.*

Contribution income statement. Income statement that groups costs into variable costs and fixed costs to highlight the contribution margin.

Contribution margin. Total revenues minus total variable costs.

Contribution margin per unit. Selling price minus the variable cost per unit.

Contribution margin percentage. Contribution margin per unit divided by selling price. Also called *contribution margin ratio.*

Contribution margin ratio. See *contribution margin percentage.*

Control. Taking actions that implement the planning decisions, deciding how to evaluate performance, and providing feedback and learning that will help future decision making.

Control chart. Graph of a series of successive observations of a particular step, procedure, or operation taken at regular intervals of time. Each observation is plotted relative to specified ranges that represent the limits within which observations are expected to fall.

Controllability. Degree of influence that a specific manager has over costs, revenues, or related items for which he or she is responsible.

Controllable cost. Any cost that is primarily subject to the influence of a given responsibility center manager for a given period.

Controller. The financial executive primarily responsible for management accounting and financial accounting. Also called *chief accounting officer.*

Conversion costs. All manufacturing costs other than direct material costs.

Cost. Resource sacrificed or forgone to achieve a specific objective.

Cost accounting. Measures, analyzes, and reports financial and nonfinancial information relating to the costs of acquiring or using resources in an organization. It provides information for both management accounting and financial accounting.

Cost Accounting Standards Board (CASB). Government agency that has the exclusive authority to make, put into effect, amend, and rescind cost accounting standards and interpretations thereof designed to achieve uniformity and consistency in regard to measurement, assignment, and allocation of costs to government contracts within the United States.

Cost accumulation. Collection of cost data in some organized way by means of an accounting system.

Cost allocation. Assignment of indirect costs to a particular cost object.

Cost-allocation base. A factor that links in a systematic way an indirect cost or group of indirect costs to a cost object.

Cost-application base. Cost-allocation base when the cost object is a job, product, or customer.

Cost assignment. General term that encompasses both (1) tracing accumulated costs that have a direct relationship to a cost object and (2) allocating accumulated costs that have an indirect relationship to a cost object.

Cost-benefit approach. Approach to decision-making and resource allocation based on a comparison of the expected benefits from attaining company goals and the expected costs.

Cost center. Responsibility center where the manager is accountable for costs only.

Cost driver. A variable, such as the level of activity or volume, that causally affects costs over a given time span.

Cost estimation. The attempt to measure a past relationship based on data from past costs and the related level of an activity.

Cost function. Mathematical description of how a cost changes with changes in the level of an activity relating to that cost.

Cost hierarchy. Categorization of indirect costs into different cost pools on the basis of the different types of cost drivers, or cost-allocation bases, or different degrees of difficulty in determining cause-and-effect (or benefits received) relationships.

Cost incurrence. Describes when a resource is consumed (or benefit forgone) to meet a specific objective.

Cost leadership. Organization's ability to achieve lower costs relative to competitors through productivity and efficiency improvements, elimination of waste, and tight cost control.

Cost management. The approaches and activities of managers to use resources to increase value to customers and to achieve organizational goals.

Cost object. Anything for which a measurement of costs is desired.

Cost of capital. See *required rate of return (RRR)*.

Cost of goods manufactured. Cost of goods brought to completion, whether they were started before or during the current accounting period.

Cost pool. A grouping of individual cost items.

Cost predictions. Forecasts about future costs.

Cost tracing. Describes the assignment of direct costs to a particular cost object.

Costs of quality (COQ). Costs incurred to prevent, or the costs arising as a result of, the production of a low-quality product.

Cost-volume-profit (CVP) analysis. Examines the behavior of total revenues, total costs, and operating income as changes occur in the units sold, the selling price, the variable cost per unit, or the fixed costs of a product.

Cumulative average-time learning model. Learning curve model in which the cumulative average time per unit declines by a constant percentage each time the cumulative quantity of units produced doubles.

Current cost. Asset measure based on the cost of purchasing an asset today identical to the one currently held, or the cost of purchasing an asset that provides services like the one currently held if an identical asset cannot be purchased.

Customer-cost hierarchy. Hierarchy that categorizes costs related to customers into different cost pools on the basis of different types of cost drivers, or cost-allocation bases, or different degrees of difficulty in determining cause-and-effect or benefits-received relationships.

Customer life-cycle costs. Focuses on the total costs incurred by a customer to acquire, use, maintain, and dispose of a product or service.

Customer-profitability analysis. The reporting and analysis of revenues earned from customers and the costs incurred to earn those revenues.

Customer-response time. Duration from the time a customer places an order for a product or service to the time the product or service is delivered to the customer.

Customer service. Providing after-sale support to customers. (6)

Decentralization. The freedom for managers at lower levels of the organization to make decisions.

Decision model. Formal method for making a choice, often involving both quantitative and qualitative analyses.

Decision table. Summary of the alternative actions, events, outcomes, and probabilities of events in a decision model.

Degree of operating leverage. Contribution margin divided by operating income at any given level of sales.

Denominator level. The denominator in the budgeted fixed overhead rate computation.

Denominator-level variance. See *production-volume variance*.

Dependent variable. The cost to be predicted.

Design of products and processes. The detailed planning and engineering of products and processes.

Design quality. Refers to how closely the characteristics of a product or service meet the needs and wants of customers.

Designed-in costs. See *locked-in costs*.

Diagnostic control systems. Lever of control that monitors critical performance variables that help managers track progress toward achieving a company's strategic goals. Managers are held accountable for meeting these goals.

Differential cost. Difference in total cost between two alternatives.

Differential revenue. Difference in total revenue between two alternatives.

Direct costing. See *variable costing*.

Direct costs of a cost object. Costs related to the particular cost object that can be traced to that object in an economically feasible (cost-effective) way.

Direct manufacturing labor costs. Include the compensation of all manufacturing labor that can be traced to the cost object (work in process and then finished goods) in an economically feasible way.

Direct material costs. Acquisition costs of all materials that eventually become part of the cost object (work in process and then finished goods), and that can be traced to the cost object in an economically feasible way.

Direct materials inventory. Direct materials in stock and awaiting use in the manufacturing process.

Direct materials mix variance. The difference between (1) budgeted cost for actual mix of the actual total quantity of direct materials used and (2) budgeted cost of budgeted mix of the actual total quantity of direct materials used.

Direct materials yield variance. The difference between (1) budgeted cost of direct materials based on the actual total quantity of direct materials used and (2) flexible-budget cost of direct materials based on the budgeted total quantity of direct materials allowed for the actual output produced.

Direct method. Cost allocation method that allocates each support department's costs to operating departments only.

Discount rate. See *required rate of return (RRR).*

Discounted cash flow (DCF) methods. Capital budgeting methods that measure all expected future cash inflows and outflows of a project as if they occurred at the present point in time.

Discounted payback method. Capital budgeting method that calculates the amount of time required for the discounted expected future cash flows to recoup the net initial investment in a project.

Discretionary costs. Arise from periodic (usually annual) decisions regarding the maximum amount to be incurred and have no measurable cause-and-effect relationship between output and resources used.

Distribution. Delivering products or services to customers.

Downsizing. An integrated approach of configuring processes, products, and people to match costs to the activities that need to be performed to operate effectively and efficiently in the present and future. Also called *rightsizing.*

Downward demand spiral. Pricing context where prices are raised to spread capacity costs over a smaller number of output units. Continuing reduction in the demand for products that occurs when the prices of competitors' products are not met and, as demand drops further, higher and higher unit costs result in more and more reluctance to meet competitors' prices.

Dual pricing. Approach to transfer pricing using two separate transfer-pricing methods to price each transfer from one subunit to another.

Dual-rate method. Allocation method that classifies costs in each cost pool into two pools (a variable-cost pool and a fixed-cost pool) with each pool using a different cost-allocation base.

Dumping. Under U.S. laws, it occurs when a non-U.S. company sells a product in the United States at a price below the market value in the country where it is produced, and this lower price materially injures or threatens to materially injure an industry in the United States.

Dysfunctional decision making. See *suboptimal decision making.*

Economic order quantity (EOQ). Decision model that calculates the optimal quantity of inventory to order under a set of assumptions.

Economic value added (EVA®). After-tax operating income minus the (after-tax) weighted-average cost of capital multiplied by total assets minus current liabilities.

Effectiveness. The degree to which a predetermined objective or target is met.

Efficiency. The relative amount of inputs used to achieve a given output level.

Efficiency variance. The difference between actual input quantity used and budgeted input quantity allowed for actual output, multiplied by budgeted price. Also called *usage variance.*

Effort. Exertion toward achieving a goal.

Engineered costs. Costs that result from a cause-and-effect relationship between the cost driver, output, and the (direct or indirect) resources used to produce that output.

Equivalent units. Derived amount of output units that (a) takes the quantity of each input (factor of production) in units completed and in incomplete units of work in process and (b) converts the quantity of input into the amount of completed output units that could be produced with that quantity of input.

Event. A possible relevant occurrence in a decision model.

Expected monetary value. See *expected value.*

Expected value. Weighted average of the outcomes of a decision with the probability of each outcome serving as the weight. Also called *expected monetary value.*

Experience curve. Function that measures the decline in cost per unit in various business functions of the value chain, such as manufacturing, marketing, distribution, and so on, as the amount of these activities increases.

External failure costs. Costs incurred on defective products after they are shipped to customers.

Facility-sustaining costs. The costs of activities that cannot be traced to individual products or services but support the organization as a whole.

Factory overhead costs. See *indirect manufacturing costs.*

Favorable variance. Variance that has the effect of increasing operating income relative to the budgeted amount. Denoted F.

Finance director. See *chief financial officer (CFO).*

Financial accounting. Measures and records business transactions and provides financial statements that are based on generally accepted accounting principles. It focuses on reporting to external parties such as investors and banks.

Financial budget. Part of the master budget that focuses on how operations and planned capital outlays affect cash. It is made up of the capital expenditures budget, the cash budget, the budgeted balance sheet, and the budgeted statement of cash flows.

Financial planning models. Mathematical representations of the relationships among operating activities, financial activities, and other factors that affect the master budget.

Finished goods inventory. Goods completed but not yet sold.

First-in, first-out (FIFO) process-costing method. Method of process costing that assigns the cost of the previous accounting period's equivalent units in beginning work-in-process inventory to the first units completed and transferred out of the process, and assigns the cost of equivalent units worked on during the current period first to complete beginning inventory, next to start and complete new units, and finally to units in ending work-in-process inventory.

Fixed cost. Cost that remains unchanged in total for a given time period, despite wide changes in the related level of total activity or volume.

Fixed overhead flexible-budget variance. The difference between actual fixed overhead costs and fixed overhead costs in the flexible budget.

Fixed overhead spending variance. Same as the fixed overhead flexible-budget variance. The difference between actual fixed overhead costs and fixed overhead costs in the flexible budget.

Flexible budget. Budget developed using budgeted revenues and budgeted costs based on the actual output in the budget period.

Flexible-budget variance. The difference between an actual result and the corresponding flexible-budget amount based on the actual output level in the budget period.

Full costs of the product. The sum of all variable and fixed costs in all business functions of the value chain (R&D, design, production, marketing, distribution, and customer service).

Goal congruence. Exists when individuals and groups work toward achieving the organization's goals. Managers working in their own best interest take actions that align with the overall goals of top management.

Gross margin percentage. Gross margin divided by revenues.

Growth component. Change in operating income attributable solely to the change in the quantity of output sold between one period and the next.

High-low method. Method used to estimate a cost function that uses only the highest and lowest observed values of the cost driver within the relevant range and their respective costs.

Homogeneous cost pool. Cost pool in which all the costs have the same or a similar cause-and-effect or benefits-received relationship with the cost-allocation base.

Hurdle rate. See *required rate of return (RRR)*.

Hybrid-costing system. Costing system that blends characteristics from both job-costing systems and process-costing systems.

Idle time. Wages paid for unproductive time caused by lack of orders, machine breakdowns, material shortages, poor scheduling, and the like.

Imputed costs. Costs recognized in particular situations but not incorporated in financial accounting records.

Incongruent decision making. See *suboptimal decision making*.

Incremental cost. Additional total cost incurred for an activity.

Incremental cost-allocation method. Method that ranks the individual users of a cost object in the order of users most responsible for the common cost and then uses this ranking to allocate cost among those users.

Incremental revenue. Additional total revenue from an activity.

Incremental revenue-allocation method. Method that ranks individual products in a bundle according to criteria determined by management (for example, sales), and then uses this ranking to allocate bundled revenues to the individual products.

Incremental unit-time learning model. Learning curve model in which the incremental time needed to produce the last unit declines by a constant percentage each time the cumulative quantity of units produced doubles.

Independent variable. Level of activity or cost driver used to predict the dependent variable (costs) in a cost estimation or prediction model.

Indirect costs of a cost object. Costs related to the particular cost object that cannot be traced to that object in an economically feasible (cost-effective) way.

Indirect manufacturing costs. All manufacturing costs that are related to the cost object (work in process and then finished goods) but that cannot be traced to that cost object in an economically feasible way. Also called *manufacturing overhead costs* and *factory overhead costs*.

Industrial engineering method. Approach to cost function estimation that analyzes the relationship between inputs and outputs in physical terms. Also called *work measurement method*.

Inflation. The decline in the general purchasing power of the monetary unit, such as dollars.

Input-price variance. See *price variance*.

Insourcing. Process of producing goods or providing services within the organization rather than purchasing those same goods or services from outside vendors.

Inspection point. Stage of the production process at which products are examined to determine whether they are acceptable or unacceptable units.

Interactive control systems. Formal information systems that managers use to focus organization attention and learning on key strategic issues.

Intercept. See *constant*.

Intermediate product. Product transferred from one subunit to another subunit of an organization. This product may either be further worked on by the receiving subunit or sold to an external customer.

Internal failure costs. Costs incurred on defective products before they are shipped to customers.

Internal rate-of-return (IRR) method. Capital budgeting discounted cash flow (DCF) method that calculates the discount rate at which the present value of expected cash inflows from a project equals the present value of its expected cash outflows.

Inventoriable costs. All costs of a product that are considered as assets in the balance sheet when they are incurred and that become cost of goods sold only when the product is sold.

Inventory management. Planning, coordinating, and controlling activities related to the flow of inventory into, through, and out of an organization.

Investment. Resources or assets used to generate income.

Investment center. Responsibility center where the manager is accountable for investments, revenues, and costs.

Job. A unit or multiple units of a distinct product or service.

Job-cost record. Source document that records and accumulates all the costs assigned to a specific job, starting when work begins. Also called *job-cost sheet*.

Job-cost sheet. See *job-cost record*.

Job-costing system. Costing system in which the cost object is a unit or multiple units of a distinct product or service called a job.

Joint costs. Costs of a production process that yields multiple products simultaneously.

Joint products. Two or more products that have high total sales values compared with the total sales values of other products yielded by a joint production process.

Just-in-time (JIT) production. Demand-pull manufacturing system in which each component in a production line is produced as soon as, and only when, needed by the next step in the production line. Also called *lean production*.

Just-in-time (JIT) purchasing. The purchase of materials (or goods) so that they are delivered just as needed for production (or sales).

Kaizen budgeting. Budgetary approach that explicitly incorporates continuous improvement anticipated during the budget period into the budget numbers.

Labor-time sheet. Source document that contains information about the amount of labor time used for a specific job in a specific department.

Lean accounting. Costing method that supports creating value for the customer by costing the entire value stream, not individual products or departments, thereby eliminating waste in the accounting process.

Lean production. See *just-in-time (JIT) production*.

Learning. Involves managers examining past performance and systematically exploring alternative ways to make better-informed decisions and plans in the future.

Learning curve. Function that measures how labor-hours per unit decline as units of production increase because workers are learning and becoming better at their jobs.

Life-cycle budgeting. Budget that estimates the revenues and business function costs of the value chain attributable to each product from initial R&D to final customer service and support.

Life-cycle costing. System that tracks and accumulates business function costs of the value chain attributable to each product from initial R&D to final customer service and support.

Line management. Managers (for example, in production, marketing, or distribution) who are directly responsible for attaining the goals of the organization.

Linear cost function. Cost function in which the graph of total costs versus the level of a single activity related to that cost is a straight line within the relevant range.

Linear programming (LP). Optimization technique used to maximize an objective function (for example, contribution margin of a mix of products), when there are multiple constraints.

Locked-in costs. Costs that have not yet been incurred but, based on decisions that have already been made, will be incurred in the future. Also called *designed-in costs*.

Main product. Product from a joint production process that has a high total sales value compared with the total sales values of all other products of the joint production process.

Make-or-buy decisions. Decisions about whether a producer of goods or services will insource (produce goods or services within the firm) or outsource (purchase them from outside vendors).

Management accounting. Measures, analyzes, and reports financial and nonfinancial information that helps managers make decisions to fulfill the goals of an organization. It focuses on internal reporting.

Management by exception. Practice of focusing management attention on areas not operating as expected and giving less attention to areas operating as expected.

Management control system. Means of gathering and using information to aid and coordinate the planning and control decisions throughout an organization and to guide the behavior of its managers and employees.

Manufacturing cells. Grouping of all the different types of equipment used to make a given product.

Manufacturing cycle efficiency (MCE). Value-added manufacturing time divided by manufacturing cycle time.

Manufacturing cycle time. See *manufacturing lead time*.

Manufacturing lead time. Duration between the time an order is received by manufacturing to the time a finished good is produced. Also called *manufacturing cycle time*.

Manufacturing overhead allocated. Amount of manufacturing overhead costs allocated to individual jobs, products, or services based on the budgeted rate multiplied by the actual quantity used of the cost-allocation base. Also called *manufacturing overhead applied*.

Manufacturing overhead applied. See *manufacturing overhead allocated*.

Manufacturing overhead costs. See *indirect manufacturing costs*.

Manufacturing-sector companies. Companies that purchase materials and components and convert them into various finished goods.

Margin of safety. Amount by which budgeted (or actual) revenues exceed breakeven revenues.

Marketing. Promoting and selling products or services to customers or prospective customers.

Market-share variance. The difference in budgeted contribution margin for actual market size in units caused solely by actual market share being different from budgeted market share.

Market-size variance. The difference in budgeted contribution margin at the budgeted market share caused solely by actual market size in units being different from budgeted market size in units.

Master budget. Expression of management's operating and financial plans for a specified period (usually a fiscal year) including a set of budgeted financial statements. Also called *pro forma statements*.

Master-budget capacity utilization. The expected level of capacity utilization for the current budget period (typically one year).

Materials requirements planning (MRP). Push-through system that manufactures finished goods for inventory on the basis of demand forecasts.

Materials-requisition record. Source document that contains information about the cost of direct materials used on a specific job and in a specific department.

Matrix method. See *reciprocal method*.

Merchandising-sector companies. Companies that purchase and then sell tangible products without changing their basic form.

Mixed cost. A cost that has both fixed and variable elements. Also called a *semivariable cost.*

Moral hazard. Describes situations in which an employee prefers to exert less effort (or to report distorted information) compared with the effort (or accurate information) desired by the owner because the employee's effort (or validity of the reported information) cannot be accurately monitored and enforced.

Motivation. The desire to attain a selected goal (the goal-congruence aspect) combined with the resulting pursuit of that goal (the effort aspect).

Multicollinearity. Exists when two or more independent variables in a multiple regression model are highly correlated with each other.

Multiple regression. Regression model that estimates the relationship between the dependent variable and two or more independent variables.

Net income. Operating income plus nonoperating revenues (such as interest revenue) minus nonoperating costs (such as interest cost) minus income taxes.

Net present value (NPV) method. Capital budgeting discounted cash flow (DCF) method that calculates the expected monetary gain or loss from a project by discounting all expected future cash inflows and outflows to the present point in time, using the required rate of return.

Net realizable value (NRV) method. Method that allocates joint costs to joint products on the basis of final sales value minus separable costs of total production of the joint products during the accounting period.

Nominal rate of return. Made up of three elements: (a) a risk-free element when there is no expected inflation, (b) a business-risk element, and (c) an inflation element.

Nonlinear cost function. Cost function in which the graph of total costs based on the level of a single activity is not a straight line within the relevant range.

Nonvalue-added cost. A cost that, if eliminated, would not reduce the actual or perceived value or utility (usefulness) customers obtain from using the product or service.

Normal capacity utilization. The level of capacity utilization that satisfies average customer demand over a period (say, two to three years) that includes seasonal, cyclical, and trend factors.

Normal costing. A costing system that traces direct costs to a cost object by using the actual direct-cost rates times the actual quantities of the direct-cost inputs and that allocates indirect costs based on the budgeted indirect-cost rates times the actual quantities of the cost-allocation bases.

Normal spoilage. Spoilage inherent in a particular production process that arises even under efficient operating conditions.

Objective function. Expresses the objective to be maximized (for example, operating income) or minimized (for example, operating costs) in a decision model (for example, a linear programming model).

On-time performance. Delivering a product or service by the time it is scheduled to be delivered.

One-time-only special order. Orders that have no long-run implications.

Operating budget. Budgeted income statement and its supporting budget schedules.

Operating department. Department that directly adds value to a product or service. Also called a *production department* in manufacturing companies.

Operating income. Total revenues from operations minus cost of goods sold and operating costs (excluding interest expense and income taxes).

Operating-income volume variance. The difference between static-budget operating income and the operating income based on budgeted profit per unit and actual units of output.

Operating leverage. Effects that fixed costs have on changes in operating income as changes occur in units sold and hence in contribution margin.

Operation. A standardized method or technique that is performed repetitively, often on different materials, resulting in different finished goods.

Operation-costing system. Hybrid-costing system applied to batches of similar, but not identical, products. Each batch of products is often a variation of a single design, and it proceeds through a sequence of operations, but each batch does not necessarily move through the same operations as other batches. Within each operation, all product units use identical amounts of the operation's resources.

Opportunity cost. The contribution to operating income that is forgone or rejected by not using a limited resource in its next-best alternative use.

Opportunity cost of capital. See *required rate of return (RRR).*

Ordering costs. Costs of preparing, issuing, and paying purchase orders, plus receiving and inspecting the items included in the orders.

Organization structure. Arrangement of lines of responsibility within the organization.

Outcomes. Predicted economic results of the various possible combinations of actions and events in a decision model.

Output unit-level costs. The costs of activities performed on each individual unit of a product or service.

Outsourcing. Process of purchasing goods and services from outside vendors rather than producing the same goods or providing the same services within the organization.

Overabsorbed indirect costs. See *overallocated indirect costs.*

Overallocated indirect costs. Allocated amount of indirect costs in an accounting period is greater than the actual (incurred) amount in that period. Also called *overapplied indirect costs* and *overabsorbed indirect costs.*

Overapplied indirect costs. See *overallocated indirect costs.*

Overtime premium. Wage rate paid to workers (for both direct labor and indirect labor) in excess of their straight-time wage rates.

Pareto diagram. Chart that indicates how frequently each type of defect occurs, ordered from the most frequent to the least frequent.

Partial productivity. Measures the quantity of output produced divided by the quantity of an individual input used.

Payback method. Capital budgeting method that measures the time it will take to recoup, in the form of expected future cash flows, the net initial investment in a project.

Peak-load pricing. Practice of charging a higher price for the same product or service when the demand for it approaches the physical limit of the capacity to produce that product or service.

Perfectly competitive market. Exists when there is a homogeneous product with buying prices equal to selling prices and no individual buyers or sellers can affect those prices by their own actions.

Period costs. All costs in the income statement other than cost of goods sold.

Physical-measure method. Method that allocates joint costs to joint products on the basis of the relative weight, volume, or other physical measure at the splitoff point of total production of these products during the accounting period.

Planning. Selecting organization goals, predicting results under various alternative ways of achieving those goals, deciding how to attain the desired goals, and communicating the goals and how to attain them to the entire organization.

Practical capacity. The level of capacity that reduces theoretical capacity by unavoidable operating interruptions such as scheduled maintenance time, shutdowns for holidays, and so on.

Predatory pricing. Company deliberately prices below its costs in an effort to drive out competitors and restrict supply and then raises prices rather than enlarge demand.

Prevention costs. Costs incurred to preclude the production of products that do not conform to specifications.

Previous-department costs. See *transferred-in costs*.

Price discount. Reduction in selling price below list selling price to encourage increases in customer purchases.

Price discrimination. Practice of charging different customers different prices for the same product or service.

Price-recovery component. Change in operating income attributable solely to changes in prices of inputs and outputs between one period and the next.

Price variance. The difference between actual price and budgeted price multiplied by actual quantity of input. Also called *input-price variance* or *rate variance*.

Prime costs. All direct manufacturing costs.

Pro forma statements. Budgeted financial statements.

Probability. Likelihood or chance that an event will occur.

Probability distribution. Describes the likelihood (or the probability) that each of the mutually exclusive and collectively exhaustive set of events will occur.

Process-costing system. Costing system in which the cost object is masses of identical or similar units of a product or service.

Product. Any output that has a positive total sales value (or an output that enables an organization to avoid incurring costs).

Product cost. Sum of the costs assigned to a product for a specific purpose.

Product-cost cross-subsidization. Costing outcome where one undercosted (overcosted) product results in at least one other product being overcosted (undercosted).

Product differentiation. Organization's ability to offer products or services perceived by its customers to be superior and unique relative to the products or services of its competitors.

Product life cycle. Spans the time from initial R&D on a product to when customer service and support is no longer offered for that product.

Product-mix decisions. Decisions about which products to sell and in what quantities.

Product overcosting. A product consumes a low level of resources but is reported to have a high cost per unit.

Product-sustaining costs. The costs of activities undertaken to support individual products regardless of the number of units or batches in which the units are produced.

Product undercosting. A product consumes a high level of resources but is reported to have a low cost per unit.

Production. Acquiring, coordinating, and assembling resources to produce a product or deliver a service.

Production-denominator level. The denominator in the budgeted manufacturing fixed overhead rate computation.

Production department. See *operating department*.

Production-volume variance. The difference between budgeted fixed overhead and fixed overhead allocated on the basis of actual output produced. Also called *denominator-level variance*.

Productivity. Measures the relationship between actual inputs used (both quantities and costs) and actual outputs produced; the lower the inputs for a given quantity of outputs or the higher the outputs for a given quantity of inputs, the higher the productivity.

Productivity component. Change in costs attributable to a change in the quantity of inputs used in the current period relative to the quantity of inputs that would have been used in the prior period to produce the quantity of current period output.

Profit center. Responsibility center where the manager is accountable for revenues and costs.

Proration. The spreading of underallocated manufacturing overhead or overallocated manufacturing overhead among ending work in process, finished goods, and cost of goods sold.

Purchase-order lead time. The time between placing an order and its delivery.

Purchasing costs. Cost of goods acquired from suppliers including incoming freight or transportation costs.

PV graph. Shows how changes in the quantity of units sold affect operating income.

Qualitative factors. Outcomes that are difficult to measure accurately in numerical terms.

Quality. The total features and characteristics of a product made or a service performed according to specifications to satisfy customers at the time of purchase and during use.

Quantitative factors. Outcomes that are measured in numerical terms.

Rate variance. See *price variance*.

Real rate of return. The rate of return demanded to cover investment risk (with no inflation). It has a risk-free element and a business-risk element.

Reciprocal method. Cost allocation method that fully recognizes the mutual services provided among all support departments. Also called *matrix method*.

Reengineering. The fundamental rethinking and redesign of business processes to achieve improvements in critical measures of performance, such as cost, quality, service, speed, and customer satisfaction.

Refined costing system. Costing system that reduces the use of broad averages for assigning the cost of resources to cost objects (jobs, products, services) and provides better measurement of the costs of indirect resources used by different cost objects—no matter how differently various cost objects use indirect resources.

Regression analysis. Statistical method that measures the average amount of change in the dependent variable associated with a unit change in one or more independent variables.

Relevant costs. Expected future costs that differ among alternative courses of action being considered.

Relevant range. Band of normal activity level or volume in which there is a specific relationship between the level of activity or volume and the cost in question.

Relevant revenues. Expected future revenues that differ among alternative courses of action being considered.

Reorder point. The quantity level of inventory on hand that triggers a new purchase order.

Required rate of return (RRR). The minimum acceptable annual rate of return on an investment. Also called the *discount rate*, *hurdle rate*, *cost of capital*, or *opportunity cost of capital*.

Research and development. Generating and experimenting with ideas related to new products, services, or processes.

Residual income (RI). Accounting measure of income minus a dollar amount for required return on an accounting measure of investment.

Residual term. The vertical difference or distance between actual cost and estimated cost for each observation in a regression model.

Responsibility accounting. System that measures the plans, budgets, actions, and actual results of each responsibility center.

Responsibility center. Part, segment, or subunit of an organization whose manager is accountable for a specified set of activities.

Return on investment (ROI). An accounting measure of income divided by an accounting measure of investment. See also *accrual accounting rate of return method*.

Revenue allocation. The allocation of revenues that are related to a particular revenue object but cannot be traced to it in an economically feasible (cost-effective) way.

Revenue center. Responsibility center where the manager is accountable for revenues only.

Revenue driver. A variable, such as volume, that causally affects revenues.

Revenue object. Anything for which a separate measurement of revenue is desired.

Revenues. Inflows of assets (usually cash or accounts receivable) received for products or services provided to customers.

Rework. Units of production that do not meet the specifications required by customers for finished units that are subsequently repaired and sold as good finished units.

Rightsizing. See *downsizing*.

Rolling budget. Budget or plan that is always available for a specified future period by adding a period (month, quarter, or year) to the period that just ended. Also called *continuous budget*.

Safety stock. Inventory held at all times regardless of the quantity of inventory ordered using the EOQ model.

Sales mix. Quantities of various products or services that constitute total unit sales.

Sales-mix variance. The difference between (1) budgeted contribution margin for the actual sales mix, and (2) budgeted contribution margin for the budgeted sales mix.

Sales-quantity variance. The difference between (1) budgeted contribution margin based on actual units sold of all products at the budgeted mix and (2) contribution margin in the static budget (which is based on the budgeted units of all products to be sold at the budgeted mix).

Sales value at splitoff method. Method that allocates joint costs to joint products on the basis of the relative total sales value at the splitoff point of the total production of these products during the accounting period.

Sales-volume variance. The difference between a flexible-budget amount and the corresponding static-budget amount.

Scrap. Residual material left over when making a product.

Selling-price variance. The difference between the actual selling price and the budgeted selling price multiplied by the actual units sold.

Semivariable cost. See *mixed cost*.

Sensitivity analysis. A what-if technique that managers use to calculate how an outcome will change if the original predicted data are not achieved or if an underlying assumption changes.

Separable costs. All costs (manufacturing, marketing, distribution, and so on) incurred beyond the splitoff point that are assignable to each of the specific products identified at the splitoff point.

Sequential allocation method. See *step-down method*.

Sequential tracking. Approach in a product-costing system in which recording of the journal entries occurs in the same order as actual purchases and progress in production.

Service department. See *support department*.

Service-sector companies. Companies that provide services or intangible products to their customers.

Service-sustaining costs. The costs of activities undertaken to support individual services.

Shrinkage costs. Costs that result from theft by outsiders, embezzlement by employees, misclassifications, and clerical errors.

Simple regression. Regression model that estimates the relationship between the dependent variable and one independent variable.

Single-rate method. Allocation method that allocates costs in each cost pool to cost objects using the same rate per unit of a single allocation base.

Slope coefficient. Coefficient term in a cost estimation model that indicates the amount by which total cost changes when a one-unit change occurs in the level of activity within the relevant range.

Source document. An original record that supports journal entries in an accounting system.

Specification analysis. Testing of the assumptions of regression analysis.

Splitoff point. The juncture in a joint-production process when two or more products become separately identifiable.

Spoilage. Units of production that do not meet the specifications required by customers for good units and that are discarded or sold at reduced prices.

Staff management. Staff (such as management accountants and human resources managers) who provide advice and assistance to line management.

Stand-alone cost-allocation method. Method that uses information pertaining to each user of a cost object as a separate entity to determine the cost-allocation weights.

Stand-alone revenue-allocation method. Method that uses product-specific information on the products in the bundle as weights for allocating the bundled revenues to the individual products.

Standard. A carefully determined price, cost, or quantity that is used as a benchmark for judging performance. It is usually expressed on a per unit basis.

Standard cost. A carefully determined cost of a unit of output.

Standard costing. Costing system that traces direct costs to output produced by multiplying the standard prices or rates by the standard quantities of inputs allowed for actual outputs produced and allocates overhead costs on the basis of the standard overhead-cost rates times the standard quantities of the allocation bases allowed for the actual outputs produced.

Standard error of the estimated coefficient. Regression statistic that indicates how much the estimated value of the coefficient is likely to be affected by random factors.

Standard error of the regression. Statistic that measures the variance of residuals in a regression analysis.

Standard input. A carefully determined quantity of input required for one unit of output.

Standard price. A carefully determined price that a company expects to pay for a unit of input.

Static budget. Budget based on the level of output planned at the start of the budget period.

Static-budget variance. Difference between an actual result and the corresponding budgeted amount in the static budget.

Step cost function. A cost function in which the cost remains the same over various ranges of the level of activity, but the cost increases by discrete amounts (that is, increases in steps) as the level of activity changes from one range to the next.

Step-down method. Cost allocation method that partially recognizes the mutual services provided among all support departments. Also called *sequential allocation method.*

Stockout costs. Costs that result when a company runs out of a particular item for which there is customer demand. The company must act to meet that demand or suffer the costs of not meeting it.

Strategic cost management. Describes cost management that specifically focuses on strategic issues.

Strategy. Specifies how an organization matches its own capabilities with the opportunities in the marketplace to accomplish its objectives.

Strategy map. A diagram that describes how an organization creates value by connecting strategic objectives in explicit cause-and-effect relationships with each other in the financial, customer, internal business process, and learning and growth perspectives.

Suboptimal decision making. Decisions in which the benefit to one subunit is more than offset by the costs or loss of benefits to the organization as a whole. Also called *incongruent decision making* or *dysfunctional decision making*.

Sunk costs. Past costs that are unavoidable because they cannot be changed no matter what action is taken. (393)

Super-variable costing. See *throughput costing*.

Supply chain. Describes the flow of goods, services, and information from the initial sources of materials and services to the delivery of products to consumers, regardless of whether those activities occur in the same organization or in other organizations.

Support department. Department that provides the services that assist other internal departments (operating departments and other support departments) in the company. Also called a *service department*.

Target cost per unit. Estimated long-run cost per unit of a product or service that enables the company to achieve its target operating income per unit when selling at the target price. Target cost per unit is derived by subtracting the target operating income per unit from the target price.

Target operating income per unit. Operating income that a company aims to earn per unit of a product or service sold.

Target price. Estimated price for a product or service that potential customers will pay.

Target rate of return on investment. The target annual operating income that an organization aims to achieve divided by invested capital.

Theoretical capacity. The level of capacity based on producing at full efficiency all the time.

Theory of constraints (TOC). Describes methods to maximize operating income when faced with some bottleneck and some nonbottleneck operations.

Throughput costing. Method of inventory costing in which only variable direct material costs are included as inventoriable costs. Also called *super-variable costing*.

Throughput margin. Revenues minus the direct material costs of the goods sold.

Time driver. Any factor in which a change in the factor causes a change in the speed of an activity.

Time value of money. Takes into account that a dollar (or any other monetary unit) received today is worth more than a dollar received at any future time.

Total factor productivity (TFP). The ratio of the quantity of output produced to the costs of all inputs used, based on current period prices.

Total-overhead variance. The sum of the flexible-budget variance and the production-volume variance.

Transfer price. Price one subunit (department or division) charges for a product or service supplied to another subunit of the same organization.

Transferred-in costs. Costs incurred in previous departments that are carried forward as the product's costs when it moves to a subsequent process in the production cycle. Also called *previous department costs*.

Trigger point. Refers to a stage in the cycle from purchase of direct materials to sale of finished goods at which journal entries are made in the accounting system.

Uncertainty. The possibility that an actual amount will deviate from an expected amount.

Underabsorbed indirect costs. See *underallocated indirect costs*.

Underallocated indirect costs. Allocated amount of indirect costs in an accounting period is less than the actual (incurred) amount in that period. Also called *underapplied indirect costs* or *underabsorbed indirect costs*.

Underapplied indirect costs. See *underallocated indirect costs*.

Unfavorable variance. Variance that has the effect of decreasing operating income relative to the budgeted amount. Denoted U.

Unit cost. Cost computed by dividing total cost by the number of units. Also called *average cost*.

Unused capacity. The amount of productive capacity available over and above the productive capacity employed to meet consumer demand in the current period.

Usage variance. See *efficiency variance*.

Value-added cost. A cost that, if eliminated, would reduce the actual or perceived value or utility (usefulness) customers obtain from using the product or service.

Value chain. The sequence of business functions in which customer usefulness is added to products or services of a company.

Value engineering. Systematic evaluation of all aspects of the value chain, with the objective of reducing costs and achieving a quality level that satisfies customers.

Value streams. All valued-added activities needed to design, manufacture, and deliver a given product or product line to customers.

Variable cost. Cost that changes in total in proportion to changes in the related level of total activity or volume.

Variable costing. Method of inventory costing in which only all variable manufacturing costs are included as inventoriable costs. Also called *direct costing*.

Variable overhead efficiency variance. The difference between the actual quantity of variable overhead cost-allocation base used and budgeted quantity of variable overhead cost-allocation base that should have been used to produce actual output, multiplied by budgeted variable overhead cost per unit of cost-allocation base.

Variable overhead flexible-budget variance. The difference between actual variable overhead costs incurred and flexible-budget variable overhead amounts.

Variable overhead spending variance. The difference between actual variable overhead cost per unit and budgeted variable overhead cost per unit of the cost-allocation base, multiplied by actual quantity of variable overhead cost-allocation base used for actual output.

Variance. The difference between actual result and expected performance.

Weighted-average process-costing method. Method of process costing that assigns the equivalent-unit cost of the work done to date (regardless of the accounting period in which it was done) to equivalent units completed and transferred out of the process and to equivalent units in ending work-in-process inventory.

Whale curve. A typically backward-bending curve that represents the results from customer profitability analysis by first ranking customers from best to worst and then plotting their cumulative profitability level.

Work-in-process inventory. Goods partially worked on but not yet completed. Also called *work in progress*.

Work in progress. See *work-in-process inventory*.

Work-measurement method. See *industrial engineering method*.

Index